XSLT

Other resources from O'Reilly

Related titles

XSLT Cookbook™	XML Hacks™
XQuery	XSLT 1.0 Pocket Reference
Learning XSLT	Relax NG
Java & XML	Unicode Explained
Schematron	XML in a Nutshell
Developing Feeds with RSS and Atom	Learning XML

oreilly.com

oreilly.com is more than a complete catalog of O'Reilly books. You'll also find links to news, events, articles, weblogs, sample chapters, and code examples.

oreillynet.com is the essential portal for developers interested in open and emerging technologies, including new platforms, programming languages, and operating systems.

Conferences

O'Reilly Media, Inc. brings diverse innovators together to nurture the ideas that spark revolutionary industries. We specialize in documenting the latest tools and systems, translating the innovator's knowledge into useful skills for those in the trenches. Visit *conferences.oreilly.com* for our upcoming events.

Safari Bookshelf (*safari.oreilly.com*) is the premier online reference library for programmers and IT professionals. Conduct searches across more than 1,000 books. Subscribers can zero in on answers to time-critical questions in a matter of seconds. Read the books on your Bookshelf from cover to cover or simply flip to the page you need. Try it today for free.

SECOND EDITION

XSLT

Doug Tidwell

XSLT, Second Edition
by Doug Tidwell

Published by O'Reilly Media, Inc., 1005 Gravenstein Highway North, Sebastopol, CA 95472.

O'Reilly books may be purchased for educational, business, or sales promotional use. Online editions are also available for most titles (*http://safari.oreilly.com*). For more information, contact our corporate/institutional sales department: 800-998-9938 or *corporate@oreilly.com*.

Editor: Simon St.Laurent
Production Editor: Sarah Schneider
Proofreader: Mary Brady

Indexer: Fred Brown
Cover Designer: Karen Montgomery
Interior Designer: David Futato
Illustrator: Robert Romano

Printing History:

June 2008:	Second Edition.
August 2001:	First Edition.

ISBN: 978-0-596-52721-1

[C]

[2/10]

1265408518

To my family—my wonderful wife, Sheri Castle, and our amazing daughter, Lily—for their love, support, and understanding. Nothing I do would be possible or meaningful without them.

...and a special thanks to our dog, Domino, who frequently and selflessly pushed his fuzzy head between my hands and keyboard to protect me from carpal tunnel syndrome. Good boy!

Table of Contents

Preface

About This Book

The goal of this book is to help you make the most of XSLT, the Extensible Stylesheet Language for Transformations. It covers both XSLT 1.0 and XSLT 2.0, along with versions 1.0 and 2.0 of XPath, the XML Path Language. The two languages are designed to work together: XPath identifies the parts of an XML document that should be transformed, and XSLT says how the transformation should be done.

The first few chapters of the book cover the features of XSLT by solving common problems using the language. Once you've mastered those techniques, the last section of the book contains a complete set of examples for all the features of XSLT and XPath. The book is designed as a tutorial for learning the language as you're getting started. Once you're comfortable with XSLT, the book can be used as a dictionary-style reference for the features and functions of the language.

Where I'm Coming From

Before we begin, it's only fair that I tell you my biases.

I Believe in Open, Platform-Neutral, Standards-Based Computing

If any part of your business life ties you down to anything closed, proprietary, or platform-specific, I encourage you to make some changes. This book shows you how to take charge of your data and move it from one place to another on your terms, and not your software vendor's. XML is shifting the balance of power from vendors to software users. If your tools force you to work in unnatural ways or refuse to let you have your data when and where you want it, you don't have to take it anymore.

I Assume You're Busy

The best review I received for the first edition of this book began, "I will never read this book." This was actually a positive review, as the reviewer went on to explain. "When

I have a problem, I grab this book off the shelf, go to the index, and within five minutes I've found the answer to my problem. Then I toss it back on the shelf."

That's exactly the kind of book I've tried to write. There are hundreds of stylesheets in this book, including examples for every XSLT element, function, and operator defined by XSLT and XPath. The first chapters of the book are prose that explain how stylesheets work and what you need to learn to be productive with XSLT. Once you're comfortable with that material, you can use the rest of the book as a dictionary-style reference.

I Don't Care Which Standards-Compliant Tools You Use

My job as an author and a teacher is to show you how to use standards-compliant tools to simplify your life. I'm not here to sell you a parser, an XSLT processor, a toaster, or anything else, so please use whatever tools you like. I encourage you to take a look at all of the tools out there and find your own preferences. As I wrote this edition of the book, I used four processors to test the examples:

- Almost all of the examples were tested with Michael Kay's excellent Saxon XSLT processor. The open source edition of Saxon supports all of the XSLT 2.0, XPath 2.0 and XQuery 1.0 specs *except* for the schema-specific functions. As the editor of the XSLT 2.0 specification, Dr. Kay's processor is currently the most complete implementation of XSLT 2.0.

  Saxon-B (the basic processor without schema support) is available here: *http://saxon.sourceforge.net/*. The SourceForge project page is at *http://sourceforge.net/projects/saxon*. Saxon is available in Java and .NET versions.

  There is also a commercial version of Saxon that includes full schema support. For more information on Saxon-SA, which is the schema-aware version, visit *http://www.saxonica.com/*.

- The XSLT engine from Altova XML Spy was also used for all of the XSLT 2.0 examples. The Altova XSLT engine, although not open source, does provide complete schema support in a no-cost product. The license for the Altova engine currently allows you to redistribute it with your own code. To get the engine and the license terms, visit *http://www.altova.com/altovaxml.html*.

- Apache's Xalan XSLT engine supports almost all of the XSLT 1.0 examples in the book. (The XSLT 1.0 stylesheets that it doesn't support are ones that use extensions written for other processors.) It's also a forwards-compatible XSLT processor, so it can work with XSLT 2.0 stylesheets.

  The Java version of the processor, Xalan-J, is available at *http://xml.apache.org/xalan-j/*. There's also a C++ version at *http://xml.apache.org/xalan-c/*.

- Microsoft's .NET framework supports XSLT 1.0, as does the MSXSL utility. One significant addition to this edition is more focus on the Microsoft platform. In addition to testing all of the XSLT 1.0 samples with the Microsoft tools, there are also XSLT extensions written in C# and EcmaScript.

The MSXSL XSLT processor is available from the Microsoft XML downloads page, *http://msdn.microsoft.com/XML/XMLDownloads/default.aspx*. There is also an XSLT processor embedded in the .NET framework; it's part of the `System.Xml.Xsl` namespace.

XSLT Is a Tool, Not a Religion

An old adage says that to a person with a hammer, everything looks like a nail. I don't claim that XSLT is the solution to every business problem you'll encounter. Chapter 1 discusses reasons why XML and XSLT were created and the design decisions behind XSLT, and it tries to identify the kinds of problems XSLT is designed to solve. All chapters in this book illustrate common scenarios in which XSLT is extremely powerful and useful.

That being said, if a particular tool does something better than XSLT does, then by all means, use that other tool. For example, XSLT has functions for sorting and grouping. If the data you're transforming comes from a relational database, it's probably far more efficient to use the `ORDER BY` and `GROUP BY` features of your database instead of sorting and grouping with XSLT. XSLT is a powerful addition to your tool box, but that doesn't mean you should throw out all your other tools.

You Shouldn't Migrate All of Your Stylesheets Just Because There's a New Version of XSLT

Anytime a new version of a language, standard, or software package comes along, deciding when or if to migrate to the new features depends on your application. If you've built a web application in which you use a web browser to process XSLT stylesheets on the client side, you can't migrate to XSLT 2.0 until all the major browsers support XSLT 2.0. That's going to be a while. On the other hand, if you use XSLT to transform your data and then send the transformed data to the client, you can use XSLT 2.0 right away. With very few exceptions, anything that worked in XSLT 1.0 works in XSLT 2.0. We cover migration in Appendix G.

XSLT 2.0 and XPath 2.0 have many new features that make your stylesheets easier to write, easier to maintain, and much more powerful. It's definitely worth your time to investigate the new features to see how many of them you can use.

How This Book Is Organized

XSLT 2.0 has added significant new features to the language, many of which are related to the changes in XPath 2.0. The biggest challenge I had as an author was figuring out how to organize the book. One approach would have been to make this an XSLT 2.0

book, writing under the assumption that everyone would migrate to XSLT 2.0 as soon as possible. I don't believe that will happen, so I didn't go that way. Instead, I tried to cover everything in terms of common tasks, things you'll probably have to do with XSLT. If there are new features in XSLT 2.0 that apply to those tasks, I mention them after explaining the concepts behind the stylesheets. Usually XSLT 2.0 makes your life much easier, so I begin the discussion by pointing out that if you're using XSLT 2.0, you've got a simpler option.

As with the first edition, this book has two parts: a series of prose chapters that cover concepts and tasks, followed by a series of appendixes that form a reference to all of the elements, functions, operators, and other details you'll need as you write stylesheets. Once you're comfortable with XSLT, you can use the appendixes as a dictionary of all things related to XSLT and XPath.

The book contains the following chapters:

Chapter 1, *Getting Started*
: Covers the basics of XML and discusses how to install the stylesheet engines used in this book.

Chapter 2, *The Obligatory Hello World Example*
: Takes a look at an XML-tagged "Hello World" document, then examines stylesheets that transform it into other things.

Chapter 3, *XPath: A Syntax for Describing Needles and Haystacks*
: Covers the basics of XPath, the language used to describe parts of an XML document. This chapter includes an in-depth discussion of the many changes introduced in XPath 2.0.

Chapter 4, *Creating Output*
: Discusses the basics of creating output, including extracting text, copying information, and numbering things.

Chapter 5, *Branching and Control Elements*
: Discusses the logic elements of XSLT (`<xsl:if>` and `<xsl:choose>`) and how they work. Also covers the new `if` operator in XPath 2.0.

Chapter 6, *Creating Links and Cross-References*
: Covers the different ways to build links between elements in XML documents. Using XPath to describe relationships between related elements is also covered.

Chapter 7, *Sorting and Grouping Elements*
: Goes over the `<xsl:sort>` element and discusses various ways to sort elements in an XML document. It also talks about how to do grouping with various XSLT elements and functions. Grouping is much simpler in XSLT 2.0; the new grouping features are covered in this chapter as well.

Chapter 8, *Combining Documents*

Discusses the `document( )` function, which allows you to combine several XML documents, then write a stylesheet that works against the collection of documents. Related functions from XSLT 2.0 are also featured.

Chapter 9, *Extending XSLT*

Explains how to write extension elements and extension functions. Although XSLT and XPath are extremely powerful and flexible, there are still times when you need to do something that isn't provided by the language itself.

The last section of the book contains reference information:

Appendix A

An alphabetical listing of all the elements defined by XSLT, with examples for those elements and how they were designed to be used.

Appendix B

A listing of various aspects of XPath, including datatypes, axes, node types, and operators.

Appendix C

An alphabetical listing of all the functions defined by XPath and XSLT.

Appendix D

Provides a brief overview of XML Schema. One of the additions to XSLT 2.0 is the ability to use XML Schemas to define datatypes and validate XML structures against them.

Appendix E

Covers the syntax and features of the regular expression language used by XPath 2.0 and XSLT 2.0.

Appendix F

Provides a handy listing of all the formatting codes used in XSLT and XPath.

Appendix G

Lists a number of considerations and approaches for migrating to XSLT 2.0.

Glossary

A glossary of terms used in XSLT, XPath, and XML in general.

Conventions Used in This Book

Items appearing in this book are sometimes given a special appearance to set them apart from the regular text. Here's how they look:

Italic

Used for citations of books and articles, commands, email addresses, introduction of terms, and URLs

`Constant width`

Used for literals, constant values, code listings, and XML markup

`Constant-width bold`

Used to indicate user input

`Constant-width italic`

Used for replaceable parameter and variable names

 This icon represents a tip, suggestion, or general note.

 This icon represents a warning or caution.

[1.0]

This text represents information that applies *only* to XSLT 1.0 and XPath 1.0.

[2.0]

This text represents information that is new in XSLT 2.0 and XPath 2.0.

[2.0 – Schema]

This text represents information that applies to schema-aware XSLT 2.0 processors.

How to Contact Us

We have tested and verified the information in this book to the best of our ability, but you may find that features have changed (or even that we have made mistakes!). Please let us know about any errors you find, as well as your suggestions for future editions, by writing to:

O'Reilly Media, Inc.
1005 Gravenstein Highway North
Sebastopol, CA 95472
800-998-9938 (in the United States or Canada)
707-829-0515 (international or local)
707-829-0104 (fax)

To ask technical questions or comment on the book, send email to:

bookquestions@oreilly.com

The web site for this book lists examples, errata, and plans for future editions. You can access this page at:

---

http://www.oreilly.com/catalog/9780596527211

For more information about our books, conferences, software, resource centers, and the O'Reilly Network, see our web site:

http://www.oreilly.com

Safari® Enabled

Safari
Books Online

When you see a Safari® Enabled icon on the cover of your favorite technology book, that means the book is available online through the O'Reilly Network Safari Bookshelf.

Safari offers a solution that's better than e-books. It's a virtual library that lets you easily search thousands of top tech books, cut and paste code samples, download chapters, and find quick answers when you need the most accurate, current information. Try it for free at *http://safari.oreilly.com*.

Acknowledgments for the Second Edition

I want to thank Jeni Tennison for being the lead reviewer of this edition. Her ability to see through to the essence of a problem and point out the simplest and most elegant way to solve it is astounding. I have blisters from smacking my forehead as I read her review comments, thinking at the time, "Of course! I should have seen that right away." Jeni, thank you.

I also benefited from Priscilla Walmsley's excellent review, especially in the appendixes that cover all the elements and functions in XSLT, XPath, and XQuery. The examples and terminology in those sections are far more useful and correct as a result.

A big thanks to Michael Kay for providing a copy of Saxon-SA to test the schema examples in the book. The entire XSLT community owes him an enormous debt for making the XSLT 2.0 spec robust, readable, and complete, and for writing the Saxon XSLT engine.

This book was written entirely in DocBook, a very powerful XML vocabulary for publishing. Two books have been invaluable as I've worked with DocBook. The first is O'Reilly's *DocBook: The Definitive Guide*, written by Norm Walsh and Leonard Mueller (available online at *http://www.oreilly.com/catalog/docbook/chapter/book/doc book.html*). If you want to know anything about DocBook, this is the place to look. The open source community also maintains an extremely sophisticated set of XSLT stylesheets that transform DocBook into a variety of other formats. For help in using the DocBook XSL, Bob Stayton's *DocBook XSL: The Complete Guide* (Sagehill Enterprises; available online at *http://sagehill.net/book-description.html*) was invaluable. Thanks to all three of these great authors.

I also want to thank the people I've worked with over the last few years. The IBM developerWorks team is still a great influence on me. I'll always think of myself as part of the developerWorks family. During my time with IBM's Developer Skills organization, I had the great pleasure of working with an incredibly talented team. That group is paid to give away as much knowledge as possible, along with free software to professors and students around the world. Finally, I want to thank the members of my current team in IBM's Software Group Strategy organization. I'm very happy to be working again for Dirk Nicol, the father of developerWorks.

I will resist the temptation to name names here in fear of forgetting someone. I hope all of you know how much you mean to me, and how much I've learned from all of you.

Finally, I want to thank Simon St.Laurent for his guidance on the second edition. Both of us were nervous about figuring out how to add XSLT 2.0 and XPath 2.0 to this book without creating a 5,000 page tome. Unfortunately, I also relied on Simon's patience as portions of the book took far longer than either of us had hoped. Simon, you're the best.

Acknowledgments from the First Edition

First and foremost, I'd like to thank the reviewers of this book. David Marston of Lotus was the lead reviewer; David, thank you so much for your comments, wisdom, and knowledge. Along the way, I also got a lot of good feedback and encouragement from Tony Colle, Slavko Malesvic, Dr. Joe Molitoris, Shane O'Donnell, Andy Piper, Sreenivas Ramarao, Mike Riley, and Willie Wheeler. This book is significantly better because of your comments and other efforts.

I'd also like to thank my teammates at developerWorks for encouraging me to undertake this project. Taking on an additional full-time job hasn't been easy, but their advice, flexibility, and understanding as I've tried to balance my responsibilities has been invaluable. Even more valuable is the fact that I'm surrounded by some of the most interesting, creative, and remarkable people I've ever known. You guys rule.

For the times I've been at home (in Raleigh, North Carolina), I've depended on my nutritional advisors at Schiano's Pizza: "Hey, you want your usual?" (Slight pause.) "Yeah, that'd be great, thanks." Nothing's as comforting as a couple of slices. If you're within a day's drive of Raleigh, I strongly encourage you to visit.

Finally, I'd like to thank the staff at O'Reilly, especially Laurie Petrycki and Simon St.Laurent. Laurie, thank you for convincing me to take on this project and for sticking with me when my ability to find the time to write was in doubt. Simon, I've enjoyed reading your books for years; it's been an honor to work with you. Your guidance, technical insight, patience, and suggestions were invaluable.

Thanks so much to all of you!

CHAPTER 1

Getting Started

In this chapter, we review the design rationale behind XSLT and XPath and discuss the basics of XML. We also talk about other web standards and how they relate to XSLT and XPath. We conclude the chapter with a brief discussion of how to set up an XSLT processor on your machine so you can work with the examples throughout the book.

The Design of XSLT

XML went from working group to entrenched buzzword in record time. Its flexibility as a language for presenting structured data made it the lingua franca for data interchange. Early adopters used programming interfaces such as the Document Object Model (DOM) and the Simple API for XML (SAX) to parse and process XML documents. As XML became mainstream, however, it was clear that the average web citizen couldn't be expected to hack Java, Visual Basic, Perl, or Python code to work with documents. What was needed was a flexible, powerful, yet relatively simple language capable of processing XML.

What the world needed was XSLT.

XSLT, the Extensible Stylesheet Language for Transformations, is an official recommendation of the World Wide Web Consortium (W3C). It provides a flexible, powerful language for transforming XML documents into something else, such as an HTML document, another XML document, a Portable Document Format (PDF) file, a Scalable Vector Graphics (SVG) file, a Virtual Reality Modeling Language (VRML) file, Java code, a flat text file, a JPEG file, or most anything you want. You write an XSLT stylesheet to define the rules for transforming an XML document, and the XSLT processor does the work.

The W3C has defined two families of standards for stylesheets. The oldest and simplest is Cascading Style Sheets (CSS), a mechanism used to define various properties of markup elements. Although CSS can be used with XML, it is most often used to style HTML documents. I can use CSS properties to define certain elements to be rendered in blue, or in 58-point type, or in boldface. That's all well and good, but there are many things that CSS can't do:

- CSS can't change the order in which elements appear in a document. If you want to sort certain elements or filter elements based on a certain property, CSS won't do the job.

- CSS can't do computations. If you want to calculate and output a value (maybe you want to add up the numeric value of all `<price>` elements in a document), CSS won't do the job.

- CSS can't combine multiple documents. If you want to combine 53 purchase order documents and print a summary of all items ordered in those purchase orders, CSS won't do the job.

 Don't take this section as a criticism of CSS; XSLT and CSS were designed for different purposes. One fairly common use of XSLT is to generate an HTML document that uses CSS. See "The XPath View of an XML Document" in Chapter 3 for an example that uses XSLT to generate CSS classes, and then uses those classes to format the HTML elements

XSLT was created to be a more powerful, flexible language for transforming documents. In this book, we go through all the features of XSLT and discuss each of them in terms of practical examples. Some of XSLT's design goals specify that:

- An XSLT stylesheet should be an XML document. This means that you can write a stylesheet that transforms a second stylesheet into another stylesheet. This kind of recursive thinking is common in XSLT.

- The XSLT language should be based on pattern matching. Most of our stylesheets consist of rules (called *templates* in XSLT) used to transform a document. Each rule says, "When you see part of a document that looks like this, here's how you convert it into something else." This is probably different from any programming you've previously done.

- XSLT should be designed to be free of side effects. In other words, XSLT is designed to be optimized so that many different stylesheet rules could be applied simultaneously. The biggest impact of this is that variables can't be modified. Once a variable is bound, you can't change its value; if variables could be changed, then processing one stylesheet rule might have side effects that impact other stylesheet rules. This is almost certainly different from any programming you've previously done.

  XSLT is heavily influenced by the design of *functional programming languages*, such as Lisp, Scheme, and Haskell. These languages also feature immutable variables. Instead of defining the templates of XSLT, functional programming languages define programs as a series of functions, each of which generates a well-defined output (free from side effects, of course) in response to a well-defined input. The goal is to execute the instructions of a given XSLT template without affecting the execution of any other XSLT template.

- Instead of looping, XSLT uses iteration and recursion. Given that variables can't be changed, how do you do something like a `for` or `do-while` loop? XSLT uses two equivalent techniques: iteration and recursion. *Iteration* means that you can write an XSLT template that says, "Get all the things that look like this, and here's what I want you to do with each of them." Although that's different from a `do-while` loop, usually what you do in a procedural language is something like, "Do this while there are any items left to process." In that case, iteration does exactly what you want.

  Recursion takes some getting used to. If you must implement something like a `for` statement (`for i=1 to 10 do`, for example), recursion is the way to go. There are a number of examples of recursion throughout the book; you can flip ahead to "Using Recursion to Do Most Anything" in Chapter 5 for more information.

Given these design goals, what are XSLT's strengths? Here are some scenarios:

- Your web site needs to deliver information to a variety of devices. You need to support ordinary desktop browsers, as well as pagers, mobile phones, and other low-resolution, low-function devices. It would be great if you could create your information in structured documents, then transform those documents into all the formats you need.

- You need to exchange data with your partners, but all of you use different database systems. It would be great if you could define a common XML data format, then transform documents written in that format into the import files you need (SQL statements, comma-separated values, etc.).

- To stay on the cutting edge, your web site gets a complete visual redesign every few months. Even though things such as server-side includes and CSS can help, they can't do everything. It would be great if your data were in a flexible format that could be transformed into any look and feel, simplifying the redesign process.

- You have documents in several different formats. All the documents are machine-readable, but it's a hassle to write programs to parse and process all of them. It would be great if you could combine all of the documents into a single format, then generate summary documents and reports based on that collection of documents. It would be even better if the report could contain calculated values, automatically generated graphics, and formatting for high-quality printing.

Throughout the book, we'll demonstrate XSLT solutions for problems just like these. Most chapters focus on particular techniques, such as sorting, grouping, and generating links between pieces of data, although we'll start with a gentle introduction to the basics.

[2.0] The Design of XSLT 2.0

XSLT 2.0 is a major enhancement to the language. XSLT 2.0 uses XPath 2.0, which itself went through many significant changes. The gap between XSLT 1.0/XPath 1.0

and XSLT 2.0/XPath 2.0 was a little over seven years (November 16, 1999 to January 23, 2007). There were two major requirements that led to the monumental amount of work required to create XSLT 2.0 and XPath 2.0:

Support for XML Schema
> XSLT and XPath now support XML Schema, which means nodes and variables can have datatypes. We can define a value to be of type `xs:dateTime`, and the XSLT processor will enforce that requirement. All XSLT 2.0 processors support the basic XML Schema datatypes. A *schema-aware processor* also supports custom datatypes. If we have a datatype named `purchaseOrder`, we can use a schema-aware processor to work with values of that type.

Integration with XQuery
> The initial work for XQuery began in 1998, and version 1.0 became a W3C Recommendation on January 23, 2007. XQuery 1.0 and XPath 2.0 share a common data model, functions, and operators. Coordinating the efforts of the XQuery, XPath, and XSLT working groups must have been a challenge.

The birthing pains of XSLT 2.0 and XPath 2.0 are behind us now, and we have a more powerful language for transforming documents. We'll discuss the changes to the language as they're relevant to our discussion of common tasks that you'll probably want to do with XSLT. All of the technical details are covered in the appendixes.

XML Basics

Almost everything we do in this book deals with XML documents. XSLT stylesheets are XML documents themselves, and they're designed to transform an XML document into something else. If you don't have much experience with XML, we'll review the basics here. For more information on XML, check out Erik T. Ray's *Learning XML* (O'Reilly, 2001) and Elliotte Rusty Harold and W. Scott Means's *XML in a Nutshell* (O'Reilly, 2001).

XML's Heritage

XML's heritage is in the Standard Generalized Markup Language (SGML). Created by Dr. Charles Goldfarb in the 1970s, SGML is widely used in high-end publishing systems. Unfortunately, SGML's perceived complexity prevented its widespread adoption across the industry (SGML also stands for "sounds great, maybe later"). SGML got a boost when Tim Berners-Lee based HTML on SGML. Overnight, the whole computing industry was using a markup language to build documents and applications.

The problem with HTML is that its tags were designed for the interaction between humans and machines. When the Web was invented in the late 1980s, that was just fine. As the Web moved into all aspects of our lives, HTML was asked to do lots of strange things. We've all built HTML pages with awkward table structures, 1-pixel

GIFs, and other nonsense just to get the page to look right in the browser. XML is designed to get us out of this rut and back into the world of structured documents.

Whatever its limitations, HTML is the most popular markup language ever created. Given its popularity, why do we need XML? Consider this extremely informative HTML element:

```
<td>12304</td>
```

What does this fascinating piece of content represent?

- Is it the postal code for Schenectady, New York?
- Is it the number of light bulbs replaced each month in Las Vegas?
- Is it the number of Volkswagens sold in Hong Kong last year?
- Is it the number of tons of steel in the Sydney Harbour Bridge?

The answer: maybe, maybe not. The point of this silly example is that there's no structure to this data. Even if we include the entire table, it takes intelligence (real, live intelligence, the kind between your ears) to make sense of this. If you saw this cell in a table next to another cell that contained the text "Schenectady," and the heading above the table read "Postal Codes for the State of New York," then as a human being, you could interpret the contents of this cell correctly. On the other hand, if you wanted to write a piece of code that took any HTML table and attempted to determine whether any of the cells in the table contained postal codes, you'd find that difficult, to say the least.

Most HTML pages have one goal in mind: the appearance of the document. Veterans of the markup industry know that this is definitely not the way to create content. The *separation of content and presentation* is a long-established tenet of the publishing industry; unfortunately, most HTML pages aren't even close to approaching this ideal. An XML document should contain information, marked up with tags that describe what all the pieces of information are, as well as the relationship between those items. Presenting the document (also known as *rendering*) involves rules and decisions separate from the document itself. As we work through dozens of sample documents and applications, you'll see how delaying the rendering decisions as long as possible has significant advantages.

Let's look at another marked-up document. Consider this:

```
<?xml version="1.0"?>
<postalcodes>
  <title>Most-used postal codes in November 2000</title>
  <item>
    <city>Schenectady</city>
    <postalcode>12304</postalcode>
    <usage-count>2039</usage-count>
  </item>
  <item>
    <city>Kuala Lumpur</city>
    <postalcode>57000</postalcode>
```

```
    <usage-count>1983</usage-count>
  </item>
  <item>
    <city>London</city>
    <postalcode>SW1P 4RG</postalcode>
    <usage-count>1722</usage-count>
  </item>
  ...
</postalcodes>
```

Although we're still in the realm of contrived examples, it would be fairly easy to write a piece of code to find the postal codes in any document that used this set of tags (as opposed to HTML's `<table>`, `<tr>`, `<td>`, etc.). Our code would look for the contents of any `<postalcode>` elements in the document. (Not to get ahead of ourselves here, but writing an XSLT stylesheet to do this might take all of 30 minutes, including a 25-minute nap.) A well-designed XML document identifies each piece of data in the document and models the relationships between those pieces of data. This means we can be confident that we're processing an XML document correctly.

Again, the key idea here is that we're separating content from presentation. Our XML document clearly delineates the pieces of data and puts them into a format we can parse easily. In this book, we illustrate a number of techniques for transforming this XML document into a variety of formats. Among other things, we can transform the item `<postalcode>12304</postalcode>` into `<td>12304</td>`.

XML Document Rules

Continuing our trip through the basics of XML, there are several rules you need to keep in mind when creating XML documents. All stylesheets we develop in this book are themselves XML documents, so all the rules of XML documents apply to everything we do. The rules are pretty simple, even though the vast majority of HTML documents don't follow them.

One important point: the XML 1.0 specification makes it clear that when an XML parser finds an XML document that breaks the rules, the parser is supposed to throw an exception and stop. The parser is not allowed to guess what the document structure should actually be. This specification avoids recreating the HTML world, where lots of ugly documents are still rendered by the average browser.

An XML document must be contained in a single element

The first element in your XML document must contain the entire document. That first element is called the *document element* or the *root element*. If more than one document element is in the document, the XML parser throws an exception. This XML document is perfectly legal:

```
<?xml version="1.0"?>
<greeting>
```

```
  Hello, World!
</greeting>
```

To be precise, this document is well-formed. XML documents are described as *well-formed* and *valid* (we'll define those terms in a minute). This XML document isn't legal at all:

```
<?xml version="1.0"?>
<greeting>
  Hello, World!
</greeting>
<greeting>
  Hey, Y'all!
</greeting>
```

There are two root elements in this document, so an XML parser refuses to process it. Also, be aware that the XML declaration (the `<?xml version="1.0"?>` part; more on this later) isn't an element at all.

All elements must be nested

If you start one element inside another, you have to end it there, too. An HTML browser is happy to render this document:

```
<b>I really, <i>really</b> like XML.</i>
```

But an XML parser will throw an exception when it sees this document. If you want the same effect, you would need to code this:

```
<b>I really, <i>really</i></b><i> like XML.</i>
```

All attributes must be quoted

You can quote the attributes with either single or double quotes. These two XML tags are equivalent:

```
<a href="http://www.oreilly.com">
<a href='http://www.oreilly.com'>
```

If you need to define an attribute that contains single or double quotes, you can use one style of quote inside the other. If you need both single and double quotes in an attribute, use the predefined entities `&quot;` for double quotes and use `&apos;` for single quotes:

```
<book title="XSLT, Second Edition" publisher="O'Reilly/">
<book title="XSLT, Second Edition" publisher='O&apos;reilly"/>
```

One more note: XML doesn't allow attributes without values. In other words, HTML elements such as `<ol compact>` aren't valid in XML. To code this element in XML, you'd have to give the attribute a value, as in `<ol compact="compact">`. (You have to do things this way in XHTML as well.)

XML tags are case-sensitive

In HTML, `<h1>` and `<H1>` are the same. In XML, they're not. If you try to end an `<h1>` element with `</H1>`, the parser will throw an exception.

All end tags are required

This is another area where most HTML documents break. Your browser doesn't care whether you don't have a `</p>` or `</br>` tag, but your XML parser does.

Empty tags can contain the end marker

In other words, these two XML fragments are identical:

```
<lily age="13"></lily>

<lily age="13"/>
```

Notice that there is nothing, not even whitespace, between the start tag and the end tag in the first example; that's what makes this an empty tag.

XML declarations

Some XML documents begin with an *XML declaration*, which is a line similar to this:

```
<?xml version="1.0" encoding="ISO-8859-1"?>
```

If no `encoding` is specified, the XML parser assumes you're using UTF-8 or UTF-16. UTF, the Unicode Transformation Format, is a Unicode standard that uses different numbers of bytes to represent virtually every character and ideograph from the world's languages. Be aware that each parser supports a different set of encodings, so you need to check your parser's documentation to find out what your options are.

Document Type Definitions (DTDs) and XML Schemas

All of the rules we've discussed so far apply to all XML documents. In addition, you can use DTDs and Schemas to define other constraints for your XML documents. DTDs and Schemas are metalanguages that let you define the characteristics of an XML vocabulary. For example, you might want to specify that any XML document describing a purchase order must begin with a `<po>` element, and the `<po>` element in turn contains a `<customer-id>` element, one or more `<item-ordered>` elements, and an `<order-date>` element. In addition, each `<item-ordered>` element must contain a `part-number` attribute and a `quantity` attribute.

Here's a sample DTD that defines the constraints we just mentioned:

```
<?xml version="1.0" encoding="UTF-8"?>

<!ELEMENT po (customer-id , item-ordered+ , order-date)>

<!ELEMENT customer-id (#PCDATA)>
```

```
<!ELEMENT item-ordered EMPTY>

<!ATTLIST item-ordered   part-number CDATA  #REQUIRED
                         quantity    CDATA  #REQUIRED >
<!ELEMENT order-date EMPTY>

<!ATTLIST order-date  day    CDATA  #REQUIRED
                      month  CDATA  #REQUIRED
                      year   CDATA  #REQUIRED >
```

And here's an XML Schema that defines the same document type:

```
<?xml version="1.0" encoding="UTF-8"?>
<xsd:schema xmlns:xsd="http://www.w3.org/2001/XMLSchema">

  <xsd:element name="po">
    <xsd:complexType>
      <xsd:sequence>
        <xsd:element ref="customer-id"/>
        <xsd:element ref="item-ordered" maxOccurs="unbounded"/>
        <xsd:element ref="order-date"/>
      </xsd:sequence>
    </xsd:complexType>
  </xsd:element>

  <xsd:element name="customer-id" type="xsd:string"/>

  <xsd:element name="item-ordered">
    <xsd:complexType>
      <xsd:attribute name="part-number" use="required">
        <xsd:simpleType>
          <xsd:restriction base="xsd:string">
            <xsd:pattern value="[0-9]{5}(-[0-9]{4})?"/>
          </xsd:restriction>
        </xsd:simpleType>
      </xsd:attribute>
      <xsd:attribute name="quantity" use="required" type="xsd:integer"/>
    </xsd:complexType>
  </xsd:element>

  <xsd:element name="order-date">
    <xsd:complexType>
      <xsd:attribute name="day" use="required">
        <xsd:simpleType>
          <xsd:restriction base="xsd:positiveInteger">
            <xsd:maxInclusive value="31"/>
          </xsd:restriction>
        </xsd:simpleType>
      </xsd:attribute>
      <xsd:attribute name="month" use="required">
        <xsd:simpleType>
          <xsd:restriction base="xsd:positiveInteger">
            <xsd:maxInclusive value="12"/>
          </xsd:restriction>
        </xsd:simpleType>
      </xsd:attribute>
```

```
<xsd:attribute name="year" use="required">
  <xsd:simpleType>
    <xsd:restriction base="xsd:gYear">
      <xsd:maxInclusive value="2100"/>
    </xsd:restriction>
  </xsd:simpleType>
</xsd:attribute>
    </xsd:complexType>
  </xsd:element>
</xsd:schema>
```

Schemas have two significant advantages over DTDs:

They can define datatypes and other complex structures that are difficult or impossible to do in a DTD

In the previous example, we defined various constraints for the data in our XML documents. We defined that the **day** attribute must be an integer between 1 and 31, and the **month** attribute must be an integer between 1 and 12. We also used a regular expression to define a **part-number** attribute as a five-digit number, optionally followed by a dash and a four-digit number. None of those things are possible in a DTD. Schemas are far more powerful than DTDs; see Appendix D for an overview of schemas and what they can do.

Schemas are themselves XML documents

Since they are XML documents, we can write XSLT stylesheets to manipulate them. For example, it would be useful to create a graphical representation of an XML Schema. We could create a hierarchical diagram to indicate which elements could appear inside other element. XML Schema also provides the **<xsd:annotation>** and **<xsd:documentation>** elements. Those elements let us add as much documentation as we want inside the schema itself. We could then use a stylesheet to transform the schema into an HTML document or PDF file, using the relationships between elements, attributes, datatypes, and other information to generate highly structured information.

The best way to define the **<order-date>** attribute would be to use the XML Schema **xsd:date** datatype:

```
<xsd:element name="order-date" type="xsd:date"/>
```

In the DTD, we separated the date into three parts so it could be sorted or formatted in different ways. With the **xsd:date** datatype, the schema ensures that the date is valid; we can use a variety of functions to sort or format the date in different ways. (We'll discuss those functions in "[2.0] Formatting Dates and Times" in Chapter 4.)

Well-formed versus valid documents

Any XML document that follows the rules described here is said to be *well-formed*. In addition, if an XML document references a set of rules that define how the document is structured (either a DTD or an XML Schema), and it follows all those rules, it is said to be a *valid* document.

All valid documents are well-formed; on the other hand, not all well-formed documents are valid.

 Be aware that XML Schema validation can be done partially; XML Schema allows us to define parts of the document that should not be validated at all. On the other hand, DTD validation fails if any part of an XML document doesn't match the DTD.

Tags versus elements

Although many people use the two terms interchangably, a tag is different from an element. A *tag* is the text between (and including) the angle brackets (< and >). There are start tags, end tags, and empty tags. A tag consists of an element name and, if it is a start tag or an empty tag, some optional attributes. (Unlike other markup languages, end tags in XML cannot contain attributes.) An *element* consists of its start and end tags and everything in between. This might include text, other elements, and comments, as well as other things such as entity references and processing instructions.

Namespaces

A final XML topic we'll mention here is *namespaces*. Namespaces are designed to distinguish between two tags that have the same name. For example, if we have an online bookstore, we could design an XML vocabulary for books. When we ship an order to a customer, the postal service requires the customer's address to be in a certain format. It's likely that both vocabularies will define a `<title>` element. Our `<title>` element refers to the title of a book, while the shipping company's `<title>` element refers to the courtesy title of a customer (Mr., Ms., Mrs., etc.). An XML order document refers to both books and customers, so we'll use a namespace to distinguish between the two `<title>` elements. Namespaces are declared as follows:

```
<xyz xmlns:books="http://www.myco.com/books"
     xmlns:addr="http://www.usps.com/addresses">
```

In this example, the `xmlns:books` attribute associates the prefix `books` with one namespace, and the `xmlns:addr` attribute associates the `paintings` prefix with another namespace. This means that a `title` element from the `books` namespace would be coded as `<books:title>`, while a `title` element from the `addr` namespace would be referred to as `<addr:title>`.

I mention namespaces here primarily because all XSLT elements we use in this book are prefixed with the `xsl` namespace prefix. All stylesheets we write begin like this:

```
<?xml version="1.0"?>
<xsl:stylesheet version="1.0"
  xmlns:xsl="http://www.w3.org/1999/XSL/Transform">
```

(Obviously a stylesheet that uses the features of XSLT 2.0 starts with `version="2.0"`.) This opening associates the `xsl` namespace prefix with the string `http://www.w3.org/1999/XSL/Transform`. The value of the namespace prefix doesn't matter; we could start our stylesheets like this:

```
<?xml version="1.0"?>
<pdq:stylesheet version="1.0"
  xmlns:pdq="http://www.w3.org/1999/XSL/Transform">
```

What matters is the string to which the namespace prefix is mapped. Also keep in mind that all XSLT stylesheets use namespace prefixes to process the XML elements they contain. By default, anything that doesn't use the `xsl` namespace prefix is not processed—instead, it's written to the result tree. We'll discuss these topics in more detail as we go through the book.

[2.0] Datatypes

XSLT 2.0 provides support for most of the datatypes defined in XML Schema. XSLT 2.0 also defines new datatypes for durations. For example, we can define an XSLT variable and specify that its datatype is `xs:integer` or `xs:dateTime`. If we're using a schema-aware XSLT 2.0 processor, we can define our own datatypes and use those just like all the datatypes defined by XML Schema and XSLT 2.0. We cover datatypes and schemas in Chapter 3.

Programming Interfaces for XML: DOM, SAX, and Others

The two most popular APIs used to parse XML documents are the *Document Object Model* (DOM) and the *Simple API for XML* (SAX). DOM is an official recommendation of the W3C (available at *http://www.w3.org/TR/REC-DOM-Level-1*), while SAX is a de facto standard created by David Megginson and others on the XML-DEV mailing list (*http://lists.xml.org/archives*). We'll discuss these two APIs briefly here. We won't use them much in this book, but learning more about them will give you some insight into how most XSLT processors work.

 See *http://www.saxproject.org/* for the SAX standard. If you'd like to learn more about the XML-DEV mailing list, send email to *mailto:xml-dev-subscribe@lists.xml.org*. You can also check out *http://lists.xml.org/archives/xml-dev/* to see the XML-DEV mailing list archives.

DOM

DOM is designed to build a tree view of your document. Remember that all XML documents must be contained in a single element. That single element then becomes the root of the tree. The DOM specification defines several language-neutral interfaces, described here:

Node

This interface is the base datatype of the DOM. `Document`, `Element`, `Attr`, `Text`, `Comment`, and `ProcessingInstruction` all extend the `Node` interface.

Document

This object contains the DOM representation of the XML document. Given a `Document` object, you can get the root of the tree (the `Document` element); from the root, you can move through the tree to find all elements, attributes, text, comments, processing instructions, etc. in the XML document.

Element

This interface represents an element in an XML document.

Attr

This interface represents an attribute of an element in an XML document.

Text

This interface represents a piece of text from the XML document. Any text in your XML document becomes a `Text` node. This means that the text of a DOM object is a child of the object, not a property of it. The text of an `Element` is represented as a `Text` child of an `Element` object; the text of an `Attr` is also represented that way.

Comment

This interface represents a comment in the XML document. A comment begins with `<!--` and ends with `-->`. The only restriction on its contents is that two consecutive hyphens (`--`) can appear only at the start or end of the comment. Other than that, a comment can include anything, such as angle brackets (`< >`), ampersands (`&`), and single or double quotation marks (`' "`).

ProcessingInstruction

This interface represents a processing instruction in the XML document. Processing instructions look like this:

```
<?xml-stylesheet href="case-study.xsl" type="text/xsl"?>
```

Processing instructions contain processor-specific information. The PI here (*PI* is XML jargon—feel free to drop this into casual conversations to impress your friends) is the standard way to associate an XSLT stylesheet with an XML document (more on this in a minute).

When you parse an XML document with a DOM parser, it:

- Creates objects (`Elements`, `Attr`, `Text`, `Comments`) representing the contents of the document. These objects implement the interfaces defined in the DOM specification.

- Arranges these objects in a tree. Each `Element` in the XML document has some properties (such as the element's name) and may also have some children.

- Parses the entire document before control returns to your code. This means that for large documents, there is a long delay while the document is parsed.

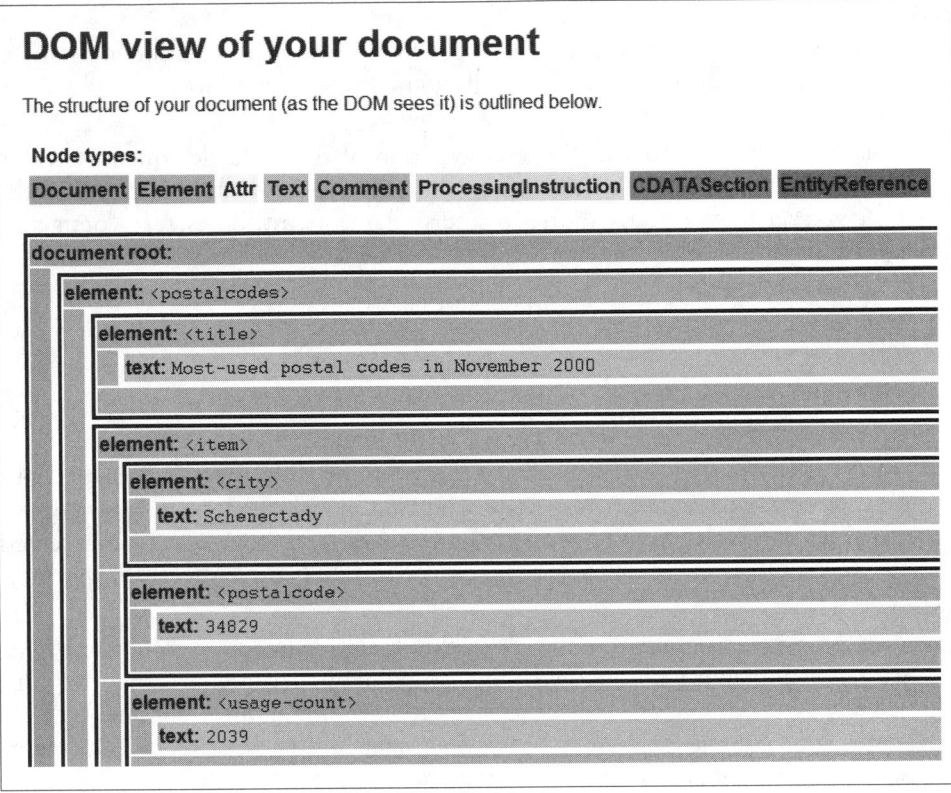

Figure 1-1. DOM tree representation of an XML document

The most significant thing about the DOM is that it is based on a tree view of your document. An XSLT processor uses a very similar tree view (with some slight differences, such as the fact that not everything we deal with in XPath and XSLT has the same root element). Understanding how a DOM parser works makes it easier to understand how an XSLT processor views your document.

A sample DOM tree. DOM, XSLT, and XPath all use tree structures to represent data from an XML document. For this reason, it's important to have at least a casual knowledge of how DOM builds a tree structure. Our earlier `<postalcodes>` document is shown as a DOM tree in Figure 1-1.

If we want to perform tasks such as find different parts of our XML document, sort the subtrees based on the first character of the text of the `<postalcode>` element, or select only the subtrees in which the text of the `<usage-count>` element has a numeric value greater than 500, we have to start at the top of the DOM tree and work our way down through the root element's descendants. When we write XSLT stylesheets, we also start at the root of the tree and work our way down.

 To be honest, the DOM tree built for our document is more complicated than our beautiful picture indicates. The whitespace characters in our document (carriage return/line feed, tabs, spaces, etc.) become Text nodes. Normally it's a good idea to remove this whitespace so the DOM tree won't be littered with these useless nodes, but I include them here to give you a sense of the XML document's structure.

SAX

The Simple API for XML was developed by David Megginson and others on the XML-DEV mailing list. It has several important differences from DOM:

- The SAX API is interactive. As a SAX parser processes your document, it sends events to your code. You don't have to wait for the parser to finish the entire document as you do with the DOM; you get events from the parser immediately. These events let you know when the parser finds the start of the document, the start of an element, some text, the end of an element, a processing instruction, the end of the document, etc.

- SAX is designed to avoid the large memory footprint of DOM. In the SAX world, you're told when the parser finds things in the XML document; it's up to you to save those things. If you don't do anything to store the data found by the parser, it goes into the bit bucket.

- SAX doesn't provide the hierarchical view of the document that DOM does. If you need to know a lot about the structure of an XML document and the context of a given element, SAX isn't much help. Each SAX event is stateless; that is, a SAX event won't tell you, "Here's some text for the `<postalcode>` element I mentioned earlier." A SAX parser only tells you, "Here's some text." If you need to know about an XML document's structure, you have to keep track of that information yourself.

The best thing about SAX is that it is interactive. Most of the transformations currently done with XSLT take place on the server. As of this writing, most XSLT processors are based on DOM parsers. In the near future, however, we'll see XSLT processors based on SAX parsers. This means that the processor can start generating results almost as soon as the parse of the source document begins, resulting in better throughput and creating the perception of faster service. Because DOM, XPath, and XSLT all use trees to represent XML documents, DOM is more relevant to our discussions here. Nevertheless, it's useful to know how SAX parsers work, especially as SAX-based XSLT processors begin to rear their speedy little heads.

Other programming interfaces

There are a number of other XML programming interfaces, including JDOM, DOM4J, and StAX. These have two important characteristics:

In-memory versus event-driven

In-memory interfaces, such as DOM, create data structures that represent the XML document. Event-driven interfaces, such as SAX, receive data from the parser as it parses the document.

Push versus pull

A push interface pushes data from the parser to the application. When the parser has some data, it uses a callback interface to push that data to the application. SAX is an example of a push interface. On the other hand, a pull interface is still event-driven, but the application tells the parser when it wants the next event. StAX, the Streaming API for XML, is an example of a pull interface. (StAX is also known as JSR 173.)

There are two other approaches we'll mention briefly. In *data binding*, an XML document is transformed into an object. The contents of the original XML document are represented as the properties of that object. Finally, a new parsing technique called *non-extractive XML processing* creates Virtual Token Descriptors that contain the offset, length, and other information of XML tokens inside the XML file itself.

The Wikipedia entry *http://en.wikipedia.org/wiki/XML#Processing_XML_files* has more detail on these approaches as well as links to various tools that implement them.

XSLT Standards

XSLT 1.0 is defined in two documents: the XSLT and XPath specifications. XSLT 2.0 and XPath 2.0, on the other hand, are defined in a set of eight documents. We'll discuss all of those specifications briefly in the next section.

XSL transformations (XSLT) version 1.0

The original standard became a recommendation of the W3C on November 16, 1999. The spec lives here: *http://www.w3.org/TR/xslt*.

XML path language (XPath) version 1.0

XPath 1.0 became a standard on the same day as XSLT 1.0. XPath began as part of XSLT. If we're going to write a stylesheet to transform an XML document, we have to have a syntax for describing different parts of that document. As the development of XSLT continued, it became obvious that XPath was useful for a variety of applications, so XPath became a separate standard. You can find the definition of XPath 1.0 at *http://www.w3.org/TR/xpath*.

XSL transformations (XSLT) version 2.0

The basic definition of XSLT 2.0 is at *http://www.w3.org/TR/xslt20/*. This document defines the elements of XSLT 2.0 and a variety of functions and also defines how XSLT 2.0 processes an XML document.

XML path language (XPath) version 2.0

The basic definition of XPath 2.0 is at *http://www.w3.org/TR/xpath20/*. XPath 2.0 is built on top of several other documents; we'll list those next.

XQuery 1.0 and XPath 2.0 Data Model (XDM)

This spec defines the way XPath 2.0, XSLT 2.0, and XQuery 1.0 organize data. It defines the information contained in the input to an XSLT 2.0 or XQuery 1.0 processor. It also defines all of the legal values for expressions in XPath 2.0, XSLT 2.0, and XQuery 1.0. You can find the spec at *http://www.w3.org/TR/xpath-datamodel/*.

XQuery 1.0 and XPath 2.0 functions and operators

This spec, also known as F&O, defines all of the functions and data operators available in XPath 2.0 and XQuery 1.0. For example, the spec defines how an `xs:yearMonthDuration` can be divided by an `xs:double` value. It also defines the `matches()` function, which determines if a value matches a regular expression. The spec is available at *http://www.w3.org/TR/xpath-functions/*.

XQuery 1.0 and XPath 2.0 formal semantics

The formal semantics spec defines a precise meaning to all of the legal expressions in XPath 2.0 and XQuery 1.0. The XQuery 1.0 and XPath 2.0 Data Model is used in those precise definitions. Possibly the least useful spec to XSLT programmers, it's available at *http://www.w3.org/TR/xquery-semantics/*.

XSLT 2.0 and XQuery 1.0 serialization

The serialization spec defines how to take an instance of the XQuery 1.0/XPath 2.0 Data Model and serialize it. For the examples in this book, we'll usually take the results generated by our XSLT stylesheet and write them to a file; the serialization spec defines how that process works. The spec is available at *http://www.w3.org/TR/xslt-xquery-serialization/*.

XQuery 1.0: an XML query language

XQuery 1.0 is a separate language that is based on XPath and other query languages. It is a superset of XPath 2.0. We won't cover XQuery in any detail in this book, but be aware that the data model, the functions, and the operators of XPath 2.0 are shared by XQuery. See *http://www.w3.org/TR/xquery/* for the complete details.

XML syntax for XQuery 1.0 (XQueryX)

One of the requirements of the XQuery working group was to provide an XML syntax for the language. XQueryX provides that syntax. It maps the XQuery grammar into XML tags. As such, it is not particularly easy or convenient for humans, but it can be very useful for various tools and utilities. The spec is available at *http://www.w3.org/ TR/xqueryx*.

XML Standards

When we talk about writing stylesheets, we'll work with two standards: XSLT and XPath. XSLT defines a set of primitives used to describe a document transformation, while XPath defines a syntax for describing locations in XML documents. When we write stylesheets, we'll use XSLT to tell the processor what to do, and we'll use XPath to tell the processor what document to do it to. Both standards are available at the W3C's web site; see *http://www.w3.org/TR/xslt* and *http://www.w3.org/TR/xpath* for more information.

There are other XML-related standards, of course. We'll discuss them here briefly, with a short mention of how (or whether) they relate to our work with XSLT and XPath.

XML 1.0

The foundation upon which everything else is built. See *http://www.w3.org/TR/REC-xml*.

XML 1.1

You can find the XML 1.1 standard at *http://www.w3.org/TR/xml11/*.

The Extensible Stylesheet Language (XSL)

Also called the *Formatting Objects specification* or *XSL-FO*, this standard deals with rendering XML elements. Although most people think of rendering as formatting for a browser or a printed page, researchers use the specification to render XML elements as Braille or as audio files. (That being said, the main market for this technology is in producing high-quality printed output.) As of this writing, the latest version of XSL is 1.1. A couple of the examples in this book use formatting objects and the Apache XML Project's Formatting Object to PDF translator (FOP) tool; see *http://xml.apache.org/ fop* for more information on FOP. For more information on XSL, see *http:// www.w3.org/TR/xsl*.

XML Schemas

In our earlier examples, we had a brief example of an XML Schema. Part 1 of the specification deals with XML document structures; it contains XML elements that define what can appear in an XML document. You use these elements to specify which elements can be nested inside others, how many times each element can appear, the attributes of those elements, and other features. Part 2 of the specification defines basic datatypes used in XML Schemas and rules for deriving new datatypes from existing ones.

The two specifications are available at *http://www.w3.org/TR/xmlschema-1* and *http://www.w3.org/TR/xmlschema-2*. For a good introduction to XML Schemas, see the XML Schema Primer, available at *http://www.w3.org/TR/xmlschema-0*.

RelaxNG

RelaxNG is a simple schema language designed as an alternative to XML Schema. One significant difference between the two is that RelaxNG avoids the many datatype definitions of XML Schema. With RelaxNG, you validate an XML document with datatype definitions imported from elsewhere (including XML Schema, for example). The home page of the OASIS RelaxNG committee is here: *http://www.oasis-open.org/committees/relax-ng/*. You can find the latest version of the spec as well as a tutorial there.

Schematron

Schematron is an elegant way to validate documents. It has a simple syntax (only six elements) and uses XPath to specify patterns in XML documents. The most interesting and most widely used implementation of Schematron is written in XSLT. For more information, including a link to the latest version of the ISO standard for Schematron, visit *http://www.schematron.com/*.

The Simple API for XML (SAX)

The SAX API defines the events and interfaces used to interact with a SAX parser. SAX and DOM are the most common APIs used to work with XML documents. See *http://www.saxproject.org/* for the complete specification.

Document Object Model (DOM)

The DOM, as we discussed earlier, is a programming API for documents. It defines a set of interfaces and methods used to view an XML document as a tree structure. XSLT and XPath use a similar tree view of XML documents. The home of the DOM is *http://www.w3.org/DOM/*. This page contains links to all of the W3C Recommendations (Levels 1, 2, and 3) and related documents. The DOM doesn't affect what we'll do here, but it's useful to have a passing knowledge of it. (The XPath data model is similar to the DOM.)

Namespaces in XML

As we mentioned earlier, namespaces provide a way to avoid name collisions when two XML elements have the same name. See *http://www.w3.org/TR/REC-xml-names/* for the version 1.0 spec; version 1.1 is at *http://www.w3.org/TR/REC-xml-names11/*.

Associating stylesheets with XML documents

It's possible to reference an XSLT stylesheet within an XML document. This specification uses processing instructions to define one or more stylesheets that should be used to transform an XML document. You can define different stylesheets to be used for different browsers. See *http://www.w3.org/TR/xml-stylesheet* for complete information. Here's the start of an XML document, with two associated stylesheets:

```
<?xml version="1.0"?>
<?xml-stylesheet href="docbook/html/docbook.xsl" type="text/xsl"?>
<?xml-stylesheet href="docbook/wap/docbook.xsl"  type="text/xsl" media="wap"?>
```

In this example, the first stylesheet is the default because it doesn't have a `media` attribute. The second stylesheet will be used when the `User-Agent` field from the HTTP header contains the string `wap`, identifying the requester of a document as a WAP browser. The advantage of this technique is that you can define several different stylesheets within a particular document and have each stylesheet generate useful results for different browser or client types. The disadvantage of this technique is that we're effectively putting rendering instructions into our XML document, something we prefer to avoid.

Scalable Vector Graphics (SVG)

The SVG specification defines an XML vocabulary for vector graphics. Described by some as "PostScript with angle brackets," it allows you to define images that can be scaled to any size or resolution. See *http://www.w3.org/TR/SVG/* for details.

XML pointer language (XPointer) version 1.0

XPointer provides a way to identify a fragment of a web resource. It uses XPath to identify fragments. The XPointer Framework is defined at *http://www.w3.org/TR/xptr-framework/*.

XML linking language (XLink) version 1.0

XLink defines an XML vocabulary for linking to other web resources within an XML document. It supports the unidirectional links we're all familiar with in HTML, as well as more sophisticated links. See *http://www.w3.org/TR/xlink/*.

Installing XSLT Processors

Before we dive in to creating stylesheets, we'll cover how to install four popular XSLT processors.

Installing Xalan

In this section, we'll go over how to install the Xalan XSLT processor. In the next chapter, we'll create our first stylesheet and use it to transform an XML document.

The installation process is pretty simple, assuming you already have a Java Runtime Environment (JRE) installed on your machine. Although very little of the code we look at in this book uses Java, the Xalan XSLT processor itself is written in Java. Once you've installed the JRE, go to *http://xml.apache.org/xalan-j/* and download the latest stable build of the code. (If you're feeling brave, feel free to download last night's build instead.)

Once the Xalan *.zip* or *.gzip* file is downloaded, unpack it and add three files to your CLASSPATH. The three files include two *.jar* files for the Xerces parser, and the *.jar* file for the Xalan stylesheet engine itself. As of this writing, the *.jar* files are named *xalan.jar*, *xercesImpl.jar*, and *xml-apis.jar*. (There's a fourth file, *bsf.jar*, that includes the Bean Scripting Framework, but we'll use that for extensions only.)

To make sure Xalan is installed correctly, go to a command prompt and type the following command:

```
java org.apache.xalan.xslt.Process
```

This is a Java class, so everything is case-sensitive. You should see an error message like this:

```
java org.apache.xalan.xslt.Process
=xslproc options:
   -IN inputXMLURL
  [-XSL XSLTransformationURL]
  [-OUT outputURL]
  [-LXCIN compiledStylesheetFileNameIn]
  [-LXCOUT compiledStylesheetFileNameOutOut]
...
```

If you get this message, you're all set! You're ready for the next chapter, in which we'll build our very first XSLT stylesheet.

Installing Saxon

As of this writing, the most complete open source XSLT 2.0 stylesheet processor is Saxon. Written by Michael Kay, the editor of the XSLT 2.0 spec, it is available at *http://saxon.sourceforge.net*. When you download the file (currently *saxonb9-0-0-2j.zip*), add *saxon9.jar* to your CLASSPATH. There are also nine other files, *saxon9-ant.jar*, *saxon9-dom.jar*, *saxon9-dom4j.jar*, *saxon9-jdom.jar*, *saxon9-s9api.jar*, *saxon9-sql.jar*, *saxon9-xom.jar*, *saxon9-xpath.jar*, and *saxon9-xqj.jar*. These *.jar* files enable additional functions; see the Saxon documentation for more information about them. For most of what we'll do in this book, *saxon9.jar* is all you'll need.

Once you've installed Saxon and updated your classpath, go to a command prompt and type the following command:

```
java net.sf.saxon.Transform
```

You should get a message like this:

```
No source file name
Saxon 9.0.0.3J from Saxonica
Usage: see http://www.saxonica.com/documentation/using-xsl/commandline.html
```

```
Options:
  -a                        Use xml-stylesheet PI, not style-doc argument
  -c:filename               Use compiled stylesheet from file
  -cr:classname             Use collection URI resolver class
  -dtd:on|off               Validate using DTD
  -expand:on|off            Expand defaults defined in schema/DTD
  -explain[:filename]       Display compiled expression tree
  -ext:on|off               Allow|Disallow external Java functions
  -im:modename              Initial mode
  -it:template              Initial template
  -l:on|off                 Line numbering for source document
  -m:classname              Use message receiver class
  -o:filename               Output file or directory
  -or:classname             Use OutputURIResolver class
  -outval:recover|fatal     Handling of validation errors on result document
  -p:on|off                 Recognize URI query parameters
  -r:classname              Use URIResolver class
  -repeat:N                 Repeat N times for performance measurement
  -s:filename               Initial source document
  -sa                       Schema-aware transformation
  ...
```

The error message will list dozens of options. Most of the time we'll simply specify the source XML file and the XSLT stylesheet.

Saxon is also available in a closed source version, Saxon-SA, that provides complete support for the XML Schema functions defined in XSLT 2.0, XPath 2.0, and XQuery 1.0. All of the examples in this book that use schema-aware functions were tested with the closed source, commercial version of Saxon.

To install the schema-aware version of Saxon, you need to add *saxon9sa.jar* to your CLASSPATH. When you purchase Saxon-SA, you'll get a *saxon-license.lic* file; put that file into the *Saxon/bin* directory and add that directory to your system PATH. The command to run the schema-aware version of Saxon is slightly different:

```
java com.saxonica.Transform
```

The version number will be different, but everything else should be the same:

```
No source file name
Saxon-SA 9.0.0.3J from Saxonica
Usage: see http://www.saxonica.com/documentation/using-xsl/commandline.html
Options:
  -a                        Use xml-stylesheet PI, not style-doc argument
  ...
```

Installing the Microsoft XSLT Processor

The most commonly used XSLT processor in the .NET world is the Microsoft XSLT processor. The best way to find the tools is to visit *http://msdn.microsoft.com/xml*. As of this writing (2008), the file you want to download is *msxsl.exe*. Put this on your system path, then go to a command prompt and type the following command:

```
msxsl
```

You'll see a message like this:

```
Microsoft (R) XSLT Processor Version 4.0

Usage: MSXSL source stylesheet [options] [param=value...] [xmlns:prefix=uri...]

Options:
    -?            Show this message
    -o filename   Write output to named file
    -m startMode  Start the transform in this mode
    -xw           Strip non-significant whitespace from source and stylesheet
...
```

In Chapter 9, we'll look at C# code that uses the XSLT processor built into the .NET framework. If we're just transforming XML documents from the command line, *msxsl.exe* is all we'll need.

Installing the Altova XSLT Engine

As of this writing (early 2008), the only zero-cost XSLT 2.0 processor that provides schema support is the Altova XSLT engine. This is the XSLT processor at the heart of Altova's XMLSpy product. It is currently a Windows-only download available under a royalty-free license at *http://www.altova.com/altovaxml*.

To install the engine, download the software (currently a setup file named *altovaxml2008.exe*) and run it. At a command prompt, type the following command:

altovaxml

You'll see a message like this:

```
AltovaXML Version 2008 sp1
Copyright (c) 1998-2007 Altova GmbH. All rights reserved.
Use of this software is subject to the license agreement at
http://www.altova.com/altovaxmldla.html


Use the xslt1 engine:
    /xslt1 <filename> /in <filename> [/param name=value] [/out <filename>]
Use the xslt2 engine:
    /xslt2 <filename> /in <filename> [/param name=value] [/out <filename>]
Use the xquery engine:
    /xquery <filename> [/in <filename>] [/param name=value] [/out <filename>]
                       [serialization options]
Use the validator:
    /validate <filename> [/schema <filename> | /dtd <filename>]
    /wellformed <filename>

Parameters:
    /validate, /v <filename>    Schema validates the specified XML file
    /wellformed, /w <filename>  Check if specified XML file is well-formed
    /xslt1 <filename>           Sets the source for XSLT1 stylesheet
    /xslt2 <filename>           Sets the source for XSLT2 stylesheet
    /xquery, /xq <filename>     Sets the source for XQuery expression
```

```
/in <filename>            Sets the source for XML data
/out <filename>           Sets the output file name
                          If omitted, data is written to stdout
/param <name>=<value>     Adds external paramter
```

Summary

In this chapter, we've gone over the basics of XML and talked about DOM and SAX, two standards that are commonly used by XSLT processors. We also talked about other technology standards and how to install several stylesheet processors. At this point, you've got everything you need to build and use your first stylesheets, which we'll do in the next chapter.

The Obligatory Hello World Example

In future chapters, we'll spend a lot of time talking about XSLT, XPath, and various advanced functions used to transform XML documents. First, though, we'll go through a short example to illustrate how stylesheets work.

Goals of This Chapter

By the end of this chapter, you should know:

- How to create a basic stylesheet
- How to use a stylesheet to transform an XML document
- How a stylesheet processor uses a stylesheet to transform an XML document
- The structure of an XSLT stylesheet

Transforming Hello World

Continuing the tradition of Hello World examples begun by Brian Kernighan and Dennis Ritchie in *The C Programming Language* (Prentice Hall, 1988), we'll transform a Hello World XML document.

Our Sample Document

First, we'll look at our sample document. This simple XML document, courtesy of the XML 1.0 specification, contains the famous friendly greeting to the world:

```
<?xml version="1.0"?>
<!-- greeting.xml -->
<greeting>
  Hello, World!
</greeting>
```

What we'd like to do is transform this fascinating document into something we can view in an ordinary household browser.

A Sample Stylesheet

Here's an XSLT stylesheet that defines how to transform the XML document:

```
<?xml version="1.0"?>
<!-- greeting.xsl -->
<xsl:stylesheet version="1.0"
  xmlns:xsl="http://www.w3.org/1999/XSL/Transform">

  <xsl:output method="html"/>

  <xsl:template match="/">
    <xsl:apply-templates select="greeting"/>
  </xsl:template>

  <xsl:template match="greeting">
    <html>
      <body>
        <h1>
          <xsl:value-of select="."/>
        </h1>
      </body>
    </html>
  </xsl:template>
</xsl:stylesheet>
```

We'll talk about these elements and what they do in just a minute. Keep in mind that the stylesheet is itself an XML document, so we have to follow all of the document rules we discussed in the previous chapter.

Transforming the XML Document

To transform the XML document using the XSLT stylesheet, run this command if you're using Xalan:

```
java org.apache.xalan.xslt.Process -in greeting.xml -xsl greeting.xsl
  -out greeting.html
```

For Saxon, the command looks like this:

```
java net.sf.saxon.Transform -o greeting.html greeting.xml greeting.xsl
```

If you're using the Schema-aware version of Saxon, the name of the Java class is different:

```
java com.saxon.Transform -o greeting.html greeting.xml greeting.xsl
```

The command for the Altova XSLT engine is:

```
altovaxml /xslt1 greeting.xsl /in greeting.xml /out greeting.html
```

Finally, if you're using Microsoft's MSXSL, type this command:

```
msxsl greeting.xml greeting.xsl -o greeting.html
```

Figure 2-1. HTML version of our Hello World file

This command transforms the document *greeting.xml*, using the templates found in the stylesheet *greeting.xsl*. The results of the transformation are written to the file *greeting.html*. Check the output file in your favorite browser to make sure the transformation worked correctly.

 This is one of the few times in this book we'll cover the syntax of the command to run a transformation. The exception to this rule will be when you need to do something more advanced (pass parameters to a stylesheet, for example). Typically, all you need to know are the filenames of the XML, XSL, and output files, and the format of the command for your stylesheet processor.

Stylesheet Results

The XSLT processor generates these results:

```
<html>
<body>
<h1>
  Hello, World!
</h1>
</body>
</html>
```

When rendered in a browser, our output document looks like Figure 2-1.

Congratulations! You've now used XSLT to transform an XML document.

How a Stylesheet Is Processed

Now that we're giddy with the excitement of having transformed an XML document, let's discuss the stylesheet and how it works. A big part of the XSLT learning curve is figuring out how stylesheets are processed. To make this clear, we'll go through the steps taken by the stylesheet processor to create the HTML document we want.

Parsing the Stylesheet

Before the XSLT processor can process your stylesheet, it has to read it. Conceptually, it doesn't matter how the XSLT processor stores the information from your stylesheet.

For our purposes, we'll just assume that the XSLT processor can magically find anything it needs in our stylesheet. (If you really must know, Xalan uses an optimized table structure to represent the stylesheet; other processors may use that approach or something else.)

Our stylesheet contains three items: an `<xsl:output>` element that specifies HTML as the output format, and two `<xsl:template>` elements that specify how parts of our XML document should be transformed.

Parsing the Transformee

Now that the XSLT processor has processed the stylesheet, it needs to read the document it's supposed to transform. The XSLT processor builds a tree view from the XML source. This tree view is what we'll keep in mind when we build our stylesheets.

Lather, Rinse, Repeat

Finally, we're ready to begin the actual work of transforming the XML document. The XSLT processor may set some properties based on your stylesheet (in the previous example, it would set its output method to HTML), then it begins processing as follows:

1. Do I have any nodes to process? The nodes to process are represented by the *context*. Initially, the context is the root of the XML document, but it changes throughout the stylesheet. We'll talk about the context extensively in the next chapter. (Note: all XSLT processors enjoy being anthropomorphized, so I'll often refer to them this way.)

While any nodes are in the context, do the following:

2. Get the next node from the context. Do I have any `<xsl:template>`s that match it? (In our example, the next node is the root node, represented in XPath syntax by /.) There is a template that matches this node—it's the one that begins `<xsl:template match="/">`.

3. If one or more `<xsl:template>`s match, pick the right one and process it. The right one is the most specific template. For example, `<xsl:template match="/html/body/h1/p">` is more specific than `<xsl:template match="p">`. (See the discussion of `<xsl:template>` in Appendix A for more information.) If no `<xsl:template>`s match, the XSLT processor uses some built-in rules. See the section "Built-in Template Rules" later in this chapter for more information.

Notice that this is a recursive processing model. We process the current node by finding the right `xsl:template` for it. That `xsl:template` may in turn invoke other `xsl:templates`, which invoke `xsl:templates` as well. This model takes some getting used to, but it is actually quite elegant once you're accustomed to it.

 If it helps, you can think of the root template (`<xsl:template match="/">`) as the `main` method in a C, C++, or Java program. No matter how much code you've written, everything starts in `main`. Similarly, no matter how many `<xsl:template>`s you've defined in your stylesheet, everything starts in `<xsl:template match="/">`.

Walking Through Our Example

Let's revisit our example and see how the XSLT processor transforms our document:

1. The XSLT stylesheet is parsed and converted into a tree structure.

2. The XML document is also parsed and converted into a tree structure. Don't worry too much about what that tree looks like or how it works; for now, just assume that the XSLT processor knows everything that's in the XML document and the XSLT stylesheet. After the first two steps are done, when we describe various things using XSLT and XPath, the processor knows what we're talking about.

3. The XSLT processor is now at the root of the XML document. This is the original context.

4. There is an `xsl:template` that matches the document root:

   ```
   <xsl:template match="/">
     <xsl:apply-templates select="greeting"/>
   </xsl:template>
   ```

   A single forward slash (/) is an *XSLT pattern* (written in *XPath*) that matches "document nodes."

5. Now the process begins again inside the `xsl:template`. Our only instruction here is to apply whatever `xsl:template`s might apply to any `greeting` elements in the current context. The current context inside this template is defined by the `match` attribute of the `xsl:template` element. This means the XSLT processor is looking for any `greeting` elements at the document root.

   Because one `greeting` element is at the document root, the XSLT processor must deal with it. (If more than one element matches in the current context, the XSLT processor deals with each one in the order in which they appear in the document; this is known as *document order*.) Looking at the `greeting` element, the `xsl:template` that applies to it is the second `xsl:template` in our stylesheet:

   ```
   <xsl:template match="greeting">
     <html>
       <body>
         <h1>
           <xsl:value-of select="."/>
         </h1>
       </body>
     </html>
   </xsl:template>
   ```

6. Now we're in the `xsl:template` for the `greeting` element. The first three elements in this `xsl:template` (`<html>`, `<body>`, and `<h1>`) are HTML elements. Because they're not defined with a namespace declaration, the XSLT processor passes those HTML elements through to the output stream unaltered.

   The middle of our `xsl:template` is an `xsl:value-of` element. This element writes the value of something to the output stream. In this case, we're using the XPath expression . (a single period) to indicate the current node. The XSLT processor looks at the current node (the `greeting` element we're currently processing) and outputs its text.

   Because our stylesheet is an XML document (we're really harping on that, aren't we?), we have to end the `<h1>`, `<body>`, and `<html>` elements here. At this point, we're done with this template, so control returns to the template that invoked us.

7. Now we're back in the template for the root element. We've processed all the `<greeting>` elements, so we're finished with this template.

8. No more elements are in the current context (there is only one root element), so the XSLT processor is done.

Stylesheet Structure

As the final part of our introduction to XSLT, we'll look at the contents of the stylesheet itself. We'll explain all the things in our stylesheet and discuss other approaches we could have taken.

The <xsl:stylesheet> Element

The `<xsl:stylesheet>` element is typically the root element of an XSLT stylesheet:

```
<xsl:stylesheet version="1.0"
  xmlns:xsl="http://www.w3.org/1999/XSL/Transform">
```

First of all, the `<xsl:stylesheet>` element defines the version of XSLT we're using, along with a definition of the `xsl` namespace. To be compliant with the XSLT specification, your stylesheet should always begin with this element, coded exactly as shown here. Some stylesheet processors, notably Xalan, issue a warning message if your `<xsl:stylesheet>` element doesn't have these two attributes with these two values. For all examples in this book, we'll start the stylesheet with this exact element, defining other namespaces as needed.

The <xsl:output> Element

Next, we specify the output method. The XSLT specification defines three output methods: `xml`, `html`, and `text`. We're creating an HTML document, so HTML is the output method we want to use. In addition to these three methods, an XSLT processor is free to define its own output methods, so check your XSLT processor's documentation to see if you have any other options:[*]

```
<xsl:output method="html"/>
```

A variety of attributes are used with the different output methods. For example, if you're using `method="xml"`, you can use `doctype-public` and `doctype-system` to define the public and system identifiers to be used in the the document type declaration. If you're using `method="xml"` or `method="html"`, you can use the `indent` attribute to control whether or not the output document is indented. The discussion of the `<xsl:output>` element in Appendix A has all the details.

Our First <xsl:template>

Our first template matches "/", the XPath expression for the document's root element:

```
<xsl:template match="/">
  <xsl:apply-templates select="greeting"/>
</xsl:template>
```

The <xsl:template> for <greeting> Elements

The second `<xsl:template>` element processes any `<greeting>` elements in our XML source document:

```
<xsl:template match="greeting">
  <html>
    <body>
      <h1>
        <xsl:value-of select="."/>
      </h1>
    </body>
  </html>
</xsl:template>
```

Built-in Template Rules

Although most stylesheets we'll develop in this book explicitly define how various XML elements should be transformed, XSLT defines several built-in template rules that apply in the absence of any specific rules. These rules have a lower priority than any other templates, so they're always overridden when you define your own templates. The built-in templates are listed here.

---

[*] *[2.0]* XSLT 2.0 also defines the `xhtml` output method.

Built-in template rule for element and document nodes

This template processes the document node and any of its children. This processing ensures that recursive processing will continue, even if no template is declared for a given element:

```
<xsl:template match="*|/">
  <xsl:apply-templates/>
</xsl:template>
```

As an example, given this document:

```
<?xml version="1.0"?>
<x>
  <y>
    <z/>
  </y>
</z>
```

The built-in template rule for element and document nodes means that we could write a stylesheet containing only a template with `match="z"` and the `<z>` element will still be processed, even if there are no template rules for the `<x>` and `<y>` elements.

Built-in template rule for modes

This template ensures that element and document nodes are processed, regardless of any mode that might be in effect. (See "Templates à la mode" in Chapter 5 for more information on the `mode` attribute.)

```
<xsl:template match="*|/" mode="x">
  <xsl:apply-templates mode="x"/>
</xsl:template>
```

Built-in template rule for text and attribute nodes

This template copies the text of all text and attribute nodes to the output tree. Be aware that you have to actually select the text and attribute nodes for this rule to be invoked:

```
<xsl:template match="text()|@*">
  <xsl:value-of select="."/>
</xsl:template>
```

Built-in template rule for comment and processing instruction nodes

This template does nothing:

```
<xsl:template match="comment()|processing-instruction()"/>
```

Built-in template rule for namespace nodes

This template also does nothing:

```
<xsl:template match="namespace()"/>
```

Top-Level Elements

To this point, we haven't actually talked about our source document or how we're going to transform it. We're simply setting up some properties for the transform. There are other elements we can put at the start of our stylesheet. Any element whose parent is the `<xsl:stylesheet>` element is called a *top-level element.* Here is a brief discussion of the other top-level elements:

`<xsl:include>` *and* `<xsl:import>`

> These elements refer to another stylesheet. The other stylesheet and all of its contents are included in the current stylesheet. The main difference between `<xsl:import>` and `<xsl:include>` is that a template, variable, or anything else imported with `<xsl:import>` has a lower priority than the things in the current stylesheet. This gives you a mechanism to subclass stylesheets, if you want to think about this from an object-oriented point of view. You can import another stylesheet that contains common templates, but any templates in the *importing* stylesheet will be used instead of any templates in the imported stylesheet. Another difference is that `<xsl:import>` can only appear at the beginning of a stylesheet, while `<xsl:include>` can appear anywhere.

`<xsl:strip-space>` *and* `<xsl:preserve-space>`

> These elements contain a space-separated list of elements from which whitespace should be removed or preserved in the output. To define these elements globally, use `<xsl:strip-space elements="*"/>` or `<xsl:preserve-space elements="*"/>`. If we want to specify that whitespace be removed for all elements except for `<greeting>` and `<salutation>` elements, we would add this markup to our stylesheet:
>
> ```
> <xsl:strip-space elements="*"/>
> <xsl:preserve-space elements="greeting
>             salutation"/>
> ```

`<xsl:key>`

> This element defines a key, which is similar to defining an index on a database. We'll talk more about the `<xsl:key>` element and the key( ) function in "Branching Elements of XSLT" in Chapter 5.

`<xsl:variable>`

> This element defines a variable. Any `<xsl:variable>` that appears as a top-level element is global to the entire stylesheet. Variables are discussed extensively in "Variables" in Chapter 5.

`<xsl:param>`

> This element defines a parameter. As with `<xsl:variable>`, any `<xsl:param>` that is a top-level element is global to the entire stylesheet. Parameters are discussed extensively in "Parameters" in Chapter 5.

Other stuff

More obscure elements that can appear as top-level elements are `<xsl:decimal-format>`, `<xsl:namespace-alias>`, and `<xsl:attribute-set>`. All are discussed in Appendix A.

Other Approaches

One mantra of the Perl community is, "There's more than one way to do it." That's true with XSLT stylesheets as well. We could have written our stylesheet like this:

```
<?xml version="1.0"?>
<!-- greeting2.xsl -->
<xsl:stylesheet version="1.0"
  xmlns:xsl="http://www.w3.org/1999/XSL/Transform">

  <xsl:output method="html"/>

  <xsl:template match="/">
    <html>
      <body>
        <xsl:apply-templates select="greeting"/>
      </body>
    </html>
  </xsl:template>

  <xsl:template match="greeting">
    <h1>
      <xsl:value-of select="."/>
    </h1>
  </xsl:template>
</xsl:stylesheet>
```

In this version, we put the wrapper elements for the HTML document in the template for the root element. One of the things you should think about as you build your stylesheets is where to put elements such as `<html>` and `<body>`. Let's say our XML document looked like this instead:

```
<?xml version="1.0"?>
<greetings>
  <greeting>Hello, World!</greeting>
  <greeting>Hey, Y'all!</greeting>
</greetings>
```

In this case, we would have to put the `<html>` and `<body>` elements in the `<xsl:template>` for the root element. If they were in the `<xsl:template>` for the `<greeting>` element, the output document would have multiple `<html>` elements, which isn't valid in an HTML document. Our updated stylesheet would look like this:

```
<?xml version="1.0"?>
<!-- multiple-greetings.xsl -->
<xsl:stylesheet version="1.0"
  xmlns:xsl="http://www.w3.org/1999/XSL/Transform">
```

```
<xsl:output method="html"/>

<xsl:template match="/">
  <html>
    <body>
      <xsl:apply-templates select="greetings/greeting"/>
    </body>
  </html>
</xsl:template>

<xsl:template match="greeting">
  <h1>
    <xsl:value-of select="."/>
  </h1>
</xsl:template>
</xsl:stylesheet>
```

Notice that we had to modify our XPath expression; what was originally `greeting` is now `greetings/greeting`. As we develop stylesheets, we'll have to make sure our XPath expressions match the document structure. When you get unexpected results, or no results, an incorrect XPath expression is usually the cause.

As a final example, we could also write our stylesheet with only one `xsl:template`:

```
<?xml version="1.0"?>
<!-- greeting3.xsl -->
<xsl:stylesheet version="1.0"
  xmlns:xsl="http://www.w3.org/1999/XSL/Transform">

  <xsl:output method="html"/>

  <xsl:template match="/">
    <html>
      <body>
        <h1>
          <xsl:value-of select="greeting"/>
        </h1>
      </body>
    </html>
  </xsl:template>
</xsl:stylesheet>
```

Although this is the shortest of our sample stylesheets, our examples will tend to feature a number of short templates, each of which defines a simple transform for a few elements. This approach makes your stylesheets much easier to understand, maintain, and reuse. The more transformations you cram into each `xsl:template`, the more difficult it is to debug your stylesheets, and the more difficult it is to reuse the templates elsewhere.

Sample Gallery

Before we get into more advanced topics, we'll transform our Hello World document in other ways. We'll look through simple stylesheets that convert our small XML document into the following things:

- A Scalable Vector Graphics (SVG) file
- A PDF file
- A Java program
- A Virtual Reality Modeling Language (VRML) file

The Hello World SVG File

Our first example will convert our Hello World document into an SVG file:

```
<?xml version="1.0"?>
<!-- svg-greeting.xsl -->
<xsl:stylesheet version="1.0"
  xmlns:xsl="http://www.w3.org/1999/XSL/Transform"
  xmlns:svg="http://www.w3.org/2000/svg">

  <xsl:template match="/">
    <svg:svg width="10cm" height="4cm">
      <svg:g>
        <svg:defs>
          <svg:radialGradient id="MyGradient"
            cx="4cm" cy="2cm" r="3cm" fx="4cm" fy="2cm">
            <svg:stop offset="0%" style="stop-color:red"/>
            <svg:stop offset="50%" style="stop-color:blue"/>
            <svg:stop offset="100%" style="stop-color:red"/>
          </svg:radialGradient>
        </svg:defs>
        <svg:rect style="fill:url(#MyGradient); stroke:black"
          x="1cm" y="1cm" width="8cm" height="2cm"/>
        <svg:text x="5.05cm" y="2.25cm" text-anchor="middle"
          style="font-family:Verdana; font-size:24;
          font-weight:bold; fill:black">
          <xsl:apply-templates select="greeting"/>
        </svg:text>
        <svg:text x="5cm" y="2.2cm" text-anchor="middle"
          style="font-family:Verdana; font-size:24;
          font-weight:bold; fill:white">
          <xsl:apply-templates select="greeting"/>
        </svg:text>
      </svg:g>
    </svg:svg>
  </xsl:template>
```

Figure 2-2. SVG version of our Hello World file

```
<xsl:template match="greeting">
  <xsl:value-of select="."/>
</xsl:template>

</xsl:stylesheet>
```

As you can see from this stylesheet, most of the code here simply sets up the structure of the SVG document. This is typical of many stylesheets; once you learn what the output format should be, you merely extract content from the XML source document and insert it into the output document at the correct spot. When we transform the Hello World document with this stylesheet, here are the results:

```
<?xml version="1.0" encoding="UTF-8"?>
<svg:svg xmlns:svg="http://www.w3.org/2000/svg" width="10cm" height="4cm">
  <svg:g>
    <svg:defs>
      <svg:radialGradient id="MyGradient" cx="4cm" cy="2cm" r="3cm"
          fx="4cm" fy="2cm">
        <svg:stop offset="0%" style="stop-color:red"/>
        <svg:stop offset="50%" style="stop-color:blue"/>
        <svg:stop offset="100%" style="stop-color:red"/>
      </svg:radialGradient>
    </svg:defs>
    <svg:rect style="fill:url(#MyGradient); stroke:black" x="1cm"
      y="1cm" width="8cm" height="2cm"/>
    <svg:text x="5.05cm" y="2.25cm" text-anchor="middle"
      style="font-family:Verdana; font-size:24; font-weight:bold; fill:black">
      Hello, World!
    </svg:text>
    <svg:text x="5cm" y="2.2cm" text-anchor="middle"
      style="font-family:Verdana; font-size:24; font-weight:bold; fill:white">
      Hello, World!
    </svg:text>
  </svg:g>
</svg:svg>
```

When rendered in an SVG viewer, our Hello World document looks like Figure 2-2.

This screen capture was made using the Adobe SVG plug-in inside the Internet Explorer browser. You can find the plug-in at *http://www.adobe.com/svg/*. (Note that many browsers now support SVG natively.)

The Hello World PDF File

To convert the Hello World file into a PDF file, we'll first convert our XML file into formatting objects. The Extensible Stylesheet Language for Formatting Objects (XSL-FO) is an XML vocabulary that describes how content should be rendered. Here is our stylesheet:

```
<?xml version="1.0"?>
<!-- fo-greeting.xsl -->
<xsl:stylesheet version="1.0"
  xmlns:xsl="http://www.w3.org/1999/XSL/Transform"
  xmlns:fo="http://www.w3.org/1999/XSL/Format">

  <xsl:output method="xml"/>

  <xsl:template match="/">
    <fo:root xmlns:fo="http://www.w3.org/1999/XSL/Format">
      <fo:layout-master-set>
        <fo:simple-page-master master-name="standard"
          margin-right="75pt" margin-left="75pt"
          page-height="11in" page-width="8.5in"
          margin-bottom="25pt" margin-top="25pt">
          <fo:region-body margin-top="50pt" margin-bottom="50pt"/>
        </fo:simple-page-master>
      </fo:layout-master-set>

      <fo:page-sequence master-reference="standard">
        <fo:flow flow-name="xsl-region-body">
          <xsl:apply-templates select="greeting"/>
        </fo:flow>
      </fo:page-sequence>
    </fo:root>
  </xsl:template>

  <xsl:template match="greeting">
    <fo:block line-height="76pt" font-size="72pt" text-align="center">
      <xsl:value-of select="."/>
    </fo:block>
  </xsl:template>

</xsl:stylesheet>
```

This stylesheet converts our Hello World document into the following XML file:

```
<?xml version="1.0" encoding="UTF-8"?>
<fo:root xmlns:fo="http://www.w3.org/1999/XSL/Format">
  <fo:layout-master-set>
    <fo:simple-page-master master-name="standard" margin-right="75pt"
      margin-left="75pt" page-height="11in" page-width="8.5in"
      margin-bottom="25pt" margin-top="25pt">
```

Figure 2-3. PDF version of our Hello World file

```
      <fo:region-body margin-top="50pt" margin-bottom="50pt"/>
    </fo:simple-page-master>
  </fo:layout-master-set>
  <fo:page-sequence master-reference="standard">
    <fo:flow flow-name="xsl-region-body">
      <fo:block line-height="76pt" font-size="72pt" text-align="center">
        Hello, World!
      </fo:block>
    </fo:flow>
  </fo:page-sequence>
</fo:root>
```

This lengthy set of tags uses formatting objects to describe the size of the page, the margins, font sizes, line heights, etc., along with the text extracted from our XML source document. Now that we have the formatting objects, we can use the Apache XML Project's FOP tool. After converting the formatting objects to PDF, the PDF file looks like Figure 2-3.

Here's the command used to convert our file of formatting objects into a PDF file:

```
java org.apache.fop.apps.Fop greeting.fo greeting.pdf
```

The Hello World Java Program

Our last two transformations don't involve XML vocabularies at all; they use XSLT to convert the Hello World document into other formats. Next, we'll transform our XML source document into the source code for a Java program. When the program is compiled and executed, it prints the message from the XML document to the console. Here's our stylesheet:

```
<?xml version="1.0"?>
<!-- java-greeting.xsl -->
<xsl:stylesheet version="1.0"
  xmlns:xsl="http://www.w3.org/1999/XSL/Transform">
```

```
    <xsl:output method="text" encoding="UTF-8"/>

    <xsl:template match="/">
        <xsl:text>
public class Greeting
{
    public static void main(String[] argv)
    {
        </xsl:text>
        <xsl:apply-templates select="greeting"/>
        <xsl:text>
    }
}
        </xsl:text>
    </xsl:template>

    <xsl:template match="greeting">
        <xsl:text>System.out.println("</xsl:text>
        <xsl:value-of select="normalize-space()"/>
        <xsl:text>");</xsl:text>
    </xsl:template>

</xsl:stylesheet>
```

(Notice that we used `<xsl:output method="text">` to generate text, not markup.) Our stylesheet produces these results:

```
public class Greeting
{
    public static void main(String[] argv)
    {
        System.out.println("Hello, World!");
    }
}
```

The class name defined in the XSLT stylesheet (`Greeting`) must be the name of the generated file. That means we have to specify the case-sensitive filename when we run the transformation. Here's how to do that with Xalan:

```
java org.apache.xalan.xslt.Process -in greeting.xml -xsl java-greeting.xsl
    -out Greeting.java
```

For Saxon, the syntax is slightly simpler:

```
java net.sf.saxon.Transform -o Greeting.java greeting.xml java-greeting.xsl
```

Again, the Schema-aware version of Saxon is slightly different:

```
java.com.saxonica.Transform -o Greeting.java greeting.xml java-greeting.xsl
```

Finally, for MSXSL and the Altova XSLT engine, the commands are:

```
msxsl -o Greeting.java greeting.xml java-greeting.xsl
```

and:

```
altovaxml /xslt1 java-greeting.xsl /in greeting.xml /out Greeting.java
```

When executed, our generated Java program looks like this:

```
C:\> java Greeting
Hello, World!
```

Although generating Java code from an XML document may seem strange, it is actually a very useful technique. The FOP tool from the Apache XML Project does this; it defines a number of properties in XML, then generates the Java source code to create class definitions and get and set methods for each of those properties.

The Hello World VRML File

For our final transformation, we'll create a VRML file from our XML source document. Here's the stylesheet that does the trick:

```
<?xml version="1.0"?>
<!-- vrml-greeting.xsl -->
<xsl:stylesheet version="1.0"
  xmlns:xsl="http://www.w3.org/1999/XSL/Transform">

  <xsl:output method="text"/>

  <xsl:template match="/">
    <xsl:text>#VRML V2.0 utf8

Shape
{
  geometry ElevationGrid
  {
    xDimension 9
    zDimension 9
    xSpacing 1
    zSpacing 1
    height
    [
      0 0 0 0 0 0 0 0 0
      0 0 0 0 0 0 0 0 0
      0 0 0 0 0 0 0 0 0
      0 0 0 0 0 0 0 0 0
      0 0 0 0 0 0 0 0 0
      0 0 0 0 0 0 0 0 0
      0 0 0 0 0 0 0 0 0
      0 0 0 0 0 0 0 0 0
      0 0 0 0 0 0 0 0 0
    ]
    colorPerVertex FALSE
    color Color
    {
      color
      [
        0 0 0, 1 1 1, 0 0 0, 1 1 1, 0 0 0, 1 1 1, 0 0 0, 1 1 1,
        1 1 1, 0 0 0, 1 1 1, 0 0 0, 1 1 1, 0 0 0, 1 1 1, 0 0 0,
        0 0 0, 1 1 1, 0 0 0, 1 1 1, 0 0 0, 1 1 1, 0 0 0, 1 1 1,
        1 1 1, 0 0 0, 1 1 1, 0 0 0, 1 1 1, 0 0 0, 1 1 1, 0 0 0,
```

```
          0 0 0, 1 1 1, 0 0 0, 1 1 1, 0 0 0, 1 1 1, 0 0 0, 1 1 1,
          1 1 1, 0 0 0, 1 1 1, 0 0 0, 1 1 1, 0 0 0, 1 1 1, 0 0 0,
          0 0 0, 1 1 1, 0 0 0, 1 1 1, 0 0 0, 1 1 1, 0 0 0, 1 1 1,
          1 1 1, 0 0 0, 1 1 1, 0 0 0, 1 1 1, 0 0 0, 1 1 1, 0 0 0,
        ]
      }
    }
  }

Transform
{
  translation 4.5 1 4
  children
  [
    Shape
    {
      geometry Text
      {
</xsl:text>
<xsl:apply-templates select="greeting"/>
<xsl:text>
        fontStyle FontStyle
        {
          justify "MIDDLE"
          style "BOLD"
        }
      }
    }
  ]
}


NavigationInfo
{
  type ["EXAMINE","ANY"]
}

Viewpoint
{
  position 4 1 10
}
    </xsl:text>
  </xsl:template>

  <xsl:template match="greeting">
    <xsl:text>string"</xsl:text>
    <xsl:value-of select="normalize-space()"/>
    <xsl:text>"</xsl:text>
  </xsl:template>

</xsl:stylesheet>
```

As with our earlier stylesheet, our VRML-generating template is mostly boilerplate, with content from the XML source document added at the appropriate point. The <xsl:apply-templates> element is replaced with the value of the <greeting> element.

Figure 2-4. One view of the VRML version of our Hello World document

Figure 2-5. Another view of the VRML version of our Hello World document

The VRML code here draws a checkerboard, then draws the text from the XML document above it, floating in midair in the center of the document. A couple of views of the VRML version of our XML document are shown in Figures 2-4 and 2-5.

The screenshots of the VRML world were generated with the Cortona VRML player. You can download the player at *http://www.parallelgraphics.com/cortona*.

Although we haven't discussed any of the specific vocabularies or file formats we've used here, hopefully you understand that you can transform your XML documents into any useful format you can think of. Through the rest of the book, we'll cover several common tasks you can solve with XSLT, all of which build on the basics we've discussed here.

Summary

Although our stylesheets here are trivial, they are much simpler than the corresponding procedural code (written in Visual Basic, C++, Java, etc.) to transform any `<greeting>` elements similarly. We've gone over the basics of what stylesheets are and how they work.

As we go through this book, we'll demonstrate the incredible range of things you can do in XSLT stylesheets, including:

- Using logic, branching, and control statements
- Sorting and grouping elements
- Linking and cross-referencing elements
- Creating master documents that embed other XML documents, then sort, filter, group, and format the combined documents.
- Adding new functions to the XSLT stylesheet processor with XSLT's extension mechanism

XSLT has an extremely active user community. To see just how active, visit the XSL-List site at *http://www.mulberrytech.com/xsl/xsl-list/index.html*.

Before we dive in to those topics, we need to talk about XPath, the syntax that describes what parts of an XML document we want to transform into all of these different things.

XPath: A Syntax for Describing Needles and Haystacks

XPath is a syntax used to describe parts of an XML document. With XPath, you can refer to the first `<para>` element, the `quantity` attribute of the `<part-number>` element, all `<first-name>` elements that contain the text `"Joe"`, and many other variations. In a stylesheet, the XSLT patterns in the `match` and `select` attributes of various elements use XPath syntax to indicate how a document should be transformed. In this chapter, we'll discuss XPath in all its glory.

XPath is designed to be used inside an attribute in an XML document. The syntax is a mix of basic programming language expressions (such as `$x*6`) and Unix-like path expressions (such as `/sonnet/author/last-name`). In addition to the basic syntax, XPath provides a set of useful functions that allow you to find out various things about the document.

One important point, though: XPath works with the parsed version of your XML document. That means that some details of the original document aren't accessible to you from XPath. For example, entity references are resolved by the XSLT processor before instructions in our stylesheet are evaluated. CDATA sections are converted to text as well. That means we have no way of knowing whether a text node in an XPath tree was in the original XML document as text, as an entity reference, or as part of a CDATA section. As you get used to thinking about your XML documents in terms of XPath expressions, this situation won't be a problem, but it may confuse you at first.

[2.0] XPath has undergone enormous changes for version 2.0. Everything that worked in XPath 1.0 still works in XPath 2.0, but there are new capabilities and operators that can greatly simplify your life if you're using an XSLT 2.0 processor. There are three major XPath 2.0 topics that we'll discuss separately in this chapter:

- In XPath 2.0's view of the world, everything is a *sequence*. A sequence replaces the concept of node-sets used in XPath 1.0. The main difference is that a sequence can contain atomic values (more on those in a minute). Be aware that nodes in the sequence (a document node, for example) can still have children. When we're working with parts of a document, it's common that our sequence is an element node with children and attributes; that one item sequence works just like the trees you know and love from XPath 1.0.

- XPath 2.0 supports *atomic values*. In XPath 1.0, everything from the parsed XML document was a node, including comments, text, and processing instructions. The type system was relatively simple; there were strings, numbers, booleans, node-sets, and something called a result tree fragment. In XPath 2.0, a sequence can contain nodes from an XML document alongside things such as the `xs:integer` value `42` or the `xs:date` value can be part of a sequence along with the nodes used in XPath 1.0. Atomic values are defined in the XML Schema spec; an atomic value is a value that can't be broken down into smaller parts. A value of type `xs:integer` or `xs:date`, for example, is an atomic value.

- XPath 2.0 supports all of the built-in datatypes of XML Schema. This means we can specify that a value must be of a particular datatype, we can create a new value of a particular datatype, and we can cast a given value to a particular datatype. If your XSLT 2.0 processor is schema-aware (more on that shortly), you can define your own datatypes and use them inside XPath along with the XML Schema datatypes. If your XSLT 2.0 processor is not schema-aware, it still supports a number of datatypes from XML Schema.

With those three exceptions, we'll discuss the changes in XPath 2.0 as we cover XPath in general.

The XPath Data Model

XPath 1.0 views an XML document as a tree of nodes. This tree is very similar to a Document Object Model (DOM) tree, so if you're familiar with the DOM, you should have some understanding of how to build basic XPath expressions. (To be precise, this is a conceptual tree; an XSLT processor or anything else that implements the XPath standard doesn't have to build an actual tree.)

[2.0] XPath 2.0 views everything as a sequence. A sequence can contain all of the nodes we cover here as well as atomic values. Whenever we're working with parsed data from an XML document, the sequences we're using are most likely nodes from the document tree, so we won't have to worry about atomic values. For now, just be aware that the underlying data model in XPath 2.0 is different; we'll cover those differences in great detail later in this chapter.

Node Types

There are seven kinds of nodes in XPath:

- The document node (one per document)
- Element nodes

- Attribute nodes
- Text nodes
- Comment nodes
- Processing instruction nodes
- Namespace nodes

We'll talk about all the different node types in terms of the following document:

```
<?xml version="1.0"?>
<?xml-stylesheet href="sonnet.xsl" type="text/xsl"?>

<!DOCTYPE sonnet [
  <!ELEMENT sonnet (auth:author, title, lines)>
  <!ATTLIST sonnet public-domain CDATA "yes"
            type (Shakespearean | Petrarchan) "Shakespearean">
  <!ELEMENT auth:author  (last-name,first-name,nationality,
                          year-of-birth?,year-of-death?)>
  <!ELEMENT last-name (#PCDATA)>
  <!ELEMENT first-name (#PCDATA)>
  <!ELEMENT nationality (#PCDATA)>
  <!ELEMENT year-of-birth (#PCDATA)>
  <!ELEMENT year-of-death (#PCDATA)>
  <!ELEMENT title (#PCDATA)>
  <!ELEMENT lines (line,line,line,line,
                   line,line,line,line,
                   line,line,line,line,
                   line,line)>
  <!ELEMENT line (#PCDATA)>
]>

<!-- Default sonnet type is Shakespearean, the other allowable  -->
<!-- type is "Petrarchan."                                      -->
<sonnet type='Shakespearean'>
  <auth:author xmlns:auth="http://www.authors.com/">
    <last-name>Shakespeare</last-name>
    <first-name>William</first-name>
    <nationality>British</nationality>
    <year-of-birth>1564</year-of-birth>
    <year-of-death>1616</year-of-death>
  </auth:author>
  <!-- Is there an official title for this sonnet?  They're
       sometimes named after the first line.                   -->
  <title>Sonnet 130</title>
  <lines>
    <line>My mistress' eyes are nothing like the sun,</line>
    <line>Coral is far more red than her lips red.</line>
    <line>If snow be white, why then her breasts are dun,</line>
    <line>If hairs be wires, black wires grow on her head.</line>
    <line>I have seen roses damasked, red and white,</line>
    <line>But no such roses see I in her cheeks.</line>
    <line>And in some perfumes is there more delight</line>
    <line>Than in the breath that from my mistress reeks.</line>
    <line>I love to hear her speak, yet well I know</line>
```

```
    <line>That music hath a far more pleasing sound.</line>
    <line>I grant I never saw a goddess go,</line>
    <line>My mistress when she walks, treads on the ground.</line>
    <line>And yet, by Heaven, I think my love as rare</line>
    <line>As any she belied with false compare.</line>
  </lines>
</sonnet>
<!-- The title of Sting's 1987 album "Nothing like the sun" is  -->
<!-- from line 1 of this sonnet.                                 -->
```

The root node

The root node is the XPath node that contains the entire document. In our example, the root node contains the `<sonnet>` element; it's not the `<sonnet>` element itself. In an XPath expression, the root node is specified with a single slash (/).

Unlike other nodes, the root node has no parent. It always has at least one child: the document element. The root node also contains comments or processing instructions that are outside the document element. In our sample, the two processing instructions named `xml-stylesheet` and `cocoon-process` are both children of the root node, as are the comments that appear before the `<sonnet>` tag and the comments that appear after it. The string value of the root node (returned by `<xsl:value-of select="/" />`), is the concatenation of all text nodes of the root node's descendants, slammed together without any spaces between them.

Element nodes

Every element in the original XML document is represented by an XPath element node. In the previous document, an element node exists for the `<sonnet>` element, the `<auth:author>` element, the `<last-name>` element, and so on. An element node's children include text nodes, element nodes, comment nodes, and processing instruction nodes that occur within that element in the original document.

An element node's string value (returned by `<xsl:value-of select="sonnet">`, for example) is the concatenation of the text of this node and all of its children, in document order (the order in which they appear in the original document). All entity references (such as `&lt;`) and character references (such as `&#xDF;`, the lowercase "sharp S" character) in the text are resolved automatically. To XPath, those characters show up as < and ß; you can't access the entity or character references from XPath.

The name of an element node (returned by the XPath `name( )` function) is the element name and any namespace in effect. In the previous example, the `name( )` of the `<sonnet>` element is `sonnet`. The `name( )` of the `<auth:author>` element is `auth:author`. Given the name of the node, XPath has functions to return the local name of the element (`author`) and the URI of the namespace associated with the node (`http://www.authors.com`). XPath 2.0 has additional functions to work with qualified names (XML Schema `xs:QName` values) directly, including functions to extract a namespace prefix and the URI associated with it.

Attribute nodes

At a minimum, an element node is the parent of one attribute node for each attribute in the XML source document. In our sample document, the element node corresponding to the `<sonnet>` element is the parent of an attribute node with a name of `type` and a value of `Shakespearean`. A couple of complications for attribute nodes exist, however:

- Although an element node is the parent of its attribute nodes, those attribute nodes are not children of their parent. The children of an element are the text, element, comment, and processing instruction nodes contained in the original element. If you want a document's attributes, you must ask for them specifically. That relationship seems odd at first, but you'll find that treating an element's attributes separately is usually what you want to do.

- If a DTD or schema defines default values for certain attributes, those attributes don't have to appear in the XML document. In our example, we declared an attribute named `public-domain` that has a default value of `yes`. The actual `<sonnet>` element doesn't have this attribute, so the value of its `public-domain` attribute is `yes`. Similarly, the default value for `type` is `Shakespearean`, so a `<sonnet>` element without a `type` attribute uses the default value.

  To make this situation even worse, an XML parser isn't required to read an external DTD. If it doesn't, then any attribute nodes that represent default values not coded in the document won't exist. Fortunately, XSLT has some branching elements (`<xsl:if>` and `<xsl:choose>`) that can help you deal with these ambiguities; we'll discuss those in Chapter 5.

- The XML 1.0 specification defines two attributes (`xml:lang` and `xml:space`) that work differently. In other words, if the `<auth:author>` element in our sample document contains the attribute `xml:lang="en-US"`, that attribute applies to all elements contained inside `<auth:author>`. Even though that attribute might apply to the `<last-name>` element, `<last-name>` won't have an attribute node named `xml:lang`. Similarly, the `xml:space` defines whether whitespace in an element should be preserved; valid values for this attribute are `preserve` and `default`. Whether these attributes are in effect for a given element or not, the only attribute nodes an element node contains are those tagged in the document and those defined with a default value in the DTD.

  We'll discuss handling whitespace in "Dealing with Whitespace" in Chapter 4. For detailed technical information on language codes and whitespace handling, see the discussions of the XPath `lang()` function in Appendix C and also the XSLT `<xsl:preserve-space>` and `<xsl:strip-space>` elements in Appendix A.

Text nodes

Text nodes are refreshingly simple; they contain text from an element. If the original text in the XML document contained entity or character references, they are resolved before the XPath text node is created. The text node is text, pure and simple. A text node is required to contain as much text as possible; the next or previous node can't be a text node.

You might have noticed that there are no CDATA nodes in this list. If your XML document contains text in a CDATA section, you can access the contents of the CDATA section as a text node. You have no way of knowing if a given text node was originally a CDATA section. Similarly, all entity references are resolved before anything in your stylesheet is evaluated, so you have no way of knowing if a given piece of text originally contained entity references.

Comment nodes

A comment node is also very simple—it has value but no name. Every comment in the source document (except for comments in the DTD) becomes a comment node. The value of the comment node is everything inside the comment—everything between the opening `<!--` and the closing `-->`.

Processing instruction nodes

A processing instruction node has two parts: a name (returned by the `name( )` function) and a string value. The string value is everything after the name, including whitespace, but not including the `?>` that closes the processing instruction.

Namespace nodes

Namespace nodes are almost never used in XSLT stylesheets; they exist primarily for the XSLT processor's benefit. Remember that the declaration of a namespace (such as `xmlns:auth="http://www.authors.net"`), even though it looks like an attribute in the XML source, becomes a namespace node, not an attribute node. Every element in the scope of a namespace declaration has a namespace node. In our sonnet, for example, every node in the `<auth:author>` node has a namespace node.

[2.0] In XPath 2.0, support for namespace nodes is optional.

Node Tests

XPath also has *node tests*. A node test looks like a function, but is used to match certain types of nodes. A node test works like a predicate in that it returns only nodes that meet certain criteria. XPath 1.0 has four node tests:

`node( )`
> Matches all nodes. The test `node( )` is true for every kind of node.

`text( )`
> Matches text nodes only.

`comment( )`
> Matches comment nodes.

`processing-instruction( )`

Matches processing instruction nodes. If this node test includes a string, it matches processing instruction nodes with that name. For example, `processing-instruction('cocoon-process')` matches processing instruction nodes that begin with `<?cocoon-process>`.

`*`

Matches all the nodes along a particular axis (we'll cover axes shortly). For example, `child::*` matches all the element children of a node, whereas `attribute::*` matches all the attributes of a node.

`NCName:*`

Matches all the nodes in a particular namespace. In our sonnet, `auth:*` matches any element that has the namespace URI `http://www.authors.com/`.

[2.0] New node tests in XPath 2.0

XPath 2.0 uses all of the node tests from XPath 1.0. It also defines several new node tests:

`element( )`

Matches any element. Using this node test without arguments is similar to `select="*"` in XPath 1.0. The difference is that in XPath 2.0, we can use the `element( )` node test to check the name and datatype of an item. For example, `element(author)` matches any elements named `<author>`. The two-argument version of this node test allows us to find elements that match a particular datatype. The node test `element(date-of-birth, xs:gYear)` matches all `<date-of-birth>` elements whose datatype is `xs:gYear`. (That includes datatypes derived from `xs:gYear`.) Finally, we can use a wildcard for the element name to find all of the elements of a particular datatype. `element(*, xs:gYear)` matches all elements with a datatype of `xs:gYear`.

`schema-element(author)`

Matches any element named `<author>` whose datatype matches the datatype of the `<author>` element declared in a schema. Unlike all the other node tests defined in XPath 1.0 and 2.0, it is an error to use this node test without an argument.

`attribute( )`

Matches any attribute. Using this node test without arguments is similar to `select="@*"` in XPath 1.0. As with `element( )`, we can use `attribute( )` to check the name and datatype of an item. The node test `attribute(public-domain)` matches any attributes named `public-domain`, regardless of the datatype. `attribute(public-domain, xs:string)` matches only attributes named `public-domain` with a datatype of `xs:string`. Finally, using a wildcard for the *attribute* name returns all the attributes that match a particular datatype. For example, `attribute(*, xs:decimal)` matches all attributes whose datatype is `xs:decimal`, regardless of the name of the attribute.

`*:NCName`

> Matches all the nodes with a particular local name. In our sonnet, `*:author` matches the `<auth:author>` element; it would also match the elements `<xyz:author>` and `<author>`. The match occurs regardless of the namespace URI *or* whether an element has a namespace URI at all.

`document-node( )`

> Matches document nodes. The node test `document-node(element(sonnet))` matches a document node with a single element child (`<sonnet>`). The document node can also contain comments or processing instructions, but it can only contain a single element node.

 *[2.0]* Although `item( )` looks like a node test, it is used only as a datatype. For example, the variable `<xsl:variable name="something" as="item( )">` defines a variable that can contain a single value. The variable can contain any node or atomic type.

[2.0] Sequences and Atomic Values

Working with the XPath 2.0 data model is probably the biggest change in XSLT 2.0. We'll mention the changes to the model as we go along, but we'll discuss three topics outright: sequences, atomic values, and schema support. We'll look at sequences and atomic values now and discuss schema support later in this chapter.

A *sequence* is, well, a sequence of items. Those items might be nodes from an XML document, or they might be simple values such as `'June'` or `3.14`. A sequence has an order and a length. You can use XPath 2.0 functions to see how many items are in a sequence, you can retrieve a subset of the items in the sequence, and you can insert or delete items at a particular point in the sequence. Here is a variable that contains a sequence:

```
<!-- sequences1.xsl -->
...
<xsl:variable name="months" as="xs:string*"
  select="('January', 'February', 'March', 'April',
           'May', 'June', 'July', 'August',
           'September', 'October', 'November',
           'December')"/>
```

There are several things to point out here. First of all, notice that we used the new `as` attribute to define the datatype of this variable. The asterisk here means that the variable can have any number of values. If we defined this variable with the datatype `xs:string`, the variable `$months` could only be a single `xs:string`. The code here would cause a fatal error.

The values in the sequence are all atomic values. An atomic value is a simple value, as opposed to a node. A sequence can contain atomic values, as in our example here; it can also use XPath to select nodes from an XML document. Here's an example that creates a sequence with atomic values and information from an XML document:

```
<!-- sequences2.xsl -->
<xsl:stylesheet version="2.0"
  xmlns:xs="http://www.w3.org/2001/XMLSchema"
  xmlns:xsl="http://www.w3.org/1999/XSL/Transform">

  <xsl:output method="text"/>

  <xsl:template match="/">
    <xsl:variable name="cities" as="xs:string*">
      <xsl:sequence select="addressbook/address/city"/>
      <xsl:sequence select="('London', 'Adelaide', 'Rome')"/>
      <xsl:sequence select="('Jakarta', 'Sao Paulo', 'Timbuktu')"/>
    </xsl:variable>
    <xsl:text>Our customers live in these cities:&#xA;&#xA;</xsl:text>
    <xsl:value-of select="$cities" separator="&#xA;"/>
  </xsl:template>

</xsl:stylesheet>
```

Notice that the variable here contains an `<xsl:sequence>` element to select the `<city>` elements, followed by two `<xsl:sequence>` elements that select three strings each. The value of the sequence `$cities` has 12 items when used with the following document:

```
<!-- names.xml -->
<addressbook>

  <address>
    <name>
      <title>Mr.</title>
      <first-name>Chester Hasbrouck</first-name>
      <last-name>Frisby</last-name>
    </name>
    <street>1234 Main Street</street>
    <city>Sheboygan</city>
    <state>WI</state>
    <zip>48392</zip>
  </address>
...
    <city>Skunk Haven</city>
...
    <city>Winter Harbor</city>
...
    <city>Skunk Haven</city>
...
    <city>Boylston</city>
...
    <city>Lynn</city>
    <state>MA</state>
    <zip>02930</zip>
  </address>
</addressbook>
```

The output from the stylesheet looks like this:

```
Our customers live in these cities:

Sheboygan
Skunk Haven
Winter Harbor
Skunk Haven
Boylston
Lynn
London
Adelaide
Rome
Jakarta
Sao Paulo
Timbuktu
```

The sequence has 12 items: 6 items from the `<city>` elements in the XML document, and 6 values from the `<xsl:sequence>` elements that contain strings. The sequence has a datatype of `xs:string*`, which means *all of the items in the sequence are converted to* `xs:string` *values.* Even though we used the pattern `/addressbook/address/city` to select the nodes, the contents of the sequence are strings. If we change the datatype of the sequence to `item( )*`, things work differently:

```
<!-- sequences3.xsl -->
...
    <xsl:variable name="cities" as="item()*">
      <xsl:sequence select="addressbook/address/city"/>
      <xsl:sequence select="('London', 'Adelaide', 'Rome')"/>
      <xsl:sequence select="('Jakarta', 'Sao Paulo', 'Timbuktu')"/>
    </xsl:variable>
    <xsl:for-each select="$cities">
      <xsl:choose>
        <xsl:when test=". instance of element()">
          <xsl:text>        Node: </xsl:text>
        </xsl:when>
        <xsl:otherwise>
          <xsl:text>Atomic value: </xsl:text>
        </xsl:otherwise>
      </xsl:choose>
      <xsl:value-of select="."/>
      <xsl:text>&#xA;</xsl:text>
    </xsl:for-each>
...
```

This stylesheet now contains 12 items, 6 of which are element nodes, 6 of which are strings. Instead of simply writing the value of each item in the sequence, we use the new `instance of` operator to see whether an item is an element or an atomic value. The results look like this:

```
Our customers live in these cities:

        Node: Sheboygan
        Node: Skunk Haven
        Node: Winter Harbor
```

```
            Node: Skunk Haven
            Node: Boylston
            Node: Lynn
   Atomic value: London
   Atomic value: Adelaide
   Atomic value: Rome
   Atomic value: Jakarta
   Atomic value: Sao Paulo
   Atomic value: Timbuktu
<xsl:variable name="cities" as="xs:string*">
  <xsl:sequence
    select="(/addressbook/address/city,
            ('London', 'Adelaide', 'Rome'),
            ('Jakarta', 'Sao Paulo', 'Timbuktu'))"/>
</xsl:variable>
```

Location Paths

One of the most common uses of XPath is to create *location paths*. A location path describes the location of something in an XML document. The pattern `/addressbook/address/city` describes the location of the elements we want to select. We'll use location paths as patterns to find parts of the XML document, then we'll use XPath expressions to manipulate them. But before we dive in to the wonders of location paths, we need to discuss the *context*.

The Context

One of the most important concepts in XPath is the context. Everything we do in XPath is interpreted with respect to the context. You can think of an XML document as a hierarchy of directories in a filesystem. In our sonnet example, we could imagine that `sonnet` is a directory at the root level of the filesystem. The `sonnet` directory would, in turn, contain directories named `auth:author`, `title`, and `lines`. In this example, the context would be the current directory. If I go to a command line and execute a particular command (such as `dir *.xsl`), the results I get vary depending on the current directory. Similarly, the results of evaluating an XPath expression will probably vary based on the context.

[1.0] The XPath 1.0 context

Most of the time, we can think of the context as the node in the tree from which any expression is evaluated. To be completely accurate, the context consists of five things:

- The *context node* (the "current directory"). The XPath expression is evaluated from this node.

- Two integers, the *context position* and the *context size*. These integers are important when we're processing a group of nodes. For example, we could write an XPath expression that selects all of the `<li>` elements in a given document. The context size refers to the number of `<li>` items selected by that expression, and the context position refers to the position of the `<li>` we're currently processing.

- A set of *variables*. This set includes names and values of all variables that are currently in scope.

- A set of all the *functions* available to XPath expressions. Some of these functions are defined by the XPath and XSLT standards themselves; others might be extension functions defined by whomever created the stylesheet. (You'll read more about extension functions in Chapter 9.)

- A set of all the *namespace declarations* currently in scope.

Having said all that, most of the time you can ignore everything but the context node. To use our command-line analogy one more time, if you're at a command line, you have a current directory; you also have (depending on your operating system) a number of environment variables defined. For most commands, you can focus on the current directory and ignore the environment variables.

[2.0] The XPath 2.0 context

As you would expect, the context in XPath 2.0 is more complicated. With support for XML Schema, dates, times, collations, and functions, there are many more things XPath 2.0 has to track.

The specs talk about two things: the *static context* and the *dynamic context*. The static context is the information that's available before an expression is evaluated. That information doesn't change during the evaluation of the expression. The base URI, the default collation, and the variables, namespaces, and schemas in scope are all part of the static context. The context item, the context position, and the context size are all part of the dynamic context. Most of the time we'll be concerned with the dynamic context, but we can access all of the parts of the context whenever we need them.

The static context contains:

- Whether the processor is in *XPath 1.0 compatibility mode*. This is `true` or `false`.

- The set of *statically known namespaces*. Each item in the set is a prefix and a namespace URI.

- The *default namespace for elements and types*. This is either a namespace URI or "none."

- The *default namespace for functions*. This is either a namespace URI or "none."

- The set of *in-scope schema definitions*. These include the schema types, elements, and attributes that are currently in scope.

- The set of *variables* that are in scope.

- The *static type of the context item*.

- The *function signatures* that are currently in scope. These include the namespace and arity (number of parameters) of each function, along with the static types of its parameters and results. Constructor functions are included in this set.

- The *statically known collations*. The format of collations is implementation-defined.

- The *default collation*.

- The *base URI*.

- A set of *statically known documents*. This refers to the documents available through the doc( ) function. See "[2.0] The doc() and doc-available() Functions" in Chapter 8 for more details on the doc( ) function.

- A set of *statically known collections*. See the description of the [2.0] collection( ) function in Appendix C for more information about collections.

- The *statically known default collection type*. The default collection type is node( )* unless an XSLT processor has set it to some other value. Again, see the description of the [2.0] collection( ) function in Appendix C for more information about collections.

The dynamic context contains everything in the static context, plus:

- The *context item*. This is similar to the context node in XPath 1.0, with the difference that the context item can be an atomic value. In XPath 1.0, you could always ask for the parent of the context node. If you try that in XPath 2.0, the processor raises an exception unless the context item is a node.

- The *context position*. This works the same way it did in XPath 1.0; the position( ) function returns the context position.

- The *context size*. Again, this works the same way it did in XPath 1.0; the last( ) function returns the context size.

- The set of *variable values* that are in scope.

- The set of *function implementations* in scope.

- The *current dateTime*. This value doesn't change during the execution of an expression.

- The *implicit timezone*. The new [2.0] implicit-timezone( ) function (see Appendix C) returns this value.

- The set of *available documents* accessible through the [2.0] doc( ) function (see Appendix C).

- The set of *available collections* accessible through the [2.0] collection( ) function (see Appendix C).

- The *default collection* returned by calling the [2.0] collection( ) function without any arguments.

Simple Location Paths

Now that we've talked about what a context is and why it matters, we'll look at some location paths. We'll start with a variety of simple paths; as we go along, we'll look at more complex location paths that use all the various features of XPath. We already looked at one of the simplest XSLT patterns:

```
<xsl:template match="/">
```

This template selects the root node of the document. We saw another simple XPath expression in the `<xsl:value-of>` element:

```
<xsl:value-of select="."/>
```

This template selects the context node, represented by a period. To complete our tour of very simple location paths, we can use the double period (`..`) to select the *parent* of the context node:

```
<xsl:value-of select=".."/>
```

All these XPath expressions have one thing in common: they don't use element names. As you might have noticed in our Hello World example, you can use element names to select elements that have a particular name:

```
<xsl:apply-templates select="greeting"/>
```

In this example, we select all of the `<greeting>` elements in the current context and apply the appropriate template to each of them. Turning to our XML sonnet, we can create location paths that specify more than one level in the document hierarchy:

```
<xsl:apply-templates select="lines/line"/>
```

This example selects all `<line>` elements that are contained in any `<lines>` elements in the current context. If the current context doesn't have any `<lines>` elements, then this expression returns an empty node-set. If the current context has plenty of `<lines>` elements, but none of them contain any `<line>` elements, this expression also returns an empty node-set.

Relative and Absolute Expressions

The XPath specification talks about two kinds of XPath expressions, *relative* and *absolute*. Our previous example is a relative XPath expression because the nodes it specifies depend on the current context. An absolute XPath expression begins with a slash (/), which tells the XSLT processor to start at the root of the document, regardless of the current context. In other words, you can evaluate an absolute XPath expression from any context node you want, and the results will be the same. Here's an absolute XPath expression:

```
<xsl:apply-templates select="/sonnet/lines/line"/>
```

The good thing about an absolute expression is that you don't have to worry about the context node. Another benefit is that it makes it easy for the XSLT processor to find all nodes that match this expression: what we've said in this expression is that there must be a `<sonnet>` element at the root of the document, that element must contain at least one `<lines>` element, and that at least one of those `<lines>` elements must contain at least one `<line>` element. If any of those conditions fail, the XSLT processor can stop looking through the tree and return an empty node-set.

A disadvantage of using absolute XPath expressions is that it makes your templates more difficult to reuse. Both of these templates process `<line>` elements, but the second one is more difficult to reuse:

```
<xsl:template match="line">
  ...
</xsl:template>

<xsl:template match="/sonnet/lines/line">
  ...
</xsl:template>
```

If the second template has wonderful code for processing `<line>` elements, but your document contains `<line>` elements that don't match the absolute XSLT pattern, you can't reuse that template. (On the other hand, the XSLT processor has less work to do with the pattern `/sonnet/lines/line`; we've told the processor exactly where to look for the elements we care about.) In general, you should use absolute expressions only if you need special processing for a specific case. If `<line>` elements that match the pattern `/sonnet/lines/line` should be processed differently, use the absolute pattern in the `match` attribute. If you don't need to process those `<line>`s differently, don't use the absolute pattern. Keep these things in mind as you design your templates.

Selecting Things Besides Elements with Location Paths

Up until now, we've discussed XPath expressions that used either element names (`/sonnet/lines/line`) or special characters (`/` or `..`) to select elements from an XML document. Obviously, XML documents contain things other than elements; we'll talk about how to select those other things here.

Selecting attributes

To select an attribute, use the at-sign (@) along with the attribute name. In our sample sonnet, you can select the `type` attribute of the `<sonnet>` element with the XPath expression `/sonnet/@type`. If the context node is the `<sonnet>` element itself, then the relative XPath expression `@type` does the same thing.

Selecting the text of an element

To select the text of an element, simply refer to it in your expression. The element `<xsl:value-of select="/sonnet/auth:author/last-name"/>` returns `Shakespeare` for our sample sonnet. You can also use the `string( )` function, although that's typically not necessary.

These XSLT instructions:

```
<xsl:value-of select="/sonnet/something_else:author/first-name"/>
<xsl:text> </xsl:text>
<xsl:value-of select="/sonnet/something_else:author/last-name/string()"/>
```

generate these results:

```
William Shakespeare
```

Be aware that getting the text of an element with children probably doesn't do what you want. For example, the element `<xsl:value-of select="/sonnet/auth:author"/>` returns the string `ShakespeareWilliamBritish15641616`. All of the text descendants of the `<auth:author>` node are concatenated together. To format these nodes more attractively, you'll have to deal with them individually.

Finally, there is a `text( )` node test that selects the text node children of the context item. That being said, you almost never want to use it. Getting the node's text the way we illustrated here is the best way to go.

Selecting comments, processing instructions, and namespace nodes

By this point, we've covered most of the document components you're ever likely to select with an XPath expression. You can use a couple of other XPath node tests to describe parts of an XML document. The `comment( )` and `processing-instruction( )` node tests allow you to select comments and processing instructions from the XML document. Going back to our sample sonnet, the XPath expression `/processing-instruction( )` returns the two processing instructions (named `xml-stylesheet` and `cocoon-process`). The expression `/sonnet/comment( )` returns the comment node that begins, "Is there an official title for this sonnet?" (That's the only comment in the `<sonnet>` element itself; the other comments are outside the root element.)

Processing comment nodes in this way can actually be useful. If you've entered comments into an XML document, you can use the `comment( )` node test to display your comments only when you want. Here's an XSLT template you could use:

```
<xsl:template match="comment()">
  <span class="comment">
    <p><xsl:value-of select="."/></p>
  </span>
</xsl:template>
```

Elsewhere in your stylesheet, you could define CSS attributes to print comments in a large, bold, purple font. To remove all comments from your output document, simply go to your stylesheet and have the template that handles comments do nothing. (You could also just remove the template; the default template for comments does nothing.)

XPath has one other kind of node—the rarely used *namespace node*. To retrieve namespace nodes, you have to use the *namespace axis*; we'll discuss axes in the "Axes" section later in this chapter. One note about namespace nodes, if you ever have to use them: when matching namespace nodes, the namespace prefix isn't important. As an example, our sample sonnet used the `auth` namespace prefix, which maps to the value `http://www.authors.com/`. If a stylesheet uses the namespace prefix `writers` to refer to the same URL, then the XPath expression `/sonnet/writers:*` would return the `<auth:author>` element. Even though the namespace prefixes are different, the URLs they refer to are the same. Most likely the only time you'll care about the namespace prefix itself is when you're looking for a particular namespace node. The name of the namespace node is the prefix. In almost all cases, you'll use the namespace URI to find what you're looking for.

Having said all that, the chances that you'll ever need to use namespace nodes are pretty slim.

Using Wildcards

XPath features three wildcards:

The asterisk (*)
> Selects all element nodes in the current context. Be aware that the asterisk wildcard selects element nodes only; attributes, text nodes, comments, or processing instructions aren't included. You can also use a namespace prefix with an asterisk. In our sample sonnet, the XPath expression `auth:*` returns all element nodes in the current context that are associated with the namespace URL `http://www.authors.com/`.
>
> *[2.0]* XPath 2.0 lets us use a wildcard as a namespace prefix. The XPath expression `*:author` returns all element nodes in the current context that have a local name of `author`, regardless of their namespace. In XPath 2.0, both `auth:*` and `*:author` are legal; in XPath 1.0, looking for `*:author` causes a fatal error.

> As always, searching for a matching namespace is based on the namespace URL, not the prefix. For example, assume the namespace URL `http://www.authors.com/` is associated with the prefix `auth` in the XML document and the prefix `something_else` in our stylesheet. Looking for `something_else:*` in the stylesheet returns all of the elements with the `auth` prefix in the XML document.

The at-sign and asterisk (@*)
> Selects all attribute nodes in the current context. You can use a namespace prefix with the attribute wildcard. In our sample sonnet, `@auth:*` returns all attribute nodes in the current context that are associated with the namespace URL `http://www.authors.com`. (There aren't any attributes associated with the `auth` namespace; if we added an element such as `<first-name auth:nickname="Bill">William</first-name>`, the `auth:nickname` would match this expression.)

[2.0] As with elements, XPath 2.0 lets us use a wildcard for the namespace prefix. The expressions `@auth:*` and `@*:nickname` are both legal in XPath 2.0. In XPath 1.0, using a wildcard for the namespace prefix is a fatal error.

The `node( )` *node test*

Selects all nodes in the current context, regardless of type. This includes elements, text, comments, processing instructions, attributes, and namespace nodes.

In addition to these wildcards, XPath includes the double slash (`//`), which indicates that zero or more elements may occur between the slashes. For example, the XPath expression `//line` selects all `<line>` elements, regardless of where they appear in the document. This is an absolute XPath expression because it begins with a slash. You can also use the double slash at any point in an XPath expression; the expression `/sonnet/descendant-or-self::node( )/line` selects all `<line>` elements that are descendants of the `<sonnet>` element at the root of the XML document. The expressions `/sonnet//line` and `/sonnet/descendant-or-self::node( )/line` are equivalent. (`descendant-or-self` is an *axis*; we'll talk more about those next.)

The double slash (`//`) is a very powerful operator, but be aware that it can make your stylesheets incredibly inefficient. If we use the XPath expression `//line`, the XSLT processor has to check every node in the document to see whether there are any `<line>` elements. The more specific you can be in your XPath expressions, the less work the XSLT processor has to do and the faster your stylesheets will execute. Thinking back to our filesystem metaphor, if I go to a Windows command prompt and type **dir/s c:*.xsl**, the operating system has to look in every subdirectory for any *.xsl* files that might be there. However, if I type **dir/s c:\doug\projects\stylesheets*.xsl**, the operating system has far fewer places to look, and the command will execute much faster.

Axes

To this point, we've been able to select child elements, attributes, text, comments, and processing instructions with some fairly simple XPath expressions. Obviously, we might want to select many other things, such as:

- All ancestors of the context node
- All descendants of the context node
- All previous siblings or following siblings of the context node (siblings are nodes that have the same parent)

To select these things, XPath provides a number of *axes* (plural of axis) that let you specify various collections of nodes. There are 13 axes in all; we'll discuss all of them here, even though most won't be particularly useful to you. To use an axis in an XPath expression, type the name of the axis, a double colon (`::`), and the name of the element you want to select, if any.

Before we define all of the axes, though, we need to talk about XPath's unabbreviated syntax.

Unabbreviated syntax

To this point, all the XPath expressions we've looked at used the XPath *abbreviated syntax*. Most of the time, that's what you'll use; however, most of the lesser-used axes can only be specified with the unabbreviated syntax. For example, when we wrote an XPath expression to select all of the `<line>` elements in the current context, we used the abbreviated syntax:

```
<xsl:apply-templates select="line"/>
```

If you really enjoy typing, you can use the unabbreviated syntax to specify that you want all the `<line>` children of the current context:

```
<xsl:apply-templates select="child::line"/>
```

We'll go through all of the axes now, pointing out which ones have an abbreviated syntax.

Axis roll call

The following list contains all of the axes defined by the XPath standard, with a brief description of each:

`child` axis

> Contains the children of the context node. As we've already mentioned, the XPath expression `child::lines/child::line` is equivalent to `lines/line`. If an XPath expression (such as `sonnet`) doesn't have an axis specifier, the `child` axis is used by default. The children of the context node include all comment, element, processing instruction, and text nodes. Attribute and namespace nodes are not considered children of the context node.

`parent` axis

> Contains the parent of the context node, if there is one. (If the context node is the root node, the parent axis returns an empty node-set.) As a step in an XPath expression, the parent axis can be abbreviated with the double period (`..`); this moves up to the current node's parent. If the `<first-name>` and `<last-name>` elements are both children of the `<author>` element and the context node is the `<first-name>` element, the expressions `../last-name`, `parent::author/last-name` and `parent::*/last-name` are equivalent. If the context node does not have a parent, this axis returns an empty node-set.

`self` axis

> Contains the context node itself. As a step in an XPath expression, the `self` axis can be abbreviated with a single period (`.`). The expressions `.`, `self::node( )`, and `self::*` are equivalent in XSLT 1.0.

[2.0] In XSLT 2.0, the self axis selects the context *item*, which might not be a node. If the context item is an atomic value, the expressions `self::node( )` and `self::*` cause the XSLT processor to raise an error. In this case, the only way to access the self axis is with a period. If the context item is a node, the self axis works just as it did in XSLT 1.0.

`attribute` axis

> Contains the attributes of the context node. If the context node is not an element node, this axis is empty. The `attribute` axis can be abbreviated with the at sign (@). The expressions `attribute::type` and `@type` are equivalent.

`ancestor` axis

> Contains the parent of the context node, the parent's parent, etc. The `ancestor` axis always contains the root node unless the context node is the root node.

`ancestor-or-self` axis

> Contains the context node, its parent, its parent's parent, and so on. This axis always includes the root node.

`descendant` axis

> Contains all children of the context node, all children of all the children of the context node, and so on. The children are all of the comment, element, processing instruction, and text nodes beneath the context node. In other words, the `descendant` axis does not include attribute or namespace nodes. (As we discussed earlier, although an attribute node has an element node as a parent, an attribute node is not considered a child of that element.)

`descendant-or-self` axis

> Contains the context node and all the children of the context node, all the children of all the children of the context node, all the children of the children of all the children of the context node, and so on. As always, the children of the context node include all comment, element, processing instruction, and text nodes; attribute and namespace nodes are not included.

`preceding-sibling` axis

> Contains all preceding siblings of the context node; in other words, all nodes that have the same parent as the context node and appear before the context node in the XML document. If the context node is an attribute node or a namespace node, the `preceding-sibling` axis is empty.

`following-sibling` axis

> Contains all the following siblings of the context node; in other words, all nodes that have the same parent as the context node and appear after the context node in the XML document. If the context node is an attribute node or a namespace node, the `following-sibling` axis is empty.

`preceding` axis

> Contains all nodes that appear before the context node in the document, except ancestors, attribute nodes, and namespace nodes.

---

following axis

> Contains all nodes that appear after the context node in the document, except descendants, attribute nodes, and namespace nodes.

namespace axis

> Contains the namespace nodes of the context node. If the context node is not an element node, this axis is empty.

Predicates

There's one more aspect of XPath expressions that we haven't discussed: *predicates*. These are filters that restrict the nodes selected by an XPath expression. Each predicate is evaluated and converted to a Boolean value (either **true** or **false**). If the predicate is **true** for a given node, that node will be selected; otherwise, it isn't. Predicates always appear inside square brackets ([ ]). Here's an example:

```
<xsl:apply-templates select="line[position() = 7]"/>
```

This expression selects the seventh `<line>` element in the current context. If there are six or fewer `<line>` elements in the current context, this XPath expression returns an empty node-set. Several things can be part of a predicate; we'll go through them here.

Numbers in predicates

Instead of using the **position( )** function, we can use a number. For example, the XPath expression `line[7]` selects the seventh `<line>` element in the context node; this means exactly the same thing as `line[position( ) = 7]`. XPath also provides the boolean **and** and **or** operators as well as the union operator (|) to combine predicates. The expression `line[position( )=3 and @style]` matches all `<line>` elements that occur third and that have a **style** attribute, while `line[position( )=3 or @style]` matches all `<line>` elements that either occur third or have a **style** attribute.

You can use more than one predicate if you like; `line[3][@style]` or `line[@style][3]` are both legal. They aren't equivalent, however. Predicates are evaluated from left to right. The XSLT processor handles the first pattern by selecting all of the `<line>` nodes that appear third in a set of sibling `<line>` nodes, then selecting all of those nodes that have a **style** attribute. For the second pattern, the processor selects all the `<line>` elements that have a **style** attribute, then selects the third node from that sequence. The first pattern can match any number of nodes, while the second pattern will never match more than one. In general, the first predicate filters the nodes, the second predicate filters the nodes that made it past the first predicate, and then the third predicate filters the nodes that made it past the second, and so forth.

Functions in predicates

In addition to numbers, we can use XPath and XSLT functions inside predicates. Here are some examples:

line[last( )]
> Selects the last <line> element in the current context.

line[position( ) mod 2 = 0]
> Selects all even-numbered <line> elements. (The mod operator returns the remainder after a division; the position of any even-numbered element divided by 2 has a remainder of 0.)

sonnet[@type="Shakespearean"]
> Selects all <sonnet> elements that have a type attribute with the value Shakespearean. Note that double versus single quotes are not significant; this XPath expression matches either <sonnet type="Shakespearean"> or <sonnet type='Shakespearean'>.

ancestor::table[@border="1"]
> Selects all <table> ancestors of the current context that have a border attribute with the value 1.

count(/body/table[@border="1"])
> Returns the number of <table> elements with a border attribute equal to 1 that are children of <body> elements that are children of the root node. Notice that in this case we're using a predicate as part of the location path.

Attribute Value Templates

Although they're technically defined in the XSLT specification (in XSLT 1.0 section 7.6.2 and XSLT 2.0 section 5.6), we'll discuss attribute value templates here. An attribute value template (sometimes abbreviated as AVT) is an XPath expression that is evaluated, and the result of that evaluation replaces the attribute value template. For example, we could create an HTML <table> element like this:

```
<table border="{@size}"/>
```

In this example, the XPath expression @size is evaluated, and its value, whatever that happens to be, is inserted into the output tree as the value of the border attribute. Attribute value templates can be used in any literal result elements in your stylesheet (for HTML elements and other things that aren't part of the XSLT namespace, for example). You can also use attribute value templates in the following XSLT attributes:

- The name and namespace attributes of the <xsl:attribute> element
- The name and namespace attributes of the <xsl:element> element
- The format, lang, letter-value, grouping-separator, and grouping-size attributes of the <xsl:number> element
- The name attribute of the <xsl:processing-instruction> element
- The lang, data-type, order, and case-order attributes of the <xsl:sort> element

[2.0] XSLT 2.0 can use AVTs in several additional places:

- The `regex` and `flags` attributes of the new [2.0] `<xsl:analyze-string>` element
- The `name`, `namespace`, and `separator` attributes of the `<xsl:attribute>` element (just as in XSLT 1.0)
- The `name` and `namespace` attributes of the `<xsl:element>` element (just as in XSLT 1.0)
- The `collation` attribute of the new [2.0] `<xsl:for-each-group>` element
- The `terminate` attribute of the `<xsl:message>` element
- The `name` attribute of the [2.0] `<xsl:namespace>` element
- The `format`, `lang`, `letter-value`, `ordinal`, `grouping-separator`, and `grouping-size` attributes of the `<xsl:number>` element (`ordinal` is new in XSLT 2.0; all the others are unchanged from XSLT 1.0)
- The `name` attribute of the `<xsl:processing-instruction>` element
- The `format`, `href`, `method`, `byte-order-mark`, `cdata-section-elements`, `doctype-public`, `doctype-system`, `encoding`, `escape-uri-attributes`, `include-content-type`, `indent`, `media-type`, `normalization-form`, `omit-xml-declaration`, `standalone`, `undeclare-prefixes`, and `output-version` attributes of the new [2.0] `<xsl:result-document>` element
- The `lang`, `order`, `collation`, `stable`, `case-order`, and `data-type` attributes of the `<xsl:sort>` element (`collation` and `stable` are new for XSLT 2.0)
- The `separator` attribute of the `<xsl:value-of>` element (a new attribute in XSLT 2.0)

Datatypes

One of the major additions to XPath 2.0 is support for the XML Schema datatype system. The XPath 1.0 and 2.0 data models are so different we'll discuss them in separate sections. In general, most statements that worked in XPath 1.0 still work in XSLT 2.0. On the other hand, any XPath 2.0 statement that uses the new datatyping features won't work at all in XPath 1.0.

Datatypes in XPath 1.0

In XPath 1.0, an expression returns one of four datatypes:

`node-set`
> Represents a set of nodes. The set can be empty or it can contain any number of nodes.

`boolean`
> Represents the value `true` or `false`. Be aware that the `true` or `false` strings have no special meaning or value in XPath; see "Converting to boolean values" in Chapter 5 for a more detailed discussion of these.

number

Represents a floating-point number. All numbers in XPath and XSLT are implemented as floating-point numbers; the `integer` (or `int`) datatype does not exist in XPath and XSLT. Specifically, all numbers are implemented as IEEE 754 floating-point numbers, which is the same standard used by the Java `float` and `double` primitive types. In addition to ordinary numbers, there are five special values for numbers: positive and negative infinity, positive and negative zero, and `NaN`, the special symbol for anything that is not a number.

string

Represents zero or more characters, as defined in the XML specification.

These datatypes are usually simple, and with the exception of node-sets, converting between types is usually straightforward. We won't discuss these datatypes in any more detail here; instead, we'll discuss datatypes and conversions as we need them to do specific tasks.

Datatypes in XPath 2.0

The XPath 2.0 data model is perhaps the most significant change to writing XSLT version 2.0 stylesheets. We'll cover the datatypes supported by XPath 2.0. XPath 2.0 supports all of the basic datatypes defined in XML Schema, and a schema-aware XSLT 2.0 processor lets you create your own datatypes. We'll start with the basic datatypes; *these are the only datatypes supported by a basic XSLT processor*. To support other datatypes, including datatypes we define (`po:purchaseOrder`, for example) and derived types defined in XML Schema (such as `xs:nonNegativeInteger`), you need a schema-aware XSLT processor.

We've already looked at using `<xsl:variable name="sample" select="'3'" as="xs:integer"/>` as a way of creating an `xs:integer` value. XPath 2.0 also provides *constructor functions*, described in the following list. For example, `<xsl:variable name="sample" select="xs:integer(3)"/>` creates a new `xs:integer` value, whereas `<xsl:variable name="birthday" select="xs:date('1995-04-21')"/>` creates a new `xs:date` value:

xs:string

The `xs:string` datatype represents a string. Every datatype supported by XPath 2.0 has a *string representation*. If you want to see how a datatype looks as a string, the XSLT `<xsl:value-of>` element will do the trick. You can convert anything to a string by using the constructor function `xs:string( )`. The constructor is the equivalent of the Java `toString( )` method that's inherited by every class.

xs:boolean

As in XSLT 1.0, the string values `true` and `false` don't have any special meaning. To work with the boolean values themselves, XPath provides the `true( )` and `false( )` functions; they return the corresponding boolean values. See "Converting to boolean values" in Chapter 5 for a more detailed discussion of these values. You can also use the `xs:boolean()` constructor to create boolean values. `xs:boolean(1)` creates the value `true`, while `xs:boolean(0)` creates the value `false`.

`xs:decimal`

XML Schema defines an `xs:decimal` value as a numeric value consisting of decimal digits (`&#x30;` through `&#x39;`), beginning with an optional plus or minus sign. *An `xs:decimal` cannot contain an exponent.* The XML Schema spec states that an implementation must support a minimum of 18 decimal digits. The values `42`, `8.37284`, and `–83982.22` are all legal `xs:decimal` values.

`xs:float` *and* `xs:double`

The `xs:float` and `xs:double` datatypes are based on the IEEE single-precision and double-precision floating-point types, respectively. Unlike `xs:decimal`, `xs:float` and `xs:double` values can have exponents. There are three special values of `xs:float` and `xs:double`: `INF` (infinity), `–INF` (negative infinity), and `NaN` (not a number). The values `42`, `8.37284`, `–83982.22`, `–8.39822e4`, `INF`, and `–0` are all valid values for an `xs:float` or `xs:double`.

`xs:integer`

An integer is a number without a decimal point or digits after it. An integer can include a plus or minus sign (`+` or `-`) to indicate a negative value; without either, the integer is assumed to be positive.

`xs:duration`

An `xs:duration` represents a span of time. It has six components: year, month, day, hour, minute, and second. The XML Schema spec states that an implementation should support at least a four-digit year and a seconds value with at least three decimal points (millisecond precision). A duration of 1 year, 7 months, 18 days, 4 hours, 27 minutes, and 3.673 seconds is written as `P1Y7M18DT4H27M3.673S`.

Date and time values

There are three datatypes for dates and times: `xs:date`, `xs:time`, and `xs:dateTime`. The format of a date is `YYYY-MM-DD`, as in `1995-04-21` for April 21st, 1995. A time value is in the format `hh:mm:ss.sss`, so `17:38:22.183` is the same as 22.183 seconds past 5:38 p.m.

Both `xs:date` and `xs:time` values have an optional time zone indicator, shown by a plus or minus sign (`+` | `-`) that indicates that the date or time is some number of hours ahead or behind Coordinated Universal Time (UTC, also known as Greenwich Mean Time). For example, during the winter (when Daylight Savings Time is not in effect), the time zone on the East coast of the United States is `-05:00`. Be aware that if the XSLT processor normalizes a date or time value, parts of the value can change. The time value `17:30:22.183-05:00` is the same as the time value `00:30:22.183Z` (a date or time value that ends with `Z` has been normalized to UTC).

Finally, an `xs:dateTime` value is the combination of an `xs:date` and an `xs:time`. The written representation of an `xs:dateTime` has a `T` between the two portions. To combine our earlier examples, `1995-04-21T17:38:22.183-05:00` is 22.183 seconds past 5:38 p.m. on April 21st, 1995, five hours behind UTC. That value is equivalent to `1995-04-22T00:38:22.183Z`.

Be aware that `xs:date`, `xs:time`, and `xs:dateTime` can have negative values.

Parts of date and time values

XML Schema defines the datatypes `xs:gYearMonth`, `xs:gYear`, `xs:gMonthDay`, `gDay`, and `gMonth`. Examples of these values, in order, are `1995-04` for April, 1995; `1995` for the year 1995; `--04-21` for the 21st day of April; `---21` for the 21st day of a month; and `--04` for April.

`xs:hexBinary` *and* `xs:base64Binary`

The `xs:hexBinary` datatype is a string composed of binary octets. In other words, it must contain only pairs of hexadecimal digits (`[0-9a-fA-F]`). The `xs:base64Binary` datatype uses base 64 encoding to represent binary data. It is also a string. An `xs:base64Binary` value consists of the 65 characters defined in RFC2045: [0-9a-zA-Z], the plus sign (+), the forward slash (/), and the equals sign (=), along with whitespace characters. (The RFC is available at *http://www.ietf.org/rfc/rfc2045.txt.*)

`xs:anyURI`

An `xs:anyURI` value is any string that forms a valid URI as defined by RFC 2396 (and later updated by RFC2732). The RFCs are available at *http://www.ietf.org/rfc/rfc2396.txt* and *http://www.ietf.org/rfc/rfc2732.txt.*

`xs:QName`

An `xs:QName` (qualified name) is an XML name qualified with a namespace prefix. For example, `auth:author` is a qualified name. To use an `xs:QName` in a stylesheet, the namespace prefix must be in scope.

`xs:anyType` *and* `xs:anySimpleType`

The datatype `xs:anyType` is considered the base datatype (called the *ur-type* in the XML Schema datatypes spec) from which all other datatypes are derived. A value of `xs:anyType` can contain any data; it is not constrained in any way.

The `xs:anySimpleType` datatype is a restricted version of `xs:anyType`; an `xs:anySimpleType` value can be any legal value for any of the primitive datatypes defined in XML Schema. A *primitive datatype* is a datatype that is not defined in terms of another. The `xs:float` datatype is a primitive datatype, so an `xs:float` value would be considered `xs:anySimpleType`. On the other hand, `xs:integer` is not a simple type; it is defined in terms of `xs:float`.

The following datatypes were added by the XPath 2.0 and XQuery 1.0 Data Model spec. They are supported along with all of the datatypes defined by XML Schema:

`xs:yearMonthDuration` *and* `xs:dayTimeDuration`

These two types were added to the XML Schema datatypes namespace by the XPath 2.0 and XQuery 1.0 Data Model spec. They represent the two halves of an `xs:duration`. An `xs:yearMonthDuration` is some number of years, months, and days, whereas an `xs:dayTimeDuration` is some number of days, hours, minutes, and seconds. Both of these datatypes can have negative values. The duration 12 years and 2 months is written as P12Y2M. Note that an xs:yearMonthDuration doesn't have a days component. The duration 4 days, 7 hours, 47 minutes, and 32.883 seconds is written as P4DT7H47M32.883S.

xs:untyped *and* xs:untypedAtomic

These datatypes are defined by the XPath 2.0 and XQuery 1.0 Data Model spec. A node that has not been validated has a dynamic type of xs:untyped, whereas an atomic value that has not been validated has a dynamic type of xs:untypedAtomic.

xs:anyAtomicType

In XPath 2.0 and XQuery 1.0, all simple types have xs:anyAtomicType as their base type. For example, xs:integer, xs:boolean, and xs:string are all derived from xs:anyAtomicType.

XPath Operators

XPath supports a number of operators that make your expressions more powerful. We'll look at each of them here.

[1.0] The first two sections here cover all of the XPath 1.0 operators except the vertical bar (|), the union operator. Only the vertical bar is supported in XPath 1.0; the new union keyword is supported only in XPath 2.0. See the section "[2.0] Set Operators— except, intersect, and union" later in this chapter for the details of the union operator (|) and the union keyword.

[2.0] In XPath 2.0, some operators work with dates, times, and durations. For example, you can add 12 hours to an xs:dayTimeDuration if you want. We cover the operators and features specific to XPath 2.0 after looking at the features common to XPath 1.0 and 2.0.

Mathematical Operators

The mathematical operators available in XPath are pretty limited. We'll use two stylesheets to illustrate how the operators work; the first indicates how an operator works in XSLT 1.0 and the second indicates how it works in XSLT 2.0. We'll cover the stylesheets in detail for the first operator (the plus sign), then simply refer to those examples throughout this section.

Addition (+)

The plus sign adds two numbers.

[1.0] In an XSLT 1.0 stylesheet, the processor attempts to convert each operand to a number. The following XPath expressions all work in XPath 1.0:

```
<?xml version="1.0"?>
<!-- addition-1_0.xsl -->
```

```
<xsl:stylesheet version="1.0"
  xmlns:xsl="http://www.w3.org/1999/XSL/Transform"
  xmlns:xs="http://www.w3.org/2001/XMLSchema">

  <xsl:output method="text"/>

  <xsl:template match="/">
    <xsl:text>Tests of addition in XPath 1.0&#xA;</xsl:text>
    <xsl:text>&#xA;  9 + 3 = </xsl:text>
    <xsl:value-of select="9 + 3"/>
    <xsl:text>&#xA;  9 + 3.8 = </xsl:text>
    <xsl:value-of select="9 + 3.8"/>
    <xsl:text>&#xA;  9 + '4' = </xsl:text>
    <xsl:value-of select="9 + '4'"/>
    <xsl:text>&#xA;  9 + 'Q' = </xsl:text>
    <xsl:value-of select="9 + 'Q'"/>
    <xsl:text>&#xA;  9 + true() = </xsl:text>
    <xsl:value-of select="9 + true()"/>
    <xsl:text>&#xA;  9 + false() = </xsl:text>
    <xsl:value-of select="9 + false()"/>
  </xsl:template>
</xsl:stylesheet>
```

Here are the stylesheet results:

```
Tests of addition in XPath 1.0

  9 + 3 = 12
  9 + 3.8 = 12.8
  9 + '4' = 13
  9 + 'Q' = NaN
  9 + true() = 10
  9 + false() = 9
```

Notice that XSLT 1.0 converts a string ('4') to a number. If the string can't be converted
to a number ('Q'), the result is NaN, or not a number. The boolean values returned by
the functions true( ) and false( ) are converted to the numbers 1 and 0, respectively.

[2.0] XSLT 2.0 is much more strict. The two operands must be compatible datatypes.
Changing the stylesheet to <xsl:stylesheet version="2.0" ...> causes the stylesheet
to fail. The first two operations (9 + 3 and 9 + 3.8) work, but none of the others do.
To fix the problem, we can use the number( ) function to convert the values to numbers.
The updated stylesheet looks like this:

```
<?xml version="1.0"?>
<!-- addition-2_0.xsl -->
<xsl:stylesheet version="2.0"
  xmlns:xsl="http://www.w3.org/1999/XSL/Transform"
  xmlns:xs="http://www.w3.org/2001/XMLSchema">

  <xsl:output method="text"/>

  <xsl:template match="/">
    <xsl:text>Tests of addition in XPath 2.0&#xA;</xsl:text>
    <xsl:text>&#xA;  9 + 3 = </xsl:text>
```

```
  <xsl:value-of select="9 + 3"/>
  <xsl:text>&#xA;   9 + 3.8 = </xsl:text>
  <xsl:value-of select="9 + 3.8"/>
  <xsl:text>&#xA;   9 + number('4') = </xsl:text>
  <xsl:value-of select="9 + number('4')"/>
  <xsl:text>&#xA;   9 + number('Q') = </xsl:text>
  <xsl:value-of select="9 + number('Q')"/>
  <xsl:text>&#xA;   9 + number(true()) = </xsl:text>
  <xsl:value-of select="9 + number(true())"/>
  <xsl:text>&#xA; 9 + number(false()) = </xsl:text>
  <xsl:value-of select="9 + number(false())"/>
 </xsl:template>
</xsl:stylesheet>
```

Now that we explicitly cast each value to a number, the stylesheet generates the same results as the XSLT 1.0 stylesheet:

```
Tests of addition in XPath 2.0

9 + 3 = 12
9 + 3.8 = 12.8
9 + number('4') = 13
9 + number('Q') = NaN
9 + number(true()) = 10
9 + number(false()) = 9
```

A final option is to add the XSLT 2.0 attribute `version="1.0"` to any of the `<xsl:value-of>` elements. This works in an XSLT 2.0 stylesheet:

```
<xsl:value-of select="9 + '4'" version="1.0"/>
```

This generates the value **13**. The **version** attribute can be added to any XSLT element to specify that it should be processed as if it were in an XSLT 1.0 stylesheet.

> If the values we're adding are nodes instead of atomic values, the dynamic typing from XPath 1.0 works the same way. For example, we can use this subtraction to find Shakespeare's age:
>
> ```
> <xsl:value-of select="/sonnet/auth:author/year-of-death -
>                       /sonnet/auth:author/year-of-birth"/>
> ```
>
> We're subtracting two nodes here, so both of them are converted to numbers and subtracted. Trying to do the same thing with two strings doesn't work in XSLT 2.0:
>
> ```
> <xsl:value-of select="'1616' - '1564'"/>
> ```

[2.0] In XPath 2.0, the plus sign can be used to add combinations of dates, times, and durations. You can use the plus sign to add the following:

- Two `xs:yearMonthDuration`s
- Two `xs:dayTimeDuration`s
- An `xs:yearMonthDuration` to an `xs:dateTime`

- An xs:dayTimeDuration to an xs:dateTime
- An xs:yearMonthDuration to an xs:date
- An xs:dayTimeDuration to an xs:date
- An xs:dayTimeDuration to an xs:time.

(Notice that you can't add an xs:yearMonthDuration to an xs:time.)

Here is a stylesheet with examples of all the supported types of addition:

```
<?xml version="1.0"?>
<!-- addition-datesTimesDurations.xsl -->
<xsl:stylesheet version="2.0"
  xmlns:xsl="http://www.w3.org/1999/XSL/Transform"
  xmlns:xs="http://www.w3.org/2001/XMLSchema">

<xsl:output method="text"/>

<xsl:variable name="yMD1" as="xs:yearMonthDuration"
  select="xs:yearMonthDuration('P1Y8M')"/>
<xsl:variable name="yMD2" as="xs:yearMonthDuration"
  select="xs:yearMonthDuration('P2Y7M')"/>
<xsl:variable name="dTD1" as="xs:dayTimeDuration"
  select="xs:dayTimeDuration('P5DT9H23M12S')"/>
<xsl:variable name="dTD2" as="xs:dayTimeDuration"
  select="xs:dayTimeDuration('P3DT16H12M17S')"/>
<xsl:variable name="dT" as="xs:dateTime"
  select="xs:dateTime('1995-04-21T00:47:00')"/>
<xsl:variable name="d" as="xs:date"
  select="xs:date('1995-04-21')"/>
<xsl:variable name="t" as="xs:time"
  select="xs:time('17:03:00')"/>

<xsl:template match="/">
  <xsl:text>More tests of addition in XPath 2.0:</xsl:text>
  <xsl:text>&#xA;&#xA;  Two xs:yearMonthDurations:&#xA;     </xsl:text>
  <xsl:value-of select="($yMD1, '+', $yMD2, '=', $yMD1 + $yMD2)"/>
  <xsl:text>&#xA;&#xA;  Two xs:dayTimeDurations:&#xA;     </xsl:text>
  <xsl:value-of select="($dTD1, '+', $dTD2, '=', $dTD1 + $dTD2)"/>
  <xsl:text>&#xA;&#xA;  An xs:yearMonthDuration and an </xsl:text>
  <xsl:text>xs:dateTime:&#xA;     </xsl:text>
  <xsl:value-of select="($dT, '+', $yMD1, '=', $dT + $yMD1)"/>
  <xsl:text>&#xA;&#xA;  An xs:dayTimeDuration and an </xsl:text>
  <xsl:text>xs:dateTime:&#xA;     </xsl:text>
  <xsl:value-of select="($dT, '+', $dTD1, '=', $dT + $dTD1)"/>
  <xsl:text>&#xA;&#xA;  An xs:yearMonthDuration and an </xsl:text>
  <xsl:text>xs:date:&#xA;     </xsl:text>
  <xsl:value-of select="($d, '+', $yMD1, '=', $d + $yMD1)"/>
  <xsl:text>&#xA;&#xA;  An xs:dayTimeDuration and an </xsl:text>
  <xsl:text>xs:date:&#xA;     </xsl:text>
  <xsl:value-of select="($d, '+', $dTD1, '=', $d + $dTD1)"/>
  <xsl:text>&#xA;&#xA;  An xs:dayTimeDuration and an </xsl:text>
  <xsl:text>xs:time:&#xA;     </xsl:text>
  <xsl:value-of select="($t, '+', $dTD1, '=', $t + $dTD1)"/>
```

```
    </xsl:template>
  </xsl:stylesheet>
```

Here are the results:

```
More tests of addition in XPath 2.0:

  Two xs:yearMonthDurations:
    P1Y8M + P2Y7M = P4Y3M

  Two xs:dayTimeDurations:
    P5DT9H23M12S + P3DT16H12M17S = P9DT1H35M29S

  An xs:yearMonthDuration and an xs:dateTime:
    1995-04-21T00:47:00 + P1Y8M = 1996-12-21T00:47:00

  An xs:dayTimeDuration and an xs:dateTime:
    1995-04-21T00:47:00 + P5DT9H23M12S = 1995-04-26T10:10:12

  An xs:yearMonthDuration and an xs:date:
    1995-04-21 + P1Y8M = 1996-12-21

  An xs:dayTimeDuration and an xs:date:
    1995-04-21 + P5DT9H23M12S = 1995-04-26

  An xs:dayTimeDuration and an xs:time:
    17:03:00 + P5DT9H23M12S = 02:26:12
```

Subtraction (−)

Given two numbers, the minus sign subtracts the second number from the first. Using subtraction in our sample stylesheets, we get these results:

```
Tests of XPath subtraction in XSLT 1.0

9 - 3 = 6
9 - 3.8 = 5.2
9 - '4' = 5
9 - 'Q' = NaN
9 - true() = 8
9 - false() = 9
```

We get the same results in an XSLT 2.0 stylesheet by casting each of the arguments to numbers or by using the version attribute.

[2.0] In XPath 2.0, the minus sign can be used to subtract durations from each other and from xs:date, xs:dateTime, and xs:time values. We can use the minus sign to subtract:

- One xs:yearMonthDuration from another
- One xs:dayTimeDuration from another
- An xs:yearMonthDuration from an xs:dateTime
- An xs:dayTimeDuration from an xs:dateTime

- An `xs:yearMonthDuration` from an `xs:date`
- An `xs:dayTimeDuration` from an `xs:date`
- An `xs:dayTimeDuration` from an `xs:time`.

Replacing the plus signs with minus signs in our previous stylesheet gives us these results:

```
More tests of subtraction in XPath 2.0:

  One xs:yearMonthDuration from another:
    P1Y8M - P2Y7M = -P11M

  One xs:dayTimeDuration from another:
    P5DT9H23M12S - P3DT16H12M17S = P1DT17H10M55S

  An xs:yearMonthDuration from an xs:dateTime:
    1995-04-21T00:47:00 - P1Y8M = 1993-08-21T00:47:00

  An xs:yearMonthDuration from an xs:dateTime:
    1995-04-21T00:47:00 - P1Y8M = 1993-08-21T00:47:00

  An xs:dayTimeDuration from an xs:dateTime:
    1995-04-21T00:47:00 - P5DT9H23M12S = 1995-04-15T15:23:48

  An xs:yearMonthDuration from an xs:date:
    1995-04-21 - P1Y8M = 1993-08-21

  An xs:dayTimeDuration from an xs:date:
    1995-04-21 - P5DT9H23M12S = 1995-04-15

  An xs:dayTimeDuration from an xs:time:
    17:03:00 - P5DT9H23M12S = 07:39:48
```

Notice that the first subtraction returns the *negative* value –P11M.

Multiplication (*)

Given two numbers, the multiplication sign multiplies the first number by the second. Again, using the * operator in our stylesheets gives us these results:

```
Tests of XPath multiplication in XPath 1.0

  9 * 3 = 27
  9 * 3.8 = 34.199999999999996
  9 * '4' = 36
  9 * 'Q' = NaN
  9 * true() = 9
  9 * false() = 0
```

The results in XPath 2.0 are cleaner; `34.19999...` is rounded to `34.2`:

```
Tests of XPath multiplication in XPath 2.0

  9 * 3 = 27
  9 * 3.8 = 34.2
```

```
9 * number('4') = 36
9 * number('Q') = NaN
9 * number(true()) = 9
9 * number(false()) = 0
```

[2.0] In XPath 2.0, you can multiply xs:yearMonthDurations and xs:dayTimeDurations by numeric values:

```
<?xml version="1.0"?>
<!-- multiplication-datesTimesDurations.xsl -->
<xsl:stylesheet version="2.0"
  xmlns:xsl="http://www.w3.org/1999/XSL/Transform"
  xmlns:xs="http://www.w3.org/2001/XMLSchema">

  <xsl:output method="text"/>

  <xsl:variable name="yMD1" as="xs:yearMonthDuration"
    select="xs:yearMonthDuration('P1Y8M')"/>
  <xsl:variable name="dTD1" as="xs:dayTimeDuration"
    select="xs:dayTimeDuration('P24DT08H00M00S')"/>

  <xsl:template match="/">
    <xsl:text>More tests of multiplication in XPath 2.0:</xsl:text>
    <xsl:text>&#xA;&#xA;  A xs:yearMonthDuration multiplied </xsl:text>
    <xsl:text>by a number:&#xA;    </xsl:text>
    <xsl:value-of select="($yMD1, '* 3 =', $yMD1 * 3)"/>
    <xsl:text>&#xA;&#xA;  A xs:dayTimeDuration multiplied </xsl:text>
    <xsl:text>by a number:&#xA;    </xsl:text>
    <xsl:value-of select="($dTD1, '* 10.5 =', $dTD1 * 10.5)"/>
  </xsl:template>
</xsl:stylesheet>
```

The results look like this:

```
More tests of multiplication in XPath 2.0:

  A xs:yearMonthDuration multiplied by a number:
    P1Y8M * 3 = P5Y

  A xs:dayTimeDuration multiplied by a number:
    P24DT8H * 10.5 = P255DT12H
```

(Technically, the numeric value should be an xs:double, but XSLT 2.0 converts the numeric value 3 automatically.)

Division (div)

Given two numbers, the division sign divides the first number by the second. In most programming languages, the division operator is the slash (/), but XPath uses the slash as a separator in location paths, so we use the more verbose div operator instead. Using div in our stylesheets, here are the results for XPath 1.0:

```
Tests of XPath div in XPath 1.0

  9 div 3 = 3
```

```
9 div 3.8 = 2.368421052631579
9 div '4' = 2.25
9 div 'Q' = NaN
9 div true() = 9
9 div false() = INF
```

The results for XPath 2.0 are very similar:

```
Tests of XPath div in XPath 2.0

9 div 3 = 3
9 div 3.8 = 2.368421052631578947
9 div number('4') = 2.25
9 div number('Q') = NaN
9 div number(true()) = 9
9 div number(false()) = INF
```

Notice that the value `9 div false( )`, equivalent to `9 div 0`, returns the value `INF` (infinity). Dividing by zero is not a fatal error, as you might expect.

[2.0] You can also divide durations in four different ways:

- Divide an `xs:yearMonthDuration` by an `xs:double`
- Divide one `xs:yearMonthDuration` by another
- Divide an `xs:dayTimeDuration` by an `xs:double`
- Divide one `xs:dayTimeDuration` by another

We'll use this stylesheet:

```
<?xml version="1.0"?>
<!-- div-datesTimesDurations.xsl -->
<xsl:stylesheet version="2.0"
  xmlns:xsl="http://www.w3.org/1999/XSL/Transform"
  xmlns:xs="http://www.w3.org/2001/XMLSchema">

<xsl:output method="text"/>

<xsl:variable name="yMD1" as="xs:yearMonthDuration"
  select="xs:yearMonthDuration('P1Y8M')"/>
<xsl:variable name="yMD2" as="xs:yearMonthDuration"
  select="xs:yearMonthDuration('P0Y5M')"/>
<xsl:variable name="dTD1" as="xs:dayTimeDuration"
  select="xs:dayTimeDuration('P24DT08H00M00S')"/>
<xsl:variable name="dTD2" as="xs:dayTimeDuration"
  select="xs:dayTimeDuration('P0DT4H00M00S')"/>

<xsl:template match="/">
  <xsl:text>More tests of division in XPath 2.0:</xsl:text>
  <xsl:text>&#xA;&#xA;  A xs:yearMonthDuration divided </xsl:text>
  <xsl:text>by a number:&#xA;    </xsl:text>
  <xsl:value-of select="($yMD1, 'div 4 =', $yMD1 div 4)"/>
  <xsl:text>&#xA;&#xA;  One xs:yearMonthDuration divided </xsl:text>
  <xsl:text>by another:&#xA;    </xsl:text>
  <xsl:value-of select="($yMD1, 'div', $yMD2, '=', $yMD1 div $yMD2)"/>
  <xsl:text>&#xA;&#xA;  A xs:dayTimeDuration divided </xsl:text>
```

```
    <xsl:text>by a number:&#xA;    </xsl:text>
    <xsl:value-of select="($dTD1, 'div 4.5 =', $dTD1 div 4.5)"/>
    <xsl:text>&#xA;&#xA;  One xs:dayTimeDuration divided </xsl:text>
    <xsl:text>by another:&#xA;    </xsl:text>
    <xsl:value-of select="($dTD1, 'div', $dTD2, '=', $dTD1 div $dTD2)"/>
  </xsl:template>
</xsl:stylesheet>
```

The results look like this:

```
More tests of division in XPath 2.0:

  A xs:yearMonthDuration divided by a number:
    P1Y8M div 4 = P5M

  One xs:yearMonthDuration divided by another:
    P1Y8M div P5M = 4

  A xs:dayTimeDuration divided by a number:
    P24DT8H div 4.5 = P5DT9H46M40S

  One xs:dayTimeDuration divided by another:
    P24DT8H div PT4H = 146
```

[2.0] Integer division (idiv)

XPath 2.0 introduces the `idiv` operator for integer division. The rules for integer division in XPath 2.0 are different from the rules you might know from C++ and Java; no rounding is done if there is any remainder from the division. Changing our earlier `div` example to use `idiv`, we have to remove a couple of error cases:

```
<?xml version="1.0"?>
<!-- idiv.xsl -->
<xsl:stylesheet version="2.0"
  xmlns:xsl="http://www.w3.org/1999/XSL/Transform">

  <xsl:output method="text"/>

  <xsl:template match="/">
    <xsl:text>Tests of idiv in XPath 2.0&#xA;</xsl:text>
    <xsl:text>&#xA;  9 idiv 3 = </xsl:text>
    <xsl:value-of select="9 idiv 3"/>
    <xsl:text>&#xA;  9 idiv 3.8 = </xsl:text>
    <xsl:value-of select="9 idiv 3.8"/>
    <xsl:text>&#xA;  9 idiv number('4') = </xsl:text>
    <xsl:value-of select="9 idiv number('4')"/>
    <!-- Causes a fatal error -->
    <!-- <xsl:value-of select="9 idiv number('Q')"/> -->
    <xsl:text>&#xA;  9 idiv number(true()) = </xsl:text>
    <xsl:value-of select="9 idiv number(true())"/>
    <!-- Causes a fatal error -->
    <!-- <xsl:value-of select="9 idiv number(false())"/> -->
  </xsl:template>
</xsl:stylesheet>
```

Compare these results to those for the `div` operator:

```
Tests of idiv in XPath 2.0

9 idiv 3 = 3
9 idiv 3.8 = 2
9 idiv number('4') = 2
9 idiv number(true()) = 9
```

As you can see, no rounding is done.

Modulo (mod)

The `mod` operator returns the remainder of a division. Here are the results for XPath 1.0:

```
Tests of the mod operator in XPath 1.0

9 mod 3 = 0
9 mod 3.8 = 1.4000000000000004
9 mod '4' = 1
9 mod 'Q' = NaN
9 mod true() = 0
9 mod false() = NaN
```

The results for XPath 2.0 are very similar:

```
Tests of the mod operator in XPath 2.0

9 mod 3 = 0
9 mod 3.8 = 1.4
9 mod number('4') = 1
9 mod number('Q') = NaN
9 mod number(true()) = 0
9 mod number(false()) = NaN
```

When we use `mod` to divide by zero, we get the value `NaN` (not a number). This is the same result we get when we divide by something that can't be converted to a number (`'Q'`, for example).

The most common use of the `mod` operator is to cycle through a set of values. For example, say we want a stylesheet that generates different background colors for rows of a table. We want to alternate between white and gray backgrounds. We can use the `mod` operator for this:

```xml
<xsl:attribute name="bgcolor">
  <xsl:choose>
    <xsl:when test="position() mod 2 = 1">
      <xsl:text>white</xsl:text>
    </xsl:when>
    <xsl:otherwise>
      <xsl:text>gray</xsl:text>
    </xsl:otherwise>
  </xsl:choose>
</xsl:attribute>
```

The position of the first item is 1. The remainder of dividing 1 by 2 is 1, so the first row will have a white background. For every alternate row, the remainder will be 0, which means the background color will be gray. To alternate between five different values, you would write tests such as position( ) mod 5 = 1, position( ) mod 5 = 2, and so on.

Unary minus (–x)

The unary minus sign returns the negation of its operand. Here is a stylesheet that illustrates how it works:

```
<?xml version="1.0"?>
<!-- unary-minus.xsl -->
<xsl:stylesheet version="2.0"
  xmlns:xsl="http://www.w3.org/1999/XSL/Transform"
  xmlns:xs="http://www.w3.org/2001/XMLSchema">

  <xsl:output method="text"/>

  <xsl:template match="/">
    <xsl:variable name="x" as="xs:integer" select="xs:integer(-10)"/>

    <xsl:text>An example of the unary minus </xsl:text>
    <xsl:text>operator:&#xA;    </xsl:text>
    <xsl:value-of select="('$x =', $x, '&#xA;   -$x = ', -$x)"/>
  </xsl:template>

</xsl:stylesheet>
```

The results look like this:

```
An example of the unary minus operator:
    $x = -10
   -$x =  10
```

Some details from the Functions and Operators spec: if the argument is an xs:integer or xs:decimal, the negation of 0 or 0.0 is 0 and 0.0, respectively. If the argument is an xs:float or xs:double, NaN returns NaN, 0.0E0 returns –0.0E0, –0.0E0 returns 0.0E0, INF returns –INF, and –INF returns INF.

Unary plus (+x)

The unary plus operator returns its operand with the sign unchanged. It makes no change to the operand, but it is included for completeness. Changing the stylesheet we used for unary minus, we get these results:

```
An example of the unary plus operator:
    $x = -10
   +$x = -10
```

Boolean Operators

XPath provides several boolean operators. They're all straightforward (in XPath 1.0, anyway), so we'll just list them here.

 When you're working with boolean expressions in XPath, remember that the values `'true'` and `'false'` are just strings. If you need to use the boolean values, use the functions `true( )` and `false( )`. Simply using `true` in an XPath expression means a node whose name is `true`, which is almost certainly not what you want. To emphasize the point, we'll refer to the boolean values with their functions.

As we saw in the section on mathematical operators, converting `true( )` and `false( )` to numbers returns `1` and `0`, respectively. XPath defines rules for converting different datatypes to boolean values. See "Converting to boolean values" in Chapter 5 for all the details.

Comparing expressions

There are several operators from XPath 1.0 (and 2.0) that compare expressions. We'll look at those here:

= *(equal)*
: Given two expressions, returns `true( )` if the two expressions evaluate to the same value, and returns `false( )` otherwise.

!= *(not equal)*
: Given two expressions, returns `true( )` if the two expressions do not evaluate to the same value, and returns `false( )` otherwise.

< *or* < *(less than)*
: Given two expressions, returns `true( )` if the first expression evaluates to a value less than the second. Otherwise, it returns `false( )`. The less than operator is usually escaped with < so that it doesn't look like the opening arrow of an XML tag.

<= *or* <= *(less than or equal)*
: Given two expressions, returns `true( )` if the first expression evaluates to a value less than or equal to the second. Otherwise, it returns `false( )`. The less than or equal operator is usually escaped with <= so that it doesn't look like the start of an XML element named =.

> *or* > *(greater than)*
: Given two expressions, returns `true( )` if the first expression evaluates to a value greater than the second. Otherwise, it returns `false( )`. The greater than operator can be escaped with > so that it doesn't look like the closing arrow of an XML tag.

>= or >= (greater than or equal)

> Given two expressions, returns `true( )` if the first expression evaluates to a value greater than or equal to the second. Otherwise, it returns `false( )`. The greater than or equal operator can be escaped with `&gt;=`.

and

> Given two expressions, returns `true( )` if both expressions evaluate to `true( )`. If either evaluates to `false( )`, then and returns `false( )`.

or

> Given two expressions, returns `true( )` if either expression evaluates to `true( )`. If both values evaluate to `false( )`, then or returns `false( )`.

For a boolean not operation, XPath provides the `not( )` function. The not keyword doesn't exist in XPath. See the `not( )` function in Appendix C for the details.

> Many programming languages define specific rules for evaluating boolean operators such as and and or. For example, many languages state that the first term is evaluated before the second, and that the second term is not evaluated if the overall result is known after the first term is evaluated. (If the first term evaluates to `false( )`, the result of an and expression is `false( )`; if the first term evaluates to `true( )`, the result of an or expression is `true( )`.) XPath does not define these rules, so XSLT processors are free to implement and and or as they see fit.

[2.0] Comparing atomic values

As we discussed earlier, XPath 2.0 introduces the concept of atomic values. There are six new operators that allow us to compare values:

eq

> Determines whether two values are equal.

ge

> Determines whether the first value is greater than or equal to the second.

gt

> Determines whether the first value is greater than the second.

le

> Determines whether the first value is less or equal to the second.

lt

> Determines whether the first value is less than the second.

ne

> Determines whether two values are not equal.

The eq and ne operators work on any of the following datatypes:

- Numeric values (`xs:decimal`, `xs:double`, `xs:float`, `xs:integer`)

- Boolean values
- Durations (`xs:duration`, `xs:yearMonthDuration`, `xs:dayTimeDuration`)
- Dates and times (`xs:date`, `xs:time`, `xs:dateTime`)
- Parts of dates (`xs:gYear`, `xs:gYearMonth`, `xs:gMonth`, `xs:gMonthDay`, `xs:gDay`)
- QNames (`xs:QName`)
- Binary data (`xs:hexBinary`, `xs:base64Binary`)
- Notations (`xs:NOTATION`)

The `ge`, `gt`, `le`, and `lt` operators support fewer datatypes:

- Numeric values (`xs:decimal`, `xs:double`, `xs:float`, `xs:integer`)
- Boolean values
- Durations (`xs:duration`, `xs:yearMonthDuration`, `xs:dayTimeDuration`)
- Dates and times (`xs:date`, `xs:time`, `xs:dateTime`)

The operators for comparing values work slightly differently than the general comparisons. Value comparisons are stricter because they require the two operands to be the same type. Given these XML elements:

```
...
<brand>
  <name>Callebaut</name>
  <units>8203</units>
</brand>
...
```

the expression `brand[1]/units gt 10000` raises an error because we're comparing an untyped value and an integer. We need to compare two integers here, so we must either convert the value of the `<units>` element to a number or use an XML Schema to identify the element as an `xs:integer`. If we use the general comparison operators to compare the values (`brand[1]/units > 10000`), it works just fine. To use the value comparison operators, the expression `xs:integer(brand[1]) gt 10000` works as well, although it requires us to cast the value ourselves.

The general comparison operators (`=`, `!=`, `<=`, `>=`, `<` and `>`) can compare nodes and sequences in addition to values, so you'll probably use them far more often. Just be aware that XPath 2.0 gives you new comparison operators that work on atomic values; they're very useful if you're working with values instead of nodes or sequences.

[2.0] Comparing sequences

And speaking of comparing sequences, that works differently than you might think. When comparing a sequence to a value, the XSLT processor compares the value to each value in the sequence. If the comparison is true for *any* value in the sequence, the operation returns *true*. We'll use an XML document of chocolate sales for our examples:

```
<?xml version="1.0" encoding="utf-8"?>
<!-- chocolate.xml -->
<report month="8" year="2006">
  <title>Chocolate bar sales</title>
  <brand>
    <name>Lindt</name>
    <units>27408</units>
  </brand>
  <brand>
    <name>Callebaut</name>
    <units>8203</units>
  </brand>
  <brand>
    <name>Valrhona</name>
    <units>22101</units>
  </brand>
  <brand>
    <name>Perugina</name>
    <units>14336</units>
  </brand>
  <brand>
    <name>Ghirardelli</name>
    <units>19268</units>
  </brand>
</report>
```

Here's the stylesheet we'll use to demonstrate comparisons with sequences:

```
<?xml version="1.0" encoding="utf-8"?>
<!-- compare-sequences.xsl -->
<xsl:stylesheet version="2.0"
  xmlns:xsl="http://www.w3.org/1999/XSL/Transform"
  xmlns:xs="http://www.w3.org/2001/XMLSchema">

  <xsl:output method="text"/>

  <xsl:template match="/">
    <xsl:text>&#xA;Comparing sequences with values:</xsl:text>
    <xsl:text>&#xA;  Sales figures (/report/brand/units):</xsl:text>s
    <xsl:text>&#xA;    </xsl:text>
    <xsl:value-of select="/report/brand/units" separator=", "/>
    <xsl:text>&#xA;&#xA;    /report/brand/units &gt; 27408 : </xsl:text>
    <xsl:value-of select="/report/brand/units &gt; 27408"/>
    <xsl:text>&#xA;    /report/brand/units &gt;= 27408 : </xsl:text>
    <xsl:value-of select="/report/brand/units &gt;= 27408"/>
    <xsl:text>&#xA;    /report/brand/units &lt; 8203  : </xsl:text>
    <xsl:value-of select="/report/brand/units &lt; 8203"/>
    <xsl:text>&#xA;    /report/brand/units &lt;= 8203  : </xsl:text>
    <xsl:value-of select="/report/brand/units &lt;= 8203"/>
    <xsl:text>&#xA;    /report/brand/units =  22101 : </xsl:text>
    <xsl:value-of select="/report/brand/units = 22101"/>
    <xsl:text>&#xA;    /report/brand/units =  17905 : </xsl:text>
    <xsl:value-of select="/report/brand/units = 17905"/>
    <xsl:text>&#xA;  not(/report/brand/units =  17905): </xsl:text>
    <xsl:value-of select="not(/report/brand/units = 17905)"/>
```

```
<xsl:text>&#xA;&#xA;Comparing two sequences:</xsl:text>
<xsl:variable name="testSequence1" as="xs:integer*"
  select="(8203, 22101, 27408, 19268, 14336)"/>
<xsl:text>&#xA;  $testSequence1 (xs:integer*):&#xA;   </xsl:text>
<xsl:value-of select="$testSequence1" separator=", "/>
<xsl:text>&#xA;    $testSequence1 = /report/brand/units: </xsl:text>
<xsl:value-of select="$testSequence1 = /report/brand/units"/>

<xsl:variable name="testSequence2" as="xs:integer*"
  select="(19268, 17, 95, 6, 42)"/>
<xsl:text>&#xA;&#xA;  $testSequence2 (xs:integer*):&#xA;    </xsl:text>
<xsl:value-of select="$testSequence2" separator=", "/>
<xsl:text>&#xA;    $testSequence2 = /report/brand/units: </xsl:text>
<xsl:value-of select="$testSequence2 = /report/brand/units"/>
<xsl:text>&#xA;    $testSequence2 &lt; /report/brand/units: </xsl:text>
<xsl:value-of select="$testSequence2 &lt; /report/brand/units"/>
<xsl:text>&#xA;    $testSequence2 &gt; /report/brand/units: </xsl:text>
<xsl:value-of select="$testSequence2 &gt; /report/brand/units"/>

<xsl:variable name="testSequence3" as="xs:string*"
  select="('blue', 'white', '19268')"/>
<xsl:text>&#xA;&#xA;  $testSequence3 (xs:string*):&#xA;    </xsl:text>
<xsl:value-of select="$testSequence3" separator=", "/>
<xsl:text>&#xA;    $testSequence3 = /report/brand/units: </xsl:text>
<xsl:value-of select="$testSequence3 = /report/brand/units"/>

<xsl:variable name="testSequence4" as="xs:yearMonthDuration*"
  select="(xs:yearMonthDuration('P3Y8M'),
          xs:yearMonthDuration('P4Y8M'),
          xs:yearMonthDuration('P2Y9M'))"/>
<xsl:text>&#xA;&#xA;  $testSequence4 (xs:yearMonthDuration*):</xsl:text>
<xsl:text>&#xA;    (</xsl:text>
<xsl:value-of select="$testSequence4" separator=", "/>
<xsl:text>)&#xA;  $testSequence4 &gt; </xsl:text>
<xsl:text>xs:yearMonthDuration('P4Y7M'): </xsl:text>
<xsl:value-of select="$testSequence4 > xs:yearMonthDuration('P4Y7M')"/>
  </xsl:template>

</xsl:stylesheet>
```

The results look like this:

```
Comparing sequences with values:
  Sales figures (/report/brand/units):
    27408, 8203, 22101, 14336, 19268

      /report/brand/units >  27408 : false
      /report/brand/units >= 27408 : true
      /report/brand/units <  8203  : false
      /report/brand/units <= 8203  : true
      /report/brand/units =  22101 : true
      /report/brand/units =  17905 : false
  not(/report/brand/units =  17905): true

Comparing two sequences:
  $testSequence1 (xs:integer*):
```

```
  (8203, 22101, 27408, 19268, 14336)
$testSequence1 = /report/brand/units: true

$testSequence2 (xs:integer*):
  (19268, 17, 95, 6, 42)
$testSequence2 = /report/brand/units: true
$testSequence2 < /report/brand/units: true
$testSequence2 > /report/brand/units: true

$testSequence3 (xs:string*):
  (blue, white, 19268)
$testSequence3 = /report/brand/units: true

$testSequence4 (xs:yearMonthDuration*):
 (P3Y8M, P4Y8M, P2Y9M)
$testSequence4 > xs:yearMonthDuration('P4Y7M'): true
```

In the first set of comparisons, we're comparing the sequence matched by /report/ brand/units to individual values. The comparison /report/brand/units > 27408 is false because there are no values in the sequence greater than 27408. When we change the operator to >=, the comparison is true. For test of equality, if any value in the sequence matches the value we're comparing, the result is true. Also notice that we used the not( ) function to reverse the result here; the != operator would do the same thing.

For the next three examples, we're comparing two sequences. In the first, we're comparing the sequence $testSequence1 to the sequence matched by /report/brand/ units. The two sequences have the same five values, although they're in different orders. The two sequences are considered equal in this comparison, although only one value has to match for that to be true. Comparing the sequence from the XML document to $testSequence2 makes this clear; although the two sequences have only one value in common, they are considered equal. In addition, comparing $testSequence2 with other operators, we can see that $testSequence is less than, equal to, and greater than the sequence matched by /report/brand/units. This isn't intuitive, but that's how it works.

The difference in the third example is that $testSequence3 is a sequence of xs:strings. Because we're not using an XML Schema, the values from the XML document are untyped. The XSLT processor automatically converted the values from the document to xs:integers in the previous two examples, and it converts them to xs:strings here. The sequence ('blue', 'white', '19268') matches because converting the untyped value of the parsed <units>19268</units> element to a string creates the value '19268'.

The final example here demonstrates comparisons with a sequence of xs:yearMonthDurations. We create a sequence of three values, and then compare it to the value xs:yearMonthDuration('P4Y7M'). Because one of the values is greater than 4 years, 7 months, this returns true.

More sophisticated operations on sequences are possible. See the sections "[2.0] Quantified Expressions—some and every" and "[2.0] Set Operators—except, intersect, and union" later in this chapter.

[2.0] Conditional Expressions—if, then, and else

One of the less elegant features of XSLT is its if-then-else logic. If I want to test one condition (a simple if), I use <xsl:if>. If I want to change that to test more than one condition or add an else case, I have to use <xsl:choose>, <xsl:when>, and <xsl:otherwise>. (We cover those elements in Chapter 5.) XPath 2.0 gives us the extremely useful if operator. We can now do if-then-else logic inside the XPath expression itself.

For comparison, here's how we do things in XSLT 1.0:

```
<?xml version="1.0"?>
<!-- if-1_0.xsl -->
<xsl:stylesheet version="1.0"
  xmlns:xsl="http://www.w3.org/1999/XSL/Transform">

  <xsl:param name="x" select="'10'"/>

  <xsl:output method="text"/>

  <xsl:template match="/">
    <xsl:text>&#xA;An example of if-then-else logic in XSLT 1.0:</xsl:text>
    <xsl:text>&#xA;&#xA;  If $x is larger than 10, print 'Big', </xsl:text>
    <xsl:text>&#xA;    otherwise print 'Little'</xsl:text>
    <xsl:text>&#xA;&#xA;          </xsl:text>
    <xsl:choose>
      <xsl:when test="$x &gt; 10">
        <xsl:text>Big</xsl:text>
      </xsl:when>
      <xsl:otherwise>
        <xsl:text>Little</xsl:text>
      </xsl:otherwise>
    </xsl:choose>
    <xsl:text>&#xA;</xsl:text>
  </xsl:template>

</xsl:stylesheet>
```

We look at the value of $x and write Big if it's larger than 10; otherwise, we write Little. Pretty simple stuff, but the <xsl:choose> element takes up 8 lines here. To do the same thing in XSLT 2.0, it's much simpler:

```
<?xml version="1.0"?>
<!-- if-2_0.xsl -->
<xsl:stylesheet version="2.0"
  xmlns:xsl="http://www.w3.org/1999/XSL/Transform">

  <xsl:param name="x" select="10"/>

  <xsl:output method="text"/>

  <xsl:template match="/">
    ...
    <xsl:value-of select="if ($x &gt; 10) then 'Big' else 'Little'"/>
```

```
    ...
  </xsl:template>

</xsl:stylesheet>
```

We've accomplished the same result with a single XPath expression.

There are two important details to remember when using the `if` operator: the expression we're testing must be enclosed in parentheses, and we *always* have to use the `else` keyword.

[2.0] Iterators Over Sequences—The for Operator

Given XSLT 2.0's emphasis on sequences, it makes sense that we would have an operator to iterate through all the values of a sequence. Just as the `if` operator lets you put the logic of `<xsl:choose>` into an XPath expression, the `for` operator gives XPath expressions the power of `<xsl:for-each>`. Here is a stylesheet with an example:

```
<?xml version="1.0"?>
<!-- for.xsl -->
<xsl:stylesheet version="2.0"
  xmlns:xsl="http://www.w3.org/1999/XSL/Transform"
  xmlns:xs="http://www.w3.org/2001/XMLSchema">

  <xsl:output method="text"/>

  <xsl:variable name="English-months" as="xs:string*"
    select="('January', 'February', 'March', 'April',
             'May', 'June', 'July', 'August',
             'September', 'October', 'November',
             'December')"/>
  <xsl:variable name="German-months" as="xs:string*"
    select="('Januar', 'Februar', 'März', 'April',
             'Mai', 'Juni', 'Juli', 'August',
             'September', 'Oktober', 'November',
             'Dezember')"/>

  <xsl:template match="/">
    <xsl:value-of
      select="for $m in ($English-months, $German-months) return
                if (starts-with($m, 'J'))
                  then concat ($m, ' starts with J!&#xA;')
                  else ''"
      separator=""/>
  </xsl:template>

</xsl:stylesheet>
```

[2.0] Quantified Expressions—some and every

XPath 2.0 provides the `some` and `every` operators to perform a test against a sequence. The `some` operator returns `true` if the test is true for at least one item in the sequence, while **every** returns `false` if the test is false for at least one item in the sequence. Here is an example of the two operators:

```
<?xml version="1.0"?>
<!-- some-every.xsl -->
<xsl:stylesheet version="2.0"
  xmlns:xsl="http://www.w3.org/1999/XSL/Transform"
  xmlns:xs="http://www.w3.org/2001/XMLSchema">

  <xsl:output method="text"/>

  <xsl:variable name="English-months" as="xs:string*"
    select="('January', 'February', 'March', 'April',
             'May', 'June', 'July', 'August',
             'September', 'October', 'November',
             'December')"/>

  <xsl:template match="/">
    <xsl:text>&#xA;An example of the XPath 2.0 every and </xsl:text>
    <xsl:text>some operators:&#xA;&#xA;</xsl:text>
    <xsl:text>  If ANY month name has a string-length() </xsl:text>
    <xsl:text>&#xA;    greater than 4, print 'Yes,' otherwise</xsl:text>
    <xsl:text>&#xA;    print 'No'&#xA;&#xA;         </xsl:text>

    <xsl:value-of
      select="if (some $m in $English-months satisfies
                 (string-length($m) &gt; 4)) then 'Yes' else 'No'"/>

    <xsl:text>&#xA;</xsl:text>
    <xsl:text>&#xA;&#xA;  If EVERY month name has a string-</xsl:text>
    <xsl:text>length() &#xA;    greater than 4, print 'Yes,' </xsl:text>
    <xsl:text>otherwise&#xA;    print 'No'&#xA;&#xA;         </xsl:text>

    <xsl:value-of
      select="if (every $m in $English-months satisfies
                 (string-length($m) &gt; 4)) then 'Yes' else 'No'"/>

    <xsl:text>&#xA;</xsl:text>
  </xsl:template>

</xsl:stylesheet>
```

We have a sequence containing the months of the year in English, and we use **some** and **every** against that sequence. We're testing to see whether each month name has a `string-length( )` greater than 4. The **some** expression returns `true`, while the **every** expression returns `false`. This stylesheet is written to illustrate the new operands; it doesn't use anything from an XML document. In a more normal case, we would use **some** and **every** against an XPath expression that selected nodes from an XML document. If you replace the variable `$English-months` with `/sonnet/lines/line` in the two preceding expressions, both will evaluate to `true`, assuming you use the stylesheet to process `sonnet.xml`.

Complications of the some and every Operators

It's entirely possible that the sequence you're testing is empty. If your expression is `some $m in /sonnet/lines/words` (or anything that returns an empty sequence), the `some` operator returns `false`, while the `every` operator returns `true`. This less-than-intuitive result is defined by the XPath 2.0 and XQuery 1.0 Functions and Operators specification (Section 3.9, if you want to take a look). These results for empty sequences make more sense if you think about a simple way to evaluate these operators:

- For the `some` operator, assume the result is `false`. As we evaluate the test against each item in the sequence, if the test is ever `true`, we stop evaluating the items and return `true`. If we get to the end of the sequence and we haven't found any item for which the test is `true`, we'll return `false`.

- For the `every` operator, assume the result is `true`. As we evaluate the test against each item in the sequence, if the test is ever `false`, we stop evaluating the items and return `false`. If we get to the end of the sequence and we haven't found any item for which the test is `false`, we'll return `true`.

A complication of this rule is that a `some` or `every` expression might contain a fatal error if all of the items in the test sequence were evaluated. The XPath spec does not define any required behavior here. If an XSLT processor tests items only until it knows the value of `some` or `every`, those errors might never be encountered. Here are two examples from the XPath spec:

```
some $x in (1, 2, "cat") satisfies $x * 2 = 4
every $x in (1, 2, "cat") satisfies $x * 2 = 4
```

If an XSLT processor evaluates the items in the sequence from the first to the last, and it stops evaluating items as soon as it determines the final result, the fatal error `"cat" * 2` won't happen. The test is `true` for the value 2, so `some` returns `true`. The test is `false` for the value 1, so `every` returns `false`.

The XPath specification does not say how a processor must implement `some` and `every`, nor does it specify the order in which items in the sequence are evaluated. A processor's internal structures might make it simpler to start at the end of the sequence; if so, both of these expressions would generate a fatal error. The most ominous implication of this behavior is that the fatal error might happen intermittently based on the input data. You can avoid this by using the datatyping operators, which we'll discuss soon. (You can also avoid this if your data has been validated before it gets to the XSLT processor, assuming you trust your data source implicitly....)

[2.0] Range Expressions—The to Operator

To create sequences of integers, XPath 2.0 introduces the `to` operator. For example, here is a short stylesheet that creates a sequence of five integers and a reversed sequence of five integers, then prints the values of the sequences:

```
<?xml version="1.0"?>
<!-- to.xsl -->
```

```
<xsl:stylesheet version="2.0"
  xmlns:xsl="http://www.w3.org/1999/XSL/Transform"
  xmlns:xs="http://www.w3.org/2001/XMLSchema">

  <xsl:output method="text"/>

  <xsl:variable name="some-numbers" as="xs:integer*"
    select="1 to 5"/>

  <xsl:variable name="reversed-numbers" as="xs:integer*"
    select="reverse(1 to 5)"/>

  <xsl:template match="/">
    <xsl:value-of select="$some-numbers" separator=", "/>
    <xsl:text>
</xsl:text>
    <xsl:value-of select="$reversed-numbers" separator=", "/>
  </xsl:template>

</xsl:stylesheet>
```

The to operator creates only sequences of integers. If the second number is lower than the first (10 to 1, for example), the result is an empty sequence. If the second number is the same as the first (such as 10 to 10), the result is a sequence that contains that single integer.

Be aware that the to operator can be used as part of a larger sequence. For example, we could create the sequence (1 to 17, 65 to 100). Finally, if you need to create a sequence of numbers in descending order, you can use the [2.0] reverse( ) function (see Appendix C) to reverse the sequence of integers created with the to operator.

The results of this stylesheet look like this:

```
1, 2, 3, 4, 5
5, 4, 3, 2, 1
```

[2.0] Constructor Functions

XPath 2.0 introduces the idea of *constructor functions*, which are similar to constructor functions in object-oriented languages. As with object-oriented languages, the name of the constructor function is the name of the datatype. Here's how to create a value of type xs:date:

```
<xsl:variable name="birthday" select="xs:date('1995-04-21')"/>
```

This takes the string 1995-04-21 and creates a new value of type xs:date. This can cause runtime errors, as you would expect. A stylesheet that contains this instruction won't run at all:

```
<xsl:variable name="birthday" select="xs:date('next Tuesday')"/>
```

This is a static error because the stylesheet processor knows this instruction will fail. On the other hand, we'll get a runtime error if we send bad data to the `xs:date` constructor while the stylesheet is being processed:

```
<xsl:variable name="birthday" select="xs:date(@birthday)"/>
```

This uses the `birthday` attribute of the current node to create a new `xs:date` value. If that attribute contains a value that can be cast as a `xs:date`, everything is fine; if the attribute doesn't contain valid data, we get a runtime error.

[2.0] Datatype Operators—instance of, castable as, cast as, and treat as

As you would expect, a language that supports datatypes and constructors also has operators to convert a value from one type to another. XPath 2.0 provides four operators: `instance of`, `castable as`, `cast as`, and `treat as`. We'll cover those here.

instance of

The `instance of` operator lets us see whether a value is an instance of a particular datatype. Here are some examples:

```
<?xml version="1.0"?>
<!-- instance-of.xsl -->
<xsl:stylesheet version="2.0"
  xmlns:xsl="http://www.w3.org/1999/XSL/Transform"
  xmlns:xs="http://www.w3.org/2001/XMLSchema">

  <xsl:output method="text"/>

  <xsl:template match="/">
    <xsl:text>&#xA;Some tests of the "instance of" operator:</xsl:text>

    <xsl:text>&#xA;&#xA;  '1995-04-21' instance of xs:date: </xsl:text>
    <xsl:value-of select="'1995-04-21' instance of xs:date"/>
    <xsl:text>&#xA;  xs:date('1995-04-21') instance of xs:date: </xsl:text>
    <xsl:value-of select="xs:date('1995-04-21') instance of xs:date"/>
    <xsl:text>&#xA;&#xA;  3 instance of xs:integer: </xsl:text>
    <xsl:value-of select="3 instance of xs:integer"/>
    <xsl:text>&#xA;  '3' instance of xs:integer: </xsl:text>
    <xsl:value-of select="'3' instance of xs:integer"/>
    <xsl:text>&#xA;  number('3') instance of xs:integer: </xsl:text>
    <xsl:value-of select="number('3') instance of xs:integer"/>
    <xsl:text>&#xA;  number('3') instance of xs:double: </xsl:text>
    <xsl:value-of select="number('3') instance of xs:double"/>
    <xsl:text>&#xA;  xs:integer('3') instance of xs:integer: </xsl:text>
    <xsl:value-of select="xs:integer('3') instance of xs:integer"/>
    <xsl:text>&#xA;  'e' instance of xs:integer: </xsl:text>
    <xsl:value-of select="'e' instance of xs:integer"/>

  </xsl:template>
</xsl:stylesheet>
```

The results of the stylesheet are:

```
Some tests of the "instance of" operator:

    '1995-04-21' instance of xs:date: false
    xs:date('1995-04-21') instance of xs:date: true

    3 instance of xs:integer: true
    '3' instance of xs:integer: false
    number('3') instance of xs:integer: false
    number('3') instance of xs:double: true
    xs:integer('3') instance of xs:integer: true
    'e' instance of xs:integer: false
```

For the first test, we're asking whether the string value 1995-04-21 is an instance of xs:date. This is false; XPath doesn't automatically try to cast the string as an xs:date. In the second test, we use the xs:date constructor function to create a new xs:date value with the string. This test is true.

The last six tests here check the xs:integer datatype. The atomic value 3, as we would expect, is an xs:integer. The string '3' is not an xs:integer, even though we can cast it as one (we'll look at casting next). In addition to casting, another way to convert a string to a numeric value is to use the number( ) function. The number( ) function returns an xs:double, so instance of xs:integer is false. Using the constructor function xs:integer( ) returns an xs:integer, of course. Finally, the value 'e' isn't an xs:integer and can't be cast as one.

cast as

The instance of operator tells us about the datatype of a value; it doesn't actually convert the value to the appropriate datatype. There are times when we want to take a value of a particular datatype and create the equivalent value of another. In other programming languages, this is done by *casting*. XPath 2.0 provides the cast as operator to do just that. Here are a few examples:

```
<?xml version="1.0"?>
<!-- cast-as.xsl -->
<xsl:stylesheet version="2.0"
  xmlns:xsl="http://www.w3.org/1999/XSL/Transform"
  xmlns:xs="http://www.w3.org/2001/XMLSchema">

<xsl:output method="text"/>

<xsl:template match="/">
  <xsl:text>&#xA;Some tests of the "cast as" operator:</xsl:text>

  <xsl:text>&#xA;&#xA;  '1995-04-21' cast as xs:date: </xsl:text>
  <xsl:value-of select="'1995-04-21' cast as xs:date"/>
  <xsl:text>&#xA;  '3' cast as xs:integer: </xsl:text>
  <xsl:value-of select="'3' cast as xs:integer"/>
  <xsl:text>&#xA;  3 cast as xs:integer: </xsl:text>
  <xsl:value-of select="3 cast as xs:integer"/>
```

```
<xsl:text>&#xA;    'e' cast as xs:integer: </xsl:text>
<xsl:text>[causes a fatal error if we try it]</xsl:text>

    </xsl:template>
</xsl:stylesheet>
```

In this sample, we cast the string **1995-04-21** to an **xs:date**. This works without a hitch, as do the next two tests. The fourth test, **'3' cast as xs:integer**, fails if we try to execute it. The stylesheet won't run at all because this is a static error. Here are the results:

```
Some tests of the "cast as" operator:

'1995-04-21' cast as xs:date: 1995-04-21
'3' cast as xs:integer: 3
3 cast as xs:integer: 3
'e' cast as xs:integer: [causes a fatal error if we try it]
```

As you'd expect, it's a dynamic error if we extract a value from an XML source document and try to cast it to a datatype that won't work. If only we had a way to see if **cast as** would work before we actually tried it, we could avoid dynamic errors....

castable as

The **castable as** operator lets us see whether a given cast will work. If it won't, we can respond to that gracefully instead of having our stylesheet fail. Here's how we use castable as:

```
<?xml version="1.0"?>
<!-- castable-as.xsl -->
<xsl:stylesheet version="2.0"
  xmlns:xsl="http://www.w3.org/1999/XSL/Transform"
  xmlns:xs="http://www.w3.org/2001/XMLSchema">

  <xsl:output method="text"/>

  <xsl:template match="/">
    <xsl:text>&#xA;Some tests of the "castable as" operator:</xsl:text>

    <xsl:text>&#xA;&#xA;    '1995-04-21' castable as xs:date: </xsl:text>
    <xsl:value-of select="'1995-04-21' castable as xs:date"/>
    <xsl:text>&#xA;    '3' castable as xs:integer: </xsl:text>
    <xsl:value-of select="'3' castable as xs:integer"/>
    <xsl:text>&#xA;    3 castable as xs:integer: </xsl:text>
    <xsl:value-of select="3 castable as xs:integer"/>
    <xsl:text>&#xA;    'e' castable as xs:integer: </xsl:text>
    <xsl:value-of select="'e' castable as xs:integer"/>

    </xsl:template>
</xsl:stylesheet>
```

With the **castable as** operator, we can see whether a cast will work before we try it. If it's not going to work (we can't convert **e** to an **xs:integer**), we can do something else in our stylesheet. Here are the results from our stylesheet:

```
Some tests of the "castable as" operator:

    '1995-04-21' castable as xs:date: true
    '3' castable as xs:integer: true
    3 castable as xs:integer: true
    'e' castable as xs:integer: false
```

treat as

There is one more operator XPath gives us: the **treat as** operator. This one is a little harder to grasp. To understand why it's needed, we'll have to talk about *static types* and *dynamic types*. A static datatype is the type of a value as it is declared. A dynamic type may be more specific than the static type; more often they're the same. To take an example from the XPath 2.0 spec, the static type of a variable could be **xs:integer***, yet its dynamic type could be **xs:integer**. Here's an example:

```
<xsl:variable name="integerSequence" as="xs:integer+" select="(3)"/>
```

The variable **$integerSequence** is a sequence of one or more integers. In this instance, however, **$integerSequence** is also a single integer. Here's an example in which we treat a sequence of integers as a single integer:

```
<?xml version="1.0"?>
<!-- treat-as.xsl -->
<xsl:stylesheet version="2.0"
  xmlns:xsl="http://www.w3.org/1999/XSL/Transform"
  xmlns:xs="http://www.w3.org/2001/XMLSchema">

  <xsl:output method="text"/>

  <xsl:variable name="numbers" as="xs:integer*">
    <xsl:sequence select="/numbers/number"/>
  </xsl:variable>

  <xsl:template match="/">
    <xsl:variable name="number" as="xs:integer"
      select="$numbers treat as xs:integer"/>

    <xsl:text>&#xA;An example of the XPath 2.0 treat as </xsl:text>
    <xsl:text>operator:&#xA;&#xA;</xsl:text>
    <xsl:text>  Treat a sequence of integers as a single integer:</xsl:text>
    <xsl:text>&#xA;          </xsl:text>

    <xsl:value-of select="$number"/>
  </xsl:template>

</xsl:stylesheet>
```

Here we have a variable that consists of a sequence of values of `<number>` elements in an XML document. If there is only one number in the sequence, the stylesheet works. If the sequence isn't a singleton (it's empty or has more than one integer), we get a runtime error. This XML document, for example, doesn't cause any problems:

```
<?xml version="1.0" encoding="utf-8"?>
<!-- numbers.xml -->
<numbers>
  <number>3</number>
</numbers>
```

Adding more `<number>` elements (or using a document that doesn't have any `<number>` elements at all) causes a runtime error. The `treat as` operator tells the XSLT processor not to worry about the inconsistencies between datatypes (`xs:integer*` versus `xs:integer`), but it puts the burden on us to make sure the dynamic type of the data is correct. To do that, of course, we can use the `cast as` and `castable as` operators.

[2.0] Set Operators—except, intersect, and union

One weakness of XPath 1.0 was the inability to compare sets of nodes. If we selected two node-sets with two XPath 1.0 expressions, it was difficult to tell which nodes were in both sets and which were in one set but not the other. XPath 2.0 has two new set operators, `except` and `intersect`. If you enjoy extra typing, XPath 2.0 also adds the `union` operator, a synonym for the vertical bar operator (|) in XPath 1.0. (The vertical bar is still supported in XPath 2.0.)

Be aware that these operators work only on sequences of nodes. If you try to use them with sequences that contain atomic values, you'll get an error.

As we discuss these operators, we'll use this XML document:

```
<?xml version="1.0" encoding="utf-8"?>
<!-- books.xml -->
<favorite-books>
  <booklist>
    <book isbn="0596000537"
      favorite="Doug Sheri">XSLT</book>
    <book isbn="0141439777"
      favorite="Doug">Tristram Shandy</book>
    <book isbn="0142437298"
      favorite="Doug">Herzog</book>
    <book isbn="0679762108"
      favorite="Doug Sheri">The Sportswriter</book>
    <book isbn="0143035479"
      favorite="Sheri">The Girls' Guide to Hunting and Fishing</book>
    <book isbn="0375724443"
      favorite="Sheri">Ava's Man</book>
  </booklist>
</favorite-books>
```

We'll select two sequences in our sample stylesheets: the books I like (the `favorite` attribute contains the string `Doug`) and the books my wife likes (the `favorite` attribute contains the string `Sheri`). We'll use those two sequences to illustrate the set operators.

The except, intersect, and union operators compare *the nodes themselves*, not the values of those nodes. If two different nodes have the same value, they are still two different nodes. These operators help you select different nodes, not different values. If you're curious about the values of the nodes, the new [2.0] distinct-values( ) function (see Appendix C) will probably be useful.

Here is a sample stylesheet for the except operator:

```
<?xml version="1.0"?>
<!-- except.xsl -->
<xsl:stylesheet version="2.0"
  xmlns:xsl="http://www.w3.org/1999/XSL/Transform">

  <xsl:output method="text"/>

  <xsl:variable name="Dougs-favorites" as="node()*">
    <xsl:sequence
      select="/favorite-books/booklist
              /book[contains(@favorite, 'Doug')]"/>
  </xsl:variable>

  <xsl:variable name="Sheris-favorites" as="node()*">
    <xsl:sequence
      select="/favorite-books/booklist
              /book[contains(@favorite, 'Sheri')]"/>
  </xsl:variable>

  <xsl:template match="/">
    <xsl:text>&#xA;Books Doug likes but Sheri doesn't:</xsl:text>
    <xsl:text>&#xA;&#xA;   </xsl:text>

    <xsl:for-each select="$Dougs-favorites except $Sheris-favorites">
      <xsl:sort select="."/>
      <xsl:value-of select="."/>
      <xsl:text>&#xA;   </xsl:text>
    </xsl:for-each>
  </xsl:template>

</xsl:stylesheet>
```

The other sample stylesheets are identical, but they use the intersect and union operators instead.

except

The except operator returns all of the nodes that are in the first sequence but not in the second. Given our two sequences, the expression $Dougs-favorites except $Sheris-favorites generates these results:

```
Books Doug likes but Sheri doesn't:
```

```
    Herzog
    Tristram Shandy
```

intersect

Given two sequences of nodes, `intersect` returns a sequence containing all of the nodes in both sequences. *All duplicate nodes are removed*; each node appears only once. The `intersect` operator returns these results:

```
<!-- intersect.xsl -->
...
    <xsl:for-each select="$Dougs-favorites intersect $Sheris-favorites">
...

Books we both like:

  The Sportswriter
  XSLT
```

union

The `union` operator returns a node-set containing all nodes in both sets. As with the `intersect` operator, all duplicates are removed. Using the `union` operator gives us these results:

```
<!-- union.xsl -->
...
    <xsl:for-each select="$Dougs-favorites union $Sheris-favorites">
...

All the books we like:

  Ava's Man
  Herzog
  The Girls' Guide to Hunting and Fishing
  The Sportswriter
  Tristram Shandy
  XSLT
```

As we noted earlier, the vertical bar (|) operator is still supported. Changing the stylesheet from:

```
<xsl:for-each select="$Dougs-favorites union $Sheris-favorites">
```

to:

```
<xsl:for-each select="$Dougs-favorites | $Sheris-favorites">
```

generates the same results.

To emphasize the point that these operators compare nodes, not their values, we could change the structure of our list of books:

```
<favorite-books>
  <favorites person="Doug">
    <book isbn="0679762108">The Sportswriter</book>
```

```
        </favorites>
    <favorites person="Sheri">
        <book isbn="0679762108">The Sportswriter</book>
    </favorites>
</favorite-books>
```

The two `<book>` elements here have identical values, but they are two different nodes. The `except`, `intersect`, and `union` operators treat them as such.

[2.0] Node Operators

XPath 2.0 defines three new operators to work with nodes: the `is` operator, the node-before operator (`<<`), and the node-after operator (`>>`).

The is operator

The `is` operator compares two nodes to see whether they are the same. This compares the nodes themselves, not their values. Continuing our example from the previous section, here's a stylesheet that illustrates how the operator works:

```
<?xml version="1.0"?>
<!-- is.xsl -->
<xsl:stylesheet version="2.0"
    xmlns:xsl="http://www.w3.org/1999/XSL/Transform">

  <xsl:output method="text"/>

  <xsl:variable name="Dougs-favorites" as="node()*">
    <xsl:sequence
      select="/favorite-books/booklist
              /book[contains(@favorite, 'Doug')]"/>
  </xsl:variable>

  <xsl:variable name="Sheris-favorites" as="node()*">
    <xsl:sequence
      select="/favorite-books/booklist
              /book[contains(@favorite, 'Sheri')]"/>
  </xsl:variable>

  <xsl:template match="/">
    <xsl:text>A test of the is operator:</xsl:text>
    <xsl:text>&#xA;  Comparing the first nodes of </xsl:text>
    <xsl:text>the sequences:&#xA;</xsl:text>

    <xsl:value-of
      select="if (subsequence($Dougs-favorites, 1, 1) is
                  subsequence($Sheris-favorites, 1, 1))
              then '   The first nodes are the same!&#xA;'
              else '   The first nodes aren''t the same!&#xA;'"/>

    <xsl:text>  Reversing one sequence and trying it </xsl:text>
    <xsl:text>again:&#xA;</xsl:text>
```

```
<xsl:value-of
  select="if (subsequence($Dougs-favorites, 1, 1) is
              subsequence(reverse($Sheris-favorites), 1, 1))
          then '    The first nodes are the same!&#xA;'
          else '    The first nodes aren''t the same!&#xA;'"/>
</xsl:template>

</xsl:stylesheet>
```

This stylesheet creates two sequences of nodes, then compares the first nodes of each sequence. In the first example, the nodes are the same. In the second example, we reverse the order of one of the sequences, so the nodes are not the same. (Of course, if each sequence contained only one item, **is** would still return **true**.) Here are the results:

```
A test of the is operator:

Comparing the first nodes of the sequences:
  The first nodes are the same!
Reversing one sequence and trying it again:
  The first nodes aren't the same!
```

node-after (>>)

The node-after operator compares two nodes. If the first node occurs after the second, node-after returns **true**; otherwise, it returns **false**. The expression **node1 >> node1** returns **false**, as you would expect; a node can't appear after itself. Here's a sample stylesheet:

```
<?xml version="1.0"?>
<!-- node-after.xsl -->
<xsl:stylesheet version="2.0"
  xmlns:xsl="http://www.w3.org/1999/XSL/Transform">

<xsl:output method="text"/>

<xsl:variable name="Dougs-favorites" as="node()*">
  <xsl:sequence
    select="/favorite-books/booklist
            /book[contains(@favorite, 'Doug')]"/>
</xsl:variable>

<xsl:template match="/">
  <xsl:text>A test of the node-after (>>) operator:</xsl:text>
  <xsl:text>&#xA;&#xA;  Comparing nodes from </xsl:text>
  <xsl:text>the sequence:&#xA;</xsl:text>

  <xsl:value-of
    select="if (subsequence($Dougs-favorites, 1, 1) >>
                subsequence($Dougs-favorites, 2, 1))
            then '    node1 >> node2 = true&#xA;'
            else '    node1 >> node2 = false&#xA;'"/>
  <xsl:value-of
    select="if (subsequence($Dougs-favorites, 2, 1) >>
                subsequence($Dougs-favorites, 1, 1))
```

```
            then '    node2 >> node1 = true&#xA;'
            else '    node2 >> node1 = false&#xA;'"/>
        <xsl:value-of
          select="if (subsequence($Dougs-favorites, 1, 1) >>
                      subsequence($Dougs-favorites, 1, 1))
            then '    node1 >> node1 = true&#xA;'
            else '    node1 >> node1 = false&#xA;'"/>
      </xsl:template>

    </xsl:stylesheet>
```

The nodes in the sequence $Dougs-favorites are in document order, so node1 >> node2 returns false and node2 >> node1 returns true. In the third example, we compare the node to itself. A node can't appear before itself, so node1 >> node1 returns false. Here are the results:

```
A test of the node-after (>>) operator:

  Comparing nodes from the sequence:
    node1 >> node2 = false
    node2 >> node1 = true
    node1 >> node1 = false
```

node-before (<<)

The node-before operator compares two nodes and returns true if the first node appears in the document before the second. Replacing the node-after operator with the node-before operator in our previous stylesheet gives these results:

```
A test of the node-before (<<) operator:

  Comparing nodes from the sequence:
    node1 << node2 = true
    node2 << node1 = false
    node1 << node1 = false
```

 Although the specs define the node-before operator as <<, we have to escape the less-than sign inside an XPath expression. The expressions in the stylesheet use the node-before operator in the form node1 << node2.

[2.0] Comments in XPath Expressions

Another addition to the XPath 2.0 syntax is the ability to add comments. Using delightfully happy syntax, a comment begins with (: and ends with :). We'll use a stylesheet with a complicated if statement:

```
<?xml version="1.0"?>
<!-- comments.xsl -->
<xsl:stylesheet version="2.0"
  xmlns:xsl="http://www.w3.org/1999/XSL/Transform">
```

```
<xsl:output method="text"/>

<xsl:template match="/">
  <xsl:for-each select="cars/make">
    <xsl:text>&#xA;  Car: </xsl:text>
    <xsl:value-of select="."/>
    <xsl:text> - </xsl:text>
    <xsl:value-of
      select="(: Most of our cars are from North America,
                  so we look there first :)
              if (@geography = 'North America') then
                'Domestic car'

              (: Next, see if the car is from Europe :)
              else if (@geography = 'Europe') then
                'Import from Europe'

              (: Check for Asia :)
              else if (@geography = 'Asia') then
                &quot;It's from Asia&quot;

              (: If it's anything else, just say
                'We don't know' :)
              else
                'We don''t know!'"/>

  </xsl:for-each>
</xsl:template>

</xsl:stylesheet>
```

The stylesheet has three **if** statements that check the value of the **geography** attribute of an element. We've used spacing and comments liberally here to make the code more legible. In the last comment, you can see that we don't have to escape quote marks inside the comment, although we do have to handle them appropriately outside the comment. For one quote that contains an apostrophe, we wrap the text in double quotes (`&quot;It's from Asia&quot;`). For the next quote, we use a doubled apostrophe (`'We don''t know!'`) to display the text.

Here's the XML document we'll transform:

```
<?xml version="1.0"?>
<!-- carlist-geography.xml -->
<cars>
  <make geography="Europe">Alfa Romeo</make>
  <make geography="Europe">Bentley</make>
  <make geography="North America">Chevrolet</make>
  <make geography="North America">Dodge</make>
  <make geography="North America">GMC</make>
  <make geography="Asia">Honda</make>
  <make geography="Asia">Isuzu</make>
  <make geography="?">Quantum</make>
</cars>
```

The output looks like this:

```
Car: Alfa Romeo - Import from Europe
Car: Bentley - Import from Europe
Car: Chevrolet - Domestic car
Car: Dodge - Domestic car
Car: GMC - Domestic car
Car: Honda - Import from Asia
Car: Isuzu - Import from Asia
Car: Quantum - We don't know!
```

These comments work only within an XPath statement; you can't use them to comment out parts of your stylesheet. Comments can also be nested. If we wanted to remove the `if` statement that checks for European cars, we could comment out that entire section of the XPath expression:

```
(: (: Next, see if the car is from Europe :)

else if (@geography = 'Europe') then
  'Import from Europe' :)
```

This comment includes our earlier comment and the `if` statement. XPath comments are more convenient than XML comments, which cannot be nested.

[2.0] Types of XSLT 2.0 Processors

The XSLT 2.0 spec defines two types of XSLT 2.0 processors:

Schema-aware processors
> A *schema-aware* XSLT 2.0 processor supports user-defined schemas. In other words, we can use XML Schema to define our own datatypes and document structures, then ask the processor to validate values or nodes against that schema.

Basic processors
> A *basic* XSLT 2.0 processor supports only the datatypes defined in the XML Schema Datatypes spec, with a few extra datatypes added by the XPath 2.0 and XQuery 1.0 Data Model spec. We covered all of those datatypes earlier in this chapter.

For a brief introduction to XML Schema, as well as a short discussion of how schemas are used in XSLT 2.0 stylesheets, see Appendix D.

The XPath View of an XML Document

Before we leave the subject of XPath, we'll look at a stylesheet that generates a pictorial view of a document. The stylesheet has to distinguish between all of the different XPath node types, including any `namespace` nodes.

Output View

Figure 3-1 shows the output of our stylesheet. In this graphical view of the document, the nested HTML tables illustrate which nodes are contained inside of others, as well as the sequence in which these nodes occur in the original document. In the section of the document visible in Figure 3-1, the root of the document contains, in order, two processing instructions and two comments, followed by the `<sonnet>` element and two more comments. The `<sonnet>` element, in turn, contains two attributes and an `<auth:author>` element. The `<auth:author>` element contains a namespace node and an element.

Be aware that if you throw a very large XML document at this stylesheet, you'll get an HTML file with hundreds, perhaps thousands of tables. It's possible that your XSLT processor will run out of memory before it's finished with the document. For example, using this stylesheet to process the XML source of the Function Reference appendix creates an HTML file with more than 17,000 tables.

The Stylesheet

Now we'll take a look at the stylesheet and how it works. The stylesheet creates a number of nested tables to illustrate the XPath view of the document. We begin by writing the basic HTML elements to the output stream, defining some CSS styles and creating a legend for our nested tree view. Having created the legend for our document, we select all the different types of nodes and represent them:

```
<xsl:for-each select="*|comment()|processing-instruction()|text()">
    ...
</xsl:for-each>
```

It's very important to understand the difference between the XPath *document root* and the XML *root element*. In our XML sonnet, there are processing instructions and comments outside the root element. The document root contains those processing instructions and comments in addition to the `<sonnet>` element itself. In a location path, `/` represents the document root, while `/sonnet` represents the root element in our XML document. (The more general expression `/*` represents the root element in any document.)

[2.0] The situation is even more complicated in XPath 2.0, where you have to distinguish between a node type (document node, element node, etc.) and the *role* the node plays: nodes of any type can be at the root of a document. It's only in well-formed XML documents that we can say that the root node is a document node and its only element child is the document element. All that being said, if you're transforming XML documents, this situation will come up very rarely.

The `select` attribute in the template for the document root doesn't include attributes (`@*`) or namespace nodes (`namespace::*`) because those can't be defined on a document

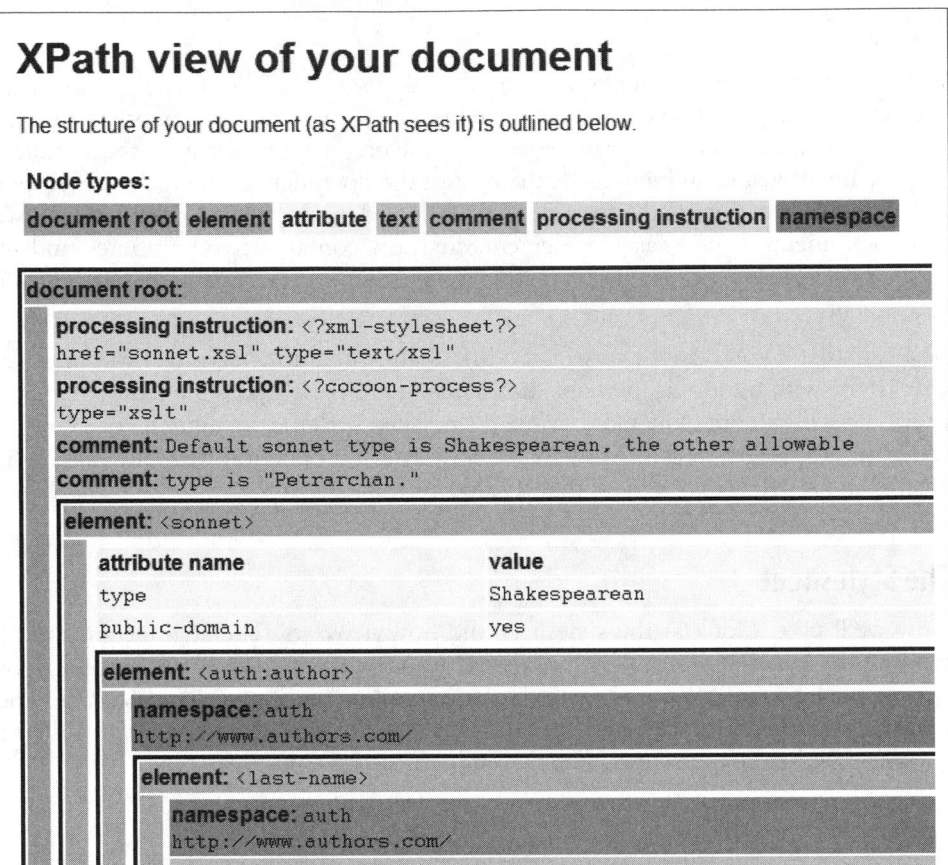

XPath view of your document

The structure of your document (as XPath sees it) is outlined below.

Node types:

document root element attribute text comment processing instruction namespace

document root:

processing instruction: `<?xml-stylesheet?>`
`href="sonnet.xsl" type="text/xsl"`

processing instruction: `<?cocoon-process?>`
`type="xslt"`

comment: Default sonnet type is Shakespearean, the other allowable

comment: type is "Petrarchan."

element: `<sonnet>`

attribute name	value
type	Shakespearean
public-domain	yes

element: `<auth:author>`

namespace: auth
http://www.authors.com/

element: `<last-name>`

namespace: auth
http://www.authors.com/

text: Shakespeare

Figure 3-1. XPath tree view of an XML document

root. If you try to select attributes or namespace nodes at the document root, some XSLT processors (Saxon, for example) give you a warning message.

The rest of the stylesheet has templates to handle each of the types of nodes. Most of them print the type of node followed by the content of that node. The only template with any complexity is the element template. We create a new table row, and then put a nested table inside the row. When we create the new table row, we use the HTML `title` and `alt` attributes. Whenever the user pauses his mouse over part of the table, a pop up appears that indicates the ancestry of the element represented in that part of the table. Here's how we create the value for the `title` and `alt` attributes:

```
<xsl:variable name="title">
  <xsl:for-each select="ancestor-or-self::*">
    <xsl:text>/</xsl:text>
    <xsl:value-of select="name()"/>
  </xsl:for-each>
```

Figure 3-2. Pop-up text shows the ancestry of each element

```
    </xsl:variable>
    <tr title="{$title}" alt="{$title}">
```

The `ancestor-or-self` axis returns all of the ancestors of the current node plus the current node itself. Even though the `ancestor-or-self` axis returns nodes that occur before the current node, the nodes it returns are in document order. In other words, the first element in the sequence returned by `ancestor-or-self` axis is the root element. Figure 3-2 shows how the pop up looks.

For this example, the sequence of nodes returned by `ancestor-or-self` are the `<sonnet>`, `<auth:author>`, and `<last-name>` elements, in that order.

The next step in processing an element is to look for attributes and namespace definitions. An element is the only type of node that can contain these. Here's how we look for them:

```
<table border="0" width="100%">
  <xsl:if test="count(@*) &gt; 0">
    <tr>
      <td>
        <table width="100%">
          <tr class="attribute">
            <td width="20%">
              <b>attribute name</b>
            </td>
            <td>
              <b>value</b>
            </td>
          </tr>
          <xsl:for-each select="@*">
            <tr class="attribute">
              <td width="20%">
                <span class="literal">
                  <xsl:value-of select="name()"/>
                </span>
              </td>
              <td>
```

```
                <span class="literal">
                    <xsl:value-of select="."/>
                </span>
            </td>
        </tr>
    </xsl:for-each>
    </table>
    </td>
    </tr>
</xsl:if>
...
```

To illustrate the structure of the document, we create a table for each element. If that element in turn contains other elements, we put those in separate tables as well. After creating the table, we check for any attribute nodes (`count(@*) &gt; 0`). If there are any attributes, we create a new table to list them.

Once all the attributes have been processed, we look for all the namespace nodes and list them as well. To do this, we employ the rarely used `namespace` axis:

```
<xsl:for-each select="namespace::*">
  <xsl:if test="name() != 'xml'">
    <xsl:call-template name="namespace-node"/>
  </xsl:if>
</xsl:for-each>
```

 We don't display the `xml` namespace prefix because it's always defined and always associated with the namespace URI `http://www.w3.org/XML/ 1998/namespace`. For a namespace node, the `name( )` function returns the namespace prefix. The value of a namespace node (`<xsl:value-of select="."/>`) is its URI. If we were looking for a namespace node that could be associated with any prefix, we would test the value of the namespace node instead. For example, this namespace definintion:

```
xmlns:sample="http://www.w3c.org/1999/XSL/Transform"
```

associates the XSLT namespace with the prefix `sample`. If we wanted to see whether the XSLT namespace were defined, we would have to use the value of the namespace node instead of simply looking for the usual prefix `xsl`.

Finally, we use `<xsl:apply-templates>` to process everything contained in the element:

```
<xsl:apply-templates select="node()"/>
```

Here's the complete stylesheet:

```
<?xml version="1.0" encoding="utf-8"?>
<!--xpath-1_0-tree-diagram.xsl -->
<xsl:stylesheet version="1.0"
  xmlns:xsl="http://www.w3.org/1999/XSL/Transform"
  xmlns:xs="http://www.w3.org/2001/XMLSchema">

  <xsl:output method="html"/>
```

```
<xsl:template match="/">
  <html>
    <head>
      <title>XPath view of your document</title>
      <style type="text/css">
        <xsl:comment>
          .literal   { font-family: Courier, monospace; }
          .docroot   { background-color: #99CCCC; }
          .element   { background-color: #CCCC99; }
          .attribute { background-color: #FFFF99; }
          .text      { background-color: #FFCC99; }
          .comment   { background-color: #CCCCFF; }
          .pi        { background-color: #99FF99; }
          .namespace { background-color: #CC99CC; }
          .box       { border: solid black 3px; }
        </xsl:comment>
      </style>
    </head>
    <body style="font-family: sans-serif;">
      <h1>XPath view of your document</h1>
      <p>
        The structure of your document (as XPath sees it)
        is outlined below.
      </p>
      <table cellspacing="5" cellpadding="2" border="0">
        <tr>
          <td colspan="7">
            <b>Node types:</b>
          </td>
        </tr>
        <tr>
          <td class="docroot"><b>document root</b></td>
          <td class="element"><b>element</b></td>
          <td class="attribute"><b>attribute</b></td>
          <td class="text"><b>text</b></td>
          <td class="comment"><b>comment</b></td>
          <td class="pi"><b>processing instruction</b></td>
          <td class="namespace"><b>namespace</b></td>
        </tr>
      </table>
      <br/>
      <table width="100%" class="box" bgcolor="#FFFFFF"
        title="document root" alt="document root">
        <tr class="docroot">
          <td colspan="3">
            <b>document root:</b>
          </td>
        </tr>
        <tr>
          <td width="15" class="docroot"></td>
          <td>
            <table width="100%">
              <xsl:apply-templates
                select="*|comment()|processing-instruction()|text()"/>
```

```
          </table>
        </td>
        <td width="15" class="docroot"></td>
      </tr>
      <tr class="docroot">
        <td colspan="3"> </td>
      </tr>
    </table>
  </body>
</html>
</xsl:template>

<xsl:template match="comment()">
  <tr>
    <td class="comment">
      <b>comment: </b>
      <span class="literal">
        <xsl:value-of select="."/>
      </span>
    </td>
  </tr>
</xsl:template>

<xsl:template match="processing-instruction()">
  <tr>
    <td class="pi">
      <b>processing instruction: </b>
      <span class="literal">
        <xsl:text>&lt;?</xsl:text>
        <xsl:value-of select="name()"/>
        <xsl:text>?&gt;</xsl:text>
        <br/>
        <xsl:value-of select="."/>
      </span>
    </td>
  </tr>
</xsl:template>

<xsl:template match="text()">
  <xsl:if test="string-length(normalize-space(.))">
    <tr>
      <td class="text" width="100%">
        <b>text: </b>
        <span class="literal">
          <xsl:value-of select="."/>
        </span>
      </td>
    </tr>
  </xsl:if>
</xsl:template>

<xsl:template name="namespace-node">
  <tr>
    <td class="namespace">
      <b>namespace: </b>
```

```
        <span class="literal">
          <xsl:value-of select="name()"/>
        </span>
        <br/>
        <span class="literal">
          <xsl:value-of select="."/>
        </span>
      </td>
    </tr>
</xsl:template>

<xsl:template match="*">
  <xsl:variable name="title">
    <xsl:for-each select="ancestor-or-self::*">
      <xsl:text>/</xsl:text>
      <xsl:value-of select="name()"/>
    </xsl:for-each>
  </xsl:variable>
  <tr title="{$title}" alt="{$title}">
    <td>
      <table class="box" width="100%">
        <tr>
          <td class="element" colspan="3" valign="top">
            <b>element: </b>
            <span class="literal">
              <xsl:text>&lt;</xsl:text>
              <xsl:value-of select="name()"/>
              <xsl:text>&gt;</xsl:text>
            </span>
          </td>
        </tr>
        <tr>
          <td class="element" width="15">  </td>
          <td>
            <table border="0" width="100%">
              <xsl:if test="count(@*) &gt; 0">
                <tr>
                  <td>
                    <table width="100%">
                      <tr class="attribute">
                        <td width="20%">
                          <b>attribute name</b>
                        </td>
                        <td>
                          <b>value</b>
                        </td>
                      </tr>
                      <xsl:for-each select="@*">
                        <tr class="attribute">
                          <td width="20%">
                            <span class="literal">
                              <xsl:value-of select="name()"/>
                            </span>
                          </td>
                          <td>
```

```
                     <span class="literal">
                        <xsl:value-of select="."/>
                     </span>
                  </td>
               </tr>
            </xsl:for-each>
          </table>
        </td>
      </tr>
    </xsl:if>
    <xsl:for-each select="namespace::*">
      <xsl:if test="name() != 'xml'">
        <xsl:call-template name="namespace-node"/>
      </xsl:if>
    </xsl:for-each>
    <xsl:apply-templates select="node()"/>
  </table>
</td>
<td bgcolor="#CCCC99" width="15"> </td>
</tr>
<tr>
  <td colspan="3" bgcolor="#CCCC99"> </td>
</tr>
      </table>
    </td>
  </tr>
</xsl:template>

</xsl:stylesheet>
```

Before we leave this example, a couple of other techniques are worth mentioning here. First, notice that we used CSS to format some of the output. XSLT and CSS aren't mutually exclusive; you can use XSLT to generate CSS as part of an HTML page, as we demonstrated here. Second, we used wildcard expressions such as * and @* to process all the elements and attributes in our document. Use of these expressions allows us to apply this stylesheet to any XML document, regardless of the tags it uses. Because we use these wildcard expressions, we have to use the name( ) function to get the name of the element or attribute we're currently working with. Third, notice that we used conditional logic and the expression count(@*) > 0 to determine whether a given element has attributes. We'll talk more about conditional logic in Chapter 5.

Summary

We've covered the basics of XPath. Hopefully, at this point you're comfortable with the idea of writing XPath expressions to describe parts of an XML document. As we go through the following chapters, you'll see XPath expressions used in a variety of ways, all of which build on the basics we've discussed here. When you're debugging a stylesheet, you'll probably spend most of your time making sure your XPath expressions select the right data. Very few of the things we'll do in the rest of the book are possible without precise XPath expressions.

CHAPTER 4

Creating Output

Goals of This Chapter

By the end of this chapter, you should know how to:

- Generate text
- Number things, including numbering at multiple levels
- Format numbers
- *[2.0]* Format dates and times
- Use `<xsl:copy>` and `<xsl:copy-of>` to copy nodes from the input document to the output document
- Deal with whitespace

Generating Text

The first thing we'll cover is how to put text in the output. Just putting some text out there is simple enough, but we'll look at some more advanced techniques that we'll explore throughout the book. We'll look at two elements in particular: `<xsl:text>` and `<xsl:value-of>`. We'll use these to create an HTML document that contains a table of contents for an XML document. Here's the XML document we'll use:

```
<?xml version="1.0"?>
<!-- toc_source.xml -->
<article>
  <title>Creating output</title>
  <body>
    <heading1>Generating text</heading1>
    <heading1>Numbering things</heading1>
    <heading1>Formatting numbers</heading1>
    <heading1>Copying nodes from the input document to the output</heading1>
    <heading1>Handling whitespace</heading1>
  </body>
</article>
```

Creating Simple Text

There are many times you need to write some text to the output. In the first example we'll build in this chapter, we want to create HTML that looks like this:

```
<h1>Table of Contents</h1>
<h2>Generating text</h2>
<h2>Numbering things</h2>
<h2>Formatting numbers</h2>
<h2>Copying nodes from the input document to the output</h2>
<h2>Handling whitespace</h2>
```

In this output document, the text of each item in the table is the text of a particular element in the XML source. The text Table of Contents, however, is the same each time. To generate this text, we'll use the <xsl:text> element. We'll start our stylesheet by generating that text:

```
<xsl:template match="/">
  <h1>
    <xsl:text>Table of Contents</xsl:text>
  </h1>
  ...
</xsl:template>
```

All we did here was insert a string in our output document. To make things even simpler, we could have done this:

```
<xsl:template match="/">
  <h1>Table of Contents</h1>
  ...
</xsl:template>
```

For any non-XSLT element in a stylesheet (<h1>, for example), XSLT's default behavior is to simply pass that element to the output. Normally we'll use <xsl:text> when we need complete control over whitespace or when we're creating text output instead of a marked-up document such as an HTML file.

In these examples, we simply wrote text to our output document; most often we'll combine text with values from our source document. For example, we might want to generate an HTML document that looks like this:

```
<h1>Table of Contents</h1>
<p>This document contains <b>5</b> chapters:</p>
<h2>Generating text</h2>
<h2>Numbering things</h2>
...
```

The paragraph we added contains text as well as a value, which is the number of chapters in our source document. To output values such as this or the title of each chapter we need the <xsl:value-of> element, which we'll look at in just a minute.

 Before we move on to the `<xsl:value-of>` element, a quick note: if we were writing Java or C# code to create the output document, we wouldn't put literal text such as `Table of Contents` in the code itself. We'd load that string at runtime from a file of translated strings. That would let us use the same code to create a table of contents in English, Japanese, Polish, or whatever language we need. Setting up stylesheets to do the same thing is complicated, but we'll discuss how to do just that later in "The document() Function" in Chapter 8.

Outputting the Value of Something

Creating a simple text string is easy: we just use the `<xsl:text>` element. However, in any stylesheet you write, you'll probably need to output the value of something from the XML source. That's what the `<xsl:value-of>` element is for. In the example stylesheet we're building, we want to transform this element in the XML source:

```
<heading1>Generating text</heading1>
```

into this HTML element in the output:

```
<h2>Generating text</h2>
```

In other words, we want to take every `<heading1>` element and transform it into an HTML `<h2>` element that contains the value of the `<heading1>` element. Here's a template that does just that:

```
<xsl:template match="heading1">
  <h2>
    <xsl:value-of select="."/>
  </h2>
</xsl:template>
```

To generate our earlier paragraph that contains the number of chapters, we'll use `<xsl:value-of>` with the XPath `count()` function:

```
<p>
  This document contains
  <xsl:value-of select="count(/article/body/heading1)"/>
  chapters.
</p>
```

This bit of XSLT creates the following HTML paragraph:

```
<p>
    This document contains
    5
    chapters.

</p>
```

An HTML browser normalizes the whitespace before rendering it, as shown in Figure 4-1.

Figure 4-1. HTML normalizes whitespace before displaying a document

If we needed more control over the output, we could use `<xsl:value-of>` and `<xsl:text>` together:

```
<p>
  <xsl:text>This document contains </xsl:text>
  <xsl:value-of select="count(/article/body/heading1)"/>
  <xsl:text> chapters.</xsl:text>
</p>
```

This generates an HTML paragraph without any extra whitespace:

```
<p>This document contains 5 chapters.</p>
```

Notice that we had to put blank spaces inside the `<xsl:text>` elements so there would be spaces around the number 5. Finally, a simpler, but far less readable alternative would be to run all of the text and the `<xsl:value-of>` element together on a single line:

```
<p>This document contains <xsl:value-of select="count(/article/body...
```

HTML browsers typically handle whitespace the way you want; for other types of output, dealing with whitespace is a significant issue. We'll talk more about whitespace a little later.

[2.0] Changes to <xsl:value-of> in XSLT 2.0

In XSLT 2.0, `<xsl:value-of>` has a `separator` attribute. If the `select` attribute is a sequence of items, those items are output in sequence, with the value of the `separator` attribute between them. We'll look at a couple of examples that use `separator` here.

First of all, here's a short XML document that lists different automobile manufacturers and some of the cars they make:

```
<?xml version="1.0" encoding="utf-8"?>
<!-- cars.xml -->
<cars>
  <manufacturer name="Chevrolet">
    <car>Cavalier</car>
    <car>Corvette</car>
    <car>Impala</car>
    <car>Malibu</car>
  </manufacturer>
```

```
    <manufacturer name="Ford">
      <car>Pinto</car>
      <car>Mustang</car>
      <car>Taurus</car>
    </manufacturer>
    <manufacturer name="Volkswagen">
      <car>Beetle</car>
      <car>Jetta</car>
      <car>Passat</car>
      <car>Touraeg</car>
    </manufacturer>
  </cars>
```

Our first `<xsl:value-of>` element uses the **separator** attribute to list all of the manufacturers, separated by commas:

```
<?xml version="1.0" encoding="utf-8"?>
<!-- value-of_2_0.xsl -->
<xsl:stylesheet version="2.0"
  xmlns:xsl="http://www.w3.org/1999/XSL/Transform">

  <xsl:output method="text"/>

  <xsl:template match="/">
    <xsl:value-of select="cars/manufacturer/@name" separator=", "/>
  </xsl:template>

</xsl:stylesheet>
```

Transforming our XML document with this stylesheet gives us the following results:

```
Chevrolet, Ford, Volkswagen
```

The **separator** attribute is useful in this case because it is inserted after every value except the last. In XSLT 1.0, we have to do something like this:

```
<?xml version="1.0" encoding="utf-8"?>
<!-- value-of_1_0.xsl -->
<xsl:stylesheet version="1.0"
  xmlns:xsl="http://www.w3.org/1999/XSL/Transform">

  <xsl:output method="text"/>

  <xsl:template match="/">
    <xsl:for-each select="cars/manufacturer/@name">
      <xsl:value-of select="."/>
      <xsl:if test="not(position()=last())">
        <xsl:text>, </xsl:text>
      </xsl:if>
    </xsl:for-each>
  </xsl:template>

</xsl:stylesheet>
```

After we output each item, we have to see whether that item is the last; if not, we insert our separator with `<xsl:text>`. The `<xsl:for-each>` and `<xsl:if>` elements aren't necessary in XSLT 2.0; the `separator` attribute makes it much easier to create the output we want.

We can use the `separator` attribute with sequences as well. Here's an example that uses a sequence of `xs:string`s and a sequence created with XPath 2.0's new `to` operator:

```
<?xml version="1.0"?>
<!-- value-of_sequences.xsl -->
<xsl:stylesheet version="2.0"
  xmlns:xsl="http://www.w3.org/1999/XSL/Transform"
  xmlns:xs="http://www.w3.org/2001/XMLSchema">

  <xsl:output method="text"/>

  <xsl:variable name="months" as="xs:string*"
    select="'January', 'February', 'March', 'April',
            'May', 'June', 'July', 'August',
            'September', 'October', 'November', 'December'"/>

  <xsl:template match="/">
    <xsl:value-of select="1 to 7" separator=", "/>
    <xsl:text>&#xA;</xsl:text>
    <xsl:value-of select="$months" separator="&#xA;"/>
  </xsl:template>

</xsl:stylesheet>
```

This stylesheet generates the following results:

```
1, 2, 3, 4, 5, 6, 7
January
February
March
April
May
June
July
August
September
October
November
December
```

Numbering Things

XSLT provides the `<xsl:number>` element to number the parts of a document. (It can also be used to format a numeric value; more on that later.) In general, `<xsl:number>` counts something. We'll look at a variety of examples here.

To fully illustrate how `<xsl:number>` works, we'll need an XML document with some things to count. We'll reuse our list of cars from the previous section:

```
<?xml version="1.0" encoding="utf-8"?>
<!-- cars.xml -->
```

```
<cars>
  <manufacturer name="Chevrolet">
    <car>Cavalier</car>
    <car>Corvette</car>
    <car>Impala</car>
    <car>Malibu</car>
  </manufacturer>
  <manufacturer name="Ford">
    <car>Pinto</car>
    <car>Mustang</car>
    <car>Taurus</car>
  </manufacturer>
  <manufacturer name="Volkswagen">
    <car>Beetle</car>
    <car>Jetta</car>
    <car>Passat</car>
    <car>Touraeg</car>
  </manufacturer>
</cars>
```

We'll use `<xsl:number>` in several different ways to illustrate the various options we have in numbering things. We'll start with something simple:

```
<?xml version="1.0" encoding="utf-8"?>
<!-- number1.xsl -->
<xsl:stylesheet version="1.0"
  xmlns:xsl="http://www.w3.org/1999/XSL/Transform">

  <xsl:output method="html"/>

  <xsl:template match="/">
    <html>
      <head>
        <title>Automobile manufacturers and their cars</title>
      </head>
      <body>
        <xsl:for-each select="cars/manufacturer">
          <p>
            <xsl:number format="1. "/>
            <xsl:value-of select="@name"/>
          </p>
        </xsl:for-each>
      </body>
    </html>
  </xsl:template>

</xsl:stylesheet>
```

We get this HTML document:

```
<html>
  <head>
    <meta http-equiv="Content-Type" content="text/html; charset=UTF-8">
    <title>Automobile manufacturers and their cars</title>
  </head>
  <body>
```

```
      <p>1. Chevrolet</p>
      <p>2. Ford</p>
      <p>3. Volkswagen</p>
    </body>
  </html>
```

This is about the simplest example of `<xsl:number>` that you can write. (You could leave off the `format` attribute, but you'd get paragraphs such as `<p>1Chevrolet</p>`—probably not what you want.) Changing the stylesheet to use `format="a. "` generates these paragraphs:

```
      <p>a. Chevrolet</p>
      <p>b. Ford</p>
      <p>c. Volkswagen</p>
```

Here's what we get with `format="i. "`:

```
      <p>i. Chevrolet</p>
      <p>ii. Ford</p>
      <p>iii. Volkswagen</p>
```

The `<xsl:number>` element has lots of other attributes and capabilities; we'll look at the most common ones here. (See the complete description of the `<xsl:number>` element in Appendix A.) Here's an example that uses the `value` attribute:

```
<?xml version="1.0" encoding="utf-8"?>
<!-- number2.xsl -->
<xsl:stylesheet version="1.0"
  xmlns:xsl="http://www.w3.org/1999/XSL/Transform">

  <xsl:output method="html"/>

  <xsl:template match="/">
    <html>
      <head>
        <title>Automobile manufacturers and their cars</title>
      </head>
      <body>
        <xsl:for-each select="cars/manufacturer">
          <p>
            <xsl:text>Cars produced by </xsl:text>
            <xsl:value-of select="@name"/>
            <xsl:text>: </xsl:text>
            <xsl:number value="count(car)" format="01"/>
          </p>
        </xsl:for-each>
      </body>
    </html>
  </xsl:template>

</xsl:stylesheet>
```

This stylesheet generates this HTML document:

```
<html>
    <head>
```

```
      <meta http-equiv="Content-Type" content="text/html; charset=UTF-8">
      <title>Automobile manufacturers and their cars</title>
   </head>
   <body>
      <p>Cars produced by Chevrolet: 04</p>
      <p>Cars produced by Ford: 03</p>
      <p>Cars produced by Volkswagen: 04</p>
   </body>
</html>
```

In this case, we could have used `<xsl:value-of select="count(car)"/>` to get similar results, but `<xsl:number>` lets us format the number as we want.

Using `<xsl:number>` with the `format` attribute is a good way to format any value, whether it comes from the XML source or not. For example, this markup:

```
<xsl:number value="1965" format="I"/>
```

produces the text `MCMLXV`.

As you'd expect, there are more powerful things we can do. Here's an example that uses the `level` and `count` attributes:

```
<?xml version="1.0" encoding="utf-8"?>
<!-- number3.xsl -->
<xsl:stylesheet version="1.0"
  xmlns:xsl="http://www.w3.org/1999/XSL/Transform">

  <xsl:output method="text"/>

  <xsl:template match="/">
    <xsl:text>Automobile manufacturers and their cars&#xA;</xsl:text>
    <xsl:for-each select="cars/manufacturer">
      <xsl:number count="manufacturer" format="1. "/>
      <xsl:value-of select="@name"/>
      <xsl:text>&#xA;</xsl:text>
      <xsl:for-each select="car">
        <xsl:number count="manufacturer|car" level="multiple"
          format="1.1. "/>
        <xsl:value-of select="."/>
        <xsl:text>&#xA;</xsl:text>
      </xsl:for-each>
    </xsl:for-each>
  </xsl:template>

</xsl:stylesheet>
```

This stylesheet gives us the following text document:

```
Automobile manufacturers and their cars
1. Chevrolet
1.1. Cavalier
1.2. Corvette
1.3. Impala
1.4. Malibu
2. Ford
2.1. Pinto
```

```
2.2. Mustang
2.3. Taurus
3. Volkswagen
3.1. Beetle
3.2. Jetta
3.3. Passat
3.4. Touraeg
```

The `count` attribute tells the XSLT processor what elements to count, and `level="multiple"` counts the manufacturers at one level and the cars per manufacturer at another. Notice that in the second `<xsl:for-each<` element we used the attribute `count="manufacturer|car"`, even though we're looking only at `<car>` elements. That's because the number 3.2 means the second `<car>` from the third `<manufacturer>`. If we don't include the manufacturers in our count, we won't get the results we want.

The values for `level` are `single`, `multiple`, and `any`. The value `single`, the default, counts only an item's siblings, while `multiple` counts an item along with any of its ancestors (that's what we did in the previous example). `level="any"` counts an item along with everything that occurred before it in the document, whether it's an ancestor of the current item or not. Here's an example that uses `level="any"`:

```
<?xml version="1.0" encoding="utf-8"?>
<!-- number4.xsl -->
<xsl:stylesheet version="1.0"
  xmlns:xsl="http://www.w3.org/1999/XSL/Transform">

  <xsl:output method="text"/>

  <xsl:template match="/">
    <xsl:text>Automobile manufacturers and their cars&#xA;</xsl:text>
    <xsl:for-each select="cars/manufacturer">
      <xsl:number count="manufacturer|car" level="any" format="1. "/>
      <xsl:value-of select="@name"/>
      <xsl:text>&#xA;</xsl:text>
      <xsl:for-each select="car">
        <xsl:number count="manufacturer|car" level="any" format="1. "/>
        <xsl:value-of select="."/>
        <xsl:text>&#xA;</xsl:text>
      </xsl:for-each>
    </xsl:for-each>
  </xsl:template>

</xsl:stylesheet>
```

Here we use an identical `<xsl:number>` element in both places. We're counting all of the `<manufacturer>` and `<car>` elements, so we need to use `level="any"` and `count="manufacturer|car"` in both places. Here are the results:

```
Automobile manufacturers and their cars
1. Chevrolet
2. Cavalier
3. Corvette
4. Impala
5. Malibu
```

6. Ford
7. Pinto
8. Mustang
9. Taurus
10. Volkswagen
11. Beetle
12. Jetta
13. Passat
14. Touraeg

Also keep in mind that you can use `<xsl:number>` at isolated times. Here's a contrived example that counts only even-numbered cars from each manufacturer:

```
<?xml version="1.0" encoding="utf-8"?>
<!-- number5.xsl -->
<xsl:stylesheet xmlns:xsl="http://www.w3.org/1999/XSL/Transform"
                version="1.0">

  <xsl:output method="text"/>

  <xsl:template match="/">
    <xsl:text>Automobile manufacturers and their cars&#xA;</xsl:text>
    <xsl:for-each select="cars/manufacturer">
      <xsl:value-of select="@name"/>
      <xsl:text>&#xA;</xsl:text>
      <xsl:for-each select="car">
        <xsl:text>  </xsl:text>
        <xsl:if test="(position() mod 2) = 0">
          <xsl:number count="manufacturer|car" level="multiple"
            format="1.1. "/>
        </xsl:if>
        <xsl:value-of select="."/>
        <xsl:text>&#xA;</xsl:text>
      </xsl:for-each>
    </xsl:for-each>
  </xsl:template>

</xsl:stylesheet>
```

To select only even-numbered items, we use the XPath `mod` operator. If we divide the position of the current element by 2 and the result is zero, we know we have an even-numbered item. This stylesheet gives us the following list:

```
Automobile manufacturers and their cars
Chevrolet
  Cavalier
  1.2. Corvette
  Impala
  1.4. Malibu
Ford
  Pinto
  2.2. Mustang
  Taurus
Volkswagen
  Beetle
  3.2. Jetta
```

```
Passat
3.4. Touraeg
```

In this example, we used `<xsl:number>` only for even-numbered cars from each manufacturer, and we never used `<xsl:number>` for the `<manufacturer>` element at all. Despite
that, the `<xsl:number>` element calculates the correct value based on the position of the
current item in the source document.

That can lead to some complications, however. If we sort the source document as we
process it, our numbers look a little strange. We'll add a `<xsl:sort>` element to our
stylesheet:

```
<?xml version="1.0" encoding="utf-8"?>
<!-- number6.xsl -->
<xsl:stylesheet version="1.0"
  xmlns:xsl="http://www.w3.org/1999/XSL/Transform">

  <xsl:output method="text"/>

  <xsl:template match="/">
    <xsl:text>Automobile manufacturers and their cars&#xA;</xsl:text>
    <xsl:for-each select="cars/manufacturer">
      <xsl:value-of select="@name"/>
      <xsl:text>&#xA;</xsl:text>
      <xsl:for-each select="car">
        <xsl:sort select="."/>
        <xsl:text>  </xsl:text>
        <xsl:if test="(position() mod 2) = 0">
          <xsl:number count="manufacturer|car" level="multiple"
            format="1.1. "/>
        </xsl:if>
        <xsl:value-of select="."/>
        <xsl:text>&#xA;</xsl:text>
      </xsl:for-each>
    </xsl:for-each>
  </xsl:template>

</xsl:stylesheet>
```

And our results look like this:

```
Automobile manufacturers and their cars
Chevrolet
  Cavalier
  1.2. Corvette
  Impala
  1.4. Malibu
Ford
  Mustang
  2.1. Pinto
  Taurus
Volkswagen
  Beetle
  3.2. Jetta
```

```
    Passat
    3.4. Touraeg
```

The number for `Pinto` isn't what we expected. That's because the `position( )` function is based on the current (sorted) context, while the numbering we're doing is based on the original document order. In the sorted order `Pinto` is the second item, so the `test` of our `<xsl:if>` element is true. When we use `<xsl:number>`, however, `Pinto` is the first `<car>` in the source document. The result is the number `2.1` instead of the `2.2` we expected.

It's not pretty, but here's a stylesheet that fixes the problem. We use `<xsl:number>` to count `<manufacturer>` elements; that generates the first part of the number. Next we use `position( )` to output the position of the *sorted* element. The stylesheet looks like this:

```
<?xml version="1.0" encoding="utf-8"?>
<!-- number7.xsl -->
<xsl:stylesheet version="1.0"
  xmlns:xsl="http://www.w3.org/1999/XSL/Transform">

  <xsl:output method="text"/>

  <xsl:template match="/">
    <xsl:text>Automobile manufacturers and their cars&#xA;</xsl:text>
    <xsl:for-each select="cars/manufacturer">
      <xsl:value-of select="@name"/>
      <xsl:text>&#xA;</xsl:text>
      <xsl:for-each select="car">
        <xsl:sort select="."/>
        <xsl:text>  </xsl:text>
        <xsl:if test="(position() mod 2) = 0">
          <xsl:number count="manufacturer" level="multiple"
            format="1."/>
          <xsl:value-of select="position()"/>
          <xsl:text>. </xsl:text>
        </xsl:if>
        <xsl:value-of select="."/>
        <xsl:text>&#xA;</xsl:text>
      </xsl:for-each>
    </xsl:for-each>
  </xsl:template>

</xsl:stylesheet>
```

This numbers the `Pinto` using the sorted order:

```
Automobile manufacturers and their cars
Chevrolet
  Cavalier
  1.2. Corvette
  Impala
  1.4. Malibu
Ford
  Mustang
  2.2. Pinto
```

```
    Taurus
Volkswagen
  Beetle
  3.2. Jetta
  Passat
  3.4. Touraeg
```

We used `<xsl:number>` to count the position of the current car within the current man-ufacturer.

[2.0] Changes to `<xsl:number>` in XSLT 2.0

There are some changes to the `<xsl:number>` element in XSLT 2.0. First of all, three new formats have been added: w, W, and Ww. Those formats produce words in the default language on your machine (there's also a lang attribute you can use to change the language). Here's an example:

```
<?xml version="1.0" encoding="utf-8"?>
<xsl:stylesheet xmlns:xsl="http://www.w3.org/1999/XSL/Transform"
                version="2.0">

  <xsl:output method="text"/>

  <xsl:template match="/">
    <xsl:text>Automobile manufacturers and their cars&#xA;</xsl:text>
    <xsl:for-each select="cars/manufacturer">
      <xsl:value-of select="@name"/>
      <xsl:text>&#xA;</xsl:text>
      <xsl:for-each select="car">
        <xsl:text>  Car </xsl:text>
        <xsl:number count="car" level="single" format="w"/>
        <xsl:text>: </xsl:text>
        <xsl:value-of select="."/>
        <xsl:text>&#xA;</xsl:text>
      </xsl:for-each>
    </xsl:for-each>
  </xsl:template>

</xsl:stylesheet>
```

This stylesheet produces this text:

```
Automobile manufacturers and their cars
Chevrolet
  Car one: Cavalier
  Car two: Corvette
  Car three: Impala
  Car four: Malibu
Ford
  Car one: Pinto
  Car two: Mustang
  Car three: Taurus
Volkswagen
  Car one: Beetle
```

```
Car two: Jetta
Car three: Passat
Car four: Touraeg
```

Using the format W produces the numbers ONE, TWO, THREE, and so forth, while the format Ww produces One, Two, Three.

Another difference is the addition of the `select` attribute. Normally `<xsl:number>` numbers the current node; you can use the `select` attribute to generate the number for another node.

XSLT 2.0 also adds the `ordinal` attribute; `ordinal="yes"` combined with `format="1"` generates 1st, 2nd, 3rd, while `ordinal="yes"` combined with `format="Ww"` generates First, Second, Third. The `ordinal` attribute has many different options that depend on the `lang` attribute and the `format` attribute; as you would expect, each XSLT 2.0 processor supports a different set of languages and options for the `ordinal` attribute. See your processor's documentation for information on what capabilities are available.

Finally, XSLT 2.0 signals an error if your `<xsl:number>` element has incompatible attributes. For example, you can't have a `select` attribute and a `value` attribute. In XSLT 1.0, the extra attributes were ignored.

 Appendix F has a complete description of all the formatting codes for numbers, dates, times, and durations.

Formatting Decimal Numbers

We've already seen several ways of formatting decimal numbers using `<xsl:number>`. However, if we're going to work with numbers, we'll almost certainly have to deal with decimals. XSLT defines the `format-number( )` function and the `<xsl:decimal-format>` element to do just that. We'll use `<xsl:decimal-format>` to define a pattern for formatting numbers, and then we'll use `format-number( )` to apply a pattern to a number.

This stylesheet has several examples of `<xsl:decimal-format>` and `format-number( )`:

```
<?xml version="1.0" encoding="utf-8"?>
<!-- decimal-format.xsl -->
<xsl:stylesheet version="1.0"
  xmlns:xsl="http://www.w3.org/1999/XSL/Transform">

<xsl:output method="text"/>

<!-- This format has no name, so it's assumed to be the default. -->
<xsl:decimal-format decimal-separator="," grouping-separator="."/>

<xsl:decimal-format name="us_default"/>

<xsl:decimal-format name="other_options" NaN="[not a number]"
```

```
                infinity="unfathomably huge"/>

    <xsl:decimal-format name="hash_mark" digit="!"/>

    <xsl:template match="/">
      <xsl:text>&#xA;Tests of &lt;xsl:decimal-format&gt; and </xsl:text>
      <xsl:text>format-number():</xsl:text>
      <xsl:text>&#xA;&#xA;  1. format-number(3728493.3882, </xsl:text>
      <xsl:text>'#.###,##') : </xsl:text>
      <xsl:value-of
        select="format-number(3728493.3882, '#.###,##')"/>

      <xsl:text>&#xA;&#xA;  2. format-number(3728493.3882, </xsl:text>
      <xsl:text>'#,###.##', 'us_default') : </xsl:text>
      <xsl:value-of
        select="format-number(3728493.3882, '#,###.##', 'us_default')"/>

      <xsl:text>&#xA;&#xA;  3. format-number(number(1) div 0, '#.#') : </xsl:text>
      <xsl:value-of select="format-number(number(1) div 0, '#.#')"/>

      <xsl:text>&#xA;&#xA;  4. format-number(number(1) div 0, '#.#', </xsl:text>
      <xsl:text>'other_options') : &#xA;        </xsl:text>
      <xsl:value-of
        select="format-number(number(1) div 0, '#.#', 'other_options')"/>

      <xsl:text>&#xA;&#xA;  5. format-number(number('blue') * </xsl:text>
      <xsl:text>number('orange'), '#') : </xsl:text>
      <xsl:value-of
        select="format-number(number('blue') * number('orange'), '#')"/>

      <xsl:text>&#xA;&#xA;  6. format-number(number('blue') * </xsl:text>
      <xsl:text>number('orange'), '#', 'other_options') : </xsl:text>
      <xsl:text>&#xA;        </xsl:text>
      <xsl:value-of
        select="format-number(number('blue') * number('orange'), '#',
                'other_options')"/>

      <xsl:text>&#xA;&#xA;  7. format-number(42, '#!', </xsl:text>
      <xsl:text>'hash_mark') : </xsl:text>
      <xsl:value-of select="format-number(42, '#!', 'hash_mark')"/>
    </xsl:template>

  </xsl:stylesheet>
```

When we run this stylesheet against any document, we get this output:

```
    Tests of <xsl:decimal-format> and format-number():

    1. format-number(3728493.3882, '#.###,##') : 3.728.493,39

    2. format-number(3728493.3882, '#,###.##', 'us_default') : 3,728,493.39

    3. format-number(number(1) div 0, '#.#') : Infinity

    4. format-number(number(1) div 0, '#.#', 'other_options') :
        unfathomably huge
```

```
5. format-number(number('blue') * number('orange'), '#') : NaN

6. format-number(number('blue') * number('orange'), '#', 'other_options') :
   [not a number]

7. format-number(42, '#!', 'hash_mark') : #42
```

This is an XSLT 1.0 stylesheet, but changing the `version` attribute to `2.0` generates the same results. We'll discuss each line in the output and point out some differences in the way XSLT 2.0 processes numbers as we go.

1. This example formats a number using the default format we defined. Because our stylesheet has a `<xsl:decimal-format>` element without a name, this format is used unless the name of another `<xsl:decimal-format>` element is used. We defined the default format to use periods as the thousands separator and a comma as the decimal point. Notice that to get this to work we had to use the period and comma appropriately in the formatting string. The numeric value itself uses the decimal point as usual.

2. This is the same example as before, only we pass the name of a number format as the third argument. Notice that the decimal format `us_default` doesn't have any attributes; that means it uses a period as the decimal point and a comma as the thousands separator.

3. This generates the default value for infinity, which is the string `Infinity`. In XSLT 1.0, the expression `1 div 0` generates the same result.

   [2.0] In XSLT 2.0, any value that is an `xs:integer` or `xs:decimal` cannot have the value infinity, so `1 div 0` won't run at all. Calling the function `number(1)` converts `1` into the `xs:double` equivalent, so `number(1) div 0` works. (That's a lot of work to divide a number by zero, but it does explain some of the details of how math works in XSLT 2.0.)

4. This generates the value for infinity defined in the number format `other_options`. The same details apply here as in the previous example; the expression `1 div 0` doesn't work in XSLT 2.0.

5. This generates `NaN`. In XSLT 1.0, the expression `'blue' * 'orange'` generates the same result.

   [2.0] In XSLT 2.0, the expression `'blue' * 'orange'` doesn't work because the multiplication symbol requires two numbers. Using the `number()` function turns each of the strings into the numeric value `NaN`. To generate `NaN` in XSLT 2.0, `number('NaN')` does the trick, as do `number('blue')`, `number('orange')`, and `number('any old string at all')`.

6. This generates `[not a number]`, the value defined in the number format `other_options`. (The same restrictions for XSLT 2.0 apply here as well.)

7. This generates #42. This uses the number format `hash_mark`, which defines an exclamation point as the digit character in the picture string. This allows us to put the hash mark into the picture string.

[2.0] Formatting Dates and Times

XSLT 2.0 adds three new formatting functions, `format-date( )`, `format-time( )`, and `format-dateTime( )`. We'll take `xs:date`, `xs:time`, and `xs:dateTime` values and format them in some useful way.

You can call each of these functions in two ways. The simplest is to pass the function a value and a formatting string. If you need more detail, the second way of calling these functions requires you to specify a language, a calendar, and a country as well. The XSLT 2.0 specification lists more than 25 different calendars used around the world, and there are hundreds of combinations of language and country codes. Look at the documentation for your XSLT processor to see which calendars, languages, and countries it supports.

Our first example is pretty simple. We'll create a stylesheet that uses the XPath functions `current-date( )`, `current-time( )`, and `current-dateTime( )`:

```
<?xml version="1.0" encoding="utf-8"?>
<!-- datetime1.xsl -->
<xsl:stylesheet version="2.0"
  xmlns:xsl="http://www.w3.org/1999/XSL/Transform">

  <xsl:output method="text"/>

  <xsl:template match="/">
    <xsl:text>&#xA;Tests of date and time formatting:&#xA;</xsl:text>
    <xsl:text>&#xA;  The current date is </xsl:text>
    <xsl:value-of select="format-date(current-date(),
                     '[M01]/[D01]/[Y0001]')"/>
    <xsl:text>&#xA;  The current time is </xsl:text>
    <xsl:value-of select="format-time(current-time(),
                     '[H01]:[m01] [z]')"/>
    <xsl:text>&#xA;  It's currently </xsl:text>
    <xsl:value-of select="format-dateTime(current-dateTime(),
                     '[h1]:[m01] [P] on [MNn] [D].')"/>
  </xsl:template>

</xsl:stylesheet>
```

This stylesheet produces this text:

```
Tests of date and time formatting:

The current date is 03/08/2006
The current time is 22:27 GMT-5
It's currently 10:27 p.m. on March 8.
```

In this stylesheet, `M01` produces the two-digit month, `D01` produces the two-digit day, and `Y0001` produces the four-digit year. `H01` produces the 2-digit hour in a 24-hour clock, `m01` produces the 2-digit minutes, `z` produces the time zone, `h1` produces the 1- or 2-digit hour in a 12-hour clock, and `P` generates `a.m.` or `p.m.` Finally, `MNn` generates the capitalized name of the month.

The formatting codes used by the `<xsl:number>` element can be used in the picture string for these functions. Here's another stylesheet that uses more of those formatting codes:

```
<?xml version="1.0" encoding="utf-8"?>
<!-- datetime2.xsl -->
<xsl:stylesheet version="2.0"
  xmlns:xsl="http://www.w3.org/1999/XSL/Transform"
  xmlns:xs="http://www.w3.org/2001/XMLSchema">

  <xsl:output method="text"/>

  <xsl:template match="/">
    <xsl:text>&#xA;More tests of date and time formatting:&#xA;</xsl:text>
    <xsl:text>&#xA;  Today is the </xsl:text>
    <xsl:value-of select="format-date(current-date(),
                          '[Dwo] day of [MNn], [Y0001]')"/>
    <xsl:text>&#xA;  Right now is the </xsl:text>
    <xsl:value-of select="format-time(current-time(),
                          '[m1o] minute of the [Hwo] hour of the day.')"/>
    <xsl:text>&#xA;  It's currently </xsl:text>
    <xsl:value-of select="format-dateTime(current-dateTime(),
                          '[h01]:[m01] [P] on [FNn] the [D1o].')"/>
    <xsl:text>&#xA;  Today is the </xsl:text>
    <xsl:value-of select="format-date(current-date(),
                          '[dwo]')"/>
    <xsl:text> day of the year. </xsl:text>
    <xsl:text>&#xA;  December 25, 1960 in German: </xsl:text>
    <xsl:value-of select="format-date(xs:date('1960-12-25'),
                          '[D] [MNn,3-3] [Y0001]', 'de',
                          'AD', 'DE')"/>
  </xsl:template>

</xsl:stylesheet>
```

This stylesheet generates this text:

```
More tests of date and time formatting:

  Today is the eighth day of March, 2006
  Right now is the 28th minute of the twenty-second hour of the day.
  It's currently 10:28 p.m. on Wednesday the 8th.
  Today is the sixty-seventh day of the year.
  December 25, 1960 in German: 25 Dez 1960
```

Here are the explanations for all the formatting codes in this example:

Dwo

The word for the ordinal value of the day

MNn
> The capitalized name of the month

Y0001
> The four-digit year

m1o
> The numeric ordinal of the minute

Hwo
> The hour, expressed as an ordinal word

h01
> The 2-digit hour in a 24-hour clock

m01
> The 2-digit minute

P
> The a.m. or p.m. indicator

FNn
> The capitalized name of the day of the week

D1o
> The numeric ordinal of the day

dwo
> The day of the year, expressed as an ordinal word

D
> The numeric day of the month

MNn,3-3
> The capitalized name of the month, returned in a string that's at least three characters long, but no more than three characters long

For the last call to `format-date( )`, we used the five-option version of the function, passing in the language, calendar and country codes. The formatting codes defined by XSLT give you a wide range of options for formatting the different components of dates and times.

Using <xsl:copy> and <xsl:copy-of>

As you transform your XML input document into something else, you'll often want to just copy a given element to the output document. XSLT provides two elements that do this: `<xsl:copy>` and `<xsl:copy-of>`. We'll discuss them here and go through several stylesheets that use these elements to create output.

A Stylesheet That Reproduces Its Input Document

To start our examples, we'll look at a stylesheet that generates a document equal to the input document. (This is sometimes called an *identity transform*.) The stylesheet is short and sweet:

```
<?xml version="1.0"?>
<!-- copy-of.xsl -->
<xsl:stylesheet version="1.0"
  xmlns:xsl="http://www.w3.org/1999/XSL/Transform">

  <xsl:template match="/">
    <xsl:copy-of select="*"/>
  </xsl:template>
</xsl:stylesheet>
```

That's all we have to do. Our template simply says to start with the document element of the input document and copy it to the output. `<xsl:copy-of>` does a *deep copy* of a node, so the root node and all of its children are copied to the output. If any of the root node's descendants are element nodes with attributes, the attributes are copied as well. (Remember, an element's attributes aren't considered children.)

We'll test our stylesheet against this document:

```
<?xml version="1.0"?>
<!-- sonnet.xml -->
<sonnet type='Shakespearean'>
  <auth:author xmlns:auth="http://www.authors.com/">
    <last-name>Shakespeare</last-name>
    <first-name>William</first-name>
    <nationality>British</nationality>
    <year-of-birth>1564</year-of-birth>
    <year-of-death>1616</year-of-death>
  </auth:author>
  <!-- Is there an official title for this sonnet?  They're
       sometimes named after the first line.               -->
  <title>Sonnet 130</title>
  <lines>
    <line>My mistress' eyes are nothing like the sun,</line>
    <line>Coral is far more red than her lips red.</line>
    <line>If snow be white, why then her breasts are dun,</line>
    <line>If hairs be wires, black wires grow on her head.</line>
    <line>I have seen roses damasked, red and white,</line>
    <line>But no such roses see I in her cheeks.</line>
    <line>And in some perfumes is there more delight</line>
    <line>Than in the breath that from my mistress reeks.</line>
    <line>I love to hear her speak, yet well I know</line>
    <line>That music hath a far more pleasing sound.</line>
    <line>I grant I never saw a goddess go,</line>
    <line>My mistress when she walks, treads on the ground.</line>
    <line>And yet, by Heaven, I think my love as rare</line>
    <line>As any she belied with false compare.</line>
  </lines>
</sonnet>
```

The results look like this:

```
<?xml version="1.0" encoding="UTF-8"?><!-- sonnet.xml --><sonnet type="Shakespearean">
  <auth:author xmlns:auth="http://www.authors.com/">
    <last-name>Shakespeare</last-name>
    <first-name>William</first-name>
    <nationality>British</nationality>
    <year-of-birth>1564</year-of-birth>
    <year-of-death>1616</year-of-death>
  </auth:author>
  <!-- Is there an official title for this sonnet?  They're
       sometimes named after the first line.                -->
  <title>Sonnet 130</title>
  <lines>
    <line>My mistress' eyes are nothing like the sun,</line>
    <line>Coral is far more red than her lips red.</line>
    <line>If snow be white, why then her breasts are dun,</line>
    <line>If hairs be wires, black wires grow on her head.</line>
    <line>I have seen roses damasked, red and white,</line>
    <line>But no such roses see I in her cheeks.</line>
    <line>And in some perfumes is there more delight</line>
    <line>Than in the breath that from my mistress reeks.</line>
    <line>I love to hear her speak, yet well I know</line>
    <line>That music hath a far more pleasing sound.</line>
    <line>I grant I never saw a goddess go,</line>
    <line>My mistress when she walks, treads on the ground.</line>
    <line>And yet, by Heaven, I think my love as rare</line>
    <line>As any she belied with false compare.</line>
  </lines>
</sonnet>
```

The result document looks almost exactly like the original. The `<sonnet>` element no longer begins on a separate line, and the XML declaration now includes `encoding="UTF-8"`. Also notice that the single quotes around the `type` attribute are now double quotes. These are changes from the text of the original XML document, but semantically the two are the same. Notice four things in particular that were copied to the output document:

- The comment before the document element
- The `type` attribute of the `<sonnet>` element
- The comment in the middle of the document
- The namespace declaration on the `<auth:author>` element

 Earlier in our discussion we made a point of talking about the root node rather than the document element. The root node here contains two things: the comment outside the document element and the document element itself. Everything in the XML source is a descendant of the root node; the document element isn't always the root node's only child.

We'll look at the `<xsl:copy>` element next and see how it handles (or doesn't handle) our input document.

A Stylesheet That Doesn't Quite Reproduce Its Input Document

Now we'll look at a similar stylesheet that uses `<xsl:copy>` instead. Again, our stylesheet is very simple:

```
<?xml version="1.0"?>
<!-- copy1.xsl -->
<xsl:stylesheet version="1.0"
  xmlns:xsl="http://www.w3.org/1999/XSL/Transform">

  <xsl:template match="/">
    <xsl:copy/>
  </xsl:template>
</xsl:stylesheet>
```

You probably noticed that the stylesheet is shorter. Unlike `<xsl:copy-of>`, the `<xsl:copy>` element doesn't have a `select` attribute. (It has some other attributes in XSLT 2.0; it didn't have any at all in XSLT 1.0.) Here are the results when we use this stylesheet:

```
<?xml version="1.0" encoding="UTF-8"?>
```

Hmmm. It appears that `<xsl:copy>` didn't actually copy anything. While that makes for a small, concise document, it's probably not what we wanted. (This is the result you get from Xalan; Saxon doesn't generate anything at all.) One thing to remember here is that the document root is *not* the root element that contains the XML data in our document. An XML document can contain comments and processing instructions that are outside the root element; those comments and PIs are part of the XPath document root. So, if we want to copy anything, we need to create a template for the root element. Here's another attempt at a stylesheet:

```
<?xml version="1.0"?>
<!-- copy2.xsl -->
<xsl:stylesheet version="1.0"
  xmlns:xsl="http://www.w3.org/1999/XSL/Transform">

  <xsl:template match="/">
    <xsl:apply-templates select="*"/>
  </xsl:template>

  <xsl:template match="*">
    <xsl:copy/>
  </xsl:template>
</xsl:stylesheet>
```

And here are the results we get:

```
<?xml version="1.0" encoding="UTF-8"?><sonnet/>
```

Well, at least we have the `<sonnet>` element, but we don't have any of its children. We also lost the `type` attribute of the `<sonnet>` element. Using `<xsl:copy>` to copy our document requires using the `<xsl:for-each>` element to copy all the attributes of each element we're copying. Here's how the latest iteration of our stylesheet looks:

```
<?xml version="1.0"?>
<!-- copy3.xsl -->
<xsl:stylesheet version="1.0"
  xmlns:xsl="http://www.w3.org/1999/XSL/Transform">

  <xsl:template match="/">
    <xsl:apply-templates select="*"/>
  </xsl:template>

  <xsl:template match="*">
    <xsl:copy>
      <xsl:for-each select="@*">
        <xsl:copy/>
      </xsl:for-each>
      <xsl:apply-templates/>
    </xsl:copy>
  </xsl:template>
</xsl:stylesheet>
```

We used `<xsl:for-each>` to copy all of the attributes that an element might have. This stylesheet comes pretty close to duplicating the input document:

```
<?xml version="1.0" encoding="UTF-8"?><sonnet type="Shakespearean">
  <auth:author xmlns:auth="http://www.authors.com/">
    <last-name>Shakespeare</last-name>
    <first-name>William</first-name>
    <nationality>British</nationality>
    <year-of-birth>1564</year-of-birth>
    <year-of-death>1616</year-of-death>
  </auth:author>

  <title>Sonnet 130</title>
  <lines>
    <line>My mistress' eyes are nothing like the sun,</line>
    <line>Coral is far more red than her lips red.</line>
    <line>If snow be white, why then her breasts are dun,</line>
    <line>If hairs be wires, black wires grow on her head.</line>
    <line>I have seen roses damasked, red and white,</line>
    <line>But no such roses see I in her cheeks.</line>
    <line>And in some perfumes is there more delight</line>
    <line>Than in the breath that from my mistress reeks.</line>
    <line>I love to hear her speak, yet well I know</line>
    <line>That music hath a far more pleasing sound.</line>
    <line>I grant I never saw a goddess go,</line>
    <line>My mistress when she walks, treads on the ground.</line>
    <line>And yet, by Heaven, I think my love as rare</line>
    <line>As any she belied with false compare.</line>
  </lines>
</sonnet>
```

Even this version of the stylesheet doesn't copy comments or processing instructions. Notice that the output has a blank line in place of the comment in the original document. If we wanted to handle comments and processing instructions, we'd have to change the match and select attributes to make sure they were processed.

The point of these examples is that <xsl:copy> *forces you do to most of the work yourself.* You have complete control over what exactly gets copied, but that comes at a price. If you wanted only to copy certain elements, such as all <customer> elements with an <address> element in which the <province> element has a value of PEI, <xsl:copy> gives you the control to do that.

Before we go on to more complicated examples that use <xsl:copy>, be aware that we could use the XPath node( ) test. This stylesheet:

```
<?xml version="1.0"?>
<!-- copy-identity.xsl -->
<xsl:stylesheet version="1.0"
  xmlns:xsl="http://www.w3.org/1999/XSL/Transform">

  <xsl:template match="node()|@*">
    <xsl:copy>
      <xsl:apply-templates select="node()|@*"/>
    </xsl:copy>
  </xsl:template>
</xsl:stylesheet>
```

accomplishes the same thing as the <xsl:copy-of> stylesheet we looked at earlier.

For an example that needs that contol, we'll look a stylesheet that copies only the <author> information and the title of the sonnet. This stylesheet uses a separate template to make sure nothing happens to the <lines> element that contains the poem:

```
<?xml version="1.0"?>
<!-- copy4.xsl -->
<xsl:stylesheet version="1.0"
  xmlns:xsl="http://www.w3.org/1999/XSL/Transform">

<xsl:template match="/">
  <xsl:apply-templates select="*"/>
</xsl:template>

<xsl:template match="*">
  <xsl:copy>
    <xsl:for-each select="@*">
      <xsl:copy/>
    </xsl:for-each>
    <xsl:apply-templates/>
  </xsl:copy>
</xsl:template>

<xsl:template match="lines"/>
```

```
</xsl:stylesheet>
```

Our template for the `<lines>` element is empty; because it doesn't contain anything, it doesn't generate any output. That means our output should contain everything except the `<lines>` element and its children. The results look like this:

```
<?xml version="1.0" encoding="UTF-8"?><sonnet type="Shakespearean">
  <auth:author xmlns:auth="http://www.authors.com/">
    <last-name>Shakespeare</last-name>
    <first-name>William</first-name>
    <nationality>British</nationality>
    <year-of-birth>1564</year-of-birth>
    <year-of-death>1616</year-of-death>
  </auth:author>

  <title>Sonnet 130</title>

</sonnet>
```

The results contain all of the `<auth:author>` and `<title>` information, along with some extra whitespace. (Feel free to change the stylesheet to delete that whitespace if you want.) We couldn't do this with `<xsl:copy-of>`; `<xsl:copy>` gives us the control to do what we want. If we added more elements to our `<sonnet>` schema, this stylesheet would still copy everything except the `<lines>` elements and its children.

Our last stylesheet used an empty `<xsl:template>` for the `<lines>` element. That means all other elements, text, and attributes are copied to the output; our stylesheet defines what should *not* be copied to the output. Creating a stylesheet that defines what *should* be copied is more complex:

```
<?xml version="1.0"?>
<!-- copy5.xsl -->
<xsl:stylesheet version="1.0"
  xmlns:xsl="http://www.w3.org/1999/XSL/Transform"
  xmlns:auth="http://www.authors.com/">

  <xsl:template match="sonnet">
    <xsl:copy>
      <xsl:copy-of select="@*"/>
      <xsl:apply-templates select="auth:author|title"/>
    </xsl:copy>
  </xsl:template>

  <xsl:template match="*">
    <xsl:copy>
      <xsl:copy-of select="@*"/>
      <xsl:apply-templates/>
    </xsl:copy>
  </xsl:template>

</xsl:stylesheet>
```

There are a couple of complications here. First of all, to specify that we want to copy the namespace-qualified element `<auth:author>`, we have to define that namespace in the stylesheet. Next, we list the two child elements of the `<sonnet>` element. Finally, we create a generic template that copies whatever elements are processed. Using the built-in template rules, the `<auth:author>` and `<title>` elements *and all their descendants* are processed with the generic template. We never process the `<lines>` element, so we get the results we want:

```
<?xml version="1.0" encoding="UTF-8"?><sonnet type="Shakespearean"><auth:author
xmlns:auth="http://www.authors.com/">
    <last-name>Shakespeare</last-name>
    <first-name>William</first-name>
    <nationality>British</nationality>
    <year-of-birth>1564</year-of-birth>
    <year-of-death>1616</year-of-death>
  </auth:author><title>Sonnet 130</title></sonnet>
```

We've looked at the two elements XSLT uses for copying: `<xsl:copy-of>` and `<xsl:copy>`. Use `<xsl:copy-of>` when you want a deep copy of an element, including its children and its attributes. On the other hand, `<xsl:copy>` forces you to choose exactly what gets copied. If you need that control, use `<xsl:copy>`; otherwise, use `<xsl:copy-of>`.

Dealing with Whitespace

One of the challenges of working with any XML document is processing whitespace, especially when want want to generate output other than HTML. As we noted earlier, an HTML browser renders both of these paragraphs the same way:

```
<p>
   This document contains
   5
   chapters.

</p>
<p>This document contains 5 chapters.</p>
```

If we generated these two paragraphs as text, however, they would appear as differently in print as they do in the HTML source. We'll look at several techniques for controlling whitespace in this section.

Whitespace Basics

Before we begin, it's worth defining the four characters that the XML spec defines as whitespace:

- The *tab* character (	)
- The *newline* character (
)

- The *carriage return* character (`&#xD;`)
- The *space* character (`&#x20;`)

We'll use this modified version of our car list to illustrate how XML parsers and XSLT processors work with whitespace:

```
<?xml version="1.0" encoding="utf-8"?>
<!-- carlist_whitespace.xml -->
<cars>
  <manufacturer name="            Chevrolet

">
    <car>Cavalier</car>
    <car>Corvette</car>
    <car>Impala</car>
    <car>Monte



Carlo</car>
  </manufacturer>
</cars>
```

From an XML parser's perspective, there are a number of whitespace-only nodes (nodes that contain only whitespace characters) in this document. The `<cars>` element contains a whitespace-only node with the newline character and the tab or spaces before the `<manufacturer>` tag, the node for the `<manufacturer>` element, and a whitespace-only node with the newline character after the `</manufacturer>` tag. Similarly, the `<manufacturer>` element contains whitespace-only nodes between the various `<car>` elements.

The XML parser doesn't remove any whitespace-only nodes, so we can always use them in our stylesheets. Put another way, the data model used by the XSLT processor contains the whitespace-only nodes from the XML source. The one exception to this is in an XSLT 2.0 processor that validates the XML source against a schema. If the schema indicates that an element can only contain other elements, any whitespace-only nodes contained in those elements are removed.

An XSLT processor doesn't know if the XML parser validated the document or not, so it assumes any whitespace nodes delievered by the XML parser must be significant. We'll use our sample stylesheet for the `<xsl:copy-of>` element to see what we get from our document. Processing our short list of cars with this stylesheet:

```
<?xml version="1.0"?>
<!-- copy-of.xsl -->
<xsl:stylesheet version="1.0"
  xmlns:xsl="http://www.w3.org/1999/XSL/Transform">

  <xsl:template match="/">
    <xsl:copy-of select="."/>
  </xsl:template>
</xsl:stylesheet>
```

gives us this XML document:

```
<?xml version="1.0" encoding="UTF-8"?><!-- carlist_whitespace.xml --><cars>
    <manufacturer name="            Chevrolet  ">
      <car>Cavalier</car>
      <car>Corvette</car>
      <car>Impala</car>
      <car>Monte



Carlo</car>
    </manufacturer>
</cars>
```

There's only one change in the processed version of the document: The newline characters were replaced with spaces in the value of the `name` attribute of the `<manufacturer>` element. All the whitespace nodes were preserved.

Using `<xsl:preserve-space>` and `<xsl:strip-space>`

The XSLT spec gives us two ways of dealing with whitespace nodes. We can use the `<xsl:preserve-space>` and `<xsl:strip-space>` nodes to keep or delete whitespace. Here's a slightly modified version of our stylesheet:

```
<?xml version="1.0"?>
<!-- copy-of-whitespace.xsl -->
<xsl:stylesheet version="1.0"
  xmlns:xsl="http://www.w3.org/1999/XSL/Transform">

  <xsl:preserve-space elements="manufacturer"/>
  <xsl:strip-space elements="cars"/>

  <xsl:template match="/">
    <xsl:copy-of select="."/>
  </xsl:template>
</xsl:stylesheet>
```

Here's what we get when we process our list of cars with the modified stylesheet:

```
<?xml version="1.0" encoding="UTF-8"?><!-- carlist_whitespace.xml --><cars>
        <manufacturer name="            Chevrolet  ">
      <car>Cavalier</car>
      <car>Corvette</car>
      <car>Impala</car>
      <car>Monte



Carlo</car>
    </manufacturer></cars>
```

In the result document, the whitespace nodes inside the `<cars>` element have been removed, while all the whitespace inside the `<manufacturer>` element has been preserved. (The complete text of the `<manufacturer>` element scrolls off the right side of the page.) You can use `<xsl:preserve-space>` and `<strip-space>` with wildcards as well:

```
<xsl:preserve-space elements="cars manufacturer"/>
<xsl:strip-space elements="*"/>
```

This tells the XSLT processor to strip whitespace nodes on all the elements except the `<cars>` and `<manufacturer>` elements. The `elements` attribute can contain an asterisk or a space-separated list of element names.

 Because whitespace-only nodes are always preserved, there's no need to use `<xsl:preserve-space elements="*"/>`. Using `<xsl:strip-space elements="*"/>` as we have here means whitespace-only nodes are removed by default. We have to specify the mixed content elements in which whitespace is significant, but removing as many whitespace-only nodes as possible can make the node tree much smaller for a large document with lots of whitespace.

You can also use wildcards for namespace-qualified elements. For example, `elements="auth:*"` means all elements in the `auth` namespace. *[2.0]* In XSLT 2.0, you can also use `elements="*:car`" to specify all `<car>` elements, regardless of their namespace.

The `<xsl:preserve-space>` and `<strip-space>` elements give us control over which whitespace nodes will be processed by our stylesheet. If we want to copy that whitespace directly to the output document, we can use the `<xsl:copy-of>` and `<xsl:copy>` elements as we discussed earlier.

A final note: the XML spec defines the little-used `xml:space` attribute. If an element in the XML source document contains the attribute `xml:space="preserve"`, all whitespace in that element is preserved, regardless of any `<xsl:strip-space>` elements our stylesheet might have.

The normalize-space( ) function

Another useful technique for controlling whitespace is the `normalize-space( )` function. In our previous example, we used `<xsl:preserve-space>` and `<xsl:strip-space>` to control whitespace nodes in various elements, but we still have quite a bit of whitespace in the `name` attribute and the last `<car>` in the list. To clean up the whitespace, we can use the `normalize-space( )` function. It does three things:

- It removes all leading spaces.
- It removes all trailing spaces.
- It replaces any group of consecutive whitespace characters with a single space.

We'll use `normalize-space( )` in this stylesheet:

```
<?xml version="1.0"?>
<!-- normalize-space.xsl -->
<xsl:stylesheet version="1.0"
  xmlns:xsl="http://www.w3.org/1999/XSL/Transform">

  <xsl:template match="/">
    <xsl:apply-templates />
  </xsl:template>

  <xsl:template match="*">
    <xsl:copy>
      <xsl:for-each select="@*">
        <xsl:attribute name="{name()}">
          <xsl:value-of select="normalize-space()"/>
        </xsl:attribute>
      </xsl:for-each>
      <xsl:apply-templates/>
    </xsl:copy>
  </xsl:template>

  <xsl:template match="text()">
    <xsl:value-of select="normalize-space()"/>
  </xsl:template>

</xsl:stylesheet>
```

This stylesheet generates these crowded results:

```
<?xml version="1.0" encoding="UTF-8"?><cars><manufacturer name="Chevr
olet"><car>Cavalier</car><car>Corvette</car><car>Impala</car><car>Mon
te Carlo</car></manufacturer></cars>
```

This removes all the extraneous whitespace from the name attribute and the `<car>` element; it also effectively removes the whitespace-only text nodes.

A Simple Technique for Adding Whitespace to Text Output

Whenever we generate text output, we usually need to control line breaks. Programming languages have facilities for this; in Java, for example, we can use `System.out.print( )`, `System.out.println( )`, or even `System.out.print("\n\n")` to put line breaks exactly where we need them.

The simplest way to do this in an XSLT stylesheet is to use the character entities for the newline (`&#xA;`) and tab (`&#x9;`) characters. We've used this technique with the newline character throughout this chapter. As a further example, here's a stylesheet that uses all three character entities in the `separator` attribute of the `<xsl:value-of>` element:

```
<?xml version="1.0" encoding="utf-8"?>
<xsl:stylesheet xmlns:xsl="http://www.w3.org/1999/XSL/Transform"
                version="2.0">

  <xsl:output method="text"/>

  <xsl:template match="/">
```

```
<xsl:text>&#xA;Values separated with newlines:&#xA;&#xA;</xsl:text>
<xsl:value-of select="1 to 7" separator="&#xA;"/>

<xsl:text>&#xA;&#xA;Values separated with tabs:&#xA;&#xA;</xsl:text>
<xsl:value-of select="1 to 7" separator="&#x9;"/>

<xsl:text>&#xA;&#xA;Values separated with spaces:&#xA;&#xA;</xsl:text>
<xsl:value-of select="1 to 7" separator="&#x20;"/>
  </xsl:template>

</xsl:stylesheet>
```

This stylesheet generates these results:

```
Values separated with newlines:

1
2
3
4
5
6
7

Values separated with tabs:

1       2       3       4       5       6       7

Values separated with spaces:

1 2 3 4 5 6 7
```

Summary

This chapter has covered the various ways you can generate output from your XSLT stylesheets. You'll use those basic techniques in every stylesheet you write. The main challenge as we go forward is learning how to select and organize the elements you want to process. You might need logic to select elements that have certain properties or you might need to sort or group elements before you process them. You might need to use special functions not defined in XSLT or XPath. You might need to write output to more than one document. Future chapters will address all of those topics.

Whatever your stylesheet does, you'll ultimately use the output methods in this chapter.

CHAPTER 5

Branching and Control Elements

So far, we've done some straightforward transformations and we've been able to do some reasonably sophisticated things. To do truly useful work, though, we'll need to use logic in our stylesheets. In this chapter, we'll discuss the XSLT elements that allow you to do just that. Although you'll see several XML elements that look like constructs from other programming languages, they're not exactly the same. As we go along, we'll discuss what makes XSLT different and how to do common tasks with your stylesheets.

Goals of This Chapter

By the end of this chapter, you should:

- Know the XSLT elements used for branching and control
- Understand the differences between XSLT's branching elements and similar constructs in other programming languages
- Know how to invoke XSLT templates by name and how to pass parameters to them, if you want
- Know how to use XSLT variables
- Understand how changes in XSLT 2.0 affect the way parameters and variables work
- Understand how to use recursion to get around the "limitations" of XSLT's branching and control elements

Branching Elements of XSLT

Three XSLT elements are used for branching: `<xsl:if>`, `<xsl:choose>`, and `<xsl:for-each>`. The first two are much like the `if` and `case` statements you may be familiar with from other languages, but the `for-each` element is significantly different from the `for` or `do-while` structures in other languages. We'll discuss all of them here.

The <xsl:if> Element

The <xsl:if> element looks like this:

```
<xsl:if test="count(zone) > 2">
  <xsl:text>Applicable zones: </xsl:text>
  <xsl:apply-templates select="zone"/>
</xsl:if>
```

The <xsl:if> element, surprisingly enough, implements an if statement. The element has only one attribute: test. If the value of test evaluates to the boolean value true, then all elements inside the <xsl:if> are processed. If test evaluates to false, then the contents of the <xsl:if> element are ignored. (If you want to implement an if-then-else statement, see the section "The <xsl:choose> Element" later in this chapter.)

Notice that we used the character > in the value of the test attribute. If you need to use the less-than operator (<), you'll have to use the < entity. The same holds true for the less-than-or-equal operator (<=).

Converting to boolean values

The <xsl:if> element is pretty simple, but it's the first time we've had to deal with *boolean values*. These values will come up later, so we might as well discuss them here. Attributes such as the test attribute of the <xsl:if> element convert whatever their values happen to be into a boolean value. If that boolean value is true, the <xsl:if> element is processed. (The <xsl:when> element, which we'll discuss in the section "The <xsl:choose> Element" later in this chapter, has a test attribute as well.)

[1.0] Here's the rundown of how various datatypes are converted to boolean values:

number
> If a number is positive or negative zero, it is false. If a numeric value is NaN (not a number; if I try to use the string "blue" as a number, the result is NaN), it is false. If a number has any other value, it is true.

node-set
> An empty node-set is false, a nonempty node-set is true.

string
> A zero-length string is false; a string whose length is not zero is true.

These rules are defined in Section 4.3 of the XPath 1.0 specification.

[2.0] For XSLT 2.0, things are more complicated. The value returned, as you'd expect, is an xs:boolean. Here's how different datatypes are converted to xs:boolean values:

- A singleton of any numeric type is false if its value is zero or NaN (not a number); everything else is true.

- A singleton of type xs:string, xs:anyURI, xs:untypedAtomic, or any type derived from them is true if the argument has a length greater than zero.

- The value of a singleton of type `xs:boolean` (or of a type derived from `xs:boolean`) is simply used as is.
- A sequence whose first item is a node is `true`.
- An empty sequence is `false`.
- Converting any other datatype to `xs:boolean` causes the XSLT processor to raise an error. For example, an `xs:date` can't be converted to `true` or `false`.

Boolean examples

Here are some examples that illustrate how boolean values evaluate the `test` attribute:

`<xsl:if test="count(zone) &gt;= 2">`

> This is a boolean expression because it uses the greater-than-or-equal boolean operator. If the `count( )` function returns a value greater than or equal to 2, the `test` attribute is `true`. Otherwise, the `test` attribute is `false`.

`<xsl:if test="$x">`

> The variable `$x` is evaluated and converted to a boolean value using the rules we just covered. The result, of course, depends on the value of `$x` and how it is converted to a boolean value.

`<xsl:if test="true( )">`

> The boolean function `true( )` always returns the boolean value `true`. Therefore, this `test` attribute is always `true`.

`<xsl:if test="true">`

> This example is a trick. This `test` attribute is `true` only if there is at least one `<true>` element that's a child of the context node. The XSLT processor interprets the value `true` as an XPath expression that specifies all `<true>` elements in the current context. The strings `true` and `false` don't have any special significance in XSLT.

`<xsl:if test="'true'">`

> This `test` attribute is always `true`. Notice that in this case we used single quotes inside double quotes to specify that this is a literal string, not an element name. This `test` attribute is always `true` because the string has a length greater than zero, *not* because its value happens to be the word "true."

`<xsl:if test="'false'">`

> Another trick example; this `test` attribute is always `true`. As before, we used single quotes inside double quotes to specify that this is a literal string. Because the string has a length greater than zero, the `test` attribute is always `true`. The value of the nonempty string, confusing as it is, doesn't matter.

`<xsl:if test="not(3)">`

> This `test` attribute is always `false`. The literal 3 evaluates to `true`, so its negation is `false`. On the other hand, the expressions `not(0)` and `not(-0)` are always `true`.

```
<xsl:if test="false( )">
```
This test attribute is always false. The boolean function false( ) always returns the boolean value false.

```
<xsl:if test="section/section">
```
The XPath expression section/section returns a node-set. If the current context contains one or more <section> elements that contain a <section> element in turn, the test attribute is true. If no such elements exist in the current context, the test attribute is false.

The <xsl:choose> Element

The <xsl:choose> element is logically equivalent to an if-then-else statement, although it has the feel of a case or switch statement in other programming languages. An <xsl:choose> contains at least one <xsl:when> element (logically equivalent to an <xsl:if> element), with an optional <xsl:otherwise> element (logically equivalent to an else in other programming languages). The test attribute of each <xsl:when> element is evaluated until the XSLT processor finds one that evaluates to true. When that happens, the contents of that <xsl:when> element are evaluated. (Unlike a case or switch element, each <xsl:when> is a separate test.) If none of the <xsl:when> elements have a test that is true, the contents of the <xsl:otherwise> element (if there is one) are processed.

<xsl:choose> example

Here's a sample <xsl:choose> element that sets the background color of the table's rows. If the bgcolor attribute is coded on the <table-row> element, the value of that attribute is used as the color; otherwise, the sample uses the position( ) function and the mod operator to cycle the colors between black, green, red, and blue:

```
<xsl:template match="table-row">
  <tr>
    <xsl:attribute name="bgcolor">
     <xsl:choose>
        <xsl:when test="@bgcolor">
          <xsl:value-of select="@bgcolor"/>
        </xsl:when>
        <xsl:when test="position() mod 4 = 0">
          <xsl:text>black</xsl:text>
        </xsl:when>
        <xsl:when test="position() mod 4 = 1">
          <xsl:text>green</xsl:text>
        </xsl:when>
        <xsl:when test="position() mod 4 = 2">
          <xsl:text>red</xsl:text>
        </xsl:when>
        <xsl:otherwise>
          <xsl:text>blue</xsl:text>
        </xsl:otherwise>
     </xsl:choose>
```

```
        </xsl:attribute>
        <xsl:apply-templates select="*"/>
      </tr>
    </xsl:template>
```

In this sample, we use `<xsl:choose>` to generate the value of the `bgcolor` attribute of the `<tr>` element. Our first test is to see whether the `bgcolor` attribute of the `<table-row>` element exists; if it does, we use that value for the background color and the `<xsl:otherwise>` and other `<xsl:when>` elements are ignored. (If the `bgcolor` attribute is coded, the XPath expression `@bgcolor` returns a node-set containing a single attribute node.)

The next three `<xsl:when>` elements check the position of the current `<table-row>` element. The use of the `mod` operator here is the most efficient way to cycle between the various options. Finally, we use an `<xsl:otherwise>` element to specify `blue` as the default case. If `position( ) mod 4 = 3`, the background color will be `blue`.

There are a couple of minor details to note. In this example, we could replace the `<xsl:otherwise>` element with `<xsl:when test="position( ) mod 4 = 3">`; that is logically equivalent to the example as coded previously. For obfuscation bonus points, we could code the second `<xsl:when>` element as `<xsl:when test="not(position( ) mod 4)">`. (Remember that the boolean negation of zero is `true`.)

The `<xsl:for-each>` Element

If you want to process all the nodes that match a certain criteria, you can use the `<xsl:for-each>` element. Be aware that this isn't a traditional `for` loop; you can't ask the XSLT processor to do something like this:

```
for i = 1 to 10 do
```

The `<xsl:for-each>` element lets you select a set of nodes, and then do something with each of them. Let me mention again that this is not the same as a traditional `for` loop. Another important point is that the current node changes with each iteration through the `<xsl:for-each>` element. We'll go through some examples to illustrate this.

 You can use the XSLT 2.0 `to` operator to do something similar (`select="1 to 10"`). When you're working with XSLT, it's better to think of `<xsl:for-each>` as an iterator rather than a traditional `for` loop.

`<xsl:for-each>` example

Here's a sample that selects all `<section>` elements inside a `<tutorial>` element and then uses a second `<xsl:for-each>` element to select all the `<panel>` elements inside each `<section>` element:

```
<xsl:template match="tutorial">
  <xsl:for-each select="section">
```

```
<h1>
  <xsl:text>Section </xsl:text>
  <xsl:value-of select="position()"/>
  <xsl:text>. </xsl:text>
  <xsl:value-of select="title"/>
</h1>
<ul>
  <xsl:for-each select="panel">
    <li>
      <xsl:value-of select="position()"/>
      <xsl:text>. </xsl:text>
      <xsl:value-of select="title"/>
    </li>
  </xsl:for-each>
</ul>
  </xsl:for-each>
</xsl:template>
```

Given this XML document:

```
<tutorial>
  <section>
    <title>Gene Splicing for Young People</title>
    <panel>
      <title>Introduction</title>
      <!-- ... -->
    </panel>
    <panel>
      <title>Discovering the secrets of life and creation</title>
      <!-- ... -->
    </panel>
    <panel>
      <title>"I created him for good, but he's turned out evil!"</title>
      <!-- ... -->
    </panel>
    <panel>
      <title>When angry mobs storm your castle</title>
      <!-- ... -->
    </panel>
  </section>
</tutorial>
```

The previous template produces these results:

```
<h1>Section 1. Gene Splicing for Young People</h1>
<ul>
  <li>1. Introduction</li>
  <li>2. Discovering the secrets of life and creation</li>
  <li>3. "I created him for good, but he's turned out evil!"</li>
  <li>4. When angry mobs storm your castle</li>
</ul>
```

Each time a select attribute is processed, it is evaluated in terms of the current node. As the XSLT processor cycles through all the <section> and <panel> elements, each of them in turn becomes the current node. By using iteration, we've generated a table of contents with a very simple template.

Invoking Templates by Name

Up to this point, we've always used XSLT's `<xsl:apply-templates>` element to invoke other templates. You can think of this as a limited form of *polymorphism;* a single instruction is invoked a number of times, and the XSLT processor uses each node in the node-set to determine which `<xsl:template>` to invoke. Most of the time, this is what we want. However, sometimes we want to invoke a particular template. XSLT allows us to do this with the `<xsl:call-template>` element.

How It Works

To invoke a template by name, two things have to happen:

- The template you want to invoke has to have a `name`.
- You use the `<xsl:call-template>` element to invoke the named template.

Here's how to do this. Say we have a template named *createMasthead* that creates the masthead of a web page. Whenever we create an HTML page for our web site, we want to invoke the *createMasthead* template to create the masthead. Here's what our stylesheet would look like:

```
<xsl:template name="createMasthead">
  <!-- interesting stuff that generates the masthead goes here -->
</xsl:template>
...
<xsl:template match="/">
  <html>
    <head>
      <title><xsl:value-of select="title"/></title>
    </head>
    <body>
      <xsl:call-template name="createMasthead"/>
...
```

Named templates are extremely useful for defining commonly used markup. For example, say you're using an XSLT stylesheet to create web pages with a particular look and feel. You can write named templates that create the header, footer, navigation areas, or other items that define how your web page will look. Every time you need to create a web page, simply use `<xsl:call-template>` to invoke those templates and create the look and feel you want.

Even better, if you put those named templates in a separate stylesheet and import the stylesheet (with either `<xsl:import>` or `<xsl:include>`), you can create a set of stylesheets that generate the look and feel of the web site you want. If you decide to redesign your web site, redesign the stylesheets that define the common graphical and layout elements. Change those stylesheets, regenerate your web site, and voila! You will see an instantly updated web site.

Templates à la mode

The XSLT `<xsl:template>` element has a `mode` attribute that lets you process the same set of nodes several times. For example, we might want to process `<h1>` elements one way when we generate a table of contents, and another way when we process the document as a whole. We could use the `mode` attribute to define different templates for different purposes:

```
<xsl:template match="h1" mode="build-toc">
  <!-- Template to process the <h1> element for table of contents -->
</xsl:template>

<xsl:template match="h1" mode="process-text">
  <!-- Template to process the <h1> element along with the rest  -->
  <!-- of the document                                           -->
</xsl:template>
```

We can then start applying templates with the `mode` attribute:

```
<xsl:template match="/">
  <html>
    <body>
      <h1>Table of Contents</h1>
      <ul>
        <xsl:apply-templates select="h1" mode="build-toc"/>
      </ul>
      <xsl:apply-templates select="*" mode="process-text"/>
    </body>
  </html>
</xsl:template>
```

This style of coding makes maintenance much easier; if the table of contents isn't generated correctly, the templates with `mode="build-toc"` are the obvious place to start debugging. (We discuss the `mode` attribute in more detail in the section "New values for the mode attribute" later in this chapter.)

Parameters

The XSLT `<xsl:param>` and `<xsl:with-param>` elements allow you to pass parameters to a template. You can pass templates with either the `<call-template>` element or the `<apply-templates>` element; we'll discuss the details in this section.

Defining a Parameter in a Template

To define a parameter in a template, use the `<xsl:param>` element. Here's an example of a template that defines two parameters:

```
<xsl:template name="calcuateArea">
  <xsl:param name="width"/>
  <xsl:param name="height"/>
```

```
  <xsl:value-of select="$width * $height"/>
</xsl:template>
```

Conceptually, this is a lot like writing code in a traditional programming language, isn't it? Our template here defines two parameters, width and height, and outputs their product.

If you want, you can define a default value for a parameter. There are two ways to define a default value; the simplest is to use a select attribute on the <xsl:param> element:

```
<template name="addTableCell">
  <xsl:param name="bgColor" select="'blue'"/>
  <xsl:param name="width" select="150"/>
  <xsl:param name="content"/>
  <td width="{$width}" bgcolor="{$bgColor}">
    <xsl:apply-templates select="$content"/>
  </td>
</template>
```

In this example, the default values of the parameters bgColor and width are 'blue' and 150, respectively. If we invoke this template without specifying values for these parameters, the default values are used. Also notice that we generated the values of the width and bgcolor attributes of the HTML <td> tag with attribute value templates, the values in curly braces. For more information, see the section "Attribute Value Templates" in Chapter 3.

One thing to note about this example is that the content parameter doesn't have a default value here; we're assuming that content contains the nodes to be processed and put inside the table cell. If the value of content is an empty string, calling <xsl:apply-templates select="$content"/> causes an error. To be on the safe side, we could add an <xsl:if> element here to create an empty table cell if content is an empty string. As an exercise for the reader, feel free to make this code more robust....

Notice that in the previous example, we put single quotes around the value blue, but we didn't do it around the value 150. Without the single quotes around blue, the XSLT processor assumes we want to select all the <blue> elements in the current context, which is probably not what we want. The XSLT processor is clever enough to realize that the value 150 can't be an XML element name (the XML 1.0 Specification says element names can't begin with numbers), so we don't need the single quotes around a numeric value.

Try to keep this in mind when you're using parameters. You'll probably forget it at some point, and you'll probably go nuts trying to figure out the strange behavior you're getting from the XSLT processor.

The second way to define a default value for a parameter is to include content inside the <xsl:param> element:

```
<template name="addTableCell">
  <xsl:param name="bgColor">
```

```
  <xsl:text>blue</xsl:text>
</xsl:param>
<xsl:param name="width">
  <xsl:value-of select="7+8"/><xsl:text>0</xsl:text>
</xsl:param>
<xsl:param name="content"/>
<td width="{$width}" bgcolor="{$bgColor}">
  <xsl:apply-templates select="$content"/>
</td>
</template>
```

In this example, we used `<xsl:text>` and `<xsl:value-of>` elements to define the default values of the parameters. Out of sheer perverseness, we defined the value of width as the concatenation of the numeric expression 7+8, followed by the string "0". The result of the numeric expression, 15, is converted to a string, and then that string is concatenated with the string 0 This example produces the string 150, which will be converted into a number as necessary.

Passing Parameters

If we invoke a template by name, which is similar to calling a subroutine, we'll need to pass parameters to those templates. We do this with the `<xsl:with-param>` element. For example, let's say we want to call a template named *draw-box*, and then pass the parameters startX, startY, endX, and endY to it. Here's what we'd do:

```
<xsl:call-template name="draw-box">
  <xsl:with-param name="startX" select="50"/>
  <xsl:with-param name="startY" select="50"/>
  <xsl:with-param name="endX" select="97"/>
  <xsl:with-param name="endY" select="144"/>
</xsl:call-template>
```

In this sample, we've called the template named draw-box with the four parameters we mentioned earlier. Notice that up until now, `<xsl:call-template>` has always been an empty tag; here, though, the parameters are the content of the `<xsl:call-template>` element. (If you want, you can do the same thing with `<xsl:apply-templates>`.)

If we're going to pass parameters to a template, we have to set up the template so that it expects the parameters we're passing. To do this, we'll use the `<xsl:param>` element inside the template. Here are some examples:

```
<xsl:template name="draw-box">
  <xsl:param name="startX"/>
  <xsl:param name="startY" select="'0'"/>
  <xsl:param name="endX">
    10
  </xsl:param>
  <xsl:param name="endY">
    10
  </xsl:param>
  ...
</xsl:template>
```

A couple of notes about the `<xsl:param>` element:

- If you define any `<xsl:param>` elements in a template, they must be the first thing in the template.

- The `<xsl:param>` element allows you to define a default value for the parameter. If the calling template doesn't supply a value, the default is used instead. The last three `<xsl:param>` elements in our previous example define default values.

- The `<xsl:param>` element has the same content model as `<xsl:variable>`. With no content and no select attribute, the default value of the parameter is an empty string (""). With a `select` attribute, the default value of the parameter is the value of the select attribute. If the `<xsl:param>` element contains content, the default value of the parameter is the content of the `<xsl:param>` element.

Global Parameters

XSLT allows you to define parameters whose scope is the entire stylesheet. You can define default values for these parameters, and you can pass values to those parameters externally to the stylesheet. Before we talk about how to pass in values for *global parameters*, we'll show you how to create them. Any parameters that are top-level elements (any `<xsl:param>` elements whose parent is `<xsl:stylesheet>`) are global parameters. Here's an example:

```
<?xml version="1.0"?>
<!-- params.xsl -->
<xsl:stylesheet version="1.0"
  xmlns:xsl="http://www.w3.org/1999/XSL/Transform">

  <xsl:output method="text"/>

  <xsl:param name="startX"/>
  <xsl:param name="baseColor"/>

  <xsl:template match="/">
    <xsl:text>&#xA;Global parameters example&#xA;&#xA;</xsl:text>

    <xsl:text>The value of startX is: </xsl:text>
    <xsl:value-of select="$startX"/>
    <xsl:text>&#xA;The value of baseColor is: </xsl:text>
    <xsl:value-of select="$baseColor"/>
    <xsl:text>&#xA;</xsl:text>
  </xsl:template>

</xsl:stylesheet>
```

How you pass values for global parameters depends on the XSLT processor you're using. We'll go through some examples here for all the usual suspects. Let's say we want to pass the numeric value 50 as the value for startX, and the string value magenta as the default value for baseColor. The following list describes the commands you'd use to do that:

Xalan

To pass global parameters to Xalan, you can define them on the Xalan command line:

```
java org.apache.xalan.xslt.Process -in blank.xml -xsl params.xsl
    -param startX 50 -param baseColor magenta
```

(This command should be on a single line.)

Saxon

Saxon supports external parameters like this:

```
java net.sf.saxon.Transform blank.xml params.xsl startX=50 baseColor=magenta
```

Microsoft's XSLT tools

Here's how you pass external parameters to Microsoft's XSLT tools:

```
msxsl blank.xml params.xsl startX=50 baseColor=magenta
```

Altova

If you're using the Altova XML engine, you pass external parameters like this:

```
altovaxml /xslt1 params.xsl /in blank.xml /param startX=50 /param
baseColor='magenta'
```

Notice that we have to put single quotes around the text value `magenta`.

Using this stylesheet with any XML document and any of the XSLT processors listed here produces these results:

```
Global parameters example

The value of startX is: 50
The value of baseColor is: magenta
```

Setting global parameters in a Java program

If your XSLT engine supports the Transformation API for XML (TrAX), you can embed the XSLT processor and set global parameters in your code. Here's an example that uses TrAX support:

```
import java.io.File;
import javax.xml.transform.Transformer;
import javax.xml.transform.TransformerConfigurationException;
import javax.xml.transform.TransformerException;
import javax.xml.transform.TransformerFactory;
import javax.xml.transform.stream.StreamResult;
import javax.xml.transform.stream.StreamSource;

public class GlobalParameters
{
  public static void parseAndProcess(String sourceID,
                                     String xslID,
                                     String outputID)
  {
    try
```

```
    {
      TransformerFactory tfactory = TransformerFactory.newInstance();

      Transformer transformer
        = tfactory.newTransformer(new StreamSource(xslID));

      // Use the setParameter method to set global parameters
      transformer.setParameter("startX", new Integer(50));
      transformer.setParameter("baseColor", "magenta");

      transformer.transform(new StreamSource(sourceID),
                            new StreamResult(outputID));
    }
    catch (TransformerConfigurationException tce)
    {
      System.err.println("Exception: " + tce);
    }
    catch (TransformerException te)
    {
      System.err.println("Exception: " + te);
    }
  }

  public static void main(String argv[])
    throws java.io.IOException,
           org.xml.sax.SAXException
  {
    GlobalParameters gp = new GlobalParameters();
    gp.parseAndProcess(argv[0], argv[1], argv[2]);
  }
}
```

Notice that we used the **setParameter** method to set global parameters for the
Transformer object before we invoke the **transform** method. This transformation generates the following results in *output.text*:

```
Global parameters example

The value of startX is: 50
The value of baseColor is: magenta
```

Setting global parameters in .NET

The .NET framework provides the **XsltArgumentList** object for setting global stylesheet
parameters. As with the Java example, the code is straightforward:

```
using System;
using System.Collections.Generic;
using System.Text;
using System.Xml;
using System.Xml.Xsl;

namespace com.oreilly.xslt
{
  class XsltGlobalParameters
```

```
{
  static void Main(string[] args)
  {
    // Create the stylesheet object and the XMLWriter that
    // writes the output to a file
    XslCompiledTransform stylesheet = new XslCompiledTransform();
    XmlTextWriter xWriter =
      new XmlTextWriter(args[2], Encoding.UTF8);

    // Use an XsltSettings object that allows executing scripts
    // (we need this for extensions), then load the stylesheet
    XsltSettings settings = new XsltSettings(true, true);
    stylesheet.Load(args[1], settings, new XmlUrlResolver());

    // We pass global parameters to the stylesheet with an
    // XsltArgumentList object.
    XsltArgumentList argList = new XsltArgumentList();
    argList.AddParam("startX", "", 50);
    argList.AddParam("baseColor", "", "magenta");

    // With everything in place, we call the Transform() method
    // to do the work...
    stylesheet.Transform(args[0], argList, xWriter);
  }
}
}
```

We create an **XslCompiledTransform** object, and then use an **XsltArgumentList** object to set parameters for the stylesheet. Once everything is set, we use the **Transform( )** method of the **XslCompiledTransform** class. This generates the same results we saw with the Java code:

```
Global parameters example

The value of startX is: 50
The value of baseColor is: magenta
```

[2.0] Important Differences in XSLT 2.0

There are some changes to the way parameters and modes work in XSLT 2.0. We'll cover those here. To summarize, the key differences are:

- The **mode** attribute features three new values: **#all**, **#current**, and **#default**.

- If you pass a parameter to a template, and that parameter is not defined in that template, an XSLT 2.0 processor will give you an error message and stop. In XSLT 1.0, the undefined parameters were simply ignored.

- XSLT 2.0 adds the attribute **required="yes"** to define that a value must be passed for a parameter.

- You can specify the datatype and/or the structure of a parameter. If a parameter must be an **xs:date** or a sequence of at least one element, you can specify that.

- XSLT 2.0 defines a new kind of parameter called a *tunnel parameter*. Tunnel parameters help you avoid sloppy coding practices that you were often forced into with XSLT 1.0.

New values for the mode attribute

In XSLT 2.0, there are three new values for the mode attribute:

#all
> For `<xsl:template>`, we can use the value `mode="#all"`. This specifies that a given template matches all modes. However, if the current mode is `"toc"`, a template with `mode="toc"` is invoked instead of a template with `mode="#all"`.

#current
> For the `<xsl:apply-templates>` element, we can use the value `mode="#current"` to invoke other templates using the current mode. This effectively uses the current mode as a parameter.

#default
> The `<xsl:apply-templates>` and `<xsl:template>` elements can use `mode="#default"`. The default mode is unnamed.

Another difference in XSLT 2.0: the value of the mode attribute can be a space-separated list of mode names. In XSLT 1.0, you could only specify one mode at a time.

See the definition of the `<xsl:apply-templates>` element in Appendix A for a complete example of these new features.

Undefined parameters are illegal

In XSLT 1.0, you can pass as many parameters to a template as you want. If you pass two parameters to a template that defines only one parameter, the extra parameter is simply ignored. You won't even get a warning or error message from the XSLT processor. Here's an example:

```
<?xml version="1.0"?>
<!-- parameters-1_0.xsl -->
<xsl:stylesheet version="1.0"
  xmlns:xsl="http://www.w3.org/1999/XSL/Transform">

  <xsl:output method="text"/>

  <xsl:template match="/">
    <xsl:call-template name="test">
      <xsl:with-param name="param1" select="'57'"/>
      <xsl:with-param name="param2" select="'93'"/>
    </xsl:call-template>
  </xsl:template>

  <xsl:template name="test">
    <xsl:param name="param1"/>
    <xsl:text>Value of $param1: </xsl:text>
```

```
    <xsl:value-of select="$param1"/>
  </xsl:template>

</xsl:stylesheet>
```

In this example, the template for the document root calls a named template, passing it two parameters. The parameter `param2` isn't defined in the named template. With an XSLT 1.0 processor, this is *not* an error. Here's the output you get from Xalan-J 2.7.0, which is an XSLT 1.0 processor:

```
java org.apache.xalan.xslt.Process -xsl parameters-1_0.xsl
Value of $param1: 57
```

Using the same stylesheet with Saxon 9.0.0.3, which is an XSLT 2.0 processor, gives these results:

```
java net.sf.saxon.Transform blank.xml parameters-1_0.xsl
Warning: Running an XSLT 1.0 stylesheet with an XSLT 2.0 processor
Value of $param1: 57
```

Saxon gives us a warning message that we're running an XSLT 1.0 stylesheet, but it ignores the extra parameter as it should when it's processing a stylesheet in XSLT 1.0 mode. However, if we change the **version** attribute of the **<xsl:stylesheet>** tag to look like this:

```
<xsl:stylesheet xmlns:xsl="http://www.w3.org/1999/XSL/Transform"
                version="2.0">
```

Saxon processes this as an XSLT 2.0 stylesheet:

```
java net.sf.saxon.Transform blank.xml parameters-2_0.xsl
Error at xsl:call-template on line 9 of file:/C:/parameters-2_0.xsl:
  XTSE0680: Parameter param2 is not declared in the called template
Failed to compile stylesheet. 1 error detected.
```

An XSLT 2.0 stylesheet processor stops the transformation as soon as it finds the undefined parameter.

Finally, if we run the XSLT 2.0 stylesheet with Xalan, it ignores the **version="2.0"** attribute entirely and processes the stylesheet as you'd expect an XSLT 1.0 processor to do:

```
java org.apache.xalan.xslt.Process -xsl parameters-2_0.xsl
Value of $param1: 57
```

You might have noticed in the preceding code that when we processed the stylesheet with Xalan, we specified only our stylesheet. Saxon, on the other hand, requires that we specify both an XML file and an XSLT stylesheet. The contents of the file *blank.xml* are the single empty element `<blank/>`.

An alternative would be to give the template a name (`<xsl:template match="/" name="main">`) and invoke it using Saxon's `-it` option:

```
java net.sf.saxon.Transform -it main parameters_1.0.xsl
Warning: Running an XSLT 1.0 stylesheet with an XSLT 2.0 processor
Value of $param1: 57
```

The `-it` option lets you specify the named template where the transformation should begin.

Required parameters

XSLT 2.0 adds a `required` attribute to the `<xsl:param>` element. Valid values are `yes` and `no`, as you'd expect. If a parameter is required, the `<xsl:param>` element *must not* have a `select` attribute.

Here's an example of a required parameter:

```
<?xml version="1.0" encoding="utf-8"?>
<!-- required_parameters.xsl -->
<xsl:stylesheet version="2.0"
  xmlns:xsl="http://www.w3.org/1999/XSL/Transform">

  <xsl:output method="text"/>

  <xsl:template match="/">
    <xsl:call-template name="date-formatter">
      <xsl:with-param name="date" select="current-date()"/>
    </xsl:call-template>
  </xsl:template>

  <xsl:template name="date-formatter">
    <xsl:param name="date" required="yes"/>
    <xsl:value-of select="format-date($date, '[M01]/[D01]/[Y0001]')"/>
  </xsl:template>

</xsl:stylesheet>
```

In this stylesheet, the `date` parameter is required; if we try to invoke this template without passing the required parameter, the XSLT processor will refuse to run our stylesheet. This would be a good place to use XSLT 2.0's datatyping support (more on this next); the XSLT processor forces us to use the required parameter, but it doesn't check its datatype. If the parameter we pass to the `format-date()` function is not an `xs:date`, the XSLT processor throws an error. (This stylesheet uses the `current-date()` function to generate the parameter, so we know we'll always have the correct datatype.)

A final restriction on `<xsl:param>` is that you can't use the **required** and **select** attributes on the same parameter. Remember, the **select** attribute defines a default value in case a parameter isn't passed to the template. On the other hand, the **required** attribute says that the parameter *must* be passed to the template.

Datatyping support

The `<xsl:param>`, `<xsl:with-param>`, and `<xsl:variable>` elements have an optional **as** attribute that define the datatype and/or structure of a parameter or variable. As an example, here's a parameter that must be an **xs:date**:

```
<?xml version="1.0" encoding="utf-8"?>
<!-- datatype_parameters.xsl -->
<xsl:stylesheet version="2.0"
  xmlns:xsl="http://www.w3.org/1999/XSL/Transform"
  xmlns:xs="http://www.w3.org/2001/XMLSchema">

  <xsl:output method="text"/>

  <xsl:template match="/">
    <xsl:call-template name="date-formatter">
      <xsl:with-param name="date" select="current-date()"/>
    </xsl:call-template>
  </xsl:template>

  <xsl:template name="date-formatter">
    <xsl:param name="date" as="xs:date" required="yes"/>
    <xsl:value-of select="format-date($date, '[M01]/[D01]/[Y0001]')"/>
  </xsl:template>

</xsl:stylesheet>
```

 Typically we're concerned about the datatype of a parameter, but we can also define the parameter's structure. The attribute `as="element( )+"` says the parameter must be a sequence of one or more element nodes, while `as="element(*, xs:date)+"` says that the parameter must be a sequence of one or more element nodes, each of which has the datatype `xs:date`.

In this stylesheet, we're calling a named template. The `<xsl:param>` element in the named template tells the XSLT processor that the parameter is required, and that its datatype must be the XML Schema **date** type. When we run this stylesheet with an XSLT 2.0 processor, we get these results:

```
java net.sf.saxon.Transform blank.xml datatype_parameters.xsl
03/02/2008
```

The XSLT 2.0 stylesheet engine has taken the value of our parameter and formatted it according to the picture clause used in the **format-date( )** function.

If the parameter's datatype doesn't match the datatype required by the template, an error will occur. For example, if we change the stylesheet so that we call the template with bad data:

```
<xsl:call-template name="date-formatter">
  <xsl:with-param name="date" select="'blue'"/>
</xsl:call-template>
```

we'll get an error:

```
Error at xsl:with-param on line 11 of file:/C:/datatype_parameters.xsl:
  XTTE0570: Required item type of value of variable $date is xs:date;
  supplied value has item type xs:string
Failed to compile stylesheet. 1 error detected.
```

The stylesheet engine doesn't even process the entire stylesheet because the parameter's value (the string blue) clearly doesn't match the required datatype. If we generated the value of the parameter dynamically and the generated value wasn't an xs:date, we would get a runtime error that would stop the transformation.

Tunnel parameters

The use of parameters in XSLT 1.0 can lead to sloppy programming in a couple of ways. First of all, you don't have to worry so much about the "signature" of the template you're invoking. You can pass the exact number of parameters to the template, none at all, or twice as many. The XSLT 1.0 processor will probably do what you want, but if a parameter isn't set correctly, it can be difficult to figure out where the problem lies. XSLT 2.0's requirement that you pass the exact number of parameters makes for much cleaner code.

The second problem is when you need to pass a parameter that might eventually be used by another template. As an example, say we have a stylesheet that generates HTML from DocBook. DocBook features hundreds of elements, so we'll just look at templates for a few DocBook elements here. We'll take a DocBook document and create two HTML files. Each HTML file will contain the major section headings (sect1/title), along with all of the code listings in the source document (DocBook <programlisting> elements). We'll run this transformation twice, generating normal-sized text in one document and larger text in the second.

Here's what our stylesheet looks like *without* tunnel parameters:

```
<?xml version="1.0" encoding="utf-8"?>
<!-- normal_parameters.xsl -->
<xsl:stylesheet version="2.0"
  xmlns:xsl="http://www.w3.org/1999/XSL/Transform">

  <xsl:output method="html"/>

  <xsl:template match="/">
    <xsl:result-document href="regular-type.html" method="html">
      <html>
        <xsl:apply-templates select="*|text()">
```

```xsl
        <xsl:with-param name="code-font-size" select="'14'"/>
      </xsl:apply-templates>
    </html>
  </xsl:result-document>
  <xsl:result-document href="larger-type.html" method="html">
    <html>
      <xsl:apply-templates select="*|text()">
        <xsl:with-param name="code-font-size" select="'20'"/>
      </xsl:apply-templates>
    </html>
  </xsl:result-document>
</xsl:template>

<xsl:template match="chapter">
  <xsl:param name="code-font-size"/>
  <head>
    <title><xsl:value-of select="title"/></title>
  </head>
  <body>
    <xsl:apply-templates select="*[not(name() = 'title')]|text()">
      <xsl:with-param name="code-font-size" select="$code-font-size"/>
    </xsl:apply-templates>
  </body>
</xsl:template>

<xsl:template match="programlisting">
  <xsl:param name="code-font-size"/>
  <pre>
    <span>
      <xsl:attribute name="style">
        <xsl:text>font-family:monospace; font-size:</xsl:text>
        <xsl:value-of select="$code-font-size"/>
        <xsl:text>;</xsl:text>
      </xsl:attribute>
      <xsl:apply-templates select="*|text()">
        <xsl:with-param name="code-font-size" select="$code-font-size"/>>
      </xsl:apply-templates>
    </span>
  </pre>
</xsl:template>

<xsl:template match="sect1/title">
  <xsl:param name="code-font-size"/>
  <h1>
    <xsl:apply-templates select="*|text()">
      <xsl:with-param name="code-font-size" select="$code-font-size"/>
    </xsl:apply-templates>
  </h1>
</xsl:template>

<!-- A useful stylesheet would have dozens more templates here... -->
<xsl:template match="*">
  <xsl:param name="code-font-size"/>
  <xsl:apply-templates select="*">
    <xsl:with-param name="code-font-size" select="$code-font-size"/>
```

```
    </xsl:apply-templates>
  </xsl:template>

</xsl:stylesheet>
```

This stylesheet generates the output we want, creating the result documents **regular-type.html** and **larger-type.html**. An excerpt from **regular-type.html** looks like this:

```
    <h1>Goals of This Chapter</h1>

    <h1>Branching Elements of XSLT</h1><pre>
<span style="font-family:monospace; font-size:14;">
&lt;xsl:if test="count(zone) &gt; 2"&gt;
  &lt;xsl:text&gt;Applicable zones: &lt;/xsl:text&gt;
  &lt;xsl:apply-templates select="zone"/&gt;
&lt;/xsl:if&gt;</span></pre><pre>
<span style="font-family:monospace; font-size:14;">
&lt;xsl:template match="table-row"&gt;
  &lt;tr&gt;
    &lt;xsl:attribute name="bgcolor"&gt;
      &lt;xsl:choose&gt;
```

The file **larger-type.html** is identical, with the exception that the **style** attribute contains **font-size:20;** instead of **font-size:14;**. However, the stylesheet is messy, and maintenance will be more difficult than it should be. Notice how many templates have this structure:

```
<xsl:template match="whatever">
  <xsl:param name="code-font-size"/>

  <!-- Do something with the current element, -->
  <!-- then process its descendants           -->

  <xsl:apply-templates select="*|text()">
    <!-- Pass the code-font-size parameter, just in case -->
    <!-- we need it later -->
    <xsl:with-param name="code-font-size" select="$code-font-size"/>
  </xsl:apply-templates>
</xsl:template>
```

The problem is that everytime we use **<xsl:apply-templates>**, we have to pass along the **code-font-size** variable just in case a template somewhere down the line needs it. Any of the elements for which we've written templates might have **<programlisting>** as a descendant, so we don't have any choice. To make things even worse, every time we add a new template to our stylesheet, we have to add the same **<xsl:param>** and **<xsl:with-param>** markup. If we suddenly had three more parameters that we needed to pass around in this way, our stylesheet would become very convoluted, and every change to the stylesheet could introduce errors if we don't remember to make the same changes to all the affected templates.

And that's where tunnel parameters come in.

Tunnel parameters are similar to *dynamically scoped variables* in functional programming languages such as Haskell and Scheme. In those languages, a variable may go in and out of scope as one function invokes another. In XSLT 2.0, when you create a tunnel parameter, that parameter is passed on to each template that's directly or indirectly invoked. As one template invokes another during processing, any template anywhere can use that tunnel parameter simply by referring to it as a tunnel parameter. Here's how the stylesheet looks with tunnel parameters:

```
<?xml version="1.0" encoding="utf-8"?>
<!-- tunnel_parameters.xsl -->
<xsl:stylesheet version="2.0"
  xmlns:xsl="http://www.w3.org/1999/XSL/Transform">

  <xsl:output method="html"/>

  <xsl:template match="/">
    <xsl:result-document href="regular-type.html" method="html">
      <html>
        <xsl:apply-templates select="*|text()">
          <xsl:with-param name="code-font-size" select="'14'"
            tunnel="yes"/>
        </xsl:apply-templates>
      </html>
    </xsl:result-document>
    <xsl:result-document href="larger-type.html" method="html">
      <html>
        <xsl:apply-templates select="*|text()">
          <xsl:with-param name="code-font-size" select="'20'"
            tunnel="yes"/>
        </xsl:apply-templates>
      </html>
    </xsl:result-document>
  </xsl:template>

  <xsl:template match="chapter">
    <head>
      <title><xsl:value-of select="title"/></title>
    </head>
    <body>
      <xsl:apply-templates select="*[not(name() = 'title')]|text()"/>
    </body>
  </xsl:template>

  <xsl:template match="programlisting">
    <xsl:param name="code-font-size" tunnel="yes"/>
    <pre>
      <span>
        <xsl:attribute name="style">
          <xsl:text>font-family:monospace; font-size:</xsl:text>
          <xsl:value-of select="$code-font-size"/>
          <xsl:text>;</xsl:text>
        </xsl:attribute>
        <xsl:apply-templates select="*|text()"/>
      </span>
```

```
      </pre>
    </xsl:template>

    <xsl:template match="sect1/title">
      <h1>
        <xsl:apply-templates select="*|text()"/>
      </h1>
    </xsl:template>

    <!-- A useful stylesheet would have dozens more templates here... -->
    <xsl:template match="*">
      <xsl:apply-templates select="*"/>
    </xsl:template>

  </xsl:stylesheet>
```

Notice how tunnel parameters have simplified the code. In the root template, we're passing a tunnel parameter as we tell the XSLT processor to transform all of the descendant elements. Each time a subsequent template invokes another template, whether through `<apply-templates>` or `<call-template>`, the tunnel parameters are silently passed along. The only time we use the parameter is in the only place we need it: the template for the `programlisting` element.

A couple of syntax notes: first of all, the `<xsl:with-param>` element that declares the parameter must have `tunnel="yes"` to be a tunnel parameter. Secondly, the template that wants to use the tunnel parameter must have the `tunnel="yes"` attribute on the `<xsl:param>` element that defines the parameter. If the parameter definition doesn't include `tunnel="yes"`, the XSLT processor assumes that the parameter is a new variable local to that template.

It might have occurred to you that we could solve this problem with a global parameter. That's true, although there are a couple of disadvantages to this method. First of all, we would like to limit the number of global parameters. Adding a global parameter just so we can use it anywhere we need it isn't good form.

The second problem is that we can't change the value of the global parameter. In our example here, we would have to create two global variables, one for each value we'd like to use in the stylesheet. Using tunnel parameters lets us set the value of `code-font-size` each time we want to process our source document. With tunnel parameters, our stylesheet is easier to write, easier to debug, and easier to maintain.

Variables

If we use logic to control the flow of our stylesheets, we'll probably want to store temporary results along the way. In other words, we'll need to use variables. XSLT provides the `<xsl:variable>` element, which allows you to store a value and associate it with a name.

The `<xsl:variable>` element can be used in three ways. The simplest form of the element creates a new variable whose value is an empty string (""). Here's how it looks:

```
<xsl:variable name="x"/>
```

This element creates a new variable named x, whose value is an empty string. (Please hold your applause until the end of the section.)

You can also create a variable by adding a `select` attribute to the `<xsl:variable>` element:

```
<xsl:variable name="favouriteColour" select="'blue'"/>
```

In this case, we've set the value of the variable to be the string "blue". Notice that we put single quotes around the value. These quotes ensure that the literal value `blue` is used as the value of the variable. If we had left out the single quotes, this would mean the value of the variable is the node-set (or sequence) of all the `<blue>` elements in the context node, which definitely isn't what we want here.

 Be aware that single quotes around numeric values are significant. The value 35 represents a numeric value (it's a number in XSLT 1.0, and an `xs:integer` in XSLT 2.0), while the value `'35'` represents the *string* 35. That might seem like a minor distinction, but it has a major impact on how your stylesheet works, especially in XSLT 2.0.

The third way to use the `<xsl:variable>` element is to put content inside it. Here's a brief example:

```
<xsl:variable name="y">
  <xsl:choose>
    <xsl:when test="$x &gt; 7">
      <xsl:text>13</xsl:text>
    </xsl:when>
    <xsl:otherwise>
      <xsl:text>15</xsl:text>
    </xsl:otherwise>
  </xsl:choose>
</xsl:variable>
```

In this more complicated example, the content of the variable y depends on the test attribute of the `<xsl:when>` element. This is the equivalent of this procedural programming construct:

```
int y;
if (x > 7)
  y = 13;
else
  y = 15;
```

Are These Things Really Variables?

Although these XSLT variables are called variables, they're not variables in the traditional sense of procedural programming languages such as C++ or Java. Remember that earlier we said one goal behind the design of the stylesheet language is to avoid side effects in execution? Well, one of the most common side effects used in most procedural languages is changing the value of a variable. If we write our stylesheet so that the results depend on the varying values of different variables, the stylesheet engine would be forced to evaluate the templates in a certain order.

XSLT variables are more like variables in the traditional mathematical sense. In mathematics, we can define a function called `square(x)` that returns the value of a number (represented by *x*) multiplied by itself. In other words, `square(2.5)` returns `6.25`. In this context, we understand that *x* can be any number; we also understand that the `square` function can't change the value of *x*.

It takes a while to get used to this concept, but you'll get there. Trust me on this.

Variable Scope

An `<xsl:variable>` element is scoped to the element that contains it. If an `<xsl:variable>` element is a top-level element (its parent is `<xsl:stylesheet>`), it is global, and its value is visible everywhere in the stylesheet. You can also use an `<xsl:variable>` element within an `<xsl:template>` to override the value of a global variable locally.

Using Recursion to Do Most Anything

Writing an XSLT stylesheet is different from programming in other languages. If you didn't believe that before, you probably do now. We'll finish this chapter with a couple of examples that demonstrate how to use recursion to solve the kinds of problems that you're probably used to solving with procedural programming languages. We'll also look at some new features of XSLT 2.0 and XPath 2.0 that allow you to avoid recursion in some situations.

Implementing a String Replace Function

To demonstrate how to use recursion to solve problems, we'll write a string replace function. This is sometimes useful when you need to escape certain characters or substrings in your output. The stylesheet we'll develop here transforms an XML document into a set of SQL statements that will be executed at a Windows command prompt. We have to do several things:

Put a caret (^) in front of all ampersands (&)

On the Windows NT and Windows 2000 command prompt, the ampersand means that the current command has ended and another is beginning. For example, this command creates a new directory called *xslt* and changes the current directory to the newly created one:

```
mkdir xslt & chdir xslt
```

If we create a SQL statement that contains an ampersand, we'll need to escape the ampersand so it's processed as a literal character, not as an operator. If we insert the value `Jones & Son` as the value of the company field in a row of the database, we need to change it to `Jones ^& Son` before we try to run the SQL command.

Put a caret (^) in front of all vertical bars (|)

The vertical bar is the pipe operator on Windows systems, so we need to escape it if we want it interpreted as literal text instead of an operator.

Replace any single quote (') with two single quotes ('')

This is a requirement of our database system.

Procedural design

Three functions we could use in our template are `concat( )`, `substring-before( )`, and `substring-after( )`. To replace an ampersand with a caret and an ampersand, this would do the trick:

```
<xsl:value-of select="concat(substring-before(., '&amp;'), '^&amp;',
                      substring-after(., '&amp;'))"/>
```

The obvious problem with this step is that it replaces only the first occurrence of the ampersand. If there are two ampersands, or three, or three hundred, we need to call this method once for each ampersand in the original string. Because of the way variables work, we can't do what we'd do in a procedural language:

```
private static String strChange(String string, String from, String to)
{
  String before = "", after = "";
  int    index;

  index = string.indexOf(from);
  while (index >= 0)
  {
    before = string.substring(0, index);
    after = string.substring(index + from.length());
    string = before + to + after;

    index = string.indexOf(from, index + to.length());
  }

  return string;
}
```

XSLT doesn't have any simple way to iterate through the characters of the string, so we'll use recursion instead.

Recursive design

To implement a string replace function with recursion, we'll take this approach:

- If the whole string *does contain* the substring we want to replace, we do the following:

  1. Return the first part of the whole string—everything before the substring we want to replace.

  2. Return the replacement substring.

  3. Return the result of calling our function with the last part of the whole string—everything after the first occurrence of the substring we want to replace. *This is the recursive part of our design.*

- If the whole string *does not contain* the substring we want to replace, we simply return the whole string.

If the substring we're replacing occurs in the whole string, we call the substring replace function on the last of the string. The key here, as with all recursive functions, is that we have an *exit case*, a condition in which we don't recurse. Eventually we'll call our recursive function with a string that doesn't contain the substring we're replacing.

Here's the design in pseudocode:

```
replaceSubstring(originalString, substring, replacementString)
{
  if (contains(originalString, substring))
  {
    return
      (substring-before(originalString, substring) +
       replacementString +
       replaceSubstring(substring-after(originalString, substring),
                        substring, replacementString));
  }
  else
    return originalString;
}
```

In the recursive approach, the function calls itself whenever there's at least one occurrence of the substring. Each time the function calls itself, the `originalString` parameter is a little smaller, until eventually we've processed the complete string. Here's the complete stylesheet:

```
<?xml version="1.0"?>
<!-- string_replace-1_0.xsl -->
<xsl:stylesheet version="1.0"
  xmlns:xsl="http://www.w3.org/1999/XSL/Transform">

  <xsl:output method="text"/>
```

```
<xsl:template match="/">
  <xsl:apply-templates select="ul/li"/>
</xsl:template>

<xsl:template match="li">
  <xsl:variable name="single-quote">
    <xsl:text>&apos;</xsl:text>
  </xsl:variable>
  <xsl:variable name="two-quotes">
    <xsl:text>&apos;&apos;</xsl:text>
  </xsl:variable>

  <xsl:variable name="sub1">
    <xsl:call-template name="replace-substring">
      <xsl:with-param name="original" select="."/>
      <xsl:with-param name="substring" select="'&amp;'"/>
      <xsl:with-param name="replacement" select="'^&amp;'"/>
    </xsl:call-template>
  </xsl:variable>

  <xsl:variable name="sub2">
    <xsl:call-template name="replace-substring">
      <xsl:with-param name="original" select="$sub1"/>
      <xsl:with-param name="substring" select="'|'"/>
      <xsl:with-param name="replacement" select="'^|'"/>
    </xsl:call-template>
  </xsl:variable>

  <xsl:call-template name="replace-substring">
    <xsl:with-param name="original" select="$sub2"/>
    <xsl:with-param name="substring" select="$single-quote"/>
    <xsl:with-param name="replacement" select="$two-quotes"/>
  </xsl:call-template>
  <xsl:text>&#xA;</xsl:text>
</xsl:template>

<xsl:template name="replace-substring">
  <xsl:param name="original" />
  <xsl:param name="substring" />
  <xsl:param name="replacement" />
  <xsl:choose>
    <xsl:when test="contains($original, $substring)">
      <xsl:value-of
        select="substring-before($original, $substring)" />
      <xsl:value-of select="$replacement" />
      <xsl:call-template name="replace-substring">
        <xsl:with-param name="original"
          select="substring-after($original, $substring)" />
        <xsl:with-param
          name="substring" select="$substring" />
        <xsl:with-param
          name="replacement" select="$replacement" />
      </xsl:call-template>
    </xsl:when>
```

```
      <xsl:otherwise>
        <xsl:value-of select="$original" />
      </xsl:otherwise>
    </xsl:choose>
  </xsl:template>

</xsl:stylesheet>
```

We create the variable **$sub1** by replacing all of the ampersands in the original text with a caret and an ampersand. We create the variable **$sub2** by replacing all of the vertical bars in **$sub1** with a caret and a vertical bar. Finally we use **$sub2** in our third call to the **replace-substring** template. The third call to the template doubles all the single quotes. Notice that the third call isn't inside an **<xsl:variable>** element, so it is written to the output.

Given this XML input document:

```
<?xml version="1.0" encoding="utf-8"?>
<!-- testlines.xml -->
<ul>
  <li>This is a test &amp; I hope it works | fails gracefully</li>
  <li>Some techniques are simpler &amp; easier than recursion</li>
  <li>Will I enjoy next Tuesday's meeting?</li>
</ul>
```

Our recursive template returns these results:

```
This is a test ^& I hope it works ^| fails gracefully
Some techniques are simpler ^& easier than recursion
Will I enjoy next Tuesday''s meeting?
```

This style of programming takes some getting used to, but whatever you want to do can usually be done. Our example here is a good illustration of the techniques we've discussed in this chapter, including branching statements, variables, invoking templates by name, and passing parameters.

[2.0] Using the XPath 2.0 replace( ) Function to Avoid Recursion

Because string manipulation is a common task in transforming documents, XPath 2.0 provides the very useful **replace( )** function. This lets us provide the original string, the string we want to replace, and the string we want substituted in its place. To review our earlier example, we want to make three replacements in our text:

- Any ampersand (&) should have a caret added in front of it (^&).
- Any vertical bar (|) should have a caret added in front of it (^|).
- Any single quote (') should be replaced with two single quotes ('').

Our stylesheet to perform these tasks looks like this:

```
<?xml version="1.0"?>
<!-- string_replace-2_0.xsl -->
<xsl:stylesheet version="2.0"
```

```
  xmlns:xsl="http://www.w3.org/1999/XSL/Transform">

  <xsl:output method="text"/>

  <xsl:template match="/">
    <xsl:apply-templates select="ul/li"/>
  </xsl:template>

  <xsl:template match="li">
    <xsl:variable name="sub1" select="replace(., '&amp;', '^&amp;')"/>
    <xsl:variable name="sub2" select="replace($sub1, '\|', '^|')"/>
    <xsl:value-of select='replace($sub2, "&apos;", "&apos;&apos;")'/>
    <xsl:text>&#xA;</xsl:text>
  </xsl:template>

</xsl:stylesheet>
```

We get the same results we got from our much longer XSLT 1.0 stylesheet:

```
This is a test ^& I hope it works ^| fails gracefully
Some techniques are simpler ^& easier than recursion
Will I enjoy next Tuesday''s meeting?
```

This example is far simpler than the recursive technique we used in the XSLT 1.0 stylesheet. Both of them generate the same results, but the code in the XSLT 2.0 stylesheet is much easier to understand.

> A quick note about the syntax we used to escape all the single quotes in the XSLT 2.0 stylesheet: our technique was to use the single quote (apostrophe) entity within double quotes. In XPath 2.0, single quotes can be escaped by doubling them in an XPath expression, so we also could have written our call to the replace( ) function like this:
>
> ```
> <xsl:value-of select="replace($sub2, '''', ''''''')"/>
> ```
>
> This syntax is really confusing, but it works.

A Stylesheet That Emulates a for Loop

We stressed earlier that the xsl:for-each element is not a for loop; it's merely an iterator across a group of nodes. However, if you simply must implement a for loop, there's a way to do it. (Get ready to use recursion, though.)

Template Design

Our design here is to create a named template that will take some arguments, and then act as a for loop processor. If you think about a traditional for loop, it has several properties:

One or more initialization statements

These statements are processed before the `for` loop begins. Typically the initialization statements refer to an *index variable* that is used to determine whether the loop should continue.

An increment statement

This statement specifies how the index variable should be updated after each pass through the loop.

A boolean expression

If the expression is `true`, the loop continues; if it is ever `false`, the loop exits.

Let's take a sample from the world of Java and C++:

```
for (int i=0; i<length; i++)
```

In this scintillating example, the initialization statement is `i=0`, the index variable (the variable whose value determines whether we're done or not) is `i`, the boolean expression we use to test whether the loop should continue is `i<length`, and the increment statement is `i++`.

For our purposes here, we're going to make several simplifying assumptions. (Feel free, dear reader, to make the example as complicated as you wish.) Here are the shortcuts we'll take:

- Rather than use an initialization statement, we'll require the caller to set the value of the local variable `i` when it invokes our `for` loop processor. This value is passed as a parameter, so it can be calculated by an XPath expression.

- Rather than specify an increment statement such as `i++`, we'll require the caller to set the value of the local variable `increment`. The default value for this variable is `1`; it can be any negative or positive integer, however. The value of this variable will be added to the current value of `i` after each iteration through our loop.

- Rather than allow any conceivable boolean expression, we'll require the caller to pass in two parameters; `operator` and `testValue`. The allowable values for the `operator` variable are =, < (coded as `&lt;`), > (coded as `&gt;`), !=, <= (coded as `&lt;=`), and >= (coded as `&gt;=`). We're doing things this way because there isn't a way to ask the XSLT processor to evaluate a literal (such as `i<length`) as if it were part of the stylesheet.

Implementation

We'll define four global parameters for our stylesheet:

```
<xsl:param name="i"         select="1"/>
<xsl:param name="increment" select="1"/>
<xsl:param name="operator"  select="'<='"/>
<xsl:param name="testValue" select="10"/>
```

The default values defined here correspond to the C++ or Java statement `for (i = 1; i <= 10; i++)`. We also have a `match="/"` template that invokes our `for` loop processor:

```
<xsl:template match="/">
  <xsl:call-template name="for-loop">
    <xsl:with-param name="i"         select="$i"/>
    <xsl:with-param name="increment" select="$increment"/>
    <xsl:with-param name="operator"  select="$operator"/>
    <xsl:with-param name="testValue" select="$testValue"/>
  </xsl:call-template>
</xsl:template>
```

In the `for-loop` template, our first task is to determine whether the condition is true. We do this by calculating a boolean value with several `<xsl:when>` elements, each of which looks like the one below:

```
<xsl:variable name="testPassed">
  <xsl:choose>
    <xsl:when test="$operator = '!='">
      <xsl:if test="$i != $testValue">
        <xsl:text>true</xsl:text>
      </xsl:if>
    </xsl:when>
    ...
  </xsl:choose>
</xsl:variable>
```

If the variable `$testPassed` is `true`, the `for-loop` template calls itself again. Before the `<xsl:call-template>` instruction, we can put whatever logic we want. For our sample, we simply write the current value of `$i` to the output.

The Complete Example

Here's the complete stylesheet:

```
<?xml version="1.0"?>
<!-- for-loop.xsl -->
<xsl:stylesheet version="1.0"
  xmlns:xsl="http://www.w3.org/1999/XSL/Transform">

  <xsl:output method="text"/>

  <xsl:param name="i" select="1"/>
  <xsl:param name="increment" select="1"/>
  <xsl:param name="operator" select="'&lt;='"/>
  <xsl:param name="testValue" select="10"/>

  <xsl:template match="/">
    <xsl:call-template name="for-loop">
      <xsl:with-param name="i"         select="$i"/>
      <xsl:with-param name="increment" select="$increment"/>
      <xsl:with-param name="operator"  select="$operator"/>
      <xsl:with-param name="testValue" select="$testValue"/>
    </xsl:call-template>
  </xsl:template>
```

```
<xsl:template name="for-loop">
  <xsl:param name="i"/>
  <xsl:param name="increment"/>
  <xsl:param name="operator"/>
  <xsl:param name="testValue"/>

  <xsl:variable name="testPassed">
    <xsl:choose>
      <xsl:when test="$operator = '!='">
        <xsl:if test="$i != $testValue">
          <xsl:text>true</xsl:text>
        </xsl:if>
      </xsl:when>
      <xsl:when test="$operator = '&lt;='">
        <xsl:if test="$i &lt;= $testValue">
          <xsl:text>true</xsl:text>
        </xsl:if>
      </xsl:when>
      <xsl:when test="$operator = '&gt;='">
        <xsl:if test="$i &gt;= $testValue">
          <xsl:text>true</xsl:text>
        </xsl:if>
      </xsl:when>
      <xsl:when test="$operator = '='">
        <xsl:if test="$i = $testValue">
          <xsl:text>true</xsl:text>
        </xsl:if>
      </xsl:when>
      <xsl:when test="$operator = '&lt;'">
        <xsl:if test="$i &lt; $testValue">
          <xsl:text>true</xsl:text>
        </xsl:if>
      </xsl:when>
      <xsl:when test="$operator = '&gt;'">
        <xsl:if test="$i &gt; $testValue">
          <xsl:text>true</xsl:text>
        </xsl:if>
      </xsl:when>
      <xsl:otherwise>
        <xsl:message terminate="yes">
          <xsl:text>Sorry, the for-loop emulator only </xsl:text>
          <xsl:text>handles six operators &#xA;</xsl:text>
          <xsl:text>(&lt; | &gt; | = | &lt;= | &gt;= | !=).  </xsl:text>
          <xsl:text>The value </xsl:text>
          <xsl:value-of select="$operator"/>
          <xsl:text> is not allowed.&#xA;</xsl:text>
        </xsl:message>
      </xsl:otherwise>
    </xsl:choose>
  </xsl:variable>

  <xsl:if test="$testPassed='true'">
    <!-- Put your logic here, whatever it might be.  For the purpose     -->
    <!-- of our example, we'll just write some text to the output stream. -->
```

```
<xsl:text>Value of i=</xsl:text>
<xsl:value-of select="$i"/>
<xsl:text>&#xA;</xsl:text>

<!-- Your logic should end here; don't change the rest of this    -->
<!-- template!                                                     -->

<!-- Now for the important part: we increment the index variable and -->
<!-- loop.  Notice that we're passing the incremented value, not    -->
<!-- changing the variable itself.                                  -->

<xsl:call-template name="for-loop">
  <xsl:with-param name="i"         select="$i + $increment"/>
  <xsl:with-param name="increment" select="$increment"/>
  <xsl:with-param name="operator"  select="$operator"/>
  <xsl:with-param name="testValue" select="$testValue"/>
</xsl:call-template>
    </xsl:if>
  </xsl:template>

</xsl:stylesheet>
```

Running the stylesheet with the default parameter values creates these exciting results:

```
Value of i=1
Value of i=2
Value of i=3
Value of i=4
Value of i=5
Value of i=6
Value of i=7
Value of i=8
Value of i=9
Value of i=10
```

Using the parameters i=10, increment="-1", operator=">=" and testValue=0, we get these results:

```
Value of i=10
Value of i=9
Value of i=8
Value of i=7
Value of i=6
Value of i=5
Value of i=4
Value of i=3
Value of i=2
Value of i=1
Value of i=0
```

The quotes around the values of increment and operator are necessary when passing those values from the command line to the XSLT processor. As a final test, here are the results for i=10, increment="-2", operator=">" and testValue=0:

```
Value of i=10
Value of i=8
Value of i=6
Value of i=4
Value of i=2
```

If you want to modify the **for** loop to do something useful, put your code between these comments:

```
<!-- Put your logic here, whatever it might be. For the purpose    -->
<!-- of our example, we'll just write some text to the output stream. -->


<!-- Your logic should end here; don't change the rest of this      -->
<!-- template!                                                       -->
```

Summary

We've covered a lot of ground in this chapter, haven't we? We've gone over all of the basic elements you need to add logic and branching to your stylesheets. We discussed some of the similarities between XSLT and other programming languages you might know; more importantly, we discussed how XSLT is different from most of the code you've probably written. In particular, the use of recursion and the principles of variables that don't change takes some getting used to. Despite the learning curve, most of the common tasks you'll need to do will be similar to the exercises we've gone through in this chapter. Now that we've covered these basic elements, we'll talk about links and references, discovering ways to build links between different parts of an XML document.

Creating Links and Cross-References

If you're creating a web site, publishing a book, or processing an XML-based purchase order, chances are many pieces of information will refer to other things. This chapter discusses several ways to link XML elements. It reviews three techniques:

- Using the XML `ID`, `IDREF`, and `IDREFS` datatypes
- Doing more advanced linking with the `key( )` function
- Generating links in unstructured documents

Using the XML ID, IDREF, and IDREFS Datatypes

Our first attempt at linking will be with the XPath `id( )` function. This useful function helps us find the element that has an `ID` attribute with a particular value.

The Datatypes and How They Work

Three of the basic datatypes that are supported by XML Document Type Definitions (DTDs) and XML Schemas are `ID`, `IDREF`, and `IDREFS`. The `ID` and `IDREF` datatypes work according to two rules:

- Every attribute of datatype `ID` must be unique.
- Every value of datatype `IDREF` must match a value of an attribute of datatype `ID` somewhere in the document.

An attribute with a datatype of `IDREFS` contains one or more space-separated values, each of which must match a value of an `ID` elsewhere in the document. The `IDREFS` datatype is a list of `IDREF` values, just as its name implies.

Here is a simple DTD fragment that uses the `ID` and `IDREF` datatypes:

```
<?xml version="1.0"?>
<!-- parts-list1.xml -->
<!DOCTYPE parts-list [
<!ELEMENT parts-list     (component+, part+)>
```

```
<!ELEMENT component        (name, partref+)>
<!ATTLIST component        component-id ID #REQUIRED>

<!ELEMENT name             (#PCDATA)>

<!ELEMENT partref          EMPTY>
<!ATTLIST partref          refid IDREF #REQUIRED>

<!ELEMENT part             (name)>
<!ATTLIST part             part-id ID #REQUIRED>
]>

<parts-list>
...
</parts-list>
```

Here is the XML Schema definition of the same document type:

```
<?xml version="1.0" encoding="UTF-8"?>
<!-- parts-list.xsd -->
<xs:schema
  xmlns:xs="http://www.w3.org/2001/XMLSchema">

  <xs:element name="parts-list">
    <xs:complexType>
      <xs:sequence>
        <xs:element ref="component" minOccurs="1" maxOccurs="unbounded"/>
        <xs:element ref="part" minOccurs="1" maxOccurs="unbounded"/>
      </xs:sequence>
    </xs:complexType>
  </xs:element>

  <xs:element name="component">
    <xs:complexType>
      <xs:sequence>
        <xs:element ref="name" minOccurs="1" maxOccurs="1"/>
        <xs:element ref="partref" minOccurs="1" maxOccurs="unbounded"/>
      </xs:sequence>
      <xs:attribute name="component-id" type="xs:ID" use="required"/>
    </xs:complexType>
  </xs:element>

  <xs:element name="part">
    <xs:complexType>
      <xs:sequence>
        <xs:element ref="name" minOccurs="1" maxOccurs="1"/>
      </xs:sequence>
      <xs:attribute name="part-id" type="xs:ID" use="required"/>
    </xs:complexType>
  </xs:element>

  <xs:element name="name" type="xs:string"/>

  <xs:element name="partref">
    <xs:complexType>
      <xs:attribute name="refid" type="xs:IDREF" use="required"/>
```

```
        </xs:complexType>
      </xs:element>
    </xs:schema>
```

The DTD and the XML Schema here are semantically identical, so we won't worry about which of the two we use to validate our XML files. (There are many things you can express in XML Schema that aren't possible in DTDs, but in this case the two documents mean the exact same thing.) Here we're using the `ID` and `IDREF` datatypes. We'll take a quick look at the lesser-used `IDREFS` datatype; for our purposes, we process `IDREFS` the same way.

 We'll discuss this in more detail later in this chapter, but be aware that you have to validate the XML document for any attributes to be assigned the `ID`, `IDREF`, and `IDREFS` datatypes. If you can't wait to read the details, you can skip ahead to the section "[2.0] The idref() Function" later in this chapter.

To sum up how our parts list document works, a valid `<parts-list>` has one or more `<component>` elements, followed by one or more `<part>` elements. The `<component>` and `<part>` elements are required to have an `ID` attribute (`component-id` or `part-id`, respectively). There's also a `<partref>` element with a required attribute of type `IDREF`; the value of that attribute, named `refid`, must match the value of an `ID` element somewhere in the parts list.

Our first look at linking parts of a document together will use these nicely structured documents.

Linking Parts of an XML Document

To illustrate the value of linking, we'll use a document that defines several `<component>` and `<part>` elements. Each `<component>` uses some number of `<part>`s. Because our XML document contains `ID` and `IDREF` values, we can link different parts of the document together.

Here's how our document looks:

```
<?xml version="1.0"?>
<!-- parts-list1.xml -->
<!DOCTYPE parts-list [
...
]>

<parts-list>
  <component component-id="C28392-33-TT">
    <name>Turnip Twaddler</name>
    <partref refid="P81952-26-PK"/>
    <partref refid="P86679-52-SP"/>
    <partref refid="P81472-68-FD"/>
    <partref refid="P88107-39-GT"/>
```

```
    </component>
...
    <component component-id="C28772-63-OB">
      <name>Olive Bruiser</name>
      <partref refid="P80228-21-PT"/>
      <partref refid="P82387-85-PA"/>
    </component>

    <part part-id="P80228-21-PT">
      <name>Pitter</name>
    </part>
...
    <part part-id="P86994-25-RC">
      <name>Ribbon Curler</name>
    </part>
</parts-list>
```

Our first task will be to look at each `<component>` and list the names of the `<part>`s that
it uses. Each of the `refid` attributes of each of the `<partref>` elements refers to the `id`
attribute of a `<part>` element.

A Stylesheet That Uses the id( ) Function

Let's look at our desired output. What we want is a simple text document that lists all
of the part names for each component, which should look like this:

```
Here is a test of the id() function:

    Turnip Twaddler (component #C28392-33-TT) uses these parts:
      Spanner
      Feather Duster
      Grommet
      Paring Knife

    Prawn Goader (component #C28813-70-PG) uses these parts:
      Paring Knife
      Mucilage
      Ribbon Curler

...

    Olive Bruiser (component #C28772-63-OB) uses these parts:
      Pitter
      Patter
```

The stylesheet to generate these results is pretty straightforward:

```
<?xml version="1.0"?>
<!-- id1.xsl -->
<xsl:stylesheet version="2.0"
  xmlns:xsl="http://www.w3.org/1999/XSL/Transform">

  <xsl:output method="text"/>

  <xsl:template match="/">
```

```
<xsl:text>&#xA;Here is a test of the id() </xsl:text>
<xsl:text>function:&#xA;</xsl:text>

<xsl:for-each select="/parts-list/component">
  <xsl:text>&#xA;  </xsl:text>
  <xsl:value-of select="name"/>
  <xsl:text> (component #</xsl:text>
  <xsl:value-of select="@component-id"/>
  <xsl:text>) uses these parts:&#xA;    </xsl:text>
  <xsl:for-each select="id(partref/@refid)">
    <xsl:value-of select="name"/>
    <xsl:text>&#xA;    </xsl:text>
  </xsl:for-each>
</xsl:for-each>
    </xsl:template>
  </xsl:stylesheet>
```

We call the id( ) function, which returns a node-set/sequence of all the nodes that
match all of the **refid** attributes of the **<partref>** elements in each component. Each
item in the node-set is the actual **<part>** element, so the XPath expression
select="name" returns the name of the part (the text of the **<name>** child element).

> The **id**( ) and **idref**( ) functions both have a two-argument version. The
> second argument for both functions is a node. That parameter tells the
> XSLT processor to look in the document that contains the node instead
> of the document that contains the context item. You probably won't
> need this option, but it's there.

Before we move on to more complicated examples, we'll look at a slightly different
XML document, which uses attributes of type **IDREFS** instead of **IDREF**. Here's what it
looks like:

```
<?xml version="1.0"?>
<!-- parts-list2.xml -->
<!DOCTYPE parts-list [
<!ELEMENT parts-list        (component+, part+)>

<!ELEMENT component         (name, partref)>
<!ATTLIST component         component-id ID #REQUIRED>

<!ELEMENT name              (#PCDATA)>

<!ELEMENT partref           EMPTY>
<!ATTLIST partref           refid IDREFS #REQUIRED>

<!ELEMENT part              (name) >
<!ATTLIST part              part-id ID #REQUIRED>
]>

<parts-list>
  <component component-id="C28392-33-TT">
    <name>Turnip Twaddler</name>
```

```
        <partref
          refid="P81952-26-PK P86679-52-SP P81472-68-FD P88107-39-GT"/>
      </component>
      <component component-id="C28813-70-PG">
        <name>Prawn Goader</name>
        <partref refid="P81952-26-PK P80499-43-MC P86994-25-RC"/>
      </component>
  ...
  </parts-list>
```

Even though the structure of this XML document is different, we can use the same stylesheet against it. *We get the same results, even though the datatype of the attribute has changed.* When we call the `id()` function with an argument such as `P81952-PK P86679-52-SP ...`, the `id()` function treats each space-separated string as a separate ID. The value of any `ID` attribute must be a valid XML name, which means it can't contain spaces. That's why this works. (We'll talk more about valid XML names in a little while.)

We've written a stylesheet that goes from an `IDREF` to the element that has that particular `ID`. Next we'll write a stylesheet that goes from an `ID` to all of the references to it. We'll list each `<part>` in our document, and then list all of the `<component>`s that use it. The challenge is in the XPath expression; given the `ID` of a `<part>`, how do we find all of the `<component>`s that have a `<partref>` element with a `refid` attribute? Here's the stylesheet:

```
<?xml version="1.0"?>
<!-- id2.xsl -->
<xsl:stylesheet version="1.0"
    xmlns:xsl="http://www.w3.org/1999/XSL/Transform">

  <xsl:output method="text"/>

  <xsl:template match="/">
    <xsl:text>&#xA;Here is a test of the id() </xsl:text>
    <xsl:text>function in reverse:&#xA;</xsl:text>

    <xsl:for-each select="/parts-list/part">
      <xsl:text>&#xA;  </xsl:text>
      <xsl:value-of select="name"/>
      <xsl:text> (part #</xsl:text>
      <xsl:value-of select="@part-id"/>
      <xsl:text>) is used in these products:&#xA;</xsl:text>
      <xsl:for-each
        select="/parts-list/component
                [partref/@refid=current()/@part-id]">
        <xsl:value-of select="name"/>
        <xsl:if test="position() != last()">
          <xsl:text>&#xA;    </xsl:text>
        </xsl:if>
      </xsl:for-each>
      <xsl:text>&#xA;</xsl:text>
    </xsl:for-each>
```

```
    </xsl:template>
  </xsl:stylesheet>
```

The XPath expression in the `<xsl:for-each>` is more complicated here; we'll take a closer look at it.

```
/parts-list/component[partref/@refid=current()/@part-id]
```

The expression returns all of the `<component>` elements for which the predicate expression is true. The predicate expression specifies that the component has at least one `<partref>` child element whose `refid` attribute matches the `part-id` attribute of the current node.

The predicate is comparing two values, even though it looks like a location path with three parts. One of the values is `partref/@refid`, the set of `refid` attributes from all the `<partref>` elements in a given `<component>`. The other value is `current( )/@part-id`, the value of the `part-id` attribute of the current node. Every value inside the predicate refers to a `<component>` element; the `current( )` function refers to the current `<part>` element we're processing. That `<part>` element is selected by the first `<xsl:for-each>` element in the template.

Here are the results of the stylesheet:

```
Here is a test of the id() function in reverse:

  Pitter (part #P80228-21-PT) is used in these products:
    Olive Bruiser

  Patter (part #P82387-85-PA) is used in these products:
    Olive Bruiser

  Spanner (part #P86679-52-SP) is used in these products:
    Turnip Twaddler
    Clam Teaser
    Lemon Snubber

  Feather Duster (part #P81472-68-FD) is used in these products:
    Turnip Twaddler
    Clam Teaser
    Cucumber Decorating Kit
...
```

Inside the inner `<xsl:for-each>` element, the XPath expression `name` returns the name of the current `<component>`. We could have written the inner `<xsl:for-each>` element like this:

```
<xsl:for-each
  select="/parts-list/component/partref
          [@refid=current()/@part-id]">
  <xsl:value-of select="../name"/>
```

This generates the same results, but the expression to select the name of the component is slightly more complicated. The `select` attribute of the `<xsl:for-each>` element returns a node-set of `<partref>` elements, so we have to use `../name` to get the name of the component. If you find yourself writing lots of complicated expressions inside a `<xsl:for-each>` element, you should see whether you can rewrite the `<for-each>` element's XPath expression to simplify your stylesheet.

[2.0] The idref( ) Function

In the previous stylesheet, it was tedious to use the `id( )` function in reverse, going from something with a given `ID` to the elements that reference it. Because this is a fairly common task, XSLT 2.0 adds the `idref( )` function. Given an ID, `idref( )` returns all of the elements that reference it. Here's a simple stylesheet that works with our parts list:

```
<?xml version="1.0"?>
<!-- idref.xsl -->
<xsl:stylesheet version="2.0"
  xmlns:xsl="http://www.w3.org/1999/XSL/Transform">

  <xsl:output method="text"/>

  <xsl:template match="/">
    <xsl:text>&#xA;Here is a test of the idref() </xsl:text>
    <xsl:text>function:&#xA;</xsl:text>

    <xsl:for-each select="/parts-list/part">
      <xsl:text>&#xA;  </xsl:text>
      <xsl:value-of select="name"/>
      <xsl:text> (part #</xsl:text>
      <xsl:value-of select="@part-id"/>
      <xsl:text>) is used in these products:&#xA;</xsl:text>
      <xsl:value-of select="idref(@part-id)/../../name"
        separator="&#xA;"/>
      <xsl:text>&#xA;</xsl:text>
    </xsl:for-each>
  </xsl:template>
</xsl:stylesheet>
```

In this stylesheet, we can do everything with a single `<xsl:value-of>` element. Notice that the `idref( )` function returns the matching *attributes*; that's why we use the XPath expression `idref(@part-id)/../../name` to get the name of the component. The parent of the attribute is a `<partref>` element and its parent is a `<component>`. The component's `<name>` child is what we want here.

Finally, the new `idref( )` function works with the `IDREFS` datatype, just like `id( )`.

Generating HTML Documents with Links

Before we leave the topic of IDs, we'll look at a more complicated stylesheet—one that generates HTML. We want to list all the components and parts in our document, and we want to create hyperlinks between them. So, we'll list the components and the parts they use; each part name will be a link to a description of that part. We'll do the same thing when we list each part and the components that use it. Our source document has changed slightly for the purposes of our next few examples:

```
<?xml version="1.0"?>
<!-- parts-list3.xml -->
<!DOCTYPE parts-list [
<!ELEMENT parts-list        (component+, part+, supplier+)>

<!ELEMENT component         (name, partref+, description)>
<!ATTLIST component         component-id ID #REQUIRED>

<!ELEMENT name              (#PCDATA)>

<!ELEMENT partref           EMPTY>
<!ATTLIST partref           refid IDREF #REQUIRED>

<!ELEMENT part              (name, description)>
<!ATTLIST part              part-id ID #REQUIRED
                            supplier CDATA #REQUIRED>

<!ELEMENT description       (#PCDATA|partref)*>

<!ELEMENT supplier          (name)>
<!ATTLIST supplier          country CDATA #REQUIRED
                            vendor-id CDATA #REQUIRED>
]>

<parts-list>
  <component component-id="C28392-33-TT">
    <name>Turnip Twaddler</name>
    <partref refid="P81952-26-PK"/>
    <partref refid="P86679-52-SP"/>
    <partref refid="P81472-68-FD"/>
    <partref refid="P88107-39-GT"/>
    <description>
      If you've got turnips to twaddle, this is the tool for you!
      Comes with a <partref refid="P81472-68-FD"/>.
    </description>
  </component>
  <component component-id="C28100-38-CT">
    <name>Clam Teaser</name>
    <partref refid="P81472-68-FD"/>
    <partref refid="P86994-25-RC"/>
    <partref refid="P86679-52-SP"/>
    <description>
      Everyone knows they're proverbially happy, but what to
      do with a shy clam?  Bring recalcitrant mollusks out of
      their shells with this entertaining gadget.  Includes a
      festive <partref refid="P86994-25-RC"/>.
    </description>
  </component>

...

  <part part-id="P80228-21-PT" supplier="4839">
```

```
    <name>Pitter</name>
    <description>
      Removes pits from olives and cherries in no time at all.
    </description>
  </part>
  <part part-id="P82387-85-PA" supplier="2983">
    <name>Patter</name>
    <description>
      We're not sure what these things do, but people seem
      to like 'em.
    </description>
  </part>

...

  <supplier country="Great Britain" vendor-id="4839">
    <name>Acme Products, Inc.</name>
  </supplier>
  <supplier country="Germany" vendor-id="2983">
    <name>Deutschland Excelsior Gmbh</name>
  </supplier>
  <supplier country="Great Britain" vendor-id="5910">
    <name>Unlimited Spanners Ltd.</name>
  </supplier>
</parts-list>
```

There are a couple of differences here. First of all, we've added a `<description>` element
to every `<component>` and `<part>`. To complicate things, some of the descriptions contain
a `<partref>` element. Notice that the `<partref>` element doesn't have any text. That
means the name of a given part is defined in one place only; if we change the name of
a part, the part name will automatically be updated every place we use it. Finally, we've
added some `<supplier>` elements and put `country` and `vendor-id` attributes on each
part. We'll use those when we talk about keys and key functions.

To generate the HTML document we want, we need to create link points. The description of every component and part should have an HTML anchor
(`<a name="...">`), so we can link to those descriptions. Because the parts and components have unique IDs already, we'll use those IDs as the names of the link points. That
means we know how to create a link point for each component and part, and we know
how to link to a given part or component.

Here's the stylesheet:

```
<?xml version="1.0"?>
<!-- id-html.xsl -->
<xsl:stylesheet version="1.0"
  xmlns:xsl="http://www.w3.org/1999/XSL/Transform">

  <xsl:output method="html"/>

  <xsl:template match="/">
    <html>
      <head>
```

```
        <title>Our Catalog</title>
      </head>
      <body style="font-family: sans-serif;">
        <h1>Our Catalog</h1>
        <p>Here's a look at everything in our catalog:</p>
        <h2 style="background: #66FF66;">Components</h2>
        <xsl:apply-templates select="/parts-list/component"/>
        <h2 style="background: #6666FF;">Parts</h2>
        <xsl:apply-templates select="/parts-list/part"/>
      </body>
    </html>
</xsl:template>

<xsl:template match="component">
  <a name="{@component-id}"/>
  <h3>
    <xsl:value-of select="name"/>
  </h3>
  <p>
    <xsl:apply-templates select="description"/>
  </p>
  <p>
    <xsl:value-of select="name"/>
    <xsl:text> uses these parts:</xsl:text>
  </p>
  <ul>
    <xsl:for-each select="partref">
      <li>
        <xsl:apply-templates select="."/>
      </li>
    </xsl:for-each>
  </ul>
</xsl:template>

<xsl:template match="description">
  <xsl:apply-templates select="*|text()"/>
</xsl:template>

<xsl:template match="partref">
  <a href="{concat('#', @refid)}">
    <xsl:value-of select="id(@refid)/name"/>
  </a>
</xsl:template>

<xsl:template match="part">
  <a name="{@part-id}"/>
  <h3>
    <xsl:value-of select="name"/>
  </h3>
  <p>
    <xsl:apply-templates select="description"/>
  </p>
  <p>
    <xsl:value-of select="name"/>
    <xsl:text> is used in these components:</xsl:text>
```

```
      </p>
      <ul>
        <xsl:for-each select="/parts-list/component
                              [partref/@refid=current()/@part-id]">
          <li>
            <a href="{concat('#', @component-id)}">
              <xsl:value-of select="name"/>
            </a>
          </li>
        </xsl:for-each>
      </ul>
    </xsl:template>

  </xsl:stylesheet>
```

Here's how we create the link points:

```
<a name="{@part-id}"/>
```

This generates the HTML markup `<a name="C28392-33-TT"/>` for the first `<component>` in the document. Whenever we need to create a link *to* that component, the markup is pretty straightforward:

```
<a href="{concat('#', @component-id)}">
  <xsl:value-of select="name"/>
</a>
```

This generates the HTML markup `<a href="#C28392-33-TT">Turnip Twaddler</a>` for any reference to the Turnip Twaddler. If your document uses `ID`, `IDREF`, and `IDREFS` attributes, creating links with this technique is easy.

Figure 6-1 shows how the HTML document looks.

Limitations of IDs

To this point, we've been able to generate cross-references easily. There are some limitations of the `ID` datatype and the `id( )` function, though:

- If you want to use the `ID` datatype, you have to declare the attributes that use that datatype in your DTD or schema. Unfortunately, if your DTD is defined externally to your XML document, the XML parser isn't required to read it. If the DTD isn't read, then the parser has no idea that a given attribute is of type `ID`. Similarly, if you're using a schema, you have to make sure your XSLT processor validates your XML document against the schema to ensure that the `ID`, `IDREF`, and `IDREFS` datatypes are used correctly.

- You must define the `ID`, `IDREF`, and `IDREFS` relationship in the XML document. It would be nice to have the XML document define the data only, with the relationships between parts of the document defined externally (say, in a stylesheet). That way, if you need to define a new relationship between parts of the document, you could do it by creating a new stylesheet, and you wouldn't have to modify your

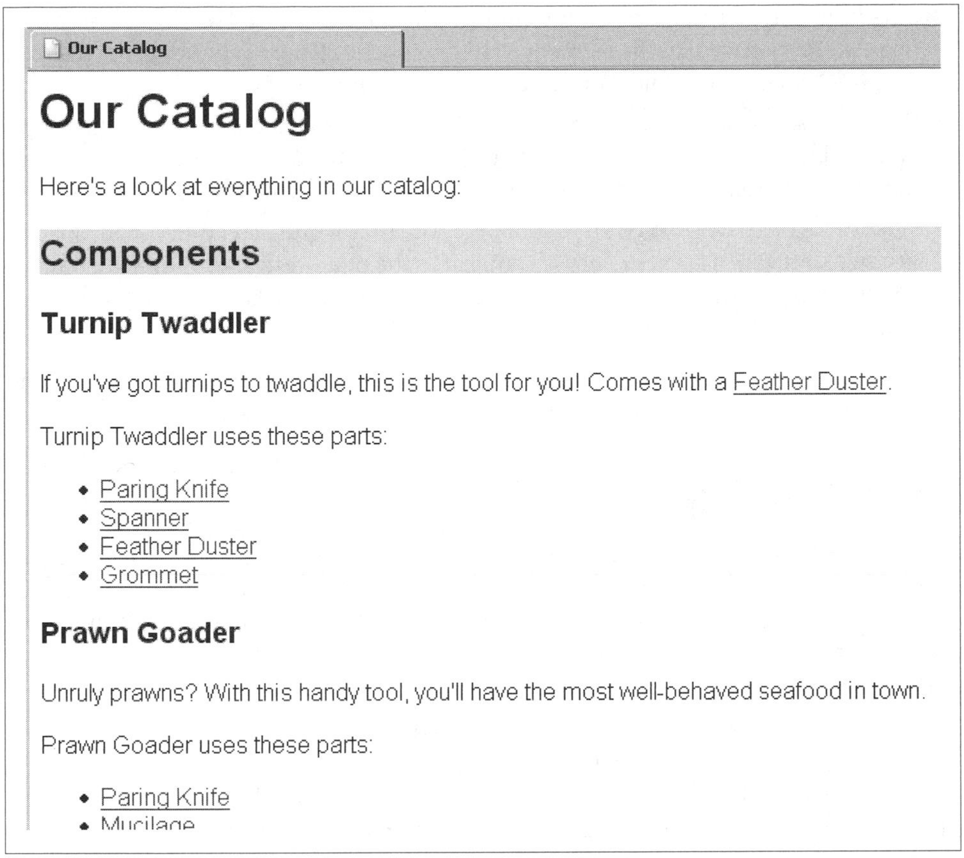

Our Catalog

Here's a look at everything in our catalog:

Components

Turnip Twaddler

If you've got turnips to twaddle, this is the tool for you! Comes with a <u>Feather Duster</u>.

Turnip Twaddler uses these parts:

- <u>Paring Knife</u>
- <u>Spanner</u>
- <u>Feather Duster</u>
- <u>Grommet</u>

Prawn Goader

Unruly prawns? With this handy tool, you'll have the most well-behaved seafood in town.

Prawn Goader uses these parts:

- <u>Paring Knife</u>
- <u>Mucilage</u>

Figure 6-1. HTML file with generated hyperlinks

XML document. It becomes unwieldy quickly if you have to change the XML document structure every time you need to define a new relationship between parts of the document.

- An element can have at most one attribute of type ID. If you'd like to refer to the same element in more than one way, you can't use the id( ) function.

- Any given ID value can be found on one element at most. If you'd like to refer to more than one element with a single value, you can't use the id( ) function for that, either.

- Only one set of IDs exists for the entire document. In other words, if you declare the attributes component-id and part-id to be of type ID, the value of a component-id must be unique across all the attributes of type ID. It is illegal in this case for a component-id to be the same as a part-id, even though those attributes might belong to different elements.

- If you're using a DTD, an ID can only be an attribute of an XML element. The only way you can use the id( ) function to refer to another element is through its attribute of type ID. If you want to find another element based on an attribute that isn't an ID, or based on the element's content or the element's children, and so on, the id( ) function is of no use whatsoever.

- If you're using an XML schema, you can define an element with a datatype of xs:ID. This means you can use the id( ) function to find an element. This is an improvement on the situation, but it does require a schema-aware XSLT parser.

- The value of an ID must be an XML name. In other words, it can't contain spaces, it can't start with a number, and it's subject to the other restrictions of XML names. (Section 2.3 of the XML Recommendation defines these restrictions; see *http://www.w3.org/TR/REC-xml* if you'd like more information.)

To get around all of these limitations, XSLT defines the `<xsl:key>` element and the key( ) function. We'll discuss them now.

XSLT's Key Facility

Now that we've covered the id( ) function in great detail, we'll move on to XSLT's key( ) function and the `<xsl:key>` element. Each `<xsl:key>` element effectively creates an index of the document. You can then use that index to find all elements that have a particular property. Once the key is created, we can use the key( ) function to retrieve parts of the document.

For example, if you have a database of (U.S. postal) addresses, you might want to index that database by the people's last names, by the states in which they live, by their zip codes, etc. Each index takes a certain amount of time to build, but it saves processing time later. (Be aware that it can take a significant amount of memory to create a key, particularly for very large documents.) If you want to find all the people who live in the state of Idaho, you can use the index to find all those people directly; you don't have to search the entire database.

We'll discuss the details of how the key facility works, and then we'll compare it to the id( ) function.

Defining a Key with <xsl:key>

You define a key( ) function with the `<xsl:key>` element:

```
<xsl:key name="supplier-by-country" match="supplier" use="@country"/>
<xsl:key name="part-by-supplier" match="part" use="@supplier"/>
```

The key has three attributes:

name
> This attribute is used to refer to this particular key. When you want to find parts of your XML document, use the name to indicate the key you want to use.

`match`

Containing an XPath expression, this attribute specifies what part of the document you want to index. In our sample here, we've created two keys: one for retrieving `<supplier>`s and one for retrieving `<part>`s.

`use`

Containing another XPath expression, this attribute is interpreted in the context of the `match` attribute. In other words, the first `<xsl:key>` element here, named `supplier-by-country`, creates an index of all the `<supplier>` elements, and uses the `country` attribute to retrieve them. The second `<xsl:key>` element, named `part-by-supplier`, creates an index of all the `<part>` elements and uses the `supplier` attribute to find them.

[2.0] XSLT 2.0 adds a fourth attribute, `collation`. This allows us to specify a set of rules for how values are compared. To cite a frequent example from the specs, the German word for *street* can be spelled *Strasse* or *Straße*. Using a German collation for the key function causes those to words to be the same, despite the fact that they are clearly different strings.

The XSLT 1.0 specification specifically states that the `match` and `use` attributes can't contain variables.

Generating Links with the key( ) Function

In the modified parts list document we looked at a moment ago, we added a `<supplier>` to each `<part>`. We also added a `country` attribute to the `<supplier>` element. If you look at the document structure as defined in the embedded DTD (or the external schema), you'll notice that the `vendor-id` and `country` attributes of the `<supplier>` element don't have a datatype of `ID`, and that the `supplier` attribute of the `<part>` element is not an `IDREF`.

We want to retrieve all the parts that are provided by a particular country. If we defined the `country` attribute to be of type `ID`, we could only have one supplier from each country. Clearly that's an unacceptable limitation on our document.

Now that we've created a more flexible XML document, we'll use the key( ) function to process our document. We'll use two keys here. The first retrieves all of the `<supplier>` elements that match a given country name. The second retrieves all of the `<part>` elements whose `supplier` attribute matches a given supplier's ID. Here's the stylesheet:

```
<?xml version="1.0"?>
<!-- key.xsl -->
<xsl:stylesheet version="1.0"
  xmlns:xsl="http://www.w3.org/1999/XSL/Transform">
```

```
<xsl:output method="html"/>

<xsl:param name="country-name"/>

<xsl:key name="supplier-by-country" match="supplier" use="@country"/>
<xsl:key name="part-by-supplier" match="part" use="@supplier"/>

<xsl:template match="/">
  <html>
    <head>
      <title>
        <xsl:text>Parts from </xsl:text>
        <xsl:value-of select="$country-name"/>
      </title>
    </head>
    <body style="font-family: sans-serif;">
      <h1>
        <xsl:text>Parts from </xsl:text>
        <xsl:value-of select="$country-name"/>
      </h1>
      <xsl:choose>
        <xsl:when test="key('supplier-by-country', $country-name)">
          <xsl:apply-templates select="key('supplier-by-country', $country-name)"/>
        </xsl:when>

        <xsl:otherwise>
          <p>Sorry, we don't get any parts from that country!</p>
        </xsl:otherwise>
      </xsl:choose>
    </body>
  </html>
</xsl:template>

<xsl:template match="supplier">
  <h2>
    <xsl:value-of select="name"/>
  </h2>
  <p>
    <xsl:value-of select="name"/>
    <xsl:text> supplies these parts:</xsl:text>
  </p>
  <ul>
    <xsl:for-each select="key('part-by-supplier', @vendor-id)">
      <li>
        <b>
          <xsl:value-of select="name"/>
        </b>
        <xsl:text>:  </xsl:text>
        <xsl:apply-templates select="description"/>
      </li>
    </xsl:for-each>
  </ul>
</xsl:template>

</xsl:stylesheet>
```

Our stylesheet takes an external parameter named `country-name` (defined at the top of the stylesheet) and returns all of the parts supplied by companies based in that country. The first time we use the `key( )` function, we see whether there are any values that match the external parameter:

```
<xsl:when test="key('country-index', $country-name)">
  <xsl:for-each select="key('country-index', $country-name)">
    <xsl:apply-templates select="."/>
  </xsl:for-each>
</xsl:when>
```

The key `country-index` returns all of the `<supplier>` elements that match the given `$country-name`. Assuming there's at least one, we process it (if there's not at least one, the expression evaluates to `false`). Processing the `<supplier>` element uses the other key:

```
<xsl:for-each select="key('part-index', @vendor-id)">
```

This returns all of the `<part>` elements whose `supplier` attribute matches the `vendor-id` attribute of the current `<supplier>`.

Notice that the attribute we're using to retrieve matching nodes can contain spaces. If `country` were of datatype `ID`, it could not have the value `"Great Britain"`. This is one of the advantages of keys. A `country-name` of `"Great Britain"` gives us the HTML document shown in Figure 6-2.

Advantages of the key( ) Function

Now that we've taken the `key( )` function through its paces, you can see that it has several advantages:

- The `key( )` function is defined in a stylesheet. That means I can define any number of relationships between parts of an XML document at any time. If I need to define a new relationship tomorrow, I don't have to change my XML documents.

- Any number of `key( )` functions can be defined for a given element. In our parts list example, we could define `key( )` functions for the values of the `vendor-id`, `part-id`, and `component-id` attributes. We could also create `key( )` functions based on the text of various elements or their children. If we used `ID`s instead of the `key( )` function, we would be limited to a single index based on the value of the single attribute of the `ID` datatype.

  To sum up the advantages for this point, an element can have more than one `key( )` defined against it, and that key doesn't have to be based on an attribute. The key can be based on the element's text, the text of child elements, or other constructs.

- Any number of elements can match a given value. Taking another look at our example, when we use the `key( )` function to find all the parts from a particular country, the `key( )` function returns a node-set that can have any number of nodes.

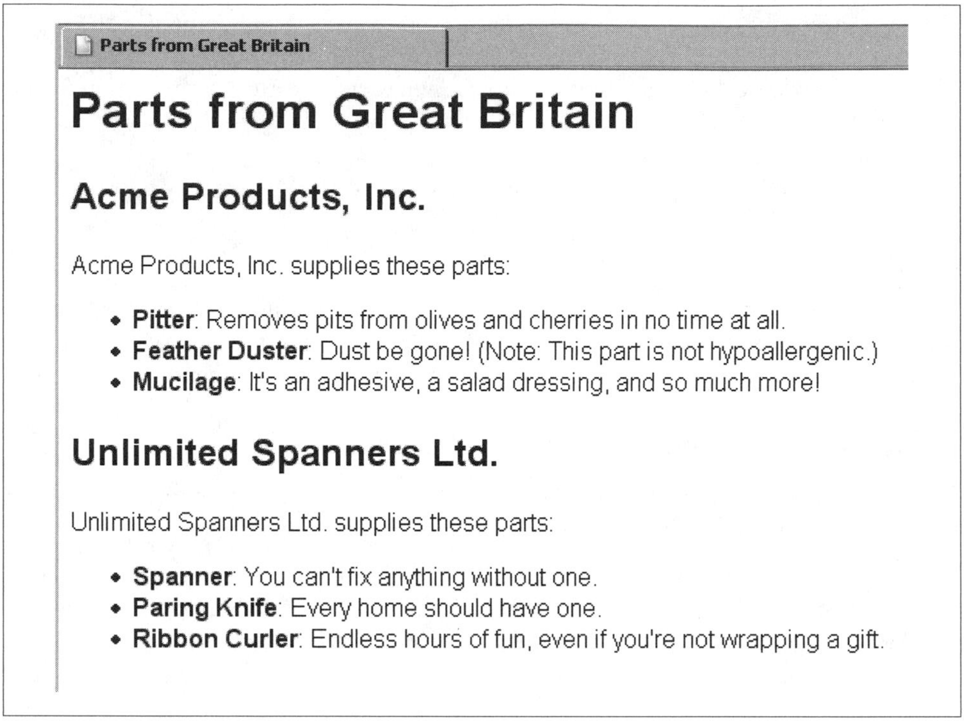

Parts from Great Britain

Parts from Great Britain

Acme Products, Inc.

Acme Products, Inc. supplies these parts:

- **Pitter**: Removes pits from olives and cherries in no time at all.
- **Feather Duster**: Dust be gone! (Note: This part is not hypoallergenic.)
- **Mucilage**: It's an adhesive, a salad dressing, and so much more!

Unlimited Spanners Ltd.

Unlimited Spanners Ltd. supplies these parts:

- **Spanner**: You can't fix anything without one.
- **Paring Knife**: Every home should have one.
- **Ribbon Curler**: Endless hours of fun, even if you're not wrapping a gift.

Figure 6-2. All the parts from our suppliers in Great Britain

If we use an ID instead, legally there can be only one element that matches a given country.

- The value we use to look up elements in the key function isn't constrained to be an XML name. If we use the ID datatype, its value can't contain spaces, among other constraints.

Normally you'll use the two-argument version of the key( ) function. We pass the name of the key and the value we're looking for, and the matching items are returned. There's also a three-argument version of the function that lets you limit values returned by the function to a particular set of nodes. See the description of the key( ) function in Appendix C for more information.

Generating Links in Unstructured Documents

Before we leave the topic of linking, we'll discuss one more useful technique. So far, all of this chapter's examples have been structured nicely. When there was a relationship between two pieces of information, we had an ID and IDREF pair to match them. What happens if the XML document you're transforming isn't written that way? Fortunately, we can use the key( ) function and the generate-id( ) function to create structure where there isn't any.

An Unstructured XML Document in Need of Links

For our example here, we'll take out all of the `id` and `refid` attributes that have served us well so far. This is a contrived example, but it demonstrates how we can use the `key( )` and `generate-id( )` functions to generate links between parts of our document.

In our new sample document, we've stripped out the references that tied things together so neatly before:

```
<?xml version="1.0"?>
<!-- parts-list4.xml -->
<parts-list>
  <component>
    <name>Turnip Twaddler</name>
    <partref>Paring Knife</partref>
    <partref>Spanner</partref>
    <partref>Feather Duster</partref>
    <partref>Grommet</partref>
    <description>
      If you've got turnips to twaddle, this is the tool for you!
      Comes with a <partref>Feather Duster</partref>.
    </description>
  </component>

  ...

  <part>
    <name>Pitter</name>
    <description>
      Removes pits from olives and cherries in no time at all.
    </description>
  </part>
  <part>
    <name>Patter</name>
    <description>
      We're not sure what these things do, but people seem
      to like 'em.
    </description>
  </part>
  ...
</parts-list>
```

We've removed all of the IDs and IDREFs in the document. For elements such as `<partref>` that formerly used attributes to link parts of the document together, we simply use the text of the item we're referring to. To generate the cross-references we created before, we'll need to do three things:

1. Define two keys for all parts and components. One key lets us get the `<part>` that matches a given name, and the other lets us find a `<component>` with a `<partref>` child whose text matches a given name.

2. Generate a new ID for each `<component>` and `<part>` we find.

3. For each `<component>`, use one key to retrieve the `<part>` nodes that match a particular name. For each `<part>`, we use the other key to retrieve the `<component>` nodes that refer to the current part. We'll use `generate-id( )` to create the IDs for us.

We'll go through the relevant parts of the stylesheet. First, we define the two keys we'll use:

```
<xsl:key name="parts-index" match="part/name" use="."/>
<xsl:key name="component-index" match="component" use="partref"/>
```

The first key returns the `<name>` element that matches a given part name. Notice that the `match` attribute means we're getting the `<name>` element; if we want the `<part>` element itself, we would have to use the parent axis on the node returned by the `key( )` function. (We don't need to access the `<part>` element in our stylesheet; that's why we set up the key this way.)

The second key returns the `<component>` element that has a `<partref>` that matches a given part name. What we get from the `key( )` function is the `<component>`, the parent of both the `<partref>` element that contains the part name we're looking for and the `<name>` element that we'll want to insert into our HTML document.

The next step is to create an ID for each `<component>` and `<part>`:

```
<xsl:template match="component">
  <a name="{generate-id(name)}"/>
  ...
</xsl:template>
...
<xsl:template match="part">
  <a name="{generate-id(name)}"/>
  ...
</xsl:template>
```

In both cases, we're generating an ID based on the text of the `<name>` child of the given element. We're using the names of parts and components throughout our stylesheet, so basing the IDs on the `<name>` elements makes things simpler.

Now we need to process all of the `<partref>`s under a given `<component>`. Here's how that works:

```
<ul>
  <xsl:for-each select="partref">
    <li>
      <a href="{concat('#', generate-id(key('parts-index', .)[1]))}">
        <xsl:value-of select="."/>
      </a>
    </li>
  </xsl:for-each>
</ul>
```

We generate the `href` attribute of the link by generating an ID of the first match from the `key( )` function. The `parts-index` key returns the `<name>` element that matches a string; that string in this case is the text value of the current element.

 Notice that we used the predicate expression [1] to specify the first element from the node-set or sequence. This is good practice for XSLT 1.0, because it makes it clear exactly which node we want. However, this is crucial for XSLT 2.0, because it is a fatal error to pass a sequence with more than one node to the key() function in an XSLT 2.0 stylesheet.

The final task is to create the links from each <part> to all of the <component>s that use it. Here's how that code looks:

```
<ul>
  <xsl:for-each select="key('component-index', name)">
    <li>
      <a href="{concat('#', generate-id(name))}">
        <xsl:value-of select="name"/>
      </a>
    </li>
  </xsl:for-each>
</ul>
```

Remember, the component-index key returns the <component> element. The <component> is the parent of both the <partref> elements and the <name> element. The search term we pass to the key is the name of the current part. When we get the <component> back from the key, we use its <name> child to generate an ID and to write the name of the component.

Here's the complete stylesheet:

```
<?xml version="1.0"?>
<!-- generate-id.xsl -->
<xsl:stylesheet version="1.0"
  xmlns:xsl="http://www.w3.org/1999/XSL/Transform">

  <xsl:output method="html"/>

  <xsl:key name="parts-index" match="part/name" use="."/>
  <xsl:key name="component-index" match="component" use="partref"/>

  <xsl:template match="/">
    <html>
      <head>
        <title>Our Catalog</title>
      </head>
      <body style="font-family: sans-serif;">
        <h1>Our Catalog</h1>
        <p>Here's a look at everything in our catalog:</p>
        <h2 style="background: #66FF66;">Components</h2>
        <xsl:apply-templates select="/parts-list/component"/>
        <h2 style="background: #6666FF;">Parts</h2>
        <xsl:apply-templates select="/parts-list/part"/>
      </body>
    </html>
  </xsl:template>
```

```
<xsl:template match="component">
  <a name="{generate-id(name)}"/>
  <h3>
    <xsl:value-of select="name"/>
  </h3>
  <p>
    <xsl:apply-templates select="description"/>
  </p>
  <p>
    <xsl:value-of select="name"/>
    <xsl:text> uses these parts:</xsl:text>
  </p>
  <ul>
    <xsl:for-each select="partref">
      <li>
        <a href="{concat('#', generate-id(key('parts-index', .)[1]))}">
          <xsl:value-of select="."/>
        </a>
      </li>
    </xsl:for-each>
  </ul>
</xsl:template>

<xsl:template match="description">
  <xsl:apply-templates select="*|text()"/>
</xsl:template>

<xsl:template match="component/description/partref">
  <a href="{concat('#', generate-id(key('parts-index', .)[1]))}">
    <xsl:value-of select="."/>
  </a>
</xsl:template>

<xsl:template match="part">
  <a name="{generate-id(name)}"/>
  <h3>
    <xsl:value-of select="name"/>
  </h3>
  <p>
    <xsl:apply-templates select="description"/>
  </p>
  <p>
    <xsl:value-of select="name"/>
    <xsl:text> is used in these components:</xsl:text>
  </p>
  <ul>
    <xsl:for-each select="key('component-index', name)">
      <li>
        <a href="{concat('#', generate-id(name))}">
          <xsl:value-of select="name"/>
        </a>
      </li>
    </xsl:for-each>
  </ul>
```

```
    </xsl:template>

</xsl:stylesheet>
```

Looking at the HTML output in a browser, the document looks exactly the same as our earlier stylesheet. The HTML source code is slightly different, of course:

```
<a name="d1e31"></a>
<h3>Prawn Goader</h3>
<p>
  Unruly prawns?  With this handy tool, you'll have the most
  well-behaved seafood in town.
</p>
<p>Prawn Goader uses these parts:</p>
<ul>
  <li><a href="#d1e181">Paring Knife</a></li>
  <li><a href="#d1e190">Mucilage</a></li>
  <li><a href="#d1e199">Ribbon Curler</a></li>
</ul>
```

All of the names of the anchor points were generated by the XSLT processor. Using a different XSLT processor will probably generate different values for these IDs, but they'll still work. It's even possible that rerunning a document and stylesheet through the same processor will generate different values. (We'll cover all the details of the generate-id( ) function in the next section.)

Using the key( ) and generate-id( ) functions, we've been able to create IDs and references automatically. This approach isn't perfect; we have to make sure the text of the <partref> element matches the text of the part's <name> exactly. Despite that, generate-id( ) can help you add some structure to your documents.

The generate-id( ) Function

Before we leave the topic of linking, we'll go over the details of the generate-id( ) function. This function takes a node-set as its argument, and it works as follows:

- For a given transformation, every time generate-id( ) is invoked against a given node, it returns the same ID. The ID doesn't change while you're doing a given transformation. If you run the transformation again tomorrow, there's no guarantee that generate-id( ) will generate the same ID that it generated today. As long as the XSLT processor is running, however, generate-id( ) returns the same ID for the same node every time.

- If you invoke generate-id( ) against two different nodes, the two generated IDs will be different.

- *[1.0]* Given a node-set, generate-id( ) returns an ID for the node in the node-set that occurs first in document order.

  [2.0] It is a fatal error in XSLT 2.0 to pass a sequence of more than one item to generate-id( ).

- If the node-set you pass to the function is empty (you invoke `generate-id(fleeber)`, and there are no `<fleeber>` elements in the current context), `generate-id( )` returns an empty string.

- If no node-set is passed in (you invoke `generate-id( )`), the function generates an ID for the context node.

> The `generate-id( )` function is not required to check whether an ID it generates duplicates an ID that's already in the document. In other words, if your document has an attribute of type `ID` with a value of `sdk3829a`, there's a possibility that an ID returned by `generate-id( )` will also be `sdk3829a`. It's not likely, but be aware that it could happen.

Summary

In this chapter, we've examined several ways to generate links and cross-references between different parts of a document. If your XML document has a reasonable amount of structure, you can use the `id( )` and `key( )` functions to define many different relationships between the parts of a document. Even if your XML document isn't structured, you may be able to use `key( )` and `generate-id( )` to create simple references. In the next chapter, we'll look at sorting and grouping—two more ways to organize the information in our XML documents.

Sorting and Grouping Elements

By now, I hope you're convinced that you can use XSLT to convert big piles of XML data into other useful things. Our examples to this point have pretty much gone through the XML source in what's referred to as *document order*. We'd like to go through our XML documents in a couple of other common ways, though:

- We could sort some or all of the XML elements, then generate output based on the sorted elements.
- We could group the data, selecting all elements that have some property in common, then sorting the groups of elements.

We'll give several examples of these operations in this chapter.

Sorting Data with <xsl:sort>

The simplest way to rearrange our XML elements is to use the `<xsl:sort>` element. This element temporarily rearranges a collection of elements based on criteria we define in our stylesheet.

Our First Example

For our first example, we'll have a set of U.S. postal addresses that we want to sort. (No chauvinism is intended here; obviously every country has different conventions for mailing addresses. We just needed a short sample document that can be sorted in many useful ways.) Here's our original document:

```
<?xml version="1.0"?>
<!-- names.xml -->
<addressbook>
  <address>
    <name>
      <title>Mr.</title>
      <first-name>Chester Hasbrouck</first-name>
      <last-name>Frisby</last-name>
    </name>
```

```
      <street>1234 Main Street</street>
      <city>Sheboygan</city>
      <state>WI</state>
      <zip>48392</zip>
  </address>
  <address>
    <name>
      <first-name>Mary</first-name>
      <last-name>Backstayge</last-name>
    </name>
    <street>283 First Avenue</street>
    <city>Skunk Haven</city>
    <state>MA</state>
    <zip>02718</zip>
  </address>
  <address>
    <name>
      <title>Ms.</title>
      <first-name>Natalie</first-name>
      <last-name>Attired</last-name>
    </name>
    <street>707 Breitling Way</street>
    <city>Winter Harbor</city>
    <state>ME</state>
    <zip>00218</zip>
  </address>
  <address>
    <name>
      <first-name>Harry</first-name>
      <last-name>Backstayge</last-name>
    </name>
    <street>283 First Avenue</street>
    <city>Skunk Haven</city>
    <state>MA</state>
    <zip>02718</zip>
  </address>
  <address>
    <name>
      <first-name>Mary</first-name>
      <last-name>McGoon</last-name>
    </name>
    <street>103 Bryant Street</street>
    <city>Boylston</city>
    <state>VA</state>
    <zip>27318</zip>
  </address>
  <address>
    <name>
      <title>Ms.</title>
      <first-name>Amanda</first-name>
      <last-name>Reckonwith</last-name>
    </name>
    <street>930-A Chestnut Street</street>
    <city>Lynn</city>
    <state>MA</state>
```

```
      <zip>02930</zip>
    </address>
</addressbook>
```

We'd like to generate a list of these addresses, sorted by `<last-name>`. We'll use the magical `<xsl:sort>` element to do the work. Our stylesheet looks like this:

```
<?xml version="1.0"?>
<!-- namesorter1.xsl -->
<xsl:stylesheet version="1.0"
  xmlns:xsl="http://www.w3.org/1999/XSL/Transform">

  <xsl:output method="text"/>

  <xsl:template match="/">
    <xsl:for-each select="addressbook/address">
      <xsl:sort select="name/last-name"/>
      <xsl:if test="name/title">
        <xsl:value-of select="name/title"/>
        <xsl:text> </xsl:text>
      </xsl:if>
      <xsl:value-of select="name/first-name"/>
      <xsl:text> </xsl:text>
      <xsl:value-of select="name/last-name"/>
      <xsl:text>&#xA;</xsl:text>
      <xsl:value-of select="street"/>
      <xsl:text>&#xA;</xsl:text>
      <xsl:value-of select="city"/>
      <xsl:text>, </xsl:text>
      <xsl:value-of select="state"/>
      <xsl:text>   </xsl:text>
      <xsl:value-of select="zip"/>
      <xsl:text>&#xA;</xsl:text>
      <xsl:text>&#xA;</xsl:text>
    </xsl:for-each>
  </xsl:template>
</xsl:stylesheet>
```

The heart of our stylesheet is the `<xsl:for-each>` and `<xsl:sort>` elements. The `<xsl:for-each>` element selects the items with which we'll work, and the `<xsl:sort>` element rearranges them before we write them out. (Notice that we use `<xsl:if>` to determine whether a given customer has a courtesy title.)

Notice that we're using `<xsl:output method="text"/>` to generate a text file. (Feel free to generate an HTML file or something more complicated if you want.) Here are the results we get from our first attempt at sorting:

```
Ms. Natalie Attired
707 Breitling Way
Winter Harbor, ME  00218

Mary Backstayge
283 First Avenue
Skunk Haven, MA  02718
```

```
Harry Backstayge
283 First Avenue
Skunk Haven, MA  02718

Mr. Chester Hasbrouck Frisby
1234 Main Street
Sheboygan, WI  48392

Mary McGoon
103 Bryant Street
Boylston, VA  27318

Ms. Amanda Reckonwith
930-A Chestnut Street
Lynn, MA  02930
```

As you can see from the output, the addresses in our original document were sorted by last name. All we had to do was add `<xsl:sort>` to our stylesheet, and all the elements were magically reordered. If you aren't convinced that XSLT can increase your programmer productivity, try writing the Java code and DOM method calls to do the same thing.

We can improve on our stylesheet by sorting addresses by `<first-name>` within `<last-name>`. In our last example, Mary Backstayge should appear after Harry Backstayge. Here's how we can modify our stylesheet to use more than one sort key:

```
<?xml version="1.0"?>
<!-- namesorter2.xsl -->
...
<xsl:template match="/">
  <xsl:for-each select="addressbook/address">
    <xsl:sort select="name/last-name"/>
    <xsl:sort select="name/first-name"/>
    ...
```

We've simply added a second `<xsl:sort>` element to our stylesheet. This element does what we want; it sorts the `<address>` elements by `<first-name>` within `<last-name>`.

Now our output is better:

```
Ms. Natalie Attired
707 Breitling Way
Winter Harbor, ME  00218

Harry Backstayge
283 First Avenue
Skunk Haven, MA  02718

Mary Backstayge
283 First Avenue
Skunk Haven, MA  02718

Mr. Chester Hasbrouck Frisby
1234 Main Street
```

```
Sheboygan, WI  48392

Mary McGoon
103 Bryant Street
Boylston, VA  27318

Ms. Amanda Reckonwith
930-A Chestnut Street
Lynn, MA  02930
```

The Details on the <xsl:sort> Element

Now that we've seen a couple of examples of how <xsl:sort> works, we'll go over its
syntax, its attributes, and where you can use it.

What's the deal with that syntax?

I'm so glad you asked that question. One thing the XSLT working group could have
done is something like this:

```
<xsl:for-each select="addressbook/address" sort-key-1="name/last-name"
    sort-key-2="name/first-name"/>
```

The problem with this approach is that no matter how many **sort-key-x** attributes you
define, out of sheer perverseness, someone will cry out that they really need the
sort-key-8293 attribute. To avoid this messy issue, the XSLT designers decided to let
you specify the sort keys by using a number of <xsl:sort> elements. The first is the
primary sort key, the second is the secondary sort key, the 8293rd one is the eight-
thousand-two-hundred-and-ninety-third sort key, etc.

Well, that's why the syntax looks the way it does, but how does it actually work? When
I first saw this syntax:

```
<xsl:for-each select="addressbook/address">
  <xsl:sort select="name/last-name"/>
  <xsl:sort select="name/first-name"/>
  ...
</xsl:for-each>
```

I thought it meant that all the nodes were sorted during each iteration through the
<xsl:for-each> element. That seemed incredibly inefficient; if you've sorted all
the nodes, why re-sort them each time through the <xsl:for-each> element? Actually,
the XSLT processor handles all <xsl:sort> elements before it does anything, then it
processes the <xsl:for-each> element as if the <xsl:sort> elements weren't there.

It's less efficient, but if it makes you feel better about the syntax, you could write the
stylesheet like this:

```
<xsl:template match="/">
  <xsl:for-each select="addressbook/address">
    <xsl:sort select="name/last-name"/>
    <xsl:sort select="name/first-name"/>
```

```
      <xsl:for-each select=".">  <!-- This is slower, but it works -->
        <xsl:apply-templates/>
      </xsl:for-each>
    </xsl:for-each>
  </xsl:template>
```

(Don't actually do this. I'm only trying to make a point.) This stylesheet generates the same results as our earlier one.

Another approach is to use the `<xsl:sort>` element within `<xsl:apply-templates>`. Here's a stylesheet that does that:

```
<?xml version="1.0"?>
<!-- namesorter3.xsl -->
<xsl:stylesheet version="1.0"
  xmlns:xsl="http://www.w3.org/1999/XSL/Transform">

  <xsl:output method="text"/>

  <xsl:template match="/">
    <xsl:apply-templates select="addressbook/address">
      <xsl:sort select="name/last-name"/>
      <xsl:sort select="name/first-name"/>
    </xsl:apply-templates>
  </xsl:template>

  <xsl:template match="address">
    <xsl:if test="name/title">
      <xsl:value-of select="name/title"/>
      <xsl:text> </xsl:text>
    </xsl:if>
    <xsl:value-of select="name/first-name"/>
    <xsl:text> </xsl:text>
    <xsl:value-of select="name/last-name"/>
    <xsl:text>&#xA;</xsl:text>
    <xsl:value-of select="street"/>
    <xsl:text>&#xA;</xsl:text>
    <xsl:value-of select="city"/>
    <xsl:text>, </xsl:text>
    <xsl:value-of select="state"/>
    <xsl:text>   </xsl:text>
    <xsl:value-of select="zip"/>
    <xsl:text>&#xA;</xsl:text>
    <xsl:text>&#xA;</xsl:text>
  </xsl:template>

</xsl:stylesheet>
```

Using `<xsl:sort>` inside `<xsl:apply-templates>` generates the same results as our previous stylesheet.

Attributes

The `<xsl:sort>` element has several attributes; we'll discuss the most useful ones here. The discussion of the `<xsl:sort>` element in Appendix A has complete details on all of the attributes.

select

> The `select` attribute defines the characteristic we'll use for sorting. Its contents is an XPath expression, so you can select elements, text, attributes, comments, ancestors, etc. As always, the XPath expression defined in `select` is evaluated in terms of the element that contains it. In other words, in this example:

```
<xsl:template match="/">
  <xsl:apply-templates select="addressbook/address">
    <xsl:sort select="name/last-name"/>
    <xsl:sort select="name/first-name"/>
  </xsl:apply-templates>
</xsl:template>
```

> In this example, the `select` attributes of the `<xsl:sort>` elements are interpreted from the `addressbook/address` expression. That means `select="name/last-name"` refers to a `<last-name>` element inside a `<name>` inside an `<address>` element that's inside an `<addressbook>` element.

data-type

> The `data-type` attribute can have three values:

> - `data-type="text"`
> - `data-type="number"`
> - A `data-type="QName"` that identifies a particular datatype. How a given datatype is supported (or if it's supported at all) is implementation-defined.

> The XSLT specification defines the behavior for `data-type="text"` and `data-type="number"`. Consider this XML document:

```
<?xml version="1.0"?>
<!-- numberlist.xml -->
<numberlist>
  <number>127</number>
  <number>23</number>
  <number>10</number>
</numberlist>
```

> We'll sort these values using the default datatype of text (we could specify `data-type="text"` to get the same results):

```
<?xml version="1.0"?>
<!-- sort-datatype-text.xsl -->
<xsl:stylesheet version="1.0"
  xmlns:xsl="http://www.w3.org/1999/XSL/Transform">

  <xsl:output method="text"/>
```

```
    <xsl:template match="/">
      <xsl:for-each select="numberlist/number">
        <xsl:sort select="."/>
        <xsl:value-of select="."/>
        <xsl:text>&#xA;</xsl:text>
      </xsl:for-each>
    </xsl:template>
</xsl:stylesheet>
```

When we treat the values of these elements as text, here are the results:

```
10
127
23
```

We get this result because a text-based sort puts anything that starts with a "1" before anything that starts with a "2." If we change the `<xsl:sort>` element to be `<xsl:sort select="." data-type="number"/>`:

```
<?xml version="1.0"?>
<!-- sort-datatype-number1.xsl -->
...
    <xsl:template match="/">
      <xsl:for-each select="numberlist/number">
        <xsl:sort select="." data-type="number"/>
        ...
```

we get these results:

```
10
27
123
```

(See `sort-datatype-number1.xsl` for the complete stylesheet.)

If you use something else here (`data-type="floating-point"`, for example), what the XSLT processor does is anybody's guess. The XSLT specification allows for other values here, but it's up to the XSLT processor to decide how (or if) it wants to process those values. Check your processor's documentation to see whether it does anything relevant or useful for values other than `data-type="text"` or `data-type="number"`.

A final note: if you're using `data-type="number"`, and any of the values aren't numbers, those nonnumeric values will sort before the numeric values. That means that if you're using `order="ascending"`, the nonnumeric values appear first; if you use `order="descending"`, the nonnumeric values appear last.

```
<?xml version="1.0"?>
<!-- badnumberlist.xml -->
<numberlist>
  <number>127</number>
  <number>23</number>
  <number>zzz</number>
  <number>10</number>
```

```
<number>yyy</number>
</numberlist>
```

Given this less-than-perfect data, here are the correctly sorted results:

```
zzz
yyy
10
23
127
```

Notice that the nonnumeric values were not sorted; they simply appear in the output document in the order in which they were encountered.

[2.0] The **data-type** attribute is deprecated in XSLT 2.0. The preferred way of sorting typed data in XSLT 2.0 is to specify the datatype in the **select** attribute of the **<xsl:sort>** element itself. For example, specifying **<xsl:sort select="xs:integer(.)"/>** forces all of the items that we're sorting to be cast as integers:

```
<?xml version="1.0"?>
<!-- sort-datatype-number2.xsl -->
<xsl:stylesheet version="2.0"
  xmlns:xsl="http://www.w3.org/1999/XSL/Transform"
  xmlns:xs="http://www.w3.org/2001/XMLSchema">

  <xsl:output method="text"/>

  <xsl:template match="/">
    <xsl:for-each select="numberlist/number">
      <xsl:sort select="xs:integer(.)"/>
      <xsl:value-of select="."/>
      <xsl:text>&#xA;</xsl:text>
    </xsl:for-each>
  </xsl:template>
</xsl:stylesheet>
```

Be aware that using this XSLT 2.0 stylesheet with *badnumberlist.xml* causes a runtime error. Calling **xs:integer('zzz')** doesn't work.

order

> You can order the sort as **order="ascending"** or **order="descending"**. The default is **order="ascending"**.

case-order

> This attribute can have two values. **case-order="upper-first"** means that upper-case letters sort before lowercase letters, and **case-order="lower-first"** means that lowercase letters sort first. The **case-order** attribute is used only when the **data-type** attribute is **text**. The default value depends on the value of the soon-to-be-discussed **lang** attribute.

lang

> This attribute defines the language of the sort keys. The valid values for this attribute are the same as those for the **xml:lang** attribute defined in Section 2.12 of

the XML 1.0 specification. The language codes are those commonly used in Java programming, Unix locales, and other places where ISO language and country namings are defined. For example, `lang="en"` means "English," `lang="en-US"` means "U.S. English," and `lang="en-GB"` means "U.K. English." Without the `lang` attribute (it's rarely used in practice), the XSLT processor determines the default language from the system environment.

Where can you use <xsl:sort>?

The `<xsl:sort>` element can appear inside the `<xsl:apply-templates>` and `<xsl:for-each>` elements.

[2.0] In XSLT 2.0, you can also use `<xsl:sort>` inside the new `<xsl:for-each-group>` and `<xsl:perform-sort>` elements; more on those later in this chapter.

If you use one or more `<xsl:sort>` elements, they must appear first. If you try something like this, you'll get an exception from the XSLT processor:

```
<xsl:for-each select="addressbook/address">
  <xsl:sort select="name/last-name"/>
  <xsl:value-of select="name/title"/>
  <xsl:sort select="name/first-name"/> <!-- NOT LEGAL! -->
  ...
```

Another Example

We've pretty much covered the `<xsl:sort>` element at this point. To add another wrinkle to our example, we'll change the stylesheet so the `xsl:sort` element acts upon a subset of the addresses, and then sorts that subset. We'll sort only the addresses from states that start with the letter M. As you'd expect, we'll do this magic with an XPath expression that limits the elements to be sorted:

```
<?xml version="1.0"?>
<!-- namesorter4.xsl -->
<xsl:stylesheet version="1.0"
  xmlns:xsl="http://www.w3.org/1999/XSL/Transform">

  <xsl:output method="text" indent="no"/>

  <xsl:template match="/">
    <xsl:for-each select="addressbook/address[starts-with(state, 'M')]">
      <xsl:sort select="name/last-name"/>
      <xsl:sort select="name/first-name"/>
      <xsl:if test="name/title">
        <xsl:value-of select="name/title"/>
        <xsl:text> </xsl:text>
      </xsl:if>
      <xsl:value-of select="name/first-name"/>
      <xsl:text> </xsl:text>
      <xsl:value-of select="name/last-name"/>
      <xsl:text>&#xA;</xsl:text>
      <xsl:value-of select="street"/>
```

```
        <xsl:text>&#xA;</xsl:text>
        <xsl:value-of select="city"/>
        <xsl:text>, </xsl:text>
        <xsl:value-of select="state"/>
        <xsl:text>  </xsl:text>
        <xsl:value-of select="zip"/>
        <xsl:text>&#xA;</xsl:text>
        <xsl:text>&#xA;</xsl:text>
      </xsl:for-each>
    </xsl:template>
</xsl:stylesheet>
```

Here are the results—only those addresses from states beginning with the letter M, sorted by first name within last name:

```
Ms. Natalie Attired
707 Breitling Way
Winter Harbor, ME  00218

Harry Backstayge
283 First Avenue
Skunk Haven, MA  02718

Mary Backstayge
283 First Avenue
Skunk Haven, MA  02718

Ms. Amanda Reckonwith
930-A Chestnut Street
Lynn, MA  02930
```

Notice that in the `xsl:for-each` element, we used a predicate in our XPath expression so that only addresses containing `<state>` elements whose contents begin with M are selected. This example starts us on the path to grouping nodes.

We could do some other things here:

- We could generate output that prints all the unique zip codes, along with the number of addresses that have those zip codes.
- For each unique zip code (or state, or last name, etc.) we could sort on a field and list all addresses with that zip code.

We'll discuss these topics in just a moment. Before we move on to the topic of grouping, we'll go over the new `<xsl:perform-sort>` element.

[2.0] The <xsl:perform-sort> Element

As we discussed in Chapter 3, XSLT 2.0 introduces the concept of a *sequence*, which is a group of nodes or atomic values. That sequence is typically created during stylesheet processing, usually as a variable. You can use the `<xsl:perform-sort>` element to sort a sequence. Everything we've discussed about sorting applies to `<xsl:perform-sort>`; we'll look at some examples here.

There are two ways to use `<xsl:perform-sort>`: you can give it an existing sequence and use `<xsl:perform-sort>` to sort that sequence, or you can use `<xsl:perform-sort>` to both create the sequence and sort it. For our first example, we'll create a sequence of all the `<city>` elements and use `<xsl:perform-sort>` to sort it:

```
<?xml version="1.0"?>
<!-- perform-sort1.xsl -->
<xsl:stylesheet version="2.0"
  xmlns:xs="http://www.w3.org/2001/XMLSchema"
  xmlns:xsl="http://www.w3.org/1999/XSL/Transform">

  <xsl:output method="text"/>

  <xsl:template match="/">
    <xsl:variable name="sortedCities" as="xs:string*">
      <xsl:perform-sort select="addressbook/address/city">
        <xsl:sort select="."/>
      </xsl:perform-sort>
    </xsl:variable>
    <xsl:text>Our customers live in these cities:&#xA;&#xA;</xsl:text>
    <xsl:value-of select="$sortedCities" separator="&#xA;"/>
  </xsl:template>

</xsl:stylesheet>
```

The **select** attribute of `<xsl:perform-sort>` defines the sequence to be sorted. When we use this stylesheet against our address book, here are the results:

```
Our customers live in these cities:

Boylston
Lynn
Sheboygan
Skunk Haven
Skunk Haven
Winter Harbor
```

We can also use the new `<xsl:sequence>` element to create the sequence inside `<xsl:perform-sort>`:

```
<?xml version="1.0"?>
<!-- perform-sort2.xsl -->
<xsl:stylesheet version="2.0"
  xmlns:xs="http://www.w3.org/2001/XMLSchema"
  xmlns:xsl="http://www.w3.org/1999/XSL/Transform">

  <xsl:output method="text"/>

  <xsl:template match="/">
    <xsl:variable name="sortedCities" as="xs:string*">
      <xsl:perform-sort>
        <xsl:sort select="."/>
        <xsl:sequence select="addressbook/address/city"/>
      </xsl:perform-sort>
    </xsl:variable>
```

```
    <xsl:text>Our customers live in these cities:&#xA;&#xA;</xsl:text>
    <xsl:value-of select="$sortedCities" separator="&#xA;"/>
  </xsl:template>

</xsl:stylesheet>
```

There's not much point in doing things this way, but this stylesheet produces the same results. Putting the XPath expression on the `<xsl:perform-sort>` is much simpler. The contents of an `<xsl:perform-sort>` element must start with one or more `<xsl:sort>` elements. In our second example, we're not using the `select` attribute, so we use an `<xsl:sequence>` element to select some data to sort. `<xsl:perform-sort>` creates the entire sequence, and then it uses the `<xsl:sort>` elements inside it to sort the sequence.

If we want to make our customer database look more international, we can add more `<xsl:sequence>` elements to select more data:

```
<?xml version="1.0"?>
<!-- perform-sort3.xsl -->
<xsl:stylesheet version="2.0"
  xmlns:xs="http://www.w3.org/2001/XMLSchema"
  xmlns:xsl="http://www.w3.org/1999/XSL/Transform">

  <xsl:output method="text"/>

  <xsl:template match="/">
    <xsl:variable name="sortedCities" as="xs:string*">
      <xsl:perform-sort>
        <xsl:sort select="."/>
        <xsl:apply-templates select="addressbook/address/city"/>
        <xsl:sequence select="('London', 'Adelaide', 'Rome')"/>
        <xsl:sequence select="('Jakarta', 'Sao Paulo', 'Timbuktu')"/>
      </xsl:perform-sort>
    </xsl:variable>
    <xsl:text>Our customers live in these cities:&#xA;&#xA;</xsl:text>
    <xsl:value-of select="$sortedCities" separator="&#xA;"/>
  </xsl:template>

</xsl:stylesheet>
```

Now we have the impressive results we were hoping for:

```
Our customers live in these cities:

Adelaide
Boylston
Jakarta
London
Lynn
Rome
Sao Paulo
Sheboygan
Skunk Haven
Skunk Haven
Timbuktu
Winter Harbor
```

The point of this example is that you can combine multiple sequences of values and have `<xsl:perform-sort>` to sort all of the elements from all of those sequences. In this example, the first sequence is created with `<xsl:apply-templates>`; this uses the built-in stylesheet rules to return the names of the cities. The other two sequences are created with sequences of string values. The combination of `<xsl:perform-sort>` and `<xsl:sort>` produce a single sorted sequence of all the values.

Another important point about `<xsl:perform-sort>`: it always returns a sequence. If the variable `sortedCities` was defined with a datatype of `xs:string` (instead of `xs:string*`), the stylesheet would raise an error if there were no cities, or if there was more than one city.

Finally, if we want to remove the duplicate values from the sequence, we can use the XPath 2.0 function `distinct-values( )`:

```
<?xml version="1.0"?>
<!-- perform-sort4.xsl -->
<xsl:stylesheet version="2.0"
  xmlns:xs="http://www.w3.org/2001/XMLSchema"
  xmlns:xsl="http://www.w3.org/1999/XSL/Transform">

  <xsl:output method="text"/>

  <xsl:template match="/">
    <xsl:variable name="sortedCities" as="xs:string*">
      <xsl:perform-sort>
        <xsl:sort select="."/>
        <xsl:apply-templates select="addressbook/address/city"/>
        <xsl:sequence select="('London', 'Adelaide', 'Rome')"/>
        <xsl:sequence select="('Jakarta', 'Sao Paulo', 'Timbuktu')"/>
      </xsl:perform-sort>
    </xsl:variable>
    <xsl:text>Our customers live in these cities:&#xA;&#xA;</xsl:text>
    <xsl:value-of select="distinct-values($sortedCities)"
      separator="&#xA;"/>
  </xsl:template>

</xsl:stylesheet>
```

Now our results list the lovely town of Skunk Haven once only:

```
Our customers live in these cities:

Adelaide
Boylston
Jakarta
London
Lynn
Rome
Sao Paulo
Sheboygan
Skunk Haven
Timbuktu
Winter Harbor
```

Notice that we call `distinct-values( )` against the entire sequence after it's been generated. If we called `distinct-values( )` on each of the `<xsl:sequence>` elements, that would only eliminate duplicate values in each individual sequence.

Grouping Nodes

When grouping nodes, we sort things to get them into a certain order, and then we group all items that have the same value for the sort key (or keys). We'll use `xsl:sort` for this grouping, and then use variables or functions such as `key( )` or `generate-id( )` to finish the job.

[2.0] XSLT 2.0 has new elements and functions that make grouping much easier. If you're using XSLT 2.0, feel free to skip ahead to the section "[2.0] New Grouping Syntax in XSLT 2.0" later in this chapter.

Our First Attempt

For our first example, we'll take our list of addresses and group them. We'll look for all unique values of the `<zip>` element and list the addresses that match each one. We'll sort the list by zip code, then go through the list. If a given item doesn't match the previous zip code, we'll print out a heading; if it does match, we'll just print out the address. Here's our first attempt:

```
<?xml version="1.0"?>
<!-- namegrouper1.xsl -->
<xsl:stylesheet version="1.0"
  xmlns:xsl="http://www.w3.org/1999/XSL/Transform">

  <xsl:output method="text"/>

  <xsl:template match="/">
    <xsl:text>Addresses grouped by zip code &#xA;</xsl:text>
    <xsl:for-each select="addressbook/address">
      <xsl:sort select="zip"/>
      <xsl:if test="zip!=preceding-sibling::address[1]/zip">
        <xsl:text>&#xA;Zip code </xsl:text>
        <xsl:value-of select="zip"/>
        <xsl:text> (</xsl:text>
        <xsl:value-of select="city"/>
        <xsl:text>, </xsl:text>
        <xsl:value-of select="state"/>
        <xsl:text>): &#xA;</xsl:text>
      </xsl:if>
      <xsl:if test="name/title">
        <xsl:value-of select="name/title"/>
        <xsl:text> </xsl:text>
      </xsl:if>
      <xsl:value-of select="name/first-name"/>
      <xsl:text> </xsl:text>
      <xsl:value-of select="name/last-name"/>
```

```
      <xsl:text>&#xA;</xsl:text>
      <xsl:value-of select="street"/>
      <xsl:text>&#xA;&#xA;</xsl:text>
    </xsl:for-each>
  </xsl:template>
</xsl:stylesheet>
```

Our approach in this stylesheet consists of two steps:

1. Sort the addresses by zip code:

   ```
   <xsl:sort select="zip"/>
   ```

2. For each address, if its zip code doesn't match the previous one, print out a heading, and then print out the addresses that match it:

   ```
   <xsl:if test="zip!=preceding-sibling::address[1]/zip">
     <xsl:text>&#xA;Zip code </xsl:text>
     ...
   ```

   (Remember that `preceding-sibling` returns a `NodeSet/Sequence`, so `preceding-sibling::address[1]` represents the first preceding sibling.)

That sounds reasonable, doesn't it? Let's take a look at the results:

```
Addresses grouped by zip code

Zip code 00218 (Winter Harbor, ME):
Ms. Natalie Attired
707 Breitling Way


Zip code 02718 (Skunk Haven, MA):
Mary Backstayge
283 First Avenue


Zip code 02718 (Skunk Haven, MA):
Harry Backstayge
283 First Avenue


Zip code 02930 (Lynn, MA):
Ms. Amanda Reckonwith
930-A Chestnut Street


Zip code 27318 (Boylston, VA):
Mary McGoon
103 Bryant Street

Mr. Chester Hasbrouck Frisby
1234 Main Street
```

Yes, that certainly seemed like a good approach, but there's one major problem: *it doesn't work.*

Looking at our results, there are two things wrong: one of the addresses (Mr. Chester Hasbrouck Frisby) is incorrectly grouped under the heading for Boylston, Virginia, and there are two groups for Skunk Haven, Massachusetts. The problem here is that the axes work with the *document order*, not the sorted order we've created inside the `<xsl:for-each>` element.

As straightforward as our logic seemed, we'll have to find another way.

A Brute-Force Approach

One thing we could do is make the transformation in two passes; we could write an intermediate stylesheet to sort the names and generate a new XML document, and then use the stylesheet we've already written, because document order and sorted order will be the same. Here's how that intermediate stylesheet would look:

```
<?xml version="1.0"?>
<!-- namegrouper2a.xsl -->
<xsl:stylesheet version="1.0"
  xmlns:xsl="http://www.w3.org/1999/XSL/Transform">

  <xsl:output method="xml" indent="no"/>

  <xsl:strip-space elements="*"/>

  <xsl:template match="/">
    <addressbook>
      <xsl:for-each select="addressbook/address">
        <xsl:sort select="name/zip"/>
        <xsl:copy-of select="."/>
      </xsl:for-each>
    </addressbook>
  </xsl:template>
</xsl:stylesheet>
```

This stylesheet generates a new `<addressbook>` document that has all of the `<address>` elements sorted correctly. We can then run our original stylesheet against the sorted document and get results that are closer to what we want:

```
Addresses grouped by zip code
Ms. Natalie Attired
707 Breitling Way


Zip code 02718 (Skunk Haven, MA):
Harry Backstayge
283 First Avenue

Mary Backstayge
283 First Avenue


Zip code 02930 (Lynn, MA):
Ms. Amanda Reckonwith
```

```
930-A Chestnut Street


Zip code 27318 (Boylston, VA):
Mary McGoon
103 Bryant Street


Zip code 48392 (Sheboygan, WI):
Mr. Chester Hasbrouck Frisby
1234 Main Street
```

There's one more problem here: we don't have a heading for the first group. Natalie Attired lives in Winter Harbor, Maine, but there's no heading for Winter Harbor. The answer is to change our XPath expression slightly to see whether this is the first <address> element:

```
<?xml version="1.0"?>
<!-- namegrouper2b.xsl -->
<xsl:stylesheet version="1.0"
  xmlns:xsl="http://www.w3.org/1999/XSL/Transform">

  <xsl:output method="text" indent="no"/>

  <xsl:template match="/">
    <xsl:text>Addresses grouped by zip code &#xA;</xsl:text>
    <xsl:for-each select="addressbook/address">
      <xsl:sort select="zip"/>
      <xsl:if test="position() = 1 or
                    zip!=preceding-sibling::address[1]/zip">
        <xsl:text>&#xA;Zip code </xsl:text>
        <xsl:value-of select="zip"/>
...
```

If this is the first <address> element, there is no preceding-sibling. Our test condition always returns false, and the heading for the first address never prints.

Our pair of stylesheets works, but it's not very elegant. Even worse, it's really slow because we have to stop in the middle and write a file out to disk, then read that data back in. We'll find a way to group elements in a single stylesheet, but we'll have to do it with a different technique.

Grouping with <xsl:variable>

We mentioned earlier that sometimes <xsl:variable> is useful for grouping, so let's try that approach. We'll save the value of the <zip> element each time through the <xsl:for-each> element and use preceding-sibling in a slightly different way. Here's how attempt number three looks:

```
<?xml version="1.0"?>
<!-- namegrouper3.xsl -->
<xsl:stylesheet version="1.0"
  xmlns:xsl="http://www.w3.org/1999/XSL/Transform">
```

```
<xsl:output method="text" indent="no"/>

<xsl:template match="/">
  <xsl:text>Addresses sorted by zip code&#xA;</xsl:text>
  <xsl:for-each select="addressbook/address">
    <xsl:sort select="zip"/>
    <xsl:variable name="lastZip" select="zip"/>
    <xsl:if test="not(preceding-sibling::address[zip=$lastZip])">
      <xsl:text>Zip code </xsl:text>
      <xsl:value-of select="zip"/>
      <xsl:text>: &#xA;</xsl:text>
      <xsl:for-each select="/addressbook/address[zip=$lastZip]">
        <xsl:sort select="name/last-name"/>
        <xsl:sort select="name/first-name"/>
        <xsl:if test="name/title">
          <xsl:value-of select="name/title"/>
          <xsl:text> </xsl:text>
        </xsl:if>
        <xsl:value-of select="name/first-name"/>
        <xsl:text> </xsl:text>
        <xsl:value-of select="name/last-name"/>
        <xsl:text>&#xA;</xsl:text>
        <xsl:value-of select="street"/>
        <xsl:text>&#xA;&#xA;</xsl:text>
      </xsl:for-each>
    </xsl:if>
  </xsl:for-each>
</xsl:template>
</xsl:stylesheet>
```

This stylesheet generates what we want:

```
Addresses sorted by Zip Code
Zip code 00218:
Ms. Natalie Attired
707 Breitling Way

Zip code 02718:
Harry Backstayge
283 First Avenue

Mary Backstayge
283 First Avenue

Zip code 02930:
Ms. Amanda Reckonwith
930-A Chestnut Street

Zip code 27318:
Mary McGoon
103 Bryant Street

Zip code 48392:
Mr. Chester Hasbrouck Frisby
1234 Main Street
```

So why does this approach work when our first attempt didn't? The answer is that we don't count on the sorted order of the elements to generate the output. The downside of this approach is that we go through several steps to get the results we want:

1. We sort all the addresses by zip code:

   ```
   <xsl:sort select="zip"/>
   ```

2. We store the current <zip> element's value in the variable lastZip:

   ```
   <xsl:variable name="lastZip" select="zip"/>
   ```

3. For each <zip> element, we look at all of its preceding siblings to see whether this is the first time we've encountered this particular value (stored in lastZip). If it is, there won't be any preceding siblings that match.

   ```
   <xsl:if test="not(preceding-sibling::address[zip=$lastZip])">
   ```

4. If this is the first time we've encountered this value in the <zip> element, we go back and reselect all <address> elements with <zip> children that match this value. Once we have that group, we sort them by first name within last name and print each address.

   ```
   <xsl:for-each select="/addressbook/address[zip=$lastZip]">
     <xsl:sort select="name/last-name"/>
     <xsl:sort select="name/first-name"/>
   ```

So, we've found a way to get the results we want, but it's really inefficient. We sort the data, then we look at each zip code in sorted order, then see whether we've encountered that value before in document order, and then we reselect all the items that match the current zip code and resort them before we write them out.

This has reasonable performance when we're grouping the six elements in our sample document, but the amount of work the XSLT processor has to do increases exponentially as the number of elements we're grouping increases. There's got to be a better way, right? Actually there is, and we discuss it in the next section. Read on....

The <xsl:key> Approach

In this section, we'll look at using <xsl:key> to group items in an XML document. This approach is commonly referred to as the "Muench method," after Oracle XML Evangelist (and O'Reilly author) Steve Muench, who first suggested this technique. The Muench method has three steps:

1. Define a key for the property we want to use for grouping.

2. Select all of the nodes we want to group. We'll do some tricks with the key( ) and generate-id( ) functions to find the unique grouping values.

3. For each unique grouping value, use the key( ) function to retrieve all nodes that match it. We can further sort those nodes if we want.

Well, that's how the technique works—let's start building the stylesheet that makes the magic happen. The first step, creating a key function, is easy. Here's how it looks:

```
<xsl:key name="zipcodes" match="address" use="zip"/>
```

This `<xsl:key>` element defines a new index called `zipcodes`. It indexes `<address>` elements based on the value of the `<zip>` element they contain.

Now that we've defined our `key`, we're ready for the complicated part. We use the `key()` and `generate-id()` functions together. Here's the syntax, which we'll discuss extensively in a minute:

```
<xsl:for-each select="//address[generate-id(.)=
  generate-id(key('zipcodes', zip)[1])]">
```

OK, let's start digging through this syntax. We're selecting all `<address>` elements in which the automatically generated `id` matches the automatically generated `id` of the first node returned by the `key()` function when we ask for all `<address>` elements that match the current `<zip>` element.

Well, that's clear as crystal, isn't it? Let me try to explain that again from a slightly different perspective.

For each `<address>`, we use the `key()` function to retrieve all `<address>`es that have the same `<zip>`. We then take the first node from that node-set. Finally, we use the `generate-id()` function to generate an `id` for both nodes. If the two generated `id`s are identical, then the two nodes are the same.

Whew. Let me catch my breath.

If this `<address>` matches the first node returned by the `key()` function, then we know we've found the first `<address>` that matches this grouping value. Selecting all of the first values (remember, our previous predicate ends with [1]) gives us a node-set of some number of `<address>` elements, each of which contains one of the unique grouping values we need.

That's how the Muench method works. At this point, we've got a way to generate a node-set that contains all of the unique grouping values; now we need to process those nodes. From this point, we'll do several things, all of which are comparatively simple:

1. Sort all nodes based on the grouping property. In this example, the property is the `<zip>` element. We start by selecting the first occurrence of every unique `<zip>` element in the document, and then we sort those `<zip>` elements. Here's how it looks in the stylesheet:

   ```
   <xsl:for-each
     select="//address[generate-id(.)=generate-id(key('zipcodes', zip)[1])]">
     <xsl:sort select="zip"/>
   ```

2. The outer `<xsl:for-each>` element selects all the unique values of the `<zip>` element. Next, we use the `key()` function to retrieve all `<address>` elements that match the current `<zip>` element:

```
<xsl:for-each select="key('zipcodes', zip)">
```

3. The `key( )` function gives us a node-set of all matching `<address>` elements. For each group, we sort the group based on the `<last-name>` and `<first-name>` elements, print the heading, and then print each address.

To improve the looks of our output, our final stylesheet will use the techniques we've been building to create an HTML file. Here's the complete listing:

```
<?xml version="1.0"?>
<!-- namegrouper4.xsl -->
<xsl:stylesheet version="1.0"
  xmlns:xsl="http://www.w3.org/1999/XSL/Transform">

  <xsl:output method="html"/>

  <xsl:key name="zipcodes" match="address" use="zip"/>

  <xsl:template match="/">
    <html>
      <head>
        <title>Customers grouped by Zip code</title>
      </head>
      <body style="font-family: sans-serif;">
        <table border="1" cellpadding="5">
          <xsl:for-each select="//address[generate-id(.)=
                                 generate-id(key('zipcodes', zip)[1])]">
            <xsl:sort select="zip"/>
            <xsl:for-each select="key('zipcodes', zip)">
              <xsl:sort select="name/last-name"/>
              <xsl:sort select="name/first-name"/>
              <tr>
                <xsl:if test="position() = 1">
                  <td style="background: #66FF66; text-align: center;
                             vertical-align: middle; font-weight: bold;"
                    rowspan="{count(key('zipcodes', zip))}">
                    <xsl:text>Zip code </xsl:text>
                    <br/>
                    <span style="font-size: 150%;">
                      <xsl:value-of select="zip"/>
                    </span>
                    <br/>
                    <xsl:value-of select="city"/>
                    <xsl:text>, </xsl:text>
                    <xsl:value-of select="state"/>
                  </td>
                </xsl:if>
                <td style="text-align: right; vertical-align: middle;">
                  <xsl:value-of select="name/first-name"/>
                  <xsl:text> </xsl:text>
                  <span style="font-weight: bold; font-size: 125%;">
                    <xsl:value-of select="name/last-name"/>
                  </span>
                </td>
                <td>
                  <xsl:value-of select="street"/>
```

Figure 7-1. HTML document with grouped items

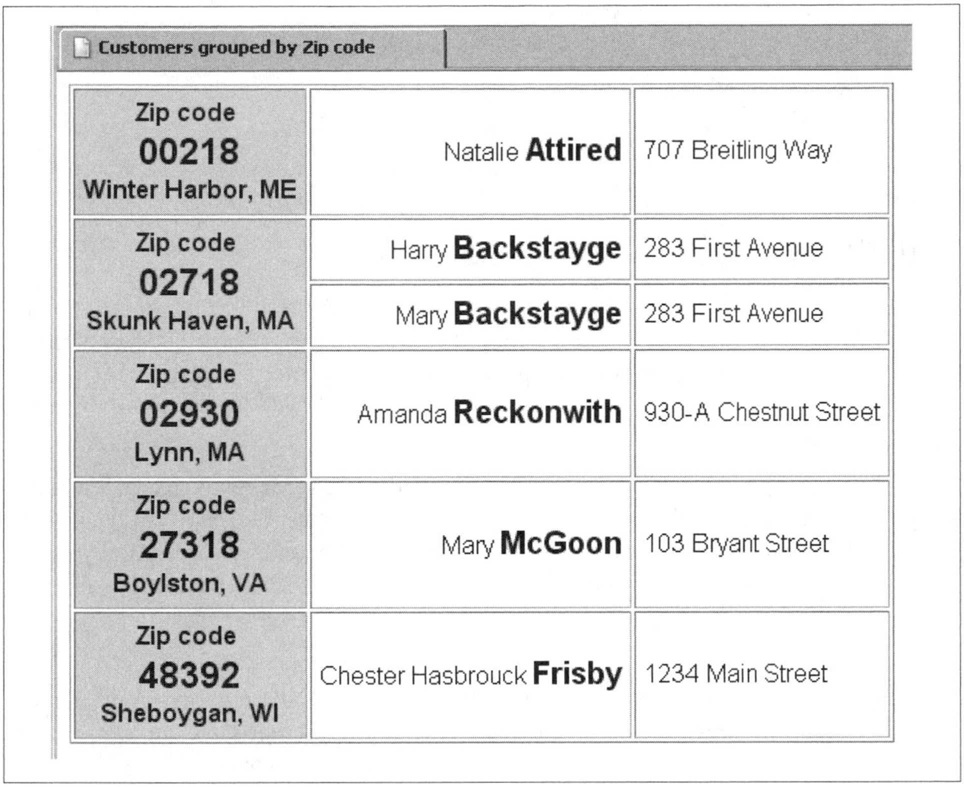

```
                </td>
              </tr>
            </xsl:for-each>
          </xsl:for-each>
        </table>
      </body>
    </html>
  </xsl:template>

</xsl:stylesheet>
```

Notice how the two `<xsl:for-each>` and the various `<xsl:sort>` elements work together. The outer `<xsl:for-each>` element selects the unique values of the `<zip>` element and sorts them; the inner `<xsl:for-each>` element selects all `<address>` elements that match the current `<zip>` element, and then sorts them by `<last-name>` and `<first-name>`.

When we view the generated HTML document in a browser, it looks like Figure 7-1.

The left column contains a table cell for each zip code. That means we need a `rowspan` attribute based on the size of the current group. The logic looks like this:

```
<xsl:if test="position() = 1">
  <td valign="center" bgcolor="#999999"
```

```
  rowspan="{count(key('zipcodes', zip))}">
  <b>
    <xsl:text>Zip code </xsl:text>
    <xsl:value-of select="zip"/>
  </b>
</td>
</xsl:if>
```

[2.0] New Grouping Syntax in XSLT 2.0

In 2001, the XSL Working Group released a document entitled "XSLT Requirements Version 2.0." More than half of the document came under the heading *"Must Simplify Grouping."* (I can't imagine how the group would have met a requirement named *"Must Make Grouping More Complicated and Confusing."*) We'll take a look at those changes in this section.

XSLT 2.0's grouping functions are built around the `<xsl:for-each-group>` element. Within this element, we'll use the new XSLT functions `current-group( )` and `current-grouping-key( )` to work with the data we're grouping. There are four mutually exclusive attributes for the `<xsl:for-each-group>` element, each of which performs a different style of grouping:

group-by

> This is the most common type of grouping. We use an XPath expression to define what identifies a group (all of the `<address>` elements that have the same `<zip>` code, for example), so we can then iterate through each group.

group-adjacent

> This approach is useful when you want to build a group containing all the adjacent nodes that match an XPath expression. As an example, we'll take all the adjacent `<p>` elements in a document, convert each one to an `<li>` element, and put `<ul>` and `</ul>` tags around the entire group.

group-starting-with

> The `group-starting-with` attribute defines an XPath expression that identifies the start of a group. Once a group starts, every element is added to the group until the start of another group is found. `group-starting-with` and `group-ending-with` are most often used when adding structure to an HTML document.

group-ending-with

> This defines an XPath expression that identifies the end of a group. When using `group-ending-with`, `<xsl:for-each-group>` creates a new group as it begins processing nodes. Whenever the end of a group is found, the XSLT processor closes that group and starts another.

Keep in mind that everything you can do with grouping in XSLT 2.0 is possible in XSLT 1.0—it's just that the markup you'll have to write and maintain in XSLT 1.0 is much more complicated. If you already have a working XSLT 1.0 stylesheet that uses the

---

Muench method to do grouping, there's no reason to change the stylesheet if you don't want to.

The Most Common Grouping Style: group-by

As we just mentioned, everything we'll do with grouping in XSLT 2.0 revolves around the new `<xsl:for-each-group>` element. This works much like `<xsl:for-each>`. In `<xsl:for-each>`, in each iteration we process an item in a sequence; with `<xsl:for-each-group>`, in each iteration we process a group. Thinking back to our addresses example, each group represents a unique zip code. When using `<xsl:for-each-group>`, the first group would be 00218, the second group would be 02718, and so forth.

To repeat from our discussion of the Muench method, we needed to do three things to group items in XSLT 1.0:

1. Define a `key` for the property we want to use for grouping.
2. Select all of the nodes we want to group. We'll do some tricks with the `key()` and `generate-id()` functions to find the unique grouping values.
3. For each unique grouping value, use the `key()` function to retrieve all nodes that match it. Because the `key()` function returns a node-set, we can do further sorts on the set of nodes that match any given grouping value.

With XSLT 2.0, we need to do the same basic things, but we don't have to get bogged down with `key()` and `generate-id()`. Our tasks are as follows:

1. Define an XPath expression for the property we want to use for grouping. All we have to do is define the XPath expression—we don't need a `key`.
2. Select all of the nodes we want to group. We select all the nodes with an XPath expression. The XSLT processor takes all the items that match this expression and groups them using the grouping property we defined.
3. Instead of dealing with each unique value of the property we're using for grouping, we use `current-group()` to deal with each group. The `current-group()` function returns a sequence, so we can sort the members of each group however we like. If we need the value of the grouping key, the `current-grouping-key()` function does what we want.

Accomplishing these tasks in XSLT 2.0 is pretty straightforward. We do steps one and two with the `<xsl:for-each-group>` element:

```
<xsl:for-each-group select="//address" group-by="zip">
```

The elements we're grouping are all of the `<address>` elements in the document. The property we're using for grouping is the value of the `<zip>` element.

For the third step, we use `current-group()` to deal with each group in turn. Here's the complete stylesheet:

```
<?xml version="1.0"?>
<!-- for-each-group_group-by.xsl -->
<xsl:stylesheet version="2.0"
  xmlns:xsl="http://www.w3.org/1999/XSL/Transform">

  <xsl:output method="html" include-content-type="no"/>

  <xsl:template match="/">
    <table border="1" cellpadding="5" style="font-family: sans-serif;">
      <xsl:for-each-group select="//address" group-by="zip">
        <xsl:sort select="current-grouping-key()"/>
        <xsl:for-each select="current-group()">
          <xsl:sort select="name/last-name"/>
          <xsl:sort select="name/first-name"/>
          <tr>
            <xsl:if test="position() = 1">
              <td valign="center" bgcolor="#999999"
                rowspan="{count(current-group())}">
                <b>
                  <xsl:text>Zip code </xsl:text>
                  <xsl:value-of select="current-grouping-key()"/>
                </b>
              </td>
            </xsl:if>
            <td align="right">
              <xsl:value-of select="name/first-name"/>
              <xsl:text> </xsl:text>
              <b><xsl:value-of select="name/last-name"/></b>
            </td>
            <td>
              <xsl:value-of select="street"/>
              <xsl:text>, </xsl:text>
              <xsl:value-of select="city"/>
              <xsl:text>, </xsl:text>
              <xsl:value-of select="state"/>
              <xsl:text> </xsl:text>
              <xsl:value-of select="zip"/>
            </td>
          </tr>
        </xsl:for-each>
      </xsl:for-each-group>
    </table>
  </xsl:template>

</xsl:stylesheet>
```

There are several things worth discussing inside the `<xsl:for-each-group>` element:

1. First of all, we use `<xsl:sort select="current-grouping-key()"/>` to put the groups themselves in order. This `<xsl:sort>` element sorts the *groups* based on their grouping keys. The items inside each group aren't rearranged at all.

2. Next, we use `<xsl:for-each select="current-group">` to iterate through each item in the current group. (Remember, `current-group()` returns the sequence of nodes that make up the current group.)

3. Within each group, we sort things by `<last-name>` and `<first-name>`.

4. The last significant thing we do is create the first column to display the current grouping key. We get the current value of the grouping key with the `current-grouping-key( )` function. To calculate the `rowspan` attribute, we use an attribute value template with `count(current-group( ))` to get the number of nodes that match the current grouping key.

Comparing this stylesheet with the Muench method version, most of the code is the same; after all, we're building the same HTML document here. However, there are some differences that make the v2.0 stylesheet simpler to create and maintain:

- It's much easier to specify what we're grouping. In the v2.0 stylesheet, we're simply specify the element we're grouping:

    ```
    [2.0] select="//address"
    ```

    ```
    [1.0] select="//address[generate-id(.)=generate-id(key('zipcodes', zip)[1])]">
    ```

- It's much easier to keep up with the current group. In the v2.0 stylesheet, the `current-group( )` and `current-grouping-key( )` functions let us work with the current group and the value we used to create it. In the v1.0 stylesheet, we have to respecify them each time. Here's how we process all the elements in the current group:

    ```
    [2.0] <xsl:for-each select="current-group()">
    ```

    ```
    [1.0] <xsl:for-each select="key('zipcodes', zip)">
    ```

As another example, finding the size of the current group is much simpler. In the v1.0 stylesheet, we have to redefine what the current group is each time we refer to it. When we need the number of items in the current group, we have to do the same thing:

    ```
    [2.0] rowspan="{count(current-group()}"
    ```

    ```
    [1.0] rowspan="{count(key('zipcodes', zip))}"
    ```

It's conceptually simpler to get the value of the grouping key in the v2.0 stylesheet, although it's arguable how much of an advantage that actually is in this example. (Comparing the two stylesheets, we typed `<xsl:value-of select="current-grouping-key( )"/>` in v2.0, but only `<xsl:value-of select="zip"/>` in v1.0.) If the key value were much more complicated, the advantage of `current-grouping-key( )` would be greater.

Also keep in mind that if we change the grouping key in a v1.0 stylesheet, we have to find all the instances of the grouping key and change them. In a v2.0 stylesheet, the grouping key is defined in one place; we still use `current-grouping-key( )` regardless of the changes to the key. This simplifies maintenance.

- We don't have to define an `<xsl:key>` separate from the grouping code. That's a minor point, but it does simplify maintenance.

Another Type of Grouping: group-adjacent

With the `group-adjacent` approach, we'll create a group based on some number of elements that are together in the source document. Our example input document is an HTML document that features groups of paragraphs together:

```
<?xml version="1.0"?>
<!-- group-adjacent_input.html -->
<html>
  <body>
    <h2>Steps for grouping in the Muench method</h2>
    <p>Define a <code>key</code> for the property we want
    to use for grouping.</p>
    <p>Select all of the nodes ...</p>
    <p>For each unique grouping value, ...</p>
    <h2>Steps for grouping in XSLT 2.0</h2>
    <p>Define an XPath expression ...</p>
    <p>Select all of the nodes we want to group ...</p>
    <p>Instead of dealing with each ...</p>
  </body>
</html>
```

This is text from earlier in this chapter, displayed here as HTML. (This book is written entirely in DocBook, an XML vocabulary with a very well-defined structure.) What we want to do is convert any sequence of paragraphs into an unordered list (`<ul>`), with each paragraph converted into a list item (`<li>`). We'll use `group-adjacent` to do that. Our stylesheet looks like this:

```
<?xml version="1.0"?>
<!-- for-each-group_group-adjacent.xsl -->
<xsl:stylesheet version="2.0"
  xmlns:xsl="http://www.w3.org/1999/XSL/Transform">

  <xsl:output method="html" include-content-type="no"/>

  <xsl:template match="/">
    <html>
      <head>
        <title>Grouping with group-adjacent</title>
      </head>
      <body style="font-family: sans-serif;">
        <h1>Grouping with group-adjacent</h1>
        <xsl:for-each-group select="html/body/*"
          group-adjacent="boolean(self::p)">
          <xsl:choose>
            <xsl:when test="current-grouping-key()">
              <ul>
                <xsl:for-each select="current-group()">
                  <li>
                    <xsl:copy-of select="@*"/>
                    <xsl:apply-templates select="*|text()"/>
                  </li>
                </xsl:for-each>
              </ul>
```

```
        </xsl:when>
        <xsl:otherwise>
          <xsl:for-each select="current-group()">
            <xsl:apply-templates select="."/>
          </xsl:for-each>
        </xsl:otherwise>
      </xsl:choose>
    </xsl:for-each-group>
  </body>
</html>
</xsl:template>

<xsl:template match="*">
  <xsl:copy>
    <xsl:copy-of select="@*"/>
    <xsl:apply-templates/>
  </xsl:copy>
</xsl:template>

</xsl:stylesheet>
```

When we're using `group-adjacent`, the value of the `group-adjacent` attribute generates an *atomic value* for each item in the list. In other words, the grouping key for each item is defined by the `group-adjacent` attribute. In the previous example, any `<p>` element has a grouping key of `true`; everything else has a grouping key of `false`. After we've defined the grouping key for each item, the XSLT 2.0 processor creates the groups. Each group contains the maximum number of adjacent items with a particular grouping key. To see the grouping keys, we can add an `<xsl:message>` to display them. We'll add this message:

```
<xsl:for-each-group select="html/body/*"
  group-adjacent="boolean(self::p)">
  <xsl:message terminate="no">
    <xsl:for-each select="current-group()">
      <xsl:text>current-grouping-key() = </xsl:text>
      <xsl:value-of select="current-grouping-key()"/>
      <xsl:text>&#xA;</xsl:text>
    </xsl:for-each>
  </xsl:message>
  ...
```

When we run the stylesheet with our sample document, here's what shows up in the console:

```
current-grouping-key() = false

current-grouping-key() = true
current-grouping-key() = true
current-grouping-key() = true

current-grouping-key() = false

current-grouping-key() = true
```

```
current-grouping-key() = true
current-grouping-key() = true
```

For each group, we print out the grouping key for each item in that group. As you'd expect, we have four groups. The first group contains the `<h2>` element at the start of the document, and the second group contains the three adjacent `<p>` elements that follow it. The second `<h2>` is the third group, and the fourth group is the three adjacent `<p>` elements at the end. When we run the stylesheet, the generated HTML document looks like this:

```
<html>
  <head>
    <title>Grouping with group-adjacent</title>
  </head>
  <body>
    <h1>Grouping with group-adjacent</h1>
    <h2>Steps for grouping in the Muench method</h2>
    <ul>
      <li>Define a <code>key</code> for the property we want
        to use for grouping.</li>
      <li>Select all of the nodes. ...</li>
      <li>For each unique grouping value, ...</li>
    </ul>
    <h2>Steps for grouping in XSLT 2.0</h2>
    <ul>
      <li>Define an XPath expression ...</li>
      <li>Select all of the nodes we want to group ...</li>
      <li>Instead of dealing with each ...</li>
    </ul>
  </body>
</html>
```

The items are now grouped just the way we want. We've converted all of the adjacent `<p>` elements and replaced them with an unordered list in which each `<p>` is now a list item. Each group contains the maximum number of adjacent `<p>` elements, so we can put each group inside a `<ul>` element.

Before we move on to the final two ways of grouping, we'll look at a more advanced example. We'll change our source HTML document slightly to add some `<p>` elements that should be processed differently. Here's how our new HTML document looks:

```
<?xml version="1.0"?>
<!-- group-adjacent_input2.html -->
<html>
  <body>
    <!-- Here's some sample text from the chapter "Sorting
         and Grouping". -->
    <h2>Steps for grouping in the Muench method</h2>
    <p class="item">Define a <code>key</code> for the property we want
    to use for grouping.</p>
    <p class="item">Select all of the nodes ...</p>
    <p class="note">This can be really complicated.</p>
    <p class="note">Many people don't enjoy this method.</p>
    <p class="note">XSLT 2.0 attempts to make grouping simpler.</p>
```

```
    <p class="item">For each unique grouping value ...</p>
    <h2>Steps for grouping in XSLT 2.0</h2>
    <p class="item">Define an XPath expression ...</p>
    <p class="item">Select all of the nodes ...</p>
    <p class="note">This is much easier than it used to be.</p>
    <p class="item">Instead of dealing with each ...</p>
  </body>
</html>
```

We now have two classes of `<p>` elements. Those with `class="item"` will be processed just as before. The `class="note"` elements will be put in an ordered list. To add another layer of complexity to our example, we'll number all of the `class="note"` items sequentially throughout the document. In other words, if the first group of adjacent `class="note"` elements has three members, we want to start numbering the next group of `class="note"` elements at four. Here's the stylesheet, which we'll discuss in detail in just a minute:

```
<?xml version="1.0"?>
<!-- for-each-group_group-adjacent2.xsl -->
<xsl:stylesheet version="2.0"
  xmlns:xsl="http://www.w3.org/1999/XSL/Transform">

  <xsl:output method="html" include-content-type="no"/>

  <xsl:template match="/">
    <html>
      <head>
        <title>Grouping with group-adjacent</title>
      </head>
      <body style="font-family: sans-serif;">
        <h1>Grouping with group-adjacent</h1>
        <xsl:for-each-group select="html/body/*"
          group-adjacent="if (self::p[@class='item']) then 1
                          else if (self::p[@class='note']) then 2
                          else 3">
          <xsl:choose>

            <!-- group for <p class="item"> -->
            <xsl:when test="current-grouping-key() = 1">
              <ul>
                <xsl:for-each select="current-group()">
                  <li>
                    <xsl:copy-of select="@*[not(name()='class')]"/>
                    <xsl:apply-templates select="*|text()"/>
                  </li>
                </xsl:for-each>
              </ul>
            </xsl:when>

            <!-- group for <p class="note"> -->
            <xsl:when test="current-grouping-key() = 2">
              <xsl:variable name="starting-point">
                <xsl:number count="p[@class='note']"
                  level="any" format="1"/>
```

```
        </xsl:variable>
        <table border="0" cellpadding="5" width="40%">
          <tr>
            <td width="10%">
              <p><xsl:text>&#x20;</xsl:text></p>
            </td>
            <td style="background: #CCCCCC;">
              <p style="font-weight: bold;">
                <xsl:value-of
                    select="if (count(current-group()) gt 1)
                            then 'Notes'
                            else 'Note'"/>
              </p>
              <ol start="{$starting-point}">
                <xsl:for-each select="current-group()">
                  <li>
                    <xsl:copy-of select="@*[not(name()='class')]"/>
                    <xsl:apply-templates select="*|text()"/>
                  </li>
                </xsl:for-each>
              </ol>
            </td>
          </tr>
        </table>
      </xsl:when>

      <!-- group for everything else -->
      <xsl:otherwise>
        <xsl:for-each select="current-group()">
          <xsl:apply-templates select="."/>
        </xsl:for-each>
      </xsl:otherwise>
    </xsl:choose>
  </xsl:for-each-group>
  </body>
  </html>
</xsl:template>

<xsl:template match="*">
  <xsl:copy>
    <xsl:copy-of select="@*"/>
    <xsl:apply-templates/>
  </xsl:copy>
</xsl:template>

</xsl:stylesheet>
```

First of all, notice that our `group-adjacent` attribute is significantly more complicated.
We're using integer values here instead of `true` and `false` because we have more than
two groups. (Remember, the grouping key for `group-adjacent` can be any atomic value;
it doesn't have to be `true` or `false`.) Here's the `<xsl:for-each-group>` element:

```
group-adjacent="if (self::p[@class='item']) then 1
                else if (self::p[@class='note']) then 2
                else 3"
```

So any `<p class="item">` element has a grouping key of 1, any `<p class="note">` element has a grouping key of 2, and everything else has a grouping key of 3. Adding an `<xsl:message>` to the stylesheet as we did before, we can list the grouping keys:

```
current-grouping-key() = 3

current-grouping-key() = 1
current-grouping-key() = 1

current-grouping-key() = 2
current-grouping-key() = 2
current-grouping-key() = 2

current-grouping-key() = 1
current-grouping-key() = 1

current-grouping-key() = 3

current-grouping-key() = 1
current-grouping-key() = 1

current-grouping-key() = 2

current-grouping-key() = 1
```

Aside from the fact that we have three groups instead of two, the main complication here is how we process items in the second group. For the first group of `<p class="note">` elements, we could simply use an ordered list (`<ol>`) element to number the items in the group. For every other group, we have to determine where to start numbering. This means we have to find the position of the first `<p class="note">` element in all of the `<p class="note">` elements to see where a particular group starts. If a group begins with the 38th `<p class="note">` element, we need to generate `<ol start="38">` in the HTML output document. `<xsl:number>` is perfect for this task.

For each group of `<p class="note">` elements, we have three tasks:

1. Generate a heading for the notes. If there is more than one item in the current group, the heading is `<h3>Notes</h3>`; otherwise, it is `<h3>Note</h3>`.

2. Generate the `start` attribute for the `<ol>` element. We use `<xsl:number>` to count all of the `<p class="note">` elements and tell us the position of the first item in the group.

3. Process the item itself. This means putting the current paragraph into a list item (`<li>`) element and processing its attributes and children.

Our first step is to generate the heading text. Fortunately, this is pretty simple; we use XPath 2.0's `if` operator:

```
<p style="font-weight: bold;">
  <xsl:value-of
      select="if (count(current-group()) gt 1)
              then 'Notes'
```

```
                else 'Note'"/>
    </p>
```

We also use the new XPath **gt** operator to compare the size of the current group—
count(current-group( ))—to the number **1**. If the current group has more than one
item, the heading text is **Notes**; otherwise, it is **Note**.

Now that our first step is complete, we'll create a variable with the value of the **<ol>**
start attribute:

```
    <xsl:variable name="starting-point">
      <xsl:number count="p[@class='note']" level="any" format="1"/>
    </xsl:variable>
```

Notice that we're using **format="1"** to create a numeric value. From an XSLT point of
view, we don't have to worry about the datatype of the value. (There's no need to add
as="xs:integer" to the **<xsl:variable>** element.) The HTML renderer treats this value
as a number and uses it accordingly.

The last step is simply to output the new **<ol>** element (using the **$starting-point**
variable we just initialized) and process the **<p>** element as before:

```
    <ol start="{$starting-point}">
      <xsl:for-each select="current-group()">
        <li>
          <xsl:copy-of select="@*[not(name()='class')]"/>
          <xsl:apply-templates select="*|text()"/>
        </li>
      </xsl:for-each>
    </ol>
```

We copy all of the attributes of the HTML **<p>** element *except* the **class** attribute.
Having copied the attributes, we use **<xsl:apply-templates>** to process anything that
might be in the original paragraph. As in our earlier stylesheet, we used an attribute
value template to include the **start** attribute on the **<ol>** element.

Our generated HTML document looks like Figure 7-2.

Grouping using group-starting-with

The next grouping type we'll use is **group-starting-with**. With this attribute, we'll
specify the node or condition that starts a new group. From that point, every item goes
into the new group until another starting node or condition is found. After that, the
XSLT processor closes the current group and starts a new one.

We'll use this approach to add some structure to another HTML document. In this
case, we want to create a group around every **<h1>** element. We'll use the file *group-
adjacent_input.html* from our earlier example.

We'll transform this markup into DocBook, which uses a containment strategy instead
of HTML's sequential approach. In other words, in HTML a level 1 heading (**<h1>**)

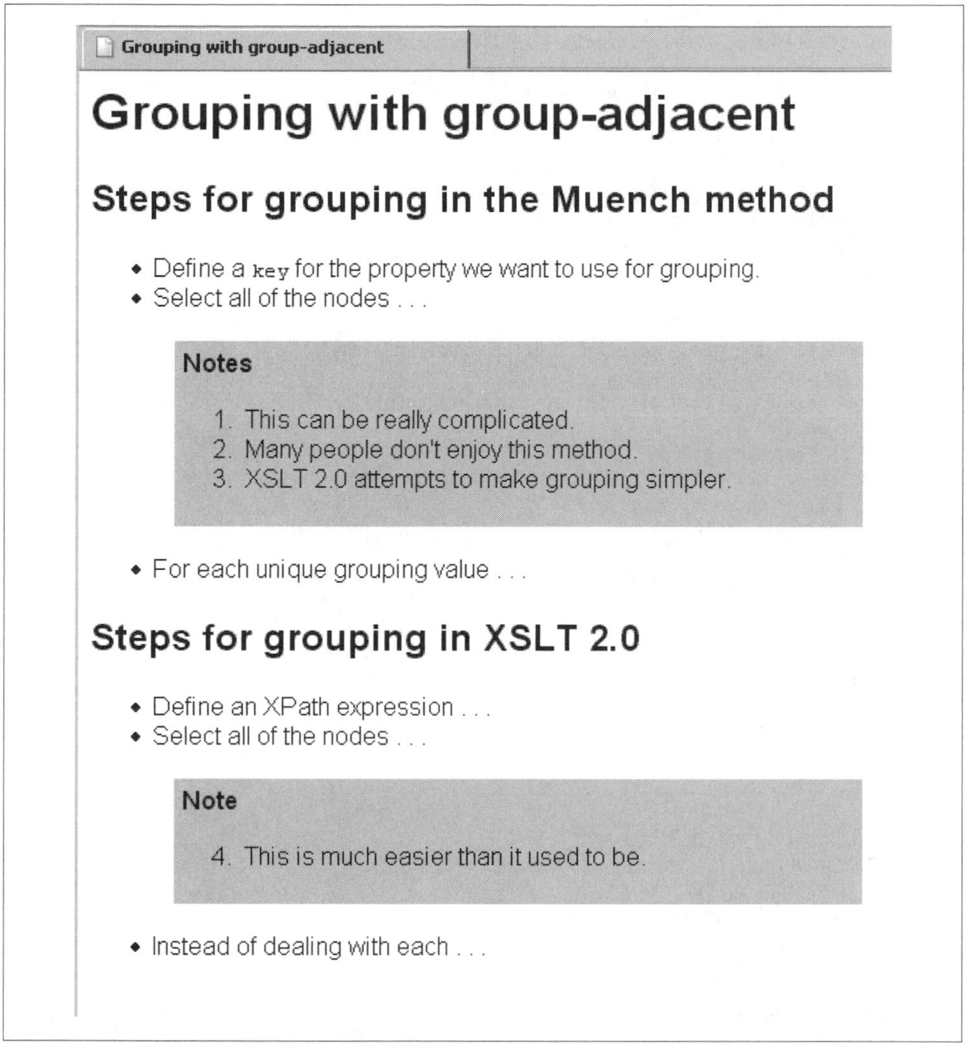

> **Grouping with group-adjacent**
>
> # Grouping with group-adjacent
>
> ## Steps for grouping in the Muench method
>
> - Define a `key` for the property we want to use for grouping.
> - Select all of the nodes . . .
>
> > **Notes**
> >
> > 1. This can be really complicated.
> > 2. Many people don't enjoy this method.
> > 3. XSLT 2.0 attempts to make grouping simpler.
>
> - For each unique grouping value . . .
>
> ## Steps for grouping in XSLT 2.0
>
> - Define an XPath expression . . .
> - Select all of the nodes . . .
>
> > **Note**
> >
> > 4. This is much easier than it used to be.
>
> - Instead of dealing with each . . .

Figure 7-2. HTML document with grouped and sequentially numbered items

stands on its own. We can assume that the first `<h1>` starts a section and that the next `<h1>` ends this section, but there's no guarantee that an HTML document is structured that way.

In DocBook, a level 1 heading is part of a section, not a standalone element. The section starts with a `<sect1>` tag and contains everything through the `</sect1>` tag, including a `<title>` element that contains the text we'd normally put on the HTML `<h1>` element.

Here's how our stylesheet looks:

```
<?xml version="1.0"?>
<!-- for-each-group_group-starting-with.xsl -->
```

```
<xsl:stylesheet version="2.0"
  xmlns:xsl="http://www.w3.org/1999/XSL/Transform">

  <xsl:output method="xml" indent="yes"/>

  <xsl:template match="/">
    <chapter>
      <title>Grouping in XSLT</title>
      <xsl:apply-templates select="html/body"/>
    </chapter>
  </xsl:template>

  <xsl:template match="body">
    <xsl:for-each-group select="*" group-starting-with="h1">
      <sect1>
        <xsl:apply-templates select="current-group()"/>
      </sect1>
    </xsl:for-each-group>
  </xsl:template>

  <xsl:template match="h1">
    <title>
      <xsl:apply-templates/>
    </title>
  </xsl:template>

  <xsl:template match="p">
    <para>
      <xsl:apply-templates/>
    </para>
  </xsl:template>

  <xsl:template match="*">
    <xsl:copy>
      <xsl:copy-of select="@*"/>
      <xsl:apply-templates/>
    </xsl:copy>
  </xsl:template>

</xsl:stylesheet>
```

Our well-structured results look like this:

```
<?xml version="1.0" encoding="UTF-8"?>
<chapter>
   <title>Grouping in XSLT</title>
   <sect1>
      <h2>Steps for grouping in the Muench method</h2>
      <para>Define a <code>key</code> for the property we want
   to use for grouping.</para>
      <para>Select all of the nodes ...</para>
      <para>For each unique grouping value, ...</para>
      <h2>Steps for grouping in XSLT 2.0</h2>
      <para>Define an XPath expression ...</para>
      <para>Select all of the nodes we want to group ...</para>
      <para>Instead of dealing with each ...</para>
```

```
        </sect1>
    </chapter>
```

In the generated DocBook code, each `<h1>` becomes the start of a `<sect1>` element. The text of the `<h1>` becomes the `<title>` of the section, each HTML `<p>` element becomes a DocBook `<para>` element, and everything else is copied as is to the output.

Grouping Using group-ending-with

The last grouping style is `group-ending-with`. This is similar to `group-starting-with`, only we're specifying the condition that *ends* each group. We'll use this technique to insert items into a three-column HTML table. Each row in the table is created from a group; each group will have no more than three members. We handle the special case of a row with less than three members (`count(current-group( )) lt 3`) by using a simplified version of our list of cars:

```
<?xml version="1.0"?>
<!-- carlist.xml -->
<cars>
  <make>Alfa Romeo</make>
  <make>Bentley</make>
  <make>Chevrolet</make>
  <make>Dodge</make>
  <make>Eagle</make>
  <make>Ford</make>
  <make>GMC</make>
  <make>Honda</make>
  <make>Isuzu</make>
  <model>Javelin</model>
  <model>K-Car</model>
  <make>Lincoln</make>
  <make>Mercedes</make>
  <make>Nash</make>
  <make>Opel</make>
  <make>Pontiac</make>
  <model>Quantum</model>
  <model>Rambler</model>
  <make>Studebaker</make>
</cars>
```

There are 19 cars in our list, so the final group should have only one item in it. Here's the stylesheet:

```
<?xml version="1.0"?>
<!-- for-each-group_group-ending-with.xsl -->
<xsl:stylesheet version="2.0"
  xmlns:xsl="http://www.w3.org/1999/XSL/Transform">

  <xsl:output method="html" include-content-type="no"/>

  <xsl:template match="/">
    <html>
      <head>
```

```
        <title>Car Makes and Models</title>
      </head>
      <body style="font-family: sans-serif;">
        <h1>Car Makes and Models</h1>
        <p>Here are the car makes and models in
        our input document.</p>
        <table border="1" cellpadding="5">
          <xsl:apply-templates select="cars"/>
        </table>
      </body>
    </html>
  </xsl:template>

  <xsl:template match="cars">
    <xsl:for-each-group select="make|model"
      group-ending-with="*[position() mod 3 = 0]">
      <tr>
        <xsl:apply-templates select="current-group()"/>
        <xsl:if test="count(current-group()) lt 3">
          <td style="background: #CCCCCC;"
            colspan="{3 - count(current-group())}">
          </td>
        </xsl:if>
      </tr>
    </xsl:for-each-group>
  </xsl:template>

  <xsl:template match="make">
    <td style="font-weight: bold;">
      <xsl:apply-templates/>
    </td>
  </xsl:template>

  <xsl:template match="model">
    <td style="font-style: italic; font-weight: bold;">
      <xsl:apply-templates/>
    </td>
  </xsl:template>

</xsl:stylesheet>
```

Figure 7-3 displays our results.

The grouping key depends on the position of each element. In our input document, all of the items we're grouping (the `<make>` and `<model>` elements) are at the same level of the document, so the position( ) function tells us what we need to know. The position( ) returns the position of an item within a sequence. In other words, the element `<xsl:for-each-group select="make|model" group-by="*[position( ) mod 3 = 0]">` creates a sequence containing all `<make>` and `<model>` elements. Calling position( ) returns an item's position in that sequence.

That covers all of the new grouping options in XSLT 2.0. As we said before, all of the things we did here can be done in XSLT 1.0, but the XSLT 2.0 syntax makes it much easier to create and maintain stylesheets that do complicated grouping.

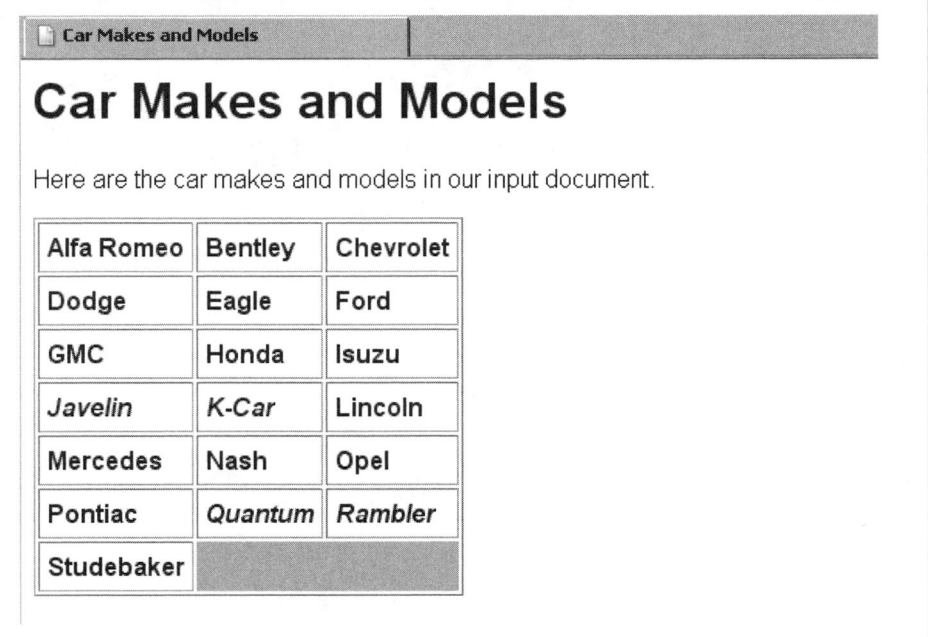

Figure 7-3. HTML document with items grouped into columns

Summary

In this chapter, we've gone over all of the common techniques used for sorting and grouping elements, including the new features available in XSLT 2.0. Regardless of the kinds of stylesheets you'll need to write in your XML projects, you'll probably use these techniques in everything you do. Now that we've covered how to sort and group elements, the next chapter will talk about how to work with multiple documents; that topic builds on what we've covered here.

CHAPTER 8

Combining Documents

One of XSLT's most powerful features is the document( ) function, which lets you combine documents. You can use parts of a document (specified with XPath expressions, of course) to identify other documents. You can then open those documents and perform stylesheet functions on the combination of those documents. In this chapter, we'll cover the document( ) function in all its glory.

[2.0] XSLT 2.0 and XPath 2.0 provide three new functions for combining documents: doc( ), collection( ), and unparsed-text( ). The doc( ) function, defined by XPath 2.0, is similar to the document( ) function, though less powerful. The collection( ) function, also defined by XPath 2.0, allows us to add collections of nodes provided by an XSLT processor. The kinds of nodes provided can vary from one processor to the next. Finally, the unparsed-text( ) function lets us add raw text to the data we're processing in our stylesheet. When combined with features such as tokenization and regular expressions, unparsed-text( ) gives us many new ways of manipulating data. We'll look at these new functions at the end of this chapter.

The document( ) Function

A common task in writing stylesheets is combining data from different documents. We'll start by using the document( ) function to parse and process multiple XML documents. We'll start our discussion with XML-tagged purchase orders that look like this:

```
<?xml version="1.0"?>
<!-- po38295.xml -->
<purchase-order id="38295">
  <date year="2001" month="9" day="8"/>
  <customer id="4738" level="Basic">
    <address type="business">
      <name>
        <title>Ms.</title>
        <first-name>Amanda</first-name>
        <last-name>Reckonwith</last-name>
      </name>
      <street>930-A Chestnut Street</street>
```

```
      <city>Lynn</city>
      <state>MA</state>
      <zip>02930</zip>
    </address>
    <address type="ship-to"/>
  </customer>
  <items>
    <item part-no="23813-03-CDK">
      <name>Cucumber Decorating Kit</name>
      <qty>1</qty>
      <price>29.95</price>
    </item>
  </items>
</purchase-order>
```

If we had a few dozen documents like this, we might want to view the collection of purchase orders in a number of ways. We could view them sorted (or even grouped) by customer, by part number, by the amount of the total order, by the state to which they were shipped, etc. One way to do this would be to write code that worked directly with the Document Object Model. We could parse each document, retrieve its DOM tree, and then use DOM functions to order and group the various DOM trees, display certain parts of the DOM trees, etc. Because this is an XSLT book, though, you probably won't be surprised to learn that XSLT provides a function to handle most of the heavy lifting for us.

We'll start with a simple example that uses the document() function. We'll assume that we have several purchase orders and that we want to combine them into a single report document. One thing we can do is create a *master document* that references all the purchase orders we want to include in the report. Here's what that master document might look like:

```
<?xml version="1.0"?>
<!-- polist.xml -->
<report>
  <title>Selected Purchase Orders</title>
  <po filename="po38292.xml"/>
  <po filename="po38293.xml"/>
  <po filename="po38294.xml"/>
  <po filename="po38295.xml"/>
</report>
```

We'll fill in the details of our stylesheet as we go along, but the first several stylesheets we'll create will use the document() function to open multiple input files. Once we've opened those files, we can use the templates in our stylesheet to transform their contents.

For our first stylesheet, we'll use the filename attribute as the argument to the document() function. The simplest thing we can do is open each purchase order, then write its details to the output stream. The key to our stylesheet is this call to the document() function:

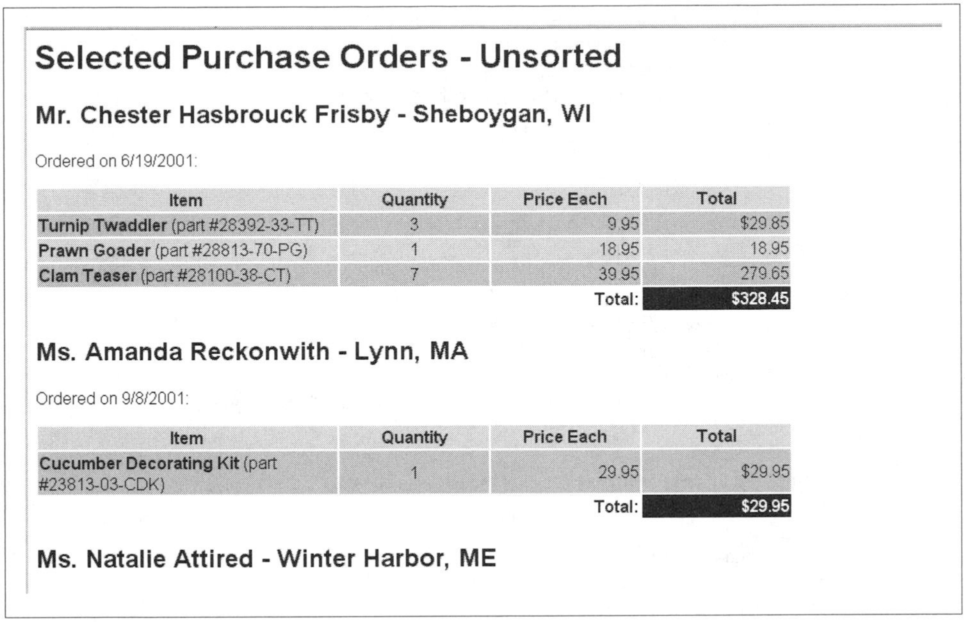

Selected Purchase Orders - Unsorted

Mr. Chester Hasbrouck Frisby - Sheboygan, WI

Ordered on 6/19/2001:

Item	Quantity	Price Each	Total
Turnip Twaddler (part #28392-33-TT)	3	9.95	$29.85
Prawn Goader (part #28813-70-PG)	1	18.95	18.95
Clam Teaser (part #28100-38-CT)	7	39.95	279.65
		Total:	$328.45

Ms. Amanda Reckonwith - Lynn, MA

Ordered on 9/8/2001:

Item	Quantity	Price Each	Total
Cucumber Decorating Kit (part #23813-03-CDK)	1	29.95	$29.95
		Total:	$29.95

Ms. Natalie Attired - Winter Harbor, ME

Figure 8-1. Document generated from multiple input files

```
<xsl:for-each select="/report/po">
  <xsl:apply-templates
    select="document(@filename)/purchase-order"/>
</xsl:for-each>
```

When we process our master document with this stylesheet, the results look like Figure 8-1.

The most notable thing about our results is that we've been able to generate a document that contains the contents of several other documents. To keep our example short, we've only combined four purchase orders, but there's no limit (beyond the physical limits of our machine) to the number of documents we could combine. Best of all, we didn't have to modify any of the individual purchase orders to generate our report.

Here's the complete stylesheet:

```
<?xml version="1.0"?>
<!-- masterdox1.xsl -->
<xsl:stylesheet version="1.0"
  xmlns:xsl="http://www.w3.org/1999/XSL/Transform">

  <xsl:output method="html"/>

  <xsl:template match="/">
    <html>
      <head>
        <title><xsl:value-of select="/report/title"/></title>
      </head>
      <body style="font-family: sans-serif;">
```

```
      <h1>Selected Purchase Orders - Unsorted</h1>
      <xsl:for-each select="/report/po">
        <xsl:apply-templates
          select="document(@filename)/purchase-order"/>
      </xsl:for-each>
    </body>
  </html>
</xsl:template>

<xsl:template match="purchase-order">
  <h2>
    <xsl:value-of
      select="customer/address[@type='business']/name/title"/>
    <xsl:text> </xsl:text>
    <xsl:value-of
      select="customer/address[@type='business']/name/first-name"/>
    <xsl:text> </xsl:text>
    <xsl:value-of
      select="customer/address[@type='business']/name/last-name"/>
    <xsl:text> - </xsl:text>
    <xsl:value-of
      select="customer/address[@type='business']/city"/>
    <xsl:text>, </xsl:text>
    <span style="font-weight: bold;">
      <xsl:value-of
        select="customer/address[@type='business']/state"/>
    </span>
  </h2>
  <p>
    <xsl:text>Ordered on </xsl:text>
    <xsl:value-of select="date/@month"/>
    <xsl:text>/</xsl:text>
    <xsl:value-of select="date/@day"/>
    <xsl:text>/</xsl:text>
    <xsl:value-of select="date/@year"/>
    <xsl:text>:</xsl:text>
  </p>
  <table width="80%" border="0">
    <tr style="background: #66FF66;">
      <th>Item</th>
      <th>Quantity</th>
      <th>Price Each</th>
      <th>Total</th>
    </tr>
    <xsl:for-each select="items/item">
      <tr>
        <xsl:attribute name="style">
          <xsl:text>background: </xsl:text>
          <xsl:choose>
            <xsl:when test="position() mod 2">
              <xsl:text>#CCCCFF</xsl:text>
            </xsl:when>
            <xsl:otherwise>
              <xsl:text>#66FF66</xsl:text>
            </xsl:otherwise>
```

```
        </xsl:choose>
        <xsl:text>;</xsl:text>
      </xsl:attribute>
      <td width="40%">
        <span style="font-weight: bold;">
          <xsl:value-of select="name"/>
        </span>
        <xsl:text> (part #</xsl:text>
        <xsl:value-of select="@part-no"/>
        <xsl:text>)</xsl:text>
      </td>
      <td style="text-align: center;" width="20%">
        <xsl:value-of select="qty"/>
      </td>
      <td style="text-align: right;" width="20%">
        <xsl:value-of select="price"/>
      </td>
      <td style="text-align: right;" width="20%">
        <xsl:choose>
          <xsl:when test="position()=1">
            <xsl:value-of
              select="format-number(price * qty, '$#,###.00')"/>
          </xsl:when>
          <xsl:otherwise>
            <xsl:value-of
              select="format-number(price * qty, '#,###.00')"/>
          </xsl:otherwise>
        </xsl:choose>
      </td>
    </tr>
  </xsl:for-each>
  <tr style="font-weight: bold;">
    <td colspan="3" style="text-align: right;">
      Total:
    </td>
    <td style="text-align: right; color: white; background: black;">
      <xsl:variable name="orderTotal">
        <xsl:call-template name="sumItems">
          <xsl:with-param name="items" select="items/item" />
        </xsl:call-template>
      </xsl:variable>
      <xsl:value-of
        select="format-number($orderTotal, '$#,###.00')"/>
    </td>
  </tr>
</table>
</xsl:template>

<xsl:template name="sumItems">
  <xsl:param name="items" />
  <xsl:param name="runningTotal" select="0" />
  <xsl:choose>
    <xsl:when test="$items">
      <xsl:variable name="firstItemSubtotal"
        select="$items[1]/qty * $items[1]/price" />
```

```
        <xsl:call-template name="sumItems">
          <xsl:with-param name="items" select="$items[position() > 1]" />
          <xsl:with-param name="runningTotal"
            select="$runningTotal + $firstItemSubtotal" />
        </xsl:call-template>
      </xsl:when>
      <xsl:otherwise>
        <xsl:value-of select="$runningTotal" />
      </xsl:otherwise>
    </xsl:choose>
  </xsl:template>

</xsl:stylesheet>
```

An Aside: Doing Math with Recursion

While we're here, we'll also mention the recursive technique we used to calculate the total for each purchase order. At first glance, this seems like a perfect opportunity to use the sum( ) function. We want to add the total of the price of each item multiplied by its quantity. We could try to invoke the sum( ) function like this:

```
<xsl:value-of select="sum(item/qty*item/price)"/>
```

Unfortunately, the sum( ) function simply takes the node-set passed to it, converts each item in the node-set to a number, and then returns the sum of all of those numbers. The expression item/qty*item/price, while a perfectly valid XPath expression, isn't a valid node-set. With that in mind, we have to create a recursive <xsl:template> to do the work for us. There are a couple of techniques worth mentioning here; we'll go through them in the order we used them in our stylesheet.

[2.0] If you're using an XSLT 2.0 processor, you can use new functions of XPath 2.0 to avoid recursion altogether. XSLT 2.0 makes this stylesheet much simpler and shorter; we discuss all the details in the last section of this chapter. If you're using an XSLT 2.0 processor and you don't really care how recursion works, feel free to skip ahead.

Recursive design

First, we pass the set of all <items> elements to our recursive template:

```
<xsl:variable name="orderTotal">
  <xsl:call-template name="sumItems">
    <xsl:with-param name="items" select="items/item" />
  </xsl:call-template>
</xsl:variable>
```

Our recursive template is named sumItems; the value it returns becomes the value of the variable $orderTotal. Within the recursive template, we use two parameters. One is the variable containing all of the <item> elements; the other is the total of all items we've processed so far. The first time we call the template, of course, this value is zero. (We gave the parameter a default value so we don't have to worry about it when we call the template for the first time.) Here are the two parameters to our template:

```
<xsl:template name="sumItems">
  <xsl:param name="items" />
  <xsl:param name="runningTotal" select="0" />
```

The body of our recursive template is an `<xsl:choose>` element. If the `$items` variable contains at least one node, we calculate the total for the current item (the price of the item multiplied by the quantity):

```
<xsl:when test="$items">
  <xsl:variable name="firstItemSubtotal"
    select="$items[1]/qty * $items[1]/price" />
```

Thinking back to how variables are converted to boolean values, a node-set (or sequence, if we're in XSLT 2.0) that starts with at least one node is `true`. Notice also that we're calculating the subtotal for the first item (`$items[1]`) only. Now that we've calculated the value of the current item, our template calls itself:

```
<xsl:call-template name="sumItems">
  <xsl:with-param name="items" select="$items[position() > 1]" />
  <xsl:with-param name="runningTotal"
    select="$runningTotal + $firstItemSubtotal" />
</xsl:call-template>
```

Notice that the `$items` parameter passed to the next invocation of the template contains everything after the first item (`position() > 1`). The parameter `$runningTotal` is the previous value of the parameter plus the total for the current item.

The template calls itself until eventually the parameter `$items` is empty. That means the attribute `test="$items"` returns `false`, so the `<xsl:otherwise>` branch of the `<xsl:choose>` element is taken. That branch uses `<xsl:value-of>` to output the final value. (All other invocations of the `sumItems` template don't output anything.)

Here's the complete recursive template:

```
<xsl:template name="sumItems">
  <xsl:param name="items" />
  <xsl:param name="runningTotal" select="0" />
  <xsl:choose>
    <xsl:when test="$items">
      <xsl:variable name="firstItemSubtotal"
        select="$items[1]/qty * $items[1]/price" />
      <xsl:call-template name="sumItems">
        <xsl:with-param name="items" select="$items[position() > 1]" />
        <xsl:with-param name="runningTotal"
          select="$runningTotal + $firstItemSubtotal" />
      </xsl:call-template>
    </xsl:when>
    <xsl:otherwise>
      <xsl:value-of select="$runningTotal" />
    </xsl:otherwise>
  </xsl:choose>
</xsl:template>
```

Recursion is a common technique in XSLT 1.0 stylesheets. XSLT 2.0 eliminates the need for recursion in many cases (more on that in a minute), but recursion is sometimes the only way to solve problems in XSLT. Knowing how to use this technique will serve you well.

Using format-number( ) to control output

The final nicety in our stylesheet is that we use the XSLT `format-number( )` function to display the total for the current purchase order. We've already discussed how we set the value of the variable `$orderTotal` to be the output of the template named `sumItems`; once the variable is set, we use `format-number` to display it with a currency sign, commas, and two decimal places:

```
<xsl:value-of select="format-number($order-total, '$#,###.00')"/>
```

Base URIs and the document( ) Function

In our previous stylesheet, we used the `document( )` function to select some number of nodes from the original source document (our list of purchase orders), and then open those files. There are a number of ways to invoke the `document( )` function; we'll discuss them briefly here.

The most common way to use the `document( )` function is as we just did. We use an XPath expression to describe a node-set; the `document( )` function takes each node in the node-set, converts it to a string, and then uses that string as a URI. So, when we passed a node-set containing the `filename` attributes in the list of purchase orders, each one is used as a URI. If those URIs are relative references (i.e., they don't begin with a protocol such as `http`), the XSLT processor needs a base URI. If the argument is a node, the base URI of the node is used to resolve the relative reference. If the argument is a string, as it is here, the base URI of the stylesheet is used.

Every node in the XPath source tree is associated with a *base URI*. When using the `document( )` function, the base URI is important for resolving references to various resources specified with relative links.

 Here I'll offer more detail about base URIs than you're ever likely to need: If a given node is an element or processing instruction node, and that node occurs in an external entity, then the base URI for that node is the base URI of the external entity. If an element or processing instruction node does not occur in an external entity, then its base URI is the base URI of the document in which it appears. The base URI of a document node is the base URI of the document itself, and the base URI of an attribute, comment, namespace, or text node is the base URI of that node's parent.

To set the base URI of a node in an XML source document, use the `xml:base` attribute. If a given node doesn't have a base URI, the XSLT processor looks at the node's ancestors (the node's parent, then the node's parent's parent, and so forth) until it finds an `xml:base` attribute. If neither a node nor its ancestors have a `xml:base` attribute, the base URI of the stylesheet is used. See the definition of the `base-uri( )` function for more information on base URIs.

If the `document( )` function has two arguments, the second must be a node-set. The first argument is processed as just described. The second argument is used to set the base URI. The base URI of the first node in the node-set (or sequence, in XSLT 2.0) is the base URI. The two-argument form of the `document( )` function isn't used often, but it's there if you need it.

In our example, we're using strings without any particular protocol (we're using `po38293.xml` instead of `http://.../po38293.xml`). You can also pass a URL to the `document( )` function. If we wanted to open a particular resource, we could simply pass the name of the resource:

```
document('http://www.ibm.com/developerworks/news/dw_dwtp.rss')
```

This action would open this particular resource and process it. Be aware that XSLT processors are required to either signal an error and halt *or* return an empty node-set if a resource can't be found. XSLT processors also don't have to support any particular protocols (`http`, `ftp`, etc.); you have to check the documentation of your XSLT processor to see what protocols are supported.

Finally, a special case occurs when you pass an empty string to the `document( )` function. As we've discussed the various combinations of arguments that can be passed to the function, we've gone over the rules for resolving URIs. When we call `document('')`, the XSLT processor parses the current stylesheet and returns a single node—the root node of the stylesheet itself. This technique is very useful for processing lookup tables in a stylesheet, which we'll discuss later in this chapter.

The document( ) Function and Sorting

Up to now, we've written a simple XML document that contains references to other XML documents, then we created a stylesheet that combines all those referenced XML documents into a single output document. That's all well and good, but we'll probably want to do more advanced things. For example, it might be useful to generate a document that lists all items ordered across all purchase orders. It might also be useful to sort all the purchase orders by the state to which they were shipped or by the last name of the customer. We'll go through some of these scenarios to illustrate the design challenges we face when generating documents from multiple input files.

Our first challenge will be to generate a listing of all purchase orders and sort them by state, then by city within state. This isn't terribly difficult; we'll simply use the `<xsl:sort>` element in conjunction with the `document( )` function. Here's the heart of our new stylesheet:

```
<?xml version="1.0"?>
<!-- masterdox2.xsl -->
<xsl:stylesheet version="1.0"
  xmlns:xsl="http://www.w3.org/1999/XSL/Transform">
...
<xsl:apply-templates
  select="document(/report/po/@filename)/purchase-order">
  <xsl:sort select="customer/address/state"/>
  <xsl:sort select="customer/address/city"/>
</xsl:apply-templates>
```

Here we're selecting all of the `<purchase-order>` elements and sorting them by the values of their `<state>` and `<city>` elements. Figure 8-2 shows our output document, sorted by the value of the `<state>` element (the state abbreviation) in each purchase order.

Notice that we're sorting purchase orders by the state *abbreviation*, not the actual state name; we'll address that in our next example.

Implementing Lookup Tables

We mentioned earlier that calling the `document( )` function with an empty string enabled us to access the nodes in the stylesheet itself. We can use this behavior to implement a lookup table. As an example, we'll create a lookup table that associates an abbreviation such as ME with the state name Maine. We can then use the value from the lookup table as the sort key. More attentive readers might have noticed in our previous example that although the abbreviation MA does indeed sort before the abbreviation ME, a sorted list of the state names themselves would put Maine (abbreviation ME) before Massachusetts (abbreviation MA).

First, we'll create our lookup table. We'll use the fact that a stylesheet can have any element as a top-level element, provided that element is namespace-qualified to

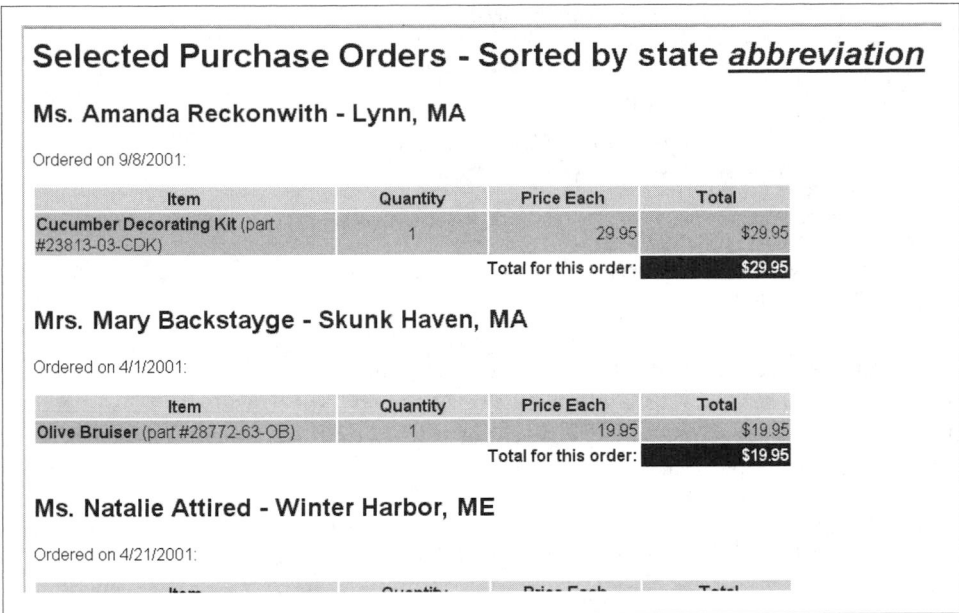

Selected Purchase Orders - Sorted by state _abbreviation_

Ms. Amanda Reckonwith - Lynn, MA

Ordered on 9/8/2001:

Item	Quantity	Price Each	Total
Cucumber Decorating Kit (part #23813-03-CDK)	1	29.95	$29.95
		Total for this order:	$29.95

Mrs. Mary Backstayge - Skunk Haven, MA

Ordered on 4/1/2001:

Item	Quantity	Price Each	Total
Olive Bruiser (part #28772-63-OB)	1	19.95	$19.95
		Total for this order:	$19.95

Ms. Natalie Attired - Winter Harbor, ME

Ordered on 4/21/2001:

Item	Quantity	Price Each	Total

Figure 8-2. Purchase orders sorted by state abbreviation

distinguish it from the `xsl:` namespace reserved for stylesheets. Here's the namespace prefix definition and part of the lookup table that uses it:

```
<?xml version="1.0"?>
<!-- masterdox3.xsl -->
<xsl:stylesheet version="1.0"
  xmlns:xsl="http://www.w3.org/1999/XSL/Transform"
  xmlns:states="http://www.usps.com/ncsc/lookups/abbreviations.html"
  exclude-result-prefixes="states">

<states:name abbrev="AL">Alabama</states:name>
<states:name abbrev="AK">Alaska</states:name>
<states:name abbrev="AS">American Samoa</states:name>
<!-- Many state names deleted for brevity -->
<states:name abbrev="WV">West Virginia</states:name>
<states:name abbrev="WI">Wisconsin</states:name>
<states:name abbrev="WY">Wyoming</states:name>
```

(The namespace mapped to the `states` prefix is the URL for the official list of state abbreviations from the United States Postal Service, although it could be any string.)

To look up values in our table, we'll use the `document( )` function to return the root node of our stylesheet, then we'll look for a `<states:name>` element with a `abbrev` attribute that matches the value of the current `<state>` element in the purchase order we're currently processing. Here's the somewhat convoluted syntax that performs this magic:

```
<body style="font-family: sans-serif;">
  <h1>
```

```
        Selected Purchase Orders - Sorted by state
        <span style="font-style: italic;
                    text-decoration: underline;">name</span>
    </h1>
    <xsl:for-each
      select="document(/report/po/@filename)/purchase-order
              /customer/address/state">
      <xsl:sort
        select="document('')/*/states:name[@abbrev=current()]"/>
      <xsl:sort select="../city"/>
      <xsl:apply-templates select="ancestor::purchase-order"/>
    </xsl:for-each>
</body>
```

Notice that we use the `document( )` function twice; once to open the document referred to by the `filename` attribute, and once to open the stylesheet itself. We also need to discuss the XPath expression in the `select` attribute of the `<xsl:sort>` element. There are four significant parts to this expression:

`document('')`
    Returns the root node of the current stylesheet.

`/*/`
    Indicates that what follows must be a top-level element of the stylesheet. This syntax starts at the root of the document and has a single element. For our current stylesheet, we could have written the XPath expression like this:

    ```
    select="document('')/xsl:stylesheet/
            states:name[@abbrev=current()]"
    ```

    Because the root element of a stylesheet can be either `<xsl:stylesheet>` or `<xsl:transform>`, it's better to use the asterisk.

`states:name`
    We're looking for a `name` element in the `states:` namespace.

`[@abbrev=current( )]`
    Means that the `abbrev` attribute of the current `<states:name>` element has the same value as the current node. We have to use the XSLT `current( )` function here because we want the current node, not the context node. Inside the predicate expression, the current node is the `<state>` element that we're processing, whereas the context node is the `<states:name>` element that contains the `abbrev` attribute that we evaluate.

Notice that the `<xsl:stylesheet>` element contains the `exclude-result-prefixes` attribute to ensure the output document doesn't declare the `states:` prefix. We use only elements in this namespace to implement the lookup table; we certainly don't need to have the `states:` namespace defined in the HTML output document.

As with any stylesheet, we can write our XPath expressions in different manners. Here is one way to access the lookup table:

```
<xsl:for-each
  select="document(/report/po/@filename)/purchase-order
          /customer/address/state">
  <xsl:sort
    select="document('')/*/states:name[@abbrev=current()]"/>
  <xsl:sort select="../city"/>
  <xsl:apply-templates select="ancestor::purchase-order"/>
</xsl:for-each>
```

And here's another:

```
<xsl:for-each
  select="document(/report/po/@filename)/purchase-order">
  <xsl:sort
    select="document('')/*/states:name
            [@abbrev=current()/customer/address/state]"/>
  <xsl:sort select="customer/address/city"/>
  <xsl:apply-templates select="."/>
</xsl:for-each>
```

Both of these listings do the same thing, but they specify parts of the document in different ways. The first example creates a `<xsl:for-each>` for all of the `<state>` elements; the second uses the `<purchase-order>` elements. In each case, the remaining XPath expressions are written from a different position in the node tree. Given a `<state>` element, the related `<city>` element is at `../city`, and we have to use the `ancestor` axis to process the `<purchase-order>`. If we base our `<xsl:for-each>` on the `<purchase-order>` element, we specify the `<city>` element with `customer/address/city`. In the second example, specifying the `<purchase-order>` is done with a dot.

Both of the samples are similarly complex, but you should always be on the lookout for simpler ways to write your XPath expressions. If every XPath expression inside an `<xsl:for-each>` or `<xsl:template>` element is very complex, you might be able to change the outermost expression and simplify your stylesheet.

Figure 8-3 shows the output from the stylesheet with a lookup table.

Notice that now the purchase orders have been sorted by the actual name of the state referenced in the address, not by the state's abbreviation. Lookup tables are an extremely useful side effect of the way the `document('')` function works. You could place a lookup table in another file and use the `document()` function to load that information from the other file, but the technique we've employed here is the most common way to implement lookup tables.

Grouping Across Multiple Documents

Our final task will be to group our collection of purchase orders. We'll create a new listing that groups all the purchase orders by the state to which they were shipped. We'll use the grouping technique we used earlier in Chapter 7.

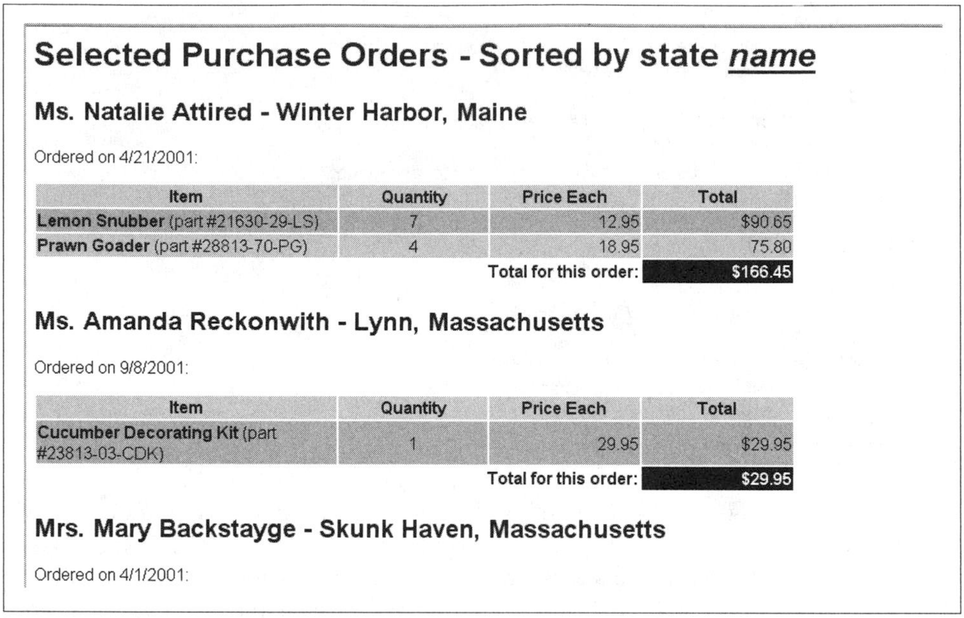

Selected Purchase Orders - Sorted by state *name*

Ms. Natalie Attired - Winter Harbor, Maine

Ordered on 4/21/2001:

Item	Quantity	Price Each	Total
Lemon Snubber (part #21630-29-LS)	7	12.95	$90.65
Prawn Goader (part #28813-70-PG)	4	18.95	75.80
		Total for this order:	$166.45

Ms. Amanda Reckonwith - Lynn, Massachusetts

Ordered on 9/8/2001:

Item	Quantity	Price Each	Total
Cucumber Decorating Kit (part #23813-03-CDK)	1	29.95	$29.95
		Total for this order:	$29.95

Mrs. Mary Backstayge - Skunk Haven, Massachusetts

Ordered on 4/1/2001:

Figure 8-3. Purchase orders sorted by state name

We'll define an XSLT key( ) for all of the `<state>` values in our set of purchase orders. We'll also create a variable that stores all of these orders. By reading all of the purchase orders into a variable, we won't have to call the document( ) function every time we need to access a particular purchase order. With those two structures in place, we'll be ready to do grouping just as we did in the last chapter.

To get things started, here's how we define the key( ):

```
<xsl:key name="po-key" match="purchase-order"
  use="customer/address/state"/>
```

And here's how we load all of the purchase order documents into a variable:

```
<xsl:variable name="purchase-orders"
  select="document(/report/po/@filename)/purchase-order"/>
```

Now that we have a variable that contains all of the nodes from all of the purchase orders, we're ready to process them. We'll go through these steps:

1. Start an `<xsl:for-each>` element to process all of the nodes in the variable `$purchase-orders`.

2. Sort the purchase orders by state name. As with our previous stylesheet, this means using the document('') function to retrieve the state name that matches the abbreviation in the purchase order.

3. Save the value of the current `<state>` in a variable.

4. Use the key( ) function to save into a variable all of the purchase orders from the current state.

5. If this is the first time we've seen this particular state (we'll use generate-id( ) here), use `<xsl:apply-templates>` to process all the purchase orders that match the current state. When we call `<xsl:apply-templates>`, we'll sort all the purchase orders for that state by city before we process them.

Here's the significant portion of the stylesheet; the template for processing the `<purchase-order>` element is unchanged from our previous stylesheets:

```
<?xml version="1.0"?>
<!-- masterdox4.xsl -->
<xsl:stylesheet version="1.0"
  xmlns:xsl="http://www.w3.org/1999/XSL/Transform"
  xmlns:states="http://www.usps.com/ncsc/lookups/abbreviations.html"
  exclude-result-prefixes="states">

...

<xsl:for-each select="$purchase-orders">
  <xsl:sort
    select="document('')/*/states:name
            [@abbrev=current()/customer/address/state]"/>
  <xsl:variable name="currentState"
    select="customer/address/state"/>
  <xsl:variable name="currentStatePOs"
    select="$purchase-orders/key('po-key', $currentState)"/>
  <xsl:if
    test="generate-id() = generate-id($currentStatePOs[1])">
    <h2 style="color: white; background: black;">
      Purchase Orders from
      <xsl:value-of
        select="document('')/*/states:name
                [@abbrev=$currentState]"/>
    </h2>
    <xsl:apply-templates select="$currentStatePOs">
      <xsl:sort select="customer/address/city"/>
    </xsl:apply-templates>
  </xsl:if>
</xsl:for-each>
```

Notice that we used the key( ) function to retrieve all of the `<purchase-order>`s that are from the current state. All of those orders are stored in a variable. To determine whether we're seeing a purchase order for the first time, we generate an ID for the current order (generate-id( )) and compare that to the generated ID for the first item in the set of purchase orders for the current state (generate-id($currentStatePOs[1])). If the two generated IDs are the same, we know that we're seeing a state name for the first time.

The result of our hard work looks like Figure 8-4.

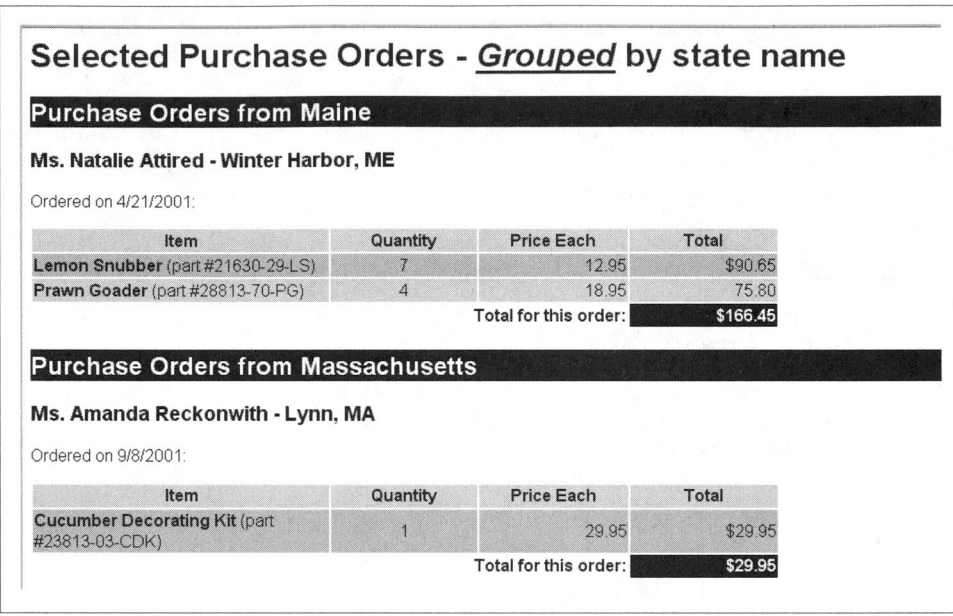

Figure 8-4. *Purchase orders grouped by state name*

[2.0] Using XSLT 2.0 to Simplify Things

We've mentioned several times in this chapter that XSLT 2.0 has capabilities that can greatly simplify our stylesheet. We'll look at those techniques in this section.

The XSLT 1.0 stylesheet we've developed here has several areas ripe for improvement:

- We have to use the XSLT 1.0 grouping technique. We can avoid this clumsiness by using XSLT 2.0's `<xsl:for-each-group>` to do the grouping for us. The XSLT processor does the work of finding all of the unique state values, simplifying our lives significantly.

- We have to use recursion to calculate the total of each purchase order. We can use new features of XPath 2.0 to calculate the total in one simple expression.

- Although the `document('')` technique we used works, it's a convoluted way of doing things. We can replace it with an XSLT function that takes a state abbreviation as input and returns the full name of that state. This gives us a much simpler syntax. Calling `getStateName()` is much easier to understand and maintain than `document('')/*/states:name[@abbrev=$next-state]`.

- It's a minor point, but we have to use an `<xsl:choose>` element in a couple of places. We can use the `if` operator defined in the XPath 2.0 and XQuery 1.0 Functions and Operators spec to simplify the stylesheet. Instead of `<xsl:choose>`, `<xsl:when>`, and `<xsl:otherwise>`, we'll use `if`, `then`, and `else`.

- Another minor point is that the date of each purchase order is stored in the XML source as a set of three attributes. We can use XSLT 2.0's support for XML Schema datatypes to create an `xs:date`, and then use the power of the `format-date( )` function to format the date more elegantly.

With these things in mind, we'll start simplifying our stylesheet.

Grouping by Distinct Values

One problem in our final XSLT 1.0 stylesheet is that we have to find all the distinct state values in all the purchase orders. We use the Muench method to do this, but the code is more difficult to write and maintain. To simplify things, we can use `<xsl:for-each-group>` to do everything at once. When using the `group-by` attribute, `<xsl:for-each-group>` automatically finds all of the unique values of the `<state>` element. Here's a fragment of the code:

```
<xsl:for-each-group
  select="document(/report/po/@filename)/purchase-order"
  group-by="customer/address/state">
  <xsl:sort
    select="states:getStateName(current-grouping-key())"/>
```

The `<xsl:for-each-group>` element groups all of the `<purchase-order>` elements by the value of their `<state>` elements. The `<xsl:sort>` sorts the groups by the actual state names: `current-grouping-key( )` returns the value of the current `<state>` element, and `states:getStateName( )` is an XSLT function (we'll discuss this in the later section, "Implementing Lookup Tables with <xsl:function>").

Comparing this stylesheet to our final XSLT 1.0 stylesheet, we've used these two elements to replace roughly 15 lines of code. Even better, the new code is much simpler and easier to maintain.

 Because `<xsl:for-each-group>` finds all of the unique values of `<state>` for us, we don't have to worry about finding them ourselves. If we did need to find the set of unique values, XPath 2.0 and XQuery 1.0 provide the `distinct-values( )` function. Here's how we would get a list of unique states with XSLT 2.0:

```
<xsl:variable name="list-of-unique-states" as="xs:string*">
  <xsl:perform-sort>
    <xsl:sort select="states:getStateName(.)"/>
    <xsl:sequence
      select="distinct-values(document(/report/po/@filename)
              /purchase-order/customer/address/state)"/>
```

```
        </xsl:perform-sort>
      </xsl:variable>
```

We create a variable of type `xs:string*`. That means our variable will be a sequence of strings, each of which is a unique state abbreviation. Next we use the new `<xsl:perform-sort>` element to sort our unique values by state name, not abbreviation. Inside `<xsl:perform-sort>`, we have the `<xsl:sort>` element, which sorts all of the values by state name, and the `<xsl:sequence>` element, which selects the distinct values of all the `<state>` elements. (We're using the `states:getStateName()` function.)

It's great that XSLT 2.0 gives us this powerful yet simple technique; it's even better that `<xsl:for-each-group>` simplifies things so we don't have to use it here at all.

Doing Math Without Recursion

Our original stylesheet had to use recursion to calculate the total of each purchase order. We passed all of the `<item>` elements to a recursive template, which returned the total for the purchase order after processing all of the `<item>`s. In XSLT 2.0, we can use a simple XPath expression to do all that work for us. Here's the single line of code:

```
<xsl:value-of
  select="format-number(sum(items/item/(qty * price)),
         '$#,###.00')"/>
```

That's it. XPath 2.0's support for mathematical expressions inside path expressions makes this ridiculously easy. We replaced maybe 20 lines of code with just 1.

Implementing Lookup Tables with <xsl:function>

Using `document('')` to implement lookup tables is a workable approach, but we can simplify things with an XSLT function. With a function, we can invoke `getStateName()` to resolve a state abbreviation to a state name; that's much simpler than invoking `document('')/*/states:name[@abbrev=current()]` or something similar. Here's how our function looks:

```
<xsl:function name="states:getStateName" as="xs:string">
  <xsl:param name="abbr" as="xs:string"/>
  <xsl:variable name="abbreviations" as="xs:string*"
    select="'AL', 'AK', 'AS', 'AZ', 'AR', 'CA', 'CO', 'CT',
<!-- state abbreviations removed for brevity -->
           'WV', 'WI', 'WY'"/>
  <xsl:variable name="stateNames" as="xs:string*"
    select="'Alabama', 'Alaska', 'American Samoa','Arizona',
<!-- state names removed for brevity -->
           'West Virginia', 'Wisconsin', 'Wyoming'"/>
  <xsl:variable name="index"
    select="if (count(index-of($abbreviations, $abbr)) gt 0)
           then subsequence(index-of($abbreviations, $abbr), 1, 1)
           else 0"/>
```

```
<xsl:value-of
   select="if ($index gt 0)
           then string(subsequence($stateNames, $index, 1))
           else ''"/>
</xsl:function>
```

Our function takes a single string, a state abbreviation, as a parameter, and it returns a single string. It uses two variables to store our data; $abbreviations is a sequence of all state abbreviations, and $stateNames is a sequence of all state names. The positions of items in the two sequences match each other. If the abbreviation passed to the function matches the fifth item in the $abbreviations sequence, the name of the state is the fifth item in the $stateNames sequence.

To calculate the position of the matching abbreviation, we use the XPath 2.0 and XQuery 1.0 index-of( ) function. This returns a sequence of xs:integers, each of which represents the index of a match. We use the count( ) function to count the number of items in the sequence returned by index-of( ). If the abbreviation passed to the function matches something in the $abbreviations sequence, the size of the sequence will be greater than zero (actually, we know the size will be either one or zero). To get the index of the matching item, we have to use the new subsequence( ) function to retrieve the first item in the sequence. If none of the abbreviations match the parameter, the index is zero.

Having calculated the index of the matching abbreviation, we return the appropriate state name. If the value of $index is greater than zero, we use subsequence( ) to return the appropriate item from the $stateNames sequence. If the $index is zero (we get a state abbreviation we've never heard of), we return an empty string.

Notice that we simplify our code here by using the XPath 2.0 and XQuery 1.0 if operator. We could do this with <xsl:choose>, <xsl:when>, and <xsl:otherwise>, but if is much simpler. Also notice that we used the gt comparison operator; we can do that because we're comparing two atomic values here. We could have used > or > with the same results.

Now that we have our function defined, states:getStateName('AL') returns Alabama. We can use this greatly simplified syntax wherever we need it. This puts all of the logic for resolving state abbreviations into one place in the stylesheet, instead of forcing us to use document('') with the appropriate XPath expression wherever we need it.

Using if Instead of <xsl:choose>

Although the XSLT elements <xsl:if>, <xsl:choose>, <xsl:when>, and <xsl:otherwise> provide the same function as the if-then-else functions of most programming languages, they're much more verbose. We can use the XPath 2.0 and XQuery 1.0 if operator to simplify things.

Our XSLT 1.0 stylesheet uses `<xsl:choose>` in two places: to choose the background color of table rows, and to change the decimal format for currency amounts in the first row of each purchase order. Here's the first `<xsl:choose>`:

```
<tr>
  <xsl:attribute name="style">
    <xsl:text>background: </xsl:text>
    <xsl:choose>
      <xsl:when test="position() mod 2">
        <xsl:text>#CCCCFF</xsl:text>
      </xsl:when>
      <xsl:otherwise>
        <xsl:text>#66FF66</xsl:text>
      </xsl:otherwise>
    </xsl:choose>
    <xsl:text>;</xsl:text>
  </xsl:attribute>
</tr>
```

We create an attribute named `style`. If this is an odd-numbered row (`position() mod 2` is `1`, which evaluates to `true`), we set the background color to `#CCCCFF`; otherwise, we set it to `#66FF66`. In our XSLT 2.0 stylesheet, we can replace those elements with this attribute value template:

```
<tr style="{if (position() mod 2)
            then 'background: #CCCCFF;'
            else 'background: #66FF66;'}">
```

The other place we use `<xsl:choose>` is to choose a decimal format. Here's how we do it in XSLT 2.0:

```
<xsl:value-of
  select="if (position() = 1)
          then format-number(price * qty, '$#,###.00')
          else format-number(price * qty, '#,###.00')"/>
```

In both cases, we've replaced several elements with a single `if` statement inside an attribute.

Using the format-date( ) Function

Our last enhancement is to use the new `format-date( )` function to format the date of the purchase order. This is an addition to the function of our XSLT 1.0 stylesheet; everything else we've done here has duplicated XSLT 1.0 function in a much simpler way. The date of each purchase order is stored as three attributes named `year`, `month`, and `day`. We'll use the values of those three attributes to create a new `xs:date` value, then we'll use `format-date( )` to format the value.

To create a new `xs:date` value, we need a string in the format `yyyy-mm-dd`. `xs:date('2006-10-10')` is a valid call to the `xs:date` constructor. To complicate things, the month and day values *must* have two digits. In other words, `xs:date('2006-9-8')` raises an error. Our purchase orders don't necessarily have two-digit month and day values, so we'll have to write code to add a leading zero if either value is less than 10. Here's how we do this:

```
<xsl:variable name="monthValue" as="xs:string"
  select="if (date/@month &lt; 10)
          then concat('0', date/@month)
          else date/@month"/>
<xsl:variable name="dayValue" as="xs:string"
  select="if (date/@day &lt; 10)
          then concat('0', date/@day)
          else date/@day"/>
```

We compare the value of the attributes to 10; if they're smaller, we add the string '0' to the value. (Notice that the two variables we're creating here are of datatype xs:string.) In this code, we have to use the < operator because we're comparing a node to a number. If we want to use the lt operator, we'd have to code if (number(date/@day) lt 10).

Once we've normalized the month and day values, we can create our xs:date value and format it. Here's the rest of the code:

```
<xsl:variable name="orderDate" as="xs:date"
  select="xs:date(concat(date/@year, '-',
          $monthValue, '-', $dayValue))"/>
<xsl:value-of
  select="format-date($orderDate, '[FNn], [MNn] [D1], [Y]')"/>
```

The date-formatting codes here format the date 2006-10-10 as Tuesday, October 10, 2006. To do this in XSLT 1.0, we would have to create a lookup table to convert month numbers to their text equivalents. We would also need a lookup table for the names of the days of the week, although we'd have to write an extension function to figure out that the 10th of October, 2006 occurred on a Tuesday.

The Complete XSLT 2.0 Solution

Here's how our final stylesheet looks in XSLT 2.0:

```
<?xml version="1.0"?>
<!-- masterdox5.xsl -->
<xsl:stylesheet version="2.0"
  xmlns:xsl="http://www.w3.org/1999/XSL/Transform"
  xmlns:xs="http://www.w3.org/2001/XMLSchema"
  xmlns:states="http://www.usps.com/ncsc/lookups/abbreviations.html"
  exclude-result-prefixes="xs states">

  <xsl:variable name="purchase-orders"
    select="document(/report/po/@filename)/purchase-order"/>

  <xsl:function name="states:getStateName" as="xs:string">
    <xsl:param name="abbr" as="xs:string"/>
    <xsl:variable name="abbreviations" as="xs:string*"
      select="'AL', 'AK', 'AS', 'AZ', 'AR', 'CA', 'CO', 'CT',
<!-- state abbreviations removed for brevity -->
```

```
                'WV', 'WI', 'WY'"/>
    <xsl:variable name="stateNames" as="xs:string*"
      select="'Alabama', 'Alaska', 'American Samoa','Arizona',
<!-- state names removed for brevity -->
                'West Virginia', 'Wisconsin', 'Wyoming'"/>
    <xsl:variable name="index"
      select="if (count(index-of($abbreviations, $abbr)) gt 0)
              then subsequence(index-of($abbreviations, $abbr), 1, 1)
              else 0"/>
    <xsl:value-of
      select="if ($index gt 0)
              then string(subsequence($stateNames, $index, 1))
              else ''"/>
</xsl:function>

<xsl:output method="html"/>

<xsl:template match="/">
  <html>
    <head>
      <title><xsl:value-of select="/report/title"/></title>
    </head>
    <body style="font-family: sans-serif;">
      <h1>
        Selected Purchase Orders -
        <span style="font-style: italic;
                     text-decoration: underline;">Grouped</span>
        by state name
      </h1>
      <xsl:for-each-group
        select="$purchase-orders" group-by="customer/address/state">
        <xsl:sort
          select="states:getStateName(current-grouping-key())"/>
        <h2 style="color: white; background: black;">
          Purchase Orders from
          <xsl:value-of
            select="states:getStateName(current-grouping-key())"/>
        </h2>
        <xsl:for-each select="current-group()">
          <xsl:sort select="customer/address/city"/>
          <xsl:apply-templates select="."/>
        </xsl:for-each>
      </xsl:for-each-group>
    </body>
  </html>
</xsl:template>

<xsl:template match="purchase-order">
  <h3>
    <xsl:value-of
      select="customer/address[@type='business']/name/title"/>
    <xsl:text> </xsl:text>
    <xsl:value-of
      select="customer/address[@type='business']/name/first-name"/>
    <xsl:text> </xsl:text>
```

```
  <xsl:value-of
    select="customer/address[@type='business']/name/last-name"/>
  <xsl:text> - </xsl:text>
  <xsl:value-of
    select="customer/address[@type='business']/city"/>
  <xsl:text>, </xsl:text>
  <span style="font-weight: bold;">
    <xsl:value-of
      select="customer/address[@type='business']/state"/>
  </span>
</h3>
<p>
  <xsl:text>Ordered on </xsl:text>
  <xsl:variable name="monthValue" as="xs:string"
    select="if (date/@month &lt; 10)
             then concat('0', date/@month)
             else date/@month"/>
  <xsl:variable name="dayValue" as="xs:string"
    select="if (date/@day &lt; 10)
             then concat('0', date/@day)
             else date/@day"/>
  <xsl:variable name="orderDate" as="xs:date"
    select="xs:date(concat(date/@year, '-',
                           $monthValue, '-', $dayValue))"/>
  <xsl:value-of
    select="format-date($orderDate, '[FNn], [MNn] [D1], [Y]')"/>
  <xsl:text>:</xsl:text>
</p>
<table width="80%" border="0">
  <tr style="background: #66FF66;">
    <th>Item</th>
    <th>Quantity</th>
    <th>Price Each</th>
    <th>Total</th>
  </tr>
  <xsl:for-each select="items/item">
    <tr style="{if ((position() mod 2) = 1)
               then 'background: #CCCCFF;'
               else 'background: #66FF66;'}">
      <td width="40%">
        <span style="font-weight: bold;">
          <xsl:value-of select="name"/>
        </span>
        <xsl:text> (part #</xsl:text>
        <xsl:value-of select="@part-no"/>
        <xsl:text>)</xsl:text>
      </td>
      <td style="text-align: center;" width="20%">
        <xsl:value-of select="qty"/>
      </td>
      <td style="text-align: right;" width="20%">
        <xsl:value-of select="price"/>
      </td>
      <td style="text-align: right;" width="20%">
        <xsl:value-of
```

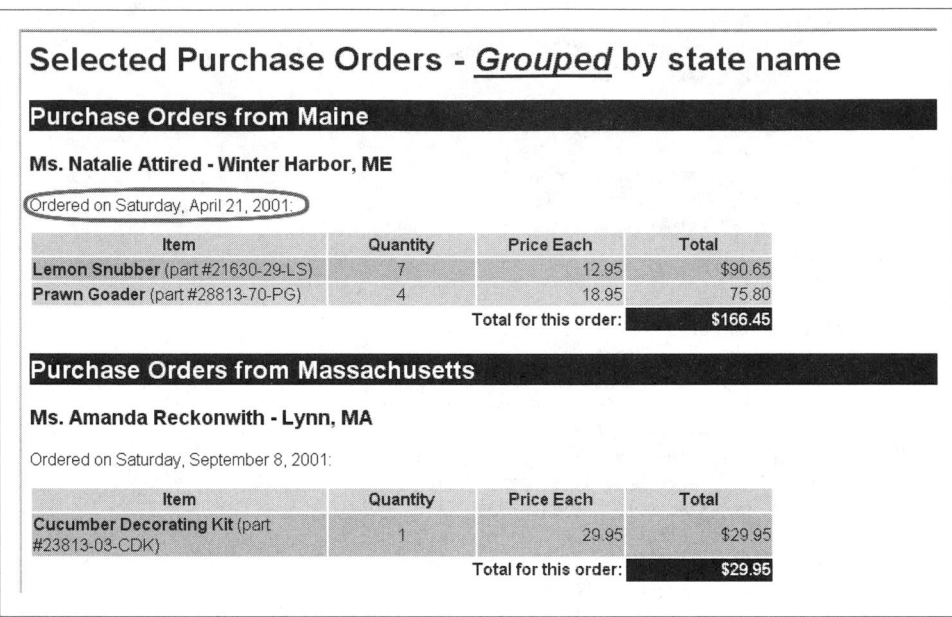

Figure 8-5. *Purchase orders grouped by state name—XSLT 2.0 version*

```
                        select="if (position() = 1)
                                then format-number(price * qty, '$#,###.00')
                                else format-number(price * qty, '#,###.00')"/>
            </td>
          </tr>
        </xsl:for-each>
        <tr style="font-weight: bold;">
          <td colspan="3" style="text-align: right;">
            Total for this order:
          </td>
          <td align="right" style="color: white; background: black;">
            <xsl:value-of
              select="format-number(sum(items/item/(qty * price)),
                                    '$#,###.00')"/>
          </td>
        </tr>
      </table>
    </xsl:template>

  </xsl:stylesheet>
```

The results of our stylesheet are as shown in Figure 8-5.

Notice that the dates are formatted differently than they were in the XSLT 1.0 version; with that exception, the output is identical, even though the stylesheet is much shorter.

[2.0] The doc( ) and doc-available( ) Functions

XSLT 2.0 provides a new function, `doc( )`, that is very similar to the `document( )` function, but that is simpler in a couple of ways. First of all, the `document( )` function can take a node-set or sequence as its first argument, whereas `doc( )` takes a single string. In our earlier stylesheets, we created a variable containing all of the nodes from all of the documents referenced in our list of purchase orders:

```
<xsl:variable name="purchase-orders"
  select="document(/report/po/@filename)/purchase-order"/>
```

This returns a sequence of `purchase-order` nodes, each of which has the structure defined in the purchase order. We can use the variable `$purchase-orders` in an `<xsl:for-each>` or `<xsl:for-each-group>` element. A stylesheet that contains this markup raises an error if there is more than one `<po>` element in the source document:

```
<!-- This doesn't work with our sample document -->
<xsl:variable name="purchase-orders"
  select="doc(/report/po/@filename)/purchase-order"/>
```

If we want to use the `doc( )` function, there are several things we could do. We could specify a particular `<po>` element:

```
<xsl:variable name="purchase-orders"
  select="doc(/report/po[2]/@filename)/purchase-order"/>
```

A more practical solution would be to put the `doc( )` function into an `<xsl:for-each>` element:

```
<xsl:for-each select="/report/po">
  <xsl:variable name="purchase-orders"
    select="doc(@filename)/purchase-order"/>
</xsl:for-each>
```

We could also change our input document so that it has only a single `<po>` element; although that's hardly a worthwhile solution, the `doc( )` function would in fact work.

To contrast the two functions, the `doc( )` function returns the document node of a single XML document, while the `document( )` function can return a set of nodes from multiple documents. In most cases, you'll want to use the more flexible `document( )` function instead.

Second, we mentioned that the `document( )` function has an optional second argument to set a base URI for resolving relative URLs. *The `doc( )` function doesn't have this option*; the base URI is always the base URI of the stylesheet.

The final difference between `doc( )` and `document( )` is that the `document( )` function supports fragment identifiers in the URL, whereas *the `doc( )` function does not*. If your processor uses fragment identifiers, the `document( )` function can return specific nodes in a document rather than simply returning the document node.

```
<!-- This is legal: -->
<xsl:variable name="mainContent"
```

```
      select="document('http://www.ibm.com/developerworks/index.html#main')"/>

  <!-- This is not: -->
  <xsl:variable name="mainContent"
      select="doc('http://www.ibm.com/developerworks/index.html#main')"/>
```

Here's a small excerpt of our first stylesheet (`masterdox1.xsl`), rewritten to use `doc()` instead of `document()`:

```
  <?xml version="1.0"?>
  <!-- doc.xsl -->
  <xsl:stylesheet version="2.0"
    xmlns:xsl="http://www.w3.org/1999/XSL/Transform">

    <xsl:output method="html"/>

    <xsl:template match="/">
      <html>
        <head>
          <title><xsl:value-of select="/report/title"/></title>
        </head>
        <body style="font-family: sans-serif;">
          <h1>Selected Purchase Orders - Unsorted</h1>
          <xsl:for-each select="/report/po">
            <xsl:apply-templates
              select="doc(@filename)/purchase-order"/>
          </xsl:for-each>
        </body>
      </html>
    </xsl:template>
  ...
```

We've structured our stylesheet so that each `filename` attribute is passed to the `doc()` function as a single string. This gives us the same results as the original stylesheet; rewriting this chapter's more complicated stylesheets to use `doc()` instead of `document()` would be more difficult.

As a companion to the `doc()` function, XPath 2.0 and XQuery 1.0 provide the `doc-available()` function. This returns `true` if a given URL is available; it returns `false` otherwise. Here's a simple stylesheet that uses this function:

```
  <?xml version="1.0"?>
  <!-- doc-available.xsl -->
  <xsl:stylesheet version="2.0"
    xmlns:xsl="http://www.w3.org/1999/XSL/Transform">

    <xsl:output method="text"/>

    <xsl:template match="/">
      <xsl:text>&#xA;Tests of the doc-available() function:&#xA;</xsl:text>

      <xsl:text>&#xA;  doc-available('polist.xml') = </xsl:text>
      <xsl:value-of select="doc-available('polist.xml')"/>

      <xsl:text>&#xA;&#xA;  doc-available('polist2.xml') = </xsl:text>
```

```
        <xsl:value-of select="doc-available('polist2.xml')"/>
      </xsl:template>

    </xsl:stylesheet>
```

This stylesheet generates these results:

```
Tests of the doc-available() function:

  doc-available('polist.xml') = true

  doc-available('polist2.xml') = false
```

You can use the doc-available( ) function to see whether opening a particular URL would raise an error. If doc-available( ) returns true, it's safe to use the doc( ) function to open the requested URL.

> Be aware that the argument to doc-available( ) has the same restrictions as the argument to doc( ). If you pass an argument to doc-available( ) that isn't legal for doc( ) (the aforementioned expression doc(/report/ po/@filename)/purchase-order, for example), doc-available( ) returns false.
>
> To sum it up, if doc-available( ) returns true, then document( ) will work; on the other hand, if doc-available( ) returns false, it's possible that document( ) will still work. XSLT 2.0 doesn't have a document-available( ) function.

[2.0] The collection( ) Function

The collection( ) function takes a string as its argument and returns a collection of nodes. Defined as part of the XPath 2.0 spec, it gives us the ability to use a URI to retrieve a collection of documents. How those documents are stored (or whether they're really documents at all) is implementation-dependent. In particular, the spec mentions accessing data in a relational database as a possible implementation of the collection( ) function. The fact that the string passed to the function can be generated and can contain parameters makes collection( ) very flexible.

We'll look at a short example here. Here's the document we'll pass to the collection( ) function:

```
<?xml version="1.0"?>
<!-- polist.xml -->
<collection>
  <doc href="po38292.xml"/>
  <doc href="po38293.xml"/>
  <doc href="po38294.xml"/>
  <doc href="po38295.xml"/>
</collection>
```

This is very similar to the list of purchase orders we worked with earlier in this chapter. The stylesheet that invokes the `collection( )` function looks like this:

```
<?xml version="1.0"?>
<!-- collection.xsl -->
<xsl:stylesheet version="2.0"
  xmlns:xsl="http://www.w3.org/1999/XSL/Transform">

  <xsl:output method="text"/>

  <xsl:template match="/">
    <xsl:text>&#xA;A test of the collection() function:</xsl:text>

    <xsl:variable name="docPile" as="node()*"
      select="collection('polist.xml')"/>

    <xsl:text>&#xA;&#xA;  The customers in the </xsl:text>
    <xsl:text>collection are: &#xA;    </xsl:text>
    <xsl:for-each select="$docPile/purchase-order/customer">
      <xsl:sort select="address/name/last-name"/>
      <xsl:value-of
        select="address/name/title,
                address/name/first-name,
                address/name/last-name"
        separator=" "/>
      <xsl:text>    &#xA;    </xsl:text>
    </xsl:for-each>
  </xsl:template>

</xsl:stylesheet>
```

The stylesheet extracts the nodes from the `collection( )` function and stores them in the variable `$docPile`. Once we have the nodes from the collection, we sort all of the customers in all of those purchase orders by last name, and then write them out. The results look like this:

```
A test of the collection() function:

  The customers in the collection are:
    Ms. Natalie Attired
    Mrs. Mary Backstayge
    Mr. Chester Hasbrouck Frisby
    Ms. Amanda Reckonwith
```

See the definition of the [2.0] `collection( )` function in Appendix C for a more complete discussion.

[2.0] The unparsed-text( ) and unparsed-text-available( ) Functions

The last new function for combining documents is the `unparsed-text( )` function. This lets you read in text from a URL. That text is not parsed, letting you read in text documents, comma-separated values, or even HTML documents that aren't well-formed XML. What's more, you can combine unparsed-text( ) with other new features such as the tokenize( ) function or the <xsl:analyze-string> element to process that text and transform it in a useful way.

As an example, we'll read in a file of comma-separated values and output them as an HTML table of addresses. Here's the comma-separated file, *unparsed-text.csv*:

```
Mr.,Chester Hasbrouck,Frisby,1234 Main Street,Sheboygan,WI,48392
Ms.,Natalie,Attired,707 Breitling Way,Winter Harbor,ME,00218
Ms.,Amanda,Reckonwith,930-A Chestnut Street,Lynn,MA,02930
Mrs.,Mary,Backstayge,283 First Avenue,Skunk Haven,MA,02718
```

We'll go through three simple steps to process this data. First, we'll use the tokenize( ) function to get each line of the file. Next, we'll use tokenize( ) to get each comma-separated value. Finally, we'll take each value and transform it appropriately. Using the comma-separated file we've listed here, the third comma-separated value in each line is the customer's last name, the seventh value is the zip code, and so forth.

To process the file one line at a time, we'll use this technique, courtesy of the XSLT 2.0 spec:

```
<xsl:for-each
    select="tokenize(unparsed-text('addresses.csv'), '\r?\n')">
```

The <xsl:for-each> element processes the file one line at a time, while the regular expression \r?\n matches a line end. (As the spec points out, unparsed-text( ) doesn't normalize line endings, so we have to allow for an optional carriage return, indicated by \r?.)

Within <xsl:for-each>, we tokenize each line. This is easy because we're simply looking for the values between the commas. The tokenize( ) function returns a sequence, so we put that sequence into a variable:

```
<xsl:variable name="tokens" select="tokenize(., ',')"/>
```

Before we process the comma-separated values, we use the count( ) function to make sure the tokenizer found anything. If the CSV file contains a blank line, the number of tokens for that line will be zero; we'll want to ignore that line and move on to the next one. The rest of the stylesheet uses the subsequence( ) function to retrieve the particular values we want.

Here's the complete stylesheet that processes the CSV file:

```
<?xml version="1.0"?>
<!-- unparsed-text.xsl -->
<xsl:stylesheet version="2.0"
  xmlns:xsl="http://www.w3.org/1999/XSL/Transform">

  <xsl:output method="html"/>

  <xsl:template match="/">
    <html>
```

```
      <head>
        <title>Customer Addresses</title>
      </head>
      <body style="font-family: sans-serif;">
        <h1>Customer Addresses</h1>
        <table width="60%" border="0">
          <tr style="background: #66FF66;">
            <th>Name</th>
            <th>Street</th>
            <th>City</th>
            <th>State</th>
            <th>Zip</th>
          </tr>
          <xsl:for-each
            select="tokenize(unparsed-text('addresses.csv'), '\r?\n')">
            <xsl:variable name="tokens" select="tokenize(., ',')"/>
            <xsl:if test="count($tokens)">
              <tr style="{if (position() mod 2)
                          then 'background: #CCCCFF;'
                          else 'background: #66FF66;'}">
                <td width="40%">
                  <xsl:value-of
                    select="subsequence($tokens, 1, 2)" separator=" "/>
                  <xsl:text> </xsl:text>
                  <span style="font-weight: bold; font-size: 125%;">
                    <xsl:value-of select="subsequence($tokens, 3, 1)"/>
                  </span>
                </td>
                <td width="20%">
                  <xsl:value-of select="subsequence($tokens, 4, 1)"/>
                </td>
                <td width="20%">
                  <xsl:value-of select="subsequence($tokens, 5, 1)"/>
                </td>
                <td width="10%" style="text-align: center;">
                  <xsl:value-of select="subsequence($tokens, 6, 1)"/>
                </td>
                <td width="10%" style="text-align: center;">
                  <xsl:value-of select="subsequence($tokens, 7, 1)"/>
                </td>
              </tr>
            </xsl:if>
          </xsl:for-each>
        </table>
      </body>
    </html>
  </xsl:template>

</xsl:stylesheet>
```

The results look like Figure 8-6.

Notice that we selected the first two tokens (the customer's courtesy title and first name) as a sequence, and then wrote them out with the attribute **separator=" "**. If a customer

Customer Addresses

Name	Street	City	State	Zip
Mr. Chester Hasbrouck **Frisby**	1234 Main Street	Sheboygan	WI	48392
Ms. Natalie **Attired**	707 Breitling Way	Winter Harbor	ME	00218
Ms. Amanda **Reckonwith**	930-A Chestnut Street	Lynn	MA	02930
Mrs. Mary **Backstayge**	283 First Avenue	Skunk Haven	MA	02718

Figure 8-6. HTML document generated from a file of comma-separated values

doesn't have a courtesy title, our stylesheet doesn't insert an unnecessary space before the customer's first name.

The `unparsed-text( )` function has an optional second argument to specify the encoding of the document located at the URL. For example, if the file *addresses.csv* used the UTF-16 encoding, we would use `unparsed-text('addresses.csv', 'utf-16')` to read the file.

You can use the `unparsed-text( )` function to import an XML or HTML file without parsing it. See the definition of the `unparsed-text( )` function for more examples.

Analogous to the `doc-available( )` function is the new `unparsed-text-available( )` function. It returns `true` if the unparsed text located at a given URL is available; it returns `false` otherwise.

Summary

This chapter completes our tour of the XSLT and XPath functions that work with multiple documents. These powerful functions allow us to generate an output document containing elements from many different input documents. In our examples here, we generated several views of those input documents, but many more combinations might be useful. The biggest benefit of these functions is that they allows us to define views of multiple documents that are separate from those documents themselves. As we need to define other views, we don't have to change our input documents.

We also looked at using the new `unparsed-text( )` function to read non-XML data and add it to our result documents. The functions we've discussed here can save you a tremendous amount of development time in generating reports and other summarizing documents.

CHAPTER 9

Extending XSLT

To this point, we've spent a lot of time learning how to use the built-in features of XSLT and XPath to get things done. We've also talked about the somewhat unusual processing model that makes life challenging for programmers from the world of procedural languages (a.k.a. Earth). But what do you do if you still can't do everything with XSLT and XPath?

In this chapter, we'll discuss the XSLT extension mechanism that allows you to add new functions and elements to the language. The XSLT standard doesn't define all of the details about how these things should work, so there are some differences between processors. The good news is that if you write an extension function or element that works with your favorite processor, another vendor can't do something sinister to prevent your functions or elements from working. The less good news is that if you decide to change XSLT processors, you'll probably have to change your code.

Along the way, we'll also discuss the EXSLT project, whose goals are to provide a common library of extension functions that work across different XSLT processors.

The examples in this chapter are written for the Java-based Saxon and Xalan processors, and for the .NET framework (using C#). We'll discuss how to write stylesheets that can work with multiple processors, and we'll briefly look at the differences between the various APIs supported by those processors. In addition, the Xalan-J processor supports Apache's Bean Scripting Framework (BSF), which means we can write extensions in Jython (also known as JPython), JavaScript, Jacl, and any other language supported by the BSF.

The XSLT Extension Mechanism

The XSLT standard defines two kinds of extensions: extension elements and extension functions. The spec also defines *fallback processing*, a way for stylesheets to respond gracefully when extension elements and functions aren't available. (Fallback processing also applies when we ask an XSLT 1.0 processor to process an XSLT 2.0 stylesheet.) We'll talk about these items briefly, and then we'll move on to some examples that illustrate the full range of extensions and fallback processing.

Keep in mind that the XSLT specs define how the extension mechanism should work; they *do not* define how it should be implemented. As we'll see throughout this chapter, different XSLT processors implement extensions in different ways. For example, a Java-based XSLT processor might use a Java class to implement an extension function or extension element, while a .NET XSLT processor might use a .NET class to do the same thing. How those classes are specified varies from one processor to the next.

Extension Elements

An extension element is an element that should be processed by a piece of code external to the XSLT processor. The implementation details vary from one XSLT processor to the next, as you'd expect. We'll discuss how an extension element can access the XPath representation of our XML source document, how (or if) it can process attribute value templates, how it can generate output, and how (or if) it can move through the XPath tree to manipulate the source document. We'll demonstrate various APIs to do all of these things; the APIs, of course, vary quite a bit between processors. Finally, although XSLT processors typically provide an extension writer with access to the XML source, the standard doesn't define a set of functions or access methods that must be supported.

Extension Functions

As you might guess, an extension function is defined in a piece of code accessed from the XSLT stylesheet. In some cases, that function is written in a scripting language in the stylesheet itself. In those instances, the scripting code is contained in an XML element that is not in the XSLT namespace. In other cases, the function is in a separate file that is loaded by the XSLT processor at runtime. The code for the function might be written in a scripting language or it might be written in a compiled language.

Regardless of how the extension function is written or accessed, you can pass values to the function and the function can return a result. That result can be any of the datatypes supported by XPath. In addition, XSLT processors are free to allow extension functions to return other datatypes, although those other datatypes must be handled by some other function that does return one of XPath's datatypes.

Fallback Processing

The final part of XSLT's extension mechanism uses the `<xsl:fallback>` element. This element is processed whenever an XSLT processor doesn't support the surrounding element. For example, the `<xsl:result-document>` element is new in XSLT 2.0. We can put an `<xsl:fallback>` element inside `<xsl:result-document>`. If we pass the stylesheet to an XSLT 1.0 processor, it won't support the `<xsl:result-document>` element. The XSLT 1.0 processor will look inside the `<xsl:result-document>` for an `<xsl:fallback>` element; if it finds one, it will process the contents of `<xsl:fallback>`. As we'll see a little later in this chapter, `<xsl:fallback>` can itself contain an `<xsl:fallback>`

element. The `<xsl:fallback>` element gives the XSLT processor a chance to respond gracefully when it can't perform the requested task.

Namespaces for Extensions

XSLT extension elements and extension functions must have a namespace prefix different from the XSLT namespace prefix. For example, here's the start of a stylesheet that declares several namespace prefixes:

```
<?xml version="1.0"?>
<xsl:stylesheet version="1.0"
  xmlns:xsl="http://www.w3.org/1999/XSL/Transform"
  xmlns:svg="http://www.w3.org/2000/svg"
  xmlns:xalan-java="http://xml.apache.org/xslt/java"
  xmlns:saxon-java="java:java.lang.Math"
  extension-element-prefixes="xalan-java saxon-java">
```

By default, the XSLT processor copies all of the non-XSLT namespaces to the output document. That means the `svg`, `xalan-java`, and `saxon-java` namespaces will be defined in the output. In this example, we're generating an SVG document using extensions associated with the `xalan-java` and `saxon-java` namespaces. We don't need our extension namespaces defined in the output document, so we use the `extension-element-prefixes` attribute to make sure they aren't in the generated document. The `svg` namespace, on the other hand, will appear in the output document, which is exactly what we want.

[2.0] Creating New Functions with `<xsl:function>`

XSLT 2.0 adds the `<xsl:function>` element. This lets you define your own functions in the stylesheet itself. This is the simplest extension that we'll examine in this chapter; the extension itself is in the same file and same syntax as the stylesheet, and the standard is very clear on how the function is defined and invoked. We'll use a simple stylesheet that creates a table in which the background color of each cell cycles through four different colors. Given the position of the current item, our function will return one of the four values.

To define a function, there are several things we have to do: define a (non-XSLT) namespace for the function, name the function, define what datatype it returns, and define the name and datatype of any parameters the function has. Defining a namespace is simple enough, although we need to remember to put our namespace prefix in the `exclude-result-prefixes` attribute of `<xsl:stylesheet>`. We'll call our function `getBackgroundColor`, and it will return an `xs:string` naming the background color of each table cell. Finally, the input to our function is an `xs:integer` of the position of the current item. The function looks like this:

```
<xsl:function name="sample:getBackgroundColor" as="xs:string">
  <xsl:param name="pos" as="xs:integer"/>
```

```
    <xsl:value-of select="$colors[($pos mod count($colors)) + 1]"/>
  </xsl:function>
```

The function is in the `sample` namespace, it returns a string, and it takes an integer as its only parameter. It references the variable `$colors` to retrieve a color name. Rather than use an XML document for input, we'll create a sequence of numbers and put each one in a table cell. Here's the stylesheet:

```
<?xml version="1.0" encoding="utf-8"?>
<!-- simple-function.xsl -->
<xsl:stylesheet version="2.0"
  xmlns:xsl="http://www.w3.org/1999/XSL/Transform"
  xmlns:xs="http://www.w3.org/2001/XMLSchema"
  xmlns:sample="http://www.oreilly.com/catalog/xslt"
  exclude-result-prefixes="xs sample">

  <xsl:output method="html" include-content-type="no"/>

  <xsl:variable name="colors" as="xs:string *"
    select="('green', 'grey', 'blue', 'red')"/>

  <xsl:template match="/">
    <html>
      <head>
        <title>A table with different background colors</title>
      </head>
      <body style="font-family: sans-serif;">
        <h1 style="font-size: 28;">
          A table with different background colors:
        </h1>
        <table border="3" cellpadding="5" cellspacing="5" width="50%">
          <tr>
            <xsl:for-each select="1 to 12">
              <td style="font-size: 48; color: black;
                         font-weight: bold; text-align: center;"
                bgcolor="{sample:getBackgroundColor(position())}">
                <xsl:value-of select="."/>
              </td>
            </xsl:for-each>
          </tr>
        </table>
      </body>
    </html>
  </xsl:template>

  <xsl:function name="sample:getBackgroundColor" as="xs:string">
    <xsl:param name="pos" as="xs:integer"/>
    <xsl:value-of select="$colors[($pos mod count($colors)) + 1]"/>
  </xsl:function>

</xsl:stylesheet>
```

In this example, we use the XPath 2.0 `to` operator to create a sequence of values, and then we invoke the `getBackgroundColor` function to set the background color of each table cell. Figure 9-1 shows how the results look in a browser.

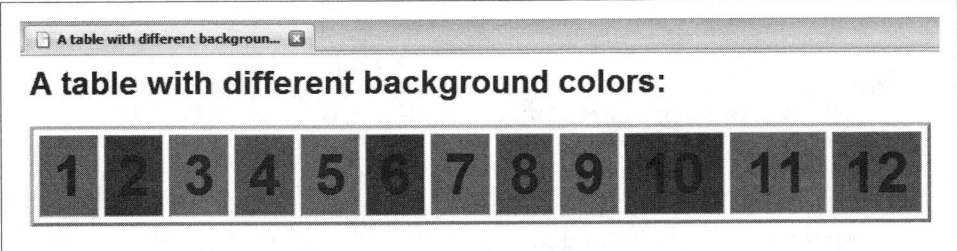

Figure 9-1. Results generated with <xsl:function>

To do the equivalent of this in XSLT 1.0, we would have to use logic like this:

```
<xsl:choose>
  <xsl:when test="position() mod 4 = 0">
    <!-- background color is xxx -->
  </xsl:when>
  <xsl:when test="position() mod 4 = 1">
    <!-- background color is xxx -->
  </xsl:when>
  ...
</xsl:choose>
```

This code is more verbose and is also less maintainable. If we change the number of colors in the sequence, we would have to change the XSLT 1.0 code. Our XSLT 2.0 function, on the other hand, uses the length of the sequence as part of its calculations, so we could add as many colors to the list as we'd like without changing the function code.

Example: Generating Multiple Output Files

The whole point of extensions is to allow you to add new capabilities to the XSLT processor. One of the most common needs is the ability to generate multiple output documents. As we saw earlier, the `document()` function allows you to have multiple input documents—but XSLT 1.0 doesn't give us any way to create these. Saxon's support for XSLT 2.0 includes the `<xsl:result-document>` element, which lets us generate multiple output documents. Although Xalan doesn't support XSLT 2.0, it does support an extension element (`<redirect:write>`) that does the same thing. We'll look at a stylesheet that uses `<xsl:fallback>` to generate useful results regardless of the processor we're using. If we're using Saxon or Xalan, we'll get multiple output documents that are hyperlinked together; if we're using any other processor, we'll get a single HTML file that contains the same information.

Here's the source document we'll use:

```
<?xml version="1.0"?>
<!-- chapters.xml -->
<book>
  <title>XSLT Topics</title>
  <chapter>
```

```
    <title>XPath</title>
    <para>If this chapter had any text, it would appear here.</para>
  </chapter>
  <chapter>
    <title>Stylesheet Basics</title>
    <para>If this chapter had any text, it would appear here.</para>
  </chapter>
...
  <chapter>
    <title>Combining XML Documents</title>
    <para>If this chapter had any text, it would appear here.</para>
  </chapter>
</book>
```

In addition to the `<xsl:fallback>` element, our stylesheet also uses the `element-available( )` function to determine what elements are available. If we can't generate multiple output documents (i.e., the elements we need aren't available), we create a single HTML file. If the elements are available, we first create a single HTML file with hyperlinks to the individual HTML files that we'll create later in the stylesheet. When we create the individual files, we'll use the `<xsl:result-document>` and `<redirect:write>` elements with `<xsl:fallback>` to handle with XSLT processors that don't support those elements.

Let's go through the relevant parts of this example. To begin with, our `<xsl:stylesheet>` element defines the `redirect` namespace prefix and tells the XSLT engine that the prefix will be used to refer to an extension element:

```
<?xml version="1.0" encoding="utf-8"?>
<!-- multiple-output-files.xsl -->
<xsl:stylesheet version="2.0"
  xmlns:xsl="http://www.w3.org/1999/XSL/Transform"
  xmlns:redirect="org.apache.xalan.xslt.extensions.Redirect"
  extension-element-prefixes="redirect">
```

The `extension-element-prefixes` attribute tells the XSLT processor that any element or function name with the `redirect` namespace prefix should be handled by an extension. When the processor encounters something from this namespace, it loads a piece of code and tells it to handle the request from the stylesheet. If we don't tell the XSLT processor that `redirect` is an extension element prefix, Xalan-J throws an error.

The syntax of everything we've done so far is according to the standard, although there's a fair amount of latitude in what the XSLT engines do with the information we've defined. For example, when defining the `redirect` namespace, Xalan uses the value as a Java classname. In other words, Xalan attempts to load the class `org.apache.xalan.xslt.extensions.Redirect` when it encounters an extension element or function defined with this namespace.

In the first part of our stylesheet, we use the `element-available( )` function to see whether the XSLT processor supports the XSLT 2.0 element `<result-document>`. In the second part, we tell the processor what to do, and we include `<xsl:fallback>` elements in case the processor doesn't support XSLT 2.0.

The first part of the stylesheet looks like this:

```
<xsl:choose>
  <xsl:when test="element-available('xsl:result-document')">
    <-- Create an external link and a list item for each <chapter> -->
  </xsl:when>
  <xsl:when test="element-available('redirect:write')">
    <-- Create an external link and a list item for each <chapter> -->
  </xsl:when>
  <xsl:otherwise>
    <-- Create an internal link and a list item for each <chapter> -->
  </xsl:otherwise>
</xsl:choose>
```

For the first two branches, we generate a link of the form `<a href="chaptern.html">`, where *n* is the position of the current chapter. For the last branch, we generate a link of the form `<a href="#chaptern">`. If the processor can generate multiple output files, we'll generate a link to that separate file; otherwise, we'll create a link to a section of the current document.

The second part of the stylesheet looks like this:

```
<xsl:result-document method="html"
  include-content-type="no"
  href="{concat('chapter', position(), '.html')}">
  <-- Create a separate HTML file for each <chapter> -->
  <xsl:fallback>
    <redirect:write select="concat('chapter', position(), '.html')">
      <-- Create a separate HTML file for each <chapter> -->
      <xsl:fallback>
        <-- Create a named anchor, an <h1> and a paragraph >
      </xsl:fallback>
    </redirect:write>
  </xsl:fallback>
</xsl:result-document>
```

We ask the XSLT processor to use the `<xsl:result-document>` element. If we're not using an XSLT 2.0 processor, this won't work, so the processor tries to use the `<xsl:fallback>` element. If we're using Xalan-J, the `<redirect:write>` element is supported; if not, the processor uses the last `<xsl:fallback>` element.

If our XSLT processor can generate multiple output files, the HTML document appears as in Figure 9-2.

Clicking on any of the links here takes us to one of the generated files. Each separate file looks as shown in Figure 9-3.

If the XSLT processor can't generate multiple output files, we get a single file that contains all of the text of all of the chapters. The document starts with a set of links to each section in the document, as shown in Figure 9-4.

Here's the complete stylesheet:

```
<?xml version="1.0" encoding="utf-8"?>
<!-- multiple-output-files.xsl -->
```

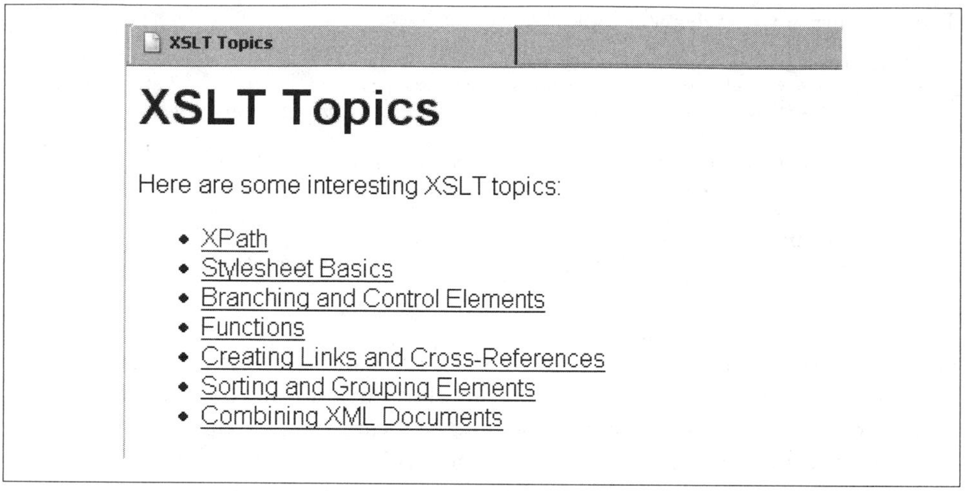

![XSLT Topics window]

XSLT Topics

Here are some interesting XSLT topics:

- XPath
- Stylesheet Basics
- Branching and Control Elements
- Functions
- Creating Links and Cross-References
- Sorting and Grouping Elements
- Combining XML Documents

Figure 9-2. HTML file with links to multiple output files

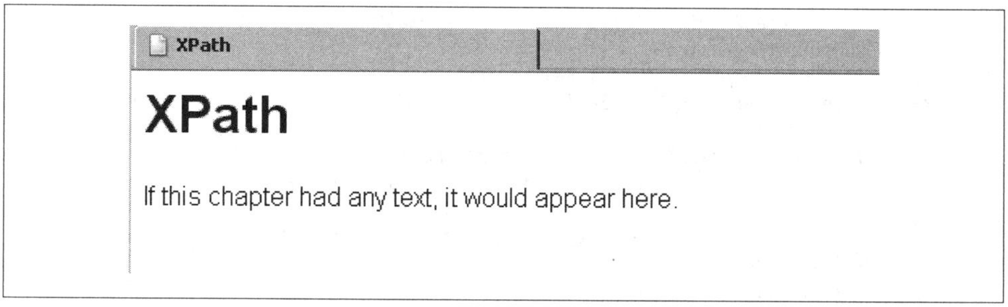

![XPath window]

XPath

If this chapter had any text, it would appear here.

Figure 9-3. An individual HTML output file

```
<xsl:stylesheet version="2.0"
  xmlns:xsl="http://www.w3.org/1999/XSL/Transform"
  xmlns:redirect="org.apache.xalan.xslt.extensions.Redirect"
  extension-element-prefixes="redirect">

<xsl:output method="html"/>

<xsl:template match="/">
  <html>
    <head>
      <xsl:comment>
        <xsl:text>Results generated by </xsl:text>
        <xsl:value-of select="system-property('xsl:vendor')"/>
      </xsl:comment>
      <title><xsl:value-of select="book/title"/></title>
    </head>
    <body style="font-family: sans-serif;">
      <h1><xsl:value-of select="book/title"/></h1>
      <p>Here are some interesting XSLT topics:</p>
      <ul>
```

XPath

If this chapter had any text, it would appear here.

Stylesheet Basics

If this chapter had any text, it would appear here.

Figure 9-4. A single HTML output file that contains all the text of all the chapters

```
<xsl:choose>
  <xsl:when test="element-available('xsl:result-document')">
    <xsl:apply-templates select="book/chapter" mode="separate-files"/>
  </xsl:when>
  <xsl:when test="element-available('redirect:write')">
    <xsl:apply-templates select="book/chapter" mode="separate-files"/>
  </xsl:when>
  <xsl:otherwise>
    <xsl:for-each select="book/chapter">
      <li>
        <a href="{concat('#chapter', position())}">
          <xsl:value-of select="title"/>
        </a>
      </li>
    </xsl:for-each>
  </xsl:otherwise>
</xsl:choose>
</ul>

<xsl:for-each select="book/chapter">
  <xsl:result-document method="html"
    include-content-type="no"
    href="{concat('chapter', position(), '.html')}">
    <xsl:apply-templates select="." mode="create-html-file"/>

    <xsl:fallback>
      <redirect:write
        select="concat('chapter', position(), '.html')">
        <xsl:apply-templates select="." mode="create-html-file"/>

        <xsl:fallback>
          <a name="{concat('chapter', position())}"/>
```

```
          <h1>
            <xsl:value-of select="title"/>
          </h1>
          <xsl:apply-templates select="*[position() > 1]"/>
        </xsl:fallback>
      </redirect:write>
    </xsl:fallback>
  </xsl:result-document>
</xsl:for-each>
        </body>
      </html>
    </xsl:template>

    <xsl:template match="chapter" mode="separate-files">
      <li>
        <a href="{concat('chapter', position(), '.html')}">
          <xsl:value-of select="title"/>
        </a>
      </li>
    </xsl:template>

    <xsl:template match="chapter" mode="create-html-file">
      <html>
        <head>
          <title><xsl:value-of select="title"/></title>
        </head>
        <body style="font-family: sans-serif;">
          <h1><xsl:value-of select="title"/></h1>
          <xsl:apply-templates select="*[position() > 1]"/>
        </body>
      </html>
    </xsl:template>

</xsl:stylesheet>
```

Notice that the stylesheet is a version 2.0 stylesheet. Telling an XSLT 1.0 processor that a stylesheet is an XSLT 2.0 stylesheet causes it to process the stylesheet in forwards-compatible mode. This means that it will ignore certain things that are errors in XSLT 1.0, and that it will go to the `<xsl:fallback>` element if it finds an element in the XSLT namespace that it doesn't recognize.

If you change the stylesheet to `version="1.0"`, Xalan (or MSXSL or whatever XSLT 1.0 processor you're using) raises a fatal error because the `<xsl:result-document>` element isn't defined in XSLT 1.0 either. If you're using *anything* from XSLT 2.0, be sure your `<xsl:stylesheet>` element clearly says so with the attribute `version="2.0"`.

In this relatively simple example, we've broken a single XML document into multiple HTML files, we've generated useful filenames for all of them, and we've automatically built hyperlinks to the different HTML files. For now, we've simply discussed how to *use* an extension; we'll talk about how to write your own extension next.

Creating Custom Collations

The XSLT 2.0 spec uses collations in several places. A collation defines how characters are sorted and compared. English doesn't have any accented characters or character sequences that sort as separate letters, so that's not an issue if all your documents are in English. Even if English is your native language, it's likely you'll need to work with documents written in other languages. In that case, characters such as the Spanish *ch* (considered a separate letter, the letter *che*) or accented characters such as the German umlaut-u, which can be written as *ü* or *ue*, become important in sorting and comparing words.

As with extension functions, the XSLT 2.0 spec defines attributes that can be used to indicate where custom collations can be used, but it doesn't define how to identify a particular piece of code that does the work. Because Saxon has taken the lead in implementing these functions, we'll focus on accessing custom collations in Saxon here. We'll look at two of these collations. The first sorts Spanish words so that *ch* sorts as a separate letter between *c* and *d*. The second collation compares German words so that *Müller* and *Mueller* are considered identical.

Your author is in no way a speaker of Spanish or German, so please pardon any incorrect statements about the languages themselves. The point here is to illustrate how to create extensions that implement custom collations and then use those extensions for sorting and comparing text in your stylesheets.

The traditional Spanish collation, the one we'll implement here, treats *ch*, *ll*, and *ñ* as separate letters that sort after *c*, *l*, and *n* respectively. However, much of the Spanish speaking world now uses the modern Spanish collation, defined by the Association of Spanish Language Academies (*La Asociación de Academias de Lingua Española*). The modern Spanish collation doesn't treat ch or ll as special characters; they sort as they would in English. The letter *ñ* still sorts after the letter *n*.

There are three collations for sorting German: DIN-1, DIN-2, and Austrian. (The DIN standards are defined by the standards body *Deutsches Institut Für Normung*.) The collation used varies from one country to the next. Typically DIN-1 is used for sorting words, although in Switzerland, it's also used for sorting names. DIN-2, the collation algorithm we'll implement here, is used for sorting names in Germany. Austria uses the Austrian collation, although it seems to be disappearing in favor of the DIN-2 rules. The main complication for the DIN-2 algorithm that we'll implement here is that ä is equal to ae, ö is equal to oe, ß is equal to ss, and ü is equal to ue. Our code has to realize that two characters in one word can be equivalent to one character in another word.

I believe the code samples here are correct implementations of the traditional Spanish and DIN-2 collation algorithms.

Using a Custom Collation for Sorting

To get started, we'll sort a short list of words:

```
<?xml version="1.0"?>
<!-- words.xml -->
<wordlist>
  <word>campo</word>
  <word>luna</word>
  <word>ciudad</word>
  <word>llaves</word>
  <word>chihuahua</word>
  <word>arroz</word>
  <word>limonada</word>
</wordlist>
```

This document contains Spanish words that are sorted differently than they would be in English. We'll write a stylesheet that uses two `<xsl:template>`s to illustrate how our extension function works. Here's the stylesheet:

```
<?xml version="1.0"?>
<!-- custom-collation1.xsl -->
<xsl:stylesheet version="2.0"
  xmlns:xsl="http://www.w3.org/1999/XSL/Transform"
  xmlns:xs="http://www.w3.org/2001/XMLSchema">

  <xsl:output method="text"/>

  <xsl:template match="/">
    <xsl:text>Test of sorting with custom collations:&#xA;&#xA;</xsl:text>
    <xsl:variable name="items" as="xs:string*" select="wordlist/word"/>
    <xsl:text>Word list in original order:&#xA;&#xA;</xsl:text>
    <xsl:value-of select="$items" separator="&#xA;"/>
    <xsl:text>&#xA;</xsl:text>
    <xsl:call-template name="ascending-alpha-sort">
      <xsl:with-param name="items" select="$items"/>
    </xsl:call-template>
    <xsl:call-template name="spanish-alpha-sort">
      <xsl:with-param name="items" select="$items"/>
    </xsl:call-template>
  </xsl:template>

  <xsl:template name="ascending-alpha-sort">
    <xsl:param name="items"/>
    <xsl:text>&#xA;Ascending text sort:&#xA;</xsl:text>
    <xsl:for-each select="$items">
      <xsl:sort/>
      <xsl:value-of select="."/>
      <xsl:text>&#xA;</xsl:text>
    </xsl:for-each>
  </xsl:template>

  <xsl:template name="spanish-alpha-sort">
    <xsl:param name="items"/>
    <xsl:text>&#xA;Spanish alpha sort:&#xA;</xsl:text>
```

```
    <xsl:for-each select="$items">
      <xsl:sort
        collation="{concat('http://saxon.sf.net/collation?',
                    'class=com.oreilly.xslt.SpanishCollation;')}"/>
      <xsl:value-of select="."/>
      <xsl:text>&#xA;</xsl:text>
    </xsl:for-each>
  </xsl:template>

</xsl:stylesheet>
```

 We have to use an attribute value template as the value of the collation attribute because we used the concat function to keep the code listing within the page. If we had coded this in a single line (collation="http://saxon.sf.net...."), the curly braces would not be necessary. If you aren't worried about how your stylesheets look when printed out, simply put everything as a long string and avoid concat and the curly braces altogether.

We use Saxon's scheme for identifying the class that performs the custom collation. (We used concat( ) to combine the two halves of the string so the listing fits on the page; normally you'd have the 70-character attribute value as a single string.) Saxon requires a particular URL, followed by a question mark and the keyword class=. Whatever follows class= is used as the name of the Java class. If that class can't be found or loaded, you'll get a fatal error. Here's the code for the extension that implements the custom collation:

```
/**
 * SpanishCollation.java
 */

package com.oreilly.xslt;

import java.text.ParseException;
import java.text.RuleBasedCollator;

public class SpanishCollation extends RuleBasedCollator
{
  public SpanishCollation() throws ParseException
  {
    super(traditionalSpanishRules);
  }

  private static String smallnTilde  = new String("\u00F1");
  private static String capitalNTilde = new String("\u00D1");

  private static String traditionalSpanishRules =
    ("< a,A < b,B < c,C < ch, cH, Ch, CH " +
     "< d,D < e,E < f,F < g,G < h,H < i,I " +
     "< j,J < k,K < l,L < ll, lL, Ll, LL " +
     "< m,M < n,N " +
```

```
         "< " + smallnTilde + "," + capitalNTilde + " " +
         "< o,O < p,P < q,Q < r,R < s,S < t,T " +
         "< u,U < v,V < w,W < x,X < y,Y < z,Z");
    }
```

The string `traditionalSpanishRules` contains the rules for character comparisons. Notice that it defines special cases for ch, ll, Ñ, and ñ. To create a custom collation, all we
have to implement is the string that defines the collation rules, then pass that to the
constructor of the `RuleBasedCollator` class. See the JDK documentation for all the details of the `java.text.RuleBasedCollator` class.

When we run the stylesheet against our document, it lists the words as they appear in
the document, and then it calls two templates that sort the words. The first uses the
default collation, so the words are sorted according to the rules of English. (English is
the default collation on *my* machine; your machine might be different.) The second
template invokes our Java class to do the comparisons between characters. The results
are different for the two templates:

```
Test of sorting with custom collations:

Word list in original order:

campo
luna
ciudad
llaves
chihuahua
arroz
limonada

Ascending text sort:
arroz
campo
chihuahua
ciudad
limonada
llaves
luna

Spanish alpha sort:
arroz
campo
ciudad
chihuahua
limonada
luna
llaves
```

As you can see, sorting the word list with the `SpanishCollation` class gives us different
results. `Chihuahua` sorts after `ciudad`, and `llaves` sorts after `luna`.

Using a Custom Collation for Comparing Text

The other way of using custom collations is in comparing text. Obviously comparing strings is part of sorting, but the new `compare( )` function in XQuery 1.0 and XPath 2.0 lets you compare two strings. To use an example from the XSLT 2.0 spec, the German word for *street* can be spelled *Straße* or *Strasse*. A simple character comparison defines sees these as two different strings; we'll use a collation function that recognizes the two words as being equal.

Here's the complete code:

```
/**
 * GermanCollation.java
 */

package com.oreilly.xslt;

import java.text.ParseException;
import java.text.RuleBasedCollator;

public class GermanCollation extends RuleBasedCollator
{
  public GermanCollation() throws ParseException
  {
    super(traditionalGermanRules);
  }

  private static String sharpS   = new String("\u00DF");
  private static String uppercaseUmlautA = new String("\u00C4");
  private static String lowercaseUmlautA = new String("\u00E4");
  private static String uppercaseUmlautO = new String("\u00D6");
  private static String lowercaseUmlautO = new String("\u00F6");
  private static String uppercaseUmlautU = new String("\u00DC");
  private static String lowercaseUmlautU = new String("\u00FC");

  private static String traditionalGermanRules =
    ("< a,A " +
     "<" + lowercaseUmlautA + "=ae " +
     "<" + uppercaseUmlautA + "=AE " +
     "< b,B < c,C < d,D < e,E < f,F " +
     "< g,G < h,H < i,I < j,J < k,K " +
     "< l,L < m,M < n,N < o,O " +
     "<" + lowercaseUmlautO + "=oe " +
     "<" + uppercaseUmlautO + "=OE " +
     "< p,P < q,Q < r,R < s,S " +
     "< ss=" + sharpS +
     "< t,T < u,U " +
     "<" + lowercaseUmlautU + "=ue " +
     "<" + uppercaseUmlautU + "=UE " +
     "< v,V < w,W < x,X < y,Y < z,Z");
  }
```

In the code, we define that certain strings are equal. There are seven special rules *that are defined in* our class; each of them is defined with an equals sign in the traditionalGermanRules string. (In the SpanishCollation class, we used a greater-than sign to indicate the sorting order.) Here is a stylesheet that compares two spellings of the German word for *street*:

```
<?xml version="1.0"?>
<!-- custom-collation2.xsl -->
<xsl:stylesheet version="2.0"
  xmlns:xsl="http://www.w3.org/1999/XSL/Transform"
  xmlns:xs="http://www.w3.org/2001/XMLSchema">

  <xsl:output method="text"/>

  <xsl:template match="/">
    <xsl:variable name="string1" select="'Stra&#xDF;e'"/>
    <xsl:variable name="string2" select="'Strasse'"/>

    <xsl:text>&#xA;Here is a test of the compare() </xsl:text>
    <xsl:text>function, using &#xA;</xsl:text>
    <xsl:text>  an extension function to compare German </xsl:text>
    <xsl:text>characters:&#xA;&#xA;</xsl:text>

    <xsl:text>  compare('</xsl:text>
    <xsl:value-of select="$string1"/>
    <xsl:text>', '</xsl:text>
    <xsl:value-of select="$string2"/>
    <xsl:text>') = </xsl:text>
    <xsl:value-of select="compare($string1, $string2)"/>
    <xsl:text>&#xA;</xsl:text>

    <xsl:text>  compare('</xsl:text>
    <xsl:value-of select="$string1"/>
    <xsl:text>', '</xsl:text>
    <xsl:value-of select="$string2"/>
    <xsl:text>', [German collation]) = </xsl:text>
    <xsl:value-of
      select="compare($string1, $string2,
              concat('http://saxon.sf.net/collation?',
                     'class=com.oreilly.xslt.GermanCollation;'))"/>
    <xsl:text>&#xA;</xsl:text>
  </xsl:template>

</xsl:stylesheet>
```

Here are the results:

```
Here is a test of the compare() function, using
  an extension function to compare German characters:

  compare('Straße', 'Strasse') = 1
  compare('Straße', 'Strasse', [German collation]) = 0
```

In the compare( ) function, a value of 1 means the first string sorts after the second, a value of -1 means the first string sorts before the second, and a value of 0 means the two strings are equal. In our results here, using the German collation indicates that

Straße and *Strasse* are identical, even though they're clearly two different sequences of characters.

Generating Hidden Word Graphics

A frequent abuse of the Web is scripts that attempt to create dozens of email accounts or buy hundreds of concert tickets by parsing HTML forms and responding to them. To counteract this, many web sites now feature hidden word graphics that contain a word along with visual noise (in our case, lines drawn through the text) so that only a human can read the word. This ensures that only a human can use the form. We'll look at an XSLT extension function that, given a word, generates a hidden word graphic and a web page.

Given a secret word, our extension function creates a graphic containing that word and an HTML form that displays the graphic and asks the user to type the word hidden in the graphic. (Obviously, a complete solution would generate the server-side code, transient cookies, and other things to process the form, but that's beyond what we'll cover here. Our focus is on how to create the XSLT extension that creates the graphic.)

Our stylesheet looks like this:

```
<?xml version="1.0"?>
<!-- hidden-word-test.xsl -->
<xsl:stylesheet version="1.0"
    xmlns:xsl="http://www.w3.org/1999/XSL/Transform"
  xmlns:saxon="java:com.oreilly.xslt.HiddenWord"
  xmlns:xalan="xalan://com.oreilly.xslt.HiddenWord"
  xmlns:ora="http://www.oreilly.com/xslt"
  extension-element-prefixes="saxon xalan ora">

<xsl:output method="html"/>

<xsl:template match="/">
  <html>
    <head>
      <title>
        Test of hidden word generator
      </title>
    </head>
    <body style="font-family: sans-serif;">
        <h1>Test of hidden word generator</h1>
      <xsl:comment>
        This <form> doesn't have a method or action
        attribute; a real form would, of course...
      </xsl:comment>
      <xsl:variable name="createGraphic">
        <xsl:choose>
          <xsl:when test="function-available('saxon:createJPEG')">
            <xsl:value-of select="saxon:createJPEG('hidden.jpg',
                                   'giraffe', 48, 200, 100)"/>
          </xsl:when>
```

```
        <xsl:when test="function-available('xalan:createJPEG')">
          <xsl:value-of select="xalan:createJPEG('hidden.jpg',
                             'monkey', 48, 200, 100)"/>
        </xsl:when>
        <xsl:when test="function-available('ora:createJPEG')">
          <xsl:value-of select="ora:createJPEG('hidden.jpg',
                             'okapi', 48, 200, 100)"/>
        </xsl:when>
        <xsl:otherwise>
          <xsl:value-of select="1"/>
        </xsl:otherwise>
      </xsl:choose>
    </xsl:variable>
    <form align="center">
      <p>Enter the word hidden in the graphic below:</p>
      <xsl:choose>
        <xsl:when test="number($createGraphic)">
          <p style="font-style: italic; font-size: 150%;">
            <xsl:text>Sorry, the image function isn't available.</xsl:text>
          </p>
        </xsl:when>
        <xsl:otherwise>
          <p>
            <img src="hidden.jpg" width="200" height="100" border="3"/>
          </p>
        </xsl:otherwise>
      </xsl:choose>
      <p>
        <input type="text" name="hiddenWord" size="20" maxlength="20"/>
      </p>
      <p>
        <input type="submit" value="Submit"/>
      </p>
    </form>
  </body>
</html>
  </xsl:template>

</xsl:stylesheet>
```

Our stylesheet uses the function-available( ) function to check for each version of the extension function. If we're running the Saxon processor, the first <xsl:when> returns true, the second branch is true if we're running Xalan, and the third <xsl:when> is true if we're running the .NET processor. That assumes, of course, that the appropriate libraries are accessible. If the Java runtime can't find the class, function-available( ) returns false.

Notice that the <xsl:choose> element is inside a <xsl:variable>. Our extension function returns 0 if the function is available and it works correctly. If none of the functions are avilable, the value of our variable is 1; the functions themselves can return a nonzero return code if something goes wrong.

Putting this code inside a variable lets the extension functions return a value that isn't written to the output document. At the bottom of the stylesheet, the test `number($createGraphic)` converts the value returned by the extension function to a number. If the value isn't zero, we print an error message. Otherwise, we generate the form that contains the generated graphic.

Java Version

The two Java-based processors use the same code; the stylesheet simply uses the Saxon and Xalan conventions to identify the extension class. The extension function takes as its input the secret word, the name of the created JPEG file, the font size for the text, and the width and height of the JPEG file. Given those parameters, the code chooses a font at random and creates a blank canvas of the requested size. The Java code then checks to make sure the selected font exists (because Java runs on so many non-Windows platforms, we need to make sure). Once the font is set, we measure the dimensions of the secret word written in the font at the requested font size. If the word is too wide to fit into the graphic, we reduce the font size by 2 points until the word fits inside the canvas.

Once the font and font size are set, we draw the word on the canvas and finish by drawing random lines over the text. When we've drawn everything on the canvas, a couple of lines of Java code write the canvas out to a JPEG file. The last few lines of code here handle any exceptions that might occur. Here's the complete listing:

```
/*
 * HiddenWord.java
 */

package com.oreilly.xslt;

import java.awt.BasicStroke;
import java.awt.Color;
import java.awt.Font;
import java.awt.FontMetrics;
import java.awt.Graphics2D;
import java.awt.GraphicsEnvironment;
import java.awt.Rectangle;
import java.awt.font.LineMetrics;
import java.awt.image.BufferedImage;
import java.io.FileNotFoundException;
import java.io.FileOutputStream;
import java.io.IOException;
import java.util.Random;

import com.sun.image.codec.jpeg.ImageFormatException;
import com.sun.image.codec.jpeg.JPEGCodec;
import com.sun.image.codec.jpeg.JPEGImageEncoder;

// This class creates a JPEG that contains a hidden word.
public class HiddenWord
```

```java
{
  // Three fonts likely to installed on any system...
  // If you want to generate hidden words in a non-Latin language,
  // you'll need to change the font names.
  public static String[] fontNames = {"Arial", "Times", "Verdana"};

  // createJPEG() is the name of the extension function.
  public static int createJPEG(String secretWord,
                               String outputFilename,
                               Double dFontSize,
                               Double dWidth,
                               Double dHeight)
    throws IOException, FileNotFoundException,
      ImageFormatException, Exception
  {
    int rc = 0;

    try
    {
      int fontSize = dFontSize.intValue();
      int width = dWidth.intValue();
      int height = dHeight.intValue();

      // Create a new BufferedImage.  We'll use it as a canvas;
      // we draw the hidden word and the lines that obscure it
      // onto the canvas, then write it out to a JPEG file.
      BufferedImage bi =
        new BufferedImage(width, height,
                          BufferedImage.TYPE_3BYTE_BGR);

      Random r = new Random();
      String fontName = fontNames[r.nextInt(fontNames.length)];

      // Fill the new graphic with a white background
      Graphics2D g = bi.createGraphics();
      g.setColor(Color.WHITE);
      g.fill(new Rectangle(0, 0, width, height));
      g.setColor(Color.BLACK);

      int fontStyle = Font.BOLD;
      int textWidth = 0;
      int textHeight = 0;

      // Now we have to load the font.  There's a chance the
      // font we selected isn't available, so we look through
      // the list of fonts until we find the one we're looking for.
      // If the font we want isn't available, we use Arial.
      // This is much more complicated than the .NET version,
      // where we assume the fonts are installed on every Windows
      // system.
      GraphicsEnvironment ge = GraphicsEnvironment.
                               getLocalGraphicsEnvironment();
      Font allFonts[] = ge.getAllFonts();
      Font chosenFont = new Font("Arial", fontStyle, fontSize);
      g.setFont(chosenFont);
```

```
FontMetrics fm = g.getFontMetrics();

boolean fontNotFound = true;
int j = 0;
while (fontNotFound && (j < allFonts.length))
{
  if (allFonts[j].getFontName().contains(fontName))
  {
    chosenFont = allFonts[j].deriveFont(fontStyle, fontSize);
    if (!chosenFont.getFontName().equalsIgnoreCase(fontName))
    {
      fontStyle = Font.PLAIN;
      chosenFont = allFonts[j].deriveFont(fontStyle, fontSize);
    }
    g.setFont(chosenFont);
    fm = g.getFontMetrics();

    // We look at the width and height of the word as drawn in
    // the current font.  If it's too big to fit into the graphic
    // canvas, we reduce the font size and try it again.
    textWidth = fm.stringWidth(secretWord);
    while (textWidth > width && fontSize > 2)
    {
      fontSize -= 2;
      chosenFont = allFonts[j].deriveFont(fontStyle, fontSize);
      g.setFont(chosenFont);
      fm = g.getFontMetrics();
      textWidth = fm.stringWidth(secretWord);
    }
    if (fontSize < 1)
      chosenFont = allFonts[j].deriveFont(fontStyle, 12);

    g.setFont(chosenFont);
    fontNotFound = false;
  }
  else
    j++;
}

// Now we draw the string onto the canvas.  We use the dimensions of
// the canvas itself and the dimensions of the string to center the
// text in the graphic.
fm = g.getFontMetrics(chosenFont);
LineMetrics lm =
  chosenFont.getLineMetrics(secretWord, g.getFontRenderContext());
textHeight = (int)lm.getAscent();
textWidth = fm.stringWidth(secretWord);
g.drawString(secretWord, (width - textWidth) / 2,
             textHeight + 30);

// Now we'll draw some lines at random to obscure the text.
g.setStroke(new BasicStroke((float)2.0));

for (int i = 0; i < width / 30; i++)
  g.drawLine(0, r.nextInt(height), width, r.nextInt(height));
```

```
      int numLines = java.lang.Math.max(height, width) / 30;
      for (int i = 0; i < numLines; i++)
      {
        int nextX = r.nextInt(width);
        g.drawLine(nextX, 0, nextX, height);
        int nextY = r.nextInt(height);
        g.drawLine(0, nextY, width, nextY);
      }

      for (int i = 0; i < height / 20; i++)
        g.drawLine(r.nextInt(width), 0, r.nextInt(width), height);

      // We've drawn everything on the canvas that we wanted, so we'll
      // write the contents of the canvas out to a JPEG file.
      FileOutputStream fos = new FileOutputStream(outputFilename);
      JPEGImageEncoder encoder = JPEGCodec.createJPEGEncoder(fos);
      encoder.encode(bi);
      fos.flush();
      fos.close();
    }
    catch (FileNotFoundException fnfe)
    {
      rc = 4;
      System.err.println(fnfe);
    }
    catch (IOException ioe)
    {
      rc = 8;
      System.err.println(ioe);
    }
    catch (Exception e)
    {
      rc = 12;
      System.err.println(e);
    }

    return rc;
  }
}
```

The generated HTML form looks like Figure 9-5.

To illustrate how text sizing works, Figure 9-6 shows a hidden word graphic with a much longer word.

As you can see, the font size has been reduced so that the word fits inside the graphic.

.NET Version

The .NET version works similarly, although we need two C# files to use the extension. The first creates the XslCompiledTransform object and associates the extension function with it. The second file actually implements the extension, creating the hidden word graphic.

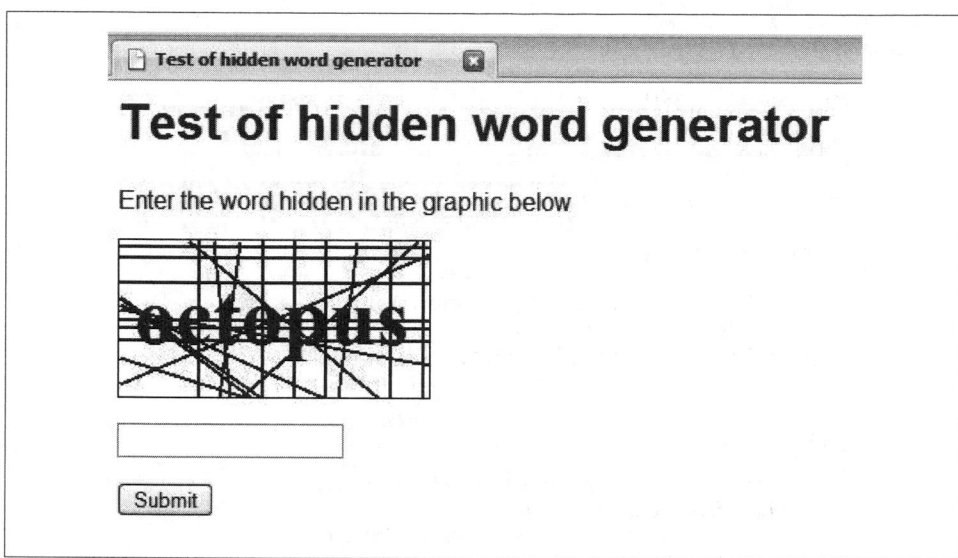

Figure 9-5. The HTML form with a hidden word graphic

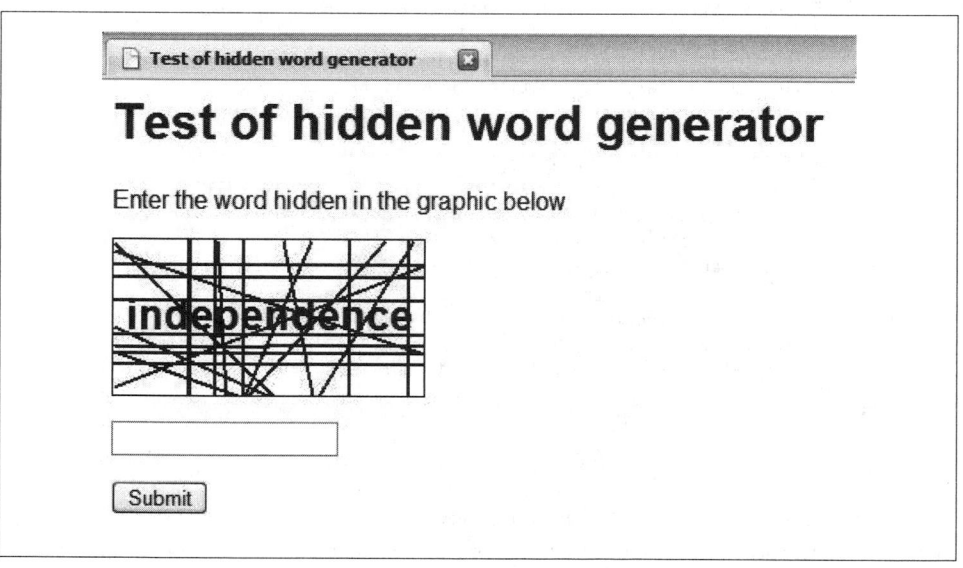

Figure 9-6. The HTML form with a longer hidden word

Here's the first C# file, which sets up the transformation object:

```
/*
 * Main.cs
 */

using System;
using System.Text;
```

```
using System.Xml;
using System.Xml.Xsl;

namespace com.oreilly.xslt
{
  class MainClass
  {
    static void Main(string[] args)
    {
      if (args.Length < 3)
      {
        System.Console.WriteLine("\nUsage: HiddenWordExample xml-file " +
          "xsl-file output-file");
        System.Console.WriteLine("\n  Example: HiddenWordExample " +
          "blank.xml hidden-word-test.xsl results.html");
      }
      else
      {
        // Create the stylesheet object and the XMLWriter that
        // writes the output to a file
        XslCompiledTransform stylesheet = new XslCompiledTransform();
        XmlTextWriter xWriter =
            new XmlTextWriter(args[2], Encoding.UTF8);

        // Use an XsltSettings object that allows executing scripts
        // (we need this for extensions), then load the stylesheet
        XsltSettings settings = new XsltSettings(true, true);
        stylesheet.Load(args[1], settings, new XmlUrlResolver());

        // Create an extension object
        HiddenWord hw = new HiddenWord();

        // We set up the extension function with an XsltArgumentList object.
        XsltArgumentList argList = new XsltArgumentList();
        argList.AddExtensionObject("http://www.oreilly.com/xslt", hw);

        // With everything in place, we call the Transform() method
        // to do the work...
        stylesheet.Transform(args[0], argList, xWriter);
      }
    }
  }
}
```

The C# file that creates the XslCompiledTransform has to define the object that implements the extension function (an instance of the HiddenWord class) and associate it with a namespace (http://www.oreilly.com/xslt). The namespace defined in the C# code must match the namespace defined in the stylesheet. When this code is built as an *.exe* file, it takes three arguments: the names of the input XML, the stylesheet, and the result files. If the user doesn't provide at least three arguments, we print an error message to avoid an IndexOutOfRange exception.

Now that we've set up the transformation, here's the actual code for the extension object. Although the methods and system objects are different from the Java version, the flow of the code is the same:

```
/*
 * HiddenWord.cs
 */

using System;
using System.Text;
using System.Xml;
using System.Xml.Xsl;
using System.Drawing;

// This class creates a JPEG that contains a hidden word.

namespace com.oreilly.xslt
{
  class HiddenWord
  {
    // Three fonts likely to be installed on a Windows system...
    // If you want to generate hidden words in a non-Latin language,
    // you'll need to change the font names.
    private static String[] fontNames = { "Arial", "Times", "Verdana" };

    // createJPEG() is the name of the extension function.
    public int createJPEG(String outputFilename,
                          String secretWord, Double dFontSize,
                          Double dWidth, Double dHeight)
    {
      int rc = 0;

      int fontSize = (int)dFontSize;
      int width = (int)dWidth;
      int height = (int)dHeight;

      Random r = new Random();

      String fontName = fontNames[r.Next(fontNames.Length)];

      // Create a new Bitmap.  We'll draw our text and graphics
      // onto the Bitmap, then write it out to a JPEG file.
      Bitmap pic = new Bitmap(width, height);
      Graphics context = Graphics.FromImage(pic);

      // First, fill the graphic with a white background
      SolidBrush brush = new SolidBrush(Color.White);
      context.FillRectangle(brush, 0, 0, width, height);

      // Load the randomly chosen font
      Font currentFont = new Font(fontName, fontSize, FontStyle.Bold);

      // Get the size of the word in the current font.  If it's too big
      // for the word to fit into the graphic, reduce the font size
      // until it fits.
```

```csharp
        SizeF textSize = context.MeasureString(secretWord, currentFont);
        float textWidth = textSize.Width;

        while (textWidth > width && fontSize > 2)
        {
          fontSize -= 2;
          currentFont = new Font(fontName, fontSize, FontStyle.Bold);
          textSize = context.MeasureString(secretWord, currentFont);
          textWidth = textSize.Width;
        }
        if (fontSize < 1)
          currentFont = new Font(fontName, 12, FontStyle.Bold);

        float textHeight = textSize.Height;
        brush.Color = Color.Black;

        // Now draw the string onto the bitmap.  We center the text
        // by using the dimensions of the bitmap and the dimensions
        // of the string as drawn in the current font.
        context.DrawString(secretWord, currentFont, brush,
            (width - textWidth) / 2, (height - textHeight) / 2);

        // Now we draw some lines on the bitmap.  We generate the start
        // and endpoints of the lines at random.
        Pen pen = new Pen(Color.Black, (float)3);
        for (int i = 0; i < width / 30; i++)
          context.DrawLine(pen, 0, r.Next(height), width, r.Next(width));

        int numLines = Math.Max(height, width) / 30;
        for (int i = 0; i < numLines; i++)
        {
          int nextX = r.Next(width);
          context.DrawLine(pen, nextX, 0, nextX, height);
          int nextY = r.Next(height);
          context.DrawLine(pen, 0, nextY, width, nextY);
        }

        for (int i = 0; i < height / 20; i++)
          context.DrawLine(pen, r.Next(width), 0, r.Next(width), height);

        // Now we've drawn everything on the bitmap, so we write it out
        // to a file, using the JPEG format
        pic.Save(outputFilename, System.Drawing.Imaging.ImageFormat.Jpeg);

        return rc;
      }
    }
  }
```

As you can see, the C# code follows the same basic pattern as the Java code. We create a new canvas, reduce the font size until the given word fits inside the graphic, and then draw the text and the lines that obfuscate it and write it out to a JPEG file.

In this example, we demonstrated how to create JPEG graphics from text inside a stylesheet. We could have selected a secret word as a global parameter to the stylesheet, or we could have selected something from an XML input document. As we mentioned, a complete solution would generate the server-side code to validate the word typed in by the user. Another thing to keep in mind is that the fonts we used here won't work for secret words written in non-Latin languages (Russian, Japanese, Greek, Chinese, Korean, and so forth). You could change the font names inside the code, or you could modify the stylesheet and the extension function to pass the font name as an argument from the stylesheet.

Example: Generating an SVG Pie Chart

As we outlined the functions and operators available in XPath and XSLT, you probably noticed that the mathematical functions at your disposal are rather limited, even in XSLT 2.0. In this example, we'll write an extension that provides a variety of trigonometric functions. We'll do this in several ways:

- We'll use the extension mechanisms in Xalan and Saxon to call static methods in the `java.lang.Math` class.
- We'll use the trigonometric functions in the EXSLT `math` library (more on EXSLT later).
- We'll use the Bean Scripting Framework, an interesting piece of code from the Apache Jakarta project that lets us write extension functions in a variety of scripting languages, including JRuby, JavaScript, Jython, and Jacl.
- We'll use classes from the .NET library to extend the Microsoft XSLT processor.

We'll start this section by building the stylesheet once, and then we'll discuss what's different in each iteration. Our scenario is that we want to generate a Scalable Vector Graphics (SVG) pie chart from an XML document. This document contains the sales figures for different stores of a company; we need to calculate the dimensions of the various slices of the pie graph for our SVG document. Here's the XML source we'll be working with:

```
<?xml version="1.0" encoding="utf-8"?>
<!-- chocolate-sales.xml -->
<report month="8" year="2006">
  <caption>
    <heading>Chocolate bar sales</heading>
    <subheading>(units)</subheading>
  </caption>
  <store>
    <name>Carrboro</name>
    <brand name="Lindt">27408</brand>
    <brand name="Callebaut">8203</brand>
    <brand name="Valrhona">22101</brand>
    <brand name="Perugina">14336</brand>
    <brand name="Ghirardelli">19268</brand>
  </store>
  <store>
```

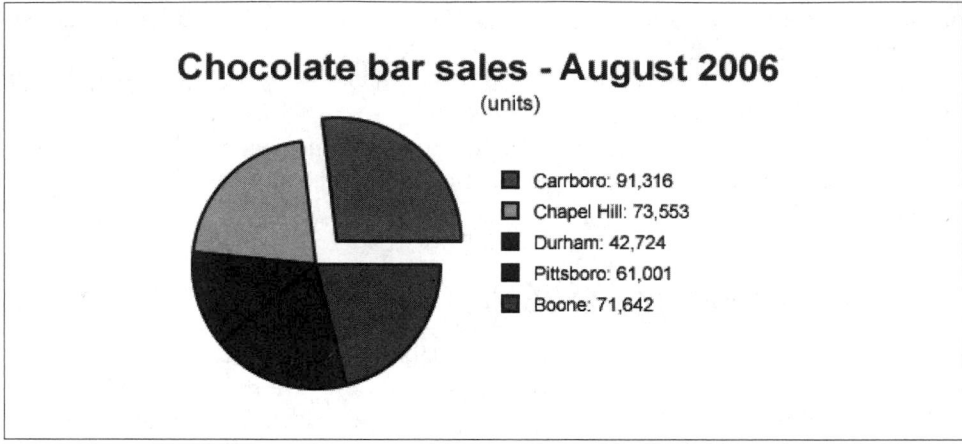

Figure 9-7. Our SVG pie chart

```
        <name>Chapel Hill</name>
        <brand name="Lindt">28503</brand>
        <brand name="Valrhona">7287</brand>
        <brand name="Perugina">12077</brand>
        <brand name="Ghirardelli">8392</brand>
        <brand name="Callebaut">17294</brand>
      </store>

  ...

      </store>
    </report>
```

Our goal is to create an SVG file that looks like Figure 9-7.

To make our pie chart really useful, we'll take advantage of the scripting support available in the Adobe SVG Viewer. We'll generate the graphics of the chart, as well as EcmaScript functions to display additional detail. For example, moving the mouse over a slice of the pie shows the details for a particular store, as shown in Figure 9-8.

We'll take advantage of SVG's functions for line joins and other details that let our chart look as professional as possible. For example, we can zoom in on the graph, and the shapes and lines and text still look sharp, as shown in Figure 9-9.

 The EcmaScript code we generate here is compatible with the Adobe SVG Viewer only; currently, Firefox displays the SVG pie chart, but it doesn't support any of the interactivity provided by the EcmaScript code.

XPath's limited math functions won't allow us to calculate the dimensions of the various arcs that make up the pie chart, so we'll use extension functions to solve this

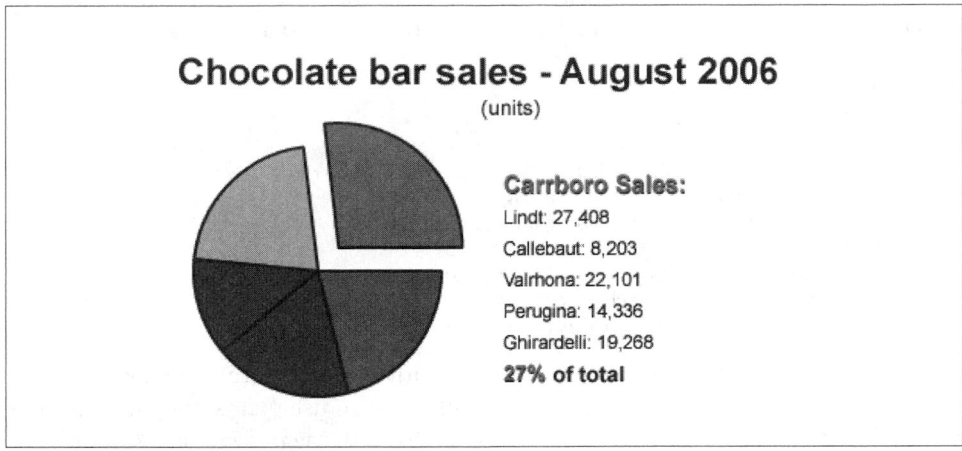

Figure 9-8. SVG chart changes in response to mouse events

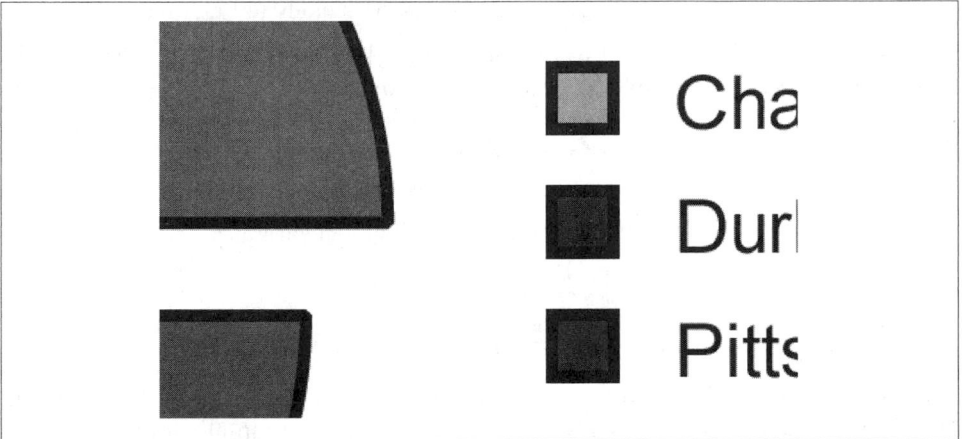

Figure 9-9. The pie chart scales to any resolution

problem. Fortunately for us, Java provides all the basic trigonometric functions we need in the `java.lang.Math` class. Even better, Xalan and Saxon make it easy for us to load this class and execute the static methods we need (`sin( )`, `cos( )` and `toRadians( )`). For the .NET case, we'll add a CDATA section containing EcmaScript code that the .NET XSLT processor can interpret.

> EcmaScript is the name for the version of JavaScript standardized by the European Computer Manufacturers Association. We'll use the term "EcmaScript" here because the examples in the SVG spec use `<script type="text/ecmascript">` (although most people use the terms "Ecma-Script" and "JavaScript" interchangeably).

We'll go over the relevant details as they appear in the stylesheet. First, we have to declare our namespace prefixes, just as we did when we used an extension element:

```
<?xml version="1.0"?>
<!-- piechart.xsl -->
<xsl:stylesheet version="1.0"
  xmlns:xsl="http://www.w3.org/1999/XSL/Transform"
  extension-element-prefixes="xalan-java saxon-java msxsl ora months"
  xmlns:svg="http://www.w3.org/2000/svg"
  xmlns:xalan-java="http://xml.apache.org/xslt/java"
  xmlns:saxon-java="java:java.lang.Math"
  xmlns:msxsl="urn:schemas-microsoft-com:xslt"
  xmlns:ora="http://www.oreilly.com/xslt"
  xmlns:months="http://www.oreilly.com/xslt/months">
```

We associated the `xalan-java` namespace prefix with the string `http://xml.apache.org/xslt/java`; Xalan uses this string to load Java classes and use their static methods. For Saxon support, we associated the `saxon-java` prefix with `java:java.lang.Math`. Notice that the two processors use different methods to load Java classes. The XSLT spec doesn't define any rules for how the namespace URIs are used to identify code that should be loaded by the processor, so each processor is likely to be different.

We also defined the `msxsl` and `ora` namespaces. The `msxsl` namespace lets us add EcmaScript directly to the stylesheet; we'll use the `ora` namespace to access that code. Finally, we define the `months` namespace. The stylesheet will contain a number of `<months:month>` elements, each of which defines the English name of a month of the year.

Next we define the output method and a couple of global variables:

```
<xsl:output method="xml"/>

<xsl:variable name="totalSales" select="sum(//brand)"/>
<xsl:variable name="stores" select="count(/report/store)"/>
```

Because SVG is an XML vocabulary, our output method is `xml`. The variable `$totalSales` is the total of all sales of all brands of chocolate in all stores, while the variable `$stores` is the number of stores in the report. We could recalculate these values every time we need them, but it's simpler to store them in global variables.

Next we define the `match="/"` template. This defines the `<svg>` element that contains our entire SVG document. Here's what the start of the template looks like:

```
<svg:svg width="450" height="300" version="1.1"
  baseProfile="full"
  xmlns="http://www.w3.org/2000/svg"
  xmlns:xlink="http://www.w3.org/1999/xlink"
  xmlns:ev="http://www.w3.org/2001/xml-events">
```

We're defining the dimensions of the SVG graphic and the version of SVG we're using, along with some namespaces the SVG interpreter needs. Now it's time to generate the EcmaScript functions that make our pie chart interactive. The original display of the pie chart shows the slices of the pie and a legend. Each slice of the pie is in a different color, and the legend identifies the store associated with each piece of the pie and the total sales at each store. In addition, a pie slice for the first store in the XML source document is detached from the rest of the pie chart (this is sometimes called an "exploded" slice).

The EcmaScript code uses two state variables. The first is a boolean variable (`detailsViewOn`) that indicates whether the legend area is displaying the default legend or the detailed sales numbers for a particular store. The second is an integer (`currentStore`) that represents the number of the store whose detailed sales figures are currently displayed. The way the pie chart responds to mouse events is determined by the values of these two variables.

Here's what the EcmaScript functions do:

- When the user moves the mouse over a particular slice of the pie:
  — If the legend area of the chart *is not* permanently displaying the details for a particular store (`detailsViewOn` = `false`), the legend is replaced with the detailed sales numbers for the store associated with that slice of the pie.
  — If the legend area of the chart *is* permanently displaying the details for a particular store (`detailsViewOn` = `true`), nothing happens.

- When the user moves the mouse out of a particular slice of the pie:
  — If the legend area of the chart *is not* permanently displaying the details for a particular store (`detailsViewOn` = `false`), then the detailed sales numbers for the store associated with the slice of pie are replaced with the default legend.
  — If the legend area of the chart *is* permanently displaying the details for a particular store (`detailsViewOff` = `true`), nothing happens.

- When the user clicks on a particular slice of the pie:
  — If the legend area of the chart *is not* permanently displaying the details for a particular store (`detailsViewOn` = `false`), display the detailed sales numbers in place of the default legend, set `detailsViewOn` = `true` and set the value of the current store (`currentStore` = `x`, where `x` is the number of the current store).
  — If the legend area of the chart *is* permanently displaying the details for a particular store (`detailsViewOn` = `true`) *and* the store number corresponding to the clicked-upon slice is the same as the current store, then set `detailsViewOn` = `false` and set the value of the current store to `0`.
  — If the legend area of the chart *is* permanently displaying the details for a particular store (`detailsViewOn` = `true`), but the store number corresponding to the clicked-upon slice *is not the same* as the current slice, set the value of the current store to the new value and replace the legend area with the detailed sales numbers for the new current store.

To sum up the behavior of the pie chart, the user can mouse over a slice of the pie to see detailed sales figures for a particular store. The user can click on a slice of pie to see the details for that store permanently. Once the details for a particular store are displayed permanently, the user can click on another slice of the pie to see that store's details permanently, or they can click on the current store to return to the original display. (I hope that's clear; it's easy to figure out how the code works by interacting with it.)

We'll define three functions (mouse_over( ), mouse_out( ), and click( )) that handle the mouse events we care about. Here they are:

```
<svg:script type="text/ecmascript">
  <xsl:text disable-output-escaping="yes">

detailsViewOn = false;
currentStore = 0;

function mouse_over(selectedItem, totalItems)
{
  if (!detailsViewOn || selectedItem == currentStore)
  {
    for (i = 1; totalItems >= i; i++)
    {
      obj = svgDocument.getElementById("details" + i);
      obj.setAttributeNS(null, "visibility", "hidden");
      obj = svgDocument.getElementById("legend" + i);
      obj.setAttributeNS(null, "visibility", "hidden");
    }

    obj = svgDocument.getElementById("details" + selectedItem);
    obj.setAttributeNS(null, "visibility", "visible");
  }
}

function mouse_out(totalItems)
{
  if (!detailsViewOn)
  {
    for (i = 1; totalItems >= i; i++)
    {
      obj = svgDocument.getElementById("details" + i);
      obj.setAttributeNS(null, "visibility", "hidden");
      obj = svgDocument.getElementById("legend" + i);
      obj.setAttributeNS(null, "visibility", "visible");
    }
  }
}

function click(selectedItem, totalItems)
{
  if (selectedItem != currentStore)
  {
    currentStore = selectedItem;
    mouse_over(selectedItem, totalItems);
    detailsViewOn = true;
  }
```

```
    else
    {
      obj = svgDocument.getElementById("details" + selectedItem);
      if (obj.getAttributeNS(null, "visibility") == "visible")
      {
        detailsViewOn = false;
        currentStore = 0;
      }
      else
      {
        currentStore = selectedItem;
        mouse_over(selectedItem, totalItems);
        detailsViewOn = true;
      }
    }
  }
}
        //        </xsl:text></svg:script>
      <xsl:text>&#xA;</xsl:text>
```

Notice that we used `disable-output-escaping` so we don't have to worry about greater-than or less-than signs tripping up the XML parser.

> If you're writing script code in an HTML file, you should write it inside a comment, allowing browsers that don't support scripting to safely ignore the code. The end of the script code should look like this:
>
> ```
>     ...
>         else
>         {
>           currentItem = selectedItem;
>           mouse_over(selectedItem, totalItems);
>           detailsViewOn = true;
>         }
>       }
>     }
>     //       -->
> ```
>
> The double slash at the end of the script is a comment, which tells the scripting engine to ignore the `-->` at the end of the `<xsl:comment>` element. Without this slash, some processors attempt to process the end of the comment and issue an error message; after all, the `--` looks like the decrement operator. Keep this in mind when you're generating script code with your stylesheets; if you don't, you'll have trouble tracking down the occasional errors that occur in some browsers.

One more thing to note about generating EcmaScript code: in some cases you may want to put the code in a separate file. SVG allows you to put the EcmaScript code in a separate file and reference it from the SVG. (We did this in the first edition of this book.) Given the current state of the Adobe SVG Viewer, it's much simpler to put the Ecma-Script code in the same file.

Now that we've created the EcmaScript code we need, we create the title and subtitle for the pie chart:

```
<!-- Generate the title and subtitle.  We draw the title and -->
<!-- subtitle on the chart, and we set the <svg:title> element -->
<!-- in the SVG document itself. -->
<xsl:variable name="titleText">
  <xsl:value-of select="/report/caption/heading"/>
  <xsl:text> - </xsl:text>
  <xsl:choose>
    <xsl:when test="function-available('math:cos')">
      <xsl:variable name="dateString">
        <xsl:text>--</xsl:text>
        <xsl:if test="string-length(/report/@month) = 1">
          <xsl:text>0</xsl:text>
        </xsl:if>
        <xsl:value-of select="/report/@month"/>
        <xsl:text>--</xsl:text>
      </xsl:variable>
      <xsl:value-of
        select="dates-and-times:month-name($dateString)"/>
      <xsl:text> </xsl:text>
    </xsl:when>
    <xsl:otherwise>
      <xsl:value-of select="/report/@month"/>
      <xsl:text>/</xsl:text>
    </xsl:otherwise>
  </xsl:choose>
  <xsl:value-of select="/report/@year"/>
</xsl:variable>

<svg:title>
  <xsl:value-of select="$titleText"/>
</svg:title>
<svg:text font-size="24px" text-anchor="start"
  font-weight="bold" x="10" y="40">
  <xsl:value-of select="$titleText"/>
</svg:text>
<svg:text font-size="14px" text-anchor="middle" y="60" x="225">
  <xsl:value-of select="/report/caption/subheading"/>
</svg:text>
```

Notice that we draw the text on the SVG canvas and also create an `<svg:title>` element for the SVG document. When the SVG document is rendered in a browser, this is treated as the title for the document. It's analogous to the HTML `<title>` element.

Now we're finally ready to process the `<store>` elements. Each `<store>` element contains the sales details for a particular store. We'll process each of these elements three ways:

1. First we create the pie slice. We'll look at the details in a minute, but our primary task here is to calculate the dimensions of the slice and to add the appropriate `onmouseover`, `onmouseout`, and `onclick` attributes. We do this in the `<xsl:template match="store" mode="pie">` template.

2. Next we create this store's entry in the legend. The legend has a colored square filled with the color for the current store, its name, and its total sales. The legend

entry for each store is drawn 20 pixels below the previous store's entry. We do this in the `<xsl:template match="store" mode="legend">` template.

3. Finally we create the detailed sales figures for the current store. The details view includes the name of the store, the sales of each brand at that store, and the current store's sales as a percentage of the total sales. Everything in the details view is drawn with the attribute `visibility="hidden"`. The details for a particular store are hidden until a particular mouse event occurs. This is done in the `<xsl:template match="store" mode="details">` template.

We'll go through these steps in detail now:

1. First of all, we need to draw the pie slice. This is done with an `<svg:path>` element. We'll use the trigonometry functions to calculate the angles of the edges of the pie slices, and we'll use SVG to draw a smooth arc between the outer endpoints of the edges. SVG also handles the details of joining the lines and filling the slice with a particular color.

2. For each slice of the pie, we calculate certain values and pass them as parameters to the `mode="pie"` template. First, we determine the color of the slice and the total sales for this particular store. We use the `position()` function and the `mod` operator to calculate the color, and we use the `sum()` function to calculate the sales for this store.

3. If this is the first slice of the pie, we'll explode it. That means that the first slice will be offset from the rest of the pie. We will set the variable `$explode` as follows:

   ```
   <xsl:variable name="explode" select="position()=1"/>
   ```

4. The last value we calculate is the total sales of all previous stores. When we draw each slice of the pie, we rotate the coordinate axis a certain number of degrees. The amount of the rotation depends on how much of the total sales have been drawn so far. In other words, if we've drawn exactly 50% of the total sales, we'll rotate the axis 180 degrees (50% of 360). Rotating the axis simplifies the trigonometry we have to do. To calculate our total sales, we use the `preceding-sibling` axis:

   ```
   <xsl:with-param name="runningTotal"
     select="sum(preceding-sibling::store/brand)"/>
   ```

5. Once we've calculated all the variables we need, we invoke the template:

   ```
   <xsl:apply-templates select="." mode="pie">
     <xsl:with-param name="color" select="$color"/>
     <xsl:with-param name="storeSales" select="$storeSales"/>
     <xsl:with-param name="totalSales" select="$totalSales"/>
     <xsl:with-param name="runningTotal"
       select="sum(preceding-sibling::store/brand)"/>
     <xsl:with-param name="stores" select="$stores"/>
     <xsl:with-param name="explode" select="$explode"/>
   </xsl:apply-templates>
   ```

6. Inside the template itself, our first step is to calculate the angle in radians of the current slice of the pie. This is the first time we use one of our extension functions:

```
<xsl:variable name="currentAngle">
  <xsl:choose>
    <xsl:when
      test="function-available('xalan-java:java.lang.Math.toRadians')">
      <xsl:value-of
        select="xalan-java:java.lang.Math.toRadians(
                ($storeSales div $totalSales) * 360.0)"/>
    </xsl:when>
    <xsl:when
      test="function-available('saxon-java:toRadians')">
      <xsl:value-of
        select="saxon-java:toRadians(
                ($storeSales div $totalSales) * 360.0)"/>
    </xsl:when>
    <xsl:when test="function-available('ora:cos')">
      <xsl:value-of
        select="($storeSales div $totalSales) *
                6.28318530717958647692528676655559"/>
    </xsl:when>
    <xsl:otherwise>
      <xsl:message terminate="yes">
        <xsl:text>Sorry, this stylesheet can't generate any </xsl:text>
        <xsl:text>useful results &#xA;  without trigonometric </xsl:text>
        <xsl:text>functions available. </xsl:text>
      </xsl:message>
    </xsl:otherwise>
  </xsl:choose>
</xsl:variable>
```

In calculating the value of the variable, we use the XSLT function-available( ) function. If we're processing this stylesheet with Xalan, the functions in the xalan-java namespace will be available. If we're using Saxon, the functions in the saxon-java namespace will be available. If we're using the .NET processor, the functions in the ora namespace will be available. If none of these functions are available, we terminate the processor. We can't generate a pie chart without trigonometric functions, so we exit.

The $currentAngle variable stores the angle in radians of the current pie slice. In other words, if the current store has 25% of the total sales for the company, we convert 90 degrees into radians and use that value to draw the slice of the pie. (We have to use radians because that's what the Java cos( ) and sin( ) functions require.) We'll use this value later with the cos( ) and sin( ) functions.

7. Now we're finally ready to draw the pie slice. We'll do this with an SVG <path> element. Here's what one looks like; we'll discuss what the attributes mean in a minute:

```
<svg:path
  fill="blue"
  stroke="black"
  stroke-width="2px"
  fillrule="evenodd"
  stroke-linejoin="bevel"
```

```
onmouseout="mouse_out(5);"
onmouseover="mouse_over(3, 5);"
onclick="click(3, 5);"
transform="translate(100,160)  rotate(-219.65188868902763)"
d="M 80 0 A 80 80 0 0 0 34.3848056509693 -72.23354581041326 L 0 0 Z "/>
```

This intimidating element was generated by this equally intimidating stylesheet fragment:

```
<svg:path fill="{$color}" stroke="black" stroke-width="2px"
    fillrule="evenodd" stroke-linejoin="bevel">
  <xsl:attribute name="onmouseout">
    <xsl:text>mouse_out(</xsl:text>
    <xsl:value-of select="$stores"/>
    <xsl:text>);</xsl:text>
  </xsl:attribute>
  <xsl:attribute name="transform">
    <xsl:choose>
      <xsl:when test="$explode">
        <xsl:text>translate(</xsl:text>
        <xsl:choose>
          <xsl:when
            test="function-available('xalan-java:java.lang.Math.cos')">
            <xsl:value-of
              select="(xalan-java:java.lang.Math.cos(
                      $currentAngle div 2) * 20) + 100"/>
            <xsl:text>,</xsl:text>
            <xsl:value-of
              select="(xalan-java:java.lang.Math.sin($currentAngle div 2)
                      * -20) + 160"/>
          </xsl:when>
          <xsl:when
            test="function-available('saxon-java:cos')">
            <xsl:value-of
              select="(saxon-java:cos($currentAngle div 2) * 20) + 100"/>
            <xsl:text>,</xsl:text>
            <xsl:value-of
              select="(saxon-java:sin($currentAngle div 2) * -20) + 160"/>
          </xsl:when>
          <xsl:when test="function-available('ora:cos')">
            <xsl:value-of
              select="(ora:cos($currentAngle div 2) * 20) + 100"/>
            <xsl:text>,</xsl:text>
            <xsl:value-of
              select="(ora:sin($currentAngle div 2) * -20) + 160"/>
          </xsl:when>
        </xsl:choose>
        <xsl:text>) </xsl:text>
      </xsl:when>
      <xsl:otherwise>
        <xsl:text>translate(100,160) </xsl:text>
      </xsl:otherwise>
    </xsl:choose>
    <xsl:text> rotate(</xsl:text>
    <xsl:value-of select="-1 * (($runningTotal div $totalSales) * 360.0)"/>
    <xsl:text>)</xsl:text>
  </xsl:attribute>
```

```
      </xsl:attribute>
      <xsl:attribute name="onmouseover">
        <xsl:text>mouse_over(</xsl:text>
        <xsl:value-of select="$position"/>
        <xsl:text>, </xsl:text>
        <xsl:value-of select="$stores"/>
        <xsl:text>);</xsl:text>
      </xsl:attribute>
      <xsl:attribute name="onclick">
        <xsl:text>click(</xsl:text>
        <xsl:value-of select="$position"/>
        <xsl:text>, </xsl:text>
        <xsl:value-of select="$stores"/>
        <xsl:text>);</xsl:text>
      </xsl:attribute>
      <xsl:attribute name="d">
        <xsl:text>M 80 0 A 80 80 0 </xsl:text>
        <xsl:choose>
          <xsl:when test="$currentAngle > 3.14">
            <xsl:text>1 </xsl:text>
          </xsl:when>
          <xsl:otherwise>
            <xsl:text>0 </xsl:text>
          </xsl:otherwise>
        </xsl:choose>
        <xsl:text>0 </xsl:text>
        <xsl:choose>
          <xsl:when test="function-available('xalan-java:java.lang.Math.cos')">
            <xsl:value-of
              select="xalan-java:java.lang.Math.cos($currentAngle) * 80"/>
            <xsl:text> </xsl:text>
            <xsl:value-of
              select="xalan-java:java.lang.Math.sin($currentAngle) * -80"/>
          </xsl:when>
          <xsl:when test="function-available('saxon-java:cos')">
            <xsl:value-of select="saxon-java:cos($currentAngle) * 80"/>
            <xsl:text> </xsl:text>
            <xsl:value-of select="saxon-java:sin($currentAngle) * -80"/>
          </xsl:when>
          <xsl:when test="function-available('ora:cos')">
            <xsl:value-of
              select="ora:cos($currentAngle) * 80"/>
            <xsl:text> </xsl:text>
            <xsl:value-of
              select="ora:sin($currentAngle) * -80"/>
          </xsl:when>
        </xsl:choose>
        <xsl:text> L 0 0 Z </xsl:text>
      </xsl:attribute>
    </svg:path>
```

We'll cover the attributes of the SVG element in order. The fill attribute defines what color to use when filling the path. stroke defines the color of the line used to draw the path, and stroke-width defines the width of that line. fillrule and stroke-linejoin define details of how a path is filled and how lines are joined.

Next we generate the calls to our script functions. If this is the third slice (out of five) of the pie, calls to the script functions look like this:

```
onmouseout="mouse_out(5);"
onmouseover="mouse_over(3, 5);"
onclick="click(3, 5);"
```

The `mouse_out` function takes as its argument the number of slices of pie. It makes all of the details view elements hidden, and it makes the legend elements visible. (Those elements have `id`s of `legend1`, `details1`, and so forth.) `mouse_over` takes the value of the current slice of pie (the one that has the mouse over it) and the number of slices of pie. The `click` function also takes the value of the current slice of pie and the number of slices.

The real work begins with the `transform` attribute. It contains two operators, `translate` and `rotate`. What we're doing with the `transform` attribute is changing the position of the point (`0,0`) and the direction of the X and Y axes. We'll move and rotate the origin so the first side of the slice of the pie is along the X axis. (Trust me, it simplifies the math.)

That brings us to the gloriously cryptic d attribute. This attribute contains a number of drawing commands; in our previous example, we move the current point to (`80,0`) (`M` stands for move), and then we draw an elliptical arc (`A` stands for arc) with various properties. Finally, we draw a line (`L` stands for line) from the current point (the end of our arc) to the origin, and then we use the `Z` command, which closes the path by drawing a line from wherever we are to wherever we started.

If you really must know what the properties of the `A` command are, they are the two radii of the ellipse, the degrees by which the x-axis should be rotated, two parameters called the large-arc-flag and the sweep-flag that determine how the arc is drawn, and the x- and y-coordinates of the end of the arc. In our example here, the two radii of the ellipse are the same (we want the pie to be round, not elliptical). Next is the x-axis rotation, which is `0`. After that is the large-arc-flag, which is `1` if this particular slice of the pie is greater than 180 degrees: it's `0` otherwise. The sweep-flag is `0`, and the last two parameters, the x- and y-coordinates of the end point, are calculated. See the SVG specification for more details on the `path` and `shape` elements.

8. Our next task is to draw all of the legends. We'll create a separate legend for each slice of the pie. Initially, all of the separate legends will be invisible (`<g style="visibility:hidden">`, in SVG parlance); as we mouse over the various slices of the pie, different legends will become visible or invisible.

When we apply our template, we pass in several parameters, including the color of the box in the legend entry and the y-coordinate offset where the legend entry should be drawn. We call this template once for each `<store>` element, ensuring that our legend identifies each slice of the pie, regardless of how many slices there are. For each slice, we draw a box filled with the appropriate color and write the name of the store next to it. We increment the y-coordinate by 20 pixels for each

Figure 9-10. An item in the legend

item in the legend. To enable the EcmaScript functions we mentioned earlier, we give each item in the legend an ID: legend1 for the first slice, legend2 for the second, and so on.

Here's the template:

```
<xsl:template match="store" mode="legend">
  <xsl:param name="color" select="'red'"/>
  <xsl:param name="storeSales" select="'0'"/>
  <xsl:param name="y-legend-offset" select="'0'"/>
  <xsl:param name="position" select="'1'"/>

  <svg:g id="legend{$position}">

    <svg:text font-size="12px" text-anchor="start" x="240">
      <xsl:attribute name="y">
        <xsl:value-of select="$y-legend-offset"/>
      </xsl:attribute>
      <xsl:value-of select="name"/>
      <xsl:text>: </xsl:text>
      <xsl:value-of select="format-number($storeSales, '#,###.#')"/>
    </svg:text>

    <svg:path stroke="black" stroke-width="2px" fill="{$color}">
      <xsl:attribute name="d">
        <xsl:text>M 220 </xsl:text>
        <xsl:value-of select="$y-legend-offset - 10"/>
        <xsl:text> L 220 </xsl:text>
        <xsl:value-of select="$y-legend-offset"/>
        <xsl:text> L 230 </xsl:text>
        <xsl:value-of select="$y-legend-offset"/>
        <xsl:text> L 230 </xsl:text>
        <xsl:value-of select="$y-legend-offset - 10"/>
        <xsl:text> Z</xsl:text>
      </xsl:attribute>
    </svg:path>
  </svg:g>
</xsl:template>
```

An individual legend appears as in Figure 9-10.

A final note: we use the SVG group element (`<svg:g>`) here to group several items. Each group contains some text, and the colored box that indicates which slice of the pie represents each store in the company. By putting these into a group and giving that group a name, we can set the `visibility` property of the group and make everything it contains visible or invisible.

9. Our final task is to draw the details for each store of the company. The name of the store and this store's percentage of the total sales are drawn in the same color as its slice of the pie. For each brand sold by this store, we list the brand and its sales. (See Figure 9-11 to see exactly how this looks.) As we did with the template for drawing the legend, we put several items together in an SVG group. Here's the template:

```
<xsl:template match="store" mode="details">
  <xsl:param name="color"/>
  <xsl:param name="y-legend-offset"/>
  <xsl:param name="storeSales"/>
  <xsl:param name="totalSales"/>

  <svg:g visibility="hidden" id="details{$position}">
    <svg:text font-size="16px" font-weight="bold" text-anchor="start"
      fill="black" x="220.5" y="{$y-legend-offset + .5}">
      <xsl:value-of select="name"/><xsl:text> Sales:</xsl:text>
    </svg:text>
    <svg:text font-size="16px" font-weight="bold" text-anchor="start"
      fill="{$color}" x="220" y="{$y-legend-offset}">
      <xsl:value-of select="name"/><xsl:text> Sales:</xsl:text>
    </svg:text>
    <xsl:for-each select="brand">
      <svg:text font-size="12px" text-anchor="start" x="220"
        y="{$y-legend-offset + (position() * 20)}">
        <xsl:value-of select="@name"/>
        <xsl:text>: </xsl:text>
        <xsl:value-of select="format-number(., '#,###.#')"/>
      </svg:text>
    </xsl:for-each>
    <svg:text font-size="14px" font-weight="bold" text-anchor="start"
      fill="black" x="220.5"
      y="{$y-legend-offset + 20.5 + (count(brand) * 20)}">
      <xsl:value-of
        select="format-number($storeSales div $totalSales, '##%')"/>
      <xsl:text> of total</xsl:text>
    </svg:text>
    <svg:text font-size="14px" font-weight="bold" text-anchor="start"
      fill="{$color}" x="220"
      y="{$y-legend-offset + 20 + (count(brand) * 20)}">
      <xsl:value-of
        select="format-number($storeSales div $totalSales, '##%')"/>
    </svg:text>
  </svg:g>
</xsl:template>
```

Notice that we draw this item to be invisible (`visibility="hidden"`); we'll use our JavaScript effects to make the various legends and details visible or hidden. In our stylesheet, we draw the title of the current store using the same color we used for the slice of the pie, followed by the sales figures for each product sold in this store and the percentage of total sales. The details for each brand are drawn 20 pixels below the previous one, and the final line that indicates the percentage of sales delivered by this particular store is written 20 pixels below the final brand.

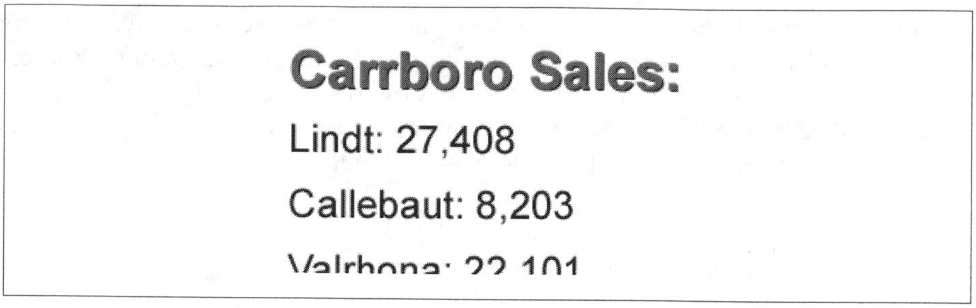

Carrboro Sales:

Lindt: 27,408

Callebaut: 8,203

Valrhona: 22,101

Figure 9-11. Sales details for a particular store

The sales details for a particular store appear as in Figure 9-11.

One subtle detail to note: we draw the name of the store and its percentage of sales twice, once in black and then once in the store's color. The black is .5 pixels down and to the right of the colored text in the foreground, which gives the display a nice shading effect.

Here's the complete stylesheet:

```
<?xml version="1.0"?>
<!-- piechart.xsl -->
<xsl:stylesheet version="1.0"
  xmlns:xsl="http://www.w3.org/1999/XSL/Transform"
  extension-element-prefixes="xalan-java saxon-java msxsl ora months"
  xmlns:svg="http://www.w3.org/2000/svg"
  xmlns:xalan-java="http://xml.apache.org/xslt/java"
  xmlns:saxon-java="java:java.lang.Math"
  xmlns:msxsl="urn:schemas-microsoft-com:xslt"
  xmlns:ora="http://www.oreilly.com/xslt"
  xmlns:months="http://www.oreilly.com/xslt/months">

  <months:month sequence="1">January</months:month>
  <months:month sequence="2">February</months:month>
  <months:month sequence="3">March</months:month>
  <months:month sequence="4">April</months:month>
  <months:month sequence="5">May</months:month>
  <months:month sequence="6">June</months:month>
  <months:month sequence="7">July</months:month>
  <months:month sequence="8">August</months:month>
  <months:month sequence="9">September</months:month>
  <months:month sequence="10">October</months:month>
  <months:month sequence="11">November</months:month>
  <months:month sequence="12">December</months:month>

  <msxsl:script implements-prefix="ora" language="C#">
    <![CDATA[
    public double cos(double d)
    {
      return Math.Round(Math.Cos(d), 4);
    }

    public double sin(double d)
```

```
      {
        return Math.Round(Math.Sin(d), 4);
      }
  ]]>
</msxsl:script>

<xsl:output method="xml"/>

<xsl:variable name="totalSales" select="sum(//brand)"/>
<xsl:variable name="stores" select="count(/sales/store)"/>

<xsl:template match="/">
  <svg:svg width="450" height="300" version="1.1"
    baseProfile="full"
    xmlns="http://www.w3.org/2000/svg"
    xmlns:xlink="http://www.w3.org/1999/xlink"
    xmlns:ev="http://www.w3.org/2001/xml-events">
    <xsl:comment>
      ECMAScript to handle mouse events
    </xsl:comment>

    <!-- Our generated SVG file has three functions: -->
    <!-- - mouse_over normally displays the details for a store -->
    <!--   in place of the legend. -->
    <!-- - mouse_out normally restores the legend when the mouse -->
    <!--   leaves a slice of the pie. -->
    <!-- - click handles a mouse click on a given slice of pie. -->
    <!--   If this is the first time we've clicked on this slice, -->
    <!--   this slice becomes the current item, and its sales -->
    <!--   details are displayed until the user clicks on another -->
    <!--   slice of pie. -->
    <!--   If this is the second time we've clicked on this slice, -->
    <!--   the details view is switched off and the normal mouse -->
    <!--   behavior returns. -->

    <svg:script type="text/ecmascript">
      <xsl:text disable-output-escaping="yes">

detailsViewOn = false;
currentItem = 0;

function mouse_over(selectedItem, totalItems)
{
  if (!detailsViewOn || selectedItem == currentItem)
  {
    for (i = 1; totalItems >= i; i++)
    {
      obj = svgDocument.getElementById("details" + i);
      obj.setAttributeNS(null, "visibility", "hidden");
      obj = svgDocument.getElementById("legend" + i);
      obj.setAttributeNS(null, "visibility", "hidden");
    }

    obj = svgDocument.getElementById("details" + selectedItem);
    obj.setAttributeNS(null, "visibility", "visible");
```

```
        }
      }

      function mouse_out(totalItems)
      {
        if (!detailsViewOn)
        {
          for (i = 1; totalItems >= i; i++)
          {
            obj = svgDocument.getElementById("details" + i);
            obj.setAttributeNS(null, "visibility", "hidden");
            obj = svgDocument.getElementById("legend" + i);
            obj.setAttributeNS(null, "visibility", "visible");
          }
        }
      }

      function click(selectedItem, totalItems)
      {
        if (selectedItem != currentItem)
        {
          currentItem = selectedItem;
          mouse_over(selectedItem, totalItems);
          detailsViewOn = true;
        }
        else
        {
          obj = svgDocument.getElementById("details" + selectedItem);
          if (obj.getAttributeNS(null, "visibility") == "visible")
          {
            detailsViewOn = false;
            currentItem = 0;
          }
          else
          {
            currentItem = selectedItem;
            mouse_over(selectedItem, totalItems);
            detailsViewOn = true;
          }
        }
      }
          //      </xsl:text></svg:script>
        <xsl:text>
</xsl:text>

        <!-- Generate the title and subtitle.  We draw the title and -->
        <!-- subtitle on the chart, and we set the <svg:title> element -->
        <!-- in the SVG document itself. -->
        <xsl:variable name="titleText">
          <xsl:value-of select="/report/caption/heading"/>
          <xsl:text> - </xsl:text>
          <xsl:value-of
            select="document('')/*/months:month
                        [@sequence=current()/report/@month]"/>
          <xsl:text> </xsl:text>
```

```
      <xsl:value-of select="/report/@year"/>
  </xsl:variable>

  <svg:title>
    <xsl:value-of select="$titleText"/>
  </svg:title>
  <svg:text font-size="24px" text-anchor="start"
    font-weight="bold" x="10" y="40">
    <xsl:value-of select="$titleText"/>
  </svg:text>
  <svg:text font-size="14px" text-anchor="middle" y="60" x="225">
    <xsl:value-of select="/report/caption/subheading"/>
  </svg:text>

  <xsl:variable name="totalSales" select="sum(//brand)"/>
  <xsl:variable name="stores" select="count(/report/store)"/>

  <xsl:for-each select="/report/store">
    <xsl:variable name="storeSales" select="sum(brand)"/>
    <xsl:variable name="color">
      <xsl:choose>
        <xsl:when test="(position() mod 6) = 1">
          <xsl:text>red</xsl:text>
        </xsl:when>
        <xsl:when test="(position() mod 6) = 2">
          <xsl:text>orange</xsl:text>
        </xsl:when>
        <xsl:when test="(position() mod 6) = 3">
          <xsl:text>purple</xsl:text>
        </xsl:when>
        <xsl:when test="(position() mod 6) = 4">
          <xsl:text>blue</xsl:text>
        </xsl:when>
        <xsl:when test="(position() mod 6) = 5">
          <xsl:text>green</xsl:text>
        </xsl:when>
        <xsl:otherwise>
          <xsl:text>gray</xsl:text>
        </xsl:otherwise>
      </xsl:choose>
    </xsl:variable>
    <xsl:variable name="explode" select="position()=1"/>

    <!-- Create the pie slice for each store -->
    <xsl:apply-templates select=".">
      <xsl:with-param name="color" select="$color"/>
      <xsl:with-param name="storeSales" select="$storeSales"/>
      <xsl:with-param name="totalSales" select="$totalSales"/>
      <xsl:with-param name="runningTotal"
        select="sum(preceding-sibling::store/brand)"/>
      <xsl:with-param name="stores" select="$stores"/>
      <xsl:with-param name="explode" select="$explode"/>
      <xsl:with-param name="position" select="position()"/>
    </xsl:apply-templates>
```

```
      <!-- Create the legend entry for each store -->
      <xsl:apply-templates select="." mode="legend">
        <xsl:with-param name="color" select="$color"/>
        <xsl:with-param name="storeSales" select="$storeSales"/>
        <xsl:with-param name="y-legend-offset"
          select="90 + (position() * 20)"/>
        <xsl:with-param name="position" select="position()"/>
      </xsl:apply-templates>

      <!-- Create the (initially hidden) sales details for -->
      <!-- each store -->
      <xsl:apply-templates select="." mode="details">
        <xsl:with-param name="color" select="$color"/>
        <xsl:with-param name="position" select="position()"/>
        <xsl:with-param name="y-legend-offset" select="110"/>
        <xsl:with-param name="storeSales" select="$storeSales"/>
        <xsl:with-param name="totalSales" select="$totalSales"/>
      </xsl:apply-templates>

    </xsl:for-each>
  </svg:svg>
</xsl:template>

<!-- For each store, create the pie slice (<svg:path>) and the -->
<!-- onmouseover(), onmouseout(), and onclick() event handlers. -->
<xsl:template match="store">
  <xsl:param name="color" select="'red'"/>
  <xsl:param name="runningTotal" select="'0'"/>
  <xsl:param name="totalSales" select="'0'"/>
  <xsl:param name="storeSales" select="'0'"/>
  <xsl:param name="stores" select="'5'"/>
  <xsl:param name="explode"/>
  <xsl:param name="position" select="'1'"/>

  <xsl:variable name="currentAngle">
    <xsl:choose>
      <xsl:when
        test="function-available('xalan-java:java.lang.Math.toRadians')">
        <xsl:value-of
          select="xalan-java:java.lang.Math.toRadians(
                  ($storeSales div $totalSales) * 360.0)"/>
      </xsl:when>
      <xsl:when
        test="function-available('saxon-java:toRadians')">
        <xsl:value-of
          select="saxon-java:toRadians(
                  ($storeSales div $totalSales) * 360.0)"/>
      </xsl:when>
      <xsl:when test="function-available('ora:cos')">
        <xsl:value-of
          select="($storeSales div $totalSales) *
                  6.283185307179586476925286766559"/>
      </xsl:when>
      <xsl:otherwise>
        <xsl:message terminate="yes">
```

```
        <xsl:text>Sorry, this stylesheet can't generate any </xsl:text>
        <xsl:text>useful results
without trigonometric </xsl:text>
        <xsl:text>functions available. </xsl:text>
      </xsl:message>
    </xsl:otherwise>
  </xsl:choose>
</xsl:variable>

<svg:path fill="{$color}" stroke="black" stroke-width="2px"
    fillrule="evenodd" stroke-linejoin="bevel">
  <xsl:attribute name="onmouseout">
    <xsl:text>mouse_out(</xsl:text>
    <xsl:value-of select="$stores"/>
    <xsl:text>);</xsl:text>
  </xsl:attribute>
  <xsl:attribute name="transform">
    <xsl:choose>
      <xsl:when test="$explode">
        <xsl:text>translate(</xsl:text>
        <xsl:choose>
          <xsl:when
            test="function-available('xalan-java:java.lang.Math.cos')">
            <xsl:value-of
              select="(xalan-java:java.lang.Math.cos(
                      $currentAngle div 2) * 20) + 100"/>
            <xsl:text>,</xsl:text>
            <xsl:value-of
              select="(xalan-java:java.lang.Math.sin($currentAngle div 2)
                      * -20) + 160"/>
          </xsl:when>
          <xsl:when
            test="function-available('saxon-java:cos')">
            <xsl:value-of
              select="(saxon-java:cos($currentAngle div 2) * 20) + 100"/>
            <xsl:text>,</xsl:text>
            <xsl:value-of
              select="(saxon-java:sin($currentAngle div 2) * -20) + 160"/>
          </xsl:when>
          <xsl:when test="function-available('ora:cos')">
            <xsl:value-of
              select="(ora:cos($currentAngle div 2) * 20) + 100"/>
            <xsl:text>,</xsl:text>
            <xsl:value-of
              select="(ora:sin($currentAngle div 2) * -20) + 160"/>
          </xsl:when>
        </xsl:choose>
        <xsl:text>) </xsl:text>
      </xsl:when>
      <xsl:otherwise>
        <xsl:text>translate(100,160) </xsl:text>
      </xsl:otherwise>
    </xsl:choose>
    <xsl:text> rotate(</xsl:text>
    <xsl:value-of select="-1 * (($runningTotal div $totalSales) * 360.0)"/>
```

```
          <xsl:text>)</xsl:text>
        </xsl:attribute>
        <xsl:attribute name="onmouseover">
          <xsl:text>mouse_over(</xsl:text>
          <xsl:value-of select="$position"/>
          <xsl:text>, </xsl:text>
          <xsl:value-of select="$stores"/>
          <xsl:text>);</xsl:text>
        </xsl:attribute>
        <xsl:attribute name="onclick">
          <xsl:text>click(</xsl:text>
          <xsl:value-of select="$position"/>
          <xsl:text>, </xsl:text>
          <xsl:value-of select="$stores"/>
          <xsl:text>);</xsl:text>
        </xsl:attribute>
        <xsl:attribute name="d">
          <xsl:text>M 80 0 A 80 80 0 </xsl:text>
          <xsl:choose>
            <xsl:when test="$currentAngle > 3.14">
              <xsl:text>1 </xsl:text>
            </xsl:when>
            <xsl:otherwise>
              <xsl:text>0 </xsl:text>
            </xsl:otherwise>
          </xsl:choose>
          <xsl:text>0 </xsl:text>
          <xsl:choose>
            <xsl:when test="function-available('xalan-java:java.lang.Math.cos')">
              <xsl:value-of
                select="xalan-java:java.lang.Math.cos($currentAngle) * 80"/>
              <xsl:text> </xsl:text>
              <xsl:value-of
                select="xalan-java:java.lang.Math.sin($currentAngle) * -80"/>
            </xsl:when>
            <xsl:when test="function-available('saxon-java:cos')">
              <xsl:value-of select="saxon-java:cos($currentAngle) * 80"/>
              <xsl:text> </xsl:text>
              <xsl:value-of select="saxon-java:sin($currentAngle) * -80"/>
            </xsl:when>
            <xsl:when test="function-available('ora:cos')">
              <xsl:value-of
                select="ora:cos($currentAngle) * 80"/>
              <xsl:text> </xsl:text>
              <xsl:value-of
                select="ora:sin($currentAngle) * -80"/>
            </xsl:when>
          </xsl:choose>
          <xsl:text> L 0 0 Z </xsl:text>
        </xsl:attribute>
      </svg:path>
</xsl:template>

<!-- For each store, create an entry in the legend -->
<xsl:template match="store" mode="legend">
```

```
<xsl:param name="color" select="'red'"/>
<xsl:param name="storeSales" select="'0'"/>
<xsl:param name="y-legend-offset" select="'0'"/>
<xsl:param name="position" select="'1'"/>

<svg:g id="legend{$position}">

  <svg:text font-size="12px" text-anchor="start" x="240">
    <xsl:attribute name="y">
      <xsl:value-of select="$y-legend-offset"/>
    </xsl:attribute>
    <xsl:value-of select="name"/>
    <xsl:text>: </xsl:text>
    <xsl:value-of select="format-number($storeSales, '#,###.#')"/>
  </svg:text>

  <svg:path stroke="black" stroke-width="2px" fill="{$color}">
    <xsl:attribute name="d">
      <xsl:text>M 220 </xsl:text>
      <xsl:value-of select="$y-legend-offset - 10"/>
      <xsl:text> L 220 </xsl:text>
      <xsl:value-of select="$y-legend-offset"/>
      <xsl:text> L 230 </xsl:text>
      <xsl:value-of select="$y-legend-offset"/>
      <xsl:text> L 230 </xsl:text>
      <xsl:value-of select="$y-legend-offset - 10"/>
      <xsl:text> Z</xsl:text>
    </xsl:attribute>
  </svg:path>
</svg:g>
</xsl:template>

<!-- For each store, create the hidden list of sales details -->
<xsl:template match="store" mode="details">
  <xsl:param name="color" select="black"/>
  <xsl:param name="position" select="'0'"/>
  <xsl:param name="y-legend-offset"/>
  <xsl:param name="storeSales"/>
  <xsl:param name="totalSales"/>

  <svg:g visibility="hidden" id="details{$position}">
    <svg:text font-size="16px" font-weight="bold" text-anchor="start"
      fill="black" x="220.5">
      <xsl:attribute name="y">
        <xsl:value-of select="$y-legend-offset + .5"/>
      </xsl:attribute>
      <xsl:value-of select="name"/><xsl:text> Sales:</xsl:text>
    </svg:text>
    <svg:text font-size="16px" font-weight="bold" text-anchor="start"
      fill="{$color}" x="220">
      <xsl:attribute name="y">
        <xsl:value-of select="$y-legend-offset"/>
      </xsl:attribute>
      <xsl:value-of select="name"/><xsl:text> Sales:</xsl:text>
    </svg:text>
```

```
        <xsl:for-each select="brand">
          <svg:text font-size="12px" text-anchor="start" x="220">
            <xsl:attribute name="y">
              <xsl:value-of select="$y-legend-offset + (position() * 20)"/>
            </xsl:attribute>
            <xsl:value-of select="@name"/>
            <xsl:text>: </xsl:text>
            <xsl:value-of select="format-number(., '#,###.#')"/>
          </svg:text>
        </xsl:for-each>
        <svg:text font-size="14px" font-weight="bold" text-anchor="start"
          fill="black" x="220.5"
          y="{$y-legend-offset + 20.5 + (count(brand) * 20)}">
          <xsl:value-of select="format-number($storeSales div $totalSales, '##%')"/>
          <xsl:text> of total</xsl:text>
        </svg:text>
        <svg:text font-size="14px" font-weight="bold" text-anchor="start"
          fill="{$color}" x="220"
          y="{$y-legend-offset + 20 + (count(brand) * 20)}">
          <xsl:value-of select="format-number($storeSales div $totalSales, '##%')"/>

        </svg:text>
      </svg:g>
    </xsl:template>

  </xsl:stylesheet>
```

In this example, we've used XSLT extension functions to add new capabilities to the XSLT processor. We needed a couple of simple trigonometric functions, and Saxon and Xalan's ability to use existing Java classes made adding new capabilities simple. You can use this technique to invoke static methods of Java classes anywhere you need them. Best of all, we didn't have to write any Java code to make this happen.

Writing Extensions in Other Languages

One of the nice features of Xalan-J's extension mechanism is that it supports the Bean Scripting Framework (BSF), an open source library from the Apache Software Foundation that allows you to execute code written in a variety of scripting languages. We'll take the SVG stylesheet we just discussed and implement it again, writing the extension functions in a variety of other languages. For our first example, we'll look at all the details of defining and invoking BSF extension functions; for the subsequent examples, we'll simply highlight the differences.

The Bean Scripting Framework supports many languages, including JRuby, Jython, Groovy, Jacl, NetRexx, PerlScript, Tcl, and VBScript. If you're using a Microsoft platform, BSF also supports Windows Script Technologies, so you may have even more choices if you're running some flavor of Windows.

Using the BSF requires two files on your CLASSPATH—*bsf.jar*, which is available at *http://jakarta.apache.org/bsf/index.html*, and *commons-logging-1.1.jar*, which is available at *http://jakarta.apache.org/commons/logging/*—in addition to the JAR files for the language you're using. We'll point out those requirements as we go. Also be aware that system requirements can change; earlier versions of the BSF did not require the logging component.

Jython

We'll start our tour of BSF-supported languages with Jython, an implementation of Python written in Java. As you would expect, we must do several things to identify our extension code to Xalan. We'll cover them, and then look at the source of the extension functions. First we need to define the namespace prefixes we'll use:

```
<!-- piechart-jython.xsl -->
<xsl:stylesheet version="1.0"
  xmlns:xsl="http://www.w3.org/1999/XSL/Transform"
  xmlns:svg="http://www.w3.org/2000/svg"
  xmlns:months="http://www.oreilly.com/xslt/months"
  xmlns:lxslt="http://xml.apache.org/xslt"
  xmlns:jython-extension="http://www.jython.org"
  extension-element-prefixes="jython-extension"
  exclude-result-prefixes="lxslt">
```

We're generating SVG markup, so we need to define the svg namespace. The months namespace is for the <months> elements we use for a document('') lookup table (for variety's sake, we'll avoid using the EXSLT extensions here). For the last two namespaces, lxslt is the namespace Xalan uses to invoke the Bean Scripting Framework, and jython-extension is the prefix we use to identify the extension functions written in Jython.

In this example, we associated the jython-extension namespace prefix with the URI http://www.jython.org, which is the home page for the Jython project. The URI could be anything. The crucial identifier for the BSF is the name of the language, as we'll see in just a minute.

Our code goes in a <lxslt:component> element:

```
<lxslt:component prefix="jython-extension"
  functions="cos sin">
  <lxslt:script lang="jython">
import math

def cos(d):
  return math.cos(d)

def sin(d):
  return math.sin(d)
  </lxslt:script>
</lxslt:component>
```

The `prefix` attribute of the `<lxslt:component>` element associates the code with a namespace prefix, while the `functions` attribute lists the extension functions provided by this code. The `<lxslt:script>` element contains the actual code. *The `lang` attribute of the `<lxslt:script>` element is case-sensitive and must match the name of a language known to the implementation of the Bean Scripting Framework you're using.* Changing the `lang` attribute to `Jython` causes a fatal error.

Now that we've packaged and labeled our Jython code correctly, all we have to do is invoke it:

```
<xsl:value-of
  select="(jython-extension:cos(number($currentAngle div 2)) * 20) + 100"/>
```

Other than the `jython-extension` extension before the function call, the rest of our stylesheet is exactly the same. The `cos( )` and `sin( )` functions are part of the Python `math` library, so all we have to do was invoke them.

To use these extension functions, your `CLASSPATH` must contain *jython.jar*, available at *http://www.jython.org*, in addition to *bsf.jar* and *commons-logging-1.1.jar*.

We'll move on to other languages now, looking at the script and the `CLASSPATH` setup for each.

JRuby

JRuby is an implementation of the popular Ruby language written in Java. We define the namespace prefix `jruby-extension` and associate it with the URI `http://jruby.codehaus.org`. Here's the JRuby code:

```
<?xml version="1.0"?>
<!-- piechart-jruby.xsl -->
<xsl:stylesheet version="1.0"
  xmlns:xsl="http://www.w3.org/1999/XSL/Transform"
  xmlns:svg="http://www.w3.org/2000/svg"
  xmlns:months="http://www.oreilly.com/xslt/months"
  xmlns:lxslt="http://xml.apache.org/xslt"
  xmlns:jruby-extension="http://jruby.codehaus.org"
  extension-element-prefixes="jruby-extension"
  exclude-result-prefixes="lxslt">
...
  <lxslt:component prefix="jruby-extension"
    functions="cos sin">
    <lxslt:script lang="ruby">
      def cos(d)
        Math::cos(d)
      end

      def sin(d)
        Math::sin(d)
      end
    </lxslt:script>
  </lxslt:component>
```

To use these extension functions, your CLASSPATH must contain *jruby.jar*, available at *http://jruby.codehaus.org*, in addition to *bsf.jar* and *commons-logging-1.1.jar*.

 The magic `lang` attribute value here is `ruby`. Using `JRuby`, `jruby`, or `Ruby`, all of which are reasonable choices, causes a runtime error.

JavaScript

We'll use Mozilla's Rhino JavaScript engine to illustrate JavaScript support. We define the namespace prefix `javascript-extension` and associate it with the URI `http://www.mozilla.org/rhino`. The JavaScript code looks like this:

```
<?xml version="1.0"?>
<!-- piechart-javascript.xsl -->
<xsl:stylesheet version="1.0"
  xmlns:xsl="http://www.w3.org/1999/XSL/Transform"
  xmlns:svg="http://www.w3.org/2000/svg"
  xmlns:months="http://www.oreilly.com/xslt/months"
  xmlns:lxslt="http://xml.apache.org/xslt"
  xmlns:javascript-extension="http://www.mozilla.org/rhino"
  extension-element-prefixes="javascript-extension"
  exclude-result-prefixes="lxslt">
...
  <lxslt:component prefix="javascript-extension"
    functions="cos sin">
    <lxslt:script lang="javascript">
      function cos(d)
      {
        return Math.cos(d);
      }

      function sin(d)
      {
        return Math.sin(d);
      }
    </lxslt:script>
  </lxslt:component>
```

To use these extension functions, your CLASSPATH must contain *js.jar*, available at *http://www.mozilla.org/rhino*, in addition to *bsf.jar* and *commons-logging-1.1.jar*.

Jacl

Jacl is a Tcl (Tool Command Language) interpreter written entirely in Java. We define the namespace prefix `jacl-extension` and associate it with the URI `http://tcljava.sourceforge.net`. The code is straightforward:

```
<?xml version="1.0"?>
<!-- piechart-jacl.xsl -->
```

```
<xsl:stylesheet version="1.0"
  xmlns:xsl="http://www.w3.org/1999/XSL/Transform"
  xmlns:svg="http://www.w3.org/2000/svg"
  xmlns:months="http://www.oreilly.com/xslt/months"
  xmlns:lxslt="http://xml.apache.org/xslt"
  xmlns:jacl-extension="http://tcljava.sourceforge.net"
  extension-element-prefixes="jacl-extension"
  exclude-result-prefixes="lxslt">
...
  <lxslt:component prefix="jacl-extension"
    functions="cos sin">
    <lxslt:script lang="jacl">
      proc cos {d}  {expr cos($d)}
      proc sin {d}  {expr sin($d)}
    </lxslt:script>
  </lxslt:component>
```

To use these extension functions, your CLASSPATH must contain *jacl.jar* and *tclja va.jar*, available at *http://tcljava.sourceforge.net*, in addition to *bsf.jar* and *commons-logging-1.1.jar*.

Using Extension Functions from the EXSLT Library

Earlier we mentioned the EXSLT project, an effort to define a common set of XSLT extension functions. For our next example, we'll use functions from the EXSLT library. Both Saxon and Xalan have EXSLT support built in, so it's very easy to use extensions from the EXSLT library.

 Although a number of XSLT processors support EXSLT, be aware that EXSLT is implemented inconsistently between processors. Not all processors support all functions, and not all functions have the same signature or results.

EXSLT provides eight categories of functions:

Common
    Common functions for data typing and for working with node-sets. These are in the http://exslt.org/common namespace.

Dates and times
    Functions for manipulating dates and times. These are in the http://exslt.org/dates-and-times namespace.

Dynamic
    Functions to dynamically evaluate XPath expressions. These are in the http://exslt.org/dynamic namespace.

Functions

Extension elements and functions that allow you to define your own functions. These are in the `http://exslt.org/functions` namespace.

Math

Functions for trigonometry, exponentiation, logarithms, and other miscellaneous mathematical functions. These are in the `http://exslt.org/math` namespace.

Random

A single function (`random-sequence( )`) that generates a sequence of random values between 0 and 1. It is in the `http://exslt.org/random` namespace.

Regular expressions

Functions that work with regular expressions. These are in the `http://exslt.org/regular-expressions` namespace.

Sets

Functions to calculate the difference and intersection between sets. These are in the `http://exslt.org/sets` namespace.

Strings

Functions for manipulating strings. These are in the `http://exslt.org/strings` namespace.

Many of the EXSLT functions and elements have been added as part of the language for XSLT 2.0. The EXSLT effort represents the most requested features missing in XSLT 1.0, so it's not surprising that EXSLT would have a strong impact on the design and features of XSLT 2.0.

You should also be aware that just because an XSLT processor supports EXSLT, it might not support all of the functions defined at `http://exslt.org`. There are also minor differences between the implementations, so beware.

We'll use EXSLT for three things: the `cos( )` and `sin( )` functions we used earlier, and the `month-name( )` function to get the name of the current month. Using `month-name( )` means we won't have to have the `<months:month>` elements we've used until now.

To keep this discussion short, we'll only look at the parts of the EXSLT stylesheet that are different from our original pie chart stylesheet. First of all, the `<xsl:stylesheet>` element has different namespace declarations, as you'd expect:

```
<?xml version="1.0"?>
<!-- piechart-exslt.xsl -->
<xsl:stylesheet version="1.0"
  xmlns:xsl="http://www.w3.org/1999/XSL/Transform"
  xmlns:svg="http://www.w3.org/2000/svg"
  xmlns:math="http://exslt.org/math"
  xmlns:dates-and-times="http://exslt.org/dates-and-times"
  extension-element-prefixes="dates-and-times math">
```

In our example, we're testing the availability of the math and date/time extension functions from EXSLT. The EXSLT functions are in two different namespaces, so we define the `dates-and-times` and `math` prefixes in addition to the ones we used earlier.

Using the `month-name( )` function takes some work. Here's how we use it:

```
<xsl:choose>
  <xsl:when test="function-available('math:cos')">
    <xsl:variable name="dateString">
      <xsl:text>--</xsl:text>
      <xsl:if test="string-length(/report/@month) = 1">
        <xsl:text>0</xsl:text>
      </xsl:if>
      <xsl:value-of select="/report/@month"/>
      <xsl:text>--</xsl:text>
    </xsl:variable>
    <xsl:value-of
      select="dates-and-times:month-name($dateString)"/>
    <xsl:text> </xsl:text>
    <xsl:value-of select="/report/@year"/>
  </xsl:when>
  <xsl:otherwise>
    <xsl:value-of select="/report/@month"/>
    <xsl:text>/</xsl:text>
    <xsl:value-of select="/report/@year"/>
  </xsl:otherwise>
</xsl:choose>
```

If the `dates-and-times:month-name( )` function is available, we use it to get the name of the month of the report. To get the name of the month, the implementations of the `month-name( )` function that ship with Xalan and Saxon require a string in the format `--MM--`. (That's the only format that works with both processors, at any rate. Each processor might work with other formats, but we'll keep our stylesheet simple by using one format for both processors.) We create a variable named `$dateString` that matches this format; if the value of the `month` attribute of the `<report>` element is one character long, we'll put a zero in front of it. If the EXSLT functions are available, `month-name('--08--')` returns `August`. If the functions aren't available, the stylesheet uses the `month` attribute directly and creates a heading such as `8/2006`.

Notice that the `function-available( )` call tests for the `math:cos` function. Calling `function-available('dates-and-times:month-name')` in Xalan-J 2.7.0 currently returns `false`, even though the function is available. Testing for the EXSLT function `math:cos` does return `true`, so that's what we use here; all that really matters is support for EXSLT.

Another difference is that EXSLT doesn't define a `toRadians( )` function, so we have to define that ourselves. Here's the difference between the EXLST version and the Saxon extension version:

```
<xsl:when test="function-available('math:cos')">
  <xsl:value-of
    select="($storeSales div $totalSales) *
```

```
                6.28318530717958647692528866766559"/>
    </xsl:when>
    <xsl:when
      test="function-available('saxon-java:toRadians')">
      <xsl:value-of
        select="saxon-java:toRadians(
                ($storeSales div $totalSales) * 360.0)"/>
    </xsl:when>
```

The rest of the stylesheet is basically the same. Here's how we generate the two coordinates for the SVG `translate( )` function, for example:

```
    <xsl:when test="function-available('math:cos')">
      <xsl:value-of
        select="(math:cos($currentAngle div 2) * 20) + 100"/>
      <xsl:text>,</xsl:text>
      <xsl:value-of
        select="(math:sin($currentAngle div 2) * -20) + 160"/>
    </xsl:when>
```

Accessing a Database with an Extension Element

The first edition of this book included an extension element that accessed an SQL database. Since that time, the Saxon and Xalan processors have added extension libraries that do this for us. We'll look at how to use those extensions here.

Our example here uses the open source Apache Derby database, available at *http:// db.apache.org/derby/*. Here are the Derby commands and SQL statements that create and populate the database:

```
    connect 'jdbc:derby://localhost:1527/books;create=true';
    create schema doug;
    set schema doug;
    create table compbks (ISBN varchar(10) primary key, title varchar(50),
      author varchar(50), pages int, price double, publisher varchar(50));
    insert into compbks values ('0596527217', 'XSLT', 'Doug Tidwell',
      800, 49.95, 'O''Reilly');
    insert into compbks values ('0974152129', 'DocBook XSL: The Complete Guide',
      'Bob Strayton', 560, 49.95, 'Sagehill Enterprises');
    insert into compbks values ('1565925807', 'DocBook: The Definitive Guide',
      'Norman Walsh and Leonard Muellner', 652, 39.95, 'O''Reilly');
    insert into compbks values ('0596009747', 'XSLT Cookbook', 'Sal Mangano',
      751, 49.95, 'O''Reilly');
    insert into compbks values ('0596003277', 'Learning XSLT',
      'Michael Fitzgerald', 352, 34.95, 'O''Reilly');
```

We create a database named books and a table named compbks, then we insert five rows into the table.

 Saxon's SQL support requires a username that must match the database schema; that's why we create the database schema **doug** and associate it with the database. It also requires a password value, which must be at least one character; we'll look at those details in just a minute.

Accessing a Database in Saxon

The Saxon XSLT processor provides a set of extension elements that provide SQL functions. There are extension elements to connect and disconnect from a database, to run a database query, and to do updates, inserts, and deletes on database tables. To keep our example simple, we'll use `<sql:connection>` element to connect to a database, then we'll use `<sql:query>` to select items from the database and `<sql:close>` to close the connection.

Here's the complete stylesheet:

```
<?xml version="1.0"?>
<!-- saxon-sql.xsl -->
<xsl:stylesheet version="1.0"
  xmlns:xsl="http://www.w3.org/1999/XSL/Transform"
  xmlns:sql="java:/net.sf.saxon.sql.SQLElementFactory"
  xmlns:saxon="http://saxon.sf.net/"
  extension-element-prefixes="saxon sql">

  <xsl:output method="html"/>

  <xsl:template match="/">

    <!-- Create the JDBC connection -->
    <xsl:variable name="connection"
      as="java:java.sql.Connection"
      xmlns:java="http://saxon.sf.net/java-type">
      <sql:connect database="jdbc:derby://localhost:1527/books"
        driver="org.apache.derby.jdbc.ClientDriver"
        user="doug"
        password="x"/>
    </xsl:variable>

    <!-- Run the query -->
    <xsl:variable name="queryResults">
      <sql:query connection="$connection" table="compbks"
        column="*" row-tag="tr" column-tag="td"/>
    </xsl:variable>

    <html>
      <head>
        <title>Computer books in our database</title>
      </head>
      <body style="font-family: sans-serif;">
        <h1>Computer books in our database</h1>
        <p>Here are the
        <xsl:value-of select="count($queryResults/tr)"/>
```

```
          computer books we have in stock:</p>
          <table border="1" cellpadding="5">
            <tr>
              <th>ISBN</th>
              <th>Title</th>
              <th>Author</th>
              <th>Pages</th>
              <th>List price</th>
              <th>Publisher</th>
            </tr>
            <xsl:copy-of select="$queryResults"/>
          </table>
        </body>
      </html>

      <!-- Close the connection -->
      <sql:close connection="$connection"/>
    </xsl:template>

  </xsl:stylesheet>
```

We use the Saxon extension elements in three places. First, we create the database connection with the `<sql:connect>` element. We have to specify the URL of the database, the Java JDBC driver we use to access the database, and a username and password. Note that both the username and password must be at least one character long. Even if your database isn't password protected (the Derby database we use here isn't), you still have to provide a username and password. To complicate things further, the username must match the name of the database schema. That's why we created the database schema **doug** when we created the Derby database.

The second extension element we use is `<sql:query>`. This is where we actually run the query and get the result set. The variable `$queryResults` contains a tree of elements representing the result set. In our example here, we specify the name of the database table, the columns to return (our example here means **select** *, although we could be more specific if we wanted), and the elements used for the rows and columns in the results. We're generating an HTML table here, so we use **tr** and **td**.

After using the `<sql:query>` element, the variable `$queryResults` contains a tree of elements that represent the results of the database query. We use the count( ) function to indicate how many books were found in the query, then we create our table. We use the HTML `<table>`, `<tr>`, and `<th>` elements to set up the table, then we copy the `$queryResults` variable to the output.

Once the HTML table is built, we use the `<sql:close>` element to close the database connection.

The results of our stylesheet appear as in Figure 9-12.

ISBN	TITLE	AUTHOR	PAGES	PRICE	
0596527217	XSLT	Doug Tidwell	800	49.95	O'l
0974152129	DocBook XSL: The Complete Guide	Bob Strayton	560	49.95	Sa
1565925807	DocBook: The Definitive Guide	Norman Walsh and Leonard Muellner	652	39.95	O'l
0596009747	XSLT Cookbook	Sal Mangano	751	49.95	O'l
0596003277	Learning XSLT	Michael Fitzgerald	352	34.95	O'l

Figure 9-12. An HTML table built with Saxon's SQL extension elements

> Be sure your CLASSPATH contains the classes for the Saxon SQL extension package and the JDBC driver classes; otherwise, your stylesheets won't work.

Saxon's SQL extension elements are built on JDBC, so they're extremely flexible. For example, to use this stylesheet with DB2, the only thing we have to change is the attributes of the `<sql:connect>` element:

```
<?xml version="1.0"?>
<!-- saxon-sql2.xsl -->
<xsl:stylesheet version="1.0"
  xmlns:xsl="http://www.w3.org/1999/XSL/Transform"
  xmlns:sql="java:/net.sf.saxon.sql.SQLElementFactory"
  xmlns:saxon="http://saxon.sf.net/"
  extension-element-prefixes="saxon sql">

  ...

    <!-- Create the JDBC connection -->
    <xsl:variable name="connection"
      as="java:java.sql.Connection"
      xmlns:java="http://saxon.sf.net/java-type">
      <sql:connect database="jdbc:db2:books"
        driver="COM.ibm.db2.jdbc.app.DB2Driver"
        user="Skippy"
        password="xxxxxxxx"/>
    </xsl:variable>

  ...

</xsl:stylesheet>
```

The DB2 version of the database is password-protected, so we have to provide a username and password that are defined on the system. We changed one element, and now our stylesheet is accessing a completely different data source. As with any database, we have to know the JDBC driver class and the URL format for the database, but that's the only change between the two stylesheets. The results of the new stylesheet, though, are exactly the same.

 Be aware that the name of the JDBC driver class is case-sensitive. If you ask for the class com.ibm.db2... instead of COM.ibm.db2..., you'll get a runtime error.

Accessing a Database in Xalan

Xalan provides a set of extension functions that give us access to any JDBC data source. The extension functions we'll use are sql:new( ) to create a new database connection, sql:query( ) to execute a query, and sql:close( ) to close the connection. In addition, we'll use the function sql:disableStreamingMode( ) to get around a "feature" of the Xalan SQL library.

Here's the stylesheet:

```
<?xml version="1.0"?>
<!-- xalan-sql.xsl -->
<xsl:stylesheet version="1.0"
  xmlns:xsl="http://www.w3.org/1999/XSL/Transform"
  xmlns:sql="org.apache.xalan.lib.sql.XConnection"
  extension-element-prefixes="sql">

  <xsl:output method="html"/>

  <xsl:template match="/">

    <!-- Create the JDBC connection -->
    <xsl:variable name="books"
      select="sql:new('org.apache.derby.jdbc.ClientDriver',
              'jdbc:derby://localhost:1527/books')"/>

    <!-- Workaround for a bug in Xalan's SQL extension? -->
    <xsl:variable name="streaming"
      select="sql:disableStreamingMode($books)"/>

    <!-- Run the query -->
    <xsl:variable name="queryResults"
      select="sql:query($books, 'select * from doug.compbks')"/>

    <html>
      <head>
        <title>Computer books in our database</title>
      </head>
      <body style="font-family: sans-serif;">
        <h1>Computer books in our database</h1>
        <p>Here are the
        <xsl:value-of select="count($queryResults/sql/row-set/row)"/>
```

```
    computer books we have in stock:</p>
    <table border="1" cellpadding="5">
      <tr>
        <xsl:for-each select="$queryResults/sql/metadata/column-header">
          <th>
            <xsl:value-of select="@column-label"/>
          </th>
        </xsl:for-each>
      </tr>
      <xsl:apply-templates select="$queryResults/sql/row-set/row"/>
    </table>
  </body>
</html>

<!-- Close the connection -->
<xsl:value-of select="sql:close($books)"/>
</xsl:template>

<xsl:template match="row">
  <tr>
    <xsl:apply-templates select="col"/>
  </tr>
</xsl:template>

<xsl:template match="col">
  <td>
    <xsl:value-of select="text()"/>
  </td>
</xsl:template>

</xsl:stylesheet>
```

We start by creating a variable named $books that represents the connection to the database. Notice that the Xalan SQL library doesn't require us to provide a username and password; we simply specify the JDBC driver class name and the database URL. The sql:disableStreamingMode($books) call lets us access all of the results in the result set. Without this, the result set never has more than one result. Xalan-J 2.7.0 works this way, it's possible that future versions of the Xalan SQL library will work more sensibly.

Notice that the Xalan library gives us access to the information provided by the Java ResultSetMetaData class. In this case, we're using the column headers defined in our database, defined in the XPath hierarchy sql/metadata/column-header. Each column header is displayed in a <th> element inside the table. The Saxon SQL library doesn't provide this information, although it would be simple to extend the source code to do so.

Also notice that Xalan gives us more flexibility in the query statement. We could add an ORDER BY or GROUP BY clause to the statement if we want. The table name is specified differently here as well. Notice that we're asking for the table doug.compbks, which refers to the table named compbks that's in the doug database schema. If we simply ask for the table `compbks`, the JDBC driver tells us that table doesn't exist. (Remember, we had to add the `doug` schema so the Saxon stylesheet would work.)

Once we've generated the headings for the columns in the table, it's time to process everything in the result set. The rows and columns from the result set are returned in a `<row-set>` element; each row is in a `<row>` element inside the `<row-set>`, and each column is in a `<col>` inside a `<row>`. The templates we define for the `<row>` and `<col>` elements are straightforward. The results are exactly the same as those for the stylesheets that used the Saxon SQL extensions.

To complete this short tour of the Xalan SQL extensions, we'll look at a second stylesheet that accesses a DB2 database. The differences, as you'd expect, are slight:

```
<?xml version="1.0"?>
<!-- xalan-sql2.xsl -->
<xsl:stylesheet version="1.0"
  xmlns:xsl="http://www.w3.org/1999/XSL/Transform"
  xmlns:sql="org.apache.xalan.lib.sql.XConnection"
  extension-element-prefixes="sql">

  ...

    <!-- Create the JDBC connection -->
    <xsl:variable name="books"
      select="sql:new('COM.ibm.db2.jdbc.app.DB2Driver',
                'jdbc:db2:books', 'Skippy', 'xxxxxxxx')"/>

    ...

    <!-- Run the query -->
    <xsl:variable name="queryResults"
      select="sql:query($books, 'select * from compbks')"/>

  ...

</xsl:stylesheet>
```

We have to specify a different JDBC driver class and a database URL in a different format. This version of the `sql:new( )` function accepts a username and password as two of its parameters. The other difference here is that we don't specify a database schema name for the database table. The default database schema in DB2 is the name of the user who created the database, so we can simply ask for the table `compbks`. If the table was created under another database schema, we would have to include the schema name here.

Creating a Photo Album with an Extension Element

As a final example, we'll create an extension element that generates an HTML table that displays all of the photographs in a given directory. The extension element takes three parameters: the directory, how many images are displayed on each row of the

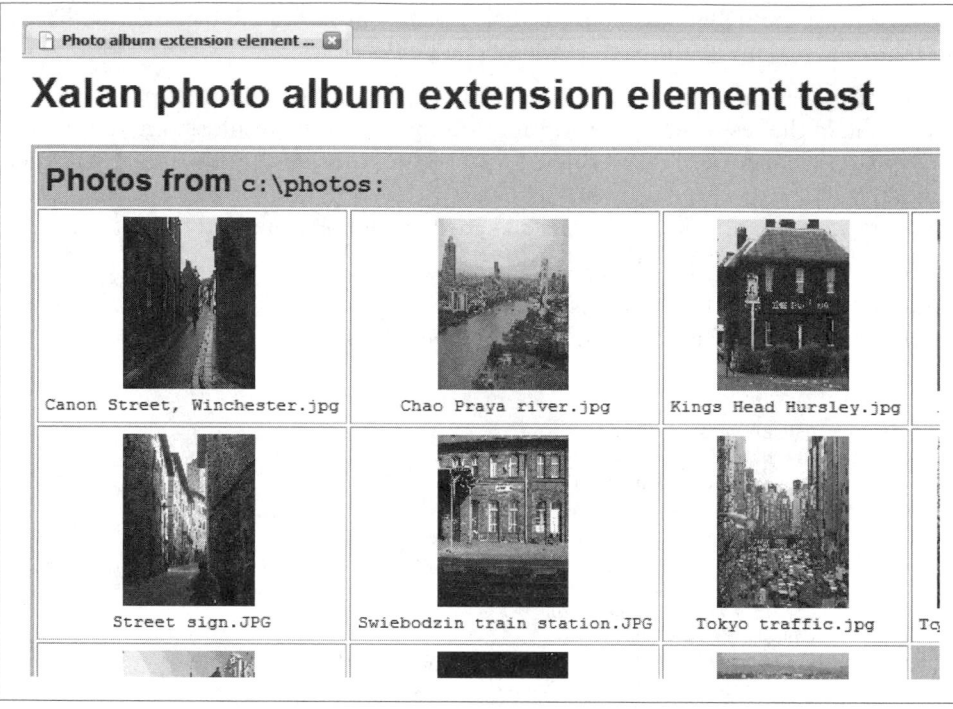

Figure 9-13. A photo album generated by an extension element

table, and whether the filename should be displayed under the photograph. The generated table displays a reduced version of each photograph; each small photo is a link to the actual file. The generated file looks like Figure 9-13.

We'll look at three versions of this extension here. The first two are written in Java, one version for Xalan and one version for Saxon. These two processors use different mechanisms to access the code; they also have different mechanisms to return the tree of HTML elements back to the stylesheet. The third version is written in C# for the .NET platform. The .NET version is written as an extension *function* rather than an element, although it still returns the tree of HTML elements we need. The HTML generated by the three implementations is the same.

All of the versions of our extension use this XML source file:

```
<?xml version="1.0"?>
<!-- photo-album.xml -->
<photo-album
  directory="c:\photos"
  imagesPerRow="5"
  includeFilenames="yes"/>
```

The XML source contains the three parameters we need for our extension: the directory that contains the images, the number of images per row, and whether to include the filenames in the table. As we'll see, the extension code varies widely in the three examples, but the input data and the HTML output is the same.

The overall flow of the code is the same in all three extensions:

1. Get the attributes from the extension element. In some cases, we'll do that in the stylesheet; in others, the extension element will be able to get its own parameters.

2. See whether the requested directory exists. If it doesn't, create a table that includes a message such as "Directory doesn't exist."

3. Assuming the directory exists, see whether there are any images inside it. If it doesn't exist, create a table that includes a message such as "Directory doesn't contain any images."

4. Assuming the directory exists and contains some images, create a table with `<img>` elements that reference those images.

Xalan Java Version

We'll start with the Xalan Java version of the extension. The return type of the extension element is `org.w3c.dom.Element`. To start with, we'll look at the XSLT stylesheet that controls everything:

```
<?xml version="1.0"?>
<!-- xalan-photo-album.xsl -->
<xsl:stylesheet version="1.0"
  xmlns:xsl="http://www.w3.org/1999/XSL/Transform"
  xmlns:xpa="xalan://com.oreilly.xslt.xalan.XalanPhotoAlbumExtension"
  extension-element-prefixes="xpa">

  <xsl:output method="html"/>

  <xsl:template match="photo-album">
    <html>
      <head>
        <title>Photo album extension element test</title>
      </head>
      <body style="font-family: sans-serif;">
        <xsl:choose>
          <xsl:when test="element-available('xpa:XalanPhotoAlbum')">
            <h1>Xalan photo album extension element test</h1>
            <xpa:XalanPhotoAlbum/>
          </xsl:when>
          <xsl:otherwise>
            <p>
              <i>[Sorry, the photo album function is not available.]</i>
            </p>
          </xsl:otherwise>
        </xsl:choose>
      </body>
    </html>
  </xsl:template>
```

```
    </xsl:stylesheet>
```

Here's the code for the extension element:

```java
/*
 * XalanPhotoAlbumExtension.java
 * Created on Nov 28, 2006 by Doug Tidwell
 */

package com.oreilly.xslt.xalan;

import java.io.File;

import javax.xml.parsers.DocumentBuilder;
import javax.xml.parsers.DocumentBuilderFactory;
import javax.xml.parsers.ParserConfigurationException;

import org.apache.xalan.extensions.XSLProcessorContext;
import org.apache.xalan.templates.ElemExtensionCall;
import org.w3c.dom.Document;
import org.w3c.dom.Element;

//This class creates a photo album with all of the images in a
//given directory.
public class XalanPhotoAlbumExtension
{
  // XalanPhotoAlbum is the name of the extension element.  Notice that
  // it returns an Element node; that node is inserted into the output tree.
  public static Element XalanPhotoAlbum(XSLProcessorContext context,
      ElemExtensionCall elem)
    throws ParserConfigurationException
  {
    Element contextNode = (Element) context.getContextNode();

    // For parameters, we get the name of the directory, the number of
    // images per row, and whether the names of the files should be displayed.

    int imagesPerRowValue;
    try
    {
      imagesPerRowValue =
        Integer.parseInt(contextNode.getAttribute("imagesPerRow"));
    }
    catch (NumberFormatException nfe)
    {
      imagesPerRowValue = 5;
    }

    String directoryName = contextNode.getAttribute("directory");

    boolean includeFilenamesFlag =
      (contextNode.getAttribute("includeFilenames").
          equalsIgnoreCase("yes"));

    // We're building a DOM tree, so we create a Document and some
```

```java
// elements beforehand.  We'll return a <table> element that
// contains the images or an error message if something goes wrong.
DocumentBuilderFactory dbf = DocumentBuilderFactory.newInstance();
DocumentBuilder db = dbf.newDocumentBuilder();
Document doc = db.newDocument();

Element a = null, br = null, img = null, span = null,
table = null, td = null, tr = null;

table = doc.createElement("table");
table.setAttribute("border", "3");
table.setAttribute("cellpadding", "5");

File dir = new File(directoryName);

// Return an error message if the directory doesn't exist
if (!dir.exists())
{
  tr = doc.createElement("tr");

  td = doc.createElement("td");
  td.setAttribute("style", "font-weight:bold; font-size: 150%");

  td.appendChild(doc.createTextNode("The directory "));

  span = doc.createElement("span");
  span.setAttribute("style", "font-family: monospace;");
  span.appendChild(doc.createTextNode(directoryName));
  td.appendChild(span);

  td.appendChild(doc.createTextNode(" does not exist!"));
  tr.appendChild(td);
  table.appendChild(tr);
}
else
{
  // Use the filename filter to find the images
  String[] graphicsFiles = dir.list(new GraphicsFilenameFilter());
  int numFiles = 0;
  if (graphicsFiles != null)
    numFiles = graphicsFiles.length;

  // Return an error message if the directory doesn't contain
  // any images
  if (numFiles == 0)
  {
    tr = doc.createElement("tr");

    td = doc.createElement("td");
    td.setAttribute("style", "font-weight:bold; font-size: 150%");

    td.appendChild(doc.createTextNode("The directory "));

    span = doc.createElement("span");
    span.setAttribute("style", "font-family: monospace;");
```

```
    span.appendChild(doc.createTextNode(directoryName));
    td.appendChild(span);

    td.appendChild(doc.createTextNode(" doesn't contain any images!"));
    tr.appendChild(td);
    table.appendChild(tr);
}

// We've got images, so let's process 'em...
else
{
    tr = doc.createElement("tr");

    td = doc.createElement("td");
    td.setAttribute("colspan", String.valueOf(imagesPerRowValue));
    td.setAttribute("style",
                    "font-weight:bold; background: #CCCCCC; " +
                    "font-size: 150%");
    td.appendChild(doc.createTextNode("Photos from "));

    span = doc.createElement("span");
    span.setAttribute("style", "font-family: monospace;");
    span.appendChild(doc.createTextNode(directoryName + ":"));
    td.appendChild(span);

    tr.appendChild(td);
    table.appendChild(tr);

    int filesProcessed = 0;
    boolean emptyColumnNotCreated = true;

    while (filesProcessed < numFiles)
    {
        tr = doc.createElement("tr");
        for (int i = 0; i < imagesPerRowValue; i++)
        {
            if (filesProcessed < numFiles)
            {
                td = doc.createElement("td");
                td.setAttribute("style", "text-align: center;");

                String qualifiedFilename = "file:\\\\\" +
                directoryName + File.separatorChar +
                graphicsFiles[filesProcessed];

                a = doc.createElement("a");
                a.setAttribute("href", qualifiedFilename);

                img = doc.createElement("img");
                img.setAttribute("src", qualifiedFilename);
                img.setAttribute("width", "100px");
                img.setAttribute("height", "130px");
                img.setAttribute("border", "0");
                a.appendChild(img);
```

```
          td.appendChild(a);

          if (includeFilenamesFlag)
          {
            br = doc.createElement("br");
            td.appendChild(br);

            span = doc.createElement("span");
            span.setAttribute("style", "font-family: monospace;");
            span.appendChild(doc.createTextNode
                              (graphicsFiles[filesProcessed]));
            td.appendChild(span);
          }
          tr.appendChild(td);
          filesProcessed++;
        }
        // we've listed all the files, so create an empty column
        else if (emptyColumnNotCreated)
        {
          td = doc.createElement("td");
          td.setAttribute("colspan",
                              String.valueOf(imagesPerRowValue - i));
          td.setAttribute("bgcolor", "#CCCCCC");
          tr.appendChild(td);
          emptyColumnNotCreated = false;
        }
      }
      table.appendChild(tr);
    }
  }
  return table;
}
}
```

Notice that the extension element receives two arguments from Xalan:
`org.apache.xalan.extensions.XSLTProcessorContext` and `org.apache.xalan.tem` `plates.ElemExtensionCall`. We use the `XSLTProcessorContext` to access the `<photo-album>` element in the XML source document. Xalan and Saxon provide similar context objects to extension elements and functions, although they have different structures, methods, and capabilities.

If you've written Java code to manipulate the Document Object Model (DOM), you'll recognize the techniques at work here. We create a DOM element named `table`, then a DOM element named `tr`, then some DOM elements named `td`, then we put text or `img` elements inside them, and so forth. It's tedious, as DOM code typically is, but it's straightforward.

When we create a `td` element, for example, we create an `a` element, and then we set its attributes. Next, we create an `img` element and set the `img` element's attributes. When the `img` element is complete, we add it to the `a` element, then we add the `a` element to the `td` element. If the XML source specified that we should include the filenames in the

HTML table, we create a text node that contains the filename and add it to the td element. When the td element is complete, we add it to the tr element; when the tr is complete, we add it to the table element. At the end of the code, the table element is complete, so we return that element to the XSLT processor. The processor then uses that element and all of its children in the output document.

To simplify the Java code, we use a Java FilenameFilter that selects only the files we want. The extension element invoked this class with this line of Java code:

```
String[] graphicsFiles = dir.list(new GraphicsFilenameFilter());
```

If it's not a graphical file, we don't want to put it into the album. Here's the code for the filter:

```java
/*
 * GraphicsFilenameFilter.java
 * Created on Nov 28, 2006 by Doug Tidwell
 */

package com.oreilly.xslt.xalan;
// The filename filter for Saxon is identical except for the package
// name (com.oreilly.xslt.saxon)

import java.io.File;
import java.io.FilenameFilter;

public class GraphicsFilenameFilter implements FilenameFilter
{
  public boolean accept(File dir, String name)
  {
    String lcName = name.toLowerCase();
    if (lcName.endsWith(".jpg")  ||
        lcName.endsWith(".jpeg") ||
        lcName.endsWith(".png")  ||
        lcName.endsWith(".gif")  ||
        lcName.endsWith(".bmp"))
      return true;
    else
      return false;
  }

}
```

If the filename extension is .jpg, .jpeg, .png, .gif or .bmp, it will pass the filter. Any file that doesn't pass the filter doesn't appear in our list of filenames. We use the filename filter when we create the list of files we have to process:

```
String[] graphicsFiles = dir.list(new GraphicsFilenameFilter());
```

 We're assuming that any file with the appropriate extension is actually an image. More ambitious readers are welcome to add code that actually opens each file to verify that it is an image. Another useful feature would be to check the dimensions of the images and create a thumbnail that preserves the aspect ratio. Finally, JPEG files can contain metadata about the date and time that the picture was taken; displaying that information in the HTML output would be a nice touch as well.

Saxon Java Version

The Saxon extension element is considerably more complicated than the Xalan version. We have to create a class that implements the `net.sf.saxon.style.ExtensionElement Factory` interface. That class is responsible for processing the attributes of the `<SaxonPhotoAlbum>` element, including processing any attribute value templates that are in the element. Here's the short file that performs this step:

```
/*
 * PhotoAlbumElementFactory.java
 * Created on Nov 28, 2006 by Doug Tidwell
 */

package com.oreilly.xslt.saxon;

import net.sf.saxon.style.ExtensionElementFactory;

public class PhotoAlbumElementFactory
  implements ExtensionElementFactory
{
  public Class getExtensionClass(String elementName)
  {
    if (elementName.equals("SaxonPhotoAlbum"))
      return SaxonPhotoAlbum.class;
    return null;
  }
}
```

Notice that the code returns the `class` object for the `SaxonPhotoAlbum` class. Saxon uses that object to actually create a `SaxonPhotoAlbum` object that processes the element in the stylesheet:

```
/*
 * SaxonPhotoAlbum.java
 * Created on Nov 28, 2006 by Doug Tidwell
 */

package com.oreilly.xslt.saxon;

import java.io.File;

import net.sf.saxon.event.Receiver;
import net.sf.saxon.event.ReceiverOptions;
import net.sf.saxon.expr.Expression;
```

```java
import net.sf.saxon.expr.SimpleExpression;
import net.sf.saxon.expr.XPathContext;
import net.sf.saxon.instruct.Executable;
import net.sf.saxon.om.NamePool;
import net.sf.saxon.style.ExtensionInstruction;
import net.sf.saxon.style.StandardNames;
import net.sf.saxon.trans.XPathException;

public class SaxonPhotoAlbum
  extends ExtensionInstruction
{
  Expression directory;
  Expression imagesPerRow;
  Expression includeFilenames;

  @Override
  public void prepareAttributes() throws XPathException
  {
    String directoryAttr = attributeList.getValue("", "directory");
    if (directoryAttr == null)
    {
      compileError("The directory attribute is required.", "");
      directoryAttr = "";
    }
    directory = makeAttributeValueTemplate(directoryAttr);

    String imagesPerRowAttr =
      attributeList.getValue("", "imagesPerRow");
    if (imagesPerRowAttr == null)
      imagesPerRowAttr = "5";
    imagesPerRow = makeAttributeValueTemplate(imagesPerRowAttr);

    String includeFilenamesAttr =
      attributeList.getValue("", "includeFilenames");
    if (includeFilenamesAttr == null)
      includeFilenamesAttr = "no";
    includeFilenames = makeAttributeValueTemplate(includeFilenamesAttr);
  }

  @Override
  public Expression compile(Executable arg0) throws XPathException
  {
    SaxonPhotoAlbumInstruction spa =
      new SaxonPhotoAlbumInstruction(directory,
                                     imagesPerRow,
                                     includeFilenames);
    return spa;
  }

  private static class SaxonPhotoAlbumInstruction
    extends SimpleExpression {

    private static final long serialVersionUID = 1184239671886575198L;
    public static final int DIRECTORY = 0;
    public static final int IMAGES_PER_ROW = 1;
```

```java
public static final int INCLUDE_FILENAMES = 2;

public SaxonPhotoAlbumInstruction(Expression directory,
    Expression imagesPerRow, Expression includeFilenames)
{
  Expression[] subs = {directory, imagesPerRow, includeFilenames};
  setArguments(subs);
}

/**
 * A subclass must provide one of the methods evaluateItem(),
 * iterate(), or process(). This method indicates which of
 * the three is provided.
 */

public int getImplementationMethod()
{
    return Expression.PROCESS_METHOD;
}

public String getExpressionType()
{
    return "spa:SaxonPhotoAlbum";
}

public void process(XPathContext context) throws XPathException
{
  String directoryName =
    arguments[DIRECTORY].evaluateAsString(context);

  int imagesPerRowValue = 5;
  try
  {
    imagesPerRowValue =
        Integer.parseInt(arguments[IMAGES_PER_ROW].
                        evaluateAsString(context));
  }
  catch (NumberFormatException nfe)
  {
    imagesPerRowValue = 5;
  }
  if (!(imagesPerRowValue > 0))
  {
    imagesPerRowValue = 5;
  }

  boolean includeFilenamesFlag =
    arguments[INCLUDE_FILENAMES].evaluateAsString(context)
    .equals("yes");

  NamePool pool = context.getController().getNamePool();
  int anchorCode = pool.allocate("", "", "a");
  int borderCode = pool.allocate("", "", "border");
  int brCode = pool.allocate("", "", "br");
  int cellpaddingCode = pool.allocate("", "", "cellpadding");
```

```
int colspanCode = pool.allocate("", "", "colspan");
int heightCode = pool.allocate("", "", "height");
int hrefCode = pool.allocate("", "", "href");
int imgCode = pool.allocate("", "", "img");
int spanCode = pool.allocate("", "", "span");
int srcCode = pool.allocate("", "", "src");
int styleCode = pool.allocate("", "", "style");
int tableCode = pool.allocate("", "", "table");
int colCode = pool.allocate("", "", "td");
int rowCode = pool.allocate("", "", "tr");
int widthCode = pool.allocate("", "", "width");

Receiver out = context.getReceiver();

// start <table>
out.startElement(tableCode, StandardNames.XDT_UNTYPED, locationId, 0);
out.attribute(borderCode, StandardNames.XDT_UNTYPED,
              "3", locationId, 0);
out.attribute(cellpaddingCode, StandardNames.XDT_UNTYPED,
              "5", locationId, 0);

String[] graphicsFiles;
int numFiles = 0;

File dir = new File(directoryName);

// Return an error message if the directory doesn't exist
if (!dir.exists())
{
  // start <tr>
  out.startElement(rowCode, StandardNames.XDT_UNTYPED, locationId, 0);

  // start <td>
  out.startElement(colCode, StandardNames.XDT_UNTYPED, locationId, 0);
  out.attribute(styleCode, StandardNames.XDT_UNTYPED,
                "font-weight: bold; font-size: 150%;", locationId, 0);
  out.characters("The directory ", locationId, 0);

  // start <span>
  out.startElement(spanCode, StandardNames.XDT_UNTYPED, locationId, 0);
  out.attribute(styleCode, StandardNames.XDT_UNTYPED,
                "font-family: monospace;", locationId, 0);
  out.characters(directoryName, locationId, 0);
  out.endElement(); // end <span>

  out.characters(" does not exist!", locationId, 0);
  out.endElement(); // end <td>

  out.endElement(); // end <tr>
}
else
{
  // Use the filename filter to find the images
  graphicsFiles = dir.list(new GraphicsFilenameFilter());
  if (graphicsFiles != null)
```

```
    numFiles = graphicsFiles.length;

// Return an error message if the directory doesn't contain
// any images
if (numFiles == 0)
{
  // start <tr>
  out.startElement(rowCode, StandardNames.XDT_UNTYPED, locationId, 0);
  // start <td>
  out.startElement(colCode, StandardNames.XDT_UNTYPED, locationId, 0);
  out.attribute(styleCode, StandardNames.XDT_UNTYPED,
                "font-weight: bold; background: #CCCCCC; " +
                "font-size: 150%;",
                locationId, 0);
  out.characters("The directory ", locationId, 0);
  // start <span>
  out.startElement(spanCode, StandardNames.XDT_UNTYPED, locationId, 0);
  out.attribute(styleCode, StandardNames.XDT_UNTYPED,
                "font-family: monospace;", locationId, 0);
  out.characters(directoryName, locationId, 0);
  out.endElement(); // end <span>
  out.characters(" doesn't contain any images!", locationId, 0);

  out.endElement(); // end <td>

  out.endElement(); // end <tr>
}

// We've got images, so let's process 'em...
else
{
  // start <tr>
  out.startElement(rowCode, StandardNames.XDT_UNTYPED, locationId, 0);

  // start <td>
  out.startElement(colCode, StandardNames.XDT_UNTYPED, locationId, 0);
  out.attribute(colspanCode, StandardNames.XDT_UNTYPED, String
      .valueOf(imagesPerRowValue), locationId, 0);
  out.attribute(styleCode, StandardNames.XDT_UNTYPED,
                "font-weight: bold; background: #CCCCCC; "
                    + "font-size: 150%;", locationId, 0);
  out.characters("Photos from ", locationId, 0);

  // start <span>
  out.startElement(spanCode, StandardNames.XDT_UNTYPED, locationId, 0);
  out.attribute(styleCode, StandardNames.XDT_UNTYPED,
                "font-family: monospace;", locationId, 0);
  out.characters(directoryName + ":", locationId, 0);
  out.endElement(); // end <span>

  out.endElement(); // end <td>

  out.endElement(); // end <tr>
}
```

```
int filesProcessed = 0;
boolean emptyColumnNotCreated = true;

while (filesProcessed < numFiles)
{
  // start <tr>
  out.startElement(rowCode, StandardNames.XDT_UNTYPED, locationId, 0);

  for (int i = 0; i < imagesPerRowValue; i++)
  {
    if (filesProcessed < numFiles)
    {
      // start <td>
      out.startElement(colCode, StandardNames.XDT_UNTYPED, locationId,
                       0);
      out.attribute(styleCode, StandardNames.XDT_UNTYPED,
                    "text-align: center;", locationId, 0);

      String qualifiedFilename = "file:\\\\" + directoryName
          + File.separatorChar + graphicsFiles[filesProcessed];

      // start <a>
      out.startElement(anchorCode, StandardNames.XDT_UNTYPED,
                       locationId, 0);
      out.attribute(hrefCode, StandardNames.XDT_UNTYPED,
                    qualifiedFilename, locationId, 0);

      // start <img>
      out.startElement(imgCode, StandardNames.XDT_UNTYPED, locationId,
                       0);
      out.attribute(widthCode, StandardNames.XDT_UNTYPED, "100px",
                    locationId, 0);
      out.attribute(heightCode, StandardNames.XDT_UNTYPED, "130px",
                    locationId, 0);
      out.attribute(srcCode, StandardNames.XDT_UNTYPED,
                    qualifiedFilename, locationId, 0);
      out.attribute(borderCode, StandardNames.XDT_UNTYPED, "0",
                    locationId, 0);
      out.endElement(); // end <img>

      out.endElement(); // end <a>

      if (includeFilenamesFlag)
      {
        // start <br>
        out.startElement(brCode, StandardNames.XDT_UNTYPED, locationId,
                         0);
        out.endElement(); // end <br>

        // start <span style="font-family: monospace">
        out.startElement(spanCode, StandardNames.XDT_UNTYPED,
                         locationId, 0);
        out.attribute(styleCode, StandardNames.XDT_UNTYPED,
                      "font-family: monospace;", locationId, 0);
        out.characters(graphicsFiles[filesProcessed], locationId, 0);
```

```
              out.endElement(); // end <span>
            }
            out.endElement(); // end <td>
            filesProcessed++;
          }
          // We've listed all the files, so create an empty column
          else if (emptyColumnNotCreated)
          {
            // start <td>
            out.startElement(colCode, StandardNames.XDT_UNTYPED, locationId,
                             0);
            out.attribute(styleCode, StandardNames.XDT_UNTYPED,
                          "background: #CCCCCC;", locationId, 0);
            out.attribute(colspanCode, StandardNames.XDT_UNTYPED,
                          String.valueOf(imagesPerRowValue - i),
                          locationId, 0);
            out.characters(" ", locationId,
                           ReceiverOptions.DISABLE_ESCAPING);
            out.endElement(); // end <td>
            emptyColumnNotCreated = false;
          }
        }
        out.endElement(); // end <tr>
      }
    }
    out.endElement(); // end <table>
  }
}
```

As with the Xalan extension, Saxon provides us with a context object—in this case, a Saxon `net.sf.saxon.expr.XPathContext`. The Saxon extension works similarly to the Xalan extension, creating elements and attributes and returning them as a tree structure. There are differences, though; to start, we need to define a Saxon `NamePool`:

```
NamePool pool = context.getController().getNamePool();
int anchorCode = pool.allocate("", "", "a");
int borderCode = pool.allocate("", "", "border");
int brCode = pool.allocate("", "", "br");
int cellpaddingCode = pool.allocate("", "", "cellpadding");
...
```

We're defining the names of the elements and attributes we're going to create. Next, we use the `out` object to create the various elements of the table. The `out` object is a Saxon `net.sf.saxon.event.Receiver` object that we retrieve from the `XPathContext`. We use `out` to create the elements, attributes, and text nodes. The four methods we use from the `Receiver` class are `startElement( )`, `attribute( )`, `characters( )`, and `endElement( )`. Notice that the `endElement( )` method doesn't take any parameters; it simply ends whatever element is being created. The code is commented to indicate whenever an element is started or ended.

As we mentioned with the Xalan version of this extension, we use a `FilenameFilter` to select only the image files.

.NET Version

The .NET version of the photo album is slightly different. We'll implement the extension as an extension *function*, not as an extension element. We'll do this to show an alternate technique for creating nodes in the output tree.

Our extension function creates a DOM tree that contains all of the HTML elements needed for the output tree. The Xalan and Saxon versions of this extension `element` replace the extension element in the stylesheet with the appropriate generated nodes. In the .NET environment, our extension function returns a DOM tree that is added to the result tree.

Here's the code for the extension function. It follows the same basic procedure as the other versions of the extension: use system functions to get the list of files and then create the DOM elements for the HTML table:

```
/*
 * PhotoAlbum.cs
 * Created on Nov 28, 2006 by Doug Tidwell
 */

using System;
using System.IO;
using System.Text;
using System.Xml;

// This class creates a photo album with all of the images in a
// given directory.
namespace com.oreilly.xslt
{
  class PhotoAlbum
  {
    // getPhotoListing is the name of the extension function.  Notice
    // that it returns an XMLNode; that node is inserted into the
    // output tree.
    public XmlNode getPhotoListing(String dirName,
                                   String imgPerRow,
                                   String incFilenames)
    {
      // For parameters, we get the name of the directory, the number
      // of images per row, and whether the names of the files should
      // be displayed.
      int imagesPerRow = int.Parse(imgPerRow);
      Boolean includeFilenames = (incFilenames.Equals("yes"));

      // We're building a DOM tree, effectively, so we create some
      // elements beforehand.
      XmlElement anchorEl, breaklineEl, imageEl, spanEl,
          tableEl, tableDataEl, tableRowEl;
      XmlNode textNode;

      XmlDocument doc = new XmlDocument();
      XmlDocumentFragment df = doc.CreateDocumentFragment();
      tableEl = doc.CreateElement("table");
```

```
tableEl.SetAttribute("border", "3");
tableEl.SetAttribute("cellpadding", "5");

Boolean directoryExists = true;

System.Collections.ArrayList allGraphicsFiles =
    new System.Collections.ArrayList();

// We add all of the JPEG, PNG, GIF and BMP files in the
// specified directory.  Windows isn't case-sensitive, so
// the code is slightly simpler than the Java version.
try
{
  allGraphicsFiles.InsertRange(allGraphicsFiles.Count,
      System.IO.Directory.GetFiles(dirName, "*.jpg"));
  allGraphicsFiles.InsertRange(allGraphicsFiles.Count,
      System.IO.Directory.GetFiles(dirName, "*.jpeg"));
  allGraphicsFiles.InsertRange(allGraphicsFiles.Count,
      System.IO.Directory.GetFiles(dirName, "*.png"));
  allGraphicsFiles.InsertRange(allGraphicsFiles.Count,
      System.IO.Directory.GetFiles(dirName, "*.gif"));
  allGraphicsFiles.InsertRange(allGraphicsFiles.Count,
      System.IO.Directory.GetFiles(dirName, "*.bmp"));
}

// Return an error message if the directory doesn't exist
catch (System.IO.DirectoryNotFoundException dnfe)
{
  directoryExists = false;
  tableRowEl = doc.CreateElement("tr");
  tableDataEl = doc.CreateElement("td");
  tableDataEl.SetAttribute("style", "font-weight: bold; " +
      "font-size: 150%;");
  textNode = doc.CreateTextNode("The directory ");
  tableDataEl.AppendChild(textNode);
  spanEl = doc.CreateElement("span");
  spanEl.SetAttribute("style", "font-family: monospace;");
  spanEl.AppendChild(doc.CreateTextNode(dirName));
  tableDataEl.AppendChild(spanEl);
  textNode = doc.CreateTextNode(" doesn't exist!");
  tableDataEl.AppendChild(textNode);
  tableRowEl.AppendChild(tableDataEl);
  tableEl.AppendChild(tableRowEl);
  df.AppendChild(tableEl);
}

int numFiles = allGraphicsFiles.Count;

if (directoryExists)
{
  // Return an error message if the directory doesn't contain
  // any images
  if (numFiles == 0)
  {
    tableRowEl = doc.CreateElement("tr");
```

```
      tableDataEl = doc.CreateElement("td");
      tableDataEl.SetAttribute("style", "font-weight: bold; " +
          "font-size: 150%;");
      textNode = doc.CreateTextNode("The directory ");
      tableDataEl.AppendChild(textNode);
      spanEl = doc.CreateElement("span");
      spanEl.SetAttribute("style", "font-family: monospace;");
      spanEl.AppendChild(doc.CreateTextNode(dirName));
      tableDataEl.AppendChild(spanEl);
      textNode =
          doc.CreateTextNode(" doesn't contain any images!");
      tableDataEl.AppendChild(textNode);
      tableRowEl.AppendChild(tableDataEl);
      tableEl.AppendChild(tableRowEl);
      df.AppendChild(tableEl);
  }

  // We've got some images, so let's process 'em...
  else
  {
      // First we create a table row for the header.
      tableRowEl = doc.CreateElement("tr");
      tableDataEl = doc.CreateElement("td");
      tableDataEl.SetAttribute("colspan", imgPerRow);
      tableDataEl.SetAttribute("style", "font-weight: bold; " +
          "background: #CCCCCC; font-size: 150%;");
      tableDataEl.AppendChild(doc.CreateTextNode("Photos from "));
      spanEl = doc.CreateElement("span");
      spanEl.SetAttribute("style", "font-family: monospace;");
      spanEl.AppendChild(doc.CreateTextNode(dirName + ":"));
      tableDataEl.AppendChild(spanEl);
      tableRowEl.AppendChild(tableDataEl);
      tableEl.AppendChild(tableRowEl);

      // Now we process all of the files.  The emptyColumnNotCreated
      // flag tells us whether the blank cell has been created.
      // If there are five images per row and there are 47 images,
      // the last row will contain a blank cell with a colspan of 3.
      // We only create that blank cell once.
      int filesProcessed = 0;
      Boolean emptyColumnNotCreated = true;

      // We look through all of the files
      while (filesProcessed < numFiles)
      {
        tableRowEl = doc.CreateElement("tr");

        // Process the next {imagesPerRow} images
        for (int i = 0; i < imagesPerRow; i++)
        {
          if (filesProcessed < numFiles)
          {
            tableDataEl = doc.CreateElement("td");
            tableDataEl.SetAttribute("style", "text-align: center;");
            String qualifiedFilename = "file:\\\\\" +
```

```
            allGraphicsFiles[filesProcessed];
          anchorEl = doc.CreateElement("a");
          imageEl = doc.CreateElement("img");
          imageEl.SetAttribute("src", qualifiedFilename);
          imageEl.SetAttribute("width", "100px");
          imageEl.SetAttribute("height", "130px");
          imageEl.SetAttribute("border", "0");
          anchorEl.AppendChild(imageEl);
          tableDataEl.AppendChild(anchorEl);

          if (includeFilenames)
          {
            breaklineEl = doc.CreateElement("br");
            tableDataEl.AppendChild(breaklineEl);

            // We use FileInfo to get the filename without the path.
            FileInfo fi =
              new FileInfo((String)allGraphicsFiles[filesProcessed]);
            spanEl = doc.CreateElement("span");
            spanEl.SetAttribute("style", "font-family: monospace;");
            spanEl.AppendChild(doc.CreateTextNode(fi.Name));
            tableDataEl.AppendChild(spanEl);
          }
          tableRowEl.AppendChild(tableDataEl);
          filesProcessed++;
        }

        // If we've processed all of the files and we haven't
        // created the empty column, we'll do that now.
        else if (emptyColumnNotCreated)
        {
          tableDataEl = doc.CreateElement("td");
          Int32 colspan = (imagesPerRow - i);
          tableDataEl.SetAttribute("colspan", colspan.ToString());
          tableDataEl.SetAttribute("style", "background: #CCCCCC;");
          tableRowEl.AppendChild(tableDataEl);
          emptyColumnNotCreated = false;
        }
      }

      // Throughout this code, we create elements and append them to
      // the appropriate parent element.
      tableEl.AppendChild(tableRowEl);
    }
    df.AppendChild(tableEl);
  }
}

// Once we've finished, we have a node-set that contains all of the
// HTML elements we need.  That is returned to the caller, which
// then inserts those nodes into the output stream.
return df;
  }
 }
}
```

The DOM code is more similar to the Xalan extension than to the Saxon one. We're using .NET classes, but the overall flow of the code is similar to the two Java extensions. We collect the filenames, create a table, create a cell for each graphic, and then return the table element. In this case, we return a .NET `XmlDocumentFragment`.

Now that we have our extension function defined, we need a stylesheet that invokes it. As we've seen before, we need to define a namespace for the extension:

```
<?xml version="1.0" encoding="utf-8" ?>
<xsl:stylesheet version="1.0"
  xmlns:xsl="http://www.w3.org/1999/XSL/Transform"
  xmlns:ora="http://www.oreilly.com/xslt"
  extension-element-prefixes="ora">

  <xsl:output method="html"/>

  <xsl:template match="/">
    <html>
      <head>
        <title>Photo album extension function test</title>
      </head>
      <body style="font-family: sans-serif;">
        <h1>
          <xsl:text>.Net Photo album extension function test</xsl:text>
        </h1>
        <xsl:variable name="album"
                      select="ora:getPhotoListing(/photo-album/@directory,
                      /photo-album/@imagesPerRow,
                      /photo-album/@includeFilenames)"/>
        <xsl:copy-of select="$album"/>
      </body>
    </html>
  </xsl:template>

</xsl:stylesheet>
```

Because our .NET implementation is an extension function, we assign its value to a variable. Once the variable (a result tree fragment) is created, we use `<xsl:copy-of>` to copy everything in the variable to the output tree.

As with our earlier .NET examples, we need a C# file that creates an `XslCompiledTransformation` object. We also create a `PhotoAlbum` object and associate it with the namespace prefix defined in our stylesheet. The final step is to create an `XsltArgumentList` that ties everything together. Here's the code:

```
/*
 * Main.cs
 * Created Nov 22, 2006 by Doug Tidwell
 */

using System;
using System.Text;
using System.Xml;
using System.Xml.Xsl;
```

```
namespace com.oreilly.xslt
{
  class MainClass
  {
    static void Main(string[] args)
    {
      // Create the stylesheet object and the XMLWriter that
      // writes the output to a file
      XslCompiledTransform stylesheet = new XslCompiledTransform();
      XmlTextWriter xWriter =
          new XmlTextWriter(args[2], Encoding.UTF8);

      // Use an XsltSettings object that allows executing scripts
      // (we need this for extensions), then load the stylesheet
      XsltSettings settings = new XsltSettings(true, true);
      stylesheet.Load(args[1], settings, new XmlUrlResolver());

      // Create an extension object
      PhotoAlbum pa = new PhotoAlbum();

      // We add the PhotoAlbum object as an extension object to the
      // XsltArgumentList.
      XsltArgumentList argList = new XsltArgumentList();
      argList.AddExtensionObject("http://www.oreilly.com/xslt", pa);

      // With everything in place, we call the Transform() method
      // to do the work...
      stylesheet.Transform(args[0], argList, xWriter);
    }
  }
}
```

Notice that the namespace defined in the stylesheet, http://www.oreilly.com/xslt, is the same namespace we use in the XsltArgumentList we create in the C# code. If these two don't match, the .NET XSLT processor won't be able to find the extension class.

When everything works together, the results appear as in Figure 9-14.

Most digital cameras produce JPEG files that contain EXIF (Exchangeable Image Format) tags. Those tags contain information such as the model of camera used to take the picture, the date and time of the picture, and other aspects. If you'd like to delve into all the details of an EXIF-tagged JPEG file, see the EXIF Tag Parsing Library here: *http://sourceforge.net/projects/libexif*. Enhancing the extension so that those details appear in the table (or are displayed in a small window when you move the mouse over the picture) would be a nice addition to the code.

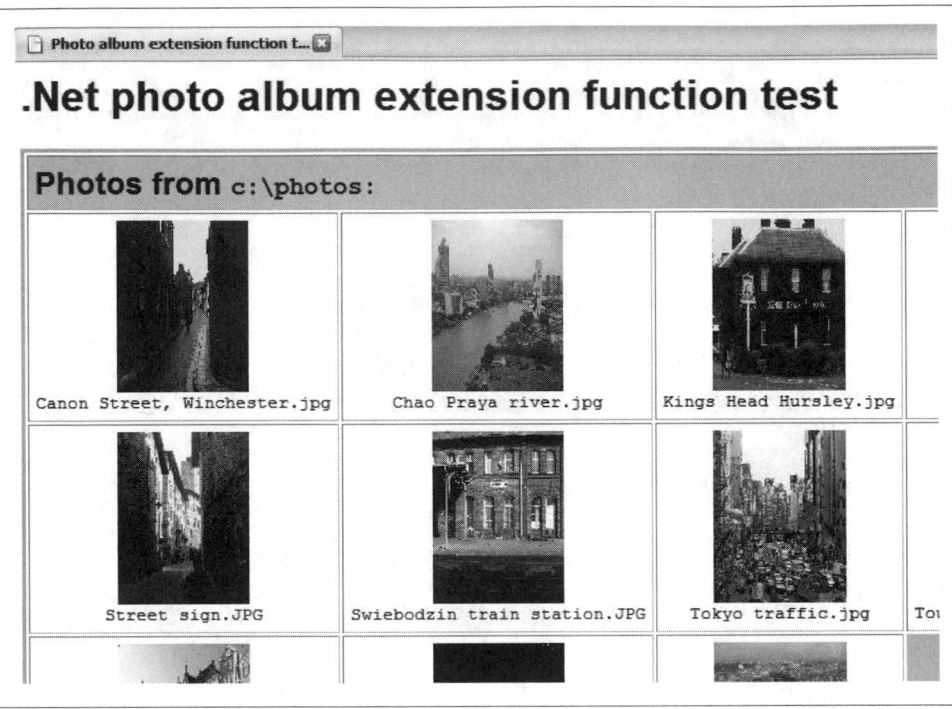

Figure 9-14. A photo album generated by a .NET extension function

Summary

In this chapter, we've run the gamut of extension functions and extension elements, demonstrating how to add sophisticated processing power to our stylesheets. We've generated many output files from a stylesheet, created JPEGs dynamically, created interactive graphics, interacted with databases, and generated HTML files created with data retrieved from the filesytem.

In terms of XSLT itself, we've created both extension elements and extension functions, and we've returned simple values as well as trees of DOM objects. Most importantly, we've demonstrated how to access the XML source document and the extension code in a variety of ways, using different platforms, languages, and XSLT processors. If you master these techniques, there's practically nothing you can't do in your stylesheets.

XSLT Reference

This chapter is a complete reference to all the elements defined in the XSLT specification. To keep the examples simple, most of them generate plain text instead of XML, HTML, or XHTML. That allows us to focus on the XSLT itself instead generating CSS properties, HTML tables, or other details. Where an XML, HTML, or XHTML example is more instructive, we'll use it of course, but most stylesheets are as simple as possible.

[2.0] Attributes common to all XSLT elements

There are six standard attributes that can be used on any XSLT element; we'll define them here rather than redefine them for every XSLT element. While these attributes can be used on any XSLT element, they are normally used on elements such as `<xsl:stylesheet>` and `<xsl:template>`.

Attributes

`version`

> Defines the version of XSLT used to process this element. This is useful when you want a particular XSLT element to be processed using the rules of a particular version of the standard. For example, `<xsl:value-of select="1 div 0"/>` works differently in XSLT 1.0 and 2.0. XSLT 2.0 treats this as a fatal error, while XSLT 1.0 returns `Infinity`. Using `<xsl:value-of version="1.0" ...>` ensures that version 1.0 processing is used.

> Although the `<xsl:output>` element has a `version` attribute, it specifies the value of the `version` attribute in the output. For example, `<xsl:output method="xml" version="1.1">` creates a result document with an XML declaration of `<?xml version="1.1" ...?>`.

`exclude-result-prefixes`

> Lists the prefixes of namespaces that should not be copied to the output. Typically used on the `<xsl:stylesheet>` element only.

`extension-element-prefixes`

> Defines the namespace prefixes that identify extension elements. The XSLT processor uses these namespaces to identify code that provides additional processing. Typically used on the `<xsl:stylesheet>` element only.

`xpath-default-namespace`

> Defines the default namespace used in XPath expressions and patterns. If you're transforming a document that uses a default namespace (`http://www.oreilly.com`, for example), you must namespace-qualify the names of any elements in that document. Defining `xpath-default-namespace="http://www.oreilly.com"` tells XPath to use this namespace as the default for element and type names in XPath expressions. If the documents you're transforming use different default namespaces in different parts of the document, you can use this attribute to change the default XPath namespace. This is typically used on the `<xsl:stylesheet>` element only.

`default-collation`

> A series of space-separated URIs that define the default collation sequence. The default collation sequence is used by `<xsl:key>` and `<xsl:for-each-group>`, but it does not affect the collation used by `<xsl:sort>`. The way collation sequences are defined varies from one XSLT processor to another, so check your processor's documentation for information on defining a collation sequence.

`use-when`

> Defines a statement involving a `system-property` that must be true for this XSLT element to be processed. As an example, using the function `system-property('xsl:is-schema-aware')` lets you determine whether the XSLT processor is schema-aware.

[2.0] <xsl:analyze-string>

Allows you to compare a string and a regular expression.

Changes in XSLT 2.0

`<xsl:analyze-string>` is new to XSLT 2.0.

Category

Instruction.

Required Attributes

`select`

> An XPath expression that defines the string to be analyzed. The expression is converted to a string if necessary.

`regex`

The regular expression. Regular expressions commonly use curly braces ({ and }), which XSLT interprets as the start and end of an attribute value template. For this reason, any curly braces in a regular expression must be doubled. For example, the regular expression `"[0-9]{{5}}"` matches a five-digit number, while `"[0-9]{5}"` matches a one-digit number followed by the number 5.

 It is a fatal error if the regular expression matches a zero-length string. See Appendix E for more details.

Optional Attribute

`flags`

The `flags` attribute modifies how the regular expression is processed. There are four different flags:

s

Regular expressions are evaluated in what the specs refer to as "dot-all" mode. When this flag is used, the dot operator (.) matches any character. Under normal processing (without the s flag), the dot operator matches any character *except* the newline character (#xA). This flag is useful when you want to match strings that might include a newline character.

m

Regular expressions are evaulated in multiline mode. By default, the meta-character (^) matches the start of the entire string, while $ matches the end of the entire string. In multiline mode, ^ matches the start of any line within the string and $ matches the end of any line within the string.

i

Regular expressions are evaluated in case-insensitive mode. The regular expression `"a"` matches both `"a"` and `"A"`.

Note that Unicode issues can complicate this greatly. For example, the XQuery 1.0 and XPath 2.0 Functions and Operators spec gives the example of the Unicode sign for degrees Kelvin (K), which is the letter `"K"`. The combination of `regex="k"` and `flags="i"` matches the Kelvin sign as well as the letters `"k"` (k) and `"K"` (K).

Other Unicode characters don't convert to letters. For example, the Unicode symbol for the Roman numeral I (Ⅰ) looks like the letter I, but does not convert to that. Fortunately, these complications are beyond the scope of this book.

x

All whitespace characters (#x9, #xA, #xD, and #x20) are removed from the regular expression before any comparison is done. In other words, with the x flag, the regular expressions "John Smith" and "JohnSmith" are the same. This flag is useful when you want to break a long regular expression into multiple lines to make it easier to read.

The flags can be combined in any order. The attributes flags="xis" and flags="six" work exactly the same way.

Content

`<xsl:analyze-string>` can contain a single, optional `<xsl:matching-substring>` element and/or a single, optional `<xsl:non-matching-substring>` element. If both `<xsl:matching-substring>` and `<xsl:non-matching-substring>` are included, the `<xsl:matching-substring>` element must appear first. In other words, all three of these `<xsl:analyze-string>` elements are valid:

```
<xsl:analyze-string select="." regex="a">
  <xsl:matching-substring>...</xsl:matching-substring>
</xsl:analyze-string>

<xsl:analyze-string select="." regex="a">
  <xsl:non-matching-substring>...</xsl:non-matching-substring>
</xsl:analyze-string>

<xsl:analyze-string select="." regex="a">
  <xsl:matching-substring>...</xsl:matching-substring>
  <xsl:non-matching-substring>...</xsl:non-matching-substring>
</xsl:analyze-string>
```

The `<xsl:analyze-string>` element can also contain any number of `<xsl:fallback>` elements. If your XSLT 1.0 processor supports forwards-compatible mode, `<xsl:fallback>` lets you define how the processor should respond when the `<xsl:analyze-string>` element is not supported. You could have a stylesheet structured like this:

```
<xsl:analyze-string...>
  <xsl:matching-substring>...</xsl:matching-substring>
  <xsl:fallback>
    <!-- Instructions for a 1.0 processor -->
  </xsl:fallback>
</xsl:analyze-string>
```

A forwards-compatible XSLT 1.0 processor will see the `<xsl:analyze-string>` element, which it cannot process. Whenever the processor finds an unsupported element in the xsl: namespace, it looks inside that element for an `<xsl:fallback>` element. If it finds one, the processor attempts to process whatever is inside `<xsl:fallback>`.

Appears in

`<xsl:analyze-string>` appears inside a template.

Defined in

XSLT section 15, "Regular Expressions."

Regular expressions in XSLT 2.0, XPath 2.0, and XQuery 1.0 are based on the syntax defined in the XML Schema standard; see Appendix F, "Regular Expressions," in *XML Schema Part 2: Datatypes* for the complete syntax. The XQuery 1.0 and XPath 2.0 Functions and Operators spec defines extensions to the XML Schema regular expression syntax in section 7.6, "String Functions that Use Pattern Matching."

Example

Here is an example of `<xsl:analyze-string>` that uses a regular expression to convert U.S. and Canadian telephone numbers of the form 999-999-9999 to the form +1 (999) 999-9999:

```
<?xml version="1.0" encoding="utf-8"?>
<!-- analyze-string1.xsl -->
<xsl:stylesheet version="2.0"
  xmlns:xsl="http://www.w3.org/1999/XSL/Transform">

  <xsl:output method="text"/>

  <xsl:template match="/">
    <xsl:for-each select="phonelist/phonenumber">
      <xsl:analyze-string select="."
      regex="([0-9]{{3}})-(\p{{Nd}}{{3}})-([0-9]{{4}})">
        <xsl:matching-substring>
          <xsl:text>&#xA;+1 (</xsl:text>
          <xsl:value-of select="regex-group(1)"/>
          <xsl:text>) </xsl:text>
          <xsl:value-of select="regex-group(2)"/>
          <xsl:text>-</xsl:text>
          <xsl:value-of select="regex-group(3)"/>
        </xsl:matching-substring>
        <xsl:non-matching-substring>
          <xsl:text>&#xA;   Unrecognized phone number: </xsl:text>
          <xsl:value-of select="."/>
        </xsl:non-matching-substring>
      </xsl:analyze-string>
    </xsl:for-each>
  </xsl:template>

</xsl:stylesheet>
```

Our stylesheet uses the regular expression ([0-9]{{3}})-(\p{{Nd}}{{3}})-([0-9]{{4}}). This creates three `regex-group`s; each group is enclosed in a set of parentheses. The code \p{{Nd}} uses the named character group Nd to refer to numeric digits. See Appendix E for a list of named character groups.

When we use this stylesheet with this list of phone numbers:

```
<?xml version="1.0" encoding="utf-8"?>
<!-- phonelist.xml -->
<phonelist>
  <phonenumber>919-555-1212</phonenumber>
  <phonenumber>(919) 555-1212</phonenumber>
```

```
<phonenumber>212.555.1212</phonenumber>
<phonenumber>617-555-1212</phonenumber>
<phonenumber>+86 555-1212</phonenumber>
</phonelist>
```

we get these results:

```
+1 (919) 555-1212
   Unrecognized phone number: (919) 555-1212
   Unrecognized phone number: 212.555.1212
+1 (617) 555-1212
   Unrecognized phone number: +86 555-1212
```

When our regular expression matches, `regex-group(1)` represents the area code, `regex-group(2)` represents the exchange, and `regex-group(3)` represents the last four digits of the phone number.

If you need to retrieve all of the string that matched the regular expression, `regex-group(0)` does the trick. (Using a dot `"."` does the same thing.) In the previous example, using `regex-group(0)` for the first phone number returns `919-555-1212`.

In some circles, it's fashionable to use periods instead of dashes to separate the sections of a phone number. To handle this, we could change our regular expression to match both periods and dashes:

```
<xsl:analyze-string select="."
  regex="([0-9]{{3}})(-|\.)([0-9]{{3}})(-|\.)([0-9]{{4}})">
```

We replaced the dashes in the original expression with `(-|.)`. This expression matches the third `<phonenumber>` element in addition to the first and fourth, but the output doesn't look right:

```
+1 (919) --555
   Unrecognized phone number: (919) 555-1212
+1 (212) .-555
+1 (617) --555
   Unrecognized phone number: +86 555-1212
```

The problem is that we've created two more groups in the regular expression. We need to change our stylesheet to use `regex-group(1)`, `regex-group(3)`, and `regex-group(5)`:

```
<?xml version="1.0" encoding="utf-8"?>
<!-- analyze-string2.xsl -->
<xsl:stylesheet version="2.0"
  xmlns:xsl="http://www.w3.org/1999/XSL/Transform">

  <xsl:output method="text"/>

  <xsl:template match="/">
    <xsl:for-each select="phonelist/phonenumber">
      <xsl:analyze-string select="."
        regex="([0-9]{{3}})(-|\.)([0-9]{{3}})(-|\.)([0-9]{{4}})">
        <xsl:matching-substring>
          <xsl:text>&#xA;+1 (</xsl:text>
          <xsl:value-of select="regex-group(1)"/>
          <xsl:text>) </xsl:text>
          <xsl:value-of select="regex-group(3)"/>
```

```
        <xsl:text>-</xsl:text>
        <xsl:value-of select="regex-group(5)"/>
      </xsl:matching-substring>
      <xsl:non-matching-substring>
        <xsl:text>&#xA;   Unrecognized phone number: </xsl:text>
        <xsl:value-of select="."/>
      </xsl:non-matching-substring>
    </xsl:analyze-string>
  </xsl:for-each>
</xsl:template>

</xsl:stylesheet>
```

Now our updated stylesheet gives us the correct results:

```
+1 (919) 555-1212
   Unrecognized phone number: (919) 555-1212
+1 (212) 555-1212
+1 (617) 555-1212
   Unrecognized phone number: +86 555-1212
```

In our discussion of the i flag, we mentioned the example of the Kelvin sign (#x212A;) as a special Unicode character that matches the letter K. Here's a stylesheet to test that, if you'd like:

```
<?xml version="1.0" encoding="utf-8"?>
<!-- analyze-string3.xsl -->
<xsl:stylesheet version="2.0"
  xmlns:xsl="http://www.w3.org/1999/XSL/Transform">

  <xsl:output method="text"/>

  <xsl:template match="/">
    <xsl:analyze-string select="'&#x212A;'"
      regex="k" flags="i">
      <xsl:matching-substring>
        <xsl:text>It matches!</xsl:text>
      </xsl:matching-substring>
      <xsl:non-matching-substring>
        <xsl:text>It doesn't match!</xsl:text>
      </xsl:non-matching-substring>
    </xsl:analyze-string>
  </xsl:template>

</xsl:stylesheet>
```

For a final example, we'll illustrate what happens with an incorrectly written regular expression. We stated earlier that any curly braces ({ and }) must be doubled. The regular expression [0-9]{{5}} matches a five-digit number, while the incorrectly written expression [0-9]{5} matches a two-digit number ending in 5. (The attribute value template {5} evaluates to the string 5.) Here's the stylesheet we'll use:

```
<?xml version="1.0" encoding="utf-8"?>
<!-- analyze-string4.xsl -->
<xsl:stylesheet version="2.0"
  xmlns:xsl="http://www.w3.org/1999/XSL/Transform">
```

```
<xsl:output method="text"/>

<xsl:template match="/">
  <xsl:text>Test of an incorrectly written regex:&#xA;&#xA;</xsl:text>
  <xsl:call-template name="bad-regex">
    <xsl:with-param name="test-value" select="'37174'"/>
  </xsl:call-template>
  <xsl:call-template name="bad-regex">
    <xsl:with-param name="test-value" select="'95'"/>
  </xsl:call-template>
</xsl:template>

<xsl:template name="bad-regex">
  <xsl:param name="test-value" required="yes"/>
  <xsl:value-of select="$test-value"/>
  <xsl:analyze-string select="$test-value" regex="[0-9]{5}">
    <xsl:matching-substring>
      <xsl:text> matches!&#xA;</xsl:text>
    </xsl:matching-substring>
    <xsl:non-matching-substring>
      <xsl:text> doesn't match!&#xA;</xsl:text>
    </xsl:non-matching-substring>
  </xsl:analyze-string>
</xsl:template>

</xsl:stylesheet>
```

Running this stylesheet against any XML document generates these results:

```
Test of an incorrectly written regex:

37174 doesn't match!
95 matches!
```

The value 95 matches the poorly written expression, whereas the expected 37174 doesn't.

See Also

Appendix E provides complete details on the way regular expressions work in XPath 2.0. Also see the definitions of the following elements and functions: [2.0] `matches( )`, [2.0] `<xsl:matching-substring>`, [2.0] `<xsl:non-matching-substring>`, [2.0] `regex-group( )`, [2.0] `replace( )`, and [2.0] `tokenize( )`.

`<xsl:apply-imports>`

Allows you to apply to the current node a template imported from another stylesheet.

Category

Instruction.

Required Attributes

None.

Optional Attributes

None.

Content

[1.0] None. `<xsl:apply-imports>` is an empty element.

[2.0] In XSLT 2.0, `<xsl:apply-imports>` can contain zero or more `<xsl:with-param>` elements to pass parameters to an imported template. If you pass extra parameters to an imported template, they are ignored. However, if you don't pass a **required** parameter to an imported template, the XSLT processor throws an error.

Appears in

`<xsl:apply-imports>` appears inside a template.

Defined in

[1.0] XSLT section 5.6, "Overriding Template Rules."

[2.0] XSLT section 6.7, "Overriding Template Rules."

Example

Here is a short XML file we'll use to illustrate `<xsl:apply-imports>`:

```
<?xml version="1.0" encoding="utf-8"?>
<!-- codelisting.xml -->
<chapter>
  <title>Some really great code</title>
  <para>Here is one of my favorite code listings:</para>
  <programlisting>
public class HelloWorld
{
  public static void main(String[] args)
  {
    System.out.println("Hello, World!");
  }
}
  </programlisting>
  <para>I wrote that code all by myself!</para>
</chapter>
```

Our main stylesheet has template rules for the four DocBook elements (`<chapter>`, `<title>`, `<para>`, and `<programlisting>`) in our sample document:

```
<?xml version="1.0"?>
<!-- apply-imports.xsl -->
<xsl:stylesheet version="1.0"
  xmlns:xsl="http://www.w3.org/1999/XSL/Transform">

  <xsl:import href="imported.xsl"/>

  <xsl:preserve-space elements="programlisting"/>

  <xsl:output method="html"/>
```

```
<xsl:template match="chapter">
  <html>
    <head>
      <title>
        <xsl:value-of select="title"/>
      </title>
    </head>
    <body>
      <xsl:apply-templates select="*"/>
    </body>
  </html>
</xsl:template>

<xsl:template match="title">
  <h1>
    <xsl:value-of select="."/>
  </h1>
</xsl:template>

<xsl:template match="para">
  <p>
    <xsl:apply-templates select="*|text()"/>
  </p>
</xsl:template>

<xsl:template match="programlisting">
  <div style="font-size: 125%; font-weight:bold;
              font-family: monospace;">
    <xsl:apply-imports />
  </div>
</xsl:template>

</xsl:stylesheet>
```

Here's the stylesheet we'll import:

```
<?xml version="1.0"?>
<!-- imported.xsl -->
<xsl:stylesheet version="1.0"
  xmlns:xsl="http://www.w3.org/1999/XSL/Transform">

  <xsl:template match="programlisting">
    <pre>
      <xsl:value-of select="."/>
    </pre>
  </xsl:template>

</xsl:stylesheet>
```

Our imported stylesheet puts `<pre>` tags around any `<programlisting>` it finds. The main stylesheet puts the `<programlisting>` inside a `<div>` that changes the font properties. When we process the XML document with the main stylesheet, we get these results:

```
<!-- codelisting.html -->
<html>
```

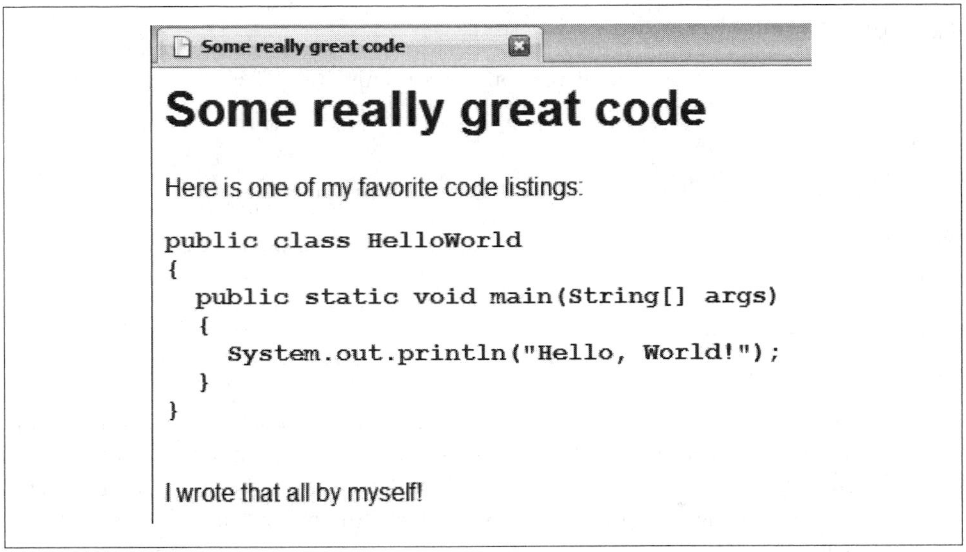

Figure A-1. HTML generated using a template imported from another stylesheet

```
    <head>
        <meta http-equiv="Content-Type" content="text/html; charset=UTF-8">
        <title>Some really great code</title>
    </head>
    <body>
        <h1>Some really great code</h1>
        <p>Here is one of my favorite code listings:</p>
        <div style="font-size: 125%; font-weight:bold;
                    font-family: monospace;"><pre>
public class HelloWorld
{
  public static void main(String[] args)
  {
    System.out.println("Hello, World!");
  }
}
    </pre></div>
        <p>I wrote that all by myself!</p>
    </body>
</html>
```

The HTML output contains a `<div>` element created by the main stylesheet and a `<pre>` element created by the imported stylesheet (see Figure A-1). If you replace `<xsl:apply-imports />` with `<xsl:value-of select="."/>`, the code listing will be run together on a single line.

See Also

The description of the [2.0] `<xsl:next-match>` element.

\<xsl:apply-templates\>

Instructs the XSLT processor to apply the appropriate templates to a node-set or sequence.

Category

Instruction.

Required Attributes

None.

Optional Attributes

select

> Contains an XPath expression that selects the nodes to which templates should be applied. Valid values include * to select all the *element* children of the current node. Without this attribute, `<xsl:apply-templates>` selects all of the children of the current node, including text, processing instructions, and comments. The instructions `<xsl:apply-templates />` and `<xsl:apply-templates select="node( )"/>` are equivalent.

mode

> Defines a *processing mode*, which is a convenient syntax that lets you write specific templates for specific purposes. For example, you could write an `<xsl:template>` with `mode="toc"` to process a node for the table of contents of a document, and write other `<xsl:template>`s with `mode="print"`, `mode="online"`, `mode="index"`, etc. to process the same information for different purposes.
>
> *[2.0]* In XSLT 2.0, there are two special values for the `mode` attribute when used with the `<xsl:apply-templates>` element:

> #default
>> Matches the default mode

> #current
>> Matches the current mode

Content

The `<xsl:apply-templates>` element can contain any number of `<xsl:sort>` and `<xsl:with-param>` elements. In many cases, `<xsl:apply-templates>` is an empty element.

Appears in

`<xsl:apply-templates>` appears inside a template.

Defined in

[1.0] XSLT section 5.4, "Applying Template Rules."

[2.0] XSLT section 6.3, "Applying Template Rules."

Example

Here is a stylesheet that processes the same nodes in three different ways. We invoke each template with a mode attribute. We'll use our list of cars as our sample document:

```
<?xml version="1.0" encoding="utf-8"?>
<!-- cars.xml -->
<cars>
  <manufacturer name="Chevrolet">
    <car>Cavalier</car>
    <car>Corvette</car>
    <car>Impala</car>
    <car>Malibu</car>
  </manufacturer>
  <manufacturer name="Ford">
    <car>Pinto</car>
    <car>Mustang</car>
    <car>Taurus</car>
  </manufacturer>
  <manufacturer name="Volkswagen">
    <car>Beetle</car>
    <car>Jetta</car>
    <car>Passat</car>
    <car>Touraeg</car>
  </manufacturer>
</cars>
```

Here's our stylesheet:

```
<?xml version="1.0" encoding="utf-8"?>
<!-- apply-templates1.xsl -->
<xsl:stylesheet xmlns:xsl="http://www.w3.org/1999/XSL/Transform"
                version="1.0">

  <xsl:output method="html"/>

  <xsl:template match="/">
    <html>
      <head>
        <title>Using the mode attribute</title>
      </head>
      <body style="font-family: sans-serif;">
        <table style="text-align: center;" border="1">
          <tr style="font-weight: bold; font-size: 150%;">
            <td width="30%">Default mode</td>
            <td width="30%">Blue mode</td>
            <td width="30%">Red mode</td>
          </tr>
          <tr>
            <td>
              <p>
                <xsl:apply-templates
                  select="/cars/manufacturer"/>
              </p>
            </td>
            <td>
```

```
            <p>
              <xsl:apply-templates mode="blue"
                select="/cars/manufacturer"/>
            </p>
          </td>
          <td>
            <p>
              <xsl:apply-templates mode="red"
                select="/cars/manufacturer"/>
            </p>
          </td>
        </tr>
      </table>
    </body>
  </html>
</xsl:template>

<xsl:template match="manufacturer">
  <div style="color: green; font-style: italic; font-size: 125%;">
    <xsl:apply-templates select="car"/>
  </div>
</xsl:template>

<xsl:template match="manufacturer" mode="blue">
  <div style="color: blue; font-weight: bold;">
    <xsl:apply-templates select="car"/>
  </div>
</xsl:template>

<xsl:template match="manufacturer" mode="red">
  <div style="color: red; font-family: monospace; font-weight: bold;
              font-size: 150%;">
    <xsl:apply-templates select="car"/>
  </div>
</xsl:template>

<xsl:template match="car">
  <xsl:value-of select="."/>
  <br/>
</xsl:template>

</xsl:stylesheet>
```

Our stylesheet generates an HTML document that looks like Figure A-2.

The first template doesn't have a mode attribute, so it is the default template.

[2.0] Next we'll take a look at the new features of the mode attribute in XSLT 2.0. This stylesheet uses the #default, #current, and #all values of the mode attribute:

```
<?xml version="1.0" encoding="utf-8"?>
<!-- apply-templates2.xsl -->
<xsl:stylesheet xmlns:xsl="http://www.w3.org/1999/XSL/Transform"
                version="2.0">

  <xsl:output method="html"/>
```

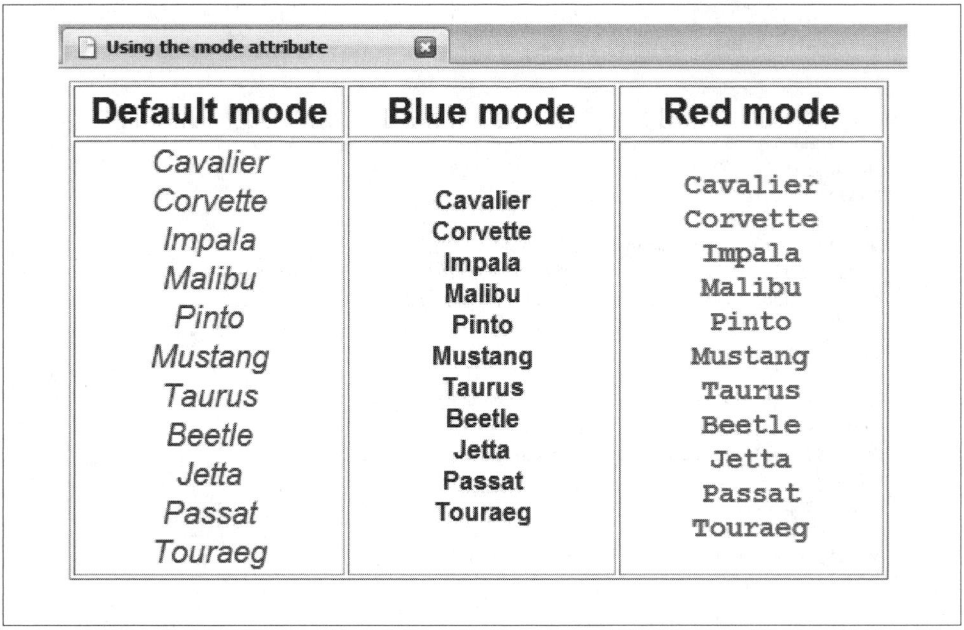

Figure A-2. HTML generated using templates with different modes

```
<xsl:template match="/">
  <html>
    <head>
      <title>Using the mode attribute</title>
    </head>
    <body style="font-family: sans-serif;">
      <table style="text-align: center;" border="1">
        <tr style="font-weight: bold; font-size: 150%;">
          <td width="30%">Default mode</td>
          <td width="30%">Blue mode</td>
          <td width="30%">Red mode</td>
        </tr>
        <tr>
          <td>
            <p>
              <xsl:apply-templates mode="#default"
                select="/cars/manufacturer"/>
            </p>
          </td>
          <td>
            <p>
              <xsl:apply-templates mode="blue"
                select="/cars/manufacturer"/>
            </p>
          </td>
          <td>
            <p>
              <xsl:apply-templates mode="red"
```

```
                            select="/cars/manufacturer"/>
            </p>
          </td>
        </tr>
      </table>
    </body>
  </html>
</xsl:template>

<xsl:template match="manufacturer">
  <div style="color: green; font-style: italic; font-size: 125%">
    <xsl:apply-templates select="car" mode="#current"/>
  </div>
</xsl:template>

<xsl:template match="manufacturer" mode="blue red">
  <div style="color: blue; font-weight: bold;">
    <xsl:apply-templates select="car" mode="#current"/>
  </div>
</xsl:template>

<xsl:template match="car" mode="#all">
  <xsl:value-of select="."/>
  <br/>
</xsl:template>

<xsl:template match="car" mode="red" priority="1">
  <div style="color: red; font-size: 125%; font-family: serif;">
    <xsl:value-of select="."/>
    <br/>
  </div>
</xsl:template>

</xsl:stylesheet>
```

In XSLT 2.0, the mode attribute on `<xsl:apply-templates>` can have the new values `#current` or `#default`. The mode attribute on `<xsl:template>` can have the new values `#all` or `#default`. Our sample stylesheet uses all of the new values:

- In the `match="/"` template, we use `<xsl:apply-templates>` with the modes `#default`, blue, and red. The only difference between the three `<xsl:apply-template>` elements is the mode.

- The first `match="manufacturer"` template doesn't have a mode attribute, so it applies to the default mode. When we use `<xsl:apply-templates mode="#default" ...>`, this template is the one that gets invoked.

- The second `match="manufacturer"` template has a mode of blue red. This template is invoked whenever the mode is blue or red.

- Both of the `match="manufacturer"` templates use `<xsl:apply-templates mode="#current" ...>` to process the `<car>` elements. The current mode is effectively passed as a parameter to the XSLT processor, telling it which template to apply.

- The first `match="car"` template is defined with `mode="#all"`, so it is the default template invoked by both of the `<xsl:apply-templates mode="#current" ...>` elements.
- The final `match="car"` template is defined with `mode="red"`. To make sure it is a better match than the `mode="#all"` template, we add the attribute `priority="1"`. Without this, Saxon displays an "Ambiguous rule match" warning, even though it invokes the `mode="red"` template when the `red` mode is in effect. The Altova XML engine doesn't issue any warnings—it simply invokes the template with `mode="red"`.

Starting with the `match="/"` template, our stylesheet called a variety of templates with three different modes to generate the output document. The three modes formatted the same information in three different ways. This stylesheet produces the same HTML document as the previous stylesheet.

See Also

The description of the `<xsl:template>` element.

<xsl:attribute>

Allows you to create an attribute in the output document. Using the `<xsl:attribute>` instruction allows you to determine the name or content of an attribute at runtime. You can build the attribute's name or value from parts of the input document, hardcoded text, values returned by functions, global variables, and any other value you can access from your stylesheet. You can also use `<xsl:if>` to determine whether the attribute should be created at all.

Category

Instruction.

Required Attribute

name

> The `name` attribute defines the name of the attribute created by the `<xsl:attribute>` element. (No matter how you try to say this, talking about the attributes of the `<xsl:attribute>` element is confusing, isn't it?)

Optional Attributes

namespace

> The `namespace` attribute defines the namespace URI that should be used for this attribute in the output document. You don't have control over the namespace prefix used; the only thing you specify with the `namespace` attribute is the namespace's URI.

[2.0] `select`

> An XPath expression that defines the content of this attribute. If the `<xsl:attribute>` element has a `select` attribute, the element must be empty.

[2.0] `separator`

> Defines the characters that separate multiple values generated by the `<xsl:attribute>` instruction. If `<xsl:attribute>` has a `select` attribute, the default value is a single space (`#x20`). Without a `select` attribute, the default value is a zero-length string (`""`). The `separator` attribute overrides the default value whether `select` is used or not.

[2.0 – Schema] `type`

> Defines the datatype of this attribute. The datatype can be any of the built-in datatypes, or it can be a datatype defined in a schema if you have a schema-aware XSLT 2.0 processor.
>
> The `type` and `validation` attributes are mutually exclusive.

[2.0 – Schema] `validation`

> Defines how the value of the new attribute will be validated. The `validation` attribute has four values: `strict`, `lax`, `preserve`, or `strip`. Because we're creating an attribute, as opposed to an element or a result document, some of the details of the `validation` attribute don't apply.
>
> The values `strip` and `preserve` have no effect. These two values define whether the type annotation of the attribute should be stripped from or preserved in the generated attribute. For an attribute, no validation is done, and the type annotation of the attribute is `xs:untypedAtomic`.
>
> `validation="strict"` means that the XSLT processor looks in all the declared schemas for a global attribute declaration (`<xs:attribute>`) with the same name as this attribute. It is a fatal error if the processor can't find a matching `<xs:attribute>`. Assuming the processor finds the declaration of the attribute, it validates the generated value against the attribute's declaration.
>
> The final value, `validation="lax"`, works just like `validation="strict"`, except that no error occurs if the processor can't find the declaration of the attribute in any declared schemas. In that case, the type annotation of the attribute is `xs:untypedAtomic`.
>
> The `validation` and `type` attributes are mutually exclusive.

Content

You can build the contents of an attribute with any elements that generate a *[1.0]* node-set or a *[2.0]* sequence. The `<xsl:choose>`, `<xsl:text>`, `<xsl:value-of>`, and *[2.0]* `<xsl:sequence>` elements all fit this description.

Appears in

`<xsl:attribute>` appears inside a template.

Defined in

[1.0] XSLT section 7.1.3, "Creating Attributes with `xsl:attribute`."

[2.0] XSLT section 11.3, "Creating Attribute Nodes Using `xsl:attribute`."

Example

For this example, we want to create an HTML table from the following XML document:

```
<?xml version="1.0"?>
<!-- albums.xml -->
<list xml:lang="en">
  <title>Albums I've bought recently:</title>
  <listitem>The Sacred Art of Dub</listitem>
  <listitem>Only the Poor Man Feel It</listitem>
  <listitem>Excitable Boy</listitem>
  <listitem xml:lang="sw">Aki Special</listitem>
  <listitem xml:lang="en-gb">Combat Rock</listitem>
  <listitem xml:lang="zu">Talking Timbuktu</listitem>
  <listitem xml:lang="jz">The Birth of the Cool</listitem>
</list>
```

We'll create a table that has each `<listitem>` in a separate row in the right column of the table, and a single cell with `rowspan` equal to the number of `<listitem>` elements in the XML document on the left. Clearly we can't hardcode a value for the `rowspan` attribute because the number of `<listitem>`s can change. This stylesheet uses `<xsl:attribute>` to do what we want:

```
<?xml version="1.0"?>
<!-- attribute1.xsl -->
<xsl:stylesheet version="1.0"
  xmlns:xsl="http://www.w3.org/1999/XSL/Transform">

<xsl:output method="html"/>

<xsl:template match="/">
  <html>
    <head>
      <title><xsl:value-of select="list/title"/></title>
    </head>
    <body style="font-family: sans-serif;">
      <xsl:apply-templates select="list"/>
    </body>
  </html>
</xsl:template>

<xsl:template match="list">
  <table border="1" cellpadding="5" cellspacing="5">
    <tr>
      <td style="background: black; color: white;
              font-weight: bold; font-size: 125%;"
              width="100" align="right">
        <xsl:if test="count(listitem) > 1">
          <xsl:attribute name="rowspan">
            <xsl:value-of select="count(listitem)"/>
          </xsl:attribute>
```

```
        </xsl:if>
        <xsl:value-of select="title"/>
      </td>
      <td>
        <xsl:value-of select="listitem[1]"/>
      </td>
    </tr>
    <xsl:for-each select="listitem[position() > 1]">
      <tr>
        <td>
          <xsl:value-of select="."/>
        </td>
      </tr>
    </xsl:for-each>
  </table>
</xsl:template>

</xsl:stylesheet>
```

Here is the generated HTML document:

```
<!-- attribute.html -->
<html>
  <head>
    <meta http-equiv="Content-Type" content="text/html; charset=UTF-8">
    <title>Albums I've bought recently:</title>
  </head>
  <body style="font-family: sans-serif;">
    <table border="1" cellpadding="5" cellspacing="5">
      <tr>
        <td style="background: black; color: white;
                   font-weight: bold; font-size: 125%;"
              width="100" align="right" rowspan="7">
          Albums I've bought recently:</td>
        <td>The Sacred Art of Dub</td>
      </tr>
      <tr>
        <td>Only the Poor Man Feel It</td>
      </tr>
      ...
    </table>
  </body>
</html>
```

Notice that the `<td>` element had several attributes hardcoded on it; those attributes are combined with the attribute we created with `<xsl:attribute>`. You can have as many `<xsl:attribute>` elements as you want, but all the `<xsl:attribute>` elements must appear before anything else in the template. Figure A-3 shows how our generated HTML document looks.

Be aware that in this instance, we could have used an attribute-value template. You could generate the value of the `rowspan` attribute like this:

```
<td bgcolor="black" rowspan="{count(listitem)}"
    width="100" align="right">
```

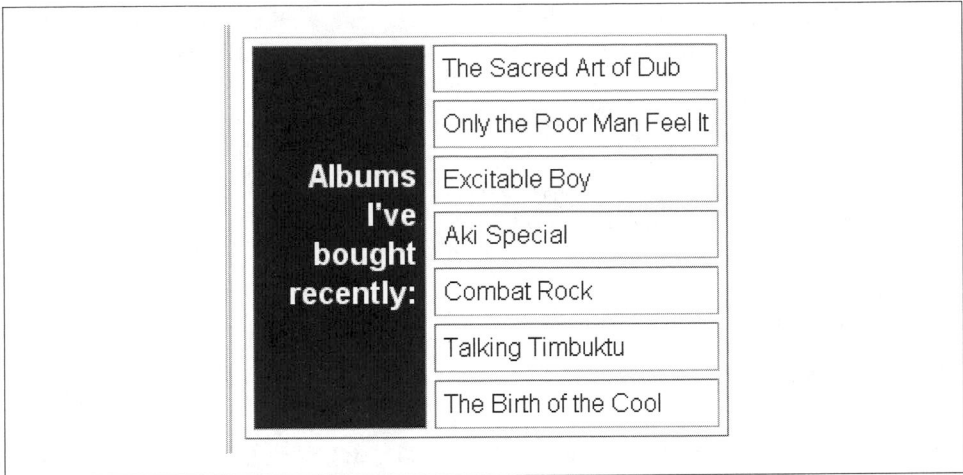

Figure A-3. Document with generated attributes

The expression in curly braces ({}) is evaluated and replaced with whatever its value happens to be. In this case, count(listitem) returns the number 7, which becomes the value of the rowspan attribute. The one difference here is that the rowspan is generated when there is only one <listitem> element.

[2.0] Next we'll look at a brief example that illustrates the new select and separator attributes. This short stylesheet uses an XPath 2.0 range expression (a "to" expression) to assign a sequence of values to the example attribute:

```
<?xml version="1.0" encoding="utf-8"?>
<!-- attribute2.xsl -->
<xsl:stylesheet version="2.0"
  xmlns:xsl="http://www.w3.org/1999/XSL/Transform">

  <xsl:output method="xml" omit-xml-declaration="yes"/>

  <xsl:template match="/">
    <sampledoc>
      <xsl:attribute name="example" select="1 to 7" separator=", "/>
    </sampledoc>
  </xsl:template>

</xsl:stylesheet>
```

This stylesheet generates the following very short document:

```
<sampledoc example="1, 2, 3, 4, 5, 6, 7"/>
```

The XSLT 2.0 separator attribute means you don't have to write logic like this:

```
<xsl:for-each>
  <xsl:value-of select="."/>
  <xsl:if test="position() != last()">
    <xsl:text>, </xsl:text>
  </xsl:if>
</xsl:for-each>
```

[2.0 – Schema] For a final example, we'll use the schema-aware attributes of `<xsl:attribute>`. Our stylesheet contains an imported schema that defines a new datatype; we'll use `<xsl:attribute>` to create attributes of that datatype. Here's the stylesheet:

```
<?xml version="1.0" encoding="utf-8"?>
<!-- attribute3.xsl -->
<xsl:stylesheet version="2.0"
  xmlns:xsl="http://www.w3.org/1999/XSL/Transform"
  xmlns:zip="http://www.oreilly.com/xslt/zip"
  xmlns:xs="http://www.w3.org/2001/XMLSchema"
  exclude-result-prefixes="xs">

  <xsl:output method="xml" indent="yes"/>

  <xsl:import-schema namespace="http://www.oreilly.com/xslt/zip">
    <xsd:schema
      xmlns="http://www.oreilly.com/xslt/zip"
      targetNamespace="http://www.oreilly.com/xslt/zip"
      xmlns:xsd="http://www.w3.org/2001/XMLSchema">

      <xsd:simpleType name="zipcode">
        <xsd:restriction base="xsd:string">
          <xsd:pattern value="[0-9]{5}(-[0-9]{4})?"/>
        </xsd:restriction>
      </xsd:simpleType>
    </xsd:schema>
  </xsl:import-schema>

  <xsl:template match="/">
    <postcodes>
      <xsl:for-each select="postcodes/postcode">
        <postcode>
          <xsl:choose>
            <xsl:when test=". castable as zip:zipcode">
              <xsl:attribute name="zip:zip" type="zip:zipcode">
                <xsl:value-of select=". cast as zip:zipcode"/>
              </xsl:attribute>
            </xsl:when>
            <xsl:otherwise>
              <xsl:attribute name="other" type="xs:string">
                <xsl:value-of select="."/>
              </xsl:attribute>
            </xsl:otherwise>
          </xsl:choose>
        </postcode>
      </xsl:for-each>
    </postcodes>
  </xsl:template>

</xsl:stylesheet>
```

We'll use this stylesheet to process this document:

```
<?xml version="1.0" encoding="utf-8"?>
<!-- postcodes.xml -->
<postcodes>
```

```
    <postcode>3S8 EOX</postcode>
    <postcode>37174</postcode>
    <postcode>NSW 3829</postcode>
    <postcode>27516</postcode>
  </postcodes>
```

The stylesheet uses the XPath `castable as` operator to determine whether a value from the source document can be cast as a `zip:zipcode` value. If the value can be cast, we create a new attribute with the datatype `zip:zipcode`. Here are the results:

```
<?xml version="1.0" encoding="UTF-8"?>
<postcodes xmlns:zip="http://www.oreilly.com/xslt/zip">
    <postcode other="3S8 EOX"/>
    <postcode zip:zip="37174"/>
    <postcode other="NSW 3829"/>
    <postcode zip:zip="27516"/>
</postcodes>
```

Two of the generated attributes are namespace-qualified and contain values of the appropriate datatype.

<xsl:attribute-set>

Allows you to define a group of attributes for the output. You can then reference the entire attribute set with its name, rather than create all attributes individually.

Category

Top-level element.

Required Attribute

name
> Defines the name of this attribute set.

Optional Attribute

use-attribute-sets
> Lists one or more attribute sets that should be used by this attribute set. If you specify more than one set, separate their names with whitespace characters. You can use this attribute to embed other `<xsl:attribute-set>`s in this one, but be aware that an `<xsl:attribute-set>` that directly or indirectly embeds itself results in an error. In other words, if attribute set A embeds attribute set B, and attribute set B embeds attribute set C, and attribute set C embeds attribute set A, the XSLT processor signals an error.

Content

One or more `<xsl:attribute>` elements.

Appears in

`<xsl:attribute-set>` is a top-level element and can only appear as a child of `<xsl:stylesheet>`.

Defined in

[1.0] XSLT section 7.1.4, "Named Attribute Sets."

[2.0] XSLT section 10.2, "Named Attribute Sets."

Example

We'll use a stylesheet with three `<xsl:attribute-set>`s. The first set defines a `style` attribute with some CSS properties, the second defines a couple of HTML `<table>` attributes and uses the first set, while the third defines a traditional HTML element and a CSS `style` attribute.

```
<?xml version="1.0"?>
<!-- attribute-set.xsl -->
<xsl:stylesheet version="1.0"
  xmlns:xsl="http://www.w3.org/1999/XSL/Transform">

  <xsl:output method="html"/>

  <xsl:attribute-set name="bold-table">
    <xsl:attribute name="style">
      font-weight: bold;
    </xsl:attribute>
  </xsl:attribute-set>

  <xsl:attribute-set name="spacious-table"
    use-attribute-sets="bold-table">
    <xsl:attribute name="cellpadding">8</xsl:attribute>
    <xsl:attribute name="cellspacing">8</xsl:attribute>
  </xsl:attribute-set>

  <xsl:attribute-set name="reverse-table">
    <xsl:attribute name="bgcolor">black</xsl:attribute>
    <xsl:attribute name="style">color: white;</xsl:attribute>
  </xsl:attribute-set>

  <xsl:template match="/">
    <html>
      <head>
        <title><xsl:value-of select="/list/title"/></title>
      </head>
      <body style="font-family: sans-serif;">
        <xsl:apply-templates select="*"/>
      </body>
    </html>
  </xsl:template>

  <xsl:template match="list">
    <h1><xsl:value-of select="title"/></h1>
    <table xsl:use-attribute-sets="spacious-table" border="2">
      <xsl:for-each select="listitem">
```

```
        <tr>
          <td xsl:use-attribute-sets="reverse-table">
            <xsl:value-of select="."/>
          </td>
        </tr>
      </xsl:for-each>
    </table>
    <h1>Here's the same table with different attribute sets:</h1>
    <table border="2" xsl:use-attribute-sets="bold-table">
      <xsl:for-each select="listitem">
        <tr>
          <td>
            <xsl:value-of select="."/>
          </td>
        </tr>
      </xsl:for-each>
    </table>
  </xsl:template>

</xsl:stylesheet>
```

Notice that you have to namespace-qualify the `xsl:use-attribute-sets` attribute so that the XSLT processor will handle it. If you just use `use-attribute-sets`, the XSLT processor copies that attribute to the HTML output without processing it at all.

Our stylesheet creates two tables from a list of items, using a different set of named attribute sets each time. We'll apply our stylesheet to one of our usual XML documents:

```
<?xml version="1.0"?>
<!-- albums.xml -->
<list>
  <title>A few of my favorite albums</title>
  <listitem>A Love Supreme</listitem>
  <listitem>Beat Crazy</listitem>
  <listitem>You Could Have it So Much Better</listitem>
  <listitem>Kind of Blue</listitem>
  <listitem>London Calling</listitem>
  <listitem>Remain in Light</listitem>
  <listitem>The Joshua Tree</listitem>
  <listitem>The Indestructible Beat of Soweto</listitem>
</list>
```

Our stylesheet produces this HTML:

```
<html>
  <head>
    <meta http-equiv="Content-Type" content="text/html; charset=UTF-8">
    <title>Albums I've bought recently:</title>
  </head>
  <body>
    <h1>Albums I've bought recently:</h1>
    <table style="font-weight: bold; font-family: sans-serif;"
              cellpadding="8" cellspacing="8" border="2">
      <tr>
        <td bgcolor="black" style="color: white;">The Sacred Art of Dub</td>
      </tr>
```

Figure A-4. Tables created with two different attribute sets

```
        ...
        <tr>
            <td bgcolor="black" style="color: white;">The Birth of the Cool</td>
        </tr>
    </table>
    <h1>Here's the same table with different attribute sets:</h1>
    <table style="font-weight: bold; font-family: sans-serif;" border="2">
        <tr>
            <td>The Sacred Art of Dub</td>
        </tr>
        ...
        <tr>
            <td>The Birth of the Cool</td>
        </tr>
    </table>
    </body>
</html>
```

The two tables look like Figure A-4.

Be aware that any attribute coded on an element takes precedence over an attribute added to that element by `xsl:use-attribute-sets`. For example, if we have this element:

```
<table cellpadding="3" xsl:use-attribute-sets="spacious-table" ...>
```

The `cellpadding` attribute in the `spacious-table` attribute set does not apply. The XSLT processor generates this `<table>` element:

```
<table cellpadding="3" cellspacing="8" ...>
```

`<xsl:call-template>`

Invokes a particular template by name. If you have output that you need to generate often, you can put the markup that creates that output into a named template and invoke that template whenever you want.

Category

Instruction.

Required Attribute

name
> The name of the template you're invoking.

Optional Attributes

None.

Content

This element can contain any number of optional `<xsl:with-param>` elements.

Appears in

`<xsl:call-template>` appears inside a template.

Defined in

[1.0] XSLT section 6, "Named Templates."

[2.0] XSLT section 10.1, "Named Templates."

Example

Invoking named templates with `<xsl:call-template>` is a great way to create modular stylesheets. We'll use named templates to format our document of chocolate sales:

```
<?xml version="1.0" encoding="utf-8"?>
<!-- chocolate.xml -->
<report month="8" year="2006">
  <title>Chocolate bar sales</title>
  <brand>
    <name>Lindt</name>
    <units>27408</units>
```

```
    </brand>
    <brand>
      <name>Callebaut</name>
      <units>8203</units>
    </brand>
    <brand>
      <name>Valrhona</name>
      <units>22101</units>
    </brand>
    <brand>
      <name>Perugina</name>
      <units>14336</units>
    </brand>
    <brand>
      <name>Ghirardelli</name>
      <units>19268</units>
    </brand>
</report>
```

Here is our stylesheet with named templates:

```
<?xml version="1.0"?>
<!-- call-template.xsl -->
<xsl:stylesheet version="1.0"
  xmlns:xsl="http://www.w3.org/1999/XSL/Transform">

  <xsl:output method="html"/>

  <xsl:template match="report">
    <html>
      <head>
        <xsl:call-template name="report-title">
          <xsl:with-param name="in-heading" select="true()"/>
          <xsl:with-param name="title" select="title"/>
        </xsl:call-template>
      </head>
      <body>
        <xsl:call-template name="insert-header"/>
        <xsl:call-template name="report-title">
          <xsl:with-param name="in-heading" select="false()"/>
          <xsl:with-param name="title" select="title"/>
        </xsl:call-template>
        <table cellpadding="5">
          <xsl:call-template name="table-heading"/>
          <xsl:apply-templates select="brand"/>
        </table>
        <xsl:call-template name="insert-footer"/>
      </body>
    </html>
  </xsl:template>

  <xsl:template name="insert-header">
    <p style="font-size: 75%; font-style: italic;">
      This confidential report is the property of DougCo, Inc.
    </p>
    <hr/>
```

```
      </xsl:template>

      <xsl:template name="report-title">
        <xsl:param name="in-heading"/>
        <xsl:param name="title"/>
        <xsl:choose>
          <xsl:when test="$in-heading">
            <title><xsl:value-of select="$title"/></title>
          </xsl:when>
          <xsl:otherwise>
            <h1><xsl:value-of select="$title"/></h1>
          </xsl:otherwise>
        </xsl:choose>
      </xsl:template>

      <xsl:template name="table-heading">
        <tr>
          <td style="background: black; color: white; font-weight: bold;">
            Brand</td>
          <td style="background: black; color: white; font-weight: bold;">
            Sales</td>
        </tr>
      </xsl:template>

      <xsl:template name="insert-footer">
        <hr/>
        <p style="font-size: 75%; font-style: italic;">
          © Copyright 2008, DougCo, Inc.
        </p>
      </xsl:template>

      <xsl:template match="brand">
        <tr>
          <td><xsl:value-of select="name"/></td>
          <td><xsl:value-of select="units"/></td>
        </tr>
      </xsl:template>

    </xsl:stylesheet>
```

Our stylesheet uses four different named templates. The templates `insert-header`, `table-heading`, and `insert-footer` make it easy to insert commonly used markup into the output. In practice, templates such as this would be imported from another stylesheet. If dozens of reports, web pages, or other documents used the same header and footer, we could store that markup in one place and add it wherever we needed with a simple `<xsl:call-template>` instruction.

The other named template, `insert-title`, uses two parameters. The first parameter tells the named template whether we're in the `<head>` section of the HTML document; the second parameter is the name of the report title. Depending on the value of `in-heading`, the template generates a `<title>` element or a `<h1>` element.

Here is the HTML file generated by the stylesheet:

```
<html>
  <head>
    <META http-equiv="Content-Type" content="text/html; charset=UTF-8">
    <title>Chocolate bar sales</title>
  </head>
  <body>
    <p style="font-size: 75%; font-style: italic;">
      This confidential report is the property of DougCo, Inc.
    </p>
    <hr>
    <h1>Chocolate bar sales</h1>
    <table cellpadding="5">
      <tr>
        <td style="background: black; color: white; font-weight: bold;">
          Brand
        </td>
        <td style="background: black; color: white; font-weight: bold;">
          Sales
        </td>
      </tr>
      <tr>
        <td>Lindt</td><td>27408</td>
      </tr>
      <tr>
        <td>Callebaut</td><td>8203</td>
      </tr>
      <tr>
        <td>Valrhona</td><td>22101</td>
      </tr>
      <tr>
        <td>Perugina</td><td>14336</td>
      </tr>
      <tr>
        <td>Ghirardelli</td><td>19268</td>
      </tr>
    </table>
    <hr>
    <p style="font-size: 75%; font-style: italic;">
      &copy; Copyright 2007, DougCo, Inc.
    </p>
  </body>
</html>
```

The results look like Figure A-5.

[2.0] In XSLT 2.0, there are changes to the rules for passing parameters to templates:

- In XSLT 1.0, you could pass as many parameters as you wanted to a template; any extra parameters (parameters not defined in the called template) were ignored. In XSLT 2.0, this is a fatal error.

- In XSLT 2.0, the `<xsl:param>` element has a `required` attribute. It is a fatal error to call a template without passing values for all of the required parameters.

- XSLT 2.0 introduces the concept of tunnel parameters. See the section "Tunnel parameters" in Chapter 5 for more information on tunnel parameters.

Figure A-5. HTML document generated with named templates

[2.0] <xsl:character-map>

Defines a set of characters, each of which should be replaced by a string of characters. This allows you to put nonstandard characters in the values of elements and attributes. An <xsl:character-map> works much like an XML <!ENTITY> declaration. Use a <xsl:character-map> in place of the disable-output-escaping attributes of <xsl:text> and <xsl:value-of> defined in XSLT 1.0. (Using the disable-output-escaping attribute is deprecated in XSLT 2.0.)

Category

Declaration.

Required Attribute

name

    The name of this character map.

Optional Attribute

use-character-maps

    The space-separated names of any character maps included in this character map. As you would expect, it is a fatal error if a character map includes itself, directly or indirectly. It is also a fatal error if a character map attempts to include a character map that does not exist.

Content

Zero or more `<xsl:output-character>` elements.

Appears in

`<xsl:character-map>` appears as a child of the `<xsl:stylesheet>` element.

Defined in

XSLT section 20, "Serialization."

Example

We'll define a simple example that has a couple of useful functions. First of all, we'll create a character mapping that replaces tab characters (`&#x9;`) with two spaces; tab characters are often displayed as eight characters wide, which can cause problems when displaying indented code listings. We'll also create a couple of graphics that should be displayed in place of certain characters. Here's the XML source we'll use:

```
<?xml version="1.0" encoding="utf-8"?>
<!-- special-characters.xml -->
<char-test>
  <tabs>public class HelloWorld {
        public static void main(String[] args) {
                System.out.println("Hello, World!");
        }
}</tabs>
  <special-char>&#x2780;</special-char>
  <special-char>&#x2781;</special-char>
</char-test>
```

Our stylesheet replaces the tab characters with two spaces, and it replaces the first two characters with graphics. (The Unicode characters `&#x2780;` through `&#x2789;` are the circled numbers 1 through 10 in a sans-serif fonti.e., ① through ⑩.) Here's the stylesheet:

```
<?xml version="1.0" encoding="utf-8"?>
<!-- character-map1.xsl -->
<xsl:stylesheet version="2.0"
  xmlns:xsl="http://www.w3.org/1999/XSL/Transform">

  <xsl:output method="html" use-character-maps="sample"/>

  <xsl:character-map name="sample" use-character-maps="circles">
    <xsl:output-character character="&#x9;" string="  "/>
  </xsl:character-map>

  <xsl:character-map name="circles">
    <xsl:output-character character="&#x2780;"
      string="&lt;img src='images/circle1.gif'
      width='28' height='28'/&gt;"/>
    <xsl:output-character character="&#x2781;"
      string="&lt;img src='images/circle2.gif'
      width='28' height='28'/&gt;"/>
  </xsl:character-map>
```

```
<xsl:template match="char-test">
  <html>
    <head>
      <title>A test of some special characters</title>
    </head>
    <body style="font-family: sans-serif;">
      <h1>A test of some special characters</h1>
      <xsl:apply-templates select="*"/>
    </body>
  </html>
</xsl:template>

<xsl:template match="tabs">
  <pre style="font-size: 150%; font-weight: bold;">
    <xsl:value-of select="."/>
  </pre>
</xsl:template>

<xsl:template match="special-char">
  <p style="font-size: 200%;">
    <xsl:text>Here's a special character: </xsl:text>
    <xsl:value-of select="."/>
  </p>
</xsl:template>

</xsl:stylesheet>
```

Notice that our stylesheet simply outputs the value of the `<tabs>` or `<special-char>` elements. The `<xsl:output>` element and its `use-character-maps="sample"` attribute take care of transforming the characters for us. The `<xsl:character-map>` named `sample` defines a single replacement, and it also uses `<xsl:character-map name="circles">`. The combination of defining a character map and referencing it on the `<xsl:output>` element makes everything happen.

Also notice that the substitutions in the `circles` character map replace a character with HTML markup—an `<img>` element. The HTML document looks like this:

```
<html>
  <head>
    <meta http-equiv="Content-Type" content="text/html; charset=UTF-8">
    <title>A test of some special characters</title>
  </head>
  <body style="font-family: sans-serif;">
    <h1>A test of some special characters</h1>
    <pre style="font-size: 150%;
    font-weight: bold;">public class HelloWorld {
  public static void main(String[] args) {
    System.out.println("Hello, World!");
  }
}</pre><p style="font-size: 200%;">
    Here's a special character:
    <img src='images/circle1.gif' width='28' height='28'/></p>
  <p style="font-size: 200%;">
    Here's a special character:
    <img src='images/circle2.gif' width='28' height='28'/></p>
```

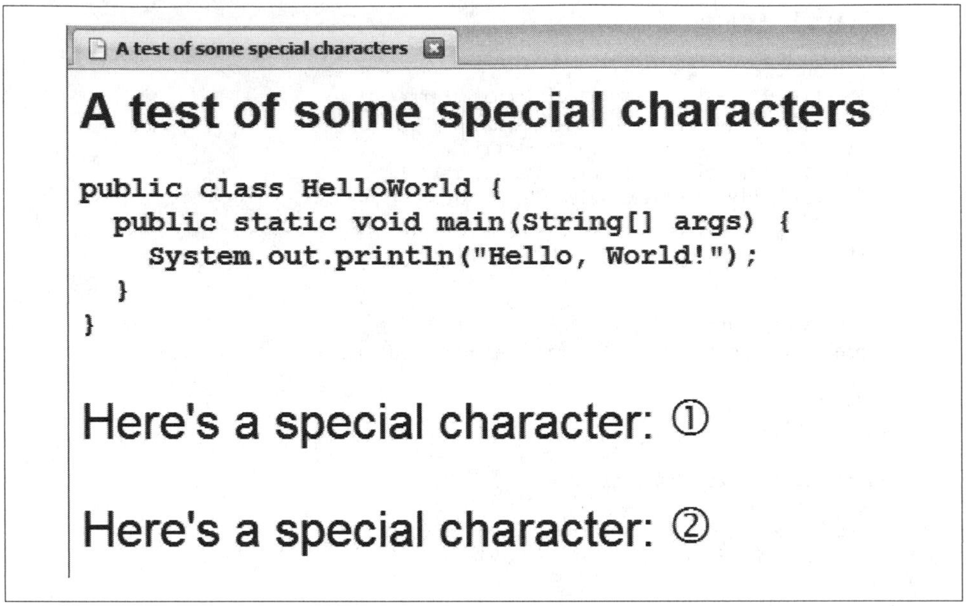

Figure A-6. HTML generated with character maps

```
      </body>
  </html>
```

When displayed in a browser, the circled numbers appear, as shown in Figure A-6.

Another common use of `<xsl:character-map>` is to convert a newline character (
) to a carriage return and line feed (
), but that's not a visually compelling demo. If you need to do that, the `<xsl:output-character>` element looks like this:

```
    <xsl:output-character character="&#xA;" string="&#xD;&#xA;"/>
```

Finally, the XSLT 2.0 spec mentions creating Java Server Pages (JSPs) as an example. JSPs use angle brackets in a way that is not valid XML or HTML. We can define a character map that looks like this:

```
    <?xml version="1.0" encoding="utf-8"?>
    <!-- character-map2.xsl -->
    <xsl:stylesheet version="2.0"
      xmlns:xsl="http://www.w3.org/1999/XSL/Transform">

      <xsl:output method="html" use-character-maps="jsp"/>

      <xsl:character-map name="jsp">
        <xsl:output-character character="«" string="&lt;%="/>
        <xsl:output-character character="»" string="%&gt;"/>
      </xsl:character-map>

      <xsl:template match="jsp-test">
        <html>
          <head>
            <title>A test of some special characters</title>
```

```
        </head>
        <body style="font-family: sans-serif;">
          <h1>Generating a .jsp page</h1>
          <p>Here's the value of a JSP function:
            <xsl:apply-templates select="text()"/>
          </p>
        </body>
      </html>
    </xsl:template>

</xsl:stylesheet>
```

Using this XML input file:

```
<?xml version="1.0" encoding="utf-8"?>
<!-- jsp-test.xml -->
<jsp-test>« new java.util.Date() »</jsp-test>
```

generates these results:

```
<html>
    <head>
        <meta http-equiv="Content-Type" content="text/html; charset=UTF-8">
        <title>A test of some special characters</title>
    </head>
    <body style="font-family: sans-serif;">
        <h1>Generating a .jsp page</h1>
        <p>Here's the value of a JSP function:
            <%= new java.util.Date() %>
        </p>
    </body>
</html>
```

<xsl:choose>

The <xsl:choose> element is XSLT's construct for if-then-else processing.

Category

Instruction.

Required Attributes

None.

Optional Attributes

None.

Content

Contains one or more <xsl:when> elements. It can also contain a single <xsl:otherwise> element. If it is present, the <xsl:otherwise> element must be the last element inside <xsl:choose>.

Appears in

`<xsl:choose>` appears inside a template.

Defined in

[1.0] XSLT section 9.2, "Conditional Processing with `xsl:choose`."

[2.0] XSLT section 8.2, "Conditional Processing with `xsl:choose`."

Example

Here's an example that uses `<xsl:choose>` to select the background color for the rows of an HTML table. We cycle among four different values, using `<xsl:choose>` to determine the value of the `style` attribute in the generated HTML document. Here's the XML document we'll use:

```
<?xml version="1.0"?>
<!-- albums.xml -->
<list xml:lang="en">
  <title>Albums I've bought recently:</title>
  <listitem>The Sacred Art of Dub</listitem>
  <listitem>Only the Poor Man Feel It</listitem>
  <listitem>Excitable Boy</listitem>
  <listitem xml:lang="sw">Aki Special</listitem>
  <listitem xml:lang="en-gb">Combat Rock</listitem>
  <listitem xml:lang="zu">Talking Timbuktu</listitem>
  <listitem xml:lang="jz">The Birth of the Cool</listitem>
</list>
```

And here's our stylesheet:

```
<?xml version="1.0"?>
<!-- choose.xsl -->
<xsl:stylesheet version="1.0"
  xmlns:xsl="http://www.w3.org/1999/XSL/Transform">

  <xsl:output method="html"/>

  <xsl:template match="/">
    <html>
      <head>
        <title>
          <xsl:value-of select="list/title"/>
        </title>
      </head>
      <body style="font-family: sans-serif; color: white;">
        <h1 style="color: black;">
          <xsl:value-of select="list/title"/>
        </h1>
        <table border="1" cellpadding="5"
          style="font-weight: bold;">
          <xsl:for-each select="list/listitem">
            <tr>
              <td>
                <xsl:attribute name="style">
                  <xsl:choose>
                    <xsl:when test="position() mod 4 = 0">
```

```
              <xsl:text>background: yellow; color: black;</xsl:text>
            </xsl:when>
            <xsl:when test="position() mod 4 = 1">
              <xsl:text>background: blue;</xsl:text>
            </xsl:when>
            <xsl:when test="position() mod 4 = 2">
              <xsl:text>background: white; color: black;</xsl:text>
            </xsl:when>
            <xsl:otherwise>
              <xsl:text>background: black;</xsl:text>
            </xsl:otherwise>
          </xsl:choose>
        </xsl:attribute>
        <xsl:value-of select="."/>
      </td>
    </tr>
  </xsl:for-each>
  </table>
  </body>
  </html>
  </xsl:template>

</xsl:stylesheet>
```

We use `<xsl:choose>` to generate the style attribute of each generated `<td>` element. Here's the generated HTML document, which cycles through the various background colors:

```
<html>
  <head>
    <meta http-equiv="Content-Type" content="text/html; charset=UTF-8">
    <title>Albums I've bought recently:</title>
  </head>
  <body style="font-family: sans-serif; color: white;">
    <h1 style="color: black;">Albums I've bought recently:</h1>
    <table border="1" cellpadding="5" style="font-weight: bold;">
      <tr>
        <td style="background: blue;">The Sacred Art of Dub</td>
      </tr>
      ...
      <tr>
        <td style="background: black;">The Birth of the Cool</td>
      </tr>
    </table>
  </body>
</html>
```

When rendered, our HTML document looks like Figure A-7.

<xsl:comment>

Allows you to create a comment in the output document. Comments are sometimes used to add legal notices, disclaimers, or information about when the output document was created.

Figure A-7. Using <xsl:choose> to cycle among background colors

Another useful application of the `<xsl:comment>` element is generating CSS definitions or JavaScript code in an HTML document.

Category

Instruction.

Required Attributes

None.

Optional Attribute

[2.0] `select`

An XPath expression that generates content for the comment. If this attribute is not present, the contents of the `<xsl:comment>` element are used instead. If the `select` attribute is not present and the `<xsl:comment>` element is empty, an empty comment is generated. It is a fatal error for an `<xsl:comment>` element to have a `select` attribute and contain content.

Content

A *[1.0]* node-set or *[2.0]* sequence constructor.

Appears in

`<xsl:comment>` appears in a template.

Defined in

[1.0] XSLT section 7.4, "Creating Comments."

[2.0] XSLT section 11.8, "Creating Comments."

Example

Here's a stylesheet that generates a comment to define CSS styles in an HTML document:

```
<?xml version="1.0"?>
<!-- comment.xsl -->
<xsl:stylesheet version="1.0"
  xmlns:xsl="http://www.w3.org/1999/XSL/Transform">

  <xsl:output method="html"/>

  <xsl:template match="/">
    <html>
      <head>
        <title>XSLT and CSS Demo</title>
        <style>
          <xsl:comment>
            p.big    {font-size: 125%; font-weight: bold;}
            p.odd    {color: purple; font-weight: bold;}
            p.even   {color: blue; font-style: italic; font-weight: bold;}
          </xsl:comment>
        </style>
      </head>
      <body style="font-family: sans-serif;">
        <xsl:apply-templates select="list/title"/>
        <xsl:apply-templates select="list/listitem"/>
      </body>
    </html>
  </xsl:template>

  <xsl:template match="title">
    <p class="big"><xsl:value-of select="."/></p>
  </xsl:template>

  <xsl:template match="listitem">
    <xsl:choose>
      <xsl:when test="position() mod 2">
        <p class="odd"><xsl:value-of select="."/></p>
      </xsl:when>
      <xsl:otherwise>
        <p class="even"><xsl:value-of select="."/></p>
      </xsl:otherwise>
    </xsl:choose>
  </xsl:template>

</xsl:stylesheet>
```

This stylesheet creates three CSS styles inside an HTML comment. We'll apply the stylesheet to this document:

```
<?xml version="1.0"?>
<!-- albums.xml -->
<list xml:lang="en">
  <title>Albums I've bought recently:</title>
```

Figure A-8. A document with CSS properties defined in comment nodes

```
<listitem>The Sacred Art of Dub</listitem>
<listitem>Only the Poor Man Feel It</listitem>
<listitem>Excitable Boy</listitem>
<listitem xml:lang="sw">Aki Special</listitem>
<listitem xml:lang="en-gb">Combat Rock</listitem>
<listitem xml:lang="zu">Talking Timbuktu</listitem>
<listitem xml:lang="jz">The Birth of the Cool</listitem>
</list>
```

The stylesheet applies one CSS style to the `<title>` element and alternates between two CSS styles for the `<listitem>`s. Here's the generated HTML:

```
<html>
  <head>
    <meta http-equiv="Content-Type" content="text/html; charset=UTF-8">
    <title>XSLT and CSS Demo</title><style>
      <!--
        p.big     {font-size: 125%; font-weight: bold;}
        p.odd     {color: purple; font-weight: bold;}
        p.even    {color: blue; font-style: italic; font-weight: bold;}
      --></style></head>
  <body style="font-family: sans-serif;">
    <p class="big">Albums I've bought recently:</p>
    <p class="odd">The Sacred Art of Dub</p>
    <p class="even">Only the Poor Man Feel It</p>
    <p class="odd">Excitable Boy</p>
    <p class="even">Aki Special</p>
    <p class="odd">Combat Rock</p>
    <p class="even">Talking Timbuktu</p>
    <p class="odd">The Birth of the Cool</p>
  </body>
</html>
```

When rendered, the document looks like Figure A-8.

[2.0] To use the `select` attribute added in XSLT 2.0, we could add this `<xsl:comment>` element to our stylesheet:

```
<xsl:comment select="concat('The second album is ', list/listitem[2])"/>
```

This generates the following comment in the HTML output:

```
<!--The second album is Only the Poor Man Feel It-->
```

 If you're using `<xsl:comment>` to generate JavaScript code, end your code with a JavaScript comment, like this:

```
<SCRIPT type="text/javascript">
<xsl:comment> // Hide this code from older browsers
  function iOver(image)
  {
    if (browser="N3") document[image].src=eval(image + "over.src");
  }
  // </xsl:comment>
</SCRIPT>
```

Putting the two slashes in the last line creates a JavaScript comment. That means the JavaScript interpreter ignores the `-->` that appears at the end of the comment.

`<xsl:copy>`

By default, `<xsl:copy>` makes a shallow copy of a node. The `<xsl:copy>` instruction copies only the current node and its namespace nodes; attribute or child nodes are not copied. `<xsl:copy>` gives you fine-grained control over the copying process, but it requires you to do more work. You can use `<xsl:copy>` to copy any kind of node, including comment or attribute nfodes.

Category
Instruction.

Required Attributes
None.

Optional Attributes
`use-attribute-sets`
> Lists one or more attribute sets that should be used by this element. If you specify more than one attribute set, separate their names with whitespace characters. See the description of the `<xsl:attribute-set>` element for more information.

[2.0] `copy-namespaces`
> Defines whether namespaces should be copied. This applies only when copying an element node. Allowed values are `yes` (the default) and `no`.

[2.0] `inherit-namespaces`

> Defines whether this element and its children inherit the current namespace nodes. Valid values are **yes** (the default) and **no**.

[2.0 – Schema] `type`

> Defines the datatype of the copied element. The datatype can be any of the built-in datatypes, or it can be a datatype defined in a schema if you have a schema-aware XSLT 2.0 processor.
>
> The `type` and `validation` attributes are mutually exclusive.

[2.0 – Schema] `validation`

> Defines how the value of the copied node will be validated. The `validation` attribute has four values: `strict`, `lax`, `preserve`, or `strip`.
>
> `validation="strict"` means that the XSLT processor looks in all the declared schemas for an attribute or element declaration (`<xs:attribute>` or `<xs:element>`) with the same name as the copied node. It is a fatal error if the processor can't find a matching declaration. Assuming the processor finds the declaration of the node, it validates the copied node's value against its declaration.
>
> `validation="lax"` works just like `validation="strict"`, except that no error occurs if the processor can't find the declaration of the copied node in any of the declared schemas. In that case, the type annotation of the element is `xs:untyped`.
>
> The effects of `validation="preserve"` depend on the kind of node being copied. If the copied node is an attribute, its type annotation is preserved. For element nodes, the copied node will have the type annotation of `xs:anyType`. The type annotations of any nodes contained by the copied element are preserved. No schema validation is done.
>
> `validation="strip"` replaces the type annotation of the copied attribute and element nodes with `xs:untypedAtomic` and `xs:untyped`, respectively. Any attribute and element nodes contained in the copied node have their type annotations replaced with `xs:untypedAtomic` and `xs:untyped` as well.
>
> The `validation` and `type` attributes are mutually exclusive.

Content

An XSLT template.

Appears in

`<xsl:copy>` appears in a template.

Defined in

[1.0] XSLT section 7.5, "Copying."

[2.0] XSLT section 11.9.1, "Shallow Copying."

Example

We'll demonstrate `<xsl:copy>` with an example that copies an element to the result tree. Our first stylesheet simply copies the document element:

```
<?xml version="1.0"?>
<!-- copy1.xsl -->
<xsl:stylesheet version="1.0"
  xmlns:xsl="http://www.w3.org/1999/XSL/Transform">

  <xsl:output method="xml"/>

  <xsl:template match="*">
    <xsl:copy/>
  </xsl:template>

</xsl:stylesheet>
```

We'll test our stylesheet with the following XML document:

```
<?xml version="1.0" encoding="utf-8"?>
<!-- albums.xml -->
<list xml:lang="en">
  <title>Albums I've bought recently:</title>
  <listitem>The Sacred Art of Dub</listitem>
  <listitem>Only the Poor Man Feel It</listitem>
  <listitem>Excitable Boy</listitem>
  <listitem xml:lang="sw">Aki Special</listitem>
  <listitem xml:lang="en-gb">Combat Rock</listitem>
  <listitem xml:lang="zu">Talking Timbuktu</listitem>
  <listitem xml:lang="jz">The Birth of the Cool</listitem>
</list>
```

We don't do anything to copy any of the children or attributes of the document element, so our results are very short:

```
<?xml version="1.0" encoding="UTF-8"?><list/>
```

To get more results, we need to copy the children of each element. Here is our stylesheet:

```
<?xml version="1.0"?>
<!-- copy2.xsl -->
<xsl:stylesheet version="1.0"
  xmlns:xsl="http://www.w3.org/1999/XSL/Transform">

  <xsl:output method="xml"/>

  <xsl:template match="*">
    <xsl:copy>
      <xsl:apply-templates/>
    </xsl:copy>
  </xsl:template>

</xsl:stylesheet>
```

Here are the results:

```
<?xml version="1.0" encoding="UTF-8"?><list>
  <title>Albums I've bought recently:</title>
  <listitem>The Sacred Art of Dub</listitem>
  <listitem>Only the Poor Man Feel It</listitem>
  <listitem>Excitable Boy</listitem>
  <listitem>Aki Special</listitem>
  <listitem>Combat Rock</listitem>
  <listitem>Talking Timbuktu</listitem>
  <listitem>The Birth of the Cool</listitem>
</list>
```

Although we have more results, we still don't have any attributes in the result document. The `<xsl:copy>` does a shallow copy, which gives you complete control over the output (unlike `<xsl:copy-of>`). The downside of having this control is that you must explicitly specify any child nodes or attribute nodes you want to copy. (Because attribute nodes aren't considered children of their parent element, we would have to specifically select and copy them.) This stylesheet doesn't copy comment nodes or processing instructions either; we would have to add more markup to handle them.

Compare this example to the example for the `<xsl:copy-of>` element.

The `<xsl:copy>` instruction is also useful inside a template that matches more than one element. We'll use our document of chocolate sales figures:

```
<?xml version="1.0" encoding="utf-8"?>
<!-- chocolate.xml -->
<report month="8" year="2006">
  <title>Chocolate bar sales</title>
  <brand>
    <name>Lindt</name>
    <units>27408</units>
  </brand>
  <brand>
    <name>Callebaut</name>
    <units>8203</units>
  </brand>
  <brand>
    <name>Valrhona</name>
    <units>22101</units>
  </brand>
  <brand>
    <name>Perugina</name>
    <units>14336</units>
  </brand>
  <brand>
    <name>Ghirardelli</name>
    <units>19268</units>
  </brand>
</report>
```

Our stylesheet uses `<xsl:copy>` to copy just the `<brand>` and `<name>` elements:

```
<?xml version="1.0"?>
<!-- copy3.xsl -->
<xsl:stylesheet version="1.0"
  xmlns:xsl="http://www.w3.org/1999/XSL/Transform">
```

```
<xsl:output method="xml"/>

<xsl:template match="report">
  <brands>
    <xsl:apply-templates select="brand"/>
  </brands>
</xsl:template>

<xsl:template match="brand|name|units">
  <xsl:copy>
    <xsl:apply-templates/>
  </xsl:copy>
</xsl:template>

</xsl:stylesheet>
```

The stylesheet creates a new `<brands>` element, and then copies all of the `<brand>` elements and their children. Here are the results:

```
<?xml version="1.0" encoding="UTF-8"?><report><brand>
    <name>Lindt</name>
    <units>27408</units>
  </brand><brand>
    <name>Callebaut</name>
    <units>8203</units>
  </brand><brand>
    <name>Valrhona</name>
    <units>22101</units>
  </brand><brand>
    <name>Perugina</name>
    <units>14336</units>
  </brand><brand>
    <name>Ghirardelli</name>
    <units>19268</units>
  </brand></report>
```

Notice that the text nodes of the selected elements are processed by the default stylesheet rule, which copies the text to the output.

`<xsl:copy-of>`

Creates a deep copy of a node.

Category

Instruction.

Required Attribute

select

Contains an XPath expression that defines the nodes to be copied to the output document.

Optional Attributes

[2.0] `copy-namespaces`

> Defines whether namespaces should be copied. This applies only when copying an element node. Allowed values are `yes` (the default) and `no`.

[2.0 – Schema] `type`

> Defines the datatype of the copied node. The datatype can be any of the built-in datatypes, or it can be a datatype defined in a schema if you have a schema-aware XSLT 2.0 processor.
>
> The `type` and `validation` attributes are mutually exclusive.

[2.0 – Schema] `validation`

> Defines how the value of the copied node will be validated. The `validation` attribute has four values: `strict`, `lax`, `preserve`, or `strip`.
>
> `validation="strict"` means that the XSLT processor looks in all the declared schemas for a node declaration (`<xs:attribute>` or `<xs:element>`) with the same name as this node. It is a fatal error if the processor can't find a matching declaration. Assuming the processor finds the declaration of the attribute or element node, it validates the generated value against its declaration in the schema.
>
> `validation="lax"` works just like `validation="strict"`, except that no error occurs if the processor can't find the declaration of the node in any of the declared schemas. In that case, the type annotation of a copied attribute or element is `xs:untypedAtomic` or `xs:untyped`, respectively.
>
> The value `validation="preserve"` means that all the copied nodes will have their type annotations preserved.
>
> Finally, `validation="strip"` removes all of the type annotations from all of the copied nodes. The copied attribute nodes will have a type annotation of `xs:untypedAtomic` and the copied element nodes will have a type annotation of `xs:untyped`.
>
> The `validation` and `type` attributes are mutually exclusive.

Content

None. `<xsl:copy-of>` is an empty element.

Appears in

`<xsl:copy-of>` appears inside a template.

Defined in

[1.0] XSLT section 11.3, "Using Values of Variables and Parameters with `xsl:copy-of`."

[2.0] XSLT section 11.9.2, "Deep Copy."

Example

We'll demonstrate `<xsl:copy-of>` with a simple stylesheet that copies the input document to the result tree. Here is our stylesheet:

```
<?xml version="1.0"?>
<!-- copy-of.xsl -->
<xsl:stylesheet version="1.0"
  xmlns:xsl="http://www.w3.org/1999/XSL/Transform">

  <xsl:output method="xml"/>

  <xsl:template match="/">
    <xsl:copy-of select="."/>
  </xsl:template>

</xsl:stylesheet>
```

We'll test our stylesheet with the following document:

```
<?xml version="1.0"?>
<!-- albums.xml -->
<list xml:lang="en">
  <title>Albums I've bought recently:</title>
  <listitem>The Sacred Art of Dub</listitem>
  <listitem>Only the Poor Man Feel It</listitem>
  <listitem>Excitable Boy</listitem>
  <listitem xml:lang="sw">Aki Special</listitem>
  <listitem xml:lang="en-gb">Combat Rock</listitem>
  <listitem xml:lang="zu">Talking Timbuktu</listitem>
  <listitem xml:lang="jz">The Birth of the Cool</listitem>
</list>
```

When we transform the XML document, the results are strikingly similar to the input document:

```
<?xml version="1.0" encoding="UTF-8"?><!-- albums.xml --><list xml:lang="en">
  <title>Albums I've bought recently:</title>
  <listitem>The Sacred Art of Dub</listitem>
  <listitem>Only the Poor Man Feel It</listitem>
  <listitem>Excitable Boy</listitem>
  <listitem xml:lang="sw">Aki Special</listitem>
  <listitem xml:lang="en-gb">Combat Rock</listitem>
  <listitem xml:lang="zu">Talking Timbuktu</listitem>
  <listitem xml:lang="jz">The Birth of the Cool</listitem>
</list>
```

The only differences between the two documents is that some whitespace has been removed and the stylesheet engine has added an **encoding** to the XML declaration. Semantically the two documents are identical. Compare this to the example for the `<xsl:copy>` element.

Be aware that this element works somewhat differently for XSLT 1.0 and 2.0:

[1.0]:

- If the **select** attribute identifies a result-tree fragment, the complete fragment is copied to the result tree.

- If select identifies a node-set, all nodes in the node-set are copied to the result tree in document order. Unlike `<xsl:copy>`, the node is copied in its entirety, including any namespace nodes, attribute nodes, and child nodes.
- If the `select` attribute identifies something other than a result-tree fragment or a node-set, it is converted to a string and inserted into the result tree.

[2.0]:

- If the `select` attribute identifies an element, that element and all of its descendants and attributes are copied to the output. By default, the element's namespace nodes are copied as well, although that can be changed with the `copy-namespaces` attribute.
- If the `select` attribute points to a document node, that document node and all of its descendants are copied to the output.
- All other types of nodes (attribute, namespace, text, comment, or processing instruction nodes) are copied to the output.
- Finally, atomic values are appended to the result sequence.

`<xsl:decimal-format>`

Defines a number format to be used when writing numeric values to the output document. If the `<decimal-format>` does not have a `name`, it is assumed to be the default number format used for all calls to the `format-number( )` function. On the other hand, if a number format is named, it can be referenced from the `format-number( )` function.

Category

Top-level element.

Required Attributes

None.

Optional Attributes

`name`
: Gives a name to this format.

`decimal-separator`
: Defines the character (usually either a period or comma) used as the decimal point. This character is used both in the format string and in the output. The default value is the period character (`.`).

`grouping-separator`
: Defines the character (usually either a period or comma) used as the thousands separator. This character is used both in the format string and in the output. The default value is the comma (`,`).

infinity

Defines the string used to represent infinity. Be aware that XSLT's number facilities support both positive and negative infinity. This string is used only in the output. The default value is the string `"Infinity"`.

minus-sign

Defines the character used as the minus sign. This character is used only in the output. The default value is the hyphen character (-, `&#x2D;`).

NaN

Defines the string displayed when the value to be formatted is not a number. This string is used only in the output; the default value is the string `"NaN"`.

percent

Defines the character used as the percent sign. This character is used both in the format string and in the output. The default value is the percent sign (%).

per-mille

Defines the character used as the per-mille sign. This character is used both in the format string and in the output. The default value is the Unicode per-mille character (‰, `&#x2030;`).

zero-digit

Defines the character used for the digit zero. This character is used both in the format string and in the output. The default is the digit zero (0).

digit

Defines the character used in the format string to stand for a digit. The default is the number sign character (#).

pattern-separator

Defines the character used to separate the positive and negative subpatterns in a pattern. The default value is the semicolon (;). This character is used only in the format string.

Content

None. `<xsl:decimal-format>` is an empty element.

Appears in

`<xsl:decimal-format>` is a top-level element and can appear only as a child of `<xsl:stylesheet>`.

Defined in

[1.0] XSLT section 12.3, "Number Formatting."

[2.0] XSLT section 16.4.1, "Defining a Decimal Format."

Example

Here is a stylesheet that defines two `<decimal-format>`s:

```
<?xml version="1.0" encoding="ISO-8859-1" ?>
<!-- decimal-format.xsl -->
<xsl:stylesheet version="1.0"
  xmlns:xsl="http://www.w3.org/1999/XSL/Transform">

  <xsl:output method="text"/>

f  <xsl:decimal-format name="f1"
    decimal-separator=":"
    grouping-separator="/"/>

  <xsl:decimal-format name="f2"
    infinity="Really, really big"
    NaN="[not a number]"/>

  <xsl:template match="/">
    <xsl:text>&#xA;Tests of the &lt;decimal-format&gt; element:</xsl:text>

    <xsl:text>&#xA;&#xA;    format-number(1528.3, '#/###:00', 'f1')=</xsl:text>
    <xsl:value-of select="format-number(1528.3, '#/###:00;-#/###:00', 'f1')"/>
    <xsl:text>&#xA;    format-number(1 div 0, '###,###.00', 'f2')=</xsl:text>
    <xsl:value-of select="format-number(1 div 0, '###,###.00', 'f2')"/>
    <xsl:text>&#xA;    format-number(blue div orange, '#.##', 'f2')=</xsl:text>
    <xsl:value-of select="format-number(blue div orange, '#.##', 'f2')"/>
    <xsl:text>&#xA;&#xA;**************************************</xsl:text>
    <xsl:text>&#xA;Sales report for </xsl:text>
    <xsl:value-of select="/report/@month"/>
    <xsl:text>/</xsl:text>
    <xsl:value-of select="/report/@year"/>
    <xsl:text>&#xA;&#xA;</xsl:text>
    <xsl:variable name="totalSales" select="sum(/report/brand/units)"/>
    <xsl:for-each select="report/brand">
      <xsl:value-of select="name"/>
      <xsl:text>: &#xA;    </xsl:text>
      <xsl:value-of select="format-number(units, '##,###')"/>
      <xsl:text> bars sold, </xsl:text>
      <xsl:value-of select="format-number(units div $totalSales, '##%')"/>
      <xsl:text> of all sales.</xsl:text>
      <xsl:text>&#xA;</xsl:text>
      <xsl:text>&#xA;</xsl:text>
    </xsl:for-each>
    <xsl:text>Total sales: </xsl:text>
    <xsl:value-of select="format-number($totalSales, '##,###')"/>
    <xsl:text> bars.&#xA;</xsl:text>
  </xsl:template>

</xsl:stylesheet>
```

We'll use this stylesheet against the following document:

```
<?xml version="1.0" encoding="utf-8"?>
<!-- chocolate.xml -->
<report month="8" year="2006">
  <title>Chocolate bar sales</title>
  <brand>
    <name>Lindt</name>
```

```
      <units>27408</units>
   </brand>
   <brand>
      <name>Callebaut</name>
      <units>8203</units>
   </brand>
   <brand>
      <name>Valrhona</name>
      <units>22101</units>
   </brand>
   <brand>
      <name>Perugina</name>
      <units>14336</units>
   </brand>
   <brand>
      <name>Ghirardelli</name>
      <units>19268</units>
   </brand>
</report>
```

When we use an XSLT 1.0 processor with this document and stylesheet, the results are as follows:

```
Tests of the <decimal-format> element:

    format-number(1528.3, '#/###:00', 'f1')=1/528:30
    format-number(1 div 0, '###,###.00', 'f2')=Really, really big
    format-number(blue div orange, '#.##', 'f2')=[not a number]


**************************************
Sales report for 8/2006

Lindt:
    27,408 bars sold, 30% of all sales.

Callebaut:
    8,203 bars sold, 9% of all sales.

Valrhona:
    22,101 bars sold, 24% of all sales.

Perugina:
    14,336 bars sold, 16% of all sales.

Ghirardelli:
    19,268 bars sold, 21% of all sales.

Total sales: 91,316 bars.
```

[2.0] As we've seen numerous times, XSLT 2.0 is more strict in the things it will accept. A stylesheet with **1 div 0** will not run. If you need to use the XSLT 1.0 behavior in an XSLT 2.0 stylesheet, remember that you can use the **version** attribute on any XSLT 2.0 element:

```
<?xml version="1.0" encoding="ISO-8859-1" ?>
<!-- decimal-format2.xsl -->
```

```
<xsl:stylesheet version="2.0"
  xmlns:xsl="http://www.w3.org/1999/XSL/Transform">
...
    <xsl:text>&#xA;    format-number(1 div 0, '###,###.00', 'f2')=</xsl:text>
    <xsl:value-of version="1.0"
      select="format-number(1 div 0, '###,###.00', 'f2')"/>
...
</xsl:stylesheet>
```

Here we've changed the `version` attribute of the `<xsl:stylesheet>` element to `2.0`, but added `version="1.0"` to the `<xsl:value-of>` element later in the stylesheet. This gives us the XSLT 1.0 behavior for this one element, which means we'll get the value `Really, really big` when we divide by zero. If we use the default XSLT 2.0 behavior, the stylesheet throws an exception and no useful output is generated.

 In XSLT 2.0, be aware that dividing an `xs:double` by zero returns `Infinity`, while dividing an `xs:integer` or `xs:decimal` by zero is a run-time error. If we change the stylesheet to read `xs:double(1) div xs:double(0)`, the stylesheet would run without errors, generating the same results (`Infinity`) as an XSLT 1.0 stylesheet that uses `1 div 0`.

See "[2.0] Attributes common to all XSLT elements" earlier in this appendix for more information about the `version` attribute and other attributes that can be added to any XSLT element.

[2.0] <xsl:document>

Allows you to create a new document node. This element is useful for validating the document node against a schema. The document node created by `<xsl:document>` is not meant to be serialized (written to disk); if that's what you want to do, use `<xsl:result-document>` instead.

Category

Instruction.

Required Attributes

None.

Optional Attributes

[2.0 – Schema] `type`
    Defines the datatype of the root element node created by this element. To validate a document node, it must have as its children a single element node, no text nodes and zero or more comment and processing instruction nodes. If the document node doesn't have this structure, the XSLT processor throws an error.

    The `type` and `validation` attributes are mutually exclusive.

[2.0 – Schema] `validation`

> Defines how the value of the new element will be validated. The `validation` attribute has four values: `strict`, `lax`, `preserve`, or `strip`. To validate a document node with `strict` or `lax`, the document node must have as its children a single element node, no text nodes, and zero or more comment and processing instruction nodes. If the document node doesn't have this structure, the XSLT processor throws an error if you use `strict` or `lax`.
>
> `validation="strict"` means that the XSLT processor looks in all the declared schemas for an element declaration (`<xs:element>`) with the same name as the single element node that is a child of this document node. It is a fatal error if the processor can't find a matching `<xs:element>`. Assuming the processor finds the declaration of the element node, it validates the generated value against the element's declaration.
>
> `validation="lax"` works just like `validation="strict"`, except that no error occurs if the processor can't find the declaration of the element in any of the declared schemas. In that case, the type annotation of the element is `xs:untyped`.
>
> The value `validation="preserve"` means the type annotations of the single element node and all its children and attributes will be preserved without changes. No schema validation is done.
>
> Finally, `validation="strip"` sets the type annotation of the single element node to `xs:untyped`. All of the elements children and attributes have their type annotations set to `xs:untyped` for elements and to `xs:untypedAtomic` for attributes. No schema validation is done.
>
> The `validation` and `type` attributes are mutually exclusive.

Content

A sequence constructor.

Appears in

`<xsl:document>` appears inside a template.

Defined in

[2.0] XSLT section 11.5, "Creating Document Nodes."

Example

We'll create a document node and give it some content. The node will be a `<name>` element, as defined in our purchase order schema:

```
<?xml version="1.0" encoding="UTF-8"?>
<!-- po.xsd -->
<xs:schema
  xmlns="http://www.oreilly.com/xslt"
  targetNamespace="http://www.oreilly.com/xslt"
  xmlns:xs="http://www.w3.org/2001/XMLSchema">
```

```
<xs:element name="purchase-order">
  ...
</xs:element>

...

<xs:element name="name">
  <xs:complexType>
    <xs:sequence>
      <xs:element ref="title"
        minOccurs="0" maxOccurs="1"/>
      <xs:element ref="first-name"
        minOccurs="1" maxOccurs="1"/>
      <xs:element ref="last-name"
        minOccurs="1" maxOccurs="1"/>
    </xs:sequence>
  </xs:complexType>
</xs:element>

<xs:element name="title" type="xs:string"/>
<xs:element name="first-name" type="xs:string"/>
<xs:element name="last-name" type="xs:string"/>

</xs:schema>
```

Here is our stylesheet:

```
<?xml version="1.0"?>
<!-- document.xsl -->
<xsl:stylesheet version="1.0"
  xmlns:xsl="http://www.w3.org/1999/XSL/Transform"
  xmlns="http://www.oreilly.com/xslt"
  xmlns:po="http://www.oreilly.com/xslt">

  <xsl:output method="xml" indent="yes"/>

  <xsl:import-schema namespace="http://www.oreilly.com/xslt"
    schema-location="po.xsd" />

  <xsl:template match="/">
    <xsl:document validation="lax">
      <xsl:element name="name">
        <xsl:element name="title">
          <xsl:text>Mr.</xsl:text>
        </xsl:element>
        <xsl:element name="first-name">
          <xsl:text>Kent Lyle</xsl:text>
        </xsl:element>
        <xsl:element name="last-name">
          <xsl:text>Birdley</xsl:text>
        </xsl:element>
      </xsl:element>
    </xsl:document>
  </xsl:template>
```

```
</xsl:stylesheet>
```

We're using `validation="lax"` here. That means the XSLT processor will validate the document node that contains the `<name>` element if it can find an XML schema that defines the `<name>` element. If we take out the `<xsl:import-schema>` element, the `<xsl:document>` element still works. If we take out the `<xsl:import-schema>` element and change the `<xsl:document>` to `validation="strict"`, the stylesheet fails because it can't find a declaration for `<name>`.

Here are the results of the stylesheet:

```
<?xml version="1.0" encoding="UTF-8"?>
<name xmlns="http://www.oreilly.com/xslt">
   <title>Mr.</title>
   <first-name>Kent Lyle</first-name>
   <last-name>Birdley</last-name>
</name>
```

In this case, we've simply written the contents of the `<xsl:document>` element to the output. A more common use of `<xsl:document>` is to store the document node in a variable, and then use that validated variable elsewhere in the stylesheet.

Note that we can use the `<xsl:document>` element to create a document node that is not well-formed. Here's a sample stylesheet that does just that:

```
<?xml version="1.0"?>
<!-- document2.xsl -->
<xsl:stylesheet version="1.0"
  xmlns:xsl="http://www.w3.org/1999/XSL/Transform">

  <xsl:output method="text"/>

  <xsl:variable name="ill-formed" as="node()*">
    <xsl:document>
      <xsl:element name="title">
        <xsl:text>Mr.</xsl:text>
      </xsl:element>
      <xsl:element name="first-name">
        <xsl:text>Kent Lyle</xsl:text>
      </xsl:element>
      <xsl:element name="last-name">
        <xsl:text>Birdley</xsl:text>
      </xsl:element>
    </xsl:document>
  </xsl:variable>

  <xsl:template match="/">
    <xsl:text>&#xA;A document node that isn't well formed:</xsl:text>
    <xsl:text>&#xA;&#xA;  Is this a document node? </xsl:text>
    <xsl:value-of select="if ($ill-formed instance of document-node())
                           then 'Yes!'
                           else 'No!'"/>
    <xsl:text>&#xA;  Number of child elements: </xsl:text>
    <xsl:value-of select="count($ill-formed/*)"/>

    <xsl:result-document method="xml" href="ill-formed.xml">
```

```
    <xsl:copy-of select="$ill-formed"/>
  </xsl:result-document>
</xsl:template>

</xsl:stylesheet>
```

This stylesheet creates a variable named `$ill-formed` that has three elements at the root of the document. We use the `document-node( )` node test to make sure this is, in fact, a document node, and then we print the number of children that the document node has:

```
A document node that isn't well formed:

  Is this a document node? Yes!
  Number of child elements: 3
```

Finally we use the `<xsl:result-document>` element to write our illegal markup to a file. The file `ill-formed.xml` looks like this:

```
<?xml version="1.0" encoding="UTF-8"?>
<title>Mr.</title>
<first-name>Kent Lyle</first-name>
<last-name>Birdley</last-name>
```

Typically a document node has a single child that represents the document element; in this case, we've sidestepped the XML parser to create markup that isn't legal. Although this situation is uncommon, be aware that a stylesheet might generate a document node that has more than one child.

<xsl:element>

Allows you to create an element in the output document. It works similarly to the `<xsl:attribute>` element.

Category

Instruction.

Required Attribute

name

> Defines the name of this element. A value of `name="Fred"` produces a `<Fred>` element in the output document.

Optional Attributes

namespace

> Defines the namespace used for this element.

use-attribute-sets

> Lists one or more attribute sets that should be used by this element. If you specify more than one attribute set, separate their names with whitespace characters.

[2.0] `inherit-namespaces`

> Defines whether this element and its children inherit the current namespace nodes. Valid values are **yes** (the default) and **no**.

[2.0 – Schema] `type`

> Defines the datatype of this element. The datatype can be any of the built-in datatypes or it can be a datatype defined in a schema if you have a schema-aware XSLT 2.0 processor.

> The `type` and `validation` attributes are mutually exclusive.

[2.0 – Schema] `validation`

> Defines how the value of the new element will be validated. The `validation` attribute has four values: `strict`, `lax`, `preserve`, or `strip`.

> `validation="strict"` means that the XSLT processor looks in all the declared schemas for an element declaration (`<xs:element>`) with the same name as this element. If the processor can't find a matching `<xs:element>`, it is a fatal error. Assuming the processor finds the declaration of the element, it validates the generated element's value against its declaration.

> `validation="lax"` works just like `validation="strict"`, except that no error occurs if the processor can't find the declaration of the element in any of the declared schemas. In that case, the type annotation of the element is `xs:untyped`.

> The value `validation="preserve"` means the created element will have a type annotation of `xs:anyType`, and the type annotations of any nodes that the new element contains will be preserved without any changes. No schema validation is done.

> Finally, `validation="strip"` creates a new element of type `xs:anyType`, and any nodes the new element contains will have their type annotations replaced with `xs:untyped` for elements and with `xs:untypedAtomic` for attributes. No schema validation is done.

> The `validation` and `type` attributes are mutually exclusive.

Content

An XSLT template.

Appears in

`<xsl:element>` appears inside a template.

Defined in

[1.0] XSLT section 7.1.2, "Creating Elements with `xsl:element`."

[2.0] XSLT section 11.2, "Creating Element Nodes using `xsl:element`."

Example

We'll use a generic stylesheet that copies the input document to the result tree, with one exception: all attributes in the original documents are converted to child elements in the result tree. The name of the new element will be the name of the attribute, and its text will be the value of the attribute. Because we don't know the name of the attribute until we process the XML source document, we must use the `<xsl:element>` element to create the result tree. Here's how our stylesheet looks:

```
<?xml version="1.0"?>
<!-- element.xsl -->
<xsl:stylesheet version="1.0"
  xmlns:xsl="http://www.w3.org/1999/XSL/Transform">

  <xsl:output method="xml"/>

  <xsl:template match="*">
    <xsl:element name="{name()}">
      <xsl:for-each select="@*">
        <xsl:element name="{name()}">
          <xsl:value-of select="."/>
        </xsl:element>
      </xsl:for-each>
      <xsl:apply-templates select="*|text()"/>
    </xsl:element>
  </xsl:template>

</xsl:stylesheet>
```

This stylesheet uses the `<xsl:element>` element in two places: first to create a new element with the same name as the original element, and second to create a new element with the same name as each attribute. We'll apply the stylesheet to this document:

```
<?xml version="1.0"?>
<!-- albums.xml -->
<list xml:lang="en">
  <title>Albums I've bought recently:</title>
  <listitem>The Sacred Art of Dub</listitem>
  <listitem>Only the Poor Man Feel It</listitem>
  <listitem>Excitable Boy</listitem>
  <listitem xml:lang="sw">Aki Special</listitem>
  <listitem xml:lang="en-gb">Combat Rock</listitem>
  <listitem xml:lang="zu">Talking Timbuktu</listitem>
  <listitem xml:lang="jz">The Birth of the Cool</listitem>
</list>
```

Our results look like this:

```
<?xml version="1.0" encoding="UTF-8"?><list><xml:lang>en</xml:lang>
  <title>Albums I've bought recently:</title>
  <listitem>The Sacred Art of Dub</listitem>
  <listitem>Only the Poor Man Feel It</listitem>
  <listitem>Excitable Boy</listitem>
  <listitem><xml:lang>sw</xml:lang>Aki Special</listitem>
  <listitem><xml:lang>en-gb</xml:lang>Combat Rock</listitem>
  <listitem><xml:lang>zu</xml:lang>Talking Timbuktu</listitem>
  <listitem><xml:lang>jz</xml:lang>The Birth of the Cool</listitem>
</list>
```

The `<xsl:element>` element created all the elements in the output document, including the `<xml:lang>` elements created from the `xml:lang` attributes.

[2.0 – Schema] Now we'll look at an example that uses XSLT 2.0's schema features. We'll use the `validation` attribute of `<xsl:element>` to make sure the element we create is valid according to our purchase order schema. We'll start with an XML file that contains similar data to our purchase order format:

```
<?xml version="1.0" encoding="utf-8"?>
<!-- create-po.xml -->
<po order-num="38292">
  <customer id="4738" standing="Platinum">
    <address>
      <name>
        <courtesy>Mr.</courtesy>
        <given-name>Chester Hasbrouck</given-name>
        <surname>Frisby</surname>
      </name>
      <street>1234 Main Street</street>
      <city>Sheboygan</city>
      <state>WI</state>
      <zip>48392</zip>
    </address>
  </customer>
  <line-items>
    <line-item>
      <partnum>28392-33-TT</partnum>
      <partname>Turnip Twaddler</partname>
      <quantity>3</quantity>
      <price>9.95</price>
    </line-item>
    <line-item>
      <partnum>28100-38-CT</partnum>
      <partname>Clam Teaser</partname>
      <quantity>7</quantity>
      <price>39.95</price>
    </line-item>
  </line-items>
</po>
```

We'll use `<xsl:element>` to create a new purchase order using the data in this document. We also have to generate a `<date>` element as the first child of `<purchase-order>`. Here's the stylesheet:

```
<?xml version="1.0"?>
<!-- element2.xsl -->
<xsl:stylesheet version="2.0"
  xmlns:xsl="http://www.w3.org/1999/XSL/Transform"
  xmlns:xs="http://www.w3.org/2001/XMLSchema"
  xmlns="http://www.oreilly.com/xslt"
  xmlns:po="http://www.oreilly.com/xslt"
  exclude-result-prefixes="xs po">

  <xsl:import-schema namespace="http://www.oreilly.com/xslt"
    schema-location="po.xsd" />
```

```
<xsl:output method="xml" indent="yes"/>

<xsl:variable name="now" as="xs:date" select="current-date()"/>

<xsl:template match="po">
  <xsl:element name="purchase-order" validation="strict">
    <xsl:attribute name="id" select="@order-num"/>
    <date>
      <xsl:attribute name="year" select="year-from-date($now)"/>
      <xsl:attribute name="month" select="month-from-date($now)"/>
      <xsl:attribute name="day" select="day-from-date($now)"/>
    </date>
    <customer>
      <xsl:attribute name="id" select="customer/@id"/>
      <xsl:attribute name="level" select="customer/@standing"/>
      <xsl:apply-templates select="customer/address"/>
    </customer>
    <xsl:apply-templates select="line-items"/>
  </xsl:element>
</xsl:template>

<xsl:template match="address">
  <address>
    <xsl:attribute name="type" select="'business'"/>
    <xsl:apply-templates select="name"/>
    <street>
      <xsl:value-of select="street"/>
    </street>
    <city>
      <xsl:value-of select="city"/>
    </city>
    <state>
      <xsl:value-of select="state"/>
    </state>
    <zip>
      <xsl:value-of select="zip"/>
    </zip>
  </address>
</xsl:template>

<xsl:template match="line-items">
  <items>
    <xsl:for-each select="line-item">
      <item>
        <xsl:attribute name="part-no" select="partnum"/>
        <partname>
          <xsl:value-of select="partname"/>
        </partname>
        <qty>
          <xsl:value-of select="quantity"/>
        </qty>
        <price>
          <xsl:value-of select="price"/>
        </price>
```

```
        </item>
      </xsl:for-each>
    </items>
  </xsl:template>

  <xsl:template match="name">
    <name>
      <xsl:if test="courtesy">
        <title>
          <xsl:value-of select="courtesy"/>
        </title>
      </xsl:if>
      <first-name>
        <xsl:value-of select="given-name"/>
      </first-name>
      <last-name>
        <xsl:value-of select="surname"/>
      </last-name>
    </name>
  </xsl:template>

</xsl:stylesheet>
```

This stylesheet uses `<xsl:element>` and `<xsl:attribute>` to build a purchase order from scratch. The `validation="strict"` attribute means the generated `<purchase-order>` element must be a valid purchase order when compared to the schema in *po.xsd*. If the stylesheet attempts to add anything to the generated `<purchase-order>` that violates the purchase order schema, the stylesheet engine throws an exception and stops. The stylesheet generates this XML:

```
<?xml version="1.0" encoding="UTF-8"?>
<purchase-order xmlns="http://www.oreilly.com/xslt" id="38292">
  <date year="2008" month="3" day="2"/>
  <customer id="4738" level="Platinum">
    <address type="business">
      <name>
        <title>Mr.</title>
        <first-name>Chester Hasbrouck</first-name>
        <last-name>Frisby</last-name>
      </name>
      <street>1234 Main Street</street>
      <city>Sheboygan</city>
      <state>WI</state>
      <zip>48392</zip>
    </address>
  </customer>
  <items>
    <item part-no="28392-33-TT">
      <partname>Turnip Twaddler</partname>
      <qty>3</qty>
      <price>9.95</price>
    </item>
    <item part-no="28100-38-CT">
      <partname>Clam Teaser</partname>
      <qty>7</qty>
```

```
            <price>39.95</price>
        </item>
    </items>
</purchase-order>
```

Notice that the generated document uses the default namespace of http://www.oreilly.com/ xslt. This is the namespace associated with the imported schema; the fact that it is declared as the default namespace in the stylesheet means it is copied to the output element. Also notice that the stylesheet uses exclude-result-prefixes to keep the po and xs prefixes out of the generated document. The default namespace of the generated purchase order is http:// www.oreilly.com/xslt, as it should be.

We create the <date> element with the current-date( ) function. To see what happens when validation fails, take out the <date> element. You'll see an error message like this:

```
XTTE1510: In content of element <purchase-order>: The content model does
    not allow element <customer> to appear here. Expected:
    {http://www.oreilly.com/xslt}date (See
    http://www.w3.org/TR/xmlschema-1/#cvc-complex-type clause 2.4)
Transformation failed: Run-time errors were reported
```

In this case, the <purchase-order> element isn't generated because it isn't valid without the <date> element in the right place.

<xsl:fallback>

Defines a template that should be used when an XSLT processor finds an instruction in the stylesheet that it can't process. Fallback processing can be triggered by an extension element that relies on code that can't be found. It is also invoked when an XSLT 1.0 processor working in forward processing mode encounters an XSLT 2.0 element.

Category
Instruction.

Required Attributes
None.

Optional Attributes
None.

Content
An XSLT template.

Appears in
<xsl:fallback> appears inside a template.

Defined in
[1.0] XSLT section 15, "Fallback."

[2.0] XSLT section 18, "Extensibility and Fallback."

Example

Here is a stylesheet that uses `<xsl:fallback>` to terminate the transformation if an extension element can't be found:

```
<?xml version="1.0"?>
<!-- fallback.xsl -->
<xsl:stylesheet version="1.0"
  xmlns:xsl="http://www.w3.org/1999/XSL/Transform"
  xmlns:db="xalan://DatabaseExtension"
  extension-element-prefixes="db">

  <xsl:output method="html"/>

  <xsl:template match="/">
    <html>
      <head>
        <title><xsl:value-of select="report/title"/></title>
      </head>
      <body>
        <h1><xsl:value-of select="report/title"/></h1>
        <xsl:for-each select="report/section">
          <h2><xsl:value-of select="title"/></h2>
          <xsl:for-each select="dbaccess">
            <db:accessDatabase>
              <xsl:fallback>
                <p>Sorry, the database library is not available!</p>
              </xsl:fallback>
            </db:accessDatabase>
          </xsl:for-each>
        </xsl:for-each>
      </body>
    </html>
  </xsl:template>

</xsl:stylesheet>
```

We'll use this stylesheet against this XML document:

```
<?xml version="1.0"?>
<!-- use-db.xml -->
<report>
  <title>HR employee listing</title>
  <section>
    <title>Employees by department</title>
    <dbaccess driver="COM.ibm.db2.jdbc.app.DB2Driver"
      database="jdbc:db2:sample" tablename="employee" where="*"
      fieldnames='workdept as "Department", lastname as "Last Name",
                  firstnme as "First Name"'
      order-by="workdept" group-by="workdept, lastname, firstnme"/>
  </section>
</report>
```

When we use this stylesheet to transform a document, the `<xsl:fallback>` element is processed if the extension element can't be found. If the element isn't available, you'll get these results:

```
<html>
  <head>
    <META http-equiv="Content-Type" content="text/html; charset=UTF-8">
    <title>HR employee listing</title>
  </head>
  <body>
    <h1>HR employee listing</h1>
    <h2>Employees by department</h2>
    <p>Sorry, the database library is not available!</p>
  </body>
</html>
```

In this case, the extension element is `<dbaccess>`. This example was originally written for the Xalan processor; in Xalan, the value of an extension element prefix's URI is a Java class name. If, for whatever reason, the class `DatabaseExtension` can't be loaded, the `<xsl:fallback>` element is processed instead.

Note that the `<xsl:fallback>` element is processed only when the extension element can't be found; if the code that implements that extension element is found, but fails, that error must be handled some other way. Also be aware that the gracefulness of stylesheet termination will vary from one XSLT processor to the next.

`<xsl:for-each>`

XSLT's iteration operator. This element has a `select` attribute that selects some nodes from the current context. The contents of the `<xsl:for-each>` element are then evaluated using each of the selected nodes. (*[2.0]* In XSLT 2.0, the `select` attribute selects items, which can include atomic values as well as nodes.)

Category

Instruction.

Required Attribute

`select`
    Contains an XPath expression that selects nodes from the current context.

Optional Attributes

None.

Content

`<xsl:for-each>` contains a template that is evaluated against each of the selected nodes. The `<xsl:for-each>` element can contain one or more `<xsl:sort>` elements to order the selected nodes before they are processed. All `<xsl:sort>` elements must appear first, before the template begins.

Appears in

`<xsl:for-each>` appears inside a template.

Defined in

[1.0] XSLT section 8, "Repetition."

[2.0] XSLT section 7, "Repetition."

Example

We'll demonstrate the `<xsl:for-each>` element with the following stylesheet:

```
<?xml version="1.0"?>
<!-- for-each.xsl -->
<xsl:stylesheet version="1.0"
  xmlns:xsl="http://www.w3.org/1999/XSL/Transform">

  <xsl:output method="text"/>

  <xsl:template match="/">
    <xsl:text>&#xA;Here is a moderately long list:
</xsl:text>
    <xsl:variable name="listitems" select="list/listitem"/>
    <xsl:call-template name="processListitems">
      <xsl:with-param name="items" select="$listitems"/>
    </xsl:call-template>
  </xsl:template>

  <xsl:template name="processListitems">
    <xsl:param name="items"/>
    <xsl:for-each select="$items">
      <xsl:value-of select="position()"/>
      <xsl:text>.  </xsl:text>
      <xsl:value-of select="."/>
      <xsl:text>&#xA;</xsl:text>
    </xsl:for-each>
  </xsl:template>

</xsl:stylesheet>
```

In this stylesheet, we use an `<xsl:param>` named `items` to illustrate the `<xsl:for-each>` element. The `items` parameter contains some number of `<listitem>` elements from the XML source document; the `<xsl:for-each>` element iterates through all those elements and processes each one. We'll use our stylesheet with the following XML document:

```
<?xml version="1.0"?>
<!-- albums.xml -->
<list xml:lang="en">
  <title>Albums I've bought recently:</title>
  <listitem>The Sacred Art of Dub</listitem>
  <listitem>Only the Poor Man Feel It</listitem>
  <listitem>Excitable Boy</listitem>
  <listitem xml:lang="sw">Aki Special</listitem>
  <listitem xml:lang="en-gb">Combat Rock</listitem>
  <listitem xml:lang="zu">Talking Timbuktu</listitem>
```

```
    <listitem xml:lang="jz">The Birth of the Cool</listitem>
</list>
```
When we run the transformation, here are the results:
```
Here is a moderately long list:
1.   The Sacred Art of Dub
2.   Only the Poor Man Feel It
3.   Excitable Boy
4.   Aki Special
5.   Combat Rock
6.   Talking Timbuktu
7.   The Birth of the Cool
```
The `<xsl:for-each>` element iterated through all the `<listitem>` elements from the XML source document and processed each one.

[2.0] <xsl:for-each-group>

Takes the items in a sequence and puts them into groups. There are four different ways of defining groups, each of which are explained in detail below. The grouping is done based on a common value or by a pattern that the first or last item in the group must match. Be aware that it is possible for an item in the original sequence to be put into more than one group.

Category

Instruction.

Required Attribute

select
>   An XPath expression that determines the items to be grouped.

Optional Attributes

group-by
>   Defines a common value that all items in a group must share. For example, group-by="state" creates a group for each unique value of the `<state>` element. All items in a given group will have the same value for `<state>`.

group-adjacent
>   Defines an expression that is evaluated for every item in the sequence. If the value of that expression for the current item is the same as the value of that expression for the previous item, then the current item is put into the same group as the previous item. If not, the current item becomes the first item in a new group.

group-starting-with
>   Defines a pattern that indicates the start of a new group. When an item matching that pattern is found, a new group is started, and all subsequent items are put into the same group until another item that matches the pattern is found.

`group-ending-with`

> Defines a pattern that indicates the end of the current group. When an item matching that pattern is found, the current group is closed. The next item in the sequence is put into a new group.

Keep in mind that `group-by`, `group-adjacent`, `group-starting-with`, and `group-ending-with` are mutually exclusive.

`collation`

> Defines the collation sequence used to compare grouping keys. The way collation sequences are defined can vary from one XSLT processor to another, so check your processor's documentation for the details.
>
> The `collation` attribute can only be used with `group-by` or `group-adjacent`. It is an error to use it with `group-starting-with` or `group-ending-with`.

Content

Zero or more `<xsl:sort>` elements and a sequence constructor.

Appears in

Any sequence constructor.

Defined in

XSLT section 14, "Grouping."

Example

We'll look at four examples here to illustrate the four types of grouping. We'll start with `group-by`, the most common type of grouping. We'll use a simplified list of customer addresses:

```
<?xml version="1.0"?>
<!-- simplified-names.xml -->
<addressbook>
  <address>
    <first-name>Chester Hasbrouck</first-name>
    <last-name>Frisby</last-name>
    <city>Sheboygan</city>
    <state>WI</state>
  </address>
  <address>
    <first-name>Mary</first-name>
    <last-name>Backstayge</last-name>
    <city>Skunk Haven</city>
    <state>MA</state>
  </address>
  <address>
    <first-name>Natalie</first-name>
    <last-name>Attired</last-name>
    <city>Winter Harbor</city>
    <state>ME</state>
```

```
    </address>
    <address>
      <first-name>Harry</first-name>
      <last-name>Backstayge</last-name>
      <city>Skunk Haven</city>
      <state>MA</state>
    </address>
    <address>
      <first-name>Mary</first-name>
      <last-name>McGoon</last-name>
      <city>Boylston</city>
      <state>VA</state>
    </address>
    <address>
      <first-name>Amanda</first-name>
      <last-name>Reckonwith</last-name>
      <city>Lynn</city>
      <state>MA</state>
    </address>
</addressbook>
```

We'll use **group-by** to group these addresses by state. Here's the stylesheet:

```
<?xml version="1.0"?>
<!-- for-each-group1.xsl -->
<xsl:stylesheet version="2.0"
  xmlns:xsl="http://www.w3.org/1999/XSL/Transform">

  <xsl:output method="text"/>

  <xsl:template match="/">
    <xsl:text>Customers grouped by state&#xA;&#xA;</xsl:text>
    <xsl:for-each-group select="/addressbook/address" group-by="state">
      <xsl:sort select="state"/>
      <xsl:text>  State = </xsl:text>
      <xsl:value-of select="current-grouping-key()"/>
      <xsl:text>&#xA;</xsl:text>
      <xsl:for-each select="current-group()">
        <xsl:text>&#x9;</xsl:text>
        <xsl:value-of select="(first-name, last-name)"
          separator=" "/>
        <xsl:text>, </xsl:text>
        <xsl:value-of select="city"/>
        <xsl:text>&#xA;</xsl:text>
      </xsl:for-each>
    </xsl:for-each-group>
  </xsl:template>

</xsl:stylesheet>
```

Our stylesheet generates these results:

```
Customers grouped by state

  State = MA
        Mary Backstayge, Skunk Haven
        Harry Backstayge, Skunk Haven
```

```
        Amanda Reckonwith, Lynn
    State = ME
        Natalie Attired, Winter Harbor
    State = VA
        Mary McGoon, Boylston
    State = WI
        Chester Hasbrouck Frisby, Sheboygan
```

The `<xsl:sort>` element after `<xsl:for-each-group>` sorts the groups themselves. For each group a heading is printed, and then the contents of each group are handled by `<xsl:for-each select="current-group()">`. If we take out the `<xsl:sort>` element to order the groups, our output is different. Our customers are still grouped correctly, but the groups are in a different order:

```
Customers grouped by state

    State = WI
        Chester Hasbrouck Frisby, Sheboygan
    State = MA
        Mary Backstayge, Skunk Haven
        Harry Backstayge, Skunk Haven
        Amanda Reckonwith, Lynn
    State = ME
        Natalie Attired, Winter Harbor
    State = VA
        Mary McGoon, Boylston
```

Because we didn't sort the groups, they appear in the order in which each state first appeared.

For `group-adjacent`, we define an expression that returns a value for each item in the sequence. To keep our example simple, we'll use `group-adjacent` to return `true()` or `false()`. Within the sequence, all adjacent items that have the same value are put into the same group. We're looking for groups of adjacent `<p>` elements in an HTML document; we'll convert them to `<ul>` elements in which each `<p>` element is transformed into a list item. Here's the HTML source:

```
<?xml version="1.0"?>
<!-- grouping-input.html -->
<html>
  <body>
    <!-- Here's some sample text from the chapter "Sorting
         and Grouping". -->
    <h1>Steps for grouping in the Muench method</h1>
    <p>Define a <code>key</code> for the property we want
    to use for grouping.</p>
    <p>Select all of the nodes ...</p>
    <p>For each unique grouping value, ...</p>
    <h1>Steps for grouping in XSLT 2.0</h1>
    <p>Define an XPath expression ...</p>
    <p>Select all of the nodes we want to group ...</p>
    <p>Instead of dealing with each ...</p>
  </body>
</html>
```

We'll use this stylesheet to do the grouping:

```
<?xml version="1.0"?>
<!-- for-each-group2.xsl -->
<xsl:stylesheet version="2.0"
  xmlns:xsl="http://www.w3.org/1999/XSL/Transform">

  <xsl:output method="html" include-content-type="no"/>

  <xsl:template match="/">
    <html>
      <head>
        <title>Grouping with group-adjacent</title>
      </head>
      <body>
        <xsl:for-each-group select="html/body/*"
          group-adjacent="boolean(self::p)">
          <xsl:choose>
            <xsl:when test="current-grouping-key()">
              <ul>
                <xsl:for-each select="current-group()">
                  <li><xsl:apply-templates select="*|text()"/></li>
                </xsl:for-each>
              </ul>
            </xsl:when>
            <xsl:otherwise>
              <xsl:apply-templates select="current-group()" />
            </xsl:otherwise>
          </xsl:choose>
        </xsl:for-each-group>
      </body>
    </html>
  </xsl:template>

  <xsl:template match="*">
    <xsl:copy>
      <xsl:for-each select="@*">
        <xsl:copy/>
      </xsl:for-each>
      <xsl:apply-templates/>
    </xsl:copy>
  </xsl:template>

</xsl:stylesheet>
```

Our stylesheet yields these results:

```
<html>
  <head>
    <title>Grouping with group-adjacent</title>
  </head>
  <body>
    <h1>Steps for grouping in the Muench method</h1>
    <ul>
      <li>Define a <code>key</code> for the property we want
          to use for grouping.
      </li>
      <li>Select all of the nodes ...</li>
```

```
            <li>For each unique grouping value, ...</li>
        </ul>
        <h1>Steps for grouping in XSLT 2.0</h1>
        <ul>
            <li>Define an XPath expression ...</li>
            <li>Select all of the nodes we want to group ...</li>
            <li>Instead of dealing with each ...</li>
        </ul>
    </body>
</html>
```

The `group-adjacent` attribute is an XPath expression that returns a value. In this case, any `<p>` element returns `true( )`, while everything else returns `false( )`. The value of `group-adjacent` can be a much more complicated expression. See the discussion of "Another Type of Grouping: group-adjacent" in Chapter 6 for more detail.

Our third grouping example uses `group-starting-with`. In this example, we'll use each `<h1>` element as the start of a section. Each `<h1>` element will start a group; everything up until the next `<h1>` element will be in the same group. We'll create a DocBook output document in which the `<h1>`, and everything that follows it is in a `<sect1>` element. (We'll reuse our HTML document from the `group-adjacent` example.) Here's our `group-starting-with` stylesheet:

```
<?xml version="1.0"?>
<!-- for-each-group3.xsl -->
<xsl:stylesheet version="2.0"
  xmlns:xsl="http://www.w3.org/1999/XSL/Transform">

  <xsl:output method="xml" indent="yes"/>

  <xsl:template match="/">
    <chapter>
      <title>Grouping in XSLT</title>
      <xsl:apply-templates select="html/body"/>
    </chapter>
  </xsl:template>

  <xsl:template match="body">
    <xsl:for-each-group select="*" group-starting-with="h1">
      <sect1>
        <xsl:apply-templates select="current-group()"/>
      </sect1>
    </xsl:for-each-group>
  </xsl:template>

  <xsl:template match="h1">
    <title>
      <xsl:apply-templates/>
    </title>
  </xsl:template>

  <xsl:template match="p">
    <para>
      <xsl:apply-templates/>
    </para>
  </xsl:template>
```

```
<xsl:template match="*">
  <xsl:copy>
    <xsl:for-each select="@*">
      <xsl:copy/>
    </xsl:for-each>
    <xsl:apply-templates/>
  </xsl:copy>
</xsl:template>

</xsl:stylesheet>
```

Our stylesheet generates a DocBook document in which each `<h1>` and everything following it is now a `<sect1>` element:

```
<?xml version="1.0" encoding="UTF-8"?>
<chapter>
  <title>Grouping in XSLT</title>
  <sect1>
    <title>Steps for grouping in the Muench method</title>
    <para>Define a <code>key</code> for the property we want
  to use for grouping.</para>
    <para>Select all of the nodes ...</para>
    <para>For each unique grouping value, ...</para>
  </sect1>
  <sect1>
    <title>Steps for grouping in XSLT 2.0</title>
    <para>Define an XPath expression ...</para>
    <para>Select all of the nodes we want to group ...</para>
    <para>Instead of dealing with each ...</para>
  </sect1>
</chapter>
```

The text of the HTML `<h1>` becomes a DocBook `<title>` element, and each HTML `<p>` element becomes a DocBook `<para>` element.

Our final example is for `group-ending-with`. In this example, we'll take a list of elements and put them into three columns. The ending condition is each third element (`position( )` `mod 3 = 0`). We'll use this list of cars:

```
<?xml version="1.0"?>
<!-- carlist.xml -->
<cars>
  <make>Alfa Romeo</make>
  <make>Bentley</make>
  <make>Chevrolet</make>
  <make>Dodge</make>
  <make>Eagle</make>
  <make>Ford</make>
  <make>GMC</make>
  <make>Honda</make>
  <make>Isuzu</make>
  <model>Javelin</model>
  <model>K-Car</model>
  <make>Lincoln</make>
  <make>Mercedes</make>
```

```
    <make>Nash</make>
    <make>Opel</make>
    <make>Pontiac</make>
    <model>Quantum</model>
    <model>Rambler</model>
    <make>Studebaker</make>
  </cars>
```

Here's our stylesheet:

```
<?xml version="1.0"?>
<!-- for-each-group4.xsl -->
<xsl:stylesheet version="2.0"
  xmlns:xsl="http://www.w3.org/1999/XSL/Transform"
  xmlns:xs="http://www.w3.org/2001/XMLSchema"
  exclude-result-prefixes="xs">

  <xsl:output method="html"/>

  <xsl:template match="/">
    <html>
      <head>
        <title>Car Makes and Models</title>
      </head>
      <body style="font-family: sans-serif;">
        <h1>Car Makes and Models</h1>
        <p>Here are the car makes and models in
        our input document.</p>
        <table border="1" cellpadding="5">
          <xsl:apply-templates select="cars"/>
        </table>
      </body>
    </html>
  </xsl:template>

  <xsl:template match="cars">
    <xsl:for-each-group select="make|model"
      group-ending-with="*[position() mod 3 = 0]">
    <tr>
      <xsl:choose>
        <xsl:when test="count(current-group()) = 3">
          <xsl:for-each select="current-group()">
            <xsl:apply-templates select="."/>
          </xsl:for-each>
        </xsl:when>
        <xsl:when test="count(current-group()) = 2">
          <xsl:apply-templates select="current-group()[1]"/>
          <xsl:apply-templates select="current-group()[2]"/>
          <td bgcolor="#CCCCCC">
            &#x20;&#x20;
          </td>
        </xsl:when>
        <xsl:otherwise>
          <xsl:apply-templates select="current-group()[1]"/>
          <td bgcolor="#CCCCCC" colspan="2">
            &#x20;&#x20;
```

```
              </td>
            </xsl:otherwise>
          </xsl:choose>
        </tr>
      </xsl:for-each-group>
    </xsl:template>

    <xsl:template match="make">
      <td style="font-weight: bold;">
        <xsl:apply-templates/>
      </td>
    </xsl:template>

    <xsl:template match="model">
      <td style="font-style: italic; font-weight: bold;">
        <xsl:apply-templates/>
      </td>
    </xsl:template>

  </xsl:stylesheet>
```

Our results look like this:

```
<html>
  <head>
    <title>Car Makes and Models</title>
  </head>
  <body style="font-family: sans-serif;">
    <h1>Car Makes and Models</h1>
    <p>Here are the car makes and models in
      our input document.
    </p>
    <table border="1" cellpadding="5">
      <tr>
        <td style="font-weight: bold;">Alfa Romeo</td>
        <td style="font-weight: bold;">Bentley</td>
        <td style="font-weight: bold;">Chevrolet</td>
      </tr>
      ...
      <tr>
        <td style="font-weight: bold;">Studebaker</td>
        <td bgcolor="#CCCCCC" colspan="2"></td>
      </tr>
    </table>
  </body>
</html>
```

The elements in the list of cars have been written to our HTML table in groups of three. Notice that the last group has only one element, so that row of the table features a cell with the last element followed by a blank, gray cell with colspan="2". The document appears as shown in Figure A-9.

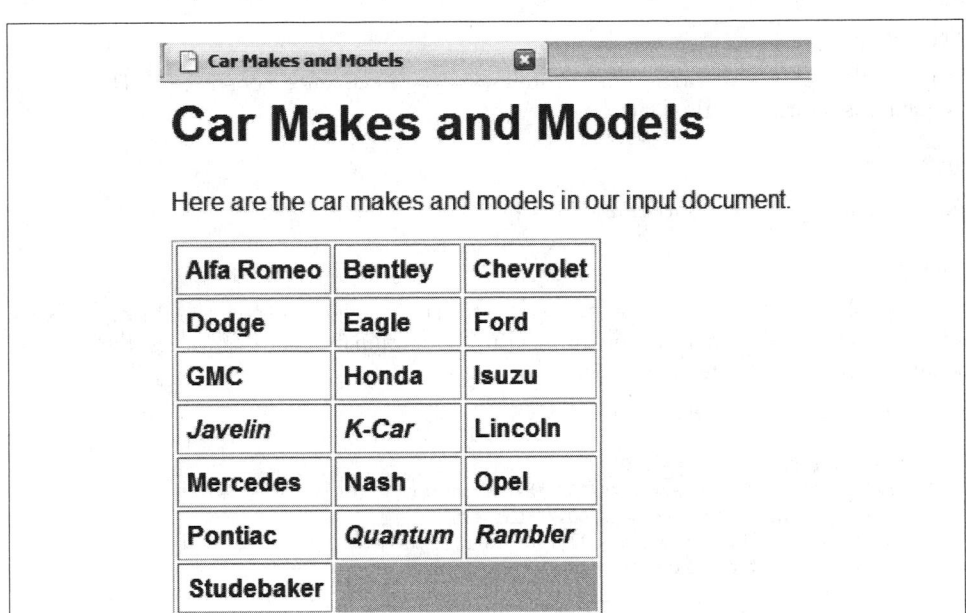

Figure A-9. Items grouped with group-ending-with

[2.0] <xsl:function>

Defines a function that can be used in XPath expressions in the stylesheet.

Category

Declaration.

Required Attribute

name

> The name of the stylesheet function.

Optional Attributes

as

> Defines the datatype returned by this function.

override

> Defines whether this function should override another function with the same name and the same number of arguments that is provided by the processor outside the scope of the stylesheet. override="yes", the default value, means this function will be used (it overrides the other function); override="no" means the other function will be used.

Content

Any number of `<xsl:param>` elements, followed by a sequence constructor. The created sequence is returned by the function.

Defined in

XSLT section 10.3, "Stylesheet Functions."

Example

This stylesheet uses three `<xsl:function>`s to return the background color, font size, and style of various HTML elements. Putting the logic into a function means we can access the function from an attribute value template. Here's the stylesheet:

```
<?xml version="1.0" encoding="utf-8"?>
<!-- function.xsl -->
<xsl:stylesheet version="2.0"
  xmlns:xsl="http://www.w3.org/1999/XSL/Transform"
  xmlns:xs="http://www.w3.org/2001/XMLSchema"
  xmlns:sample="http://www.oreilly.com/catalog/xslt"
  exclude-result-prefixes="xs sample">

  <xsl:output method="html" include-content-type="no"/>

  <xsl:variable name="colors" as="xs:string *"
    select="('yellow', 'white', 'blue')"/>

  <xsl:variable name="fontSizes" as="xs:integer *"
    select="(18, 24, 36)"/>

  <xsl:variable name="styles" as="xs:string *"
    select="('color: black;', 'color: black;',
            'color: white; font-weight: bold;')"/>

  <xsl:template match="/">
    <html>
      <head>
        <title><xsl:value-of select="/list/title"/></title>
      </head>
      <body style="font-family: sans-serif;">
        <h1 style="font-size: 48;"><xsl:value-of select="/list/title"/></h1>
        <table border="3" cellpadding="5" cellspacing="5" width="50%">
          <tr>
            <xsl:for-each select="/list/listitem">
              <td style="font-size: {sample:getFontSize(position())};
                         {sample:getStyle(position())}"
                bgcolor="{sample:getColor(position())}">
                <xsl:value-of select="."/>
              </td>
            </xsl:for-each>
          </tr>
        </table>
      </body>
    </html>
  </xsl:template>
```

```
<xsl:function name="sample:getColor" as="xs:string">
  <xsl:param name="pos" as="xs:integer"/>
  <xsl:value-of select="$colors[($pos mod count($colors)) + 1]"/>
</xsl:function>

<xsl:function name="sample:getStyle" as="xs:string">
  <xsl:param name="pos" as="xs:integer"/>
  <xsl:value-of select="$styles[($pos mod count($styles)) + 1]"/>
</xsl:function>

<xsl:function name="sample:getFontSize" as="xs:integer">
  <xsl:param name="pos" as="xs:integer"/>
  <xsl:value-of select="$fontSizes[($pos mod count($fontSizes)) + 1]"/>
</xsl:function>

</xsl:stylesheet>
```

Our functions work with the variables `colors` and `fontSizes`. These are defined as sequences of strings and integers, respectively. We call the `getColor( )` and `getFontSize( )` functions with the position of the current node; the functions use the `mod` operator to determine the item in the sequence that should be returned.

Notice that we add 1 to the index of the item returned by our functions. *The first item in a sequence is at position one, not zero.* Also, to make the code easier to maintain, we use the `count( )` function to determine the second operand for the `mod` operator. If we add more colors or font sizes to our sequences, we won't have to change our function definitions to match the new size.

We'll use this stylesheet to transform our list of albums:

```
<?xml version="1.0"?>
<!-- albums.xml -->
<list xml:lang="en">
  <title>Albums I've bought recently:</title>
  <listitem>The Sacred Art of Dub</listitem>
  <listitem>Only the Poor Man Feel It</listitem>
  <listitem>Excitable Boy</listitem>
  <listitem xml:lang="sw">Aki Special</listitem>
  <listitem xml:lang="en-gb">Combat Rock</listitem>
  <listitem xml:lang="zu">Talking Timbuktu</listitem>
  <listitem xml:lang="jz">The Birth of the Cool</listitem>
</list>
```

The generated HTML document looks like this:

```
<html>
  <head>
    <title>Albums I've bought recently:</title>
  </head>
  <body style="font-family: sans-serif;">
    <h1 style="font-size: 48;">Albums I've bought recently:</h1>
    <table border="3" cellpadding="5" cellspacing="5" width="50%">
      <tr>
        <td style="font-size: 24;
          color: black;" bgcolor="white">The Sacred Art of Dub</td>
```

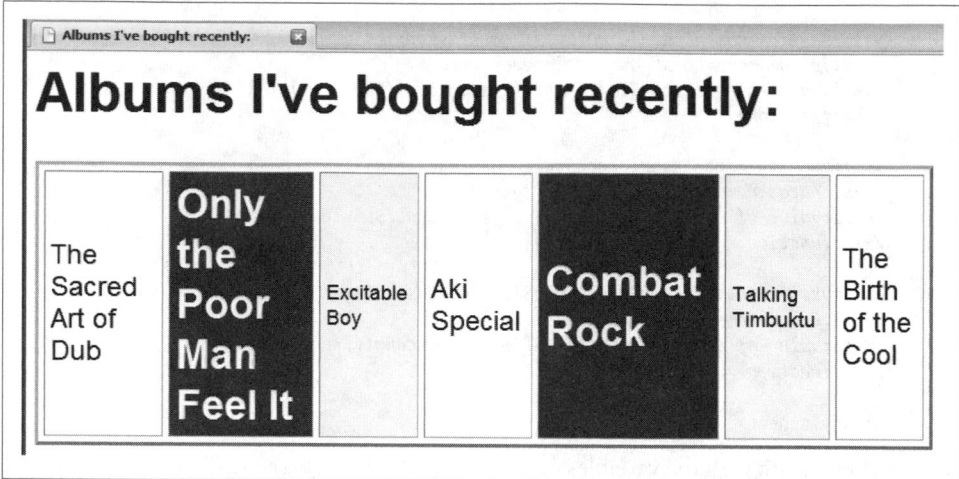

Figure A-10. An HTML table generated with the help of XSLT functions

```
            <td style="font-size: 36;
              color: white; font-weight: bold;" bgcolor="blue">
              Only the Poor Man Feel It</td>
            <td style="font-size: 18;
              color: black;" bgcolor="yellow">Excitable Boy</td>
            <td style="font-size: 24;
              color: black;" bgcolor="white">Aki Special</td>
            <td style="font-size: 36;
              color: white; font-weight: bold;" bgcolor="blue">Combat Rock</td>
            <td style="font-size: 18;
              color: black;" bgcolor="yellow">Talking Timbuktu</td>
            <td style="font-size: 24;
              color: black;" bgcolor="white">The Birth of the Cool</td>
          </tr>
        </table>
      </body>
    </html>
```

The values for the bgcolor and style attributes are generated by the XSLT functions we defined. When viewed in a browser, the output document appears as shown in Figure A-10.

XSLT functions can make your stylesheets much simpler and easier to maintain. In our XSLT 2.0 stylesheet, we used this markup to create the bgcolor attribute:

```
    bgcolor="{sample:getColor(position())}"
```

Here's how you do the same thing in XSLT 1.0:

```
    <xsl:attribute name="bgcolor">
      <xsl:choose>
        <xsl:when test="position() mod 3 = 0">
          <xsl:text>yellow</xsl:text>
        </xsl:when>
        <xsl:when test="position() mod 3 = 1">
          <xsl:text>white</xsl:text>
        </xsl:when>
```

```
      <xsl:otherwise>
         <xsl:text>blue</xsl:text>
      </xsl:otherwise>
   </xsl:choose>
</xsl:attribute>
```

<xsl:if>

Implements an `if` statement. It contains a `test` attribute and an XSLT template. If the `test` attribute evaluates to the boolean value `true`, the XSLT template is processed. This element implements an `if` statement only; if you need an if-then-else statement, use the `<xsl:choose>` element with a single `<xsl:when>` and a single `<xsl:otherwise>`.

Category

Instruction.

Required Attribute

`test`
> Contains a boolean expression. If it evaluates to the boolean value `true`, then the XSLT template inside the `<xsl:if>` element is processed.

Optional Attributes

None.

Content

An XSLT template.

Appears in

`<xsl:if>` appears inside a template.

Defined in

[1.0] XSLT section 9.1, "Conditional Processing with `xsl:if`."

[2.0] XSLT section 8.1, "Conditional Processing with `xsl:if`."

Example

We'll illustrate the `<xsl:if>` element with the following stylesheet:

```
<?xml version="1.0"?>
<!-- if.xsl -->
<xsl:stylesheet version="1.0"
  xmlns:xsl="http://www.w3.org/1999/XSL/Transform">

  <xsl:output method="text"/>

  <xsl:template match="/">
    <xsl:text>&#xA;</xsl:text>
```

```
<xsl:text>Here are the odd-numbered items from the list:</xsl:text>
<xsl:text>&#xA;</xsl:text>
<xsl:for-each select="list/listitem">
  <xsl:if test="(position() mod 2) = 1">
    <xsl:number format="1. "/>
    <xsl:value-of select="."/>
    <xsl:text>&#xA;</xsl:text>
  </xsl:if>
</xsl:for-each>
</xsl:template>

</xsl:stylesheet>
```

This stylesheet uses the `<xsl:if>` element to see whether a given `<listitem>`'s position is an odd number. If it is, we write it to the result tree. We'll test our stylesheet with this XML document:

```
<?xml version="1.0"?>
<!-- albums.xml -->
<list>
  <title>A few of my favorite albums</title>
  <listitem>A Love Supreme</listitem>
  <listitem>Beat Crazy</listitem>
  <listitem>You Could Have it So Much Better</listitem>
  <listitem>Kind of Blue</listitem>
  <listitem>London Calling</listitem>
  <listitem>Remain in Light</listitem>
  <listitem>The Joshua Tree</listitem>
  <listitem>The Indestructible Beat of Soweto</listitem>
</list>
```

When we run this transformation, here are the results:

```
Here are the odd-numbered items from the list:
1. A Love Supreme
3. You Could Have it So Much Better
5. London Calling
7. The Joshua Tree
```

<xsl:import>

Allows you to import the templates found in another XSLT stylesheet. Unlike `<xsl:include>`, all templates imported with `<xsl:import>` have a lower priority than those in the including stylesheet. Another difference between `<xsl:include>` and `<xsl:import>` is that `<xsl:include>` can appear anywhere in a stylesheet, whereas `<xsl:import>` can appear only at the beginning.

Category

Top-level element.

Required Attribute

href
> Defines the URI of the imported stylesheet.

Optional Attributes

None.

Content

None. `<xsl:import>` is an empty element.

Appears in

`<xsl:import>` is a top-level element and can appear only as a child of `<xsl:stylesheet>`.

Defined in

[1.0] XSLT section 2.6.2, "Stylesheet Import."

[2.0] XSLT section 3.10.3, "Stylesheet Import."

Example

Here is a simple stylesheet that we'll import:

```
<?xml version="1.0"?>
<!-- listitem.xsl -->
<xsl:stylesheet version="1.0"
  xmlns:xsl="http://www.w3.org/1999/XSL/Transform">

  <xsl:output method="text"/>

  <xsl:template match="/">
    <xsl:text>&#xA;</xsl:text>
    <xsl:apply-templates select="list/title"/>
    <xsl:apply-templates select="list/listitem"/>
  </xsl:template>

  <xsl:template match="title">
    <xsl:value-of select="."/>
    <xsl:text>: </xsl:text>
    <xsl:text>&#xA;</xsl:text>
    <xsl:text>&#xA;</xsl:text>
  </xsl:template>

  <xsl:template match="listitem">
    <xsl:text>HERE IS LISTITEM NUMBER </xsl:text>
    <xsl:value-of select="position()"/>
    <xsl:text>:  </xsl:text>
    <xsl:value-of select="."/>
    <xsl:text>&#xA;</xsl:text>
  </xsl:template>

</xsl:stylesheet>
```

To illustrate how `<xsl:import>` works, we'll test this stylesheet with this document:

```xml
<?xml version="1.0"?>
<!-- albums.xml -->
<list>
  <title>A few of my favorite albums</title>
  <listitem>A Love Supreme</listitem>
  <listitem>Beat Crazy</listitem>
  <listitem>You Could Have it So Much Better</listitem>
  <listitem>Kind of Blue</listitem>
  <listitem>London Calling</listitem>
  <listitem>Remain in Light</listitem>
  <listitem>The Joshua Tree</listitem>
  <listitem>The Indestructible Beat of Soweto</listitem>
</list>
```

When we process our XML source document with this stylesheet, here are the results:

```
A few of my favorite albums:

HERE IS LISTITEM NUMBER 1:  A Love Supreme
HERE IS LISTITEM NUMBER 2:  Beat Crazy
HERE IS LISTITEM NUMBER 3:  You Could Have it So Much Better
HERE IS LISTITEM NUMBER 4:  Kind of Blue
HERE IS LISTITEM NUMBER 5:  London Calling
HERE IS LISTITEM NUMBER 6:  Remain in Light
HERE IS LISTITEM NUMBER 7:  The Joshua Tree
HERE IS LISTITEM NUMBER 8:  The Indestructible Beat of Soweto
```

Now we'll use `<xsl:import>` to import our first stylesheet into a second one:

```xml
<?xml version="1.0"?>
<!-- import.xsl -->
<xsl:stylesheet version="1.0"
  xmlns:xsl="http://www.w3.org/1999/XSL/Transform">

  <xsl:import href="listitem.xsl"/>

  <xsl:output method="text"/>

  <xsl:template match="/">
    <xsl:text>&#xA;</xsl:text>
    <xsl:apply-templates select="list/title"/>
    <xsl:apply-templates select="list/listitem"/>
  </xsl:template>

  <xsl:template match="listitem">
    <xsl:value-of select="position()"/>
    <xsl:text>.  </xsl:text>
    <xsl:value-of select="."/>
    <xsl:text>&#xA;</xsl:text>
  </xsl:template>

</xsl:stylesheet>
```

Here are the results created by our second stylesheet:

```
A few of my favorite albums:

1.  A Love Supreme
2.  Beat Crazy
3.  You Could Have it So Much Better
4.  Kind of Blue
5.  London Calling
6.  Remain in Light
7.  The Joshua Tree
8.  The Indestructible Beat of Soweto
```

Notice that both stylesheets had a template with `match="listitem"`. The template in the imported stylesheet has a lower priority, so it is not used. Only the imported stylesheet has a template with `match="title"`, so the imported template is used for the `<title>` element.

See Also

The descriptions of the `<xsl:include>`, `<xsl:apply-imports>`, and [2.0] `<xsl:next-match>` elements.

[2.0 – Schema] <xsl:import-schema>

Allows you to import an XML Schema. The schema is imported and processed before any input documents are processed. This allows you to define datatypes and validation rules before the XSLT processor begins to transform the input document. *This element is only supported by schema-aware XSLT 2.0 processors.*

Category

Top-level element.

Required Attributes

None.

Optional Attributes

`namespace`

> The namespace used by the imported schema. Any templates or XPath functions can use this namespace to indicate that an element or value is defined by that schema.

`schema-location`

> A URI reference to the schema document. If a stylesheet imports *and uses* a schema, it is a fatal error if the schema can't be found. An XSLT processor is allowed to ignore the error if you import a schema but never use it.
>
> The `<xsl:import-schema>` element can include the `<xs:schema>` element itself. It is a fatal error if an `<xsl:import-schema>` element contains a `<xs:schema>` and has a `schema-location` attribute.

Content

None of the elements from the XSLT namespace can appear inside `<xsl:import-schema>`. If `<xsl:import-schema>` has any contents, it will likely be an `<xs:schema>` element that in turn defines datatypes and elements. Again, it is an error for an `<xsl:import-schema>` element to contain content and have a `schema-location` attribute.

Appears in

`<xsl:import-schema>` is a top-level element and can only appear as a child of `<xsl:stylesheet>`.

Defined in

[2.0] XSLT section 3.14, "Importing Schema Components."

Example

We'll illustrate `<xsl:import-schema>` with the purchase order schema that we've used several times throughout the book. Here's a valid purchase order:

```
<?xml version="1.0"?>
<!-- good-po.xml -->
<purchase-order id="38292"
  xmlns="http://www.oreilly.com/xslt">
  <date year="2001" month="6" day="19"/>
  <customer id="4738" level="Platinum">
    <address type="business">
      <name>
        <title>Mr.</title>
        <first-name>Chester Hasbrouck</first-name>
        <last-name>Frisby</last-name>
      </name>
      <street>1234 Main Street</street>
      <city>Sheboygan</city>
      <state>WI</state>
      <zip>48392</zip>
    </address>
  </customer>
  <items>
    <item part-no="28392-33-TT">
      <partname>Turnip Twaddler</partname>
      <qty>3</qty>
      <price>9.95</price>
    </item>
    <item part-no="28100-38-CT">
      <partname>Clam Teaser</partname>
      <qty>7</qty>
      <price>39.95</price>
    </item>
  </items>
</purchase-order>
```

Now we'll use `<xsl:import-schema>` to read the schema file and the XML document, and then see whether the XML document is an instance of the `<po:purchase-order>` element defined in the schema:

```
<?xml version="1.0"?>
<!-- import-schema.xsl -->
<xsl:stylesheet version="2.0"
  xmlns:xsl="http://www.w3.org/1999/XSL/Transform"
  xmlns:po="http://www.oreilly.com/xslt">

  <xsl:import-schema namespace="http://www.oreilly.com/xslt"
    schema-location="po.xsd" />

  <xsl:output method="text"/>

  <xsl:template match="schema-element(po:purchase-order)">
    <xsl:text>&#xA;This is a test of the &lt;xsl:import-</xsl:text>
    <xsl:text>schema&gt; element.&#xA;&#xA;</xsl:text>
    <xsl:text>Here are all the items in this purchase </xsl:text>
    <xsl:text>order:&#xA;</xsl:text>
    <xsl:for-each select="po:items/po:item">
      <xsl:text>  * </xsl:text>
      <xsl:value-of select="po:partname"/>
      <xsl:text>&#xA;</xsl:text>
    </xsl:for-each>
  </xsl:template>

</xsl:stylesheet>
```

Notice that in addition to importing the schema, we use the `schema-element` node test in the `match` attribute. That means the template only matches validated `<po:purchase-order>` elements. Here are the results:

```
This is a test of the <xsl:import-schema> element.

Here are all the items in this purchase order:
  * Turnip Twaddler
  * Clam Teaser
```

In the schema itself, the `targetNamespace` attribute and the default namespace (`xmlns=`) match the `namespace` attribute of the `<xsl:import-schema>` element in the stylesheet. In order to refer to the elements in the purchase order, we associate the prefix `po` with that namespace. Whenever we want to refer to elements in the purchase order namespace, we use the prefix (`po:purchase-order`, for example). If the namespace URIs don't match, the stylesheet won't work.

Here's an alternate version of the stylesheet, in which the `<xsl:import-schema>` element contains the schema itself. It generates the same results as the previous version:

```
<?xml version="1.0"?>
<!-- import-schema2.xsl -->
<xsl:stylesheet version="2.0"
  xmlns="http://www.oreilly.com/xslt"
  xmlns:xsl="http://www.w3.org/1999/XSL/Transform"
  xmlns:po="http://www.oreilly.com/xslt"
```

```
      xmlns:xs="http://www.w3.org/2001/XMLSchema">

    <xsl:import-schema namespace="http://www.oreilly.com/xslt">
      <xs:schema
        targetNamespace="http://www.oreilly.com/xslt"
        xmlns:xs="http://www.w3.org/2001/XMLSchema">

        <xs:element name="purchase-order">
          <xs:complexType>
            <xs:sequence>
              <xs:element ref="date"
                minOccurs="1" maxOccurs="1"/>
              <xs:element ref="customer"
                minOccurs="1" maxOccurs="1"/>
              <xs:element ref="items"
                minOccurs="1" maxOccurs="1"/>
            </xs:sequence>
            <xs:attribute name="id" type="xs:string"/>
          </xs:complexType>
        </xs:element>

        ...

      </xs:schema>
    </xsl:import-schema>

    <xsl:output method="text"/>

    <xsl:template match="schema-element(po:purchase-order)">
      <xsl:text>&#xA;This is a test of the <xsl:import-</xsl:text>
      <xsl:text>schema> element.&#xA;&#xA;</xsl:text>
      <xsl:text>Here are all the items in this purchase </xsl:text>
      <xsl:text>order:&#xA;</xsl:text>
      <xsl:for-each select="po:items/po:item">
        <xsl:text>  * </xsl:text>
        <xsl:value-of select="po:partname"/>
        <xsl:text>&#xA;</xsl:text>
      </xsl:for-each>
    </xsl:template>

  </xsl:stylesheet>
```

<xsl:include>

Allows you to include another XSLT stylesheet. This element allows you to put common transformations in a separate stylesheet, then include the templates from that stylesheet at any time. Unlike `<xsl:import>`, all templates included with `<xsl:include>` have the same priority as those in the including stylesheet. Another difference is that `<xsl:include>` can appear anywhere in a stylesheet, whereas `<xsl:import>` must appear at the beginning.

Category

Top-level element.

Required Attribute

`href`

    The URI of the included stylesheet.

Optional Attributes

None.

Content

None. `<xsl:include>` is an empty element.

Appears in

`<xsl:include>` is a top-level element and can appear only as a child of `<xsl:stylesheet>`.

Defined in

[1.0] XSLT section 2.6.1, "Stylesheet Inclusion."

[2.0] XSLT section 3.10.2, "Stylesheet Inclusion."

Example

The `<xsl:include>` element is a good way to break your stylesheets into smaller pieces; those smaller pieces are often easier to reuse. Here's a short stylesheet that includes another:

```
<?xml version="1.0"?>
<!-- include.xsl -->
<xsl:stylesheet version="1.0"
  xmlns:xsl="http://www.w3.org/1999/XSL/Transform">

  <xsl:include href="include-stylesheet.xsl"/>

  <xsl:output method="text"/>

  <xsl:template match="/">
    <xsl:value-of select="/report/title"/>
    <xsl:text>&#xA;&#xA;</xsl:text>
    <xsl:for-each select="report/brand">
      <xsl:text>   </xsl:text>
      <xsl:value-of select="name"/>
      <xsl:text>:   </xsl:text>
      <xsl:value-of select="format-number(units, '##,###')"/>
      <xsl:text> bars sold. </xsl:text>
      <xsl:text>&#xA;</xsl:text>
    </xsl:for-each>
    <xsl:text>&#xA;Total sales: </xsl:text>
    <xsl:value-of
      select="format-number(sum(/report/brand/units), '##,###')"/>
    <xsl:text> bars.&#xA;&#xA;</xsl:text>
    <xsl:value-of select="$copyright"/>
  </xsl:template>

</xsl:stylesheet>
```

And here is the stylesheet that it includes:

```
<?xml version="1.0"?>
<!-- included-stylesheet.xsl -->
<xsl:stylesheet version="1.0"
  xmlns:xsl="http://www.w3.org/1999/XSL/Transform">

  <xsl:variable name="copyright">
    <xsl:text>(C) Copyright 2007 DougCo Incorporated.</xsl:text>
  </xsl:variable>

</xsl:stylesheet>
```

The included stylesheet defines a variable, $copyright, that has some commonly used text. We might have dozens of stylesheets that have a copyright notice; we can use this included stylesheet to make sure all of our generated documents include this notice. When we need to change the notice (on the first of January, example), we change it in one place. This technique is also very useful for defining sets of CSS properties that can be replaced or swapped out with very little effort.

Here are the results of our stylesheet:

```
Chocolate bar sales

  Lindt - 27,408 bars sold.
  Callebaut - 8,203 bars sold.
  Valrhona - 22,101 bars sold.
  Perugina - 14,336 bars sold.
  Ghirardelli - 19,268 bars sold.

Total sales: 91,316 bars.

(C) Copyright 2007 DougCo Incorporated.
```

The variable $copyright contains the text as defined in the included stylesheet.

<xsl:key>

Defines an index against the current document. The element is defined with three attributes: a name, which names this index; a match, an XPath expression that describes the nodes to be indexed; and a use attribute, an XPath expression that defines the property used to create the index. Much like database indexes can improve the performance of a database application, keys can improve the performance of a stylesheet.

Category

Top-level element.

Required Attributes

name

Defines a name for this key.

`match`

Represents an XPath expression that defines the nodes to be indexed by this key.

`use`

Represents an XPath expression that defines the property of the indexed nodes that will be used to retrieve nodes from the index.

[2.0] In XSLT 2.0, this attribute is optional. The `<xsl:key>` element can contain a sequence constructor that creates or selects the nodes to be indexed.

Optional Attributes

[1.0] None

In XSLT 1.0, `<xsl:key>` doesn't have any optional attributes.

[2.0] `collation`

The `collation` attribute defines the collation sequence used to determine whether two key values are equal.

Content

[1.0] None

In XSLT 1.0, the `<xsl:key>` element is empty.

[2.0] A sequence constructor

In XSLT 2.0, the `<xsl:key>` element can contain any sequence constructor. It is an error if a `<xsl:key>` element has both content and a `use` attribute.

Appears in

`<xsl:key>` is a top-level element and can only appear as a child of `<xsl:stylesheet>`.

Defined in

[1.0] XSLT section 12.2, "Keys."

[2.0] XSLT section 16.3, "Keys."

Example

For an example, we'll use our simplified list of customers:

```
<?xml version="1.0"?>
<!-- simplified-names.xml -->
<addressbook>
  <address>
    <first-name>Chester Hasbrouck</first-name>
    <last-name>Frisby</last-name>
    <city>Sheboygan</city>
    <state>WI</state>
  </address>
  <address>
    <first-name>Mary</first-name>
    <last-name>Backstayge</last-name>
    <city>Skunk Haven</city>
```

```
        <state>MA</state>
      </address>
      <address>
        <first-name>Natalie</first-name>
        <last-name>Attired</last-name>
        <city>Winter Harbor</city>
        <state>ME</state>
      </address>
      <address>
        <first-name>Harry</first-name>
        <last-name>Backstayge</last-name>
        <city>Skunk Haven</city>
        <state>MA</state>
      </address>
      <address>
        <first-name>Mary</first-name>
        <last-name>McGoon</last-name>
        <city>Boylston</city>
        <state>VA</state>
      </address>
      <address>
        <first-name>Amanda</first-name>
        <last-name>Reckonwith</last-name>
        <city>Lynn</city>
        <state>MA</state>
      </address>
    </addressbook>
```

Here is a stylesheet that defines a `<xsl:key>` against our list of customers:

```
<?xml version="1.0"?>
<!-- key.xsl -->
<xsl:stylesheet version="1.0"
    xmlns:xsl="http://www.w3.org/1999/XSL/Transform">

  <xsl:output method="text"/>

  <xsl:param name="searchState"/>

  <xsl:key name="customersByState" match="address" use="state"/>

  <xsl:template match="/">
    <xsl:text>All customers in </xsl:text>
    <xsl:value-of select="$searchState"/>
    <xsl:text>&#xA;&#xA;</xsl:text>
    <xsl:for-each select="key('customersByState', $searchState)">
      <xsl:value-of select="first-name"/>
      <xsl:text> </xsl:text>
      <xsl:value-of select="last-name"/>
      <xsl:text>, </xsl:text>
      <xsl:value-of select="city"/>
      <xsl:text>&#xA;</xsl:text>
    </xsl:for-each>
  </xsl:template>

</xsl:stylesheet>
```

We define our key with a name of `customersByState`, we use the key to index all of the `<address>` elements in our document, and we use the value of the `<state>` element as the index property. Here's how our stylesheet responds when we invoke the XSLT processor with the input parameter `state=MA`:

```
All customers in MA

Mary Backstayge, Skunk Haven
Harry Backstayge, Skunk Haven
Amanda Reckonwith, Lynn
```

Asking for all the customers in Wisconsin (`state=WI`) uses our `<xsl:key>` to retrieve different values:

```
All customers in WI

Chester Hasbrouck Frisby, Sheboygan
```

Finally, it's not an error if the key doesn't find any values. Here's a list of all our customers in Hawaii:

```
All customers in HI
```

[2.0] <xsl:matching-substring>

Defines what to do when a string matches a regular expression. The regular expression is defined on the `regex` attribute of the `<xsl:analyze-string>` element that contains the `<xsl:matching-substring>` element.

Category

Instruction (this is effectively part of the `<xsl:analyze-string>` element).

Required Attributes

None.

Optional Attributes

None.

Content

A sequence constructor.

Appears in

The `<xsl:analyze-string>` element.

Defined in

XSLT section 15, "Regular Expressions."

Example

Here is an example of `<xsl:analyze-string>` that uses a regular expression to convert U.S. and Canadian telephone numbers of the form 999-999-9999 to the form +1 (999) 999-9999:

```
<?xml version="1.0" encoding="utf-8"?>
<!-- analyze-string1.xsl -->
<xsl:stylesheet xmlns:xsl="http://www.w3.org/1999/XSL/Transform"
                version="2.0">

  <xsl:output method="text"/>

  <xsl:template match="/">
    <xsl:for-each select="phonelist/phonenumber">
      <xsl:analyze-string select="."
        regex="([0-9]{{3}})-([0-9]{{3}})-([0-9]{{4}})">
        <xsl:matching-substring>
          <xsl:text>&#xA;+1 (</xsl:text>
          <xsl:value-of select="regex-group(1)"/>
          <xsl:text>) </xsl:text>
          <xsl:value-of select="regex-group(2)"/>
          <xsl:text>-</xsl:text>
          <xsl:value-of select="regex-group(3)"/>
        </xsl:matching-substring>
      </xsl:analyze-string>
    </xsl:for-each>
  </xsl:template>

</xsl:stylesheet>
```

Our stylesheet uses the regular expression ([0-9]{{3}})-([0-9]{{3}})-([0-9]{{4}}), which creates three regex-groups. (Each set of parentheses represents a regex-group.) When we use this stylesheet with this list of phone numbers:

```
<?xml version="1.0" encoding="utf-8"?>
<!-- phonelist.xml -->
<phonelist>
  <phonenumber>919-555-1212</phonenumber>
  <phonenumber>(919) 555-1212</phonenumber>
  <phonenumber>212.555.1212</phonenumber>
  <phonenumber>617-555-1212</phonenumber>
  <phonenumber>+86 555-1212</phonenumber>
</phonelist>
```

we get these results:

```
+1 (919) 555-1212
+1 (617) 555-1212
```

Of the five phone numbers in our input document, only two matched the regular expression. This example of `<xsl:analyze-string>` contains only an `<xsl:matching-substring>` element; `<xsl:analyze-string>` can also contain an `<xsl:non-matching-substring>` element.

See Also

The [2.0] `<xsl:analyze-string>` and [2.0] `<xsl:analyze-string>` elements.

\<xsl:message\>

Sends a message. How the message is sent can vary from one XSLT processor to the next, but it's typically written to the standard output device. This element is useful for debugging stylesheets.

Category

Instruction.

Required Attributes

None.

Optional Attributes

terminate
> If this attribute has the value **yes**, the XSLT processor stops execution after issuing this message. The default value for this attribute is **no**; if the `<xsl:message>` doesn't terminate the processor, the message is sent and processing continues.
>
> *[2.0]* In XSLT 2.0, the value of the `terminate` attribute can be an attribute value template, allowing its value to be calculated at runtime.

[2.0] select
> An XPath expression that defines the content of this message.

Content

An XSLT template.

Appears in

`<xsl:message>` appears inside a template.

Defined in

[1.0] XSLT section 13, "Messages."

[2.0] XSLT section 17, "Messages."

Example

Here's a stylesheet that uses the `<xsl:message>` element to trace the transformation of an XML document. We'll use our list of recently purchased albums again:

```
<?xml version="1.0"?>
<!-- albums.xml -->
<list xml:lang="en">
  <title>Albums I've bought recently:</title>
  <listitem>The Sacred Art of Dub</listitem>
  <listitem>Only the Poor Man Feel It</listitem>
  <listitem>Excitable Boy</listitem>
  <listitem xml:lang="sw">Aki Special</listitem>
  <listitem xml:lang="en-gb">Combat Rock</listitem>
```

```
      <listitem xml:lang="zu">Talking Timbuktu</listitem>
      <listitem xml:lang="jz">The Birth of the Cool</listitem>
    </list>
```

We'll list all of the purchased albums in an HTML table, with the background color of each row cycling through various colors. Our stylesheet uses `<xsl:message>` elements to indicate the background color of each row in the table:

```
<?xml version="1.0"?>
<!-- message.xsl -->
<xsl:stylesheet version="1.0"
  xmlns:xsl="http://www.w3.org/1999/XSL/Transform">

  <xsl:output method="html"/>

  <xsl:template match="/">
    <html>
      <head>
        <title>
          <xsl:value-of select="list/title"/>
        </title>
      </head>
      <body style="font-family: sans-serif; color: white;">
        <h1 style="color: black;">
          <xsl:value-of select="list/title"/>
        </h1>
        <table border="1" cellpadding="5"
          style="font-weight: bold;">
          <xsl:for-each select="list/listitem">
            <tr>
              <td>
                <xsl:attribute name="style">
                  <xsl:choose>
                    <xsl:when test="position() mod 4 = 0">
                      <xsl:text>background: yellow; color: black;</xsl:text>
                      <xsl:message terminate="no">
                        <xsl:text>Background color is yellow</xsl:text>
                        </xsl:message>
                    </xsl:when>
                    <xsl:when test="position() mod 4 = 1">
                      <xsl:text>background: blue;</xsl:text>
                      <xsl:message terminate="no">
                        <xsl:text>Background color is blue</xsl:text>
                        </xsl:message>
                    </xsl:when>
                    <xsl:when test="position() mod 4 = 2">
                      <xsl:text>background: white; color: black;</xsl:text>
                      <xsl:message terminate="no">
                        <xsl:text>Background color is white</xsl:text>
                        </xsl:message>
                    </xsl:when>
                    <xsl:otherwise>
                      <xsl:text>background: black;</xsl:text>
                      <xsl:message terminate="no">
                        <xsl:text>Background color is black</xsl:text>
                        </xsl:message>
```

```
                </xsl:otherwise>
              </xsl:choose>
            </xsl:attribute>
            <xsl:value-of select="."/>
          </td>
        </tr>
      </xsl:for-each>
    </table>
  </body>
</html>
</xsl:template>

</xsl:stylesheet>
```

Note that the XSLT specification doesn't define how the message is issued. When we use this stylesheet with Saxon 8.8J, we get these results:

```
Background color is blue
Background color is white
Background color is black
Background color is yellow
Background color is blue
Background color is white
Background color is black
```

Running this stylesheet with Xalan gives us the same messages, along with information about which line in the stylesheet generated those messages:

```
file:///c:/message.xsl; Line #34; Column #51; Background color is blue
file:///c:/message.xsl; Line #40; Column #51; Background color is white
file:///c:/message.xsl; Line #46; Column #51; Background color is black
file:///c:/message.xsl; Line #28; Column #51; Background color is yellow
file:///c:/message.xsl; Line #34; Column #51; Background color is blue
file:///c:/message.xsl; Line #40; Column #51; Background color is white
file:///c:/message.xsl; Line #46; Column #51; Background color is black
```

[2.0] <xsl:namespace>

Allows you to create a namespace node in the result tree.

Category

Instruction.

Required Attribute

name

> The namespace prefix.

Optional Attribute

select

> An XPath expression that defines the value of the namespace itself. If you don't use the select attribute, the <xsl:namespace> element must contain content.

Content

The `<xsl:namespace>` element must have content or a **select** attribute; it is an error if it has both or neither. It is also an error if the `<xsl:namespace>` element evaluates to a zero-length string.

Appears in

`<xsl:namespace>` appears inside a template.

Defined in

[2.0] XSLT section 11.7, "Creating Namespace Nodes."

Example

Courtesy of the XSLT 2.0 spec, here is a stylesheet with a literal result element that contains an `<xsl:namespace>` element:

```
<?xml version="1.0"?>
<!-- namespace.xsl -->
<xsl:stylesheet version="1.0"
  xmlns:xsl="http://www.w3.org/1999/XSL/Transform">

  <xsl:output method="xml" indent="yes"/>

  <xsl:template match="/">
    <data xsi:type="xs:integer"
      xmlns:xsi="http://www.w3.org/2001/XMLSchema-instance">
      <xsl:namespace name="xs"
        select="'http://www.w3.org/2001/XMLSchema'"/>
      <xsl:text>42</xsl:text>
    </data>
  </xsl:template>

</xsl:stylesheet>
```

Notice that the value of the **select** attribute is in single quotes inside double quotes; without the single quotes, this would select any `<http://www.w3.org/2001/XMLSchema>` elements, causing an error.

The results of this stylesheet look like this:

```
<?xml version="1.0" encoding="UTF-8"?>
<data xmlns:xsi="http://www.w3.org/2001/XMLSchema-instance"
      xmlns:xs="http://www.w3.org/2001/XMLSchema"
      xsi:type="xs:integer">42</data>
```

We could have written the stylesheet without the **select** attribute, putting the value of the namespace inside the `<xsl:namespace>` element:

```
<?xml version="1.0"?>
<!-- namespace2.xsl -->
<xsl:stylesheet version="1.0"
  xmlns:xsl="http://www.w3.org/1999/XSL/Transform">
```

```
<xsl:output method="xml" indent="yes"/>

<xsl:template match="/">
  <data xsi:type="xs:integer"
    xmlns:xsi="http://www.w3.org/2001/XMLSchema-instance">
    <xsl:namespace name="xs">
      <xsl:text>http://www.w3.org/2001/XMLSchema</xsl:text>
    </xsl:namespace>
    <xsl:text>42</xsl:text>
  </data>
</xsl:template>

</xsl:stylesheet>
```

Finally, we could generate the same results with a stylesheet that doesn't use `<xsl:namespace>` at all:

```
<?xml version="1.0"?>
<!-- namespace3.xsl -->
<xsl:stylesheet version="1.0"
  xmlns:xsl="http://www.w3.org/1999/XSL/Transform">

  <xsl:output method="xml" indent="yes"/>

  <xsl:template match="/">
    <data xsi:type="xs:integer"
      xmlns:xsi="http://www.w3.org/2001/XMLSchema-instance"
      xmlns:xs="http://www.w3.org/2001/XMLSchema">
      <xsl:text>42</xsl:text>
    </data>
  </xsl:template>

</xsl:stylesheet>
```

The only time you're likely to use `<xsl:namespace>` is when you're creating a new element with `<xsl:element>` and you want to define a namespace on the new element, particularly if that namespace is used in content. (If that namespace is used in the names of elements or attributes, it would be copied to the result element automatically.)

<xsl:namespace-alias>

Allows you to define an alias for a namespace when using the namespace directly would complicate processing. This seldom-used element is the simplest way to write a stylesheet that generates another stylesheet.

Category

Top-level element.

Required Attributes

`result-prefix`
>   Defines the prefix for the namespace referred to by the alias. This prefix must be declared in the stylesheet, regardless of whether any elements in the stylesheet use it.

`stylesheet-prefix`
>   Defines the prefix used in the stylesheet to refer to the namespace.

[2.0] In XSLT 2.0, you can use the value `#default` for either the `result-prefix` or `stylesheet-prefix` attributes. As you would expect, it is an error if there is no default namespace. (A default namespace is defined with `xmlns=`.)

Optional Attributes

None.

Content

None. `<xsl:namespace-alias>` is an empty element.

Appears in

`<xsl:namespace-alias>` is a top-level element and can appear only as a child of `<xsl:stylesheet>`.

Defined in

[1.0] XSLT section 7.1.1, "Literal Result Elements."

[2.0] XSLT section 11.1.4, "Namespace Aliasing."

Example

As we mentioned before, this element is normally used to create an XSLT stylesheet that generates another stylesheet. Use `<xsl:namespace-alias>` when you want the output to contain an element or attribute that would normally be handled by the XSLT processor.

Our sample here creates a stylesheet that generates another stylesheet that copies any input document to the output. Here's our original stylesheet that uses `<xsl:namespace-alias>`:

```
<?xml version="1.0"?>
<!-- namespace-alias.xsl -->
<xsl:stylesheet version="1.0"
  xmlns:xsl="http://www.w3.org/1999/XSL/Transform"
  xmlns:xslout="[anything but the XSL namespace]">

  <xsl:output method="xml" indent="yes"/>

  <xsl:namespace-alias stylesheet-prefix="xslout"
    result-prefix="xsl"/>

  <xsl:template match="/">
    <xslout:stylesheet version="1.0">
```

```
      <xslout:output method="xml"/>
      <xslout:template match="/">
        <xslout:copy-of select="."/>
      </xslout:template>
    </xslout:stylesheet>
  </xsl:template>

</xsl:stylesheet>
```

When we run this stylesheet with any XML document at all, we get a new stylesheet:

```
<?xml version="1.0" encoding="UTF-8"?>
<xsl:stylesheet xmlns:xsl="http://www.w3.org/1999/XSL/Transform" version="1.0">
   <xsl:output method="xml"/>
   <xsl:template match="/">
      <xsl:copy-of select="."/>
   </xsl:template>
</xsl:stylesheet>
```

In our original stylesheet, we use `<xsl:namespace-alias>` to make sure the XSLT processor doesn't treat the XSLT elements we want to copy to the output stylesheet as instructions. Notice that when we define the namespace we'll be using as the alias, that namespace *cannot* be the same as the XSLT namespace. If it is, the XSLT processor will process our `<xslout:` elements as XSLT elements, defeating the purpose of using `<xsl:namespace-alias>`.

In the generated stylesheet, notice that the namespace value is the namespace associated with the `result-prefix` defined in the `<xsl:namespace-alias>` element. Be aware that the actual prefix in the generated stylesheet might not be `xsl` as it is here. Saxon generates a prefix of `xsl`, while Xalan uses the prefix `xslout` that we used in our original stylesheet. Regardless of the prefix, the generated stylesheet works the same.

[2.0] To illustrate using the default namespace with `<xsl:namespace-alias>`, we'll look at two stylesheets, one of which uses `result-prefix="#default"` and one of which uses `stylesheet-prefix="#default"`. Here is the first stylesheet:

```
<?xml version="1.0"?>
<!-- namespace-alias-2.xsl -->
<stylesheet version="1.0"
  xmlns="http://www.w3.org/1999/XSL/Transform"
  xmlns:xslout="[anything but the XSL namespace]">

  <output method="xml" indent="yes"/>

  <namespace-alias stylesheet-prefix="xslout"
    result-prefix="#default"/>

  <template match="/">
    <xslout:stylesheet version="1.0">
      <xslout:output method="xml"/>
      <xslout:template match="/">
        <xslout:copy-of select="."/>
      </xslout:template>
    </xslout:stylesheet>
  </template>
```

```
    </stylesheet>
```

The output from this stylesheet looks like this:

```
<?xml version="1.0" encoding="UTF-8"?>
<stylesheet xmlns="http://www.w3.org/1999/XSL/Transform" version="1.0">
    <output method="xml"/>
    <template match="/">
        <copy-of select="."/>
    </template>
</stylesheet>
```

The original stylesheet and the generated stylesheet work because all of the XSLT elements are in the default namespace, `http://www.w3.org/1999/XSL/Transform`.

Here is the second stylesheet:

```
<?xml version="1.0"?>
<!-- namespace-alias-3.xsl -->
<xsl:stylesheet version="1.0"
  xmlns="[anything but the XSL namespace]"
  xmlns:xsl="http://www.w3.org/1999/XSL/Transform">

  <xsl:output method="xml" indent="yes"/>

  <xsl:namespace-alias stylesheet-prefix="#default"
    result-prefix="xsl"/>

  <xsl:template match="/">
    <stylesheet version="1.0">
      <output method="xml"/>
      <template match="/">
        <copy-of select="."/>
      </template>
    </stylesheet>
  </xsl:template>

</xsl:stylesheet>
```

The output from this stylesheet looks more typical:

```
<?xml version="1.0" encoding="UTF-8"?>
<xsl:stylesheet xmlns:xsl="http://www.w3.org/1999/XSL/Transform" version="1.0">
    <xsl:output method="xml"/>
    <xsl:template match="/">
        <xsl:copy-of select="."/>
    </xsl:template>
</xsl:stylesheet>
```

[2.0] <xsl:next-match>

Tells the XSLT processor to select a template that is the next lowest in priority than the current template. This works similarly to `<xsl:apply-imports>`, although `<xsl:next-match>` works with all templates, including those in the main stylesheet and in any stylesheets included or imported. Using `<xsl:next-match>` allows you to set up templates that work like overridden methods in object-oriented languages; using `<xsl:next-match>` is conceptually the same as calling `super( )` in a Java program.

Category

Instruction.

Required Attributes

None.

Optional Attributes

None.

Content

Any number of `<xsl:with-param>` and `<xsl:fallback>` elements.

Appears in

`<xsl:next-match>` appears inside a template.

Defined in

[2.0] XSLT section 6.7, "Overriding Template Rules."

Example

For our example, we'll create some templates to process this HTML document:

```
<!-- element-discussion.html -->
<html>
  <head>
    <title>Interesting new XSLT elements</title>
  </head>
  <body>
    <h1>Interesting new XSLT elements</h1>
    <p>XSLT 2.0 has lots of interesting new elements.
    We'll mention a couple of them here. </p>
    <h1>The <code>&lt;xsl:next-match&gt;</code> element</h1>
    <p>One of the most interesting new elements in XSLT 2.0
    is <code>&lt;xsl:next-match&gt;</code>. </p>
    <h1>The <code>&lt;xsl:perform-sort&gt;</code> element</h1>
    <p>Don't forget about <code>&lt;xsl:perform-sort&gt;</code>,
    though.  It's very interesting as well.</p>
  </body>
</html>
```

Our example document has HTML `<code>` elements. Some of them are inside `<h1>` elements, others are inside `<p>` elements. To illustrate how `<xsl:next-match>` works, we'll create two different templates to process the `<code>` elements. The basic template puts the text of the element into a monospaced font; the overriding template changes the color of the `<code>` element if it occurs inside an `<h1>` element. Here's the stylesheet:

```
<?xml version="1.0"?>
<!-- next-match.xsl -->
<xsl:stylesheet version="2.0"
  xmlns:xsl="http://www.w3.org/1999/XSL/Transform">

  <xsl:output method="html"/>

  <xsl:template match="html">
    <html>
      <head>
        <title>
          <xsl:value-of select="head/title"/>
        </title>
      </head>
      <body style="font-family: sans-serif;">
        <xsl:apply-templates select="body/*"/>
      </body>
    </html>
  </xsl:template>

  <xsl:template match="h1/code">
    <span style="color: red;">
      <xsl:next-match/>
    </span>
  </xsl:template>

  <xsl:template match="code">
    <span style="font-family: monospace;">
      <xsl:apply-templates select="*|text()"/>
    </span>
  </xsl:template>

  <xsl:template match="h1">
    <h1>
      <xsl:apply-templates select="*|text()"/>
    </h1>
  </xsl:template>

  <xsl:template match="p">
    <p>
      <xsl:apply-templates select="*|text()"/>
    </p>
  </xsl:template>

</xsl:stylesheet>
```

The key to using `<xsl:next-match>` is that the templates involved have different priorities. In our example here, the different priorities are set by the default XSLT precedence rules. A more specific rule always has precedence over a less specific one, so the highest priority rule for a `<code>` element inside an `<h1>` element is the `match="h1/code"` template. Using `<xsl:next-match>` inside that template invokes the next template in priority order—the template with `match="code"`.

The way our stylesheet is written, the default behavior of processing a `<code>` element is to create a `<span>` element that uses a monospaced font. The more specific (and therefore higher priority) template creates a `<span>` element that sets the font color to red. If we want to use a different font for all `<code>` elements, we would only have to change the `match="code"` template that sets the `font-family` property. Here are the results of our stylesheet:

```
<html>
   <head>
      <meta http-equiv="Content-Type" content="text/html; charset=UTF-8">
      <title>Interesting new XSLT elements</title>
   </head>
   <body style="font-family: sans-serif;">
      <h1>Interesting new XSLT elements</h1>
      <p>XSLT 2.0 has lots of interesting new elements.
         We'll mention a couple of them here.
      </p>
      <h1>The <span style="color: red;">
        <span style="font-family: monospace;">
        &lt;xsl:next-match&gt;</span>
        </span> element
      </h1>
      <p>One of the most interesting new elements in XSLT 2.0
         is <span style="font-family: monospace;">
        &lt;xsl:next-match&gt;</span>.
      </p>
      <h1>The <span style="color: red;">
        <span style="font-family: monospace;">
        &lt;xsl:perform-sort&gt;</span>
        </span> element
      </h1>
      <p>Don't forget about <span style="font-family: monospace;">
        &lt;xsl:perform-sort&gt;</span>,
        though.  It's very interesting as well.
      </p>
   </body>
</html>
```

The output looks like Figure A-11.

[2.0] <xsl:non-matching-substring>

Defines what to do when a string doesn't match a regular expression. The regular expression is defined on the `regex` attribute of the `<xsl:analyze-string>` element that contains the `<xsl:non-matching-substring>` element.

Category

Instruction (this is effectively part of the `<xsl:analyze-string>` element).

Required Attributes

None.

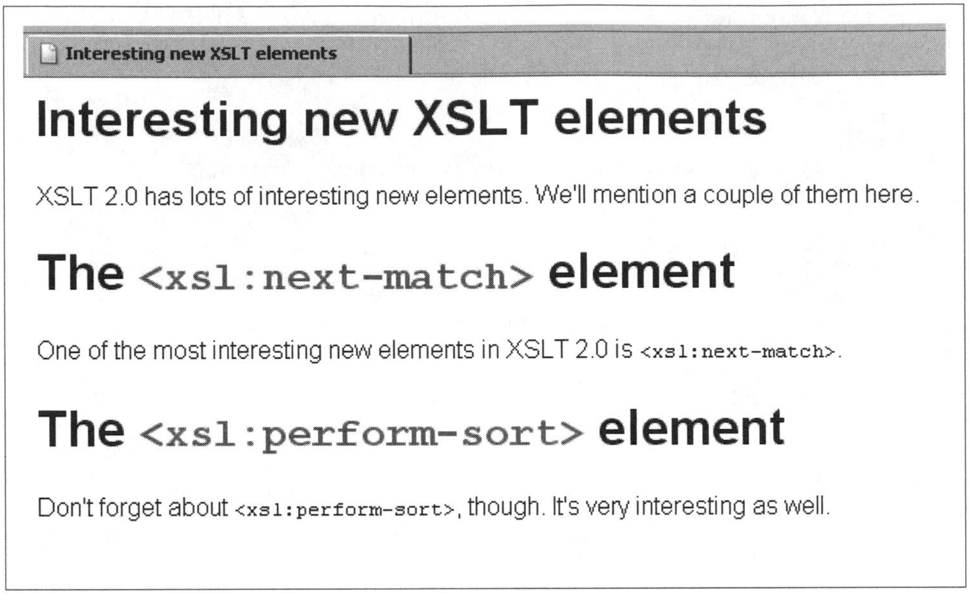

Figure A-11. HTML generated with <xsl:next-match>

Optional Attributes

None.

Content

A sequence constructor.

Appears in

The `<xsl:analyze-string>` element.

Defined in

XSLT section 15, "Regular Expressions."

Example

Here is an example of `<xsl:analyze-string>` that uses a regular expression to convert U.S. and Canadian telephone numbers of the form 999-999-9999 to the form +1 (999) 999-9999:

```
<?xml version="1.0" encoding="utf-8"?>
<!-- non-matching-substring.xsl -->
<xsl:stylesheet version="2.0"
  xmlns:xsl="http://www.w3.org/1999/XSL/Transform">

  <xsl:output method="text"/>

  <xsl:template match="/">
    <xsl:for-each select="phonelist/phonenumber">
      <xsl:analyze-string select="."
```

```
        regex="([0-9]{{3}})-([0-9]{{3}})-([0-9]{{4}})">
        <xsl:non-matching-substring>
          <xsl:text>&#xA;    Unrecognized phone number: </xsl:text>
          <xsl:value-of select="."/>
        </xsl:non-matching-substring>
      </xsl:analyze-string>
    </xsl:for-each>
  </xsl:template>

</xsl:stylesheet>
```

Our stylesheet uses the regular expression ([0-9]{{3}})-([0-9]{{3}})-([0-9]{{4}}). When we use this stylesheet with this list of phone numbers:

```
<?xml version="1.0" encoding="utf-8"?>
<!-- phonelist.xml -->
<phonelist>
  <phonenumber>919-555-1212</phonenumber>
  <phonenumber>(919) 555-1212</phonenumber>
  <phonenumber>212.555.1212</phonenumber>
  <phonenumber>617-555-1212</phonenumber>
  <phonenumber>+86 555-1212</phonenumber>
</phonelist>
```

we get these results:

```
    Unrecognized phone number: (919) 555-1212
    Unrecognized phone number: 212.555.1212
    Unrecognized phone number: +86 555-1212
```

This example of `<xsl:analyze-string>` contains only an `<xsl:non-matching-substring>` element; `<xsl:analyze-string>` can also contain an `<xsl:matching-substring>` element.

See Also

The [2.0] `<xsl:analyze-string>` element and the [2.0] `<xsl:matching-substring>` element.

`<xsl:number>`

Displays a number. It is most often used to number parts of a document, although it can also be used to format a numeric value.

Category

Instruction.

Required Attributes

None.

Optional Attributes

count

> The count attribute is an XPath pattern that defines what should be counted. If the count attribute isn't specified, it counts nodes with the same name as the current node.

level

> This attribute defines what levels of the source tree should be considered when numbering elements. The three valid values for this attribute are single, multiple, and any:

single

> Counts items at one level only. The XSLT processor goes to the first node in the ancestor-or-self axis that matches the count attribute, and then counts that node plus all its preceding siblings that also match the count attribute. This is the default value.

multiple

> Counts items at multiple levels. The XSLT processor looks at all the ancestors of the current node and at the current node itself, and then it selects all nodes that match the count attribute.

any

> Includes all of the current node's ancestors (as level="multiple" does) as well as all elements in the preceding axis.

> In all of these cases, if the from attribute is used, the only ancestors that are examined are descendants of the nearest ancestor that matches the from attribute. In other words, with from="h1", the only nodes considered for counting are those that appear under the nearest <h1> attribute.

from

> The from attribute is an XPath pattern that defines where counting starts. For example, from="h1" means that counting should begin at the previous <h1> element.

value

> An expression that is converted to a number. Using this attribute is a quick way to format a number; the element <xsl:number value="7" format="i:"/> returns the string "vii:".

> If the value attribute is specified, none of the count, level, from, or select attributes may be used.

format

> The format attribute defines the format of the generated number:

format="1"

> Formats a sequence of numbers as 1 2 3 4 5 6 7 8 9 10 11 ....

`format="01"`

Formats a sequence of numbers as 01 02 03 04 ... 09 10 11 ... 99 100 101 ....

`format="a"`

Formats a sequence of numbers as a b c d e f ... x y z aa ab ac ....

`format="A"`

Formats a sequence of numbers as A B C D E F ... X Y Z AA AB AC ....

`format="i"`

Formats a sequence of numbers as i ii iii iv v vi vii viii ix x ....

`format="I"`

Formats a sequence of numbers as I II III IV V VI VII VIII IX X ....

[2.0] `format="w"`

Formats a sequence of numbers as words. When used with `ordinal="yes"` and `lang="en"`, it formats a sequence of numbers as `first second third fourth` .... If `ordinal="yes"` is not specified, it formats a sequence of numbers as `one two three four` .... If a given `format`, `ordinal`, and `lang` combination is not supported, the XSLT processor is required to format the numbers as 1 2 3 4 5 ... as a last resort.

[2.0] `format="Ww"`

Formats a sequence of numbers as words. When used with `ordinal="yes"` and `lang="en"`, it formats a sequence of numbers as `First Second Third Fourth` .... If `ordinal="yes"` is not specified, it formats a sequence of numbers as `One Two Three Four` .... If a given `format`, `ordinal`, and `lang` combination is not supported, the XSLT processor is required to format the numbers as 1 2 3 4 5 ... as a last resort.

`format="anything else"`

How this works depends on the XSLT processor you're using. The XSLT specification lists several other numbering schemes (`format="&#0E51;"` for Thai numbering, for example); check your XSLT processor's documentation to see which formats it supports. If the XSLT processor doesn't support the numbering scheme you requested, the XSLT spec requires that it use `format="1"` as the default.

[2.0] `lang`

The `lang` attribute defines the language whose alphabet should be used. Different XSLT processors support different language values, so check the documentation of your favorite XSLT processor for more information.

`letter-value`

This attribute has the value `alphabetic` or `traditional`. There are a number of languages in which two letter-based numbering schemes are used; one assigns numeric values in alphabetic sequence, while the other uses a tradition native to that language. (Roman numerals—a letter-based numbering scheme that doesn't use an alphabetic order—are one example.) The default for this attribute is `alphabetic`.

grouping-separator

This attribute is the character that should be used between groups of digits in a generated number. The default is the comma (`,`).

grouping-size

This attribute defines the number of digits that appear in each group; the default is `3`.

[2.0] ordinal

Defines that ordinal numbers should be used; valid values are `yes` and `no`. The `ordinal`, `format`, and `lang` attributes work together. For example, `ordinal="yes"`, `format="1"`, and `lang="en"` produces the sequence `1st 2nd 3rd 4th`. With `format="w"` the sequence is `first second third fourth`. `format="Ww"` produces `First Second Third Fourth`. If the combination of `ordinal`, `format`, and `lang` is not supported, the XSLT processor is required to generate cardinal numbers (`1 2 3 4`) instead. See the documentation for your XSLT processor to find out which language and format combinations it supports for the `ordinal` attribute.

[2.0] select

Selects a node to be numbered. This allows you to select a node other than the context node.

Content

None. `<xsl:number>` is an empty element.

Appears in

`<xsl:number>` appears inside a template.

Defined in

[1.0] XSLT section 7.7, "Numbering."

[2.0] XSLT section 12, "Numbering."

Example

To fully illustrate how `<xsl:number>` works, we'll need an XML document with many things to count. Here's the document we'll use:

```
<?xml version="1.0"?>
<!-- items-to-number.xml -->
<book>
  <chapter><title>Alfa Romeo</title>
    <sect1><title>Bentley</title></sect1>
    <sect1><title>Chevrolet</title>
      <sect2><title>Dodge</title>
        <sect3><title>Eagle</title></sect3>
      </sect2>
    </sect1>
```

```
    </chapter>
    <chapter><title>Ford</title>
      <sect1><title>GMC</title>
        <sect2><title>Honda</title>
          <sect3><title>Isuzu</title></sect3>
          <sect3><title>Javelin</title></sect3>
          <sect3><title>K-Car</title></sect3>
          <sect3><title>Lincoln</title></sect3>
        </sect2>
        <sect2><title>Mercedes</title></sect2>
        <sect2><title>Nash</title>
          <sect3><title>Opel</title></sect3>
          <sect3><title>Pontiac</title></sect3>
        </sect2>
        <sect2><title>Quantum</title>
          <sect3><title>Rambler</title></sect3>
          <sect3><title>Studebaker</title></sect3>
        </sect2>
      </sect1>
      <sect1><title>Toyota</title></sect1>
    </chapter>
</book>
```

We'll use `<xsl:number>` in several different ways to illustrate the various options we have in numbering things. We'll look at several short stylesheets and their results. Here's the first one:

```
<?xml version="1.0"?>
<!-- number1.xsl -->
<xsl:stylesheet version="1.0"
  xmlns:xsl="http://www.w3.org/1999/XSL/Transform">

  <xsl:output method="text"/>

  <xsl:template match="book">
    <xsl:for-each select="chapter|.//sect1|.//sect2|.//sect3">
      <xsl:number level="multiple" count="chapter|sect1|sect2|sect3"
          format="1.1.1.1. "/>
      <xsl:value-of select="title"/>
      <xsl:text>&#xA;</xsl:text>
    </xsl:for-each>
  </xsl:template>

</xsl:stylesheet>
```

Here are our results:

```
1. Alfa Romeo
1.1. Bentley
1.2. Chevrolet
1.2.1. Dodge
1.2.1.1. Eagle
2. Ford
2.1. GMC
2.1.1. Honda
2.1.1.1. Isuzu
2.1.1.2. Javelin
2.1.1.3. K-Car
```

```
2.1.1.4. Lincoln
2.1.2. Mercedes
2.1.3. Nash
2.1.3.1. Opel
2.1.3.2. Pontiac
2.1.4. Quantum
2.1.4.1. Rambler
2.1.4.2. Studebaker
2.2. Toyota
```

Here we use `level="multiple"` to count the `<chapter>`, `<sect1>`, `<sect2>`, and `<sect3>` elements. Numbering these at multiple levels gives us a dotted decimal number for each element. We can look at the number next to `Studebaker` and know that it is the second `<sect3>` element inside the fourth `<sect2>` element inside the first `<sect1>` element inside the second `<chapter>` element.

In the stylesheet, we use `<xsl:for-each>` to select the items we want to list, and we use `<xsl:number>` to number them. As we'll see in a minute, we don't have to select all the items in the `<xsl:for-each>` for them to be numbered correctly. If we wrote an XPath expression that selected just the `<sect3>` element with `<title>Studebaker</title>`, the output would be `2.1.4.2 Studebaker`, just as it is earlier.

Our next stylesheet uses `level="any"` to count all of the `<chapter>`, `<sect1>`, `<sect2>`, and `<sect3>` elements in order. The stylesheet looks like this:

```
<?xml version="1.0"?>
<!-- number2.xsl -->
<xsl:stylesheet version="1.0"
  xmlns:xsl="http://www.w3.org/1999/XSL/Transform">

  <xsl:output method="text"/>

  <xsl:template match="book">
    <xsl:for-each select="chapter|.//sect1|.//sect2|.//sect3">
      <xsl:number level="any" count="chapter|sect1|sect2|sect3"
        format="1. "/>
      <xsl:value-of select="title"/>
      <xsl:text>&#xA;</xsl:text>
    </xsl:for-each>
  </xsl:template>

</xsl:stylesheet>
```

The results are straightforward:

```
1. Alfa Romeo
2. Bentley
3. Chevrolet
4. Dodge
5. Eagle
6. Ford
7. GMC
8. Honda
9. Isuzu
10. Javelin
11. K-Car
```

```
12. Lincoln
13. Mercedes
14. Nash
15. Opel
16. Pontiac
17. Quantum
18. Rambler
19. Studebaker
20. Toyota
```

Stylesheet *number3.xsl* uses `level="single"` to count the elements at each level. This means that the fourth `<sect3>` element inside a given `<sect2>` element will be numbered with a **4** (or *iv* or D or whatever the appropriate value would be). Notice that the number used for each element is the same as the last number beside each element in Test 1.

```
<?xml version="1.0"?>
<!-- number3.xsl -->
<xsl:stylesheet version="1.0"
  xmlns:xsl="http://www.w3.org/1999/XSL/Transform">

  <xsl:output method="text"/>

  <xsl:template match="book">
    <xsl:for-each select="chapter|.//sect1|.//sect2|.//sect3">
      <xsl:number level="single" count="chapter|sect1|sect2|sect3"
        format="1.1.1.1. "/>
      <xsl:value-of select="title"/>
      <xsl:text>&#xA;</xsl:text>
    </xsl:for-each>
  </xsl:template>

</xsl:stylesheet>
```

These results are less useful, but here they are:

```
1. Alfa Romeo
1. Bentley
2. Chevrolet
1. Dodge
1. Eagle
2. Ford
1. GMC
1. Honda
1. Isuzu
2. Javelin
3. K-Car
4. Lincoln
2. Mercedes
3. Nash
1. Opel
2. Pontiac
4. Quantum
1. Rambler
2. Studebaker
2. Toyota
```

Stylesheet *number4.xsl* does a couple of things differently: first, it uses the uppercase-alpha and lowercase-roman numbering styles. Second, it counts elements at multiple levels (for the `<chapter>`, `<sect1>`, and `<sect2>` elements), but we process only the `<sect2>` elements. Even though we output only the title text for the `<sect2>` elements, we can still generate the appropriate multilevel numbers:

```
<?xml version="1.0"?>
<!-- number4.xsl -->
<xsl:stylesheet version="1.0"
  xmlns:xsl="http://www.w3.org/1999/XSL/Transform">

  <xsl:output method="text"/>

  <xsl:template match="book">
    <xsl:for-each select=".//sect2">
      <xsl:number level="multiple" count="chapter|sect1|sect2"
        format="I-A-i: "/>
      <xsl:value-of select="title"/>
      <xsl:text>&#xA;</xsl:text>
    </xsl:for-each>
  </xsl:template>

</xsl:stylesheet>
```

Because we're numbering only the `<sect2>` elements, our output is much shorter:

```
I-B-i: Dodge
II-A-i: Honda
II-A-ii: Mercedes
II-A-iii: Nash
II-A-iv: Quantum
```

As we mentioned before, the elements we selected with the `<xsl:for-each>` element are numbered correctly, even though we don't reference the elements around them.

number5.xsl generates numbers similarly to *number4.xsl*, except that it uses the `from` attribute. We generate numbers for `<sect3>` elements in four stages. First, we count the `<chapter>` ancestors, starting at the first `<book>` ancestor; then we count the `<sect1>` ancestors, starting at the first `<chapter>` ancestor, etc.:

```
<?xml version="1.0"?>
<!-- number5.xsl -->
<xsl:stylesheet version="1.0"
  xmlns:xsl="http://www.w3.org/1999/XSL/Transform">

  <xsl:output method="text"/>

  <xsl:template match="book">
    <xsl:for-each select=".//sect3">
      <xsl:number level="any" from="book" count="chapter" format="1."/>
      <xsl:number level="any" from="chapter" count="sect1" format="1."/>
      <xsl:number level="any" from="sect1" count="sect2" format="1."/>
      <xsl:number level="any" from="sect2" count="sect3" format="1. "/>
      <xsl:value-of select="title"/>
      <xsl:text>&#xA;</xsl:text>
    </xsl:for-each>
```

```
    </xsl:template>

  </xsl:stylesheet>
```

Our results are similar to those for *number4.xsl*:

```
1.2.1.1. Eagle
2.1.1.1. Isuzu
2.1.1.2. Javelin
2.1.1.3. K-Car
2.1.1.4. Lincoln
2.1.3.1. Opel
2.1.3.2. Pontiac
2.1.4.1. Rambler
2.1.4.2. Studebaker
```

For stylesheet *number6.xsl* we start counting at 1000. We use the `grouping-separator` attribute here as well:

```
<?xml version="1.0"?>
<!-- number6.xsl -->
<xsl:stylesheet version="1.0"
  xmlns:xsl="http://www.w3.org/1999/XSL/Transform">

  <xsl:output method="text"/>

  <xsl:template match="book">
    <xsl:for-each select="chapter|.//sect1|.//sect2|.//sect3">
      <xsl:variable name="value1">
        <xsl:number level="any" count="chapter|sect1|sect2|sect3"/>
      </xsl:variable>
      <xsl:number value="$value1 + 999"
        grouping-separator="," grouping-size="3"/>
      <xsl:text>. </xsl:text>
      <xsl:value-of select="title"/>
      <xsl:text>&#xA;</xsl:text>
    </xsl:for-each>
  </xsl:template>

</xsl:stylesheet>
```

To start counting at 1000, we use a variable to store the number generated by `<xsl:number>`. Next we use `<xsl:number>` again to output that value plus 999. The output looks like this:

```
1,000. Alfa Romeo
1,001. Bentley
1,002. Chevrolet
1,003. Dodge
1,004. Eagle
1,005. Ford
1,006. GMC
1,007. Honda
1,008. Isuzu
1,009. Javelin
1,010. K-Car
1,011. Lincoln
1,012. Mercedes
```

```
1,013. Nash
1,014. Opel
1,015. Pontiac
1,016. Quantum
1,017. Rambler
1,018. Studebaker
1,019. Toyota
```

In stylesheet *number7.xsl*, we number items from the first and second `<sect1>` elements
(`<sect1>` elements whose `position( )` is less than 3) in the second `<chapter>` element:

```
<?xml version="1.0"?>
<!-- number7.xsl -->
<xsl:stylesheet version="1.0"
  xmlns:xsl="http://www.w3.org/1999/XSL/Transform">

  <xsl:output method="text"/>

  <xsl:template match="book">
    <xsl:for-each select="chapter[2]/sect1[position() < 3]">
      <xsl:for-each select="chapter|.//sect1|.//sect2|.//sect3">
        <xsl:number level="multiple" count="chapter|sect1|sect2|sect3"
          format="1.1.1.1. "/>
        <xsl:value-of select="title"/>
        <xsl:text>&#xA;</xsl:text>
      </xsl:for-each>
    </xsl:for-each>
  </xsl:template>

</xsl:stylesheet>
```

The results look like this:

```
2.1.1. Honda
2.1.1.1. Isuzu
2.1.1.2. Javelin
2.1.1.3. K-Car
2.1.1.4. Lincoln
2.1.2. Mercedes
2.1.3. Nash
2.1.3.1. Opel
2.1.3.2. Pontiac
2.1.4. Quantum
2.1.4.1. Rambler
2.1.4.2. Studebaker
```

This style of numbering is useful for a partial table of contents.

[2.0] Now we'll look at some of the new features added in XSLT 2.0. To keep the output
short, we'll only count the `<sect2>` elements as we did in stylesheet *number4.xsl*. First, we'll
use the `ordinal` attribute:

```
<?xml version="1.0"?>
<!-- number8.xsl -->
<xsl:stylesheet version="2.0"
  xmlns:xsl="http://www.w3.org/1999/XSL/Transform">
```

```
<xsl:output method="text"/>

<xsl:template match="book">
  <xsl:for-each select=".//sect2">
    <xsl:number level="any" count="chapter|sect1|sect2|sect3"
      format="Ww - " ordinal="yes"/>
    <xsl:value-of select="title"/>
    <xsl:text>&#xA;</xsl:text>
  </xsl:for-each>
</xsl:template>

</xsl:stylesheet>
```

The wordy output looks like this:

```
Fourth - Dodge
Eighth - Honda
Thirteenth - Mercedes
Fourteenth - Nash
Seventeenth - Quantum
```

Now we'll use the combination of **format** and **lang**:

```
<?xml version="1.0"?>
<!-- number9.xsl -->
<xsl:stylesheet version="2.0"
  xmlns:xsl="http://www.w3.org/1999/XSL/Transform">

  <xsl:output method="text"/>

  <xsl:template match="book">
    <xsl:for-each select=".//sect2">
      <xsl:number level="any" count="chapter|sect1|sect2|sect3"
        format="w - " lang="de"/>
      <xsl:value-of select="title"/>
      <xsl:text>&#xA;</xsl:text>
    </xsl:for-each>
  </xsl:template>

</xsl:stylesheet>
```

Using this stylesheet with Saxon, our cardinal numbers appear in German:

```
vier - Dodge
acht - Honda
dreizehn - Mercedes
vierzehn - Nash
siebzehn - Quantum
```

If we request a combination of **format**, **ordinal**, and **lang** that the XSLT processor doesn't support, the processor reverts to its default behavior. We'll use *number10.xsl* to see what Saxon does when we ask for cardinal numbers in Polish:

```
<?xml version="1.0"?>
<!-- number10.xsl -->
<xsl:stylesheet version="2.0"
  xmlns:xsl="http://www.w3.org/1999/XSL/Transform">
```

```
<xsl:output method="text"/>

<xsl:template match="book">
  <xsl:for-each select=".//sect2">
    <xsl:number level="any" count="chapter|sect1|sect2|sect3"
      format="w - " lang="pl"/>
      <xsl:value-of select="title"/>
      <xsl:text>&#xA;</xsl:text>
  </xsl:for-each>
</xsl:template>

</xsl:stylesheet>
```

Saxon doesn't support Polish, so we get our numbers in English:

```
four - Dodge
eight - Honda
thirteen - Mercedes
fourteen - Nash
seventeen - Quantum
```

For our last example, we'll use format="๑" (Thai numbering) and ordinal="yes":

```
<?xml version="1.0"?>
<!-- number11.xsl -->
<xsl:stylesheet version="2.0"
  xmlns:xsl="http://www.w3.org/1999/XSL/Transform">

  <xsl:output method="html"/>

  <xsl:template match="book">
    <html>
      <head>
        <title>Thai numbering</title>
      </head>
      <body style="font-family: sans-serif;">
        <h1>Thai numbering</h1>
        <p style="font-size: 150%">
          <xsl:for-each select=".//sect2">
            <xsl:number level="any" count="sect2"
              format="&#x0E51; "/>
            <xsl:value-of select="title"/>
            <br/>
          </xsl:for-each>
        </p>
      </body>
    </html>
  </xsl:template>

</xsl:stylesheet>
```

This stylesheet generates an HTML document that counts all of the `<sect2>` elements and uses Thai numbering:

```
<html>
  <head>
    <meta http-equiv="Content-Type" content="text/html; charset=UTF-8">
```

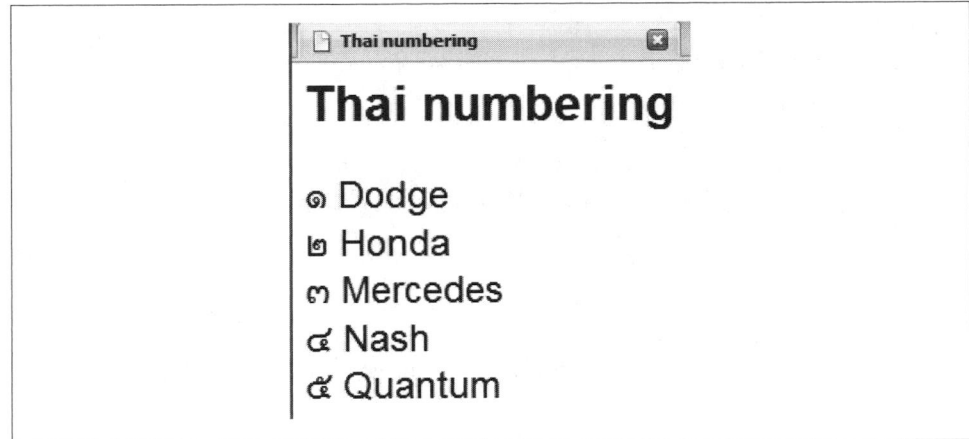

Figure A-12. A list with Thai numbering

```
        <title>Thai numbering</title>
    </head>
    <body style="font-family: sans-serif;">
        <h1>Thai numbering</h1>
        <p style="font-size: 150%">&#x0E51; Dodge<br>
        &#x0E52; Honda<br>&#x0E53; Mercedes<br>
        &#x0E54; Nash<br>&#x0E55; Quantum<br></p>
    </body>
</html>
```

When formatted in a browser, the document appears as in Figure A-12.

\<xsl:otherwise\>

Defines the `else` or `default` case in an `<xsl:choose>` element. This element always appears inside an `<xsl:choose>` element, and it must always appear last.

Category

Subinstruction (`<xsl:otherwise>` always appears as part of an `<xsl:choose>` element).

Required Attributes

None.

Optional Attributes

None.

Content

A template.

Appears in

The `<xsl:choose>` element.

Defined in

[1.0] XSLT section 9.2, "Conditional Processing with `xsl:choose`."

[2.0] XSLT section 8.2, "Conditional Processing with `xsl:choose`."

Example

Here's an example that uses `<xsl:choose>` to select the background and foreground colors for the rows of an HTML table. We cycle among four different values, using `<xsl:otherwise>` to determine the default value of the `style` attribute in the generated HTML document. Here's the XML document we'll use:

```
<?xml version="1.0"?>
<!-- albums.xml -->
<list xml:lang="en">
  <title>Albums I've bought recently:</title>
  <listitem>The Sacred Art of Dub</listitem>
  <listitem>Only the Poor Man Feel It</listitem>
  <listitem>Excitable Boy</listitem>
  <listitem xml:lang="sw">Aki Special</listitem>
  <listitem xml:lang="en_GB">Combat Rock</listitem>
  <listitem xml:lang="zu">Talking Timbuktu</listitem>
  <listitem xml:lang="jz">The Birth of the Cool</listitem>
</list>
```

And here's our stylesheet:

```
<?xml version="1.0"?>
<!-- otherwise.xsl -->
<xsl:stylesheet version="1.0"
    xmlns:xsl="http://www.w3.org/1999/XSL/Transform">

  <xsl:output method="html"/>

  <xsl:template match="/">
    <html>
      <head>
        <title>
          <xsl:value-of select="list/title"/>
        </title>
      </head>
      <body style="font-family: sans-serif; color: white;">
        <h1 style="color: black;">
          <xsl:value-of select="list/title"/>
        </h1>
        <table border="1" cellpadding="5"
          style="font-weight: bold;">
          <xsl:for-each select="list/listitem">
            <tr>
              <td>
                <xsl:attribute name="style">
                  <xsl:choose>
```

```
      <xsl:when test="position() mod 4 = 0">
        <xsl:text>background: yellow; color: black;</xsl:text>
      </xsl:when>
      <xsl:when test="position() mod 4 = 1">
        <xsl:text>background: blue;</xsl:text>
      </xsl:when>
      <xsl:when test="position() mod 4 = 2">
        <xsl:text>background: white; color: black;</xsl:text>
      </xsl:when>
      <xsl:otherwise>
        <xsl:text>background: black;</xsl:text>
      </xsl:otherwise>
    </xsl:choose>
  </xsl:attribute>
  <xsl:value-of select="."/>
</td>
      </tr>
    </xsl:for-each>
  </table>
  </body>
  </html>
</xsl:template>

</xsl:stylesheet>
```

Here's the generated HTML document, which cycles through the various background and foreground colors:

```
<html>
  <head>
    <META http-equiv="Content-Type" content="text/html; charset=UTF-8">
    <title>Albums I've bought recently:</title>
  </head>
  <body style="font-family: sans-serif; color: white;">
    <h1 style="color: black;">Albums I've bought recently:</h1>
    <table border="1" cellpadding="5" style="font-weight: bold;">
      <tr>
        <td style="background: blue;">The Sacred Art of Dub</td>
      </tr>
      <tr>
        <td style="background: white; color: black;">Only the Poor Man Feel It</td>
      </tr>
      <tr>
        <td style="background: black;">Excitable Boy</td>
      </tr>
      <tr>
        <td style="background: yellow; color: black;">Aki Special</td>
      </tr>
      ...
    </table>
  </body>
</html>
```

When rendered, our HTML document looks like Figure A-13.

Figure A-13. Using <xsl:when> and <xsl:otherwise> to cycle among background colors

Notice that every fourth row has a style of "`background:black;`". That value is generated by the `<xsl:otherwise>` element.

Defines the characteristics of an output document.

Category

Top-level element.

Required Attributes

None.

Optional Attributes

method

Typically has one of four values: `xml`, `html`, `xhtml`, or `text`. This value indicates the type of document that is generated. An XSLT processor can add other values to this list; how those values affect the generated document is determined by the XSLT processor. The default value is `xml` unless the root element of the output document is `<html>`.

[1.0] In XSLT 1.0, there are only three output methods defined in the standard: `xml`, `html`, and `text`. *[2.0]* In XSLT 2.0, `xhtml` has been added as an output method that must be supported by an XSLT processor. Individual processors are still free to add other values as well. To simplify our discussion here, we'll discuss `xhtml` as

one of the standard output types without constantly reminding you that it's not available in XSLT 1.0.

version

Defines the version of the XML, HTML, or XHTML output document. This attribute is ignored with method="text".

 The version attribute of the <xsl:output> element works differently from the version attribute that is legal on every XSLT element in XSLT 2.0. See "[2.0] Attributes common to all XSLT elements" earlier in this appendix for more details.

encoding

Defines the value of the encoding specified in the XML declaration in the output document. This attribute is ignored with method="text".

omit-xml-declaration

Defines whether the XML declaration is omitted in the output document. Allowable values are yes and no; the default is no. This attribute is used only with method="xml" and method="xhtml".

standalone

Defines the value of the standalone attribute of the XML declaration in the output document. Valid values are yes and no. This attribute is used only with method="xml" and method="xhtml".

[2.0] In XSLT 2.0, the value omit is also allowed. Coding standalone="omit" means the output document will not have a value for standalone.

doctype-public

Defines the value of the PUBLIC attribute of the DOCTYPE declaration in the output document. This attribute defines the public identifier of the output document's DTD. This attribute is ignored with method="text".

doctype-system

Defines the value of the SYSTEM attribute of the DOCTYPE declaration in the output document. It defines the system identifier of the output document's DTD. This attribute is ignored with method="text".

cdata-section-elements

Lists the elements whose content should be written as CDATA sections in the output document. All restrictions and escaping conventions of CDATA sections are handled by the XSLT processor. If you need to list more than one element, separate the element names with one or more whitespace characters. This attribute is used only with method="xml" and method="xhtml".

indent

Specifies whether the tags in the output document should be indented. Allowable values are yes and no. This attribute is used only with method="xml", method="html", or method="xhtml", and the XSLT processor is not required to honor it. The default value is yes for method="html" and method="xhtml", and no for method="xml".

media-type

Defines the MIME type of the output document. The default value is text/xml for method="xml", text/html for method="html" and method="xhtml", and text/plain for method="text".

[2.0] name

Names this output specification. The new [2.0] <xsl:result-document> element can use its format attribute to refer to this name. If your stylesheet uses <xsl:result-document> to create multiple output documents, you can define an output specification with the name attribute and use it wherever you need it.

[2.0] byte-order-mark

Defines whether or not a byte-order mark is written to the output. Valid values are yes and no. The default is yes if the encoding is UTF-16, but the default for UTF-8 varies from one XSLT processor to the next. The default is no for every other encoding.

[2.0] escape-uri-attributes

Defines whether HTML and XHTML attributes with URI values should have special characters replaced with their hex equivalents. For example, if a URI contains spaces, the escaped value of the URI replaces each spaces with %20.

[2.0] include-content-type

Defines whether the content type should be written to the output document. Valid values are yes and no; the default is yes. As an example, if include-content-type is used for method="html", the element <meta http-equiv="Content-Type" content="text/html; charset=UTF-8"> is added to the <head> element of the HTML document.

[2.0] normalization-form

Defines how Unicode characters should be normalized. Valid values are NFC, NFD, NFKC, NFKD, fully-normalized, and none. XSLT processors are free to support other values as well; see your processor's documentation to find out whether it supports any other normalization forms.

[2.0] undeclare-prefixes

Defines whether the output document should include namespace undeclarations (an *undeclaration* associates a namespace prefix with an empty string, as in xmlns:doug=""). Valid values are yes and no, and this attribute has meaning only with method="xml" and when the version attribute is 1.1 or higher. See section 20 of the XSLT 2.0 specification for the complete details on this obscure attribute.

[2.0] use-character-maps

Defines a space-separated list of named character maps (created with the [2.0] <xsl:character-map> that should be used when creating the output document).

Content

None. `<xsl:output>` is an empty element.

Appears in

`<xsl:output>` is a top-level element and can only appear as a child of `<xsl:stylesheet>`.

Defined in

[1.0] XSLT section 16, "Output."

[2.0] XSLT section 20, "Serialization."

Example

To illustrate the four output methods defined in the XSLT specification, we'll create four stylesheets, each of which uses one of the four methods. We'll use the following XML document in all four examples:

```
<?xml version="1.0"?>
<!-- albums.xml -->
<list xml:lang="en">
  <title>Albums I've bought recently:</title>
  <listitem>The Sacred Art of Dub</listitem>
  <listitem>Only the Poor Man Feel It</listitem>
  <listitem>Excitable Boy</listitem>
  <listitem xml:lang="sw">Aki Special</listitem>
  <listitem xml:lang="en-gb">Combat Rock</listitem>
  <listitem xml:lang="zu">Talking Timbuktu</listitem>
  <listitem xml:lang="jz">The Birth of the Cool</listitem>
</list>
```

We'll now look at our stylesheets and the results produced by each. First, let's look at the `method="xml"` stylesheet:

```
<?xml version="1.0"?>
<!-- output1.xsl -->
<xsl:stylesheet version="1.0"
  xmlns:xsl="http://www.w3.org/1999/XSL/Transform">

  <xsl:output method="xml" indent="yes" encoding="ISO-8859-1"/>

  <xsl:template match="/">
    <catalog>
      <xsl:for-each select="/list/listitem">
        <album>
          <xsl:apply-templates/>
        </album>
      </xsl:for-each>
    </catalog>
  </xsl:template>

</xsl:stylesheet>
```

This stylesheet generates the following results:

```
<?xml version="1.0" encoding="ISO-8859-1"?>
<catalog>
   <album>The Sacred Art of Dub</album>
   <album>Only the Poor Man Feel It</album>
   <album>Excitable Boy</album>
   <album>Aki Special</album>
   <album>Combat Rock</album>
   <album>Talking Timbuktu</album>
   <album>The Birth of the Cool</album>
</catalog>
```

The output document has the encoding we specified in our stylesheet, and the output document has been indented. (Specifying indent="no" generates an XML document that's unreadable, although well-formed.)

Now let's look at the HTML version:

```
<?xml version="1.0"?>
<!-- output2.xsl -->
<xsl:stylesheet version="1.0"
  xmlns:xsl="http://www.w3.org/1999/XSL/Transform">

  <xsl:output method="html" encoding="ISO-8859-1"/>

  <xsl:template match="/">
    <html>
      <head>
        <title><xsl:value-of select="/list/title"/></title>
      </head>
      <body>
        <h1><xsl:value-of select="/list/title"/></h1>
        <p>
          <xsl:for-each select="/list/listitem">
            <xsl:number format="1. "/>
            <xsl:value-of select="."/>
            <br/>
          </xsl:for-each>
        </p>
      </body>
    </html>
  </xsl:template>

</xsl:stylesheet>
```

Here is the HTML document generated by this stylesheet:

```
<html>
   <head>
      <meta http-equiv="Content-Type" content="text/html;
charset=ISO-8859-1">
      <title>Albums I've bought recently:</title>
   </head>
   <body>
      <h1>Albums I've bought recently:</h1>
      <p>1. The Sacred Art of Dub<br>2. Only the Poor Man
Feel It<br>3. Excitable Boy<br>4. Aki Special<br>5.
Combat Rock<br>6. Talking Timbuktu<br>7. The Birth of the
```

```
Cool<br></p>
    </body>
</html>
```

(We added line breaks to make the listing legible.) Notice that the XSLT processor has automatically inserted a `<META>` element in the `<head>` of our HTML document. The `<br>` elements are old-fashioned `<br>` tags. Even though this style of XSLT output results in a document that is not well-formed XML (or XHTML), the document works with existing HTML browsers.

To generate valid XHTML, we'll use `method="xhtml"`:

```
<?xml version="1.0"?>
<!-- output3.xsl -->
<xsl:stylesheet version="2.0"
  xmlns:xsl="http://www.w3.org/1999/XSL/Transform">

  <xsl:output
    method="xhtml"
    encoding="ISO-8859-3"
    doctype-public="-//W3C//DTD XHTML 1.0 Strict//EN"
    doctype-system="http://www.w3.org/TR/xhtml1/DTD/xhtml1-strict.dtd"/>

  <xsl:template match="/">
    <html>
      <head>
        <title><xsl:value-of select="/list/title"/></title>
      </head>
      <body>
        <h1><xsl:value-of select="/list/title"/></h1>
        <p>
          <xsl:for-each select="/list/listitem">
            <xsl:number format="1. "/>
            <xsl:value-of select="."/>
            <br/>
          </xsl:for-each>
        </p>
      </body>
    </html>
  </xsl:template>

</xsl:stylesheet>
```

Our results look like this:

```
<?xml version="1.0" encoding="ISO-8859-3"?>
<!DOCTYPE html
  PUBLIC "-//W3C//DTD XHTML 1.0 Strict//EN" "http://www.w3.org
/TR/xhtml1/DTD/xhtml1-strict.dtd">
<html>
    <head>
        <title>Albums I've bought recently:</title>
    </head>
    <body>
        <h1>Albums I've bought recently:</h1>
        <p>1. The Sacred Art of Dub
            <br></br>2. Only the Poor Man Feel It
```

```
            <br></br>3. Excitable Boy
            <br></br>4. Aki Special
            <br></br>5. Combat Rock
            <br></br>6. Talking Timbuktu
            <br></br>7. The Birth of the Cool
            <br></br>
        </p>
      </body>
    </html>
```

(We added a line break in the DOCTYPE declaration; originally it appeared on a single long line.) Our <br> elements are well-formed XML now.

Our final stylesheet uses method="text":

```
<?xml version="1.0"?>
<!-- output4.xsl -->
<xsl:stylesheet version="1.0"
  xmlns:xsl="http://www.w3.org/1999/XSL/Transform">

  <xsl:output method="text"
    encoding="ISO-8859-3"
    indent="yes"
    omit-xml-declaration="no"
    standalone="yes"
    doctype-public="-//W3C//DTD XHTML 1.0 Strict//EN"
    doctype-system="http://www.w3.org/TR/xhtml1/DTD/xhtml1-strict.dtd"/>

  <xsl:template match="/">
    <html>
      <head>
        <title><xsl:value-of select="/list/title"/></title>
      </head>
      <body>
        <h1><xsl:value-of select="/list/title"/></h1>
        <p>
          <xsl:for-each select="/list/listitem">
            <xsl:number format="1. "/>
            <xsl:value-of select="."/>
            <br/>
          </xsl:for-each>
        </p>
      </body>
    </html>
  </xsl:template>

</xsl:stylesheet>
```

Here are the results, such as they are, from this stylesheet:

```
Albums I've bought recently:Albums I've bought recently:1. The Sacred
Art of Dub2. Only the Poor Man Feel It3. Excitable Boy4. Aki Special5.
Combat Rock6. Talking Timbuktu7. The Birth of the Cool
```

(As before, we inserted line breaks so the document would fit on the page.) These results are basically worthless. Why weren't our carefully coded HTML elements and all the information we put on the <xsl:output> element written to the text document? The reason is that the

---

`method="text"` outputs only text nodes to the result tree, and it ignores most of the attributes of `<xsl:output>`. Even though we requested that various HTML elements be generated along the way, they're ignored because we specified `method="text"`.

[2.0] <xsl:output-character>

Defines a symbol and a string that should replace it. This is similar to an XML `<!ENTITY>` declaration.

Category

Declaration (this is effectively part of the `<xsl:character-map>` element).

Required Attributes

`character`
> The character to be replaced.

`string`
> The string that replaces the character.

Optional Attributes

None.

Content

None. `<xsl:output-character>` is an empty element.

Appears in

The `<xsl:character-map>` element.

Defined in

XSLT section 20, "Serialization."

Example

We'll repeat a small section of our example from the description of the `<xsl:character-map>` element. Here is a stylesheet that replaces two circled number characters (Unicode code points ૜ and ૝) with graphics:

```
<?xml version="1.0" encoding="utf-8"?>
<!-- character-map2.xsl -->
<xsl:stylesheet version="2.0"
  xmlns:xsl="http://www.w3.org/1999/XSL/Transform">

  <xsl:output method="html" use-character-maps="circles"/>

  <xsl:character-map name="circles">
    <xsl:output-character character="&#x2780;"
      string="&lt;img src='images/circle1.gif'
```

```
      width='28' height='28'/&gt;"/>
    <xsl:output-character character="&#x2781;"
      string="&lt;img src='images/circle2.gif'
      width='28' height='28'/&gt;"/>
  </xsl:character-map>

  <xsl:template match="char-test">
    <html>
      <head>
        <title>A test of some special characters</title>
      </head>
      <body style="font-family: sans-serif;">
        <h1>A test of some special characters</h1>
        <xsl:apply-templates select="*"/>
      </body>
    </html>
  </xsl:template>

  <xsl:template match="special-char">
    <p style="font-size: 200%;">
      <xsl:text>Here's a special character: </xsl:text>
      <xsl:value-of select="."/>
    </p>
  </xsl:template>

</xsl:stylesheet>
```

We'll transform this tabbed code listing:

```
<?xml version="1.0" encoding="utf-8"?>
<!-- special-characters2.xml -->
<char-test>
  <special-char>&#x2780;</special-char>
  <special-char>&#x2781;</special-char>
</char-test>
```

Our result document has replaced the circled numbers with graphics:

```
<html>
   <head>
      <meta http-equiv="Content-Type" content="text/html; charset=UTF-8">
      <title>A test of some special characters</title>
   </head>
   <body style="font-family: sans-serif;">
      <h1>A test of some special characters</h1>
      <p style="font-size: 200%;">Here's a special character:
      <img src='images/circle1.gif' width='28' height='28'/></p>
      <p style="font-size: 200%;">Here's a special character:
      <img src='images/circle2.gif'width='28' height='28'/></p>
   </body>
</html>
```

This is a useful way of replacing characters that aren't displayable on every browser. Our HTML document appears as in Figure A-14.

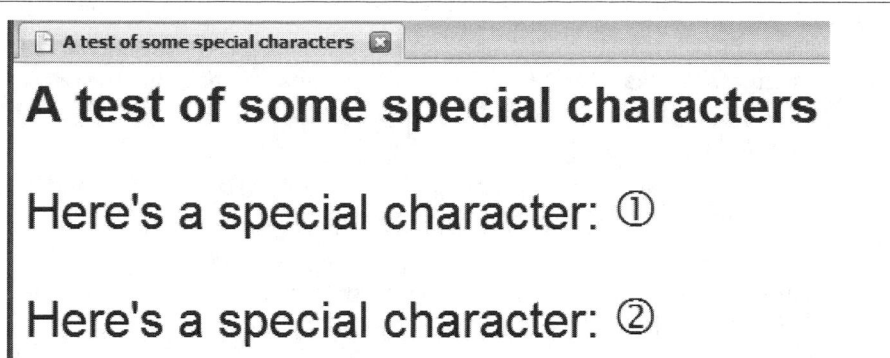

Figure A-14. HTML document generated with character maps

<xsl:param>

Defines the name and value of a parameter to be used in a stylesheet. This element can appear as a top-level element or inside the `<xsl:template>` element. If the `<xsl:param>` appears as a top-level element, it is a global parameter, visible to all areas of the stylesheet. The default value of the parameter can be defined in one of two ways: specified in the `select` attribute or defined inside the `<xsl:param>` element itself. *[2.0]* In XSLT 2.0, `<xsl:param>` can also appear inside the new `<xsl:function>` element.

Category

Instruction.

Required Attribute

name
: Defines the name of this parameter.

Optional Attributes

select
: Contains an XPath expression that defines the value of this parameter.

[2.0 – Schema] as
: Defines the datatype of this parameter. The datatype can be any of the built-in types or, if you have a schema-aware XSLT processor, a datatype defined in an XML Schema. For example, `as="xs:integer"` specifies a parameter that is a single integer, and `as="xs:string*"` specifies a parameter that is a sequence of zero or more strings. With a schema-aware XSLT processor, `as="schema-element(po:purchase-order)"` means that the parameter must be a valid `po:purchase-order`.

[2.0] `required`

> Defines whether this parameter is required. Valid values are **yes** and **no**. If this is a parameter for an `<xsl:function>`, this attribute must not be defined. For stylesheet and template parameters, the default value is that the parameter is optional (`required="no"`).
>
> It is a static error if an `<xsl:param>` element has a `required` attribute and a default value. Required parameters cannot have a `select` attribute, and they must be empty.
>
> It is also a static error to use the `required` attribute on a parameter defined in an `<xsl:function>` element.

[2.0] `tunnel`

> Defines whether this is a tunnel parameter. Valid values are **yes** and **no**, with **no** being the default. (For an in-depth discussion of tunnel parameters, see "Tunnel parameters" in Chapter 5.)

Content

If the `select` attribute is used, `<xsl:param>` must be empty. Otherwise, it contains an XSLT template.

[2.0] In XSLT 2.0, this rule is enforced much more strictly. It is a static error if a nonempty `<xsl:param>` element has a `select` attribute.

Appears in

`<xsl:stylesheet>` and `<xsl:template>`. If an `<xsl:param>` appears as a child of `<xsl:style sheet>`, then it is a global parameter visible throughout the stylesheet. XSLT doesn't define the way global parameters are passed to the XSLT processor, so check the documentation for your processor to see how this is done. (See "Global Parameters" in Chapter 5 for an overview of how to pass parameters to the most popular XSLT processors.)

[2.0] In XSLT 2.0, `<xsl:param>` can also appear in the new `<xsl:function>` element.

Defined in

[1.0] XSLT section 11, "Variables and Parameters."

[2.0] XSLT section 9, "Variables and Parameters."

Example

This stylesheet that defines several `<xsl:param>` elements, both global and local. Notice that one of the parameters is a node-set; parameters can be of any XPath or XSLT datatype. Here's the stylesheet:

```
<?xml version="1.0"?>
<!-- param.xsl -->
<xsl:stylesheet version="1.0"
  xmlns:xsl="http://www.w3.org/1999/XSL/Transform">

  <xsl:output method="text"/>
```

```
<xsl:param name="favoriteNumber" select="23"/>
<xsl:param name="favoriteColor"/>


<xsl:template match="/">
  <xsl:text>&#xA;</xsl:text>
  <xsl:value-of select="list/title"/>
  <xsl:text>&#xA;</xsl:text>
  <xsl:variable name="listitems" select="list/listitem"/>
  <xsl:call-template name="processListItems">
    <xsl:with-param name="items" select="$listitems"/>
    <xsl:with-param name="color" select="'yellow'"/>
    <xsl:with-param name="number" select="$favoriteNumber"/>
  </xsl:call-template>
</xsl:template>

<xsl:template name="processListItems">
  <xsl:param name="items"/>
  <xsl:param name="color" select="'blue'"/>

  <xsl:for-each select="$items">
    <xsl:value-of select="position()"/>
    <xsl:text>.  </xsl:text>
    <xsl:value-of select="."/>
    <xsl:text>&#xA;</xsl:text>
  </xsl:for-each>

  <xsl:text>&#xA;</xsl:text>

  <xsl:text>Your favorite color is </xsl:text>
  <xsl:value-of select="$favoriteColor"/>
  <xsl:text>.</xsl:text>
  <xsl:text>&#xA;</xsl:text>
  <xsl:text>The color passed to this template is </xsl:text>
  <xsl:value-of select="$color"/>
  <xsl:text>.</xsl:text>
  <xsl:text>&#xA;</xsl:text>
</xsl:template>

</xsl:stylesheet>
```

We'll use this stylesheet to transform the following document:

```
<?xml version="1.0"?>
<!-- albums.xml -->
<list>
  <title>A few of my favorite albums</title>
  <listitem>A Love Supreme</listitem>
  <listitem>Beat Crazy</listitem>
  <listitem>You Could Have it So Much Better</listitem>
  <listitem>Kind of Blue</listitem>
  <listitem>London Calling</listitem>
  <listitem>Remain in Light</listitem>
  <listitem>The Joshua Tree</listitem>
```

```
    <listitem>The Indestructible Beat of Soweto</listitem>
  </list>
```

Here are the results:

```
A few of my favorite albums
1.   A Love Supreme
2.   Beat Crazy
3.   You Could Have it So Much Better
4.   Kind of Blue
5.   London Calling
6.   Remain in Light
7.   The Joshua Tree
8.   The Indestructible Beat of Soweto


Your favorite color is purple.
The color passed to this template is yellow.
```

Notice that when we call the template processListItems, we passed in three parameters, only two of which are defined inside the template. In XSLT 1.0, the undefined parameters are simply ignored; in XSLT 2.0, this is a fatal error. If we change the stylesheet to <xsl:stylesheet version="2.0" ..., the stylesheet won't run at all. Also notice that the parameter $items is a node-set, so we can use the parameter in an <xsl:for-each> element.

To generate the previous results, we passed the value purple to the XSLT processor. If you're using Saxon, the command line looks like this:

```
java net.sf.saxon.Transform albums.xml param.xsl favoriteColor=purple
```

With Xalan-J, the value is passed like this:

```
java org.apache.xalan.xslt.Process -in albums.xml -xsl param.xsl
  -param favoriteColor purple
```

(The command should be entered on a single line.) See "Global Parameters" in Chapter 5 for a more complete discussion of global parameters and how they can be set for various XSLT processors.

As a further example, here's an XSLT 2.0 stylesheet that uses required parameters, including a required global parameter that must be specified when the stylesheet is invoked:

```
<?xml version="1.0"?>
<!-- param2.xsl -->
<xsl:stylesheet version="2.0"
  xmlns:xsl="http://www.w3.org/1999/XSL/Transform"
  xmlns:xs="http://www.w3.org/2001/XMLSchema">

  <xsl:output method="text"/>

  <xsl:param name="favoriteNumber"
    required="yes" as="xs:integer"/>

  <xsl:template match="/">
    <xsl:text>&#xA;</xsl:text>
    <xsl:value-of select="list/title"/>
    <xsl:text>&#xA;</xsl:text>
    <xsl:variable name="listitems" select="list/listitem"/>
```

```
    <xsl:call-template name="processListItems">
      <xsl:with-param name="items" select="$listitems"/>
    </xsl:call-template>
  </xsl:template>

  <xsl:template name="processListItems">
    <xsl:param name="items" required="yes"/>

    <xsl:for-each select="$items">
      <xsl:value-of select="position()"/>
      <xsl:text>.  </xsl:text>
      <xsl:value-of select="."/>
      <xsl:text>&#xA;</xsl:text>
    </xsl:for-each>

    <xsl:text>&#xA;</xsl:text>

    <xsl:text>Your favorite number is </xsl:text>
    <xsl:value-of select="$favoriteNumber"/>
    <xsl:text>.</xsl:text>
    <xsl:text>&#xA;</xsl:text>
  </xsl:template>

</xsl:stylesheet>
```

This generates results similar to our earlier stylesheet, but the required parameter is enforced. We'll look at four invocations of this stylesheet with Saxon. For the first, we won't supply the required parameter at all:

```
C:\>java net.sf.saxon.Transform albums.xml param2.xsl
Error
  XTDE0050: No value supplied for required parameter favoriteNumber
Transformation failed: Run-time errors were reported
```

Next we'll specify a value for the required parameter, but that value isn't an integer:

```
C:\>java net.sf.saxon.Transform albums.xml param2.xsl favoriteNumber=yellow
Validation error
  FORG0001: Cannot convert string "yellow" to an integer
Transformation failed: Run-time errors were reported
```

Now we'll supply a valid number, but we mistype the variable name. Variables in XSLT are case-sensitive, so favoritenumber and favoriteNumber are two different variables.

```
C:\>java net.sf.saxon.Transform albums.xml param2.xsl favoritenumber=23
Error
  XTDE0050: No value supplied for required parameter favoriteNumber
Transformation failed: Run-time errors were reported
```

Finally, we provide the required parameter with a valid value, and everything works:

```
C:\>java net.sf.saxon.Transform albums.xml param2.xsl favoriteNumber=23

Albums I've bought recently:
1.  The Sacred Art of Dub
2.  Only the Poor Man Feel It
3.  Excitable Boy
```

```
        4.  Aki Special
        5.  Combat Rock
        6.  Talking Timbuktu
        7.  The Birth of the Cool

        Your favorite number is 23.
```

[2.0] <xsl:perform-sort>

Sorts a sequence. The sequence to be sorted can be defined with the `select` attribute, or it can be constructed inside the `<xsl:perform-sort>` element itself.

Category

Instruction

Required Attributes

None.

Optional Attribute

`select`

> An XPath expression that defines the items to be sorted. If the `select` attribute is present, the `<xsl:perform-sort>` element can only contain `<xsl:sort>` and `<xsl:fallback>` elements. In other words, with a `select` attribute, the `<xsl:perform-sort>` element is not allowed to construct a sequence of items because the `select` attribute has already specified one.

Content

`<xsl:perform-sort>` contains one or more `<xsl:sort>` elements, along with any number of `<xsl:fallback>` elements. If the `select` attribute is not defined, `<xsl:perform-sort>` can contain a sequence constructor. If there is no `select` attribute and the `<xsl:perform-sort>` element doesn't create a sequence, the result is an empty sequence.

Appears in

Any XSLT element whose content model is a sequence constructor or any literal result element.

Defined in

XSLT section 13.2, "Creating a Sorted Sequence."

Example

We'll start with an `<xsl:perform-sort>` element that uses a `select` attribute to produce a sorted sequence. Here is our stylesheet:

```
<?xml version="1.0"?>
<!-- perform-sort4.xsl -->
```

```
<xsl:stylesheet version="2.0"
  xmlns:xsl="http://www.w3.org/1999/XSL/Transform"
  xmlns:xs="http://www.w3.org/2001/XMLSchema">

  <xsl:output method="text"/>

  <xsl:variable name="vendorsInOrder" as="xs:string*">
    <xsl:perform-sort select="/report/brand/name">
      <xsl:sort select="."/>
    </xsl:perform-sort>
  </xsl:variable>

  <xsl:template match="/">
    <xsl:text>We sell these brands of chocolate:&#xA;&#xA;</xsl:text>
    <xsl:value-of select="$vendorsInOrder" separator="&#xA;"/>
  </xsl:template>

</xsl:stylesheet>
```

We'll use this stylesheet to process our document of chocolate bar sales:

```
<?xml version="1.0" encoding="utf-8"?>
<!-- chocolate.xml -->
<report month="8" year="2006">
  <title>Chocolate bar sales</title>
  <brand>
    <name>Lindt</name>
    <units>27408</units>
  </brand>
  <brand>
    <name>Callebaut</name>
    <units>8203</units>
  </brand>
  <brand>
    <name>Valrhona</name>
    <units>22101</units>
  </brand>
  <brand>
    <name>Perugina</name>
    <units>14336</units>
  </brand>
  <brand>
    <name>Ghirardelli</name>
    <units>19268</units>
  </brand>
</report>
```

Here are our results:

```
We sell these brands of chocolate:

Callebaut
Ghirardelli
Lindt
Perugina
Valrhona
```

The `select` attribute of our `<xsl:perform-sort>` element creates a sequence of all of the `<name>` elements in our input document. The names of those elements are sorted and returned as a sequence, which is then stored in the variable `vendorsInOrder`. Be aware that `<xsl:perform-sort>` returns a sequence of zero or one or more items.

The `<xsl:sort>` elements can be arbitrarily complex. In this example, the sequence we're creating is still based on the brand names, but the sort order is determined by the sales of each brand:

```
<?xml version="1.0"?>
<!-- perform-sort5.xsl -->
<xsl:stylesheet version="2.0"
  xmlns:xsl="http://www.w3.org/1999/XSL/Transform"
  xmlns:xs="http://www.w3.org/2001/XMLSchema">

  <xsl:output method="text"/>

  <xsl:variable name="vendorsInOrder" as="xs:string*">
    <xsl:perform-sort select="/report/brand/name">
      <xsl:sort select="../units"
        data-type="number" order="descending"/>
    </xsl:perform-sort>
  </xsl:variable>

  <xsl:template match="/">
    <xsl:text>Here are our best-selling brands:&#xA;&#xA;</xsl:text>
    <xsl:value-of select="$vendorsInOrder" separator="&#xA;"/>
  </xsl:template>

</xsl:stylesheet>
```

Now our results are different:

```
Here are our best-selling brands:

Lindt
Valrhona
Ghirardelli
Perugina
Callebaut
```

We're still using the `select` attribute to define the items in our sequence, but we're sorting them with a more complicated key. For an example of an `<xsl:perform-sort>` element that doesn't use the `select` attribute, we'll use `<xsl:sequence>` to select nodes instead:

```
<?xml version="1.0"?>
<!-- perform-sort6.xsl -->
<xsl:stylesheet version="2.0"
  xmlns:xsl="http://www.w3.org/1999/XSL/Transform"
  xmlns:xs="http://www.w3.org/2001/XMLSchema">

  <xsl:output method="text"/>

  <xsl:variable name="vendorsInOrder" as="xs:string*">
    <xsl:perform-sort>
      <xsl:sort select="../units"
```

```
              data-type="number" order="descending"/>
            <xsl:sequence select="/report/brand/name"/>
          </xsl:perform-sort>
        </xsl:variable>

        <xsl:template match="/">
          <xsl:text>Here are our best-selling brands:&#xA;&#xA;</xsl:text>
          <xsl:value-of select="$vendorsInOrder" separator="&#xA;"/>
        </xsl:template>

      </xsl:stylesheet>
```

This gives the same results as before, although the syntax looks strange. Within `<xsl:perform-sort>`, one or more `<xsl:sort>` elements must appear first. Those elements define the sort key for the sequence of items created inside the `<xsl:perform-sort>` element itself. We could generate a more complicated sequence if we want:

```
<?xml version="1.0"?>
<!-- perform-sort7.xsl -->
<xsl:stylesheet version="2.0"
  xmlns:xsl="http://www.w3.org/1999/XSL/Transform"
  xmlns:xs="http://www.w3.org/2001/XMLSchema">

  <xsl:output method="text"/>

  <xsl:variable name="vendorsInOrder" as="xs:string*">
    <xsl:perform-sort>
      <xsl:sort select="."
        data-type="number" order="descending"/>
      <xsl:sequence select="/report/brand/units"/>
      <xsl:sequence select="('3829', '28852', '18831')"/>
    </xsl:perform-sort>
  </xsl:variable>

  <xsl:template match="/">
    <xsl:text>Here are our sales figures:&#xA;&#xA;</xsl:text>
    <xsl:value-of select="$vendorsInOrder" separator="&#xA;"/>
  </xsl:template>

</xsl:stylesheet>
```

We've added some bogus sales data to make our figures look better. The results here show that we added extra values to the sequence before it was sorted:

```
Here are our sales figures:

28852
27408
22101
19268
18831
14336
8203
3829
```

These are sorted in reverse order because we used the attribute `order="descending"` on the `<xsl:sort>` element.

<xsl:preserve-space>

Defines the source document elements for which whitespace should be preserved.

Category

Top-level element.

Required Attribute

`elements`

Contains a space-separated list of source document elements for which nonsignificant whitespace should be preserved. *Nonsignificant whitespace* typically means text nodes that contain nothing but whitespace; whitespace that appears in and around text is always preserved. The `elements` attribute can also contain the value *, which means whitespace should be preserved in all elements not specified in a `<xsl:strip-space>` element. (Although `<xsl:preserve-space elements="*"/>` is legal, there's no need to ever use this. XSLT preserves whitespace text nodes by default.) It is also valid to specify `elements="po:*"` to specify all elements in the `po` namespace.

[2.0] In XSLT 2.0, the `elements` attribute can use wildcards for the namespace prefix. For example, the value `elements="*:title"` refers to all `<title>` elements, regardless of their namespaces. As with XSLT 1.0, the value `elements="dc:*"` refers to all elements in the `dc` namespace.

 The XML spec defines the seldom used attribute `xml:space`. The `xml:space` attribute can have the values `preserve` or `default`. If `xml:space="preserve"` applies to a given element in the XML source, all whitespace is preserved, regardless of any `<xsl:preserve-space>` or `<xsl:strip-space>` elements.

Optional Attributes

None.

Content

None. `<xsl:preserve-space>` is an empty element.

Appears in

`<xsl:preserve-space>` is a top-level element and can only appear as a child of `<xsl:stylesheet>`.

Defined in

[1.0] XSLT section 3.4, "Whitespace Stripping."

[2.0] XSLT section 4.4, "Stripping Whitespace from a Source Tree."

Example

We'll illustrate how `<preserve-space>` works with the following stylesheet:

```
<?xml version="1.0"?>
<!-- preserve-space.xsl -->
<xsl:stylesheet version="1.0"
  xmlns:xsl="http://www.w3.org/1999/XSL/Transform">

  <xsl:output method="text"/>

  <xsl:strip-space elements="*"/>
  <xsl:preserve-space elements="listing"/>

  <xsl:template match="/">
    <xsl:text>&#xA;</xsl:text>
    <xsl:value-of select="/code-sample/title"/>
    <xsl:text>&#xA;</xsl:text>
    <xsl:for-each select="/code-sample/listing">
      <xsl:value-of select="."/>
    </xsl:for-each>
  </xsl:template>

</xsl:stylesheet>
```

We'll use this stylesheet to process the following document:

```
<?xml version="1.0" encoding="utf-8"?>
<!-- whitespace.xml -->
<code-sample>
  <title>Conditional variable initialization:</title>
  <listing>
    <type>int</type><var> y</var><endstmt>;</endstmt>
    <type>int</type><var> x</var><endstmt>;</endstmt>

    <var>y</var> <op>=</op> <const>23</const><endstmt>;</endstmt>

    <block>
      <keyword>if</keyword> (<var>y</var> <comp>></comp> <const>10</const>)
        <var>x</var> <op>=</op> <const>5</const><endstmt>;</endstmt>
      <keyword>else </keyword>
      <keyword>if</keyword> (<var>y</var> <comp>></comp> <const>5</const>)
        <var>x</var> <op>=</op> <const>3</const><endstmt>;</endstmt>
      <keyword>else </keyword>
        <var>x</var> <op>=</op> <const>1</const><endstmt>;</endstmt>
    </block>
  </listing>
</code-sample>
```

When we process this document with our stylesheet, we get these results:

```
Conditional variable initialization:

    int y;
    int x;

    y = 23;

    if (y>10)
        x=5;else if (y>5)
        x=3;else x=1;
```

The `<xsl:strip-space>` element strips the whitespace off all the elements in the document, so we use `<xsl:preserve-space>` to preserve whitespace inside the `<listing>` element. Notice that the whitespace inside the `<block>` element was stripped. The `<xsl:preserve-space>` element is useful when you need to exclude an element from whitespace stripping; by default, no whitespace is stripped from any nodes. Compare this example to the one for the `<strip-space>` element.

`<xsl:processing-instruction>`

Creates a processing instruction in the output document.

Category

Instruction.

Required Attribute

name
> Defines the name (also known as the target) of this processing instruction.

Optional Attribute

[2.0] select
> Defines an expression that creates the data for the processing instruction. If the select attribute is used, the `<xsl:processing-instruction>` must be empty.

Content

An XSLT template. The contents of the template become the data of the processing instruction.

Appears in

`<xsl:processing-instruction>` appears inside a template.

Defined in

[1.0] XSLT section 7.3, "Creating Processing Instructions."

[2.0] XSLT section 11.6, "Creating Processing Instructions."

Example

We'll demonstrate a stylesheet that adds a processing instruction to an XML document. The processing instruction will associate the stylesheet *docbook.xsl* with this XML document. Here is our stylesheet:

```
<?xml version="1.0"?>
<!-- processing-instruction.xsl -->
<xsl:stylesheet version="1.0"
  xmlns:xsl="http://www.w3.org/1999/XSL/Transform">

  <xsl:output method="xml"/>

  <xsl:template match="/">
    <xsl:processing-instruction name="xml-stylesheet">href="docbook/
html/docbook.xsl" type="text/xsl"</xsl:processing-instruction>
    <xsl:copy-of select="."/>
  </xsl:template>

</xsl:stylesheet>
```

(The `<xsl:processing-instruction>` element should all be on one line.) This stylesheet simply uses the `<xsl:copy-of>` element to copy the input document to the result tree, adding a processing instruction along the way. We'll use our stylesheet with this XML document:

```
<?xml version="1.0"?>
<!-- greeting.xml -->
<greeting>
  Hello, World!
</greeting>
```

When we run this transformation, here are the results:

```
<?xml version="1.0" encoding="UTF-8"?>
<?xml-stylesheet href="docbook/html/docbook.xsl" type="text/xsl"?>
<greeting>
  Hello, World!
</greeting>
```

Note that the contents of a processing instruction are text. Even though the processing instruction we just generated looks like it contains two attributes, you can't create the processing instruction like this:

```
<?xml version="1.0"?>
<!-- processing-instruction-doesnt-work.xsl -->
<xsl:stylesheet version="1.0"
  xmlns:xsl="http://www.w3.org/1999/XSL/Transform">
  <xsl:output method="xml"/>

  <xsl:template match="/">
    <xsl:processing-instruction name="xml-stylesheet">

      <!-- This doesn't work!  You can't put <xsl:attribute>
           elements inside a <xsl:processing-instruction> element. -->

      <xsl:attribute name="href">
        <xsl:text>docbook/html/docbook.xsl</xsl:text>
```

```
          </xsl:attribute>
          <xsl:attribute name="type">
            <xsl:text>text/xsl</xsl:text>
          </xsl:attribute>
        </xsl:processing-instruction>
        <xsl:copy-of select="."/>
      </xsl:template>

    </xsl:stylesheet>
```

If you try this, Xalan throws an exception. Saxon doesn't throw an exception, but it doesn't generate a valid processing instruction, either.

[2.0] <xsl:result-document>

Creates a final result tree. Typically a result tree is written to a file, although an XSLT 2.0 processor is not required to be able to do so. The <xsl:result-document> instruction is useful for generating multiple files from a single stylesheet. It also makes it possible to generate the name of the output file at runtime.

Category

Instruction.

Required Attributes

None.

Optional Attributes

format

> Refers to an output specification defined on a named <xsl:output> element. You can define properties such as an output method or a character encoding, then reuse those output specifications by referencing the name attribute of the appropriate <xsl:output> element.

href

> Defines the URI of this result document. Typically this is used to define a filename for the result document, although an XSLT processor is free to use this URI any way it chooses.

[2.0 – Schema] type

> Defines the datatype of the document element. The datatype can be any of the built-in datatypes, or it can be a datatype defined in a schema if you have a schema-aware XSLT 2.0 processor.
>
> The type and validation attributes are mutually exclusive.

[2.0 – Schema] validation

> Defines how the new document element will be validated. The validation attribute has four values: strict, lax, preserve, or strip.

`validation="strict"` means that the XSLT processor looks in all the declared schemas for an element declaration (`<xs:element>`) with the same name as the document element. It is a fatal error if the processor can't find a matching `<xs:element>`. Assuming the processor finds the declaration of the element, it validates the new document against the document element's declaration.

`validation="lax"` works just like `validation="strict"`, except that no error occurs if the processor can't find the declaration of the element in any of the in-scope schemas. In that case, the type annotation of the document element is `xs:untyped`.

The value `validation="preserve"` means the created element will have a type annotation of `xs:anyType`, and the type annotations of any nodes the new document element contains will be retained without changes. No schema validation is done.

Finally, `validation="strip"` means that the new document element will have a type annotation of `xs:anyType`.

The `validation` and `type` attributes are mutually exclusive.

method
>   Defines the output method for this result tree. Valid values are `xml`, `html`, `xhtml`, and `text`. XSLT processors are free to support other methods as well; check your processors documentation to see whether it supports any other output methods.

byte-order-mark
>   Defines whether or not a byte-order mark is written to the output. Valid values are `yes` and `no`. The default is `yes` if the `encoding` is `UTF-16`, but the default for `UTF-8` can vary from one XSLT processor to the next. The default is `no` for every other encoding.

cdata-section-elements
>   Lists the elements that should be written as CDATA sections in the output document. All restrictions and escaping conventions of CDATA sections are handled by the XSLT processor. If you need to list more than one element, separate the element names with one or more whitespace characters. This attribute is used only with `method="xml"` and `method="xhtml"`.

doctype-public
>   Defines the value of the PUBLIC attribute of the DOCTYPE declaration in the output document. This attribute defines the public identifier of the output document's DTD. This attribute is ignored with `method="text"`.

doctype-system
>   Defines the value of the SYSTEM attribute of the DOCTYPE declaration in the output document. It defines the system identifier of the output document's DTD. This attribute is ignored with `method="text"`.

encoding
>   Defines the value of the `encoding` attribute of the XML declaration in the output document. This attribute is ignored with `method="text"`.

escape-uri-attributes

Defines whether HTML and XHTML attributes with URI values should have special characters replaced with their hex equivalents. For example, if a URI contains spaces, the escaped value of the URI replaces each space with %20.

include-content-type

Defines whether the content type should be written to the output document. Valid values are yes and no; the default is yes. As an example, if include-content-type is used for method="html", the element <meta http-equiv="Content-Type" content="text/html; charset=UTF-8"> is added to the <head> element of the HTML document.

indent

Defines whether or not elements in the result tree should be indented. Valid values are yes and no. This attribute is ignored for method="text".

media-type

Defines the MIME type of the output document. The default value is text/xml for method="xml", text/html for method="html" and method="xhtml", and text/plain for method="text".

normalization-form

Valid values are NFC, NFD, NFKC, NFKD, fully-normalized, and none. XSLT processors are free to support other values as well; see your processor's documentation to find out whether it supports any other normalization forms.

omit-xml-declaration

Defines whether or not the result tree should include an XML declaration. Valid values are yes and no; the default is no.

standalone

Defines whether or not the XML declaration should include standalone. Valid values are yes (the declaration includes standalone="yes"), no (the declaration includes standalone="no"), and ([2.0]) omit (the declaration does not contain standalone at all).

undeclare-prefixes

Defines whether the output document should include namespace undeclarations (an undeclaration associates a namespace prefix with an empty string, as in xmlns:doug=""). Valid values are yes and no. See section 20 of the XSLT 2.0 specification for the complete details on this obscure attribute.

use-character-maps

Defines a space-separated list of named character maps that should be used when creating the output document.

output-version

Overrides the version attribute on the <xsl:output> element.

Content

A sequence constructor.

Appears in

An `<xsl:template>`.

Defined in

XSLT section 19.1, "Creating Final Result Trees."

Example

We'll illustrate the power of `<xsl:result-document>` with this small DocBook document:

```
<?xml version="1.0"?>
<!-- chapters.xml -->
<book>
  <title>XSLT Topics</title>
  <chapter>
    <title>XPath</title>
    <para>If this chapter had any text, it would appear here.</para>
  </chapter>
  <chapter>
    <title>Stylesheet Basics</title>
    <para>If this chapter had any text, it would appear here.</para>
  </chapter>
  <chapter>
    <title>Branching and Control Elements</title>
    <para>If this chapter had any text, it would appear here.</para>
  </chapter>
  <chapter>
    <title>Functions</title>
    <para>If this chapter had any text, it would appear here.</para>
  </chapter>
  <chapter>
    <title>Creating Links and Cross-References</title>
    <para>If this chapter had any text, it would appear here.</para>
  </chapter>
  <chapter>
    <title>Sorting and Grouping Elements</title>
    <para>If this chapter had any text, it would appear here.</para>
  </chapter>
  <chapter>
    <title>Combining XML Documents</title>
    <para>If this chapter had any text, it would appear here.</para>
  </chapter>
</book>
```

We'll use a stylesheet to create several documents. First of all, we'll create a single HTML file that lists all of the titles of the chapters defined here. Each chapter title will be a link to a separate HTML file created with `<xsl:result-document>`. We'll use `<xsl:result-document>` to create a separate HTML file from each `<chapter>` element. Here's the stylesheet:

```
<?xml version="1.0" encoding="utf-8"?>
<!-- result-document.xsl -->
<xsl:stylesheet version="2.0"
  xmlns:xsl="http://www.w3.org/1999/XSL/Transform">

  <xsl:output method="html" include-content-type="no"/>

  <xsl:template match="/">
    <html>
      <head>
        <title><xsl:value-of select="book/title"/></title>
      </head>
      <body>
        <h1><xsl:value-of select="book/title"/></h1>
        <p>Here are some interesting XSLT topics:</p>
        <ul>
          <xsl:for-each select="book/chapter">
            <li>
              <a href="{concat('chapter', position(), '.html')}">
                <xsl:value-of select="title"/>
              </a>
            </li>
          </xsl:for-each>
        </ul>
        <xsl:for-each select="book/chapter">
          <xsl:result-document method="html"
            include-content-type="no"
            href="{concat('chapter', position(), '.html')}">
            <html>
              <head>
                <title><xsl:value-of select="title"/></title>
              </head>
              <body>
                <h1><xsl:value-of select="title"/></h1>
                <xsl:apply-templates select="*[position() > 1]"/>
              </body>
            </html>
          </xsl:result-document>
        </xsl:for-each>
      </body>
    </html>
  </xsl:template>

  <xsl:template match="para">
    <p><xsl:apply-templates select="*|text()"/></p>
  </xsl:template>

</xsl:stylesheet>
```

Our stylesheet begins by creating the main HTML document. It uses `<xsl:for-each
select="book/chapter">` to create a list item and link for each `<chapter>` in the original docu-
ment. It then uses another `<xsl:for-each>` element that uses `<xsl:result-document>` to create
a new document for each `<chapter>`.

Notice that in the stylesheet we use the attribute value template {concat('chapter', position( ), '.html')} to create filenames and links. We could have required an identifying attribute on each <chapter> element, but it's simpler to use this naming convention to create the files and links. The fourth <chapter> is in the file *chapter4.html*. The main HTML file looks like this:

```
<html>
   <head>
      <title>XSLT Topics</title>
   </head>
   <body>
      <h1>XSLT Topics</h1>
      <p>Here are some interesting XSLT topics:</p>
      <ul>
         <li><a href="chapter1.html">XPath</a></li>
         <li><a href="chapter2.html">Stylesheet Basics</a></li>
         <li><a href="chapter3.html">Branching and Control Elements</a></li>
         <li><a href="chapter4.html">Functions</a></li>
         <li><a href="chapter5.html">Creating Links and Cross-References</a></li>
         <li><a href="chapter6.html">Sorting and Grouping Elements</a></li>
         <li><a href="chapter7.html">Combining XML Documents</a></li>
      </ul>
   </body>
</html>
```

Each individual HTML file looks something like this:

```
<html>
   <head>
      <title>XPath</title>
   </head>
   <body>
      <h1>XPath</h1>
      <p>If this chapter had any text, it would appear here.</p>
   </body>
</html>
```

In a browser, the main HTML file appears as in Figure A-15.

Clicking on one of the links takes us to one of the individual documents created by <xsl:result-document>, as shown in Figure A-16.

The <xsl:result-document> element officially replaces a common extension element from most XSLT 1.0 processors. Performing this task with an XSLT 1.0 processor required calls to a processor-specific extension element that created multiple output files. See the example "The document() Function and Sorting" in Chapter 9 for a complete discussion of the most common XSLT 1.0 mechanisms.

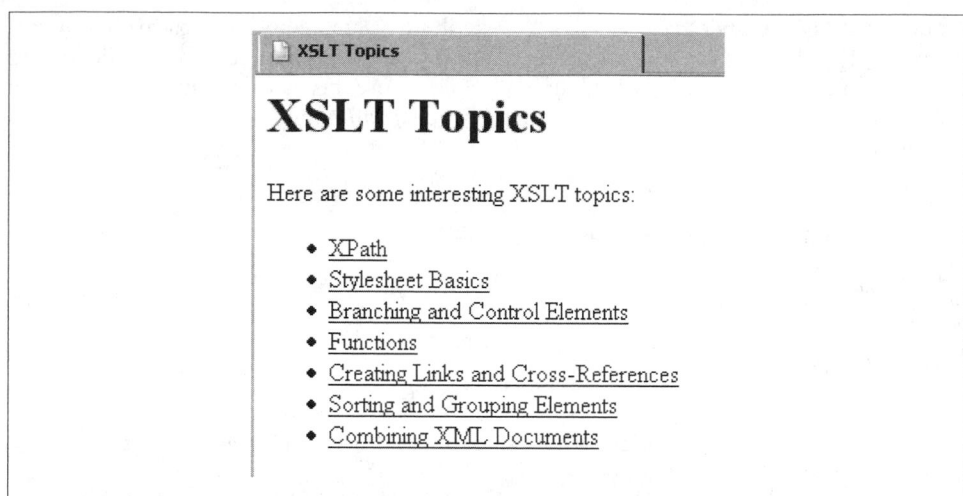

Figure A-15. An HTML file that links to documents created by <xsl:result-document>

Figure A-16. One of the documents created by <xsl:result-document>

[2.0] <xsl:sequence>

Creates a sequence of nodes and/or atomic values.

Category

Instruction.

Required Attribute

select
    An XPath expression that determines the content of the sequence.

Optional Attributes

None.

Content

Zero or more `<xsl:fallback>` elements. The `<xsl:fallback>` element specifies processing that should take place in the case of an element that the XSLT processor doesn't support. They are most commonly written for XSLT 1.0 processors operating in forwards-compatible mode.

Appears in

A template.

Defined in

XSLT section 11.10, "Constructing Sequences."

Example

We'll use a simple example here that creates a sequence inside an `<xsl:variable>`. Here's the stylesheet:

```
<?xml version="1.0" encoding="utf-8"?>
<!-- sequence.xsl -->
<xsl:stylesheet version="2.0"
  xmlns:xsl="http://www.w3.org/1999/XSL/Transform"
  xmlns:xs="http://www.w3.org/2001/XMLSchema">

  <xsl:output method="text"/>

  <xsl:template match="/">
    <xsl:variable name="sales" as="xs:integer*">
      <xsl:for-each select="/report/brand/units">
        <xsl:if test=". > 10000">
          <xsl:sequence select="."/>
        </xsl:if>
      </xsl:for-each>
    </xsl:variable>

    <xsl:value-of select="/report/title"/>
    <xsl:text>&#xA;&#xA;Sales figures: </xsl:text>
    <xsl:value-of select="$sales" separator=", "/>
    <xsl:text>&#xA;&#xA;Sequence total:    &#9;</xsl:text>
    <xsl:value-of select="format-number(sum($sales), '$#,###.00')"/>
    <xsl:text>&#xA;Sequence average:&#9;</xsl:text>
    <xsl:value-of select="format-number(avg($sales), '$#,###.00')"/>
  </xsl:template>

</xsl:stylesheet>
```

Inside the `<xsl:for-each>` element, each `<xsl:sequence>` creates a one-node sequence. The value of the variable is the sequence of `xs:integer`s created from all the items (nodes and atoms) generated by the `<xsl:sequence>` elements. (In other words, everything selected by a `<xsl:sequence>` is cast to an `xs:integer` before it becomes part of the variable.) We'll run this stylesheet against our report of chocolate sales:

```
<?xml version="1.0" encoding="utf-8"?>
<!-- chocolate.xml -->
<report month="8" year="2006">
```

```
<title>Chocolate bar sales</title>
<brand>
  <name>Lindt</name>
  <units>27408</units>
</brand>
<brand>
  <name>Callebaut</name>
  <units>8203</units>
</brand>
<brand>
  <name>Valrhona</name>
  <units>22101</units>
</brand>
<brand>
  <name>Perugina</name>
  <units>14336</units>
</brand>
<brand>
  <name>Ghirardelli</name>
  <units>19268</units>
</brand>
</report>
```

Our stylesheet creates a sequence of all the `<units>` elements larger than 10000. It gives these results:

```
Chocolate bar sales

Sales figures:  27408, 22101, 14336, 19268

Sequence total:        $83,113.00
Sequence average:      $20,778.25
```

Remember that a sequence can have any combination of nodes and atomic values. If we'd like to make our sales figures look better, we could change the declaration of the variable to add more items to the sequence:

```
<!-- sequence2.xsl -->
...
<xsl:variable name="sales" as="xs:integer*">
  <xsl:for-each select="/report/brand/units">
    <xsl:if test=". > 10000">
      <xsl:sequence select="."/>
    </xsl:if>
  </xsl:for-each>
  <xsl:sequence select="(80000, 75000, 65000)"/>
</xsl:variable>
...
```

Our calculations now include the extra numbers, so our sales figures look much better:

```
Chocolate bar sales

Sales figures:  27408, 22101, 14336, 19268, 80000, 75000, 65000

Sequence total:        $303,113.00
Sequence average:      $43,301.86
```

Remember, the variable that contains the sequence is of type `xs:integer*`, so all of the selected nodes and atomic values are cast to `xs:integer`s before they become part of the variable.

\<xsl:sort>

Defines a sort key for the current context. The first `<xsl:sort>` defines the primary sort key, the second `<xsl:sort>` defines the secondary sort key, etc. You can have as many `<xsl:sort>` elements as you need.

Category

Subinstruction.

Required Attributes

None.

Optional Attributes

`select`
> Determines the nodes to be sorted. You can also omit the `select` attribute and use the contents of the `<xsl:sort>` element to define the nodes to be sorted.

`lang`
> A string that defines the language used by the sort. The language codes are defined in RFC1766, available at *http://www.ietf.org/rfc/rfc1766.txt*. Not all processors support all languages, so check your XSLT processor's documentation.

`data-type`
> An attribute that defines the type of the items to be sorted. Allowable values are `number` and `text`; the default is `text`. An XSLT processor has the option of supporting other values as well. Sorting the values `32 10 120` with `data-type="text"` returns `10 120 32`, while `data-type="number"` returns `10 32 120`.
>
> *[2.0]* In XSLT 2.0, you can specify a QName that represents some other datatype. How (or if) that value is processed can vary from one XSLT processor to another.

`order`
> An attribute that defines the order of the sort. Allowable values are `ascending` and `descending`.

`case-order`
> An attribute that defines the order in which upper- and lowercase letters are sorted. Allowable values are `upper-first` and `lower-first`.

[2.0] `collation`
> The collation order used by this sort. For example, in Spanish, the single letter *ll* sorts after the two letters *lz*, so English collating rules don't sort Spanish words correctly.

This value is a URI; how that URI is used to specify a particular language value varies from one XSLT processor to the next. Keep in mind that if an XSLT 2.0 processor does not support the collation order you requested, the processor uses its default collation.

[2.0] `stable`

Valid values are `yes` and `no`; the default is `yes`. Only the first `<xsl:sort>` element can have a `stable` attribute. If `stable="yes"`, any elements with the same sort value stay in their original order in the document. For example, if we sort these elements:

```
<statelist>
  <title>U.S. Road trips I've made recently</title>
  <state year="2006" month="4">California</state>
  <state year="2005" month="12">Texas</state>
  <state year="2006" month="2">Washington</state>
  <state year="2006" month="3">California</state>
</statelist>
```

and if we sort by the `year` attribute and the value of the `<state>` element (the `month` attribute is ignored), the first and last elements here have the same sort value. With `stable="yes"`, the two trips to California will stay in their original document order. If you go out of your way to code `stable="no"`, the XSLT processor is not required to keep the nodes in their original order.

Content

[1.0] None.

[2.0] In XSLT 2.0, you can use the content of the `<xsl:sort>` element to define the nodes to be sorted. As you would expect, it is a fatal error to have both a `select` attribute and content inside `<xsl:sort>`. If neither is specified, it defaults to the current context node, which is equivalent to `select="."`

Appears in

`<xsl:apply-templates>` and `<xsl:for-each>`.

[2.0] In XSLT 2.0, `<xsl:sort>` can appear in the new `<xsl:for-each-group>` and `<xsl:perform-sort>` elements as well.

Defined in

[1.0] XSLT section 10, "Sorting."

[2.0] XSLT section 13, "Sorting."

Example

We'll illustrate `<xsl:sort>` with this stylesheet:

```
<?xml version="1.0"?>
<!-- sort.xsl -->
<xsl:stylesheet version="1.0"
  xmlns:xsl="http://www.w3.org/1999/XSL/Transform">
```

```
<xsl:output method="text"/>

<xsl:template match="/">
  <xsl:text>&#xA;</xsl:text>
  <xsl:call-template name="ascending-alpha-sort">
    <xsl:with-param name="items" select="/sample/textlist/listitem"/>
  </xsl:call-template>
  <xsl:call-template name="ascending-alpha-sort">
    <xsl:with-param name="items" select="/sample/numericlist/listitem"/>
  </xsl:call-template>
  <xsl:call-template name="ascending-numeric-sort">
    <xsl:with-param name="items" select="/sample/numericlist/listitem"/>
  </xsl:call-template>
  <xsl:call-template name="descending-alpha-sort">
    <xsl:with-param name="items" select="/sample/textlist/listitem"/>
  </xsl:call-template>
  <xsl:call-template name="category-sort">
    <xsl:with-param name="items" select="/sample/textlist/listitem"/>
  </xsl:call-template>
</xsl:template>

<xsl:template name="ascending-alpha-sort">
  <xsl:param name="items"/>
  <xsl:text>Ascending text sort:</xsl:text>
  <xsl:text>&#xA;</xsl:text>
  <xsl:for-each select="$items">
    <xsl:sort select="."/>
    <xsl:value-of select="."/>
    <xsl:text>&#xA;</xsl:text>
  </xsl:for-each>
  <xsl:text>&#xA;</xsl:text>
</xsl:template>

<xsl:template name="descending-alpha-sort">
  <xsl:param name="items"/>
  <xsl:text>Descending text sort:</xsl:text>
  <xsl:text>&#xA;</xsl:text>
  <xsl:for-each select="$items">
    <xsl:sort select="." order="descending"/>
    <xsl:value-of select="."/>
    <xsl:text>&#xA;</xsl:text>
  </xsl:for-each>
  <xsl:text>&#xA;</xsl:text>
</xsl:template>

<xsl:template name="ascending-numeric-sort">
  <xsl:param name="items"/>
  <xsl:text>Ascending numeric sort:</xsl:text>
  <xsl:text>&#xA;</xsl:text>
  <xsl:for-each select="$items">
    <xsl:sort select="." data-type="number"/>
    <xsl:value-of select="."/>
    <xsl:text>&#xA;</xsl:text>
  </xsl:for-each>
```

```
    <xsl:text>&#xA;</xsl:text>
  </xsl:template>

  <xsl:template name="category-sort">
    <xsl:param name="items"/>
    <xsl:text>Ascending category sort:</xsl:text>
    <xsl:text>&#xA;</xsl:text>
    <xsl:for-each select="$items">
      <xsl:sort select="@category"/>
      <xsl:sort select="."/>
      <xsl:value-of select="."/>
      <xsl:text>&#xA;</xsl:text>
    </xsl:for-each>
    <xsl:text>&#xA;</xsl:text>
  </xsl:template>

</xsl:stylesheet>
```

Our stylesheet defines four named templates, each of which sorts `<listitem>`s in a different order or with a different **data-type**. Notice that the fourth template, **category-sort**, sorts by an attribute first, then by the value of the current item. We'll use this stylesheet against this document:

```
<?xml version="1.0"?>
<!-- items-to-sort.xml -->
<sample>
  <numericlist>
    <listitem>1</listitem>
    <listitem>3</listitem>
    <listitem>23</listitem>
    <listitem>120</listitem>
    <listitem>2</listitem>
  </numericlist>
  <textlist>
    <listitem category="number">3</listitem>
    <listitem category="fruit">apple</listitem>
    <listitem category="fruit">orange</listitem>
    <listitem category="foreign-fruit">dragonfruit</listitem>
    <listitem category="foreign-fruit">carambola</listitem>
  </textlist>
  <datelist>
    <listitem>2006-12-25</listitem>
    <listitem>1995-04-21</listitem>
    <listitem>1965-06-19</listitem>
    <listitem>2007-01-01</listitem>
  </datelist>
  <spanishlist>
    <listitem>campo</listitem>
    <listitem>luna</listitem>
    <listitem>ciudad</listitem>
    <listitem>llaves</listitem>
    <listitem>chihuahua</listitem>
    <listitem>arroz</listitem>
    <listitem>limonada</listitem>
```

```
        </spanishlist>
    </sample>
```

Here are the results:

```
Ascending text sort:
3
apple
carambola
dragonfruit
orange

Ascending text sort:
1
120
2
23
3

Ascending numeric sort:
1
2
3
23
120

Descending text sort:
orange
dragonfruit
carambola
apple
3

Ascending category sort:
carambola
dragonfruit
apple
orange
3
```

Notice that the `data-type="numeric"` attribute causes data to be sorted in numeric order.

[2.0] To illustrate some of the new features of XSLT 2.0, we'll sort this data with another stylesheet. One template casts the children of `<datelist>` into `xs:date` values, and then sorts those values. Another template uses a custom collation to sort the children of `<spanishlist>` using a custom collation. Here's the stylesheet:

```
<?xml version="1.0"?>
<!-- sort2.xsl -->
<xsl:stylesheet version="2.0"
  xmlns:xsl="http://www.w3.org/1999/XSL/Transform"
  xmlns:xs="http://www.w3.org/2001/XMLSchema">

  <xsl:output method="text"/>

  <xsl:template match="/">
```

```
    <xsl:text>&#xA;</xsl:text>
    <xsl:variable name="date-sequence" as="xs:date*">
      <xsl:for-each select="/sample/datelist/listitem">
        <xsl:value-of select="xs:date(.)"/>
      </xsl:for-each>
    </xsl:variable>
    <xsl:call-template name="ascending-date-sort">
      <xsl:with-param name="items" select="$date-sequence"/>
    </xsl:call-template>
    <xsl:call-template name="spanish-alpha-sort">
      <xsl:with-param name="items" select="/sample/spanishlist/listitem"/>
    </xsl:call-template>
    <xsl:call-template name="ascending-alpha-sort">
      <xsl:with-param name="items" select="/sample/spanishlist/listitem"/>
    </xsl:call-template>
</xsl:template>

<xsl:template name="ascending-date-sort">
  <xsl:param name="items" as="xs:date*"/>
  <xsl:text>Ascending date sort:</xsl:text>
  <xsl:text>&#xA;</xsl:text>
  <xsl:for-each select="$items">
    <xsl:sort/>
    <xsl:value-of select="."/>
    <xsl:text>&#xA;</xsl:text>
  </xsl:for-each>
  <xsl:text>&#xA;</xsl:text>
</xsl:template>

<xsl:template name="ascending-alpha-sort">
  <xsl:param name="items"/>
  <xsl:text>Ascending text sort:</xsl:text>
  <xsl:text>&#xA;</xsl:text>
  <xsl:for-each select="$items">
    <xsl:sort/>
    <xsl:value-of select="."/>
    <xsl:text>&#xA;</xsl:text>
  </xsl:for-each>
  <xsl:text>&#xA;</xsl:text>
</xsl:template>

<xsl:template name="spanish-alpha-sort">
  <xsl:param name="items"/>
  <xsl:text>Spanish alpha sort:</xsl:text>
  <xsl:text>&#xA;</xsl:text>
  <xsl:for-each select="$items">
    <xsl:sort
      collation="{concat('http://saxon.sf.net/collation?',
                  'class=com.oreilly.xslt.SpanishCollation;')}"/>
    <xsl:value-of select="."/>
    <xsl:text>&#xA;</xsl:text>
  </xsl:for-each>
  <xsl:text>&#xA;</xsl:text>
</xsl:template>
```

```
</xsl:stylesheet>
```

The results look like this:

```
Ascending date sort:
1965-06-19
1995-04-21
2006-12-25
2007-01-01

Spanish alpha sort:
arroz
campo
ciudad
chihuahua
limonada
luna
llaves

Ascending text sort:
arroz
campo
chihuahua
ciudad
limonada
llaves
luna
```

The dates are sorted as `xs:date` values, even though those results are the same as a text sort. For the Spanish collation, we specify the Java class that compares strings to determine the sort order. The way the Java class is specified here is specific to the Saxon XSLT 2.0 processor. Check the documentation of your XSLT processor to see how (or if) it supports custom collations.

See Chapter 9 for a discussion of "Creating Custom Collations."

<xsl:strip-space>

Defines the source-document elements for which nonsignificant whitespace should be removed.

Category

Top-level element.

Required Attribute

elements

> Contains a space-separated list of element names or node tests for which nonsignificant whitespace should be removed. *Nonsignificant whitespace* typically means text nodes that contain nothing but whitespace; whitespace that appears in and around text is always preserved. The `elements` attribute can also contain the

value *, which means whitespace should be removed from all elements not specified in an `<xsl:preserve-space>` element. The value `elements="auth:*"` is also legal; this specifies all elements in the `auth` namespace.

[2.0] In XSLT 2.0, the `elements` attribute can also use wildcards for the namespace prefix. For example, the value `*:title` refers to all `<title>` elements, regardless of their namespaces.

 The XML spec defines the seldom used attribute `xml:space`. The `xml:space` attribute can have the values `preserve` or `default`. If `xml:space="preserve"` applies to a given element in the XML source, all whitespace is preserved, regardless of any `<xsl:preserve-space>` or `<xsl:strip-space>` elements.

Optional Attributes

None.

Content

None. `<xsl:strip-space>` is an empty element.

Appears in

`<xsl:strip-space>` is a top-level element and can only appear as a child of `<xsl:stylesheet>`.

Defined in

[1.0] XSLT section 3.4, "Whitespace Stripping."

[2.0] XSLT section 4.4, "Stripping Whitespace from a Source Tree."

Example

We'll illustrate the `<xsl:strip-space>` element with the following stylesheet:

```
<?xml version="1.0"?>
<!-- strip-space.xsl -->
<xsl:stylesheet version="1.0"
  xmlns:xsl="http://www.w3.org/1999/XSL/Transform">

  <xsl:output method="text"/>

  <xsl:strip-space elements="*"/>

  <xsl:template match="/">
    <xsl:text>&#xA;</xsl:text>
    <xsl:value-of select="/code-sample/title"/>
    <xsl:text>&#xA;</xsl:text>
    <xsl:for-each select="/code-sample/listing">
      <xsl:value-of select="."/>
    </xsl:for-each>
  </xsl:template>
```

```
    </xsl:stylesheet>
```

We'll use this stylesheet to process the following document:

```xml
<?xml version="1.0" encoding="utf-8"?>
<!-- whitespace.xml -->
<code-sample>
  <title>Conditional variable initialization:</title>
  <listing>
    <type>int</type><var> y</var><endstmt>;</endstmt>
    <type>int</type><var> x</var><endstmt>;</endstmt>

    <var>y</var> <op>=</op> <const>23</const><endstmt>;</endstmt>

    <block>
      <keyword>if</keyword> (<var>y</var> <comp>></comp> <const>10</const>)
        <var>x</var> <op>=</op> <const>5</const><endstmt>;</endstmt>
      <keyword>else </keyword>
      <keyword>if</keyword> (<var>y</var> <comp>></comp> <const>5</const>)
        <var>x</var> <op>=</op> <const>3</const><endstmt>;</endstmt>
      <keyword>else </keyword>
        <var>x</var> <op>=</op> <const>1</const><endstmt>;</endstmt>
    </block>
  </listing>
</code-sample>
```

Here are the results:

```
Conditional variable initialization:
int y;int x;y=23;if (y>10)
        x=5;else if (y>5)
        x=3;else x=1;
```

Notice that all the extra whitespace from all the elements has been removed. This includes the space between the various elements contained inside `<listing>`, such as `<keyword>`, `<const>`, and `<var>`. Wherever the `<listing>` element has nonwhitespace characters between elements (a semicolon or parenthesis, for example), that text node and all the whitespace it contains are preserved. Those text nodes are the reason why some whitespace appears in our results. If we went to the extreme of putting every character inside an element, all of the text inside the `<listing>` element would run together.

Compare this to the example for `<xsl:preserve-space>`.

`<xsl:stylesheet>`

The root element of an XSLT stylesheet. It is identical to the `<xsl:transform>` element, which was included in the XSLT specification for historical purposes.

Category

Contains the entire stylesheet.

Required Attributes

version

> Indicates the version of XSLT that the stylesheet requires. For XSLT version 1.0, its value should always be 1.0. As later versions of the XSLT specification are defined, the required values for the version attribute will be defined along with them.
>
> *[2.0]* In XSLT version 2.0, this value should be 2.0. The XSLT 2.0 spec defines stricter rules for handling the version attribute than the XSLT 1.0 spec. To avoid complications, you should use the values 1.0 and 2.0.
>
> XSLT 2.0 also allows you to specify the version attribute on any XSLT element. If you want to use version 1.0 processing for a given portion of your stylesheet, you can define version="1.0" for that portion of the stylesheet. For example, the `<xsl:decimal-format>` element works differently in XSLT 2.0, so you could use `<xsl:decimal-format version="1.0">` to process the element according to the rules of XSLT 1.0.

xmlns:xsl

> Defines the URI for the XSL namespace. For both XSLT version 1.0 and XSLT version 2.0, this attribute's value must be http://www.w3.org/1999/XSL/Transform. (Although this is a namespace declaration, not an attribute, it is required. Your stylesheet won't work without it.)

Optional Attributes

id

> Defines an ID for this stylesheet.

extension-element-prefixes

> Defines any namespace prefixes used to invoke extension elements. Multiple namespace prefixes are separated by whitespace.

exclude-result-prefixes

> Defines namespace prefixes whose declarations should not be sent to the output document. Multiple namespace prefixes are separated by whitespace.

[2.0] xpath-default-namespace

> Defines the default namespace used by XPath functions and operators. If you're transforming a document that uses a default namespace (http://www.oreilly.com, for example), you must normally namespace-qualify the names of any elements in your XPath expressions. Defining xpath-default-namespace="http://www.oreilly.com" tells XPath to use this namespace as the default. By using this on any element in your stylesheet, you can have different default XPath namespaces in different sections of your stylesheet.

[2.0] default-validation

> Defines the default value for the validation attribute of the `<xsl:document>`, `<xsl:element>`, `<xsl:attribute>`, `<xsl:copy>`, `<xsl:copy-of>`, and `<xsl:result-`

document> elements. Allowed values for this attribute are preserve and strip. If this attribute is not coded, the default value is strip.

[2.0] default-collation

A series of space-separated URIs that define the default collation sequence. This sequence is used by <xsl:key> and <xsl:for-each-group>, but it does not affect the collation used by <xsl:sort>. The way collation sequences are defined varies from one XSLT processor to another, so check your processor's documentation for information on defining a collation sequence.

[2.0] input-type-annotations

Defines whether datatype information should be preserved in the output. Valid values for this attribute are preserve, strip, and unspecified; the default value is unspecified.

Content

This element contains the entire stylesheet. The following elements can be children of <xsl:stylesheet>:

```
<xsl:attribute-set>
[2.0] [2.0] <xsl:character-map>
<xsl:decimal-format>
[2.0] [2.0] <xsl:function>
<xsl:import>
[2.0] [2.0 – Schema] <xsl:import-schema>
<xsl:include>
<xsl:key>
<xsl:namespace-alias>
<xsl:output>
<xsl:param>
<xsl:preserve-space>
<xsl:strip-space>
<xsl:template>
<xsl:variable>
```

Appears in

None. <xsl:stylesheet> is the root element of the stylesheet.

Defined in

[1.0] XSLT section 2.2, "Stylesheet Element."

[2.0] XSLT section 3.6, "Stylesheet Element."

Example

For a simple example, we'll use the Hello World document from the XML 1.0 specification:

```
<?xml version="1.0"?>
<greeting>
  Hello, World!
</greeting>
```

We'll transform our document with this stylesheet:

```
<?xml version="1.0"?>
<!-- stylesheet.xsl -->
<xsl:stylesheet version="1.0"
  xmlns:xsl="http://www.w3.org/1999/XSL/Transform">

  <xsl:output method="html"/>

  <xsl:template match="/">
    <xsl:apply-templates select="greeting"/>
  </xsl:template>

  <xsl:template match="greeting">
    <html>
      <body>
        <h1>
          <xsl:value-of select="."/>
        </h1>
      </body>
    </html>
  </xsl:template>

</xsl:stylesheet>
```

When we transform our document with this stylesheet, here are the results:

```
<html>
<body>
<h1>
  Hello, World!
</h1>
</body>
</html>
```

[2.0] XSLT 2.0 added the xpath-default-namespace attribute to simplify working with documents that have a default namespace. Here's a modified version of our chocolate sales document that uses a default namespace:

```
<?xml version="1.0" encoding="utf-8"?>
<!-- chocolate-default-namespace.xml -->
<report month="8" year="2006"
  xmlns="http://www.oreilly.com">
  <title>Chocolate bar sales</title>
  <brand>
    <name>Lindt</name>
    <units>27408</units>
  </brand>
  <brand>
    <name>Callebaut</name>
    <units>8203</units>
  </brand>
```

```
  <brand>
    <name>Valrhona</name>
    <units>22101</units>
  </brand>
  <brand>
    <name>Perugina</name>
    <units>14336</units>
  </brand>
  <brand>
    <name>Ghirardelli</name>
    <units>19268</units>
  </brand>
</report>
```

Here's a simple stylesheet to list the sales figures for each brand:

```
<?xml version="1.0"?>
<!-- stylesheet2.xsl -->
<xsl:stylesheet version="2.0"
  xmlns:xsl="http://www.w3.org/1999/XSL/Transform">

  <xsl:output method="text"/>

  <xsl:template match="/">
    <xsl:text>Here are this month's sales figures:&#xA;&#xA;</xsl:text>
    <xsl:for-each select="/report/brand">
      <xsl:value-of select="name"/>
      <xsl:text>&#x9;</xsl:text>
      <xsl:value-of select="units"/>
      <xsl:text>&#xA;</xsl:text>
    </xsl:for-each>
  </xsl:template>

</xsl:stylesheet>
```

And here are our disappointing results:

```
Here are this month's sales figures:
```

We don't get any results because we don't specify the namespace of our element names in our XPath expressions. If we add xpath-default-namespace to the <xsl:stylesheet> element:

```
<xsl:stylesheet version="2.0"
  xmlns:xsl="http://www.w3.org/1999/XSL/Transform"
  xpath-default-namespace="http://www.oreilly.com">
```

we get the results we want:

```
Here are this month's sales figures:

Lindt    27408
Callebaut    8203
Valrhona     22101
Perugina     14336
Ghirardelli  19268
```

\<xsl:template\>

Defines an output template. Templates that begin `<xsl:template match="x"` define a transformation for a given element. Templates that begin `<xsl:template name="x"` define a set of output elements that are processed whenever the template is invoked by name. All `<xsl:template>` elements must have either the `match` or the `name` attribute defined. Although not common, it is also possible to create `<xsl:template>` elements that have both a `match` and a `name`.

Category

Top-level element.

Required Attributes

None; however, an `<xsl:template>` must contain a `match` attribute, a `name` attribute, or both.

Optional Attributes

match
> A pattern that defines the elements for which this template should be invoked. For example, `<xsl:template match="xyz">` defines a template for processing `<xyz>` elements.

name
> An attribute that names this template. Named templates are invoked with the `<xsl:call-template>` element.

mode
> An attribute that defines a mode for this template. A *mode* is a convenient syntax that allows you to write specific templates for specific purposes. For example, we could write an `<xsl:template>` with `mode="toc"` to process a node for the table of contents of a document, and we could write other `<xsl:template>`s with `mode="print"`, `mode="online"`, `mode="index"`, etc. to process the same information for different purposes.
>
> *[2.0]* In XSLT 2.0, the `mode` attribute can use the value `#default` to indicate that this template applies to the default mode, or use `#all` to indicate that this template applies to all modes. XSLT 2.0 also allows you to specify multiple mode names separated by whitespace. It is an error if you use the `mode` attribute on a template that doesn't have a `match` attribute.

priority
> An attribute that assigns a numeric priority to this template. The value can be any numeric value except `Infinity`. If the XSLT processor cannot determine which template to use (in other words, more than one template has the same default priority), the `priority` attribute allows you to define a tiebreaker. Keep in mind that you can simply use the `priority` attribute to raise the priority of a given template.

[2.0] In XSLT 2.0, it is an error if you use the `priority` attribute on a named template.

[2.0] **as**

Defines the datatype of the result of the template. If this attribute is omitted, the template can return any datatype.

Content

An XSLT template.

Appears in

`<xsl:template>` is a top-level element and can only appear as a child of `<xsl:stylesheet>`.

Defined in

[1.0] XSLT section 5.3, "Defining Template Rules."

[2.0] XSLT section 6.1, "Defining Template Rules."

Example

We'll use the Hello World document from the XML 1.0 specification for our example:

```
<?xml version="1.0"?>
<greeting>
  Hello, World!
</greeting>
```

We'll transform our document with this stylesheet:

```
<?xml version="1.0"?>
<!-- stylesheet.xsl -->
<xsl:stylesheet version="1.0"
  xmlns:xsl="http://www.w3.org/1999/XSL/Transform">

  <xsl:output method="html"/>

  <xsl:template match="/">
    <xsl:apply-templates select="greeting"/>
  </xsl:template>

  <xsl:template match="greeting">
    <html>
      <body>
        <h1>
          <xsl:value-of select="."/>
        </h1>
      </body>
    </html>
  </xsl:template>

</xsl:stylesheet>
```

This simple stylesheet has two templates, one of which matches the root node (or document node in XSLT 2.0), and one of which matches the `<greeting>` element (`match="greeting"`).

```
<html>
<body>
<h1>
  Hello, World!
</h1>
</body>
</html>
```

<xsl:text>

Allows you to write literal text to the output document. The main benefit of the `<xsl:text>` element is that it gives you complete control over whitespace in the output.

Category

Instruction.

Required Attributes

None.

Optional Attribute

`disable-output-escaping`

> Defines whether special characters are escaped when they are written to the output document. For example, if the literal text contains the character >, it is normally written to the output document as >. If you code `disable-output-escaping="yes"`, the character > is written instead. Note that If you're using `<xsl:output method="text">`, this attribute is ignored because output escaping is not done for the `text` output method.
>
> *[2.0]* In XSLT 2.0, this attribute is deprecated. Instead you should use the new [2.0] `<xsl:character-map>` element.

Content

Literal text and entity references (
, for example). These are known collectively as PCDATA, or *parsed character data*.

Appears in

`<xsl:text>` appears inside a template.

Defined in

[1.0] XSLT section 7.2, "Creating Text."

[2.0] XSLT section 11.4.2, "Creating Text Nodes Using `xsl:text`."

Example

This sample stylesheet generates text with `<xsl:text>`. We intermingle `<xsl:text>` and `<xsl:value-of>` elements to create a coherent sentence. In this case, we simply generate a text document, but this technique works equally well to create the text of an HTML or XML element. Here is the stylesheet:

```
<?xml version="1.0"?>
<!-- text.xsl -->
<xsl:stylesheet version="1.0"
  xmlns:xsl="http://www.w3.org/1999/XSL/Transform">

  <xsl:output method="html"/>

  <xsl:template match="/">
    <html>
      <head>
        <title>Test of &lt;xsl:text&gt;</title>
      </head>
      <body style="font-family: sans-serif;">
        <!-- disable-output-escaping="no" by default -->
        <h1>Test of &lt;xsl:text&gt;</h1>
        <p>
          <xsl:text>Your document contains </xsl:text>
          <xsl:value-of select="count(//*)"/>
          <xsl:text> elements and </xsl:text>
          <xsl:value-of select="count(//@*)"/>
          <xsl:text> attributes.  </xsl:text>
        </p>
        <p>
          <xsl:text
            disable-output-escaping="yes">&lt;Have a great day!&gt;</xsl:text>
        </p>
      </body>
    </html>
  </xsl:template>

</xsl:stylesheet>
```

Given this XML document:

```
<?xml version="1.0"?>
<!-- albums.xml -->
<list xml:lang="en">
  <title>Albums I've bought recently:</title>
  <listitem>The Sacred Art of Dub</listitem>
  <listitem>Only the Poor Man Feel It</listitem>
  <listitem>Excitable Boy</listitem>
  <listitem xml:lang="sw">Aki Special</listitem>
  <listitem xml:lang="en-gb">Combat Rock</listitem>
  <listitem xml:lang="zu">Talking Timbuktu</listitem>
  <listitem xml:lang="jz">The Birth of the Cool</listitem>
</list>
```

Our stylesheet produces this HTML document:

```
<html>
   <head>
      <meta http-equiv="Content-Type" content="text/html; charset=UTF-8">
      <title>Test of &lt;xsl:text&gt;</title>
   </head>
   <body style="font-family: sans-serif;">
      <h1>Test of &lt;xsl:text&gt;</h1>
      <p>Your document contains 9 elements and 5 attributes.  </p>
      <p><Have a great day!></p>
   </body>
</html>
```

If you view this document in a browser, the browser ignores the unknown `<Have>` element in the second paragraph. Using the `disable-output-escaping` attribute lets you generate text that is not valid (or even well-formed) HTML, XML, or XHTML, and it should be used as a last resort in an XSLT 1.0 stylesheet.

<xsl:transform>

This is a synonym for `<xsl:stylesheet>`. It was included in the XSLT 1.0 spec for historical purposes. Its attributes, content, and all other properties are the same as those for `<xsl:style sheet>`. See the "`<xsl:stylesheet>`" section for more information.

Category

Instruction.

<xsl:value-of>

Calculates the value of an XPath expression, converts that value to a text node and then writes the value to the result tree.

Category

Instruction.

Required Attribute

select

The XPath expression that is evaluated and written to the output.

[2.0] In XSLT 2.0, this attribute is optional. The `<xsl:value-of>` element must have either a `select` attribute or it must contain content. It is an error if it contains neither or both.

Optional Attributes

disable-output-escaping

An attribute that defines whether special characters are escaped when written to the output document. For example, if the literal text contains the character >, it is normally written to the output document as `&gt;`. If you code `disable-output-escaping="yes"`, the character > is written instead. The XSLT processor uses this attribute only if you use the `html` or `xml` output methods. If you use `<xsl:output method="text">`, the attribute is ignored becasue output escaping is not done for the `text` output method. See the "`<xsl:text>`" section for a more thorough discussion of the `disable-output-escaping` attribute.

[2.0] In XSLT 2.0, this attribute is deprecated. You should use a character map instead; see the discussion of the [2.0] `<xsl:character-map>` element for more information.

[2.0] separator

Defines the characters that separate multiple values generated by the `select` attribute. The default value is a single space (`#x20`). The value of the `separator` attribute appears after all of the values except the last.

 Be aware that in XSLT 1.0, `<xsl:value-of>` selects the first item in a node-set and discards all the others. In XSLT 2.0, all of the nodes are output with the separator between them.

Content

None. `<xsl:value-of>` is an empty element.

[2.0] In XSLT 2.0, `<xsl:value-of>` can contain content; that content is evaluated and written to the output.

Appears in

`<xsl:value-of>` appears inside a template.

Defined in

[1.0] XSLT section 7.6.1, "Generating Text with `xsl:value-of`."

[2.0] XSLT section 11.4.3, "Generating Text with `xsl:value-of`."

Example

We'll use the `<xsl:value-of>` element to generate some text. Here is our stylesheet:

```
<?xml version="1.0"?>
<!-- value-of.xsl -->
<xsl:stylesheet version="1.0"
  xmlns:xsl="http://www.w3.org/1999/XSL/Transform">

  <xsl:output method="text"/>

  <xsl:template match="/">
    <xsl:text>Your document contains </xsl:text>
    <xsl:value-of select="count(//*)"/>
    <xsl:text> elements and </xsl:text>
```

```
    <xsl:value-of select="count(//@*)"/>
    <xsl:text> attributes.&#xA;Have a great day!</xsl:text>
  </xsl:template>

</xsl:stylesheet>
```

We'll use this XML document as input:

```
<?xml version="1.0"?>
<!-- albums.xml -->
<list xml:lang="en">
  <title>Albums I've bought recently:</title>
  <listitem>The Sacred Art of Dub</listitem>
  <listitem>Only the Poor Man Feel It</listitem>
  <listitem>Excitable Boy</listitem>
  <listitem xml:lang="sw">Aki Special</listitem>
  <listitem xml:lang="en-gb">Combat Rock</listitem>
  <listitem xml:lang="zu">Talking Timbuktu</listitem>
  <listitem xml:lang="jz">The Birth of the Cool</listitem>
</list>
```

Here are the results:

```
Your document contains 9 elements and 5 attributes.
Have a great day!
```

[2.0] Before we leave the `<xsl:value-of>` element, we'll look at its new capabilities. Here's a short stylesheet that uses a nonempty `<xsl:value-of>` and the `separator` attribute:

```
<?xml version="1.0"?>
<!-- value-of2.xsl -->
<xsl:stylesheet version="2.0"
  xmlns:xsl="http://www.w3.org/1999/XSL/Transform">

  <xsl:output method="text"/>

  <xsl:template match="/">
    <xsl:value-of>
      <xsl:text>Here is a list of the </xsl:text>
      <xsl:value-of select="count(//*)"/>
      <xsl:text> elements in your document:&#xA;&#xA;</xsl:text>
    </xsl:value-of>
    <xsl:value-of select="//*/name()" separator="&#xA;"/>
  </xsl:template>

</xsl:stylesheet>
```

Processing *albums.xml* with our new stylesheet generates these results:

```
Here is a list of the 9 elements in your document:

list
title
listitem
listitem
listitem
listitem
listitem
```

```
listitem
listitem
```

The first paragraph is generated by an `<xsl:value-of>` element that contains three elements, one of which is another `<xsl:value-of>` element. The rest of the document is generated by a single `<xsl:value-of>` statement that uses the handy **separator** attribute. If we wanted to do the same thing in XSLT 1.0, we would have to replace the following line:

```
<xsl:value-of select="//*/name()" separator="&#xA;"/>
```

with this more complicated markup:

```
<xsl:for-each select="//*">
  <xsl:value-of select="name()"/>
  <xsl:if test="position() != last()">
    <xsl:text>&#xA;</xsl:text>
  </xsl:if>
</xsl:for-each>
```

<xsl:variable>

Defines a variable. If `<xsl:variable>` occurs as a top-level element, it is a global variable that is accessible throughout the stylesheet. Otherwise, the variable is local and exists only in the element that contains the `<xsl:variable>`. The value of the variable can be defined in one of two ways: specified in the **select** attribute or defined in an XSLT template inside the `<xsl:variable>` element itself. If neither method is used, the value of the variable is an empty string.

Category

Either a top-level element or an instruction.

Required Attribute

name
> An attribute that names this variable.

Optional Attributes

select
> An XPath expression that defines the value of this variable.

[2.0 – Schema] as
> The datatype of the variable. For example, `<xsl:variable name="age" as="xs:integer" select="11"/>` defines a new variable of type `xs:integer`. It is an error if the supplied value can't be converted to the specified type; using the attribute `select="'really, really old'"` here would cause an error. If you're using a schema-aware XSLT processor, you can use your own datatypes.

Content

The `<xsl:variable>` element can be empty or it can contain an XSLT template. It is a fatal error if it contains both content and a `select` attribute.

Appears in

`<xsl:stylesheet>` as a top-level element or in a template.

Defined in

[1.0] XSLT section 11, "Variables and Parameters."

[2.0] XSLT section 9, "Variables and Parameters."

Example

Here is a stylesheet that defines a number of variables:

```
<?xml version="1.0"?>
<!-- variable.xsl -->
<xsl:stylesheet version="1.0"
  xmlns:xsl="http://www.w3.org/1999/XSL/Transform">

  <xsl:output method="text"/>

  <xsl:variable name="favoriteNumber" select="23"/>
  <xsl:variable name="favoriteColor" select="'blue'"/>
  <xsl:variable name="complicatedVariable">
    <xsl:choose>
      <xsl:when test="count(//listitem) > 10">
        <xsl:text>really long list</xsl:text>
      </xsl:when>
      <xsl:when test="count(//listitem) > 5">
        <xsl:text>moderately long list</xsl:text>
      </xsl:when>
      <xsl:otherwise>
        <xsl:text>fairly short list</xsl:text>
      </xsl:otherwise>
    </xsl:choose>
  </xsl:variable>

  <xsl:template match="/">
    <xsl:text>Hello!  Your favorite number is </xsl:text>
    <xsl:value-of select="$favoriteNumber"/>
    <xsl:text>.&#xA;Your favorite color is </xsl:text>
    <xsl:value-of select="$favoriteColor"/>
    <xsl:text>.&#xA;&#xA;Here is a </xsl:text>
    <xsl:value-of select="$complicatedVariable"/>
    <xsl:text>:&#xA;</xsl:text>
    <xsl:variable name="listitems" select="list/listitem"/>
    <xsl:call-template name="processListItems">
      <xsl:with-param name="items" select="$listitems"/>
    </xsl:call-template>
  </xsl:template>
```

```
<xsl:template name="processListItems">
  <xsl:param name="items"/>
  <xsl:variable name="favoriteColor">
    <xsl:text>chartreuse</xsl:text>
  </xsl:variable>

  <xsl:text>    (Your favorite color is now </xsl:text>
  <xsl:value-of select="$favoriteColor"/>
  <xsl:text>.)&#xA;</xsl:text>
  <xsl:for-each select="$items">
    <xsl:value-of select="position()"/>
    <xsl:text>.  </xsl:text>
    <xsl:value-of select="."/>
    <xsl:text>&#xA;</xsl:text>
  </xsl:for-each>
</xsl:template>

</xsl:stylesheet>
```

We'll use our stylesheet to transform the following document:

```
<?xml version="1.0"?>
<!-- albums.xml -->
<list xml:lang="en">
  <title>Albums I've bought recently:</title>
  <listitem>The Sacred Art of Dub</listitem>
  <listitem>Only the Poor Man Feel It</listitem>
  <listitem>Excitable Boy</listitem>
  <listitem xml:lang="sw">Aki Special</listitem>
  <listitem xml:lang="en-gb">Combat Rock</listitem>
  <listitem xml:lang="zu">Talking Timbuktu</listitem>
  <listitem xml:lang="jz">The Birth of the Cool</listitem>
</list>
```

Here are the results of our transformation:

```
Hello!  Your favorite number is 23.
Your favorite color is blue.

Here is a moderately long list:
    (Your favorite color is now chartreuse.)
1.  The Sacred Art of Dub
2.  Only the Poor Man Feel It
3.  Excitable Boy
4.  Aki Special
5.  Combat Rock
6.  Talking Timbuktu
7.  The Birth of the Cool
```

In XSLT 1.0, having two variables at the same level with the same name is an error. It's also an error to define an <xsl:variable> and an <xsl:param> with the same name at the same level. Neither of these conditions is an error in XSLT 2.0.

Several things are worth mentioning in our stylesheet. First, notice that when we defined values for the first two variables (favoriteNumber and favoriteColor), we had to quote the string blue, but didn't have to quote 23. If we don't quote blue, the XSLT processor assumes we mean the node-set (or sequence) of all the <blue> elements in the context node. That's obviously not what we want.

 Be aware that single quotes around numeric values are significant. The value 35 represents a numeric value (it's a number in XSLT 1.0 and an xs:integer in XSLT 2.0), while the value '35' represents the *string* 35. That might seem like a minor distinction, but it has a major impact on how your stylesheet works, especially in XSLT 2.0.

Also notice that we have two variables named favoriteColor. One is a global variable because its parent is the <xsl:stylesheet> element; the other is a local variable because it is defined in a <xsl:template>. When we access favoriteColor in the match="/" template, it has one value; when we access it inside the name="processListItems" template, it has another.

Using an <xsl:choose> element to initialize an <xsl:variable> is a common technique. This technique is the equivalent of this procedural programming construct:

```
String complicatedVariable;

if (count(listitems) > 10)
  complicatedVariable = "really long list";
else if (count(listitems)) > 5)
  complicatedVariable = "moderately long list";
else
  complicatedVariable = "fairly short list";
```

Notice that a variable can be any of the XPath or XSLT variable types, including a *[1.0]* node-set or *[2.0]* sequence. When we call the processListItems template, the parameter we pass to it is a variable containing the node-set of all the <listitem> elements in our document. Inside the processListItems template, our variable (which is now technically a parameter) can be used inside an <xsl:for-each> element.

[2.0] For a final example, we'll use the as attribute to show how datatyping works. Here is a simple stylesheet:

```
<?xml version="1.0"?>
<!-- variable2.xsl -->
<xsl:stylesheet version="2.0"
  xmlns:xsl="http://www.w3.org/1999/XSL/Transform"
  xmlns:xs="http://www.w3.org/2001/XMLSchema">

<xsl:output method="text"/>

<xsl:variable name="numberOne" as="xs:integer" select="23"/>
<xsl:variable name="numberTwo" as="xs:double" select="2.718281828459"/>
<xsl:variable name="numberThree" as="xs:float" select="$numberTwo"/>
<xsl:variable name="numberFour" as="xs:integer"
  select="xs:integer($numberTwo)"/>
<xsl:variable name="dateValue" as="xs:date" select="xs:date('1995-04-21')"/>
<xsl:variable name="whatever" as="xs:integer" select="xs:integer(42)"/>
```

```
<xsl:template match="/">
  <xsl:call-template name="bob">
    <xsl:with-param name="whatever" select="xs:integer(8)"/>
  </xsl:call-template>
  <xsl:text>&#xA;whatever&#x9;</xsl:text>
  <xsl:value-of select="$whatever"/>
  <xsl:text>&#xA;</xsl:text>
</xsl:template>

<xsl:template name="bob">
  <xsl:param name="whatever" as="xs:integer"/>
  <xsl:variable name="whatever" as="xs:integer" select="xs:integer(4)"/>
  <xsl:variable name="whatever" as="xs:integer" select="xs:integer(98)"/>
  <xsl:text>Hello!  The values of your variables are:&#xA;</xsl:text>
  <xsl:text>&#xA;numberOne&#x9;</xsl:text>
  <xsl:value-of select="$numberOne"/>
  <xsl:text>&#xA;numberTwo&#x9;</xsl:text>
  <xsl:value-of select="$numberTwo"/>
  <xsl:text>&#xA;numberThree&#x9;</xsl:text>
  <xsl:value-of select="$numberThree"/>
  <xsl:text>&#xA;numberFour&#x9;</xsl:text>
  <xsl:value-of select="$numberFour"/>
  <xsl:text>&#xA;dateValue&#x9;</xsl:text>
  <xsl:value-of select="$dateValue"/>
  <xsl:text>&#xA;whatever&#x9;</xsl:text>
  <xsl:value-of select="$whatever"/>
  <xsl:text>&#xA;</xsl:text>
</xsl:template>

</xsl:stylesheet>
```

When we run this stylesheet, here are the results:

```
Hello!  The values of your variables are:

numberOne      23
numberTwo      2.718281828459
numberThree    2.7182817
numberFour     2
dateValue      1995-04-21
whatever       98

whatever       42
```

Notice that we had to use the xs:date constructor to create a valid date, and that we lost several digits of accuracy when we copied the double value of numberTwo to the float value of numberThree. We also had to use the xs:integer constructor to cast the double value of numberTwo to the integer required by numberFour.

The <xsl:variable> elements here are all initialized with literal values, so if you change them to something that's not valid (assigning 'blue' to the xs:integer value $numberOne, for example), the stylesheet won't run at all. If the values of the variables are set while the stylesheet is running, you'll get a fatal error if your stylesheet tries to set a variable with the wrong kind of data.

The variable $whatever is used several times in this stylesheet. Because variables and parameters can shadow each other in XSLT 2.0, the value of $whatever is the last value defined in the current context. Within the named template, the value of $whatever is 98, the last value assigned to that name. The fact that $whatever was previously assigned the values 4 (as a local variable), 8 (as a parameter), and 42 (as a global variable) doesn't matter. When the stylesheet returns to the calling template, the value of $whatever is now 42. The parameter passed to our named template and the local variables inside the named template are no longer in scope.

 A complication of variables in XSLT 2.0: if you create a variable containing nodes and specify the datatype with the **as** attribute, the variable works as you would expect. However, if you don't use the **as** attribute, the variable is a new document node whose children are the nodes in the variable. Section 9.4 of the XSLT 2.0 spec discusses this in more detail. In general, it's best to use the **as** attribute.

<xsl:when>

Defines one branch of an `<xsl:choose>` element; `<xsl:choose>` is equivalent to an if-then-else statement.

Category

Subinstruction (`<xsl:when>` always appears as a child of an `<xsl:choose>` element).

Required Attribute

test

    Contains a boolean expression that is evaluated. If the expression evaluates to `true`, the contents of the `<xsl:when>` element are processed; otherwise, the contents of `<xsl:when>` are ignored. When evaluating an `<xsl:choose>` element, the XSLT processor examines each `<xsl:when>` until it finds one whose `test` attribute evaluates to `true`. That `<xsl:when>` element is processed and all subsequent `<xsl:when>` elements are ignored. Within an `<xsl:choose>` element, at most one `<xsl:when>` element will be processed.

Optional Attributes

None.

Content

An XSLT template.

Appears in

The `<xsl:choose>` element only.

Defined in

[1.0] XSLT section 9.2, "Conditional Processing with xsl:choose."

[2.0] XSLT section 8.2, "Conditional Processing with xsl:choose."

Example

Here's an example that uses `<xsl:choose>` to select the background color for the rows of an HTML table. We cycle among four different values, using `<xsl:when>` to determine the value of the style attribute in the generated HTML document. Here's the XML document we'll use:

```
<?xml version="1.0"?>
<!-- albums.xml -->
<list xml:lang="en">
  <title>Albums I've bought recently:</title>
  <listitem>The Sacred Art of Dub</listitem>
  <listitem>Only the Poor Man Feel It</listitem>
  <listitem>Excitable Boy</listitem>
  <listitem xml:lang="sw">Aki Special</listitem>
  <listitem xml:lang="en_GB">Combat Rock</listitem>
  <listitem xml:lang="zu">Talking Timbuktu</listitem>
  <listitem xml:lang="jz">The Birth of the Cool</listitem>
</list>
```

And here's our stylesheet:

```
<?xml version="1.0"?>
<!-- when.xsl -->
<xsl:stylesheet version="1.0"
  xmlns:xsl="http://www.w3.org/1999/XSL/Transform">

  <xsl:output method="html"/>

  <xsl:template match="/">
    <html>
      <head>
        <title>
          <xsl:value-of select="list/title"/>
        </title>
      </head>
      <body style="font-family: sans-serif; color: white;">
        <h1 style="color: black;">
          <xsl:value-of select="list/title"/>
        </h1>
        <table border="1" cellpadding="5"
          style="font-weight: bold;">
          <xsl:for-each select="list/listitem">
            <tr>
              <td>
                <xsl:attribute name="style">
                  <xsl:choose>
                    <xsl:when test="position() mod 4 = 0">
                      <xsl:text>background: yellow; color: black;</xsl:text>
                    </xsl:when>
                    <xsl:when test="position() mod 4 = 1">
                      <xsl:text>background: blue;</xsl:text>
```

```
        </xsl:when>
        <xsl:when test="position() mod 4 = 2">
          <xsl:text>background: white; color: black;</xsl:text>
        </xsl:when>
        <xsl:otherwise>
          <xsl:text>background: black;</xsl:text>
        </xsl:otherwise>
      </xsl:choose>
    </xsl:attribute>
    <xsl:value-of select="."/>
  </td>
</tr>
      </xsl:for-each>
    </table>
  </body>
</html>
</xsl:template>

</xsl:stylesheet>
```

Here's the generated HTML document, which cycles through the various background colors:

```
<html>
  <head>
    <META http-equiv="Content-Type" content="text/html; charset=UTF-8">
    <title>Albums I've bought recently:</title>
  </head>
  <body style="font-family: sans-serif; color: white;">
    <h1 style="color: black;">Albums I've bought recently:</h1>
    <table border="1" cellpadding="5" style="font-weight: bold;">
      <tr>
        <td style="background: blue;">The Sacred Art of Dub</td>
      </tr>
      <tr>
        <td style="background: white; color: black;">Only the Poor Man Feel It</td>
      </tr>
      <tr>
        <td style="background: black;">Excitable Boy</td>
      </tr>
      <tr>
        <td style="background: yellow; color: black;">Aki Special</td>
      </tr>
      ...
    </table>
  </body>
</html>
```

The table cells with styles of "background: yellow; color: black;", "background: blue;", and "background: white; color: black;" are generated by <xsl:when> elements, while "background: black;" is generated by the <xsl:otherwise> element.

When rendered, our HTML document looks like Figure A-17.

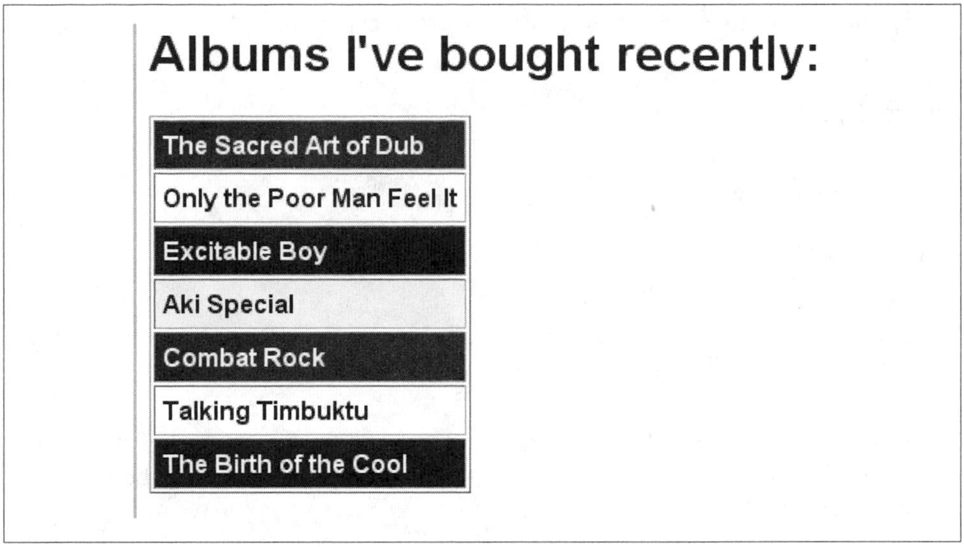

Figure A-17. Generating different background colors with <xsl:when>

<xsl:with-param>

Defines a parameter to be passed to a template. When the template is invoked, values can be passed in for the parameter.

Category

Subinstruction; `<xsl:with-param>` always appears inside the `<xsl:apply-templates>` or `<xsl:call-template>` element.

[2.0] In XSLT 2.0, it can also appear inside the new `<xsl:apply-imports>` and `<xsl:next-match>` elements.

Description

`<xsl:with-param>` defines a parameter to be passed to a template. When a template is invoked, values can be passed in for its parameters. The value of a parameter can be defined in one of three ways:

- If the `<xsl:with-param>` element is empty and does not contain a select attribute, then no value is passed to the template.
- If the `<xsl:with-param>` element is empty and has a select attribute, the value of the parameter is the value of the select attribute.
- If the `<xsl:with-param>` element is not empty, the value of the parameter is the result of processing its contents.

If no value is passed to the template (`<xsl:with-param name="x"/>`), then the default value of the parameter, if any, is used instead. The default value of the parameter is defined on the `<xsl:param>` element inside the `<xsl:template>` itself; see the description of the `<xsl:param>` element for more details.

Required Attribute

name
> Names this parameter.

Optional Attributes

select
> An XPath expression that defines the value of this parameter. It is a fatal error if `<xsl:with-param>` has a `select` attribute and contains content.

[2.0 – Schema] as
> Defines the datatype of this parameter. The datatype can be any of the built-in datatypes, or, if you have a schema-aware XSLT 2.0 processor, it can be a datatype defined in a schema.

[2.0] tunnel
> Defines whether this is a tunnel parameter. Valid values are yes and no, with no being the default.

Content

The `<xsl:with-param>` element can be empty or it can contain an XSLT template. It is a fatal error if `<xsl:with-param>` contains content and has a `select` attribute.

Appears in

`<xsl:apply-templates>`, `<xsl:call-template>`, *[2.0]* `<xsl:apply-imports>`, and *[2.0]* `<xsl:next-match>`.

Defined in

[1.0] XSLT section 11.6, "Passing Parameters to Templates."

[2.0] XSLT section 10.1.1, "Passing Parameters to Templates."

Example

Here is a stylesheet with a number of parameters. Notice that some parameters are global and defined outside the stylesheet:

```
<?xml version="1.0"?>
<!-- with-param.xsl -->
<xsl:stylesheet version="1.0"
  xmlns:xsl="http://www.w3.org/1999/XSL/Transform">

  <xsl:output method="text"/>

  <xsl:param name="favoriteNumber" select="23"/>
  <xsl:param name="favoriteColor"/>
```

```
<xsl:template match="/">
  <xsl:text>&#xA;</xsl:text>
  <xsl:value-of select="list/title"/>
  <xsl:text>&#xA;</xsl:text>
  <xsl:variable name="listitems" select="list/listitem"/>
  <xsl:call-template name="processListItems">
    <xsl:with-param name="items" select="$listitems"/>
    <xsl:with-param name="color" select="'yellow'"/>
    <xsl:with-param name="number" select="$favoriteNumber"/>
  </xsl:call-template>
</xsl:template>

<xsl:template name="processListItems">
  <xsl:param name="items"/>
  <xsl:param name="color" select="'blue'"/>

  <xsl:for-each select="$items">
    <xsl:value-of select="position()"/>
    <xsl:text>.  </xsl:text>
    <xsl:value-of select="."/>
    <xsl:text>&#xA;</xsl:text>
  </xsl:for-each>

  <xsl:text>&#xA;</xsl:text>

  <xsl:text>Your favorite color is </xsl:text>
  <xsl:value-of select="$favoriteColor"/>
  <xsl:text>.</xsl:text>
  <xsl:text>&#xA;</xsl:text>
  <xsl:text>The color passed to this template is </xsl:text>
  <xsl:value-of select="$color"/>
  <xsl:text>.</xsl:text>
  <xsl:text>&#xA;</xsl:text>
</xsl:template>

</xsl:stylesheet>
```

We'll use this stylesheet to transform this document:

```
<?xml version="1.0"?>
<!-- albums.xml -->
<list xml:lang="en">
  <title>Albums I've bought recently:</title>
  <listitem>The Sacred Art of Dub</listitem>
  <listitem>Only the Poor Man Feel It</listitem>
  <listitem>Excitable Boy</listitem>
  <listitem xml:lang="sw">Aki Special</listitem>
  <listitem xml:lang="en-gb">Combat Rock</listitem>
  <listitem xml:lang="zu">Talking Timbuktu</listitem>
  <listitem xml:lang="jz">The Birth of the Cool</listitem>
</list>
```

Our stylesheet contains two global parameters (favoriteNumber and favoriteColor), and it defines a default value for favoriteNumber. The stylesheet also passes a parameter from the match="/" template to the name="processListItems" template; that parameter contains a node-set. Here are the results of the transformation:

```
Albums I've bought recently:
1.   The Sacred Art of Dub
2.   Only the Poor Man Feel It
3.   Excitable Boy
4.   Aki Special
5.   Combat Rock
6.   Talking Timbuktu
7.   The Birth of the Cool

Your favorite color is orange.
The color passed to this template is yellow.
```

Notice that when we call the template `processListItems`, we pass in three parameters, only two of which are defined inside the template. In XSLT 1.0, the undefined parameters are simply ignored; in XSLT 2.0, this is a fatal error. If we change the stylesheet to `<xsl:stylesheet version="2.0" ...>`, the stylesheet won't run at all. Also notice that the parameter `$items` is a node-set, so we can use the parameter in an `<xsl:for-each>` element.

To generate these results with Saxon, we use this command:

```
java net.sf.saxon.Transform albums.xml with-param.xsl favoriteColor=orange
```

To generate these results with Xalan, we use this command:

```
java org.apache.xalan.xslt.Process -in albums.xml -xsl with-param.xsl
    -param favoriteColor orange
```

(The command should be entered on a single line.) See "Global Parameters" in Chapter 5 for a complete discussion of global parameters and how you define them for various XSLT processors.

[2.0 – Schema] We'll wrap up with an example of `<xsl:with-param>` that uses schema support. We'll use a parameter whose datatype must be `zipcode`. Here's the XML Schema that defines the datatype:

```
<?xml version="1.0" encoding="UTF-8"?>
<!-- zip.xsd -->
<xsd:schema
  xmlns="http://www.oreilly.com/xslt/zip"
  targetNamespace="http://www.oreilly.com/xslt/zip"
  xmlns:xsd="http://www.w3.org/2001/XMLSchema">

  <xsd:simpleType name="zipcode">
    <xsd:restriction base="xsd:string">
      <xsd:pattern value="[0-9]{5}(-[0-9]{4})?"/>
    </xsd:restriction>
  </xsd:simpleType>
</xsd:schema>
```

Here's the stylesheet that looks for a valid `zipcode`:

```
<?xml version="1.0"?>
<!-- with-param2.xsl -->
<xsl:stylesheet version="2.0"
  xmlns:xsl="http://www.w3.org/1999/XSL/Transform"
  xmlns:zip="http://www.oreilly.com/xslt/zip"
  xmlns="http://www.oreilly.com/xslt/zip"
```

```
      xmlns:po="http://www.oreilly.com/xslt">

  <xsl:import-schema namespace="http://www.oreilly.com/xslt/zip"
    schema-location="zip.xsd" />

  <xsl:import-schema namespace="http://www.oreilly.com/xslt"
    schema-location="po.xsd" />

  <xsl:output method="text"/>

  <xsl:template match="/">
    <xsl:choose>
      <xsl:when
        test="/po:purchase-order/po:customer/po:address/po:zip
              castable as zip:zipcode">
        <xsl:call-template name="postalCode">
          <xsl:with-param name="zip" as="zip:zipcode"
            select="/po:purchase-order/po:customer/po:address/po:zip"/>
        </xsl:call-template>
      </xsl:when>
      <xsl:otherwise>
        <xsl:text>The &lt;zip&gt; element isn't valid!&#xA;</xsl:text>
      </xsl:otherwise>
    </xsl:choose>
  </xsl:template>

  <xsl:template name="postalCode">
    <xsl:param name="zip" as="zip:zipcode"/>
    <xsl:text>The value </xsl:text>
    <xsl:value-of select="$zip"/>
    <xsl:text> is a valid Zip code!&#xA;</xsl:text>
  </xsl:template>

</xsl:stylesheet>
```

When we use this template against a valid `<po:purchase-order>` whose `<zip>` element can be cast as a `zip:zipcode` value, we use `<xsl:with-param>` to pass a parameter of type `zip:zipcode`. We'll use this purchase order again:

```
<?xml version="1.0"?>
<!-- good-po.xml -->
<purchase-order id="38292"   xmlns="http://www.oreilly.com/xslt">
  <date year="2001" month="6" day="19"/>
  <customer id="4738" level="Platinum">
    <address type="business">
      ...
      <zip>48392</zip>
    </address>
  </customer>
  <items>
  ...
  </items>
</purchase-order>
```

The less-than-exciting results look like this:

```
The value 48392 is a valid Zip code!
```

Notice that we imported two schemas, one for the `zip:zipcode` datatype and one for the `<po:purchase-order>` element, although these could have been in the same file. If the elements in the purchase order are in a namespace, we would have to use the `po:` prefix on all the elements in the purchase order or else use `xpath-default-namespace`. Our stylesheet uses the XPath `castable as` operator to verify that the value of the `<po:zip>` element can be cast as a `zip:zipcode` value. That means we use the `<xsl:with-param>` and `<xsl:param>` elements only if the data is valid. If it is, we create the parameter, knowing that the `as` attributes will be satisfied.

One final point: the `as` attribute can only contain sequence types. Specifically, the `as` attribute can't refer to complex types declared in an XML Schema. We could rewrite our purchase order schema to have a `purchase-order` complex type. To use it on the `as` attribute, we would have to code `as="element(*, po:purchase-order)"`.

XPath Reference

This appendix contains reference information from the XPath specification, including node types, axes, operators, and datatypes.

XPath Node Types

There are seven types of nodes in XPath. (They're called *node kinds* in XPath 2.0.) We'll stick to the reference material here; for more information on the different node types, see our earlier discussion of "The XPath Data Model" in Chapter 3.

The Root Node

The root node is the root of the tree. Unlike all other nodes, it does not have a parent. Its children are the root element for the document, as are any comments or processing instructions that appear outside the document element. The root node does not have an expanded name. It is known as the *document node* in XPath 2.0.

Element Nodes

Each element in the original XML document is represented by an element node. The expanded name of the element is its local name, combined with any namespace that is in effect for the element. You can access the different parts of the element name with the `name( )`, `local-name( )`, and `namespace-uri( )` functions. Here is an element from an XML document:

```
<xyz:report xmlns:xyz="http://www.xyz.com/">
```

The values of the three functions for this element node are:

```
name( )
    xyz:report
local-name( )
    report
```

```
namespace-uri( )
    http://www.xyz.com/
```

Attribute Nodes

Attributes of elements in the XML document become XPath attribute nodes. An attribute has an expanded name, just as an element node has. The attribute nodes of a given element node are the attributes explicitly coded on the XML element and any attributes defined with default values in the DTD.

Taking a different approach from the Document Object Model, an element node is the parent of its attributes, although the attributes are not the children of the element. In other words, selecting all the children of an element node does not select any attribute nodes that the element node might have.

Text Nodes

Text nodes simply contain text from an element. If the original text in the XML document contained character or entity references, they are resolved before the XPath text node is created. Similarly, any existing CDATA sections appear as text nodes. You have no way of knowing if a given portion of a text node was originally a character or entity reference or a CDATA section.

Comment Nodes

A comment node is also very simple; it contains some text. Every comment in the source document (except for any comments in the DTD) becomes a comment node. The text of the comment node (returned with `<xsl:value-of select=".">`) contains everything inside the comment except the opening `<!--` and the closing `-->`.

Processing-Instruction Nodes

A processing-instruction node has two parts: a name (returned by the `name( )` function) and a string value. The string value is everything after the name, including the whitespace, but not including the `?>` that closes the processing instruction.

Namespace Nodes

Namespace nodes are almost never used in XSLT stylesheets; they exist primarily for the XSLT processor's benefit. One thing to keep in mind is that the declaration of a namespace (such as `xmlns:auth="http://www.authors.net"`), even though it looks like an attribute in the XML source, becomes a namespace node and not an attribute node. Namespace nodes exist for both the namespace prefixes that are defined and any default namespaces.

XPath Node Tests

XPath defines several node tests that can be used to select nodes from the source tree. These node tests allow you to select nodes that can't be selected any other way. (Although they look and work like functions, they are technically node tests.) The node tests are described here:

text( )
> Selects all the text-node children of the context node.

comment( )
> Selects all the comment-node children of the context node.

processing-instruction( )
> Selects all the processing-instruction children of the context node. Unlike the other node tests defined here, processing-instruction( ) can have an optional argument; processing-instruction('xml-stylesheet') selects all processing instructions with a name of xml-stylesheet.

node( )
> Returns all nodes, regardless of type. Using this node test selects all element nodes, attribute nodes, processing-instruction nodes, etc. (Be aware that using node( ) on the child axis does *not* return any attribute nodes, because attributes are not considered child nodes.)

[2.0] attribute( )
> Returns any attribute. When used with an attribute name (attribute(public-domain)), it returns all attributes with the specified name. When used with an attribute name and a datatype (attribute(public-domain, xs:boolean)), it returns all attributes with that specified name and datatype. Finally, when used with a wildcard for the attribute name (attribute(*, xs:boolean)), it returns all attributes with the specified datatype.

[2.0] element( )
> Returns any element. When used with an element name (element(author)), it returns all elements with the specified name. When used with an element name and a datatype (element(year-of-birth, xs:gYear)), it returns all elements with that specified name and datatype. Finally, when used with a wildcard for the element name (element(*, xs:gYear)), it returns all elements with the specified datatype.

[2.0] schema-element(name)
> Given the name of an element globally declared in an XML Schema, returns the elements with the same name and the same datatype as the schema-defined element. It also returns all the elements in the specified element's substitution group. Appendix D discusses "Substitution Groups" in more detail.

[2.0] document-node( )
> Matches document nodes. The node test can include a name; the test document-node(element(sonnet)) returns a document node whose root element is <sonnet>.

 *[2.0]* Although `item( )` looks like a node test, it is only used as a datatype. For example, the variable `<xsl:variable name="something" as="item( )">` defines a variable that can contain a single value. The variable can contain any node or atomic type.

XPath Axes

The XPath specification defines 13 different axes; each axis contains various nodes. The nodes that are in a given axis depend on the context node. All 13 axes, excerpted from our more involved discussion in "The XPath Data Model" in Chapter 3, are listed here.

`child` *axis*

> Contains the children of the context node. As we've already mentioned, the XPath expressions `child::lines/child::line` and `lines/line` are equivalent. If an XPath expression (such as `sonnet`) doesn't have an axis specifier, the `child` axis is used by default.

`parent` *axis*

> Contains the parent of the context node, if there is one. (If the context node is the root node, the `parent` axis returns an empty node-set.) As a step in an XPath expression, the `parent` axis can be abbreviated with the double period (`..`); this moves up to the current node's parent. If the `<first-name>` and `<last-name>` elements are both children of the `<author>` element, and the context node is the `<first-name>` element, the expressions `../last-name`, `parent::author/last-name` and `parent::*/last-name` are equivalent. If the context node does not have a parent, this axis returns an empty node-set.

`self` *axis*

> Contains the context node itself. As a step in an XPath expression, the `self` axis can be abbreviated with a single period (`.`). The expressions `.`, `self::node( )`, and `self::*` are equivalent in XSLT 1.0.
>
> *[2.0]* In XSLT 2.0, the `self` axis selects the context *item*, which might not be a node. If the context item is an atomic value, the expressions `self::node( )` and `self::*` cause the XSLT processor to raise an error. In this case, the only way to access the `self` axis is with a period. If the context item is a node, the `self` axis works just as it did in XSLT 1.0.

`attribute` *axis*

> Contains the attributes of the context node. If the context node is not an element node, this axis is empty. The `attribute` axis can be abbreviated with the at sign (`@`). The expressions `attribute::type` and `@type` are equivalent.

ancestor *axis*

> Contains the parent of the context node, the parent's parent, and so on. The ancestor axis always contains the root node, unless the context node is the root node.

ancestor-or-self *axis*

> Contains the context node, its parent, its parent's parent, and so on. This axis always includes the root node.

descendant *axis*

> Contains all children of the context node, all children of all the children of the context node, and so on. Be aware that the descendant axis does not include any attribute or namespace nodes. (As we discussed earlier, an attribute node has an element node as its parent, even though the attribute node is not considered a child of its parent.)

descendant-or-self *axis*

> Contains the context node and all children of the context node, all children of all the children of the context node, and so on.

preceding-sibling *axis*

> Contains all of the preceding siblings of the context node—in other words, all nodes that have the same parent as the context node and appear before the context node in the XML document. If the context node is an attribute node or a namespace node, the preceding-sibling axis is empty.

following-sibling *axis*

> Contains all of the following siblings of the context node—in other words, all nodes that have the same parent as the context node and appear after the context node in the XML document. If the context node is an attribute node or a namespace node, the following-sibling axis is empty.

preceding *axis*

> Contains all nodes that appear before the context node in the document, except any ancestors, attribute nodes, and namespace nodes.

following *axis*

> Contains all nodes that appear after the context node in the document, except any descendants, attribute nodes, and namespace nodes.

namespace *axis*

> Contains the namespace nodes of the context node. If the context node is not an element node, this axis is empty.

> *[2.0]* The namespace axis is deprecated in XPath 2.0.

The five axes ancestor, descendant, following, preceding, and self partition everything in the XML document (with the exception of any attribute or namespace nodes). Any node in the XPath tree appears in one of these five axes, and the five axes do not overlap.

The XPath Context

The context in an XPath expression consists of several things:

Context node

> The node currently being evaluated. *[2.0]* If the context item is a node, the context node is the same as the context item. If the context item is an atomic value, the context node is undefined.

[2.0] Context item

> The item currently being evaluated. This is the equivalent of the context node in XPath 1.0; the name reflects the fact that the context can be focused on an atomic value instead of a node.

Context position

> A nonzero positive integer that indicates the position of the context node within the set of context nodes. The XPath function `position( )` returns the context position.

Context size

> A nonzero positive integer that indicates the number of nodes in the current context. The XPath function `last( )` returns the context size.

Variable bindings

> A set of variables that are in scope for the current context. Each one is represented by a variable name and an object that represents its value.

Functions

> A set of functions visible to the current context. Each function is represented by a mapping between a function name and the actual code to be invoked. Each function takes zero or more arguments and returns a single result. XPath defines a number of core functions that are always available; XSLT defines additional functions that go beyond those defined in the XPath specification. Any extension functions defined in the stylesheet are visible as well.

Namespace declarations

> The set of namespace declarations visible to the current context. Each one consists of a namespace prefix and the URI with which it is associated.

[2.0] Default namespace

> The default namespace is defined by the `xpath-default-namespace` attribute. If no such attribute exists on any elements that enclose the context item, the default namespace is null, regardless of any default namespace declarations (`xmlns="..."`) in the stylesheet.

[2.0] Documents and collections

> The XPath 2.0 context also includes information about available documents, available collections, and the default collection. The functions `doc( )`, `doc-available( )`, and `collection( )` functions work with documents and collec-

tions of nodes. See the discussions of the [2.0] `doc( )` function, the [2.0] `doc-available( )` function, and the [2.0] `collection( )` function for more details.

[2.0] Miscellaneous information

Given the added complexity of XPath 2.0 and XSLT 2.0, there are a number of other things stored in the context. Many of them apply only in certain situations (the current group is meaningful only when we're grouping data, for example), so they're listed briefly here:

- The current template rule.

- The current template mode.

- The current group and current grouping key.

- The current captured substrings (used within `<xsl:analyze-string>`).

- The output state, which indicates whether output is being written to a result tree or a data structure. For example, within an `<xsl:variable>` element, the output state is to a data structure.

- The implicit timezone.

- The set of named keys, used by the `key( )` function.

- The set of named decimal formats, used by the `format-number( )` function.

- The values of all the system properties, used by the `system-property( )` function.

- The set of available elements, used by the `element-available( )` function.

- The set of all known collations.

- The default collation.

- The base URI of the containing element. This is returned by the XPath `base-uri( )` function.

- The set of in-scope schema definitions.

XPath 1.0 Datatypes

XPath 1.0 and XSLT 1.0 define five datatypes, described in the list that follows. The `result tree fragment` type is defined by XSLT 1.0 and is specific to transformations; the other four are defined by XPath and are generic to any technology that uses XPath. The four XPath datatypes are tersely defined in section 1 of the XPath specification; section 11.1 of the XSLT specification defines result tree fragments.

`node-set`

A set of nodes. The set can be empty or it can contain any number of nodes.

[2.0] In XSLT 2.0, the `node-set` has been replaced by the sequence.

boolean

The value `true` or `false`. Be aware that the strings `true` and `false` have no special meaning or value in XPath. If you need to use the boolean values themselves, use the functions `true( )` and `false( )`.

number

A floating-point number. All numbers in XPath and XSLT 1.0 are implemented as floating-point numbers; the `integer` or `int` datatype does not exist in XPath and XSLT 1.0. To be specific, all numbers are implemented as IEEE 754 floating-point numbers, the same standard used by the Java `float` and `double` primitive types. In addition to ordinary numbers, there are five special values for numbers: positive and negative infinity, positive and negative zero, and `NaN`, the special symbol for anything that is not a number.

string

Zero or more characters, as defined in the XML specification.

result tree fragment

A temporary tree. You can create one with an `<xsl:variable>` element that uses content (instead of the `select` attribute) to initialize its value. A result tree fragment can be copied to the result tree with the `<xsl:copy-of>` element. It may also be converted to a string with the `<xsl:value-of>` element.

[2.0] In XSLT 2.0, the `result tree fragment` datatype no longer exists. There is no difference between a tree constructed from an input document and a tree constructed using a variable.

[2.0] XPath 2.0 Datatypes

XML Schema defines 19 primitive datatypes, and five others (`xs:anyAtomicType`, `xs:untyped`, `xs:untypedAtomic`, `xs:dayTimeDuration`, and `xs:yearMonthDuration`) were added to the XML Schema namespace by the XQuery 1.0 and XPath 2.0 Data Model spec. We'll review those briefly here.

XPath 1.0 used the `node-set` datatype as its basic data structure; XPath 2.0 uses sequences. Like a `node-set`, a *sequence* can contain the node types we covered earlier in this appendix, but it can also contain atomic values of the types listed here.

Here are the 24 datatypes:

xs:anyAtomicType

The base type for all primitive atomic types, such as `xs:integer` or `xs:string`. This datatype was added by XQuery 1.0 and XPath 2.0.

xs:anyURI

A Uniform Resource Identifier. The value can be absolute or relative, and it can also have a fragment reference identifier. The value should follow the rules for URI syntax as defined in RFC 2396 and amended in RFC 2732.

`xs:base64Binary`

> Arbitrary binary data represented using the Base64 alphabet defined in RFC 2045. Legal characters are the basic alpha characters and digits [`a-zA-Z0-9`], along with the plus sign (`+`), the forward slash (`/`), and the equals sign (`=`). An `xs:base64Binary` value can also contain any number of whitespace characters.

`xs:boolean`

> The value `true` or `false`. In XSLT and XPath, the strings `"true"` and `"false"` have no special meaning. To generate boolean values, use the functions `true()` and `false()` instead.

`xs:date`

> A date with four components: year, month, day, and an optional timezone. The format of a complete `xs:date` value is `1995-04-21-05:00`, where `1995` is the year, `04` is the month, `21` is the day, and `-05:00` is the timezone. An optional minus sign can appear before the year, indicating a date before the current era.

> Be aware that the values for month and day must be two digits long, and the value for the year must be at least four digits long. The value `1995-4-21` is illegal. The seconds can be specified to any number of decimal places.

`xs:dateTime`

> A date and time with seven components: year, month, day, hours, minutes, seconds, and an optional timezone. The format of a complete `xs:dateTime` value is `1995-04-21T00:05:32.6-05:00`, where `1995` is the year, `04` is the month, `21` is the day, `00` is the hours, `05` is the minutes, `32.6` is the seconds, and `-05:00` is the timezone. An optional minus sign can appear before the year, indicating a date and time before the current era.

> Be aware that the values for month, day, hours, minutes and seconds must be two digits long, and the value for the year must be at least four digits long. The value `1995-4-21T00:5:32.6` is illegal. The seconds can be specified to any number of decimal places.

`xs:dayTimeDuration`

> A new datatype defined by XQuery 1.0 and XPath 2.0. It is derived from `xs:duration` and can only contain the days, hours, minutes, and seconds components of an `xs:duration`. For example, `P2DT4H32M12.83S` is a duration of 2 days, 4 hours, 32 minutes, and 12.83 seconds.

`xs:decimal`

> A sequence of digits with a decimal point. An `xs:decimal` is allowed to have a leading sign (`-` or `+`). In addition, if there is no fractional portion of the number, the decimal point can be omitted. Sample `xs:decimal` values are `210`, `12678967.543233`, `-1.23`, and `+100000.00`.

`xs:double`

> A number based on the IEEE double-precision 64-bit floating-point type. Like `xs:decimal`, `xs:double` values can have a leading sign (`-` or `+`). If there is no fractional

portion of the number, the decimal point can be omitted. An `xs:double` can also have an exponent, represented by E or e, followed by the exponent. The exponent must be an integer.

There are three special values for `xs:double`: INF, -INF, and NaN. They represent positive infinity, negative infinity, and not a number. Sample `xs:double` values are -1E4, 1267.43233E12, 12.78e-2, 12, -0, 0, and INF.

xs:duration

An `xs:duration` is a six-dimensional period of time, with the six dimensions of years, months, days, hours, minutes and seconds. The string P2Y3M2DT7H52M23.8S is a duration of 2 years, 3 months, 2 days, 7 hours, 52 minutes, and 23.8 seconds. The P character is always required. The T character separates the date portion from the time portion and can be omitted if none of the time components are specified. In other words, P2Y3M is a duration of 2 years and 3 months. If any component of the duration is zero, it may be omitted, although at least one portion of the duration must be specified. For example, PT2H is a duration of 2 hours, as is P0Y0M0DT2H0M0S.

xs:float

A number based on the IEEE single-precision 32-bit floating-point type. Like `xs:decimal`, `xs:float` values can have a leading sign (- or +). If there is no fractional portion of the number, the decimal point can be omitted. `xs:float` can also have an exponent, represented by E or e, followed by the exponent. The exponent must be an integer.

There are three special values for `xs:float`: INF, -INF, and NaN. They represent positive infinity, negative infinity, and not a number. Sample `xs:float` values are -1E4, 1267.43233E12, 12.78e-2, 12, -0, 0, and INF.

xs:gDay

A specific day. It is specified as three dashes followed by the two-digit day, such as ---21. A timezone is allowed.

xs:gMonth

A specific month. It is specified as two dashes followed by the two-digit month, such as --04. A timezone is allowed.

xs:gMonthDay

A specific day in a specific month. An `xs:gMonthDay` is specified as two dashes, the two-digit month, a dash, and the two-digit day, such as --04-21. A timezone is allowed.

xs:gYear

A specific year. It is specified as number with at least four digits, such as 1995. The year can have a leading minus sign, and a timezone is allowed.

xs:gYearMonth

A specific month in a specific year. It is specified in the format 1995-04. The year value must be at least four digits and can have a leading minus sign. The month value must be two digits. A timezone is allowed.

`xs:hexBinary`

Arbitrary hex-encoded binary data. Each binary octet in the original data is represented as two hexadecimal digits (`[a-fA-F0-9]`).

`xs:NOTATION`

This rarely used datatype represents the `NOTATION` attribute type defined in the XML specification.

`xs:QName`

Consists of a namespace name (sometimes defined with a namespace prefix) and a local name.

`xs:string`

A sequence of characters.

`xs:time`

A time with four components: hours, minutes, seconds, and an optional timezone. The format of a complete `xs:time` value is `00:05:32.6-05:00`, where `00` is the hours, `05` is the minutes, `32.6` is the seconds, and `-05:00` is the timezone.

Be aware that the values for hours, minutes, and seconds must be two digits long. The seconds can be specified to any number of decimal places.

`xs:untyped`

The datatype of an element that has not been validated. If an element is validated in skip mode, that element's type is `xs:untyped` as well. This datatype was added by XQuery 1.0 and XPath 2.0.

`xs:untypedAtomic`

An untyped atomic value. Text that has not been assigned a more specific type is considered `xs:untypedAtomic`, as is any attribute validated in skip mode. Text from an input document that did not have a schema is `xs:untypedAtomic`, for example. This datatype was added by XQuery 1.0 and XPath 2.0.

`xs:yearMonthDuration`

A new datatype defined by XQuery 1.0 and XPath 2.0. It is derived from `xs:duration` and can contain only the year and month components of an `xs:duration`. For example, `P2Y3M` is a duration of two years and three months.

 Be aware that you do not have to have a schema-aware XSLT 2.0 processor to use these basic datatypes. You can use the `cast as`, `castable as`, and `instance of` operators with all of these datatypes. What you can't do without a schema-aware XSLT processor is define your own datatypes in a schema, and then use those datatypes with these operators.

Operators and Keywords

Here is the complete list of operators and keywords in XPath:

!= *(not equal)*
> Compares its two operands and returns `true` if the first operand is not equal to the second. (Complete details on how comparisons work are in the section "Boolean Operators" in Chapter 3.)

( )
> Contains a parenthesized expression. In addition to using parentheses in mathematical expressions, parentheses are required around test conditions in the `if` operator.

* *(occurrence indicator)*
> Represents zero or more of an item.

* *(multiplication)*
> Multiplies its two operands together. In XPath 1.0, the two operands must be numbers or values that can be converted to numbers.
>
> *[2.0]* In XPath 2.0, we can multiply `xs:yearMonthDuration`s and `xs:dayTimeDuration`s by numeric values. Valid combinations are:
>
> - `xs:yearMonthDuration * xs:double`
> - `xs:dayTimeDuration * xs:double`

+ *(occurrence indicator)*
> Represents zero or one of an item.

+ *(addition)*
> Adds its two operands. In XPath 1.0, the two operands must be numbers or values that can be converted to numbers.
>
> *[2.0]* In XPath 2.0, we can add dates, times, and durations in addition to numeric values. Valid combinations are:
>
> - `xs:yearMonthDuration + xs:yearMonthDuration`
> - `xs:dayTimeDuration + xs:dayTimeDuration`
> - `xs:dateTime + xs:yearMonthDuration`
> - `xs:dateTime + xs:dayTimeDuration`
> - `xs:date + xs:yearMonthDuration`
> - `xs:date + xs:dayTimeDuration`
> - `xs:time + xs:dayTimeDuration`

+ *(unary plus)*
> Returns its operand with the sign unchanged. This operator doesn't change its operand at all.

[2.0], *(sequence operator)*

The comma operator concatenates items into a sequence. For example, using `select="((1, 2, 3), (4, 5), 6)"` creates the new sequence (1, 2, 3, 4, 5, 6).

– (unary minus)

Returns the negation of its operand.

– (subtraction)

Subtracts its second operand from the first. In XPath 1.0, the two operands must be numbers or values that can be converted to numbers.

[2.0] In XPath 2.0, we can subtract dates, times, and durations in addition to numeric values. Valid combinations are:

- `xs:yearMonthDuration - xs:yearMonthDuration`
- `xs:dayTimeDuration - xs:dayTimeDuration`
- `xs:dateTime - xs:yearMonthDuration`
- `xs:dateTime - xs:dayTimeDuration`
- `xs:date - xs:yearMonthDuration`
- `xs:date - xs:dayTimeDuration`
- `xs:time - xs:dayTimeDuration`

/ (location step)

Represents a step in an location path.

// (location step)

Represents zero or more levels in a location path.

< (less than)

Compares its two operands and returns `true` if the first operand is less than the second. (Complete details on how comparisons work are in the section "Boolean Operators" in Chapter 3.)

[2.0]<< (node-before)

Compares two nodes and returns `true` if the first node appears before the second in the source document. Returns `false` otherwise, including the case in which the two nodes are the same. Because an attribute in XSLT can't contain a left bracket, this operator must be coded `&lt;&lt;`.

<= (less than or equal to)

Compares its two operands and returns `true` if the first operand is less than or equal to the second. (Complete details on how comparisons work are in the section "Boolean Operators" in Chapter 3.)

= (equal to)

Compares its two operands and returns `true` if the first operand is equal to the second. (Complete details on how comparisons work are in the section "Boolean Operators" in Chapter 3.)

> (greater than)

Compares its two operands and returns `true` if the first operand is greater than the second. (Complete details on how comparisons work are in the section "Boolean Operators" in Chapter 3.)

[2.0] >> (node-after)

Compares two nodes and returns `true` if the first node appears after the second in the source document. Returns `false` otherwise, including the case in which the two nodes are the same.

>= (greater than or equal to)

Compares its two operands and returns `true` if the first operand is greater than or equal to the second. (Complete details on how comparisons work are in the section "Boolean Operators" in Chapter 3.)

? (occurrence indicator)

Represents zero or one of an item.

[ ]

Contains a predicate in an XPath expression.

| (union)

Compares two node-sets and returns a node-set containing all of the nodes from both node-sets. *[2.0]* In XPath 2.0, the vertical bar is identical to the `union` operator.

and

Given two expressions, returns `true` if both are `true`. Returns false if either is `false`.

[2.0] cast as

Casts a value to another type. Be aware that `cast as` causes a fatal error if the value can't be cast to the new type. For example, `"'Lily' cast as xs:integer"` causes a fatal error. To check whether `cast as` will work, use the `castable as` operator first.

[2.0] castable as

Determines whether a value can be cast as another value type. The expression `"'3' castable as xs:integer"` is `true`. As you'd expect, `"'Lily' castable as xs:integer"` is `false`. Unlike the `cast as` operator, `castable as` doesn't actually cast the value. It simply lets us know whether the cast will work.

div (division)

Divides its first operand by the second. In XPath 1.0, the two operands must be numbers or values that can be converted to numbers.

[2.0] In XPath 2.0, we can divide durations:

- `xs:yearMonthDuration div xs:double`
- `xs:yearMonthDuration div xs:yearMonthDuration`
- `xs:dayTimeDuration div xs:double`
- `xs:dayTimeDuration div xs:dayTimeDuration`

[2.0] eq *(equal to)*

Compares two atomic values and returns `true` if the two values are equal. The `eq` operator can be used to compare the following *datatypes*:

- Numeric values (`xs:decimal`, `xs:double`, `xs:float`, `xs:integer`)
- String values
- Boolean values
- Durations (`xs:duration`, `xs:yearMonthDuration`, `xs:dayTimeDuration`)
- Dates and times (`xs:date`, `xs:time`, `xs:dateTime`)
- Parts of dates (`xs:gYear`, `xs:gYearMonth`, `xs:gMonth`, `xs:gMonthDay`, `xs:gDay`)
- QNames (`xs:QName`)
- Binary data (`xs:hexBinary`, `xs:base64Binary`)
- Notations (`xs:NOTATION`)

[2.0] every

Given a sequence and a test condition, returns `true` if every item in the sequence satisfies the condition. The operator is written as `every $x in $sequence satisfies [test condition for $x]`.

[2.0] except

Compares two sequences of nodes and returns a sequence containing the nodes that appear in the first sequence but not the second. All duplicate nodes are removed. The **except** operator compares the nodes themselves, not their values.

[2.0] for

This operator is an iterator across a sequence. The operator, written as `for $x in $sequence return ...`, iterates through all the values in `$sequence`. For each iteration through the sequence, the value `$x` represents the current value.

[2.0] ge *(greater than or equal to)*

Compares two atomic values and returns `true` if the first value is greater than or equal to the second. The `ge` operator can be used to compare the following datatypes:

- Numeric values (`xs:decimal`, `xs:double`, `xs:float`, `xs:integer`)
- String values
- Boolean values
- Durations (`xs:yearMonthDuration` and `xs:dayTimeDuration`, but *not* `xs:duration`)
- Dates and times (`xs:date`, `xs:time`, `xs:dateTime`)

[2.0] gt *(greater than)*

Compares two atomic values and returns `true` if the first value is greater than the second. The **gt** operator can be used to compare the following datatypes:

- Numeric values (`xs:decimal`, `xs:double`, `xs:float`, `xs:integer`)
- String values

- Boolean values
- Durations (`xs:yearMonthDuration` and `xs:dayTimeDuration`, but *not* `xs:duration`)
- Dates and times (`xs:date`, `xs:time`, `xs:dateTime`)

[2.0] `idiv` *(integer division)*

Divides its first operand by the second. Any remainder is discarded, and the integer portion is returned.

[2.0] `if`

Evaluates an expression, then performs one action or another depending on whether the expression evaluated to `true` or `false`. The expression must be (in parentheses), and there must be a `then` and an `else`.

[2.0] `instance of`

Determines whether an argument is an instance of a particular datatype. The expression `"3 instance of xs:integer"` is `true`; `"'j' instance of xs:integer"` is `false`.

[2.0] `intersect`

Compares two sequences of nodes and returns a sequence containing the nodes that appear in both sequences. All duplicate nodes are removed. The `intersect` operator compares the nodes themselves, not their values.

[2.0] `is`

Compares two nodes and returns `true` if they are *the same node*. If two different nodes have the same values, `node1 is node2` returns `false`. The `is` operator compares the nodes, not their values.

[2.0] `le` *(less than or equal to)*

Compares two atomic values and returns `true` if the first value is less than or equal to the second. The `le` operator can be used to compare the following datatypes:

- Numeric values (`xs:decimal`, `xs:double`, `xs:float`, `xs:integer`)
- String values
- Boolean values
- Durations (`xs:yearMonthDuration` and `xs:dayTimeDuration`, but *not* `xs:duration`)
- Dates and times (`xs:date`, `xs:time`, `xs:dateTime`)

[2.0] `lt` *(less than)*

Compares two atomic values and returns `true` if the first value is less than the second. The `lt` operator can be used to compare the following datatypes:

- Numeric values (`xs:decimal`, `xs:double`, `xs:float`, `xs:integer`)
- String values
- Boolean values
- Durations (`xs:yearMonthDuration` and `xs:dayTimeDuration`, but *not* `xs:duration`)
- Dates and times (`xs:date`, `xs:time`, `xs:dateTime`)

mod *(modulus)*

Divides its first operand by the second and returns the remainder.

[2.0] ne *(not equal to)*

Compares two atomic values and returns `true` if the two values are *not* equal. The ne operator can be used to compare the following datatypes:

- Numeric values (`xs:decimal`, `xs:double`, `xs:float`, `xs:integer`)
- Boolean values
- String values
- Durations (`xs:duration`, `xs:yearMonthDuration`, `xs:dayTimeDuration`)
- Dates and times (`xs:date`, `xs:time`, `xs:dateTime`)
- Parts of dates (`xs:gYear`, `xs:gYearMonth`, `xs:gMonth`, `xs:gMonthDay`, `xs:gDay`)
- QNames (`xs:QName`)
- Binary data (`xs:hexBinary`, `xs:base64Binary`)
- Notations (`xs:NOTATION`)

or

Given two expressions, returns `true` if either or both are `true`. Returns `false` if both are `false`.

[2.0] some

Given a sequence and a test condition, returns `true` if at least one item in the sequence satisfies the condition. The operator is written `some $x in $sequence sat isfies [test condition for $x]`.

[2.0] to *(range)*

Creates a sequence of integers. The expression `1 to 10` creates a sequence of 10 integers, ordered `1, 2, 3...`.

[2.0] treat as

Disables XPath 2.0's static type checking. If `$a` is of type `xs:integer*` and a function needs a parameter of type `xs:integer`, we can use the expression `$a treat as xs:integer` to get around the static type checking. At runtime, if `$a` is a sequence of one `xs:integer`, `treat as` works without any errors. On the other hand, if `$a` is anything else, including an empty sequence, a runtime error occurs.

[2.0] union

Compares two sequences of nodes and returns a sequence containing all of the nodes from both sequences. All duplicate nodes are removed. The `union` operator compares the nodes themselves, not their values.

Operator Precedence—XPath 1.0

Here is the precedence of operators in XPath 1.0, arranged from lowest to highest:

- or
- and
- =, !=, <, <=, >, >=
- + (addition), - (subtraction)
- * (multiplication), div, mod
- |
- - (unary minus), + (unary plus)
- /, //
- [ ], ( ), { }

[2.0] Operator Precedence—XQuery 1.0 and XPath 2.0

Here is the precedence of operators in XQuery 1.0 and XPath 2.0, arranged from lowest to highest:

- , (comma)
- for, some, every, if
- or
- and
- eq, ne, lt, le, gt, ge, =, !=, <, <=, >, >=, is, <<, >>
- to
- + (addition), - (subtraction)
- * (multiplication), div, idiv, mod
- union, |
- intersect, except
- instance of
- treat as
- castable as
- cast as
- - (unary minus), + (unary plus)
- ?, * (occurrence indicator), + (occurrence indicator)
- /, //
- [ ], ( ), { }

XSLT, XPath, and XQuery Function Reference

This section lists all functions defined by XSLT 1.0 and 2.0, XPath 1.0 and 2.0, and XQuery 1.0.

Kinds of Functions

Including the new functions added by XSLT 2.0 and XPath 2.0, there are now more than 100 useful functions. The following presents a categorized list of them.

Accessor Functions

XPath 2.0 provides accessor functions to expose certain properties of items, sequences, and documents:

- [2.0] `base-uri( )`
- [2.0] `data( )`
- [2.0] `document-uri( )`
- [2.0 – Schema] `nilled( )`
- [2.0] `node-name( )`
- `string( )`

Boolean Functions

These functions work with Boolean values:

- `false( )`
- `not( )`
- `true( )`

Constructor Functions

There are two functions for creating `xs:dateTime` and `xs:QName` values:

- [2.0] `dateTime( )`
- [2.0] `QName( )`

Context Functions

The XPath *context* has a number of properties. These functions allow us to access those properties:

- [2.0] `collection( )`
- `current( )`
- [2.0] `current-date( )`
- [2.0] `current-dateTime( )`
- [2.0] `current-time( )`
- [2.0] `default-collation( )`
- `element-available( )`
- `function-available( )`
- [2.0] `implicit-timezone( )`
- `last( )`
- `position( )`
- [2.0] `static-base-uri( )`
- [2.0] `type-available( )`

 The functions `element-available( )`, `function-available( )`, and [2.0] `type-available( )` are actually defined in XSLT 2.0.

Cross-Referencing and Grouping Functions

These functions help you resolve unique identifiers and references between elements and attributes:

- [2.0] `current-group( )`
- [2.0] `current-grouping-key( )`
- `generate-id( )`
- `id( )`

- [2.0] `idref( )`
- `key( )`

Date, Time, and Duration Functions

These functions let you work with date, time and duration values. These are the XML Schema types `xs:date`, `xs:dateTime`, `xs:dayTimeDuration`, `xs:duration`, `xs:time`, and `xs:yearMonthDuration`:

- [2.0] `adjust-date-to-timezone( )`
- [2.0] `adjust-dateTime-to-timezone( )`
- [2.0] `adjust-time-to-timezone( )`
- [2.0] `day-from-date( )`
- [2.0] `day-from-dateTime( )`
- [2.0] `days-from-duration( )`
- [2.0] `format-date( )`
- [2.0] `format-dateTime( )`
- [2.0] `format-time( )`
- [2.0] `hours-from-dateTime( )`
- [2.0] `hours-from-duration( )`
- [2.0] `hours-from-time( )`
- [2.0] `minutes-from-dateTime( )`
- [2.0] `minutes-from-duration( )`
- [2.0] `minutes-from-time( )`
- [2.0] `month-from-date( )`
- [2.0] `month-from-dateTime( )`
- [2.0] `months-from-duration( )`
- [2.0] `seconds-from-dateTime( )`
- [2.0] `seconds-from-duration( )`
- [2.0] `seconds-from-time( )`
- [2.0] `timezone-from-date( )`
- [2.0] `timezone-from-dateTime( )`
- [2.0] `timezone-from-time( )`
- [2.0] `year-from-date( )`
- [2.0] `year-from-dateTime( )`
- [2.0] `years-from-duration( )`

 The [2.0] `format-date( )`, [2.0] `format-dateTime( )`, and [2.0] `format-time( )` functions are defined in XSLT 2.0.

Node Functions

These functions perform operations on nodes:

- `lang( )`
- `local-name( )`
- `name( )`
- `namespace-uri( )`
- `number( )`
- [2.0] `root( )`

Numeric Functions

These functions work with numeric values. Some of them work with a single number, while others work with node-sets or sequences:

- [2.0] `abs( )`
- [2.0] `avg( )`
- `ceiling( )`
- `floor( )`
- `format-number( )`
- [2.0] `max( )`
- [2.0] `min( )`
- `round( )`
- [2.0] `round-half-to-even( )`
- `sum( )`

QName Functions

These functions work with QNames (the XML Schema datatype `xs:QName`):

- [2.0] `in-scope-prefixes( )`
- [2.0] `local-name-from-QName( )`
- [2.0] `namespace-uri-for-prefix( )`
- [2.0] `namespace-uri-from-QName( )`
- [2.0] `prefix-from-QName( )`

- [2.0] `QName( )`
- [2.0] `resolve-QName( )`

Regular Expression Functions

These functions are part of the regular expression support in XSLT 2.0 and XPath 2.0:

- [2.0] `matches( )`
- [2.0] `regex-group( )`
- [2.0] `replace( )`
- [2.0] `tokenize( )`

Sequence or Node-Set Functions

These functions work with *[1.0]* node-sets or *[2.0]* sequences:

- [2.0] `avg( )`
- `boolean( )`
- `count( )`
- [2.0] `deep-equal( )`
- [2.0] `distinct-values( )`
- [2.0] `doc-available( )`
- [2.0] `doc( )`
- [2.0] `empty( )`
- [2.0] `exactly-one( )`
- [2.0] `exists( )`
- [2.0] `index-of( )`
- [2.0] `insert-before( )`
- [2.0] `max( )`
- [2.0] `min( )`
- [2.0] `one-or-more( )`
- [2.0] `remove( )`
- [2.0] `reverse( )`
- [2.0] `subsequence( )`
- `sum( )`
- [2.0] `unordered( )`
- [2.0] `zero-or-one( )`

String Functions

These functions help you manipulate strings:

- [2.0] `codepoint-equal( )`
- [2.0] `codepoints-to-string( )`
- [2.0] `compare( )`
- `concat( )`
- `contains( )`
- [2.0] `encode-for-uri( )`
- [2.0] `ends-with( )`
- [2.0] `escape-html-uri( )`
- [2.0] `iri-to-uri( )`
- [2.0] `lower-case( )`
- [2.0] `matches( )`
- `normalize-space( )`
- [2.0] `normalize-unicode( )`
- [2.0] `replace( )`
- `starts-with( )`
- [2.0] `string-join( )`
- `string-length( )`
- [2.0] `string-to-codepoints( )`
- `substring-after( )`
- `substring-before( )`
- `substring( )`
- [2.0] `tokenize( )`
- `translate( )`
- [2.0] `upper-case( )`

Miscellaneous Functions

Here are functions that don't fit under any other category:

- [2.0] `collection( )`
- [2.0] `doc-available( )`
- [2.0] `doc( )`
- `document( )`
- [2.0] `error( )`

- [2.0] `resolve-uri( )`
- `system-property( )`
- [2.0] `trace( )`
- [2.0] `unparsed-entity-public-id( )`
- `unparsed-entity-uri( )`
- [2.0] `unparsed-text-available( )`
- [2.0] `unparsed-text( )`

Collation Functions

There are several functions that allow you to specify a collation function that compares or sorts text based on the conventions of specific languages. (All of these have been listed previously as string or sequence functions. This subset contains all the functions that work with collations.)

- [2.0] `compare( )`
- `contains( )`
- [2.0] `deep-equal( )`
- [2.0] `distinct-values( )`
- [2.0] `index-of( )`
- `substring-after( )`
- `substring-before( )`

[2.0] abs()

Returns the absolute value of a numeric argument.

Syntax

```
numeric? abs(numeric?)
```

Input

A numeric value.

Output

The absolute value of the given numeric value.

Defined in

XQuery 1.0 and XPath 2.0 Functions and Operators section 6.4, "Functions on Numeric Values."

Example

Here's a short stylesheet that tests the abs( ) function:

```
<?xml version="1.0"?>
<!-- abs.xsl -->
<xsl:stylesheet version="2.0"
  xmlns:xsl="http://www.w3.org/1999/XSL/Transform"
  xmlns:xs="http://www.w3.org/2001/XMLSchema">

  <xsl:output method="text"/>

  <xsl:template match="/">
    <xsl:text>&#xA;Here are some tests of the abs() function:&#xA;</xsl:text>
    <xsl:text>&#xA;  abs(7) = </xsl:text>
    <xsl:value-of select="abs(7)"/>
    <xsl:text>&#xA;  abs(-7) = </xsl:text>
    <xsl:value-of select="abs(-7)"/>
    <xsl:text>&#xA;  abs(0) = </xsl:text>
    <xsl:value-of select="abs(0)"/>
    <xsl:text>&#xA;  abs(-0) = </xsl:text>
    <xsl:value-of select="abs(-0)"/>

    <!-- An XSLT 2.0 processor won't run this example at all. -->
    <!-- <xsl:value-of select="abs('x')"/> -->

    <xsl:variable name="testSequence" as="xs:integer*" select="1 to 10"/>
    <xsl:text>&#xA;  $testSequence = </xsl:text>
    <xsl:value-of select="$testSequence" separator=", "/>
    <xsl:text>&#xA;  abs(count($testSequence)) = </xsl:text>
    <xsl:value-of select="abs(count($testSequence))"/>
  </xsl:template>

</xsl:stylesheet>
```

Here are the results:

```
Here are some tests of the abs() function:

  abs(7) = 7
  abs(-7) = 7
  abs(0) = 0
  abs(-0) = 0
  $testSequence = 1, 2, 3, 4, 5, 6, 7, 8, 9, 10
  abs(count($testSequence)) = 10
```

The last call to abs( ) uses the count( ) function to create a numeric value. As we mentioned in a comment in the stylesheet, any attempt to pass a nonnumeric value to the abs( ) function is a static error. You can uncomment the line <xsl:value-of select="abs('x')"/> and try it yourself if you like.

[2.0] adjust-date-to-timezone()

Adjusts an xs:date value to a particular timezone.

Syntax

```
xs:date? adjust-date-to-timezone(xs:date?)
xs:date? adjust-date-to-timezone(xs:date?, $timezone as xs:dayTimeDuration)
```

Input

An optional xs:date value and an optional xs:dayTimeDuration. If no xs:date is provided, the empty sequence is returned. If an xs:dayTimeDuration is provided, the date is adjusted to the timezone it contains; otherwise, the XSLT processor uses the default timezone as returned by [2.0] implicit-timezone( ). Finally, if the timezone provided by the xs:dayTimeDuration is the empty sequence, the function returns the date with the timezone information removed.

Output

An xs:date value adjusted to the appropriate timezone.

Defined in

XQuery 1.0 and XPath 2.0 Functions and Operators section 10.7, "Timezone Adjustment Functions on Dates and Time Values."

Example

Here's a stylesheet that uses the adjust-date-to-timezone( ) in several ways:

```
<?xml version="1.0"?>
<!-- adjust-date-to-timezone.xsl -->
<xsl:stylesheet version="2.0"
  xmlns:xsl="http://www.w3.org/1999/XSL/Transform"
  xmlns:xs="http://www.w3.org/2001/XMLSchema">

<xsl:output method="text"/>

<xsl:template match="/">
  <xsl:variable name="gmt" select="xs:dayTimeDuration('PT0H')"/>
  <xsl:variable name="est" select="xs:dayTimeDuration('-PT5H')"/>
  <xsl:variable name="cst" select="xs:dayTimeDuration('-PT6H')"/>
  <xsl:variable name="minusTen" select="xs:dayTimeDuration('-PT10H')"/>

  <xsl:variable name="LilysBirthday" as="xs:date"
    select="xs:date('1995-04-21')"/>
  <xsl:variable name="format"
    select="'[FNn], [MNn] [D1], [Y0001]'"/>

  <xsl:text>&#xA;Here are some tests of the </xsl:text>
  <xsl:text>adjust-date-to-timezone() function:&#xA;</xsl:text>

  <xsl:text>&#xA;  My daughter was born on &#x9;</xsl:text>
  <xsl:value-of
    select="format-date($LilysBirthday, $format)"/>
  <xsl:text>&#xA;    adjusted to GMT: &#x9;&#x9;</xsl:text>
  <xsl:value-of
    select="format-date(
            adjust-date-to-timezone($LilysBirthday, $gmt),
            $format)"/>
```

```
<xsl:text>&#xA;    adjusted to EST: &#x9;&#x9;</xsl:text>
<xsl:value-of
  select="format-date
          (adjust-date-to-timezone($LilysBirthday, $est),
          $format)"/>

<xsl:text>&#xA;    adjusted to CST: &#x9;&#x9;</xsl:text>
<xsl:value-of
  select="format-date
          (adjust-date-to-timezone($LilysBirthday, $cst),
          $format)"/>

<xsl:text>&#xA;&#xA;  </xsl:text>
<xsl:text>The current date in the default timezone is: </xsl:text>
<xsl:text>&#xA;&#x9;&#x9;&#x9;&#x9;</xsl:text>
<xsl:value-of
  select="format-date(
          adjust-date-to-timezone(current-date()),
          $format)"/>

<xsl:text>&#xA;    adjusted to GMT: &#x9;&#x9;</xsl:text>
<xsl:value-of
  select="format-date
          (adjust-date-to-timezone(current-date(), $gmt),
          $format)"/>

<xsl:text>&#xA;    adjusted to GMT-10: &#x9;</xsl:text>
<xsl:value-of
  select="format-date(
          adjust-date-to-timezone(current-date(), $minusTen),
          $format)"/>
</xsl:template>

</xsl:stylesheet>
```

Here are the results from this stylesheet:

```
Here are some tests of the adjust-date-to-timezone() function:

My daughter was born on       Friday, April 21, 1995
    adjusted to GMT:          Friday, April 21, 1995
    adjusted to EST:          Friday, April 21, 1995
    adjusted to CST:          Friday, April 21, 1995

The current date in the default timezone is:
                              Thursday, November 16, 2007
    adjusted to GMT:          Thursday, November 16, 2007
    adjusted to GMT-10:       Wednesday, November 15, 2007
```

Notice that we used the format-date( ) function to print the xs:date values.

See Also

The definitions of the [2.0] adjust-dateTime-to-timezone( ), [2.0] adjust-time-to-timezone( ), and [2.0] format-date( ) functions.

[2.0] adjust-dateTime-to-timezone()

Adjusts an xs:dateTime value to a particular timezone.

Syntax

```
xs:dateTime? adjust-dateTime-to-timezone(xs:dateTime?)
xs:dateTime? adjust-dateTime-to-timezone(xs:dateTime?,
                                $timezone as xs:dayTimeDuration?)
```

Inputs

An optional xs:dateTime value and an optional xs:dayTimeDuration. If no xs:dateTime is provided, the empty sequence is returned. If an xs:dayTimeDuration is supplied, the xs:dateTime value is adjusted to the timezone it contains. Otherwise, adjust-dateTime-to-timezone( ) adjusts the xs:dateTime value to the default timezone as returned by [2.0] implicit-timezone( ). Finally, if the timezone provided is the empty sequence, the function returns the xs:dateTime with the timezone information removed.

Output

The given xs:dateTime value adjusted to the appropriate timezone.

Defined in

XQuery 1.0 and XPath 2.0 Functions and Operators section 10.7, "Timezone Adjustment Functions on Dates and Time Values."

Example

This stylesheet uses adjust-dateTime-to-timezone( ) in several different ways. The default timezone here is GMT -4, representing Eastern Daylight Time (EDT).

```
<?xml version="1.0"?>
<!-- adjust-datetime-to-timezone.xsl -->
<xsl:stylesheet version="2.0"
  xmlns:xsl="http://www.w3.org/1999/XSL/Transform"
  xmlns:xs="http://www.w3.org/2001/XMLSchema">

<xsl:output method="text"/>

<xsl:template match="/">
  <xsl:variable name="gmt" select="xs:dayTimeDuration('PT0H')"/>
  <xsl:variable name="est" select="xs:dayTimeDuration('-PT5H')"/>
  <xsl:variable name="cst" select="xs:dayTimeDuration('-PT6H')"/>
  <xsl:variable name="minusTen" select="xs:dayTimeDuration('-PT10H')"/>

  <xsl:variable name="LilysBirthday" as="xs:dateTime"
    select="xs:dateTime('1995-04-21T00:43:00-05:00')"/>
  <xsl:variable name="format"
    select="'[FNn], [MNn] [D1], [Y0001], at [h1]:[m01]:[s01]'"/>

  <xsl:text>&#xA;Here are some tests of the </xsl:text>
  <xsl:text>adjust-dateTime-to-timezone() function:&#xA;</xsl:text>
```

```
<xsl:text>&#xA;   My daughter was born on &#x9;</xsl:text>
<xsl:value-of
  select="format-dateTime($LilysBirthday, $format)"/>
<xsl:text>&#xA;      adjusted to GMT: &#x9;&#x9;</xsl:text>
<xsl:value-of
  select="format-dateTime(
            adjust-dateTime-to-timezone($LilysBirthday, $gmt),
            $format)"/>

<xsl:text>&#xA;      adjusted to EST: &#x9;&#x9;</xsl:text>
<xsl:value-of
  select="format-dateTime
            (adjust-dateTime-to-timezone($LilysBirthday, $est),
            $format)"/>

<xsl:text>&#xA;      adjusted to CST: &#x9;&#x9;</xsl:text>
<xsl:value-of
  select="format-dateTime
            (adjust-dateTime-to-timezone($LilysBirthday, $cst),
            $format)"/>

<xsl:text>&#xA;&#xA;   </xsl:text>
<xsl:text>The current time in the default timezone is: </xsl:text>
<xsl:text>&#xA;   &#x9;&#x9;&#x9;&#x9;</xsl:text>
<xsl:value-of
  select="format-dateTime(
            adjust-dateTime-to-timezone(current-dateTime()),
            $format)"/>

<xsl:text>&#xA;      adjusted to GMT: &#x9;&#x9;</xsl:text>
<xsl:value-of
  select="format-dateTime
            (adjust-dateTime-to-timezone(current-dateTime(), $gmt),
            $format)"/>

<xsl:text>&#xA;      adjusted to GMT-10: &#x9;</xsl:text>
<xsl:value-of
  select="format-dateTime(
            adjust-dateTime-to-timezone(current-dateTime(), $minusTen),
            $format)"/>
</xsl:template>

</xsl:stylesheet>
```

Here are the results of our stylesheet:

```
Here are some tests of the adjust-dateTime-to-timezone() function:

My daughter was born on      Friday, April 21, 1995, at 12:43:00
   adjusted to GMT:          Friday, April 21, 1995, at 5:43:00
   adjusted to EST:          Friday, April 21, 1995, at 12:43:00
   adjusted to CST:          Thursday, April 20, 1995, at 11:43:00

The current time in the default timezone is:
                            Thursday, November 16, 2006, at 3:34:29
```

```
adjusted to GMT:          Thursday, November 16, 2006, at 8:34:29
adjusted to GMT-10:       Wednesday, November 15, 2006, at 10:34:29
```

The default timezone is considered part of the context; you can invoke the function `implicit-timezone( )` to get the default. See the definition of the [2.0] `implicit-timezone( )` function for more information. Also notice that we used the `format-dateTime( )` function to format the `xs:dateTime` values.

See Also

The definitions of the [2.0] `adjust-date-to-timezone( )`, [2.0] `adjust-time-to-timezone( )`, and [2.0] `format-dateTime( )` functions.

[2.0] adjust-time-to-timezone()

Adjusts an `xs:time` value to a particular timezone.

Syntax

```
xs:time? adjust-time-to-timezone(xs:time?)
xs:time? adjust-time-to-timezone(xs:time?, $timezone as xs:dayTimeDuration?)
```

Input

An optional `xs:time` value and an optional `xs:dayTimeDuration`. If no `xs:date` is provided, the empty sequence is returned. If an `xs:dayTimeDuration` is provided, the `xs:time` value is adjusted to the timezone contained in the `xs:dayTimeDuration`; otherwise, the XSLT processor uses the default timezone as returned by [2.0] `implicit-timezone( )`. Finally, if the timezone provided by the `xs:dayTimeDuration` is the empty sequence, the function returns the `xs:time` with the timezone information removed.

Output

The given `xs:time` value adjusted to the appropriate timezone.

Defined in

XQuery 1.0 and XPath 2.0 Functions and Operators section 10.7, "Timezone Adjustment Functions on Dates and Time Values."

Example

The following stylesheet tests the `adjust-time-to-timezone( )` function:

```
<?xml version="1.0"?>
<!-- adjust-time-to-timezone.xsl -->
<xsl:stylesheet version="2.0"
  xmlns:xsl="http://www.w3.org/1999/XSL/Transform"
  xmlns:xs="http://www.w3.org/2001/XMLSchema">

  <xsl:output method="text"/>

  <xsl:template match="/">
```

```
<xsl:variable name="gmt" select="xs:dayTimeDuration('PT0H')"/>
<xsl:variable name="est" select="xs:dayTimeDuration('-PT5H')"/>
<xsl:variable name="cst" select="xs:dayTimeDuration('-PT6H')"/>
<xsl:variable name="minusTen" select="xs:dayTimeDuration('-PT10H')"/>

<xsl:variable name="LilysBirthday" as="xs:time"
  select="xs:time('00:43:00-05:00')"/>
<xsl:variable name="format"
  select="'[h1]:[m01]:[s01] [P]'"/>

<xsl:text>&#xA;Here are some tests of the </xsl:text>
<xsl:text>adjust-time-to-timezone() function:&#xA;</xsl:text>

<xsl:text>&#xA;  My daughter was born at &#x9;</xsl:text>
<xsl:value-of
  select="format-time($LilysBirthday, $format)"/>
<xsl:text>&#xA;    adjusted to GMT: &#x9;&#x9;</xsl:text>
<xsl:value-of
  select="format-time(
          adjust-time-to-timezone($LilysBirthday, $gmt),
          $format)"/>

<xsl:text>&#xA;    adjusted to EST: &#x9;&#x9;</xsl:text>
<xsl:value-of
  select="format-time
          (adjust-time-to-timezone($LilysBirthday, $est),
          $format)"/>

<xsl:text>&#xA;    adjusted to CST: &#x9;&#x9;</xsl:text>
<xsl:value-of
  select="format-time
          (adjust-time-to-timezone($LilysBirthday, $cst),
          $format)"/>

<xsl:text>&#xA;&#xA;  </xsl:text>
<xsl:text>The current time in the default timezone is: </xsl:text>
<xsl:text>&#xA;  &#x9;&#x9;&#x9;&#x9;</xsl:text>
<xsl:value-of
  select="format-time(
          adjust-time-to-timezone(current-time()),
          $format)"/>

<xsl:text>&#xA;    adjusted to GMT: &#x9;&#x9;</xsl:text>
<xsl:value-of
  select="format-time
          (adjust-time-to-timezone(current-time(), $gmt),
          $format)"/>

<xsl:text>&#xA;    adjusted to GMT-10: &#x9;</xsl:text>
<xsl:value-of
  select="format-time(
          adjust-time-to-timezone(current-time(), $minusTen),
          $format)"/>
</xsl:template>
```

```
</xsl:stylesheet>
```

Here are the stylesheet results:

```
Here are some tests of the adjust-time-to-timezone() function:

My daughter was born at      12:43:00 a.m.
   adjusted to GMT:          5:43:00 a.m.
   adjusted to EST:          12:43:00 a.m.
   adjusted to CST:          11:43:00 p.m.

The current time in the default timezone is:
                             3:35:44 a.m.
   adjusted to GMT:          8:35:44 a.m.
   adjusted to GMT-10:       10:35:44 p.m.
```

Notice that we used the `format-time( )` function to print the `xs:time` values.

See Also

The definitions of the [2.0] `adjust-date-to-timezone( )`, [2.0] `adjust-dateTime-to-timezone( )`, and [2.0] `format-time( )` functions.

[2.0] avg()

Given a sequence, returns the average value of the items in the sequence.

Syntax

```
xs:anyAtomicType? avg(xs:anyAtomicType*)
```

Input

A sequence of values.

Output

The average of the given sequence. You can calculate averages for six different datatypes: `xs:integer`, `xs:double`, `xs:decimal`, `xs:float`, `xs:yearMonthDuration`, and `xs:dayTimeDuration`.

Given a sequence of numeric values, the XSLT processor returns the average of those numbers, converting datatypes as necessary. Given a sequence of durations, the XSLT processor returns the average of those durations.

The `avg( )` function assumes you'll send it a sequence containing sensible data; if not, the XSLT processor throws an error. Asking for the average of the sequence (`42, 57, 'blue'`) returns an error, as you'd expect.

Some notes about how the `avg( )` function works:

- To calculate the average of a sequence of durations, all the values must be `xs:dayTimeDuration`s or `xs:yearMonthDuration`s. You can't mix the two types of durations; if you do, the XSLT processor throws an error.

- If all the items in the sequence are of type `xs:untypedAtomic`, the XSLT processor attempts to cast each value to `xs:double`. If *any* item in the sequence can't be converted to an `xs:double`, the XSLT processor throws an error.

- Finally, if you pass the **avg( )** function the empty sequence, the function returns the empty sequence. Although you're not giving the function any useful data in this case, the XSLT processor doesn't throw an error.

Defined in

XQuery 1.0 and XPath 2.0 Functions and Operators section 15.4, "Aggregate Functions."

Example

Here's a stylesheet that calculates the averages of several sequences:

```
<?xml version="1.0"?>
<!-- avg.xsl -->
<xsl:stylesheet version="2.0"
  xmlns:xsl="http://www.w3.org/1999/XSL/Transform"
  xmlns:xs="http://www.w3.org/2001/XMLSchema">

  <xsl:output method="text"/>

  <xsl:template match="/">
    <xsl:variable name="seq1" select="(3, 5, 18)"/>
    <xsl:variable name="seq2" select="(3, 5, 48.273, 2.9e3)"/>

    <xsl:variable name="value1" as="xs:integer" select="42"/>
    <xsl:variable name="value2" as="xs:double" select="2718.28E-3"/>
    <xsl:variable name="value3" as="xs:float" select="98.6"/>
    <xsl:variable name="value4" as="xs:decimal" select="2.54"/>
    <xsl:variable name="seq3"
      select="($value1, $value2, $value3, $value4)"/>

    <xsl:variable name="seq4"
      select="(xs:yearMonthDuration('P3Y8M'),
              xs:yearMonthDuration('P4Y2M'),
              xs:yearMonthDuration('P6Y4M'))"/>
    <xsl:variable name="seq5"
      select="(xs:dayTimeDuration('P2DT4H23M12.2S'),
              xs:dayTimeDuration('P3DT8H17M'),
              xs:dayTimeDuration('P3D'))"/>

    <xsl:text>&#xA;Here are some tests of the avg() function:&#xA;</xsl:text>

    <xsl:text>&#xA;  avg(</xsl:text>
    <xsl:value-of select="$seq1" separator=", "/>
    <xsl:text>) = </xsl:text>
    <xsl:value-of select="format-number(avg($seq1), '#.###')"/>
```

```
<xsl:text>&#xA;&#xA;  avg(</xsl:text>
<xsl:value-of select="$seq2" separator=", "/>
<xsl:text>) = </xsl:text>
<xsl:value-of select="format-number(avg($seq2), '#.###')"/>

<xsl:text>&#xA;&#xA;  avg(</xsl:text>
<xsl:value-of select="$seq3" separator=", "/>
<xsl:text>) = </xsl:text>
<xsl:value-of select="format-number(avg($seq3), '#.###')"/>

<xsl:text>&#xA;&#xA;  avg(</xsl:text>
<xsl:value-of select="$seq4" separator=", "/>
<xsl:text>) = </xsl:text>
<xsl:value-of select="avg($seq4)"/>

<xsl:text>&#xA;&#xA;    In text, the average of</xsl:text>
<xsl:for-each select="$seq4">
  <xsl:text>&#xA;        </xsl:text>
  <xsl:value-of select="years-from-duration(.)"/>
  <xsl:text> years and </xsl:text>
  <xsl:value-of select="months-from-duration(.)"/>
  <xsl:text> months (</xsl:text>
  <xsl:value-of select="."/>
  <xsl:text>)</xsl:text>
</xsl:for-each>

<xsl:text>&#xA;   is </xsl:text>
<xsl:value-of select="years-from-duration(avg($seq4))"/>
<xsl:text> years and </xsl:text>
<xsl:value-of select="months-from-duration(avg($seq4))"/>
<xsl:text> months (</xsl:text>
<xsl:value-of select="avg($seq4)"/>
<xsl:text>).</xsl:text>

<xsl:text>&#xA;&#xA;  avg(</xsl:text>
<xsl:value-of select="$seq5" separator=", "/>
<xsl:text>) = </xsl:text>
<xsl:variable name="avg5" select="avg($seq5)"/>
<xsl:value-of select="$avg5"/>

<xsl:text>&#xA;&#xA;    In text, the average of</xsl:text>
<xsl:for-each select="$seq5">
  <xsl:text>&#xA;        </xsl:text>
  <xsl:value-of select="days-from-duration(.)"/>
  <xsl:text> days, </xsl:text>
  <xsl:value-of select="hours-from-duration(.)"/>
  <xsl:text> hours, </xsl:text>
  <xsl:value-of select="minutes-from-duration(.)"/>
  <xsl:text> minutes and </xsl:text>
  <xsl:value-of
    select="format-number(seconds-from-duration(.), '#.##')"/>
  <xsl:text> seconds (</xsl:text>
  <xsl:value-of select="."/>
  <xsl:text>)</xsl:text>
</xsl:for-each>
```

```
    <xsl:text>&#xA;    is </xsl:text>
      <xsl:value-of select="days-from-duration($avg5)"/>
      <xsl:text> days, </xsl:text>
      <xsl:value-of select="hours-from-duration($avg5)"/>
      <xsl:text> hours, </xsl:text>
      <xsl:value-of select="minutes-from-duration($avg5)"/>
      <xsl:text> minutes and </xsl:text>
      <xsl:value-of
        select="format-number(seconds-from-duration($avg5), '#.##')"/>
      <xsl:text> seconds.</xsl:text>

  </xsl:template>

</xsl:stylesheet>
```

Here are the results from this stylesheet:

```
Here are some tests of the avg() function:

  avg(3, 5, 18) = 8.667

  avg(3, 5, 48.273, 2900) = 739.068

  avg(42, 2.71828, 98.6, 2.54) = 36.465

  avg(P3Y8M, P4Y2M, P6Y4M) = P4Y9M

    In text, the average of
      3 years and 8 months (P3Y8M)
      4 years and 2 months (P4Y2M)
      6 years and 4 months (P6Y4M)
    is 4 years and 9 months (P4Y9M).

  avg(P2DT4H23M12.2S, P3DT8H17M, P3D) = P2DT20H13M24.066666S

    In text, the average of
      2 days, 4 hours, 23 minutes and 12.2 seconds (P2DT4H23M12.2S)
      3 days, 8 hours, 17 minutes and 0 seconds (P3DT8H17M)
      3 days, 0 hours, 0 minutes and 0 seconds (P3D)
    is 2 days, 20 hours, 13 minutes and 24.07 seconds.
```

The stylesheet demonstrates five different types of sequences. The first is all integers, and the second is a sequence of numbers. All the values in the first two sequences can be converted to numbers, so the results are what we expect. The third sequence features four numeric values, each of which is a different numeric type (xs:integer, xs:decimal, xs:float, and xs:double). The last two sequences are made up of the two types of durations. The stylesheet also uses functions such as years-from-duration( ), and format-number( ) to format the data.

The sequence (3, 5, '18') won't work because one of the items in the sequence is a string. Although the string '18' could obviously be converted to a number with the number( ) function, the avg( ) function puts the burden on us to make sure all the literal values in the sequence are numbers or durations. However, if the sequence contains untyped values (nodes read in from a document that doesn't use a schema, for example), the XSLT processor attempts to cast all of those values to xs:double. If any of them can't be cast to xs:double, the XSLT processor raises an error.

A final note: if you want to store a numeric average in a typed variable, the xs:double datatype is the most flexible. Using the most restrictive numeric type, xs:integer, is a really bad idea. For example, the XSLT processor binds this variable without complaint:

```
<xsl:variable name="avg1" as="xs:integer" select="avg((3, 5, 4))"/>
```

On the other hand, this generates a static error:

```
<xsl:variable name="avg2" as="xs:integer" select="avg((3, 5, 18))"/>
```

If we use avg( ) to set the value of an integer variable dynamically, the XSLT processor throws an error if the returned value isn't an xs:integer. We could get this to work by casting the result to an xs:integer:

```
<xsl:variable name="avg2" as="xs:integer"
  select="xs:integer(avg((3, 5, 18)))"/>
```

[2.0] base-uri()

Returns the base URI of a given node.

Syntax

```
xs:anyURI? base-uri(node()?)
xs:anyURI? base-uri()
```

Input

A node. Without an argument, base-uri( ) returns the base URI of the context item.

Output

The base URI of the given node.

The base-uri( ) function works with the XML Base specification. By default the base URI is the URI of the XML document itself, but a document can change that by using the xml:base attribute on any element.

If a given node does not have a base URI property and the node has a parent, base-uri( ) looks at the node's ancestors. The function attempts to find the base URI of the node's parent, then its parent's parent, and so forth, until it either finds a base URI property or reaches a node that does not have a parent. If no base URI property can be found, base-uri( ) returns the empty sequence. If the argument to base-uri( ) is the empty sequence, the function returns the empty sequence.

Defined in

XQuery 1.0 and XPath 2.0 Functions and Operators section 2, "Accessors."

Example

Here's a revised version of our list of cars. Notice that the <manufacturer> elements all use the xml:base attribute to define a new base URI:

```
<?xml version="1.0" encoding="utf-8"?>
<!-- xmlbase.xml -->
<cars>
  <manufacturer name="Chevrolet"
    xml:base="http://www.chevrolet.com/">
    <car>Cavalier</car>
    <car>Corvette</car>
    <car>Impala</car>
    <car>Malibu</car>
  </manufacturer>
  <manufacturer name="Ford"
    xml:base="http://www.ford.com/">
    <car>Pinto</car>
    <car>Mustang</car>
    <car>Taurus</car>
  </manufacturer>
  <manufacturer name="Volkswagen"
    xml:base="http://www.vw.com/">
    <car>Beetle</car>
    <car>Jetta</car>
    <car>Passat</car>
    <car>Touraeg</car>
  </manufacturer>
</cars>
```

We'll test the base-uri( ) function with this stylesheet:

```
<?xml version="1.0"?>
<!-- base-uri.xsl -->
<xsl:stylesheet version="2.0"
  xmlns:xsl="http://www.w3.org/1999/XSL/Transform">

  <xsl:output method="text"/>

  <xsl:template match="/">
    <xsl:text>&#xA;Tests of the base-uri() function:</xsl:text>

    <xsl:text>&#xA;&#xA;  The base URI for the </xsl:text>
    <xsl:text>document root is:&#xA;    </xsl:text>
    <xsl:value-of select="base-uri()"/>

    <xsl:text>&#xA;&#xA;  The base URI for the </xsl:text>
    <xsl:text>&lt;cars&gt; element is:&#xA;    </xsl:text>
    <xsl:value-of select="base-uri(cars)"/>

    <xsl:for-each select="/cars/manufacturer">
      <xsl:text>&#xA;&#xA;  The base URI for the </xsl:text>
      <xsl:text>manufacturer named </xsl:text>
      <xsl:value-of select="@name"/>
      <xsl:text>: &#xA;    </xsl:text>
      <xsl:value-of select="base-uri()"/>
```

```
      </xsl:for-each>
    </xsl:template>

  </xsl:stylesheet>
```

When running this stylesheet against our modified list of cars, we get these results:

```
Tests of the base-uri() function:

  The base URI for the document root is:
    file:/C:/projects/XSLTbookV2/AppendixC/xmlbase.xml

  The base URI for the <cars> element is:
    file:/C:/projects/XSLTbookV2/AppendixC/xmlbase.xml

  The base URI for the manufacturer named Chevrolet:
    http://www.chevrolet.com/

  The base URI for the manufacturer named Ford:
    http://www.ford.com/

  The base URI for the manufacturer named Volkswagen:
    http://www.vw.com/
```

The base-uri() function would be very useful if we were generating links from this XML document. Here's a stylesheet that creates links for the <car> elements using the base-uri() function:

```
<?xml version="1.0"?>
<!-- base-uri2.xsl -->
<xsl:stylesheet version="2.0"
  xmlns:xsl="http://www.w3.org/1999/XSL/Transform">

  <xsl:output method="html" include-content-type="no"/>

  <xsl:template match="/">
    <html>
      <head>
        <title>Here are some cars</title>
      </head>
      <body>
        <h1>Here are some cars:</h1>
        <xsl:apply-templates select="cars/manufacturer"/>
      </body>
    </html>
  </xsl:template>

  <xsl:template match="manufacturer">
    <h2>
      <xsl:value-of select="@name"/>
    </h2>
    <ul>
      <xsl:for-each select="car">
        <li>
          <a href="{concat(base-uri(), ., '.html')}">
            <xsl:value-of select="."/>
```

```
            </a>
          </li>
        </xsl:for-each>
      </ul>
    </xsl:template>

  </xsl:stylesheet>
```

To generate the links, we use an attribute value template and the concat( ) function to combine the value of the base URI, the value of the current element (the dot represents the `<car>` we're currently processing), and the string .html. This generates a series of links that look like this:

```
<h2>Volkswagen</h2>
<ul>
    <li><a href="http://www.vw.com/Beetle.html">Beetle</a></li>
    <li><a href="http://www.vw.com/Jetta.html">Jetta</a></li>
    <li><a href="http://www.vw.com/Passat.html">Passat</a></li>
    <li><a href="http://www.vw.com/Touraeg.html">Touraeg</a></li>
</ul>
```

Our assumption here is that the base URI property ends with a slash, as all the xml:base attributes in our source document did. More robust code would check the value returned by base-uri( ) and concatenate a slash if necessary.

boolean()

Converts its argument to a boolean value.

Syntax

```
[1.0] boolean boolean(object)
[2.0] xs:boolean boolean(item()*)
```

Inputs

An object. The object is converted to a boolean value. This conversion is described in the following subsection.

Output

[1.0] The boolean value corresponding to the input object. Objects are converted to boolean values as follows:

- A number is true if and only if it is not zero, negative zero, or NaN (not a number).

- A node-set is true if and only if it is not empty.

- A string is true if and only if its length is greater than zero.

- All other datatypes are converted in a way specific to those datatypes.

[2.0] For XSLT 2.0, things are more complicated. The value returned, as you'd expect, is an xs:boolean. Here's how the argument to boolean( ) is converted to a boolean value:

- If the argument is a singleton of any numeric type, boolean( ) returns false if the value is zero or NaN (not a number); everything else returns true.

- If the argument is a singleton of type xs:string, xs:anyURI, xs:untypedAtomic, or any type derived from them, boolean( ) returns true if the argument has a length greater than zero.

- If the argument is a singleton of type xs:boolean (or of a type derived from xs:boolean), boolean( ) simply returns the argument as is.

- If the argument is a sequence whose first item is a node, boolean( ) returns true.

- If the argument is the empty sequence, boolean( ) returns false.

- If the argument is anything else (xs:date, xs:time, or a sequence of multiple atomic values, for example), boolean( ) raises an error.

Defined in

[1.0] XPath section 4.3, "Boolean Functions."

[2.0] XQuery 1.0 and XPath 2.0 Functions and Operators section 15.1, "General Functions and Operators on Sequences."

Example

We'll use our sales document to illustrate the boolean( ) function:

```
<?xml version="1.0" encoding="utf-8"?>
<!-- chocolate.xml -->
<report month="8" year="2006">
  <title>Chocolate bar sales</title>
  <brand>
    <name>Lindt</name>
    <units>27408</units>
  </brand>
  <brand>
    <name>Callebaut</name>
    <units>8203</units>
  </brand>
  <brand>
    <name>Valrhona</name>
    <units>22101</units>
  </brand>
  <brand>
    <name>Perugina</name>
    <units>14336</units>
  </brand>
  <brand>
    <name>Ghirardelli</name>
    <units>19268</units>
  </brand>
</report>
```

Here's our stylesheet:

```
<?xml version="1.0"?>
<!-- boolean.xsl -->
<xsl:stylesheet version="1.0"
  xmlns:xsl="http://www.w3.org/1999/XSL/Transform">

  <xsl:output method="text"/>

  <xsl:template match="/">
    <xsl:text>&#xA;</xsl:text>
    <xsl:text>Tests of the boolean() function:</xsl:text>

    <xsl:text>&#xA;&#xA;  boolean(true()) = </xsl:text>
    <xsl:value-of select="boolean(true())"/>

    <xsl:text>&#xA;  boolean(true) = </xsl:text>
    <xsl:value-of select="boolean(true)"/>

    <xsl:text>&#xA;  boolean('false') = </xsl:text>
    <xsl:value-of select="boolean('false')"/>

    <xsl:text>&#xA;  boolean('7') = </xsl:text>
    <xsl:value-of select="boolean('7')"/>

    <xsl:text>&#xA;  boolean(7) = </xsl:text>
    <xsl:value-of select="boolean(7)"/>

    <xsl:text>&#xA;  boolean(/report/brand/units[. > 20000]) = </xsl:text>
    <xsl:value-of select="boolean(/report/brand/units[. > 20000])"/>
  </xsl:template>

</xsl:stylesheet>
```

Here are the results:

```
Tests of the boolean() function:

  boolean(true()) = true
  boolean(true) = false
  boolean('false') = true
  boolean('7') = true
  boolean(7) = true
  boolean(/report/brand/units[. > 20000]) = true
```

For the first test, the argument is a call to the true( ) function, which always returns true. Because this is a boolean value already, the boolean( ) function simply returns that value as is. For the second test, we're asking for all the <true> elements in the current context; there are no <true> elements, so this is false. The argument of the third and fourth tests are strings whose length is greater than zero, so boolean( ) returns true. The fifth argument is a number greater than zero, so it is true as well.

The final example uses an XPath statement to select all of the <units> elements in our sales report that have a numeric value greater than 20000. Because this selects at least one node, boolean( ) returns true. This works in XSLT 1.0 because it generates a node-set with at least one member, and it works in XSLT 2.0 because it creates a sequence whose first member is a node. If we changed the expression to look for sales figures greater than 30000, boolean( ) would return false.

Here's a stylesheet that uses XSLT 2.0's rules to process various sequences:

```
<?xml version="1.0"?>
<!-- boolean2.xsl -->
<xsl:stylesheet version="2.0"
  xmlns:xsl="http://www.w3.org/1999/XSL/Transform">

  <xsl:output method="text"/>

  <xsl:template match="/">
    <xsl:text>&#xA;</xsl:text>
    <xsl:text>Tests of the boolean() function:</xsl:text>

    <xsl:text>&#xA;&#xA;  boolean(()) = </xsl:text>
    <xsl:value-of select="boolean(())"/>

    <xsl:variable name="testSequence1" as="item()*">
      <xsl:sequence select="(3)"/>
    </xsl:variable>

    <xsl:text>&#xA;&#xA;  $testSequence1 = (</xsl:text>
    <xsl:value-of select="$testSequence1" separator=", "/>
    <xsl:text>)&#xA;  boolean($testSequence1) = </xsl:text>
    <xsl:value-of select="boolean($testSequence1)"/>

    <xsl:variable name="testSequence2" as="item()*">
      <xsl:sequence select="/report/brand/units"/>
      <xsl:sequence select="(3, 4, 5)"/>
    </xsl:variable>

    <xsl:text>&#xA;&#xA;  $testSequence2 = (</xsl:text>
    <xsl:value-of select="$testSequence2" separator=", "/>
    <xsl:text>)&#xA;  boolean($testSequence2) = </xsl:text>
    <xsl:value-of select="boolean($testSequence2)"/>
  </xsl:template>

</xsl:stylesheet>
```

Here are the results:

```
Tests of the boolean() function:

  boolean(()) = false

  $testSequence1 = (3)
  boolean($testSequence1) = true

  $testSequence2 = (27408, 8203, 22101, 14336, 19268, 3, 4, 5)
  boolean($testSequence2) = true
```

There are three different tests here. For the first test, we pass the boolean( ) function the empty sequence, so the result is false. In the second test, we pass a singleton numeric value to boolean( ); because that value is nonzero, the result is true. In the final test, the argument we use is a sequence that contains five `<units>` nodes, followed by three numeric values. Because the first item in the sequence is a node, `boolean( )` returns `true`.

In this stylesheet, if we define `$testSequence1` to have more than one item, the stylesheet would fail to compile. Any sequence we send to `boolean( )` must be a singleton or a sequence whose first value is a node. For the second sequence, `$testSequence2`, we can add as many items of as many different types as we like, as long as the first item is a node. If there were no nodes that matched the expression `/report/brand/units`, the first node in the sequence would be the atomic value 3, so the stylesheet would generate a runtime error.

See "Converting to boolean values" in Chapter 5 for more examples and information.

ceiling()

Returns the smallest integer that is not less than the argument.

Syntax

```
[1.0] number? ceiling(number?)
[2.0] numeric? ceiling(numeric?)
```

Inputs

A number.

[1.0] If the argument is not a number, it is transformed into a number as if it had been processed by the `number( )` function. If the argument cannot be transformed into a number, the `ceiling( )` function returns the value `NaN` (not a number).

[2.0] In XSLT 2.0, the argument must be one of the four numeric types (`xs:float`, `xs:decimal`, `xs:double`, or `xs:integer`). If it is not, the XSLT processor raises an error. The result of the `ceiling( )` function will be of the same type as the argument.

Output

The smallest integer that is not less than the argument.

[1.0] In XSLT 1.0, `ceiling( )` returns `NaN` if the argument cannot be converted to a number.

[2.0] In XSLT 2.0, `ceiling( )` raises an error if the argument cannot be converted to a number.

Defined in

[1.0] XPath section 4.4, "Number Functions."

[2.0] XQuery 1.0 and XPath 2.0 Functions and Operators section 6.4, "Functions on Numeric Values."

Example

The following stylesheet shows the results of invoking the `ceiling( )` function against a variety of values. We'll use this XML document as input:

```
<?xml version="1.0" encoding="utf-8"?>
<!-- chocolate.xml -->
```

```
<report month="8" year="2006">
  <title>Chocolate bar sales</title>
  <brand>
    <name>Lindt</name>
    <units>27408</units>
  </brand>
  <brand>
    <name>Callebaut</name>
    <units>8203</units>
  </brand>
  <brand>
    <name>Valrhona</name>
    <units>22101</units>
  </brand>
  <brand>
    <name>Perugina</name>
    <units>14336</units>
  </brand>
  <brand>
    <name>Ghirardelli</name>
    <units>19268</units>
  </brand>
</report>
```

Here's the stylesheet that uses the `ceiling( )` function:

```
<?xml version="1.0"?>
<!-- ceiling.xsl -->
<xsl:stylesheet version="2.0"
  xmlns:xsl="http://www.w3.org/1999/XSL/Transform">

  <xsl:output method="text"/>

  <xsl:template match="/">
    <xsl:text>&#xA;Tests of the ceiling() function:&#xA;&#xA;</xsl:text>

    <xsl:text>  ceiling(7.983) = </xsl:text>
    <xsl:value-of select="ceiling(7.983)"/>

    <xsl:text>&#xA;  ceiling(-7.893) = </xsl:text>
    <xsl:value-of select="ceiling(-7.893)"/>

    <xsl:text>&#xA;  ceiling(avg(/report/brand/units)) = </xsl:text>
    <xsl:value-of select="ceiling(avg(/report/brand/units))"/>

    <xsl:text>&#xA;  ceiling('blue') = </xsl:text>
    <xsl:value-of version="1.0" select="ceiling('blue')"/>

  </xsl:template>

</xsl:stylesheet>
```

When we transform the XML document with our stylesheet, here are the results:

```
Tests of the ceiling() function:

  ceiling(7.983) = 8
```

```
ceiling(-7.893) = -7
ceiling(avg(/report/brand/units)) = 18264
ceiling('blue') = NaN
```

For the last test of the `ceiling( )` function, we specified `version="1.0"` on the `<xsl:value-of>` element. In XSLT 1.0 mode, we get the result `NaN` (not a number). If we process this `<xsl:value-of>` element in XSLT 2.0 mode, the stylesheet won't run at all.

[2.0] codepoint-equal()

Determines whether two strings are equal, based on their Unicode codepoints.

Syntax

```
xs:boolean? codepoint-equal(xs:string?, xs:string?)
```

Inputs

Two `xs:string`s to be compared.

Output

This function returns `true` or `false` depending on whether the two strings are equal using the Unicode code point collation. This function allows you to compare `xs:anyURI` values without having to specify a collation. If either argument is the empty sequence, the result is the empty sequence.

Defined in

XQuery 1.0 and XPath 2.0 Functions and Operators section 7.3, "Equality and Comparison of Strings."

Example

Here is a short stylesheet that tests strings to see whether they are equal:

```
<?xml version="1.0"?>
<!-- codepoint-equal.xsl -->
<xsl:stylesheet version="2.0"
  xmlns:xsl="http://www.w3.org/1999/XSL/Transform"
  xmlns:xs="http://www.w3.org/2001/XMLSchema">

  <xsl:output method="text"/>

  <xsl:template match="/">
    <xsl:text>&#xA;Tests of the codepoint-equal() function:&#xA;</xsl:text>

    <xsl:text>&#xA;  codepoint-equal('A', 'A') = </xsl:text>
    <xsl:value-of select="codepoint-equal('A', 'A')"/>

    <xsl:text>&#xA;  codepoint-equal('A', '&amp;#x41;') = </xsl:text>
    <xsl:value-of select="codepoint-equal('A', '&amp;#x41;')"/>

    <xsl:text>&#xA;  codepoint-equal('A', '&amp;#65;') = </xsl:text>
```

```
<xsl:value-of select="codepoint-equal('A', '&#65;')"/>

<xsl:text>&#xA;  codepoint-equal('Strasse', 'Stra&amp;#xDF;e') = </xsl:text>
<xsl:value-of select="codepoint-equal('Strasse', 'Stra&#xDF;e')"/>
</xsl:template>

</xsl:stylesheet>
```

Here are the stylesheet results:

```
Tests of the codepoint-equal() function:

codepoint-equal('A', 'A') = true
codepoint-equal('A', '&#x41;') = true
codepoint-equal('A', '&#65;') = true
codepoint-equal('Strasse', 'Straße') = false
```

The first three tests compare the capital letter *A* with itself and with the hexadecimal and decimal representations of itself. The last test compares two spellings of the German word *Strasse*, one of which uses *ss* and one of which uses the German "sharp-s" character (ß). In the Unicode code point collation, these two strings are not equal.

There are some functions in XPath 2.0 and XSLT 2.0 that allow us to specify different collation algorithms (one in which ss and ß are equal, for example). See the definitions of the functions [2.0] `compare( )`, `contains( )`, [2.0] `deep-equal( )`, [2.0] `distinct-values( )`, [2.0] `ends-with( )`, [2.0] `index-of( )`, [2.0] `max( )`, [2.0] `min( )`, `starts-with( )`, `substring-after( )`, and `substring-before( )` for examples.

[2.0] codepoints-to-string()

Converts a sequence of Unicode codepoints to a string.

Syntax

```
xs:string codepoints-to-string(xs:integer*)
```

Inputs

A sequence of `xs:integer`s, each of which represents a Unicode codepoint.

Output

An `xs:string` created by concatenating the given codepoints. If the input argument is the empty sequence, `codepoints-to-string( )` returns a zero-length string. If any codepoint in the argument is not a legal XML character, the XSLT processor raises an error.

Defined in

XQuery 1.0 and XPath 2.0 Functions and Operators section 7.2, "Functions to Assemble and Disassemble Strings."

Example

Here's a short stylesheet that converts sequences of integers into strings:

```
<?xml version="1.0"?>
<!-- codepoints-to-string.xsl -->
<xsl:stylesheet version="2.0"
  xmlns:xsl="http://www.w3.org/1999/XSL/Transform"
  xmlns:xs="http://www.w3.org/2001/XMLSchema">

  <xsl:output method="text"/>

  <xsl:template match="/">
    <xsl:text>&#xA;Tests of the codepoints-to-string() </xsl:text>
    <xsl:text>function:&#xA;</xsl:text>

    <xsl:text>&#xA;  codepoints-to-string</xsl:text>
    <xsl:text>((76, 105, 108, 121)) = </xsl:text>
    <xsl:value-of
      select="codepoints-to-string((76, 105, 108, 121))"/>

    <xsl:text>&#xA;  codepoints-to-string</xsl:text>
    <xsl:text>((83, 116, 114, 97, 223, 101)) = </xsl:text>
    <xsl:value-of
      select="codepoints-to-string((83, 116, 114, 97, 223, 101))"/>
  </xsl:template>

</xsl:stylesheet>
```

The stylesheet generates these results:

```
Tests of the codepoints-to-string() function:

  codepoints-to-string((76, 105, 108, 121)) = Lily
  codepoints-to-string((83, 116, 114, 97, 223, 101)) = Straße
```

We mentioned earlier that if any codepoint in the input sequence is not a valid XML character, the XSLT processor throws an error. As an example, `codepoints-to-string((0))` causes the XSLT processor to crash; feel free to try this in your spare time.

[2.0] collection()

Returns a collection of nodes. This expands on the capabilities of the `document()` function defined in XSLT 1.0.

Syntax

```
node()* collection(xs:string?)
```

Input

An optional `xs:string` specifying the URI of a collection. If no string is given, the default collection is returned.

Output

The specified collection of nodes. If no collection name is given, the default collection is returned. The details of the URI format and what kinds of resources can be accessed are implementation-dependent.

Defined in

XQuery 1.0 and XPath 2.0 Functions and Operators section 15.5, "Functions and Operators that Generate Sequences."

Example

For our example, we'll use Saxon's implementation that allows us to load an XML document referencing other XML documents. The structure of the collection document is:

```
<?xml version="1.0"?>
<!-- polist.xml -->
<collection>
  <doc href="po38292.xml"/>
  <doc href="po38293.xml"/>
  <doc href="po38294.xml"/>
  <doc href="po38295.xml"/>
</collection>
```

When loading this document with the collection( ) function, Saxon looks at the href attributes of all the <doc> elements and considers each one a document URI. Saxon then opens and parses those documents and adds their nodes to the collection. Each document URI in our example points to a purchase order document structured like this:

```
<?xml version="1.0" ?>
<!-- po38293.xml -->
<purchase-order id="38293">
  <date year="2001" month="9" day="8"/>
  <customer id="4738" level="Basic">
    <address type="business">
      <name>
        <title>Ms.</title>
        <first-name>Amanda</first-name>
        <last-name>Reckonwith</last-name>
      </name>
      <street>930-A Chestnut Street</street>
      <city>Lynn</city>
      <state>MA</state>
      <zip>02930</zip>
    </address>
    <address type="ship-to"/>
  </customer>
  <items>
    <item part-no="23813-03-CDK">
      <name>Cucumber Decorating Kit</name>
      <qty>1</qty>
      <price>29.95</price>
    </item>
  </items>
</purchase-order>
```

When the file *polist.xml* is processed, our collection contains four document elements, each of which represents a purchase order. We can then use XSLT and XPath to work with all the nodes in the collection. Here is the stylesheet that loads the collection and works with it:

```
<?xml version="1.0"?>
<!-- collection.xsl -->
<xsl:stylesheet version="2.0"
  xmlns:xsl="http://www.w3.org/1999/XSL/Transform">

  <xsl:output method="text"/>

  <xsl:template match="/">
    <xsl:text>&#xA;A test of the collection() function:</xsl:text>

    <xsl:variable name="docPile" as="node()*"
      select="collection('polist.xml')"/>

    <xsl:text>&#xA;&#xA;  The customers in the </xsl:text>
    <xsl:text>collection are: &#xA;     </xsl:text>
    <xsl:for-each select="$docPile/purchase-order/customer">
      <xsl:sort select="address/name/last-name"/>
      <xsl:value-of
        select="address/name/title,
                address/name/first-name,
                address/name/last-name"
        separator=" "/>
      <xsl:text>&#xA;     </xsl:text>
    </xsl:for-each>
  </xsl:template>

</xsl:stylesheet>
```

Running the stylesheet gives us these results:

```
A test of the collection() function:

The customers in the collection are:
   Ms. Natalie Attired
   Mrs. Mary Backstayge
   Mr. Chester Hasbrouck Frisby
   Ms. Amanda Reckonwith
```

We loaded the collection and stored the document nodes of each of the files in the variable docPile. Once the collection is loaded, we can work with the nodes in the collection, even though they don't share a common document root. In the sample stylesheet, we listed all of the customers in all of the purchase orders in the collection. We used <xsl:for-each> to iterate through the purchase orders, and we used <xsl:sort> to list the customers by their last names.

Remember that most of the details of the collection( ) function are implementation-defined. Saxon's use of the <collection> and <doc> elements are not part of the spec; neither is the feature that let us load the collection document by typing the name of the file. See the documentation for your XSLT processor for the details of how it implements the collection( ) function.

[2.0] compare()

Compares two xs:strings and returns -1, 0, or 1, depending on whether the first string is less than, equal to, or greater than the second.

Syntax

```
xs:integer? compare(xs:string?, xs:string?)
xs:integer? compare(xs:string?, xs:string?, $collation as xs:string)
```

Inputs

Two xs:strings and an optional collation.

Output

The numeric value -1, 0, or 1, depending on whether the first string is less than, equal to, or greater than the second. The optional $collation argument names a collation used for comparing the two strings. To quote an example from the XSLT 2.0 spec, in a collation for German characters, *Strasse* and *Straße* are equal; in other collations they are not. If either string is the empty sequence, compare( ) returns the empty sequence.

Defined in

XQuery 1.0 and XPath 2.0 Functions and Operators section 7.3, "Equality and Comparison of Strings."

Example

Here's a stylesheet that uses compare( ) in several different ways:

```
<?xml version="1.0"?>
<!-- compare1.xsl -->
<xsl:stylesheet version="2.0"
  xmlns:xsl="http://www.w3.org/1999/XSL/Transform">

  <xsl:output method="text"/>

  <xsl:template match="/">
    <xsl:text>&#xA;Here are some tests of the compare() </xsl:text>
    <xsl:text>function:&#xA;</xsl:text>

    <xsl:text>&#xA;  compare('Lily', 'lily') = </xsl:text>
    <xsl:value-of select="compare('Lily', 'lily')"/>

    <xsl:text>&#xA;  compare('Lily', 'Lily') = </xsl:text>
    <xsl:value-of select="compare('Lily', 'Lily')"/>

    <xsl:text>&#xA;  compare('Lily', </xsl:text>
    <xsl:text>'&amp;#x4C;&amp;#x69;&amp;#x6C;&amp;#x79;') = </xsl:text>
    <xsl:value-of select="compare('Lily', '&#x4C;&#x69;&#x6C;&#x79;')"/>

    <xsl:text>&#xA;  compare('Lily', 'Doug') = </xsl:text>
    <xsl:value-of select="compare('Lily', 'Doug')"/>
```

```
<xsl:text>&#xA;&#xA;  if (not(compare('Lily', 'Lily'))) : </xsl:text>
<xsl:value-of select="if (not(compare('Lily', 'Lily')))
                      then 'The two test strings are equal!'
                      else 'The two test strings aren''t equal!'"/>
</xsl:template>

</xsl:stylesheet>
```

Here are the results:

```
Here are some tests of the compare() function:

compare('Lily', 'lily') = -1
compare('Lily', 'Lily') = 0
compare('Lily', '&#x4C;&#x69;&#x6C;&#x79;') = 0
compare('Lily', 'Doug') = 1

if (not(compare('Lily', 'Lily'))) : The two test strings are equal!
```

The first four tests of the compare( ) function compared strings, with the third test using character entities instead of the actual text. In the fifth test, we used compare( ) in a boolean expression; if the two strings are equal, compare( ) returns 0. The expression not(compare( )) is an awkward way of saying, "If these two strings are not unequal."

Keep in mind that we could use any of the comparison operators in XPath, either the operators for atomic values (eq, ne, gt, lt, ge, and le) or the more general operators (=, !=, >, <, >=, and <=). The only time you're required to use the compare( ) function is when you need to specify a collation.

Speaking of which, we'll look at a final example that uses a collation function. The German word for *street* can be spelled two ways: *Strasse* and *Straße*. We'll compare the two words twice, once using the default collation and once using a German collation provided by an extension function. Here's the stylesheet:

```
<?xml version="1.0"?>
<!-- compare2.xsl -->
<xsl:stylesheet version="2.0"
  xmlns:xsl="http://www.w3.org/1999/XSL/Transform"
  xmlns:xs="http://www.w3.org/2001/XMLSchema">

<xsl:output method="text"/>

<xsl:template match="/">
  <xsl:variable name="string1" select="'Stra&#xDF;e'"/>
  <xsl:variable name="string2" select="'Strasse'"/>

  <xsl:text>&#xA;Here are more tests of the compare() </xsl:text>
  <xsl:text>function:&#xA;</xsl:text>

  <xsl:text>  compare('</xsl:text>
  <xsl:value-of select="$string1"/>
  <xsl:text>', '</xsl:text>
  <xsl:value-of select="$string2"/>
  <xsl:text>') = </xsl:text>
  <xsl:value-of select="compare($string1, $string2)"/>
  <xsl:text>&#xA;</xsl:text>
```

```
<xsl:text>  compare('</xsl:text>
<xsl:value-of select="$string1"/>
<xsl:text>', '</xsl:text>
<xsl:value-of select="$string2"/>
<xsl:text>', [German collation]) = </xsl:text>
<xsl:value-of
  select="compare($string1, $string2,
          concat('http://saxon.sf.net/collation?',
                 'class=com.oreilly.xslt.GermanCollation;'))"/>
<xsl:text>&#xA;</xsl:text>
</xsl:template>

</xsl:stylesheet>
```

Here are the results:

```
Here are more tests of the compare() function:
  compare('Straße', 'Strasse') = 1
  compare('Straße', 'Strasse', [German collation]) = 0
```

As you can see, the two spellings are different in the default collation, but they're equal when we use the German collation. (To keep the listing within the margins of the page, we used the concat( ) function to combine the two halves of the Saxon collation URI.) See "The document() Function and Sorting" in Chapter 8 for more information.

concat()

Takes all of its arguments and concatenates them. Any arguments that are not strings are converted to strings as if processed by the string( ) function.

Syntax

```
[1.0] string concat(string, string, string*)
[2.0] xs:string concat(xs:anyAtomicType?, xs:anyAtomicType?, ...)
```

Inputs

Two or more strings. The concat( ) function is unique in that it may have any number of arguments.

[2.0] In XSLT 2.0, the arguments passed to the concat( ) function can be any atomic type. All of the values are converted to strings. If any of the arguments is the empty sequence, it is treated as a zero-length string. It is an error if any argument is a sequence with a length greater than 1.

Output

The concatenation of all of the input values.

Defined in

[1.0] XPath section 4.2, "String Functions."

[2.0] XQuery 1.0 and XPath 2.0 Functions and Operators section 7.4, "Functions on String Values."

Example

We'll use this XML file to demonstrate how concat( ) works:

```
<?xml version="1.0"?>
<!-- albums.xml -->
<list xml:lang="en">
  <title>Albums I've bought recently:</title>
  <listitem>The Sacred Art of Dub</listitem>
  <listitem>Only the Poor Man Feel It</listitem>
  <listitem>Excitable Boy</listitem>
  <listitem xml:lang="sw">Aki Special</listitem>
  <listitem xml:lang="en-gb">Combat Rock</listitem>
  <listitem xml:lang="zu">Talking Timbuktu</listitem>
  <listitem xml:lang="jz">The Birth of the Cool</listitem>
</list>
```

In our stylesheet, we'll use the concat( ) function to create filenames for various HTML files. The filenames are composed from three pieces of information, concatenated by the concat( ) function:

```
<?xml version="1.0"?>
<!-- concat.xsl -->
<xsl:stylesheet version="1.0"
  xmlns:xsl="http://www.w3.org/1999/XSL/Transform">

  <xsl:output method="text"/>

  <xsl:template match="/">
    <xsl:text>&#xA;Tests of the concat() function: &#xA;</xsl:text>
    <xsl:for-each select="list/listitem">
      <xsl:text>&#xA;  See the file </xsl:text>
      <xsl:value-of select="concat('album', position(), '.html')"/>
      <xsl:text> to see the details of &#xA;    the album "</xsl:text>
      <xsl:value-of select="."/>
      <xsl:text>."&#xA;</xsl:text>
    </xsl:for-each>
  </xsl:template>

</xsl:stylesheet>
```

Our stylesheet generates these results:

```
Tests of the concat() function:

  See the file album1.html to see the details of
    the album "The Sacred Art of Dub."

  See the file album2.html to see the details of
    the album "Only the Poor Man Feel It."

  See the file album3.html to see the details of
    the album "Excitable Boy."
  ...
```

[2.0] To illustrate how `concat( )` combines atomic values in XSLT 2.0, here's another stylesheet:

```
<?xml version="1.0"?>
<!-- concat2.xsl -->
<xsl:stylesheet version="2.0"
  xmlns:xsl="http://www.w3.org/1999/XSL/Transform"
  xmlns:xs="http://www.w3.org/2001/XMLSchema">

  <xsl:output method="text"/>

  <xsl:template match="/">
    <xsl:text>&#xA;Another test of the concat() function: &#xA;</xsl:text>

    <xsl:text>&#xA;  concat(3, 4, current-time(), 'blue', </xsl:text>
    <xsl:text>/list/title) = &#xA;     </xsl:text>
    <xsl:value-of
      select="concat(3, 4, current-time(), 'blue', /list/title)"/>
  </xsl:template>

</xsl:stylesheet>
```

When used with our XML input document, the stylesheet produces these results:

```
Another test of the concat() function:

  concat(3, 4, current-time(), 'blue', /list/title) =
     3416:23:12.217-04:00blueAlbums I've bought recently:
```

This concatenates the numbers 3 and 4, the `xs:time` value returned by the `current-time( )` function, the string blue, and the `<title>` element from the input document. All of those values are converted to strings and concatenated.

All the arguments to `concat( )` must be atomic values or sequences of zero or one items. The stylesheet works with our XML input document because there is only one node in the document that matches the XPath expression `/list/title`. If we change the XPath expression to `/list/listitem`, it selects more than one node, and the XSLT processor raises an error. To concatenate sequences of multiple items, use the *[2.0]* `string-join( )` function.

contains()

Determines whether the first argument string contains the second.

Syntax

```
[1.0] boolean contains(string, string)
[2.0] xs:boolean contains(xs:string?, xs:string?)
[2.0] xs:boolean contains(xs:string?, xs:string?, $collation as xs:string)
```

Inputs

Two strings. If the first string contains the second string, the function returns the boolean value `true`. *[2.0]* In XSLT 2.0, there is an optional third argument—the name of a collation that specifies how strings in different languages are compared.

Output

The boolean value `true` if the first argument contains the second; `false` otherwise. If the second string is a zero-length string, `contains( )` returns `true`. If the first string is a zero-length string, `contains( )` returns `false`.

Defined in

[1.0] XPath section 4.2, "String Functions."

[2.0] XQuery 1.0 and XPath 2.0 Functions and Operators section 7.5, "Functions Based on Substring Matching."

Example

This stylesheet uses the `replace-substring` named template. It passes three arguments to the `replace-substring` template: the original string, the substring to be searched for in the original string, and the substring to replace the target substring in the original string. The `replace-substring` template uses the `contains( )`, `substring-after( )`, and `substring-before( )` functions.

Here is our sample stylesheet. It replaces all occurrences of `World` with the string `"Mundo"`:

```
<?xml version="1.0"?>
<!-- contains1.xsl -->
<xsl:stylesheet version="1.0"
  xmlns:xsl="http://www.w3.org/1999/XSL/Transform">

  <xsl:output method="text"/>

  <xsl:template match="/">
    <xsl:text>&#xA;A test of the contains() function:&#xA;&#xA;</xsl:text>
    <xsl:text>  Replacing 'World' with 'Mundo' in </xsl:text>
    <xsl:text>'Hello World!': &#xA;    </xsl:text>
    <xsl:variable name="test">
      <xsl:call-template name="replace-substring">
        <xsl:with-param name="original">Hello World!</xsl:with-param>
        <xsl:with-param name="substring">World</xsl:with-param>
        <xsl:with-param name="replacement">Mundo</xsl:with-param>
      </xsl:call-template>
    </xsl:variable>
    <xsl:value-of select="$test"/>
  </xsl:template>

  <xsl:template name="replace-substring">
    <xsl:param name="original" />
    <xsl:param name="substring" />
    <xsl:param name="replacement" />
    <xsl:choose>
      <xsl:when test="contains($original, $substring)">
        <xsl:value-of select="substring-before($original, $substring)" />
        <xsl:value-of select="$replacement" />
        <xsl:call-template name="replace-substring">
          <xsl:with-param name="original"
            select="substring-after($original, $substring)" />
```

```
        <xsl:with-param name="substring" select="$substring" />
        <xsl:with-param name="replacement" select="$replacement" />
      </xsl:call-template>
    </xsl:when>
    <xsl:otherwise>
      <xsl:value-of select="$original" />
    </xsl:otherwise>
  </xsl:choose>
</xsl:template>

</xsl:stylesheet>
```

In this example, we're replacing one substring with another. To do this, we use three functions (contains( ), substring-after( ), and substring-before( )) and a recursive named template (replace-substring). Our recursive template takes three strings as input: the original string, the string to be replaced, and the replacement string itself. If the original string doesn't contain the string to be replaced, our named template returns the entire string. Otherwise, the template calls itself recursively, using three arguments: the portion of the string after the string to be replaced, the string to be replaced, and the replacement string. Put another way, if the named template finds the string to be replaced, it invokes itself on the rest of the string. The substring-after function is a key part of the named template.

The stylesheet produces these results, regardless of the XML document used as input:

```
Hello Mundo!
```

[2.0] In our first example, we used XSLT 1.0, so we created a tail-recursive named procedure that uses contains( ), substring-after( ), and substring-before( ) to replace one substring with another. In XSLT 2.0, we can use the very useful replace( ) function instead:

```
<?xml version="1.0"?>
<!-- replace2.xsl -->
<xsl:stylesheet version="2.0"
  xmlns:xsl="http://www.w3.org/1999/XSL/Transform">

  <xsl:output method="text"/>

  <xsl:template match="/">
    <xsl:text>&#xA;A test of the replace() function:&#xA;&#xA;</xsl:text>
    <xsl:text>  Replacing 'World' with 'Mundo' in </xsl:text>
    <xsl:text>'Hello World!': &#xA;     </xsl:text>
    <xsl:value-of select="replace('Hello World', 'World', 'Mundo')"/>
  </xsl:template>

</xsl:stylesheet>
```

This stylesheet generates the same results as our XSLT 1.0 stylesheet, but with far less code.

As a final example, we'll illustrate the use of a collation function:

```
<?xml version="1.0"?>
<!-- contains2.xsl -->
<xsl:stylesheet version="1.0"
  xmlns:xsl="http://www.w3.org/1999/XSL/Transform">

  <xsl:output method="text"/>
```

```
<xsl:template match="/">
  <xsl:variable name="string1"
    select="'Sch&#xF6;naicherstra&#xDF;e'"/>
  <xsl:variable name="string2" select="'strasse'"/>

  <xsl:text>&#xA;Another test of the contains() </xsl:text>
  <xsl:text>function:&#xA;&#xA;</xsl:text>

  <xsl:text>  contains('</xsl:text>
  <xsl:value-of select="$string1"/>
  <xsl:text>', '</xsl:text>
  <xsl:value-of select="$string2"/>
  <xsl:text>') = </xsl:text>
  <xsl:value-of select="contains($string1, $string2)"/>
  <xsl:text>&#xA;</xsl:text>

  <xsl:text>  contains('</xsl:text>
  <xsl:value-of select="$string1"/>
  <xsl:text>', '</xsl:text>
  <xsl:value-of select="$string2"/>
  <xsl:text>', [German collation]) = </xsl:text>
  <xsl:value-of
    select="contains($string1, $string2,
            concat('http://saxon.sf.net/collation?',
                   'class=com.oreilly.xslt.GermanCollation;'))"/>
  <xsl:text>&#xA;</xsl:text>
</xsl:template>

</xsl:stylesheet>
```

Here are the results:

```
Another test of the contains() function:

  contains('Schönaicherstraße', 'strasse') = false
  contains('Schönaicherstraße', 'strasse', [German collation]) = true
```

The German word for *street* can be spelled either *Strasse* or *Straße*. In this stylesheet, using the German collation respects this difference; the default collation does not. (To keep the listing within the margins of the page, we used the **concat( )** function to combine the two halves of the Saxon collation URI.) See "The document() Function and Sorting" in Chapter 8 for more information.

count()

Counts the number of nodes in a given *[1.0]* node-set or *[2.0]* sequence.

Syntax

```
[1.0] number count(node-set)
[2.0] xs:integer count(item()*)
```

Inputs

A node-set or sequence.

Output

The number of items in the node-set or sequence. *[2.0]* If the argument is the empty sequence, count( ) returns 0.

Defined in

[1.0] XPath section 4.1, "Node Set Functions."

[2.0] XQuery 1.0 and XPath 2.0 Functions and Operators section 15.4, "Aggregate Functions."

Examples

Here's the XML document we'll use to illustrate the count( ) function:

```
<?xml version="1.0" encoding="utf-8"?>
<!-- chocolate.xml -->
<report month="8" year="2006">
  <title>Chocolate bar sales</title>
  <brand>
    <name>Lindt</name>
    <units>27408</units>
  </brand>
  <brand>
    <name>Callebaut</name>
    <units>8203</units>
  </brand>
  <brand>
    <name>Valrhona</name>
    <units>22101</units>
  </brand>
  <brand>
    <name>Perugina</name>
    <units>14336</units>
  </brand>
  <brand>
    <name>Ghirardelli</name>
    <units>19268</units>
  </brand>
</report>
```

And our stylesheet that illustrates the count( ) function:

```
<?xml version="1.0"?>
<!-- count.xsl -->
<xsl:stylesheet version="1.0"
  xmlns:xsl="http://www.w3.org/1999/XSL/Transform">

  <xsl:output method="text"/>

  <xsl:template match="/">
    <xsl:text>&#xA;Tests of the count() function:&#xA;&#xA;</xsl:text>
```

```
<xsl:text>  Our store sells </xsl:text>
<xsl:value-of select="count(/report/brand)"/>
<xsl:text> different brands of chocolate.</xsl:text>
<xsl:text>&#xA;&#xA;  For the last month, </xsl:text>
<xsl:value-of select="count(/report/brand[units > 20000])"/>
<xsl:text> brand(s) sold more than 20,000 units,</xsl:text>
<xsl:text>&#xA;    and all but </xsl:text>
<xsl:value-of select="count(/report/brand[units &lt; 10000])"/>
<xsl:text> brand(s) sold 10,000 units or more.</xsl:text>

<xsl:text>&#xA;&#xA;  Here are the brands we sell: </xsl:text>
<xsl:for-each select="/report/brand">
  <xsl:text>&#xA;    Brand </xsl:text>
  <xsl:value-of select="position()"/>
  <xsl:text> of </xsl:text>
  <xsl:value-of select="count(/report/brand)"/>
  <xsl:text>: </xsl:text>
  <xsl:value-of select="name"/>
</xsl:for-each>
</xsl:template>

</xsl:stylesheet>
```

Here are the results of our stylesheet:

```
Tests of the count() function:

  Our store sells 5 different brands of chocolate.

  For the last month, 2 brand(s) sold more than 20,000 units,
    and all but 1 brand(s) sold 10,000 units or more.

  Here are the brands we sell:
    Brand 1 of 5: Lindt
    Brand 2 of 5: Callebaut
    Brand 3 of 5: Valrhona
    Brand 4 of 5: Perugina
    Brand 5 of 5: Ghirardelli
```

We use the count( ) function in several different ways here. In the first sentence, the number 5 is the count of <brand> elements in the document. In the second sentence, we use count( ) with XPath predicates to count only <brand> elements whose <units> children have certain values. Finally, in the list of the brands we sell, we use the position( ) and count( ) functions together to create the "Brand x of y" text.

There are two things to notice. First of all, the stylesheet begins with <xsl:stylesheet version="1.0". This stylesheet works with both XSLT 1.0 and 2.0 processors. Secondly, we used < for the less-than symbol (<); the value of an attribute can't contain a less-than sign.

Here's a short stylesheet to illustrate how count( ) works with sequences in XSLT 2.0:

```
<?xml version="1.0"?>
<!-- count2.xsl -->
<xsl:stylesheet version="2.0"
  xmlns:xsl="http://www.w3.org/1999/XSL/Transform"
```

```
    xmlns:xs="http://www.w3.org/2001/XMLSchema">

    <xsl:output method="text"/>

    <xsl:template match="/">
      <xsl:text>&#xA;Tests of the count() function:&#xA;&#xA;</xsl:text>

      <xsl:variable name="salesFigures" as="xs:integer*">
        <xsl:sequence select="/report/brand/units"/>
      </xsl:variable>

      <xsl:text>  Our store sells </xsl:text>
      <xsl:value-of select="count($salesFigures)"/>
      <xsl:text> different brands of chocolate.</xsl:text>
      <xsl:text>&#xA;&#xA;  For the last month, </xsl:text>
      <xsl:value-of select="count($salesFigures[. > 20000])"/>
      <xsl:text> brand(s) sold more than 20,000 units,</xsl:text>
      <xsl:text>&#xA;    and all but </xsl:text>
      <xsl:value-of select="count($salesFigures[. &lt; 10000])"/>
      <xsl:text> brand(s) sold 10,000 units or more.</xsl:text>
    </xsl:template>

  </xsl:stylesheet>
```

We create a sequence of **xs:integer**s here, and then use the **count( )** function to count the items in the sequence. Just as we did with the first stylesheet, we use predicates to select certain values from the sequence. Here are the results:

```
Tests of the count() function:

  Our store sells 5 different brands of chocolate.

  For the last month, 2 brand(s) sold more than 20,000 units,
    and all but 1 brand(s) sold 10,000 units or more.
```

In the second stylesheet, our sequence contains the **xs:integer** values of the **<units>** elements in our source document, so the XPath predicate uses the current node (.) in the comparison expression: count($salesFigures[. > 20000]. In our first stylesheet, we could have written count(/report/brand[units < 10000]) as count(/report/brand/units[. < 10000] to get the same results with a similar XPath expression.

---

current()

Returns a node-set that has the current node as its only member.

Syntax

```
[1.0] node-set current()
[2.0] item() current()
```

Inputs

None.

Output

[1.0] A node-set that has the current node as its only member. Most of the time, the current node is no different than the context node.

[2.0] This function, used inside an XPath expression, returns the item that was the context item when the expression was invoked.

In XSLT 1.0 and 2.0, the current node/item is almost always the same as the context node/item. For example, the two XPath expressions below are always the same:

```
<xsl:value-of select="current()"/>
<xsl:value-of select="."/>
```

Within a predicate expression, however, the current node and the context node are usually different.

Defined in

[1.0] XSLT section 12.4, "Miscellaneous Additional Functions."

[2.0] XSLT section 16.6, "Miscellaneous Additional Functions."

Example

We'll use the **current( )** function along with a lookup table. We'll transform a modified version of our chocolate sales figures:

```
<?xml version="1.0" encoding="utf-8"?>
<!-- chocolate-by-month.xml -->
<report year="2006">
  <title>Chocolate bar sales by month</title>
  <sales month="08" total="91316"/>
  <sales month="09" total="82911"/>
  <sales month="10" total="128587"/>
  <sales month="11" total="79244"/>
  <sales month="12" total="113606"/>
</report>
```

Here's our stylesheet. It has a lookup table of month names; we'll use the lookup table to replace the month attribute with the name of the corresponding month. The stylesheet does the same transform three times, once with the **current( )** function and twice without it:

```
<?xml version="1.0"?>
<!-- current.xsl -->
<xsl:stylesheet version="1.0"
    xmlns:xsl="http://www.w3.org/1999/XSL/Transform"
    xmlns:months="http://www.months.com">

    <months:name sequence="01">January</months:name>
    <months:name sequence="02">February</months:name>
    <months:name sequence="03">March</months:name>
    <months:name sequence="04">April</months:name>
    <months:name sequence="05">May</months:name>
    <months:name sequence="06">June</months:name>
    <months:name sequence="07">July</months:name>
    <months:name sequence="08">August</months:name>
```

```
<months:name sequence="09">September</months:name>
<months:name sequence="10">October</months:name>
<months:name sequence="11">November</months:name>
<months:name sequence="12">December</months:name>

<xsl:output method="text"/>

<xsl:template match="/">
  <xsl:text>&#xA;Tests of the current() function:&#xA;</xsl:text>

  <xsl:text>&#xA;  Using the current() function:&#xA;</xsl:text>
  <xsl:text>&#xA;    Chocolate bar sales for </xsl:text>
  <xsl:value-of select="/report/@year"/>
  <xsl:text>: &#xA;</xsl:text>

  <xsl:for-each select="/report/sales">
    <xsl:text>&#xA;      </xsl:text>
    <xsl:value-of
      select="document('')/*/months:name[@sequence=current()/@month][1]"/>
    <xsl:text> - Total sales = </xsl:text>
    <xsl:value-of select="format-number(@total, '##,###')"/>
  </xsl:for-each>

  <xsl:text>&#xA;&#xA;  Without the current() function:&#xA;</xsl:text>
  <xsl:text>&#xA;    Chocolate bar sales for </xsl:text>
  <xsl:value-of select="/report/@year"/>
  <xsl:text>: &#xA;</xsl:text>

  <xsl:for-each select="/report/sales">
    <xsl:text>&#xA;      </xsl:text>
    <xsl:value-of
      select="document('')/*/months:name[@sequence=./@month][1]"/>
    <xsl:text> - Total sales = </xsl:text>
    <xsl:value-of select="format-number(@total, '##,###')"/>
  </xsl:for-each>

  <xsl:text>&#xA;&#xA;  Another test without the current() </xsl:text>
  <xsl:text>function:&#xA;</xsl:text>
  <xsl:text>&#xA;    Chocolate bar sales for </xsl:text>
  <xsl:value-of select="/report/@year"/>
  <xsl:text>: &#xA;</xsl:text>

  <xsl:for-each select="/report/sales">
    <xsl:text>&#xA;      </xsl:text>
    <xsl:value-of
      select="document('')/*/months:name[@sequence=./@sequence][1]"/>
    <xsl:text> - Total sales = </xsl:text>
    <xsl:value-of select="format-number(@total, '##,###')"/>
  </xsl:for-each>
</xsl:template>

</xsl:stylesheet>
```

Here are the results:

```
Tests of the current() function:

  Using the current() function:

    Chocolate bar sales for 2006:

        August - Total sales = 91,316
        September - Total sales = 82,911
        October - Total sales = 128,587
        November - Total sales = 79,244
        December - Total sales = 113,606

  Without the current() function:

    Chocolate bar sales for 2006:

        - Total sales = 91,316
        - Total sales = 82,911
        - Total sales = 128,587
        - Total sales = 79,244
        - Total sales = 113,606

  Another test without the current() function:

    Chocolate bar sales for 2006:

        January - Total sales = 91,316
        January - Total sales = 82,911
        January - Total sales = 128,587
        January - Total sales = 79,244
        January - Total sales = 113,606
```

The first test works correctly because we use the current( ) function. This function returns the <sales> element we're currently processing. Within the predicate expression, we have to use current( ) to get that element. The <xsl:value-of> element outputs the text of the <months:name> element whose sequence attribute matches the month attribute of the current <sales> element.

Notice that we end the XPath expression with another predicate, [1], to make sure we select only the first match. That doesn't matter in XSLT 1.0, because <xsl:value-of> uses only the first node in the node-set. XSLT 2.0, however, uses *all* the items that match. Because of the structure of our XML source document, only one item matches in the first test, but that might not be the case for all XML source documents. For that reason, specifying exactly which node you want to use is a good habit to get into, especially if you're going to migrate XSLT 1.0 stylesheets to XSLT 2.0.

The second and third tests don't work because we don't use the current( ) function. In the second test, our XPath expression is document('')/*/months:name[@sequence=./@month][1]. The dot here represents the <months:name> element we're evaluating, *not* the current <sales> element. The XPath predicate [@sequence=./@month] doesn't match anything, because there aren't any <months:name> elements that have a month attribute.

The point of the third test is to illustrate what the dot operator (the context node) actually represents. The predicate [@sequence=./@sequence] wouldn't match anything if the dot represented the <sales> element we're currently processing; there aren't any <sales> elements with a sequence attribute. Because the dot represents the <months:name> element, there is a match. We specified that XSLT should output the first item ([1]), so every month is January.

A final note about the predicate specifying that we use the first item: in the first test, we could leave out the [1] predicate because the XPath expression matches only one node based on our XML source document. In the second test, we could leave out the [1] predicate because there weren't any matches. In the third test, however, leaving out the [1] predicate and changing the stylesheet version to 2.0 gives these results:

```
Another test without the current() function:

Chocolate bar sales for 2006:

    January February March April May June July August September Octo
ber November December - Total sales = 91,316
    January February March April May June July August September Octo
ber November December - Total sales = 82,911
    January February March April May June July August September Octo
ber November December - Total sales = 128,587
    January February March April May June July August September Octo
ber November December - Total sales = 79,244
    January February March April May June July August September Octo
ber November December - Total sales = 113,606
```

In XSLT 2.0, <xsl:value-of> uses all of the nodes that match, not just the first.

[2.0] current-date()

Returns the current date as an xs:date value.

Syntax

```
xs:date current-date()
```

Inputs

None.

Output

An xs:date value set to the current time on the system. The returned value is set to the default timezone. (You can get the details of the default timezone with the implicit-timezone( ) function). *The current-date( ) function returns the same value throughout the processing of the stylesheet.* If you call current-date( ) a dozen times throughout your stylesheet, the function returns the same value each time.

Defined in

XQuery 1.0 and XPath 2.0 Functions and Operators section 16, "Context Functions."

Example

Here is a stylesheet that displays the current date. It uses the `current-date( )`, `format-date( )`, and `implicit-timezone( )` functions.

```
<?xml version="1.0"?>
<!-- current-date.xsl -->
<xsl:stylesheet version="2.0"
  xmlns:xsl="http://www.w3.org/1999/XSL/Transform">

  <xsl:output method="text"/>

  <xsl:template match="/">
    <xsl:text>The current date is </xsl:text>
    <xsl:value-of
      select="format-date(current-date(),
              '[FNn], the [D1o] of [MNn], [Y01]')"/>
    <xsl:text>&#xA;&#xA;The implicit timezone for the </xsl:text>
    <xsl:text>current context is: </xsl:text>
    <xsl:value-of select="implicit-timezone()"/>
    <xsl:text>&#xA;&#xA;The timezone extracted from the </xsl:text>
    <xsl:text>current date is: </xsl:text>
    <xsl:value-of select="timezone-from-date(current-date())"/>
  </xsl:template>

</xsl:stylesheet>
```

Here are the stylesheet's results:

```
The current date is Thursday, the 6th of July, 06

The implicit timezone for the current context is: -PT4H

The timezone extracted from the current date is: -PT4H
```

Notice that the implicit timezone retrieved with the `implicit-timezone( )` function is the same timezone we extracted from the current date. The *implicit timezone* is a component of all the `xs:date`, `xs:dateTime`, and `xs:time` values created without specifying a particular timezone.

[2.0] current-dateTime()

Returns the current date and time as an `xs:dateTime` value.

Syntax

```
xs:dateTime current-dateTime()
```

Inputs

None.

Output

An `xs:dateTime` value set to the current date and time on the system. The returned value is set to the default timezone. (You can get the details of the default timezone with the context function `implicit-timezone( )`). *The current-dateTime( ) function returns the same value throughout the processing of the stylesheet.* If you call `current-dateTime( )` a dozen times throughout your stylesheet, the function returns the same value each time.

Defined in

XQuery 1.0 and XPath 2.0 Functions and Operators section 16, "Context Functions."

Example

Here is a stylesheet that displays the current date and time. It uses the `current-dateTime( )`, `format-dateTime( )` and `implicit-timezone( )` functions.

```
<?xml version="1.0"?>
<!-- current-datetime.xsl -->
<xsl:stylesheet version="2.0"
  xmlns:xsl="http://www.w3.org/1999/XSL/Transform">

  <xsl:output method="text"/>

  <xsl:template match="/">
    <xsl:text>The current date and time is </xsl:text>
    <xsl:value-of
      select="format-dateTime(current-dateTime(),
              '[h]:[mO1] [Pn] on [FNn], the [D1o] of [MNn], [Y]')"/>
    <xsl:text>&#xA;&#xA;The implicit timezone for the </xsl:text>
    <xsl:text>current context is: </xsl:text>
    <xsl:value-of select="implicit-timezone()"/>
    <xsl:text>&#xA;&#xA;The timezone extracted from the </xsl:text>
    <xsl:text>current date and time is: </xsl:text>
    <xsl:value-of select="timezone-from-dateTime(current-dateTime())"/>
  </xsl:template>

</xsl:stylesheet>
```

The results of this stylesheet are:

```
The current date and time is 6:43 a.m. on Thursday, the 6th of July, 2006

The implicit timezone for the current context is: -PT4H

The timezone extracted from the current date and time is: -PT4H
```

Notice that the implicit timezone retrieved with the `implicit-timezone( )` function is the same timezone we extracted from the current date and time. The implicit timezone is a component of all the `xs:date`, `xs:dateTime`, and `xs:time` values created without specifying a particular timezone.

[2.0] current-group()

Returns all the items that are included in the current group.

Syntax

```
item()* current-group()
```

Inputs

None.

Output

The set of items that are included in the current group. This function is only useful inside the `<xsl:for-each-group>` element. Calling `current-group( )` outside `<xsl:for-each-group>` returns the empty sequence.

Defined in

XSLT 2.0 section 14, "Grouping."

Example

We'll use a simplified version of our address book document to illustrate the `current-group( )` function:

```
<?xml version="1.0"?>
<!-- simple-addresses.xml -->
<addressbook>
  <address>
    <name>Mr. Chester Hasbrouck Frisby</name>
    <city>Sheboygan</city>
    <state>WI</state>
  </address>
  <address>
    <name>Mary Backstayge</name>
    <city>Skunk Haven</city>
    <state>MA</state>
  </address>
  <address>
    <name>Ms. Natalie Attired</name>
    <city>Winter Harbor</city>
    <state>ME</state>
  </address>
  <address>
    <name>Harry Backstayge</name>
    <city>Skunk Haven</city>
    <state>MA</state>
  </address>
  <address>
    <name>Mary McGoon</name>
    <city>Boylston</city>
    <state>VA</state>
  </address>
  <address>
    <name>Ms. Amanda Reckonwith</name>
    <city>Lynn</city>
    <state>MA</state>
```

```
        </address>
    </addressbook>
```

We'll group these names by `<state>` with this stylesheet:

```
<?xml version="1.0"?>
<!-- current-group.xsl -->
<xsl:stylesheet version="2.0"
    xmlns:xsl="http://www.w3.org/1999/XSL/Transform">

    <xsl:output method="text"/>

    <xsl:template match="/">
        <xsl:text>&#xA;Here's a test of the </xsl:text>
        <xsl:text>current-group() function:&#xA;</xsl:text>
        <xsl:text>&#xA;  Customers grouped by state</xsl:text>

        <xsl:for-each-group select="//address" group-by="state">
            <xsl:sort select="state"/>
            <xsl:text>&#xA;&#xA;    Customers in </xsl:text>
            <xsl:value-of select="current-grouping-key()"/>
            <xsl:text>:</xsl:text>

            <xsl:for-each select="current-group()">
                <xsl:text>&#xA;        </xsl:text>
                <xsl:value-of select="name"/>
                <xsl:text> of </xsl:text>
                <xsl:value-of select="city"/>
            </xsl:for-each>
        </xsl:for-each-group>
    </xsl:template>

</xsl:stylesheet>
```

In this example, we're grouping the people in our address book by the state they live in. The groups are selected by the `<xsl:for-each-group>` element. Within this element, we use `current-group()` in an `<xsl:for-each>` element to iterate through all the items in the current group.

Running our stylesheet against our simplified address book generates these results:

```
Here's a test of the current-group() function:

Customers grouped by state:

    Customers in MA:
        Mary Backstayge of Skunk Haven
        Harry Backstayge of Skunk Haven
        Ms. Amanda Reckonwith of Lynn

    Customers in ME:
        Ms. Natalie Attired of Winter Harbor

    Customers in VA:
        Mary McGoon of Boylston
```

```
Customers in WI:
   Mr. Chester Hasbrouck Frisby of Sheboygan
```

We could make our stylesheet more sophisticated by using the count( ) function with current-group( ). If we have more than one customer in a state (count(current-group( )) > 1), our heading could be Customers in MA. For states that have only one customer (count(current-group( )) = 1), our heading could be Our only customer in ME.

[2.0] current-grouping-key()

Returns the value used to select the current group.

Syntax

```
xs:anyAtomicType? current-grouping-key()
```

Inputs

None.

Output

The value used to select the items in the current group. The current-grouping-key( ) function is only useful inside an <xsl:for-each-group> element with a group-by or group-adjacent attribute. Calling current-grouping-key( ) anywhere else returns the empty sequence.

Defined in

XSLT 2.0 section 14, "Grouping."

Example

We'll use a simplified version of our address book document to illustrate the current-grouping-key( ) function:

```
<?xml version="1.0"?>
<!-- simple-addresses.xml -->
<addressbook>
  <address>
    <name>Mr. Chester Hasbrouck Frisby</name>
    <city>Sheboygan</city>
    <state>WI</state>
  </address>
  <address>
    <name>Mary Backstayge</name>
    <city>Skunk Haven</city>
    <state>MA</state>
  </address>
  <address>
    <name>Ms. Natalie Attired</name>
    <city>Winter Harbor</city>
    <state>ME</state>
  </address>
  <address>
```

```
      <name>Harry Backstayge</name>
      <city>Skunk Haven</city>
      <state>MA</state>
    </address>
    <address>
      <name>Mary McGoon</name>
      <city>Boylston</city>
      <state>VA</state>
    </address>
    <address>
      <name>Ms. Amanda Reckonwith</name>
      <city>Lynn</city>
      <state>MA</state>
    </address>
  </addressbook>
```

We'll group these names by `<state>` with this stylesheet:

```
<?xml version="1.0"?>
<!-- current-grouping-key.xsl -->
<xsl:stylesheet version="2.0"
  xmlns:xsl="http://www.w3.org/1999/XSL/Transform">

  <xsl:output method="text"/>

  <xsl:template match="/">
    <xsl:text>&#xA;Here's a test of the </xsl:text>
    <xsl:text>current-grouping-key() function:&#xA;</xsl:text>
    <xsl:text>&#xA;  Customers grouped by state</xsl:text>

    <xsl:for-each-group select="//address" group-by="state">
      <xsl:sort select="state"/>
      <xsl:text>&#xA;&#xA;    Customers in </xsl:text>
      <xsl:value-of select="current-grouping-key()"/>
      <xsl:text>:</xsl:text>

      <xsl:for-each select="current-group()">
        <xsl:text>&#xA;        </xsl:text>
        <xsl:value-of select="name"/>
        <xsl:text> of </xsl:text>
        <xsl:value-of select="city"/>
      </xsl:for-each>
    </xsl:for-each-group>
  </xsl:template>

</xsl:stylesheet>
```

In this example, we're grouping the people in our address book by the state they live in. In the heading for each group, we output the grouping value (the state) with current-grouping-key( ) in the heading for each state:

```
Here's a test of the current-grouping-key() function:

  Customers grouped by state:

    Customers in MA:
```

```
        Mary Backstayge of Skunk Haven
        Harry Backstayge of Skunk Haven
        Ms. Amanda Reckonwith of Lynn

    Customers in ME:
        Ms. Natalie Attired of Winter Harbor

    Customers in VA:
        Mary McGoon of Boylston

    Customers in WI:
        Mr. Chester Hasbrouck Frisby of Sheboygan
```

[2.0] current-time()

Returns an `xs:time` object set to the current time.

Syntax

```
    xs:time current-time()
```

Inputs

None.

Output

An `xs:time` value set to the current time on the system. The returned value is set to the default timezone. (You can get the details of the default timezone with the context function `implicit-timezone( )`). *The `current-time( )` function returns the same value throughout the processing of the stylesheet.* If you call `current-time( )` a dozen times throughout your stylesheet, the function returns the same value each time.

Defined in

XQuery 1.0 and XPath 2.0 Functions and Operators section 2, "Accessors."

Example

Here is a stylesheet that displays the current time. It uses the `current-time( )`, `format-time( )`, and `implicit-timezone( )` functions:

```
    <?xml version="1.0"?>
    <!-- current-time.xsl -->
    <xsl:stylesheet version="2.0"
      xmlns:xsl="http://www.w3.org/1999/XSL/Transform">

      <xsl:output method="text"/>

      <xsl:template match="/">
        <xsl:text>The current time is </xsl:text>
        <xsl:value-of
          select="format-time(current-time(),
                  '[h]:[m01] [Pn]')"/>
```

```
<xsl:text>&#xA;&#xA;The implicit timezone for the </xsl:text>
<xsl:text>current context is: </xsl:text>
<xsl:value-of select="implicit-timezone()"/>
<xsl:text>&#xA;&#xA;The timezone extracted from the </xsl:text>
<xsl:text>current date and time is: </xsl:text>
<xsl:value-of select="timezone-from-time(current-time())"/>
  </xsl:template>

</xsl:stylesheet>
```

The exciting results from this stylesheet look like this:

```
The current time is 6:49 a.m.

The implicit timezone for the current context is: -PT4H

The timezone extracted from the current date and time is: -PT4H
```

Notice that the implicit timezone retrieved with the `implicit-timezone( )` function is the same timezone we extracted from the current time. The implicit timezone is a component of all the `xs:date`, `xs:dateTime`, and `xs:time` values created without specifying a particular timezone.

[2.0] data()

Given a sequence of items, returns a sequence of atomic values that represent the set of items.

Syntax

```
xs:anyAtomicType* data(item()*)
```

Inputs

A sequence of items.

Output

A sequence in which each item in the input sequence has been converted to an atomic value. If an item in the input sequence is an atomic value, it is returned as is in the result sequence. For nodes, any item with a datatype is converted to an atomic value and returned in the result sequence.

Defined in

XQuery 1.0 and XPath 2.0 Functions and Operators section 2, "Accessors."

Example

Here is a stylesheet that creates a sequence of atoms and elements and lists them, identifying atomic values versus elements in the sequence. Next, the stylesheet lists the sequence returned by the `data( )` function:

```
<?xml version="1.0"?>
<!-- data.xsl -->
<xsl:stylesheet version="2.0"
  xmlns:xsl="http://www.w3.org/1999/XSL/Transform"
```

```
              xmlns:xs="http://www.w3.org/2001/XMLSchema"
              xmlns:datatest="http://www.oreilly.com">

  <xsl:output method="text"/>

  <xsl:template match="/">

    <!-- Before we test the data() function, we create a sequence. -->
    <xsl:variable name="testSequence" as="item()*">
      <xsl:sequence select="(3, 4, 5)"/>
      <xsl:element name="currentDate">
        <xsl:value-of select="current-date()"/>
      </xsl:element>
      <xsl:element name="currentTime">
        <xsl:value-of select="current-time()"/>
      </xsl:element>
      <xsl:element name="integerTest">
        <xsl:value-of select="xs:integer(8)"/>
      </xsl:element>
      <xsl:sequence select="('blue', 'red')"/>
      <xsl:element name="floatTest1">
        <xsl:value-of select="xs:float(3.14)"/>
      </xsl:element>
      <xsl:element name="floatTest2">
        <xsl:value-of select="xs:float(42)"/>
      </xsl:element>
      <xsl:element name="dateTest">
        <xsl:value-of select="xs:date('1995-04-21')"/>
      </xsl:element>
    </xsl:variable>

    <xsl:text>&#xA;Here is a test of the data() </xsl:text>
    <xsl:text>function:&#xA;</xsl:text>

    <xsl:text>&#xA;  Our original sequence is:&#xA;&#xA;    </xsl:text>
    <xsl:value-of
      select="for $i in (1 to count($testSequence))
              return (datatest:print-item(
              subsequence($testSequence, $i, 1)))"
      separator="&#xA;    "/>

    <xsl:text>&#xA;&#xA;  Passing our sequence to data() </xsl:text>
    <xsl:text>gives us:&#xA;&#xA;    </xsl:text>

    <xsl:variable name="atomicSequence" as="item()*"
      select="data($testSequence)"/>
    <xsl:value-of
      select="for $i in (1 to count($atomicSequence))
              return (datatest:print-item(
              subsequence($atomicSequence, $i, 1)))"
      separator="&#xA;    "/>
  </xsl:template>

  <!-- Given an item(), this function returns a string -->
  <!-- describing that item. -->
```

```
<xsl:function name="datatest:print-item" as="xs:string">
  <xsl:param name="item" as="item()"/>
  <xsl:choose>
    <xsl:when test="$item instance of element()">
      <xsl:value-of
        select="concat('Element:          &lt;', name($item), '&gt;', $item,
                '&lt;/', name($item), '&gt;')"/>
    </xsl:when>
    <xsl:otherwise>
      <xsl:value-of
        select="concat('Atomic value:     ', $item)"/>
    </xsl:otherwise>
  </xsl:choose>
</xsl:function>

</xsl:stylesheet>
```

Here are the results:

```
Here is a test of the data() function:

Our original sequence is:

    Atomic value:   3
    Atomic value:   4
    Atomic value:   5
    Element:        <currentDate>2008-03-04-05:00</currentDate>
    Element:        <currentTime>23:58:38.609-05:00</currentTime>
    Element:        <integerTest>8</integerTest>
    Atomic value:   blue
    Atomic value:   red
    Element:        <floatTest1>3.14</floatTest1>
    Element:        <floatTest2>42</floatTest2>
    Element:        <dateTest>1995-04-21</dateTest>

Passing our sequence to data() gives us:

    Atomic value:   3
    Atomic value:   4
    Atomic value:   5
    Atomic value:   2008-03-04-05:00
    Atomic value:   23:58:38.609-05:00
    Atomic value:   8
    Atomic value:   blue
    Atomic value:   red
    Atomic value:   3.14
    Atomic value:   42
    Atomic value:   1995-04-21
```

The test sequence we create has 11 items, 5 of which are atoms and 6 of which are elements. We pass each item in the sequence to our datatest:print-item( ) function. This function looks at the type of the item. If it is an element( ), the function returns a string that includes the opening tag for the element, its value, and its closing tag. For atoms, the function simply returns the atom's value. All of the strings returned by datatest:print-item( ) are labeled with `Element:` or `Atom:` so we can see whether each item is an atom or an element. This shows us the contents of the original sequence.

After listing all the atoms and elements in the original sequence, we use the `data( )` function to convert our original sequence to a sequence of atomic values. Calling our `datatest:print-item( )` against each item in the new sequence shows that it is composed of atoms only.

In our stylesheet, we invoke our `datatest:print-item( )` function against each item with the following XPath expression:

```
select="for $i in (1 to count($testSequence))
        return (datatest:print-item(
        subsequence($testSequence, $i, 1)))"
```

This expression uses the new XPath `for` instruction to iterate over the items in the sequence (`count($testSequence)`). For each item, we return the `xs:string` value returned by our `datatest:print-item( )` function. To keep the stylesheet organized, we have the relatively complicated XPath expressions in the `match="/"` template, and we create a function to handle the repetitive task of printing each item.

If we want, we can create an XPath expression that does the work of the function as well. Here's what that code looks like:

```
<!-- data2.xsl -->
...
    <xsl:for-each select="$testSequence">
      <xsl:value-of
        select="if (. instance of node())
                then concat('Element:        &lt;', name(.),
                            '&gt;', ., '&lt;/', name(.), '&gt;')
                else concat('Atomic value:    ', .)"/>
      <xsl:text>&#xA;    </xsl:text>
    </xsl:for-each>
...
    <xsl:variable name="atomicSequence" as="item()*"
      select="data($testSequence)"/>
    <xsl:for-each select="$atomicSequence">
      <xsl:value-of
        select="if (. instance of item())
                then concat('Atomic value:    ', .)
                else concat('Element:        &lt;', name(.),
                            '&gt;', ., '&lt;/', name(.), '&gt;')"/>
      <xsl:text>&#xA;    </xsl:text>
    </xsl:for-each>
...
```

This works, but it requires us to duplicate the `if-then-else` logic wherever we want to print a sequence. It's much better to use an `<xsl:function>` to do the repetitive work. There's another concern: an XSLT processor can give warnings about the type safety of the calls to the `name( )` function. If we change the processing of `$atomicSequence` so that it begins `. instance of node( )`, we get a static error and the stylesheet won't work. To avoid this, it's simpler to put the code into a function.

[2.0] dateTime()

This is a special constructor function that lets you create an xs:dateTime value from an xs:date and xs:time.

Syntax

```
xs:dateTime? dateTime(xs:date?, xs:time?)
```

Inputs

An xs:date value and an xs:time value.

Output

A new xs:dateTime value based on the two input values. If either input value is the empty sequence, xs:dateTime( ) returns the empty sequence. The timezone of the xs:dateTime result is calculated as follows:

- If neither argument has a timezone, the result does not have a timezone.
- If one of the arguments has a timezone or if both arguments have the same timezone, the result has that timezone.
- If the two arguments have different timezones, the XSLT processor raises an error.

Defined in

XQuery 1.0 and XPath 2.0 Functions and Operators section 5, "Constructor Functions."

Example

This stylesheet uses the values from the current-date( ) and current-time( ) functions to create a new xs:dateTime value:

```
<?xml version="1.0"?>
<!-- datetime.xsl -->
<xsl:stylesheet version="2.0"
  xmlns:xsl="http://www.w3.org/1999/XSL/Transform"
  xmlns:xs="http://www.w3.org/2001/XMLSchema">

  <xsl:output method="text"/>

  <xsl:template match="/">
    <xsl:text>&#xA;Creating an xs:dateTime with an </xsl:text>
    <xsl:text>xs:date and xs:time:</xsl:text>
    <xsl:variable name="currentDate" as="xs:date" select="current-date()"/>
    <xsl:variable name="currentTime" as="xs:time" select="current-time()"/>
    <xsl:text>&#xA;&#xA;  The current date is: </xsl:text>
    <xsl:value-of select="$currentDate"/>
    <xsl:text>&#xA;&#xA;  The current time is: </xsl:text>
    <xsl:value-of select="$currentTime"/>

    <xsl:variable name="currentDateTime"
      select="dateTime($currentDate, $currentTime)"/>
```

```
<xsl:text>&#xA;&#xA;   The new xs:dateTime is: </xsl:text>
<xsl:value-of select="$currentDateTime"/>
<xsl:text>&#xA;&#xA;   The new xs:dateTime value can be </xsl:text>
<xsl:text>written as &#xA;     </xsl:text>
<xsl:value-of
   select="format-dateTime($currentDateTime,
             '[h]:[m01] [Pn] on [FNn], the [D1o] of [MNn], [Y0001]')"/>
</xsl:template>

</xsl:stylesheet>
```

Here are the results:

```
Creating an xs:dateTime with an xs:date and xs:time:

  The current date is: 2006-11-16-05:00

  The current time is: 03:48:09.888-05:00

  The new xs:dateTime is: 2006-11-16T03:48:09.888-05:00

  The new xs:dateTime value can be written as
     3:48 a.m. on Thursday, the 16th of November, 2006
```

[2.0] day-from-date()

Given an xs:date value, returns its day value.

Syntax

```
xs:integer? day-from-date(xs:date?)
```

Input

An xs:date value.

Output

An xs:integer representing the day component of the given xs:date value. If the input argument is the empty sequence, this function returns the empty sequence.

Defined in

XQuery 1.0 and XPath 2.0 Functions and Operators section 10.5, "Component Extraction Functions on Durations, Dates and Times."

Example

This stylesheet demonstrates the day-from-date( ) function:

```
<?xml version="1.0"?>
<!-- day-from-date.xsl -->
<xsl:stylesheet version="2.0"
  xmlns:xsl="http://www.w3.org/1999/XSL/Transform"
  xmlns:xs="http://www.w3.org/2001/XMLSchema">

  <xsl:output method="text"/>
```

```
<xsl:template match="/">
  <xsl:text>&#xA;Extracting the day from an xs:date:</xsl:text>
  <xsl:variable name="currentDate" as="xs:date" select="current-date()"/>
  <xsl:text>&#xA;&#xA;The current date is: </xsl:text>
  <xsl:value-of select="$currentDate"/>

  <xsl:text>&#xA;&#xA;  The current day: </xsl:text>
  <xsl:value-of select="day-from-date($currentDate)"/>
  <xsl:text>&#xA;    In words: </xsl:text>
  <xsl:value-of select="format-date($currentDate, '[DWw]')"/>
  <xsl:text>&#xA;    In German: </xsl:text>
  <xsl:value-of select="format-date($currentDate, '[Dw]', 'de', (), ())"/>
  <xsl:text>&#xA;    It's the </xsl:text>
  <xsl:value-of select="format-date($currentDate, '[dwo]')"/>
  <xsl:text> day of the year.</xsl:text>
</xsl:template>

</xsl:stylesheet>
```

The stylesheet creates these results:

```
Extracting the day from an xs:date:

The current date is: 2006-11-16-05:00

  The current day: 16
    In words: Sixteen
    In German: sechszehn
    It's the three hundred and twentieth day of the year.
```

Notice that some of the results were generated by the day-from-date( ) extraction function, while other results were generated by using format-date( ) with a format string that selected only the day component of the xs:date value.

See Also

The definitions of the [2.0] format-date( ), [2.0] month-from-date( ), [2.0] timezone-from-date( ), and [2.0] year-from-date( ) functions.

[2.0] day-from-dateTime()

Given an xs:dateTime value, returns its day value.

Syntax

```
xs:integer? day-from-dateTime(xs:dateTime?)
```

Inputs

An xs:dateTime value.

Output

An `xs:integer` representing the day component of the given `xs:dateTime` value. If the input argument is the empty sequence, this function returns the empty sequence.

Defined in

XQuery 1.0 and XPath 2.0 Functions and Operators section 10.5, "Component Extraction Functions on Durations, Dates and Times."

Example

This stylesheet demonstrates the `day-from-dateTime( )` function:

```
<?xml version="1.0"?>
<!-- day-from-datetime.xsl -->
<xsl:stylesheet version="2.0"
  xmlns:xsl="http://www.w3.org/1999/XSL/Transform"
  xmlns:xs="http://www.w3.org/2001/XMLSchema">

  <xsl:output method="text"/>

  <xsl:template match="/">
    <xsl:text>&#xA;Extracting the day from an xs:dateTime:</xsl:text>
    <xsl:variable name="currentDateTime" as="xs:dateTime"
      select="current-dateTime()"/>
    <xsl:text>&#xA;&#xA;The current date and time is: </xsl:text>
    <xsl:value-of select="$currentDateTime"/>

    <xsl:text>&#xA;&#xA;  The current day: </xsl:text>
    <xsl:value-of select="day-from-dateTime($currentDateTime)"/>
    <xsl:text>&#xA;    In words: </xsl:text>
    <xsl:value-of select="format-dateTime($currentDateTime, '[DWw]')"/>
    <xsl:text>&#xA;    In German words: </xsl:text>
    <xsl:value-of
      select="format-dateTime($currentDateTime, '[Dw]', 'de', (), ())"/>
    <xsl:text>&#xA;    It's the </xsl:text>
    <xsl:value-of select="format-dateTime($currentDateTime, '[dwo]')"/>
    <xsl:text> day of the year.</xsl:text>
  </xsl:template>

</xsl:stylesheet>
```

The stylesheet creates these results:

```
Extracting the day from an xs:dateTime:

The current date and time is: 2006-11-16T04:04:46.811-05:00

  The current day: 16
    In words: Sixteen
    In German words: sechszehn
    It's the three hundred and twentieth day of the year.
```

Notice that some of the results were generated by the day-from-dateTime( ) function, while others were generated by using format-dateTime( ) with a format string that selected only the day component of the xs:dateTime value.

See Also

The definitions of the [2.0] format-dateTime( ), [2.0] hours-from-dateTime( ), [2.0] minutes-from-dateTime( ), [2.0] month-from-dateTime( ), [2.0] seconds-from-dateTime( ), [2.0] time zone-from-dateTime( ), and [2.0] year-from-dateTime( ) functions.

[2.0] days-from-duration()

Given an xs:duration value, returns the number of days in that duration.

Syntax

```
xs:integer? days-from-duration(xs:duration?)
```

Inputs

A xs:duration.

Output

An xs:integer representing the days component of the given xs:duration. Be aware that for an xs:yearMonthDuration, this function always returns 0 because there is no days component of an xs:yearMonthDuration. Also, if the input argument is the empty sequence, this function returns the empty sequence.

Defined in

XQuery 1.0 and XPath 2.0 Functions and Operators section 10.5, "Component Extraction Functions on Durations, Dates and Times."

Example

This stylesheet demonstrates the days-from-duration( ) function with all three types of durations:

```
<?xml version="1.0"?>
<!-- days-from-duration.xsl -->
<xsl:stylesheet version="2.0"
  xmlns:xsl="http://www.w3.org/1999/XSL/Transform"
  xmlns:xs="http://www.w3.org/2001/XMLSchema">

<xsl:output method="text"/>

<xsl:template match="/">
  <xsl:text>&#xA;Extracting the days component from durations:</xsl:text>

  <xsl:variable name="sampleDuration" as="xs:duration"
    select="xs:duration('P3Y8M2DT4H23M12.2S')"/>
  <xsl:variable name="sampleYearMonthDuration" as="xs:yearMonthDuration"
```

```
          select="xs:yearMonthDuration('P3Y8M')"/>
      <xsl:variable name="sampleDayTimeDuration" as="xs:dayTimeDuration"
          select="xs:dayTimeDuration('P2DT4H23M12.2S')"/>

      <xsl:text>&#xA;&#xA;  A sample xs:duration: </xsl:text>
      <xsl:value-of select="$sampleDuration"/>
      <xsl:text>&#xA;    The days component of this duration is </xsl:text>
      <xsl:value-of select="days-from-duration($sampleDuration)"/>
      <xsl:text>.</xsl:text>

      <xsl:text>&#xA;&#xA;  A sample xs:yearMonthDuration: </xsl:text>
      <xsl:value-of select="$sampleYearMonthDuration"/>
      <xsl:text>&#xA;    The days component of this duration is </xsl:text>
      <xsl:value-of select="days-from-duration($sampleYearMonthDuration)"/>
      <xsl:text>.</xsl:text>

      <xsl:text>&#xA;&#xA;  A sample xs:dayTimeDuration: </xsl:text>
      <xsl:value-of select="$sampleDayTimeDuration"/>
      <xsl:text>&#xA;    The days component of this duration is </xsl:text>
      <xsl:value-of select="days-from-duration($sampleDayTimeDuration)"/>
      <xsl:text>.</xsl:text>
  </xsl:template>

</xsl:stylesheet>
```

This stylesheet generates these results:

```
Extracting the days component from durations:

  A sample xs:duration: P3Y8M2DT4H23M12.2S
    The days component of this duration is 2.

  A sample xs:yearMonthDuration: P3Y8M
    The days component of this duration is 0.

  A sample xs:dayTimeDuration: P2DT4H23M12.2S
    The days component of this duration is 2.
```

Notice that calling days-from-duration( ) against xs:yearMonthDuration returns 0, as we mentioned earlier.

See Also

The definitions of the [2.0] hours-from-duration( ), [2.0] minutes-from-duration( ), [2.0] months-from-duration( ), [2.0] seconds-from-duration( ), and [2.0] years-from-duration( ) functions.

[2.0] deep-equal()

Compares two sequences of items to see whether they and all their descendants are equal.

Syntax

```
xs:boolean deep-equal(item()*, item()*)
xs:boolean deep-equal(item()*, item()*, $collation as xs:string)
```

Inputs

Two sequences of items. An optional third argument identifies a collation that should be used when comparing string values. (The collation is not used when comparing node names, so `<strasse>` and `<straße>` are never equal, even though a German collation might find those string values to be the same.)

Output

`true` if the items are *deep-equal* to each other; `false` otherwise. Given the variety of types of items in XSLT 2.0, the rules for two sequences being deep-equal are somewhat complicated:

- If both values are empty sequences, `deep-equal()` returns `true`.
- If the two values are sequences of different lengths (`count($value1)` != `count($value2)`), `deep-equal()` returns `false`.
- If the two values are nodes of different kinds (an element and an attribute, for example), `deep-equal()` returns `false`.
- If the two values are document nodes, they are equal only if `$value1/(*|text())` is deep-equal to `$value2/(*|text())`.
- If the two values are element nodes, they must have the same name and the same number of attributes. Also, those attributes must have the same values, and children must all be deep-equal.
- The remaining node types (attributes, processing instructions, comments, and text) are straightforward. For attributes and processing instructions, they must have the same name and the same values. For comments and text, their string values must be equal.

Defined in

XQuery 1.0 and XPath 2.0 Functions and Operators section 15.3, "Equals, Union, Intersection and Except."

Example

We'll use our chocolate sales document to test the `deep-equal()` function:

```xml
<?xml version="1.0" encoding="utf-8"?>
<!-- chocolate.xml -->
<report month="8" year="2006">
  <title>Chocolate bar sales</title>
  <brand>
    <name>Lindt</name>
    <units>27408</units>
  </brand>
  <brand>
    <name>Callebaut</name>
```

```
      <units>8203</units>
    </brand>
    <brand>
      <name>Valrhona</name>
      <units>22101</units>
    </brand>
    <brand>
      <name>Perugina</name>
      <units>14336</units>
    </brand>
    <brand>
      <name>Ghirardelli</name>
      <units>19268</units>
    </brand>
  </report>
```

Here is a stylesheet that compares several different values. Notice that deep-equal( ) compares both atoms and nodes.

```
<?xml version="1.0"?>
<!-- deep-equal.xsl -->
<xsl:stylesheet version="2.0"
  xmlns:xsl="http://www.w3.org/1999/XSL/Transform"
  xmlns:xs="http://www.w3.org/2001/XMLSchema">

  <xsl:output method="text"/>

  <xsl:variable name="testTree" as="node()*">
    <ora:report month="8" year="2006"
      xmlns:ora="http://www.oreilly.com">
      <ora:title>Chocolate bar sales</ora:title>
      <ora:brand>
        <ora:name>Lindt</ora:name>
        <ora:units>27408</ora:units>
      </ora:brand>
    </ora:report>

    <dw:report month="8" year="2006"
      xmlns:dw="http://www.oreilly.com">
      <dw:title>Chocolate bar sales</dw:title>
      <dw:brand>
        <dw:name>Lindt</dw:name>
        <dw:units>27408</dw:units>
      </dw:brand>
    </dw:report>

    <report month="8" year="2006">
      <title>Chocolate bar sales</title>
      <brand>
        <name>Lindt</name>
        <units>27408</units>
      </brand>
    </report>

    <address>
      <company>IBM Boeblingen</company>
```

```
      <street>Schoenaicherstrasse 220</street>
    </address>

    <address>
      <company>IBM B&#xF6;blingen</company>
      <street>Sch&#xF6;naicherstra&#xDF;e 220</street>
    </address>
</xsl:variable>

<xsl:variable name="sequence1" as="item()*">
  <xsl:sequence select="(3, 4, 5)"/>
</xsl:variable>

<xsl:variable name="sequence2" as="item()*">
  <xsl:sequence select="(3, 5, 4)"/>
</xsl:variable>

<xsl:variable name="sequence3" as="item()*">
  <xsl:sequence select="(3, 4, 5)"/>
</xsl:variable>

<xsl:template match="/">
  <xsl:text>&#xA;Tests of the deep-equal() function:</xsl:text>

  <xsl:text>&#xA;&#xA;  $sequence1 = (</xsl:text>
  <xsl:value-of select="$sequence1" separator=", "/>
  <xsl:text>)</xsl:text>
  <xsl:text>&#xA;  $sequence2 = (</xsl:text>
  <xsl:value-of select="$sequence2" separator=", "/>
  <xsl:text>)</xsl:text>
  <xsl:text>&#xA;  $sequence3 = (</xsl:text>
  <xsl:value-of select="$sequence3" separator=", "/>
  <xsl:text>)</xsl:text>

  <xsl:text>&#xA;&#xA;  deep-equal(</xsl:text>
  <xsl:text>$sequence1, $sequence2) = </xsl:text>
  <xsl:value-of select="deep-equal($sequence1, $sequence2)"/>

  <xsl:text>&#xA;&#xA;  deep-equal(</xsl:text>
  <xsl:text>$sequence1, $sequence3) = </xsl:text>
  <xsl:value-of select="deep-equal($sequence1, $sequence3)"/>

  <xsl:text>&#xA;&#xA;  deep-equal(</xsl:text>
  <xsl:text>subsequence($sequence1, 3, 1), &#xA;</xsl:text>
  <xsl:text>             subsequence($sequence2, 2, 1) = </xsl:text>
  <xsl:value-of
    select="deep-equal(subsequence($sequence1, 3, 1),
            subsequence($sequence2, 2, 1))"/>

  <xsl:text>&#xA;&#xA;  Comparing the first two </xsl:text>
  <xsl:text>subtrees in $testTree:</xsl:text>
  <xsl:text>&#xA;    deep-equal(subsequence($testTree, 1, 1),&#xA;</xsl:text>
  <xsl:text>              subsequence($testTree, 2, 1)) = </xsl:text>
  <xsl:value-of
    select="deep-equal(subsequence($testTree, 1, 1),
```

```
                    subsequence($testTree, 2, 1))"/>

    <xsl:text>&#xA;&#xA;  Comparing part of our input </xsl:text>
    <xsl:text>document to &#xA;       part of the third subtree </xsl:text>
    <xsl:text>in $testTree:</xsl:text>
    <xsl:text>&#xA;    deep-equal(/report/brand[1]/units,$#xA;</xsl:text>
    <xsl:text>                  subsequence($testTree, 3, 1)</xsl:text>
    <xsl:text>/brand[1]/units) = </xsl:text>
    <xsl:value-of
       select="deep-equal(/report/brand[1]/units,
                 subsequence($testTree, 3, 1)/brand[1]/units)"/>

    <xsl:text>&#xA;&#xA;  Comparing two German addresses:</xsl:text>
    <xsl:text>&#xA;    deep-equal(subsequence($testTree, 4, 1),&#xA;</xsl:text>
    <xsl:text>                subsequence($testTree, 5, 1)) = </xsl:text>
    <xsl:value-of
       select="deep-equal(subsequence($testTree, 4, 1),
                 subsequence($testTree, 5, 1))"/>

    <xsl:text>&#xA;&#xA;  Comparing two German addresses </xsl:text>
    <xsl:text>using German collation: </xsl:text>
    <xsl:text>&#xA;    deep-equal(subsequence($testTree, 4, 1),&#xA;</xsl:text>
    <xsl:text>                 subsequence($testTree, 5, 1), &#xA;</xsl:text>
    <xsl:text>                 $GermanCollation) = </xsl:text>
    <xsl:value-of
       select="deep-equal(subsequence($testTree, 4, 1),
                 subsequence($testTree, 5, 1),
                 concat('http://saxon.sf.net/collation?',
                     'class=com.oreilly.xslt.GermanCollation;'))"/>
  </xsl:template>

</xsl:stylesheet>
```

The results are:

```
    Tests of the deep-equal() function:

      $sequence1 = (3, 4, 5)
      $sequence2 = (3, 5, 4)
      $sequence3 = (3, 4, 5)

      deep-equal($sequence1, $sequence2) = false

      deep-equal($sequence1, $sequence3) = true

      deep-equal(subsequence($sequence1, 3, 1),
                subsequence($sequence2, 2, 1) = true

    Comparing the first two subtrees in $testTree:
      deep-equal(subsequence($testTree, 1, 1),
                subsequence($testTree, 2, 1)) = true

    Comparing part of our input document to
        part of the third subtree in $testTree:
      deep-equal(/report/brand[1]/units,
                subsequence($testTree, 3, 1)/brand[1]/units) = true
```

```
Comparing two German addresses:
   deep-equal(subsequence($testTree, 4, 1),
              subsequence($testTree, 5, 1)) = false

Comparing two German addresses using German collation:
   deep-equal(subsequence($testTree, 4, 1),
              subsequence($testTree, 5, 1),
              $GermanCollation) = true
```

We start by creating a variable that contains three root nodes. The first two are identical except for different namespace prefixes. The third root node in $testTree is similar to part of our chocolate sales document. We also create three sequences of atomic values. We compare the sequences of atoms with each other, and we compare one item from $sequence1 with one item from $sequence2.

Comparing the first two root nodes in $testTree, they are in fact deep-equal to each other because the namespace prefix doesn't matter. Both prefixes map to the same URI, so the two root nodes are the same. If the two nodes use the same prefixes, but those two identical prefixes map to two different URLs, those two nodes would not be deep-equal to each other.

Next, we compare the <units> element from the first <brand> element in the third root node in $testTree with the similar element from our input document. The two nodes are deep-equal to each other.

Finally, we use the two <address> elements in $testTree. Using the default collation, the text values IBM Boeblingen and IBM Böblingen are different, as are Schoenaicherstrasse 220 and Schönaicherstraße 220. Using the German collation, those strings are the same, so deep-equal( ) returns true. (To keep the listing within the margins of the page, we used the concat( ) function to combine the two halves of the Saxon collation URI.) See "The document( ) Function and Sorting" in Chapter 8 for more information.

[2.0] default-collation()

Returns a string that represents the default collation.

Syntax

```
xs:string default-collation()
```

Inputs

None.

Output

An xs:string that represents the default collation.

Defined in

XQuery 1.0 and XPath 2.0 Functions and Operators section 16, "Context Functions."

Example

Here's a stylesheet that simply displays the default collation:

```
<?xml version="1.0"?>
<!-- default-collation.xsl -->
<xsl:stylesheet version="2.0"
  xmlns:xsl="http://www.w3.org/1999/XSL/Transform">

  <xsl:output method="text"/>

  <xsl:template match="/">
    <xsl:text>&#xA;The default collation is: &#xA;  </xsl:text>
    <xsl:value-of select="default-collation()"/>
  </xsl:template>

</xsl:stylesheet>
```

The results are:

```
The default collation is:
  http://www.w3.org/2005/xpath-functions/collation/codepoint
```

The default collation, as defined in the XQuery 1.0 and XPath 2.0 Functions and Operators spec, is the Unicode code point collation. That collation is associated with the URI http://www.w3.org/2005/xpath-functions/collation/codepoint, and all implementations of XPath 2.0 and XQuery 1.0 are required to support it. Implementors are free to support other collation schemes, and each processor can define its own mechanisms for associating a URI with a particular collation. Each processor can define its own default collation as well.

A final note: the default collation can be overridden in functions that specify a collation sequence, such as compare( ), deep-equal( ), ends-with( ), or max( ).

[2.0] distinct-values()

Given a sequence, returns a new sequence containing one copy of each unique value in the original sequence.

Syntax

```
xs:anyAtomicType* distinct-values(xs:anyAtomicType*)
xs:anyAtomicType* distinct-values(xs:anyAtomicType*, $collation as xs:string)
```

Inputs

A sequence of atomic values. distinct-values( ) also has an optional argument specifying a collation algorithm. If present, the collation algorithm is used to determine whether two values are different from each other.

Output

A sequence containing only one copy of each atomic value in the original sequence. Some minor complications are as follows:

- When `distinct-values( )` returns its result sequence, the order in which the unique values are returned is implementation-defined. Also, within a group of values that have the same value, *which* value is returned is implementation-defined.

- If the input sequence is the empty sequence, the empty sequence is returned. Passing the empty sequence to `distinct-values( )` does not raise an error.

- When comparing `xs:float` and `xs:double` values, positive zero and negative zero are considered equal. Also, if there are numbers with the value `NaN` (not a number), only one of those values will be in the result sequence.

- When comparing `xs:date`, `xs:dateTime`, and `xs:time` values, if those values don't have a timezone component, their timezone is considered to be the timezone returned by the `implicit-timezone( )` function. Also be aware that `xs:date`, `xs:dateTime`, and `xs:time` values can be equal even though their timezone values are different. Noon in one timezone might be equal to 9 a.m. in another, for example.

Defined in

XQuery 1.0 and XPath 2.0 Functions and Operators section 15.1, "General Functions and Operators on Sequences."

Example

We'll start with our simplified address book to illustrate the `distinct-values( )` function:

```xml
<?xml version="1.0"?>
<!-- simple-addresses.xml -->
<addressbook>
  <address>
    <name>Mr. Chester Hasbrouck Frisby</name>
    <city>Sheboygan</city>
    <state>WI</state>
  </address>
  <address>
    <name>Mary Backstayge</name>
    <city>Skunk Haven</city>
    <state>MA</state>
  </address>
  <address>
    <name>Ms. Natalie Attired</name>
    <city>Winter Harbor</city>
    <state>ME</state>
  </address>
  <address>
    <name>Harry Backstayge</name>
    <city>Skunk Haven</city>
    <state>MA</state>
  </address>
  <address>
    <name>Mary McGoon</name>
    <city>Boylston</city>
    <state>VA</state>
```

```
        </address>
        <address>
          <name>Ms. Amanda Reckonwith</name>
          <city>Lynn</city>
          <state>MA</state>
        </address>
      </addressbook>
```

Here's a simple stylesheet that lists the distinct values of the `<state>` elements in the XML source document:

```
<?xml version="1.0"?>
<!-- distinct-values1.xsl -->
<xsl:stylesheet version="2.0"
  xmlns:xsl="http://www.w3.org/1999/XSL/Transform"
  xmlns:xs="http://www.w3.org/2001/XMLSchema">

  <xsl:output method="text"/>

  <xsl:template match="/">
    <xsl:text>&#xA;Here is a test of the distinct-values() </xsl:text>
    <xsl:text>function:&#xA;</xsl:text>

    <xsl:text>&#xA;  The states in the source </xsl:text>
    <xsl:text>document are:&#xA;    </xsl:text>
    <xsl:value-of
      select="/addressbook/address/state"
      separator=", "/>

    <xsl:text>&#xA;&#xA;  The unique states </xsl:text>
    <xsl:text>is:&#xA;    </xsl:text>
    <xsl:value-of
      select="distinct-values(/addressbook/address/state)"
      separator=", "/>
  </xsl:template>

</xsl:stylesheet>
```

Here are the results:

```
Here is a test of the distinct-values() function:

  The states in the source document are:
    WI, MA, ME, MA, VA, MA

  The unique states is:
    WI, MA, ME, VA
```

In this example, the values returned by `distinct-values()` are returned in document order, although other XSLT processors might return those values in sorted order or some other way.

Here's a stylesheet that compares some of the special cases we mentioned earlier:

```
<?xml version="1.0"?>
<!-- distinct-values2.xsl -->
<xsl:stylesheet version="2.0"
  xmlns:xsl="http://www.w3.org/1999/XSL/Transform"
```

```
xmlns:xs="http://www.w3.org/2001/XMLSchema">

<xsl:output method="text"/>

<xsl:template match="/">
  <xsl:text>&#xA;Here are some tests of the </xsl:text>
  <xsl:text>distinct-values() </xsl:text>
  <xsl:text>function:&#xA;</xsl:text>

  <xsl:text>&#xA;  A sequence of xs:time values:</xsl:text>
  <xsl:variable name="timeSequence" as="xs:time*">
    <xsl:sequence
      select="(xs:time('00:43:00-06:00'),
               xs:time('01:43:00-05:00'),
               xs:time('02:43:00'),
               xs:time('07:35:00'),
               current-time())"/>
  </xsl:variable>

  <xsl:text>&#xA;&#xA;    </xsl:text>
  <xsl:value-of
    select="distinct-values($timeSequence)"
    separator="&#xA;    "/>

  <xsl:text>&#xA;&#xA;  A sequence of integer values:</xsl:text>
  <xsl:variable name="numberSequence" as="xs:integer*">
    <xsl:sequence select="(3, 8, (2 + 1), -0, 0)"/>
  </xsl:variable>

  <xsl:text>&#xA;    </xsl:text>
  <xsl:value-of
    select="distinct-values($numberSequence)"
    separator=", "/>
</xsl:template>

</xsl:stylesheet>
```

The results from this stylesheet look like this:

```
Here are some tests of the distinct-values() function:

  A sequence of xs:time values:

    00:43:00-06:00
    07:35:00
    06:23:05.19-04:00

  A sequence of integer values:
    3, 8, 0
```

In the first sequence, we compare five different xs:time values. The first three are actually equal; they represent the same time in three different zones. Notice that the third xs:time value uses the implicit timezone; you'll get different results if you run this stylesheet on a machine that isn't set to the GMT-4 timezone. The fourth and fifth values are different, so there are three values in the output sequence. We used Saxon for this example; for duplicate values, it returns the first one it finds.

For the second sequence, we have several numeric values. The values 3 and (2 + 1) are identical, and -0 and 0 are the same as well. Notice that in this case the value in the output sequence is the second zero value, not the first. (Saxon normalizes negative zero to zero, although this is implementation-defined.)

As a final example, we'll use a collation function. Here is the stylesheet:

```
<?xml version="1.0"?>
<!-- distinct-values3.xsl -->
<xsl:stylesheet version="2.0"
  xmlns:xsl="http://www.w3.org/1999/XSL/Transform"
  xmlns:xs="http://www.w3.org/2001/XMLSchema">

  <xsl:output method="text"/>

  <xsl:template match="/">
    <xsl:text>&#xA;A final test of the </xsl:text>
    <xsl:text>distinct-values() function:&#xA;&#xA;</xsl:text>

    <xsl:variable name="testStrings" as="xs:string*">
      <xsl:sequence
        select="'street', 'Strasse', 'Stra&#xDF;e'"/>
    </xsl:variable>

    <xsl:text>  The test sequence: &#xA;    </xsl:text>
    <xsl:value-of select="$testStrings" separator=", "/>
    <xsl:text>&#xA;  distinct-values($testStrings):</xsl:text>
    <xsl:text>&#xA;    </xsl:text>
    <xsl:value-of select="distinct-values($testStrings)"
      separator=", "/>

    <xsl:text>&#xA;  distinct-values($testStrings, </xsl:text>
    <xsl:text>[German collation]):&#xA;    </xsl:text>
    <xsl:value-of
      select="distinct-values($testStrings,
              concat('http://saxon.sf.net/collation?',
                     'class=com.oreilly.xslt.GermanCollation;'))"
      separator=", "/>
  </xsl:template>

</xsl:stylesheet>
```

Here are the results:

```
A final test of the distinct-values() function:

The test sequence:
  street, Strasse, Straße
distinct-values($testStrings):
  street, Strasse, Straße
distinct-values($testStrings, [German collation]):
  street, Strasse
```

The German sharp-s character (ß) is equivalent to ss. The default collation doesn't recognize this, but our custom collation does. (To keep the listing within the margins of the page, we used the concat( ) function to combine the two halves of the Saxon collation URI.) See "The document() Function and Sorting" in Chapter 8 for more information.

[2.0] doc()

Given a URI, returns a document node representing the contents of that URI.

Syntax

```
document-node()? doc($uri as xs:string?)
```

Inputs

A URI. The format of the URI is implementation-defined.

Output

A document node that represents the contents of the requested URI.

Defined in

XQuery 1.0 and XPath 2.0 Functions and Operators section 15.5, "Functions and Operators that Generate Sequences."

Example

Here is an example that uses Saxon's support for simple filenames as URIs. We'll invoke the doc( ) function to load this XML document:

```
<?xml version="1.0"?>
<!-- polist.xml -->
<collection>
  <doc href="po38292.xml"/>
  <doc href="po38293.xml"/>
  <doc href="po38294.xml"/>
  <doc href="po38295.xml"/>
</collection>
```

Here's our stylesheet:

```
<?xml version="1.0"?>
<!-- doc.xsl -->
<xsl:stylesheet version="2.0"
  xmlns:xsl="http://www.w3.org/1999/XSL/Transform">

  <xsl:output method="text"/>

  <xsl:template match="/">
    <xsl:text>&#xA;A test of the doc() function:</xsl:text>

    <xsl:text>&#xA;&#xA;  Here are all the purchase orders </xsl:text>
    <xsl:text>listed in polist.xml:</xsl:text>
    <xsl:for-each select="doc('polist.xml')/collection/doc">
```

```
      <xsl:text>&#xA;    </xsl:text>
      <xsl:value-of select="@href"/>
    </xsl:for-each>
  </xsl:template>

</xsl:stylesheet>
```

We use the doc( ) function to load the file *polist.xml*, and then we use `<xsl:for-each>` to process the contents of the document we just loaded. Here are the results:

```
A test of the doc() function:

Here are all the purchase orders listed in polist.xml:
    po38292.xml
    po38293.xml
    po38294.xml
    po38295.xml
```

Notice that we use the doc( ) function in an XPath expression. We iterate through all the <doc> elements in the source file using the document root returned by the doc( ) function. We could also use the doc( ) function to open each of the documents referenced in the *polist.xml* file.

See Also

The [2.0] collection( ), [2.0] doc-available( ), and document( ) functions and the discussion of "[2.0] The doc() and doc-available() Functions" in Chapter 8.

[2.0] doc-available()

Tests to see if a given document node is available.

Syntax

```
xs:boolean doc-available($uri as xs:string)
```

Inputs

The URI of a document.

Output

This function returns `true` if the doc( ) function can successfully load the requested URI. If the argument cannot be converted to an `xs:anyURI`, the XSLT processor raises an error. Otherwise, doc-available( ) returns `false`. The format of the URI is implementation-defined.

Defined in

XQuery 1.0 and XPath 2.0 Functions and Operators section 15.5, "Functions and Operators that Generate Sequences."

Example

Here's a short stylesheet that tests whether two documents are available. This uses Saxon's support for simple filenames as URIs:

```
<?xml version="1.0"?>
<!-- doc-available.xsl -->
<xsl:stylesheet version="2.0"
  xmlns:xsl="http://www.w3.org/1999/XSL/Transform">

  <xsl:output method="text"/>

  <xsl:template match="/">
    <xsl:text>&#xA;Tests of the doc-available() function:&#xA;</xsl:text>

    <xsl:text>&#xA;  doc-available('polist.xml') = </xsl:text>
    <xsl:value-of select="doc-available('polist.xml')"/>

    <xsl:text>&#xA;&#xA;  doc-available('polist2.xml') = </xsl:text>
    <xsl:value-of select="doc-available('polist2.xml')"/>
  </xsl:template>

</xsl:stylesheet>
```

Here are the results:

```
Tests of the doc-available() function:

  doc-available('polist.xml') = true

  doc-available('polist2.xml') = false
```

The file *polist.xml* exists in the current directory and can be loaded by Saxon; the file *polist2.xml* does not exist in the current directory.

Many of the details of the `doc-available( )` function are implementation-defined. See the documentation for your XSLT processor to see how it implements `doc-available( )` and what URI formats it supports.

---

document()

Allows you to process multiple source documents in a single stylesheet. This extremely powerful and flexible function is discussed extensively in Chapter 7, so we'll only include a brief overview of the function here.

Syntax

```
[1.0] node-set document(object, node-set?)
[2.0] node()* document(item()*)
[2.0] node()* document(item()*, node())
```

Inputs

The `document( )` function most commonly takes a string as its argument; that string is treated as a URI, and the XSLT processor attempts to open that URI and parse it. If the string is empty (the function call is `document('')`), the `document()` function parses the stylesheet itself. See "Grouping Nodes" in Chapter 7 for all the details on the parameters to the `document()` function.

[2.0] In XSLT 2.0, the `document()` function can also take a second argument, a node used to find the base URI property of the requested documents. The base URI of the node is combined with the resource names in the first argument to form a complete URI.

Output

A *[1.0]* node-set or *[2.0]* sequence containing the nodes identified by the input argument. Again, Chapter 7 has all the details, so we won't rehash them here.

Defined in

[1.0] XSLT section 12.1, "Multiple Source Documents."

[2.0] XSLT section 16.1, "Multiple Source Documents."

Example

The following example uses the `document()` function with an empty string to implement a lookup table. Here is our XML document:

```
<?xml version="1.0"?>
<!-- polist.xml -->
<collection>
  <doc href="po38292.xml"/>
  <doc href="po38293.xml"/>
  <doc href="po38294.xml"/>
  <doc href="po38295.xml"/>
</collection>
```

We'll use the `document()` function against each `href` attribute in this XML file. Calling `document()` returns a set of nodes representing the referenced document. Each `href` points to a purchase order document that is something like this:

```
<?xml version="1.0" ?>
<!-- po38293.xml -->
<purchase-order id="38293">
  <date year="2001" month="9" day="8"/>
  <customer id="4738" level="Basic">
    <address type="business">
      <name>
        <title>Ms.</title>
        <first-name>Amanda</first-name>
        <last-name>Reckonwith</last-name>
      </name>
      <street>930-A Chestnut Street</street>
      <city>Lynn</city>
      <state>MA</state>
      <zip>02930</zip>
    </address>
    <address type="ship-to"/>
  </customer>
  <items>
```

```
    <item part-no="23813-03-CDK">
      <name>Cucumber Decorating Kit</name>
      <qty>1</qty>
      <price>29.95</price>
    </item>
  </items>
</purchase-order>
```

We want our stylesheet to find all of the purchase orders in which a customer ordered more than one item. Here's how the stylesheet looks:

```
<?xml version="1.0"?>
<!-- document.xsl -->
<xsl:stylesheet version="1.0"
  xmlns:xsl="http://www.w3.org/1999/XSL/Transform">

  <xsl:output method="text"/>

  <xsl:template match="/">
    <xsl:text>&#xA;A test of the document() function:&#xA;</xsl:text>

    <xsl:for-each select="/collection/doc">
      <xsl:variable name="latestDoc" select="document(@href)"/>
      <xsl:if
        test="count($latestDoc/purchase-order/items/item) &gt; 1">
        <xsl:text>&#xA;   </xsl:text>
        <xsl:value-of
          select="$latestDoc/purchase-order/customer/
                  address/name/first-name"/>
        <xsl:text> </xsl:text>
        <xsl:value-of
          select="$latestDoc/purchase-order/customer/
                  address/name/last-name"/>
        <xsl:text>&#xA;     ordered </xsl:text>
        <xsl:value-of
          select="count($latestDoc/purchase-order/items/item)"/>
        <xsl:text> items on </xsl:text>
        <xsl:value-of
          select="$latestDoc/purchase-order/date/@month"/>
        <xsl:text>/</xsl:text>
        <xsl:value-of
          select="$latestDoc/purchase-order/date/@day"/>
        <xsl:text>/</xsl:text>
        <xsl:value-of
          select="$latestDoc/purchase-order/date/@year"/>
        <xsl:text> - see P.O. #</xsl:text>
        <xsl:value-of
          select="$latestDoc/purchase-order/@id"/>
      </xsl:if>
    </xsl:for-each>
  </xsl:template>

</xsl:stylesheet>
```

Running the stylesheet gives us these results:

```
A test of the document() function:

Chester Hasbrouck Frisby
    ordered 3 items on 6/19/2001 - see P.O. #38292
Natalie Attired
    ordered 2 items on 4/21/2001 - see P.O. #38294
```

The stylesheet has used the document( ) function to open all of the purchase orders referenced in *polist.xml*. For any orders in which the customer ordered more than one item (count($latestDoc/purchase-order/items/item) > 1), we print out a few details from the purchase order. Notice that we re-initialize the variable $latestDoc as we iterate through all of the href attributes; if we find a document that we want to process, storing the tree in a variable means we don't have to call document( ) over and over to get the information we need.

[2.0] document-uri()

Given a node, returns the document URI property for that node.

Syntax

```
xs:anyURI? document-uri(node()?)
```

Inputs

A node.

Output

If the node is not a document node, document-uri( ) returns the empty sequence. Otherwise, it returns the document URI property for the node. If the argument is the empty sequence, document-uri( ) returns the empty sequence.

Defined in

XQuery 1.0 and XPath 2.0 Functions and Operators section 2, "Accessors."

Example

Here's a short stylesheet that returns the document URI for the XML document we're processing:

```
<?xml version="1.0"?>
<!-- document-uri.xsl -->
<xsl:stylesheet version="2.0"
  xmlns:xsl="http://www.w3.org/1999/XSL/Transform">

  <xsl:output method="text"/>

  <xsl:template match="/">
    <xsl:text>&#xA;A test of the document-uri() function:</xsl:text>

    <xsl:text>&#xA;&#xA;  The document URI for the </xsl:text>
```

```
      <xsl:text>root element is:&#xA;    </xsl:text>
      <xsl:value-of select="document-uri(/)"/>
    </xsl:template>

</xsl:stylesheet>
```

When we run this stylesheet against the file *blank.xml*, here are the results:

```
A test of the document-uri() function:

The document URI for the root element is:
   file:/C:/projects/XSLTbookV2/AppendixC/blank.xml
```

element-available()

Determines if a given element is available to the XSLT processor. This function allows you to design stylesheets that react gracefully if a particular extension element is not available to process an XML document.

Syntax

```
[1.0] boolean element-available($elementName as string)
[2.0] xs:boolean element-available($elementName as xs:string)
```

Inputs

The element's name. The name should be qualified with a namespace; if the namespace URI is the same as the XSLT namespace URI, then the element name refers to an element defined by XSLT. Otherwise, the name refers to an extension element. If the element name has a null namespace URI, then the `element-available` function returns `false`. *[2.0]* If the argument cannot be converted to a valid QName, the XSLT processor raises an error.

Output

The boolean value `true` if the element is available; `false` otherwise.

Defined in

[1.0] XSLT section 15, "Fallback."

[2.0] XSLT section 18.2, "Extension Instructions."

Example

We'll illustrate the `element-available( )` function with the following XML document:

```
<?xml version="1.0"?>
<!-- chapterlist.xml -->
<book>
  <title>XSLT</title>
  <chapter>
    <title>Getting Started</title>
    <para>If this chapter had any text, it would appear here.</para>
  </chapter>
  <chapter>
```

```
      <title>The Hello World Example</title>
      <para>If this chapter had any text, it would appear here.</para>
    </chapter>
    ...
    <chapter>
      <title>Combining XML Documents</title>
      <para>If this chapter had any text, it would appear here.</para>
    </chapter>
  </book>
```

Our stylesheet attempts to use the Xalan-J <redirect:write> to write each <chapter> to a
different file. If that element is not available, we write all of the information to a single HTML
file. Here's the stylesheet:

```
<?xml version="1.0"?>
<!-- element-available.xsl -->
<xsl:stylesheet version="1.0"
  xmlns:xsl="http://www.w3.org/1999/XSL/Transform"
  xmlns:redirect="org.apache.xalan.xslt.extensions.Redirect"
  extension-element-prefixes="redirect">

  <xsl:output method="html"/>

  <xsl:template match="/">
    <xsl:choose>
      <xsl:when test="element-available('redirect:write')">
        <xsl:for-each select="/book/chapter">
          <redirect:write select="concat('chapter', position(), '.html')">
            <html>
              <head>
                <title><xsl:value-of select="title"/></title> ·
              </head>
              <body>
                <h1><xsl:value-of select="title"/></h1>
                <xsl:apply-templates select="para"/>
                <xsl:if test="not(position()=1)">
                  <p>
                    <a href="chapter{position()-1}.html">Previous</a>
                  </p>
                </xsl:if>
                <xsl:if test="not(position()=last())">
                  <p>
                    <a href="chapter{position()+1}.html">Next</a>
                  </p>
                </xsl:if>
              </body>
            </html>
          </redirect:write>
        </xsl:for-each>
      </xsl:when>
      <xsl:otherwise>
        <html>
          <head>
            <title><xsl:value-of select="/book/title"/></title>
          </head>
          <xsl:for-each select="/book/chapter">
```

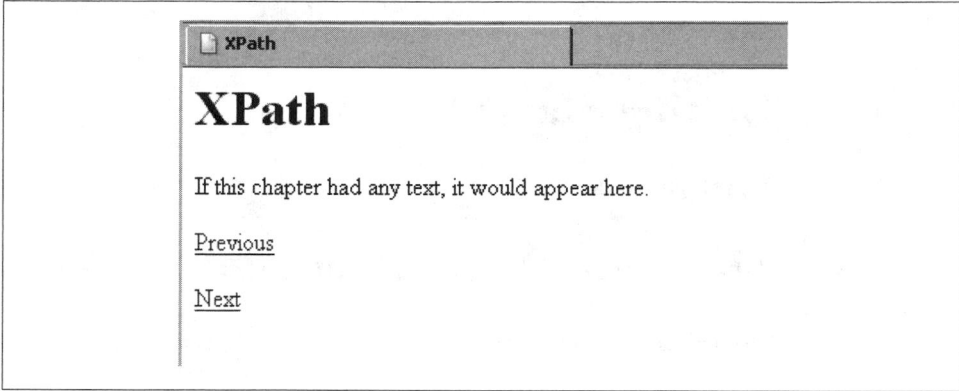

Figure C-1. Sample HTML output file

```
            <h1><xsl:value-of select="title"/></h1>
            <xsl:apply-templates select="para"/>
          </xsl:for-each>
        </html>
      </xsl:otherwise>
    </xsl:choose>
  </xsl:template>

  <xsl:template match="para">
    <p><xsl:apply-templates select="*|text()"/></p>
  </xsl:template>

</xsl:stylesheet>
```

If the `<redirect:write>` element is available, we'll get a separate file for each `<chapter>` element. Those files look like this:

```
<html>
  <head>
    <meta http-equiv="Content-Type" content="text/html; charset=utf-8">
    <title>XPath</title>
  </head>
  <body>
    <h1>XPath</h1>
    <p>If this chapter had any text, it would appear here.</p>
    <p><a href="chapter2.html">Previous</a></p>
    <p><a href="chapter4.html">Next</a></p>
  </body>
</html>
```

When rendered in a browser, the file looks like Figure C-1.

Clicking on the Previous link takes you to the file *chapter2.html*, while clicking on the Next link takes you to *chapter4.html*.

Although the format of the message is slightly different, the output in the multiple HTML files is the same.

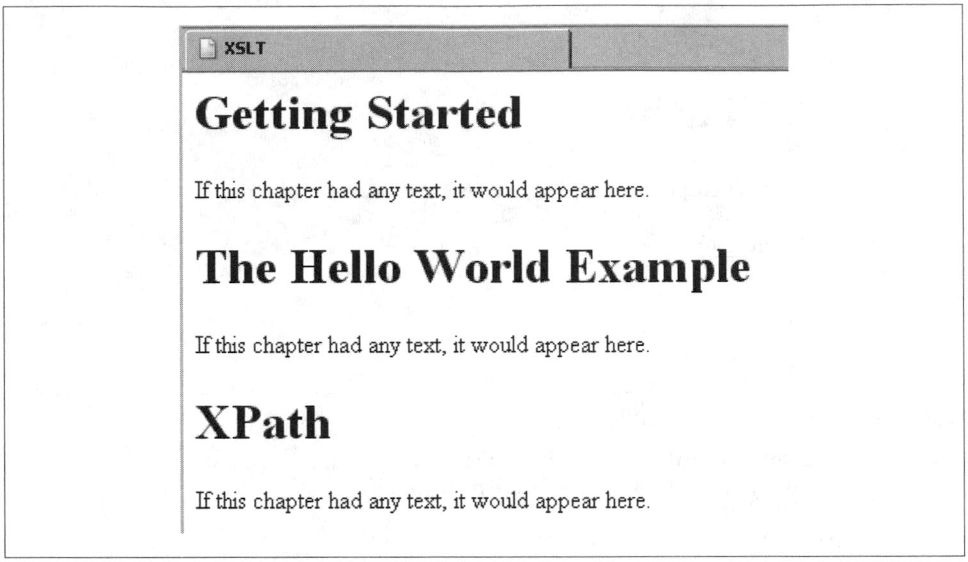

Getting Started

If this chapter had any text, it would appear here.

The Hello World Example

If this chapter had any text, it would appear here.

XPath

If this chapter had any text, it would appear here.

Figure C-2. HTML document listing all chapters

If we use Saxon, which doesn't have the `<redirect:write>` element, we get a single HTML file that looks like this:

```
<html>
  <head>
    <meta http-equiv="Content-Type" content="text/html; charset=UTF-8">
    <title>XSLT</title>
  </head>
  <h1>Getting Started</h1>
  <p>If this chapter had any text, it would appear here.</p>
  ...
  <h1>Combining XML Documents</h1>
  <p>If this chapter had any text, it would appear here.</p>
</html>
```

When rendered, our output looks like Figure C-2.

MSXSL and the AltovaXML engine generate the same results.

In this example, the `element-available( )` function allows us to determine what processing capabilities are available and to respond gracefully to whatever we find.

[2.0] empty()

Given a sequence, returns `true` if the argument is the empty sequence, `false` otherwise.

Syntax

```
xs:boolean empty(item()*)
```

Inputs

A sequence of items.

Output

true if the argument is the empty sequence; false otherwise. Although empty($sequence) and count($sequence) = 0 are logically equivalent, empty( ) is likely to be more efficient.

Defined in

XQuery 1.0 and XPath 2.0 Functions and Operators section 15.1, "General Functions and Operators on Sequences."

Example

This stylesheet illustrates the empty( ) function:

```
<?xml version="1.0"?>
<!-- empty.xsl -->
<xsl:stylesheet version="2.0"
  xmlns:xsl="http://www.w3.org/1999/XSL/Transform"
  xmlns:xs="http://www.w3.org/2001/XMLSchema">

  <xsl:output method="text"/>

  <xsl:template match="/">

    <xsl:variable name="emptySequence" as="item()*">
      <xsl:sequence select="()"/>
    </xsl:variable>

    <xsl:variable name="singleton" as="item()*">
      <xsl:sequence select="(3)"/>
    </xsl:variable>

    <xsl:variable name="longSequence" as="item()*">
      <xsl:sequence
        select="(3, 4, 5, current-date(), current-time(), 8, 'blue',
                'red', xs:float(3.14), 42, xs:date('1995-04-21'))"/>
    </xsl:variable>

    <xsl:text>&#xA;Here are some tests of the empty() </xsl:text>
    <xsl:text>function:&#xA;</xsl:text>

    <xsl:text>&#xA;  Our first sequence is:&#xA;&#xA;    </xsl:text>
    <xsl:value-of select="$emptySequence" separator="&#xA;    "/>
    <xsl:text>&#xA;&#xA;</xsl:text>
    <xsl:value-of select="if (empty($emptySequence))
                          then 'This is the empty sequence!'
                          else 'This is not the empty sequence!'"/>
    <xsl:text>&#xA;&#xA;</xsl:text>

    <xsl:text>&#xA;  Our next sequence is:&#xA;&#xA;    </xsl:text>
    <xsl:value-of select="$singleton" separator="&#xA;    "/>
    <xsl:text>&#xA;&#xA;</xsl:text>
```

```
<xsl:value-of select="if (empty($singleton))
                      then 'This is the empty sequence!'
                      else 'This is not the empty sequence!'"/>
<xsl:text>&#xA;&#xA;</xsl:text>

<xsl:text>&#xA;  Our final sequence is:&#xA;&#xA;   </xsl:text>
<xsl:value-of select="$longSequence" separator="&#xA;   "/>
<xsl:text>&#xA;&#xA;</xsl:text>
<xsl:value-of select="if (empty($longSequence))
                      then 'This is the empty sequence!'
                      else 'This is not the empty sequence!'"/>
<xsl:text>&#xA;&#xA;</xsl:text>

</xsl:template>

</xsl:stylesheet>
```

The stylesheet generates these results:

```
Here are some tests of the empty() function:

  Our first sequence is:


This is the empty sequence!


  Our next sequence is:
   3

This is not the empty sequence!


  Our final sequence is:
   3
   4
   5
   2008-03-04-05:00
   11:04:14.25-05:00
   8
   blue
   red
   3.14
   42
   1995-04-21

This is not the empty sequence!
```

[2.0] encode-for-uri()

Given a string, encodes that string for use in a URI.

Syntax

```
xs:string encode-for-uri($uri-part as xs:string?)
```

Input

A string containing the value to be escaped.

Output

The input string with the appropriate characters escaped as percent-encoded values. All characters are escaped *except* the following: upper- and lowercase letters A-Z, the digits 0-9, the hyphen-minus character ("-" or `&#x2D;`), the underscore or low-line character ("_" or `&#x5F;`), the period or full stop ("." or `&#2E;`), and the tilde ("~" or `&#x7E;`). For example, the space character, `&#x20`, is escaped as `%20`. All hexadecimal digits are in uppercase, so the character `&#xe1;` (á, a lowercase a with an acute accent) is escaped as `%E1`.

Keep in mind that the `encode-for-uri( )` function escapes every character, so you should use it to escape only the parts of a URI that need to be escaped. For example, calling `encode-for-uri('http://www.oreilly.com/')` returns `http%3A%2F%2Fwww.oreilly.com%2F`, which is almost certainly *not* what you want.

If the value of the argument is the empty sequence, a zero-length string is returned.

Defined in

XQuery 1.0 and XPath 2.0 Functions and Operators section 7.4, "Functions on String Values."

Example

Here's a stylesheet that features two examples courtesy of the XQuery 1.0 and XPath 2.0 Functions and Operators spec:

```
<?xml version="1.0" encoding="utf-8"?>
<!-- encode-for-uri.xsl -->
<xsl:stylesheet version="2.0"
  xmlns:xsl="http://www.w3.org/1999/XSL/Transform">

  <xsl:output method="text"/>

  <xsl:template match="/">
    <xsl:text>&#xA;Tests of the encode-for-uri() function:</xsl:text>

    <xsl:text>&#xA;&#xA;  encode-for-uri</xsl:text>
    <xsl:text>('http://www.oreilly.com/') = &#xA;    </xsl:text>
    <xsl:value-of
      select="encode-for-uri('http://www.oreilly.com/')"/>

    <xsl:text>&#xA;&#xA;  concat('http://www.example.com/', </xsl:text>
    <xsl:text>&#xA;          encode-for-uri</xsl:text>
    <xsl:text>('~b&#xE9;b&#xE9;')) = &#xA;    </xsl:text>
    <xsl:value-of
      select="concat('http://www.example.com/',
              encode-for-uri('~b&#xE9;b&#xE9;'))"/>

    <xsl:text>&#xA;&#xA;  concat('http://www.example.com/', </xsl:text>
    <xsl:text>&#xA;          encode-for-uri</xsl:text>
    <xsl:text>('100% organic')) = &#xA;    </xsl:text>
    <xsl:value-of
```

```
    select="concat('http://www.example.com/',
            encode-for-uri('100% organic'))"/>
  </xsl:template>

</xsl:stylesheet>
```

The stylesheet generates these results:

```
Tests of the encode-for-uri() function:

  encode-for-uri('http://www.oreilly.com/') =
    http%3A%2F%2Fwww.oreilly.com%2F

  concat('http://www.example.com/',
      encode-for-uri('~bébé')) =
    http://www.example.com/~b%C3%A9b%C3%A9

  concat('http://www.example.com/',
      encode-for-uri('100% organic')) =
    http://www.example.com/100%25%20organic
```

See Also

The descriptions of the [2.0] `escape-html-uri( )` and [2.0] `iri-to-uri( )` functions.

[2.0] ends-with()

Given two strings and an optional collation, returns `true` if the first string ends with the characters of the second string.

Syntax

```
xs:boolean ends-with(xs:string?, xs:string?)
xs:boolean ends-with(xs:string?, xs:string?, $collation as xs:string)
```

Inputs

Two strings and an optional name of a collation algorithm. A collation algorithm defines how characters are compared; to take an example from the specs, a collation algorithm might define that the characters **ss** and the German **ß** (sharp-s) character are the same.

Output

Assuming both arguments are not zero-length strings, if the first string ends with the second, `ends-with( )` returns the boolean value `true`; otherwise, it returns `false`. If the second string is a zero-length string, `ends-with( )` returns `true`. If the first string *and* the second string are both zero-length strings, `ends-with( )` returns true. If the first string is a zero-length string but the second string is not, `ends-with( )` returns `false`.

Defined in

XQuery 1.0 and XPath 2.0 Functions and Operators section 7.5, "Functions Based on Substring Matching."

Example

Here's a short stylesheet that demonstrates how the ends-with( ) function works:

```
<?xml version="1.0" encoding="utf-8"?>
<!-- ends-with1.xsl -->
<xsl:stylesheet version="2.0"
  xmlns:xsl="http://www.w3.org/1999/XSL/Transform">

  <xsl:output method="text"/>

  <xsl:template match="/">
    <xsl:variable name="string1" select="'Have a nice day'"/>
    <xsl:variable name="string2" select="'Have a nice day!'"/>
    <xsl:variable name="string3" select="'day'"/>

    <xsl:text>&#xA;A test of the ends-with() function:&#xA;</xsl:text>

    <xsl:text>  ends-with('</xsl:text>
    <xsl:value-of select="$string1"/>
    <xsl:text>', '</xsl:text>
    <xsl:value-of select="$string3"/>
    <xsl:text>') = </xsl:text>
    <xsl:value-of select="ends-with($string1, $string3)"/>
    <xsl:text>&#xA;</xsl:text>

    <xsl:text>  ends-with('</xsl:text>
    <xsl:value-of select="$string2"/>
    <xsl:text>', '</xsl:text>
    <xsl:value-of select="$string3"/>
    <xsl:text>') = </xsl:text>
    <xsl:value-of select="ends-with($string2, $string3)"/>
    <xsl:text>&#xA;</xsl:text>
  </xsl:template>

</xsl:stylesheet>
```

Here are the results:

```
A test of the ends-with() function:
  ends-with('Have a nice day', 'day') = true
  ends-with('Have a nice day!', 'day') = false
```

The ends-with function is one of several that can contain an optional collation. How that collation is specified varies from one processor to the next. In Saxon this is done with a URI that includes the name of the Java class that performs the collation. Here's an example that compares the German words *Straße* and *Strasse*. In the default collation, these two words are different; using the German collation, they're the same. Here's the stylesheet:

```
<?xml version="1.0" encoding="utf-8"?>
<!-- ends-with2.xsl -->
<xsl:stylesheet version="2.0"
  xmlns:xsl="http://www.w3.org/1999/XSL/Transform">

  <xsl:output method="text"/>

  <xsl:template match="/">
```

```
<xsl:variable name="string1" select="'Stra&#xDF;e'"/>
<xsl:variable name="string2" select="'Strasse'"/>

<xsl:text>&#xA;A test of the ends-with() function:&#xA;</xsl:text>

<xsl:text>  ends-with('</xsl:text>
<xsl:value-of select="$string1"/>
<xsl:text>', '</xsl:text>
<xsl:value-of select="$string2"/>
<xsl:text>') = </xsl:text>
<xsl:value-of select="ends-with($string1, $string2)"/>
<xsl:text>&#xA;</xsl:text>

<xsl:text>  ends-with('</xsl:text>
<xsl:value-of select="$string1"/>
<xsl:text>', '</xsl:text>
<xsl:value-of select="$string2"/>
<xsl:text>', [German collation]) = </xsl:text>
<xsl:value-of
  select="ends-with($string1, $string2,
          concat('http://saxon.sf.net/collation?',
                  'class=com.oreilly.xslt.GermanCollation;'))"/>
<xsl:text>&#xA;</xsl:text>
  </xsl:template>

</xsl:stylesheet>
```

And here are the results:

```
A test of the ends-with() function:
  ends-with('Straße', 'Strasse') = false
  ends-with('Straße', 'Strasse', [German collation]) = true
```

Using the collation we defined, the two spellings of Strasse are the same; using the default collation, they're not. (To keep the listing within the margins of the page, we used the concat() function to combine the two halves of the Saxon collation URI.) See "The document() Function and Sorting" in Chapter 8 for more information.

[2.0] error()

Raises an error. This is equivalent to throwing an exception in Java, C++, Ruby, and other languages.

Syntax

```
none error()
none error($error as xs:QName)
none error($error as xs:QName?, $description as xs:string)
none error($error as xs:QName?, $description as xs:string,
          $error-object as item()*)
```

Inputs

This function has four different signatures. The three optional parameters defined in the "Syntax" section are the QName associated with the error, an xs:string, and a sequence of items. How these inputs are processed is implementation-defined, so useful or appropriate values for these arguments vary from one processor to the next.

Output

This function never returns. The `error( )` function returns an error to the external processing environment. How (or if) the QName, string, and sequence of items passed to this function are delivered to the environment is implementation-defined.

Defined in

XQuery 1.0 and XPath 2.0 Functions and Operators section 3, "The Error Function." In addition, Appendix C of this spec defines a number of error conditions and codes. For example, `err:FODT0003` is the error code for a timezone value that is not valid. The `err` namespace is bound to the URI `http://www.w3.org/2005/xqt-errors`—we'll use this in our examples. You're free to create your own error codes and messages if you like.

Example

We'll look at four stylesheets that throw errors, one for each of the four method signatures of the `error( )` function. Here's the first, which we simply call `error( )`:

```
<?xml version="1.0"?>
<!-- error1.xsl -->
<xsl:stylesheet version="2.0"
  xmlns:xsl="http://www.w3.org/1999/XSL/Transform">

  <xsl:output method="text"/>

  <xsl:template match="/">
    <xsl:text>&#xA;Test #1 of the error() function:</xsl:text>

    <xsl:value-of select="error()"/>
  </xsl:template>

</xsl:stylesheet>
```

Our results look like this:

```
FOER0000: Error signalled by application call on error()
Transformation failed: Run-time errors were reported
```

The error code here, `FOER0000`, is defined in the XQuery 1.0 and XPath 2.0 Functions and Operators spec as "Unidentified error."

For our second attempt, we use a QName that refers to a specific error code from the spec:

```
<?xml version="1.0"?>
<!-- error2.xsl -->
<xsl:stylesheet version="2.0"
  xmlns:xsl="http://www.w3.org/1999/XSL/Transform">

  <xsl:output method="text"/>

  <xsl:template match="/">
    <xsl:text>&#xA;Test #2 of the error() function:</xsl:text>
```

```
    <xsl:value-of
      select="error(QName('http://www.w3.org/2005/xqt-errors',
              'err:FORX0004'))"/>
  </xsl:template>

</xsl:stylesheet>
```

Our results:

```
    FORX0004: Error signalled by application call on error()
Transformation failed: Run-time errors were reported
```

These results have a specific error code, FORX0004. We'll move on to our third example, in which we add a descriptive string to the call to error( ):

```
    <?xml version="1.0"?>
    <!-- error3.xsl -->
    <xsl:stylesheet version="2.0"
      xmlns:xsl="http://www.w3.org/1999/XSL/Transform">

      <xsl:output method="text"/>

      <xsl:template match="/">
        <xsl:text>&#xA;Test #3 of the error() function:</xsl:text>

        <xsl:value-of
          select="error(QName('http://www.w3.org/2005/xqt-errors',
                  'err:FORX0004'),
                  'Invalid replacement string.')"/>
      </xsl:template>

    </xsl:stylesheet>
```

The results here are more informative; the error message includes our string:

```
    FORX0004: Invalid replacement string.
Transformation failed: Run-time errors were reported
```

The specs define error code FORX0004 as "Invalid replacement string," so that's what we put into our error string. With Saxon, whatever string we pass to the error( ) function is put into the output, so we're free to put more information in the string if we want.

Our final example includes an item—in this case, an xs:dateTime value:

```
    <?xml version="1.0"?>
    <!-- error4.xsl -->
    <xsl:stylesheet version="2.0"
      xmlns:xsl="http://www.w3.org/1999/XSL/Transform">

      <xsl:output method="text"/>

      <xsl:template match="/">
        <xsl:text>&#xA;Test #4 of the error() function:</xsl:text>

        <xsl:value-of
          select="error(QName('http://www.w3.org/2005/xqt-errors',
                  'err:FORX0004'),
```

```
                'Invalid replacement string.',
                current-dateTime())"/>
    </xsl:template>

</xsl:stylesheet>
```

Here our results are exactly what they were before:

```
    FORX0004: Invalid replacement string.
    Transformation failed: Run-time errors were reported
```

Looking into the Saxon documentation, it seems the sequence of items we can pass to the error( ) function are intended for more advanced techniques than simply writing messages to the console. The saxon:try( ) function, available in the schema-aware version of Saxon, appears to have access to this data. Again, virtually all of the details of how the error( ) function work are implementation-defined, so check your processor's documentation for more information.

[2.0] escape-html-uri()

Given an HTML URI, returns that URI with its non-ASCII characters escaped as UTF-8 characters.

Syntax

```
    xs:string escape-html-uri(xs:string?)
```

Inputs

An xs:string representing an HTML URI.

Output

The input string with all characters outside the range   to ~ escaped as UTF-8 characters. When a character is converted to UTF-8, it is represented as octets in the form %HH, where HH is the hexadecimal representation of the octet. The hexadecimal characters generated by escape-html-uri( ) are in uppercase. This function conforms to the rules for escaping non-ASCII characters defined in the HTML 4.0 spec.

If argument is the empty sequence, a zero-length string is returned.

Defined in

XQuery 1.0 and XPath 2.0 Functions and Operators section 7.4, "Functions on String Values."

Example

This stylesheet uses escape-html-uri( ) to correctly encode characters in the URI (in this case é, a lowercase e with an acute accent) as UTF-8. (This example was taken from the XQuery 1.0 and XPath 2.0 Functions and Operators spec.)

```
    <?xml version="1.0" encoding="UTF-8"?>
    <!-- escape-html-uri.xsl -->
    <xsl:stylesheet version="1.0"
```

```
xmlns:xsl="http://www.w3.org/1999/XSL/Transform">

<xsl:output method="text"/>

<xsl:template match="/">
  <xsl:text>&#xA;Tests of the escape-html-uri() function:</xsl:text>

  <xsl:text>&#xA;&#xA;  escape-html-uri</xsl:text>
  <xsl:text>('http://www.example.com/~bébé') = &#xA;      </xsl:text>
  <xsl:value-of
    select="escape-html-uri('http://www.example.com/~bébé')"/>
</xsl:template>

</xsl:stylesheet>
```

The results look like this:

```
Tests of the escape-html-uri() function:

escape-html-uri('http://www.example.com/~bébé') =
    http://www.example.com/~b%C3%A9b%C3%A9
```

Notice that the single-byte character in the original URL (é) has been replaced by a two-byte UTF-8 character (%C3%A9) in the output.

See Also

The descriptions of the [2.0] encode-for-uri( ) and [2.0] iri-to-uri( ) functions.

[2.0] exactly-one()

Raises an error unless its argument is a singleton, a sequence containing exactly one item. Be aware that exactly-one( ) terminates processing. For a more flexible approach, use the count( ) function to determine the cardinality of a sequence.

Syntax

```
item()+ exactly-one(item()*)
```

Inputs

A sequence.

Outputs

If the input sequence contains exactly one item, the input sequence is returned. Otherwise, exactly-one( ) raises an error.

Defined in

XQuery 1.0 and XPath 2.0 Functions and Operators section 15.2, "Functions That Test the Cardinality of Sequences." More details about this function can be found in XQuery 1.0 and XPath 2.0 Formal Semantics section 7.2, "Standard Functions with Specific Static Typing Rules."

Example

The exactly-one( ) function is useful for working with XSLT 2.0's static typing. Any sequence can be empty, a singleton, or have multiple items. If we need to test the cardinality of the sequence at runtime, the exactly-one( ) function can enforce the restriction that a sequence must be a singleton. However, exactly-one( ) terminates stylesheet processing if its argument doesn't have exactly one item, so it's far more flexible to use the count( ) function to check the number of items in a sequence before working with it.

Here is a short stylesheet that invokes the exactly-one( ) function with a singleton:

```
<?xml version="1.0"?>
<!-- exactly-one.xsl -->
<xsl:stylesheet version="2.0"
  xmlns:xsl="http://www.w3.org/1999/XSL/Transform">

  <xsl:output method="text"/>

  <xsl:template match="/">

    <xsl:text>&#xA;Here is a test of the exactly-one() </xsl:text>
    <xsl:text>function:&#xA;</xsl:text>

    <xsl:variable name="singleton" as="item()*">
      <xsl:sequence select="0"/>
    </xsl:variable>

    <xsl:text>&#xA;  Our sequence is:&#xA;&#xA;    </xsl:text>
    <xsl:value-of select="$singleton" separator="&#xA;    "/>

    <xsl:if test="count(exactly-one($singleton))">
      <xsl:text>&#xA;&#xA;  Our test sequence has exactly </xsl:text>
      <xsl:text>one item!&#xA;</xsl:text>
    </xsl:if>
  </xsl:template>

</xsl:stylesheet>
```

In the test attribute of the <xsl:if> element we need to use exactly-one( ) to generate a boolean value. Here's a simple, yet incorrect, way to do this:

```
<xsl:if test="exactly-one($singleton)">  <!-- doesn't work! -->
```

If the exactly-one( ) function doesn't raise an error, it returns a sequence with exactly one item. It would seem that a one-item sequence would always be true, but that's not the case. In our example here, the singleton sequence (0) evaluates to false because the atomic value 0 is false. Using the count( ) function ensures that we get a meaningful result. (With a singleton sequence, count( ) always returns 1, which is always true.)

Also keep in mind that many datatypes cannot be converted to boolean values. If our singleton were the sequence (xs:date('1995-04-21')), the XSLT processor would raise an error because xs:date values cannot be converted to boolean.

At any rate, here are the results:

```
Here is a test of the exactly-one() function:

  Our sequence is:

    0

  Our test sequence has exactly one item!
```

See Also

The descriptions of the count( ), [2.0] empty( ), [2.0] one-or-more( ), and the [2.0] zero-or-one( ) functions and the XPath 2.0 treat as operater (in the section "[2.0] Datatype Operators —instance of, castable as, cast as, and treat as" in Chapter 3).

[2.0] exists()

Returns true if the input sequence is nonempty; false otherwise.

Syntax

```
xs:boolean exists(item()*)
```

Input

A sequence of items.

Output

If the sequence of items is not empty, exists( ) returns true; otherwise, it returns false.

Defined in

XQuery 1.0 and XPath 2.0 Functions and Operators section 15.1, "General Functions and Operators on Sequences."

Example

This simple stylesheet uses the exists( ) function against three sequences. The first sequence is the empty sequence, the second is a singleton, and the third is a longer sequence:

```
<?xml version="1.0"?>
<!-- exists.xsl -->
<xsl:stylesheet version="2.0"
  xmlns:xsl="http://www.w3.org/1999/XSL/Transform"
  xmlns:xs="http://www.w3.org/2001/XMLSchema">

  <xsl:output method="text"/>

  <xsl:template match="/">

    <xsl:text>&#xA;Here is a test of the exists() </xsl:text>
    <xsl:text>function:&#xA;&#xA;  </xsl:text>

    <xsl:variable name="emptySequence" as="item()*">
```

```
    <xsl:sequence select="()"/>
  </xsl:variable>

  <xsl:variable name="singleton" as="item()*">
    <xsl:sequence select="(3)"/>
  </xsl:variable>

  <xsl:variable name="longSequence" as="item()*">
    <xsl:sequence
      select="(3, 4, 5, current-date(), current-time(), 8, 'blue',
              'red', xs:float(3.14), 42, xs:date('1995-04-21'))"/>
  </xsl:variable>

  <xsl:choose>
    <xsl:when test="exists($emptySequence)">
      <xsl:text>The empty sequence does exist!</xsl:text>
    </xsl:when>
    <xsl:otherwise>
      <xsl:text>The empty sequence doesn't exist!</xsl:text>
    </xsl:otherwise>
  </xsl:choose>

  <xsl:text>&#xA;  </xsl:text>
  <xsl:value-of select="if (exists($singleton))
                        then 'The singleton sequence does exist!'
                        else 'The singleton sequence doesn''t exist!'"/>

  <xsl:text>&#xA;  </xsl:text>
  <xsl:value-of select="if (exists($longSequence))
                        then 'The long sequence does exist!'
                        else 'The long sequence doesn''t exist!'"/>
  </xsl:template>

</xsl:stylesheet>
```

Notice that the first test of **exists( )** does if-then-else logic with the XSLT 1.0 `<choose>` element, while the other tests use the **exists( )** function in XPath 2.0's **if** statement. The results from the stylesheet look like this:

```
Here is a test of the exists() function:

The empty sequence doesn't exist!
The singleton sequence does exist!
The long sequence does exist!
```

false()

Always returns the boolean value **false**. Remember that the strings "true" and "false" don't have any special significance in XSLT; any string with a length greater than zero is true. This function (and the **true( )** function) allow you to generate boolean values when you need them.

Syntax

```
[1.0] boolean false()
[2.0] xs:boolean false()
```

Inputs

None.

Output

The boolean value `false`.

Defined in

XPath section 4.3, "Boolean Functions."

[2.0] XQuery 1.0 and XPath 2.0 Functions and Operators Section 9.1, "Additional Boolean Constructor Functions."

Example

Here's a brief example that uses the `false( )` function:

```
<?xml version="1.0"?>
<!-- false.xsl -->
<xsl:stylesheet version="1.0"
  xmlns:xsl="http://www.w3.org/1999/XSL/Transform">

  <xsl:output method="text"/>

  <xsl:template match="/">
    <xsl:text>&#xA;A test of the false() function:&#xA;&#xA;</xsl:text>

    <xsl:text>  false() returned </xsl:text>
    <xsl:value-of select="false()"/>
    <xsl:text>!</xsl:text>
  </xsl:template>
</xsl:stylesheet>
```

When using this stylesheet against any XML document, it generates this less-than exciting result:

```
A test of the false() function:

  false() returned false!
```

---

floor()

Returns the largest integer that is not greater than the argument.

Syntax

```
[1.0] number floor(number)
[2.0] numeric? floor(numeric?)
```

Inputs

A number.

[1.0] If the argument is not a number, it is transformed into a number as if it had been processed by the `number( )` function. If the argument cannot be transformed into a number, the `floor( )` function returns the value NaN (not a number).

[2.0] In XSLT 2.0, the argument must be one of the four numeric types (`xs:float`, `xs:decimal`, `xs:double`, or `xs:integer`). If it is not, the XSLT processor raises an error. The result of the `floor( )` function will be of the same type as the argument.

In XSLT 2.0, the argument must be a number. If it is not, the XSLT processor raises an error.

Output

The largest integer that is not less than the argument.

[1.0] In XSLT 1.0, `floor( )` returns NaN if the argument cannot be converted to a number.

[2.0] In XSLT 2.0, `floor( )` raises an error if the argument cannot be converted to a number.

Defined in

[1.0] XPath section 4.4, "Number Functions."

[2.0] XQuery 1.0 and XPath 2.0 Functions and Operators section 6.4, "Functions on Numeric Values."

Example

The following stylesheet shows the results of invoking the `floor( )` function against a variety of values:

```
<?xml version="1.0"?>
<!-- floor.xsl -->
<xsl:stylesheet version="2.0"
  xmlns:xsl="http://www.w3.org/1999/XSL/Transform">

  <xsl:output method="text"/>

  <xsl:template match="/">
    <xsl:text>&#xA;Tests of the floor() function:&#xA;&#xA;</xsl:text>

    <xsl:text>  floor(7.983) = </xsl:text>
    <xsl:value-of select="floor(7.983)"/>

    <xsl:text>&#xA;  floor(-7.893) = </xsl:text>
    <xsl:value-of select="floor(-7.893)"/>

    <xsl:text>&#xA;  floor('blue') = </xsl:text>
    <xsl:value-of version="1.0" select="floor('blue')"/>

  </xsl:template>

</xsl:stylesheet>
```

When we transform the XML document with our stylesheet, here are the results:

```
Tests of the floor() function:

    floor(7.983) = 7
    floor(-7.893) = -8
    floor('blue') = NaN
```

For the last test of the floor( ) function, we specified version="1.0" on the <xsl:value-of> element. In XSLT 1.0 mode, we get the result NaN (not a number). If we process this <xsl:value-of> element in XSLT 2.0 mode, the stylesheet won't run at all. If you change the entire stylesheet to XSLT version 1.0, you'll have to take the version attribute off of the <xsl:value-of> element.

[2.0] format-date()

Formats an xs:date value according to a format string.

Syntax

```
xs:string? format-date(xs:date?, xs:string)
xs:string? format-date(xs:date?, xs:string, $language as xs:string?,
                       $calendar as xs:string?,
                       $country as xs:string?)
```

Inputs

In the first form of this function, an optional xs:date value and a formatting string. If the xs:date value is omitted, the current date is used. In the second form of this function, you can supply strings that represent the preferred language, calendar, and country codes for the output value.

The following codes are defined for the formatting string. The default values are how the processor interprets codes without any modifiers. In other words, [Y] is the same as [Y1]. The codes are:

Y

The year. The default value is [Y1], which generates a four-digit year.

M

The month in the year. The default value is [M1], which generates a one- or two-digit numeric month.

D

The day in the month. The default value is [D1], which generates a one- or two-digit numeric day.

d

The day in the year. The default value is [d1], which generates a one-, two-, or three-digit day (if the date is July 26 of a nonleap year, this generates 207, for example).

F

The day in the week. The default value is [Fn], which generates the lowercase word representing the day of the week (wednesday, for example).

W

The week in the year. The default value is [W1], which generates the one- or two-digit number of the week in the year.

w

The week in the month. The default value is [w1], which generates the one-digit number of the week in the month.

Z

The timezone as an offset from UTC. The default value is [Z1], which generates the hour and minute offset from UTC (-04:00, for example).

z

The timezone as an offset from GMT. The default value is [z1], which generates the offset from GMT (GMT-4, for example).

For complete details on the formatting strings for dates, times, and numbers, see Appendix F.

Output

A string representing the xs:date formatted according to the format string. If the xs:date argument is the empty sequence, the empty sequence is returned.

Defined in

XSLT section 16.5, "Formatting Dates and Times."

Example

This stylesheet illustrates many different ways to format an xs:date and its various components:

```
<?xml version="1.0"?>
<!-- format-date.xsl -->
<xsl:stylesheet version="2.0"
  xmlns:xsl="http://www.w3.org/1999/XSL/Transform"
  xmlns:xs="http://www.w3.org/2001/XMLSchema">

  <xsl:output method="text"/>

  <xsl:template match="/">
    <xsl:text>&#xA;Tests of the format-date() function:&#xA;</xsl:text>

    <xsl:variable name="today" select="current-date()"/>
    <xsl:text>&#xA;  The current date is: </xsl:text>
    <xsl:value-of select="$today"/>
    <xsl:variable name="longFormat"
      select="concat('Today is [FNn], [MNn] [D1], [Y], &#xA;        ',
              'the [D1o] day of the [W1o] week of the year,',
              '&#xA;        the [w1o] week of the month,',
              '&#xA;        in the [zWw] time zone.')"/>
```

```
<xsl:text>&#xA;&#xA;    The year - format-date</xsl:text>
<xsl:text>($today, '[Y]'): </xsl:text>
<xsl:value-of select="format-date($today, '[Y1111]')"/>
<xsl:text>&#xA;&#xA;    The two-digit year - </xsl:text>
<xsl:text>format-date($today, '[Y11]'): </xsl:text>
<xsl:value-of select="format-date($today, '[Y11]')"/>
<xsl:text>&#xA;&#xA;    The month - format-date(</xsl:text>
<xsl:text>$today, '[M11]'): </xsl:text>
<xsl:value-of select="format-date($today, '[M11]')"/>
<xsl:text>&#xA;&#xA;    The month in German words - </xsl:text>
<xsl:text>format-date($today, '[MWw]', 'de', (), ()): </xsl:text>
<xsl:text>&#xA;       </xsl:text>
<xsl:value-of
  select="format-date($today, '[MWw]', 'de', (), ())"/>
<xsl:text>&#xA;&#xA;    The day in words - format-date(</xsl:text>
<xsl:text>$today, '[DWw]'): &#xA;       </xsl:text>
<xsl:value-of select="format-date($today, '[DWw]')"/>
<xsl:text>&#xA;&#xA;    The day in German words - </xsl:text>
<xsl:text>format-date($today, '[Dw]', 'de', (), ()): </xsl:text>
<xsl:text>&#xA;       </xsl:text>
<xsl:value-of select="format-date($today, '[Dw]', 'de', (), ())"/>
<xsl:text>&#xA;&#xA;    Using format-date($today, '[dwo]'):</xsl:text>
<xsl:text>&#xA;       It's the </xsl:text>
<xsl:value-of select="format-date($today, '[dwo]')"/>
<xsl:text> day of the year.</xsl:text>
<xsl:text>&#xA;&#xA;    Using format-date($today, '[d1o]'):</xsl:text>
<xsl:text>&#xA;       It's the </xsl:text>
<xsl:value-of select="format-date($today, '[d1o]')"/>
<xsl:text> day of the year.</xsl:text>

<xsl:text>&#xA;&#xA;  The grand finale:</xsl:text>
<xsl:text>&#xA;     </xsl:text>
<xsl:value-of select="format-date($today, $longFormat)"/>
  </xsl:template>

</xsl:stylesheet>
```

The results look like this:

```
Tests of the format-date() function:

  The current date is: 2006-07-26-04:00

    The year - format-date($today, '[Y]'): 2006

    The two-digit year - format-date($today, '[Y11]'): 06

    The month - format-date($today, '[M11]'): 07

    The month in German words - format-date($today, '[MWw]', 'de', (), ()):
       Sieben

    The day in words - format-date($today, '[DWw]'):
       Twenty Six
```

```
    The day in German words - format-date($today, '[Dw]', 'de', (), ()):
      sechsundzwanzig

    Using format-date($today, '[dwo]'):
      It's the two hundred and seventh day of the year.

    Using format-date($today, '[d1o]'):
      It's the 207th day of the year.

  The grand finale:
    Today is Wednesday, July 26, 2006,
      the 26th day of the 30th week of the year,
      the 4th week of the month,
      in the GMT-4 time zone.
```

Notice that we used the language code de for two of the examples. With the different combinations of modifiers, we printed out the components of a date in numbers and words, both in cardinal and ordinal formats. Also notice that we stored the formatting string in a variable so we could use it whenever we want.

[2.0] format-dateTime()

Formats an xs:dateTime value according to a format string.

Syntax

```
xs:string? format-dateTime(xs:dateTime?, $picture as xs:string)
xs:string? format-dateTime(xs:dateTime?, $picture as xs:string,
                           $language as xs:string?,
                           $calendar as xs:string?,
                           $country as xs:string?)
```

Inputs

In the first form of this function, an optional xs:dateTime value and a formatting string. If the xs:dateTime value is omitted, the current date and time is used. In the second form of this function, you can supply strings that represent the preferred language, calendar, and country codes for the output value.

The following codes are defined for the formatting string:

Y

The year. The default value is [Y1], which generates a four-digit year.

M

The month in the year. The default value is [M1], which generates a one- or two-digit numeric month.

D

The day in the month. The default value is [D1], which generates a one- or two-digit numeric day.

d

The day in the year. The default value is [d1], which generates a one-, two-, or three-digit day (if the date is July 26 of a nonleap year, this generates 207, for example).

F

The day in the week. The default value is [Fn], which generates the lowercase word representing the day of the week (wednesday, for example).

W

The week in the year. The default value is [W1], which generates the one- or two-digit number of the week in the year.

w

The week in the month. The default value is [w1], which generates the one-digit number of the week in the month.

H

The hour in the day, in a 24-hour clock. The default value is [H1], which generates the one- or two-digit number of the hour in the day. Note that this value will never be greater than 23.

h

The hour in the day, in a 12-hour clock. The default value is [h1], which generates the one- or two-digit number of the hour in the day.

P

The AM/PM marker. The default value is [Pn], which generates the AM/PM marker in lowercase (a.m. or p.m.).

m

The minute in the hour. The default value is [m01], which generates the two-digit minute in the hour.

s

The second in the minute. The default value is [s01], which generates the two-digit second in the minute.

f

The fractional seconds. The default value is [f1], which generates the fractional seconds to three decimal places.

Z

The timezone as an offset from UTC. The default value is [Z1], which generates the hour and minute offset from UTC (-04:00, for example).

z

The timezone as an offset from GMT. The default value is [z1], which generates the offset from GMT (GMT-4, for example).

For complete details on the formatting strings for dates, times, and numbers, see Appendix F.

Output

A string representing the xs:dateTime formatted according to the format string. If the xs:dateTime argument is the empty sequence, the empty sequence is returned.

Defined in

XSLT section 16.5, "Formatting Dates and Times."

Example

This stylesheet illustrates many different ways to format an xs:dateTime and its various components:

```
<?xml version="1.0"?>
<!-- format-dateTime.xsl -->
<xsl:stylesheet version="2.0"
  xmlns:xsl="http://www.w3.org/1999/XSL/Transform"
  xmlns:xs="http://www.w3.org/2001/XMLSchema">

  <xsl:output method="text"/>

  <xsl:template match="/">
    <xsl:text>&#xA;Tests of the format-dateTime() function:&#xA;</xsl:text>

    <xsl:variable name="today" select="current-dateTime()"/>
    <xsl:text>&#xA;   The current date and time is: </xsl:text>
    <xsl:value-of select="$today"/>
    <xsl:variable name="longFormat"
      select="concat('It''s [h1]:[m11] [P] on ',
              '[FNn], [MNn] [D1], [Y], &#xA;        ',
              'the [D1o] day of the [W1o] week of the year,',
              '&#xA;        the [w1o] week of the month,',
              '&#xA;        in the [zWw] time zone.')"/>

    <xsl:text>&#xA;&#xA;   The year - format-dateTime</xsl:text>
    <xsl:text>($today, '[Y]'): </xsl:text>
    <xsl:value-of select="format-dateTime($today, '[Y]')"/>
    <xsl:text>&#xA;&#xA;   The hour (12-hour clock) - </xsl:text>
    <xsl:text>format-dateTime($today, '[h] [PN]'): </xsl:text>
    <xsl:value-of select="format-dateTime($today, '[h] [PN]')"/>
    <xsl:text>&#xA;&#xA;   The minutes - format-dateTime(</xsl:text>
    <xsl:text>$today, '[m11]'): </xsl:text>
    <xsl:value-of select="format-dateTime($today, '[m11]')"/>
    <xsl:text>&#xA;&#xA;   The seconds - format-dateTime(</xsl:text>
    <xsl:text>$today, '[s11].[f1111]): </xsl:text>
    <xsl:value-of select="format-dateTime($today, '[s11].[f1111]')"/>
    <xsl:text>&#xA;&#xA;   The complete time - format-dateTime(</xsl:text>
    <xsl:text>$today, '[h]:[m11]:[s11] [P]'): &#xA;        </xsl:text>
    <xsl:value-of
      select="format-dateTime($today, '[h]:[m11]:[s11] [P]')"/>
    <xsl:text>&#xA;&#xA;   The day in words - format-dateTime(</xsl:text>
    <xsl:text>$today, '[FNn]'): &#xA;        </xsl:text>
    <xsl:value-of select="format-dateTime($today, '[FNn]')"/>

    <xsl:text>&#xA;&#xA;   The grand finale:</xsl:text>
```

```
<xsl:text>&#xA;    </xsl:text>
<xsl:value-of select="format-dateTime($today, $longFormat)"/>
</xsl:template>

</xsl:stylesheet>
```

Here are the results:

```
Tests of the format-dateTime() function:

  The current date and time is: 2006-07-26T13:58:25.790-04:00

    The year - format-dateTime($today, '[Y]'): 2006

    The hour (12-hour clock) - format-dateTime($today, '[h] [PN]'): 1 P.M.

    The minutes - format-dateTime($today, '[m11]'): 58

    The seconds - format-dateTime($today, '[s11].[f1111]): 25.7900

    The complete time - format-dateTime($today, '[h]:[m11]:[s11] [P]'):
      1:58:25 p.m.

    The day in words - format-dateTime($today, '[FNn]'):
      Wednesday

  The grand finale:
    It's 1:58 p.m. on Wednesday, July 26, 2006,
      the 26th day of the 30th week of the year,
      the 4th week of the month,
      in the GMT-4 time zone.
```

format-number()

Takes a number and formats it as a string.

Syntax

```
[1.0] string format-number($value as number, $picture as string,
                           $formatName as string?)
[2.0] xs:string format-number($value as numeric, $picture as xs:string,
                              $formatName as xs:string?)
```

Inputs

The number to be formatted and the format pattern string are required. The third argument is the optional name of a decimal format; if the third argument is not supplied, the default decimal format is used.

[2.0] The numeric argument must be one of the four numeric types (xs:float, xs:decimal, xs:double, or xs:integer). If it is not a numeric type or cannot be converted to one, the XSLT processor raises an error. The XSLT processor also raises an error if the named decimal format does not exist.

Output

The number, formatted according to the rules supplied by the other arguments. The special characters used in the second argument are:

#

Represents a digit. Trailing or leading zeroes are not displayed. Formatting the number **4.0** with the string **#.##** returns the string **4**.

0

Represents a digit. Unlike the **#** character, the **0** always displays a zero. Formatting the number **4.1** with the string **#.00** returns the string **4.10**.

.

Represents the decimal point.

–

Represents the minus sign.

,

Is the grouping separator.

;

Separates the positive-number pattern from the negative-number pattern.

%

Indicates that a number should be displayed as a percentage. The value will be multiplied by 100, then displayed as a percentage. Formatting the number **.76** with the string **##%** returns the string **76%**.

\u2030

Is the Unicode character for the per-thousand (per-mille) sign. The value will be multiplied by 1000, then displayed as a per mille. Formatting the number **.768** with the string **###\u2030** returns the string **768‰**.

For complete details on the formatting strings for dates, times and numbers, see Appendix F.

The third argument, if given, must be the name of an `<xsl:decimal-format>` element. The `<xsl:decimal-format>` element lets you define the character that should be used for the decimal point and the grouping separator, the string used to represent infinity, and other formatting options. See the discussion of the `<xsl:decimal-format>` element in Appendix A for more information.

Defined in

[1.0] XSLT section 12.3, "Number Formatting."

[2.0] XSLT section 16.4, "Number Formatting."

Example

The following stylesheet uses the `format-number( )` function in various ways:

```
<?xml version="1.0"?>
<!-- format-number.xsl -->
```

```
<xsl:stylesheet version="1.0"
  xmlns:xsl="http://www.w3.org/1999/XSL/Transform">

  <xsl:output method="text"/>

  <xsl:decimal-format name="f1"
    decimal-separator=":"
    grouping-separator="/"/>

  <xsl:decimal-format name="f2"
    infinity="Really, really big"
    NaN="[not a number]"/>

  <xsl:template match="/">
    <xsl:text>&#xA;Tests of the format-number() </xsl:text>
    <xsl:text>function:&#xA;&#xA;</xsl:text>

    <xsl:text>  1. format-number(528.3, '#.#;-#.#')=</xsl:text>
    <xsl:value-of
      select="format-number(528.3, '#.#;-#.#')"/>
    <xsl:text>&#xA;  2. format-number(528.3, </xsl:text>
    <xsl:text>'0,000.00;-0,000.00')=</xsl:text>
    <xsl:value-of
      select="format-number(528.3, '0,000.00;-0,000.00')"/>
    <xsl:text>&#xA;  3. format-number(-23528.3, </xsl:text>
    <xsl:text>'$#,###.00;($#,###.00)')=</xsl:text>
    <xsl:value-of
      select="format-number(-23528.3, '$#,###.00;($#,###.00)')"/>
    <xsl:text>&#xA;  4. format-number(1528.3, </xsl:text>
    <xsl:text>'#/###:00', 'f1')=</xsl:text>
    <xsl:value-of
      select="format-number(1528.3, '#/###:00;-#/###:00', 'f1')"/>
    <xsl:text>&#xA;  5. format-number(1 div 0, </xsl:text>
    <xsl:text>'###,###.00', 'f2')=</xsl:text>
    <xsl:value-of
      select="format-number(1 div 0, '###,###.00', 'f2')"/>
    <xsl:text>&#xA;  6. format-number(blue div orange, </xsl:text>
    <xsl:text>'#.##', 'f2')=</xsl:text>
    <xsl:value-of
      select="format-number(blue div orange, '#.##', 'f2')"/>
    <xsl:text>&#xA;&#xA;  </xsl:text>

    <xsl:value-of select="report/title"/>
    <xsl:text> - </xsl:text>
    <xsl:value-of select="report/@month"/>
    <xsl:text>/</xsl:text>
    <xsl:value-of select="report/@year"/>
    <xsl:text>&#xA;&#xA;</xsl:text>

    <xsl:variable name="totalSales"
      select="sum(/report/brand/units)"/>

    <xsl:for-each select="report/brand">
      <xsl:text>     </xsl:text>
      <xsl:value-of select="name"/>
```

```
        <xsl:text> - </xsl:text>
        <xsl:value-of select="format-number(units, '##,###')"/>
        <xsl:text> bars sold, </xsl:text>
        <xsl:value-of
          select="format-number(units div $totalSales, '##%')"/>
        <xsl:text> of all sales.&#xA;</xsl:text>
      </xsl:for-each>

      <xsl:text>&#xA;  Total sales: </xsl:text>
      <xsl:value-of
        select="format-number(sum(/report/brand/units), '##,###')"/>
  </xsl:template>

</xsl:stylesheet>
```

We'll use this XML document with our stylesheet:

```
<?xml version="1.0" encoding="utf-8"?>
<!-- chocolate.xml -->
<report month="8" year="2006">
  <title>Chocolate bar sales</title>
  <brand>
    <name>Lindt</name>
    <units>27408</units>
  </brand>
  ...
  <brand>
    <name>Ghirardelli</name>
    <units>19268</units>
  </brand>
</report>
```

When we run this stylesheet, here are the results:

```
Tests of the format-number() function:

  1. format-number(528.3, '#.#;-#.#')=528.3
  2. format-number(528.3, '0,000.00;-0,000.00')=0,528.30
  3. format-number(-23528.3, '$#,###.00;($#,###.00)')=($23,528.30)
  4. format-number(1528.3, '#/###:00', 'f1')=1/528:30
  5. format-number(1 div 0, '###,###.00', 'f2')=Really, really big
  6. format-number(blue div orange, '#.##', 'f2')=[not a number]

Chocolate bar sales - 8/2006

  Lindt - 27,408 bars sold, 30% of all sales.
  Callebaut - 8,203 bars sold, 9% of all sales.
  Valrhona - 22,101 bars sold, 24% of all sales.
  Perugina - 14,336 bars sold, 16% of all sales.
  Ghirardelli - 19,268 bars sold, 21% of all sales.

  Total sales: 91,316
```

The first three examples use format-number( ) to control the decimal places, commas, and the format of negative numbers. The fourth example uses the <decimal-format> named f1, which uses a slash (/) as a grouping separator and a colon (:) as the decimal point.

Examples 5 and 6 cause problems in XSLT 2.0. Example 5 doesn't work because division by zero is a fatal error for `xs:integer` values in XSLT 2.0. Example 6 doesn't work because the `div` operator requires numeric operands. If you want XSLT 1.0 processing in an XSLT 2.0 stylesheet, you can add the `version="1.0"` attribute to any `<xsl:value-of>` element that needs it:

```
<xsl:value-of version="1.0"
  select="format-number(1 div 0, '###,###.00', 'f2')"/>
```

The last set of examples extracts data from our document of chocolate bar sales, formatting the total sales of each bar. We also generate the percentage of total sales for each brand and print the total sales for all brands.

[2.0] format-time()

Given an `xs:time` value and a format string, returns the formatted time value.

Syntax

```
xs:string format-time(xs:time?, $picture as xs:string)
xs:string format-time(xs:time?, $picture as xs:string,
                      $language as xs:string?,
                      $calendar as xs:string?,
                      $country as xs:string?)
```

Inputs

In the first form of this function, an optional `xs:time` value and a formatting string. If the `xs:time` value is omitted, the current time is used. In the second form of this function, you can supply strings that represent the preferred language, calendar, and country codes for the output value.

The following codes are defined for the formatting string:

H

> The hour in the day, in a 24-hour clock. The default value is [H1], which generates the one- or two-digit number of the hour in the day. Note that this value will never be greater than 23.

h

> The hour in the day, in a 12-hour clock. The default value is [h1], which generates the one- or two-digit number of the hour in the day.

P

> The AM/PM marker. The default value is [Pn], which generates the AM/PM marker in lowercase (a.m. or p.m.).

m

> The minute in the hour. The default value is [m01], which generates the two-digit minute in the hour.

s

The second in the minute. The default value is [s01], which generates the two-digit second in the minute.

f

The fractional seconds. The default value is [f1], which generates the fractional seconds to three decimal places.

Z

The timezone as an offset from UTC. The default value is [Z1], which generates the hour and minute offset from UTC (-04:00, for example).

z

The timezone as an offset from GMT. The default value is [z1], which generates the offset from GMT (GMT-4, for example).

For complete details on the formatting strings for dates, times, and numbers, see Appendix F.

Output

A string representing the xs:time formatted according to the format string. If the xs:time argument is the empty sequence, the empty sequence is returned.

Defined in

XSLT section 16.5, "Formatting Dates and Times."

Example

Here's a stylesheet that uses format-time( ) in several different ways:

```
<?xml version="1.0"?>
<!-- format-time.xsl -->
<xsl:stylesheet version="2.0"
  xmlns:xsl="http://www.w3.org/1999/XSL/Transform"
  xmlns:xs="http://www.w3.org/2001/XMLSchema">

  <xsl:output method="text"/>

  <xsl:template match="/">
    <xsl:text>&#xA;Tests of the format-time() function:&#xA;</xsl:text>

    <xsl:variable name="now" select="current-time()"/>
    <xsl:text>&#xA;  The current date and time is: </xsl:text>
    <xsl:value-of select="$now"/>
    <xsl:variable name="longFormat"
      select="concat('It''s [h1]:[m11]:[s11] [P] ',
              'in the [zWw] time zone.')"/>

    <xsl:text>&#xA;&#xA;   The hour (24-hour clock) - </xsl:text>
    <xsl:text>format-time($now, '[H]'): </xsl:text>
    <xsl:value-of select="format-time($now, '[H]')"/>
    <xsl:text>&#xA;&#xA;   The minutes - format-time(</xsl:text>
    <xsl:text>$now, '[m11]'): </xsl:text>
    <xsl:value-of select="format-time($now, '[m11]')"/>
```

```
<xsl:text>&#xA;&#xA;    Using format-time(</xsl:text>
<xsl:text>$now, '[mWwo]'): &#xA;    It's the </xsl:text>
<xsl:value-of select="format-time($now, '[mWwo]')"/>
<xsl:text> minute of the hour.</xsl:text>
<xsl:text>&#xA;&#xA;    The time - format-time(</xsl:text>
<xsl:text>$now, '[H]:[m11]'): &#xA;        </xsl:text>
<xsl:value-of
   select="format-time($now, '[H]:[m11]')"/>

<xsl:text>&#xA;&#xA;  The grand finale:</xsl:text>
<xsl:text>&#xA;    </xsl:text>
<xsl:value-of select="format-time($now, $longFormat)"/>
</xsl:template>

</xsl:stylesheet>
```

Here are the results:

```
Tests of the format-time() function:

  The current date and time is: 14:10:00.028-04:00

  The hour (24-hour clock) - format-time($now, '[H]'): 14

  The minutes - format-time($now, '[m11]'): 10

  Using format-time($now, '[mWwo]'):
    It's the Tenth minute of the hour.

  The time - format-time($now, '[H]:[m11]'):
    14:10

The grand finale:
  It's 2:10:00 p.m. in the GMT-4 time zone.
```

function-available()

Determines if a given function is available to the XSLT processor. This function allows you to design stylesheets that react gracefully if a particular extension function is not available.

Syntax

```
[1.0] boolean function-available($functionName as string)
[2.0] xs:boolean function-available($functionName as xs:string,
                                    $arity as xs:integer?)
```

Inputs

The function's name. The name is usually qualified with a namespace; if the namespace of the function name is nonnull, the function is an extension function. Otherwise, the function is assumed to be one of the functions defined in the XSLT or XPath specifications.

[2.0] XSLT 2.0's version of this function also has an *arity* argument. This lets you specify how many parameters a function accepts. For example, function-available('ora:greatFunction',

2) might return true, while function-available('ora:greatFunction', 3) might return false. If you try to call function-available('me:my-function', 2) with an XSLT 1.0 processor, you'll get a runtime error.

Output

The boolean value true if the function is available; false otherwise.

Defined in

[1.0] XSLT section 15, "Fallback."

[2.0] XSLT section 18.1, "Extension Functions."

Example

We'll use the following XML document to test the function-available( ) function:

```
<?xml version="1.0"?>
<!-- favorites.xml -->
<list>
  <title>A few of my favorite albums</title>
  <listitem>A Love Supreme</listitem>
  <listitem>Beat Crazy</listitem>
  <listitem>Here Come the Warm Jets</listitem>
  <listitem>Kind of Blue</listitem>
  <listitem>London Calling</listitem>
  <listitem>Remain in Light</listitem>
  <listitem>The Joshua Tree</listitem>
  <listitem>The Indestructible Beat of Soweto</listitem>
</list>
```

Here's our stylesheet:

```
<?xml version="1.0"?>
<!-- function-available.xsl -->
<xsl:stylesheet version="2.0"
  xmlns:xsl="http://www.w3.org/1999/XSL/Transform"
  xmlns:jpeg="class:JPEGWriter"
  extension-element-prefixes="jpeg">

  <xsl:output method="text"/>

  <xsl:template match="/">
    <xsl:text>&#xA;A test of function-avilable():&#xA;&#xA;</xsl:text>
    <xsl:for-each select="list/listitem">
      <xsl:choose>
        <xsl:when test="function-available('jpeg:buildJPEGFile')">
          <xsl:value-of
            select="jpeg:buildJPEGFile(., 'titlebar.jpg',
            concat('album', position(), '.jpg'),
            'Verdana Bold Italic', 20, 12, 20, '000000')"/>
          <xsl:text>See the file </xsl:text>
          <xsl:value-of select="concat('album', position(), '.jpg')"/>
          <xsl:text> to see the title of album #</xsl:text>
          <xsl:value-of select="position()"/>
          <xsl:text>&#xA;</xsl:text>
```

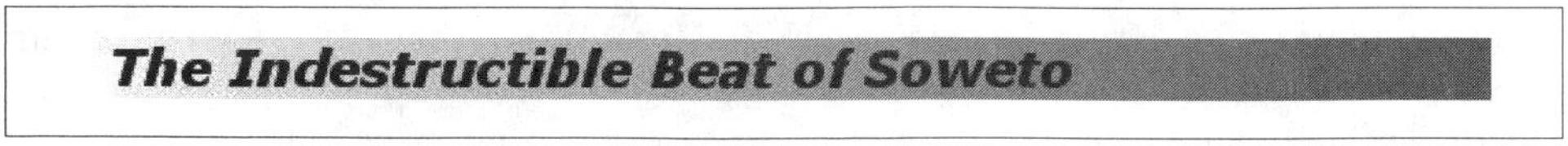

Figure C-3. Generated graphic for the eighth <listitem> element

```
      </xsl:when>
      <xsl:otherwise>
        <xsl:value-of select="position()"/>
        <xsl:text>. </xsl:text>
        <xsl:value-of select="."/>
        <xsl:text>&#xA;</xsl:text>
      </xsl:otherwise>
    </xsl:choose>
  </xsl:for-each>
</xsl:template>

</xsl:stylesheet>
```

> *Be aware that the mechanism for defining, referencing, and building extension functions varies from one processor to another.* The example here uses Xalan-J's mechanism. We create a new namespace (`jpeg`) and define its URI as `class:JPEGWriter`. When we ask whether a function in the `jpeg` namespace is available, Xalan-J attempts to load a Java class named `JPEGWriter`. If that class can't be found, `function-available( )` returns `false`. If the class is found, Xalan-J looks in the class and returns `true` if that Java class contains a method with the requested name (`buildJPEGFile`, in this example).
>
> Also be aware that `function-available( )` is not required to check the signature of the method. In our example, if Xalan-J finds the class and a method with the name we requested, it returns `true`. That doesn't mean that Xalan-J checked the number and type of arguments that we're passing to the function to see whether they're correct. If they aren't correct, we'll get a runtime error.

In our stylesheet, if the `buildJPEGFile( )` function is available, we'll invoke it to create JPEG files for the titles of all our favorite albums. If the function is not available, we'll simply write those titles to the output stream. Here are the results we get when the `buildJPEGFile( )` function is available:

```
See the file album1.jpg to see the title of album #1
See the file album2.jpg to see the title of album #2
See the file album3.jpg to see the title of album #3
See the file album4.jpg to see the title of album #4
See the file album5.jpg to see the title of album #5
See the file album6.jpg to see the title of album #6
See the file album7.jpg to see the title of album #7
See the file album8.jpg to see the title of album #8
```

All album titles (the text of the `<listitem>` elements) are converted to JPEG graphics. In this example, the file *album8.jpg* looks like Figure C-3.

If the XSLT processor can't load the extension function (maybe we're using Saxon, which doesn't load extension classes this way; maybe the *.class* file isn't on the classpath; maybe we misspelled the function name, etc.), we get these results instead:

1. A Love Supreme
2. Beat Crazy
3. Here Come the Warm Jets
4. Kind of Blue
5. London Calling
6. Remain in Light
7. The Joshua Tree
8. The Indestructible Beat of Soweto

generate-id()

Generates a unique ID (an XML name) for a given node. If no node-set is given, generate-id( ) generates an ID for the context node.

Syntax

```
[1.0] string generate-id(node-set?)
[2.0] xs:string generate-id()
[2.0] xs:string generate-id(node()?)
```

Inputs

[1.0] An optional node-set. If no node-set is given, this function generates an ID for the context node. If the node-set is empty, generate-id( ) returns an empty string.

[2.0] An optional node. If no node is given, this function generates an ID for the context node. If the argument is the empty sequence, the result is a zero-length string.

In XSLT 1.0, passing a node-set to the generate-id( ) function generated a unique ID for the first item in the node-set; all nodes after the first were ignored. *In XSLT 2.0, it is an error to pass a sequence with more than one node to* generate-id( ).

Output

A unique ID, or an empty string if an empty node-set is given. Several things about the generate-id( ) function are important to know:

- For a given transformation, every time you invoke generate-id( ) against a given node, the XSLT processor must return the same ID. The ID can't change while you're doing a transformation. If you ask the XSLT processor to transform your document with this stylesheet tomorrow, there's no guarantee that generate-id( ) will generate the same ID the second time around. All of tomorrow's calls (during one transformation) to generate-id( ) will generate the same ID, but that ID might not be the one generated today.

- The generate-id( ) function is not required to check whether its generated ID duplicates an ID that's already in the document. In other words, if an element in your document has an attribute of type ID with the value sdk3829a, there's a remote possibility that an ID returned by generate-id( ) would have the value sdk3829a. It's not likely, but it could happen.

- If you invoke generate-id( ) against two different nodes, the two generated IDs must be different.

- *[1.0]* Given a node-set, generate-id( ) returns an ID for the node in the node-set that occurs first in document order.

  [2.0] Given a sequence, an XSLT 2.0 processor raises an error if that sequence contains more than one item.

- If the node-set you pass to the function is empty (you invoke generate-id(fleeber), but there are no <fleeber> elements in the current context), generate-id( ) returns an empty string.

Defined in

[1.0] XSLT section 12.4, "Miscellaneous Additional Functions."

[2.0] XSLT section 16.6, "Miscellaneous Additional Functions."

Example

We'll use our report of chocolate bar sales as the input to our stylesheet:

```
<?xml version="1.0" encoding="utf-8"?>
<!-- chocolate.xml -->
<report month="8" year="2006">
  <title>Chocolate bar sales</title>
  <brand>
    <name>Lindt</name>
    <units>27408</units>
  </brand>
  <brand>
    <name>Callebaut</name>
    <units>8203</units>
  </brand>
  <brand>
    <name>Valrhona</name>
    <units>22101</units>
  </brand>
  <brand>
    <name>Perugina</name>
    <units>14336</units>
  </brand>
  <brand>
    <name>Ghirardelli</name>
    <units>19268</units>
  </brand>
</report>
```

Our stylesheet generates a new ID for each node in our source document. Just to make sure the XSLT processor generates the same node each time, we generate a new ID for each node again. The two generated IDs should match for each node:

```
<?xml version="1.0"?>
<xsl:stylesheet version="1.0"
  xmlns:xsl="http://www.w3.org/1999/XSL/Transform">

  <xsl:output method="text"/>

  <xsl:template match="/">
    <xsl:text>&#xA;A test of the generate-id() </xsl:text>
    <xsl:text>function:&#xA;&#xA;</xsl:text>

    <xsl:text>  We'll generate IDs for every node </xsl:text>
    <xsl:text>in the XML source:&#xA;&#xA;</xsl:text>
    <xsl:for-each select="//*">
      <xsl:text>    Node name: &lt;</xsl:text>
      <xsl:value-of select="name()"/>
      <xsl:text>&gt; - generated id: </xsl:text>
      <xsl:value-of select="generate-id()"/>
      <xsl:text>&#xA;</xsl:text>
    </xsl:for-each>

    <xsl:text>&#xA;  Now we'll try it again...&#xA;&#xA;</xsl:text>
    <xsl:for-each select="//*">
      <xsl:text>    Node name: &lt;</xsl:text>
      <xsl:value-of select="name()"/>
      <xsl:text>&gt; - generated id: </xsl:text>
      <xsl:value-of select="generate-id()"/>
      <xsl:text>&#xA;</xsl:text>
    </xsl:for-each>
  </xsl:template>

</xsl:stylesheet>
```

Our stylesheet generates these results:

```
A test of the generate-id() function:

  We'll generate IDs for every node in the XML source:

    Node name: <report> - generated id: d1e2
    Node name: <title> - generated id: d1e4
    Node name: <brand> - generated id: d1e7
    Node name: <name> - generated id: d1e9
    Node name: <units> - generated id: d1e12
    Node name: <brand> - generated id: d1e16
    Node name: <name> - generated id: d1e18
    Node name: <units> - generated id: d1e21
    Node name: <brand> - generated id: d1e25
    Node name: <name> - generated id: d1e27
    Node name: <units> - generated id: d1e30
    Node name: <brand> - generated id: d1e34
    Node name: <name> - generated id: d1e36
    Node name: <units> - generated id: d1e39
    Node name: <brand> - generated id: d1e44
    Node name: <name> - generated id: d1e46
    Node name: <units> - generated id: d1e49
```

```
Now we'll try it again...

   Node name: <report> - generated id: d1e2
   Node name: <title> - generated id: d1e4
   Node name: <brand> - generated id: d1e7
   Node name: <name> - generated id: d1e9
   Node name: <units> - generated id: d1e12
   Node name: <brand> - generated id: d1e16
   Node name: <name> - generated id: d1e18
   Node name: <units> - generated id: d1e21
   Node name: <brand> - generated id: d1e25
   Node name: <name> - generated id: d1e27
   Node name: <units> - generated id: d1e30
   Node name: <brand> - generated id: d1e34
   Node name: <name> - generated id: d1e36
   Node name: <units> - generated id: d1e39
   Node name: <brand> - generated id: d1e44
   Node name: <name> - generated id: d1e46
   Node name: <units> - generated id: d1e49
```

The IDs generated each time are the same. Be aware that other processors generate IDs differently. The first ID generated by Xalan-J is N10002, while the first ID generated by AltovaXML is idreport220739936.

[2.0] hours-from-dateTime()

Given an xs:dateTime value, returns its hours value.

Syntax

```
xs:integer? hours-from-dateTime(xs:dateTime?)
```

Inputs

An xs:dateTime value.

Output

An xs:integer representing the hours component of the given xs:dateTime value. If the input argument is the empty sequence, this function returns the empty sequence.

Defined in

XQuery 1.0 and XPath 2.0 Functions and Operators section 10.5, "Component Extraction Functions on Durations, Dates and Times."

Example

This stylesheet demonstrates the hours-from-dateTime( ) function:

```
<?xml version="1.0"?>
<!-- hours-from-datetime.xsl -->
<xsl:stylesheet version="2.0"
  xmlns:xsl="http://www.w3.org/1999/XSL/Transform"
```

```
xmlns:xs="http://www.w3.org/2001/XMLSchema">

<xsl:output method="text"/>

<xsl:template match="/">
  <xsl:text>&#xA;Extracting the hour from an xs:dateTime:</xsl:text>
  <xsl:variable name="currentDateTime" as="xs:dateTime"
    select="current-dateTime()"/>
  <xsl:text>&#xA;&#xA;  The current date and time is: </xsl:text>
  <xsl:value-of select="$currentDateTime"/>

  <xsl:text>&#xA;&#xA;  The current hour is: </xsl:text>
  <xsl:value-of select="hours-from-dateTime($currentDateTime)"/>
  <xsl:text>&#xA;    Also known as </xsl:text>
  <xsl:value-of select="format-dateTime($currentDateTime, '[h] [Pn]')"/>
  <xsl:text>&#xA;    or </xsl:text>
  <xsl:value-of select="format-dateTime($currentDateTime, '[H] [ZN]')"/>
  <xsl:text>&#xA;    or </xsl:text>
  <xsl:value-of select="format-dateTime($currentDateTime, '[H] [z]')"/>
</xsl:template>

</xsl:stylesheet>
```

The stylesheet creates these results:

```
Extracting the hour from an xs:dateTime:

  The current date and time is: 2006-11-16T04:17:15.778-05:00

  The current hour is: 4
    Also known as 4 a.m.
    or 4 EST
    or 4 GMT-5
```

Notice that some of the results were generated by the `hours-from-dateTime( )` function, while others were generated by using `format-dateTime( )` with a format string that selected only the hours component of the `xs:dateTime` value.

See Also

The definitions of the [2.0] `day-from-dateTime( )`, [2.0] `format-dateTime( )`, [2.0] `minutes-from-dateTime( )`, [2.0] `month-from-dateTime( )`, [2.0] `seconds-from-dateTime( )`, [2.0] `time zone-from-dateTime( )`, and [2.0] `year-from-dateTime( )` functions.

[2.0] hours-from-duration()

Given an `xs:duration` value, returns the number of hours in that duration.

Syntax

```
xs:integer? hours-from-duration(xs:duration?)
```

Inputs

An `xs:duration`.

Output

An `xs:integer` representing the hours component of the given `xs:duration`. Be aware that for an `xs:yearMonthDuration`, this function always returns 0 because there is no hours component of an `xs:yearMonthDuration`. Also, if the input argument is the empty sequence, this function returns the empty sequence.

Defined in

XQuery 1.0 and XPath 2.0 Functions and Operators section 10.5, "Component Extraction Functions on Durations, Dates and Times."

Example

This stylesheet demonstrates the `hours-from-duration()` function with all three types of durations:

```
<?xml version="1.0"?>
<!-- hours-from-duration.xsl -->
<xsl:stylesheet version="2.0"
  xmlns:xsl="http://www.w3.org/1999/XSL/Transform"
  xmlns:xs="http://www.w3.org/2001/XMLSchema">

  <xsl:output method="text"/>

  <xsl:template match="/">
    <xsl:text>&#xA;Extracting the hours component from durations:</xsl:text>

    <xsl:variable name="sampleDuration" as="xs:duration"
      select="xs:duration('P3Y8M2DT4H23M12.2S')"/>
    <xsl:variable name="sampleYearMonthDuration" as="xs:yearMonthDuration"
      select="xs:yearMonthDuration('P3Y8M')"/>
    <xsl:variable name="sampleDayTimeDuration" as="xs:dayTimeDuration"
      select="xs:dayTimeDuration('P2DT4H23M12.2S')"/>

    <xsl:text>&#xA;&#xA;  A sample xs:duration: </xsl:text>
    <xsl:value-of select="$sampleDuration"/>
    <xsl:text>&#xA;    The hours component of this duration is </xsl:text>
    <xsl:value-of select="hours-from-duration($sampleDuration)"/>
    <xsl:text>.</xsl:text>

    <xsl:text>&#xA;&#xA;  A sample xs:yearMonthDuration: </xsl:text>
    <xsl:value-of select="$sampleYearMonthDuration"/>
    <xsl:text>&#xA;    The hours component of this duration is </xsl:text>
    <xsl:value-of select="hours-from-duration($sampleYearMonthDuration)"/>
    <xsl:text>.</xsl:text>

    <xsl:text>&#xA;&#xA;  A sample xs:dayTimeDuration: </xsl:text>
    <xsl:value-of select="$sampleDayTimeDuration"/>
    <xsl:text>&#xA;    The hours component of this duration is </xsl:text>
    <xsl:value-of select="hours-from-duration($sampleDayTimeDuration)"/>
```

```
        <xsl:text>.</xsl:text>
    </xsl:template>

</xsl:stylesheet>
```

This stylesheet generates these results:

```
Extracting the hours component from durations:

   A sample xs:duration: P3Y8M2DT4H23M12.2S
     The hours component of this duration is 4.

   A sample xs:yearMonthDuration: P3Y8M
     The hours component of this duration is 0.

   A sample xs:dayTimeDuration: P2DT4H23M12.2S
     The hours component of this duration is 4.
```

Notice that calling hours-from-duration( ) against xs:yearMonthDuration returns 0.

See Also

The definitions of the [2.0] days-from-duration( ), [2.0] minutes-from-duration( ), [2.0] months-from-duration( ), [2.0] seconds-from-duration( ), and [2.0] years-from-duration( ) functions.

[2.0] hours-from-time()

Given an xs:time value, returns its hours component.

Syntax

```
    xs:integer? hours-from-time(xs:time?)
```

Input

An xs:time value.

Output

An xs:integer representing the hours component of the given xs:time value. If the argument is the empty sequence, this function returns the empty sequence.

Defined in

XQuery 1.0 and XPath 2.0 Functions and Operators section 10.5, "Component Extraction Functions on Durations, Dates and Times."

Example

This stylesheet uses hours-from-time( ) against the current time:

```
<?xml version="1.0"?>
<!-- hours-from-time.xsl -->
<xsl:stylesheet version="2.0"
```

```
xmlns:xsl="http://www.w3.org/1999/XSL/Transform"
xmlns:xs="http://www.w3.org/2001/XMLSchema">

<xsl:output method="text"/>

<xsl:template match="/">
  <xsl:text>&#xA;Extracting the hours component from an xs:time:</xsl:text>
  <xsl:variable name="currentTime" as="xs:time" select="current-time()"/>
  <xsl:text>&#xA;&#xA;  The current time is: </xsl:text>
  <xsl:value-of select="$currentTime"/>

  <xsl:text>&#xA;&#xA;  The current hour is: </xsl:text>
  <xsl:value-of select="hours-from-time($currentTime)"/>
  <xsl:text>&#xA;    Also known as </xsl:text>
  <xsl:value-of select="format-time($currentTime, '[h] [Pn]')"/>
  <xsl:text>, </xsl:text>
  <xsl:value-of select="format-time($currentTime, '[H] [ZN]')"/>
  <xsl:text>, or </xsl:text>
  <xsl:value-of select="format-time($currentTime, '[H] [z]')"/>
</xsl:template>

</xsl:stylesheet>
```

The stylesheet creates these results:

```
Extracting the hours component from an xs:time:

  The current time is: 17:02:52.515-05:00

  The current hour is: 17
    Also known as 5 p.m., 17 EST, or 17 GMT-5
```

Notice that the first result was generated by the hours-from-time( ) function, while the other results were generated by the format-time( ) function with a format string that selected the hours component from the xs:time value.

See Also

The definitions of the [2.0] format-time( ), [2.0] minutes-from-time( ), [2.0] seconds-from-time( ), and [2.0] timezone-from-time( ) functions.

---

id()

Returns the node in the source tree whose ID attribute matches the value(s) passed in as input.

Syntax

```
[1.0] node-set id(object)
[2.0] element()* id(xs:string*)
[2.0] element()* id(xs:string*, node())
```

Inputs

[1.0] An object. If the input object is a node-set, the result is a node-set that contains the result of applying the id( ) function to the string value of each node in the argument node-set. Usually, the argument is some other node type, which is (or is converted to) a string. That string is then used as the search value while all attributes of type ID are searched.

[2.0] An xs:string and an optional node. If the optional node argument is present, the processor looks for those values in the document that contains that node.

In both XSLT 1.0 and 2.0, if the string value contains multiple values separated by spaces, each space-separated value is used as a search argument for the id( ) function. Our examples here use both simple strings and strings with multiple values.

Remember that a limitation of the XML ID datatype is that a single set of names across all attributes is declared to be of type ID. The XSLT key( ) function and the associated <xsl:key> element address this and other limitations; see the description of the key( ) function earlier in this appendix and the description of the <xsl:key> element in Appendix A for more information.

Output

[1.0] A node-set containing all nodes whose attributes of type ID match the string values of the input node-set.

[2.0] A sequence containing all the nodes that have an ID value equal to one of the values specified in the search string.

> In a validated XML document, only one node will match each search value; the value of an ID attribute must be unique across all ID attributes in the document. Given that an XSLT processor is not required to validate an XML document, it is possible that the node-set or sequence will have more than one match for each search value.

Defined in

[1.0] XPath section 4.1, "Node Set Functions."

[2.0] XQuery 1.0 and XPath 2.0 Functions and Operators section 15.5, "Functions and Operators that Generate Sequences."

Example

For our example, we'll use a list of components and parts with an embedded DTD. We'll list each component, followed by the name of each part used by that component. The id( ) function lets us retrieve the <part> element with the specific ID; from there we can get the name of the part.

 This is the exact opposite of the example for the XSLT 2.0 `idref( )` function. In that example, we take each `<part>` and list all of the components that reference it.

Here's our XML document:

```xml
<?xml version="1.0"?>
<!-- parts-list1.xml -->
<!DOCTYPE parts-list [
<!ELEMENT parts-list        (component+, part+)>

<!ELEMENT component         (name, partref+)>
<!ATTLIST component         component-id ID #REQUIRED>

<!ELEMENT name              (#PCDATA)>

<!ELEMENT partref           EMPTY>
<!ATTLIST partref           refid IDREF #REQUIRED>

<!ELEMENT part              (name)>
<!ATTLIST part              part-id ID #REQUIRED
                            price CDATA #REQUIRED
                            source CDATA #REQUIRED>

]>

<parts-list>
  <component component-id="C28392-33-TT">
    <name>Turnip Twaddler</name>
    <partref refid="P81952-26-PK"/>
    <partref refid="P86679-52-SP"/>
    <partref refid="P81472-68-FD"/>
    <partref refid="P88107-39-GT"/>
  </component>
...
  <component component-id="C28772-63-OB">
    <name>Olive Bruiser</name>
    <partref refid="P80228-21-PT"/>
    <partref refid="P82387-85-PA"/>
  </component>

  <part part-id="P80228-21-PT" price="3.28" source="us">
    <name>Pitter</name>
  </part>
...
  <part part-id="P86994-25-RC" price="4.28" source="gb">
    <name>Ribbon Curler</name>
  </part>
</parts-list>
```

We'll use this stylesheet to resolve the references:

```xml
<?xml version="1.0"?>
<!-- id.xsl -->
<xsl:stylesheet version="2.0"
```

```
          xmlns:xsl="http://www.w3.org/1999/XSL/Transform">

        <xsl:output method="text"/>

        <xsl:template match="/">
          <xsl:text>&#xA;Here is a test of the id() </xsl:text>
          <xsl:text>function:&#xA;</xsl:text>

          <xsl:for-each select="/parts-list/component">
            <xsl:sort select="name"/>
            <xsl:text>&#xA;   </xsl:text>
            <xsl:value-of select="name"/>
            <xsl:text> (part #</xsl:text>
            <xsl:value-of select="@component-id"/>
            <xsl:text>) uses these parts:&#xA;    </xsl:text>
            <xsl:for-each select="id(partref/@refid)">
              <xsl:value-of select="name"/>
              <xsl:text>&#xA;    </xsl:text>
            </xsl:for-each>
          </xsl:for-each>
        </xsl:template>
      </xsl:stylesheet>
```

Our stylesheet generates these results:

```
Here is a test of the id() function:

  Clam Teaser (part #C28100-38-CT) uses these parts:
    Spanner
    Feather Duster
    Ribbon Curler

  Cucumber Decorating Kit (part #C23813-03-CDK) uses these parts:
    Feather Duster
    Paring Knife
    Mucilage
    Ribbon Curler

  Lemon Snubber (part #C21630-29-LS) uses these parts:
    Spanner
    Grommet
    Paring Knife

  Olive Bruiser (part #C28772-63-OB) uses these parts:
    Pitter
    Patter

  Prawn Goader (part #C28813-70-PG) uses these parts:
    Paring Knife
    Mucilage
    Ribbon Curler

  Turnip Twaddler (part #C28392-33-TT) uses these parts:
    Spanner
    Feather Duster
```

```
     Grommet
     Paring Knife
```

If the argument to the `id( )` function is a string, each space-separated token in the string is assumed to be a separate ID. That means we can use `id( )` with the datatype `IDREFS` as well. Here's a modified version of our source document that uses an `IDREFS` attribute:

```
<?xml version="1.0"?>
<!-- parts-list2.xsl -->
<!DOCTYPE parts-list [
<!ELEMENT parts-list       (component+, part+)>

<!ELEMENT component        (name, partref)>
<!ATTLIST component        component-id ID #REQUIRED>

<!ELEMENT name             (#PCDATA)>

<!ELEMENT partref          EMPTY>
<!ATTLIST partref          refid IDREFS #REQUIRED>

<parts-list>
  <component component-id="C28392-33-TT">
    <name>Turnip Twaddler</name>
    <partref
      refid="P81952-26-PK P86679-52-SP P81472-68-FD P88107-39-GT"/>
  </component>
...
  <part part-id="P80228-21-PT" price="3.28" source="us">
    <name>Pitter</name>
  </part>
...
</parts-list>
```

The only change here is that the **refid** attribute of the `<partref>` element is of datatype `IDREFS`. Despite that change, we can transform *parts-list2.xsl* with the same stylesheet and get the same results.

The value of any attribute of type `ID`, `IDREF`, and `IDREFS` must be valid XML names. A ID value of `86679-52-SP` is *not* a valid XML name, so an XSLT processor that validates the XML source document might not generate any results for that particular value. To see how this can cause problems, change all of the IDs so that they start with a number, and then run them through the Saxon XSLT processor. The results look like this:

```
Here is a test of the id() function:

Turnip Twaddler (part #28392-33-TT) uses these parts:

Prawn Goader (part #28813-70-PG) uses these parts:

Clam Teaser (part #28100-38-CT) uses these parts:

Cucumber Decorating Kit (part #23813-03-CDK) uses these parts:
```

```
Lemon Snubber (part #21630-29-LS) uses these parts:

Olive Bruiser (part #28772-63-OB) uses these parts:
```

When transforming the document with Saxon, we don't get any results. Using the Saxon -v flag to validate the XML source gives us dozens of messages like this:

```
Error on line 59 column 56 of file:/C:/XSLT20/AppendixC/parts-list3.xml:
  SXXP0003: Error reported by XML parser: Attribute value "80228-21-PT"
  of type ID must be an NCName when namespaces are enabled.
```

Changing the XML source document so that all of the IDs are valid XML names gives us the results we expect.

Keep this in mind if you're unable to get the id( ) *function working; it's a subtle error that can be hard to debug.* Using the current tools as of early 2008, Xalan and the Altova XML engine ignore the bad IDs, while MSXSL and Saxon don't generate any useful results.

[2.0] idref()

Given a sequence of ID values, returns a sequence containing all the nodes with an IDREF value matching one of the given IDs.

Syntax

```
node()* idref(xs:string*)
node()* idref(xs:string*, node())
```

Inputs

A sequence of xs:strings, each of which represents an ID value. If the node( ) argument is supplied, the XSLT processor looks for matching IDREF and IDREFS values in the document that contains that node. Without the node( ) argument, the processor looks in the document that contains the context node.

Outputs

A sequence of nodes, each of which has an IDREF or IDREFS value that matches one of the given IDs. The nodes are returned in document order, and any duplicate nodes are removed.

Defined in

XQuery 1.0 and XPath 2.0 Functions and Operators section 15.5, "Functions and Operators that Generate Sequences."

Example

For our example, we'll use a list of components and parts with an embedded DTD. We'll list each part, followed by the name of each component that uses that part. The idref( ) function lets us retrieve the <component> element with the specific ID; from there we can get the name of the component.

This is the exact opposite of the example for the id( ) function. In that example, we take each <component> and list all of the parts that it uses.

To illustrate the idref( ) function, we'll use an XML document with an embedded DTD. (This allows us to demonstrate the function without requiring a schema-aware XSLT processor.) Here is a fragment of the document:

```
<?xml version="1.0"?>
<!-- parts-list1.xml -->
<!DOCTYPE parts-list [
<!ELEMENT parts-list      (component+, part+)>

<!ELEMENT component       (name, partref+)>
<!ATTLIST component       component-id ID #REQUIRED>

<!ELEMENT name            (#PCDATA)>

<!ELEMENT partref         EMPTY>
<!ATTLIST partref         refid IDREF #REQUIRED>

<!ELEMENT part            (name)>
<!ATTLIST part            part-id ID #REQUIRED
                          price CDATA #REQUIRED
                          source CDATA #REQUIRED>

]>

<parts-list>
  <component component-id="C28392-33-TT">
    <name>Turnip Twaddler</name>
    <partref refid="P81952-26-PK"/>
    <partref refid="P86679-52-SP"/>
    <partref refid="P81472-68-FD"/>
    <partref refid="P88107-39-GT"/>
  </component>
...
  <component component-id="C28772-63-OB">
    <name>Olive Bruiser</name>
    <partref refid="P80228-21-PT"/>
    <partref refid="P82387-85-PA"/>
  </component>

  <part part-id="P80228-21-PT" price="3.28" source="us">
    <name>Pitter</name>
  </part>
...
  <part part-id="P86994-25-RC" price="4.28" source="gb">
    <name>Ribbon Curler</name>
  </part>
</parts-list>
```

Our document has a list of components; each component has an component-id attribute, a <name>, and a <partrefs> element. Each <partrefs> element has a refids attribute that refers to some number `<part>` elements. The rules of the ID, IDREF, and IDREFS datatypes (or `xs:ID`, `xs:IDREF`, and `xs:IDREFS` in an XML Schema) are:

- Any attribute of type ID (`xs:ID`) must have a unique value. That value must be unique across all ID attributes. In other words, in our sample document, the `component-id` attribute of a `<component>` element can't have the same value as the `part-id` attribute of a `<part>` element.

- Any attribute of type IDREF (`xs:IDREF`) must have a value that matches an ID attribute somewhere in the document.

- Any attribute of type IDREFS (`xs:IDREFS`) must have a space-separated set of IDREF values.

Our stylesheet is pretty simple; it lists all the `<part>` items in the document, then it uses the `idrefs()` function to find all the `<component>`s that use that part. Here's the stylesheet:

```
<?xml version="1.0"?>
<!-- idref.xsl -->
<xsl:stylesheet version="2.0"
  xmlns:xsl="http://www.w3.org/1999/XSL/Transform"
  xmlns:xs="http://www.w3.org/2001/XMLSchema">

  <xsl:output method="text"/>

  <xsl:template match="/">
    <xsl:text>&#xA;Here is a test of the idref() </xsl:text>
    <xsl:text>function:&#xA;</xsl:text>

    <xsl:for-each select="/parts-list/part">
      <xsl:sort select="name"/>
      <xsl:text>&#xA;   </xsl:text>
      <xsl:value-of select="name"/>
      <xsl:text> (part #</xsl:text>
      <xsl:value-of select="@part-id"/>
      <xsl:text>) is used in these products:&#xA;    </xsl:text>
      <xsl:value-of select="idref(@part-id)/../../name"
        separator="&#xA;    "/>
      <xsl:text>&#xA;</xsl:text>
    </xsl:for-each>
  </xsl:template>
</xsl:stylesheet>
```

When we use the `idref()` function here, we pass in the value of the `part-id` attribute for the current `<part>` element. The `idref()` function returns the sequence of all the attributes of type IDREF whose values contain the current `part-id`.

Keep in mind that `idref()` returns a sequence of the attributes themselves, not their parents. That's why our XPath expression to print the value of each product is `idref(@part-id)/../../name`. The `idref()` function returns the sequence of the `refid` attribute nodes that match. To get the name of each product, we first get the `refid`'s parent and the `<partref>` element, then we get its parent and the `<component>` element, and finally we get its `<name>` child. Here are the results:

```
Here is a test of the idref() function:

  Feather Duster (part #P81472-68-FD) is used in these products:
    Turnip Twaddler
    Clam Teaser
    Cucumber Decorating Kit

  Grommet (part #P88107-39-GT) is used in these products:
    Turnip Twaddler
    Lemon Snubber

  Mucilage (part #P80499-43-MC) is used in these products:
    Prawn Goader
    Cucumber Decorating Kit

  Paring Knife (part #P81952-26-PK) is used in these products:
    Turnip Twaddler
    Prawn Goader
    Cucumber Decorating Kit
    Lemon Snubber

  Patter (part #P82387-85-PA) is used in these products:
    Olive Bruiser

  Pitter (part #P80228-21-PT) is used in these products:
    Olive Bruiser

  Ribbon Curler (part #P86994-25-RC) is used in these products:
    Prawn Goader
    Clam Teaser
    Cucumber Decorating Kit

  Spanner (part #P86679-52-SP) is used in these products:
    Turnip Twaddler
    Clam Teaser
    Lemon Snubber
```

One thing our sample document doesn't address is attributes of datatype `IDREFS` (`xs:IDREFS`). If we want, we could also design our `<component>` element like this:

```
<?xml version="1.0"?>
<!-- parts-list2.xml -->
<!DOCTYPE parts-list [
<!ELEMENT parts-list      (component+, part+)>

<!ELEMENT component       (name, partref)>
<!ATTLIST component       component-id ID #REQUIRED>

<!ELEMENT name            (#PCDATA)>

<!ELEMENT partref         EMPTY>
<!ATTLIST partref         refid IDREFS #REQUIRED>
```

```
<!ELEMENT part              (name) >
<!ATTLIST part              part-id ID #REQUIRED
                            price CDATA #REQUIRED
                            source CDATA #REQUIRED>
]>

<parts-list>
  <component component-id="C28392-33-TT">
    <name>Turnip Twaddler</name>
    <partref
      refid="P81952-26-PK P86679-52-SP P81472-68-FD P88107-39-GT"/>
  </component>
...
  <part part-id="P80228-21-PT" price="3.28" source="us">
    <name>Pitter</name>
  </part>
  <part part-id="P82387-85-PA" price="6.92" source="us">
    <name>Patter</name>
  </part>
...
</parts-list>
```

In this case, the `refid` attribute has a datatype of IDREFS (`xs:IDREFS`). That means the attribute has a whitespace-separated list of IDREF values. Because of the way `idref( )` works, we can use the stylesheet against this differently structured document and get the same results. The file *parts-list2.xml* changed how the references to the part IDs were structured, but it didn't change how or where the part IDs themselves were defined. That means the `idref( )` function still returns the results we want.

Using `idref( )`, we've retrieved all the uses of each of the `<part>`s in our inventory.

 Keep in mind that values for ID, IDREF, and IDREFS datatypes must be valid XML names. IDs that start with a number can cause unpredictable results. See the note at the end of the discussion of the `id( )` function earlier in this appendix for all the details on this issue.

[2.0] implicit-timezone()

Returns the implicit timezone used when creating new `xs:date`, `xs:dateTime`, and `xs:time` values.

Syntax

    xs:dayTimeDuration **implicit-timezone()**

Inputs

None.

Outputs

An `xs:dayTimeDuration` that contains the implicit timezone.

Defined in

XQuery 1.0 and XPath 2.0 Functions and Operators section 16, "Context Functions."

Example

Here's a stylesheet that retrieves the implicit timezone as an `xs:dayTimeDuration`:

```
<?xml version="1.0"?>
<!-- implicit-timezone.xsl -->
<xsl:stylesheet version="2.0"
  xmlns:xsl="http://www.w3.org/1999/XSL/Transform">

  <xsl:output method="text"/>

  <xsl:template match="/">
    <xsl:text>&#xA;Using the implicit-timezone() function:&#xA;&#xA;</xsl:text>
    <xsl:text>  The implicit timezone for the current context is: </xsl:text>
    <xsl:value-of select="implicit-timezone()"/>
  </xsl:template>

</xsl:stylesheet>
```

The stylesheet generates these results:

```
Using the implicit-timezone() function:

  The implicit timezone for the current context is: -PT5H
```

The results for Bangalore and London, respectively, look like this:

```
  The implicit timezone for the current context is: PT5H30M
...
  The implicit timezone for the current context is: PT0S
```

[2.0] in-scope-prefixes()

Given an element, returns a sequence of all the namespace prefixes in scope for that element.

Syntax

```
xs:string* in-scope-prefixes(element())
```

Inputs

An element.

Outputs

A sequence of `xs:strings` listing the namespace prefixes that are in scope for that element.

Defined in

XQuery 1.0 and XPath 2.0 Functions and Operators section 11.2, "Operators and Functions Related to QNames."

Example

To illustrate the `in-scope-prefixes( )` function, we'll reuse our Shakespearean sonnet:

```
<?xml version="1.0"?>
<!-- sonnet.xml -->
<sonnet type='Shakespearean'>
  <auth:author xmlns:auth="http://www.authors.com/">
    <last-name>Shakespeare</last-name>
    <first-name>William</first-name>
    <nationality>British</nationality>
    <year-of-birth>1564</year-of-birth>
    <year-of-death>1616</year-of-death>
  </auth:author>
  <!-- Is there an official title for this sonnet?  They're
       sometimes named after the first line.                -->
  <title>Sonnet 130</title>
  <lines>
    <line>My mistress' eyes are nothing like the sun,</line>
    <line>Coral is far more red than her lips red.</line>
    <line>If snow be white, why then her breasts are dun,</line>
    <line>If hairs be wires, black wires grow on her head.</line>
    <line>I have seen roses damasked, red and white,</line>
    <line>But no such roses see I in her cheeks.</line>
    <line>And in some perfumes is there more delight</line>
    <line>Than in the breath that from my mistress reeks.</line>
    <line>I love to hear her speak, yet well I know</line>
    <line>That music hath a far more pleasing sound.</line>
    <line>I grant I never saw a goddess go,</line>
    <line>My mistress when she walks, treads on the ground.</line>
    <line>And yet, by Heaven, I think my love as rare</line>
    <line>As any she belied with false compare.</line>
  </lines>
</sonnet>
```

We'll use this stylesheet to list the namespace prefixes in scope for each element in the document:

```
<?xml version="1.0"?>
<!-- in-scope-prefixes.xsl -->
<xsl:stylesheet version="2.0"
  xmlns:xsl="http://www.w3.org/1999/XSL/Transform">

  <xsl:output method="text"/>

  <xsl:template match="/">
    <xsl:text>&#xA;A test of the in-scope-prefixes() function:</xsl:text>

    <xsl:for-each select="//*">
      <xsl:text>&#xA;    In-scope prefixes for &lt;</xsl:text>
      <xsl:value-of select="name()"/>
```

```
        <xsl:text>&gt;: </xsl:text>
        <xsl:value-of select="in-scope-prefixes(.)" separator=", "/>
      </xsl:for-each>
    </xsl:template>

  </xsl:stylesheet>
```

Here are the results:

```
A test of the in-scope-prefixes() function:
    In-scope prefixes for <sonnet>: xml
    In-scope prefixes for <auth:author>: xml, auth
    In-scope prefixes for <last-name>: xml, auth
    In-scope prefixes for <first-name>: xml, auth
    In-scope prefixes for <nationality>: xml, auth
    In-scope prefixes for <year-of-birth>: xml, auth
    In-scope prefixes for <year-of-death>: xml, auth
    In-scope prefixes for <title>: xml
    In-scope prefixes for <lines>: xml
    In-scope prefixes for <line>: xml
    In-scope prefixes for <line>: xml
    In-scope prefixes for <line>: xml
    In-scope prefixes for <line>: xml
    In-scope prefixes for <line>: xml
    In-scope prefixes for <line>: xml
    In-scope prefixes for <line>: xml
    In-scope prefixes for <line>: xml
    In-scope prefixes for <line>: xml
    In-scope prefixes for <line>: xml
    In-scope prefixes for <line>: xml
    In-scope prefixes for <line>: xml
    In-scope prefixes for <line>: xml
    In-scope prefixes for <line>: xml
```

The xml namespace prefix is always in scope; as the XSLT processor goes through the source document, the auth prefix goes in and out of scope.

[2.0] index-of()

Given a sequence and a search argument, returns a sequence of integers indicating the position(s) of the search argument in the sequence.

Syntax

```
xs:integer* index-of($sequenceParam as xs:anyAtomicType*,
                     $searchParam as xs:anyAtomicType)
xs:integer* index-of($sequenceParam as xs:anyAtomicType*,
                     $searchParam as xs:anyAtomicType,
                     $collation as xs:string)
```

Inputs

A sequence of atomic values and a search argument (also an atomic value). The optional third argument specifies the URL of a collation to be used when comparing the search argument to the values in the sequence.

Outputs

A sequence of `xs:integer`s representing the position(s) of the search argument in the sequence.

If the search sequence is the empty sequence or if no values in the sequence match the search argument, `index-of()` returns the empty sequence. Also, when comparing the search argument to values in the sequence, the processor uses the rules defined for the **eq** operator for each datatype. If the **eq** operator is not defined for a given datatype, all values of that datatype will not be considered equal to the search argument.

Defined in

XQuery 1.0 and XPath 2.0 Functions and Operators section 15.1, "General Functions and Operators on Sequences."

Example

Here is a short stylesheet that uses the `index-of()` function:

```
<?xml version="1.0"?>
<!-- index-of.xsl -->
<xsl:stylesheet version="2.0"
  xmlns:xsl="http://www.w3.org/1999/XSL/Transform"
  xmlns:xs="http://www.w3.org/2001/XMLSchema">

  <xsl:output method="text"/>

  <xsl:template match="/">

    <xsl:variable name="now" as="xs:time"
      select="current-time()"/>

    <xsl:variable name="testSequence1" as="item()*">
      <xsl:sequence
        select="(3, 4, 5, 'blue', $now, current-date(), 8, 'blue',
                'Strasse', 'Stra&#xDF;e')"/>
    </xsl:variable>

    <xsl:text>&#xA;Here's a test of the index-of() </xsl:text>
    <xsl:text>function:&#xA;</xsl:text>

    <xsl:text>&#xA;  Our first test sequence ($testSequence1) </xsl:text>
    <xsl:text>is:&#xA;        </xsl:text>
    <xsl:value-of select="$testSequence1" separator="&#xA;        "/>
    <xsl:text>&#xA;&#xA;</xsl:text>

    <xsl:text>    $now = </xsl:text>
    <xsl:value-of select="$now"/>
    <xsl:text>&#xA;&#xA;</xsl:text>
```

```
<xsl:text>     index-of($testSequence1, 3) = (</xsl:text>
<xsl:value-of
  select="index-of($testSequence1, 3)" separator=", "/>
<xsl:text>)&#xA;&#xA;</xsl:text>

<xsl:text>     index-of($testSequence1, 'red') = (</xsl:text>
<xsl:value-of
  select="index-of($testSequence1, 'red')" separator=", "/>
<xsl:text>)&#xA;&#xA;</xsl:text>

<xsl:text>     index-of($testSequence1, 'blue') = (</xsl:text>
<xsl:value-of
  select="index-of($testSequence1, 'blue')" separator=", "/>
<xsl:text>)&#xA;&#xA;</xsl:text>

<xsl:text>     index-of($testSequence1, $now) = (</xsl:text>
<xsl:value-of
  select="index-of($testSequence1, $now)" separator=", "/>
<xsl:text>)</xsl:text>

<xsl:text>&#xA;&#xA;     index-of($testSequence1, </xsl:text>
<xsl:text>'stra&#xDF;e') = (</xsl:text>
<xsl:value-of
  select="index-of($testSequence1, 'Strasse')"
  separator=", "/>
<xsl:text>)&#xA;</xsl:text>

<xsl:text>&#xA;     index-of($testSequence1, </xsl:text>
<xsl:text>'stra&#xDF;e', [German collation]) = (</xsl:text>
<xsl:value-of
  select="index-of($testSequence1, 'Stra&#xDF;e',
          concat('http://saxon.sf.net/collation?',
                 'class=com.oreilly.xslt.GermanCollation;'))"
  separator=", "/>
<xsl:text>)&#xA;</xsl:text>
  </xsl:template>

</xsl:stylesheet>
```

Here are the results:

```
Here's a test of the index-of() function:

  Our first test sequence ($testSequence1) is:
     3
     4
     5
     blue
     15:04:18.841-05:00
     2006-11-23-05:00
     8
     blue
     Strasse
     Straße
```

```
$now = 15:04:18.841-05:00

index-of($testSequence1, 3) = (1)

index-of($testSequence1, 'red') = ()

index-of($testSequence1, 'blue') = (4, 8)

index-of($testSequence1, $now) = (5)

index-of($testSequence1, 'Strasse') = (9)

index-of($testSequence1, 'Strasse', [German collation]) = (9, 10)
```

Notice that we stored the current time in the variable $now. Technically we don't have to do this because the current-time( ) function is stable; in other words, every time you call it during a single transformation, it returns the same result.

Also notice that we used a custom collation in the last call to index-of( ). In German, *Strasse* and *Straße* are two ways to spell the same word. The default collation doesn't recognize this, but our custom collation does. (To keep the listing within the margins of the page, we used the concat( ) function to combine the two halves of the Saxon collation URI.) See "The document() Function and Sorting" in "The document() Function and Sorting for more information.

[2.0] insert-before()

Allows you to create a new sequence by inserting items into an existing sequence.

Syntax

```
item()* insert-before($target as item()*, $position as xs:integer,
                       $inserts as item()*)
```

Inputs

A sequence, an xs:integer (a position), and a second sequence.

Outputs

A new sequence in which the second sequence has been inserted into the first sequence before the item at the requested position.

The rules for insert-before( ) are what you'd expect. If the first sequence is empty, the second sequence is returned unchanged. If the second sequence is empty, the first sequence is returned unchanged. If the position is less than 1, the processor inserts the second sequence at the start of the first. Finally, if the position is greater than the number of items in the first sequence, the second sequence is inserted at the end of the first.

Defined in

XQuery 1.0 and XPath 2.0 Functions and Operators section 15.1, "General Functions and Operators on Sequences."

Example

Here's a stylesheet that uses `insert-before( )` in several ways:

```
<?xml version="1.0"?>
<!-- insert-before.xsl -->
<xsl:stylesheet version="2.0"
  xmlns:xsl="http://www.w3.org/1999/XSL/Transform"
  xmlns:xs="http://www.w3.org/2001/XMLSchema">

  <xsl:output method="text"/>

  <xsl:template match="/">

    <xsl:variable name="longSequence" as="item()*">
      <xsl:sequence
        select="(3, 4, 5, current-date(), current-time(), 8, 'blue')"/>
    </xsl:variable>

    <xsl:variable name="shortSequence" as="item()*"
      select="(current-dateTime(), xs:yearMonthDuration('P3Y8M'))"/>

    <xsl:text>&#xA;Here's a test of the insert-before() </xsl:text>
    <xsl:text>function:&#xA;</xsl:text>

    <xsl:text>&#xA;  Our first sequence ($longSequence) </xsl:text>
    <xsl:text>is:&#xA;        </xsl:text>
    <xsl:value-of select="$longSequence" separator="&#xA;        "/>

    <xsl:text>&#xA;&#xA;  Our second sequence ($shortSequence) </xsl:text>
    <xsl:text>is:&#xA;        </xsl:text>
    <xsl:value-of select="$shortSequence" separator="&#xA;        "/>

    <xsl:text>&#xA;&#xA;    Test 1. insert-before($longSequence, </xsl:text>
    <xsl:text>3, (23)) </xsl:text>
    <xsl:text>= &#xA;        </xsl:text>
    <xsl:value-of select="insert-before($longSequence, 3, (23))"
      separator="&#xA;        "/>

    <xsl:text>&#xA;&#xA;    Test 2. insert-before($longSequence, </xsl:text>
    <xsl:text>4, $shortSequence) </xsl:text>
    <xsl:text>= &#xA;        </xsl:text>
    <xsl:value-of
      select="insert-before($longSequence, 4, $shortSequence)"
      separator="&#xA;        "/>

    <xsl:text>&#xA;&#xA;    Test 3. insert-before($longSequence, </xsl:text>
    <xsl:text>4, $shortSequence) </xsl:text>
    <xsl:text>= &#xA;        </xsl:text>
    <xsl:value-of
      select="insert-before($longSequence, 4, $shortSequence)"
      separator="&#xA;        "/>

    <xsl:text>&#xA;&#xA;    Test 4. insert-before($longSequence, 0, </xsl:text>
    <xsl:text>$shortSequence) </xsl:text>
    <xsl:text>= &#xA;        </xsl:text>
```

```
<xsl:value-of select="insert-before($longSequence, 0, $shortSequence)"
    separator="&#xA;        "/>

<xsl:text>&#xA;&#xA;     Test 5. insert-before($longSequence, 42, </xsl:text>
<xsl:text>$shortSequence) </xsl:text>
<xsl:text>= &#xA;        </xsl:text>
<xsl:value-of select="insert-before($longSequence, 42, $shortSequence)"
    separator="&#xA;        "/>

<xsl:text>&#xA;&#xA;     Creating a new variable based on </xsl:text>
<xsl:text>&#xA;          </xsl:text>
<xsl:text>insert-before($longSequence, 4, $shortSequence): </xsl:text>
<xsl:text>&#xA;        </xsl:text>
<xsl:text>updatedSequence = insert-before($longSequence, 4, </xsl:text>
<xsl:text>$shortSequence) : &#xA;        </xsl:text>
<xsl:variable name="updatedSequence" as="item()*"
    select="insert-before($longSequence, 4, $shortSequence)"/>
<xsl:text>&#xA;     Test 6. $updatedSequence = &#xA;        </xsl:text>
<xsl:value-of select="$updatedSequence" separator="&#xA;        "/>

  </xsl:template>

</xsl:stylesheet>
```

The results are:

```
Here's a test of the insert-before() function:

  Our first sequence ($longSequence) is:
      3
      4
      5
      2006-07-25-04:00
      04:24:21.216-04:00
      8
      blue

  Our second sequence ($shortSequence) is:
      2006-07-25T04:24:21.216-04:00
      P3Y8M

    Test 1. insert-before($longSequence, 3, (23)) =
      3
      4
      23
      5
      2006-07-25-04:00
      04:31:23.383-04:00
      8
      blue

    Test 2. insert-before($longSequence, 4, $shortSequence) =
      3
      4
      5
      2006-07-25T04:24:21.216-04:00
```

```
P3Y8M
2006-07-25-04:00
04:24:21.216-04:00
8
blue
```

Test 3. insert-before($longSequence, 4, $shortSequence) =
```
  3
  4
  5
  2006-07-25T04:24:21.216-04:00
  P3Y8M
  2006-07-25-04:00
  04:24:21.216-04:00
  8
  blue
```

Test 4. insert-before($longSequence, 0, $shortSequence) =
```
  2006-07-25T04:24:21.216-04:00
  P3Y8M
  3
  4
  5
  2006-07-25-04:00
  04:24:21.216-04:00
  8
  blue
```

Test 5. insert-before($longSequence, 42, $shortSequence) =
```
  3
  4
  5
  2006-07-25-04:00
  04:24:21.216-04:00
  8
  blue
  2006-07-25T04:24:21.216-04:00
  P3Y8M
```

Creating a new variable based on
    insert-before($longSequence, 4, $shortSequence):
    updatedSequence = insert-before($longSequence, 4, $shortSequence) :

Test 6. $updatedSequence =
```
  3
  4
  5
  2006-07-25T04:24:21.216-04:00
  P3Y8M
  2006-07-25-04:00
  04:24:21.216-04:00
  8
  blue
```

We start the stylesheet by listing the two sequences we'll be using. For our first test, we hardcode a sequence (a singleton containing the value 23) and insert it. Test 2 inserts the short sequence into the longer one before position 4 and returns the new sequence. Test 3 illustrates that calling insert-before( ) doesn't change the original sequence; it merely returns a new sequence with the requested items inserted.

Tests 4 and 5 show what happens when the position is out of range. Specifying a position of 0 inserts the second sequence at the start of the first, while a position of 42 inserts the second sequence at the end of the first. Finally, test 6 stores the new sequence in a variable.

[2.0] iri-to-uri()

Given a string containing an Internationalized Resource Identifier (IRI), this function converts it to a URI. URI syntax allows only a subset of roughly 60 ASCII characters, which is inadequate for most of the world's languages. IRI syntax addresses this problem; this function translates IRI syntax to URI syntax.

Syntax

```
xs:string iri-to-uri(xs:string?)
```

Inputs

An xs:string containing an IRI.

Outputs

An xs:string with the appropriate characters escaped so that they are legal for a URI. (If you want all the details, see RFC 3987, Internationalized Resource Identifiers [IRIs], available at *http://www.ietf.org/rfc/rfc3987.txt*. For the details of URI syntax, see RFC 3986, Uniform Resource Identifiers [URI]: Generic Syntax, available at *http://www.ietf.org/rfc/rfc3986.txt*.)

This function does *not* escape the percent character (%). If you want to use this function, you must escape all the percent signs yourself (calling replace-string($string, '%', '%25') will do the trick) before you call iri-to-uri( ).

If the value of the argument is the empty sequence, a zero-length string is returned.

Defined in

XQuery 1.0 and XPath 2.0 Functions and Operators section 7.4, "Functions on String Values."

Example

Here are two examples from the spec:

```
<?xml version="1.0" encoding="utf-8"?>
<!-- iri-to-uri.xsl -->
<xsl:stylesheet version="2.0"
  xmlns:xsl="http://www.w3.org/1999/XSL/Transform">

  <xsl:output method="text"/>
```

```
Tests of the iri-to-uri() function:

iri-to-uri('http://www.example.com/00/Weather/CA/Los Angeles#ocean') =
  http://www.example.com/00/Weather/CA/Los%20Angeles#ocean

iri-to-uri('http://www.example.com/~bébé') =
  http://www.example.com/~b%C3%A9b%C3%A9
iri-to-uri('http://www.example.co.jp/家') =
  http://www.example.co.jp/%E5%AE%B6
```

Figure C-4. Sample with illegal URI characters escaped

```
<xsl:template match="/">
  <xsl:text>&#xA;Tests of the iri-to-uri() function:</xsl:text>

  <xsl:text>&#xA;&#xA;  iri-to-uri('http://www.example.com/</xsl:text>
  <xsl:text>00/Weather/CA/Los Angeles#ocean') = &#xA;     </xsl:text>
  <xsl:value-of
    select="iri-to-uri('http://www.example.com/00/Weather/CA/Los Angeles#ocean')"/>

  <xsl:text>&#xA;&#xA;  iri-to-uri('http://www.example.com/</xsl:text>
  <xsl:text>~b&#xE9;b&#xE9;') = &#xA;     </xsl:text>
  <xsl:value-of
    select="iri-to-uri('http://www.example.com/~b&#xE9;b&#xE9;')"/>

  <!-- The character &#x5BB6; is Japanese for "home," I hope... -->
  <xsl:text>&#xA;&#xA;  iri-to-uri('http://www.example.co.jp/</xsl:text>
  <xsl:text>&#x5BB6;') = &#xA;     </xsl:text>
  <xsl:value-of
    select="iri-to-uri('http://www.example.co.jp/&#x5BB6;')"/>
</xsl:template>

</xsl:stylesheet>
```

As seen in Figure C-4, the IRIs are translated into URIs.

In the first example, the space was encoded as %20; in the second, the character *é* was encoded as the two-byte UTF-8 sequence %C3%A9.

The Japanese character in the last example (家) was correctly encoded as the three-byte UTF-8 sequence %E5%AE%B6. (I believe this is the character for "home," but I'm not 100% sure.)

See Also

The descriptions of the [2.0] encode-for-uri( ) and [2.0] escape-html-uri( ) functions.

key()

References a relation defined with an `<xsl:key>` element. Conceptually, the key( ) function works similarly to the id( ) function, although keys are more flexible than IDs.

Syntax

```
[1.0] node-set key(string, object)
[2.0] node()* key(xs:string, xs:anyAtomicType*)
[2.0] node()* key(xs:string, xs:anyAtomicType*, node())
```

Inputs

[1.0] The name of the key (defined by an `<xsl:key>` element) and an object. If the object is a node-set, then the key( ) function applies itself to the string value of each node in the node-set and returns the node-set of the result of all those key( ) function invocations. If the object is any other type, it is converted to a string as if by a call to the string( ) function.

[2.0] The name of the key (an `xs:string`) and a sequence of search values. An optional third argument limits the search to all the nodes that have the specified node as an `ancestor-or-self` node. The third argument lets us limit the search results to a particular group of nodes.

Output

[1.0] A node-set containing the nodes in the same document as the context node whose values for the requested key match the search argument(s). In other words, if our stylesheet has an `<xsl:key>` element that defines a key named `postalcodes` based on the `<postalcode>` child of all `<address>` elements in the current document, the function call `key(postalcodes, '34829')` returns a node-set containing all the `<address>` elements with a `<postalcode>` element whose value is `34829`.

[2.0] A sequence of nodes, each of which matches one of the values in the sequence of search values. How those nodes match the search arguments is determined by the specified key.

 *[2.0]* Keep in mind that any untyped values in the sequence of search values will be compared as strings. If the key you're using defined `xs:date` values as the index property, your string values will never match and key( ) will always return the empty sequence. In this case, only search values of type `xs:date` will return any results.

Defined in

[1.0] XSLT section 12.2, "Keys."

[2.0] XSLT section 16.3, "Keys."

Example

To illustrate the power of the key( ) function, we'll use this document:

```
<?xml version="1.0"?>
<!-- simplified-names.xml -->
```

```
<addressbook>
  <address>
    <first-name>Chester Hasbrouck</first-name>
    <last-name>Frisby</last-name>
    <city>Sheboygan</city>
    <state>WI</state>
  </address>
  <address>
    <first-name>Mary</first-name>
    <last-name>Backstayge</last-name>
    <city>Skunk Haven</city>
    <state>MA</state>
  </address>
  <address>
    <first-name>Natalie</first-name>
    <last-name>Attired</last-name>
    <city>Winter Harbor</city>
    <state>ME</state>
  </address>
  <address>
    <first-name>Harry</first-name>
    <last-name>Backstayge</last-name>
    <city>Skunk Haven</city>
    <state>MA</state>
  </address>
  <address>
    <first-name>Mary</first-name>
    <last-name>McGoon</last-name>
    <city>Boylston</city>
    <state>VA</state>
  </address>
  <address>
    <first-name>Amanda</first-name>
    <last-name>Reckonwith</last-name>
    <city>Lynn</city>
    <state>MA</state>
  </address>
</addressbook>
```

Here's the stylesheet we'll use to process this document. Notice that we define a key to index customer addresses by state:

```
<?xml version="1.0"?>
<!-- key-function.xsl -->
<xsl:stylesheet version="1.0"
  xmlns:xsl="http://www.w3.org/1999/XSL/Transform">

  <xsl:output method="text"/>

  <xsl:param name="searchState"/>

  <xsl:key name="customersByState" match="address" use="state"/>

  <xsl:template match="/">
    <xsl:text>&#xA;A test of the key() function:&#xA;</xsl:text>
    <xsl:text>&#xA;  All customers in </xsl:text>
```

```
<xsl:value-of select="$searchState"/>
<xsl:text>&#xA;&#xA;    </xsl:text>
<xsl:for-each select="key('customersByState', $searchState)">
  <xsl:value-of select="first-name"/>
  <xsl:text> </xsl:text>
  <xsl:value-of select="last-name"/>
  <xsl:text>, </xsl:text>
  <xsl:value-of select="city"/>
  <xsl:text>&#xA;    </xsl:text>
</xsl:for-each>
</xsl:template>

</xsl:stylesheet>
```

Running our stylesheet with a `$searchState` parameter of `MA` gives these results:

```
A test of the key() function:

All customers in MA

    Mary Backstayge, Skunk Haven
    Harry Backstayge, Skunk Haven
    Amanda Reckonwith, Lynn
```

A search parameter of `WI` finds only one customer:

```
A test of the key() function:

All customers in WI

    Chester Hasbrouck Frisby, Sheboygan
```

lang()

Determines whether a given language string is the same as, or is a sublanguage of, the language of the context node, as defined by an `xml:lang` attribute.

Syntax

```
[1.0] boolean lang(string)
[2.0] xs:boolean lang(xs:string?)
[2.0] xs:boolean lang(xs:string?, node())
```

Inputs

A string representing a language code. If the context node has a language of `xml:lang="en-us"`, invoking the `lang( )` function with any of the values `en`, `EN`, and `en-us` returns the boolean value `true`, while invoking `lang( )` with the value `en-gb` returns the boolean value `false`.

Output

If the argument string is the same as, or is a sublanguage of, the context node's language, `lang( )` returns the boolean value `true`. If the context node does not have an `xml:lang` attribute, then the value of the `xml:lang` attribute of its nearest ancestor is used instead. If there is no such attribute, then the `lang( )` function returns the boolean value `false`. When comparing the language code of the context node with the argument string, the `lang( )` function ignores case.

Defined in

[1.0] XPath section 4.3, "Boolean Functions."

[2.0] XQuery 1.0 and XPath 2.0 Functions and Operators section 14, "Functions and Operators on Nodes."

Example

Here is an XML document that uses language codes:

```
<?xml version="1.0"?>
<!-- albums.xml -->
<list xml:lang="en">
  <title>Albums I've bought recently:</title>
  <listitem>The Sacred Art of Dub</listitem>
  <listitem>Only the Poor Man Feel It</listitem>
  <listitem>Excitable Boy</listitem>
  <listitem xml:lang="sw">Aki Special</listitem>
  <listitem xml:lang="en-gb">Combat Rock</listitem>
  <listitem xml:lang="zu">Talking Timbuktu</listitem>
  <listitem xml:lang="jz">The Birth of the Cool</listitem>
</list>
```

Here's a stylesheet that uses the `lang( )` function:

```
<?xml version="1.0"?>
<!-- lang.xsl -->
<xsl:stylesheet version="1.0"
  xmlns:xsl="http://www.w3.org/1999/XSL/Transform">

  <xsl:output method="text"/>

  <xsl:template match="/">
    <xsl:text>&#xA;A test of the lang() function:&#xA;&#xA;</xsl:text>
    <xsl:for-each select="list/listitem">
      <xsl:choose>
        <xsl:when test="lang('EN')">
          <xsl:text>  Here's an English-language album: </xsl:text>
        </xsl:when>
        <xsl:otherwise>
          <xsl:text>  -------> Here's some World music: </xsl:text>
        </xsl:otherwise>
      </xsl:choose>
      <xsl:value-of select="."/>
      <xsl:text>&#xA;</xsl:text>
    </xsl:for-each>
  </xsl:template>

</xsl:stylesheet>
```

Finally, here are the results:

```
A test of the lang() function:

    Here's an English-language album: The Sacred Art of Dub
    Here's an English-language album: Only the Poor Man Feel It
    Here's an English-language album: Excitable Boy
    -------> Here's some World music: Aki Special
    Here's an English-language album: Combat Rock
    -------> Here's some World music: Talking Timbuktu
    -------> Here's some World music: The Birth of the Cool
```

Notice that the search argument of EN matches both en, the default language, and en-gb, the code for U.K. English.

last()

Returns the position of the last node in the current context. This function is useful for defining templates for the last occurrence of a given element or for testing whether a given node is the last in the node-set to which it belongs.

Syntax

```
[1.0] number last()
[2.0] xs:integer last()
```

Inputs

None.

Output

A number equal to the number of nodes in the current context. For example, if the current context contains 12 <li> nodes, last( ) returns 12.

Defined in

[1.0] XPath section 4.1, "Node Set Functions."

[2.0] XQuery 1.0 and XPath 2.0 Functions and Operators section 16, "Context Functions."

Example

We'll use the last( ) function to handle the last item in a list in a special way. Here's the XML document we'll use:

```
<?xml version="1.0"?>
<!-- albums.xml -->
<list xml:lang="en">
  <title>Albums I've bought recently:</title>
  <listitem>The Sacred Art of Dub</listitem>
  <listitem>Only the Poor Man Feel It</listitem>
  <listitem>Excitable Boy</listitem>
  <listitem xml:lang="sw">Aki Special</listitem>
  <listitem xml:lang="en-gb">Combat Rock</listitem>
  <listitem xml:lang="zu">Talking Timbuktu</listitem>
```

```
    <listitem xml:lang="jz">The Birth of the Cool</listitem>
</list>
```

Here is the stylesheet that handles the last `<listitem>` in the list differently:

```
<?xml version="1.0"?>
<!-- last.xsl -->
<xsl:stylesheet version="1.0"
  xmlns:xsl="http://www.w3.org/1999/XSL/Transform">

  <xsl:output method="text"/>

  <xsl:template match="/">
    <xsl:text>&#xA;A test of the last() function:&#xA;</xsl:text>
    <xsl:for-each select="list/listitem">
      <xsl:text>&#xA;   </xsl:text>
      <xsl:if test="position()=last()">
        <xsl:text>&#xA;   LAST, but not least:  </xsl:text>
      </xsl:if>
      <xsl:value-of select="."/>
    </xsl:for-each>
  </xsl:template>

</xsl:stylesheet>
```

When we transform the XML document with this stylesheet, here are the results:

```
A test of the last() function:

   The Sacred Art of Dub
   Only the Poor Man Feel It
   Excitable Boy
   Aki Special
   Combat Rock
   Talking Timbuktu

   LAST, but not least:  The Birth of the Cool
```

local-name()

Returns the local part of the first node in the argument node-set.

Syntax

```
[1.0] string local-name(node-set?)
[2.0] xs:string local-name()
[2.0] xs:string local-name(node()?)
```

Inputs

A node-set. If the node-set is empty, the function returns an empty string. If the node-set is omitted, the function uses a node-set with the context node as its only member.

Output

A string corresponding to the local name of the first element in the argument node-set. If the node-set is empty, the `local-name( )` function returns an empty string.

[2.0] In XSLT 2.0, it is a fatal error if the argument contains more than one node.

Defined in

[1.0] XPath section 4.1, "Node Set Functions."

[2.0] XQuery 1.0 and XPath 2.0 Functions and Operators section 14, "Functions and Operators on Nodes."

Example

We'll use our Shakespearean sonnet to test the `local-name( )` function:

```
<?xml version="1.0"?>
<!-- sonnet.xml -->
<sonnet type='Shakespearean'>
  <auth:author xmlns:auth="http://www.authors.com/">
    <last-name>Shakespeare</last-name>
    <first-name>William</first-name>
    <nationality>British</nationality>
    <year-of-birth>1564</year-of-birth>
    <year-of-death>1616</year-of-death>
  </auth:author>
  <!-- Is there an official title for this sonnet?  They're
       sometimes named after the first line.                -->
  <title>Sonnet 130</title>
  <lines>
    <line>My mistress' eyes are nothing like the sun,</line>
    <line>Coral is far more red than her lips red.</line>
    <line>If snow be white, why then her breasts are dun,</line>
    <line>If hairs be wires, black wires grow on her head.</line>
    <line>I have seen roses damasked, red and white,</line>
    <line>But no such roses see I in her cheeks.</line>
    <line>And in some perfumes is there more delight</line>
    <line>Than in the breath that from my mistress reeks.</line>
    <line>I love to hear her speak, yet well I know</line>
    <line>That music hath a far more pleasing sound.</line>
    <line>I grant I never saw a goddess go,</line>
    <line>My mistress when she walks, treads on the ground.</line>
    <line>And yet, by Heaven, I think my love as rare</line>
    <line>As any she belied with false compare.</line>
  </lines>
</sonnet>
```

Here's the short stylesheet we'll use:

```
<?xml version="1.0"?>
<!-- local-name.xsl -->
<xsl:stylesheet version="1.0"
  xmlns:xsl="http://www.w3.org/1999/XSL/Transform">

  <xsl:output method="text"/>
```

```
  <xsl:template match="/">
    <xsl:text>&#xA;A test of the local-name() function:&#xA;</xsl:text>

    <xsl:for-each select="//*">
      <xsl:text>&#xA;    The local name for &lt;</xsl:text>
      <xsl:value-of select="name()"/>
      <xsl:text>&gt;: </xsl:text>
      <xsl:value-of select="local-name(.)"/>
    </xsl:for-each>
  </xsl:template>

</xsl:stylesheet>
```

Here are the results from the stylesheet:

```
A test of the local-name() function:

    The local name for <sonnet>: sonnet
    The local name for <auth:author>: author
    The local name for <last-name>: last-name
    The local name for <first-name>: first-name
    The local name for <nationality>: nationality
    The local name for <year-of-birth>: year-of-birth
    The local name for <year-of-death>: year-of-death
    The local name for <title>: title
    The local name for <lines>: lines
    The local name for <line>: line
    The local name for <line>: line
    The local name for <line>: line
    The local name for <line>: line
    The local name for <line>: line
    The local name for <line>: line
    The local name for <line>: line
    The local name for <line>: line
    The local name for <line>: line
    The local name for <line>: line
    The local name for <line>: line
    The local name for <line>: line
    The local name for <line>: line
    The local name for <line>: line
```

[2.0] local-name-from-QName()

Given an xs:QName value, returns its local name.

Syntax

```
xs:NCName? local-name-from-QName(xs:QName?)
```

Input

An xs:QName value.

Output

The local name portion of the given `QName`. This is returned as an `xs:NCName`, or "noncolonized" name. If the argument is the empty sequence, `local-name-from-QName()` returns the empty sequence.

Defined in

XQuery 1.0 and XPath 2.0 Functions and Operators section 11.2, "Operators and Functions Related to QNames."

Example

Here is a short stylesheet that uses `local-name-from-QName()`:

```
<?xml version="1.0"?>
<!-- local-name-from-qname.xsl -->
<xsl:stylesheet version="2.0"
  xmlns:xsl="http://www.w3.org/1999/XSL/Transform"
  xmlns:xs="http://www.w3.org/2001/XMLSchema">

  <xsl:output method="text"/>

  <xsl:template match="/">
    <xsl:text>&#xA;Tests of the local-name-from-QName() </xsl:text>
    <xsl:text>function:&#xA;</xsl:text>

    <xsl:variable name="testQName1" as="xs:QName"
      select="QName('http://www.authors.com', 'auth:author')"/>

    <xsl:text>&#xA;  QName('http://www.authors.com', </xsl:text>
    <xsl:text>'auth:author') = </xsl:text>
    <xsl:value-of select="$testQName1"/>

    <xsl:text>&#xA;    The local name associated with </xsl:text>
    <xsl:text>this QName: "</xsl:text>
    <xsl:value-of select="local-name-from-QName($testQName1)"/>
    <xsl:text>"</xsl:text>

    <xsl:variable name="testQName2" as="xs:QName"
      select="QName('', 'sonnet')"/>

    <xsl:text>&#xA;&#xA;  QName('', 'sonnet') = </xsl:text>
    <xsl:value-of select="$testQName2"/>

    <xsl:text>&#xA;    The local name associated with </xsl:text>
    <xsl:text>this QName: "</xsl:text>
    <xsl:value-of select="local-name-from-QName($testQName2)"/>
    <xsl:text>"</xsl:text>

  </xsl:template>

</xsl:stylesheet>
```

The straightforward results look like this:

```
Tests of the local-name-from-QName() function:

  QName('http://www.authors.com', 'auth:author') = auth:author
    The local name associated with this QName: "author"

  QName('', 'sonnet') = sonnet
    The local name associated with this QName: "sonnet"
```

[2.0] lower-case()

Given a string, returns the lowercased version of that string.

Syntax

```
xs:string lower-case(xs:string)
```

Inputs

An `xs:string` value.

Outputs

An `xs:string` in which all of the uppercase letters in the original string have been converted to lowercase. Any character that was originally in lowercase and any character that does not have an lowercase value is returned as is. If the value of the argument is the empty sequence, a zero-length string is returned.

Accented characters and other features of the world's languages mean that changing the case of a string might change its length. Also be aware that `lower-case()` and `upper-case()` are not always the inverse of each other in some languages. All of the case conversion rules are defined by the Unicode standard, and XSLT processors are expected to conform with those rules.

Defined in

XQuery 1.0 and XPath 2.0 Functions and Operators section 7.4, "Functions on String Values."

Example

Here is a stylesheet that illustrates the `lower-case()` function. Notice that we're using `<xsl:output method="xml" encoding="UTF-8"/>` to make sure the character set is handled properly:

```
<?xml version="1.0" encoding="UTF-8"?>
<!-- lower-case.xsl -->
<xsl:stylesheet version="2.0"
  xmlns:xsl="http://www.w3.org/1999/XSL/Transform">

  <xsl:output method="xml" encoding="UTF-8" indent="yes"/>

  <xsl:template match="/">
    <testcase>
```

```
      <heading>Tests of the lower-case() function:</heading>
      <test>
        <label>lower-case('Lily') = </label>
        <result><xsl:value-of select="lower-case('Lily')"/></result>
      </test>
      <test>
        <label>lower-case('LILY') = </label>
        <result><xsl:value-of select="lower-case('LILY')"/></result>
      </test>
      <test>
        <label>lower-case('lily') = </label>
        <result><xsl:value-of select="lower-case('lily')"/></result>
      </test>
      <test>
        <label>lower-case('JALAPEÑO') = </label>
        <result><xsl:value-of select="lower-case('JALAPEÑO')"/></result>
      </test>
    </testcase>
  </xsl:template>

</xsl:stylesheet>
```

The results look like this:

```
<?xml version="1.0" encoding="UTF-8"?>
<testcase>
  <heading>Tests of the lower-case() function:</heading>
  <test>
    <label>lower-case('Lily') = </label>
    <result>lily</result>
  </test>
  <test>
    <label>lower-case('LILY') = </label>
    <result>lily</result>
  </test>
  <test>
    <label>lower-case('lily') = </label>
    <result>lily</result>
  </test>
  <test>
    <label>lowercase('JALAPEÑO') = </label>
    <result>jalapeño</result>
  </test>
</testcase>
```

[2.0] matches()

Determines whether a given string matches a given regular expression.

Syntax

```
xs:boolean matches($input as xs:string?, $pattern as xs:string)
xs:boolean matches($input as xs:string?, $pattern as xs:string,
                   $flags as xs:string)
```

Inputs

An input string and a regular expression. The `matches()` function also supports an optional string defining flags that modify how the regular expression is processed.

Outputs

`true` if the string matches the regular expression; `false` otherwise.

Regular expressions are extremely powerful, so there are a number of details about how they work:

- If `$input` is the empty sequence, it is interpreted as a zero-length string. The `matches()` function can still return `true` in this situation. For example, `matches((), '.?')` is `true`, as is `matches('', '.?')`.

- Regular expression matching does not use collations; the characters' Unicode code points are compared. Cases in which different characters are considered equal in the world's languages are not taken into account.

- Unless you use the `^` (start of line) or `$` (end of line) characters as anchors in your regular expression, a string is considered a match if any part of it matches the regular expression.

- Unlike regular expressions used in the `<xsl:analyze-string>` element, curly braces (`{` and `}`) are not doubled. (Curly braces used inside the `regex` attribute of `<xsl:analyze-string>` must be doubled so they aren't interpreted as attribute value templates.)

- The `$flags` parameter modifies how the regular expression is processed. There are four different flags:

  s

    Regular expressions are evaluated in what the specs refer to as "dot-all" mode. When this flag is used, the dot operator (`.`) matches any character. Under normal processing (without the `s` flag), the dot operator matches any character *except* the newline character (`&#xA;`). This flag is useful when you want to match strings that might include a newline character.

  m

    Regular expressions are evaluated in multiline mode. By default, the metacharacter (`^`) matches the start of the entire string, while `$` matches the end of the entire string. In multiline mode, `^` matches the start of any line within the string and `$` matches the end of any line within the string.

  i

    Regular expressions are evaluated in case-insensitive mode. The regular expression `"a"` matches both `"a"` and `"A"`.

    Note that Unicode issues can complicate this greatly. For example, the XQuery 1.0 and XPath 2.0 Functions and Operators spec gives the example of the Unicode sign for degrees Kelvin (`&#x212A;`), which is the letter `"K"`. The combination of regex="k" and flags="i" matches the Kelvin sign as well as the letters "k" (k) and "K" (K).

Other Unicode characters don't convert to letters. For example, the Unicode symbol for the Roman numeral I (ࡰ) looks like the letter I, but does not convert to one.

x

All whitespace characters (	,
, , and) are removed from the regular expression before any comparison is done. In other words, with the x flag, the regular expressions "John Smith" and "JohnSmith" are the same. This flag is useful when you want to break a long regular expression into multiple lines to make it easier to read.

The flags can be combined in any order. The parameters 'xis' and 'six' work exactly the same way.

Defined in

XQuery 1.0 and XPath 2.0 Functions and Operators section 7.6, "String Functions that Use Pattern Matching."

Example

Here is a stylesheet that uses the matches( ) function:

```
<?xml version="1.0"?>
<!-- matches.xsl -->
<xsl:stylesheet version="2.0"
  xmlns:xsl="http://www.w3.org/1999/XSL/Transform"
  xmlns:xs="http://www.w3.org/2001/XMLSchema">

  <xsl:output method="text"/>

  <xsl:template match="/">

    <xsl:variable name="string1"
      select="concat('Now is the time for all good men&#xA;',
              'and women &#xA;',
              'to aid the party.')"/>

    <xsl:text>&#xA;Here's a test of the matches() </xsl:text>
    <xsl:text>function:&#xA;</xsl:text>

    <xsl:text>&#xA;  $string1 = &#xA;</xsl:text>
    <xsl:value-of select="$string1"/>

    <xsl:text>&#xA;&#xA;  Test 1. matches($string1, </xsl:text>
    <xsl:text>'Now.*men') = </xsl:text>
    <xsl:value-of select="matches($string1, 'Now.*men')"/>

    <xsl:text>&#xA;&#xA;  Test 2. matches($string1, </xsl:text>
    <xsl:text>'Now.*men$') = </xsl:text>
    <xsl:value-of select="matches($string1, 'Now.*men$')"/>
```

```
<xsl:text>&#xA;&#xA;  Test 3. matches($string1, </xsl:text>
<xsl:text>'Now.*men$', 'm') = </xsl:text>
<xsl:value-of select="matches($string1, 'Now.*men$', 'm')"/>

<xsl:text>&#xA;&#xA;  Test 4. matches($string1, </xsl:text>
<xsl:text>'women $', 'm') = </xsl:text>
<xsl:value-of select="matches($string1, 'women $', 'm')"/>

<xsl:text>&#xA;&#xA;  Test 5. matches($string1, </xsl:text>
<xsl:text>'party.$') = </xsl:text>
<xsl:value-of select="matches($string1, 'party.$')"/>

<xsl:text>&#xA;&#xA;  Test 6. matches($string1, </xsl:text>
<xsl:text>'^and' 'm') = </xsl:text>
<xsl:value-of select="matches($string1, '^and', 'm')"/>

<xsl:text>&#xA;&#xA;  Test 7. matches($string1, </xsl:text>
<xsl:text>'women .?to' 's') = </xsl:text>
<xsl:value-of select="matches($string1, 'women .?to', 's')"/>

  </xsl:template>

</xsl:stylesheet>
```

Here are the results:

```
Here's a test of the matches() function:

  $string1 =
Now is the time for all good men
and women
to aid the party.

  Test 1. matches($string1, 'Now.*men') = true

  Test 2. matches($string1, 'Now.*men$') = false

  Test 3. matches($string1, 'Now.*men$', 'm') = true

  Test 4. matches($string1, 'women $', 'm') = true

  Test 5. matches($string1, 'party.$') = true

  Test 6. matches($string1, '^and' 'm') = true

  Test 7. matches($string1, 'women .?to' 's') = true
```

Our sample string contains two line breaks so we can test the ^ and $ characters along with the flags. The regular expression in test 1 is the characters 'Now' followed by zero or more characters, followed by the characters 'men'. Test 2 specifies that 'men' should be the last three characters in the string; that's clearly not the case here. In test 3, we specify that the expression should be processed in multiline mode (using the 'm' flag), so 'men
' is considered a match for 'men$'.

In test 4, we look for the characters `'women '`, at the end of a line. Because we're using multiline mode, this matches. Notice that we had to include the space character at the end of the line; `'women$'` does not match here. Test 5 specifies the characters `'party.'` at the end of the string. We're not in multiline mode, but that's OK; the last characters in the string are `'party.'` Test 6 looks for the characters `'and'` at the start of a line; because we're in multiline mode, this works.

Finally, we look for the characters `'women '` followed by a single optional character followed by the characters `'to'`. We're using "dot all" mode here (we specified the `'s'` flag), so this is a match. The single optional character here is a newline, which matches when the `'s'` flag is in effect.

See Also

Appendix E has complete details on the way regular expressions work in XPath 2.0. Also see the definitions of the following elements and functions: [2.0] `<xsl:analyze-string>`, [2.0] `<xsl:matching-substring>`, [2.0] `<xsl:non-matching-substring>`, [2.0] `regex-group( )`, [2.0] `replace( )`, and [2.0] `tokenize( )`.

[2.0] max()

Returns the largest value in a given sequence.

Syntax

```
xs:anyAtomicType max(xs:anyAtomicType*)
xs:anyAtomicType max(xs:anyAtomicType*, $collation as xs:string)
```

Input

A sequence of values.

Output

The maximum value in the given sequence. The `max( )` function works with the following types of values: numeric values (`xs:integer`, `xs:double`, `xs:decimal`, and `xs:float`), `xs:string`, `xs:boolean`, `xs:date`, `xs:dateTime`, `xs:time`, `xs:yearMonthDuration`, and `xs:dayTimeDuration` (but *not* `xs:duration`).

Given a sequence of numeric values, the XSLT processor returns the largest number, converting datatypes as necessary. Given a sequence of durations, the XSLT processor returns the longest of those durations. Given a sequence of strings, the XSLT processor returns the string that appears last in sorted order.

The `max( )` function assumes you'll send it a sequence containing sensible data; if not, the XSLT processor throws an error. Asking for the maximum value in the sequence (`xs:dayTimeDuration('P3DT8H17M')`, `38`, `'football'`) returns an error, as you'd expect.

Details about how the `max( )` function works are as follows:

- To find the longest of a sequence of durations, the values must all be `xs:dayTimeDuration`s, or they must all be `xs:yearMonthDuration`s. You can't mix the two types of durations; if you do, the XSLT processor throws an error.

- If any of the items in the sequence are of type `xs:untypedAtomic`, the XSLT processor attempts to cast it to `xs:double`. If the item can't be converted to `xs:double`, the XSLT processor throws an error.

- When comparing `xs:string` values, the default collation is used unless you specify another.

- Finally, if you pass the `max()` function the empty sequence, it returns the empty sequence. Although you're not giving the function any useful data in this case, the XSLT processor doesn't throw an error.

Defined in

XQuery 1.0 and XPath 2.0 Functions and Operators section 15.4, "Aggregate Functions."

Example

Here's a stylesheet that finds the maximum value in several different types of sequences:

```
<?xml version="1.0"?>
<!-- max.xsl -->
<xsl:stylesheet version="2.0"
  xmlns:xsl="http://www.w3.org/1999/XSL/Transform"
  xmlns:xs="http://www.w3.org/2001/XMLSchema">

  <xsl:output method="text"/>

  <xsl:template match="/">
    <xsl:variable name="seq1" select="(3, 5, 18)"/>
    <xsl:variable name="seq2" select="(3, 5, 48.273, 2.9e3)"/>

    <xsl:variable name="value1" as="xs:integer" select="42"/>
    <xsl:variable name="value2" as="xs:double" select="2718.28E-3"/>
    <xsl:variable name="value3" as="xs:float" select="98.6"/>
    <xsl:variable name="value4" as="xs:decimal" select="2.54"/>
    <xsl:variable name="seq3"
      select="($value1, $value2, $value3, $value4)"/>

    <xsl:variable name="seq4"
      select="(xs:yearMonthDuration('P3Y8M'),
              xs:yearMonthDuration('P4Y2M'),
              xs:yearMonthDuration('P6Y4M'))"/>
    <xsl:variable name="seq5"
      select="(xs:dayTimeDuration('P2DT4H23M12.2S'),
              xs:dayTimeDuration('P3DT8H17M'),
              xs:dayTimeDuration('P3D'))"/>

    <xsl:text>&#xA;Here are some tests of the max() function:&#xA;</xsl:text>

    <xsl:text>&#xA;  max(</xsl:text>
    <xsl:value-of select="$seq1" separator=", "/>
```

```
<xsl:text>) = </xsl:text>
<xsl:value-of select="format-number(max($seq1), '#.###')"/>

<xsl:text>&#xA;&#xA;  max(</xsl:text>
<xsl:value-of select="$seq2" separator=", "/>
<xsl:text>) = </xsl:text>
<xsl:value-of select="format-number(max($seq2), '#.###')"/>

<xsl:text>&#xA;&#xA;  max(</xsl:text>
<xsl:value-of select="$seq3" separator=", "/>
<xsl:text>) = </xsl:text>
<xsl:value-of select="format-number(max($seq3), '#.###')"/>

<xsl:text>&#xA;&#xA;  max(</xsl:text>
<xsl:value-of select="$seq4" separator=", "/>
<xsl:text>) = </xsl:text>
<xsl:value-of select="max($seq4)"/>

<xsl:text>&#xA;&#xA;  In text, the maximum of</xsl:text>
<xsl:for-each select="$seq4">
  <xsl:text>&#xA;      </xsl:text>
  <xsl:value-of select="years-from-duration(.)"/>
  <xsl:text> years and </xsl:text>
  <xsl:value-of select="months-from-duration(.)"/>
  <xsl:text> months (</xsl:text>
  <xsl:value-of select="."/>
  <xsl:text>)</xsl:text>
</xsl:for-each>

<xsl:text>&#xA;    is </xsl:text>
<xsl:value-of select="years-from-duration(max($seq4))"/>
<xsl:text> years and </xsl:text>
<xsl:value-of select="months-from-duration(max($seq4))"/>
<xsl:text> months (</xsl:text>
<xsl:value-of select="max($seq4)"/>
<xsl:text>).</xsl:text>

<xsl:text>&#xA;&#xA;  max(</xsl:text>
<xsl:value-of select="$seq5" separator=", "/>
<xsl:text>) = </xsl:text>
<xsl:variable name="max5" select="max($seq5)"/>
<xsl:value-of select="$max5"/>

<xsl:text>&#xA;&#xA;  In text, the maximum of</xsl:text>
<xsl:for-each select="$seq5">
  <xsl:text>&#xA;      </xsl:text>
  <xsl:value-of select="days-from-duration(.)"/>
  <xsl:text> days, </xsl:text>
  <xsl:value-of select="hours-from-duration(.)"/>
  <xsl:text> hours, </xsl:text>
  <xsl:value-of select="minutes-from-duration(.)"/>
  <xsl:text> minutes and </xsl:text>
  <xsl:value-of
    select="format-number(seconds-from-duration(.), '#.##')"/>
  <xsl:text> seconds (</xsl:text>
```

```
          <xsl:value-of select="."/>
          <xsl:text>)</xsl:text>
       </xsl:for-each>

       <xsl:text>&#xA;    is </xsl:text>
       <xsl:value-of select="days-from-duration($max5)"/>
       <xsl:text> days, </xsl:text>
       <xsl:value-of select="hours-from-duration($max5)"/>
       <xsl:text> hours, </xsl:text>
       <xsl:value-of select="minutes-from-duration($max5)"/>
       <xsl:text> minutes and </xsl:text>
       <xsl:value-of
          select="format-number(seconds-from-duration($max5), '#.##')"/>
       <xsl:text> seconds.</xsl:text>

    </xsl:template>

 </xsl:stylesheet>
```

Here are the results from this stylesheet:

```
Here are some tests of the max() function:

  max(3, 5, 18) = 18

  max(3, 5, 48.273, 2900) = 2900

  max(42, 2.71828, 98.6, 2.54) = 98.6

  max(P3Y8M, P4Y2M, P6Y4M) = P6Y4M

    In text, the maximum of
       3 years and 8 months (P3Y8M)
       4 years and 2 months (P4Y2M)
       6 years and 4 months (P6Y4M)
    is 6 years and 4 months (P6Y4M).

  max(P2DT4H23M12.2S, P3DT8H17M, P3D) = P3DT8H17M

    In text, the maximum of
       2 days, 4 hours, 23 minutes and 12.2 seconds (P2DT4H23M12.2S)
       3 days, 8 hours, 17 minutes and 0 seconds (P3DT8H17M)
       3 days, 0 hours, 0 minutes and 0 seconds (P3D)
    is 3 days, 8 hours, 17 minutes and 0 seconds.
```

The stylesheet demonstrates five different types of sequences. The first is all integers and the second is a sequence of numbers. All the values in the first two sequences can be converted to numbers, so the results are what we expect. The third sequence features four numeric values, each of which has a specific numeric type. The last two sequences are made up of the two types of durations. The stylesheet also uses functions such as `years-from-duration( )` and `format-number( )` to format the data.

Here's a short example that illustrates using a custom collation:

```
<?xml version="1.0"?>
<!-- max2.xsl -->
```

```
<xsl:stylesheet version="2.0"
  xmlns:xsl="http://www.w3.org/1999/XSL/Transform"
  xmlns:xs="http://www.w3.org/2001/XMLSchema">

  <xsl:output method="text"/>

  <xsl:template match="/">
    <xsl:variable name="seq1"
      select="('strasse', 'stra&#xDF;e')"/>
    <xsl:variable name="seq2" select="reverse($seq1)"/>

    <xsl:text>&#xA;Here are some tests of the max() function:&#xA;</xsl:text>

    <xsl:text>&#xA;  max(</xsl:text>
    <xsl:value-of select="$seq1" separator=", "/>
    <xsl:text>) = </xsl:text>
    <xsl:value-of select="max($seq1)"/>

    <xsl:text>&#xA;  max(</xsl:text>
    <xsl:value-of select="$seq1" separator=", "/>
    <xsl:text> [German collation]) = </xsl:text>
    <xsl:value-of
      select="max($seq1,
                  concat('http://saxon.sf.net/collation?',
                         'class=com.oreilly.xslt.GermanCollation;'))"/>

    <xsl:text>&#xA;  max(</xsl:text>
    <xsl:value-of select="$seq2" separator=", "/>
    <xsl:text> [German collation]) = </xsl:text>
    <xsl:value-of
      select="max($seq2,
                  concat('http://saxon.sf.net/collation?',
                         'class=com.oreilly.xslt.GermanCollation;'))"/>

  </xsl:template>

</xsl:stylesheet>
```

Here are the results:

```
Here are some tests of the max() function:

  max(strasse, straße) = straße
  max(strasse, straße [German collation]) = strasse
  max(straße, strasse [German collation]) = straße
```

Using the default collation, these two strings are not equal. In the first example, **straße** sorts after **strasse**, so that's the value returned by the max( ) function. In the final two examples, the two strings are considered equal by the German collation. In Saxon 9.0.0.3J, max( ) returns the maximum value that appears first in the sequence. This is implementation dependent; XSLT processors are allowed to return any of the equal maximum values.

[2.0] min()

Returns the smallest value in a given sequence.

Syntax

```
xs:anyAtomicType min(xs:anyAtomicType*)
xs:anyAtomicType min(xs:anyAtomicType*, $collation as xs:string)
```

Input

A sequence of values. The optional collation is only used if the items in the sequence are xs:strings.

Output

The minimum value in the given sequence. The min( ) function works with the following types of values: numeric values (xs:integer, xs:double, xs:decimal, and xs:float), xs:string, xs:boolean, xs:date, xs:dateTime, xs:time, xs:yearMonthDuration, and xs:dayTimeDuration (but *not* xs:duration).

Given a sequence of numeric values, the XSLT processor returns the smallest number, converting datatypes as necessary. Given a sequence of durations, the XSLT processor returns the shortest of those durations. Given a sequence of strings, the XSLT processor returns the string that appears first in sorted order.

The min( ) function assumes you'll send it a sequence containing sensible data; if not, the XSLT processor throws an error. Asking for the minimum value in the sequence (xs:year MonthDuration('P4Y2M'), 'strawberry', 3.14) returns an error, as you'd expect.

Some notes about how the min( ) function works are as follows:

- To find the shortest of a sequence of durations, the values must all be xs:dayTimeDurations, or they must all be xs:yearMonthDurations. You can't mix the two types of durations; if you do, the XSLT processor throws an error.

- If any of the items in the sequence are of type xs:untypedAtomic, the XSLT processor attempts to cast it to xs:double. If the item can't be converted to an xs:double, the XSLT processor throws an error.

- When comparing xs:string values, the default collation is used unless you specify another.

- Finally, if you pass the min( ) function the empty sequence, it returns the empty sequence. Although you're not giving the function any useful data in this case, the XSLT processor doesn't throw an error.

Defined in

XQuery 1.0 and XPath 2.0 Functions and Operators section 15.4, "Aggregate Functions."

Example

Here's a stylesheet that finds the minimum value in several different types of sequences:

```
<?xml version="1.0"?>
<!-- min.xsl -->
<xsl:stylesheet version="2.0"
  xmlns:xsl="http://www.w3.org/1999/XSL/Transform"
  xmlns:xs="http://www.w3.org/2001/XMLSchema">

  <xsl:output method="text"/>

  <xsl:template match="/">
    <xsl:variable name="seq1" select="(3, 5, 18)"/>
    <xsl:variable name="seq2" select="(3, 5, 48.273, 2.9e3)"/>

    <xsl:variable name="value1" as="xs:integer" select="42"/>
    <xsl:variable name="value2" as="xs:double" select="2718.28E-3"/>
    <xsl:variable name="value3" as="xs:float" select="98.6"/>
    <xsl:variable name="value4" as="xs:decimal" select="2.54"/>
    <xsl:variable name="seq3"
      select="($value1, $value2, $value3, $value4)"/>

    <xsl:variable name="seq4"
      select="(xs:yearMonthDuration('P3Y8M'),
               xs:yearMonthDuration('P4Y2M'),
               xs:yearMonthDuration('P6Y4M'))"/>
    <xsl:variable name="seq5"
      select="(xs:dayTimeDuration('P2DT4H23M12.2S'),
               xs:dayTimeDuration('P3DT8H17M'),
               xs:dayTimeDuration('P3D'))"/>
    <xsl:variable name="seq6"
      select="('red', 'white', 'blue')"/>

    <xsl:text>&#xA;Here are some tests of the min() function:&#xA;</xsl:text>

    <xsl:text>&#xA;  min(</xsl:text>
    <xsl:value-of select="$seq1" separator=", "/>
    <xsl:text>) = </xsl:text>
    <xsl:value-of select="format-number(min($seq1), '#.###')"/>

    <xsl:text>&#xA;&#xA;  min(</xsl:text>
    <xsl:value-of select="$seq2" separator=", "/>
    <xsl:text>) = </xsl:text>
    <xsl:value-of select="format-number(min($seq2), '#.###')"/>

    <xsl:text>&#xA;&#xA;  min(</xsl:text>
    <xsl:value-of select="$seq3" separator=", "/>
    <xsl:text>) = </xsl:text>
    <xsl:value-of select="format-number(min($seq3), '#.###')"/>

    <xsl:text>&#xA;&#xA;  min(</xsl:text>
    <xsl:value-of select="$seq4" separator=", "/>
    <xsl:text>) = </xsl:text>
    <xsl:value-of select="min($seq4)"/>

    <xsl:text>&#xA;&#xA;   In text, the minimum of</xsl:text>
    <xsl:for-each select="$seq4">
      <xsl:text>&#xA;        </xsl:text>
```

```
    <xsl:value-of select="years-from-duration(.)"/>
    <xsl:text> years and </xsl:text>
    <xsl:value-of select="months-from-duration(.)"/>
    <xsl:text> months (</xsl:text>
    <xsl:value-of select="."/>
    <xsl:text>)</xsl:text>
  </xsl:for-each>

  <xsl:text>&#xA;    is </xsl:text>
  <xsl:value-of select="years-from-duration(min($seq4))"/>
  <xsl:text> years and </xsl:text>
  <xsl:value-of select="months-from-duration(min($seq4))"/>
  <xsl:text> months (</xsl:text>
  <xsl:value-of select="min($seq4)"/>
  <xsl:text>).</xsl:text>

  <xsl:text>&#xA;&#xA;  min(</xsl:text>
  <xsl:value-of select="$seq5" separator=", "/>
  <xsl:text>) = </xsl:text>
  <xsl:variable name="min5" select="min($seq5)"/>
  <xsl:value-of select="$min5"/>

  <xsl:text>&#xA;&#xA;   In text, the minimum of</xsl:text>
  <xsl:for-each select="$seq5">
    <xsl:text>&#xA;      </xsl:text>
    <xsl:value-of select="days-from-duration(.)"/>
    <xsl:text> days, </xsl:text>
    <xsl:value-of select="hours-from-duration(.)"/>
    <xsl:text> hours, </xsl:text>
    <xsl:value-of select="minutes-from-duration(.)"/>
    <xsl:text> minutes and </xsl:text>
    <xsl:value-of
      select="format-number(seconds-from-duration(.), '#.##')"/>
    <xsl:text> seconds (</xsl:text>
    <xsl:value-of select="."/>
    <xsl:text>)</xsl:text>
  </xsl:for-each>

  <xsl:text>&#xA;   is </xsl:text>
  <xsl:value-of select="days-from-duration($min5)"/>
  <xsl:text> days, </xsl:text>
  <xsl:value-of select="hours-from-duration($min5)"/>
  <xsl:text> hours, </xsl:text>
  <xsl:value-of select="minutes-from-duration($min5)"/>
  <xsl:text> minutes and </xsl:text>
  <xsl:value-of
    select="format-number(seconds-from-duration($min5), '#.##')"/>
  <xsl:text> seconds.</xsl:text>

  <xsl:text>&#xA;&#xA;  min(</xsl:text>
  <xsl:value-of select="$seq6" separator=", "/>
  <xsl:text>) = </xsl:text>
  <xsl:value-of select="min($seq6)"/>

</xsl:template>
```

```
        </xsl:stylesheet>
```

Here are the results from this stylesheet:

```
Here are some tests of the min() function:

  min(3, 5, 18) = 3

  min(3, 5, 48.273, 2900) = 3

  min(42, 2.71828, 98.6, 2.54) = 2.54

  min(P3Y8M, P4Y2M, P6Y4M) = P3Y8M

    In text, the minimum of
      3 years and 8 months (P3Y8M)
      4 years and 2 months (P4Y2M)
      6 years and 4 months (P6Y4M)
    is 3 years and 8 months (P3Y8M).

  min(P2DT4H23M12.2S, P3DT8H17M, P3D) = P2DT4H23M12.2S

    In text, the minimum of
      2 days, 4 hours, 23 minutes and 12.2 seconds (P2DT4H23M12.2S)
      3 days, 8 hours, 17 minutes and 0 seconds (P3DT8H17M)
      3 days, 0 hours, 0 minutes and 0 seconds (P3D)
    is 2 days, 4 hours, 23 minutes and 12.2 seconds.
```

The stylesheet demonstrates six different types of sequences. The first is all integers and the second is a sequence of numbers. All the values in the first two sequences can be converted to numbers, so the results are what we expect. The third sequence features four numeric values, each of which has a specific numeric type. The next two sequences are made up of the two types of durations, and the final sequence is made up of strings. The stylesheet also uses functions such as years-from-duration( ) and format-number( ) to format the data.

Here's a short example that illustrates using a custom collation:

```
<?xml version="1.0"?>
<!-- min2.xsl -->
<xsl:stylesheet version="2.0"
  xmlns:xsl="http://www.w3.org/1999/XSL/Transform"
  xmlns:xs="http://www.w3.org/2001/XMLSchema">

<xsl:output method="text"/>

<xsl:template match="/">
  <xsl:variable name="seq1"
    select="('stra&#xDF;e', 'strasse')"/>
  <xsl:variable name="seq2" select="reverse($seq1)"/>

  <xsl:text>&#xA;Here are some tests of the min() function:&#xA;</xsl:text>

  <xsl:text>&#xA;  min(</xsl:text>
  <xsl:value-of select="$seq1" separator=", "/>
  <xsl:text>) = </xsl:text>
```

```
<xsl:value-of select="min($seq1)"/>

<xsl:text>&#xA;  min(</xsl:text>
<xsl:value-of select="$seq1" separator=", "/>
<xsl:text> [German collation]) = </xsl:text>
<xsl:value-of
  select="min($seq1,
          concat('http://saxon.sf.net/collation?',
                 'class=com.oreilly.xslt.GermanCollation;'))"/>

<xsl:text>&#xA;  min(</xsl:text>
<xsl:value-of select="$seq2" separator=", "/>
<xsl:text> [German collation]) = </xsl:text>
<xsl:value-of
  select="min($seq2,
          concat('http://saxon.sf.net/collation?',
                 'class=com.oreilly.xslt.GermanCollation;'))"/>

  </xsl:template>

</xsl:stylesheet>
```

Here are the results:

```
Here are some tests of the min() function:

min(strasse, straße) = strasse
min(straße, strasse [German collation]) = straße
min(strasse, straße [German collation]) = strasse
```

Using the default collation, these two strings are not equal. In the first example, strasse sorts before straße, so that's the value returned by the min( ) function. In the final two examples, the two strings are considered equal by the German collation. In Saxon 9.0.0.3J, min( ) returns the minimum value that appears first in the sequence. This is implementation dependent; XSLT processors are allowed to return any of the equal minimum values.

[2.0] minutes-from-dateTime()

Given an xs:dateTime, returns its minutes value.

Syntax

```
xs:integer? minutes-from-dateTime(xs:dateTime?)
```

Inputs

An xs:dateTime value.

Output

An xs:integer representing the minutes component of the given xs:dateTime value. If the argument is the empty sequence, this function returns the empty sequence.

Defined in

XQuery 1.0 and XPath 2.0 Functions and Operators section 10.5, "Component Extraction Functions on Durations, Dates and Times."

Example

This stylesheet demonstrates the minutes-from-dateTime( ) function:

```
<?xml version="1.0"?>
<!-- minutes-from-datetime.xsl -->
<xsl:stylesheet version="2.0"
  xmlns:xsl="http://www.w3.org/1999/XSL/Transform"
  xmlns:xs="http://www.w3.org/2001/XMLSchema">

  <xsl:output method="text"/>

  <xsl:template match="/">
    <xsl:text>&#xA;Extracting the minutes from an xs:dateTime:</xsl:text>
    <xsl:variable name="currentDateTime" as="xs:dateTime"
      select="current-dateTime()"/>
    <xsl:text>&#xA;&#xA;  The current date and time is: </xsl:text>
    <xsl:value-of select="$currentDateTime"/>

    <xsl:text>&#xA;&#xA;  The current minute is: </xsl:text>
    <xsl:value-of select="minutes-from-dateTime($currentDateTime)"/>
  </xsl:template>

</xsl:stylesheet>
```

The stylesheet creates these results:

```
Extracting the minutes from an xs:dateTime:

  The current date and time is: 2006-11-16T04:34:19.921-05:00

  The current minute is: 34
```

See Also

The definitions of the [2.0] day-from-dateTime( ), [2.0] format-dateTime( ), [2.0] hours-from-dateTime( ), [2.0] month-from-dateTime( ), [2.0] seconds-from-dateTime( ), [2.0] timezone-from-dateTime( ), and [2.0] year-from-dateTime( ) functions.

[2.0] minutes-from-duration()

Given an xs:duration value, returns the number of minutes in that duration.

Syntax

```
xs:integer? minutes-from-duration(xs:duration?)
```

Inputs

An xs:duration value.

Output

An `xs:integer` representing the minutes component of the given `xs:duration`. Be aware that for an `xs:yearMonthDuration`, this function always returns 0 because there is no minutes component of an `xs:yearMonthDuration`. Also, if the argument is the empty sequence, this function returns the empty sequence.

Defined in

XQuery 1.0 and XPath 2.0 Functions and Operators section 10.5, "Component Extraction Functions on Durations, Dates and Times."

Example

This stylesheet demonstrates the `minutes-from-duration( )` function with all three types of durations:

```
<?xml version="1.0"?>
<!-- minutes-from-duration.xsl -->
<xsl:stylesheet version="2.0"
  xmlns:xsl="http://www.w3.org/1999/XSL/Transform"
  xmlns:xs="http://www.w3.org/2001/XMLSchema">

  <xsl:output method="text"/>

  <xsl:template match="/">
    <xsl:text>&#xA;Extracting the minutes component from durations:</xsl:text>

    <xsl:variable name="sampleDuration" as="xs:duration"
      select="xs:duration('P3Y8M2DT4H23M12.2S')"/>
    <xsl:variable name="sampleYearMonthDuration" as="xs:yearMonthDuration"
      select="xs:yearMonthDuration('P3Y8M')"/>
    <xsl:variable name="sampleDayTimeDuration" as="xs:dayTimeDuration"
      select="xs:dayTimeDuration('P2DT4H23M12.2S')"/>

    <xsl:text>&#xA;&#xA;  A sample xs:duration: </xsl:text>
    <xsl:value-of select="$sampleDuration"/>
    <xsl:text>&#xA;    The minutes component of this duration is </xsl:text>
    <xsl:value-of select="minutes-from-duration($sampleDuration)"/>
    <xsl:text>.</xsl:text>

    <xsl:text>&#xA;&#xA;  A sample xs:yearMonthDuration: </xsl:text>
    <xsl:value-of select="$sampleYearMonthDuration"/>
    <xsl:text>&#xA;    The minutes component of this duration is </xsl:text>
    <xsl:value-of select="minutes-from-duration($sampleYearMonthDuration)"/>
    <xsl:text>.</xsl:text>

    <xsl:text>&#xA;&#xA;  A sample xs:dayTimeDuration: </xsl:text>
    <xsl:value-of select="$sampleDayTimeDuration"/>
    <xsl:text>&#xA;    The minutes component of this duration is </xsl:text>
    <xsl:value-of select="minutes-from-duration($sampleDayTimeDuration)"/>
    <xsl:text>.</xsl:text>
  </xsl:template>

</xsl:stylesheet>
```

This stylesheet generates these results:

```
Extracting the minutes component from durations:

  A sample xs:duration: P3Y8M2DT4H23M12.2S
    The minutes component of this duration is 23.

  A sample xs:yearMonthDuration: P3Y8M
    The minutes component of this duration is 0.

  A sample xs:dayTimeDuration: P2DT4H23M12.2S
    The minutes component of this duration is 23.
```

Extracting the minutes component from an `xs:yearMonthDuration` returns 0, as you'd expect.

See Also

The definitions of the [2.0] `days-from-duration( )`, [2.0] `hours-from-duration( )`, [2.0] `months-from-duration( )`, [2.0] `seconds-from-duration( )`, and [2.0] `years-from-duration( )` functions.

[2.0] minutes-from-time()

Given an `xs:time` value, returns its minutes component.

Syntax

```
xs:integer? minutes-from-time(xs:time?)
```

Input

An `xs:time` value.

Output

An `xs:integer` representing the minutes component of the given `xs:time` value. If the argument is the empty sequence, this function returns the empty sequence.

Defined in

XQuery 1.0 and XPath 2.0 Functions and Operators section 10.5, "Component Extraction Functions on Durations, Dates and Times."

Example

Here's a stylesheet that uses `minutes-from-time( )`:

```
<?xml version="1.0"?>
<!-- minutes-from-time.xsl -->
<xsl:stylesheet version="2.0"
  xmlns:xsl="http://www.w3.org/1999/XSL/Transform"
  xmlns:xs="http://www.w3.org/2001/XMLSchema">

  <xsl:output method="text"/>
```

```
<xsl:template match="/">
  <xsl:text>&#xA;Extracting the minutes component from an xs:time:</xsl:text>
  <xsl:variable name="currentTime" as="xs:time" select="current-time()"/>
  <xsl:text>&#xA;&#xA;  The current time is: </xsl:text>
  <xsl:value-of select="$currentTime"/>

  <xsl:text>&#xA;&#xA;  The current minute is: </xsl:text>
  <xsl:value-of select="minutes-from-time($currentTime)"/>
  <xsl:text>, the </xsl:text>
  <xsl:value-of select="format-time($currentTime, '[mwo]')"/>
  <xsl:text> minute of the hour.</xsl:text>
</xsl:template>

</xsl:stylesheet>
```

The stylesheet creates these results:

```
Extracting the minutes component from an xs:time:

  The current time is: 04:39:49.875-05:00

  The current minute is: 39, the thirty-ninth minute of the hour.
```

Notice that the first result was generated by the minutes-from-time( ) function, while the second result was generated by using format-time( ) with a format string that selected the minutes component from the xs:time value.

See Also

The definitions of the [2.0] format-time( ), [2.0] hours-from-time( ), [2.0] seconds-from-time( ), and [2.0] timezone-from-time( ).

[2.0] month-from-date()

Given an xs:date value, returns its month value.

Syntax

```
xs:integer? month-from-date(xs:date?)
```

Input

An xs:date value.

Output

An xs:integer representing the month component of the given xs:date value. If the argument is the empty sequence, this function returns the empty sequence.

Defined in

XQuery 1.0 and XPath 2.0 Functions and Operators section 10.5, "Component Extraction Functions on Durations, Dates and Times."

Example

This stylesheet demonstrates the `month-from-date( )` function:

```
<?xml version="1.0"?>
<!-- month-from-date.xsl -->
<xsl:stylesheet version="2.0"
  xmlns:xsl="http://www.w3.org/1999/XSL/Transform"
  xmlns:xs="http://www.w3.org/2001/XMLSchema">

  <xsl:output method="text"/>

  <xsl:template match="/">
    <xsl:text>&#xA;Extracting the month from an xs:date:</xsl:text>
    <xsl:variable name="currentDate" as="xs:date" select="current-date()"/>
    <xsl:text>&#xA;&#xA;The current date is: </xsl:text>
    <xsl:value-of select="$currentDate"/>

    <xsl:text>&#xA;&#xA;  The current month: </xsl:text>
    <xsl:value-of select="month-from-date($currentDate)"/>
    <xsl:text>&#xA;     In English: </xsl:text>
    <xsl:value-of select="format-date($currentDate, '[MNn]')"/>
    <xsl:text>&#xA;     In German: </xsl:text>
    <xsl:value-of select="format-date($currentDate, '[MNn]', 'de', (), ())"/>
    <xsl:text>&#xA;     It's the </xsl:text>
    <xsl:value-of select="format-date($currentDate, '[M1o]')"/>
    <xsl:text> month of the year.</xsl:text>
  </xsl:template>

</xsl:stylesheet>
```

The stylesheet creates these results:

```
Extracting the month from an xs:dateTime:

The current date and time is: 2006-07-05T12:38:00.877-05:00

  The current month: 7
     In English: July
     In German: Juli
     It's the 7th month of the year.
```

Notice that the first result was generated by the `month-from-date( )` function, while the other results were generated by using `format-date( )` with a format string that selected only the month component of the `xs:date` value.

See Also

The definitions of the [2.0] `day-from-date( )`, [2.0] `format-date( )`, [2.0] `timezone-from-date( )`, and [2.0] `year-from-date( )` functions.

[2.0] month-from-dateTime()

Given an xs:dateTime value, returns its month value.

Syntax

```
xs:integer? month-from-dateTime(xs:dateTime?)
```

Inputs

An xs:dateTime value.

Output

An xs:integer representing the month component of the given xs:dateTime value. If the argument is the empty sequence, this function returns the empty sequence.

Defined in

XQuery 1.0 and XPath 2.0 Functions and Operators section 10.5, "Component Extraction Functions on Durations, Dates and Times."

Example

This stylesheet demonstrates the month-from-dateTime( ) function:

```
<?xml version="1.0"?>
<!-- month-from-datetime.xsl -->
<xsl:stylesheet version="2.0"
  xmlns:xsl="http://www.w3.org/1999/XSL/Transform"
  xmlns:xs="http://www.w3.org/2001/XMLSchema">

  <xsl:output method="text"/>

  <xsl:template match="/">
    <xsl:text>&#xA;Extracting the month from an xs:dateTime:</xsl:text>
    <xsl:variable name="currentDateTime" as="xs:dateTime"
      select="current-dateTime()"/>
    <xsl:text>&#xA;&#xA;The current date and time is: </xsl:text>
    <xsl:value-of select="$currentDateTime"/>

    <xsl:text>&#xA;&#xA;  The current month: </xsl:text>
    <xsl:value-of select="month-from-dateTime($currentDateTime)"/>
    <xsl:text>&#xA;    In English: </xsl:text>
    <xsl:value-of select="format-dateTime($currentDateTime, '[MNn]')"/>
    <xsl:text>&#xA;    In German: </xsl:text>
    <xsl:value-of select="format-dateTime($currentDateTime, '[MNn]', 'de', (), ())"/>
    <xsl:text>&#xA;    It's the </xsl:text>
    <xsl:value-of select="format-dateTime($currentDateTime, '[M1o]')"/>
    <xsl:text> month of the year.</xsl:text>
  </xsl:template>

</xsl:stylesheet>
```

The stylesheet creates these results:

```
Extracting the month from an xs:dateTime:

The current date and time is: 2006-11-16T04:42:47.481-05:00

  The current month: 11
    In English: November
    In German: November
    It's the 11th month of the year.
```

Notice that some of the results were generated by the month-from-dateTime( ) function, while other results were generated by using format-dateTime( ) with a format string that selected only the month component of the xs:dateTime value.

See Also

The definitions of the [2.0] day-from-dateTime( ), [2.0] format-dateTime( ), [2.0] hours-from-dateTime( ), [2.0] minutes-from-dateTime( ), [2.0] seconds-from-dateTime( ), [2.0] timezone-from-dateTime( ), and [2.0] year-from-dateTime( ) functions.

[2.0] months-from-duration()

Given an xs:duration value, returns the number of months in that duration.

Syntax

```
xs:integer? months-from-duration(xs:duration?)
```

Inputs

An xs:duration value.

Output

An xs:integer representing the months component of the given xs:duration. Be aware that for an xs:dayTimeDuration, this function always returns 0 because there is no months component of an xs:dayTimeDuration. Also, if the argument is the empty sequence, this function returns the empty sequence.

Defined in

XQuery 1.0 and XPath 2.0 Functions and Operators section 10.5, "Component Extraction Functions on Durations, Dates and Times."

Example

This stylesheet demonstrates the months-from-duration( ) function with all three types of durations:

```
<?xml version="1.0"?>
<!-- months-from-duration.xsl -->
<xsl:stylesheet version="2.0"
  xmlns:xsl="http://www.w3.org/1999/XSL/Transform"
  xmlns:xs="http://www.w3.org/2001/XMLSchema">
```

```
<xsl:output method="text"/>

<xsl:template match="/">
  <xsl:text>&#xA;Extracting the months component from durations:</xsl:text>

  <xsl:variable name="sampleDuration" as="xs:duration"
    select="xs:duration('P3Y8M2DT4H23M12.2S')"/>
  <xsl:variable name="sampleYearMonthDuration" as="xs:yearMonthDuration"
    select="xs:yearMonthDuration('P3Y8M')"/>
  <xsl:variable name="sampleDayTimeDuration" as="xs:dayTimeDuration"
    select="xs:dayTimeDuration('P2DT4H23M12.2S')"/>

  <xsl:text>&#xA;&#xA;  A sample xs:duration: </xsl:text>
  <xsl:value-of select="$sampleDuration"/>
  <xsl:text>&#xA;    The months component of this duration is </xsl:text>
  <xsl:value-of select="months-from-duration($sampleDuration)"/>
  <xsl:text>.</xsl:text>

  <xsl:text>&#xA;&#xA;  A sample xs:yearMonthDuration: </xsl:text>
  <xsl:value-of select="$sampleYearMonthDuration"/>
  <xsl:text>&#xA;    The months component of this duration is </xsl:text>
  <xsl:value-of select="months-from-duration($sampleYearMonthDuration)"/>
  <xsl:text>.</xsl:text>

  <xsl:text>&#xA;&#xA;  A sample xs:dayTimeDuration: </xsl:text>
  <xsl:value-of select="$sampleDayTimeDuration"/>
  <xsl:text>&#xA;    The months component of this duration is </xsl:text>
  <xsl:value-of select="months-from-duration($sampleDayTimeDuration)"/>
  <xsl:text>.</xsl:text>
</xsl:template>

</xsl:stylesheet>
```

This stylesheet generates these results:

```
Extracting the months component from durations:

  A sample xs:duration: P3Y8M2DT4H23M12.2S
    The months component of this duration is 8.

  A sample xs:yearMonthDuration: P3Y8M
    The months component of this duration is 8.

  A sample xs:dayTimeDuration: P2DT4H23M12.2S
    The months component of this duration is 0.
```

As you can see from the results, extracting the months component from an xs:dayTimeDuration returns 0.

See Also

The definitions of the [2.0] days-from-duration( ), [2.0] hours-from-duration( ), [2.0] minutes-from-duration( ), [2.0] seconds-from-duration( ), and the [2.0] years-from-duration( ) functions.

name()

Returns the qualified name of a node. The qualified name includes the appropriate namespace prefix. For information on the namespace URI (not the prefix), XPath provides the namespace-uri( ) function.

Syntax

```
[1.0] string name(node-set?)
[2.0] xs:string name(node()?)
```

Inputs

[1.0] An optional node-set. If the node-set is present, the XSLT 1.0 processor invokes the name( ) function against the first node in the node-set. If no node-set is given, the name( ) function applies to the context node.

[2.0] An optional node sequence. *In XSLT 2.0, it is an error to call the* name( ) *function with a sequence containing more than one node.* If the node sequence is not present, the name( ) function applies to the context node.

Output

The qualified name of the node. If the argument to the name( ) function is empty (say we use select="item" where there are no <item> elements, for example), name( ) returns an empty string.

Defined in

[1.0] XPath section 4.1, "Node Set Functions."

[2.0] XQuery 1.0 and XPath 2.0 Functions and Operators section 14, "Functions and Operators on Nodes."

Example

Here is the XML document we'll use to demonstrate the name( ) function:

```
<?xml version="1.0"?>
<!-- sonnet.xml -->
<sonnet type='Shakespearean'>
  <auth:author xmlns:auth="http://www.authors.com/">
    <last-name>Shakespeare</last-name>
    <first-name>William</first-name>
    <nationality>British</nationality>
    <year-of-birth>1564</year-of-birth>
    <year-of-death>1616</year-of-death>
  </auth:author>
  <!-- Is there an official title for this sonnet?  They're
       sometimes named after the first line.              -->
  <title>Sonnet 130</title>
  <lines>
    <line>My mistress' eyes are nothing like the sun,</line>
    <line>Coral is far more red than her lips red.</line>
    <line>If snow be white, why then her breasts are dun,</line>
```

```
        <line>If hairs be wires, black wires grow on her head.</line>
        <line>I have seen roses damasked, red and white,</line>
        <line>But no such roses see I in her cheeks.</line>
        <line>And in some perfumes is there more delight</line>
        <line>Than in the breath that from my mistress reeks.</line>
        <line>I love to hear her speak, yet well I know</line>
        <line>That music hath a far more pleasing sound.</line>
        <line>I grant I never saw a goddess go,</line>
        <line>My mistress when she walks, treads on the ground.</line>
        <line>And yet, by Heaven, I think my love as rare</line>
        <line>As any she belied with false compare.</line>
    </lines>
</sonnet>
```

We'll use this stylesheet to output the value of the name( ) function for each node in the XML document:

```
<?xml version="1.0"?>
<!-- name.xsl -->
<xsl:stylesheet version="1.0"
  xmlns:xsl="http://www.w3.org/1999/XSL/Transform">

  <xsl:output method="text"/>

  <xsl:template match="/">
    <xsl:text>&#xA;A test of the name() function:&#xA;</xsl:text>

    <xsl:for-each select="//*">
      <xsl:text>&#xA;  Element </xsl:text>
      <xsl:number level="any" count="*"/>
      <xsl:text>: </xsl:text>
      <xsl:value-of select="name()"/>
    </xsl:for-each>
  </xsl:template>

</xsl:stylesheet>
```

When we transform the XML document with this stylesheet, here are the results:

```
A test of the name() function:

  Element 1: sonnet
  Element 2: auth:author
  Element 3: last-name
  Element 4: first-name
  Element 5: nationality
  Element 6: year-of-birth
  Element 7: year-of-death
  Element 8: title
  Element 9: lines
  Element 10: line
  Element 11: line
  Element 12: line
  Element 13: line
  Element 14: line
  Element 15: line
  Element 16: line
```

```
Element 17: line
Element 18: line
Element 19: line
Element 20: line
Element 21: line
Element 22: line
Element 23: line
```

Here's a slightly more advanced version in which we use the XSLT 2.0 `<xsl:sequence>` element to select a sequence of nodes from the document. We store that sequence in a variable, and then iterate through the values of the variable and print the names of the elements:

```
<?xml version="1.0"?>
<!-- name2.xsl -->
<xsl:stylesheet version="2.0"
  xmlns:xsl="http://www.w3.org/1999/XSL/Transform"
  xmlns="http://www.oreilly.com/xslt"
  xmlns:auth="http://www.authors.com/">

  <xsl:output method="text"/>

  <xsl:template match="/">
    <xsl:text>&#xA;Tests of the name() function:&#xA;</xsl:text>

    <xsl:variable name="authorDetails" as="element()*"
      select="/sonnet/auth:author/*"/>
    <xsl:for-each select="$authorDetails">
      <xsl:text>&#xA;  Element </xsl:text>
      <xsl:value-of select="position()"/>
      <xsl:text>: </xsl:text>
      <xsl:value-of select="name()"/>
    </xsl:for-each>
  </xsl:template>

</xsl:stylesheet>
```

(Notice that the sequence is stored in a variable with type `element( )*`, and that we had to define the `auth` namespace in the stylesheet.) The results contain the names of all the elements that appear below the `<auth:author>` element in the source document:

```
Tests of the name() function:

Element 1: last-name
Element 2: first-name
Element 3: nationality
Element 4: year-of-birth
Element 5: year-of-death
```

As we mentioned earlier, it is an error in XSLT 2.0 to pass more than one node to the `name( )` function. (In XSLT 1.0, the processor simply used the first node in the node-set and ignored everything else.) It is possible to pass a variable with type `element( )*` to the `name( )` function, but that sequence cannot contain more than one member. For example, the following is legal in XSLT 2.0:

```
<xsl:variable name="salesFigures" as="element()*"
  select="/report/brand[1]/*[2]"/>
<xsl:value-of select="name($salesFigures)"/>
```

This is legal because the XPath expression in the `<xsl:variable>` element selects only a single node. This code, however, causes the XSLT 2.0 processor to raise an error:

```
<xsl:variable name="salesFigures" as="element()*"
  select="/report/brand[1]/*"/>
<xsl:value-of select="name($salesFigures)"/>
```

This is an error because the XPath expression selects more than one node from our sample document. If we change the XML source document so that there is only one node under the first `<brand>` element, the stylesheet would work.

namespace-uri()

Returns the namespace URI of the argument node.

Syntax

```
[1.0] string namespace-uri(node-set?)
[2.0] xs:anyURI namespace-uri()
[2.0] xs:anyURI namespace-uri(node()?)
```

Inputs

[1.0] A node-set. If the node-set is omitted, the `namespace-uri()` function creates a node-set that has the context node as its only member.

[2.0] A node. If the node is omitted, the `namespace-uri()` function is evaluated against the context item. If the input is a sequence with more than one node, the XSLT processor raises an error.

Output

[1.0] The namespace URI of the first node in the argument node-set. If the argument node-set is empty, the first node has no namespace URI, or the first node has a namespace URI that is null, an empty string is returned.

[2.0] The namespace URI of the argument node. If the argument is the empty sequence, the argument has no namespace URI or the node has a namespace URI that is null, an empty string is returned.

Be aware that the `namespace-uri()` function returns an empty string for all nodes other than element and attribute nodes.

Defined in

[1.0] XPath section 4.1, "Node Set Functions."

[2.0] XQuery 1.0 and XPath 2.0 Functions and Operators section 14, "Functions and Operators on Nodes."

Example

We'll use a slightly modified version of our Shakespearean sonnet to illustrate the `namespace-uri( )` function:

```
<?xml version="1.0"?>
<!-- sonnet-namespace.xml -->
<sonnet type='Shakespearean'
  xmlns="http://www.oreilly.com/xslt">
  <author xmlns="http://www.authors.com/">
    <last-name>Shakespeare</last-name>
    <first-name>William</first-name>
    <nationality>British</nationality>
    <year-of-birth>1564</year-of-birth>
    <year-of-death>1616</year-of-death>
  </author>
  <!-- Is there an official title for this sonnet?  They're
       sometimes named after the first line.                -->
  <title>Sonnet 130</title>
  <lines>
    <line>My mistress' eyes are nothing like the sun,</line>
    <line>Coral is far more red than her lips red.</line>
    <line>If snow be white, why then her breasts are dun,</line>
    <line>If hairs be wires, black wires grow on her head.</line>
    <line>I have seen roses damasked, red and white,</line>
    <line>But no such roses see I in her cheeks.</line>
    <line>And in some perfumes is there more delight</line>
    <line>Than in the breath that from my mistress reeks.</line>
    <line>I love to hear her speak, yet well I know</line>
    <line>That music hath a far more pleasing sound.</line>
    <line>I grant I never saw a goddess go,</line>
    <line>My mistress when she walks, treads on the ground.</line>
    <line>And yet, by Heaven, I think my love as rare</line>
    <line>As any she belied with false compare.</line>
  </lines>
</sonnet>
```

The sonnet has been modified so that it has a default namespace (`http://www.oreilly.com/`).
Our sample stylesheet goes through any XML document and invokes `namespace-uri( )` against
every element and attribute node in the document. Here's the stylesheet:

```
<?xml version="1.0"?>
<!-- namespace-uri.xsl -->
<xsl:stylesheet version="1.0"
  xmlns:xsl="http://www.w3.org/1999/XSL/Transform">

  <xsl:output method="text"/>

  <xsl:template match="/">
    <xsl:text>&#xA;A test of the namespace-uri() function:&#xA;&#xA;</xsl:text>

    <xsl:for-each select="//*">
      <xsl:text>  Namespace URI for &lt;</xsl:text>
      <xsl:value-of select="node-name(.)"/>
      <xsl:text>&gt;: </xsl:text>
      <xsl:value-of select="namespace-uri()"/>
```

```
<xsl:text>&#xA;</xsl:text>
<xsl:for-each select="@*">
  <xsl:text>    Namespace URI for attribute "</xsl:text>
  <xsl:value-of select="node-name(.)"/>
  <xsl:text>": </xsl:text>
  <xsl:value-of select="namespace-uri()"/>
  <xsl:text>&#xA;</xsl:text>
</xsl:for-each>
    </xsl:for-each>
  </xsl:template>

</xsl:stylesheet>
```

Here are the results of our stylesheet:

```
A test of the namespace-uri() function:

Namespace URI for <sonnet>: http://www.oreilly.com/xslt
  Namespace URI for attribute "type":
Namespace URI for <author>: http://www.authors.com/
Namespace URI for <last-name>: http://www.authors.com/
Namespace URI for <first-name>: http://www.authors.com/
Namespace URI for <nationality>: http://www.authors.com/
Namespace URI for <year-of-birth>: http://www.authors.com/
Namespace URI for <year-of-death>: http://www.authors.com/
Namespace URI for <title>: http://www.oreilly.com/xslt
Namespace URI for <lines>: http://www.oreilly.com/xslt
Namespace URI for <line>: http://www.oreilly.com/xslt
Namespace URI for <line>: http://www.oreilly.com/xslt
Namespace URI for <line>: http://www.oreilly.com/xslt
Namespace URI for <line>: http://www.oreilly.com/xslt
Namespace URI for <line>: http://www.oreilly.com/xslt
Namespace URI for <line>: http://www.oreilly.com/xslt
Namespace URI for <line>: http://www.oreilly.com/xslt
Namespace URI for <line>: http://www.oreilly.com/xslt
Namespace URI for <line>: http://www.oreilly.com/xslt
Namespace URI for <line>: http://www.oreilly.com/xslt
Namespace URI for <line>: http://www.oreilly.com/xslt
Namespace URI for <line>: http://www.oreilly.com/xslt
Namespace URI for <line>: http://www.oreilly.com/xslt
```

In our modified sonnet, the `<author>` element declares a new default namespace, so all of the elements inside it return the default namespace. Outside the `<author>` element, the original default namespace comes back into scope.

[2.0] namespace-uri-for-prefix()

Given a namespace prefix and an element, returns the URI associated with that prefix.

Syntax

```
xs:anyURI? namespace-uri-for-prefix($prefix as xs:string?,
                                    $element as element())
```

Inputs

A namespace prefix and an element. If the prefix is an empty string, the URI for the default namespace is returned, assuming a default namespace is in scope.

Output

The URI associated with the namespace prefix for the given element.

Defined in

XQuery 1.0 and XPath 2.0 Functions and Operators section 11.2, "Operators and Functions Related to QNames."

Example

For an example, we'll reuse our Shakespearean sonnet:

```
<?xml version="1.0"?>
<!-- sonnet.xml -->
<sonnet type='Shakespearean'>
  <auth:author xmlns:auth="http://www.authors.com/">
    <last-name>Shakespeare</last-name>
    <first-name>William</first-name>
    <nationality>British</nationality>
    <year-of-birth>1564</year-of-birth>
    <year-of-death>1616</year-of-death>
  </auth:author>
  <!-- Is there an official title for this sonnet?  They're
       sometimes named after the first line.              -->
  <title>Sonnet 130</title>
  <lines>
    <line>My mistress' eyes are nothing like the sun,</line>
    <line>Coral is far more red than her lips red.</line>
    <line>If snow be white, why then her breasts are dun,</line>
    <line>If hairs be wires, black wires grow on her head.</line>
    <line>I have seen roses damasked, red and white,</line>
    <line>But no such roses see I in her cheeks.</line>
    <line>And in some perfumes is there more delight</line>
    <line>Than in the breath that from my mistress reeks.</line>
    <line>I love to hear her speak, yet well I know</line>
    <line>That music hath a far more pleasing sound.</line>
    <line>I grant I never saw a goddess go,</line>
    <line>My mistress when she walks, treads on the ground.</line>
    <line>And yet, by Heaven, I think my love as rare</line>
    <line>As any she belied with false compare.</line>
  </lines>
</sonnet>
```

And here's our stylesheet:

```
<?xml version="1.0" encoding="UTF-8"?>
<!-- namespace-uri-for-prefix.xsl -->
<xsl:stylesheet version="2.0"
  xmlns:xsl="http://www.w3.org/1999/XSL/Transform">

  <xsl:output method="text"/>
```

```
<xsl:template match="/">
  <xsl:text>&#xA;Tests of the namespace-uri-for-prefix() </xsl:text>
  <xsl:text>function:&#xA;</xsl:text>

  <xsl:text>&#xA;  namespace-uri-for-prefix</xsl:text>
  <xsl:text>('auth', //last-name) = "</xsl:text>
  <xsl:value-of
    select="namespace-uri-for-prefix('auth', //last-name)"/>
  <xsl:text>"</xsl:text>

  <xsl:text>&#xA;  namespace-uri-for-prefix</xsl:text>
  <xsl:text>('auth', //*:author) = "</xsl:text>
  <xsl:value-of
    select="namespace-uri-for-prefix('auth', //*:author)"/>
  <xsl:text>"</xsl:text>

  <xsl:text>&#xA;  namespace-uri-for-prefix</xsl:text>
  <xsl:text>('auth', /sonnet) = "</xsl:text>
  <xsl:value-of
    select="namespace-uri-for-prefix('auth', /sonnet)"/>
  <xsl:text>"</xsl:text>
</xsl:template>

</xsl:stylesheet>
```

Here are the results:

```
Tests of the namespace-uri-for-prefix() function:

  namespace-uri-for-prefix('auth', //last-name) = "http://www.authors.com/"
  namespace-uri-for-prefix('auth', //*:author) = "http://www.authors.com/"
  namespace-uri-for-prefix('auth', /sonnet) = ""
```

In our stylesheet, we're looking for the URI for the prefix auth. In the first test of namespace-uri-for-prefix( ), the auth prefix is in scope for the <auth:author> element and everything inside it, so XSLT returns the URL associated with it. For the second test, we choose to use a wildcard in the XPath expression. (The function call namespace-uri-for-prefix('auth', //auth:author) requires us to define the auth namespace in our stylesheet.) Finally, the last example returns an empty string because the auth prefix is not in scope for the <sonnet> element.

This stylesheet was written with knowledge of the XML document. A more complicated example would use a function such as in-scope-prefixes( ) to retrieve a sequence of prefixes, and then use namespace-uri-for-prefix( ) to retrieve the URI associated with each prefix.

There are other complications: It is a fatal error to pass the empty sequence or a sequence of more than one item as the second argument. That's not a problem here because we wrote our stylesheet knowing there were <last-name>, <auth:author>, and <sonnet> elements in the document, and that each of them occurred once.

As always, feel free to implement a more robust stylesheet for your own amusement.

[2.0] namespace-uri-from-QName()

Given an `xs:QName` value, returns the namespace URI associated with that `QName`.

Syntax

```
xs:anyURI? namespace-uri-from-QName(xs:QName?)
```

Input

An `xs:QName` value.

Output

The namespace URI associated with this `QName`. If the argument is the empty sequence, the empty sequence is returned. If the `QName` is not in a namespace, a zero-length string is returned.

Defined in

XQuery 1.0 and XPath 2.0 Functions and Operators section 11.2, "Operators and Functions Related to QNames."

Example

We'll reuse our Shakespearean sonnet as our XML input document here:

```
<?xml version="1.0"?>
<!-- sonnet.xml -->
<sonnet type='Shakespearean'>
  <auth:author xmlns:auth="http://www.authors.com/">
    <last-name>Shakespeare</last-name>
    <first-name>William</first-name>
    <nationality>British</nationality>
    <year-of-birth>1564</year-of-birth>
    <year-of-death>1616</year-of-death>
  </auth:author>
  <!-- Is there an official title for this sonnet?  They're
       sometimes named after the first line.              -->
  <title>Sonnet 130</title>
  <lines>
    <line>My mistress' eyes are nothing like the sun,</line>
    <line>Coral is far more red than her lips red.</line>
    <line>If snow be white, why then her breasts are dun,</line>
    <line>If hairs be wires, black wires grow on her head.</line>
    <line>I have seen roses damasked, red and white,</line>
    <line>But no such roses see I in her cheeks.</line>
    <line>And in some perfumes is there more delight</line>
    <line>Than in the breath that from my mistress reeks.</line>
    <line>I love to hear her speak, yet well I know</line>
    <line>That music hath a far more pleasing sound.</line>
    <line>I grant I never saw a goddess go,</line>
    <line>My mistress when she walks, treads on the ground.</line>
    <line>And yet, by Heaven, I think my love as rare</line>
    <line>As any she belied with false compare.</line>
  </lines>
</sonnet>
```

Here is our stylesheet:

```
<?xml version="1.0" encoding="UTF-8"?>
<!-- namespace-uri-from-QName.xsl -->
<xsl:stylesheet version="2.0"
  xmlns:xsl="http://www.w3.org/1999/XSL/Transform"
  xmlns:xs="http://www.w3.org/2001/XMLSchema">

  <xsl:output method="text"/>

  <xsl:template match="/">
    <xsl:text>&#xA;Tests of the namespace-uri-from-QName() </xsl:text>
    <xsl:text>function:&#xA;</xsl:text>

    <xsl:variable name="testQName1" as="xs:QName"
      select="resolve-QName('auth:last-name',
              /sonnet/*:author/last-name)"/>
    <xsl:text>&#xA;  testQName1 = resolve-QName('auth:last-name', </xsl:text>
    <xsl:text>/sonnet/*:author/last-name)</xsl:text>
    <xsl:text>&#xA;  namespace-uri-from-QName($testQName1) = "</xsl:text>
    <xsl:value-of select="namespace-uri-from-QName($testQName1)"/>
    <xsl:text>"</xsl:text>

    <xsl:variable name="testQName2" as="xs:QName"
      select="resolve-QName('something-else', /sonnet)"/>
    <xsl:text>&#xA;&#xA;  testQName2 = resolve-QName('</xsl:text>
    <xsl:text>something-else', /sonnet)</xsl:text>
    <xsl:text>&#xA;  namespace-uri-from-QName($testQName2) = "</xsl:text>
    <xsl:value-of select="namespace-uri-from-QName($testQName2)"/>
    <xsl:text>"</xsl:text>

    <xsl:variable name="testQName3" as="xs:QName"
      select="QName('http://www.authors.com/', 'pfx:writer')"/>
    <xsl:text>&#xA;&#xA;  testQName3 = QName('http://www.</xsl:text>
    <xsl:text>authors.com/', 'pfx:writer')&#xA;</xsl:text>
    <xsl:text>  namespace-uri-from-QName($testQName3) = "</xsl:text>
    <xsl:value-of select="namespace-uri-from-QName($testQName3)"/>
    <xsl:text>"</xsl:text>

  </xsl:template>

</xsl:stylesheet>
```

Here are our results:

```
Tests of the namespace-uri-from-QName() function:

  testQName1 = resolve-QName('auth:last-name', /sonnet/*:author/last-name)
  namespace-uri-from-QName($testQName1) = "http://www.authors.com/"

  testQName2 = resolve-QName('something-else', /sonnet)
  namespace-uri-from-QName($testQName2) = ""

  testQName3 = QName('http://www.authors.com/', 'pfx:writer')
  namespace-uri-from-QName($testQName3) = "http://www.authors.com/"
```

The argument to the namespace-uri-from-QName( ) function *must* be an xs:QName. In this stylesheet, we create QNames with the resolve-QName( ) function and the QName( ) constructor function.

For the first test, we create a QName with a qualified element name of auth:last-name. The element (the second argument to resolve-QName( )) is the <last-name> element in our sonnet. The resolve-QName( ) function returns a QName with a local name of last-name, a namespace prefix of auth, and a namespace URI of http://www.authors.com/. If there are no nodes that match the XPath expression /sonnet/*:author/last-name, the call to resolve-QName( ) fails. The call also fails if the auth prefix is not declared for the <last-name> element.

The second test of namespace-uri-from-QName( ) uses an unprefixed element name in the call to resolve-QName( ). The XML document doesn't have a default namespace, so our QName has an empty string for its namespace prefix and namespace URI.

For the final test, we use the QName( ) function to create a QName from scratch. The two arguments to the function are the namespace URI and an element name—in this case, a prefixed element name. The resulting QName has a local name of writer, a namespace prefix of pfx, and a namespace URI of http://www.authors.com/.

We'll look at a couple more examples, but this time we'll use a version of the sonnet that *does* have a default namespace:

```
<?xml version="1.0"?>
<!-- sonnet-default-namespace.xml -->
<sonnet type='Shakespearean'
  xmlns="http://www.oreilly.com/xslt">
  <auth:author xmlns:auth="http://www.authors.com/">
    <last-name>Shakespeare</last-name>
    <first-name>William</first-name>
    <nationality>British</nationality>
    <year-of-birth>1564</year-of-birth>
  ...
</sonnet>
```

The default namespace in the new version of our sonnet is http://www.oreilly.com/xslt. Now we need to modify our stylesheet:

```
<?xml version="1.0" encoding="UTF-8"?>
<!-- namespace-uri-from-QName2.xsl -->
<xsl:stylesheet version="2.0"
  xmlns:xsl="http://www.w3.org/1999/XSL/Transform"
  xmlns:xs="http://www.w3.org/2001/XMLSchema">

  <xsl:output method="text"/>

  <xsl:template match="/">
    <xsl:text>&#xA;Tests of the namespace-uri-from-QName() </xsl:text>
    <xsl:text>function:&#xA;</xsl:text>

    <xsl:variable name="testQName1" as="xs:QName"
      select="resolve-QName('auth:last-name',
              /*:sonnet/*:author/*:last-name)"/>
    <xsl:text>&#xA;  testQName1 = resolve-QName('auth:last-name', </xsl:text>
    <xsl:text>/*:sonnet/*:author/*:last-name)</xsl:text>
```

```
<xsl:text>&#xA;  namespace-uri-from-QName($testQName1) = "</xsl:text>
<xsl:value-of select="namespace-uri-from-QName($testQName1)"/>
<xsl:text>"</xsl:text>

<xsl:variable name="testQName2" as="xs:QName"
  select="resolve-QName('something-else', /*:sonnet)"/>
<xsl:text>&#xA;&#xA;  testQName2 = resolve-QName('</xsl:text>
<xsl:text>something-else', /*:sonnet)</xsl:text>
<xsl:text>&#xA;  namespace-uri-from-QName($testQName2) = "</xsl:text>
<xsl:value-of select="namespace-uri-from-QName($testQName2)"/>
<xsl:text>"</xsl:text>
  </xsl:template>

</xsl:stylesheet>
```

Now we get slightly different results:

```
Tests of the namespace-uri-from-QName() function:

testQName1 = resolve-QName('auth:last-name', /*:sonnet/*:author/*:last-name)
namespace-uri-from-QName($testQName1) = "http://www.authors.com/"

testQName2 = resolve-QName('something-else', /*:sonnet)
namespace-uri-from-QName($testQName2) = "http://www.oreilly.com/xslt"
```

The difference in these results is that we get a namespace URI for the QName we created without a prefix. Our modified sonnet has a default namespace, so we get the value of that namespace.

The change in our stylesheet is that we had to use asterisks to refer to items in the http://www.oreilly.com/xslt namespace. In other words, we had to replace /sonnet/*:auth/last-name with /*:sonnet/*:auth/*:last-name. One way of referring to the default namespace from the XML document would be to declare it with a namespace prefix in our stylesheet.

Another approach is that we could give the sonnet's default namespace a prefix in our stylesheet:

```
<?xml version="1.0" encoding="UTF-8"?>
<!-- namespace-uri-from-QName3.xsl -->
<xsl:stylesheet version="2.0"
  xmlns:xsl="http://www.w3.org/1999/XSL/Transform"
  xmlns:xs="http://www.w3.org/2001/XMLSchema"
  xmlns:ora="http://www.oreilly.com/xslt">

<xsl:output method="text"/>

<xsl:template match="/">
  <xsl:text>&#xA;Tests of the namespace-uri-from-QName() </xsl:text>
  <xsl:text>function:&#xA;</xsl:text>

  <xsl:variable name="testQName1" as="xs:QName"
    select="resolve-QName('auth:last-name',
            /ora:sonnet/*:author/ora:last-name)"/>
  ...
  </xsl:template>

</xsl:stylesheet>
```

This gives us results similar to those in our second stylesheet:

```
Tests of the namespace-uri-from-QName() function:

  testQName1 = resolve-QName('auth:last-name',
                             /ora:sonnet/*:author/ora:last-name)
  namespace-uri-from-QName($testQName1) = "http://www.authors.com/"

  testQName2 = resolve-QName('something-else', /ora:sonnet)
  namespace-uri-from-QName($testQName2) = "http://www.oreilly.com/xslt"
```

We associated the `ora` namespace prefix with the default namespace in the XML source document. Whenever we use the `ora` prefix in our stylesheet, it refers to the `http://www.oreilly.com/xslt` namespace. That's the default namespace of the XML document we're processing, so we can use a specific namespace instead of a wildcard.

[2.0 – Schema] nilled()

Returns `true` if a given element has been nilled, `false` otherwise. If the argument is not an element, `nilled( )` returns the empty sequence.

Syntax

```
xs:boolean? nilled(node()?)
```

Inputs

A node.

Outputs

If the given node has been nilled (meaning it has the attribute `xsi:nil="true"`), this function returns `true`; otherwise it returns `false`. Calling `nilled( )` with the empty sequence returns the empty sequence.

The `nilled( )` function works only with schema-aware processors, and only if the document is using a schema. The schema can be imported into the stylesheet with `<xsl:import-schema>`, or the XML document can use the `xsi:schemaLocation` or `xsi:noNamespaceSchemaLocation` attributes. If no schema is associated with the XML document, all of the nodes in the document will have datatypes, and the `nilled( )` function will always return `false`.

Defined in

XQuery 1.0 and XPath 2.0 Functions and Operators section 2, "Accessors."

Example

Here is a very short XML document that we'll use to demonstrate the `nilled( )` function:

```
<?xml version="1.0" encoding="utf-8"?>
<!-- person.xml -->
<person
  xmlns="http://www.oreilly.com/xslt"
  xmlns:xsi="http://www.w3.org/2001/XMLSchema-instance"
   xsi:schemaLocation="http://www.oreilly.com/xslt person.xsd">

  <name>Doug Tidwell</name>
  <age>42</age>
  <birthday xsi:nil="true"/>
</person>
```

Notice that we've defined a schema, *person.xsd*. That schema says that the `<birthday>` element can be nilled:

```
<?xml version="1.0" encoding="UTF-8"?>
<!-- person.xsd -->
<xs:schema
  xmlns="http://www.oreilly.com/xslt"
  targetNamespace="http://www.oreilly.com/xslt"
  xmlns:xs="http://www.w3.org/2001/XMLSchema">

  <xs:element name="person">
    <xs:complexType>
      <xs:sequence>
        <xs:element ref="name"/>
        <xs:element ref="age"/>
        <xs:element ref="birthday"/>
      </xs:sequence>
    </xs:complexType>
  </xs:element>

  <xs:element name="name" type="xs:string"/>
  <xs:element name="age" type="xs:positiveInteger"/>
  <xs:element name="birthday" type="xs:date" nillable="true"/>

</xs:schema>
```

The XML document has specified that the `<birthday>` element is nil, and the schema specified that the element is nillable. We'll use this stylesheet to illustrate the `nilled()` function at work:

```
<?xml version="1.0"?>
<!-- nilled.xsl -->
<xsl:stylesheet version="2.0"
  xmlns:xsl="http://www.w3.org/1999/XSL/Transform"
  xmlns:po="http://www.oreilly.com/xslt">

  <xsl:output method="text"/>
  <xsl:import-schema namespace="http://www.oreilly.com/xslt"
    schema-location="person.xsd"/>

  <xsl:template match="/">
    <xsl:text>&#xA;A test of the nilled() function:&#xA;</xsl:text>

    <xsl:for-each select="//*">
      <xsl:text>&#xA;    Element &lt;</xsl:text>
```

```
        <xsl:value-of select="name()"/>
        <xsl:text>&gt; </xsl:text>
        <xsl:value-of select="if (nilled(.))
                              then '===>>> IS nilled!'
                              else 'is not nilled!'"/>
    </xsl:for-each>
  </xsl:template>

</xsl:stylesheet>
```

Here are the results:

```
A test of the nilled() function:

    Element <person> is not nilled!
    Element <name> is not nilled!
    Element <age> is not nilled!
    Element <birthday> ===>>> IS nilled!
```

[2.0] node-name()

Returns an expanded QName for nodes that can have names.

Syntax

```
xs:QName? node-name(node()?)
```

Input

A node.

Outputs

For nodes that are allowed to have names, returns the node name. For other kinds of nodes (comment nodes, for example), node-name( ) returns the empty sequence. If the argument to node-name( ) is the empty sequence, the function returns the empty sequence, as you'd expect.

Defined in

XQuery 1.0 and XPath 2.0 Functions and Operators section 2, "Accessors."

Example

We'll use this stylesheet to illustrate how the node-name( ) function works with different kinds of nodes:

```
<?xml version="1.0"?>
<!-- node-name.xsl -->
<xsl:stylesheet version="2.0"
  xmlns:xsl="http://www.w3.org/1999/XSL/Transform">

  <xsl:output method="text"/>

  <xsl:template match="/">
```

```
    <xsl:text>&#xA;Here's a test of the node-name() </xsl:text>
    <xsl:text>function:&#xA;</xsl:text>

    <xsl:apply-templates
      select="*|comment()|processing-instruction()|text()"/>
</xsl:template>

<xsl:template match="*">
  <xsl:text>&#xA;</xsl:text>
  <xsl:text>  Element node: node-name(.) = '</xsl:text>
  <xsl:value-of select="node-name(.)"/>
  <xsl:if test="prefix-from-QName(node-name(.))">
    <xsl:text>'&#xA;    Prefix: '</xsl:text>
    <xsl:value-of select="prefix-from-QName(node-name(.))"/>
  </xsl:if>
  <xsl:text>'&#xA;    Local name: '</xsl:text>
  <xsl:value-of select="local-name-from-QName(node-name(.))"/>
  <xsl:if test="namespace-uri-from-QName(node-name(.))">
    <xsl:text>'&#xA;    Namespace URI: '</xsl:text>
    <xsl:value-of select="namespace-uri-from-QName(node-name(.))"/>
  </xsl:if>
  <xsl:text>'&#xA;</xsl:text>

  <xsl:if test="count(@*)">
    <xsl:for-each select="@*">
      <xsl:text>    Attribute node: node-name(.) = '</xsl:text>
      <xsl:value-of select="node-name(.)"/>
      <xsl:text>'&#xA;</xsl:text>
    </xsl:for-each>
  </xsl:if>

  <xsl:for-each select="namespace::*">
    <xsl:call-template name="namespace-node"/>
  </xsl:for-each>

  <xsl:for-each
    select="*|comment()|processing-instruction()|text()">
    <xsl:apply-templates select="."/>
  </xsl:for-each>
</xsl:template>

<xsl:template match="comment()">
  <xsl:text>&#xA;</xsl:text>
  <xsl:text>  Comment node: node-name(.) = '</xsl:text>
  <xsl:value-of select="node-name(.)"/>
  <xsl:text>'&#xA;</xsl:text>
</xsl:template>

<xsl:template match="processing-instruction()">
  <xsl:text>&#xA;</xsl:text>
  <xsl:text>  Processing instruction node: </xsl:text>
  <xsl:text>node-name(.) = '</xsl:text>
  <xsl:value-of select="node-name(.)"/>
  <xsl:text>'&#xA;</xsl:text>
</xsl:template>
```

```
<xsl:template match="text()">
  <xsl:if test="string-length(normalize-space(.))">
    <xsl:text>  Text node: node-name(.) = '</xsl:text>
    <xsl:value-of select="node-name(.)"/>
    <xsl:text>'&#xA;</xsl:text>
  </xsl:if>
</xsl:template>

<xsl:template name="namespace-node">
  <xsl:if test="string(node-name(.)) != 'xml'">
    <xsl:text>  Namespace node: node-name(.) = '</xsl:text>
    <xsl:value-of select="node-name(.)"/>
    <xsl:text>'&#xA;</xsl:text>
  </xsl:if>
</xsl:template>

</xsl:stylesheet>
```

We'll test this stylesheet with a slightly modified version of our Shakespearean sonnet (we added a processing instruction at the top):

```
<?xml version="1.0"?>
<!-- sonnet-pi.xml -->
<?xml-stylesheet href="node-name.xsl" type="text/xsl"?>
<!-- This is a slightly modified version of our usual sonnet. -->
<sonnet type='Shakespearean'>
  <auth:author xmlns:auth="http://www.authors.com/">
    <last-name>Shakespeare</last-name>
    <first-name>William</first-name>
    <nationality>British</nationality>
    <year-of-birth>1564</year-of-birth>
    <year-of-death>1616</year-of-death>
  </auth:author>
  <!-- Is there an official title for this sonnet?  They're
       sometimes named after the first line.                -->
  <title>Sonnet 130</title>
  <lines>
    <line>My mistress' eyes are nothing like the sun,</line>
    <line>Coral is far more red than her lips red.</line>
    <line>If snow be white, why then her breasts are dun,</line>
    <line>If hairs be wires, black wires grow on her head.</line>
    <line>I have seen roses damasked, red and white,</line>
    <line>But no such roses see I in her cheeks.</line>
    <line>And in some perfumes is there more delight</line>
    <line>Than in the breath that from my mistress reeks.</line>
    <line>I love to hear her speak, yet well I know</line>
    <line>That music hath a far more pleasing sound.</line>
    <line>I grant I never saw a goddess go,</line>
    <line>My mistress when she walks, treads on the ground.</line>
    <line>And yet, by Heaven, I think my love as rare</line>
    <line>As any she belied with false compare.</line>
  </lines>
</sonnet>
```

Our example is a generic stylesheet that works with any XML document. For our sonnet, it generates this output:

```
Here's a test of the node-name() function:

  Comment node: node-name(.) = ''

  Processing instruction node: node-name(.) = 'xml-stylesheet'

  Comment node: node-name(.) = ''

  Element node: node-name(.) = 'sonnet'
    Local name: 'sonnet'
    Attribute node: node-name(.) = 'type'

  Element node: node-name(.) = 'auth:author'
    Prefix: 'auth'
    Local name: 'author'
    Namespace URI: 'http://www.authors.com/'
  Namespace node: node-name(.) = 'auth'

  Element node: node-name(.) = 'last-name'
    Local name: 'last-name'
  Namespace node: node-name(.) = 'auth'
  Text node: node-name(.) = ''

  Element node: node-name(.) = 'first-name'
    Local name: 'first-name'
  Namespace node: node-name(.) = 'auth'
  Text node: node-name(.) = ''

  ...

  Comment node: node-name(.) = ''

  Element node: node-name(.) = 'title'
    Local name: 'title'
  Text node: node-name(.) = ''

  Element node: node-name(.) = 'lines'
    Local name: 'lines'

  Element node: node-name(.) = 'line'
    Local name: 'line'
  Text node: node-name(.) = ''

  Element node: node-name(.) = 'line'
    Local name: 'line'
  Text node: node-name(.) = ''
  ...
```

Notice that element, attribute, processing instruction, and namespace nodes have names, whereas comment and text nodes don't. Also notice that the document has a processing instruction and a comment node that are outside the root element; those are available in the match="/" template.

The node-name( ) function returns an xs:QName. An xs:QName has three parts: the prefix, the local name, and the namespace URI. All elements have a local name, but as you can see from our results here, many elements do not have a prefix or namespace URI. XPath 2.0 provides several functions to work with xs:QNames. In this stylesheet, we use prefix-from-QName( ), local-name-from-QName( ), and namespace-uri-from-QName( ) to get the three parts.

Finally, the <?xml-stylesheet ... processing instruction defines the default stylesheet for processing this XML document. When you invoke an XSLT processor, it typically requires the name of an XML file and a stylesheet. The processor normally uses the stylesheet you specify and ignores the processing instruction. If you want the XSLT processor to use the default stylesheet, there is usually an option to do so. (With Saxon, the -a option does the trick.) Check your processor's documentation for details.

normalize-space()

Removes extra whitespace from its argument string.

Syntax

```
[1.0] string normalize-space(string?)
[2.0] xs:string normalize-space(xs:string?)
```

Inputs

An optional string. If the argument is omitted, the normalize-space( ) function uses the string value of the context node.

[2.0] If the argument is the empty sequence, normalize-space( ) returns a zero-length string.

Output

The argument string, with whitespace removed as follows:

- All leading whitespace is removed.
- All trailing whitespace is removed.
- Within the string, any sequence of whitespace characters is replaced with a single space.

If the string is all whitespace, a zero-length string is returned.

[2.0] In XSLT 2.0, passing the empty sequence to normalize-space( ) returns the empty sequence.

Defined in

[1.0] XPath section 4.2, "String Functions."

[2.0] XQuery 1.0 and XPath 2.0 Functions and Operators section 7.4, "Functions on String Values."

Example

Here is a short example that demonstrates how `normalize-space( )` works:

```
<?xml version="1.0"?>
<!-- normalize-space1.xsl -->
<xsl:stylesheet version="1.0"
  xmlns:xsl="http://www.w3.org/1999/XSL/Transform">

  <xsl:output method="text"/>

  <xsl:variable name="newline">
    <xsl:text>&#xA;</xsl:text>
  </xsl:variable>

  <xsl:variable name="testString">
    <xsl:text>                 This
is


a string
that had        &#x9;&#x9;    lots of

&#xA;&#xA;&#xA;
whitespace.

</xsl:text>
    </xsl:variable>

  <xsl:template match="/">
    <xsl:text>&#xA;Tests of the normalize-space() function:</xsl:text>

    <xsl:text>&#xA;&#xA;  normalize-space('      </xsl:text>
    <xsl:text>Hello,           World!')="</xsl:text>
    <xsl:value-of
      select="normalize-space('      Hello,           World!')"/>
    <xsl:text>"</xsl:text>
    <xsl:text>&#xA;  normalize-space($newline)="</xsl:text>
    <xsl:value-of select="normalize-space($newline)"/>
    <xsl:text>"&#xA;</xsl:text>
    <xsl:text>  normalize-space($testString)=&#xA;    "</xsl:text>
    <xsl:value-of select="normalize-space($testString)"/>
    <xsl:text>"</xsl:text>
  </xsl:template>

</xsl:stylesheet>
```

The stylesheet generates this output:

```
Tests of the normalize-space() function:

  normalize-space('      Hello,           World!')="Hello, World!"
  normalize-space($newline)=""
  normalize-space($testString)=
    "This is a string that had lots of whitespace."
```

In the first and third tests of `normalize-space( )`, the whitespace was removed as advertised, with the intermingled spaces, tabs (`&#x9;`) and newlines (`&#xA;`) inside the string replaced with a single space. In the second test, the variable has a value of `&#xA;`. This is a string containing only whitespace, so the space-normalized version of the string is a zero-length string.

Here's another stylesheet that tests the XSLT 2.0 behavior when calling `normalize-space( )` with the empty sequence as input:

```
<?xml version="1.0"?>
<!-- normalize-space2.xsl -->
<xsl:stylesheet version="2.0"
  xmlns:xsl="http://www.w3.org/1999/XSL/Transform">

  <xsl:output method="text"/>

  <xsl:template match="/">
    <xsl:text>&#xA;A test of the normalize-space() function:</xsl:text>

    <xsl:text>&#xA;&#xA;  normalize-space(())="</xsl:text>
    <xsl:value-of select="normalize-space(())"/>
    <xsl:text>"</xsl:text>
  </xsl:template>

</xsl:stylesheet>
```

The results are as exciting as you'd expect:

```
A test of the normalize-space() function:

  normalize-space(())=""
```

[2.0] normalize-unicode()

Given a string, this function returns that string with its characters converted to a particular Unicode normalization form.

Syntax

```
xs:string normalize-unicode(xs:string?)
xs:string normalize-unicode(xs:string?, $normalizationForm as xs:string)
```

Inputs

The string to be normalized. You can optionally specify a second string naming a normalization form. The Unicode normalization forms are `NFC`, `NFD`, `NFKC`, `NFKD`, and `FULLY-NORMALIZED`.

In general, the Unicode normalization forms deal with how combining characters are processed. As an example, the A-ring character (Å) can be a single character (`&#xC5;`) or an uppercase A (A) followed by a combining ring above character (`&#x30A;`). These two representations are semantically equivalent, but different at a character level. Unicode normalization converts the different representations to the same form so they can be compared.

All conforming processors must support the NFC format. They are also free to support any or all of the other formats defined by Unicode, and they can support their own formats if they want.

If you'd like to know more, see Unicode Standard Annex #15, Unicode Normalization Forms, available at *http://www.unicode.org/unicode/reports/tr15/*.

Outputs

The input string, with its characters converted to the appropriate Unicode normalization form. If the value of the first argument is the empty sequence, normalize-unicode( ) returns a zero-length string.

Defined in

XQuery 1.0 and XPath 2.0 Functions and Operators section 7.4, "Functions on String Values."

Example

Here is a very short example that compares the two character strings just mentioned:

```
<?xml version="1.0"?>
<!-- normalize-unicode.xsl -->
<xsl:stylesheet version="2.0"
  xmlns:xsl="http://www.w3.org/1999/XSL/Transform"
  xmlns:xs="http://www.w3.org/2001/XMLSchema">

  <xsl:output method="text"/>

  <xsl:template match="/">
    <xsl:text>&#xA;Here is a test of the normalize-</xsl:text>
    <xsl:text>unicode() function:&#xA;</xsl:text>

    <xsl:text>&#xA;  compare('&#xC5', </xsl:text>
    <xsl:text>'&#x41;&#x30A;') = </xsl:text>
    <xsl:value-of select="compare('&#xC5;', '&#x41;&#x30A;')"/>

    <xsl:text>&#xA;&#xA;  compare(normalize-unicode</xsl:text>
    <xsl:text>('&#xC5'),&#xA;          normalize-unicode(</xsl:text>
    <xsl:text>'&#x41;&#x30A;')) = </xsl:text>
    <xsl:value-of
      select="compare(normalize-unicode('&#xC5;'),
              normalize-unicode('&#x41;&#x30A;'))"/>
  </xsl:template>

</xsl:stylesheet>
```

Here are the results:

```
Here is a test of the normalize-unicode() function:

  compare('&#xC5', '&#x41;&#x30A;') = 1

  compare(normalize-unicode('&#xC5'),
          normalize-unicode('&#x41;&#x30A;')) = 0
```

In the first comparison, the two strings are not equal. In the second comparison, the Unicode normalized versions of the string are equal.

not()

Returns the negation of its argument. If the argument is not a boolean value already, it is converted to a boolean value using the rules described in the **boolean( )** function entry.

Syntax

```
[1.0] boolean not(boolean)
[2.0] xs:boolean not(item()*)
```

Inputs

A boolean value, or more commonly, an XPath expression that evaluates to a boolean value.

Output

false if the input parameter is **true**; **true** if the input parameter is **false**.

Defined in

[1.0] XPath section 4.3, "Boolean Functions."

[2.0] XQuery 1.0 and XPath 2.0 Functions and Operators section 9.3, "Functions on Boolean Values."

Example

To demonstrate the not( ) function, we'll use the same stylesheet and XML document we used for the **boolean( )** function. Here's our XML document:

```
<?xml version="1.0" encoding="utf-8"?>
<!-- chocolate.xml -->
<report month="8" year="2006">
  <title>Chocolate bar sales</title>
  <brand>
    <name>Lindt</name>
    <units>27408</units>
  </brand>
  <brand>
    <name>Callebaut</name>
    <units>8203</units>
  </brand>
  <brand>
    <name>Valrhona</name>
    <units>22101</units>
  </brand>
  <brand>
    <name>Perugina</name>
    <units>14336</units>
  </brand>
  <brand>
```

```
        <name>Ghirardelli</name>
        <units>19268</units>
      </brand>
    </report>
```

We'll process this document with the following stylesheet, which uses not( ) instead of boolean( ). The boolean( ) function converts its argument to a boolean value; the not( ) function implicitly uses boolean( ) to convert its argument to a boolean value, and then negates it.

```
<?xml version="1.0"?>
<!-- not.xsl -->
<xsl:stylesheet version="1.0"
  xmlns:xsl="http://www.w3.org/1999/XSL/Transform">

  <xsl:output method="text"/>

  <xsl:template match="/">
    <xsl:text>&#xA;Tests of the not() function:</xsl:text>

    <xsl:text>&#xA;&#xA;  not((true()) = </xsl:text>
    <xsl:value-of select="not(true())"/>

    <xsl:text>&#xA;  not(true) = </xsl:text>
    <xsl:value-of select="not(true)"/>

    <xsl:text>&#xA;  not('false') = </xsl:text>
    <xsl:value-of select="not('false')"/>

    <xsl:text>&#xA;  not('7') = </xsl:text>
    <xsl:value-of select="not('7')"/>

    <xsl:text>&#xA;  not(/report/brand/units[. > 20000]) = </xsl:text>
    <xsl:value-of select="not(/report/brand/units[. > 20000])"/>
  </xsl:template>

</xsl:stylesheet>
```

Here are the results:

```
Tests of the not() function:

  not((true()) = false
  not(true) = true
  not('false') = false
  not('7') = false
  not(/report/brand/units[. > 20000]) = false
```

As you'd expect, these results are the exact opposite of the results we got when we tested the boolean( ) function. For the first test, the argument is a call to the true( ) function, which always returns true. The negation of true is false. For the second test, we're asking for all the <true> elements in the current context; there are no <true> elements, so this is false and its negation is true. The argument of the third test is a string whose length is greater than zero, so not( ) returns false (a nonzero-length string is true). Similarly, the argument of the fourth test is a string whose length is greater than zero, so not( ) returns false here as well.

The final example uses an XPath statement to select all of the `<units>` elements in our sales report that have a numeric value greater than 20000. Because this selects at least one node, the expression is `true` and `not( )` returns `false`. This works in XSLT 1.0 because it generates a node-set with at least one member, and it works in XSLT 2.0 because it creates a sequence whose first item is a node. If we change the expression to look for sales figures greater than 30000, `not( )` would return `true`.

number()

Converts its argument to a number.

Syntax

```
[1.0] number number(object?)
[2.0] xs:double number()
[2.0] xs:double number(xs:anyAtomicType)
```

Inputs

[1.0] An object.

[2.0] An `xs:anyAtomicType` value.

Output

A number. If no argument is passed to the `number` function, the context item is used. The specific rules for converting the argument to a number are different for XSLT 1.0 and 2.0.

[1.0] Here are the rules for XSLT 1.0:

- If the argument is a boolean value, the value `true` is converted to the number 1; the value `false` is converted to the number 0.

- If the argument is a node-set, the node-set is converted to a string as if it were passed to the `string( )` function, and then that string is converted to a number like any other string. (Remember that the `string( )` function returns the string value of the first node in the node-set.)

- If the argument is a string, it is converted as follows:

  — If the string consists of optional whitespace, followed by an optional minus sign (-), followed by a number, followed by whitespace, it is converted to the floating-point value nearest to the mathematical value represented by the string. (The IEEE 754 standard defines a `round-to-nearest` rule; see the standard for more information.)

  — Any other string is converted to the value `NaN` (not a number).

- XSLT 1.0 processors are allowed to support other datatypes. If the argument is any other type, it is converted to a number in a way that depends on that type. See the documentation for your XSLT processor to find out what other types are supported and how they are converted to numbers.

[2.0] Because XSLT 2.0 supports more datatypes, the rules are more complicated:

- If the argument is already an `xs:double`, it is returned unchanged.
- If the argument is an `xs:boolean`, `true` is returned as `1.0E0` and `false` is returned as `0.0E0`.
- If the argument an `xs:float`, `xs:decimal`, or `xs:integer`, it is converted to an `xs:double` and returned. If the argument is an `xs:float` and is one of the `xs:float` values `INF`, `-INF`, `NaN`, positive zero, or negative zero, it is returned as the `xs:double` version of those values.
- If the argument is the empty sequence, `NaN` (not a number) is returned.
- If the argument (or the context node, if there isn't an argument) can't be converted to an `xs:double`, `NaN` is returned. (The `xs:date`, `xs:dateTime`, and `xs:time` datatypes can't be converted to numbers, for example.)

Defined in

[1.0] XPath section 4.4, "Number Functions."

[2.0] XQuery 1.0 and XPath 2.0 Functions and Operators section 14, "Functions and Operators on Nodes."

Example

We'll use our document of chocolate bar sales to illustrate the `number()` function:

```
<?xml version="1.0" encoding="utf-8"?>
<!-- chocolate.xml -->
<report month="8" year="2006">
  <title>Chocolate bar sales</title>
  <brand>
    <name>Lindt</name>
    <units>27408</units>
  </brand>
  <brand>
    <name>Callebaut</name>
    <units>8203</units>
  </brand>
  <brand>
    <name>Valrhona</name>
    <units>22101</units>
  </brand>
  <brand>
    <name>Perugina</name>
    <units>14336</units>
  </brand>
  <brand>
    <name>Ghirardelli</name>
    <units>19268</units>
  </brand>
</report>
```

We'll test the `number()` function with a variety of arguments:

```
<?xml version="1.0"?>
<!-- number.xsl -->
<xsl:stylesheet version="1.0"
  xmlns:xsl="http://www.w3.org/1999/XSL/Transform">

  <xsl:output method="text"/>

  <xsl:template match="/">
    <xsl:text>&#xA;Tests of the number() function:</xsl:text>

    <xsl:text>&#xA;&#xA;  number(true()) = </xsl:text>
    <xsl:value-of select="number(true())"/>
    <xsl:text>&#xA;&#xA;  number(false()) = </xsl:text>
    <xsl:value-of select="number(false())"/>
    <xsl:text>&#xA;&#xA;  number(/report/brand[2]/units) = </xsl:text>
    <xsl:value-of select="number(/report/brand[2]/units)"/>
    <xsl:text>&#xA;&#xA;  number(//units) = </xsl:text>
    <xsl:value-of select="number(//units)"/>
    <xsl:text>&#xA;&#xA;  number(/report/title) = </xsl:text>
    <xsl:value-of select="number(/report/title)"/>
  </xsl:template>

</xsl:stylesheet>
```

The output of our stylesheet looks like this:

```
Tests of the number() function:

  number(true()) = 1

  number(false()) = 0

  number(/report/brand[2]/units) = 8203

  number(//units) = 27408

  number(/report/title) = NaN
```

This is an XSLT 1.0 stylesheet, so the expression `number(//units)` works in an XSLT 2.0 processor running in XSLT 1.0 compatibility mode. In XSLT 2.0, the processor raises an error if we pass more than one node to the `number( )` function. Here's a slightly different stylesheet designed for XSLT 2.0:

```
<?xml version="1.0"?>
<!-- number2.xsl -->
<xsl:stylesheet version="2.0"
  xmlns:xsl="http://www.w3.org/1999/XSL/Transform">

  <xsl:output method="text"/>

  <xsl:template match="/">
    <xsl:text>&#xA;Tests of the number() function:</xsl:text>

    <xsl:text>&#xA;&#xA;  number(true()) = </xsl:text>
    <xsl:value-of select="number(true())"/>
    <xsl:text>&#xA;&#xA;  number(false()) = </xsl:text>
```

```
<xsl:value-of select="number(false())"/>
<xsl:text>&#xA;&#xA;  number(/report/brand[2]/units) = </xsl:text>
<xsl:value-of select="number(/report/brand[2]/units)"/>
<xsl:text>&#xA;&#xA;  number((//units)[1]) = </xsl:text>
<xsl:value-of select="number((//units)[1])"/>
<xsl:text>&#xA;&#xA;  number(/report/title) = </xsl:text>
<xsl:value-of select="number(/report/title)"/>
<xsl:text>&#xA;&#xA;  number(current-date()) = </xsl:text>
<xsl:value-of select="number(current-date())"/>
<xsl:text>&#xA;&#xA;  number(current-time()) = </xsl:text>
<xsl:value-of select="number(current-time())"/>
    </xsl:template>

  </xsl:stylesheet>
```

Notice that we had to change the number(//units) call to number((//units)[1]). This retrieves all of the <units> elements at all levels of the document and selects the first one. At any rate, here are the results:

```
Tests of the number() function:

  number(true()) = 1

  number(false()) = 0

  number(/report/brand[2]/units) = 8203

  number((//units)[1]) = 27408

  number(/report/title) = NaN

  number(current-date()) = NaN

  number(current-time()) = NaN
```

Notice that the xs:date and xs:time values are returned as NaN.

[2.0] one-or-more()

Raises an error unless its argument is a sequence containing one or more items. This function can be used as a form of type checking. For example, we might have an <addressbook> element that's required to have at least one <address> element. We could call one-or-more(address) with an <addressbook> element as the current item; if at least one <address> element isn't present, the XSLT processor would raise an error.

Syntax

```
item()+ one-or-more(item()*)
```

Inputs

A sequence. If that sequence doesn't have at least one item, one-or-more( ) raises an error.

Outputs

Assuming the input sequence has at least one item, one-or-more( ) returns that sequence. If the input sequence is the empty sequence, one-or-more( ) raises an error.

Defined in

XQuery 1.0 and XPath 2.0 Functions and Operators section 15.2, "Functions That Test the Cardinality of Sequences." More details about this function can be found in XQuery 1.0 and XPath 2.0 Formal Semantics section 7.2, "Standard Functions with Specific Static Typing Rules."

Example

Here's a simple stylesheet that illustrates the one-or-more( ) function:

```
<?xml version="1.0"?>
<!-- one-or-more.xsl -->
<xsl:stylesheet version="2.0"
  xmlns:xsl="http://www.w3.org/1999/XSL/Transform"
  xmlns:xs="http://www.w3.org/2001/XMLSchema">

  <xsl:output method="text"/>

  <xsl:template match="/">

    <xsl:variable name="testSequence" as="item()*">
      <xsl:sequence
        select="(3, 4, 5, current-date(), current-time(), 8, 'blue',
                'red', xs:float(3.14), 42, xs:date('1995-04-21'))"/>
    </xsl:variable>

    <xsl:text>&#xA;Here is a test of the one-or-more() </xsl:text>
    <xsl:text>function:&#xA;</xsl:text>

    <xsl:text>&#xA;  Our sequence is:&#xA;&#xA;    </xsl:text>
    <xsl:value-of select="$testSequence" separator="&#xA;    "/>

    <xsl:if test="count(one-or-more($testSequence))">
      <xsl:text>&#xA;&#xA;  Our test sequence has one or </xsl:text>
      <xsl:text>more items!</xsl:text>
    </xsl:if>

  </xsl:template>

</xsl:stylesheet>
```

Here are the results of our stylesheet:

```
Here is a test of the one-or-more() function:

  Our sequence is:

    3
    4
    5
```

```
2006-07-22-04:00
23:04:38.183-04:00
8
blue
red
3.14
42
1995-04-21
```

```
Our test sequence has one or more items!
```

Notice that we use the count( ) function in the test attribute of the <xsl:if> element. At first glance, it seems like this would be a reasonable way to write the <xsl:if> element:

```
<xsl:if test="one-or-more($testSequence)">  <!-- doesn't work! -->
```

The one-or-more( ) function returns the input sequence, assuming it has at least one value. The XSLT processor attempts to convert the contents of the test attribute to a boolean. If the sequence returned by one-or-more( ) is a single item *or* its first item is a node, this works. However, our example sequence would cause the XSLT processor to raise an error. A sequence of more than one item whose first item is an atom can't be converted to a boolean value. That's why we have to write the <xsl:if> element like this:

```
<xsl:if test="count(one-or-more($testSequence))"/>
```

The XSLT processor converts the numeric value returned by count( ) into a boolean value. That value will always be at least 1, so the test attribute evaluates to true anytime the one-or-more( ) function works.

See Also

The descriptions of the [2.0] exactly-one( ) and [2.0] zero-or-one( ) functions.

---

position()

Returns the position of the context item within the sequence of items currently being processed.

Syntax

```
[1.0] number position()
[2.0] xs:integer position()
```

Inputs

None.

Output

A number equal to the position of the current node in the sequence of items currently being processed. For example, if the current node is the fifth <li> being processed, position( ) returns 5.

Defined in

[1.0] XPath section 4.1, "Node Set Functions."

[2.0] XQuery 1.0 and XPath 2.0 Functions and Operators section 16, "Context Functions."

Examples

This example uses the `position( )` function to create a `style` attribute for the cells of an HTML table. The background colors cycle through the options `black`, `gray`, and `white`, while the foreground colors cycle through `white`, `white`, and `black`. Here's the XML document we'll use:

```
<?xml version="1.0"?>
<!-- albums.xml -->
<list xml:lang="en">
  <title>Albums I've bought recently:</title>
  <listitem>The Sacred Art of Dub</listitem>
  <listitem>Only the Poor Man Feel It</listitem>
  <listitem>Excitable Boy</listitem>
  <listitem xml:lang="sw">Aki Special</listitem>
  <listitem xml:lang="en-gb">Combat Rock</listitem>
  <listitem xml:lang="zu">Talking Timbuktu</listitem>
  <listitem xml:lang="jz">The Birth of the Cool</listitem>
</list>
```

We'll use this stylesheet to generate our HTML document:

```
<?xml version="1.0"?>
<!-- position.xsl -->
<xsl:stylesheet version="1.0"
  xmlns:xsl="http://www.w3.org/1999/XSL/Transform">

  <xsl:output method="html"/>

  <xsl:template match="/">
    <html>
      <head>
        <title>
          <xsl:value-of select="/list/title"/>
        </title>
      </head>
      <body style="font-family: sans-serif;">
        <h1>
          <xsl:value-of select="/list/title"/>
        </h1>
        <table border="1" cellpadding="5">
          <xsl:for-each select="/list/listitem">
            <xsl:variable name="style">
              <xsl:text>color: </xsl:text>
              <xsl:choose>
                <xsl:when test="position() mod 3 = 1">white</xsl:when>
                <xsl:when test="position() mod 3 = 2">white</xsl:when>
                <xsl:otherwise>black</xsl:otherwise>
              </xsl:choose>
              <xsl:text>; background: </xsl:text>
              <xsl:choose>
                <xsl:when test="position() mod 3 = 1">black</xsl:when>
```

```
        <xsl:when test="position() mod 3 = 2">gray</xsl:when>
        <xsl:otherwise>white</xsl:otherwise>
      </xsl:choose>
      <xsl:text>;</xsl:text>
    </xsl:variable>
    <tr style="{$style}">
      <td>
        <b><xsl:value-of select="."/></b>
      </td>
    </tr>
  </xsl:for-each>
</table>
      </body>
    </html>
  </xsl:template>

</xsl:stylesheet>
```

We use the **position( )** function to cycle through the different background and foreground colors. Our stylesheet generates the following results:

```
<html>
  <head>
    <meta http-equiv="Content-Type" content="text/html; charset=UTF-8">
    <title>Albums I've bought recently:</title>
  </head>
  <body style="font-family: sans-serif;">
    <h1>Albums I've bought recently:</h1>
    <table border="1" cellpadding="5">
      <tr style="color: white; background: black;">
        <td><b>The Sacred Art of Dub</b></td>
      </tr>
      <tr style="color: white; background: gray;">
        <td><b>Only the Poor Man Feel It</b></td>
      </tr>
      <tr style="color: black; background: white;">
        <td><b>Excitable Boy</b></td>
      </tr>
      <tr style="color: white; background: black;">
        <td><b>Aki Special</b></td>
      </tr>
      <tr style="color: white; background: gray;">
        <td><b>Combat Rock</b></td>
      </tr>
      <tr style="color: black; background: white;">
        <td><b>Talking Timbuktu</b></td>
      </tr>
      <tr style="color: white; background: black;">
        <td><b>The Birth of the Cool</b></td>
      </tr>
    </table>
  </body>
</html>
```

When rendered, the HTML file looks like Figure C-5.

Figure C-5. HTML file displaying items with different background colors

[2.0] prefix-from-QName()

Given an `xs:QName` value, returns its namespace prefix.

Syntax

```
xs:NCName? prefix-from-QName(xs:QName?)
```

Input

An `xs:QName` value.

Output

An `xs:NCName` ("noncolonized" name) representing the prefix from the `QName`. If the `QName` doesn't have a prefix or the `xs:QName` argument is the empty sequence, `prefix-from-QName( )` returns the empty sequence.

Defined in

XQuery 1.0 and XPath 2.0 Functions and Operators section 11.2, "Operators and Functions Related to QNames."

Example

As usual, when we're working with namespaces, we'll use our Shakespearean sonnet as our XML input document:

```
<?xml version="1.0"?>
<!-- sonnet.xml -->
```

```
<sonnet type='Shakespearean'>
  <auth:author xmlns:auth="http://www.authors.com/">
    <last-name>Shakespeare</last-name>
    <first-name>William</first-name>
    <nationality>British</nationality>
    <year-of-birth>1564</year-of-birth>
    <year-of-death>1616</year-of-death>
  </auth:author>
  <!-- Is there an official title for this sonnet?  They're
       sometimes named after the first line.                -->
  <title>Sonnet 130</title>
  <lines>
    <line>My mistress' eyes are nothing like the sun,</line>
    <line>Coral is far more red than her lips red.</line>
    <line>If snow be white, why then her breasts are dun,</line>
    <line>If hairs be wires, black wires grow on her head.</line>
    <line>I have seen roses damasked, red and white,</line>
    <line>But no such roses see I in her cheeks.</line>
    <line>And in some perfumes is there more delight</line>
    <line>Than in the breath that from my mistress reeks.</line>
    <line>I love to hear her speak, yet well I know</line>
    <line>That music hath a far more pleasing sound.</line>
    <line>I grant I never saw a goddess go,</line>
    <line>My mistress when she walks, treads on the ground.</line>
    <line>And yet, by Heaven, I think my love as rare</line>
    <line>As any she belied with false compare.</line>
  </lines>
</sonnet>
```

Here is our stylesheet:

```
<?xml version="1.0"?>
<!-- prefix-from-qname.xsl -->
<xsl:stylesheet version="2.0"
  xmlns:xsl="http://www.w3.org/1999/XSL/Transform"
  xmlns:xs="http://www.w3.org/2001/XMLSchema">

  <xsl:output method="text"/>

  <xsl:template match="/">
    <xsl:text>&#xA;Tests of the prefix-from-QName() </xsl:text>
    <xsl:text>function:&#xA;</xsl:text>

    <xsl:variable name="testQName1" as="xs:QName"
      select="resolve-QName('auth:last-name',
              /sonnet/*:author/last-name)"/>
    <xsl:text>&#xA;  testQName1 = resolve-QName('auth:last-name', </xsl:text>
    <xsl:text>/sonnet/*:author/last-name)</xsl:text>
    <xsl:text>&#xA;   prefix-from-QName($testQName1) = "</xsl:text>
    <xsl:value-of select="prefix-from-QName($testQName1)"/>
    <xsl:text>"</xsl:text>

    <xsl:variable name="testQName2" as="xs:QName"
      select="resolve-QName('something-else', /sonnet)"/>
    <xsl:text>&#xA;&#xA;  testQName2 = resolve-QName('</xsl:text>
    <xsl:text>something-else', /sonnet)</xsl:text>
```

```
<xsl:text>&#xA;  prefix-from-QName($testQName2) = "</xsl:text>
<xsl:value-of select="prefix-from-QName($testQName2)"/>
<xsl:text>"</xsl:text>

<xsl:variable name="testQName3" as="xs:QName"
  select="QName('http://www.authors.com/', 'pfx:writer')"/>
<xsl:text>&#xA;&#xA;  testQName3 = QName('http://www.</xsl:text>
<xsl:text>authors.com/', 'pfx:writer')&#xA;</xsl:text>
<xsl:text>  prefix-from-QName($testQName3) = "</xsl:text>
<xsl:value-of select="prefix-from-QName($testQName3)"/>
<xsl:text>"</xsl:text>

</xsl:template>

</xsl:stylesheet>
```

And here are our results:

```
Tests of the prefix-from-QName() function:

  testQName1 = resolve-QName('auth:last-name', /sonnet/*:author/last-name)
  prefix-from-QName($testQName1) = "auth"

  testQName2 = resolve-QName('something-else', /sonnet)
  prefix-from-QName($testQName2) = ""

  testQName3 = QName('http://www.authors.com/', 'pfx:writer')
  prefix-from-QName($testQName3) = "pfx"
```

The argument to the `prefix-from-QName()` function *must* be an `xs:QName`. In this stylesheet, we create `QName`s with the `resolve-QName()` function and the `QName()` constructor function.

For the first test, we create a `QName` with a prefixed element name of `auth:last-name`. The context for resolving the `QName` (the second argument to `resolve-QName()`) is the `<last-name>` element in our sonnet. The `resolve-QName()` function returns a `QName` with a local name of `last-name`, a namespace prefix of `auth`, and a namespace URI of `http://www.authors.com/`. If there are no nodes that match the XPath expression `/sonnet/*:author/last-name`, the call to `resolve-QName()` fails. The call also fails if the `auth` prefix is not defined for the `<last-name>` element.

The second test of `prefix-from-QName()` uses an unprefixed element name in the call to `resolve-QName()`. The XML document doesn't have a default namespace, so our `QName` has an empty string for its namespace prefix and namespace URI.

For the final test, we use the `QName()` constructor function to create a `QName` from scratch. The two arguments to the constructor function are the namespace URI and an element name—in this case, a prefixed element name. The resulting `QName` has a local name of `writer`, a namespace prefix of `pfx`, and a namespace URI of `http://www.authors.com/`.

[2.0] QName()

This is a constructor function that allows you to create a new `QName`.

Syntax

```
xs:QName QName($paramURI as xs:string?, $paramQName as xs:string)
```

Inputs

Two `xs:string`s. The first string is the namespace URI of the `QName`, and the second is the string value of the `QName`. If the second string contains a colon (`:`), the substring before the colon is the namespace prefix of the `QName` and the substring after the colon is the local name. For example, if the second string is `auth:author`, the namespace prefix is `auth` and the local name is `author`.

The namespace URI string can be a zero-length string or the empty sequence, meaning this `QName` does not belong to a namespace. In this case, the XSLT processor raises an error if the second string contains a colon. (In other words, you can't have a namespace prefix if you don't have a namespace URI.)

Output

An `xs:QName` value.

Defined in

XQuery 1.0 and XPath 2.0 Functions and Operators section 11.1, "Additional Constructor Functions for QNames."

Example

Here is a stylesheet that creates several `QName`s, and then uses various functions to print the details of those `QName`s:

```
<?xml version="1.0"?>
<!-- qname.xsl -->
<xsl:stylesheet version="2.0"
  xmlns:xsl="http://www.w3.org/1999/XSL/Transform"
  xmlns:xs="http://www.w3.org/2001/XMLSchema">

  <xsl:output method="text"/>

  <xsl:template match="/">
    <xsl:text>&#xA;Tests of the QName() constructor function:&#xA;</xsl:text>

    <xsl:variable name="testQName1" as="xs:QName"
      select="QName('http://www.authors.com', 'auth:author')"/>

    <xsl:text>&#xA;  testQName1 = QName('http://www.</xsl:text>
    <xsl:text>authors.com', 'auth:author')</xsl:text>
    <xsl:text>&#xA;  prefix-from-QName</xsl:text>
    <xsl:text>($testQName1) = "</xsl:text>
    <xsl:value-of select="prefix-from-QName($testQName1)"/>
    <xsl:text>"&#xA;  local-name-from-QName($testQName1) = "</xsl:text>
    <xsl:value-of select="local-name-from-QName($testQName1)"/>
    <xsl:text>"&#xA;  namespace-uri-from-QName($testQName1) = "</xsl:text>
    <xsl:value-of select="namespace-uri-from-QName($testQName1)"/>
    <xsl:text>"</xsl:text>
```

```
<xsl:variable name="testQName2" as="xs:QName"
  select="QName('', 'sonnet')"/>

<xsl:text>&#xA;&#xA;  testQName2 = QName('', 'sonnet')</xsl:text>
<xsl:text>&#xA;  prefix-from-QName</xsl:text>
<xsl:text>($testQName2) = "</xsl:text>
<xsl:value-of select="prefix-from-QName($testQName2)"/>
<xsl:text>"&#xA;  local-name-from-QName($testQName2) = "</xsl:text>
<xsl:value-of select="local-name-from-QName($testQName2)"/>
<xsl:text>"&#xA;  namespace-uri-from-QName($testQName2) = "</xsl:text>
<xsl:value-of select="namespace-uri-from-QName($testQName2)"/>
<xsl:text>"</xsl:text>

<xsl:variable name="testQName3" as="xs:QName"
  select="QName('http://www.authors.com/', 'writer')"/>

<xsl:text>&#xA;&#xA;  testQName3 = QName('http://www.</xsl:text>
<xsl:text>authors.com/', 'writer')</xsl:text>
<xsl:text>&#xA;  prefix-from-QName</xsl:text>
<xsl:text>($testQName3) = "</xsl:text>
<xsl:value-of select="prefix-from-QName($testQName3)"/>
<xsl:text>"&#xA;  local-name-from-QName($testQName3) = "</xsl:text>
<xsl:value-of select="local-name-from-QName($testQName3)"/>
<xsl:text>"&#xA;  namespace-uri-from-QName($testQName3) = "</xsl:text>
<xsl:value-of select="namespace-uri-from-QName($testQName3)"/>
<xsl:text>"</xsl:text>

</xsl:template>

</xsl:stylesheet>
```

Here are the results:

```
Tests of the QName() constructor function:

    testQName1 = QName('http://www.authors.com', 'auth:author')
    prefix-from-QName($testQName1) = "auth"
    local-name-from-QName($testQName1) = "author"
    namespace-uri-from-QName($testQName1) = "http://www.authors.com"

    testQName2 = QName('', 'sonnet')
    prefix-from-QName($testQName2) = ""
    local-name-from-QName($testQName2) = "sonnet"
    namespace-uri-from-QName($testQName2) = ""

    testQName3 = QName('http://www.authors.com/', 'writer')
    prefix-from-QName($testQName3) = ""
    local-name-from-QName($testQName3) = "writer"
    namespace-uri-from-QName($testQName3) = "http://www.authors.com/"
```

Our stylesheet creates three QNames, and then retrieves the namespace prefix, local name, and namespace URI for each one. For the first test, we create a QName with a prefixed element name of auth:last-name. The second test has an empty namespace and an unprefixed element name, and the third test has a namespace URI but no element prefix.

[2.0] regex-group()

When using a regular expression to process a string, this function returns portions of the analyzed string based on groups in the regular expression. This function is used inside the `<xsl:matching-substring>` element only.

Syntax

```
xs:string regex-group(xs:integer)
```

Inputs

An `xs:integer` representing a section of the regular expression.

Output

The portion of the analyzed string that matches the specified portion of the regular expression. A portion of a regular expression must be in parentheses to be considered a group.

Here are some notes about how `regex-group( )` works:

- Calling `regex-group(0)` returns the entire matching substring, including characters that don't belong to any group.

- If the requested portion of the regular expression exists, but doesn't match anything in the analyzed string, `regex-group( )` returns a zero-length string. (In other words, the group is optional in the regular expression.)

- If the requested portion of the regular expression exists, but it matches the zero-length portion of the analyzed string, `regex-group( )` returns a zero-length string.

- If the requested portion of the regular expression doesn't exist (we call `regex-group(4)` when the regular expression has only three groups, for example), `regex-group( )` returns a zero-length string.

- Finally, `regex-group( )` returns a zero-length string if the group number is a negative integer.

Defined in

XSLT 2.0 section 15, "Regular Expressions."

Example

We'll use a simplified version of one of the stylesheets we used to demonstrate the `<xsl:analyze-string>` element:

```
<?xml version="1.0" encoding="utf-8"?>
<!-- regex-group.xsl -->
<xsl:stylesheet version="2.0"
  xmlns:xsl="http://www.w3.org/1999/XSL/Transform">

  <xsl:output method="text"/>

  <xsl:template match="/">
```

```
<xsl:text>Formatted phone numbers:&#xA;</xsl:text>
<xsl:for-each select="phonelist/phonenumber">
  <xsl:analyze-string select="."
    regex="([0-9]{{3}})-([0-9]{{3}})-([0-9]{{4}})">
    <xsl:matching-substring>
      <xsl:text>&#xA;  The data </xsl:text>
      <xsl:value-of select="regex-group(0)"/>
      <xsl:text> matches.  </xsl:text>
      <xsl:text>&#xA;     The formatted phone number is: +1 (</xsl:text>
      <xsl:value-of select="regex-group(1)"/>
      <xsl:text>) </xsl:text>
      <xsl:value-of select="regex-group(2)"/>
      <xsl:text>-</xsl:text>
      <xsl:value-of select="regex-group(3)"/>
    </xsl:matching-substring>
  </xsl:analyze-string>
</xsl:for-each>
</xsl:template>

</xsl:stylesheet>
```

We're using a regular expression to analyze telephone numbers. The regular expression ([0-9]{{3}})-([0-9]{{3}})-([0-9]{{4}}) contains three groups: ([0-9]{{3}}), ([0-9]{{3}}), and ([0-9]{{4}}). The two dashes between the groups are not in parentheses, so they are not part of any group.

We'll use this stylesheet to process this very simple document:

```
<?xml version="1.0" encoding="utf-8"?>
<!-- simple-phonelist.xml -->
<phonelist>
  <phonenumber>Doug's number is 919-555-1212</phonenumber>
  <phonenumber>617-555-1212</phonenumber>
</phonelist>
```

And here are the results:

```
Formatted phone numbers:

  The data 919-555-1212 matches.
     The formatted phone number is: +1 (919) 555-1212
  The data 617-555-1212 matches.
     The formatted phone number is: +1 (617) 555-1212
```

For each matching string, regex-group(0) returns the entire matching string, regex-group(1) returns the area code (we're using the Canadian and U.S. phone number format here), regex-group(2) returns the exchange and regex-group(3) returns the last four digits of the phone number. Notice that the output of regex-group(0) is the entire matching string, including the two dashes that don't belong to any matching group. In the first line of the XML source file, regex-group(0) *doesn't* return the characters outside the matching string, just the part of the string that matches the regular expression.

Finally, if our regular expression allows a two- or three-letter state or province abbreviation at the end of the phone number (we used the regular expression ([0-9]{{3}})-([0-9]{{3}})-([0-9]{{4}})([A-Z]{{2,3}})?), regex-group(4) would return a zero-length string for both

<phonenumber> elements in our sample document. Although the match technically exists, it doesn't contain any data. In this case, we could use `string-length(regex-group(4))` to see whether the match contains any data.

See Also

The definition of the [2.0] `<xsl:analyze-string>` element.

[2.0] remove()

Given a sequence and a position, removes the item at the requested position.

Syntax

```
item()* remove($target as item()*, $position as xs:integer)
```

Inputs

A sequence and an `xs:integer`.

Outputs

This function returns the input sequence with the item at the requested position removed. If the position is less than **1** or greater than the length of the sequence, the sequence is returned unchanged. Finally, if the sequence is the empty sequence, the empty sequence is returned.

Defined in

XQuery 1.0 and XPath 2.0 Functions and Operators section 15.1, "General Functions and Operators on Sequences."

Example

To illustrate the **remove( )** function, we'll look at three short stylesheets. Each stylesheet uses a different type of sequence. The first stylesheet uses a singleton sequence:

```
<?xml version="1.0"?>
<!-- remove1.xsl -->
<xsl:stylesheet version="2.0"
  xmlns:xsl="http://www.w3.org/1999/XSL/Transform"
  xmlns:xs="http://www.w3.org/2001/XMLSchema">

<xsl:output method="text"/>

<xsl:template match="/">

  <xsl:variable name="singleton" as="item()*">
    <xsl:sequence select="(3)"/>
  </xsl:variable>

  <xsl:text>&#xA;Here is a test of the remove() </xsl:text>
  <xsl:text>function:&#xA;</xsl:text>

  <xsl:text>&#xA;  Our sequence ($singleton) </xsl:text>
```

```
<xsl:text>is:&#xA;        </xsl:text>
<xsl:value-of select="$singleton" separator="&#xA;      "/>
<xsl:text>&#xA;&#xA;    remove($singleton, 0) = </xsl:text>
<xsl:value-of select="remove($singleton, 0)"
   separator="&#xA;      "/>
<xsl:text>&#xA;&#xA;    remove($singleton, 7) = </xsl:text>
<xsl:value-of select="remove($singleton, 7)"
   eparator="&#xA;      "/>
<xsl:text>&#xA;&#xA;    remove($singleton, 1) = </xsl:text>
<xsl:value-of select="remove($singleton, 1)"
   separator="&#xA;      "/>
<xsl:text>&#xA;&#xA;    empty(remove($singleton, 1)) = </xsl:text>
<xsl:value-of select="empty(remove($singleton, 1))"/>

   </xsl:template>

</xsl:stylesheet>
```

Here are the results:

```
Here is a test of the remove() function:

Our sequence ($singleton) is:
    3

remove($singleton, 0) = 3

remove($singleton, 7) = 3

remove($singleton, 1) =

empty(remove($singleton, 1)) = true
```

In our results, removing an item at positions 0 and 7 doesn't change the sequence at all. Removing the first item from a singleton returns the empty sequence, as you would expect. As a final test, we use the empty( ) function to show that removing one item from a singleton does, in fact, return the empty sequence.

Our next test of the remove( ) function uses a longer sequence that contains a variety of datatypes:

```
<?xml version="1.0"?>
<!-- remove2.xsl -->
<xsl:stylesheet version="2.0"
  xmlns:xsl="http://www.w3.org/1999/XSL/Transform"
  xmlns:xs="http://www.w3.org/2001/XMLSchema">

<xsl:output method="text"/>

<xsl:template match="/">

  <xsl:variable name="longSequence" as="item()*">
    <xsl:sequence
      select="(3, 4, 5, current-date(), current-time(), 8, 'blue',
              'red', xs:float(3.14), 42, xs:date('1995-04-21'))"/>
  </xsl:variable>
```

```
<xsl:text>&#xA;Here's another test of the remove() </xsl:text>
<xsl:text>function:&#xA;</xsl:text>

<xsl:text>&#xA;  Our sequence ($longSequence) </xsl:text>
<xsl:text>is:&#xA;        </xsl:text>
<xsl:value-of select="$longSequence" separator="&#xA;        "/>
<xsl:text>&#xA;&#xA;    Test 1. remove($longSequence, 1) </xsl:text>
<xsl:text>= &#xA;        </xsl:text>
<xsl:value-of select="remove($longSequence, 1)"
   separator="&#xA;        "/>
<xsl:text>&#xA;&#xA;    Test 2. remove($longSequence, 1) =</xsl:text>
<xsl:text>&#xA;         [We're running this test again to show the </xsl:text>
<xsl:text>variable didn't change]&#xA;        </xsl:text>
<xsl:value-of select="remove($longSequence, 1)"
   separator="&#xA;        "/>
<xsl:text>&#xA;&#xA;    Test 3. remove(remove($longSequence, 7), 1) </xsl:text>
<xsl:text>= &#xA;        </xsl:text>
<xsl:value-of select="remove(remove($longSequence, 7), 1)"
   separator="&#xA;        "/>

<xsl:text>&#xA;&#xA;    Creating a new variable based on </xsl:text>
<xsl:text>remove($longSequence, 1): &#xA;        </xsl:text>
<xsl:text>updatedSequence = remove($longSequence, 1): &#xA;        </xsl:text>
<xsl:variable name="updatedSequence" as="item()*"
   select="remove($longSequence, 1)"/>
<xsl:text>&#xA;    Test 4. $updatedSequence = &#xA;        </xsl:text>
<xsl:value-of select="$updatedSequence" separator="&#xA;        "/>

  </xsl:template>

</xsl:stylesheet>
```

The somewhat longwinded results look like this:

```
Here's another test of the remove() function:

  Our sequence ($longSequence) is:
      3
      4
      5
      2006-07-25-04:00
      03:14:18.783-04:00
      8
      blue
      red
      3.14
      42
      1995-04-21

  Test 1. remove($longSequence, 1) =
      4
      5
      2006-07-25-04:00
      03:14:18.783-04:00
      8
```

```
blue
red
3.14
42
1995-04-21

Test 2. remove($longSequence, 1) =
   [We're running this test again to show the variable didn't change]
   4
   5
   2006-07-25-04:00
   03:14:18.783-04:00
   8
   blue
   red
   3.14
   42
   1995-04-21

Test 3. remove(remove($longSequence, 7), 1) =
   4
   5
   2006-07-25-04:00
   03:31:45.859-04:00
   8
   red
   3.14
   42
   1995-04-21

Creating a new variable based on remove($longSequence, 1):
   updatedSequence = remove($longSequence, 1):

Test 4. $updatedSequence =
   4
   5
   2006-07-25-04:00
   03:14:18.783-04:00
   8
   blue
   red
   3.14
   42
   1995-04-21
```

Our stylesheet begins by listing the items in the sequence. In our first test, removing the first item returns a sequence in which the first item (3) has been removed. Next, we call remove( ) against the same sequence. The results are the same. Remember, variables in XSLT don't change; they can be initialized, but not changed. We can call remove($longSequence, 1) as many times as we want, but the results will always be the same. If we want to "remove" an item permanently, we need to store the sequence returned by remove( ) in a variable.

In our third test we nest calls to remove( ) to remove the first and seventh items. If we wanted to remove the first two items, it would be more efficient to use subsequence($longSequence,

3). Because we're removing items that aren't adjacent, the nested calls to `remove( )` are the way to go.

The fourth example stores the results of the `remove( )` function in a variable. That variable's type is `item( )*` as well. Here are three ways of creating the new variable:

```
<!-- Simplest approach -->
<xsl:variable name="updatedSequence1" as="item()*"
  select="remove($longSequence, 1)"/>

<!-- This works... -->
<xsl:variable name="updatedSequence2" as="item()*">
  <xsl:sequence select="remove($longSequence, 1)"/>
</xsl:variable>

<!-- Doesn't work! -->
<xsl:variable name="updatedSequence3" as="item()*">
  <xsl:value-of select="remove($longSequence, 1)"/>
</xsl:variable>
```

The first approach is the simplest; it's what we used in our stylesheet. The second approach works and is useful if we need to add multiple items to this sequence. *The third approach doesn't work.* The `<xsl:value-of>` element inserts *the string value* of the subsequence, with the values separated by spaces. This creates a sequence of one item:

```
$updatedSequence3 =
4 5 2006-07-25-04:00 03:20:35.815-04:00 8 blue red 3.14 42 1995-04-21
```

Using `<xsl:value-of>` seems like a reasonable approach, but it doesn't work. Be sure to use `<xsl:sequence>` instead. (I'm mentioning that here because I've made the same mistake; hopefully, you can learn from my absent-mindedness.)

Our last example illustrates `remove( )` with the empty sequence:

```
<?xml version="1.0"?>
<!-- remove3.xsl -->
<xsl:stylesheet version="2.0"
  xmlns:xsl="http://www.w3.org/1999/XSL/Transform"
  xmlns:xs="http://www.w3.org/2001/XMLSchema">

<xsl:output method="text"/>

<xsl:template match="/">

  <xsl:variable name="emptySequence" as="item()*">
    <xsl:sequence select="()"/>
  </xsl:variable>

  <xsl:text>&#xA;Here's a final test of the remove() </xsl:text>
  <xsl:text>function:&#xA;</xsl:text>

  <xsl:text>&#xA;  Our sequence ($emptySequence) is </xsl:text>
  <xsl:text>empty:&#xA;        empty($emptySequence) = </xsl:text>
  <xsl:value-of select="empty($emptySequence)"/>
  <xsl:text>&#xA;&#xA;        remove($emptySequence, 1) = </xsl:text>
  <xsl:value-of select="remove($emptySequence, 1)"/>
```

```
<xsl:text>&#xA;&#xA;          empty(remove($emptySequence, 1)) </xsl:text>
<xsl:text>= </xsl:text>
<xsl:value-of select="empty(remove($emptySequence, 1))"/>

</xsl:template>

</xsl:stylesheet>
```

Our last set of results are:

```
Here's a final test of the remove() function:

  Our sequence ($emptySequence) is empty:
     empty($emptySequence) = true

     remove($emptySequence, 1) =

     empty(remove($emptySequence, 1)) = true
```

[2.0] replace()

Given an input string, a regular expression, and a replacement string, replaces all matches of the regular expression in the input string with the replacement string.

Syntax

```
xs:string replace($input as xs:string?, $pattern as xs:string,
                  $replacement as xs:string)
xs:string replace($input as xs:string?, $pattern as xs:string,
                  $replacement as xs:string, $flags as xs:string)
```

Inputs

Three strings; the first string is the original string, the second is a regular expression, and the third is a replacement string. There is also an optional fourth string that specifies flags for how the regular expression should be processed.

> It is a fatal error if a regular expression matches a zero-length string. See Appendix E for more details.

Outputs

An updated string in which all matches of the regular expression have been replaced with the replacement string.

Here are the details about how **replace( )** actually works:

- If the regular expression doesn't match anything in the input string, the input string is returned unchanged.

- If the regular expression matches two overlapping strings in the input string, only the first match is replaced.

- Regular expression matching does not use collations; the characters' Unicode code points are compared. Cases in which different characters are considered equal in the world's languages are not taken into account.

- The input string and the replacement string can both be zero-length strings. If the input string is a zero-length string, a zero-length string is returned. If the replacement string is zero-length, any matches for the regular expression are deleted. The regular expression cannot be a zero-length string, nor can it match a zero-length string (`matches("", $pattern, $replacement)` can't be true, in other words). Assuming the input string is not of zero length, it *is* acceptable for a captured substring to be of zero length.

  If the expression `matches("", $pattern, $replacement)` is `true`, an error is raised. For example, using the pattern `'.?'` with any input string raises an error because this pattern matches a zero-length string.

- Unlike regular expressions used in the `<xsl:analyze-string>` element, curly braces (`{` and `}`) are not doubled. (Curly braces used inside the `regex` attribute of `<xsl:analyze-string>` must be doubled so they aren't interpreted as attribute value templates.)

- There are special features and requirements for the replacement string:

  — A literal dollar sign (`$`) symbol must be escaped as `\$`, and a literal backslash (`\`) must be escaped as `\\`. An error is raised if a dollar sign is not preceded by a backslash or followed by at least one digit (`[0-9]`). An error is also raised if a backslash is not part of a pair of backslashes (`\\`) or an escaped dollar sign (`\$`).

  — Within the replacement string, you can use the notation `$N` to indicate the portion of the input string that matches the Nth parenthesized portion of the regular expression. (This capability is similar to the `regex-group( )` function.) Here is a regular expression we'll use in our example; it represents the pattern for a 16-digit credit card number:

    `([0-9]{4})-([0-9]{4})-([0-9]{4})-([0-9]{4})`

  There are four parenthesized groups here. (The hyphens between the parentheses aren't in any group.) Given the credit card number `1234-5678-9101-1121`, `$1` represents `1234`, `$2` represents `5678`, `$3` represents `9101`, and `$4` represents `1121`.

  — The notation `$0` refers to the entire string matched by the regular expression. In our example, that happens to be the entire input string, but that's not always the case.

  — If a given regular expression group doesn't match anything in the input string, its value is a zero-length string.

—If you use a single-digit $N expression and that digit is greater than the number of regular expression groups, a zero-length string is returned. In our example, $7 would produce a zero-length string.

—Whenever you use the $N notation, the processor assumes every consecutive digit after the dollar sign refers to a group in the regular expression. If that's not the case, it uses the largest number of digits possible, and then the rest of the digits are written to the output.

For example, if we use $417 in our earlier example, this would generate 112117. $4 is the longest expression that matches anything, so the remaining digits (17) are output along with the match. If our regular expression has 41 groups, this would be interpreted as $41 followed immediately by a 7.

- If a regular expression specifies more than one alternative, and more than one of those alternatives match at the same position in the input, the first alternative in the regular expression is the one that's used. Here's an example from the spec:

```
replace("abcd", "(ab)|(a)", "[1=$1][2=$2]") = "[1=ab][2=]cd"
```

The first alternative in the regular expression (ab) is considered the match, so $1 is ab and $2 is a zero-length string. This is true even though the second alternative is shorter than the first.

- Finally, the $flags parameter modifies how the regular expression is processed. There are four different flags:

s

Regular expressions are evaluated in what the specs refer to as "dot-all" mode. When this flag is used, the dot operator (.) matches any character. Under normal processing (without the s flag), the dot operator matches any character *except* the newline character (&#xA). This flag is useful when you want to match strings that might include a newline character.

m

Regular expressions are evaulated in multiline mode. By default, the meta-character (^) matches the start of the entire string, while $ matches the end of the entire string. In multiline mode, ^ matches the start of any line within the string and $ matches the end of any line within the string.

i

Regular expressions are evaluated in case-insensitive mode. The regular expression "a" matches both "a" and "A".

Note that Unicode issues can complicate this greatly. For example, the XQuery 1.0 and XPath 2.0 Functions and Operators spec gives the example of the Unicode sign for degrees Kelvin (K), which is the letter "K". The combination of regex="k" and flags="i" matches the Kelvin sign as well as the letters "k" (k) and "K" (K).

Other Unicode characters don't convert to letters. For example, the Unicode symbol for the Roman numeral I (ࡰ) looks like the letter I, but does not convert to one. Fortunately, these complications are beyond the scope of this book.

x

All whitespace characters (	,
, , and) are removed from the regular expression before any comparison is done. In other words, with the x flag, the regular expressions "John Smith" and "JohnSmith" are the same. This flag is useful when you want to break a long regular expression into multiple lines to make it easier to read.

The flags can be combined in any order. The parameters 'xis' and 'six' work exactly the same way.

Defined in

XQuery 1.0 and XPath 2.0 Functions and Operators section 7.6, "String Functions that use Pattern Matching."

Example

Here is a stylesheet with several tests of the replace( ) function:

```
<?xml version="1.0"?>
<!-- replace.xsl -->
<xsl:stylesheet version="2.0"
  xmlns:xsl="http://www.w3.org/1999/XSL/Transform"
  xmlns:xs="http://www.w3.org/2001/XMLSchema">

  <xsl:output method="text"/>

  <xsl:template match="/">

    <xsl:variable name="string1"
      select="concat('Now is the time for all good men and ',
              'women to aid the party.')"/>
    <xsl:variable name="string2" as="xs:string"
      select="'Visa # 1234-5678-9101-1121'"/>

    <xsl:text>&#xA;Here's a test of the replace() </xsl:text>
    <xsl:text>function:&#xA;</xsl:text>

    <xsl:text>&#xA;  $string1 = &#xA;    </xsl:text>
    <xsl:value-of select="$string1"/>

    <xsl:text>&#xA;&#xA;  Test 1. replace($string1, </xsl:text>
    <xsl:text>'men', 'boys') = &#xA;    </xsl:text>
    <xsl:value-of select="replace($string1, 'men', 'boys')"/>

    <xsl:text>&#xA;&#xA;  Test 2. replace($string1, </xsl:text>
    <xsl:text>' men', ' boys') = &#xA;    </xsl:text>
    <xsl:value-of select="replace($string1, ' men', ' boys')"/>
```

```
<xsl:text>&#xA;&#xA;   Test 3. replace($string1, </xsl:text>
<xsl:text>'wombats', 'weasels') = &#xA;   </xsl:text>
<xsl:value-of select="replace($string1, 'wombats', 'weasels')"/>

<xsl:text>&#xA;&#xA;   $string2 = &#xA;   </xsl:text>
<xsl:value-of select="$string2"/>

<xsl:text>&#xA;&#xA;   Test 4. replace($string2, </xsl:text>
<xsl:text>&#xA;                 </xsl:text>
<xsl:text>'([0-9]{4}-)([0-9]{4}-)([0-9]{4}-)([0-9]{4})', </xsl:text>
<xsl:text>&#xA;                 </xsl:text>
<xsl:text>'XXXX-XXXX-XXXX-$4') = &#xA;   </xsl:text>
<xsl:value-of
  select="replace($string2,
          '([0-9]{4})-([0-9]{4})-([0-9]{4})-([0-9]{4})',
          'XXXX-XXXX-XXXX-$4')"/>

<xsl:text>&#xA;&#xA;   Test 5. replace($string2, </xsl:text>
<xsl:text>&#xA;                     </xsl:text>
<xsl:text>'([0-9]{4}-)([0-9]{4}-)([0-9]{4}-)([0-9]{4})', </xsl:text>
<xsl:text>&#xA;                     </xsl:text>
<xsl:text>'$0 -> XXXX-XXXX-XXXX-$4') = &#xA;   </xsl:text>
<xsl:value-of
  select="replace($string2,
          '([0-9]{4})-([0-9]{4})-([0-9]{4})-([0-9]{4})',
          '$0 -> XXXX-XXXX-XXXX-$4')"/>

</xsl:template>

</xsl:stylesheet>
```

Here are the results:

```
Here's a test of the replace() function:

  $string1 =
  Now is the time for all good men and women to aid the party.

  Test 1. replace($string1, 'men', 'boys') =
  Now is the time for all good boys and woboys to aid the party.

  Test 2. replace($string1, ' men', ' boys') =
  Now is the time for all good boys and women to aid the party.

  Test 3. replace($string1, 'wombats', 'weasels') =
  Now is the time for all good men and women to aid the party.

  $string2 =
  Visa # 1234-5678-9101-1121

  Test 4. replace($string2,
              '([0-9]{4}-)([0-9]{4}-)([0-9]{4}-)([0-9]{4})',
              'XXXX-XXXX-XXXX-$4') =
  Visa # XXXX-XXXX-XXXX-1121

  Test 5. replace($string2,
```

```
          '([0-9]{4})-([0-9]{4})-([0-9]{4})-([0-9]{4})',
          '$0 -> XXXX-XXXX-XXXX-$4') =
Visa # 1234-5678-9101-1121 -> XXXX-XXXX-XXXX-1121
```

Tests 1, 2, and 3 are pretty straightforward. Test 1 replaces text in the input string, but it doesn't work exactly the way we want. Test 2 uses a slightly modified pattern and replacement string to get more useful results. Test 3 returns the input string without any changes because the pattern does not match.

Tests 4 and 5 use the substring feature to display matching text from the original string. In both cases, we're using `replace( )` to hide all but the last four digits of the credit card number. Both tests use the fourth matching substring (`$4`), while test 5 also uses `$0` to display the entire matching string.

See Also

Appendix E has complete details on the way regular expressions work in XPath 2.0. Also see the definitions of the following elements and functions: [2.0] `<xsl:analyze-string>`, [2.0] `matches( )`, [2.0] `<xsl:matching-substring>`, [2.0] `<xsl:non-matching-substring>`, [2.0] `regex-group( )`, and [2.0] `tokenize( )`.

[2.0] resolve-QName()

This is a function that constructs a `QName`. Given an `xs:string` in the format of a (optionally prefixed) name and an element, this function returns a `QName`. The prefix of the name, if any, is resolved using the namespaces in scope for the given element.

Syntax

```
xs:QName? resolve-QName($qname as xs:string?, $element as element())
```

Inputs

An `xs:string` that is a valid XML name (it can contain a namespace prefix as well) and an element.

Outputs

A new `xs:QName` value.

Defined in

XQuery 1.0 and XPath 2.0 Functions and Operators section 11.1, "Additional Constructor Functions for QNames."

Example

To create a new `QName` value with `resolve-QName( )`, we'll revisit our Shakespearean sonnet:

```
<?xml version="1.0"?>
<!-- sonnet.xml -->
<sonnet type='Shakespearean'>
  <auth:author xmlns:auth="http://www.authors.com/">
```

```
      <last-name>Shakespeare</last-name>
      <first-name>William</first-name>
      <nationality>British</nationality>
      <year-of-birth>1564</year-of-birth>
      <year-of-death>1616</year-of-death>
    </auth:author>
    <!-- Is there an official title for this sonnet?  They're
         sometimes named after the first line.               -->
    <title>Sonnet 130</title>
    <lines>
      <line>My mistress' eyes are nothing like the sun,</line>
      <line>Coral is far more red than her lips red.</line>
      <line>If snow be white, why then her breasts are dun,</line>
      <line>If hairs be wires, black wires grow on her head.</line>
      <line>I have seen roses damasked, red and white,</line>
      <line>But no such roses see I in her cheeks.</line>
      <line>And in some perfumes is there more delight</line>
      <line>Than in the breath that from my mistress reeks.</line>
      <line>I love to hear her speak, yet well I know</line>
      <line>That music hath a far more pleasing sound.</line>
      <line>I grant I never saw a goddess go,</line>
      <line>My mistress when she walks, treads on the ground.</line>
      <line>And yet, by Heaven, I think my love as rare</line>
      <line>As any she belied with false compare.</line>
    </lines>
  </sonnet>
```

Here is our stylesheet:

```
<?xml version="1.0"?>
<!-- resolve-qname.xsl -->
<xsl:stylesheet version="2.0"
  xmlns:xsl="http://www.w3.org/1999/XSL/Transform"
  xmlns:xs="http://www.w3.org/2001/XMLSchema">

  <xsl:output method="text"/>

  <xsl:template match="/">
    <xsl:text>&#xA;Tests of the resolve-QName() function:&#xA;</xsl:text>

    <xsl:variable name="testQName1" as="xs:QName"
      select="resolve-QName('auth:last-name',
              /sonnet/*:author/last-name)"/>

    <xsl:text>&#xA;  testQName1 = resolve-QName('auth:</xsl:text>
    <xsl:text>last-name', /sonnet/author/last-name)</xsl:text>
    <xsl:text>&#xA;   prefix-from-QName</xsl:text>
    <xsl:text>($testQName1) = "</xsl:text>
    <xsl:value-of select="prefix-from-QName($testQName1)"/>
    <xsl:text>"&#xA;  local-name-from-QName($testQName1) = "</xsl:text>
    <xsl:value-of select="local-name-from-QName($testQName1)"/>
    <xsl:text>"&#xA;  namespace-uri-from-QName($testQName1) = "</xsl:text>
    <xsl:value-of select="namespace-uri-from-QName($testQName1)"/>
    <xsl:text>"&#xA;</xsl:text>

    <xsl:variable name="testQName2" as="xs:QName"
```

```
        select="resolve-QName('something-else', /sonnet)"/>

    <xsl:text>&#xA;  testQName2 = resolve-QName('something-</xsl:text>
    <xsl:text>else', /sonnet)</xsl:text>
    <xsl:text>&#xA;  prefix-from-QName</xsl:text>
    <xsl:text>($testQName2) = "</xsl:text>
    <xsl:value-of select="prefix-from-QName($testQName2)"/>
    <xsl:text>"&#xA;  local-name-from-QName($testQName2) = "</xsl:text>
    <xsl:value-of select="local-name-from-QName($testQName2)"/>
    <xsl:text>"&#xA;  namespace-uri-from-QName($testQName2) = "</xsl:text>
    <xsl:value-of select="namespace-uri-from-QName($testQName2)"/>
    <xsl:text>"</xsl:text>

    <!-- This raises an error; the 'auth' prefix isn't in scope for -->
    <!-- the <sonnet> element. -->
    <!--    <xsl:variable name="testQName3" as="xs:QName"
              select="resolve-QName('auth:new-element', /sonnet)"/> -->
  </xsl:template>

</xsl:stylesheet>
```

And here are the results:

```
Tests of the resolve-QName() function:

  testQName1 = resolve-QName('auth:last-name', /sonnet/author/last-name)
  prefix-from-QName($testQName1) = "auth"
  local-name-from-QName($testQName1) = "last-name"
  namespace-uri-from-QName($testQName1) = "http://www.authors.com/"

  testQName2 = resolve-QName('something-else', /sonnet)
  prefix-from-QName($testQName2) = ""
  local-name-from-QName($testQName2) = "something-else"
  namespace-uri-from-QName($testQName2) = ""
```

In our first use of `resolve-QName( )`, we created a variable of datatype `xs:QName` that used the `auth` prefix in the scope of the `<last-name>` element. Notice that the `auth` prefix is actually defined on the `<last-name>`'s parent, but it is in scope. Once we've created the `QName`, we use the `*-from-QName( )` functions to display its parts.

The second example here creates a `QName` that doesn't have a namespace. We're using a local name that doesn't have a prefix, so the `prefix-from-QName( )` function returns a zero-length string. The second argument to `resolve-QName( )` is a `<sonnet>` element. Our sonnet doesn't have a default namespace, so our `QName` isn't in a namespace.

Finally, the commented-out code in the stylesheet attempts to use the `auth` namespace at the root element (`/sonnet`). The `auth` namespace is not in scope at the root element, so this call to `resolve-QName( )` raises an error.

[2.0] resolve-uri()

Resolves a relative URI against an absolute URI.

Syntax

```
xs:anyURI? resolve-uri($relative as xs:string?)
xs:anyURI? resolve-uri($relative as xs:string?, $base as xs:string)
```

Inputs

An xs:string representing a relative URI. An optional xs:string containing an absolute URI is accepted as well. If no absolute URI is given, the base URI from the static context is used.

Outputs

An xs:anyURI containing the resolved URI. If the second argument is not provided and no base URI is defined in the current context, an error is raised. If either input string is not a valid URI, an error is raised. If the relative URI is an absolute URI, it is returned unchanged. Finally, if the relative URI is the empty sequence, the empty sequence is returned.

Defined in

XQuery 1.0 and XPath 2.0 Functions and Operators section 8, "Functions on anyURI."

Example

Here is a stylesheet that resolves two URIs. In one we use the base URI from the static context, while in the other we supply an absolute URI.

```
<?xml version="1.0"?>
<!-- resolve-uri.xsl -->
<xsl:stylesheet version="2.0"
  xmlns:xsl="http://www.w3.org/1999/XSL/Transform">

  <xsl:output method="text"/>

  <xsl:template match="/">
    <xsl:text>&#xA;Tests of the resolve-uri() function:</xsl:text>

    <xsl:text>&#xA;&#xA;  The static base URI for the </xsl:text>
    <xsl:text>document root is:&#xA;     </xsl:text>
    <xsl:value-of select="static-base-uri()"/>

    <xsl:text>&#xA;&#xA;  The base URI for the </xsl:text>
    <xsl:text>document root is:&#xA;     </xsl:text>
    <xsl:value-of select="base-uri()"/>

    <xsl:text>&#xA;&#xA;  resolve-uri('doug.html') = </xsl:text>
    <xsl:text>&#xA;     </xsl:text>
    <xsl:value-of select="resolve-uri('doug.html')"/>

    <xsl:text>&#xA;&#xA;  resolve-uri('doug.html', </xsl:text>
    <xsl:text>'http://www.oreilly.com/') = </xsl:text>
    <xsl:text>&#xA;     </xsl:text>
    <xsl:value-of
      select="resolve-uri('doug.html', 'http://www.oreilly.com/')"/>

  </xsl:template>
```

```
</xsl:stylesheet>
```

(We use the `static-base-uri( )` function to print out the static base URI for the transformation and use the `base-uri( )` function to print out the base URI property before we use the `resolve-uri( )` function.) The results look like this:

```
Tests of the resolve-uri() function:

  The static base URI for the document root is:
    file:/C://resolve-uri.xsl

  The base URI for the document root is:
    file:/C://chocolate.xml

  resolve-uri('doug.html') =
    file:/C:/doug.html

  resolve-uri('doug.html', 'http://www.oreilly.com/') =
    http://www.oreilly.com/doug.html
```

We get these results when invoking this stylesheet against the file *chocolate.xml*. That file's location on the file system becomes the base URI for the document. The first test creates a URI for a document in the same directory as our input document. The second test takes the name of a resource and the URL of a web site and combines them to create a URI.

[2.0] reverse()

Given a sequence of items, returns a sequence with the items in reverse order.

Syntax

```
item()* reverse(item()*)
```

Inputs

A sequence of items. If the sequence is the empty sequence, the empty sequence is returned.

Outputs

A sequence with the input items in reverse order.

Defined in

XQuery 1.0 and XPath 2.0 Functions and Operators section 15.1, "General Functions and Operators on Sequences."

Example

Here is a short stylesheet that creates a sequence and prints it, and then prints the sequence again after invoking the `reverse( )` function against it:

```
<?xml version="1.0"?>
<!-- reverse.xsl -->
<xsl:stylesheet version="2.0"
```

```
      xmlns:xsl="http://www.w3.org/1999/XSL/Transform"
      xmlns:xs="http://www.w3.org/2001/XMLSchema"
      xmlns:datatest="http://www.oreilly.com">

      <xsl:output method="text"/>

      <xsl:template match="/">

        <xsl:variable name="testSequence" as="item()*">
          <xsl:sequence
            select="(3, 4, 5, current-date(), current-time(), 8, 'blue',
                    'red', xs:float(3.14), 42, xs:date('1995-04-21'))"/>
        </xsl:variable>

        <xsl:text>&#xA;Here is a test of the reverse() </xsl:text>
        <xsl:text>function:&#xA;</xsl:text>

        <xsl:text>&#xA;  Our original sequence is:&#xA;&#xA;     </xsl:text>
        <xsl:value-of select="$testSequence" separator="&#xA;     "/>

        <xsl:text>&#xA;&#xA;  Passing our sequence to reverse() </xsl:text>
        <xsl:text>gives us:&#xA;&#xA;     </xsl:text>

        <xsl:value-of select="reverse($testSequence)" separator="&#xA;     "/>
      </xsl:template>

    </xsl:stylesheet>
```

Here are the results:

```
    Here is a test of the reverse() function:

      Our original sequence is:

        3
        4
        5
        2006-07-22-04:00
        13:48:23.256-04:00
        8
        blue
        red
        3.14
        42
        1995-04-21

      Passing our sequence to reverse() gives us:

        1995-04-21
        42
        3.14
        red
        blue
        8
        13:48:23.256-04:00
        2006-07-22-04:00
```

```
5
4
3
```

Remember that variables don't change, so the original sequence still exists. If we want to use the reversed sequence, we would have to store it in a new variable.

[2.0] root()

Given a node, returns the root of the tree to which the node belongs.

Syntax

```
node() root()
node() root(node()?)
```

Inputs

An optional node. If no node is provided, the context node is used.

Outputs

The root of the tree to which the node (or the context node, if the call was **root( )**) belongs. This will usually be a document node, but that isn't always the case.

If an argument is provided, and that argument is the empty sequence, the empty sequence is returned. Also, if the argument itself is a document node, the argument is simply returned.

Defined in

XQuery 1.0 and XPath 2.0 Functions and Operators section 14, "Functions and Operators on Nodes."

Example

To test the **root( )** function, we'll take another look at our list of favorite albums:

```
<?xml version="1.0"?>
<!-- favorites.xml -->
<list>
  <title>A few of my favorite albums</title>
  <listitem>A Love Supreme</listitem>
  <listitem>Beat Crazy</listitem>
  <listitem>Here Come the Warm Jets</listitem>
  <listitem>Kind of Blue</listitem>
  <listitem>London Calling</listitem>
  <listitem>Remain in Light</listitem>
  <listitem>The Joshua Tree</listitem>
  <listitem>The Indestructible Beat of Soweto</listitem>
</list>
```

We'll use this stylesheet to test the **root( )** function:

```
<?xml version="1.0"?>
<!-- root.xsl -->
```

```
<xsl:stylesheet version="2.0"
  xmlns:xsl="http://www.w3.org/1999/XSL/Transform"
  xmlns:xs="http://www.w3.org/2001/XMLSchema"
  xmlns:ora="http://www.oreilly.com">

  <xsl:output method="text"/>

  <xsl:template match="/">
    <xsl:text>&#xA;Tests of the root() function:</xsl:text>

    <xsl:variable name="testTree" as="node()*">
      <report month="8" year="2006">
        <title>Chocolate bar sales</title>
        <brand>
          <name>Lindt</name>
          <units>27408</units>
        </brand>
      </report>
      <otherReport month="9" year="2006">
        <title>Chocolate bar sales</title>
        <brand>
          <name>Callebaut</name>
          <units>8203</units>
        </brand>
      </otherReport>
    </xsl:variable>

    <xsl:text>&#xA;&#xA;  1. root(//listitem[3]):</xsl:text>
    <xsl:text>&#xA;</xsl:text>
    <xsl:value-of
      select="ora:doc-node-test(root(//listitem[3]))"/>

    <xsl:text>&#xA;&#xA;  2. root(subsequence($testTree, 1, 1)):</xsl:text>
    <xsl:text>&#xA;</xsl:text>
    <xsl:value-of
      select="ora:doc-node-test(root(subsequence($testTree, 1, 1)))"/>

    <xsl:text>&#xA;&#xA;  3. root(subsequence($testTree, 2)):</xsl:text>
    <xsl:text>&#xA;</xsl:text>
    <xsl:value-of
      select="ora:doc-node-test(root(subsequence($testTree, 2, 1)))"/>

    <xsl:text>&#xA;&#xA;  4. root():</xsl:text>
    <xsl:text>&#xA;</xsl:text>
    <xsl:value-of
      select="ora:doc-node-test(root())"/>

  </xsl:template>

  <xsl:function name="ora:doc-node-test" as="xs:string">
    <xsl:param name="node" as="node()*"/>
    <xsl:choose>
      <xsl:when test="empty($node)">
        <xsl:value-of select="'        [empty sequence]'"/>
      </xsl:when>
```

```
      <xsl:when test="$node instance of document-node()">
        <xsl:value-of
          select="concat('        This IS a document node.&#xA;',
                  '        root node''s name: &lt;',
                node-name($node/*[1]),
                '&gt;')"/>
      </xsl:when>
      <xsl:otherwise>
        <xsl:value-of
          select="concat('        This IS NOT a document node.&#xA;',
                  '        root node''s name: &lt;',
                node-name($node),
                '&gt;')"/>
      </xsl:otherwise>
    </xsl:choose>
  </xsl:function>

</xsl:stylesheet>
```

Notice that we define a variable named testTree that contains two elements; you can't have two root elements in an XML document, but it is legal in a variable. We'll use this variable to demonstrate calls to root( ) that don't return a document node.

Our stylesheet uses an <xsl:function> to refactor out the code that processes the various root elements. Given a sequence, our function ora:doc-node-test( ) first checks to see whether the sequence is the empty sequence. (For example, if we use this stylesheet to transform an XML document that doesn't contain three <listitem> elements, the sequence is empty.)

Assuming the sequence is not empty, we use the document-node( ) node test to see whether it is a document node. If it is, we print the name of its first child element. A document node can technically contain more than one child, so we use the node test $node/*[1] to select its first child node. (See the discussion of the [2.0] <xsl:document> element in Appendix A for an example of a document node with more than one child element.) If this is not a document node, we simply pass the node itself to the node-name( ) function.

> To make our stylesheet more robust, we could write the XPath expres-
> sion like this:
>
> ```
> <xsl:when test="($node treat as node()) instance of document-node()">
> ```
>
> The variable $node has a type of node( )*; the treat as instruction casts
> it to a type of node( ). We could also use the exactly-one( ) function to
> ensure the sequence has only one item. Our stylesheet makes sure that
> we only call the ora:doc-node-test( ) function with a singleton.

Now that we've discussed the function, we'll look at the four tests of the root( ) function. The first use of root( ) gets the root item of the third <listitem> element in the context item. The second and third calls to root( ) use the two root nodes in the variable $testTree. While both of them have root nodes, neither root node is a document node. For the last use of root( ), we send the root of the context item, which is the root node of the XML document we're transforming.

Here are the results we get:

```
Tests of the root() function:

    1. root(//listitem[3]):
          This IS a document node.
          root node's name: <list>

    2. root(subsequence($testTree, 1, 1)):
          This IS NOT a document node.
          root node's name: <report>

    3. root(subsequence($testTree, 2)):
          This IS NOT a document node.
          root node's name: <otherReport>

    4. root():
          This IS a document node.
          root node's name: <list>
```

round()

Returns the integer closest to the argument.

Syntax

```
[1.0] number? round(number?)
[2.0] numeric? round(numeric?)
```

Inputs

[1.0] A number. If the argument is not a number, it is converted to a number as if it were passed to the number( ) function.

[2.0] In XSLT 2.0, the argument for round( ) must be a number (xs:integer, xs:float, xs:decimal, or xs:double, or a datatype derived from them). If the argument is not a number, the XSLT processor raises an error. For example, if the argument is an untyped value read in from an XML document that doesn't use a schema, it must be cast to a numeric value before it is passed to round( ).

Output

The integer that is closest to the argument. If two numbers are equally close to the argument (1 and 2 are equally close to 1.5), the number closest to positive infinity is returned. Various argument values are handled as follows:

- If the argument is positive infinity, then positive infinity is returned.
- If the argument is negative infinity, then negative infinity is returned.
- If the argument is positive zero, then positive zero is returned.
- If the argument is negative zero, then negative zero is returned.
- If the argument is between zero and -0.5, then negative zero is returned.

- If the argument is NaN (not a number), the round( ) function returns NaN.

[2.0] In XSLT 2.0, the output value has the same datatype as the input value. In other words, the function round(xs:integer) returns an xs:integer, while round(xs:float) returns an xs:float.

Defined in

[1.0] XPath section 4.4, "Number Functions."

[2.0] XQuery 1.0 and XPath 2.0 Functions and Operators section 6.4, "Functions on Numeric Values."

Example

The following stylesheet shows the results of invoking the round( ) function against a variety of values. We'll use this XML document as input:

```
<?xml version="1.0" encoding="utf-8"?>
<!-- chocolate.xml -->
<report month="8" year="2006">
  <title>Chocolate bar sales</title>
  <brand>
    <name>Lindt</name>
    <units>27408</units>
  </brand>
  <brand>
    <name>Callebaut</name>
    <units>8203</units>
  </brand>
  <brand>
    <name>Valrhona</name>
    <units>22101</units>
  </brand>
  <brand>
    <name>Perugina</name>
    <units>14336</units>
  </brand>
  <brand>
    <name>Ghirardelli</name>
    <units>19268</units>
  </brand>
</report>
```

Here's the stylesheet that uses the round( ) function:

```
<?xml version="1.0"?>
<!-- round1.xsl -->
<xsl:stylesheet version="1.0"
  xmlns:xsl="http://www.w3.org/1999/XSL/Transform">

  <xsl:output method="text"/>

  <xsl:template match="/">
    <xsl:text>&#xA;Tests of the round() function:&#xA;&#xA;</xsl:text>
```

```
<xsl:text>  round(7.983) = </xsl:text>
<xsl:value-of select="round(7.983)"/>

<xsl:text>&#xA;  round(-7.893) = </xsl:text>
<xsl:value-of select="round(-7.893)"/>

<xsl:text>&#xA;  round(avg(/report/brand/units)) = </xsl:text>
<xsl:value-of select="round(avg(/report/brand/units))"/>

<xsl:text>&#xA;  round('blue') = </xsl:text>
<xsl:value-of select="round('blue')"/>

  </xsl:template>

</xsl:stylesheet>
```

When we process our XML document with this stylesheet, the results are:

```
Tests of the round() function:

  round(7.983) = 8
  round(-7.893) = -8
  round(avg(/report/brand/units)) = 18263
  round('blue') = NaN
```

If we change the `<xsl:stylesheet>` element to have version="2.0", the stylesheet won't run at all because round('blue') is a static error. We can add version="1.0" to the `<xsl:value-of>` element so the element is processed in XSLT 1.0 mode. We can also use the number() function to convert blue to a number. Here's how the stylesheet looks:

```
<?xml version="1.0"?>
<!-- round2.xsl -->
<xsl:stylesheet version="2.0"
  xmlns:xsl="http://www.w3.org/1999/XSL/Transform">

  <xsl:template match="/">
    ...
    <xsl:text>&#xA;  [1.0] round('blue') = </xsl:text>
         <xsl:value-of version="1.0" select="round('blue')"/>

    <xsl:text>&#xA;  round(number('blue')) = </xsl:text>
    <xsl:value-of select="round(number('blue'))"/>
  </xsl:template>

</xsl:stylesheet>
```

The results are similar:

```
Tests of the round() function:
  ...
  [1.0] round('blue') = NaN
  round(number('blue')) = NaN
```

[2.0] round-half-to-even()

Returns the integer closest to the argument, with the exception that any value that ends with **.5** is rounded to the nearest *even* number.

Syntax

```
numeric? round-half-to-even(numeric?)
numeric? round-half-to-even(numeric?, $precision as xs:integer)
```

Inputs

A numeric value and an optional `xs:integer` specifying the number of digits of precision to be used in the calculation. The numeric value must be of type `xs:float`, `xs:double`, `xs:decimal`, or `xs:integer`. If it is not, the XSLT processor raises an error.

Output

The integer closest to the argument, with values ending in **.5** rounded to the nearest even number. With that exception, `round-half-to-even( )` works the same as `round( )`:

- If the argument is positive infinity, then positive infinity is returned.
- If the argument is negative infinity, then negative infinity is returned.
- If the argument is positive zero, then positive zero is returned.
- If the argument is negative zero, then negative zero is returned.
- If the argument is between zero and **-0.5**, then negative zero is returned.
- If the argument is `NaN` (not a number), then `NaN` is returned.

If the `$precision` argument is used, the XSLT processor returns the number closest to the value that is a multiple of 10 to the power of *minus* `$precision`. The value **-2** rounds the number to the nearest **100**, while the value **2** rounds the number to the nearest **.01**.

The output value has the same datatype as the input value. In other words, the function `round-half-to-even(xs:integer)` returns an `xs:integer`, while `round-half-to-even(xs:float)` returns an `xs:float`.

Defined in

XQuery 1.0 and XPath 2.0 Functions and Operators section 6.4, "Functions on Numeric Values."

Example

Here is a simple stylesheet that illustrates how `round-half-to-even( )` works:

```
<?xml version="1.0"?>
<!-- round-half-to-even.xsl -->
<xsl:stylesheet version="2.0"
  xmlns:xsl="http://www.w3.org/1999/XSL/Transform">

  <xsl:output method="text"/>
```

```
<xsl:template match="/">
  <xsl:text>&#xA;Tests of the round-half-to-even() function:&#xA;</xsl:text>

  <xsl:text>&#xA;  round-half-to-even(-0.5) = </xsl:text>
  <xsl:value-of select="round-half-to-even(-0.5)"/>

  <xsl:text>&#xA;  round-half-to-even(0.5) = </xsl:text>
  <xsl:value-of select="round-half-to-even(0.5)"/>

  <xsl:text>&#xA;  round-half-to-even(1.5) = </xsl:text>
  <xsl:value-of select="round-half-to-even(1.5)"/>

  <xsl:text>&#xA;  round-half-to-even(2.5) = </xsl:text>
  <xsl:value-of select="round-half-to-even(2.5)"/>

  <xsl:text>&#xA;  round-half-to-even(number('NaN')) = </xsl:text>
  <xsl:value-of select="round-half-to-even(number('NaN'))"/>

  <xsl:text>&#xA;  round-half-to-even</xsl:text>
  <xsl:text>(avg(/report/brand/units)) = </xsl:text>
  <xsl:value-of select="round-half-to-even(avg(/report/brand/units))"/>

  <xsl:text>&#xA;  round-half-to-even</xsl:text>
  <xsl:text>(avg(/report/brand/units), -2) = </xsl:text>
  <xsl:value-of
    select="round-half-to-even(avg(/report/brand/units), -2)"/>
</xsl:template>

</xsl:stylesheet>
```

The stylesheet generates these results:

```
Tests of the round-half-to-even() function:

  round-half-to-even(-0.5) = 0
  round-half-to-even(0.5) = 0
  round-half-to-even(1.5) = 2
  round-half-to-even(2.5) = 2
  round-half-to-even(avg(/report/brand/units)) = 18263
  round-half-to-even(avg(/report/brand/units), -2) = 18300
```

Notice the effect of the $precision argument in the last line. The average sales figure has been rounded to the nearest multiple of 100 (10 to the power of minus -2).

[2.0] seconds-from-dateTime()

Given an xs:dateTime value, returns its seconds value.

Syntax

```
xs:decimal? seconds-from-dateTime(xs:dateTime?)
```

Inputs

An xs:dateTime value.

Output

An `xs:decimal` representing the seconds component of the given `xs:dateTime` value. If the argument is the empty sequence, this function returns the empty sequence.

Defined in

XQuery 1.0 and XPath 2.0 Functions and Operators section 10.5, "Component Extraction Functions on Durations, Dates and Times."

Example

This stylesheet demonstrates the `seconds-from-dateTime( )` function:

```
<?xml version="1.0"?>
<!-- seconds-from-datetime.xsl -->
<xsl:stylesheet version="2.0"
  xmlns:xsl="http://www.w3.org/1999/XSL/Transform"
  xmlns:xs="http://www.w3.org/2001/XMLSchema">

  <xsl:output method="text"/>

  <xsl:template match="/">
    <xsl:text>&#xA;Extracting the seconds from an xs:dateTime:</xsl:text>
    <xsl:variable name="currentDateTime" as="xs:dateTime"
      select="current-dateTime()"/>
    <xsl:text>&#xA;&#xA;  The current date and time is: </xsl:text>
    <xsl:value-of select="$currentDateTime"/>

    <xsl:text>&#xA;&#xA;  The current seconds are: </xsl:text>
    <xsl:value-of select="seconds-from-dateTime($currentDateTime)"/>
    <xsl:text>, &#xA;    usually written as a whole number (</xsl:text>
    <xsl:value-of select="format-dateTime($currentDateTime, '[s01]')"/>
    <xsl:text>)</xsl:text>
  </xsl:template>

</xsl:stylesheet>
```

The stylesheet creates these results:

```
Extracting the seconds from an xs:dateTime:

  The current date and time is: 2006-11-16T05:02:55.438-05:00

  The current seconds are: 55.438,
    usually written as a whole number (55)
```

See Also

The definitions of the [2.0] `day-from-dateTime( )`, [2.0] `format-dateTime( )`, [2.0] `hours-from-dateTime( )`, [2.0] `minutes-from-dateTime( )`, [2.0] `month-from-dateTime( )`, [2.0] `timezone-from-dateTime( )`, and [2.0] `year-from-dateTime( )` functions.

[2.0] seconds-from-duration()

Given an xs:duration value, returns the number of seconds in that duration.

Syntax

```
xs:decimal? seconds-from-duration(xs:duration?)
```

Inputs

An xs:duration value.

Output

An xs:decimal representing the seconds component of the given xs:duration. Be aware that for an xs:yearMonthDuration, this function always returns 0 because there is no seconds component of an xs:yearMonthDuration. Also, if the argument is the empty sequence, this function returns the empty sequence.

Defined in

XQuery 1.0 and XPath 2.0 Functions and Operators section 10.5, "Component Extraction Functions on Durations, Dates and Times."

Example

This stylesheet demonstrates the seconds-from-duration( ) function with all three types of durations:

```
<?xml version="1.0"?>
<!-- seconds-from-duration.xsl -->
<xsl:stylesheet version="2.0"
  xmlns:xsl="http://www.w3.org/1999/XSL/Transform"
  xmlns:xs="http://www.w3.org/2001/XMLSchema">

  <xsl:output method="text"/>

  <xsl:template match="/">
    <xsl:text>&#xA;Extracting the seconds component from durations:</xsl:text>

    <xsl:variable name="sampleDuration" as="xs:duration"
      select="xs:duration('P3Y8M2DT4H23M12.2S')"/>
    <xsl:variable name="sampleYearMonthDuration" as="xs:yearMonthDuration"
      select="xs:yearMonthDuration('P3Y8M')"/>
    <xsl:variable name="sampleDayTimeDuration" as="xs:dayTimeDuration"
      select="xs:dayTimeDuration('P2DT4H23M12.2S')"/>

    <xsl:text>&#xA;&#xA;  A sample xs:duration: </xsl:text>
    <xsl:value-of select="$sampleDuration"/>
    <xsl:text>&#xA;    The seconds component of this duration is </xsl:text>
    <xsl:value-of select="seconds-from-duration($sampleDuration)"/>
    <xsl:text>.</xsl:text>

    <xsl:text>&#xA;&#xA;  A sample xs:yearMonthDuration: </xsl:text>
    <xsl:value-of select="$sampleYearMonthDuration"/>
```

```
<xsl:text>&#xA;     The seconds component of this duration is </xsl:text>
<xsl:value-of select="seconds-from-duration($sampleYearMonthDuration)"/>
<xsl:text>.</xsl:text>

<xsl:text>&#xA;&#xA;  A sample xs:dayTimeDuration: </xsl:text>
<xsl:value-of select="$sampleDayTimeDuration"/>
<xsl:text>&#xA;     The seconds component of this duration is </xsl:text>
<xsl:value-of select="seconds-from-duration($sampleDayTimeDuration)"/>
<xsl:text>.</xsl:text>
</xsl:template>

</xsl:stylesheet>
```

This stylesheet generates these results:

```
Extracting the seconds component from durations:

  A sample xs:duration: P3Y8M2DT4H23M12.2S
  The seconds component of this duration is 12.2.

  A sample xs:yearMonthDuration: P3Y8M
  The seconds component of this duration is 0.

  A sample xs:dayTimeDuration: P2DT4H23M12.2S
  The seconds component of this duration is 12.2.
```

As we mentioned earlier, extracting the seconds component from an xs:yearMonthDuration returns 0.

See Also

The definitions of the [2.0] days-from-duration( ), [2.0] hours-from-duration( ), [2.0] minutes-from-duration( ), [2.0] months-from-duration( ), and [2.0] years-from-duration( ) functions.

[2.0] seconds-from-time()

Given an xs:time value, returns its seconds component.

Syntax

```
xs:decimal? seconds-from-time(xs:time?)
```

Input

An xs:time value.

Output

An xs:decimal representing the seconds component of the given xs:time value. If the argument is the empty sequence, this function returns the empty sequence.

Defined in

XQuery 1.0 and XPath 2.0 Functions and Operators section 10.5, "Component Extraction Functions on Durations, Dates and Times."

Example

Here is a short stylesheet that uses the seconds-from-time( ) function:

```
<?xml version="1.0"?>
<!-- seconds-from-time.xsl -->
<xsl:stylesheet version="2.0"
  xmlns:xsl="http://www.w3.org/1999/XSL/Transform"
  xmlns:xs="http://www.w3.org/2001/XMLSchema">

  <xsl:output method="text"/>

  <xsl:template match="/">
    <xsl:text>&#xA;Extracting the seconds component from an xs:time:</xsl:text>
    <xsl:variable name="currentTime" as="xs:time" select="current-time()"/>
    <xsl:text>&#xA;&#xA;  The current time is: </xsl:text>
    <xsl:value-of select="$currentTime"/>

    <xsl:text>&#xA;&#xA;  The current seconds are: </xsl:text>
    <xsl:value-of select="seconds-from-time($currentTime)"/>
    <xsl:text>, &#xA;    usually written as a whole number (</xsl:text>
    <xsl:value-of select="format-time($currentTime, '[s01]')"/>
    <xsl:text>)</xsl:text>
  </xsl:template>

</xsl:stylesheet>
```

The stylesheet generates these results:

```
Extracting the seconds component from an xs:time:

  The current time is: 05:07:40.307-05:00

  The current seconds are: 40.307,
    usually written as a whole number (40)
```

Notice that the first result was generated by the seconds-from-time( ) function, while the second was generated by format-time( ).

See Also

The definitions of the [2.0] hours-from-time( ), [2.0] format-time( ), [2.0] minutes-from-time( ), [2.0] seconds-from-time( ), and [2.0] timezone-from-time( ) functions.

---

starts-with()

Determines whether the first argument string begins with the second argument.

Syntax

```
[1.0] boolean starts-with(string, string)
[2.0] xs:boolean starts-with(xs:string, xs:string)
[2.0] xs:boolean starts-with(xs:string, xs:string, $collation as xs:string)
```

Inputs

Two strings.

[2.0] In XSLT 2.0, there is an optional third argument—the name of a collation that specifies how strings are compared.

Output

Assuming both arguments are not zero-length strings, if the first string begins with the second, `starts-with( )` returns the boolean value `true`; otherwise, it returns `false`. If the second string is a zero-length string, `starts-with( )` returns `true`. If the first string *and* the second string are both zero-length strings, `starts-with( )` returns `true`. If the first string is a zero-length string but the second string is not, `starts-with( )` returns `false`.

Defined in

[1.0] XPath section 4.2, "String Functions."

[2.0] XQuery 1.0 and XPath 2.0 Functions and Operators section 7.5, "Functions Based on Substring Matching."

Example

We'll use this sample XML document:

```
<?xml version="1.0"?>
<!-- favorites.xml -->
<list>
  <title>A few of my favorite albums</title>
  <listitem>A Love Supreme</listitem>
  <listitem>Beat Crazy</listitem>
  <listitem>Here Come the Warm Jets</listitem>
  <listitem>Kind of Blue</listitem>
  <listitem>London Calling</listitem>
  <listitem>Remain in Light</listitem>
  <listitem>The Joshua Tree</listitem>
  <listitem>The Indestructible Beat of Soweto</listitem>
</list>
```

This stylesheet outputs the contents of all `<listitem>` elements that begin with the string "The":

```
<?xml version="1.0"?>
<!-- starts-with.xsl -->
<xsl:stylesheet version="1.0"
  xmlns:xsl="http://www.w3.org/1999/XSL/Transform">

  <xsl:output method="text"/>

  <xsl:template match="/">
```

```
<xsl:text>&#xA;A test of the starts-with() </xsl:text>
<xsl:text>function:&#xA;&#xA;</xsl:text>
<xsl:for-each select="list/listitem[starts-with(., 'The')]">
  <xsl:number count="listitem" format="1. "/>
  <xsl:value-of select="."/>
  <xsl:text>&#xA;</xsl:text>
</xsl:for-each>
  </xsl:template>

</xsl:stylesheet>
```

Our stylesheet generates these results:

```
A test of the starts-with() function:

7. The Joshua Tree
8. The Indestructible Beat of Soweto
```

We used `starts-with()` inside an XPath predicate expression to select all of the `<listitem>` nodes that begin with `The`.

The `<xsl:number>` element indicates the position of each item in the original list. Using `position()` to generate item numbers labels the items as 1 and 2 because these are the only two nodes being processed inside the `<xsl:for-each>` element.

[2.0] The `starts-with` function is one of several that can contain an optional collation. How that collation is specified varies from one processor to the next. In Saxon this is done with a URI that includes the name of the Java class that performs the collation. Here's an example that compares the German words *Straße* and *Strasse*. In the default collation, these two words are different; using the German collation, they're the same. Here's the stylesheet:

```
<?xml version="1.0" encoding="utf-8"?>
<!-- starts-with2.xsl -->
<xsl:stylesheet version="2.0"
  xmlns:xsl="http://www.w3.org/1999/XSL/Transform">

  <xsl:output method="text"/>

  <xsl:template match="/">
    <xsl:variable name="string1" select="'Stra&#xDF;e'"/>
    <xsl:variable name="string2" select="'Strasse'"/>

    <xsl:text>&#xA;A test of the starts-with() function:&#xA;</xsl:text>

    <xsl:text>  starts-with('</xsl:text>
    <xsl:value-of select="$string1"/>
    <xsl:text>', '</xsl:text>
    <xsl:value-of select="$string2"/>
    <xsl:text>') = </xsl:text>
    <xsl:value-of select="starts-with($string1, $string2)"/>
    <xsl:text>&#xA;</xsl:text>

    <xsl:text>  starts-with('</xsl:text>
    <xsl:value-of select="$string1"/>
    <xsl:text>', '</xsl:text>
    <xsl:value-of select="$string2"/>
```

```
  <xsl:text>', [German collation]) = </xsl:text>
  <xsl:value-of
    select="starts-with($string1, $string2,
            concat('http://saxon.sf.net/collation?',
                   'class=com.oreilly.xslt.GermanCollation;'))"/>
  <xsl:text>&#xA;</xsl:text>
</xsl:template>

</xsl:stylesheet>
```

And here are the results:

```
A test of the starts-with() function:
  starts-with('Straße', 'Strasse') = false
  starts-with('Straße', 'Strasse', [German collation]) = true
```

Using the collation we defined, the two spellings of Strasse are the same; using the default collation, they're not. (To keep the listing within the margins of the page, we used the concat( ) function to combine the two halves of the Saxon collation URI.) See "The document() Function and Sorting" in Chapter 8 for more information.

[2.0] static-base-uri()

Returns the value of the base URI property from the static context. The base URI property can change from one XML element to the next, but static-base-uri( ) returns the same value regardless of the location in the input document. In Saxon-J 9.0.0.3, the static base URI is the base URI of the stylesheet. Altova XML works similarly, although the format of the URI is not exactly the same.

Syntax

```
xs:anyURI? static-base-uri()
```

Inputs

None.

Outputs

An xs:anyURI that represents the static base URI. If the base URI property is not defined in the static context, static-base-uri( ) returns the empty sequence.

Defined in

XQuery 1.0 and XPath 2.0 Functions and Operators section 16, "Context Functions."

Example

To illustrate how static-base-uri( ) works, we'll reuse our earlier document that used the xml:base attribute to define different base URIs throughout the document:

```
<?xml version="1.0" encoding="utf-8"?>
<!-- xmlbase.xml -->
<cars>
```

```
<manufacturer name="Chevrolet"
   xml:base="http://www.chevrolet.com/">
   <car>Cavalier</car>
   <car>Corvette</car>
   <car>Impala</car>
   <car>Malibu</car>
</manufacturer>
<manufacturer name="Ford"
   xml:base="http://www.ford.com/">
   <car>Pinto</car>
   <car>Mustang</car>
   <car>Taurus</car>
</manufacturer>
<manufacturer name="Volkswagen"
   xml:base="http://www.vw.com/">
   <car>Beetle</car>
   <car>Jetta</car>
   <car>Passat</car>
   <car>Touraeg</car>
</manufacturer>
</cars>
```

Here's our stylesheet. We call the **static-base-uri( )** function at the document root, and we also call it for the **<manufacturer>** elements that change the base URI:

```
<?xml version="1.0"?>
<!-- static-base-uri.xsl -->
<xsl:stylesheet version="2.0"
   xmlns:xsl="http://www.w3.org/1999/XSL/Transform">

  <xsl:output method="text"/>

  <xsl:template match="/">
    <xsl:text>&#xA;Tests of the static-base-uri() function:</xsl:text>

    <xsl:text>&#xA;&#xA;  The static base URI for the </xsl:text>
    <xsl:text>document root is:&#xA;    </xsl:text>
    <xsl:value-of select="static-base-uri()"/>
    <xsl:text>&#xA;&#xA;</xsl:text>

    <xsl:for-each select="/cars/manufacturer">
      <xsl:text>  The static base URI for manufacturer </xsl:text>
      <xsl:value-of select="@name"/>
      <xsl:text> is: &#xA;    </xsl:text>
      <xsl:value-of select="static-base-uri()"/>
      <xsl:text>&#xA;</xsl:text>
    </xsl:for-each>
  </xsl:template>

</xsl:stylesheet>
```

Here are our results:

```
Tests of the static-base-uri() function:

  The static base URI for the document root is:
    file:/C://static-base-uri.xsl
```

```
The static base URI for manufacturer Chevrolet is:
   file:/C://static-base-uri.xsl
The static base URI for manufacturer Ford is:
   file:/C://static-base-uri.xsl
The static base URI for manufacturer Volkswagen is:
   file:/C://static-base-uri.xsl
```

As you can see, the `static-base-uri( )` function always returns the same value (the URI of the stylesheet), regardless of where we are in the XML document or whether any `xml:base` attributes have been defined.

string()

Returns the string value of the argument.

Syntax

```
[1.0] string string(object)
[2.0] xs:string string(item()?)
```

Inputs

An *[1.0]*object or *[2.0]* item. The argument is converted to a string as described in the following subsection.

Output

[1.0] A string. The input argument is converted to a string as follows:

- If the argument is a node-set, the first node in the node-set is converted to a string. (The first node in the node-set is the one that occurs first in document order.) For an element or root node, this means all of its text content. For an attribute, this means its value.

- If the argument is a number, it is converted to a string as follows:

  — The value NaN is converted to the string `"NaN"`.

  — Positive zero is converted to the string `"0"`.

  — Negative zero is converted to the string `"0"`.

  — Positive infinity is converted to the string `"Infinity"`.

  — Negative infinity is converted to the string `"-Infinity"`.

  — An integer is converted to a string representing that integer, using no decimal point and no leading zeros. If the integer is negative, it will be preceded by a minus sign (-).

  — Any other number is converted to a string with a decimal point—at least one number before the decimal point and at least one number after the decimal point. If the number is negative, it will be preceded by a minus sign (-). There will not be any leading zeros before the decimal point (with the possible exception of the one required digit before the decimal point). After the decimal point, there will be only as many digits as needed to distinguish this number from all other numeric values defined by the IEEE 754 standard, the same standard used by the Java `float` and `double` types.

- If the argument is a boolean value, the value `true` is represented by the string `"true"` and the value `false` is represented by the string `"false"`.

- If the argument is any other type, it is converted to a string in a way that depends on that type. See the documentation for your XSLT processor to find out what other types are supported and how they are converted to strings.

[2.0] An `xs:string`. Because XSLT 2.0 supports more datatypes than XSLT 1.0, it's not surprising that the rules for converting values to strings are more complicated. The rules are:

- If the item is an `xs:string` or any datatype derived from `xs:string`, the argument is returned without any changes.

- If the item is a sequence, it must be either the empty sequence or a singleton. *It is an error to call* `string( )` *with a sequence containing more than one item.* This is a major change from XSLT 1.0, in which `string( )` (and a number of other functions) simply took the first item in the node-set and processed it. If you are migrating an XSLT 1.0 stylesheet to XSLT 2.0, you'll have to change this code:

  ```
  <xsl:value-of select="string(items/item/price)"/>
  ```

  to this:

  ```
  <xsl:value-of select="string((items/item/price)[1])"/>
  ```

  If the `string( )` function doesn't have an argument, the context item is used. In other words, `string( )` is the same as `string(.)`. Calling `string( )` with the empty sequence returns a zero-length string.

- If the item is numeric (`xs:integer`, `xs:decimal`, `xs:float`, or `xs:double`, or anything derived from them), it is converted to a string using these rules:

  —If the value is NaN (not a number), it is converted to the string `"NaN"`.

  —If the value is positive infinity, it is converted to the string `"INF"`.

  —If the value is negative infinity, it is converted to the string `"-INF"`.

  —If the value is positive zero, it is converted to the string `0`.

  —If the value is negative zero, it is converted to the string `-0`.

  The XQuery 1.0 and XPath 2.0 Functions and Operators spec goes into exhaustive detail about how various numeric datatypes are converted to strings. For example, an `xs:integer` value will not have a decimal point when it is converted to a string. There are also rules for how a mantissa and an exponent can be formatted, how `xs:decimal` values with no digits after the decimal point are handled, and many, many other rules. See the spec for all the details.

- If the item is an `xs:date`, `xs:time`, or `xs:dateTime`, the string value is the default form of those datatypes. For example, an `xs:date` is represented as `YYYY-MM-DD-Z` in most cases (the `-Z` represents the timezone if one is defined), an `xs:time` is represented as `HH:MM:SS-Z` (where `Z` represents the timezone), and a `xs:dateTime` is represented as `YYYY-MM-DDTHH:MM:SS-Z`.

  The `string()` function returns the raw form of these types; the `format-date()`, `format-dateTime()`, and `format-time()` functions are more useful ways of converting these datatypes to strings.

- If the item is an `xs:dayTimeDuration`, `xs:yearMonthDuration`, or a basic `xs:duration`, the string value is the default format. An `xs:dayTimeDuration` is represented as `P2DT4H23M12.2S` (2 days, 4 hours, 23 minutes, and 12.2 seconds), for example. The functions `days-from-duration()`, `hours-from-duration()`, `minutes-from-duration()`, `months-from-duration()`, `seconds-from-duration()`, and `years-from-duration()` are much more useful ways of converting these datatypes to strings.

- If the item is an `xs:anyURI`, it is returned as its string value. None of the characters in the string value are escaped.

- For any other XML Schema datatypes that have a default format (typically known as the canonical representation), they are converted to `xs:string` values using that default format. The process for converting any datatypes that do not have a canonical representation to strings is implementation-defined.

Defined in

[1.0] XPath section 4.2, "String Functions."

[2.0] XQuery 1.0 and XPath 2.0 Functions and Operators section 2, "Accessors," with the rules for converting datatypes to strings defined in section 17.1.2, "Casting to `xs:string` and `xs:untypedAtomic`."

Example

We'll use our document of chocolate bar sales to test the `string()` function:

```
<?xml version="1.0" encoding="utf-8"?>
<!-- chocolate.xml -->
<report month="8" year="2006">
  <title>Chocolate bar sales</title>
  <brand>
    <name>Lindt</name>
    <units>27408</units>
  </brand>
  <brand>
    <name>Callebaut</name>
    <units>8203</units>
  </brand>
  <brand>
    <name>Valrhona</name>
    <units>22101</units>
```

```
    </brand>
    <brand>
      <name>Perugina</name>
      <units>14336</units>
    </brand>
    <brand>
      <name>Ghirardelli</name>
      <units>19268</units>
    </brand>
  </report>
```

We'll test the **string( )** function with a variety of arguments:

```
<?xml version="1.0"?>
<!-- string.xsl -->
<xsl:stylesheet version="1.0"
  xmlns:xsl="http://www.w3.org/1999/XSL/Transform">

  <xsl:output method="text"/>

  <xsl:template match="/">
    <xsl:text>&#xA;Tests of the string() function:</xsl:text>

    <xsl:text>&#xA;&#xA;  string(count(/report/brand)) = </xsl:text>
    <xsl:value-of select="string(count(/report/brand))"/>

    <xsl:text>&#xA;&#xA;  string(true()) = </xsl:text>
    <xsl:value-of select="string(true())"/>

    <xsl:text>&#xA;&#xA;  string(count(/report</xsl:text>
    <xsl:text>/brand/units[. &gt; 20000])) = </xsl:text>
    <xsl:value-of
      select="string(count(/report/brand/units[. &gt; 20000]))"/>

    <xsl:text>&#xA;&#xA;  string(/report/brand/units</xsl:text>
    <xsl:text>[. &gt; 20000][1]/../name) = </xsl:text>
    <xsl:value-of
      select="string(/report/brand/units[. &gt; 20000][1]/../name)"/>
  </xsl:template>

</xsl:stylesheet>
```

Here are the results of our stylesheet:

```
Tests of the string() function:

  string(count(/report/brand)) = 5

  string(true()) = true

  string(count(/report/brand/units[. > 20000])) = 2

  string(/report/brand/units[. > 20000][1]/../name) = Lindt
```

[2.0] Converting a value to a string is usually pretty straightforward. Here is another stylesheet that converts some of XSLT 2.0's datatypes to strings:

```
<?xml version="1.0"?>
<!-- string2.xsl -->
<xsl:stylesheet version="2.0"
  xmlns:xsl="http://www.w3.org/1999/XSL/Transform"
  xmlns:xs="http://www.w3.org/2001/XMLSchema">

  <xsl:output method="text"/>

  <xsl:template match="/">
    <xsl:text>&#xA;More tests of the string() function:</xsl:text>

    <xsl:text>&#xA;&#xA;  string(xs:double(2718.28E-3)) = </xsl:text>
    <xsl:value-of select="string(xs:double(2718.28E-3))"/>

    <xsl:text>&#xA;&#xA;  string(current-time()) = </xsl:text>
    <xsl:value-of select="string(current-time())"/>

    <xsl:text>&#xA;&#xA;  string(xs:yearMonthDuration</xsl:text>
    <xsl:text>('P3Y8M')) = </xsl:text>
    <xsl:value-of
      select="string(xs:yearMonthDuration('P3Y8M'))"/>

    <xsl:text>&#xA;&#xA;  string(xs:date('1995-04-21')) = </xsl:text>
    <xsl:value-of
      select="string(xs:date('1995-04-21'))"/>

    <xsl:variable name="topBrands" as="xs:string*"
      select="/report/brand/units[. &gt; 15000]/../name/string()"/>
    <xsl:text>&#xA;&#xA;  Top-selling brands: &#xA;    </xsl:text>
    <xsl:value-of select="$topBrands" separator=", "/>
  </xsl:template>

</xsl:stylesheet>
```

Here are the results:

```
More tests of the string() function:

  string(xs:double(2718.28E-3)) = 2.71828

  string(current-time()) = 06:38:08.438-04:00

  string(xs:yearMonthDuration('P3Y8M')) = P3Y8M

  string(xs:date('1995-04-21')) = 1995-04-21

  Top-selling brands:
    Lindt, Valrhona, Ghirardelli
```

The stylesheet also uses the string( ) function as the last step in an XPath expression. The expression /report/brand/units[. > 15000]/../name/string( ) finds all of the <units> elements with a value greater than 15000, and then converts the text of their sibling <name> elements into strings, returning a sequence of strings. Outputting this sequence with the <xsl:value-of> element lists the three brands (Lindt, Valrhona, and Ghirardelli).

[2.0] string-join()

Given a sequence of strings and a separator string, returns a string containing each string from the sequence, separated by the second string.

Syntax

```
xs:string string-join(xs:string*, xs:string)
```

Inputs

A sequence of xs:strings and a string used as a separator.

Outputs

An xs:string that contains all of the strings in the sequence, separated by the second argument. If the second string is a zero-length string, the strings in the sequence are concatenated without a separator. If the sequence is the empty sequence, string-join( ) returns a zero-length string.

Defined in

XQuery 1.0 and XPath 2.0 Functions and Operators section 7.4, Functions on String Values.

Example

Here is a stylesheet that tests the string-join( ) function:

```
<?xml version="1.0"?>
<!-- string-join.xsl -->
<xsl:stylesheet version="2.0"
  xmlns:xsl="http://www.w3.org/1999/XSL/Transform"
  xmlns:xs="http://www.w3.org/2001/XMLSchema">

  <xsl:output method="text"/>

  <xsl:template match="/">
    <xsl:text>&#xA;A test of the string-join() function:&#xA;</xsl:text>

    <xsl:variable name="testSequence" as="xs:string*">
      <xsl:sequence
        select="('Brooklyn', 'Manhattan', 'Williamsburg',
                'George Washington', 'Tribeca')"/>
    </xsl:variable>

    <xsl:text>&#xA;  Our sequence of strings:&#xA;    </xsl:text>
    <xsl:value-of select="$testSequence" separator="&#xA;    "/>

    <xsl:text>&#xA;&#xA;  string-join($testSequeqnce, ' - ') = </xsl:text>
    <xsl:text>&#xA;    </xsl:text>
    <xsl:value-of select="string-join($testSequence, ' - ')"/>

    <xsl:text>&#xA;&#xA;  Courtesy of the specs, here's </xsl:text>
    <xsl:text>another example:&#xA;&#xA;    Ancestors of all </xsl:text>
    <xsl:text>the elements:&#xA;       using string-join&#xA;</xsl:text>
```

```
    <xsl:text>              (for $i in unordered</xsl:text>
    <xsl:text>(ancestor-or-self::*) return name($i), </xsl:text>
    <xsl:text>&#xA;              '/'):&#xA;</xsl:text>

    <xsl:for-each select="//*">
      <xsl:text>&#xA;      </xsl:text>
      <xsl:value-of
        select="string-join(for $i in ancestor-or-self::*
               return name($i), '/')"/>
    </xsl:for-each>
  </xsl:template>

</xsl:stylesheet>
```

Here are the results:

```
A test of the string-join() function:

  Our sequence of strings:
    Brooklyn
    Manhattan
    Williamsburg
    George Washington
    Tribeca

  string-join($testSequeqnce, ' - ') =
    Brooklyn - Manhattan - Williamsburg - George Washington - Tribeca

  Courtesy of the specs, here's another example:

  Ancestors of all the elements:
    using string-join
          (for $i in unordered(ancestor-or-self::*) return name($i),
          '/'):

    report
    report/title
    report/brand
    report/brand/name
    report/brand/units
    report/brand
    report/brand/name
    report/brand/units
    report/brand
    report/brand/name
    report/brand/units
    report/brand
    report/brand/name
    report/brand/units
    report/brand
    report/brand/name
    report/brand/units
```

string-length()

Returns the number of characters in the string passed in as the argument to this function. If no argument is specified, the context node is converted to a string and the length of that string is returned.

Syntax

```
[1.0] number string-length(string?)
[2.0] xs:integer string-length()
[2.0] xs:integer string-length(string?)
```

Inputs

An optional string.

Output

The number of characters defined in the string (an `xs:integer` in XSLT 2.0). If no string is specified as an argument, the context node is used. In other words, `string-length( )` and `string-length(.)` are equivalent.

[2.0] If the string is the empty sequence, the value `0` is returned.

Defined in

[1.0] XPath section 4.2, "String Functions."

[2.0] XQuery 1.0 and XPath 2.0 section 7.4, "Functions on String Values."

Example

The following example demonstrates the results of invoking the `string-length( )` function against various argument types. Here's the XML document we'll use for our example:

```
<?xml version="1.0" encoding="utf-8"?>
<!-- chocolate.xml -->
<report month="8" year="2006">
  <title>Chocolate bar sales</title>
  <brand>
    <name>Lindt</name>
    <units>27408</units>
  </brand>
  <brand>
    <name>Callebaut</name>
    <units>8203</units>
  </brand>
  <brand>
    <name>Valrhona</name>
    <units>22101</units>
  </brand>
  <brand>
    <name>Perugina</name>
    <units>14336</units>
  </brand>
  <brand>
```

```
      <name>Ghirardelli</name>
      <units>19268</units>
    </brand>
  </report>
```

We'll process this document with the following stylesheet:

```
<?xml version="1.0"?>
<!-- string-length.xsl -->
<xsl:stylesheet version="1.0"
  xmlns:xsl="http://www.w3.org/1999/XSL/Transform">

  <xsl:output method="text"/>

  <xsl:template match="/">
    <xsl:text>&#xA;Tests of the string-length() function:</xsl:text>

    <xsl:text>&#xA;&#xA;    string-length() = </xsl:text>
    <xsl:value-of select="string-length()"/>
    <xsl:text>&#xA;    string-length(/report) = </xsl:text>
    <xsl:value-of select="string-length(/report)"/>
    <xsl:text>&#xA;    string-length(/report/brand[1]) = </xsl:text>
    <xsl:value-of select="string-length(/report/brand[1])"/>
    <xsl:text>&#xA;    string-length(/report/brand[1]/name) = </xsl:text>
    <xsl:value-of select="string-length(/report/brand[1]/name)"/>

    <xsl:text>&#xA;</xsl:text>
    <xsl:for-each select="/report/brand">
      <xsl:text>&#xA;    The name of brand #</xsl:text>
      <xsl:value-of select="position()"/>
      <xsl:text>, </xsl:text>
      <xsl:value-of select="name"/>
      <xsl:text>, has </xsl:text>
      <xsl:value-of select="string-length(name)"/>
      <xsl:text> characters.</xsl:text>
    </xsl:for-each>
  </xsl:template>

</xsl:stylesheet>
```

Here are the results of our stylesheet:

```
Tests of the string-length() function:

    string-length() = 168
    string-length(/report) = 168
    string-length(/report/brand[1]) = 23
    string-length(/report/brand[1]/name) = 5

    The name of brand #1, Lindt, has 5 characters.
    The name of brand #2, Callebaut, has 9 characters.
    The name of brand #3, Valrhona, has 8 characters.
    The name of brand #4, Perugina, has 8 characters.
    The name of brand #5, Ghirardelli, has 11 characters.
```

When we invoked the **string-length( )** function without any arguments, the root node (in XSLT 2.0, the document node) was converted to a string, and then the length of that string was returned. (The context node is the root node at this point.) The string length of the root element (`<report>`) has the same value because there is no text outside the `<report>` element. Remember, the string value of any node is the concatenation of all the text in that node and all of its descendants.

[2.0] string-to-codepoints()

Converts a string into a sequence of Unicode codepoints.

Syntax

```
xs:integer* string-to-codepoints(xs:string?)
```

Inputs

An `xs:string`.

Output

A sequence of `xs:integer`s, each of which represents a Unicode codepoint. If the input string is of zero length or is the empty sequence, the empty sequence is returned.

Defined in

XQuery 1.0 and XPath 2.0 Functions and Operators section 7.2, "Functions to Assemble and Disassemble Strings."

Example

Here's a short stylesheet that converts strings into sequences of integers:

```
<?xml version="1.0" encoding="UTF-8"?>
<!-- string-to-codepoints.xsl -->
<xsl:stylesheet version="2.0"
  xmlns:xsl="http://www.w3.org/1999/XSL/Transform"
  xmlns:xs="http://www.w3.org/2001/XMLSchema">

  <xsl:output method="text"/>

  <xsl:template match="/">
    <xsl:text>&#xA;Tests of the string-to-codepoints() </xsl:text>
    <xsl:text>function:&#xA;</xsl:text>

    <xsl:text>&#xA;  string-to-codepoints('Lily') = </xsl:text>
    <xsl:value-of
      select="string-to-codepoints('Lily')" separator=", " />

    <xsl:text>&#xA;  string-to-codepoints('Straße') = </xsl:text>
    <xsl:value-of
      select="string-to-codepoints('Straße')" separator=", "/>
  </xsl:template>

</xsl:stylesheet>
```

The stylesheet generates these results:

```
Tests of the string-to-codepoints() function:

  string-to-codepoints('Lily') = 76, 105, 108, 121
  string-to-codepoints('Straße') = 83, 116, 114, 97, 223, 101
```

[2.0] subsequence()

Returns a contiguous portion of a sequence.

Syntax

```
item()* subsequence($sourceSeq as item()*, $startingLoc as xs:double)
item()* subsequence($sourceSeq as item()*, $startingLoc as xs:double,
                    $length as xs:double)
```

Inputs

A sequence and a starting position. An optional third argument specifies the number of items to be returned. The second and third arguments are xs:doubles because many numeric operations on untyped data return xs:double.

Some details about how the two numeric arguments work:

- If the starting position is larger than the number of items in the sequence, the empty sequence is returned.

- If the sequence is the empty sequence, the empty sequence is returned.

Outputs

A new sequence containing the specified items.

Defined in

XQuery 1.0 and XPath 2.0 Functions and Operators section 15.1, "General Functions and Operators on Sequences."

Example

Here's a stylesheet that illustrates how subsequence( ) works:

```
<?xml version="1.0"?>
<!-- subsequence.xsl -->
<xsl:stylesheet version="2.0"
  xmlns:xsl="http://www.w3.org/1999/XSL/Transform"
  xmlns:xs="http://www.w3.org/2001/XMLSchema">

  <xsl:output method="text"/>

  <xsl:template match="/">

    <xsl:variable name="testSequence" as="item()*">
      <xsl:sequence select="(3, 4, 5)"/>
```

```
        <xsl:element name="currentDate">
          <xsl:value-of select="current-date()"/>
        </xsl:element>
        <xsl:element name="currentTime">
          <xsl:value-of select="current-time()"/>
        </xsl:element>
        <xsl:element name="integerTest">
          <xsl:value-of select="xs:integer(8)"/>
        </xsl:element>
        <xsl:sequence select="('blue', 'red')"/>
        <xsl:element name="floatTest1">
          <xsl:value-of select="xs:float(3.14)"/>
        </xsl:element>
        <xsl:element name="floatTest2">
          <xsl:value-of select="xs:float(42)"/>
        </xsl:element>
        <xsl:element name="dateTest">
          <xsl:value-of select="xs:date('1995-04-21')"/>
        </xsl:element>
</xsl:variable>

<xsl:variable name="emptySequence" as="item()*">
  <xsl:sequence select="()"/>
</xsl:variable>

<xsl:text>&#xA;Here is a test of the subsequence() </xsl:text>
<xsl:text>function:&#xA;</xsl:text>

<xsl:text>&#xA;  Our original sequence is:&#xA;&#xA;     </xsl:text>
<xsl:value-of select="$testSequence"
  separator="&#xA;     "/>

<xsl:text>&#xA;&#xA;  subsequence($testSequence, 8) = </xsl:text>
<xsl:text>&#xA;     </xsl:text>
<xsl:value-of select="subsequence($testSequence, 8)"
  separator="&#xA;     "/>

<xsl:text>&#xA;&#xA;  subsequence($testSequence, 3, 3) = </xsl:text>
<xsl:text>&#xA;     </xsl:text>
<xsl:value-of select="subsequence($testSequence, 3, 3)"
  separator="&#xA;     "/>

<xsl:text>&#xA;&#xA;  subsequence($testSequence, 1, 1) = </xsl:text>
<xsl:text>&#xA;     </xsl:text>
<xsl:value-of select="subsequence($testSequence, 1, 1)"
  separator="&#xA;     "/>

<xsl:text>&#xA;&#xA;  subsequence($testSequence, -1, 3) = </xsl:text>
<xsl:text>&#xA;     </xsl:text>
<xsl:value-of select="subsequence($testSequence, -1, 3)"
  separator="&#xA;     "/>

<xsl:text>&#xA;&#xA;  subsequence($testSequence, 14, 2) = </xsl:text>
<xsl:text>&#xA;     </xsl:text>
<xsl:value-of select="subsequence($testSequence, 14, 2)"
```

```
      separator="&#xA;     "/>

   <xsl:text>&#xA;&#xA;  subsequence($testSequence, 2.3, 1.7) = </xsl:text>
   <xsl:text>&#xA;     </xsl:text>
   <xsl:value-of select="subsequence($testSequence, 2.3, 1.7)"
      separator="&#xA;     "/>

   <xsl:text>&#xA;&#xA;  subsequence($emptySequence, 1) = </xsl:text>
   <xsl:text>&#xA;     </xsl:text>
   <xsl:value-of select="subsequence($emptySequence, 1)"/>
   </xsl:template>

</xsl:stylesheet>
```

Here are the results:

```
Here is a test of the subsequence() function:

  Our original sequence is:

    3
    4
    5
    2007-02-19-05:00
    11:19:24.734-05:00
    8
    blue
    red
    3.14
    42
    1995-04-21

  subsequence($testSequence, 8) =
    red
    3.14
    42
    1995-04-21

  subsequence($testSequence, 3, 3) =
    5
    2007-02-19-05:00
    11:19:24.734-05:00

  subsequence($testSequence, 1, 1) =
    3

  subsequence($testSequence, -1, 3) =
    3

  subsequence($testSequence, 14, 2) =


  subsequence($testSequence, 2.3, 1.7) =
    4
    5
```

```
subsequence($emptySequence, 1) =
```

In the first example, we start at the eighth item in the sequence and return all of the subsequent items. Next, we start at the third item and return items 3, 4, and 5. To return a single item, we use 1, 1 to get one item starting at the first item. Using a negative start position can actually return items, as we see in the example -1, 3. The three items we're requesting are items –1, 0, and 1. Item 1 is the only one that exists, so that's what subsequence( ) returns. In the next example, the starting position of 14 returns the empty sequence because there are less than 14 items. Using decimals for the numeric arguments means they are rounded to the nearest whole number, so this is the same as 2, 2. Finally, calling subsequence( ) against the empty sequence returns the empty sequence.

substring()

Returns a portion of a given string.

Syntax

```
[1.0] string substring($sourceString as string, $startingLoc as number,
                        $length as number?)
[2.0] xs:string substring($sourceString as xs:string?,
                          $startingLoc as xs:double)
[2.0] xs:string substring($sourceString as xs:string?,
                          $startingLoc as xs:double,
                          $length as xs:double)
```

Inputs

The substring( ) function takes a string and one or two numbers as arguments. The string is the string from which the substring will be extracted. The second argument is used as the starting position of the returned substring, and the optional third argument specifies how many characters are returned.

Output

With two arguments (a string and a starting position), the substring( ) function returns all characters in the string whose position is greater than or equal to the starting position. *Be aware that the first character in a string is at position 1, not 0.*

With three arguments (a string, a starting position, and a length), the substring( ) function returns all characters in the string whose position is greater than or equal to the starting position or whose position is less than the starting position *plus* the length.

Normally, the arguments to the substring( ) function are integers, although they may be floating-point numbers or more complicated expressions. In the case of floating-point numbers, the number is converted to an integer by the round( ) function.

Defined in

[1.0] XPath section 4.2, "String Functions."

[2.0] XQuery 1.0 and XPath 2.0 Functions and Operators section 7.4, "Functions on String Values."

Example

Here's the stylesheet we'll use to demonstrate the **substring( )** function:

```
<?xml version="1.0"?>
<!-- substring.xsl -->
<xsl:stylesheet version="1.0"
  xmlns:xsl="http://www.w3.org/1999/XSL/Transform">

  <xsl:output method="text"/>

  <xsl:template match="/">
    <xsl:text>&#xA;Tests of the substring() function:</xsl:text>

    <xsl:text>&#xA;&#xA;  1. substring('Now is the time', 4)     = "</xsl:text>
    <xsl:value-of select="substring('Now is the time', 4)"/>
    <xsl:text>"&#xA;</xsl:text>
    <xsl:text>  2. substring('Now is the time', 4, 6)  = "</xsl:text>
    <xsl:value-of select="substring('Now is the time', 4, 6)"/>
    <xsl:text>"&#xA;</xsl:text>

    <!-- Xalan chokes on this example, Saxon and MSXSL don't. -->
    <xsl:text>  3. substring('Now is the time', 8, -6) = "</xsl:text>
    <xsl:value-of select="substring('Now is the time', 8, -6)"/>
    <xsl:text>"&#xA;</xsl:text>
    <xsl:text>  4. substring('Now is the time', -3, 6) = "</xsl:text>
    <xsl:value-of select="substring('Now is the time', -3, 6)"/>
    <xsl:text>"&#xA;</xsl:text>
    <xsl:text>  5. substring('Now is the time', 54, 6) = "</xsl:text>
    <xsl:value-of select="substring('Now is the time', 54, 6)"/>
    <xsl:text>"&#xA;&#xA;</xsl:text>
    <xsl:text>  6. substring('Now is the time', 1.7, 6.4) = "</xsl:text>
    <xsl:value-of select="substring('Now is the time', 1.7, 6.4)"/>
    <xsl:text>"&#xA;</xsl:text>
    <xsl:text>  7. substring('Now is the time', 1.7, 6.5) = "</xsl:text>
    <xsl:value-of select="substring('Now is the time', 1.7, 6.5)"/>
    <xsl:text>"&#xA;&#xA;</xsl:text>
    <xsl:text>  count(document('')//*) = </xsl:text>
    <xsl:value-of select="count(document('')//*)"/>
    <xsl:text>&#xA;&#xA;  8. substring('Here is a really, </xsl:text>
    <xsl:text>really, really long string',</xsl:text>
    <xsl:text>&#xA;     count(document('')//*)) = "</xsl:text>
    <xsl:value-of
      select="substring('Here is a really, really, really long string',
              count(document('')//*))"/>
    <xsl:text>"&#xA;</xsl:text>
  </xsl:template>

</xsl:stylesheet>
```

When using the Saxon or MSXSL processor, here are the results:

```
Tests of the substring() function:

  1. substring('Now is the time', 4) = " is the time"
  2. substring('Now is the time', 4, 6) = " is th"
  3. substring('Now is the time', 8, -6) = ""
  4. substring('Now is the time', -3, 6) = "No"
  5. substring('Now is the time', 54, 6) = ""

  6. substring('Now is the time', 1.7, 6.4) = "ow is "
  7. substring('Now is the time', 1.7, 6.5) = "ow is t"

  count(document('')//*) = 32

  8. substring('Here is a really, really, really long string',
     count(document('')//*)) = "y long string"
```

We'll look at each test case individually:

1. The first test case returns all the characters whose position is >= 4.

2. The second test case returns all the characters whose position is >= 4 and < 10. (Remember, the starting value and the length are added together to determine the upper bound of the substring.)

3. The third test case returns all the characters whose position is >= 8 and < 2. This useless range of characters is, of course, empty.

4. This test returns all the characters whose position is >= –3 and < 3. Even though starting from a negative position seems as though it would return nothing, positions 1 and 2 fall into the requested range.

5. This test returns nothing because the starting position is greater than the length of the string.

6. This test case uses floating-point numbers for the starting position and the length. The two numbers are rounded, meaning this is equivalent to substring('Now is the time', 2, 6). All characters whose positions are >= 2 and < 8 are returned.

7. This test case also uses floating-point numbers. In this case, the second number (6.5) is rounded to 7, making this equivalent to substring('Now is the time', 2, 7). Characters whose positions are >= 2 and < 9 are returned.

8. For the final two test cases, we use a more complicated XPath expression (count(document('')//*)) to generate a number. This value is the number of elements in the stylesheet itself. This test case returns all characters whose position is >= 36.

A final note: Xalan raises an error with the example substring('Now is the time', 8, –6):

```
XSLT Error (javax.xml.transform.TransformerException):
java.lang.StringIndexOutOfBoundsException:
String index out of range: -6
```

Although this is an error in Xalan's implementation, it does make the point that passing unreasonable data to a function can lead to unpleasant results.

substring-after()

Given a data string and a search string, returns the portion of the data string after the first occurrence of the search string. If the search string is not found, the substring-after( ) function returns a zero-length string.

Syntax

```
[1.0] string substring-after(string, string)
[2.0] xs:string substring-after(xs:string?, xs:string?)
[2.0] xs:string substring-after(xs:string?, xs:string?,
                                $collation as xs:string)
```

Inputs

Two strings. The first string is the data string to be searched, and the second is the search string. substring-after( ) looks for the search string in the data string.

[2.0] In XSLT 2.0, there is an optional third argument: the name of a collation that specifies how strings are compared.

Output

The portion of the data string that occurs after the first occurrence of the search string. If the search string does not appear in the data string, the function returns an empty string. If the second string is a zero-length string, substring-after( ) returns a zero-length string. The function also returns a zero-length string if the first string is shorter than the second string.

Defined in

[1.0] XPath section 4.2, "String Functions."

[2.0] XQuery 1.0 and XPath 2.0 Functions and Operators section 7.5, "Functions Based on Substring Matching."

Example

Here is a sample stylesheet that uses substring-after( ):

```
<?xml version="1.0"?>
<!-- substring-after1.xsl -->
<xsl:stylesheet version="1.0"
  xmlns:xsl="http://www.w3.org/1999/XSL/Transform">

  <xsl:output method="text"/>

  <xsl:template match="/">
    <xsl:text>&#xA;A test of the substring-after() </xsl:text>
    <xsl:text>function:&#xA;&#xA;</xsl:text>

    <xsl:text>  substring-after('Abracadabra', </xsl:text>
```

```
    <xsl:text>'bra')   = "</xsl:text>
    <xsl:value-of
      select="substring-after('Abracadabra', 'bra')"/>
    <xsl:text>"&#xA;</xsl:text>

    <xsl:text>  substring-after('Abracadabra', </xsl:text>
    <xsl:text>'abra') = "</xsl:text>
    <xsl:value-of
      select="substring-after('Abracadabra', 'abra')"/>
    <xsl:text>"&#xA;</xsl:text>

    <xsl:text>  substring-after('Abracadabra', </xsl:text>
    <xsl:text>'A')     = "</xsl:text>
    <xsl:value-of
      select="substring-after('Abracadabra', 'A')"/>
    <xsl:text>"&#xA;</xsl:text>

    <xsl:text>  substring-after('Abracadabra', </xsl:text>
    <xsl:text>'A')     = "</xsl:text>
    <xsl:value-of
      select="substring-after('Abracadabra', 'a')"/>
    <xsl:text>"&#xA;</xsl:text>

    <xsl:text>  substring-after('Abracadabra', </xsl:text>
    <xsl:text>'')       = "</xsl:text>
    <xsl:value-of
      select="substring-after('Abracadabra', '')"/>
    <xsl:text>"&#xA;</xsl:text>
  </xsl:template>

</xsl:stylesheet>
```

The stylesheet produces these results:

```
A test of the substring-after() function:

  substring-after('Abracadabra', 'bra')  = "cadabra"
  substring-after('Abracadabra', 'abra') = ""
  substring-after('Abracadabra', 'A')    = "bracadabra"
  substring-after('Abracadabra', 'A')    = "cadabra"
  substring-after('Abracadabra', '')      = "Abracadabra"
```

As a second example, here's an XSLT 2.0 stylesheet that uses a custom collation:

```
<?xml version="1.0"?>
<!-- substring-after2.xsl -->
<xsl:stylesheet version="1.0"
  xmlns:xsl="http://www.w3.org/1999/XSL/Transform">

  <xsl:output method="text"/>

  <xsl:template match="/">
    <xsl:text>&#xA;Another test of the substring-after() </xsl:text>
    <xsl:text>function:&#xA;&#xA;</xsl:text>

    <xsl:text>  substring-after('Schoenaicherstrasse', </xsl:text>
    <xsl:text>'Sch&#xF6;n') = &#xA;      "</xsl:text>
```

```
<xsl:value-of
  select="substring-after('Schoenaicherstrasse', 'Sch&#xF6;n')"/>
<xsl:text>"&#xA;</xsl:text>

<xsl:text>  substring-after('Schoenaicherstrasse', </xsl:text>
<xsl:text>'Sch&#xF6;n', [German collation]) = &#xA;     "</xsl:text>
<xsl:value-of
  select="substring-after('Schoenaicherstrasse', 'Sch&#xF6;n',
          concat('http://saxon.sf.net/collation?',
                 'class=com.oreilly.xslt.GermanCollation;'))"/>
<xsl:text>"&#xA;</xsl:text>
  </xsl:template>

</xsl:stylesheet>
```

The stylesheet generates these results:

```
Another test of the substring-after() function:

  substring-after('Schoenaicherstrasse', 'Schön') =
     ""

  substring-after('Schoenaicherstrasse', 'Schön', [German collation]) =
     "aicherstrasse"
```

The German umlaut-o character (ö) is equivalent to *oe*. The default collation doesn't recognize this, but our custom collation does. (To keep the listing within the margins of the page, we used the concat( ) function to combine the two halves of the Saxon collation URI.) See "The document() Function and Sorting" in Chapter 8 for more information.

substring-before()

Given a data string and a search string, returns the portion of the data string before the first occurrence of the search string. If the search string is not found, the substring-before( ) function returns a zero-length string.

Syntax

```
[1.0] string substring-before(string, string)
[2.0] xs:string substring-before(xs:string?, xs:string?)
[2.0] xs:string substring-before(xs:string?, xs:string?,
                                 $collation as xs:string)
```

Inputs

Two strings. The first string is the string to be searched, and the second is the string to be searched for in the first string.

[2.0] In XSLT 2.0, there is an optional third argument: the name of a collation that specifies how strings are compared.

Output

The portion of the data string that occurs before the first occurrence of the search string. If the search string does not appear in the data string, the function returns an empty string. If the second string is a zero-length string, `substring-before( )` returns a zero-length string. The function also returns a zero-length string if the first string is shorter than the second string.

Defined in

[1.0] XPath section 4.2, "String Functions."

[2.0] XQuery 1.0 and XPath 2.0 Functions and Operators section 7.5, "Functions Based on Substring Matching."

Example

Here is a sample stylesheet that uses `substring-before( )`:

```
<?xml version="1.0"?>
<!-- substring-before1.xsl -->
<xsl:stylesheet version="1.0"
  xmlns:xsl="http://www.w3.org/1999/XSL/Transform">

  <xsl:output method="text"/>

  <xsl:template match="/">
    <xsl:text>&#xA;A test of the substring-before() </xsl:text>
    <xsl:text>function:&#xA;&#xA;</xsl:text>

    <xsl:text>  substring-before('Abracadabra', </xsl:text>
    <xsl:text>'abra')         = "</xsl:text>
    <xsl:value-of
      select="substring-before('Abracadabra', 'abra')"/>
    <xsl:text>"&#xA;</xsl:text>

    <xsl:text>  substring-before('Abracadabra', </xsl:text>
    <xsl:text>'Abracadabra') = "</xsl:text>
    <xsl:value-of
      select="substring-before('Abracadabra', 'Abracadabra')"/>
    <xsl:text>"&#xA;</xsl:text>

    <xsl:text>  substring-before('Abracadabra', </xsl:text>
    <xsl:text>'A')            = "</xsl:text>
    <xsl:value-of
      select="substring-before('Abracadabra', 'A')"/>
    <xsl:text>"&#xA;</xsl:text>

    <xsl:text>  substring-before('Abracadabra', </xsl:text>
    <xsl:text>'a')            = "</xsl:text>
    <xsl:value-of
      select="substring-before('Abracadabra', 'a')"/>
    <xsl:text>"&#xA;</xsl:text>

    <xsl:text>  substring-before('Abracadabra', </xsl:text>
    <xsl:text>'')             = "</xsl:text>
    <xsl:value-of
      select="substring-before('Abracadabra', '')"/>
    <xsl:text>"&#xA;</xsl:text>
  </xsl:template>
```

```
</xsl:stylesheet>
```

The stylesheet produces these results:

```
A test of the substring-before() function:

  substring-before('Abracadabra', 'abra')       = "Abracad"
  substring-before('Abracadabra', 'Abracadabra') = ""
  substring-before('Abracadabra', 'A')           = ""
  substring-before('Abracadabra', 'a')           = "Abr"
  substring-before('Abracadabra', '')            = ""
```

As a second example, here's an XSLT 2.0 stylesheet that uses a custom collation:

```
<?xml version="1.0"?>
<!-- substring-before2.xsl -->
<xsl:stylesheet version="1.0"
  xmlns:xsl="http://www.w3.org/1999/XSL/Transform">

  <xsl:output method="text"/>

  <xsl:template match="/">
    <xsl:text>&#xA;Another test of the substring-before() </xsl:text>
    <xsl:text>function:&#xA;&#xA;</xsl:text>

    <xsl:text>  substring-before('Schoenaicherstrasse', </xsl:text>
    <xsl:text>'stra&#xDF;e') = &#xA;    "</xsl:text>
    <xsl:value-of
      select="substring-before('Schoenaicherstrasse', 'stra&#xDF;e')"/>
    <xsl:text>"&#xA;</xsl:text>

    <xsl:text>  substring-before('Schoenaicherstrasse', </xsl:text>
    <xsl:text>'stra&#xDF;e', [German collation]) = &#xA;    "</xsl:text>
    <xsl:value-of
      select="substring-before('Schoenaicherstrasse', 'stra&#xDF;e',
              concat('http://saxon.sf.net/collation?',
                     'class=com.oreilly.xslt.GermanCollation;'))"/>
    <xsl:text>"&#xA;</xsl:text>
  </xsl:template>

</xsl:stylesheet>
```

The stylesheet generates these results:

```
Another test of the substring-before() function:

  substring-before('Schoenaicherstrasse', 'straße') =
    ""
  substring-before('Schoenaicherstrasse', 'straße', [German collation]) =
    "Schoenaicher"
```

The German sharp-s character (ß) is equivalent to ss. The default collation doesn't recognize this, but our custom collation does. (To keep the listing within the margins of the page, we used the concat( ) function to combine the two halves of the Saxon collation URI.) See "The document() Function and Sorting" in Chapter 8 for more information.

sum()

Converts all nodes in the argument node-set to numbers, and then returns the sum of all of those numbers.

Syntax

```
[1.0] number sum(node-set)
[2.0] xs:anyAtomicType sum(xs:anyAtomicType)
[2.0] xs:anyAtomicType sum(xs:anyAtomicType, $empty as xs:anyAtomicType)
```

Inputs

[1.0] A node-set. Any node in the node-set that is not a number is converted to a number as if it were passed to the `number()` function, after which the numeric values of all of the nodes are summed.

[2.0] A sequence of atomic values, plus an optional value that is returned when the first argument to `sum()` is the empty sequence.

Output

[1.0] The sum of the numeric values of all of the nodes in the argument node-set. If any node in the argument node-set cannot be converted to a number, the `sum()` function returns `NaN`.

[2.0] Given a sequence of numeric values, `sum()` returns the sum of those values. Given a sequence of durations, `sum()` returns the sum of those durations. As you'd expect from XSLT 2.0, there are some complications to consider:

- To calculate the sum of a sequence of durations, the durations must all be `xs:dayTimeDuration`s, or they must all be `xs:yearMonthDuration`s. You can't mix the two types of durations; if you do, the XSLT processor raises an error.
- If any of the items in the sequence are of type `xs:untypedAtomic`, the XSLT processor attempts to cast it to `xs:double`. If it can't be converted to an `xs:double`, the XSLT processor raises an error.
- If you pass a nonempty sequence to `sum()` and the sum is `0`, the function returns `0`.
- Passing the empty sequence to `sum()` returns `0` by default. If for some reason you'd like the empty sequence to return some other value, such as the string `"Not applicable"`, you can specify the optional `$empty` argument. That argument, if it exists, is returned when you call `sum()` with the empty sequence.

Defined in

[1.0] XPath section 4.4, "Number Functions."

[2.0] XQuery 1.0 and XPath 2.0 Functions and Operators section 15.4, "Aggregate Functions."

Example

We'll demonstrate the `sum()` function against the following XML document:

```
<?xml version="1.0" encoding="utf-8"?>
<!-- chocolate.xml -->
<report month="8" year="2006">
  <title>Chocolate bar sales</title>
  <brand>
    <name>Lindt</name>
    <units>27408</units>
  </brand>
  <brand>
    <name>Callebaut</name>
    <units>8203</units>
  </brand>
  <brand>
    <name>Valrhona</name>
    <units>22101</units>
  </brand>
  <brand>
    <name>Perugina</name>
    <units>14336</units>
  </brand>
  <brand>
    <name>Ghirardelli</name>
    <units>19268</units>
  </brand>
</report>
```

Here is a very simple stylesheet that uses the sum( ) function:

```
<?xml version="1.0"?>
<!-- sum.xsl -->
<xsl:stylesheet version="1.0"
  xmlns:xsl="http://www.w3.org/1999/XSL/Transform">

  <xsl:output method="text"/>

  <xsl:template match="/">
    <xsl:text>&#xA;A test of the sum() function:&#xA;&#xA;</xsl:text>

    <xsl:text>  Total chocolate bar sales this quarter: </xsl:text>
    <xsl:value-of
      select="format-number(sum(/report/brand/units), '###,###')"/>
  </xsl:template>

</xsl:stylesheet>
```

Processing the XML document with this stylesheet generates these results:

```
A test of the sum() function:

  Total chocolate bar sales this quarter: 91,316
```

We used the format-number( ) function to format the value returned by the sum( ) function.

Here's an XSLT 2.0 stylesheet that uses the sum( ) function against a variety of sequences:

```
<?xml version="1.0"?>
<!-- sum2.xsl -->
<xsl:stylesheet version="2.0"
```

```
xmlns:xsl="http://www.w3.org/1999/XSL/Transform"
xmlns:xs="http://www.w3.org/2001/XMLSchema">

<xsl:output method="text"/>

<xsl:template match="/">
  <xsl:variable name="seq1" select="(3, 5, 18)"/>
  <xsl:variable name="seq2" select="(3, 5, 48.273, 2.9e3)"/>

  <xsl:variable name="value1" as="xs:integer" select="42"/>
  <xsl:variable name="value2" as="xs:double" select="2718.28E-3"/>
  <xsl:variable name="value3" as="xs:float" select="98.6"/>
  <xsl:variable name="value4" as="xs:decimal" select="2.54"/>
  <xsl:variable name="seq3"
    select="($value1, $value2, $value3, $value4)"/>

  <xsl:variable name="seq4"
    select="(xs:yearMonthDuration('P3Y8M'),
             xs:yearMonthDuration('P4Y2M'),
             xs:yearMonthDuration('P6Y4M'))"/>
  <xsl:variable name="seq5"
    select="(xs:dayTimeDuration('P2DT4H23M12.2S'),
             xs:dayTimeDuration('P3DT8H17M'),
             xs:dayTimeDuration('P3D'))"/>

  <xsl:text>Here are some tests of the sum() function:&#xA;</xsl:text>

  <xsl:text>&#xA;  sum(</xsl:text>
  <xsl:value-of select="$seq1" separator=", "/>
  <xsl:text>) = </xsl:text>
  <xsl:value-of select="format-number(sum($seq1), '#.###')"/>

  <xsl:text>&#xA;&#xA;  sum(</xsl:text>
  <xsl:value-of select="$seq2" separator=", "/>
  <xsl:text>) = </xsl:text>
  <xsl:value-of select="format-number(sum($seq2), '#.###')"/>

  <xsl:text>&#xA;&#xA;  sum(</xsl:text>
  <xsl:value-of select="$seq3" separator=", "/>
  <xsl:text>) = </xsl:text>
  <xsl:value-of select="format-number(sum($seq3), '#.###')"/>

  <xsl:text>&#xA;&#xA;  sum(</xsl:text>
  <xsl:value-of select="$seq4" separator=", "/>
  <xsl:text>) = </xsl:text>
  <xsl:value-of select="sum($seq4)"/>

  <xsl:text>&#xA;&#xA;    In text, the sum of</xsl:text>
  <xsl:for-each select="$seq4">
    <xsl:text>&#xA;      </xsl:text>
    <xsl:value-of select="years-from-duration(.)"/>
    <xsl:text> years and </xsl:text>
    <xsl:value-of select="months-from-duration(.)"/>
    <xsl:text> months (</xsl:text>
    <xsl:value-of select="."/>
```

```
      <xsl:text>)</xsl:text>
    </xsl:for-each>

    <xsl:text>&#xA;    is </xsl:text>
    <xsl:value-of select="years-from-duration(sum($seq4))"/>
    <xsl:text> years and </xsl:text>
    <xsl:value-of select="months-from-duration(sum($seq4))"/>
    <xsl:text> months (</xsl:text>
    <xsl:value-of select="sum($seq4)"/>
    <xsl:text>).</xsl:text>

    <xsl:text>&#xA;&#xA;  sum(</xsl:text>
    <xsl:value-of select="$seq5" separator=", "/>
    <xsl:text>) = </xsl:text>
    <xsl:variable name="sum5" select="sum($seq5)"/>
    <xsl:value-of select="$sum5"/>

    <xsl:text>&#xA;&#xA;    In text, the sum of</xsl:text>
    <xsl:for-each select="$seq5">
      <xsl:text>&#xA;      </xsl:text>
      <xsl:value-of select="days-from-duration(.)"/>
      <xsl:text> days, </xsl:text>
      <xsl:value-of select="hours-from-duration(.)"/>
      <xsl:text> hours, </xsl:text>
      <xsl:value-of select="minutes-from-duration(.)"/>
      <xsl:text> minutes and </xsl:text>
      <xsl:value-of
        select="format-number(seconds-from-duration(.), '#.##')"/>
      <xsl:text> seconds (</xsl:text>
      <xsl:value-of select="."/>
      <xsl:text>)</xsl:text>
    </xsl:for-each>

    <xsl:text>&#xA;    is </xsl:text>
    <xsl:value-of select="days-from-duration($sum5)"/>
    <xsl:text> days, </xsl:text>
    <xsl:value-of select="hours-from-duration($sum5)"/>
    <xsl:text> hours, </xsl:text>
    <xsl:value-of select="minutes-from-duration($sum5)"/>
    <xsl:text> minutes and </xsl:text>
    <xsl:value-of
      select="format-number(seconds-from-duration($sum5), '#.##')"/>
    <xsl:text> seconds.</xsl:text>

    <xsl:text>&#xA;&#xA;  sum(()) = </xsl:text>
    <xsl:value-of select="sum(())"/>

    <xsl:text>&#xA;&#xA;  sum((), 'Not applicable') = </xsl:text>
    <xsl:value-of select="sum((), 'Not applicable')"/>

    <xsl:text>&#xA;&#xA;  sum((3, -3), 'Not applicable') = </xsl:text>
    <xsl:value-of select="sum((3, -3), 'Not applicable')"/>

  </xsl:template>
```

```
    </xsl:stylesheet>
```

Here are the results from the XSLT 2.0 stylesheet:

```
Here are some tests of the sum() function:

  sum(3, 5, 18) = 26

  sum(3, 5, 48.273, 2900) = 2956.273

  sum(42, 2.71828, 98.6, 2.54) = 145.858

  sum(P3Y8M, P4Y2M, P6Y4M) = P14Y2M

    In text, the sum of
      3 years and 8 months (P3Y8M)
      4 years and 2 months (P4Y2M)
      6 years and 4 months (P6Y4M)
    is 14 years and 2 months (P14Y2M).

  sum(P2DT4H23M12.2S, P3DT8H17M, P3D) = P8DT12H40M12.2S

    In text, the sum of
      2 days, 4 hours, 23 minutes and 12.2 seconds (P2DT4H23M12.2S)
      3 days, 8 hours, 17 minutes and 0 seconds (P3DT8H17M)
      3 days, 0 hours, 0 minutes and 0 seconds (P3D)
    is 8 days, 12 hours, 40 minutes and 12.2 seconds.

  sum(()) = 0

  sum((), 'Not applicable') = Not applicable

  sum((3, -3), 'Not applicable') = 0
```

system-property()

Returns the value of the system property named by the argument to the function.

Syntax

```
[1.0] object system-property(string)
[2.0] xs:string system-property(xs:string)
```

Inputs

The three properties defined by the XSLT 1.0 specification must be supported by all XSLT 1.0 processors; XSLT 2.0 processors must support the five additional properties defined in the XSLT 2.0 spec. Other properties may be supported by individual processors, although vendors are not allowed to add more properties in the xsl: namespace.

All XSLT processors must support three system properties:

`xsl:version`

> A floating-point number representing the version of XSLT implemented by this XSLT processor. This property is equivalent to the numeric value **1.0**, although some XSLT processors (Xalan, for example) return the value **1**. XSLT 2.0 processors must report the version as a floating-point number such as **2.0**.

`xsl:vendor`

> A string identifying the vendor of this XSLT processor.

`xsl:vendor-url`

> A string containing the URL identifying the vendor of the XSLT processor. This string is typically the home page of the vendor's web site.

[2.0] The XSLT 2.0 specification defines five additional properties that must be supported by all XSLT 2.0 processors:

`xsl:product-name`

> The vendor's name for the processor. The XSLT 2.0 specification recommends that this name remain constant from one release of the product to the next, although this is not a requirement.

`xsl:product-version`

> The vendor-defined version of the processor. The XSLT 2.0 spec does not require that the version be in any particular format.

`xsl:is-schema-aware`

> Returns the string **yes** if the XSLT processor is schema-aware; returns the string **no** otherwise.

`xsl:supports-serialization`

> Returns the string **yes** if the XSLT processor supports serialization; returns the string **no** otherwise.

`xsl:supports-backwards-compatibility`

> Returns the string **yes** if the XSLT processor supports backwards compatibility for earlier versions of XSLT; returns the string **no** otherwise.

Output

The value of the queried property.

Defined in

[1.0] XSLT section 12.4, "Miscellaneous Additional Functions."

[2.0] XSLT section 16.6, "Miscellaneous Additional Functions."

Example

Here is a stylesheet that queries the properties defined by XSLT 1.0:

```
<?xml version="1.0"?>
<!-- system-property1.xsl -->
<xsl:stylesheet version="1.0"
```

```
  xmlns:xsl="http://www.w3.org/1999/XSL/Transform">

  <xsl:output method="text"/>

  <xsl:template match="/">
    <xsl:text>&#xA;A test of the system-property() function:</xsl:text>
    <xsl:text>&#xA;&#xA;  xsl:version = "</xsl:text>
    <xsl:value-of select="system-property('xsl:version')"/>
    <xsl:text>"&#xA;</xsl:text>
    <xsl:text>  xsl:vendor = "</xsl:text>
    <xsl:value-of select="system-property('xsl:vendor')"/>
    <xsl:text>"&#xA;</xsl:text>
    <xsl:text>  xsl:vendor-url = "</xsl:text>
    <xsl:value-of select="system-property('xsl:vendor-url')"/>
    <xsl:text>"</xsl:text>
  </xsl:template>

</xsl:stylesheet>
```

We'll process this stylesheet with the Saxon processor:

```
A test of the system-property() function:

  xsl:version = "2.0"
  xsl:vendor = "SAXON 9.0.0.3 from Saxonica"
  xsl:vendor-url = "http://www.saxonica.com/"
```

Running this stylesheet with Xalan-J gives these results:

```
A test of the system-property() function:

  xsl:version = "1"
  xsl:vendor = "Apache Software Foundation (Xalan XSLTC)"
  xsl:vendor-url = "http://xml.apache.org/xalan-j"
```

The Microsoft XSLT processor generates these values:

```
A test of the system-property() function:

  xsl:version = "1"
  xsl:vendor = "Microsoft"
  xsl:vendor-url = "http://www.microsoft.com"
```

Finally, we'll use the Altova XML engine in XSLT 1.0 mode:

```
A test of the system-property() function:

  xsl:version = "1"
  xsl:vendor = "Altova GmbH"
  xsl:vendor-url = "http://www.altova.com"
```

In XSLT 2.0 mode, the Altova processor returns `xsl:version = "2.0"`.

Here's a stylesheet that tests for the XSLT 2.0 properties as well:

```
<?xml version="1.0"?>
<!-- system-property2.xsl -->
<xsl:stylesheet version="2.0"
  xmlns:xsl="http://www.w3.org/1999/XSL/Transform">
```

```
<xsl:output method="text"/>

<xsl:template match="/">
  <xsl:text>&#xA;A test of the system-property() function:</xsl:text>
  <xsl:text>&#xA;&#xA;  xsl:version = "</xsl:text>
  <xsl:value-of select="system-property('xsl:version')"/>
  <xsl:text>"&#xA;</xsl:text>
  <xsl:text>  xsl:vendor = "</xsl:text>
  <xsl:value-of select="system-property('xsl:vendor')"/>
  <xsl:text>"&#xA;</xsl:text>
  <xsl:text>  xsl:vendor-url = "</xsl:text>
  <xsl:value-of select="system-property('xsl:vendor-url')"/>
  <xsl:text>"&#xA;&#xA;XSLT 2.0 properties:&#xA;&#xA;</xsl:text>
  <xsl:text>  xsl:product-name = "</xsl:text>
  <xsl:value-of select="system-property('xsl:product-name')"/>
  <xsl:text>"&#xA;</xsl:text>
  <xsl:text>  xsl:product-version = "</xsl:text>
  <xsl:value-of select="system-property('xsl:product-version')"/>
  <xsl:text>"&#xA;</xsl:text>
  <xsl:text>  xsl:is-schema-aware = "</xsl:text>
  <xsl:value-of select="system-property('xsl:is-schema-aware')"/>
  <xsl:text>"&#xA;</xsl:text>
  <xsl:text>  xsl:supports-serialization = "</xsl:text>
  <xsl:value-of
    select="system-property('xsl:supports-serialization')"/>
  <xsl:text>"&#xA;</xsl:text>
  <xsl:text>  xsl:supports-backwards-compatibility = "</xsl:text>
  <xsl:value-of
    select="system-property('xsl:supports-backwards-compatibility')"/>
  <xsl:text>"</xsl:text>
</xsl:template>

</xsl:stylesheet>
```

When processing this stylesheet with Saxon-B, the non-schema-aware processor, the results look like this:

```
A test of the system-property() function:

  xsl:version = "2.0"
  xsl:vendor = "SAXON 9.0.0.3 from Saxonica"
  xsl:vendor-url = "http://www.saxonica.com/"

XSLT 2.0 properties:

  xsl:product-name = "SAXON"
  xsl:product-version = "9.0.0.3"
  xsl:is-schema-aware = "no"
  xsl:supports-serialization = "yes"
  xsl:supports-backwards-compatibility = "yes"
```

The same stylesheet with the schema-aware version (Saxon-SA) generates these results:

```
A test of the system-property() function:

  xsl:version = "2.0"
```

```
xsl:vendor = "SAXON 9.0.0.3 from Saxonica"
xsl:vendor-url = "http://www.saxonica.com/"
```

XSLT 2.0 properties:

```
xsl:product-name = "SAXON"
xsl:product-version = "SA 9.0.0.3"
xsl:is-schema-aware = "yes"
xsl:supports-serialization = "yes"
xsl:supports-backwards-compatibility = "yes"
```

Processing the stylesheet with the Altova XML engine in XSLT 2.0 mode gives these results:

```
A test of the system-property() function:

xsl:version = "2.0"
xsl:vendor = "Altova GmbH"
xsl:vendor-url = "http://www.altova.com"
```

XSLT 2.0 properties:

```
xsl:product-name = "Altova XSLT Engine"
xsl:product-version = "2007"
xsl:is-schema-aware = "yes"
xsl:supports-serialization = "yes"
xsl:supports-backwards-compatibility = "no"
```

Finally, XSLT processors are free to support other properties. The Java version of Saxon, for example, supports the Java system properties. Here's a stylesheet that queries some of those properties:

```
<?xml version="1.0"?>
<!-- system-property3.xsl -->
<xsl:stylesheet version="2.0"
  xmlns:xsl="http://www.w3.org/1999/XSL/Transform">

  <xsl:output method="text"/>

  <xsl:template match="/">
    <xsl:text>&#xA;Getting Java system properties with </xsl:text>
    <xsl:text>system-property():</xsl:text>
    <xsl:text>&#xA;&#xA;  java.version = "</xsl:text>
    <xsl:value-of select="system-property('java.version')"/>
    <xsl:text>"&#xA;  path.separator = "</xsl:text>
    <xsl:value-of select="system-property('path.separator')"/>
    <xsl:text>"&#xA;  file.separator = "</xsl:text>
    <xsl:value-of select="system-property('file.separator')"/>
    <xsl:text>"&#xA;  user.name = "</xsl:text>
    <xsl:value-of select="system-property('user.name')"/>
    <xsl:text>"&#xA;  user.country = "</xsl:text>
    <xsl:value-of select="system-property('user.country')"/>
    <xsl:text>"</xsl:text>
  </xsl:template>

</xsl:stylesheet>
```

Here are the results Saxon returns:

Getting Java system properties with system-property():

```
java.version = "1.5.0_10"
path.separator = ";"
file.separator = "\"
user.name = "Skippy"
user.country = "US"
```

Using this stylesheet with Altova returns blank values for all of the Java properties.

[2.0] timezone-from-date()

Given an xs:date value, returns its timezone component.

Syntax

```
xs:dayTimeDuration? timezone-from-date(xs:date?)
```

Input

An xs:date value.

Output

An xs:dayTimeDuration that represents the timezone component of the given xs:date value. If the argument is the empty sequence, this function returns the empty sequence.

Defined in

XQuery 1.0 and XPath 2.0 Functions and Operators section 10.5, "Component Extraction Functions on Durations, Dates and Times."

Example

This stylesheet illustrates the timezone-from-date( ) function:

```
<?xml version="1.0"?>
<!-- timezone-from-date.xsl -->
<xsl:stylesheet version="2.0"
  xmlns:xsl="http://www.w3.org/1999/XSL/Transform"
  xmlns:xs="http://www.w3.org/2001/XMLSchema">

  <xsl:output method="text"/>

  <xsl:template match="/">
    <xsl:text>&#xA;Extracting the timezone from an xs:date:</xsl:text>
    <xsl:variable name="currentDate" as="xs:date" select="current-date()"/>
    <xsl:text>&#xA;&#xA;  The current date is: </xsl:text>
    <xsl:value-of select="$currentDate"/>

    <xsl:text>&#xA;&#xA;  The current timezone is: </xsl:text>
    <xsl:value-of select="timezone-from-date($currentDate)"/>
    <xsl:text>&#xA;    The timezone is also known as </xsl:text>
    <xsl:value-of select="format-date($currentDate, '[ZN]')"/>
  </xsl:template>
```

```
</xsl:stylesheet>
```

The stylesheet creates these results:

```
Extracting the timezone from an xs:date:

  The current date is: 2006-11-16-05:00

  The current timezone is: -PT5H
    The timezone is also known as EST
```

Notice that the first result was generated by the timezone-from-date( ) function, while the second was generated using format-date( ) with a format string that selected only the timezone component of the xs:date value.

See Also

The definitions of the [2.0] day-from-date( ), [2.0] format-date( ), [2.0] month-from-date( ), and [2.0] year-from-date( ) functions.

[2.0] timezone-from-dateTime()

Given an xs:dateTime value, returns its timezone.

Syntax

```
xs:dayTimeDuration? timezone-from-dateTime(xs:dateTime?)
```

Inputs

An xs:dateTime value.

Output

An xs:dayTimeDuration representing the timezone of the given xs:dateTime value. If the argument is the empty sequence, this function returns the empty sequence.

Defined in

XQuery 1.0 and XPath 2.0 Functions and Operators section 10.5, "Component Extraction Functions on Durations, Dates and Times."

Example

This stylesheet demonstrates the timezone-from-dateTime( ) function:

```
<?xml version="1.0"?>
<!-- timezone-from-datetime.xsl -->
<xsl:stylesheet version="2.0"
  xmlns:xsl="http://www.w3.org/1999/XSL/Transform"
  xmlns:xs="http://www.w3.org/2001/XMLSchema">

  <xsl:output method="text"/>
```

```
<xsl:template match="/">
  <xsl:text>&#xA;Extracting the timezone from an xs:dateTime:</xsl:text>
  <xsl:variable name="currentDateTime" as="xs:dateTime"
    select="current-dateTime()"/>
  <xsl:text>&#xA;&#xA;  The current date and time is: </xsl:text>
  <xsl:value-of select="$currentDateTime"/>

  <xsl:text>&#xA;&#xA;  The current timezone is: </xsl:text>
  <xsl:value-of select="timezone-from-dateTime($currentDateTime)"/>
  <xsl:text>&#xA;    The timezone is also known as </xsl:text>
  <xsl:value-of select="format-dateTime($currentDateTime, '[ZN]')"/>

</xsl:template>

</xsl:stylesheet>
```

The stylesheet creates these results:

```
Extracting the timezone from an xs:dateTime:

  The current date and time is: 2006-11-16T05:13:44.431-05:00

  The current timezone is: -PT5H
    The timezone is also known as EST
```

Notice that the first result was generated by the `timezone-from-dateTime( )` function, while the second was generated by using `format-dateTime( )` with a format string that selected only the timezone component of the `xs:dateTime` value.

See Also

The definitions of the [2.0] `day-from-dateTime( )`, [2.0] `format-dateTime( )`, [2.0] `hours-from-dateTime( )`, [2.0] `minutes-from-dateTime( )`, [2.0] `month-from-dateTime( )`, [2.0] `seconds-from-dateTime( )`, and [2.0] `year-from-dateTime( )` functions.

[2.0] timezone-from-time()

Given an `xs:time` value, returns its timezone component.

Syntax

```
xs:dayTimeDuration? timezone-from-time(xs:time?)
```

Input

An `xs:time` value.

Output

An `xs:dayTimeDuration` value representing the timezone component of the given `xs:time` value. If the argument is the empty sequence, this function returns the empty sequence.

Defined in

XQuery 1.0 and XPath 2.0 Functions and Operators section 10.5, "Component Extraction Functions on Durations, Dates and Times."

Example

This stylesheet illustrates the timezone-from-time( ) function:

```
<?xml version="1.0"?>
<!-- timezone-from-time.xsl -->
<xsl:stylesheet version="2.0"
  xmlns:xsl="http://www.w3.org/1999/XSL/Transform"
  xmlns:xs="http://www.w3.org/2001/XMLSchema">

  <xsl:output method="text"/>

  <xsl:template match="/">
    <xsl:text>&#xA;Extracting the timezone from an xs:time:</xsl:text>
    <xsl:variable name="currentTime" as="xs:time" select="current-time()"/>
    <xsl:text>&#xA;&#xA;  The current time is: </xsl:text>
    <xsl:value-of select="$currentTime"/>

    <xsl:text>&#xA;&#xA;  The current timezone is: </xsl:text>
    <xsl:value-of select="timezone-from-time($currentTime)"/>
    <xsl:text>&#xA;    The timezone is also known as </xsl:text>
    <xsl:value-of select="format-time($currentTime, '[ZN]')"/>
  </xsl:template>

</xsl:stylesheet>
```

The stylesheet creates these results:

```
Extracting the timezone component from an xs:time:

  The current time is: 05:15:30.423-05:00

  The current timezone is: -PT5H
    The timezone is also known as EST
```

Notice that the first result was generated by timezone-from-time( ), while the second was generated with the format-time( ) function and a format string that selected the timezone component of the xs:time.

See Also

The definitions of the [2.0] hours-from-time( ), [2.0] format-time( ), [2.0] minutes-from-dateTime( ), and [2.0] seconds-from-time( ) functions.

[2.0] tokenize()

Breaks a string into a sequence of strings, using a regular expression as a separator.

Syntax

```
xs:string* tokenize($input as xs:string?, $pattern as xs:string)
xs:string* tokenize($input as xs:string?, $pattern as xs:string,
                    $flags as xs:string)
```

Inputs

A string to be tokenized and a regular expression. The `tokenize()` function also accepts a third string containing flags that change how the regular expression is evaluated.

 It is a fatal error if a regular expression matches a zero-length string. See Appendix E for more details.

Outputs

A sequence of `xs:string`s, each of which represents a token parsed from the original string. The returned strings do not contain the separator.

Here are the full details of how `tokenize()` works:

- If the first string is the empty sequence or a zero-length string, the empty sequence is returned.

- If the regular expression doesn't match anything in the input string, a singleton sequence containing the original input string is returned.

- If the regular expression matches the start of the string, the first string in the returned sequence will be an empty string (""). Similarly, if the regular expression matches the end of the string, the last string in the returned sequence will be an empty string.

- If the regular expression matches two overlapping strings in the input string, only the first match is replaced.

- The regular expression cannot be a zero-length string, nor can it match a zero-length string (in other words, `matches("", $pattern, $replacement)` can't be true). Assuming the input string is not of zero length, it *is* acceptable for a captured substring to be of zero length.

  If the expression `matches("", $pattern, $replacement)` is `true`, an error is raised. For example, using the pattern `'.?'` with any input string raises an error because this pattern matches a zero-length string.

- Regular expression matching does not use collations; the characters' Unicode code points are compared. Cases in which different characters are considered equal in the world's languages are not taken into account.

- Unlike regular expressions used in the `<xsl:analyze-string>` element, curly braces ({ and }) are not doubled. (Curly braces used inside the `regex` attribute of

`<xsl:analyze-string>` must be doubled so they aren't interpreted as attribute value templates.)

- If a regular expression specifies more than one alternative, and more than one of those alternatives match at the same position in the input, the first alternative in the regular expression is the one that's used. To quote an example from the spec, `tokenize("abracadabra", "(ab)|(a)")` returns (`""`, `"r"`, `"c"`, `"d"`, `"r"`, `""`).

  The first alternative in the regular expression (`ab`) is considered the match in this situation, even though the second alternative (`a`) also matches.

- Finally, the third parameter modifies how the regular expression is processed. There are four different flags:

  s

  > Regular expressions are evaluated in what the specs refer to as "dot-all" mode. When this flag is used, the dot operator (`.`) matches any character. Under normal processing (without the s flag), the dot operator matches any character *except* the newline character (`&#xA`). This flag is useful when you want to match strings that might include a newline character.

  m

  > Regular expressions are evaulated in multiline mode. By default, the meta-character (`^`) matches the start of the entire string, while `$` matches the end of the entire string. In multiline mode, `^` matches the start of any line within the string, and `$` matches the end of any line within the string.

  i

  > Regular expressions are evaluated in case-insensitive mode. The regular expression `"a"` matches both `"a"` and `"A"`.
  >
  > Note that Unicode issues can complicate this greatly. For example, the XQuery 1.0 and XPath 2.0 Functions and Operators spec gives the example of the Unicode sign for degrees Kelvin (`&#x212A`), which is the letter `"K"`. The combination of `regex="k"` and `flags="i"` matches the Kelvin sign as well as the letters `"k"` (`&#x6B`) and `"K"` (`&#x4B`).
  >
  > Other Unicode characters don't convert to letters. For example, the Unicode symbol for the Roman numeral I (`&#2160`) looks like the letter I, but does not convert to one. Fortunately, these complications are beyond the scope of this book.

  x

  > All whitespace characters (`&#x9`, `&#xA`, `&#xD`, and `&#x20`) are removed from the regular expression before any comparison is done. In other words, with the x flag, the regular expressions `"John Smith"` and `"JohnSmith"` are the same. This flag is useful when you want to break a long regular expression into multiple lines to make it easier to read.

The flags can be combined in any order. The parameters `'xis'` and `'six'` work exactly the same way.

Defined in

XQuery 1.0 and XPath 2.0 Functions and Operators section 7.6, "String Functions that use Pattern Matching."

Example

Here's the stylesheet we'll use to illustrate how `tokenize( )` works:

```
<?xml version="1.0"?>
<!-- tokenize.xsl -->
<xsl:stylesheet version="2.0"
  xmlns:xsl="http://www.w3.org/1999/XSL/Transform"
  xmlns:xs="http://www.w3.org/2001/XMLSchema">

  <xsl:output method="text"/>

  <xsl:template match="/">

    <xsl:variable name="string1"
      select="concat('Now is the time for all good men&#xA;',
              'and women &#xA;',
              'to aid the party.')"/>

    <xsl:variable name="string2" as="xs:string"
      select="'Visa # 1234-5678-9101-1121'"/>

    <xsl:text>&#xA;Here are some tests of the </xsl:text>
    <xsl:text>tokenize() function:&#xA;</xsl:text>

    <xsl:text>&#xA;  $string1 = &#xA;</xsl:text>
    <xsl:value-of select="$string1"/>

    <xsl:text>&#xA;&#xA;  $string2 = &#xA;</xsl:text>
    <xsl:value-of select="$string2"/>

    <xsl:text>&#xA;&#xA;  tokenize($string1, </xsl:text>
    <xsl:text>'&amp;#xA;') = </xsl:text>
    <xsl:text>&#xA;     ('</xsl:text>
    <xsl:value-of select="tokenize($string1, '&#xA;')"
      separator="',&#xA;      '"/>
    <xsl:text>')&#xA;     count() = </xsl:text>
    <xsl:value-of select="count(tokenize($string1, '&#xA;'))"/>

    <xsl:text>&#xA;&#xA;  tokenize($string2, '-') = </xsl:text>
    <xsl:text>&#xA;     ('</xsl:text>
    <xsl:value-of
      select="tokenize($string2, '-')" separator="', '"/>
    <xsl:text>')&#xA;     count() = </xsl:text>
    <xsl:value-of select="count(tokenize($string2, '-'))"/>

    <xsl:text>&#xA;&#xA;  tokenize($string2, </xsl:text>
    <xsl:text>'(Visa # )|-') = </xsl:text>
    <xsl:text>&#xA;     ('</xsl:text>
    <xsl:value-of
      select="tokenize($string2, '(Visa # )|-')" separator="', '"/>
```

```
<xsl:text>')&#xA;    count() = </xsl:text>
<xsl:value-of select="count(tokenize($string2, '(Visa #)|-'))"/>

</xsl:template>

</xsl:stylesheet>
```

Here are the results:

```
Here are some tests of the tokenize() function:

 $string1 =
Now is the time for all good men
and women
to aid the party.

 $string2 =
Visa # 1234-5678-9101-1121

 tokenize($string1, '&#xA;') =
   ('Now is the time for all good men',
    'and women ',
    'to aid the party.')
   count() = 3

 tokenize($string2, '-') =
   ('Visa # 1234', '5678', '9101', '1121')
   count() = 4

 tokenize($string2, '(Visa # )|-') =
   ('', '1234', '5678', '9101', '1121')
   count() = 5
```

In the first test, we tokenized a string by its newline characters (
). Note that we don't have to use the 's' flag here because we're not looking for characters at the start or end of a line; we're simply looking for newline characters. For the second test, we broke our credit card number into four pieces. Unfortunately, the first token is 'Visa # 1234', which isn't what we wanted. To get just the four segments of numbers, we need to rewrite our regular expression as we did in test 3. Because the pattern 'Visa # ' matches the start of the string, the first token we get is a zero-length string.

The count( ) function displays how many tokens are in each sequence.

See Also

Appendix E has complete details on the way regular expressions work in XPath 2.0. Also see the definitions of the following elements and functions: [2.0] <xsl:analyze-string>, [2.0] matches( ), [2.0] <xsl:matching-substring>, [2.0] <xsl:non-matching-substring>, [2.0] regex-group( ), and [2.0] replace( ).

[2.0] trace()

Outputs diagnostic messages useful in tracing the processing of a stylesheet.

Syntax

```
item()* trace($value as item()*, $label as xs:string)
```

Inputs

A sequence of items and an `xs:string`. The string is typically something such as `The value of $x is:`. A diagnostic message containing that string and the value of the items in the sequence can be very useful in tracing the processing of the stylesheet.

Outputs

The output of the `trace( )` function is the input sequence of items. They are returned without changes.

In addition, `trace( )` converts the sequence of items into an `xs:string`. That string and the second argument are typically combined into a diagnostic message. *Almost all of the details of the `trace( )` function are implementation-dependent.* The format of the diagnostic message, the destination of the diagnostic message, and the order in which calls to the `trace( )` function are evaluated can vary from one processor to the next.

Defined in

XQuery 1.0 and XPath 2.0 Functions and Operators section 4, "The Trace Function."

Example

This stylesheet is a smaller version of the stylesheet we used to illustrate the `data( )` function. We want to create trace messages each time we invoke the `datatest:print-item( )` function we created. Here's the stylesheet:

```
<?xml version="1.0"?>
<!-- trace.xsl -->
<xsl:stylesheet version="2.0"
  xmlns:xsl="http://www.w3.org/1999/XSL/Transform"
  xmlns:xs="http://www.w3.org/2001/XMLSchema"
  xmlns:datatest="http://www.oreilly.com">

<xsl:output method="text"/>

<xsl:template match="/">

  <xsl:variable name="testSequence" as="item()*">
    <xsl:sequence select="(3)"/>
    <xsl:element name="currentDate">
      <xsl:value-of select="current-date()"/>
    </xsl:element>
    <xsl:element name="currentTime">
      <xsl:value-of select="current-time()"/>
    </xsl:element>
    <xsl:element name="integerTest">
      <xsl:value-of select="xs:integer(8)"/>
    </xsl:element>
    <xsl:sequence select="('blue', 'red')"/>
    <xsl:element name="floatTest1">
```

```
      <xsl:value-of select="xs:float(3.14)"/>
    </xsl:element>
    <xsl:element name="floatTest2">
      <xsl:value-of select="xs:float(42)"/>
    </xsl:element>
    <xsl:element name="dateTest">
      <xsl:value-of select="xs:date('1995-04-21')"/>
    </xsl:element>
  </xsl:variable>

  <xsl:text>&#xA;Here is a test of the </xsl:text>
  <xsl:text>trace() function:</xsl:text>

  <xsl:value-of
    select="for $i in (1 to count($testSequence))
            return (datatest:print-item(
            subsequence($testSequence, $i, 1)))"/>
</xsl:template>

<xsl:function name="datatest:print-item" as="xs:string">
  <xsl:param name="item" as="item()"/>
  <xsl:choose>
    <xsl:when test="$item instance of element()">
      <xsl:analyze-string regex="!!!.?"
        select="string(trace($item, 'trace() element '))">
        <xsl:matching-substring></xsl:matching-substring>
      </xsl:analyze-string>
    </xsl:when>
    <xsl:otherwise>
      <xsl:analyze-string regex="!!!.?"
        select="string(trace($item, 'trace()  atom '))">
        <xsl:matching-substring></xsl:matching-substring>
      </xsl:analyze-string>
    </xsl:otherwise>
  </xsl:choose>
  <xsl:text> </xsl:text>
</xsl:function>

</xsl:stylesheet>
```

Our stylesheet creates a sequence of items, and then calls our datatest:print-item( ) function. When we invoke this with Saxon, we get these results:

```
trace()  atom : xs:integer: 3
trace()  element : element(currentDate, untyped): currentDate
trace()  element : element(currentTime, untyped): currentTime
trace()  element : element(integerTest, untyped): integerTest
trace()  atom : xs:string: blue
trace()  atom : xs:string: red
trace()  element : element(floatTest1, untyped): floatTest1
trace()  element : element(floatTest2, untyped): floatTest2
trace()  element : element(dateTest, untyped): dateTest

Here is a test of the trace() function:
```

3

```
2006-12-19-05:00
17:13:55-05:00
8
blue
red
3.14
42
1995-04-21
```

Notice that all of the **trace( )** messages are output before any of the <xsl:text> or <xsl:value-of> elements. The format of the messages and the order in which calls to **trace( )** are handled is implementation-dependent. Running the same stylesheet with the Altova XML engine produces a slightly different output:

```
trace()   atom 3
trace()   element <currentDate>2006-12-19-05:00</currentDate>
trace()   element <currentTime>17:30:28-05:00</currentTime>
trace()   element <integerTest>8</integerTest>
trace()   atom blue
trace()   atom red
trace()   element <floatTest1>3.14</floatTest1>
trace()   element <floatTest2>42</floatTest2>
trace()   element <dateTest>1995-04-21</dateTest>

Here is a test of the trace() function:

3
...
```

Again, all of the **trace( )** messages appear before the other output.

translate()

Allows you to convert individual characters in a string from one value to another. In many languages, this function is powerful enough to convert characters from one case to another. (*[2.0]* For case conversions, XQuery 1.0 and XPath 2.0 provide the more powerful **lower-case( )** and **upper-case( )** functions.)

Syntax

> *[1.0]* string **translate(***string, $mapString as string, $transString as string***)**
> *[2.0]* xs:string **translate(***xs:string?, $mapString as xs:string,*
>   *$transString as xs:string***)**

Inputs

Three strings. The first is the original, untranslated string, and the second and third strings define the characters to be converted.

Output

The original string, translated as follows:

- If a character in the original string appears in the second argument string (the mapping string), it is replaced with the corresponding character in the third argument string (the translation string).

  In other words, `translate('CAR', 'ABCDE', 'EXHQF')` returns HER. Going through the characters of the first string in order, C is the third character in the mapping string, so it is replaced with H, the third character in the translation string. The next character of the first string, A, is the first character in the mapping string, so it is replaced with E, the first character in the translation string. Finally, the last character of the first string, R, doesn't appear in the second string, so it is not modified at all.

- If a character in the original string appears in the second argument string and there is no corresponding character in the third argument string (the second argument string is longer than the third), then that character is deleted.

  In other words, `translate('CAR, 'ABCDER', 'EXHQF')` returns HE. The first two characters are translated as before. The last letter of the original string, R, is the sixth character of the mapping string. Because there is no sixth character in the translation string, the letter is deleted.

- If a character in the second argument string appears more than once, the first occurrence determines the replacement character.

- If the third argument string is longer than the second argument string, the extra characters are ignored.

- If the second string is a zero-length string, the original string is returned unchanged.

- *[2.0]* If the value of the first argument is the empty sequence, a zero-length string is returned.

Defined in

[1.0] XPath section 4.2, "String Functions."

[2.0] XQuery 1.0 and XPath 2.0 Functions and Operators section 7.4, "Functions on String Values."

Example

Here's a stylesheet with several examples of the `translate( )` function:

```
<?xml version="1.0"?>
<!-- translate.xsl -->
<xsl:stylesheet version="1.0"
  xmlns:xsl="http://www.w3.org/1999/XSL/Transform">

  <xsl:output method="text"/>

  <xsl:template match="/">
    <xsl:text>&#xA;Tests of the translate() function:</xsl:text>

    <xsl:text>&#xA;&#xA;  Convert a string to uppercase:</xsl:text>
```

```
<xsl:text>&#xA;    translate('Lily', </xsl:text>
<xsl:text>'abcdefghijklmnopqrstuvwxyz', </xsl:text>
<xsl:text>&#xA;                'ABCDEFGHIJKLMNOPQRSTUVWXYZ')=</xsl:text>
<xsl:value-of
  select="translate('Lily', 'abcdefghijklmnopqrstuvwxyz',
                    'ABCDEFGHIJKLMNOPQRSTUVWXYZ')"/>
<xsl:text>&#xA;&#xA;  Convert a string to lowercase:</xsl:text>
<xsl:text>&#xA;    translate('Lily', </xsl:text>
<xsl:text>'ABCDEFGHIJKLMNOPQRSTUVWXYZ', </xsl:text>
<xsl:text>&#xA;                'abcdefghijklmnopqrstuvwxyz')=</xsl:text>
<xsl:value-of
  select="translate('Lily', 'ABCDEFGHIJKLMNOPQRSTUVWXYZ',
                    'abcdefghijklmnopqrstuvwxyz')"/>
<xsl:text>&#xA;&#xA;  Remove parentheses, spaces, and dashes </xsl:text>
<xsl:text>from a U.S. phone number:</xsl:text>
<xsl:text>&#xA;    translate('(555) 555-1212', '() -', '')=</xsl:text>
<xsl:value-of select="translate('(555) 555-1212', '() -', '')"/>
<xsl:text>&#xA;&#xA;  Replace all but the last four digits of a </xsl:text>
<xsl:text>credit card number with Xs:&#xA;</xsl:text>
<xsl:variable name="credit" select="'1234 5678 9101 1810'"/>
<xsl:text>    $credit='</xsl:text>
<xsl:value-of select="$credit"/>
<xsl:text>'</xsl:text>
<xsl:text>&#xA;    translate(substring($credit, 1, 15), </xsl:text>
<xsl:text>'1234567890 ', 'XXXXXXXXX-')</xsl:text>
<xsl:text>&#xA;    substring($credit, 16)</xsl:text>
<xsl:text>&#xA;&#xA;    The first part is </xsl:text>
<xsl:value-of
  select="translate(substring($credit, 1, 15), '1234567890 ',
                    'XXXXXXXXX-')"/>
<xsl:text>&#xA;    The second part is </xsl:text>
<xsl:value-of select="substring($credit, 16)"/>
<xsl:text>&#xA;    Here's how they look together: &#xA;    </xsl:text>
<xsl:value-of
  select="translate(substring($credit, 1, 15), '1234567890 ',
                    'XXXXXXXXX-')"/>
<xsl:value-of select="substring($credit, 16)"/>
  </xsl:template>

</xsl:stylesheet>
```

When we use this stylesheet with any XML document, here are the results:

```
Tests of the translate() function:

  Convert a string to uppercase:
    translate('Lily', 'abcdefghijklmnopqrstuvwxyz',
            'ABCDEFGHIJKLMNOPQRSTUVWXYZ')=LILY

  Convert a string to lowercase:
    translate('Lily', 'ABCDEFGHIJKLMNOPQRSTUVWXYZ',
            'abcdefghijklmnopqrstuvwxyz')=lily

  Remove parentheses, spaces, and dashes from a U.S. phone number:
    translate('(555) 555-1212', '() -', '')=5555551212
```

```
Replace all but the last four digits of a credit card number with Xs:
  $credit='1234 5678 9101 1810'
  translate(substring($credit, 1, 15), '1234567890 ', 'XXXXXXXXXX-')
  substring($credit, 16)

The first part is XXXX-XXXX-XXXX-
The second part is 1810
Here's how they look together:
  XXXX-XXXX-XXXX-1810
```

true()

Always returns the boolean value **true**. Remember that the strings **"true"** and **"false"** don't have any special significance in XSLT. This function (and the **false( )** function) allow you to generate boolean values when you need them.

Syntax

```
[1.0] boolean true()
[2.0] xs:boolean true()
```

Inputs

None.

Output

The boolean value **true**.

Defined in

[1.0] XPath section 4.3, "Boolean Functions."

[2.0] XQuery 1.0 and XPath 2.0 Functions and Operators section 9.1, "Additional Boolean Constructor Functions."

Example

Here's a brief example that uses the **true( )** function:

```
<?xml version="1.0"?>
<!-- true.xsl -->
<xsl:stylesheet version="1.0"
  xmlns:xsl="http://www.w3.org/1999/XSL/Transform">

  <xsl:output method="text"/>

  <xsl:template match="/">
    <xsl:text>&#xA;A test of the true() function:&#xA;&#xA;</xsl:text>

    <xsl:text>  true() returned </xsl:text>
    <xsl:value-of select="true()"/>
    <xsl:text>!</xsl:text>
  </xsl:template>
</xsl:stylesheet>
```

When using this stylesheet against any XML document, it generates this less-than-exciting result:

```
A test of the true() function:

  true() returned true!
```

[2.0] type-available()

Given the name of a datatype, returns **true** if that datatype is known to the XSLT processor.

Syntax

```
xs:boolean type-available($typeName as xs:string)
```

Input

An xs:string containing the name of a datatype.

Output

The xs:boolean value **true** if the datatype is known to the XSLT processor; **false** otherwise.

Defined in

XSLT 2.0 section 18.1.4, "Testing Availability of Types."

Example

Here's a short stylesheet that checks the availability of two datatypes. The first datatype is defined to all XSLT 2.0 processors, while the second datatype is defined in a schema and therefore requires a schema-aware processor.

```
<?xml version="1.0"?>
<!-- type-available.xsl -->
<xsl:stylesheet version="2.0"
  xmlns:xs="http://www.w3.org/2001/XMLSchema"
  xmlns:age="http://www.oreilly.com/xslt"
  xmlns:xsl="http://www.w3.org/1999/XSL/Transform">

  <xsl:output method="text"/>

  <xsl:template match="/">
    <xsl:text>&#xA;A test of the type-available() function:&#xA;</xsl:text>
    <xsl:text>&#xA;    xs:integer is available:  </xsl:text>
    <xsl:value-of select="type-available('xs:integer')"/>
    <xsl:text>&#xA;    age:age-type is available:  </xsl:text>
    <xsl:value-of select="type-available('age:age-type')"/>
  </xsl:template>

</xsl:stylesheet>
```

Notice that we have to declare the namespace prefixes for the datatypes. Because there is no <xsl:import-schema> element, only the first datatype is available:

```
A test of the type-available() function:

    xs:integer is available:  true
    age:age-type is available:  false
```

If we import a schema into the stylesheet, a schema-aware processor will find other types available:

```
<?xml version="1.0"?>
<!-- type-available2.xsl -->
<xsl:stylesheet version="2.0"
  xmlns:xs="http://www.w3.org/2001/XMLSchema"
  xmlns:age="http://www.oreilly.com/xslt"
  xmlns:xsl="http://www.w3.org/1999/XSL/Transform">

  <xsl:output method="text"/>

  <xsl:import-schema namespace="http://www.oreilly.com/xslt">
    <xs:schema
      targetNamespace="http://www.oreilly.com/xslt"
      xmlns:xs="http://www.w3.org/2001/XMLSchema">
      <xs:simpleType name="age-type">
        <xs:restriction base="xs:integer">
          <xs:minInclusive value="0"/>
          <xs:maxInclusive value="130"/>
        </xs:restriction>
      </xs:simpleType>
    </xs:schema>
  </xsl:import-schema>
  ...
</xsl:stylesheet>
```

With the schema imported, the stylesheet tells us the second datatype is available:

```
A test of the type-available() function:

    xs:integer is available:  true
    age:age-type is available:  true
```

[2.0] unordered()

Given a sequence, returns those items in an implementation-defined order.

Syntax

```
item()* unordered(item()*)
```

Inputs

A sequence of items.

Outputs

A sequence containing the same items as the input sequence, but in an order determined by the XSLT processor.

Defined in

XQuery 1.0 and XPath 2.0 Functions and Operators section 15.1, "General Functions and Operators on Sequences."

Example

The unordered( ) function is a way of telling the XSLT processor that we don't care how items are sequenced. In some cases, this can improve the performance of the XSLT processor. As an example, we'll look at the ancestors of an element in two ways. Using the normal approach, the ancestors appear in document order. When using unordered( ) with Saxon, the ancestors appear in the reverse order. Most likely, Saxon is taking advantage of its internal data structures to start at a node and list its ancestors from the innermost level of the document outward. Using the same stylesheet with AltovaXML, the ancestors appear in document order in both cases.

We'll reuse one of our purchase orders as our input document:

```
<?xml version="1.0" ?>
<!-- po38293.xml -->
<purchase-order id="38293">
  <date year="2001" month="9" day="8"/>
  <customer id="4738" level="Basic">
    <address type="business">
      <name>
        <title>Ms.</title>
        <first-name>Amanda</first-name>
        <last-name>Reckonwith</last-name>
      </name>
      <street>930-A Chestnut Street</street>
      <city>Lynn</city>
      <state>MA</state>
      <zip>02930</zip>
    </address>
    <address type="ship-to"/>
  </customer>
  <items>
    <item part-no="23813-03-CDK">
      <name>Cucumber Decorating Kit</name>
      <qty>1</qty>
      <price>29.95</price>
    </item>
  </items>
</purchase-order>
```

We'll display the ancestors of the `<first-name>` element, selecting them once with a normal XPath expression and selecting them a second time with the unordered( ) function. Here's the stylesheet:

```
<?xml version="1.0"?>
<!-- unordered.xsl -->
<xsl:stylesheet version="2.0"
  xmlns:xsl="http://www.w3.org/1999/XSL/Transform"
  xmlns:xs="http://www.w3.org/2001/XMLSchema">
```

```
<xsl:output method="text"/>

<xsl:template match="/">

  <xsl:text>&#xA;Here is a test of the unordered() </xsl:text>
  <xsl:text>function:&#xA;</xsl:text>

  <xsl:for-each select="//first-name">
    <xsl:text>&#xA;   Element &lt;first-name&gt;</xsl:text>
    <xsl:value-of select="."/>
    <xsl:text>&lt;/first-name&gt;:&#xA;    </xsl:text>
    <xsl:text>&#xA;    Ancestors:&#xA;      </xsl:text>
    <xsl:value-of select="ancestor::*/name()" separator=", "/>
    <xsl:text>&#xA;&#xA;    Unordered ancestors:&#xA;      </xsl:text>
    <xsl:value-of select="unordered(ancestor::*/name())"
      separator=", "/>
  </xsl:for-each>

</xsl:template>

</xsl:stylesheet>
```

Here are the results:

```
Here is a test of the unordered() function:

   Element <first-name>Amanda</first-name>:

    Ancestors:
      purchase-order, customer, address, name

    Unordered ancestors:
      name, address, customer, purchase-order
```

The first time we select the ancestors of the element, they appear in document order. The second time, the ancestors appear in what is presumably the most efficient way for Saxon to find them.

[2.0] unparsed-entity-public-id()

Returns the public ID of the unparsed entity with the specified name. If there is no such entity, unparsed-entity-public-id( ) returns an empty string.

Syntax

```
xs:string unparsed-entity-public-id(xs:string)
```

Input

The name of the unparsed entity.

Output

The public ID of the unparsed entity with the specified name.

Defined in

XSLT 2.0 section 16.6, "Miscellaneous Additional Functions."

Example

Unparsed entities are rarely used; they typically refer to non-XML data, as in the entity author-picture defined in this XML document:

```
<?xml version="1.0"?>
<!-- unparsed-entity.xml -->
<!DOCTYPE book [
  <!ENTITY author-picture PUBLIC "-//OReilly//Author Images//DT"
    "dougtidwell.jpg" NDATA JPEG>
]>

<book>
  <prolog cover-image="author-picture"/>
  <body>
    <p>Pretend that lots of useful content appears here.</p>
  </body>
</book>
```

We'll use this stylesheet to return the public ID of our unparsed entity:

```
<?xml version="1.0"?>
<!-- unparsed-entity-public-id.xsl -->
<xsl:stylesheet version="2.0"
  xmlns:xsl="http://www.w3.org/1999/XSL/Transform">

  <xsl:output method="text"/>

  <xsl:template match="/">
    <xsl:text>&#xA;A test of the unparsed-entity-</xsl:text>
    <xsl:text>public-id() function:</xsl:text>

    <xsl:text>&#xA;&#xA;    </xsl:text>
    <xsl:text>The public ID of the cover image is:&#xA;    </xsl:text>
    <xsl:value-of
      select="unparsed-entity-public-id(/book/prolog/@cover-image)"/>
    <xsl:text>.&#xA;</xsl:text>
  </xsl:template>

</xsl:stylesheet>
```

When we transform the XML document with our stylesheet, the results look like this:

```
A test of the unparsed-entity-public-id() function:

    The public ID of the cover image is:
    -//OReilly//Author Images//DT.
```

unparsed-entity-uri()

Returns the URI of the unparsed entity with the specified name. If there is no such entity, unparsed-entity-uri returns an empty string.

Syntax

```
[1.0] string unparsed-entity-uri(string)
[2.0] xs:anyURI unparsed-entity-uri(xs:string)
```

Inputs

The name of the unparsed entity.

Output

The URI of the unparsed entity with the specified name.

Defined in

[1.0] XSLT section 12.4, "Miscellaneous Additional Functions."

[2.0] XSLT section 16.6, "Miscellaneous Additional Functions."

Example

Unparsed entities are rarely used; they typically refer to non-XML data, as in the entity **author-picture** in this XML document:

```
<?xml version="1.0"?>
<!-- unparsed-entity.xml -->
<!DOCTYPE book [
  <!ENTITY author-picture PUBLIC "-//OReilly//Author Images//DT"
    "dougtidwell.jpg" NDATA JPEG>
]>

<book>
  <prolog cover-image="author-picture"/>
  <body>
    <p>Pretend that lots of useful content appears here.</p>
  </body>
</book>
```

We'll use this stylesheet to get the public URI of our unparsed entity:

```
<?xml version="1.0"?>
<!-- unparsed-entity-uri.xsl -->
<xsl:stylesheet version="1.0"
  xmlns:xsl="http://www.w3.org/1999/XSL/Transform">

  <xsl:output method="text"/>

  <xsl:template match="/">
    <xsl:text>&#xA;A test of the unparsed-entity-</xsl:text>
    <xsl:text>uri() function:</xsl:text>

    <xsl:text>&#xA;&#xA;    </xsl:text>
```

```
    <xsl:text>The URI of the cover image is:&#xA;        </xsl:text>
    <xsl:value-of
      select="unparsed-entity-uri(/book/prolog/@cover-image)"/>
    <xsl:text>.&#xA;</xsl:text>
  </xsl:template>

</xsl:stylesheet>
```

When we transform the XML document with our stylesheet, the results look like this:

```
A test of the unparsed-entity-uri() function:

  The URI of the cover image is:
      file:/C:/projects/XSLTbookV2/AppendixC/dougtidwell.jpg.
```

The URI of the unparsed entity is based on the base URI of the XML document itself.

[2.0] unparsed-text()

Given a URI, returns the unparsed text of the resources identified by that URI.

Syntax

```
xs:string unparsed-text($href as xs:string)
xs:string unparsed-text($href as xs:string, $encoding as xs:string)
```

Inputs

An `xs:string` specifying the URI of the requested document. An optional second string specifies the document's encoding.

Output

An `xs:string` that contains the unparsed text of the URI.

Defined in

XSLT 2.0 section 16.2, "Reading Text Files."

Example

In this example, we'll generate an HTML page. Part of the page is a standard header and footer; those will be inserted into the document as unparsed text. If we use the `collection( )`, `doc( )`, or `document( )` functions, the data we read would have to be well-formed XML. Using `unparsed-text( )` instead, we can read documents that aren't necessarily well-formed (most HTML documents, for example) and use them.

We'll use our document of chocolate bar sales as the XML input document:

```
<?xml version="1.0" encoding="utf-8"?>
<!-- chocolate.xml -->
<report month="8" year="2006">
  <title>Chocolate bar sales</title>
  <brand>
    <name>Lindt</name>
```

```
        <units>27408</units>
      </brand>
      <brand>
        <name>Callebaut</name>
        <units>8203</units>
      </brand>
      <brand>
        <name>Valrhona</name>
        <units>22101</units>
      </brand>
      <brand>
        <name>Perugina</name>
        <units>14336</units>
      </brand>
      <brand>
        <name>Ghirardelli</name>
        <units>19268</units>
      </brand>
  </report>
```

We'll generate an HTML report from this document. Our stylesheet uses unparsed-text( ) to import an HTML header and footer:

```
<?xml version="1.0"?>
<!-- unparsed-text.xsl -->
<xsl:stylesheet version="2.0"
  xmlns:xsl="http://www.w3.org/1999/XSL/Transform">

  <xsl:output method="html"/>

  <xsl:variable name="reportTitle">
    <xsl:value-of select="/report/title"/>
    <xsl:text> for </xsl:text>
    <xsl:value-of select="/report/@month"/>
    <xsl:text>/</xsl:text>
    <xsl:value-of select="/report/@year"/>
  </xsl:variable>

  <xsl:template match="/">
    <html>
      <head>
        <title>
          <xsl:value-of select="$reportTitle"/>
        </title>
      </head>
      <body style="font-family: sans-serif;">
        <xsl:value-of
          select="unparsed-text('header.html')"
          disable-output-escaping="yes"/>
        <xsl:apply-templates select="*|text()"/>
        <xsl:value-of
          select="unparsed-text('footer.html')"
          disable-output-escaping="yes"/>
      </body>
    </html>
  </xsl:template>
```

```
<xsl:template match="title">
  <h1>
    <xsl:value-of select="$reportTitle"/>
  </h1>
</xsl:template>

<xsl:template match="brand">
  <h2>
    <xsl:value-of select="name"/>
    <xsl:text> : </xsl:text>
    <xsl:value-of select="units"/>
  </h2>
</xsl:template>

</xsl:stylesheet>
```

Notice that we used the `disable-output-escaping` attribute on `<xsl:value-of>`. Without this attribute, the markup we import is displayed as `&lt;td&gt;This header was generated....` That means the text we import is treated as text, not as markup to be processed by the browser.

The document *header.html* looks like this:

```
<!-- header.html -->
<table width=33% border=1>
  <tr style="background: lightgray;">
    <td style="text-align: center;
               font-weight: bold;">
      This header was generated by<br>
      <code>unparsed-text()</code>, using a
      stylesheet from <br>O'Reilly's
      <cite>XSLT</cite>, 2nd edition.
    </td>
  </tr>
</table>
```

Notice that our HTML document features unquoted attributes on the `<table>` element and old-style `<br>` elements. Despite those violations of XML syntax, we can still import this document and use it in our results.

(With the exception of the word "footer" in place of "header," the file *footer.html* is exactly the same.)

Our completed document appears as in Figure C-6.

Another great use of the `unparsed-text( )` function is reading structured data formats such as comma-separated values. See the discussion in the section "[2.0] The unparsed-text() and unparsed-text-available() Functions" in Chapter 8 for a complete example.

[2.0] unparsed-text-available()

Given a URI, returns `true` if that document is available, `false` otherwise. This function allows you to check the existence and availability of a document before you attempt to open it with

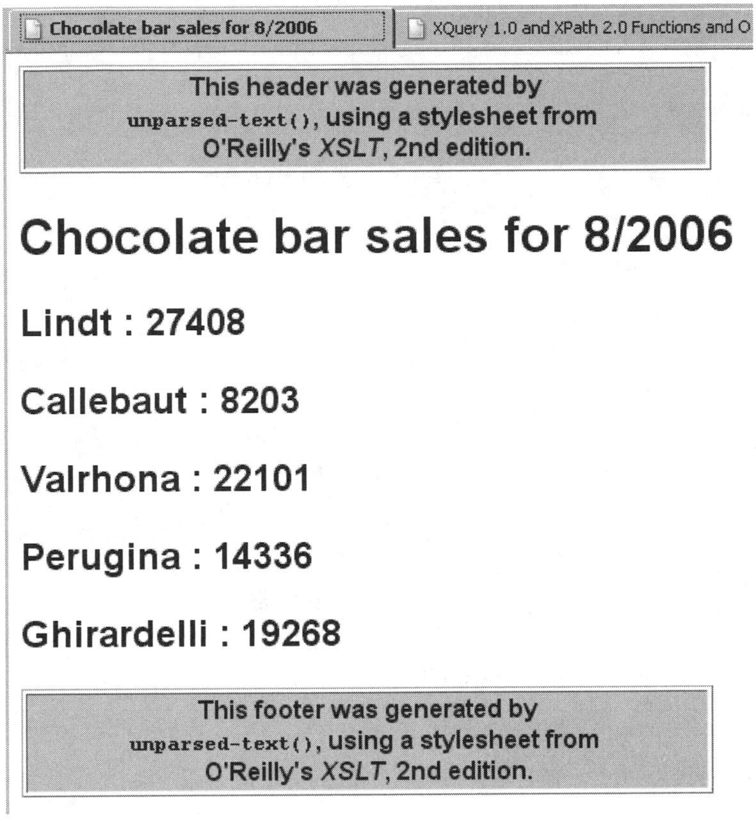

Figure C-6. HTML file created with the unparsed-text( ) function

unparsed-text( ). If you attempt to open a document that is unavailable, the XSLT processor raises a fatal error.

Syntax

```
xs:boolean unparsed-text-available(xs:string)
xs:boolean unparsed-text-available(xs:string, xs:string)
```

Inputs

An xs:string specifying the URI of the requested document. An optional second string specifies the document's encoding.

Output

true if the document is unavailable; false otherwise.

Defined in

XSLT 2.0 section 16.2, "Reading Text Files."

Example

Here's a short stylesheet that checks to see whether three different files are available:

```
<?xml version="1.0"?>
<!-- unparsed-text-available.xsl -->
<xsl:stylesheet version="2.0"
  xmlns:xsl="http://www.w3.org/1999/XSL/Transform">

  <xsl:output method="text"/>

  <xsl:template match="/">

    <xsl:text>&#xA;Here are some tests of the </xsl:text>
    <xsl:text>unparsed-text-available() function:</xsl:text>

    <xsl:text>&#xA;&#xA;  unparsed-text-available</xsl:text>
    <xsl:text>('header.html') = </xsl:text>
    <xsl:value-of
      select="unparsed-text-available('header.html')"/>

    <xsl:text>&#xA;&#xA;  unparsed-text-available</xsl:text>
    <xsl:text>('disclaimer.html') = </xsl:text>
    <xsl:value-of
      select="unparsed-text-available('disclaimer.html')"/>

    <xsl:text>&#xA;&#xA;  unparsed-text-available</xsl:text>
    <xsl:text>('footer.html') = </xsl:text>
    <xsl:value-of
      select="unparsed-text-available('footer.html')"/>

  </xsl:template>

</xsl:stylesheet>
```

The results are:

```
Here are some tests of the unparsed-text-available() function:

  unparsed-text-available('header.html') = true

  unparsed-text-available('disclaimer.html') = false

  unparsed-text-available('footer.html') = true
```

The second file isn't available, but the first and third files are.

[2.0] upper-case()

Given a string, returns the uppercased version of that string.

Syntax

```
xs:string upper-case(xs:string?)
```

Inputs

An `xs:string` value.

Outputs

An `xs:string` in which all of the lowercase letters in the original string have been converted to uppercase. Any character that was originally in uppercase and any character that does not have an uppercase value is returned as is. If the value of the argument is the empty sequence, a zero-length string is returned.

Accented characters and other features of the world's languages mean that changing the case of a string might change its length. Also be aware that `upper-case( )` and `lower-case( )` are not always the inverse of each other in some languages. All of the case-conversion rules are defined by the Unicode standard, and XSLT processors are expected to conform with those rules.

Defined in

XQuery 1.0 and XPath 2.0 Functions and Operators section 7.4, "Functions on String Values."

Example

Here is a stylesheet that illustrates the `upper-case( )` function. Notice that we're using `<xsl:output method="xml" encoding="UTF-8"/>` to make sure the character set is handled properly:

```
<?xml version="1.0" encoding="UTF-8"?>
<!-- upper-case.xsl -->
<xsl:stylesheet version="2.0"
  xmlns:xsl="http://www.w3.org/1999/XSL/Transform">

  <xsl:output method="xml" encoding="UTF-8" indent="yes"/>

  <xsl:template match="/">
    <testcase>
      <heading>Tests of the upper-case() function:</heading>
      <test>
        <label>upper-case('Lily') = </label>
        <result><xsl:value-of select="upper-case('Lily')"/></result>
      </test>
      <test>
        <label>upper-case('LILY') = </label>
        <result><xsl:value-of select="upper-case('LILY')"/></result>
      </test>
      <test>
        <label>upper-case('lily') = </label>
        <result><xsl:value-of select="upper-case('lily')"/></result>
      </test>
      <test>
        <label>uppercase('jalapeño') = </label>
        <result><xsl:value-of select="upper-case('jalapeño')"/></result>
      </test>
    </testcase>
  </xsl:template>
```

```
    </xsl:stylesheet>
```

The results look like this:

```
<?xml version="1.0" encoding="UTF-8"?>
<testcase>
   <heading>Tests of the upper-case() function:</heading>
   <test>
      <label>upper-case('Lily') = </label>
      <result>LILY</result>
   </test>
   <test>
      <label>upper-case('LILY') = </label>
      <result>LILY</result>
   </test>
   <test>
      <label>upper-case('lily') = </label>
      <result>LILY</result>
   </test>
   <test>
      <label>uppercase('jalapeño') = </label>
      <result>JALAPEÑO</result>
   </test>
</testcase>
```

[2.0] year-from-date()

Given an xs:date value, returns its year component.

Syntax

```
xs:integer? year-from-date(xs:date?)
```

Input

An xs:date value.

Output

An xs:integer representing the year component of the given xs:date value. If the argument is the empty sequence, this function returns the empty sequence.

Defined in

XQuery 1.0 and XPath 2.0 Functions and Operators section 10.5, "Component Extraction Functions on Durations, Dates and Times."

Example

This stylesheet demonstrates the year-from-date( ) function:

```
<?xml version="1.0"?>
<!-- year-from-date.xsl -->
<xsl:stylesheet version="2.0"
```

```
xmlns:xsl="http://www.w3.org/1999/XSL/Transform"
xmlns:xs="http://www.w3.org/2001/XMLSchema">

<xsl:output method="text"/>

<xsl:template match="/">
  <xsl:text>&#xA;Extracting the year from an xs:date:</xsl:text>
  <xsl:variable name="currentDate" as="xs:date" select="current-date()"/>
  <xsl:text>&#xA;&#xA;  The current date is: </xsl:text>
  <xsl:value-of select="$currentDate"/>

  <xsl:text>&#xA;&#xA;  The current year: </xsl:text>
  <xsl:value-of select="year-from-date($currentDate)"/>
  <xsl:text>&#xA;    In words: </xsl:text>
  <xsl:value-of select="format-date($currentDate, '[YWw]')"/>
  <xsl:text>&#xA;    In German: </xsl:text>
  <xsl:value-of select="format-date($currentDate, '[YWw]', 'de', (), ())"/>
</xsl:template>

</xsl:stylesheet>
```

The stylesheet creates these exciting results:

```
Extracting the year from an xs:date:

  The current date is: 2006-11-16-05:00

  The current year: 2006
    In words: Two Thousand and Six
    In German: Zweitausend Sechs
```

See Also

The definitions of the [2.0] day-from-date( ), [2.0] format-date( ), [2.0] month-from-date( ), and [2.0] timezone-from-date( ) functions.

[2.0] year-from-dateTime()

Given an xs:dateTime value, returns its year value.

Syntax

```
xs:integer? year-from-dateTime(xs:dateTime?)
```

Inputs

An xs:dateTime value.

Output

An xs:integer representing the year component of the given xs:dateTime value. If the argument is the empty sequence, this function returns the empty sequence.

Defined in

XQuery 1.0 and XPath 2.0 Functions and Operators section 10.5, "Component Extraction Functions on Durations, Dates and Times."

Example

This stylesheet demonstrates the year-from-dateTime( ) function:

```
<?xml version="1.0"?>
<!-- year-from-datetime.xsl -->
<xsl:stylesheet version="2.0"
  xmlns:xsl="http://www.w3.org/1999/XSL/Transform"
  xmlns:xs="http://www.w3.org/2001/XMLSchema">

  <xsl:output method="text"/>

  <xsl:template match="/">
    <xsl:text>&#xA;Extracting the year from an xs:dateTime:</xsl:text>
    <xsl:variable name="currentDateTime" as="xs:dateTime"
      select="current-dateTime()"/>
    <xsl:text>&#xA;&#xA;The current date and time is: </xsl:text>
    <xsl:value-of select="$currentDateTime"/>

    <xsl:text>&#xA;&#xA;  The current year: </xsl:text>
    <xsl:value-of select="year-from-dateTime($currentDateTime)"/>
    <xsl:text>&#xA;    In words: </xsl:text>
    <xsl:value-of select="format-dateTime($currentDateTime, '[YWw]')"/>
    <xsl:text>&#xA;    In German: </xsl:text>
    <xsl:value-of
      select="format-dateTime($currentDateTime, '[YWw]', 'de', (), ())"/>
  </xsl:template>

</xsl:stylesheet>
```

The stylesheet creates these results:

```
The current date and time is: 2006-11-16T05:18:20.187-05:00

  The current year: 2006
    In words: Two Thousand and Six
    In German: Zweitausend Sechs
```

See Also

The definitions of the [2.0] day-from-dateTime( ), [2.0] format-dateTime( ), [2.0] hours-from-dateTime( ), [2.0] minutes-from-dateTime( ), [2.0] month-from-dateTime( ), [2.0] seconds-from-dateTime( ), and [2.0] timezone-from-dateTime( ) functions.

[2.0] years-from-duration()

Given an xs:duration value, returns the number of years in that duration.

Syntax

```
xs:integer? years-from-duration(xs:duration?)
```

Inputs

An xs:duration value.

Output

An xs:integer representing the years component of the given xs:duration. Be aware that for an xs:dayTimeDuration, this function always returns 0 because there is no years component of an xs:dayTimeDuration. Also, if the argument is the empty sequence, this function returns the empty sequence.

Defined in

XQuery 1.0 and XPath 2.0 Functions and Operators section 10.5, "Component Extraction Functions on Durations, Dates and Times."

Example

This stylesheet demonstrates the years-from-duration( ) function with all three types of durations:

```
<?xml version="1.0"?>
<!-- years-from-duration.xsl -->
<xsl:stylesheet version="2.0"
  xmlns:xsl="http://www.w3.org/1999/XSL/Transform"
  xmlns:xs="http://www.w3.org/2001/XMLSchema">

  <xsl:output method="text"/>

  <xsl:template match="/">
    <xsl:text>&#xA;Extracting the years component from durations:</xsl:text>

    <xsl:variable name="sampleDuration" as="xs:duration"
      select="xs:duration('P3Y8M2DT4H23M12.2S')"/>
    <xsl:variable name="sampleYearMonthDuration" as="xs:yearMonthDuration"
      select="xs:yearMonthDuration('P3Y8M')"/>
    <xsl:variable name="sampleDayTimeDuration" as="xs:dayTimeDuration"
      select="xs:dayTimeDuration('P2DT4H23M12.2S')"/>

    <xsl:text>&#xA;&#xA;  A sample xs:duration: </xsl:text>
    <xsl:value-of select="$sampleDuration"/>
    <xsl:text>&#xA;    The years component of this duration is </xsl:text>
    <xsl:value-of select="years-from-duration($sampleDuration)"/>
    <xsl:text>.</xsl:text>

    <xsl:text>&#xA;&#xA;  A sample xs:yearMonthDuration: </xsl:text>
    <xsl:value-of select="$sampleYearMonthDuration"/>
    <xsl:text>&#xA;    The years component of this duration is </xsl:text>
    <xsl:value-of select="years-from-duration($sampleYearMonthDuration)"/>
    <xsl:text>.</xsl:text>

    <xsl:text>&#xA;&#xA;  A sample xs:dayTimeDuration: </xsl:text>
```

```
<xsl:value-of select="$sampleDayTimeDuration"/>
<xsl:text>&#xA;    The years component of this duration is </xsl:text>
<xsl:value-of select="years-from-duration($sampleDayTimeDuration)"/>
<xsl:text>.</xsl:text>
</xsl:template>

</xsl:stylesheet>
```

Here are the results from this stylesheet:

```
Extracting the years component from durations:

  A sample xs:duration: P3Y8M2DT4H23M12.2S
  The years component of this duration is 3.

  A sample xs:yearMonthDuration: P3Y8M
  The years component of this duration is 3.

  A sample xs:dayTimeDuration: P2DT4H23M12.2S
  The years component of this duration is 0.
```

As you can see, extracting the years component from an `xs:dayTimeDuration` returns 0.

See Also

The definitions of the [2.0] `days-from-duration( )`, [2.0] `hours-from-duration( )`, [2.0] `minutes-from-duration( )`, [2.0] `months-from-duration( )`, and [2.0] `seconds-from-duration( )` functions.

[2.0] zero-or-one()

Raises an error unless its argument is a sequence containing zero or one items. For example, if a `<name>` element can have at most one `<title>` child, `zero-or-one(title)` would raise an error if a `<name>` element had the wrong number of `<title>` elements. Be aware that `zero-or-one( )` terminates processing; for a more flexible approach, use the `count( )` function to determine the cardinality of a sequence.

Syntax

```
item()? zero-or-one(item()*)
```

Inputs

A sequence of items. The sequence must either be empty or a singleton.

Outputs

This function returns the input sequence, assuming it has zero or one items. If the input sequence has more than one item, the `zero-or-one( )` function raises an error.

Defined in

XQuery 1.0 and XPath 2.0 Functions and Operators section 15.2, "Functions That Test the Cardinality of Sequences." More details about this function can be found in XQuery 1.0 and

XPath 2.0 Formal Semantics section 7.2, "Standard Functions with Specific Static Typing Rules."

Example

We'll look at a trivial example that illustrates the **zero-or-one( )** function. Invoking **zero-or-one( )** with a sequence containing more than one item raises an error. Here's the stylesheet:

```
<?xml version="1.0"?>
<!-- zero-or-one.xsl -->
<xsl:stylesheet version="2.0"
  xmlns:xsl="http://www.w3.org/1999/XSL/Transform"
  xmlns:xs="http://www.w3.org/2001/XMLSchema">

  <xsl:output method="text"/>

  <xsl:template match="/">

    <xsl:variable name="emptySequence" as="item()*">
      <xsl:sequence select="()"/>
    </xsl:variable>

    <xsl:variable name="singleton" as="item()*">
      <xsl:sequence select="(3)"/>
    </xsl:variable>

    <xsl:text>&#xA;Here are two tests of the zero-or-one() </xsl:text>
    <xsl:text>function:&#xA;</xsl:text>

    <xsl:text>&#xA;  Calling zero-or-one() with the empty </xsl:text>
    <xsl:text>sequence:&#xA;    </xsl:text>

    <xsl:if test="count(zero-or-one($emptySequence) &lt; 2)">
      <xsl:text>&#xA;    Our sequence has zero or one items!</xsl:text>
    </xsl:if>

    <xsl:text>&#xA;&#xA;  Calling zero-or-one() with a </xsl:text>
    <xsl:text>singleton:&#xA;</xsl:text>
    <xsl:text>&#xA;    Our sequence is:&#xA;      </xsl:text>
    <xsl:value-of select="$singleton" separator="&#xA;    "/>

    <xsl:if test="count(zero-or-one($singleton) &lt; 2)">
      <xsl:text>&#xA;&#xA;    Our sequence has zero or one items!</xsl:text>
    </xsl:if>
  </xsl:template>

</xsl:stylesheet>
```

Notice that we use the **count( )** function to create a boolean value here. Converting a sequence into a boolean value directly won't work here. If the sequence is the empty sequence, the XSLT 2.0 processor evaluates that as **false**, which is the opposite of what we want. Even if the sequence has one member, there are still problems; the sequence (0) evaluates as **false**, and the sequence (**xs:date('1995-04-21')**) raises an error. The best way to get a boolean value here is to see whether the size of the returned sequence is **< 2**.

The stylesheet generates these results:

```
Here are two tests of the zero-or-one() function:

  Calling zero-or-one() with the empty sequence:

    Our sequence has zero or one items!

  Calling zero-or-one() with a singleton:

    Our sequence is:
     3

    Our sequence has zero or one items!
```

Calling zero-or-one( ) with the empty sequence or a singleton returns the input sequence; calling zero-or-one( ) with anything else raises an error.

See Also

The descriptions of the count( ), [2.0] empty( ), [2.0] exactly-one( ), and the [2.0] one-or-more( ) functions and the discussion of the XPath 2.0 treat as operator in the section "[2.0] Datatype Operators—instance of, castable as, cast as, and treat as" in Chapter 3.

XML Schema Overview

This appendix is a brief overview of XML Schema. For in-depth information about XML Schemas, I highly recommend Eric van der Vlist's *XML Schema*, published by O'Reilly. The *XML Schema Primer* at the W3C is very useful as well.

We'll cover three topics in this appendix. First, we'll look at how to declare elements and attributes in XML Schema. Next we'll go through the many ways to create types. Finally, we'll look at how to use XML Schemas in XSLT stylesheets. The focus here is on the aspects of XML Schema that apply to XSLT. A schema-aware XSLT processor can use a schema to validate a document or element. If we're working with types declared in an XML Schema, a schema-aware processor can use those datatypes just like `xs:string`, `xs:date`, or any other basic datatype.

Declaring Elements and Attributes

The most common task in XML Schema is declaring elements and attributes. We'll start with an empty element, then move on to more sophisticated things.

Creating an Empty Element

Here's how we create an empty element:

```
<?xml version="1.0" encoding="UTF-8"?>
<!-- empty1.xsd -->
<xs:schema
  xmlns="http://www.oreilly.com/xslt"
  targetNamespace="http://www.oreilly.com/xslt"
  xmlns:xs="http://www.w3.org/2001/XMLSchema">

  <xs:element name="empty1">
    <xs:complexType/>
  </xs:element>

</xs:schema>
```

That's it. The empty `<xs:complexType>` means that our element can't have any attributes and it can't have any content. It's not terribly useful, but that's how it works. An XML document that uses this schema looks like this:

```
<?xml version="1.0" encoding="utf-8"?>
<!-- empty1.xml -->
<empty1
  xmlns="http://www.oreilly.com/xslt"
  xmlns:xsi="http://www.w3.org/2001/XMLSchema-instance"
  xsi:schemaLocation="http://www.oreilly.com/xslt empty1.xsd"/>
```

Although we said our empty element couldn't contain attributes, it looks like we have three of them here. The first two (`xmlns` and `xmlns:xsi`) are actually namespace declarations, not attributes. The `xsi:schemaLocation` attribute (it actually *is* an attribute) associates the XML Schema with our document. In the schema, the `targetNamespace` attribute defines the namespace used by this schema; it's also the default namespace (`xmlns="http://www.oreilly.com/xslt"`) in the schema and the XML document. To tie everything together, the `xsi:schemaLocation` attribute in our XML document tells the XML parser where to find the schema that defines what a valid document looks like.

There are other ways of using namespaces, but we won't cover them in any detail here. For example, our XML document could look like this:

```
<ora:empty1
  xmlns:ora="http://www.oreilly.com/xslt"
  xmlns:xsi="http://www.w3.org/2001/XMLSchema-instance"
  xsi:schemaLocation="http://www.oreilly.com/xslt empty1.xsd"/>
```

We took out the default namespace and declared a namespace prefix that matches the namespace in the XML Schema. Because the XML document doesn't have a default namespace, we have to qualify all of the elements with the namespace prefix that matches the target namespace of the schema. That's why our element is now `<ora:empty1>` instead of `<empty1>`.

Creating an Empty Element with Attributes

Our next step is to create an attribute for our empty element. To do that, we declare what XML Schema refers to as a *complex type*:

```
<?xml version="1.0" encoding="UTF-8"?>
<!-- empty2.xsd -->
<xs:schema
  xmlns="http://www.oreilly.com/xslt"
  targetNamespace="http://www.oreilly.com/xslt"
  xmlns:xs="http://www.w3.org/2001/XMLSchema">

  <xs:element name="empty2">
    <xs:complexType>
      <xs:attribute name="color"/>
    </xs:complexType>
  </xs:element>
```

```
    </xs:schema>
```

The XML document is slightly more interesting now:

```
<?xml version="1.0" encoding="utf-8"?>
<!-- empty2.xml -->
<empty2
  xmlns="http://www.oreilly.com/xslt"
  xmlns:xsi="http://www.w3.org/2001/XMLSchema-instance"
  xsi:schemaLocation="http://www.oreilly.com/xslt empty2.xsd"
  color="blue"/>
```

We simply declared an attribute with a name here. We could have declared a datatype for the attribute; we'll do that soon.

Creating an Element with Text

To create an element that's actually useful, we'll want to let it contain something. We'll start by simply creating an element whose type is `xs:string`:

```
<?xml version="1.0" encoding="UTF-8"?>
<!-- content1.xsd -->
<xs:schema
  xmlns="http://www.oreilly.com/xslt"
  targetNamespace="http://www.oreilly.com/xslt"
  xmlns:xs="http://www.w3.org/2001/XMLSchema">

  <xs:element name="content1" type="xs:string"/>

</xs:schema>
```

Notice that we didn't use `<xs:complexType>` this time. We simply said our element was a string. Here's a valid document for this schema:

```
<?xml version="1.0" encoding="utf-8"?>
<!-- content1.xml -->
<content1
  xmlns="http://www.oreilly.com/xslt"
  xmlns:xsi="http://www.w3.org/2001/XMLSchema-instance"
  xsi:schemaLocation="http://www.oreilly.com/xslt content1.xsd">
Our element now contains some text!  It's getting more useful
all the time.
</content1>
```

Creating an Element with Text and Attributes

Now we'll create an element that has both text and attributes. Remember, in order to create attributes, we have to create an `<xs:complexType>`, so we have to create a new type based on `xs:string`. Here's how we do that:

```
<?xml version="1.0" encoding="UTF-8"?>
<!-- content2.xsd -->
<xs:schema
```

```
  xmlns="http://www.oreilly.com/xslt"
  targetNamespace="http://www.oreilly.com/xslt"
  xmlns:xs="http://www.w3.org/2001/XMLSchema">

  <xs:element name="content2">
    <xs:complexType>
      <xs:simpleContent>
        <xs:extension base="xs:string">
          <xs:attribute name="color" type="xs:string"/>
        </xs:extension>
      </xs:simpleContent>
    </xs:complexType>
  </xs:element>

</xs:schema>
```

Our new element is a complex type, but it uses what XML Schema refers to as *simple content*. In other words, this element is an extension of a simple type, xs:string. The extension to the simple type is that we're adding an attribute. Here's how our document looks now:

```
<?xml version="1.0" encoding="utf-8"?>
<!-- content2.xml -->
<content2
  xmlns="http://www.oreilly.com/xslt"
  xmlns:xsi="http://www.w3.org/2001/XMLSchema-instance"
  xsi:schemaLocation="http://www.oreilly.com/xslt content2.xsd"
  color="blue">
Our element now contains some text!  It's getting more useful
all the time.
</content2>
```

Creating an Element with Mixed Content

For our final example, we'll create an element with mixed content. *Mixed content* means this element can contain text and other elements. Here's an expanded schema that declares a second element; the first element can contain any combination of text and the second element:

```
<?xml version="1.0" encoding="UTF-8"?>
<!-- content3.xsd -->
<xs:schema
  xmlns="http://www.oreilly.com/xslt"
  targetNamespace="http://www.oreilly.com/xslt"
  xmlns:xs="http://www.w3.org/2001/XMLSchema">

  <xs:element name="content3">
    <xs:complexType mixed="true">
      <xs:sequence minOccurs="0" maxOccurs="unbounded">
        <xs:element ref="emphasis"/>
      </xs:sequence>
      <xs:attribute name="color" type="xs:string"/>
    </xs:complexType>
  </xs:element>
```

```
<xs:element name="emphasis" type="xs:string"/>

</xs:schema>
```

Now we've declared a complex type that contains mixed content, an element, and an attribute. Here's a valid document in our new schema:

```
<?xml version="1.0" encoding="utf-8"?>
<!-- content3.xml -->
<content3
  xmlns="http://www.oreilly.com/xslt"
  xmlns:xsi="http://www.w3.org/2001/XMLSchema-instance"
  xsi:schemaLocation="http://www.oreilly.com/xslt content3.xsd"
  color="blue">
Our element <emphasis>now</emphasis> contains some text!
It's getting <emphasis>more useful</emphasis> all the time.
</content3>
```

One final detail: in the schema, we declared the `<emphasis>` element outside the complex type and referred to it in the declaration of the `<content3>` element. If we had declared `<emphasis>` like this:

```
<xs:complexType mixed="true">
  <xs:sequence minOccurs="0" maxOccurs="unbounded">
    <xs:element name="emphasis" type="xs:string"/>
    ...
```

we would get the same results, but we couldn't reuse the `<emphasis>` element anywhere else. In all our examples from now on, we'll declare elements globally and reference them where we need them. (A *globally declared element* is an `<xs:element>` whose parent is the `<xs:schema>` element.)

Defining Datatypes

Some of the elements and attributes we've created to this point use the built-in XML Schema datatypes. The ability to define our own types is a powerful feature of the language. Custom datatypes are the feature most directly related to XSLT. With a schema-aware processor, we can use our own datatypes for validation. We'll cover the ways to create datatypes in the next section.

 We don't cover the basic datatypes (`xs:string`, `xs:integer`, etc.) used by XML Schema here. See the discussion of "*[2.0]* XPath 2.0 Datatypes" in Appendix B for all the details on those datatypes.

Anonymous Types

Everything we've done to this point has used anonymous types. That means we used `<xs:simpleType>` or `<xs:complexType>`, but we didn't give those types a name. That was

OK for our simple schemas because we didn't want to reuse those datatypes outside the element in which they were defined. From now on, we'll give our datatypes a name so we can use them whenever we need to. Here's the difference between an anonymous type and a named type:

```
<?xml version="1.0" encoding="UTF-8"?>
<!-- content4.xsd -->
<xs:schema
  xmlns="http://www.oreilly.com/xslt"
  targetNamespace="http://www.oreilly.com/xslt"
  xmlns:xs="http://www.w3.org/2001/XMLSchema">

  <xs:element name="content4a">
    <xs:complexType>
      <xs:simpleContent>
        <xs:extension base="xs:string">
          <xs:attribute name="color" type="xs:string"/>
        </xs:extension>
      </xs:simpleContent>
    </xs:complexType>
  </xs:element>

  <xs:complexType name="content4b-type">
    <xs:simpleContent>
      <xs:extension base="xs:string">
        <xs:attribute name="color" type="xs:string"/>
      </xs:extension>
    </xs:simpleContent>
  </xs:complexType>

  <xs:element name="content4b" type="content4b-type"/>

</xs:schema>
```

The first element in the schema, `<content4a>`, uses an anonymous type. The second element has the exact same structure, but it uses the named datatype we created. The difference, of course, is that we can use the named datatype anywhere, while the anonymous type exists only inside the declaration of element `<content4a>`.

Groups

There are three kinds of groups we can define in an XML Schema: `<xs:sequence>` groups, `<xs:choice>` groups, and `<xs:all>` groups. Normally these groups are inside the declaration of a type or element, but we can also use the `<xs:group>` element to create a group separately and refer to it as we need it.

The most flexible group is a choice group. A *choice group* contains a list of elements, only one of which may appear in a valid XML document. Although that sounds restrictive, we can say that a choice group can appear zero or more times, and we can put it in a mixed content model. For example, here's a choice group that says a `<p>` element can contain text and any combination of `<a>`, `<b>`, `<br>`, `<code>`, `<i>`, or `<img>` elements:

```
<?xml version="1.0" encoding="UTF-8"?>
<!-- paragraph.xsd -->
<xs:schema
  xmlns="http://www.oreilly.com/xslt"
  targetNamespace="http://www.oreilly.com/xslt"
  xmlns:xs="http://www.w3.org/2001/XMLSchema">

  <xs:element name="a">
    <xs:complexType>
      <xs:simpleContent>
        <xs:extension base="xs:string">
          <xs:attribute name="href" type="xs:string"/>
        </xs:extension>
      </xs:simpleContent>
    </xs:complexType>
  </xs:element>

  <xs:element name="b">
    <xs:complexType mixed="true">
      <xs:choice minOccurs="0" maxOccurs="unbounded">
        <xs:element ref="a"/>
        <xs:element ref="br"/>
        <xs:element ref="code"/>
        <xs:element ref="i"/>
      </xs:choice>
    </xs:complexType>
  </xs:element>

  <xs:element name="br"/>

  <xs:element name="code">
    <xs:complexType mixed="true">
      <xs:choice minOccurs="0" maxOccurs="unbounded">
        <xs:element ref="a"/>
        <xs:element ref="b"/>
        <xs:element ref="br"/>
        <xs:element ref="i"/>
      </xs:choice>
    </xs:complexType>
  </xs:element>

  <xs:element name="i">
    <xs:complexType mixed="true">
      <xs:choice minOccurs="0" maxOccurs="unbounded">
        <xs:element ref="a"/>
        <xs:element ref="b"/>
        <xs:element ref="br"/>
        <xs:element ref="code"/>
      </xs:choice>
    </xs:complexType>
  </xs:element>

  <xs:element name="img">
    <xs:complexType>
      <xs:attribute name="href" type="xs:string"/>
```

```
      </xs:complexType>
    </xs:element>

    <xs:element name="p">
      <xs:complexType mixed="true">
        <xs:choice minOccurs="0" maxOccurs="unbounded">
          <xs:element ref="a"/>
          <xs:element ref="b"/>
          <xs:element ref="br"/>
          <xs:element ref="code"/>
          <xs:element ref="i"/>
        </xs:choice>
      </xs:complexType>
    </xs:element>

  </xs:schema>
```

All of the elements that have mixed content can also contain any number of elements from the `<xs:choice>`. This schema gives us a great deal of flexibility; we can have a `<p>` element that contains text that contains a `<code>` element, which in turn contains a `<b>` element, which in turn contains an `<i>` element.

Next we'll look at sequence groups. A sequence group is defined with `<xs:sequence>` and contains a list of elements that must appear in the sequence in which they are listed. We can `minOccurs="0"` to indicate that some of the elements are optional. Here's a schema that defines elements that must appear inside a `<person>` element:

```
<?xml version="1.0" encoding="UTF-8"?>
<!-- person.xsd -->
<xs:schema
  xmlns="http://www.oreilly.com/xslt"
  targetNamespace="http://www.oreilly.com/xslt"
  xmlns:xs="http://www.w3.org/2001/XMLSchema">

  <xs:element name="person">
    <xs:complexType>
      <xs:sequence>
        <xs:element ref="name"/>
        <xs:element ref="age"/>
        <xs:element ref="birthday"/>
      </xs:sequence>
    </xs:complexType>
  </xs:element>

  <xs:element name="name" type="xs:string"/>
  <xs:element name="age" type="xs:positiveInteger"/>
  <xs:element name="birthday" type="xs:date"/>

</xs:schema>
```

This schema says that any `<person>` element must contain a `<name>` element, an `<age>` element, and a `<birthday>` element. The elements must occur in this order, and all of them are required.

The final kind of group we'll look at is the `<xs:all>` group. An `<xs:all>` group contains a list of elements. All of the elements in the list must appear once, although the order in which they appear doesn't matter. We can define some of the elements as being optional by using `minOccurs="0"` if necessary. The only legal values for `minOccurs` and `maxOccurs` are `0` and `1`. Here's a schema with an `<xs:all>` group:

```
<?xml version="1.0" encoding="UTF-8"?>
<!-- person-all.xsd -->
<xs:schema
  xmlns="http://www.oreilly.com/xslt"
  targetNamespace="http://www.oreilly.com/xslt"
  xmlns:xs="http://www.w3.org/2001/XMLSchema">

  <xs:element name="person">
    <xs:complexType>
      <xs:all>
        <xs:element ref="name"/>
        <xs:element ref="age"/>
        <xs:element ref="birthday"/>
      </xs:all>
    </xs:complexType>
  </xs:element>

  <xs:element name="name" type="xs:string"/>
  <xs:element name="birthday" type="xs:date" nillable="true"/>
  <xs:element name="age" type="xs:positiveInteger"/>

</xs:schema>
```

The three elements here can occur in any order, but all three must occur. Here's an XML document that's valid against this schema:

```
<?xml version="1.0" encoding="utf-8"?>
<!-- person-all.xml -->
<person
  xmlns="http://www.oreilly.com/xslt"
  xmlns:xsi="http://www.w3.org/2001/XMLSchema-instance"
  xsi:schemaLocation="http://www.oreilly.com/xslt person-all.xsd">
  <age>42</age>
  <birthday>1965-06-19</birthday>
  <name>Doug Tidwell</name>
</person>
```

There is one important restriction on `<xs:all>` groups. The elements defined or referenced inside the group can only be individual elements. You can't use a group to add multiple elements to the group—you have to do that individually.

One more thing before we leave the topic of groups: XML Schema defines the `<xs:group>` element. We can use it to define a group of elements or to reference a group of elements defined elsewhere. Here's an example:

```
<?xml version="1.0" encoding="UTF-8"?>
<!-- group.xsd -->
<xs:schema
```

```
  xmlns="http://www.oreilly.com/xslt"
  targetNamespace="http://www.oreilly.com/xslt"
  xmlns:xs="http://www.w3.org/2001/XMLSchema">

  <xs:element name="person">
    <xs:complexType>
      <xs:group ref="person-elements"/>
    </xs:complexType>
  </xs:element>

  <xs:group name="person-elements">
    <xs:sequence>
      <xs:element ref="name"/>
      <xs:element ref="birthday"/>
      <xs:element ref="age"/>
    </xs:sequence>
  </xs:group>

  <xs:element name="name" type="xs:string"/>
  <xs:element name="birthday" type="xs:date"/>
  <xs:element name="age" type="xs:positiveInteger"/>

</xs:schema>
```

We define a named group and refer to it in the definition of the `<person>` element.

Creating New Datatypes by Restriction

A common way to create new datatypes is to restrict the values of another datatype. We'll look at three approaches: ranges, enumerations, and regular expressions.

For our first example, we'll use a range to define a datatype called `age` based on `xs:integer`. We would like for the `age` datatype to have a value between `0` and `130`. (We're being optimistic about longevity here.) Here's how we define a range of valid values:

```
<?xml version="1.0" encoding="UTF-8"?>
<!-- person1.xsd -->
<xs:schema
  xmlns="http://www.oreilly.com/xslt"
  targetNamespace="http://www.oreilly.com/xslt"
  xmlns:xs="http://www.w3.org/2001/XMLSchema">

  <xs:element name="person">
    <xs:complexType>
      <xs:sequence>
        <xs:element ref="name"/>
        <xs:element ref="age"/>
      </xs:sequence>
      <xs:attribute name="eyeColor" type="xs:string"/>
    </xs:complexType>
  </xs:element>

  <xs:element name="name" type="xs:string"/>
```

```
<xs:simpleType name="age-type">
  <xs:restriction base="xs:integer">
    <xs:minInclusive value="0"/>
    <xs:maxInclusive value="130"/>
  </xs:restriction>
</xs:simpleType>

<xs:element name="age" type="age-type"/>

</xs:schema>
```

We've defined a new datatype, age-type, and we've used it as the datatype for the element <age>. Here's a valid document for this schema:

```
<?xml version="1.0" encoding="utf-8"?>
<!-- person1.xml -->
<person
  xmlns="http://www.oreilly.com/xslt"
  xmlns:xsi="http://www.w3.org/2001/XMLSchema-instance"
  xsi:schemaLocation="http://www.oreilly.com/xslt person1.xsd"
  eyeColor="brown">
  <name>Doug Tidwell</name>
  <age>42</age>
</person>
```

If the value of <age> is outside the range we defined, this document won't validate.

We'll continue developing our person schema by limiting the value of the eyeColor attribute. For simplicity's sake, we'll limit this attribute to four colors. We do that with an enumeration:

```
<?xml version="1.0" encoding="UTF-8"?>
<!-- person2.xsd -->
...
      <xs:attribute name="eyeColor" type="eyeColor-type"/>
    </xs:complexType>
  </xs:element>

  <xs:simpleType name="eyeColor-type">
    <xs:restriction base="xs:string">
      <xs:enumeration value="blue"/>
      <xs:enumeration value="brown"/>
      <xs:enumeration value="gray"/>
      <xs:enumeration value="green"/>
    </xs:restriction>
  </xs:simpleType>
  ...
```

If the value of the eyeColor attribute is anything other than the four values defined here, validation fails.

For a final use of restrictions, we'll use a regular expression. The regular expression defines what valid data looks like; if a value of that type doesn't match the regular expression, validation fails. Here's a datatype defined with a regular expression:

```
<?xml version="1.0" encoding="UTF-8"?>
<!-- person3.xsd -->
...
  <xs:element name="driversLicense" type="driversLicense-type"/>
...
  <xs:simpleType name="driversLicense-type">
    <xs:restriction base="xs:string">
      <xs:pattern value="[A-Z]{2}-[0-9]{4}-[0-9]{6}"/>
    </xs:restriction>
  </xs:simpleType>
...
```

Here's a document that's valid according to this schema:

```
<?xml version="1.0" encoding="utf-8"?>
<!-- person3.xml -->
<person
  xmlns="http://www.oreilly.com/xslt"
  xmlns:xsi="http://www.w3.org/2001/XMLSchema-instance"
  xsi:schemaLocation="http://www.oreilly.com/xslt person3.xsd"
  eyeColor="brown">
  <name>Doug Tidwell</name>
  <age>42</age>
  <driversLicense>NC-3821-388297</driversLicense>
</person>
```

(Notice that we defined the element that uses the datatype before the datatype itself. The order in which you define things in the schema doesn't matter.)

Because we've defined our own datatypes through restriction, validation fails if `<age>` is outside the defined range, *or* `eyeColor` isn't one of our four colors, *or* `<driversLicense>` doesn't match our regular expression. Because all of these datatypes are named, we can reuse them wherever we need them.

Creating New Datatypes by Extension

Another way to create new datatypes is through extension. The most common example of this is adding an attribute to a simple type. The XML Schema spec says that simple types (`xs:string`, `xs:integer`, etc.) can't have attributes. We can create a complex type that allows an element to have content of type `xs:integer` and have an attribute. Here's how the schema looks:

```
<?xml version="1.0" encoding="UTF-8"?>
<!-- extension.xsd -->
<xs:schema
  xmlns="http://www.oreilly.com/xslt"
  targetNamespace="http://www.oreilly.com/xslt"
  xmlns:xs="http://www.w3.org/2001/XMLSchema">

  <xs:simpleType name="currency-type">
    <xs:restriction base="xs:string">
      <xs:enumeration value="USD"/>
      <xs:enumeration value="GBP"/>
```

```
      <xs:enumeration value="CNY"/>
      <xs:enumeration value="EUR"/>
    </xs:restriction>
  </xs:simpleType>

  <xs:complexType name="price-type">
    <xs:simpleContent>
      <xs:extension base="xs:decimal">
        <xs:attribute name="currency" type="currency-type"/>
      </xs:extension>
    </xs:simpleContent>
  </xs:complexType>

  <xs:element name="price" type="price-type"/>

</xs:schema>
```

Now we have an element whose content must be an `xs:decimal`, while it must also have an attribute named currency. Here's a valid document for this schema:

```
<?xml version="1.0" encoding="utf-8"?>
<!-- extension.xml -->
<price
  xmlns="http://www.oreilly.com/xslt"
  xmlns:xsi="http://www.w3.org/2001/XMLSchema-instance"
  xsi:schemaLocation="http://www.oreilly.com/xslt extension.xsd"
  currency="USD">
438.92
</price>
```

If we change the content of the element to be `akd482.58`, validation fails.

Casting Between Datatypes

It is possible to cast an atomic value from one atomic datatype to another. We can't do that with complex types, but it does work for atomic types. Here's a short example that illustrates this:

```
<?xml version="1.0"?>
<!-- typecasting.xsl -->
<xsl:stylesheet version="2.0"
  xmlns:xs="http://www.w3.org/2001/XMLSchema"
  xmlns:age="http://www.oreilly.com/xslt"
  xmlns:xsl="http://www.w3.org/1999/XSL/Transform">

  <xsl:output method="text"/>

  <xsl:import-schema namespace="http://www.oreilly.com/xslt">
    <xs:schema
      targetNamespace="http://www.oreilly.com/xslt"
      xmlns:xs="http://www.w3.org/2001/XMLSchema">
      <xs:simpleType name="age-type">
        <xs:restriction base="xs:integer">
          <xs:minInclusive value="0"/>
          <xs:maxInclusive value="130"/>
```

```
        </xs:restriction>
      </xs:simpleType>
    </xs:schema>
  </xsl:import-schema>

  <xsl:template match="/">
    <xsl:variable name="age" as="age:age-type"
      select="age:age-type(42)"/>
    <xsl:variable name="age-int" as="xs:integer"
      select="$age cast as xs:integer"/>
    <xsl:variable name="float-age" as="age:age-type"
      select="xs:float(42.0) cast as age:age-type"/>
    <xsl:value-of select="$age, $age-int, $float-age"
      separator=", "/>
  </xsl:template>
</xsl:stylesheet>
```

The three variables at the bottom of the stylesheet are of datatypes `age:age-type`, `xs:integer`, and `xs:float`. Because all of these are numeric types, we can cast a value from one type to another. We still have to follow the restrictions for each datatype; the statement `xs:float(148.3) cast as age:age-type` fails at runtime. Casting `xs:float(48.3)` to an `age:age-type` creates a new `age:age-type` value of 48.

To "cast" to or from a complex type, we have to build the complex type ourselves. In other words, to create a new complex type, we have to use `<xsl:element>` to create and validate the complex type, filling in the elements and attributes of the complex type appropriately. See the second example of the `<xsl:element>` element in Appendix A for more details.

Creating List Types

Another datatype we can create is a list type. A list type references a datatype; the new list type allows space-separated values of that type. We'll add a new datatype called `state-abbr` to our schema, then create a list type based on it. Here's the schema:

```
<?xml version="1.0" encoding="UTF-8"?>
<!-- list.xsd -->
<xs:schema
  xmlns="http://www.oreilly.com/xslt"
  targetNamespace="http://www.oreilly.com/xslt"
  xmlns:xs="http://www.w3.org/2001/XMLSchema">

  <xs:element name="person">
    <xs:complexType>
      <xs:sequence>
        <xs:element ref="name"/>
        <xs:element ref="birthday"/>
        <xs:element ref="age"/>
        <xs:element ref="priorAddresses"/>
      </xs:sequence>
    </xs:complexType>
  </xs:element>
```

```
<xs:simpleType name="state-abbr-type">
  <xs:restriction base="xs:string">
    <xs:length value="2"/>
  </xs:restriction>
</xs:simpleType>

<xs:simpleType name="state-abbr-list-type">
  <xs:list itemType="state-abbr-type"/>
</xs:simpleType>

<xs:element name="name" type="xs:string"/>
<xs:element name="birthday" type="xs:date"/>
<xs:element name="age" type="xs:positiveInteger"/>
<xs:element name="priorAddresses">
  <xs:complexType>
    <xs:attribute name="states" type="state-abbr-list-type"/>
  </xs:complexType>
</xs:element>

</xs:schema>
```

Now we have an attribute named **states** whose content is a list of one or more state abbreviations. Here's a valid document:

```
<?xml version="1.0" encoding="utf-8"?>
<!-- list.xml -->
<person
  xmlns="http://www.oreilly.com/xslt"
  xmlns:xsi="http://www.w3.org/2001/XMLSchema-instance"
  xsi:schemaLocation="http://www.oreilly.com/xslt list.xsd">
  <name>Doug Tidwell</name>
  <birthday>1965-06-19</birthday>
  <age>42</age>
  <priorAddresses states="GA TN NC"/>
</person>
```

Creating Union Types

A union type references two or more datatypes. The valid content of a union type is a value from one of those datatypes. We'll create another schema that defines a list of zipcodes, then create a union type that allows the **states** attribute to be either a list of state abbreviations or a list of zipcodes. Here's an excerpt from the schema:

```
<?xml version="1.0" encoding="UTF-8"?>
<!-- union.xsd -->
...
  <xs:simpleType name="zipcode">
    <xs:restriction base="xs:integer">
      <xs:pattern value="[0-9]{5}"/>
    </xs:restriction>
  </xs:simpleType>

  <xs:simpleType name="zipcode-list-type">
```

```
              <xs:list itemType="zipcode"/>
            </xs:simpleType>

            <xs:simpleType name="state-abbr-type">
              <xs:restriction base="xs:string">
                <xs:length value="2"/>
              </xs:restriction>
            </xs:simpleType>

            <xs:simpleType name="state-abbr-list-type">
              <xs:list itemType="state-abbr-type"/>
            </xs:simpleType>

            <xs:simpleType name="address-union-type">
              <xs:union memberTypes="state-abbr-list-type zipcode-list-type"/>
            </xs:simpleType>
            ...
            <xs:element name="priorAddresses">
              <xs:complexType>
                <xs:attribute name="states" type="address-union-type"/>
              </xs:complexType>
            </xs:element>

          </xs:schema>
```

And here's a valid document for this schema:

```
          <?xml version="1.0" encoding="utf-8"?>
          <!-- union.xml -->
          <person
            xmlns="http://www.oreilly.com/xslt"
            xmlns:xsi="http://www.w3.org/2001/XMLSchema-instance"
            xsi:schemaLocation="http://www.oreilly.com/xslt union.xsd">
            <name>Doug Tidwell</name>
            <birthday>1965-06-19</birthday>
            <age>42</age>
            <priorAddresses states="27516 37174 30606"/>
          </person>
```

A **states** attribute that contains a list of zip codes or a list of state abbreviations is legal. What we *can't* do is combine the two. The following is illegal:

```
          <!-- Not valid! -->
          <priorAddresses states="27516 37174 30606 NC TN GA"/>
```

Substitution Groups

A substitution group is a set of elements that can be substituted for each other. We'll add an <address> element to our schema, then we'll define two types of address that can be used instead. Here's the schema:

```
          <?xml version="1.0" encoding="UTF-8"?>
          <!-- substitute.xsd -->
          <xs:schema
            xmlns="http://www.oreilly.com/xslt"
```

```
    targetNamespace="http://www.oreilly.com/xslt"
    xmlns:xs="http://www.w3.org/2001/XMLSchema">

    <xs:element name="person">
      <xs:complexType>
        <xs:sequence>
          <xs:element ref="name"/>
          <xs:element ref="birthday"/>
          <xs:element ref="age"/>
          <xs:element ref="address"/>
        </xs:sequence>
      </xs:complexType>
    </xs:element>

    <xs:element name="name" type="xs:string"/>
    <xs:element name="birthday" type="xs:date"/>
    <xs:element name="age" type="xs:positiveInteger"/>

    <xs:element name="address" type="xs:string"/>
    <xs:element name="businessAddress" type="xs:string"
      substitutionGroup="address"/>
    <xs:element name="residentialAddress" type="xs:string"
      substitutionGroup="address"/>

</xs:schema>
```

The schema defines two additional elements, `<businessAddress>` and `<residentialAddress>`, that can be substituted for `<address>`. Notice that the two additional elements use the `substitutionGroup` attribute to reference the element they can replace. Also, all of the elements are the same type. Here's a valid XML document:

```
<?xml version="1.0" encoding="utf-8"?>
<!-- substitute.xml -->
<person
  xmlns="http://www.oreilly.com/xslt"
  xmlns:xsi="http://www.w3.org/2001/XMLSchema-instance"
  xsi:schemaLocation="http://www.oreilly.com/xslt substitute.xsd">
  <name>Doug Tidwell</name>
  <birthday>1965-06-19</birthday>
  <age>42</age>
  <address>4013 Corporate Parkway</address>
</person>
```

This document is valid as well:

```
<?xml version="1.0" encoding="utf-8"?>
<!-- substitute2.xml -->
<person
...
  <businessAddress>4013 Corporate Parkway</businessAddress>
</person>
```

And so is this:

```
<?xml version="1.0" encoding="utf-8"?>
<!-- substitute3.xml -->
```

```
<person
...
  <residentialAddress>1234 Main Street</residentialAddress>
</person>
```

Abstract Elements and Datatypes

Our final topic is the use of *abstract elements and datatypes*. An abstract element or datatype works like an abstract class in object-oriented programming languages. We define the abstract class, but we have to create a subclass to actually use it. In terms of XML Schema, we'll be creating new elements and datatypes based on the abstract ones.

In our first example, we'll define an abstract element and its properties, and then use our substitution group as before. The only change to the schema is that we've added `abstract="true"` to the definition of the `<address>` element:

```
<?xml version="1.0" encoding="UTF-8"?>
<!-- abstract1.xsd -->
<xs:schema
...
  <xs:element name="address" type="xs:string" abstract="true"/>

  <xs:element name="businessAddress" type="xs:string"
    substitutionGroup="address"/>
  <xs:element name="residentialAddress" type="xs:string"
    substitutionGroup="address"/>
...
```

The effect of the abstract element is that we're forcing the document to contain either a `<businessAddress>` or a `<residentialAddress>`. This document is valid:

```
<?xml version="1.0" encoding="utf-8"?>
<!-- abstract1.xml -->
<person
  xmlns="http://www.oreilly.com/xslt"
  xmlns:xsi="http://www.w3.org/2001/XMLSchema-instance"
  xsi:schemaLocation="http://www.oreilly.com/xslt abstract1.xsd">
  <name>Doug Tidwell</name>
  <birthday>1965-06-19</birthday>
  <age>42</age>
  <businessAddress>4013 Corporate Parkway</businessAddress>
</person>
```

If this document used the `<address>` element instead of `<businessAddress>`, it would not be valid.

Finally, we'll look at an abstract datatype. In this example, we'll define an abstract datatype named `state-or-province-type` and an element of that type named `<state-or-province>`. We'll then define two nonabstract extensions of those types called `province-type` and `state-type`. The `<xsl:state-or-province>` elements in our sample document will use the `xsi:type` attribute to declare the element to be of a nonabstract type:

```
<?xml version="1.0" encoding="UTF-8"?>
<!-- abstract2.xsd -->
<xs:schema
  xmlns="http://www.oreilly.com/xslt"
  targetNamespace="http://www.oreilly.com/xslt"
  xmlns:xs="http://www.w3.org/2001/XMLSchema">

  <xs:element name="person">
    <xs:complexType>
      <xs:sequence>
        <xs:element ref="name"/>
        <xs:element ref="birthday"/>
        <xs:element ref="age"/>
        <xs:element ref="state-or-province"
          minOccurs="2" maxOccurs="2"/>
      </xs:sequence>
    </xs:complexType>
  </xs:element>

  <xs:element name="name" type="xs:string"/>
  <xs:element name="birthday" type="xs:date"/>
  <xs:element name="age" type="xs:positiveInteger"/>

  <xs:element name="address" type="xs:string"/>

  <xs:complexType name="state-or-province-type" abstract="true"/>

  <xs:complexType name="state-type">
    <xs:complexContent>
      <xs:extension base="state-or-province-type">
        <xs:attribute name="state-abbr">
          <xs:simpleType>
            <xs:restriction base="xs:string">
              <xs:enumeration value="NC"/>
              <xs:enumeration value="TN"/>
              <xs:enumeration value="GA"/>
              <!-- Other states left out -->
            </xs:restriction>
          </xs:simpleType>
        </xs:attribute>
      </xs:extension>
    </xs:complexContent>
  </xs:complexType>

  <xs:complexType name="province-type">
    <xs:complexContent>
      <xs:extension base="state-or-province-type">
        <xs:attribute name="province-abbr">
          <xs:simpleType>
            <xs:restriction base="xs:string">
              <xs:enumeration value="NS"/>
              <xs:enumeration value="BC"/>
              <xs:enumeration value="PEI"/>
              <!-- Other provinces left out -->
            </xs:restriction>
```

```
            </xs:simpleType>
          </xs:attribute>
        </xs:extension>
      </xs:complexContent>
    </xs:complexType>

    <xs:element name="state-or-province" type="state-or-province-type"/>

  </xs:schema>
```

The two datatypes we define extend the abstract datatype by adding an attribute. Each attribute is restricted with an enumeration. The `state-type` datatype has a `state-abbr` attribute that can only contain values from our enumeration; the same is true for the `province-type` datatype and its `province-abbr` attribute.

Here's a valid XML document:

```
<?xml version="1.0" encoding="utf-8"?>
<!-- abstract2.xml -->
<person
  xmlns="http://www.oreilly.com/xslt"
  xmlns:xsi="http://www.w3.org/2001/XMLSchema-instance"
  xsi:schemaLocation="http://www.oreilly.com/xslt abstract2.xsd">
  <name>Doug Tidwell</name>
  <birthday>1965-06-19</birthday>
  <age>42</age>
  <state-or-province xsi:type="province-type" province-abbr="NS"/>
  <state-or-province xsi:type="state-type" state-abbr="NC"/>
</person>
```

(For the sake of illustration, we changed the `minOccurs` attribute on the `<state-or-province>` element so we could use both nonabstract datatypes here.) Because the `<state-or-province>` element is declared with an abstract datatype, we have to use the `xsi:type` attribute to declare a nonabstract datatype for the element.

Using an XML Schema in a Stylesheet

Now that we've covered how schemas work, we'll take a look at how to use them in XSLT. The `<xsl:import-schema>` element lets us import an XML Schema into our stylesheet directly. In addition to `<xsl:import-schema>`, an XML document can reference a schema with the `xsi:noNamespaceSchemaLocation` or `xsi:schemaLocation` attributes. If our stylesheet is set up correctly, the XSLT processor can use the referenced schema to validate data.

Importing XML Schemas with <xsl:import-schema>

The `<xsl:import-schema>` element allows you to import an XML Schema. The schema is imported and processed before any input documents are processed. This allows you to define datatypes and validation rules before the XSLT processor begins to transform the input document. *This element is only supported by schema-aware XSLT 2.0 processors.*

The element has two optional parameters: `namespace`, which defines the namespace URI for the schema, and `schema-location`, which contains the URI of the schema file itself. `<xsl:import-schema>` can use `schema-location` to import a file, or it can contain the actual XML Schema within the stylesheet. We'll look at a couple of examples here; for more complete examples, see the discussion of the [2.0 – Schema] `<xsl:import-schema>` element.

The simplest way to import a schema into a stylesheet is to use the URI:

```
<?xml version="1.0"?>
<!-- import-schema.xsl -->
<xsl:stylesheet version="2.0"
  xmlns:xsl="http://www.w3.org/1999/XSL/Transform"
  xmlns:po="http://www.oreilly.com/xslt">

  <xsl:import-schema namespace="http://www.oreilly.com/xslt"
    schema-location="po.xsd" />

  <xsl:output method="text"/>

  <xsl:template match="schema-element(po:purchase-order)">
    <xsl:text>&#xA;This is a test of the &lt;xsl:import-</xsl:text>
    <xsl:text>schema&gt; element.&#xA;&#xA;</xsl:text>
    <xsl:text>Here are all the items in this purchase </xsl:text>
    <xsl:text>order:&#xA;</xsl:text>
    <xsl:for-each select="po:items/po:item">
      <xsl:text>  * </xsl:text>
      <xsl:value-of select="po:partname"/>
      <xsl:text>&#xA;</xsl:text>
    </xsl:for-each>
  </xsl:template>

  <xsl:template match="*">
    <xsl:message terminate="yes">
      <xsl:text>This is not a valid purchase order!</xsl:text>
    </xsl:message>
  </xsl:template>

</xsl:stylesheet>
```

Notice that the imported schema is associated with a namespace URI, which in turn is associated with the prefix `po`. The XSLT pattern uses the `schema-element(po:purchase-order)` node test to find all of the elements named `<purchase-order>` with a namespace URI of `http://www.oreilly.com/xslt`. Given that starting point, the stylesheet finds all of the `<item>` elements in the purchase order. The output looks like this:

```
This is a test of the <xsl:import-schema> element.

Here are all the items in this purchase order:
```

```
        * Turnip Twaddler
        * Clam Teaser
```

The second template in our stylesheet matches anything *except* a valid purchase order. If the root element doesn't have the correct name and namespace URI, the second template stops the processor.

We can use `<xsl:import-schema>` with the schema embedded inside the XSLT stylesheet as well:

```
<?xml version="1.0"?>
<!-- import-schema2.xsl -->
<xsl:stylesheet version="2.0"
  xmlns="http://www.oreilly.com/xslt"
  xmlns:xsl="http://www.w3.org/1999/XSL/Transform"
  xmlns:po="http://www.oreilly.com/xslt"
  xmlns:xs="http://www.w3.org/2001/XMLSchema">

  <xsl:import-schema namespace="http://www.oreilly.com/xslt">
    <xs:schema
      targetNamespace="http://www.oreilly.com/xslt"
      xmlns:xs="http://www.w3.org/2001/XMLSchema">

      <xs:element name="purchase-order">
        <xs:complexType>
          <xs:sequence>
            <xs:element ref="date"
              minOccurs="1" maxOccurs="1"/>
            <xs:element ref="customer"
              minOccurs="1" maxOccurs="1"/>
            <xs:element ref="items"
              minOccurs="1" maxOccurs="1"/>
          </xs:sequence>
          <xs:attribute name="id" type="xs:string"/>
        </xs:complexType>
      </xs:element>

      <xs:element name="date">
        <xs:complexType>
          <xs:attribute name="year" type="xs:integer"/>
          <xs:attribute name="month" type="xs:integer"/>
          <xs:attribute name="day" type="xs:integer"/>
        </xs:complexType>
      </xs:element>
  ...
    </xs:schema>
  </xsl:import-schema>
  ...
  <xsl:template match="schema-element(po:purchase-order)">
    ...
</xsl:stylesheet>
```

It is a fatal error to have an `<xsl:import-schema>` element that has a `select` attribute and content.

Using XML Schemas Without Namespaces

To use an XML Schema without `<xsl:import-schema>`, we have to tie the XML, the schema, and the stylesheet together. We'll start by doing this without namespaces, beginning with the `xsi:noNamespaceSchemaLocation` attribute in our XML document:

```
<?xml version="1.0"?>
<!-- parts-list-schema-no-ns.xml -->
<parts-list
  xmlns:xsi="http://www.w3.org/2001/XMLSchema-instance"
  xsi:noNamespaceSchemaLocation="parts-list-no-ns.xsd">
  <component component-id="C28392-33-TT">
    <name>Turnip Twaddler</name>
    <partref refid="P81952-26-PK"/>
    <partref refid="P86679-52-SP"/>
    ...
```

The schema doesn't specify a default namespace:

```
<?xml version="1.0" encoding="UTF-8"?>
<!-- parts-list-no-ns.xsd -->
<xs:schema
  xmlns:xs="http://www.w3.org/2001/XMLSchema">

  <xs:element name="parts-list">
    <xs:complexType>
      <xs:sequence>
        <xs:element ref="component" minOccurs="1" maxOccurs="unbounded"/>
        ...
```

The only prefix we used here is the one for XML Schema itself. The XML file and the schema are now in sync and namespace-free, so our stylesheet is straightforward:

```
<?xml version="1.0"?>
<!-- id-schema-no-ns.xsl -->
<xsl:stylesheet version="1.0"
  xmlns:xsl="http://www.w3.org/1999/XSL/Transform">

  <xsl:output method="text"/>
  ...
    <xsl:for-each select="/parts-list/part">
      <xsl:text>&#xA;  </xsl:text>
      <xsl:value-of select="name"/>
      <xsl:text> (part #</xsl:text>
      <xsl:value-of select="@part-id"/>
      <xsl:text>) is used in these products:&#xA;    </xsl:text>
      <xsl:for-each
        select="/parts-list/component
                [partref/@refid=current()/@part-id]">
        <xsl:value-of select="name"/>
        ...
```

Because we're not using namespaces, we don't have to qualify anything in our XPath expressions. Next we'll look at using a schema with namespaces.

Using XML Schemas with Namespaces

If we're using an XML Schema with a namespace, we have to make sure the three files
(*.xml*, *.xsd*, and *.xsl*) are in sync. It's slightly more complicated, as you'd expect. First
of all, the XML file needs to have a default namespace:

```
<?xml version="1.0"?>
<!-- parts-list-schema-ns.xml -->
<parts-list xmlns="http://www.oreilly.com/xslt"
  xmlns:xsi="http://www.w3.org/2001/XMLSchema-instance"
  xsi:schemaLocation="http://www.oreilly.com/xslt
                      parts-list-schema-ns.xsd">
  <component component-id="C28392-33-TT">
    <name>Turnip Twaddler</name>
    <partref refid="P81952-26-PK"/>
    ...
```

Notice that we've defined the default namespace (`xmlns=`) as `http://www.oreilly.com/`
`xslt`. The `xsi:schemaLocation` attribute has two parts, separated by whitespace: the
namespace URI and the URI of the schema itself. The schema file uses the same default
namespace:

```
<?xml version="1.0" encoding="UTF-8"?>
<!-- parts-list-schema-ns.xsd -->
<xs:schema
  xmlns="http://www.oreilly.com/xslt"
  targetNamespace="http://www.oreilly.com/xslt"
  xmlns:xs="http://www.w3.org/2001/XMLSchema">

  <xs:element name="parts-list">
    <xs:complexType>
      <xs:sequence>
        <xs:element ref="component" minOccurs="1" maxOccurs="unbounded"/>
        <xs:element ref="part" minOccurs="1" maxOccurs="unbounded"/>
        ...
```

We also use the XML Schema attribute `targetNamespace`; it has the same value as the
default namespace. Finally, we need to use the namespace in the XSLT file. We define
`http://www.oreilly.com/xslt` as the default namespace and define a prefix for that
namespace as well:

```
<?xml version="1.0"?>
<!-- id-schema-ns.xsl -->
<xsl:stylesheet version="1.0"
  xmlns:xsl="http://www.w3.org/1999/XSL/Transform"
  xmlns="http://www.oreilly.com/xslt"
  xmlns:pl="http://www.oreilly.com/xslt">

  <xsl:output method="text"/>

  <xsl:template match="/">
    <xsl:text>&#xA;Here is a test of the id() </xsl:text>
    <xsl:text>function in reverse:&#xA;</xsl:text>
```

```
<xsl:for-each select="/pl:parts-list/pl:part">
  <xsl:text>&#xA;  </xsl:text>
  <xsl:value-of select="pl:name"/>
  <xsl:text> (part #</xsl:text>
  <xsl:value-of select="@part-id"/>
  <xsl:text>) is used in these products:&#xA;    </xsl:text>
  <xsl:for-each
    select="/pl:parts-list/pl:component
            [pl:partref/@refid=current()/@part-id]">
    <xsl:value-of select="pl:name"/>
```

Because we've defined namespaces in our schema, we have to create a namespace prefix
for that namespace and use it whenever we refer to elements in the XML document. If
we change the stylesheet to look for `<parts-list>` elements instead of `<pl:parts-
list>` elements, the stylesheet won't work. It's more difficult to use a schema with
namespaces, but you don't always have a choice.

To address this problem, XSLT 2.0 adds the `xpath-default-namespace` attribute. In our
previous stylesheet, we defined a namespace and a namespace prefix, then used the
prefix in all of our XPath statements. With `xpath-default-namespace`, we don't have to
do that:

```
<?xml version="1.0"?>
<!-- id-schema-ns2.xsl -->
<xsl:stylesheet version="2.0"
  xmlns:xsl="http://www.w3.org/1999/XSL/Transform"
  xmlns="http://www.oreilly.com/xslt"
  xpath-default-namespace="http://www.oreilly.com/xslt">

  <xsl:output method="text"/>

  <xsl:template match="/">
    <xsl:text>&#xA;Here is a test of the id() </xsl:text>
    <xsl:text>function in reverse:&#xA;</xsl:text>

    <xsl:for-each select="/parts-list/part">
      <xsl:text>&#xA;  </xsl:text>
      <xsl:value-of select="name"/>
      <xsl:text> (part #</xsl:text>
      <xsl:value-of select="@part-id"/>
      <xsl:text>) is used in these products:&#xA;    </xsl:text>
      <xsl:for-each
        select="/parts-list/component
                [partref/@refid=current()/@part-id]">
        <xsl:value-of select="name"/>
        <xsl:if test="position() != last()">
          <xsl:text>&#xA;    </xsl:text>
        </xsl:if>
      </xsl:for-each>
      <xsl:text>&#xA;</xsl:text>
    </xsl:for-each>
  </xsl:template>
</xsl:stylesheet>
```

By adding `xpath-default-namespace` to our stylesheet, our XPath expressions are much simpler.

Be aware that you can add this attribute to any element in the XSLT namespace. For example, we could remove `xpath-default-namespace` from the `<xsl:stylesheet>` element and write our stylesheet like this:

```
<?xml version="1.0"?>
<!-- id-schema-ns3.xsl -->
<xsl:stylesheet version="2.0"
  xmlns:xsl="http://www.w3.org/1999/XSL/Transform"
  xmlns="http://www.oreilly.com/xslt">
...
    <xsl:for-each select="/parts-list/part"
      xpath-default-namespace="http://www.oreilly.com/xslt">
      <xsl:text>&#xA;  </xsl:text>
      <xsl:value-of select="name"/>
...
</xsl:stylesheet>
```

This gives us the same results as before. If you're using data from different namespaces (maybe you're reading more than one XML document as input), redefining the default XPath namespace as needed makes your XPath expressions much simpler. Most of the time, though, you'll just use it on `<xsl:stylesheet>`.

[2.0] Regular Expressions

The regular expression language used by XSLT 2.0, XPath 2.0, and XQuery 1.0 is a superset of the XML Schema regular expression language. Regular expressions are used in the XSLT 2.0 [2.0] `<xsl:analyze-string>` element and the XPath 2.0 and XQuery 1.0 functions [2.0] `matches( )`, [2.0] `replace( )`, and [2.0] `tokenize( )`.

This appendix defines the syntax and capabilities of regular expressions in XSLT 2.0, XPath 2.0, and XQuery 1.0. The details of regular expressions are defined in XQuery 1.0 and XPath 2.0 Functions and Operators section 7.6, "String Functions that Use Pattern Matching."

 *[XPath]* The Functions and Operators spec extends the XML Schema regular expression in several ways. Features unique to the XPath 2.0 and XQuery 1.0 regular expression language are indicated with the text *[XPath]*.

Simple Expressions

The simplest regular expression is just a string of text. The regular expression `abc` matches the string `abc`. We're merely searching for a series of characters inside some data. For this case, `contains('abc', 'abc')` does the same thing.

Regular expressions exist to do far more than search for a literal string; they help us find data that matches a pattern. We can use character sets to specify groups of characters. The regular expression `[abc]d` matches two characters in which the first character is `a`, `b`, or `c`, followed by the character `d`.

We can also negate a character set, asking for all the characters *not* in the character set. To do this, add a caret (`^`) to the start of the character set. The regular expression `[^abc]d` matches two characters in which the first character is anything except `a`, `b`, or `c`, followed by `d`.

Ranges give us a shorthand way of defining character sets. The character set `[0-9]` specifies the digits 0 through 9, while the character set `[a-zA-Z]` specifies all of the unaccented letters used in Western European languages. A range can be negated just like any other character set; [^0-9] specifies anything except the digits.

Ranges can also be subtracted from each other. The range [A-Z-[IOQ]] matches any unaccented uppercase letter except I, O, or Q.

Subexpressions

It's often useful to split a regular expression into subexpressions. A subexpression is surrounded by parentheses, and can be modified by a quantifier to define how often (or if) an expression can occur. For example, this regular expression matches a phone number in the format 999-999-9999:

    ([0-9]{3})-([0-9]{3})-([0-9]{4})

The regular expression has three subexpressions, each of which matches a group of digits. XSLT 2.0 provides the regex-group( ) function to retrieve the part of the analyzed string that matches a particular subexpression. Here's an example:

```
<?xml version="1.0" encoding="utf-8"?>
<!-- subexpressions1.xsl -->
<xsl:stylesheet version="2.0"
  xmlns:xsl="http://www.w3.org/1999/XSL/Transform">

  <xsl:output method="text"/>

  <xsl:template match="/">
    <xsl:analyze-string select="'Call me at 919-555-1212, please.'"
      regex="([0-9]{{3}})-(\p{{Nd}}{{3}})-([0-9]{{4}})">
      <xsl:matching-substring>
        <xsl:text>The matching substring is '</xsl:text>

        <!-- <xsl:value-of select="."/> does the same thing here -->
        <xsl:value-of select="regex-group(0)"/>
        <xsl:text>'&#xA;</xsl:text>
        <xsl:text>The formatted string is '</xsl:text>
        <xsl:value-of
          select="'(', regex-group(1), ') ', regex-group(2),
                   '-', regex-group(3), '''')"
          separator=""/>
      </xsl:matching-substring>
    </xsl:analyze-string>
  </xsl:template>

</xsl:stylesheet>
```

(The curly braces in this example are doubled so that the XSLT processor knows this is not an attribute value template.) Notice that the regular expression contains two hyphens that are not part of any subexpression. The function regex-group(0) returns the entire portion of the string that matches. That means everything from the first character that matches the regular expression to the last character that matches the regular expression. In our test string here, regex-group(0) returns 919-555-1212, but

---

not any of the other characters in the string. (Asking for the context item does the same thing.) That includes the two hyphens that aren't in any of the subexpressions. Here are the results of the stylesheet:

```
The matching substring is '919-555-1212'
The formatted string is '(919) 555-1212'
```

Calling regex-group( ) with a negative number or with a number larger than the number of subexpressions returns an empty string.

The replace( ) function provides a mechanism similar to regex-group( ). Within the replacement string, the dollar sign ($) references the matches to different subexpressions. As you would expect, $1 returns the match for the first subexpression, $2 returns the match for the second subexpression, and $0 returns the entire matching string. Here's the replace( ) version of our previous example:

```
<?xml version="1.0" encoding="utf-8"?>
<!-- subexpressions2.xsl -->
<xsl:stylesheet version="2.0"
  xmlns:xsl="http://www.w3.org/1999/XSL/Transform">

  <xsl:output method="text"/>

  <xsl:template match="/">
    <xsl:text>The string '</xsl:text>
    <xsl:value-of
      select="replace('Call me at 919-555-1212, please',
              '([0-9]{3})-([0-9]{3})-([0-9]{4})',
              '$0')"/>
    <xsl:text>' contains a match!&#xA;</xsl:text>
    <xsl:text>The version with all the replacements: &#xA;  </xsl:text>
    <xsl:value-of
      select="replace('Call me at 919-555-1212, please',
              '([0-9]{3})-([0-9]{3})-([0-9]{4})',
              '($1) $2-$3')"/>
  </xsl:template>

</xsl:stylesheet>
```

The first call to the replace( ) function simply uses the $0 operator. This string is identical to the original string. The replace( ) function replaces only the part of the string that matches, so replacing the part that matches with the part that matches doesn't change anything. The second call to replace( ) formats the phone number as we want. We put the area code ($1) inside parentheses, followed by a space, the exchange ($2), a dash, and the last four digits ($3). The results look like this:

```
The string 'Call me at 919-555-1212, please' contains a match!
The version with all the replacements:
  Call me at (919) 555-1212, please
```

There is one important difference between regex-group( ) and replace( ). Calling regex-group( ) with a group number that does not exist returns an empty string. With the dollar sign, the XSLT 2.0 engine interprets the rightmost digits as literal characters, continuing this process until only a single digit is left. If that single digit is greater than the number of subexpressions, that digit is replaced with an empty string. To quote an example from the spec, if there are five subexpressions, $23 returns the value of the second subexpression followed by the number 3. Using $63 with the same regular expression simply returns the value 3.

Quantifiers

A quantifier specifies how many times (or if) something occurs. There are three quantifier characters and a syntax for specifying quantities more explicitly. For example, (a|b)?c matches ac, bc, and c, because the question mark indicates zero or one instances of a pattern. Here are all the quantifiers and their syntax:

?

Zero or one of a pattern.

*

Zero or more of a pattern.

+

One or more of a pattern.

{x}

The pattern must occur exactly x times. The pattern (a|b){3} matches aaa and abb, but not ab.

{x,}

The pattern must occur at least x times. The pattern (a|b){3,} matches aaa and aaaaaaaaa, but not aa.

{x,y}

The pattern must occur at least x times, but no more than y times. The pattern (a|b){2,5} matches aa and aaa, but not aaaaaa.

[XPath] Reluctant Quantifiers

By default, a regular expression or subexpression matches the longest possible string. The quantifiers +, *, and ? match as many characters as possible. Adding a question mark to the end of a quantifier causes the expression or subexpression to match the *shortest* possible string. The quantifiers are modified as follows:

a+?

Matches a once

a??

> Matches a, either once or not at all (works only in the matches( ) function; more on this later in this section)

a*?

> Matches a, zero times or once (works only in the matches( ) function; more on this later in this section)

a{x}?

> Matches a, exactly x times (in this case the reluctant qualifier doesn't change anything)

a{x,}?

> Matches a exactly x times (the comma is irrelevant—a reluctant quantifier matches only the minimum length)

a{x,y}?

> Matches a exactly x times (the second number, y, is irrelevant—a reluctant quantifier matches only the minimum length)

As an example, we'll use the replace( ) function. We'll put square brackets around each match in the original string. The normal quantifier and the reluctant quantifier work differently, as we'll see. Here's the stylesheet:

```
<?xml version="1.0" encoding="utf-8"?>
<!-- reluctant.xsl -->
<xsl:stylesheet version="2.0"
  xmlns:xsl="http://www.w3.org/1999/XSL/Transform">

  <xsl:output method="text"/>

  <xsl:template match="/">
    <xsl:text>Original string: 'Call me at 19195551212'&#xA;</xsl:text>
    <xsl:text>  replace($x, '([0-9]+)', '[$1]'):&#xA;    </xsl:text>
    <xsl:value-of
      select="replace('Call me at 19195551212',
              '([0-9]+)',
              '[$1]')"/>
    <xsl:text>&#xA;</xsl:text>
    <xsl:text>  replace($x, '(([0-9])+?)', '[$1]'):&#xA;    </xsl:text>
    <xsl:value-of
      select="replace('Call me at 19195551212',
              '(([0-9])+?)',
              '[$1]')"/>
    <xsl:text>&#xA;</xsl:text>
    <xsl:text>  replace($x, '(([0-9]){2,4}?)', '[$1]'):&#xA;    </xsl:text>
    <xsl:value-of
      select="replace('Call me at 19195551212',
              '(([0-9]){2,4}?)',
              '[$1]')"/>
  </xsl:template>

</xsl:stylesheet>
```

Here are the results:

```
Original string: 'Call me at 19195551212'
  replace($x, '([0-9]+)', '[$1]'):
    Call me at [19195551212]
  replace($x, '(([0-9])+?)', '[$1]'):
    Call me at [1][9][1][9][5][5][5][1][2][1][2]
  replace($x, '(([0-9]){2,4}?)', '[$1]'):
    Call me at [19][19][55][51][21]2
```

With the normal quantifier (([0-9]+)), the entire string of digits is matched. The single match appears between square brackets. In the second example, the reluctant qualifier ((([0-9])+?)) matches each digit separately, so there are square brackets around each digit. The final example reluctantly matches two to four digits, which means each match is two digits long. Notice that the last number in the string isn't part of a match at all.

 With the exception of the matches( ) function, it is illegal to have an expression that matches a zero-length string. The reluctant qualifiers a??, a*?, a{0}?, a{0,}?, and a{0,5}? all match nothing at all. If you use a regular expression that matches a zero-length string anywhere except the matches( ) function, the XSLT processor throws a static error.

Processing Modes

There are four flags that change how regular expressions are evaluated:

s

Regular expressions are evaluated in what the specs refer to as "dot-all" mode. When this flag is used, the dot operator (.) matches any character. Under normal processing (without the s flag), the dot operator matches any character *except* the newline character (#xA). This flag is useful when you want to match strings that might include a newline character.

 Perl and other languages refer to this as "single-line" mode; that's why the abbreviation for "dot-all" mode is s.

m

Regular expressions are evaulated in multiline mode. By default, the metacharacter (^) matches the start of the entire string, while $ matches the end of the entire string. In multiline mode, ^ matches the start of any line within the string, and $ matches the end of any line within the string.

i

Regular expressions are evaluated in case-insensitive mode. The regular expression "a" matches both "a" and "A".

Note that Unicode issues can complicate this greatly. For example, the XQuery 1.0 and XPath 2.0 Functions and Operators spec gives the example of the Unicode sign for degrees Kelvin (K), which is the letter "K". The combination of `regex="k"` and `flags="i"` matches the Kelvin sign as well as the letters "k" (k) and "K" (K).

Other Unicode characters don't convert to letters. For example, the Unicode symbol for the Roman numeral I (Ⅰ) looks like the letter I, but does not convert to one.

x

All whitespace characters (#x9, #xA, #xD and #x20) are removed from the regular expression before any comparison is done. In other words, with the x flag, the regular expressions `"John Smith"` and `"JohnSmith"` are the same. This flag is useful when you want to break a long regular expression into multiple lines to make it easier to read.

The flags can be combined in any order. The attributes `flags="xis"` and `flags="six"` work exactly the same way.

[XPath] Anchors

In XML Schema, regular expressions are anchored; in other words, the regular expression is assumed to start at the beginning of the text and end at the end of the text. That means the expression abc matches only the three-character string abc. If there are any extra characters before or after the letters abc, XML Schema does not consider the string a match.

The regular expression language in XPath 2.0 doesn't work that way. When we use any of the regular expression functions or elements, a string matches if it contains the regular expression *anywhere* inside it. In other words, using XPath's regular expression language, both abc and I know my abc's match the expression abc. XPath provides the traditional anchor operators used in other regular expression languages. The caret (^) matches the start of the string, while the dollar sign ($) matches the end of the string. If multiline mode is on (-m), the caret matches the start of the string and any character immediately following a newline. Similarly, in multiline mode, the dollar sign matches the end of the string and any character immediately before a newline.

Here's an example that illustrates how the anchors work:

```
<?xml version="1.0" encoding="utf-8"?>
<!-- anchors.xsl -->
<xsl:stylesheet version="2.0"
  xmlns:xsl="http://www.w3.org/1999/XSL/Transform">

  <xsl:output method="text"/>

  <xsl:template match="/">
    <xsl:text>matches('abcdefghij', 'cde'): </xsl:text>
```

```
<xsl:value-of
  select="if (matches('abcdefghij', 'cde'))
          then 'It''s a match!'
          else 'No match'"/>
<xsl:text>&#xA;matches('abcdefghij', 'cde$'): </xsl:text>
<xsl:value-of
  select="if (matches('abcdefghij', 'cde$'))
          then 'It''s a match!'
          else 'No match'"/>
<xsl:text>&#xA;matches('abcdefghij', 'hij$'): </xsl:text>
<xsl:value-of
  select="if (matches('abcdefghij', 'hij$'))
          then 'It''s a match!'
          else 'No match'"/>
<xsl:text>&#xA;matches('ab&amp;#xA;cdefghij', '^cde', 'm'): </xsl:text>
<xsl:value-of
  select="if (matches('ab&#xA;cdefghij', '^cde', 'm'))
          then 'It''s a match!'
          else 'No match'"/>
  </xsl:template>

</xsl:stylesheet>
```

The first example doesn't use an anchor at all, so matches( ) returns true. The second test looks for the characters cde at the end of the string, which means matches( ) is false. In the third example, hij is at the end of the string, so we have a match. In the final example, we insert a newline character (
) inside the string and use multiline mode. Looking for cde at the start of a line succeeds. Here are the results of the stylesheet:

```
matches('abcdefghij', 'cde'): It's a match!
matches('abcdefghij', 'cde$'): No match
matches('abcdefghij', 'hij$'): It's a match!
matches('ab&#xA;cdefghij', '^cde', 'm'): It's a match!
```

If you want your regular expressions to work the way they do in XML Schema, simply surround your regular expressions with ^ and $. The expression ^abc$ matches the three-character string abc, while the expression abc matches any string of any length that contains the three characters abc at least once.

Back-references

A back-reference allows you to refer to a previously matched subexpression *within the regular expression itself*. As an example, say you want to find words that begin and end with the same two letters. The expression ([a-z]{2})(.*)\1 does the trick. The \1 represents whatever two characters matched the first subexpression. The back-reference \2 represents the match for the second subexpression, \3 represents the match for the third subexpression, and so on. (Notice that although the references go backwards, counting subexpressions goes from left to right.)

Here's a sample stylesheet:

```
<?xml version="1.0" encoding="utf-8"?>
<!-- back-reference.xsl -->
<xsl:stylesheet version="2.0"
  xmlns:xsl="http://www.w3.org/1999/XSL/Transform">

  <xsl:output method="text"/>

  <xsl:template match="/">
    <xsl:text>Using back-references to find words that begin &#xA;</xsl:text>
    <xsl:text>  and end with the same two letters:&#xA;&#xA;</xsl:text>
    <xsl:text>  replace($x, '([a-z]{2})(.*)\1', '$1--$2--$1')&#xA;</xsl:text>
    <xsl:text>    edited:    </xsl:text>
    <xsl:value-of
      select="replace('edited', '([a-z]{2})(.*)\1', '$1--$2--$1')"/>
    <xsl:text>&#xA;    editor:    </xsl:text>
    <xsl:value-of
      select="replace('editor', '([a-z]{2})(.*)\1', '$1--$2--$1')"/>
    <xsl:text>&#xA;    educated:  </xsl:text>
    <xsl:value-of
      select="replace('educated', '([a-z]{2})(.*)\1', '$1--$2--$1')"/>
    <xsl:text>&#xA;    orator:    </xsl:text>
    <xsl:value-of
      select="replace('orator', '([a-z]{2})(.*)\1', '$1--$2--$1')"/>
  </xsl:template>

</xsl:stylesheet>
```

The stylesheet generates these results:

```
Using back-references to find words that begin
  and end with the same two letters:

  replace($x, '([a-z]{2})(.*)\1', '$1--$2--$1')
    edited:    ed--it--ed
    editor:    editor
    educated:  ed--ucat--ed
    orator:    or--at--or
```

For the words **edited**, **educated**, and **orator**, the regular expression matches. The `replace( )` function writes out the two letters at the start and end of the word, with whatever was in between them offset by double hyphens. The word **editor** doesn't match the regular expression, so it isn't changed.

Metacharacters

Within a regular expression, most characters represent themselves. For example, the regular expression **A** represents a capital A. There are, of course, special characters that are processed differently:

.

By default, this matches any character except the newline character. In dot-all mode, this matches the newline character as well.

^

By default, this represents the beginning of the string literal. In multiline mode, this represents the beginning of a line within the string.

[XPath] Use of the caret to indicate that the beginning of a string or line is an addition to the regular expression syntax defined by XML Schema.

The caret can also be used inside a character class expression to indicate the negation of that character set. For example, [a-f] represents the letters a through f, while [^a-f] represents every character *except* the letters a through f.

$

[XPath] By default, this represents the end of the string literal. In multiline mode, this represents the end of a line within the string.

\

Escapes the following character.

|

The union operator. The expression A|B matches both A and B. It does not match AB.

?

Zero or one of a pattern. For example, A[A-Z]?Z matches AZ and ABZ, but not ABCZ.

*

Zero or more of a pattern. For example, A[A-Z]* matches any string of uppercase basic Latin characters that starts with A and is followed by zero or more uppercase Latin characters. The strings A, ABC, AA, and AREALLYLONGSTRING all match this expression.

+

One or more of a pattern. For example, A[A-Z]+ matches any string of uppercase basic Latin characters that starts with A and is followed by one or more uppercase characters. The strings AA, AD, and ADD match this expression, but A does not.

(

Starts a subexpression. For example, in the expression A(BCD)+, the parentheses define the subexpression BCD, which can appear once or not at all. This expression matches A and ABCD.

)

Ends a subexpression.

[

Begins a character class expression. For example, the expression [a-f] refers to the letters a through f.

-

Within square brackets, separates the upper and lower bounds of a range. For example, [a-f] represents the letters a through f. The expressions [a-f] and a|b|c|d|e|f are equivalent.

]

Ends a character class expression.

{

Starts a named category, block, or quantifier. For example, \p{IsThai} specifies the set of all Thai characters (฀ to ๿), while \p{Lu} specifies all upper-case letters.

Quantifiers can have three forms: {x}, {x,}, and {x,y}, where x and y are integers and y is greater than x. The quantifier {2} means something must occur exactly two times, {2,} means at least two times, and {2,5} means two to five times. The expression (AB|AC|AD){2,5} matches ACAB and ACADACADAB, but not AB or ABABABA BABAB.

}

Ends a named category, block, or quantifier.

> Because curly braces ({ and }) identify attribute value templates, you must use double curly braces for a regular expression inside an attribute. For example, if you want to look for a five-digit number with the `<xsl:analyze-string>` element, you would code this:
>
> ```
> <xsl:analyze-string select="." regex="[0-9]{{5}}" ...>
> ```
>
> If you don't double the curly braces inside an attribute, the regular expression [0-9]{5} (single curly braces) is interpreted as a single digit followed by the number 5.
>
> On the other hand, when using a regular expression in a function call, you *don't* use double curly braces. To replace a five-digit number with dashes, you would code this:
>
> ```
> <xsl:value-of select="replace(., [0-9]{5}, '-----')"/>
> ```

Single-Character Escapes

The regular expression language provides escapes for some special characters. They are:

\n

The newline character (
)

\r

The return character ()

\t

The tab character (	)

\\

The backslash character (\)

\|

The vertical bar character (|)

\\.
   A period (.)

\\-
   The hyphen or minus character (-)

\\^
   The circumflex accent (^)

\\?
   A question mark (?)

*
   An asterisk (*)

\\+
   The plus sign (+)

\\{
   A left curly bracket ({)

\\}
   A right curly bracket (})

\\(
   A left parenthesis (()

\\)
   A right parenthesis ())

\\[
   A left square bracket ([)

\\]
   A right square bracket (])

Multiple-Character Escapes

There are also escapes that represent multiple characters. They are:

\\s
   Any whitespace character

\\S
   Anything other than a whitespace character

\\d
   Any digit

\\D
   Anything other than a digit

\\w
   Any word character. Word characters are all characters except the punctuation, separator and other characters (the character groups defined with P, Z and C).

`\W`

Anything other than a word character.

`\i`

Any character that can be the first letter of an XML name. That includes the underscore (_), the colon (:), and characters of all the world's languages defined as letters in the XML specification.

`\I`

Anything other than a character that can be the first letter of an XML name.

`\c`

Any character that can be used in an XML name. That includes all of the characters that can appear as the first character (`\i`), plus the period (.), hyphen (-), and the characters defined as digits, combining characters and extenders in the XML specification.

`\C`

Anything other than a character that can be used in an XML name.

`\p`

A character in the following named character group. For example, `\p{Nd}` matches a numeric digit, while `\p{IsThai}` matches a Thai character.

`\P`

Anything other than a character in the following named character group. For example, `\P{Nd}` matches anything except a numeric digit, while `\P{IsThai}` matches anything except a Thai character.

Character Groups

For convenience, we can use character groups to stand for groups of characters. Specifying L is simpler than specifying all letters, particularly if you have to allow for the many thousands of characters defined in the Unicode standard. The character groups are used with the `\p` and `\P` operators; `\p{L}` means all letters, while `\P{L}` means everything *except* letters. The character groups and their names are defined in the Unicode Character Database, available online here: *http://www.unicode.org/Public/UNIDATA/UCD.html*.

The following lists are the character groups.

Letters

L

All letters.

Lu

All uppercase letters.

Ll

All lowercase letters.

Lt

Letters in titlecase, such as &#1C5;, which is a single character that combines a capital letter D with a small z that has a caron.

Lm

Modifiers (characters such as ª, which is the feminine ordinal indicator [ª]).

Lo

Other letters, including ideographs. The Hebrew letter alef (א) is an example.

Marks

M

All marks.

Mn

Nonspacing marks (characters such as ́, which is the Unicode combining acute accent).

Mc

Spacing combining marks.

Me

Enclosing marks.

Numbers

N

All numbers, including alternate forms such as circled (Unicode character ①, which is the circled digit one) and parenthesized (Unicode character ⑴, the parenthesized digit one).

Nd

Decimal digits (as opposed to Ⅶ, which is the Unicode character for the Roman numeral seven).

Nl

Numbers as letters (as opposed to digits; the aforementioned Unicode character Ⅶ character applies here).

No

Other numeric characters, such as ½, which is the single character for the fraction ½.

Punctuation

P

All punctuation characters.

Pc

Connector characters, such as _, which is the underscore character.

Pd

Dashes, such as the hyphen-minus character, -.

Ps

Opening (start) characters, such as a left curly bracket ({).

Pe

Closing characters, such as a right curly bracket (}).

Pi

Initial quote marks. Be aware that in some languages, an initial quote mark might actually be in the set of closing characters (Pe). As an example, quotations in Swedish begin and end with a double closing quotation mark (ȝ). In that case, the initial quote mark would not be found by searching for Pi.

Pf

Final quote marks. As with initial quote marks, a character used as a final quote mark in a particular language can be from the set of opening or closing characters.

Po

Other punctuation marks.

Separators

Z

All separators

Zs

Space characters, such as an em space (Unicode character) or an en space (Unicode character)

Zl

The line separator character (Unicode character  )

Zp

The paragraph separator character (Unicode character  )

Symbols

S

All symbols

Sm

Math symbols

Sc
> Currency symbols

Sk
> Modifiers

So
> Other symbols

Everything Else

C
> All others

Cc
> Control characters

Cf
> Formatting characters

Co
> Private use (reserved by Unicode)

Cn
> Not assigned

 The Unicode standard also defines a class of "surrogate" characters, `Cs`. These characters don't apply to XML documents; by the time a document is parsed, the surrogate characters no longer exist. For this reason, `Cs` is not a valid character group.

Block Escapes

A block escape is a simple way to refer to a range of characters that have some property in common. Each block escape has a name; to use a block name, prepend `Is` to it. Block escapes are used with the `\p` and `\P` operators. For example, the expression `\p{IsThai}` refers to the Thai characters (`&#x0E00` – `&#x0E7F`). The expression `\P{IsThai}` refers to everything except Thai characters. The block names are listed here in the format defined in the XML Schema spec.

Table E-1 shows the complete list of block escapes. This table was generated from version 5.0.0 of the file *blocks.txt*. The list of block escape names is part of the Unicode Character Database; see *http://www.unicode.org/* for the latest version of the Unicode standard.

Table E-1. Block escape names

Block name	Starting character	Ending character
BasicLatin	&#x0000	&#x007F
Latin-1Supplement	&#x0080	&#x00FF
LatinExtended-A	&#x0100	&#x017F
LatinExtended-B	&#x0180	&#x024F
IPAExtensions	&#x0250	&#x02AF
SpacingModifierLetters	&#x02B0	&#x02FF
CombiningDiacriticalMarks	&#x0300	&#x036F
GreekandCoptic	&#x0370	&#x03FF
Cyrillic	&#x0400	&#x04FF
CyrillicSupplement	&#x0500	&#x052F
Armenian	&#x0530	&#x058F
Hebrew	&#x0590	&#x05FF
Arabic	&#x0600	&#x06FF
Syriac	&#x0700	&#x074F
ArabicSupplement	&#x0750	&#x077F
Thaana	&#x0780	&#x07BF
NKo	&#x07C0	&#x07FF
Devanagari	&#x0900	&#x097F
Bengali	&#x0980	&#x09FF
Gurmukhi	&#x0A00	&#x0A7F
Gujarati	&#x0A80	&#x0AFF
Oriya	&#x0B00	&#x0B7F
Tamil	&#x0B80	&#x0BFF
Telugu	&#x0C00	&#x0C7F
Kannada	&#x0C80	&#x0CFF
Malayalam	&#x0D00	&#x0D7F
Sinhala	&#x0D80	&#x0DFF
Thai	&#x0E00	&#x0E7F
Lao	&#x0E80	&#x0EFF
Tibetan	&#x0F00	&#x0FFF
Myanmar	&#x1000	&#x109F
Georgian	&#x10A0	&#x10FF
HangulJamo	&#x1100	&#x11FF
Ethiopic	&#x1200	&#x137F

Block name	Starting character	Ending character
EthiopicSupplement	&#x1380	&#x139F
Cherokee	&#x13A0	&#x13FF
UnifiedCanadianAboriginalSyllabics	&#x1400	&#x167F
Ogham	&#x1680	&#x169F
Runic	&#x16A0	&#x16FF
Tagalog	&#x1700	&#x171F
Hanunoo	&#x1720	&#x173F
Buhid	&#x1740	&#x175F
Tagbanwa	&#x1760	&#x177F
Khmer	&#x1780	&#x17FF
Mongolian	&#x1800	&#x18AF
Limbu	&#x1900	&#x194F
TaiLe	&#x1950	&#x197F
NewTaiLue	&#x1980	&#x19DF
KhmerSymbols	&#x19E0	&#x19FF
Buginese	&#x1A00	&#x1A1F
Balinese	&#x1B00	&#x1B7F
PhoneticExtensions	&#x1D00	&#x1D7F
PhoneticExtensionsSupplement	&#x1D80	&#x1DBF
CombiningDiacriticalMarksSupplement	&#x1DC0	&#x1DFF
LatinExtendedAdditional	&#x1E00	&#x1EFF
GreekExtended	&#x1F00	&#x1FFF
GeneralPunctuation	&#x2000	&#x206F
SuperscriptsandSubscripts	&#x2070	&#x209F
CurrencySymbols	&#x20A0	&#x20CF
CombiningDiacriticalMarksforSymbols	&#x20D0	&#x20FF
LetterlikeSymbols	&#x2100	&#x214F
NumberForms	&#x2150	&#x218F
Arrows	&#x2190	&#x21FF
MathematicalOperators	&#x2200	&#x22FF
MiscellaneousTechnical	&#x2300	&#x23FF
ControlPictures	&#x2400	&#x243F
OpticalCharacterRecognition	&#x2440	&#x245F
EnclosedAlphanumerics	&#x2460	&#x24FF
BoxDrawing	&#x2500	&#x257F

Block name	Starting character	Ending character
BlockElements	&#x2580	&#x259F
GeometricShapes	&#x25A0	&#x25FF
MiscellaneousSymbols	&#x2600	&#x26FF
Dingbats	&#x2700	&#x27BF
MiscellaneousMathematicalSymbols-A	&#x27C0	&#x27EF
SupplementalArrows-A	&#x27F0	&#x27FF
BraillePatterns	&#x2800	&#x28FF
SupplementalArrows-B	&#x2900	&#x297F
MiscellaneousMathematicalSymbols-B	&#x2980	&#x29FF
SupplementalMathematicalOperators	&#x2A00	&#x2AFF
MiscellaneousSymbolsandArrows	&#x2B00	&#x2BFF
Glagolitic	&#x2C00	&#x2C5F
LatinExtended-C	&#x2C60	&#x2C7F
Coptic	&#x2C80	&#x2CFF
GeorgianSupplement	&#x2D00	&#x2D2F
Tifinagh	&#x2D30	&#x2D7F
EthiopicExtended	&#x2D80	&#x2DDF
SupplementalPunctuation	&#x2E00	&#x2E7F
CJKRadicalsSupplement	&#x2E80	&#x2EFF
KangxiRadicals	&#x2F00	&#x2FDF
IdeographicDescriptionCharacters	&#x2FF0	&#x2FFF
CJKSymbolsandPunctuation		&#x303F
Hiragana	&#x3040	&#x309F
Katakana	&#x30A0	&#x30FF
Bopomofo	&#x3100	&#x312F
HangulCompatibilityJamo	&#x3130	&#x318F
Kanbun	&#x3190	&#x319F
BopomofoExtended	&#x31A0	&#x31BF
CJKStrokes	&#x31C0	&#x31EF
KatakanaPhoneticExtensions	&#x31F0	&#x31FF
EnclosedCJKLettersandMonths	&#x3200	&#x32FF
CJKCompatibility	&#x3300	&#x33FF
CJKUnifiedIdeographsExtensionA	&#x3400	&#x4DBF
YijingHexagramSymbols	&#x4DC0	&#x4DFF
CJKUnifiedIdeographs	&#x4E00	&#x9FFF

Block name	Starting character	Ending character
YiSyllables	&#xA000	&#xA48F
YiRadicals	&#xA490	&#xA4CF
ModifierToneLetters	&#xA700	&#xA71F
LatinExtended-D	&#xA720	&#xA7FF
SylotiNagri	&#xA800	&#xA82F
Phags-pa	&#xA840	&#xA87F
HangulSyllables	&#xAC00	&#xD7AF
HighSurrogates	&#xD800	&#xDB7F
HighPrivateUseSurrogates	&#xDB80	&#xDBFF
LowSurrogates	&#xDC00	&#xDFFF
PrivateUseArea	&#xE000	&#xF8FF
CJKCompatibilityIdeographs	&#xF900	&#xFAFF
AlphabeticPresentationForms	&#xFB00	&#xFB4F
ArabicPresentationForms-A	&#xFB50	&#xFDFF
VariationSelectors	&#xFE00	&#xFE0F
VerticalForms	&#xFE10	&#xFE1F
CombiningHalfMarks	&#xFE20	&#xFE2F
CJKCompatibilityForms	&#xFE30	&#xFE4F
SmallFormVariants	&#xFE50	&#xFE6F
ArabicPresentationForms-B	&#xFE70	&#xFEFF
HalfwidthandFullwidthForms	&#xFF00	&#xFFEF
Specials	&#xFFF0	&#xFFFF
LinearBSyllabary	&#x10000	&#x1007F
LinearBIdeograms	&#x10080	&#x100FF
AegeanNumbers	&#x10100	&#x1013F
AncientGreekNumbers	&#x10140	&#x1018F
OldItalic	&#x10300	&#x1032F
Gothic	&#x10330	&#x1034F
Ugaritic	&#x10380	&#x1039F
OldPersian	&#x103A0	&#x103DF
Deseret	&#x10400	&#x1044F
Shavian	&#x10450	&#x1047F
Osmanya	&#x10480	&#x104AF
CypriotSyllabary	&#x10800	&#x1083F
Phoenician	&#x10900	&#x1091F

Block name	Starting character	Ending character
Kharoshthi	&#x10A00	&#x10A5F
Cuneiform	&#x12000	&#x123FF
CuneiformNumbersandPunctuation	&#x12400	&#x1247F
ByzantineMusicalSymbols	&#x1D000	&#x1D0FF
MusicalSymbols	&#x1D100	&#x1D1FF
AncientGreekMusicalNotation	&#x1D200	&#x1D24F
TaiXuanJingSymbols	&#x1D300	&#x1D35F
CountingRodNumerals	&#x1D360	&#x1D37F
MathematicalAlphanumericSymbols	&#x1D400	&#x1D7FF
CJKUnifiedIdeographsExtensionB	&#x20000	&#x2A6DF
CJKCompatibilityIdeographsSupplement	&#x2F800	&#x2FA1F
Tags	&#xE0000	&#xE007F
VariationSelectorsSupplement	&#xE0100	&#xE01EF
SupplementaryPrivateUseArea-A	&#xF0000	&#xFFFFF
SupplementaryPrivateUseArea-B	&#x100000	&#x10FFFF

You can find the latest list of block names and the characters they contain at Unicode.org in the file *blocks.txt*.

XSLT Formatting Codes

This appendix lists the formatting codes for numbers, dates, and times used in XSLT. These codes are used in the following elements and functions:

- `format-date( )`, `format-time( )` and `format-dateTime( )`, defined in XSLT 2.0 section 16.5, "Formatting Dates and Times."

- The `format` attribute of the `<xsl:number>` element, defined in XSLT 1.0 section 7.7, "Numbering." The capabilities of the `format` attribute were enhanced in XSLT 2.0 section 12, "Numbering."

- The `<xsl:decimal-format>` element, defined in XSLT 1.0 section 12.3, "Number Formatting."

- The `format-number( )` function, defined in XSLT 1.0 and XSLT 2.0.

Most of the formatting codes for numbers were defined in XSLT 1.0. The main additions for number formatting added by XSLT 2.0 are the ordinal and language options. The date and time formatting functions were added in XSLT 2.0. There are three types of formatting codes we'll list here:

- The date and time format codes defined by the ISO 8601 standard for the representation of dates and times. You use these format codes for creating new `xs:date`, `xs:time`, `xs:dateTime`, `xs:duration`, `xs:dayTimeDuration`, and `xs:yearMonthDuration` values.

- The date and time formatting codes defined in XSLT 2.0 section 16.5, "Formatting Dates and Times." Use these codes to format parts of `xs:date`, `xs:time`, `xs:dateTime`, `xs:duration`, `xs:dayTimeDuration`, and `xs:yearMonthDuration` values.

- The numbering formatting codes defined in XSLT 1.0 section 7.7, "Numbering," and section 12.3, "Number Formatting." These codes were extended in XSLT 2.0 section 12, "Numbering," and section 16.4, "Number Formatting."

Formatting Codes for Numbers

The following subsections detail the codes for formatting numbers. These are used by the `<xsl:decimal-format>` and `<xsl:number>` elements and by the `format-number()` function.

Parts of Numbers

Table F-1 describes the characters that represent parts of a number. They are used by the `format-number()` function and by the `<xsl:decimal-format>` element.

Table F-1. Number formatting codes

Code	Meaning
#	Represents a digit. Trailing or leading zeroes are not displayed. Formatting the number 4.0 with the string `"#.##"` returns the string `"4"`.
0	Represents a digit. Unlike the # character, the 0 always displays a zero. Formatting the number 4.1 with the string `"#.00"` returns the string `"4.10"`.
.	Represents the decimal point.
-	Represents the minus sign.
,	Is the grouping separator.
;	Separates the positive-number pattern from the negative-number pattern.
%	Indicates that a number should be displayed as a percentage. The value is multiplied by 100, and then displayed as a percentage. Formatting the number `.76` with the string `"##%"` returns the string `"76%"`.
\u2030	Is the Unicode character for the per-thousand (per-mille) sign. The value will be multiplied by 1000, and then displayed as a per mille. Formatting the number `.768` with the string `"###\u2030"` returns the string `"768‰"`.

Parts of Decimal Formats

The `<xsl:decimal-format>` element lets us define named formats for decimal numbers. Each named format is a group of settings for the properties discussed in Table F-2.

Table F-2. Parts of decimal formats

Part name	Meaning	Default value
name	Gives a name to this format.	N/A
decimal-separator	Defines the character (usually either a period or comma) used as the decimal point. This character is used both in the format string and in the output.	. (period)
grouping-separator	Defines the character (usually either a period or comma) used as the thousands separator. This character is used both in the format string and in the output.	, (comma)
infinity	Defines the string used to represent infinity. Be aware that XSLT's number facilities support both positive and negative infinity. This string is used only in the output.	Infinity

Part name	Meaning	Default value
minus-sign	Defines the character used as the minus sign. This character is used only in the output.	–(hyphen,-)
NaN	Defines the string displayed when the value to be formatted is not a number. This string is used only in the output.	NaN
percent	Defines the character used as the percent sign. This character is used both in the format string and in the output.	% (percent sign)
per-mille	Defines the character used as the per-mille sign. This character is used both in the format string and in the output.	‰ (Unicode per-mille character, ‰).
zero-digit	Defines the character used for the digit zero. This character is used both in the format string and in the output.	0 (zero)
digit	Defines the character used in the format string to stand for a digit.	#
pattern-separator	Defines the character used to separate the positive and negative subpatterns in a pattern. This character is used only in the format string.	; (semicolon)

Formatting Codes for Dates and Times

Parts of Dates and Times

Table F-3 describes the codes defined for the different parts of xs:date, xs:dateTime, and xs:time values.

Table F-3. Parts of dates and times

Specifier	Meaning	Default presentation modifier
Y	Year (absolute value)	1
M	Month in year	1
D	Day in month	1
d	Day in year	1
F	Day of week	n
W	Week in year	1
w	Week in month	1
H	Hour in day (24 hours)	1
h	Hour in half-day (12 hours)	1
P	a.m./p.m. marker	n
m	Minute in hour	01
s	Second in minute	01
f	Fractional seconds	1
Z	Timezone as a time offset from UTC—or if an alphabetic modifier is present, the conventional name of a timezone (such as PST)	1

Specifier	Meaning	Default presentation modifier
z	Timezone as a time offset using GMT—for example, GMT+1	1
C	Calendar: the name or abbreviation of a calendar name	n
E	Era: the name of a baseline for the numbering of years—for example, the reign of a monarch	n

Presentation Modifiers

A presentation modifier is a code that defines how a part of a date or time value should be displayed. For example, FNn displays the day of the week as the capitalized name of the day, using the current language. If your system is set up to use English and the calendar used in the United States, the name of the day of the week (FNn) for 15 August 2007 is Wednesday. The formatting code FWw displays the numeric value Four. Using German with the same codes on the same date displays the values Mittwoch and Drei (Wednesday is the third day of the week in the European calendar). Table F-4 describes the presentation modifiers.

Table F-4. Presentation modifiers

Modifier	Meaning
1	The value as a number with one or more digits: 0, 1, 2, 3, 4, ….
01	The value as a number with two or more digits: 00, 01, 02, … 09, 10, 11, … 99, 100, 101, ….
(Other numeric values)	An XSLT processor is free to support other numbering schemes. To quote an example from the spec, a formatting code of ๑ tells the processor to use Thai numbering. See the documentation for your processor to see which numbering schemes it supports.
A	The value as an uppercase letter: A, B, C, … Z, AA, AB, AC, ….
a	The value as a lowercase letter: a, b, c, … z, aa, ab, ac, ….
I	The value as an uppercase roman numeral: I, II, III, IV, V, VI, VII, VIII, IX, X, ….
i	The value as an lowercase roman numeral: i, ii, iii, iv, v, vi, vii, viii, ix, x, ….
n	The name of the component in lowercase. Applies only to components that have names, such as the day of the week (F), the month of the year (M), and the time zone (Z).
N	The name of the component in uppercase. Applies only to components that have names, such as the day of the week (F), the month of the year (M), and the time zone (Z).
Nn	The name of the component in title case. Applies only to components that have names, such as the day of the week (F), the month of the year (M), and the time zone (Z).
w	The value as a word in lowercase: one, two, three, four, ….
W	The value as a word in uppercase: ONE, TWO, THREE, FOUR, ….
Ww	The value as a word in title case: One, Two, Three, Four, ….

Calendars

These are the calendar names defined in the XSLT 2.0 specification. In addition to the values listed in Table F-5, an XSLT processor is free to implement support for other calendars. The abbreviation for any calendar not listed in the table must be qualified with a namespace prefix. Check the documentation for your XSLT processor to see which calendars it supports.

Table F-5. Calendars

Abbreviation	Calendar
AD	Anno Domini (Christian Era)
AH	Anno Hegirae (Muhammedan Era)
AME	Mauludi Era (solar years since Mohammed's birth)
AM	Anno Mundi (Jewish Calendar)
AP	Anno Persici
AS	Aji Saka Era (Java)
BE	Buddhist Era
CB	Cooch Behar Era
CE	Common Era
CL	Chinese Lunar Era
CS	Chula Sakarat Era
EE	Ethiopian Era
FE	Fasli Era
ISO	ISO 8601 calendar
JE	Japanese Calendar
KE	Khalsa Era (Sikh calendar)
KY	Kali Yuga
ME	Malabar Era
MS	Monarchic Solar Era
NS	Nepal Samwat Era
OS	Old Style (Julian Calendar)
RS	Rattanakosin (Bangkok) Era
SE	Saka Era
SH	Mohammedan Solar Era (Iran)
SS	Saka Samvat
TE	Tripurabda Era
VE	Vikrama Era
VS	Vikrama Samvat Era

XSLT 2.0 Migration Guide

This appendix contains some hits and suggestions for migrating your XSLT 1.0 stylesheets to XSLT 2.0. Most XSLT 1.0 stylesheets will work with an XSLT 2.0 processor, but there are a few errors you need to watch for. We'll also look at some of the new features in XSLT 2.0. If none of the new features in XSLT 2.0 and XPath 2.0 provide any value for you, there's no reason to migrate your stylesheets. (It's very unlikely that nothing in XSLT 2.0 and XPath 2.0 can help you, but still....)

Powerful New Features in XSLT 2.0 and XPath 2.0

We'll discuss some of the most important new features in XSLT 2.0 and XPath 2.0. This isn't a complete list, but it should give you an idea of whether XSLT 2.0 will simplify your stylesheets and applications.

Recursion Isn't Necessary Nearly as Often

In XSLT 1.0 stylesheets, tail recursion was a common technique. String replacement, for example, requires a recursive template that replaces the first instance of a substring, and then reinvokes itself with the remainder of the string. In XSLT 2.0, you can use the `replace()` function. Recursive templates are much more difficult to write and maintain; if you can replace them with simpler code in an XSLT 2.0 stylesheet, it's worth it. See the section "[2.0] Using the XPath 2.0 replace() Function to Avoid Recursion" in Chapter 5 for a more detailed example. Another good example is in the section "Doing Math Without Recursion" in Chapter 8.

Grouping Is Much, Much Easier

Grouping in XSLT 2.0 is orders of magnitude easier than it was in XSLT 1.0. The `<xsl:for-each-group>` element can make your code as much as 80% smaller, depending on the complexity of your XSLT 1.0 stylesheets. If your existing stylesheets do grouping, the new grouping support in XSLT 2.0 can make them much more elegant. See the section "[2.0] New Grouping Syntax in XSLT 2.0" in Chapter 7 for all the details.

Datatypes and XML Schemas Are Supported

If type checking and validation are important to your application, moving to XSLT 2.0 is a must. A basic XSLT 2.0 processor supports all the basic datatypes of XML Schema, while a schema-aware processor lets you define your own datatypes and use them in your stylesheets. Datatypes and schema support are discussed in Chapter 3.

Regular Expressions Are Supported

Although XSLT 1.0 supports functions such as `contains( )`, `substring-before( )`, and `substring-after( )`, these are no substitute for regular expressions. The regular expression support in XSLT 2.0 is very powerful and flexible. See the discussions of the [2.0] `<xsl:analyze-string>` element and the [2.0] `matches( )`, [2.0] `replace( )`, and [2.0] `tokenize( )` functions for the details on regular expression support. Appendix E has a complete overview of the regular expression syntax used in XSLT 2.0 and XPath 2.0.

Potential Errors

There are several differences between XSLT 1.0 and XSLT 2.0 that can cause fatal errors. If you're going to migrate your 1.0 stylesheets to 2.0, you'll need to handle all of those differences.

Passing Undefined Parameters with <xsl:call-template> Causes an Error

In XSLT 1.0, you could use `<xsl:call-template>` to invoke a template with as many parameters as you wanted. If any of those parameters weren't defined in the template, they were ignored. In XSLT 2.0, using `<xsl:call-template>` with an undefined parameter causes a fatal error.

 It's *not* an error to pass undefined parameters with `<xsl:apply-templates>`, `<xsl:apply-imports>`, or `<xsl:next-match>`.

Many times XSLT 1.0 stylesheets passed extra parameters because they might eventually be needed by another template. Every time another template was invoked (via `<xsl:apply-templates>` or `<xsl:call-template>`), the extra parameters were passed along. XSLT 2.0 features much more sophisticated *tunnel parameters*. A tunnel parameter isn't passed to each template, so it makes your stylesheets much cleaner. See the section "Tunnel parameters" in Chapter 5 for more information.

This potential problem is a static error. That means the XSLT 2.0 processor can tell whether you're passing the wrong number of parameters to a template without actually transforming an XML document.

Math Works Differently in Some Cases

XSLT 1.0 featured a simple `number` datatype. Math operations, particularly anything dealing with division by zero, work differently in XSLT 2.0.

To make things more complicated, XSLT 2.0 handles different kinds of numbers differently. Dividing an `xs:integer` or `xs:decimal` by zero is a fatal error, while dividing an `xs:double` or `xs:float` returns `INF` (infinity).

The simplest way to avoid this error is to add `version="1.0"` to the element. That causes the XSLT 2.0 processor to evaluate the expression in XSLT 1.0 mode, so your stylesheets will behave as they always have.

```
<xsl:variable version="1.0" name="ratio"
  select="$orders div $returns"/>
```

A more sophisticated approach is to use the new XPath `if` operator. For example, you could change the code like this:

```
<xsl:variable name="ratio"
  select="if ($returns != 0) then
          $orders div $returns else
          0"/>
```

If the value of `$returns` is not equal to zero, we perform the calculation; otherwise, we return zero.

Division works with six datatypes: `xs:integer`, `xs:decimal`, `xs:float`, `xs:double`, `xs:yearMonthDuration`, and `xs:dayTimeDuration`. Here's a stylesheet that illustrates how division by zero works:

```
<?xml version="1.0"?>
<!-- divide-by-zero.xsl -->
<xsl:stylesheet version="2.0"
  xmlns:xs="http://www.w3.org/2001/XMLSchema"
  xmlns:xsl="http://www.w3.org/1999/XSL/Transform">

  <xsl:output method="text"/>

  <xsl:template match="/">
    <xsl:text>&#xA;Division by zero in XSLT 2.0:&#xA;&#xA;</xsl:text>

    <xsl:text>&lt;xsl:value-of select="1 div 0"/&gt;&#xA;</xsl:text>
    <xsl:text>   [fatal error]&#xA;&#xA;</xsl:text>
    <xsl:text>&lt;xsl:value-of select="1.0 div 0.0"/&gt;&#xA;</xsl:text>
    <xsl:text>   [fatal error]&#xA;&#xA;</xsl:text>
    <xsl:text>&lt;xsl:value-of select="xs:integer(1) </xsl:text>
    <xsl:text>div xs:integer(0)"/&gt;&#xA;</xsl:text>
    <xsl:text>   [fatal error]&#xA;&#xA;</xsl:text>
    <xsl:text>&lt;xsl:value-of select="xs:decimal(1.0) </xsl:text>
    <xsl:text>div xs:decimal(0.0)"/&gt;&#xA;</xsl:text>
    <xsl:text>   [fatal error]&#xA;&#xA;</xsl:text>
    <xsl:text>&lt;xsl:value-of select="xs:double(1.0) </xsl:text>
    <xsl:text>div xs:double(0.0)"/&gt;&#xA;   </xsl:text>
    <xsl:value-of
```

```
      select="(xs:double(1.0) div xs:double(0.0), '&#xA;&#xA;')"/>
    <xsl:text>&lt;xsl:value-of select="xs:float(1.0) </xsl:text>
    <xsl:text>div xs:float(0.0)"/&gt;&#xA;  </xsl:text>
    <xsl:value-of
      select="(xs:float(1.0) div xs:float(0.0), '&#xA;&#xA;')"/>

    <xsl:text>Dividing durations by zero:&#xA;&#xA;</xsl:text>
    <xsl:text>&lt;xsl:value-of select="xs:yearMonthDuration</xsl:text>
    <xsl:text>('P3Y4M') div xs:double(0.0)"/&gt;&#xA; </xsl:text>
    <xsl:text>  [fatal error]&#xA;&#xA;</xsl:text>
    <xsl:text>&lt;xsl:value-of select="xs:yearMonthDuration</xsl:text>
    <xsl:text>('P3Y4M') div &#xA;                       </xsl:text>
    <xsl:text>xs:yearMonthDuration('P0Y0M')"/&gt;&#xA; </xsl:text>
    <xsl:text>  [fatal error]&#xA;&#xA;</xsl:text>
    <xsl:text>&lt;xsl:value-of select="xs:dayTimeDuration</xsl:text>
    <xsl:text>('P3DT8H') div xs:double(0.0)"/&gt;&#xA; </xsl:text>
    <xsl:text>  [fatal error]&#xA;&#xA;</xsl:text>
    <xsl:text>&lt;xsl:value-of select="xs:dayTimeDuration</xsl:text>
    <xsl:text>('P3DT8H') div &#xA;                       </xsl:text>
    <xsl:text>xs:dayTimeDuration('P0DT0H')"/&gt;&#xA; </xsl:text>
    <xsl:text>  [fatal error]&#xA;&#xA;</xsl:text>
  </xsl:template>

</xsl:stylesheet>
```

As we noted before, dividing `xs:double` or `xs:float` by zero returns `INF`; everything else causes a fatal error. Dividing `xs:yearMonthDuration` or `xs:dayTimeDuration` by zero or by an interval of length zero also causes a fatal error.

It's possible division by zero will be a static error, but it's far more likely to occur at runtime. If you migrate your stylesheet to use XSLT 2.0's math processing, you'll need to test your code to make sure any division by zero error cases are handled correctly.

Type Checking Is Much Stricter

XSLT 1.0 had a very simple type system. The support for XML Schema in XSLT 2.0 means type checking is much stricter. For example, in XSLT 1.0, this statement works:

```
<xsl;value-of select="substring-before(12345, 3)"/>
```

This returns the value `12`, which causes a static error in XSLT 2.0. To get this function to work in XSLT 2.0, we have to write it like this:

```
<xsl;value-of select="substring-before(string(12345), string(3))"/>
```

As you migrate your stylesheets from XSLT 1.0 to 2.0, you'll find yourself explicitly casting values such as this quite often.

Calling Some Functions with More Than One Node Causes an Error

In XSLT 1.0, there were a number of functions that took a node as an argument. If we passed more than one node to the function, it simply took the first node and ignored the rest. XSLT 2.0 is much more strict; passing more than one node to a function that requires a single node is a fatal error. You can certainly make the argument that using the argument `/purchase-order/items/item` when you really mean `/purchase-order/items/item[1]` is sloppy code. Whether you agree with that opinion or not, XSLT 2.0 forces you to pass a single node to the function.

The XSLT 1.0 and XPath 1.0 functions `generate-id( )`, `local-name( )`, `name( )`, `namespace-uri( )`, `number( )`, and `string( )` require a single node in XSLT 2.0. To avoid any problems, simply add the predicate `[1]` to your stylesheets as you migrate them. In addition, if you use an XPath expression to select nodes for the `concat( )` function, that XPath expression cannot return more than a single node. The expression `concat('#1. ', /report/brand/name)` throws an error in XSLT 2.0 if more than one node matches the XPath expression. On the other hand, `concat('#1. ', (/report/brand/name)[1])` always works.

This is a dynamic error. It can be difficult to catch if your XPath expressions typically select only one node. That means the error condition occurs in the rare case that the XPath expression returns more than one node. If you need only one node, changing your expression from `x/y/z` to `(x/y/z)[1]` is the best way to go.

Approaches to Migration

There are several approaches to migrating your stylesheets to XSLT 2.0. We'll outline them here.

Write (or Rewrite) Your Stylesheets from Scratch

Obviously this is the most drastic option. If you don't have a large investment in XSLT 1.0 code, you can start writing XSLT 2.0 stylesheets from scratch. It's more likely that you would replace a few stylesheets used in parts of your application, and then use your expertise and experience to rewrite larger and more sophisticated stylesheets.

This requires a significant commitment in development resources and training. Having the resources to develop stylesheets from scratch is one thing; those resources need to understand all of the new features of XSLT 2.0 and how to take advantage of them.

Change the Version to 2.0 and See What Happens

The simplest approach to migration is to change the `version` attribute of the `<xsl:stylesheet>` element to `2.0`. If you have any static errors, the XSLT 2.0 processor will flag those immediately. You can then fix the errors or use `version="1.0"` on specific XSLT elements so the XSLT 2.0 processor will use backwards-compatible mode.

If you use this approach, it's important to check for the dynamic errors we covered in the previous section. If you add `version="2.0"` to your stylesheet and it runs with an

XML document, that doesn't mean it will run with every document. As with any modi-fied code, testing is crucial before you put your stylesheet into production.

Replace Awkward XSLT 1.0 Code with XSLT 2.0 Features

A less drastic way to migrate to XSLT 2.0 is to look through your stylesheets for tem-plates that could be replaced with XSLT 2.0 features. For example, if you have a re-cursive template to do string replacement, replacing that with the new `replace()` func-tion will simplify your code. (It's likely it will perform better as well.) Anything that uses recursion or extension functions is a candidate for replacement with XSLT 2.0.

Another thing to look for is using variables extensively. If you use a variable to store the result generated by a named template, consider replacing the named template with an `<xsl:function>`. Using an XSLT 2.0 function means you can invoke the code inside an XPath expression. The function call can replace the variable and the named template with a single step.

If the templates in your stylesheet pass many parameters, consider using tunnel parameters. As stylesheets grow in complexity and power, it's common for every tem-plate to accept one or more parameters, and then pass those parameters on to any templates it invokes. The stylesheet needs to pass those parameters to every template in case they're needed somewhere. Tunnel parameters make your code much cleaner and simplify maintenance.

Mix XSLT 1.0 and XSLT 2.0 in the Same Stylesheet

A very useful technique for XSLT 2.0 migration is to process parts of the stylesheet in XSLT 1.0 or XSLT 2.0 mode. The simplest way to do this is to create an stylesheet with `version="2.0"`, adding `version="1.0"` to templates as needed. (Remember, the `version` attribute can be used on any XSLT element except `<xsl:output>`.) This lets you migrate your stylesheet in stages without worrying about dynamic errors. If your style-sheet depends on math being processed using XSLT 1.0 rules, you can set that section of the stylesheet to use `version="1.0"`. As your XSLT 2.0 experience grows, you can address the XSLT 1.0 sections of the stylesheet and migrate them to XSLT 2.0.

Don't Migrate at All

This is the cheapest and fastest solution. If your stylesheets aren't good candidates for using the new features of XSLT 2.0, there's no real reason to migrate. Having said that, it's unlikely that any sophisticated stylesheet can't be improved by any of the new features.

The architecture of your application can determine whether you should migrate. If you application sends XML data and an XSLT stylesheet down to a browser, that browser has to have an XSLT 2.0-compliant processor. There aren't any browsers that have XSLT 2.0 support built in, so it could be a while before migration is an option for you.

Glossary

A

absolute location path

A location path that begins with /, followed by one or more location steps separated by /. All location paths that begin with / are evaluated from the root node, so they always return the same result, regardless of the context node. Compare with *location path* and *relative location path*.

ancestor

A node that appears above a given node. Ancestors include a node's parent, its parent's parent, its parent's parent's parent, etc. XPath also defines the `ancestor` axis, which includes a node's parent, its parent's parent, its parent's parent's parent, etc., but not the node itself. Contrast with *parent*.

[2.0] arity

The number of parameters required by a function.

[2.0] atomic value

A value from one of the atomic datatypes defined by XML Schema (or a datatype derived from one of those types). `xs:integer`, `xs:dayTimeDuration`, and `xs:string` are examples of atomic datatypes.

attribute node

The XPath node type that represents an attribute from an XML document. Attributes are different from other nodes because an attribute node is not considered a child of the element node that contains it. Despite this fact, the element node is considered the parent of the attribute node.

attribute set

A named group of attributes. You can create an attribute set (with the `<xsl:attribute-set>` element), then reference that attribute set elsewhere. For more information, see the description of the `<xsl:attribute-set>` element in Appendix A.

attribute value template

An expression that contains an XPath expression in curly braces ({}). The XPath expression is evaluated at runtime, and its value replaces the expression. For an example of an attribute value template, see the discussion of the `<xsl:attribute>` element in Appendix A; Chapter 3 contains a complete discussion of attribute value templates.

axis

A relationship between the context node and other nodes in the document. XPath defines 13 different axes; see "Axes" in Chapter 3 for a complete discussion of them.

B

base URI

The URI associated with every node in the XPath source tree. In certain circumstances, the base URI is used to resolve references to other resources. If a given node is an element or processing-instruction node and that node occurs in an external entity, then the base URI for that node is the base URI of the external entity. If an element or processing-instruction node does not occur in an external entity, then its base URI is the base URI of the document in which it appears. The base URI of a document node is the base URI of the document itself, and the base URI of an attribute, comment, namespace, or text node is the base URI of that node's parent.

C

[2.0] cast

The conversion of a value from one atomic type to another.

CDATA section

A section of an XML document in which all markup is ignored. A CDATA section begins with the characters `<![CDATA[`, and ends with the characters `]]>`. If two right brackets appear in the content of a CDATA section, they must be escaped. Within a stylesheet, determining whether a given text node was originally a CDATA section is not possible. It is possible to generate certain elements as CDATA sections with the `cdata-section-elements` attribute of the `<xsl:output>` element.

child

An immediate descendant of a given node. Contrast with *descendant*. `child` is also the name of one of the XPath axes. The children of a node include all comment, element, processing-instruction, and text nodes. Attribute nodes and namespace nodes are not considered children.

[2.0] codepoint

A number that represents a Unicode character. For example, the number `x20AC` is the codepoint for the Euro sign (€).

[2.0] codepoint collation

The collation that simply compares strings according to their codepoint values. This is the default collation used by all XSLT processors.

[2.0] collation

A set of rules defining how string values should be compared. In XSLT 2.0 and XPath 2.0, processors have the option to support

special collations that allow comparisons based on various languages. For example, the German word for street can be spelled *Strasse* or *Straße*; a custom collation might define those two strings as equal.

comment node

A node that represents a comment from the original XML document. This is one of the seven kinds of nodes defined by XPath.

[2.0] complex type

Any datatype defined with XML Schema that can have children or attributes.

[2.0] constructor function

A function used to create an atomic value of a particular datatype. The name of the function is the name of the datatype; the function `xs:integer()` is a constructor function for the `xs:integer` datatype.

context

A data structure that determines how XPath expressions are evaluated.

[1.0] In XPath 1.0, the context consists of five items: the context node, a pair of non-zero positive integers (the context position and context size), a set of variable bindings, a function library, and the set of namespace declarations that are in scope.

[2.0] In XPath 2.0, the context includes everything from the XPath 1.0 context plus several other items. These include the datatypes and namespaces currently in scope. See "The XPath Context" in Appendix B for a complete description of everything in the context.

[2.0] context item

The item from which all XPath expressions are evaluated. In XPath 2.0, if the context item is a node, the context node and the context item are the same. If the context item is an atomic value, the context node is undefined.

context node

The node from which all XPath expressions are evaluated. The context node is analogous to the current directory at a command prompt; all commands you type at a command prompt are evaluated in terms of the current directory. Compare with *current node*.

[2.0] In XPath 2.0, the context node is undefined if the context item is an atomic value. If the context item is a node, the context node and the context item are the same.

context position

[1.0] A nonzero positive integer that indicates the position of the current node. The context position is always less than or equal to the context size.

[2.0] A nonzero positive integer that indicates the position of the current item within the sequence of items currently being processed.

context size

[1.0] The number of nodes in the current node list.

[2.0] The number of items in the sequence of items currently being processed.

current node

[1.0] The node currently being processed. The node is defined by the `select` attribute of the `<xsl:apply-templates>` or `<xsl:for-each>` elements. Except within a predicate expression, the current node and the context node are the same.

[2.0] The item currently being processed.

current node list

The list of nodes selected by the `select` attribute of the `<xsl:apply-templates>` or `<xsl:for-each>` element currently being processed. By default, the current node list is in document order, but it may be reordered with one or more `<xsl:sort>` elements.

[2.0] In XPath 2.0, the current node list is referred to as "the sequence of items currently being processed" in lieu of the term "current node list."

D

descendant

A given node's children, its children's children, its children's children's children, etc. **descendant** is also the name of one of the axes defined by XPath. Contrast with *child*.

document element

The element in the XML source document that contains the entire XML document. The node that represents the document element is a child of the root node; the root node and the element node for the document element are not the same.

document node

In a tree created from a well-formed XML document, the root node will be a document node with exactly one element node as its child. That element node represents the document element, and does not have any text nodes as children. An XML parser will only create document nodes from well-formed XML documents. However, it is possible within an XSLT stylesheet to create a document node that is not well-formed. See the discussion of the `<xsl:document>` element for an example.

document order

The order in which a set of nodes appeared in the XML source document.

[2.0] dynamic context

The portion of the *context* that can change during the evaluation of a stylesheet or XPath expression. The context item, context size, and context position are all part of the dynamic context. See "[2.0] The XPath 2.0 context" in Chapter 3 for a complete description of everything in the context. Compare with [2.0] static context.

E

element node

An XPath node that represents an element from the XML source document.

empty sequence

A sequence that contains zero items.

encoding

A set of characters, referenced in the XML declaration to describe the characters used in a particular document. The range of values for encodings is defined in *http://www.ietf.org/rfc/rfc2278.txt*. The range of values supported by a given XML parser or XSLT processor varies.

expanded name

The complete name of an element or attribute, including the local name and a possibly null namespace URI.

extension element

An element in an XSLT stylesheet whose namespace prefix references an extension. The XSLT specification defines how extension elements are identified in the stylesheet, but does not specify how they are implemented. Extension elements are implemented with a piece of code that is referenced in the stylesheet; each XSLT processor defines how that code is invoked to handle the transformation of the extension element. See Chapter 8 for an extensive discussion of extension elements and extension functions.

extension function

A function whose namespace prefix references an extension. The XSLT specification defines how extension functions are identified in the stylesheet, but does not specify how they are implemented. Extension functions are implemented with a piece of code that is referenced in the stylesheet; each XSLT processor defines how that code is invoked to handle the invocation of the extension function. See Chapter 9 for an extensive discussion of extension elements and extension functions.

F

fallback processing

Processing designed to handle the absence of an extension element or an extension function gracefully. This processing is typically accomplished with the `element-available( )` or the `function-available( )` function. When either function returns false, a stylesheet can respond gracefully to the absence of the requested function. XSLT also defines the `<xsl:fallback>` element, which can be used when an extension element is not available.

final result tree

A tree that forms part of the final output of a transformation. Once created, the contents of the final result tree are not accessible within the stylesheet itself.

I

ID

One of the basic datatypes defined by the XML specification. (It is also defined as type `xs:ID` in XML Schema.) In an XML document, one attribute of an element can be declared to be of type `ID`; this means that the value of that attribute must be unique across all attributes of type `ID` for all elements in the document. No more than one attribute on a given element can be of type `ID`. Attributes of type `ID` are useful for generating cross-references with the `id( )` function. See Chapter 5 for an extensive discussion of the `ID`, `IDREF`, and `IDREFS` datatypes.

IDREF

One of the basic datatypes defined by the XML specification. (It is also defined as type `xs:IDREF` in XML Schema.) In an XML document, an attribute declared to be of type `IDREF` must have a value that matches an `ID` attribute elsewhere in the document. Attributes of type `IDREF` are useful for generating cross-references with the `id( )` function. See Chapter 5 for an extensive discussion of the `ID`, `IDREF`, and `IDREFS` datatypes.

IDREFS

One of the basic datatypes defined by the XML specification. (It is also defined as type `xs:IDREFS` in XML Schema.) In an XML document, an `IDREFS` attribute must contain one or more whitespace-separated values, each of which matches an `ID` attribute elsewhere in the document. Attributes of type `IDREFS` are useful for generating cross-references with the `id( )` function. See Chapter 5 for an extensive discussion of the `ID`, `IDREF`, and `IDREFS` datatypes.

[2.0] item

A value that is either an atomic value or a node.

K

key

A key is similar to a database index. It has three components: a *name*, used to identify the key (specified with the `name` attribute of the `<xsl:key>` element); the *nodes*, which will be returned by the key (specified with the `use` attribute of the `<xsl:key>` element); and the *values*, used to search for things in the key (specified with the `match` attribute of the `<xsl:key>` element).

The key `<key name="language-index" match="defn" use="@language"/>`, for example, defines a new key named `language-index`. Given a value for the `language` attribute, the key returns all `<defn>` elements whose `language` attributes match the given value. See "Branching Elements of XSLT" in Chapter 5 for a complete discussion of keys and how they are used.

L

literal result element (LRE)

An element in an XSLT stylesheet that does not belong to the XSLT namespace and is not an extension element. Literal elements are simply copied to the result tree.

local name

The nonqualified portion of an element or attribute name. For example, in the element `<xsl:template>`, `template` is the local name.

location path

An XPath expression that selects a set of nodes relative to the context node. Compare with *absolute location path* and *relative location path*.

location step

Consists of three parts: an axis name, a node test, and zero or more predicate expressions. There are three location steps in the following XPath expression: `preceding-sibling::region/product[@name="Sandpiper"]/text( )`.

The first location step is `preceding-sibling::region`; it has an axis name of `preceding-sibling` and a node test of `region`. It selects all `<region>` elements that are preceding siblings of the context node. It does not have a predicate expression.

The second location step, which is `product[@name="Sandpiper"]`, has an axis name of `child`, the default axis. Its node test is `product` and it has the predicate `[@name="Sandpiper"]`. It selects all `<product>` children of the previous location step that have an attribute named `name` with a value of `Sandpiper`.

The third location step, `text( )`, has an axis name of `child` and a node test of `text( )`. It selects all text node children of the previous location step. It does not have a predicate expression.

M

mode

An XSLT feature that allows an element to be processed multiple times, using a different template and producing a different result each time. See the discussion of the `<xsl:apply-templates>` element in Appendix A for a detailed example of modes.

N

namespace

A collection of element and attribute names that are associated with a URI.

namespace declaration

Part of an XML document that defines a namespace for a particular part of the document. Namespace declarations appear as XML attributes. A namespace declaration that begins `xmlns=` defines the default namespace, while a declaration that begins `xmlns:prefix` defines a namespace with a prefix.

namespace node

The XPath node type that corresponds to a namespace declaration in an XML document.

namespace prefix

Part of a qualified name used to associate an element or attribute with a namespace URI.

namespace URI

The URI associated with a collection of element and attribute names.

NCName

An XML noncolonized name, used for local names and namespace prefixes. An NCName must start with a letter or an underscore (_).

node test

An XPath expression that selects certain nodes. The expressions `child::*`, `para`, and `@id` select all child nodes, all `<para>` child nodes, and any attribute named `id`, respectively. Four node tests—`text( )`, `comment( )`, `node( )`, and `processing-instruction( )`— look like functions, even though they technically aren't. (*[2.0]* XSLT 2.0 also includes the `document-node( )` node test.) See "XPath Node Tests" in Appendix B for a complete listing of XPath node tests.

O

output escaping

The process of changing reserved characters (such as <, >, and &) into their entity references (such as <, >, and &).

P

parameter

An XSLT mechanism used to bind a name to a value, defined with the `<xsl:param>` element. The difference between a parameter and a variable is that the value specified in the definition of a parameter is a default value. When the template or stylesheet that contains the parameter is invoked, the default value can be overridden. Like variables, though, once the value of a parameter is set, it cannot be changed.

parent

A node that appears immediately above a given node. A parent is a node's first ancestor. XPath also defines the `parent` axis, which contains a node's parent. With the exception of the root node, all nodes in an input document have a parent. Contrast with *ancestor*.

path expression

An expression that selects nodes from a tree. The expression is composed of some number of *steps*. The nodes returned by a path expression appear in *document order* with any duplicates removed.

pattern

A condition that a given node may or may not match. The syntax for a pattern is a subset of the syntax for XPath expressions. Patterns are used in the XSLT elements `<xsl:template>`, `<xsl:key>`, `<xsl:number>`, and `<xsl:for-each-group>`.

predicate expression

An XPath expression that appears in square brackets ([ ]). Predicate expressions filter a *[1.0]* node-set or *[2.0]* sequence, selecting only nodes that match the expression in square brackets. See "Predicates" in Chapter 3 for more information.

prefix

An abbreviation for *namespace prefix*.

[2.0] primitive type

XML Schema defines 19 primitive types. In the XPath 2.0 data model, these are all defined as subtypes of `xs:anyAtomicType`. (The 19 primitive types are `xs:boolean`, `xs:string`, `xs:decimal`, `xs:double`, `xs:float`, `xs:QName`, `xs:anyURI`, `xs:hexBinary`, `xs:base64Binary`, `xs:date`, `xs:time`, `xs:date Time`, `xs:gYear`, `xs:gYearMonth`, `xs:gMonth`, `xs:gMonthDay`, `xs:gDay`, `xs:duration`, and `xs:NOTATION`.) XPath also adds `xs:untypedAtomic`, the datatype of any value that has not been validated against a schema or cast to a primitive type.

processing instruction

Part of an XML document containing instructions for applications. Here is a sample processing instruction:

```
<?xml-stylesheet href="docbook/html/
    docbook.xsl" type="text/xsl"?>
```

This processing instruction associates an XSLT stylesheet with an XML document. See "Document Object Model (DOM)" in Chapter 1 for a complete discussion of processing instructions.

processing-instruction node

The XPath node type that represents a processing instruction from an XML document.

Q

qualified name

An element or attribute name that may be qualified with a namespace prefix. The format of a qualified name is `prefix:local-name`, where the optional `prefix` and `local-name` are both NCNames. In an XSLT stylesheet, `<xsl:template>` is a prefixed qualified name, while `<template>` is not. The names in an XSLT stylesheet (variable names, template names, mode names, etc.) are qualified names, whether they have prefixes or not. Note that if the default namespace is null (`xmlns=""`), an unprefixed QName will not have a namespace.

QName

An abbreviation for *qualified name*.

R

[2.0] regular expression

A pattern used to analyze strings. Regular expressions can be used in the XPath 2.0 functions `matches()`, `replace()`, and `tokenize()`, as well as the XSLT 2.0 instruction `<xsl:analyze-string>`.

relative location path

A location path that consists of one or more location steps separated by /, but not

starting with /. Compare with *location path* and *absolute location path*.

[1.0] result-tree fragment

A fragment of the result tree that can be associated with a variable in XSLT 1.0. See "XPath 1.0 Datatypes" in Appendix B for a more complete discussion of result-tree fragments. *[2.0]* In XSLT 2.0, the result-tree fragment has been replaced with the sequence.

root node

The XPath node that represents the root of an XML document. Note that the root node is not the same as the element node for the document element. The root node is specified with the XPath expression /. The children of the root node are the element node for the document element, as well as any comments or processing instructions that occur outside the document element. *[2.0]* In XSLT 2.0, root nodes that represent an XML document are called document nodes.

S

sequence

An ordered collection of *items*.

sibling

Two nodes that have the same parent. XPath defines the `preceding-sibling` and `following-sibling` axes.

[2.0] static context

The portion of the *context* that is known before an XML source document is processed. See "[2.0] The XPath 2.0 context" in Chapter 3 for a complete description of everything in the context. Compare with [2.0] dynamic context.

static error

An error that can be detected before an XML source document is processed.

step

A portion of a path expression that navigates from one node to another. An axis step, a node test, and a predicate are all steps in an path expression.

stylesheet

An XML document, written with the XSLT vocabulary, that specifies how an XML document should be transformed.

T

template

A rule in an XSLT stylesheet that defines how part of an XML document should be transformed. Templates are defined with the `<xsl:template>` element.

text node

A group of characters from an XML document. Text nodes are one of the seven types of nodes defined by XPath. The XPath specification states that as much text as possible must be combined into a single text node. In other words, a text node will never have a preceding or following sibling that is also a text node.

top-level element

An element whose parent is the `<xsl:stylesheet>` element.

[2.0] tunnel parameter

Within a template, a tunnel parameter is automatically passed on to any templates called by that template. The tunnel parameter is passed on recursively to any further templates that may be invoked along the way.

[2.0] type annotation

The datatype associated with every element and attribute node. Type annotations are added to element and attribute nodes when they are validated by a schema. Any nodes that are not validated with a schema have the datatype `xs:untyped`; any attribute that is not validated has the datatype `xs:untypedAtomic`.

U

unparsed entity

A resource in an XML document whose contents may or may not be text, and if text, may not be XML. Every unparsed entity has an associated XML notation. See the discussion of the `unparsed-entity-uri( )` function in Appendix C for more details on unparsed entities.

[2.0] unparsed text

Text that is returned by the `unparsed-text( )` function. As the name implies, this text is not parsed in any way, so it may or may not be valid XML, well-formed XML, or any kind of markup at all.

URI

Uniform Resource Identifier, a generalized version of the URLs used on the Web. URIs are defined by RFC 2396 and only support roughly 60 ASCII characters. Internationalized Resource Identifiers (IRIs), defined by RFC 3987, are supported by XSLT 2.0 and support a much wider range of characters. The XPath 2.0 `iri-to-uri( )` function converts an IRI to a URI as a convenience.

V

valid document

An XML document that follows the basic rules of XML documents and additionally follows all rules of its associated document type definition or schema. See "XML Document Rules" in Chapter 1 for a complete discussion of the XML document rules; "Document Type Definitions (DTDs) and XML Schemas," also in Chapter 1, discusses document type definitions and schemas.

validation

The process of comparing a node against a schema. If the node is valid, that node and all its children and attributes are assigned a datatype based on the node definitions in the schema.

variable

An XSLT mechanism used to bind a name to a value, defined with the `<xsl:variable>` element. Variables are different from parameters because parameters can have default values. One significant difference between XSLT variables and variables in most other programming languages is that once an XSLT variable is bound, its value cannot be changed. See "Variables" in Chapter 5 for a complete discussion of the `<xsl:variable>` element and how it is used.

W

well-formed document

An XML document that follows the basic rules of XML syntax. See "XML Document Rules" in Chapter 1 for a complete discussion of those rules.

whitespace

One of four characters: space (`&#x20;`), tab (`&#x09;`), return (`&#x0D;`), or linefeed (`&#x0A;`).

X

XML declaration

Part of an XML document that defines the version of XML being used and the encoding of the document. Although the XML declaration looks like a processing instruction, it is not. For that reason, you cannot access the XML declaration from an XSLT stylesheet or an XPath expression.

Index

Symbols

We'd like to hear your suggestions for improving our indexes. Send email to *index@oreilly.com*.

\w escape character, 908

\W escape character, 909

\[left square bracket escape character, 908

\\ backslash escape character, 907

\] right square bracket escape characters, 908

\{ left curly brace escape character, 908

\| vertical bar escape character, 907

\} right curly brace escape character, 908

] (square bracket) metacharacter, 907

^ (carat) metacharacter, 906

{ (left curly brace) metacharacter, 907

{} (curly braces)
in regular expressions, 363

| (vertical bar) union operator, 98, 99, 558, 561, 906

} (right curly brace) metacharacter, 907

() (parentheses) parenthesized expression operator, 556

A

absolute expressions
XPath, 58

absolute location path
defined, 933

absolute XPath expressions, 62

abstract datatypes
about, 888–890

abstract elements
about, 888–890

abs() function, 569–570

accessor functions
list of, 563

addition (+) operator, 556

addition operator
XPath, 71

adjust-date-to-timezone() function, 570–572

adjust-dateTime-to-timezone() function, 573–575

adjust-time-to-timezone() function, 575–577

Altova XSLT engine
about, xii
commands for Hello World example, 26, 40
global parameters, 156
installing, 23

ancestor axis, 64, 549

ancestor-or-self axis, 64, 107, 549

ancestor::table[] predicate, 66

ancestors

defined, 933

anchors, 903–904

and operator, 558

anonymous datatype, 875

APIs (see SAX (Simple API for XML))

arity
defined, 933

as attribute, 52, 435, 489, 525, 540, 544

asterisk (*) as attribute, 52

asterisk (*) metacharacter, 906

asterisk (*) multiplication operator, 556

asterisk (*) occurrence indicator operator, 556

asterisk (*) quantifier character, 900

asterisk (*) escape character, 908

atomic values
comparing, 83
defined, 933
group-adjacent attribute, 233
sequence, 215–219
XPath 2.0, 46, 52

attr interface, 13

attribute axis, 64, 548

attribute nodes
about, 49
built-in template rules, 32
defined, 546, 933

attribute sets
defined, 933
<xsl:attribute-set> element, 383

attribute value templates
collation for sorting, 289
defined, 933

attributes
common attributes, 361
declaring, 192
elements with, 873
empty elements with, 872
list of by element, 362–544
output methods, 31
quotes, 7
selecting, 59
XPath, 45
<xsl:sort element>, 211

attribute() node test, 51, 547

avg() function, 577–581

axes, xviii
(see also specific axes)
defined, 933
list of in XPath, 63

current() function, 605–609

D

d attribute, 315
D formatting code, 132
D1o formatting code, 132
dashes (Pd) character group, 911
data binding
    defined, 16
data model
    XPath, 46–54
data-type attribute, 211, 511
databases
    extension elements, 333–339
    Xalan XSLT processor, 337–339
datatype operators
    XPath 2.0, 93–97
datatypes, xviii
    (see also built-in datatypes; list types of XML Schema; union types; specific datatype)
    converting to boolean values, 146
    defining, 875–890
    for division, 927
    parameters, 158
    XML ID, IDREF and IDREFS, 181–194
    in XML schemas, 10
    XPath, 67–71, 551–555
    XPath 2.0, 926
    XSLT 2.0, 12, 162, 926
data() function, 617–620
date functions
    defined, 330
    list of, 565
dates
    formatting, 130–132, 921–923
dates-and-times:month-name() function, 332
dateTime() function, 621–622
day-from-dateTime() function, 623–625
day-from-date() function, 622–623
days-from-duration() function, 625–626
debugging, xviii
    (see also errors)
    stylesheets, 35
decimal digits (Nd) character group, 910
decimal numbers
    formatting, 127–130
decimal-separator attribute, 408
declarations (see namespace declarations; XML declarations)

declaring, xviii
    (see also defining)
    attributes, 192
    elements, 871–875
deep-equal() function, 626–631
default collation sequences
    URIs, 362
default namespace
    XPath context, 550
default values
    attributes, 49
    parameters, 155
default-collation attribute, 362, 521
default-collation() function, 631–632
default-validation attribute, 520
defining, xviii
    (see also declaring)
    datatypes, 875–890
depoint-equal() function, 590–591
descendant axis, 64, 549
descendant-or-self axis, 64
descendants
    defined, 935
design goals (see features)
digit attribute, 409
digits (see numbers)
disable-output-escaping attribute, 526, 528
distinct-values() function, 218, 632–637
div (division) operator, 558
division
    datatypes, 927
division operator, xviii
    (see also integer division (idiv) operator)
    XPath, 77
doc-available() function, 269–271, 638–639
DocBook documents
    converting to HTML, 163
    using group-starting-with attribute, 238
    <xsl:for-each-group> element, 431
doctype-public attribute, 481, 503
doctype-system attribute, 481, 503
document elements
    defined, 6, 935
document interface, 13
document nodes, xviii
    (see also root nodes)
    built-in template rules, 32
    defined, 935
Document Object Model (see DOM)

not equal (!=) operator, 556
not equal to (ne) operator, 561
not() function, 83, 759–761
number datatype
    conversion to boolean values, 146
    defined, 68, 552
    errors in math operations, 927
<number> elements, 96
numbering
    document parts, 118–127
numbers, xviii
    (see also decimal numbers)
    errors in math operations, 927
    formatting codes, 920–921
    in predicates, 65
    \d any digit escape character, 908
numbers (N) character groups, 910
numbers as letters (Nl) character group, 910
number() function, 761–764
numeric functions
    list of, 566
numeric values
    single quotes, 168

O

objects (see formatting objects)
occurrence indicator (*) operator, 556
occurrence indicator (+) operator, 556
occurrence indicator (?) operator, 558
omit-xml-declaration attribute, 481, 504
one-or-more() function, 764–766
opening (Ps) character group, 911
operations (see mathematical operations)
operators, xviii
    (see also boolean operators, datatype
    operators; mathematical operators; set
    operators)
    precedence in XPath, 562
    XPath, 71–102, 556–561
    XQuery 1.0 and XPath 2.0, 17
or operator, 561
order attribute, 213, 511
order of operations
    boolean operators in XPath, 83
ordinal attribute, 127, 468
other letters (Lo) character group, 910
other numeric characters (No) character group,
    910

other punctuation marks (Po) character group,
    911
output, 113–144
    dates and times, 130–132
    decimal numbers, 127–130
    by function, 569–870
    multiple files, 281–286
    numbering document parts, 118–125
    text, 113–118
    whitespace, 139–144
    <xsl:copy> and <xsl:copy-of> elements,
        132–139
output escaping
    defined, 938
output methods
    <xsl:output> element, 30, 480–487
output view
    of XML documents, 105
output-version attribute, 504
override attribute, 435

P

P character groups, 911
P formatting code, 132
paragraph separator (Zp) character group, 911
parameters, xviii, 152–167
    (see also global parameters; tunnel
    parameters)
    defined, 938
    defining in templates, 152
    passing to templates, 154, 158
    <xsl:param> element, 33
    XSLT 2.0, 158–167
parent
    defined, 938
parent axis, 63, 548
parentheses escape characters, 908
parenthesis metacharacter, 906
parenthesized expression operator, 556
parents
    axes, 63–65
    element nodes and attribute nodes, 49
parsing
    multiple XML documents, 245–253
    stylesheets, 27
    whitespace-only nodes, 140
    XML documents, 6, 13
    and XPath, 45
partial XML schema validation, 11

About the Author

Doug Tidwell is a senior programmer at IBM. He has more than a sixth of a century of programming experience, and has been working with markup languages for more than a decade. He was a speaker at the first XML conference in 1997 and has taught XML classes around the world. His job as a cyber evangelist is to look busy and to help people use new technologies to solve problems. Using a pair of zircon-encrusted tweezers, he holds a master's degree in computer science from Vanderbilt University and a bachelor's degree in English from the University of Georgia. He lives in Raleigh, North Carolina, with his wife and their daughter Lily.

Colophon

The animal on the cover of *XSLT*, Second Edition, is a Jabiru (*Jabiru mycteria*). Standing up to five feet tall and with a wingspan of eight feet, this wading stork is the largest flying bird in the western hemisphere. The bird's habitat ranges from southern Mexico to northern Argentina, and much of its migrating population is found in Belize from November through July. Its habitat generally includes coastal areas, savannas, and marshes, and it feeds on freshwater wildlife such as frogs, fish, and even snakes. Its plumage is mostly white, but its head, neck, and beak are jet black. A featherless red pouch at the base of its neck gives the Jabiru its name, which means "swollen neck" in the Tupi-Guarani language.

The Jabiru population has steadily decreased over the past decades due to hunting and deforestation, but some areas of Central America have seen a recovery in the bird's numbers. It is currently considered a species of least concern by the World Conservation Union, an improvement from a status of near-threatened in 1988.

The cover image is an original antique engraving from the 19th century. The cover font is Adobe's ITC Garamond. The text font is Linotype Birka, the heading font is Adobe Myriad Condensed, and the code font is LucasFont's TheSansMonoCondensed.

Related Titles from O'Reilly

XML

Developing Feeds with RSS & Atom

Java and XML, *3rd Edition*

Java and XSLT

Learning XML, *2nd Edition*

Learning XSLT

Perl and XML

Practical RDF

Programming Jabber

Programming Web Services with SOAP

Python & XML

SAX2

SVG Essentials

Unicode Explained

Web Services Essentials

XForms Essentials

XML Hacks

XML in a Nutshell, *3rd Edition*

XML Pocket Reference, *3rd Edition*

XML Schema

Xpath and Xpointer

XQuery

XSLT, *2nd Edition*

XSLT Cookbook, *2nd Edition*

XSLT 1.0 Pocket Reference

O'REILLY®

Our books are available at most retail and online bookstores.

To order direct: 1-800-998-9938 • *order@oreilly.com* • *www.oreilly.com*

Online editions of most O'Reilly titles are available by subscription at *safari.oreilly.com*

The New Millennium Reader

The New Millennium Reader

FOURTH EDITION

Stuart Hirschberg
Rutgers University

Terry Hirschberg

PEARSON

Prentice
Hall

Upper Saddle River, New Jersey 07458

Library of Congress Cataloging-in-Publication Data

The new millennium reader / [compiled by] Stuart Hirschberg, Terry Hirschberg.— 4th ed.
  p. cm.
  Includes bibliographical references and index.
  ISBN 0-13-191849-4
  1. College readers. 2. English language—Rhetoric—Problems, exercises, etc. 3. Report writing—
Problems, exercises, etc. I. Hirschberg, Stuart II. Hirschberg. Terry.

PE1417.N48 2006
808'.0427–dc22

                                                                              2004053496

Editorial Director: Leah Jewell
Senior Acquisitions Editor: Brad Potthoff
Acquisitions Assistant: Steven Kyritz
VP/Director, Production and Manufacturing:
  Barbara Kittle
Production Editor: Joan E. Foley
Production Assistant: Marlene Gassler
Copyeditor: Kathryn Graehl
Text Permissions Specialist: Frederick Courtright
Manufacturing Manager: Nick Sklitsis
Assistant Manufacturing Manager: Mary Ann
  Gloriande
Director, Marketing: Brandy Dawson
Marketing Manager: Kate Stewart
Marketing Assistant: Kara Pottle
Media Production Manager: Lynn Pearlman
Media Editor: Christy Pepper

Director, Image Resource Center: Melinda Reo
Manager, Image Rights and Permissions: Zina
  Arabia
Manager, Visual Research: Beth Brenzel
Manager, Cover Visual Research & Permissions:
  Karen Sanatar
Image Permissions Coordinator: Michelina Viscusi
Image Researcher: Linda Sykes
Director, Creative Design: Leslie Osher
Senior Art Director: Anne B. Nieglos
Interior and Cover Designer: Jill Lehan
Cover Art: Grace Hartigan, American, born 1922.
  "Billboard," 1957. Painting oil on canvas, ab-
  straction. 78½ × 87 in. (199.4 × 221.0 cm.)
  LR in black: [Hartigan '57]. The Minneapolis
  Institute of Arts, The Julia B. Bigelow Fund.

This book was set in 10/12 Sabon by Pine Tree Composition, Inc., and was printed and bound by R. R. Donnelley, Inc. Covers were printed by The Lehigh Press.

For permission to use copyrighted material, grateful acknowledgment is made to the copyright holders on pages 709-714, which are considered an extension of this copyright page.

Pearson Education LTD.
Pearson Education Singapore, Pte. Ltd
Pearson Education, Canada, Ltd
Pearson Education-Japan
Pearson Education Australia PTY, Limited

Pearson Education North Asia Ltd
Pearson Educación de Mexico, S.A.de C.V.
Pearson Education Malaysia, Pte. Ltd
Pearson Education, Upper Saddle River, NJ

10 9 8 7 6 5 4 3 2 1

ISBN 0-13-191849-4

ARGUMENTATION AND PERSUASION

Arguments That Define and Draw Distinctions

Arguments That Establish Causes and Draw Consequences

Arguments That Make Value Judgments

Arguments That Propose Solutions

AUTOBIOGRAPHY

BIOGRAPHY

IRONY, HUMOR, AND SATIRE

SPEECHES

INTERVIEWS

PREFACE

The fourth edition of *The New Millennium Reader* is intended for first-year composition, intermediate and advanced composition courses, and courses that consider the essay as a form of literature.

The book introduces students to major traditions in essay writing and explores the relationship between the writer's voice and stylistics features that express the writer's attitude toward his or her personal experiences. The text also provides guidance for students in developing skills in critical reading and writing, with a strong emphasis on argumentation.

The New Millennium Reader provides thought-provoking and engaging models of writing by scholars, researchers, and scientists that show writing is essential to learning in all academic fields of study.

The eighty-eight nonfiction selections, which are new to this edition, have been chosen for their interest, reading level, and length and include a broad range of topics, authors, disciplines, and cross-cultural perspectives.

Many of the longer readings are included because of their value in allowing students to observe the development of ideas and to enhance their own skills in reading comprehension and writing their own essays.

The readings shed light on myriad subjects—from ancient Egypt to genetically engineered goats; from the sinking of the *Titanic* to the FDR Memorial; from the lowly pencil to The Sims; from the American Civil War to Richard Nixon's "Checkers" Speech and the events of September 11, 2001; from Niagara Falls to the McDonald's marketing strategy for children; from ballet to Nazi Germany; from autism to advertising; from Marcel Proust's "madeleine" to fetal alcohol syndrome; from shopping malls to Harry Potter.

The text is thematically organized in order to bridge the gap between the expressive essays students traditionally read and their own life experiences. Selections drawn from memoirs, scholarly essays, and biographies illustrate how writers move through, and beyond, personal experiences and adapt what they write for different audiences.

The book includes 142 selections by classic, modern, and contemporary authors whose work, in many cases, provides the foundation of the broader intellectual heritage of a college education.

Chapters are organized by themes that have traditionally elicited compelling expressive essays and thoughtful arguments and include accounts of personal growth, nature writing, prison literature, and narratives of religious and philosophical exploration. *The New Millennium Reader* is rich in a variety of perspectives by African-American, Native American, Asian-American, and Hispanic writers and offers cross-cultural and regional works as well as a core of selections by classic authors, more than forty percent of them women.

The sixteen short stories (ten new to this edition), thirty-two poems (six new to this edition), and two new plays amplify the themes in each chapter in ways that introduce students to techniques and forms that writers have traditionally used in the fields of fiction, poetry, and drama.

NEW TO THIS EDITION

We have thoroughly updated all eleven chapters and have provided a thought-provoking quotation at the beginning of each chapter.

We have added more than seventy color illustrations (from photographs to billboard art, and from film stills to drawings, paintings, and other images) that enhance the impact of the themes and selections. We have also added a new section ("Reading and Analyzing Visual Texts") to the Introduction, which shows students how to think about visuals rhetorically, and we link this discussion with "Thinking Critically About the Image" in each of the eleven chapters.

In the Rhetorical Contents, we have classified arguments into the categories traditionally used by teachers of writing. We have also created a descriptive Glossary (keyed to bolded terms), with examples drawn from the works, and an Index of First Lines of Poems.

CHAPTER DESCRIPTIONS

The eleven chapters cover a wide range from the sphere of reflections on personal experience, family life, and influential people, to descriptions of memorable places, discussions of the value of education and perspectives on language, and consideration of issues in popular culture. Various selections contemplate our place in nature, history in the making, the pursuit of justice, the impact of technology, the artistic impulse, and matters of ethics, philosophy, and religion.

- Chapter 1, "Reflections on Experience," introduces candid, introspective reminiscences by writers who want to understand the meaning of important personal events that proved to be decisive turning points in their lives.
- Chapter 2, "Influential People and Memorable Places," introduces portraits of people important to the writers, presents an invaluable opportunity to study the methods biographers use, and explores the role that landscapes and natural and architectural wonders have played in the lives of the writers.
- Chapter 3, "The Value of Education," attests to the value of literacy and looks at the role education plays in different settings as a vehicle for self-discovery and at questions raised by censorship and the Internet.
- Chapter 4, "Perspectives on Language," explores the social impact of language and how it defines ethnic identity; the importance of being able to communicate; and the dangers of language used to manipulate attitudes, beliefs, and emotions, whether in the form of propaganda or advertising.
- Chapter 5, "Issues in Popular Culture," touches on broad issues of contemporary concern, including child abuse, consumerism, television news, gay marriage, eating disorders, the plight of the elderly, racism, and the hidden dimension of the fast-food industry.
- Chapter 6, "Our Place in Nature," looks at the tradition of nature writing and offers investigations of animal behavior and parallels in humans, explores the complex interactions of living things, and explains the ecosystem of the oceans.
- Chapter 7, "History in the Making," brings to life important social, economic, and political events of the past and addresses the question of how historians shape our perceptions of the past in ways that influence the present.

- Chapter 8, "The Pursuit of Justice," draws on firsthand testimonies by writers whose accounts combine eyewitness reports, literary texts, and historical records in the continuing debate over the allegiance individuals owe their government and the protection of individual rights that citizens expect in return.
- Chapter 9, "The Impact of Technology," examines the extent of our culture's dependence on technology and energy, and the mixed blessings that scientific innovations, including cyberspace and genetic engineering, will bequeath to future generations.
- Chapter 10, "The Artistic Impulse," considers how artists deepen and enrich our knowledge of human nature and experience through their distinctive contributions in particular societies and how art changes from age to age and culture to culture.
- Chapter 11, "Matters of Ethics, Philosophy, and Religion," focuses on universal questions of faith, good and evil, obedience to authority, and basic questions about the meaning and value of life as applied to specific contemporary issues of abortion, ethics and personal choice, religious tenets and taboos, and allocation of environmental resources.

EDITORIAL APPARATUS

An introduction, "Reading in the Various Genres," discusses the crucial skills of reading for ideas and organization and introduces students to the basic rhetorical techniques writers use in developing their essays. This introduction also shows students how to approach important elements in appreciating and analyzing short fiction, poetry, drama, and the rhetoric of visual texts.

Chapter introductions discuss the theme of each chapter and its relation to the individual selections. A biographical sketch preceding each selection gives background information on the writer's life and identifies the personal and literary context in which the selection was written.

Questions for discussion and writing at the end of each selection are designed to encourage readers to discover relationships between their personal experiences and those described by the writers in the text, to explore points of agreement in areas of conflict sparked by the viewpoint of the authors, and to provide ideas for further inquiry and writing. These questions ask students to think critically about the content, meaning, and purpose of each selection; students will evaluate the author's rhetorical strategy, voice projected in relationship to his or her audience, evidence cited, and underlying assumptions. The writing suggestions afford opportunities for personal and expressive writing as well as expository and persuasive writing.

Images within each chapter, including the full-page image at the opening of each chapter, are accompanied by prompts or questions that ask students to connect that image to the corresponding selection or chapter theme.

Connection questions at the end of each chapter link each selection with other readings in that chapter and with readings throughout the book to afford students the opportunity to explore multiple perspectives on the same topic.

The Rhetorical Contents is included to enhance the usefulness of the text by permitting students to study the form (the rhetorical mode employed) of the selections as well as their content and themes. A Glossary, an Index of First Lines of Poems, and an Index of Authors and Titles also are provided to enhance the usefulness of this text.

INSTRUCTOR'S MANUAL

An accompanying Instructor's Manual provides (1) guidance on how to approach each selection; (2) sample syllabi and suggestions for organizing courses with different kinds of focus (argumentation, cultural studies, writing across the curriculum); (3) background information about each essay, with definitions of terms that may be unfamiliar to students; (4) detailed answers to the discussion and writing questions; (5) additional essay topics for writing and research; (6) supplemental resources (bibliographies and Web sites) for students who wish to follow up on any of the authors or issues for in-depth study; and (7) alternative tables of contents by secondary themes, disciplines, and subjects.

A Companion Web site at www.prenhall.com/hirschberg provides additional chapter exercises, links, and activities that reinforce and build upon the material presented in the text.

WRITER'S ONEKEY

Use *Writer's OneKey* to enhance your composition classes. Everything in one place on the Web for students and instructors, including:

- Personal tutoring available to students
- Paper review tool and research tools, including the *New York Times* archive
- Visual analysis exercises
- Mini-handbook
- And much more . . .

A free subscription to *Writer's OneKey* can be packaged with each copy of this text by specifying ISBN 0-13-155686-X. See www.prenhall.com/writersonekey for details.

PRENTICE HALL POCKET READERS

Every reading in our pocket readers has withstood the test of time and teaching, making each one the perfect companion for any writing course (limit one free reader per package). To package this text with . . .

ARGUMENT: A Prentice Hall Pocket Reader, by Christy Desmet, Deborah Miller, and Kathy Houff, specify package ISBN 0-13-155657-6.

LITERATURE: A Prentice Hall Pocket Reader, by Mary Balkun, specify package ISBN 0-13-155658-4.

PATTERNS: A Prentice Hall Pocket Reader, by Dorothy Minor, specify package ISBN 0-13-155659-2.

THEMES: A Prentice Hall Pocket Reader, by Clyde Moneyhun, specify package ISBN 0-13-155660-6.

WRITING ACROSS THE CURRICULUM: A Prentice Hall Pocket Reader, by Stephen Brown, specify package ISBN 0-13-168969-X.

THE NEW AMERICAN WEBSTER HANDY COLLEGE DICTIONARY

To order this text packaged with a free dictionary, specify ISBN 0-13-154888-3.

THE NEW AMERICAN ROGET'S COLLEGE THESAURUS

To order this text packaged with a free thesaurus, specify ISBN 0-13-154887-5.

ACKNOWLEDGMENTS

No expression of thanks can adequately convey our gratitude to those teachers of composition who offered thoughtful comments and suggestions on changes for this edition: John R. Turner, Scott Community College; Paul Vantine, Cameron University; and Joanne Vickers, Ohio Dominican College.

Once again, we want to thank Leah Jewell, Editorial Director, whose continuing enthusiasm and guidance made it a pleasure to work on this fourth edition.

Also for their dedication and skill, we owe much to the able staff at Prentice Hall, especially to our editor, Brad Potthoff, and his assistant, Steve Kyritz. We were indeed fortunate to have Joan Foley as our production editor and Kathryn Graehl as our copyeditor. We would also like to thank Linda Sykes for her splendid work in obtaining the visual images and once again to our permissions editor, Fred Courtright. Thanks go as well to the staff at Chatham Public Library, especially Judy Lean.

Stuart Hirschberg
Terry Hirschberg

11 MATTERS OF ETHICS, PHILOSOPHY, AND RELIGION   626

CONTENTS

1   REFLECTIONS ON EXPERIENCE   28

RHETORICAL CONTENTS

COMPARISON AND CONTRAST

PROCESS ANALYSIS

CLASSIFICATION

6   OUR PLACE IN NATURE   322

The New Millennium Reader

Reading in the Various Genres

READING ESSAYS

As a literary **genre,** the **essay** harks back to the form invented four hundred years ago by the French writer Michel Montaigne, who called his writings *essais* (attempts) because they were intended less as accounts of objective truth than as personal disclosures of a mind exploring its own attitudes, values, and assumptions on a diverse range of subjects. The essayist speaks directly without the mediation of imagined characters and events.

Essayists invite us to share the dramatic excitement of an observant and sensitive mind struggling to understand and clarify an issue that is of great importance to the writer. We feel the writer trying to reconcile opposing impulses to evolve a viewpoint that takes into account known facts as well as personal values.

READING FOR IDEAS AND ORGANIZATION

One of the most important skills to have is the ability to survey unfamiliar articles, essays, or excerpts and come away with an accurate understanding of what the author wanted to communicate and of how the material is organized. On the first and in subsequent readings of any of the selections in this text, especially the longer ones, pay particular attention to the title, look closely at the introductory and concluding paragraphs (with special emphasis on the author's statement or restatement of central ideas), identify the headings and subheadings (and determine the relationship between these and the title), and locate any unusual terms necessary to fully understand the author's concepts.

As you first read through an essay, you might look for cues that enable you to recognize the main parts or help you to perceive its overall **organization.** Once you find the main **thesis,** underline it. Then work your way through fairly rapidly, identifying the main ideas and the sequence in which they are presented. As you identify an important idea, ask yourself how this idea relates to the thesis statement you underlined or to the idea expressed in the title.

FINDING A THESIS

Finding a thesis involves discovering the idea that serves as the focus of the essay. The thesis is often stated in the form of a single sentence that asserts the author's response to an issue that an **audience** might respond to in different ways. For example, in "The Lowest Animal" (Ch. 6), Mark Twain presents his assessment of human nature:

> In the course of my experiments I convinced myself that among the animals man is the only one that harbors insults and injuries, broods over them, waits till a chance offers, then takes revenge. The passion of revenge is unknown to the higher animals.

The thesis represents the writer's view of a subject or **topic** from a certain perspective. Here Twain states a view that serves as a focus for his essay.

Writers often place the thesis in the first paragraph or group of paragraphs so that the readers will be able to perceive the relationship between the supporting evidence and this main idea.

As you read, you might wish to underline the topic sentence or main idea of each paragraph or section (since key ideas are often developed over the course of several paragraphs). Jot it down in your own words in the margins, identify supporting statements and **evidence** (such as examples, statistics, and the testimony of authorities), and try to discover how the author organizes the material to support the development of important ideas. To identify supporting material, look for any ideas more specific than the main idea that is used to support it.

Pay particular attention to important transitional words, phrases, or paragraphs to better see the relationships among major sections of the selection. Noticing how certain words or phrases act as **transitions** to link paragraphs or sections together will dramatically improve your reading comprehension. Also look for section summaries, where the author draws together several preceding ideas.

Writers use certain words to signal the starting point of an **inductive** or **deductive** chain of reasoning. If you detect any of the following terms, look for the main idea they introduce:

since	as shown by	for the reason that
because	inasmuch as	may be inferred from
for	otherwise	may be derived from
as	as indicated by	may be deduced from
follows from	the reason is that	in view of the fact that

An especially important category of words includes signals that the author will be stating a conclusion. Words to look for are the following:

therefore	in summary
hence	which shows that
thus	which means that
so	and which entails
accordingly	consequently
in consequence	proves that

it follows that	as a result
we may infer	which implies that
I conclude that	which allows us to infer
in conclusion	points to the conclusion that

You may find it helpful to create a running dialogue with the author in the margins, posing and then trying to answer the basic questions *who, what, where, when,* and *why,* and to note your observations on how the main idea of the article is related to the title. You can later use these notes to evaluate how effectively any specific section contributes to the overall line of thought.

Organization of the Essay   Writers use a variety of means in an **introduction** to attract readers' interest, at the same time explicitly stating or at least implying the probable thesis. Some writers find that a brief story or anecdote is an ideal way to focus the audience's attention on the subject, as does Jill Nelson in "Number One!" (Ch. 1):

> That night I dream about my father, but it is really more a memory than a dream. "Number one! Not two! Number one!" my father intones from the head of the breakfast table. The four of us sit at attention, two on each side of the ten-foot teak expanse, our brown faces rigid. At the foot, my mother looks up at my father, the expression on her face a mixture of pride, anxiety and could it be, boredom? I am twelve. It is 1965.

Other writers use the strategy of opening with an especially telling or apt quotation. Writers may also choose to introduce their essays in many other ways, by defining key terms, offering a prediction, posing a thoughtful question, or providing a touch of humor.

Even though the introductory paragraph is the most logical place to state the thesis, one can also expect to find the central assertion of the essay in the title, as, for example, in William A. Henry III's argument "In Defense of Elitism" (Ch. 3), which decries what he perceives to be a lowering of national educational standards in the interest of encouraging everyone to attend college.

The main portion of the essay presents and develops the main points the writer wishes to communicate. A wide range of strategies may be used, depending on the kind of point the writer is making and the form the supporting evidence takes to demonstrate the likelihood of the writer's thesis.

The **conclusion** of an essay may serve a variety of purposes. The writer may restate the thesis after reviewing the most convincing points or close with an appeal to the needs and values of the specific audience. This sense of closure can be achieved in many different ways. For instance, the conclusion can echo the ideas stated in the opening paragraph, or it can present a compelling image. Other writers choose to end on a note of reaffirmation and challenge or with irony or a striking **paradox.** The most traditional ending sums up points raised in the essay, although usually not in as impressive a fashion, as does David Rothenberg's ending in "How the Web Destroys the Quality of Students' Research Papers" (Ch. 3):

> Knowledge does not emerge in a vacuum, but we do need silence and space for sustained thought. Next semester, I'm going to urge my students to turn off their glowing boxes and think, if only once in a while.

Supporting Evidence   An important part of critical reading depends on your ability to identify and evaluate how the writer develops the essay in order to **support** the thesis. The most common patterns of thinking are known as the **rhetorical modes.** For example, writers might describe how something looks, narrate an experience, analyze how something works, provide examples, define important terms, create a classification, compare and contrast, create an analogy, or explore what caused something. To clarify and support the thesis, writers also use a wide variety of evidence, including examples drawn from personal experience, the testimony of experts, statistical data, and case histories.

Describing   Writers use **description** for a variety of purposes, ranging from portraying the appearance of people, objects, events, or scenes to revealing the writer's feelings and reactions to those people, objects, events, or scenes. Gayle Pemberton in "Antidisestablishmentarianism" (Ch. 2) accomplishes this in her description of her grandmother, an intimidating woman who taught Pemberton to be independent and think for herself:

> She disliked white people, black people in the aggregate and pretty much individually too, children—particularly female children—her daughter, her husband, my mother, Episcopalianism, Catholicism, Judaism and Dinah Shore. She had a hot temper and a mean streak. . . . Grandma scared the daylights out of me.

We learn that her grandmother's curmudgeon-like attitude proved invaluable in helping Pemberton deal with the white society in which she grew up.

Perhaps the most useful method of arranging details within a description is the technique of focusing on an impression that dominates the entire scene. This main impression can center on a prominent physical feature, a tower or church steeple, or a significant psychological trait, such as Pemberton's grandmother's "take no shit" attitude. A skillful writer will often arrange a description around this central impression, in much the same way a good photographer will locate a focal point for pictures. Jack London, who was a journalist and novelist, uses this technique in "The San Francisco Earthquake" (Ch. 7) in his description of how San Francisco residents reacted to the devastating earthquake of 1906:

> Before the flames, throughout the night, fled tens of thousands of homeless ones. Some were wrapped in blankets. Others carried bundles of bedding and dear household treasures. Sometimes a whole family was harnessed to a carriage or delivery wagon that was weighted down with their possessions. Baby buggies, toy wagons, and go-carts were used as trucks, while every other person was dragging a trunk. Yet everybody was gracious. The most perfect courtesy obtained. Never, in all San Francisco's history, were her people so kind and courteous as on this night of terror.

A wealth of specific descriptive details re-creates the sights and sounds of the conflagration. Yet, the primary impression London communicates is that the citizens of San Francisco displayed forbearance and rare courtesy toward one another in the most trying of circumstances.

Description is more effective when the writer arranges details to produce a certain effect, such as **suspense**, empathy, or surprise. Agnes De Mille, a renowned choreographer, does this in "Pavlova" (Ch. 10) when she describes the great Russian ballerina, so that her readers can share the moment when De Mille decided to become a dancer herself. De Mille's description draws the reader's attention to Pavlova's physical appearance, gestures, style of performance, and the response she produced in her audiences. Through a multitude of evocative details we can "see" Pavlova's slight figure, minuscule slipper size, graceful limbs and neck, and accelerated hummingbird-like movements. De Mille carefully structures her description to present Pavlova first at rest, a diminuative figure who seems insignificant, and then to depict her in motion, when Pavlova magically becomes larger than life through her dancing.

Narrating   Another essential technique often used by writers is **narration.** Narrative relates a series of events or a significant experience by telling about it in chronological order. The events related through narrative can entertain, inform, or dramatize an important moment. For example, in "West with the Night" (Ch. 1), Beryl Markham tells us of the moment on her epic cross-Atlantic flight when she faced a life-and-death decision. By relating the events of the flight as they led to this crucial moment, Markham provides her readers with a coherent framework in which to interpret the events of her story.

Effective narration focuses on a single significant action that dramatically changes the relationship of the writer (or main character) to family, friends, or environment. A significant experience may be defined as a situation in which something important to the writer or to the people he or she is writing about is at stake.

Narratives are usually written from the **point of view** of a **first-person** narrator, as in the case of Beryl Markham:

> It is dark already and I am over the south of Ireland. There are the lights of Cork and the lights are wet; they are drenched in Irish rain, and I am above them and dry.

Events can also be related through a second-person point of view ("you") or through a more objective third-person ("he," "she," "they") point of view.

Narration can take the form of an anecdote (such as Markham's) or as a historical account synthesized from journals, logs, diaries, and even interviews, such as that compiled by Hanson W. Baldwin (in "R.M.S. *Titanic*," Ch. 7). Baldwin's account of the events leading up to and after the moment when the *Titanic* struck an iceberg is shaped to emphasize the poignancy and irony of this catastrophe. For example, Baldwin recounts the following event:

> 12:45 A.M. Murdock, in charge on the starboard side, eyes tragic, but calm and cool, orders boat No. 7 lowered. The women hang back: they want no boat ride on an ice-strewn sea; the *Titanic* is unsinkable. The men encourage them, explain that this is just a precautionary measure: "We'll see you again at breakfast."

We notice how skillfully Baldwin creates a composite that includes the actions of those who were there along with what was actually said at the time. Baldwin uses narration to summarize, explain, interpret, and dramatize an important moment in history.

Narratives offer writers means by which they can discover the meaning of experiences through the process of writing about them. For Mikhal Gilmore (in "My Brother, Gary Gilmore," Ch. 2), the need to understand his family history became an overpowering motivation that led him to write his **autobiography:**

Over the years, many people have judged me by my brother's actions as if in coming from a family that yielded a murderer I must be formed by the same causes, the same sins, must by my brother's actions be responsible for the violence that resulted, and bear the mark of a frightening and shameful heritage. It's as if there is guilt in the fact of the blood-line itself. Maybe there is.

In these more personal, autobiographical narratives (see, for example, Fritz Peters, Jill Nelson, Richard Rhodes, Annie Dillard, Agnes De Mille, and Sabine Reichel), the need to clarify and interpret one's past requires the writer to reconstruct the meaning and significance of experiences *whose importance may not have been appreciated at the time they occurred.*

Just as individuals can discover the meaning of past experiences through the process of writing about them, so writers use narration to focus on important moments of collective self-revelation. Sabine Reichel in "Learning What Was Never Taught" (Ch. 3) draws on records and eyewitness accounts (including her own memories) from the post-Nazi era for specific details to re-create the scene for her readers, and she summarizes necessary background information to provide a context for her account.

Illustrating with Examples   Providing good **examples** is an essential part of effective writing. A single well-chosen example or a range of illustrations can provide clear cases that illustrate, document, and substantiate a writer's thesis. The report of a memorable incident, an account drawn from records, eyewitness reports, and a personal narrative account of a crucial incident are all important ways examples can document the authenticity of the writer's thesis.

One extremely effective way of substantiating a claim is by using a **case history,** that is, an in-depth account of the experiences of one person that typifies the experience of many people in the same situation. Dennis Smith, an author and former firefighter, uses this technique in his account of September 11, 2001, "Report from Ground Zero" (Ch. 7). The experience of a battalion chief, Joe Pfeifer, stands for the experiences of hundreds of the police, firefighters, and emergency service personnel who went to the World Trade Center on that morning. Smith begins by telling us something about Chief Pfeifer and then follows him as he attempts to make his way through the rubble to help survivors:

> All the firefighters are now staring upward, as is a film crew that is shooting a documentary about firefighters. It is a plane. Chief Pfeifer's gaze follows the path of the plane, and he has a clear view as it crashes into the north tower of the World Trade Center, near the top, somewhere around the ninetieth floor.

By selecting one person to represent hundreds of rescuers and thousands of victims, Smith brings into human terms an event that otherwise would be beyond the reader's comprehension.

Defining   Yet another rhetorical pattern often used by writers is **definition.** Definition is a useful way of specifying the basic nature of any phenomenon, idea, or thing. Definition is the method of clarifying the meaning of key terms, either in the thesis or elsewhere in the essay. In some cases, writers may develop an entire essay to explore the **connotations** accrued by an unusual or controversial term or to challenge preconceptions attached to a familiar term. Besides eliminating **ambiguity** or defining a term important to the development of the essay, definitions can be used persuasively to influence perceptions, as Rosemarie Garland-Thomson does for the term *disability* in "The FDR Memorial: Who Speaks from the Wheelchair?" (Ch. 4):

> Even more important, to have the first two words a visitor encounters at the memorial be "Franklin's illness" presents disability in a way that doubly violates the spirit of equality. "Illness" is a synonym for impairment, a term that disability scholars and activists use to denote functional limitation. "Disability," on the other hand, is a term we use to describe the system of representation that produces discriminatory attitudes and barriers to full integration. In essence, "impairment" and "illness" are about bodily differences, whereas "disability" is about the social and political context in which our bodies operate.

Dividing and Classifying   Writers also divide and classify a subject on the basis of important similarities. **Classification and division** is used to sort, group, and collect things into categories, or classes, that are based on one or more criteria. The criteria are features that members of the group all have in common. The purposes of the classifier determine which specific features are selected as the basis of the classification. Thus, classification is, first and foremost, an intellectual activity based on discovering generic characteristics shared by members of a group, according to the interests of the writer. Effective classifications shed light on the nature of what is being classified by identifying significant features, using these features as criteria in a systematic way, dividing phenomena into at least two different classes on the basis of these criteria, and presenting the results logically and consistently. For example, in "The Rhetoric of Advertising" (Ch. 4), Stuart Hirschberg classifies the techniques advertisers use according to the traditional rhetorical strategies identified by Aristotle:

> Seen in this way, ads appear as mini-arguments whose strategies and techniques of persuasion can be analyzed just like a written argument. We can discover which elements are designed to appeal to the audience's emotions (*pathos* according to Aristotle), which elements make their appeal in terms of reasons, evidence, or logic (*logos*), and how the advertiser goes about winning credibility . . . in terms of the spokesperson employed to speak on behalf of the product (the *ethos* dimension).

If we can identify the specific techniques advertisers use, the author believes, we will be less likely to be manipulated into buying things we don't need.

Comparing and Contrasting   Another way of arranging a discussion of similarities and differences relies on the rhetorical method of **comparison and contrast.** Using this method, the writer compares and contrasts relevant points about one subject with corresponding aspects of another. For example, in "Concerning Egypt" (Ch. 7), Herodotus compares unfamiliar Egyptian customs to the corresponding, but different, customs of his countrymen:

> In other countries the priests have long hair, in Egypt their heads are shaven; elsewhere it is customary, in mourning for near relations to cut their hair close: the Egyptians, who wear no hair at any other time, when they lose a relative, let their beards and the hair of their heads grow long.

The comparative method serves Herodotus well as a way of getting his audience to perceive basic differences between the two cultures (Egypt and Greece).

Comparisons may be arranged structurally in one of two ways. In one method, the writer discusses all the relevant points of one subject and then covers the same ground for the second. Writers may use transitional words like *although, however, but, on the other hand, instead of, different from,* and *as opposed to* to indicate contrast. Words used to show comparisons include *similarly, likewise,* and *in the same way.* Comparisons may also be arranged point by point to create a continual contrast from sentence to sentence between relevant aspects of two subjects. Comparisons may also evaluate two subjects. The writer contrasts sets of qualities and decides between the two on the basis of some stipulated criteria.

Dramatic contrast is a favorite device of satirists, who expose hypocrisy by reminding people of what they really do, as opposed to what they profess. In "The Lowest Animal" (Ch. 6), Mark Twain contrasts the behavior of humans with that of animals in comparable situations in order to deflate the high opinion the human species has of itself. Each of Twain's "experiments" is meant to show the preponderance in humans of such traits as greed and cruelty, and to **parody** the interpretation of Darwin's theory (then currently popular) that humans were the apex of all living species.

Although Twain's "experiments" are hypothetical and meant to underscore ironic insights, the comparative technique is indispensable as a way of structuring real scientific experiments. Such is the case in a fascinating study reported by Constance Holden in "Identical Twins Reared Apart" (Ch. 9), which followed nine sets of identical twins who had been separated at birth, raised in different environments, and then reunited. Holden reports what happened when one of the sets of twins, Oskar and Jack, first saw each other:

> Similarities started cropping up as soon as Oskar arrived at the airport. Both were wearing wire-rimmed glasses and mustaches, both sported two-pocket shirts with epaulets. They shared idiosyncrasies galore: they like spicy foods and sweet liqueurs, are absentminded, have a habit of falling asleep in front of the television, think it's funny to sneeze in a crowd of strangers, flush the toilet before using it, store rubber bands on their wrists, read magazines from back to front, dip buttered toast in their coffee.

Holden's analysis of different characteristics and traits is developed through a point-by-point comparison of striking similarities in behavior between each of the nine sets of twins. For Holden, the number and range of similarities shared by each set of twins argues for the overwhelming importance of heredity, rather than environment, in shaping human behavior.

Figurative Comparisons and Analogies   **Figurative language** rather than literal comparisons reveal the writer's feelings about the subject. Figurative comparisons can take the form of **metaphors** that identify two different things with each other, as in Annie Dillard's description in "So, This Was Adolescence" (Ch. 1): "I was what they called a live wire." They can also take the form of **similes** that use the word *like* or *as* to relate two seemingly unrelated things, as in Gayle Pemberton's description in "Antidisestablishmentarianism" (Ch. 2): "He was a thin, small-boned man who looked to me far more *like* an Indian chief than *like* a black man."

The ability to create compelling images in picturesque language is an important element in communicating a writer's thoughts, feelings, and experiences. Creating a vivid picture or image in an audience's mind requires writers to use metaphors, similes, and other figures of speech. **Imagery** works by evoking a vivid picture in the audience's imagination. A simile compares one object or experience to another by using *like* or *as*. A metaphor applies a word or phrase to an object it does not literally denote in order to suggest the comparison. To be effective, metaphors must look at things in a fresh light to let the reader see a familiar subject in a new way.

Analogy, which is a comparison between two basically different things that have some points in common, is an extraordinarily useful tool that writers use to clarify subjects that otherwise might prove to be difficult to understand, unfamiliar, or hard to visualize. The greater the numbers of similarities that the writer is able to draw between what the audience finds familiar and the newer complex idea the writer is trying to clarify, the more successful the analogy. For example, Garrett Hardin in "Lifeboat Ethics" (Ch. 11) compares an affluent country to a lifeboat that is already almost full of people and compares immigrants from poor countries to people in the water who desperately wish to get into the lifeboat: "Since the boat has an unused excess capacity of ten more passengers, we could admit just ten more to it. But which ten do we let in?"

Hardin's tactics are based on getting his audience to agree that a country has a limited capacity to support a population, just as there are only so many seats in a lifeboat, and that if those begging for admission are taken into "our boat," the boat will swamp and everyone will drown.

In addition to clarifying abstract concepts and processes, analogies are ideally suited to transmit religious truths in the form of parables and metaphors. An aptly chosen metaphor can create a memorable image capable of conveying truth in a way that is permanent and vivid.

An effective analogy provides a way to shed new light on hidden, difficult, or complex ideas by relating them to everyday human experience. One of the most famous analogies ever conceived, Plato's "Allegory of the Cave" (Ch. 11), uses a series of comparisons to explore how lifelong conditioning deludes people into mistaking illusions for reality:

> Behold! Human beings living in an underground den, which had a mouth open toward the light and reaching all along the den; here they have been from their childhood, and have their legs and necks chained so that they cannot move, and can only see before them, being prevented by the chains from turning around their heads. Above and behind them is a fire blazing at a distance.

Plato explains that in this den the prisoners, who have never seen anything outside the cave, mistake shadows cast on the wall by reflected firelight for realities. If some were free to leave the cave, they would be dazzled by the sunlight. It is ironic, says Plato, that once their eyes had adjusted to the light, they would be unable, if they then returned to the cave, to see as well as the others. Moreover, if they persisted in trying to lead their fellow prisoners out of the cave into the light, the others would find their claim of greater light outside the cave ridiculous. Thus, each element in the analogy—the fire, the prisoners, the shadows, the dazzling light—offers an unparalleled means for grasping the Platonic ideal of truth as a greater reality beyond the illusory shadows of what we mistake as the "real" world.

Thus, analogies are extraordinarily useful to natural and social scientists, poets, and philosophers as an intellectual strategy and rhetorical technique for clarifying difficult subjects, explaining unfamiliar terms and processes, transmitting religious truths through parables, and spurring creativity in problem solving by opening the mind to new ways of looking at things.

Process Analysis   One of the most effective ways to clarify the nature of something is to explain how it works. **Process analysis** divides a complex procedure into separate and easy-to-understand steps in order to explain how something works, how something happened, or how an action should be performed. Process analysis requires the writer to include all necessary steps in the procedure and to demonstrate how each step is related to preceding and subsequent steps in the overall sequence. To be effective, process analysis should emphasize the significance of each step in the overall sequence and help the reader understand how each step emerges from the preceding stage and flows into the next.

For example, in "To Make Them Stand in Fear" (Ch. 8), Kenneth M. Stampp, a noted historian, investigates a past era in our country's history when blacks were brought to America as slaves. Stampp analyzes the instructions given by manuals that told slaveowners, step-by-step, how to break the spirit of newly transported blacks in order to change them into "proper" slaves:

> Here, then, was the way to produce the perfect slave: accustom him to rigid discipline, demand from him unconditional submission, impress upon him his innate inferiority, develop in him a paralyzing fear of white men, train him to adopt the master's code of good behavior, and instill in him a sense of complete dependence. This, at least, was the goal.

Stampp's analysis of source documents reveals that slaveowners used behavior modification techniques to produce "respectful" and "docile" slaves. The process began with a series of measures designed to enforce external discipline. Later on, attention shifted to measures designed to encourage psychological conditioning so that, in theory at least, the slave would control himself or herself through internalized perceptions of inferiority.

Causal Analysis   Whereas process analysis explains *how* something works, **causal analysis** seeks to discover *why* something happened, or why it will happen, by dividing an ongoing stream of events into causes and effects. Writers may proceed from a given effect and seek to discover what cause or chain of causes could have produced the observed effect, or to show how further effects will flow from a known cause.

Causal analysis is an invaluable analytical technique used in many fields of study. Because of the complexity of causal relationships, writers try to identify, as precisely as possible, the contributory factors in any causal sequence. The direct or immediate causes of the event are those most likely to have triggered the actual event. Yet, behind direct causes may lie indirect or remote causes that set the stage or create the framework in which the event could occur. By the same token, long-term future effects are much more difficult to identify than are immediate, short-term effects.

This technique of distinguishing between predisposing and triggering causes is used by Aldous Huxley, political essayist and author of *Brave New World* (1932), to answer the question of why one particular segment of the German population was so easily swayed by Hitler's rhetoric:

> Hitler made his strongest appeal to those members of the lower middle classes who had been ruined by the inflation of 1923, and then ruined all over again by the depression of 1929 and the following years. "The masses" of whom he speaks were these bewildered, frustrated and chronically anxious millions.

In this passage from "Propaganda Under a Dictatorship" (Ch. 4), Huxley uses causal analyis to emphasize that the people most likely to yield to **propaganda** were those whose security had been destroyed by previous financial disasters. That is, previous cycles of financial instability (the disastrous inflation of 1923 and the depression of 1929) played a crucial role in predisposing the lower middle classes, those whose security was most affected by the financial turmoil, to become receptive to Hitler's propaganda. Hitler, says Huxley, used techniques of propaganda—mass marches, repetition of slogans, scapegoating—to manipulate the segment of the population that was the least secure and the most fearful.

It is most important that causal analysis demonstrate the means (sometimes called the *agency*) by which an effect could have been produced. Writers are obligated to show how the specific causes they identify could have produced the effects in question.

Solving a Problem   Although not a rhetorical strategy as such, writers use techniques for **problem solving** to identify difficulties and apply theoretical models. Defining constraints, employing various search techniques, and checking solutions against relevant criteria are an important part of all academic and professional research.

The problem-solving process usually involves recognizing and defining the problem, using various search techniques to discover a solution, verifying the solution, and communicating it to a particular audience, who might need to know the history of the problem, the success or failure of previous attempts to solve it, and other relevant information.

Recognizing the Existence and Nature of the Problem   The first step in solving a problem is recognizing that a problem exists. Often, the magnitude of the problem is obvious from serious effects that the problem is causing. For example, in his analysis of the dangers posed by pollution, Thor Heyerdahl in "How to Kill an Ocean" (Ch. 6) describes the disastrous effects that already have beset the Great Lakes and alerts us to how vulnerable the ocean is, a concept that most people would find hard to believe:

> In the long run the ocean can be affected by the continued discharge of all modern man's toxic waste. One generation ago no one would have thought that the giant lakes of America could be polluted. Today they are, like the largest lakes of Europe. A few years ago the public was amazed to learn that industrial and urban refuse had killed the fish in Lake Erie. The enormous lake was dead.

Heyerdahl uses this dramatic evidence to persuade his readers to relinquish their concept of the ocean as a body of water so immense that it is immune to pollution.

Defining the Problem   When the problem has been clearly perceived, it is often helpful to present it as a single, clear-cut example. William A. Henry III in "In Defense of Elitism" (Ch. 3) uses the following situation to define the need for a more realistic view of who should go to college:

> U.S. colleges go on blithely "educating" many more prospective managers and professionals than the country is likely to need. In my own field, there are typically more students majoring in journalism at any given moment than there are journalists employed at all the daily newspapers in the U.S.

The way Henry frames this problem provides a context in which to understand the problem and a way to identify the most important criterion—efficiency in education—by which to evaluate solutions.

Verifying the Solution   When at last a solution is found after researchers have used various search techniques, it must meet all the tests specific to the problem and take into account all pertinent data uncovered during the search. For example, Lawrence Osborne reports in "Got Silk" (Ch. 9) that scientists had succeeded in genetically mixing spider genes with West African Dwarf goats to produce a transgenic species whose milk would contain spider silk, one of the strongest natural materials, with a host of useful applications:

> It occurred to Turner . . . that, theoretically, one could introduce foreign genes into an animal's mammary gland and get any given protein out of the animal without killing it, much as one milks a cow.

In his article, Osborne describes how the researchers (1) analyzed the nature of the problem, (2) created a set of procedures to solve it, (3) allocated resources for the most productive investigations, and (4) verified the result of their experiment, according to scientific criteria.

Argumentation and Persuasion   Some of the most interesting and effective writing you will read takes the form of **arguments** that seek to persuade a specific audience (colleagues, fellow researchers, or the general public) of the validity of a proposition or claim through logical reasoning supported by facts, examples, data, or other kinds of evidence.

The purpose of argument is the **persuasion** of an audience to accept the validity or probability of an idea, proposition, or claim. Essentially, a **claim** is an assertion that would be met with skepticism if it were not supported with sound evidence and persuasive reasoning. Formal arguments differ from assertions based on likes and dislikes or personal opinion. Unlike questions of personal taste, arguments rest on evidence, whether in the form of facts, examples, the testimony of experts, or statistics, which can be brought forward to objectively prove or disprove the thesis in question.

Readers expect that evidence cited to substantiate or refute assertions will be sound, accurate, and relevant and that conclusions will be drawn from this evidence according to the guidelines of logic. Readers also expect that the writer arguing in support of a proposition will acknowledge and answer objections put forth by the opposing side and will provide compelling evidence to support the writer's own position.

Although arguments explore important issues and espouse specific theories, the forms in which arguments appear vary according to the style and format of individual disciplines. Evidence in different fields of study can appear in a variety of formats, including laws, precedents, the interpretation of statistics, or the citation of authorities. The means used in constructing arguments depend on the audience within the discipline being addressed, the nature of the thesis being proposed, and the accepted methodology for that particular area of study.

In the liberal arts, critics evaluate and interpret works of fine art; review music, dance, drama, and film; and write literary analyses (see Aaron Copland's "Film Music," Ch. 10). Philosophers probe the moral and ethical implications of people's actions and advocate specific ways of meeting the ethical challenges posed by new technologies (see David Ewing Duncan's "DNA as Destiny," Ch. 9). Historians interpret political, military, and constitutional events; analyze their causes; and theorize about how the past influences the present (see Kenneth M. Stampp's "To Make Them Stand in Fear," Ch. 8).

In the political and social sciences, lawyers and constitutional scholars argue for specific ways of applying legal and constitutional theory to everyday problems (see Jonathan Kozol's "The Human Cost of an Illiterate Society," Ch. 3). Economists debate issues related to changes wrought by technology, distribution of income, unemployment, and commerce (see Juliet B. Schor's "The Culture of Consumerism," Ch. 5).

Political scientists look into how effectively governments initiate and manage social change, and they ask basic questions about the limits of governmental intrusion into individual rights (see Steven E. Barkan and Lynne L. Snowden's "Defining and Countering Terrorism," Ch. 8). Sociologists analyze statistics and trends to evaluate how successfully institutions accommodate social change (see Barbara Ehrenreich's "Nickel-and-Dimed," Ch. 8).

In the sciences, biologists as well as biochemists, zoologists, botanists, and other natural scientists propose theories to explain the interdependence of living things with their natural environment (see Gunjan Sinha's "You Dirty Vole," Ch. 6). Psychologists champion hypotheses based on physiological, experimental, social, and clinical research to explain various aspects of human behavior. Physicists, as well as mathematicians, astronomers, engineers, and computer scientists, put forward and defend hypotheses about the basic laws underlying manifestations of the physical world, from the microscopic to the cosmic (see the excerpt from Bill Gates's "The Road Ahead," Ch. 9).

Evaluating Tone   An important ability to develop in critical reading is making inferences about the writer from clues in the text. Looking beyond the facts to see what those facts imply requires readers to look carefully at writers' word choices, their level of knowledge, their use of personal experience, and the skill with which various elements of an essay are arranged. Inferences about a writer's frame of reference and values go beyond what is on the page and can help us get a sense of what the writer is like as a person.

Tone is a crucial element in establishing a writer's credibility. Tone is produced by the combined effect of word choice, sentence structure, and the writer's success in adapting his or her particular **voice** to the subject, the audience, and the occasion. When we try to identify and analyze the tone of a work, we are seeking to hear the actual "voice" of the author in order to understand how the writer intended the work to be perceived. It is important for writers to know what image of themselves they project. Writers should consciously decide on the particular style and tone that best suit the audience, the occasion, and the specific subject matter of the argument.

For example, Martin Luther King, Jr.'s speech "I Have a Dream" (Ch. 8) was delivered when King led a march of 250,000 people through Washington, D.C., to the Lincoln Memorial on the centennial of Lincoln's Emancipation Proclamation. The persuasive techniques that King uses are well suited to adapt his message of nonviolent protest to both his audience and the occasion.

King reminds his audience that the civil rights movement puts into action basic ideas contained in the Constitution. King reaffirms minority rights as a way of renewing aspirations put forward by the Founding Fathers of the United States and uses figurative language drawn from the Emancipation Proclamation and the Bible to reinforce his audience's emotional resolve to continue in their quest for equal rights:

> I say to you today, my friends, even though we face the difficulties of today and tomorrow, I still have a dream. It is a dream deeply rooted in the American dream. I have a dream that one day this nation will rise up and live out the true meaning of its creed: "We hold these truths to be self-evident, that all men are created equal." I have a dream that one day, on the red hills of Georgia, sons of former slaves and the sons of former slaveowners will be able to sit down together at the table of brotherhood.

The effectiveness of this speech depends in large part on the audience's sense of King as a man of high moral character. In arguments that appeal to the emotions as well as to the intellect, the audience's perception of the speaker as a person of the highest ethics, good character, and sound reason amplifies the logic of the discourse.

Irony, Humor, and Satire   A particular kind of tone encountered in many essays is called **irony.** Writers adopt this rhetorical strategy to express a discrepancy between opposites, between the ideal and the real, between the literal and the implied, and most often between the way things are and the way the writer thinks things ought to be.

Sometimes it is difficult to pick up the fact that not everything the writer says is intended to be taken literally. Authors occasionally say the opposite of what they mean to catch the attention of the reader. If your first response to an ironic statement is "Can the writer really be serious?" look for signals that the writer means the opposite of what is being said. One clear signal that the author is being ironic is a noticeable disparity between the tone and the subject. For example, Jonathan Swift in his essay "A Modest Proposal" (Ch. 8) presents a narrator who offers in a most reasonable, matter-of-fact way a proposal that Ireland solve its economic problems by slaughtering and exporting one-year-old children as foodstuffs.

Satire is an enduring form of argument that uses parody, irony, and caricature to poke fun at a subject, an idea, or a person. Tone is especially important in satire. The satirist frequently creates a mask, or **persona,** that is very different from the author's real self in order to shock the audience into a new awareness about an established institution or custom. Satirical works by Mark Twain (Ch. 6) and Umberto Eco (Ch. 9) assail folly, greed, corruption, pride, self-righteous complacency, cultural pretensions, hypocrisy, and other permanent targets of the satirist's pen.

RESPONDING TO WHAT YOU READ

When reading an essay that seems to embody a certain value system, try to examine any **assumptions** or beliefs the writer expects the audience to share. How are these assumptions related to the author's purpose? If you do not agree with these assumptions, has the writer provided sound reasons and evidence to persuade you to change your mind?

You might describe the author's tone or voice and try to assess how much it contributed to the essay. How effectively does the writer use authorities, statistics, or examples to support the claim? Does the author identify the assumptions or **values** on which his or her views are based? Are they ones with which you would agree or disagree? To what extent does the author use the emotional connotations of language to try to persuade the reader? Do you see anything unworkable or disadvantageous about the solutions offered as an answer to the problem the essay addresses? All these and many other ways of analyzing someone else's essay can be used to create your own. Here are some specific guidelines to help you.

When evaluating an essay, consider what the author's **purpose** is in writing it. Is it to inform, explain, solve a problem, make a recommendation, amuse, enlighten, or achieve some combination of these goals? How is the tone, or voice, the author projects related to the purpose in writing the essay?

You may find it helpful to write short summaries after each major section to determine whether you understand what the writer is trying to communicate. These summaries can then serve as a basis for an analysis of how successfully the author employs reasons, examples, statistics, and expert testimony to support and develop main points.

For example, if the essay you are analyzing cites authorities to support a claim, assess whether the authorities bring the most timely opinions to bear on the subject or display any obvious biases, and determine whether they are experts in that particular field. Watch for experts described as "often quoted" or "highly placed reliable sources" without accompanying names, credentials, or appropriate documentation. If the experts cited offer what purports to be a reliable interpretation of facts, consider whether the writer also quotes equally trustworthy experts who hold opposing views.

If statistics are cited to support a point, judge whether they derive from verifiable and trustworthy sources. Also, evaluate whether the author has interpreted them in ways that are beneficial to the case, whereas someone who held an opposing view could interpret them quite differently. If real-life examples are presented to support the author's opinions, determine whether they are representative or whether they are too atypical to be used as evidence. If the author relies on hypothetical examples or analogies to dramatize ideas that otherwise would be hard to grasp, judge whether these examples are too far-fetched to back up the claims being made. If the essay depends on the stipulated definition of a term that might be defined in different ways, check whether the author provides clear reasons to indicate why one definition rather than another is preferable.

As you list observations about the various elements of the article you are analyzing, take a closer look at the underlying assumptions and see whether you can locate and distinguish between those assumptions that are explicitly stated and those that are implicit. Once the author's assumptions or **premises** are identified, you can compare them with your own beliefs about the subject, determine whether these assumptions are commonly held, and make a judgment as to their validity. Would you readily agree with these assumptions? If not, has the author provided sound reasons and supporting evidence to persuade you to change your mind?

MARKING AS YOU READ

The most effective way to think about what you read is to make notes as you read. Making notes as you read forces you to go slowly and think carefully about each sentence. This process is sometimes called *annotating the text*, and all you need is a pen or a pencil. There are as many styles of annotating as there are readers, and you will discover your own favorite technique once you have done it a few times. Some readers prefer to underline major points or statements and jot down their reactions to them in the margin. Others prefer to summarize each paragraph or section to help them follow the author's line of thinking. Other readers circle key words or phrases necessary to understand the main ideas. Feel free to use your notes as a kind of conversation with the text. Ask questions. Express doubts. Mark unfamiliar words or phrases to look up later. If the paragraphs are not already numbered, you might wish to number them as you go to help you keep track of your responses. Try to distinguish the main ideas from supporting points and examples. Most important, go slowly and think about what you are reading. Try to discover whether the author makes a credible case for the conclusions reached. One last point: Take a close look at the idea expressed in the title before and after you read the essay to see how it relates to the main idea.

KEEPING A READING JOURNAL

The most effective way to keep track of your thoughts and impressions and to review what you have learned is to start a reading journal. The comments you record in your journal may express your reflections, observations, questions, and reactions to the essays you read. Normally, your journal would not contain lecture notes from class. A reading journal will allow you to keep a record of your progress during the term and can also reflect insights you gain during class discussions and questions you may want to ask, as well as unfamiliar words you intend to look up. Keeping a reading journal becomes a necessity if your composition course requires you to write a research paper that will be due at the end of the semester. Keep in mind that your journal is not something that will be corrected or graded, although some instructors may wish you to share your entries with the class.

Turning Annotations into Journal Entries   Although there is no set form for what a journal should look like, reading journals are most useful for converting your brief annotations into more complete entries that explore in depth your reactions to what you have read. Interestingly, the process of turning your annotations into journal entries will often produce surprising insights that will give you a new perspective.

Summarizing   Reading journals may also be used to record summaries of the essays you read. The value of summarizing is that it requires you to pay close attention to the reading in order to distinguish the main points from the supporting details. Summarizing tests your understanding of the material by requiring you to restate concisely the author's main ideas in your own words. First, create a list composed of sentences that express in your own words the essential idea of each paragraph or of each group of related paragraphs. Your previous underlining of topic sentences, main ideas, and key terms (as part of the process of critical reading) will help you follow the author's line of thought. Next, whittle down this list still further by eliminating repetitive ideas. Then formulate a thesis statement that expresses the main idea in the article. Start your summary with this thesis statement, and combine your notes so that the summary flows together and reads easily.

Remember that summaries should be much shorter (usually no longer than half a page) than the original text (whether the original is one page or twenty pages long) and should accurately reflect the central ideas of the article in as few words as possible. Try not to intrude your own opinions or critical evaluations into the summary. Besides requiring you to read the original piece more closely, summaries are necessary first steps in developing papers that synthesize materials from different sources. The test for a good summary, of course, is whether a person reading it without having read the original article would get an accurate, balanced, and complete account of the original material.

Using Your Reading Journal to Generate Ideas for Writing   You can use all the material in your reading journal (annotations converted to journal entries, reflections, observations, questions, rough and final summaries) to relate your own ideas to the ideas of the person who wrote the essay you are reading. Here are several different kinds of strategies you can use as you analyze an essay in order to generate material for your own:

1. What is missing in the essay? Information that is not mentioned is often just as significant as information the writer chose to include. First, you must already have summarized the main points in the article. Then, make up another list of points that are not discussed, that is, missing information that you would have expected an article of this kind to cover or touch on. Write down the possible reasons why this missing material has been omitted, censored, or downplayed. What possible purpose could the author have had? Look for vested interests or biases that could explain why information of a certain kind is missing.

2. You might analyze an essay in terms of what you already knew and what you didn't know about the issue. To do this, simply make a list of what concepts were already familiar to you and a second list of information or concepts that were new to you. Then write down three to five questions you would like answered about this new information and make a list of possible sources you might consult.

3. You might consider whether the author presents a solution to a problem. List the short-term and long-term consequences of the action the writer recommends. You might wish to evaluate the solution to see whether positive short-term benefits would be offset by possible negative long-term consequences not mentioned by the author. This might provide you with a starting point for your own essay.

4. After clearly stating what the author's position on an issue is, try to imagine other people in that society or culture who would view the same issue from a different perspective. How would the concerns of these people be different from those of the writer? Try to think of as many different people, representing as many different perspectives, as you can. Now, try to think of a solution that would satisfy both the author and at least one other person who holds a different viewpoint. Try to imagine that you are an arbitrator negotiating an agreement. How would your recommendation require both parties to compromise and reach an agreement?

READING FICTION

Works of **fiction** communicate intense, complex, deeply felt responses to human experiences that speak to the heart, mind, body, and imagination.

Although the range of situations that stories can offer is limitless, what makes any particular story enjoyable is the writer's capacity to present an interesting **plot**, believable characters, and convincing dialogue. The nature of the original events matters less than the writer's ability to make us feel the impact of this experience intellectually, physically, and emotionally. The writer who uses language in skillful and precise ways allows us to share the perceptions and feelings of people different from ourselves. Works of fiction not only can take us to parts of the world we may never have the opportunity to visit but can deepen our emotional capacity to understand what life is like for others in conditions very different from our own. We become more conscious of ourselves as individual human beings when our imaginations and emotions are fully involved. We value a story when through it we touch the aspirations, motives, and feelings of other people in diverse personal and cultural situations.

Works of fiction, as distinct from biographies and historical accounts, are imaginative works that tell a story. Fiction writers use language to re-create the emotional flavor of experiences and are free to restructure their accounts in ways that will create suspense and even build conflict. They can add to or take away from the known facts, expand or compress time, invent additional imaginative details, or even invent new characters or a narrator through whose eyes the story is told.

The oldest works of fiction took the form of **myths** and legends that described the exploits of heroes and heroines, gods and goddesses, and supernatural beings. Other ancient forms of literature include **fables** (stating explicit lessons using animal characters), **folk tales, fairy tales,** and **parables** (using analogies to suggest rather than state moral points or complex philosophical concepts) of the kind related by Jesus in the New Testament.

The modern short story differs from earlier narrative forms in emphasizing life as most people know it. The **short story** originated in the nineteenth century as a brief fictional prose narrative that was designed to be read in a single sitting. In a short story, all the literary elements of plot, **character(s), setting,** and the author's distinctive use of language work together to create a single effect. Short stories usually describe the experiences of one or two characters over the course of a series of related events. Realistic stories present sharply etched pictures of characters in real settings reacting to kinds of crises with which readers can identify. The emotions, reactions, perceptions, and motivations of the characters are explored in great detail. **Realism** is reflected in short stories ranging from Kate Chopin's "Désirée's Baby" (Ch. 5), written in the nineteenth century, through Raymond Carver's "Neighbors" (Ch. 2) to, most recently, Irene Zabytko's "Home Soil" (Ch. 7).

Other writers, reacting against the prevailing conventions of realistic fiction, create a kind of story in which everyday reality is not presented directly but is filtered through the perceptions, associations, and emotions of the main character. In these *nonrealistic* stories, the normal chronology of events is displaced by a psychological narrative that reflects the ebb and flow of the characters' feelings and associations. Nonrealistic stories may include fantastic, bizarre, or supernatural elements as well. We can see this alternative to the realistic story in Edgar Allan Poe's "The Masque of the Red Death" (Ch. 6) and in Joaquim María Machado de Assis's "A Canary's Ideas" (Ch. 3).

Although it is something we have done most of our lives, when we look at it closely reading is a rather mysterious activity. The individual interpretations readers bring to characters and events in the text make every story mean something slightly different to every reader. There are, however, some strategies all readers use: We instinctively draw on our own knowledge of human relationships in interpreting characters and incidents, we simultaneously draw on clues in the text to anticipate what will happen next, and we continuously revise our past impressions as we encounter new information.

At what points in the work were you required to imagine or anticipate what would happen next? How did you make use of the information the author gave you to generate a **hypothesis** about what lay ahead? To what extent do your own circumstances—gender, age, race, class, and culture—differ from those of the characters in the story, poem, or play? How might your reading of the text differ from that of other readers? Has the writer explored all the possibilities raised within the work? Has the writer missed any opportunities that you as the writer would have explored?

The New Millennium Reader offers works drawn from many cultural contexts reflecting diverse styles and perspectives. Fiction produced in the second half of the twentieth century differs in a number of important ways from that produced before World War II. Writers in this postmodern period avoid seeing events as having only one meaning and produce works that represent reality in unique, complex, and highly individual ways.

Contemporary writers have a great deal to say about the forces that shape ethnic, sexual, and racial identity in various cultural contexts. Unlike traditional works that presented social dilemmas in order to resolve them, **postmodernist** works underscore the difficulty of integrating competing ethnic, sexual, and racial identities within a single culture. This is especially apparent in Irene Zabytko's "Home Soil" (Ch. 7) and Andre Dubus's "The Fat Girl" (Ch. 1). Other writers address the ways different cultures define gender roles and class relationships in terms of power and powerlessness. These issues are explored in Kate Chopin's "Désirée's Baby" (Ch. 5) and Liliana Heker's "The Stolen Party" (Ch. 8).

READING POETRY

Poetry differs from other genres in that a **poem** achieves its effects with fewer words, compressing details into carefully organized forms in which sounds, words, and images work together to create a single intense experience. Poetry uses language in ways that communicate experience rather than simply give information. The difference between prose and poetry emerges quite clearly when you compare a **stanza** from Grace Caroline Bridges's poem "Lisa's Ritual, Age 10" (Ch. 5) with the same words punctuated as a sentence in prose:

> The wall is steady while she falls away: first the hands lost arms dissolving feet gone the legs disjointed body cracking down the center like a fault she falls inside slides down like dust like kitchen dirt slips off the dustpan into noplace a place where nothing happens, nothing ever happened.

Notice how in this **free verse** stanza from the poem the arrangement of the words and lines creates an entirely different relationship:

> The wall is steady
> while she falls   away:
>   first the hands   lost
> arms dissolving   feet gone
> the legs   dis-   jointed
>   body cracking down
>   the center like a fault
>   she falls inside
>   slides down like
>   dust   like kitchen dirt
>   slips off

> the dustpan into
>
>   noplace
>
> a place where
> nothing happens,
> nothing ever happened.

The way the words are arranged communicates the experience of the child's detachment, alienation, and sense of shock, whereas the same words in prose merely describe it.

Because it communicates an extraordinarily compressed moment of thought, feeling, or experience, poetry relies on figurative language, connotation, imagery, sound, and **rhythm.** Poetry evokes emotional associations through images whose importance is underscored by a rhythmic beat or pulse. Patterns of sounds and images emphasize and underscore distinct thoughts and emotions, appealing simultaneously to the heart, mind, and imagination. The rhythmic beat provides the sensuous element coupled with imagery that appeals to the senses and touches the heart. At the same time, the imagination is stimulated through unexpected combinations and perceptions and figurative language (similes, metaphors, **personification**) that allow the reader to see things in new ways. Because these effects work simultaneously, the experience of a poem is concentrated and intense.

Like fiction, poems may have a narrator (called a **speaker**), a particular point of view, and a distinctive tone and **style.**

Learning to enjoy what poetry has to offer requires the reader to pay close attention to specific linguistic details of sound and rhythm, **rhyme** and **meter, assonance** and **consonance, alliteration,** connotations of words, and the sensations, feelings, memories, and associations that these words evoke. After reading a poem, preferably aloud, try to determine who the speaker is. What situation does the poem describe? How might the title provide insight into the speaker's predicament? What attitude does the poet project toward the events described in the poem? Observe the language used by the speaker. What emotional state of mind is depicted? You might look for recurrent references to a particular subject and see whether these references illuminate some psychological truth.

Although it has a public use, poetry mainly unfolds private joys, tragedies, and challenges common to all people, such as the power of friendship, value of self-discovery, bondage of outworn traditions, delight in nature's beauty, devastation of war, achievement of self-respect, and despair over failed dreams. The universal elements in poetry bridge gaps in time and space and tie people together in expressing emotions shared by all people in different times, places, and cultures.

READING DRAMA

Drama, unlike fiction and poetry, is meant to be performed on a stage. The **script** of a play includes **dialogue** (conversation between two or more characters)—or a **monologue** (lines spoken by a single character to the audience)—and the playwright's stage directions.

Although the dramatist makes use of plot, characters, setting, and language, the nature of drama limits the playwright to presenting the events from an objective point of view. There are other important differences between short stories, novels, and drama as well. The dramatist must restrict the action in the play to what can be shown on the stage in two or three hours. Since plays must hold the attention of an audience, playwrights prefer obvious rather than subtle conflicts, clearly defined sequences of action, and fast-paced

exposition that is not weighed down by long descriptive or narrative passages. Everything in drama has to be shown directly, concretely, through vivid images of human behavior.

The **structure** of most plays begins with an exposition or introduction that introduces the characters, shows their relationship to one another, and provides the background information necessary for the audience or reader to understand the main conflict of the play. The essence of drama is **conflict.** Conflict is produced when an individual pursuing an objective meets with resistance either from another person, from society, from nature, or from an internal aspect of that individual's own personality. In the most effective plays, the audience can see the central conflict through the eyes of each character in the play. As the play proceeds, complications make the problem more difficult to solve and increase suspense as to whether the **protagonist,** or main character, or the opposing force (referred to as the **antagonist**) will triumph. In the **climax** of the play, the conflict reaches the height of emotional intensity, and one side achieves a decisive advantage over the other. This **crisis** is often the moment of truth, when characters see themselves and the situation clearly for the first time. The end of the play, or conclusion, explores the implications of the nature of the truth that has been realized and what the consequences will be.

Reading the script of a play is a very different kind of experience from seeing it performed on the stage. From a script containing dialogue and brief descriptions, you must visualize what the characters look like and sound like and imagine how they relate to one another. For example, try to imagine the following scene from *Trifles* by Susan Glaspell (Ch. 8). It dramatizes the beginning of an investigation of the murder of Mr. John Wright under circumstances that seem to point to his wife.

COUNTY ATTORNEY. And what did Mrs. Wright do when she knew that you had gone for the coroner?

HALE. She moved from that chair to this one over here (*Pointing to a small chair in the corner.*) and just sat there with her hands held together and looking down. I got a feeling that I ought to make some conversation, so I said I had come in to see if John wanted to put in a telephone, and at that she started to laugh, and then she stopped and looked at me—scared. (*The County Attorney, who has had his notebook out, makes a note.*) I dunno, maybe it wasn't scared. I wouldn't like to say it was. Soon Harry got back, and then Dr. Lloyd came, and you, Mr. Peters, and so I guess that's all I know that you don't.

COUNTY ATTORNEY. (*Looking around.*) I guess we'll go upstairs first—and then out to the barn and around there. (*To the Sheriff.*) You're convinced that there was nothing important here—nothing that would point to any motive.

SHERIFF. Nothing here but kitchen things.

How do you stage this **scene** in your mind? What do the County Attorney, a neighboring farmer (Mr. Hale), and the Sheriff look like? What are they wearing? Keep in mind that Hale is a farmer and might be dressed in overalls while the County Attorney might be in a suit and the Sheriff in a uniform. What do their voices sound like? How do you imagine the interior of the farmhouse where this conversation takes place? What emotions are reflected in the faces of each at various points in the scene? In all of these and countless other details, the reader must play a vital role in bringing the scene to life by making the kinds of decisions that would be delegated to the director, the set designer, the costume designer, and the actors in a stage production.

LITERARY WORKS IN CONTEXT

Since no short story, poem, drama, or essay is written in a vacuum, a particularly useful way of studying works of **literature** entails discovering the extent to which a work reflects or incorporates the historical, cultural, literary, and personal contexts in which it was written. Although works vary in what they require readers to know already, in most cases knowing more about the **context** in which the work was written will enhance the reader's understanding and enjoyment. For this reason, the information contained in the biographical sketches that precede each selection can be quite useful.

Investigating the psychological or **biographical context** in which the work was written assumes that the facts of an author's life are particularly relevant to a full understanding of the work. For example, the predicament confronting the speaker in Linda Pastan's poem "Ethics" (Ch. 11) articulates a problem the poet confronted in her own life. Similarly, we can assume that Charlotte Perkins Gilman's account of the narrator's decline into madness in her story "The Yellow Wallpaper" (Ch. 1) grew out of the author's own experiences. Despite the presumed relevance of an author's life, especially if the work seems highly autobiographical, we should remember that literature does not simply report events; it imaginatively re-creates experience.

The information that precedes each selection can be useful in a number of ways. For example, the reader can better understand a single story, poem, or play by comparing how an author has treated similar subjects and concerns in other works. Speeches, interviews, lectures, and essays by authors often provide important insights into the contexts in which a particular literary work was created. For example, Linda Hogan's humanistic perspective in her essay "Waking Up the Rake" (Ch. 6) is also apparent in her poem "Workday" (Ch. 3).

Placing individual works within the author's total repertoire is another way of studying works in their context. You can compare different works by the same author or compare different stages in the composition of the same work by studying subsequent revisions in different published versions of a story, poem, or play. Authors often address themselves to the important political and social issues of their time. For example, Bruce Springsteen's song "Streets of Philadelphia" (Ch. 5) can be understood as a protest against society's treatment of those with AIDS in its poignant depiction of the consequences in the lives of those afflicted with this disease.

In studying the **social context** of a work, ask yourself what dominant social values the work dramatizes, and try to determine whether the author approves or disapproves of particular social values by the way in which the characters are portrayed. Or you might analyze how the author describes or draws upon the manners, mores, customs, rituals, or codes of conduct of a specific society at a particular time, as does Kate Chopin in "Désirée's Baby" (Ch. 5), a story that dramatizes the human consequences of racism in the South at the turn of the nineteenth century.

Studying the **historical context** in which a work is written means identifying how features of the work reveal important historical, political, economic, social, intellectual, or religious currents and problems of the time. Think how useful it would be, for example, to know what issues were at stake in Cyprus in the 1950s and how they are reflected in Panos Ioannides's story "Gregory" (Ch. 8).

In an analysis of any work, the title, names of characters, references to places and events, or topical **allusions** may provide important clues to the work's original sources. For example, has the writer chosen to interweave historical incidents and figures with characters and events of his or her own creation and, if so, to what effect? In any case, simply knowing more about the circumstances under which a work was written will add to your enjoyment and give you a broader understanding of the essay, short story, poem, or play.

READING AND ANALYZING VISUAL TEXTS

A prominent feature of this anthology is that visual images accompany some of the readings. They are quite similar to those you see every day, often without really noticing them. They can include items as diverse as pop-up ads on the Internet, book covers, photos in travel brochures, reproductions of works of art, still life photography, architectural layouts, greeting cards, postcards, editorial cartoons and caricatures, catalogue photos of products, magazine covers, ads for nonprofit organizations, spreads in fashion magazines, menu photos in restaurants, postage stamps, billboards, announcements on park benches and bus shelters, displays of childrens' drawings in banks and supermarkets, personal snapshots, photos that accompany articles in newspapers, bumper stickers, concert programs and playbills, CD covers, film posters, matchbook covers, designer logos, and, of course, images in textbooks like this one.

In addition to these purely visual images, we are innundated by images (on television, in films, and on Web pages) whose effectiveness is enhanced by sound and movement. Fortunately, many of the same considerations that help us analyze a written text can also serve us in analyzing the rhetoric of visual texts.

For every visual image, the first question to ask is, who is the likely *audience?* The general public? Or some specialized segment of the general population, such as children, teenagers, senior citizens, parents, young professionals, baby boomers, men, women, or particular ethnic or racial groups? What might this intended audience be expected to know, believe, or feel about this particular image? For example, if you compare the ads on different kinds of television shows—soap operas, late-night talk shows, Monday night football, Saturday morning cartoons, cooking shows—you will observe different kinds of products being advertised and, correspondingly, different marketing appeals targeted for specific audiences.

The next thing to determine is the *purpose* for which the visual image was created. As with written texts, images may explain or inform, persuade, or entertain. Unlike the case in written texts, however, one of these usually predominates. For example, news photographs are primarily intended to inform an audience by showing events and persons. Ads obviously are intended to persuade while most films and television shows are intended to entertain.

We can look at an image to see how it illustrates a *subject* or topic. Looked at in this way, the image serves the same function as clear-cut examples do in a written text. They clarify, illustrate, or support the main idea. For example, does a CD cover show a picture of the performer(s), or does it show an image that evokes a feeling or expresses a theme? Does an ad show a product in a literal way, or does it use images of celebrities, supermodels, or prominent athletes to promote the product's mystique? Or is the ad intended to offset criticism (as with oil or chemical companies) by highlighting the company's efforts to protect the environment?

In general, visual texts are much more closely tied to specific *occasions* than are written texts. For example, does a cartoon strip reflect a current issue? Is a billboard or bumper sticker part of a political campaign? Does an ad introduce a new product or take advantage of a current trend? Is a public sculpture intended to commemorate a famous person or notable event?

Last, what does the image suggest about the *artist or creator* who designed the image for a given audience, purpose, and occasion? This is analogous to analyzing a written text where the author is known, or at least is knowable.

ELEMENTS OF DESIGN

We analyze written texts in terms of rhetorical techniques. So, too, in understanding visual texts we can analyze the formal elements of design (balance, proportion, movement, contrast, and unity) according to basic principles that determine how we "read" an image in both a literal and figurative sense.

Our feeling that a design is *balanced* is determined by how symmetical or asymmetrical the image is; if the top and bottom or right and left sides are of equal proportion or mirror each other, the effect is one of stability. For example, see the sheet music cover for the film *Philadelphia;* its right and left sides mirror each other. The effect is formal and static (and aptly communicates the conventional society in which an AIDS victim, Tom Hanks, and his lawyer, Denzel Washington, fight for equal rights). By contrast, an asymmetrical design will suggest informality and dynamic movement, as does the publicity photo for Beyoncé.

Next, the relative size of elements in a design will create a sense of *proportion* and determine what we notice first, second, and so on. By adjusting these elements, the designer can suggest an implicit agenda as to what is most important and least important.

We are accustomed to reading a page of text, and our sense of *movement* is created by the fact that we read from left to right and from top to bottom. However, the size and arrangment of elements in a visual text can make us scan differently. Horizontal and vertical lines in a two-dimensional image will suggest stability and lack of movement, whereas diagonal or angular lines imply movement and energy. For example, Beyoncé's photo appears to catch her in a dynamic gesture that emphasizes her energy as both singer and dancer, whereas a static pose would have simply shown her as a singer.

Visual images can also suggest an agenda through *contrast* of size, shape, and color and by placing the subject in sharp focus in the foreground.

When an image is effective, all the preceding elements (balance, proportion, movement, and contrast) work together to produce a feeling of *unity,* a sense that the image is complete in and of itself. Most ads are designed to function this way.

READING IMAGES AS CULTURAL SIGNS

Beyond these rhetorical elements (audience, purpose, topic, occasion, and designer or artist) and the principles of design that create moods and communicate messages, visual texts can also be **read** as signs for what they reveal about the surrounding **culture.**

Cultural **signs** can include artifacts, objects, events, images, products, gestures, sounds, or indeed almost anything that when analyzed reveals something meaningful about a culture, its assumptions, values, beliefs, and struggles. The process of "decoding" these underlying meanings requires us to move from a literal analysis of the design principles in art reproductions, photographs, advertisements, and cartoons in order to discover the explicit and implicit messages conveyed and to think critically about the agendas of those who wish to influence our behavior.

SEMIOTICS

The study of images for what they suggest about our culture puts us in a situation similar to that of anthropologists who discover and try to decipher the meaning of artifacts. Just as anthropologists have to form hypotheses about the context within which these objects and artifacts have meaning, so practitioners of **semiotics** (the study of signs) always try to recontextualize the meaning of any single sign or image by putting

it in a broader cultural context. We do this by identifying the current themes, and issues of the moment that are reflected in the image (or visual text) and by becoming
aware of the larger underlying system in which the sign functions. The key to interpreting ads and other cultural artifacts is to mentally link them to the associations,
similarities, and differences that collectively make up that particular sign system (in
the next image for example, the themes are finance, the Internet, religion, and vacations
at the beach).

ANALYZING AN ADVERTISEMENT

Just how this works can be seen by analyzing a rather interesting **advertisement** that
appeared a few years ago for a financial service offered by an Internet portal, Yahoo!
Since the ad is selling a service ("up-to-the-minute financial news. Stock quotes. Market Research. 24 hours a day") rather than a product, it uses an amusing photograph
of nuns jumping in the surf to promote its financial Web site. The design of the ad is
highly effective: As we scan the page, we read the small text in the upper left-hand corner (with the alliteration of "rolling" or "wallowing") and see the happy users of the
service (who are nuns). The text suggests a stark choice of either rolling in the surf or
wallowing in self-pity. The nuns' sense of buoyancy and elation is suggested by the
large floating circle that contains the scene. The ad tells the story that the nuns clicked
on Yahoo! (indicated by the icon), acted on timely information, and, in the words of
the caption, "got out before the market crashed." Notice how the outlined thin rectangle

Get that "I got out before the market crashed" feeling.

Yahoo! Finance

contrasts with the radiating circles, to underscore the contrast between anxiety and relief. The radiating circles emanating from the Yahoo! icon reinforce the positive associations of interconnectedness and timely information.

As a cultural sign, the ad makes us smile because it is incongruous that (1) nuns would be as materialistic as the rest of us and that (2) they would be frolicking in the surf in their habits. Underlying the ad are a number of sign systems that take the form of visual puns. We "surf" the Internet, and the choice of nuns conspicuously singles out a group that renounced materialism and "got out" of the materialistic world. This ad appeared when the dot-com bubble was about to burst, and thus the need for such a financial service was certainly timely. Also notice (in the lower right-hand corner) that the advertisers use the name of the service as a verb and reinforce the sense of euphoria implicit in the term (Yahoo!) in the accompanying picture. As we can see from this ad, images are really another form of text that tell stories about ourselves, our culture, and our world.

Pablo Picasso, **The Dream (La Reve),** *January 24, 1932.*
Oil on canvas, 130 × 97 cm. Private collection. Art Resource, NY. © ARS, NY.

Reflections on Experience

I am being frank about myself in this book. I tell of my first mistake on page 850.

HENRY KISSINGER, THE OBSERVER (LONDON)

THE AUTHORS IN THIS CHAPTER ARE MOTIVATED by the desire to understand crucial life experiences and to share them with others. For example, the essays by Fritz Peters, Douchan Gersi, and Nasdijj explore moments that proved to be decisive turning points in the authors' lives. Jill Nelson, Annie Dillard, Judith Ortiz Cofer, and Marcel Proust recover pivotal memories that illuminate the directions their lives have taken. An essay by Beryl Markham draws us into the private world of a pioneering aviator.

In works of fiction writers can add to known facts, expand or compress events, build suspense, and invent characters including a narrator to tell the story. For example, Charlotte Perkins Gilman creates a story that parallels her own experiences as a young woman who suffered postpartum depression. So, too, Andre Dubus explores the lifelong consequences for a young girl of the social pressures to be thin.

The poems in this chapter are personal reminiscences that allow us to share the perceptions of the speaker. In a sonnet, William Shakespeare discovers that the memory of someone he loved gave his life meaning. Barbara Kingsolver gives us a profound insight into alienation, and Anna Kamieńska explores the fleeting nature of human existence. Sara Teasdale realizes that being independent and self-sufficient were the values she cherished most.

NONFICTION

Jill Nelson

. . . .

Jill Nelson, born in 1952, is a native New Yorker and a graduate of the City College of New York and Columbia University's School of Journalism. A journalist for fifteen years, she is a frequent contributor to Essence, U.S.A. Weekend, the Village Voice, *and* Ms. *In 1986 she went to work for* The Washington Post's *new Sunday magazine as the only black woman reporter in a bastion of elite journalism, an experience she described in* Volunteer Slavery: My Authentic Negro Experience *(1993). Her latest books are* Straight, No Chaser: How I Became a Grown-Up Black Woman *(1997) and* Sexual Healing *(2003). In "Number One!" she reflects on the importance of her father's influence on her life.*

NUMBER ONE!

That night I dream about my father, but it is really more a memory than a dream.

"Number one! Not two! Number one!" my father intones from the head of the breakfast table. The four of us sit at attention, two on each side of the ten-foot teak expanse, our brown faces rigid. At the foot, my mother looks up at my father, the expression on her face a mixture of pride, anxiety, and, could it be, boredom? I am twelve. It is 1965.

"You kids have got to be, not number two," he roars, his dark face turning darker from the effort to communicate. He holds up his index and middle fingers. "But number—" here, he pauses dramatically, a preacher going for revelation, his four children a rapt congregation, my mother a smitten church sister. "Number one!"

These last words he shouts while lowering his index finger. My father has great, big black hands, long, perfectly shaped fingers with oval nails so vast they seem landscapes all their own. The half moons leading to the cuticle take up most of the nail and seem ever encroaching, threatening to swallow up first his fingertips, then his whole hand. I always wondered if he became a dentist just to mess with people by putting those enormous fingers in their mouths, each day surprising his patients and himself by the delicacy of the work he did.

Years later my father told me that when a woman came to him with an infant she   5
asserted was his, he simply looked at the baby's hands. If they lacked the size, enormous nails, and half-moon cuticles like an ocean eroding the shore of the fingers, he dismissed them.

Early on, what I remember of my father were Sunday morning breakfasts and those hands, index finger coyly lowering, leaving the middle finger standing alone.

When he shouted "Number one!" that finger seemed to grow, thicken and harden, thrust up and at us, a phallic symbol to spur us, my sister Lynn, fifteen, brothers Stanley and Ralph, thirteen and nine, on to greatness, to number oneness. My father's rich, heavy voice rolled down the length of the table, breaking and washing over our four trembling bodies.

When I wake up I am trembling again, but it's because the air conditioner, a luxury in New York but a necessity in D.C., is set too high. I turn it down, check on Misu,[1] light a cigarette, and think about the dream.

It wasn't until my parents had separated and Sunday breakfasts were no more that I faced the fact that my father's symbol for number one was the world's sign language for "fuck you." I know my father knew this, but I still haven't figured out what he meant by it. Were we to become number one and go out and fuck the world? If we didn't, would life fuck us? Was he intentionally sending his children a mixed message? If so, what was he trying to say?

I never went to church with my family. While other black middle-class families journeyed to Baptist church on Sundays, both to thank the Lord for their prosperity and donate a few dollars to the less fortunate brethren they'd left behind, we had what was reverentially known as "Sunday breakfast." That was our church.

In the dining room of the eleven-room apartment we lived in, the only black family in a building my father had threatened to file a discrimination suit to get into, my father delivered the gospel according to him. The recurring theme was the necessity that each of us be "number one," but my father preached about whatever was on his mind: current events, great black heroes, lousy black sell-outs, our responsibility as privileged children, his personal family history.

His requirements were the same as those at church: that we be on time, not fidget, hear and heed the gospel, and give generously. But Daddy's church boasted no collection plate; dropping a few nickels into a bowl would have been too easy. Instead, my father asked that we absorb his lessons and become what he wanted us to be, number one. He never told us what that meant or how to get there. It was years before I was able to forgive my father for not being more specific. It was even longer before I understood and accepted that he couldn't be.

Like most preachers, my father was stronger on imagery, oratory, and instilling fear than he was on process. I came away from fifteen years of Sunday breakfasts knowing that to be number two was not enough, and having no idea what number one was or how to become it, only that it was better.

When I was a kid, I just listened, kept a sober face, and tried to understand what was going on. Thanks to my father, my older sister Lynn and I, usually at odds, found spiritual communion. The family dishwashers, our spirits met wordlessly as my father talked. We shared each other's anguish as we watched egg yolk harden on plates, sausage fat congeal, chicken livers separate silently from gravy.

We all had our favorite sermons. Mine was the "Rockefeller wouldn't let his dog shit in our dining room" sermon.

"You think we're doing well?" my father would begin, looking into each of our four faces. We knew better than to venture a response. For my father, even now, conversations are lectures. Please save your applause—and questions—until the end.

"And we are," he'd answer his own query. "We live on West End Avenue, I'm a professional, your mother doesn't have to work, you all go to private school, we go to

10

15

Martha's Vineyard in the summer. But what we have, we have because 100,000 other black people haven't made it. Have nothing! Live like dogs!"

My father has a wonderfully expressive voice. When he said dogs, you could almost hear them whimpering. In my head, I saw an uncountable mass of black faces attached to the bodies of mutts, scrambling to elevate themselves to a better life. For some reason, they were always on 125th Street, under the Apollo Theatre marquee. Years later, when I got political and decided to be the number-one black nationalist, I was thrilled by the notion that my father might have been inspired by Claude McKay's[2] poem that begins, "If we must die, let it not be like dogs."

"There is a quota system in this country for black folks, and your mother and me were allowed to make it," my father went on. It was hard to imagine anyone allowing my six-foot-three, suave, smart, take-no-shit father to do anything. Maybe his use of the word was a rhetorical device.

"Look around you," he continued. With the long arm that supported his heavy   20
hand he indicated the dining room. I looked around. At the eight-foot china cabinet gleaming from the weekly oiling administered by Margie, our housekeeper, filled to bursting with my maternal grandmother's china and silver. At the lush green carpeting, the sideboard that on holidays sagged from the weight of cakes, pies, and cookies, at the paintings on the walls. We were living kind of good, I thought. That notion lasted only an instant.

My father's arm slashed left. It was as though he had stripped the room bare. I could almost hear the china crashing to the floor, all that teak splintering, silver clanging.

"Nelson Rockefeller wouldn't let his dog shit in here!" my father roared. "What we have, compared to what Rockefeller and the people who rule the world have, is nothing. Nothing! Not even good enough for his dog. You four have to remember that and do better than I have. Not just for yourselves, but for our people, black people. You have to be number one."

My father went on, but right about there was where my mind usually started drifting. I was entranced by the image of Rockefeller's dog—which I imagined to be a Corgi or Afghan or Scottish Terrier—bladder and rectum full to bursting, sniffing around the green carpet of our dining room, refusing to relieve himself.

The possible reasons for this fascinated me. Didn't he like green carpets? Was he used to defecating on rare Persian rugs and our 100 percent wool carpeting wasn't good enough? Was it because we were black? But weren't dogs colorblind?

I've spent a good part of my life trying to figure out what my father meant by   25
number one. Born poor and dark in Washington, I think he was trying, in his own way, to protect us from the crushing assumptions of failure that he and his generation grew up with. I like to think he was simply saying, like the army, "Be all that you can be," but I'm still not sure. For years, I was haunted by the specter of number two gaining on me, of never having a house nice enough for Rockefeller dog shit, of my father's middle finger admonishing me. It's hard to move forward when you're looking over your shoulder.

---

[2]*Claude McKay (1889–1948)*: African-American poet.

When I was younger, I didn't ask my father what he meant. By the time I was confident enough to ask, my father had been through so many transformations—from dentist to hippie to lay guru—that he'd managed to forget, or convince himself he'd forgotten, those Sunday morning sermons. When I brought them up he'd look blank, his eyes would glaze over, and he'd say something like, "Jill, what are you talking about? With your dramatic imagination you should have been an actress."

But I'm not an actress. I'm a journalist, my father's daughter. I've spent a good portion of my life trying to be a good race woman and number one at the same time. Tomorrow, I go to work at the *Washington Post* magazine, a first. Falling asleep, I wonder if that's the same as being number one.

Questions for Discussion and Writing

1. What message did Jill Nelson's father wish to instill during their Sunday breakfasts?
2. How has Nelson's life been influenced by her attempt to understand and act on her father's advice?
3. Is there a member of your family who has been particularly influential in shaping your attitudes and expectations? Describe this person, and give some examples of how your life has been changed because of the expectations.

Fritz Peters

Fritz Peters's (1916–1979) association with the philosopher and mystic George Gurdjieff began when Peters attended a school founded by Gurdjieff in Fontainebleau, France, where he spent four and a half years between 1924 and 1929. His experiences with Gurdjieff were always unpredictable and often enigmatic and rewarding. Peters wrote two books about his experiences, Boyhood with Gurdjieff *(1964) and* Gurdjieff Remembered *(1965). In the following essay, Peters reveals the highly unconventional methods Gurdjieff used to compel his protégé to develop compassion.*

BOYHOOD WITH GURDJIEFF

The Saturday evening after Gurdjieff's return from America, which had been in the middle of the week, was the first general "assembly" of everyone at the Prieuré,[1] in the study-house. The study-house was a separate building, originally an airplane hangar. There was a linoleum-covered raised stage at one end. Directly in front of the stage there was a small, hexagonal fountain, equipped electrically so that various coloured lights played on the water. The fountain was generally used only during the playing of music on the piano which was to the left of the stage as one faced it.

The main part of the building, from the stage to the entrance at the opposite end, was carpeted with oriental rugs of various sizes, surrounded by a small fence which made a large, rectangular open space. Cushions, covered by fur rugs, surrounded the sides of this rectangle in front of the fence, and it was here that most of the students

---

[1]*Prieuré:* a priory; a large chateau in Fountainebleau, France, where G. I. Gurdjieff conducted his school.

would normally sit. Behind the fence, at a higher level, were built-up benches, also covered with Oriental rugs, for spectators. Near the entrance of the building there was a small cubicle, raised a few feet from the floor, in which Gurdjieff habitually sat, and above this there was a balcony which was rarely used and then only for "important" guests. The cross-wise beams of the ceiling had painted material nailed to them, and the material hung down in billows, creating a cloud-like effect. It was an impressive interior—with a church-like feeling about it. One had the impression that it would be improper, even when it was empty, to speak above a whisper inside the building.

On that particular Saturday evening, Gurdjieff sat in his accustomed cubicle, Miss Madison sat near him on the floor with her little black book on her lap, and most of the students sat around, inside the fence, on the fur rugs. New arrivals and "spectators" or guests were on the higher benches behind the fence. Mr. Gurdjieff announced that Miss Madison would go over all the "offences" of all the students and that proper "punishments" would be meted out to the offenders. All of the children, and perhaps I, especially, waited with bated breath as Miss Madison read from her book, which seemed to have been arranged, not alphabetically, but according to the number of offences committed. As Miss Madison had warned me, I led the list, and the recitation of my crimes and offences was a lengthy one.

Gurdjieff listened impassively, occasionally glancing at one or another of the offenders, sometimes smiling at the recital of a particular misdemeanour, and interrupting Miss Madison only to take down, personally, the actual number of individual black marks. When she had completed her reading, there was a solemn, breathless silence in the room and Gurdjieff said, with a heavy sigh, that we had all created a great burden for him. He said then that he would give out punishments according to the number of offences committed. Naturally, I was the first one to be called. He motioned to me to sit on the floor before him and then had Miss Madison re-read my offences in detail. When she had finished, he asked me if I admitted all of them. I was tempted to refute some of them, at least in part, and to argue extenuating circumstances, but the solemnity of the proceedings and the silence in the room prevented me from doing so. Every word that had been uttered had dropped on the assemblage with the clarity of a bell. I did not have the courage to voice any weak defence that might have come to my mind, and I admitted that the list was accurate.

With another sigh, and shaking his head at me as if he was very much put upon, ⁵ he reached into his pocket and pulled out an enormous roll of bills. Once again, he enumerated the number of my crimes, and then laboriously peeled off an equal number of notes. I do not remember exactly how much he gave me—I think it was ten francs for each offence—but when he had finished counting, he handed me a sizeable roll of francs. During this process, the entire room practically screamed with silence. There was not a murmur from anyone in the entire group, and I did not even dare to glance in Miss Madison's direction.

When my money had been handed to me, he dismissed me and called up the next offender and went through the same process. As there were a great many of us, and there was not one individual who had not done something, violated some rule during his absence, the process took a long time. When he had gone through the list, he turned to Miss Madison and handed her some small sum—perhaps ten francs, or the equivalent of one "crime" payment—for her, as he put it, "conscientious fulfilment of her obligations as director of the Prieuré."

We were all aghast; we had been taken completely by surprise, of course. But the main thing we all felt was a tremendous compassion for Miss Madison. It seemed to me a senselessly cruel, heartless act against her. I have never known Miss Madison's feelings about this performance; except for blushing furiously when I was paid, she showed no obvious reaction to anything at all, and even thanked him for the pittance he had given her.

The money that I had received amazed me. It was, literally, more money than I had ever had at one time in my life. But it also repelled me. I could not bring myself to do anything with it. It was not until a few days later, one evening when I had been summoned to bring coffee to Gurdjieff's room, that the subject came up again. I had had no private, personal contact with him—in the sense of actually talking to him, for instance—since his return. That evening—he was alone—when I had served him his coffee, he asked me how I was getting along; how I felt. I blurted out my feelings about Miss Madison and about the money that I felt unable to spend.

He laughed at me and said cheerfully that there was no reason why I should not spend the money any way I chose. It was my money, and it was a reward for my activity of the past winter. I said I could not understand why I should have been rewarded for having been dilatory about my jobs and having created only trouble.

Gurdjieff laughed again and told me that I had much to learn. 10

"What you not understand," he said, "is that not everyone can be troublemaker, like you. This important in life—is ingredient, like yeast for making bread. Without trouble, conflict, life become dead. People live in status-quo, live only by habit, automatically, and without conscience. You good for Miss Madison. You irritate Miss Madison all time—more than anyone else, which is why you get most reward. Without you, possibility for Miss Madison's conscience fall asleep. This money should really be reward from Miss Madison, not from me. You help keep Miss Madison alive."

I understood the actual, serious sense in which he meant what he was saying, but I said that I felt sorry for Miss Madison, that it must have been a terrible experience for her when she saw us all receiving those rewards.

He shook his head at me, still laughing. "You not see or understand important thing that happen to Miss Madison when give money. How you feel at time? You feel pity for Miss Madison, no? All other people also feel pity for Miss Madison, too."

I agreed that this was so.

"People not understand about learning," he went on. "Think necessary talk all 15 time, that learn through mind, through words. Not so. Many things can only learn with feeling, even from sensation. But because man talk all time—use only formulatory centre—people not understand this. What you not see other night in studyhouse is that Miss Madison have new experience for her. Is poor woman, people not like, people think she funny—they laugh at. But other night, people not laugh. True, Miss Madison feel uncomfortable, feel embarrassed when I give money, feel shame perhaps. But when many people also feel for her sympathy, pity, compassion, even love, she understand this but not right away with mind. She feel, for first time in life, sympathy from many people. She not even know then that she feel this, but her life change; with you, I use you like example, last summer you hate Miss Madison. Now you not hate, you not think funny, you feel sorry. You even like Miss Madison. This good for her even if she not know right away—you will show; you cannot hide this from her, even if wish, cannot hide. So she now have friend, when used to be enemy. This good thing which I do for Miss Madison. I not concerned she understand this now—someday she understand and make her feel warm in heart. This unusual experience—this warm feeling—for such personality as Miss Madison who not have charm, who not friendly in self. Someday, perhaps even soon, she have good feeling because many people feel sorry, feel compassion for her. Someday she even understand what I do and even like me for this. But this kind learning take long time."

I understood him completely and was very moved by his words. But he had not finished.

"Also good thing for you in this," he said. "You young, only boy still, you not care about other people, care for self. I do this to Miss Madison and you think I do bad thing. You feel sorry, you not forget, you think I do bad thing to her. But now you understand not so. Also, good for you, because you feel about other person—you identify with Miss Madison, put self in her place, also regret what you do. Is necessary put self in place of other person if wish understand and help. This good for your conscience, this way is possibility for you learn not hate Miss Madison. All people same—stupid, blind, human. If I do bad thing, this make you learn love other people, not just self."

Questions for Discussion and Writing

1. How did Gurdjieff's allotment of rewards violate conventional expectations? What consequences did this have in changing Peters's view of Miss Madison?
2. What knowledge of human nature is implied in Gurdjieff's ability to create such an emotionally challenging event?
3. Write about a personal experience that forced you to completely reevaluate your attitude toward another person or group.

Beryl Markham

Beryl Markham (1902–1986) achieved renown when she became the first person to fly solo across the Atlantic from England to America (a journey of over twenty-one hours). Hemingway said of her, "She can write rings around all of us who consider ourselves as writers." In this final chapter of West with the Night *(1942), Markham describes the harrowing conditions of this flight.*

How does Beryl Markham identify herself in this photo?

WEST WITH THE NIGHT

I have seldom dreamed a dream worth dreaming again, or at least none worth recording. Mine are not enigmatic dreams; they are peopled with characters who are plausible and who do plausible things, and I am the most plausible amongst them. All the characters in my dreams have quiet voices like the voice of the man who telephoned me at Elstree one morning in September of nineteen-thirty-six and told me that there was rain and strong head winds over the west of England and over the Irish Sea, and that there were variable winds and clear skies in mid-Atlantic and fog off the coast of Newfoundland.

"If you are still determined to fly the Atlantic this late in the year," the voice said, "the Air Ministry suggests that the weather it is able to forecast for tonight, and for tomorrow morning, will be about the best you can expect."

The voice had a few others things to say, but not many, and then it was gone, and I lay in bed half-suspecting that the telephone call and the man who made it were only parts of the mediocre dream I had been dreaming. I felt that if I closed my eyes the unreal quality of the message would be re-established, and that, when I opened them again, this would be another ordinary day with its usual beginning and its usual routine.

But of course I could not close my eyes, nor my mind, nor my memory. I could lie there for a few moments—remembering how it had begun, and telling myself, with senseless repetition, that by tomorrow morning I should either have flown the Atlantic to America—or I should not have flown it. In either case this was the day I would try.

I could stare up at the ceiling of my bedroom in Aldenham House, which was a   5 ceiling undistinguished as ceilings go, and feel less resolute than anxious, much less brave than foolhardy. I could say to myself, "You needn't do it, of course," knowing at the same time that nothing is so inexorable as a promise to your pride.

I could ask, "Why risk it?" as I have been asked since, and I could answer, "Each to his element." By his nature a sailor must sail, by his nature a flyer must fly. I could compute that I had flown a quarter of a million miles; and I could foresee that, so long as I had a plane and the sky was there, I should go on flying more miles.

There was nothing extraordinary in this. I had learned a craft and had worked hard learning it. My hands had been taught to seek the controls of a plane. Usage had taught them. They were at ease clinging to a stick, as a cobbler's fingers are in repose grasping an awl. No human pursuit achieves dignity until it can be called work, and when you can experience a physical loneliness for the tools of your trade, you see that the other things—the experiments, the irrelevant vocations, the vanities you used to hold—were false to you.

Record flights had actually never interested me very much for myself. There were people who thought that such flights were done for admiration and publicity, and worse. But of all the records—from Louis Blériot's first crossing of the English Channel in nineteen hundred and nine, through and beyond Kingsford Smith's flight from San Francisco to Sydney, Australia—none had been made by amateurs, nor by novices, nor by men or women less than hardened to failure, or less than masters of their trade. None of these was false. They were a company that simple respect and simple ambition made it worth more than an effort to follow.

The Carberrys (of Seramai) were in London and I could remember everything about their dinner party—even the menu. I could remember June Carberry and all her guests, and the man named McCarthy, who lived in Zanzibar,[1] leaning across the table and saying, "J. C., why don't you finance Beryl for a record flight?"

I could lie there staring lazily at the ceiling and recall J. C.'s dry answer: "A num-   10 ber of pilots have flown the North Atlantic, west to east. Only Jim Mollison has done it alone the other way—from Ireland. Nobody has done it alone from England—man or woman. I'd be interested in that, but nothing else. If you want to try it, Burl, I'll back

---

[1]*Zanzibar:* an island off the east coast of Africa.

you. I think Edgar Percival could build a plane that would do it, provided you can fly it. Want to chance it?"

"Yes."

I could remember saying that better than I could remember anything—except J. C.'s almost ghoulish grin, and her remark that sealed the agreement: "It's a deal, Burl. I'll furnish the plane and you fly the Atlantic—but, gee, I wouldn't tackle it for a million. Think of all that black water! Think how cold it is!"

And I had thought of both.

I had thought of both for a while, and then there had been other things to think about. I had moved to Elstree, half-hour's flight from the Percival Aircraft Works at Gravesend, and almost daily for three months now I had flown down to the factory in a hired plane and watched the Vega Gull they were making for me. I had watched her birth and watched her growth. I had watched her wings take shape, and seen wood and fabric moulded to her ribs to form her long, sleek belly, and I had seen her engine cradled into her frame, and made fast.

The Gull had a turquoise-blue body and silver wings. Edgar Percival had made her   15
with care, with skill, and with worry—the care of a veteran flyer, the skill of a master designer, and the worry of a friend. Actually the plane was a standard sport model with a range of only six hundred and sixty miles. But she had a special undercarriage built to carry the weight of her extra oil and petrol tanks. The tanks were fixed into the wings, into the centre section, and into the cabin itself. In the cabin they formed a wall around my seat, and each tank had a petcock of its own. The petcocks were important.

"If you open one," said Percival, "without shutting the other first, you may get an airlock. You know the tanks in the cabin have no gauges, so it may be best to let one run completely dry before opening the next. Your motor might go dead in the interval—but she'll start again. She's a De Havilland Gipsy—and Gipsys never stop."

I had talked to Tom. We had spent hours going over the Atlantic chart, and I had realized that the tinker of Molo, now one of England's great pilots, had traded his dreams and had got in return a better thing. Tom had grown older too; he had jettisoned a deadweight of irrelevant hopes and wonders, and had left himself a realistic code that had no room for temporizing or easy sentiment.

"I'm glad you're going to do it, Beryl. It won't be simple. If you can get off the ground in the first place, with such an immense load of fuel, you'll be alone in that plane about a night and a day—mostly night. Doing it east to west, the wind's against you. In September, so is the weather. You won't have a radio. If you misjudge your course only a few degrees, you'll end up in Labrador or in the sea—so don't misjudge anything."

Tom could still grin. He had grinned; he had said: "Anyway, it ought to amuse you to think that your financial backer lives on a farm called 'Place of Death' and your plane is being built at 'Gravesend.' If you were consistent, you'd christen the Gull 'The Flying Tombstone.' "

I hadn't been that consistent. I had watched the building of the plane and I had   20
trained for the flight like an athlete. And now, as I lay in bed, fully awake, I could still hear the quiet voice of the man from the Air Ministry intoning, like the voice of a dispassionate court clerk: ". . . the weather for tonight and tomorrow . . . will be about the best you can expect." I should have liked to discuss the flight once more with Tom

before I took off, but he was on a special job up north. I got out of bed and bathed and put on my flying clothes and took some cold chicken packed in a cardboard box and flew over to the military field at Abingdon, where the Vega Gull waited for me under the care of the R.A.F. I remember that the weather was clear and still.

Jim Mollison lent me his watch. He said: "This is not a gift. I wouldn't part with it for anything. It got me across the North Atlantic and the South Atlantic too. Don't lose it—and, for God's sake, don't get it wet. Salt water would ruin the works."

Brian Lewis gave me a life-saving jacket. Brian owned the plane I had been using between Elstree and Gravesend, and he had thought a long time about a farewell gift. What could be more practical than a pneumatic jacket that could be inflated through a rubber tube?

"You could float around in it for days," said Brian. But I had to decide between the life-saver and warm clothes. I couldn't have both, because of their bulk, and I hate the cold, so I left the jacket.

And Jock Cameron, Brian's mechanic, gave me a sprig of heather. If it had been a whole bush of heather, complete with roots growing in an earthen jar, I think I should have taken it, bulky or not. The blessing of Scotland, bestowed by a Scotsman, is not to be dismissed. Nor is the well-wishing of a ground mechanic to be taken lightly, for these men are the pilot's contact with reality.

It is too much that with all those pedestrian centuries behind us we should, in a few 25 decades, have learned to fly; it is too heady a thought, too proud a boast. Only the dirt on a mechanic's hands, the straining vise, the splintered bolt of steel underfoot on the hanger floor—only these and such anxiety as the face of a Jock Cameron can hold for a pilot and his plane before a flight, serve to remind us that, not unlike the heather, we too are earth-bound. We fly, but we have not "conquered" the air. Nature presides in all her dignity, permitting us the study and the use of such of her forces as we may understand. It is when we presume to intimacy, having been granted only tolerance, that the harsh stick falls across our impudent knuckles and we rub the pain, staring upward, startled by our ignorance.

"Here is a sprig of heather," said Jock, and I took it and pinned it into a pocket of my flying jacket.

There were press cars parked outside the field at Abingdon, and several press planes and photographers, but the R.A.F. kept everyone away from the grounds except technicians and a few of my friends.

The Carberrys had sailed for New York a month ago to wait for me there. Tom was still out of reach with no knowledge of my decision to leave, but that didn't matter so much, I thought. It didn't matter because Tom was unchanging—neither a fair-weather pilot nor a fairweather friend. If for a month, or a year, or two years we sometimes had not seen each other, it still hadn't mattered. Nor did this. Tom would never say, "You should have let me know." He assumed that I had learned all that he had tried to teach me, and for my part, I thought of him, even then, as the merest student must think of his mentor. I could sit in a cabin overcrowded with petrol tanks and set my course for North America, but the knowledge of my hands on the controls would be Tom's knowledge. His words of caution and words of guidance, spoken so long ago, so many times, on bright mornings over the veldt or over a forest, or with a far mountain visible at the tip of our wing, would be spoken again, if I asked.

So it didn't matter, I thought. It was silly to think about.

You can live a lifetime and, at the end of it, know more about other people than 30
you know about yourself. You learn to watch other people, but you never watch yourself because you strive against loneliness. If you read a book, or shuffle a deck of cards,
or care for a dog, you are avoiding yourself. The abhorrence of loneliness is as natural as wanting to live at all. If it were otherwise, men would never have bothered to
make an alphabet, nor to have fashioned words out of what were only animal sounds,
nor to have crossed continents—each man to see what the other looked like.

Being alone in an aeroplane for even so short a time as a night and a day, irrevocably alone, with nothing to observe but your instruments and your own hands in
semi-darkness, nothing to contemplate but the size of your small courage, nothing to
wonder about but the beliefs, the faces, and the hopes rooted in your mind—such an
experience can be as startling as the first awareness of a stranger walking by your side
at night. You are the stranger.

It is dark already and I am over the south of Ireland. There are the lights of Cork
and the lights are wet; they are drenched in Irish rain, and I am above them and dry. I
am above them and the plane roars in a sobbing world, but it imparts no sadness to
me. I feel the security of solitude, the exhilaration of escape. So long as I can see the
lights and imagine the people walking under them, I feel selfishly triumphant, as if I
have eluded care and left even the small sorrow of rain in other hands.

It is a little over an hour now since I left Abingdon. England, Wales, and the Irish
Sea are behind me like so much time used up. On a long flight distance and time are
the same. But there had been a moment when Time stopped—and Distance too. It was
the moment I lifted the blue-and-silver Gull from the aerodrome, the moment the photographers aimed their cameras, the moment I felt the craft refuse its burden and strain
toward the earth in sullen rebellion, only to listen at last to the persuasion of stick and
elevators, the dogmatic argument of blueprints that said she *had* to fly because the figures proved it.

So she had flown, and once airborne, once she had yielded to the sophistry of a
draughtsman's board, she had said, "There: I have lifted the weight. Now, where are
we bound?"—and the question had frightened me.

"We are bound for a place thirty-six hundred miles from here—two thousand 35
miles of it unbroken ocean. Most of the way it will be night. We are flying west with
the night."

So there behind me is Cork; and ahead of me is Berehaven Lighthouse. It is the
last light, standing on the last land. I watch it, counting the frequency of its flashes—
so many to the minute. Then I pass it and fly out to sea.

The fear is gone now—not overcome nor reasoned away. It is gone because something else has taken its place; the confidence and the trust, the inherent belief in the security of land underfoot—now this faith is transferred to my plane, because the land
has vanished and there is no other tangible thing to fix faith upon. Flight is but momentary escape from the eternal custody of earth.

Rain continues to fall, and outside the cabin it is totally dark. My altimeter says
that the Atlantic is two thousand feet below me, my Sperry Artificial Horizon says that
I am flying level. I judge my drift at three degrees more than my weather chart suggests,

and fly accordingly. I am flying blind. A beam to follow would help. So would a radio—but then, so would clear weather. The voice of the man at the Air Ministry had not promised storm.

I feel the wind rising and the rain falls hard. The smell of petrol in the cabin is so strong and the roar of the plane so loud that my senses are almost deadened. Gradually it becomes unthinkable that existence was ever otherwise.

At ten o'clock P.M. I am flying along the Great Circle Course for Harbour Grace,   40
Newfoundland, into a forty-mile headwind at a speed of one hundred and thirty miles an hour. Because of the weather, I cannot be sure of how many more hours I have to fly, but I think it must be between sixteen and eighteen.

At ten-thirty I am still flying on the large cabin tank of petrol, hoping to use it up and put an end to the liquid swirl that has rocked the plane since my take-off. The tank has no gauge, but written on its side is the assurance: "This tank is good for four hours."

There is nothing ambiguous about such a guaranty. I believe it, but at twenty-five minutes to eleven, my motor coughs and dies, and the Gull is powerless above the sea.

I realize that the heavy drone of the plane has been, until this moment, complete and comforting silence. It is the actual silence following the last splutter of the engine that stuns me. I can't feel any fear; I can't feel anything. I can only observe with a kind of stupid disinterest that my hands are violently active and know that, while they move, I am being hypnotized by the needle of my altimeter.

I suppose that the denial of natural impulse is what is meant by "keeping calm," but impulse has reason in it. If it is night and you are sitting in an aeroplane with a stalled motor, and there are two thousand feet between you and the sea, nothing can be more reasonable than the impulse to pull back your stick in the hope of adding to that two thousand, if only by a little. The thought, the knowledge, the law that tells you that your hope lies not in this, but in a contrary act—the act of directing your impotent craft toward the water—seems a terrifying abandonment, not only of reason, but of sanity. Your mind and your heart reject it. It is your hands—your stranger's hands—that follow with unfeeling precision the letter of the law.

I sit there and watch my hands push forward on the stick and feel the Gull respond   45
and begin its dive to the sea. Of course it is a simple thing; surely the cabin tank has run dry too soon. I need only to turn another petcock . . .

But it is dark in the cabin. It is easy to see the luminous dial of the altimeter and to note that my height is now eleven hundred feet, but it is not easy to see a petcock that is somewhere near the floor of the plane. A hand gropes and reappears with an electric torch, and fingers, moving with agonizing composure, find the petcock and turn it; and I wait.

At three hundred feet the motor is still dead, and I am conscious that the needle of my altimeter seems to whirl like the spoke of a spindle winding up the remaining distance between the plane and the water. There is some lightning, but the quick flash only serves to emphasize the darkness. How high can waves reach—twenty feet, perhaps? Thirty?

It is impossible to avoid the thought that this is the end of my flight, but my reactions are not orthodox; the various incidents of my entire life do not run through my mind like a motion-picture film gone mad. I only feel that all this has happened before—

and it has. It has all happened a hundred times in my mind, in my sleep, so that now I am not really caught in terror; I recognize a familiar scene, a familiar story with its climax dulled by too much telling.

I do not know how close to the waves I am when the motor explodes to life again. But the sound is almost meaningless. I see my hand easing back on the stick, and I feel the Gull climb up into the storm, and I see the altimeter whirl like a spindle again, paying out the distance between myself and the sea.

The storm is strong. It is comforting. It is like a friend shaking me and saying, 50 "Wake up! You were only dreaming."

But soon I am thinking. By simple calculation I find that my motor had been silent for perhaps an instant more than thirty seconds.

I ought to thank God—and I do, though indirectly. I thank Geoffrey De Havilland who designed the indomitable Gipsy, and who, after all, must have been designed by God in the first place.

A lighted ship—the daybreak—some steep cliffs standing in the sea. The meaning of these will never change for pilots. If one day an ocean can be flown within an hour, if men can build a plane that so masters time, the sight of land will be no less welcome to the steersman of that fantastic craft. He will have cheated laws that the cunning of science has taught him how to cheat, and he will feel his guilt and be eager for the sanctuary of the soil.

I saw the ship and the daybreak, and then I saw the cliffs of Newfoundland wound in ribbons of fog. I felt the elation I had so long imagined, and I felt the happy guilt of having circumvented the stern authority of the weather and the sea. But mine was a minor triumph; my swift Gull was not so swift as to have escaped unnoticed. The night and the storm had caught her and we had flown blind for nineteen hours.

I was tired now, and cold. Ice began to film the glass of the cabin windows and the 55 fog played a magician's game with the land. But the land was there. I could not see it, but I had seen it. I could not afford to believe that it was any land but the land I wanted. I could not afford to believe that my navigation was at fault, because there was no time for doubt.

South to Cape Race, west to Sydney on Cape Breton Island. With my protractor, my map, and my compass, I set my new course, humming the ditty that Tom had taught me: "Variation West—magnetic best. Variation East—magnetic least." A silly rhyme, but it served to placate, for the moment, two warring poles—the magnetic and the true. I flew south and found the lighthouse of Cape Race protruding from the fog like a warning finger. I circled twice and went on over the Gulf of Saint Lawrence.

After a while there would be New Brunswick, and then Maine—and then New York. I could anticipate. I could almost say, "Well, if you stay awake, you'll find it's only a matter of time now"—but there was no question of staying awake. I was tired and I had not moved an inch since that uncertain moment at Abingdon when the Gull had elected to rise with her load and fly, but I could not have closed my eyes. I could sit there in the cabin, walled in glass and petrol tanks, and be grateful for the sun and the light, and the fact that I could see the water under me. They were almost the last waves I had to pass. Four hundred miles of water, and then the land again—Cape

Breton. I would stop at Sydney to refuel and go on. It was easy now. It would be like stopping at Kisumu and going on.

Success breeds confidence. But who has a right to confidence except the Gods? I had a following wind, my last tank of petrol was more than three-quarters full, and the world was as bright to me as if it were a new world, never touched. If I had been wiser, I might have known that such moments are, like innocence, short-lived. My engine began to shudder before I saw the land. It died, it spluttered, it started again and limped along. It coughed and spat black exhaust toward the sea.

There are words for everything. There was a word for this—airlock, I thought. This had to be an airlock because there was petrol enough. I thought I might clear it by turning on and turning off all the empty tanks, and so I did that. The handles of the petcocks were sharp little pins of metal, and when I had opened and closed them a dozen times, I saw that my hands were bleeding and that the blood was dropping on my maps and on my clothes, but the effort wasn't any good. I coasted along on a sick and halting engine. The oil pressure and the oil temperature gauges were normal, the magnetos working, and yet I lost altitude slowly while the realization of failure seeped into my heart. If I made the land, I should have been the first to fly the North Atlantic from England, but from my point of view, from a pilot's point of view, a forced landing was failure because New York was my goal. If only I could land and then take off, I would make it still . . . if only, if only . . .

The engine cuts again, and then catches, and each time it spurts to life I climb as   60
high as I can get, and then it splutters and stops and I glide once more toward the water, to rise again and descend again, like a hunting sea bird.

I find the land. Visibility is perfect now and I see land forty or fifty miles ahead. If I am on my course, that will be Cape Breton. Minute after minute goes by. The minutes almost materialize; they pass before my eyes like links in a long slow-moving chain, and each time the engine cuts, I see a broken link in the chain and catch my breath until it passes.

The land is under me. I snatch my map and stare at it to confirm my whereabouts. I am, even at my present crippled speed, only twelve minutes from Sydney Airport, where I can land for repairs and then go on.

The engine cuts once more and I begin to glide, but now I am not worried; she will start again, as she has done, and I will gain altitude and fly into Sydney.

But she doesn't start. This time she's dead as death; the Gull settles earthward and it isn't any earth I know. It is black earth stuck with boulders and I hang above it, on hope and on a motionless propeller. Only I cannot hang above it long. The earth hurries to meet me, I bank, turn, and side-slip to dodge the boulders, my wheels touch, and I feel them submerge. The nose of the plane is engulfed in mud, and I go forward striking my head on the glass of the cabin front, hearing it shatter, feeling blood pour over my face.

I stumble out of the plane and sink to my knees in muck and stand there foolishly   65
staring, not at the lifeless land, but at my watch.

Twenty-one hours and twenty-five minutes.

Atlantic flight, Abingdon, England, to a nameless swamp—nonstop.

A Cape Breton Islander found me—a fisherman trudging over the bog saw the Gull with her tail in the air and her nose buried, and then he saw me floundering in the embracing soil of his native land. I had been wandering for an hour and the black mud had got up to my waist and the blood from the cut in my head had met the mud halfway.

From a distance, the fisherman directed me with his arms and with shouts toward the firm places in the bog, and for another hour I walked on them and came toward him like a citizen of Hades blinded by the sun, but it wasn't the sun; I hadn't slept for forty hours.

He took me to his hut on the edge of the coast and I found that built upon the   70 rocks there was a little cubicle that housed an ancient telephone—put there in case of shipwrecks.

I telephoned to Sydney Airport to say that I was safe and to prevent a needless search being made. On the following morning I did step out of a plane at Floyd Bennett Field and there was a crowd of people still waiting there to greet me, but the plane I stepped from was not the Gull, and for days while I was in New York I kept thinking about that and wishing over and over again that it had been the Gull, until the wish lost its significance, and time moved on, overcoming many things it met on the way.

Questions for Discussion and Writing

1. What motivates Markham and explains her compulsion to succeed?
2. How would you characterize Markham's personality as it emerges in her account? What sort of relationship did she have with her fellow pilots?
3. Do you consider Markham a workaholic? What distinguishes workaholics from other hard workers? Would you consider yourself one? Why or why not?

Marcel Proust

• •

Marcel Proust (1871–1922), the French novelist, is undisputably one of the great literary figures of the twentieth century. He was born in Auteuil, France; graduated from the Sorbonne; and briefly served in the French Army (where he was ranked seventy-third in a company of seventy-four). As a young man, he was active in the Paris social scene and became friends with Anatole France and other literary celebrities. His health deteriorated so greatly (from asthma and bronchitis) that from 1905 until his death in 1922 he lived as an invalid, spending most of his days propped up in bed, with the windows closed and shuttered, in the now famous cork-lined room.

The paradox of Proust is that, although so enfeebled, he undertook and created the most astounding and monumental novel, Remembrance of Things Past, *in seven volumes (3,300 pages in the English translation). The first volume appeared in 1913, and the succeeding six parts (three were published after his death) contain a wealth of brilliant social and psychological observations expressed in rich metaphors and meticulous and intricate prose. The selection reprinted here consists of the last pages of the "Overture" from volume 1, "Swann's Way," and contains the most famous passage in Proust (the madeleine cake dipped in tea) that explores the connection between the conscious and unconscious mind.*

THE BODILY MEMORY

I feel that there is much to be said for the Celtic belief that the souls of those whom we have lost are held captive in some inferior being, in an animal, in a plant, in some inanimate object, and so effectively lost to us until the day (which to many never comes) when we happen to pass by the tree or to obtain possession of the object which forms their prison. Then they start and tremble, they call us by our name, and as soon as we have recognised their voice the spell is broken. We have delivered them: they have overcome death and return to share our life.

And so it is with our own past. It is a labour in vain to attempt to recapture it: all the efforts of our intellect must prove futile. The past is hidden somewhere outside the realm, beyond the reach of intellect, in some material object (in the sensation which that material object will give us) which we do not suspect. And as for that object, it depends on chance whether we come upon it or not before we ourselves must die.

Many years had elapsed during which nothing of Combray,[1] save what was comprised in the theatre and the drama of my going to bed there, had any existence for me, when one day in winter, as I came home, my mother, seeing that I was cold, offered me some tea, a thing I did not ordinarily take. I declined at first, and then, for no particular reason, changed my mind. She sent out for one of those short, plump little cakes called 'petites madeleines,' which look as though they had been moulded in the fluted scallop of a pilgrim's shell. And soon, mechanically, weary after a dull day with the prospect of a depressing morrow. I raised to my lips a spoonful of the tea in which I had soaked a morsel of the cake. No sooner had the warm liquid, and the crumbs with it, touched my palate than a shudder ran through my whole body, and I stopped, intent upon the extraordinary changes that were taking place. An exquisite pleasure had invaded my senses, but individual, detached, with no suggestion of its origin. And at once the vicissitudes of life had become indifferent to me, its disasters innocuous, its brevity illusory—this new sensation having had on me the effect which love has of filling me with a precious essence; or rather this essence was not in me, it was myself. I had ceased now to feel mediocre, accidental, mortal. Whence could it have come to me, this all-powerful joy? I was conscious that it was connected with the taste of tea and cake, but that it infinitely transcended those savours, could not, indeed, be of the same nature as theirs. Whence did it come? What did it signify? How could I seize upon and define it?

I drink a second mouthful, in which I find nothing more than in the first, a third, which gives me rather less than the second. It is time to stop; the potion is losing its magic. It is plain that the object of my quest, the truth, lies not in the cup but in myself. The tea has called up in me, but does not itself understand, and can only repeat indefinitely with a gradual loss of strength, the same testimony; which I, too, cannot interpret, though I hope at least to be able to call upon the tea for it again and to find it there presently, intact and at my disposal, for my final enlightenment. I put down my cup and examine my own mind. It is for it to discover the truth. But how? What an abyss of uncertainty whenever the mind feels that some part of it has strayed beyond

---

[1]*Combray:* The village where the hero of *Remembrance of Things Past* spent much of his childhood. The title is drawn from Shakespeare's *Sonnet 30* (see page 88).

its own borders; when it, the seeker, is at once the dark region through which it must go seeking, where all its equipment will avail it nothing. Seek? More than that: create. It is face to face with something which does not so far exist, to which it alone can give reality and substance, which it alone can bring into the light of day.

And I begin again to ask myself what it could have been, this unremembered state which brought with it no logical proof of its existence, but only the sense that it was a happy, that it was a real state in whose presence other states of consciousness melted and vanished. I decide to attempt to make it reappear. I retrace my thoughts to the moment at which I drank the first spoonful of tea. I find again the same state, illumined by no fresh light. I compel my mind to make one further effort, to allow and recapture once again the fleeting sensation. And that nothing may interrupt it in its course I shut out every obstacle, every extraneous idea, I stop my ears and inhibit all attention to the sounds which come from the next room. And then, feeling that my mind is growing fatigued without having any success to report, I compel it for a change to enjoy that distraction which I have just denied it, to think of other things, to rest and refresh itself before the supreme attempt. And then for the second time I clear an empty space in front of it. I place in position before my mind's eye the still recent taste of that first mouthful, and I feel something start within me, something that leaves its resting-place and attempts to rise, something that has been embedded like an anchor at a great depth; I do not know yet what it is, but I can feel it mounting slowly; I can measure the resistance. I can hear the echo of great spaces traversed.

Undoubtedly what is thus palpitating in the depths of my being must be the image, the visual memory which, being linked to that taste, has tried to follow it into my conscious mind. But its struggles are too far off, too much confused; scarcely can I perceive the colourless reflection in which are blended the uncapturable whirling medley of radiant hues, and I cannot distinguish its form, cannot invite it, as the one possible interpreter, to translate to me the evidence of its contemporary, its inseparable paramour, the taste of cake soaked in tea; cannot ask it to inform me what special circumstance is in question, of what period in my past life.

Will it ultimately reach the clear surface of my consciousness, this memory, this old, dead moment which the magnetism of an identical moment has travelled so far to importune, to disturb, to raise up out of the very depths of my being? I cannot tell. Now that I feel nothing, it has stopped, has perhaps gone down again into its darkness, from which who can say whether it will ever rise? Ten times over I must essay the task, must lean down over the abyss. And each time the natural laziness which deters us from every difficult enterprise, every work of importance, has urged me to leave the thing alone, to drink my tea and to think merely of the worries of to-day and of my hopes for to-morrow, which let themselves be pondered over without effort or distress of mind.

And suddenly the memory returns. The taste was that of the little crumb of madeleine which on Sunday mornings at Combray (because on those mornings I did not go out before church-time), when I went to say good day to her in her bedroom, my aunt Léonie used to give me, dipping it first in her own cup of real or of lime-flower tea. The sight of the little madeleine had recalled nothing to my mind before I tasted it; perhaps because I had so often seen such things in the interval, without tasting them, on the trays in pastry-cooks' windows, that their image had disociated itself from those Combray days to take its place among others more recent; perhaps because of those memories, so long abandoned and put out of mind, nothing now survived, everything was scattered; the forms of things, including that of the little scallop-shell of pastry, so richly sensual under its severe, religious folds, were either obliterated or had been so long dormant as to have lost the power of expansion which would have allowed them to resume their place in my consciousness. But when from a long-distant past nothing subsists, after the people are dead, after the things are broken and scattered, still, alone, more fragile, but with more vitality, more unsubstantial, more persistent, more faithful, the smell and taste of things remain poised a long time, like souls, ready to remind us, waiting and hoping for their moment, amid the ruins of all the rest; and bear unfaltering, in the tiny and almost impalpable drop of their essence, the vast structure of recollection.

And once I had recognized the taste of the crumb of madeleine soaked in her decoction of lime-flowers which my aunt used to give me (although I did not yet know and must long postpone the discovery of why this memory made me so happy) immediately the old grey house upon the street, where her room was, rose up like the scenery of a theatre to attach itself to the little pavilion, opening on to the garden, which had been built out behind it for my parents (the isolated panel which until that moment had been all that I could see); and with the house the town, from morning to night and in all weathers, the Square where I was sent before luncheon, the streets along which I used to run errands, the country roads we took when it was fine. And just as the Japanese amuse themselves by filling a porcelain bowl with water and steeping in it little crumbs of paper which until then are without character or form, but, the moment they become wet, stretch themselves and bend, take on colour and distinctive shape, become flowers or houses or people, permanent and recognisable, so in that moment all the flowers in our garden and in M. Swann's park, and the water-lilies on the Vivonne and the good folk of the village and their little dwellings and the parish church and the whole of Combray and of its surroundings, taking their proper shapes and growing solid, sprang into being, town and gardens alike, from my cup of tea.

Questions for Discussion and Writing

1. How did the madeline cake dipped in tea function as a sensory trigger to unlock past memories?
2. How does the narrator's experience illustrate the difference between an "intellectual memory" and the "bodily memory" that recovers a past experience as if it were happening in the present? How does Proust's elaborate style mirror the difficulty of retrieving the past?
3. Proust says that one's personal past is often "beyond the reach of intellect" and may be held captive "in some material object (in the sensation which that material object will give us)" Have you ever recovered a past memory through some sensory trigger? Describe your experience.

Douchan Gersi

. . . .

Douchan Gersi is the producer of the National Geographic *television series called* Discovery. *He has traveled extensively throughout the Philippines, New Zealand, the Polynesian Islands, the Melanesian Islands, the Sahara, Africa, New Guinea, and Peru. "Initiated into an Iban Tribe of Headhunters," from his book* Explorer *(1987), tells of the harrowing initiation process he underwent to become a member of the Iban tribe in Borneo. He subsequently wrote* Out of Africa *with Maroussia Gersi (1989). His works include* Faces in the Smoke: An Eyewitness Experience of Voodoo *(1991) and, most recently,* Une vie de maharajah *[The Life of a Maharajah] (2003). Gersi's account introduces us to the mode of life of the Iban, a people whose customs, including intertribal warfare and headhunting, have remained unchanged for centuries.*

An accomplished Iban man not only would be proficient in argument and courageous in hunting but also would be skillful in woodcarving. The traditional Iban dwelling is the longhouse (which is nearly always built by the bank of a navigable river), a semipermanent structure housing twenty or more families in separate apartments. The longhouse is decorated with drums, gongs, weavings, and hanging skulls from days gone by.

What does this group photo of the Iban tribe in their longhouse suggest about the life that might await Douchan Gersi?

INITIATED INTO AN IBAN TRIBE OF HEADHUNTERS

The hopeful man sees success where others see shadows and storm.

—O. S. Marden

Against Tawa's excellent advice I asked the chief if I could become a member of their clan. It took him a while before he could give me an answer, for he had to question the spirits of their ancestors and wait for their reply to appear through different omens: the flight of a blackbird, the auguries of a chick they sacrificed. A few days after the question, the answer came:

"Yes . . . but!"

The "but" was that I would have to undergo their initiation. Without knowing exactly what physical ordeal was in store, I accepted. I knew I had been through worse and survived. It was to begin in one week.

Late at night I was awakened by a girl slipping into my bed. She was sweet and already had a great knowledge of man's morphology. Like all the others who came and "visited" me this way every night, she was highly skilled in the arts of love. Among the Iban, only unmarried women offer sexual hospitality, and no one obliged these women to offer me their favors. Sexual freedom ends at marriage. Unfaithfulness—except during yearly fertility celebrations when everything, even incest at times, is permitted—is punished as an offense against their matrimonial laws.

As a sign of respect to family and the elders, sexual hospitality is not openly practiced. The girls always came when my roommates were asleep and left before they awoke. They were free to return or give their place to their girlfriends.

The contrast between the violence of some Iban rituals and the beauty of their art, their sociability, their kindness, and their personal warmth has always fascinated me. I also witnessed that contrast among a tribe of Papuans (who, besides being headhunters, practice cannibalism) and among some African tribes. In fact, tribes devoted to cannibalism and other human sacrifices are often among the most sociable of people, and their art, industry, and trading systems are more advanced than other tribes that don't have these practices.

For my initiation, they had me lie down naked in a four-foot-deep pit filled with giant carnivorous ants. Nothing held me there. At any point I could easily have escaped, but the meaning of this rite of passage was not to kill me. The ritual was intended to test my courage and my will, to symbolically kill me by the pain in order for me to be reborn as a man of courage. I am not sure what their reactions would have been if I had tried to get out of the pit before their signal, but it occurred to me that although the ants might eat a little of my flesh, the Iban offered more dramatic potentials.

Since I wore, as Iban do, a long piece of cloth around my waist and nothing more, I had the ants running all over my body. They were everywhere. The pain of the ants' bites was intense, so I tried to relax to decrease the speed of my circulation and therefore the effects of the poison. But I couldn't help trying to get them away from my face where they were exploring every inch of my skin. I kept my eyes closed, inhaling through my almost closed lips and exhaling through my nose to chase them away from there.

I don't know how long I stayed in the pit, waiting with anguish for the signal which would end my ordeal. As I tried to concentrate on my relaxing, the sound of the beaten

5

gongs and murmurs of the assistants watching me from all around the pit started to disappear into a chaos of pain and loud heartbeat.

Then suddenly I heard Tawa and the chief calling my name. I removed once more 10 the ants wandering on my eyelids before opening my eyes and seeing my friends smiling to indicate that it was over. I got out of the pit on my own, but I needed help to rid myself of the ants, which were determined to eat all my skin. After the men washed my body, the shaman applied an herbal mixture to ease the pain and reduce the swellings. I would have quit and left the village then had I known that the "pit" experience was just the hors d'oeuvre.

The second part of the physical test started early the next morning. The chief explained the "game" to me. It was Hide and Go Seek Iban-style. I had to run without any supplies, weapons, or food, and for three days and three nights escape a group of young warriors who would leave the village a few hours after my departure and try to find me. If I were caught, my head would be used in a ceremony. The Iban would have done so without hate. It was simply the rule of their life. Birth and death. A death that always engenders new life.

When I asked, "What would happen if someone refused this part of the initiation?" the chief replied that such an idea wasn't possible. Once one had begun, there was no turning back. I knew the rules governing initiations among the cultures of tradition but never thought they would be applied to me. Whether or not I survived the initiation, I would be symbolically killed in order to be reborn among them. I had to die from my present time and identity into another life. I was aware that, among some cultures, initiatory ordeals are so arduous that young initiates sometimes really die. These are the risks if one wishes to enter into another world.

I was given time to get ready and the game began. I ran like hell without a plan or, it seemed to me, a prayer of surviving. Running along a path I had never taken, going I knew not where, I thought about every possible way I could escape from the young warriors. To hide somewhere. But where? Climb a tree and hide in it? Find a hole and squeeze in it? Bury myself under rocks and mud? But all of these seemed impossible. I had a presentiment they would find me anyway. So I ran straight ahead, my head going crazy by dint of searching for a way to safely survive the headhunters.

I would prefer staying longer with ants, I thought breathlessly. It was safer to stay among them for a whole day since they were just simple pain and fear compared to what I am about to undergo. I don't want to die.

For the first time I realized the real possibility of death—no longer in a romantic 15 way, but rather at the hands of butchers.

Ten minutes after leaving the long house, I suddenly heard a call coming from somewhere around me. Still running, I looked all around trying to locate who was calling, and why. At the second call I stopped, cast my gaze about, and saw a woman's head peering out from the bushes. I recognized her as one of my pretty lovers. I hesitated, not knowing if she were part of the hunting party or a goddess come to save me. She called again. I thought, God, what to do? How will I escape from the warriors? As I stood there truly coming into contact with my impossible situation, I began to panic. She called again. With her fingers she showed me what the others would do if they caught me. Her forefinger traced an invisible line from one side of her throat to the other. If someone was going to kill me, why not her? I joined her and found out she was in a lair. I realized I had entered the place where the tribe's women go to hide during their menstruation. This area is taboo for men. Each woman has her own refuge. Some have shelters made of branches, others deep covered holes hidden behind bushes with enough space to eat and sleep and wait until their time is past.

She invited me to make myself comfortable. That was quite difficult since it was just large enough for one person. But I had no choice. And after all, it was a paradise compared to what I would have undergone had I not by luck crossed this special ground.

Nervously and physically exhausted by my run and fear and despair, I soon fell asleep. Around midnight I woke. She gave me rice and meat. We exchanged a few words. Then it was her turn to sleep.

The time I spent in the lair with my savior went fast. I tried to sleep all day long, an escape from the concerns of my having broken a taboo. And I wondered what would happen to me if the headhunters were to learn where I spent the time of my physical initiation.

Then, when it was safe, I snuck back to the village . . . in triumph. I arrived before   20
the warriors, who congratulated and embraced me when they returned. I was a head-hunter at last.

I spent the next two weeks quietly looking at the Iban through new eyes. But strangely enough, instead of the initiation putting me closer to them, it had the opposite effect. I watched them more and more from an anthropological distance: my Iban brothers became an interesting clan whose life I witnessed but did not really share. And then suddenly I was bored and yearned for my own tribe. When Tawa had to go to an outpost to exchange pepper grains for other goods, I took a place aboard his canoe. Two days later I was in a small taxi-boat heading toward Sibu, the first leg in civilization on my voyage home.

I think of them often. I wonder about the man I tried to cure. I think about Tawa and the girl who saved my life, and all the others sitting on the veranda. How long will my adopted village survive before being destroyed like all the others in the way of civilization? And what has become of those who marked my flesh with the joy of their lives and offered me the best of their souls? If they are slowly vanishing from my memories, I know that I am part of the stories they tell. I know that my life among them will be perpetuated until the farthest tomorrow. Now I am a story caught in a living legend of a timeless people.

Questions for Discussion and Writing

1. What do the unusual sexual customs and hospitality bestowed on outsiders suggest about the different cultural values of the Iban? Do these customs suggest that the initiation would be harsher or milder than Gersi expected?

2. At what point did Gersi realize that his former ideas about being accepted by the tribe were unrealistic and that his present situation was truly life-endangering? How is the narrative shaped to put the reader through the same suspenseful moments that Gersi experienced? Speculate about why Gersi's life-and-death

initiation, rather than bringing him closer to the Iban, as he expected, actually made him more distant from them.

3. Have you ever gone through an initiation ritual to become part of an organization, club, fraternity, or sorority? Describe your experiences and how you felt before, during, and after this initiation. How can other rituals, such as being confirmed in the Catholic church or becoming a bar or bat mitzvah in Judaism, be analyzed as an initiation rite?

Annie Dillard

Annie Dillard was born in 1945 in Pittsburgh. She is the author of nine books, including An American Childhood *(1987), where this essay originally appeared;* The Writing Life *(1989); and* Holy the Firm *(1977). In 1975,* Pilgrim at Tinker Creek *was awarded the Pulitzer Prize in nonfiction. Dillard's writing appears in* Atlantic, Harper's, The New York Times Magazine, *the* Yale Review, American Heritage, *and many anthologies. She has received numerous grants and awards, including grants from the Guggenheim Foundation and the National Endowment for the Arts. Dillard's latest book is* For the Time Being *(1999). She currently lives in Connecticut with her husband, Robert D. Richardson, Jr., who is a biographer of Thoreau and Emerson, and her daughter, Rosie.*

SO, THIS WAS ADOLESCENCE

When I was fifteen, I felt it coming; now I was sixteen, and it hit. My feet had imperceptibly been set on a new path, a fast path into a long tunnel like those many turnpike tunnels near Pittsburgh, turnpike tunnels whose entrances bear on brass plaques a roll call of those men who died blasting them. I wandered witlessly forward and found myself going down, and saw the light dimming; I adjusted to the slant and dimness, traveled further down, adjusted to greater dimness, and so on. There wasn't a whole lot I could do about it, or about anything. I was going to hell on a handcart, that was all, and I knew it and everyone around me knew it, and there it was.

I was growing and thinning, as if pulled. I was getting angry, as if pushed. I morally disapproved most things in North America, and blamed my innocent parents for them. My feelings deepened and lingered. The swift moods of early childhood—each formed by and suited to its occasion—vanished. Now feelings lasted so long they left stains. They arose from nowhere, like winds or waves, and battered at me or engulfed me.

When I was angry, I felt myself coiled and longing to kill someone or bomb something big. Trying to appease myself, during one winter I whipped my bed every afternoon with my uniform belt. I despised the spectacle I made in my own eyes—whipping the bed with a belt, like a creature demented—and I often began halfheartedly, but I did it daily after school as a desperate discipline, trying to rid myself and the innocent world of my wildness. It was like trying to beat back the ocean.

Sometimes in class I couldn't stop laughing; things were too funny to be borne. It began then, my surprise that no one else saw what was so funny.

I read some few books with such reverence I didn't close them at the finish, but only moved the pile of pages back to the start, without breathing, and began again. I read   5 one such book, an enormous novel, six times that way—closing the binding between sessions, but not between readings.

On the piano in the basement I played the maniacal "Poet and Peasant Overture"[1] so loudly, for so many hours, night after night, I damaged the piano's keys and strings. When I wasn't playing this crashing overture, I played boogie-woogie, or something else, anything else in octaves—otherwise, it wasn't loud enough. My fingers were so strong I could do push-ups with them. I played one piece with my fists. I banged on a steel-stringed guitar till I bled, and once on a particularly piercing rock-and-roll downbeat I broke straight through one of Father's snare drums.

I loved my boyfriend so tenderly, I thought I must transmogrify into vapor. It would take spectroscopic analysis to locate my molecules in thin air. No possible way of holding him was close enough. Nothing could cure this bad case of gentleness except, perhaps, violence: maybe if he swung me by the legs and split my skull on a tree? Would that ease this insane wish to kiss too much his eyelids' outer corners and his temples, as if I could love up his brain?

I envied people in books who swooned. For two years I felt myself continuously swooning and continuously unable to swoon; the blood drained from my face and eyes and flooded my heart; my hands emptied, my knees unstrung, I bit at the air for something worth breathing—but I failed to fall, and I couldn't find the way to black out. I had to live on the lip of a waterfall, exhausted.

When I was bored I was first hungry, then nauseated, then furious and weak. "Calm yourself," people had been saying to me all my life. Since early childhood I had tried one thing and then another to calm myself, on those few occasions when I truly wanted to. Eating helped; singing helped. Now sometimes I truly wanted to calm myself. I couldn't lower my shoulders; they seemed to wrap around my ears. I couldn't lower my voice although I could see the people around me flinch. I waved my arm in class till the very teachers wanted to kill me.

I was what they called a live wire. I was shooting out sparks that were digging a   10 pit around me, and I was sinking into that pit. Laughing with Ellin at school recess, or driving around after school with Judy in her jeep, exultant, or dancing with my boyfriend to Louis Armstrong[2] across a polished dining-room floor, I got so excited I looked around wildly for aid; I didn't know where I should go or what I should do with myself. People in books split wood.

When rage or boredom reappeared, each seemed never to have left. Each so filled me with so many years' intolerable accumulation it jammed the space behind my eyes, so I couldn't see. There was no room left even on my surface to live. My rib cage was so taut I couldn't breathe. Every cubic centimeter of atmosphere above my shoulders and head was heaped with last straws. Black hatred clogged my very blood. I couldn't peep, I couldn't wiggle or blink; my blood was too mad to flow.

---

[1]*"Poet and Peasant Overture"*: written (1846) by the Austrian composer Franz von Suppé for *Dichter un Bauer,* a comedy with song.   [2]*Louis "Satchmo" Armstrong (1900–1971):* black American jazz trumpeter, singer, and bandleader known for his improvisational genius.

For as long as I could remember, I had been transparent to myself, unselfconscious, learning, doing, most of every day. Now I was in my own way; I myself was a dark object I could not ignore. I couldn't remember how to forget myself. I didn't want to think about myself, to reckon myself in, to deal with myself every livelong minute on top of everything else—but swerve as I might, I couldn't avoid it. I was a boulder blocking my own path. I was a dog barking between my own ears, a barking dog who wouldn't hush.

So this was adolescence. Is this how the people around me had died on their feet—inevitably, helplessly? Perhaps their own selves eclipsed the sun for so many years the world shriveled around them, and when at last their inescapable orbits had passed through these dark egoistic years it was too late, they had adjusted.

Must I then lose the world forever, that I had so loved? Was it all, the whole bright and various planet, where I had been so ardent about finding myself alive, only a passion peculiar to children, that I would outgrow even against my will?

Questions for Discussion and Writing

1. How does Dillard understand the nature of the crisis she experienced during her adolescence?

2. What images are especially effective in communicating her perception of this crisis? Does her attitude change over the course of the essay?

3. Compare Dillard's experience of adolescence with your own. How were your experiences and hers different, and in what ways were they similar?

4. Does this oil painting by Paul Kaleja titled *Adolescence* say the same thing about growing up that Annie Dillard does?

Judith Ortiz Cofer

Judith Ortiz Cofer, a poet and novelist, was born in 1952 in Hormigueros, Puerto Rico, and was educated at Augusta College, Florida Atlantic University, and Oxford University. Her published work includes the collections of poetry Peregrina *(1985),* Terms of Survival *(1987), and* Reaching for the Mainland and Selected New Poems *(1996) and a novel,* The Line of the Sun *(1989). She also wrote* An Island Like You: Stories of the Barrio *(1995);* Year of Our Revolution: New and Selected Stories and Poems *(1998); and* Woman in Front of the Sun: On Becoming a Writer *(2001); and* The Meaning of Consuelo *(2003). "The Myth of the Latin Woman: I Just Met a Girl Named Maria," which first appeared in* The Latin Deli: Prose and Poetry *(1993), explores the destructive effects of the Latina stereotype.*

THE MYTH OF THE LATIN WOMAN: I JUST MET A GIRL NAMED MARIA

On a bus trip to London from Oxford University where I was earning some graduate credits one summer, a young man, obviously fresh from a pub, spotted me and as
if struck by inspiration went down on his knees in the aisle. With both hands over his
heart he broke into an Irish tenor's rendition of "Maria" from *West Side Story.*[1] My
politely amused fellow passengers gave his lovely voice the round of gentle applause it
deserved. Though I was not quite as amused, I managed my version of an English smile:
no show of teeth, no extreme contortions of the facial muscles—I was at this time of
my life practicing reserve and cool. Oh, that British control, how I coveted it. But
"Maria" had followed me to London, reminding me of a prime fact of my life: you can
leave the island, master the English language, and travel as far as you can, but if you
are a Latina, especially one like me who so obviously belongs to Rita Moreno's gene
pool, the island travels with you.

This is sometimes a very good thing—it may win you that extra minute of someone's attention. But with some people, the same things can make *you* an island—not
a tropical paradise but an Alcatraz, a place nobody wants to visit. As a Puerto Rican
girl living in the United States and wanting like most children to "belong," I resented
the stereotype that my Hispanic appearance called forth from many people I met.

Growing up in a large urban center in New Jersey during the 1960s, I suffered
from what I think of as "cultural schizophrenia." Our life was designed by my parents
as a microcosm of their *casas* on the island. We spoke in Spanish, ate Puerto Rican
food bought at the *bodega,* and practiced strict Catholicism at a church that allotted
us a one-hour slot each week for mass, performed in Spanish by a Chinese priest trained
as a missionary for Latin America.

As a girl I was kept under strict surveillance by my parents, since my virtue and
modesty were, by their cultural equation, the same as their honor. As a teenager I was
lectured constantly on how to behave as a proper *señorita.* But it was a conflicting
message I received, since the Puerto Rican mothers also encouraged their daughters to
look and act like women and to dress in clothes our Anglo friends and their mothers
found too "mature" and flashy. The difference was, and is, cultural; yet I often felt hu-
miliated when I appeared at an American friend's party wearing a dress more suitable
to a semi-formal than to a playroom birthday celebration. At Puerto Rican festivities,
neither the music nor the colors we wore could be too loud.

I remember Career Day in our high school, when teachers told us to come dressed   5
as if for a job interview. It quickly became obvious that to the Puerto Rican girls "dressing up" meant wearing their mother's ornate jewelry and clothing, more appropriate
(by mainstream standards) for the company Christmas party than as daily office attire.
That morning I had agonized in front of my closet, trying to figure out what a "career
girl" would wear. I knew how to dress for school (at the Catholic school I attended,
we all wore uniforms), I knew how to dress for Sunday mass, and I knew what dresses
to wear for parties at my relatives' homes. Though I do not recall the precise details

---

[1]*West Side Story:* a musical (1957) by Leonard Bernstein and Arthur Laurents, which featured the song "I
Just Met a Girl Named Maria."

of my Career Day outfit, it must have been a composite of these choices. But I remember a comment my friend (an Italian American) made in later years that coalesced my impressions of that day. She said that at the business school she was attending, the Puerto Rican girls always stood out for wearing "everything at once." She meant, of course, too much jewelry, too many accessories. On that day at school we were simply made the negative models by the nuns, who were themselves not credible fashion experts to any of us. But it was painfully obvious to me that to the others, in their tailored skirts and silk blouses, we must have seemed "hopeless" and "vulgar." Though I now know that most adolescents feel out of step much of the time, I also know that for the Puerto Rican girls of my generation that sense was intensified. The way our teachers and classmates looked at us that day in school was just a taste of the cultural clash that awaited us in the real world, where prospective employers and men on the street would often misinterpret our tight skirts and jingling bracelets as a "come-on."

Mixed cultural signals have perpetuated certain stereotypes—for example, that of the Hispanic woman as the "hot tamale" or sexual firebrand. It is a one-dimensional view that the media have found easy to promote. In their special vocabulary, advertisers have designated "sizzling" and "smoldering" as the adjectives of choice for describing not only the foods but also the women of Latin America. From conversations in my house I recall hearing about the harassment that Puerto Rican women endured in factories where the "boss-men" talked to them as if sexual innuendo was all they understood, and worse, often gave them the choice of submitting to their advances or being fired.

It is custom, however, not chromosomes, that leads us to choose scarlet over pale pink. As young girls, it was our mothers who influenced our decisions about clothes and colors—mothers who had grown up on a tropical island where the natural environment was a riot of primary colors, where showing your skin was one way to keep cool as well as to look sexy. Most important of all, on the island, women perhaps felt freer to dress and move more provocatively since, in most cases, they were protected by the traditions, mores, and laws of a Spanish/Catholic system of morality and machismo whose main rule was: *You may look at my sister, but if you touch her I will kill you.* The extended family and church structure could provide a young woman with a circle of safety in her small pueblo on the island; if a man "wronged" a girl, everyone would close in to save her family honor.

My mother has told me about dressing in her best party clothes on Saturday nights and going to the town's plaza to promenade with her girlfriends in front of the boys they liked. The males were thus given an opportunity to admire the women and to express their admiration in the form of *piropos:* erotically charged street poems they composed on the spot. (I have myself been subjected to a few *piropos* while visiting the island, and they can be outrageous, although custom dictates that they must never cross into obscenity.) This ritual, as I understand it, also entails a show of studied indifference on the woman's part; if she is "decent," she must not acknowledge the man's impassioned words. So I do understand how things can be lost in translation. When a Puerto Rican girl dressed in her idea of what is attractive meets a man from the mainstream culture who has been trained to react to certain types of clothing as a sexual signal, a clash is likely to take place. I remember the boy who took me to my first formal dance leaning over to plant a sloppy, over-eager kiss painfully on my mouth; when

I didn't respond with sufficient passion, he remarked resentfully: "I thought you Latin girls were supposed to mature early," as if I were expected to *ripen* like a fruit or vegetable, not just grow into womanhood like other girls.

It is surprising to my professional friends that even today some people, including those who should know better, still put others "in their place." It happened to me most recently during a stay at a classy metropolitan hotel favored by young professional couples for weddings. Late one evening after the theater, as I walked toward my room with a colleague (a woman with whom I was coordinating an arts program), a middle-aged man in a tuxedo, with a young girl in satin and lace on his arm, stepped directly into our path. With his champagne glass extended toward me, he exclaimed "Evita!"[2]

Our way blocked, my companion and I listened as the man half-recited, half-   10
bellowed "Don't Cry for Me, Argentina." When he finished, the young girl said: "How about a round of applause for my daddy?" We complied, hoping this would bring the silly spectacle to a close. I was becoming aware that our little group was attracting the attention of the other guests. "Daddy" must have perceived this too, and he once more barred the way as we tried to walk past him. He began to shout-sing a ditty to the tune of "La Bamba"—except the lyrics were about a girl named Maria whose exploits rhymed with her name and gonorrhea. The girl kept saying "Oh, Daddy" and looking at me with pleading eyes. She wanted me to laugh along with the others. My companion and I stood silently waiting for the man to end his offensive song. When he finished, I looked not at him but at his daughter. I advised her calmly never to ask her father what he had done in the army. Then I walked between them and to my room. My friend complimented me on my cool handling of the situation, but I confessed that I had really wanted to push the jerk into the swimming pool. This same man—probably a corporate executive, well-educated, even worldly by most standards—would not have been likely to regale an Anglo woman with a dirty song in public. He might have checked his impulse by assuming that she could be somebody's wife or mother, or at least *somebody* who might take offense. But, to him, I was just an Evita or a Maria: merely a character in his cartoon-populated universe.

Another facet of the myth of the Latin woman in the United States is the menial, the domestic—Maria the housemaid or countergirl. It's true that work as domestics, as waitresses, and in factories is all that's available to women with little English and few skills. But the myth of the Hispanic menial—the funny maid, mispronouncing words and cooking up a spicy storm in a shiny California kitchen—has been perpetuated by the media in the same way that "Mammy" from *Gone with the Wind* became America's idea of the black woman for generations. Since I do not wear my diplomas around my neck for all to see, I have on occasion been sent to that "kitchen" where some think I obviously belong.

One incident has stayed with me, though I recognize it as a minor offense. My first public poetry reading took place in Miami, at a restaurant where a luncheon was being held before the event. I was nervous and excited as I walked in with notebook in hand.

---

[2]*Evita:* a musical about Eva Duarte de Perón, the former first lady of Argentina, opened on Broadway in 1979; "Don't Cry for Me, Argentina" is a song from the musical.

An older woman motioned me to her table, and thinking (foolish me) that she wanted me to autograph a copy of my newly published slender volume of verse, I went over. She ordered a cup of coffee from me, assuming that I was the waitress. (Easy enough to mistake my poems for menus, I suppose.) I know it wasn't an intentional act of cruelty. Yet of all the good things that happened later, I remember that scene most clearly, because it reminded me of what I had to overcome before anyone would take me seriously. In retrospect I understand that my anger gave my reading fire. In fact, I have almost always taken any doubt in my abilities as a challenge, the result most often being the satisfaction of winning a convert, of seeing the cold, appraising eyes warm to my words, the body language change, the smile that indicates I have opened some avenue for communication. So that day as I read, I looked directly at that woman. Her lowered eyes told me she was embarrassed at her faux pas, and when I willed her to look up at me, she graciously allowed me to punish her with my full attention. We shook hands at the end of the reading and I never saw her again. She has probably forgotten the entire incident, but maybe not.

Yet I am one of the lucky ones. There are thousands of Latinas without the privilege of an education or the entrees into society that I have. For them life is a constant struggle against the misconceptions perpetuated by the myth of the Latina. My goal is to try to replace the old stereotypes with a much more interesting set of realities. Every time I give a reading, I hope the stories I tell, the dreams and fears I examine in my work, can achieve some universal truth that will get my audience past the particulars of my skin color, my accent, or my clothes.

I once wrote a poem in which I called all Latinas "God's brown daughters." This poem is really a prayer of sorts, offered upward, but also, through the human-to-human channel of art, outward. It is a prayer for communication and for respect. In it, Latin women pray "in Spanish to an Anglo God / with a Jewish heritage," and they are "fervently hoping / that if not omnipotent, / at least He be bilingual."

Questions for Discussion and Writing

1. What characteristics define, from Cofer's perspective, the "Maria" stereotype? How has this stereotype been a source of discomfort for Cofer personally? What use does she make of her personal experience to support her thesis?
2. Have you ever been perceived in stereotyped ways? What steps, if any, did you take to correct this misimpression?
3. At different points in her narrative, Cofer enters the minds of others to see things from their perspective. Try choosing a person you know whose point of view differs from yours, and write a first-person narrative describing the way the world looks to him or her.

Nasdijj

• •

Nasdijj was born in 1950 in the Southwest into a family of migrant workers. He has lived among the Tewa, the Chippawa, the Navajo, and the Mescalero Apache people. Nasdijj has been writing for over twenty years and has supported himself by being a reporter and a teacher. His name is Athabaskan for "to become again." This chapter from his memoir first appeared in June 1999 in Esquire *and was later named as a finalist for the National Magazine Award. In it, he tells of his adopted son's struggle with fetal alcohol syndrome and what Nasdijj learned from him in their all too brief time together.*

THE BLOOD RUNS LIKE A RIVER THROUGH MY DREAMS

My son is dead. I didn't say my adopted son is dead. He was my son.

My son was a Navajo. He lived six years. Those were the best six years of my life.

The social workers didn't tell me about the fetal alcohol syndrome when they brought my son to the hogan I was living in on the Navajo Nation. Perhaps they didn't know. The diagnosis would come later. As a newborn, Tommy Nothing Fancy looked like any other newborn wrapped in his diaper and his blankies, with his tiny fist in his mouth. Had the Indian social worker said the words "fetal alcohol syndrome," I don't know if I would have done any of it differently.

In the beginning there were no bad things in his head. That would come later. In the beginning he was perfect, even if he was a little small, underweight, and premature. He cried a lot, too. He was perfect to me. I would tie him to his Navajo cradleboard and walk him around, bouncing his growing demons briefly to sleep. We were frequently up all night.

My wife was exhausted.   5

The doctors at the Indian Health Service said it was nothing. Probably gas.

My solution for coping with the demons of my son was to take them fishing. It worked.

Fishing was this place where I could stand in the middle of the river with Tommy Nothing Fancy strapped to the cradleboard, which I wore on my back. The sun would warm him, and he would sleep. The wind would wake him up, and he would wiggle and kick and giggle and wail with all the voices and singing of the river. He didn't stay tied to the cradleboard very long. As soon as he could walk, he was fishing.

Fishermen will tell you that fishing is about more than catching fish. Fishing with my son was like surrendering myself to the talons of some wondrous beast. Death is always the uncharted logic of its wars, the punished boy child who has been terribly burned, disfigured, standing like an Aztec priest under his father's infinity.

I took Tommy Nothing Fancy fishing everywhere. We fished the lakes of Canada 10
from a canoe. We fished the Colorado, the San Juan, the Rio Grande. We fished in the Sea of Cortès. I will never forget the look on Tommy's face the day I pulled in a bluefin tuna off the coast of Key West. That such a beast could exist was an awesome discovery both frightening and fascinating to my son.

Fishing was our antidote to keep from falling into the blackness Tommy knew was there gnawing at his bones like an animal. A gravity to all his many failures.

When Tommy Nothing Fancy became agitated, he would go outside and sit in Old Big Wanda. Instead of climbing the walls, he would pretend to drive, although he could not see over the steering wheel. I watched the steering wheel go back and forth, sometimes violently. He couldn't hurt Old Big Wanda, and he couldn't take her anywhere, either. I could always immobilize the truck. So I allowed this. He must have driven that old vehicle through a thousand adventures. What he liked best about it was the fact that it was the truck that took us fishing.

We're not really sure when the seizures started, because he could have been having small ones and we didn't know it. The seizures were controlled by medication. For a while.

The demons always came back to turn Tommy Nothing Fancy inside out.

The doctors at the Indian Health Service didn't think it was gas anymore. Now it had a name. They see a lot of fetal alcohol syndrome at the Indian Health Service. You treat the symptoms. There is no cure.

We had a Navajo *hataalii* (medicine man) come to the hogan for sings.

Tommy was surrounded and nurtured by his culture.

My son didn't want to die in a hospital.

He hated hospitals. Hospitals were boring and invasive. People in hospitals were always making him pull his pants down so they could give him shots. My son was very shy.

We did not speak directly of death. Even now, writing about it feels like some amorphous thing come in from the snow and the cold.

For my son, hospitals were analogous to torture.

He kept begging me to save him from the hospitals.

Perhaps he was begging me to save him from death.

I was never very good as a dad. I failed badly. I knew it. Tommy knew it.

I always tried to give him what he wanted. I gave him a stuffed bear once. He called it Poochie. I gave him cowboy boots when he could walk, because I knew he wanted cowboy boots. I gave him toys. I gave him a real fishing rod. Not the cheap, breakable kind of fake kiddie fishing rod you might give a child to pretend with. Fishing was the one place where we did not pretend. We really were fishermen.

I gave him a real Eagle Claw fly-fishing rod. I took him to Canada, where we went brook trout fishing. It was the trip of a lifetime. My son kept fidgeting with his tackle because he wanted it to be perfect. Too many things in a man's life are never perfect; his tackle did not have to be one of them. My son caught a three-pound female brown that fell for a Muddler Minnow in the acid tan waters of the Asheweig River. The rolling hills surrounding the river were lush and green with spruce and tamarack and poplar.

Every man who has a son should give something of himself. This is what the sons are really looking for. I didn't have much, but I had a dog, I had a truck, I had fishing rods. I had upriver treks to Straight Lake Camp, I had pieces of the wilderness, I had Sleeping Spirit Falls, and I had Thunder Bay.

We swam beneath the falls.

At night we cuddled in our sleeping bags and laughed at the dog, who growled when she thought she heard a bear.

It was Tommy's notion that we name the dog Navajo.

I laughed and said okay.

She went back and forth between the two of us like a gentle conduit between his demons and my determination to tame them.

Death, to the Navajo, is like the cold wind that blows across the mesa from the north. We do not speak of it. But I must break with this tradition of silence, because the silence is ill fitting when it comes to FAS, and the fact that so many Indian children have this horrible affliction must be articulated.

This disease is my enemy. A fetus is damaged when the mother drinks alcohol. Any alcohol. It's that simple.

But men drink.   35

I have listened to many Indian women say this, and they believe it, because it's true.

When pregnant women drink alcohol, there are serious consequences. Our biologies are not the same.

The male body does not nurture fetuses.

But Indian babies do not count. They do not matter. All the old, vicious morality that accompanies the stereotypical image of the inebriated Indian rises to this issue the way a hungry salmon rises to a fly.

There is very little quality to the lives of children who have FAS.   40

Sometimes none.

I have FAS. Not as badly as Tommy Nothing Fancy had it. My version of the disease manifests itself in some rather severe learning disabilities. All my craziness, my inability to deal with authority, my perceptual malfunctions (I can read entire books upside down), my upside-down imagery, and my rage come from FAS. I have never held a real job for more than a year of my life. Reading and writing are torture for me, so I could understand how they were torture for my son.

I cannot recall my mother ever being completely sober. And there it is.

I am still trying to find ways to forgive her. It's hard. To date, I have mainly failed.

Tribal social-work agencies are overwhelmed with children who have FAS, and   45
there are few Indian people willing to adopt these children.

White people are no longer allowed to adopt Indian children. In their wisdom, the tribes attempt to prevent these adoptions. Yet the number of Indian children who have FAS and who need homes, real homes with real families, is often a daunting challenge for the tribes to keep up with. I knew what I was getting into when I adopted my son. I knew the risks. I knew the possibilities. Life on the reservation was nothing new to me.

When People Who Should Know made the point that fetal alcohol syndrome is a racial epidemic on Indian reservations, they were not exaggerating.

My son kicked holes in the wall once. I have yet to fix the holes.

In many ways he was like the wolves among us.

And he could bite.   50

The Bureau of Indian Affairs school down the dirt road from my hogan held a Western Dance Night, a fundraiser, which turned into a drunken brawl. Drunk Navajo and beer cans all over the parking lot of an elementary school. These were the parents of the Navajo children who attended the school. It was a bad example for the kids to see. When I talk to my Navajo friends about how such drinking is inappropriate—not in a bar, but in an elementary school—they sincerely, honestly look at me as if they have no idea what I'm talking about.

Old Stoneface lives.

These are people I love. These are *my* people. These are the people my mother came from. These are the people who call themselves the Diné.

So I just pick up the beer cans, and my heart breaks.

Indians are only doing it to themselves.

Remember: it was done to us long before we started doing it to ourselves. Remember.

When you drive through White People Town there's a big sign downtown that encourages Navajo to drink "desert wine."

In moderation, of course.

Not long ago, another Navajo drunk was found underneath this sign, frozen to death in a ditch.

There are varying degrees of FAS. I have seen children with cases so bad their bodies are twisted like pretzels and they are confined to wheelchairs. Many of them are completely nonverbal.

They can't communicate.

They live life in a diaper.

FAS affects individual children differently. There is no way to predict what it will do to you next.

FAS seems to be mainly neurological. With Tommy Nothing Fancy it was manifested in epileptic seizures and out-of-control behavior. He was the terror of schools and teachers and bus drivers and nurses. I thought I could see him getting duller with every seizure. One seizure was so severe they had to put the boy under general anesthesia. Life under general anesthesia—asleep—is no life.

The seizures seemed to be eating away at his brain. Watching him get duller and duller was the hardest part of it. There had been a time when this child had an edge as sharp as the edge on a razor.

He was smart.

He was an uppity Indian.

He knew things.

You have them while you can. And then you don't have them anymore.

Patty-cake, patty-cake, baker's man, roll'em and roll'em as fast as you can.

He knew he was slowly dying, even though we had never discussed it openly in such specific terms. But he knew.

The slowness was killing both of us.

He was forgetting things now. He took a walk down the dirt road and got lost, and I found him in the woods crying. It was dangerous to let him out of my sight.

More seizures led to more trips to the hospital.

"I don't want to be in a hospital," he said.

"Where do you want to be?" I asked.

Then toss them up in the oven to bake.

"I want to go fishing," he said.

We are still swimming underneath Sleeping Spirit Falls. The water roaring and tumbling.

The social worker, who always seems very tired, leaves you with this living bundle of blankets, diapers, booties, baby powder, formula, crying, kicking, fists balled up with those tiny fingers. The eyes aren't focused yet—and one never will be—and the first thing you do is inspect the goods.

Naked.

Indian babies are brown and soft, and almost purple when they scream.

Suck that little fist.

Chickenpox was fun.

I didn't know that when the pox comes, it forms horrible little scabs all over your   85
penis. I would bathe him in a bath of water and baking soda. Already the sound of water
seemed to soothe him.

If someone had said to me in the beginning, "fetal alcohol syndrome," I can't say
I would not have done this. I *would* have done this. I loved him from the moment the
social worker brought the bundle to my door. I was his dad.

I never thought of him as adopted. I thought of him as mine.

There were times when I could have sworn I had given birth to the little shit.

Bus drivers hated him. Teachers hated him. Nurses hated him.

His dog loved him. She often slept at the foot of his bed.   90

I was not good about sharing him. Even with the woman who was my wife at the time.

Now I had a fishing buddy.

The sound of water would stop his crying.

The doctors tell me it was unusual that he lived as long as he did. I know this:
Tommy Nothing Fancy lived as long as he did, all the way to the age of six, because I
took such good care of him. We were inseparable. I taught him how to fish. But the
enthusiasm was completely his.

I still have his tackle box. I cannot open it. Perhaps someday I will.   95

The stuff inside will be perfect.

. . .

My wife wanted Tommy to die in a hospital. I do not blame her for feeling this way.
Institutions like hospitals lend the illusion of control. Americans have turned birth and
death into the landscape of the experts. My wife was a modern Indian. She wanted
Tommy Nothing Fancy to die surrounded by his family and by a medical community
with its own agenda. It was the normal, modern thing to do. Perhaps they could save
him. Perhaps not.

Tommy Nothing Fancy wanted to die with his dad and his dog while fishing in
the Rio Hondo.

I know because in his own way he told me so.

My wife hated me for telling her this. She begged. She pleaded. She screamed. She   100
pounded the walls.

But the hospitals and the doctors had never made Tommy better. They seemed
helpless in the face of the damage that had been done.

Our marriage could not withstand the stress. We are now divorced. I understand the
anguish I put her through. But Tommy Nothing Fancy did not want to die in a hospital.

I took my son fishing in the Rio Hondo. Our dog loved to romp around the rocks
of the Rio Hondo gorge. She barked at crows.

The place where the Rio Hondo runs free and crystal clear, paradise lost, again, is
filled with spectacular brown trout. It is a place where the sun glitters golden on the
gravel of the riverbed, and life with all its prowess, its struggle, its tenacity, and its
yielding exists in a turbulent crescendo all around you as it rushes downstream, un-
hindered by the complicated likes of man. I was catching brown trout. I was thinking

about cooking them for dinner over our campfire when Tommy Nothing Fancy fell. All that shaking. It was as if a bolt of lightning surged out of control through the damaged brain of my son. It wasn't fair. He was just a little boy who liked to fish. I went to him like I had gone to him a thousand times before. I was holding him when he died. He just stopped breathing. CPR was not effective. The two of us were wet. The dog licked him, barked, and ran in circles. The fish escaped.

Back into the river.   105

Just the soft sound of the river, with its unruly grandeur and its fluid savvy.

I carried Tommy Nothing Fancy to my truck and put him in the back on a blanket.

We are so alone now.

No more patty-cake.

I made a second trip to retrieve his tackle. I could not leave this perfection behind.   110

He was so flawed. But his fishing tackle was sublime.

The pediatric neurologist at the hospital had seen FAS deaths before.

"He died fishing," I said.

He had lived fishing, too. I was glad I could give him that. Anyone could have given him hospitals. I was not anyone. I was Tommy Nothing Fancy's father.

We are still swimming under the water at Sleeping Spirit Falls. The water roaring   115 and tumbling. The blood runs like a river through my dreams.

The dog and I drove back to the Navajo Nation that night by ourselves. The shadows of the mountains loomed before us. *Patty-cake, patty-cake, baker's man, roll 'em and roll 'em as fast as you can.* It took me a long, long time before I could cry, and when I did, I thought the universe had ended. First gear is mainly torque. Second gear turns corners. Third gear gets you on the highway. Fourth gear lets you fly. Learning to release him is going to take me some time.

Questions for Discussion and Writing

1. Describe the bond that existed between the author and his adopted son, Tommy Nothing Fancy, and what their fishing trips meant to both of them.

2. Why is it important to understand fetal alcohol syndrome and its devastating personal and cultural effects among Native Americans?

3. In your opinion, could this autobiographical account have served as a kind of catharsis for Nasdijj? Explain your answer. Why was it important for Nasdijj that his son spend his last moments on a fishing trip rather than in a hospital?

FICTION

Charlotte Perkins Gilman

Charlotte Perkins Gilman (1860–1935) was born in Hartford, Connecticut, into a family that, despite their poverty, made every attempt to give her the advantages of an education. She married an artist, Charles Stetson, in 1884, and after the birth of their daughter the following year, she suffered a nervous breakdown. Her struggle with depression brought her to the attention of an eminent neurologist, whose prescription for a "rest cure" had disastrous consequences (parallel to those experienced by the narrator in "The Yellow Wallpaper"). In later life, she became an advocate for social and political reform. Her book Women and Economics *(1898) anticipated the work of such feminists as Simone de Beauvoir, a half-century later. She promoted her views through public lectures and in her magazine,* The Forerunner, *which she edited from 1909 to 1916.*

THE YELLOW WALLPAPER

It is very seldom that mere ordinary people like John and myself secure ancestral halls for the summer.

A colonial mansion, a hereditary estate, I would say a haunted house and reach the height of romantic felicity—but that would be asking too much of fate!

Still I will proudly declare that there is something queer about it.

Else, why should it be let so cheaply? And why have stood so long untenanted?

John laughs at me, of course, but one expects that.   5

John is practical in the extreme. He has no patience with faith, an intense horror of superstition, and he scoffs openly at any talk of things not to be felt and seen and put down in figures.

John is a physician, and *perhaps*—(I would not say it to a living soul, of course, but this is dead paper and a great relief to my mind)—*perhaps* that is one reason I do not get well faster.

You see, he does not believe I am sick! And what can one do?

If a physician of high standing, and one's own husband, assures friends and relatives that there is really nothing the matter with one but temporary nervous depression—a slight hysterical tendency—what is one to do?

My brother is also a physician, and also of high standing, and he says the same thing.   10

So I take phosphates or phosphites—whichever it is—and tonics, and air and exercise, and journeys, and am absolutely forbidden to "work" until I am well again.

Personally, I disagree with their ideas.

Personally, I believe that congenial work, with excitement and change, would do me good.

But what is one to do?

I did write for a while in spite of them; but it *does* exhaust me a good deal—having to be so sly about it, or else meet with heavy opposition.   15

I sometimes fancy that in my condition, if I had less opposition and more society and stimulus—but John says the very worst thing I can do is to think about my condition, and I confess it always makes me feel bad.

So I will let it alone and talk about the house.

The most beautiful place! It is quite <u>alone</u>, standing <u>well back from the road</u>, quite three miles from the village. It makes me think of English places that you read about, for there are hedges and <u>walls</u> and <u>gates</u> that <u>lock,</u> and lots of separate little houses for the gardeners and people.

There is a *delicious* garden! I never saw such a garden—large and shady, full of box-bordered paths, and lined with long grape-covered arbors with seats under them.

There were greenhouses, too, but they are all <u>broken</u> now.   20

There was some legal trouble, I believe, something about the heirs and coheirs; anyhow, the place has been <u>empty for years</u>.

That spoils my ghostliness, I am afraid, but I don't care—there is something <u>strange</u> about the house—I can feel it.

I even said so to John one moonlight evening, but he said what I felt was a draught, and shut the window.

I get <u>unreasonably angry</u> with John sometimes. I'm sure I <u>never used to be so sensitive</u>. I <u>think it is due to this nervous condition.</u>

But John says if I feel so I shall neglect proper <u>self-control</u>; so I take pains to con- 25
trol myself—before him at least, and that makes me very tired.

I don't like our room a bit. I wanted one downstairs that opened on the piazza and had roses all over the window, and such pretty old-fashioned chintz hangings! But John would not hear of it.

He said there was only one window and not room for two beds, and no near room for him if he took another.

He is very careful and loving, and hardly lets me stir without special direction.

I have a schedule prescription for each hour in the day; he takes all care from me, and so I feel basely ungrateful not to value it more.

He said he came here solely on my account, that I was to have perfect rest and all 30
the air I could get. "Your exercise depends on your strength, my dear," said he, "and your food somewhat on your appetite; but air you can absorb all the time." So we took the nursery at the top of the house.

It is a big, airy room, the whole floor nearly, with windows that look all ways, and air and sunshine galore. It was nursery first and then playroom and gymnasium, I should judge; for the <u>windows are barred</u> for little children, and there are rings and things in the walls.

The paint and paper look as if a boys' school had used it. It is <u>stripped off</u>—the paper—in great patches all around the head of my bed, about as far as I can reach, and in a great place on the other side of the room low down. I never saw a worse paper in my life. One of those <u>sprawling flamboyant patterns committing every artistic sin</u>.

It is <u>dull</u> enough to <u>confuse the eye in</u> following, pronounced enough to <u>constantly irritate and provoke study</u>, and when you follow the lame <u>uncertain</u> curves for a little distance they <u>suddenly commit suicide</u>—plunge off at outrageous angles, destroy themselves in unheard-of contradictions.

The color is repellent, almost revolting: a smouldering unclean yellow, strangely faded by the slow-turning sunlight. It is a dull yet lurid orange in some places, a sickly sulphur tint in others.

No wonder the children hated it! I should hate it myself if I had to live in this room long. 35

There comes John, and I must put this away—he hates to have me write a word.

[margin note: 2 wks after]
[note above: time line]

We have been here two weeks, and I haven't felt like writing before, since that first day.

I am sitting by the window now, up in this atrocious nursery, and there is nothing to hinder my writing as much as I please, save lack of strength.

John is away all day, and even some nights when his cases are serious.

I am glad my case is not serious! 40

But these nervous troubles are dreadfully depressing.

John does not know how much I really suffer. He knows there is no reason to suffer, and that satisfies him.

Of course it is only nervousness. It does weigh on me so not to do my duty in any way!

I meant to be such a help to John, such a real rest and comfort, and here I am a comparative burden already! *[note: Guilt]*

Nobody would believe what an effort it is to do what little I am able—to dress 45 and entertain, and order things.

It is fortunate Mary is so good with the baby. Such a dear baby!

And yet I *cannot* be with him, it makes me so nervous.

I suppose John never was nervous in his life. He laughs at me so about this wallpaper!

At first he meant to repaper the room, but afterward he said that I was letting it get the better of me, and that nothing was worse for a nervous patient than to give way to such fancies.

He said that after the wallpaper was changed it would be the heavy bedstead, and 50 then the barred windows, and then that gate at the head of the stairs, and so on.

"You know the place is doing you good," he said, "and really, dear, I don't care to renovate the house just for a three months' rental."

"Then do let us go downstairs," I said. "There are such pretty rooms there."

Then he took me in his arms and called me a blessed little goose, and said he would go down cellar, if I wished, and have it whitewashed into the bargain.

But he is right enough about the beds and windows and things.

It is as airy and comfortable room as any one need wish, and, of course, I would 55 not be so silly as to make him uncomfortable just for a whim.

I'm really getting quite fond of the big room, all but that horrid paper.

Out of one window I can see the garden—those mysterious deep-shaded arbors, the riotous old-fashioned flowers, and bushes and gnarly trees.

Out of another I get a lovely view of the bay and a little private wharf belonging to the estate. There is a beautiful shaded lane that runs down there from the house. I always fancy I see people walking in these numerous paths and arbors, but John has cautioned me not to give way to fancy in the least. He says that with my imaginative power and habit of story-making, a nervous weakness like mine is sure to lead to all manner of excited fancies, and that I ought to use my will and good sense to check the tendency. So I try.

I think sometimes that if I were only well enough to write a little it would relieve the press of ideas and rest me.

But I find I get pretty tired when I try.

It is so discouraging not to have any advice and companionship about my work. When I get really well, John says we will ask Cousin Henry and Julia down for a long visit; but he says he would as soon put fireworks in my pillow-case as to let me have those stimulating people about now.

I wish I could get well faster.

But I must not think about that. This paper looks to me as if it *knew* what a vicious influence it had!

There is a recurrent spot where the pattern lolls like a broken neck and two bulbous eyes stare at you upside down.

I get positively angry with the impertinence of it and the everlastingness. Up and down and sideways they crawl, and those absurd unblinking eyes are everywhere. There is one place where two breadths didn't match, and the eyes go all up and down the line, one a little higher than the other.

I never saw so much expression in an inanimate thing before, and we all know how much expression they have! I used to lie awake as a child and get more entertainment and terror out of blank walls and plain furniture than most children could find in a toy-store.

I remember what a kindly wink the knobs of our big old bureau used to have, and there was one chair that always seemed like a strong friend.

I used to feel that if any of the other things looked too fierce I could always hop into that chair and be safe.

The furniture in this room is no worse than inharmonious, however, for we had to bring it all from downstairs. I suppose when this was used as a playroom they had to take the nursery things out, and no wonder! I never saw such ravages as the children have made here.

The wallpaper, as I said before, is torn off in spots, and it sticketh closer than a brother—they must have had perseverance as well as hatred.

Then the floor is scratched and gouged and splintered, the plaster itself is dug out here and there, and this great heavy bed, which is all we found in the room, looks as if it had been through the wars.

But I don't mind it a bit—only the paper.

There comes John's sister. Such a dear girl as she is, and so careful of me! I must not let her find me writing.

She is a perfect and enthusiastic housekeeper, and hopes for no better profession. I verily believe she thinks it is the writing which made me sick!

But I can write when she is out, and see her a long way off from these windows.

There is one that commands the road, a lovely shaded winding road, and one that just looks off over the country. A lovely country, too, full of great elms and velvet meadows.

This wallpaper has a kind of sub-pattern in a different shade, a particularly irritating one, for you can only see it in certain lights, and not clearly then.

But in the places where it isn't faded and where the sun is just so—I can see a strange, provoking, formless sort of figure that seems to skulk about behind that silly and conspicuous front design.

There's sister on the stairs!

Well, the Fourth of July is over! The people are all gone, and I am tired out. John   80 thought it might do me good to see a little company, so we just had mother and Nellie and the children down for a week.

Of course I didn't do a thing. Jennie sees to everything now.

But it tired me all the same.

John says if I don't pick up faster he shall send me to Weir Mitchell[1] in the fall.

But I don't want to go there at all. I had a friend who was in his hands once, and she says he is just like John and my brother, only more so!

Besides, it is such an undertaking to go so far.   85

I don't feel as if it was worth while to turn my hand over for anything, and I'm getting dreadfully fretful and querulous.

I cry at nothing, and cry most of the time.

Of course I don't when John is here, or anybody else, but when I am alone.

And I am alone a good deal just now. John is kept in town very often by serious cases, and Jennie is good and lets me alone when I want her to.

So I walk a little in the garden or down that lovely lane, sit on the porch under the   90 roses, and lie down up here a good deal.

I'm getting really fond of the room in spite of the wallpaper. Perhaps *because* of the wallpaper.

It dwells in my mind so!

I lie here on this great immovable bed—it is nailed down, I believe—and follow that pattern about by the hour. It is as good as gymnastics, I assure you. I start, we'll say, at the bottom, down in the corner over there where it has not been touched, and I determine for the thousandth time that I *will* follow that pointless pattern to some sort of a conclusion.

I know a little of the principle of design, and I know this thing was not arranged on any laws of radiation, or alternation, or repetition, or symmetry, or anything else that I ever heard of.

It is repeated, of course, by the breadths, but not otherwise.   95

Looked at in one way each breadth stands alone; the bloated curves and flourishes—a kind of "debased Romanesque"[2] with delirium tremens go waddling up and down in isolated columns of fatuity.

But, on the other hand, they connect diagonally, and the sprawling outlines run off in great slanting waves of optic horror, like a lot of wallowing sea-weeds in full chase.

The whole thing goes horizontally, too, at least it seems so, and I exhaust myself in trying to distinguish the order of its going in that direction.

---

[1]*Dr. Silas Weir Mitchell:* nineteenth-century physician known for his treatment of psychosomatic illnesses.
[2]*Romanesque:* a style of art and architecture that prevailed throughout Europe from the mid-eleventh to the mid-twelfth centuries and that made use of Roman architectural features such as the rounded arch and the barrel vault.

They have used a horizontal breadth for a frieze, and that adds wonderfully to the confusion.

There is one end of the room where it is almost intact, and there, when the crosslights fade and the low sun shines directly upon it, I can almost fancy radiation after all—the interminable grotesque seems to form around a common center and rush off in headlong plunges of equal distraction.

It makes me tired to follow it. I will take a nap, I guess.

I don't know why I should write this.

I don't want to.

I don't feel able.

And I know John would think it absurd. But I *must* say what I feel and think in some way—it is such a relief!

But the effort is getting to be greater than the relief.

Half the time now I am awfully lazy, and lie down ever so much. John says I mustn't lose my strength, and has me take cod liver oil and lots of tonics and things, to say nothing of ale and wine and rare meat.

Dear John! He loves me very dearly, and hates to have me sick. I tried to have a real earnest reasonable talk with him the other day, and tell him how I wish he would let me go and make a visit to Cousin Henry and Julia.

But he said I wasn't able to go, nor able to stand it after I got there; and I did not make out a very good case for myself, for I was crying before I had finished.

It is getting to be a great effort for me to think straight. Just this nervous weakness, I suppose.

And dear John gathered me up in his arms, and just carried me upstairs and laid me on the bed, and sat by me and read to me till it tired my head.

He said I was his darling and his comfort and all he had, and that I must take care of myself for his sake, and keep well.

He says no one but myself can help me out of it, that I must use my will and self-control and not let any silly fancies run away with me.

There's one comfort—the baby is well and happy, and does not have to occupy this nursery with the horrid wallpaper.

If we had not used it, that blessed child would have! What a fortunate escape! Why, I wouldn't have a child of mine, an impressionable little thing, live in such a room for worlds.

I never thought of it before, but it is lucky that John kept me here after all; I can stand it so much easier than a baby, you see.

Of course I never mention it to them any more—I am too wise—but I keep watch for it all the same.

There are things in that paper that nobody knows but me, or ever will.

Behind that outside pattern the dim shapes get clearer every day.

It is always the same shape, only very numerous.

And it is like a woman stooping down and creeping about behind that pattern. I don't like it a bit. I wonder—I begin to think—I wish John would take me away from here!

It is so hard to talk with John about my case, because he is so wise, and because he loves me so.

But I tried it last night.

It was moonlight. The moon shines in all around just as the sun does.

I hate to see it sometimes, it creeps so slowly, and always comes in by one window　125
or another.

John was asleep and I hated to waken him, so I kept still and watched the moonlight on that undulating wallpaper till I felt creepy.

The faint figure behind seemed to shake the pattern, just as if she wanted to get out.

I got up softly and went to feel and see if the paper *did* move, and when I came
back John was awake.

"What is it, little girl?" he said. "Don't go walking about like that—you'll get cold."

I thought it was a good time to talk, so I told him that I really was not gaining　130
here, and that I wished he would take me away.

"Why, darling!" said he, "our lease will be up in three weeks, and I can't see how
to leave before.

"The repairs are not done at home, and I cannot possibly leave town just now. Of
course if you were in any danger, I could and would, but you really are better, dear,
whether you can see it or not. I am a doctor, dear, and I know. You are gaining flesh
and color, your appetite is better, I feel really much easier about you."

"I don't weigh a bit more," said I, "nor as much; and my appetite may be better
in the evening when you are here, but it is worse in the morning when you are away!"

"Bless her little heart!" said he with a big hug. "She shall be as sick as she pleases! But
now let's improve the shining hours by going to sleep, and talk about it in the morning!"

"And you won't go away?" I asked gloomily.　135

"Why, how can I, dear? It is only three weeks more and then we will take a nice little trip of a few days while Jennie is getting the house ready. Really, dear, you are better!"

"Better in body perhaps—" I began, and stopped short, for he sat up straight and
looked at me with such a stern, reproachful look that I could not say another word.

"My darling," said he, "I beg of you, for my sake and for our child's sake, as well
as for your own, that you will never for one instant let that idea enter your mind! There
is nothing so dangerous, so fascinating, to a temperament like yours. It is a false and
foolish fancy. Can you not trust me as a physician when I tell you so?"

So of course I said no more on that score, and we went to sleep before long. He
thought I was asleep first, but I wasn't, and lay there for hours trying to decide whether
that front pattern and the back pattern really did move together or separately.

On a pattern like this, by daylight, there is a lack of sequence, a defiance of law,　140
that is a constant irritant to a normal mind.

The color is hideous enough, and unreliable enough, and infuriating enough, but
the pattern is torturing.

You think you have mastered it, but just as you get well under way in following,
it turns a back-somersault and there you are. It slaps you in the face, knocks you down,
and tramples upon you. It is like a bad dream.

The outside pattern is a florid arabesque, reminding one of a fungus. If you can
imagine a toadstool in joints, an interminable string of toadstools, budding and sprouting in endless convolutions—why, that is something like it.

That is, sometimes!

There is one marked peculiarity about this paper, a thing nobody seems to notice   145
but myself, and that is that it changes as the light changes.

When the sun shoots in through the east window—I always watch for that first
long, straight ray—it changes so quickly that I never can quite believe it.

That is why I watch it always.

By moonlight—the moon shines in all night when there is a moon—I wouldn't
know it was the same paper.

At night in any kind of light, in twilight, candlelight, lamplight, and worst of all
by moonlight, it becomes bars! The outside pattern, I mean, and the woman behind it
is as plain as can be.

I didn't realize for a long time what the thing was that showed behind, that dim   150
sub-pattern, but now I am quite sure it is a woman.

By daylight she is subdued, quiet. I fancy it is the pattern that keeps her so still. It
is so puzzling. It keeps me quiet by the hour.

I lie down ever so much now. John says it is good for me, and to sleep all I can.

Indeed he started the habit by making me lie down for an hour after each meal.

It is a very bad habit I am convinced, for you see I don't sleep.

And that cultivates deceit, for I don't tell them I'm awake—oh, no!   155

The fact is I am getting a little afraid of John.

He seems very queer sometimes, and even Jennie has an inexplicable look.

It strikes me occasionally, just as a scientific hypothesis, that perhaps it is the paper!

I have watched John when he did not know I was looking, and come into the room
suddenly on the most innocent excuses, and I've caught him several times *looking at
the paper!* And Jennie too. I caught Jennie with her hand on it once.

She didn't know I was in the room, and when I asked her in a quiet, a very quiet   160
voice, with the most restrained manner possible, what she was doing with the paper,
she turned around as if she had been caught stealing, and looked quite angry—asked
me why I should frighten her so!

Then she said that the paper stained everything it touched, that she had found yellow smooches on all my clothes and John's and she wished we would be more careful!

Did not that sound innocent? But I know she was studying that pattern, and I am
determined that nobody shall find it out but myself!

Life is very much more exciting now than it used to be. You see, I have something
more to expect, to look forward to, to watch. I really do eat better, and am more quiet
than I was.

John is so pleased to see me improve! He laughed a little the other day, and said I
seemed to be flourishing in spite of my wallpaper.

I turned it off with a laugh. I had no intention of telling him it was *because* of the   165
wallpaper—he would make fun of me. He might even want to take me away.

I don't want to leave now until I have found it out. There is a week more, and I
think that will be enough.

I'm feeling ever so much better!

I don't sleep much at night, for it is so interesting to watch developments; but I sleep
a good deal in the daytime.

In the daytime it is tiresome and perplexing.

There are always new shoots on the fungus, and new shades of yellow all over it.   170
I cannot keep count of them, though I have tried conscientiously.

It is the strangest yellow, that wallpaper! It makes me think of all the yellow things
I ever saw—not beautiful ones like buttercups, but old, foul, bad yellow things.

But there is something else about that paper—the smell! I noticed it the moment
we came into the room, but with so much air and sun it was not bad. Now we have
had a week of fog and rain, and whether the windows are open or not, the smell is here.

It creeps all over the house.

I find it hovering in the dining-room, skulking in the parlor, hiding in the hall,
lying in wait for me on the stairs.

It gets into my hair.   175

Even when I go to ride, if I turn my head suddenly and surprise it—there is that smell!

Such a peculiar odor, too! I have spent hours in trying to analyze it, to find what
it smelled like.

It is not bad—at first—and very gentle, but quite the subtlest, most enduring odor
I ever met.

In this damp weather it is awful, I wake up in the night and find it hanging over me.

It used to disturb me at first. I thought seriously of burning the house—to   180
reach the smell.

But now I am used to it. The only thing I can think of that it is like is the *color* of
the paper! A yellow smell.

There is a very funny mark on this wall, low down, near the mopboard. A streak
that runs round the room. It goes behind every piece of furniture, except the bed, a
long, straight, even *smooch*, as if it had been rubbed over and over.

I wonder how it was done and who did it, and what they did it for. Round and
round and round—round and round and round—it makes me dizzy!

I really have discovered something at last.

Through watching so much at night, when it changes so, I have finally found out.   185

The front pattern *does* move—and no wonder! The woman behind shakes it!

Sometimes I think there are a great many women behind, and sometimes only one,
and she crawls around fast, and her crawling shakes it all over.

Then in the very bright spots she keeps still, and in the very shady spots she just
takes hold of the bars and shakes them hard.

And she is all the time trying to climb through. But nobody could climb through
that pattern—it strangles so; I think that is why it has so many heads.

They get through and then the pattern strangles them off and turns them upside   190
down, and makes their eyes white!

If those heads were covered or taken off it would not be half so bad.

I think that woman gets out in the daytime!

And I'll tell you why—privately—I've seen her!

I can see her out of every one of my windows!

It is the same woman, I know, for she is always creeping, and most women do not   195
creep by daylight.

I see her in that long shaded lane, creeping up and down. I see her in those dark grape arbors, creeping all around the garden.

I see her on that long road under the trees, creeping along, and when a carriage comes she hides under the blackberry vines.

I don't blame her a bit. It must be very humiliating to be caught creeping by daylight!

I always lock the door when I creep by daylight. I can't do it at night, for I know John would suspect something at once.

And John is so queer now that I don't want to irritate him. I wish he would take another room! Besides, I don't want anybody to get that woman out at night but myself.   200

I often wonder if I could see her out of all the windows at once.

But, turn as fast as I can, I can only see out of one at one time.

And though I always see her, she *may* be able to creep faster than I can turn! I have watched her sometimes away off in the open country, creeping as fast as a cloud shadow in a wind.

If only that top pattern could be gotten off from the under one! I mean to try it, little by little.

I have found out another funny thing, but I shan't tell it this time! It does not do   205
to trust people too much.

There are only two more days to get this paper off, and I believe John is beginning to notice. I don't like the look in his eyes.

And I heard him ask Jennie a lot of professional questions about me. She had a very good report to give.

She said I slept a good deal in the daytime.

John knows I don't sleep very well at night, for all I'm so quiet!

He asked me all sorts of questions, too, and pretended to be very loving and kind.   210
As if I couldn't see through him!

Still, I don't wonder he acts so, sleeping under this paper for three months.

It only interests me, but I feel sure John and Jennie are affected by it.

Hurrah! This is the last day, but it is enough. John is to stay in town over night, and won't be out until this evening.

Jennie wanted to sleep with me—the sly thing; but I told her I should undoubtedly   215
rest better for a night all alone.

That was clever, for really I wasn't alone a bit! As soon as it was moonlight and that poor thing began to crawl and shake the pattern, I got up and ran to help her.

I pulled and she shook, I shook and she pulled, and before morning we had peeled off yards of that paper.

A strip about as high as my head and half around the room.

And then when the sun came and that awful pattern began to laugh at me, I declared I would finish it today!

We go away tomorrow, and they are moving all my furniture down again to leave   220
things as they were before.

Jennie looked at the wall in amazement, but I told her merrily that I did it out of pure spite at the vicious thing.

She laughed and said she wouldn't mind doing it herself, but I must not get tired.
How she betrayed herself that time!

But I am here, and no person touches this paper but Me—not *alive!*

She tried to get me out of the room—it was too patent! But I said it was so quiet   225
and empty and clean now that I believed I would lie down again and sleep all I could,
and not to wake me even for dinner—I would call when I woke.

So now she is gone, and the servants are gone, and the things are gone, and there
is nothing left but that great bedstead nailed down, with the canvas mattress we found
on it.

We shall sleep downstairs tonight, and take the boat home tomorrow.

I quite enjoy the room, now it is bare again.

How those children did tear about here!

This bedstead is fairly gnawed!   230

But I must get to work.

I have locked the door and thrown the key down into the front path.

I don't want to go out, and I don't want to have anybody come in, till John
comes.

I want to astonish him.

I've got a rope up here that even Jennie did not find. If that woman does get out,   235
and tries to get away, I can tie her!

But I forgot I could not reach far without anything to stand on!

This bed will *not* move!

I tried to lift and push it until I was lame, and then I got so angry I bit off a little
piece at one corner—but it hurt my teeth.

Then I peeled off all the paper I could reach standing on the floor. It sticks horribly and the pattern just enjoys it! All those strangled heads and bulbous eyes and waddling fungus growths just shriek with derision!

I am getting angry enough to do something desperate. To jump out of the window   240
would be admirable exercise, but the bars are too strong even to try.

Besides I wouldn't do it. Of course not. I know well enough that a step like that
is improper and might be misconstrued.

I don't like to *look* out of the windows even—there are so many of those creeping
women, and they creep so fast.

I wonder if they all come out of that wallpaper as I did?

But I am securely fastened now by my well-hidden rope—you don't get *me* out in
the road there!

I suppose I shall have to get back behind the pattern when it comes night, and that   245
is hard!

It is so pleasant to be out in this great room and creep around as I please!

I don't want to go outside. I won't, even if Jennie asks me to.

For outside you have to creep on the ground, and everything is green instead of
yellow.

But here I can creep smoothly on the floor, and my shoulder just fits in that long
smooch around the wall, so I cannot lose my way.

Why there's John at the door!   250

It is no use, young man, you can't open it!

How he does call and pound!

Now he's crying to Jennie for an axe.

It would be a shame to break down that beautiful door!

"John, dear!" said I in the gentlest voice. "The key is down by the front steps, 255 under a plantain leaf!"

That silenced him for a few moments.

Then he said, very quietly indeed, "Open the door, my darling!"

"I can't," said I. "The key is down by the front door under a plantain leaf!" And then I said it again, several times, very gently and slowly, and said it so often that he had to go and see, and he got it of course, and came in. He stopped short by the door.

"What is the matter?" he cried. "For God's sake, what are you doing!"

I kept on creeping just the same, but I looked at him over my shoulder. 260

"I've got out at last," said I, "in spite of you and Jennie! And I've pulled off most of the paper, so you can't put me back!"

Now why should that man have fainted? But he did, and right across my path by the wall, so that I had to creep over him every time!

Questions for Discussion and Writing

1. What role does the narrator's husband (who is also her physician) play in her psychological deterioration?
2. How does the yellow wallpaper in the story and the narrator's attitude toward it reflect her decline into madness?
3. Does the narrator in the story elicit your sympathy? Why or why not? In what respects is the story still a timely one, even though it was written in 1892?

Andre Dubus

· ·

Andre Dubus (1936–1999) was born in Lake Charles, Louisiana. He graduated from McNeese State College and joined the Marine Corps, in which he served until 1964. After studying creative writing at the University of Iowa, he taught at Bradford College in Massachusetts from 1966 until 1984. His many collections of short fiction include The Cage Keeper and Other Stories *(1989), and* Dancing After Hours *(1996). His short story "Killings" was adapted for the 2001 film* In the Bedroom. *"The Fat Girl" first appeared in* Adultery and Other Choices *(1975).*

THE FAT GIRL

Her name was Louise. Once when she was sixteen a boy kissed her at a barbecue; he was drunk and he jammed his tongue into her mouth and ran his hands up and down her hips. Her father kissed her often. He was thin and kind and she could see in his eyes when he looked at her the lights of love and pity.

It started when Louise was nine. You must start watching what you eat, her mother would say. I can see you have my metabolism. Louise also had her mother's pale blond hair. Her mother was slim and pretty, carried herself erectly, and ate very little. The two of them would eat bare lunches, while her older brother ate sandwiches and potato chips, and then her mother would sit smoking while Louise eyed the bread box, the pantry, the refrigerator. Wasn't that good, her mother would say. In five years you'll be in high school and if you're fat the boys won't like you; they won't ask you out. Boys were as far away as five years, and she would go to her room and wait for nearly an hour until she knew her mother was no longer thinking of her, then she would creep into the kitchen and, listening to her mother talking on the phone, or her footsteps upstairs, she would open the bread box, the pantry, the jar of peanut butter. She would put the sandwich under her shirt and go outside or to the bathroom to eat it.

Her father was a lawyer and made a lot of money and came home looking pale and happy. Martinis put color back in his face, and at dinner he talked to his wife and two children. Oh give her a potato, he would say to Louise's mother. She's a growing girl. Her mother's voice then became tense: If she has a potato she shouldn't have dessert. She should have both, her father would say, and he would reach over and touch Louise's cheek or hand or arm.

In high school she had two girlfriends and at night and on weekends they rode in a car or went to movies. In movies she was fascinated by fat actresses. She wondered why they were fat. She knew why she was fat: she was fat because she was Louise. Because God had made her that way. Because she wasn't like her friends Joan and Marjorie, who drank milk shakes after school and were all bones and tight skin. But what about those actresses, with their talents, with their broad and profound faces? Did they eat as heedlessly as Bishop Humphries and his wife who sometimes came to dinner and, as Louise's mother said, gorged between amenities? Or did they try to lose weight, did they go about hungry and angry and thinking of food? She thought of them eating lean meats and salads with friends, and then going home and building strange large sandwiches with French bread. But mostly she believed they did not go through these failures; they were fat because they chose to be. And she was certain of something else too: she could see it in their faces: they did not eat secretly. Which she did: her creeping to the kitchen when she was nine became, in high school, a ritual of deceit and pleasure. She was a furtive eater of sweets. Even her two friends did not know her secret.

Joan was thin, gangling, and flat-chested; she was attractive enough and all she needed was someone to take a second look at her face, but the school was large and there were pretty girls in every classroom and walking all the corridors, so no one ever needed to take a second look at Joan. Marjorie was thin too, an intense, heavy-smoking girl with brittle laughter. She was very intelligent, and with boys she was shy because she knew she made them uncomfortable, and because she was smarter than they were and so could not understand or could not believe the levels they lived on. She was to have a nervous breakdown before earning her Ph.D. in philosophy at the University of California, where she met and married a physicist and discovered within herself an untrammelled passion: she made love with her husband on the couch, the carpet, in the bathtub, and on the washing machine. By that time much had happened to her and she never thought of Louise. Joan would finally stop growing and begin moving with grace and confidence. In college she would have two lovers and then several more during   5 the six years she spent in Boston before marrying a middle-aged editor who had two sons in their early teens, who drank too much, who was tenderly, boyishly grateful for her love, and whose wife had been killed while rock-climbing in New Hampshire with her lover. She would not think of Louise either, except in an earlier time, when lovers were still new to her and she was ecstatically surprised each time one of them loved her and, sometimes at night, lying in a man's arms, she would tell how in high school no one dated her, she had been thin and plain (she would still believe that: that she had been plain; it had never been true) and so had been forced into the weekend and night-time company of a neurotic smart girl and a shy fat girl. She would say this with self-pity exaggerated by Scotch and her need to be more deeply loved by the man who held her.

She never eats, Joan and Marjorie said of Louise. They ate lunch with her at school, watched her refusing potatoes, ravioli, fried fish. Sometimes she got through the cafeteria line with only a salad. That is how they would remember her: a girl whose hapless body was destined to be fat. No one saw the sandwiches she made and took to her room when she came home from school. No one saw the store of Milky Ways, Butterfingers, Almond Joys, and Hersheys far back on her closet shelf, behind the stuffed animals of her childhood. She was not a hypocrite. When she was out of the house she truly believed she was dieting; she forgot about the candy, as a man speaking into his office dictaphone may forget the lewd photographs hidden in an old shoe in his closet. At other times, away from home, she thought of the waiting candy with near lust. One night driving home from a movie, Marjorie said: "You're lucky you don't smoke; it's in*cred*ible what I go through to hide it from my parents." Louise turned to her a smile which was elusive and mysterious; she yearned to be home in bed, eating chocolate in the dark. She did not need to smoke; she already had a vice that was insular and destructive. . . .

She brought it with her to college. She thought she would leave it behind. A move from one place to another, a new room without the haunted closet shelf, would do for her what she could not do for herself. She packed her large dresses and went. For two weeks she was busy with registration, with shyness, with classes; then she began to feel at home. Her room was no longer like a motel. Its walls had stopped watching her, she felt they were her friends, and she gave them her secret. Away from her mother, she did not have to be as elaborate; she kept the candy in her drawer now.

The school was in Massachusetts, a girls' school. When she chose it, when she and her father and mother talked about it in the evenings, everyone so carefully avoided the word boys that sometimes the conversations seemed to be about nothing but boys. There are no boys there, the neuter words said; you will not have to contend with that. In her father's eyes were pity and encouragement; in her mother's was disappointment, and her voice was crisp. They spoke of courses, of small classes where Louise would get more attention. She imagined herself in those small classes; she saw herself as a teacher would see her, as the other girls would; she would get no attention.

The girls at the school were from wealthy families, but most of them wore the uniform of another class: blue jeans and work shirts, and many wore overalls. Louise bought some overalls, washed them until the dark blue faded, and wore them to classes. In the cafeteria she ate as she had in high school, not to lose weight nor even to sustain her lie, but because eating lightly in public had become as habitual as good manners.

Everyone had to take gym, and in the locker room with the other girls, and wearing shorts on the volleyball and badminton courts, she hated her body. She liked her body most when she was unaware of it: in bed at night, as sleep gently took her out of her day, out of herself. And she liked parts of her body. She liked her brown eyes and sometimes looked at them in the mirror: they were not shallow eyes, she thought; they were indeed windows of a tender soul, a good heart. She liked her lips and nose, and her chin, finely shaped between her wide and sagging cheeks. Most of all she liked her long pale blond hair, she liked washing and drying it and lying naked on her bed, smelling of shampoo, and feeling the soft hair at her neck and shoulders and back.

Her friend at college was Carrie, who was thin and wore thick glasses and often   10 at night she cried in Louise's room. She did not know why she was crying. She was crying, she said, because she was unhappy. She could say no more. Louise said she was unhappy too, and Carrie moved in with her. One night Carrie talked for hours, sadly and bitterly, about her parents and what they did to each other. When she finished she hugged Louise and they went to bed. Then in the dark Carrie spoke across the room: "Louise? I just wanted to tell you. One night last week I woke up and smelled chocolate. You were eating chocolate, in your bed. I wish you'd eat it in front of me, Louise, whenever you feel like it."

Stiffened in her bed, Louise could think of nothing to say. In the silence she was afraid Carrie would think she was asleep and would tell her again in the morning or tomorrow night. Finally she said okay. Then after a moment she told Carrie if she ever wanted any she could feel free to help herself; the candy was in the top drawer. Then she said thank you.

They were roommates for four years and in the summers they exchanged letters. Each fall they greeted with embraces, laughter, tears, and moved into their old room, which had been stripped and cleansed of them for the summer. Neither girl enjoyed summer. Carrie did not like being at home because her parents did not love each other. Louise lived in a small city in Louisiana. She did not like summer because she had lost touch with Joan and Marjorie; they saw each other, but it was not the same. She liked being with her father but with no one else. The flicker of disappointment in her mother's eyes at the airport was a vanguard of the army of relatives and acquaintances who awaited her: they would see her on the streets, in stores, at the country club, in her home, and in theirs; in the first moments of greeting, their eyes would tell her she was still fat Louise, who had been fat as long as they could remember, who had gone to college and returned as fat as ever. Then their eyes dismissed her, and she longed for school and Carrie, and she wrote letters to her friend. But that saddened her too. It wasn't simply that Carrie was her only friend, and when they finished college they might never see each other again. It was that her existence in the world was so divided; it had begun when she was a child creeping to the kitchen; now that division was much sharper, and her friendship with Carrie seemed disproportionate and perilous. The world she was destined to live in had nothing to do with the intimate nights in their room at school.

In the summer before their senior year, Carrie fell in love. She wrote to Louise about him, but she did not write much, and this hurt Louise more than if Carrie had shown the joy her writing tried to conceal. That fall they returned to their room; they were still close and warm, Carrie still needed Louise's ears and heart at night as she spoke of her parents and her recurring malaise whose source the two friends never discovered. But on most weekends Carrie left, and caught a bus to Boston where her boyfriend studied music. During the week she often spoke hesitantly of sex; she was not sure if she liked it. But Louise, eating candy and listening, did not know whether Carrie was telling the truth or whether, as in her letters of the past summer, Carrie was keeping from her those delights she may never experience.

Then one Sunday night when Carrie had just returned from Boston and was unpacking her overnight bag, she looked at Louise and said: "I was thinking about you. On the bus coming home tonight." Looking at Carrie's concerned, determined face, Louise prepared herself for humiliation. "I was thinking about when we graduate. What you're going to do. What's to become of you. I want you to be loved the way I love you. Louise, if I help you, *really* help you, will you go on a diet?"

Louise entered a period of her life she would remember always, the way some people remember having endured poverty. Her diet did not begin the next day. Carrie told her to eat on Monday as though it were the last day of her life. So for the first time since grammar school Louise went into a school cafeteria and ate everything she wanted. At breakfast and lunch and dinner she glanced around the table to see if the other girls noticed the food on her tray. They did not. She felt there was a lesson in this, but it lay beyond her grasp. That night in their room she ate the four remaining candy bars. During the day Carrie rented a small refrigerator, bought an electric skillet, an electric broiler, and bathroom scales. 15

On Tuesday morning Louise stood on the scales, and Carrie wrote in her notebook: *October 14: 184 lbs.* Then she made Louise a cup of black coffee and scrambled one egg and sat with her while she ate. When Carrie went to the dining room for breakfast, Louise walked about the campus for thirty minutes. That was part of the plan. The campus was pretty, on its lawns grew at least one of every tree native to New England, and in the warm morning sun Louise felt a new hope. At noon they met in their room, and Carrie broiled her a piece of hamburger and served it with lettuce. Then while Carrie ate in the dining room Louise walked again. She was weak with hunger and she felt queasy. During her afternoon classes she was nervous and tense, and she chewed her pencil and tapped her heels on the floor and tightened her calves. When she returned to her room late that afternoon, she was so glad to see Carrie that she embraced her; she had felt she could not bear another minute of hunger, but now with Carrie she knew she could make it at least through tonight. Then she would sleep and face tomorrow when it came. Carrie broiled her a steak and served it with lettuce. Louise studied while Carrie ate dinner, then they went for a walk.

That was her ritual and her diet for the rest of the year, Carrie alternating fish and chicken breasts with the steaks for dinner, and every day was nearly as bad as the first. In the evenings she was irritable. In all her life she had never been afflicted by ill temper and she looked upon it now as a demon which, along with hunger, was taking possession of her soul. Often she spoke sharply to Carrie. One night during their after-dinner walk Carrie talked sadly of night, of how darkness made her more aware of herself, and at night she did not know why she was in college, why she studied, why she was walking the earth with other people. They were standing on a wooden foot bridge, looking down at a dark pond. Carrie kept talking; perhaps soon she would cry. Suddenly Louise said: "I'm sick of lettuce. I never want to see a piece of lettuce for the rest of my life. I hate it. We shouldn't even buy it, it's immoral."

Carrie was quiet. Louise glanced at her, and the pain and irritation in Carrie's face soothed her. Then she was ashamed. Before she could say she was sorry, Carrie turned to her and said gently: "I know. I know how terrible it is."

Carrie did all the shopping, telling Louise she knew how hard it was to go into a supermarket when you were hungry. And Louise was always hungry. She drank diet soft drinks and started smoking Carrie's cigarettes, learned to enjoy inhaling, thought of cancer and emphysema but they were as far away as those boys her mother had talked about when she was nine. By Thanksgiving she was smoking over a pack a day and her weight in Carrie's notebook was one hundred and sixty-two pounds. Carrie was afraid if Louise went home at Thanksgiving she would lapse from the diet, so Louise spent the vacation with Carrie, in Philadelphia. Carrie wrote her family about the diet, and told Louise that she had. On the phone to Philadelphia, Louise said: "I feel like a bedwetter. When I was a little girl I had a friend who used to come spend the night and Mother would put a rubber sheet on the bed and we all pretended there wasn't a rubber sheet and that she hadn't wet the bed. Even me, and I slept with her." At Thanksgiving dinner she lowered her eyes as Carrie's father put two slices of white meat on her plate and passed it to her over the bowls of steaming food.

When she went home at Christmas she weighed a hundred and fifty-five pounds; at the airport her mother marveled. Her father laughed and hugged her and said: "But now there's less of you to love." He was troubled by her smoking but only mentioned it once; he told her she was beautiful and, as always, his eyes bathed her with love. During the long vacation her mother cooked for her as Carrie had, and Louise returned to school weighing a hundred and forty-six pounds. 20

Flying north on the plane she warmly recalled the surprised and congratulatory eyes of her relatives and acquaintances. She had not seen Joan or Marjorie. She thought of returning home in May, weighing the hundred and fifteen pounds which Carrie had in October set as their goal. Looking toward the stoic days ahead, she felt strong. She thought of those hungry days of fall and early winter (and now: she was hungry now: with almost a frown, almost a brusque shake of the head, she refused peanuts from the stewardess): those first weeks of the diet when she was the pawn of an irascibility which still, conditioned to her ritual as she was, could at any moment take command of her. She thought of the nights of trying to sleep while her stomach growled. She thought of her addiction to cigarettes. She thought of the people at school: not one teacher, not one girl, had spoken to her about her loss of weight, not even about her absence from meals. And without warning her spirit collapsed. She did not feel strong, she did not feel she was committed to and within reach of achieving a valuable goal. She felt that somehow she had lost more than pounds of fat; that some time during her dieting she had lost herself too. She tried to remember what it had felt like to be Louise before she had started living on meat and fish, as an unhappy adult may look sadly in the memory of childhood for lost virtues and hopes. She looked down at the earth far below, and it seemed to her that her soul, like her body aboard the plane, was in some rootless flight. She neither knew its destination nor where it had departed from; it was on some passage she could not even define.

During the next few weeks she lost weight more slowly and once for eight days Carrie's daily recording stayed at a hundred and thirty-six. Louise woke in the morning thinking of one hundred and thirty-six and then she stood on the scales and they echoed her. She became obsessed with that number, and there wasn't a day when she didn't say it aloud, and through the days and nights the number stayed in her mind, and if a teacher had spoken those digits in a classroom she would have opened her mouth to speak. What if that's me, she said to Carrie. I mean what if a hundred and thirty-six is my real weight and I just can't lose anymore. Walking hand-in-hand with her despair was a longing for this to be true, and that longing angered her and wearied her, and every day she was gloomy. On the ninth day she weighed a hundred and thirty-five and a half pounds. She was not relieved; she thought bitterly of the months ahead, the shedding of the last twenty and a half pounds.

On Easter Sunday, which she spent at Carrie's, she weighed one hundred and twenty pounds, and she ate one slice of glazed pineapple with her ham and lettuce. She did not enjoy it: she felt she was being friendly with a recalcitrant enemy who had once tried to destroy her. Carrie's parents were laudative. She liked them and she wished they would touch sometimes, and look at each other when they spoke. She guessed they would divorce when Carrie left home, and she vowed that her own marriage would be one of affection and tenderness. She could think about that now: marriage. At school she had read in a Boston paper that this summer the cicadas would come out of their seventeen-year hibernation on Cape Cod, for a month they would mate and then die, leaving their young to burrow into the ground where they would stay for seventeen years. That's me, she had said to Carrie. Only my hibernation lasted twenty-one years.

Often her mother asked in letters and on the phone about the diet, but Louise answered vaguely. When she flew home in late May she weighed a hundred and thirteen pounds, and at the airport her mother cried and hugged her and said again and again: You're so *beaut*iful. Her father blushed and bought her a martini. For days her relatives and acquaintances congratulated her, and the applause in their eyes lasted the entire summer, and she loved their eyes, and swam in the country club pool, the first time she had done this since she was a child.

She lived at home and ate the way her mother did and every morning she weighed herself on the scales in her bathroom. Her mother liked to take her shopping and buy her dresses and they put her old ones in the Goodwill box at the shopping center; Louise thought of them existing on the body of a poor woman whose cheap meals kept her fat. Louise's mother had a photographer come to the house, and Louise posed on the couch and standing beneath a live oak and sitting in a wicker lawn chair next to an azalea bush. The new clothes and the photographer made her feel she was going to another country or becoming a citizen of a new one. In the fall she took a job of no consequence, to give herself something to do.

Also in the fall a young lawyer joined her father's firm, he came one night to dinner, and they started seeing each other. He was the first man outside her family to kiss her since the barbecue when she was sixteen. Louise celebrated Thanksgiving not with rice dressing and candied sweet potatoes and mince meat and pumpkin pies, but by giving Richard her virginity which she realized, at the very last moment of its existence, she had embarked on giving him over thirteen months ago, on that Tuesday in October when Carrie had made her a cup of black coffee and scrambled one egg. She wrote this to Carrie, who replied happily by return mail. She also, through glance and smile and innuendo, tried to tell her mother too. But finally she controlled that impulse, because Richard felt guilty about making love with the daughter of his partner and friend. In the spring they married. The wedding was a large one, in the Episcopal church, and Carrie flew from Boston to be maid of honor. Her parents had recently separated and she was living with the musician and was still victim of her unpredictable malaise. It overcame her on the night before the wedding, so Louise was up with her until past three and woke next morning from a sleep so heavy that she did not want to leave it.

Richard was a lean, tall, energetic man with the metabolism of a pencil sharpener. Louise fed him everything he wanted. He liked Italian food and she got recipes from her mother and watched him eating spaghetti with the sauce she had only tasted, and ravioli and lasagna, while she ate antipasto with her chianti. He made a lot of money and borrowed more and they bought a house whose lawn sloped down to the shore of a lake; they had a wharf and a boathouse, and Richard bought a boat and they took friends waterskiing. Richard bought her a car and they spent his vacations in Mexico, Canada, the Bahamas, and in the fifth year of their marriage they went to Europe and, according to their plan, she conceived a child in Paris. On the plane back, as she looked out the window and beyond the sparkling sea and saw her country, she felt that it was waiting for her, as her home by the lake was, and her parents, and her good friends who rode in the boat and waterskied; she thought of the accumulated warmth and pelf of her marriage, and how by slimming her body she had bought into the pleasures of the nation. She felt cunning, and she smiled to herself, and took Richard's hand.

But these moments of triumph were sparse. On most days she went about her routine of leisure with a sense of certainty about herself that came merely from not thinking. But there were times, with her friends, or with Richard, or alone in the house, when she was suddenly assaulted by the feeling that she had taken the wrong train and arrived at a place where no one knew her, and where she ought not to be. Often, in bed with Richard, she talked of being fat: "I was the one who started the friendship with Carrie, I chose her, I started the conversations. When I understood that she was my friend I understood something else: I had chosen her for the same reason I'd chosen Joan and Marjorie. They were all thin. I was always thinking about what people saw when they looked at me and I didn't want them to see two fat girls. When I was alone I didn't mind being fat but then I'd have to leave the house again and then I didn't want to look like me. But at home I didn't mind except when I was getting dressed to go out of the house and when Mother looked at me. But I stopped looking at her when she looked at me. And in college I felt good with Carrie; there weren't any boys and I didn't have any other friends and so when I wasn't with Carrie I thought about her and I tried to ignore the other people around me, I tried to make them not exist. A lot of the time I could do that. It was strange, and I felt like a spy."

If Richard was bored by her repetition he pretended not to be. But she knew the story meant very little to him. She could have been telling him of a childhood illness, or wearing braces, or a broken heart at sixteen. He could not see her as she was when she was fat. She felt as though she were trying to tell a foreign lover about her life in the United States, and if only she could command the language he would know and love all of her and she would feel complete. Some of the acquaintances of her childhood were her friends now, and even they did not seem to remember her when she was fat.

Now her body was growing again, and when she put on a maternity dress for the first time she shivered with fear. Richard did not smoke and he asked her, in a voice   30 just short of demand, to stop during her pregnancy. She did. She ate carrots and celery instead of smoking, and at cocktail parties she tried to eat nothing, but after her first drink she ate nuts and cheese and crackers and dips. Always at these parties Richard had talked with his friends and she had rarely spoken to him until they drove home. But now when he noticed her at the hors d'oeuvres table he crossed the room and, smiling, led her back to his group. His smile and his hand on her arm told her he was doing his clumsy, husbandly best to help her through a time of female mystery.

She was gaining weight but she told herself it was only the baby, and would leave with its birth. But at other times she knew quite clearly that she was losing the discipline she had fought so hard to gain during her last year with Carrie. She was hungry now as she had been in college, and she ate between meals and after dinner and tried to eat only carrots and celery, but she grew to hate them, and her desire for sweets was as vicious as it had been long ago. At home she ate bread and jam and when she shopped for groceries she bought a candy bar and ate it driving home and put the wrapper in her purse and then in the garbage can under the sink. Her cheeks had filled out, there was loose flesh under her chin, her arms and legs were plump, and her mother was concerned. So was Richard. One night when she brought pie and milk to the living room where they were watching television, he said: "You already had a piece. At dinner."

She did not look at him.

"You're gaining weight. It's not all water, either. It's fat. It'll be summertime. You'll want to get into your bathing suit."

The pie was cherry. She looked at it as her fork cut through it; she speared the piece and rubbed it in the red juice on the plate before lifting it to her mouth.

"You never used to eat pie," he said. "I just think you ought to watch it a bit. It's 35 going to be tough on you this summer."

In her seventh month, with a delight reminiscent of climbing the stairs to Richard's apartment before they were married, she returned to her world of secret gratification. She began hiding candy in her underwear drawer. She ate it during the day and at night while Richard slept, and at breakfast she was distracted, waiting for him to leave.

She gave birth to a son, brought him home, and nursed both him and her appetites. During this time of celibacy she enjoyed her body through her son's mouth; while he suckled she stroked his small head and back. She was hiding candy but she did not conceal her other indulgences: she was smoking again but still she ate between meals, and at dinner she ate what Richard did, and coldly he watched her, he grew petulant, and when the date marking the end of their celibacy came they let it pass. Often in the afternoons her mother visited and scolded her and Louise sat looking at the baby and said nothing until finally, to end it, she promised to diet. When her mother and father came for dinners, her father kissed her and held the baby and her mother said nothing about Louise's body, and her voice was tense. Returning from work in the evenings Richard looked at a soiled plate and glass on the table beside her chair as if detecting traces of infidelity, and at every dinner they fought.

"Look at you," he said. "Lasagna, for God's sake. When are you going to start? It's not simply that you haven't lost any weight. You're gaining. I can see it. I can feel it when you get in bed. Pretty soon you'll weigh more than I do and I'll be sleeping on a trampoline."

"You never touch me anymore."

"I don't want to touch you. Why should I? Have you *looked* at yourself?"   40

"You're cruel," she said. "I never knew how cruel you were."

She ate, watching him. He did not look at her. Glaring at his plate, he worked with fork and knife like a hurried man at a lunch counter.

"I bet you didn't either," she said.

That night when he was asleep she took a Milky Way to the bathroom. For a while she stood eating in the dark, then she turned on the light. Chewing, she looked at herself in the mirror; she looked at her eyes and hair. Then she stood on the scales and looking at the numbers between her feet, one hundred and sixty-two, she remembered when she had weighed a hundred and thirty-six pounds for eight days. Her memory of those eight days was fond and amusing, as though she were recalling an Easter egg hunt when she was six. She stepped off the scales and pushed them under the lavatory and did not stand on them again.

It was summer and she bought loose dresses and when Richard took friends out   45 on the boat she did not wear a bathing suit or shorts; her friends gave her mischievous glances, and Richard did not look at her. She stopped riding on the boat. She told them she wanted to stay with the baby, and she sat inside holding him until she heard the boat leave the wharf. Then she took him to the front lawn and walked with him in the shade of the trees and talked to him about the blue jays and mockingbirds and cardinals she saw on their branches. Sometimes she stopped and watched the boat out on the lake and the friend skiing behind it.

Every day Richard quarreled, and because his rage went no further than her weight and shape, she felt excluded from it, and she remained calm within layers of flesh and spirit, and watched his frustration, his impotence. He truly believed they were arguing about her weight. She knew better: she knew that beneath the argument lay the question of who Richard was. She thought of him smiling at the wheel of his boat, and long ago courting his slender girl, the daughter of his partner and friend. She thought of Carrie telling her of smelling chocolate in the dark and, after that, watching her eat it night after night. She smiled at Richard, teasing his anger.

He is angry now. He stands in the center of the living room, raging at her, and he wakes the baby. Beneath Richard's voice she hears the soft crying, feels it in her heart, and quietly she rises from her chair and goes upstairs to the child's room and takes him from the crib. She brings him to the living room and sits holding him in her lap, pressing him gently against the folds of fat at her waist. Now Richard is pleading with her. Louise thinks tenderly of Carrie broiling meat and fish in their room, and walking with her in the evenings. She wonders if Carrie still has the malaise. Perhaps she will come for a visit. In Louise's arms now the boy sleeps.

"I'll help you," Richard says. "I'll eat the same things you eat."

But his face does not approach the compassion and determination and love she had seen in Carrie's during what she now recognizes as the worst year of her life. She can remember nothing about that year except hunger, and the meals in her room. She is hungry now. When she puts the boy to bed she will get a candy bar from her room. She will eat it here, in front of Richard. This room will be hers soon. She considers the possibilities: all these rooms and the lawn where she can do whatever she wishes. She knows he will leave soon. It has been in his eyes all summer. She stands, using one hand to pull herself out of the chair. She carries the boy to his crib, feels him against her large breasts, feels that his sleeping body touches her soul. With a surge of vindication and relief she holds him. Then she kisses his forehead and places him in the crib. She goes to the bedroom and in the dark takes a bar of candy from her drawer. Slowly she descends the stairs. She knows Richard is waiting but she feels his departure so happily that, when she enters the living room, unwrapping the candy, she is surprised to see him standing there.

Questions for Discussion and Writing

1. What factors explain why being thin becomes so important to Louise? How do her mother and father communicate very different messages about this?
2. Why is Louise's relationship with Carrie one of the most important ones in her life?
3. Why does Louise return to being fat after she has married Richard and had a child and established a life she presumably wanted?
4. Write a caption to a snapshot or an e-mailed photo of a family member or friend, and then write a short paragraph describing the person, the circumstances, and how the picture and the caption work together.

POETRY

William Shakespeare

*William Shakespeare (1564–1616) was born in Stratford-upon-Avon, the son of a prosperous merchant, and received his early education at Stratford Grammar School. In 1582, he married Anne Hathaway and over the next twenty years established himself as a professional actor and playwright in London. Shakespeare's **sonnets,** of which there are 154, were probably written in the 1590s but were first published in 1609. The fourteen lines of the Shakespearean sonnet fall into three quatrains and a couplet rhyming abab cdcd efef gg. They hint at a story involving a young man, a "dark lady," and the poet himself, together with a "rival poet." Sonnet 30 expresses a variation on a familiar theme: the encroachment of time, loss, and death, and the undying power of love and friendship to resist these devastations.*

SONNET 30: WHEN TO THE SESSIONS OF SWEET SILENT THOUGHT

When to the sessions[1] of sweet silent thought
I summon up remembrance of things past,
I sigh the lack of many a thing I sought,
And with old woes new wail my dear time's waste.
Then can I drown an eye, unused to flow,   5
For precious friends hid in death's dateless[2] night,
And weep afresh love's long since cancelled[3] woe,
And moan th' expense of many a vanished sight.
Then can I grieve at grievances forgone,
And heavily from woe to woe tell o'er   10
The sad account of fore-bemoanèd moan,
Which I new pay as if not paid before.
    But if the while I think on thee, dear friend,
    All losses are restored, and sorrows end.

Questions for Discussion and Writing

1. What power does Shakespeare attribute to the person who is the object of love and friendship in this sonnet?
2. What does this sonnet imply about the importance of love to withstand the destructive effects of time and physical and emotional changes?
3. Do you feel the same way Shakespeare does, that is, that love has the power to obliterate the destructive effects of time and loss? Describe an experience that made you realize this.

Barbara Kingsolver

· ·

Barbara Kingsolver was born in 1955 in Annapolis, Maryland, and was raised in rural Kentucky. She received her B.A. from DePauw University (1977) and a master's degree in biology from the University of Arizona (1981). She had a career as a journalist and technical writer before turning to fiction and poetry in the 1980s. Her novels include The Poisonwood Bible *(1998) and* Prodigal Summer *(2000). Kingsolver's collections of poetry include* Another America *(1991), in which the following poem first appeared. She has also written nonfiction works, including* Holding the Line *(1989) and* High Tide in Tucson *(1995), and a collection of short stories,* Homeland *(1989). Her poetry is passionate and blends personal commentary with insight into contemporary patterns of family relationships. Her most recent work is a volume of essays,* Small Wonder *(2002).*

---

[1]*Sessions:* as in a court of law.   [2]*Dateless:* endless.   [3]ll. 7–14: The financial metaphor, as in a court case, continues through *cancelled, expense* (loss), *tell* (count), *account, pay, losses,* etc.

THIS HOUSE I CANNOT LEAVE

My friend describes the burglar:
how he touched her clothes, passed through rooms
leaving himself there,
staining the space
between walls, a thing she can see.   5
She doesn't care what he took, only
that he has driven her out, she can't
stay in this house
she loved, scraped the colors of four families
from the walls and painted with her own,   10
and planted things.
She is leaving fruit trees behind.

She will sell, get out, maybe
another neighborhood.
                    People say   15
Get over it. The market isn't good. They advise
that she think about cash to mortgage
and the fruit trees

but the trees have stopped growing for her.

I offer no advice.   20
I tell her I know, she will leave. I am thinking
of the man who broke and entered

me.

Of the years it took to be home again
in this house I cannot leave.   25

Questions for Discussion and Writing

1. How does the speaker apply the problem that confronts her friend to her own life? What important differences make the speaker's situation more poignant?
2. Why is the metaphor of a house that has been burglarized a particularly apt **symbol** to describe the speaker's predicament?
3. In your opinion, why doesn't the speaker offer the same sensible advice as the other friends? What advice would you have given?

Anna Kamieńska

Anna Kamieńska (1920–1986), a Polish poet, translator, critic, essayist, and editor, was the author of numerous collections of original and translated poetry (from Russian and other Slavic languages) as well as of anthologies, books for children, and collections of interpretations of poems. Initially a poet of peasant themes and moral concerns, she underwent a spiritual metamorphosis in the early 1970s, becoming an important poet of religious experience. A posthumous collection of her poetry is Two Darknesses, *translated by Tomasz P. Krzeszowski and Desmond Graham (1994). "Funny" (1973), translated by Mieczyslaw Jastrun, offers a wryly thought-provoking view of the human condition.*

FUNNY

What's it like to be a human
the bird asked

I myself don't know
it's being held prisoner by your skin
while reaching infinity   5
being a captive of your scrap of time
while touching eternity
being hopelessly uncertain
and helplessly hopeful
being a needle of frost   10
and a handful of heat
breathing in the air
and choking wordlessly
it's being on fire
with a nest made of ashes   15
eating bread
while filling up on hunger
it's dying without love
it's loving through death

That's funny said the bird   20
and flew effortlessly up into the air

Questions for Discussion and Writing

1. How is the poem developed between a set of opposing values represented by the condition of the bird and the condition of humanity?
2. If the bird side of the equation is represented through the image of effortlessness, what details suggest the difficulties, uncertainties, and precariousness of the human condition? How does Kamieńska use irony to suggest the enormous gap between the bird and the human, especially in relationship to the title? Why would the human condition be "funny" from the bird's point of view?
3. How would you go about explaining to someone who didn't possess a particular sense (sight, hearing) or was color-blind what it is like to see, to hear, or to see colors? What analogies or metaphors would you choose to use in your explanation?

Sara Teasdale

• •

Sara Teasdale (1884–1933) was raised and educated in St. Louis and traveled to Europe and the Near East. After returning to the United States, she settled in New York and lived a life very similar to the independent "solitary" she describes in this poem. Her published works include Rivers to the Sea *(1915) and* Love Songs *(1917).* Love Songs *went through five editions in one year and won Teasdale a special Pulitzer award, the first given to a book of poetry.*

THE SOLITARY

My heart has grown rich with the passing of years,
  I have less need now than when I was young

To share myself with every comer
  Or shape my thoughts into words with my tongue.

It is one to me that they come or go   5
  If I have myself and the drive of my will,
And strength to climb on a summer night
  And watch the stars swarm over the hill.

Let them think I love them more than I do,
  Let them think I care, though I go alone;   10
If it lifts their pride, what is it to me
  Who am self-complete as a flower or a stone.

Questions for Discussion and Writing

1. In what way has the speaker changed from when she was young?
2. How does the speaker feel toward the way others perceive her?
3. Do you believe it is possible or desirable for someone to become as "self-complete as a flower or a stone"? Why, or why not? Alternatively, you might consider whether people become more self-sufficient as they grow older.

Thinking Critically About the Image

Pablo Picasso (1881–1973), Spanish painter, sculptor, and graphic artist, worked in France. A foremost figure in twentieth-century art, he was renowned for his technical virtuosity and originality, especially for his development of Cubism, in which three-dimensional subjects are frgamented and redefined from several points of view simultaneously. *The Dream* depicts a young woman, Marie-Therese Walter (who Picasso used as a model in many of his paintings), in a state of reverie. Turn the picture clockwise to the side to gain an unexpected view.

1. How does Picasso's choice of subject, colors, **surreal** and overlapping angles of representation convey a dreamlike mood?
2. How does this picture illustrate the way Picasso expresses a reflection on experience by using a new method of representation?
3. What might the young woman be thinking and feeling as she drifts into sleep?

Connections

Chapter 1: Reflections on Experience

Jill Nelson,   *Number One!*
In what ways do both Nelson and Judith Ortiz Cofer strive to transcend socially restrictive expectations linked to race and ethnicity?

Fritz Peters,   *Boyhood with Gurdjieff*
Compare Gurdjieff's seemingly unfair method for teaching compassion with Jesus's teaching parable about the laborers in the vineyard (Ch. 11).

Beryl Markham,   *West with the Night*
Compare the reasons why Markham and Douchan Gersi subject themselves to life-endangering challenges that most people would not choose to encounter.

Marcel Proust,   *The Bodily Memory*
How do events in the present trigger past memories that overwhelm the speakers in Proust's account and in Barbara Kingsolver's "This House I Cannot Leave"?

Douchan Gersi,   *Initiated into an Iban Tribe of Headhunters*
Compare the experiences, expectations, and outcomes in Gersi's account with those of Herodotus in "Concerning Egypt" (Ch. 7).

Annie Dillard, *So, This Was Adolescence*
Compare the reflections of Dillard on the uncertainties of adolescence with those of the character Connie in Joyce Carol Oates's story "Where Are You Going, Where Have You Been?" (Ch. 11).

Judith Ortiz Cofer, *The Myth of the Latin Woman: I Just Met a Girl Named Maria*
In what respects are the narrator in Charlotte Perkins Gilman's story and Cofer in this account encouraged to think less of themselves because of prevailing social and cultural stereotypes?

Nasdijj, *The Blood Runs Like a River Through My Dreams*
How does Nasdijj's account provide another perspective to Jared Diamond's essay "Why Do We Smoke, Drink, and Use Dangerous Drugs?" (Ch. 6)?

Charlotte Perkins Gilman, *The Yellow Wallpaper*
Compare the very different expectations the narrators set for themselves in Gilman's story and in Beryl Markham's account.

Andre Dubus, *The Fat Girl*
To what extent are the protagonists in the stories by Charlotte Perkins Gilman and Dubus victims of society's expectations in different eras?

William Shakespeare, *Sonnet 30: When to the Sessions of Sweet Silent Thought*
What contrasting perspectives do Shakespeare and Sara Teasdale bring to the theme of being capable of love?

Barbara Kingsolver, *This House I Cannot Leave*
Compare the ideology of the image of confinement in both Charlotte Perkins Gilman's story and Kingsolver's poem.

Anna Kamieńska, *Funny*
In what way do both Kamieńska and Joaquim María Machado de Assis in "A Canary's Ideas" (Ch. 3) use birds to express an ironic perspective on the human condition?

Sara Teasdale, *The Solitary*
How is the theme of self-reliance developed in Teasdale's poem and in Nasreddin Hodja's story "Do As You Please" (Ch. 11)?

Vincent Van Gogh, **The Café Terrace on the Place du Forum, Arles, at Night,** *1888.*
Oil on canvas. Cat. 232. Erich Lessing/Art Resource, NY. Rijksmuseum Kroeller-Mueller, Otterlo, The Netherlands.

Influential People and Memorable Places

Who shall set a limit to the influence of a human being?
—RALPH WALDO EMERSON, "POWER," THE CONDUCT OF LIFE

THE AUTHORS IN THIS CHAPTER REFLECT ON the influence of parents, friends, teachers, and others in shaping their lives. As you read the accounts by Maya Angelou, Gayle Pemberton, Mikhal Gilmore, and Fatima Mernissi, you might ask yourself how much of your personality, outlook, and expectations are the direct result of knowing someone who was important to you.

The writers of the essays identify defining qualities and character traits, and they also relate important incidents that enable us to understand why each of the people they describe had such an impact on their lives. In other essays, places, not people, play a decisive role in eliciting unique responses. The landscapes and architectural wonders described by Richard Keller Simon, William Zinsser, and Joseph Addison transport us to the mega shopping mall, Niagara Falls, and Westminster Abbey. George Carlin satirizes Americans' dependence on their "stuff," especially when traveling to a strange place.

In the first story, by Raymond Carver, a couple vicariously enter the lives of their friends who are out of town. A story by Bessie Head reveals the impact of a seven-year drought on a family in Botswana.

The poems in this chapter deepen our emotional capacity to understand the often inexpressible dimensions of human relationships. The poems by Cathy Song and Robert Hayden give intimate portraits of a daughter and her mother and a son and his father. The influence of an important place can be observed in William Wordsworth's deeply felt tribute to the city of London.

NONFICTION

Maya Angelou

• •

Maya Angelou was born in 1928 in St. Louis, Missouri, and attended public schools in Arkansas and California. In her widely varied career, she has been a streetcar conductor, a successful singer, an actress, and a teacher. She is the author of several volumes of poetry and ten plays for stage, screen, and television, but she is best known for her autobiography, a work still in progress (five volumes of which have been published). "Liked for Myself" originally appeared in the first volume of this autobiography, I Know Why the Caged Bird Sings *(1970). Her most recent works are* Even the Stars Look Lonesome *(1997),* Heart of a Woman *(1997), and* Angelina of Italy *(2004).*

LIKED FOR MYSELF

For nearly a year, I sopped around the house, the Store, the school and the church, like an old biscuit, dirty and inedible. Then I met, or rather got to know, the lady who threw me my first life line.

Mrs. Bertha Flowers was the aristocrat of Black Stamps. She had the grace of control to appear warm in the coldest weather, and on the Arkansas summer days it seemed she had a private breeze which swirled around, cooling her. She was thin without the taut look of wiry people, and her printed voile dresses and flowered hats were as right for her as denim overalls for a farmer. She was our side's answer to the richest white woman in town.

Her skin was a rich black that would have peeled like a plum if snagged, but then no one would have thought of getting close enough to Mrs. Flowers to ruffle her dress, let alone snag her skin. She didn't encourage familiarity. She wore gloves too.

I don't think I ever saw Mrs. Flowers laugh, but she smiled often. A slow widening of her thin black lips to show even, small white teeth, then the slow effortless closing. When she chose to smile on me, I always wanted to thank her. The action was so graceful and inclusively benign.

She was one of the few gentlewomen I have ever known, and has remained throughout my life the measure of what a human being can be. . . .   5

One summer afternoon, sweet-milk fresh in my memory, she stopped at the Store to buy provisions. Another Negro woman of her health and age would have been expected to carry the paper sacks home in one hand, but Momma said, "Sister Flowers, I'll send Bailey up to your house with these things."

She smiled that slow dragging smile, "Thank you, Mrs. Henderson. I'd prefer Marguerite, though." My name was beautiful when she said it. "I've been meaning to talk to her, anyway." They gave each other age-group looks. . . .

There was a little path beside the rocky road, and Mrs. Flowers walked in front swinging her arms and picking her way over the stones.

She said, without turning her head, to me, "I hear you're doing very good school work, Marguerite, but that it's all written. The teachers report that they have trouble getting you to talk in class." We passed the triangular farm on our left and the path widened to allow us to walk together. I hung back in the separate unasked and unanswerable questions.

"Come and walk along with me, Marguerite." I couldn't have refused even if I 10 wanted to. She pronounced my name so nicely. Or more correctly, she spoke each word with such clarity that I was certain a foreigner who didn't understand English could have understood her.

"Now no one is going to make you talk—possibly no one can. But bear in mind, language is man's way of communicating with his fellow man and it is language alone which separates him from the lower animals." That was a totally new idea to me, and I would need time to think about it.

"Your grandmother says you read a lot. Every chance you get. That's good, but not good enough. Words mean more than what is set down on paper. It takes the human voice to infuse them with the shades of deeper meaning."

I memorized the part about the human voice infusing words. It seemed so valid and poetic.

She said she was going to give me some books and that I not only must read them, I must read them aloud. She suggested that I try to make a sentence sound in as many different ways as possible.

"I'll accept no excuse if you return a book to me that has been badly handled." My 15 imagination boggled at the punishment I would deserve if in fact I did abuse a book of Mrs. Flowers'. Death would be too kind and brief.

The odors in the house surprised me. Somehow I had never connected Mrs. Flowers with food or eating or any other common experience of common people. There must have been an outhouse, too, but my mind never recorded it.

The sweet scent of vanilla had met us as she opened the door.

"I made tea cookies this morning. You see, I had planned to invite you for cookies and lemonade so we could have this little chat. The lemonade is in the icebox."

It followed that Mrs. Flowers would have ice on an ordinary day, when most families in our town bought ice late on Saturdays only a few times during the summer to be used in the wooden ice-cream freezers.

She took the bags from me and disappeared through the kitchen door. I looked 20 around the room that I had never in my wildest fantasies imagined I would see. Browned photographs leered or threatened from the walls and the white, freshly done curtains pushed against themselves and against the wind. I wanted to gobble up the room entire and take it to Bailey, who would help me analyze and enjoy it.

"Have a seat, Marguerite. Over there by the table." She carried a platter covered with a tea towel. Although she warned that she hadn't tried her hand at baking sweets for some time, I was certain that like everything else about her the cookies would be perfect.

They were flat round wafers, slightly browned on the edges and butter-yellow in the center. With the cold lemonade they were sufficient for childhood's lifelong diet. Remembering my manners, I took nice little lady-like bites off the edges. She said she had made them expressly for me and that she had a few in the kitchen that I could take home to my brother. So I jammed one whole cake in my mouth and the rough crumbs scratched the insides of my jaws, and if I hadn't had to swallow, it would have been a dream come true.

As I ate she began the first of what we later called "my lessons in living." She said that I must always be intolerant of ignorance but understanding of illiteracy. That some people, unable to go to school, were more educated and even more intelligent than college professors. She encouraged me to listen carefully to what country people called mother wit. That in those homely sayings was couched the collective wisdom of generations.

When I finished the cookies she brushed off the table and brought a thick, small book from the bookcase. I had read *A Tale of Two Cities*[1] and found it up to my standards as a romantic novel. She opened the first page and I heard poetry for the first time in my life.

"It was the best of times and the worst of times . . ." Her voice slid in and curved   25
down through and over the words. She was nearly singing. I wanted to look at the pages. Were they the same that I had read? Or were there notes, music, lined on the pages, as in a hymn book? Her sounds began cascading gently. I knew from listening to a thousand preachers that she was nearing the end of her reading, and I hadn't really heard, heard to understand, a single word.

"How do you like that?"

It occurred to me that she expected a response. The sweet vanilla flavor was still on my tongue and her reading was a wonder in my ears. I had to speak.

I said, "Yes, ma'am." It was the least I could do, but it was the most also.

"There's one more thing. Take this book of poems and memorize one for me. Next time you pay me a visit, I want you to recite."

I have tried often to search behind the sophistication of years for the enchantment   30
I so easily found in those gifts. The essence escapes but its aura remains. To be allowed, no, invited, into the private lives of strangers, and to share their joys and fears, was a chance to exchange the Southern bitter wormwood for a cup of mead with Beowulf[2] or a hot cup of tea and milk with Oliver Twist.[3] When I said aloud, "It is a far, far better thing that I do, than I have ever done . . ." tears of love filled my eyes at my selfishness.

On that first day, I ran down the hill and into the road (few cars ever came along it) and had the good sense to stop running before I reached the Store.

I was liked, and what a difference it made. I was respected not as Mrs. Henderson's grandchild or Bailey's sister but for just being Marguerite Johnson.

Childhood's logic never asks to be proved (all conclusions are absolute). I didn't question why Mrs. Flowers had singled me out for attention, nor did it occur to me that Momma might have asked her to give me a little talking to. All I cared about was that

---

[1]*A Tale of Two Cities (1859):* written by Charles Dickens (1812–1870), one of the great English writers of fiction, begins with the familiar lines "It was the best of times, it was the worst of times"; set against the background of the French Revolution, which Dickens researched with the aid of his friend Thomas Carlyle's *History of the French Revolution* (1837).   [2]*Beowulf:* the oldest English epic, in alliterative verse, probably composed in the early eighth century; drawn from Scandinavian history.   [3]*Oliver Twist (1838):* Dickens's second novel, which tells the story of an orphan living in the seamy underside of London's criminal world.

she had made tea cookies for *me* and read to *me* from her favorite book. It was enough to prove that she liked me.

Questions for Discussion and Writing

1. What insights about attitudes toward race at that time does Angelou's account provide, as revealed in the conversations between Marguerite and Mrs. Flowers?
2. What do you think Angelou means by "mother wit"? How does it differ from formal education?
3. How did the way Bertha Flowers treated Marguerite help her gain self-esteem?

Gayle Pemberton

• •

Gayle Pemberton (b. 1948) is the William R. Kenan Professor of the Humanities at Wesleyan University and chair of the African-American Studies Department. She was raised in Chicago and Ohio, received a Ph.D. in English and American literature at Harvard University, and has served as the associate director of African-American Studies at Princeton University. Pemberton has taught at Smith, Reed, and Bowdoin Colleges. The following chapter, drawn from her memoir The Hottest Water in Chicago *(1992), recounts the influential role her grandmother played in her life.*

ANTIDISESTABLISHMENTARIANISM

Okay, so where's Gloria Lockerman?[1] I want to know. Gloria Lockerman was partially responsible for ruining my life. I might never have ended up teaching literature if it had not been for her. I don't want to "call her out." I just want to know how things are, what she's doing. Have things gone well, Gloria? How's the family? What's up?

Gloria Lockerman, in case you don't recall, won scads of money on "The $64,000 Question."[2] Gloria Lockerman was a young black child, like me, but she could spell anything. Gloria Lockerman became my nemesis with her ability, her a-n-t-i-d-i-s-e-s-t-a-b-l-i-s-h-m-e-n-t-a-r-i-a-n-i-s-m.

My parents, my sister, and I shared a house in Dayton, Ohio, with my father's mother and her husband, my stepgrandfather, during the middle fifties. Sharing is an overstatement. It was my grandmother's house. Our nuclear group ate in a makeshift kitchen in the basement; my sister and I shared a dormer bedroom, and my parents actually had a room on the main floor of the house—several parts of which were off-limits. These were the entire living room, anywhere within three feet of Grandma's

---

[1]*Gloria Lockerman:* the African-American twelve-year-old from Baltimore who won $32,000 with her spelling abilities on *The $64,000 Question.* [2]*The $64,000 Question* was a phenomenally popular big-money quiz show that aired in the mid-1950s. In the first six months of this show, the sales of Revlon (the show's sponsor) rose 54 percent. The following year, Revlon's sales tripled.

African violets, the windows and venetian blinds, anything with a doily on it, the re-frigerator, and the irises in the backyard.

It was an arrangement out of necessity, given the unimpressive state of our com-bined fortunes, and it did not meet with anyone's satisfaction. To make matters worse, we had blockbusted a neighborhood. So, for the first year, I integrated the local ele-mentary school—a thankless and relatively inhuman experience. I remember one day taking the Sunday paper route for a boy up the block who was sick. It was a beauti-ful spring day, dewy, warm. I walked up the three steps to a particular house and placed the paper on the stoop. Suddenly, a full-grown man, perhaps sixty or so, appeared with a shotgun aimed at me and said that if he ever saw my nigger ass on his porch again he'd blow my head off, I know—typical American grandfather.

Grandma liked spirituals, preferably those sung by Mahalia Jackson. She was not   5
a fan of gospel and I can only imagine what she'd say if she were around to hear what's passing for inspirational music these days. She also was fond of country singers, and any of the members of "The Lawrence Welk Show." ("That Jimmy. Oh, I love the way he sings. He's from Iowa.") She was from Iowa, Jimmy was from Iowa, my father was from Iowa. She was crazy about Jimmy Dean too, and Tennessee Ernie Ford, and "Gun-smoke." She could cook with the finest of them and I wish I could somehow recreate her Parkerhouse rolls, but I lack bread karma. Grandma liked flowers (she could make anything bloom) and she loved her son.

She disliked white people, black people in the aggregate and pretty much individ-ually too, children—particularly female children—her daughter, her husband, my mother, Episcopalianism, Catholicism, Judaism, and Dinah Shore. She had a hot tem-per and a mean streak. She also suffered from several nagging ailments: high blood pressure, ulcers, an enlarged heart, ill-fitting dentures, arteriosclerosis, and arthritis—enough to make anyone hot tempered and mean, I'm sure. But to a third grader, such justifications and their subtleties were ultimately beyond me and insufficient, even though I believe I understood in part the relationship between pain and personality. Grandma scared the daylights out of me. I learned to control my nervous stomach enough to keep from getting sick daily. So Grandma plus school plus other family woes and my sister still predicting the end of the world every time the sirens went off—Grandma threatened to send her to a convent—made the experience as a whole some-thing I'd rather forget, but because of the mythic proportions of family, can't.

I often think that it might have been better had I been older, perhaps twenty years older, when I knew Grandma. But I realize that she would have found much more wrong with me nearing thirty than she did when I was eight or nine. When I was a child, she could blame most of my faults on my mother. Grown, she would have had no recourse but to damn me to hell.

Ah, but she is on the gene. Grandma did everything fast. She cooked, washed, cleaned, moved—everything was at lightning speed. She passed this handicap on to me, and I have numerous bruises, cuts, and burns to show for it. Watching me throw pots and pans around in the creation of a meal, my mother occasionally calls me by my grandmother's first name. I smile back, click my teeth to imitate a slipping upper, and say something unpleasant about someone.

Tuesday nights were "The $64,000 Question" nights, just as Sundays we watched Ed Sullivan and Saturdays were reserved for Lawrence Welk and "Gunsmoke." We would all gather around the television in what was a small, informal family section between the verboten real living room and the mahogany dining table and chairs, used only three or four times a year. I don't remember where I sat, but it wasn't on the floor since that wasn't allowed either.

As we watched these television programs, once or twice I sat briefly on Grandma's 10 lap. She was the world's toughest critic. No one was considered worthy, apart from the above-mentioned. To her, So-and-So or Whosits could not sing, dance, tell a joke, read a line—nothing. In her hands "Ted Mack's Amateur Hour" would have lasted three minutes. She was willing to forgive only very rarely—usually when someone she liked gave a mediocre performance on one of her favorite shows.

I must admit that Grandma's style of teaching critical thinking worked as well as some others I've encountered. My father had a different approach. Throughout my youth he would play the music of the thirties and forties. His passion was for Billie Holiday, with Ella Fitzgerald, Peggy Lee, Sarah Vaughan, and a few others thrown in for a touch of variety. He enjoyed music, and when he wanted to get some musical point across, he would talk about some nuance of style that revealed the distinction be-tween what he called "really singing" and a failure. He would say, "Now, listen to that there. Did you catch it? Hear what she did with that note?" With Grandma it was more likely to be:

"Did you hear that?"

"What?" I might ask.

"That. What she just sang."

"Yes." 15

"Well, what do you think of it?"

"It's okay, I guess."

"Well, that was garbage. She can't sing a note. That stinks. She's a fool."

Message across. We all choose our own pedagogical techniques.

Game shows are, well, game shows. I turned on my television the other day, and 20 as I clicked through channels looking for something to watch I stopped long enough to hear an announcer say that the guest contestant was going to do something or other in 1981. Reruns of game shows? Well, why not? What difference does it make if the whole point is to watch people squirm, twist, sweat, blare, weep, convulse to get their hands on money and gifts, even if they end up being just "parting gifts?" (I won some of them myself once: a bottle of liquid Johnson's Wax, a box of Chunkies, a beach towel with the name of a diet soda on it, plus a coupon for a case of the stuff, and sev-eral boxes of Sugar Blobs—honey-coated peanut butter, marshmallow, and chocolate flavored crispies, dipped in strawberry flavoring for that special morning taste treat!)

Game shows in the fifties were different, more exciting. I thought the studio sets primitive even when I was watching them then. The clock on "Beat the Clock," the coat and crown on "Queen for a Day"—nothing like that mink on "The Big Payoff" that Bess Meyerson modeled—and that wire card flipper on "What's My Line" that John Charles Daly used—my, was it flimsy looking. The finest set of all, though, was on "The $64,000 Question." Hal March would stand outside the isolation booth, the door closing on the likes of Joyce Brothers, Catherine Kreitzer, and Gloria Lockerman, the music would play, and the clock would begin ticking down, like all game show clocks: *TOOT-toot-TOOT-tootTOOT-toot-BUZZZZZZ.*

There were few opportunities to see black people on television in those days. I had watched "Amos 'n' Andy" when we lived in Chicago. But that show was a variation on a theme. Natives running around or jumping up and down or looking menacing in African adventure movies; shuffling, subservient, and clowning servants in local color movies (or any other sort); and "Amos 'n' Andy" were all the same thing: the perpetuation of a compelling, deadly, darkly humorous, and occasionally laughable idea. Nonfictional blacks on television were limited to Sammy Davis, Jr., as part of the Will Mastin Trio and afterward, or Peg Leg Bates on "The Ed Sullivan Show" on Sunday, or the entertainers who might show up on other variety shows, or Nat King Cole during his fifteen-minute program. Naturally, the appearance of Gloria Lockerman caused a mild sensation as we watched "The $64,000 Question," all assembled.

"Look at her," Grandma said.

I braced myself for the torrent of abuse that was about to be leveled at the poor girl.

"You ought to try to be like that," Grandma said.   25

"Huh?" I said.

"What did you say?"

"Yes, ma'am."

I was shocked, thrown into despair. I had done well in school, as well as could be hoped. I was modestly proud of my accomplishments, and given the price I was paying every day—and paying in silence, for I never brought my agonies at school home with me—I didn't need Gloria Lockerman thrown in my face. Gloria Lockerman, like me, on television, spelling. I was perennially an early-round knockout in spelling bees.

My sister understands all of this. Her own story is slightly different and she says   30
she'll tell it all one day herself. She is a very good singer and has a superb ear; with our critical training, what more would she need? Given other circumstances, she might have become a performer herself. When she was about eleven Leslie Uggams was on Arthur Godfrey's "Talent Scouts" and was soon to be tearing down the "Name That Tune" runway, ringing the bell and becoming moderately famous. No one ever held Leslie Uggams up to my sister for image consciousness-raising. But my sister suffered nevertheless. She could outsing Leslie Uggams and probably run as fast; she knew the songs and didn't have nearly so strange a last name. But, there she was, going nowhere in the Middle West, and there was Leslie Uggams on her way to "Sing Along With Mitch." To this day, my sister mumbles if she happens to see Leslie Uggams on television—before she can get up to change the channel—or hears someone mention her name. I told her I saw Leslie Uggams in the flesh at a club in New York. She was sitting at a table, just like the rest of us, listening with pleasure to Barbara Cook. My sister swore at me.

Grandma called her husband "Half-Wit." He was a thin, small-boned man who looked to me far more like an Indian chief than like a black man. He was from Iowa too, but that obviously did not account for enough in Grandma's eyes. He had a cracking tenor voice, a head full of dead straight black hair, reddish, dull brown skin, and large sad, dark brown eyes. His craggy face also reminded me of pictures I'd seen of Abraham Lincoln—but, like all political figures and American forefathers, Lincoln, to my family, was fair game for wisecracks, so that resemblance did Grandpa no good either. And for reasons that have gone to the grave with both of them, he was the most thoroughly henpecked man I have ever heard of, not to mention seen.

Hence, domestic scenes had a quality of pathos and high humor as far as I was concerned. My sister and I called Grandpa "Half-Wit" when we were alone together, but that seemed to have only a slight effect on our relations with him and our willingness to obey him—though I cannot recall any occasions calling for his authority. Grandma was Grandma, Half-Wit was Half-Wit—and we lived with the two of them. I have one particularly vivid memory of Grandma, an aficionada of the iron skillet, chasing him through the house waving it in the air, her narrow, arthritis-swollen wrist and twisted knuckles turning the heavy pan as if it were a lariat. He didn't get hurt; he was fleet of foot and made it out the back door before she caught him. My father's real father had been dead since the thirties and divorced from Grandma since the teens—so Half-Wit had been in place for quite some years and was still around to tell the story, if he had the nerve.

Grandma had a glass menagerie, the only one I've seen apart from performances of the Williams[3] play. I don't think she had a unicorn, but she did have quite a few pieces. From a distance of no less than five feet I used to squint at the glass forms, wondering what they meant to Grandma, who was herself delicate of form but a powerhouse of strength, speed, and temper. I also wondered how long it would take me to die if the glass met with some unintended accident caused by me. Real or imagined unpleasantries, both in the home and outside of it, helped develop in me a somewhat melancholic nature. And even before we had moved to Ohio I found myself laughing and crying at the same time.

In the earlier fifties, in Chicago, I was allowed to watch such programs as "The Ernie Kovacs Show," "Your Show of Shows," "The Jackie Gleason Show," "The Red Skelton Show," and, naturally, "I Love Lucy." I was continually dazzled by the skits and broad humor, but I was particularly taken with the silent sketches, my favorite comedians as mime artists: Skelton[4] as Freddy the Freeloader, Caesar and Coca[5] in a number of roles, thoroughly outrageous Kovacs acts backed by Gershwin's "Rialto Ripples." My father was a very funny man and a skillful mime. I could tell when he watched Gleason's Poor Soul that he identified mightily with what was on the screen. It had nothing to do with self-pity. My father had far less of it than other men I've met with high intelligence, financial and professional stress, and black faces in a white world. No, my father would even say that we were all poor souls; it was the human condition. His mimicking of the Gleason character—head down, shoulders tucked, stomach sagging, feet splayed—served as some kind of release. I would laugh and cry watching either of them.

But my absolute favorite was Martha Raye, who had a way of milking the fine 35
line between tragedy and comedy better than most. I thought her eyes showed a combination of riotous humor and terror. Her large mouth contorted in ways that seemed to express the same two emotions. Her face was a mask of profound sadness. She did for me what Sylvia Sidney did for James Baldwin. In *The Devil Finds Work*,[6] Baldwin says, "Sylvia Sidney was the only American film actress who reminded me of a

---

[3]*The Glass Menagerie* (1945), by the American playwright Tennessee Williams.   [4]*Red Skelton (1913–1997):* popular comedian on radio and television.   [5]*Sid Caesar (b. 1922):* American comedian and actor who starred in television's *Your Show of Shows* (1950–1954) with Imogene Coca, actress, comedian (1908–2001).
[6]*The Devil Finds Works: An Essay* (1976): written by James Baldwin (1924–1987).

colored girl, or woman—which is to say that she was the only American film actress who reminded me of reality." The reality Raye conveyed to me was of how dreams could turn sour in split-seconds, and how underdogs, even when winning, often had to pay abominable prices. She also could sing a jazz song well, with her husky scat phrasing, in ways that were slightly different from those of my favorite singers, and almost as enjoyable.

There were no comedic or dramatic images of black women on the screen—that is, apart from Sapphire and her mother on "Amos 'n' Andy." And knowing Grandma and Grandpa taught me, if nothing else suggested it, that what I saw of black life on television was a gross burlesque—played to the hilt with skill by black actors, but still lacking reality.

Black female singers who appeared on television were, like their music, sacrosanct, and I learned from their styles, lyrics, and improvisations, lessons about life that mime routines did not reveal. Still, it was Martha Raye, and occasionally Lucille Ball and Imogene Coca at their most absurd, that aligned me with my father and his Poor Soul, and primed me to both love and despise Grandma and to see that in life most expressions, thoughts, acts, and intentions reveal their opposite polarities simultaneously.

Grandma died in 1965. I was away, out of the country, and I missed her funeral—which was probably a good idea since I might have been tempted to strangle some close family friend who probably would have launched into a "tsk, tsk, tsk" monologue about long-suffering grandmothers and impudent children. But, in another way, I'm sorry I didn't make it. Her funeral might have provided some proper closure for me, might have prompted me to organize her effect on my life sooner than I did, reconciling the grandmother who so hoped I would be a boy that she was willing to catch a Constellation or a DC-3 to witness my first few hours, but instead opted to take the bus when she heard the sad news, with the grandmother who called me "Sally Slap-cabbage" and wrote to me and my sister regularly, sending us the odd dollar or two, until her death.

I remember coming home from school, getting my jelly sandwich and wolfing it down, and watching "The Mickey Mouse Club," my favorite afternoon show, since there was no afternoon movie. I had noticed and had been offended by the lack of black children in the "Club," but the cartoons, particularly those with Donald Duck, were worth watching. On this particular episode—one of the regular guest act days—a group of young black children, perhaps nine or ten of them, came on and sang, with a touch of dancing, "Old MacDonald Had a Farm," in an up-tempo, jazzy version. In spite of the fact that usually these guest days produced some interesting child acts, I became angry with what I saw. I felt patronized, for myself and for them. Clearly a couple of them could out-sing and out-dance any Mouseketeer—something that wasn't worth giving a thought to—but this performance was gratuitous, asymmetrical, a non-sequitur, like Harpo Marx marching through the Negro section in *A Day at the Races*,[7] blowing an imaginary horn and exciting the locals to much singing, swinging, and dancing to a charming ditty called "Who Dat Man?"

---

[7]*A Day at the Races:* popular 1937 Marx Brothers movie about inmates turned loose in a sanitarium.

I must have mumbled something as I watched the group singing "Old MacDon- 40
ald." Grandma, passing through, took a look at what was on the screen, and at me,
turned off the television, took my hand, led me to her kitchen, and sat me down at the
table where she and Half-Wit ate, poured me some milk, and without so much as a blink
of her eye, said, "Pay no attention to that shit."

Questions for Discussion and Writing

1. How do the circumstances Pemberton describes (especially, her grandmother's response to Gloria Lockerman) explain why Pemberton remembers her so fondly?
   What life lessons did Pemberton learn from her grandmother?
2. What traits does Pemberton possess as a writer? How would you characterize the
   voice that you hear in this essay? How did her grandmother's influence shape her
   personality and contribute to her literary style?
3. In your opinion, do television shows accurately reflect (or fail to reflect) African-
   American life in the United States today?
4. Find an old photo and analyze the details that provide information about the social, economic, historical, and cultural context in which it was taken.

Mikhal Gilmore

· ·

*Mikhal Gilmore was born in 1951 in Salt Lake City, Utah, and grew up in Portland,
Oregon. He is a senior writer at* Rolling Stone *magazine. "My Brother, Gary Gilmore"
first appeared in* Granta *(Autumn 1991) and served as the basis for his prize-winning autobiography,* Shot Through the Heart *(1994). His most recent work (with Ron Kenner) is*
Manson: The Unholy Trail of Charlie and the Family *(2000).*

MY BROTHER, GARY GILMORE

I am the brother of a man who murdered innocent men. His name was Gary
Gilmore. After his conviction and sentencing, he campaigned to end his own life, and
in January 1977 he was shot to death by a firing-squad in Draper, Utah. It was the
first execution in America in over a decade.

Over the years, many people have judged me by my brother's actions as if in coming from a family that yielded a murderer I must be formed by the same causes, the same
sins, must by my brother's actions be responsible for the violence that resulted, and
bear the mark of a frightening and shameful heritage. It's as if there is guilt in the fact
of the blood-line itself. Maybe there is.

Pictures in the family scrap-book show my father with his children. I have only
one photograph of him and Gary together. Gary is wearing a sailor's cap. He has his
arms wrapped tightly around my father's neck, his head bent towards him, a look of
broken need on his face. It is heart-breaking to look at this picture—not just for the

look on Gary's face, the look that was the stamp of his future, but also for my father's expression: pulling away from my brother's cheek, he is wearing a look of distaste.

When my brother Gaylen was born in the mid forties, my father turned all his love on his new, beautiful brown-eyed son. Gary takes on a harder aspect in the pictures around this time. He was beginning to keep a greater distance from the rest of the family. Six years later, my father turned his love from Gaylen to me. You don't see Gary in the family pictures after that.

Gary had nightmares. It was always the same dream: he was being beheaded.   5

In 1953, Gary was arrested for breaking windows. He was sent to a juvenile detention home for ten months, where he saw young men raped and beaten. Two years later, at age fourteen, he was arrested for car theft and sentenced to eighteen months in jail. I was four years old.

When I was growing up I did not feel accepted by, or close to, my brothers. By the time I was four or five, they had begun to find life and adventure outside the home. Frank, Gary and Gaylen signified the teenage rebellion of the fifties for me. They wore their hair in greasy pompadours and played Elvis Presley and Fats Domino records. They dressed in scarred motorcycle jackets and brutal boots. They smoked cigarettes, drank booze and cough syrup, skipped—and quit—school, and spent their evenings hanging out with girls in tight sweaters, racing souped-up cars along country roads outside Portland, or taking part in gang rumbles. My brothers looked for a forbidden life—the life they had seen exemplified in the crime lore of gangsters and killers. They studied the legends of violence. They knew the stories of John Dillinger, Bonnie and Clyde, and Leopold and Loeb; mulled over the meanings of the lives and executions of Barbara Graham, Bruno Hauptmann, Sacco and Vanzetti, the Rosenbergs; thrilled to the pleading of criminal lawyers like Clarence Darrow and Jerry Giesler. They brought home books about condemned men and women, and read them avidly.

I remember loving my brothers fiercely, wanting to be a part of their late-night activities and to share in their laughter and friendship. I also remember being frightened of them. They looked deadly, beyond love, destined to hurt the world around them.

Gary came home from reform school for a brief Christmas visit. On Christmas night I was sitting in my room, playing with the day's haul of presents, when Gary wandered in. "Hey Mike, how you doing?" he asked, taking a seat on my bed. "Think I'll just join you while I have a little Christmas cheer." He had a six-pack of beer with him and was speaking in a bleary drawl. "Look partner, I want to have a talk with you." I think it was the first companionable statement he ever made to me. I never expected the intimacy that followed and could not really fathom it at such a young age. Sitting on the end of my bed, sipping at his Christmas beer, Gary described a harsh, private world and told me horrible, transfixing stories: about the boys he knew in the detention halls, reform schools and county farms where he now spent most of his time; about the bad boys who had taught him the merciless codes of his new life; and about the soft boys who did not have what it took to survive that life. He said he had shared a cell with one of the soft boys, who cried at night, wanting to disappear into nothing, while Gary held him in his arms until the boy finally fell into sleep, sobbing.

Then Gary gave me some advice. "You have to learn to be hard. You have to learn   10 to take things and feel nothing about them: no pain, no anger, nothing. And you have to realize, if anybody wants to beat you up, even if they want to hold you down and kick you, you have to let them. You can't fight back. You *shouldn't* fight back. Just lie down in front of them and let them beat you, let them kick you. Lie there and let them do it. It is the only way you will survive. If you don't give in to them, they will kill you."

He set aside his beer and cupped my face in his hands. "You have to remember this, Mike," he said. "Promise me. Promise me you'll be a man. Promise me you'll let them beat you." We sat there on that winter night, staring at each other, my face in his hands, and as Gary asked me to promise to take my beatings, his bloodshot eyes began to cry. It was the first time I had seen him shed tears.

I promised: Yes, I'll let them kick me. But I was afraid—afraid of betraying Gary's plea.

Gary and Gaylen weren't at home much. I came to know them mainly through their reputations, through the endless parade of grim policemen who came to the door trying to find them, and through the faces and accusations of bail bondsman and lawyers who arrived looking sympathetic and left disgusted. I knew them through many hours spent in waiting-rooms at city and county jails, where my mother went to visit them, and through the numerous times I accompanied her after midnight to the local police station on Milwaukie's Main Street to bail out another drunken son.

I remember being called into the principal's office while still in grammar school, and being warned that the school would never tolerate my acting as my brothers did; I was told to watch myself, that my brothers had already used years of the school district's good faith and leniency, and that if I was going to be like them, there were other schools I could be sent to. I came to be seen as an extension of my brothers' reputations. Once, I was waiting for a bus in the centre of the small town when a cop pulled over. "You're one of the Gilmore boys, aren't you? I hope you don't end up like those two. I've seen enough shitheads from your family." I was walking down the local main highway when a car pulled over and a gang of older teenage boys piled out, surrounding me, "Are you Gaylen Gilmore's brother?" one of them asked. They shoved me into the car, drove me a few blocks to a deserted lot and took turns punching me in the face. I remembered Gary's advice—"You can't fight back; you *shouldn't* fight back"— and I let them beat me until they were tired. Then they spat on me, got back in their car and left.

I cried all the way back home, and I hated the world. I hated the small town I lived in, its ugly, mean people. For the first time in my life I hated my brothers. I felt that my future would be governed by them, that I would be destined to follow their lives whether I wanted to or not, that I would never know any relief from shame and pain and disappointment. I felt a deep impulse to violence: I wanted to rip the faces off the boys who had beat me up. "I want to kill them," I told myself. "I want to *kill* them"— and as I realized what it was I was saying, and why I was feeling that way, I only hated my world, and my brothers, more.

Frank Gilmore, Sr. died on 30 June 1962. Gary was in Portland's Rocky Butte Jail, and the authorities denied his request to attend the funeral. He tore his cell apart; he smashed a light bulb and slashed his wrists. He was placed in "the hole"—solitary confinement—on the day of father's funeral. Gary was twenty-one. I was eleven.

I was surprised at how hard my mother and brothers took father's death. I was surprised they loved him enough to cry at all. Or maybe they were crying for the love he

15

had so long withheld, and the reconciliation that would be forever denied them. I was the only one who didn't cry. I don't know why, but I never cried over my father's death—not then, and not now.

With my father's death Gary's crimes became more desperate, more violent. He talked a friend into helping him commit armed robbery. Gary grabbed the victim's wallet while the friend held a club; he was arrested a short time later, tried and found guilty. The day of his sentencing, during an afternoon when my mother had to work, he called me from the Clackamas County Courthouse. "How you doing partner? I just wanted to let you and mom know: I got sentenced to fifteen years."

I was stunned. "Gary, what can I do for you?" I asked. I think it came out wrong, as if I was saying: I'm busy; what do you *want?*

"I . . . I didn't really want anything," Gary said, his voice broken. "I just wanted   20 to hear your voice. I just wanted to say goodbye. You know, I won't be seeing you for a few years. Take care of yourself." We hadn't shared anything so intimate since that Christmas night, many years before.

I didn't have much talent for crime (neither did my brothers, to tell the truth), but I also didn't have much appetite for it. I had seen what my brothers' lives had brought them. For years, my mother had told me that I was the family's last hope for redemption. "I want one son to turn out right, *one* son I don't have to end up visiting in jail, one son I don't have to watch in court as his life is sentenced away, piece by piece." After my father's death, she drew me closer to her and her religion, and when I was twelve, I was baptized a Mormon. For many years, the Church's beliefs helped to provide me with a moral center and a hope for deliverance that I had not known before.

I think culture and history helped to save me. I was born in 1951, and although I remember well the youthful explosion of the 1950s, I was too young to experience it the way my brothers did. The music of Elvis Presley and others had represented and expressed my brothers' rebellion: it was hard-edged, with no apparent ideology. The music was a part of my childhood, but by the early sixties the spirit of the music had been spent.

Then, on 9 February 1964 (my thirteenth birthday, and the day I joined the Mormon priesthood), the Beatles made their first appearance on the Ed Sullivan Show. My life would never be the same. The Beatles meant a change, they promised a world that my parents and brothers could not offer. In fact, I liked the Beatles in part because they seemed such a departure from the world of my brothers, and because my brothers couldn't abide them.

The rock culture and youth politics of the sixties allowed their adherents to act out a kind of ritualized criminality: we could use drugs, defy authority, or contemplate violent or destructive acts of revolt, we told ourselves, *because we had a reason to.* The music aimed to foment a sense of cultural community, and for somebody who had felt as disenfranchised by his family as I did, rock and roll offered not just a sense of belonging but empowered me with new ideals. I began to find rock's morality preferable to the Mormon ethos, which seemed rigid and severe. One Sunday in the summer of 1967, a member of the local bishopric—a man I admired, and had once regarded as something of a father figure—drove over to our house and asked me to step outside for a talk. He told me that he and other church leaders had grown concerned about my changed appearance—the new length of my hair and my style of dressing—and felt it was an unwelcome influence on other young Mormons. If I did not reject the new youth culture, I would no longer be welcome in church.

On that day a line was drawn. I knew that rock and roll had provided me with a new creed and a sense of courage. I believed I was taking part in a rebellion that mattered—or at least counted for more than my brothers' rebellions. In the music of the Rolling Stones or Doors or Velvet Underground, I could participate in darkness without submitting to it, which is something Gary and Gaylen had been unable to do. I remember their disdain when I tried to explain to them why Bob Dylan was good, why he mattered. It felt great to belong to a different world from them.

And I did: my father and Gaylen were dead; Gary was in prison and Frank was broken. I thought of my family as a cursed outfit, plain and simple, and I believed that the only way to escape its debts and legacies was to leave it. In 1969 I graduated from high school—the only member of my family to do so. The next day, I moved out of the house in Milwaukie and, with some friends, moved into an apartment near Portland State University, in downtown Portland.

In the summer of 1976, I was working at a record store in downtown Portland, making enough money to pay my rent and bills. I was also writing free-lance journalism and criticism, and had sold my first reviews and articles to national publications, including *Rolling Stone*.

On the evening of 30 July, having passed up a chance to go drinking with some friends, I headed home. *The Wild Bunch*, Peckinpah's genuflection to violence and honor, was on television, and as I settled back on the couch to watch it, I picked up the late edition of *The Oregonian*. I almost passed over a page-two item headlined OREGON MAN HELD IN UTAH SLAYINGS, but then something clicked inside me, and I began to read it. "Gary Mark Gilmore, 35, was charged with the murders of two young clerks during the hold-up of a service station and a motel." I read on, dazed, about how Gary had been arrested for killing Max Jensen and Ben Bushnell on consecutive nights. Both men were Mormons, about the same age as I, and both left wives and children behind.

I dropped the paper to the floor. I sat on the couch the rest of the night, alternately staring at *The Wild Bunch* and re-reading the sketchy account. I felt shocks of rage, remorse and guilt—as if I were partly responsible for the deaths. I had been part of an uninterested world that had shut Gary away. I had wanted to believe that Gary's life and mine were not entwined, that what had shaped him had not shaped me.

It had been a long time since I had written or visited Gary. After his resentencing in 1972, I heard news of him from my mother. In January 1975, Gary was sent to the federal penitentiary in Marion, Illinois. After his transfer, we exchanged a few perfunctory letters. In early April 1976, I learned of the Oregon State Parole Board's decision to parole Gary from Marion to Provo, Utah, rather than transfer him back to Oregon. The transaction had been arranged between the parole board, Brenda Nicol (our cousin) and her father, our uncle Vernon Damico, who lived in Provo. I remember thinking that Gary's being paroled into the heart of one of Utah's most devout and severe Mormon communities was not a great idea.

Between his release and those fateful nights in July, Gary held a job at Uncle Vernon's shoe store, and he met and fell in love with Nicole Barrett, a beautiful young woman with two children. But Gary was unable to deny some old, less wholesome appetites. Almost immediately after his release, he started drinking heavily and taking

Fiorinal, a muscle and headache medication that, in sustained doses, can cause severe mood swings and sexual dysfunction. Gary apparently experienced both reactions. He became more violent. Sometimes he got rough with Nicole over failed sex, or over what he saw as her flirtations. He picked fights with other men, hitting them from behind, threatening to cave in their faces with a tire iron that he twirled as handily as a baton. He lost his job and abused his Utah relatives. He walked into stores and walked out again with whatever he wanted under his arm, glaring at the cashiers, challenging them to try to stop him. He brought guns home, and sitting on the back porch would fire them at trees, fences, the sky. "Hit the sun," he told Nicole. "See if you can make it sink." Then he hit Nicole with his fist one too many times, and she moved out.

Gary wanted her back. He told a friend that he thought he might kill her.

On a hot night in late July, Gary drove over to Nicole's mother's house and persuaded Nicole's little sister, April, to ride with him in his white pick-up truck. He wanted her to join him in looking for her sister. They drove for hours, listening to the radio, talking aimlessly, until Gary pulled up by a service station in the small town of Orem. He told April to wait in the truck. He walked into the station, where twenty-six-year-old attendant Max Jensen was working alone. There were no other cars there. Gary pulled a .22 automatic from his jacket and told Jensen to empty the cash from his pockets. He took Jensen's coin changer and led the young attendant around the back of the station and forced him to lie down on the bathroom floor. He told Jensen to place his hands under his stomach and press his face to the ground. Jensen complied and offered Gary a smile. Gary pointed the gun at the base of Jensen's skull. "This one is for me," Gary said, and he pulled the trigger. And then: "This one is for Nicole," and he pulled the trigger again.

The next night, Gary walked into the office of a motel just a few doors away from his uncle Vernon's house in Provo. He ordered the man behind the counter, Ben Bushnell, to lie down on the floor, and then he shot him in the back of the head. He walked out with the motel's cashbox under his arm and tried to stuff the pistol under a bush. But it discharged, blowing a hole in his thumb.

Gary decided to get out of town. First he had to take care of his thumb. He drove to   35
the house of a friend named Craig and telephoned his cousin. A witness had recognized Gary leaving the site of the second murder, and the police had been in touch with Brenda. She had the police on one line, Gary on another. She tried to stall Gary until the police could set up a road-block. After they finished speaking, Gary got into his truck and headed for the local airport. A few miles down the road, he was surrounded by police cars and a SWAT team. He was arrested for Bushnell's murder and confessed to the murder of Max Jensen.

Gary's trial began some months later. The verdict was never in question. Gary didn't help himself when he refused to allow his attorneys to call Nicole as a defense witness. Gary and Nicole had been reconciled; she felt bad for him and visited him in jail every day for hours. Gary also didn't help his case by staring menacingly at the jury members or by offering belligerent testimony on his own behalf. He was found guilty. My mother called me on the night of Gary's sentencing, 7 October, to tell me that he had received the death penalty. He told the judge he would prefer being shot to being hanged.

On Saturday 15 January, I saw Gary for the last time. Camera crews were camped in the town of Draper, preparing for the finale.

During our other meetings that week, Gary had opened with friendly remarks or a joke or even a handstand. This day, though, he was nervous and was eager to deny it. We were separated by a glass partition. "Naw, the noise in this place gets to me sometimes, but I'm as cool as a cucumber," he said, holding up a steady hand. The muscles in his wrists and arms were taut and thick as rope.

Gary showed me letters and pictures he'd received, mainly from children and teenage girls. He said he always tried to answer the ones from the kids first, and he read one from an eight-year-old boy: "I hope they put you some place and make you live forever for what you did. You have no right to die. With all the malice in my heart. [*name*.]"

"Man, that one shook me up for a long time," he said.   40

I asked him if he'd replied to it.

"Yeah, I wrote, 'You're too young to have malice in your heart. I had it in mine at a young age and look what it did for me.'"

Gary's eyes nervously scanned some letters and pictures, finally falling on one that made him smile. He held it up. A picture of Nicole. "She's pretty, isn't she?" I agreed. "I look at this picture every day. I took it myself; I made a drawing from it. Would you like to have it?"

I said I would. I asked him where he would have gone if he had made it to the airport the night of the second murder.

"Portland."   45

I asked him why.

Gary studied the shelf in front of him. "I don't want to talk about that night any more," he said. "There's no point in talking about it."

"Would you have come to see me?"

He nodded. For a moment his eyes flashed the old anger. "And what would *you* have done if I'd come to you?" he asked. "If I had come and said I was in trouble and needed help, needed a place to stay? Would *you* have taken me in? Would you have hidden me?"

The question had been turned back on me. I couldn't speak. Gary sat for a long   50
moment, holding me with his eyes, then said steadily: "I think I was coming to kill you. I think that's what would have happened; there may have been no choice for you, no choice for me." His eyes softened. "Do you understand why?"

I nodded. Of course I understood why: I had escaped the family—or at least thought I had. Gary had not.

I felt terror. Gary's story could have been mine. Then terror became relief—Jensen and Bushnell's deaths, and Gary's own impending death, had meant my own safety. I finished the thought, and my relief was shot through with guilt and remorse. I felt closer to Gary than I'd ever felt before. I understood why he wanted to die.

The warden entered Gary's room. They discussed whether Gary should wear a hood for the execution.

I rapped on the glass partition and asked the warden if he would allow us a final handshake. At first he refused but consented after Gary explained it was our final visit, on the condition that I agree to a skin search. After I had been searched by two guards, two other guards brought Gary around the partition. They said that I would have to roll up my sleeve past my elbow, and that we could not touch beyond a handshake. Gary grasped my hand, squeezed it tight and said, "Well, I guess this is it." He leaned over and kissed me on the cheek.

On Monday morning, 17 January, in a cannery warehouse out behind Utah State   55
Prison, Gary met his firing-squad. I was with my mother and brother and girl-friend
when it happened. Just moments before, we had seen the morning newspaper with the
headline EXECUTION STAYED. We switched on the television for more news. We saw a
press conference. Gary's death was being announced.

There was no way to be prepared for that last see-saw of emotion. You force yourself to live through the hell of knowing that somebody you love is going to die in an
expected way, at a specific time and place, and that there is nothing you can do to
change that. For the rest of your life, you will have to move around in a world that
wanted this death to happen. You will have to walk past people every day who were
heartened by the killing of somebody in your family—somebody who you knew had
long before been murdered emotionally.

You turn on the television, and the journalist tells you how the warden put a black
hood over Gary's head and pinned a small, circular cloth target above his chest, and how
five men pumped a volley of bullets into him. He tells you how the blood flowed from
Gary's devastated heart and down his chest, down his legs, staining his white pants
scarlet and dripping to the warehouse floor. He tells you how Gary's arm rose slowly
at the moment of the impact, how his fingers seemed to wave as his life left him.

Shortly after Gary's execution, *Rolling Stone* offered me a job as an assistant editor at their Los Angeles bureau. It was a nice offer. It gave me the chance to get away
from Portland and all the bad memories it represented.

I moved to Los Angeles in April 1977. It was not an easy life at first. I drank a
pint of whisky every night, and I took Dalmane, a sleeping medication that interfered
with my ability to dream—or at least made it hard to remember my dreams. There
were other lapses: I was living with one woman and seeing a couple of others. For a
season or two my writing went to hell. I didn't know what to say or how to say it; I
could no longer tell if I had anything *worth* writing about. I wasn't sure how you made
words add up. Instead of writing, I preferred reading. I favoured hard-boiled crime
fiction—particularly the novels of Ross Macdonald—in which the author tried to solve
murders by explicating labyrinthine family histories. I spent many nights listening to
punk rock. I liked the music's accommodation with a merciless world. One of the most
famous punk songs of the period was by the Adverts. It was called "Gary Gilmore's
Eyes." What would it be like, the song asked, to see the world through Gary Gilmore's
dead eyes? Would you see a world of murder?

All around me I had Gary's notoriety to contend with. During my first few months   60
in LA—and throughout the years that followed—most people asked me about my
brother. They wanted to know what Gary was like. They admired his bravado, his
hardness. I met a woman who wanted to sleep with me because I was his brother. I tried
to avoid these people.

I also met women who, when they learned who my brother was, would not see me
again, not take my calls again. I received letters from people who said I should not be
allowed to write for a young audience. I received letters from people who thought I
should have been shot alongside my brother.

There was never a time without a reminder of the past. In 1979, Norman Mailer's
The Executioner's Song was published. At the time, I was living with a woman I loved
very much. As she read the book, I could see her begin to wonder about who she was

sleeping with, about what had come into her life. One night, a couple of months after the book had been published, we were watching *Saturday Night Live*. The guest host was doing a routine of impersonations. He tied a bandana around his eyes and glee-fully announced his next subject: "Gary Gilmore!" My girl-friend got up from the sofa and moved into the bedroom, shutting the door. I poured a glass of whisky. She came out a few minutes later. "I'm sorry," she said, "I can't live with you any more. I can't stand being close to all this stuff." She was gone within a week.

I watched as a private and troubling event continued to be the subject of public sen-sation and media scrutiny; I watched my brother's life—and in some way, my life—be-come too large to control. I tried not to surrender to my feelings because my feelings wouldn't erase the pain or shame or bad memories or unresolved love and hate. I was waiting to be told what to feel.

Only a few months before, I had gone through one of the worst times of my life—my brief move to Portland and back. What had gone wrong, I realized, was because of my past, something that had been set in motion long before I was born. It was what Gary and I shared, more than any blood tie: we were both heirs to a legacy of nega-tion that was beyond our control or our understanding. Gary had ended up turning the nullification outward—on innocents, on Nicole, on his family, on the world and its ideas of justice, finally on himself. I had turned the ruin inward. Outward or inward—either way, it was a powerfully destructive legacy, and for the first time in my life, I came to see that it had not really finished its enactment. To believe that Gary had absorbed all the family's dissolution, or that the worst of that rot had died with him that morn-ing in Draper, Utah, was to miss the real nature of the legacy that had placed him be-fore those rifles: what that heritage or patrimony was about, and where it had come from.

We tend to view murders as solitary ruptures in the world around us, outrages that need to be attributed and then punished. There is a motivation, a crime, an arrest, a trial, a verdict and a punishment. Sometimes—though rarely—that punishment is death. The next day, there is another murder. The next day, there is another. There has been no punishment that breaks the pattern, that stops this custom of one murder fol-lowing another. 65

Murder has worked its way into our consciousness and our culture in the same way that murder exists in our literature and film: we consume each killing until there is another, more immediate or gripping one to take its place. When *this* murder story is finished, there will be another to intrigue and terrify that part of the world that has survived it. And then there will be another. Each will be a story, each will be treated and reported and remembered as a unique incident. Each murder will be solved, but murder itself will never be solved. You cannot solve murder without solving the human heart or the history that has rendered that heart so dark and desolate.

This murder story is told from inside the house where murder was born. It is the house where I grew up, and it is a house that I have never been able to leave.

As the night passed, I formed an understanding of what I needed to do. I would go back into my family—into its stories, its myths, its memories, its inheritance—and find the real story and hidden propellants behind it. I wanted to climb into the family story in the same way I've always wanted to climb into a dream about the house where we all grew up.

In the dream, it is always night. We are in my father's house—a charred-brown, 1950s-era home. Shingled, two-story and weather-worn, it is located on the far outskirts of a dead-end American town, pinioned between the night-lights and smoking chimneys of towering industrial factories. A moonlit stretch of railroad track forms the border to a forest I am forbidden to trespass. A train whistle howls in the distance. No train ever comes.

People move from the darkness outside the house to the darkness inside. They are   70
my family. They are all back from the dead. There is my mother, Bessie Gilmore, who, after a life of bitter losses, died spitting blood, calling the names of her father and her husband—men who had long before brutalized her hopes and her love—crying to them for mercy, for a passage into the darkness that she had so long feared. There is my brother Gaylen, who died young of knife-wounds, as his new bride sat holding his hand, watching the life pass from his sunken face. There is my brother Gary, who murdered innocent men in rage against the way life had robbed him of time and love, and who died when a volley of bullets tore his heart from his chest. There is my brother Frank, who became quieter and more distant with each new death, and who was last seen in the dream walking down a road, his hands rammed deep into his pockets, a look of uncomprehending pain on his face. There is my father, Frank, Sr., dead of the ravages of lung cancer. He is in the dream less often than the other family members, and I am the only one happy to see him.

One night, years into the same dream, Gary tells me why I can never join my family in its comings and goings, why I am left alone sitting in the living-room as they leave: it is because I have not yet entered death. I cannot follow them across the tracks, into the forest where their real lives take place, until I die. He pulls a gun from his coat pocket. He lays it on my lap. There is a door across the room, and he moves towards it. Through the door is the night. I see the glimmer of the train tracks. Beyond them, my family.

I do not hesitate. I pick the pistol up. I put its barrel in my mouth. I pull the trigger. I feel the back of my head erupt. It is a softer feeling than I expected. I feel my teeth fracture, disintegrate and pass in a gush of blood out of my mouth. I feel my life pass out of my mouth, and in that instant, I collapse into nothingness. There is darkness, but there is no beyond. There is *never* any beyond, only the sudden, certain rush of extinction. I know that it is death I am feeling—that is, I know this is how death must truly feel and I know that this is where beyond ceases to be a possibility.

I have had the dream more than once, in various forms. I always wake up with my heart hammering hard, hurting after being torn from the void that I know is the gateway to the refuge of my ruined family. Or is it the gateway to hell? Either way, I want to return to the dream, but in the haunted hours of the night there is no way back.

Questions for Discussion and Writing

1. What can you infer from Mikhal's account about why Gary committed the murders?
2. What consequences have his brother Gary's crimes had on Mikhal's life? How would you characterize the relationship that the brothers had before and after the murders?

3. Describe an experience in which you were a "victim of guilt by association" and were blamed for something done by a sibling or other relative. Are there any mysterious or shady characters in your lineage? What are they reputed to have done?
4. You might wish to read Norman Mailer's account of Gary Gilmore in *The Executioner's Song* (1979).

Fatima Mernissi

Fatima Mernissi is a scholar of Middle Eastern history and culture who was born in 1940 in Fez, Morocco. Her childhood was unusual in that she was raised in a harem (which means "forbidden" in Arabic). Her experiences there became the subject of her book Dreams of Trespass: Tales of a Harem Girlhood *(1994), in which the following essay first appeared. Mernissi also wrote* Scheherazade Goes West: Different Cultures, Different Harems *(2001).*

To what extent does this photograph of a harem door communicate the same sense of seclusion that Mernissi describes?

MOONLIT NIGHTS OF LAUGHTER

On Yasmina's farm, we never knew when we would eat. Sometimes, Yasmina only remembered at the last minute that she had to feed me, and then she would convince me that a few olives and a piece of her good bread, which she had baked at dawn, would be enough. But dining in our harem in Fez[1] was an entirely different story. We ate at strictly set hours and never between meals.

To eat in Fez, we had to sit at our prescribed places at one of the four communal tables. The first table was for the men, the second for the important women, and the third for the children and less important women, which made us happy, because that meant that Aunt Habiba could eat with us. The last table was reserved for the domestics and anyone who had come in late, regardless of age, rank, or sex. That table was often overcrowded, and was the last chance to get anything to eat at all for those who had made the mistake of not being on time.

Eating at fixed hours was what Mother hated most about communal life. She would nag Father constantly about the possibility of breaking loose and taking our immediate family to live apart. The nationalists advocated the end of seclusion and the veil, but they did not say a word about a couple's right to split off from their larger family. In fact, most of the leaders still lived with their parents. The male nationalist movement supported the liberation of women, but had not come to grips with the idea of the elderly living by themselves, nor with couples splitting off into separate households. Neither idea seemed right, or elegant.

Mother especially disliked the idea of a fixed lunch hour. She always was the last to wake up, and liked to have a late, lavish breakfast which she prepared herself with a lot of flamboyant defiance, beneath the disapproving stare of Grandmother Lalla Mani. She would make herself scrambled eggs and *baghrir,* or fine crêpes, topped with pure honey and fresh butter, and, of course, plenty of tea. She usually ate at exactly eleven, just as Lalla Mani was about to begin her purification ritual for the noon prayer. And after that, two hours later at the communal table, Mother was often absolutely unable to eat lunch. Sometimes she would skip it altogether, especially when she wanted to annoy Father, because to skip a meal was considered terribly rude and too openly individualistic.

Mother dreamed of living alone with Father and us kids. "Whoever heard of ten   5
birds living together squashed into a single nest?" she would say. "It is not natural to live in a large group, unless your objective is to make people feel miserable." Although Father said that he was not really sure how the birds lived, he still sympathized with Mother, and felt torn between his duty towards the traditional family and his desire to make her happy. He felt guilty about breaking up the family solidarity, knowing only too well that big families in general, and harem life in particular, were fast becoming relics of the past. He even prophesied that in the next few decades, we would become like the Christians, who hardly ever visited their old parents. In fact, most of my uncles who had already broken away from the big house barely found the time to visit their mother, Lalla Mani, on Fridays after prayer anymore. "Their kids do not kiss

----

[1]*Fez:* a city in northern Morocco, established 808 A.D.

hands either," ran the constant refrain. To make matters worse, until very recently, all my uncles had lived in our house, and had only split away when their wives' opposition to communal life had become unbearable. That is what gave Mother hope.

The first to leave the big family was Uncle Karim, Cousin Malika's father. His wife loved music and liked to sing while being accompanied by Uncle Karim, who played the lute beautifully. But he would rarely give in to his wife's desire to spend an evening singing in their salon, because his older brother Uncle Ali thought it unbecoming for a man to sing or play a musical instrument. Finally, one day, Uncle Karim's wife just took her children and went back to her father's house, saying that she had no intention of living in the communal house ever again. Uncle Karim, a cheerful fellow who had himself often felt constrained by the discipline of harem life, saw an opportunity to leave and took it, excusing his actions by saying that he preferred to give in to his wife's wishes rather than forfeit his marriage. Not long after that, all my other uncles moved out, one after the other, until only Uncle Ali and Father were left. So Father's departure would have meant the death of our large family. "As long as [my] Mother lives," he often said, "I wouldn't betray the tradition."

Yet Father loved his wife so much that he felt miserable about not giving in to her wishes and never stopped proposing compromises. One was to stock an entire cupboardful of food for her, in case she wanted to discreetly eat sometimes, apart from the rest of the family. For one of the problems in the communal house was that you could not just open a refrigerator when you were hungry and grab something to eat. In the first place, there were no refrigerators back then. More importantly, the entire idea behind the harem was that you lived according to the group's rhythm. You could not just eat when you felt like it. Lalla Radia, my uncle's wife, had the key to the pantry, and although she always asked after dinner what people wanted to eat the next day, you still had to eat whatever the group—after lengthy discussion—decided upon. If the group settled on couscous with chick-peas and raisins, then that is what you got. If you happened to hate chick-peas and raisins, you had no choice but to shut up and settle for a frugal dinner composed of a few olives and a great deal of discretion.

"What a waste of time," Mother would say. "These endless discussions about meals! Arabs would be much better off if they let each individual decide what he or she wanted to swallow. Forcing everyone to share three meals a day just complicates things. And for what sacred purpose? None of course." From there, she would go on to say that her whole life was an absurdity, that nothing made sense, while Father would say that he could not just break away. If he did, tradition would vanish: "We live in difficult times, the country is occupied by foreign armies, our culture is threatened. All we have left is these traditions." This reasoning would drive Mother nuts: "Do you think that by sticking together in this big, absurd house, we will gain the strength we need to throw the foreign armies out? And what is more important anyway, tradition or people's happiness?" That would put an abrupt end to the conversation. Father would try to caress her hand but she would take it away. "This tradition is choking me," she would whisper, tears in her eyes.

So Father kept offering compromises. He not only arranged for Mother to have her own food stock, but also brought her things he knew she liked, such as dates, nuts, almonds, honey, flour, and fancy oils. She could make all the desserts and cookies she wanted, but she was not supposed to prepare a meat dish or a major meal. That would have meant the beginning of the end of the communal arrangement. Her flamboyantly prepared individual breakfasts were enough of a slap in the face to the rest of the family. Every once in a long while, Mother *did* get away with preparing a complete lunch or a dinner, but she had to not only be discreet about it but also give it some sort of exotic overtone. Her most common ploy was to camouflage the meal as a nighttime picnic on the terrace.

These occasional tête-à-tête dinners on the terrace during moonlit summer nights   10
were another peace offering that Father made to help satisfy Mother's yearning for privacy. We would be transplanted to the terrace, like nomads, with mattresses, tables, trays, and my little brother's cradle, which would be set down right in the middle of everything. Mother would be absolutely out of her mind with joy. No one else from the courtyard dared to show up, because they understood all too well that Mother was fleeing from the crowd. What she most enjoyed was trying to get Father to depart from his conventional self-controlled pose. Before long, she would start acting foolishly, like a young girl, and soon, Father would chase her all around the terrace, when she challenged him, "You can't run anymore, you have grown too old! All you're good for now is to sit and watch your son's cradle." Father, who had been smiling up to that point, would look at her at first as if what she had just said had not affected him at all. But then his smile would vanish, and he would start chasing her all over the terrace, jumping over tea-trays and sofas. Sometimes both of them made up games which included my sister and Samir (who was the only one of the rest of the family allowed to attend our moonlit gatherings) and myself. More often, they completely forgot about the rest of the world, and we children would be sneezing all the next day because they had forgotten to put blankets on us when we had gone to sleep that night.

After these blissful evenings, Mother would be in an unusually soft and quiet mood for a whole week. Then she would tell me that whatever else I did with my life, I had to take her revenge. "I want my daughters' lives to be exciting," she would say, "very exciting and filled with one hundred percent happiness, nothing more, nothing less." I would raise my head, look at her earnestly, and ask what one hundred percent happiness meant, because I wanted her to know that I intended to do my best to achieve it. Happiness, she would explain, was when a person felt good, light, creative, content, loving and loved, and free. An unhappy person felt as if there were barriers crushing her desires and the talents she had inside. A happy woman was one who could exercise all kinds of rights, from the right to move to the right to create, compete, and challenge, and at the same time could feel loved for doing so. Part of happiness was to be loved by a man who enjoyed your strength and was proud of your talents. Happiness was also about the right to privacy, the right to retreat from the company of others and plunge into contemplative solitude. Or to sit by yourself doing nothing for a whole day, and not give excuses or feel guilty about it either. Happiness was to be with loved ones, and yet still feel that you existed as a separate being, that you were not there just to make them happy. Happiness was when there was a balance between what you gave and what you took. I then asked her how much happiness she had in her life, just to get an idea, and she said that it varied according to the days. Some days she had only five percent; others, like the evenings we spent with Father on the terrace, she had full-blown one hundred percent happiness.

Aiming at one hundred percent happiness seemed a bit overwhelming to me, as a young girl, especially since I could see how much Mother labored to sculpt her moments of happiness. How much time and energy she put into creating those wonderful moonlit evenings sitting close to Father, talking softly in his ear, her head on his shoulder! It seemed quite an accomplishment to me because she had to start working on him days ahead of time, and then she had to take care of all the logistics, like the cooking and the moving of the furniture. To invest so much stubborn effort just to achieve a few hours of happiness was impressive, and at least I knew it could be done. But how, I wondered, was I going to create such a high level of excitement for an entire lifetime? Well, if Mother thought it was possible, I should certainly give it a try.

"Times are going to get better for women now, my daughter," she would say to me. "You and your sister will get a good education, and you'll walk freely in the streets and discover the world. I want you to become independent, independent and happy. I want you to shine like moons. I want your lives to be a cascade of serene delights. One hundred percent happiness. Nothing more, nothing less." But when I asked her for more details about how to create that happiness, Mother would grow very impatient. "You have to work at it. One develops the muscles for happiness, just like for walking and breathing."

So every morning, I would sit on our threshold, contemplating the deserted courtyard and dreaming about my beautiful future, a cascade of serene delights. Hanging on to the romantic moonlit terrace evenings, challenging your beloved man to forget about his social duties, relax and act foolish and gaze at the stars while holding your hand, I thought, could be one way to go about developing muscles for happiness. Sculpting soft nights, when the sound of laughter blends with the spring breezes, could be another.

But those magical evenings were rare, or so they seemed. During the days, life took 15 a much more rigid and disciplined turn. Officially, there was no jumping around or foolishness allowed in the Mernissi household—all that was confined to clandestine times and spaces, such as late afternoons in the courtyard when the men were out, or evenings on the deserted terraces.

Questions for Discussion and Writing

1. How did Mernissi's mother manage to create a private family dinner despite the restrictions of communal life?
2. What expectations did Mernissi's mother have for her daughter, and how did she express them?
3. Discuss what the issue of privacy means to you and how this value translates into your everyday life.
4. As a research project, investigate how harems are depicted in films, television, and fairy tales. In what ways do these portrayals differ from Mernissi's description? In a short essay, discuss the significance of the Western myth of the harem as exotic. You might consult Edward Said's classic work *Orientalism* (1978), a lively analysis of how the West has created cultural stereotypes about the East.

Richard Keller Simon

• •

A clear sign that malls are a vital feature of modern culture can be inferred from the fact that the largest mall in the world, located in Bloomington, Minnesota, has had more visitors than Disney World. Richard Keller Simon has looked at the function of the mall from a new perspective. Simon describes how the modern shopping mall incorporates and updates garden designs of the past to create a self-enclosed world devoted to consumption. Simon is professor of English and director of the humanities program at California Polytechnic State University, San Luis Obispo. He is the author of The Labyrinth of the Comic *(1986) and* Trash Culture: Popular Culture and the Great Tradition *(1999), in which this selection first appeared.*

THE SHOPPING MALL AND THE FORMAL GARDEN

The contemporary shopping mall is a great formal garden of American culture, a commercial space that shares fundamental characteristics with many of the great garden styles of Western history. Set apart from the rest of the world as a place of earthly delight like the medieval walled garden; filled with fountains, statuary, and ingeniously devised machinery like the Italian Renaissance garden; designed on grandiose and symmetrical principles like this seventeenth-century French garden; made up of the fragments of cultural and architectural history like the eighteenth-century irregular English garden; and set aside for the public like the nineteenth-century American park, the mall is the next phase of this garden history, a synthesis of all these styles that have come before. But it is now joined with the shopping street, or at least a sanitized and standardized version of one, something never before allowed within the garden. In this latest version of the earthly paradise, people live on the goods of the consumer economy peacefully, pleasurably, and even with sophisticated complexity, for although their pleasure comes from buying and everything is set up to facilitate that pleasure, the garden itself is no simple place. Nordstrom has come to Eden. There were dangers and temptations in the very first garden, of course, and the delights dangled before us have been equally powerful. We have moved from the knowledge of good and evil to the joys of shopping.

Visitors learn the meanings of consumer society at the mall, not only in the choices they make in their purchases but also in the symbol systems they walk through, just as visitors to those earlier gardens were invited to learn about the meanings of their own times from the pastoral adventures presented to them. Like the formal garden, the shopping mall is a construct of promenades, walls, vistas, mounts, labyrinths, fountains, statues, archways, trees, grottoes, theaters, flowering plants and shrubs, trellises, and assorted reproductions from architectural history, all artfully arranged. Some of these features, such as the mount, have undergone technological or economic modification. The mount—the manmade earthworks designed to present a vista of the garden to the visitor and typically reached by path or staircase—was a standard part of garden design from the Middle Ages to the eighteenth century. This has been replaced by the escalator, which rises at key points in the enclosed central parts of the mall, where it presents a similar vista of the space to the visitor, who is now lifted dramatically from the floor below by unseen forces without any effort on his or her part. And this, in its turn, is only the modification of a standard feature from Italian Renaissance gardens, the elaborate hydraulic machinery or automata that engineers had devised to move statues about in striking dramatic tableaux. Now in the mall it is the visitors who are moved about by the escalators, becoming themselves the actors in a tableau we might title "modern shopping." Combining the mount with the automata, the mall then encloses this machinery in two or three stories of space, topped with skylights. The result is something like Houston's Galleria Mall, a massive, three-story, enclosed mall topped with skylights. This, in turn, is an updated version of Henry VIII's great garden at Hampton Court, where a mount was topped by a three-story glass arbor surrounded by figures of the king's beasts and royal crown. We have dispensed with the beasts and crown; joggers now run on the roof of the Galleria. But the mount in the king's garden allowed the visitor to look both inside and outside of his garden; the escalator within the enclosed mall of the Galleria, by contrast, only allows the visitor to look at the inside space.

Similarly, the labyrinth—the maze of pathways or hedges that confounded the visitor's attempts to find an easy way out and was a favorite device of Renaissance gardens—is now the cleverly laid out pattern of aisles with department stores, which can be designed to discourage the visitor's easy exit. Shoppers simply cannot find a way out. A decade ago Bloomingdale's in the Willow Grove Mall in suburban Philadelphia received so many complaints from irate shoppers lost in its mazes that finally small, discreet exit signs were posted. What might have originated in the mazes of the early Christian Church, which penitents traveled on their knees while praying at particular points, was first moved outside into the garden, where it was secularized, and has now become thoroughly commodified, a journey in which purchases have replaced prayers. Buy enough and we will let you out.

Played against the maze and labyrinth in the Renaissance garden were the axial and radial avenues that began as extensions of hallways of the palace and ended in suitably grand natural vistas. Played against the department store maze in the mall are the axial and radial avenues that begin as extensions of hallways of one anchor department store and end in the grand vistas of the entrances to other anchor department stores.

The kitchen garden, that area of the formal garden closest to the house and set   5
aside for the production of food, has become the food court, that area of the mall set aside for the consumption of food. The statues—the assorted imitations of Greek and Roman models, portraits of contemporary royalty, or stylized representations of the ancient virtues—have become mannequins decked out in fashionable clothing, the generalized imitations of consumers in their most beautiful, heroic, and changeable poses, portraits of contemporary anonymous life that we should see as stylized representations of the modern virtues: pose, flexibility, nubility, interchangeability, emotional absence. The generalized faces on the statues are now the empty faces of the mannequins. And the various architectural antiquities that became a feature of eighteenth-century English irregular gardens—the miscellaneous copies of Greek temples, Gothic ruins, Japanese pagodas, Roman triumphal arches, and Italian grottoes—are now represented not

so much by the miscellaneous architectural reproductions that appear seasonally in the mall, as in the Easter Bunny's cottage or Santa's Workshop, but much more profoundly by many of the stores themselves, which present idealized versions of architectural and cultural history to the consumer; the Victorian lingerie shop, the high modernist fur salon, the nineteenth-century Western goods store, the Mexican restaurant, the country store designed as a red barn, the dark bar designed as a grotto. Also present in smaller details—in the grand staircase, the wall of mirrors, the plush carpeting, the man playing the white grand piano—are echoes of the 1930s movie set; in the merry-go-round, the popcorn cart, and the clown with balloons, the echoes of funland. The eighteenth-century garden included such historical reproductions in an effort to make sense of its past and to accommodate its cultural inheritances to new situations. One can say the same about the mall's inclusion of historical recollections. If we judge this to be playful and parodic, then we can also call the space postmodern, but if it is only a nostalgic recovery of history, we cannot. This can be a tricky thing. The mall's appropriation of history into idealized spaces of consumption can be a nostalgia or parody, or both at the same time.

The Stanford Shopping Center near Palo Alto presents such a parodic and nostalgic bricolage of cultural and architectural history: Crabtree and Evelyn with its images of eighteenth-century life; Laura Ashley with its images of Romantic and early Victorian life; Victoria's Secret, the late Victorian whorehouse with overtones of French fashion; Banana Republic, the late Victorian colonial outfitter; the Disney Store with its images of 1940s art; and The Nature Company, closest to the sixteenth century and the rise of science in its stock of simple instruments and decor of simple observations of nature. One walks through the images of history just as one did in the formal garden, but now they can be appropriated through the act of consuming. One buys images but learns "history." It is a clean, neat, middle-class version of history without the homeless of a downtown big city, and thus a retreat from the frenzy of urban life and of contemporary history, which is exactly what the formal garden was designed to be. To one side is an alley devoted to food: a lavishly idealized greengrocer, a pseudo-Italian coffee bar, and Max's Opera Café, a reproduction of a grand nineteenth-century cafe in Vienna—but what one finds when one wanders inside is not real or ersatz Vienna, but a glorified Jewish deli. Here the history of central Europe is rewritten as it might have been.

In one Renaissance garden a grotto dedicated to Venus and voluptuous pleasure was juxtaposed with one dedicated to Diana and virtuous pleasure. In another a Temple of Ancient Virtue was contrasted with one representing Modern Virtue. In a similar manner the visitor to the modern garden at Stanford is presented with choices between Victoria's Secret, the shop of voluptuous pleasure, and Westminster Lace, the shop of virtuous pleasure and chastity, but he or she does not have to choose between the Temple of Modern Virtue, the modern shopping center itself, or the Temple of Ancient Virtue, the remnants of the gardens of the past, because the mall artfully combines both.

We are almost at an end of our catalogue of garden elements. In fact, the only standard feature of garden design not present in the modern mall, either in original or in modified form, is the hermitage ruin, a favorite eighteenth-century architectural device designed to allow the visitor to pretend to be a hermit, to be alone and to meditate. There are only two places where a visitor can be alone in the mall: in the lavatories and in the clothing store changing room, but even there one can find surveillance cameras. Meditation and isolation are not virtues encouraged by the modern garden because, interestingly enough, given the opportunity, too many consumers will not meditate there at all, but try to steal whenever they can.

The shopping mall is, of course, quite an imperfect paradise, but the fault does not lie so much with the garden as with the shopping street it has come to assimilate. It is true that there are very few trees in these postmodern gardens, and those that do appear are typically confined in antipastoral concrete planters, but such subordination of nature has occurred before in garden history. Plants were incidental to the Renaissance garden, where visitors instead were expected to direct their attention to the grottoes, fountains, and various mechanical automata.

By bringing the mundane world of commerce into the garden, along with its attendant ills, the mall appears to be inverting the fundamental purposes of many of those earlier gardens as places of repose and contemplation, of escape from the mundane world. Conspicuous consumption has replaced quiet repose. But many of the great styles of garden history have been practical, if not precisely in this way, for example, the *ferme ornée* or eighteenth-century ornamented working farm with its fields, kitchen gardens, orchards, and pastures placed beside the more decorative and formal elements of the garden. These were gardens that had their practical commercial aspects. But although the mall is a far more commercial place than the practical garden, the shift has not so much destroyed the garden—for most of history a space set aside for the rich—as adapted it to new social and economic realities, and it thus can be seen as the appropriate garden for a consumer-oriented culture. In the formal gardens of the past, where nature was rearranged to fit the aesthetic taste of the period, one walked through the landscape contemplating the vistas and approaching the beautiful. In the shopping mall, where nature is similarly rearranged to fit the commercial needs of the period, one walks through the landscape, now contemplating not the vistas of nature, which have been completely blocked out, but rather the vistas presented by the entrances to the anchor department stores, and now approaching not the beautiful but rather the commodities by means of which one can become beautiful. These are practical times. The aristocrat who walked down the path of the garden admired the flowers and smelled their scents; the consumer who walks down the path of the shopping mall buys the flower scents in bottles and then smells like the flower or the musk ox. The focus has shifted from the individual in reverie facing an artificial version of nature to the individual in excitement facing a garden of consumer products. In the eighteenth century the visitor to the garden was expected to feel the elevation of his or her soul. It is unlikely that the visitor to the modern mall has a comparable experience.

Questions for Discussion and Writing

1. What kinds of features found in traditional gardens reappear in the modern shopping mall, and how are they now geared to promote consumption? Why would the hermitage (a place to meditate) be irrelevant in the modern mall?
2. Although Simon is describing a specific mall outside Palo Alto, California what kinds of themes, stores, and fantasy worlds reappear in malls everywhere?

3. Analyze the physical layout of the mall that you frequent the most in terms of how it is designed to provide a congenial environment for spending time with friends and boosting your purchases.

4. How does the ability to buy things online (such as bidding for goods on eBay) create a virtual mall in which a competitive auction-like atmosphere encourages consumerism?

How does the photo of a shopping mall in Los Angeles illustrate Simon's thesis?

William Zinsser

* *

William Zinsser was born in 1922 and graduated from Princeton University in 1944. He joined the staff of the New York Herald Tribune *in 1946 and worked there until 1959, first as a feature editor and then as a drama editor and film critic. He taught at Yale University between 1971 and 1979 and is the author of numerous books, including* Pop Goes America *(1966),* On Writing Well *(1976), and* American Places: A Writer's Pilgrimage to Fifteen of This Country's Most Visited and Cherished Sites *(1992), in which "Niagara Falls" first appeared.* Easy to Remember: The Great American Songwriters and Their Songs *(2000) and* Spring Training *(2003) are his most recent works.*

NIAGARA FALLS

Walden Pond and the Concord writers got me thinking about America's great natural places, and I decided to visit Niagara Falls and Yellowstone Park next. I had been reminded that one of the most radical ideas that Emerson and Thoreau and the other Trancendentalists[1] lobbed into the 19th-century American air was that nature was not an enemy to be feared and repelled, but a spiritual force that the people of a young nation should embrace and take nourishment from. The goal, as Thoreau put it in his essay "Walking," was to become "an inhabitant, or a part and parcel of Nature, rather than a member of society," and it occurred to me that the long and powerful hold of Niagara and Yellowstone on the American imagination had its roots in the gratifying news from Concord that nature was a prime source of uplift, improvement and the "higher" feelings.

---

[1]*Transcendentalism*: a philosophy emphasizing the intuitive and spiritual above the empirical.

Niagara Falls existed only in the attic of my mind where collective memory is stored: scraps of songs about honeymooning couples, vistas by painters who tried to get the plummeting waters to hold still, film clips of Marilyn Monroe running for her life in *Niagara,* odds and ends of lore about stuntmen who died going over the falls, and always, somewhere among the scraps, a boat called *Maid of the Mist,* which took tourists . . . where? Behind the falls? *Under* the falls? Death hovered at the edge of the images in my attic, or at least danger. But I had never thought of going to see the place itself. That was for other people. Now I wanted to be one of those other people.

One misconception I brought to Niagara Falls was that it consisted of two sets of falls, which had to be viewed separately. I would have to see the American falls first and then go over to the Canadian side to see *their* falls, which, everyone said, were better. But nature hadn't done anything so officious, as I found when the shuttle bus from the Buffalo airport stopped and I got out and walked, half running, down a path marked FALLS. The sign was hardly necessary; I could hear that I was going in the right direction.

Suddenly all the images of a lifetime snapped into place—all the paintings and watercolors and engravings and postcards and calendar lithographs. The river does indeed split into two cataracts, divided by a narrow island called Goat Island, but it was man who put a boundary between them. The eye can easily see them as one spectacle: first the straight line of the American falls, then the island, then the much larger, horseshoe-shaped curve of the Canadian falls. The American falls, 1,060 feet across, are majestic but relatively easy to process—water cascading over a ledge. The Canadian falls, 2,200 feet across, are elusive. Water hurtles over them in such volume that the spray ascends from their circular base as high as the falls themselves, 185 feet, hiding them at the heart of the horseshoe. If the Canadian falls are "better," it's not only because they are twice as big but because they have more mystery, curled in on themselves. Whatever is behind all that spray will remain their secret.

My vantage point for this first glimpse was a promenade that overlooks the falls   5 on the American side—a pleasantly landscaped area that has the feeling of a national park; there was none of the souvenir-stand clutter I expected. My strongest emotion as I stood and tried to absorb the view was that I was very glad to be there. So *that's* what they look like! I stayed at the railing for a long time, enjoying the play of light on the tumbling waters; the colors, though the day was gray, were subtle and satisfying. My thoughts, such as they were, were banal—vaguely pantheistic, poor man's Wordsworth. My fellow sightseers were equally at ease, savoring nature with 19th-century serenity, taking pictures of each other against the cataracts. (More Kodak film is sold here than at any place except the Taj Mahal.) Quite a few of the tourists appeared to be honeymooners; many were parents with children; some were elementary school teachers with their classes. I heard some foreign accents, but on the whole it was—as it always has been—America-on-the-road. The old icon was still worth taking the kids to see. Today more people visit Niagara Falls than ever before: 10 million a year.

Far below, in the gorge where the river reassembles after its double descent, I saw a small boat bobbing in the turbulent water, its passengers bunched at the railing in blue slickers. Nobody had to tell me it was the *Maid of the Mist*—I heard it calling. I took the elevator down to the edge of the river. Even there, waiting at the dock, I could hardly believe that such a freakish trip was possible—or even prudent. What if the boat capsized? What if its engine stopped? What if . . . ? But when the *Maid of the Mist* arrived, there was no question of not getting on it. I was just one more statistic proving the falls' legendary pull—the force that has beckoned so many daredevils to their death and that compels so many suicides every year to jump.

On the boat, we all got blue raincoats and put them on with due seriousness. The *Maid of the Mist* headed out into the gorge and immediately sailed past the American falls. Because these falls have famously fallen apart over the years and dumped large chunks of rock at their base, the water glances off the rubble and doesn't churn up as much spray as a straight drop would generate. That gave us a good view of the falls from a fairly close range and got us only moderately wet.

Next we sailed past Goat Island. There I saw a scene so reminiscent of a Japanese movie in its gauzy colors and stylized composition that I could hardly believe it wasn't a Japanese movie. Filtered through the mist, a straggling line of tourists in yellow raincoats was threading its way down a series of wooden stairways and catwalks to reach the rocks in front of the American falls. They were on a tour called "Cave of the Winds," so named because in the 19th century it was possible to go behind the falls into various hollowed-out spaces that have since eroded. Even today nobody gets closer to the falls, or gets wetter, than these stair people. I watched them as I might watch a colony of ants: small yellow figures doggedly following a zigzag trail down a steep embankment to some ordained goal. The sight took me by surprise and was surprisingly beautiful.

Leaving the ants, we proceeded to the Canadian falls. Until then the *Maid of the Mist* had struck me as a normal excursion boat, the kind that might take sightseers around Manhattan. Suddenly it seemed very small. By now we had come within the outer circle of the horseshoe. On both sides of our boat, inconceivable amounts of water were rushing over the edge from the height of a 15-story building. I thought of the word I had seen in so many articles about Niagara's stuntmen: they were going to "conquer" the falls. Conquer! No such emanations were felt in our crowd. Spray was pelting our raincoats, and we peered out at each other from inside our hoods—eternal tourists bonded together by some outlandish event voluntarily entered into. (Am I really riding down the Grand Canyon on a burro? Am I really about to be charged by an African rhino?) The *Maid of the Mist* showed no sign of being afraid of the Canadian falls; it headed straight into the cloud of spray at the heart of the horseshoe. How much farther were we going to go? The boat began to rock in the eddying water. I felt a twinge of fear.

In the 19th-century literature of Niagara Falls, one adjective carries much of the   10
baggage: "sublime." Today it's seldom heard, except in bad Protestant hymns. But for a young nation eager to feel emotions worthy of God's mightiest wonders, the word had a precise meaning—"a mixture of attraction and terror," as the historian Elizabeth McKinsey puts it. Tracing the theory of sublimity to mid-18th-century aestheticians such as Edmund Burke[2]—in particular, to Burke's *Philosophical Enquiry into the Origin*

---

[2]*Edmund Burke (1729–1797):* an Irish statesman, orator, and writer.

of Our Ideas of the Sublime and Beautiful—Professor McKinsey says that the experience of early visitors to Niagara Falls called for a word that would go beyond mere awe and fear. "Sublime" was the perfect answer. It denoted "a new capacity to appreciate the beauty and grandeur of potentially terrifying natural objects." Anybody could use it, and everybody did.

Whether I was having sublime feelings as I looked up at the falls I will leave to some other aesthetician. By any name, however, I was thinking: This is an amazing place to be. I wasn't having a 19th-century rapture, but I also wasn't connected in any way to 20th-century thought. I was somewhere in a late-Victorian funk, the kind of romanticism that induced Hudson River School[3] artists to paint a rainbow over Niagara Falls more often than they saw one there. Fortunately, in any group of Americans there will always be one pragmatist to bring us back to earth. Just as I was becoming edgy at the thought of being sucked into the vortex, the man next to me said that he had been measuring our progress by the sides of the gorge and we weren't making any progress at all. Even with its engines at full strength, the *Maid of the Mist* was barely holding its own. That was a sufficiently terrifying piece of news, and when the boat finally made a U-turn I didn't protest. A little sublime goes a long way.

The first *Maid of the Mist* took tourists to the base of the horseshoe falls in 1846. Now, as the mist enveloped our *Maid,* I liked the idea that I was in the same spot and was having what I assume were the same feelings that those travelers had almost 150 years ago. I liked the idea of a tourist attraction so pure that it doesn't have to be tricked out with improvements. The falls don't tug on our sense of history or on our national psyche. They don't have any intellectual content or take their meaning from what was achieved there. They just do what they do.

"When people sit in the front of that boat at the foot of the falls they get a little philosophical," said Christopher M. Glynn, marketing director of the Maid of the Mist Corporation. "They think: There's something bigger than I am that put *this* together. A lot of them have heard about the Seven Wonders of the World, and they ask, 'Is this one of them?'" Glynn's father, James V. Glynn, owner and president of the company, which has been owned by only two families since 1889, often has his lunch on the boat and talks with grandfathers and grandmothers who first visited Niagara on their honeymoon. "Usually," he told me, "they only saw the falls from above. Down here it's a totally different perspective, and they find the power of the water almost unbelievable. You're seeing one of God's great works when you're in that horseshoe."

Most Americans come to the falls as a family, said Ray H. Wigle of the Niagara Falls Visitors and Convention Bureau. "They wait until the kids are out of school to visit places like this and the Grand Canyon and Yellowstone. They say, "This is part of your education—to see these stupendous works of nature." On one level today's tourists are conscious of 'the environment,' and they're appreciative of the magnificence of the planet and the fact that something like this has a right to exist by itself—unlike early tourists, who felt that nature was savage and had to be tamed and utilized. But deep down there's still a primal response to uncivilized nature that doesn't change

---

[3]*Hudson River School artists:* a group of 29 nineteenth-century landscape painters in New York state who depicted romantic views of the Catskill Mountains using contrasts of light and dark.

from one century to another. 'I never realized it was like this!' I hear tourists say all the time, and when they turn away from their first look at the falls—when they first connect again with another person—there's always a delighted smile on their face that's universal and childish."

I spent two days at Niagara, looking at the falls at different times of day and night,   15
especially from the Canadian side, where the view of both cataracts across the gorge is the most stunning and—as so many artists have notified us—the most pictorial. Even when I wasn't looking at them, even when I was back in my hotel room, I was aware of them, a low rumble in the brain. They are always *there*. Some part of us, as Americans, has known that for a long time.

Sightseers began coming to Niagara in sizable numbers when the railroads made it easy for them to get there, starting in 1836 with the opening of the Lockport & Niagara Falls line, which brought families traveling on the Erie Canal. Later, workers came over from Rochester on Sunday afternoon after church, and passengers taking Lake Erie steamers came over for a few hours from Buffalo. To stroll in the park beside the falls was an acceptable Victorian thing to do. No other sublime experience of such magnitude was available. People might have heard of the Grand Canyon or the Rockies, but they couldn't get there; vacations were too short and transportation was too slow.

So uplifting were the falls deemed to be that they became a rallying point after the Civil War for religious leaders, educators, artists and scientists eager to preserve them as a sacred grove for the public. This meant wresting them back from the private owners who had bought the adjacent land from New York State, putting up mills, factories and tawdry souvenir shops, and charging admission for a view of God's handiwork through holes in the fence. That the state had sold off its land earlier was not all that surprising; before the Concord poets and philosophers suggested otherwise, the notion that nature should be left intact and simply appreciated was alien to the settler mentality. Land was meant to be cleared, civilized and put to productive use.

Two men in particular inspired the "Free Niagara!" movement: the painter Frederic Edwin Church and the landscape architect Frederick Law Olmsted,[4] designer of New York's great Central Park. Church's seven-foot-long *Niagara,* which has been called the greatest American painting, drew such worshipful throngs when it was first exhibited in a Broadway showroom in 1857—thousands came every day—that it was sent on a tour of England, where it was unanimously praised by critics, including the sainted John Ruskin.[5] If America could produce such a work, there was hope for the colonies after all. Back home, the painting made a triumphal tour of the South in 1858–59 and was reproduced and widely sold as a chromolithograph. More than any other image, it fixed the falls in the popular imagination as having powers both divine and patriotic: "an earthly manifestation of God's attributes" and a prophecy of "the nation's collective aspirations." Iconhood had arrived; Niagara Falls began to appear

---

[4]*Frederick Edwin Church (1826–1900):* American painter, member of the Hudson River school. *Frederick Law Olmsted (1822–1903):* American landscape architect and writer who designed Central Park in Manhattan and Prospect Park in Brooklyn.   [5]*John Ruskin (1819–1900):* English critic and social theorist.

in posters and advertisements as the symbol of America. Only the Statue of Liberty would dislodge it.

Olmsted, the other man who shaped Niagara's aesthetic, proposed the heretical idea of a public park next to the falls and on the neighboring islands, in which nature would be left alone. This was counter to the prevailing European concept of a park as a formal arrangement of paths and plantings. In the 1870s Olmsted and a coalition of zealous Eastern intellectuals launched a campaign of public meetings, pamphlets, articles and petitions urging state officials to buy back the land and raze everything that man had put on it. Massive political opposition greeted their effort. Not only were the owners of the land rich and influential; many citizens felt that the government in a free society had no right to say, "In the public interest we're taking this land back." The fight lasted 15 years and was narrowly won in 1885 with the creation of the Niagara Reservation, America's first state park. (One hundred thousand people came on opening day.) Olmsted's hands-off landscaping, which preserved the natural character of the area and kept essential roads and buildings unobtrusive, became a model for parks in many other parts of the country.

Gradually, however, the adjacent hotels and commercial enterprises began to go to   20 seed, as aging resorts will, and in the early 1960s Mayor E. Dent Lackey of Niagara Falls, New York, decided that only a sharp upgrading of the American side would enable his city to attract enough tourists to keep it healthy. Sublimity was no longer the only option for honeymooners; they could fly to Bermuda as easily as they could fly to Buffalo. Mayor Lackey, riding the 1960s' almost religious belief in urban renewal, tore down much of the "falls area." Like so much '60s renewal, the tearing down far outraced the building back up, but today the new pieces are finally in place: a geological museum, an aquarium, a Native American arts and crafts center, a glass-enclosed botanical garden with 7,000 tropical specimens, an "Artpark," a shopping mall and other such placid amenities. Even the new Burger King is tasteful. The emphasis is on history, culture, education and scenery.

By contrast, over on the Canadian side, a dense thoroughfare called Clifton Hill offers a Circus World, a Ripley's Believe It or Not Museum, a House of Frankenstein, a Guinness Book of Records Museum, several wax museums, a Ferris wheel, a miniature golf course and other such amusements. The result of Mayor Lackey's faith that Americans still want to feel the higher feelings is that tourism has increased steadily ever since he got the call.

> Niag'ra Falls, I'm falling for you,
> Niag'ra Falls, with your rainbow hue,
> Oh, the Maid of the Mist
> Has never been kissed,
> Niag'ra, I'm falling for you.

This terrible song is typical of the objects I found in the local-history section of the Niagara Falls Public Library, along with 20,000 picture postcards, 15,000 stereopticon slides, books by writers as diverse as Jules Verne and William Dean Howells,[6] and

---

[6] *William Dean Howells (1837–1920):* introduced realism and naturalism into American literature. *Their Wedding Journey* (1882) was Howell's first novel about a delightful honeymoon to Niagara Falls.

thousands of newspaper and magazine articles. Together, for two centuries, they have sent America the message WISH YOU WERE HERE!, sparing no superlative. Howells, in his novel *Their Wedding Journey,* in 1882, wrote: "As the train stopped, Isabel's heart beat with a child-like exultation, as I believe everyone's heart must who is worthy to arrive at Niagara." Describing the place where Isabel and Basil got off the train as a "sublime destination," Howells says: "Niagara deserves almost to rank with Rome, the metropolis of history and religion; with Venice, the chief city of sentiment and fantasy. In either you are at once made at home by a perception of its greatness . . . and you gratefully accept its sublimity as a fact in no way contrasting with your own insignificance."

What the library gets asked about most often, however, is the "stunts and stunters," according to Donald E. Loker, its local-history specialist. "Just yesterday," he told me, "I got a call from an advertising agency that wanted to use Annie Taylor in an ad campaign." Mrs. Taylor was a schoolteacher who went over the falls in a barrel on October 4, 1901, and survived the plunge, unlike her cat, which she had previously sent over in her barrel for a trial run. Thereby she became the first person to conquer the falls—and also one of the last. Most of the other conquerors tried their luck once too often. Today there is a ban on stunts, but not on ghosts. "Didn't somebody tightrope over this?" is one question that tour guides always get. "People want to see the scene," one of the guides told me. "They want to know: "How did he do it?""

Of all those glory-seekers, the most glorious was Jean François Gravelet, known as the great Blondin. A Frenchman trained in the European circus, he came to America in 1859 under the promotional arm of P. T. Barnum and announced that he would cross the Niagara gorge on a tightrope on June 30, 1859. "Blondin was too good a showman to make the trip appear easy," Philip Mason writes in a booklet called "Niagara and the Daredevils." "His hesitations and swayings began to build a tension that soon had the huge crowd gripped in suspense." In the middle he stopped, lowered a rope to the *Maid of the Mist,* pulled up a bottle and sat down to have a drink. Continuing toward the Canadian shore, "he paused, steadied the balancing pole and suddenly executed a back somersault. Men screamed, women fainted. Those near the rope wept and begged him to come in. . . . For the rest of the fabulous summer of 1859 he continued to provide thrills for the huge crowds that flocked to Niagara to see him. Never content to merely to repeat his last performance, Blondin crossed his rope on a bicycle, walked it blindfolded, pushed a wheelbarrow, cooked an omelet in the center, and made the trip with his hands and feet manacled."

I left the library and went back to the falls for a final look. Far below and far away   25 I saw a tiny boat with a cluster of blue raincoats on its upper deck, vanishing into a tall cloud of mist at the center of the horseshoe falls. Then I didn't see it any more. Would it ever come back out? Historical records going back to 1846 said that it would.

Questions for Discussion and Writing

1. What role have writers, philosophers, and painters played in the emergence of Niagara Falls as a tourist attraction?
2. How effective do you find Zinsser's method of interweaving personal experiences with documented historical facts?

3. Describe another natural wonder that elicits from you the same kinds of reactions and feelings that Niagara Falls did from Zinsser.

4. How does this view of Niagara Falls from the *Maid of the Mist* illustrate why this natural wonder has become one of the world's most popular tourist attractions?

Joseph Addison

* *

English essayist and journalist, Joseph Addison (1672–1719) had a distinguished career as a diplomat, member of Parliament, and secretary of state. But he is best known for his collaboration with Richard Steele on the periodicals The Tatler *(1709–1710) and* The Spectator *(1711–1712, 1714). His sparkling and perceptive observations on different aspects of society are well worth revisiting. In the following essay from* The Spectator *(Number 26, dated Friday, March 30, 1711), Addison takes us through the famous Gothic cathedral in London where all English monarchs have been crowned since William I (1027–1087) and where kings, statesmen, poets, and others of distinction, including Addison himself, are buried.*

REFLECTIONS IN WESTMINSTER ABBEY

When I am in a serious humour, I very often walk by myself in Westminster-abbey; where the gloominess of the place, and the use to which it is applied, with the solemnity of the building, and the condition of the people who lie in it, are apt to fill the mind with a kind of melancholy, or rather thoughtfulness, that is not disagreeable. I yesterday passed a whole afternoon in the churchyard, the cloisters, and the church, amusing myself with the tomb-stones and inscriptions that I met with in those several regions of the dead. Most of them recorded nothing else of the buried person, but that he was born upon one day, and died upon another; the whole history of his life being comprehended in those epitaphs, which are written with great elegance of expression and justness of thought, and therefore do honour to the living as well as the dead. As a foreigner is very apt to conceive an idea of the ignorance or politeness of a nation from the turn of their public monuments and inscriptions, they should be submitted to the perusal of men of learning and genius before they are put in execution. Sir Cloudesley Shovel's monument has very often given me great offence. Instead of the brave rough English admiral, which was the distinguishing character of that plain gallant man, he is represented on his tomb by the figure of a beau, dressed in a long periwig, and reposing himself upon velvet cushions, under a canopy of state. The inscription is answerable to the monument; for instead of celebrating the many remarkable actions he had performed in the service of his country, it acquaints us only with the manner of his death, in which it was impossible for him to reap any honour. The Dutch, whom we are apt to despise for want of genius, show an infinitely greater taste of antiquity and politeness in their buildings and works of this nature, than what we meet with in those of our own country. The monuments of their admirals, which have been erected at the public expense, represent them like themselves, and are adorned with rostral crowns and naval ornaments, with beautiful festoons of sea-weed, shells, and coral.

But to return to our subject. I have left the repository of our English kings for the contemplation of another day, when I shall find my mind disposed for so serious an amusement. I know that entertainments of this nature are apt to raise dark and dismal thoughts in timorous minds, and gloomy imaginations; but for my own part, though I am always serious, I do not know what it is to be melancholy; and can therefore take a view of nature, in her deep and solemn scenes, with the same pleasure as in her most gay and delightful ones. By this means I can improve myself with those objects, which others consider with terror. When I look upon the tombs of the great, every emotion of envy dies in me; when I read the epitaphs of the beautiful, every inordinate desire goes out; when I meet with the grief of parents upon a tombstone, my heart melts with compassion; when I see the tomb of the parents themselves, I consider the vanity of grieving for those whom we must quickly follow. When I see kings lying by those who deposed them, when I consider rival wits placed side by side, or the holy men that divided the world with their contests and disputes, I reflect with sorrow and astonishment on the little competitions, factions, and debates of mankind. When I read the several dates of the tombs, of some that died yesterday, and some six hundred years ago, I consider that great day when we shall all of us be contemporaries, and make our appearance together.

Questions for Discussion and Writing

1. In what respects do Addison's activities and reactions seem to be a bit eccentric?
2. What function does **humor** serve in this account? Is it out of place considering the circumstance? Why or why not?
3. Pay a visit to a public monument in your town or community and compose your own "Reflections." you might wish to emulate some of the dis-

tinctive features of Addison's syntax (for example, how is parallelism used in the second paragraph?).

4. How does this view of the South Transept and Poet's Corner in Westminster Abbey convey the scene that elicited Addison's observations?

George Carlin

George Carlin's social criticism, presented in the guise of stand-up comedy, has made him one of the most successful performers over the past forty years. He was awarded the Lifetime Achievement Award in 2001 at the 15th Annual American Comedy Awards. In this classic monologue, reprinted from Brain Droppings *(1997), Carlin looks at our love-hate relationship with our possessions. Carlin's hilarious monologue will strike many people as being right on target. His latest works are* Napalm and Silly Putty *(2001) and* When Will Jesus Bring the Pork Chops? *(2004).*

George Carlin on stage in 2004 delivering his unique form of social commentary.

A PLACE FOR YOUR STUFF

Hi! How are ya? You got your stuff with you? I'll bet you do. Guys have stuff in their pockets; women have stuff in their purses. Of course, some women have pockets, and some guys have purses. That's okay. There's all different ways of carryin' your stuff.

Then there's all the stuff you have in your car. You got stuff in the trunk. Lotta different stuff: spare tire, jack, tools, old blanket, extra pair of sneakers. Just in case you wind up barefoot on the highway some night.

And you've got other stuff in your car. In the glove box. Stuff you might need in a hurry: flashlight, map, sunglasses, automatic weapon. You know. Just in case you wind up barefoot on the highway some night.

So stuff is important. You gotta take care of your stuff. You gotta have a *place* for your stuff. Everybody's gotta have a place for their stuff. That's what life is all about, tryin' to find a place for your stuff! That's all your house is: a place to keep your stuff. If you didn't have so much stuff, you wouldn't *need* a house. You could just walk around all the time.

A house is just a pile of stuff with a cover on it. You can see that when you're tak-   5
ing off in an airplane. You look down and see all the little piles of stuff. Everybody's got his own little pile of stuff. And they lock it up! That's right! When you leave your house, you gotta lock it up. Wouldn't want somebody to come by and *take* some of your stuff. 'Cause they always take the *good* stuff! They don't bother with that crap you're saving. Ain't nobody interested in your fourth-grade arithmetic papers. *National Geographics,* commemorative plates, your prize collection of Navajo underwear; they're not interested. They just want the good stuff; the shiny stuff; the electronic stuff.

So when you get right down to it, your house is nothing more than a place to keep your stuff . . . while you go out and get . . . *more stuff.* 'Cause that's what this country is all about. Tryin' to get more stuff. Stuff you don't want, stuff you don't need, stuff that's poorly made, stuff that's overpriced. Even stuff you can't afford! Gotta keep on gettin' more stuff. Otherwise someone else might wind up with more stuff. Can't let that happen. Gotta have the most stuff.

So you keep gettin' more and more stuff, and puttin' it in different places. In the closets, in the attic, in the basement, in the garage. And there might even be some stuff you left at your parents' house: baseball cards, comic books, photographs, souvenirs. Actually, your parents threw that stuff out long ago.

So now you got a houseful of stuff. And, even though you might like your house, you gotta move. Gotta get a bigger house. Why? Too much stuff! And that means you gotta move all your stuff. Or maybe, put some of your stuff in storage. Storage! Imagine that. There's a whole industry based on keepin' an eye on other people's stuff.

Or maybe you could sell some of your stuff. Have a yard sale, have a garage sale! Some people drive around all weekend just lookin' for garage sales. They don't have enough of their own stuff, they wanna buy other people's stuff.

Or you could take your stuff to the swap meet, the flea market, the rummage sale,   10
or the auction. There's a lotta ways to get rid of stuff. You can even give your stuff away. The Salvation Army and Goodwill will actually come to your house and pick up your stuff and give it to people who don't have much stuff. It's part of what economists call the Redistribution of Stuff.

OK, enough about your stuff. Let's talk about other people's stuff. Have you ever noticed when you visit someone else's house, you never quite feel at home? You know why? No room for your stuff! Somebody *else's* stuff is all over the place. And what crummy stuff it is! "God! Where'd they get *this* stuff?"

And you know how sometimes when you're visiting someone, you unexpectedly have to stay overnight? It gets real late, and you decide to stay over? So they put you in a bedroom they don't use too often . . . because Grandma died in it eleven years ago! And they haven't moved any of her stuff? Not even the vaporizer?

Or whatever room they put you in, there's usually a dresser or a nightstand, and there's never any room on it for your stuff. Someone else's shit is on the dresser! Have you noticed that their stuff is shit, and your shit is stuff? "Get this shit off of here, so I can put my stuff down!" Crap is also a form of stuff. Crap is the stuff that belongs to the person you just broke up with. "When are you comin' over here to pick up the rest of your crap?"

Now let's talk about traveling. Sometimes you go on vacation, and you gotta take some of your stuff. Mostly stuff to wear. But which stuff should you take? Can't take all your stuff. Just the stuff you really like; the stuff that fits you well that month. In effect, on vacation, you take a smaller, "second version" of your stuff.

Let's say you go to Honolulu for two weeks. You gotta take two big suitcases of stuff. Two weeks, two big suitcases. That's the stuff you check onto the plane. But you also got your carry-on stuff, plus the stuff you bought in the airport. So now you're all set to go. You got stuff in the overhead rack, stuff under the seat, stuff in the seat pocket, and stuff in your lap. And let's not forget the stuff you're gonna steal from the airline: silverware, soap, blanket, toilet paper, salt and pepper shakers. Too bad those headsets won't work at home. 15

And so you fly to Honolulu, and you claim your stuff—if the airline didn't drop it in the ocean—and you go to the hotel, and the first thing you do is put away your stuff. There's lots of places in a hotel to put your stuff.

"I'll put some stuff in here, you put some stuff in there. Hey, don't put your stuff in *there!* That's my stuff! Here's another place! Put some stuff in here. And there's another place! Hey, you know what? We've got more places than we've got stuff! We're gonna hafta go out and buy . . . *more stuff!!!*"

Finally you put away all your stuff, but you don't quite feel at ease, because you're a long way from home. Still, you sense that you must be OK, because you do have some of your stuff with you. And so you relax in Honolulu on that basis. That's when your friend from Maui calls and says, "Hey, why don't you come over to Maui for the weekend and spend a couple of nights over here?"

Oh no! Now whaddya bring? Can't bring all this stuff. You gotta bring an even *smaller* version of your stuff. Just enough stuff for a weekend on Maui. The "third version" of your stuff.

And, as you're flyin' over to Maui, you realize that you're really spread out now: You've got stuff all over the world!! Stuff at home, stuff in the garage, stuff at your parents' house (maybe), stuff in storage, stuff in Honolulu, and stuff on the plane. Supply lines are getting longer and harder to maintain! 20

Finally you get to your friends' place on Maui, and they give you a little room to sleep in, and there's a nightstand. Not much room on it for your stuff, but it's OK because you don't have much stuff now. You got your 8×10 autographed picture of Drew Carey, a large can of gorgonzola-flavored Cheez Whiz, a small, unopened packet of brown confetti, a relief map of Corsica, and a family-size jar of peppermint-flavored, petrified egg whites. And you know that even though you're a long way from home, you must be OK because you do have a good supply of peppermint-flavored, petrified egg whites. And so you begin to relax in Maui on that basis. That's when your friend says, "Hey, I think tonight we'll go over to the other side of the island and visit my sister. Maybe spend the night over there."

Oh no! Now whaddya bring? Right! You gotta bring an even smaller version. The "fourth version" of your stuff. Just the stuff you *know* you're gonna need: Money, keys, comb, wallet, lighter, hankie, pen, cigarettes, contraceptives, Vaseline, whips, chains, whistles, dildos, and a book. Just the stuff you *hope* you're gonna need. Actually, your friend's sister probably has her own dildos.

By the way, if you go to the beach while you're visiting the sister, you're gonna have to bring—that's right—an even smaller version of your stuff: the "fifth version." Cigarettes and wallet. That's it. You can always borrow someone's suntan lotion. And then suppose, while you're there on the beach, you decide to walk over to the refreshment stand to get a hot dog? That's right, my friend! Number six! The most important version of your stuff: your wallet! Your wallet contains the only stuff you really can't do without.

Well, by the time you get home you're pretty fed up with your stuff and all the problems it creates. And so about a week later, you clean out the closet, the attic, the basement, the garage, the storage locker, and all the other places you keep your stuff, and you get things down to manageable proportions. Just the right amount of stuff to lead a simple and uncomplicated life. And that's when the phone rings. It's a lawyer. It seems your aunt has died . . . and left you all her stuff. Oh no! Now whaddya do? Right. You do the only thing you can do. The honorable thing. You tell the lawyer to stuff it.

Questions for Discussion and Writing

1. According to Carlin, how has the accumulation of "stuff" come to define our culture? What forms does this obsession take? Why do people view their "stuff" differently than the "stuff" that belongs to others?

2. How does Carlin's example of what to take on a vacation in Hawaii illustrate his thesis that we are dependent on our "stuff" to provide an identify?

3. As an experiment, count how many times you either hear or use the word "stuff" in the course of a day, and write a page or two that adds to Carlin's monologue. What could an archaeologist of the future tell about our culture from the contents of your most cluttered drawer or closet?

4. How does the greeting card shown here exaggerate George Carlin's thesis? Who would you give this card to?

FICTION

Raymond Carver

Raymond Carver (1938–1988) grew up in a logging town in Oregon and was educated at Humboldt State College (B.A., 1963) and at the University of Iowa, where be studied creative writing. He first received recognition in the 1970s with the publication of stories in the New Yorker, Esquire, *and the* Atlantic Monthly. *His first collection of short stories,* Will You Please Be Quiet, Please? *(1976), was nominated for the National Book Award. Subsequent collections include* What We Talk About When We Talk About Love *(1981),* Cathedral *(1983), and* Where I'm Calling From *(1988), in which "Neighbors" first appeared. A posthumous book of Carver's poetry,* All of Us, *was published in 1998. "Neighbors" displays Carver's conversational style and unique gift for getting to the heart of human relationships.*

NEIGHBORS

Bill and Arlene Miller were a happy couple. But now and then they felt they alone among their circle had been passed by somehow, leaving Bill to attend to his bookkeeping duties and Arlene occupied with secretarial chores. They talked about it sometimes, mostly in comparison with the lives of their neighbors, Harriet and Jim Stone. It seemed to the Millers that the Stones lived a fuller and brighter life. The Stones were always going out for dinner, or entertaining at home, or traveling about the country somewhere in connection with Jim's work.

The Stones lived across the hall from the Millers. Jim was a salesman for a machine-parts firm and often managed to combine business with pleasure trips, and on this occasion the Stones would be away for ten days, first to Cheyenne, then on to St. Louis to visit relatives. In their absence, the Millers would look after the Stones' apartment, feed Kitty, and water the plants.

Bill and Jim shook hands beside the car. Harriet and Arlene held each other by the elbows and kissed lightly on the lips.

"Have fun," Bill said to Harriet.

"We will," said Harriet. "You kids have fun too."   5

Arlene nodded.

Jim winked at her. "Bye, Arlene. Take good care of the old man."

"I will," Arlene said.

"Have fun," Bill said.

"You bet," Jim said, clipping Bill lightly on the arm. "And thanks again, you guys."   10

The Stones waved as they drove away, and the Millers waved too.

"Well, I wish it was us," Bill said.

"God knows, we could use a vacation," Arlene said. She took his arm and put it around her waist as they climbed the stairs to their apartment.

After dinner Arlene said, "Don't forget. Kitty gets liver flavor the first night." She stood in the kitchen doorway folding the handmade tablecloth that Harriet had bought for her last year in Santa Fe.

Bill took a deep breath as he entered the Stones' apartment. The air was already   15
heavy and it was vaguely sweet. The sunburst clock over the television said half past
eight. He remembered when Harriet had come home with the clock, how she had
crossed the hall to show it to Arlene, cradling the brass case in her arms and talking
to it through the tissue paper as if it were an infant.

Kitty rubbed her face against his slippers and then turned onto her side, but jumped
up quickly as Bill moved to the kitchen and selected one of the stacked cans from the
gleaming drainboard. Leaving the cat to pick at her food, he headed for the bathroom.
He looked at himself in the mirror and then closed his eyes and then looked again. He
opened the medicine chest. He found a container of pills and read the label—*Harriet
Stone. One each day as directed*—and slipped it into his pocket. He went back to the
kitchen, drew a pitcher of water, and returned to the living room. He finished watering, set the pitcher on the rug, and opened the liquor cabinet. He reached in back for
the bottle of Chivas Regal. He took two drinks from the bottle, wiped his lips on his
sleeve, and replaced the bottle in the cabinet.

Kitty was on the couch sleeping. He switched off the lights, slowly closing and
checking the door. He had the feeling he had left something.

"What kept you?" Arlene said. She sat with her legs turned under her, watching
television.

"Nothing. Playing with Kitty," he said, and went over to her and touched her breasts.

"Let's go to bed, honey," he said.   20

The next day Bill took only ten minutes of the twenty-minute break allotted for
the afternoon and left at fifteen minutes before five. He parked the car in the lot just
as Arlene hopped down from the bus. He waited until she entered the building, then
ran up the stairs to catch her as she stepped out of the elevator.

"Bill! God, you scared me. You're early," she said.

He shrugged. "Nothing to do at work," he said.

She let him use her key to open the door. He looked at the door across the hall before following her inside.

"Let's go to bed," he said.   25

"Now?" She laughed. "What's gotten into you?"

"Nothing. Take your dress off." He grabbed for her awkwardly, and she said,
"Good God, Bill."

He unfastened his belt.

Later they sent out for Chinese food, and when it arrived they ate hungrily, without speaking, and listened to records.

"Let's not forget to feed Kitty," she said.   30

"I was just thinking about that," he said. "I'll go right over."

He selected a can of fish flavor for the cat, then filled the pitcher and went to water.
When he returned to the kitchen, the cat was scratching in her box. She looked at him
steadily before she turned back to the litter. He opened all the cupboards and examined the canned goods, the cereals, the packaged foods, the cocktail and wine glasses,
the china, the pots and pans. He opened the refrigerator. He sniffed some celery, took
two bites of cheddar cheese, and chewed on an apple as he walked into the bedroom.

The bed seemed enormous, with a fluffy white bedspread draped to the floor. He pulled out a nightstand drawer, found a half-empty package of cigarettes and stuffed them into his pocket. Then he stepped to the closet and was opening it when the knock sounded at the front door.

He stopped by the bathroom and flushed the toilet on his way.

"What's been keeping you?" Arlene said. "You've been over here more than an hour."

"Have I really?" he said.   35

"Yes, you have," she said.

"I had to go to the toilet," he said.

"You have your own toilet," she said.

"I couldn't wait," he said.

That night they made love again.   40

In the morning he had Arlene call in for him. He showered, dressed, and made a light breakfast. He tried to start a book. He went out for a walk and felt better. But after a while, hands still in his pockets, he returned to the apartment. He stopped at the Stones' door on the chance he might hear the cat moving about. Then he let himself in at his own door and went to the kitchen for the key.

Inside it seemed cooler than his apartment, and darker too. He wondered if the plants had something to do with the temperature of the air. He looked out the window, and then he moved slowly through each room considering everything that fell under his gaze, carefully, one object at a time. He saw ashtrays, items of furniture, kitchen utensils, the clock. He saw everything. At last he entered the bedroom, and the cat appeared at his feet. He stroked her once, carried her into the bathroom, and shut the door.

He lay down on the bed and stared at the ceiling. He lay for a while with his eyes closed, and then he moved his hand under his belt. He tried to recall what day it was. He tried to remember when the Stones were due back, and then he wondered if they would ever return. He could not remember their faces or the way they talked and dressed. He sighed and with effort rolled off the bed to lean over the dresser and look at himself in the mirror.

He opened the closet and selected a Hawaiian shirt. He looked until he found Bermudas, neatly pressed and hanging over a pair of brown twill slacks. He shed his own clothes and slipped into the shorts and the shirt. He looked in the mirror again. He went to the living room and poured himself a drink and sipped it on his way back to the bedroom. He put on a blue shirt, a dark suit, a blue and white tie, black wing-tip shoes. The glass was empty and he went for another drink.

In the bedroom again, he sat on a chair, crossed his legs, and smiled, observing   45
himself in the mirror. The telephone rang twice and fell silent. He finished the drink and took off the suit. He rummaged through the top drawers until he found a pair of panties and a brassiere. He stepped into the panties and fastened the brassiere, then looked through the closet for an outfit. He put on a black and white checkered skirt and tried to zip it up. He put on a burgundy blouse that buttoned up the front. He considered her shoes, but understood they would not fit. For a long time he looked out the living-room window from behind the curtain. Then he returned to the bedroom and put everything away.

He was not hungry. She did not eat much, either. They looked at each other shyly and smiled. She got up from the table and checked that the key was on the shelf and then she quickly cleared the dishes.

He stood in the kitchen doorway and smoked a cigarette and watched her pick up the key.

"Make yourself comfortable while I go across the hall," she said. "Read the paper or something." She closed her fingers over the key. He was, she said, looking tired.

He tried to concentrate on the news. He read the paper and turned on the television. Finally he went across the hall. The door was locked.

"It's me. Are you still there, honey?" he called.   50

After a time the lock released and Arlene stepped outside and shut the door. "Was I gone so long?" she said.

"Well, you were," he said.

"Was I?" she said. "I guess I must have been playing with Kitty."

He studied her, and she looked away, her hand still resting on the doorknob.

"It's funny," she said. "You know—to go in someone's place like that."   55

He nodded, took her hand from the knob, and guided her toward their own door. He let them into their apartment.

"It *is* funny," he said.

He noticed white lint clinging to the back of her sweater, and the color was high in her cheeks. He began kissing her on the neck and hair and she turned and kissed him back.

"Oh, damn," she said. "Damn, damn," she sang, girlishly clapping her hands. "I just remembered. I really and truly forgot to do what I went over there to do. I didn't feed Kitty or do any watering." She looked at him. "Isn't that stupid?"

"I don't think so," he said. "Just a minute. I'll get my cigarettes and go back with you."   60

She waited until he had closed and locked their door, and then she took his arm at the muscle and said. "I guess I should tell you. I found some pictures."

He stopped in the middle of the hall. "What kind of pictures?"

"You can see for yourself," she said, and she watched him.

"No kidding." He grinned. "Where?"

"In a drawer," she said.   65

"No kidding," he said.

And then she said, "Maybe they won't come back," and was at once astonished at her words.

"It could happen," he said, "Anything could happen."

"Or maybe they'll come back and . . ." but she did not finish.

They held hands for the short walk across the hall, and when he spoke she could   70
barely hear his voice.

"The key," he said. "Give it to me."

"What?" she said, She gazed at the door.

"The key," he said. "You have the key."

"My God," she said, "I left the key inside."

He tried the knob. It was locked. Then she tried the knob. It would not turn. Her   75
lips were parted, and her breathing was hard, expectant. He opened his arms and she moved into them.

"Don't worry," he said into her ear. "For God's sake, don't worry."

They stayed there. They held each other. They leaned into the door as if against a wind, and braced themselves.

Questions for Discussion and Writing

1. How does the opening of the story define Bill and Arlene Miller's neighbors (the Stones) as people to be envied? How does house-sitting for the Stones change Bill and Arlene's relationship?
2. How does the progression of incidents suggest that the Millers (especially Bill) are getting carried away with stepping outside their lives? Although Carver does not tell us, what can you infer is going on in the minds of Bill and Arlene at the end of the story (they have forgotten to water the plants and feed the cat, and they have left the key locked inside)?
3. Would you consider letting the Millers house-sit for you? Why or why not? To what extent is the success of the story due to most people's desire (even if they do not act on it) to look into the cabinets, drawers, and closets of others, if given the opportunity?

Bessie Head

. . . .

Bessie Head (1937–1986) was born of mixed parentage in Pietermaritzburg, South Africa. She was taken from her mother at birth, raised by foster parents until she was thirteen, and then placed in a mission orphanage. In 1961, newly married, she left South Africa to escape apartheid and settled on an agricultural commune in Serowe, Botswana, where she lived until her death in 1986. Among her publications are the novels When Rain Clouds Gather *(1969),* Maru *(1971), and* A Question of Power *(1974), acclaimed as one of the first psychological accounts of a black woman's experience, as well as* A Collector of Treasures and Other Botswana Village Tales *(1977). She is also the author of two histories:* Serowe: Village of the Rain Wind *(1981) and* A Bewitched Crossroad *(1985). "Looking for a Rain God" (1977) is based on a shocking local newspaper report. Head dramatizes how a seven-year drought creates conflicts between ancient tribal rituals and contemporary moral codes.*

LOOKING FOR A RAIN GOD

It is lonely at the lands where the people go to plough. These lands are vast clearings in the bush, and the wild bush is lonely too. Nearly all the lands are within walking distance from the village. In some parts of the bush where the underground water is very near the surface, people made little rest camps for themselves and dug shallow wells to quench their thirst while on their journey to their own lands. They experienced all kinds of things once they left the village. They could rest at shady watering places full of lush, tangled trees with delicate pale-gold and purple wildflowers springing up between soft green moss and the children could hunt around for wild figs and any berries that might be in season. But from 1958, a seven-year drought fell upon the land and even the watering places began to look as dismal as the dry open thornbush country; the leaves of the trees curled up and withered; the moss became dry and hard and, under the shade of the tangled trees, the ground turned a powdery black and white, because there was no rain. People said rather humorously that if you tried to catch the rain in a cup it would only fill a teaspoon. Toward the beginning of the seventh year of drought, the summer had become an anguish to live through. The air was so dry and moisture-free that it burned the skin. No one knew what to do to escape the heat and tragedy was in the air. At the beginning of that summer, a number of men just went out of their homes and hung themselves to death from trees. The majority of the people had lived off crops, but for two years past they had all returned from the lands with only their rolled-up skin blankets and cooking utensils. Only the charlatans, incanters, and witch doctors made a pile of money during this time because people were always turning to them in desperation for little talismans and herbs to rub on the plough for the crops to grow and the rain to fall.

The rains were late that year. They came in early November, with a promise of good rain. It wasn't the full, steady downpour of the years of good rain but thin, scanty, misty rain. It softened the earth and a rich growth of green things sprang up everywhere for the animals to eat. People were called to the center of the village to hear the proclamation of the beginning of the ploughing season; they stirred themselves and whole families began to move off to the lands to plough.

The family of the old man, Mokgobja, were among those who left early for the lands. They had a donkey cart and piled everything onto it, Mokgobja—who was over seventy years old; two girls, Neo and Boseyong; their mother Tiro and an unmarried sister, Nesta; and the father and supporter of the family, Ramadi, who drove the donkey cart. In the rush of the first hope of rain, the man, Ramadi, and the two women, cleared the land of thornbush and then hedged their vast ploughing area with this same thornbush to protect the future crop from the goats they had brought along for milk. They cleared out and deepened the old well with its pool of muddy water and still in this light, misty rain, Ramadi inspanned[1] two oxen and turned the earth over with a hand plough.

The land was ready and ploughed, waiting for the crops. At night, the earth was alive with insects singing and rustling about in search of food. But suddenly, by mid-November, the rain flew away; the rain clouds fled away and left the sky bare. The sun danced dizzily in the sky, with a strange cruelty. Each day the land was covered in a haze of mist as the sun sucked up the last drop of moisture out of the earth. The family sat down in despair, waiting and waiting. Their hopes had run so high; the goats had started producing milk, which they had eagerly poured on their porridge, now they ate plain porridge with no milk. It was impossible to plant the corn, maize, pumpkin, and watermelon seeds in the dry earth. They sat the whole day in the shadow of the huts and even stopped thinking, for the rain had fled away. Only the children, Neo and Boseyong, were quite happy in their little-girl world. They carried on with their game of making house like their mother and chattered to each other in light, soft tones. They made children from sticks around which they tied rags, and scolded them severely in an exact imitation of their own mother. Their voices could be heard scolding

---

[1]*inspanned*: yoked together.

the day long: "You stupid thing, when I send you to draw water, why do you spill half of it out of the bucket!" "You stupid thing! Can't you mind the porridge pot without letting the porridge burn!" And then they would beat the rag dolls on their bottoms with severe expressions.

The adults paid no attention to this; they did not even hear the funny chatter; they sat waiting for rain; their nerves were stretched to breaking-point willing the rain to fall out of the sky. Nothing was important, beyond that. All their animals had been sold during the bad years to purchase food, and of all their herd only two goats were left. It was the women of the family who finally broke down under the strain of waiting for rain. It was really the two women who caused the death of the little girls. Each night they started a weird, high-pitched wailing that began on a low, mournful note and whipped up to a frenzy. Then they would stamp their feet and shout as though they had lost their heads. The men sat quiet and self-controlled; it was important for men to maintain their self-control at all times but their nerve was breaking too. They knew the women were haunted by the starvation of the coming year.

Finally, an ancient memory stirred in the old man, Mokgobja. When he was very young and the customs of the ancestors still ruled the land, he had been witness to a rain-making ceremony. And he came alive a little, struggling to recall the details which had been buried by years and years of prayer in a Christian church. As soon as the mists cleared a little, he began consulting in whispers with his youngest son, Ramadi. There was, he said, a certain rain god who accepted only the sacrifice of the bodies of children. Then the rain would fall; then the crops would grow, he said. He explained the ritual and as he talked, his memory became a conviction and he began to talk with unshakable authority. Ramadi's nerves were smashed by the nightly wailing of the women and soon the two men began whispering with the two women. The children continued their game: "You stupid thing! How could you have lost the money on the way to the shop! You must have been playing again!"

After it was all over and the bodies of the two little girls had been spread across the land, the rain did not fall. Instead, there was a deathly silence at night and the devouring heat of the sun by day. A terror, extreme and deep, overwhelmed the whole family. They packed, rolling up their skin blankets and pots, and fled back to the village.

People in the village soon noted the absence of the two little girls. They had died at the lands and were buried there, the family said. But people noted their ashen, terror-stricken faces and a murmur arose. What had killed the children, they wanted to know? And the family replied that they had just died. And people said amongst themselves that it was strange that the two deaths had occurred at the same time. And there was a feeling of great unease at the unnatural looks of the family. Soon the police came around. The family told them the same story of death and burial at the lands. They did not know what the children had died of. So the police asked to see the graves. At this, the mother of the children broke down and told everything.

Throughout that terrible summer the story of the children hung like a dark cloud of sorrow over the village, and the sorrow was not assuaged when the old man and Ramadi were sentenced to death for ritual murder. All they had on the statute books was that ritual murder was against the law and must be stamped out with the death penalty. The subtle story of strain and starvation and breakdown was inadmissible evidence at court; but all the people who lived off crops knew in their hearts that only a hair's breadth had saved them from sharing a fate similar to that of the Mokgobja family. They could have killed something to make the rain fall.

Questions for Discussion and Writing

1. How does Head lay the psychological groundwork for what otherwise would come as a shock—the choice of the two young girls as sacrificial victims? How do the girls appear to other members of the family when everyone must conserve food and water?

2. Why doesn't Head withhold knowledge of the ending in telling the story? How does knowing what happened shift the focus of the story from *what* to *how* it might have occurred? How does the unceasing drought reactivate a belief that leads to the slaughter and dismemberment of the girls to produce rain?

3. What does Head mean when she ends the story by stating that other villagers "could have killed something to make the rain fall"? What does this imply about her attitude toward the murderers and their plight?

POETRY

Cathy Song

Born in 1955 in Honolulu, Hawaii, of Chinese and Korean ancestry, Cathy Song was educated at Wellesley and Boston University. Her poetry is collected in Picture Bride *(1983), in which "The Youngest Daughter" first appeared. Song's work focuses on family relationships, and in this poem she explores the intricacies of a mother–daughter relationship. Her most recent collection of poetry is* The Lamp of Bliss *(2001).*

THE YOUNGEST DAUGHTER

The sky has been dark
for many years.
My skin has become as damp
and pale as rice paper
and feels the way
mother's used to before the drying sun
parched it out there in the fields.

Lately, when I touch my eyelids,
my hands react as if

5

I had just touched something   10
hot enough to burn.
My skin, aspirin colored,
tingles with migraine. Mother
has been massaging the left side of my face
especially in the evenings   15
when the pain flares up.

This morning
her breathing was graveled,
her voice gruff with affection
when I wheeled her into the bath.   20
She was in a good humor,
making jokes about her great breasts,
floating in the milky water
like two walruses,
flaccid and whiskered around the nipples.   25
I scrubbed them with a sour taste
in my mouth, thinking:
six children and an old man
have sucked from those brown nipples.

I was almost tender   30
when I came to the blue bruises
that freckle her body,
places where she had been injecting insulin
for thirty years. I soaped her slowly,
she sighed deeply, her eyes closed.   35
It seems it has always
been like this: the two of us
in this sunless room,
the splashing of the bathwater.

In the afternoons   40
when she has rested,
she prepares our ritual of tea and rice,
garnished with a shred of gingered fish,
a slice of pickled turnip,
a token for my white body.   45
We eat in the familiar silence.
She knows I am not to be trusted,
even now planning my escape.
As I toast to her health
with the tea she has poured,   50
a thousand cranes curtain the window,
fly up in a sudden breeze.

Questions for Discussion and Writing

1. How would you characterize the relationship between the mother and daughter in this poem? For how long has this relationship existed in this way? What, in your view, is the significance of the title, "The Youngest Daughter," in explaining the situation the poem describes, in light of the fact that the speaker has five siblings?
2. What details suggest the strain the daughter is experiencing in finally deciding to make her escape and leave?
3. Do you know children who have submerged their own identities and possibilities for an independent life in the interest of caring for an infirm parent or other relative? If you have ever been involved in a relationship as a child similar to the one between the mother and daughter in the poem, did you react as the daughter did? Discuss your experiences.

Robert Hayden

• •

Robert Hayden (1913–1980) was born in Detroit and educated at Wayne State University and the University of Michigan. He taught for more than twenty years at Fisk University before becoming a professor of English at the University of Michigan. He was elected to the National Academy of American Poets in 1975 and served twice as the poetry consultant to the Library of Congress. His volumes of poetry include A Ballad of Remembrance (1962), Words in Mourning Time (1970), and Angle of Ascent (1975). "Those Winter Sundays" (1962) is a finely etched depiction of the speaker's change in attitude toward his father.

THOSE WINTER SUNDAYS

Sundays too my father got up early
and put his clothes on in the blueblack cold,
then with cracked hands that ached
from labor in the weekday weather made
banked fires blaze. No one ever thanked him.   5

I'd wake and hear the cold splintering, breaking,
When the rooms were warm, he'd call,
and slowly I would rise and dress,
fearing the chronic angers of that house,

Speaking indifferently to him,   10
who had driven out the cold
and polished my good shoes as well.

What did I know, what did I know
of love's austere and lonely offices?

Questions for Discussion and Writing

1. How does Hayden make use of the contrast in imagery between cold and warmth to underscore the shift in the speaker's attitude?
2. What has made the speaker realize, now that he has grown up, how much his father really cared for him?
3. In a short essay, discuss the poem's dominant emotion. Have you ever come to realize that someone cared for you in ways not obvious to you at the time? Describe your experience.
4. Compare a candid informal photo with a formal posed photograph of yourself or someone else, and in a short paragraph discuss the different aspects of the subject that emerge from each of these two pictures.

William Wordsworth

*William Wordsworth (1770–1850) was born in a village on the edge of the Lake District in England. He attended St. John's College, Cambridge, in 1787, and began a series of walking tours of Switzerland and France that fired his imagination and are reflected in his autobiographical poem "The Prelude" (1805). He lived in France from 1791 to 1792 at the height of the French Revolution. In 1797 he began a lifelong friendship with the younger poet Samuel Coleridge, a creative association that led in 1798 to the publication of a groundbreaking volume of poems—*Lyrical Ballads—*whose down-to-earth style and everyday subjects set English poetry on a new course. Wordsworth's ability to communicate heartfelt reactions to inspiring landscapes and to see spiritual depths in everyday scenes is well illustrated in the poem "Composed upon Westminster Bridge, September 3, 1802."*

COMPOSED UPON WESTMINSTER BRIDGE,[1] SEPTEMBER 3, 1802

Earth has not anything to show more fair:
Dull would he be of soul who could pass by
A sight so touching in its majesty:
This City now doth, like a garment, wear
The beauty of the morning; silent, bare,   5
Ships, towers, domes, theatres, and temples lie
Open unto the fields, and to the sky;
All bright and glittering in the smokeless air.

---

[1] *Westminster Bridge;* bridge over the Thames near the Houses of Parliament in London.

Never did sun more beautifully steep
In his first splendour, valley, rock, or hill;   10
Ne'er saw I, never felt, a calm so deep!
The river glideth at his own sweet will:
Dear God! the very houses seem asleep;
And all that mighty heart is lying still!

Does this modern-day photograph of Westminster Bridge by Jeremy Horner evoke the same feeling as Wordsworth's poem?

Questions for Discussion and Writing

1. What sights and emotions touch the poet as he stands upon Westminster Bridge in early morning?
2. What effect does Wordsworth achieve by ascribing human qualities to the city?
3. Try your hand at writing a short poem about a place that has inspired you, personifying the features of the scene you find most compelling.

Thinking Critically About the Image

Vincent Van Gogh (1853–1890) was a Dutch Postimpressionist painter. A majority of his works were produced in twenty-nine months of frenzied activity that ended with his suicide. *The Café Terrace on the Place du Forum, Arles, at Night* is the first of three paintings done in Arles, France, which feature starlit skies. It is one of his most acclaimed works. The tranquil atmosphere Van Gogh depicts (which he painted on the spot) is unique in his art. This memorable place still stands and was remodeled in 1995 to appear the way it does in Van Gogh's painting. *Lust for Life* (1956) is a highly fictionalized but colorful film based on Van Gogh's life.

1. Did you notice that Van Gogh created a night picture without any black in it?
2. How do the horse and carriage serve as a center of the work toward which all the lines of composition point?
3. How do the different elements in the picture combine to suggest a peaceful night in a small town? Is it a place you would like to visit?

Connections

Chapter 2: Influential People and Memorable Places

Maya Angelou,   *Liked for Myself*
How are Angelou and Fatima Mernissi encouraged to transcend existing societal restrictions related to race and gender by strong female figures in their lives?

Gayle Pemberton,   *Antidisestablishmentarianism*
Compare the roles that Pemberton's grandmother and Mrs. Flowers in Maya Angelou's memoir play as influential figures in the lives of the two girls.

Mikhail Gilmore,   *My Brother, Gary Gilmore*
How does Gilmore's narrative raise the questions of heredity and environment discussed by David Ewing Duncan in "DNA As Destiny" (Ch. 9)?

Fatima Mernissi,   *Moonlit Nights of Laughter*
In what ways do both Mernissi and Gayle Pemberton benefit from the free-spirited, independent thinking of their mother and grandmother, respectively?

Richard Keller Simon,   *The Shopping Mall and the Formal Garden*
What features of the shopping mall described by Simon set it apart from the world as a secluded enclave similar to that of the harem as described by Fatima Mernissi?

William Zinsser,   *Niagara Falls*
What comparable intangible meanings do Zinsser and Richard Keller Simon find embodied in Niagara Falls and the modern shopping mall, although one is natural and the other is artificial?

Joseph Addison,   *Reflections in Westminster Abbey*
Compare and contrast the funeral customs described by Addison with those of ancient Egypt described by Herodotus in "Concerning Egypt" (Ch. 7).

George Carlin,   *A Place for Your Stuff*
How does Raymond Carver's story reverse Carlin's assumption that our own "stuff" is more desirable than that of our neighbors?

Raymond Carver,   *Neighbors*
What variation does Carver's story offer on Margaret Atwood's "Happy Endings" (Ch. 5)?

Bessie Head,   *Looking for a Rain God*
How can Head's story be thought of as a worst-case scenario of Garrett Hardin's "Lifeboat Ethics" (Ch. 11)?

Cathy Song,   *The Youngest Daughter*
Compare the real or perceived expectations of the daughters in Jill Nelson's essay "Number One!" (Ch. 1) and Song's poem.

Robert Hayden,   *Those Winter Sundays*
In what different ways do the parents in the poems by Cathy Song and Hayden express their love for their children, and how does each speaker react?

William Wordsworth,   *Composed upon Westminster Bridge, September 3, 1802*
In what ways do both William Zinsser's description of Niagara Falls and Wordsworth's description of the city of London evoke feelings of the sublime?

***Jean-Honoré Fragonard, A Young Girl Reading**, c. 1776.*
Gift of Mrs. Mellon Bruce in memory of her father, Andrew W. Mellon. Photograph © 2004 Board of Trustees, National Gallery of Art, Washington, DC. Oil on Canvas, .811 × .648 cm. (32 × 25 ½ in.); framed: 1.049 × .895 × .022 cm. (41 5/16 × 35 ¼ × ⅞ in.).

The Value of Education

The old believe everything. The middle-aged suspect everything. The young know everything.

—OSCAR WILDE, *THE PICTURE OF DORIAN GRAY*

As the essays in this chapter make clear, education is primarily a liberating experience. Yet, the accounts by Frederick Douglass and Sabine Reichel attest to the ingenuity and determination that are often required in getting an education. Essays by William A. Henry III, John Milton, Nat Hentoff, and Judy Blume confront some basic questions: (1) What constitutes an educated person? (2) What role should education play in society? (3) Does censorship have any role in a free society?

An essay by Jonathan Kozol explores the consequences for society when many citizens are unable to read or write. David Rothenberg explores a contrasting dilemma: has the Internet, paradoxically, decreased students' capacity for doing independent research?

In the fictional work by Joaquim María Machado de Assis, the author spins a thought-provoking tale about the consequences when one's avocation becomes an obsession.

The poems by Francis E. W. Harper and Linda Hogan offer intensely personal reflections on the value of education, especially for minorities.

NONFICTION

Frederick Douglass

. . . .

Frederick Douglass (1817–1895) was born into slavery in Maryland, where he worked as a field hand and servant. In 1838, after previous failed attempts to escape, for which he was beaten and tortured, he successfully made his way to New York by using the identity papers of a freed black sailor. There he adopted the last name of Douglass and subsequently settled in New Bedford, Massachusetts. Douglass was the first black American to rise to prominence as a national figure. He gained renown as a speaker for the Massachusetts Anti-Slavery League and was an editor for the North Star, *an abolitionist paper, from 1847 to 1860. He was a friend to John Brown, helped convince President Lincoln to issue the Emancipation Proclamation, and became ambassador to several foreign countries.* The Narrative of the Life of Frederick Douglass, an American Slave *(1845) is one of the most illuminating of the many slave narratives written during the nineteenth century. "Learning to Read and Write," drawn from this autobiography, reveals Douglass's ingenuity in manipulating his circumstances so as to become literate.*

LEARNING TO READ AND WRITE

I lived in Master Hugh's family about seven years. During this time, I succeeded in learning to read and write. In accomplishing this, I was compelled to resort to various stratagems. I had no regular teacher. My mistress, who had kindly commenced to instruct me, had, in compliance with the advice and direction of her husband, not only ceased to instruct, but had set her face against my being instructed by any one else. It is due, however, to my mistress to say of her, that she did not adopt this course of treatment immediately. She at first lacked the depravity indispensable to shutting me up in mental darkness. It was at least necessary for her to have some training in the exercise of irresponsible power, to make her equal to the task of treating me as though I were a brute.

My mistress was, as I have said, a kind and tender-hearted woman; and in the simplicity of her soul she commenced, when I first went to live with her, to treat me as she supposed one human being ought to treat another. In entering upon the duties of a slaveholder, she did not seem to perceive that I sustained to her the relation of a mere chattel, and that for her to treat me as a human being was not only wrong, but dangerously so. Slavery proved as injurious to her as it did to me. When I went there, she was a pious, warm, and tender-hearted woman. There was no sorrow or suffering for which she had not a tear. She had bread for the hungry, clothes for the naked, and comfort for every mourner that came within her reach. Slavery soon proved its ability to divest her of these heavenly qualities. Under its influence, the tender heart became stone, and the lamb-like disposition gave way to one of tiger-like fierceness. The first step in her downward course was in her ceasing to instruct me. She now commenced to practise her husband's precepts. She finally became even more violent in her opposition than her husband himself. She was not satisfied with simply doing as well as he had commanded; she seemed anxious to do better. Nothing seemed to make her more angry than to see me with a newspaper. She seemed to think that here lay the danger. I have had her rush at me with a face made all up of fury, and snatch from me a newspaper, in a manner that fully revealed her apprehension. She was an apt woman; and a little experience soon demonstrated, to her satisfaction, that education and slavery were incompatible with each other.

From this time I was most narrowly watched. If I was in a separate room any considerable length of time, I was sure to be suspected of having a book, and was at once called to give an account of myself. All this, however, was too late. The first step had been taken. Mistress, in teaching me the alphabet, had given me the *inch,* and no precaution could prevent me from taking the *ell.*[1]

The plan which I adopted, and the one by which I was most successful, was that of making friends of all the little white boys whom I met in the street. As many of these as I could, I converted into teachers. With their kindly aid, obtained at different times and in different places, I finally succeeded in learning to read. When I was sent on errands, I always took my book with me, and by going one part of my errand quickly, I found time to get a lesson before my return. I used also to carry bread with me, enough of which was always in the house, and to which I was always welcome; for I was much better off in this regard than many of the poor white children in our neighborhood. This bread I used to bestow upon the hungry little urchins, who, in return, would give me that more valuable bread of knowledge. I am strongly tempted to give the names of two or three of those little boys, as a testimonial of the gratitude and affection I bear them; but prudence forbids;—not that it would injure me, but it might embarrass them; for it is almost an unpardonable offence to teach slaves to read in this Christian country. It is enough to say of the dear little fellows, that they lived on Philpot Street, very near Durgin and Bailey's ship-yard. I used to talk this matter of slavery over with them. I would sometimes say to them, I wished I could be as free as they would be when they got to be men. "You will be free as soon as you are twenty-one, *but I am a slave for life!* Have not I as good a right to be free as you have?" These words used to trouble them; they would express for me the liveliest sympathy, and console me with the hope that something would occur by which I might be free.

I was now about twelve years old, and the thought of being *a slave for life* began   5 to bear heavily upon my heart. Just about this time, I got hold of a book entitled "The Columbian Orator."[2] Every opportunity I got, I used to read this book. Among much of other interesting matter, I found in it a dialogue between a master and his slave. The slave was represented as having run away from his master three times. The dialogue represented the conversation which took place between them, when the slave was retaken the third time. In this dialogue, the whole argument in behalf of slavery was brought forward by the master, all of which was disposed of by the slave. The slave was made to say some very smart as well as impressive things in reply to his master—things

---

[1]*ell:* a measurement equal to 1.14 meters.   [2]*The Columbian Orator (1797):* written by Caleb Bingham. It was one of the first readers used in New England schools.

which had the desired though unexpected effect; for the conversation resulted in the voluntary emancipation of the slave on the part of the master.

In the same book, I met with one of Sheridan's mighty speeches on and in behalf of Catholic emancipation. These were choice documents to me. I read them over and over again with unabated interest. They gave tongue to interesting thoughts of my own soul, which had frequently flashed through my mind, and died away for want of utterance. The moral which I gained from the dialogue was the power of truth over the conscience of even a slaveholder. What I got from Sheridan was a bold denunciation of slavery, and a powerful vindication of human rights. The reading of these documents enabled me to utter my thoughts, and to meet the arguments brought forward to sustain slavery; but while they relieved me of one difficulty, they brought on another even more painful than the one of which I was relieved. The more I read, the more I was led to abhor and detest my enslavers. I could regard them in no other light than a band of successful robbers, who had left their homes, and gone to Africa, and stolen us from our homes, and in a strange land reduced us to slavery. I loathed them as being the meanest as well as the most wicked of men. As I read and contemplated the subject, behold! that very discontentment which Master Hugh had predicted would follow my learning to read had already come, to torment and sting my soul to unutterable anguish. As I writhed under it, I would at times feel that learning to read had been a curse rather than a blessing. It had given me a view of my wretched condition, without the remedy. It opened my eyes to the horrible pit, but to no ladder upon which to get out. In moments of agony, I envied my fellow-slaves for their stupidity. I have often wished myself a beast. I preferred the condition of the meanest reptile to my own. Any thing, no matter what, to get rid of thinking! It was this everlasting thinking of my condition that tormented me. There was no getting rid of it. It was pressed upon me by every object within sight or hearing, animate or inanimate. The silver trump of freedom had roused my soul to eternal wakefulness. Freedom now appeared, to disappear no more forever. It was heard in every sound, and seen in every thing. It was ever present to torment me with a sense of my wretched condition. I saw nothing without seeing it, I heard nothing without hearing it, and felt nothing without feeling it. It looked from every star, it smiled in every calm, breathed in every wind, and moved in every storm.

I often found myself regretting my own existence, and wishing myself dead; and but for the hope of being free, I have no doubt but that I should have killed myself, or done something for which I should have been killed. While in this state of mind, I was eager to hear any one speak of slavery. I was a ready listener. Every little while, I could hear something about the abolitionists. It was some time before I found what the word meant. It was always used in such connections as to make it an interesting word to me. If a slave ran away and succeeded in getting clear, or if a slave killed his master, set fire to a barn, or did any thing very wrong in the mind of a slaveholder, it was spoken of as the fruit of *abolition*. Hearing the word in this connection very often, I set about learning what it meant. The dictionary afforded me little or no help. I found it was "the act of abolishing," but then I did not know what was to be abolished. Here I was perplexed. I did not dare to ask any one about its meaning, for I was satisfied that it was something they wanted me to know very little about. After a patient waiting, I got one of our city papers, containing an account of the number of petitions from the north, praying for the abolition of slavery in the District of Columbia, and of the slave trade between the States. From this time I understood the words *abolition* and *abolitionist,* and always drew near when that word was spoken, expecting to hear something of importance to myself and fellow-slaves. The light broke in upon me by degrees. I went one day down on the wharf of Mr. Waters; and seeing two Irishmen unloading a scow of stone, I went, unasked, and helped them. When we had finished, one of them came to me and asked me if I were a slave. I told him I was. He asked, "Are ye a slave for life?" I told him that I was. The good Irishman seemed to be deeply affected by the statement. He said to the other that it was a pity so fine a little fellow as myself should be a slave for life. He said it was a shame to hold me. They both advised me to run away to the north; that I should find friends there, and that I should be free. I pretended not to be interested in what they said, and treated them as if I did not understand them; for I feared they might be treacherous. White men have been known to encourage slaves to escape, and then, to get the reward, catch them and return them to their masters. I was afraid that these seemingly good men might use me so; but I nevertheless remembered their advice, and from that time I resolved to run away. I looked forward to a time at which it would be safe for me to escape. I was too young to think of doing so immediately; besides, I wished to learn how to write, as I might have occasion to write my own pass. I consoled myself with the hope that I should one day find a good chance. Meanwhile, I would learn to write.

The idea as to how I might learn to write was suggested to me by being in Durgin and Bailey's ship-yard, and frequently seeing the ship carpenters, after hewing, and getting a piece of timber ready for use, write on the timber the name of that part of the ship for which it was intended. When a piece of timber was intended for the larboard side, it would be marked thus—"L." When a piece was for the starboard side, it would be marked thus—"S." A piece for the larboard side forward, would be marked thus—"L. F." When a piece was for starboard side forward, it would be marked thus—"S. F." For larboard aft, it would be marked thus—"L. A." For starboard aft, it would be marked thus—"S. A." I soon learned the names of these letters, and for what they were intended when placed upon a piece of timber in the ship-yard. I immediately commenced copying them, and in a short time was able to make the four letters named. After that, when I met with any boy who I knew could write, I would tell him I could write as well as he. The next word would be, "I don't believe you. Let me see you try it." I would then make the letters which I had been so fortunate as to learn, and ask him to beat that. In this way I got a good many lessons in writing, which it is quite possible I should never have gotten in any other way. During this time, my copy-book was the board fence, brick wall, and pavement; my pen and ink was a lump of chalk. With these, I learned mainly how to write. I then commenced and continued copying the italics in *Webster's Spelling Book,* until I could make them all without looking on the book. By this time, my little Master Thomas had gone to school, and learned how to write, and had written over a number of copy-books. These had been brought home, and shown to some of our near neighbors, and then laid aside. My mistress used to go to class meeting at the Wilk Street meetinghouse every Monday afternoon, and leave me to take care of the house. When left thus, I used to spend the time in writing in the spaces left in Master Thomas's copy-book, copying what he had written. I continued to do this until I could write a hand very similar to that of Master Thomas. Thus, after a long, tedious effort for years, I finally succeeded in learning how to write.

Questions for Discussion and Writing

1. What effect did the institution of slavery have on Douglass's relationship with the mistress of the household when she initially wanted to help him become literate?
2. Douglass writes that "education and slavery were incompatible with each other." How does this account illustrate his belief? What ingenious methods did Douglass devise to obtain knowledge of reading and writing?
3. What would your life be like if you could not read or write? Describe a day in your life, providing specific examples that would dramatize this condition.

Jonathan Kozol

. . . .

Jonathan Kozol was born in Boston in 1936 and graduated from Harvard in 1958. He was a Rhodes scholar at Oxford University and has taught at numerous colleges, including Yale. His many books on education and literacy include Death at an Early Age *(1967);* Illiterate America *(1985), from which the following selection is taken;* Rachel and Her Children *(1988);* Savage Inequalities *(1991);* Amazing Grace: The Lives of Children and the Conscience of a Nation *(1995); and most recently,* Ordinary Resurrections: Children in the Years of Hope *(2000).*

THE HUMAN COST OF AN ILLITERATE SOCIETY

PRECAUTIONS, READ BEFORE USING.
Poison: Contains sodium hydroxide (caustic soda-lye).
Corrosive: Causes severe eye and skin damage, may cause blindness.
Harmful or fatal if swallowed.
If swallowed, give large quantities of milk or water.
Do not induce vomiting.
Important: Keep water out of can at all times to prevent contents from violently erupting. . . .
                                                                    —Warning on a can of Drano

Questions of literacy, in Socrates' belief, must at length be judged as matters of morality. Socrates could not have had in mind the moral compromise peculiar to a nation like our own. Some of our Founding Fathers did, however, have this question in their minds. One of the wisest of those Founding Fathers (one who may not have been most compassionate but surely was more prescient than some of his peers) recognized the special dangers that illiteracy would pose to basic equity in the political construction that he helped to shape.

"A people who mean to be their own governors," James Madison wrote, "must arm themselves with the power knowledge gives. A popular government without popular information or the means of acquiring it, is but a prologue to a farce or a tragedy, or perhaps both."

Tragedy looms larger than farce in the United States today. Illiterate citizens seldom vote. Those who do are forced to cast a vote of questionable worth. They cannot make informed decisions based on serious print information. Sometimes they can be alerted to their interests by aggressive voter education. More frequently, they vote for a face, a smile, or a style, not for a mind or character or body of beliefs.

The number of illiterate adults exceeds by 16 million the entire vote cast for the winner in the 1980 presidential contest. If even one third of all illiterates could vote, and read enough and do sufficient math to vote in their self-interest, Ronald Reagan would not likely have been chosen president. There is, of course, no way to know for sure. We do know this: Democracy is a mendacious term when used by those who are prepared to countenance the forced exclusion of one third of our electorate. So long as 60 million people are denied significant participation, the government is neither of nor for, nor by, the people. It is a government, at best, of those two thirds whose wealth, skin color, or parental privilege allows them opportunity to profit from the provocation and instruction of the written word.

The undermining of democracy in the United States is one "expense" that sensi-   5
tive Americans can easily deplore because it represents a contradiction that endangers citizens of all political positions. The human price is not so obvious at first.

Since I first immersed myself within this work I have often had the following dream: I find that I am in a railroad station or a large department store within a city that is utterly unknown to me and where I cannot understand the printed words. None of the signs or symbols is familiar. Everything looks strange: like mirror writing of some kind. Gradually I understand that I am in the Soviet Union. All the letters on the walls around me are Cyrillic. I look for my pocket dictionary but I find that it has been mislaid. Where have I left it? Then I recall that I forgot to bring it with me when I packed my bags in Boston. I struggle to remember the name of my hotel. I try to ask somebody for directions. One person stops and looks at me in a peculiar way. I lose the nerve to ask. At last I reach into my wallet for an ID card. The card is missing. Have I lost it? Then I remember that my card was confiscated for some reason, many years before. Around this point, I wake up in a panic.

This panic is not so different from the misery that millions of adult illiterates experience each day within the course of their routine existence in the U.S.A.

Illiterates cannot read the menu in a restaurant.

They cannot read the cost of items on the menu in the *window* of the restaurant before they enter.

Illiterates cannot read the letters that their children bring home from their teach-   10
ers. They cannot study school department circulars that tell them of the courses that their children must be taking if they hope to pass the SAT exams. They cannot help with homework. They cannot write a letter to the teacher. They are afraid to visit in the classroom. They do not want to humiliate their child or themselves.

Illiterates cannot read instructions on a bottle of prescription medicine. They cannot find out when a medicine is past the year of safe consumption; nor can they read of allergenic risks, warnings to diabetics, or the potential sedative effect of certain kinds of nonprescription pills. They cannot observe preventive health care admonitions. They cannot read about "the seven warning signs of cancer" or the indications of blood-sugar fluctuations or the risks of eating certain foods that aggravate the likelihood of cardiac arrest.

Illiterates live, in more than literal ways, an uninsured existence. They cannot understand the written details on a health insurance form. They cannot read the waivers that they sign preceding surgical procedures. Several women I have known in Boston have entered a slum hospital with the intention of obtaining a tubal ligation and have emerged a few days later after having been subjected to a hysterectomy. Unaware of their rights, incognizant of jargon, intimidated by the unfamiliar air of fear and atmosphere of ether that so many of us find oppressive in the confines even of the most attractive and expensive medical facilities, they have signed their names to documents they could not read and which nobody, in the hectic situation that prevails so often in those overcrowded hospitals that serve the urban poor, had even bothered to explain.

Childbirth might seem to be the last inalienable right of any female citizen within a civilized society. Illiterate mothers, as we shall see, already have been cheated of the power to protect their progeny against the likelihood of demolition in deficient public schools and, as a result, against the verbal servitude within which they themselves exist. Surgical denial of the right to bear that child in the first place represents an ultimate denial, an unspeakable metaphor, a final darkness that denies even the twilight gleamings of our own humanity. What greater violation of our biological, our biblical, our spiritual humanity could possibly exist than that which takes place nightly, perhaps hourly these days, within such overburdened and benighted institutions as the Boston City Hospital? Illiteracy has many costs; few are so irreversible as this.

Even the roof above one's head, the gas or other fuel for heating that protects the residents of northern city slums against the threat of illness in the winter months become uncertain guarantees. Illiterates cannot read the lease that they must sign to live in an apartment which, too often, they cannot afford. They cannot manage check accounts and therefore seldom pay for anything by mail. Hours and entire days of difficult travel (and the cost of bus or other public transit) must be added to the real cost of whatever they consume. Loss of interest on the check accounts they do not have, and could not manage if they did, must be regarded as another of the excess costs paid by the citizen who is excluded from the common instruments of commerce in a numerate society.

"I couldn't understand the bills," a woman in Washington, D.C., reports, "and   15 then I couldn't write the checks to pay them. We signed things we didn't know what they were."

Illiterates cannot read the notices that they receive from welfare offices or from the IRS. They must depend on word-of-mouth instruction from the welfare worker—or from other persons whom they have good reason to mistrust. They do not know what rights they have, what deadlines and requirements they face, what options they might choose to exercise. They are half-citizens. Their rights exist in print but not in fact.

Illiterates cannot look up numbers in a telephone directory. Even if they can find the names of friends, few possess the sorting skills to make use of the yellow pages; categories are bewildering and trade names are beyond decoding capabilities for millions of nonreaders. Even the emergency numbers listed on the first page of the phone book—

"Ambulance," "Police," and "Fire"—are too frequently beyond the recognition of nonreaders.

Many illiterates cannot read the admonition on a pack of cigarettes. Neither the Surgeon General's warning nor its reproduction on the package can alert them to the risks. Although most people learn by word of mouth that smoking is related to a number of grave physical disorders, they do not get the chance to read the detailed stories which can document this danger with the vividness that turns concern into determination to resist. They can see the handsome cowboy or the slim Virginia lady lighting up a filter cigarette; they cannot heed the words that tell them that this product is (not "may be") dangerous to their health. Sixty million men and women are condemned to be the unalerted, high-risk candidates for cancer.

Illiterates do not buy "no-name" products in the supermarkets. They must depend on photographs or the familiar logos that are printed on the packages of brand-name groceries. The poorest people, therefore, are denied the benefits of the least costly products.

Illiterates depend almost entirely upon label recognition. Many labels, however, are not easy to distinguish. Dozens of different kinds of Campbell's soup appear identical to the nonreader. The purchaser who cannot read and does not dare to ask for help, out of the fear of being stigmatized (a fear which is unfortunately realistic), frequently comes home with something which she never wanted and her family never tasted. [20]

Illiterates cannot read instructions on a pack of frozen food. Packages sometimes provide an illustration to explain the cooking preparations; but illustrations are of little help to someone who must "boil water, drop the food—*within* its plastic wrapper—in the boiling water, wait for it to simmer, instantly remove."

Even when labels are seemingly clear, they may be easily mistaken. A woman in Detroit brought home a gallon of Crisco for her children's dinner. She thought that she had bought the chicken that was pictured on the label. She had enough Crisco now to last a year—but no more money to go back and buy the food for dinner.

Recipes provided on the packages of certain staples sometimes tempt a semiliterate person to prepare a meal her children have not tasted. The longing to vary the uniform and often starchy content of low-budget meals provided to the family that relies on food stamps commonly leads to ruinous results. Scarce funds have been wasted and the food must be thrown out. The same applies to distribution of food-surplus produce in emergency conditions. Government inducements to poor people to "explore the ways" by which to make a tasty meal from tasteless noodles, surplus cheese, and powdered milk are useless to nonreaders. Intended as benevolent advice, such recommendations mock reality and foster deeper feelings of resentment and of inability to cope. (Those, on the other hand, who cautiously refrain from "innovative" recipes in preparation of their children's meals must suffer the opprobrium of "laziness," "lack of imagination. . . .")

Illiterates cannot travel freely. When they attempt to do so, they encounter risks that few of us can dream of. They cannot read traffic signs and, while they often learn to recognize and to decipher symbols, they cannot manage street names which they haven't seen before. The same is true for bus and subway stops. While ingenuity can sometimes help a man or woman to discern directions from familiar landmarks, buildings, cemeteries, churches, and the like, most illiterates are virtually immobilized. They seldom wander past the streets and neighborhoods they know. Geographical paralysis becomes a bitter metaphor for their entire existence. They are immobilized in almost every sense we can imagine. They can't move up. They can't move out. They cannot see beyond. Illiterates may take an oral test for drivers' permits in most sections of America. It is a questionable concession. Where will they go? How will they get there? How will they get home? Could it be that some of us might like it better if they stayed where they belong?

Travel is only one of many instances of circumscribed existence. Choice, in almost   25
all its facets, is diminished in the life of an illiterate adult. Even the printed TV schedule, which provides most people with the luxury of preselection, does not belong within the arsenal of options in illiterate existence. One consequence is that the viewer watches only what appears at moments when he happens to have time to turn the switch. Another consequence, a lot more common, is that the TV set remains in operation night and day. Whatever the program offered at the hour when he walks into the room will be the nutriment that he accepts and swallows. Thus, to passivity, is added frequency— indeed, almost uninterrupted continuity. Freedom to select is no more possible here than in the choice of home or surgery or food.

"You don't choose," said one illiterate woman. "You take your wishes from somebody else." Whether in perusal of a menu, selection of highways, purchase of groceries, or determination of affordable enjoyment, illiterate Americans must trust somebody else: a friend, a relative, a stranger on the street, a grocery clerk, a TV copywriter.

"All of our mail we get, it's hard for her to read. Settin' down and writing a letter, she can't do it. Like if we get a bill . . . we take it over to my sister-in-law. . . . My sister-in-law reads it."

Billing agencies harass poor people for the payment of the bills for purchases that might have taken place six months before. Utility companies offer an agreement for a staggered payment schedule on a bill past due. "You have to trust them," one man said. Precisely for this reason, you end up by trusting no one and suspecting everyone of possible deceit. A submerged sense of distrust becomes the corollary to a constant need to trust. "They are cheating me . . . I have been tricked . . . I do not know . . ."

Not knowing: This is a familiar theme. Not knowing the right word for the right thing at the right time is one form of subjugation. Not knowing the world that lies concealed behind those words is a more terrifying feeling. The longitude and latitude of one's existence are beyond all easy apprehension. Even the hard, cold stars within the firmament above one's head begin to mock the possibilities for self-location. Where am I? Where did I come from? Where will I go?

"I've lost a lot of jobs," one man explains. "Today, even if you're a janitor, there's   30
still reading and writing. . . . They leave a note saying, 'Go to room so-and-so . . .' You can't do it. You can't read it. You don't know."

"The hardest thing about it is that I've been places where I didn't know where I was. You don't know where you are. . . . You're lost."

"Like I said: I have two kids. What do I do if one of my kids starts choking? I go running to the phone . . . I can't look up the hospital phone number. That's if we're at home. Out on the street, I can't read the sign. I get to a pay phone. 'Okay, tell us where you are. We'll send an ambulance.' I look at the street sign. Right there, I can't tell you what it says. I'd have to spell it out, letter for letter. By that time, one of my kids would be dead. . . . These are the kinds of fears you go with, every single day . . ."

"Reading directions, I suffer with. I work with chemicals. . . . That's scary to begin with . . ."

"You sit down. They throw the menu in front of you. Where do you go from there? Nine times out of ten you say, 'Go ahead. Pick out something for the both of us.' I've eaten some weird things, let me tell you!"

Menus. Chemicals. A child choking while his mother searches for a word she does not know to find assistance that will come too late. Another mother speaks about the inability to help her kids to read: "I can't read to them. Of course that's leaving them out of something they should have. Oh, it matters. You *believe* it matters! I ordered all these books. The kids belong to a book club. Donny wanted me to read a book to him. I told Donny: 'I can't read.' He said: 'Mommy, you sit down. I'll read it to you.' I tried it one day, reading from the pictures. Donny looked at me. He said, 'Mommy, that's not right.' He's only five. He knew I couldn't read . . .' "

A landlord tells a woman that her lease allows him to evict her if her baby cries and causes inconvenience to her neighbors. The consequence of challenging his words conveys a danger which appears, unlikely as it seems, even more alarming than the danger of eviction. Once she admits that she can't read, in the desire to maneuver for the time in which to call a friend, she will have defined herself in terms of an explicit impotence that she cannot endure. Capitulation in this case is preferable to self-humiliation. Resisting the definition of oneself in terms of what one cannot do, what others take for granted, represents a need so great that other imperatives (even one so urgent as the need to keep one's home in winter's cold) evaporate and fall away in face of fear. Even the loss of home and shelter, in this case, is not so terrifying as the loss of self.

"I come out of school. I was sixteen. They had their meetings. The directors meet. They said that I was wasting their school paper. I was wasting pencils . . ."

Another illiterate, looking back, believes she was not worthy of her teacher's time. She believes that it was wrong of her to take up space within her school. She believes that it was right to leave in order that somebody more deserving could receive her place.

Children choke. Their mother chokes another way: on more than chicken bones.

People eat what others order, know what others tell them, struggle not to see themselves as they believe the world perceives them. A man in California speaks about his own loss of identity, of self-location, definition:

"I stood at the bottom of the ramp. My car had broke down on the freeway. There was a phone. I asked for the police. They was nice. They said to tell them where I was. I looked up at the signs. There was one that I had seen before. I read it to them: ONE WAY STREET. They thought it was a joke. I told them I couldn't read. There was other signs above the ramp. They told me to try. I looked around for somebody to help. All the cars was going by real fast. I couldn't make them understand that I was lost. The cop was nice. He told me: 'Try once more.' I did my best. I couldn't read. I only knew the sign above my head. The cop was trying to be nice. He knew that I was trapped. 'I can't send out a car to you if you can't tell me where you are.' I felt afraid. I nearly cried. I'm forty-eight years old. I only said: 'I'm on a one-way street . . .' "

The legal problems and the courtroom complications that confront illiterate adults have been discussed above. The anguish that may underlie such matters was brought home to me this year while I was working on this book. I have spoken, in the introduction, of a sudden phone call from one of my former students, now in prison for a criminal offense. Stephen is not a boy today. He is twenty-eight years old. He called to ask me to assist him in his trial, which comes up next fall. He will be on trial for murder. He has just knifed and killed a man who first enticed him to his home, then cheated him, and then insulted him—as "an illiterate subhuman."

Stephen now faces twenty years to life. Stephen's mother was illiterate. His grandparents were illiterate as well. What parental curse did not destroy was killed off finally by the schools. Silent violence is repaid with interest. It will cost us $25,000 yearly to maintain this broken soul in prison. But what is the price that has been paid by Stephen's victim? What is the price that will be paid by Stephen?

Perhaps we might slow down a moment here and look at the realities described above. This is the nation that we live in. This is a society that most of us did not create but which our President and other leaders have been willing to sustain by virtue of malign neglect. Do we possess the character and courage to address a problem which so many nations, poorer than our own, have found it natural to correct?

The answers to these questions represent a reasonable test of our belief in the   45
democracy to which we have been asked in public school to swear allegiance.

Questions for Discussion and Writing

1. What kinds of limitations beset an illiterate person and limit his or her ability to function in everyday life? What examples best dramatize the costs of illiteracy in personal rather than statistical terms?
2. In Kozol's view, why would an illiterate society be more likely to become less democratic? How persuasive do you find his analysis?
3. Imagine what a typical day in your life would be like if you could not read or write. Keep a record of all your activities, and describe how each would be different if you were illiterate.

William A. Henry III

. . . .

William A. Henry III (1950–1994) was the drama critic for Time *magazine and frequently wrote on social issues. Henry's belief that an antielitist trend in American society has debased higher education is developed in his last book,* In Defense of Elitism *(1994). The following excerpt from this book first appeared in the August 29, 1994, issue of* Time.

IN DEFENSE OF ELITISM

While all the major social changes in post-war America reflect egalitarianism of some sort, no social evolution has been more willfully egalitarian than opening the academy. Half a century ago, a high school diploma was a significant credential, and college was a privilege for the few. Now high school graduation is virtually automatic for adolescents outside the ghettos and barrios, and college has become a normal way station in the average person's growing up. No longer a mark of distinction or proof of achievement, a college education is these days a mere rite of passage, a capstone to adolescent party time.

Some 63% of all American high school graduates now go on to some form of further education, according to the Department of Commerce's *Statistical Abstract of the United States,* and the bulk of those continuing students attain at least an associate's degree. Nearly 30% of high school graduates ultimately receive a four-year baccalaureate degree. A quarter or so of the population may seem, to egalitarian eyes, a small and hence elitist slice. But by world standards this is inclusiveness at its most extreme— and its most peculiarly American.

For all the socialism of British or French public policy and for all the paternalism of the Japanese, those nations restrict university training to a much smaller percentage of their young, typically 10% to 15%. Moreover, they and other First World nations tend to carry the elitism over into judgments about precisely which institution one attends. They rank their universities, colleges and technical schools along a prestige hierarchy much more rigidly gradated—and judged by standards much more widely accepted—than Americans ever impose on their jumble of public and private institutions.

In the sharpest divergence from American values, these other countries tend to separate the college-bound from the quotidian masses[1] in early adolescence, with scant hope for a second chance. For them, higher education is logically confined to those who displayed the most aptitude for lower education.

The opening of the academy's doors has imposed great economic costs on the   5 American people while delivering dubious benefits to many of the individuals supposedly being helped. The total bill for higher education is about $150 billion per year, with almost two-thirds of that spent by public institutions run with taxpayer funds. Private colleges and universities also spend the public's money. They get grants for research and the like, and they serve as a conduit for subsidized student loans—many of which are never fully repaid. President Clinton refers to this sort of spending as an investment in human capital. If that is so, it seems reasonable to ask whether the investment pays a worthwhile rate of return. At its present size, the American style of mass higher education probably ought to be judged a mistake—and one based on a giant lie.

Why do people go to college? Mostly to make money. This reality is acknowledged in the mass media, which are forever running stories and charts showing how much a college degree contributes to lifetime income (with the more sophisticated publications very occasionally noting the counterweight costs of tuition paid and income forgone during the years of full-time study).

But the equation between college and wealth is not so simple. College graduates unquestionably do better on average economically than those who don't go at all. At the extremes, those with five or more years of college earn about triple the income of

---

[1]*quotidian masses:* common, standard, or ordinary.

those with eight or fewer years of total schooling. Taking more typical examples, one finds that those who stop their educations after earning a four-year degree earn about 1½ times as much as those who stop at the end of high school. These outcomes, however, reflect other things besides the impact of the degree itself. College graduates are winners in part because colleges attract people who are already winners—people with enough brains and drive that they would do well in almost any generation and under almost any circumstances, with or without formal credentialing.

The harder and more meaningful question is whether the mediocrities who have also flooded into colleges in the past couple of generations do better than they otherwise would have. And if they do, is it because college actually made them better employees or because it simply gave them the requisite credential to get interviewed and hired? The U.S. Labor Department's Bureau of Labor Statistics reports that about 20% of all college graduates toil in fields not requiring a degree, and this total is projected to exceed 30% by the year 2005. For the individual, college may well be a credential without being a qualification, required without being requisite.

For American society, the big lie underlying higher education is akin to Garrison Keillor's description of the children in Lake Wobegon:[2] they are all above average. In the unexamined American Dream rhetoric promoting mass higher education in the nation of my youth, the implicit vision was that one day everyone, or at least practically everyone, would be a manager or a professional. We would use the most elitist of all means, scholarship, toward the most egalitarian of ends. We would all become chiefs; hardly anyone would be left a mere Indian. On the surface, this New Jerusalem appears to have arrived. Where half a century ago the bulk of jobs were blue collar, now a majority are white or pink collar. They are performed in an office instead of on a factory floor. If they still tend to involve repetition and drudgery, at least they do not require heavy lifting.

But the wages for them are going down virtually as often as up. And as a great   10
many disappointed office workers have discovered, being better educated and better dressed at the workplace does not transform one's place in the pecking order. There are still plenty more Indians than chiefs. Lately, indeed, the chiefs are becoming even fewer. The major focus of the "downsizing" of recent years has been eliminating layers of middle management—much of it drawn from the ranks of those lured to college a generation or two ago by the idea that a degree would transform them from the mediocre to magisterial.

Yet U.S. colleges blithely go on "educating" many more prospective managers and professionals than the country is likely to need. In my own field, there are typically more students majoring in journalism at any given moment than there are journalists employed at all the daily newspapers in the U.S. A few years ago, there were more students enrolled in law school than there were partners in all law firms. As trends shift, there have been periodic oversupplies of M.B.A.-wielding financial analysts, of grade school and high school teachers, of computer programmers, even of engineers.

---

[2]*Lake Wobegon:* an imaginary and idealized town in Minnesota known to listeners of the national weekly radio show *The Prairie Home Companion* hosted by Garrison Keillor.

Inevitably many students of limited talent spend huge amounts of time and money pursuing some brass-ring occupation, only to see their dreams denied. As a society America considers it cruel not to give them every chance at success. It may be more cruel to let them go on fooling themselves.

Just when it should be clear that the U.S. is already probably doing too much to entice people into college, Bill Clinton is suggesting it do even more. In February 1994, for example, the President asserted that America needs a greater fusion between academic and vocational training in high school—not because too many mediocre people misplaced on the college track are failing to acquire marketable vocational skills, but because too many people on the vocational track are being denied courses that will secure them admission to college. Surely what Americans need is not a fusion of the two tracks but a sharper division between them, coupled with a forceful program for diverting intellectual also-rans out of the academic track and into the vocational one. That is where most of them are heading in life anyway. Why should they wait until they are older and must enroll in high-priced proprietary vocational programs of often dubious efficacy—frequently throwing away not only their own funds but federal loans in the process—because they emerged from high school heading nowhere and knowing nothing that is useful in the marketplace?

If the massive numbers of college students reflected a national boom in love of learning and a prevalent yen for self-improvement, America's investment in the classroom might make sense. There are introspective qualities that can enrich any society in ways beyond the material. But one need look no further than the curricular wars to understand that most students are not looking to broaden their spiritual or intellectual horizons. Consider three basic trends, all of them implicit rejections of intellectual adventure. First, students are demanding courses that reflect and affirm their own identities in the most literal way. Rather than read a Greek dramatist of 2,000 years ago and thrill to the discovery that some ideas and emotions are universal, many insist on reading writers of their own gender or ethnicity or sexual preference, ideally writers of the present or the recent past.

The second trend, implicit in the first, is that the curriculum has shifted from being what professors desire to teach to being what students desire to learn. Nowadays colleges have to hustle for students by truckling trendily. If the students want media-studies programs so they can all fantasize about becoming TV news anchors, then media studies will abound. There are in any given year some 300,000 students enrolled in undergraduate communications courses.

Of even greater significance than the solipsism of students and the pusillanimity of teachers is the third trend, the sheer decline in the amount and quality of work expected in class. In an egalitarian environment the influx of mediocrities relentlessly lowers the general standards at colleges to levels the weak ones can meet. When my mother went to Trinity College in Washington in the early 1940s, at a time when it was regarded more as a finishing school for nice Catholic girls than a temple of discipline, an English major there was expected to be versed in Latin, Anglo-Saxon and medieval French. A course in Shakespeare meant reading the plays, all 37 of them. In today's indulgent climate, a professor friend at a fancy college told me as I was writing this chapter, taking a half semester of Shakespeare compels students to read exactly four plays. "Anything more than one a week," he explained, "is considered too heavy a load."

This probably should not be thought surprising in an era when most colleges, even prestigious ones, run some sort of remedial program for freshmen to learn the reading and writing skills they ought to have developed in junior high school—not to mention an era when many students vociferously object to being marked down for spelling or grammar. Indeed, all the media attention paid to curriculum battles at Stanford, Dartmouth and the like obscures the even bleaker reality of American higher education. As Russell Jacoby points out in his book *Dogmatic Wisdom,* most students are enrolled at vastly less demanding institutions, where any substantial reading list would be an improvement.

My modest proposal is this: Let us reduce, over perhaps a five-year span, the number of high school graduates who go on to college from nearly 60% to a still generous 33%. This will mean closing a lot of institutions. Most of them, in my view, should be community colleges, current or former state teachers' colleges and the like. These schools serve the academically marginal and would be better replaced by vocational training in high school and on-the-job training at work. Two standards should apply in judging which schools to shut down. First, what is the general academic level attained by the student body? That might be assessed in a rough-and-ready way by requiring any institution wishing to survive to give a standardized test—say, the Graduate Record Examination—to all its seniors. Those schools whose students perform below the state norm would face cutbacks or closing. Second, what community is being served? A school that serves a high percentage of disadvantaged students (this ought to be measured by family finances rather than just race or ethnicity) can make a better case for receiving tax dollars than one that subsidizes the children of the prosperous, who have private alternatives. Even ardent egalitarians should recognize the injustice of taxing people who wash dishes or mop floors for a living to pay for the below-cost public higher education of the children of lawyers so that they can go on to become lawyers too.

Some readers may find it paradoxical that a book arguing for greater literacy and intellectual discipline should lead to a call for less rather than more education. Even if college students do not learn all they should, the readers' counterargument would go, surely they learn something, and that is better than learning nothing. Maybe it is. But at what price? One hundred fifty billion dollars is awfully high for deferring the day when the idle or ungifted take individual responsibility and face up to their fate. Ultimately it is the yearning to believe that anyone can be brought up to college level that has brought colleges down to everyone's level.

Questions for Discussion and Writing

1. How, according to Henry, has a misguided egalitarianism led to present abuses in the educational system in the United States? Do the inferences Henry draws from statistics appear to support his claim?
2. How does Henry counter the widely perceived claim that a college degree leads to better-paying jobs?

3. In your opinion, do Henry's recommendations about separating college from vocational skills training make sense? Why, or why not?

4. Does this 1997 *New Yorker* cartoon by Boris Drucker reflect the state of affairs at your school? To what extent does it support William A. Henry III's argument? What does the image add to the words in this cartoon?

"I'm glad we won, and I hope that someday we'll have a university that our football team can be proud of."

Richard Rodriguez

* *

Richard Rodriguez was born in 1944 in San Francisco, where he grew up as a child of Spanish-speaking Mexican-American parents. Rodriguez pursued graduate studies at the University of California at Berkeley and received a Fulbright fellowship to the Warburg Institute in London to study English Renaissance literature. He is an editor at Pacific News Service and in 1997 received the George Foster Peabody Award for his NewsHour *essays on American life. His autobiography,* Hunger of Memory: The Education of Richard Rodriguez *(1982), received the Christopher Award. He has also written* Days of Obligation: An Argument with My Mexican Father *(1992) and* Brown: The Last Discovery of America *(2003) as well as many articles for the* Wall Street Journal, *the* New York Times, The American Scholar, Time, *and other publications. "On Becoming a Chicano" reveals his sense of estrangement from his culture when he entered an academic English-speaking environment.*

ON BECOMING A CHICANO

Today I am only technically the person I once felt myself to be—a Mexican-American, a Chicano. Partly because I had no way of comprehending my racial identity except in this technical sense, I gave up long ago the cultural consequences of being a Chicano.

The change came gradually but early. When I was beginning grade school, I noted to myself the fact that the classroom environment was so different in its styles and assumptions from my own family environment that survival would essentially entail a choice between both worlds. When I became a student, I was literally "remade"; neither I nor my teachers considered anything I had known before as relevant. I had to forget most of what my culture had provided, because to remember it was a disadvantage. The past and its cultural values became detachable, like a piece of clothing grown heavy on a warm day and finally put away.

Strangely, the discovery that I have been inattentive to my cultural past has arisen because others—student colleagues and faculty members—have started to assume that I am a Chicano. The ease with which the assumption is made forces me to suspect that the label is not meant to suggest cultural, but racial, identity. Nonetheless, as a graduate student and a prospective university faculty member, I am routinely expected to assume intellectual leadership *as a member of a racial minority.* Recently, for example, I heard the moderator of a panel discussion introduce me as "Richard Rodriguez, a Chicano intellectual." I wanted to correct the speaker—because I felt guilty representing a non-academic cultural tradition that I had willingly abandoned. So I can only guess what it would have meant to have retained my culture as I entered the classroom, what it would mean for me to be today a "Chicano intellectual." (The two words juxtaposed excite me; for years I thought a Chicano had to decide between being one or the other.)

Does the fact that I barely spoke any English until I was nine, or that as a child I felt a surge of self-hatred whenever a passing teenager would yell a racial slur, or that I saw my skin darken each summer—do any of these facts shape the ideas which I have or am capable of having? Today, I suspect they do—in ways I doubt the moderator who referred to me as a "Chicano intellectual" intended. The peculiar status of being a "Chicano intellectual" makes me grow restless at the thought that I have lost at least as much as I have gained through education.

I remember when, 20 years ago, two grammar-school nuns visited my childhood   5
home. They had come to suggest—with more tact than was necessary, because my parents accepted without question the church's authority—that we make a greater effort to speak as much English around the house as possible. The nuns realized that my brothers and I led solitary lives largely because we were barely able to comprehend English in a school where we were the only Spanish-speaking students. My mother and father complied as best they could. Heroically, they gave up speaking to us in Spanish—the language that formed so much of the family's sense of intimacy in an alien world—and began to speak a broken English. Instead of Spanish sounds, I began hearing sounds that were new, harder, less friendly. More important, I was encouraged to respond in English.

The change in language was the most dramatic and obvious indication that I would become very much like the "gringo"—a term which was used descriptively rather than perjoratively in my home—and unlike the Spanish-speaking relatives who largely constituted my preschool world. Gradually, Spanish became a sound freighted with only a kind of sentimental significance, like the sound of the bedroom clock I listened to in my aunt's house when I spent the night. Just as gradually, English became the language I came not to *hear* because it was the language I used every day, as I gained access to a new, larger society. But the memory of Spanish persisted as a reminder of the society I had left. I can remember occasions when I entered a room and my parents were speaking to one another in Spanish; seeing me they shifted into their more formalized English. Hearing them speak to me in English troubled me. The bonds their voices once secured were loosened by the new tongue.

This is not to suggest that I was being *forced* to give up my Chicano past. After the initial awkwardness of transition, I committed myself, fully and freely, to the culture of the classroom. Soon what I was learning in school was so antithetical to what my parents knew and did that I was careful about the way I talked about myself at the evening dinner table. Occasionally, there were moments of childish cruelty: a son's condescending to instruct either one of his parents about a "simple" point of English pronunciation or grammar.

Social scientists often remark, about situations such as mine, that children feel a sense of loss as they move away from their working-class identifications and models. Certainly, what I experienced, others have also—whatever their race. Like other generations of, say, Polish-American or Irish-American children coming home from college, I was to know the silence that ensues so quickly after the quick exchange of news and the dwindling of common interests.

In addition, however, education seemed to mean not only a gradual dissolving of familial and class ties but also a change of racial identity. The new language I spoke was only the most obvious reason for my associating the classroom with "gringo" society. The society I knew as Chicano was barely literate—in English *or* Spanish—and so impatient with either prolonged reflection or abstraction that I found the academic environment a sharp contrast. Sharpening the contrast was the stereotype of the Mexican as a mental inferior. (The fear of this stereotype has been so deep that only recently have I been willing to listen to those, like D. H. Lawrence, who celebrate the "non-cerebral" Mexican as an alternative to the rational and scientific European man.) Because I did not know how to distinguish the healthy non-rationality of Chicano culture from the mental incompetency of which Chicanos were unjustly accused, I was willing to abandon my non-mental skiffs in order to disprove the racist's stereotype.

I was wise enough not to feel proud of the person education had helped me to become. I knew that education had led me to repudiate my race. I was frequently labeled a *pocho*, a Mexican with gringo pretensions, not only because I could not speak Spanish but also because I would respond in English with precise and careful sentences. Uncles would laugh good-naturedly, but I detected scorn in their voices. For my grandmother, the least assimilated of my relations, the changes in her grandson since entering school were expecially troubling. She remains today a dark and silently critical figure in my memory, a reminder of the Mexican-Indian ancestry that somehow my educational success has violated.

Nonetheless, I became more comfortable reading or writing careful prose than talking to a kitchen filled with listeners, withdrawing from situations to reflect on their significance rather than grasping for meaning at the scene. I remember, one August evening, slipping away from a gathering of aunts and uncles in the backyard, going into a bedroom tenderly lighted by a late sun, and opening a novel about life in nineteenth-century England. There, by an open window, reading, I was barely conscious of the sounds of laughter outside.

With so few fellow Chicanos in the university, I had no chance to develop an alternative consciousness. When I spent occasional weekends tutoring lower-class Chicano teenagers or when I talked with Mexican-American janitors and maids around

10

the campus, there was a kind of sympathy—a sense, however privately held—that we knew something about one another. But I regarded them all primarily as people from my past. The maids reminded me of my aunts (similarly employed); the students I tutored reminded me of my cousins (who also spoke English with barrio accents).

When I was young, I was taught to refer to my ancestry as Mexican-American. *Chicano* was a word used among friends or relatives. It implied a familiarity based on shared experience. Spoken casually, the term easily became an insult. In 1968 the word *Chicano* was about to become a political term. I heard it shouted into microphones as Third World groups agitated for increased student and faculty representation in higher education. It was not long before I *became* a Chicano in the eyes of students and faculty members. My racial identity was assumed for only the simplest reasons: my skin color and last name.

On occasion I was asked to account for my interests in Renaissance English literature. When I explained them, declaring a need for cultural assimilation, on the campus, my listener would disagree. I sensed suspicion on the part of a number of my fellow minority students. When I could not imitate Spanish pronunciations or the dialect of the barrio, when I was plainly uninterested in wearing ethnic costumes and could not master a special handshake that minority students often used with one another, they knew I was different. And I was. I was assimilated into the culture of a graduate department of English. As a result, I watched how in less than five years nearly every minority graduate student I knew dropped out of school, largely for cultural reasons. Often they didn't understand the value of analyzing literature in professional jargon, which others around them readily adopted. Nor did they move as readily to lofty heights of abstraction. They became easily depressed by the seeming uselessness of talk they heard around them. "It's not for real," I still hear a minority student murmur to herself and perhaps to me, shaking her head slowly, as we sat together in a class listening to a discussion on punctuation in a Renaissance epic.

I survived—thanks to the accommodation I had made long before. In fact, I prospered, partly as a result of the political movement designed to increase the enrollment of minority students less assimilated than I in higher education. Suddenly grants, fellowships, and teaching offers became abundant.   15

In 1972 I went to England on a Fulbright scholarship. I hoped the months of brooding about racial identity were behind me. I wanted to concentrate on my dissertation, which the distractions of an American campus had not permitted. But the freedom I anticipated did not last for long. Barely a month after I had begun working regularly in the reading room of the British Museum, I was surprised, and even frightened, to have to acknowledge that I was not at ease living the rarefied life of the academic. With my pile of research file cards growing taller, the mass of secondary materials and opinions was making it harder for me to say anything original about my subject. Every sentence I wrote, every thought I had, became so loaded with qualifications and footnotes that it said very little. My scholarship became little more than an exercise in caution. I had an accompanying suspicion that whatever I did manage to write and call my dissertation would be of little use. Opening books so dusty that they must not have been used in decades, I began to doubt the value of writing what only a few people would read.

Obviously, I was going through the fairly typical crisis of the American graduate student. But with one difference: After four years of involvement with questions of racial identity, I now saw my problems as a scholar in the context of the cultural issues that had been raised by my racial situation. So much of what my work in the British Museum lacked, my parents' culture possessed. They were people not afraid to generalize or to find insights in their generalities. More important, they had the capacity to make passionate statements, something I was beginning to doubt my dissertation would ever allow me to do. I needed to learn how to trust the use of "I" in my writing the way they trusted its use in their speech. Thus developed a persistent yearning for the very Chicano culture that I had abandoned as useless.

Feelings of depression came occasionally but forcefully. Some days I found my work so oppressive that I had to leave the reading room and stroll through the museum. One afternoon, appropriately enough, I found myself in an upstairs gallery containing Mayan and Aztec sculptures. Even there the sudden yearning for a Chicano past seemed available to me only as nostalgia. One morning, as I was reading a book about Puritan autobiography, I overheard two Spaniards whispering to one another. I did not hear what they said, but I did hear the sound of their Spanish—and it embraced me, filling my mind with swirling images of a past long abandoned.

I returned from England, disheartened, a few months later. My dissertation was coming along well, but I did not know whether I wanted to submit it. Worse, I did not know whether I wanted a career in higher education. I detested the prospect of spending the rest of my life in libraries and classrooms, in touch with my past only through the binoculars nostalgia makes available. I knew that I could not simply recreate a version of what I would have been like had I not become an academic. There was no possibility of going back. But if the culture of my birth was to survive, it would have to animate my academic work. That was the lesson of the British Museum.

I frankly do not know how my academic autobiography will end. Sometimes I   20 think I will have to leave the campus, in order to reconcile my past and present. Other times, more optimistically, I think that a kind of negative reconciliation is already in progress, that I can make creative use of my sense of loss. For instance, with my sense of the cleavage between past and present, I can, as a literary critic, identify issues in Renaissance pastoral—a literature which records the feelings of the courtly when confronted by the alternatives of rural and rustic life. And perhaps I can speak with unusual feeling about the price we must pay, or have paid, as a rational society for confessing seventeenth-century Cartesian[1] faiths. Likewise, because of my sense of cultural loss, I may be able to identify more readily than another the ways in which language has meaning simply as sound and what the printed word can and cannot give us. At the very least, I can point up the academy's tendency to ignore the cultures beyond its own horizons.

February 1974

On my job interview the department chairman has been listening to an oral version of what I have just written. I tell him he should be very clear about the fact that

---

[1]*Cartesian:* refers to René Descartes (1596–1650), the French philosopher who emphasized rationalization and logic and extended mathematical methods to all fields of human knowledge. He is known for the phrase "I think, therefore I am."

I am not, at the moment, confident enough to call myself a Chicano. Perhaps I never will be. But as I say all this, I look at the interviewer. He smiles softly. Has he heard what I have been trying to say? I wonder. I repeat: I have lost the ability to bring my past into my present; I do not know how to be a Chicano reader of Spenser or Shakespeare. All that remains is a desire for the past. He sighs, preoccupied, looking at my records. Would I be interested in teaching a course on the Mexican novel in translation? Do I understand that part of my duties would require that I become a counselor of minority students? What was the subject of that dissertation I did in England? Have I read the book on the same subject that was just published this month?

Behind the questioner, a figure forms in my imagination: my grandmother, her face solemn and still.

Questions for Discussion and Writing

1. How did working on his dissertation in England reinforce a sense of lost contact with his Hispanic heritage that Rodriguez first experienced in grade school? How does the title express his need to repossess those values he had once discarded?
2. Of what advantage is it to Rodriguez to organize his essay employing extended comparisons and contrasts?
3. In a short essay, discuss the advantages and disadvantages of permitting students to use Spanish or some other native language in school rather than English. If you are the only one in your family who is fluent in English, what challenges do you face because of your role as translator and intermediary?
4. Create a visual essay (with or without captions) that illustrates your experiences at college through physical artifacts such as a daily planner; tickets to games and theater productions; exams and quizzes; asignments; headlines from your school newspaper; lecture notes; posters for events on campus; photos of yourself, friends, and your dorm room; and anything else that would give a picture of your life at school.

Sabine Reichel

Sabine Reichel was born in Hamburg, Germany, in 1946, to a German actor and a Lithuanian artist. She grew up in West Germany (now Germany) and since 1965 has had a varied career as clothing designer, freelance journalist, contributor of film criticism, lecturer, filmmaker, and social worker active in projects caring for homeless children. She immigrated to the United States in 1976. Dissatisfied with the silence she and others of her generation encountered concerning the systematic slaughter of European Jews by Hitler and the Nazis, Reichel spent six months interviewing soldiers and teachers whose lives seemed to her to represent Germany's amnesia. The autobiographical essay that resulted was published under the title What Did You Do in the War, Daddy? *(1989). In this chapter from that book, Reichel describes the moral complacency of those of her parents' generation who refused to acknowledge the realities of the Nazi era and its lingering effects in contemporary Germany.*

Learning What Was Never Taught

I remember Herr Stock and Fräulein Lange without much affection. Partly because they weren't extraordinary people, partly because they failed their profession. They were my history teachers, ordinary civil servants, singled out to bring the tumultuous events of European history into perspective for a classroom of bored German schoolkids.

As it happened, Hitler and the Third Reich were the subjects under discussion when we were about fourteen years old, which is not to say that we discussed anything at all. I always thought that the decision to study the subject then was the result of a carefully calculated estimate by the school officials—as if German students were emotionally and intellectually ready to comprehend and digest the facts about Nazi Germany at exactly the age of 14.3. I learned much later that it had nothing to do with calculation; it was a matter of sequence. German history is taught chronologically, and Hitler was there when we were fourteen, whether we were ready or not.

Teaching this particular period was a thankless, though unavoidable, task. It was accompanied by sudden speech impediments, hoarse voices, uncontrollable coughs, and sweaty upper lips. A shift of mood would creep into the expansive lectures about kings and conquerors from the old ages, and once the Weimar Republic came to an end our teachers lost their proud diction.

We knew what it meant. We could feel the impending disaster. Only a few more pages in the history book, one last nervous swallowing, and then in a casual but controlled voice, maybe a touch too loud, Fräulein Lange would ask, "We are now getting to a dark chapter in German history. I'm sure you all know what I mean?"

We did, because each of us had already skimmed through the whole book count- 5 less times in search of exotic material and, naturally, had come across the man with the mustache. We knew that she was referring to the terrible time between 1933 and 1945 when Germany fell prey to a devil in brown disguise. There were fifteen pages devoted to the Third Reich, and they were filled with incredible stories about a mass movement called National Socialism which started out splendidly and ended in a catastrophe for the whole world.

And then there was an extra chapter, about three-quarters of a page long. It was titled "The Extermination of the Jews," and I had read it in my room at home many times. I always locked the door because I didn't want anybody to know what I was reading. Six million Jews were killed in concentration camps, and as I read about Auschwitz and the gas chambers a wave of feelings—fearful fascination mingled with disgust—rushed over me. But I kept quiet. What monsters must have existed then. I was glad it had all happened in the past and that the cruel Germans were gone, because, as the book pointed out, the ones responsible were punished. I couldn't help feeling alarmed by something I couldn't put my finger on. How could so many innocent people be murdered?

There was no explanation for my unspoken questions, no answers in Fräulein Lange's helpless face. She seemed embarrassed and distraught, biting her lip and looking down at her orthopedic shoes while trying to summarize the Third Reich in fifty minutes. That worked out to one minute for every one million people killed in World War II . . . and twenty-six lines for six million Jews, printed on cheap, yellowish paper in a German history book published in 1960. An efficient timesaver, the German way.

We never read that particular chapter aloud with our teacher as we did with so many other ones. It was the untouchable subject, isolated and open to everyone's personal interpretation. There was a subtle, unspoken agreement between teacher and student not to dig into something that would cause discomfort on all sides. Besides, wanting to have known more about concentration camps as a student would have been looked upon as sick.

All things must come to an end, however, and once the Third Reich crumbled in our classroom to the sound of hastily turning pages, the suffocating silence was lifted. Everybody seemed relieved, especially Fräulein Lange, who became her jolly old self again. She had survived two world wars, she would survive a bunch of unappreciative teenagers.

In her late fifties in 1960, Fräulein Lange was a tiny, wrinkled woman who matched   10
my idea of the institutional matron right down to her baggy skirt, steel-gray bun at the nape of her neck, and seamed stockings. She also had a trying predilection for Gutenberg, the inventer of movable type, whom we got to know more intimately than Hitler. But she did her duty, more or less. German teachers had to teach history whether they liked it or not.

The teachers of my time had all been citizens of the Third Reich and therefore participants in an epoch that only a few years after its bitter collapse had to be discussed in a neutral fashion. But what could they possibly have said about this undigested, shameful subject to a partly shocked, partly bored class of adolescents? They had to preserve their authority in order to appear credible as teachers. Yet they were never put to the test. A critical imagination and unreasonable curiosity were unwelcome traits in all the classrooms of my twelve years in school. There was no danger that a precocious student would ever corner a teacher and demand more facts about the Nazis; they could walk away unscathed. We didn't ask our parents at home about the Nazis; nor did we behave differently in school.

The truth was that teachers were not allowed to indulge in private views of the Nazi past. There were nationwide guidelines for handling this topic, including one basic rule: The Third Reich and Adolf Hitler should be condemned unequivocally, without any specific criticism or praise. In reality, however, there were basically three ways to deal with the German past: (1) to go through the chapter as fast as possible, thereby avoiding any questions and answers; (2) to condemn the past passionately in order to deflate any suspicion about personal involvement; (3) to subtly legitimate the Third Reich by pointing out that it wasn't really as bad as it seemed; after all, there were the *Autobahnen*.[1]

But no matter what the style of prevarication, the German past was always presented as an isolated, fatal accident, and so the possibility of investigating the cause of such a disaster was, of course, eliminated. Investigating crimes reinforces guilt. If something is programmatically depicted as black and bad, one doesn't look for different shades and angles. The Third Reich was out of reach for us; it couldn't be cut down to size.

I wonder now what could have been accomplished by a teacher who had taken part in the war—as a soldier, or a Nazi, or an anti-Nazi—and who talked candidly about his personal experience. But that never happened. Instead we were showered

---

[1]*Autobahnen:* an extensive network of freeways without mandatory speed limits, constructed during the Third Reich.

with numbers and dates. A few million dead bodies are impossible to relate to; raw numbers don't evoke emotions. Understanding is always personal. Only stories that humanized the numbers might have reached us. Had we been allowed to draw a connection between ourselves and the lives of other people, we might have been able to identify and feel compassion. But we were not aware of how blatantly insufficiently the past was handled in school because we resented the subject as much as the teacher who was somewhat entangled in it. Teenagers generally have little interest in history lessons; we learned facts and dates in order to pass a test or get a good grade and weren't convinced that comprehension of the warp and woof of historical events made any difference to the world or anybody in particular.

Another history teacher in a new school I attended in 1962 took an activist approach, mixing pathos and drama into a highly entertaining theatrical performance. To introduce highlights of the Third Reich there was no finer actor than Herr Stock. His voice was angry, his brows furrowed, and his fist was raised when he talked about the Führer's ferocious reign. Some of the more outgoing male teachers might even mimic parts of a Hitler speech. Yet when it came time to discuss the war itself, everything went downhill. His hands stopped moving, his voice became reproachful—no more victories to report. His saddest expression was reserved for the tragic end of "Germany under National Socialist dictatorship." It was time for the untouchable chapter again, the chapter that made Herr Stock nervously run his hands over his bald head, clear his throat, and mumble something about "six million Jews." It was the chapter that made him close the book with a clap, turn his back to the class, and announce with a palpable sigh of relief, "Recess."

In our next history lesson that chapter was usually forgotten, and nobody followed up with any questions. Happy to have escaped interrogation, Herr Stock turned the pages quickly, ignoring "unpleasantries" like capitulation, denazification, and the humiliating aftermath of a defeated nation. The dark clouds were gone, the past had been left behind, and he turned jocular and voluble again.

But Herr Stock wasn't really talking to us, he was rather trying to convince us of something, assuming the stance of a prosecutor. For him, the scandal wasn't the casualties of World War II, but the resulting partition of Germany and the malevolence of the Russians. Rage, anger, and disappointment over the lost war, always repressed or directed at others, could be openly displayed now, disguised as righteousness. "They" had stolen parts of Germany—no word of what we stole from other countries. The Russians were war criminals; the Germans were victims.

If I had been unexpectedly curious about Nazi Germany, I would have received little help from my history books. The conclusions to be drawn from a twelve-year catastrophe packed with enough dramatic material to fill a library were reduced to a few cryptic phrases: "The Germans showed very little insight" and "No real feelings of contrition were expressed." Teachers and history books were their own best examples of how to eviscerate the Nazi terror without ever really trying to come to terms with it.

But a new chapter, a new era, and a magic word—*Wirtschaftswunder*[2]—soon revived our classroom and inspired another patriotic performance by Herr Stock. The

15

---

[2]*Wirtschaftswunder:* "wonder of economics," the name given to the phenomenal recovery of the German economy after World War II.

undisputed star of German history education in the sixties was the remarkable recon-
struction of postwar Germany. Now here was something an old schoolteacher could
sink his teeth into. Gone were stutters and coughs. A nation of survivors had rolled up
its sleeves, and Herr Stock had certainly been one of them. Here was a chance to re-
habilitate Germany and put some gloss over its rotten core. Postwar Germany was a
genuine communal construction, a well-made product, mass-manufactured by and for
the tastes of the former citizens of the Reich. Every German with two functioning hands
had taken part in rebuilding Germany, and history teachers all over the country waxed
nostalgic about the united strength, the grim determination, and the close camaraderie
that had helped build up Germany brick by brick.

We schoolchildren couldn't have cared less about these achievements. We were all   20
born under occupation; the postwar years were ours too and the memories of ruins
and poverty were just as indelible—if not as traumatic—as they had been for our parents. But in his enthusiasm he overlooked the fact that his words were falling on deaf
ears: we didn't like Herr Stock; nor did we trust or admire him. In all this excitement
about the "economic miracle," another, even greater miracle was conveniently left unexplained. On page 219 of my history book, Germany was described as a nation living happily under National Socialism and a seemingly accepted Führer without any
visible crisis of conscience. Yet only fourteen pages later the same *Volk*[3] is depicted in
the midst of an entirely different world, miraculously denazified and retrained, its mur-
derous past neatly tucked away behind a tattered but nevertheless impenetrable veil of
forgetfulness.

How did they do it? The existing Federal Republic of Germany is only one state
away from the Nazi Reich. Where did they unload the brown ballast? The role change
from obedient Nazi citizen to obedient *Bundes*[4] citizen went too smoothly from "*Sieg
Heil!*" to democracy, and from marching brown uniforms to marching gray flannel suits.
Where was the genuine substance which had initially constituted the basic foundation
and ideology of the Third Reich? Could it still be there, hidden, repressed, put on ice?

Such questions were never asked, or encouraged. The schoolteachers that I encountered were a uniformly intimidating group of people (with one glorious exception):
older men and women who demanded respect, order, and obedience. They were always
curbing my curiosity with the clobbering logic of people who get paid for controlling
outbursts of independent thinking. Their assessment of my character in report cards
read: "She talks too much and could accomplish more if she would be more diligent."

Even though prohibited when I went to school, corporal punishment in many forms
was still practiced with parental support, and my own classroom recollections are thick
with thin-lipped, hawk-eyed, bespectacled men and women with mercilessly firm hands
ready to take up the switch.

I always felt powerless toward teachers, and all of these emotions crystallized in
1983, when I was preparing to interview one of them. I couldn't help feeling a little triumphant. I was asking the questions now because I had discovered a slight spot on
their white vests, something I couldn't see clearly when I was young and under their

---

[3]*Volk:* "people" or "folk," as in Volkswagen (literally, "people's car."   [4]*Bundes:* "federal," an adjective.

control. Now I had the power to make them nervous. My victory over German authority seemed complete. A schoolgirl's revenge?

But that wasn't all. I had a genuine interest in finding out how teachers in Germany 25 feel today about their past failures. Had they found new ways to justify their damaging elisions, euphemisms, and omissions? More than any other age group, my generation was in desperate need not only of historical education but also of some form of emotional assistance from the adults who were linked to that not so distant yet unspeakable past.

In a way, I was looking for Herr Stock. But teachers as mediocre as he and Fräulein Lange had little to contribute to the kind of discussion I had in mind. I wanted the perspective of a teacher who had at least attempted to come to grips with his past. I was lucky to find one in Cäsar Hagener, a seventy-six-year-old former teacher and history professor. Hagener lives with his wife in a cozy, old-fashioned house with a garden in a suburb of Hamburg, in a quiet, safe neighborhood with lots of trees, many dachshunds, and little activity. He owns the type of one-family house, surrounded by a fence, that was commonly built in the thirties. A German house must have a fence. A house without a fence is disorderly, like a coat with a missing button.

Cäsar Hagener exuded integrity and an appealing friendliness—yet I found it impossible to forget that he had also been a teacher in the Third Reich. Hitler had envisioned a training program that would make every German youth "resilient as leather, fast as a weasel, and hard as Krupp steel." He believed that "too much education spoils the youth." (Not surprisingly, after a few years of dictatorship 30 percent of the university professors, including Jews, had left the country.)

In 1933, Cäsar Hagener was a teacher of pedagogy and history at a liberal school in Hamburg, and when he heard that Hitler was appointed Reichs Chancellor he happened to be studying *Das Kapital*[5] together with some left-wing colleagues. "My friend said to me, 'It'll be over in no time. When you and I write a history book in twenty years, the Nazis will only be a footnote.' "

Even a skillful dictator like Hitler couldn't turn a country upside down overnight, and school life changed slowly under the Nazis. "But after 1934, the Nazis began to investigate the teachers' adaptation to the new order. Some were fired, and some were retrained in special camps. We had, of course, some 'overnight' Nazis who were strutting around in uniform, which didn't impress the students, who were quite critical. Later, in 1937, the young teachers were told to join the Nazi Party or else, so I joined the Party. Still, the first years of National Socialism were almost bearable."

However, at least once a week, teachers and students had to muster for the rais- 30 ing of the swastika flag and the singing of the "Horst-Wessel-Lied" or other Nazi songs. The Führer's speeches were required listening on the popular *Volksempfänger* for teachers and older students, while the nazified text in the new schoolbooks read like this: "If a mental patient costs 4 Reichsmarks a day in maintenance, a cripple 5.50, and a criminal 3.50, and about 50,000 of these people are in our institutions, how much does it cost our state at a daily rate of 4 Reichsmarks—and how many marriage loans of 1,000 Reichsmarks per couple could have been given out instead?"

---

[5]*Das Kapital:* the classic text by Karl Marx (1867) published in English in 1887 and edited by Frederick Engels.

The new features of Nazi education like race hygiene and heredity theory were given different degrees of importance in different schools. Hagener prepared himself: "I made sure to get a class with school beginners because children of that age weren't taught history or any of that Nazi nonsense. Besides, as a teacher, you were pretty much independent in your classroom and could make your own decision about what to say and what to skip. There were ways of getting around the obnoxious Nazi ideology."

The first public action by the Nazis right after January 1933 was to purge public and school libraries of "Jewish and un-German elements," leaving empty spaces on the shelves, since new "literature" wasn't written yet and new schoolbooks, adapted to the Nazis' standards, weren't printed until 1936. That same year they initiated compulsory membership in the Hitler Youth, starting at the age of ten with boys organized into Jungvolk and Hitler Jungen and girls and young women into the Bund Deutscher Mädel (League of German Girls). What the Reich of the future needed were fearless, proud men of steel and yielding, fertile women—preferably blond—not effete intellectuals.

"The children can't be blamed for having been enthusiastic members of the Hitler Youth," Cäsar Hagener points out. "They grew up with that ideology and couldn't be expected to protect themselves from National Socialism; to do so, children would have had to be unaffected by all outside influences. It was their world, and the Hitler Youth programs were very attractive, with sports, contests, and decorations. It was possible for the son of a Communist or a Social Democrat to become a highly decorated Hitler Youth leader. I accuse the teachers who didn't perceive what was going on, and who taught Nazi ideology and glorified war, of having failed their profession."

In the last years of the war there was not much academic activity in Germany. The Nazi state was concerned with other problems besides education. Many schools were destroyed by bombs and virtually all Germans between fifteen and sixty years of age— Cäsar Hagener was drafted in 1940—were mobilized for the *Endkampf* (the final struggle) by the end of 1944. Hunger, death, and the will to survive prevailed over culture and education. Who needs to know algebra when the world is falling apart?

In 1945 denazification fever broke out in the defeated nation and reversed the roles of master and servant. For over a decade the country had been straining to purge itself of "un-German elements," and now the occupying powers were trying to purge it of all Nazi elements. Yet their efforts only exposed the unfeasibility of such a gargantuan task, since it involved much more than just the Nazi Party and the SS. Twelve years under the swastika had produced all kinds of "literature," art, music, film—indeed, a whole society had to be taken apart and its guiding principles destroyed. Naturally, reforming the educational system was a high priority, and millions of schoolbooks were thrown out, but some had to be preserved. The specially assigned Allied education officers decided which schoolbooks could still be used (after tearing out a Nazi-contaminated page or censoring a suspicious chapter or two). The approved books were stamped, and were circulated until new ones could be printed, which wasn't until the early fifties.

"The British, our occupiers, did everything wrong, because nothing could be worked out intellectually. They came over here with certain expectations and this incredibly bad image of the enemy, and they were very surprised to find their task not as easy as they had thought. They tried to control the situation by being very strict."

Reforming the faculty was even more problematic, since many teachers had been forced to join the Nazi Party and it wasn't always easy to tell who was a "real" Nazi and who wasn't. As a rule of thumb, those who appeared to have cooperated unwillingly were permitted to continue teaching, younger teachers who had been educated under the Nazi regime were retrained in special seminars, while those who had been active supporters were barred from teaching for as long as two years.

Cäsar Hagener still gets angry over how easily former colleagues were rehired. "After 1945, nobody seemed to remember what a Nazi was, and people who I knew were definitely Nazis by nature landed on top again. I was one of a group of young teachers who protested violently against this tendency—and I felt like a McCarthy witch-hunter. I saw these people as criminals who did a lot of harm to us teachers."

Still, the main consideration was that teachers were badly needed. The war had wiped out a whole generation of young men, and keeping professionals from their profession in Germany after 1945 was as uneconomical as it was impractical: what was left was what Germany's children got. It's safe to say that by 1950 almost all teachers were back in schools and universities regardless of their past.

In the years immediately following the war, the few schools that were not badly damaged were overcrowded with children of all ages and several grades gathered together in one room. There was cardboard in place of windows, and opening umbrellas inside the school on rainy days was as natural as being sent home for a "cold-weather holiday" because there was no heat. The teacher had to be a good-humored ringmaster, innovative and full of stories; because of the book shortage, he had to know his lessons by heart. The students also needed good memories, because there wasn't any paper. Arithmetic and grammar assignments were often written down on the margins of newspapers. 40

It might have been the only time in Germany when school lessons were extemporaneous, personal, and an accurate reflection of real life. School was suddenly a popular place where humanity prevailed over theory. Teachers were not merely authority figures but people who had been harmed by the war just like the students and their families, and much of the time was spent discussing how to steal potatoes and coal and other survival tactics, which were more pressing than Pythagoras.

How did a teacher in those years explain history while it was happening? The change from "Nazis are good" to "Nazis are bad" must have been a confusing experience for the uprooted, disillusioned children of the Third Reich. Children weren't denazified. They had to adapt to "democracy" without shedding a brown skin. All the values they had learned to defend so passionately crumbled before their eyes and the reality they once trusted was rearranged silently, without their consent. The glorious, thunderous Third Reich was a gyp. The Jews weren't "*Volks* enemy number one" anymore. And as for the Führer, he wasn't a superhuman hero, but a vicious little coward, a maniac who wanted to exterminate a whole people and almost succeeded. What irreparable mistrust must have become lodged in the minds of all these young Germans whose youth was trampled flat by goose-stepping jackboots.

But teachers didn't explain history at all. "I'm afraid to say that it didn't occur to the students to bring up Adolf in any form. We had all survived and dealt mostly with the effects of the war in a practical sense. I tried to do nice, positive things with the children, who had it bad enough as it was," Cäsar Hagener explains, and adds, almost surprised, "It is amazing how extremely apolitical we were. Any reflection was impossible under the circumstances, because everything was defined in terms of the struggle of daily life, which had a dynamic all by itself."

He also knows why the adolescents of the fifties and sixties were as uninquisitive as their teachers and parents were silent. "There was strong resentment toward the grown-ups. The teenagers had a fine sense for the things that didn't quite fit together with the Nazis. I didn't have any luck with my own three sons; they frustrated my desire to talk about the past by calling it lecturing, so I ended up talking about it mostly in foreign countries, where the people seemed to be more interested in it."

Things have changed radically during the last twenty years. There has been a   45
small revolution in the German classroom. While teachers after the war were much younger and more outspoken than their predecessors, students became rebellious and undisciplined.

Cäsar Hagener remembers his school days. "My own generation and my students lived in a very strict and conformist structure which existed much earlier than 1933. Sure, there were provocative and rebellious personalities, but this phenomenon of developing an independent mind is new. Today it wouldn't be possible to stand in front of a class in uniform and in all seriousness talk about racial theory. The students would die laughing."

German students today often know more facts about the Third Reich than both their parents and the immediate postwar generation and are not afraid to ask questions. Yet their interest in Nazism is strictly intellectual, and they generally succeed in remaining emotionally detached. They don't know yet that they can't escape the past. Tragically, almost all of Cäsar Hagener's contemporaries have managed to escape their Nazi past. In his opinion: "You can't put a whole nation on the couch. I find my own contemporaries just plain terrible and I don't have much contact with many old friends anymore. In their eyes I'm too critical, a guy who fouls his own nest and who can't see the good sides of the Nazi era—which infuriates and bores me at the same time. They reject the radical examination of the past. But it's necessary, since we know better than most that terrible things can and did happen."

Questions for Discussion and Writing

1. From the narrator's perspective, what was odd about the way in which the Holocaust was taught? How did her search for a satisfactory explanation about this event change her relationship with her family and school authorities?
2. How did Reichel's interview with Herr Hagener provide insights into the pressures to which teachers were subjected and give her some of the answers she sought?
3. You might rent the subtitled acclaimed German film *The Nasty Girl* (1990), which is based on Reichel's account, and compare it with her essay. How does each genre treat the same events differently?

David Rothenberg

David Rothenberg (b. 1962) is an associate professor of philosophy at the New Jersey Institute of Technology in Newark, New Jersey. He is the editor of Terra Nova: Journal of Nature and Culture *and has written* Hand's End: Technology and the Limits of Nature

(1993). In 2001, Rothenberg edited with Marta Ulvaeus The Book of Music and Nature: An Anthology of Sounds, Words, Thoughts; Writing on Water *and* World and the Wild. *This essay first appeared in the* Chronicle of Higher Education *in August 1997. His latest work is* Always the Mountains *(2002).*

HOW THE WEB DESTROYS THE QUALITY OF STUDENTS' RESEARCH PAPERS

Sometimes I look forward to the end-of-semester rush, when students' final papers come streaming into my office and mailbox. I could have hundreds of pages of original thought to read and evaluate. Once in a while, it is truly exciting, and brilliant words are typed across pages in response to a question I've asked the class to discuss.

But this past semester was different. I noticed a disturbing decline in both the quality of the writing and the originality of the thoughts expressed. What had happened since last fall? Did I ask worse questions? Were my students unusually lazy? No. My class had fallen victim to the latest easy way of writing a paper: doing their research on the World Wide Web.

It's easy to spot a research paper that is based primarily on information collected from the Web. First, the bibliography cites no books, just articles or pointers to places in that virtual land somewhere off any map: http://www.etc. Then a strange preponderance of material in the bibliography is curiously out of date. A lot of stuff on the Web that is advertised as timely is actually at least a few years old. (One student submitted a research paper last semester in which all of his sources were articles published between September and December 1995; that was probably the time span of the Web page on which he found them.)

Another clue is the beautiful pictures and graphs that are inserted neatly into the body of the student's text. They look impressive, as though they were the result of careful work and analysis, but actually they often bear little relation to the precise subject of the paper. Cut and pasted from the vast realm of what's out there for the taking, they masquerade as original work.

Accompanying them are unattributed quotes (in which one can't tell who made   5 the statement or in what context) and curiously detailed references to the kinds of things that are easy to find on the Web (pages and pages of federal documents, corporate propaganda, or snippets of commentary by people whose credibility is difficult to assess). Sadly, one finds few references to careful, in-depth commentaries on the subject of the paper, the kind of analysis that requires a book, rather than an article, for its full development.

Don't get me wrong, I'm no neo-Luddite.[1] I am as enchanted as anyone else by the potential of this new technology to provide instant information. But too much of what passes for information these days is simply *advertising* for information. Screen after screen shows you where you can find out more, how you can connect to this place or that. The acts of linking and networking and randomly jumping from here to there become as exciting or rewarding as actually finding anything of intellectual value.

---

[1]*neo-Luddite:* referring to English weavers who protested the arrival of mechanized looms at the dawn of the Industrial Revolution. Thus, neo-Luddites are those who fear technology.

Search engines, with their half-baked algorithms, are closer to slot machines than to library catalogues. You throw your query to the wind, and who knows what will come back to you? You may get 234,468 supposed references to whatever you want to know. Perhaps one in a thousand might actually help you. But it's easy to be side-tracked or frustrated as you try to go through those Web pages one by one. Unfortunately, they're not arranged in order of importance.

What I'm describing is the hunt-and-peck method of writing a paper. We all know that word processing makes many first drafts look far more polished than they are. If the paper doesn't reach the assigned five pages, readjust the margin, change the font size, and . . . voila! Of course, those machinations take up time that the student could have spent revising the paper. With programs to check one's spelling and grammar now standard features on most computers, one wonders why students make any mistakes at all. But errors are as prevalent as ever, no matter how crisp the typeface. Instead of becoming perfectionists, too many students have become slackers, preferring to let the machine do their work for them.

What the Web adds to the shortcuts made possible by word processing is to make research look too easy. You toss a query to the machine, wait a few minutes, and suddenly a lot of possible sources of information appear on your screen. Instead of books that you have to check out of the library, read carefully, understand, synthesize, and then tactfully excerpt, these sources are quips, blips, pictures, and short summaries that may be downloaded magically to the dorm-room computer screen. Fabulous! How simple! The only problem is that a paper consisting of summaries of summaries is bound to be fragmented and superficial, and to demonstrate more of a random montage than an ability to sustain an argument through 10 to 15 double-spaced pages.

Of course, you can't blame the students for ignoring books. When college libraries are diverting funds from books to computer technology that will be obsolete in two years at most, they send a clear message to students: Don't read, just connect. Surf. Download. Cut and paste. Originality becomes hard to separate from plagiarism if no author is cited on a Web page. Clearly, the words are up for grabs, and students much prefer the fabulous jumble to the hard work of stopping to think and make sense of what they've read. 10

Libraries used to be repositories of words and ideas. Now they are, seen as centers for the retrieval of information. Some of this information comes from other, bigger libraries, in the form of books that can take time to obtain through interlibrary loan. What happens to the many students (some things never change) who scramble to write a paper the night before it's due? The computer screen, the gateway to the world sitting right on their desks, promises instant access—but actually offers only a pale, two-dimensional version of a real library.

But it's also my fault. I take much of the blame for the decline in the quality of student research in my classes. I need to teach students how to read, to take time with language and ideas, to work through arguments, to synthesize disparate sources to come up with original thought. I need to help my students understand how to assess sources to determine their credibility, as well as to trust their own ideas more than snippets of thought that materialize on a screen. The placelessness of the Web leads to an ethereal randomness of thought. Gone are the pathways of logic and passion, the sense of the progress of an argument. Chance holds sway, and it more often misses than hits. Judgment must be taught, as well as the methods of exploration.

I'm seeing my students' attention spans wane and their ability to reason for themselves decline. I wish that the university's computer system would crash for a day, so that I could encourage them to go outside, sit under a tree, and read a really good book—from start to finish. I'd like them to sit for a while and ponder what it means to live in a world where some things get easier and easier so rapidly that we can hardly keep track of how easy they're getting, while other tasks remain as hard as ever—such as doing research and writing a good paper that teaches the writer something in the process. Knowledge does not emerge in a vacuum, but we do need silence and space for sustained thought. Next semester, I'm going to urge my students to turn off their glowing boxes and think, if only once in a while.

Questions for Discussion and Writing

1. According to Rothenberg, how has the process by which students write research papers been changed by the Internet? What traditional skills does he feel have been lost?
2. To what extent does Rothenberg's argument depend on establishing a causal connection between students' use of the Internet and the declining quality of research papers? In your opinion, has he made a good case? Why or why not?
3. Does Rothenberg's characterization of the deficiencies now apparent in research papers correspond to your own experiences? What do you do to avoid the many defects Rothenberg identifies?

John Milton

• •

The English poet John Milton (1608–1674) named his 1644 pamphlet Areopagitica *after a speech delivered by Isocrates, an Athenian orator (436–338 B.C.) who argued for the right to write, speak, and publish freely. Milton was urging his contemporaries (Presbyterians, who, in 1643, tried to quiet the political opposition by imposing censorship) to censor only those books that were atheistic or libelous. As you read the following piece (originally given as a speech in Parliament), notice the inventive analogy Milton creates between homicide and censorship.*

AREOPAGITICA:[1] DEFENSE OF BOOKS

I deny not, but that it is of greatest concernment in the Church and Commonwealth, to have a vigilant eye how books demean themselves as well as men; and thereafter to confine, imprison, and do sharpest justice on them as malefactors. For books are not absolutely dead things, but do contain a potency of life in them to be as active

---

[1]*Areopagus:* the oldest, most respectable council of ancient Athens.

as that soul was whose progeny they are; nay, they do preserve as in a vial the purest efficacy and extraction of that living intellect that bred them. I know they are as lively, and as vigorously productive, as those fabulous dragon's teeth; and being sown up and down, may chance to spring up armed men. And yet, on the other hand, unless wariness be used, as good almost kill a man as kill a good book. Who kills a man kills a reasonable creature, God's image; but he who destroys a good book, kills reason itself, kills the image of God, as it were in the eye. Many a man lives a burden to the earth; but a good book is the precious life-blood of a master spirit, embalmed and treasured up on purpose to a life beyond life. 'Tis true, no age can restore a life, whereof perhaps there is no great loss; and revolutions of ages do not oft recover the loss of a rejected truth, for the want of which whole nations fare the worse.

We should be wary therefore what persecutions we raise against the living labours of public men, how we spill that seasoned life of man, preserved and stored up in books; since we see a kind of homicide may be thus committed, sometimes a martyrdom, and if it extend to the whole impression, a kind of massacre; whereof the execution ends not in the slaying of an elemental life, but strikes at that ethereal and fifth essence, the breath of reason itself, slays an immortality rather than a life. But lest I should be condemned of introducing licence, while I oppose licensing, I refuse not the pains to be so much historical, as will serve to show what hath been done by ancient and famous commonwealths against this disorder, till the very time that this project of licensing crept out of the inquisition, was catched up by our prelates, and hath caught some of our presbyters.

In Athens, where books and wits were ever busier than in any other part of Greece, I find but only two sorts of writings which the magistrate cared to take notice of; those either blasphemous and atheistical, or libellous. Thus the books of Protagoras,[2] were by the judges of Areopagus commanded to be burnt, and himself banished the territory for a discourse begun with his confessing not to know "whether there were gods, or whether not." And against defaming, it was agreed that none should be traduced by name, as was the manner of Vetus Comoedia,[3] whereby we may guess how they censured libelling. And this course was quick enough, as Cicero writes, to quell both the desperate wits of other atheists, and the open way of defaming, as the event showed. Of other sects and opinions, though tending to voluptuousness, and the denying of Divine Providence, they took no heed.

Therefore we do not read that either Epicurus,[4] or that libertine school of Cyrene, or what the Cynic impudence uttered, was ever questioned by the laws. Neither is it recorded that the writings of those old comedians were suppressed, though the acting of them were forbid; and that Plato commended the reading of Aristophanes, the loosest of them all, to his royal scholar Dionysius, is commonly known, and may be excused, if holy Chrysostom,[5] as is reported, nightly studied so much the same author and had the art to cleanse a scurrilous vehemence into the style of a rousing sermon.

---

[2]*Protagoras of Abdera:* a sophist banished from Athens for his atheism in 415 B.C.   [3]*Vetus Comoedia:* the "old comedy" of Athens that lampooned public figures.   [4]*Epicurus:* a hedonist (341–270 B.C.) condemned by Milton.   [5]*Chrysostom:* reference to the patriarch of Constantinople who died in A.D. 407 and was depicted as open-minded by Milton.

Questions for Discussion and Writing

1. According to Milton, why may preventing a book from being published or censoring it after it has been published do as much injury as murdering a human being? Do you find this argument persuasive? Why or why not?
2. How does Milton use references to Athenian society to support his argument?
3. Are there some books that should never be published (for example, those that argue the Holocaust never existed)? Why or why not? Conversely, could any book ever be as valuable as a human life (keep in mind this would include the Bible, the Koran, and other religious documents as well as CPR manuals)? Explain your answer.

Nat Hentoff

. . . .

A former board member of the American Civil Liberties Union, Nat Hentoff is a writer and an adjunct associate professor at New York University. He was born in 1925 in Boston. Hentoff graduated from Northeastern in 1945 and did postgraduate work at Harvard and the Sorbonne. He is a regular contributor to such publications as the Washington Post, *the* Progressive, *the* Village Voice, *and* The New Yorker. *Collections of his work include* The First Freedom *(1980). "'Speech Codes' on the Campus and Problems of Free Speech" first appeared in the Fall 1991 issue of* Dissent. *His most recent works are* Listen to the Stories: Nat Hentoff on Jazz and Country Music *(2000) and* The War on the Bill of Rights and the Gathering Resistance *(2003).*

"SPEECH CODES" ON THE CAMPUS AND PROBLEMS OF FREE SPEECH

During three years of reporting on anti-free-speech tendencies in higher education, I've been at more than twenty colleges and universities—from Washington and Lee and Columbia to Mesa State in Colorado and Stanford.

On this voyage of initially reverse expectations—with liberals fiercely advocating censorship of "offensive" speech and conservatives merrily taking the moral high ground as champions of free expression—the most dismaying moment of revelation took place at Stanford.

An Ecumenical Call for a Harsh Code

In the course of a two-year debate on whether Stanford, like many other universities, should have a speech code punishing language that might wound minorities, women, and gays, a letter appeared in the *Stanford Daily*. Signed by the African-American Law Students Association, the Asian-American Law Students Association, and the Jewish Law Students Association, the letter called for a harsh code. It reflected the letter and the spirit of an earlier declaration by Canetta Ivy, a black leader of student government at Stanford during the period of the great debate. "We don't put as many restrictions on freedom of speech," she said, "as we should."

Reading the letter by this rare ecumenical body of law students (so pressing was the situation that even Jews were allowed in), I thought of twenty, thirty years from now. From so bright a cadre of graduates, from so prestigious a law school would come some of the law professors, civic leaders, college presidents, and even maybe a Supreme Court justice of the future. And many of them would have learned—like so many other university students in the land—that censorship is okay provided your motives are okay.

The debate at Stanford ended when the president, Donald Kennedy, following the   5
prevailing winds, surrendered his previous position that once you start telling people what they can't say, you will end up telling them what they can't think. Stanford now has a speech code.

This is not to say that these gags on speech—every one of them so overboard and vague that a student can violate a code without knowing he or she has done so—are invariably imposed by student demand. At most colleges, it is the administration that sets up the code. Because there have been racist or sexist or homophobic taunts, anonymous notes or graffiti, the administration feels it must *do something*. The cheapest, quickest way to demonstrate that it cares is to appear to suppress racist, sexist, homophobic speech.

"The Pall of Orthodoxy"

Usually, the leading opposition among the faculty consists of conservatives—when there is opposition. An exception at Stanford was law professor Gerald Gunther, arguably the nation's leading authority on constitutional law. But Gunther did not have much support among other faculty members, conservative or liberal.

At the University of Buffalo Law School, which has a code restricting speech, I could find just one faculty member who was against it. A liberal, he spoke only on condition that I not use his name. He did not want to be categorized as a racist.

On another campus, a political science professor, for whom I had great respect after meeting and talking with him years ago, has been silent—students told me—on what Justice William Brennan once called "the pall of orthodoxy" that has fallen on his campus.

When I talked to him, the professor said, "It doesn't happen in my class. There's   10
no 'politically correct' orthodoxy here. It may happen in other places at this university, but I don't know about that." He said no more.

One of the myths about the rise of P.C. (politically correct) is that, coming from the left, it is primarily intimidating conservatives on campus. Quite the contrary. At almost every college I've been, conservative students have their own newspaper, usually quite lively and fired by a muckraking glee at exposing "politically correct" follies on campus.

By and large, those most intimidated—not so much by the speech codes themselves but by the Madame Defarge–like spirit behind them—are liberal students and those who can be called politically moderate.

I've talked to many of them, and they no longer get involved in class discussions when their views would go against the grain of P.C. righteousness. Many, for instance, have questions about certain kinds of affirmative action. They are not partisans of Jesse Helms or David Duke, but they wonder whether progeny of middle-class black families should get scholarship preference. Others have a question about abortion.

Most are not pro-life, but they believe that fathers should have a say in whether the fetus should be sent off into eternity.

Self-Censorship

Jeff Shesol, a recent graduate of Brown and now a Rhodes scholar at Oxford, became nationally known while at Brown because of his comic strip, "Thatch," which, not too kindly, parodied P.C. students. At a forum on free speech at Brown before he left, Shesol said he wished he could tell the new students at Brown to have no fear of speaking freely. But he couldn't tell them that, he said, advising the new students to stay clear of talking critically about affirmative action or abortion, among other things, in public.

At that forum, Shesol told me, he said that those members of the left who regard dis-   15
sent from their views as racist and sexist should realize that they are discrediting their goals. "They're honorable goals," said Shesol, "and I agree with them. I'm against racism and sexism. But these people's tactics are obscuring the goals. And they've resulted in Brown's no longer being an open-minded place." There were hisses from the audience.

Students at New York University Law School have also told me that they censor themselves in class. The kind of chilling atmosphere they describe was exemplified as a case assigned for a moot court competition became subject to denunciation when a sizable number of law students said it was too "offensive" and would hurt the feelings of gay and lesbian students. The case concerned a divorced father's attempt to gain custody of his children on the grounds that their mother had become a lesbian. It was against P.C. to represent the father.

Although some of the faculty responded by insisting that you learn to be a lawyer by dealing with all kinds of cases, including those you personally find offensive, other faculty members supported the rebellious students, praising them for their sensitivity. There was little public opposition from the other students to the attempt to suppress the case. A leading dissenter was a member of the conservative Federalist Society.

What is P.C. to white students is not necessarily P.C. to black students. Most of the latter did not get involved in the N.Y.U. protest, but throughout the country many black students do support speech codes. A vigorous exception was a black Harvard law school student during a debate on whether the law school should start punishing speech. A white student got up and said that the codes are necessary because without them, black students would be driven away from colleges and thereby deprived of the equal opportunity to get an education.

A black student rose and said that the white student had a hell of a nerve to assume that he—in the face of racist speech—would pack up his books and go home. He's been familiar with that kind of speech all his life, and he had never felt the need to run away from it. He'd handled it before and he could again.

The black student then looked at his white colleague and said that it was conde-   20
scending to say that blacks have to be "protected" from racist speech. "It is more racist and insulting," he emphasized, "to say that to me than to call me a nigger."

But that would appear to be a minority view among black students. Most are convinced they do need to be protected from wounding language. On the other hand, a good many black student organizations on campus do not feel that Jews have to be protected from wounding language.

Presence of Anti-Semitism

Though it's not much written about in reports of the language wars on campus, there is a strong strain of anti-Semitism among some—not all, by any means—black students. They invite such speakers as Louis Farrakhan, the former Stokely Carmichael (now Kwame Touré), and such lesser but still burning bushes as Steve Cokely, the Chicago commentator who has declared that Jewish doctors inject the AIDS virus into black babies. That distinguished leader was invited to speak at the University of Michigan.

The black student organization at Columbia University brought to the campus Dr. Khallid Abdul Muhammad. He began his address by saying: "My leader, my teacher, my guide is the honorable Louis Farrakhan. I thought that should be said at Columbia Jewniversity."

Many Jewish students have not censored themselves in reacting to this form of political correctness among some blacks. A Columbia student, Rachel Stoll, wrote a letter to the *Columbia Spectator*: "I have an idea. As a white Jewish American, I'll just stand in the middle of a circle comprising . . . Khallid Abdul Muhammad and assorted members of the Black Students Organization and let them all hurl large stones at me. From recent events and statements made on this campus, I gather this will be a good cheap method of making these people feel good."

At UCLA, a black student magazine printed an article indicating there is considerable truth to the *Protocols of the Elders of Zion*.[1] For months, the black faculty, when asked their reactions, preferred not to comment. One of them did say that the black students already considered the black faculty to be insufficiently militant, and the professors didn't want to make the gap any wider. Like white liberal faculty members on other campuses, they want to be liked—or at least not too disliked.

Along with quiet white liberal faculty members, most black professors have not opposed the speech codes. But unlike the white liberals many honestly do believe that minority students have to be insulated from barbed language. They do not believe—as I have found out in a number of conversations—that an essential part of an education is to learn to demystify language, to strip it of its ability to demonize and stigmatize you. They do not believe that the way to deal with bigoted language is to answer it with more and better language of your own. This seems very elementary to me, but not to the defenders, black and white, of the speech codes.

"Fighting Words"

Consider University of California president David Gardner. He has imposed a speech code on all the campuses in his university system. Students are to be punished—and this is characteristic of the other codes around the country—if they use "fighting words"— derogatory references to "race, sex, sexual orientation, or disability."

The term "fighting words" comes from a 1942 Supreme Court decision, *Chaplinsky v. New Hampshire*, which ruled that "fighting words" are not protected by the First Amendment. That decision, however, has been in disuse at the High Court for many years. But it is thriving on college campuses.

---

[1]*Protocols of the Elders of Zion:* a document forged c. 1897 alleging that an international Jewish conspiracy was plotting the overthrow of Christian civilization.

In the California code, a word becomes "fighting" if it is directly addressed to "any ordinary person" (presumably, extraordinary people are above all this). These are the kinds of words that are "inherently likely to provoke a violent action, *whether or not they actually do.*" (Emphasis added.)

Moreover, he or she who fires a fighting word at any ordinary person can be reprimanded or dismissed from the university because the perpetrator should "reasonably know" that what he or she has said will interfere with the "victim's ability to pursue effectively his or her education or otherwise participate fully in university programs and activities."

Asked Gary Murikami, chairman of the Gay and Lesbian Association at the University of California, Berkeley: "What does it mean?"

Among those—faculty, law professors, college administrators—who insist such codes are essential to the university's purpose of making *all* students feel at home and thereby able to concentrate on their work, there has been a celebratory resort to the Fourteenth Amendment.

That amendment guarantees "equal protection of the laws" to all, and that means to all students on campus. Accordingly, when the First Amendment rights of those engaging in offensive speech clash with the equality rights of their targets under the Fourteenth Amendment, the First Amendment must give way.

This is the thesis, by the way, of John Powell, legal director of the American Civil Liberties Union, even though that organization has now formally opposed all college speech codes—after a considerable civil war among and within its affiliates.

The battle of the amendments continues, and when harsher codes are called for at some campuses, you can expect the Fourteenth Amendment—which was not intended to censor *speech*—will rise again.

A precedent has been set at, of all places, colleges and universities, that the principle of free speech is merely situational. As college administrators change, so will the extent of free speech on campus. And invariably, permissible speech will become more and more narrowly defined. Once speech can be limited in such subjective ways, more and more expression will be included in what is forbidden.

Freedom of Thought

One of the exceedingly few college presidents who speaks out on the consequences of the anti-free-speech movement is Yale University's Benno Schmidt:

> Freedom of thought must be Yale's central commitment. It is not easy to embrace. It is, indeed, the effort of a lifetime. . . . Much expression that is free may deserve our contempt. We may well be moved to exercise our own freedom to counter it or to ignore it. But universities cannot censor or suppress speech, no matter how obnoxious in content, without violating their justification for existence. . . .

> On some other campuses in this country, values of civility and community have been offered by some as paramount values of the university, even to the extent of superseding freedom of expression.

> Such a view is wrong in principle and, if extended, is disastrous to freedom of thought. . . . The chilling effects on speech of the vagueness and open-ended nature of many universities'

prohibitions . . . are compounded by the fact that these codes are typically enforced by faculty and students who commonly assert that vague notions of community are more important to the academy than freedom of thought and expression. . . .

This is a flabby and uncertain time for freedom in the United States.

On the Public Broadcasting System in June 1991, I was part of a Fred Friendly panel at Stanford University in a debate on speech codes versus freedom of expression. The three black panelists strongly supported the codes. So did the one Asian-American on the panel. But then so did Stanford law professor Thomas Grey, who wrote the Stanford code, and Stanford president Donald Kennedy, who first opposed and then embraced the code. We have a new ecumenicism of those who would control speech for the greater good. It is hardly a new idea, but the mix of advocates is rather new.

But there are other voices. In the national board debate at the ACLU on college speech codes, the first speaker—and I think she had a lot to do with making the final vote against codes unanimous—was Gwen Thomas.

A black community college administrator from Colorado, she is a fiercely persist- 40
ent exposer of racial discrimination.

She started by saying, "I have always felt as a minority person that we have to protect the rights of all because if we infringe on the rights of any persons, we'll be next.

"As for providing a nonintimidating educational environment, our young people have to learn to grow up on college campuses. We have to teach them how to deal with adversarial situations. They have to learn how to survive offensive speech they find wounding and hurtful." Gwen Thomas is an educator—an endangered species in higher education.

Questions for Discussion and Writing

1. With which of the assumptions underlying the imposition of speech codes does Hentoff disagree? How do Hentoff's experiences or examples from campuses around the country challenge the presumed benefits of speech codes?
2. How does Hentoff frame the debate about whether the First or the Fourteenth Amendment ought to be given more consideration?
3. Does your own experience in classrooms confirm or disprove Hentoff's contention that the chilling effects on campuses have mostly been felt by students with moderate views? Have you ever felt inhibited from discussing issues because of the circumstances described by Hentoff?

Judy Blume

· ·

Judy Blume (b. 1938), a writer of juvenile and adult fiction, has often been in the position she discusses—that of having her books for children censored, including Are You There God? It's Me, Margaret *(1970),* Blubber *(1974), and* Tiger Eyes *(1981). She is also the editor of* Places I Never Meant to Be: Original Stories by Censored Writers *(1999). Blume's recent works include* Double Fudge *(2002), a continuation of her very popular series. This editorial, which first appeared in the* New York Times *on October 22, 1999,*

How does the imagery in this film still from Harry Potter and the Sorcerer's Stone *(2001) place him in the context of traditional sorcerers, albeit in a benign guise?*

defends the phenomenally successful Harry Potter series against those who wish to ban it from school libraries.

IS HARRY POTTER EVIL?

I happened to be in London last summer on the very day *Harry Potter and the Prisoner of Azkaban,* the third book in the wildly popular series by J. K. Rowling, was published. I couldn't believe my good fortune. I rushed to the bookstore to buy a copy, knowing this simple act would put me up there with the best grandmas in the world. The book was still months away from publication in the United States, and I have an 8-year-old grandson who is a big Harry Potter fan.

It's a good thing when children enjoy books, isn't it? Most of us think so. But like many children's books these days, the Harry Potter series has recently come under fire. In Minnesota, Michigan, New York, California and South Carolina, parents who feel the books promote interest in the occult have called for their removal from classrooms and school libraries.

I knew this was coming. The only surprise is that it took so long—as long as it took for the zealots who claim they're protecting children from evil (and evil can be found lurking everywhere these days) to discover that children actually like these books. If children are excited about a book, it must be suspect.

I'm not exactly unfamiliar with this line of thinking, having had various books of mine banned from schools over the last 20 years. In my books, it's reality that's seen as corrupting. With Harry Potter, the perceived danger is fantasy. After all, Harry and his classmates attend the celebrated Hogwarts School of Witchcraft and Wizardry. According to certain adults, these stories teach witchcraft, sorcery and satanism. But hey, if it's not one "ism," it's another. I mean Madeleine L'Engle's *A Wrinkle in Time* has been targeted by censors for promoting New Ageism, and Mark Twain's *Adventures of Huckleberry Finn* for promoting racism. Gee, where does that leave the kids?

The real danger is not in the books, but in laughing off those who would ban them. 5 The protests against Harry Potter follow a tradition that has been growing since the early 1980's and often leaves school principals trembling with fear that is then passed down to teachers and librarians.

What began with the religious right has spread to the politically correct. (Remember the uproar in Brooklyn last year when a teacher was criticized for reading a book entitled *Nappy Hair* to her class?) And now the gate is open so wide that some parents believe they have the right to demand immediate removal of any book for any reason from school or classroom libraries. The list of gifted teachers and librarians who find their jobs in jeopardy for defending their students' right to read, to imagine, to question, grows every year.

My grandson was bewildered when I tried to explain why some adults don't want their children reading about Harry Potter. "But that doesn't make any sense!" he said. J. K. Rowling is on a book tour in America right now. She's probably befuddled by the brouhaha, too. After all, she was just trying to tell a good story.

My husband and I like to reminisce about how, when we were 9, we read straight through L. Frank Baum's Oz series, books filled with wizards and witches. And you know what those subversive tales taught us? That we loved to read! In those days I used to dream of flying. I may have been small and powerless in real life, but in my imagination I was able to soar.

At the rate we're going, I can imagine next year's headline: "'Goodnight Moon'[1] Banned for Encouraging Children to Communicate With Furniture." And we all know where that can lead, don't we?

Questions for Discussion and Writing

1. Why is Blume alarmed by the growing trend of parents petitioning school libraries to remove children's books from their shelves? How does she characterize those who want books (such as the Harry Potter series) to be banned because of fantasy elements that "teach" witchcraft, sorcery, and satanism?

2. How does Blume structure her editorial to stress the growing nature of this trend and its apparent indiscriminate hysteria? What tools (such as mockery) does she use to make her case?

3. The issue is whether parents have the right to demand that schools censor their children's reading materials. In your opinion, do they, and if so, how should they exercise this right? There are numerous Web sites devoted to the Harry Potter censorship controversy. Check one of these and compare its statements with your own views.

---

[1]*Goodnight Moon:* A classic work in children's literature by Margaret Wise Brown, with illustrations by Clement Hurd; first published in 1947.

FICTION

Joaquim María Machado de Assis

Joáquim María Machado de Assis (1839–1908) was born in Rio de Janeiro, where he lived most of his life. His first great success was Epitaph of a Small Winner *(1881), written from a startlingly original point of view, namely, the posthumous memoirs of the narrator, Braz Cubas—a tongue-in-cheek account of his life.*

Machado's second novel, Philosopher or Dog? *(1891), and his acknowledged masterpiece,* Dom Casmurro *(1900), both feature protagonists who are reflective skeptics tinged with madness. These unreliable narrators are a feature of his work. His close attention to the protagonist's stream of consciousness, his cool irony, unexpected juxtaposition of times, characters, and value systems conveyed in a forceful, unique style anticipate many features of the twentieth-century novel. He is now acknowledged by critics to be a master of the early modern novel, the equal of Gustave Flaubert and Henry James. His complete works fill thirty-one volumes, and he is the author of over a hundred short stories, of which "A Canary's Ideas," translated by Jack Schmitt and Lorie Ishimatsu (1976), is typical. In this story, an egocentric, reasoning canary forms his impression of the universe according to what surrounds him at the moment.*

A Canary's Ideas

A man by the name of Macedo, who had a fancy for ornithology, related to some friends an incident so extraordinary that no one took him seriously. Some came to believe he had lost his mind. Here is a summary of his narration.

At the beginning of last month, as I was walking down the street, a carriage darted past me and nearly knocked me to the ground. I escaped by quickly side-stepping into a secondhand shop. Neither the racket of the horse and carriage nor my entrance stirred the proprietor, dozing in a folding chair at the back of the shop. He was a man of shabby appearance: his beard was the color of dirty straw, and his head was covered by a tattered cap which probably had not found a buyer. One could not guess that there was any story behind him, as there could have been behind some of the objects he sold, nor could one sense in him that austere, disillusioned sadness inherent in the objects which were remnants of past lives.

The shop was dark and crowded with the sort of old, bent, broken, tarnished, rusted articles ordinarily found in secondhand shops, and everything was in that state of semidisorder befitting such an establishment. This assortment of articles, though banal, was interesting. Pots without lids, lids without pots, buttons, shoes, locks, a black shirt, straw hats, fur hats, picture frames, binoculars, dress coats, a fencing foil, a stuffed dog, a pair of slippers, gloves, nondescript vases, epaulets, a velvet satchel, two hatracks, a slingshot, a thermometer, chairs, a lithographed portrait by the late Sisson, a backgammon board, two wire masks for some future Carnival—all this and more, which I either did not see or do not remember, filled the shop in the area around the door, propped up, hung, or displayed in glass cases as old as the objects inside them. Further inside the shop were many objects of similar appearance. Predominant were the large objects—chests of drawers, chairs, and beds—some of which were stacked on top of others which were lost in the darkness.

I was about to leave, when I saw a cage hanging in the doorway. It was as old as everything else in the shop, and I expected it to be empty so it would fit in with the general appearance of desolation. However, it wasn't empty. Inside, a canary was hopping about. The bird's color, liveliness, and charm added a note of life and youth to that heap of wreckage. It was the last passenger of some wrecked ship, who had arrived in the shop as complete and happy as it had originally been. As soon as I looked at the bird, it began to hop up and down, from perch to perch, as if it meant to tell me that a ray of sunshine was frolicking in the midst of that cemetery I'm using this image to describe the canary only because I'm speaking to rhetorical people, but the truth is that the canary thought about neither cemetery nor sun, according to what it told me later. Along with the pleasure the sight of the bird brought me I felt indignation regarding its destiny and softly murmured these bitter words.

"What detestable owner had the nerve to rid himself of this bird for a few cents?   5 Or what indifferent soul, not wishing to keep his late master's pet, gave it away to some child, who sold it so he could make a bet on a soccer game?"

The canary, sitting on top of its perch, trilled this reply.

"Whoever you may be, you're certainly not in your right mind. I had no detestable owner, nor was I given to any child to sell. Those are the delusions of a sick person. Go and get yourself cured, my friend . . ."

"What?" I interrupted, not having had time to become astonished. "So your master didn't sell you to this shop? It wasn't misery or laziness that brought you, like a ray of sunshine, to this cemetery?"

"I don't know what you mean by 'sunshine' or 'cemetery.' If the canaries you've seen use the first of those names, so much the better, because it sounds pretty, but really, I'm sure you're confused."

"Excuse me, but you couldn't have come here by chance, all alone. Has your mas-   10 ter always been that man sitting over there?"

"What master? That man over there is my servant. He gives me food and water every day, so regularly that if I were to pay him for his services, it would be no small sum, but canaries don't pay their servants. In fact, since the world belongs to canaries, it would be extravagant for them to pay for what is already in the world."

Astonished by these answers, I didn't know what to marvel at more—the language or the ideas. The language, even though it entered my ears as human speech, was uttered by the bird in the form of charming trills. I looked all around me so I could determine if I were awake and saw that the street was the same, and the shop was the same dark, sad, musty place. The canary, moving from side, was waiting for me to speak. I then asked if it were lonely for the infinite blue space . . .

"But, my dear man," trilled the canary, "what does 'infinite blue space' mean?"

"But, pardon me, what do you think of this world? What is the world to you?"

"The world," retorted the canary, with a certain professional air, "is a secondhand   15 shop with a small rectangular bamboo cage hanging from a nail. The canary is lord of the cage it lives in and the shop that surrounds it. Beyond that, everything is illusion and deception."

With this, the old man woke up and approached me, dragging his feet. He asked me if I wanted to buy the canary. I asked if he had acquired it in the same way he had acquired the rest of the objects he sold and learned that he had bought it from a barber, along with a set of razors.

"The razors are in very good condition," he said.

"I only want the canary."

I paid for it, ordered a huge, circular cage of wood and wire, and had it placed on the veranda of my house so the bird could see the garden, the fountain, and a bit of blue sky.

It was my intention to do a lengthy study of this phenomenon, without saying anything to anyone until I could astound the world with my extraordinary discovery. I began by alphabetizing the canary's language in order to study its structure, its relation to music, the bird's appreciation of aesthetics; its ideas and recollections. When this philological and psychological analysis was done, I entered specifically into the study of canaries: their origin, their early history, the geology and flora of the Canary Islands, the bird's knowledge of navigation, and so forth. We conversed for hours while I took notes, and it waited, hopped about, and trilled.

As I have no family other than two servants, I ordered them not to interrupt me, even to deliver a letter or an urgent telegram or to inform me of an important visitor. Since they both knew about my scientific pursuits, they found my orders perfectly natural and did not suspect that the canary and I understood each other.

Needless to say, I slept little, woke up two or three times each night, wandered about aimlessly, and felt feverish. Finally, I returned to my work in order to reread, add, and emend. I corrected more than one observation, either because I had misunderstood something or because the bird had not expressed it clearly. The definition of the world was one of these. Three weeks after the canary's entrance into my home, I asked it to repeat to me its definition of the world.

"The world," it answered, "is a sufficiently broad garden with a fountain in the middle, flowers, shrubbery, some grass, clear air and a bit of blue up above. The canary, lord of the world, lives in a spacious cage, white and circular, from which it looks out on the rest of the world. Everything else is illusion and deception."

The language of my treatise also suffered some modifications, and I saw that certain conclusions which had seemed simple were actually presumptuous. I still could not write the paper I was to send to the National Museum, the Historical Institute, and the German universities, not due to a lack of material but because I first had to put together all my observations and test their validity. During the last few days, I neither left the house, answered letters, nor wanted to hear from friends or relatives. The canary was everything to me. One of the servants had the job of cleaning the bird's cage and giving it food and water every morning. The bird said nothing to him, as if it knew the man was completely lacking in scientific background. Besides, the service was no more than cursory, as the servant was not a bird lover.

One Saturday I awoke ill, my head and back aching. The doctor ordered complete rest. I was suffering from an excess of studying and was not to read or even think; nor was I even to know what was going on in the city or the rest of the outside world. I remained in this condition for five days. On the sixth day I got up, and only then did I find out that the canary, while under the servant's care, had flown out of its cage. My first impulse was to strangle the servant—I was choking with indignation and collapsed into my chair, speechless and bewildered. The guilty man defended himself, swearing he had been careful, but the wily bird had nevertheless managed to escape.

"But didn't you search for it?"

"Yes, I did, sir. First it flew up to the roof, and I followed it. It flew to a tree, and then who knows where it hid itself? I've been asking around since yesterday. I asked the neighbors and the local farmers, but no one has seen the bird."

I suffered immensely. Fortunately, the fatigue left me within a few hours, and I was soon able to go out to the veranda and the garden. There was no sign of the canary. I ran everywhere, making inquiries and posting announcements, all to no avail. I had already gathered my notes together to write my paper, even though it would be disjointed and incomplete, when I happened to visit a friend who had one of the largest and most beautiful estates on the outskirts of town. We were taking a stroll before dinner when this question was trilled to me:

"Greetings, Senhor Macedo, where have you been since you disappeared?"

It was the canary, perched on the branch of a tree. You can imagine how I reacted   30 and what I said to the bird. My friend presumed I was mad, but the opinions of friends are of no importance to me. I spoke tenderly to the canary and asked it to come home and continue our conversations in that world of ours, composed of a garden, a fountain, a veranda, and a white circular cage.

"What garden? What fountain?"

"The world, my dear bird."

"What world? I see you haven't lost any of your annoying professorial habits. The world," it solemnly concluded, "is an infinite blue space, with the sun up above."

Indignant, I replied that if I were to believe what it said, the world could be anything—it had even been a secondhand shop . . .

"A secondhand shop?" it trilled to its heart's content. "But is there really such a   35 thing as a secondhand shop?"

Questions for Discussion and Writing

1. In what different circumstances does the narrator encounter the canary? How does the canary redefine its conception of the world to suit each new environment in which it finds itself?
2. What details in the description of Macedo suggest that he sees the canary as a vehicle for self-aggrandizement in the world of ornithology?
3. In what sense might the canary be seen as having a view of life that Macedo lacks and would like to possess? In what way does the narrator's extensive study and observation of the canary suggest that he has become obsessed with writing his treatise?

POETRY

Francis E. W. Harper

Francis Ellen Watkins Harper (1824–1911) was born in Baltimore, the daughter of free blacks. She attended a school run by her uncle and worked as a seamstress and as a teacher. In the 1850s she began actively working and lecturing for the abolitionist cause. Her writing includes Poems on Miscellaneous Subjects *(1854), a volume of antislavery verse that sold 12,000 copies by 1858 and went through some 20 editions;* Sketches of Southern Life *(1872); and a novel,* Iola Leroy *(1892), recognized as the first novel by a black author to describe Reconstruction.*

LEARNING TO READ

Very soon the Yankee teachers
Came down and set up school;
But, oh! how the Rebs did hate it,—
It was agin' their rule.

Our masters always tried to hide   5
Book learning from our eyes;
Knowledge didn't agree with slavery—
'Twould make us all too wise.

But some of us would try to steal
A little from the book,   10
And put the words together,
And learn by hook or crook.

I remember Uncle Caldwell,
Who took pot liquor[1] fat
And greased the pages of his book,   15
And hid it in his hat

And had his master ever seen
The leaves upon his head,
He'd have thought them greasy papers,
But nothing to be read.   20

And there was Mr. Turner's Ben,
Who heard the children spell,
And picked the words right up by heart,
And learned to read 'em well.

---

[1]*pot liquor:* broth in which meat and/or vegetables have cooked.

Well, the Northern folks kept sending   25
The Yankee teachers down;
And they stood right up and helped us,
Though Rebs did sneer and frown.

And, I longed to read my Bible,
For precious words it said;   30
But when I begun to learn it,
Folks just shook their heads,

And said there is no use trying,
Oh! Chloe, you're too late;
But as I was rising sixty,   35
I had no time to wait.

So I got a pair of glasses,
And straight to work I went,
And never stopped till I could read
The hymns and Testament.   40

Then I got a little cabin
A place to call my own—
And I felt as independent
As the queen upon her throne.

Questions for Discussion and Writing

1. What kind of danger did learning to read pose to the system of slavery?
2. What function do the examples of slaves learning to read serve in Harper's poem?
3. What motivates Chloe to learn to read? In what ways does reading change her life for the better?

Linda Hogan

Linda Hogan, Chickasaw poet, novelist, and essayist, was born in 1947 in Denver, Colorado, and grew up in Oklahoma. She taught American Indian studies at the University of Minnesota from 1984–1991 and she is currently professor of American studies and American Indian studies at the University of Colorado. Her poetry has been collected in Seeing through the Sun *(1985), which received an American Book Award from the Before Columbus Foundation;* The Book of Medicines *(1993); and* Solar Storms *(1996). She has also published short stories, one of which, "Aunt Moon's Young Man," was featured in* Best American Short Stories *(1989). Her novel* Mean Spirit *was nominated for a Pulitzer Prize (1990). Hogan's latest works are* The Woman Who Watches over the World: A Native Memoir *(2001) and (with Brenda Peterson)* Sightings: The Gray Whale's Mysterious Journey *(2002). In "Workday" she uses the occasion of a bus ride she took when returning from working at the University of Colorado to explore the gap between Native Americans and her middle-class white coworkers.*

WORKDAY

I go to work
though there are those who were missing today
from their homes.
I ride the bus
and I do not think of children without food   5
or how my sisters are chained to prison beds.

I go to the university
and out for lunch
and listen to the higher-ups
tell me all they have read   10
about Indians
and how to analyze this poem.
They know us
better than we know ourselves.

I ride the bus home   15
and sit behind the driver.
We talk about the weather
and not enough exercise.
I don't mention Victor Jara's[1] mutilated hands
or men next door   20
in exile
or my own family's grief over the lost child.

When I get off the bus
I look back at the light in the windows
and the heads bent   25
and how the women are all alone
in each seat
framed in the windows
and the men are coming home,
then I see them walking on the Avenue,   30
the beautiful feet,

the perfect legs
even with their spider veins,
the broken knees
with pins in them,   35
the thighs with their cravings,
the pelvis
and small back

---

[1]*Victor Jara:* Chilean folksinger and political activist (1932–1973) instrumental in the election of Salvador Allende. Jara was arrested, tortured, and beaten, his hands and wrists broken, before being machine-gunned to death after the coup by Augusto Pinochet.

with its soft down,
the shoulders which bend forward   40
and forward and forward
to protect the heart from pain.

Questions for Discussion and Writing

1. How does the poem raise the question of whether the speaker has irrevocably lost touch with her own people by working at a university where she is little more than a token Native American?
2. What kind of connection does the speaker feel with the Native American laborers on the bus?
3. What images express the speaker's grief at the psychological and physical costs for Native Americans trying to survive in contemporary American society?

Thinking Critically About the Image

Jean-Honoré Fragonard (1732–1806), a French painter whose polished, delicate scenes are praised for his fluid brush strokes, is known for the vitality of his portraits and landscapes depicting the gaiety of the age of Louis XV. This portrait, *A Young Girl Reading,* was painted quickly, in less than an hour. Fragonard reveals a girl intently focused on the world opened up to her by reading, before she is cast into the real world of domesticity.

1. What do you think the young girl is reading—a work of philosophy, her Bible, or a novel?
2. How do the soft colors and curves add to the mood of quiet intensity?
3. How does this painting dissolve the boundaries between a sketch and a finished painting, and why is this condition appropriate for a girl who is in the process of becoming an adult?

Connections

Chapter 3: The Value of Education

Frederick Douglass,   *Learning to Read and Write*
How do both Douglass and Jonathan Kozol emphasize the empowerment that literacy produces?

Jonathan Kozol, *The Human Cost of an Illiterate Society*
In what sense is the predicament facing an illiterate person comparable to that of the characters Betty and Bill in David Ives's play *Sure Thing* (Ch. 5) as they try to navigate in an always changing social situation?

William A. Henry III, *In Defense of Elitism*
To what extent is the situation Henry describes analogous to the "tragedy of the commons" discussed by Garrett Hardin in "Lifeboat Ethics" (Ch. 11)?

Richard Rodriguez, *On Becoming a Chicano*
Discuss the ambivalence both Rodriguez and Linda Hogan feel in relationship to losing touch with their cultures as they advance in the academic world.

Sabine Reichel, *Learning What Was Never Taught*
In what sense might education in postwar Germany, as examined by Reichel, represent an extention of "Propaganda Under a Dictatorship" described by Aldous Huxley (Ch. 4)?

David Rothenberg, *How the Web Destroys the Quality of Students' Research Papers*
Compare the different perspectives on using the Web by Rothenberg and Bill Gates in the excerpt from "The Road Ahead" (Ch. 9).

John Milton, *Areopagitica: Defense of Books*
What limits, if any, should be placed on speech, according to Milton and Judy Blume in "Is Harry Potter Evil?" (Ch. 3)?

Nat Hentoff, *"Speech Codes" on the Campus and Problems of Free Speech*
Compare Hentoff's view on censorship with John Milton's view, expressed four hundred years earlier, in "Areopagitica: Defense of Books."

Judy Blume, *Is Harry Potter Evil?*
To what extent do Blume and Eric Schlosser in "Kid Kustomers" (Ch. 5) discuss the controversial issue of marketing strategies directed at children?

Joaquim María Machado de Assis, *A Canary's Ideas*
How do Machado de Assis and Anna Kamieńska in "Funny" (Ch. 1) use birds in their works to symbolize a dispassionate perception of human life?

Francis E. W. Harper, *Learning to Read*
Compare the views of Harper and Peggy Seeger in "I'm Gonna Be an Engineer" (Ch. 9) on empowerment for women.

Linda Hogan, *Workday*
In what ways do Hogan and Bertolt Brecht in "A Worker Reads History" (Ch. 7) adopt viewpoints of those who are thought of as marginal in relationship to mainstream society?

CHAPTER 4

Paul Gaugin, Ta Matete *("The Market"), 1892.*
Erich Lessing/Art Resource, NY. Kunstmuseum, Basel, Switzerland.

Perspectives on Language

The limits of my language are the limits of my world.
—Ludwig Wittgenstein, *Tractatus Logico-Philosophicus*

THE SELECTIONS IN THIS CHAPTER ATTEST TO the value of literacy and the importance of being able to communicate. Personal accounts by Helen Keller and Temple Grandin are particularly fascinating in demonstrating how the creation of an identity depends on language. Alison Lurie broadens our concept of what language is and analyzes how clothing can make statements about who we are and how we wish to be perceived. Aldous Huxley reveals how propaganda has been used to deceive by manipulating emotions and beliefs. Rosemarie Garland-Thomson in her essay broadens our concept of the social dimensions of language used to define "disability."

Deborah Tannen inquires into the reasons men and women have so much difficulty in communicating with each other. George Lakoff and Stuart Hirschberg deal with contemporary social issues connected with language: Do metaphors used to express anger contain scenarios that govern our actions? Should we take another look at the rhetorical techniques advertisers use so successfully?

Anthony Burgess, in his short work of fiction, invents a dialect to depict the gap in social class between his narrator, a violent teenager, and the doctors who are treating him.

The poem by Ted Hughes offers a witty commentary on the elusive nature of language through his mythic creation, Crow.

NONFICTION

Helen Keller

Helen Keller (1880–1968) was born, without handicaps, in Alabama; she contracted a disease at the age of nineteen months that left her both blind and deaf. Because of the extraordinary efforts of Annie Sullivan, Keller overcame her isolation and learned what words meant. She graduated with honors from Radcliffe and devoted most of her life to helping the blind and deaf through the American Foundation for the Blind. She was awarded the Presidential Medal of Freedom by Lyndon Johnson in 1964. "The Day Language Came into My Life" is taken from her autobiography, The Story of My Life *(1902). This work served as the basis for a film,* The Unconquered *(1954), and the acclaimed play by William Gibson,* The Miracle Worker *(1959), which was subsequently made into a movie with Anne Bancroft and Patty Duke.*

THE DAY LANGUAGE CAME INTO MY LIFE

The most important day I remember in all my life is the one on which my teacher, Anne Mansfield Sullivan, came to me. I am filled with wonder when I consider the immeasurable contrast between the two lives which it connects. It was the third of March 1887, three months before I was seven years old.

On the afternoon of that eventful day, I stood on the porch, dumb, expectant. I guessed vaguely from my mother's signs and from the hurrying to and fro in the house that something unusual was about to happen, so I went to the door and waited on the steps. The afternoon sun penetrated the mass of honeysuckle that covered the porch and fell on my upturned face. My fingers lingered almost unconsciously on the familiar leaves and blossoms which had just come forth to greet the sweet southern spring. I did not know what the future held of marvel or surprise for me. Anger and bitterness had preyed upon me continually for weeks and a deep languor had succeeded this passionate struggle.

Have you ever been at sea in a dense fog, when it seemed as if a tangible white darkness shut you in, and the great ship, tense and anxious, groped her way toward the shore with plummet and sounding-line, and you waited with beating heart for something to happen? I was like that ship before my education began, only I was without compass or sounding-line and had no way of knowing how near the harbor was. "Light! give me light!" was the wordless cry of my soul, and the light of love shone on me in that very hour.

I felt approaching footsteps. I stretched out my hand as I supposed to my mother. Someone took it, and I was caught up and held close in the arms of her who had come to reveal all things to me, and, more than all things else, to love me.

The morning after my teacher came she led me into her room and gave me a doll. 5
The little blind children at the Perkins Institution had sent it and Laura Bridgman had dressed it; but I did not know this until afterward. When I had played with it a little

while, Miss Sullivan slowly spelled into my hand the word "d-o-l-l." I was at once in-terested in this finger play and tried to imitate it. When I finally succeeded in making the letters correctly I was flushed with childish pleasure and pride. Running down-stairs to my mother I held up my hand and made the letters for doll. I did not know that I was spelling a word or even that words existed; I was simply making my fingers go in monkeylike imitation. In the days that followed I learned to spell in this un-comprehending way a great many words, among them *pin, hat, cup* and a few verbs like *sit, stand* and *walk.* But my teacher had been with me several weeks before I un-derstood that everything has a name.

One day, while I was playing with my new doll, Miss Sullivan put my big rag doll into my lap also, spelled "d-o-l-l" and tried to make me understand that "d-o-l-l" applied to both. Earlier in the day we had had a tussle over the words "m-u-g" and "w-a-t-e-r." Miss Sullivan had tried to impress it upon me that "m-u-g" is *mug* and that "w-a-t-e-r" is *water,* but I persisted in confounding the two. In despair she had dropped the subject for the time, only to renew it at the first opportunity. I became impatient at her repeated attempts and, seizing the new doll, I dashed it upon the floor. I was keenly delighted when I felt the fragments of the broken doll at my feet. Neither sor-row nor regret followed my passionate outburst. I had not loved the doll. In the still, dark world in which I lived there was no strong sentiment or tenderness. I felt my teacher sweep the fragments to one side of the hearth, and I had a sense of satisfaction that the cause of my discomfort was removed. She brought me my hat, and I knew I was going out into the warm sunshine. This thought, if a wordless sensation may be called a thought, made me hop and skip with pleasure.

We walked down the path to the well-house, attracted by the fragrance of the hon-eysuckle with which it was covered. Some one was drawing water and my teacher placed my hand under the spout. As the cool stream gushed over one hand she spelled into the other the word *water,* first slowly, then rapidly. I stood still, my whole attention fixed upon the motions of her fingers. Suddenly I felt a misty consciousness as of something forgotten—a thrill of returning thought; and somehow the mystery of language was re-vealed to me. I knew then that "w-a-t-e-r" meant the wonderful cool something that was flowing over my hand. The living word awakened my soul, gave it light, hope, joy, set it free! There were barriers still, it is true, but barriers that could in time be swept away.

I left the well-house eager to learn. Everything had a name, and each name gave birth to a new thought. As we returned to the house every object which I touched seemed to quiver with life. That was because I saw everything with the strange, new sight that had come to me. On entering the door I remembered the doll I had broken. I felt my way to the hearth and picked up the pieces. I tried vainly to put them together. Then my eyes filled with tears; for I realized what I had done, and for the first time I felt repentance and sorrow.

I learned a great many new words that day. I do not remember what they all were; but I do know that *mother, father, sister, teacher* were among them—words that were to make the world blossom for me, "like Aaron's rod, with flowers." It would have been difficult to find a happier child than I was as I lay in my crib at the close of that event-ful day and lived over the joys it had brought me, and for the first time longed for a new day to come.

Questions for Discussion and Writing

1. Why is it important for the reader to understand Keller's state of mind in the days preceding the events she describes?
2. How did Keller's understanding of language when she became conscious of the meaning of words differ from her previous experience of spelling them by rote?
3. How does the episode of the broken doll reveal how much Keller was transformed by the experience she describes?

Temple Grandin

. . . .

Temple Grandin has a Ph.D. in animal science from the University of Illinois. She has designed many of the livestock-handling facilities in the United States and in other countries. What makes her achievement astounding is the fact that she is autistic and is one of the few who have overcome this neurological impairment enough to communicate with others. The following selection is drawn from her autobiography, Thinking in Pictures: And Other Reports from My Life with Autism *(1996). She has written (with Catherine Johnson)* Animals in Translation: Using the Mysteries of Autism to Decode Animal Behavior *(2005).*

THINKING IN PICTURES

Processing Nonvisual Information

Autistics[1] have problems learning things that cannot be thought about in pictures. The easiest words for an autistic child to learn are nouns, because they directly relate to pictures. Highly verbal autistic children like I was can sometimes learn how to read with phonics. Written words were too abstract for me to remember, but I could laboriously remember the approximately fifty phonetic sounds and a few rules. Lower-functioning children often learn better by association, with the aid of word labels attached to objects in their environment. Some very impaired autistic children learn more easily if words are spelled out with plastic letters they can feel.

Spatial words such as "over" and "under" had no meaning for me until I had a visual image to fix them in my memory. Even now, when I hear the word "under" by itself, I automatically picture myself getting under the cafeteria tables at school during an air-raid drill, a common occurrence on the East Coast during the early fifties. The first memory that any single word triggers is almost always a childhood memory. I can remember the teacher telling us to be quiet and walking single-file into the cafeteria, where six or eight children huddled under each table. If I continue on the same train of thought, more and more associative memories of elementary school emerge. I can remember the teacher scolding me after I hit Alfred for putting dirt on my shoe. All of

---

[1]*autism:* a condition characterized by a delay in the acquisition of speech, resistance to change of any kind, obsessive repetitive body movements, and a withdrawal into fantasy.

these memories play like video-tapes in the VCR in my imagination. If I allow my mind to keep associating, it will wander a million miles away from the word "under," to submarines under the Antarctic and the Beatles song "Yellow Submarine." If I let my mind pause on the picture of the yellow submarine, I then hear the song. As I start humming the song and get to the part about people coming on board, my association switches to the gangway of a ship I saw in Australia.

I also visualize verbs. The word "jumping" triggers a memory of jumping hurdles at the mock Olympics held at my elementary school. Adverbs often trigger inappropriate images—"quickly" reminds me of Nestle's Quik—unless they are paired with a verb, which modifies my visual image. For example, "he ran quickly" triggers an animated image of Dick from the first-grade reading book running fast, and "he walked slowly" slows the image down. As a child, I left out words such as "is," "the," and "it," because they had no meaning by themselves. Similarly, words like "of" and "an" made no sense. Eventually I learned how to use them properly, because my parents always spoke correct English and I mimicked their speech patterns. To this day certain verb conjugations, such as "to be," are absolutely meaningless to me.

When I read, I translate written words into color movies or I simply store a photo of the written page to be read later. When I retrieve the material, I see a photocopy of the page in my imagination. I can then read it like a TelePrompTer. It is likely that Raymond, the autistic savant depicted in the movie *Rain Man,* used a similar strategy to memorize telephone books, maps, and other information. He simply photocopied each page of the phone book into his memory. When he wanted to find a certain number, he just scanned pages of the phone book that were in his mind. To pull information out of my memory, I have to replay the video. Pulling facts up quickly is sometimes difficult, because I have to play bits of different videos until I find the right tape. This takes time.

When I am unable to convert text to pictures, it is usually because the text has no concrete meaning. Some philosophy books and articles about the cattle futures market are simply incomprehensible. It is much easier for me to understand written text that describes something that can be easily translated into pictures. The following sentence from a story in the February 21, 1994, issue of *Time* magazine, describing the Winter Olympics figure-skating championships, is a good example: "All the elements are in place—the spotlights, the swelling waltzes and jazz tunes, the sequined sprites taking to the air." In my imagination, I see the skating rink and skaters. However, if I ponder too long on the word "elements," I will make the inappropriate association of a periodic table on the wall of my high school chemistry classroom. Pausing on the word "sprite" triggers an image of a Sprite can in my refrigerator instead of a pretty young skater.

Teachers who work with autistic children need to understand associative thought patterns. An autistic child will often use a word in an inappropriate manner. Sometimes these uses have a logical associative meaning and other times they don't. For example, an autistic child might say the word "dog" when he wants to go outside. The word "dog" is associated with going outside. In my own case, I can remember both logical and illogical use of inappropriate words. When I was six, I learned to say "prosecution." I had absolutely no idea what it meant, but it sounded nice when I said it, so I used it as an exclamation every time my kite hit the ground. I must have baffled more than a few people who heard me exclaim "Prosecution!" to my downward-spiraling kite.

Discussions with other autistic people reveal similar visual styles of thinking about tasks that most people do sequentially. An autistic man who composes music told me that he makes "sound pictures" using small pieces of other music to create new compositions. A computer programmer with autism told me that he sees the general pattern of the program tree. After he visualizes the skeleton for the program, he simply writes the code for each branch. I use similar methods when I review scientific literature and troubleshoot at meat plants. I take specific findings or observations and combine them to find new basic principles and general concepts.

My thinking pattern always starts with specifics and works toward generalization in an associational and nonsequential way. As if I were attempting to figure out what the picture on a jigsaw puzzle is when only one third of the puzzle is completed, I am able to fill in the missing pieces by scanning my video library. Chinese mathematicians who can make large calculations in their heads work the same way. At first they need an abacus, the Chinese calculator, which consists of rows of beads on wires in a frame. They make calculations by moving the rows of beads. When a mathematician becomes really skilled, he simply visualizes the abacus in his imagination and no longer needs a real one. The beads move on a visualized video abacus in his brain.

Abstract Thought

Growing up, I learned to convert abstract ideas into pictures as a way to understand them. I visualized concepts such as peace or honesty with symbolic images. I thought of peace as a dove, an Indian peace pipe, or TV or newsreel footage of the signing of a peace agreement. Honesty was represented by an image of placing one's hand on the Bible in court. A news report describing a person returning a wallet with all the money in it provided a picture of honest behavior.

The Lord's Prayer was incomprehensible until I broke it down into specific visual   10
images. The power and the glory were represented by a semicircular rainbow and an electrical tower. These childhood visual images are still triggered every time I hear the Lord's Prayer. The words "thy will be done" had no meaning when I was a child, and today the meaning is still vague. Will is a hard concept to visualize. When I think about it, I imagine God throwing a lightning bolt. Another adult with autism wrote that he visualized "Thou art in heaven" as God with an easel above the clouds. "Trespassing" was pictured as black and orange no trespassing signs. The word "Amen" at the end of the prayer was a mystery: a man at the end made no sense.

As a teenager and young adult I had to use concrete symbols to understand abstract concepts such as getting along with people and moving on to the next steps of my life, both of which were always difficult. I knew I did not fit in with my high school peers, and I was unable to figure out what I was doing wrong. No matter how hard I tried, they made fun of me. They called me "workhorse," "tape recorder," and "bones" because I was skinny. At the time I was able to figure out why they called me "workhorse" and "bones," but "tape recorder" puzzled me. Now I realize that I must have sounded like a tape recorder when I repeated things verbatim over and over. But back then I just could not figure out why I was such a social dud. I sought refuge in doing things I was good at, such as working on reroofing the barn or practicing my riding prior to a horse show. Personal relationships made absolutely no sense to me until I developed visual symbols of doors and windows. It was then that I started to understand concepts such as learning the give-and-take of a relationship. I still wonder what would have happened to me if I had not been able to visualize my way in the world.

How does this Time *magazine cover by Steve Liss dramatize the growing frequency and increased public awareness of the disability that Temple Grandin discusses?*

Questions for Discussion and Writing

1. What limitations does Grandin confront in trying to understand abstract ideas and to communicate with other people? What problems did she encounter in high school because of this limitation?

2. In order to explain the radical difference of the way autistics think about things and understand words, Grandin uses analogies. Which of these analogies did you find most effective?

3. Try to translate a passage about an abstract idea (for example, charity or love) by thinking in pictures instead of words. What images did you use to represent these abstract ideas? What insight did this exercise give you into the world of autism?

Deborah Tannen

. . . .

Deborah Tannen teaches linguistics at Georgetown University. She has written many books on the difficulties of communicating across cultural, class, ethnic, and gender boundaries, including You Just Don't Understand: Women and Men in Conversation *(1990) and* The Argument Culture *(1998). The following essay from this book originally appeared in the* Washington Post *(1990). Tannen explains why men and women talk at cross-purposes and don't really listen to each other. Tannen's latest book is* Conversational Style: Analyzing Talk Among Friends *(2005).*

SEX, LIES, AND CONVERSATION

I was addressing a small gathering in a suburban Virginia living room—a women's group that had invited men to join them. Throughout the evening, one man had been particularly talkative, frequently offering ideas and anecdotes, while his wife sat silently beside him on the couch. Toward the end of the evening, I commented that women frequently complain that their husbands don't talk to them. This man quickly concurred. He gestured toward his wife and said, "She's the talker in our family." The room burst into laughter; the man looked puzzled and hurt. "It's true," he explained. "When I come home from work I have nothing to say. If she didn't keep the conversation going, we'd spend the whole evening in silence."

This episode crystallizes the irony that although American men tend to talk more than women in public situations, they often talk less at home. And this pattern is wreaking havoc with marriage.

The pattern was observed by political scientist Andrew Hacker in the late '70s. Sociologist Catherine Kohler Riessman reports in her new book *Divorce Talk* that most of the women she interviewed—but only a few of the men—gave lack of communication as the reason for their divorces. Given the current divorce rate of nearly 50 percent, that amounts to millions of cases in the United States every year—a virtual epidemic of failed conversation.

In my own research, complaints from women about their husbands most often focused not on tangible inequities such as having given up the chance for a career to accompany a husband to his, or doing far more than their share of daily life-support work like cleaning, cooking, social arrangements and errands. Instead, they focused on communication: "He doesn't listen to me," "He doesn't talk to me." I found, as Hacker observed years before, that most wives want their husbands to be, first and foremost, conversational partners, but few husbands share this expectation of their wives.

In short, the image that best represents the current crisis is the stereotypical cartoon scene of a man sitting at the breakfast table with a newspaper held up in front of his face, while a woman glares at the back of it, wanting to talk. 5

Linguistic Battle of the Sexes

How can women and men have such different impressions of communication in marriage? Why the widespread imbalance in their interests and expectations?

In the April issue of *American Psychologist,* Stanford University's Eleanor Maccoby reports the results of her own and other's research showing that children's development is most influenced by the social structure of peer interactions. Boys and girls tend to play with children of their own gender, and their sex-separate groups have different organizational structures and interactive norms.

I believe these systematic differences in childhood socialization make talk between women and men like cross-cultural communication, heir to all the attraction and pitfalls of that enticing but difficult enterprise. My research on men's and women's conversations uncovered patterns similar to those described for children's groups.

For women, as for girls, intimacy is the fabric of relationships, and talk is the thread from which it is woven. Little girls create and maintain friendships by exchanging secrets; similarly, women regard conversation as the cornerstone of friendship. So a woman expects her husband to be a new and improved version of a best friend. What is important is not the individual subjects that are discussed but a sense of closeness, of a life shared, that emerges when people tell their thoughts, feelings, and impressions.

Bonds between boys can be as intense as girls', but they are based less on talking, more on doing things together. Since they don't assume talk is the cement that binds a relationship, men don't know what kind of talk women want and they don't miss it when it isn't there.

Boy's groups are larger, more inclusive, and more hierarchical, so boys must struggle to avoid the subordinate position in the group. This may play a role in women's complaints that men don't listen to them. Some men really don't like to listen, because being the listener makes them feel one-down, like a child listening to adults or an employee to a boss.

But often when women tell men, "You aren't listening," and the men protest, "I am," the men are right. The impression of not listening results from misalignments in the mechanics of conversation. The misalignment begins as soon as a man and a woman take physical positions. This became clear when I studied videotapes made by psychologist Bruce Dorval of children and adults talking to their same-sex best friends. I found that at every age, the girls and women faced each other directly, their eyes anchored on each other's faces. At every age, the boys and men sat at angles to each other and looked elsewhere in the room, periodically glancing at each other. They were obviously attuned to each other, often mirroring each other's movements. But the tendency of men to face away can give women the impression they aren't listening even when they are. A young woman in college was frustrated: Whenever she told her boyfriend she wanted to talk to him, he would lie down on the floor, close his eyes, and put his arm over his face. This signaled to her, "He's taking a nap." But he insisted he was listening extra hard. Normally, he looks around the room, so he is easily distracted. Lying down and covering his eyes helped him concentrate on what she was saying.

Analogous to the physical alignment that women and men take in conversation is their topical alignment. The girls in my study tended to talk at length about one topic, but the boys tended to jump from topic to topic. The second-grade girls exchanged

10

stories about people they knew. The second-grade boys teased, told jokes, noticed things in the room and talked about finding games to play. The sixth-grade girls talked about problems with a mutual friend. The sixth-grade boys talked about 55 different topics, none of which extended over more than a few turns.

Listening to Body Language

Switching topics is another habit that gives women the impression men aren't listening, especially if they switch to a topic about themselves. But the evidence of the 10th-grade boys in my study indicates otherwise. The 10th-grade boys sprawled across their chairs with bodies parallel and eyes straight ahead, rarely looking at each other. They looked as if they were riding in a car, staring out the windshield. But they were talking about their feelings. One boy was upset because a girl had told him he had a drinking problem, and the other was feeling alienated from all his friends.

Now, when a girl told a friend about a problem, the friend responded by asking   15
probing questions and expressing agreement and understanding. But the boys dismissed each other's problems. Todd assured Richard that his drinking was "no big problem" because "sometimes you're funny when you're off your butt." And when Todd said he felt left out, Richard responded, "Why should you? You know more people than me."

Women perceive such responses as belittling and unsupportive. But the boys seemed satisfied with them. Whereas women reassure each other by implying, "You shouldn't feel bad because I've had similar experiences," men do so by implying, "You shouldn't feel bad because your problems aren't so bad."

There are even simpler reasons for women's impression that men don't listen. Linguist Lynette Hirschman found that women make more listener-noise, such as "mhm," "uhuh," and "yeah," to show "I'm with you." Men, she found, more often give silent attention. Women who expect a stream of listener-noise interpret silent attention as no attention at all.

Women's conversational habits are as frustrating to men as men's are to women. Men who expect silent attention interpret a stream of listener-noise as overreaction or impatience. Also, when women talk to each other in a close, comfortable setting, they often overlap, finish each other's sentences and anticipate what the other is about to say. This practice, which I call "participatory listenership," is often perceived by men as interruption, intrusion and lack of attention.

A parallel difference caused a man to complain about his wife, "She just wants to talk about her own point of view. If I show her another view, she gets mad at me." When most women talk to each other, they assume a conversationalist's job is to express agreement and support. But many men see their conversational duty as pointing out the other side of an argument. This is heard as disloyalty by women, and refusal to offer the requisite support. It is not that women don't want to see other points of view, but that they prefer them phrased as suggestions and inquiries rather than as direct challenges.

In his book *Fighting for Life,* Walter Ong points out that men use "agonistic" or   20
warlike, oppositional formats to do almost anything; thus discussion becomes debate, and conversation a competitive sport. In contrast, women see conversation as a ritual

means of establishing rapport. If Jane tells a problem and June says she has a similar one, they walk away feeling closer to each other. But this attempt at establishing rapport can backfire when used with men. Men take too literally women's ritual "troubles talk," just as women mistake men's ritual challenges for real attack.

The Sounds of Silence

These differences begin to clarify why women and men have such different expectations about communication in marriage. For women, talk creates intimacy. Marriage is an orgy of closeness: you can tell your feelings and thoughts, and still be loved. Their greatest fear is being pushed away. But men live in a hierarchical world, where talk maintains independence and status.They are on guard to protect themselves from being put down and pushed around.

This explains the paradox of the talkative man who said of his silent wife, "She's the talker." In the public setting of a guest lecture, he felt challenged to show his intelligence and display his understanding of the lecture. But at home, where he has nothing to prove and no one to defend against, he is free to remain silent. For his wife, being home means she is free from the worry that something she says might offend someone, or spark disagreement, or appear to be showing off; at home she is free to talk.

The communication problems that endanger marriage can't be fixed by mechanical engineering. They require a new conceptual framework about the role of talk in human relationships. Many of the psychological explanations that have become second nature may not be helpful, because they tend to blame either women (for not being assertive enough) or men (for not being in touch with their feelings). A sociolinguistic approach by which male-female conversation is seen as cross-cultural communication allows us to understand the problem and forge solutions without blaming either party.

Once the problem is understood, improvement comes naturally, as it did to the young woman and her boyfriend who seemed to go to sleep when she wanted to talk. Previously, she had accused him of not listening, and he had refused to change his behavior, since that would be admitting fault. But then she learned about and explained to him the differences in women's and men's habitual ways of aligning themselves in conversation. The next time she told him she wanted to talk, he began, as usual, by lying down and covering his eyes. When the familiar negative reaction bubbled up, she reassured herself that he really was listening. But then he sat up and looked at her. Thrilled, she asked why. He said, "You like me to look at you when we talk, so I'll try to do it." Once he saw their differences as cross-cultural rather than right and wrong, he independently altered his behavior.

Women who feel abandoned and deprived when their husbands won't listen to or 25 report daily news may be happy to discover their husbands trying to adapt once they understand the place of small talk in women's relationships. But if their husbands don't adapt, the women may still be comforted that for men, this is not a failure of intimacy. Accepting the difference, the wives may look to their friends or family for that kind of talk. And husbands who can't provide it shouldn't feel their wives have made unreasonable demands. Some couples will still decide to divorce, but at least their decisions will be based on realistic expectations.

In these times of resurgent ethnic conflicts, the world desperately needs cross-cultural understanding. Like charity, successful cross-cultural communication should begin at home.

Questions for Discussion and Writing

1. What different objectives do men and women pursue in conversations? How do these differences reveal themselves in verbal and nonverbal behavior?
2. How do the extended examples Tannen presents about two specific couples illustrate her thesis?
3. Evaluate her suggestions for improving communication between men and women. In your opinion, would they work? Why or why not?

George Lakoff

George Lakoff is a professor of linguistics at the University of California at Berkeley. He is coauthor (with Rafael Nuñez) of Where Mathematics Come From *(2000) and (with Mark Johnson) of* Metaphors We Live By *(2003). Lakoff is also the author of* Moral Politics: How Liberals and Conservatives Think *(2nd ed., 2002),* Don't Think of an Elephant *(2004), and* Women, Fire, and Dangerous Things: What Categories Reveal About the Mind *(1987), from which the following excerpts are drawn. Lakoff believes that rather than being simple expressions of feeling, the language used to express anger reveals a number of scenarios (anger/appeasement, anger/retribution) that determine not only how we express anger but how we think about it. A disturbing manifestation of how we conceptualize and express anger can be seen in metaphors that result in blaming the victim.*

ANGER

The Conceptualization of Feeling

Emotions are often considered to be feelings alone, and as such they are viewed as being devoid of conceptual content. As a result, the study of emotions is usually not taken seriously by students of semantics and conceptual structure. A topic such as the logic of emotions would seem on this view to be a contradiction in terms, since emotions, being devoid of conceptual content, would give rise to no inferences at all, or at least none of any interest.

I would like to argue that the opposite is true, that emotions have an extremely complex conceptual structure, which gives rise to a wide variety of nontrivial inferences. The work I will be presenting is based on joint research by myself and Zoltán Kövecses. Kövecses had suggested that the conceptual structure of emotions could be studied in detail using techniques devised by Mark Johnson and myself for the systematic investigation of expressions that are understood metaphorically. English has an extremely large range of such expressions. What we set out to do was to study them systematically to see if any coherent conceptual structure emerged.

At first glance, the conventional expressions used to talk about anger seem so diverse that finding any coherent system would seem impossible. For example, if we look up *anger* in, say, *Roget's University Thesaurus,* we find about three hundred entries, most of which have something or other to do with anger, but the thesaurus doesn't tell us exactly what. Many of these are idioms, and they seem too diverse to reflect any coherent cognitive model. Here are some sample sentences using such idioms:

- He *lost his cool.*
- She was *looking daggers* at me.
- I almost *burst a blood vessel.*
- He was *foaming at the mouth.*
- You're beginning to *get to me.*
- You make my *blood boil.*
- He's *wrestling* with his anger.
- Watch out! He's *on a short fuse.*
- He's just *letting off steam.*
- Don't *get a hernia!*
- Try to *keep a grip on yourself.*
- Don't *fly off the handle.*
- When I told him, he *blew up.*
- He *channeled* his anger into something constructive.
- He was *red with anger.*
- He was *blue in the face.*
- He *appeased* his anger.
- He was *doing a slow burn.*
- He *suppressed* his anger.
- She kept *bugging* me.
- When I told my mother, *she had a cow.*

What do these expressions have to do with anger, and what do they have to do with each other? We will be arguing that they are not random. When we look at inferences among these expressions, it becomes clear that there must be a systematic structure of some kind. We know, for example, that someone who is foaming at the mouth has lost his cool. We know that someone who is looking daggers at you is likely to be doing a slow burn or be on a short fuse. We know that someone whose blood is boiling has not had his anger appeased. We know that someone who has channeled his anger into something constructive has not had a cow. How do we know these things? Is it just that each idiom has a literal meaning and the inferences are based on the literal meanings? Or is there something more going on? What we will try to show is that there is a coherent conceptual organization underlying all these expressions and that much of it is metaphorical and metonymical in nature.

Metaphor and Metonymy

The analysis we are proposing begins with the common folk theory of the physiolog-   5
ical effects of anger:

> The physiological effects of anger are increased body heat, increased internal pres-
> sure (blood pressure, muscular pressure), agitation, and interference with ac-
> curate perception.
> As anger increases, its physiological effects increase.
> There is a limit beyond which the physiological effects of anger impair normal
> functioning.
> We use this folk theory in large measure to tell when someone is angry on the basis
> of their appearance—as well as to signal anger or hide it. In doing this, we make
> use of a general metonymic principle:
> The physiological effects of an emotion stand for the emotion.
> Given this principle, the folk theory given above yields a system of metonymies
> for anger:

Body heat

- Don't get *hot under the collar.*
- Billy's a *hothead.*
- They were having a *heated argument.*
- When the cop gave her a ticket, she got all *hot and bothered* and started cursing.

Internal pressure

- Don't get a *hernia!*
- When I found out, I almost *burst a blood vessel.*
- He almost had a *hemorrhage.*

Increased body heat and/or blood pressure is assumed to cause redness in the face and
neck area, and such redness can also metonymically indicate anger.

Redness in face and neck area

- She was *scarlet with rage.*
- He got *red with anger.*
- He was *flushed with anger.*

Agitation

- She was *shaking* with anger.
- I was *hopping mad.*
- He was *quivering with rage.*
- He's *all worked up.*
- There's no need to get so *excited* about it!
- She's *all wrought up.*
- You look *upset.*

Interference with accurate perception

- She was *blind with rage.*
- I was beginning to *see red.*
- I was so mad I *couldn't see straight.*

Each of these expressions indicate the presence of anger via its supposed physiological effects.

The folk theory of physiological effects, especially the part that emphasizes HEAT, forms the basis of the most general metaphor for anger: ANGER IS HEAT. There are two versions of this metaphor, one where the heat is applied to fluids, the other where it is applied to solids. When it is applied to fluids, we get: ANGER IS THE HEAT OF A FLUID IN A CONTAINER. The specific motivation for this consists of the HEAT, INTERNAL PRESSURE, and AGITATION parts of the folk theory. When ANGER IS HEAT is applied to solids, we get the version ANGER IS FIRE, which is motivated by the HEAT and REDNESS aspects of the folk theory of physiological effects.

As we will see shortly, the fluid version is much more highly elaborated. The reason for this, we surmise, is that in our overall conceptual system we have the general metaphor:

The body is a container for the emotions.

- He was *filled* with anger.
- She couldn't *contain* her joy.
- She was *brimming* with rage.
- Try to get your anger *out of your system.*

The ANGER IS HEAT metaphor, when applied to fluids, combines with the metaphor THE BODY IS A CONTAINER FOR THE EMOTIONS to yield the central metaphor of the system:

Anger is the heat of a fluid in a container.

- You make my *blood boil.*
- *Simmer* down!
- I had reached the *boiling point.*
- Let him *stew.*

A historically derived instance of this metaphor is:

- She was *seething with rage.*

Although most speakers do not now use *seethe* to indicate physical boiling, the boiling image is still there when *seethe* is used to indicate anger. Similarly, *pissed off* is used only to refer to anger, not to the hot liquid under pressure in the bladder. Still, the effectiveness of the expression seems to depend on such an image.

When there is no heat, the liquid is cool and calm. In the central metaphor, cool and calmness corresponds to lack of anger.

- Keep *cool.*
- Stay *calm.* . . .

Let us now turn to the question of what issues the central metaphor addresses and what kind of ontology of anger it reveals. The central metaphor focuses on the fact that anger can be intense, that it can lead to a loss of control, and that a loss of control can be dangerous. Let us begin with intensity. Anger is conceptualized as a mass, and takes the grammar of mass nouns, as opposed to count nouns:

> Thus, you can say
> > How much anger has he got in him?
> but not
> > How many angers does he have in him?

Anger thus has the ontology of a mass entity, that is, it has a scale indicating its amount, it exists when the amount is greater than zero, and it goes out of existence when the amount falls to zero. In the central metaphor, the scale indicating the amount of anger is the heat scale. But, as the central metaphor indicates, the anger scale is not open-ended; it has a limit. Just as a hot fluid in a closed container can only take so much heat before it explodes, so we conceptualize the anger scale as having a limit point. We can only bear so much anger before we explode, that is, lose control. This has its correlates in our folk theory of physiological effects. As anger gets more intense the physiological effects increase and those increases interfere with our normal function. Body heat, blood pressure, agitation, and interference with perception cannot increase without limit before our ability to function normally becomes seriously impaired, and we lose control over our functioning. In the folk model of anger, loss of control is dangerous, both to the angry person and to those around him. In the central metaphor, the danger of loss of control is understood as the danger of explosion. . . .

The ANGER IS AN OPPONENT metaphor is constituted by the following correspondences: 10

Source: STRUGGLE   Target: ANGER

- The opponent is anger.
- Winning is controlling anger.
- Losing is having anger control you.
- Surrender is allowing anger to take control of you.
- The pool of resources needed for winning is the energy needed to control anger.

One thing that is left out of this account so far is what constitutes "appeasement." To appease an opponent is to give in to his demands. This suggests that anger has demands. We will address the question of what these demands are below.

The OPPONENT metaphor focuses on the issue of control and the danger of loss of control to the angry person himself. There is another metaphor that focuses on the issue of control, but its main aspect is the danger to others. It is a very widespread metaphor in Western culture, namely, PASSIONS ARE BEASTS INSIDE A PERSON. According to this metaphor, there is a part of each person that is a wild animal. Civilized people are supposed to keep that part of them private, that is, they are supposed to keep the animal inside them. In the metaphor, loss of control is equivalent to the animal getting loose. And the behavior of a person who has lost control is the behavior of a wild animal. There are versions of this metaphor for the various passions—desire, anger, etc. In the case of anger, the beast presents a danger to other people.

Anger is a dangerous animal.

- He has a *ferocious* temper.
- He has a *fierce* temper.
- It's dangerous to *arouse* his anger.
- That *awakened* my ire.
- His anger *grew.*
- He has a *monstrous* temper.
- He *unleashed* his anger.
- Don't let your anger *get out of hand,*
- He *lost his grip* on his anger.
- His anger is *insatiable.*

An example that draws on both the FIRE and DANGEROUS ANIMAL metaphors is:

- He was *breathing fire.*

The image here is of a dragon, a dangerous animal that can devour you with fire.

The DANGEROUS ANIMAL metaphor portrays anger as a sleeping animal that it is dangerous to awaken, as something that can grow and thereby become dangerous, as something that has to be held back, and as something with a dangerous appetite. . . .

As in the case of the OPPONENT metaphor, our analysis of the DANGEROUS ANIMAL metaphor leaves an expression unaccounted for—"insatiable." This expression indicates that the animal has an appetite. This "appetite" seems to correspond to the "demands" in the OPPONENT metaphor, as can be seen from the fact that the following sentences entail each other:

- Harry's anger is *insatiable.*
- Harry's anger cannot be *appeased.*

To see what it is that anger demands and has an appetite for, let us turn to expressions that indicate causes of anger. Perhaps the most common group of expressions that indicate anger consists of conventionalized forms of annoyance: minor pains, burdens placed on domestic animals, etc. Thus we have the metaphor:

The cause of anger is a physical annoyance.

- Don't be *a pain in the ass.*
- Get *off my back!*
- You don't have to *ride me so hard.*
- You're *getting under my skin.*
- He's *a pain in the neck.*
- Don't *be a pest!*

These forms of annoyance involve an offender and a victim. The offender is at fault. The victim, who is innocent, is the one who gets angry.

There is another set of conventionalized expressions used to speak of, or to, peo- 15
ple who are in the process of making someone angry. These are expressions of terri-
toriality, in which the cause of anger is viewed as a trespasser.

Causing anger is trespassing.

- You're beginning to *get to* me.
- Get *out of here!*
- Get *out of my sight!*
- *Leave me alone!*
- This is where I *draw the line!*
- Don't *step on my toes!*

Again, there is an offender (the cause of anger) and a victim (the person who is getting
angry). The offense seems to constitute some sort of injustice. This is reflected in the
conventional wisdom:

- Don't get *mad*, get *even!*

In order for this saying to make sense, there has to be some connection between anger
and retribution. Getting even is equivalent to balancing the scales of justice. The saying assumes a model in which injustice leads to anger and retribution can alleviate or
prevent anger. In short, what anger "demands" and has an "appetite" for is revenge.
This is why warnings and threats can count as angry behavior:

- If I get mad, watch out!
- Don't get me angry, or you'll be sorry.

The angry behavior is, in itself, viewed as a form of retribution.
   We are now in a position to make sense of another metaphor for anger:

Anger is a burden.

- Unburdening himself of his anger gave him a sense of *relief.*
- After I lost my temper, I felt *lighter.*
- He *carries* his anger around with him.
- He *has a chip on his shoulder.*
- You'll feel better if you *get it off your chest.*

In English, it is common for responsibilities to be metaphorized as burdens. There are
two kinds of responsibilities involved in the folk model of anger that has emerged so
far. The first is a responsibility to control one's anger. In cases of extreme anger, this
may place a considerable burden on one's "inner resources." The second comes from
the model of retributive justice that is built into our concept of anger; it is the responsibility to seek vengeance. What is particularly interesting is that these two responsibilities are in conflict in the case of angry retribution: If you take out your anger on
someone, you are not meeting your responsibility to control your anger, and if you

don't take out your anger on someone, you are not meeting your responsibility to provide retribution. The slogan "Don't get mad, get even!" offers one way out: retribution without anger. The human potential movement provides another way out by suggesting that letting your anger out is okay. But the fact is that neither of these solutions is the cultural norm. It should also be mentioned in passing that the human potential movement's way of dealing with anger by sanctioning its release is not all that revolutionary. It assumes almost all of our standard folk model and metaphorical understanding and makes one change: sanctioning the "release." . . .

The metaphors and metonymies that we have investigated so far converge on a certain prototypical cognitive model of anger. It is not the only model of anger we have; in fact, there are quite a few. But as we shall see, all of the others can be characterized as minimal variants of the model that the metaphors converge on. The model has a temporal dimension and can be conceived of as a scenario with a number of stages. We will call this the "prototypical scenario"; it is similar to what De Sousa calls the "paradigm scenario." We will be referring to the person who gets angry as S, short for the self.

Stage 1: Offending Event

There is an offending event that displeases S. There is a wrongdoer who intentionally does something directly to S. The wrongdoer is at fault and S is innocent. The offending event constitutes an injustice and produces anger in S. The scales of justice can only be balanced by some act of retribution. That is, the intensity of retribution must be roughly equal to the intensity of offense. S has the responsibility to perform such an act of retribution.

Stage 2: Anger

Associated with the entity anger is a scale that measures its intensity. As the intensity of anger increases, S experiences physiological effects: increase in body heat, internal pressure, and physical agitation. As the anger gets very intense, it exerts a force upon S to perform an act of retribution. Because acts of retribution are dangerous and/or socially unacceptable, S has a responsibility to control his anger. Moreover, loss of control is damaging to S's own well-being, which is another motivation for controlling anger.

Stage 3: Attempt at Control

S attempts to control his anger.

Stage 4: Loss of Control

Each person has a certain tolerance for controlling anger. That tolerance can be viewed as the limit point on the anger scale. When the intensity of anger goes beyond that limit, S can no longer control his anger. S exhibits angry behavior and his anger forces him to attempt an act of retribution. Since S is out of control and acting under coercion, he is not responsible for his actions.

Stage 5: Act of Retribution

S performs the act of retribution. The wrongdoer is the target of the act. The intensity of retribution roughly equals the intensity of the offense and the scales are balanced again. The intensity of anger drops to zero.

At this point, we can see how the various conceptual metaphors we have discussed all map onto a part of the prototypical scenario and how they jointly converge on that scenario. This enables us to show exactly how the various metaphors are related to one another and how they function together to help characterize a single concept.

Questions for Discussion and Writing

1. How do the metaphorical systems used to express anger project (a) physiological effects, (b) equivalence with heat, (c) equivalence with insanity, (d) equivalence with dangerous animals, and (e) anger at an opponent? What did Lakoff discover about the way systems of metaphors interact?
2. Lakoff cites the "folk theory of physiological effects" as a kind of commonsense, homespun value system that makes it possible to understand the hidden connection between related metaphors used to express anger. How does Lakoff use this folk theory of anger, structured on the concept of a protagonist and antagonist, to examine the rationale for acted-out aggression?
3. What metaphors underlie the reporting of sports? As a research project, analyze the verbs (for example, *maul, jolt, blast*) sportwriters use in reporting scores of football, basketball, and other games to discover the systems of metaphors (for example, those that value speed) and what they suggest about our culture.
4. Find a photo that expresses an emotion that surprises you, makes you laugh, or makes you see things from a different perspective, and supply a metaphor that communicates the feeling in the picture.

Alison Lurie

• •

Alsion Lurie (b. 1926) is the Frederic J. Whiton Professor of American Literature at Cornell University, where she teaches writing and children's literature. She is the author of several books of nonfiction and fiction, including Foreign Affairs *(1984), for which she was awarded a Pulitzer Prize in 1985. Her latest works are* The Last Resort *(1998),* Imaginary Friends *(1998), and* Familiar Spirits: A Memoir of James Merrill and David Jackson *(2001). "The Language of Clothes" first appeared in* Human Ecology *(Spring 1991).*

THE LANGUAGE OF CLOTHES

For thousands of years human beings have communicated with one another first in the language of dress. Long before I am near enough to talk to you on the street, in a meeting, or at a party, you announce your sex, age and class to me through what you are wearing—and very possibly give me important information (or misinformation) as to your occupation, origin, personality, opinions, tastes, sexual desires and current mood. I may not be able to put what I observe into words, but I register the information unconsciously; and you simultaneously do the same for me. By the time we meet and converse we have already spoken to each other in an older and more universal language.

The statement that clothing is a language, though made occasionally with the air of a man finding a flying saucer in his backyard, is not new. Balzac, in *Daughter of Eve* (1830), observed that dress is a "continual manifestation of intimate thoughts, a language, a symbol." Today, as semiotics becomes fashionable, sociologists tell us that fashion too is a language of signs, a nonverbal system of communication.

None of these theorists, however, has gone on to remark what seems obvious: that if clothing is a language, it must have a vocabulary and a grammar like other languages. Of course, as with human speech, there is not a single language of dress, but many: some (like Dutch and German) closely related and others (like Basque) almost unique. And within every language of clothes there are many different dialects and accents, some almost unintelligible to members of the mainstream culture. Moreover, as with speech, each individual has his own stock of words and employs personal variations of tone and meaning.

The vocabulary of dress includes not only items of clothing, but also hair styles, accessories, jewelry, makeup and body decoration. Theoretically at least this vocabulary is as large as or larger than that of any spoken tongue, since it includes every garment, hair style, and type of body decoration ever invented. In practice, of course, the sartorial resources of an individual may be very restricted. Those of a sharecropper, for instance, may be limited to five or ten "words" from which it is possible to create only a few "sentences" almost bare of decoration and expressing only the most basic concepts. A so-called fashion leader, on the other hand, may have several hundred "words" at his or her disposal, and thus be able to form thousands of different "sentences" that will express a wide range of meanings. Just as the average English-speaking person knows many more words than he or she will ever use in conversation, so all of us are able to understand the meaning of styles we will never wear.

Magical Clothing

Archaeologists digging up past civilizations and anthropologists studying primitive tribes have come to the conclusion that, as Rachel Kemper [*Costume*] puts it, "Paint, ornament, and rudimentary clothing were first employed to attract good animistic powers and to ward off evil." When Charles Darwin visited Tierra del Fuego, a cold, wet, disagreeable land plagued by constant winds, he found the natives naked except for feathers in their hair and symbolic designs painted on their bodies. Modern Australian bushmen, who may spend hours decorating themselves and their relatives with patterns in colored clay, often wear nothing else but an amulet or two.

However skimpy it may be, primitive dress almost everywhere, like primitive speech, is full of magic. A necklace of shark's teeth or a girdle of cowrie shells or feathers serves the same purpose as a prayer or spell, and may magically replace—or more often supplement—a spoken charm. In the first instance a form of *contagious* magic is at work: the shark's teeth are believed to endow their wearer with the qualities of a fierce and successful fisherman. The cowrie shells, on the other hand, work through *sympathetic* magic: since they resemble the female sexual parts, they are thought to increase or preserve fertility.

In civilized society today belief in the supernatural powers of clothing—like belief in prayers, spells and charms—remains widespread, though we denigrate it with the name "superstition." Advertisements announce that improbable and romantic events will follow the application of a particular sort of grease to our faces, hair or bodies; they claim that members of the opposite (or our own) sex will be drawn to us by the smell of a particular soap. Nobody believes those ads, you may say. Maybe not, but we behave as though we did: look in your bathroom cabinet.

The supernatural garments of European folk tales—the seven-league boots, the cloaks of invisibility and the magic rings—are not forgotten, merely transformed, so that today we have the track star who can only win a race in a particular hat or shoes, the plain-clothes cop who feels no one can see him in his raincoat and the wife who takes off her wedding ring before going to a motel with her lover.

Sympathetic or symbolic magic is also often employed, as when we hang crosses, stars or one of the current symbols of female power and solidarity around our necks, thus silently involving the protection of Jesus, Jehovah or Astarte. Such amulets, of course, may be worn to announce our allegiance to some faith or cause rather than as a charm. Or they may serve both purposes simultaneously—or sequentially. The crucifix concealed below the parochial-school uniform speaks only to God until some devilish force persuades its wearer to remove his or her clothes; then it acts—or fails to act—as a warning against sin as well as a protective talisman.

Articles of clothing, too, may be treated as if they had mana, the impersonal supernatural force that tends to concentrate itself in objects. When I was in college it was common to wear a particular "lucky" sweater, shirt or hat to final examinations, and this practice continues today. Here it is usually contagious magic that is at work: the chosen garment has become lucky by being worn on the occasion of some earlier success, or has been given to its owner by some favored person. The wearing of such magical garments is especially common in sports, where they are often publicly credited with bringing their owners luck. Their loss or abandonment is thought to cause injury as well as defeat. Actors also believe ardently in the magic of clothes, possibly because they are so familiar with the near-magical transforming power of theatrical costume.

10

Fashion and Status

Clothing designed to show the social position of its wearer has a long history. Just as the oldest languages are full of elaborate titles and forms of address, so for thousands of years certain modes have indicated high or royal rank. Many societies passed decrees known as *sumptuary laws* to prescribe or forbid the wearing of specific styles by specific classes of persons. In ancient Egypt only those in high position could wear sandals; the Greeks and Romans controlled the type, color and number of garments worn and the sorts of embroidery with which they could be trimmed. During the Middle Ages almost every aspect of dress was regulated at some place or time—though not always with much success. The common features of all sumptuary laws—like that of edicts, against the use of certain words—seem to be that they are difficult to enforce for very long.

Laws about what could be worn by whom continued to be passed in Europe until about 1700. But as class barriers weakened and wealth could be more easily and rapidly converted into gentility, the system by which color and shape indicated social status began to break down. What came to designate high rank instead was the evident cost of a costume: rich materials, superfluous trimmings and difficult-to-care-for styles, or as Thorstein Veblen later put it [in *The Theory of the Leisure Class*], Conspicuous Waste and Conspicuous Leisure. As a result, it was assumed that the people you met would be dressed as lavishly as their income permitted. In Fielding's *Tom Jones,* for instance, everyone judges strangers by their clothing and treats them accordingly; this is presented as natural. It is a world in which rank is very exactly indicated by costume, from the rags of Molly the gamekeeper's daughter to Sophia Western's riding habit "which was so very richly laced" that "Partridge and the postboy instantly started from their chairs, and my landlady fell to her curtsies, and her ladyships, with great eagerness." The elaborate wigs characteristic of this period conferred status partly because they were both expensive to buy and expensive to maintain.

By the early eighteenth century the social advantages of conspicuous dress were such that even those who could not afford it often spent their money on finery. This development was naturally deplored by supporters of the status quo. In Colonial America the Massachusetts General Court declared its "utter detestation and dislike, that men or women of mean condition, should take upon them the garb of Gentlemen, by wearing Gold or Silver lace, or Buttons, or Points at their knees, or to walk in great Boots; or Women of the same rank to wear Silk or Tiffiny hoods, or Scarfes. . . ." What "men or women of mean condition"—farmers or artisans—were supposed to wear were coarse linen or wool, leather aprons, deerskin jackets, flannel petticoats and the like.

To dress above one's station was considered not only foolishly extravagant, but deliberately deceptive. In 1878 an American etiquette book complained,

> It is . . . unfortunately the fact that, in the United States, but too much attention is paid to dress by those who have neither the excuse of ample means nor of social claims. . . . We Americans are lavish, generous, and ostentatious. The wives of our wealthy men are glorious in garb as are princesses and queens. They have a right so to be. But when those who can ill afford to wear alpaca persist in arraying themselves in silk . . . the matter is a sad one.

Color and Pattern

Certain sorts of information about other people can be communicated in spite of a language barrier. We may not be able to understand Welsh or the thick Southern dialect of the Mississippi delta, but when we hear a conversation in these tongues we can tell at once whether the speakers are excited or bored, cheerful or miserable, confident or frightened. In the same way, some aspects of the language of clothes can be read by almost anyone.

The first and most important of these signs, and the one that makes the greatest and most immediate impact, is color. Merely looking at different colors, psychologists have discovered, alters our blood pressure, heartbeat and rate of respiration, just as hearing a harsh noise or a harmonious musical chord does. When somebody approaches from a distance the first thing we see is the hue of his clothes; the closer he comes, the more space this hue occupies in our visual field and the greater its effect on our nervous system. Loud, clashing colors, like loud noises or loud voices, may actually hurt our eyes or give us a headache; soft, harmonious hues, like music and soft voices, thrill or soothe us. Color in dress is also like tone of voice in speech in that it can completely alter the meaning of what is "said" by other aspects of the costume: style, fabric and trimmings. Just as the words "Do you want to dance with me?" can be whispered shyly or flung as a challenge, so the effect of a white evening dress is very different from that of a scarlet one of identical fabric and pattern. In certain circumstances some hues, like some tones of voice, are beyond the bounds of polite discourse. A bride in a black wedding dress, or a stockbroker greeting his clients in a shocking-pink three-piece suit, would be like people screaming aloud.

Although color often indicates mood, it is not by any means an infallible guide. For one thing, convention may prescribe certain hues. The urban businessman must wear a navy blue, dark gray or (in certain regions) brown or tan suit, and can express his feelings only through his choice of shirt and tie, or tie alone; and even here the respectable possibilities may be very limited. Convention also alters the meaning of colors according to the place and time at which they are worn. Vermilion in the office is not the same as vermilion at a disco; and hot weather permits the wearing of pale hues that would make one look far more formal and fragile in midwinter.

There are other problems. Some people may avoid colors they like because of the belief or illusion that they are unbecoming, while others may wear colors they normally dislike for symbolic reason: because they are members or fans of a certain football team, for instance. In addition, some fashionable types may select certain hues merely because they are "in" that year.

Finally, it should be noted that the effect of any color in dress is modified by the colors that accompany it. In general, therefore, the following remarks should be taken as applying mainly to costumes composed entirely or almost entirely of a single hue.

The mood of a crowd, as well as that of an individual, can often be read in the colors of clothing. In the office of a large corporation, or at a professional convention, there is usually a predominance of conventional gray, navy, beige, tan and white—suggesting a general attitude of seriousness, hard work, neutrality, propriety and status. The same group of people at a picnic are a mass of lively, relaxed blue, red and brown, with touches of yellow and green. In the evening, at a disco, they shimmer under the rotating lights in dramatic combinations of purple, crimson, orange, turquoise, gold, silver and black.

Apart from the chameleon, man is the only animal who can change his skin to suit his background. Indeed, if he is to function successfully he must do so. The individual whose clothes do not fall within the recognized range of colors for a given situation attracts attention, usually (though not always) unfavorable attention. When a child puts its pet chameleon down on the earth and it does not turn brown, we know the creature is seriously ill. In the same way, men or women who begin to come to work in a conservative office wearing disco hues and a disco mood are regarded with anxiety and suspicion. If they do not blush a respectable beige, navy or gray within a reasonable length of time, their colleagues know that they will not be around for long.

Questions for Discussion and Writing

1. In what way, according to Lurie, is clothing a kind of language that can be analyzed to discover both the wearer's and the surrounding culture's values? In the past, how did clothing and adornment serve magical purposes?
2. What factors related to social class have determined which kinds of clothes could or could not be worn in particular societies in different eras? As a research project, you might investigate the evolution of blue jeans and their class-related values at different points in history—from sturdy miner's clothes to chic designer apparel.
3. Go through your wardrobe and classify items of clothes you wear according to the "statement" you wish to make in different contexts. Should high school students be required to wear uniforms? Why or why not?
4. Take a photo of a friend or acquaintance (of course, with his or her permission) that focuses on a distinctive item of clothing or a tattoo, piercing, jewelry, hairstyle, or accessory, and write a short paragraph analyzing the personal, generational, and cultural significance of this feature.

Rosemarie Garland-Thomson

• •

Rosemarie Garland-Thomson is a disabilities study scholar and professor of English at Howard University. She has written extensively on disability in literature and culture, and her essays have appeared in many journals. She is the author of Extraordinary Bodies: Figuring Physical Disability in American Culture and Literature *(1997) and has edited* Freakery: Cultural Spectacles of the Extraordinary Body *(1996) and most recently has coedited (with Sharon L. Snyder and Brenda Jo Brueggemann)* Disability Studies: Enabling the Humanities *(2002). In 1999, Garland-Thomson codirected the first National Endowment for the Humanities Summer Institute for Disability Studies in the Humanities. In the following essay, she discusses the controversy over an inscription proposed for the national memorial to President Franklin Delano Roosevelt.*

THE FDR MEMORIAL: WHO SPEAKS FROM THE WHEELCHAIR?

As public spaces transformed into collective stories, memorials are inherently controversial. Didactic narratives about who we are and what we believe, they span generations and vast differences in human perceptions, bringing to light all sorts of divisions in the national "we." One of those divides has occurred between a group of scholars in disability studies and the designers of the Franklin Delano Roosevelt Memorial in Washington. The five-year struggle over the collective story told by the F.D.R. memorial ended only this month, when President Clinton dedicated an addition to the memorial. The controversy—and, unfortunately, its not entirely satisfactory conclusion—tells us much about disability in American culture, about disability studies, and about ourselves.

Even before its dedication, on May 2, 1997, the memorial had splintered the national "we." The original monument consisted of four granite-walled outdoor "rooms," which narrated F.D.R.'s presidency with inscriptions of his own words and with nine bronze bas-reliefs and statues, representing scenes of his presidency, all intermingled with pools, waterfalls, and greenery.

The segment of the American "we" representing disability-rights activists and scholars in disability studies had wanted to avoid repeating the persistent stereotypes of disability—the ones that tell us that disability is a shameful personal problem relegated to the private realm of charity and medicine, but inappropriate in the public sphere.

We had wanted the memorial to tell the story of a man who was both disabled by polio and president of the United States for 12 years; to claim F.D.R. as a disabled public figure who represented not just the 15 percent of the U.S. population who have disabilities, but everyone, since we will all become disabled if we live long enough. The memorial's present and future audiences, we had argued, would consist of people whose consciousness had been transformed by civil-rights movements that included the disability-rights movement, and by legislation like the Americans with Disabilities Act, the landmark law that mandates full integration of people with disabilities into American society.

But the only statue that even remotely referred to F.D.R.'s disability showed him   5 seated, covered by a cape, on a chair with small wheels barely peeking out. The threat of protests by disability activists at the memorial's dedication convinced President Clinton to seek an addition, and the designers agreed—the first time that an existing national memorial was to be changed. Maya Lin's controversial Vietnam Veterans Memorial was augmented with representational figures of soldiers, but those traditionally heroic statues only flank, rather than fundamentally change, the somber black-granite slab and the space of meditation and mourning it creates.

The bold mandate to reimagine F.D.R. as at once heroic and disabled has now been realized. A new "room" at the entrance to the present memorial contains a simple, life-size bronze statue depicting Roosevelt seated in his wheelchair, wearing his trademark rumpled suit, pince-nez, and fedora. It differs from the regal, robed, larger-than-life figure represented in the third room, where the ample cloak erases and denies the mark of his disability. The new statue witnesses the simple humanity of the great leader and registers it as the universality of disability. It also marks today's historical moment, when disability defined as a civil-rights issue is superseding disability as a medical or charitable issue.

Yet the controversy continues, because the story that the new "room" of the F.D.R. memorial tells is still fraught with contradiction. At issue is the phrasing of the words inscribed on the granite wall behind the new statue of F.D.R. A group of us from the field of disability studies had been invited to recommend potential quotations, from which the designers were to choose an inscription. As historians and literary critics who traffic in words, we relished the chance to influence the way that people present and future would understand disability. The memorial's other inscriptions are illustrious words that enrich the story told by the spaces and the statues. F.D.R.'s eloquent verbal commitments to equality are literally set in stone, shaping the story of his presidency and of the nation itself. One powerful quotation reads, "We must scrupulously guard the civil rights and civil liberties of all citizens, whatever their background. We must remember that any oppression, any injustice, any hatred, is a wedge designed to attack our civilization." We wanted the new addition to continue the theme of equal rights that is the hallmark of both the disability-rights movement and the F.D.R. memorial.

We had a story about disability that we wanted the new room to tell. We sought to offer a quotation as crisp, powerful, and unambiguous as the bold "I hate war" chiseled into the wall above the tumbled stones that suggest the blasted buildings of World War II while creating a majestic waterfall that implies transcendence.

F.D.R.'s strategy in the Depression had been to alter the environment to meet the needs of the people. That was parallel, we reasoned, to the idea that people with disabilities need a material situation that accommodates the differences of their bodies or minds. So we looked for a quotation to convey the idea that political equality and access to the workplace for people with disabilities requires a leveling of the playing field—both literally, in the case of wheelchair users like F.D.R., and metaphorically, for those of us who need other accommodations to be fully integrated into the public sphere.

We also wanted to tell the story of a determined man who used a wheelchair, and whose use of it influenced the world around him. As scholars in disability studies, we examine disability as a cultural concept that shapes history, belief, art, literature, and other aspects of culture. We saw F.D.R. as someone whose disability shaped him and who, in turn, shaped his own world and the world that has come after. We looked for a quotation telling that story about disability while eschewing stereotypical stories about courageous people who overcame their disabilities or found serenity through suffering.

Enough of those oppressive narratives dominate public thought and circulate in telethons, fiction, and sentimental tracts. The F.D.R. memorial should offer up an accomplished leader, not a cheerful or chastened cripple.

To provide criteria for selecting the inscription in the new room, we suggested three themes that should be emphasized, and three that should be avoided. We sought a quotation, first of all, that would advance the idea that disability is integral to a person's character and life experience, rather than a defect to be eliminated. Second, we wanted a quotation suggesting that the experience of disability can enrich a life, foster leadership, and create a sense of community. Third, in keeping with the human scale of the statue, we searched for words hinting that F.D.R.'s disability made him an accessible—rather than a lofty—hero. In other words, we recommended that any new inscription present disability as a common, yet influential, human experience, one that can be integrated into a meaningful and full life.

Conversely, we argued that the quotation should avoid the stereotypical narrative that disability is a tragic experience to be overcome. Discrimination, more than impairment, is what people with disabilities have to surmount. Our second caveat was more complex: In keeping with our conviction that disability should be viewed as a political issue of rights and access, we intended to circumvent the idea that disability is simply a matter of having an individual impairment to contend with. Recasting social attitudes and removing environmental barriers are more important for improving the lives of people with disabilities than are their own spunk, saintliness, iron will, or the generosity of others. Third—the most subtle point to convey—we strove to dispel the pervasive attitude that disabled people warrant attention only to provide lessons or inspirations to others. We wanted to focus on how F.D.R. himself experienced

10

disability, rather than turn him into a homily for the nondisabled that inspires pity and admiration—or gratitude that they are not themselves disabled.

Gracing the humble but commanding statue of a disabled F.D.R. with a quotation that could do all of that political and cultural work was challenging. After reviewing more than 100 possibilities, consulting with other scholars and disability activists, and, at times, disagreeing among ourselves, we offered a unanimous recommendation to the designers, trusting that they would understand and support our criteria: "We know that equality of individual ability has never existed and never will, but we do insist that equality of opportunity still must be sought." Combined with the image of a U.S. president using a wheelchair, those words sent the unequivocal message that disability is an issue of equal opportunity.

To our dismay, however, the designers and the other people advising them selected   15
an inscription for the new room of the F.D.R. memorial that has exactly the effect we'd hoped to avoid. Disregarding our recommendation, they instead used a quotation from Eleanor Roosevelt: "Franklin's illness gave him strength and courage he had not had before. He had to think out the fundamentals of living and learn the greatest of all lessons—infinite patience and never-ending persistence." That quotation is compelling, and it even fulfills some of our criteria, because it interprets F.D.R.'s disability as a positive influence on his life. Indeed, we had offered it along with several others as a possible addition that might augment our recommended choice. But we did not want it to be the only story of disability that the memorial would tell.

Alone, Eleanor Roosevelt's words undermine disability-rights goals. To begin with, we believe that F.D.R. should speak for himself. Too often, others have spoken for and about people with disabilities. In the old way of understanding disability people with disabilities were silenced while the authority to define them and to narrate their experience was appropriated by medical experts, service providers, or family members. Having another person speak for F.D.R. repeats the humiliating experience of being ignored that people with disabilities often endure. A quotation from his wife also reinforces the myth that F.D.R. denied his disability—especially since nowhere else in the memorial do quotations from anyone but him appear.

Even more important, to have the first two words a visitor encounters at the memorial be "Franklin's illness" presents disability in a way that doubly violates the spirit of equality. "Illness" is a synonym for impairment, a term that disability scholars and activists use to denote functional limitation. "Disability," on the other hand, is a term we use to describe the system of representation that produces discriminatory attitudes and barriers to full integration. In essence, "impairment" and "illness" are about bodily differences, whereas "disability" is about the social and political context in which our bodies operate. The distinction is much the same as the one that scholars often draw between "sex" and "gender." "Illness" locates the story of disability in hospitals and rehabilitation centers. We want the story of disability to be placed in independent-living centers. To object to "illness" is not to fault Eleanor Roosevelt for being politically incorrect; rather, it is to suggest that the way we view disability in 2001 and beyond has changed from the way it was imagined in 1949. After all, a memorial should not simply replicate the past, but use history to create a future vision.

"Franklin's illness" also personalizes rather than politicizes disability. While the quotation the designers propose is certainly moving, it tells the stereotypical, apolitical story of disability as an individual catastrophe, psychological adjustment, and moral chastening. Impairment is a private problem that an individual must overcome, not a public problem of environmental and attitudinal barriers that can be removed through legislation, policy, and education. Moreover, opening with this quotation places the F.D.R. memorial in the genre of public works intended for collective grieving—like war memorials, the AIDS Memorial Quilt, the Oklahoma City National Memorial, or plaques for sailors lost at sea.

In our debate with the designers, they asserted that their quotation would make F.D.R. "very personal, very accessible." But they confused their intent to humanize F.D.R. with personalizing his disability. The inscription that now flanks the statue encourages visitors to respond with sympathy, admiration, and charity rather than with support for equal access and integration. A more effective way to humanize F.D.R. would be to suggest that his impairment reinforced his commitment to the universal mandate for "equality of opportunity," a point to which our recommended quotation alludes.

The designers also mistakenly justified the choice of their text on aesthetic grounds. 20 The story of "Franklin's illness" as well as of his "strength," "courage," "patience," and "persistence" would create an aesthetically differentiated and inspirational space, they argued in commenting on our recommendation. The new room was to be a "prologue." In reality, that suggests separating the personal story of disability from the political content of the memorial's other rooms. The quotation clings to the stubborn stereotypes of disability that still feel comfortable to many Americans, simply because those ideas are so easily recognizable. A wheelchair-using F.D.R., spoken about by others, is segregated within his own memorial. That denies the political work of disability-rights activists and scholars, who have sought to eliminate precisely such segregation.

Many of us in disability studies wish to register our dissent from the choice of the inscription for the new room of the F.D.R. memorial. Pleased as we are with the statue itself, we worry that this memorial to our first markedly disabled president ultimately replicates the segregation and privatization of disability. The inscription undermines the work of disability-rights advocates who worked so hard to make the new room a reality. It tells the story that disability is separate from politics—a personal problem rather than a public political struggle.

In the year 2001, we are on the cultural cusp of a new way to understand disability. The memorial's figures, spaces, and, particularly, its words implicitly instruct visitors in how they should imagine disability. In the controversy over the F.D.R. memorial, our evolving national narrative of disability was played out as a quarrel between aesthetics and politics. But underneath, the disagreement was a struggle between familiar old stories and bold new ones, between moving stories about personal suffering and empowering ones about social equality. While the designers of the F.D.R. memorial have laudably affirmed disability with the depiction of the president using a wheelchair, they did not succeed in rewriting the story of disability in terms that will resonate for future generations.

The addition to the F.D.R. memorial suggests two conflicting stories: yesterday's story of disability as a personal failing overcome by individual effort, and today's and tomorrow's story of disability as an issue of civil rights, integration, and diversity. Our national disability politics has come a long way since the 1930's. Shouldn't our national aesthetics now take up the challenge to transform the meaning of disability?

How does this photo by the National Organization on Disability publicize the importance of having a statue of FDR in his wheelchair?

Questions for Discussion and Writing

1. In what way was the addition of a life-size bronze statue showing Roosevelt in his wheelchair to the already completed memorial an attempt to change public perception about the meaning of disability?
2. How does Garland-Thomson use the quotation from Eleanor Roosevelt to highlight the traditional "story" the public associated with disabilities and to suggest why a newer "story" was needed?
3. To what extent have public memorials stemming from the 9/11 attacks on the World Trade Center reflected some of the same tensions between realistic and idealistic representation that the FDR Memorial illustrates?
4. For further research on FDR you might consult Hugh Gregory Gallagher's *FDR's Splendid Deception* (1985).

Aldous Huxley

* *

Aldous Huxley (1894–1963) was born in Surrey, England, and was educated at Eton and Balliol College, Oxford. Despite a serious eye disease, Huxley read with the aid of a magnifying glass and graduated from Oxford in 1915 with honors in English literature, after which he joined the staff of the Atheneum. *His brilliant social satires and wide-ranging essays on architecture, science, music, history, philosophy, and religion explore the relationship between humans and society.* Brave New World *(1932) is his best-known satire on how futuristic mass technology will achieve a sinister utopia of scientific breeding and conditioned happiness. Huxley's other works include* Eyeless in Gaza *(1936),* After Many a Summer *(1939),* Time Must Have a Stop *(1944), and* Ape and Essence *(1948).* The Doors of Perception *(1954),* Heaven and Hell *(1956), and* Island *(1962) can be seen as attempts to search in new spiritual directions—through mysticism, mescaline, and parapsychology—as a reaction to the grim future he so devastatingly portrayed. In "Propaganda under a Dictatorship," from* Brave New World Revisited *(1958), Huxley reveals how the manipulation of language in the propaganda of Nazi Germany conditioned the thoughts and behavior of the masses.*

PROPAGANDA UNDER A DICTATORSHIP

At his trial after the Second World War, Hitler's Minister for Armaments, Albert Speer, delivered a long speech in which, with remarkable acuteness, he described the Nazi tyranny and analyzed its methods. "Hitler's dictatorship," he said, "differed in one fundamental point from all its predecessors in history. It was the first dictatorship in the present period of modern technical development, a dictatorship which made complete use of all technical means for the domination of its own country. Through technical devices like the radio and the loudspeaker, eighty million people were deprived of independent thought. It was thereby possible to subject them to the will of one man. . . . Earlier dictators needed highly qualified assistants even at the lowest level—men who could think and act independently. The totalitarian system in the period of modern technical development can dispense with such men; thanks to modern methods of communication, it is possible to mechanize the lower leadership. As a result of this there has arisen the new type of the uncritical recipient of orders."

In the Brave New World of my prophetic fable technology had advanced far beyond the point it had reached in Hitler's day; consequently the recipients of orders were far less critical than their Nazi counterparts, far more obedient to the order-giving elite. Moreover, they had been genetically standardized and postnatally conditioned to perform their subordinate functions, and could therefore be depended upon to behave almost as predictably as machines. . . . This conditioning of "the lower leadership" is already going on under the Communist dictatorships. The Chinese and the Russians are not relying merely on the indirect effects of advancing technology; they are working directly on the psychophysical organisms of their lower leaders, subjecting minds and bodies to a system of ruthless and, from all accounts, highly effective conditioning. "Many a man," said Speer, "has been haunted by the nightmare that one day nations might be dominated by technical means. That nightmare was almost realized in Hitler's totalitarian system." Almost, but not quite. The Nazis did not have time—and perhaps did not have the intelligence and the necessary knowledge—to brainwash and condition their lower leadership. This, it may be, is one of the reasons why they failed.

Since Hitler's day the armory of technical devices at the disposal of the would-be dictator has been considerably enlarged. As well as the radio, the loudspeaker, the moving picture camera and the rotary press, the contemporary propagandist can make use of television to broadcast the image as well as the voice of his client, and can record both image and voice on spools of magnetic tape. Thanks to technological progress, Big Brother can now be almost as omnipresent as God. Nor is it only on the technical front that the hand of the would-be dictator has been strengthened. Since Hitler's day a great deal of work has been carried out in those fields of applied psychology and neurology which are the special province of the propagandist, the indoctrinator and the brainwasher. In the past these specialists in the art of changing people's minds were empiricists. By a method of trial and error they had worked out a number of techniques and procedures, which they used very effectively without, however, knowing precisely why they were effective. Today the art of mind-control is in process of becoming a science. The practitioners of this science know what they are doing and why. They are guided in their work by theories and hypotheses solidly established on a massive foundation of experimental evidence. Thanks to the new insights and the new techniques made possible by these insights, the nightmare that was "all but realized in Hitler's totalitarian system" may soon be completely realizable.

But before we discuss these new insights and techniques let us take a look at the nightmare that so nearly came true in Nazi Germany. What were the methods used by Hitler and Goebbels[1] for "depriving eighty million people of independent thought and subjecting them to the will of one man"? And what was the theory of human nature upon which those terrifyingly successful methods were based? These questions can be answered, for the most part, in Hitler's own words. And what remarkably clear and astute words they are! When he writes about such vast abstractions as Race and History and Providence, Hitler is strictly unreadable. But when he writes about the German masses and the methods he used for dominating and directing them, his style changes. Nonsense gives place to sense, bombast to a hard-boiled and cynical lucidity. In his philosophical lucubrations Hitler was either cloudily daydreaming or reproducing other people's half-baked notions. In his comments on crowds and propaganda he was writing of things he knew by firsthand experience. In the words of his ablest biographer, Mr. Alan Bullock, "Hitler was the greatest demagogue in history." Those who add, "only a demagogue," fail to appreciate the nature of political power in an age of mass politics. As he himself said, "To be a leader means to be able to move the masses." Hitler's aim was first to move the masses and then, having pried them loose from their traditional loyalties and moralities, to impose upon them (with the hypnotized consent of the majority) a new authoritarian order of his own devising. "Hitler," wrote Hermann Rauschning in 1939, "has a deep respect for the Catholic church and the Jesuit order; not because of their Christian doctrine, but because of the 'machinery' they have elaborated and controlled, their hierarchical system, their extremely clever tactics, their knowledge of human nature and their wise use of human weaknesses in ruling over

---

[1] *Joseph Paul Goebbels (1897–1945):* the propaganda minister under Hitler, a master of the "big lie."

believers." Ecclesiasticism without Christianity, the discipline of a monastic rule, not for God's sake or in order to achieve personal salvation, but for the sake of the State and for the greater glory and power of the demagogue turned Leader—this was the goal toward which the systematic moving of the masses was to lead.

Let us see what Hitler thought of the masses he moved and how he did the moving. The first principle from which he started was a value judgment: the masses are utterly contemptible. They are incapable of abstract thinking and uninterested in any fact outside the circle of their immediate experience. Their behavior is determined, not by knowledge and reason, but by feelings and unconscious drives. It is in these drives and feelings that "the roots of their positive as well as their negative attitudes are implanted." To be successful a propagandist must learn how to manipulate these instincts and emotions. "The driving force which has brought about the most tremendous revolutions on this earth has never been a body of scientific teaching which has gained power over the masses, but always a devotion which has inspired them, and often a kind of hysteria which has urged them into action. Whoever wishes to win over the masses must know the key that will open the door of their hearts." . . . In post-Freudian jargon, of their unconscious.

Hitler made his strongest appeal to those members of the lower middle classes who had been ruined by the inflation of 1923, and then ruined all over again by the depression of 1929 and the following years. "The masses" of whom he speaks were these bewildered, frustrated and chronically anxious millions. To make them more masslike, more homogeneously subhuman, he assembled them, by the thousands and the tens of thousands, in vast halls and arenas, where individuals could lose their personal identity, even their elementary humanity, and be merged with the crowd. A man or woman makes direct contact with society in two ways: as a member of some familial, professional or religious group, or as a member of a crowd. Groups are capable of being as moral and intelligent as the individuals who form them; a crowd is chaotic, has no purpose of its own and is capable of anything except intelligent action and realistic thinking. Assembled in a crowd, people lose their powers of reasoning and their capacity for moral choice. Their suggestibility is increased to the point where they cease to have any judgment or will of their own. They become very excitable, they lose all sense of individual or collective responsibility, they are subject to sudden accesses of rage, enthusiasm and panic. In a word, a man in a crowd behaves as though he had swallowed a large dose of some powerful intoxicant. He is a victim of what I have called "herd-poisoning." Like alcohol, herd-poison is an active, extraverted drug. The crowd-intoxicated individual escapes from responsibility, intelligence and morality into a kind of frantic, animal mindlessness.

During his long career as an agitator, Hitler had studied the effects of herd-poison and had learned how to exploit them for his own purposes. He had discovered that the orator can appeal to those "hidden forces" which motivate men's actions, much more effectively than can the writer. Reading is a private, not a collective activity. The writer speaks only to individuals, sitting by themselves in a state of normal sobriety. The orator speaks to masses of individuals, already well primed with herd-poison. They are at his mercy and, if he knows his business, he can do what he likes with them. As an orator, Hitler knew his business supremely well. He was able, in his own words, "to follow the lead of the great mass in such a way that from the living emotion to his hearers the apt word which he needed would be suggested to him and in its turn this would go straight to the heart of his hearers." Otto Strasser called him a "loudspeaker, proclaiming the most secret desires, the least admissible instincts, the sufferings and personal revolts of a whole nation." Twenty years before Madison Avenue embarked upon "Motivational Research," Hitler was systematically exploring and exploiting the secret fears and hopes, the cravings, anxieties and frustrations of the German masses. It is by manipulating "hidden forces" that the advertising experts induce us to buy their wares—a toothpaste, a brand of cigarettes, a political candidate. And it is by appealing to the same hidden forces—and to others too dangerous for Madison Avenue to meddle with—that Hitler induced the German masses to buy themselves a Fuehrer, an insane philosophy and the Second World War.

Unlike the masses, intellectuals have a taste for rationality and an interest in facts. Their critical habit of mind makes them resistant to the kind of propaganda that works so well on the majority. Among the masses "instinct is supreme, and from instinct comes faith. . . . While the healthy common folk instinctively close their ranks to form a community of the people" (under a Leader, it goes without saying) "intellectuals run this way and that, like hens in a poultry yard. With them one cannot make history; they cannot be used as elements composing a community." Intellectuals are the kind of people who demand evidence and are shocked by logical inconsistencies and fallacies. They regard oversimplification as the original sin of the mind and have no use for the slogans, the unqualified assertions and sweeping generalizations which are the propagandist's stock in trade. "All effective propaganda," Hitler wrote, "must be confined to a few bare necessities and then must be expressed in a few stereotyped formulas." These stereotyped formulas must be constantly repeated, for "only constant repetition will finally succeed in imprinting an idea upon the memory of a crowd." Philosophy teaches us to feel uncertain about the things that seem to us self-evident. Propaganda, on the other hand, teaches us to accept as self-evident matters about which it would be reasonable to suspend our judgment or to feel doubt. The aim of the demagogue is to create social coherence under his own leadership. But, as Bertrand Russell has pointed out, "systems of dogma without empirical foundations, such as scholasticism, Marxism and fascism, have the advantage of producing a great deal of social coherence among their disciples." The demagogic propagandist must therefore be consistently dogmatic. All his statements are made without qualification. There are no grays in his picture of the world; everything is either diabolically black or celestially white. In Hitler's words, the propagandist should adopt "a systematically one-sided attitude towards every problem that has to be dealt with." He must never admit that he might be wrong or that people with a different point of view might be even partially right. Opponents should not be argued with; they should be attacked, shouted down, or, if they become too much of a nuisance, liquidated. The morally squeamish intellectual may be shocked by this kind of thing. But the masses are always convinced that "right is on the side of the active aggressor."

Such, then, was Hitler's opinion of humanity in the mass. It was a very low opinion. Was it also an incorrect opinion? The tree is known by its fruits, and a theory of human nature which inspired the kind of techniques that proved so horribly effective must contain at least an element of truth. Virtue and intelligence belong to human beings as individuals freely associating with other individuals in small groups. So do sin and stupidity. But the subhuman mindlessness to which the demagogue makes his appeal, the moral imbecility on which he relies when he goads his victims into action, are characteristic not of men and women as individuals, but of men and women in masses. Mindlessness and moral idiocy are not characteristically human attributes; they are symptoms of herd-poisoning. In all the world's higher religions, salvation and enlightenment are for individuals. The kingdom of heaven is within the mind of a person, not within the collective mindlessness of a crowd. Christ promised to be present where two or three are gathered together. He did not say anything about being present where thousands are intoxicating one another with herd-poison. Under the Nazis enormous numbers of people were compelled to spend an enormous amount of time marching in serried ranks from point A to point B and back again to point A. "This keeping of the whole population on the march seemed to be a senseless waste of time and energy. Only much later," adds Hermann Rauschning, "was there revealed in it a subtle intention based on a well-judged adjustment of ends and means. Marching diverts men's thoughts. Marching kills thought. Marching makes an end of individuality. Marching is the indispensable magic stroke performed in order to accustom the people to a mechanical, quasi-ritualistic activity until it becomes second nature."

From his point of view and at the level where he had chosen to do his dreadful 10 work, Hitler was perfectly correct in his estimate of human nature. To those of us who look at men and women as individuals rather than as members of crowds, or of regimented collectives, he seems hideously wrong. In an age of accelerating overpopulation, of accelerating overorganization and even more efficient means of mass communication, how can we preserve the integrity and reassert the value of the human individual? This is a question that can still be asked and perhaps effectively answered. A generation from now it may be too late to find an answer and perhaps impossible, in the stifling collective climate of that future time, even to ask the question.

Questions for Discussion and Writing

1. In Huxley's view, why was one particular segment of the German population so vulnerable to Hitler's propaganda techniques? What role did the inflation of 1923 and the Depression of 1929 play in setting the stage for Hitler's rise to power?
2. What propaganda techniques did Hitler use to manipulate the masses? What was Hitler's opinion of the masses he manipulated?
3. What are some of the more telling examples of contemporary propaganda techniques of stereotypes, slogans, slanting, or guilt (or virtue) by association mentioned by Huxley? What present-day examples used by politicians can you identify?

Stuart Hirschberg

Stuart Hirschberg teaches English at Rutgers University, Newark, and is the author of scholarly works on W. B. Yeats and Ted Hughes. He is also the editor and coeditor (with Terry Hirschberg) of anthologies, including this book; One World, Many Cultures *(5th ed., 2004);* Every Day, Everywhere: Global Perspectives on Popular Culture *(2002);* Past to Present: Ideas that Changed Our World *(2003); and* Discovering the Many Worlds of Literature *(2004). The following essay is drawn from* Reflections on Language *(1999).*

THE RHETORIC OF ADVERTISING

Whether ads are presented as sources of information enabling the consumer to make educated choices between products or aim at offering memorable images or witty, thoughtful, or poetic copy, the underlying intent of all advertising is to persuade specific audiences. Seen in this way, ads appear as mini-arguments whose strategies and techniques of persuasion can be analyzed just like a written argument. We can discover which elements are designed to appeal to the audience's emotions (*pathos* according to Aristotle), which elements make their appeal in terms of reasons, evidence, or logic (*logos*), and how the advertiser goes about winning credibility for itself or in terms of the spokesperson employed to speak on behalf of the product (the *ethos* dimension). Like arguments, ads can be effective if they appeal to the needs, values, and beliefs of the audience. Although the verbal and visual elements within an ad are designed to work together, we can study these elements separately. We can look at how the composition of the elements within an ad is intended to function. We can look at the role of language and how it is used to persuade. We can study how objects and settings are used to promote the audience's identification with the products being sold. We can judge ads according to the skill with which they deploy all of these resources while at the same time being critically aware of their intended effects on us.

The Techniques of Advertising

The claim the ad makes is designed to establish the superiority of the product in the minds of the audience and to create a distinctive image for the product, whether it is a brand of cigarettes, a financial service, or a type of gasoline. The single most important technique for creating this image depends on transferring ideas, attributes, or feelings from outside the product onto the product itself. In this way the product comes to represent an obtainable object or service that embodies, represents, or symbolizes a whole range of meanings. This transfer can be achieved in many ways. For example, when Nicole Kidman or Jennifer Lopez lends her glamour and beauty to the merchandising of a perfume, the consumer is meant to conclude that the perfume must be superior to other perfumes in the way that the actress embodies beauty, glamour, and sex appeal. The attempt to transfer significance can operate in two ways. It can encourage the audience to discover meanings and to correlate feelings and attributes that the advertiser wishes the product to represent in ways that allow these needs and desires to become attached to specific products. It can also prevent the correlation of thoughts or feelings that might discourage the audience from purchasing a particular product. For example, the first most instinctive response to the thought of smoking a cigarette might be linked with the idea of inhaling hot and dry smoke from what are essentially burning tobacco leaves. Thus, any associations the audience might have with burning leaves, coughing, and dry hot smoke must be short-circuited by supplying them with a whole set of other associations to receive and occupy the perceptual "slot" that might have been triggered by their first reactions. Cigarette advertisers do this in a variety of ways:

> By showing active people in outdoorsy settings, they put the thought of emphysema, shortness of breath, or lung disease very far away indeed.
> By showing cigarette packs set against the background of grass glistening with morning dew or bubbling streams or cascading waterfalls, they subtly guide the

audience's response away from what is dry, hot, congested, or burning toward what is open, airy, moist, cool, and clean.

In some brands, menthol flavoring and green and blue colors are intended to promote these associations.

Thus, ads act as do all other kinds of persuasion to intensify correlations that work to the advertiser's advantage and to suppress associations that would lessen the product's appeal.

The kinds of associations audiences are encouraged to perceive reflect a broad range of positive emotional appeals that encourage the audience to find self-esteem through the purchase of a product that by itself offers a way to meet personal and social needs. The particular approach taken in the composition of the ad, the way it is laid out, and the connotations of the advertising copy vary according to the emotional appeal of the ad.

The most common manipulative techniques are designed to make consumers want   5
to consume to satisfy deep-seated human drives. Of course, no one consciously believes that purchasing a particular kind of toothpaste, perfume, lipstick, or automobile will meet real psychological and social needs, but that is exactly how products are sold—through the promise of delivering unattainable satisfactions through tangible purchasable objects or services. In purchasing a certain product, we are offered the chance to create ourselves, our personality, and our relationships through consumption.

Emotional Appeals Used in Advertising

The emotional appeals in ads function exactly the way assumptions about value do in written arguments. They supply the unstated major premise that supplies a rationale to persuade an audience that a particular product will meet one or another of several different kinds of needs. Some ads present the purchase of a product as a means by which consumers can find social acceptance.

These ads address the consumer as "you" ("Wouldn't 'you' really rather have a Buick?"). The "you" here is plural but is perceived as being individual and personal by someone who has already formed the connection with the product. Ironically, the price of remaining in good standing with this "group" of fellow consumers requires the consumer to purchase an expensive automobile. In this sense, ads give consumers a chance to belong to social groups that have only one thing in common—the purchase of a particular product.

One variation on the emotional need to belong to a designated social group is the appeal to status or "snob appeal." Snob appeal is not new. In 1710, the *Spectator,* a popular newspaper of the time, carried an ad that read:

> An incomparable Powder for Cleaning Teeth, which has given great satisfaction to most of the Nobility Gentry in England.

Ads for scotch, expensive cars, boats, jewelry, and watches frequently place their products in upper-class settings or depict them in connection with the fine arts (sculpture, ballet, etc.). The *value warrant* in these ads encourages the consumer to imagine that the purchase of the item will confer qualities associated with the background or activities of this upper-class world onto the consumer.

In other ads the need to belong takes a more subtle form of offering the product as a   10
way to become part of a time in the past the audience might look back to with nostalgia.
Grandmotherly figures wearing aprons and holding products that are advertised as being
"like Grandma used to make" offer the consumer an imaginary past, a family tradition,
or a simpler time looked back to with warmth and sentimentality. For many years,
Smucker's preserves featured ads in which the product was an integral part of a scene emanating security and warmth, which the ad invited us to remember as if it were our own
past. Ads of this kind are often photographed through filters that present misty sepia-tone
images that carefully recreate old-fashioned kitchens with the accompanying appliances,
dishes, clothes, and hairstyles. The ads thus supply us with false memories and invite us
to insert ourselves into this imaginary past and to remember it as if it were our own. At
the furthest extreme, ads employing the appeal to see ourselves as part of a group may try
to evoke patriotic feelings so that the prospective consumer will derive the satisfactions
of good citizenship and sense of participation in being part of the collective psyche of an
entire nation. The point is that people really do have profound needs that advertisers can
exploit, but it would be a rare product indeed that could really fulfill such profound needs.

Advertisers use highly sophisticated market research techniques to enable them to
define and characterize precisely those people who are most likely to be receptive to
ads of particular kinds. The science of demographics is aided and abetted by psychological research that enables advertisers to "target" a precisely designated segment of
the general public. For example, manufacturers of various kinds of liquor can rely on
studies that inform them that vodka drinkers are most likely to read *Psychology Today*
and scotch drinkers the *New Yorker,* while readers of *Time* prefer rum and the audience for *Playboy* has a large number of readers who prefer gin. Once a market segment
with defined psychological characteristics has been identified, an individual ad can be
crafted for that particular segment and placed in the appropriate publication.

Ads, of course, can elicit responses by attempting to manipulate consumers through
negative as well as positive emotional appeals. Helen Woodward, the head copywriter
for an ad agency, once offered the following advice for ad writers trying to formulate
a new ad for baby food: "Give 'em the figures about the baby death rate—but don't
say it flatly . . . if we only had the nerve to put a hearse in the ad, you couldn't keep
the women away from the food" (Stuart Ewen, *Captains of Consciousness: Advertising and the Social Roots of Consumer Culture* [1976]). Ads of this kind must first
arouse the consumer's anxieties and then offer the product as the solution to the problem that more often than not the ad has created.

For example, an advertisement for Polaroid evokes the fear of not having taken pictures of moments that cannot be re-created and then offers the product as a form of
insurance that will prevent this calamity from occurring. Nikon does the same in claim-
ing that "a moment is called a moment because it doesn't last forever. Think of sun-
sets. A child's surprise. A Labrador's licky kiss. This is precisely why the Nikon N50
has the simple 'Simple' switch on top of the camera."

Ads for products that promise to guarantee their purchasers sex appeal, youth, health,
social acceptance, self-esteem, creativity, enlightenment, a happy family life, loving relationships, escape from boredom, vitality, and many other things frequently employ scare
tactics to frighten or worry the consumer into purchasing the product to ease his or her
fears. These ads must first make the consumer dissatisfied with the self that exists. In this

way, they function exactly as do *policy arguments* that recommend solutions to problems with measurably harmful consequences. The difference is that these kinds of ads actually are designed to arouse and then exploit the anxieties related to these problems.

Large industrial conglomerates, whether in oil, chemicals, pharmaceuticals, or agribusiness, frequently use advertising to accomplish different kinds of objectives than simply persuading the consumer to buy a particular product. These companies often seek to persuade the general public that they are not polluting the environment, poisoning the water, or causing environmental havoc in the process of manufacturing their products. The emotional appeal they use is to portray themselves as concerned "corporate citizens," vitally interested in the public good as a whole, and especially in those communities where they conduct their operations. In some cases, the ads present products as if they were directly produced from nature without being subjected to intermediary processing,

15

preservatives, and contaminants, thereby lessening concern that they produce harmful byproducts. For example, Mazola might depict a spigot producing corn oil directly inserted into an ear of corn. A Jeep might appear to have materialized out of thin air on a seemingly inaccessible mountain peak. Companies sensitive to accusations that they are polluting the air and water can mount an advertising campaign designed to prove that they are not simply exploiting the local resources (whether timber, oil, fish, coal) for profits but are genuinely interested in putting something back into the community. The folksy good-neighbor tone of these ads is designed to create a benign image of the company.

The Language of Advertising

We can see how the creation of a sense of the company's credibility as a concerned citizen corresponds to what Aristotle called the *ethos* dimension. For example, Chevron expresses concern that the light from their oil drilling operations be shielded so that spawning sea turtles won't be unintentionally misdirected and lose their way!

The appeals to logic, statements of reasons, and presentations of evidence in ads correspond to the *logos* dimension of argument. The wording of the claims is particularly important, since it determines whether companies are legally responsible for any claims they make.

Claims in advertising need to be evaluated to discover whether something is asserted that needs to be proved or is implied without actually being stated.

Claims may refer to authoritative-sounding results obtained by supposedly independent laboratories, teams of research scientists, or physicians without ever saying how these surveys were conducted, what statistical methods were used, and who interpreted the results. Ads of this kind may make an impressive-sounding quasi-scientific claim; Ivory Soap used to present itself as "99 and 44/100% pure" without answering "pure" what. Some ads use technical talk and scientific terms to give the impression of a scientific breakthrough. For example, STP claims that it added "an anti-wear agent and viscosity improvers" to your oil. The copy for L. L. Bean claims of one of its jackets that "even in brutal ice winds gusting to 80 knots this remarkable anorak kept team members who wore it warm and comfortable." It would be important to know that the team members referred to are members of the "L. L. Bean test team."

Other claims cannot be substantiated, for example, "we're the Dexter Shoe Com- 20 pany. And for nearly four decades we put a lot of Dexter Maine into every pair of shoes we make."

In an ad for lipstick, Aveda makes the claim that "it's made of rich, earthy lip colours formulated with pure plant pigment from the Uruku tree. Organically grown by indigenous people in the rain forest."

Claims may be deceptive in other ways. Of all the techniques advertisers use to influence what people believe and how they spend their money, none is more basic than the use of so-called *weasel words*. This term was popularized by Theodore Roosevelt in a speech he gave in St. Louis, May 31, 1916, when he commented that notes from the Department of State were filled with weasel words that retract the meaning of the words they are next to just as a weasel sucks the meat out of the egg.

In modern advertising parlance, a weasel word has come to mean any qualifier or comparative that is used to imply a positive quality that cannot be stated as a fact, because it cannot be substantiated. For example, if an ad claims a toothpaste will "help" stop cavities it does not obligate the manufacturer to substantiate this claim. So, too, if a product is advertised as "fighting" germs, the equivocal claim hides the fact that the product may fight and lose.

An ad for STP claimed that "no matter what kind of car you drive, STP gas treatment helps remove the water that leads to gas line freeze. And unlike gas line antifreeze, our unique gas treatment formula works to reduce intake valve deposits and prevent clogged injectors." The key words are "helps" and "works," neither of which obligates STP to be legally accountable to support the claim.

The words *virtually* (as in "virtually spotless") and *up to* or *for as long as* (as in   25 "stops coughs up to eight hours") also remove any legal obligation on the part of the manufacturer to justify the claim.

Other favorite words in the copywriter's repertoire, such as *free* and *new,* are useful in selling everything from cat food to political candidates.

The Ethical Dimension of Persuasion

As we have seen in our examination of the methods advertisers use to influence consumers, ethical questions are implicit in every act of persuasion. For example, what are we to make of a persuader whose objectives in seeking to influence an audience may be praiseworthy but who consciously makes use of distorted facts or seeks to manipulate an audience by playing on their known attitudes, values, and beliefs? Is success in persuasion the only criterion or should we hold would-be persuaders accountable to some ethical standards of responsibility about the means they use to achieve specific ends? Perhaps the most essential quality in determining whether any act of persuasion is an ethical one depends on the writer maintaining an open dialogue with different perspectives that might be advanced on a particular issue. By contrast, any act of persuasion that intentionally seeks to avoid self-criticism or challenges from competing perspectives will come across as insincere, dogmatic, deceptive, and defensive. The desire to shut down debate or control an audience's capacity to respond to the argument might well be considered unethical. The consequence of this attitude may be observed in the arguer's use of fraudulent evidence, illogical reasoning, emotionally laden irrelevant appeals, simplistic representation of the issue, or the pretense of expertise. Standards to apply when judging the ethical dimension in any act of persuasion require us to consider whether any element of coercion, deception, or manipulation is present. This becomes especially true when we look at the relationship between propaganda as a form of mass persuasion and the rhetorical means used to influence large groups of people.

Questions for Discussion and Writing

1. How do modern advertisers use traditional rhetorical techniques, identified by Aristotle, to appeal to the audiences' emotions (*pathos*), reason (*logos*), and sense of credibility (*ethos*)?
2. In what ways does advertising depend on the transfer of ideas and associations to create a sense of distinctive identity for the product or service?

3. How do the preceding ads use the techniques identified in this article to market their products? In your opinion, are these ads effective? Why or why not?
4. Analyze a company's Web site in terms of the use of *ethos, pathos,* and *logos* to promote a satisfactory consumer relationship with the product or service.
5. Make up a poster, ad, postcard, or brochure for your favorite charity or organization, including a photograph, symbol, or other graphic element.

FICTION

Anthony Burgess

Anthony Burgess (1917–1993) was remarkably prolific and an always entertaining writer of biographies, essays, and novels and was a composer of symphonic music as well. He is known for his surreal darkly comic novels, the best known of which is the futuristic A Clockwork Orange *(1962), from which the following chapter is taken. His last work was* A Mouthful of Air: Language, Languages . . . Especially English *(1992).*

This chapter is from the classic **science fiction** *novel by Burgess that is widely considered to be a masterpiece of literary invention, and yet the narrator in the story, a violent fifteen-year-old delinquent, uses language that would most certainly be judged substandard and unacceptable because of its poor grammar, neologisms, and slang. Burgess, an accomplished linguist and scholar, invented this dialect of English for his protagonist, drawing in the main on Slavic languages—traces of which can be discerned in words such as "devotchka" (attractive female) and "bolshy" (large). In fact, one of the most entertaining aspects of reading* A Clockwork Orange *is trying to guess the English language equivalent of the terms Burgess has invented.*

FROM *A CLOCKWORK ORANGE*

I could not believe, brothers, what I was told. It seemed that I had been in that vonny mesto for near ever and would be there for near ever more. But it had always been a fortnight and now they said the fortnight was near up. They said: 'Tomorrow, little friend, out out out.' And they made with the old thumb like pointing to freedom. And then the white-coated veck who had tolchocked me and who had still brought me my trays of pishcha and like escorted me to my everyday torture said: 'But you still have one real big day in front of you. It's to be your passing-out day.' And he had a leery smeck at that.

I expected this morning that I would be ittying as usual to the sinny mesto in my pyjamas and toofles and over-gown. But no. This morning I was given my shirt and underveshches and my platties of the night and my horrorshow kickboots, all lovely and washed or ironed or' polished. And I was even given my cutthroat britva that I had used in those old happy days for fillying and dratsing. So I gave with the puzzled frown at this as I got dressed, but the white-coated under-veck just like grinned and would govoreet nothing, O my brothers.

I was led quite kindly to the same old mesto, but there were changes there. Curtains had been drawn in front of the sinny screen and the frosted glass under the projection holes was no longer there, it having perhaps been pushed up or folded to the sides like blind or shutters. And where there had been just the noise of coughing kashl kashl kashl and like shadows of lewdies was now a real audience, and in this audience there were litsos I knew. There was the Staja Governor and the holy man, the charlie or charles as he was called, and the Chief Chasso and this very important and well-dressed chelloveck who was the Minister of the Interior or Inferior. All the rest I did not know. Dr Brodsky and Dr Branom were there, though not now white-coated, instead they were dressed as doctors would dress who were big enough to want to dress in the heighth of fashion. Dr Branom just stood, but Dr Brodsky stood and govoreeted in a like learned manner to all the lewdies assembled. When he viddied me coming in he said: 'Aha. At this stage, gentlemen, we introduce the subject himself. He is, as you will perceive, fit and well nourished. He comes straight from a night's sleep and a good breakfast, undrugged, unhypnotized. Tomorrow we send him with confidence out into the world again, as decent a lad as you would meet on a May morning, unvicious, unviolent, if anything—as you will observe—inclined to the kindly word and the helpful act. What a change is here, gentlemen, from the wretched hoodlum the State committed to unprofitable punishment some two years ago, unchanged after two years. Unchanged, do I say? Not quite. Prison taught him the false smile, the rubbed hands of hypocrisy, the fawning greased obsequious leer. Other vices it taught him, as well as confirming him in those he had long practised before. But, gentlemen, enough of words. Actions speak louder than. Action now. Observe, all.'

I was a bit dazed by all this govoreeting and I was trying to grasp in my mind that like all this was about me. Then all the lights went out and then there came on two like spotlights shining from the projection-squares, and one of them was full on Your Humble and Suffering Narrator. And into the other spotlight there walked a bolshy big chelloveck I had never viddied before. He had a lardy like litso and a moustache and like strips of hair pasted over his near-bald gulliver. He was about thirty or forty or fifty, some old age like that, starry. He ittied up to me and the spotlight ittied with him, and soon the two spotlights had made like one big pool. He said to me; very sneery: 'Hello heap of dirt. Pooh, you don't wash much, judging from the horrible smell.' Then, as if he was like dancing, he stamped on my nogas, left, right, then he gave me a fingernail flick on the nose that hurt like bezoomny and brought the old tears to my glazzies, then he twisted at my left ooko like it was a radio dial. I could slooshy titters and a couple of real horrorshow hawhawhaws coming from like the audience. My nose and nogas and ear-hole stung and pained like benzoomny, so I said:

'What do you do that to me for? I've never done wrong to you, brother.'   5

'Oh,' this veck said, 'I do this'—flickflicked nose again—'and that'—twisted smarting ear-hole—'and the other'—stamped nasty on right noga—'because I don't care for your horrible type. And if you want to do anything about it, start, start, please do.' Now I knew that I'd have to be real skorry and get my cutthroat britva out before this horrible killing sickness whooshed up and turned the like joy of battle into feeling I was going to snuff it. But, O brothers, as my rooker reached for the britva in my inside carman I got this like picture in my mind's glazzy of this insulting chelloveck howling for mercy with the red red krovvy all streaming out of his rot, and hot after this picture the sickness and dryness and pains were rushing to overtake, and I viddied that I'd have to change the way I felt about this rotten veck very very skorry indeed, so I felt in my carmans for cigarettes or for pretty polly, and, O my brothers, there was not either of these veshches. I said, like all howly and blubbery:

'I'd like to give you a cigarette, brother, but I don't seem to have any.' This veck went:

'Wah wah. Boohoohoo. Cry, baby.' Then he flickflick-flicked with his bolshy horny nail at my nose again, and I could slooshy very loud smecks of like mirth coming from the dark audience. I said, real desperate, trying to be nice to this insulting and hurtful veck to stop the pains and sickness coming up:

'Please let me do something for you, please.' And I felt in my carmans but could find only my cut-throat britva, so I took this out and handed it to him and said: 'Please take this, please. A little present. Please have it.' But he said:

'Keep your stinking bribes to yourself. You can't get round me that way.' And he   10
banged at my rooker and my cut-throat britva fell on the floor. So I said:

'Please, I must do something. Shall I clean your boots? Look, I'll get down and lick them.' And, my brothers, believe it or kiss my sharries, I got down on my knees and pushed my red yahzick out a mile and a half to lick his grahzny vonny boots. But all this veck did was to kick me not too hard on the rot. So then it seemed to me that it would not bring on the sickness and pain if I just gripped his ankles with my rookers tight round them and brought this grahzny bratchny down to the floor. So I did this and he got a real bolshy surprise, coming down crack amid loud laughter from the vonny audience. But viddying him on the floor I could feel the whole horrible feeling coming over me, so I gave him my rooker to lift him up skorry and up he came. Then just as he was going to give me a real nasty and earnest tolchock on the litso Dr Brodsky said:

'All right, that will do very well.' Then this horrible veck sort of bowed and danced off like an actor while the lights came up on me blinking and with my rot square for howling. Dr Brodsky said to the audience: 'Our subject is, you see, impelled towards the good by, paradoxically, being impelled towards evil. The intention to act violently is accompanied by strong feelings of physical distress. To counter these the subject has to switch to a diametrically opposed attitude. Any questions?'

'Choice,' rumbled a rich deep goloss. I viddied it belonged to the prison charlie. 'He has no real choice, has he? Self-interest, fear of physical pain, drove him to that grotesque act of self-abasement. Its insincerity was clearly to be seen. He ceases to be a wrongdoer. He ceases also to be a creature capable of moral choice.'

'These are subtleties,' like smiled Dr Brodsky. 'We are not concerned with motive, with the higher ethics. We are concerned only with cutting down crime—'

'And,' chipped in this bolshy well-dressed Minister, 'with relieving the ghastly con-   15
gestion in our prisons.'

'Hear hear,' said somebody.

There was a lot of govoreeting and arguing then and I just stood there, brothers, like completely ignored by all these ignorant bratchnies, so I creeched out:

'Me, me, me. How about me? Where do I come into all this? Am I like just some animal or dog?' And that started them off govoreeting real loud and throwing slovos at me. So I creeched louder still, creeching: 'Am I just to be like a clockwork orange?' I didn't know what made me use those slovos, brothers, which just came like without asking into my gulliver. And that shut all those vecks up for some reason for a minoota or two. Then one very thin starry professor type chelloveck stood up, his neck like all cables carrying like power from his gulliver to his plott, and he said:

'You have no cause to grumble, boy. You made your choice and all this is a consequence of your choice. Whatever now ensues is what you yourself have chosen.' And the prison charlie creeched out:

'Oh, if only I could believe that.' And you could viddy the Governor give him a look   20
like meaning that he would not climb so high in like Prison Religion as he thought he would. Then loud arguing started again, and then I could slooshy the slovo Love being thrown around, the prison charles himself creeching as loud as any about Perfect Love Casteth Out Fear and all that cal. And now Dr Brodsky said, smiling all over his litso:

Selections from Glossary of NADSAT Language

Words that don't seem to be of Russian origin are distinguished by asterisks.

bezoomny: mad	mesto: place
Bog: God	minoota: minute
bolshy: big, great	noga: foot, leg
bratchny: bastard	ooko: ear
britva: razor	pishcha: food
cal: feces	platties: clothes
carman: pocket	pletcho: shoulder
*charles, charlie: chaplain	plott: body
chasso: guard	*pretty polly: money
chelloveck: person, man, fellow	rock, rooker: hand, arm
creech: to shout or scream	rot: mouth
devotchka: girl	sharries: buttocks
dratsing: fighting	shoot: fool
*filly: to play or fool with	*sinny: cinema
glazz: eye	skorry: quick, quickly
goloss: voice	sloosh, slooshy: to hear, to listen
govoreet: to speak or talk	slovo: word
grahzny: dirty	smeck: laugh
gromky: loud	*snuff it: to die
groody: breast	*Staja: State Jail
gulliver: head	starry: ancient
horrorshow: good, well	tolchock: to hit or push; blow, beating
*in-out in-out: copulation	toofles: slippers
itty: to go	veck: (see chelloveck)
jeezny: life	veshch: thing
keeshkas: guts	viddy: to see or look
krovvy: blood	von: smell
lewdies: people	yahzick: tongue
litso: face	

'I am glad, gentlemen, this question of Love, has been raised. Now we shall see in action a manner of Love that was thought to be dead with the Middle Ages.' And then the lights went down and the spotlights came on again, one on your poor and suffering Friend and Narrator, and into the other there like rolled or sidled the most lovely young devotchka you could ever hope in all your jeezny, O my brothers, to viddy. That is to say, she had real horrorshow groodies all of which you could like viddy, she having on platties which came down down down off her pletchoes. And her nogas were like Bog in His Heaven, and she walked like to make you groan in your keeshkas, and yet her litso was a sweet smiling young like innocent litso. She came up towards me with the light like it was the like light of heavenly grace and all that cal coming with her, and the first thing that flashed into my gulliver was that I would like to have her right down there on the floor with the old in-out real savage, but skorry as a shot came the sickness, like a like detective that had been watching round a corner and now followed to make his grahzny arrest. And now the von of lovely perfume that came off her made me want to think of starting to like heave in my keeshkas, so I knew I had to think of some new like way of thinking about her before all the pain and thirstiness and horrible sickness come over me real horrorshow and proper. So I creeched out:

'O most beautiful and beauteous of devotchkas, I throw like my heart at your feet for you to like trample all over. If I had a rose I would give it to you. If it was all rainy and cally now on the ground you could have my platties to walk on so as not to cover your dainty nogas with filth and cal.' And as I was saying all this, O my brothers, I could feel the sickness like slinking back. 'Let me,' I creeched out, 'worship you and be like your helper and protector from the wicked like world.' Then I thought of the right slovo and felt better for it, saying: 'Let me be like your true knight,' and down I went again on the old knees, bowing and like scraping.

And then I felt real shooty and dim, it having been like an act again, for this devotchka smiled and bowed to the audience and like danced off, the lights coming up to a bit of applause. And the glazzies of some of these starry vecks in the audience were like popping out at this young devotchka with dirty and like unholy desire, O my brothers.

'He will be your true Christian,' Dr Brodsky was creeching out, 'ready to turn the other cheek, ready to be crucified rather than crucify, sick to the very heart at the thought even of killing a fly.' And that was right, brothers, because when he said that I thought of killing a fly and felt just that tiny bit sick, but I pushed the sickness and pain back by thinking of the fly being fed with bits of sugar and looked after like a bleeding pet and all that cal. 'Reclamation,' he creeched. 'Joy before the Angels of God.'

'The point is,' this Minister of the Inferior was saying real gromky, 'that it works.'   25

'Oh,' the prison charlie said, like sighing, 'it works all right, God help the lot of us.'

Questions for Discussion and Writing

1. In what sense does the phrase "a clockwork orange" (a Cockney phrase that Burgess said he meant to stand for "the application of a mechanistic morality to a living organism") characterize the bizarre condition into which the narrator has been transformed? What was the narrator like before he was conditioned?

2. How does the attitude of the experimenters and scientists toward the narrator differ from that of the prison chaplain? What is the significance of the chaplain's final remark?

3. How does the narrator use language differently from the way his examiners use it? You might wish to rent the 1971 film directed by Stanley Kubrick and, after viewing it, discuss the role that Burgess's invented language plays in dramatizing the differences in social class between Alec and his examiners.

4. How do the separate elements in this film poster from the 1971 film *A Clockwork Orange* convey the violent sociopathic nature of the main character, Alec?

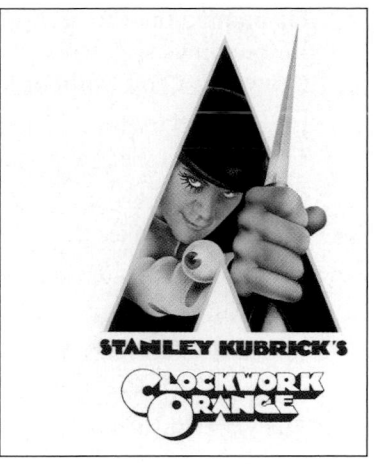

POETRY

Ted Hughes

Edward James (Ted) Hughes (1930–1998) was born in Yorkshire, England, and was educated at Cambridge University. He was married to the American poet Sylvia Plath, who committed suicide in 1963. Hughes's first volumes of verse, The Hawk in the Rain *(1957),* Lupercal *(1960), and* Wodwo *(1967), immediately brought him recognition for his ability to portray the human predicament in uncompromising ways through animal characters. His 1970 volume of poetry,* Crow, *projected a grotesque and fascinating cycle tracing the history of a lonely yet resilient figure, from before his birth through a complex allegorical journey, in which Hughes, through the character Crow, comments on the savage impulses underlying the facade of civilization. A prolific writer, Hughes produced a wide range of works, including* Gaudete *(1977),* Cave Birds *(1978),* Remains of Elmet *(1979),* Moortown *(1980),* River *(1984), and* Wolf-Watching *(1989), as well as volumes of literary criticism, essays, and poetry for children. In 1984 he was appointed Poet Laureate of Great Britain and, before his death in 1998, produced a body of work that has clearly defined him as the foremost poet writing in English. His last book was* Birthday Letters *(1998). In the following poem, drawn from* Crow, *Hughes creates a circular semantic game that puts words literally into the position of never quite catching up to an elusive reality that mocks Crow's efforts.*

CROW GOES HUNTING

Crow
Decided to try words.

He imagined some words for the job, a lovely pack—
Clear-eyed, resounding, well-trained,
With strong teeth.
You could not find a better bred lot.   5

He pointed out the hare and away went the words
Resounding.
Crow was Crow without fail, but what is a hare?

It converted itself to a concrete bunker.   10
The words circled protesting, resounding.

Crow turned the words into bombs—they blasted the bunker.
The bits of bunker flew up—a flock of starlings.

Crow turned the words into shotguns, they shot down the
                                                starlings.   15

The falling starlings turned to a cloudburst.

Crow turned the words into a reservoir, collecting the water.
The water turned into an earthquake, swallowing the
                                                reservoir.

The earthquake turned into a hare and leaped for the hill   20
Having eaten Crow's words.

Crow gazed after the bounding hare
Speechless with admiration.

Questions for Discussion and Writing

1. Why do Crow's attempts to "try words" always come up short?
2. Into what kinds of things do words transform themselves? Why is it significant that the bounding hare that Crow seeks to describe ultimately eats Crow's words?
3. What is Hughes suggesting about the capacity of language to describe reality? Have you ever had an experience where you could have been Crow hunting for the proper words?

Thinking Critically About the Image

Paul Gauguin (1848–1903), French painter and woodcut artist, at thirty-five left his career as a stockbroker and devoted himself to painting. First allied with the Impressionists, he evolved a theory of painting emphasizing flat planes and bright, non-naturalistic colors with symbolic or primitive subjects. In 1891 he went to Tahiti, where he painted some of his finest works, such as *Ta Matete* ("The Market," 1892). The scene shows girls on a bench chatting with each other in the market at Papeete.

1. How do the color harmonies in this painting add to the sense of mystery as to what the girls are saying to each other?

2. Did you notice how their posture, with heads and feet in profile and stiff conventionalized gestures, seems to suggest ancient Egyptian art?
3. Create a conversation between the figures that dramatizes the scene.

Connections

Chapter 4: Perspectives on Language

Helen Keller,   *The Day Language Came into My Life*
How might Rosemarie Garland-Thomson interpret Keller's account as a narrative of empowerment rather than of disability?

Temple Grandin,   *Thinking in Pictures*
Compare the difficulties both Grandin and Helen Keller had in surmounting their respective disabilities and their different perceptions of how language functions.

Deborah Tannen,   *Sex, Lies, and Conversation*
To what extent are Tannen's observations about different agendas between men and women illustrated in David Ives's play *Sure Thing* (Ch. 5)?

George Lakoff,   *Anger*
How do both Lakoff and Temple Grandin illustrate the concrete nature of metaphors?

Alison Lurie,   *The Language of Clothes*
How does the concept of clothes as language explain the cross-cultural confusion described by Judith Ortiz Cofer in "The Myth of the Latin Woman" (Ch. 1)?

Rosemarie Garland-Thomson,   *The FDR Memorial: Who Speaks from the Wheelchair?*
Discuss how the controversy over FDR's depiction in the memorial illustrates the way images create rather than record history, as discussed by Lance Morrow in "Imprisoning Time in a Rectangle" (Ch. 10).

Aldous Huxley,   *Propaganda Under a Dictatorship*
Examine Huxley's premise that Hitler adapted Madison Avenue techniques of advertising in light of the analysis by Stuart Hirschberg.

Stuart Hirschberg,   *The Rhetoric of Advertising*
To what extent do McDonald's and other companies that market their products for children (as described by Eric Schlosser in "Kid Kustomers," Ch. 5) apply the age-old persuasive strategies discussed by Hirschberg?

Anthony Burgess,   *A Clockwork Orange*
Compare the use and objective of behavioral conditioning as portrayed in Burgess's story and in Kenneth M. Stampp's essay "To Make Them Stand in Fear" (Ch. 8).

Ted Hughes,   *Crow Goes Hunting*
In what respects is Crow's predicament akin to the dilemma facing autistic children, as described by Temple Grandin?

Grace Hartigan, Billboard, *1957.*
Painting, oil on canvas. Abstraction. 78½ × 87 in. (199.4 × 221.0 cm) LR in black: [Hartigan '57]. The Minneapolis Institute of Arts, The Julia B. Bigelow Fund.

Issues in Popular Culture

Two things only the people anxiously desire, Bread and the Circus games.
—Juvenal, *Satires*

MANY CONTEMPORARY CONCERNS ARE TOUCHED ON BY the essays in this chapter: consumerism, TV news shows, eating disorders, racism, urban legends, addictions, AIDS, aging, the changing role of marriage, speed dating, and the worldwide influence of American culture. With a few exceptions, many of the issues overlap. For example, Juliet B. Schor and Eric Schlosser question whether consumerism has become America's dominant cultural value for children as well as adults.

Other issues include the national inability to solve problems without resorting to "quick fixes," and the resulting use of drugs; superficial news broadcasts; and the prevalence of eating disorders. Philip Slater, Neil Postman, and Steve Powers, and Rosalind Coward discuss these matters. Arthur Ashe investigates the ways race, ethnicity, and AIDs have changed our perception of celebrities in modern culture. The lasting power of urban legends, as described by Jan Harold Brunvand, further indicates our willingness to blur the lines between illusion and reality.

An essay by Barbara Kantrowitz, a short story by Margaret Atwood, and an innovative play by David Ives examine the new patterns of dating, marriage, and expectations in contemporary culture.

A classic story by Kate Chopin offers a complex and thoughtful exploration of the consequences of endemic sexism and racism.

The poetry by Grace Caroline Bridges, Marge Piercy, and Kelly Cherry and the song lyrics by Bruce Springsteen present heartfelt protests to pressing contemporary problems: child abuse, sexual stereotyping, the plight of the elderly, and the treatment of AIDS victims.

NONFICTION

Juliet B. Schor

Juliet B. Schor (b. 1955) currently is a professor of sociology at Boston College. She has written The Overworked American *(1992) and* The Overspent American *(1998), in which the following essay first appeared. Schor analyzes why what Americans previously viewed as luxuries have now become necessities. She has edited* The Consumer Society Reader *with Douglas B. Holt (2002) and is the author of* Born to Buy: The Commercialized Child and the New Consumer Culture *(2004).*

THE CULTURE OF CONSUMERISM

In 1996 a best-selling book entitled *The Millionaire Next Door* caused a minor sensation. In contrast to the popular perception of millionaire lifestyles, this book reveals that most millionaires live frugal lives—buying used cars, purchasing their suits at JC Penney, and shopping for bargains. These very wealthy people feel no need to let the world know they can afford to live much better than their neighbors.

Millions of other Americans, on the other hand, have a different relationship with spending. What they acquire and own is tightly bound to their personal identity. Driving a certain type of car, wearing particular designer labels, living in a certain kind of home, and ordering the right bottle of wine create and support a particular image of themselves to present to the world.

This is not to say that most Americans make consumer purchases solely to fool others about who they really are. It is not to say that we are a nation of crass status-seekers. Or that people who purchase more than they need are simply demonstrating a base materialism, in the sense of valuing material possessions above all else. But it is to say that, unlike the millionaires next door, who are not driven to use their wealth to create an attractive image of themselves, many of us are continually comparing our own lifestyle and possessions to those of a select group of people we respect and want to be like, people whose sense of what's important in life seems close to our own.

This aspect of our spending is not new—competitive acquisition has long been an American institution. At the turn of the century, the rich consumed conspicuously. In the early post–World War II decades, Americans spent to keep up with the Joneses, using their possessions to make the statement that they were not failing in their careers. But in recent decades, the culture of spending has changed and intensified. In the old days, our neighbors set the standard for what we had to have. They may have earned a little more, or a little less, but their incomes and ours were in the same ballpark. Their house down the block, worth roughly the same as ours, confirmed this. Today the neighbors are no longer the focus of comparison. How could they be? We may not even know them, much less which restaurants they patronize, where they vacation, and how much they spent for their living room couch.

For reasons that will become clear, the comparisons we make are no longer restricted to those in our own general earnings category, or even to those one rung above us on the ladder. Today a person is more likely to be making comparisons with, or

5

choose as a "reference group," people whose incomes are three, four, or five times his or her own. The result is that millions of us have become participants in a national culture of upscale spending. I call it the new consumerism.

Part of what's new is that lifestyle aspirations are now formed by different points of reference. For many of us, the neighborhood has been replaced by a community of coworkers, people we work alongside and colleagues in our own and related professions. And while our real-life friends still matter, they have been joined by our media "friends." (This is true both figuratively and literally—the television show *Friends* is a good example of an influential media referent.) We watch the way television families live, we read about the lifestyles of celebrities and other public figures we admire, and we consciously and unconsciously assimilate this information. It affects us.

So far so good. We are in a wider world, so we like to know that we are stacking up well against a wider population group than the people on the block. No harm in that. But as new reference groups form, they are less likely to comprise people who all earn approximately the same amount of money. And therein lies the problem. When a person who earns $75,000 a year compares herself to someone earning $90,000, the comparison is sustainable. It creates some tension, even a striving to do a bit better, to be more successful in a career. But when a reference group includes people who pull down six or even seven-figure incomes, that's trouble. When poet-waiters earning $18,000 a year, teachers earning $30,000, and editors and publishers earning six-figure incomes all aspire to be part of one urban literary referent group, which exerts pressure to drink the same brand of bottled water and wine, wear similar urban literary clothes, and appoint apartments with urban literary furniture, those at the lower economic end of the reference group find themselves in an untenable situation. Even if we choose not to emulate those who spend ostentatiously, consumer aspirations can be a serious reach.

Advertising and the media have played an important part in stretching out reference groups vertically. When twenty-somethings can't afford much more than a utilitarian studio but think they should have a New York apartment to match the ones they see on *Friends,* they are setting unattainable consumption goals for themselves, with dissatisfaction as a predictable result. When the children of affluent suburban and impoverished inner-city households both want the same Tommy Hilfiger logo emblazoned on their chests and the top-of-the-line Swoosh on their feet, it's a potential disaster. One solution to these problems emerged on the talk-show circuit recently, championed by a pair of young urban "entry-level" earners: live the *faux* life, consuming *as if* you had a big bank balance. Their strategies? Use your expense account for private entertainment, date bankers, and sneak into snazzy parties without an invitation. Haven't got the wardrobe for it? No matter. Charge expensive clothes, wear them with the tags on, and return them the morning after. Apparently the upscale life is now so worth living that deception, cheating, and theft are a small price to pay for it.

These are the more dramatic examples. Millions of us face less stark but problematic comparisons every day. People in one-earner families find themselves trying to live the lifestyle of their two-paycheck friends. Parents of modest means struggle to pay for the private schooling that others in their reference group have established as the right thing to do for their children.

Additional problems are created by the accelerating pace of product innovation. 10
To gain broader distribution for the plethora of new products, manufacturers have

gone to lifestyle marketing, targeting their pitches of upscale items at rich and nonrich alike. Gourmet cereal, a luxurious latte, or bathroom fixtures that make a statement, the right statement, are offered to people almost everywhere on the economic spectrum. In fact, through the magic of plastic, anyone can buy designer anything, at the trendiest retail shop. Or at outlet prices. That's the new consumerism. And its siren call is hard to resist.

The new consumerism is also built on a relentless ratcheting up of standards. If you move into a house with a fifties kitchen, the presumption is that you will eventually have it redone, because that's a standard that has now been established. If you didn't have air conditioning in your old car, the presumption is that when you replace it, the new one will have it. If you haven't been to Europe, the presumption is that you will get there, because you deserve to get there. And so on. In addition to the proliferation of new products (computers, cell phones, faxes, and other microelectronics), there is a continual upgrading of old ones—autos and appliances—and a shift to customized, more expensive versions, all leading to a general expansion of the list of things we have to have. The 1929 home I just moved into has a closet too shallow to fit a hanger. So the clothes face forward. The real estate agents suggested I solve the "problem" by turning the study off the bedroom into a walk-in. (Why read when you could be buying clothes?) What we want grows into what we *need*, at a sometimes dizzying rate. While politicians continue to tout the middle class as the heart and soul of American society, for far too many of us being solidly middle-class is no longer good enough.

Oddly, it doesn't seem as if we're spending wastefully, or even lavishly. Rather, many of us feel we're just making it, barely able to stay even. But what's remarkable is that this feeling is not restricted to families of limited income. It's a generalized feeling, one that exists at all levels. Twenty-seven percent of all households making more than $100,000 a year say they cannot afford to buy everything they really need. Nearly 20 percent say they "spend nearly all their income on the basic necessities of life." In the $50,000–100,000 range, 39 percent and one-third feel this way, respectively. Overall, half the population of the richest country in the world say they cannot afford everything they really need. And it's not just the poorer half.

This book is about why: About why so many middle-class Americans feel materially dissatisfied. Why they walk around with ever-present mental "wish lists" of things to buy or get. How even a six-figure income can seem inadequate, and why this country saves less than virtually any other nation in the world. It is about the ways in which, for America's middle classes, "spending becomes you," about how it flatters, enhances, and defines people in often wonderful ways, but also about how it takes over their lives. My analysis is based on new research showing that the need to spend whatever it takes to keep current within a chosen reference group—which may include members of widely disparate resources—drives much purchasing behavior. It analyzes how standards of belonging socially have changed in recent decades, and how this change has introduced Americans to highly intensified spending pressures.

And finally, it is about a growing backlash to the consumption culture, a movement of people who are downshifting—by working less, earning less, and living their consumer lives much more deliberately.

TABLE 5.1   HOW MUCH IS ENOUGH?

Statement	PERCENTAGE AGREEING WITH STATEMENT, BY INCOME						
	<$10,000	10,001–25,000	25,001–35,000	35,001–50,000	50,001–75,000	75,001–100,000	>100,000
I cannot afford to buy everything I really need	64	62	50	43	42	39	27
I spend nearly all of my money on the basic necessities of life	69	64	62	46	35	33	19

Source: Author's calculations from Merck Family Fund poll (February 1995).

Spending and Social Comparison

I am hardly the first person to have argued that consumption has a comparative, or even   15
competitive character. Ideas of this sort have a long history within economics, sociology, and other disciplines. In *The Wealth of Nations,* Adam Smith observed that even a "creditable day-laborer would be ashamed to appear in publick, without a linen shirt" and that leather shoes had become a "necessary of life" in eighteenth-century England. The most influential work on the subject, however, has been Thorstein Veblen's *Theory of the Leisure Class.* Veblen argued that in affluent societies, spending becomes the vehicle through which people establish social position. The conspicuous display of

TABLE 5.2   THE GOOD LIFE GOES UPSCALE

PERCENTAGE IDENTIFYING ITEM AS A PART OF "THE GOOD LIFE"		
	1975	1991
Vacation home	19	35
Swimming pool	14	29
Color TV	46	55
Second color TV	10	28
Travel abroad	30	39
Really nice clothes	36	44
Car	71	75
Second car	30	41
Home you own	85	87
A lot of money	38	55
A job that pays much more than average	45	60
Happy marriage	84	77
One or more children	74	73
Interesting job	69	63
Job that contributes to the welfare of society	38	38
Percentage who think they have a very good chance of achieving the "good life"	35	23

Source: Roper Center, University of Connecticut; published in *American Enterprise* (May–June 1993), p. 87.

TABLE 5.3   THE EXPANDING DEFINITION OF "NECESSITIES"

PERCENTAGE INDICATING ITEM IS A NECESSITY			
	1973	1991	1996
Second television	3	15	10
Dishwasher	10	24	13
VCR	—*	18	13
Basic cable service	—	26	17
Remote control for TV or VCR	—	23	—
Answering machine	—	20	26
Home computer	—	11	26
Microwave	—	44	32
Second automobile	20	27	37
Auto air conditioning	13	42	41
Home air conditioning	26	47	51
Television	57	74	59
Clothes dryer	54	74	62
Clothes washer	88	82	86
Automobile	90	85	93
Cellular phone	—	5	—
Housekeeper	—	4	—

*Item did not exist, was not widely in use, or was not asked about in 1973.

Source: Roper Center, University of Connecticut; 1973 and 1991 data published in *American Enterprise* (May–June 1993), p. 89.

wealth and leisure is the marker that reveals a man's income to the outside world. (Wives, by the way, were seen by Veblen as largely ornamental, useful to display a man's finest purchases—clothes, furs, and jewels.) The rich spent conspicuously as a kind of personal advertisement, to secure a place in the social hierarchy. Everyone below stood watching and, to the extent possible, emulating those one notch higher. Consumption was a trickle-down process.

The phenomenon that Veblen identified and described, conspicuous consumption by the rich and the nouveaux riches, was not new even in his own time. Spending to establish a social position has a long history. Seventeenth- and eighteenth-century Italian nobles built opulent palaces with beautiful facades and, within those facades, placed tiles engraved with the words *Pro Invidia* (To Be Envied). For centuries, aristocrats passed laws to forbid the nouveaux riches from copying their clothing styles. At the turn of the century, the wealthy published the menus of their dinner parties in the newspapers. And fifty years ago, American social climbers bought fake "ancestor portraits" to hang in their libraries.

Veblen's story made a lot of sense for the upper-crust, turn-of-the-century urban world of his day. But by the 1920s, new developments were afoot. Because productivity and output were growing so rapidly, more and more people had entered the comfortable middle classes and begun to enjoy substantial discretionary spending. And this mass prosperity eventually engendered a new socioeconomic phenomenon—a mass keeping-up process that led to convergence among consumers' acquisition goals and purchasing patterns.

The advent of mass production in the 1920s made possible an outpouring of identical consumer goods that nearly everybody wanted—and were better able to afford, thanks to declining prices. By the fifties, the Smiths had to have the Joneses' fully automatic washing machine, vacuum cleaner, and, most of all, the shiny new Chevrolet parked in the driveway. The story of this period was that people looked to their own neighborhoods for their spending cues, and the neighbors grew more and more alike in what they had. Like compared with like and strove to become even more alike.

This phenomenon was chronicled by James Duesenberry, a Harvard economist writing just after the Second World War. Duesenberry updated Veblen's trickle-down perspective in his classic discussion of "keeping up with the Joneses." In contrast to Veblen's Vanderbilts, Duesenberry's 1950s Joneses were middle-class and they lived next door, in suburban USA. Rather than seeking to best their neighbors, Duesenberry's Smiths mainly wanted to be like them. Although the ad writers urged people to be the first on the block to own a product, the greater fear in most consumers' minds during this period was that if they didn't get cracking, they might be the last to get on board.

In addition to Veblen and Duesenberry, a number of distinguished economists have emphasized these social and comparative processes in their classic accounts of consumer culture—among them, John Kenneth Galbraith, Fred Hirsch, Tibor Scitovsky, Richard Easterlin, Amartya Sen, Clair Brown, and Robert Frank. Among the most important of their messages is that consumer satisfaction, and dissatisfaction, depend less on what a person has in an absolute sense than on socially formed aspirations and expectations. Indeed, the very term "standard of living" suggests the point: the standard is a social norm. 20

By the 1970s, social trends were once again altering the nature of comparative consumption. Most obvious was the entrance of large numbers of married women into the labor force. As the workplace replaced the coffee klatch and the backyard barbecue as locations of social contact, workplace conversation became a source for information on who went where for vacation, who was having a deck put on the house, and whether the kids were going to dance class, summer camp, or karate lessons. But in the workplace, most employees are exposed to the spending habits of people across a wider economic spectrum, particularly those employees who work in white-collar settings. They have meetings with people who wear expensive suits or "real" Swiss watches. They may work with their boss, or their boss's boss, every day and find out a lot about what they and their families have.

There were also ripple effects on women who didn't have jobs. When many people lived in one-earner households, incomes throughout the neighborhood tended to be close to each other. As many families earned two paychecks, however, mothers who stayed at home or worked part-time found themselves competing with neighbors who could much more easily afford pricey restaurants, piano lessons, and two new cars. Finally, as Robert Frank and Philip Cook have argued, there has been a shift to a "winner-take-all" society: rewards within occupations have become more unequally distributed. As a group of extremely high earners emerged within occupation after occupation, they provided a visible, and very elevated, point of comparison for those who weren't capturing a disproportionate share of the earnings of the group.

Daily exposure to an economically diverse set of people is one reason Americans began engaging in more upward comparison. A shift in advertising patterns is another. Traditionally advertisers had targeted their market by earnings, using one medium or another depending on the income group they were trying to reach. They still do this. But now the huge audiences delivered by television make it the best medium for reaching just about *every* financial group. While *Forbes* readers have a much higher median income than television viewers, it's possible to reach more wealthy people on television than in the pages of any magazine, no matter how targeted its readership. A major sports event or an *ER* episode is likely to deliver more millionaires *and* more laborers than a medium aimed solely at either group. That's why you'll find ads for Lincoln town cars, Mercedes-Benz sports cars, and $50,000 all-terrain vehicles on the Super Bowl telecast. In the process, painters who earn $25,000 a year are being exposed to buying pressures never intended for them, and middle-class housewives look at products once found only in the homes of the wealthy.

Beginning in the 1970s, expert observers were declaring the death of the "belonging" process that had driven much competitive consumption and arguing that the establishment of an individual identity—rather than staying current with the Joneses—was becoming the name of the game. The new trend was to consume in a personal style, with products that signaled your individuality, your personal sense of taste and distinction. But, of course, you had to be different in the right way. The trick was to create a unique image through what you had and wore—and what you did not have and would not be seen dead in.

While the observers had identified a new stage in consumer culture, they were right   25 only to a point. People may no longer have wanted to be just like all others in their socioeconomic class, but their need to measure up within some idealized group survived. What emerged as the new standards of comparison, however, were groups that had no direct counterparts in previous times. Marketers call them clusters—groups of people who share values, orientations, and, most important, *lifestyles*. Clusters are much smaller than traditional horizontal economic strata or classes and can thereby satisfy the need for greater individuality in consumption patterns. "Yuppie" was only the most notorious of these lifestyle cluster groups. There are also middle Americans, twenty-somethings, upscale urban Asians, top one-percenters, and senior sun-seekers. We have radical feminists, comfortable capitalists, young market lions, environmentalists. Whatever.

Ironically, the shift to individuality produced its own brand of localized conformity. . . . Apparently lots of people began wanting the same "individual identity-creating" products. But this predictability, while perhaps a bit absurd, brought with it no *particular* financial problem. Seventies consumerism was manageable. The real problems started in the 1980s as an economic shift sent seismic shocks through the nation's consumer mentality. Competitive spending intensified. In a very big way.

When $18,000 Feels Luxurious: Jeff Lutz

Some Americans are pursuing another path. Want less. Live more simply. Slow down and get in touch with nature. A growing "voluntary simplicity" movement is rejecting the standard path of work and spend. This is a committed, self-conscious group of people who believe that spending less does not reduce their quality of life and may even raise it. Their experience is that *less* (spending) is *more* (time, meaning, peace of mind, financial security, ecological responsibility, physical health, friendship, appreciation of what they do spend). Seattle, long a laid-back, nature-oriented city, is home not only to Boeing and Microsoft but also to many of these individuals. I spent nearly a week there in the summer of 1996, meeting people who were living on less than $20,000 a year. Jeff Lutz was one of them.

After graduating from a small college back east, Jeff and his girlfriend Liza moved to Seattle, where they inhabit a nice, spacious old house in a middle-class neighborhood. They share the place with one friend; their rent is $312 per person. Jeff is self-employed as a medical and legal interpreter and is putting a lot of effort into "growing" his business. Nicely dressed and groomed, he doesn't look too different from other twenty-five-year-old graduates of the prep school and college he attended. But he is. Living on about $10,000 a year, he says he has basically everything he wants and will be content to live at this level of material comfort for the rest of his life. Youthful naïveté? Perhaps. But maybe not.

Lutz grew up in Mexico. His mother, a writer and social activist, went to Mexico with her parents, refugees from Franco's civil war. His father was a lawyer from New York. Family role models helped form his commitment to a frugal lifestyle. "My great-grandfather, who escaped czarist jail in Lithuania, lived in Mexico with one lightbulb and a record player. He had three photos behind his bed. One was Tolstoy, and one was Gandhi, and one was Pious XXIII."

As a teenager, Lutz went to a private school in western Massachusetts. There he 30 began to feel like "part of a herd being prodded along to do one thing after the next in semiconscious wakefulness. You go to elementary school, and then you go to junior high, and then you go to high school, and then you go to college in order to get a job, in order to compete with other people in higher salaries, in order to have more stuff. I saw really clearly in high school just where it was leading." At that point, he made up his mind about two things. First, "I needed to find a way to not be in a nine-to-five-until-I-died treadmill. I had a vision of life being much, much more than spending most of my life in a job that was somebody else's agenda." Second, "I wanted to learn how human beings could live more lightly on the earth."

His experiences in Mexico motivated these sentiments. "I spent a week with some Mazotec Indians in the mountains. And some of these kids my age, one of them had a Washington Redskins jersey. I mean, Spanish is their second language; they spoke Mazoteca, and yet they were listening to Michael Jackson and they wanted to buy my sunglasses and they wanted to buy my watch. And they wanted me to bring more sunglasses and watches so that they could resell them to their friends. It was very clear that our culture was sort of surrounding other cultures through the media. I grew up watching *The Love Boat* dubbed in Spanish."

In college, he designed his own major in environmental studies. But unlike many young people who begin their work lives enthusiastically believing they can combine improving the world with making a good salary, Lutz never really considered that path. "The things I was interested in were pretty outside the box." Near the end of his college years, he came across an article by Joe Dominguez, the creator of a nine-step program of "financial independence." Dominguez's program, contained in his best-selling book (with collaborator Vicki Robin) *Your Money or Your Life,* promises freedom from the grind of the working world, not through getting rich but by downsizing desire. Dominguez and Robin believe Americans have been trained to equate more stuff with more happiness. But that is true only up to a point, a point they feel most of us have passed. Doing it their way, you don't need to save a million dollars to retire, but just one, two, or three hundred thousand.

The program involves meticulously tracking all spending. And not just tracking it but scrutinizing it, by comparing the value of whatever you want to buy with the time it takes to earn the money for it. That calculation involves determining your real hourly wage, by taking into account all the hours you work and subtracting all job-related expenses, including the cost of your job wardrobe and takeout food because you're too tired to cook. Equipped with your real wage rate, you can figure out whether a new couch is worth three weeks of work, whether four nights in the Bahamas justify a month of earning, or whether you want to stick with the morning latte (even those half-hours add up). People who follow the program find that when they ask these questions, they spend less. Much less.

Jeff was getting close to financial independence, which entailed earning enough to spend between $800 and $1,200 per month, including health insurance. He says he does not feel materially deprived, and he is careful to point out that voluntary simplicity is not poverty. While he decided against the lattes, he does own a car and a computer, goes out to eat between one and three times a month, rents videos, has friends over for dinner, and buys his clothes both new and used. His furniture is an eclectic mix—nothing fancy, but nothing shabby either. He is convinced that "a higher standard of living will not make me happier. And I'm very clear internally. It's not a belief I picked up from somewhere." It's "something that I've gained an awareness about."

Questions for Discussion and Writing

1. According to Schor, what influence have the media had in altering the public's view of what constitutes the good life?
2. When you look at the tables of comparative statistics Schor provides about luxuries now viewed as necessities, what conclusions do you reach?
3. Would you ever consider following the example of Jeff Lutz and downsizing your expectations and lifestyle? Why or why not?

Philip Slater

* *

Philip Slater (b. 1927) has been a professor of sociology at Harvard and is author of The Pursuit of Loneliness *(1970) and* Wealth-Addiction *(1980). Slater argues that the premium Americans put on success causes many people to resort to drugs to feel better about themselves and to cope with feelings of inadequacy. Slater cites a broad range of examples from everyday life to demonstrate that advertisers exploit societal pressures in order to sell products. The following article first appeared in the* St. Paul Pioneer Press

Dispatch *(September 6, 1984). His latest book is* The Temporary Society *(revised edition with Warren G. Bennis, 1998).*

WANT-CREATION FUELS AMERICANS' ADDICTIVENESS

Imagine what life in America would be like today if the surgeon general convinced Congress that cigarettes, as America's most lethal drug, should be made illegal.

The cost of tobacco would increase 5,000 percent. Law enforcement budgets would quadruple but still be hopelessly inadequate to the task. The tobacco industry would become mob-controlled, and large quantities of Turkish tobacco would be smuggled into the country through New York and Miami.

Politicians would get themselves elected by inveighing against tobacco abuse. Some would argue shrewdly that the best enforcement strategy was to go after the growers and advertisers—making it a capital offense to raise or sell tobacco. And a great many Americans would try smoking for the first time.

Americans are individualists. We like to express our opinions much more than we like to work together. Passing laws is one of the most popular pastimes, and enforcing them one of the least. We make laws like we make New Year's resolutions—the impulse often exhausted by giving voice to it. Who but Americans would have their food grown and harvested by people who were legally forbidden to be in the country?

We are a restless, inventive, dissatisfied people. We like novelty. We like to try new   5 things. We may not want to change in any basic sense, any more than other people, but we like the illusion of movement.

We like anything that looks like a quick fix—a new law, a new road, a new pill. We like immediate solutions. We want the pain to stop, the dull mood to pass, the problem to go away. The quicker the action, the better we like it. We like confrontation better than negotiation, antibiotics better than slow healing, majority rule better than community consensus, demolition better than renovation.

When we want something we want it fast and we want it cheap. Obstacles and complications annoy us. We don't want to stop to think about side effects, the Big Picture, or how it's going to make things worse in the long run. We aren't too interested in the long run, as long as something brings more money, a promotion or a new status symbol in the short.

Our model for problem-solving is the 30-second TV commercial, in which change is produced instantaneously and there is always a happy ending. The side effects, the pollution, the wasting diseases, the slow poisoning—all these unhappy complications fall into the great void outside that 30-second frame.

Nothing fits this scenario better than drugs—legal and illegal. The same impatience that sees an environmental impact report as an annoying bit of red tape makes us highly susceptible to any substance that can make us feel better within minutes after ingesting it—whose immediate effects are more or less predictable and whose negative aspects are generally much slower to appear.

People take drugs everywhere, of course, and there is no sure way of knowing if   10 the United States has more drug abusers than other countries. The term "abuse" itself is socially defined.

The typical suburban alcoholic of the '40s and '50s and the wealthy drunks glamorized in Hollywood movies of that period were not considered "drug abusers." Nor is the ex-heroin addict who has been weaned to a lifetime addiction to Methadone.

In the 19th century, morphine addicts (who were largely middle-aged, middle-class women) maintained their genteel but often heavy addictions quite legally, with the aid of the family doctor and local druggist. Morphine only became illegal when its use spread to young, poor, black males. (This transition created some embarrassment for political and medical commentators, who argued that a distinction had to be made between "drug addicts" and "dope fiends.")

Yet addiction can be defined in a way that overrides these biases. Anyone who cannot or will not let a day pass without ingesting a substance should be considered addicted to it, and by this definition Americans are certainly addiction-prone.

It would be hard to find a society in which so great a variety of different substances have been "abused" by so many different kinds of people. There are drugs for every group, philosophy and social class: marijuana and psychedelics for the '60s counterculture, heroin for the hopeless of all periods, PCP for the angry and desperate, and cocaine for modern Yuppies and Yumpies.[1]

Drugs do, after all, have different effects, and people select the effects they want. At the lower end of the social scale people want a peaceful escape from a hopeless and depressing existence, and for this heroin is the drug of choice. Cocaine, on the other hand, with its energized euphoria and illusion of competence is particularly appealing to affluent achievers—those both obsessed and acquainted with success.   15

Addiction among the affluent seems paradoxical to outsiders. From the view-point of most people in the world an American man or woman making over $50,000 a year has everything a human being could dream of. Yet very few such people—even those with hundreds of millions of dollars—feel this way themselves. While they may not suffer the despair of the very poor, there seems to be a kind of frustration and hopelessness that seeps into all social strata in our society. The affluent may have acquired a great deal, but they seem not to have acquired what they wanted.

Most drugs—heroin, alcohol, cocaine, speed, tranquilizers, barbiturates—virtually all of them except the psychedelics and to some extent marijuana—have a numbing effect. We might then ask: Why do so many Americans need to numb themselves?

Life in modern society is admittedly harsh and confusing considering the pace for which our bodies were designed. Noise pollution alone might justify turning down our sensory volume: It's hard today even in a quiet suburb or rural setting to find respite from the harsh sound of "labor-saving" machines.

But it would be absurd to blame noise pollution for drug addiction. This rasping clamor that grates daily on our ears is only a symptom—one tangible consequence of our peculiar lifestyle. For each of us wants to be able to exert his or her will and control without having to negotiate with anyone else.

"I have a right to run my machine and do my work" even if it makes your rest impossible. "I have a right to hear my music" even if this makes it impossible to hear   20

---

[1] *Yumpies:* young, upper-middle-class professionals.

your music, or better yet, enjoy that most rare and precious of modern commodities: silence. "I have a right to make a profit" even if it means poisoning you, your children and your children's children. "I have a right to have a drink when I want to and drive my car when I want to" even if it means totaling your car and crippling your life.

This intolerance of any constraint or obstacle makes our lives rich in conflict and aggravation. Each day we encounter the noise, distress and lethal fallout of the dilemmas we brushed aside so impatiently the day before. Each day the postponed problems multiply, proliferate, metastasize—but this only makes us more aggravated and impatient than we were before. And since we're unwilling to change our ways it becomes more and more necessary to anesthetize ourselves to the havoc we've wrought.

We don't like the thought of attuning ourselves to nature or to a group or community. We like to fantasize having control over our lives, and drugs seem to make this possible. With drugs you are not only master of your fate and captain of your soul, you are dictator of your body as well.

Unwilling to respond to its own needs and wants, you goad it into activity with caffeine in the morning and slow it down with alcohol at night. If the day goes poorly, a little cocaine will set it right, and if quiet relaxation and sensual enjoyment is called for, marijuana.

Cocaine or alcohol makes a party or a performance go well. Nothing is left to chance. The quality of experience is measured by how many drugs or drinks were consumed rather than by the experience itself. Most of us are unwilling to accept the fact that life has good days and bad days. We attempt—unsuccessfully but valiantly—to postpone all the bad days until that fateful moment when the body presents us with all our IOUs, tied up in a neat bundle called cancer, heart disease, cirrhosis or whatever.

Every great sage and spiritual leader throughout history has emphasized that happiness comes not from getting more but from learning to want less. Clearly this is a hard lesson for humans, since so few have learned it.   25

But in our society we spend billions each year creating want. Covetousness, discontent and greed are taught to our children, drummed into them—they are bombarded with it. Not only through advertising, but in the feverish emphasis on success, on winning at all costs, on being the center of attention through one kind of performance or another, on being the first at something—no matter how silly or stupid (*The Guinness Book of Records*). We are an addictive society.

Addiction is a state of wanting. It is a condition in which the individual feels he or she is incomplete, inadequate, lacking, not whole, and can only be made whole by the addition of something external.

This need not be a drug. It can be money, food, fame, sex, responsibility, power, good deeds, possessions, cleaning—the addictive impulse can attach itself to anything, real or symbolic. You're addicted to something whenever you feel it completes you— that you wouldn't be a whole person without it. When you try to make sure it's always there, that there's always a good supply on hand.

Most of us are a little proud of the supposed personality defects that make addiction "necessary"—the "I can't . . . ," "I have to . . . ," "I always . . . ," "I never . . ." But such "lacks" are all delusional. It's fun to brag about not being able to live without something but it's just pomposity. We are all human, and given water, a little food, and a little warmth, we'll survive.

But it's very hard to hang onto this humanity when we're told every day that we're   30
ignorant, misguided, inadequate, incompetent and undesirable and that we will emerge
from this terrible condition only if we eat or drink or buy something, at which point
we'll magically and instantly feel better.

We may be smart enough not to believe the silly claims of the individual ad, but
can we escape the underlying message on which all of them agree? That you can only
be made whole and healthy by buying or ingesting something? Can we reasonably
complain about the amount of addiction in our society when we teach it every day?

A Caribbean worker once said, apropos of the increasing role of Western products
in the economy of his country: "Your corporations are like mosquitoes. I don't so much
mind their taking a little of my blood, but why do they have to leave that nasty itch in
its place?"

It seems futile to spend hundreds of billions of dollars trying to intercept the flow
of drugs—arresting and imprisoning those who meet the demand for them, when we
activate and nourish that demand every day. Until we get tired of encouraging the pursuit of illusory fixes and begin to celebrate and refine what we already are and have,
addictive substances will always proliferate faster than we can control them.

Questions for Discussion and Writing

1. In Slater's view, how is the quick-fix mentality responsible for
   rampant drug use and addiction in the United States?
2. Consider the definition of addiction that Slater presents. Do
   you agree or disagree with the way he frames the debate?
   Why, or why not?
3. What current ads set up hypothetically stressful situations
   and then push products as a quick and easy way to relieve
   the stress? Analyze a few of these ads.
4. To what extent have performance-enhancing drugs or steroids become an important component of sports? In your opinion, are athletes coerced into taking these
   drugs in order to remain competitive? Why or why not?
5. What grim conceit underlies Vincent Van Gogh's painting (1886), and how does this
   image ironically comment on Slater's thesis?

Jan Harold Brunvand

• •

*Jan Harold Brunvand (b. 1933) is a professor of folklore at the University of Utah and is
the author of* The Study of American Folklore: An Introduction *(1997) and* The Vanishing Hitchhiker: American Urban Legends and Their Meanings *(1981), from which the
following selection is drawn. Brunvand identifies the distinguishing features of urban legends and gives an in-depth analysis of one particular legend that has been repeated so
many times that it is thought to be true. A recent work is* Encyclopedia of Urban Legends
(2001).

URBAN LEGENDS: "THE BOYFRIEND'S DEATH"

We are not aware of our own folklore any more than we are of the grammatical rules of our language. When we follow the ancient practice of informally transmitting "lore"—wisdom, knowledge, or accepted modes of behavior—by word of mouth and customary example from person to person, we do not concentrate on the form or content of our folklore; instead, we simply listen to information that others tell us and then pass it on—more or less accurately—to other listeners. In this stream of unselfconscious oral tradition the information that acquires a clear story line is called *narrative folklore,* and those stories alleged to be true are *legends.* This, in broad summary, is the typical process of legend formation and transmission as it has existed from time immemorial and continues to operate today. It works about the same way whether the legendary plot concerns a dragon in a cave or a mouse in a Coke bottle.

It might seem unlikely that legends—*urban* legends at that—would continue to be created in an age of widespread literacy, rapid mass communications, and restless travel. While our pioneer ancestors may have had to rely heavily on oral traditions to pass the news along about changing events and frontier dangers, surely we no longer need mere "folk" reports of what's happening, with all their tendencies to distort the facts. A moment's reflection, however, reminds us of the many weird, fascinating, but unverified rumors and tales that so frequently come to our ears—killers and madmen on the loose, shocking or funny personal experiences, unsafe manufactured products, and many other unexplained mysteries of daily life. Sometimes we encounter different oral versions of such stories, and on occasion we may read about similar events in newspapers or magazines; but seldom do we find, or even seek after, reliable documentation. The lack of verification in no way diminishes the appeal urban legends have for us. We enjoy them merely as stories, and we tend at least to half-believe them as possibly accurate reports. And the legends we tell, as with any folklore, reflect many of the hopes, fears, and anxieties of our time. In short, legends are definitely part of our modern folklore—legends which are as traditional, variable, and functional as those of the past.

Folklore study consists of collecting, classifying, and interpreting in their full cultural context the many products of everyday human interaction that have acquired a somewhat stable underlying form and that are passed traditionally from person to person, group to group, and generation to generation. Legend study is a most revealing area of such research because the stories that people believe to be true hold an important place in their worldview. "If it's true, it's important" is an axiom to be trusted, whether or not the lore really *is* true or not. Simply becoming aware of this modern folklore which we all possess to some degree is a revelation in itself, but going beyond this to compare the tales, isolate their consistent themes, and relate them to the rest of the culture can yield rich insights into the state of our current civilization. . . .

Urban Legends as Folklore

Folklore subsists on oral tradition, but not all oral communication is folklore. The vast amounts of human interchange, from casual daily conversations to formal discussions in business or industry, law, or teaching, rarely constitute straight oral folklore. However, all such "communicative events" (as scholars dub them) are punctuated routinely by various units of traditional material that are memorable, repeatable, and that fit recurring social situations well enough to serve in place of original remarks. "Tradition" is the key idea that links together such utterances as nicknames, proverbs, greeting and leave-taking formulas, wisecracks, anecdotes, and jokes as "folklore"; indeed, these are a few of the best known "conversational genres" of American folklore. Longer and more complex folk forms—fairy tales, epics, myths, legends, or ballads, for example—may thrive only in certain special situations of oral transmission. All true folklore ultimately depends upon continued oral dissemination, usually within fairly homogeneous "folk groups," and upon the retention through time of internal patterns and motifs that become traditional in the oral exchanges. The corollary of this rule of stability in oral tradition is that all items of folklore, while retaining a fixed central core, are constantly changing as they are transmitted, so as to create countless "variants" differing in length, detail, style, and performance technique. Folklore, in short, consists of oral tradition in variants.

Urban legends belong to the subclass of folk narratives, legends, that—unlike fairy   5 tales—are believed, or at least believable, and that—unlike myths—are set in the recent past and involve normal human beings rather than ancient gods or demigods. Legends are folk history, or rather quasi-history. As with any folk legends, urban legends gain credibility from specific details of time and place or from references to source authorities. For instance, a popular western pioneer legend often begins something like, "My great-grandmother had this strange experience when she was a young girl on a wagon train going through Wyoming when an Indian chief wanted to adopt her. . . ." Even though hundreds of different great-grandmothers are supposed to have had the same doubtful experience (being desired by the chief because of her beautiful long blond hair), the fact seldom reaches legend-tellers; if it does, they assume that the family lore has indeed spread far and wide. This particular popular tradition, known as "Goldilocks on the Oregon Trail," interests folklorists because of the racist implications of a dark Indian savage coveting a fair young civilized woman—this legend is familiar in the *white* folklore only—and it is of little concern that the story seems to be entirely apocryphal.

In the world of modern urban legends there is usually no geographical or generational gap between teller and event. The story is *true;* it really occurred, and recently, and always to someone else who is quite close to the narrator, or at least "a friend of a friend." Urban legends are told both in the course of casual conversations and in such special situations as campfires, slumber parties, and college dormitory bull sessions. The legends' physical settings are often close by, real, and sometimes even locally renowned for other such happenings. Though the characters in the stories are usually nameless, they are true-to-life examples of the kind of people the narrators and their audience know firsthand.

One of the great mysteries of folklore research is where oral traditions originate and who invents them. One might expect that at least in modern folklore we could come up with answers to such questions, but this is seldom, if ever, the case. . . .

The Performance of Legends

Whatever the origins of urban legends, their dissemination is no mystery. The tales have traveled far and wide, and have been told and retold from person to person in the same manner that myths, fairy tales, or ballads spread in earlier cultures, with the important difference that today's legends are also disseminated by the mass media. Groups of age-mates, especially adolescents, are one important American legend channel, but other paths of transmission are among office workers and club members, as well as among religious, recreational, and regional groups. Some individuals make a point of learning every recent rumor or tale, and they can enliven any coffee break, party, or trip with the latest supposed "news." The telling of one story inspires other people to share what they have read or heard, and in a short time a lively exchange of details occurs and perhaps new variants are created.

Tellers of these legends, of course, are seldom aware of their roles as "performers of folklore." The conscious purpose of this kind of storytelling is to convey a true event, and only incidentally to entertain an audience. Nevertheless, the speaker's demeanor is carefully orchestrated, and his or her delivery is low-key and soft-sell. With subtle gestures, eye movements, and vocal inflections the stories are made dramatic, pointed, and suspenseful. But, just as with jokes, some can tell them and some can't. Passive tellers of urban legends may just report them as odd rumors, but the more active legend tellers re-create them as dramatic stories of suspense and, perhaps, humor.

"The Boyfriend's Death"

With all these points in mind [on] folklore's subject-matter style, and oral perform-   10
ance, consider this typical version of a well-known urban legend that folklorists have named "The Boyfriend's Death," collected in 1964 (the earliest documented instance of the story) by folklorist Daniel R. Barnes from an eighteen-year-old freshman at the University of Kansas. The usual tellers of the story are adolescents, and the normal setting for the narration is a college dormitory room with fellow students sprawled on the furniture and floors.

> This happened just a few years ago out on the road that turns off highway 59 by the Holiday Inn. This couple were parked under a tree out on this road. Well, it got to be time for the girl to be back at the dorm, so she told her boyfriend that they should start back. But the car wouldn't start, so he told her to lock herself in the car and he would go down to the Holiday Inn and call for help. Well, he didn't come back and he didn't come back, and pretty soon she started hearing a scratching noise on the roof of the car. "Scratch, scratch . . . scratch, scratch." She got scareder and scareder, but he didn't come back. Finally, when it was almost daylight, some people came along and stopped and helped her out of the car, and she looked up and there was her boyfriend hanging from the tree, and his feet were scraping against the roof of the car. This is why the road is called "Hangman's Road."

Here is a story that has traveled rapidly to reach nationwide oral circulation, in the process becoming structured in the typical manner of folk narratives. The traditional and fairly stable elements are the parked couple, the abandoned girl, the mysterious scratching (sometimes joined by a dripping sound and ghostly shadows on the wind-shield), the daybreak rescue, and the horrible climax. Variable traits are the precise lo-cation, the reason for her abandonment, the nature of the rescuers, murder details, and the concluding placename explanation. While "The Boyfriend's Death" seems to have captured teenagers' imaginations as a separate legend only since the early 1960s, it is clearly related to at least two older yarns, "The Hook" and "The Roommate's Death." All three legends have been widely collected by American folklorists, although only scattered examples have been published, mostly in professional journals. Exam-ination of some of these variations helps to make clear the status of the story as folk-lore and its possible meanings.

At Indiana University, a leading American center of folklore research, folk-narrative specialist Linda Dégh and her students have gathered voluminous data on urban leg-ends, especially those popular with adolescents. Dégh's preliminary published report on "The Boyfriend's Death" concerned nineteen texts collected from IU students from 1964 to 1968. Several storytellers had heard it in high school, often at parties; others had picked it up in college dormitories or elsewhere on campus. Several students ex-pressed some belief in the legend, supposing either that it had happened in their own hometowns, or possibly in other states, once as far distant as "a remote part of Al-abama." One informant reported that "she had been sworn to that the incident actu-ally happened," but another, who had heard some variations of the tale, felt that "it seemed too horrible to be true." Some versions had incorporated motifs from other popular teenage horror legends or local ghost stories. . . .

One of the Indiana texts, told in the state of Washington, localizes the story there near Moses Lake, "in the country on a road that leads to a dead-end right under a big weeping willow tree . . . about four or five miles from town." As in most American versions of the story, these specific local touches make believable what is essentially a traveling legend. In a detail familiar from other variants of "The Boyfriend's Death," the body—now decapitated—is left hanging upside down from a branch of the wil-low tree with the fingernails scraping the top of the car. Another version studied by the Indiana researcher is somewhat aberrant, perhaps because the student was told the story by a friend's parents who claimed that "it happened a long time ago, probably thirty or forty years." Here a murderer is introduced, a "crazy old lady" on whose property the couple has parked. The victim this time is skinned rather than decapi-tated, and his head scrapes the car as the corpse swings to and fro in the breezy night.

A developing motif in "The Boyfriend's Death" is the character and role of the rescuers, who in the 1964 Kansas version are merely "some people." The standard identification later becomes "the police," authority figures whose presence lends fur-ther credence to the story. They are either called by the missing teenagers' parents, or simply appear on the scene in the morning to check the car. In a 1969 variant from Leonardtown, Maryland, the police give a warning, "Miss, please get out of the car and walk to the police car with us, but don't look back." . . . In a version from Texas col-lected in 1971, set "at this lake somewhere way out in nowhere," a policeman gets an even longer line: "Young lady, we want you to get out of the car and come with us. Whatever you do, don't turn, don't turn around, just keep walking, just keep going straight and don't look back at the car." The more detailed the police instructions are, the more plausible the tale seems to become. Of course the standard rule of folk-narrative plot development now applies: the taboo must be broken (or the "interdiction violated" as some scholars put it). The girl always *does* look back, like Orpheus in the underworld, and in a number of versions her hair turns white from the shock of what she sees, as in a dozen other American legends.

In a Canadian version of "The Boyfriend's Death," told by a fourteen-year-old   15
boy from Willowdale, Ontario, in 1973, the words of the policemen are merely summarized, but the opening scene of the legend is developed more fully, with several special details, including . . . a warning heard on the car radio. The girl's behavior when left behind is also described in more detail.

> A guy and his girlfriend are on the way to a party when their car starts to give them some trouble. At that same time they catch a news flash on the radio warning all people in the area that a lunatic killer has escaped from a local criminal asylum. The girl becomes very upset and at that point the car stalls completely on the highway. The boyfriend gets out and tinkers around with the engine but can't get the car to start again. He decides that he is going to have to walk on up the road to a gas station and get a tow truck but wants his girlfriend to stay behind in the car. She is frightened and pleads with him to take her, but he says that she'll be safe on the floor of the car covered with a blanket so that anyone passing will think it is an abandoned car and not bother her. Besides he can sprint along the road and get back more quickly than if she comes with him in her high-heeled shoes and evening dress. She finally agrees and he tells her not to come out unless she hears his signal of three knocks on the window. . . .

She does hear knocks on the car, but they continue eerily beyond three; the sound is later explained as the shoes of the boyfriend's corpse bumping the car as the body swings from a limb above the car.

The style in which oral narratives are told deserves attention, for the live telling that is dramatic, fluid, and often quite gripping in actual folk performance before a sympathetic audience may seem stiff, repetitious, and awkward on the printed page. Lacking in all our examples of "The Boyfriend's Death" is the essential ingredient of immediate context—the setting of the legend-telling, the storyteller's vocal and facial expression and gestures, the audience's reaction, and the texts of other similar tales narrated at the same session. Several of the informants explained that the story was told to them in spooky situations, late at night, near a cemetery, out camping, or even "while on a hayride or out parked," occasionally near the site of the supposed murder. Some students refer to such macabre legends, therefore, as "scary stories," "screamers," or "horrors."

A widely-distributed folk legend of this kind as it travels in oral tradition acquires a good deal of its credibility and effect from the localized details inserted by individual tellers. The highway and motel identification in the Kansas text are good examples of this, and in a New Orleans version, "The Boyfriend's Death" is absorbed into a local teenage tradition about "The Grunch"—a half-sheep, half-human monster that haunts specific local sites. One teenager there reported, "A man and lady went out by the lake and in the morning they found 'em hanging upside down on a tree and they said grunches did it." Finally, rumors or news stories about missing persons or violent crimes (as mentioned in the Canadian version) can merge with urban legends, helping to support their air of truth, or giving them renewed circulation after a period of less frequent occurrence.

Even the bare printed texts retain some earmarks of effective oral tradition. Witness in the Kansas text the artful use of repetition (typical of folk narrative style): "Well, he didn't come back and he didn't come back . . . but he didn't come back." The repeated use of "well" and the building of lengthy sentences with "and" are other hallmarks of oral style which give the narrator complete control over his performance, tending to squeeze out interruptions or prevent lapses in attention among the listeners. The scene that is set for the incident—lonely road, night, a tree looming over the car, out of gas—and the sound effects—scratches or bumps on the car—contribute to the style, as does the dramatic part played by the policeman and the abrupt ending line: "She looked back, and she saw . . . !" Since the typical narrators and auditors of "The Boyfriend's Death" themselves like to "park" and may have been alarmed by rumors, strange sights and noises, or automobile emergencies (all intensified in their effects by the audience's knowing other parking legends), the abrupt, unresolved ending leaves open the possibilities of what "really happened."

Urban Legends as Cultural Symbols

Legends can survive in our culture as living narrative folklore if they contain three essential elements: a strong basic story-appeal, a foundation in actual belief, and a meaningful message or "moral." That is, popular stories like "The Boyfriend's Death" are not only engrossing tales, but also "true," or at least so people think, and they teach valuable lessons. Jokes are a living part of oral tradition, despite being fictional and often silly, because of their humor, brevity, and snappy punch lines, but legends are by nature longer, slower, and more serious. Since more effort is needed to tell and appreciate a legend than a joke, it needs more than just verbal art to carry it along. Jokes have significant "messages" too, but these tend to be disguised or implied. People tell jokes primarily for amusement, and they seldom sense their underlying themes. In legends the primary messages are quite clear and straightforward; often they take the form of explicit warnings or good examples of "poetic justice." Secondary messages in urban legends tend to be suggested metaphorically or symbolically; these may provide deeper criticisms of human behavior or social condition.

People still tell legends, therefore, and other folk take time to listen to them, not   20 only because of their inherent plot interest but because they seem to convey true, worthwhile, and relevant information, albeit partly in a subconscious mode. In other words, such stories are "news" presented to us in an attractive way, with hints of larger meanings. Without this multiple appeal few legends would get a hearing in the modern world, so filled with other distractions. Legends survive by being as lively and "factual" as the television evening news, and, like the daily news broadcasts, they tend to concern deaths, injuries, kidnappings, tragedies, and scandals. Apparently the basic human need for meaningful personal contact cannot be entirely replaced by the mass media and popular culture. A portion of our interest in what is occurring in the world must be filled by some face-to-face reports from other human beings.

On a literal level a story like "The Boyfriend's Death" simply warns young people to avoid situations in which they may be endangered, but at a more symbolic level the story reveals society's broader fears of people, especially women and the young, being alone and among strangers in the darkened world outside the security of their own home or car. Note that the young woman in the story (characterized by "her high-heeled shoes and evening dress") is shown as especially helpless and passive, cowering under the blanket in the car until she is rescued by men. Such themes recur in various forms in many other urban legends. . . .

In order to be retained in a culture, any form of folklore must fill some genuine need, whether this be the need for an entertaining escape from reality, or a desire to validate by anecdotal examples some of the culture's ideals and institutions. For legends in general, a major function has always been the attempt to explain unusual and supernatural happenings in the natural world. To some degree this remains a purpose for urban legends, but their more common role nowadays seems to be to show that the prosaic contemporary scene is capable of producing shocking or amazing occurrences which may actually have happened to friends or to near-acquaintances but which are nevertheless explainable in some reasonably logical terms. On the one hand we want our factual lore to inspire awe, and at the same time we wish to have the most fantastic tales include at least the hint of a rational explanation and perhaps even a conclusion. Thus an escaped lunatic, a possibly *real* character, not a fantastic invader from outer space or Frankenstein's monster, is said to be responsible for the atrocities committed in the gruesome tales that teenagers tell. As sometimes happens in real life, the car radio gives warning, and the police get the situation back under control. (The policemen's role, in fact, becomes larger and more commanding as the story grows in oral tradition.) Only when the young lovers are still alone and scared are they vulnerable, but society's adults and guardians come to their rescue presently.

In common with brief unverified reports ("rumors"), to which they are often closely related, urban legends gratify our desire to know about and to try to understand bizarre, frightening, and potentially dangerous or embarrassing events that *may* have happened. (In rumors and legends there is always some element of doubt concerning where and when these things *did* occur.) These floating stories appeal to our morbid curiosity and satisfy our sensation-seeking minds that demand gratification through frequent infusions of new information, "sanitized" somewhat by the positive messages. Informal rumors and stories fill in the gaps left by professional news reporting, and these marvelous, though generally false, "true" tales may be said to be carrying the folk-news—along with some editorial matter—from person to person even in today's technological world.

Questions for Discussion and Writing

1. What are the defining characteristics of urban legends and why have they had such staying power in the popular imagination? What distinguishes an urban legend from a myth or fairy tale?
2. In what ways does "The Boyfriend's Death" exhibit the variations of storyline that define the urban legend? Have you heard one of these variations? If so, how did it differ from the one Brunvand cites? Trace the features of an urban legend that you have heard, either one of those mentioned by Brunvand or another, that has been passed on as a "true" story.

3. In what way does this album suggest that Elvis's posthumous celebrity (and reported sightings) is a case of public mythmaking that corresponds to an urban legend?

Neil Postman and Steve Powers

Neil Postman (1931–2003) was University Professor, Paulette Goddard Chair of Media Ecology, and Chair of the Department of Culture and Communication at New York University. He investigated the effects of the media in books such as Amusing Ourselves to Death *(1985) and* Conscientious Objections *(1992). Most recently, he wrote* Building a Bridge to the 18th Century: How the Past Can Improve Our Future *(1999). Together with Steve Powers, an award-winning journalist with more than thirty years' experience in broadcast news, he wrote* How to Watch TV News *(1992) from which the following essay is drawn.*

Does this 1998 cartoon by Wiley Miller represent a real "non sequitur" (literally, "does not follow" in Latin)?

TV News as Entertainment

When a television news show distorts the truth by altering or manufacturing facts (through re-creations), a television viewer is defenseless even if a re-creation is properly labeled. Viewers are still vulnerable to misinformation since they will not know (at least in the case of docudramas) what parts are fiction and what parts are not. But the problems of verisimilitude posed by re-creations pale to insignificance when compared to the problems viewers face when encountering a straight (no-monkey-business) show. All news shows, in a sense, are re-creations in that what we hear and see on them are attempts to represent actual events, and are not the events themselves. Perhaps, to avoid ambiguity, we might call all news shows "re-presentations" instead of "re-creations." These re-presentations come to us in two forms: language and pictures. The question then arises: what do viewers have to know about language and pictures in order to be properly armed to defend themselves against the seductions of eloquence (to use Bertrand Russell's apt phrase)?[1] . . .

[Let us look at] the problem of pictures. It is often said that a picture is worth a thousand words. Maybe so. But it is probably equally true that one word is worth a thousand pictures, at least sometimes—for example, when it comes to understanding the world we live in. Indeed, the whole problem with news on television comes down to this: all the words uttered in an hour of news coverage could be printed on one page of a newspaper. And the world cannot be understood in one page. Of course, there is a compensation: television offers pictures, and the pictures move. Moving pictures are a kind of language in themselves, but the language of pictures differs radically from oral and written language, and the differences are crucial for understanding television news.

To begin with, pictures, especially single pictures, speak only in particularities. Their vocabulary is limited to concrete representation. Unlike words and sentences, a picture does not present to us an idea or concept about the world, except as we use language itself to convert the image to idea. By itself, a picture cannot deal with the unseen, the remote, the internal, the abstract. It does not speak of "man," only of *a* man; not of "tree," only of *a* tree. You cannot produce an image of "nature," any more than an image of "the sea." You can only show a particular fragment of the here-and-now— a cliff of a certain terrain, in a certain condition of light; a wave at a moment in time, from a particular point of view. And just as "nature" and "the sea" cannot be photographed, such larger abstractions as truth, honor, love, and falsehood cannot be talked about in the lexicon of individual pictures. For "showing of" and "talking about" are two very different kinds of processes: individual pictures give us the world as object; language, the world as idea. There is no such thing in nature as "man" or "tree." The universe offers no such categories or simplifications; only flux and infinite variety. The picture documents and celebrates the particularities of the universe's infinite variety. Language makes them comprehensible.

Of course, moving pictures, video with sound, may bridge the gap by juxtaposing images, symbols, sound, and music. Such images can present emotions and rudimentary ideas. They can suggest the panorama of nature and the joys and miseries of humankind.

---

[1]*Bertrand Russell (1872–1970):* British philosopher and mathematician known for his wit and common sense.

Picture—smoke pouring from the window, cut to people coughing, an ambulance   5
racing to a hospital, a tombstone in a cemetery.

Picture—jet planes firing rockets, explosions, lines of foreign soldiers surrendering, the American flag waving in the wind.

Nonetheless, keep in mind that when terrorists want to prove to the world that their
kidnap victims are still alive, they photograph them holding a copy of a recent newspaper. The dateline on the newspaper provides the proof that the photograph was taken on
or after that date. Without the help of the written word, film and videotape cannot portray temporal dimensions with any precision. Consider a film clip showing an aircraft carrier at sea. One might be able to identify the ship as Soviet or American, but there would
be no way of telling where in the world the carrier was, where it was headed, or when
the pictures were taken. It is only through language—words spoken over the pictures or
reproduced in them—that the image of the aircraft carrier takes on specific meaning.

Still, it is possible to enjoy the image of the carrier for its own sake. One might find
the hugeness of the vessel interesting; it signifies military power on the move. There is
a certain drama in watching the planes come in at high speeds and skid to a stop on
the deck. Suppose the ship were burning: that would be even more interesting. This leads
to an important point about the language of pictures. Moving pictures favor images
that change. That is why violence and dynamic destruction find their way onto television so often. When something is destroyed violently it is altered in a highly visible
way; hence the entrancing power of fire. Fire gives visual form to the ideas of consumption, disappearance, death—the thing that burned is actually taken away by fire.
It is at this very basic level that fires make a good subject for television news. Something was here, now it's gone, and the change is recorded on film.

Earthquakes and typhoons have the same power. Before the viewer's eyes the world
is taken apart. If a television viewer has relatives in Mexico City and an earthquake occurs there, then he or she may take a special interest in the images of destruction as a
report from a specific place and time; that is, one may look at television pictures for
information about an important event. But film of an earthquake can be interesting even
if the viewer cares nothing about the event itself. Which is only to say, as we noted
earlier, that there is another way of participating in the news—as a spectator who desires to be entertained. Actually to see buildings topple is exciting, no matter where
the buildings are. The world turns to dust before our eyes.

Those who produce television news in America know that their medium favors   10
images that move. That is why they are wary of "talking heads," people who simply
appear in front of a camera and speak. When talking heads appear on television, there
is nothing to record or document, no change in process. In the cinema the situation is
somewhat different. On a movie screen, closeups of a good actor speaking dramatically
can sometimes be interesting to watch. When Clint Eastwood narrows his eyes and
challenges his rival to shoot first, the spectator sees the cool rage of the Eastwood character take visual form, and the narrowing of the eyes is dramatic. But much of the effect of this small movement depends on the size of the movie screen and the darkness
of the theater, which make Eastwood and his every action "larger than life."

The television screen is smaller than life. It occupies about 15 percent of the viewer's
visual field (compared to about 70 percent for the movie screen). It is not set in a darkened theater closed off from the world but in the viewer's ordinary living space. This

means that visual changes must be more extreme and more dramatic to be interesting on television. A narrowing of the eyes will not do. A car crash, an earthquake, a burning factory are much better.

With these principles in mind, let us examine more closely the structure of a typical newscast, and here we will include in the discussion not only the pictures but all the nonlinguistic symbols that make up a television news show. For example, in America, almost all news shows begin with music, the tone of which suggests important events about to unfold. The music is very important, for it equates the news with various forms of drama and ritual—the opera, for example, or a wedding procession—in which musical themes underscore the meaning of the event. Music takes us immediately into the realm of the symbolic, a world that is not to be taken literally. After all, when events unfold in the real world, they do so without musical accompaniment. More symbolism follows. The sound of teletype machines can be heard in the studio, not because it is impossible to screen this noise out, but because the sound is a kind of music in itself. It tells us that data are pouring in from all corners of the globe, a sensation reinforced by the world map in the background (or clocks noting the time on different continents). The fact is that teletype machines are rarely used in TV news rooms, having been replaced by silent computer terminals. When seen, they have only a symbolic function.

Already, then, before a single news item is introduced, a great deal has been communicated. We know that we are in the presence of a symbolic event, a form of theater in which the day's events are to be dramatized. This theater takes the entire globe as its subject, although it may look at the world from the perspective of a single nation. A certain tension is present, like the atmosphere in a theater just before the curtain goes up. The tension is represented by the music, the staccato beat of the teletype machines, and often the sight of news workers scurrying around typing reports and answering phones. As a technical matter, it would be no problem to build a set in which the newsroom staff remained off camera, invisible to the viewer, but an important theatrical effect would be lost. By being busy on camera, the workers help communicate urgency about the events at hand, which suggests that situations are changing so rapidly that constant revision of the news is necessary.

The staff in the background also helps signal the importance of the person in the center, the anchor, "in command" of both the staff and the news. The anchor plays the role of host. He or she welcomes us to the newscast and welcomes us back from the different locations we visit during the filmed reports.

Many features of the newscast help the anchor to establish the impression of control. These are usually equated with production values in broadcasting. They include such things as graphics that tell the viewer what is being shown, or maps and charts that suddenly appear on the screen and disappear on cue, or the orderly progression from story to story. They also include the absence of gaps, or "dead time," during the broadcast, even the simple fact that the news starts and ends at a certain hour. These common features are thought of as purely technical matters, which a professional crew handles as a matter of course. But they are also symbols of a dominant theme of television news: the imposition of an orderly world—called "the news"—upon the disorderly flow of events.

While the form of a news broadcast emphasizes tidiness and control, its content can best be described as fragmented. Because time is so precious on television, because

15

the nature of the medium favors dynamic visual images, and because the pressures of a commercial structure require the news to hold its audience above all else, there is rarely any attempt to explain issues in depth or place events in their proper context. The news moves nervously from a warehouse fire to a court decision, from a guerrilla war to a World Cup match, the quality of the film most often determining the length of the story. Certain stories show up only because they offer dramatic pictures. Bleachers collapse in South America: hundreds of people are crushed—a perfect television news story, for the cameras can record the face of disaster in all its anguish. Back in Washington, a new budget is approved by Congress. Here there is nothing to photograph because a budget is not a physical event; it is a document full of language and numbers. So the producers of the news will show a photo of the document itself, focusing on the cover where it says "Budget of the United States of America." Or sometimes they will send a camera crew to the government printing plant where copies of the budget are produced. That evening, while the contents of the budget are summarized by a voice-over, the viewer sees stacks of documents being loaded into boxes at the government printing plant. Then a few of the budget's more important provisions will be flashed on the screen in written form, but this is such a time-consuming process—using television as a printed page—that the producers keep it to a minimum. In short, the budget is not televisable, and for that reason its time on the news must be brief. The bleacher collapse will get more time that evening.

While appearing somewhat chaotic, these disparate stories are not just dropped in the news program helter-skelter. The appearance of a scattershot story order is really orchestrated to draw the audience from one story to the next—from one section to the next—through the commercial breaks to the end of the show. The story order is constructed to hold and build the viewership rather than place events in context or explain issues in depth.

Of course, it is a tendency of journalism in general to concentrate on the surface of events rather than underlying conditions; this is as true for the newspaper as it is for the newscast. But several features of television undermine whatever efforts journalists may make to give sense to the world. One is that a television broadcast is a series of events that occur in sequence, and the sequence is the same for all viewers. This is not true for a newspaper page, which displays many items simultaneously, allowing readers to choose the order in which they read them. If newspaper readers want only a summary of the latest tax bill, they can read the headline and the first paragraph of an article, and if they want more, they can keep reading. In a sense, then, everyone reads a different newspaper, for no two readers will read (or ignore) the same items.

But all television viewers see the same broadcast. They have no choices. A report is either in the broadcast or out, which means that anything which is of narrow interest is unlikely to be included. As NBC News executive Reuven Frank once explained:

> A newspaper, for example, can easily afford to print an item of conceivable interest to only a fraction of its readers. A television news program must be put together with the assumption that each item will be of some interest to everyone that watches. Every time a newspaper includes a feature which will attract a specialized group it can assume it is adding at least a little bit to its circulation. To the degree a television news program includes an item of this sort . . . it must assume that its audience will diminish.

The need to "include everyone," an identifying feature of commercial television in   20
all its forms, prevents journalists from offering lengthy or complex explanations, or from
tracing the sequence of events leading up to today's headlines. One of the ironies of political life in modern democracies is that many problems which concern the "general
welfare" are of interest only to specialized groups. Arms control, for example, is an issue
that literally concerns everyone in the world, and yet the language of arms control and
the complexity of the subject are so daunting that only a minority of people can actually follow the issue from week to week and month to month. If it wants to act responsibly, a newspaper can at least make available more information about arms control
than most people want. Commercial television cannot afford to do so.

But even if commercial television could afford to do so, it wouldn't. The fact that
television news is principally made up of moving pictures prevents it from offering
lengthy, coherent explanations of events. A television news show reveals the world as
a series of unrelated, fragmentary moments. It does not—and cannot be expected to—
offer a sense of coherence or meaning. What does this suggest to a TV viewer? That
the viewer must come with a prepared mind—information, opinions, sense of proportion, an articulate value system. To the TV viewer lacking such mental equipment,
a news program is only a kind of rousing light show. Here a falling building, there a
five-alarm fire, everywhere the world as an object, much without meaning, connections, or continuity.

Questions for Discussion and Writing

1. According to Postman and Powers, in what different ways has television news
   been designed to emphasize spectacle over content?
2. Look at the examples of how a new U.S. budget or an arms control negotiation
   might be reported. How do they illustrate the current failings of news broadcasts?
3. Draw on this essay to analyze the form and content of a nightly TV news broadcast and evaluate the authors' conclusions.

Eric Schlosser

• •

Eric Schlosser is a contributing editor of The Atlantic. *His articles on marijuana and the
law (August and September 1994) won a National Magazine Award for reporting. He
appeared on* 60 Minutes *and is currently at work on a book about the U.S. prison system. In "Kid Kustomers" from* Fast Food Nation: The Dark Side of the All-American
Meal *(2001), Schlosser reveals how advertisers are becoming more savvy in marketing
their products toward children.*

KID KUSTOMERS

Twenty-five years ago, only a handful of American companies directed their marketing at children—Disney, McDonald's, candy makers, toy makers, manufacturers of

breakfast cereal. Today children are being targeted by phone companies, oil companies, and automobile companies as well as clothing stores and restaurant chains. The explosion in children's advertising occurred during the 1980s. Many working parents, feeling guilty about spending less time with their kids, started spending more money on them. One marketing expert has called the 1980s "the decade of the child consumer." After largely ignoring children for years, Madison Avenue began to scrutinize and pursue them. Major ad agencies now have children's divisions, and a variety of marketing firms focus solely on kids. These groups tend to have sweet-sounding names: Small Talk, Kid Connection, Kid2Kid, the Gepetto Group, Just Kids, Inc. At least three industry publications—*Youth Market Alert, Selling to Kids*, and *Marketing to Kids Report*—cover the latest ad campaigns and market research. The growth in children's advertising has been driven by efforts to increase not just current, but also future, consumption. Hoping that nostalgic childhood memories of a brand will lead to a lifetime of purchases, companies now plan "cradle-to-grave" advertising strategies. They have come to believe what Ray Kroc and Walt Disney realized long ago—a person's "brand loyalty" may begin as early as the age of two. Indeed, market research has found that children often recognize a brand logo before they can recognize their own name.

The discontinued Joe Camel ad campaign, which used a hip cartoon character to sell cigarettes, showed how easily children can be influenced by the right corporate mascot. A 1991 study published in the *Journal of the American Medical Association* found that nearly all of America's six-year-olds could identify Joe Camel, who was just as familiar to them as Mickey Mouse. Another study found that one-third of the cigarettes illegally sold to minors were Camels. More recently, a marketing firm conducted a survey in shopping malls across the country, asking children to describe their favorite TV ads. According to the CME KidCom Ad Traction Study II, released at the 1999 Kids' Marketing Conference in San Antonio, Texas, the Taco Bell commercials featuring a talking chihuahua were the most popular fast food ads. The kids in the survey also like Pepsi and Nike commercials, but their favorite television ad was for Budweiser.

The bulk of the advertising directed at children today has an immediate goal. "It's not just getting kids to whine," one marketer explained in *Selling to Kids*, "it's giving them a specific reason to ask for the product." Years ago sociologist Vance Packard described children as "surrogate salesmen" who had to persuade other people, usually their parents, to buy what they wanted. Marketers now use different terms to explain the intended response to their ads—such as "leverage," "the nudge factor," "pester power." The aim of most children's advertising is straightforward: Get kids to nag their parents and nag them well.

James U. McNeal, a professor of marketing at Texas A&M University, is considered America's leading authority on marketing to children. In his book *Kids As Customers* (1992), McNeal provides marketers with a thorough analysis of "children's requesting styles and appeals." He classifies juvenile nagging tactics into seven major categories. A *pleading* nag is one accompanied by repetitions of words like "please" or "mom, mom, mom." A *persistent* nag involves constant requests for the coveted product and may include the phrase "I'm gonna ask just one more time." *Forceful* nags are extremely pushy and may include subtle threats, like "Well, then, I'll go and ask Dad."

Demonstrative nags are the most high-risk, often characterized by full-blown tantrums in public places, breath-holding, tears, a refusal to leave the store. *Sugar-coated* nags promise affection in return for a purchase and may rely on seemingly heartfelt declarations like "You're the best dad in the world." *Threatening* nags are youthful forms of blackmail, vows of eternal hatred and of running away if something isn't bought. *Pity* nags claim the child will be heartbroken, teased, or socially stunted if the parent refuses to buy a certain item. "All of these appeals and styles may be used in combination," McNeal's research has discovered, "but kids tend to stick to one or two of each that proved most effective . . . for their own parents."

McNeal never advocates turning children into screaming, breath-holding monsters. He has been studying "Kid Kustomers" for more than thirty years and believes in a more traditional marketing approach. "The key is getting children to see a firm . . . in much the same way as [they see] mom or dad, grandma or grandpa," McNeal argues. "Likewise, if a company can ally itself with universal values such as patriotism, national defense, and good health, it is likely to nurture belief in it among children." 5

Before trying to affect children's behavior, advertisers have to learn about their tastes. Today's market researchers not only conduct surveys of children in shopping malls, they also organize focus groups for kids as young as two or three. They analyze children's artwork, hire children to run focus groups, stage slumber parties and then question children into the night. They send cultural anthropologists into homes, stores, fast food restaurants, and other places where kids like to gather, quietly and surreptitiously observing the behavior of prospective customers. They study the academic literature on child development, seeking insights from the work of theorists such as Erik Erikson and Jean Piaget. They study the fantasy lives of young children, they apply the findings in advertisements and product designs.

Dan S. Acuff—the president of Youth Market System Consulting and the author of *What Kids Buy and Why* (1997)—stresses the importance of dream research. Studies suggest that until the age of six, roughly 80 percent of children's dreams are about animals. Rounded, soft creatures like Barney, Disney's animated characters, and the Teletubbies therefore have an obvious appeal to young children. The Character Lab, a division of Youth Market System Consulting, uses a proprietary technique called Character Appeal Quadrant analysis to help companies develop new mascots. The technique purports to create imaginary characters who perfectly fit the targeted age group's level of cognitive and neurological development.

Children's clubs have for years been considered an effective means of targeting ads and collecting demographic information; the clubs appeal to a child's fundamental need for status and belonging. Disney's Mickey Mouse Club, formed in 1930, was one of the trailblazers. During the 1980s and 1990s, children's clubs proliferated, as corporations used them to solicit the names, addresses, zip codes, and personal comments of young customers. "Marketing messages sent through a club not only can be personalized," James McNeal advises, "they can be tailored for a certain age or geographical group." A well-designed and well-run children's club can be extremely good for business. According to one Burger King executive, the creation of a Burger King Kids Club in 1991 increased the sales of children's meals as much as 300 percent.

The Internet has become another powerful tool for assembling data about children. In 1998 a federal investigation of Web sites aimed at children found that 89 percent requested personal information from kids; only 1 percent required that children obtain parental approval before supplying the information. A character on the McDonald's Web site told children that Ronald McDonald was "the ultimate authority in everything." The site encouraged kids to send Ronald an e-mail revealing their favorite menu item at McDonald's, their favorite book, their favorite sports team—and their name. Fast food Web sites no longer ask children to provide personal information without first gaining parental approval; to do so is now a violation of federal law, thanks to the Children's Online Privacy Protection Act, which took effect in April of 2000.

Despite the growing importance of the Internet, television remains the primary   10
medium for children's advertising. The effects of these TV ads have long been a subject of controversy. In 1978, the Federal Trade Commission (FTC) tried to ban all television ads directed at children seven years old or younger. Many studies had found that young children often could not tell the difference between television programming and television advertising. They also could not comprehend the real purpose of commercials and trusted that advertising claims were true. Michael Pertschuk, the head of the FTC, argued that children need to be shielded from advertising that preys upon their immaturity. "They cannot protect themselves," he said, "against adults who exploit their present-mindedness."

The FTC's proposed ban was supported by the American Academy of Pediatrics, the National Congress of Parents and Teachers, the Consumers Union, and the Child Welfare League, among others. But it was attacked by the National Association of Broadcasters, the Toy Manufacturers of America, and the Association of National Advertisers. The industry groups lobbied Congress to prevent any restrictions on children's ads and sued in federal court to block Pertschuk from participating in future FTC meetings on the subject. In April of 1981, three months after the inauguration of President Ronald Reagan, an FTC staff report argued that a ban on ads aimed at children would be impractical, effectively killing the proposal. "We are delighted by the FTC's reasonable recommendation," said the head of the National Association of Broadcasters.

The Saturday-morning children's ads that caused angry debates twenty years ago now seem almost quaint. Far from being banned, TV advertising aimed at kids is now broadcast twenty-four hours a day, closed-captioned and in stereo. Nickelodeon, the Disney Channel, the Cartoon Network, and the other children's cable networks are now responsible for about 80 percent of all television viewing by kids. None of these networks existed before 1979. The typical American child now spends about twenty-one hours a week watching television—roughly one and a half months of TV every year. That does not include the time children spend in front of a screen watching videos, playing video games, or using the computer. Outside of school, the typical American child spends more time watching television than doing any other activity except sleeping. During the course of a year, he or she watches more than thirty thousand TV commercials. Even the nation's youngest children are watching a great deal of television. About one-quarter of American children between the ages of two and five have a TV in their room.

What does this 2004 photo suggest about McDonald's global marketing strategy for "Kid Kustomers"?

Questions for Discussion and Writing

1. What factors led to an upsurge in advertising directed toward children, and how is "pester power" used to influence what parents buy?
2. How does Schlosser use examples of the extraordinary lengths to which advertisers will go to obtain marketing data on what children want?
3. Advertising for children can be studied in many different ways. You might watch a Saturday morning cartoon show and observe the connection between the characters in the show and the products directly linked to them; you might study an ad specifically targeted for children and in a few paragraphs analyze the components that contribute to its effectiveness.

Rosalind Coward

* *

Rosalind Coward is a journalist and critic of contemporary culture whose books include Patriarchal Precedents: Sexuality and Social Relations *(1983);* Language and Materialism *(1985);* Female Desires: How They Are Sought, Bought, and Packaged *(1985), from which the following selection is taken;* The Whole Truth: The Myth of Alternative Health *(1989), and* Our Treacherous Hearts *(1993). Coward examines the way the ideal female body has been manufactured as an unattainable goal in contemporary American culture.*

THE BODY BEAUTIFUL

The essence of fashion is that it represents an almost annual—but usually subconsciously perceived shift in what is deemed to look good. Colour, length and shape of clothing have all changed drastically from year to year over the last few decades. What is more, there have been considerable changes in the type of woman whose beauty is taken as exemplary—the difference, for example, between Twiggy or Julie Christie in the sixties, Maria Schneider in the seventies and Nastassia Kinsky in the eighties. But this diversity of colouring, hairstyles, and dress styles disguises what has been a consistent trend in fashion for the last thirty years. The images which have bombarded us over these years leave little doubt that there is one very definite ideal, the ideal of the perfect body.

This is the one fundamental point of agreement in fashion, advertising and glamour photography; the rules are rigid and the contours agreed. There is a definite female outline which is considered the cultural ideal. This 'perfect' female body would be between five foot five and five foot eight, long-legged, tanned and vigorous looking, but above all, without a spare inch of flesh. 'Brown, slim, lively and lovely . . . that's how we would all like to see ourselves on holiday. Here are a few tips on achieving this and maintaining it.'

Ever since the sixties, with its key image of Twiggy, there has been a tendency with fashion- and beauty-writing and imagery towards the idealization of a female body with no fat on it at all. Concern with achieving this 'fashionable slimness' has become a routine part of many women's lives; dieting, watching what you eat, feeling guilty about food, and exercising affect most women to a greater or lesser degree.

The ideal outline is the silhouette which is left behind after the abolition of those areas of the body which fashion-writing designates 'problem areas.' First, bottoms:

> Female behinds—whether sexy and shapely or absolutely enormous—have long been the subject of saucy seaside postcards. But this important structure can make or mar flimsy summer clothes . . . to say nothing of beachwear. If what goes on below your back is no joke to you, join Norma Knox as she looks at ways to smooth down, gently reshape and generally improve the area between your waist and your knees.
>
> Woman's Own, *24 July 1982*

We are encouraged to 'beat saddle-bag hips' because 'pear-shaped buttocks tend to wear badly in middle age if they have lacked exercise or have been constantly flattened in over-tight trousers.' Next we learn of the disadvantages of flabby thighs. We are told to 'ride a bike and firm up *slack* calves and *floppy* thighs.' Elsewhere we learn of the horrors of loose stomach muscles and their dire consequence, 'the pot belly.' Bosoms are a little more recalcitrant but even these can be 'toned up' which means 'your bust's firmness can be improved if the circulation is encouraged.' Finally we should 'Take a Long Look at Legs.' The 'best' are 'smooth, flawless, unflabby, and golden.' But there is good news, because 'legs are leaner . . . thanks to dieting and exercise.'

And if all or any of these problem parts continue to cause you trouble, you can always resort to the knife—cosmetic surgery. Women's magazines, beauty books and beauty advice regularly give out information about this or make it the subject of light-hearted asides: 'The only known way to remove surplus body fat (short of an operation!) is to consume fewer calories.' Cosmetic surgery is offered not just for altering the shape of your nose but for cutting away bits of flesh that cling stubbornly to those problem areas.

These exhortations leave us in little doubt that the West has as constricting an ideal of female beauty and behaviour as exists in some non-European societies where clitoridectomy is practised. In the West, the ideal of sexual attractiveness is said to be upheld voluntarily, rather than inflicted by a compulsory operation to change the shape of women's anatomy. But the obsession with one particular shape, everywhere promoted by the media, is no less of a definite statement about expectations for women and their sexuality.

Confronted with the strictness of this cultural ideal, we need to understand the meanings and values attached to this shape. We also need to understand the mechanisms which engage women in a discourse so problematic for us; and we need to know how women actually perceive themselves in relation to this idealized image.

What are the values which Western society attributes to this body shape?

The shape is slim, lacking in 'excess fat' which is defined as any flesh which appears not to be muscled and firm, any flesh where you can 'pinch an inch,' as a current slimming dictum suggests. The only area where flesh is tolerated is around the breasts. The totally androgynous style of the sixties has relaxed somewhat—perhaps men couldn't stand the maternal deprivation, when it came to it. But even with breasts, the emphasis is on the 'well-rounded' and 'firm' in keeping with the bulgeless body.

The most striking aspect of this body is that it is reminiscent of adolescence; the 10 shape is a version of an immature body. This is not because with the increase in the earnings of young people, the fashion industry now has them in mind (though there may be an element of truth in this), because the ideal is not exactly a young girl. Rather it is an older woman who keeps an adolescent figure. Witness the eulogies over Jane Fonda's body; a woman of nearly fifty with the 'fantastic body' of a teenager.

This valuation of immaturity is confirmed by other practices concerned with rendering the female body sexually attractive. The practice of shaving under the arms and shaving the legs removes the very evidence that a girl has reached puberty. It is considered attractive that these 'unsightly' hairs are removed. Body hair is considered ugly and beauty advice strongly recommends shaving the body to restore prepubescent smoothness. A recent hair-removal advertisement spelled out the ideology: 'Go as Bare as You Dare. With Bikini Bare you can wear the briefest bikini, the shortest shorts or the new "thigh-high" cut swim suits with confidence.' Strange paradox here. Pubic hair appearing in its proper place is unsightly. Yet fashion is designed precisely to reveal this part.

The aim is constantly to produce smoothness, 'no razor stubble.' The aim of shaving legs is to produce these firm, lean, smooth objects which, naturally, have a far higher incidence on a rangy, sexually immature body than on an older woman.

It is no coincidence that this sexual ideal is an image which connotes powerlessness. Admittedly, the ideal is not of a demure, classically 'feminine' girl, but a vigorous and immature adolescent. Nevertheless, it is not a shape which suggests power or force. It has already been fairly widely documented how women often choose (albeit unconsciously) to remain 'fat' because of the power which somehow accrues to them. And it is certainly true that big women can be extremely imposing. A large woman who is not apologizing for her size is certainly not a figure to invite the dominant meanings which our culture attaches to femininity. She is impressive in ways that our culture's notion of the feminine cannot tolerate. Women, in other words, must always be seen as women and not as impressive Persons with definite presence.

The cultural ideal amounts to a taboo on the sexually mature woman. This taboo is closely related to other ideologies of sexually appropriate behaviour for men and women. Historically, for instance, the law has had difficulty in recognizing women as sexually responsible individuals. In the statutes of the law, in fact, it is only men who are deemed capable of committing sexual crimes, and this is not just because it is indeed men who tend to attack women. These legal ideologies are constructed on the belief that only men have an active sexuality, therefore only men can actively seek out and commit a sexual crime. Women in these discourses are defined as the sexually responsive or passive victims of men's advances. Actually (as much recent feminist writing on the law has made us realize) the *workings* of the law do embrace very definite beliefs about female sexuality. In rape cases, there are frequent attempts to establish women's culpability, to establish that women 'asked for it' in some way, and gave out messages which invited a male sexual attack. Thus even though the *statutes* of the law appear to protect women against men's active sexuality, in fact the *workings* of the law often put women on trial and interrogate them about their degree of responsibility for the attack.

The ideology in the legal treatment of rape corresponds closely with general ide-   15 ologies about masculine and feminine behaviour. It is acknowledged that women have a sexuality, but it is a sexuality which pervades their bodies almost as if *in spite of themselves*. It is up to women to protect themselves by only allowing this sexual message to be transmitted in contexts where it will be received responsibly, that is, in heterosexual, potentially permanent situations. This is why the defence of a rapist is often conducted in terms of attempting to cast doubt on a woman's sexual 'morality.' If she can be proved to have used her sexuality 'irresponsibly,' then she can be suspected of having invited the active attack of the man. It is only women who have expressed their sexuality within the safety of the heterosexual couple who can be guaranteed the protection of the law.

The sexually immature body of the current ideal fits very closely into these ideologies. For it presents a body which is sexual—it 'exudes' sexuality in its vigorous and vibrant and firm good health—but it is not the body of a woman who has an adult and powerful control over that sexuality. The image is of a highly sexualized female whose sexuality is still one of response *to* the active sexuality of a man. The ideology about adolescent sexuality is exactly the same; young girls are often seen as expressing a sexual need even if the girl herself does not know it. It is an image which feeds off the idea of a fresh, spontaneous, but essentially *responsive* sexuality.

But if this image is somewhat at variance with how the majority of women, especially the older ones, experience their sexual needs, their choices and their active wants, then how is it that this body image continues to prevail? How does that image continue to exist in women's lives, making them unhappy by upholding impossible ideals? How is it that these images have a hold when most women would also express extreme cynicism about advertising stereotypes and manipulation, not to mention knowledge of the techniques by which these body forms are sometimes achieved? (It is not just the real body that is subjected to the knife. Far more common is the cutting off of excess flesh on the photographic image.)

Perhaps the mechanism most important in maintaining women's concern with this ideal is that it is built on a *disgust* of fat and flesh. It is not just a simple case of an ideal to which some of us are close and others not, which we can take or leave. The ideal says as much about its opposite, because the war with fat and excess flesh is a war conducted in highly emotive language. And this language constructs the meanings and therefore the emotions which surround body image. The most basic point about this is that it is difficult to find a non-pejorative word to describe what after all is the average female shape in a rather sedentary culture. When it comes down to it, 'plump,' 'well-rounded,' 'full,' and so on all sound like euphemisms for fat and therefore carry negative connotations. No one wants to be plump when they could be firm; it would be like choosing to be daft when you could be bright. But perhaps more important is that language pertaining to the female body has constructed a whole regime of representations which can only result in women having a punishing and self-hating relationship with their bodies. First, there is the fragmentation of the body—the body is talked about in terms of different parts, 'problem areas,' which are referred to in the third person: 'flabby thighs . . . they.' If the ideal shape has been pared down to a lean outline, bits are bound to stick out or hang down and these become problem areas. The result is that it becomes possible, indeed, likely, for women to think about their bodies in terms of parts, separate areas, as if these parts had some separate life of their own. It means that women are presented with a fragmented sense of the body. This fragmented sense of self is likely to be the foundation for an entirely masochistic or punitive relationship with one's own body. It becomes possible to think about one's body as if it were this thing which followed one about and attached itself unevenly to the ideal outline which lingers beneath. And the dislike of the body has become pathological. The language used expresses absolute disgust with the idea of fat. Fat is like a disease: 'if you *suffer* from cellulite . . .' The cures for the disease are even worse. The body has to be hurt, made to suffer for its excess. *Company* magazine reports on 'Pinching the Fat Away.' Pummeling is regularly recommended, as is wringing out and squeezing: 'Use an oil or cream lubricant and using both hands, wring and twist the flesh as though you were squeezing out water, then use fists to iron skin upwards, kneading deeper at the fleshier thigh area.' And under the title of 'Working Hard at Looking Good' we are told about actress Kate O'Mara's 'beauty philosophy': 'I'm determined to do all I can to help myself. If I cheat on my regime, I write myself abusive notes. Anyway, all this masochistic stuff gives me a purpose in life.'

It is almost as if women had to punish themselves for existing at all, as if any manifestation of this too, too-solid flesh had to be subjected to arcane tortures and expressions of self-loathing.

I have already suggested that one of the reasons behind this self-disgust may be the conflict surrounding the cultural valuation of the sexually immature image. It seems as though women have to punish themselves for growing up, for becoming adults and flaunting their adulthood visibly about their bodies. It is as if women feel that they are too big, occupying too much space, have overgrown their apportioned limits. And a punishment is devised which internalizes the negative values which this society has for such women. It is of course sensual indulgence which is seen as the root cause for women overspilling their proper space. Women who feel themselves to be overweight also invariably have the feeling that their fatness demonstrates weakness and greed. Being fat is tantamount to walking around with a sandwich board saying, 'I can't control my appetite.'

This belief is fostered by the slimming industry and by the literature on fatness. Yudkin, for instance, in the *A–Z for Slimmers,* writes: 'It's not very nice having to admit you are fat. It's much more attractive to suppose that the extra weight isn't due to overeating but is caused by fluid retention . . .' And *Slimmer* magazine ran a spread asking whether children were helpful when their mothers were dieting. They gave a sample of the answers: 'An eight-year-old concerned about his mother's figure is Daniel Hanson of Ashford, Middlesex. "I'm not going to let my mum have any more sweets," he declared firmly. "I want her to be thin like other mums." And nine-year-old Kerry Wheeler says of her mother, "She's looking thinner now, but we can't stop her eating sweets. I have to take them away from her."'

At the heart of these caring offspring's anxieties about their mother's body shape, and at the heart of the discourses on the ideal body, lies a paradox. The *sexual* ideal of the slim, lithe, firm body is also a statement of self-denial, the absence of any other form of sensuality. This adds a further dimension to the cultural connotations of immaturity. The ideal body is also evidence of pure devotion to an aesthetic ideal of sexuality, a very limited aesthetic ideal. Ideal sexuality is limited sensuality; the ideal excludes any form of sensual pleasure which contradicts the aspiration for the perfect body. Again it is a statement about a form of sexuality over which women are assumed to have no control, since it is a statement about not having grown up and pursued other pleasures.

The ideal promoted by our culture is pretty scarce in nature; there aren't all that many mature women who can achieve this shape without extreme effort. Only the mass of advertising images, glamour photographs and so on makes us believe that just about all women have this figure. Yet the ideal is constructed artificially. There are only a very limited number of models who make it to the billboards, and the techniques of photography are all geared towards creating the illusion of this perfect body.

Somewhere along the line, most women know that the image is impossible, and corresponds to the wishes of our culture rather than being actually attainable. We remain trapped by the image, though, because our culture generates such a violent dislike of fat, fragmenting our bodies into separate areas, each of them in their own way too big. Paradoxically, though, this fragmentation also saves us from despair. Most women actually maintain an ambiguous relation to the ideal image; it is rarely rejected totally—it pervades fantasies of transforming the self. But at the same time, there's far more narcissistic self-affirmation among women than is sometimes assumed. Because of the fragmentation of the body into separate areas, most women value certain aspects of their bodies: eyes, hair, teeth, smile. This positive self-image has to be maintained against the grain for the dice are loaded against women liking themselves in this society. But such feelings do lurk there, waiting for their day, forming the basis of the escape route away from the destructive and limiting ideas which are placed on women's bodies.

What feminine body image ideal does this photo of Kate Moss convey?

Questions for Discussion and Writing

1. According to Coward, why is it significant that the female body is fragmented into separate areas women are encouraged to "fix"? What does this say about our culture? Why has the image of the immature female body become the sought-after ideal?

2. How does Coward's analysis of the language used to describe women's bodies in magazines, books, and advertising support her argument?

3. Write an essay in which you analyze the cultural messages transmitted in one striking example of advertising or the media—for example, on the popular TV show *Extreme Makeover*. To what extent do these values correspond to or differ from yours?

4. Find a fashion magazine where you think the editors have digitally slenderized the model on the cover, and write a short paragraph on the relationship between this image and Coward's thesis.

5. What is the downside of social pressure to be thin in this 1998 cartoon by Jim Borgman, and to what extent does it illustrate Coward's argument?

"I WANT TO BE THIN LIKE ALLY MCBEAL, STACKED LIKE BARBIE and ETERNALLY YOUNG LIKE A SUPERMODEL....
NOW IF YOU'LL EXCUSE ME, I HAVE TO GO VOMIT MY HAPPY MEAL."

Arthur Ashe

When Arthur Ashe (1943–1993) defeated Jimmy Connors in 1975 to win the Wimbledon singles title, he became the first black man to win the world's most prestigious grass-court tournament. A chronicle of Ashe's life includes other notable firsts, such as being the first African-American player named to the U.S. Davis Cup team in 1963 and the first black to win the U.S. Open in 1968. (The tournament is now played in the Arthur Ashe Stadium in Forest Hills, New York.) He also became the first black pro to play in South Africa's championships in 1973, when the country was still under apartheid. What makes these victories so poignant is that, during double-bypass surgery in 1983, Ashe received blood contaminated with HIV and died from AIDS ten years later. This essay, taken from his memoir, Days of Grace *(1993), written with Arnold Rampersad, contains Ashe's thoughtful reflections on the psychic toll of racism.*

THE BURDEN OF RACE

I had spent more than an hour talking in my office at home with a reporter for *People* magazine. Her editor had sent her to do a story about me and how I was coping with AIDS. The reporter's questions had been probing and yet respectful of my right to privacy. Now, our interview over, I was escorting her to the door. As she slipped on her coat, she fell silent. I could see that she was groping for the right words to express her sympathy for me before she left.

"Mr. Ashe, I guess this must be the heaviest burden you have ever had to bear, isn't it?" she asked finally.

I thought for a moment, but only a moment. "No, it isn't. It's a burden, all right. But AIDS isn't the heaviest burden I have had to bear."

"Is there something worse? Your heart attack?"

I didn't want to detain her, but I let the door close with both of us still inside.   5
"You're not going to believe this," I said to her, "but being black is the greatest burden I've had to bear."

"You can't mean that."

"No question about it. Race has always been my biggest burden. Having to live as a minority in America. Even now it continues to feel like an extra weight tied around me."

I can still recall the surprise and perhaps even the hurt on her face. I may even have surprised myself, because I simply had never thought of comparing the two conditions before. However, I stand by my remark. Race is for me a more onerous burden than AIDS. My disease is the result of biological factors over which we, thus far, have had no control. Racism, however, is entirely made by people, and therefore it hurts and inconveniences infinitely more.

Since our interview (skillfully presented as a first-person account by me) appeared in *People* in June 1992, many people have commented on my remark. A radio station in Chicago aimed primarily at blacks conducted a lively debate on its merits on the air. Most African Americans have little trouble understanding and accepting my statement, but other people have been baffled by it. Even Donald Dell, my close friend of more than thirty years, was puzzled. In fact, he was so troubled that he telephoned me in the middle of the night from Hamburg, Germany, to ask if I had been misquoted. No, I told him, I had been quoted correctly. Some people have asked me flatly, what could *you*, Arthur Ashe, possibly have to complain about? Do you want more money or fame than you already have? Isn't AIDS inevitably fatal? What can be worse than death?

The novelist Henry James suggested somewhere that it is a complex fate being an   10 American. I think it is a far more complex fate being an African American. I also sometimes think that this indeed may be one of those fates that are worse than death.

I do not want to be misunderstood. I do not mean to appear fatalistic, self-pitying, cynical, or maudlin. Proud to be an American, I am also proud to be an African American. I delight in the accomplishments of fellow citizens of my color. When one considers the odds against which we have labored, we have achieved much. I believe in life and hope and love, and I turn my back on death until I must face my end in all its finality. I am an optimist, not a pessimist. Still, a pall of sadness hangs over my life and the lives of almost all African Americans because of what we as a people have experienced historically in America, and what we as individuals experience each and every day. Whether one is a welfare recipient trapped in some blighted "housing project" in the inner city or a former Wimbledon champion who is easily recognized on the streets and whose home is a luxurious apartment in one of the wealthiest districts of Manhattan, the sadness is still there.

In some respects, I am a prisoner of the past. A long time ago, I made peace with the state of Virginia and the South. While I, like other blacks, was once barred from free association with whites, I returned time and time again, under the new rule of desegregation, to work with whites in my hometown and across the South. But segregation had achieved by that time what it was intended to achieve: It left me a marked man, forever aware of a shadow of contempt that lies across my identity and my sense of self-esteem. Subtly the shadow falls on my reputation, the way I know I am perceived; the mere memory of it darkens my most sunny days. I believe that the same is true for almost every African American of the slightest sensitivity and intelligence. Again, I don't want to overstate the case. I think of myself, and others think of me, as supremely self-confident. I know objectively that it is almost impossible for someone to be as successful as I have been as an athlete and to lack self-assurance. Still, I also know that the shadow is always there; only death will free me, and blacks like me, from its pall.

The shadow fell across me recently on one of the brightest days, literally and metaphorically, of my life. On 30 August 1992, the day before the US Open, the USTA and I together hosted an afternoon of tennis at the National Tennis Center in Flushing Meadows, New York. The event was a benefit for the Arthur Ashe Foundation for the Defeat of AIDS. Before the start, I was nervous. Would the invited stars (McEnroe, Graf, Navratilova, et al.) show up? Would they cooperate with us, or be difficult to manage? And, on the eve of a Grand Slam tournament, would fans pay to see light-hearted tennis? The answers were all a resounding yes (just over ten thousand fans turned out). With CBS televising the event live and Aetna having provided the air time, a profit was assured. The sun shone brightly, the humidity was mild, and the temperature hovered in the low 80s.

What could mar such a day? The shadow of race, and my sensitivity, or perhaps hypersensitivity, to its nuances. Sharing the main stadium box with Jeanne, Camera, and me, at my invitation, were Stan Smith, his wife Marjory, and their daughter Austin. The two little girls were happy to see one another. During Wimbledon in June, they had renewed their friendship when we all stayed near each other in London. Now Austin, seven years old, had brought Camera a present. She had come with twin dolls, one for herself, one for Camera. A thoughtful gesture on Austin's part, and on her parents' part, no doubt. The Smiths are fine, religious people. Then I noticed that Camera was playing with her doll above the railing of the box, in view of the attentive network television cameras. The doll was the problem; or rather, the fact that the doll was conspicuously a blond. Camera owns dolls of all colors, nationalities, and ethnic varieties. But she was now on national television playing with a blond doll. Suddenly I heard voices in my head, the voices of irate listeners to a call-in show on some 'black format' radio station. I imagined insistent, clamorous callers attacking Camera, Jeanne, and me.

"*Can you believe the doll Arthur Ashe's daughter was holding up at the AIDS ben-*   15
efit? Wasn't that a shame?"

"*Is that brother sick or what? Somebody ought to teach that poor child about her true black self!*"

"*What kind of role model is Arthur Ashe if he allows his daughter to be brainwashed in that way?*"

"*Doesn't the brother* understand *that he is corrupting his child's mind with notions about the superiority of the white woman? I tell you, I thought we were long past that!*"

The voices became louder in my head. Despite the low humidity, I began to squirm in my seat. What should I do? Should I say, to hell with what some people might think? I know that Camera likes her blond dolls, black dolls, brown dolls, Asian dolls, Indian dolls just about equally; I know that for a fact, because I have watched her closely. I have searched for signs of racial partiality in her, indications that she may be dissatisfied with herself, with her own color. I have seen none. But I cannot dismiss the voices. I try always to live practically, and I do not wish to hear such comments on the radio. On the other hand, I do not want Austin's gift to be sullied by an ungracious response. Finally, I act.

"Jeanne," I whisper, "we have to do something."   20

"About what?" she whispers back.

"That doll. We have to get Camera to put that doll down."

Jeanne takes one look at Camera and the doll and she understands immediately. Quietly, cleverly, she makes the dolls disappear. Neither Camera nor Austin is aware of anything unusual happening. Smoothly, Jeanne has moved them on to some other distraction.

I am unaware if Margie Smith has noticed us, but I believe I owe her an explanation. I get up and go around to her seat. Softly I tell her why the dolls have disappeared. Margie is startled, dumbfounded.

"Gosh, Arthur, I never thought about that. I never *ever* thought about anything   25
like that!"

"*You* don't have to think about it," I explain. "But it happens to us, in similar situations, all the time."

"All the time?" She is pensive now.

"All the time. It's perfectly understandable. And it certainly is not your fault. You were doing what comes naturally. But for us, the dolls make for a bit of a problem. All for the wrong reasons. It shouldn't be this way, but it is."

I return to my seat, but not to the elation I had felt before I saw that blond doll in Camera's hand. I feel myself becoming more and more angry. I am angry at the force that made me act, the force of racism in all its complexity, as it spreads into the world and creates defensiveness and intolerance among the very people harmed by racism. I am also angry with myself. I am angry with myself because I have just acted out of pure practicality, not out of morality. The moral act would have been to let Camera have her fun, because she was innocent of any wrongdoing. Instead, I had tampered with her innocence, her basic human right to act impulsively, to accept a gift from a friend in the same beautiful spirit in which it was given.

Deeply embarrassed now, I am ashamed at what I have done. I have made Camera adjust her behavior merely because of the likelihood that some people in the African American community would react to her innocence foolishly and perhaps even maliciously. I know I am not misreading the situation. I would have had telephone calls that very evening about the unsuitability of Camera's doll. Am I being a hypocrite? Yes, definitely, up to a point. I have allowed myself to give in to those people who say we must avoid even the slightest semblance of "Eurocentric" influence. But I also know what stands behind the entire situation. Racism ultimately created the state in which defensiveness and hypocrisy are our almost instinctive responses, and innocence and generosity are invitations to trouble. 30

This incident almost ruined the day for me. That night, when Jeanne and I talked about the excitement of the afternoon, and the money that would go to AIDS research and education because of the event, we nevertheless ended up talking mostly about the incident of the dolls. We also talked about perhaps its most ironic aspect. In 1954, when the Supreme Court ruled against school segregation in *Brown v. Board of Education,* some of the most persuasive testimony came from the psychologist Dr. Kenneth Clark concerning his research on black children and their pathetic preference for white dolls over black. In 1992, the dolls are still a problem.

Once again, the shadow of race had fallen on me.

Questions for Discussion and Writing

1. Given the events of August 30, 1992, why was Ashe so unnerved by seeing his young daughter play with a white doll?
2. In what sense was race a greater burden on Ashe than having AIDS? How does he explain this paradox?
3. Although this event happened some time ago, how much of Ashe's assessment of racism in America is still pertinent in and out of sports?

Barbara Kantrowitz

Barbara Kantrowitz, the lead editor[1] for this article, which appeared in the March 1, 2004 issue of Newsweek International, *has been an editor and writer at* Newsweek *since 1985. She has written many cover stories on education and family issues and has won numerous awards. Kantrowitz, who is a graduate of Cornell University and the Columbia University Graduate School of Journalism, is also a published fiction writer. The debate over same-sex marriage and the proposed constitutional amendment to prohibit it is a signal that the institution of marriage is undergoing a radical transformation both here and abroad.*

THE NEW FACE OF MARRIAGE

Los Angeles actresses Alice Dodd and Jillian Armenante got married four years ago at a raucous wedding in New Jersey before 250 friends and family members. Even so, when San Francisco Mayor Gavin Newsom began issuing same-sex marriage licenses in mid-February—in open defiance of California law—the couple drove 650 kilometers north and waited in line for seven hours at city hall to tie the knot again. "Uncle Sam couldn't make it to our first wedding," says Armenante. "We thought it would be nice if he came to our second." They were among the more than 3,000 gay and lesbian couples that had exchanged vows by the end of last week, even though it's still not clear whether their marriages will stand up in court.

To supporters of gay rights, the scene was deeply moving: elderly men and women who had spent a lifetime waiting to make their unions legal, parents with infants in their arms, middle-aged lawyers and doctors. But to opponents, the peaceful scene was a provocative call to arms. American conservatives say San Francisco is proof of the anarchy they've predicted if officials act on their own before the legal debate over gay marriage is settled. "There are millions of Americans angry and disgusted by what they see on the TV—two brides, two grooms, but not a man and a woman," says Randy Thomasson, executive director of the Campaign for California Families, which is fighting the San Francisco marriages in court. "This is the new civil war in America."

The issue threatens to be a defining one in the current U.S. presidential election. Under pressure from his evangelical Christian supporters, President George W. Bush has been dancing around it for months. Although he keeps reiterating his view that marriage should be limited to the union of a man and a woman, he has stopped short of a full public endorsement of a constitutional amendment that would ban same-sex weddings. His most likely Democratic opponent, Massachusetts Sen. John Kerry, has said he opposes gay marriage but thinks the issue is up to each state to decide.

The debate is gaining momentum. Civil unions between same-sex couples are currently legal in only one state—Vermont—but at the end of last week officials in New Mexico's Sandoval County began issuing licenses to gays before being shut down by

---

[1]With Brad Stone, Pat Wingert, Karen Springen, Julie Scelfo, Barry Brown, Liat Radcliffe, Stefan Theil, Melissa Roberts, Kay Itoi, Mac Margolis, Peter Hudson, and bureau reports.

the state's attorney general. The next move will most likely be in court, not only in California, but also in Massachusetts, where the state's Supreme Judicial Court essentially legalized gay marriage in November. State officials have until mid-May to say how they will comply.

Much of the rest of the world is watching America's struggle with curiosity. In many places, same-sex marriage is simply a ho-hum issue. Last week even the 81-year-old king of Cambodia, Norodom Sihanouk, said that as a "liberal democracy," his country should allow gays and lesbians to marry. The Netherlands became the first country to legalize same-sex marriages, in 2001; Belgium followed earlier last year, as did two Canadian provinces, Ontario and British Columbia. In Brazil, stable gay and lesbian couples can inherit from each other and claim one another as dependents in tax returns. In the Argentine province Rio Negro and the capital of Buenos Aires, new laws allow registered gay couples to qualify for family welfare payments. While critics contend that same-sex weddings will destroy the "sanctity" of traditional unions, many scholars say that it's actually heterosexual couples who are radically redefining marriage. Many countries, including Norway, Sweden, Denmark and its province Greenland, have registered partnership laws that extend some benefits of marriage to unmarried couples, both gay and straight. Germany has quietly expanded rights for cohabitating couples, while in 1998, France approved the Pacte Civil de Solidarite—a kind of intermediate step between casual cohabitation and formal marriage that provides tax and health benefits. "There is no way to turn back the wheel," says sociologist Dieter Bruhl of Germany's University of Oldenburg. "Today marriage is an institution at the free disposal of individualized members of a highly differentiated society."

Across the world, the old model—marriage and then kids—has given way to a dizzying array of family arrangements that reflect more lenient attitudes about cohabitation, divorce and illegitimate births. University of Chicago sociologist Linda Waite, author of *The Case for Marriage,* says that gay couples are "really swimming against the tide. What they want is something that maybe heterosexual couples take for granted: the social, religious and legal recognition of a union."

On the other hand, this increasingly diverse family album could be one reason why the push for gay marriage has struck a nerve among some social conservatives. The institution of marriage is so battered that many consider gay unions the last straw, says Princeton historian Hendrik Hartog, author of *Man and Wife in America.* "They see gay marriage as a boundary case," he says—in other words, a step too far.

Marriage rates are tumbling virtually everywhere. In 1990, eight out of every 1,000 Brazilians got married; a decade later that number had dropped to 5.7. In Europe as well, marriage rates are plummeting and illegitimate births are increasingly common. Divorce rates are rising; Germany's divorce rate reached a record high last year—and new marriages approached a record low. "We've moved from de jure to de facto marriage," says Kathleen Kiernan of the London School of Economics. She estimates that 50 percent of 25- to 34-year-olds in Europe are cohabiting. The numbers are highest, perhaps 70 percent, in Scandinavia, especially Sweden. The Swedes have even created their own term for someone who cohabits: "sambo," or "living together": a word that appears on official forms besides the options "married" and "single." Another new word, "sarbo," refers to people who consider themselves a couple but live apart.

In many countries, women see little reason to forgo their newly won independence. The number of thirtysomething single women in Japan has increased drastically in recent years. "They don't have a good reason to get married or, rather, a good reason to put a stop to their single lives," says Keiko Oshima, chief planner at Gauss Life Psychology Institute, a marketing agency in Tokyo. A Yomiuri Shimbun survey conducted in August found that 52 percent of people believed that a woman could be happy without marriage. The same poll found that only 45 percent thought that a man became a "real man" when he had his own family. Nearly one in three Tokyo women in their 30s is unmarried, in a culture where getting married at 25 was once the norm.

Establishing a family used to involve four steps: a marital ceremony, moving in together, beginning a sex life and finally having children. Today couples pick and choose not only the steps but also which will come first. Thirty years ago, says Kiernan, only five of 19 European countries reported 10 percent or more of children born out of wedlock. Today only Greece remains below that threshold, and the European average has jumped to 30 percent.   10

Those figures are of great concern to researchers, who say that children suffer without the emotional and economic support of two parents—and thrive when reared in stable two-parent families. Married couples tend to have more assets, live longer and are better adjusted emotionally than their single counterparts. Fewer money worries may contribute to that well-being, but having someone around to watch out for you also helps, says Evelyn Lehrer, a professor of economics at the University of Illinois.

While the decline of marriage may seem to portend some kind of social cataclysm, scholars say the institution has always been in flux, responding to the particular needs of different eras. "Throughout much of history, if you acted like you were married, then you were treated like you were married," says marriage historian Stephanie Coontz of Evergreen State University in Washington. Religion, a major part of the current defense of "traditional" marriage, didn't even enter the picture, Coontz says, until the ninth century, and then only to prevent European aristocrats from marrying close relatives. The goal was to make sure noble families didn't consolidate too much power. (Commoners could still hook up with anyone they fancied.)

Even in modern times, traditional marriage has never been a universal institution. Carlos Eroles, a lecturer in social work at the University of Buenos Aires, says that throughout Argentina's history, the lower classes and especially farm laborers tended to cohabit, while the upper classes married. Marriage became more widespread after the influx of millions of immigrants from Spain and Italy, both conservative Roman Catholic countries, during the nineteenth and early twentieth centuries.

What's most amazing, perhaps, is that the ideal of marriage has such staying power. The push by gay activists to gain equal rights in marriage was initially motivated by the desire to obtain the legal benefits of being a spouse, such as health insurance and inheritance rights. But many say that it's equally important to make a public statement of affection and commitment—a view of marriage that crosses political and social boundaries. In 1998, Australian Jackie Stricker married Dr. Kerryn Phelps under a chuppah (the Jewish marriage canopy) in a Park Avenue apartment. "The rabbi read verses from the Book of Ruth: 'Where you go, I will go'," Stricker recalls. "It was incredibly romantic." The two women are now back in Australia, where gay couples have some limited rights but can't legally marry. "No group in any society should be grateful for crumbs from the table masquerading as grand gestures," says Phelps. "I feel robbed of the language of being married, of being the daughter-in-law, the wife, the aunt, the stepmother." And when the law says "You can't," the sweetest words are "I do."

Questions for Discussion and Writing

1. What are the pros and cons of legalizing same-sex marriage, according to the authors?
2. How do the authors provide a context for this discussion by citing a wide range of statistics and customs regarding the institution of marriage worldwide? To what extent have other countries moved in the direction of allowing same-sex marriages that the United States is just starting to consider?
3. In your opinion, was this issue a major factor in the 2004 presidential election? Why or why not?

FICTION

Kate Chopin

Kate Chopin (1851–1904) is best known for her novel The Awakening, *published in 1899, which created enormous public controversy by its realistic treatment of the psychological and sexual awakening of the female protagonist. The collections of Chopin's short stories based on her experiences while living in rural Louisiana are* Bayou Folk *(1894) and* A Night in Acadie *(1897). Her short story "Désirée's Baby" (1899) is widely recognized as a small masterpiece of psychological realism.*

DÉSIRÉE'S BABY

As the day was pleasant, Madame Valmondé drove over to L'Abri to see Désirée and the baby.

It made her laugh to think of Désirée with a baby. Why, it seems but yesterday that Désirée was little more than a baby herself; when Monsieur in riding through the gateway of Valmondé had found her lying asleep in the shadow of the big stone pillar.

The little one awoke in his arms and began to cry for "Dada." That was as much as she could do or say. Some people thought she might have strayed there of her own accord, for she was of the toddling age. The prevailing belief was that she had been purposely left by a party of Texans, whose canvas-covered wagons, late in the day, had crossed the ferry that Coton Maïs kept, just below the plantation. In time Madame Valmondé abandoned every speculation but the one that Désirée had been sent to her by a beneficent Providence to be the child of her affection, seeing that she was without child of the flesh. For the girl grew to be beautiful and gentle, affectionate and sincere—the idol of Valmondé.

It was no wonder, when she stood one day against the stone pillar in whose shadow she had lain asleep, eighteen years before, that Armand Aubigny riding by and seeing her there, had fallen in love with her. That was the way all the Aubignys fell in love, as if struck by a pistol shot. The wonder was that he had not loved her before; for he had known her since his father brought him home from Paris, a boy of eight, after his mother died there. The passion that awoke in him that day, when he saw her at the gate, swept along like an avalanche, or like a prairie fire, or like anything that drives head-long over all obstacles.

Madame Valmondé bent her portly figure over Désirée and kissed her, holding her an instant tenderly in her arms. Then she turned to the child.

"This is not the baby!" she exclaimed, in startled tones. French was the language spoken at Valmondé in those days.

"I knew you would be astonished," laughed Désirée, "at the way he has grown. The little *cochon de lait!*[1] Look at his legs, mamma, and his hands and fingernails,—real fingernails. Zandrine had to cut them this morning. Isn't it true, Zandrine?"

The woman bowed her turbaned head majestically, "Mais si, Madame."

"And the way he cries," went on Désirée, "is deafening. Armand heard him the other day as far away as La Blanche's cabin."

Madame Valmondé had never removed her eyes from the child. She lifted it and walked with it over to the window that was lightest. She scanned the baby narrowly, then looked as searchingly at Zandrine, whose face was turned to gaze across the fields.

"Yes, the child has grown, has changed," said Madame Valmondé, slowly, as she replaced it beside its mother. "What does Armand say?"

Désirée's face became suffused with a glow that was happiness itself.

"Oh, Armand is the proudest father in the parish, I believe, chiefly because it is a boy, to bear his name; though he says not—that he would have loved a girl as well. But I know it isn't true. I know he says that to please me. And mamma," she added, drawing Madame Valmondé's head down to her, and speaking in a whisper, "he hasn't punished one of them—not one of them—since baby is born. Even Négrillon, who pretended to have burnt his leg that he might rest from work—he only laughed, and said Négrillon was a great scamp. Oh, mamma, I'm so happy; it frightens me."

What Désirée said was true. Marriage, and later the birth of his son, had softened Armand Aubigny's imperious and exacting nature greatly. This was what made the gentle Désirée so happy, for she loved him desperately. When he frowned she trembled, but loved him. When he smiled, she asked no greater blessing of God. But Armand's dark, handsome face had not often been disfigured by frowns since the day he fell in love with her.

When the baby was about three months old, Désirée awoke one day to the conviction that there was something in the air menacing her peace. It was at first too subtle to grasp. It had only been a disquieting suggestion; an air of mystery among the blacks; unexpected visits from far-off neighbors who could hardly account for their coming. Then a strange, an awful change in her husband's manner, which she dared not ask him to explain. When he spoke to her, it was with averted eyes, from which the old love light seemed to have gone out. He absented himself from home; and when there, avoided her presence and that of her child, without excuse. And the very spirit of Satan

---

[1] *cochon de lait:* literally "pig of milk"—a big feeder.

seemed suddenly to take hold of him in his dealings with the slaves. Désirée was miserable enough to die.

She sat in her room, one hot afternoon, in her *peignoir*, listlessly drawing through her fingers the strands of her long, silky brown hair that hung about her shoulders. The baby, half naked, lay asleep upon her own great mahogany bed, that was like a sumptuous throne, with its satin-lined half canopy. One of La Blanche's little quadroon boys—half naked too—stood fanning the child slowly with a fan of peacock feathers. Désirée's eyes had been fixed absently and sadly upon the baby, while she was striving to penetrate the threatening mist that she felt closing about her. She looked from her child to the boy who stood beside him; and back again, over and over. "Ah!" It was a cry that she could not help, which she was not conscious of having uttered. The blood turned like ice in her veins, and a clammy moisture gathered upon her face.

She tried to speak to the little quadroon boy; but no sound would come, at first. When he heard his name uttered, he looked up, and his mistress was pointing to the door. He laid aside the great, soft fan, and obediently stole away, over the polished floor, on his bare tiptoes.

She stayed motionless, with gaze riveted upon her child, and her face the picture of fright.

Presently her husband entered the room, and without noticing her, went to a table and began to search among some papers which covered it.

"Armand," she called to him, in a voice which must have stabbed him, if he was human. But he did not notice. "Armand," she said again. Then she rose and tottered towards him. "Armand," she panted once more, clutching his arm, "look at our child. What does it mean? Tell me."

He coldly but gently loosened her fingers from about his arm and thrust the hand away from him. "Tell me what it means!" she cried despairingly.

"It means," he answered lightly, "that the child is not white; it means that you are not white."

A quick conception of all that this accusation meant for her nerved her with unwonted courage to deny it. "It is a lie; it is not true, I am white! Look at my hair, it is brown; and my eyes are gray, Armand, you know they are gray. And my skin is fair," seizing his wrist. "Look at my hand, whiter than yours, Armand," she laughed hysterically.

"As white as La Blanche's," he returned cruelly, and went away leaving her alone with their child.

When she could hold a pen in her hand, she sent a despairing letter to Madame Valmondé.

"My mother, they tell me I am not white. Armand has told me I am not white. For God's sake tell them it is not true. You must know it is not true. I shall die. I must die. I cannot be so unhappy, and live."

The answer that came was as brief:

"My own Désirée: Come home to Valmondé; back to your mother who loves you. Come with your child."

When the letter reached Désirée she went with it to her husband's study, and laid it open upon the desk before which he sat. She was like a stone image: silent, white, motionless after she placed it there.

In silence he ran his cold eyes over the written words. He said nothing. "Shall I go, 30
Armand?" she asked in tones sharp with agonized suspense.

"Yes, go."

"Do you want me to go?"

"Yes, I want you to go."

He thought Almighty God had dealt cruelly and unjustly with him; and felt, somehow, that he was paying Him back in kind when he stabbed thus into his wife's soul.
Moreover he no longer loved her, because of the unconscious injury she had brought
upon his home and his name.

She turned away like one stunned by a blow, and walked slowly towards the door, 35
hoping he would call her back.

"Good-by, Armand," she moaned.

He did not answer her. That was his last blow at fate.

Désirée went in search of her child. Zandrine was pacing the sombre gallery with
it. She took the little one from the nurse's arms with no word of explanation, and descending the steps, walked away, under the live-oak branches.

It was an October afternoon; the sun was just sinking. Out in the still fields the Negroes were picking cotton.

Désirée had not changed the thin white garment nor the slippers which she wore. 40
Her hair was uncovered and the sun's rays brought a golden gleam from its brown
meshes. She did not take the broad, beaten road which led to the far-off plantation of
Valmondé. She walked across a deserted field, where the stubble bruised her tender
feet, so delicately shod, and tore her thin gown to shreds.

She disappeared among the reeds and willows that grew thick along the banks of
the deep, sluggish bayou; and she did not come back again.

Some weeks later there was a curious scene enacted at L'Abri. In the centre of the
smoothly swept back yard was a great bonfire. Armand Aubigny sat in the wide hall-
way that commanded a view of the spectacle; and it was he who dealt out to a half
dozen negroes the material which kept this fire ablaze.

A graceful cradle of willow, with all its dainty furbishings, was laid upon the pyre,
which had already been fed with the richness of a priceless *layette*. Then there were silk
gowns, and velvet and satin ones added to these; laces, too, and embroideries; bon-
nets and gloves; for the *corbeille*[2] had been of rare quality.

The last thing to go was a tiny bundle of letters; innocent little scribblings that
Désirée had sent to him during the days of their espousal. There was the remnant of
one back in the drawer from which he took them. But it was not Désirée's; it was part
of an old letter from his mother to his father. He read it. She was thanking God for the
blessing of her husband's love:

"But, above all," she wrote, "night and day, I thank the good God for having so 45
arranged our lives that our dear Armand will never know that his mother, who adores
him, belongs to the race that is cursed with the brand of slavery."

---

[2]*corbeille:* a basket of linens, clothing, and accessories collected in anticipation of a baby's birth.

Questions for Discussion and Writing

1. What can you infer about Armand's character and his past behavior from the fact that he has not punished one slave since his baby was born? How does his behavior toward Désirée change after the baby is three months old? What causes this change in his behavior?
2. What did you assume Désirée would do when she realizes Armand values his social standing more than he does her? In retrospect, what clues would have **foreshadowed** the truth disclosed at the end of the story?
3. Have you ever been in a situation where someone was unaware of your racial or ethnic background and made disparaging remarks about that group? How did you feel and what did you do?

Margaret Atwood

Margaret Atwood was born in Ottawa, Ontario, in 1939. She was educated at the University of Toronto, where she came under the influence of the critic Northrup Frye, whose theories of mythical modes in literature she has adapted to her own purposes in her prolific writing of poetry, novels, and short stories. She is the author of more than twenty volumes of poetry and fiction, including The Handmaid's Tale *(1986), which was made into a film in 1989. Her short story collections include* Bluebeard's Egg and Other Stories *(1986). Her most recent works include* Alias Grace: A Novel *(1996),* A Quiet Game *(1997),* Two Solitudes *(1998),* Blind Assassin *(2001),* Negotiating with the Dead: A Writer on Writing *(2002), and* Oryx and Crake *(2003). "Happy Endings," a gleeful dissection of narrative mutations, first appeared in* Ms. *magazine in February 1983.*

HAPPY ENDINGS

John and Mary meet.
What happens next?
If you want a happy ending, try A.

A. John and Mary fall in love and get married. They both have worthwhile and remunerative jobs which they find stimulating and challenging. They buy a charming house. Real estate values go up. Eventually, when they can afford live-in help, they have two children, to whom they are devoted. The children turn out well. John and Mary have a stimulating and challenging sex life and worthwhile friends. They go on fun vacations together. They retire. They both have hobbies which they find stimulating and challenging. Eventually they die. This is the end of the story.

B. Mary falls in love with John but John doesn't fall in love with Mary. He merely uses her body for selfish pleasure and ego gratification of a tepid kind. He comes to her apartment twice a week and she cooks him dinner, you'll notice that he doesn't even consider her worth the price of a dinner out, and after he's eaten the dinner he fucks her and after that he falls asleep, while she does the dishes so he won't think she's untidy having all those dirty dishes lying around, and puts on fresh lipstick so she'll look good when he wakes up, but when he wakes up he doesn't even notice, he puts on his socks and his shorts and his pants and his shirt and his tie and his shoes, the reverse order from the one in which he took them off. He doesn't take off Mary's clothes, she takes them off herself, she acts as if she's dying for it every time, not because she likes sex exactly, she doesn't, but she wants John to think she does because if they do it often enough surely he'll get used to her, he'll come to depend on her and they will get married, but John goes out the door with hardly so much as a good-night and three days later he turns up at six o'clock and they do the whole thing over again.

Mary gets run-down. Crying is bad for your face, everyone knows that and so does Mary but she can't stop. People at work notice. Her friends tell her John is a rat, a pig, a dog, he isn't good enough for her, but she can't believe it. Inside John, she thinks, is another John, who is much nicer. This other John will emerge like a butterfly from a cocoon, a Jack from a box, a pit from a prune, if the first John is only squeezed enough.

One evening John complains about the food. He has never complained about the food before. Mary is hurt.

Her friends tell her they've seen him in a restaurant with another woman,   5
whose name is Madge. It's not even Madge that finally gets to Mary: it's the restaurant. John has never taken Mary to a restaurant. Mary collects all the sleeping pills and aspirins she can find, and takes them and a half a bottle of sherry. You can see what kind of a woman she is by the fact that it's not even whiskey. She leaves a note for John. She hopes he'll discover her and get her to the hospital in time and repent and then they can get married, but this fails to happen and she dies.

John marries Madge and everything continues as in A.

C. John, who is an older man, falls in love with Mary, and Mary, who is only twenty-two, feels sorry for him because he's worried about his hair falling out. She sleeps with him even though she's not in love with him. She met him at work. She's in love with someone called James, who is twenty-two also and not yet ready to settle down.

John on the contrary settled down long ago: this is what is bothering him. John has a steady, respectable job and is getting ahead in his field, but Mary isn't impressed by him, she's impressed by James, who has a motorcycle and a fabulous record collection. But James is often away on his motorcycle, being free. Freedom isn't the same for girls, so in the meantime Mary spends Thursday evenings with John. Thursdays are the only days John can get away.

John is married to a woman called Madge and they have two children, a charming house which they bought just before the real estate values went up, and hobbies which they find stimulating and challenging, when they have the time. John tells Mary how important she is to him, but of course he can't leave his wife because a commitment is a commitment. He goes on about this more than is necessary and Mary finds it boring, but older men can keep it up longer so on the whole she has a fairly good time.

One day James breezes in on his motorcycle with some top-grade Cali- 10 fornia hybrid and James and Mary get higher than you'd believe possible and they climb into bed. Everything becomes very underwater, but along comes John, who has a key to Mary's apartment. He finds them stoned and entwined. He's hardly in any position to be jealous, considering Madge, but nevertheless he's overcome with despair. Finally he's middle-aged, in two years he'll be bald as an egg and he can't stand it. He purchases a handgun, saying he needs it for target practice—this is the thin part of the plot, but it can be dealt with later—and shoots the two of them and himself.

Madge, after a suitable period of mourning, marries an understanding man called Fred and everything continues as in A, but under different names.

D. Fred and Madge have no problems. They get along exceptionally well and are good at working out any little difficulties that may arise. But their charming house is by the seashore and one day a giant tidal wave approaches. Real estate values go down. The rest of the story is about what caused the tidal wave and how they escape from it. They do, though thousands drown, but Fred and Madge are virtuous and lucky. Finally on high ground they clasp each other, wet and dripping and grateful, and continue as in A.

E. Yes, but Fred has a bad heart. The rest of the story is about how kind and understanding they both are until Fred dies. Then Madge devotes herself to charity work until the end of A. If you like, it can be "Madge," "cancer," "guilty and confused," and "bird watching."

F. If you think this is all too bourgeois, make John a revolutionary and Mary a counterespionage agent and see how far that gets you. Remember, this is Canada. You'll still end up with A, though in between you may get a lustful brawling saga of passionate involvement, a chronicle of our times, sort of.

You'll have to face it, the endings are the same however you slice it. Don't be deluded 15 by any other endings, they're all fake, either deliberately fake, with malicious intent to deceive, or just motivated by excessive optimism if not by downright sentimentality.

The only authentic ending is the one provided here:

John and Mary die. John and Mary die. John and Mary die.

So much for endings. Beginnings are always more fun. True connoisseurs, however, are known to favor the stretch in between, since it's the hardest to do anything with.

That's about all that can be said for plots, which anyway are just one thing after another, a what and a what and a what.

Now try How and Why.

Questions for Discussion and Writing

1. What is it that people really want when they say they want "happy endings" in fiction? What variations does Atwood provide on the conventional happy ending in choice A? Why would showing the "how" and "why" of the story be more challenging to the writer than simply stating "what" happens?

2. How does Atwood use different scenarios related to women's self-esteem to comment on the range of contemporary relationships between men and women? Where does she satirize the difference between Canadian life and books about Canadian life that readers prefer, as well as the literary talks she herself has given before book clubs?

3. In your opinion, which of the short works of fiction in this anthology achieves the best balance between predictability and surprise? Explain your answer in a page or two. You might choose Raymond Carver's "Neighbors" (Ch. 2), Joaquim María Machado de Assis's "A Canary's Ideas" (Ch. 3), Liliana Heker's "The Stolen Party" (Ch. 8), Carson McCullers's "Madame Zilensky and the King of Finland" (Ch. 10), or any other story.

POETRY

Marge Piercy

· ·

Marge Piercy was born in 1936. She received a B.A. in 1957 from the University of Michigan and an M.A. in 1958 from Northwestern University. She is a prolific novelist and poet. Piercy's novels include Going Down Fast *(1969),* Woman on the Edge of Time *(1976), and* Vida *(1979). Collections of her poetry are* Breaking Camp *(1968),* Hard Living *(1969),* To Be of Use *(1972),* Circles in the Water *(1973),* Living in the Open *(1976), and* The Art of Blessing the Day: Poems with a Jewish Theme *(1999). She recently wrote* Sleeping with Cats: A Memoir *(2002) and* The Third Child *(2003). "Barbie Doll" (1973) is typical of Piercy's satiric meditations on economic, racial, and sexual inequality in contemporary American life.*

BARBIE DOLL

This girlchild was born as usual
and presented dolls that did pee-pee
and miniature GE stoves and irons
and wee lipsticks the color of cherry candy.
Then in the magic of puberty, a classmate said: 5
You have a great big nose and fat legs.

She was healthy, tested intelligent,
possessed strong arms and back,

abundant sexual drive and manual dexterity.
She went to and fro apologizing.   10
Everyone saw a fat nose on thick legs.

She was advised to play coy,
exhorted to come on hearty,
exercise, diet, smile and wheedle.
Her good nature wore out   15
like a fan belt.
So she cut off her nose and her legs
and offered them up.

In the casket displayed on satin she lay
with the undertaker's cosmetics painted on,   20
a turned-up putty nose.
dressed in a pink and white nightie.
Doesn't she look pretty? everyone said.
Consummation at last.
To every woman a happy ending.   25

Questions for Discussion and Writing

1. How does the "girlchild" change herself in response to the advice, criticisms, and suggestions she receives?
2. How is Piercy's use of the **controlling image** of a Barbie Doll apropos of the point she is making? What is she saying about contemporary American cultural values as they shape expectations of young women?
3. What is ironic about the conclusion of the poem?
4. Pretend you are a Barbie doll (or Ken before he was dropped by Mattel and replaced by the buff Australian surfer doll, Blaine) and write a paragraph or two emphasizing the needs that you meet and the way you function as a valid role model in **popular culture.**
5. How does this Marilyn Monroe Barbie, dressed in a costume from the 1953 film *Gentleman Prefer Blondes,* suggest she, too, is an icon in popular culture?

Grace Caroline Bridges

. . . .

Grace Caroline Bridge's poetry has appeared in the Evergreen Chronicles, The Northland Review, *and* Great River Review. *"Lisa's Ritual, Age 10" was published in* Looking for Home: Women Writing About Exile *(1990). The distinctive effects of the following poem are due to Bridge's ability to communicate a child's experience of violation through words and images that re-create the shock of this trauma rather than merely describing it.*

LISA'S RITUAL, AGE 10

Afterwards when he is finished with her
lots of mouthwash helps
to get rid of her father's cigarette taste.
She runs a hot bath
  to soak away the pain   5
   like red dye leaking from her
    school dress in the washtub.
She doesn't cry.
When the bathwater cools she adds more hot.
She brushes her teeth for a long time.   10

Then she finds the corner of her room,
curls against it. There the wall is
hard and smooth
as teacher's new chalk, white
as a clean bedsheet. Smells   15
fresh. Isn't sweaty, hairy, doesn't stick
to skin. Doesn't hurt much
when she presses her small backbone
into it. The wall is steady

while she falls away: 20
 first the hands lost
arms dissolving feet gone
 the legs dis- jointed
  body cracking down
   the center like a fault   25
    she falls inside
      slides down like
dust like kitchen dirt
     slips off
 the dustpan into   30
       noplace
 a place where
nothing happens,
nothing ever happened.

When she feels the cool   35
wall against her cheek
she doesn't want to
come back. Doesn't want to
think about it.
The wall is quiet, waiting.   40
It is tall like a promise
only better.

Questions for Discussion and Writing

1. How does the way the words are arranged on the page help communicate Lisa's emotional shock and withdrawal as a result of the trauma she has experienced?
2. To what extent might the title refer not only to the physical ritual of cleansing but the psychological ritual of distancing herself from the memories?
3. Bridges apparently is familiar with the clinical symptoms of children who have been sexually abused. What features of the poem suggest that children who experience this kind of abuse may develop multiple personalities or even become schizophrenic as a way of dealing with the trauma?

Bruce Springsteen

* *

Bruce Springsteen was born 1949 in Freehold, New Jersey. He began performing in New York and New Jersey nightclubs and signed with Columbia Records in 1972. He has given numerous nationwide and international concert tours with the E-Street Band. He received the Grammy Award for best male rock vocalist in 1984, 1987, and 1994. The Academy Award and the Golden Globe Award for best original song in a film were given to him for "Streets of Philadelphia" from the film Philadelphia *(1994). His albums include* Born to Run *(1975),* Darkness on the Edge of Town *(1978),* Born in the USA *(1984),* Tunnel of Love *(1987),* Bruce Springsteen's Greatest Hits *(1995),* Live in New York City *(2001), and* The Rising *(2002).*

STREETS OF PHILADELPHIA

I was bruised and battered: I couldn't tell what I felt.
I was unrecognizable to myself.
Saw my reflection in a window and didn't know my own face.
Oh, brother are you gonna leave me wastin' away on the streets of Philadelphia.
Ain't no angel gonna greet me: it's just you and I, my friend.   5
And my clothes don't fit me no more: I walked a thousand miles
    just to slip this skin.

I walked the avenue till my legs felt like stone.
I heard the voices of friends vanished and gone.
At night I could hear the blood in my veins

Just as black and whispering as the rain   10
On the streets of Philadelphia.
Ain't no angel gonna greet me: it's just you and I, my friend.
And my clothes don't fit me no more: I walked a thousand miles
   just to slip this skin.

The night has fallen. I'm lying awake.
I can feel myself fading away.   15
So, receive me, brother, with your faithless kiss.
Or will we leave each other alone like this
On the streets of Philadelphia?

Ain't no angel gonna greet me: it's just you and I, my friend.
And my clothes don't fit me no more: I walked a thousand miles   20
   just to slip this skin.

Questions for Discussion and Writing

1. How would you characterize the voice you hear? What images convey the speaker's sense of losing himself because of having AIDS?
2. How does being recognized and acknowledged become a central **theme** in this song? At what point in the lyrics does the speaker appeal for this recognition?
3. What impact do you think this song is designed to have on those who hear it? What effect did it have on you?

Kelly Cherry

Kelly Cherry was born in 1940 in Baton Rouge, Louisiana. She received a B.A. from Mary Washington College in 1961 and an M.F.A. from the University of North Carolina at Greensboro in 1967. She is currently professor of English at the University of Wisconsin at Madison. Her works of fiction include Augusta Played: A Novel *(1998) and* The Society of Friends: Stories *(1999). Her collections of poetry are* Death and Transfiguration *(1997), in which "Alzheimer's" first appeared, and* Rising Venus *(2002).*

ALZHEIMER'S

He stands at the door, a crazy old man
Back from the hospital, his mind rattling
Like the suitcase, swinging from his hand,
That contains shaving cream, a piggy bank,
A book he sometimes pretends to read,   5
His clothes. On the brick wall beside him
Roses and columbine slug it out for space, claw the mortar.
The sun is shining, as it does late in the afternoon
In England, after rain.
Sun hardens the house, reifies it,   10

Strikes the iron grillwork like a smithy
And sparks fly off, burning in the bushes—
The rosebushes—
While the white wood trim defines solidity in space.
This is his house. He remembers it as his,   15
Remembers the walkway he built between the front room
And the garage, the rhododendron he planted in back,
The car he used to drive. He remembers himself,
A younger man, in a tweed hat, a man who loved
Music. There is no time for that now. No time for music,   20
The peculiar screeching of strings, the luxurious
Fiddling with emotion.
Other things have become more urgent.
Other matters are now of greater import, have more
Consequence, must be attended to. The first   25
Thing he must do, now that he is home, is decide who
This woman is, this old, white-haired woman
Standing here in the doorway,
Welcoming him in.

Questions for Discussion and Writing

1. What can you infer about the difference in self-awareness of the "old man" in the poem before and after the onset of Alzheimer's?
2. Why is the final image in the last three lines especially effective in communicating how much of the old man's identity and memory have been lost? How do the repeated words and clauses in the last seven lines enact the sense of urgency and desperation the old man experiences in trying to focus his thoughts?
3. How do the images in lines 15–20 serve as a flashback that makes the old man's present situation all the more tragic?

DRAMA

David Ives

David Ives (b. 1943) was born in Chicago and educated at Northwestern University and the Yale Drama School. Ives's work appears in diverse formats, including television, film, opera, and the theater. He has written several one-act plays for the annual comedy festival of Manhattan Punch Line, where Sure Thing *was performed in 1988. Six of his one-act comedies have been collected in* All in the Timing *(1994). His latest work is* Polish Joke and Other Plays *(2004). The following two-character* **farce** *is a lighthearted inventive variation on the premise that if we could take back our verbal blunders on the spot, relationships would never fail.*

Would you consider using an Internet dating service that speeds up the process, such as this one? What are the advantages and disadvantages?

SURE THING

CHARACTERS

BILL and BETTY, both in their late 20s

Setting

A café table, with a couple of chairs

Betty is reading at the table. An empty chair opposite her. Bill enters.

BILL.   Excuse me. Is this chair taken?
BETTY.   Excuse me?
BILL.   Is this taken?
BETTY.   Yes it is.
BILL.   Oh. Sorry.   5
BETTY.   Sure thing.

   (A bell rings softly.)

BILL.   Excuse me. Is this chair taken?
BETTY.   Excuse me?
BILL.   Is this taken?
BETTY.   No, but I'm expecting somebody in a minute.   10
BILL.   Oh. Thanks anyway.
BETTY.   Sure thing.

   (A bell rings softly.)

BILL.   Excuse me. Is this chair taken?

BETTY.   No, but I'm expecting somebody very shortly.

BILL.   Would you mind if I sit here till he or she or it comes?   15

BETTY.   *(Glances at her watch.)* They do seem to be pretty late . . .

BILL.   You never know who you might be turning down.

BETTY.   Sorry. Nice try, though.

BILL.   Sure thing. *(Bell.)* Is this seat taken?

BETTY.   No it's not.   20

BILL.   Would you mind if I sit here?

BETTY.   Yes I would.

BILL.   Oh. *(Bell.)* Is this chair taken?

BETTY.   No it's not.

BILL.   Would you mind if I sit here?   25

BETTY.   No. Go ahead.

BILL.   Thanks. *(He sits. She continues reading.)* Every place else seems to be taken.

BETTY.   Mm-hm.

BILL.   Great place.

BETTY.   Mm-hm.   30

BILL.   What's the book?

BETTY.   I just wanted to read in quiet, if you don't mind.

BILL.   No. Sure thing. *(Bell.)* Every place else seems to be taken.

BETTY.   Mm-hm.

BILL.   Great place for reading.   35

BETTY.   Yes, I like it.

BILL.   What's the book?

BETTY.   *The Sound and the Fury.*

BILL.   Oh. Hemingway. *(Bell.)* What's the book?

BETTY.   *The Sound and the Fury.*   40

BILL.   Oh. Faulkner.

BETTY.   Have you read it?

BILL.   Not . . . actually. I've sure read *about* it, though. It's supposed to be great.

BETTY.   It is great.

BILL.   I hear it's great. *(Small pause.)* Waiter? *(Bell.)* What's the book?   45

BETTY.   *The Sound and the Fury.*

BILL.   Oh. Faulkner.

BETTY.   Have you read it?

BILL.   I'm a Mets fan, myself. *(Bell.)*

BETTY.   Have you read it?   50

BILL.   Yeah, I read it in college.

BETTY.   Where was college?

BILL.   I went to Oral Roberts University. *(Bell.)*

BETTY.   Where was college?

BILL.   I was lying. I never really went to college. I just like to party. *(Bell.)*   55

BETTY.   Where was college?

BILL.   Harvard.

BETTY.   Do you like Faulkner?

BILL.   I love Faulkner. I spent a whole winter reading him once.

BETTY.   I've just started.   60

BILL.   I was so excited after ten pages that I went out and bought everything else he wrote. One of the greatest reading experiences of my life. I mean, all that incredible psychological understanding. Page after page of gorgeous prose. His profound grasp of the mystery of time and human existence. The smells of the earth. . . . What do you think?

BETTY.   I think it's pretty boring. *(Bell.)*

BILL.   What's the book?

BETTY.   *The Sound and the Fury.*

BILL.   Oh! Faulkner!   65

BETTY.   Do you like Faulkner?

BILL.   I love Faulkner.

BETTY.   He's incredible.

BILL.   I spent a whole winter reading him once.

BETTY.   I was so excited after ten pages that I went out and bought everything   70
else he wrote.

BILL.   All that incredible psychological understanding.

BETTY.   And the prose is so gorgeous.

BILL.   And the way he's grasped the mystery of time—

BETTY.   —and human existence. I can't believe I've waited this long to read him.

BILL.   You never know. You might not have liked him before.   75

BETTY.   That's true.

BILL.   You might not have been ready for him. You have to hit these things at the right moment or it's no good.

BETTY.   That's happened to me.

BILL.   It's all in the timing. *(Small pause.)* My name's Bill, by the way.

BETTY.   I'm Betty.   80

BILL.   Hi.

BETTY.   Hi. *(Small pause.)*

BILL.   Yes I thought reading Faulkner was . . . a great experience.

BETTY.   Yes. *(Small pause.)*

BILL.   *The Sound and the Fury* . . . *(Another small pause.)*   85

BETTY.   Well. Onwards and upwards. *(She goes back to her book.)*

BILL.   Waiter—? *(Bell.)* You have to hit these things at the right moment or it's no good.

BETTY.   That's happened to me.

BILL.   It's all in the timing. My name's Bill, by the way.

BETTY.   I'm Betty.   90

BILL.   Hi.

BETTY.   Hi.

BILL.   Do you come in here a lot?

BETTY.   Actually I'm just in town for two days from Pakistan.

BILL.   Oh. Pakistan. *(Bell.)* My name's Bill, by the way.   95

BETTY.   I'm Betty.

BILL.   Hi.

BETTY. Hi.

BILL. Do you come in here a lot?

BETTY. Every once in a while. Do you? 100

BILL. Not so much anymore. Not as much as I used to. Before my nervous break-down. *(Bell.)* Do you come in here a lot?

BETTY. Why are you asking?

BILL. Just interested.

BETTY. Are you really interested, or do you just want to pick me up?

BILL. No, I'm really interested. 105

BETTY. Why would you be interested in whether I come in here a lot?

BILL. Just . . . getting acquainted.

BETTY. Maybe you're only interested for the sake of making small talk long enough to ask me back to your place to listen to some music, or because you've just rented some great tape for your VCR, or because you've got some terrific un-known Django Reinhardt[1] record, only all you really want to do is fuck—which you won't do very well—after which you'll go into the bathroom and pee very loudly, then pad into the kitchen and get yourself a beer from the refrigerator without asking me whether I'd like anything, and then you'll proceed to lie back down beside me and confess that you've got a girlfriend named Stephanie who's away at medical school in Belgium for a year, and that you've been involved with her—*off and on*—in what you'll call a very "intricate" relationship, for about *seven YEARS*. None of which *interests* me, mister!

BILL. Okay. *(Bell.)* Do you come in here a lot?

BETTY. Every other day, I think. 110

BILL. I come in here quite a lot and I don't remember seeing you.

BETTY. I guess we must be on different schedules.

BILL. Missed connections.

BETTY. Yes. Different time zones.

BILL. Amazing how you can live right next door to somebody in this town and 115
never even know it.

BETTY. I know.

BILL. City life.

BETTY. It's crazy.

BILL. We probably pass each other in the street every day. Right in front of this place, probably.

BETTY. Yep. 120

BILL. *(Looks around.)* Well the waiters here sure seem to be in some different time zone. I can't seem to locate one anywhere. . . . Waiter! *(He looks back.)* So what do you— *(He sees that she's gone back to her book.)*

BETTY. I beg pardon?

BILL. Nothing. Sorry. *(Bell.)*

BETTY. I guess we must be on different schedules.

BILL. Missed connections. 125

---

[1]*Django Reinhardt (1910–1953):* virtuoso jazz guitar player who thrilled generations of jazz lovers.

BETTY.   Yes. Different time zones.

BILL.   Amazing how you can live right next door to somebody in this town and never even know it.

BETTY.   I know.

BILL.   City life.

BETTY.   It's crazy.   130

BILL.   You weren't waiting for somebody when I came in, were you?

BETTY.   Actually I was.

BILL.   Oh. Boyfriend?

BETTY.   Sort of.

BILL.   What's a sort-of boyfriend?   135

BETTY.   My husband.

BILL.   Ah-ha. *(Bell.)* You weren't waiting for somebody when I came in, were you?

BETTY.   Actually I was.

BILL.   Oh. Boyfriend?

BETTY.   Sort of.   140

BILL.   What's a sort-of boyfriend?

BETTY.   We were meeting here to break up.

BILL.   Mm-hm . . . *(Bell.)* What's a sort-of boyfriend?

BETTY.   My lover. Here she comes right now! *(Bell.)*

BILL.   You weren't waiting for somebody when I came in, were you?   145

BETTY.   No, just reading.

BILL.   Sort of a sad occupation for a Friday night, isn't it? Reading here, all by yourself?

BETTY.   Do you think so?

BILL.   Well sure. I mean, what's a good-looking woman like you doing out alone on a Friday night?

BETTY.   Trying to keep away from lines like that.   150

BILL.   No, listen— *(Bell.)* You weren't waiting for somebody when I came in, were you?

BETTY.   No, just reading.

BILL.   Sort of a sad occupation for a Friday night, isn't it? Reading here all by yourself?

BETTY.   I guess it is, in a way.

BILL.   What's a good-looking woman like you doing out alone on a Friday night   155
anyway? No offense, but . . .

BETTY.   I'm out alone on a Friday night for the first time in a very long time.

BILL.   Oh.

BETTY.   You see, I just recently ended a relationship.

BILL.   Oh.

BETTY.   Of rather long standing.   160

BILL.   I'm sorry. *(Small pause.)* Well listen, since reading by yourself *is* such a sad occupation for a Friday night, would you like to go elsewhere?

BETTY.   No . . .

BILL.   Do something else?

BETTY.   No thanks.

BILL.   I was headed out to the movies in a while anyway.   165

BETTY.   I don't think so.

BILL.   Big chance to let Faulkner catch his breath. All those long sentences get him pretty tired.

BETTY.   Thanks anyway.

BILL.   Okay.

BETTY.   I appreciate the invitation.   170

BILL.   Sure thing. *(Bell.)* You weren't waiting for somebody when I came in, were you?

BETTY.   No, just reading.

BILL.   Sort of a sad occupation for a Friday night, isn't it? Reading here all by yourself?

BETTY.   I guess I was trying to think of it as existentially romantic. You know—cappuccino, great literature, rainy night . . .

BILL.   That only works in Paris. We *could* hop the late plane to Paris. Get on a Con- 175
corde. Find a café . . .

BETTY.   I'm a little short on plane fare tonight.

BILL.   Darn it, so am I.

BETTY.   To tell you the truth, I was headed to the movies after I finished this section. Would you like to come along? Since you can't locate a waiter?

BILL.   That's a very nice offer, but . . .

BETTY.   Uh-huh. Girlfriend?   180

BILL.   Two, actually. One of them's pregnant, and Stephanie.—*(Bell.)*

BETTY.   Girlfriend?

BILL.   No, I don't have a girlfriend. Not if you mean the castrating bitch I dumped last night. *(Bell.)*

BETTY.   Girlfriend?

BILL.   Sort of. Sort of.   185

BETTY.   What's a sort-of girlfriend?

BILL.   My mother. *(Bell.)* I just ended a relationship, actually.

BETTY.   Oh.

BILL.   Of rather long standing.

BETTY.   I'm sorry to hear it.   190

BILL.   This is my first night out alone in a long time. I feel a little bit at sea, to tell you the truth.

BETTY.   So you didn't stop to talk because you're a Moonie, or you have some weird political affiliation—?

BILL.   Nope. Straight-down-the-ticket Republican. *(Bell.)* Straight-down-the-ticket Democrat. *(Bell.)* Can I tell you something about politics? *(Bell.)* I like to think of myself as a citizen of the universe. *(Bell.)* I'm unaffiliated.

BETTY.   That's a relief. So am I.

BILL.   I vote my beliefs.   195

BETTY.   Labels are not important.

BILL.   Labels are not important, exactly. Take me, for example. I mean, what does it matter if I had a two-point at—*(Bell.)*—three-point at—*(Bell.)*—four-point at college? Or if I did come from Pittsburgh—*(Bell.)*—Cleveland—*(Bell.)*—Westchester County?

BETTY.   Sure.

BILL.   I believe that a man is what he is. *(Bell.)* A person is what he is. *(Bell.)* A person is . . . what they are.

BETTY.   I think so too.   200

BILL.   So what if I admire Trotsky? *(Bell.)* So what if I once had a total-body lipo-
suction? *(Bell.)* So what if I don't have a penis? *(Bell.)* So what if I once spent a
year in the Peace Corps? I was acting on my convictions.

BETTY.   Sure.

BILL.   You can't just hang a sign on a person.

BETTY.   Absolutely. I'll bet you're a Scorpio. *(Many bells ring.)* Listen, I was headed
to the movies after I finished this section. Would you like to come along?

BILL.   That sounds like fun. What's playing?   205

BETTY.   A couple of the really early Woody Allen movies.

BILL.   Oh.

BETTY.   You don't like Woody Allen?

BILL.   Sure. I like Woody Allen.

BETTY.   But you're not crazy about Woody Allen.   210

BILL.   Those early ones kind of get on my nerves.

BETTY.   Uh-huh. *(Bell.)*

BILL.   *(Simultaneously.)*   BETTY.   *(Simultaneously.)*
Y'know I was headed to the—   I was thinking about—

BILL.   I'm sorry.   215

BETTY.   No, go ahead.

BILL.   I was going to say that I was headed to the movies in a little while, and . . .

BETTY.   So was I.

BILL.   The Woody Allen festival?

BETTY.   Just up the street.   220

BILL.   Do you like the early ones?

BETTY.   I think anybody who doesn't ought to be run off the planet.

BILL.   How many times have you seen *Bananas*?

BETTY.   Eight times.

BILL.   Twelve. So are you still interested? *(Long pause.)*   225

BETTY.   Do you like Entenmann's crumb cake . . . ?

BILL.   Last night I went out at two in the morning to get one. *(Small pause.)* Did
you have an Etch-a-Sketch as a child?

BETTY.   Yes! And do you like Brussels sprouts? *(Small pause.)*

BILL.   No, I think they're disgusting.

BETTY.   They *are* disgusting!   230

BILL.   Do you still believe in marriage in spite of current sentiments against it?

BETTY.   Yes.

BILL.   And children?

BETTY.   Three of them.

BILL.   Two girls and a boy.   235

BETTY.   Harvard, Vassar and Brown.

BILL.   And will you love me?

BETTY.   Yes.

BILL.   And cherish me forever?

BETTY.   Yes.   240

BILL.   Do you still want to go to the movies?

BETTY.   Sure thing.
BILL AND BETTY.   *(Together.) Waiter!*

BLACKOUT

Questions for Discussion and Writing

1. What kinds of things are "turn-offs" for both Betty and Bill? What does this imply about how difficult it is for them to find someone compatible?
2. How does Ives make the ringing bell almost into another character? What details suggests that the relationship really begins when Bill and Betty move beyond the need for scripted responses?
3. Despite its whimsical nature, what real social issues are addressed in this play? What do you think Ives meant by the title?

Thinking Critically About the Image

Grace Hartigan was born in New Jersey in 1922. She was the only woman whose work was included in the exhibition called "The New American Painting" that the Museum of Modern Art sent in 1959 to eight European countries. Hartigan was greatly influenced by the Abstract Expressionists, whose art is marked by the use of huge canvases, the harnessing of accidents that occur while painting, and a style in which paint is applied in an apparently random manner producing nonrepresentational images. In *Billboard* (1957), an oil on canvas that measures 78½ by 87 inches, Hartigan uses vivid colors and dynamic brush strokes in a seemingly chaotic but really quite unified composition to suggest the fleeting fragments of billboard images one might see while traveling down the highway.

1. What was your initial reaction to this painting—surprise, confusion? What did you first notice?
2. How does Hartigan use complementary colors to create a feeling that you can enter the painting at any point and visually walk through from one color or interesting shape to the next?
3. In what ways is this painting similar to a billboard or sign, and how is it different? What product or service would the billboard be advertising?

Connections

Chapter 5: Issues in Popular Culture

Juliet B. Schor,   *The Culture of Consumerism*
How do the values relating to body image described by Rosalind Coward support Schor's thesis about the extent to which we "buy" into the media's depiction of how we should look and what we should want to own?

Philip Slater,   *Want-Creation Fuels Americans' Addictiveness*
What factors account for the new direction that "want-creation" (as discussed by Slater) has taken, according to Juliet B. Schor?

Jan Harold Brunvand,   *Urban Legends: The Boyfriend's Death*
To what extent does Joyce Carol Oates's story "Where Are You Going, Where Have You Been?" (Ch. 11) portray an urban legend as described by Brunvand?

Neil Postman and Steve Powers,   *TV News as Entertainment*
How are the objectives of television news the opposite of those of poetry, according to Emily Dickinson in "Tell All the Truth but Tell It Slant" (Ch. 10)?

Eric Schlosser,   *Kid Kustomers*
How has "want-creation" as described by Philip Slater now been extended to include children, as discussed by Schlosser?

Rosalind Coward,   *The Body Beautiful*
Draw on the method for analyzing ads described by Stuart Hirschberg in "The Rhetoric of Advertising" (Ch. 4) and discuss whether current ads support Coward's assessment.

Arthur Ashe,   *The Burden of Race*
Given what Neil Postman and Steve Powers say about how the news on televison sensationalizes everything into entertainment, were Ashe's fears justified? Why or why not?

Barbara Kantrowitz,   *The New Face of Marriage*
Discuss how the new trend of same-sex marriage offers a contrasting perspective to Bruce Springsteen's "Streets of Philadelphia."

Kate Chopin,   *Désirée's Baby*
What features of Chopin's "Désirée's Baby" illustrate Martin Luther King, Jr.'s assessment of race relations in the United States in "I Have a Dream" (Ch. 8)?

Margaret Atwood,   *Happy Endings*
Are Americans addicted (in Philip Slater's sense of the word) to "happy endings" in fiction?

Marge Piercy,   *Barbie Doll*
How does the Barbie doll as portrayed by Piercy illustrate Coward's thesis regarding the damaging effects of society's messages about female body image?

Grace Caroline Bridges,   *Lisa's Ritual, Age 10*

If the events in Bridges's poem were investigated as a crime, what gender-based assumptions would help or hinder the inquiry? Refer to Susan Glaspell's play *Trifles* (Ch. 8).

Bruce Springsteen,   *Streets of Philadelphia*

What different perspectives on the loss of self are offered by Springsteen and by Kelly Cherry in her poem?

Kelly Cherry,   *Alzheimer's*

Compare the social view of disability in Cherry's poem with the controversy over the FDR Memorial described by Rosemarie Garland-Thomson in "The FDR Memorial: Who Speaks from the Wheelchair?" (Ch. 4).

David Ives,   *Sure Thing*

Do the aspirations of Betty and Bill in Ives's play match those described by Juliet B. Schor as being characteristic of mainstream culture?

Claude Monet, **The Artist's Garden at Giverny,** *1902.*
Oil on canvas. 89.5 × 92.3 cm. Inv. 3889. Nimatallah/Art Resource, NY. Oesterreichische Galerie, Vienna, Austria.

Our Place in Nature

Animals are not brethren, they are not underlings; they are other nations, caught with ourselves in the net of life and time.
—Henry Beston, "Autumn, Ocean, and Birds"

MANY ESSAYS IN THIS CHAPTER STAND AS classic investigations of the complex interactions of living things, the study of animal behavior, the deteriorating environment, and the value of wilderness. Linda Hogan and Thor Heyerdahl consider how exploitation of the environment and pollution of the ocean destroy the interdependence of all living things within the ecosystem. Richard Rhodes takes his readers behind the scenes at a meat-processing plant to witness what is usually hidden from public view. Gunjan Sinha reports on the latest research that reveals that the brain chemistry and mating behavior of the prairie vole are surprisingly similar to that of humans. Jared Diamond extrapolates from seemingly inexplicable displays in the animal world to equally inexplicable self-destructive human behaviors.

Alice Walker shares a personal encounter with an unusual horse that evokes parallels to the subjugation of one race by another. Mark Twain brings his satiric gifts to bear upon this chapter's central question about our place in nature.

In a harrowing tale with modern parallels, Edgar Allan Poe, the master of the macabre, projects us into the terrifying realm of the plague and the fate that awaits its victims.

Mary Oliver and Henry Wadsworth Longfellow explore the profound sense of being at one with nature while Humbert Wolfe questions our presumed superiority over lesser species.

NONFICTION

Mark Twain

Samuel Langhorne Clemens (1835–1910) was brought up in Hannibal, Missouri. After serving as a printer's apprentice, he became a steamboat pilot on the Mississippi (1857–1861) and adopted his pen name or **pseudonym** *from the leadsman's call ("mark twain" means "by the mark two fathoms") when sounding the river in shallow places. After an unsuccessful attempt to mine gold in Nevada, Twain edited the* Virginia City Enterprise. *In 1865 in the* New York Saturday Press, *Twain published "Jim Smiley and His Jumping Frog," which then became the title story of* The Celebrated Jumping Frog of Calaveras County and Other Sketches *(1867). His reputation as a humorist was enhanced by* Innocents Abroad *(1869), a comic account of his travels through France, Italy, and Palestine; and by* Roughing It *(1872), a delightful spoof of his mining adventures. His acknowledged masterpieces are* The Adventures of Tom Sawyer *(1876) and its sequel* The Adventures of Huckleberry Finn *(1885), works of great comic power and social insight. Twain's later works, including* The Man That Corrupted Hadleyburg *(1900), a fable about greed, and* The Mysterious Stranger *(1916), published six years after Twain's death, assail hypocrisy as endemic to the human condition. "The Lowest Animal" (1906) shows Twain at his most iconoclastic, formulating a scathing comparison between humans and the so-called lower animals.*

THE LOWEST ANIMAL

I have been studying the traits and dispositions of the "lower animals" (so-called), and contrasting them with the traits and dispositions of man. I find the result humiliating to me. For it obliges me to renounce my allegiance to the Darwinian theory of the Ascent of Man from the Lower Animals; since it now seems plain to me that that theory ought to be vacated in favor of a new and truer one, this new and truer one to be named the Descent of Man from the Higher Animals.

In proceeding toward this unpleasant conclusion I have not guessed or speculated or conjectured, but have used what is commonly called the scientific method. That is to say, I have subjected every postulate that presented itself to the crucial test of actual experiment, and have adopted it or rejected it according to the result. Thus I verified and established each step of my course in its turn before advancing to the next. These experiments were made in the London Zoological Gardens, and covered many months of painstaking and fatiguing work.

Before particularizing any of the experiments, I wish to state one or two things which seem to more properly belong in this place than further along. This in the interest of clearness. The massed experiments established to my satisfaction certain generalizations, to wit:

1. That the human race is of one distinct species. It exhibits slight variations—in color, stature, mental caliber, and so on—due to climate, environment, and so forth; but it is a species by itself, and not to be confounded with any other.

2. That the quadrupeds are a distinct family, also. This family exhibits variations—in color, size, food preferences and so on; but it is a family by itself.
3. That the other families—the birds, the fishes, the insects, the reptiles, etc.—are more or less distinct, also. They are in the procession. They are links in the chain which stretches down from the higher animals to man at the bottom.

Some of my experiments were quite curious. In the course of my reading I had come across a case where, many years ago, some hunters on our Great Plains organized a buffalo hunt for the entertainment of an English earl—that, and to provide some fresh meat for his larder. They had charming sport. They killed seventy-two of those great animals; and ate part of one of them and left the seventy-one to rot. In order to determine the difference between an anaconda and an earl—if any—I caused seven young calves to be turned into the anaconda's cage. The grateful reptile immediately crushed one of them and swallowed it, then lay back satisfied. It showed no further interest in the calves, and no disposition to harm them. I tried this experiment with other anacondas; always with the same result. The fact stood proven that the difference between an earl and an anaconda is that the earl is cruel and the anaconda isn't; and that the earl wantonly destroys what he has no use for, but the anaconda doesn't. This seemed to suggest that the anaconda was not descended from the earl. It also seemed to suggest that the earl was descended from the anaconda, and had lost a good deal in the transition.

I was aware that many men who have accumulated more millions of money than they can ever use have shown a rabid hunger for more, and have not scrupled to cheat the ignorant and the helpless out of their poor servings in order to partially appease that appetite. I furnished a hundred different kinds of wild and tame animals the opportunity to accumulate vast stores of food, but none of them would do it. The squirrels and bees and certain birds made accumulations, but stopped when they had gathered a winter's supply, and could not be persuaded to add to it either honestly or by chicane. In order to bolster up a tottering reputation the ant pretended to store up supplies, but I was not deceived. I know the ant. These experiments convinced me that there is this difference between man and the higher animals: he is avaricious and miserly, they are not. 5

In the course of my experiments I convinced myself that among the animals man is the only one that harbors insults and injuries, broods over them, waits till a chance offers, then takes revenge. The passion of revenge is unknown to the higher animals.

Roosters keep harems, but it is by consent of their concubines; therefore no wrong is done. Men keep harems, but it is by brute force, privileged by atrocious laws which the other sex is allowed no hand in making. In this matter man occupies a far lower place than the rooster.

Cats are loose in their morals, but not consciously so. Man, in his descent from the cat, has brought the cat's looseness with him but has left the unconsciousness behind—the saving grace which excuses the cat. The cat is innocent, man is not.

Indecency, vulgarity, obscenity—these are strictly confined to man; he invented them. Among the higher animals there is no trace of them. They hide nothing; they are not ashamed. Man, with his soiled mind, covers himself. He will not even enter a drawing room with his breast and back naked, so alive are he and his mates to indecent suggestion. Man is "The Animal that Laughs." But so does the monkey, as Mr. Darwin pointed out; and so does the Australian bird that is called the laughing jackass. No—Man is the Animal that Blushes. He is the only one that does it—or has occasion to.

At the head of this article we see how "three monks were burnt to death" a few days ago, and a prior "put to death with atrocious cruelty." Do we inquire into the details? No; or we should find out that the prior was subjected to unprintable mutilations. Man—when he is a North American Indian—gouges out his prisoner's eyes; when he is King John, with a nephew to render untroublesome, he uses a red-hot iron; when he is a religious zealot dealing with heretics in the Middle Ages, he skins his captive alive and scatters salt on his back; in the first Richard's time he shuts up a multitude of Jew families in a tower and sets fire to it; in Columbus's time he captures a family of Spanish Jews and—but that is not printable; in our day in England a man is fined ten shillings for beating his mother nearly to death with a chair, and another man is fined forty shillings for having four pheasant eggs in his possession without being able to satisfactorily explain how he got them. Of all the animals, man is the only one that is cruel. He is the only one that inflicts pain for the pleasure of doing it. It is a trait that is not known to the higher animals. The cat plays with the frightened mouse; but she has this excuse, that she does not know that the mouse is suffering. The cat is moderate—unhumanly moderate: she only scares the mouse, she does not hurt it; she doesn't dig out its eyes, or tear off its skin, or drive splinters under its nails—man-fashion; when she is done playing with it she makes a sudden meal of it and puts it out of its trouble. Man is the Cruel Animal. He is alone in that distinction.

The higher animals engage in individual fights, but never in organized masses. Man is the only animal that deals in that atrocity of atrocities, War. He is the only one that gathers his brethren about him and goes forth in cold blood and with calm pulse to exterminate his kind. He is the only animal that for sordid wages will march out, as the Hessian[1] did in our Revolution, and as the boyish Prince Napoleon did in the Zulu war, and help to slaughter strangers of his own species who have done him no harm and with whom he has no quarrel.

Man is the only animal that robs his helpless fellow of his country—takes possession of it and drives him out of it or destroys him. Man has done this in all the ages. There is not an acre of ground on the globe that is in possession of its rightful owner, or that has not been taken away from owner after owner, cycle after cycle, by force and bloodshed.

Man is the only Slave. And he is the only animal who enslaves. He has always been a slave in one form or another, and has always held other slaves in bondage under him in one way or another. In our day he is always some man's slave for wages, and does that man's work; and this slave has other slaves under him for minor wages, and they do his work. The higher animals are the only ones who exclusively do their own work and provide their own living.

Man is the only Patriot. He sets himself apart in his own country, under his own flag, and sneers at the other nations, and keeps multitudinous uniformed assassins on

---

[1]*Hessians:* the German auxiliary soldiers brought over by the British to fight the Americans during the Revolutionary War.

hand at heavy expense to grab slices of other people's countries, and keep *them* from grabbing slices of *his*. And in the intervals between campaigns he washes the blood off his hands and works for "the universal brotherhood of man"—with his mouth.

Man is the Religious Animal. He is the only Religious Animal. He is the only an- 15 imal that has the True Religion—several of them. He is the only animal that loves his neighbor as himself, and cuts his throat if his theology isn't straight. He has made a graveyard of the globe in trying his honest best to smooth his brother's path to happiness and heaven. He was at it in the time of the Caesars, he was at it in Mahomet's time, he was at it in the time of the Inquisition, he was at it in France a couple of centuries, he was at it in England in Mary's day, he has been at it ever since he first saw the light, he is at it today in Crete—as per the telegrams quoted above—he will be at it somewhere else tomorrow. The higher animals have no religion. And we are told that they are going to be left out, in the Hereafter. I wonder why? It seems questionable taste.

Man is the Reasoning Animal. Such is the claim. I think it is open to dispute. Indeed, my experiments have proven to me that he is the Unreasoning Animal. Note his history, as sketched above. It seems plain to me that whatever he is he is *not* a reasoning animal. His record is the fantastic record of a maniac. I consider that the strongest count against his intelligence is the fact that with that record back of him he blandly sets himself up as the head animal of the lot: whereas by his own standards he is the bottom one.

In truth, man is incurably foolish. Simple things which the other animals easily learn, he is incapable of learning. Among my experiments was this. In an hour I taught a cat and a dog to be friends. I put them in a cage. In another hour I taught them to be friends with a rabbit. In the course of two days I was able to add a fox, a goose, a squirrel and some doves. Finally a monkey. They lived together in peace; even affectionately.

Next, in another cage I confined an Irish Catholic from Tipperary, and as soon as he seemed tame I added a Scotch Presbyterian from Aberdeen. Next a Turk from Constantinople; a Greek Christian from Crete; an Armenian; a Methodist from the wilds of Arkansas; a Buddhist from China; a Brahman from Benares. Finally, a Salvation Army Colonel from Wapping. Then I stayed away two whole days. When I came back to note result, the cage of Higher Animals was all right, but in the other there was but a chaos of gory odds and ends of turbans and fezzes and plaids and bones and flesh— not a specimen left alive. These Reasoning Animals had disagreed on a theological detail and carried the matter to a Higher Court.

One is obliged to concede that in true loftiness of character, Man cannot claim to approach even the meanest of the Higher Animals. It is plain that he is constitutionally incapable of approaching that altitude; that he is constitutionally afflicted with a Defect which must make such approach forever impossible, for it is manifest that this defect is permanent in him, indestructible, ineradicable.

I find this Defect to be *the Moral Sense*. He is the only animal that has it. It is the 20 secret of his degradation. It is the quality *which enables him to do wrong*. It has no other office. It is incapable of performing any other function. It could never have been intended to perform any other. Without it, man could do no wrong. He would rise at once to the level of the Higher Animals.

Since the Moral Sense has but the one office, the one capacity—to enable man to do wrong—it is plainly without value to him. It is as valueless to him as is disease. In fact, it manifestly is a disease. *Rabies* is bad, but it is not so bad as this disease. Rabies enables a man to do a thing which he could not do when in a healthy state: kill his neighbor with a poisonous bite. No one is the better man for having rabies. The Moral Sense enables a man to do wrong. It enables him to do wrong in a thousand ways. Rabies is an innocent disease, compared to the Moral Sense. No one, then, can be the better man for having the Moral Sense. What, now, do we find the Primal Curse to have been? Plainly what it was in the beginning: the infliction upon man of the Moral Sense; the ability to distinguish good from evil; and with it, necessarily, the ability to *do* evil; for there can be no evil act without the presence of consciousness of it in the doer of it.

And so I find that we have descended and degenerated, from some far ancestor—some microscopic atom wandering at its pleasure between the mighty horizons of a drop of water perchance—insect by insect, animal by animal, reptile by reptile, down the long highway of smirchless innocence, till we have reached the bottom stage of development—namable as the Human Being. Below us—nothing. Nothing but the Frenchman.

Questions for Discussion and Writing

1. How are Twain's experiments—comparing human behavior to that of animals in various situations—intended to puncture some illusions the human species has about itself? In what way do each of Twain's experiments reveal that other animals are superior to humans?
2. How is the method Twain uses to organize his discussion well suited to highlight important differences between animals and humans?
3. How do Twain's experiments provide an ironic commentary on the interpretation of Darwin's thesis that places humans at the apex of all other species?

Gunjan Sinha

. . . .

Gunjan Sinha was born in Bihar, India, but grew up in Brooklyn, New York. She earned a graduate degree in molecular genetics from the University of Glasgow, Scotland, and received a degree from New York University's Science and Environmental Reporting Program in 1996. She was life sciences editor for Popular Science *for five years and in 2000 was awarded the Ray Bruner Science Writing Award. In the following essay, written in 2002, Sinha explores the mating behavior of the common prairie vole (a mouselike rodent, about seven inches long with a two-inch tail) and what it reveals about the human pattern of monogamy.*

YOU DIRTY VOLE

George is a typical Midwestern American male in the prime of his life, with an attractive spouse named Martha. George is a devoted husband, Martha an attentive wife. The couple has four young children, a typical home in a lovely valley full of corn and bean fields, and their future looks bright. But George is occasionally unfaithful. So, occasionally, is Martha. No big deal: That's just the way life is in this part of America.

This is a true story, though the names have been changed, and so, for that matter, has the species. George and Martha are prairie voles. They don't marry, of course, or think about being faithful. And a bright future for a vole is typically no more than 60 days of mating and pup-rearing that ends in a fatal encounter with a snake or some other prairie predator.

But if you want to understand more about the conflict in human relationships between faithfulness and philandering, have a peek inside the brain of this wee rodent. Researchers have been studying voles for more than 25 years, and they've learned that the mating behavior of these gregarious creatures uncannily resembles our own—including a familiar pattern of monogamous attachment: Male and female share a home and child care, the occasional dalliance notwithstanding. More important, researchers have discovered what drives the animals' monogamy: brain chemistry. And when it comes to the chemical soup that governs behavior associated with what we call love, prairie vole brains are a lot like ours.

Scientists are careful to refer to what voles engage in as "social monogamy," meaning that although voles prefer to nest and mate with a particular partner, when another vole comes courting, some will stray. And as many as 50 percent of male voles never find a permanent partner. Of course, there is no moral or religious significance to the vole's behavior—monogamous or not. Voles will be voles, because that's their nature.

Still, the parallels to humans are intriguing. "We're not an animal that finds it in   5 our best interest to screw around," says Pepper Schwartz, a sociologist at the University of Washington, yet studies have shown that at least one-third of married people cheat. In many cases, married couples struggle with the simple fact that love and lust aren't always in sync, often tearing us in opposite directions. Vole physiology and behavior reinforce the idea that love and lust are biochemically separate systems, and that the emotional tug of war many of us feel between the two emotions is perfectly natural—a two-headed biological drive that's been hardwired into our brains through millions of years of evolution.

No one knew that voles were monogamous until Lowell Getz, a now-retired professor of ecology, ethology, and evolution at the University of Illinois, began studying them in 1972. At the time, Getz wanted to figure out why the vole population would boom during certain years and then slowly go bust. He set traps in the grassy plains of Illinois and checked them a few times a day, tagging the voles he caught. What surprised him was how often he'd find the same male and female sitting in a trap together.

Voles build soft nests about 8 inches below ground. A female comes of age when she is about 30 days old: Her need to mate is then switched on as soon as she encounters an unpartnered male and sniffs his urine. About 24 hours later, she's ready to breed—with the male she just met or another unattached one if he's gone. Then, hooked, the pair will stick together through thick and thin, mating and raising young.

Getz found vole mating behavior so curious that he wanted to bring the animals into the lab to study them more carefully. But he was a field biologist, not a lab scientist, so he called Sue Carter, a colleague and neuroendocrinologist. Carter had been studying how sex hormones influence behavior, and investigating monogamy in voles dovetailed nicely with her own research. The animals were small: They made the perfect lab rats.

The scientific literature was already rich with studies on a hormone called oxytocin that is made in mammalian brains and that in some species promotes bonding between males and females and between mothers and offspring. Might oxytocin, swirling around in tiny vole brains, be the catalyst for turning them into the lifelong partners that they are?

Sure enough, when Carter injected female voles with oxytocin, they were less   10 finicky in choosing mates and practically glued themselves to their partners once they had paired. The oxytocin-dosed animals tended to lick and cuddle more than untreated animals, and they avoided strangers. What's more, when Carter injected females with oxytocin-blocking chemicals, the animals deserted their partners.

In people, not only is the hormone secreted by lactating women but studies have shown that oxytocin levels also increase during sexual arousal—and skyrocket during orgasm. In fact, the higher the level of oxytocin circulating in the blood during intercourse, the more intense the orgasm.

But there's more to vole mating than love; there's war too. Male voles are territorial. Once they bond with a female, they spend lots of time guarding her from other suitors, often sitting near the entrance of their burrow and aggressively baring their beaver-like teeth. Carter reasoned that other biochemicals must kick in after mating, chemicals that turn a once laid-back male into a territorial terror. Oxytocin, it turns out, is only part of the story. A related chemical, vasopressin, also occurs in both sexes. Males, however, have much more of it.

When Carter dosed male voles with a vasopressin-blocking chemical after mating, their feistiness disappeared. An extra jolt of vasopressin, on the other hand, boosted their territorial behavior and made them more protective of their mates.

Vasopressin is also present in humans. While scientists don't yet know the hormone's exact function in men, they speculate that it works similarly: It is secreted during sexual arousal and promotes bonding. It may even transform some men into jealous boyfriends and husbands. "The biochemistry [of attachment] is probably going to be similar in humans and in [monogamous] animals because it's quite a basic function," says Carter. Because oxytocin and vasopressin are secreted during sexual arousal and orgasm, she says, they are probably the key biochemical players that bond lovers to one another.

But monogamous animals aren't the only ones that have vasopressin and oxytocin   15 in their brains. Philandering animals do too. So what separates faithful creatures from unfaithful ones? Conveniently for scientists, the generally monogamous prairie vole has a wandering counterpart: the montane vole. When Thomas Insel, a neuroscientist at Emory University, studied the two species' vasopressin receptors (appendages on a cell that catch specific biochemicals) he found them in different places. Prairie voles have receptors for the hormone in their brains' pleasure centers; montane voles have the receptors in other brain areas. In other words, male prairie voles stick with the same partner after mating because it feels good. For montane voles, mating is a listless but necessary affair, rather like scratching an itch.

Of course, human love is much more complicated. The biochemistry of attachment isn't yet fully understood, and there's clearly much more to it than oxytocin and vasopressin. Humans experience different kinds of love. There's "compassionate love," associated with feelings of calm, security, social comfort, and emotional union. This kind of love, say scientists, is probably similar to what voles feel toward their partners and involves oxytocin and vasopressin. Romantic love—that crazy obsessive euphoria that people feel when they are "in love"—is very different, as human studies are showing.

Scientists at University College London led by Andreas Bartels recently peered inside the heads of love-obsessed college students. They took 17 young people who claimed to be in love, stuck each of them in an MRI machine, and showed them pictures of their lovers. Blood flow increased to very specific areas of the brain's pleasure center—including some of the same areas that are stimulated when people engage in addictive behaviors. Some of these same areas are also active during sexual arousal, though romantic love and sexual arousal are clearly different: Sex has more to do with hormones like testosterone, which, when given to both men and women, increases sex drive and sexual fantasies. Testosterone, however, doesn't necessarily make people fall in love with, or become attached to, the object of their attraction.

Researchers weren't particularly surprised by the parts of the lovers' brains that were active. What astonished them was that two other brain areas were suppressed—the amygdala and the right prefrontal cortex. The amygdala is associated with negative emotions like fear and anger. The right prefrontal cortex appears to be overly active in people suffering from depression. The positive emotion of love, it seems, suppresses negative emotions. Might that be the scientific basis for why people who are madly in love fail to see the negative traits of their beloved? "Maybe," says Bartels cautiously. "But we haven't proven that yet."

The idea that romantic love activates parts of the brain associated with addiction got Donatella Marazziti at Pisa University in Tuscany wondering if it might be related to obsessive compulsive disorder (OCD). Anyone who has ever been in love knows how consuming the feeling can be. You can think of nothing but your lover every waking moment. Some people with OCD have low levels of the brain chemical serotonin. Might love-obsessed people also have low serotonin levels? Sure enough, when Marazziti and her colleagues tested the blood of 20 students who were madly in love and 20 people with OCD, she found that both groups had low levels of a protein that shuttles serotonin between brain cells.

And what happens when the euphoria of "mad love" wears off? Marazziti tested 20 the blood of a few of the lovers 12 to 18 months later and found that their serotonin levels had returned to normal. That doesn't doom a couple, of course, but it suggests a biological explanation for the evolution of relationships. In many cases, romantic love turns into compassionate love, thanks to oxytocin and vasopressin swirling inside the lovers' brains. This attachment is what keeps many couples together. But because attachment and romantic love involve different biochemical processes, attachment to one person does not suppress lust for another. "The problem is, they are not always well linked," says anthropologist Helen Fisher, who has written several books on love, sex and marriage.

In the wild, about half of male voles wander the fields, never settling down with one partner. These "traveling salesmen," as Lowell Getz calls them, are always "trying to get with other females." Most females prefer to mate with their partners. But if they get the chance, some will mate with other males too. And, according to Jerry Wolff, a biologist at the University of Memphis, female voles sometimes "divorce" their partners. In the lab, he restricts three males at a time in separate but connected chambers and gives a female free range. The female has already paired with one of the males and is pregnant with his pups. Wolff says about a third of the females pick up their nesting materials and move in with a different fellow. Another third actually solicit and successfully mate with one or both of the other males, and the last third remain faithful.

Why are some voles fickle, others faithful? Vole brains differ from one creature to the next. Larry Young, a neuroscientist at Emory University, has found that some animals have more receptors for oxytocin and vasopressin than others. In a recent experiment, he injected a gene into male prairie voles that permanently upped the number of vasopressin receptors in their brains. The animals paired with females even though the two hadn't mated. "Normally they have to mate for at least 24 hours to establish a bond," he says. So the number of receptors can mean the difference between sticking around and skipping out after sex. Might these differences in brain wiring influence human faithfulness? "It's too soon to tell," Young says. But it's "definitely got us very curious."

How does evolution account for the often-conflicting experiences of love and lust, which have caused no small amount of destruction in human history? Fisher speculates that the neural systems of romantic love and attachment evolved for different reasons. Romantic love, she says, evolved to allow people to distinguish between potential mating partners and "to pursue these partners until insemination has occurred." Attachment, she says, "evolved to make you tolerate this individual long enough to raise a child." Pepper Schwartz agrees: "We're biologically wired to be socially monogamous, but it's not a good evolutionary tactic to be sexually monogamous. There need to be ways to keep reproduction going if your mate dies."

Many of our marriage customs, say sociologists, derive from the need to reconcile this tension. "As much as people love passion and romantic love," Schwartz adds, "most people also want to have the bonding sense of loyalty and friendship love as well." Marriage vows are a declaration about romantic love and binding attachment, but also about the role of rational thought and the primacy of mind and mores over impulses.

Scientists hope to do more than simply decode the biochemistry of the emotions 25
associated with love and attachment. Some, like Insel, are searching for treatments for attachment disorders such as autism, as well as pathological behaviors like stalking and violent jealousy. It is not inconceivable that someday there might be sold an attachment drug, a monogamy pill; the mind reels at the marketing possibilities.

Lowell Getz, the grandfather of all this research, couldn't be more thrilled. "I spent almost $1 million of taxpayer money trying to figure out stuff like why sisters don't make it with their brothers," he says. "I don't want to go to my grave feeling like it was a waste."

Questions for Discussion and Writing

1. What insight does Sinha offer into the biochemical triggers that are responsible for the mating behavior of the prairie vole? What parallel behaviors do human beings display that suggest an underlying biochemical matrix similar to that of the vole?
2. A good deal of Sinha's article is based on extrapolating features of the vole's behavior onto humans. This argument by analogy may be effective up to a point. In your opinion, does it break down, and if so, in what respects?
3. Are biology (hard-wired primal drives) and psychology (learned social and cultural behaviors) ultimately irreconcilable explanations for the same observed effects in human beings?

Richard Rhodes

• •

Richard Rhodes was born in 1937 in Kansas City, Kansas. After graduating with honors from Yale in 1959, he worked for Hallmark Cards and was a contributing editor for Harper's *and* Playboy *magazines. He is the author of more than fifty articles, and ten books, including* Looking for America: A Writer's Odyssey *(1979);* Making Love: An Erotic Odyssey *(1993);* Voyage of Rediscovery: A Cultural Odyssey Through Polynesia *(1995);* How to Write: Advice and Reflections *(1996); the acclaimed* The Making of the Atomic Bomb *(1987), which won the Pulitzer Prize, the National Book Award, and the National Book Critics Circle Award;* Deadly Feasts: Tracking the Secrets of a Terrifying New Plague *(1997); and* Masters of Death: The SS-Einsatzgruppen and the Invention of the Holocaust *(2002). Rhodes's ability to cut through to the essentials and follow an action from its onset to its completion is clearly seen in "Watching the Animals" (1970), an absorbing and realistic account of the processing of pigs into foodstuffs by the I-D Packing Company of Des Moines, Iowa.*

WATCHING THE ANIMALS

The loves of flint and iron are naturally a little rougher than those of the nightingale and the rose.

—*Ralph Waldo Emerson*

I remembered today about this country lake in Kansas where I live: that it is artificial, built at the turn of the century, when Upton Sinclair was writing *The Jungle,* as an ice lake. The trains with their loads of meat from the Kansas City stockyards would stop by the Kaw River, across the road, and ice the cars. "You have just dined," Emerson once told what must have been a shocked Victorian audience, "and however scrupulously the slaughterhouse is concealed in the graceful distance of miles, there is complicity, expensive races—race living at the expense of race. . . ."

The I-D Packing Company of Des Moines, Iowa: a small outfit which subcontracts from Armour the production of fresh pork. It can handle about 450 pigs an hour on its lines. No beef or mutton. No smoked hams or hot dogs. Plain fresh pork. A well-run outfit, with federal inspectors alert on all the lines.

The kind of slaughterhouse Upton Sinclair was talking about doesn't exist around here any more. The vast buildings still stand in Des Moines and Omaha and Kansas City, but the operations are gone. The big outfits used to operate on a profit margin of 1.5 per cent, which didn't give them much leeway, did it. Now they are defunct, and their buildings, which look like monolithic enlargements of concentration-camp barracks, sit empty, the hundreds of windows broken, dusty, jagged pieces of glass sticking out of the frames as if the animals heard the good news one day and leaped out the nearest exit. Even the stockyards, miles and miles of rotting, weathered board pens, floors paved fifty years ago by hand with brick, look empty, though I am told cattle receipts are up compared to what they were a few years back. The new thing is small, specialized, efficient houses out where the cattle are, in Denver, in Phoenix, in Des Moines, especially in Texas, where the weather is more favorable to fattening cattle. In Iowa the cattle waste half their feed just keeping warm in the wintertime. But in Iowa or in Texas, the point of meat-packing today is refrigeration. It's cheaper to ship cold meat than live animals. So the packing plants have gone out to the farms and ranches. They are even beginning to buy up the ranches themselves so that they won't have to depend on the irregularities of farmers and cattlemen who bring their animals in only when the price is up or the ground too wet for plowing. Farmhouses stand empty all over America. Did you know that? The city has already won, never mind how many of our television shows still depict the hardy bucolic rural. I may regret the victory, but that's my lookout. We are an urban race now, and meat is something you buy shrink-wrapped at the supermarket.

There are no stockyards inside the I-D Packing Company. The pigs arrive by trailer truck from Sioux City and other places. Sometimes a farmer brings in two or three in the back of his pickup. He unloads them into the holding pens, where they are weighed and inspected, goes into the office and picks up his check. The men, except on the killing floor, are working on the cooled carcasses of yesterday's kill anyway, so there is time to even out the line. Almost everything in a packinghouse operates on a chain line, and for maximum profit that line must be full, 450 carcasses an hour at the I-D Packing Company, perhaps 300 heavies if today is heavies day—sows, overgrown hogs. Boars presumably escape the general fate. Their flesh is flavored with rut and tastes like an unventilated gymnasium locker room.

Down goes the tail gate and out come the pigs, enthusiastic after their drive. Pigs   5
are the most intelligent of all farm animals, by actual laboratory test. Learn the fastest, for example, to push a plunger with their foot to earn a reward of pelletized feed. And not as reliable in their instincts. You don't have to call cattle to dinner. They are waiting outside the fence at 4:30 sharp, having arrived as silently as the Vietcong. But perhaps that is pig intelligence too: let you do the work, laze around until the last minute, and then charge over and knock you down before you can slop the garbage into the trough. Cattle will stroll one by one into a row of stalls and usually fill them in serial order. Not pigs. They squeal and nip and shove. Each one wants the entire meal for himself. They won't stick together in a herd, either. Shoot out all over the place, and you'd

damned better have every gate closed or they'll be in your garden and on your lawn and even in your living room, nodding by the fire.

They talk a lot, to each other, to you if you care to listen. I am not romanticizing pigs. They always scared me a little on the farm, which is probably why I watched them more closely than the other animals. They do talk: low grunts, quick squeals, a kind of hum sometimes, angry shrieks, high screams of fear.

I have great respect for the I-D Packing Company. They do a dirty job and do it as cleanly and humanely as possible, and do it well. They were nice enough to let me in the door, which is more than I can say for the Wilson people in Omaha, where I first tried to arrange a tour. What are you hiding, Wilson people?

Once into the holding pen, the pigs mill around getting to know each other. The I-D holding pens are among the most modern in the nation, my spokesman told me. Tubular steel painted tinner's red to keep it from rusting. Smooth concrete floors with drains so that the floors can be washed down hygienically after each lot of pigs is run through.

The pigs come out of the first holding pen through a gate that allows only one to pass at a time. Just beside the gate is a wooden door, and behind the door is the first worker the pigs encounter. He has a wooden box beside him filled with metal numbers, the shape of each number picked out with sharp needles. For each lot of pigs he selects a new set of numbers—2473, say—and slots them into a device like a hammer and dips it in nontoxic purple dye. As a pig shoots out of the gate he hits the pig in the side with the numbers, making a tattoo. The pig gives a grunt—it doesn't especially hurt, pigskin is thick, as you know—and moves on to one of several smaller pens where each lot is held until curtain time. The tattoo, my spokesman told me, will stay on the animal through all the killing and cleaning and cutting operations, to the very end. Its purpose is to identify any animal or lot of animals which might be diseased, so that the seller can be informed and the carcasses destroyed. Rather too proud of his tattooing process, I thought, but then, you know the tattoos I am thinking about.

It would be more dramatic, make a better story, if the killing came last, but it comes first. We crossed a driveway with more red steel fencing. Lined up behind it, pressing into it because they sensed by now that all was not well with them, were perhaps a hundred pigs. But still curious, watching us go by in our long white canvas coats. Everyone wore those, and hard plastic helmets, white helmets for the workers, yellow helmets for the foremen. I got to be a foreman.

Before they reach their end, the pigs get a shower, a real one. Water sprays from every angle to wash the farm off of them. Then they begin to feel crowded. The pen narrows like a funnel; the drivers behind urge the pigs forward, until one at a time they climb onto a moving ramp. The ramp's sides move as well as its floor. The floor is created to give the pigs footing. The sides are made of blocks of wood so that they will not bruise, and they slant inward to wedge the pigs along. Now they scream, never having been on such a ramp, smelling the smells they smell ahead. I do not want to over-dramatize, because you have read all this before. But it was a frightening experience, seeing their fear, seeing so many of them go by. It had to remind me of things no one wants to be reminded of anymore, all mobs, all death marches, all mass murders and extinctions, the slaughter of the buffalo, the slaughter of the Indian, the Inferno, Judgment Day, complicity, expensive races, race living at the expense of race. That so gentle

10

a religion as Christianity could end up in Judgment Day. That we are the most expensive of races, able in our affluence to hire others of our kind to do this terrible necessary work of killing another race of creatures so that we may feed our oxygen-rich brains. Feed our children, for that matter.

At the top of the ramp, one man. With rubber gloves on, holding two electrodes that looked like enlarged curling irons except that they sported more of those needles. As a pig reached the top, this man jabbed the electrodes into the pig's butt and shoulder, and that was it. No more pain, no more fear, no more mudholes, no more sun in the lazy afternoon. Knocked instantly unconscious, the pig shuddered in a long spasm and fell onto a stainless steel table a foot below the end of the ramp. Up came another pig, and the same result. And another, and another, 450 an hour, 3,600 a day, the belts returning below to coax another ride.

The pigs are not dead, merely unconscious. The electrodes are humane, my spokesman said, and relatively speaking, that is true. They used to gas the pigs—put them on a conveyor belt that ran through a room filled with anesthetic gas. That was humane too. The electrodes are more efficient. Anesthesia relaxes the body and loosens the bowels. The gassed pigs must have been a mess. More efficient, then, to put their bodies in spasm.

They drop to the table, and here the endless chain begins. A worker takes the nearest dangling chain by its handle as it passes. The chain is attached at the top to a belt of links, like a large bicycle chain. At the bottom the dangling chain has a metal handle like the handle on a bike. The chain runs through the handle and then attaches to the end of the handle, so that by sliding the handle the worker forms a loop. Into the loop he hooks one of the pig's hind feet. Another worker does the same with the other foot. Each has his own special foot to grab, or the pig would go down the line backwards, which would not be convenient. Once hooked into the line, the pig will stay in place by the force of its own weight.

Now the line ascends, lifting the unconscious animal into the air. The pig proceeds a distance of ten feet, where a worker standing on a platform deftly inserts a butcher knife into its throat. They call it "sticking," which it is. Then all hell breaks loose, if blood merely is hell. It gushes out, at about a 45-degree angle downward, thick as a ship's hawser, pouring directly onto the floor. Nothing is so red as blood, an incandescent red and most beautiful. It is the brightest color we drab creatures possess. Down on the floor below, with a wide squeegee on a long handle, a worker spends his eight hours a day squeegeeing that blood, some of it clotted, jellied, now, into an open drain. It is cycled through a series of pipes into a dryer, later to be made into blood meal for animal feed. 15

The line swings around a corner, high above the man with the squeegee, around the drain floor, turns left at the next corner, and begins to ascend to the floor above. This interval—thirteen seconds, I think my spokesman said, or was it thirty?—so that the carcass may drain completely before further processing. Below the carcass on the ascent is a trough like those lowered from the rear of cement trucks, there to catch the last drainings of blood.

Pigs are not skinned, as cattle are, unless you are after the leather, and we are after the meat. But the hair must be taken off, and it must first be scalded loose. Courteously, the line lowers the carcass into a long trough filled with water heated to 180 degrees. The carcass will float if given a chance, fat being lighter than water, so wooden pushers on crankshafts spaced equally along the scalding tank immerse and roll the carcasses. Near the end of the trough, my spokesman easily pulls out a tuft of hair. The line ascends again, up and away, and the carcass goes into a chamber where revolving brushes as tall as a man whisk away the hair. We pass to the other side of the chamber and find two workers with wide knives scraping off the few patches of hair that remain. The carcasses then pass through great hellish jets of yellowish-blue gas flame to singe the skin and harden it. The last step is polishing: more brushes. Our pig has turned pink and clean as a baby.

One of the small mercies of a slaughterhouse: what begins as a live animal loses all similarity as the processing goes on, until you can actually face the packaged meat at the exit door and admire its obvious flavor.

The polished carcasses swing through a door closed with rubber flaps, and there, dear friends, the action begins. Saws. Long knives. Butcher knives. Drawknives. Boning knives. Wails from the saws, large and small, that are driven by air like a dentist's drill. Shouts back and forth from the men, jokes, announcements, challenges. The temperature down to 50 degrees, everyone keen. Men start slicing off little pieces of the head right inside the door, each man his special slice, throwing them onto one of several lines that will depart for special bins. A carcass passes me and I see a bare eyeball staring, stripped of its lids. Deft knives drop the head from the neck leaving it dangling by a two-inch strip of skin. Around a corner, up to a platform, and three men gut the carcasses, great tubs of guts, each man taking the third carcass as it goes by. One of them sees me with my tape recorder and begins shouting at us something like "I am the greatest!" A crazy man, grinning and roaring at us, turning around and slipping in the knife, and out comes everything in one great load flopped onto a stainless-steel trough. And here things divide, and so must our attention.

My spokesman is proud of his chitterling machine. "I call them chitlins, but they're really chitterlings." It is the newest addition to his line. A worker separates the intestines from the other internal organs and shoves them down a slide, gray and shiny. Another worker finds one end and feeds it onto a steel tube flushed with water. Others trim off connective tissue, webbings, fat. The intestines shimmer along the tube into a washing vat, skinny up to the top of the machine where they are cooled, skinny back down where they are cooled further, and come out the other side ready for the supermarket. A worker drops them into wax buckets, pops on a lid, and packs them into shipping boxes. That is today's chitlin machine. They used to have to cool the chitlins overnight before they could be packaged. Now five men do the work of sixteen, in less time. 20

The remaining organs proceed down a waist-high conveyor; on the other side of the same walkway, the emptied carcasses pass; on a line next to the organ line the heads pass. By now all the meat has been trimmed off each head. A worker sockets them one at a time into a support like a footrest in a shoeshine parlor and a wedge neatly splits them in half. Out come the tongues, out come the brains, and at the end of the line, out come the pituitaries, each tiny gland being passed to a government inspector in white pants, white shirt, and a yellow hard hat, who looks it over and drops it into a wax bucket. All these pieces, the brain, the tongue, the oddments of sidemeat off the head and carcass, will become "by-products": hot dogs, baloney, sausage. You are what you eat.

The loudest noise in the room comes from the big air-saw used to split the carcass in half down the backbone, leaving, again, connections at the butt end and between the shoulders. Other workers trim away interior fat, and then the carcasses proceed down their chain at 50 miles an hour to the blast freezer, 25 below zero and no place for mere mortals, to be chilled overnight.

Coming out of the freezer in another part of the room is yesterday's kill, cold and solid and smooth. A worker splits apart the two sides; the hams come off and go onto their own line; the shoulders come off and go onto theirs, to be made into picnics, shoulder roasts, trotters. Away goes the valuable loin, trimmed out deftly by a worker with a drawknife. Away goes the bacon. Chunks and strips of fat go off from everywhere in buckets carried on overhead hooks to a grinder that spins out worms of fat and blows them through a tube directly to the lard-rendering vats. Who uses lard anymore, I ask my spokesman. I don't know, he says, I think we export most of it.

At the end of all these lines men package the component parts of pig into wax-paper-lined cartons, load the cartons onto pallets, forklift the pallets into spotless aluminum trailers socketed right into the walls of the building so that I do not even realize I am inside a truck until my spokesman tells me, and off they go to Armour.

Processing an animal is exactly the opposite of processing a machine: the machine starts out with components and ends up put together; the animal starts out put together and ends up components. No clearer illustration of the law of entropy has ever been devised.   25

And that is a tour of a slaughterhouse, as cheerful as I could make it.

But the men there. Half of them blacks, some Mexicans, the rest whites. It gets harder and harder to hire men for this work, even though the pay is good. The production line keeps them hopping; they take their breaks when there is a break in the line, so that the killing floor breaks first, and their break leaves an empty space ten minutes long in the endless chain, which, arriving at the gutting operation, allows the men there to break, and so on. Monday morning absenteeism is a problem, I was told. Keeping the men under control can be a problem, too, I sensed: when the line broke down briefly during my tour, the men cheered as convicts might at a state license-plate factory when the stamping machine breaks down. It cannot be heartening to kill animals all day.

There is a difference, too, between the men who work with the live animals and hot carcasses and those who cut up the cold meat, a difference I remember from my days of butchering on the farm: the killing unsettles, while the cold cutting is a craft like carpentry or plumbing and offers the satisfactions of craftsmanship. The worker with the electrodes jammed them into the animal with anger and perverse satisfaction, as if he were knocking off the enemy. The worker at the guts acted as if he were wrestling bears. The hot workers talked to themselves, yelled at each other, or else lapsed into that strained silence you meet in deeply angry men; the cold workers said little but worked with deftness and something like pride. They knew they were good, and they showed off a little, zip zip, as we toured by. They used their hands as if they knew how to handle tools, and they did.

The technology at the I-D Packing Company is humane by present standards, at least so far as the animals are concerned. Where the workers are concerned, I'm not so sure. They looked to be in need of lulling.

Beyond technology is the larger question of attitude. Butchering on the farm when 30
I was a boy had the quality of a ceremony. We would select, say, a steer, and pen it separately overnight. The next morning several of us boys—this was a boys' home as well as a farm—would walk the steer to a large compound and leave it standing, trusting as hell, near the concrete-floored area where we did the skinning and gutting. Then the farm manager, a man of great kindness and reserve, would take aim with a .22 rifle at the crosspoint of two imaginary lines drawn from the horns to the opposite eyes. And hold his bead until the steer was entirely calm, looking at him, a certain shot, because this man did not want to miss, did not want to hurt the animal he was about to kill. And we would stand in a spread-out circle, at a respectful distance, tense with the drama of it, because we didn't want him to miss either.

The shot cracked out, the bullet entered the brain, and the animal instantly collapsed. Then the farm manager handed back the rifle, took a knife, ran forward, and cut into the throat. Then we dragged the steer onto the concrete, hooked its back legs through the Achilles tendons to a cross tree, and laboriously winched it into the air with a differential pulley. Four boys usually did the work, two older, two younger. The younger boys were supposed to be learning this skill, and you held your stomach together as best you could at first while the older boys played little tricks like, when they got there in the skinning, cutting off the pizzle and whipping it around your neck, but even these crudities had their place: they accustomed you to contact with flesh and blood.

And while the older boys did their work of splitting the halves with a hacksaw, you got to take the guts, which on the farm we did not save except for the liver, the heart, and the sweetbreads, in a wheelbarrow down to the back lane where you built with wood you had probably cut yourself, a most funereal pyre. Then we doused the guts with gasoline, tossed in a match, and Whoosh! off they went. And back on the concrete, the sawing done, the older boys left the sides hanging overnight in the winter cold to firm the meat for cutting.

By now it was noon, time for lunch, and you went in with a sort of pride that you had done this important work, and there on the table was meat some other boys had killed on some other ceremonial day. It was bloody work, of course, and sometimes I have wondered how adults could ask children to do such work, but it was part of a coherent way of life, as important as plowing or seeding or mowing or baling hay. It had a context, and I was literary enough even then to understand that burning the guts had a sacrificial significance. We could always have limed them and dumped them into a ditch. Lord knows they didn't burn easily.

I never saw our farm manager more upset than the day we were getting ready to butcher five pigs. He shot one through the nose rather than through the brain. It ran screaming around the pen, and he almost cried. It took two more bullets to finish the animal off, and this good man was shaking when he had finished. "I hate that," he said to me. "I hate to have them in pain. Pigs are so damned hard to kill clean."

But we don't farm anymore. The coherence is gone. Our loves are no longer the 35
loves of flint and iron, but of the nightingale and the rose, and so we delegate our killing. Our farm manager used to sleep in the sheep barn for nights on end to be sure

he was there to help the ewes deliver their lambs, ewes being so absentminded they sometimes stop labor with the lamb only halfway out. You saw the beginning and the end on the farm, not merely the prepackaged middle. Flint and iron, friends, flint and iron. And humility, and sorrow that this act of killing must be done, which is why in those days good men bowed their heads before they picked up their forks.

Questions for Discussion and Writing

1. How does the title raise expectations that contrast ironically with the subject of Rhodes's essay? What is the significance of Emerson's phrase "race living at the expense of race" (in para. 1) in relationship to this account?
2. How does Rhodes's characterization of the pigs awaiting slaughter give you insight into their intelligence and seeming awareness of what awaits them?
3. Write a short essay exploring the increasing tendency in modern life to conceal natural processes that in the past were routinely encountered in everyday life.
4. As a project, research a process that can be explained visually. Use clip art or other images available on the Web with a software program that will allow you to add balloon captions to explain the process.

Thor Heyerdahl

* *

Thor Heyerdahl (1914–2002), the daring Norwegian explorer and anthropologist, was educated at the University of Oslo and served with the Free Norwegian Military Forces (1940–1945). His seafaring odysseys, which won him international renown, attempted to establish that the pre-Inca inhabitants of Peru could have originally sailed from Peru and settled in Polynesia. To prove this, Heyerdahl constructed a balsa raft and successfully navigated from Callao, Peru, to Tuamotu Island in the South Pacific. In later voyages, Heyerdahl sailed from Morocco in a papyrus boat, the Ra II, *to the West Indies, and in 1977–1978 he journeyed from Qurna, Iraq, to Djibouti, on the Gulf of Aden, in a boat made entirely of reeds. His fascinating adventures are recounted in* On the Hunt for Paradise *(1938),* The Kon-Tiki Expedition *(1948),* Aku-Aku *(1958), and* The Maldive Mystery *(1986), a true-life archaeological detective story. His most recent books include* Pyramids of Tucume *(1995),* Green Was the Earth on the Seventh Day *(1997), and* In the Footsteps of Adam *(2000). In "How to Kill an Ocean," which originally appeared in* Saturday Review *(1975), Heyerdahl disputes the traditional concept of a "boundless ocean" and identifies current threats that could endanger the oceans of the world.*

How to Kill an Ocean

Since the ancient Greeks maintained that the earth was round and great navigators like Columbus and Magellan demonstrated that this assertion was true, no geographical discovery has been more important than what we all are beginning to understand today: that our planet has exceedingly restricted dimensions. There is a limit to all resources. Even the height of the atmosphere and the depth of soil and water represent layers so thin that they would disappear entirely if reduced to scale on the surface of a commonsized globe.

The correct concept of our very remarkable planet, rotating as a small and fertile oasis, two-thirds covered by life-giving water, and teeming with life in a solar system otherwise unfit for man, becomes clearer for us with the progress of moon travel and modern astronomy. Our concern about the limits to human expansion increases as science produces ever more exact data on the measurable resources that mankind has in stock for all the years to come.

Because of the population explosion, land of any nature has long been in such demand that nations have intruded upon each other's territory with armed forces in order to conquer more space for overcrowded communities. During the last few years, the United Nations has convened special meetings in Stockholm, Caracas, and Geneva in a dramatic attempt to create a "Law of the Sea" designed to divide vast sections of the global ocean space into national waters. The fact that no agreement has been reached illustrates that in our ever-shriveling world there is not even ocean space enough to satisfy everybody. And only one generation ago, the ocean was considered so vast that no one nation would bother to lay claim to more of it than the three-mile limit which represented the length of a gun shot from the shore.

It will probably take still another generation before mankind as a whole begins to realize fully that the ocean is but another big lake, landlocked on all sides. Indeed, it is essential to understand this concept for the survival of coming generations. For we of the 20th century still treat the ocean as the endless, bottomless pit it was considered to be in medieval times. Expressions like "the bottomless sea" and "the boundless ocean" are still in common use, and although we all know better, they reflect the mental image we still have of this, the largest body of water on earth. Perhaps one of the reasons why we subconsciously consider the ocean a sort of bottomless abyss is the fact that all the rain and all the rivers of the world keep pouring constantly into it and yet its water level always remains unchanged. Nothing affects the ocean, not even the Amazon, the Nile, or the Ganges. We know, of course, that this imperviousness is no indicator of size, because the sum total of all the rivers is nothing but the return to its own source of the water evaporated from the sea and carried ashore by drilling clouds.

What is it really then that distinguishes the ocean from the other more restricted 5 bodies of water? Surely it is not its salt content. The Old and the New World have lakes with a higher salt percentage than the ocean has. The Aral Sea, the Dead Sea, and the Great Salt Lake in Utah are good examples. Nor is it the fact that the ocean lacks any outlet. Other great bodies of water have abundant input and yet no outlet. The Caspian Sea and Lake Chad in Central Africa are valid examples. Big rivers, among them the Volga, enter the Caspian Sea, but evaporation compensates for its lack of outlet, precisely as is the case with the ocean. Nor is it correct to claim that the ocean is open while inland seas and lakes are landlocked. The ocean is just as landlocked as any lake. It is flanked by land on all sides and in every direction. The fact that the earth is round makes the ocean curve around it just as does solid land, but a shoreline encloses the ocean on all sides and in every direction. The ocean is not even the lowest body of water on our planet. The surface of the Caspian Sea, for instance, is 85 feet below sea level, and the surface of the Dead Sea is more than 1,200 feet below sea level.

Only when we fully perceive that there is no fundamental difference between the various bodies of water on our planet, beyond the fact that the ocean is the largest of all lakes, can we begin to realize that the ocean has something else in common with all other bodies of water: it is vulnerable. In the long run the ocean can be affected by the continued discharge of all modern man's toxic waste. One generation ago no one would have thought that the giant lakes of America could be polluted. Today they are, like the largest lakes of Europe. A few years ago the public was amazed to learn that industrial and urban refuse had killed the fish in Lake Erie. The enormous lake was dead. It was polluted from shore to shore in spite of the fact that it has a constant outlet through Niagara Falls, which carries pollutants away into the ocean in a never-ending flow. The ocean receiving all this pollution has no outlet but represents a dead end, because only pure water evaporates to return into the clouds. The ocean is big; yet if 10 Lake Eries were taken and placed end to end, they would span the entire Atlantic from Africa to South America. And the St. Lawrence River is by no means the only conveyor of pollutants into the ocean. Today hardly a creek or a river in the world reaches the ocean without carrying a constant flow of nondegradable chemicals from industrial, urban, or agricultural areas. Directly by sewers or indirectly by way of streams and other waterways, almost every big city in the world, whether coastal or inland, makes use of the ocean as mankind's common sink. We treat the ocean as if we believed that it is not part of our own planet—as if the blue waters curved into space somewhere beyond the horizon where our pollutants would fall off the edge, as ships were believed to do before the days of Christopher Columbus. We build sewers so far into the sea that we pipe the harmful refuse away from public beaches. Beyond that is no man's concern. What we consider too dangerous to be stored under technical control ashore we dump forever out of sight at sea, whether toxic chemicals or nuclear waste. Our only excuse is the still-surviving image of the ocean as a bottomless pit.

It is time to ask: is the ocean vulnerable? And if so, can many survive on a planet with a dead ocean? Both questions can be answered, and they are worthy of our attention.

First, the degree of vulnerability of any body of water would of course depend on two factors: the volume of the water and the nature of the pollutants. We know the volume of the ocean, its surface measure, and its average depth. We know that it covers 71 percent of the surface of our planet, and we are impressed, with good reason, when all these measurements are given in almost astronomical figures. If we resort to a more visual image, however, the dimensions lose their magic. The average depth of all oceans is only 1,700 meters. The Empire State Building is 448 meters high. If stretched out horizontally instead of vertically, the average ocean depth would only slightly exceed the 1,500 meters than an Olympic runner can cover by foot in 3 minutes and 35 seconds. The average depth of the North Sea, however, is not 1,700 meters, but only 80 meters, and many of the buildings in downtown New York would emerge high above water level if they were built on the bottom of this sea. During the Stone Age most of the North Sea was dry land where roaming archers hunted deer and other game. In this shallow water, until only recently, all the industrial nations of Western Europe have conducted year-round routine dumping of hundreds of thousands of tons of their most toxic industrial refuse. All the world's sewers and most of its waste are dumped into waters as shallow as, or shallower than, the North Sea. An attempt was made at a recent ocean exhibition to illustrate graphically and in correct proportion the depths of the

Atlantic, the Pacific, and the Indian oceans in relation to a cross section of the planet earth. The project had to be abandoned, for although the earth was painted with a diameter twice the height of a man, the depths of the world oceans painted in proportion became so insignificant that they could not be seen except as a very thin pencil line.

The ocean is in fact remarkably shallow for its size. Russia's Lake Baikal, for instance, less than 31 kilometers wide, is 1,500 meters deep, which compares well with the average depth of all oceans. It is the vast *extent* of ocean surface that has made man of all generations imagine a correspondingly unfathomable depth.

When viewed in full, from great heights, the ocean's surface is seen to have definite, confining limits. But at sea level, the ocean seems to extend outward indefinitely, to the horizon and on into blue space. The astronauts have come back from space literally disturbed upon seeing a full view of our planet. They have seen at first hand how cramped together the nations are in a limited space and how the "endless" oceans are tightly enclosed within cramped quarters by surrounding land masses. But one need not be an astronaut to lose the sensation of a boundless ocean. It is enough to embark on some floating logs tied together, as we did with the *Kon-Tiki* in the Pacific, or on some bundles of papyrus reeds, as we did with the *Ra* in the Atlantic. With no effort and no motor we were pushed by the winds and currents from one continent to another in a few weeks.

After we abandon the outworn image of infinite space in the ocean, we are still left with many wrong or useless notions about biological life and vulnerability. Marine life is concentrated in about 4 percent of the ocean's total body of water, whereas roughly 96 percent is just about as poor in life as is a desert ashore. We all know, and should bear in mind, that sunlight is needed to permit photosynthesis for the marine plankton on which all fishes and whales directly or indirectly base their subsistence. In the sunny tropics the upper layer of light used in photosynthesis extends down to a maximum depth of 80 to 100 meters. In the northern latitudes, even on a bright summer's day, this zone reaches no more than 15 to 20 meters below the surface. Because much of the most toxic pollutants are buoyant and stay on the surface (notably all the pesticides and other poisons based on chlorinated hydrocarbons), this concentration of both life and venom in the same restricted body of water is most unfortunate.

What is worse is the fact that life is not evenly distributed throughout this thin surface layer. Ninety percent of all marine species are concentrated above the continental shelves next to land. The water above these littoral shelves represents an area of only 8 percent of the total ocean surface, which itself represents only 4 percent of the total body of water, and means that much less than half a percent of the ocean space represents the home of 90 percent of all marine life. This concentration of marine life in shallow waters next to the coasts happens to coincide with the area of concentrated dumping and the outlet of all sewers and polluted river mouths, not to mention silt from chemically treated farmland. The bulk of some 20,000 known species of fish, some 30,000 species of mollusks, and nearly all the main crustaceans lives in the most exposed waters around the littoral areas. As we know, the reason is that this is the most fertile breeding ground for marine plankton. The marine plant life, the phytoplankton, find here their mineral nutriments, which are brought down by rivers and silt and up from the ocean bottom through coastal upwellings that bring back to the surface the remains of decomposed organisms which have sunk to the bottom through the ages. When we speak of farmable land in any country, we do not include deserts or sterile rock in our calculations. Why then shall we deceive ourselves by the total size of the ocean when we know that not even 1 percent of its water volume is fertile for the fisherman?

Much has been written for or against the activities of some nations that have dumped vast quantities of nuclear waste and obsolete war gases in the sea and excused their actions on the grounds that it was all sealed in special containers. In such shallow waters as the Irish Sea, the English Channel, and the North Sea there are already enough examples of similar "foolproof" containers moving about with bottom currents until they are totally displaced and even crack open with the result that millions of fish are killed or mutilated. In the Baltic Sea, which is shallower than many lakes and which—except for the thin surface layer—has already been killed by pollution, 7,000 tons of arsenic were dumped in cement containers some 40 years ago. These containers have now started to leak. Their combined contents are three times more than is needed to kill the entire population of the earth today.

Fortunately, in certain regions modern laws have impeded the danger of dumpings; yet a major threat to marine life remains—the less spectacular but more effective ocean pollution through continuous discharge from sewers and seepage. Except in the Arctic, there is today hardly a creek or a river in the world from which it is safe to drink at the outlet. The more technically advanced the country, the more devastating the threat to the ocean. A few examples picked at random will illustrate the pollution input from the civilized world:

French rivers carry 18 billion cubic meters of liquid pollution annually into the   15
sea. The city of Paris alone discharges almost 1.2 million cubic meters of untreated effluent into the Seine every day.

The volume of liquid waste from the Federal Republic of Germany is estimated at over 9 billion cubic meters per year, or 25.4 million cubic meters per day, not counting cooling water, which daily amounts to 33.6 million cubic meters. Into the Rhine alone 50,000 tons of waste are discharged daily, including 30,000 tons of sodium chloride from industrial plants.

A report from the U.N. Economic and Social Council, issued prior to the Stockholm Conference on the Law of the Sea four years ago, states that the world had then dumped an estimated billion pounds of DDT into our environment and was adding an estimated 100 million more pounds per year. The total world production of pesticides was estimated at more than 1.3 billion pounds annually, and the United States alone exports more than 400 million pounds per year. Most of this ultimately finds its way into the ocean with winds, rain, or silt from land. A certain type of DDT sprayed on crops in East Africa a few years ago was found and identified a few months later in the Bay of Bengal, a good 4,000 miles away.

The misconception of a boundless ocean makes the man in the street more concerned about city smog than about the risk of killing the ocean. Yet the tallest chimney in the world does not suffice to send the noxious smoke away into space; it gradually sinks down, and nearly all descends, mixed with rain, snow, and silt, into the ocean. Industrial and urban areas are expanding with the population explosion all over the world, and in the United States alone, waste products in the form of smoke and noxious fumes amount to it total of 390,000 tons of pollutants every day, or 142 million tons every year.

With this immense concentration of toxic matter, life on the continental shelves would in all likelihood have been exterminated or at least severely decimated long since if the ocean had been immobile. The cause for the delayed action, which may benefit man for a few decades but will aggravate the situation for coming generations, is the well-known fact that the ocean rotates like boiling water in a kettle. It churns from east to west, from north to south, from the bottom to the surface, and down again, in perpetual motion. At a U.N. meeting one of the developing countries proposed that if ocean dumping were prohibited by global or regional law, they would offer friendly nations the opportunity of dumping in their own national waters—for a fee, of course!

It cannot be stressed too often, however, that it is nothing but a complete illusion   20
when we speak of national waters. We can map and lay claim to the ocean bottom, but not to the mobile sea above it. The water itself is in constant transit. What is considered to be the national waters of Morocco one day turns up as the national waters of Mexico soon after. Meanwhile Mexican national water is soon on its way across the North Atlantic to Norway. Ocean pollution abides by no law.

My own transoceanic drifts with the *Kon-Tiki* raft and the reed vessels *Ra I* and *II* were eye-openers to me and my companions as to the rapidity with which so-called national waters displace themselves. The distance from Peru to the Tuamotu Islands in Polynesia is 4,000 miles when it is measured on a map. Yet the *Kon-Tiki* raft had only crossed about 1,000 miles of ocean surface when we arrived. The other 3,000 miles had been granted us by the rapid flow of the current during the 101 days our crossing lasted. But the same raft voyages taught us another and less pleasant lesson: it is possible to pollute the oceans, and it is already being done. In 1947, when the balsa raft *Kon-Tiki* crossed the Pacific, we towed a plankton net behind. Yet we did not collect specimens or even see any sign of human activity in the crystal-clear water until we spotted the wreck of an old sailing ship on the reef where we landed. In 1969 it was therefore a blow to us on board the papyrus raftship *Ra* to observe, shortly after our departure from Morocco, that we had sailed into an area filled with ugly clumps of hard asphalt-like material, brownish to pitch black in color, which were floating at close intervals on or just below the water's surface. Later on, we sailed into other areas so heavily polluted with similar clumps that we were reluctant to dip up water with our buckets when we needed a good scrub-down at the end of the day. In between these areas the ocean was clean except for occasional floating oil lumps and other widely scattered refuse such as plastic containers, empty bottles, and cans. Because the ropes holding the papyrus reeds of *Ra I* together burst, the battered wreck was abandoned in polluted waters short of the island of Barbados, and a second crossing was effectuated all the way from Safi in Morocco to Barbados in the West Indies in 1970. This time a systematic day-by-day survey of ocean pollution was carried out, and samples of oil lumps collected were sent to the United Nations together with a detailed report on the observations. This was published by Secretary-General U Thant as an annex to his report to the Stockholm Conference on the Law of the Sea. It is enough here to repeat that sporadic oil clots drifted by within reach of our dip net during 43 out of the 57 days our transatlantic crossing lasted. The laboratory analysis of the various samples of oil clots collected showed a wide range in the level of nickel and vanadium content, revealing that they originated from different geographical localities. This again proves that they represent not the homogeneous spill from a leaking oil drill or from a wrecked super-tanker, but the steadily accumulating waste from the daily routine washing of sludge from the combined world fleet of tankers.

The world was upset when the *Torrey Canyon* unintentionally spilled 100,000 tons of oil into the English Channel some years ago; yet this is only a small fraction of the intentional discharge of crude oil sludge through less spectacular, routine tank cleaning. Every year more than *Torrey Canyon*'s spill of 100,000 tons of oil is intentionally pumped into the Mediterranean alone, and a survey of the sea south of Italy yielded 500 liters of solidified oil for every square kilometer of surface. Both the Americans and the Russians were alarmed by our observations of Atlantic pollution in 1970 and sent out specially equipped oceanographic research vessels to the area. American scientists from Harvard University working with the Bermuda Biological Station for Research found more solidified oil than seaweed per surface unit in the Sargasso Sea and had to give up their plankton catch because their nets were completely plugged up by oil sludge. They estimated, however, a floating stock of 86,000 metric tons of tar in the Northwest Atlantic alone. The Russians, in a report read by the representative of the Soviet Academy of Sciences at a recent pollution conference in Prague, found that pollution in the coastal areas of the Atlantic had already surpassed their tentative limit for what had been considered tolerable, and that a new scale of tolerability would have to be postulated.

The problem of oil pollution is in itself a complex one. Various types of crude oil are toxic in different degrees. But they all have one property in common: they attract other chemicals and absorb them like blotting paper, notably the various kinds of pesticides. DDT and other chlorinated hydrocarbons do not dissolve in water, nor do they sink: just as they are absorbed by plankton and other surface organisms, so are they drawn into oil slicks and oil clots, where in some cases they have been rediscovered in stronger concentrations than when originally mixed with dissolvents in the spraying bottles. Oil clots, used as floating support for barnacles, marine worms, and pelagic crabs, were often seen by us from the *Ra*, and these riders are attractive bait for filter-feeding fish and whales, which cannot avoid getting gills and baleens cluttered up by the tarlike oil. Even sharks with their rows of teeth plastered with black oil clots are now reported from the Caribbean Sea. Yet the oil spills and dumping of waste from ships represent a very modest contribution compared with the urban and industrial refuse released from land.

That the ocean, given time, will cope with it all, is a common expression of wishful thinking. The ocean has always been a self-purifying filter that has taken care of all global pollution for millions of years. Man is not the first polluter. Since the morning of time nature itself has been a giant workshop, experimenting, inventing, decomposing, and throwing away waste: the incalculable billions of tons of rotting forest products, decomposing flesh, mud, silt, and excrement. If this waste had not been recycled, the ocean would long since have become a compact soup after millions of years of death and decay, volcanic eruptions, and global erosion. Man is not the first large-scale producer, so why should he become the first disastrous polluter?

Man has imitated nature by manipulating atoms, taking them apart and group-   25
ing them together in different compositions. Nature turned fish into birds and beasts
into man. It found a way to make fruits out of soil and sunshine. It invented radar for
bats and whales, and shortwave transceivers for beetles and butterflies. Jet propulsion
was installed on squids, and unsurpassed computers were made as brains, for mankind.
Marine bacteria and plankton transformed the dead generations into new life. The
life cycle of spaceship earth is the closest one can ever get to the greatest of all inventions, *perpetuum mobile*—the perpetual-motion machine. And the secret is that nothing was composed by nature that could not be recomposed, recycled, and brought
back into service again in another form as another useful wheel in the smoothly running global machinery.

This is where man has sidetracked nature. We put atoms together into molecules
of types nature had carefully avoided. We invent to our delight immediately useful materials like plastics, pesticides, detergents, and other chemical products hitherto unavailable on planet earth. We rejoice because we can get our laundry whiter than the
snow we pollute and because we can exterminate every trace of insect life. We spray
bugs and bees, worms and butterflies. We wash and flush the detergents down the
drain out to the oysters and fish. Most of our new chemical products are not only
toxic: they are in fact created to sterilize and kill. And they keep on displaying these
same inherent abilities wherever they end up. Through sewers and seepage they all
head for the ocean, where they remain to accumulate as undesired nuts and bolts in between the cogwheels of a so far smoothly running machine. If it had not been for the
present generation, man could have gone on polluting the ocean forever with the degrad-
able waste he produced. But with ever-increasing speed and intensity we now produce
and discharge into the sea hundreds of thousands of chemicals and other products.
They do not evaporate nor do they recycle, but they grow in numbers and quantity
and threaten all marine life.

We have long known that our modern pesticides have begun to enter the flesh of
penguins in the Antarctic and the brains of polar bears and the blubber of whales in
the Arctic, all subsisting on plankton and plankton-eating crustaceans and fish in areas
far from cities and farmland. We all know that marine pollution has reached global extent in a few decades. We also know that very little or nothing is being done to stop
it. Yet there are persons who tell us that there is no reason to worry, that the ocean is
so big and surely science must have everything under control. City smog is being fought
through intelligent legislation. Certain lakes and rivers have been improved by leading
the sewers down to the sea. But where, may we ask, is the global problem of ocean pollution under control?

No breathing species could live on this planet until the surface layer of the ocean
was filled with phytoplankton, as our planet in the beginning was only surrounded
by sterile gases. These minute plant species manufactured so much oxygen that it rose
above the surface to help form the atmosphere we have today. All life on earth depended upon this marine plankton for its evolution and continued subsistence. Today,
more than ever before, mankind depends on the welfare of this marine plankton for
his future survival as a species. With the population explosion we need to harvest
even more protein from the sea. Without plankton there will be no fish. With our

rapid expansion of urban and industrial areas and the continuous disappearance of jungle and forest, we shall be ever more dependent on the plankton for the very air we breathe. Neither man nor any other terrestrial beast could have bred had plankton not preceded them. Take away this indispensable life in the shallow surface areas of the sea, and life ashore will be unfit for coming generations. A dead ocean means a dead planet.

Questions for Discussion and Writing

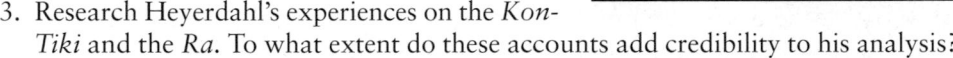

1. To what types of pollution is the ocean most vulnerable? In what respects is the popular conception of the ocean erroneous, according to Heyerdahl?
2. How does Heyerdahl use statistics and a hypothetical scenario to dramatize the ocean's vulnerability?
3. Research Heyerdahl's experiences on the *Kon-Tiki* and the *Ra*. To what extent do these accounts add credibility to his analysis?
4. Is this winning entry in a children's poster art contest more effective than artwork by a professional artist would have been? Why or why not?

Jared Diamond

Jared Diamond (b. 1937) is a professor of physiology in the medical school at the University of California at Los Angeles. He is among the world's leading scientists in the various fields of physiology, ecology, and ornithology. He received the Pulitzer Prize for nonfiction in 1998 for Guns, Germs, and Steel: The Fates of Human Societies. *The following selection originally appeared in* The Third Chimpanzee: The Evolution and Future of the Human Animal *(1992).*

WHY DO WE SMOKE, DRINK, AND USE DANGEROUS DRUGS?

Chernobyl—Formaldehyde in drywall—Lead poisoning—smog—the *Valdez* oil spill—Love Canal—asbestos—Agent Orange . . . Hardly a month goes by without our learning of yet another way in which we and our children have been exposed to toxic chemicals through the negligence of others. The public's outrage, sense of helplessness, and demand for change are growing. Why, then, do we do to ourselves what we cannot stand for others to do to us? How do we explain the paradox that many people intentionally consume, inject, or inhale toxic chemicals, such as alcohol, cocaine, and the chemicals in tobacco smoke? Why are various forms of this willful self-damage native to many contemporary societies, from primitive tribes to high-tech urbanites, and extending back into the past as far as we have written records? How did drug abuse become a hallmark virtually unique to the human species?

The problem isn't so much in understanding why we continue to take toxic chemicals once we've started. In part, that's because our drugs of abuse are addictive. Instead, the greater mystery is what impels us to start at all. Evidence for the damaging or lethal effects of alcohol, cocaine, and tobacco is by now overwhelming and familiar. Only the existence of some strong countervailing motives could explain why people consume these poisons voluntarily, even eagerly. It's as if unconscious programs were driving us to do something we know to be dangerous. What could those programs be?

Naturally, there is no single explanation: different motives carry different weight with different people and in different societies. For instance, some people drink to overcome their inhibitions or to join friends, others to deaden their feelings or drown their sorrows, still others because they like the taste of alcoholic beverages. Naturally, too, differences among human populations and social classes in their options for achieving satisfying lives largely account for geographic and class differences in chemical abuse. It's not surprising that self-destructive alcoholism is a bigger problem in high-unemployment areas of Ireland than in southeast England, or that cocaine and heroin addiction is commoner in Harlem than in affluent suburbs. One could be tempted to dismiss drug abuse as a human hallmark with obvious social and cultural causes, and in no need of a search for animal precedents.

However, none of the motives that I've just mentioned goes to the heart of the paradox of our actively seeking what we know to be harmful. In this chapter I'll propose one other contributing motive, which does address that paradox. It relates our chemical self-assaults to a wide range of seemingly self-destructive traits in animals, and to a general theory of animal signaling. It unifies a wide range of phenomena in our culture, from smoking and alcoholism to drug abuse. It has potential cross-cultural validity, for it may explain not just phenomena of the western world but also some otherwise mystifying customs elsewhere, such as kerosene drinking by Indonesian kung fu experts. I'll also reach into the past and apply the theory to the seemingly bizarre practice of ceremonial enemas in ancient Mayan civilization.

Let me begin by relating how I arrived at this idea. One day, I was abruptly   5
struck by the puzzle that companies manufacturing toxic chemicals for human use advertise their use explicitly. This business practice would seem a sure route to bankruptcy. Yet, while we don't tolerate ads for cocaine, ads for tobacco and alcohol are so widespread that we cease to regard their existence as puzzling. It hit me only after I had been living with New Guinea hunters in the jungle for many months, far from any advertising.

Day after day, my New Guinea friends had been asking me about western customs, and I had come to realize through their astonished responses how senseless many of our customs are. Then the months of fieldwork ended with one of those sudden transitions that modern transportation has made possible. On June 25 I was still in the jungle, watching a brilliant-colored male bird of paradise flap awkwardly across a clearing, dragging its three-foot-long tail behind it. On June 26 I was sitting in a Boeing 747 jet, reading the magazines and catching up on the wonders of western civilization.

I leafed through the first magazine. It fell open to a page with a photo of a tough-looking man on horseback chasing cows, and the name of a brand of cigarette in large letters below. The American in me knew what the photo was about. But part of me was still in the jungle, looking at that photo naïvely. Perhaps my reaction won't seem so strange to you if you try to imagine yourself completely unfamiliar with western society, seeing the ad for the first time, and trying to fathom the connection between chasing cows and smoking (or not smoking) cigarettes.

The naïve part of me, fresh out of the jungle, thought: such a brilliant antismoking ad! It's well known that smoking impairs athletic ability and causes cancer and early death. Cowboys are widely regarded as athletic and admirable. This ad must be a devastating new appeal by the antismoking forces, telling us that if we smoke that particular brand of cigarette, we won't be fit to be cowboys. What an effective message to our youth!

But then it became obvious that the ad had been put there by the cigarette company itself, which somehow hoped that readers would draw exactly the opposite message from the ad. How on earth did the company let its public-relations department talk it into such a disastrous miscalculation? Surely that ad would dissuade any person concerned about his/her strength and self-image from starting to smoke.

Still half immersed in the jungle, I turned to another page. There I saw a photo of   10
a whiskey bottle on a table, a man sipping presumably the bottle's contents from a glass, and an obviously fertile young woman gazing at him admiringly as if she were on the verge of sexual surrender. How can that be? I asked myself. Everyone knows that alcohol interferes with sexual function, tends to make men impotent, makes one likely to stumble, impairs judgment, and predisposes to cirrhosis of the liver and other debilitating conditions. In the immortal words of the porter in Shakespeare's *Macbeth,* "It [alcohol] provokes the desire, but it takes away the performance." A man with such performance handicaps should conceal them at all costs from a woman he aims to seduce. Why is the man in the photo intentionally displaying those handicaps? Do whiskey manufacturers think that pictures of this impaired individual will help sell their product? One could expect that Mothers Against Drunk Driving would be the ones producing such ads, and that the whiskey companies would be suing to prevent publication.

Page after page of ads flaunted the use of cigarettes or strong alcohol, and hinted at their benefits. There were even pictures of young people smoking in the presence of attractive members of the opposite sex, as if to imply that smoking too brought sexual opportunities. Yet any nonsmoker who has ever been kissed by (or tried to kiss) a smoker knows how severely the smoker's bad breath compromises his or her sex appeal. The ads paradoxically implied not just sexual benefits but also platonic friendships, business opportunities, vigor, health, and happiness, when the direct conclusion to be drawn from the ads was actually the reverse.

As the days passed and I reimmersed myself in western civilization, I gradually stopped noticing its apparently self-defeating ads. I retreated into analyzing my field data and wondering instead about an entirely different paradox, involving bird evolution. But that paradox was what led me finally to understand one rationale behind cigarette and whiskey ads.

The new paradox concerned why that male bird of paradise I had been watching on June 25 had evolved the impediment of a tail three feet long. Males of other bird of paradise species evolved other bizarre impediments, such as long plumes growing out of their eyebrows, the habit of hanging upside-down, and brilliant colors and loud calls likely to attract hawks. All those features must impair male survival, yet they also serve as the advertisements by which male birds of paradise woo female birds of paradise. Like many other biologists, I found myself wondering why male birds of paradise use such handicaps as advertisements, and why females find the handicaps attractive.

At that point I recalled a remarkable paper published in 1975 by an Israeli biologist, Amotz Zahavi. In that paper Zahavi proposed a novel general theory, still hotly debated by biologists, about the role of costly or self-destructive signals in animal behavior. For example, he attempted to explain how deleterious male traits might attract a female precisely because they constitute handicaps. On reflection, I decided that Zahavi's hypothesis might apply to the birds of paradise I studied. Suddenly I realized, with growing excitement, that his theory perhaps could also be extended to explain the paradox of our use of toxic chemicals, and our touting it in ads.

Zahavi's theory as he proposed it concerned the broad problem of animal communication. All animals need to devise quick, easily understood signals for conveying messages to their mates, potential mates, offspring, parents, rivals, and would-be predators. For example, consider a gazelle that notices a lion stalking it. It would be in the gazelle's interests to give a signal that the lion would interpret to mean, "I am a superior fast gazelle! You'll never succeed in catching me, so don't waste your time and energy on trying." Even if that gazelle really is able to outrun a lion, giving a signal that dissuades the lion from trying would save time and energy for the gazelle too.

But what signal will unequivocally tell the lion that it's hopeless? The gazelle can't take the time to run a demonstration hundred-yard dash in front of every lion that shows up. Perhaps gazelles could agree on some quick arbitrary signal that lions learn to understand: e.g., pawing the ground with the left hind foot means, "I claim that I'm fast!" However, such a purely arbitrary signal opens the door to cheating: any gazelle can easily give the signal regardless of its speed. Lions will then catch on that many slow gazelles giving the signal are lying, and lions will learn to ignore the signal. It's in the interests both of lions and of fast gazelles that the signal be believable. What type of signal could convince a lion of the gazelle's honesty?

The same dilemma arises in the problem of sexual selection and mate choice that I discussed in earlier chapters. This is especially a problem of how females pick males, since females invest more in reproduction, have more to lose, and have to be choosier. Ideally, a female should pick a male for his good genes to pass on to her offspring. Since genes themselves are hard to assess, a female should look for quick indicators of good genes in a male, and a superior male should provide such indicators. In practice, male traits such as plumage, songs, and displays usually serve as indicators. Why do males "choose" to advertise with those particular indicators, why should females trust a male's honesty and find those indicators attractive, and why do they imply good genes?

15

I've described the problem as if a gazelle or courting male voluntarily picks out some indicator from among many possible ones, and as if a lion or a female decides on reflection whether it's really a valid indicator of speed or good genes. In practice, of course, those "choices" are the result of evolution and become specified by genes. Those females who select males on the basis of indicators that really denote good male genes, and those males that use unambiguous indicators of good genes for self-advertisement, tend to leave the most offspring, as do those gazelles and lions that spare themselves unnecessary chases.

As it turns out, many of the advertising signals evolved by animals pose a paradox similar to that posed by cigarette ads. The indicators often seem not to suggest speed or good genes but instead to constitute handicaps, expenses, or sources of risk. For example, a gazelle's signal to a lion that it sees approaching consists of a peculiar behavior termed "stotting." Instead of running away as fast as possible, the gazelle runs slowly while repeatedly jumping high into the air with stiff-legged leaps. Why on earth should the gazelle indulge in this seemingly self-destructive display, which wastes time and energy and gives the lion a chance to catch up? Or think of the males of many animal species that sport large structures, such as a peacock's tail or a bird of paradise's plumes, that make movement difficult. Males of many more species have bright colors, loud songs, or conspicuous displays that attract predators. Why should a male advertise such an impediment, and why should a female like it? These paradoxes remain an important unsolved problem in animal behavior today.

Zahavi's theory goes to the heart of this paradox. According to his theory, those 20 deleterious structures and behaviors constitute valid indicators that the signaling animal is being honest in its claim of superiority, precisely *because* those traits themselves impose handicaps. A signal that entails no cost lends itself to cheating, since even a slow or inferior animal can afford to give the signal. Only costly or deleterious signals are guarantees of honesty. For example, a slow gazelle that stotted at an approaching lion would seal its fate, whereas a fast gazelle could still outrun the lion after stotting. By stotting, the gazelle boasts to the lion, "I'm so fast that I can escape you even after giving you this head start." The lion thereby has grounds for believing in the gazelle's honesty, and both the lion and the gazelle profit by not wasting time and energy on a chase whose outcome is certain.

Similarly, as applied to males displaying toward females, Zahavi's theory reasons that any male that has managed to survive despite the handicap of a big tail or conspicuous song must have terrific genes in other respects. He has proved that he must be *especially* good at escaping predators, finding food, and resisting disease. The bigger the handicap, the more rigorous the test that he has passed. The female who selects such a male is like the medieval damsel testing her knight suitors by watching them slay dragons. When she sees a one-armed knight who can still slay a dragon, she knows that she has finally found a knight with great genes. And that knight, by flaunting his handicap, is actually flaunting his superiority.

It seems to me that Zahavi's theory applies to many costly or dangerous human behaviors aimed at achieving status in general or at sexual benefits in particular. For instance, men who woo women with costly gifts and other displays of wealth are in effect saying, "I have plenty of money to support you and children, and you can believe my boast because you see how much money I'm spending now without blanching." People who show off expensive jewels, sports cars, or works of art gain status because the signal can't be faked; everyone else knows what those ostentatious objects cost. American Indians of the Pacific Northwest used to seek status by competing to give away as much wealth as possible in ceremonies known as potlatch rituals. In the days before modern medicine, tattooing was not only painful but dangerous because of the risk of infection; hence tattooed people in effect were advertising two facets of their strength, resistance to disease plus tolerance of pain. Men on the Pacific island of Malekula have traditionally showed off by the insanely dangerous practice, now imitated elsewhere by bungee jumpers, of building a high tower and jumping off it headfirst, after tying one end of some stout vines to each ankle and the other end to the top of the tower. The length of the vines is calculated to stop the braggart's plunge while his head is still a few feet above the ground. Survival guarantees that the jumper is courageous, carefully calculating, and a good builder.

Zahavi's theory can also be extended to human abuse of chemicals. Especially in adolescence and early adulthood, the age when drug abuse is most likely to begin, we are devoting much energy to asserting our status. I suggest that we share the same unconscious instinct that leads birds to indulge in dangerous displays. Ten thousand years ago, we "displayed" by challenging a lion or a tribal enemy. Today, we do it in other ways, such as by fast driving or by consuming dangerous drugs.

The messages of our old and new displays nevertheless remain the same: I'm strong and superior. Even to take drugs only once or twice, I must be strong enough to get past the burning, choking sensation of my first puff on a cigarette, or to get past the misery of my first hangover. To do it chronically and remain alive and healthy, I must be superior (so I imagine). It's a message to our rivals, our peers, our prospective mates— and to ourselves. The smoker's kiss may taste awful, and the drinker may be impotent in bed, but he or she still hopes to impress peers or attract mates by the implicit message of superiority.

Alas, the message may be valid for birds, but for us it's a false one. Like so many animals instincts in us, this one has become maladaptive in modern human society. If you can still walk after drinking a bottle of whiskey, it may prove that you have high levels of liver alcohol dehydrogenase, but it implies no superiority in other respects. If you haven't developed lung cancer after chronically smoking several packs of cigarettes daily, you may have a gene for resistance to lung cancer, but that gene doesn't convey intelligence, business acumen, or the ability to create happiness for your spouse and children. 25

It's true that animals with only brief lives and courtships have no alternative except to develop quick indicators, since prospective mates don't have enough time to measure each other's real quality. But we, with our long lives and courtships and business associations, have ample time to scrutinize each other's worth. We needn't rely on superficial, misleading indicators. Drug abuse is a classic instance of a once-useful instinct—the reliance on handicap signals—that has turned foul in us. It's that old instinct to which the tobacco and whiskey companies are directing their clever, obscene ads. If we legalized cocaine, the drug lords too would soon have ads appealing to the same instinct. You can easily picture it: the photo of the cowboy on his horse, or the suave man and the attractive maiden, above the tastefully displayed packet of white powder.

Now, let's test my theory by jumping from western industrialized society to the other side of the world. Drug abuse did not begin with the industrial revolution. Tobacco was a native American Indian crop, native alcoholic beverages are widespread in the world, and cocaine and opium came to us from other societies. The oldest preserved code of laws, that of the Babylonian king Hammurabi (1792–50 B.C.), already contained a section regulating drinking houses. Hence my theory, if it's valid, should apply to other societies as well. As an instance of its cross-cultural explanatory power, I'll cite a practice you may not have heard of: kung fu kerosene drinking.

I learned of this practice when I was working in Indonesia with a wonderful young biologist named Ardy Irwanto. Ardy and I had come to like and admire each other, and to look out for each other's well-being. At one point, when we reached a troubled area and I expressed concern about dangerous people we might encounter, Ardy assured me, "No problem, Jared. I have kung fu grade eight." He explained that he practiced the Oriental martial art of kung fu and had reached a high level of proficiency, such that he could single-handedly fight off a group of eight attackers. To illustrate, Ardy showed me a scar in his back stemming from an attack by eight ruffians. One had knifed him, whereupon Ardy broke the arms of two and the skull of a third and the remainder fled. I had nothing to fear in Ardy's company, he told me.

One evening at our campsite, Ardy walked with his drinking cup up to our jerrycans. As usual, we had two cans: a blue one for water, and a red one for kerosene for our pressure lamp. To my horror, I watched Ardy pour from the red jerrycan and raise the cup to his lips. Remembering an awful moment during a mountaineering expedition when I had taken a sip of kerosene by mistake and spent all the next day coughing it back up, I screamed to Ardy to stop. But he raised his hand and said calmly, "No problem, Jared. I have kung fu grade eight."

Ardy explained that kung fu gave him strength, which he and his fellow kung fu   30
masters tested each month by drinking a cup of kerosene. Without kung fu, of course, kerosene would make a weaker person sick: heaven forbid that I, Jared, for instance, should try it. But it did him, Ardy, no harm, because he had kung fu. He calmly retired to his tent to sip his kerosene and emerged the next morning, happy and healthy as usual.

I can't believe that kerosene did Ardy no harm. I wish that he could have found a less damaging way to make periodic tests of his preparedness. But for him and his kung fu associates, it served as an indicator of their strength and their advanced level of kung fu. Only a really robust person could get through that test. Kerosene drinking illustrates the handicap theory of toxic chemical use, in a form as startlingly repellent to us as our cigarettes and alcohol were to a horrified Ardy.

As my last example, I'll generalize my theory further by extending its applications to the past—in this case, to the civilization of Mayan Indians that flourished in Central America one or two thousand years ago. Archaeologists have been fascinated by Mayan success at creating an advanced society in the middle of tropical rain forest. Many Mayan achievements, such as their calendar, writing, astronomical knowledge, and agricultural practices, are now understood to varying degrees. But archaeologists were long puzzled by slender tubes of unknown purpose that they kept finding in Mayan excavations.

The tubes' function finally became clear with the discovery of painted vases showing scenes of the tubes' use: to administer intoxicating enemas. The vases depict a high-status figure, evidently a priest or a prince, receiving a ceremonial enema in the presence of other people. The enema tube is shown as connected to a bag of a frothy, beerlike beverage—probably containing either alcohol or hallucinogens or both, as suggested by practices of other Indian groups. Many Central and South American Indian tribes formerly practiced similar ritual enemas when first encountered by European explorers, and some still do so today. The substances known to be administered range from alcohol (made by fermenting agave sap or a tree bark) to tobacco, peyote, LSD derivatives, and mushroom-derived hallucinogens. Thus, the ritual enema is similar to our consumption of intoxicants by mouth, but there are four reasons why an enema constitutes a more effective and valid indicator of strength than does drinking.

First, it is possible to relapse into solitary drinking and thus to lose all opportunity for signaling one's high status to others. However, it is more difficult for a solitary person to administer the same beverage to himself or herself unassisted as an enema. An enema encourages one to enlist associates, and thereby automatically creates an occasion for self-advertisement. Second, more strength is required to handle alcohol as an enema than as a drink, since the alcohol goes directly into the intestine and thence to the bloodstream, and it isn't first diluted with food in the stomach. Third, drugs absorbed from the small intestine after ingestion by mouth pass first to the liver, where many drugs are detoxified before they can reach the brain and other sensitive organs. But drugs absorbed from the rectum after an enema bypass the liver. Finally, nausea may limit one's intake of drinks but not of enemas. Hence an enema seems to me a more convincing advertisement of superiority than are our whiskey ads. I recommend this concept to an ambitious public-relations firm competing for the account of one of the large distilleries.

Let's now step back and summarize the perspective on chemical abuse that I've suggested. Although frequent self-destruction by chemicals may be unique to humans, I see it as fitting into a broad pattern of animal behavior and thus as having innumerable animal precedents. All animals have had to evolve signals for quickly communicating messages to other animals. If the signals were ones that any individual animal could master or acquire, they would lend themselves to rampant cheating and hence to disbelief. To be valid and believable, a signal must be one that guarantees the honesty of the signaler, by entailing a cost, risk, or burden that only superior individuals can afford. Many animal signals that would otherwise strike us as counterproductive—such as stotting by gazelles, or costly structures and risky displays with which males court females—can be understood in this light.

It seems to me that this perspective has contributed to the evolution not only of human art but also of human chemical abuse. Both art and chemical abuse are widespread human hallmarks characteristic of most known human societies. Both beg explanation, since it's not immediately obvious why they promote our survival through natural selection, or why they help us acquire mates through sexual selection. I argued earlier that art often serves as a valid indicator of an individual's superiority or status, since art requires skill to create and requires status or wealth to acquire. But those individuals perceived by their fellows as enjoying status thereby acquire enhanced access to resources and mates. I'm arguing now that humans seek status through many other costly displays besides art, and that some of those displays (like jumping from towers, fast driving, and chemical abuse) are surprisingly dangerous. The former costly displays advertise status or wealth; the latter dangerous ones advertise that the displaying individual can master even such risks and hence must be superior.

I don't claim, though, that this perspective affords a total understanding of art or chemical abuse. As I mentioned in connection with art, complex behaviors acquire a life of their own, go far beyond their original purpose (if there ever was just a single purpose), and may even originally have served multiple functions. Just as art is now motivated far more by pleasure than by need for advertisement, chemical abuse too is now clearly much more than an advertisement. It's also a way to get past inhibitions, drown sorrows, or just enjoy a good-tasting drink.

I also don't deny that, even from an evolutionary perspective, there remains a basic difference between human abuse of chemicals and its animal precedents. Stotting, long tails, and all the animal precedents that I described involve costs, but those behaviors persist because the costs are outweighed by the benefits. A stotting gazelle loses a possible head start in a chase, but gains by decreasing the likelihood that a lion will embark on a serious chase at all. A long-tailed male bird is encumbered in finding food or escaping predators, but those survival disadvantages imposed by natural selection are more than compensated by mating advantages gained through sexual selection. The net balance is more rather than fewer offspring to pass on the male's genes. Hence these animal traits only appear to be self-destructive; they are actually self-promoting.

In the case of our chemical abuse, though, the costs outweigh the benefits. Drug addicts and drunkards not only lead shorter lives, but they lose rather than gain attractiveness in the eyes of potential mates and lose the ability to care for children. These traits don't persist because of hidden advantages outweighing costs; they persist mainly because they are chemically addicting. Overall, they are self-destructive, not self-promoting, behaviors. While gazelles may occasionally miscalculate in stotting, they don't commit suicide through addiction to the excitement of stotting. In that respect, our self-destructive abuse of chemicals diverged from its animal precursors to become truly a human hallmark.

Questions for Discussion and Writing

1. What theory does Diamond propose to explain why people intentionally inhale, inject, or consume addictive and toxic substances?
2. How does Diamond use analogies drawn from animal behavior, examples drawn from personal experience, and historical research to develop his case?
3. Do you find Diamond's thesis credible? Why or why not? Do your own experiences or observations of the behavior of others support Diamond's assertions? Explain your answer.
4. How does this picture of a male bird of paradise illustrate what led Diamond to formulate his hypothesis?

Linda Hogan

· ·

Linda Hogan, Chickasaw poet, novelist, and essayist, was born in 1947 in Denver, Colorado, and grew up in Oklahoma. She taught American Indian Studies at the University of Minnesota from 1984 to 1991 and is currently professor of American Studies and American Indian Studies at the University of Colorado. Her poetry has been collected in Seeing Through the Sun *(1985), which received an American Book Award from the Before Columbus Foundation;* The Book of Medicines *(1993); and* Solar Storms *(1996). She has also published short stories, one of which, "Aunt Moon's Young Man," was featured in* Best American Short Stories *(1989). Her novel* Mean Spirit *was nominated for a Pulitzer Prize (1990). Hogan's latest work is* The Woman Who Watches Over the World: A Native Memoir *(2001). In "Waking Up the Rake," reprinted from* Parabola, the Magazine of Myth and Tradition *(Summer 1988), Hogan reveals how even the simplest act of compassion for animals can yield unexpected spiritual rewards.*

WAKING UP THE RAKE

In the still dark mornings, my grandmother would rise up from her bed and put wood in the stove. When the fire began to burn, she would sit in front of its warmth and let down her hair. It had never been cut and it knotted down in two long braids. When I was fortunate enough to be there, in those red Oklahoma mornings, I would wake up with her, stand behind her chair, and pull the brush through the long strands of her hair. It cascaded down her back, down over the chair, and touched the floor.

We were the old and the new, bound together in front of the snapping fire, woven like a lifetime's tangled growth of hair. I saw my future in her body and face, and her past was alive in me. We were morning people, and in all of earth's mornings the new intertwines with the old. Even new, a day itself is ancient, old with earth's habit of turning over and over again.

Years later, I was sick, and I went to a traditional healer. The healer was dark and thin and radiant. The first night I was there, she also lit a fire. We sat before it, smelling the juniper smoke. She asked me to tell her everything, my life spoken in words, a case history of living, with its dreams and losses, the scars and wounds we all bear from being in the world. She smoked me with cedar smoke, wrapped a sheet around me, and put me to bed, gently, like a mother caring for her child.

The next morning she nudged me awake and took me outside to pray. We faced east where the sun was beginning its journey on our side of earth.

The following morning in red dawn, we went outside and prayed. The sun was a full orange eye rising up the air. The morning after that we did the same, and on Sunday we did likewise.   5

The next time I visited her it was a year later, and again we went through the same prayers, standing outside facing the early sun. On the last morning I was there, she left for her job in town. Before leaving, she said, "Our work is our altar."

Those words have remained with me.

Now I am a disciple of birds. The birds that I mean are eagles, owls, and hawks. I clean cages at the Birds of Prey Rehabilitation Foundation. It is the work I wanted to do, in order to spend time inside the gentle presence of the birds.

There is a Sufi saying that goes something like this: "Yes, worship God, go to church, sing praises, but first tie your camel to the post." This cleaning is the work of tying the camel to a post.

I pick up the carcasses and skin of rats, mice, and of rabbits. Some of them have   10 been turned inside out by the sharp-beaked eaters, so that the leathery flesh becomes a delicately veined coat for the inner fur. It is a boneyard. I rake the smooth fragments of bones. Sometimes there is a leg or shank of deer to be picked up.

In this boneyard, the still-red vertebrae lie on the ground beside an open rib cage. The remains of a rabbit, a small intestinal casing, holds excrement like beads in a necklace. And there are the clean, oval pellets the birds spit out, filled with fur, bone fragments and now and then, a delicate sharp claw that looks as if it were woven inside. A feather, light and soft, floats down a current of air, and it is also picked up.

Over time, the narrow human perspective from which we view things expands. A deer carcass begins to look beautiful and rich in its torn redness, the muscle and bone exposed in the shape life took on for a while as it walked through meadows and drank at creeks.

And the bone fragments have their own stark beauty, the clean white jaw bones with ivory teeth small as the head of a pin still in them. I think of medieval physicians trying to learn about our private, hidden bodies by cutting open the stolen dead and finding the splendor inside, the grace of every red organ, and the smooth, gleaming bone.

This work is an apprenticeship, and the birds are the teachers. Sweet-eyed barn owls, such taskmasters, asking us to be still and slow and to move in time with their rhythms, not our own. The short-eared owls with their startling yellow eyes require the full presence of a human. The marsh hawks, behind their branches, watch our every move.

There is a silence needed here before a person enters the bordered world the birds   15 inhabit, so we stop and compose ourselves before entering their doors, and we listen to the musical calls of the eagles, the sound of wings in air, the way their feet with sharp claws, many larger than our own hands, grab hold of a perch. Then we know we are ready to enter, and they are ready for us.

The most difficult task the birds demand is that we learn to be equal to them, to feel our way into an intelligence that is different from our own. A friend, awed at the thought of working with eagles, said, "Imagine knowing an eagle." I answered her honestly, "It isn't so much that we know the eagles. It's that they know us."

And they know that we are apart from them, that as humans we have somehow fallen from our animal grace, and because of that we maintain a distance from them, though it is not always a distance of heart. The places we inhabit, even sharing a common earth, must remain distinct and separate. It was our presence that brought most of them here in the first place, nearly all of them injured in a clash with the human world. They have been shot, or hit by cars, trapped in leg hold traps, poisoned, ensnared in wire fences. To ensure their survival, they must remember us as the enemies that we are. We are the embodiment of a paradox; we are the wounders and we are the healers.

There are human lessons to be learned here, in the work. Fritjof Capra wrote: "Doing work that has to be done over and over again helps us to recognize the natural cycles of growth and decay, of birth and death, and thus become aware of the dynamic order of the universe." And it is true, in whatever we do, the brushing of hair, the cleaning of cages, we begin to see the larger order of things. In this place, there is a constant coming to terms with both the sacred place life occupies, and with death. Like one of those early physicians who discovered the strange, inner secrets of our human bodies, I'm filled with awe at the very presence of life, not just the birds, but a horse contained in its living fur, a dog alive and running. What a marvel it is, the fine shape life takes in all of us. It is equally marvelous that life is quickly turned back to the earth-colored ants and the soft white maggots that are time's best and closest companions. To sit with the eagles and their flutelike songs, listening to the longer flute of wind sweep through the lush grasslands, is to begin to know the natural laws that exist apart from our own written ones.

One of those laws, that we carry deep inside us, is intuition. It is lodged in a place even the grave-robbing doctors could not discover. It's a blood-written code that directs us through life. The founder of this healing center, Sigrid Ueblacker, depends on this inner knowing. She watches, listens, and feels her way to an understanding of each eagle and owl. This vision, as I call it, directs her own daily work at healing the injured birds and returning them to the wild.

"Sweep the snow away," she tells me. "The Swainson's hawks should be in Argentina this time of year and should not have to stand in the snow." 20

I sweep.

And that is in the winter when the hands ache from the cold, and the water freezes solid and has to be broken out for the birds, fresh buckets carried over icy earth from the well. In summer, it's another story. After only a few hours the food begins to move again, as if resurrected to life. A rabbit shifts a bit. A mouse turns. You could say that they have been resurrected, only with a life other than the one that left them. The moving skin swarms with flies and their offspring, ants, and a few wasps, busy at their own daily labor.

Even aside from the expected rewards for this work, such as seeing an eagle healed and winging across the sky it fell from, there are others. An occasional snake, beautiful and sleek, finds its way into the cage one day, eats a mouse and is too fat to leave, so we watch its long muscular life stretched out in the tall grasses. Or, another summer day, taking branches to be burned with a pile of wood near the little creek, a large turtle with a dark and shining shell slips soundlessly into the water, its presence a reminder of all the lives beyond these that occupy us.

One green morning, an orphaned owl perches nervously above me while I clean. Its downy feathers are roughed out. It appears to be twice its size as it clacks its beak at me, warning me: stay back. Then, fearing me the way we want it to, it bolts off the perch and flies, landing by accident onto the wooden end of my rake, before it sees that a human is an extension of the tool, and it flies again to a safer place, while I return to raking.

The word "rake" means to gather or heap up, to smooth the broken ground. And   25
that's what this work is, all of it, the smoothing over of broken ground, the healing of
the severed trust we humans hold with earth. We gather it back together again with great
care, take the broken pieces and fragments and return them to the sky. It is work at the
borderland between species, at the boundary between injury and healing.

There is an art to raking, a very fine art, one with rhythm in it, and life. On the
days I do it well, the rake wakes up. Wood that came from dark dense forests seems
to return to life. The water that rose up through the rings of that wood, the minerals
of earth mined upward by the burrowing tree roots, all come alive. My own fragile
hand touches the wood, a hand full of my own life, including that which rose each
morning early to watch the sun return from the other side of the planet. Over time, these
hands will smooth the rake's wooden handle down to a sheen.

Raking. It is a labor round and complete, smooth and new as an egg, and the
rounding seasons of the world revolving in time and space. All things, even our own
heartbeats and sweat, are in it, part of it. And that work, that watching the turning over
of life, becomes a road into what is essential. Work is the country of hands, and they
want to live there in the dailiness of it, the repetition that is time's language of prayer,
a common, tongue. Everything is there, in that language, in the humblest of labor. The
rake wakes up and the healing is in it. The shadows of leaves that once fell beneath the
tree the handle came from are in that labor, and the rabbits that passed this way, on
the altar of our work. And when the rake wakes up, all earth's gods are reborn and they
dance and sing in the dusty air around us.

Questions for Discussion and Writing

1. How did Hogan's recovery from an illness lead her to devote so much time to the
   care of injured birds of prey?
2. What special significance does the title convey, and how does it summarize what
   Hogan has learned from her experiences at the shelter?
3. Would you ever volunteer your time to take care of sick or injured animals as
   Hogan did? Would you consider this a worthwhile activity? Why or why not?

Alice Walker

*Alice Walker was born in 1944 in Georgia and graduated from Sarah Lawrence College
in 1965. She has taught at Yale, Wellesley, and other colleges and has edited and published poetry, fiction, and biography. She is best known for her novel* The Color Purple
*(1982), which won the American Book Award and the Pulitzer Prize for Fiction and was
made into an Academy Award–winning movie in 1985. "Am I Blue?" was first published in her collection of essays* Living by the Word *(1988). Her recent works include*
Alice Walker Banned *(1996),* By the Light of My Father's Smile *(1998),* The Way Forward Is with a Broken Heart *(2000),* Absolute Trust in the Goodness of the Earth: New
Poems *(2003), and* Now Is the Time to Open your Heart *(2004).*

AM I BLUE?

"Ain't these tears in these eyes tellin' you?"

For about three years my companion and I rented a small house in the country that stood on the edge of a large meadow that appeared to run from the end of our deck straight into the mountains. The mountains, however, were quite far away, and between us and them there was, in fact, a town. It was one of the many pleasant aspects of the house that you never really were aware of this.

It was a house of many windows, low, wide, nearly floor to ceiling in the living room, which faced the meadow, and it was from one of these that I first saw our closest neighbor, a large white horse, cropping grass, flipping its mane, and ambling about—not over the entire meadow, which stretched well out of sight of the house, but over the five or so fenced-in acres that were next to the twenty-odd that we had rented. I soon learned that the horse, whose name was Blue, belonged to a man who lived in another town, but was boarded by our neighbors next door. Occasionally, one of the children, usually a stocky teenager, but sometimes a much younger girl or boy, could be seen riding Blue. They would appear in the meadow, climb up on his back, ride furiously for ten or fifteen minutes, then get off, slap Blue on the flanks, and not be seen again for a month or more.

There were many apple trees in our yard, and one by the fence that Blue could almost reach. We were soon in the habit of feeding him apples, which he relished, especially because by the middle of summer the meadow grasses—so green and succulent since January—had dried out from lack of rain and Blue stumbled about munching the dried stalks half-heartedly. Sometimes he would stand very still just by the apple tree, and when one of us came out he would whinny, snort loudly, or stamp the ground. This meant, of course: I want an apple.

It was quite wonderful to pick a few apples, or collect those that had fallen to the ground overnight, and patiently hold them, one by one, up to his large, toothy mouth. I remained as thrilled as a child by his flexible dark lips, huge, cubelike teeth that crunched the apples core and all, with such finality, and his high, broad-breasted *enormity*; beside which, I felt small indeed. When I was a child, I used to ride horses, and was especially friendly with one named Nan until the day I was riding and my brother deliberately spooked her and I was thrown, head first, against the trunk of a tree. When I came to, I was in bed and my mother was bending worriedly over me; we silently agreed that perhaps horseback riding was not the safest sport for me. Since then I have walked, and prefer walking to horseback riding—but I had forgotten the depth of feeling one could see in horses' eyes.

I was therefore unprepared for the expression in Blue's. Blue was lonely. Blue was horribly lonely and bored. I was not shocked that this should be the case; five acres to tramp by yourself, endlessly, even in the most beautiful of meadows—and his was— cannot provide many interesting events, and once rainy season turned to dry that was about it. No, I was shocked that I had forgotten that human animals and nonhuman animals can communicate quite well; if we are brought up around animals as children we take this for granted. By the time we are adults we no longer remember. However, the animals have not changed. They are in fact *completed* creations (at least they seem to be, so much more than we) who are not likely *to* change; it is their nature to express 5 themselves. What else are they going to express? And they do. And, generally speaking, they are ignored.

After giving Blue the apples, I would wander back to the house, aware that he was observing me. Were more apples not forthcoming then? Was that to be his sole entertainment for the day? My partner's small son had decided he wanted to learn how to piece a quilt; we worked in silence on our respective squares as I thought . . .

Well, about slavery: about white children, who were raised by black people, who knew their first all-accepting love from black women, and then, when they were twelve or so, were told they must "forget" the deep levels of communication between themselves and "mammy" that they knew. Later they would be able to relate quite calmly, "My old mammy was sold to another good family." "My old mammy was——— ———." Fill in the blank. Many more years later a white woman would say: "I can't understand these Negroes, these blacks. What do they want? They're so different from us."

And about the Indians, considered to be "like animals" by the "settlers" (a very benign euphemism for what they actually were), who did not understand their description as a compliment.

And about the thousands of American men who marry Japanese, Korean, Filipina, and other non-English-speaking women and of how happy they report they are, "*blissfully,*" until their brides learn to speak English, at which point the marriages tend to fall apart. What then did the men see, when they looked into the eyes of the women they married, before they could speak English? Apparently only their own reflections.

I thought of society's impatience with the young. "Why are they playing the music 10
so loud?" Perhaps the children have listened to much of the music of oppressed people their parents danced to before they were born, with its passionate but soft cries for acceptance and love, and they have wondered why their parents failed to hear.

I do not know how long Blue had inhabited his five beautiful, boring acres before we moved into our house; a year after we had arrived—and had also traveled to other valleys, other cities, other worlds—he was still there.

But then, in our second year at the house, something happened in Blue's life. One morning, looking out the window at the fog that lay like a ribbon over the meadow, I saw another horse, a brown one, at the other end of Blue's field. Blue appeared to be afraid of it, and for several days made no attempt to go near. We went away for a week. When we returned, Blue had decided to make friends and the two horses ambled or galloped along together, and Blue did not come nearly as often to the fence underneath the apple tree.

When he did, bringing his new friend with him, there was a different look in his eyes. A look of independence, of self-possession, of inalienable *horse*ness. His friend eventually became pregnant. For months and months there was, it seemed to me, a mutual feeling between me and the horses of justice, of peace. I fed apples to them both. The look in Blue's eyes was one of, unabashed "this is *it*ness."

It did not, however, last forever. One day, after a visit to the city, I went out to give Blue some apples. He stood waiting, or so I thought, though not beneath the tree. When I shook the tree and jumped back from the shower of apples, he made no move. I carried some over to him. He managed to half-crunch one. The rest he let fall to the ground. I dreaded looking into his eyes—because I had of course noticed that Brown, his partner, had gone—but I did look. If I had been born into slavery, and my partner had been sold or killed, my eyes would have looked like that. The children next door explained that Blue's partner had been "put with him" (the same expression that old people used, I had noticed, when speaking of an ancestor during slavery who had been impregnated by her owner) so that they could mate and she conceive. Since that was accomplished, she had been taken back by her owner, who lived somewhere else.

Will she be back? I asked.

They didn't know.

Blue was like a crazed person. Blue *was*, to me, a crazed person. He galloped furiously, as if he were being ridden, around and around his five beautiful acres. He whinnied until he couldn't. He tore at the ground with his hooves. He butted himself against his single shade tree. He looked always and always toward the road down which his partner had gone. And then, occasionally, when he came up for apples, or I took apples to him, he looked at me. It was a look so piercing, so full of grief, a look so *human*, I almost laughed (I felt too sad to cry) to think there are people who do not know that animals suffer. People like me who have forgotten, and daily forget, all that animals try to tell us. "Everything you do to us will happen to you; we are your teachers, as you are ours. We are one lesson" is essentially it, I think. There are those who never once have even considered animals' rights: those who have been taught that animals actually want to be used and abused by us, as small children "love" to be frightened, or women "love" to be mutilated and raped. . . . They are the great-grandchildren of those who honestly thought, because someone taught them this: "Women can't think," and "niggers can't faint." But most disturbing of all, in Blue's large brown eyes was a new look, more painful than the look of despair: the look of disgust with human beings, with life; the look of hatred. And it was odd what the look of hatred did. It gave him, for the first time, the look of a beast. And what that meant was that he had put up a barrier within to protect himself from further violence; all the apples in the world wouldn't change that fact.

And so Blue remained, a beautiful part of our landscape, very peaceful to look at from the window, white against the grass. Once a friend came to visit and said, looking out on the soothing view: "And it *would* have to be a *white*, horse; the very image of freedom." And I thought, yes, the animals are forced to become for us merely "images" of what they once so beautifully expressed. And we are used to drinking milk from containers showing "contented" cows, whose real lives we want to hear nothing about, eating eggs and drumsticks from "happy" hens, and munching hamburgers advertised by bulls of integrity who seem to command their fate.

As we talked of freedom and justice one day for all, we sat down to steaks. I am eating misery, I thought, as I took the first bite. And spit it out.

Questions for Discussion and Writing

1. How does Walker broaden the significance of Blue's reactions so as to suggest the comparable treatment of slaves, Native Americans, and non-English-speaking women and children? In your opinion, is this extension far-fetched or warranted?

2. In what way is Walker transformed by her experience with Blue? What does she learn from him?

3. Have you ever learned something from an animal that changed your perception of yourself or those around you? Explain your answer.

FICTION

Edgar Allan Poe

Edgar Allan Poe (1809–1849) was born in Boston, Massachusetts. He was orphaned before he was three and taken into the home of John Allan, a wealthy merchant of Richmond, Virginia. Allan later disowned Poe when he chose a literary rather than a commerical career. Poe served two years in the Army and in 1830 received an appointment to West Point, from which he was dismissed within a year for a "gross neglect of duty." He served as the editor for a series of magazines, including Southern Literary Messenger, Burton's Gentleman's Magazine, Graham's Magazine, *and later* Broadway Journal. *In 1835, Poe married his cousin, Virginia Clemm, whose fragile health was a source of concern. They moved to Philadelphia, and Poe began to be recognized for his stories, literary essays, and poems (such as "The Raven," which appeared in 1845). Virginia died of tuberculosis in 1847 and was memorialized in Poe's poem "Annabel Lee." His last years were not happy ones and he died under mysterious circumstances at forty in Baltimore, Maryland. Poe's influence on literature has been extraordinary. He incorporated symbolism and technical devices such as assonance, rhythm, and rhyme in poetry. He invented the modern detective story in tales such as "Murders in the Rue Morgue" and "The Purloined Letter," and he created many psychological short stories such as "The Tell-Tale Heart," "The Black Cat," and "The Cask of Amontillado," which communicate a sense of guilt and terror. In "The Masque of the Red Death" (1842), Poe blends a folktale with reminiscences of the devasting plagues that swept Europe in the Middle Ages, and recent memories of a cholera outbreak in Baltimore, to create a somber and elegant tale.*

THE MASQUE OF THE RED DEATH

The "Red Death" had long devastated the country. No pestilence had ever been so fatal, or so hideous. Blood was its Avatar[1] and its seal—the redness and the horror of blood. There were sharp pains, and sudden dizziness, and then profuse bleeding at the pores, with dissolution. The scarlet stains upon the body and especially upon the face of the victim, were the pest ban which shut him out from the aid and from the sympathy of his fellowmen. And the whole seizure, progress, and termination of the disease, were the incidents of half an hour.

But the Prince Prospero[2] was happy and dauntless and sagacious. When his dominions were half depopulated, he summoned to his presence a thousand hale and

---

[1]*Avatar:* An embodiment or concrete manifestation.   [2]*Prospero:* Refers to the principal character in Shakespeare's *The Tempest;* someone who is fortunate.

light-hearted friends from among the knights and dames of his court, and with these retired to the deep seclusion of one of his castellated abbeys. This was an extensive and magnificent structure, the creation of the prince's own eccentric yet august taste. A strong and lofty wall girdled it in. This wall had gates of iron. The courtiers, having entered, brought furnaces and massy hammers and welded the bolts. They resolved to leave means neither of ingress nor egress to the sudden impulses of despair or of frenzy from within. The abbey was amply provisioned. With such precautions the courtiers might bid defiance to contagion. The external world could take care of itself. In the meantime it was folly to grieve, or to think. The prince had provided all the appliances of pleasure. There were buffoons, there were improvisatori, there were ballet-dancers, there were musicians, there was Beauty, there was wine. All these and security were within. Without was the "Red Death."

It was toward the close of the fifth or sixth month of his seclusion, and while the pestilence raged most furiously abroad, that the Prince Prospero entertained his thousand friends at a masked ball of the most unusual magnificence.

It was a voluptuous scene, that masquerade. But first let me tell of the rooms in which it was held. There were seven—an imperial suite. In many palaces, however, such suites form a long and straight vista, while the folding doors slide back nearly to the walls on either hand, so that the view of the whole extent is scarcely impeded. Here the case was very different, as might have been expected from the duke's love of the *bizarre*. The apartments were so irregularly disposed that the vision embraced but little more than one at a time. There was a sharp turn at every twenty or thirty yards, and at each turn a novel effect. To the right and left, in the middle of each wall, a tall and narrow Gothic window looked out upon a closed corridor which pursued the windings of the suite. These windows were of stained glass whose color varied in accordance with the prevailing hue of the decorations of the chamber into which it opened. That at the eastern extremity was hung, for example, in blue—and vividly blue were its windows. The second chamber was purple in its ornaments and tapestries, and here the panes were purple. The third was green throughout, and so were the casements. The fourth was furnished and lighted with orange—the fifth with white—the sixth with violet. The seventh apartment was closely shrouded in black velvet tapestries that hung all over the ceiling and down the walls, falling in heavy folds upon a carpet of the same material and hue. But in this chamber only, the color of the windows failed to correspond with the decorations. The panes here were scarlet—a deep blood color. Now in no one of the seven apartments was there any lamp or candelabrum, amid the profusion of golden ornaments that lay scattered to and fro or depended from the roof. There was no light of any kind emanating from lamp or candle within the suite of chambers. But in the corridors that followed the suite, there stood, opposite to each window, a heavy tripod, bearing a brazier of fire, that projected its rays through the tinted glass and so glaringly illumined the room. And thus were produced a multitude of gaudy and fantastic appearances. But in the western or black chamber the effect of the firelight that streamed upon the dark hangings through the blood-tinted panes was ghastly in the extreme, and produced so wild a look upon the countenances of those who entered, that there were few of the company bold enough to set foot within its precincts at all.

It was in this apartment, also, that there stood against the western wall, a gigan-   5
tic clock of ebony. Its pendulum swung to and fro with a dull, heavy, monotonous
clang; and when the minute-hand made the circuit of the face, and the hour was to be
stricken, there came from the brazen lungs of the clock a sound which was clear and
loud and deep and exceedingly musical, but of so peculiar a note and emphasis that,
at each lapse of an hour, the musicians of the orchestra were constrained to pause, momentarily, in their performance, to hearken to the sound; and thus the waltzers perforce
ceased their evolutions; and there was a brief disconcert of the whole gay company; and,
while the chimes of the clock yet rang, it was observed that the giddiest grew pale, and
the more aged and sedate passed their hands over their brows as if in confused revery
or meditation. But when the echoes had fully ceased, a light laughter at once pervaded
the assembly; the musicians looked at each other and smiled as if at their own nervousness and folly, and made whispering vows, each to the other, that the next chiming
of the clock should produce in them no similar emotion; and then, after the lapse of
sixty minutes (which embrace three thousand and six hundred seconds of the Time
that flies), there came yet another chiming of the clock, and then were the same disconcert and tremulousness and meditation as before.

But, in spite of all these things, it was a gay and magnificent revel. The tastes of
the duke were peculiar. He had a fine eye for colors and effects. He disregarded the
decora[3] of mere fashion. His plans were bold and fiery, and his conceptions glowed
with barbaric lustre. There are some who would have thought him mad. His followers felt that he was not. It was necessary to hear and see and touch him to be *sure* that
he was not.

He had directed, in great part, the movable embellishments of the seven chambers,
upon occasion of this great fête,[4] and it was his own guiding taste which had given
character to the masqueraders. Be sure they were grotesque. There were much glare and
glitter and piquancy and phantasm—much of what has been since seen in "Hernani."[5]
There were arabesque figures with unsuited limbs and appointments. There were deliri-
ous fancies such as the madman fashions. There were much of the beautiful, much of
the wanton, much of the *bizarre*, something of the terrible, and not a little of that
which might have excited disgust. To and fro in the seven chambers there stalked, in
fact, a multitude of dreams. And these—the dreams—writhed in and about, taking hue
from the rooms, and causing the wild music of the orchestra to seem as the echo of their
steps. And, anon, there strikes the ebony clock which stands in the hall of the velvet.
And then, for a moment, all is still, and all is silent save the voice of the clock. The
dreams are stiff-frozen as they stand. But the echoes of the chime die away—they have
endured but an instant—and a light, half-subdued laughter floats after them as they depart. And now again the music swells, and the dreams live, and writhe to and fro more
merrily than ever, taking hue from the many-tinted windows through which stream
the rays from the tripods. But to the chamber which lies most westwardly of the seven
there are now none of the maskers who venture; for the night is waning away; and
there flows a ruddier light through the blood-colored panes; and the blackness of the

---

[3]*decora:* Current styles of adornment.　　[4]*fête:* Festive celebration.　　[5]*Hernani:* A tragedy (1830) by Victor
Hugo (1802–1885), with spectacular scenes and costumes.

sable drapery appalls; and to him whose foot falls upon the sable carpet, there comes from the near clock of ebony a muffled peal more solemnly emphatic than any which reaches *their* ears who indulge in the more remote gaieties of the other apartments.

But these other apartments were densely crowded, and in them beat feverishly the heart of life. And the revel went whirlingly on, until at length there commenced the sounding of midnight upon the clock. And then the music ceased, as I have told; and the evolutions of the waltzers were quieted; and there was an uneasy cessation of all things as before. But now there were twelve strokes to be sounded by the bell of the clock; and thus it happened, perhaps that more of thought crept, with more of time, into the meditations of the thoughtful among those who revelled. And thus, too, it happened, perhaps that before the last echoes of the last chime had utterly sunk into silence, there were many individuals in the crowd who had found leisure to become aware of the presence of a masked figure, which had arrested the attention of no single individual before. And the rumor of this new presence having spread itself whisperingly around, there arose at length from the whole company a buzz, or murmur, expressive of disapprobation and surprise—then, finally, of terror, of horror, and of disgust.

In an assembly of phantasms such as I have painted, it may well be supposed that no ordinary appearance could have excited such sensation. In truth the masquerade license of the night was nearly unlimited; but the figure in question had out-Heroded Herod,[6] and gone beyond the bounds of even the prince's indefinite decorum. There are chords in the hearts of the most reckless which cannot be touched without emotion. Even with the utterly lost, to whom life and death are equally jests, there are matters of which no jest can be made. The whole company, indeed, seemed now deeply to feel that in the costume and bearing of the stranger neither wit nor propriety existed. The figure was tall and gaunt, and shrouded from head to foot in the habiliments of the grave. The mask which concealed the visage was made so nearly to resemble the countenance of a stiffened corpse that the closest scrutiny must have had difficulty in detecting the cheat. And yet all this might have been endured, if not approved, by the mad revellers around. But the mummer had gone so far as to assume the type of the Red Death. His vesture was dabbled in *blood*—and his broad brow, with all the features of the face, was besprinkled with the scarlet horror.

When the eyes of Prince Prospero fell upon this spectral image (which, with a slow   10 and solemn movement, as if more fully to sustain its role, stalked to and fro among the waltzers) he was seen to be convulsed, in the first moment with a strong shudder either of terror or distaste; but, in the next, his brow reddened with rage.

"Who dares"—he demanded hoarsely of the courtiers who stood near him—"who dares insult us with this blasphemous mockery? Seize him and unmask him—that we may know whom we have to hang, at sunrise, from the battlements!"

It was in the eastern or blue chamber in which stood the Prince Prospero as he uttered these words. They rang throughout the seven rooms loudly and clearly, for the prince was a bold and robust man, and the music had become hushed at the waving of his hand.

---

[6]*Herod:* Quoted from Shakespeare's *Hamlet*, Act 3, scene 2, line 11; refers to unnecessary theatrics.

It was in the blue room where stood the prince, with a group of pale courtiers by his side. At first, as he spoke, there was a slight rushing movement of this group in the direction of the intruder, who, at the moment was also near at hand, and now, with deliberate and stately step, made closer approach to the speaker. But from a certain nameless awe with which the mad assumptions of the mummer had inspired the whole party, there were found none who put forth hand to seize him; so that, unimpeded, he passed within a yard of the prince's person; and, while the vast assembly, as if with one impulse, shrank from the centres of the rooms to the walls, he made his way uninterruptedly, but with the same solemn and measured step which had distinguished him from the first, through the blue chamber to the purple—through the purple to the green—through the green to the orange—through this again to the white—and even thence to the violet, ere a decided movement had been made to arrest him. It was then, however, that the Prince Prospero, maddening with rage and the shame of his own momentary cowardice, rushed hurriedly through the six chambers, while none followed him on account of a deadly terror that had seized upon all. He bore aloft a drawn dagger, and had approached, in rapid impetuosity, to within three or four feet of the retreating figure, when the latter, having attained the extremity of the velvet apartment, turned suddenly and confronted his pursuer. There was a sharp cry—and the dagger dropped gleaming upon the sable carpet, upon which, instantly afterward, fell prostrate in death the Prince Prospero. Then, summoning the wild courage of despair, a throng of the revellers at once threw themselves into the black apartment, and, seizing the mummer, whose tall figure stood erect and motionless within the shadow of the ebony clock, gasped in unutterable horror at finding the grave cerements and corpse-like mask, which they handled with so violent a rudeness, untenanted by any tangible form.

And now was acknowledged the presence of the Red Death. He had come like a thief in the night,[7] And one by one dropped the revellers in the blood-bedewed halls of their revel, and died each in the despairing posture of his fall. And the life of the ebony clock went out with that of the last of the gay. And the flames of the tripods expired. And Darkness and Decay and the Red Death held illimitable dominion over all.

Questions for Discussion and Writing

1. How does Prince Prospero react to the crisis his country confronts? Why is he so outraged by the appearance of the "masked" figure?
2. How does Poe use the progression of colors, details of lighting, and numerical symbolism to create the distinctive atmosphere of the story? How does the imagery of the last room reflect the threat from which the revelers have tried to escape? What role does the ebony clock play, and how does its appearance and sound foreshadow the outcome?
3. Is Poe depicting a mad genius or a heroic leader? In your opinion, would current leaders start behaving like Prince Prospero if their countries were threatened with a pandemic influenza, SARS, or some such disease?

---

[7] *thief in the night:* In 2 Peter 3:10: "But the day of the Lord will come as a thief in the night." Refers to an apocalypse or judgment.

4. How does this film still from *The Masque of the Red Death* (1964) suggest the lurid appeal of Poe's story and the maniacal determination of Prince Prospero?

POETRY

Mary Oliver

• •

Mary Oliver (b. 1935) grew up in Cleveland, Ohio, and was educated at Ohio State University and Vassar College. She has written numerous collections of poetry, including American Primitive *(1983), for which she received the Pulitzer Prize. Most recently, she has written* Winter Hours: Poetry, Prose, and Essays *(1999),* The Leaf and the Cloud *(2000), and* Long Life: Essays and Other Writings *(2004). Oliver currently teaches at Bennington College in Vermont. The following poem is reprinted from* Twelve Moons *(1978).*

SLEEPING IN THE FOREST

I thought the earth
remembered me, she
took me back so tenderly, arranging,
her dark skirts, her pockets
full of lichens and seeds. I slept   5
as never before, a stone
on the riverbed, nothing
between me and the white fire of the stars
but my thoughts, and they floated
light as moths among the branches   10
of the perfect trees. All night
I heard the small kingdoms breathing
around me, the insects, and the birds
who do their work in the darkness. All night
I rose and fell, as if in water, grappling   15
with a luminous doom. By morning
I had vanished at least a dozen times
into something better.

Questions for Discussion and Writing

1. How does the rhythm or pulse of this poem reinforce the sense that the speaker has blended into the world of nature?
2. In what sense does the earth seem to remember her and welcome her return?
3. The experience of being spiritually at one with nature is rare. Under what circumstances, if ever, have you felt this way?

Henry Wadsworth Longfellow

* *

Henry Wadsworth Longfellow (1807–1882) graduated from Bowdoin College in 1825 and mastered Spanish, French, Italian, German, and the Scandinavian languages. He became a professor of languages at Harvard in 1836. Longfellow is acknowledged as one of the great American poets; his works were so popular that he was able to live on the proceeds. Some of his best-known works are Evangeline *(1847) and* Paul Revere's Ride *(1863). The following poem presents a common experience, rendered with uncommon stylistic grace.*

THE SOUND OF THE SEA

The sea awoke at midnight from its sleep,
   And round the pebbly beaches far and wide
   I heard the first wave of the rising tide
Rush onward with uninterrupted sweep;
A voice out of the silence of the deep,   5
   A sound mysteriously multiplied
   As of a cataract from the mountain's side,
Or roar of winds upon a wooded steep.
   So comes to us at times, from the unknown
      And inaccessible solitudes of being,   10
         The rushing of the sea-tides of the soul;
   And inspirations, that we deem our own,
      Are some divine foreshadowing and foreseeing
         Of things beyond our reason or control.

Questions for Discussion and Writing

1. In this vividly imagined poem, what signs are there that the speaker has made contact with a mystical or religious spirit?
2. Examine the pattern of end rhymes in this poem and the way Longfellow accentuates the meaning through varying this basic pattern. Where does he use alliteration and assonance to evoke the spirit of the ocean?
3. Try to create a poem that expresses how you feel about the ocean or any other natural phenomenon, and vary the visual appearance and indentations of the lines as

Longfellow does to evoke the movement, size, shape, or defining features of what you are describing.

4. How does this postcard extoll the positive aspects of the sea, although in a different way than Longfellow?

Humbert Wolfe

Humbert Wolfe (1885–1940) was born in Milan, Italy; when he was quite young, his family moved to Bradford, England. He won academic distinction at Oxford University and began publishing poetry in the 1920s. Perhaps his best-known work is Requiem *(1927), a book of poems based on World War I. In the following poem Wolfe displays his dapper **wit** as he makes us see a commonplace creature in a new light.*

THE GRAY SQUIRREL

Like a small gray
coffeepot
sits the squirrel.
He is not

all he should be,   5
kills by dozens
trees, and eats
his red-brown cousins.

The keeper, on the
other hand,   10
who shot him, is
a Christian, and

loves his enemies,
which shows
The squirrel was not   15
one of those.

Questions for Discussion and Writing

1. How does Wolfe demonize, in a mocking way, the common squirrel while at the same time questioning the motives of the groundskeeper?
2. How does Wolfe use commonplace imagery to get his readers to really *see* a creature they might otherwise ignore?
3. According to Wolfe, who is actually more at home in nature, the squirrel or the groundskeeper? Explain your answer.

Thinking Critically About the Image

Claude Monet (1840–1926), French landscape painter and founder of Impressionism, always worked outside, painting changes in light and atmosphere caused by different times of day and seasons. He eliminated black and gray from his palette and broke down light into its color components, much as a prism does, in repeated pictures of such subjects as haystacks, the Rouen cathedral, and his garden of water lilies and flowers at his home in Giverny, forty-six miles northwest of Paris. In *The Garden at Giverny* (1902) we enter Monet's beautiful world as we travel up the path to his house.

1. How does the garden become more than a subject and almost a vehicle for Monet's unique way of seeing and painting? How does his choice of colors and arrangement of shapes create a feeling of timelessness within a moment in an environment we feel we have entered?
2. How does the painting communicate the sense that Monet was actually learning from the landscape, as compared to a studio painter who worked from memory?
3. Describe a place in nature that means as much to you as his garden at Giverny meant to Monet, creating a word "impression" of the scene.

Connections

Chapter 6: Our Place in Nature

Mark Twain, *The Lowest Animal*
How do Twain and Jonathan Swift in "A Modest Proposal" (Ch. 8) use satire to attack their targets?

Gunjan Sinha, *You Dirty Vole*
To what extent do both Sinha in her essay and Constance Holden in "Identical Twins Reared Apart" (Ch. 9) suggest that biology is destiny?

Richard Rhodes, *Watching the Animals*
Compare the literal and figurative uses of the slaughterhouse theme in Rhodes's essay and Swift's "A Modest Proposal" (Ch. 8).

Thor Heyerdahl, *How to Kill an Ocean*
How does Heyerdahl's analysis challenge the traditional poetic conception of the ocean voiced by Henry Wadsworth Longfellow in his poem?

Jared Diamond,   *Why Do We Smoke, Drink, and Use Dangerous Drugs?*
In what ways do both Diamond and Gunjan Sinha draw analogies between human and animal behavior?

Linda Hogan,   *Waking Up the Rake*
In what sense do Hogan and Bill McKibben in "It's Easy Being Green" (Ch. 9) subscribe to protecting the environment?

Alice Walker,   *Am I Blue?*
How do Walker's reflections on the racial "other" connect with insights about racism in Kate Chopin's story "Désirée's Baby" (Ch. 5), written in the previous century?

Edgar Allan Poe,   *The Masque of the Red Death*
Contrast the depiction and response to catastophes (a plague and an earthquake) in Poe's story and Jack London's "The San Francisco Earthquake" (Ch. 7).

Mary Oliver,   *Sleeping in the Forest*
In what sense do Oliver's poem and Linda Hogan's account urge readers to transcend customary perspectives about nature?

Henry Wadsworth Longfellow,   *The Sound of the Sea*
In what ways do Longfellow and Mary Oliver evoke intimations of mystical and religious forces through their reflections on the sea and the forest?

Humbert Wolfe,   *The Gray Squirrel*
How do Wolfe in this poem and Anna Kamieńska in "Funny" (Ch. 1) use animals to comment on human values?

Francisco de Goya, **The Third of May, 1808,** *1814.*
Scala/Art Resource, NY. Museo del Prado, Madrid, Spain.

History in the Making

Those who cannot remember the past are condemned to repeat it.
—GEORGE SANTAYANA, "REASON IN COMMON SENSE"

THIS CHAPTER BRINGS TO LIFE IMPORTANT EVENTS and addresses the question of how the present has been shaped by the past. Herodotus offers a glimpse into the customs of ancient Egypt. In seeking to explain past events, historians examine journals, letters, newspaper accounts, photographs, and other primary documents and draw on information provided by witnesses. Gilbert Highet analyzes the rhetorical techniques in Lincoln's Gettysburg Address to discover why it still moves audiences.

This chapter includes reports of Jack London on the aftermath of the 1906 San Francisco earthquake; Hanson W. Baldwin's reconstruction of radio messages, ship's logs, and accounts of survivors of the 1912 sinking of the *Titanic;* and an interview conducted by Maurizio Chierici with the lead pilot whose plane dropped the atomic bomb on Hiroshima, Japan, in 1945. Historians of the future will study the testimony Dennis Smith provides on the catastrophe that confronted a battalion fire chief on September 11, 2001. Historical research also underlies the social criticism of Haunani-Kay Trask's denunciation of the colonization of modern Hawaii and Stuart Hirschberg's analysis of the rhetoric of Richard Nixon's "Checker's Speech."

In Ambrose Bierce's story we experience the Civil War through the eyes of unwilling participants, and in the story by Irene Zabytko we learn what it was like to lose one's humanity during the Nazi occupation of the Ukraine.

The poems challenge us to revisit past events in unusual ways. Bertolt Brecht speaks for the unknown workers. David R. Slavitt commemorates the tragedy of the *Titanic.* Eleni Fourtouni recalls the Nazi occupation of Greece, and W. B. Yeats foresees an awakened "rough beast."

NONFICTION

Herodotus

Herodotus (484–425 B.C.), whom Cicero called the "father of history" for his detailed account of the wars between the Greeks and the Persians (500 B.C. and 479 B.C.), was born at Halicarnassus, in Caria, a province bordering the coast of Asia Minor. In order to gather materials for his monumental work, History, *he traveled widely in Greece, Macedonia, and regions that are now Bulgaria, Turkey, Israel, Iran, and Egypt.*

In "Concerning Egypt" we can observe that the expository principle Herodotus uses is that of comparison and contrast, which is well suited for understanding the unfamilar: Egyptian customs in relationship to the corresponding but different customs of the Greeks, the audience for whom he is writing. Herodotus always supports his observations with a wealth of concrete details. We learn about habits of diet, cooking, bathing, hairstyles, how parents are treated, shopping in the market, weaving practices, and a multitude of other customs that take the reader directly into the everyday lives of the ancient Egyptians.

CONCERNING EGYPT

Concerning Egypt itself I shall extend my remarks to a great length, because there is no country that possesses so many wonders, nor any that has such a number of works which defy description. Not only is the climate different from that of the rest of the world, and the rivers unlike any other rivers, but the people also, in most of their manners and customs, exactly reverse the common practice of mankind. The women attend the markets and trade, while the men sit at home at the loom; and here, while the rest of the world works the woof up the warp, the Egyptians work it down; the women likewise carry burthens upon their shoulders, while the men carry them upon their heads. They eat their food out of doors in the streets, but retire for private purposes to their houses, giving as a reason that what is unseemly, but necessary, ought to be done in secret, but what has nothing unseemly about it, should be done openly. A woman cannot serve the priestly office, either for god or goddess, but men are priests to both; sons need not support their parents unless they choose, but daughters must, whether they choose or no.

In other countries the priests have long hair, in Egypt their heads are shaven; elsewhere it is customary, in mourning, for near relations to cut their hair close: the Egyptians, who wear no hair at any other time, when they lose a relative, let their beards and the hair of their heads grow long. All other men pass their lives separate from animals, the Egyptians have animals always living with them; others make barley and wheat their food; it is a disgrace to do so in Egypt, where the grain they live on is spelt, which some call *zea*. Dough they knead with their feet; but they mix mud, and even take up dirt, with their hands. They are the only people in the world—they at least, and such as have learnt the practice from them—who use circumcision. Their men wear two garments apiece, their women but one. They put on the rings and fasten the ropes to sails inside; others put them outside. When they write or calculate, instead of going, like the Greeks, from left to right, they move their hand from right to left; and they insist, notwithstanding, that it is they who go to the right, and the Greeks who go to the left. They have two quite different kinds of writing, one of which is called sacred, the other common.

They are religious to excess, far beyond any other race of men, and use the following ceremonies:—They drink out of brazen cups, which they scour every day: there is no exception to this practice. They wear linen garments, which they are specially careful to have always fresh washed. They practise circumcision for the sake of cleanliness, considering it better to be cleanly than comely. The priests shave their whole body every other day, that no lice or other impure thing may adhere to them when they are engaged in the service of the gods. Their dress is entirely of linen, and their shoes of the papyrus plant: it is not lawful for them to wear either dress or shoes of any other material. They bathe twice every day in cold water, and twice each night; besides

Opposite: *This wall painting is from the tomb of Anhour Khaou, the chief builder of the temple complexes at Thebes. He is seated with his wife (who wears an earring) and grandchildren and a servant who brings a tiny statue of Osiris, the god of the dead (1200–1080 B.C.). How does this tomb painting give you a glimpse into the world Herodotus saw?*

which they observe, so to speak, thousands of ceremonies. They enjoy, however, not a few advantages. They consume none of their own property, and are at no expense for anything; but every day bread is baked for them of the sacred corn, and a plentiful supply of beef and of goose's flesh is assigned to each, and also a portion of wine made from the grape. Fish they are not allowed to eat; and beans—which none of the Egyptians ever sow, or eat, if they come up of their own accord, either raw or boiled—the priests will not even endure to look on, since they consider it an unclean kind of pulse. Instead of a single priest, each god has the attendance of a college, at the head of which is a chief priest, when one of these dies, his son is appointed in his room.

Male kine are reckoned to belong to Epaphus,[1] and are therefore tested in the following manner:—One of the priests appointed for the purpose searches to see if there is a single black hair on the whole body, since in that case the beast is unclean. He examines him all over, standing on his legs, and again laid upon his back; after which he takes the tongue out of his mouth, to see if it be clean in respect to the prescribed marks (what they are I will mention elsewhere); he also inspects the hairs of the tail, to observe if they grow naturally. If the animal is pronounced clean in all these various points, the priest marks him by twisting a piece of papyrus round his horns, and attaching thereto some sealing clay, which he then stamps with his own signet-ring. After this the beast is led away; and it is forbidden, under the penalty of death, to sacrifice an animal which has not been marked in this way.

The following is their manner of sacrifice:—They lead the victim, marked with their signet, to the altar where they are about to offer it, and setting the wood alight, pour a libation of wine upon the altar in front of the victim, and at the same time invoke the god. Then they slay the animal, and cutting off his head, proceed to flay the body. Next they take the head, and heaping imprecations on it, if there is a market-place and a body of Greek traders in the city, they carry it there and sell it instantly; if, however, there are no Greeks among them, they throw the head into the river. The imprecation is to this effect:—They pray that if any evil is impending either over those who sacrifice, or over universal Egypt, it may be made to fall upon that head. These practices, the imprecations upon the heads, and the libations of wine, prevail all over Egypt, and extend to victims of all sorts; and hence the Egyptians will never eat the head of any animal.

The disembowelling and burning are, however, different in different sacrifices. I will mention the mode in use with respect to the goddess whom they regard as the greatest, and honour with the chiefest festival. When they have flayed their steer they pray, and when their prayer is ended they take the paunch of the animal out entire, leaving the intestines and the fat inside the body; they then cut off the legs, the ends of the loins, the shoulders, and the neck; and having so done, they fill the body of the steer with clean bread, honey, raisins, figs, frankincense, myrrh, and other aromatics. Thus

[1]*Epaphus:* son of Zeus by Io. In a jealous fit, the goddess Hera had changed Io into a cow, who wandered finally to Egypt, where Epaphus was born and where he became king and father of a famous line of heroes. The myth has interest in relation to the religious reverence for the cow in Egypt, sacred to the goddess Isis, as Herodotus says. A goddess perhaps older than Isis, Hathor, was represented as a cow in ancient Egyptian engravings, shown as standing over the earth and giving suck to mankind from her great udders.

filled, they burn the body, pouring over it great quantities of oil. Before offering the sacrifice they fast, and while the bodies of the victims are being consumed they beat themselves. Afterwards, when they have concluded this part of the ceremony, they have the other parts of the victim served up to them for a repast.

The male kine, therefore, if clean, and the male calves, are used for sacrifice by the Egyptians universally; but the females they are not allowed to sacrifice since they are sacred to Isis.[2] The statue of this goddess has the form of a woman but with horns like a cow, resembling thus the Greek representations of Io; and the Egyptians, one and all, venerate cows much more highly than any other animal. This is the reason why no native of Egypt, whether man or woman, will give a Greek a kiss, or use the knife of a Greek, or his spit, or his cauldron, or taste the flesh of an ox, known to be pure, if it has been cut with a Greek knife. When kine die, the following is the manner of their sepulture:—The females are thrown into the river; the males are buried in the suburbs of the towns, with one or both of their horns appearing above the surface of the ground to mark the place. When the bodies are decayed, a boat comes, at an appointed time, from the island called Prosôpitis—which is a portion of the Delta, nine schoenes[3] in circumference,—and calls at the several cities in turn to collect the bones of the oxen. Prosôpitis is a district containing several cities; the name of that from which the boats come is Atarbêchis. Venus has a temple there of much sanctity. Great numbers of men go forth from this city and proceed to the other towns, where they dig up the bones, which they take away with them and bury together in one place. The same practice prevails with respect to the interment of all other cattle—the law so determining; they do not slaughter any of them.

Such Egyptians as possess a temple of the Theban Jove, or live in the Thebaïc canton, offer no sheep in sacrifice, but only goats; for the Egyptians do not all worship the same gods, excepting Isis and Osiris,[4] the latter of whom they say is the Grecian Bacchus. Those, on the contrary, who possess a temple dedicated to Mendes, or belong to the Mendesian canton, abstain from offering goats, and sacrifice sheep instead. The Thebans, and such as imitate them in their practice, give the following account of the origin of the custom:—"Hercules," they say, "wished of all things to see Jove, but Jove did not choose to be seen of him. At length, when Hercules persisted, Jove hit on a device—to flay a ram, and, cutting off his head, hold the head before him, and cover himself with fleece. In this guise he showed himself to Hercules." Therefore the Egyptians give their statues of Jupiter the face of a ram: and from them the practice has passed to the Ammonians, who are a joint colony of Egyptians and Ethiopians, speaking a language between the two; hence also, in my opinion, the latter people took their

---

[2]*Isis:* great nature-goddess, worshiped with Osiris as his sister and wife. Hathor the cow-goddess. The worship blended into and became identified with that of Isis.   [3]*nine schoenes:* a land measurement of several miles.   [4]*Osiris:* a plant-god and fertility-god, actually a "Lord of Life" like Dionysus (Bacchus), Adonis, Atys (or Attis), Tammuz, and others. He was slain in youth by his brother Set, and the pieces of his body were scattered over the land. Isis, his sister-wife, wandered everywhere searching for him and grieving, until the fragments of his body were collected and put together. Then the god was resurrected into life. This fertility myth has many parallels originally symbolizing the cycle of winter and summer, the death of vegetation and its annual renewal. Later the myth came to symbolize the more mystical belief in human resurrection and immortality.

name of Ammonians, since the Egyptian name for Jupiter is Amun. Such, then, is the reason why the Thebans do not sacrifice rams, but consider them sacred animals. Upon one day in the year, however, at the festival of Jupiter, they slay a single ram, and stripping off the fleece, cover with it the statue of that god, as he once covered himself, and then bring up to the statue of Jove an image of Hercules. When this has been done, the whole assembly beat their breasts in mourning for the ram, and afterwards bury him in a holy sepulchre. . . .

The pig is regarded among them as an unclean animal, so much so that if a man in passing accidentally touch a pig, he instantly hurries to the river, and plunges in with all his clothes on. Hence, too, the swineherds, notwithstanding that they are of pure Egyptian blood, are forbidden to enter into any of the temples, which are open to all other Egyptians; and further, no one will give his daughter in marriage to a swineherd, or take a wife from among them, so that the swineherds are forced to intermarry among themselves. They do not offer swine in sacrifice to any of their gods, excepting Bacchus and the Moon,[5] whom they honour in this way at the same time, sacrificing pigs to both of them at the same full moon, and afterwards eating of the flesh. There is a reason alleged by them for their detestation of swine at all other seasons, and their use of them at this festival, with which I am well acquainted, but which I do not think it proper to mention. The following is the mode in which they sacrifice the swine to the Moon:— As soon as the victim is slain, the tip of the tail, the spleen, and the caul are put together, and having been covered with all the fat that has been found in the animal's belly, are straightway burnt. The remainder of the flesh is eaten on the same day that the sacrifice is offered, which is the day of the full moon: at any other time they would not so much as taste it. The poorer sort, who cannot afford live pigs, form pigs of dough, which they bake and offer in sacrifice.

To Bacchus, on the eve of his feast, every Egyptian sacrifices a hog before the door   10 of his house, which is then given back to the swineherd by whom it was furnished, and by him carried away. In other respects the festival is celebrated almost exactly as Bacchic festivals are in Greece, excepting that the Egyptians have no choral dances. They also use instead of phalli[6] another invention, consisting of images a cubit high, pulled by strings, which the women carry round to the villages.

A piper goes in front, and the women follow, singing hymns in honour of Bacchus. They give a religious reason for the peculiarities of the image.

---

[5]*Bacchus and the Moon:* Osiris and Isis. Herodotus has previously suggested an identification between Osiris and the Greek Bacchus; and Isis was goddess of the moon as well as of the rest of nature (one of her emblems was the crescent moon). Pigs are one of the ancient animal symbols of reproductive fertility. In the custom Herodotus speaks of here, it is because of the fertility aspect of Osiris and Isis that pigs were sacrificed to them. The custom corresponds to that of the ancient Greeks, who threw slaughtered pigs into crevices of the earth as offerings to Persephone (daughter of Demeter, the corn-goddess). In Ireland, pigs carved out of bog oak are given as good-luck symbols. The normal Egyptian taboo on the eating of swine meat (except for the monthly sacrifice) was no doubt acquired by the Hebrews during their stay in Egypt, like the practice of circumcision.   [6]*phalli:* This religious fertility symbolism is universal. In the myth of the death and the scattering of the parts of Osiris' body, the phallus was the last to be found, and without it Osiris could not come back to life. It had fallen into the Nile, on which Egyptian agriculture depends.

Melampus,[7] the son of Amytheon, cannot (I think) have been ignorant of this ceremony—nay, he must, I should conceive, have been well acquainted with it. He it was who introduced into Greece the name of Bacchus, the ceremonial of his worship, and the procession of the phallus. He did not, however, so completely apprehend the whole doctrine as to be able to communicate it entirely, but various sages since his time have carried out his teaching to greater perfection. Still it is certain that Melampus introduced the phallus, and that the Greeks learnt from him the ceremonies which they now practise. I therefore maintain that Melampus, who was a wise man, and had acquired the art of divination, having become acquainted with the worship of Bacchus through knowledge derived from Egypt, introduced it into Greece, with a few slight changes, at the same time that he brought in various other practices. For I can by no means allow that it is by mere coincidence that the Bacchic ceremonies in Greece are so nearly the same as the Egyptian—they would then have been more Greek in their character, and less recent in their origin. Much less can I admit that the Egyptians borrowed these customs, or any other, from the Greeks. My belief is that Melampus got his knowledge of them from Cadmus the Tyrian, and the followers whom he brought from Phoenicia into the country which is now called Boeotia.[8]

Almost all the names of the gods came into Greece from Egypt. My inquiries prove that they were all derived from a foreign source, and my opinion is that Egypt furnished the greater number. For with the exception of Neptune and the Dioscûri, whom I mentioned above, and Juno, Vesta, Themis, the Graces, and the Nereids, the other gods have been known from time immemorial in Egypt. This I assert on the authority of the Egyptians themselves. The gods, with whose names they profess themselves unacquainted, the Greeks received, I believe, from the Pelasgi, except Neptune. Of him they got their knowledge from the Libyans, by whom he has been always honoured, and who were anciently the only people that had a god of the name. The Egyptians differ from the Greeks also in paying no divine honours to heroes. . . .[9]

Whence the gods severally sprang, whether or no they had all existed from eternity, what forms they bore—these are questions of which the Greeks knew nothing until the other day, so to speak. For Homer and Hesiod were the first to compose Theogonies, and give the gods their epithets, to allot them their several offices and occupations, and describe their forms; and they lived but four hundred years before my

---

[7]*Melampus:* mythological seer who understood the speech of all creatures.   [8]Cadmus, legendary founder of Thebes, was said to have brought the alphabet from Tyre in Phoenicia (on the eastern Mediterranean coast) to Greece. Boeotia was the ancient name of the country north of the Gulf of Corinth, dominated by Thebes.   [9]The Dioscûri (*dios-kuroi,* god's sons) were Castor and Pollux, sons of Zeus and Leda, conceived when Zeus met Leda in the form of a swan, and brothers of Helen and Clytemnestra. They were patrons of horsemanship, boxing, and all the athletic skills of the Olympic Games. At their death they became the constellation Gemini, the Twins. Vesta was an ancient earth-goddess who became, in the Olympian pantheon, goddess of the home and hearth. Themis was another very ancient earth-goddess, a Titaness (the Titans were nature-gods who preceded the Olympians), mother of Prometheus. The oracle at Delphi spoke through her priestesses. The Pelasgi were, so far as is known, aboriginal inhabitants of Greece, whose immense rough stonework is found in various parts of Greece. The Nereids were daughters of an ancient sea-god, Nereus, who were represented as attending the later sea-god, Poseidon, riding sea horses; they are the original "mermaids."

time, as I believe. As for the poets who are thought by some to be earlier than these, they are, in my judgment, decidedly later writers. In these matters I have the authority of the priestesses of Dodôna for the former portion of my statements; what I have said of Homer and Hesiod is my own opinion. . . .[10]

The Egyptians first made it a point of religion to have no converse with women in   15
the sacred places,[11] and not to enter them without washing, after such converse. Almost all other nations, except the Greeks and the Egyptians, act differently, regarding man as in this matter under no other law than the brutes. Many animals, they say, and various kinds of birds, may be seen to couple in the temples and the sacred precincts, which would certainly not happen if the gods were displeased at it. Such are the arguments by which they defend their practice, but I nevertheless can by no means approve of it. In these points the Egyptians are specially careful, as they are indeed in everything which concerns their sacred edifices.

Egypt, though it borders upon Libya, is not a region abounding in wild animals. The animals that do exist in the country, whether domesticated or otherwise, are all regarded as sacred. If I were to explain why they are consecrated to the several gods, I should be led to speak of religious matters, which I particularly shrink from mentioning;[12] the points whereon I have touched slightly hitherto have all been introduced from sheer necessity. Their custom with respect to animals is as follows:—For every kind there are appointed certain guardians, some male, some female, whose business it is to look after them; and this honour is made to descend from father to son. The inhabitants of the various cities, when they have made a vow to any god, pay it to his animals in the way which I will now explain. At the time of making the vow they shave the head of the child, cutting off all the hair, or else half, or sometimes a third part, which they then weigh in a balance against a sum of silver; and whatever sum the hair weighs is presented to the guardian of the animals, who thereupon cuts up some fish, and gives it to them for food—such being the stuff whereon they fed. When a man has killed one of the sacred animals, if he did it with malice prepense,[13] he is punished with death; if unwittingly, he has to pay such a fine as the priests choose to impose. When an ibis, however, or a hawk is killed, whether it was done by accident or on purpose, the man must needs die.

The number of domestic animals in Egypt is very great, and would be still greater were it not for what befalls the cats. As the females, when they have kittened, no longer seek the company of the males, these last, to obtain once more their companionship, practise a curious artifice. They seize the kittens, carry them off, and kill them, but do not eat them afterwards. Upon this the females, being deprived of their young, and longing to supply their place, seek the males once more, since they are particularly

---

[10]Modern scholars tend to accept Herodotus's date for Homer ("four hundred years before my time") as correct. Theogonies are genealogies of the gods. Dodôna was a famous oracle of Zeus in northwestern Greece.   [11]*converse . . . places:* Ritual prostitution in temple precincts, setting a symbolic example to the earth to renew its fertility, was common in ancient Greece.   [12]the sacred mysteries were not to be lightly spoken of or gossiped about, even by a historian. The famous mysteries of Eleusis (a few miles from Athens) apparently had much in common with those of Isis and Osiris in Egypt.   [13]*malice prepence:* malice aforethought.

fond of their offspring. On every occasion of a fire in Egypt the strangest prodigy occurs with the cats. The inhabitants allow the fire to rage as it pleases, while they stand about at intervals and watch these animals, which, slipping by the men or else leaping over them, rush headlong into the flames. When this happens, the Egyptians are in deep affliction. If a cat dies in a private house by a natural death, all the inmates of the house shave their eyebrows; on the death of a dog they shave the head and the whole of the body.

The cats on their decease are taken to the city of Bubastis, where they are embalmed, after which they are buried in certain sacred repositories. The dogs are interred in the cities to which they belong, also in sacred burial-places. The same practice obtains with respect to the ichneumons; the hawks and shrew-mice, on the contrary, are conveyed to the city of Buto for burial, and the ibises to Hermopolis. The bears, which are scarce in Egypt, and the wolves, which are not much bigger than foxes, they bury wherever they happen to find them lying. . . .

They have also another sacred bird called the phoenix, which I myself have never seen, except in pictures. Indeed it is a great rarity, even in Egypt, only coming there (according to the accounts of the people of Heliopolis) once in five hundred years, when the old phoenix dies. Its size and appearance, if it is like the pictures, are as follow:—The plumage is partly red, partly golden, while the general make and size are almost exactly that of the eagle. They tell a story of what this bird does, which does not seem to me to be credible: that he comes all the way from Arabia, and brings the parent bird, all plastered over with myrrh, to the temple of the Sun, and there buries the body. In order to bring him, they say, he first forms a ball of myrrh as big as he finds that he can carry; then he hollows out the ball, and puts his parent inside, after which he covers over the opening with fresh myrrh, and the ball is then of exactly the same weight as at first; so he brings it to Egypt, plastered over as I have said, and deposits it in the temple of the Sun. Such is the story they tell of the doings of this bird. . . .

With respect to the Egyptians themselves, it is to be remarked that those who live   20
in the corn country, devoting themselves, as they do, far more than any other people in the world, to the preservation of the memory of past actions, are the best skilled in history of any men that I have ever met. The following is the mode of life habitual to them:—For three successive days in each month they purge the body by means of emetics and clysters, which is done out of a regard for their health, since they have a persuasion that every disease to which men are liable is occasioned by the substances whereon they feed. Apart from any such precautions, they are, I believe, next to the Libyans, the healthiest people in the world—an effect of their climate, in my opinion, which has no sudden changes. Diseases almost always attack men when they are exposed to a change, and never more than during changes of the weather. They live on bread made of spelt, which they form into loaves called in their own tongue *cyllêstis*. Their drink is a wine which they obtain from barley, as they have no vines in their country. Many kinds of fish they eat raw, either salted or dried in the sun. Quails also, and ducks and small birds, they eat uncooked, merely first salting them. All other birds and fishes, excepting those which are set apart as sacred, are eaten either roasted or boiled.

In social meetings among the rich, when the banquet is ended, a servant carries round to the several guests a coffin, in which there is a wooden image of a corpse, carved and painted to resemble nature as nearly as possible, about a cubit or two cubits in length. As he shows it to each guest in turn, the servant says, "Gaze here, and drink and be merry; for when you die, such will you be." . . .

The Egyptian likewise discovered to which of the gods each month and day is sacred; and found out from the day of a man's birth, what he will meet with in the course of his life, and how he will end his days, and what sort of man he will be—discoveries whereof the Greeks engaged in poetry have made a use. The Egyptians have also discovered more prognostics than all the rest of mankind besides. Whenever a prodigy takes place, they watch and record the result; then, if anything similar ever happens again, they expect the same consequences. . . .

The following is the way in which they conduct their mournings and their funerals:—On the death in any house of a man of consequence, forthwith the women of the family beplaster their heads, and sometimes even their faces, with mud; and then, leaving the body indoors, sally forth and wander through the city, with their dress fastened by a band, and their bosoms bare, beating themselves as they walk. All the female relations join them and do the same. The men too, similarly begirt, beat their breasts separately. When these ceremonies are over, the body is carried away to be embalmed.

There are a set of men in Egypt who practice the art of embalming, and make it their proper business. These persons, when a body is brought to them, show the bearers various models of corpses, made in wood, and painted so as to resemble nature. The most perfect is said to be after the manner of him whom I do not think it religious to name[14] in connection with such a matter; the second sort is inferior to the first, and less costly; the third is the cheapest of all. All this the embalmers explain, and then ask in which way it is wished that the corpse should be prepared. The bearers tell them, and having concluded their bargain, take their departure, while the embalmers left to themselves, proceed to their task. The mode of embalming, according to the most perfect process, is the following:—They take first a crooked piece of iron, and with it draw out the brain through the nostrils, thus getting rid of a portion, while the skull is cleared of the rest by rinsing with drugs; next they make a cut along the flank with a sharp Ethiopian stone, and take out the whole contents of the abdomen, which they then cleanse, washing it thoroughly with palm wine, and again frequently with an infusion of pounded aromatics. After this they fill the cavity with purest bruised myrrh, with cassia, and every other sort of spicery except frankincense, and sew up the opening. Then the body is placed in natrum[15] for seventy days, and covered entirely over. After the expiration of that space of time, which must not be exceeded, the body is washed, and wrapped round, from head to foot, with bandages of fine linen cloth, smeared over with gum, which is used generally by the Egyptians in the place of glue, and in this state it is given back to the relations, who enclose it in a wooden case which they have had made for the purpose, shaped into the figure of a man. Then fastening the case, they place it in a sepulchral chamber, upright against the wall. Such is the most costly way of embalming the dead.

---

[14]*him . . . name:* undoubtedly Osiris. Though he might feel free to name Osiris in other contexts, Herodotus speaks again here as one who was under the seal of mysteries corresponding with those of Egypt.   [15]*natrum:* sodium carbonate.

If persons wish to avoid expense, and choose the second process, the following is   25
the method pursued:—Syringes are filled with oil made from the cedar-tree, which is
then, without any incision or disembowelling, injected into the abdomen. The passage
by which it might be likely to return is stopped, and the body laid in natrum the prescribed number of days. At the end of the time the cedar-oil is allowed to make its escape; and such is its power that it brings with it the whole stomach and intestines in a
liquid state. The natrum meanwhile has dissolved the flesh, and so nothing is left of the
dead body but the skin and the bones. It is returned in this condition to the relatives,
without any further trouble being bestowed upon it.

The third method of embalming, which is practised in the case of the poorer classes,
is to clear out the intestines with a clyster, and let the body lie in natrum the seventy
days, after which it is at once given to those who come to fetch it away.

The wives of men of rank are not given to be embalmed immediately after death,
nor indeed are any of the more beautiful and valued women. It is not till they have
been dead three of four days that they are carried to the embalmers. This is done to
prevent indignities from being offered them. It is said that once a case of this kind occurred; the man was detected by the information of his fellow-workman. . . .

Thus far I have spoken of Egypt from my own observation, relating what I myself
saw, the ideas that I formed, and the results of my own researches.

Questions for Discussion and Writing

1. What were the customs and rituals of the ancient Egyptians designed to achieve? How does the way that Herodotus collected material suggest that he was one of the world's first historians?

2. Why is the comparative method that Herodotus uses throughout his essay well suited to his subject and audience?

3. Herodotus describes customs that were strange to him. Write a page or two as if you were writing for someone who was not at all familiar with, for example, Easter egg hunts, tattooing, body piercing, shopping malls, fast food, fashion trends, beauty salons, or any other cultural or religious custom.

4. The entire history of Herodotus in the George Rawlinson translation is available at <http://classics.mit.edu/Herodotus/history.html>. An interactive database with more than two thousand images of the Valley of the Kings is available at <http://www.thebanmappingproject.com/>. Look at these sites and select a topic for a research project.

5. How does this postcard with its view of the Great Pyramid, outside Cairo, suggest that modern tourists still come to see these ancient sites just as Herodotus did in the fifth century?

Gilbert Highet

Gilbert Highet (1906–1978) was born in Glasgow, Scotland, and educated at the University of Glasgow and Oxford University. From 1937 to 1972 Highet was professor of Greek, Latin, and comparative literature at Columbia University. His many distinguished books include The Classical Tradition: Greek and Roman Influences on Western Literature *(1949),* The Anatomy of Satire *(1962), and* The Immortal Profession: The Joy of Teaching and Learning *(1976). He was particularly successful in bridging the gap from classicism to popular culture as an editor for the Book of the Month Club, chairman of the editorial board of* Horizon *magazine, and literary critic for* Harper's. *"The Gettysburg Address," from* A Clerk of Oxenford *(1959), shows Highet at his most illuminating in his analysis of the structure, themes, and rhetoric of Lincoln's famous speech.*

What does this 1984 Gary Larson cartoon say about our expectations regarding politicians' oratory?

THE GETTYSBURG ADDRESS

Fourscore and seven years ago our fathers brought forth on this continent, a new nation, conceived in Liberty, and dedicated to the proposition that all men are created equal.

Now we are engaged in a great civil war, testing whether that nation or any nation so conceived and so dedicated, can long endure. We are met on a great battle-field of that war. We have come to dedicate a portion of that field, as a final resting place for those who here gave their lives that that nation might live. It is altogether fitting and proper that we should do this.

But, in a larger sense, we can not dedicate—we can not consecrate—we can not hallow—this ground. The brave men, living and dead, who struggled here, have consecrated it, far above our poor power to add or detract. The world will little note, nor long remember, what we say here, but it can never forget what they did here. It is for us the living, rather, to be dedicated here to the unfinished work which they who fought here have thus far so nobly advanced. It is rather for us to be here dedicated to the great task remaining before us—that from these honored dead we take increased devotion to that cause for which they gave the last full measure of devotion—that we here highly resolve that these dead shall not have died in vain—that this nation, under God, shall have a new birth of freedom—and that government of the people, by the people, for the people, shall not perish from the earth.

Fourscore and seven years ago . . .

These five words stand at the entrance to the best-known monument of American prose, one of the finest utterances in the entire language and surely one of the greatest speeches in all history. Greatness is like granite: it is molded in fire, and it lasts for many centuries.

Fourscore and seven years ago. . . . It is strange to think that President Lincoln was looking back to the 4th of July 1776, and that he and his speech are now further removed from us than he himself was from George Washington and the Declaration of Independence. Fourscore and seven years before the Gettysburg Address, a small group of patriots signed the Declaration. Fourscore and seven years after the Gettysburg Address, it was the year 1950, and that date is already receding rapidly into our troubled, adventurous, and valiant past.

Inadequately prepared and at first scarcely realized in its full importance, the dedication of the graveyard at Gettysburg was one of the supreme moments of American history. The battle itself had been a turning point of the war. On the 4th of July 1863, General Meade repelled Lee's invasion of Pennsylvania. Although he did not follow up his victory, he had broken one of the most formidable aggressive enterprises of the Confederate armies. Losses were heavy on both sides. Thousands of dead were left on the field, and thousands of wounded died in the hot days following the battle. At first, their burial was more or less haphazard; but thoughtful men gradually came to feel that an adequate burying place and memorial were required. These were established by an interstate commission that autumn, and the finest speaker in the North was invited to dedicate them. This was the scholar and statesman Edward Everett of Harvard. He made a good speech—which is still extant: not at all academic, it is full of close strategic analysis and deep historical understanding.

Lincoln was not invited to speak, at first. Although people knew him as an effec- 5
tive debater, they were not sure whether he was capable of making a serious speech on
such a solemn occasion. But one of the impressive things about Lincoln's career is that
he constantly strove to *grow.* He was anxious to appear on that occasion and to say
something worthy of it. (Also, it has been suggested, he was anxious to remove the impression that he did not know how to behave properly—an impression which had been
strengthened by a shocking story about his clowning on the battlefield of Antietam the
previous year). Therefore when he was invited he took considerable care with his
speech. He drafted rather more than half of it in the White House before leaving, finished it in the hotel at Gettysburg the night before the ceremony (not in the train, as
sometimes reported), and wrote out a fair copy next morning.

There are many accounts of the day itself, 19 November 1863. There are many descriptions of Lincoln, all showing the same curious blend of grandeur and awkwardness, or lack of dignity, or—it would be best to call it humility. In the procession he rode
horseback: a tall lean man in a high plug hat, straddling a short horse, with his feet too
near the ground. He arrived before the chief speaker, and had to wait patiently for half
an hour or more. His own speech came right at the end of a long and exhausting ceremony, lasted less than three minutes, and made little impression on the audience. In
part this was because they were tired, in part because (as eyewitnesses said) he ended
almost before they knew he had begun, and in part because he did not speak the Address, but read it, very slowly, in a thin high voice, with a marked Kentucky accent, pro-
nouncing "to" as "toe" and dropping his final R's.

Some people of course were alert enough to be impressed. Everett congratulated
him at once. But most of the newspapers paid little attention to the speech, and some
sneered at it. The *Patriot and Union* of Harrisburg wrote, "We pass over the silly remarks of the President; for the credit of the nation we are willing . . . that they shall
no more be repeated or thought of"; and the London *Times* said, "The ceremony was
rendered ludicrous by some of the sallies of that poor President Lincoln," calling his
remarks "dull and commonplace." The first commendation of the Address came in a
single sentence of the Chicago *Tribune,* and the first discriminating and detailed praise
of it appeared in the Springfield *Republican,* the Providence *Journal,* and the Philadelphia *Bulletin.* However, three weeks after the ceremony and then again the following
spring, the editor of *Harper's Weekly* published a sincere and thorough eulogy of the
Address, and soon it was attaining recognition as a masterpiece.

> At the time, Lincoln could not care much about the reception of his words. He was ex-
> hausted and ill. In the train back to Washington, he lay down with a wet towel on his head.
> He had caught smallpox. At that moment he was incubating it, and he was stricken down
> soon after he reentered the White House. Fortunately it was a mild attack, and it evoked
> one of his best jokes: he told his visitors, "At last I have something I can give to everybody."

He had more than that to give to everybody. He was a unique person, far greater
than most people realize until they read his life with care. The wisdom of his policy,
the sources of his statesmanship—these were things too complex to be discussed in a
brief essay. But we can say something about the Gettysburg Address as a work of art.

A work of art. Yes: for Lincoln was a literary artist, trained both by others and by
himself. The textbooks he used as a boy were full of difficult exercises and skillful

devices in formal rhetoric, stressing the qualities he practiced in his own speaking: antithesis, parallelism, and verbal harmony. Then he read and reread many admirable models of thought and expression: the King James Bible, the essays of Bacon, the best plays of Shakespeare. His favorites were *Hamlet, Lear, Macbeth, Richard III,* and *Henry VIII,* which he had read dozens of times. He loved reading aloud, too, and spent hours reading poetry to his friends. (He told his partner Herndon that he preferred getting the sense of any document by reading it aloud.) Therefore his serious speeches are important parts of the long and noble classical tradition of oratory which begins in Greece, runs through Rome to the modern world, and is still capable (if we do not neglect it) of producing masterpieces.

The first proof of this is that the Gettysburg Address is full of quotations—or 10 rather of adaptations—which give it strength. It is partly religious, partly (in the highest sense) political: therefore it is interwoven with memories of the Bible and memories of American history. The first and the last words are Biblical cadences. Normally Lincoln did not say "fourscore" when he meant eighty but on this solemn occasion he recalled the important dates in the Bible—such as the age of Abram when his first son was born to him, and he was "fourscore and six years old."[1] Similarly he did not say there was a chance that democracy might die out: he recalled the somber phrasing of the Book of Job—where Bildad speaks of the destruction of one who shall vanish without a trace, and says that "his branch shall be cut off; his remembrance shall perish from the earth."[2] Then again, the famous description of our State as "government of the people, by the people, for the people" was adumbrated by Daniel Webster in 1830 (he spoke of "the people's government, made for the people, made by the people, and answerable to the people") and then elaborated in 1854 by the abolitionist Theodore Parker (as "government of all the people, by all the people, for all the people"). There is good reason to think that Lincoln took the important phrase "under God" (which he interpolated at the last moment) from Weems, the biographer of Washington; and we know that it had been used at least once by Washington himself.

Analyzing the Address further, we find that it is based on a highly imaginative theme, or group of themes. The subject is—how can we put it so as not to disfigure it?—the subject is the kinship of life and death, that mysterious linkage which we see sometimes as the physical succession of birth and death in our world, sometimes as the contrast, which is perhaps a unity, between death and immortality. The first sentence is concerned with birth:

Our *fathers brought forth a new* nation, *conceived* in liberty.

The final phrase but one expresses the hope that

this nation, under God, shall have a *new birth* of freedom.

---

[1] *"fourscore and six years old"*: Genesis 16.16.   [2] *"his branch . . . earth"*: Job 18.16–17.

And the last phrase of all speaks of continuing life as the triumph over death. Again and again throughout the speech, this mystical contrast and kinship reappear: "those who *gave their lives* that that nation might *live*," "the brave men *living* and *dead*," and so in the central assertion that the dead have already consecrated their own burial place, while "it is for us, the *living*, rather to be dedicated . . . to the great task remaining." The Gettysburg Address is a prose poem; it belongs to the same world as the great elegies, and the adagios of Beethoven. Its structure, however, is that of a skillfully contrived speech. The oratorical pattern is perfectly clear. Lincoln describes the occasion, dedicates the ground, and then draws a larger conclusion by calling on his hearers to dedicate themselves to the preservation of the Union. But within that, we can trace his constant use of at least two important rhetorical devices.

The first of these is *antithesis*: opposition, contrast. The speech is full of it. Listen:

> The world will little *note*
> nor long *remember*   what *we say* here
> but   it can never *forget*   what *they did* here.

And so in nearly every sentence: "brave men, *living* and *dead*"; "to *add* or *detract*." There is the antithesis of the Founding Fathers and the men of Lincoln's own time:

> Our *fathers brought forth* a new nation . . .
> now *we* are testing whether that nation . . . can *long endure*.

And there is the more terrible antithesis of those who have already died and those who still live to do their duty. Now, antithesis is the figure of contrast and conflict. Lincoln was speaking in the midst of a great civil war.

The other important pattern is different. It is technically called *tricolon*—the division of an idea into three harmonious parts, usually of increasing power. The most famous phrase of the Address is a tricolon:

> government of the people
> by the people
> and   for the people

The most solemn sentence is a tricolon:

> we cannot dedicate
> we cannot consecrate
> we cannot hallow this ground.

And above all, the last sentence (which has sometimes been criticized as too complex) is essentially two parallel phrases, with a tricolon growing out of the second and then producing another tricolon: a trunk, three branches, and a cluster of flowers. Lincoln says that it is for his hearers to be dedicated to the great task remaining before them. Then he goes on,

> that from these honored dead

—apparently he means "in such a way that from these honored dead"—

> we take increased devotion to that cause.

Next, he restates this more briefly:

> that we here highly resolve . . .

And now the actual resolution follows, in three parts of growing intensity:

> that these dead shall not have died in vain
> that this nation, under God, shall have a new birth of freedom

and that (one more tricolon)

> government of the people
>   by the people
>   and   for the people
> shall not perish from the earth.

Now, the tricolon is the figure which, through division, emphasizes basic harmony and unity. Lincoln used antithesis because he was speaking to a people at war. He used the tricolon because he was hoping, planning, praying for peace.

No one thinks that when he was drafting the Gettysburg Address, Lincoln deliberately looked up these quotations and consciously chose these particular patterns of thought. No, he chose the theme. From its development and from the emotional tone of the entire occasion, all the rest followed, or grew—by that marvelous process of choice and rejection which is essential to artistic creation. It does not spoil such a work of art to analyze it as closely as we have done; it is altogether fitting and proper that we should do this: for it helps us to penetrate more deeply into the rich meaning of the Gettysburg Address, and it allows us the very rare privilege of watching the workings of a great man's mind.

Questions for Discussion and Writing

1. What three principles of rhetorical organization did Lincoln utilize in creating the Gettysburg Address? How did Lincoln use these principles to speak to his audience's concerns, put the moment in a historical perspective, and motivate the listeners to begin to reunite a nation shattered by the Civil War?
2. How do the metaphors of birth and death contribute to the eloquence of Lincoln's speech? Where does he echo the language and rhythms of the Bible to give his speech a feeling of solemnity?
3. As a research project, investigate why the Battle of Gettysburg was seen as important enough for Lincoln to give his address there. What evidence is there that Lincoln realized that his speech was seen as a great one? You might wish to

analyze the rhetorical strategies in another famous speech, such as John F. Kennedy's Inaugural Address (1961).

Jack London

• •

Jack London (1876–1916) was born John Griffith Chaney in San Francisco but took the name of his stepfather, John London. His impoverished childhood bred self-reliance: He worked in a canning factory and a jute mill and as a longshoreman, robbed oyster beds as the self-styled "Prince of the Oyster Pirates," went to sea at seventeen, and took part in the Klondike gold rush of 1897. When he began writing his distinctive stories, often set in the Yukon, of the survival of men and animals in harsh environments, he drew on these experiences. He was also profoundly influenced by the works of Karl Marx, Rudyard Kipling, and Friedrich Wilhelm Nietzsche. In his novels The Call of the Wild *(1903),* The Sea Wolf *(1904),* White Fang *(1906), and* The Iron Heel *(1908), and in short stories such as "Love of Life" (1906) and "To Build a Fire" (1910), London powerfully dramatizes the conflict between barbarism and civilization. During London's short, turbulent life, his prolific output as a writer also included his work as a journalist. Among other assignments, he covered the Russo-Japanese War of 1904–1905 as a syndicated correspondent. "The San Francisco Earthquake" (1906) was the first in a series of reports on the April 18, 1906, catastrophe that London wrote for* Collier's *magazine. His straightforward descriptive style influenced later writers such as Ernest Hemingway and Sherwood Anderson.*

THE SAN FRANCISCO EARTHQUAKE

The earthquake shook down in San Francisco hundreds of thousands of dollars' worth of walls and chimneys. But the conflagration that followed burned up hundreds of millions of dollars' worth of property. There is no estimating within hundreds of millions the actual damage wrought. Not in history has a modern imperial city been so completely destroyed. San Francisco is gone. Nothing remains of it but memories and a fringe of dwelling-houses on its outskirts. Its industrial section is wiped out. Its business section is wiped out. The factories and warehouses, the great stores and newspaper buildings, the hotels and the palaces of the nabobs, are all gone. Remains only the fringe of dwelling-houses on the outskirts of what was once San Francisco.

Within an hour after the earthquake shock the smoke of San Francisco's burning was a lurid tower visible a hundred miles away. And for three days and nights this lurid tower swayed in the sky, reddening the sun, darkening the day, and filling the land with smoke.

On Wednesday morning at a quarter past five came the earthquake. A minute later the flames were leaping upward. In a dozen different quarters south of Market Street, in the working-class ghetto, and in the factories, fires started. There was no opposing the flames. There was no organization, no communication. All the cunning adjustments of a twentieth century city had been smashed by the earthquake. The streets were humped into ridges and depressions, and piled with the debris of fallen walls. The steel rails were twisted into perpendicular and horizontal angles. The telephone and telegraph systems were disrupted. And the great water-mains had burst. All the shrewd contrivances and safe-guards of man had been thrown out of gear by thirty seconds' twitching of the earth-crust.

The Fire Made Its Own Draft

By Wednesday afternoon, inside of twelve hours, half the heart of the city was gone. At that time I watched the vast conflagration from out on the bay. It was dead calm. Not a flicker of wind stirred. Yet from every side wind was pouring in upon the city. East, west, north, and south, strong winds were blowing upon the doomed city. The heated air rising made an enormous suck. Thus did the fire of itself build its own colossal chimney through the atmosphere. Day and night this dead calm continued, and yet, near to the flames, the wind was often half a gale, so mighty was the suck.

Wednesday night saw the destruction of the very heart of the city. Dynamite was   5 lavishly used, and many of San Francisco's proudest structures were crumbled by man himself into ruins, but there was no withstanding the onrush of the flames. Time and again successful stands were made by the fire-fighters, and every time the flames flanked around on either side, or came up from the rear, and turned to defeat the hard-won victory.

An enumeration of the buildings destroyed would be a directory of San Francisco. An enumeration of the buildings undestroyed would be a line and several addresses. An enumeration of the deeds of heroism would stock a library and bankrupt the Carnegie Medal fund. An enumeration of the dead will never be made. All vestiges of them were destroyed by the flames. The number of victims of the earthquake will never be known. South of Market Street, where the loss of life was particularly heavy, was the first to catch fire.

Remarkable as it may seem, Wednesday night, while the whole city crashed and roared into ruin, was a quiet night. There were no crowds. There was no shouting and yelling. There was no hysteria, no disorder. I passed Wednesday night in the path of the advancing flames, and in all those terrible hours I saw not one woman who wept, not one man who was excited, not one person who was in the slightest degree panic-stricken.

Before the flames, throughout the night, fled tens of thousands of homeless ones. Some were wrapped in blankets. Others carried bundles of bedding and dear household treasures. Sometimes a whole family was harnessed to a carriage or delivery wagon that was weighted down with their possessions. Baby buggies, toy wagons, and go-carts were used as trucks, while every other person was dragging a trunk. Yet everybody was gracious. The most perfect courtesy obtained. Never, in all San Francisco's history, were her people so kind and courteous as on this night of terror.

A Caravan of Trunks

All night these tens of thousands fled before the flames. Many of them, the poor people from the labor ghetto, had fled all day as well. They had left their homes burdened with possessions. Now and again they lightened up, flinging out upon the street clothing and treasures they had dragged for miles.

They held on longest to their trunks, and over these trunks many a strong man   10
broke his heart that night. The hills of San Francisco are steep, and up these hills, mile
after mile, were the trunks dragged. Everywhere were trunks, with across them lying
their exhausted owners, men and women. Before the march of the flames were flung
picket lines of soldiers. And a block at a time, as the flames advanced, these pickets retreated. One of their tasks was to keep the trunk-pullers moving. The exhausted creatures, stirred on by the menace of bayonets, would arise and struggle up the steep
pavements, pausing from weakness every five or ten feet.

Often, after surmounting a heart-breaking hill, they would find another wall of
flame advancing upon them at right angles and be compelled to change anew the line
of their retreat. In the end, completely played out, after toiling for a dozen hours like
giants, thousands of them were compelled to abandon their trunks. Here the shopkeepers and soft members of the middle class were at a disadvantage. But the working men dug holes in vacant lots and backyards and buried their trunks.

The Doomed City

At nine o'clock Wednesday evening I walked down through the very heart of the city.
I walked through miles and miles of magnificent buildings and towering skyscrapers.
Here was no fire. All was in perfect order. The police patrolled the streets. Every build-
ing had its watchman at the door. And yet it was doomed, all of it. There was no water.
The dynamite was giving out. And at right angles two different conflagrations were
sweeping down upon it.

At one o'clock in the morning I walked down through the same section. Everything still stood intact. There was no fire. And yet there was a change. A rain of ashes
was falling. The watchmen at the doors were gone. The police had been withdrawn.
There were no firemen, no fire engines, no men fighting with dynamite. The district had
been absolutely abandoned. I stood at the corner of Kearney and Market, in the very
innermost heart of San Francisco. Kearney Street was deserted. Half a dozen blocks
away it was burning on both sides. The street was a wall of flame, and against this
wall of flame, silhouetted sharply, were two United States cavalrymen sitting their
horses, calmly watching. That was all. Not another person was in sight. In the intact
heart of the city two troopers sat their horses and watched.

Spread of the Conflagration

Surrender was complete. There was no water. The sewers had long since been pumped
dry. There was no dynamite. Another fire had broken out further uptown, and now
from three sides conflagrations were sweeping down. The fourth side had been burned
earlier in the day. In that direction stood the tottering walls of the Examiner building,
the burned-out Call building, the smoldering ruins of the Grand Hotel, and the gutted,
devastated, dynamited Palace Hotel.

The following will illustrate the sweep of the flames and the inability of men to cal-   15
culate their spread. At eight o'clock Wednesday evening I passed through Union Square.
It was packed with refugees. Thousands of them had gone to bed on the grass.

Government tents had been set up, supper was being cooked, and the refugees were lining up for free meals.

At half-past one in the morning three sides of Union Square were in flames. The fourth side, where stood the great St. Francis Hotel, was still holding out. An hour later, ignited from top and sides, the St. Francis was flaming heavenward. Union Square, heaped high with mountains of trunks, was deserted. Troops, refugees, and all had retreated.

A Fortune for a Horse!

It was at Union Square that I saw a man offering a thousand dollars for a team of horses. He was in charge of a truck piled high with trunks for some hotel. It had been hauled here into what was considered safety, and the horses had been taken out. The flames were on three sides of the Square, and there were no horses.

Also, at this time, standing beside the truck, I urged a man to seek safety in flight. He was all but hemmed in by several conflagrations. He was an old man and he was on crutches. Said he, "Today is my birthday. Last night I was worth thirty thousand dollars. I bought five bottles of wine, some delicate fish, and other things for my birthday dinner. I have had no dinner, and all I own are these crutches."

I convinced him of his danger and started him limping on his way. An hour later, from a distance, I saw the truckload of trunks burning merrily in the middle of the street.

On Thursday morning, at a quarter past five, just twenty-four hours after the earthquake, I sat on the steps of a small residence on Nob Hill. With me sat Japanese, Italians, Chinese, and Negroes—a bit of the cosmopolitan flotsam of the wreck of the city. All about were the palaces of the nabob pioneers of Forty-nine. To the east and south, at right angles, were advancing two mighty walls of flame. 20

I went inside with the owner of the house on the steps of which I sat. He was cool and cheerful and hospitable. "Yesterday morning," he said, "I was worth six hundred thousand dollars. This morning this house is all I have left. It will go in fifteen minutes." He pointed to a large cabinet. "That is my wife's collection of china. This rug upon which we stand is a present. It cost fifteen hundred dollars. Try that piano. Listen to its tone. There are few like it. There are no horses. The flames will be here in fifteen minutes."

Outside, the old Mark Hopkins residence, a palace, was just catching fire. The troops were falling back and driving the refugees before them. From every side came the roaring of flames, the crashing of walls, and the detonations of dynamite.

The Dawn of the Second Day

I passed out of the house. Day was trying to dawn through the smoke-pall. A sickly light was creeping over the face of things. Once only the sun broke through the smoke-pall, blood-red, and showing a quarter its usual size. The smoke-pall itself, viewed from beneath, was a rose color that pulsed and fluttered with lavender shades. Then it turned to mauve and yellow and dun. There was no sun. And so dawned the second day on stricken San Francisco.

An hour later I was creeping past the shattered dome of the City Hall. Than it, there was no better exhibit of the destructive forces of the earthquake. Most of the stone had been shaken from the great dome, leaving standing the naked framework of steel. Market Street was piled high with wreckage, and across the wreckage lay the overthrown pillars of the City Hall shattered into short crosswise sections.

This section of the city, with the exception of the Mint and the Post-Office, was   25
already a waste of smoking ruins. Here and there through the smoke, creeping warily under the shadows of tottering walls, emerged occasional men and women. It was like the meeting of the handful of survivors after the day of the end of the world.

Beeves Slaughtered and Roasted

On Mission Street lay a dozen steers, in a neat row stretching across the street, just as they had been struck down by the flying ruins of the earthquake. The fire had passed through afterward and roasted them. The human dead had been carried away before the fire came. At another place on Mission Street I saw a milk wagon. A steel telegraph pole had smashed down sheer through the driver's seat and crushed the front wheels. The milkcans lay scattered around.

All day Thursday and all Thursday night, all day Friday and Friday night, the flames still raged.

Friday night saw the flames finally conquered, though not until Russian Hill and Telegraph Hill had been swept and three-quarters of a mile of wharves and docks had been licked up.

The Last Stand

The great stand of the fire-fighters was made Thursday night on Van Ness Avenue. Had they failed here, the comparatively few remaining houses of the city would have been swept. Here were the magnificent residences of the second generation of San Francisco nabobs, and these, in a solid zone, were dynamited down across the path of the fire. Here and there the flames leaped the zone, but these fires were beaten out, principally by the use of wet blankets and rugs.

San Francisco, at the present time, is like the crater of a volcano, around which are   30
camped tens of thousand of refugees. At the Presidio alone are at least twenty thousand. All the surrounding cities and towns are jammed with the homeless ones, where they are being cared for by the relief committees. The refugees were carried free by the railroads to any point they wished to go, and it is estimated that over one hundred thousand people have left the peninsula on which San Francisco stood. The Government has the situation in hand, and, thanks to the immediate relief given by the whole United States, there is not the slightest possibility of a famine. The bankers and business men have already set about making preparations to rebuild San Francisco.

Questions for Discussion and Writing

1. What examples of courteous behavior does London cite that support the impression of the civility of San Franciscans under great stress? How much of San Francisco was destroyed by subsequent fires in comparison with the damage done by

the earthquake itself? How do we know that London risked his own life to accurately report the extent of the destruction?

2. What effect does London produce by reporting the event from many different vantage points within the city? How is his description enhanced by metaphors that evoke the sounds, sights, tastes, and smells of the conflagration? How does his shift from war imagery to the metaphor of the shipwreck reflect the predicament citizens faced as survivors of the devastation?

3. How does the phrase "[my] fortune for a horse" (echoing the famous line from Shakespeare's play *Richard III,* "my kingdom for a horse") express the desperation of citizens seeking to save what little they could? Which parts of this report are enhanced by London's skill as a novelist using fictional techniques to dramatize his otherwise objective journalistic account?

4. You might wish to check the *1906 San Francisco Earthquake Photographs* Web site at <www.sfmuseum.org/1906.html>, and compare the photographs with London's account.

Hanson W. Baldwin

. . . .

Hanson W. Baldwin (1903–1991) served as military editor for the New York Times *and won the Pulitzer Prize for his reporting in 1943. Among his published works are* The Crucial Year, 1939–41: The World at War *(1976). This account was first published in* Harper's *magazine in January 1934.*

R. M. S. TITANIC

The White Star liner *Titanic,* largest ship the world had ever known, sailed from Southampton on her maiden voyage to New York on April 10, 1912. The paint on her strakes was fair and bright; she was fresh from Harland and Wolff's Belfast yards, strong in the strength of her forty-six thousand tons of steel, bent, hammered, shaped and riveted through the three years of her slow birth.

There was little fuss and fanfare at her sailing; her sister ship, the *Olympic*—slightly smaller than the *Titanic*—had been in service for some months and to her had gone the thunder of the cheers.

But the *Titanic* needed no whistling steamers or shouting crowds to call attention to her superlative qualities. Her bulk dwarfed the ships near her as longshoremen singled up her mooring lines and cast off the turns of heavy rope from the dock bollards. She was not only the largest ship afloat, but was believed to be the safest. Carlisle, her builder, had given her double bottoms and had divided her hull into sixteen watertight compartments, which made her, men thought, unsinkable. She had been built to be and had been described as a gigantic lifeboat. Her designers' dreams of a triple-screw giant, a luxurious, floating hotel, which could speed to New York at twenty-three knots, had been carefully translated from blueprints and mold-loft lines at the Belfast yards into a living reality.

The *Titanic*'s sailing from Southampton, though quiet, was not wholly uneventful. As the liner moved slowly toward the end of her dock that April day, the surge of her passing sucked away from the quay the steamer *New York*, moored just to seaward of the *Titanic*'s berth. There were sharp cracks as the manila mooring lines of the *New York* parted under the strain. The frayed ropes writhed and whistled through the air and snapped down among the waving crowd on the pier; the *New York* swung toward the *Titanic*'s bow, was checked and dragged back to the dock barely in time to avert a collision. Seamen muttered, thought it an ominous start.

Past Spithead and the Isle of Wight the *Titanic* steamed. She called at Cherbourg   5
at dusk and then laid her course for Queenstown. At 1:30 p.m. on Thursday, April 11, she stood out of Queenstown harbor, screaming gulls soaring in her wake, with 2,201 persons—men, women, and children—aboard.

Occupying the Empire bedrooms and Georgian suites of the first-class accommodations were many well-known men and women—Colonel John Jacob Astor and his young bride; Major Archibald Butt, military aide to President Taft, and his friend, Frank D. Millet, the painter; John B. Thayer, vice-president of the Pennsylvania Railroad, and Charles M. Hays, president of the Grand Trunk Railway of Canada; W. T. Stead, the English journalist; Jacques Futrelle, French novelist; H. B. Harris, theatrical manager, and Mrs. Harris; Mr. and Mrs. Isidor Straus; and J. Bruce Ismay, chairman and managing director of the White Star line.

Down in the plain wooden cabins of the steerage class were 706 immigrants to the land of promise, and trimly stowed in the great holds was a cargo valued at $420,000: oak beams, sponges, wine, calabashes, and an odd miscellany of the common and the rare.

The *Titanic* took her departure on Fastnet Light and, heading into the night, laid her course for New York. She was due at Quarantine the following Wednesday morning.

Sunday dawned fair and clear. The *Titanic* steamed smoothly toward the west, faint streamers of brownish smoke trailing from her funnels. The purser held services in the saloon in the morning; on the steerage deck aft the immigrants were playing games and a Scotsman was puffing "The Campbells Are Coming" on his bagpipes in the midst of the uproar.

At 9 A.M. a message from the steamer *Caronia* sputtered into the wireless shack: 10

Captain, Titanic—Westbound steamers report bergs growlers and field ice in 42 degrees N. from 49 degrees to 51 degrees W. 12th April.

Compliments—Barr.

It was cold in the afternoon; the sun was brilliant, but the *Titanic*, her screws turning over at 75 revolutions per minute, was approaching the Banks.

In the Marconi cabin Second Operator Harold Bride, earphones clamped on his head, was figuring accounts; he did not stop to answer when he heard MWL, Continental Morse for the nearby Leyland liner, *Californian*, calling the *Titanic*. The *Californian* had some message about three icebergs; he didn't bother then to take it down. About 1:42 P.M. the rasping spark of those days spoke again across the water. It was the *Baltic*, calling the *Titanic*, warning her of ice on the steamer track. Bride took the message down and sent it up to the bridge. The officer-of-the-deck glanced at it; sent it to the bearded master of the *Titanic*, Captain E. C. Smith, a veteran of the White Star service. It was lunch time then; the Captain, walking along the promenade deck, saw

Mr. Ismay, stopped, and handed him the message without comment. Ismay read it, stuffed it in his pocket, told two ladies about the icebergs, and resumed his walk. Later, about 7:15 P.M., the Captain requested the return of the message in order to post it in the chart room for the information of officers.

Dinner that night in the Jacobean dining room was gay. It was bitter on deck, but the night was calm and fine; the sky was moonless but studded with stars twinkling coldly in the clear air.

After dinner some of the second-class passengers gathered in the saloon, where the Reverend Mr. Carter conducted a "hymn singsong." It was almost ten o'clock and the stewards were waiting with biscuits and coffee as the group sang:

> O, hear us when we cry to Thee
>   For those in peril on the sea.

On the bridge Second Officer Lightoller—short, stocky, efficient—was relieved at   15
ten o'clock by First Officer Murdock. Lightoller had talked with other officers about the proximity of ice; at least five wireless ice warnings had reached the ship; lookouts had been cautioned to be alert; captains and officers expected to reach the field at any time after 9:30 P.M. At twenty-two knots, its speed unslackened, the *Titanic* plowed on through the night.

Lightoller left the darkened bridge to his relief and turned in. Captain Smith went to his cabin. The steerage was long since quiet; in the first and second cabins lights were going out; voices were growing still, people were asleep. Murdock paced back and forth on the bridge, peering out over the dark water, glancing now and then at the compass in front of Quatermaster Hichens at the wheel.

In the crow's nest, Lookout Frederick Fleet and his partner, Leigh, gazed down at the water, still and unruffled in the dim, starlit darkness. Behind and below them the ship, a white shadow with here and there a last winking light; ahead of them a dark and silent and cold ocean.

There was a sudden clang. "Dong-dong. Dong-dong. Dong-dong. Dong!" The metal clapper of the great ship's bell struck out 11:30. Mindful of the warnings, Fleet strained his eyes, searching the darkness for the dreaded ice. But there were only the stars and the sea.

In the wireless room, where Phillips, first operator, had relieved Bride, the buzz of the *Californian*'s set again crackled into the earphones:

Californian: "Say, old man, we are stuck here, surrounded by ice."
Titanic: "Shut up, shut up; keep out. I am talking to Cape Race; you are jamming my signals."

Then, a few minutes later—about 11:40 . . .   20
Out of the dark she came, a vast, dim, white, monstrous shape, directly in the *Titanic*'s path. For a moment Fleet doubted his eyes. But she was a deadly reality, this ghastly thing. Frantically, Fleet struck three bells—*something dead ahead*. He snatched the telephone and called the bridge:
"Iceberg! Right ahead!"
The First Officer heard but did not stop to acknowledge the message.
"Hard astarboard!"

Hichens strained at the wheel; the bow swung slowly to port. The monster was al-   25
most upon them now.

Murdock leaped to the engine-room telegraph. Bells clanged. Far below in the engine room those bells struck the first warning. Danger! The indicators on the dial faces
swung round to "Stop!" Then "Full speed astern!" Frantically the engineers turned
great valve wheels; answered the bridge bells. . . .

There was a slight shock, a brief scraping, a small list to port. Shell ice—slabs and
chunks of it—fell on the foredeck. Slowly the *Titanic* stopped.

Captain Smith hurried out of his cabin.

"What has the ship struck?"

Murdock answered, "An iceberg, sir. I hard-astarboarded and reversed the en-   30
gines, and I was going to hard-aport around it, but she was too close. I could not do
any more. I have closed the watertight doors."

Fourth Officer Boxhall, other officers, the carpenter, came to the bridge. The Captain sent Boxhall and the carpenter below to ascertain the damage.

A few lights switched on in the first and second cabins; sleepy passengers peered
through porthole glass; some casually asked the stewards:

"Why have we stopped?"

"I don't know, sir, but I don't suppose it is anything much."

In the smoking room a quorum of gamblers and their prey were still sitting round   35
a poker table; the usual crowd of kibitzers looked on. They had felt the slight jar of
the collision and had seen an eighty-foot ice mountain glide by the smoking-room windows, but the night was calm and clear, the *Titanic* was "unsinkable"; they hadn't
bothered to go on deck.

But far below, in the warren of passages on the starboard side forward, in the forward holds and boiler rooms, men could see that the *Titanic*'s hurt was mortal. In
No. 6 boiler room, where the red glow from the furnaces lighted up the naked, sweaty
chests of coal-blackened firemen, water was pouring through a great gash about two
feet above the floor plates. This was no slow leak; the ship was open to the sea; in ten
minutes there were eight feet of water in No. 6. Long before then the stokers had raked
the flaming fires out of the furnaces and had scrambled through the watertight doors
into No. 5 or had climbed up the long steel ladders to safety. When Boxhall looked at
the mail room in No. 3 hold, twenty-four feet above the keel, the mailbags were already
floating about in the slushing water. In No. 5 boiler room a stream of water spurted
into an empty bunker. All six compartments forward of No. 4 were open to the sea;
in ten seconds the iceberg's jagged claw had ripped a three-hundred-foot slash in the
bottom of the great *Titanic*.

Reports came to the bridge; Ismay in dressing gown ran out on deck in the cold,
still, starlit night, climbed up the bridge ladder.

"What has happened?"

Captain Smith: "We have struck ice."

"Do you think she is seriously damaged?"   40

Captain: "I'm afraid she is."

Ismay went below and passed Chief Engineer William Bell fresh from an inspec-
tion of the damaged compartments. Bell corroborated the Captain's statement;

hurried back down the glistening steel ladders to his duty. Man after man followed him—Thomas Andrews, one of the ship's designers, Archie Frost, the builder's chief engineer, and his twenty assistants—men who had no posts of duty in the engine room but whose traditions called them there.

On deck, in corridor and stateroom, life flowed again. Men, women, and children awoke and questioned; orders were given to uncover the lifeboats; water rose into the firemen's quarters; half-dressed stokers streamed up on deck. But the passengers—most of them—did not know that the *Titanic* was sinking. The shock of the collision had been so slight that some were not awakened by it; the *Titanic* was so huge that she must be unsinkable; the night was too calm, too beautiful, to think of death at sea.

Captain Smith half ran to the door of the radio shack. Bride, partly dressed, eyes dulled with sleep, was standing behind Phillips, waiting.

"Send the call for assistance."

The blue spark danced: "CQD—CQD—CQD—CQ—"

45

Miles away Marconi men heard. Cape Race heard it, and the steamships *La Provence* and *Mt. Temple*.

The sea was surging into the *Titanic*'s hold. At 12:20 the water burst into the seamen's quarters through a collapsed fore-and-aft wooden bulkhead. Pumps strained in the engine rooms—men and machinery making a futile fight against the sea. Steadily the water rose.

The boats were swung out—slowly; for the deckhands were late in reaching their stations, there had been no boat drill, and many of the crew did not know to what boats they were assigned. Orders were shouted; the safety valves had lifted, and steam was blowing off in a great rushing roar. In the chart house Fourth Officer Boxhall bent above a chart, working rapidly with pencil and dividers.

12:15 A.M. Boxhall's position is sent out to a fleet of vessels: "Come at once; we have struck a berg."

50

To the Cunarder *Carpathia* (Arthur Henry Rostron, Master, New York to Liverpool, fifty-eight miles away): "It's a CQD, old man. Position 41–46 N.; 50–14 W."

The blue spark dancing: "Sinking; cannot hear for noise of steam."

12:30 A.M. The word is passed: "Women and children in the boats." Stewards finish waking their passengers below; life preservers are tied on; some men smile at the precaution. "The *Titanic* is unsinkable." The *Mt. Temple* starts for the *Titanic*; the *Carpathia*, with a double watch in her stokeholds, radios, "Coming hard." The CQD changes the course of many ships—but not of one; the operator of the *Californian*, near by, has just put down his earphones and turned in.

The CQD flashes over land and sea from Cape Race to New York; newspaper city rooms leap to life and presses whir.

On the *Titanic*, water creeps over the bulkhead between Nos. 5 and 6 firerooms. She is going down by the head; the engineers—fighting a losing battle—are forced back foot by foot by the rising water. Down the promenade deck, Happy Jock Hume, the bandsman, runs with his instrument.

55

12:45 A.M. Murdock, in charge on the starboard side, eyes tragic, but calm and cool, orders boat No. 7 lowered. The women hang back; they want no boat ride on an ice-strewn sea; the *Titanic* is unsinkable. The men encourage them, explain that this is just a precautionary measure: "We'll see you again at breakfast." There is little confusion; passengers stream slowly to the boat deck. In the steerage the immigrants chatter excitedly.

A sudden sharp hiss—a streaked flare against the night; Boxhall sends a rocket toward the sky. It explodes, and a parachute of white stars lights up the icy sea. "God! Rockets!" The band plays ragtime.

No. 8 is lowered, and No. 5. Ismay, still in dressing gown, calls for women and children, handles lines, stumbles in the way of an officer, is told to "get the hell out of here." Third Officer Pitman takes charge of No. 5; as he swings into the boat Murdock grasps his hand. "Good-by and good luck, old man."

No. 6 goes over the side. There are only twenty-eight people in a lifeboat with a capacity of sixty-five.

A light stabs from the bridge; Boxhall is calling in Morse flashes, again and again,   60
to a strange ship stopped in the ice jam five to ten miles away. Another rocket drops its shower of sparks above the ice-strewn sea and the dying ship.

1:00 A.M. Slowly the water creeps higher; the fore ports of the *Titanic* are dipping into the sea. Rope squeaks through blocks; lifeboats drop jerkily seaward. Through the shouting on the decks comes the sound of the band playing ragtime.

The "Millionaires' Special" leaves the ship—boat No. 1, with a capacity of forty people, carries only Sir Cosmo and Lady Duff Gordon and ten others. Aft, the frightened immigrants mill and jostle and rush for a boat. An officer's fist flies out; three shots are fired into the air, and the panic is quelled. . . . Four Chinese sneak unseen into a boat and hide in its bottom.

1:20 A.M. Water is coming into No. 4 boiler room. Stokers slice and shovel as water laps about their ankles—steam for the dynamos, steam for the dancing spark! As the water rises, great ash hoes rake the flaming coals from the furnaces. Safety valves pop; the stokers retreat aft, and the watertight doors clang shut behind them.

The rockets fling their spendor toward the stars. The boats are more heavily loaded now, for the passengers know the *Titanic* is sinking. Women cling and sob. The great screws aft are rising clear of the sea. Half-filled boats are ordered to come alongside the cargo ports and take on more passengers, but the ports are never opened—and the boats are never filled. Others pull for the steamer's light miles away but never reach it; the light disappears, the unknown ship steams off.

The water rises and the band plays ragtime.   65

1:30 A.M. Lightoller is getting the port boats off; Murdock the starboard. As one boat is lowered into the sea a boat officer fires his gun along the ship's side to stop a rush from the lower decks. A woman tries to take her great Dane into a boat with her; she is refused and steps out of the boat to die with her dog. Millet's "little smile which played on his lips all through the voyage" plays no more; his lips are grim, but he waves good-by and brings wraps for the women.

Benjamin Guggenheim, in evening clothes, smiles and says, "We've dressed up in our best and are prepared to go down like gentlemen."

1:40 A.M. Boat 14 is clear, and then 13, 16, 15, and C. The lights still shine, but the *Baltic* hears the blue spark say, "Engine room getting flooded."

The *Olympic* signals, "Am lighting up all possible boilers as fast as can."

Major Butt helps women into the last boats and waves good-by to them. Mrs. 70
Straus puts her foot on the gunwale of a lifeboat, then she draws back and goes to her
husband: "We have been together many years; where you go I will go." Colonel John
Jacob Astor puts his young wife in a lifeboat, steps back, taps cigarette on fingernail:
"Good-by, dearie; I'll join you later."

1:45 A.M. The foredeck is under water, the fo'c'sle head almost awash; the great
stern is lifted high toward the bright stars; and still the band plays. Mr. and Mrs. Harris approach a lifeboat arm in arm.

Officer: "Ladies first, please."

Harris bows, smiles, steps back: "Of course, certainly; ladies first."

Boxhall fires the last rocket, then leaves in charge of boat No. 2.

2:00 A.M. She is dying now; her bow goes deeper, her stern higher. But there must 75
be steam. Below in the stokeholds the sweaty firemen keep steam up for the flaring
lights and the dancing spark. The glowing coals slide and tumble over the slanted grate
bars; the sea pounds behind that yielding bulkhead. But the spark dances on.

The *Asian* hears Phillips try the new signal—SOS.

Boat No. 4 has left now; boat D leaves ten minutes later. Jacques Futrelle clasps
his wife: "For God's sake, go! It's your last chance; go!" Madame Futrelle is half forced
into the boat. It clears the side.

There are about 660 people in the boats, and 1,500 still on the sinking *Titanic*.

On top of the officers' quarters men work frantically to get the two collapsibles
stowed there over the side. Water is over the forward part of A deck now; it surges up
the companionways toward the boat deck. In the radio shack, Bride has slipped a coat
and lifejacket about Phillips as the first operator sits hunched over his key, sending—
still sending—"41–46 N.; 50–14 W. CQD—CQD—SOS—SOS—"

The Captain's tired white face appears at the radio-room door: "Men, you have 80
done your full duty. You can do no more. Now, it's every man for himself." The Captain disappears—back to his sinking bridge, where Painter, his personal steward, stands
quietly waiting for orders. The spark dances on. Bride turns his back and goes into the
inner cabin. As he does so, a stoker, grimed with coal, mad with fear, steals into the
shack and reaches for the lifejacket on Phillips' back. Bride wheels about and brains
him with a wrench.

2:10 A.M. Below decks the steam is still holding, though the pressure is falling—
rapidly. In the gymnasium on the boat deck the athletic instructor watches quietly as
two gentlemen ride the bicycles and another swings casually at the punching bag. Mail
clerks stagger up the boat-deck stairways, dragging soaked mail sacks. The spark still
dances. The band still plays—but not ragtime:

> Nearer my God to Thee,
>   Nearer to Thee . . .

A few men take up the refrain; others kneel on the slanting decks to pray. Many
run and scramble aft, where hundreds are clinging above the silent screws on the great
uptilted stern. The spark still dances and the lights still flare; the engineers are on the
job. The hymn comes to its close. Bandmaster Hartley, Yorkshireman violinist, taps
his bow against a bulkhead, calls for "Autumn" as the water curls about his feet, and

the eight musicians brace themselves against the ship's slant. People are leaping from the decks into the nearby water—the icy water. A woman cries, "Oh, save me, save me!" A man answers, "Good lady, save yourself. Only God can save you now." The band plays "Autumn":

> God of Mercy and Compassion!
>   Look with pity on my pain . . .

The water creeps over the bridge where the *Titanic*'s master stands; heavily he steps out to meet it.

2:17 A.M. "CQ—" The *Virginian* hears a ragged, blurred CQ, then an abrupt stop. The blue spark dances no more. The lights flicker out; the engineers have lost their battle.

2:18 A.M. Men run about blackened decks; leap into the night; are swept into the sea by the curling wave which licks up the *Titanic*'s length. Lightoller does not leave the ship; the ship leaves him; there are hundreds like him, but only a few who live to tell of it. The funnels still swim above the water, but the ship is climbing to the perpendicular; the bridge is under and most of the foremast; the great stern rises like a squat leviathan. Men swim away from the sinking ship; others drop from the stern. 85

The band plays in the darkness, the water lapping upwards:

> Hold me up in mighty waters,
> Keep my eyes on things above,
> Righteousness, divine atonement,
> Peace and everlas . . .

The forward funnel snaps and crashes into the sea; its steel tons hammer out of existence swimmers struggling in the freezing water. Streams of sparks, of smoke and steam, burst from the after funnels. The ship upends to fifty—to sixty degrees.

Down in the black abyss of the stokeholds, of the engine rooms, where the dynamos have whirred at long last to a stop, the stokers and the engineers are reeling against hot metal, the rising water clutching at their knees. The boilers, the engine cylinders, rip from their bed plates: crash through bulkheads; rumble—steel against steel.

The *Titanic* stands on end, poised briefly for the plunge. Slowly she slides to her grave—slowly at first, and then more quickly—quickly—quickly.

2:20 A.M. The greatest ship in the world has sunk. From the calm, dark waters where the floating lifeboats move, there goes up, in the white wake of her passing, "one long continuous moan." 90

The boats that the *Titanic* had launched pulled safely away from the slight suction of the sinking ship, pulled away from the screams that came from the lips of the freezing men and women in the water. The boats were poorly manned and badly equipped, and they had been unevenly loaded. Some carried so few seamen that women bent to the oars. Mrs. Astor tugged at an oar handle; the Countess of Rothes took a tiller. Shivering stokers in sweaty, coal-blackened singlets and light trousers steered in some boats; stewards in white coats rowed in others. Ismay was in the last boat that left the ship from the starboard side; with Mr. Carter of Philadelphia and two seamen he tugged at the oars. In one of the lifeboats an Italian with a broken wrist—disguised in a woman's shawl and hat—huddled on the floor boards, ashamed now that fear had left him. In another rode the only baggage saved from the *Titanic*—the carry-all of Samuel L. Goldenberg, one of the rescued passengers.

There were only a few boats that were heavily loaded; most of those that were half empty made but perfunctory efforts to pick up the moaning swimmers, their officers and crew fearing that they would endanger the living if they pulled back into the midst of the dying. Some boats beat off the freezing victims; fear-crazed men and women struck with oars at the heads of swimmers. One woman drove her fist into the face of a half-dead man as he tried feebly to climb over the gunwale. Two other women helped him in and stanched the flow of blood from the ring cuts on his face.

One of the collapsible boats, which had floated off the top of the officers' quarters when the *Titanic* sank, was an icy haven for thirty or forty men. The boat had capsized as the ship sank; men swam to it, clung to it, climbed upon its slippery bottom, stood knee-deep in water in the freezing air. Chunks of ice swirled about their legs; their soaked clothing clutched their bodies in icy folds. Colonel Archibald Gracie was cast up there, Gracie who had leaped from the stern as the *Titanic* sank; young Thayer who had seen his father die; Lightoller who had twice been sucked down with the ship and twice blown to the surface by a belch of air; Bride, the second operator, and Phillips, the first. There were many stokers, half-naked; it was a shivering company. They stood there in the icy sea, under the far stars, and sang and prayed—the Lord's Prayer. After a while a lifeboat came and picked them off, but Phillips was dead then or died soon afterward in the boat.

Only a few of the boats had lights; only one—No. 2—had a light that was of any use to the *Carpathia,* twisting through the ice field to the rescue. Other ships were "coming hard" too; one, the *Californian,* was still dead to opportunity.

The blue sparks still danced, but not the *Titanic*'s. *Le Provence* to *Celtic:* "Nobody has heard the *Titanic* for about two hours." 95

It was 2:40 when the *Carpathia* first sighted the green light from No. 2 boat; it was 4:10 when she picked up the first boat and learned that the *Titanic* had foundered. The last of the moaning cries had just died away then.

Captain Rostron took the survivors aboard, boatload by boatload. He was ready for them, but only a small minority of them required much medical attention. Bride's feet were twisted and frozen; others were suffering from exposure; one died, and seven were dead when taken from the boats, and were buried at sea.

It was then that the fleet of racing ships learned they were too late; the *Parisian* heard the weak signals of MPA, the *Carpathia,* report the death of the *Titanic.* It was then—or soon afterward, when her radio operator put on his earphones—that the *Californian,* the ship that had been within sight as the *Titanic* was sinking, first learned of the disaster.

And it was then, in all its white-green majesty, that the *Titanic*'s survivors saw the iceberg, tinted with the sunrise, floating idly, pack ice jammed about its base, other bergs heaving slowly near by on the blue breast of the sea.

Questions for Discussion and Writing

1. In what way is the encounter between the iceberg and the *Titanic* described in ways that underscore the many ironies involved, including the naming of the ship, the handling of radio messages, and the experiences of those on board? How does Baldwin's account suggest the modern-day equivalent of a Greek tragedy, whose heroes, through a combination of fate and their tragic flaws, brought catastrophes on themselves?

2. Analyze Baldwin's narrative technique. For example, what is the effect of the considerable statistical data he provides? How effectively does he reveal the character of individual passengers and crew?

3. The sinking of the *Titantic* has assumed the dimensions of a modern-day myth and has been the subject of a number of films, including the Academy Award–winning 1997 movie and a Broadway musical. Analyze one or several of these in relationship to Baldwin's account, and discuss the subtle and not-so-subtle shifts in emphasis that are evident in these dramatizations.

Maurizio Chierici

* *

Maurizio Chierici is an Italian journalist who worked as a special correspondent for the Milan newspaper Corriere della Sera. *"The Man from Hiroshima," translated from the Italian by Wallis Wilde-Menozzi, first appeared in* Granta *in 1987. At the time Chierici interviewed him, Claude Eatherly was the only American pilot still alive who could provide a firsthand account, and some historical perspective, on the mission over Hiroshima that resulted in the dropping of the atomic bomb. Eatherly was the lead pilot who had to decide if weather conditions permitted the bomb to be dropped. Chierci discovered that Eatherly, who was a much decorated, well-respected pilot, had been irrevocably changed by this event and was tormented by guilt. Fourteen months after this interview, Eatherly committed suicide. The following interview offers an unparalled insight into the meaning of Hiroshima from the perspective of an American pilot who was part of the crew responsible for dropping the atomic bomb.*

THE MAN FROM HIROSHIMA

The protagonists of Hiroshima have no nostalgia. Even those people only remotely connected with the event have had difficult lives. All except one: Colonel Paul Tibbets, pilot of the *Enola Gay,* the plane that carried the atom bomb. On TV, serene under his white locks, he was unrepentant: 'I did my duty: I would do it again.' Tibbets is the only one to have passed these years without so much as a shiver. One of the pilots in the formation which flew over Hiroshima that day was unable to participate in the victory celebrations; he took his life three days before the official ceremony.

I knew another pilot full of problems; it wasn't at all easy to arrange to meet him. Everyone said: 'You'll need patience. But if he gave you his word, you'll hear from him sooner or later.' For days I waited and no one came. Then the pilot called to apologize.

There was fog at the airport: the plane couldn't take off. Or: he had no money and the banks were closed. He would buy the ticket tomorrow. Tomorrow came and went; there was always a different story. Eventually I made a proposal: 'Eatherly, in five days it will be Christmas. I want to be back home in Italy before then. So I'll come to see you. It's much warmer where you are than in New York, and I've never been to Texas. I'll leave this afternoon.'

'No, stay where you are,' Eatherly interrupted. 'It's hard to talk here. Being in Texas blocks me; the people inhibit me. They know me too well, and there's no love lost between us. I plan to spend the holidays in New Jersey with a friend—I'd go out of my mind staying in Waco for Christmas—so I'll come and see you.'

I waited. Hours and hours in the lobby of the Hotel St Moritz, Central Park south. Behind windows the city is grey. Great lighted clocks scan the seconds at the tops of skyscrapers. Soon it will start to snow. People rush past who have come to New York on business, and who are going home laden with presents in coloured packages, their ribbons fluttering to the ground. In this festive atmosphere I find it strange to be meeting a man who contributed to the deaths of 60,000 people and turned their city into a monument for all time.

Three hours later the man sits down on the other side of the table, a glass in his   5 hands. He is thin; his eyes are deeply marked, making his glance look old. But his hands are calm. When we shook hands I could feel they were cold and dry. He speaks first.

'How do I look?'

'I couldn't say. I've only seen your photographs. In them you seem older. And more tired and down on your luck.'

'I'm not old, or tired; only tormented. But not all the time. They have taken care of my nightmares. Right there in Waco; a doctor by the name of Parker. Grey-haired man; thin. It was heavy treatment. I don't know if their methods have changed, but the one they used with me was useless. "Give it up, Claude," Parker said, "you're not guilty. It just fell to you to pilot a plane over Hiroshima. How many other Claudes were there in the air force who would have carried out an order as important as that one? The war finished; they went home. And what was the order anyway? Look at the sky and say: *Too many clouds here. Can't see Kokura and Nagasaki. Better do Hiroshima.*" Every day for fourteen months Doctor Parker gave me more or less the same speech. In the end I had to ask not to see him any more. I'd got worse.'

'There are a lot of stories, Mr. Eatherly. Some people say you're a fake. Why?'

He doesn't answer immediately. Instead he asks if he can take advantage of my   10 hospitality: would I have another drink with him? I wouldn't like to give the impression that Eatherly was an alcoholic. He could hold a bottle of whisky without any trouble and his eyes never clouded over. They remained alert and cold, just as they had been when he entered, bringing in a little of the wind from the city.

'You mean what Will Bradfort Huie wrote? He's a journalist who spent two days with me and then wrote a book—a whole book—about my life. Who am I? I don't know. But no one can describe himself in a minute. If I asked you point blank: "Do you think of yourself as an honest person, or someone who works at giving others an impression to suit your own needs?" would you be able to demonstrate either in a minute? I doubt it. I didn't know how to answer him either.'

'Are you a pacifist as you've claimed for years?'

'I am, and sincerely so, as is any American of good will. If I were religious, I would say that pacifism springs from a Jewish or Christian consciousness, but I'm not religious, and I don't want to look a fool expounding my philosophy. I can't be religious after Hiroshima. When someone makes a trip like mine and returns alive, he either kills himself or he lives like a Trappist monk. Cloistered; praying that the world changes and that the likes of Claude Eatherly and Paul Tibbets and the scientists who worked on the bomb are never born again.'

Claude grew up in Texas, where discourse is uninformed by Edwardian whispers from New England. Hearty laughter and loud voices; every sensation seems amplified. After the Japanese bombed Pearl Harbor, Texas offered more volunteers than any other state—the yellow devils had to be punished. Eatherly was among the volunteers. The youngest of six children, and a tackle on the Texas North College football team, he had a level head and a solid way of bringing them down. He didn't miss in the air either: he shot down thirty-three planes and his career took off. After three years he became a major, and a brilliant future seemed to await the handsome man with two bravery medals on his chest. The medals were what dug his grave. In the summer of 1945, he got orders to return home, but first he had to carry out one more mission. Just one.

You don't send a soldier home for the pleasure of giving him a little of the good   15 life. In the letter he posted to his mother announcing his imminent return, Claude wrote. 'This will be the last cigarette they stick in this prisoner's mouth.' Nothing to get worried about. He went to New Mexico and joined a formation of supermen: the best, bravest, most famous pilots, all being trained in secret. They assigned him to a Boeing B-29 Superfortress that Claude christened *Straight Flush*.

The account of that morning some weeks later belongs to history. Three planes take off during the night of 6 August from Tinian in the Mariana Islands. Paul Tibbets is the group's commander. Eatherly opens the formation. There are no bombs in his plane; as for the others, no one suspects what a terrible device is hidden inside the *Enola Gay*. A bigger contrivance, they think, nothing more. Eatherly's job is to pinpoint the target with maximum accuracy. He must establish whether weather conditions allow for the centre to be Hiroshima, Kokura or Nagasaki, or whether they should continue towards secondary targets. He tells the story of that morning's events in a voice devoid of emotion which suggests that the recitation is the thousandth one.

'I had command of the lead plane, the *Straight Flush*. I flew over Hiroshima for fifteen minutes, studying the clouds covering the target—a bridge between the military zone and the city. Fifteen Japanese fighters were circling beneath me, but they're not made to fly above 29,000 feet where we were to be found. I looked up: cumulus clouds at 10,000, 12,000 metres. The wind was blowing them towards Hiroshima. Perfect weather. I could see the target clearly: the central span of the bridge. I laugh now when I think of the order: "I want only the central arch of the bridge, *only* that, you under-stand?" Even if I'd guessed that we were carrying something a bit special, the houses, the roads, the city still seemed very far away from our bomb. I said to myself: This morning's just a big scare for the Japanese.

'I transmitted the coded message, but the person who aimed the bomb made an error of 3,000 feet. Towards the city, naturally. But three thousand feet one way or the other wouldn't have made much difference: that what I thought as I watched it drop.

Then the explosion stunned me momentarily. Hiroshima disappeared under a yellow cloud. No one spoke after that. Usually when you return from a mission with everyone still alive, you exchange messages with each other, impressions, congratulations. This time the radios stayed silent; three planes close together and mute. Not for fear of the enemy, but for fear of our own words. Each one of us must have asked forgiveness for the bomb. I'm not religious and I didn't know who to ask forgiveness from, but in that moment I made a promise to myself to oppose all bombs and all wars. Never again that yellow cloud . . .'

Eatherly raises his voice. It is clear the yellow cloud accompanies him through his life. 'And what did Tibbets say?'

Tibbets has nerves of steel, but the evening afterwards he explained how he spent those minutes. They had told him to be extremely careful: he was most at risk. So when the machine gunner yelled that the shock waves were on their way, he veered to take photographs; but the aeroplane just bounced like a ping-pong ball held up by a fountain. Calm returned and Tibbets felt tired; he asked to be relieved, and fell asleep. But he talked about it that evening when the number of victims was just beginning to be known. He kept on saying: "I'm sorry guys, I did my duty. I've no regrets." And I don't have his nerves. A year later I asked to be discharged.'

'What reason did you give?'

'Exhaustion. I was exhausted. And I wanted to get married. It's risky to bring matters of conscience into it when you're in the forces. They were astounded—how could I throw away such a promising future? The day of my discharge they waved a sheet of paper in front of me. It said I would receive 237 dollars a month pension. That was good money in those days, but I turned it down. And since the regulations didn't allow me to refuse, I put it in writing that the sum was to go to war widows. The end of my relationship with flying.'

He didn't tell the rest of the story willingly. He returns to Texas where his family doesn't recognize him: thin, nervous, irascible, 24 years old. He marries the Italian girl he met in New Mexico while he was training for the final mission. Concetta Margetti had tried Hollywood and finally been reduced to selling cigarettes in a local nightclub—not perhaps the ideal wife for someone in Claude's state. But they write to each other, they get married. A war story, yes; but the war had shredded Eatherly's nerves. In the middle of the night he wakes his wife, breathless and in tears: 'Hit the ground, the yellow cloud's coming!' It goes on like this for four years. His family finally convince him to enter the psychiatric hospital in Waco as a voluntary patient. He can take walks in the park any time of the day or night. He plays golf and receives visitors. Concetta keeps him company on Sunday. His brother brings him books and a pair of running shoes.

Then the problems start. Claude forges a cheque to send to the victims of Hiroshima. He enters a bank with a toy pistol; for a few minutes the employees are terrified until Eatherly bursts out laughing. One day his move succeeds; he threatens a department store clerk with a fake gun and makes her turn over the money, which he throws from a balcony before escaping. They catch him and take him back to Waco. He's no longer a voluntary patient: now they lock him in. They accuse him of behaving in an antisocial way. (This euphemism is the last show of respect for his heroic war record.) He is confined to his room.

20

25

After fourteen months in the mental hospital he leaves, a ghost. His wife abandons him. His brother closes his bank account. Claude cannot look after himself or his money. And now the protest smoulders again. He enters a bar in Texas, armed. He threatens the people inside and gets them to put their money into the sack he is holding, just like he's seen in films. But it comes to nothing. He is handcuffed and taken to gaol in a police car. The sergeant accompanying him doesn't know who he is, only that he's an ex-pilot. I asked Eatherly how it felt to be facing a prison sentence for the first time.

I should say terrible, but it wasn't. Nothing mattered to me. I'd been in prison all the time; the door was inside me. In the police car the sergeant was staring at me. He was curious. He was thinking about some famous criminal. . . . It was a long trip. I was quiet, but his staring eyes bothered me. "Where do you come from, sergeant?" I asked him. "From Chicago." And I: "I knew you came from somewhere." I wanted to un-freeze the atmosphere, but he wasn't having it. He asked me: "It's not strictly legal, but can you talk, here in the car?" I made a yes sign.

"Where are you from?"

"From here."

"Where were you based during the war?"   30

"In the Pacific."

"I was in the Pacific too. Where did they land you?"

"Tinian, in the Marianas, special group 509."

He looked at me, stunned. "I know who you are. You're Major Eatherly! Good God, Major, how did you end up like this? You're sick, right? I read that somewhere. I'll give you a hand."

'Then they locked me up in the loony bin again.'   35

His torment went on: a poor soul, incapable of getting on with the business of life. No one understands his drama. People's aversion to him grows. Let's not forget that Eatherly lived out this difficult period in the America of Senator McCarthy—the Grand Inquisitor of frustrated nationalism. McCarthy formented a type of suspicion which reflected the cold war: the witch hunt. Eatherly becomes a witch. His passionate, if slightly naïve, criticism of the mechanisms of war is considered a threat to national security. The judges disagree over his case. The biography confected by William Bradfort Huie from less than two days of interviews weakens his defence. For Bradfort, the Major 'never saw the ball of fire, nor was he aware of the yellow wave. By the time of the explosion, he and his gunner were 100 kilometres from the site.' Returning to base he was surprised by the journalists and photographers crowding the runway where the *Enola Gay* had landed. 'If Eatherly is mad,' writes Bradfort, 'then his madness was hatched on 6 August, 1945, not from horror but from jealousy.'

'When I knew him,' Bradfort Huie continues implacably, 'he was already a fraud. Right off he asked me for five hundred dollars. He had never once attempted suicide. I spent a long time with him, and I looked at his wrists: there were no scars.'

'Is that true Claude?'

'These are not the kind of things you want to brag about. Look at my arms.' He turns up the sleeves of his jacket and unbuttons his cuffs. Two purple scars, deep and unpleasant, run towards his hands. 'I don't want you to pity me. I'm happy to have been able to talk. Now I've got to go.'

He disappeared as he had appeared, with the same suddenness. Before passing 40 through the bar door and turning out into the hall he looked back, as if he had forgotten something. 'I want to apologize for being late. And thanks for these . . .' He gestured towards the row of glasses on the table.

'It was my pleasure to meet you. Merry Christmas.'

Fourteen months later Claude Eatherly took his life.

Questions for Discussion and Writing

1. How did Claude Eatherly's decision regarding the weather conditions over Japan, on the day the atomic bomb was dropped, irrevocably alter his life?
2. What means does Chierici use, as an interviewer, to put Eatherly's story into a context that would allow the reader to understand how Eatherly's guilt took over his life?
3. Conduct an interview with someone who was involved in a momentous event, and write up your results in order to allow your readers to understand the effect this event had on the person's life.

Haunani-Kay Trask

. . . .

Haunani-Kay Trask (b. 1949), an activist, author, and poet, is a professor of Hawaiian Studies at the University of Hawai'i at Manoa. She received her Ph.D. in political science from the University of Wisconsin at Madison. The following essay originally appeared in From a Native Daughter: Colonialism and Sovereignty in Hawai'i *(1999). The essay is an impassioned argument against the abuse of Native Hawaiian rights caused by rampant tourism.*

FROM A NATIVE DAUGHTER

I am certain that most, if not all, Americans have heard of Hawai'i and have wished, at some time in their lives, to visit my Native land. But I doubt that the history of how Hawai'i came to be territorially incorporated, and economically, politically, and culturally subordinated to the United States is known to most Americans. Nor is it common knowledge that Hawaiians have been struggling for over twenty years to achieve a land base and some form of political sovereignty on the same level as American Indians. Finally, I would imagine that most Americans could not place Hawai'i or any other Pacific island on a map of the Pacific. But despite all this appalling ignorance, five million Americans will vacation in my homeland this year *and* the next, and so on, into the foreseeable capitalist future. Such are the intended privileges of the so-called American standard of living ignorance of and yet power over one's relations to Native peoples. Thanks to postwar American imperialism, the ideology that the United States has no overseas colonies and is, in fact, the champion of self-determination the world over holds no greater sway than in the United States itself. To most Americans, then, Hawai'i is *theirs:* to use, to take, and, above all, to fantasize about long after the experience.

Just five hours away by plane from California, Hawai'i is a thousand light years away in fantasy. Mostly a state of mind, Hawai'i is the image of escape from the rawness and violence of daily American life. Hawaii—the word, the vision, the sound in the mind—is the fragrance and feel of soft kindness. Above all, Hawai'i is "she," the Western image of the Native "female" in her magical allure. And if luck prevails, some of "her" will rub off on you, the visitor.

This fictional Hawai'i comes out of the depths of Western sexual sickness that demands a dark, sin-free Native for instant gratification between imperialist wars. The attraction of Hawai'i is stimulated by slick Hollywood movies, saccharine Andy Williams music, and the constant psychological deprivations of maniacal American life. Tourists flock to my Native land for escape, but they are escaping into a state of mind while participating in the destruction of a host people in a Native place.

To Hawaiians, daily life is neither soft nor kind. In fact, the political, economic, and cultural reality for most Hawaiians is hard, ugly, and cruel.

In Hawai'i, the destruction of our land and the prostitution of our culture is planned   5
and executed by multinational corporations (both foreign-based and Hawai'i-based), by huge landowners (such as the missionary-descended Castle & Cook of Dole Pineapple fame), and by collaborationist state and county governments. The ideological gloss that claims tourism to be our economic savior and the "natural" result of Hawaiian culture is manufactured by ad agencies (such as the state-supported Hawai'i Visitors Bureau) and tour companies (many of which are owned by the airlines) and spewed out to the public through complicitous cultural engines such as film, television and radio, and the daily newspaper. As for the local labor unions, both rank and file and management clamor for more tourists, while the construction industry lobbies incessantly for larger resorts.

The major public educational institution, the University of Hawai'i, funnels millions of taxpayer dollars into a School of Travel Industry Management and a business school replete with a Real Estate Center and a Chair of Free Enterprise (renamed the Walker Chair to hide the crude reality of capitalism). As the propaganda arm of the tourist industry in Hawai'i, both schools churn out studies that purport to show why Hawai'i needs more golf courses, hotels, and tourist infrastructure and how Hawaiian culture is "naturally" one of giving and entertaining.

Of course, state-encouraged commodification and prostitution of Native cultures through tourism is not unique to Hawai'i. It is suffered by peoples in places as disparate as Goa, Australia, Tahiti, and the southwestern United States. Indeed, the problem is so commonplace that international organizations—for example, the Ecumenical Coalition on Third World Tourism out of Bangkok, the Center for Responsible Tourism in California, and the Third World European Network—have banded together to help give voice to Native peoples in daily resistance against corporate tourism. My focus on Hawai'i, although specific to my own culture, would likely transfer well when applied to most Native peoples.

Despite our similarities with other major tourist destinations, the statistical picture of the effects of corporate tourism in Hawai'i is shocking:

Fact: Nearly forty years ago, at statehood, Hawai'i residents outnumbered tourists by more than 2 to 1. Today, tourists outnumber residents by 6 to 1; they outnumber Native Hawaiians by 30 to 1.[1]

Fact: According to independent economists and criminologists, "tourism has been the single most powerful factor in O'ahu's crime rate," including crimes against people and property.[2]

Fact: Independent demographers have been pointing out for years that "tourism is the major source of population growth in Hawai'i" and that "rapid growth of the tourist industry ensures the trend toward a rapidly expanded population that receives lower per capita income."[3]

Fact: The Bank of Hawai'i has reported that the average real incomes of Hawai'i residents grew only *one* percent during the period from the early seventies through the early eighties, when tourism was booming. The same held true throughout the nineties. The census bureau reports that personal income growth in Hawai'i during the same time was the lowest by far of any of the fifty American states.[4]

Fact: Groundwater supplies on O'ahu will be insufficient to meet the needs of residents and tourists by the year 2000.[5]

Fact: According to the *Honolulu Advertiser*, "Japanese investors have spent more than $7.1 billion on their acquisitions" since 1986 in Hawai'i. This kind of volume translates into huge alienations of land and properties. For example, nearly 2,000 acres of land on the Big Island of Hawai'i was purchased for $18.5 million and over 7,000 acres on Moloka'i went for $33 million. In 1989, over $1 billion was spent by the Japanese on land alone.[6]

Fact: More plants and animals from our Hawaiian Islands are now extinct or on the endangered species list than in the rest of the United States.[7]

Fact: More than 29,000 families are on the Hawaiian trust lands list, waiting for housing, pastoral, or agricultural lots.[8]

Fact: The median cost of a home on the most populated island of O'ahu is around $350,000.[9]

---

[1]Eleanor C. Nordyke, *The Peopling of Hawai'i*, 2nd ed. (Honolulu: University of Hawai'i Press, 1989), *pp. 134–172*. [2]Meda Chesney-Lind, "Salient Factors in Hawai'i's Crime Rate," University of Hawai'i School of Social Work. Available from author. [3]Nordyke, *The Peopling of Hawai'i*, pp. 134–172. [4]Bank of Hawai'i Annual Economic Report, *1984*. [5]Estimate of independent hydrologist Kate Vandemoer to community organizing group *Kupa'a He'eia*, February 1990. Water quality and groundwater depletion are two problems much discussed by state and county officials in Hawai'i but ignored when resort permits are considered. [6]*The Honolulu Advertiser*, April 8, 1990. [7]David Stannard, Testimony against West Beach Estates. Land Use Commission, State of Hawaii, January 10, 1985. [8]Department of Hawaiian Home Lands, phone interview, March *1998*. [9]*Honolulu Star-Bulletin*, May 8, 1990.

Fact: Hawai'i has by far the worst ratio of average family income to average housing costs in the country. This explains why families spend nearly 52 percent of their gross income for housing costs.[10]

Fact: Nearly one-fifth of Hawai'i's resident population is classified as *near-homeless,* that is, those for whom any mishap results in immediate on-the-street homelessness.[11]

These kinds of statistics render a very bleak picture, not at all what the posters and jingoistic promoters would have you believe about Hawai'i.

My use of the word *tourism* in the Hawai'i context refers to a mass-based, corporately controlled industry that is both vertically and horizontally integrated such that one multinational corporation owns an airline and the tour buses that transport tourists to the corporation-owned hotel where they eat in a corporation-owned restaurant, play golf, and "experience" Hawai'i on corporation-owned recreation areas and eventually consider buying a second home built on corporation land. Profits, in this case, are mostly repatriated back to the home country. In Hawai'i, these "home" countries are Japan, Taiwan, Hong Kong, Canada, Australia, and the United States. In this sense, Hawai'i is very much like a Third World colony where the local elite—the Democratic Party in our state—collaborate in the rape of Native land and people.[12]

The mass nature of this kind of tourism results in megaresort complexes on thousands of acres with demands for water and services that far surpass the needs of Hawai'i residents. These complexes may boast several hotels, golf courses, restaurants, and other "necessaries" to complete the total tourist experience. Infrastructure is usually built by the developer in exchange for county approval of more hotel units. In Hawai'i, counties bid against each other to attract larger and larger complexes. "Rich" counties, then, are those with more resorts, since they will pay more of the tax base of the county. The richest of these is the City and County of Honolulu, which encompasses the entire island of O'ahu. This island is the site of four major tourist destinations, a major international airport, and 80 percent of the resident population of Hawai'i. The military also controls nearly 30 percent of the island, with bases and airports of their own. As you might imagine, the density of certain parts of Honolulu (e.g., Waikīkī) is among the highest in the world. At the present annual visitor count, more than five million tourists pour through O'ahu, an island of only 607 square miles.

With this as a background on tourism, I want to move now into the area of cultural prostitution. *Prostitution* in this context refers to the entire institution that

10

---

[10]Bank of Hawai'i Annual Economic Report, 1984. In 1992, families probably spent closer to 60 percent of their gross income for housing costs. Billion-dollar Japanese investments and other speculation since 1984 have caused rental and purchase prices to skyrocket.   [11]This is the estimate of a state-contracted firm that surveyed the islands for homeless and near-homeless families. Testimony was delivered to the state legislature, 1990 session.   [12]For an analysis of post-statehood Hawai'i and its turn to mass-based corporate tourism, see Noel Kent, *Hawai'i: Islands Under the Influence.* For an analysis of foreign investment in Hawai'i, see *A Study of Foreign Investment and Its Impact on the State* (Honolulu: Hawai'i Real Estate Center, University of Hawaii, 1989).

defines a woman (and by extension the *female*) as an object of degraded and victimized sexual value for use and exchange through the medium of money. The *prostitute* is a woman who sells her sexual capacities and is seen, thereby, to possess and reproduce them at will, that is, by her very "nature." The prostitute and the institution that creates and maintains her are, of course, of patriarchal origin. The pimp is the conduit of exchange, managing the commodity that is the prostitute while acting as the guard at the entry and exit gates, making sure the prostitute behaves as a prostitute by fulfilling her sexual-economic functions. The victims participate in their victimization with enormous ranges of feeling, from resistance to complicity, but the force and continuity of the institution are shaped by men.

There is much more to prostitution than my sketch reveals but this must suffice, for I am interested in using the largest sense of this term as a metaphor in understanding what has happened to Hawaiian culture. My purpose is not to exact detail or fashion a model but to convey the utter degradation of our culture and our people under corporate tourism by employing *prostitution* as an analytic category.

Finally, I have chosen four areas of Hawaiian culture to examine: our homeland, our *one hānau* that is Hawai'i, our lands and fisheries, the outlying seas and the heavens; our language and dance; our familial relationships; and our women.

The *mo'olelo,* or history of Hawaiians, is to be found in our genealogies. From   15 our great cosmogonic genealogy, the *kumulipo,* derives the Hawaiian identity. The "essential lesson" of this genealogy is "the interrelatedness of the Hawaiian world, and the inseparability of its constituents parts." Thus, "the genealogy of the land, the gods, chiefs, and people intertwine one with the other, and with all aspects of the universe."[13]

In the *mo'olelo* of Papa and W,kea, "earth mother" and "sky father," our islands were born: Hawai'i, Maui, O'ahu, Kaua'i, and Ni'ihau. From their human offspring came the *taro* plant and from the *taro* came the Hawaiian people. The lessons of our genealogy are that human beings have a familial relationship to land and to the *taro,* our elder siblings or *kua'ana.*

In Hawai'i, as in all of Polynesia, younger siblings must serve and honor elder siblings who, in turn, must feed and care for their younger siblings. Therefore, Hawaiians must cultivate and husband the land that will feed and provide for the Hawaiian people. This relationship of people to land is called *mālama 'āina* or *aloha 'āina,* "care and love of the land."

When people and land work together harmoniously, the balance that results is called *pono.* In Hawaiian society, the *ali'i,* or "chiefs," were required to maintain order, an abundance of food, and good government. The *maka'āinana* or "common people," worked the land and fed the chiefs; the *ali'i* organized production and appeased the gods.

Today, *mālama'āina* is called *stewardship* by some, although that word does not convey spiritual and genealogical connections. Nevertheless, to love and make the land flourish is a Hawaiian value. *'Āina, one* of the words for "land," means "that which

---

[13]Lilikala Kame'eleihiwa, *Native Land and Foreign Desires* (Honolulu: Bishop Museum Press, 1992), p. 2.

feeds." *Kama'āina,* a term for native-born people, means "child of the land.' " Thus is the Hawaiian relationship to land both familial and reciprocal.

Hawaiian deities also spring from the land: Pele is our volcano, Kāne and Lono, 20 our fertile valleys and plains, Kanaloa our ocean and all that lives within it, and so on with the numerous gods of Hawai'i. Our whole universe, physical and metaphysical, is divine.

Within this world, the older people, or *kūpuna,* are to cherish those who are younger, the *mo'opuna.* Unstinting generosity is a prized value. Social connections between our people are through *aloha,* simply translated as "love" but carrying with it a profoundly Hawaiian sense that is, again, familial and genealogical. Hawaiians feel *aloha* for Hawai'i from whence they come and for their Hawaiian kin upon whom they depend. It is nearly impossible to feel or practice *aloha* for something that is not familial. This is why we extend familial relations to those few non-Natives whom we feel understand and can reciprocate our *aloha.* But *aloha* is freely given and freely returned; it is not and cannot be demanded or commanded. Above all, *aloha* is a cultural feeling and practice that works among the people and between the people and their land.

The significance and meaning of *aloha* underscores the centrality of the Hawaiian language or *'ōlelo,* to the culture. *'Olelo* means both "language" and "tongue;" *mo'olelo,* or "history," is that which comes from the tongue, that is, "a story." *Haole,* or white people, say that we have oral history, but what we have are stories, such as our creation story, passed on through the generations. This sense of history is different from the *haole* sense of history. To Hawaiians in traditional society, language had tremendous power, thus the phrase, *i ka 'ōlelo ke ola; i ka 'ōlelo ka make*—"in language is life, in language is death."

After nearly two thousand years of speaking Hawaiian, our people suffered the near extinction of our language through its banning by the American-imposed government in 1900, the year Hawai'i became a territory of the United States. All schools, government operations and official transactions were thereafter conducted in English, despite the fact that most people, including non-Natives, still spoke Hawaiian at the turn of the century.

Since 1970, *'ōlelo Hawai'i,* or the Hawaiian language, has undergone a tremendous revival, including the rise of language immersion schools. The state of Hawai'i now has two official languages, Hawaiian and English, and the call for Hawaiian language speakers and teachers is increasing every day.[14]

Along with the flowering of Hawaiian language has come a flowering of Hawai- 25 ian dance, especially in its ancient form, called *hula kahiko.* Dance academies, known as *hālau,* have proliferated throughout Hawai'i, as have *kumu hula;* or dance masters, and formal competitions where all-night presentations continue for three or four days to throngs of appreciative listeners. Indeed, among Pacific Islanders, Hawaiian dance is considered one of the finest Polynesian art forms today.

---

[14]See Larry Kimura, "Native Hawaiian Culture," *Native Hawaiians Study Commission Report,* vol. 1, pp. 173–197.

Of course, the cultural revitalization that Hawaiians are now experiencing and transmitting to their children is as much a *repudiation* of colonization by so-called Western civilization in its American form as it is a *reclamation* of our own past and our own ways of life. This is why cultural revitalization is often resisted and disparaged by anthropologists and others: they see very clearly that its political effect is decolonization of the mind. Thus our rejection of the nuclear family as the basic unit of society and of individualism as the best form of human expression infuriates social workers, the churches, the legal system, and educators to this day. Hawaiians continue to have allegedly "illegitimate" children, to *hānai*, or "adopt," both children and adults outside of sanctioned Western legal concepts, to hold and use land and water in a collective form rather than a private property form, and to proscribe the notion and the value that one person should strive to surpass and therefore outshine all others.

All these Hawaiian values can be grouped under the idea of *'ohana*, loosely translated as "family," but more accurately imagined as a group of both closely and distantly related people who share nearly everything, from land and food to children and status. Sharing is central to this value, since it prevents individual decline. Of course, poverty is not thereby avoided; it is only shared with everyone in the unit. The *'ohana* works effectively when the *kua'ana* relationship (elder sibling/younger sibling reciprocity) is practiced.

Finally, within the *'ohana*, our women are considered the life-givers of the nation and are accorded the respect and honor this status conveys. Our young women, like our young people in general, are the *pua*, or "flower" of our *lāhui*, or our "nation." The renowned beauty of our women, especially their sexual beauty, is not considered a commodity to be hoarded by fathers and brothers but an attribute of our people. Culturally, Hawaiians are very open and free about sexual relationships, although Christianity and organized religion have done much to damage these traditional sexual values.

With this understanding of what it means to be Hawaiian, I want to move now to the prostitution of our culture by tourism.

Hawai'i itself is the female object of degraded and victimized sexual value. Our 30
'āina, or lands, are not any longer the source of food and shelter, but the source of money. Land is now called "real estate," rather than "our mother," Papa. The American relationship of people to land is that of exploiter to exploited. Beautiful areas, once sacred to my people, are now expensive resorts; shorelines where net fishing, seaweed gathering, and crabbing occurred are more and more the exclusive domain of recreational activities such as sunbathing, wind-surfing, and jet skiing. Now, even access to beaches near hotels is strictly regulated or denied to the local public altogether.

The phrase, *mālama 'āina*—"to care for the land"—is used by government officials to sell new projects and to convince the locals that hotels can be built with a concern for "ecology." Hotel historians, like hotel doctors, are stationed in-house to soothe the visitors' stay with the pablum of invented myths and tales of the "primitive."

High schools and hotels adopt each other and funnel teenagers through major resorts for guided tours from kitchens to gardens to honeymoon suites in preparation for post-secondary school jobs in the lowest paid industry in the state. In the meantime, tourist appreciation kits and movies are distributed through the state Department of

Education to all elementary schools. One film, unashamedly titled *What's in It for Me?*, was devised to convince locals that tourism is, as the newspapers never tire of saying, "the only game in town."

Of course, all this hype is necessary to hide the truth about tourism, the awful exploitative truth that the industry is the major cause of environmental degradation, low wages, land dispossession, and the highest cost of living in the United States.

While this propaganda is churned out to local residents, the commercialization of Hawaiian culture proceeds with calls for more sensitive marketing of our Native values and practices. After all, a prostitute is only as good as her income-producing talents. These talents, in Hawaiian terms, are the *hula;* the generosity, or *aloha,* of our people; the *u'i,* or youthful beauty of our women and men, and the continuing allure of our lands and waters, that is, of our place, Hawai'i.

The selling of these talents must produce income. And the function of tourism and   35 the State of Hawaii is to convert these attributes into profit.

The first requirement is the transformation of the product, or the cultural attribute, much as a woman must be transformed to look like a prostitute—that is, someone who is complicitous in her own commodification. Thus *hula* dancers wear clownlike makeup, don costumes from a mix of Polynesian cultures, and behave in a manner that is smutty and salacious rather than powerfully erotic. The distance between the smutty and the erotic is precisely the distance between Western culture and Hawaiian culture. In the hotel version of the *hula,* the sacredness of the dance has completely evaporated, while the athleticism and sexual expression have been packaged like ornaments. The purpose is entertainment for profit rather than a joyful and truly Hawaiian celebration of human and divine nature.

The point, of course, is that everything in Hawai'i can be yours, that is, you the tourists', the non-Natives', the visitors'. The place, the people, the culture, even our identity as a "Native" people is for sale. Thus the word "Aloha" is employed as an aid in the constant hawking of things Hawaiian. In truth, this use of *aloha is* so far removed from any Hawaiian cultural context that it is, literally, meaningless.

Thus, Hawai'i, like a lovely woman, is there for the taking. Those with only a little money get a brief encounter; those with a lot of money, like the Japanese, get more. The state and counties will give tax breaks, build infrastructure, and have the governor personally welcome tourists to ensure that they keep coming. Just as the pimp regulates prices and guards the commodity of the prostitute, so the state bargains with developers for access to Hawaiian land and culture. Who builds the biggest resorts to attract the most affluent tourists gets the best deal: more hotel rooms, golf courses, and restaurants approved. Permits are fast-tracked, height and density limits are suspended, new groundwater sources are miraculously found.

Hawaiians, meanwhile, have little choice in all this. We can fill up the unemployment lines, enter the military, work in the tourist industry, or leave Hawai'i. Increasingly, Hawaiians are leaving, not by choice but out of economic necessity.

Our people who work in the industry—dancers, waiters, singers, valets, garden-   40 ers, housekeepers, bartenders, and even a few managers—make between $10,000 and $25,000 a year, an impossible salary for a family in Hawai'i. Psychologically, our young people have begun to think of tourism as the only employment opportunity, trapped as they are by the lack of alternatives. For our young women, modeling is a "cleaner" job when compared to waiting on tables or dancing in a weekly revue, but modeling feeds on tourism and the commodification of Hawaiian women. In the end, the entire employment scene is shaped by tourism.

Despite their exploitation, Hawaiians' participation in tourism raises the problem of complicity. Because wages are so low and advancement so rare, whatever complicity exists is secondary to the economic hopelessness that drives Hawaiians into the industry. Refusing to contribute to the commercialization of one's culture becomes a peripheral concern when unemployment looms.

Of course, many Hawaiians do not see tourism as part of their colonization. Thus, tourism is viewed as providing jobs, not as a form of cultural prostitution. Even those who have some glimmer of critical consciousness do not generally agree that the tourist industry prostitutes Hawaiian culture. This is a measure of the depth of our mental oppression: we cannot understand our own cultural degradation because we are living it. As colonized people, we are colonized to the extent that we are unaware of our oppression. When awareness begins, then so, too, does decolonization. Judging by the growing resistance to new hotels, to geothermal energy and manganese nodule mining, which would supplement the tourist industry, and to increases in the sheer number of tourists, I would say that decolonization has begun, but we have many more stages to negotiate on our path to sovereignty.

My brief excursion into the prostitution of Hawaiian culture has done no more than give an overview. Now that you have read a Native view, let me just leave this thought with you. If you are thinking of visiting my homeland, please do not. We do not want or need any more tourists, and we certainly do not like them. If you want to help our cause, pass this message on to your friends.

Questions for Discussion and Writing

1. Trask feels that the cumulative effects of tourism on Hawaii have been disastrous. What facts and figures does she present to support her thesis?
2. Does Trask run the risk of alienating even those who might agree with her because of her incendiary rhetorical approach? Why or why not? Did you find her approach effective? Explain your answer.
3. Trask concludes her essay by requesting prospective visitors to remain home. Would her essay have any effect on your decision to visit Hawaii if you had the opportunity to do so? Why or why not?

Stuart Hirschberg

· ·

Stuart Hirschberg teaches English at Rutgers University, Newark, and is the author of scholarly works on W. B. Yeats and Ted Hughes. He is also the editor and coeditor (with Terry Hirschberg) of anthologies, including this book; One World, Many Cultures *(5th ed., 2004);* Every Day, Everywhere: Global Perspectives on Popular Culture *(2002);* Past to Present: Ideas that Changed Our World *(2003); and* Discovering the Many Worlds of Literature *(2004). The following essay is drawn from* Reflections on Language *(1999).*

As you read the next selection, consider what this candid shot of Richard M. Nixon with Checkers tells you about his political savvy in crafting his career-saving speech.

ANALYZING THE RHETORIC OF NIXON'S "CHECKERS" SPEECH

Propaganda: The Language of Doublespeak

Ultimately, it is the intention with which words are used that determines whether any of the techniques already discussed, such as slanting, labeling, and emotionally loaded language, pose a political danger. Of themselves, strategies of persuasion are neither good nor bad, it is the purpose for which they are employed that makes them unethical and offensive. It is for this reason that the techniques of rhetorical persuasion have been decried throughout the ages. Aldous Huxley in "Propaganda Under a Dictatorship" in *Brave New World Revisited* (1958) discussed how the manipulation of language through propaganda techniques in Nazi Germany conditioned thoughts and behavior. Some of the key techniques identified by Huxley included the use of slogans, unqualified assertions, and sweeping generalizations. Huxley notes that Hitler had said "all effective propaganda must be confined to a few bare necessities and then must be expressed in a few stereotyped formulas. . . . Only constant repetition will finally succeed in imprinting an idea upon the memory of a crowd." Hitler knew that any lie can seem to be the truth if it is repeated often enough. Repeated exposure encourages a sense of acceptance and familiarity with the slogan. Hitler's use of propaganda required that all statements be made without qualification.

George Orwell commented frequently on the dangers posed by political propaganda. In his novel *1984* he coined the term *doublespeak* to show how political language could be used to deceive, beg the question, and avoid responsibility.

Doublespeak can take forms that can range from the innocuous, such as Lt. Colonel Oliver North's intention to give "a non-visual slide show" (cited in *Quarterly Review of Doublespeak* [January 1988]), to the deceptive and dangerous, such as the Pentagon's reference to the neutron bomb as "an efficient nuclear weapon that eliminates an enemy with a minimum degree of damage to friendly territory." Or consider a statement by the U.S. Army that "we do not call it 'killing,' we call it 'servicing the target'" (cited in *Quarterly Review of Doublespeak* [January 1988]). In each of these cases language is used against itself to distort and manipulate rather than to communicate.

Intensifying and Downplaying: Strategies for Persuasion

One of the most valuable ways of analyzing forms of public persuasion was suggested by Hugh Rank in "Teaching About Public Persuasion: Rationale and a Schema" (1976). Rank won the 1976 *Orwell Award* (presented by the Committee on Public Doublespeak) for his "Intensifying/Downplaying Schema." Rank observed that all acts of public persuasion are variations of what he terms *intensifying* and *downplaying*.

Persuaders use intensifying and downplaying in the following ways: (1) to intensify, focus on, or draw attention to anything that would make their case look good; (2) to intensify, focus on, or draw attention to anything that would make counterclaims or their opponent's arguments look bad; (3) to downplay, dismiss, or divert attention from any weak points that would make their case look bad; and (4) to downplay, dismiss, or divert attention from anything that would make their opponent's case look good.

What is meant by intensifying and downplaying can be seen by comparing the words a country uses to refer to actions of the enemy (by intensifying) with those words it uses to describe its own identical activities (by downplaying):

Intensifying	Downplaying
Bombing	Air support
Spying	Intelligence gathering
Invasion	Pacification
Infiltration	Reinforcement
Retreat	Strategic withdrawal

The calculated manipulation and conditioning of thought and behavior by propaganda experts is now a fact of everyday life. Professional persuaders have an unequal advantage over those whom they seek to influence and persuade. By contrast, the average citizen has never received any training in critically examining the various techniques professional persuaders use.

The three basic techniques of intensification are (1) repetition, (2) association, and (3) composition.

Repetition.   Slogans, unqualified assertions, and sweeping generalizations will seem more true if they are constantly repeated. Much of commercial advertising is built on the repetition of slogans, product logos, and brand names. Political campaigns rely on repetition of candidates' names and messages over the airwaves and on posters and bumper stickers.

Association.   Intensifying by association is a technique that is also known as virtue   10
(or guilt) by association. This strategy depends on linking an idea, person, or product with something already loved or admired (or hated and despised) by the intended audience. That is, an idea, person, or product is put into a context that already has an emotional significance for the intended audience. Once market researchers discover needs and values of a target audience, political campaigns and advertising for commercial products can exploit the audience's needs by linking their idea, candidate, or product to values already known to be appealing to the audience. Much of advertising exploits this technique of correlating feelings and emotions with purchasable objects.

Composition.   A message gains intensity when it is arranged in a clearly perceivable pattern. Arranging the message can rely on the traditional rhetorical patterns (comparison and contrast, cause and effect, process analysis, classification, analogy, narration, description, and exemplification) as well as inductive or deductive logic or any other distinctive way of grouping elements of the message.

The three basic techniques of downplaying are (1) omission, (2) diversion, and (3) confusion.

Omission.   If persuaders wish to downplay or divert attention away from an issue that is felt to be potentially damaging to their purposes, they can use the opposite of each of the intensifying techniques. If repetition is an effective way to intensify, persuaders can downplay by omitting, biasing, or slanting. Omissions can range from euphemisms that downplay serious issues to acts of overt censorship.

Diversion.   Just as persuaders intensify by associating, they can downplay by diverting attention through an emphasis on unimportant or unrelated side issues. These tactics include the *red herring, non sequitur, straw man, argumentum ad hominem, argumentum ad populum, argumentum ad misericordiam or appeal to pity, argumentum ad baculum or appeal to force, circular reasoning or begging the question*, and *appeal to ignorance*. All these techniques are used to divert or distract attention from the main issues to peripheral or entirely unrelated issues.

Confusion.   Just as a message gains intensity when it is well structured and coherent,   15
so persuaders can downplay by using a variety of techniques designed to obscure or cloud the points at issue. These techniques include the calculated use of faulty logic, including the *fallacy of complex question, false dilemma, false cause, post hoc, slippery slope*, and *faulty analogy*. Downplaying via confusion also results from the use of ambiguous terms or phrases as in the fallacies of *equivocation, amphiboly,* and *accent*, as well as the use of bureaucratese, medicalese, legalese, pentagonese, and all other jargons used to obscure or cloud the real issues.

We should realize that all these strategies of intensifying and downplaying can take place *simultaneously* during any attempt to persuade.

To see how this works in practice, we can apply Rank's "Intensifying/Downplaying Schema" to one of the most famous cases of public persuasion in this century—Richard Nixon's "Checkers" speech. Before the speech was broadcast on radio and television in Los Angeles, on September 23, 1952, Dwight Eisenhower, an immensely popular Republican presidential candidate, was going to dump Nixon as his running mate because of accusations that Nixon had accepted $18,000 in personal gifts from lobbyists. Nixon appealed for one last chance to go on television and make his case before the American public. After the speech, two million favorable telegrams were received and Nixon stayed on the ticket. This speech accomplished what it set out to do—it neutralized the charges against him and brought about a favorable public image of Nixon. After disclosing him financial assets, Nixon concluded:

> . . . That's what we have and that's what we owe. It isn't very much.
>
> But, Pat and I have the satisfaction that every dime that we've got is honestly ours. I should say this, that Pat doesn't have a mink coat, but she does have a respectable Republican cloth coat.
>
> And I always tell her that she'd look good in anything. One other thing I probably should tell you because if I don't they'll probably be saying this about me too. We did get something, a gift, after the election. A man down in Texas heard Pat on the radio mention the fact that our two youngsters would like to have a dog. And, believe it or not, the day before we left on this campaign trip, we got a message from Union Station in Baltimore saying they had a package for us. We went down to get it. You know what it was. It was a little cocker spaniel dog in a crate that he sent all the way from Texas. Black and white spotted. And our little girl Tricia the 6 year old, named it "Checkers." And you know, the kids like all kids, love the dog and I just want to say this, right now, the regardless of what they say about it, we're going to keep it.
>
> It isn't easy to come before a nationwide audience and bare your life as I have done. But I want to say some things before I conclude that I think most of you will agree on. Mr. Mitchell, the Chairman of the Democratic National Committee, made the statement that if a man couldn't afford to be in the United States Senate he shouldn't run for the Senate. And, I just want to make my position clear. I don't agree with Mr. Mitchell when he says that only a rich man should serve his government in the U.S. Senate or in the Congress. I don't believe that represents the thinking of the Democratic Party. And, I know that it doesn't represent the thinking of the Republican Party.
>
> I believe that it's fine that a man like Governor Stevenson who inherited a fortune from his father can run for President. But I also feel that it is essential in this country of ours that a man of modest means can also run for President. Because you know, remember Abraham Lincoln, you remember what he said "God must have loved the common people, he made so many of them." And now I am going to suggest some courses of conduct. First of all, you have read in the papers about other funds now, Mr. Stevenson apparently had a couple, one of them in which a group of business people paid and helped to supplement the salaries of state employees. Here is where the money went directly into their pockets. And I think what Mr. Stevenson should do should be to come before the American people as I have, give the names of the people that contributed to that fund, give the names of the people who put this money into their pockets at the same time that they were receiving money from their state government and see what favors, if any, they gave out for that. I don't condemn Mr. Stevenson for what he did, but until the facts are in, there is a doubt that will be

raised. And as far as Mr. Sparkman is concerned, I would suggest the same thing. He's had his wife on the payroll. I don't condemn him for that, but I think that he should come before the American people and indicate what outside sources of income he has had. I would suggest that under the circumstances both Mr. Sparkman and Mr. Stevenson should come before the American people as I have and make complete financial statements as to their financial history. And if they don't, it will be an admission that they have something to hide. And I think you will agree with me. Because folks, remember, a man that's to be President of the U.S., a man that's to be Vice President of the U.S. must have the confidence of all the people. And, that's why I'm doing what I'm doing and that's why I suggest that Mr.Stevenson and Mr. Sparkmen, since they are under attack, should do what they're doing [sic].

Now, let me say this, I know that this is not the last of the smears. In spite of my explanation tonight, other smears will be made. Others have been made in the past. And the purpose of the smears, I know, is this—to silence me, to make me let up. Well, they just don't know who they're dealing with. I'm going to tell you this. I remember in the dark days of the Hiss case, some of the same columnists, some of the same radio commentators who are attacking me now, and misrepresenting my position, were violently opposing me at the time I was after Alger Hiss. But I continued to fight because I knew I was right and I can say to this great television and radio audience that I have no apologies to the American people for my part in putting Alger Hiss where he is today. And as far as this is concerned, I intend to continue to fight. Why do I feel so deeply, why do I feel that in spite of the smears, the misunderstandings, the necessity for a man to come up here and bare his soul as I have? Why is it necessary for me to continue this fight? I want to tell you why, because you see, I love my country and I think my country is in danger and I think the only man that can save America at this time is the man that's running for President on my ticket, Dwight Eisenhower.

A breakdown of this speech using the intensify/downplay schema might appear as follows:

1. Nixon intensifies positive features in the following lines:
    a. "But, Pat and I have the satisfaction that every dime that we've got is honestly ours."
    b. "Pat doesn't have a mink coat, but she does have a respectable Republican cloth coat." [Virtue by association.]
    c. "And I always tell her that she'd look good in anything."
    d. "It was a little cocker spaniel dog . . . named . . . 'Checkers.' And you know, the kids like all kids, love the dog and I just want to say this, right now, that regardless of what they say about it, we're going to keep it." [Virtue by association; i.e., loves his children who love dogs, wouldn't hurt his children by sending Checkers back, implies opponents would take his children's puppy away; name Checkers has folksy connotation of people playing checkers.]
    e. "a man of modest means can also run for President." [Just plain folks appeal.]
    f. "Because you know, remember Abraham Lincoln, you remember what he said 'God must have loved the common people . . .'" [Virtue by association, plain folks appeal, and suggests a link with a respected Republican president.]
    g. "I think the only man that can save America at this time is the man that's running for President on my [sic] ticket, Dwight Eisenhower." [Virtue by association with a person already loved and admired by the voting public; although

perhaps a slip of the tongue, note how Nixon, who is the vice-presidential candidate, makes himself as important as the respected and very popular presidential candidate.]

2. Nixon intensifies the points on which his opponents might be vulnerable:
   a. "and I just want to say this, right now, that regardless of what they say about it, we're going to keep it." [Wouldn't hurt his children by sending Checkers back, with the clear implication that his opponents would.]
   b. "I don't agree with Mr. Mitchell when he says that only a rich man should serve his government in the U.S. Senate or in the Congress." [Characterizing himself as poor but honest in contrast to rich elitist Democrats.]
   c. "Mr. Stevenson apparently had a couple [of funds] . . . where the money went directly into their pockets."
   d. I don't condemn Mr. Stevenson for what he did, but until the facts are in, there is a doubt that will be raised. And as far as Mr. Sparkman is concerned, I would suggest the same thing. He's had his wife on the payroll. I don't condemn him for that . . ." [Presented as a search for the truth, Nixon accrues the added benefit of appearing to be nonjudgmental; he raises the issue while at the same time appears to deny he is doing so.]
   e. "I know that this is not the last of the smears. In spite of my explanation tonight, other smears will be made. Others have been made in the past. And the purpose of the smears . . ." [Technique of repetition, characterizing the accusation that prompted this speech as a smear.]
3. Nixon downplays potential weaknesses in his own position:
   a. "It isn't very much." [Diminishes importance of financial holdings; by implication, he would be richer if he had really been accepting money.]
   b. "One other thing I probably should tell you because if I don't they'll probably be saying this about me too." [A classic straw man maneuver since no one had or conceivably would accuse him of accepting a puppy for his little girls as a payoff.]
   c. "Because you know, remember Abraham Lincoln, you remember what he said 'God must have loved the common people . . .'" [Diverting attention with an unrelated *argumentum ad populum*.]
   d. "Mr. Sparkman and Mr. Stevenson should come before the American people as I have and make complete financial statements as to their financial history. And, if they don't, it will be an admission that they have something to hide." [Diverting attention to Stevenson and Sparkman who Nixon characterizes as being under a cloud of guilt.]
   e. "And the purpose of the smears, I know, is this—to silence me, to make me let up. Well, they just don't know who they're dealing with. I'm going to tell you this. I remember in the dark days of the Hiss case, some of the same columnists, some of the same radio commentators who are attacking me now, and misrepresenting my position, were violently opposing me at the time I was after Alger Hiss." [Diversion by attributing a false cause to confuse the issue; diversion by introducing a red herring converts the charge of financial impropriety being made against him into an occasion for characterizing "some" of his accusers as un-American.]

f. "in spite of the smears, the misunderstanding, the necessity for a man to come up here and bare his soul as I have." [Diversion through appeal to pity, fused with the common man theme.]

g. "Why is it necessary for me to continue this fight? I want to tell you why, because you see, I love my country and I think my country is in danger. . . ." [Scare tactics combined with elevation of his campaign for the vice-presidency into a holy cause to save the country.]

4. Nixon downplays what some might consider to be a point in Stevenson's favor, i.e., a man or woman wealthy at the time he or she took office might be seen as less likely to exploit power for financial gain.

a. "I believe that it's fine that a man like Governor Stevenson who inherited a fortune from his father can run for President." [In light of his earlier condemnation of Mitchell for implying that "only a rich man should serve his government" this statement is transparently false.]

Thus, we see how traditional rhetorical strategies can be intuitively mobilized by a skillful politician to downplay his own problems while intensifying doubts about his critics.

Questions for Discussion and Writing

1. How do the strategies of "intensifying" and "downplaying" operate in the "Checkers" speech? What role do logical fallacies play in diverting the audience's attention from the specific charges Nixon was fighting?

2. In your opinion, what accounts for the effectiveness of the symbolism of the cocker spaniel puppy (Checkers) and the "respectable Republican cloth coat"?

3. If you had heard this speech, would it have changed your mind about Nixon's credibility? Why or why not? What contemporary speech, editorial pronouncement, or other public rhetoric seems to call for this kind of analysis? Choose one and identify the elements of intensifying and downplaying.

Dennis Smith

• •

Dennis Smith (b. 1940) began his career as a firefighter in the New York Fire Department. In 1972, he published his first book, the New York Times *best-seller* Report from Engine Co. 82. *He is the author of nine other books, including his memoir,* A Song for Mary: An Irish-American Memory *(1999). Immediately after two hijacked jets struck the twin towers of the World Trade Center on the morning of September 11, 2001, Smith reported to Manhattan's Ladder Co. 16 to volunteer in the rescue effort.* Report from Ground Zero *(2002) is a dramatic narrative of this three-month period, a time that has permanently altered the landscape and character of America. In the following excerpt from the book, we hear the testimony of a battalion chief, Joe Pfeifer.*

Report from Ground Zero

Chief Joe Pfeifer

Battalion 1

Joe Pfeifer has been a battalion chief for five years, and has been working the downtown area with the 1st Battalion. He is a thin, athletic man, with a studious air. If you saw him in a suit, you might take him for a lawyer, or a financial expert. If you mention his name in a group of firefighters, they invariably say, "Chief Pfeifer? The best."

On this pleasant morning he is standing in his shirtsleeves at the intersection of Church Street and Lispenard Street. It is 8:48 A.M. and the day is already summer clear. He has been sent to this location with the men of Engine 7 and Ladder 1 to investigate a report of a gas leak. Ladder 8 pulls up as Chief Pfeifer takes a gas meter from his van, a small device with a long thin neck, at the end of which is a sensor. The chief circles a grating in the street with the meter until it buzzes, indicating a slight presence of gas. Sewer gas, maybe?

Suddenly a shadow falls over the street corner, and a firefighter, Steven Olsen of Ladder 1, looks up. It is accompanied by a heavy, roaring sound that is abnormal and surprising. *You never hear planes roaring over Manhattan,* Chief Pfeifer thinks. It is also much lower than it should be. All the firefighters are now staring upward, as is a film crew that is shooting a documentary about firefighters. It is a plane. Chief Pfeifer's gaze follows the path of the plane, and he has a clear view as it crashes into the north tower of the World Trade Center, near the top, somewhere around the ninetieth floor. There is no discussion among the fire companies as they rush into their trucks and speed fourteen blocks south.

In the chief's van, Chief Pfeifer hears the Manhattan dispatcher announce that a plan has gone into tower 1 of the World Trade Center. The chief reaches for the telephone.

"Battalion 1 to Manhattan."   5

"Okay," the dispatcher answers. It is John Lightsey who is working the microphone this shift.

"We have another report of a fire," Chief Pfeifer says, calmly and resolutely. He knows these are public airwaves. "It looks like a plane has steamed into the building. Transmit a third alarm. We'll have a staging area at Vesey and West streets. Have the third-alarm assignment go into that area, the second-alarm assignment go to the building."

"Ten-four," Lightsey answers.

He next hears on the radio. "Division 1 is on the air."

"Ten-four, Division 1. You have a full third-alarm assignment." Chief Pfeifer now   10
knows that Chief Hayden is on his way. He and Chief Hayden have been colleagues for a long time, and he is glad this is the deputy on assignment today.

When he reaches the staging area and steps into the street, he sees a large amount of fire and white smoke lifting from the top of the building to the sky. Behind him, Jules Naudet follows with his video camera. Chief Pfeifer pulls his heavy bunker pants over his trousers, and steps into his boots. He puts his helmet on, a leather helmet painted over with white enamel, which has been the traditional style of the FDNY for more than a hundred years. His own has a large front piece that reads, in large antiqued lettering: BATTALION CHIEF. There is a shower of debris falling, and he runs through it into the building, straight through to the elevator control bank, where he sets up a command post. He notices that all the twenty-five-foot-high windows that surround the lobby, at least in this northwest section of the building, have been blown out, and people are walking through the frames. They undoubtedly were broken upon the impact of the plane, which means the building must have shook violently.

A maintenance worker runs to him, saying, "We have a report of people trapped in a stairwell on 78." '

"Okay, 78," he answers. People have begun staggering through the lobby, badly burned, while others are running. The firefighters of Ladder 10 appear, as does an officer who reports to the chief.

"I want you to go to 78," Chief Pfeifer says.

"What floor, Chief?" the officer asks. It is almost as if he does not want to register the floor number, anticipating the length of the climb, the weight of the equipment he has to carry, and the smoke and fire that will confront him there.

"Seventy-eight."

Just then Chief Hayden arrives. The unspoken transfer of command is passed from Chief Pfeifer, even as they realize they are all in this together. The elevator control bank stands behind a five-foot marble wall, and Chief Hayden and Chief Pfeifer station themselves behind it. As firefighters report in, they speak to the chiefs as customers do over a high counter in a meat market. Civilians are running past the firefighters, leaving the lobby as the firefighters are entering it. The firefighters move more deliberately, carrying equipment and hose, for they know they have to conserve their energy to ascend the highest building in the city.

Chief Hayden and Chief Pfeifer are very focused and exacting. Not a voice is raised in any discussion between firefighters and fire chiefs. Chief Bill McGovern of Battalion 2 joins them. About thirty firefighters have gathered, patiently awaiting assignment, hose and tools at their feet. As their orders are issued they disappear into the building, and other firefighters appear, among them the men of Engine 10. In front of the elevator bank counter, the field communications unit begins to set up a portable command station consisting of a large suitcaselike piece of equipment on four legs, with a magnetic board where the list of entering fire companies can be logged. Just behind them, firefighters are dressing the windows, breaking off the dangerously hanging shards of glass.

Lieutenant Kevin Pfeifer and the men of Engine 33 arrive and report to Chief Pfeifer. The chief seems surprised to see his brother now in front of him, for he knew that Kevin had put in for a couple of weeks off, combining vacation days and mutual trading of working tours with another officer, just to study for the upcoming captain's test.

"The fire is reported," Chief Pfeifer says, "on 78 or 80." There is none of the normal joking between them. Kevin nods, needing no further information, and then the two brothers lock their eyes together for a few moments of shared and worried concern before Kevin leads his men to the stairs. Their names can be read on their bunker coats as they depart: PFEIFER, BOYLE, ARCE, MAYNARD, KING, EVANS.

Rescue 1 arrives with Captain Hatton carrying an extra bottle of air, followed by Tom Schoales and the men of Engine 4. The affiliation of firefighters is designated by the front piece of their helmets, on which is their company and badge number. A group of police officers passes through the lobby and disappears into the stairwell, all with masks, air tanks, and blue hard hats. They are carrying large nylon satchels filled with their tools and ropes. These are members of the elite emergency service unit of the NYPD.

Chief of Safety Turi has also arrived and speaks with Chief Hayden. Assistant Chief of Department Callan steps into the lobby and takes command, almost automatically. He speaks into his handy-talkie, "Battalion 7 . . . Battalion 7 . . ."

Captain Jonas and the men of Ladder 6 enter and speak momentarily with Chief Hayden and then to Chief Pfeifer. Just as they take their orders there is a loud crashing sound outdoors. Debris, some large and burning, showers down from the crash floors, hitting the ground with such force that pieces shoot into the lobby like shrapnel. Someone says, "I just saw a plane go into the other building."

Tom Von Essen, the fire commissioner, appears, but no one goes to greet him. He is on the civilian side of the department, and his counsel will not be sought by the fire chiefs.

It is 9:03 A.M. All of the chiefs have radios to their ears, and they do not seem surprised by the news of *a second plane*. Maybe it is responsible for all the burning debris outside.   25

The fire commissioner walks over to the huddled chiefs and listens for a few moments, then moves away. A firefighter from Rescue 1 is standing before the command post waiting for someone to tell him the location of his company so that he can catch up with them. Another firefighter passes with a length of folded hose on his shoulder, ninety feet long and forty pounds.

The field com firefighter says, holding a phone, "I have Battalion 2 here."

Chief Pfeifer takes the line to speak to Chief McGovern, who has now gone up into the building. Chief Hayden says to an officer, "I have a report of trapped people in this tower up on 71."

The deputy fire commissioners are now on the scene and are standing off to the side with the fire commissioner. The firefighters of Ladder 1 move to the command post, receive their orders, and then quickly advance into the building. Chief Hayden is talking in the middle of the group of fire chiefs when he is suddenly interrupted by a loud report, as if a very large shotgun has been fired. Startled, he turns toward the sound and realizes it has come from the impact of a falling body, the first person to jump on this side of the building.

An African American firefighter nearby looks profoundly pensive as he moves to   30
a wall and scans the lobby.

Deputy Commissioner Bill Feehan stops to assist a group of people in the lobby. One says, "Please take me out of here." Bill Feehan was once the chief of department, the highest uniformed rank, but today he knows that he is also on the civilian side. He directs them to proceed in the direction they are going, to keep moving, and reassures them. It is Commissioner Feehan's way, to keep everyone reassured.

The fire companies keep stepping up to the command post, as orderly as in a parade. They stop briefly as their company officer speaks to one of the chiefs to receive instruction.

Few firefighters are in the lobby at one time now, for they are all quickly and methodically dispatched to their work, going up, up, as high as the sixtieth floor. All the while there is an incessant whistling from the firefighters' Air Paks, the crashing of debris outside, and the frightful *bang, bang, bang* as the bodies begin to fall one after another.

Chief Hayden is in a discussion with the chief of safety.

"But," he is saying, "we have to get those people out!" He doesn't gesture, he doesn't flail his arms but the tension in his voice is noticeable. All the chiefs are by now beginning to appreciate the extent of the terrible scene above them, getting worse by the second.

Engine 16 comes into the lobby as more emergency police officers and EMTs move in and out of the building. A probationary firefighter, his orange front piece denoting the short period of time he has served in the department, stands alone, waiting for his officer, looking ambivalent, as if he is trying to gauge the dangers that surround him. None of the firefighters remaining on the floor are talking among themselves. As they wait for their orders, every one of them exudes an undeniable apprehension, as if they suspect, each of them, that an almost certain doom faces this group. But for now, all they really know is that this is the toughest job they have ever faced.

A voice is heard, a chief's command, "All units down to the lobby."

There is another sudden crash and breaking glass, as bodies continue to fall from the very top floors, ninety floors up, traveling at 120 miles per hour. The sound has become a part of the environment, and hardly anyone reacts to it.

A field com firefighter stands before the opened suitcase of the command unit. There is a telephone connected to it and lined boxes with titles written across the open lid: STAGING AREA, ADDRESS, ALARMS, R&R, CONTROL. In the boxes are white tags for the fire companies in both buildings.

Father Mychal Judge appears, in his turnout jacket and white helmet. He stands off to the side, his hands on his hips, careful to stay out of the way of the huddles. The loud whistling in the background is now coming in series of fours, *scheeeeee, scheeeeee, scheeeeee*. It is from the alarm packs of firefighters that are going off, what they call the personal alert alarm, designed to locate them when they are down.

Yelling is the preferred form of communication between men who are not sharing radio waves. Police officers in shirtsleeves and men from the mayor's Office of Emergency Management are all about, mostly on cell phones and handy-talkies. On a balcony above them a crowd of men and women moves forward in an orderly way. Where have they come from, a stairwell or an elevator? These are survivors. The *bangs* of the falling bodies in the plaza are now regular, and almost syncopated.

Father Judge's lips move in silent prayer as four firefighters pass him carrying a Stokes basket. The Franciscan is so focused in his mediation, so completely one with his inner voice as it is connecting with his God, that it appears he is straining himself and that the power of his prayer is outpacing the ability of his heart to keep up. Chief Pfeifer notices that the priest seems to be carrying a great burden in the midst of this disaster, and he is struck by his aloneness, praying so feverishly, like Christ in the Garden of Gethsemane. Finally, a man goes over to Father Judge and shakes his hand. "I'm Michael Angelini," he says. Father Judge is pleased to see him, for Michael's father, Joe, is a member of Rescue 1 and also the president of the department's Catholic fraternal association. "Ahh," Father Judge says. "Your mother and father were recently at my jubilee celebration. I will pray for your family, Michael." Father Judge taps him on the shoulder as well. It is the human thing. A handshake is not quite sufficient.

Michael leaves the priest's side, and Father Judge is again left alone with his prayers. He has no one to counsel, no one to console, no one to shepherd. It is only him and God now, together, trying to work the greatest emergency New York has ever seen. It is obvious that Father Judge is trying to make some agreement about the safety of his firefighters.

A Port Authority police officer in white shirtsleeves has the attention, momentarily, of the chiefs. Chief Pfeifer tells a firefighter to write TOWER I across the panel top where they are standing, the elevator control bank. Then Chief Pfeifer begins to call in his radio for 44, when a loud noise is heard, a new and odd noise, a rumble. No, it is a roar.

It is 9:59 A.M.

Chief Pfeifer looks up to the ceiling as if to concentrate his hearing. Suddenly, he turns and runs toward the escalators behind him. Four fire patrolmen in their red helmets, from the insurance-industry-supported fire patrol, are just ahead, and Chief Callan and Chief Hayden are following closely behind.   45

And in the midst of the roar, a great cloud chases them, and then envelops them, until, almost immediately, all is black. It is black as midnight. The roar has lasted only sixteen seconds, a great rumble wave, flinging a tidal wave of ash against the building. And now, just as suddenly, all is quiet. It is a profound quiet, in a profound darkness. Within this stillness the men are one with their thoughts, and asking themselves, *Am I alive?*

After a few minutes pass there is a faint rustling. People begin to call out and flashlight beams shine vaguely through the whirling dust. It is reassuring to realize they are a sign that men in the lobby have survived. It seems as if it is snowing, thick clouds of pulverized concrete mixed with pulverized marble, and computers and office chairs, and teapots, and . . .

A voice asks, "Is everybody all right?"

"Yeah, I'm okay," someone answers.

"Hey guys, we need a hand here."   50

"Right. We got four guys."

"Top of the escalator."

"Yeah. Go."

"Joe?"

"Pete, where are you, Pete?"   55

"Where are the stairs?"

"Everybody join hands. Keep together."

"We gotta get out of here."

Chief Pfeifer radios: "All units, tower 1, evacuate the building."

"Here are the stairs."   60

Chief Pfeifer takes the lead when the group sees Father Judge on the ground, and they all rush to him. Chief Pfeifer loosens the priest's collar, but he isn't breathing. The prayers have consumed all his energy, and he wasn't able to survive the shock of this catastrophe, this enveloping cloud. They work on him now, mouth to mouth, but the environment is dangerous. They can't just stay here, and they look for something to place Father Judge in, a stretcher, a Stokes basket. Michael Angelini finds a wooden board, and they carefully lay the priest's body on it, and they lift him up and out.

The powder begins to lift as the sound of crashing continues. Chief Pfeifer reaches a mezzanine and heads down a corridor, completely gray with ash.

A firefighter who is following close behind asks, "Where are we headed?"

Another *bang*.

It is a long wide corridor, the pedestrian walkway over West Street, two stories 65
above ground.

Chief Pfeifer is thinking, *The whole building came down and we have to get everyone safely out.*

Mayday, Mayday, Mayday.

He notices the blue tape strung between the columns of the corridor, as if someone had prognosticated an emergency scene.

"Battalion 1 to Division 1."

"You okay?" 70

He has raised the division and learns that they have evacuated safely through a window on the east side of West Street. He turns and walks the long corridor for the third time until he comes to a set of stairs that take him down to the street.

On West Street the rigs are parked up and down the road, the apparatus of Rescue 1, High-rise Unit 3, pumpers and ladder trucks from Manhattan and Brooklyn.

The chief hears someone say, "I can't believe this can happen."

There is an eerie, otherworldly nature to the surface of the street. It is like the soft earth beneath the boardwalk at Coney Island. But here the ground is strewn with millions of pieces of paper. It is quiet, a heavy quiet like the quiet beneath the boardwalk at night.

Just a sliver of the Vista Hotel is standing. Could it be? Tower 2, the south tower, 75
has come down, and the entire tract across West Street that had once been the tallest building in the world is now a field of rubble and raging fire, and. . . .

And people. How many people were in that building? How many cops? How many firefighters?

And Kevin, Chief Pfeifer thinks. At least Kevin is in the north tower. He lifts his radio transmitter to his mouth.

"Battalion 1 to Engine 33," he asks searchingly. "Battalion 1 to Engine 33. Lieutenant Pfeifer?"

But there is no answer.

The air above the pile that was tower 2 is a haze and now an impenetrable cloud 80
and gold with fire.

Chief Pfeifer is standing beneath the overpass on the Vesey Street side, the overpass that crosses West Street and connects the Financial Center to the World Trade Center. He surveys the site before him, and he is planning strategy.

Two trees are lying in the street, still green, but a gray green.

He walks to Vesey Street and meets with Chief Cassano and Chief Hayden, still uncertain about exactly what has happened, for smoke obscures everything. The south tower has collapsed. But all of it, half of it?

It is 10:28 A.M. when the sound, that terrible roar erupts again, as people scream, "Run, run!"

Everyone is rushing in a different direction; Chief Pfeifer heads toward the river, 85
still accompanied by the cameraman who is following him around. He doesn't see that

just behind him a policewoman has been hit by a piece of flying glass and has been thrown to the ground. Someone stops to help her as Chief Pfeifer darts between a car and a truck. The cameraman hits the ground and the chief, in his bunker gear, falls on top of him, covering him from the debris crashing all around them.

As it had before, the cloud changes from a brown haze to one of complete blackness. There is just one thought in Joe Pfeifer's mind now: *Oh, God, I want to see my family again.* He closes his eyes and waits for something to crush him.

But the din stops, and the smoke begins to lift a little lightening in color back to dirty brown. Then, suddenly, loud gunshots ring out, just down the street at Vesey and West. For one fleeting moment the thought of an invading army crosses his mind. *Now they are shooting at me.* His eyes are crusted, and he can barely see, but he makes his way back to the corner of West and Vesey.

It is almost as if snow had fallen, for the gray dust mutes all ambient sound. But, eerily, there is no sound, no screaming, not even crackling from his two radios.

He has no idea how many people are lost, or where they are, or where his brother might be. *I am out here,* he thinks, *I am more visible. My brother will come looking for me. He'll find me easily enough.* He sees the rig of Engine 33 on Vesey Street and goes to check the riding list. He knows Kevin is on the list, but, still, just to make certain, he will check everything.

Each chief has stepped out from the place he has sought for cover and heads for 90 a different area of the devastation. They seem to develop a sectoring plan without articulating or drawing it, without the formal convention. They consult with one another by radio, remaining in their separate locations, directing work, any work that advances the idea of rescue. Get the men out. Get the people out. There is no actual command structure.

Chief Pfeifer receives a communication that several firefighters are trapped in the north tower, Chief Picciotto with Captain Jonas and Ladder 6, between the second and fifth floors. But where could what used to be these floors even be? That operation lasts for several hours, and it is reassuring when the men are rescued along with a civilian man and woman.

The chief tries again and again to place a phone call to his wife, but every line he gets goes dead. He repeatedly circles the entire site looking for his brother. He doesn't see Kevin, or anyone from Engine 33. He tries to ignore the pain that is pressing at the center of his stomach, the feeling of everything sinking away.

It is 11:00 P.M.

He can't walk anymore and looks for a car, a bus, anything to take him back to the firehouse. But there is nothing, so he sets off on foot. On Duane Street, the firehouse is dark. He doesn't stop to change clothes but gets in his car and drives home to Middle Village. Because all the bridges, highways, and tunnels are closed, he has to keep presenting identification.

It is near midnight when he arrives home, covered, head to toe, with garbage and 95 soot. He goes upstairs where his wife, Ginny, rushes out, hugging him and crying, followed by his two children. The four of them stand in the hall, locked in their embrace.

He is exhausted and can barely keep his injured, beaten eyes open. He thinks of his brother, his last thought of the day. *We will find him tomorrow,* he thinks. *We will find Kevin tomorrow.*

Questions for Discussion and Writing

1. What insight does Smith's account offer into the physical and psychological challenges that faced Chief Pfeifer and other rescuers on the fateful morning of September 11, 2001?
2. How do the personal encounters Smith reports communicate the harrowing experiences of both the office workers and their would-be rescuers?
3. In a short essay, discuss the impact of the events of 9/11 on any aspect of American society.
4. How is this ad, sponsored by the Arab-American Institute and the Ad Council, intended to provide a message of tolerance?

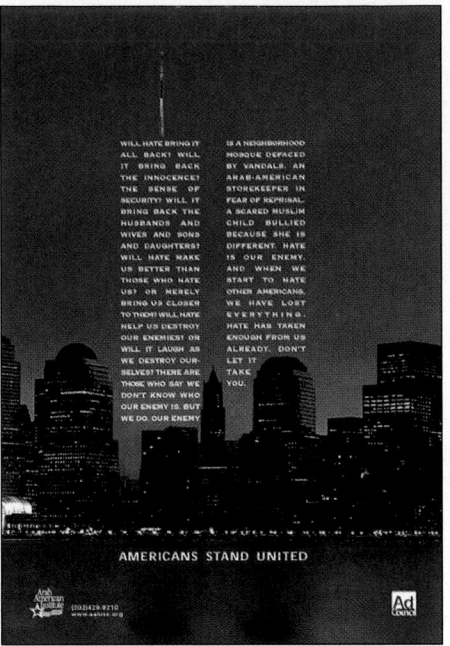

FICTION

Ambrose Bierce

Ambrose Bierce (1842–1914?) was born in rural Ohio, the youngest of a large, devout poverty-stricken family. He enlisted in the Union Army at the outbreak of the Civil War as a drummer boy, fought bravely in some of the most important battles, and rose from the rank of private to major. After the war, he became a journalist in San Francisco and wrote satiric pieces for a news weekly, of which he was soon made editor. The biting wit for which Bierce is so distinguished became his hallmark. He worked briefly in London as a journalist; after returning to the United States he wrote his famous "Prattler" column for the Argonaut *magazine. In 1887, William Randolph Hearst bought the column and placed it on the editorial page of the* Sunday Examiner. *Bierce published tales of soldiers and civilians in 1891 and later followed them with* Can Such Things Be? *(1893) and his acerbic* Devil's Dictionary *(1906). In 1913 he left for Mexico to cover the revolution and vanished without a trace. With characteristic aplomb, his last letter to a friend stated, "Goodbye, if you hear of my being stood up against a Mexican stone wall and shot to rags, please know that I think it a pretty good way to depart this life. It beats old age, disease, or falling down the cellar stairs." "An Occurrence at Owl Creek Bridge" (1890) has emerged as a classic. This haunting story reconstructs an experience so that impressions, colors, sounds, sensations, and time itself are thoroughly subordinated to the psychological state of the narrator.*

AN OCCURRENCE AT OWL CREEK BRIDGE

I

A man stood upon a railroad bridge in Northern Alabama, looking down into the swift waters twenty feet below. The man's hands were behind his back, the wrists bound with a cord. A rope loosely encircled his neck. It was attached to a stout cross-timber above his head, and the slack fell to the level of his knees. Some loose boards laid upon the sleepers supporting the metals of the railway supplied a footing for him and his executioners—two private soldiers of the Federal army, directed by a sergeant, who in civil life may have been a deputy sheriff. At a short remove upon the same temporary platform was an officer in the uniform of his rank, armed. He was a captain. A sentinel at each end of the bridge stood with his rifle in the position known as "support," that is to say, vertical in front of the left shoulder, the hammer resting on the forearm thrown straight across the chest—a normal and unnatural position, enforcing an erect carriage of the body. It did not appear to be the duty of these two men to know what was occurring at the centre of the bridge; they merely blockaded the two ends of the foot plank which traversed it.

Beyond one of the sentinels nobody was in sight; the railroad ran straight away into a forest for a hundred yards, then, curving, was lost to view. Doubtless there was an outpost further along. The other bank of the stream was open ground—a gentle acclivity crowned with a stockade of vertical tree trunks, loop-holed for rifles, with a single embrasure through which protruded the muzzle of a brass cannon commanding the bridge. Midway of the slope between bridge and fort were the spectators—a single company of infantry in line, at "parade rest," the butts of the rifles on the ground, the barrels inclining slightly backward against the right shoulder, the hands crossed upon the stock. A lieutenant stood at the right of the line, the point of his sword upon the ground, his left hand resting upon his right. Excepting the group of four at the centre of the bridge not a man moved. The company faced the bridge, staring stonily, motionless. The sentinels, facing the banks of the stream, might have been statues to adorn the bridge. The captain stood with folded arms, silent, observing the work of his subordinates but making no sign. Death is a dignitary who, when he comes announced, is to be received with formal manifestations of respect, even by those most familiar with him. In the code of military etiquette silence and fixity are forms of deference.

The man who was engaged in being hanged was apparently about thirty-five years of age. He was a civilian, if one might judge from his dress, which was that of a planter. His features were good—a straight nose, firm mouth, broad forehead, from which his long, dark hair was combed straight back, falling behind his ears to the collar of his well-fitted frock coat. He wore a moustache and pointed beard, but no whiskers; his eyes were large and dark grey and had a kindly expression which one would hardly have expected in one whose neck was in the hemp. Evidently this was no vulgar assassin. The liberal military code makes provision for hanging many kinds of people, and gentlemen are not excluded.

The preparations being complete, the two private soldiers stepped aside and each drew away the plank upon which he had been standing. The sergeant turned to the captain, saluted and placed himself immediately behind that officer, who in turn moved apart one pace. These movements left the condemned man and the sergeant standing on the two ends of the same plank, which spanned three of the cross-ties of the bridge. The end upon which the civilian stood almost, but not quite, reached a fourth. This plank had been held in place by the weight of the captain; it was now held by that of the sergeant. At a signal from the former, the latter would step aside, the plank would tilt and the condemned man go down between two ties. The arrangement commended itself to his judgment as simple and effective. His face had not been covered nor his eyes bandaged. He looked a moment at his "unsteadfast footing," then let his gaze wander to the swirling water of the stream racing madly beneath his feet. A piece of dancing driftwood caught his attention and his eyes followed it down the current. How slowly it appeared to move! What a sluggish stream!

He closed his eyes in order to fix his last thoughts upon his wife and children. The water, touched to gold by the early sun, the brooding mists under the banks at some distance down the stream, the fort, the soldiers, the piece of drift—all had distracted him. And now he became conscious of a new disturbance. Striking through the thought of his dear ones was a sound which he could neither ignore nor understand, a sharp, distinct, metallic percussion like the stroke of a blacksmith's hammer upon the anvil; it had the same ringing quality. He wondered what it was, and whether immeasurably distant or near by—it seemed both. Its recurrence was regular, but as slow as the tolling of a death knell. He awaited each stroke with impatience and—he knew not why—apprehension. The intervals of silence grew progressively longer; the delays became maddening. With their greater infrequency the sounds increased in strength and sharpness. They hurt his car like the thrust of a knife; he feared he would shriek. What he heard was the ticking of his watch.

He unclosed his eyes and saw again the water below him. "If I could free my hands," he thought, "I might throw off the noose and spring into the stream. By diving I could evade the bullets, and, swimming, vigorously, reach the bank, take to the woods, and get away home. My home, thank God, is as yet outside their lines; my wife and little ones are still beyond the invader's farthest advance."

As these thoughts, which have here to be set down in words, were flashed into the doomed man's brain rather than evolved from it, the captain nodded to the sergeant. The sergeant stepped aside.

II

Peyton Farquhar was a well-to-do planter, of an old and highly-respected Alabama family. Being a slave owner, and, like other slave owners, a politician, he was naturally an original secessionist and ardently devoted to the Southern cause. Circumstances of an imperious nature which it is unnecessary to relate here, had prevented him from taking service with the gallant army which had fought the disastrous campaigns ending with the fall of Corinth, and he chafed under the inglorious restraint, longing for the release of his energies, the larger life of the soldier, the opportunity for distinction. That opportunity, he felt, would come, as it comes to all in war time. Meanwhile he did what he could. No service was too humble for him to perform in aid of the South, no adventure too perilous for him to undertake if consistent with the character of a civilian who was at heart a soldier, and who in good faith and without too much qualification assented to at least a part of the frankly villainous dictum that all is fair in love and war.

One evening while Farquhar and his wife were sitting on a rustic bench near the entrance to his ground, a grey-clad soldier[1] rode up to the gate and asked for a drink of water. Mrs. Farquhar was only too happy to serve him with her own white hands. While she was gone to fetch the water, her husband approached the dusty horseman and inquired eagerly for news from the front.

"The Yanks are repairing the railroads," said the man, "and are getting ready for   10 another advance. They have reached the Owl Creek bridge, put it in order, and built a stockade on the other bank. The commandant has issued an order, which is posted everywhere, declaring that any civilian caught interfering with the railroad, its bridges, tunnels, or trains, will be summarily hanged. I saw the order."

"How far is it to the Owl Creek bridge?" Farquhar asked.

"About thirty miles."

"Is there no force on this side the creek?"

"Only a picket post half a mile out, on the railroad, and a single sentinel at this end of the bridge."

"Suppose a man—a civilian and student of hanging—should elude the picket   15 post and perhaps get the better of the sentinel," said Farquhar, smiling, "what could he accomplish?"

The soldier reflected. "I was there a month ago," he replied. "I observed that the flood of last winter had lodged a great quantity of driftwood against the wooden pier at this end of the bridge. It is now dry and would burn like tow."

The lady had now brought the water, which the soldier drank. He thanked her ceremoniously, bowed to her husband, and rode away. An hour later, after nightfall, he repassed the plantation, going northward in the direction from which he had come. He was a Federal scout.

III

As Peyton Farquhar fell straight downward through the bridge, he lost consciousness and was as one already dead. From this state he was awakened—ages later, it seemed to him—by the pain of a sharp pressure upon his throat, followed by a sense of suffocation. Keen, poignant agonies seemed to shoot from his neck downward through every fibre of his body and limbs. These pains appeared to flash along well-defined lines of ramification, and to beat with an inconceivably rapid periodicity. They seemed like streams of pulsating fire heating him to an intolerable temperature. As to his head, he was conscious of nothing but a feeling of fullness—of congestion. These sensations were unaccompanied by thought. The intellectual part of his nature was already effaced; he had power only to feel, and feeling was torment. He was conscious of motion. Encompassed in a luminous cloud, of which he was now merely the fiery heart,

---

[1]*grey-clad soldier:* refers to the gray uniforms worn by Confederate soldiers.

without material substance, he swung through unthinkable arcs of oscillation, like a vast pendulum. Then all at once, with terrible suddenness, the light about him shot upward with the noise of a loud plash; a frightful roaring was in his ears, and all was cold and dark. The power of thought was restored; he knew that the rope had broken and he had fallen into the stream. There was no additional strangulation; the noose about his neck was already suffocating him, and kept the water from his lungs. To die of hanging at the bottom of a river—the idea seemed to him ludicrous. He opened his eyes in the blackness and saw above him a gleam of light, but how distant, how inaccessible! He was still sinking, for the light became fainter and fainter until it was a mere glimmer. Then it began to grow and brighten, and he knew that he was rising toward the surface—knew it with reluctance, for he was now very comfortable. "To be hanged and drowned," he thought, "that is not so bad; but I do not wish to be shot. No: I will not be shot; that is not fair."

He was not conscious of an effort, but a sharp pain in his wrist apprised him that he was trying to free his hands. He gave the struggle his attention, as an idler might observe the feat of a juggler, without interest in the outcome. What splendid effort!— what magnificent, what superhuman strength! Ah, that was a fine endeavor! Bravo! The cord fell away; his arms parted and floated upward, the hands dimly seen on each side in the growing light. He watched them with a new interest as first one and then the other pounced upon the noose at his neck. They tore it away and thrust it fiercely aside, its undulations resembling those of a water-snake. "Put it back, put it back!" He thought he shouted these words to his hands, for the undoing of the noose had been succeeded by the direst pang which he had yet experienced. His neck arched horribly; his brain was on fire; his heart, which had been fluttering faintly, gave a great leap, trying to force itself out at his mouth. His whole body was racked and wrenched with an insupportable anguish! But his disobedient hands gave no heed to the command. They beat the water vigorously with quick, downward strokes, forcing him to the surface. He felt his head emerge; his eyes were blinded by the sunlight; his chest expanded convulsively, and with a supreme and crowning agony his lungs engulfed a great draught of air, which instantly he expelled in a shriek!

He was now in full possession of his physical senses. They were, indeed, preternaturally keen and alert. Something in the awful disturbance of his organic system had so exalted and refined them that they made record of things never before perceived. He felt the ripples upon his face and heard their separate sounds as they struck. He looked at the forest on the bank of the stream, saw the individual trees, the leaves and the veining of each leaf—saw the very insects upon them, the locusts, the brilliant-bodied flies, the grey spiders stretching their webs from twig to twig. He noted the prismatic colors in all the dewdrops upon a million blades of grass. The humming of the gnats that danced above the eddies of the stream, the beating of the dragon flies' wings, the strokes of the water spiders' legs, like oars which had lifted their boat—all these made audible music. A fish slid along beneath his eyes and he heard the rush of its body parting the water.

He had come to the surface facing down the stream; in a moment the visible world seemed to wheel slowly round, himself the pivotal point, and he saw the bridge, the fort, the soldiers upon the bridge, the captain, the sergeant, the two privates, his executioners. They were in silhouette against the blue sky. They shouted and gesticulated,

20

pointing at him; the captain had drawn his pistol, but did not fire; the others were un-armed. Their movements were grotesque and horrible, their forms gigantic.

Suddenly he heard a sharp report and something struck the water smartly within a few inches of his head, spattering his face with spray. He heard a second report, and saw one of the sentinels with his rifle at his shoulder, a light cloud of blue smoke rising from the muzzle. The man in the water saw the eye of the man on the bridge gazing into his own through the sights of the rifle. He observed that it was a grey eye, and remembered having read that grey eyes were keenest and that all famous marksmen had them. Nevertheless, this one had missed.

A counter swirl had caught Farquhar and turned him half round; he was again looking into the forest on the bank opposite the fort. The sound of a clear, high voice in a monotonous singsong now rang out behind him and came across the water with a distinctness that pierced and subdued all other sounds, even the beating of the ripples in his ears. Although no soldier, he had frequented camps enough to know the dread significance of that deliberate, drawling, aspirated chant; the lieutenant on shore was taking a part in the morning's work. How coldly and pitilessly—with what an even, calm intonation, presaging and enforcing tranquility in the men—with what accurately-measured intervals fell those cruel words:

"Attention, company. . . . Shoulder arms. . . . Ready. . . . Aim. . . . Fire."

Farquhar dived—dived as deeply as he could. The water roared in his ears like the voice of Niagara, yet he heard the dulled thunder of the volley, and rising again toward the surface, met shining bits of metal, singularly flattened, oscillating slowly downward. Some of them touched him on the face and hands, then fell away, continuing their descent. One lodged between his collar and neck, it was uncomfortably warm, and he snatched it out. 25

As he rose to the surface, gasping for breath, he saw that he had been a long time under water; he was perceptibly farther down stream—nearer to safety. The soldiers had almost finished reloading; the metal ramrods flashed all at one in the sunshine as they were drawn from the barrels, turned in the air, and thrust into their sockets. The two sentinels fired again, independently and ineffectually.

The hunted man saw all this over his shoulder; he was now swimming vigorously with the current. His brain was as energetic as his arms and legs; he thought with the rapidity of lightning.

"The officer," he reasoned, "will not make the martinet's error a second time. It is as easy to dodge a volley as a single shot. He has probably already given the command to fire at will. God help me, I cannot dodge them all!"

An appalling plash within two yards of him, followed by a loud rushing sound, *diminuendo,*[2] which seemed to travel back through the air to the fort and died in an explosion which stirred the very river to its deeps! A rising sheet of water, which curved over him, fell down upon him, blinded him, strangled him! The cannon had taken a hand in the game. As he shook his head free from the commotion of the smitten water, he heard the deflected shot humming through the air ahead, and in an instant it was cracking and smashing the branches in the forest beyond.

---

[2]*diminuendo:* a gradually diminishing volume, a term used in music.

"They will not do that again," he thought; "the next time they will use a charge   30
of grape. I must keep my eye upon the gun; the smoke will apprise me—the report arrives too late; it lags behind the missile. It is a good gun."

Suddenly he felt himself whirled round and round—spinning like a top. The water,
the banks, the forest, the now distant bridge, fort, and men—all were commingled and
blurred. Objects were represented by their colors only; circular horizontal streaks of
color—that was all he saw. He had been caught in a vortex and was being whirled on
with a velocity of advance and gyration which made him giddy and sick. In a few moments he was flung upon the gravel at the foot of the left bank of the stream—the southern bank—and behind a projecting point which concealed him from his enemies. The
sudden arrest of his motion, the abrasion of one of his hands on the gravel, restored him
and he wept with delight. He dug his fingers into the sand, threw it over himself in
handfuls and audibly blessed it. It looked like gold, like diamonds, rubies, emeralds; he
could think of nothing beautiful which it did not resemble. The trees upon the bank were
giant garden plants; he noted a definite order in their arrangement, inhaled the fragrance of their blooms. A strange, roseate light shone through the spaces among their
trunks, and the wind made in their branches the music of æolian harps.[3] He had no
wish to perfect his escape, was content to remain in that enchanting spot until retaken.

A whizz and rattle of grapeshot among the branches high above his head roused
him from his dream. The baffled cannoneer had fired him a random farewell. He sprang
to his feet, rushed up the sloping bank, and plunged into the forest.

All that day he travelled, laying his course by the rounding sun. The forest seemed
interminable; nowhere did he discover a break in it, not even a woodman's road. He
had not known that he lived in so wild a region. There was something uncanny in the
revelation:

By nightfall he was fatigued, footsore, famishing. The thought of his wife and children urged him on. At last he found a road which led him in what he knew to be the
right direction. It was as wide and straight as a city street, yet it seemed untravelled.
No fields bordered it, no dwelling anywhere. Not so much as the barking of a dog suggested human habitation. The black bodies of the great trees formed a straight wall on
both sides, terminating on the horizon in a point, like a diagram in a lesson in perspective. Overhead, as he looked up through this rift in the wood, shone great golden
stars looking unfamiliar and grouped in strange constellations. He was sure they were
arranged in some order which had a secret and malign significance. The wood on either side was full of singular noises, among which—once, twice, and again—he distinctly
heard whispers in an unknown tongue.

His neck was in pain, and, lifting his hand to it, he found it horribly swollen. He   35
knew that it had a circle of black where the rope had bruised it. His eyes felt congested;
he could no longer close them. His tongue was swollen with thirst; he relieved its fever
by thrusting it forward from between his teeth into the cool air. How softly the turf had
carpeted the untravelled avenue! He could no longer feel the roadway beneath his feet!

---

[3]*aeolian harp:* a musical instrument consisting of a box equipped with strings of equal length that are tuned
in unison. Such harps are placed in windows to produce harmonious tones sounded by the wind.

Doubtless, despite his suffering, he fell asleep while walking, for now he sees another scene—perhaps he has merely recovered from a delirium. He stands at the gate of his own home: All is as he left it, and all bright and beautiful in the morning sunshine. He must have travelled the entire night. As he pushes open the gate and passes up the wide white walk, he sees a flutter of female garments; his wife, looking fresh and cool and sweet, steps down from the verandah to meet him. At the bottom of the steps she stands waiting, with a smile of ineffable joy, an attitude of matchless grace and dignity. Ah, how beautiful she is! He springs forward with extended arms. As he is about to clasp her, he feels a stunning blow upon the back of the neck; a blinding white light blazes all about him, with a sound like a shock of a cannon—then all is darkness and silence!

Peyton Farquhar was dead; his body, with a broken neck, swung gently from side to side beneath the timbers of the Owl Creek bridge.

Questions for Discussion and Writing

1. If we conclude that the narrator is actually hanged at the end of the story, what clues does Bierce provide to suggest that almost everything that happens is in the mind of the main character?
2. What details does Bierce provide to signal that events as they are reported are not the same as what actually occurs? How does section II serve as a **flashback**?
3. How does Bierce convey the psychological desperation of the main character as he tries to ward off tangible signs of what is actually happening?

Irene Zabytko

Irene Zabytko was born in 1954 to a Ukrainian family in Chicago. Her fiction has won the PEN Syndicated Fiction Project, and she is the founder and publisher of Odessa-Pressa *Productions. Her most recent works are* The Sky Unwashed *(2000), a novel based on the nuclear accident in Chernobyl, Russia and* When Luba Leaves Home: Stories *(2003). The following story originally appeared in* The Perimeter of Light: Writing About the Vietnam War, *edited by Vivian Vie Balfour (1992).*

HOME SOIL

I watch my son crack his knuckles, oblivious to the somber sounds of the Old Slavonic hymns the choir behind us is singing.

We are in the church where Bohdan, my son, was baptized nineteen years ago. It is Sunday. The pungent smell of frankincense permeates the darkened atmosphere of this cathedral. Soft sun rays illuminate the stained-glass windows. I sit near the one that shows Jesus on the cross looking down on some unidentifiable Apostles who are kneeling beneath His nailed feet. In the background, a tiny desperate Judas swings from a rope, the thirty pieces of silver thrown on the ground.

There is plenty of room in my pew, but my son chooses not to sit with me. I see him staring at the round carapace of a ceiling, stoic icons staring directly back at him. For the remainder of the Mass, he lightly drums his nervous fingers on top of the cover of *My Divine Friend,* the Americanized prayer book of the Ukrainian service. He took bongo lessons before he graduated high school, and learned the basic rolls from off a record, "Let's Swing with Bongos." I think it was supposed to make him popular with the girls at parties. I also think he joined the army because he wanted the virile image men in uniforms have that the bongos never delivered. When he returned from Nam, he mentioned after one of our many conversational silences that he lost the bongos, and the record is cracked, with the pieces buried somewhere deep inside the duffel bag he still hasn't unpacked.

Bohdan, my son, who calls himself Bob, has been back for three weeks. He looks so "American" in his green tailored uniform: his spit-shined vinyl dress shoes tap against the red-cushioned kneelers. It was his idea to go to church with me. He has not been anywhere since he came home. He won't even visit my garden.

Luba, my daughter, warned me he would be moody. She works for the Voice of   5 America and saw him when he landed from Nam in San Francisco. "Just don't worry, *tato,*[1] she said to me on the telephone. "He's acting weird. Culture shock."

"Explain what you mean."

"Just, you know, strange." For a disc jockey, and a bilingual one at that, she is so inarticulate. She plays American jazz and tapes concerts for broadcasts for her anonymous compatriots in Ukraine. That's what she was doing when she was in San Francisco, taping some jazz concert. Pure American music for the huddled gold-toothed youths who risk their *komsomol* privileges and maybe their lives listening to these clandestine broadcasts and to my daughter's sweet voice. She will never be able to visit our relatives back there because American security won't allow it, and she would lose her job. But it doesn't matter. After my wife died, I have not bothered to keep up with anyone there, and I don't care if they have forgotten all about me. It's just as well.

I noticed how much my son resembled my wife when I first saw him again at the airport. He was alone, near the baggage claim ramp. He was taller than ever, and his golden hair was bleached white from the jungle sun. He inherited his mother's high cheekbones, but he lost his baby fat, causing his cheeks to jut out from his lean face as sharp as the arrowheads he used to scavenge for when he was a kid.

We hugged briefly. I felt his medals pinch through my thin shirt. "You look good, son," I tied. I avoided his eyes and concentrated on a pin shaped like an open parachute that he wore over his heart.

"Hi, *tato,*" he murmured. We spoke briefly about his flight home from San Fran-   10 cisco, how he'd seen Luba. We stood apart, unlike the other soldiers with their families who were hugging and crying on each other's shoulders in a euphoric delirium.

He grabbed his duffel bag from the revolving ramp and I walked behind him to see if he limped or showed any signs of pain. He showed nothing.

"Want to drive?" I asked, handing him the keys to my new Plymouth.

---

[1]*tato:* "Father" or "Dad."

"Nah," he said. He looked around at the cars crowding the parking lot, and I thought he seemed afraid. "I don't remember how the streets go anymore."

An usher in his best borscht-red polyester suit waits for me to drop some money into the basket. It is old Pan.[2] Medved, toothless except for the prominent gold ones he flashes at me as he pokes me with his basket.

"*Nu,* give," he whispers hoarsely, but loud enough for a well-dressed woman with   15
lacquered hair who sits in front of me to turn around and stare in mute accusation.

I take out the gray and white snakeskin wallet Bohdan brought back for me, and transfer out a ten dollar bill. I want the woman to see it before it disappears into the basket. She smiles at me and nods.

Women always smile at me like that. Especially after they see my money and find out that I own a restaurant in the neighborhood. None of the Ukies[3] go there; they don't eat fries and burgers much. But the "jackees"—the Americans—do when they're sick of eating in the cafeteria at the plastics factory. My English is pretty good for a D.P.,[4] and no one has threatened to bomb my business because they accuse me of being a no-god bohunk commie. Not yet anyway.

But the women are always impressed. I usually end up with the emigrés—some of them Ukrainians. The Polish women are the greediest for gawdy trinkets and for a man to give them money so that they can return to their husbands and children in Warsaw. I like them the best anyway because they laugh more than the other women I see, and they know how to have a good time.

Bohdan knows nothing about my lecherous life. I told the women to stay clear after my son arrived. He is so lost with women. I think he was a virgin when he joined the army, but I'm sure he isn't now. I can't ask him.

After mass ends, I lose Bohdan in the tight clusters of people leaving their pews and   20
genuflecting toward the iconostasis. He waits for me by the holy water font. It looks like a regular porcelain water fountain but without a spout. There is a sponge in the basin that is moistened with the holy water blessed by the priests here. Bohdan stands towering over the font, dabs his fingers into the sponge, but doesn't cross himself the way he was taught to do as a boy.

"What's the matter?" I ask in English. I hope he will talk to me if I speak to him in his language.

But Bohdan ignores me and watches an elderly woman gingerly entering the door of the confessional. "What she got to say? Why is she going in there?"

"Everyone has sins."

"Yeah, but who forgives?"

"God forgives," I say. I regret it because it makes me feel like a hypocrite when-   25
ever I parrot words I still find difficult to believe.

We walk together in the neighborhood; graffiti visible in the alley-ways despite the well-trimmed lawns with flowers and "bathtub" statues of the Blessed Mary smiling benevolently at us as we pass by the small bungalows. I could afford to move out of

---

[2]*Pan:* a term of respect for adult males, the equivalent of *Mr.*   [3]*Ukies:* Ukrainian Americans.   [4]*D.P.:* displaced person (war refugee).

here, out of Chicago and into some nearby cushy suburb, Skokie or something. But what for? Some smart Jewish lawyer or doctor would be my next door neighbor and find out that I'm a Ukie and complain to me about how his grandmother was raped by Petliura.[5] I've heard it before. Anyway, I like where I am. I bought a three-flat apartment building after my wife died and I live in one of the apartments rent-free. I can walk to my business, and see the past—old women in babushkas sweeping the sidewalks in front of their cherished gardens; men in Italian-made venetian-slat sandals and woolen socks rushing to a chess match at the Soyuiez, a local meeting place where the D.P.s sit for hours rehashing the war over beers and chess.

Bohdan walks like a soldier. Not exactly a march, but a stiff gait that a good posture in a rigid uniform demands. He looks masculine, but tired and worn. Two pimples are sprouting above his lip where a faint moustache is starting.

"Want a cigarette?" I ask. Soldiers like to smoke. During the forties, I smoked that horrible cheap tobacco, *mahorka*. I watch my son puff heavily on the cigarette I've given him, with his eyes partially closed, delicately cupping his hands to protect it from the wind. In my life, I have seen so many soldiers in that exact pose; they all look the same. When their faces are contorted from sucking the cigarette, there is an unmistakable shadow of vulnerability and fear of living. That gesture and stance are more eloquent than the blood and guts war stories men spew over their beers.

Pan Medved, the battered gold-toothed relic in the church, has that look. Pan Holewski, one of my tenants, has it too. I would have known it even if he never openly displayed his old underground soldier's cap that sits on a bookshelf in the living room between small Ukrainian and American flags. I see it every time I collect the rent.

I wish Bohdan could tell me what happened to him in Vietnam. What did he do? What was done to him? Maybe now isn't the time to tell me. He may never tell me. I never told anyone either.   30

I was exactly his age when I became a soldier. At nineteen, I was a student at the university in L'vov, which the Poles occupied. I was going to be a poet, to study poetry and write it, but the war broke out, and my family could not live on the romantic epics I tried to publish, so I was paid very well by the Nazis to write propaganda pamphlets. "Freedom for Ukrainians" I wrote—"Freedom for our people. Fight the Poles and Russians alongside our German brothers" and other such dreck. I even wrote light verse that glorified Hitler as the protector of the free Ukrainian nation that the Germans promised us. My writing was as naïve as my political ideas.

My new career began in a butcher shop, commandeered after the Polish owner was arrested and shot. I set my battered Underwood typewriter atop an oily wooden table where crescents of chicken feathers still clung between the cracks. Meat hooks that once held huge sides of pork hung naked in a back room, and creaked ominously like a deserted gallows whenever anyone slammed the front door. Every shred of meat had been stolen by looters after the Germans came into the city. Even the little bell that

---

[5]*Petliura:* Simeon Petliura (1879–1926), an anti-Bolshevik Ukrainian leader who was accused of responsibility for Jewish pogroms during World War I. When his forces were defeated by the Russians he went into exile in Paris, where he was ultimately assassinated by a Jewish nationalist.

shopkeepers kept at the entrance was taken. But I was very comfortable in my surroundings. I thought only about how I was to play a part in a historical destiny that my valiant words would help bring about. That delusion lasted only about a week or so until three burly Nazis came in. "*Schnell!*" they said to me, pushing me out of my chair and pointing to the windows where I saw crowds chaotically swarming about. Before I could question the soldiers, one of them shoved a gun into my hands and pushed me out into the streets. I felt so bewildered until the moment I pointed my rifle at a man who was about—I thought—to hit me with a club of some sort. Suddenly, I felt such an intense charge of power, more so than I had ever felt writing some of my best poems. I was no longer dealing with abstract words and ideas for a mythological cause; I was responsible for life and death.

I enjoyed that power, until it seeped into my veins and poisoned my soul. It was only an instant, a brief interlude, a matter of hours until that transformation occurred. I still replay that scene in my mind almost forty years after it happened, no matter what I am doing, or who I am with.

I think she was a village girl. Probably a Jew, because on that particular day, the Jews were the ones chosen to be rounded up and sent away in cattle cars. Her hair was golden red, short and wavy as was the style, and her neck was awash in freckles. It was a crowded station in the center of the town, not far from the butcher shop. There were Germans shouting and women crying and church bells ringing. I stood with that German regulation rifle I hardly knew how to handle, frozen because I was too lightheaded and excited. I too began to yell at people and held the rifle against my chest, and I was very much aware of how everyone responded to my authority.

Then, this girl appeared in my direct line of vision. Her back was straight, her shoulders tensed; she stopped in the middle of all the chaos. Simply stopped. I ran up and pushed her. I pushed her hard, she almost fell. I kept pushing her, feeling the thin material of her cheap wool jacket against my chapped eager hand; her thin muscles forced forward by my shoves. Once, twice, until she toppled into the open door of a train and fell toward a heap of other people moving deeper into the tiny confines of the stinking cattle car. She never turned around.

I should have shot her. I should have spared her from whatever she had to go through. I doubt she survived. I should have tried to find out what her name was, so I could track down her relatives and confess to them. At least in that way, they could have spat at me injustice and I would have finally received the absolution I will probably never find in this life.

I don't die. Instead, I go to the garden. It is Sunday evening. I am weeding the crop of beets and cabbages I planted in the patch in my backyard. The sun is lower, a breeze kicks up around me, but my forehead sweats. I breathe in the thick deep earth smells as the dirt crumbles and rotates against the blade of my hoe. I should destroy the honeysuckle vine that is slowly choking my plants, but the scent is so sweet, and its intoxicating perfume reminds me of a woman's gentleness.

I hoe for a while, but not for long, because out of the corner of my eye, I see Bohdan sitting on the grass tearing the firm green blades with his clenched hands. He is still wearing his uniform, all except the jacket, tie, and cap. He sits with his legs apart, his head down, ignoring the black flies that nip at his ears.

I wipe my face with a bright red bandana, which I brought with me to tie up the stalks of my drooping sunflowers. "Bohdan," I say to my son. "Why don't we go into the house and have a beer. I can finish this another time." I look at the orange sun. 'It's humid and there's too many flies—means rain will be coming."

My son is quietly crying to himself.   40

"*Tato,* I didn't know anything," he cries out. "You know, I just wanted to jump" out from planes with my parachute. I just wanted to fly . . ."

"I should have stopped you," I say more to myself than to him. Bohdan lets me stroke the thin spikes of his army regulation crew-cut which is soft and warm and I am afraid of how easily my hand can crush his skull.

I rock him in my arms the way I saw his mother embrace him when he was afraid to sleep alone.

There is not much more I can do right now except to hold him. I will hold him until he pulls away.

Questions for Discussion and Writing

1. Suddenly finding oneself with the power of life and death over other human be-ings is a harrowing experience for the narrator. How do the memories of this ex-perience bring him closer to his son, who just returned from Vietnam?
2. What means does Zabytko use to make the narrator a sympathetic character de-spite the evil he has perpetrated in the past?
3. *The Mahabarata,* a classic Indian epic (200 B.C.), suggests that just as no good man is all good, no bad man is all bad. How does "Home Soil" illustrate this insight?

POETRY

Bertolt Brecht

. . . .

Bertolt Brecht (1898–1956) was born in Augsburg, Germany; he studied medicine at Munich University and served as an orderly in a military hospital during World War I. Although he wrote poems and stories, he is best known for his dramas, such as The Three-Penny Opera *(1928, written with Kurt Weill) and* The Caucasian Chalk Circle *(1954). The following poem (translated by H. R. Hayes) is reprinted from* Selected Poems *(1947).*

A WORKER READS HISTORY

Who built the seven gates of Thebes?
The books are filled with names of kings.
Was it kings who hauled the craggy blocks of stone?

And Babylon, so many times destroyed,
Who built the city up each time? In which of Lima's houses,   5
That city glittering with gold, lived those who built it?
~~In the evening when the Chinese wall was finished~~
Where did the masons go? Imperial Rome
Is full of arcs of triumph. Who reared them up? Over whom
Did the Caesars triumph? Byzantium lives in song,   10
Were all her dwellings palaces? And even in Atlantis[1] of the legend
The night the sea rushed in,
The drowning men still bellowed for their slaves.

Young Alexander conquered India.
He alone?   15
Caesar beat the Gauls.
Was there not even a cook in his army?
Philip of Spain wept as his fleet
Was sunk and destroyed. Were there no other tears?
Frederick the Great triumphed in the Seven Years War. Who   20
Triumphed with him?

Each page a victory,

At whose expense the victory ball?
Every ten years a great man,
Who paid the piper?   25

So many particulars.
So many questions.

Questions for Discussion and Writing

1. In what way is the poem designed to make readers think about people that history books never mention? Who are they, and what role have they really played?
2. The contrast between the "great man" who appears every ten years and the faceless masses who pay the "piper" is a source of dramatic irony. What point is Brecht making with this statement?
3. A classic debate in history has been whether leaders shape history or are created by historical events. What is your view? Give an example that supports it.
4. For Web sites that provide information on any era or specific date in history, you might consult <www.thehistorynet.com>, <www.scopesys.com/anyday/>, or <www.440.com/twtd/today.html>. Look at these sites and select a topic for a research project.

---

[1]*Atlantis:* a mythical island in the Atlantic Ocean west of Gibraltar, said to have sunk into the sea.

Eleni Fourtouni

Eleni Fourtouni was born in Sparta, Greece, in 1933. Fourtouni's poetry springs from her translations of nine journals kept by Greek women political prisoners during the war in Greece. These journals were edited and compiled by Victoria Theodorou, herself an inmate of the prison and writer of one of the journals. These compilations and oral histories are called Greek Women of the Resistance. *Fourtouni's work includes a collection of poetry,* Monovassia *(1976), and an anthology she edited and translated,* Contemporary Greek Women Poets *(1978), in which "Child's Memory" first appeared. In this poem, the act of cutting off the head of a fish the narrator's young son has just caught releases submerged childhood memories of brutalities committed during the Nazi occupation.*

CHILD'S MEMORY

Every time I think of it
there's a peculiar tickle
at my throat
especially when I clean fish
the fish my blond son brings me   5
proud of his catch—
and I must cut off the heads

my hand holding the knife hesitates—
that peculiar tickle again—
I set the knife aside   10
furtively I scratch my throat

then I bring the knife down
on the thick scaly neck—
not much of a neck really—
just below the gills   15
I hack at the slippery
hulk of bass
my throat itches
my hands stink fish
they drip blood   20
my knife cuts through

the great head is off
I breathe

Once again the old image comes
into focus—   25
the proud blond soldier
his polished black boots
his spotless green uniform

his smile
the sack he lugs   30
into the schoolyards

the children gather
the soldier dips his hand inside the sack
the children hold their breath
what is it what?   35
their ink-smudged hands fly to their eyes

but we're full of curiosity
between our spread fingers we see . . .

the soldier's laughter is loud
as he pulls out   40
the heads of two Greek partisans.

quickly I rinse the blood off my knife.

Questions for Discussion and Writing

1. How does the way in which the poem begins suggest that the traumatic events of the past are never far from the speaker's consciousness?
2. What insight does the poem offer into the relationship between the local Greek population and the German army that occupied the town during World War II?
3. How does the way the poem is constructed build suspense about the unknown horrible event that still casts a shadow over the young mother's life in the present? How has the mother's relationship with her son been forever altered by the events that took place in her own childhood during wartime?

David R. Slavitt

. . . .

David R. Slavitt (b. 1935) was educated at Yale and Columbia Universities. His published works include novels, plays, several books of poetry, and translations of Greek and Roman poets. "Titanic" first appeared in Big Nose *(1983). He translated* The Latin Odes of Jean Dorat *(2000) and, from the French,* Sonnets of Love and Death: Jean de Sponde—1557–1595 *(2001) and* The Book of Lamentations: A Meditation and Translation *(2001). Slavitt currently teaches at Bennington College in Vermont. His latest work is* Aspects of the Novel: A Novel *(2003).*

TITANIC

Who does not love the *Titanic?*
If they sold passage tomorrow for the same crossing,
who would not buy?

To go down . . . We all go down, mostly
alone. But with crowds of people, friends, servants,   5
well fed, with music, with lights! Ah!

And the world, shocked, mourns, as it ought to do
and almost never does. There will be the books and movies
to remind our grandchildren who we were
and how we died, and give them a good cry.   10

Not so bad, after all. The cold
water is anesthetic and very quick.
The cries on all sides must be a comfort.

We all go: only a few, first-class.

Questions for Discussion and Writing

1. Slavitt uses the historical event of the *Titanic*'s sinking to explore the broader implications of mortality. What particular twist does he give this age-old topic?
2. To what extent is self-pity the dominant emotion Slavitt evokes, or do you find his poem ironic? Explain your reaction.
3. Would being remembered in the way Slavitt suggests the passengers on the Titanic are remembered be important to you? Why or why not?
4. What do these menus from the *Titanic* tell you about class divisions on the luxury liner, and what do they add to your understanding of Slavitt's poem?

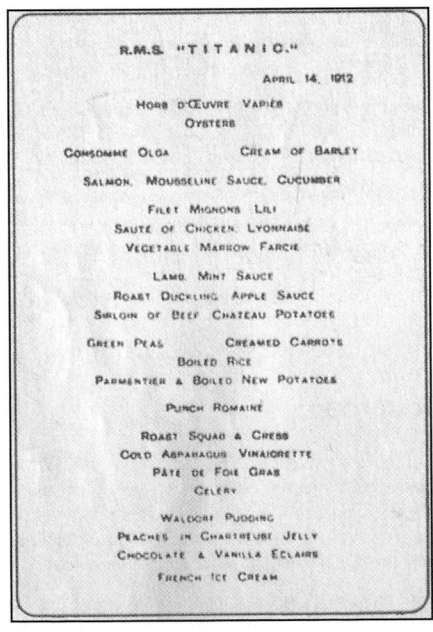

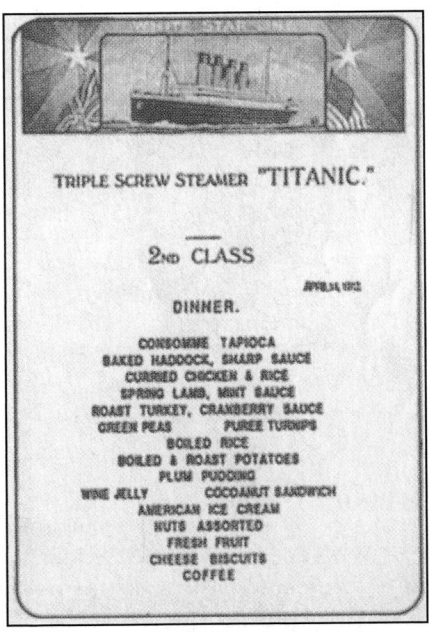

W. B. Yeats

William Butler Yeats (1865–1939), an Irish poet and playwright, was the son of the artist John Yeats. William initially studied painting and lived in London and in Sligo, where many of his poems are set. Fascinated by Irish legend and the occult, he became a leader of the Irish Literary Renaissance. The long poems in his early book, The Wanderings of Oisin *(1889), show an intense nationalism, a feeling strengthened by his hopeless passion for the Irish patriot Maude Gonne. In 1898 he helped to found the Irish Literary Theatre and later the Abbey Theatre. As he grew older, Yeats's poetry moved from transcendentalism to a more physical realism, and polarities between the physical and the spiritual are central in poems like "Sailing to Byzantium" and the "Crazy Jane" sequence. Some of his best work came late, in* The Tower *(1928) and* Last Poems *(1940). Yeats received the Nobel Prize for Literature in 1923 and is generally considered the greatest poet of the twentieth century. The extraordinary vibrancy of Yeats's later poetry can be seen in "The Second Coming" (1919), widely acknowledged to be his signature poem.*

THE SECOND COMING[1]

Turning and turning in the widening gyre
The falcon cannot hear the falconer;
Things fall apart; the centre cannot hold;
Mere anarchy is loosed upon the world,
The blood-dimmed tide is loosed, and everywhere   5
The ceremony of innocence is drowned;
The best lack all conviction, while the worst
Are full of passionate intensity.

Surely some revelation is at hand;
Surely the Second Coming is at hand.   10
The Second Coming! Hardly are those words out
When a vast image out of *Spiritus Mundi*[2]
Troubles my sight: somewhere in sands of the desert
A shape with lion body and the head of a man,
A gaze blank and pitiless as the sun,   15
Is moving its slow thighs, while all about it
Reel shadows of the indignant desert birds.
The darkness drops again; but now I know
That twenty centuries of stony sleep
Were vexed to nightmare by a rocking cradle,   20
And what rough beast, its hour come round at last,
Slouches towards Bethlehem to be born?

---

[1]*The Second Coming:* The return ("second coming") of Christ is prophesied in the New Testament (Matthew 24). Here the return is not of Jesus but of a terrifying inhuman embodiment of pre-Christian and pre-Grecian barbarism. The poem is a sharply prophetic response to the turmoil of Europe following World War I.
[2]*Spiritus Mundi* (Latin): Spirits of the World, that is, archetypal images in the "Great Memory" of the human psyche.

Questions for Discussion and Writing

1. How do the images with which the poem begins suggest to the speaker that the conditions prophesied in the New Testament (Matthew 24) signify the second coming of Christ? How does the vision that suddenly appears refute this expectation?
2. What is the relationship between the birth of Christ two thousand years before and the risen Sphinx "slouching" over the desert? How would you characterize the shift in the emotional state of the speaker throughout the course of the poem?
3. What aspects of this "rough beast" suggest to the speaker that a new age of barbarism is about to begin with the twentieth century?

Thinking Critically About the Image

Francisco de Goya (1746–1828), Spanish painter and graphic artist, was acclaimed as the greatest painter of his age. The candor of observation revealed in his works makes him the most graphic and savage of social satirists. Although he was appointed court painter to Charles III and Charles IV, his royal portraits show his disdain for his subjects. Napoleon's invasion of Spain in 1808 inspired Goya's impressive painting *The Third of May, 1808* (1814) commemorating the execution of a group of Madrid citizens. The painting reveals a powerful use of color, and we feel Goya's outrage directed toward war (depicted here for the first time as futile and ignoble): there are no heroes, only those who kill and those who are killed.

1. How does the effect of the painting depend on Goya's exclusion of everything that is irrelevant?
2. How does Goya create artistic effects through the use of color, light, and shadow, as well as gestures and facial expressions?
3. Why is it significant that we cannot see the faces of the executioners?

Connections

Chapter 7: History in the Making

Herodotus, *Concerning Egypt*
Compare the traditional religion of the ancient Egyptians as described by Herodotus with the modern religions that the Dalai Lama discusses in "The Role of Religion in Modern Society" (Ch. 11).

Gilbert Highet,   *The Gettysburg Address*
Compare the rhetorical strategies used by Lincoln with those used by Martin Luther King, Jr., in "I Have a Dream" (Ch. 8).

Jack London,   *The San Francisco Earthquake*
Compare the reactions of the survivors of the earthquake with the survivors of the *Titanic* as reported by Hanson W. Baldwin.

Hanson W. Baldwin,   *R. M. S.* Titanic
What aspects of the literal lifeboat dilemma confronting passengers on the *Titanic* does Garrett Hardin use in "Lifeboat Ethics" (Ch. 11) to explore ethical trade-offs?

Maurizio Chierici,   *The Man from Hiroshima*
How did the pressures to which Claude Eatherly was subjected illustrate Stanley Milgram's experiment described in "The Perils of Obedience" (Ch. 11)?

Haunani-Kay Trask,   *From a Native Daughter*
In what sense might Trask's analysis be considered the worker's reading of history espoused by Bertolt Brecht in his poem?

Stuart Hirschberg,   *Analyzing the Rhetoric of Nixon's "Checkers" Speech*
Contrast Nixon's speech with that of President Lincoln as analyzed by Gilbert Highet to discover how politicans can use rhetoric to reveal or conceal the truth.

Dennis Smith,   *Report from Ground Zero*
What similar methods do Smith and Jack London use to allow their readers to comprehend the magnitude of an inconceivable disaster?

Ambrose Bierce,   *An Occurrence at Owl Creek Bridge*
Bierce uses a neutral journalistic framework to set the stage for his story. After reading the account by Jack London, discuss the advantages of this method in nonfiction and fiction.

Irene Zabytko,   *Home Soil*
Compare the way Vietnam is depicted in Zabytko's story with Lance Morrow's article "Imprisoning Time in a Rectangle" (Ch. 10) and its accompanying photo by Eddie Adams.

Bertolt Brecht,   *A Worker Reads History*
In what respects do both Brecht and Stuart Hirschberg argue for a reexamination of assumptions that underlie important figures and events in history?

Eleni Fourtouni,   *Child's Memory*
In what respects do Fourtouni's poem and Irene Zabytko's story provide complementary perspectives on wartime memories triggered by events in the present?

David R. Slavitt,   *Titanic*
What different emphasis do Slavitt and Hanson W. Baldwin give to the sinking of the *Titanic*?

W. B. Yeats,   *The Second Coming*
To what extent does Dennis Smith's report on the 9/11 attacks illustrate Yeats's prediction?

Ben Shahn, Riot on Carol Street, *1944.*
Tempera on board, 71 × 51 cm; framed: 83 × 63 × 5 cm. Thyssen-Bornemisza Colletions.

The Pursuit of Justice

You only have power over people so long as you don't take everything *away from them. But when you've robbed a man of* everything *he's no longer in your power—he's free again.*

—ALEXANDER SOLZHENITSYN, *THE FIRST CIRCLE*

The allegiance individuals owe their governments, and the protection of individual rights citizens expect in return, have been subjects of intense analysis through the ages. The readings that follow continue this debate by providing accounts drawn from many different societies.

Jonathan Swift, writing in the 1700s, and Martin Luther King, Jr., writing over two centuries later, enunciate strikingly similar ideas of civil and economic freedom. A livable wage for the working poor is advocated by Barbara Ehrenreich, and the impact of terrorism is explored by Steven E. Barkan and Lynne L. Snowden.

Readings by Harriet Jacobs, Kenneth M. Stampp, and Luis Sepulveda bear witness to the consequences of the suspension of civil rights. Michael Levin creates an intriguing hypothetical case as a response to potential acts of nuclear terrorism.

Panos Ioannides's story, *Gregory,* dramatizes the emotional turmoil of a soldier during the Cypriot liberation struggle. Liliana Heker creates a story that explores impenetrable class barriers in Argentina.

The poems of W. H. Auden, Margaret Atwood, and Carolyn Forché offer a sardonic epitaph on a compliant citizen, a catalogue of the effects of wars on soldiers and the women they leave behind, and a terrifying and surreal encounter with a modern-day Central American dictator.

Trifles, a play (based on real events) by Susan Glaspell, dramatizes a criminal investigation that illustrates how the search for justice is profoundly influenced by time, place, and gender.

NONFICTION

Harriet Jacobs

Harriet Jacobs (1813–1896), also known as Linda Brent, escaped from the slavery into which she had been born and made a new life for herself in the North. She told her story, related below, "Incidents in the Life of a Slave Girl" (1861), with the assistance of Lydia Maria Child, a northern abolitionist leader. Her account has become part of the canon of American literature, history, and women's studies. In the following selection, Jacobs reveals the harrowing predicament that many female slaves found themselves in, trying to fend off their masters' lust and the ensuing jealousy of their wives.

INCIDENTS IN THE LIFE OF A SLAVE GIRL

I would ten thousand times rather that my children should be the half-starved paupers of Ireland than to be the most pampered among the slaves of America. I would rather drudge out my life on a cotton plantation, till the grave opened to give me rest, than to live with an unprincipled master and a jealous mistress. The felon's home in a penitentiary is preferable. He may repent, and turn from the error of his ways, and so find peace, but it is not so with a favorite slave. She is not allowed to have any pride of character. It is deemed a crime in her to wish to be virtuous.

Mrs. Flint possessed the key to her husband's character before I was born. She might have used this knowledge to counsel and to screen the young and the innocent among her slaves; but for them she had no sympathy. They were the objects of her constant suspicion and malevolence. She watched her husband with unceasing vigilance; but he was well practiced in means to evade it. What he could not find opportunity to say in words he manifested in signs. He invented more than were ever thought of in a deaf and dumb asylum. I let them pass, as if I did not understand what he meant; and many were the curses and threats bestowed on me for my stupidity. One day he caught me teaching myself to write. He frowned, as if he was not well pleased; but I suppose he came to the conclusion that such an accomplishment might help to advance his favorite scheme. Before long, notes were often slipped into my hand. I would return them, saying, "I can't read them, sir." "Can't you?" he replied; "then I must read them to you." He always finished the reading by asking, "Do you understand?" Sometimes he would complain of the heat of the tea room, and order his supper to be placed on a small table in the piazza. He would seat himself there with a well-satisfied smile, and tell me to stand by and brush away the flies. He would eat very slowly, pausing between the mouthfuls. These intervals were employed in describing the happiness I was so foolishly throwing away, and in threatening me with the penalty that finally awaited my stubborn disobedience. He boasted much of the forbearance he had exercised toward me, and reminded me that there was a limit to his patience. When I succeeded in avoiding opportunities for him to talk to me at home, I was ordered to come to his office, to do some errand. When there, I was obliged to stand and listen to such language as he saw fit to address to me. Sometimes I so openly expressed my contempt for him that he would become violently enraged, and I wondered why he did not strike me. Circumstanced as he was, he probably thought it was better policy to be forebearing. But the state of things grew worse and worse daily. In desperation I told him that I must and would apply to my grandmother for protection. He threatened me with death, and worse than death, if I made my complaint to her. Strange to say, I did not despair. I was naturally of a buoyant disposition, and always I had a hope of somehow getting out of his clutches. Like many a poor, simple slave before me, I trusted that some threads of joy would yet be woven into my dark destiny.

I had entered my sixteenth year, and every day it became more apparent that my presence was intolerable to Mrs. Flint. Angry words frequently passed between her and her husband. He had never punished me himself, and he would not allow anybody else to punish me. In that respect, she was never satisfied; but, in her angry moods, no terms were too vile for her to bestow upon me. Yet I, whom she detested so bitterly, had far more pity for her than he had, whose duty it was to make her life happy. I never wronged her, or wished to wrong her; and one word of kindness from her would have brought me to her feet.

After repeated quarrels between the doctor and his wife, he announced his intention to take his youngest daughter, then four years old, to sleep in his apartment. It was necessary that a servant should sleep in the same room, to be on hand if the child stirred. I was selected for that office, and informed for what purpose that arrangement had been made. By managing to keep within sight of people, as much as possible, during the daytime, I had hitherto succeeded in eluding my master, though a razor was often held to my throat to force me to change this line of policy. At night I slept by the side of my great aunt, where I felt safe. He was too prudent to come into her room. She was an old woman, and had been in the family many years. Moreover, as a married man, and a professional man, he deemed it necessary to save appearances in some degree. But he resolved to remove the obstacle in the way of his scheme; and he thought he had planned it so that he should evade suspicion. He was well aware how much I prized my refuge by the side of my old aunt, and he determined to dispossess me of it. The first night the doctor had the little child in his room alone. The next morning, I was ordered to take my station as nurse the following night. A kind Providence interposed in my favor. During the day Mrs. Flint heard of this new arrangement, and a storm followed. I rejoiced to hear it rage.

After a while my mistress sent for me to come to her room. Her first question was, 5 "Did you know you were to sleep in the doctor's room?"

"Yes, ma'am."

"Who told you?"

"My master."

"Will you answer truly all the questions I ask?"

"Yes, ma'am." 10

"Tell me, then, as you hope to be forgiven, are you innocent of what I have accused you?"

"I am."

She handed me a Bible, and said, "Lay your hand on your heart, kiss this holy book, and swear before God that you tell me the truth."

I took the oath she required, and I did it with a clear conscience.

"You have taken God's holy word to testify your innocence," said she. "If you 15 have deceived me, beware! Now take this stool, sit down, look me directly in the face, and tell me all that has passed between your master and you."

I did as she ordered. As I went on with my account her color changed frequently, she wept, and sometimes groaned. She spoke in tones so sad, that I was touched by her grief. The tears came to my eyes; but I was soon convinced that her emotions arose from anger and wounded pride. She felt that her marriage vows were desecrated, her dignity insulted; but she had no compassion for the poor victim of her husband's perfidy. She pitied herself as a martyr; but she was incapable of feeling for the condition of shame and misery in which her unfortunate, helpless slave was placed.

Yet perhaps she had some touch of feeling for me; for when the conference was ended, she spoke kindly, and promised to protect me. I should have been much comforted by this assurance if I could have had confidence in it; but my experiences in slavery had filled me with distrust. She was not a very refined woman, and had not much control over her passions. I was an object of her jealousy, and, consequently, of her hatred; and I knew I could not expect kindness or confidence from her under the circumstances in which I was placed. I could not blame her. Slaveholders' wives feel as other women would under similar circumstances. The fire of her temper kindled from small sparks, and now the flame became so intense that the doctor was obliged to give up his intended arrangement.

I knew I had ignited the torch, and I expected to suffer for it afterward; but I felt too thankful to my mistress for the timely aid she rendered me to care much about that. She now took me to sleep in a room adjoining her own. There I was an object of her especial care, though not of her especial comfort, for she spent many a sleepless night to watch over me. Sometimes I woke up, and found her bending over me. At other times she whispered in my ear, as though it was her husband who was speaking to me, and listened to hear what I would answer. If she startled me, on such occasions, she would glide stealthily away; and the next morning she would tell me I had been talking in my sleep, and ask who I was talking to. At last I began to be fearful for my life. It had been often threatened; and you can imagine, better than I can describe, what an unpleasant sensation it must produce to wake up in the dead of night and find a jealous woman bending over you. Terrible as this experience was, I had fears that it would give place to one more terrible.

My mistress grew weary of her vigils; they did not prove satisfactory. She changed her tactics. She now tried the trick of accusing my master of crime, in my presence, and gave my name as the author of the accusation. To my utter astonishment, he replied, "I don't believe it; but if she did acknowledge it, you tortured her into exposing me." Tortured into exposing him! Truly, Satan had no difficulty in distinguishing the color of his soul! I understood his object in making this false representation. It was to show me that I gained nothing by seeking the protection of my mistress; that the power was still all in his own hands. I pitied Mrs. Flint. She was a second wife, many years the junior of her husband; and the hoary-headed miscreant was enough to try the patience of a wiser and better woman. She was completely foiled, and knew not how to proceed. She would gladly have had me flogged for my supposed false oath; but, as I have already stated, the doctor never allowed anyone to whip me. The old sinner was politic.

The application of the lash might have led to remarks that would have exposed him in the eyes of his children and grandchildren. How often did I rejoice that I lived in a town where all the inhabitants knew each other! If I had been on a remote plantation, or lost among the multitude of a crowded city, I should not be a living woman at this day.

The secrets of slavery are concealed like those of the Inquisition. My master was, 20 to my knowledge, the father of eleven slaves. But did the mothers dare to tell who was the father of their children? Did the other slaves dare to allude to it, except in whispers among themselves? No, indeed! They knew too well the terrible consequences.

My grandmother could not avoid seeing things which excited her suspicions. She was uneasy about me, and tried various ways to buy me; but the never-changing answer was always repeated: "Linda does not belong to *me*. She is my daughter's property, and I have no legal right to sell her." The conscientious man! He was too scrupulous to *sell* me; but he had no scruples whatever about committing a much greater wrong against the helpless young girl placed under his guardianship, as his daughter's property. Sometimes my persecutor would ask me whether I would like to be sold. I told him I would rather be sold to anybody than to lead such a life as I did. On such occasions he would assume the air of a very injured individual, and reproach me for my ingratitude. "Did I not take you into the house, and make you the companion of my own children?" he would say. "Have I ever treated you like a Negro? I have never allowed you to be punished, not even to please your mistress. And this is the recompense I get, you ungrateful girl!" I answered that he had reasons of his own for screening me from punishment, and that the course he pursued made my mistress hate me and persecute me. If I wept, he would say, "Poor child! Don't cry! don't cry! I will make peace for you with your mistress. Only let me arrange matters in my own way. Poor, foolish girl! you don't know what is for your own good. I would cherish you. I would make a lady of you. Now go, and think of all I have promised you."

I did think of it.

Reader, I draw no imaginary pictures of southern homes. I am telling you the plain truth. Yet when victims make their escape from this wild beast of Slavery, northerners consent to act the part of bloodhounds, and hunt the poor fugitive back into his den, "full of dead men's bones, and all uncleanness." Nay, more, they are not only willing, but proud, to give their daughters in marriage to slaveholders. The poor girls have romantic notions of a sunny clime, and of the flowering vines that all the year round shade a happy home. To what disappointments are they destined! The young wife soon learns that the husband in whose hands she has placed her happiness pays no regard to his marriage vows. Children of every shade of complexion play with her own fair babies, and too well she knows that they are born unto him of his own household. Jealousy and hatred enter the flowery home, and it is ravaged of its loveliness.

Southern women often marry a man knowing that he is the father of many little slaves. They do not trouble themselves about it. They regard such children as property, as marketable as the pigs on the plantation; and it is seldom that they do not make them aware of this by passing them into the slave-trader's hand's as soon as possible, and thus getting them out of their sight. I am glad to say there are some honorable exceptions.

I have myself known two southern wives who exhorted their husbands to free 25 those slaves toward whom they stood in a "parental relation"; and their request was granted. These husbands blushed before the superior nobleness of their wives' natures. Though they had only counseled them to do that which it was their duty to do, it commanded their respect, and rendered their conduct more exemplary. Concealment was at an end, and confidence took the place of distrust.

Though this bad institution deadens the moral sense, even in white women, to a fearful extent, it is not altogether extinct. I have heard southern ladies say of Mr. Such-a-one, "He not only thinks it no disgrace to be the father of those little niggers, but he is not ashamed to call himself their master. I declare, such things ought not to be tolerated in any decent society!"

Questions for Discussion and Writing

1. In what ways did slavery create the conditions in which the kinds of events Jacobs describes could occur? How does she convey her untenable predicament vis-à-vis Dr. and Mrs. Flint and her resourcefulness in coping with it?

2. What was Jacobs's purpose in writing this narrative? How does it change assumptions that her readers might have held about the institution of slavery? In what way was slavery a morally corrupting influence on everyone involved?

3. Discuss comparable circumstances that exist today that have the same effect as those Jacobs describes, for example, sexual harassment in the workplace or illegal aliens working for families or the predicament of immigrants who are completely dependent on their employers.

Kenneth M. Stampp

. . . .

Kenneth M. Stampp was born in 1912 in Milwaukee, Wisconsin, and earned his Ph.D. from the University of Wisconsin in 1942. Stampp is the Morrison Professor of American History Emeritus at the University of California at Berkeley and has served as president of the Organization of American Historians. He has been Harmsworth Professor of American History at Oxford University and a Fulbright lecturer at the University of Munich and has received two Guggenheim fellowships. In addition to editing The Causes of the Civil War *(1974), Stampp is the author of many distinguished studies, including* And the War Came *(1950),* The Peculiar Institution: Slavery in the Antebellum South *(1956), and* The Imperiled Union *(1960). His most recent books include* America in 1857: A Nation on the Brink *(1990) and* The Causes of the Civil War *(1991). In "To Make Them Stand in Fear," taken from* The Peculiar Institution, *Stampp lets the facts of brutal exploitation speak for themselves as he describes the step-by-step process by which slavemasters in the South sought to break the spirits of newly arrived blacks.*

TO MAKE THEM STAND IN FEAR

A wise master did not take seriously the belief that Negroes were natural-born slaves. He knew better. He knew that Negroes freshly imported from Africa had to be broken to bondage; that each succeeding generation had to be carefully trained. This was no easy task, for the bondsman rarely submitted willingly. Moreover, he rarely submitted completely. In most cases there was no end to the need for control—at least not until old age reduced the slave to a condition of helplessness.

Masters revealed the qualities they sought to develop in slaves when they singled out certain ones for special commendation. A small Mississippi planter mourned the death of his "faithful and dearly beloved servant" Jack: "Since I have owned him he has been true to me in all respects. He was an obedient trusty servant. . . . I never knew him to steal nor lie and he ever set a moral and industrious example to those around him. . . . I shall ever cherish his memory." A Louisiana sugar planter lost a "very valuable Boy" through an accident: "His life was a very great one. I have always found him willing and obedient and never knew him to fail to do anything he was put to do." These were "ideal" slaves, the models slaveholders had in mind as they trained and governed their workers.

How might this ideal be approached? The first step, advised those who wrote discourses on the management of slaves, was to establish and maintain strict discipline. An Arkansas master suggested the adoption of the "Army Regulations as to the discipline in Forts." "They must obey at all times, and under all circumstances, cheerfully and with alacrity," affirmed a Virginia slaveholder. "It greatly impairs the happiness of a negro, to be allowed to cultivate an insubordinate temper. Unconditional submission is the only footing upon which slavery should be placed. It is precisely similar to the attitude of a minor to his parent, or a soldier to his general." A South Carolinian limned a perfect relationship between a slave and his master: "that the slave should know that his master is to govern absolutely, and he is to obey implicitly. That he is never for a moment to exercise either his will or judgment in opposition to a positive order."

The second step was to implant in the bondsmen themselves a consciousness of personal inferiority. They had "to know and keep their places," to "feel the difference between master and slave," to understand that bondage was their natural status. They had to feel that African ancestry tainted them, that their color was a badge of degradation. In the country they were to show respect for even their master's nonslaveholding neighbors; in the towns they were to give way on the streets to the most wretched white man. The line between the races must never be crossed, for familiarity caused slaves to forget their lowly station and to become "impudent."

Frederick Douglass explained that a slave might commit the offense of impudence in various ways: "in the tone of an answer; in answering at all; in not answering; in the expression of countenance; in the motion of the head; in the gait, manner and bearing of the slave." Any of these acts, in some subtle way, might indicate the absence of proper subordination. "In a well regulated community," wrote a Texan, "a negro takes off his hat in addressing a white man. . . . Where this is not enforced, we may always look for impudent and rebellious negroes."

The third step in the training of slaves was to awe them with a sense of their master's enormous power. The only principle upon which slavery could be maintained, reported a group of Charlestonians, was the "principle of fear." In his defense of slavery James H. Hammond admitted that this, unfortunately, was true but put the responsibility upon the abolitionists. Antislavery agitation had forced masters to strengthen their authority: "We have to rely more and more on the power of fear. . . . We are determined to continue masters, and to do so we have to draw the rein tighter and tighter day by day to be assured that we hold them in complete check." A North Carolina mistress, after subduing a troublesome domestic, realized that it was essential "to make them stand in fear"!

In this the slaveholders had considerable success. Frederick Douglass believed that most slaves stood "in awe" of white men; few could free themselves altogether from the notion that their masters were "invested with a sort of sacredness." Olmsted saw a small white girl stop a slave on the road and boldly order him to return to his plantation. The slave fearfully obeyed her command. A visitor in Mississippi claimed that a master, armed only with a whip or cane, could throw himself among a score of bondsmen and cause them to "flee with terror." He accomplished this by the "peculiar tone of authority" with which he spoke. "Fear, awe, and obedience . . . are interwoven into the very nature of the slave."

The fourth step was to persuade the bondsmen to take an interest in the master's enterprise and to accept his standards of good conduct. A South Carolina planter explained: "The master should make it his business to show his slaves, that the advancement of his individual interest, is at the same time an advancement of theirs. Once they feel this, it will require but little compulsion to make them act as it becomes them." Though slaveholders induced only a few chattels to respond to this appeal, these few were useful examples for others.

The final step was to impress Negroes with their helplessness, to create in them "a habit of perfect dependence" upon their masters. Many believed it dangerous to train slaves to be skilled artisans in the towns, because they tended to become self-reliant. Some thought it equally dangerous to hire them to factory owners. In the Richmond tobacco factories they were alarmingly independent and "insolvent." A Virginian was dismayed to find that his bondsmen, while working at an iron furnace, "got a habit of roaming about and *taking care of themselves*." Permitting them to hire their own time produced even worse results. "No higher evidence can be furnished of its baneful effects," wrote a Charlestonian, "than the unwillingness it produces in the slave, to return to the regular life and domestic control of the master."

A spirit of independence was less likely to develop among slaves kept on the land, 10 where most of them became accustomed to having their master provide their basic needs, and where they might be taught that they were unfit to look out for themselves. Slaves then directed their energies to the attainment of mere "temporary ease and enjoyment." "Their masters," Olmsted believed, "calculated on it in them—do not wish to cure it—and by constant practice encourage it."

Here, then, was the way to produce the perfect slave: accustom him to rigid discipline, demand from him unconditional submission, impress upon him his innate inferiority, develop in him a paralyzing fear of white men, train him to adopt the master's code of good behavior, and instill in him a sense of complete dependence. This, at least, was the goal.

But the goal was seldom reached. Every master knew that the average slave was only an imperfect copy of the model. He knew that some bondsmen yielded only to superior power—and yielded reluctantly. This complicated his problem of control.

Questions for Discussion and Writing

1. What kind of instructions were provided in the source manuals from which Stampp quotes? How does Stampp's use of these source documents illustrate the method historians use to reconstruct and interpret past events?
2. How is Stampp's analysis arranged to show that the conditioning process moved through separate stages, from external control of behavior to a state in which the slaves believed that what was good for the slave owners was good for them as well?
3. Why was the psychological conditioning used to produce dependency ultimately more important to the process than physical constraints? Why were slaves who could hire themselves out independently less able to be conditioned than those kept solely on one plantation?

Martin Luther King, Jr.

• •

Martin Luther King, Jr. (1929–1968), a monumental figure in the U.S. civil rights movement and a persuasive advocate of nonviolent means for producing social change, was born in Atlanta, Georgia, in 1929. He was ordained a Baptist minister in his father's church when he was eighteen and went on to earn degrees from Morehouse College (B.A., 1948), Crozer Theological Seminary (B.D., 1951), Chicago Theological Seminary (D.D., 1957), and Boston University (Ph.D., 1955; D.D. 1959). On December 5, 1955, while he was pastor of a church in Montgomery, Alabama, King focused national attention on the predicament of southern blacks by leading a citywide boycott of the segregated bus system. The boycott lasted over one year and nearly bankrupted the company. King founded the Southern Christian Leadership Conference and adapted techniques of nonviolent protest, which had been employed by Gandhi,[1] in a series of sit-ins and mass marches that were instrumental in bringing about the Civil Rights Act of 1964 and the Voting Rights Act of 1965. He was awarded the Nobel Prize for Peace in 1964 in recognition of his great achievements as the leader of the American civil rights movement. Sadly, King's affirmation of the need to meet physical violence with peaceful resistance led to his being jailed more than fourteen times, beaten, stoned, stabbed in the chest, and finally murdered in Memphis, Tennessee, on April 4, 1968. His many distinguished writings include Stride Towards Freedom: The Montgomery Story *(1958);* Letter from Birmingham Jail, *written in 1963 and published in 1968;* Why We Can't Wait *(1964);* Where Do We Go from Here: Community or Chaos? *(1967); and* The Trumpet of Conscience *(1968). "I Have a Dream" (1963) is the inspiring sermon delivered by King from the steps of the Lincoln Memorial to the nearly 250,000 people who had come to Washington, D.C., to commemorate the centennial of Lincoln's Emancipation Proclamation. Additional millions who watched on television were moved by this eloquent, noble, and impassioned plea that*

---

[1]*Gandhi: (1869–1948):* a great Indian political and spiritual leader, called Mahatma (great-souled), whose approach was one of nonviolent protest. He is regarded as the father of independent India.

the United States might fulfill its original promise of freedom and equality for all its citizens.

I HAVE A DREAM

I am happy to join with you today in what will go down in history as the greatest demonstration for freedom in the history of our nation.

Five score years ago, a great American, in whose symbolic shadow we stand today, signed the Emancipation Proclamation.[2] This momentous decree came as a great beacon light of hope to millions of Negro slaves who had been seared in the flames of withering injustice. It came as a joyous daybreak to end the long night of their captivity. But one hundred years later, the Negro is still not free. One hundred years later, the life of the Negro is still sadly crippled by the manacles of segregation and the chains of discrimination. One hundred years later, the Negro lives on a lonely island of poverty in the midst of a vast ocean of material prosperity. One hundred years later, the Negro is still anguished in the corners of American society and finds himself in exile in his own land. And so we have come here today to dramatize a shameful condition.

In a sense we have come to our nation's capital to cash a check. When the architects of our republic wrote the magnificent words of the Constitution and the Declaration of Independence, they were signing a promissory note to which every American was to fall heir. This note was the promise that all men—yes, Black men as well as white men—would be guaranteed the inalienable rights of life, liberty, and the pursuit of happiness.

It is obvious today that America has defaulted on this promissory note insofar as her citizens of color are concerned. Instead of honoring this sacred obligation, America has given the Negro people a bad check, a check which has come back marked "insufficient funds." But we refuse to believe that the bank of justice is bankrupt. We refuse to believe that there are insufficient funds in the great vaults of opportunity of this nation; and so we have come to cash this check, a check that will give us upon demand the riches of freedom and the security of justice.

We have also come to this hallowed spot to remind America of the fierce urgency   5
of *now*. This is no time to engage in the luxury of cooling off or to take the tranquilizing drug of gradualism. *Now* is the time to make real the promises of democracy. *Now* is the time to rise from the dark and desolate valley of segregation to the sunlit patch of racial justice. *Now* is the time to lift our nation from the quicksands of racial injustice to the solid rock of brotherhood. *Now* is the time to make justice a reality for all of God's children.

It would be fatal for the nation to overlook the urgency of the moment. This sweltering summer of the Negro's legitimate discontent will not pass until there is an invigorating autumn of freedom and equality. Nineteen sixty-three is not an end, but a beginning. And those who hope that the Negro needed to blow off steam and will now be content will have a rude awakening if the nation returns to business as usual. There

---

[2]*The Emancipation Proclamation:* the executive order abolishing slavery in the Confederacy that President Abraham Lincoln put into effect on January 1, 1863.

will be neither rest nor tranquility in America until the Negro is granted his citizenship rights. The whirlwinds of revolt will continue to shake the foundations of our nation until the bright day of justice emerges.

But there is something that I must say to my people who stand on the warm threshold which leads into the palace of justice. In the process of gaining our rightful place, we must not be guilty of wrongful deeds. Let us not seek to satisfy our thirst for freedom by drinking from the cup of bitterness and hatred. We must forever conduct our struggle on the high plane of dignity and discipline. We must not allow our creative protest to degenerate into physical violence. Again and again we must rise to the majestic heights of meeting physical force with soul force. And the marvelous new militancy which has engulfed the Negro community must not lead us to a distrust of all white people; for many of our white brothers, as evidenced by their presence here today, have come to realize that their destiny is tied up with our destiny, and they have come to realize that their freedom is inextricably bound to our freedom.

We cannot walk alone. And as we walk we must make the pledge that we shall always march ahead. We cannot turn back. There are those who are asking the devotees of civil rights, "When will you be satisfied?" We can never be satisfied as long as the Negro is the victim of the unspeakable horrors of police brutality. We can never be satisfied as long as our bodies, heavy with the fatigue of travel, cannot gain lodging in the motels of the highways and the hotels of the cities. We cannot be satisfied as long as the Negro's basic mobility is from a smaller ghetto to a larger one. We can never be satisfied as long as our children are stripped of their selfhood and robbed of their dignity by signs stating "For Whites Only." We cannot be satisfied as long as the Negro in Mississippi cannot vote and a Negro in New York believes he has nothing for which to vote. No, no, we are not satisfied, and we will not be satisfied until justice rolls down like waters and righteousness like a mighty stream.

I am not unmindful that some of you have come here out of great trials and tribulations. Some of you have come fresh from narrow jail cells. Some of you have come from areas where your quest for freedom left you battered by the storms of persecution and staggered by the winds of police brutality. You have been the veterans of creative suffering. Continue to work with the faith that unearned suffering is redemptive.

Go back to Mississippi, and go back to Alabama. Go back to South Carolina. Go 10 back to Georgia. Go back to Louisiana. Go back to the slums and ghettos of our northern cities, knowing that somehow this situation can and will be changed. Let us not wallow in the valley of despair.

I say to you today, my friends, even though we face the difficulties of today and tomorrow, I still have a dream. It is a dream deeply rooted in the American dream. I have a dream that one day this nation will rise up and live out the true meaning of its creed: "We hold these truths to be self-evident, that all men are created equal." I have a dream that one day, on the red hills of Georgia, sons of former slaves and the sons of former slave owners will be able to sit down together at the table of brotherhood. I have a dream that one day even the state of Mississippi, a state sweltering with the heat of injustice, sweltering with the heat of oppression, will be transformed into an oasis of freedom and justice. I have a dream that my four little children will one day live in a nation where they will not be judged by the color of their skin, but by the content of their character.

I have a dream today. I have a dream that one day down in Alabama—with its vicious racists, with its governor's lips dripping with the words of interposition and nullification—one day right there in Alabama, little Black boys and Black girls will be able to join hands with little white boys and white girls as sisters and brothers.

I have a dream today. I have a dream that one day every valley shall be exalted and every hill and mountain shall be made low, the rough places will be made plain and the crooked places will be made straight, and the glory of the Lord shall be revealed, and all flesh shall see it together.

This is our hope. This is the faith that I go back to the South with. And with this faith we will be able to hew out of the mountain of despair a stone of hope. With this faith we will be able to transform the jangling discords of our nation into a beautiful symphony of brotherhood. With this faith we will be able to work together, to play together, to struggle together, to go to jail together, to stand up for freedom together, knowing that we will be free one day.

And this will be the day—this will be the day when all of God's children will be   15
able to sing with new meaning.

> My country, 'tis of thee,
> Sweet land of liberty,
> Of thee I sing;
> Land where my fathers died,
> Land of the Pilgrims' pride,
> From every mountainside
> Let freedom ring.

And if America is to be a great nation, this must become true.

And so let freedom ring from the prodigious hilltops of New Hampshire. Let freedom ring from the mighty mountains of New York. Let freedom ring from the heightening Alleghenies of Pennsylvania. Let freedom ring from the snow-capped Rockies of Colorado. Let freedom ring from the curvaceous slopes of California.

But not only that. Let freedom ring from Stone Mountain of Georgia. Let freedom ring from Lookout Mountain of Tennessee. Let freedom ring from every hill and molehill of Mississippi. "From every mountainside let freedom ring."

And when this happens—when we allow freedom to ring, when we let it ring from every village and every hamlet, from every state and every city—we will be able to speed up that day when all of God's children, Black men and white men, Jews and Gentiles, Protestants and Catholics, will be able to join hands and sing in the words of the old Negro spiritual: "Free at last! Free at last! Thank God Almighty. We are free at last!"

Questions for Discussion and Writing

1. How did the civil rights movement express ideas of equality and freedom that were already deeply rooted in the Constitution? How did the affirmation of minority rights renew aspirations first stated by America's Founding Fathers?

2. What evidence is there that King was trying to reach many different groups of people, each with its own concerns? Where does he seem to shift his attention from one group to another?

3. What importance does King place on the idea of nonviolent protest? How do King's references to the Bible and the Emancipation Proclamation enhance the effectiveness of his speech?

Jonathan Swift

• •

Jonathan Swift (1667–1745), certainly one of the keenest minds of his age, was born in Dublin, into an impoverished family who were originally from England. He was educated at Trinity College, Dublin, with the help of his wealthy uncle, and in 1688 left Ireland and became a secretary to Sir William Temple in Moor Park, England. There he tutored Esther Johnson, Temple's ward, rumored to be Temple's illegimate daughter, who later became the "Stella" of Swift's letters and poems. He returned to Ireland in 1694, where he was ordained an Anglican priest, and spent a brief time in a parish in Belfast. Dissatisfied with this life, he returned to England and became active in the literary intellectual life of London, where he became friends with prominent figures such as Joseph Addison, Sir Richard Steele, and Alexander Pope. In 1713 he was named Dean of St. Patrick's Cathedral in Dublin. When his political ambitions in England were crushed with the defeat of the Tory party the following year, Swift returned to Ireland for good. A prolific writer of enormous brilliance, over the course of his life Swift used his pen to champion various causes and to assail those in power. From 1721 to 1725, he worked on his masterpiece, Gulliver's Travels, *a satire on human nature, which was published anonymously in 1726 and became an instant best-seller. The following essay, "A Modest Proposal," was published in 1729 and was written to protest repressive economic measures against the Irish by the Whig government in England.*

A MODEST PROPOSAL

*For Preventing the Children of
Poor People in Ireland from Being a Burden to
Their Parents or Country, and for Making
Them Beneficial to the Public*

It is a melancholy object to those who walk through this great town,[1] or travel in the country, when they see the streets, the roads, and cabin doors crowded with beggars of the female sex, followed by three, four, or six children, all in rags and importuning every passenger for an alms. These mothers, instead of being able to work for their honest livelihood, are forced to employ all their time in strolling to beg sustenance for their helpless infants; who as they grow up either turn thieves, for want of

---

[1] *this great town:* Dublin.

work, or leave their dear native country to fight for the Pretender[2] in Spain, or sell themselves to the Barbados.[3]

I think it is agreed by all parties that this prodigious number of children in the arms, or on the backs, or at the heels of their mothers, and frequently of their fathers, is, in the present deplorable state of the kingdom, a very great additional grievance; and therefore whoever could find out a fair, cheap, and easy method of making these children sound, useful members of the commonwealth would deserve so well of the public as to have his statue set up for a preserver of the nation.

But my intention is very far from being confined to provide only for the children of professed beggars: it is of a much greater extent and shall take in the whole number of infants at a certain age who are born of parents in effect as little able to support them as those who demand our charity in the streets.

As to my own part, having turned my thoughts for many years upon this important subject and maturely weighed the several schemes of other projectors, I have always found them grossly mistaken in their computation. It is true, a child just dropped from its dam may be supported by her milk for a solar year, with little other nourishment: at most not above the value of two shillings, which the mother may certainly get, or the value in scraps, by her lawful occupation of begging; and it is exactly at one year old that I propose to provide for them in such a manner, as, instead of being a charge upon their parents or the parish, or wanting food and raiment for the rest of their lives, they shall, on the contrary, contribute to the feeding and partly to the clothing of many thousands.

There is likewise another great advantage in my scheme, that it will prevent those   5
voluntary abortions and that horrid practice of women murdering their bastard children, alas! too frequent among us, sacrificing the poor innocent babes, I doubt more to avoid the expense than the shame, which would move tears and pity in the most savage and inhuman breast.

The number of souls in this kingdom being usually reckoned one million and a half, of these I calculate there may be about two hundred thousand couple whose wives are breeders; from which number I subtract thirty thousand couple; who are able to maintain their own children (although I apprehend there cannot be so many, under the present distresses of the kingdom), but this being granted, there will remain an hundred and seventy thousand breeders. I again subtract fifty thousand for those women who miscarry, or whose children die by accident or disease within the year. There only remain one hundred and twenty thousand children of poor parents annually born. The question therefore is, How this number shall be reared and provided for? which, as I have already said, under the present situation of affairs, is utterly impossible by all the methods hitherto proposed. For we can neither employ them in handicraft or agriculture; we neither build houses (I mean in the country) nor

---

[2]*the Pretender:* James Stuart (1688–1766), son of King James II, "pretender" or claimant to the throne which his father had lost in the Revolution of 1688. He was Catholic, and Ireland was loyal to him.   [3]*sell . . . Barbados:* Because of extreme poverty, many of the Irish bound or sold themselves to obtain passage to the West Indies or other British possessions in North America. They agreed to work for their new masters, usually planters, for a specified number of years.

cultivate land: they can very seldom pick up a livelihood by stealing till they arrive at six years old, except where they are of towardly[4] parts; although I confess they learn the rudiments much earlier, during which time they can, however, be properly looked upon only as probationers; as I have been informed by a principal gentleman in the county of Cavan, who protested to me that he never knew above one or two instances under the age of six, even in a part of the kingdom so renowned for the quickest proficiency in that art.

I am assured by our merchants that a boy or a girl before twelve years old is no salable commodity; and even when they come to this age they will not yield above three pounds, or three pounds and half a crown at most, on the exchange; which cannot turn to account either to the parents or kingdom, the charge of nutriment and rags having been at least four times that value.

I shall now therefore humbly propose my own thoughts, which I hope will not be liable to the least objection.

I have been assured by a very knowing American of my acquaintance in London that a young healthy child well nursed is at a year old a most delicious, nourishing, and wholesome food, whether stewed, roasted, baked, or boiled; and I make no doubt that it will equally serve in a fricassee or a ragout.[5]

I do therefore humbly offer it to public consideration that of the hundred and twenty thousand children already computed, twenty thousand may be reserved for breed, whereof only one-fourth part to be males; which is more than we allow to sheep, black cattle, or swine; and my reason is that these children are seldom the fruits of marriage, a circumstance not much regarded by our savages; therefore one male will be sufficient to serve four females. That the remaining hundred thousand may, at a year old, be offered in sale to the persons of quality and fortune through the kingdom; always advising the mother to let them suck plentifully in the last month, so as to render them plump and fat for a good table. A child will make two dishes at an entertainment for friends; and when the family dines alone, the fore or hind quarter will make a reasonable dish, and seasoned with a little pepper or salt will be very good boiled on the fourth day, especially in winter.

I have reckoned upon a medium that a child just born will weigh twelve pounds, and in a solar year, if tolerably nursed, will increase to twenty-eight pounds.

I grant this food will be somewhat dear, and therefore very proper for landlords, who, as they have already devoured most of the parents, seem to have the best title to the children.

Infant's flesh will be in season throughout the year, but more plentifully in March, and a little before and after for we are told by a grave author, an eminent French physician,[6] that fish being a prolific diet, there are more children born in Roman Catholic countries about nine months after Lent than at any other season; therefore, reckoning a year after Lent, the markets will be more glutted than usual, because the number of popish infants is at least three to one in this kingdom: and therefore it will have one other collateral advantage, by lessening the number of papists among us.

---

[4]*towardly:* dutiful; easily managed.   [5]*ragout:* (ra gü), a highly seasoned meat stew.   [6]*grave author . . . physician:* François Rabelais (c. 1494–1553), who was anything but a "grave author."

I have already computed the charge of nursing a beggar's child (in which list I reckon all cottagers, laborers, and four-fifths of the farmers) to be about two shillings per annum, rags included; and I believe no gentleman would repine to give ten shillings for the carcass of a good fat child, which, as I have said, will make four dishes of excellent nutritive meat, when he has only some particular friend or his own family to dine with him. Thus the squire will learn to be a good landlord and grow popular among his tenants; the mother will have eight shillings net profit and be fit for work till she produces another child.

Those who are more thrifty (as I must confess the times require) may flay the carcass; the skin of which artificially[7] dressed will make admirable gloves for ladies and summer boots for fine gentlemen.

As to our city of Dublin, shambles[8] may be appointed for this purpose in the most convenient parts of it, and butchers we may be assured will not be wanting; although I rather recommend buying the children alive and dressing them hot from the knife as we do roasting pigs.

A very worthy person, a true lover of his country, and whose virtues I highly esteem, was lately pleased, in discoursing on this matter, to offer a refinement upon my scheme. He said that many gentlemen of this kingdom, having of late destroyed their deer, he conceived that the want of venison might be well supplied by the bodies of young lads and maidens, not exceeding fourteen years of age nor under twelve; so great a number of both sexes in every country being now ready to starve for want of work and service; and these to be disposed of by their parents, if alive, or otherwise by their nearest relations. But with due deference to so excellent a friend and so deserving a patriot, I cannot be altogether in his sentiments; for as to the males, my American acquaintance assured me from frequent experience that their flesh was generally tough and lean, like that of our schoolboys, by continual exercise, and their taste disagreeable; and to fatten them would not answer the charge. Then as to the females, it would, I think, with humble submission be a loss to the public, because they soon would become breeders themselves: and besides, it is not improbable that some scrupulous people might be apt to censure such a practice (although indeed very unjustly), as a little bordering upon cruelty; which, I confess, has always been with me the strongest objection against any project, how well soever intended.

But in order to justify my friend, he confessed that this expedient was put into his head by the famous Psalmanazar,[9] a native of the island Formosa, who came from thence to London above twenty years ago: and in conversation told my friend that in his country when any young person happened to be put to death, the executioner sold the carcass to persons of quality as a prime dainty; and that in his time the body of a plump girl of fifteen, who was crucified for an attempt to poison the emperor, was sold to his imperial majesty's prime minister of state, and other great mandarins of the court, in joints from the gibbet, at four hundred crowns. Neither indeed can I deny

15

---

[7]*artificially:* artfully; skillfully.   [8]*shambles:* slaughterhouses.   [9]*Psalmanazar:* the imposter George Psalmanazar (c. 1679–1763), a Frenchman who passed himself off in England as a Formosan, and wrote a totally fictional "true" account of Formosa, in which he described cannibalism.

that if the same use were made of several plump girls in this town, who, without one single groat to their fortunes, cannot stir abroad without a chair, and appear at a playhouse and assemblies in foreign fineries which they never will pay for, the kingdom would not be the worse.

Some persons of a desponding spirit are in great concern about that vast number of poor people who are aged, diseased, or maimed; and I have been desired to employ my thoughts, what course may be taken to ease the nation of so grievous an encumbrance. But I am not in the least pain upon that matter, because it is very well known that they are every day dying and rotting, by cold and famine, and filth and vermin, as fast as can be reasonably expected. And as to the young laborers, they are now in almost as hopeful a condition: they cannot get work, and consequently pine away for want of nourishment to a degree that if at any time they are accidentally hired to common labor, they have not strength to perform it; and thus the country and themselves are happily delivered from the evils to come.

I have too long digressed and therefore shall return to my subject. I think the advantages, by the proposal which I have made, are obvious and many, as well as of the highest importance.

For first, as I have already observed, it would greatly lessen the number of papists, with whom we are yearly overrun, being the principal breeders of the nation, as well as our most dangerous enemies; and who stay at home on purpose to deliver the kingdom to the Pretender, hoping to take their advantage by the absence of so many good Protestants, who have chosen rather to leave their country than stay at home and pay tithes against their conscience to an Episcopal curate.[10]

Secondly, the poorer tenants will have something valuable of their own, which by law may be made liable to distress,[11] and help to pay their landlord's rent; their corn and cattle being already seized, and money a thing unknown.

Thirdly, whereas the maintenance of a hundred thousand children, from two years old and upwards, cannot be computed at less than ten shillings a piece per annum, the nation's stock will be thereby increased fifty thousand pounds per annum, beside the profit of a new dish introduced to the tables of all gentlemen of fortune in the kingdom who have any refinement in taste. And the money will circulate among ourselves, the goods being entirely of our own growth and manufacture.

Fourthly, the constant breeders, besides the gain of eight shillings sterling per annum by the sale of their children, will be rid of the charge of maintaining them after the first year.

Fifthly, this food would likewise bring great custom to taverns: where the vintners will certainly be so prudent as to procure the best receipts for dressing it to perfection, and consequently have their houses frequented by all the fine gentlemen, who justly value themselves upon their knowledge in good eating and a skilful cook, who understands how to oblige his guests, will contrive to make it as expensive as they please.

---

[10]*Protestants . . . curate:* Swift is here attacking the absentee landlords.   [11]*distress:* distraint, the legal seizure of property for payment of debts.

Sixthly, this would be a great inducement to marriage, which all wise nations have either encouraged by rewards or enforced by laws and penalties. It would increase the care and tenderness of mothers toward their children, when they were sure of a settlement for life to the poor babes, provided in some sort by the public, to their annual profit instead of expense. We should see an honest emulation among the married women, which of them could bring the fattest child to the market. Men would become as fond of their wives during the time of their pregnancy as they are now of their mares in foal, their cows in calf, or sows when they are ready to farrow; nor offer to beat or kick them (as is too frequent a practice) for fear of a miscarriage.

Many other advantages might be enumerated. For instance, the addition of some thousand carcasses in our exportation of barreled beef, the propagation of swine's flesh, and improvement in the art of making good bacon, so much wanted among us by the great destruction of pigs, too frequent at our tables; which are no way comparable in taste or magnificence to a well grown, fat, yearling child, which roasted whole will make a considerable figure at a lord mayor's feast, or any other public entertainment. But this and many others I omit, being studious of brevity.

Supposing that one thousand families in this city would be constant customers for infants' flesh, besides others who might have it at merry meetings, particularly weddings and christenings, I compute that Dublin would take off annually about twenty thousand carcasses; and the rest of the kingdom (where probably they will be sold somewhat cheaper) the remaining eighty thousand.

I can think of no one objection that will possibly be raised against this proposal, unless it should be urged that the number of people will be thereby much lessened in the kingdom. This I freely own, and it was indeed one principal design in offering it to the world. I desire the reader will observe that I calculate my remedy for this one individual kingdom of Ireland, and for no other that ever was, is, or, I think, ever can be upon earth. Therefore let no man talk to me of other expedients: of taxing our absentees at five shillings a pound: of using neither clothes nor household furniture, except what is of our own growth and manufacture: of utterly rejecting the materials and instruments that promote foreign luxury: of curing the expensiveness of pride, vanity, idleness, and gaming in our women of introducing a vein of parsimony, prudence, and temperance: of learning to love our country, in the want of which we differ even from Laplanders and the inhabitants of Topinamboo:[12] of quitting our animosities and factions, nor acting any longer like the Jews, who were murdering one another at the very moment their city was taken:[13] of being a little cautious not to sell our country and conscience for nothing: of teaching landlords to have at least one degree of mercy toward their tenants: lastly, of putting a spirit of honesty, industry, and skill into our shopkeepers; who, if a resolution could now be taken to buy only our native goods, would immediately unite to cheat and exact upon us in the price, the measure, and the goodness, nor could ever yet be brought to make one fair proposal of just dealing, though often and earnestly invited to it.[14]

---

[12]*Topinamboo:* a savage area of Brazil.   [13]*city was taken:* While the Roman Emperor Titus was besieging Jerusalem, which he took and destroyed in A.D. 70, within the city factions of fanatics were waging bloody warfare.   [14]*invited to it:* Swift had already made all these proposals in various pamphlets.

Therefore, I repeat, let no man talk to me of these and the like expedients, till he 30 has at least some glimpse of hope that there will ever be some hearty and sincere attempt to put them in practice.

But as to myself, having been wearied out for many years with offering vain, idle, visionary thoughts, and at length utterly despairing of success, I fortunately fell upon this proposal; which, as it is wholly new, so it has something solid and real, of no expense and little trouble, full in our own power, and whereby we can incur no danger in disobliging England. For this kind of commodity will not bear exportation, the flesh being of too tender a consistence to admit a long continuance in salt, although perhaps I could name a country which would be glad to eat up our whole nation without it.[15]

After all, I am not so violently bent upon my own opinion as to reject any offer proposed by wise men, which shall be found equally innocent, cheap, easy, and effectual. But before something of that kind shall be advanced in contradiction to my scheme, and offering a better, I desire the author or authors will be pleased maturely to consider two points. First, as things now stand, how they will be able to find food and raiment for an hundred thousand useless mouths and backs. And, secondly, there being a round million of creatures in human figure throughout this kingdom, whose whole subsistence put into a common stock would leave them in debt two millions of pounds sterling, adding those who are beggars by profession to the bulk of farmers, cottagers, and laborers, with their wives and children, who are beggars in effect; I desire those politicians, who dislike my overture, and may perhaps be so bold as to attempt an answer, that they will first ask the parents of these mortals, whether they would not at this day think it a great happiness to have been sold for food at a year old in the manner I prescribe, and thereby have avoided such a perpetual scene of misfortunes as they have since gone through by the oppression of landlords, the impossibility of paying rent without money or trade, the want of common sustenance, with neither house nor clothes to cover them from the inclemencies of the weather, and the most inevitable prospect of entailing the like or greater miseries upon their breed for ever.

I profess, in the sincerity of my heart, that I have not the least personal interest in endeavoring to promote this necessary work, having no other motive than the public good of my country, by advancing our trade, providing for infants, relieving the poor, and giving some pleasure to the rich. I have no children by which I can propose to get a single penny; the youngest being nine years old, and my wife past childbearing.

Questions for Discussion and Writing

1. What is a "projector," and in what sense is the narrator's proposal "modest"? At what point did you realize that Swift was being ironic and not literal?
2. How do the shocking details about life in Ireland in the early 1700s, which the narrator casually reveals, strengthen Swift's satire? To what extent does Swift criticize the Irish for not doing enough to help themselves?
3. Write your own "modest" proposal of two to three pages offering a truly offensive solution to a contemporary problem (such as corporate corruption,

---

[15]*a country . . . without it:* England; this is another way of saying, "The English are devouring the Irish."

overpayment of athletes, antismoking ordinances, obesity in children) using Swift's techniques of irony, **understatement,** and skewed statistics.

Barbara Ehrenreich

Barbara Ehrenreich is an investigative reporter who went undercover to discover the realities of the low-wage service worker. She was researching the consequences of the changes in the welfare system passed in 1995 that limited the length of time that single women with dependent children could receive benefits. The question she tried to answer was whether unskilled workers could generate an income they could live on without help from the government. As her following report reveals, the answer is no. This piece was originally published in Harper's *magazine, 1999, and later was included in her book* Nickel-and-Dimed: On (Not) Getting By in America *(2001). Her most recent book is* Global Women: Nannies, Maids, and Sex Workers in the New Economy *(2003).*

How does the photo of this demonstration for economic justice give voice to those who are usually unheard and invisible?

NICKEL-AND-DIMED: ON (NOT) GETTING BY IN AMERICA

At the beginning of June 1998 I leave behind everything that normally soothes the ego and sustains the body—home, career, companion, reputation, ATM card—for a plunge into the low-wage workforce. There, I become another, occupationally much diminished "Barbara Ehrenreich"—depicted on job-application forms as a divorced homemaker whose sole work experience consists of housekeeping in a few private homes. I am terrified, at the beginning, of being unmasked for what I am: a middle-class journalist setting out to explore the world that welfare mothers are entering, at the rate of approximately 50,000 a month, as welfare reform kicks in. Happily, though, my fears turn out to be entirely unwarranted: during a month of poverty and toil, my name goes unnoticed and for the most part unuttered. In this parallel universe where my father never got out of the mines and I never got through college, I am "baby," "honey," "blondie," and, most commonly, "girl."

My first task is to find a place to live. I figure that if I can earn $7 an hour—which, from the want ads, seems doable—I can afford to spend $500 on rent, or maybe, with severe economies, $600. In the Key West area, where I live, this pretty much confines me to flophouses and trailer homes—like the one, a pleasing fifteen-minute drive from town, that has no air-conditioning, no screens, no fans, no television, and, by way of diversion, only the challenge of evading the landlord's Doberman pinscher. The big problem with this place, though, is the rent, which at $675 a month is well beyond my reach. All right, Key West is expensive. But so is New York City, or the Bay Area, or Jackson Hole, or Telluride, or Boston, or any other place where tourists and the wealthy compete for living space with the people who clean their toilets and fry their hash browns.[1] Still, it is a shock to realize that "trailer trash" has become, for me, a demographic category to aspire to.

So I decide to make the common trade-off between affordability and convenience, and go for a $500-a-month efficiency thirty miles up a two-lane highway from the employment opportunities of Key West, meaning forty-five minutes if there's no road construction and I don't get caught behind some sun-dazed Canadian tourists. I hate the drive, along a roadside studded with white crosses commemorating the more effective head-on collisions, but it's a sweet little place—a cabin, more or less, set in the swampy back yard of the converted mobile home where my landlord, an affable TV repairman, lives with his bartender girlfriend. Anthropologically speaking, a bustling trailer park would be preferable, but here I have a gleaming white floor and a firm mattress, and the few resident bugs are easily vanquished.

Besides, I am not doing this for the anthropology. My aim is nothing so mistily subjective as to "experience poverty" or find out how it "really feels" to be a long-term low-wage worker. I've had enough unchosen encounters with poverty and the world of low-wage work to know it's not a place you want to visit for touristic purposes;

---

[1] According to the Department of Housing and Urban Development, the "fair-market rent" for an efficiency is $551 here in Monroe County, Florida. A comparable rent in the five boroughs of New York City is $704; in San Francisco, $713; and in the heart of Silicon Valley, $808. The fair-market rent for an area is defined as the amount that would be needed to pay rent plus utilities for "privately owned, decent, safe, and sanitary rental housing of a modest (non-luxury) nature with suitable amenities." [Author's note]

it just smells too much like fear. And with all my real-life assets—bank account, IRA, health insurance, multiroom home—waiting indulgently in the background, I am, of course, thoroughly insulated from the terrors that afflict the genuinely poor.

No, this is a purely objective, scientific sort of mission. The humanitarian ration-   5
ale for welfare reform—as opposed to the more punitive and stingy impulses that may actually have motivated it—is that work will lift poor women out of poverty while si-multaneously inflating their self-esteem and hence their future value in the labor mar-ket. Thus, whatever the hassles involved in finding child care, transportation, etc., the transition from welfare to work will end happily, in greater prosperity for all. Now there are many problems with this comforting prediction, such as the fact that the economy will inevitably undergo a downturn, eliminating many jobs. Even without a downturn, the influx of a million former welfare recipients into the low-wage labor mar-ket could depress wages by as much as 11.9 percent, according to the Economic Pol-icy Institute (EPI) in Washington, D.C.

But is it really possible to make a living on the kinds of jobs currently available to unskilled people? Mathematically, the answer is no, as can be shown by taking $6 to $7 an hour, perhaps subtracting a dollar or two an hour for child care, multiplying by 160 hours a month, and comparing the result to the prevailing rents. According to the National Coalition for the Homeless, for example, in 1998 it took, on average na-tionwide, an hourly wage of $8.89 to afford a one-bedroom apartment, and the Pre-amble Center for Public Policy estimates that the odds against a typical welfare recipient's landing a job at such a "living wage" are about 97 to 1. If these numbers are right, low-wage work is not a solution to poverty and possibly not even to homelessness.

It may seem excessive to put this proposition to an experimental test. As certain family members keep unhelpfully reminding me, the viability of low-wage work could be tested, after a fashion, without ever leaving my study. I could just pay myself $7 an hour for eight hours a day, charge myself for room and board, and total up the num-bers after a month. Why leave the people and work that I love? But I am an experi-mental scientist by training. In that business, you don't just sit at a desk and theorize; you plunge into the everyday chaos of nature, where surprises lurk in the most mun-dane measurements. Maybe, when I got into it, I would discover some hidden economies in the world of the low-wage worker. After all, if 30 percent of the work-force toils for less than $8 an hour, according to the EPI, they may have found some tricks as yet unknown to me. Maybe—who knows?—I would even to able to detect in myself the bracing psychological effects of getting out of the house, as promised by the welfare wonks at places like the Heritage Foundation. Or, on the other hand, maybe there would be unexpected costs—physical, mental, or financial—to throw off all my calculations. Ideally, I should do this with two small children in tow, that being the welfare average, but mine are grown and no one is willing to lend me theirs for a month-long vacation in penury. So this is not the perfect experiment, just a test of the best possible case: an unencumbered woman, smart and even strong, attempting to live more or less off the land.

On the morning of my first full day of job searching, I take a red pen to the want ads, which are auspiciously numerous. Everyone in Key West's booming "hospitality industry" seems to be looking for someone like me—trainable, flexible, and with suitably humble expectations as to pay. I know I possess certain traits that might be advantageous—I'm white and, I like to think, well-spoken and poised—but I decide on two rules: One, I cannot use any skills derived from my education or usual work—not that there are a lot of want ads for satirical essayists anyway. Two, I have to take the best-paid job that is offered me and of course do my best to hold it; no Marxist rants or sneaking off to read novels in the ladies' room. In addition, I rule out various occupations for one reason or another. Hotel front-desk clerk, for example, which to my surprise is regarded as unskilled and pays around $7 an hour, gets eliminated because it involves standing in one spot for eight hours a day. Waitressing is similarly something I'd like to avoid, because I remember it leaving me bone tired when I was eighteen, and I'm decades of varicosities and back pain beyond that now. Telemarketing, one of the first refuges of the suddenly indigent, can be dismissed on grounds of personality. This leaves certain supermarket jobs, such as deli clerk, or housekeeping in Key West's thousands of hotel and guest rooms. Housekeeping is especially appealing, for reasons both atavistic and practical: it's what my mother did before I came along, and it can't be too different from what I've been doing part-time, in my own home, all my life.

So I put on what I take to be a respectful-looking outfit of ironed Bermuda shorts and scooped-neck T-shirt and set out for a tour of the local hotels and supermarkets. Best Western, Econo Lodge, and HoJo's all let me fill out application forms, and these are, to my relief, interested in little more than whether I am a legal resident of the United States and have committed any felonies. My next step is Winn-Dixie, the supermarket, which turns out to have a particularly onerous application process, featuring a fifteen-minute "interview" by computer since, apparently, no human on the premises is deemed capable of representing the corporate point of view. I am conducted to a large room decorated with posters illustrating how to look "professional" (it helps to be white and, if female, permed) and warning of the slick promises that union organizers might try to tempt me with. The interview is multiple choice: Do I have anything, such as child-care problems, that might make it hard for me to get to work on time? Do I think safety on the job is the responsibility of management? Then, popping up cunningly out of the blue: How many dollars' worth of stolen goods have I purchased in the last year? Would I turn in a fellow employee if I caught him stealing? Finally," Are you an honest person?"

Apparently, I ace the interview, because I am told that all I have to do is show up   10 in some doctor's office tomorrow for a urine test. This seems to be a fairly general rule: if you want to stack Cheerio boxes or vacuum hotel rooms in chemically fascist America, you have to be willing to squat down and pee in front of some health worker (who has no doubt had to do the same thing herself). The wages Winn-Dixie is offering—$6 and a couple of dimes to start with—are not enough, I decide, to compensate for this indignity.[2]

---

[2]According to the *Monthly Labor Review* (November 1996), 28 percent of work sites surveyed in the service industry conduct drug tests (corporate workplaces have much higher rates), and the incidence of testing has risen markedly since the Eighties. The rate of testing is highest in the South (56 percent of work sites polled), with the Midwest in second place (50 percent). The drug most likely to be detected—marijuana, which can be detected in urine for weeks—is also the most innocuous, while heroin and cocaine are generally undetectable three days after use. Prospective employees sometimes try to cheat the tests by consuming excessive amounts of liquids and taking diuretics and even masking substances available through the Internet. [Author's note]

I lunch at Wendy's, where $4.99 gets you unlimited refills at the Mexican part of the Superbar, a comforting surfeit of refried beans and "cheese sauce." A teenage employee, seeing me studying the want ads, kindly offers me an application form, which I fill out, though here, too, the pay is just $6 and change an hour. Then it's off for a round of the locally owned inns and guest-houses. At "The Palms," let's call it, a bouncy manager actually takes me around to see the rooms and meet the existing housekeepers, who, I note with satisfaction, look pretty much like me—faded ex-hippie types in shorts with long hair pulled back in braids. Mostly, though, no one speaks to me or even looks at me except to proffer an application form. At my last stop, a palatial B&B, I wait twenty minutes to meet "Max," only to be told that there are no jobs now but there should be one soon, since "nobody lasts more than a couple weeks." (Because none of the people I talked to knew I was a reporter, I have changed their names to protect their privacy and, in some cases perhaps, their jobs.)

Three days go by like this, and, to my chagrin, no one out of the approximately twenty places I've applied calls me for an interview. I had been vain enough to worry about coming across as too educated for the jobs I sought, but no one even seems interested in finding out how overqualified I am. Only later will I realize that the want ads are not a reliable measure of the actual jobs available at any particular time. They are, as I should have guessed from Max's comment, the employers' insurance policy against the relentless turnover of the low-wage workforce. Most of the big hotels run ads almost continually, just to build a supply of applicants to replace the current workers as they drift away or are fired, so finding a job is just a matter of being at the right place at the right time and flexible enough to take whatever is being offered that day. This finally happens to me at one of the big discount hotel chains, where I go, as usual, for housekeeping and am sent, instead, to try out as a waitress at the attached "family restaurant," a dismal spot with a counter and about thirty tables that looks out on a parking garage and features such tempting fare as "Pollish [sic] sausage and BBQ sauce" on 95-degree days. Phillip, the dapper young West Indian who introduces himself as the manager, interviews me with about as much enthusiasm as if he were a clerk processing me for Medicare, the principal questions being what shifts can I work and when can I start. I mutter something about being woefully out of practice as a waitress, but he's already on to the uniform: I'm to show up tomorrow wearing black slacks and black shoes; he'll provide the rust-colored polo shirt with HEARTHSIDE embroidered on it, though I might want to wear my own shirt to get to work, ha ha. At the word "tomorrow," something between fear and indignation rises in my chest. I want to say, "Thank you for your time, sir, but this is just an experiment, you know, not my actual life."

So begins my career at the Hearthside, I shall call it, one small profit center within a global discount hotel chain, where for two weeks I work from 2:00 till 10:00 P.M. for $2.43 an hour plus tips.[3] In some futile bid for gentility, the management has barred

---

[3]According to the Fair Labor Standards Act, employers are not required to pay "tipped employees," such as restaurant servers, more than $2.13 an hour in direct wages. However, if the sum of tips plus $2.13 an hour falls below the minimum wage, or $5.15 an hour, the employer is required to make up the difference. This fact was not mentioned by managers or otherwise publicized at either of the restaurants where I worked. [Author's note]

employees from using the front door, so my first day I enter through the kitchen, where a red-faced man with shoulder-length blond hair is throwing frozen steaks against the wall and yelling, "Fuck this shit!" "That's just Jack," explains Gail, the wiry middle-aged waitress who is assigned to train me. "He's on the rag again"—a condition occasioned, in this instance, by the fact that the cook on the morning shift had forgotten to thaw out the steaks. For the next eight hours, I run after the agile Gail, absorbing bits of instruction along with fragments of personal tragedy. All food must be trayed, and the reason she's so tired today is that she woke up in a cold sweat thinking of her boyfriend, who killed himself recently in an upstate prison. No refills on lemonade. And the reason he was in prison is that a few DUIs caught up with him, that's all, could have happened to anyone. Carry the creamers to the table in a monkey bowl, never in your hand. And after he was gone she spent several months living in her truck, peeing in a plastic pee bottle and reading by candlelight at night, but you can't live in a truck in the summer, since you need to have the windows down, which means anything can get in, from mosquitoes on up.

At least Gail puts to rest any fears I had of appearing overqualified. From the first day on, I find that of all the things I have left behind, such as home and identity, what I miss the most is competence. Not that I have ever felt utterly competent in the writing business, in which one day's success augurs nothing at all for the next. But in my writing life, I at least have some notion of procedure: do the research, make the outline, rough out a draft, etc. As a server, though, I am beset by requests like bees: more iced tea here, ketchup over there, a to-go box for table fourteen, and where are the high chairs, anyway? Of the twenty-seven tables, up to six are usually mine at any time, though on slow afternoons or if Gail is off, I sometimes have the whole place to myself. There is the touch-screen computer-ordering system to master, which is, I suppose, meant to minimize server-cook contact, but in practice requires constant verbal fine-tuning: "That's gravy on the mashed, okay? None on the meatloaf," and so forth—while the cook scowls as if I were inventing these refinements just to torment him. Plus, something I had forgotten in the years since I was eighteen: about a third of a server's job is "side work" that's invisible to customers—sweeping, scrubbing, slicing, refilling, and restocking. If it isn't all done, every little bit of it, you're going to face the 6:00 P.M. dinner rush defenseless and probably go down in flames. I screw up dozens of times at the beginning, sustained in my shame entirely by Gail's support—"It's okay, baby, everyone does that sometimes"—because, to my total surprise and despite the scientific detachment I am doing my best to maintain, I care.

The whole thing would be a lot easier if I could just skate through it as Lily Tomlin in one of her waitress skits, but I was raised by the absurd Booker T. Washingtonian precept that says: If you're going to do something, do it well. In fact, "well" isn't good enough by half. Do it better than anyone has ever done it before. Or so said my father, who must have known what he was talking about because he managed to pull himself, and us with him, up from the mile-deep copper mines of Butte to the leafy suburbs of the Northeast, ascending from boilermakers to martinis before booze beat out ambition. As in most endeavors I have encountered in my life, doing it "better than anyone" is not a reasonable goal. Still, when I wake up at 4:00 A.M. in my own cold sweat, I am not thinking about the writing deadlines I'm neglecting; I'm thinking about the table whose order I screwed up so that one of the boys didn't get his kiddie meal

15

until the rest of the family had moved on to their Key Lime pies. That's the other powerful motivation I hadn't expected—the customers, or "patients," as I can't help thinking of them on account of the mysterious vulnerability that seems to have left them temporarily unable to feed themselves. After a few days at the Hearthside, I feel the service ethic kick in like a shot of oxytocin, the nurturance hormone. The plurality of my customers are hard-working locals—truck drivers, construction workers, even housekeepers from the attached hotel—and I want them to have the closest to a "fine dining" experience that the grubby circumstances will allow. No "you guys" for me; everyone over twelve is "sir" or "ma'am." I ply them with iced tea and coffee refills; I return, mid-meal, to inquire how everything is; I doll up their salads with chopped raw mushrooms, summer squash slices, or whatever bits of produce I can find that have survived their sojourn in the cold-storage room mold-free.

There is Benny, for example, a short, tight-muscled sewer repairman, who cannot even think of eating until he has absorbed a half hour of air-conditioning and ice water. We chat about hyperthermia and electrolytes until he is ready to order some finicky combination like soup of the day, garden salad, and a side of grits. There are the German tourists who are so touched by my pidgin "Willkommen" and "Ist alles gut?" that they actually tip. (Europeans, spoiled by their trade-union-ridden, high-wage welfare states, generally do not know that they are supposed to tip. Some restaurants, the Hearthside included, allow servers to "grat" their foreign customers, or add a tip to the bill. Since this amount is added before the customers have a chance to tip or not tip, the practice amounts to an automatic penalty for imperfect English.) There are the two dirt-smudged lesbians, just off their construction shift, who are impressed enough by my suave handling of the fly in the piña colada that they take the time to praise me to Stu, the assistant manager. There's Sam, the kindly retired cop, who has to plug up his tracheotomy hole with one finger in order to force the cigarette smoke into his lungs.

Sometimes I play with the fantasy that I am a princess who, in penance for some tiny transgression, has undertaken to feed each of her subjects by hand. But the non-princesses working with me are just as indulgent, even when this means flouting management rules—concerning, for example, the number of croutons that can go on a salad (six). "Put on all you want," Gail whispers," "as long as Stu isn't looking." She dips into her own tip money to buy biscuits and gravy for an out-of-work mechanic who's used up all his money on dental surgery, inspiring me to pick up the tab for his milk and pie. Maybe the same high levels of agape can be found throughout the "hospitality industry." I remember the poster decorating one of the apartments I looked at, which said "If you seek happiness for yourself you will never find it. Only when you seek happiness for others will it come to you," or words to that effect—an odd sentiment, it seemed to me at the time, to find in the dank one-room basement apartment of a bellhop at the Best Western. At the Hearthside, we utilize whatever bits of autonomy we have to ply our customers with the illicit calories that signal our love. It is our job as servers to assemble the salads and desserts, pouring the dressings and squirting the whipped cream. We also control the number of butter patties our customers get and the amount of sour cream on their baked potatoes. So if you wonder why Americans are so obese, consider the fact that waitresses both express their humanity and earn their tips through the covert distribution of fats.

Ten days into it, this is beginning to look like a livable lifestyle. I like Gail, who is "looking at fifty" but moves so fast she can alight in one place and then another without apparently being anywhere between them. I clown around with Lionel, the teenage Haitian busboy, and catch a few fragments of conversation with Joan, the svelte fortyish hostess and militant feminist who is the only one of us who dares to tell Jack to shut the fuck up. I even warm up to Jack when, on a slow night and to make up for a particularly unwarranted attack on my abilities, or so I imagine, he tells me about his glory days as a young man at "coronary school"—or do you say "culinary"?—in Brooklyn, where he dated a knock-out Puerto Rican chick and learned everything there is to know about food. I finish up at 10:00 or 10:30, depending on how much side work I've been able to get done during the shift, and cruise home to the tapes I snatched up at random when I left my real home—Marianne Faithfull, Tracy Chapman, Enigma, King Sunny Ade, the Violent Femmes—just drained enough for the music to set my cranium resonating but hardly dead. Midnight snack is Wheat Thins and Monterey Jack, accompanied by cheap white wine on ice and whatever AMC has to offer. To bed by 1:30 or 2:00, up at 9:00 or 10:00, read for an hour while my uniform whirls around in the landlord's washing machine, and then it's another eight hours spent following Mao's central instruction, as laid out in the Little Red Book, which was: Serve the people.

I could drift along like this, in some dreamy proletarian idyll, except for two things. One is management. If I have kept this subject on the margins thus far it is because I still flinch to think that I spent all those weeks under the surveillance of men (and later women) whose job it was to monitor my behavior for signs of sloth, theft, drug abuse, or worse. Not that managers and especially "assistant managers" in low-wage settings like this are exactly the class enemy. In the restaurant business, they are mostly former cooks or servers, still capable of pinch-hitting in the kitchen or on the floor, just as in hotels they are likely to be former clerks, and paid a salary of only about $400 a week. But everyone knows they have crossed over to the other side, which is, crudely put, corporate as opposed to human. Cooks want to prepare tasty meals; servers want to serve them graciously; but managers are there for only one reason—to make sure that money is made for some theoretical entity that exists far away in Chicago or New York, if a corporation can be said to have a physical existence at all. Reflecting on her career, Gail tells me ruefully that she had sworn, years ago, never to work for a corporation again. "They don't cut you no slack. You give and you give, and they take."

Managers can sit—for hours at a time if they want—but it's their job to see that   20
no one else ever does, even when there's nothing to do, and this is why, for servers, slow times can be as exhausting as rushes. You start dragging out each little chore, because if the manager on duty catches you in an idle moment, he will give you something far nastier to do. So I wipe, I clean, I consolidate ketchup bottles and recheck the cheesecake supply, even tour the tables to make sure the customer evaluation forms are all standing perkily in their places—wondering all the time how many calories I burn in these strictly theatrical exercises. When, on a particularly dead afternoon, Stu finds me glancing at a *USA Today* a customer has left behind, he assigns me to vacuum the entire floor with the broken vacuum cleaner that has a handle only two feet long, and

the only way to do that without incurring orthopedic damage is to proceed from spot to spot on your knees.

On my first Friday at the Hearthside there is a "mandatory meeting for all restaurant employees," which I attend, eager for insight into our overall marketing strategy and the niche (your basic Ohio cuisine with a tropical twist?) we aim to inhabit. But there is no "we" at this meeting. Phillip, our top manager except for an occasional "consultant" sent out by corporate headquarters, opens it with a sneer: "The break room—it's disgusting. Butts in the ashtrays, newspapers lying around, crumbs." This windowless little room, which also houses the time clock for the entire hotel, is where we stash our bags and civilian clothes and take our half-hour meal breaks. But a break room is not a right, he tells us. It can be taken away. We should also know that the lockers in the break room and whatever is in them can be searched at any time. Then comes gossip; there has been gossip; gossip (which seems to mean employees talking among themselves) must stop. Off-duty employees are henceforth barred from eating at the restaurant, because "other servers gather around them and gossip." When Phillip has exhausted his agenda of rebukes, Joan complains about the condition of the ladies' room and I throw in my two bits about the vacuum cleaner. But I don't see any backup coming from my fellow servers, each of whom has subsided into her own personal funk; Gail, my role model, stares sorrowfully at a point six inches from her nose. The meeting ends when Andy, one of the cooks, gets up, muttering about breaking up his day off for this almighty bullshit.

Just four days later we are suddenly summoned into the kitchen at 3:30 P.M., even though there are live tables on the floor. We all—about ten of us—stand around Phillip, who announces grimly that there has been a report of some "drug activity" on the night shift and that, as a result, we are now to be a "drug-free" workplace, meaning that all new hires will be tested, as will possibly current employees on a random basis. I am glad that this part of the kitchen is so dark, because I find myself blushing as hard as if I had been caught toking up in the ladies' room myself: I haven't been treated this way—lined up in the corridor, threatened with locker searches, peppered with carelessly aimed accusations—since junior high school. Back on the floor, Joan cracks, "Next they'll be telling us we can't have sex on the job." When I ask Stu what happened to inspire the crackdown, he just mutters about "management decisions" and takes the opportunity to upbraid Gail and me for being too generous with the rolls. From now on there's to be only one per customer, and it goes out with the dinner, not with the salad. He's also been riding the cooks, prompting Andy to come out of the kitchen and observe—with the serenity of a man whose customary implement is a butcher knife—that "Stu has a death wish today."

Later in the evening, the gossip crystallizes around the theory that Stu is himself the drug culprit, that he uses the restaurant phone to order up marijuana and sends one of the late servers out to fetch it for him. The server was caught, and she may have ratted Stu out or at least said enough to cast some suspicion on him, thus accounting for his pissy behavior. Who knows? Lionel, the busboy, entertains us for the rest of the shift by standing just behind Stu's back and sucking deliriously on an imaginary joint.

The other problem, in addition to the less-than-nurturing management style, is that this job shows no sign of being financially viable. You might imagine, from a comfortable distance, that people who live, year in and year out, on $6 to $10 an hour have discovered some survival stratagems unknown to the middle class. But no. It's not hard to get my co-workers to talk about their living situations, because housing, in almost every case, is the principal source of disruption in their lives, the first thing they fill you in on when they arrive for their shifts. After a week, I have compiled the following survey:

- Gail is sharing a room in a well-known downtown flophouse for which she and a roommate pay about $250 a week. Her roommate, a male friend, has begun hitting on her, driving her nuts, but the rent would be impossible alone.
- Claude, the Haitian cook, is desperate to get out of the two-room apartment he shares with his girlfriend and two other, unrelated, people. As far as I can determine, the other Haitian men (most of whom only speak Creole) live in similarly crowded situations.
- Annette, a twenty-year-old server who is six months pregnant and has been abandoned by her boyfriend, lives with her mother, a postal clerk.
- Marianne and her boyfriend are paying $170 a week for a one-person trailer.
- Jack, who is, at $10 an hour, the wealthiest of us, lives in a trailer he owns, paying only the $400-a-month lot fee.
- The other white cook, Andy, lives on his dry-docked boat, which, as far as I can tell from his loving descriptions, can't be more than twenty feet long. He offers to take me out on it, once it's repaired, but the offer comes with inquiries as to my marital status, so I do not follow up on it.
- Tina and her husband are paying $60 a night for a double room in a Days Inn. This is because they have no car and the Days Inn is within walking distance of the Hearthside. When Marianne, one of the breakfast servers, is tossed out of her trailer for subletting (which is against the trailer-park rules), she leaves her boyfriend and moves in with Tina and her husband.
- Joan, who had fooled me with her numerous and tasteful outfits (hostesses wear their own clothes), lives in a van she parks behind a shopping center at night and showers in Tina's motel room. The clothes are from thrift shops.[4]

It strikes me, in my middle-class solipsism, that there is gross improvidence in some   25
of these arrangements. When Gail and I are wrapping silverware in napkins—the only task for which we are permitted to sit—she tells me she is thinking of escaping from her roommate by moving into the Days Inn herself. I am astounded: How can she even think of paying between $40 and $60 a day? But if I was afraid of sounding like a social worker, I come out just sounding like a fool. She squints at me in disbelief, "And where am I supposed to get a month's rent and a month's deposit for an apartment?" I'd been feeling pretty smug about my $500 efficiency, but of course it was made possible only by the $1,300 I had allotted myself for start-up costs when I began my

---

[4]I could find no statistics on the number of employed people living in cars or vans, but according to the National Coalition for the Homeless's 1997 report, "Myths and Facts About Homelessness," nearly one in five homeless people (in twenty-nine cities across the nation) is employed in a full- or part-time job. [Author's note]

low-wage life: $1,000 for the first month's rent and deposit, $100 for initial groceries and cash in my pocket, $200 stuffed away for emergencies. In poverty, as in certain propositions in physics, starting conditions are everything.

There are no secret economies that nourish the poor; on the contrary, there are a host of special costs. If you can't put up the two months' rent you need to secure an apartment, you end up paying through the nose for a room by the week. If you have only a room, with a hot plate at best, you can't save by cooking up huge lentil stews that can be frozen for the week ahead. You eat fast food, or the hot dogs and styro-foam cups of soup that can be microwaved in a convenience store. If you have no money for health insurance—and the Hearthside's niggardly plan kicks in only after three months—you go without routine care or prescription drugs and end up paying the price. Gail, for example, was fine until she ran out of money for estrogen pills. She is supposed to be on the company plan by now, but they claim to have lost her application form and need to begin the paperwork all over again. So she spends $9 per migraine pill to control the headaches she wouldn't have, she insists, if her estrogen supplements were covered. Similarly, Marianne's boyfriend lost his job as a roofer because he missed so much time after getting a cut on his foot for which he couldn't afford the prescribed antibiotic.

My own situation, when I sit down to assess it after two weeks of work, would not be much better if this were my actual life. The seductive thing about waitressing is that you don't have to wait for payday to feel a few bills in your pocket, and my tips usually cover meals and gas, plus something left over to stuff into the kitchen drawer I use as a bank. But as the tourist business slows in the summer heat, I sometimes leave work with only $20 in tips (the gross is higher, but servers share about 15 percent of their tips with the bus-boys and bartenders). With wages included, this amounts to about the minimum wage of $5.15 an hour. Although the sum in the drawer is piling up, at the present rate of accumulation it will be more than a hundred dollars short of my rent when the end of the month comes around. Nor can I see any expenses to cut. True, I haven't gone the lentil-stew route yet, but that's because I don't have a large cooking pot, pot holders, or a ladle to stir with (which cost about $30 at Kmart, less at thrift stores), not to mention onions, carrots, and the indispensable bay leaf. I do make my lunch almost every day—usually some slow-burning, high-protein combo like frozen chicken patties with melted cheese on top and canned pinto beans on the side. Dinner is at the Hearthside, which offers its employees a choice of BLT, fish sandwich, or hamburger for only $2. The burger lasts longest, especially if it's heaped with gut-puckering jalapeños, but by midnight my stomach is growling again.

So unless I want to start using my car as a residence, I have to find a second, or alternative, job. I call all the hotels where I filled out housekeeping applications weeks ago—the Hyatt, Holiday Inn, Econo Lodge, Hojo's, Best Western, plus a half dozen or so locally run guesthouses. Nothing. Then I start making the rounds again, wasting whole mornings waiting for some assistant manager to show up, even dipping into places so creepy that the front-desk clerk greets you from behind bulletproof glass and sells pints of liquor over the counter. But either someone has exposed my real-life house-keeping habits—which are, shall we say, mellow—or I am at the wrong end of some infallible ethnic equation: most, but by no means all, of the working housekeepers I see on my job searches are African Americans, Spanish-speaking, or immigrants from the Central European post-Communist world, whereas servers are almost invariably white and monolingually English-speaking. When I finally get a positive response, I have been identified once again as server material. Jerry's, which is part of a well-known national family restaurant chain and physically attached here to another budget hotel chain, is ready to use me at once. The prospect is both exciting and terrifying, because, with about the same number of tables and counter seats, Jerry's attracts three or four times the volume of customers as the gloomy old Hearthside.

I start out with the beautiful, heroic idea of handling the two jobs at once, and for two days I almost do it: the breakfast/lunch shift at Jerry's, which goes till 2:00, arriving at the Hearthside at 2:10, and attempting to hold out until 10:00. In the ten minutes between jobs, I pick up a spicy chicken sandwich at the Wendy's drive-through window, gobble it down in the car, and change from khaki slacks to black, from Hawaiian to rust polo. There is a problem, though. When during the 3:00 to 4:00 P.M. dead time I finally sit down to wrap silver, my flesh seems to bond to the seat. I try to refuel with a purloined cup of soup, as I've seen Gail and Joan do dozens of times, but a manager catches me and hisses "No eating!" though there's not a customer around to be offended by the sight of food making contact with a server's lips. So I tell Gail I'm going to quit, and she hugs me and says she might just follow me to Jerry's herself.

But the chances of this are miniscule. She has left the flophouse and her annoying roommate and is back to living in her beat-up old truck. But guess what? she reports to me excitedly later that evening: Phillip has given her permission to park overnight in the hotel parking lot, as long as she keeps out of sight, and the parking lot should be totally safe, since it's patrolled by a hotel security guard! With the Hearthside offering benefits like that, how could anyone think of leaving?   30

True, I take occasional breaks from this life, going home now and then to catch up on e-mail and for conjugal visits (though I am careful to "pay" for anything I eat there), seeing *The Truman Show* with friends and letting them buy my ticket. And I still have those what-am-I-doing-here moments at work, when I get so homesick for the printed word that I obsessively reread the six-page menu. But as the days go by, my old life is beginning to look exceedingly strange. The e-mails and phone messages addressed to my former self come from a distant race of people with exotic concerns and far too much time on their hands. The neighborly market I used to cruise for produce now looks forbiddingly like a Manhattan yuppie emporium. And when I sit down one morning in my real home to pay bills from my past life, I am dazzled at the two- and three-figure sums owed to outfits like Club BodyTech and Amazon.com.

Management at Jerry's is generally calmer and more "professional" than at the Hearthside, with two exceptions. One is Joy, a plump, blowsy woman in her early thirties, who once kindly devoted several minutes to instructing me in the correct one-handed method of carrying trays but whose moods change disconcertingly from shift to shift and even within one. Then there's B.J., a.k.a. B.J.-the-bitch, whose contribution is to stand by the kitchen counter and yell, "Nita, your order's up, move it!" or, "Barbara, didn't you see you've got another table out there? Come on, girl!" Among other things, she is hated for having replaced the whipped-cream squirt cans with big plastic whipped-cream-filled baggies that have to be squeezed with both hands—because, reportedly, she saw or thought she saw employees trying to inhale the propellant gas from the squirt cans, in the hope that it might be nitrous oxide. On my third night, she pulls me aside abruptly and brings her face so close that it looks as if she's planning to butt me with her forehead. But instead of saying, "You're fired," she says, "You're doing fine." The only trouble is I'm spending time chatting with customers: "That's how they're getting you." Furthermore I am letting them "run me," which means harassment by sequential demands: you bring the ketchup and they decide they want extra Thousand Island; you bring that and they announce they now need a side of fries; and so on into distraction. Finally she tells me not to take her wrong. She tries to say things in a nice way, but you get into a mode, you know, because everything has to move so fast.[5]

I mumble thanks for the advice, feeling like I've just been stripped naked by the crazed enforcer of some ancient sumptuary law: No chatting for you, girl. No fancy service ethic allowed for the serfs. Chatting with customers is for the beautiful young college-educated servers in the downtown carpaccio joints, the kids who can make $70 to $100 a night. What had I been thinking? My job is to move orders from tables to kitchen and then trays from kitchen to tables. Customers are, in fact, the major obstacle to the smooth transformation of information into food and food into money—they are, in short, the enemy. And the painful thing is that I'm beginning to see it this way myself. There are the traditional asshole types—frat boys who down multiple Buds and then make a fuss because the steaks are so emaciated and the fries so sparse—as well as the variously impaired—due to age, diabetes, or literacy issues—who require patient nutritional counseling.

I make friends, over time, with the other "girls" who work my shift: Nita, the tattooed twenty-something who taunts us by going around saying brightly, "Have we started making money yet?" Ellen, whose teenage son cooks on the graveyard shift and who once managed a restaurant in Massachusetts but won't try out for management here because she prefers being a "common worker" and not "ordering people around." Easy-going fiftyish Lucy, with the raucous laugh, who limps toward the end of the shift because of something that has gone wrong with her leg, the exact nature of which cannot be determined without health insurance. We talk about the usual girl things—men, children, and the sinister allure of Jerry's chocolate peanut-butter cream pie—though no one, I notice, ever brings up anything potentially expensive, like shopping or movies. As at the Hearthside, the only recreation ever referred to is partying, which requires little more than some beer, a joint, and a few close friends. Still, no one here is homeless, or cops to it anyway, thanks usually to a working husband or boyfriend. All in all, we form a reliable mutual-support group: If one of us is feeling

---

[5]In *Workers in a Lean World: Unions in the International Economy* (Verso, 1997), Kim Moody cites studies finding an increase in stress-related workplace injuries and illness between the mid-1980s and the early 1990s. He argues that rising stress levels reflect a new system of "management by stress," in which workers in a variety of industries are being squeezed to extract maximum productivity, to the detriment of their health. [Author's note]

sick or overwhelmed, another one will "bev" a table or even carry trays for her. If one of us is off sneaking a cigarette or a pee,[6] the others will do their best to conceal her absence from the enforcers of corporate rationality.

But my saving human connection—my oxytocin receptor, as it were—George, the   35
nineteen-year-old, fresh-off-the-boat Czech dishwasher. We get to talking when he asks me, tortuously, how much cigarettes cost at Jerry's. I do my best to explain that they cost over a dollar more here than at a regular store and suggest that he just take one from the half-filled packs that are always lying around on the break table. But that would be unthinkable. Except for the one tiny earring signaling his allegiance to some vaguely alternative point of view, George is a perfect straight arrow—crew-cut, hard-working, and hungry for eye contact. "Czech Republic," I ask, "or Slovakia?" and he seems delighted that I know the difference. "Václav Havel," I try. "Velvet Revolution, Frank Zappa?" "Yes, yes, 1989," he says, and I realize we are talking about history.

My project is to teach George English. "How are you today, George?" I say at the start of each shift. "I am good, and how are you today, Barbara?" I learn that he is not paid by Jerry's but by the "agent" who shipped him over—$5 an hour, with the agent getting the dollar or so difference between that and what Jerry's pays dishwashers. I learn also that he shares an apartment with a crowd of other Czech "dishers," as he calls them, and that he cannot sleep until one of them goes off for his shift, leaving a vacant bed. We are having one of our ESL sessions late one afternoon when B.J. catches us at it and orders "Joseph" to take up the rubber mats on the floor near the dish-washing sinks and mop underneath. "I thought your name was George," I say loud enough for B.J. to hear as she strides off back to the counter. Is she embarrassed? Maybe a little, because she greets me back at the counter with "George, Joseph—there are so many of them!" I say nothing, neither nodding nor smiling, and for this I am punished later when I think I am ready to go and she announces that I need to roll fifty more sets of silverware and isn't it time I mixed up a fresh four-gallon batch of blue-cheese dressing? May you grow old in this place, B.J., is the curse I beam out at her when I am finally permitted to leave. May the syrup spills glue your feet to the floor.

I make the decision to move closer to Key West. First, because of the drive. Second and third, also because of the drive: gas is eating up $4 to $5 a day, and although Jerry's is as high-volume as you can get, the tips average only 10 percent, and not just for a newbie like me. Between the base pay of $2.15 an hour and the obligation to share tips with the busboys and dishwashers, we're averaging only about $7.50 an

---

[6]Until April 1998, there was no federally mandated right to bathroom breaks. According to Marc Linder and Ingrid Nygaard, authors of *Void Where Prohibited: Rest Breaks and the Right to Urinate on Company Time* (Cornell University Press, 1997), "The right to rest and void at work is not high on the list of social or political causes supported by professional or executive employees, who enjoy personal workplace liberties that millions of factory workers can only daydream about. . . . While we were dismayed to discover that workers lacked an acknowledged legal right to void at work, (the workers) were amazed by outsiders' naïve belief that their employers would permit them to perform this basic bodily function when necessary. . . . A factory worker, not allowed a break for six-hour stretches, voided into pads worn inside her uniform; and a kindergarten teacher in a school without aides had to take all twenty children with her to the bathroom and line them up outside the stall door when she voided." [Author's note]

hour. Then there is the $30 I had to spend on the regulation tan slacks worn by Jerry's servers—a setback it could take weeks to absorb. (I had combed the town's two down-scale department stores hoping for something cheaper but decided in the end that these marked-down Dockers, originally $49, were more likely to survive a daily washing.) Of my fellow servers, everyone who lacks a working husband or boyfriend seems to have a second job: Nita does something at a computer eight hours a day; another welds. Without the forty-five-minute commute, I can picture myself working two jobs and having the time to shower between them.

So I take the $500 deposit I have coming from my landlord, the $400 I have earned toward the next month's rent, plus the $200 reserved for emergencies, and use the $1,100 to pay the rent and deposit on trailer number 46 in the Overseas Trailer Park, a mile from the cluster of budget hotels that constitute Key West's version of an in-dustrial park. Number 46 is about eight feet in width and shaped like a barbell inside, with a narrow region—because of the sink and the stove—separating the bedroom from what might optimistically be called the "living" area, with its two-person table and half-sized couch. The bathroom is so small my knees rub against the shower stall when I sit on the toilet, and you can't just leap out of the bed, you have to climb down to the foot of it in order to find a patch of floor space to stand on. Outside, I am within a few yards of a liquor store, a bar that advertises "free beer tomorrow," a convenience store, and a Burger King—but no supermarket or, alas, laundromat. By reputation, the Overseas park is a nest of crime and crack, and I am hoping at least for some vibrant, multicultural street life. But desolation rules night and day, except for a thin stream of pedestrian traffic heading for their jobs at the Sheraton or 7-Eleven. There are not ex-actly people here but what amounts to canned labor, being preserved from the heat between shifts.

In line with my reduced living conditions, a new form of ugliness arises at Jerry's. First we are confronted—via an announcement on the computers through which we input orders—with the new rule that the hotel bar is henceforth off-limits to restaurant employees. The culprit, I learn through the grapevine, is the ultra-efficient gal who trained me—another trailer-home dweller and a mother of three. Something had set her off one morning, so she slipped out for a nip and returned to the floor impaired. This mostly hurts Ellen, whose habit it is to free her hair from its rubber band and drop by the bar for a couple of Zins before heading home at the end of the shift, but all of us feel the chill. Then the next day, when I go for straws, for the first time I find the dry-storage room locked. Ted, the portly assistant manager who opens it for me, explains that he caught one of the dishwashers attempting to steal something, and, unfortu-nately, the miscreant will be with us until a replacement can be found—hence the locked door. I neglect to ask what he had been trying to steal, but Ted tells me who he is—the kid with the buzz cut and the earring. You know, he's back there right now.

I wish I could say I rushed back and confronted George to get his side of the story. I wish I could say I stood up to Ted and insisted that George be given a translator and allowed to defend himself, or announced that I'd find a lawyer who'd handle the case pro bono. The mystery to me is that there's not much worth stealing in the dry-storage room, at least not in any fenceable quantity: "Is Gyorgi here, and am having

40

200—maybe 250—ketchup packets. What do you say?" My guess is that he had taken—if he had taken anything at all—some Saltines or a can of cherry-pie mix, and that the motive for taking it was hunger.

~~So why didn't I intervene? Certainly not because I was held back by the kind of~~ moral paralysis that can pass as journalistic objectivity. On the contrary, something new—something loathsome and servile—had infected me, along with the kitchen odors that I could still sniff on my bra when I finally undressed at night. In real life I am moderately brave, but plenty of brave people shed their courage in concentration camps, and maybe something similar goes on in the infinitely more congenial milieu of the low-wage American workplace. Maybe, in a month or two more at Jerry's, I might have regained my crusading spirit. Then again, in a month or two I might have turned into a different person altogether—say, the kind of person who would have turned George in. But this is not something I am slated to find out.

I can do this two-job thing, is my theory, if I can drink enough caffeine and avoid getting distracted by George's ever more obvious suffering.[7] The first few days after being caught he seemed not to understand the trouble he was in, and our chirpy little conversations had continued. But the last couple of shifts he's been listless and unshaven, and tonight he looks like the ghost we all know him to be, with dark half-moons hanging from his eyes. At one point, when I am briefly immobilized by the task of filling little paper cups with sour cream for baked potatoes, he comes over and looks as if he'd like to explore the limits of our shared vocabulary, but I am called to the floor for a table. I resolve to give him all my tips that night and to hell with the experiment in low-wage money management. At eight, Ellen and I grab a snack together standing at the mephitic end of the kitchen counter, but I can only manage two or three mozzarella sticks and lunch had been a mere handful of McNuggets. I am not tired at all, I assure myself, though it may be that there is simply no more "I" left to do the tiredness monitoring. What I would see, if I were more alert to the situation, is that the forces of destruction are already massing against me. There is only one cook on duty, a young man names Jesus ("Hay-Sue," that is) and he is new to the job. And there is Joy, who shows up to take over in the middle of the shift, wearing high heels and a long, clingy white dress and fuming as if she'd just been stood up in some cocktail bar.

Then it comes, the perfect storm. Four of my tables fill up at once. Four tables is nothing for me now, but only so long as they are obligingly staggered. As I bev table 27, tables 25, 28, and 24 are watching enviously. As I bev 25, 24 glowers because their bevs haven't even been ordered. Twenty-eight is four yuppyish types, meaning everything on the side and agonizing instructions as to the chicken Caesars. Twenty-five is a middle-aged black couple, who complain, with some justice, that the iced tea isn't fresh and the tabletop is sticky. But table 24 is the meteorological event of the century: ten

---

[7]In 1996, the number of persons holding two or more jobs averaged 7.8 million, or 6.2 percent of the workforce. It was about the same rate for men and for women (6.1 versus 6.2), though the kinds of jobs differ by gender. About two thirds of multiple jobholders work one job full-time and the other part-time. Only a heroic minority—4 percent of men and 2 percent of women—work two full-time jobs simultaneously. (From John F. Stinson Jr., "New Data on Multiple Jobholding Available from the CPS," in the *Monthly Labor Review,* March 1997.) [Author's note]

British tourists who seem to have made the decision to absorb the American experience entirely by mouth. Here everyone has at least two drinks—iced tea and milk shake, Michelob and water (with lemon slice, please)—and a huge promiscuous orgy of break-fast specials, mozz sticks, chicken strips, quesadillas; burgers with cheese and without, sides of hash browns with cheddar, with onions, with gravy, seasoned fries, plain fries, banana splits. Poor Jesus! Poor me! Because when I arrive with their first tray of food— after three prior trips just to refill bevs—Princess Di refuses to eat her chicken strips with her pancake-and-sausage special, since, as she now reveals, the strips were meant to be an appetizer. Maybe the others would have accepted their meals, but Di, who is deep into her third Michelob, insists that everything else go back while they work on their "starters." Meanwhile, the yuppies are waving me down for more decaf and the black couple looks ready to summon the NAACP.

Much of what happened next is lost in the fog of war. Jesus starts going under. The little printer on the counter in front of him is spewing out orders faster than he can rip them off, much less produce the meals. Even the invincible Ellen is ashen from stress. I bring table 24 their reheated main courses, which they immediately reject as either too cold or fossilized by the microwave. When I return to the kitchen with their trays (three trays in three trips), Joy confronts me with arms akimbo: "What is this?" She means the food—the plates of rejected pancakes, hash browns in assorted flavors, toasts, burgers, sausages, eggs. "Uh, scrambled with cheddar," I try, "and that's . . ." "NO," she screams in my face. "Is it a traditional, a super-scramble, an eye-opener?" I pre-tend to study my check for a clue, but entropy has been up to its tricks, not only on the plates but in my head, and I have to admit that the original order is beyond recon-struction. "You don't know an eye-opener from a traditional?" she demands in out-rage. All I know, in fact, is that my legs have lost interest in the current venture and have announced their intention to fold. I am saved by a yuppie (mercifully not one of mine) who chooses this moment to charge into the kitchen to bellow that his food is twenty-five minutes late. Joy screams at him to get the hell out of her kitchen, please, and then turns on Jesus in a fury, hurling an empty tray across the room for emphasis.

I leave. I don't walk out, I just leave. I don't finish my side work or pick up my credit-card tips, if any, at the cash register or, of course, ask Joy's permission to go. And the surprising thing is that you *can* walk out without permission, that the door opens, that the thick tropical night air parts to let me pass, that my car is still parked where I left it. There is no vindication in this exit, no fuck-you surge of relief, just an overwhelming, dank sense of failure pressing down on me and the entire parking lot. I had gone into this venture in the spirit of science, to test a mathematical proposition, but somewhere along the line, in the tunnel vision imposed by long shifts and relent-less concentration, it became a test of myself, and clearly I have failed. Not only had I flamed out as a housekeeper/server, I had even forgotten to give George my tips, and, for reasons perhaps best known to hardworking, generous people like Gail and Ellen, this hurts. I don't cry, but I am in a position to realize, for the first time in many years, that the tear ducts are still there, and still capable of doing their job.

When I moved out of the trailer park, I gave the key to number 46 to Gail and arranged for my deposit to be transferred to her. She told me that Joan is still living in her van and that Stu had been fired from the Hearthside. I never found out what happened to George.

In one month, I had earned approximately $1,040 and spent $517 on food, gas, toiletries, laundry, phone, and utilities. If I had remained in my $500 efficiency, I would have been able to pay the rent and have $22 left over (which is $78 less than the cash I had in my pocket at the start of the month). During this time I bought no clothing except for the required slacks and no prescription drugs or medical care (I did finally buy some vitamin B to compensate for the lack of vegetables in my diet). Perhaps I could have saved a little on food if I had gotten to a supermarket more often, instead of convenience stores, but it should be noted that I lost almost four pounds in four weeks, on a diet weighted heavily toward burgers and fries.

How former welfare recipients and single mothers will (and do) survive in the low-wage workforce, I cannot imagine. Maybe they will figure out how to condense their lives—including child-raising, laundry, romance, and meals—into the couple of hours between full-time jobs. Maybe they will take up residence in their vehicles, if they have one. All I know is that I couldn't hold two jobs and I couldn't make enough money to live on with one. And I had advantages unthinkable to many of the long-term poor—health, stamina, a working car, and no children to care for and support. Certainly nothing in my experience contradicts the conclusion of Kathryn Edin and Laura Lein, in their recent book *Making Ends Meet: How Single Mothers Survive Welfare and Low-Wage Work*, that low-wage work actually involves more hardship and deprivation than life at the mercy of the welfare state. In the coming months and years, economic conditions for the working poor are bound to worsen, even without the almost inevitable recession. As mentioned earlier, the influx of former welfare recipients into the low-skilled workforce will have a depressing effect on both wages and the number of jobs available. A general economic downturn will only enhance these effects, and the working poor will of course be facing it without the slight, but nonetheless often saving, protection of welfare as a backup.

The thinking behind welfare reform was that even the humblest jobs are morally uplifting and psychologically buoying. In reality they are likely to be fraught with insult and stress. But I did discover one redeeming feature of the most abject low-wage work—the camaraderie of people who are, in almost all cases, far too smart and funny and caring for the work they do and the wages they're paid. The hope, of course, is that someday these people will come to know what they're worth, and take appropriate action.

Questions for Discussion and Writing

1. What kinds of trade-offs and choices does Ehrenreich have to make when she becomes an unskilled worker?
2. How do the people (bosses and employees) and different environments she encounters change whatever preconceptions Ehrenreich had about the working poor?
3. Which of the issues Ehrenreich touches on, including homelessness, drug testing in the workplace, and holding two jobs just to survive, dramatize most vividly the

plight of the working poor? After reading her report, do you agree with her conclusions regarding welfare reform? Why or why not?

Luis Sepulveda

• •

The Chilean novelist Luis Sepulveda (b. 1949) was confined to prison as a political enemy under the dictatorship of Augusto Pinochet. He describes his experiences in this selection from Full Circle: A South American Journey *(1996). He has also written* The Old Man Who Read Love Stories *(1992),* The Name of the Bullfighter *(1996), and* Hot Line *(2002).*

DAISY

The military had rather inflated ideas of our destructive capacity. They questioned us about plans to assassinate all the officers in American military history, to blow up bridges and seal off tunnels, and to prepare for the landing of a terrible foreign enemy whom they could not identify.

Temuco is a sad, grey, rainy city. No-one would call it a tourist attraction, and yet the barracks of the Tucapel regiment came to house a sort of permanent international convention of sadists. The Chileans, who were the hosts, after all, were assisted in the interrogations by primates from Brazilian military intelligence—they were the worst—North Americans from the State Department, Argentinian paramilitary personnel, Italian neo-fascists and even some agents of Mossad.

I remember Rudi Weismann, a Chilean with a passion for the South and sailing, who was tortured and interrogated in the gentle language of the synagogues. This infamy was too much for Rudi, who had thrown in his lot with Israel: he had worked on a kibbutz, but in the end his nostalgia for Tierra del Fuego had brought him back to Chile. He simply could not understand how Israel could support such a gang of criminals, and though till then he had always been a model of good humour, he dried up like a neglected plant. One morning we found him dead in his sleeping bag. No need for an autopsy, his face made it clear: Rudi Weismann had died of sadness.

The commander of the Tucapel regiment—a basic respect for paper prevents me from writing his name—was a fanatical admirer of Field Marshal Rommel. When he found a prisoner he liked, he would invite him to recover from the interrogations in his office. After assuring the prisoner that everything that happened in the barracks was in the best interests of our great nation, the commander would offer him a glass of Korn—somebody used to send him this insipid, wheat-based liquor from Germany—and make him sit through a lecture on the Africa Korps. The guy's parents or grandparents were German, but he couldn't have looked more Chilean: chubby, short-legged, dark untidy hair. You could have mistaken him for a truck driver or a fruit vendor, but when he talked about Rommel he became the caricature of a Nazi guard.

At the end of the lecture he would dramatise Rommel's suicide, clicking his heels, raising his right hand to his forehead to salute an invisible flag, muttering "Adieu geliebtes Vaterland," and pretending to shoot himself in the mouth. We all hoped that one day he would do it for real.   5

There was another curious officer in the regiment: a lieutenant struggling to contain a homosexuality that kept popping out all over the place. The soldiers had nicknamed him Daisy, and he knew it.

We could all tell that it was a torment for Daisy not to be able to adorn his body with truly beautiful objects, and the poor guy had to make do with the regulation paraphernalia. He wore a .45 pistol, two cartridge clips, a commando's curved dagger, two hand grenades, a torch, a walkie-talkie, the insignia of his rank and the silver wings of the parachute corps. The prisoners and the soldiers thought he looked like a Christmas tree

This individual sometimes surprised us with generous and apparently disinterested acts—we didn't know that the Stockholm syndrome could be a military perversion. For example, after the interrogations he would suddenly fill our pockets with cigarettes or the highly prized aspirin tablets with vitamin C. One afternoon he invited me to his room.

"So you're a man of letters," he said, offering me a can of Coca-Cola.

"I've written a couple of stories. That's all," I replied.   10

"You're not here for an interrogation. I'm very sorry about what's happening, but that's what war is like. I want us to talk as one writer to another. Are you surprised? The army has produced some great men of letters. Think of Don Alonso de Ercilla y Zúñiga, for example."

"Or Cervantes," I added.

Daisy included himself among the greats. That was his problem. If he wanted adulation, he could have it. I drank the Coca-Cola and thought about Garcés, or rather, about his chicken, because, incredible as it seems, the cook had a chicken called Dulcinea,[1] the name of Don Quixote's mistress.

One morning it jumped the wall which separated the common-law prisoners from the POWs, and it must have been a chicken with deep political convictions, because it decided to stay with us. Garcés caressed it and sighed, saying: "If I had a pinch of pepper and a pinch of cumin, I'd make you a chicken marinade like you've never tasted."

"I want you to read my poems and give me your opinion, your honest opinion,"   15
said Daisy, handing me a notebook.

I left that room with my pockets full of cigarettes, caramel sweets, tea bags and a tin of U.S. Army marmalade. That afternoon I started to believe in the brotherhood of writers.

They transported us from the prison to the barracks and back in a cattle truck. The soldiers made sure there was plenty of cow shit on the floor of the truck before ordering us to lie face down with our hands behind our necks. We were guarded by four of them, with North American machine guns, one in each corner of the truck. They were almost all young guys brought down from northern garrisons, and the harsh climate of the South kept them flu-ridden and in a perpetually filthy mood. They had orders to fire on the bundles—us—at the slightest suspect movement, or on any civilian who

---

[1]*Dulcinea:* ironically refers to the object of Don Quixote's affection in the novel *Don Quixote de La Mancha* (1605) by Miguel de Cervantes (1547–1616).

tried to approach the truck. But as time wore on, the discipline gradually relaxed and they turned a blind eye to the packet of cigarettes or piece of fruit thrown from a window, or the pretty and daring girl who ran beside the truck blowing us kisses and shouting: "Don't give up, comrades! We'll win!"

Back in prison, as always, we were met by the welcoming committee organised by Doctor "Skinny" Pragnan, now an eminent psychiatrist in Belgium. First he examined those who couldn't walk and those who had heart problems, then those who had come back with a dislocation or with ribs out of place. Pragnan was expert at estimating how much electricity had been put into us on the grill, and patiently determined who would be able to absorb liquids in the next few hours. Then finally it was time to take communion: we were given the aspirin with vitamin C and an anticoagulant to prevent internal haematomas.

"Dulcinea's days are numbered," I said to Garcés, and looked for a corner in which to read Daisy's notebook.

The elegantly inscribed pages were redolent of love, honey, sublime suffering and   20
forgotten flowers. By the third page I knew that Daisy hadn't even gone to the trouble of reusing the ideas of the Mexican poet Amado Nervo—he'd simply copied out his poems word for word.

I called out to Peyuco Gálvez, a Spanish teacher, and read him a couple of lines.

"What do you think, Peyuco?"

"Amado Nervo. The book is called *The Interior Gardens.*"

I had got myself into a real jam. If Daisy found out that I knew the work of this sugary poet Nervo, then it wasn't Garcés's chicken whose days were numbered, but mine. It was a serious problem, so that night I presented it to the Council of Elders.

"Now, Daisy, would he be the passive or the active type?" enquired Iriarte.   25

"Stop it, will you. My skin's at risk here," I replied.

"I'm serious. Maybe our friend wants to have an affair with you, and giving you the notebook was like dropping a silk handkerchief. And like a fool you picked it up. Perhaps he copied out the poems for you to find a message in them. I've known queens who seduced boys by lending them *Demian*[2] by Hermann Hesse. If Daisy is the passive type, this business with Amado Nervo means he wants to test your nerve, so to speak. And if he's the active type, well, it would have to hurt less than a kick in the balls."

"Message my arse. He gave you the poems as his own, and you should say you liked them a lot. If he was trying to send a message, he should have given the notebook to Garcés; he's the only one who has an interior garden. Or maybe Daisy doesn't know about the pot plant," remarked Andrés Müller.

"Let's be serious about this. You have to say something to him, and Daisy mustn't even suspect that you know Nervo's poems," declared Pragnan.

"Tell him you liked the poems but that the adjectives strike you a bit excessive.   30
Quote Huidobro: when an adjective doesn't give life, it kills. That way you'll show him that you read his poems carefully and that you are criticising his work as a colleague," suggested Gálvez.

---

[2]*Demian (1919):* by Hermann Hesse, German novelist (1877–1962).

The Council of Elders approved of Gálvez's idea, but I spent two weeks on tenterhooks. I couldn't sleep. I wished they would come and take me to be kicked and electrocuted so I could give the damned notebook back. In those two weeks I came to hate good old Garcés:

"Listen, mate, if everything goes well, and you get a little jar of capers as well as the cumin and the pepper, we'll have such a feast with that chicken."

After a fortnight, I found myself at last stretched out face down on the mattress of cowpats with my hands behind my neck. I thought I was going mad: I was happy to be heading towards a session of the activity known as torture.

Tucapel barracks. Service Corps. In the background, the perpetual green of Cerro Ñielol, sacred to the Mapuche Indians. There was a waiting room outside the interrogation cell, like at the doctor's. There they made us sit on a bench with our hands tied behind our backs and black hoods over our heads. I never understood what the hoods were for, because once we got inside they took them off, and we could see the interrogators—the toy soldiers who, with panic-stricken faces, turned the handle of the generator, and the health officers who attached the electrodes to our anuses, testicles, gums and tongue, and then listened with stethoscopes to see who was faking and who had really passed out on the grill.

Lagos, a deacon of the Emmaus International ragmen, was the first to be interrogated that day. For a year they had been working him over to find out how the organisation had come by a couple of dozen old military uniforms which had been found in their warehouses. A trader who sold army surplus gear had donated them. Lagos screamed in pain and repeated over and over what the soldiers wanted to hear: the uniforms belonged to an invading army which was preparing to land on the Chilean coast.

I was waiting for my turn when someone took off the hood. It was Lieutenant Daisy.

"Follow me," he ordered.

We went into an office. On the desk I saw a tin of cocoa and a carton of cigarettes which were obviously there to reward my comments on his literary work.

"Did you read my poesy?" he asked, offering me a seat.

Poesy. Daisy said poesy, not poetry. A man covered with pistols and grenades can't say "poesy" without sounding ridiculous and effete. At that moment he revolted me, and I decided that even if it meant pissing blood, hissing when I spoke and being able to charge batteries just by touching them, I wasn't going to lower myself to flattering a plagiarising faggot in uniform.

"You have pretty handwriting, Lieutenant. But you know these poems aren't yours," I said, giving him back the notebook.

I saw him begin to shake. He was carrying enough arms to kill me several times over, and if he didn't want to stain his uniform, he could order someone else to do it. Trembling with anger he stood up, threw what was on the desk onto the floor and shouted:

"Three weeks in the cube. But first, you're going to visit the chiropodist, you piece of subversive shit!"

The chiropodist was a civilian, a landholder who had lost several thousand hectares in the land reform, and who was getting his revenge by participating in the interrogations as a volunteer. His speciality was peeling back toenails, which led to terrible infections.

I knew the cube. I had spent my first six months of prison there in solitary con-   45
finement: it was an underground cell, one and a half metres wide by one and a half
metres long by one and a half metres high. In the old days there had been a tannery
in the Temuco jail, and the cube was used to store fat. The walls still stank of fat,
but after a week your excrement fixed that, making the cube very much a place of
your own.

You could only stretch out across the diagonal, but the low temperatures of southern Chile, the rainwater and the soldiers' urine made you want to curl up hugging your
legs and stay like that wishing yourself smaller and smaller, so that eventually you
could live on one of the islands of floating shit, which conjured up images of dream
holidays. I was there for three weeks, running through Laurel and Hardy[3] films, remembering the books of Salgari,[4] Stevenson,[5] and London[6] word by word, playing
long games of chess, licking my toes to protect them from infection. In the cube I swore
over and over again never to become a literary critic.

Questions for Discussion and Writing

1. Sepulveda's main tormentor is a prison guard with literary aspirations, nicknamed
   Daisy. What moral, aesthetic, and practical choices does Sepulveda face?
2. Sepulveda displays surprising good humor considering the circumstances. Give
   some examples of how he gets this across in his account.
3. Plagiarism, even for those who are not prison guards, is a serious offense.
   What precautions have you taken to avoid committing plagiarism in your
   schoolwork?

Steven E. Barkan and Lynne L. Snowden

• •

*Steven E. Barkan is a professor of sociology at the University of Maine. He received a
Ph.D. from the State University of New York at Stony Brook in 1980 and has published
widely in the areas of criminology, deviant behavior, and social movements. His works
include* Protestors on Trial *(1985),* Criminology: A Sociological Understanding *(2nd ed.,
2001), and* Essentials of Criminal Justice *(with George Bryjak, 2004). Lynne L. Snowden
is an associate professor of criminal justice at the University of North Carolina at Wilm-
ington. She received a Ph.D. from the University of Delaware. The following essay is
drawn from* Collective Violence *(2001). Although it was written before September 11,
2001, it provides a useful overview of terrorism and its impact.*

---

[3]*Laurel and Hardy:* American film comedy team made up of Stan Laurel (1890–1965) and Oliver Hardy
(1892–1957).   [4]*Emilio Salgari (1862–1911):* called the Italian Jules Verne, the author of more than two hundred adventure stories and novels.   [5]*Robert Louis Stevenson (1850–1894):* Scottish novelist, poet, and essayist. Best known for *Treasure Island* (1883).   [6]*Jack London (1876–1916):* American author who created
romantic yet realistic fiction in works such as *The Call of the Wild* (1903). See his essay "The San Francisco
Earthquake" (Ch. 7).

How does the symbolism of a sea of umbrellas in Madrid, Spain, after the March 3, 2004 terrorist attack express public indignation?

DEFINING AND COUNTERING TERRORISM

Defining Terrorism

The terrorism literature is filled with discussions of the difficulties in deciding just what *terrorism* means. Not surprisingly, many definitions of terrorism exist, with one estimate putting the number at more than a hundred. This plethora underscores the problems in defining terrorism and led one analyst to despair that "a comprehensive definition of terrorism . . . does not exist nor will it be found in the foreseeable future."

This pessimistic appraisal notwithstanding, most definitions of terrorism highlight several key dimensions that characterize a given behavior or pattern of behavior as one of terrorism. Before outlining these dimensions, let's explore why the concept is so difficult to define precisely.

One problem in defining terrorism is that the word "terrorism" can be confused with words such as "terror" and "terrorize," both of which connote violence or the threat of violence and stem from the Latin term *terr(ēre)*, meaning "to frighten." (The term "terrorism" originated from the Reign of Terror that characterized the French Revolution.) Thus a common criminal commits vicious acts of violence against a terrorized victim; a violent street gang terrorizes a whole neighborhood; a stalker forces a woman to live in terror of attack. These unfortunately common, tragic acts all involve the fear that "terror" and "terrorize" connote, but they do not involve the essentially *political* activity that lies at the heart of most standard definitions of terrorism.

Another, more important definitional problem is that the word "terrorism" raises all sorts of emotions. It immediately brings to mind hideous, irrational acts of violence committed by desperate and often slovenly individuals. With this image in people's minds, terrorism takes on a negative connotation that makes it difficult to discuss the concept objectively. To complicate matters, terrorism is sometimes viewed positively by bystanders who share its goals. As is often said, "One person's terrorist is another person's freedom fighter." Thus, for example, many people in Northern Ireland, and many Irish Americans in the United States, view the Irish Republican Army (IRA) as heroes struggling valiantly against a British government that is denying Ireland its independence, whereas many others condemn the IRA's bombings and other terrorist tactics as sickening and beyond contempt. Many people in the Middle East regard the actions of the Palestinian Liberation Organization (PLO) and other terrorist groups as necessary acts of liberation, while others regard them as the worst sort of terrorism.

In a related definitional issue, the usual equation of "terrorists" and "terrorism"   5
with individuals obscures the fact that governments themselves sometimes use terrorism to achieve their ends. In both contemporary and earlier periods, nations worldwide, including the United States, have engaged in or otherwise supported acts of terrorism to achieve political ends. This chapter returns to this point shortly.

Australian terrorism expert Grant Wardlaw summarizes these definitional problems by saying that terrorism is, at heart, a "moral problem." By labeling certain behaviors as acts of terrorism and the people who commit them as terrorists, we implicitly condemn both the acts and the actors. By not labeling other, similar acts as terrorism and their perpetrators as terrorists, we implicitly approve those acts and actors. As a result, says sociologist Jack P. Gibbs, any definition of terrorism "may reflect ideological or political bias." To be useful, then, a definition of terrorism must dispassionately highlight its essential dimensions in a way that covers the various acts that comprise terrorism and the various actors that do terrorism.

This discussion suggests three dimensions that should be considered when defining terrorism: violence, fear, and political change. To the extent that this is true, the term *political terrorism* favored by some commentators is, as argued here, redundant, because terrorism necessarily implies a political component.

Many definitions that include these three dimensions abound. A simple dictionary definition would thus be "the use of violence and threats to intimidate or coerce, especially for political purposes." A definition proposed by political scientist Ted Robert Gurr goes one step further in highlighting the random, sudden nature of terrorism that makes it so frightening: "the use of *unexpected* violence to intimidate or coerce people in the pursuit of political or social objectives" (emphasis added). This definition underscores the fact that anyone—including innocent people—can be victims of terrorism and the fact that innocent people are often *the* targets of choice for terrorists. As philosopher Loren E. Lomasky observes, terrorists, unlike Robin Hood, typically don't distinguish between the guilty and the innocent or between justifiable victims and unjustifiable victims: "The enemy is only incidentally particular individuals who cross the terrorist's path; more fundamentally it is civil order."

Thus although there might not be one perfect definition of terrorism, these definitions and others like them underscore its essentially political nature, its use to provoke fear in the general population, and its use both by and against the state. Viewed dispassionately, terrorism is a violent tactic aimed at winning political objectives.

One reason terrorism is so difficult to define is that there are so many types of ter- 10 rorism. Recognizing this, scholars have developed typologies of terrorism that consolidate these many types into a much smaller number of categories. The intent is to clarify the key characteristics distinguishing one form of terrorism from another. Most typologies incorporate at least two of three important features of terrorism: its purpose, its actors and supporters, and its location. The typology favored here comes from political scientist Gurr. It has the advantage of being comprehensive but not too complex. It consists of four categories based on the "political status and situation of the perpetrators."

Gurr's first type is *vigilante terrorism,* which is committed by private citizens, for example, the Ku Klux Klan (KKK or the Klan), against other private citizens to express hatred or to resist social change. This type is the most common form of terrorism in U.S. history and is neglected in most terrorism typologies. Gurr's second type is *insurgent terrorism,* in which private citizens commit terrorism against their government to win political goals. Next is *transnational terrorism,* in which terrorists living in one nation strike inside another nation. Gurr's final category is *state terrorism.* Sometimes called *repressive terrorism,* this type is used by a government to intimidate its own citizens.

· · ·

Countering Terrorism

The terrorism literature is filled with recommendations and debates concerning the best ways to counter terrorism, and the term *counterterrorism* has made its way into popular usage. Almost all work on counterterrorism addresses only two of the four types of terrorism discussed earlier in this chapter. These two types are insurgent and transnational terrorism. As noted previously, discussions of terrorism typically ignore the vigilante variety and often neglect the state variety, and the counterterrorism literature is no exception. This section sketches the major points of the counterterrorism debate on the first two types and turns later to the latter two.

The question that all counterterrorism discussions try to answer is how can we best deal with the terrorist threat. This question is difficult to answer. As Richard E. Rubenstein observes, "Since serious terrorist movements are locally rooted and politically diverse, there is no unified terrorist threat to discuss, and no possibility of prescribing an all-purpose response. One's reaction to any particular terrorist campaign will depend on the nature of the attacking group, the precise situation presented, and one's own political ideas." Other writers also emphasize that the diversity of terrorism makes it difficult to come up with any all-encompassing solution to it. Thus Sederberg says that the response to insurgent terrorism must at a minimum consider the goals of the groups committing it and the degree to which those groups enjoy public support.

Most counterterrorism experts have answered this question by advocating a law enforcement or military approach to terrorism. In this approach, the law, legal system, and military are used to try to prevent terrorism and to punish terrorists. Here we can distinguish between offensive and defense strategies. Offensive strategies include economic and diplomatic sanctions, military strikes, harsh prison terms, and so on.

Defense strategies typically take the form of *target hardening,* which involves efforts to make potential terrorist targets secure and safe. Airport metal detectors are perhaps the most familiar example of target hardening.

How successful are such counterterrorism measures? Although target hardening has   15 helped in many cases, determined terrorists can still succeed. The effectiveness of the offensive strategies is even more debatable. Although there is some evidence that police crackdowns have weakened or eliminated some terrorist groups in the United States and Western Europe, other groups, especially in the Middle East, persist despite repeated military strikes and other punitive measures. This fact makes several experts question the value and advisability of such measures, with one saying flatly that "terrorist movements cannot be eliminated by a policy of assassination and disruption." Moreover, often these harsh measures have the unintended effect of increasing the resolve of terrorists, as well as popular support for their cause, while doing nothing to address the political, social, and economic conditions underlying at least some examples of terrorism.

Another problem raised by harsh counterterrorist measures in democratic societies is the threat they pose to civil liberties. In any democratic society, tension always exists between the goals of keeping the society safe (e.g., from crime and terrorism) and keeping the society free. As one writer notes, "Responding to terrorism exposes a conflict between our need for survival, the most urgent objective, and our commitment to democracy, our highest purpose." A recent example of the civil liberties debate surrounding counterterrorism occurred after the Oklahoma City bombing. . . . The public, media, and government at first suspected Middle Eastern terrorists, and Congress soon considered legislation designed to crack down on terrorism. Critics charged that several provisions in the legislation would cut away at civil liberties guaranteed by the Bill of Rights.

In a related area, several counterterrorism experts believe the United States and other democracies need to restrict media coverage of terrorism. In response, other observers charge that such restrictions would undermine the freedom of the press guaranteed in the First Amendment. Britain, which does not have the freedom of the press tradition that the United States enjoys, does restrict media coverage of terrorism, and observers there and elsewhere continue to debate the merits of British law in this regard.

An alternative to conventional counterterrorism measures stems from the political explanation of terrorism discussed previously and focuses on the social, economic, and political causes of terrorism. If inequality, oppression, and other such ills lie at the heart of much insurgent and transnational terrorism, then efforts to reduce or eliminate these problems should reduce terrorism. This is especially the case when terrorist groups "have a broad base of support and substantive grievances." However, such efforts are less likely to succeed when terrorist groups enjoy little public support and have goals unrelated to structural problems in their society.

Perhaps the key question concerning the use of such structural reform to deal with terrorism is whether this approach will placate terrorists and would-be terrorists or instead encourage them to commit even more terrorism. Christopher Hewitt thinks that both effects could occur. On the one hand, terrorists may regard these efforts as concessions and increase their terrorism because they perceive that their previous actions have succeeded. If so, addressing the underlying causes of terrorism may, ironically, increase it in the short run. On the other hand, addressing the social roots of terrorism may in the long run meet the intended goal of reducing or eliminating terrorist activity.

Rubenstein argues that much insurgent and transnational terrorism today derives from U.S. imperialism: "American diplomats, soldiers, and businesspeople are prime targets for terrorist attack because they are considered representatives of imperialist oppression . . . by a frighteningly broad array of groups subjected to American power." He thus feels that an end to U.S. involvement in other nations would do much to end terrorism. 20

What about vigilante terrorism and state terrorism? An examination of historical and contemporary vigilante terrorism in the United States shows that much of it takes place when economic conditions are worsening and when public officials indicate through word or deed their approval, or at least a lack of stern disapproval, of such terrorism. To the extent that both factors underlie vigilante terrorism, an improved economy and a practice of zero tolerance for such violence should help reduce, if not eliminate, it.

State terrorism is a different matter altogether. Because the government itself commits this sort of violence, we cannot count on the government to do anything about it. That is why groups such as Amnesty International continue to publicize the worst examples of governmental violence. The long-term solution to state terrorism is not easy. As Sederberg notes, it probably means that "the character of the regime itself must change." Some terrorist governments might be vulnerable to external pressure, such as economic boycotts, and thus might be induced by such pressure to at least lessen their repressiveness. As an example, the international economic boycott of South Africa, because of its notorious apartheid policy, is often cited as one factor that helped end apartheid in the 1990s.

Most often, however, external pressure is not enough to force governments to lessen or end their repression. The international community usually disagrees on using such pressure, and repressive governments typically resist. Even in South Africa, the key factor in ending apartheid was by all accounts the political struggle of the South Africans that apartheid tyrannized. For better or worse, the historical record worldwide indicates that often the only way to end state terrorism is for the people subjected to it to revolt against it. Indeed, it's fair to say that most revolutions, violent or nonviolent, in the last few centuries occurred precisely because a populace abhorred state terrorism and other governmental abuses. The fact that revolution might be necessary to end state terrorism underscores how serious and unyielding this form of terrorism is.

Conclusion

Because terrorism so often seems so senseless, it remains difficult for us to comprehend. When innocent victims die or are maimed, what purpose can terrorism serve?

In discussing terrorism, this chapter continued the theme of the preceding ones, that of the essential rationality of collective violence. If riots and revolution are violent acts of primarily rational actors protesting often grievous conditions, then so is terrorism. For better or worse, terrorism has played a central role in the struggle between political regimes and their opponents. The fact that terrorism is such a common 25 tactic in political struggle underscores its essentially political nature. This observation doesn't necessarily make terrorism any more justifiable, but at least it helps put it into an understandable context.

Questions for Discussion and Writing

1. According to the authors, what are the key features of terrorism, and why does it always involve political coercion? What trade-offs are involved (e.g., civil liberties, media restriction, right to privacy) in considering how best to counter terrorism?
2. How is Barkan and Snowden's analysis designed to provide a context for understanding what we may think is a relatively recent phenomenon, but which actually began with the French Revolution in 1789?
3. In the aftermath of September 11, 2001, and its political and military repercussions, what new events have sharpened the debate as to the nature of terrorism and how best to combat it?

Michael Levin

* *

Michael Levin (b. 1943) was educated at Michigan State University and Columbia University. From 1968 to 1980 he taught philosophy at Columbia; he is currently a professor of philosophy at City College of the City University of New York. In addition to many articles on ethics and philosophy, Levin has written Metaphysics and the Mind–Body Problem *(with Lawrence M. Thomas, 1979). His latest book is* Sexual Orientation and Human Rights *(1999). In "The Case for Torture," which first appeared in* Newsweek *(1982), Levin uses a number of intriguing hypothetical cases to challenge the conventional assumption that there are no circumstances under which torture is permissible.*

THE CASE FOR TORTURE

It is generally assumed that torture is impermissible, a throwback to a more brutal age. Enlightened societies reject it outright, and regimes suspected of using it risk the wrath of the United States.

I believe this attitude is unwise. There are situations in which torture is not merely permissible but morally mandatory. Moreover, these situations are moving from the realm of imagination to fact.

Death   Suppose a terrorist has hidden an atomic bomb on Manhattan Island which will detonate at noon on July 4 unless . . . (here follow the usual demands for money and release of his friends from jail). Suppose, further, that he is caught at 10 A.M. of the fateful day, but—preferring death to failure—won't disclose where the bomb is. What do we do? If we follow due process—wait for his lawyer, arraign him—millions of people will die. If the only way to save those lives is to subject the terrorist to the most excruciating possible pain, what grounds can there be for not doing so? I suggest there are none. In any case, I ask you to face the question with an open mind.

Torturing the terrorist is unconstitutional? Probably. But millions of lives surely outweigh constitutionality. Torture is barbaric? Mass murder is far more barbaric. Indeed, letting millions of innocents die in deference to one who flaunts his guilt is moral cowardice, an unwillingness to dirty one's hands. If *you* caught the terrorist, could you sleep nights knowing that millions died because you couldn't bring yourself to apply the electrodes?

Once you concede that torture is justified in extreme cases, you have admitted that   5
the decision to use torture is a matter of balancing innocent lives against the means needed to save them. You must now face more realistic cases involving more modest numbers. Someone plants a bomb on a jumbo jet. He alone can disarm it, and his demands cannot be met (or if they can, we refuse to set a precedent by yielding to his threats). Surely we can, we must, do anything to the extortionist to save the passengers. How can we tell 300, or 100, or 10 people who never asked to be put in danger, "I'm sorry, you'll have to die in agony, we just couldn't bring ourselves to . . ."

Here are the results of an informal poll about a third, hypothetical, case. Suppose a terrorist group kidnapped a newborn baby from a hospital. I asked four mothers if they would approve of torturing kidnappers if that were necessary to get their own newborns back. All said yes, the most "liberal" adding that she would like to administer it herself.

I am not advocating torture as punishment. Punishment is addressed to deeds irrevocably past. Rather, I am advocating torture as an acceptable measure for preventing future evils. So understood, it is far less objectionable than many extant punishments. Opponents of the death penalty, for example, are forever insisting that executing a murderer will not bring back his victim (as if the purpose of capital punishment were supposed to be resurrection, not deterrence or retribution). But torture, in the cases described, is intended not to bring anyone back but to keep innocents from being dispatched. The most powerful argument against using torture as a punishment or to secure confessions is that such practices disregard the rights of the individual. Well, if the individual is all that important—and he is—it is correspondingly important to protect the rights of individuals threatened by terrorists. If life is so valuable that it must never be taken, the lives of the innocents must be saved even at the price of hurting the one who endangers them.

Better precedents for torture are assassination and pre-emptive attack. No Allied leader would have flinched at assassinating Hitler, had that been possible. (The Allies did assassinate Heydrich.) Americans would be angered to learn that Roosevelt could have had Hitler killed in 1943—thereby shortening the war and saving millions of lives—but refused on moral grounds. Similarly, if nation A learns that nation B is about to launch an unprovoked attack, A has a right to save itself by destroying B's military capability first. In the same way, if the police can by torture save those who would otherwise die at the hands of kidnappers or terrorists, they must.

Idealism   There is an important difference between terrorists and their victims that should mute talk of the terrorists' "rights." The terrorist's victims are at risk unintentionally, not having asked to be endangered. But the terrorist knowingly initiated his actions. Unlike his victims, he volunteered for the risks of his deed. By threatening to kill for profit or idealism, he renounces civilized standards, and he can have no complaint if civilization tries to thwart him by whatever means necessary.

Just as torture is justified only to save lives (not extort confessions or recantations)   10
it is justifiably administered only to those *known* to hold innocent lives in their hands.
Ah, but how can the authorities ever be sure they have the right malefactor? Isn't there
a danger of error and abuse? Won't We turn into Them?

Questions like these are disingenuous in a world in which terrorists proclaim themselves and perform for television. The name of their game is public recognition. After all,
you can't very well intimidate a government into releasing your freedom fighters unless
you announce that it is your group that has seized its embassy. "Clear guilt" is difficult
to define, but when 40 million people see a group of masked gunmen seize an airplane
on the evening news, there is not much question about who the perpetrators are. There
will be hard cases where the situation is murkier. Nonetheless, a line demarcating the legitimate use of torture can be drawn. Torture only the obviously guilty, and only for the
sake of saving innocents, and the line between Us and Them will remain clear.

There is little danger that the Western democracies will lose their way if they choose
to inflict pain as one way of preserving order. Paralysis in the face of evil is the greater
danger. Some day soon a terrorist will threaten tens of thousands of lives, and torture
will be the only way to save them. We had better start thinking about this.

Questions for Discussion and Writing

1. Does the way in which Levin sets up the alternatives of "inflict[ing] pain as one
   way of preserving order" versus becoming paralyzed "in the face of evil" represent the choices fairly?
2. Levin displays amazing ingenuity in thinking up his hypothetical examples. For
   each of the hypothetical examples he invents, can you invent a counterexample that
   would lead to the opposite conclusion?
3. What assumptions does Levin make that if untrue would undercut his argument?
   For example, he assumes that we know we caught the correct terrorist to subject
   to the torture.
4. As a research project, investigate the official policies of various governments (for
   example, the United States, Great Britain, Pakistan) toward suspected terrorists in
   terms of limitations on torture following September 11, 2001.

FICTION

Panos Ioannides

*Panos Ioannides was born in Cyprus in 1935 and was educated in Cyprus, the United
States, and Canada. He has been the head of TV programs at Cyprus Broadcasting Corporation. Ioannides is the author of many plays, which have been staged or telecast in-
ternationally, and has written novels, short stories, and radio scripts. "Gregory" was
written in 1963 and first appeared in* The Charioteer, *a Review of Modern Greek*

Literature (1965). The English translation is by Marion Byron and Catherine Raisiz. This compelling story is based on a true incident that took place during the Cypriot Liberation struggle against the British in the late 1950s. Ioannides takes the unusual approach of letting the reader experience the torments of a soldier ordered to shoot a prisoner, Gregory, who had saved his life and was his friend.

GREGORY

My hand was sweating as I held the pistol. The curve of the trigger was biting against my finger.

Facing me, Gregory trembled.

His whole being was beseeching me, "Don't!"

Only his mouth did not make a sound. His lips were squeezed tight. If it had been me, I would have screamed, shouted, cursed.

The soldiers were watching. . . .   5

The day before, during a brief meeting, they had each given their opinions: "It's tough luck, but it has to be done. We've got no choice."

The order from Headquarters was clear: "As soon as Lieutenant Rafel's execution is announced, the hostage Gregory is to be shot and his body must be hanged from a telegraph pole in the main street as an exemplary punishment."

It was not the first time that I had to execute a hostage in this war. I had acquired experience, thanks to Headquarters which had kept entrusting me with these delicate assignments. Gregory's case was precisely the sixth.

The first time, I remember, I vomited. The second time I got sick and had a headache for days. The third time I drank a bottle of rum. The fourth, just two glasses of beer. The fifth time I joked about it, "This little guy, with the big pop-eyes, won't be much of a ghost!"

But why, dammit, when the day came did I have to start thinking that I'm not so   10
tough, after all? The thought had come at exactly the wrong time and spoiled all my disposition to do my duty.

You see, this Gregory was such a miserable little creature, such a puny thing, such a nobody, damn him.

That very morning, although he had heard over the loudspeakers that Rafel had been executed, he believed that we would spare his life because we had been eating together so long.

"Those who eat from the same mess tins and drink from the same water canteen," he said, "remain good friends no matter what."

And a lot more of the same sort of nonsense.

He was a silly fool—we had smelled that out the very first day Headquarters gave   15
him to us. The sentry guarding him had got dead drunk and had dozed off. The rest of us with exit permits had gone from the barracks. When we came back, there was Gregory sitting by the sleeping sentry and thumbing through a magazine.

"Why didn't you run away, Gregory?" we asked, laughing at him, several days later.

And he answered, "Where would I go in this freezing weather? I'm O.K. here."

So we started teasing him.

"You're dead right. The accommodations here are splendid. . . ."

"It's not so bad here," he replied. "The barracks where I used to be are like a sieve.   20
The wind blows in from every side. . . ."

We asked him about his girl. He smiled.

"Maria is a wonderful person," he told us. "Before I met her she was engaged to
a no-good fellow, a pig. He gave her up for another girl. Then nobody in the village
wanted to marry Maria. I didn't miss my chance. So what if she is second-hand. Nonsense. Peasant ideas, my friend. She's beautiful and good-hearted. What more could I
want? And didn't she load me with watermelons and cucumbers every time I passed
by her vegetable garden? Well, one day I stole some cucumbers and melons and watermelons and I took them to her. 'Maria,' I said, 'from now on I'm going to take care
of you.' She started crying and then me, too. But ever since that day she has given me
lots of trouble—jealousy. She wouldn't let me go even to my mother's. Until the day I
was recruited, she wouldn't let me go far from her apron strings. But that was just
what I wanted. . . ."

He used to tell this story over and over, always with the same words, the same
commonplace gestures. At the end he would have a good laugh and start gulping from
his water jug.

His tongue was always wagging! When he started talking, nothing could stop him.
We used to listen and nod our heads, not saying a word. But sometimes, as he was
telling us about his mother and family problems, we couldn't help wondering, "Eh,
well, these people have the same headaches in their country as we've got."

Strange, isn't it!   25

Except for his talking too much, Gregory wasn't a bad fellow. He was a marvelous
cook. Once he made us some apple tarts, so delicious we licked the platter clean. And
he could sew, too. He used to sew on all our buttons, patch our clothes, darn our socks,
iron our ties, wash our clothes. . . .

How the devil could you kill such a friend?

Even though his name was Gregory and some people on his side had killed one of
ours, even though we had left wives and children to go to war against him and his
kind—but how can I explain? He was our friend. He actually liked us! A few days before, hadn't he killed with his own bare hands a scorpion that was climbing up my
leg? He could have let it send me to hell!

"Thanks, Gregory!" I said then, "Thank God who made you. . . ."

When the order came, it was like a thunderbolt. Gregory was to be shot, it said,   30
and hanged from a telegraph pole as an exemplary punishment.

We got together inside the barracks. We sent Gregory to wash some underwear for us.

"It ain't right."

"What is right?"

"Our duty!"

"Shit!"   35

"If you dare, don't do it! They'll drag you to court-martial and then bang-bang. . . ."

Well, of course. The right thing is to save your skin. That's only logical. It's either
your skin or his. His, of course, even if it was Gregory, the fellow you've been sharing
the same plate with, eating with your fingers, and who was washing your clothes that
very minute.

What could I do? That's war. We had seen worse things.

So we set the hour.

We didn't tell him anything when he came back from the washing. He slept peace- 40
fully. He snored for the last time. In the morning, he heard the news over the loudspeaker and he saw that we looked gloomy and he began to suspect that something was
up. He tried talking to us, but he got no answers and then he stopped talking.

He just stood there and looked at us, stunned and lost. . . .

Now, I'll squeeze the trigger. A tiny bullet will rip through his chest. Maybe I'll lose my
sleep tonight but in the morning I'll wake up alive.

Gregory seems to guess my thoughts. He puts out his hand and asks, "You're kidding,
friend! Aren't you kidding?"

What a jackass! Doesn't he deserve to be cut to pieces? What a thing to ask at such a
time. Your heart is about to burst and he's asking if you're kidding. How can a body be kidding about such a thing? Idiot! This is no time for jokes. And you, if you're such a fine
friend, why don't you make things easier for us? Help us kill you with fewer qualms? If you
would get angry—curse our Virgin, our God—if you'd try to escape it would be much easier for us and for you.

So it is *now*.

Now, Mr. Gregory, you are going to pay for your stupidities wholesale. Because you
didn't escape the day the sentry fell asleep; because you didn't escape yesterday when we
sent you all alone to the laundry—we did it on purpose, you idiot! Why didn't you let me
die from the sting of the scorpion?

So now don't complain. It's all your fault, nitwit.

Eh? What's happening to him now?

Gregory is crying. Tears flood his eyes and trickle down over his cleanshaven cheeks.
He is turning his face and pressing his forehead against the wall. His back is shaking as he
sobs. His hands cling, rigid and helpless, to the wall.

Now is my best chance, now that he knows there is no other solution and turns his
face from us.

I squeeze the trigger.

Gregory jerks, His back stops shaking up and down.

I think I've finished him! How easy it is. . . . But suddenly he starts crying out loud, his
hands claw at the wall and try to pull it down. He screams, "No, no. . . ."

I turn to the others. I expect them to nod, "That's enough."

They nod, "What are you waiting for?"

I squeeze the trigger again.

The bullet smashed into his neck. A thick spray of blood spurts out.

Gregory turns. His eyes are all red. He lunges at me and starts punching me with his fists.

"I hate you, hate you . . . ," he screams.

I emptied the barrel. He fell and grabbed my leg as if he wanted to hold on.

He died with a terrible spasm. His mouth was full of blood and so were my
boots and socks.

We stood quietly, looking at him.

When we came to, we stooped and picked him up. His hands were frozen and
wouldn't let my legs go.

I still have their imprints, red and deep, as if made by a hot knife. 45

"We will hang him tonight," the men said.

"Tonight or now?" they said.
I turned and looked at them one by one.
"Is that what you all want?" I asked.
They gave me no answer.   50
"Dig a grave," I said.

Headquarters did not ask for a report the next day or the day after. The top brass were sure that we had obeyed them and had left him swinging from a pole.

They didn't care to know what happened to that Gregory, alive or dead.

Questions for Discussion and Writing

1. What in the narrator's past leads his superiors (and the narrator himself) to conclude that he is the best one for the job? Why is Gregory's innocence both a source of admiration and irritation? How does the narrator's final order reveal his inner distress?

2. Why is the story more effective because it is told from the narrator/executioner's point of view rather than from Gregory's? What details emphasize the anguish the narrator feels and the irony of the whole situation when the authorities never even inquire whether their orders have been carried out?

3. If you were in the narrator's place, what would you have done, and how would you have felt about your decision?

Liliana Heker

. . . .

Liliana Heker (b. 1943) was born in Buenos Aires, Argentina, and achieved fame in her early twenties with her first volume of short stories, Those Who Beheld the Burning Bush *(1966). Between 1977 and 1986, she was the editor of a literary magazine,* El Ornitorrinco *("The Platypus"), which served as a forum for writers during the period when Argentina was under a military dictatorship. She is also the author of a novel,* Zona de Clivage *(1988), and many short stories. "The Stolen Party" first appeared in translation in* Other Fires: Short Fiction by Latin American Women *(1985), translated by Alberto Manguel. She has also written the as yet untranslated* Fin de la Historia *(1996) and* Hermanas de Shakespeare *(1999).*

THE STOLEN PARTY

As soon as she arrived she went straight to the kitchen to see if the monkey was there. It was: what a relief! She wouldn't have liked to admit that her mother had been right. *Monkeys at a birthday?* her mother had sneered. *Get away with you, believing any nonsense you're told!* She was cross, but not because of the monkey, the girl thought; it's just because of the party.

"I don't like you going," she told her. "It's a rich people's party."

"Rich people go to Heaven too," said the girl, who studied religion at school.

"Get away with Heaven," said the mother. "The problem with you, young lady, is that you like to fart higher than your ass."

The girl didn't approve of the way her mother spoke. She was barely nine, and one of the best in her class.

"I'm going because I've been invited," she said. "And I've been invited because Luciana is my friend. So there."

"Ah yes, your friend," her mother grumbled. She paused. "Listen, Rosaura," she said at last. "That one's not your friend. You know what you are to them? The maid's daughter, that's what."

Rosaura blinked hard: she wasn't going to cry. Then she yelled: "Shut up! You know nothing about being friends!"

Every afternoon she used to go to Luciana's house and they would both finish their homework while Rosaura's mother did the cleaning. They had their tea in the kitchen and they told each other secrets. Rosaura loved everything in the big house, and she also loved the people who lived there.

"I'm going because it will be the most lovely party in the whole world, Luciana told me it would. There will be a magician, and he will bring a monkey and everything."

The mother swung around to take a good look at her child, and pompously put her hands on her hips.

"Monkeys at a birthday?" she said. "Get away with you, believing any nonsense you're told!"

Rosaura was deeply offended. She thought it unfair of her mother to accuse other people of being liars simply because they were rich. Rosaura too wanted to be rich, of course. If one day she managed to live in a beautiful palace, would her mother stop loving her? She felt very sad. She wanted to go to that party more than anything else in the world.

"I'll die if I don't go," she whispered, almost without moving her lips.

And she wasn't sure whether she had been heard, but on the morning of the party she discovered that her mother had starched her Christmas dress. And in the afternoon, after washing her hair, her mother rinsed it in apple vinegar so that it would be all nice and shiny. Before going out, Rosaura admired herself in the mirror, with her white dress and glossy hair, and thought she looked terribly pretty.

Señora Ines also seemed to notice. As soon as she saw her, she said:

"How lovely you look today, Rosaura."

Rosaura gave her starched skirt a slight toss with her hands and walked into the party with a firm step. She said hello to Luciana and asked about the monkey. Luciana put on a secretive look and whispered into Rosaura's ear: "He's in the kitchen. But don't tell anyone, because it's a surprise."

Rosaura wanted to make sure. Carefully she entered the kitchen and there she saw it: deep in thought, inside its cage. It looked so funny that the girl stood there for a while, watching it, and later, every so often, she would slip out of the party unseen and go and admire it. Rosaura was the only one allowed into the kitchen. Señora Ines had said: "You yes, but not the others, they're much too boisterous, they might break something." Rosaura had never broken anything. She even managed the jug of orange juice, carrying it from the kitchen into the dining-room. She held it carefully and didn't spill a single drop. And Señora Ines had said: "Are you sure you can manage a jug as big as that?" Of course she could manage. She wasn't a butterfingers, like the others. Like that blonde girl with the bow in her hair. As soon as she saw Rosaura, the girl with the bow had said:

"And you? Who are you?"   20

"I'm a friend of Luciana," said Rosaura.

"No," said the girl with the bow, "you are not a friend of Luciana because I'm her cousin and I know all her friends. And I don't know you."

"So what," said Rosaura. "I come here every afternoon with my mother and we do our homework together."

"You and your mother do your homework together?" asked the girl, laughing.

"I and Luciana do our homework together," said Rosaura, very seriously.   25

The girl with the bow shrugged her shoulders.

"That's not being friends," she said. "Do you go to school together?"

"No."

"So where do you know her from?" said the girl, getting impatient.

Rosaura remembered her mother's words perfectly. She took a deep breath.   30

"I'm the daughter of the employee," she said.

Her mother had said very clearly: "If someone asks, you say you're the daughter of the employee; that's all." She also told her to add: "And proud of it." But Rosaura thought that never in her life would she dare say something of the sort.

"What employee?" said the girl with the bow. "Employee in a shop?"

"No," said Rosaura angrily. "My mother doesn't sell anything in any shop, so there."

"So how come she's an employee?" said the girl with the bow.   35

Just then Señora Ines arrived saying *shh shh,* and asked Rosaura if she wouldn't mind helping serve out the hot-dogs, as she knew the house so much better than the others.

"See?" said Rosaura to the girl with the bow, and when no one was looking she kicked her in the shin.

Apart from the girl with the bow, all the others were delightful. The one she liked best was Luciana, with her golden birthday crown; and then the boys. Rosaura won the sack race, and nobody managed to catch her when they played tag. When they split into two teams to play charades, all the boys wanted her for their side. Rosaura felt she had never been so happy in all her life.

But the best was still to come. The best came after Luciana blew out the candles. First the cake. Señora Ines had asked her to help pass the cake around, and Rosaura had enjoyed the task immensely, because everyone called out to her, shouting "Me, me!" Rosaura remembered a story in which there was a queen who had the power of life or death over her subjects. She had always loved that, having the power of life or death. To Luciana and the boys she gave the largest pieces, and to the girl with the bow she gave a slice so thin one could see through it.

After the cake came the magician, tall and bony, with a fine red cape. A true ma-   40
gician: he could untie handkerchiefs by blowing on them and make a chain with links that had no openings. He could guess what cards were pulled out from a pack, and the monkey was his assistant. He called the monkey "partner." "Let's see here, partner," he would say, "Turn over a card." And, "Don't run away, partner: time to work now."

The final trick was wonderful. One of the children had to hold the monkey in his arms and the magician said he would make him disappear.

"What, the boy?" they all shouted.

"No, the monkey!" shouted back the magician.

Rosaura thought that this was truly the most amusing party in the whole world.

The magician asked a small fat boy to come and help, but the small fat boy got   45
frightened almost at once and dropped the monkey on the floor. The magician picked
him up carefully, whispered something in his ear, and the monkey nodded almost as if
he understood.

"You mustn't be so unmanly, my friend," the magician said to the fat boy.

"What's unmanly?" said the fat boy.

The magician turned around as if to look for spies.

"A sissy," said the magician. "Go sit down."

Then he stared at all the faces, one by one. Rosaura felt her heart tremble.   50

"You, with the Spanish eyes," said the magician. And everyone saw that he was
pointing at her.

She wasn't afraid. Neither holding the monkey, nor when the magician made him
vanish; not even when, at the end, the magician flung his red cape over Rosaura's head
and uttered a few magic words . . . and the monkey reappeared, chattering happily, in
her arms. The children clapped furiously. And before Rosaura returned to her seat, the
magician said:

"Thank you very much, my little countess."

She was so pleased with the compliment that a while later, when her mother came
to fetch her, that was the first thing she told her.

"I helped the magician and he said to me, "Thank you very much, my little countess."   55

It was strange because up to then Rosaura had thought that she was angry with
her mother. All along Rosaura had imagined that she would say to her: "See that the
monkey wasn't a lie?" But instead she was so thrilled that she told her mother all about
the wonderful magician.

Her mother tapped her on the head and said: "So now we're a countess!"

But one could see that she was beaming.

And now they both stood in the entrance, because a moment ago Señora Ines, smiling, had said: "Please wait here a second."

Her mother suddenly seemed worried.   60

"What is it?" she asked Rosaura.

"What is what?" said Rosaura. "It's nothing; she just wants to get the presents for
those who are leaving, see?"

She pointed at the fat boy and at a girl with pigtails who were also waiting there,
next to their mothers. And she explained about the presents. She knew, because she had
been watching those who left before her. When one of the girls was about to leave,
Señora Ines would give her a bracelet. When a boy left, Señora Ines gave him a yo-yo.
Rosaura preferred the yo-yo because it sparkled, but she didn't mention that to her
mother. Her mother might have said: "So why don't you ask for one, you blockhead?"
That's what her mother was like. Rosaura didn't feel like explaining that she'd be horribly ashamed to be the odd one out. Instead she said:

"I was the best-behaved at the party."

And she said no more because Señora Ines came out into the hall with two bags,   65
one pink and one blue.

First she went up to the fat boy, gave him a yo-yo out of the blue bag, and the fat boy left with his mother. Then she went up to the girl and gave her a bracelet out of the pink bag, and the girl with the pigtails left as well.

Finally she came up to Rosaura and her mother. She had a big smile on her face and Rosaura liked that. Señora Ines looked down at her, then looked up at her mother, and then said something that made Rosaura proud:

"What a marvellous daughter you have, Herminia."

For an instant, Rosaura thought that she'd give her two presents: the bracelet and the yo-yo. Señora Ines bent down as if about to look for something. Rosaura also leaned forward, stretching out her arm. But she never completed the movement.

Señora Ines didn't look in the pink bag. Nor did she look in the blue bag. Instead   70 she rummaged in her purse. In her hand appeared two bills.

"You really and truly earned this," she said handing them over. "Thank you for all your help, my pet."

Rosaura felt her arms stiffen, stick close to her body, and then she noticed her mother's hand on her shoulder. Instinctively she pressed herself against her mother's body. That was all. Except her eyes. Rosaura's eyes had a cold, clear look that fixed itself on Señora Ines's face.

Señora Ines, motionless, stood there with her hand outstretched. As if she didn't dare draw it back. As if the slightest change might shatter an infinitely delicate balance.

Questions for Discussion and Writing

1. In what sense might the birthday party be thought of as being unjustly "stolen"? How does Rosaura's view of herself change because of what happens at her friend's party?

2. How does Heker use Rosaura's mother as a foil for her daughter's aspirations? What events vividly foreshadow the outcome?

3. In your opinion, what is Rosaura's mother's motive—to protect her daughter from being disappointed, or to accept her real position in society? How would the same events at the party appear from the mother's perspective?

POETRY

W. H. Auden

. . . .

W. H. Auden (1907–1973) was born in York, England, the son of a distinguished physician. He was educated at Oxford, where he was part of a group of poets, including Louis MacNeice, Stephen Spender, and C. Day Lewis, who shared the goal of creating new poetic techniques to express heightened social consciousness. After graduating from Oxford in 1928, Auden spent a year in Berlin, where he was influenced by Marxist poet and playwright Bertolt Brecht. After teaching school in England and Scotland in the 1930s, he went to Spain in 1937, where he drove an ambulance for the Republicans in the war against the Fascists. He moved to the United States in 1939 and became a U.S. citizen in 1946, dividing his time between New York and Europe. He was elected professor of poetry at Oxford in 1956. The most complete edition of his poetry is the posthumously published Collected Poems *(1978). In "The Unknown Citizen" (1940), Auden satirizes a dehumanized materialistic society that requires absolute conformity of its citizens.*

THE UNKNOWN CITIZEN

*(To JS/07/M/378
This Marble Monument
Is Erected by the State)*

He was found by the Bureau of Statistics to be
One against whom there was no official complaint,
And all the reports on his conduct agree
That, in the modern sense of an old-fashioned word, he was a saint,
For in everything he did he served the Greater Community.   5
Except for the War till the day he retired
He worked in a factory and never got fired,
But satisfied his employers, Fudge Motors Inc.
Yet he wasn't a scab[1] or odd in his views,
For his Union reports that he paid his dues,   10
(Our report on his Union shows it was sound)
And our Social Psychology workers found
That he was popular with his mates and liked a drink.
The Press are convinced that he bought a paper every day
And that his reactions to advertisements were normal in every way.   15
Policies taken out in his name prove that he was fully insured,
And his Health-card shows he was once in hospital but left it cured.
Both Producers Research and High-Grade Living declare
He was fully sensible to the advantages of the Installment Plan
And had everything necessary to the Modern Man,   20
A phonograph, radio, a car and a frigidaire.
Our researchers into Public Opinion are content
That he held the proper opinions for the time of year;
When there was peace, he was for peace; when there was war, he went.
He was married and added five children to the population,   25
Which our Eugenist[2] says was the right number for a parent of his generation,
And our teachers report that he never interfered with their education.
Was he free? Was he happy? The question is absurd:
Had anything been wrong, we should certainly have heard.

---

[1]*Scab:* a worker who won't join the union or who takes a striker's job. [2]*Eugenist:* an expert in eugenics, the science of improving the human race by careful selection of parents to breed healthier, more intelligent children.

Questions for Discussion and Writing

1. Why is it significant that no official complaint was ever brought against the unknown citizen? What kind of society did he inhabit?
2. How does Auden parody the language of bureaucracy to satirize the social and political tenets of the government? What aspects of this society does he assail?
3. How might the word *unknown* in the title be interpreted? What is the significance of the questions "Was he free? Was he happy?" in line 28? What evidence, if any, does the poem give as an answer?

Margaret Atwood

Margaret Atwood was born in Ottawa, Ontario, in 1939. She was educated at the University of Toronto, where she came under the influence of the critic Northrup Frye, whose theories of mythical modes in literature she has adapted to her own purposes in her prolific writing of poetry, novels, and short stories. She is the author of more than twenty volumes of poetry and fiction, including The Handmaid's Tale *(1986), which was made into a film in 1989. Her short story collections include* Bluebeard's Egg and Other Stories *(1986). She also edited the* Oxford Book of Canadian Short Stories in English *(1987). Her most recent works include* Alias Grace: A Novel *(1996),* A Quiet Game *(1997),* Two Solitudes *(1998), and* Oryx and Crake *(2003). In the following poem from* Power Politics *(1971), Atwood depicts how the women whom soldiers leave at home change as wars change but always find themselves in the same predicament.*

AT FIRST I WAS GIVEN CENTURIES

At first I was given centuries
to wait in caves, in leather
tents, knowing you would never come back

Then it speeded up: only
several years between   5
the day you jangled off
into the mountains, and the day (it was
spring again) I rose from the embroidery
frame at the messenger's entrance.

That happened twice, or was it   10
more; and there was once, not so
long ago, you failed,
and came back in a wheelchair
with a mustache and a sunburn
and were insufferable.   15

Time before last though, I remember
I had a good eight months between

running alongside the train, skirts hitched, handing
you violets in at the window
and opening the letter; I watched   20
~~your snapshot fade for twenty years.~~

And last time (I drove to the airport
still dressed in my factory
overalls, the wrench
I had forgotten sticking out of the back   25
pocket; there you were,
zippered and helmeted, it was zero
hour, you said Be
Brave) it was at least three weeks before
I got the telegram and could start regretting.   30

But recently, the bad evenings
there are only seconds
between the warning on the radio and the
explosion; my hands
don't reach you   35

and on quieter nights
you jump up from
your chair without even touching your dinner

and I can scarcely kiss you goodbye
before you run out into the street and they shoot   40

Questions for Discussion and Writing

1. How would you describe the voice you hear, and to whom is she speaking?
2. How have circumstances changed as the poem progresses? What specific wars are alluded to in the course of the poem?
3. What new conditions imply a change in the nature of warfare over the centuries and the consequences for those left behind?

Carolyn Forché

· ·

Carolyn Forché was born in Detroit in 1950. She was educated at Michigan State University and Bowling Green University and has taught at a number of colleges. While a journalist in El Salvador from 1978 to 1980, she reported on human rights conditions for Amnesty International. Her experiences there had a profound influence on her poetry and nonfiction writings. Her poetry collections include Gathering the Tribes *(1976) and* The Country Between Us *(1981). She is also the editor of* Against Forgetting: Twentieth-Century Poetry of Witness *(1993). "The Colonel" (1978) offers a surreal portrait of the hidden terrors lurking underneath the civilized veneer of normalcy in an unnamed Central American country. She has also written* The Angel of History *(1995) and* Blue Hour *(2003).*

THE COLONEL

What you have heard is true. I was in his house. His wife
carried a tray of coffee and sugar. His daughter filed her
nails, his son went out for the night. There were daily papers,
pet dogs, a pistol on the cushion behind him. The
moon swung bare on its black cord over the house. On the   5
television was a cop show. It was in English. Broken bottles
were embedded in the walls around the house to scoop
the kneecaps from a man's legs or cut his hands to lace. On
the windows there were gratings like those in liquor
stores. We had dinner, rack of lamb, good wine, a gold bell   10
was on the table for calling the maid. The maid brought
green mangoes, salt, a type of bread. I was asked how I enjoyed
the country. There was a brief commercial in
Spanish. His wife took everything away. There was some
talk then of how difficult it had become to govern. The parrot   15
said hello on the terrace. The colonel told it to shut up,
and pushed himself from the table. My friend said to me
with his eyes: say nothing. The colonel returned with a
sack used to bring groceries home. He spilled many human
ears on the table. They were like dried peach halves. There   20
is no other way to say this. He took one of them in his
hands, shook it in our faces, dropped it into a water glass. It
came alive there, I am tired of fooling around he said. As
for the rights of anyone, tell your people they can go fuck
themselves. He swept the ears to the floor with his arm   25
and held the last of his wine in the air. Something for your
poetry, no? he said. Some of the ears on the floor caught
this scrap of his voice. Some of the ears on the floor were
pressed to the ground.

Questions for Discussion and Writing

1. What attitude toward human rights is implied by the trophies the colonel presents
   to the visitor?
2. In what way is the display of hidden terrors underneath a civilized veneer of normalcy made more effective through the surreal contrast the poem develops?
3. Discuss the ethical dilemma the visitor confronts during the meal at which human
   rights is mentioned. How does the ending of the poem reflect the speaker's
   predicament?

DRAMA

Susan Glaspell

· ·

Susan Glaspell (1882–1948) was born and raised in Davenport, Iowa, and graduated from Drake University in 1899. She worked as a reporter and wrote short stories that were published in Harper's *and* Ladies' Home Journal. *Glaspell won a Pulitzer Prize for drama in 1931 for* Alison's House, *which was based on Emily Dickinson's life. She wrote* Trifles *in 1916 for the Provincetown Players on Cape Cod, in Massachusetts. This play was based on a murder trial she had covered while working as a reporter for the* Des Moines News. Trifles *(1916) offers an instructive example of the ways in which men and women perceive events and their own roles in life in a traditional society.*

TRIFLES

CAST OF CHARACTERS

> GEORGE HENDERSON, *county attorney*
> HENRY PETERS, *sheriff*
> LEWIS HALE, *a neighboring farmer*
> MRS. PETERS
> MRS. HALE

SCENE. The kitchen in the now abandoned farmhouse of John Wright, a gloomy kitchen, and left without having been put in order—unwashed pans under the sink, a loaf of bread outside the bread-box, a dish-towel on the table—other signs of incompleted work. At the rear the outer door opens and the Sheriff comes in followed by the County Attorney and Hale. The Sheriff and Hale are men in middle life, the County Attorney is a young man; all are much bundled up and go at once to the stove. They are followed by the two women—the Sheriff's wife first; she is a slight wiry woman, a thin nervous face. Mrs. Hale is larger and would ordinarily be called more comfortable looking, but she is disturbed now and looks fearfully about as she enters. The women have come in slowly, and stand close together near the door.

COUNTY ATTORNEY. (*Rubbing his hands.*) This feels good. Come up to the fire, ladies.

MRS. PETERS. (*After taking a step forward.*) I'm not—cold.

SHERIFF. (*Unbuttoning his overcoat and stepping away from the stove as if to mark the beginning of official business.*) Now, Mr. Hale, before we move things about, you explain to Mr. Henderson just what you saw when you came here yesterday morning.

COUNTY ATTORNEY. By the way, has anything been moved? Are things just as you left them yesterday?

SHERIFF. (*Looking about.*) It's just the same. When it dropped below zero last night I thought I'd better send Frank out this morning to make a fire for us—no use 5 getting pneumonia with a big case on, but I told him not to touch anything except the stove—and you know Frank.

COUNTY ATTORNEY.   Somebody should have been left here yesterday.

SHERIFF.   Oh—yesterday. When I had to send Frank to Morris Center for that man who went crazy—I want you to know I had my hands full yesterday. I knew you could get back from Omaha by today and as long as I went over everything here myself—

COUNTY ATTORNEY.   Well, Mr. Hale, tell just what happened when you came here yesterday morning.

HALE.   Harry and I had started to town with a load of potatoes. We came along the road from my place and as I got here I said, "I'm going to see if I can't get John Wright to go in with me on a party telephone." I spoke to Wright about it once before and he put me off, saying folks talked too much anyway, and all he asked was peace and quiet—I guess you know about how much he talked himself; but I thought maybe if I went to the house and talked about it before his wife, though I said to Harry that I didn't know as what his wife wanted made much difference to John—

COUNTY ATTORNEY.   Let's talk about that later, Mr. Hale. I do want to talk about   10
that, but tell now just what happened when you got to the house.

HALE.   I didn't hear or see anything; I knocked at the door, and still it was all quiet inside. I knew they must be up, it was past eight o'clock. So I knocked again, and I thought I heard somebody say, "Come in." I wasn't sure, I'm not sure yet, but I opened the door—this door (*Indicating the door by which the two women are still standing.*) and there in the rocker—(*Pointing to it.*) sat Mrs. Wright.

(*They all look at the rocker.*)

COUNTY ATTORNEY.   What—was she doing?

HALE.   She was rockin' back and forth. She had her apron in her hand and was kind of—pleating it.

COUNTY ATTORNEY.   And how did she—look?

HALE.   Well, she looked queer.   15

COUNTY ATTORNEY.   How do you mean—queer?

HALE.   Well, as if she didn't know what she was going to do next. And kind of done up.

COUNTY ATTORNEY.   How did she seem to feel about your coming?

HALE.   Why, I don't think she minded—one way or other. She didn't pay much attention. I said, "How do, Mrs. Wright, it's cold, ain't it?" And she said, "Is it?"—and went on kind of pleating at her apron. Well, I was surprised; she didn't ask me to come up to the stove, or to set down, but just sat there, not even looking at me, so I said, "I want to see John." And then she—laughed. I guess you would call it a laugh. I thought of Harry and the team outside, so I said a little sharp: "Can't I see John?" "No," she says, kind o' dull like. "Ain't he home?" says I. "Yes," says she, "he's home." Then why can't I see him?" I asked her, out of patience. "Cause he's dead," says she. "*Dead?*" says I. She just nodded her head, not getting a bit excited, but rockin' back and forth. "Why—where is he?" says I, not knowing what to say. She just pointed upstairs—like that. (*Himself pointing to the room above.*) I got up, with the idea of going up

there. I walked from there to here—then I says, "Why, what did he die of?" "He
died of a rope round his neck," says she, and just went on pleatin' at her apron.
Well, I went out and called Harry. I thought I might—need help. We went upstairs and there he was lyin'—

COUNTY ATTORNEY. I think I'd rather have you go into that upstairs, where you can   20
point it all out. Just go on now with the rest of the story.

HALE. Well, my first thought was to get that rope off. It looked . . . (*Stops, his face
twitches.*) . . . but Harry, he went up to him, and he said, "No, he's dead all
right, and we'd better not touch anything." So we went back downstairs. She
was still sitting that same way. "Has anybody been notified?" I asked. "No,"
says she, unconcerned. "Who did this, Mrs. Wright?" said Harry. He said it
businesslike—and she stopped pleatin' of her apron. "I don't know," she says.
"You don't *know*?" says Harry. "No," says she. "Weren't you sleepin' in the
bed with him?" says Harry. "Yes," says she, "but I was on the inside." "Somebody slipped a rope round his neck and strangled him and you didn't wake up?"
says Harry. "I didn't wake up," she said after him. We must 'a looked as if we
didn't see how that could be, for after a minute she said, "I sleep sound." Harry
was going to ask her more questions but I said maybe we ought to let her tell
her story first to the coroner, or the sheriff, so Harry went fast as he could to
Rivers' place, where there's a telephone.

COUNTY ATTORNEY. And what did Mrs. Wright do when she knew that you had
gone for the coroner?

HALE. She moved from that chair to this one over here (*Pointing to a small chair in
the corner.*) and just sat there with her hands held together and looking down. I
got a feeling that I ought to make some conversation, so I said I had come in to
see if John wanted to put in a telephone, and at that she started to laugh, and
then she stopped and looked at me—scared. (*The County Attorney, who has
had his notebook out, makes a note.*) I dunno, maybe it wasn't scared. I wouldn't
like to say it was. Soon Harry got back, and then Dr. Lloyd came, and you, Mr.
Peters, and so I guess that's all I know that you don't.

COUNTY ATTORNEY. (*Looking around.*) I guess we'll go upstairs first—and then out
to the barn and around there. (*To the Sheriff.*) You're convinced that there was
nothing important here—nothing that would point to any motive.

SHERIFF. Nothing here but kitchen things.   25

(*The County Attorney, after again looking around the kitchen, opens the door of
a cupboard closet. He gets up on a chair and looks on a shelf. Pulls his hand away.*)

COUNTY ATTORNEY. Here's a nice mess.

(*The women draw nearer.*)

MRS. PETERS. (*To the other woman.*) Oh, her fruit; it did freeze. (*To the Lawyer.*)
She worried about that when it turned so cold. She said the fire'd go out and her
jars would break.

SHERIFF. Well, can you beat the women! Held for murder and worryin' about
her preserves.

COUNTY ATTORNEY.   I guess before we're through she may have something more serious than preserves to worry about.

HALE.   Well, women are used to worrying over trifles.   30

(*The two women move a little closer together.*)

COUNTY ATTORNEY.   (*With the gallantry of a young politician.*) And yet, for all their worries, what would we do without the ladies? (*The women do not unbend. He goes to the sink, takes a dipperful of water from the pail and pouring it into a basin, washes his hands. Starts to wipe them on the roller-towel, turns it for a cleaner place.*) Dirty towels! (*Kicks his foot against the pans under the sink.*) Not much of a housekeeper, would you say, ladies?

MRS. HALE.   (*Stiffly.*) There's a great deal of work to be done on a farm.

COUNTY ATTORNEY.   To be sure. And yet (*With a little bow to her.*) I know there are some Dickson county farmhouses which do not have such roller towels.

(*He gives it a pull to expose its full length again.*)

MRS. HALE.   Those towels get dirty awful quick. Men's hands aren't always as clean as they might be.

COUNTY ATTORNEY.   Ah, loyal to your sex, I see. But you and Mrs. Wright were   35
neighbors. I suppose you were friends, too.

MRS. HALE.   (*Shaking her head.*) I've not seen much of her of late years. I've not been in this house—it's more than a year.

COUNTY ATTORNEY.   And why was that? You didn't like her?

MRS. HALE.   I liked her all well enough. Farmers' wives have their hands full, Mr. Henderson. And then—

COUNTY ATTORNEY.   Yes—?

MRS. HALE.   (*Looking about.*) It never seemed a very cheerful place.   40

COUNTY ATTORNEY.   No—it's not cheerful. I shouldn't say she had the homemaking instinct.

MRS. HALE.   Well, I don't know as Wright had, either.

COUNTY ATTORNEY.   You mean that they didn't get on very well?

MRS. HALE.   No, I don't mean anything. But I don't think a place'd be any cheerfuller for John Wright's being in it.

COUNTY ATTORNEY.   I'd like to talk more of that a little later. I want to get the lay of   45
things upstairs now.

(*He goes to the left, where three steps lead to a stair door.*)

SHERIFF.   I suppose anything Mrs. Peters does'll be all right. She was to take in some clothes for her, you know, and a few little things. We left in such a hurry yesterday.

COUNTY ATTORNEY.   Yes, but I would like to see what you take, Mrs. Peters, and keep an eye out for anything that might be of use to *us*.

MRS. PETERS.   Yes, Mr. Henderson.

(*The women listen to the men's steps on the stairs, then look about the kitchen.*)

MRS. HALE.   I'd hate to have men coming into my kitchen, snooping around and criticising.

(*She arranges the pans under the sink which the Lawyer had shoved out of place.*)

MRS. PETERS.   Of course it's no more than their duty.   50

MRS. HALE.   Duty's all right, but I guess that deputy sheriff that came out to make the fire might have got a little of this on. (*Gives the roller towel a pull.*) Wish I'd thought of that sooner. Seems mean to talk about her for not having things slicked up when she had to come away in such a hurry.

MRS. PETERS.   (*Who had gone to a small table in the left rear corner of the room, and lifted one end of a towel that covers a pan.*) She had bread set.

(*Stands still.*)

MRS. HALE.   (*Eyes fixed on a loaf of bread beside the breadbox, which is on a low shelf at the other side of the room. Moves slowly toward it.*) She was going to put this in there. (*Picks up loaf, then abruptly drops it. In a manner of returning to familiar things.*) It's a shame about her fruit. I wonder if it's all gone. (*Gets up on the chair and looks.*) I think there's some here that's all right, Mrs. Peters. Yes—here; (*Holding it toward the window.*) this is cherries, too. (*Looking again.*) I declare I believe that's the only one. (*Gets down, bottle in her hand. Goes to the sink and wipes it off on the outside.*) She'll feel awful bad after all her hard work in the hot weather. I remember the afternoon I put up my cherries last summer.

(*She puts the bottle on the big kitchen table, center of the room. With a sigh, is about to sit down in the rocking-chair. Before she is seated realizes what chair it is; with a slow look at it, steps back. The chair which she has touched rocks back and forth.*)

MRS. PETERS.   Well, I must get those things from the front room closet. (*She goes to the door at the right, but after looking into the other room, steps back.*) You coming with me, Mrs. Hale? You could help me carry them.

(*They go in the other room; reappear; Mrs. Peters carrying a dress and skirt, Mrs. Hale following with a pair of shoes.*)

MRS. PETERS.   My, it's cold in there.   55

(*She puts the clothes on the big table and hurries to the stove.*)

MRS. HALE.   (*Examining the skirt.*) Wright was close. I think maybe that's why she kept so much to herself. She didn't even belong to the Ladies Aid. I suppose she felt she couldn't do her part, and then you don't enjoy things when you feel shabby. She used to wear pretty clothes and be lively, when she was Minnie Foster, one of the town girls singing in the choir. But that—oh, that was thirty years ago. This all you was to take in?

MRS. PETERS.   She said she wanted an apron. Funny thing to want, for there isn't much to get you dirty in jail, goodness knows. But I suppose just to make her feel more natural. She said they was in the top drawer in this cupboard. Yes, here. And then her little shawl that always hung behind the door. (*Opens stair door and looks.*) Yes, here it is.

(*Quickly shuts door leading upstairs.*)

MRS. HALE.   (*Abruptly moving toward her.*) Mrs. Peters?

MRS. PETERS.   Yes, Mrs. Hale?

MRS. HALE.   Do you think she did it?   60

MRS. PETERS.   (*In a frightened voice.*) Oh, I don't know.

MRS. HALE.   Well, I don't think she did. Asking for an apron and her little shawl. Worrying about her fruit.

MRS. PETERS.   (*Starts to speak, glances up, where footsteps are heard in the room above. In a low voice.*) Mr. Peters says it looks bad for her. Mr. Henderson is awful sarcastic in a speech and he'll make fun of her sayin' she didn't wake up.

MRS. HALE.   Well, I guess John Wright didn't wake when they was slipping that rope under his neck.

MRS. PETERS.   No, it's strange. It must have been done awful crafty and still. They   65
say it was such a—funny way to kill a man, rigging it all up like that.

MRS. HALE.   That's just what Mr. Hale said. There was a gun in the house. He says that's what he can't understand.

MRS. PETERS.   Mr. Henderson said coming out that what was needed for the case was a motive; something to show anger, or—sudden feeling.

MRS. HALE.   (*Who is standing by the table.*) Well, I don't see any signs of anger around here. (*She puts her hand on the dish towel which lies on the table, stands looking down at table, one half of which is clean, the other half messy.*) It's wiped to here. (*Makes a move as if to finish work, then turns and looks at loaf of bread outside the breadbox. Drops towel. In that voice of coming back to familiar things.*) Wonder how they are finding things upstairs. I hope she had it a little more red-up[1] up there. You know, it seems kind of *sneaking*. Locking her up in town and then coming out here and trying to get her own house to turn against her!

MRS. PETERS.   But Mrs. Hale, the law is the law.

MRS. HALE.   I s'pose 'tis. (*Unbuttoning her coat.*) Better loosen up your things, Mrs.   70
Peters. You won't feel them when you go out.

(*Mrs. Peters takes off her fur tippet,[2] goes to hang it on hook at back of room, stands looking at the under part of the small corner table.*)

MRS. PETERS.   She was piecing a quilt.

(*She brings the large sewing basket and they look at the bright pieces.*)

MRS. HALE.   It's log cabin pattern. Pretty, isn't it? I wonder if she was goin' to quilt it or just knot it?

(*Footsteps have been heard coming down the stairs. The Sheriff enters followed by Hale and the County Attorney.*)

---

[1]*red-up:* neat, and orderly.   [2]*tippet:* a scarf which covers the neck and shoulders.

SHERIFF.   They wonder if she was going to quilt it or just knot it!

(*The men laugh; the women look abashed.*)

COUNTY ATTORNEY.   (*Rubbing his hands over the stove.*) Frank's fire didn't do much up there, did it? Well, let's go out to the barn and get that cleared up.

(*The men go outside.*)

MRS. HALE.   (*Resentfully.*) I don't know as there's anything so strange, our takin' up   75
our time with little things while we're waiting for them to get the evidence. (*She sits down at the big table smoothing out a block with decision.*) I don't see as it's anything to laugh about.

MRS. PETERS.   (*Apologetically.*) Of course they've got awful important things on their minds.

(*Pulls up a chair and joins Mrs. Hale at the table.*)

MRS. HALE.   (*Examining another block.*) Mrs. Peters, look at this one. Here, this is the one she was working on, and look at the sewing! All the rest of it has been so nice and even. And look at this! It's all over the place! Why, it looks as if she didn't know what she was about!

(*After she has said this they look at each other, then start to glance back at the door. After an instant Mrs. Hale has pulled at a knot and ripped the sewing.*)

MRS. PETERS.   Oh, what are you doing, Mrs. Hale?

MRS. HALE.   (*Mildly.*) Just pulling out a stitch or two that's not sewed very good. (*Threading a needle.*) Bad sewing always made me fidgety.

MRS. PETERS.   (*Nervously.*) I don't think we ought to touch things.   80

MRS. HALE.   I'll just finish up this end. (*Suddenly stopping and leaning forward.*) Mrs. Peters?

MRS. PETERS.   Yes, Mrs. Hale?

MRS. HALE.   What do you suppose she was so nervous about?

MRS. PETERS.   Oh—I don't know. I don't know as she was nervous. I sometimes sew awful queer when I'm just tired. (*Mrs. Hale starts to say something, looks at Mrs. Peters, then goes on sewing.*) Well I must get these things wrapped up. They may be through sooner than we think. (*Putting apron and other things together.*) I wonder where I can find a piece of paper, and string.

MRS. HALE.   In that cupboard, maybe.   85

MRS. PETERS.   (*Looking in cupboard.*) Why, here's a bird-cage. (*Holds it up.*) Did she have a bird, Mrs. Hale?

MRS. HALE.   Why, I don't know whether she did or not—I've not been here for so long. There was a man around last year selling canaries cheap, but I don't know as she took one; maybe she did. She used to sing real pretty herself.

MRS. PETERS.   (*Glancing around.*) Seems funny to think of a bird here. But she must have had one, or why would she have a cage? I wonder what happened to it?

MRS. HALE.   I s'pose maybe the cat got it.

MRS. PETERS.   No, she didn't have a cat. She's got that feeling some people have   90
about cats—being afraid of them. My cat got in her room and she was real upset and asked me to take it out.

MRS. HALE.   My sister Bessie was like that. Queer, ain't it?

MRS. PETERS.   (*Examining the cage.*) Why, look at this door. It's broke. One hinge is pulled apart.

MRS. HALE.   (*Looking too.*) Looks as if someone must have been rough with it.

MRS. PETERS.   Why, yes.

(*She brings the cage forward and puts it on the table.*)

MRS. HALE.   I wish if they're going to find any evidence they'd be about it. I don't   95
like this place.

MRS. PETERS.   But I'm awful glad you came with me, Mrs. Hale. It would be lonesome for me sitting here alone.

MRS. HALE.   It would, wouldn't it? (*Dropping her sewing.*) But I tell you what I do wish, Mrs. Peters. I wish I had come over sometimes when *she* was here. I–(*Looking around the room.*)—wish I had.

MRS. PETERS.   But of course you were awful busy, Mrs. Hale—your house and your children.

MRS. HALE.   I could've come. I stayed away because it weren't cheerful—and that's why I ought to have come. I—I've never liked this place. Maybe because it's down in a hollow and you don't see the road. I dunno what it is, but it's a lonesome place and always was. I wish I had come over to see Minnie Foster sometimes. I can see now—

(*Shakes her head.*)

MRS. PETERS.   Well, you mustn't reproach yourself, Mrs. Hale. Somehow we just   100
don't see how it is with other folks until—something comes up.

MRS. HALE.   Not having children makes less work—but it makes a quiet house, and Wright out to work all day, and no company when he did come in. Did you know John Wright, Mrs. Peters?

MRS. PETERS.   Not to know him; I've seen him in town. They say he was a good man.

MRS. HALE.   Yes—good; he didn't drink, and kept his word as well as most, I guess, and paid his debts. But he was a hard man, Mrs. Peters. Just to pass the time of day with him—(*Shivers.*) Like a raw wind that gets to the bone. (*Pauses, her eye falling on the cage.*) I should think she would 'a wanted a bird. But what do you suppose went with it?

MRS. PETERS.   I don't know, unless it got sick and died.

(*She reaches over and swings the broken door, swings it again, both women watch it.*)

MRS. HALE.   You weren't raised round here, were you? (*Mrs. Peters shakes her*   105
head.) You didn't know—her?

MRS. PETERS.   Not till they brought her yesterday.

MRS. HALE.   She—come to think of it, she was kind of like a bird herself—real sweet and pretty, but kind of timid and—fluttery. How—she—did—change. (*Silence; then as if struck by a happy thought and relieved to get back to everyday things.*) Tell you what, Mrs. Peters, why don't you take the quilt in with you? It might take up her mind.

MRS. PETERS.   Why, I think that's a real nice idea, Mrs. Hale. There couldn't possibly be any objection to it, could there? Now, just what would I take? I wonder if her patches are in here—and her things.

(*They look in the sewing basket.*)

MRS. HALE.   Here's some red. I expect this has got sewing things in it. (*Brings out a fancy box.*) What a pretty box. Looks like something somebody would give you. Maybe her scissors are in here. (*Opens box. Suddenly puts her hand to her nose.*) Why—(*Mrs. Peters bends nearer, then turns her face away.*) There's something wrapped up in this piece of silk.

MRS. PETERS.   Why, this isn't her scissors.   110

MRS. HALE.   (*Lifting the silk.*) Oh, Mrs. Peters—it's—

(*Mrs. Peters bends closer.*)

MRS. PETERS.   It's the bird.

MRS. HALE.   (*Jumping up.*) But, Mrs. Peters—look at it! Its neck! Look at its neck! It's all—other side *to*.

MRS. PETERS.   Somebody—wrung—its—neck.

(*Their eyes meet. A look of growing comprehension, of horror. Steps are heard outside. Mrs. Hale slips box under quilt pieces, and sinks into her chair. Enter Sheriff and County Attorney. Mrs. Peters rises.*)

COUNTY ATTORNEY.   (*As one turning from serious things to little pleasantries.*) Well,   115
ladies, have you decided whether she was going to quilt it or knot it?

MRS. PETERS.   We think she was going to—knot it.

COUNTY ATTORNEY.   Well, that's interesting, I'm sure. (*Seeing the bird-cage.*) Has the bird flown?

MRS. HALE.   (*Putting more quilt pieces over the box.*) We think the—cat got it.

COUNTY ATTORNEY.   (*Preoccupied.*) Is there a cat?

(*Mrs. Hale glances in a quick covert way at Mrs. Peters.*)

MRS. PETERS.   Well, not *now*. They're superstitious, you know. They leave.   120

COUNTY ATTORNEY.   (*To Sheriff Peters, continuing an interrupted conversation.*) No sign at all of anyone having come from the outside. Their own rope. Now let's go up again and go over it piece by piece. (*They start upstairs.*) It would have to have been someone who knew just the—

(*Mrs. Peters sits down. The two women sit there not looking at one another, but as if peering into something and at the same time holding back. When they talk now it is in the manner of feeling their way over strange ground, as if afraid of what they are saying, but as if they cannot help saying it.*)

MRS. HALE.   She liked the bird. She was going to bury it in that pretty box.

MRS. PETERS.   (*In a whisper.*) When I was a girl—my kitten—there was a boy took a hatchet, and before my eyes—and before I could get there—(*Covers her face an instant.*) If they hadn't held me back I would have—(*Catches herself, looks upstairs where steps are heard, falters weakly.*)—hurt him.

MRS. HALE.   (*With a slow look around her.*) I wonder how it would seem never to
    have had any children around. (*Pause.*) No, Wright wouldn't like the bird—a
    thing that sang. She used to sing. He killed that, too.

MRS. PETERS.   (*Moving uneasily.*) We don't know who killed the bird.   125

MRS. HALE.   I knew John Wright.

MRS. PETERS.   It was an awful thing was done in this house that night, Mrs. Hale. Killing
    a man while he slept, slipping a rope around his neck that choked the life out of him.

MRS. HALE.   His neck Choked the life out of him.

(*Her hand goes out and rests on the bird-cage.*)

MRS. PETERS.   (*With rising voice.*) We don't know who killed him. We don't know.

MRS. HALE.   (*Her own feeling not interrupted.*) If there'd been years and years of noth-   130
    ing, then a bird to sing to you, it would be awful—still, after the bird was still.

MRS. PETERS.   (*Something within her speaking.*) I know what stillness is. When we
    homesteaded in Dakota, and my first baby died—after he was two years old,
    and me with no other then—

MRS. HALE.   (*Moving.*) How soon do you suppose they'll be through, looking for
    the evidence?

MRS. PETERS.   I know what stillness is. (*Pulling herself back.*) The law has got to
    punish crime, Mrs. Hale.

MRS. HALE.   (*Not as if answering that.*) I wish you'd seen Minnie Foster when she
    wore a white dress with blue ribbons and stood up there in the choir and sang.
    (*A look around the room.*) Oh, I *wish* I'd come over here once in a while! That
    was a crime! That was a crime! Who's going to punish that?

MRS. PETERS.   (*Looking upstairs.*) We mustn't—take on.   135

MRS. HALE.   I might have known she needed help! I know how things can be—for
    women. I tell you, it's queer, Mrs. Peters. We live close together and we live far
    apart. We all go through the same things—it's all just a different kind of the same
    thing. (*Brushes her eyes, noticing the bottle of fruit, reaches out for it.*) If I was you
    I wouldn't tell her her fruit was gone. Tell her it *ain't.* Tell her it's all right. Take
    this in to prove it to her. She—she may never know whether it was broke or not.

MRS. PETERS.   (*Takes the bottle, looks about for something to wrap it in; takes petti-
    coat from the clothes brought from the other room, very nervously begins winding
    this around the bottle. In a false voice.*) My, it's a good thing the men couldn't hear
    us. Wouldn't they just laugh! Getting all stirred up over a little thing like a—dead
    canary. As if that could have anything to do with—with—wouldn't they *laugh!*

(*The men are heard coming down stairs.*)

MRS. HALE.   (*Under her breath.*) Maybe they would—maybe they wouldn't.

COUNTY ATTORNEY.   No, Peters, it's all perfectly clear except a reason for doing it.
    But you know juries when it comes to women. If there was some definite thing.
    Something to show—something to make a story about—a thing that would con-
    nect up with this strange way of doing it—

(The women's eyes meet for an instant. Enter Hale from outer door.)

HALE.   Well, I've got the team[3] around. Pretty cold out there.   140

COUNTY ATTORNEY.   I'm going to stay here a while by myself. *(To the Sheriff.)* You can send Frank out for me, can't you? I want to go over everything. I'm not satisfied that we can't do better.

SHERIFF.   Do you want to see what Mrs. Peters is going to take in?

(The County Attorney goes to the table, picks up the apron, laughs.)

COUNTY ATTORNEY.   Oh, I guess they're not very dangerous things the ladies have picked out. *(Moves a few things about, disturbing the quilt pieces which cover the box. Steps back.)* No, Mrs. Peters doesn't need supervising. For that matter, a sheriff's wife is married to the law. Ever think of it that way, Mrs. Peters?

MRS. PETERS.   Not—just that way.

SHERIFF.   *(Chuckling.)* Married to the law. *(Moves toward the other room.)* I just   145
want you to come in here a minute, George. We ought to take a look at these windows.

COUNTY ATTORNEY.   *(Stoffingly.)* Oh, windows!

SHERIFF.   We'll be right out, Mr. Hale.

(Hale goes outside. The Sheriff follows the County Attorney into the other room. Then Mrs. Hale rises, hands tight together, looking intensely at Mrs. Peters, whose eyes make a slow turn, finally meeting Mrs. Hale's. A moment Mrs. Hale holds her, then her own eyes point the way to where the box is concealed. Suddenly Mrs. Peters throws back quilt pieces and tries to put the box in the bag she is wearing. It is too big. She opens box, starts to take bird out, cannot touch it, goes to pieces, stands there helpless. Sound of a knob turning in the other room. Mrs. Hale snatches the box and puts it in the pocket of her big coat. Enter County Attorney and Sheriff.)

COUNTY ATTORNEY.   *(Facetiously.)* Well, Henry, at least we found out that she was not going to quilt it. She was going to—what is it you call it, ladies?

MRS. HALE.   *(Her hand against her pocket.)* We call it—knot it, Mr. Henderson.

CURTAIN

Questions for Discussion and Writing

1. In what dramatic ways do the men (the County Attorney and the Sheriff) look for clues and draw conclusions differently from the women (Mrs. Hale and Mrs. Peters)? To what does the title of the play refer, and why is it ironic?

2. How does Glaspell use natural objects (for example, the birdcage and the dead canary) as symbols to establish and reinforce important ideas? How does the char-

---

[3]*team:* team of horses drawing a wagon.

acterization of John Wright help explain what happens to him and allow us to understand how marrying him changed Minnie Foster? Would the play have been more effective if she were a speaking character? Why or why not?

3. In what sense can this play be considered a feminist work that comments on issues in the early twentieth century?

Thinking Critically About the Image

Ben Shahn (1898–1969), American painter and graphic artist, was born in Lithuania and emigrated to the United States in 1906. He created striking posters and important murals and is known as a social realist. His works in both realistic and abstract styles were often inspired by news reports, narrating themes of class struggle and social reform. *Riot on Carol Street* (1944, tempera on board) transcends the narrow genre of political art to create a powerful work that communicates Shahn's outrage over the treatment of workers in this era in America. A helpless crowd of women demanding fair wages has been blocked from entering the fortress-like administrative offices in which men in shirtsleeves are looking at the protest with bored disapproval.

1. How does the fact that there is no door to the building, or even a window that is opened, symbolize the contrast between the exploited women workers and the powerful bosses inside who cannot be reached?

2. How do the eerie black and white funnels atop the building assume a symbolic function, seeming to reflect the condescension of the bosses as they look down on the women demonstrating below?

3. How do Shahn's choice of colors and the disproportionate size of the office building when compared with the protesters enhance the mood of rage over the treatment of workers?

Connections

Chapter 8: The Pursuit of Justice

Harriet Jacobs, *Incidents in the Life of a Slave Girl*
In what ways do Jacobs and Martin Luther King, Jr., address the idea of justice as a fundamental human right for African Americans?

Kenneth M. Stampp, *To Make Them Stand in Fear*
What insights into the psychology of the colonizers and the colonized are offered by Stampp and Haunani-Kay Trask in "From a Native Daughter" (Ch. 7)?

Martin Luther King, Jr., *I Have a Dream*
Would you call Jill Nelson's "Number One!" (Ch. 1) a success story in terms of King's expectations for African Americans? Why or why not?

Jonathan Swift, *A Modest Proposal*
In what ways do Swift and Barbara Ehrenreich assail economic injustices?

Barbara Ehrenreich, *Nickel-and-Dimed: On (Not) Getting By in America*
How do both Ehrenreich and Liliana Heker view events from the perspective of the underclass?

Luis Sepulveda, *Daisy*
Compare and contrast the pressures to which Sepulveda and Harriet Jacobs are subjected and the way they respond.

Steven E. Barkan and Lynne L. Snowden, *Defining and Countering Terrorism*
To what extent are the problems diagnosed by Barkan and Snowden regarding terrorism addressed by Michael Levin in his hypothetical case study?

Michael Levin, *The Case for Torture*
What would an ethicist such as Philip Wheelwright ("The Meaning of Ethics," Ch. 11) say about Levin's proposal?

Panos Ioannides, *Gregory*
In what sense is the speaker's dilemma in this story comparable to that confronting Luis Sepulveda's narrator in "Daisy"?

Liliana Heker, *The Stolen Party*
Contrast Heker's story with Maya Angelou's "Liked for Myself" (Ch. 2) in terms of the enhanced or diminished self-esteem of the protagonists.

W. H. Auden, *The Unknown Citizen*
In what respects might Ehrenreich as the narrator in her account be characterized as "the unknown citizen" of Auden's poem?

Margaret Atwood, *At First I Was Given Centuries*
How does Dennis Smith's "Report from Ground Zero" (Ch. 7) illustrate the inevitable outcome in Atwood's poem?

Carolyn Forché, *The Colonel*
In what ways are the attitudes and actions of the colonel in Forché's poem comparable to the jailer in Luis Sepulveda's "Daisy"?

Susan Glaspell, *Trifles*
How does Glaspell's play dramatize Deborah Tannen's observations in "Sex, Lies, and Converstion" (Ch. 4) about the different objectives of men and women?

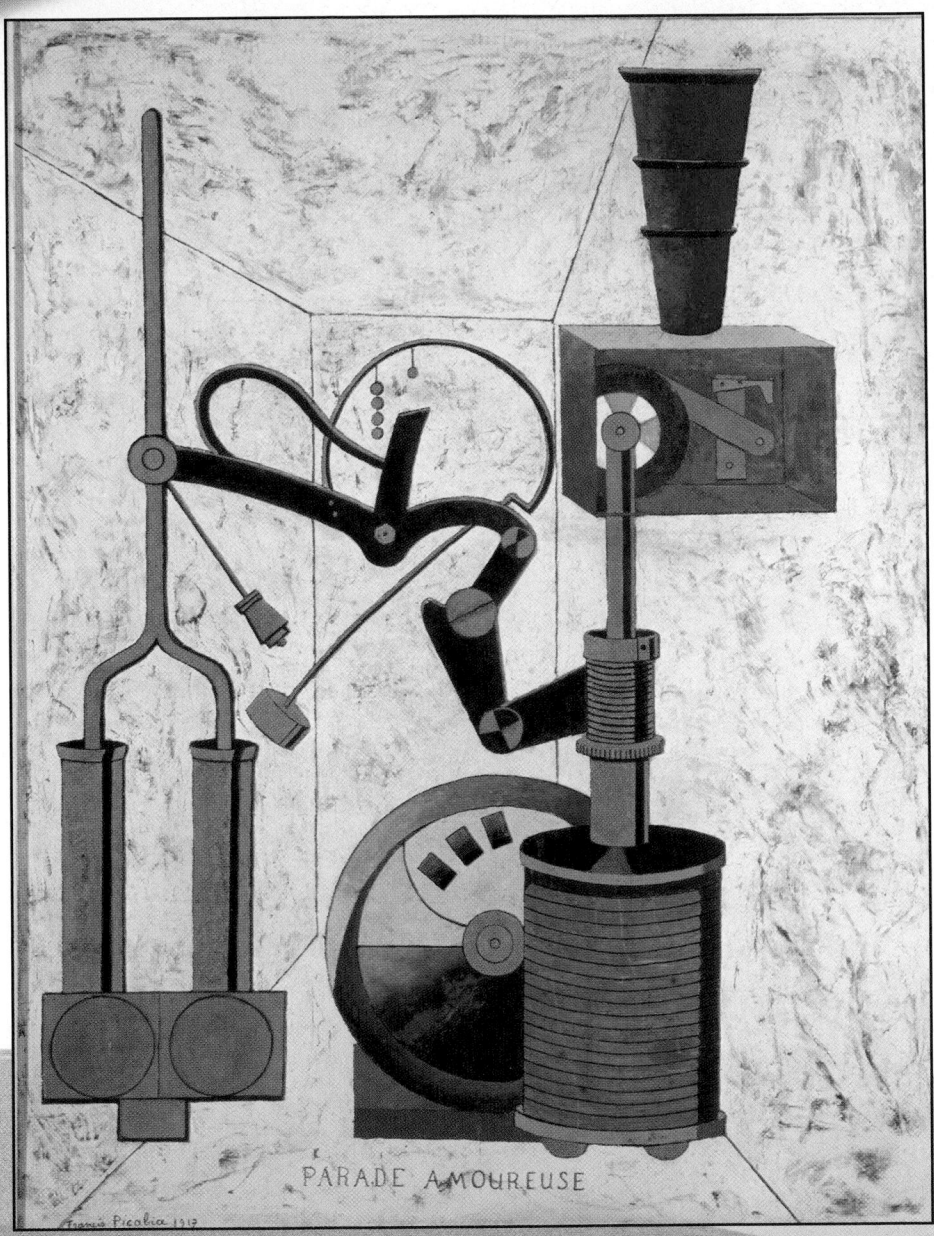

Francis Picabia, Parade Amoureuse, *1917.*
© ARS, NY. Bridgenman-Giraudon/Art Resource, NY. Private collection, Chicago, IL, USA.

The Impact of Technology

Modern man, if he dared to be articulate about his concept of heaven, would describe a vision which would look like the biggest department store in the world, showing new things and gadgets, and himself having plenty of money with which to buy them. He would wander around open-mouthed in this heaven of gadgets and commodities provided only that there were ever more and newer things to buy, and perhaps that his neighbors were just a little less privileged than he.

—ERICH FROMM, "ALIENATION"

THE SELECTIONS IN THIS CHAPTER EXAMINE THE extent to which culture and society depend on scientific discoveries and technological developments. Without scientific research, we would not have televisions, personal computers, DVDs, microwave ovens, cellular telephones, fax machines, the World Wide Web, and a host of other inventions. However, new genetic screening capabilities raise a number of profoundly important ethical and legal issues that are explored by David Ewing Duncan. Lawrence Osborne also considers the practical effects and moral issues of animal experimentation in his report on genetically modified goats. Constance Holden offers a thoughtful analysis of the role heredity plays in shaping human behavior.

Essays by Umberto Eco, Bill McKibben, LynNell Hancock, Bill Gates, and Henry Petroski offer invaluable insights into the effects of our dependence on technology, the virtues of new hybrid electric cars, the social consequences of cyberspace, and the ubiquitous, humble pencil.

Chet Williamson, in his thought-provoking story, dramatizes the unnerving effect of mass-market solicitations that are all too personal.

Walt Whitman's poem offers a different perspective on astronomy, and Peggy Seeger's ironic ballad comments on the opportunities women have to become engineers in the new technological world.

NONFICTION

David Ewing Duncan

• •

David Ewing Duncan is a contributing editor to Wired; *he has written for the* Atlantic Monthly, Harper's *magazine,* Discover, *and* Smithsonian *and was a longtime correspondent for* Life *magazine. He is the author of* Hernando De Soto: A Savage Quest in the Americas *(1997), the best-selling* Calendar: Humanity's Epic Struggle to Determine a True and Accurate Year *(1998), and other books. He was a special producer for ABC's* Nightline *and* 20/20 *and a producer for* Discovery *television. In the following article (which first appeared in* Wired *in November 2002 and was selected for the AAAS Journalism Award in 2003) Duncan discovers that new genetic screening capabilities will provide us (and our insurance companies) with more knowledge than we might wish to possess about our biologically fated predispositions to a wide range of diseases.*

DNA AS DESTINY

I feel naked. Exposed. As if my skin, bone, muscle tissue, cells, have all been peeled back, down to a tidy swirl of DNA. It's the basic stuff of life, the billions of nucleotides that keep me breathing, walking, craving, and just being. Eight hours ago, I gave a few cells, swabbed from inside my cheek, to a team of geneticists. They've spent the day extracting DNA and checking it for dozens of hidden diseases. Eventually, I will be tested for hundreds more. They include, as I will discover, a nucleic time bomb ticking inside my chromosomes that might one day kill me.

For now I remain blissfully ignorant, awaiting the results in an office at Sequenom, one of scores of biotech startups incubating in the canyons north of San Diego. I'm waiting to find out if I have a genetic proclivity for cancer, cardiac disease, deafness, Alzheimer's, or schizophrenia.

This, I'm told, is the first time a healthy human has ever been screened for the full gamut of genetic disease markers. Everyone has errors in his or her DNA, glitches that may trigger a heart spasm or cause a brain tumor. I'm here to learn mine.

Waiting, I wonder if I carry some sort of Pandora gene, a hereditary predisposition to peek into places I shouldn't. Morbid curiosity is an occupational hazard for a writer, I suppose, but I've never been bothered by it before. Yet now I find myself growing nervous and slightly flushed. I can feel my pulse rising, a cardiovascular response that I will soon discover has, for me, dire implications.

In the coming days, I'll seek a second opinion, of sorts. Curious about where my 5 genes come from, I'll travel to Oxford and visit an "ancestral geneticist" who has agreed to examine my DNA for links back to progenitors whose mutations have been passed on to me. He will reveal the seeds of my individuality and the roots of the diseases that may kill me—and my children.

For now, I wait in an office at Sequenom, a sneak preview of a trip to the DNA doctor, circa 2008. The personalized medicine being pioneered here and elsewhere prefigures a day when everyone's genome will be deposited on a chip or stored on a gene card tucked into a wallet. Physicians will forecast illnesses and prescribe preventive drugs custom-fitted to a patient's DNA, rather than the one-size-fits-all pharmaceuticals that people take today. Gene cards might also be used to find that best suited career, or a DNA-compatible mate, or, more darkly, to deny someone jobs, dates, and meds because their nucleotides don't measure up. It's a scenario Andrew Niccol imagined in his 1997 film, *Gattaca,* where embryos in a not-too-distant future are bioengineered for perfection and where genism—discrimination based on one's DNA—condemns the lesser-gened to scrubbing toilets.

The *Gattaca*-like engineering of defect-free embryos is at least twenty or thirty years away, but Sequenom and others plan to take DNA testing to the masses in just a year or two. The prize: a projected $5 billion market for personalized medicine by 2006 and billions, possibly hundreds of billions, more for those companies that can translate the errors in my genome and yours into custom pharmaceuticals.

Sitting across from me is the man responsible for my gene scan: Andi Braun, chief medical officer at Sequenom. Tall and sinewy, with a long neck, glasses, and short gray hair, Braun, forty-six, is both jovial and German. Genetic tests are already publicly available for Huntington's disease and cystic fibrosis, but Braun points out that these illnesses are relatively rare. "We are targeting diseases that impact millions," he says in a deep Bavarian accent, envisioning a day when genetic kits that can assay the whole range of human misery will be available at Wal-Mart, as easy to use as a home pregnancy test.

But a kit won't tell me if I'll definitely get a disease, just if I have a bum gene. What Sequenom and others are working toward is pinning down the probability that, for example, a colon cancer gene will actually trigger a tumor. To know this, Braun must analyze the DNA of thousands of people and tally how many have the colon cancer gene, how many actually get the disease, and how many don't. Once these data are gathered and crunched, Braun will be able to tell you, for instance, that if you have the defective gene, you have a 40 percent chance, or maybe a 75 percent chance, of getting the disease by age fifty, or ninety. Environmental factors such as eating right—or wrong—and smoking also weigh in. "It's a little like predicting the weather," says Charles Cantor, the company's cofounder and chief scientific officer.

Braun tells me that, for now, his tests offer only a rough sketch of my genetic future. 10 "We can't yet test for everything, and some of the information is only partially understood," he says. It's a peek more through a rudimentary eyeglass than a Hubble Space Telescope. Yet I will be able to glimpse some of the internal programming bequeathed to me by evolution and that I, in turn, have bequeathed to my children—Sander, Danielle, and Alex, ages fifteen, thirteen, and seven. They are a part of this story, too. Here's where I squirm, because as a father I pass on not only the ingredients of life to my children but the secret codes of their demise—just as I have passed on my blue eyes and a flip in my left brow that my grandmother called "a little lick from God." DNA is not only the book of life, it is also the book of death, says Braun: "We're all going to die, *ja?*"

Strictly speaking, Braun is not looking for entire genes, the long strings of nucleotides that instruct the body to grow a tooth or create white blood cells to attack an incoming virus. He's after single nucleotide polymorphisms, or SNPs (pronounced "snips"), the tiny genetic variations that account for nearly all differences in humans.

Imagine DNA as a ladder made of rungs—3 billion in all—spiraling upward in a double helix. Each step is a base pair, designated by two letters from the nucleotide alphabet of G, T, A, and C. More than 99 percent of these base pairs are identical in all humans, with only about one in a thousand SNPs diverging to make us distinct. For instance, you might have a CG that makes you susceptible to diabetes, and I might have a CG, which makes it far less likely I will get this disease.

This is all fairly well known: Genetics 101. What's new is how startups like Sequenom have industrialized the SNP identification process. Andi Braun and Charles Cantor are finding thousands of new SNPs a day, at a cost of about a penny each.

Braun tells me that there are possibly a million SNPs in each person, though only a small fraction are tightly linked with common ailments. These disease-causing SNPs are fueling a biotech bonanza; the hope is that after finding them, the discoverers can design wonder drugs. In the crowded SNP field, Sequenom vies with Iceland-based deCode Genetics and American companies such as Millennium Pharmaceuticals, Orchid BioSciences, and Celera Genomics, as well as multinationals like Eli Lilly and Roche Diagnostics. "It's the Oklahoma Land Grab right now," says Toni Schuh, Sequenom's CEO.

The sun sets outside Braun's office as my results arrive, splayed across his computer   15
screen like tarot cards. I'm trying to maintain a steely, reportorial facade, but my heart continues to race.

Names of SNPs pop up on the screen: connexin 26, implicated in hearing loss; factor V leiden, which causes blood clots; and alpha-1 antitrypsin deficiency, linked to lung and liver disease. Beside each SNP are codes that mean nothing to me: 13q11-q12, 1q23, 14q32.1. Braun explains that these are addresses on the human genome, the P.O. box numbers of life. For instance, 1q23 is the address for a mutant gene that causes vessels to shrink and impede the flow of blood—it's on chromosome 1. Thankfully, my result is negative. "So, David, you will not get the varicose veins. That's good, *ja?*" says Braun. One gene down, dozens to go.

Next up is the hemochromatosis gene. This causes one's blood to retain too much iron, which can damage the liver. As Braun explains it, somewhere in the past, an isolated human community lived in an area where the food was poor in iron. Those who developed a mutation that stores high levels of iron survived, and those who didn't became anemic and died, failing to reproduce. However, in these iron-rich times, hemochromatosis is a liability. Today's treatment? Regular bleeding. "You tested negative for this mutation," says Braun. "You do not have to be bled."

I'm also clean for cystic fibrosis and for a SNP connected to lung cancer.

Then comes the bad news. A line of results on Braun's monitor shows up red and is marked "MT," for mutant type. My body's programming code is faulty. There's a glitch in my system. Named ACE (for angiotensin-I converting enzyme), this SNP means my body makes an enzyme that keeps my blood pressure spiked. In plain English, I'm a heart attack risk.

My face drains of color as the news sinks in. I'm not only defective, but down the   20
road, every time I get anxious about my condition, I'll know that I have a much higher

chance of dropping dead. I shouldn't be surprised, since I'm told everyone has some sort of disease-causing mutation. Yet I realize that my decision to take a comprehensive DNA test has been based on the rather ridiculous assumption that I would come out of this with a clean genetic bill of health. I almost never get sick, and, at age forty-four, I seldom think about my physical limitations or death. This attitude is buttressed by a family largely untouched by disease. The women routinely thrive into their late eighties and nineties. One great-aunt lived to age one hundred and one; she used to bake me cupcakes in her retirement home when I was a boy. And some of the Duncan menfolk are pushing ninety-plus. My parents, now entering their seventies, are healthy. In a flash of red MTs, I'm glimpsing my own future, my own mortality. I'm slated to keel over, both hands clutching at my heart.

"Do you have any history in your family of high blood pressure or heart disease?" asks Matthew McGinniss, a Sequenom geneticist standing at Braun's side.

"No," I answer, trying to will the color back into my face. Then a second MT pops up on the screen—another high blood pressure mutation. My other cardiac indicators are OK, which is relatively good news, though I'm hardly listening now. I'm already planning a full-scale assault to learn everything I can about fighting heart disease—until McGinniss delivers an unexpected pronouncement. "These mutations are probably irrelevant," he says. Braun agrees: "It's likely that you carry a gene that keeps these faulty ones from causing you trouble—DNA that we have not yet discovered."

The SNPs keep rolling past, revealing more mutations, including a type 2 diabetes susceptibility, which tells me I may want to steer clear of junk food. More bad news: I don't have a SNP called CCR5 that prevents me from acquiring HIV, nor one that seems to shield smokers from lung cancer. "*Ja*, that's my favorite," says Braun, himself a smoker. "I wonder what Philip Morris would pay for that."

By the time I get home, I realize that all I've really learned is, I might get heart disease, and I could get diabetes. And I should avoid smoking and unsafe sex—as if I didn't already know this. Obviously, I'll now watch my blood pressure, exercise more, and lay off the Cap'n Crunch. But beyond this, I have no idea what to make of the message Andi Braun has divined from a trace of my spit.

Looking for guidance, I visit Ann Walker, director of the Graduate Program for   25
Genetic Counseling at the University of California at Irvine. Walker explains the whats and hows, and the pros and cons, of DNA testing to patients facing hereditary disease, pregnant couples concerned with prenatal disorders, and anyone else contemplating genetic evaluation. It's a tricky job because, as I've learned, genetic data are seldom clear-cut.

Take breast cancer, Walker says. A woman testing positive for BRCA1, the main breast cancer gene, has an 85 percent chance of actually getting the cancer by age seventy, a wrenching situation, since the most effective method of prevention is a double mastectomy. What if a woman has the operation and it turns out she's among those 15 percent who carry the mutation but will never get the cancer? Not surprisingly, one study, conducted in Holland, found that half of the healthy women whose mothers developed breast cancer opt not to be tested for the gene, preferring ignorance and closer monitoring. Another example is the test for APoE, the Alzheimer's gene. Since the affliction has no cure, most people don't want to know their status. But some do. A positive result, says Walker, allows them to put their affairs in order and prepare for their own dotage. Still, the news can be devastating. One biotech executive told me that a cousin of his committed suicide when he tested positive for Huntington's, having seen the disease slowly destroy his father.

Walker pulls out a chart and asks about my family's medical details, starting with my grandparents and their brothers and sisters: what they suffered and died from, and when. My Texas grandmother died at ninety-two after a series of strokes. My ninety-one-year-old Missouri grandmom was headed to a vacation in Mexico with her eighty-eight-year-old second husband when she got her death sentence—ovarian cancer. The men died younger: my grandfathers in their late sixties, though they both have brothers still alive and healthy in their nineties. To the mix, Walker adds my parents and their siblings, all of whom are alive and healthy in their sixties and seventies; then my generation; and finally our children. She looks up and smiles: "This is a pretty healthy group."

Normally, Walker says, she would send me home. Yet I'm sitting across from her, not because my parents carry some perilous SNP, but as a healthy man who is after a forecast of future maladies. "We have no real training yet for this," she says, and tells me the two general rules of genetic counseling: No one should be screened unless there is an effective treatment or readily available counseling; and the information should not bewilder people or present them with unnecessary trauma.

Many worry that these prime directives may be ignored by Sequenom and other startups that need to launch products to survive. FDA testing for new drugs can take up to ten years, and many biotech firms feel pressure to sell something in the interim. "Most of these companies need revenue," says the University of Pennsylvania's Arthur Caplan, a top bioethicist. "And the products they've got now are diagnostic. Whether they are good ones, useful ones, necessary ones, accurate ones, seems less of a concern than that they be sold." Caplan also notes that the FDA does not regulate these tests. "If it was a birth control test, the FDA would be all over it."

I ask Caplan about the *Gattaca* scenario of genetic discrimination. Will a woman dump me if she finds out about my ACE? Will my insurance company hike my rate? "People are denied insurance and jobs right now," he says, citing sickle cell anemia, whose sufferers and carriers, mostly black, have faced job loss and discrimination. No federal laws exist to protect us from genism, or from insurers and employers finding out our genetic secrets. "Right now, you're likely going to be more disadvantaged than empowered by genetic testing," says Caplan.

After probing my genetic future, I jet to England to investigate my DNA past. Who are these people who have bequeathed me this tainted bloodline? From my grandfather Duncan, an avid genealogist, I already know that my paternal ancestors came from Perth, in south-central Scotland. We can trace the name back to an Anglican priest murdered in Glasgow in 1680 by a mob of Puritans. His six sons escaped and settled in Shippensburg, Pennsylvania, where their descendants lived until my great-great-grandfather moved west to Kansas City in the 1860s.

In an Oxford restaurant, over a lean steak and a heart-healthy merlot, I talk with geneticist Bryan Sykes, a linebacker-sized fifty-five-year-old with a baby face and an impish smile. He's a molecular biologist at the university's Institute of Molecular Medicine and the author of the best-selling *Seven Daughters of Eve*. Sykes first made headlines in 1994 when he used DNA to directly link a 5,000-year-old body discovered frozen and intact in an Austrian glacier to a twentieth-century Dorset woman named Marie Mosley. This stunning genetic connection between housewife and hunter-gatherer launched Sykes's career as a globe-trotting genetic gumshoe. In 1995, he confirmed that bones dug up near Ekaterinburg, Russia, were the remains of Czar Nicholas II and his family by comparing the body's DNA with that of the czar's living relatives, including Britain's Prince Philip. Sykes debunked explorer Thor Heyerdahl's *Kon-Tiki* theory by tracing Polynesian genes to Asia, not the Americas, and similarly put the lie to the *Clan of the Cave Bear* hypothesis, which held that the Neanderthal interbred with our ancestors, the Cro-Magnon, when the two subspecies coexisted in Europe 15,000 years ago.

Sykes explains to me that a bit of DNA called mtDNA is key to his investigations. A circular band of genes residing separately from the twenty-three chromosomes of the double helix, mtDNA is passed down solely through the maternal line. Sykes used mtDNA to discover something astounding: Nearly every European can be traced back to just seven women living 10,000 to 45,000 years ago. In his book, Sykes gives these seven ancestors hokey names and tells us where they most likely lived: Ursula, in Greece (circa 43,000 B.C.), and Velda, in northern Spain (circa 15,000 B.C.), to name two of the "seven daughters of Eve." (Eve was the ur-mother who lived 150,000 years ago in Africa.)

Sykes has taken swab samples from the cheeks of more than 10,000 people, charging $220 to individually determine a person's mtDNA type. "It's not serious genetics," Sykes admits, "but people like to know their roots. It makes genetics less scary and shows us that, through our genes, we are all very closely related." He recently expanded his tests to include non-Europeans. The Asian daughters of Eve are named Emiko, Nene, and Yumio, and their African sisters are Lamia, Latifa, and Ulla, among others.

Before heading to England, I had mailed Sykes a swab of my cheek cells. Over our desserts in Oxford he finally offers up the results. "You are descended from Helena," he pronounces. "She's the most common daughter of Eve, accounting for some 40 percent of Europeans." He hands me a colorful certificate, signed by him, that heralds my many-times-great-grandma and tells me that she lived 20,000 years ago in the Dordogne Valley of France. More interesting is the string of genetic letters from my mtDNA readout that indicate I'm mostly Celtic, which makes sense. But other bits of code reveal traces of Southeast Asian DNA, and even a smidgen of Native American and African.

This doesn't quite have the impact of discovering that I'm likely to die of a heart attack. Nor am I surprised about the African and Indian DNA, since my mother's family has lived in the American South since the seventeenth century. But Southeast Asian? Sykes laughs. "We are all mutts," he says. "There is no ethnic purity. Somewhere over the years, one of the thousands of ancestors who contributed to your DNA had a child with someone from Southeast Asia." He tells me a story about a blond, blue-eyed surfer from Southern California who went to Hawaii to apply for monies awarded only to those who could prove native Hawaiian descent. The grant-givers laughed—until his DNA turned up traces of Hawaiian.

The next day, in Sykes's lab, we have one more test: running another ancestry marker in my Y chromosome through a database of 10,000 other Ys to see which

35

profile is closest to mine. If my father was in the database, his Y chromosome would be identical, or possibly one small mutation off. A cousin might deviate by one tick. Someone descended from my native county of Perth might be two or three mutations removed, indicating that we share a common ancestor hundreds of years ago. Sykes tells me these comparisons are used routinely in paternity cases. He has another application. He is building up Y-chromosome profiles of surnames: men with the same last name whose DNA confirms that they are related to common ancestors.

After entering my mtDNA code into his laptop, Sykes looks intrigued, then surprised, and suddenly moves to the edge of his seat. Excited, he reports that the closest match is, incredibly, him—Bryan Sykes! "This has never happened," he says, telling me that I am a mere one mutation removed from him, and two from the average profile of a Sykes. He has not collected DNA from many other Duncans, he says, though it appears as if sometime in the past 400 years a Sykes must have ventured into Perth and then had a child with a Duncan. "That makes us not-so-distant cousins," he says. We check a map of Britain on his wall, and sure enough, the Sykes family's homeland of Yorkshire is less than 200 miles south of Perth.

The fact that Sykes and I are members of the same extended family is just a bizarre coincidence, but it points to applications beyond simple genealogy. "I've been approached by the police to use my surnames data to match up with DNA from an unknown suspect found at a crime scene," says Sykes. Distinctive genetic markers can be found at the roots of many family trees. "This is possible, to narrow down a pool of suspects to a few likely surnames. But it's not nearly ready yet."

Back home in California, I'm sweating on a StairMaster at the gym, wondering about my heart. I wrap my hands around the grips and check my pulse: 129. Normal. I pump harder and top out at 158. Also normal. I think about my visit a few days earlier—prompted by my gene scan—to Robert Superko, a cardiologist. After performing another battery of tests, he gave me the all clear—except for one thing. Apparently, I have yet another lame heart gene, the atherosclerosis susceptibility gene ATHS, a SNP that causes plaque in my cardiac bloodstream to build up if I don't exercise far more than average—which I do, these days, as a slightly obsessed biker and runner. "As long as you exercise, you'll be fine," Superko advised, a bizarre kind of life sentence that means that I must pedal and jog like a madman or face—what? A triple bypass?

Pumping on the StairMaster, I nudge the setting up a notch, wishing, in a way, that I either knew for sure I was going to die on, say, February 17, 2021, or that I hadn't been tested at all. As it is, the knowledge that I have an ACE and ATHS deep inside me will be nagging me every time I get short of breath.

The last results from my DNA workup have also come in. Andi Braun has tested me for seventy-seven SNPs linked to lifespan in order to assess when and how I might get sick and die. He has given me a score of .49 on his scale. It indicates a lifespan at least 20 percent longer than that of the average American male, who, statistically speaking, dies in his seventy-fourth year. I will likely live, then, to the age of eighty-eight. That's forty-four years of StairMaster to go.

Braun warns that this figure does not take into account the many thousands of other SNPs that affect my life, not to mention the possibility that a piano could fall on my head.

That night, I put my seven-year-old, Alex, to bed. His eyes droop under his bright white head of hair as I finish reading *Captain Underpants* aloud. Feeling his little heart beating as he lies next to me on his bed, I wonder what shockers await him inside his nucleotides, half of which I gave him. As I close the book and then sing him to sleep, I wonder if he has my culprit genes. I don't know, because he hasn't been scanned. For now, he and the rest of humanity are living in nearly the same blissful ignorance as Helena did in long-ago Dordogne. But I do know one thing: Alex has my eyebrow, the "lick of God." I touch his flip in the dark, and touch mine. He stirs, but it's not enough to wake him.

Questions for Discussion and Writing

1. What did Duncan learn about the new capabilities for screening and detecting genetic disease markers when his DNA was examined? According to Duncan, what implications does this new technology have for society in many different spheres?
2. What does Duncan's article gain by making him the guinea pig (he was the first healthy human ever to be screened) whose discoveries became very personal?
3. In a short essay, discuss some of the social implications (positive and negative) of this new technology, and state whether you would volunteer to be screened.
4. What current science-fiction films explore the public's ambivalence toward new technologies as *Jurassic Park* (1993) did with genetic engineering and *28 Days Later* (2003) did with a laboratory-produced virus that crossed species and infected humanity?

LynNell Hancock

. . . .

LynNell Hancock is a journalist and director of the Prudential Fellowship for Children and the News at Columbia University. She has written articles on public education for Newsweek, *where the following essay first appeared on February 27, 1995. Most recently, she has written* Hands to Work: The Story of Three Families Racing the Welfare Clock *(2002).*

THE HAVES AND THE HAVE-NOTS

Aaron Smith is a teenager on the techno track. In America's breathless race to achieve information nirvana, the senior from Issaqua, a middle-class district east of Seattle, has the hardware and hookups to run the route. Aaron and 600 of his fellow students at Liberty High School have their own electronic-mail addresses. They can log on to the Internet every day, joining only about 15 percent of America's schoolchildren who can now forage on their own for documents in European libraries or chat with experts around the world. At home, the 18-year-old e-mails his teachers, when he is not prowling the World Wide Web to track down snowboarding conditions on his favorite Cascade Mountain passes. "We have the newest, greatest thing," Aaron says.

On the opposite coast, in Boston's South End, Marilee Colon scoots a mouse along a grimy Apple pad, playing a Kid Pix game on an old black-and-white terminal. It's

Wednesday at a neighborhood center, Marilee's only chance to poke around on a computer. Her mom, a secretary at the center, can't afford one in their home. Marilee's public-school classroom doesn't have any either. The 10-year-old from Roxbury depends on the United South End Settlement Center and its less than state-of-the-art Macs and IBMs perched on mismatched desks. Marilee has never heard of the Internet. She is thrilled to double-click on the stick of dynamite and watch her teddy-bear creation fly off the screen. "It's fun blowing it up," says the delicate fifth grader, twisting a brown ponytail around her finger.

Certainly Aaron was born with a stack of statistical advantages over Marilee. He is white and middle class and lives with two working parents who both have higher degrees. Economists say the swift pace of hightech advances will only drive a further wedge between these youngsters. To have an edge in America's job search, it used to be enough to be well educated. Now, say the experts, it's critical to be digital. Employees who are adept at technology "earn roughly 10 to 15 percent higher pay," according to Alan Krueger, chief economist for the U.S. Labor Department. Some argue that this pay gap has less to do with technology than with industries' efforts to streamline their work forces during the recession. . . . Still, nearly every American business from Wall Street to McDonald's requires some computer knowledge. Taco Bell is modeling its cash registers after Nintendo controls, according to Rosabeth Moss Kanter. The "haves" says the Harvard Business School professor, will be able to communicate around the globe. The "have-nots" will be consigned to the "rural backwater of the information society."

Like it or not, America is a land of inequities. And technology, despite its potential to level the social landscape, is not yet blind to race, wealth and age. The richer the family, the more likely it is to own and use a computer, according to 1993 census data. White families are three times as likely as blacks or Hispanics to have computers at home. Seventy-four percent of Americans making more than $75,000 own at least one terminal, but not even one third of all Americans own computers. A small fraction— only about 7 percent—of students' families subscribe to online services that transform the plastic terminal into a telecommunications port.

At least in public schools, the computer gap is closing. More than half the students 5 have some kind of computer, even if it's obsolete. But schools with the biggest concentration of poor children have the least equipment, according to Jeanne Hayes of Quality Education Data. Ten years ago schools had one computer for every 125 children, according Hayes. Today that figure is one for 12.

Though the gap is slowly closing, technology is advancing so fast, and at such huge costs, that it's nearly impossible for cash-strapped municipalities to catch up. Seattle is taking bids for one company to wire each ZIP code with fiber optics, so everyone— rich or poor—can hook up to video, audio and other multimedia services. Estimated cost: $500 million. Prosperous Montgomery Country, Maryland, has an $81 million plan to put every classroom online. Next door, the District of Columbia public schools have the same ambitious plan but less than $1 million in the budget to accomplish it.

New ideas—and demands—for the schools are announced every week. The '90s populist slogan is no longer "A chicken in every pot" but "A computer on every desk." Vice President Al Gore has appealed to the telecommunications industry to cut costs and wire all schools, a task Education Secretary Richard Riley estimates will cost $10 billion. House Speaker Newt Gingrich stumbled into the discussion with a suggestion that every poor family get a laptop from Uncle Sam. Rep. Ed Markey wants a computer sitting on every school desk within 10 years. "The opportunities are enormous," Markey says.

Enormous, yes, but who is going to pay for them? Some successful school projects have relied heavily on the kindness of strangers. In Union City, N.J., school officials renovated the guts of a 100-year-old building five years ago, overhauling the curriculum and wiring every classroom in Christopher Columbus Middle School for high tech. Bell Atlantic provided wiring free and agreed to give each student in last year's seventh-grade class a computer to take home. Even parents, most of whom are South American immigrants, can use their children's computers to e-mail the principal in Spanish. He uses translation software and answers them electronically. The results have shown up in test scores. In a school where 80 percent of the children are poor, reading, math, attendance and writing scores are now the best in the district. "We believe that technology will improve our everyday life," says principal Bob Fazio. "And that other schools will piggyback and learn from us."

Still, for every Christopher Columbus, there are far more schools like Jordan High School in South-Central Los Angeles. Only 30 computers in the school's lab, most of them 12 to 15 years old, are available for Jordan's 2,000 students, many of whom live in the nearby Jordan Downs housing project. "I am teaching these kids on a system that will do them no good in the real world when they get out there," says Robert Doornbos, Jordan's computer-science instructor. "The school system has not made these kids' getting on the Information Highway a priority."

Donkey Kong   Having enough terminals to go around is one problem. But another   10 important question is what the equipment is used for. Not much beyond rote drills and word processing, according to Linda Roberts, a technology consultant for the U.S. Department of Education. A 1992 National Assessment of Educational Progress survey found that most fourth-grade math students were using computers to play games, "like Donkey Kong." By the eighth grade, most math students weren't using them at all.

Many school officials think that access to the Internet could become the most effective equalizer in the educational lives of students. With a modem attached, even most ancient terminals can connect children in rural Mississippi to universities in Asia. A Department of Education report last week found that 35 percent of schools have at least one computer with a modem. But only half the schools let students use it. Apparently administrators and teachers are hogging the Info Highway for themselves.

There is another gap to be considered. Not just between rich and poor, but between the young and the used-to-be-young. Of the 100 million Americans who use computers at home, school or work, nearly 60 percent are 17 or younger, according to the census. Children, for the most part, rule cyberspace, leaving the over-40 set to browse through the almanac.

The gap between the generations may be the most important, says MIT guru Nicholas Negroponte, author of the new book *Being Digital*. Adults are the true "digitally homeless, the needy," he says. In other words, adults like Debbie Needleman,

43, an office manager at Wallpaper Warehouse in Natick, Massachusetts, are wary of the digital age. "I really don't mind that the rest of the world passes me by as long as I can still earn a living," she says.

These aging choose-nots become a more serious issue when they are teachers in schools. Even if schools manage to acquire state-of-the-art equipment, there is no guarantee that trained adults will be available to understand them. This is something that tries Aaron Smith's patience. "A lot of my teachers are quite illiterate," says Aaron, the fully equipped Issaqua teenager. "You have to explain it to them real slow to make sure they understand everything." Fast or slow, Marilee Colon, Roxbury's fifth-grade computer lover, would like her chance to understand everything too.

Questions for Discussion and Writing

1. According to Hancock, although publicized as a democratizing tool, the computer has dramatically separated the haves from the have-nots. What factors determine who has access to this technology?
2. How does Hancock's comparison of schoolchildren dramatize her thesis? Why is she critical of articles that expound on the glories of computer literacy?
3. In your experience, have computers had the kind of democratizing effect that was promised? Why or why not?

Constance Holden

• •

Constance Holden (b. 1941) is a writer for Science *magazine, whose column "News and Comment" discusses the implications of issues in the forefront of scientific research. Holden is particularly interested in questions about the relationship between mind and body. "Identical Twins Reared Apart," from* Science *(March 1980), reports on a comparative study, conducted by Thomas J. Bouchard at the University of Minnesota, which pointed to the importance of heredity rather than environment in shaping human behavior. Holden develops a point-by-point comparison of the striking similarities in behavior between nine sets of identical twins who were separated at birth, reared in different environments, and then brought together.*

IDENTICAL TWINS REARED APART

Bridget and Dorothy are 39-year-old British housewives, identical twins raised apart who first met each other a little over a year ago. When they met, to take part in Thomas Bouchard's twin study at the University of Minnesota, the manicured hands of each bore seven rings. Each also wore two bracelets on one wrist and a watch and a bracelet on the other. Investigators in Bouchard's study, the most extensive investigation ever made of identical twins reared apart, are still bewitched by the seven rings. Was it coincidence, the result of similar influences, or is this small sign of affinity a true, even inevitable, manifestation of the mysterious and infinitely complex interaction of the genes the two women have in common?

Investigators have been bemused and occasionally astonished at similarities between long-separated twins, similarities that prevailing dogma about human behavior would ordinarily attribute to common environmental influences. How is it, for example, that two men with significantly different upbringings came to have the same authoritarian personality? Or another pair to have similar histories of endogenous depression? Or still another pair to have virtually identical patterns of headaches?

These are only bits and pieces from a vast amount of data, none of it yet analyzed, being collected by the University of Minnesota twin study that began last March. So provocative have been some of the cases that the study has already received much attention in the press, and it is bound to get a lot more. The investigation is extremely controversial, aimed, as it is, directly at the heart of the age-old debate about heredity versus environment. Identical twins reared apart have been objects of scrutiny in the past, notably in three studies conducted in England, Denmark, and the United States. An indication of the sensitivity of this subject is the fact that the last one in this country was completed more than 40 years ago,[1] although the rarity of cases has also made this type of research rather exotic. The Minnesota investigators, however, have been able to locate more twin pairs than they expected. So far they have processed nine pairs of identical or monozygotic twins (as well as several pairs of fraternal or dizygotic twins used as controls) and, owing to the publicity given the project, have managed to locate 11 additional pairs to take part in the study.

The Minnesota study is unprecedented in its scope, using a team of psychologists, psychiatrists, and medical doctors to probe and analyze every conceivable aspect of the twins' life histories, medical histories and physiology, tastes, psychological inclinations, abilities, and intelligence. It began when Bouchard, a psychologist who specializes in investigating individual differences, heard of a pair of twins separated from birth, both coincidentally named Jim by their adoptive families, who were reunited at the age of 39. Bouchard did not have to look far to set up his study team, as Minnesota is a hotbed of twin research. There, ready to go to work, were Irving Gottesman, a behavioral geneticist who has spent his career studying twins and whose particular interest is the etiology of schizophrenia; psychologist David Lykken, who has been looking at the brain waves of twins for 10 years; psychologist Auke Tellegen, who recently completed a new personality questionnaire that is being used on the twins; and psychiatrist Leonard Heston, who has studied heritability of mental disorders with adopted children.

Bouchard has taken an eclectic approach in developing the battery of exercises 5 through which the twins are run. Each pair goes through 6 days of intensive testing. In addition to detailed medical histories including diet, smoking, and exercise, the twins are given electrocardiograms, chest x-rays, heart stress tests, and pulmonary exams. They are injected with a variety of substances to determine allergies. They are wired to electroencephalographs to measure their brain wave responses to stimuli in the form of tones of varying intensity, and given other psychophysiological tests to measure such responses as reaction times. Several handedness tests are given to ascertain laterality.

---

[1] A. H. Newman, F. N. Freeman, and K. J. Holzinger wrote up their study of 19 twin pairs in a 1937 book, *Twins: A Study of Heredity and Environment.*

The physiological probes are interspersed with several dozen pencil-and-paper tests, which over the week add up to about 15,000 questions; these cover family and childhood environment, fears and phobias, personal interests, vocational interests, values, reading and TV viewing habits, musical interests, aesthetic judgement tests, and color preferences. They are put through three comprehensive psychological inventories. Then there is a slew of ability tests: the Wechsler Adult Intelligence Scale (the main adult IQ test) and numerous others that reveal skills in information processing, vocabulary, spatial abilities, numerical processing, mechanical ability, memory, and so forth. Throughout the 6 days there is much overlap and repetition in the content of questions, the intent being to "measure the same underlying factor at different times," says Bouchard. Mindful of charges of investigator bias in the administration of IQ tests in past twin studies, Bouchard has contracted with outside professionals to come in just for the purpose of administering and scoring the Wechsler intelligence test.

And the upshot of all this probing? Although the data have not yet been interpreted, there have already been some real surprises. Bouchard told *Science:* "I frankly expected far more differences [between twins] than we have found so far. I'm a psychologist, not a geneticist. I want to find out how the environment works to shape psychological traits." But the most provocative morsels that have so far become available are those that seem to reveal genetic influences at work.

Take the "Jim twins," as they have come to be known. Jim Springer and Jim Lewis were adopted as infants into working-class Ohio families. Both liked math and did not like spelling in school. Both had law enforcement training and worked part-time as deputy sheriffs. Both vacationed in Florida, both drove Chevrolets. Much has been made of the fact that their lives are marked by a trail of similar names. Both had dogs named Toy. Both married and divorced women named Linda and had second marriages with women named Betty. They named their sons James Allan and James Alan, respectively. Both like mechanical drawing and carpentry. They have almost identical drinking and smoking patterns. Both chew their fingernails down to the nubs.

But what investigators thought "astounding" was their similar medical histories. In addition to having hemorrhoids and identical pulse and blood pressure and sleep patterns, both had inexplicably put on 10 pounds at the same time in their lives. What really gets the researchers is that both suffer from "mixed headache syndrome"—a combination tension headache and migraine. The onset occurred in both at the age of 18. They have these late-afternoon headaches with the same frequency and same degree of disability, and the two used the same terms to describe the pain.

The twins also have their differences. One wears his hair over his forehead, the   10 other has it slicked back with sideburns. One expresses himself better orally, the other in writing. But although the emotional environments in which they were brought up were different, the profiles on their psychological inventories were much alike.

Another much-publicized pair are 47-year-old Oskar Stöhr and Jack Yufe. These two have the most dramatically different backgrounds of all the twins studied. Born in Trinidad of a Jewish father and a German mother, they were separated shortly after birth. The mother took Oskar back to Germany, where he was raised as a Catholic and a Nazi youth by his grandmother. Jack was raised in the Caribbean, as a Jew, by his father, and spent part of his youth on an Israeli kibbutz. The two men now lead markedly different lives. Oskar is an industrial supervisor in Germany, married, a devoted union man, a skier. Jack runs a retail clothing store in San Diego, is separated, and describes himself as a workaholic.

But similarities started cropping up as soon as Oskar arrived at the airport. Both were wearing wire-rimmed glasses and mustaches, both sported two-pocket shirts with epaulets. They share idiosyncrasies galore: they like spicy foods and sweet liqueurs, are absentminded, have a habit of falling asleep in front of the television, think it's funny to sneeze in a crowd of strangers, flush the toilet before using it, store rubber bands on their wrists, read magazines from back to front, dip buttered toast in their coffee. Oskar is domineering toward women and yells at his wife, which Jack did before he was separated. Oskar did not take all the tests because he speaks only German (some are scheduled to be administered to him in German), but the two had very similar profiles on the Minnesota Multiphastic Personality Inventory (the MMPI was already available in German). Although the two were raised in different cultures and speak different languages, investigator Bouchard professed himself struck by the similarities in their mannerisms, the questions they asked, their "temperament, tempo, the way they do things"—which are, granted, relatively intangible when it comes to measuring them. Bouchard also thinks the two supply "devastating" evidence against the feminist contention that children's personalities are shaped differently according to the sex of those who rear them, since Oskar was raised by women and Jack by men.

Other well-publicized twin pairs are Bridget and Dorothy, the British housewives with the seven rings, and Barbara and Daphne, another pair of British housewives. Both sets are now in their late 30's and were separated during World War II. Bridget and Dorothy are of considerable interest because they were raised in quite different socioeconomic settings—the class difference turns out mainly to be reflected in the fact that the one raised in modest circumstances has bad teeth. Otherwise, say the investigators, they share "striking similarities in all areas," including another case of coincidence in naming children. They named their sons Richard Andrew and Andrew Richard, respectively, and their daughters Catherine Louise and Karen Louise. (Bouchard is struck by this, as the likelihood of such a coincidence would seem to be lessened by the fact that names are a joint decision by husband and wife.) On ability and IQ tests the scores of the sisters were similar, although the one raised in the lower class setting had a slightly higher score.

The other British twins, Daphne and Barbara, are fondly remembered by the investigators as the "giggle sisters." Both were great gigglers, particularly together, when they were always setting each other off. Asked if there were any gigglers in their adoptive families, both replied in the negative. The sisters also shared identical coping mechanisms in the face of stress: they ignored it, managed to "read out" such stimuli. In keeping with this, both flatly avoided conflict and controversy—neither, for example, had any interest in politics. Such avoidance of conflict is "classically regarded as learned behavior," says Bouchard. Although the adoptive families of the two women were not terribly different, "we see more differences within families than between these two."

Only fragmentary information is available so far from the rest of the nine sets of   15
twins, but it supplies abundant food for new lines of inquiry. Two 57-year-old women, for example, developed adult-onset diabetes at the same time in their lives. One of a pair of twins suffers from a rare neurological disease that has always been thought to be genetic in origin. Another area where identical twins differ is in their allergies.

Psychiatrically, according to Heston, who conducts personal interviews with all the twins, there has been remarkable agreement. "Twins brought up together have very high concordance in psychiatric histories," he says. (For example, if one identical twin has schizophrenia, the other one stands a 45 percent chance of developing it.) But what is surprising is that "what we see [with the twins in the study] is pretty much the same as in twins brought up together." By and large, he says, they share very similar phobias, and he has noted more than one case where both twins had histories of endogenous depression. In one case, twins who had been brought up in different emotional environments—one was raised in a strict disciplinarian household, the other had a warm, tolerant, loving mother—showed very similar neurotic and hypochondriacal traits. Says Heston, "things that I would never have thought of—mild depressions, phobias—as being in particular genetically mediated . . . now, at least, there are grounds for a very live hypothesis" on the role of genes not only in major mental illnesses, where chemistry clearly plays a part, but in lesser emotional disturbances.

Other odds and ends:

Two men brought up in radically different environments—one an uneducated manual laborer, the other highly educated and cosmopolitan—turned out to be great raconteurs. (They did, however, have very different IQ scores. The numbers are confidential but the difference was close to the largest difference on record for identical twins, 24 points.)

One of the greatest areas of discordance for twins was smoking. Of the nine pairs, there were four in which one twin smoked and the other did not. No one has an explanation for this. But, surprisingly, in at least one case a lifelong heavy smoker came out just as well on the pulmonary exam and heart stress test as did the nonsmoker.

In a couple of cases, one of a twin pair wore glasses and the other did not. But when their eyes were checked, it was found that both members of each pair required the same correction.

In the fascinating tidbit category: One pair of female twins was brought together briefly as children. Each wore her favorite dress for the occasion. The dresses were identical.

What is to be made of all this? As Tellegen warns, any conclusions at this point are "just gossip." The similarities are somehow more fascinating than the differences, and it could well be that the subjective impression they make on the investigators is heavier than is justified. Nonetheless, even the subjective impressions offer fertile grounds for speculation. Bouchard, for example, thinks that the team may discover that identical twins have a built-in penchant for a certain level of physical exertion. The latest pair to visit the laboratory, for example—23-year-old males—both eschew exercise (although both are thin as rails).

Lykken, who does the tests on the twins' central nervous systems, uses the case of the seven rings as an example for one of his tentative ideas. Fondness for rings is obviously not hereditary, but groups of unrelated genes on different chromosomes, producing pretty hands and other characteristics, may combine to result in beringedness. These traits, called idiographic—meaning particular to an individual rather than shared across a population—may not be as much a result of chance as has been thought. "There are probably other traits that are idiographic that may be almost inevitable given the [gene] combinations. . . . More of these unique characteristics than we previously thought may be determined by a particular combination of genes." Lykken adds, "People get so upset when you suggest that the wiring diagram can influence the mind." But to believe otherwise "requires a naïve dualism . . . an assumption that mental events occur independent of the physical substrate."

Such talk begins to sound pretty deterministic, but Lykken insists that when the 20 mass of data has been ordered "there will be material that will make environmentalists very happy and material that will make hereditarians very happy." One thing that will not make the environmentalists happy is the fact that IQ seems to have a high degree of heritability, as indicated by the fact that of all the tests administered to identical twins separately reared, IQ shows the highest concordance. It is even higher than the introversion-extroversion personality trait, a venerable measure in psychological testing that shows higher concordance than other conventional categories such as sense of well-being, responsibility, dominance, and ego strength.

As several investigators mentioned to *Science,* the scores of identical twins on many psychological and ability tests are closer than would be expected for the same person taking the same test twice. Lykken also found this to be true of brain wave tracings, which is probably the most direct evidence that identical twins are almost identically wired. Several researchers also felt that there is something to the idea that identical twins reared apart may be even more similar in some respects than those reared together. The explanation is simple: competition between the two is inevitable; hence if the stronger or taller of the two excels at sports, the other twin, even if equal in inclination and ability, will avoid sports altogether in order not to be overshadowed. Or one twin will choose to be a retiring type in order not to compete with his extroverted sibling. In short, many twins, in the interest of establishing their individuality, tend to exaggerate their differences.

Although the tentativeness of the findings so far must be repeatedly emphasized, at least one of the Minnesota researchers believes it may be safe to hypothesize that only extreme differences in environment result in significant differences between identical twins. Lykken says, after observing so many similarities, that it is tempting to conclude that "native ability will show itself over a broad range" of backgrounds. So either a seriously impoverished or a greatly enriched environment is required "to significantly alter its expression."

Such an idea, if it gained broad acceptance, would have major impacts on social policies. But Bouchard wants to keep his study separate from politics, emphasizing instead that the research is "very much exploratory."

The data, once assembled and analyzed, should provide a gold mine of new hypotheses. If a great many pairs of twins are collected, says Bouchard, they may be able to present the findings quantitatively, otherwise, the findings will be in the form of case histories. Tellegen, however, whose main interest is the methodology, says "we want to invent methods for analyzing traits in an objective manner, so we can get statistically cogent conclusions from a single case." He points out that psychoanalytic theory was developed from intensive study of small numbers of people and that behavioral psychologist B. F. Skinner similarly was able to develop his theories by studying small numbers of animals. Take the twins with the identical headache syndromes: with just one pair of twins the door is opened to a new field of research.

The twin study may also make it clear that estimating the relative contribution of heredity and environment to mental and psychological traits can never be boiled down to percentages. Some people, for example, may have authoritarian personalities no matter what their upbringing; the authoritarianism of others may be directly traceable to their environment. Similarly, with intelligence, some people may be smart or dumb regardless of outside influences, whereas the intelligence of others may be extremely malleable. Theoretically, variations from individual to individual in malleability and susceptibility may be so great that any attempt to make a generalization about the relative contribution of "innate" characteristics to a certain trait across a population would have no meaning.

Twin studies have been regarded with suspicion in some quarters because, according to Gottesman, the behavioral geneticist who worked with James Shields in England, they were "originally used to prove a genetic point of view." The most notorious of these were the studies of Cyril Burt on intelligence of twins reared separately, which were subsequently discredited. But, says Gottesman, "this study is a continuation of the efforts of Shields and Nielson[2] to challenge received wisdom about the roles of genes and environment." Everyone, observes Gottesman, "seems to have made up their minds one way or the other." With such a dearth of data of the kind that can only be obtained by studying persons with identical genes raised in different environments, people have been free to be as dogmatic as they please.

Bouchard had a devil of a time getting funding for his study. Various probes at the National Institutes of Health were discouraged on the grounds that the study was too multidisciplinary for any institute to embrace it. He finally got some money from the National Science Foundation.

Although the ultimate conclusions of the study may well be susceptible to sensationalizing, Gordon Allen of the National Institute of Mental Health, head of the International Twin Society, does not believe it will find any "new and unique answers." The sample will not be large enough for that, and besides, too few of the twin pairs were reared in environments so radically different as to bring genetically based behavioral similarities into stark relief.

The most solid and unequivocal evidence will be that supplied by the physiological findings. Although the similarities are the most titillating to most observers, it is the discordances that will be the most informative. For any difference between a pair of identical twins is "absolute proof that that is not completely controlled by heredity."

At this point, no one can make any generalizations beyond that made by James Shields, who died last year. Shields wrote that the evidence so far showed that "MZ [monozygotic] twins do not have to be brought up in the same subtly similar family environment for them to be alike." He concluded, "I doubt if MZ's will ever be numerous and representative enough to provide the main evidence about environment,

---

[2]*Nielson:* Niels Juel-Nielsen, a psychiatrist at the University of Odense in Denmark.

or about genetics, but . . . they can give unique real-life illustrations of some of the many possible pathways from genes to human behavior—and so will always be of human and scientific interest."

Questions for Discussion and Writing

1. What types of similarities did researchers discover in studying the nine sets of identical twins who were reunited after having been separated at birth and reared in different environments? Which set of twins did you find the most fascinating—the Jims, Oskar and Jack, Bridget and Dorothy, or Daphne and Barbara—and why?
2. In a study of this type, would physiological similarities (such as a predisposition to migraine headaches) be more significant than psychological similarities (such as personal taste in clothes, food, colors, etc.)? Why, or why not?
3. How did Holden's article influence your thinking about whether heredity or environment is more important in shaping human behavior? Using any one set of twins, discuss how the point-by-point similarities in behavior were or were not persuasive in establishing the overriding importance of heredity.
4. Should twins be raised so as to emphasize their differences or brought up to be as alike as possible (for example, dressed identically)? Which approach would you use if you were the parent of twins?
5. If you discovered that you had a twin from whom you were separated at birth, and you had the opportunity to meet this person, would you do so? Why or why not?
6. According to their publicist, Mary-Kate and Ashley Olsen no longer wish to be referred to as the Olsen twins. What might their reasons be?

Lawrence Osborne

Lawrence Osborne (b. 1958) was educated at Cambridge and Harvard universities. He has been a contributor to the New York Times Magazine, Salon, *and the* New York Observer *and has written a novel,* Ania Malina *(1986); a travelogue,* Paris Dreambook *(1992); a book about autism,* American Normal *(2002); and* The Accidental Connoisseur *(2004). In the following essay (2002), Osborne reports on a farm where genetically modified goats produce the silk of spiders in their milk.*

How do Webster and Pete, the world's first goats to have spider genes (in 2002), foreshadow the transgenic future discussed by Osborne?

GOT SILK

As soon as I walk into the humid goat shed in my Tyvek suit and sterilized boots, a dozen Nubians run up to the fence and begin sniffing at me, their Roman noses dilated with fervent curiosity. "They're a little frisky," a technician explains, shooing them back toward their playpen toys. "It's artificial insemination time, you know."

The technician, a young woman in galoshes named Annie Bellemare, and two colleagues are playing a trick on a long-bearded billy goat. Leading him up to a female in heat, they let him mount her; but at the last moment, they whip out a warmed, rubber-lined bottle and have him discharge into it. "There," they cry, holding up a phial of goat semen. "Good boy!"

I look around the pen. Hundreds of sly-looking, inquisitive goats are staring at me intently. They seem unexceptional enough, but the goats that are being bred here are far from ordinary. This is a so-called transgenic farm—a place where animal species are either cloned or genetically mixed to create medically useful substances—owned and run by a firm named Nexia Biotechnologies. It is housed on a former maple-sugar farm in rural Quebec, not far from the remote hamlet of St.-Telesphore. Nexia's facility is one of only three transgenic farms in the world. (One of the company's rivals, PPL Therapeutics, runs the farm in Scotland that collaborated in the production of the famous sheep clone, Dolly.)

Out here in this tough French-speaking farming country, however, hardly anybody gets worked up about the fact that on the old St.-Telesphore sugar farm, a new chapter in biotechnology is being written. Nexia scientists are pursuing a bizarre experiment straight out of *The Island of Dr. Moreau*, H. G. Wells's dark science-fiction fable of a mad scientist who breeds experimental animals on his private preserve.

"Oh, it's not that weird," Nexia's president and CEO, Jeffrey D. Turner, says as   5
we walk around the pens, being nibbled constantly by aroused goats. "What we're doing here is ingeniously simple," he says. "We take a single gene from a golden orb-weaving spider and put it into a goat egg. The idea is to make the goat secrete spider silk into its milk."

Milk silk?

Turner, a bouncy 43-year-old scientist turned biotech entrepreneur, makes a sweeping gesture at his bleating production units. "Spider silk is practically the world's strongest material," he explains. "It's much stronger than steel—five times as strong. We're going to make fishing lines out of it."

I raise my eyebrows dubiously.

"Yes. Biodegradable fishing lines. Or maybe tennis racket strings." He grows even more animated. "You could make hundreds of things out of spider silk, if only you could produce enough of it. Biodegradable sutures for surgery . . . replacement ligaments or tendons . . . hemostatic dressings . . . fashion. We call our product BioSteel."

Turner isn't simply fantasizing. Nexia foresees tapping into the $500 million mar-   10
ket for fishing materials as well as the $1.6 billion market for industrial fibers in the near future. And the haute-couture world is already intrigued by a nearly weightless gossamer-like fabric. But the real gold mine might be body armor: the Pentagon is working with Nexia to develop a prototype of a new kind of vest that might be made entirely out of goat silk. The vest would be only a little thicker than nylon, but it could stop a bullet dead.

"It's nothing short of a revolution," Turner exclaims. "This special silk is the first transgenic material ever made. The amazing thing, however, is that we're changing the world from a tiny low-rent sugar farm, and our only machinery is a goat."

Turner is very affectionate with his goats. A number of different species are being tested for the spider-gene project. In one pen a gang of floppy-eared Nubians frolic and duel, raising themselves on their back legs and then clashing foreheads. Next door live the Saanens from Switzerland, all of them white, rather meeker and well mannered, quietly cocking their heads at the sound of human voices. Across the way stand a dozen West African Dwarf goats (once used by the Hamburg Zoo as food for big cats from Africa).

"We use West African Dwarf goats because they're sexually active all year round," Turner says. "Unlike American goats, which are only active in the fall and spring." He winks. "The African goats get sexually mature in three months. This helps reach the output potential quicker."

Turner once again admires his flock. "You could call them Spidergoats," he says. "But that would give people misconceptions. They're only 1/70,000th spider, after all. When it comes down to it, they're just normal goats with one spider gene in them. They're just goats." He pauses. "Mostly."

Scientists have been tinkering with the DNA of animals for years. Researchers have   15
inserted into rhesus monkeys the gene that makes jellyfish glow in the dark; they've produced chickens that never grow feathers. But only recently have they begun to develop large-scale industrial plans for these creatures. For example, a company in Georgia

called ProLinia has cloned cattle and hogs to produce more genetically desirable breeding stock. After scientists at Johns Hopkins produced enormous "supermice" by removing the gene that limits muscle growth, researchers have scrambled to create the same results in sheep, pigs and chickens.

Inevitably, some bioethicists are alarmed by these projects. And Turner agrees that some of these experiments are creepy.

"Why do we need cloned sheep?" he asks. "What the hell's the use of millions of cloned sheep? Dolly was a scientific stunt." He tells me that Nexia's project is less about altering nature than harnessing it. The company's goal isn't to create weird goats; they're merely a means of producing useful quantities of spider silk, a simple substance created eons ago by natural evolution. Turner says that what Nexia is really up to isn't mere genetic engineering, it's "biomimicry."

In her 1997 book, *Biomimicry,* Janine M. Benyus observed that while humans create synthetic materials by means of high temperatures and pressures ("heat, beat and treat" methods, as they are known), nature does so under life-friendly conditions. That is to say, in water, at room temperature and without harsh chemicals. "Nature's crystals are finer, more densely packed, more intricately structured and better suited to their tasks than our ceramics and metals are suited to ours," Benyus observes. Inspired by this, materials scientists are now looking to merge biology and engineering—the natural and human-made.

"In the future, animals will be our factories," Turner says as we plod through the facility. "Very cheap factories."

This is a land of silos and bleached cherry-red barns, somewhere between the St.   20
Lawrence and Ottawa Rivers. "We need to be where people aren't," Turner explains. Nexia's converted *cabane a sucre* and the surrounding land, purchased five years ago from a local farmer, look sweetly ordinary. But the new facilities are meticulously de-contaminated. The company's corporate headquarters are just 15 miles down the road, rising from the flatlands of Vaudreuil-Dorion like a futuristic castle keep. Inside, the corridors are freshly carpeted and sunlit; the labs are shiny and uncluttered and stocked with the latest gadgets. These labs are known as "Class-100,000 rooms," which means that each cubic yard of air contains less than 100,000 motes of dust. Staff members proudly show me the latest PCR (polymerase chain reaction) machines—the photo-copiers of the gene world—that look like high-tech adding machines. Pinned to the walls are some curious images derived from what is known as FISH analysis. (The acronym stands for Fluorescent In Situ Hybridization.) These images show the goat genes as ghostly strands of dark orange, inside which one can clearly see the bright yellow segments of alien spider silk genes. Nearby are cute pinups of Nexia's original four transgenic goats, Willow, Bay, Santiago and Zeus.

Nexia used cloning to make its four founder animals, though the descendant animals are allowed to breed sexually. One pic shows Willow, Canada's first transgenic farm animal, posing coquettishly on a little orange plastic bobbin. I am told that she is, in fact, 1/70,000th human. This is because she has been specifically engineered to manufacture proteins for use in medical drugs like clot-busters, another source of income for Nexia. I look at her closely. Am I going mad or do I detect a human gleam in her eye?

How does a spider gene get into goat milk in the first place? Nexia uses two common spider specimens, *Araneus diadematus* (the common garden spider) and *Nephila clavipes* (the golden orb weaver, native to many tropical forests). The spiders are frozen in liquid nitrogen, then ground into a brown powder. Since every cell of a spider contains the precious silk-producing genes, it's easy to extract them. These genes are then tested in the "Charlotte machine," what Turner calls a "synthetic goat" that tests whether or not the gene will function inside an actual goat.

Next, the gene is altered. A "genetic switch" is added, which programs the gene to "turn on" only inside the mammary gland of its new female host during lactation. The altered gene is then pushed on a fine glass pipette into a goat egg. The baby goat will have a spider gene present in each of its cells (its eyes, ears and hooves will all be part spider), but only in the mammary glands of female goats will the silk gene actually spring to life. The goat will eventually start lactating a kind of silk-milk mixture, which looks and tastes just like normal milk.

This milk is first skimmed of fat, and salt is added to make the silk proteins curdle into thin whitish particles that promptly sink to the bottom. After the residue has been removed from the milk, a little water is added to this sediment until it turns into a golden-tinged syrup. This silk concentrate is known to scientists as "spin dope" and is more or less identical to what is inside a spider's belly. Now completely stripped from its milky context, the syrupy raw silk is ready for spinning.

Nexia's labs are packed with odd machines that replicate a spider's anatomy. First there is an extrusion machine, a strange-looking three-foot-tall apparatus bristling with aluminum pipes, designed to force the raw silk material through a tiny hole. As the silk comes out through this aperture, it is immediately stretched inside a long steel bathtub—at full tilt, roughly a hundred yards of it an hour.

Then the silk, which is transparently shiny with a white tinge, is taken to a spinner and strung out between two spindles a yard apart, which stretch the threads out as finely as possible. The idea is to do what a spider does naturally: subject the silk to tremendous stretching, or "shearing." This not only elongates it but actually strengthens the material as well. After being spun and wound around a plastic bobbin, some of the threads are then passed to a tensile tester, which measures their strength. In the production room, Turner hands me a few 20-micron-wide strands, frail as gossamer. The difficulty, he says, is making the silk as evenly as a spider does.

As we pass through yet more rooms filled with liquid nitrogen tanks where frozen goat semen and ova are stored, Turner explains to me the enigmatic inner world of spiders and their miraculous silk and their connection to modern needs.

Four hundred million years ago, he begins excitedly, spiders were doing just fine as ground hunters until one day bugs started flying. "The spider's evolution comes out of a kind of arms race between spiders and bugs. The bugs start flying to get away from the spiders, so the spiders have to come up with a new weapon." Most spider species died out, but a few developed a new talent, namely, spinning webs. The silk had to both be invisible to a bug's vision and virtually indestructible. Only spiders capable of making superfine, powerful silk survived—a perfect example of evolutionary pressure.

What's special about spider silk, as opposed to silk from worms, is that it is a unique liquid crystal. And that's what's magical, says Turner. "Liquid crystals are the Holy Grail of material sciences. They make for incredibly tough, light, strong materials with phenomenal properties. It's way beyond anything we humans can make. Milled steel pales next to it."

But the complexity of arachnid silk is also what is problematic about it, from the   30
point of view of biomimicry. Spider-silk proteins consist of very long strings of amino
acids that are difficult to decode, and little is known of how spiders actually unravel
them and spin them into threads. A spider, moreover, constructs its web methodically
out of different kinds of silk. It builds diagonal support lines called "dragline silk"
(which it also uses to hoist itself around its web) and then inner wheels called "the
capture spiral" made from a more viscid, sticky silk. Dragline silk, says Turner, is the
"best stopping material you've ever seen," but how it's actually made inside a small orb
weaver's abdomen remains mysterious. And whereas spiders produce up to seven kinds
of silk proteins, BioSteel, as yet, contains only one.

As a result, BioSteel doesn't have all the resistant strength of spider silk—yet. Part
of the mystery of spider silk's tremendous strength, current research suggests, lies in the
spinning rather than in the internal chemistry of the silk itself. It seems that the silk proteins self-assemble as they are squeezed out of the spider's glands much like toothpaste
being squeezed out of a tube. The stretching spontaneously causes the proteins to line
up and lock into each other. "That's why we've spent so much money on these extrusion machines," Turner says. "The secret is in the spinning."

In any case, the properties of spider silk have long been recognized. Fishermen in
India have always prized it for the making of their nets; American Civil War soldiers
frequently used it as a surgical dressing. The problem lay always in getting sufficient
quantities of it. Whereas silkworms are peaceful herbivores and can easily be farmed,
spiders are aggressive territorial carnivores that need plenty of space and solitude. In
farm conditions, they moodily attack and eat each other.

Farming zillions of spiders, then, is far too tricky. But farming peaceable goats is
a cinch. Yet how to get the desirable material from a rather nasty predator like a spider into the reproductive system of a kindly animal like a Nubian goat? Enter the odd
subject of mammary glands.

The mammary gland is a perfect natural factory for the synthesizing and production of proteins. It occurred to Turner, who had been working on lactation at McGill
University's animal sciences department in the mid-to-late '80s, that, theoretically, one
could introduce foreign genes into an animal's mammary gland and get any given protein out of the animal without killing it, much as one milks a cow. Given the enormous
expense of manufacturing drugs artificially, transgenic animals offered a brilliant way
to make dirt-cheap drugs; $50,000 worth of proteins could be extracted from a few
buckets of milk at a cost of about $12 of hay! The logic seemed irresistible: the udder
as factory outlet.

In 1993, Turner was approached by the two venture-capitalist godfathers of   35
Canada's budding biotech industry, Bernard Coupal and Ed Rygiel. They had heard of
his work at McGill and were interested in finding a way to create a transgenic goat.
But where most transgenics is concentrated on making drugs, Turner, Coupal and Rygiel eventually wondered if it might not be more practical, and less risky, to concentrate on materials. For one thing, they realized, it's almost impossible for small
companies to manufacture drugs. But a simple material that doesn't need FDA approval is quite another thing. And when they considered the possible uses of spider
silk, they were astounded.

"Humans never think about size," Turner says. "If an animal doesn't make stuff on a scale we understand, we just ignore it. But insects and marine animals, although they're tiny, make incredible materials that we could use. Who's to say we can't?"

Nexia doesn't only farm goats in St.-Telesphore. It also has ambitious plans to turn an old Air Force base on the American side of the border into its mass-production facility for BioSteel. As I approach this decommissioned base just outside Plattsburgh, New York, I look through the miles of lonely fencing at the old concrete bunkers where nuclear missiles were most likely housed. They rise from the ground like ancient tombs covered with grass. A few floppy-eared Nubian goats stand incongruously on top of them, wagging their tails and bleating.

Nexia's sympathetic farm manager, Thomas Ballma, tells me that the goats just love rolling down the grassy sides in summer. "We can't hardly control them," he says as he shows me the inside of a newly refurbished bunker coated with epoxy paint. Inside the 80-foot-long cave our voices echo ominously as he points out with some pride the new ventilation ducts and electric cables. Nexia is trying to breed as many goats here as it can. From the present 302 goats they hope to have 1,500 a year from now.

We wander into one of the inhabited bunkers, where dozens of mop-haired Angoras jump to attention. Then they come trundling over to us en masse, licking our hands and cocking their heads inquisitively. I remark that the country music playing on the loud-speakers is rather loud. Is that Dolly Parton?

"Oh, they love Dolly Parton," Ballma says. "Country music has the steadiest beat.   40
It keeps them calm and happy. Heavy metal, though, gets them agitated."

A shipment of goats has just arrived from Georgia, and as we stroll around the gigantic half-abandoned base, Ballma tells me how Nexia has revitalized the sagging post–Cold War economy of Plattsburgh. "It's been a godsend," he admits. "Even though it seems a little improbable. I've been raising goats for years, I love them, so at first the idea of making them secrete spider silk kind of weirded me out. But now I understand it. It's not what people think."

"Not Dr. Moreau?" I ask.

"No! We're just making fishing nets here. It's pretty normal, really."

As we stand in the old air-control tower overlooking the base I can hear a faint bleating of happy goats. From nuclear bombs to transgenic goats, it seems a strange progression, I say.

"Sure," he replies. "But perhaps it's just our own cleverness that weirds us out."   45

Questions for Discussion and Writing

1. The genetic engineering that produces transgenic animals (such as the goat) offers a preview that raises basic questions about corporations that invent and control new life forms as well as a myriad of bioethical concerns. Where does Osborne touch on these anxieties?

2. How does Osborne's language reflect the optimism and anxieties of this new field? How do the *Spider-Man* films fictionalize this research?

3. If you could genetically engineer your future children to possess any traits you wished, would you do so? Why or why not? If so, what would these characteristics be?

Umberto Eco

. . . .

Umberto Eco (b. 1932) is a professor of semiotics at the University of Bologna, Italy. His innovative novels include The Name of the Rose *(1994) and* The Island of the Day Before *(1995). In addition to scholarly works such as* Kant and the Platypus *(1999), Eco has written collections of popular essays, including* How to Travel with a Salmon *(1995), in which the following essay first appeared. Eco's latest works include* Five Moral Pieces, *translated by Alastair McEwen (2001), and* Baudolino, *translated by William Weaver (2002).*

HOW NOT TO USE THE FAX MACHINE AND THE CELLULAR PHONE

The fax machine is truly a great invention. For anyone still unfamiliar with it, the fax works like this: you insert a letter, you dial the number of the addressee, and in the space of a few minutes the letter has reached its destination. And the machine isn't just for letters: it can send drawings, plans, photographs, pages of complicated figures impossible to dictate over the telephone. If the letter is going to Australia, the cost of the transmission is no more than that of an intercontinental call of the same duration. If the letter is being sent from Milan to Saronno, it costs no more than a directly dialed call. And bear in mind that a call from Milan to Paris, in the evening hours, costs about a thousand lire. In a country like ours, where the postal system, by definition, doesn't work, the fax machine solves all your problems. Another thing many people don't know is that you can buy a fax for your bedroom, or a portable version for travel, at a reasonable price. Somewhere between a million five and two million lire. A considerable amount for a toy, but a bargain if your work requires you to correspond with many people in many different cities.

Unfortunately, there is one inexorable law of technology, and it is this: when revolutionary inventions become widely accessible, they cease to be accessible. Technology is inherently democratic, because it promises the same services to all; but it works only if the rich are alone in using it. When the poor also adopt technology, it stops working. A train used to take two hours to go from A to B; then the motor car arrived, which could cover the same distance in one hour. For this reason cars were very expensive. But as soon as the masses could afford to buy them, the roads became jammed, and the trains started to move faster. Consider how absurd it is for the authorities constantly to urge people to use public transport, in the age of the automobile; but with public transport, by consenting not to belong to the elite, you get where you're going before members of the elite do.

In the case of the automobile, before the point of total collapse was reached, many decades went by. The fax machine, more democratic (in fact, it costs much less than a car), achieved collapse in less than a year. At this point it is faster to send something through the mail. Actually, the fax encourages such postal communications. In the old days, if you lived in Medicine Hat, and you had a son in Brisbane, you wrote him once a week and you telephoned him once a month. Now, with the fax, you can send him, in no time, the snapshot of his newborn niece. The temptation is irresistible. Furthermore, the world is inhabited by people, in an ever-increasing number, who want to tell you something that is of no interest to you: how to choose a smarter investment, how to purchase a given object, how to make them happy by sending them a check, how to fulfill yourself completely by taking part in a conference that will improve your professional status. All of these people, the moment they discover you have a fax, and unfortunately there are now fax directories, will trample one another underfoot in their haste to send you, at modest expense, unrequested messages.

As a result, you will approach your fax machine every morning and find it swamped with messages that have accumulated during the night. Naturally, you throw them away without having read them. But suppose someone close to you wants to inform you that you have inherited ten million dollars from an uncle in America, but on condition that you visit a notary before eight o'clock: if the well-meaning friend finds the line busy, you don't receive the information in time. If someone *has* to get in touch with you, then, he has to do so by mail. The fax is becoming the medium of trivial messages, just as the automobile has become the means of slow travel, for those who have time to waste and want to spend long hours in gridlocked traffic, listening to Mozart or Dire Straits.

Finally, the fax introduces a new element into the dynamics of nuisance. Until   5
today, the bore, if he wanted to irritate you, paid (for the phone call, the postage stamp, the taxi to bring him to your doorbell). But now you contribute to the expense, because you're the one who buys the fax paper.

How can you react? I have already had letterhead printed with the warning "Unsolicited faxes are automatically destroyed," but I don't think that's enough. If you want my advice, I'd suggest keeping your fax disconnected. If someone has to send you something, he has to call you first and ask you to connect the machine. Of course, this can overload the telephone line. It would be best for the person who has to send a fax to write you first. Then you can answer, "Send your message via fax Monday at 5.05.27 P.M., Greenwich mean time, when I will connect the machine for precisely four minutes and thirty-six seconds."

It is easy to take cheap shots at the owners of cellular phones. But before doing so, you should determine to which of the five following categories they belong.

First come the handicapped. Even if their handicap is not visible, they are obliged to keep in constant contact with their doctor or the 24-hour medical service. All praise, then, to the technology that has placed this beneficent instrument at their service. Second come those who, for serious professional reasons, are required to be on call in case of emergency (fire chiefs, general practitioners, organ-transplant specialists always awaiting a fresh corpse, or President Bush, because if he is ever unavailable, the world falls into the hands of Quayle). For them the portable phone is a harsh fact of life, endured, but hardly enjoyed. Third, adulterers. Finally, for the first time in their lives, they are able to receive messages from their secret lover without the risk that family members, secretaries, or malicious colleagues will intercept the call. It suffices that the number be known only to him and her (or to him and him, or to her and her: I can't think of any other possible combinations). All three categories listed above are entitled to our respect. Indeed, for the first two we are willing to be disturbed even while dining in a restaurant, or during a funeral; and adulterers are very discreet, as a rule.

Two other categories remain. These, in contrast, spell trouble (for us and for themselves as well). The first comprises those persons who are unable to go anywhere unless they have the possibility of chattering about frivolous matters with the friends and relations they have just left. It is hard to make them understand why they shouldn't do it. And finally, if they cannot resist the compulsion to interact, if they cannot enjoy their moments of solitude and become interested in what they themselves are doing at that moment, if they cannot avoid displaying their vacuity and, indeed, make it their trademark, their emblem, well, the problem must be left to the psychologist. They irk us, but we must understand their terrible inner emptiness, be grateful we are not as they are, and forgive them—without, however, gloating over our own superior natures, and thus yielding to the sins of spiritual pride and lack of charity. Recognize them as your suffering neighbor, and turn the other ear.

In the last category (which includes, on the bottom rung of the social ladder, the 10
purchasers of fake portable phones) are those people who wish to show in public that they are greatly in demand, especially for complex business discussions. Their conversations, which we are obliged to overhear in airports, restaurants, or trains, always involve monetary transactions, missing shipments of metal sections, an unpaid bill for a crate of neckties, and other things that, the speaker believes, are very Rockefellerian.

Now, helping to perpetuate the system of class distinctions is an atrocious mechanism ensuring that, thanks to some atavistic proletarian defect, the nouveau riche, even when he earns enormous sums, won't know how to use a fish knife or will hang a plush monkey in the rear window of his Ferrari or put a San Gennaro on the dashboard of his private jet, or (when speaking his native Italian) use English words like "management." Therefore he will not be invited by the Duchesse de Guermantes (and he will rack his brain trying to figure out why not; after all, he has a yacht so long it could almost serve as a bridge across the English Channel).

What these people don't realize is that Rockefeller doesn't need a portable telephone; he has a spacious room full of secretaries so efficient that at the very worst, if his grandfather is dying, the chauffeur comes and whispers something in his ear. The man with power is the man who is not required to answer every call; on the contrary, he is always—as the saying goes—in a meeting. Even at the lowest managerial level, the two symbols of success are a key to the executive washroom and a secretary who asks, "Would you care to leave a message?"

So anyone who flaunts a portable phone as a symbol of power is, on the contrary, announcing to all and sundry his desperate, subaltern position, in which he is obliged to snap to attention, even when making love, if the CEO happens to telephone; he has to pursue creditors day and night to keep his head above water; and he is persecuted by the bank, even at his daughter's First Holy Communion, because of an overdraft. The fact that he uses, ostentatiously, his cellular phone is proof that he doesn't know these things, and it is the confirmation of his social banishment, beyond appeal.

Questions for Discussion and Writing

1. For Eco, what is ironic about the elevated value these gadgets have for us?
2. Do you agree with Eco's point that people who use cellular phones as a way of displaying their importance are ironically advertising quite the opposite? Explain your answer.
3. In your opinion, should the use of cellular phones be restricted in public places such as theaters and restaurants? Why or why not? Based on your experiences, what effects have the cellular phone and the fax machine had on business and social interactions? What gadgets (such as the Palm Pilot) have now come to represent status? Write your own Eco-like spoof on one of these.

Bill McKibben

· ·

Bill McKibben (b. 1960) is best known as the author of an international best-seller about global warming, The End of Nature *(1989). He publishes regularly in the* Atlantic Monthly, Harper's Magazine, *and the* New York Review of Books. *His most recent work is* Enough: Staying Human in an Engineered Age *(2003). He is currently a scholar-in-residence at Middlebury College. In the following essay, which first appeared in* Mother Jones *(July/August 2002), McKibben relates his experiences with his new hybrid electric car. He inveighs against the shortsighted addiction Americans have by driving SUVs and other energy-wasting, inefficient practices so pervasive in our culture.*

IT'S EASY BEING GREEN

The more I surveyed my new car, the happier I got. "New car" is one of those phrases that make Americans unreasonably happy to begin with. And this one—well, it was a particularly shiny metallic blue. Better yet, it was the first Honda Civic hybrid electric sold in the state of Vermont: I'd traded in my old Civic (40 miles to the gallon), and now the little screen behind the steering wheel was telling me that I was getting 50, 51, 52 miles to the gallon. Even better yet, I was doing nothing strange or difficult or conspicuously ecological. If you didn't know there was an electric motor assisting the small gas engine—well, you'd never know. The owner's manual devoted far more space to the air bags and the heating system. It didn't look goofily Jetsonish like Honda's first hybrid, the two-seater Insight introduced in 2000. Instead, it looked like a Civic, the most vanilla car ever produced. "Our goal was to make it look, for lack of a better word, normal," explained Kevin Bynoe, spokesman for American Honda.

And the happier I got, the angrier I got. Because, as the Honda and a raft of other recent developments powerfully proved, energy efficiency, energy conservation, and renewable energy are ready for prime time. No longer the niche province of incredibly noble backyard tinkerers distilling biodiesel from used vegetable oil or building homes from Earth rammed into tires, the equipment and attitudes necessary to radically transform our energy system are now mainstream enough for those of us too lazy or too busy to try anything that seems hard. And yet the switch toward sensible energy still isn't happening. A few weeks before I picked up my car, an overwhelming bipartisan vote in the Senate had rejected calls to increase the mileage of the nation's new car fleet by 2015—to increase it to 36 mpg, not as good as the Civic I'd traded in to buy this hybrid. The administration was pressing ahead with its plan for more drilling and refining. The world was suffering the warmest winter in history as more carbon dioxide pushed global temperatures ever higher. And people were dying in conflicts across wide swaths of the world, the casualties—at least in some measure—of America's insatiable demand for energy.

In other words, the gap between what we could be doing and what we are doing has never been wider. Consider:

- The Honda I was driving was the third hybrid model easily available in this country, following in the tire tracks of the Insight and the Toyota Prius. They take regular gas, they require nothing in the way of special service, and they boast waiting lists. And yet Detroit, despite a decade of massive funding from the Clinton administration, can't sell you one. Instead, after September 11, the automakers launched a massive campaign (zero financing, red, white, and blue ads) to sell existing stock, particularly the gas-sucking SUVs that should by all rights come with their own little Saudi flags on the hood.

- Even greater boosts in efficiency can come when you build or renovate a home. Alex Wilson, editor of *Environmental Building News,* says the average American house may be 20 percent more energy efficient than it was two decades ago, but simple tweaks like better windows and bulkier insulation could save 30 to 50 percent more energy with "very little cost implication." And yet building codes do almost nothing to boost such technologies, and the Bush administration is fighting to roll back efficiency gains for some appliances that Clinton managed to push through. For instance, air-conditioner manufacturers recently won a battle in the Senate to let them get away with making their machines only 20 percent more efficient, not the 30 percent current law demands. The difference in real terms? Sixty new power plants across the country by 2030.

- Or consider electric generation. For a decade or two, environmentalists had their fingers crossed when they talked about renewables. It was hard to imagine most Americans really trading in their grid connection for backyard solar panels with their finicky batteries. But such trade-offs are less necessary by the day. Around the world, wind power is growing more quickly than any other form of energy—Denmark, Germany, Spain, and India all generate big amounts of their power from ultra-modern wind turbines. But in this country, where the never-ending breeze across the High Plains could generate twice as much electricity as the country uses, progress has been extraordinarily slow. (North Dakota, the windiest state in the union, has exactly four turbines.) Wind power is finally beginning to get some serious attention from the energy industry, but the technology won't live up to its potential until politicians stop subsidizing fossil fuels and give serious boosts to the alternatives.

And not all those politicians are conservative, either. In Massachusetts, even some true progressives, like the gubernatorial candidate Robert Reich, can't bring themselves to endorse a big wind installation proposed for six miles off Cape Cod. They have lots of arguments, most of which boil down to NIVOMD (Not in View of My Deck), a position particularly incongruous since Cape Cod will sink quickly beneath the Atlantic unless every weapon in the fight against global warming is employed as rapidly as possible.

What really haunts energy experts is the sense that, for the first time since the oil 5 shocks of the early 1970s, the nation could have rallied around the cause of energy conservation and renewable alternatives last fall. In the wake of September 11, they agree, the president could have announced a pair of national goals—capture Osama and free ourselves from the oil addiction that leaves us endlessly vulnerable. "President Bush's failure will haunt me for decades," says Alan Durning, president of Northwest Environment Watch. "Bush had a chance to advance, in a single blow, three pressing national priorities: national security, economic recovery, and environmental protection. All the stars were aligned." If only, says Brent Blackwelder, president of Friends of the Earth, Bush had set a goal, like JFK and the space program. "We could totally get off oil in three decades." Instead, the president used the crisis to push for drilling in the Arctic National Wildlife Refuge, a present to campaign contributors that would yield a statistically insignificant new supply ten years down the road.

It's not just new technologies that Bush could have pushed, of course. Americans were, at least for a little while, in the mood to do something, to make some sacrifice, to rally around some cause. In the words of Charles Komanoff, a New York energy analyst, "The choice is between love of oil and love of country," and at least "in the initial weeks after September 11, it seemed that Americans were awakening at last to the true cost of their addiction to oil." In an effort to take advantage of that political window, Komanoff published a booklet showing just how simple it would be to cut America's oil use by 5 or 10 percent—not over the years it will take for the new technologies to really kick in, but over the course of a few weeks and with only minor modifications to our way of life.

For instance, he calculated, we could save 7 percent of the gasoline we use simply by eliminating one car trip in fourteen. The little bit of planning required to make sure you visit the grocery store three times a week instead of four would leave us with endlessly more oil than sucking dry the Arctic. Indeed, Americans are so energy-profligate that even minor switches save significant sums—if half the drivers in two-car households switched just a tenth of their travel to their more efficient vehicle, we'd instantly save 1 percent of our oil. Keep the damn Explorer; just leave it in the driveway once a week and drive the Camry.

A similar menu of small changes—cutting back on one airplane trip in seven, turning down the thermostat two degrees, screwing in a few compact fluorescent bulbs—and all of a sudden our endlessly climbing energy usage begins to decline. Impossible? Americans won't do it? Look at California. With the threat of power shortages looming and with some clever incentives provided by government and utilities, Californians last year found an awful lot of small ways to save energy that really added up: 79 percent reported taking some steps, and a third of households managed to cut their electric use by more than 20 percent. Not by becoming a Third World nation (the state's economy continued to grow), not by living in caves, not by suffering—but by turning off the lights when they left the room. In just the first six months of 2001, the Colorado energy guru Amory Lovins pointed out recently, "customers wiped out California's previous five to ten years of demand growth." Now the same companies that were scrambling to build new plants for the Golden State a year ago are backing away from their proposals, spooked by the possibility of an energy glut.

It's only in Washington, in fact, that nobody gets it. If you go to Europe or Asia, you'll find nations increasingly involved in planning for a different energy future: Every industrial country but the United States signed on to the Kyoto agreement at the last international conference on global warming, and some of those nations may actually meet their targets for carbon dioxide reductions. The Dutch consumer demand for green power outstrips even the capacity of their growing wind farms, while the Germans have taken the logical step of raising taxes on carbon-based fuels and eliminating them on renewable sources. Reducing fossil fuel use is an accepted, inevitable part of the political process on the Continent, the same way that "fighting crime" is in this country, and Europeans look with growing disgust at the depth of our addiction—only the events of September 11 saved America from a wave of universal scorn when Bush backed away from the Kyoto pact.

And in state capitols and city halls around this country, local leaders are begin-   10
ning to act as well. Voters in San Francisco last year overwhelmingly approved an initiative to require municipal purchases of solar and wind power; in Seattle, the mayor's office announced an ambitions plan to meet or beat the Kyoto targets within the confines of the city and four suburbs.

Perhaps such actions might be expected in San Francisco and Seattle. But in June of 2001, the Chicago city government signed a contract with Commonwealth Edison to buy 10 percent of its power from renewables, a figure due to increase to 20 percent in five years. And in Salt Lake City, of all places, Mayor Rocky Anderson announced on the opening day of the Winter Olympics that his city, too, was going to meet the Kyoto standards—already, in fact, crews were at work changing lightbulbs in street lamps and planning new mass transit.

Even many big American corporations have gone much further than the Bush administration. As Alex Wilson, the green building expert, points out, "Corporations are pretty good at looking at the bottom line, which is directly affected by operating costs. They're good with numbers." If you can make your product with half the energy, well, that's just as good as increasing sales—and if you can put a windmill on the cover of your annual report, that's gravy.

In short, what pretty much everyone outside the White House has realized is this: The great economic shift of this century will be away from fossil fuels and toward renewable energy. That shift will happen with or without George W. Bush—there are too many reasons, from environmental to economic to geopolitical necessity, for it not to. But American policy can slow down the transition, perhaps by decades, and that is precisely what the administration would like to see. They have two reasons: One is the enormous debt they owe to the backers of their political careers, those coal and oil and gas guys who dictated large sections of the new energy policy. Those industries want to wring every last penny from their mines, their drill rigs, and their refineries—

and if those extra decades mean that the planet's temperature rises a few degrees, well, that's business.

The other reason is just as powerful, though—it's the fear that Americans will blame their leaders if prices for gas go up too quickly. It's not an idle fear—certainly it was shared by Bill Clinton, who did nothing to stem the nation's love affair with SUVs, and by Al Gore, who, during his presidential campaign, demanded that the Strategic Petroleum Reserve be opened to drive down prices at the pump. But that's what makes Bush's post-September silence on this issue so sad. For once a U.S. president had the chance to turn it all around—to say that this was a sacrifice we needed to make and one that any patriot would support. It's tragically likely he will have the same opportunity again in the years ahead, and tragically unlikely that he will take it.

In the meantime, there's work to be done in statehouses and city halls. And at the car lot—at least the ones with the Honda and Toyota signs out front. "This Civic has a slightly different front end and a roof-mounted antenna," says Honda's Bynoe. "But other than that, it looks like a regular Civic, and it drives like one too. It's not necessarily for hard-core enviros. You don't have to scream about it at the top of your lungs. It's just a car." But a very shiny blue. And I just came back from a trip to Boston: 59 miles to the gallon.

Questions for Discussion and Writing

1. According to McKibben, how easy would it actually be for Americans to free themselves from their national "oil addiction"? Why didn't reforms take hold and become permanent after September 11, 2001?
2. How effectively does McKibben communicate his sense of bafflement as to why Americans tolerate such a self-serving, backward energy policy from both car companies and the government? Does his anger seem justified? Why or why not?
3. Of the suggestions (large and small) McKibben argues for, which seem the most plausible? Explain your answer.

Bill Gates

* *

Bill Gates (b. 1956) attended Harvard, where he wrote some of the first computer software programs. In 1975 (with Paul Allen), Gates started the company Microsoft, of which he is the chief executive officer. He is the author of The Road Ahead *(1995), from which the following selection is drawn, and of* Business @ the Speed of Thought: Using a Digital Nervous System *with Collins Hemingway (1999).*

How does this photo present Bill Gates as an educator as well as a visionary entrepreneur?

FROM *THE ROAD AHEAD*

I wrote my first software program when I was thirteen years old. It was for playing tic-tac-toe. The computer I was using was huge and cumbersome and slow and absolutely compelling. Letting a bunch of teenagers like me and my friend Paul Allen loose on a computer was the idea of the Mothers' Club at Lakeside, the private school I attended. The mothers decided that the proceeds from a rummage sale should be used to install a terminal and buy computer time for students, a pretty amazing choice at the time in Seattle—and one I'll always be grateful for.

I realized later part of the appeal was that here was an enormous, expensive, grown-up machine and we, the kids, could control it. We were too young to drive or to do any of the other fun-seeming adult activities, but we could give this big machine orders and it would always obey. It's feedback you don't get from many other things. That was the beginning of my fascination with software. And to this day it still thrills me to know that if I can get the program right it will always work perfectly, every time, just the way I told it to.

My parents paid my tuition at Lakeside and gave me money for books, but I had to take care of my own computer-time bills. This is what drove me to the commercial side of the software business. A bunch of us, including Paul, got entry-level software programming jobs. For high school students the pay was extraordinary—about $5,000 each summer, part in cash and the rest in computer time. One of the programs I wrote was the one that scheduled students in classes. I surreptitiously added a few instructions and found myself nearly the only guy in a class full of girls.

As a college sophomore, I stood in Harvard Square with Paul and pored over the description of a kit computer in *Popular Electronics* magazine. As we read excitedly about the first truly personal computer, Paul and I didn't know exactly how it would be used, but we were sure it would change us and the world of computing. We were right. The personal-computer revolution happened and it has affected millions of lives. It has led us to places we had barely imagined.

The Next Revolution

Now that computing is astoundingly inexpensive and computers inhabit every part of 5 our lives, we stand at the brink of another revolution. This one will involve unprecedentedly inexpensive communication; all the computers will join together to communicate with us and for us. Interconnected globally, they will form a network, which is being called the information highway. A direct precursor is the present Internet, which is a group of computers joined and exchanging information using current technology.

The revolution in communications is just beginning. It will take place over several decades, and will be driven by new "applications"—new tools, often meeting currently unforeseen needs. During the next few years, major decisions will have to be made by governments, companies, and individuals. These decisions will have an impact on the way the highway will roll out and how much benefit those deciding will realize. It is crucial that a broad set of people—not just technologists or those who happen to be in the computer industry—participate in the debate about how this technology should be shaped. If that can be done, the highway will serve the purposes users want. Then it will gain broad acceptance and become a reality.

In the United States, the connecting of all these computers has been compared to another massive project: the gridding of the country with interstate highways, which began during the Eisenhower era. This is why the new network was dubbed the "information superhighway." The highway metaphor isn't quite right, though. The phrase suggests landscape and geography, a distance between points, and embodies the implication that you have to travel to get from one place to another. In fact, one of the most remarkable aspects of this new communications technology is that it will eliminate distance. It won't matter if someone you're contacting is in the next room or on another continent, because this highly mediated network will be unconstrained by miles and kilometers.

A different metaphor that I think comes closer to describing a lot of the activities that will take place is that of the ultimate market. Markets from trading floors to malls are fundamental to human society, and I believe this new one will eventually be the world's central department store. It will be where we social animals will sell, trade, invest, haggle, pick stuff up, argue, meet new people, and hang out. Think of the hustle and bustle of the New York Stock Exchange or a farmers' market or of a bookstore full of people looking for fascinating stories and information. All manner of human activity takes place, from billion-dollar deals to flirtations.

The highway will enable capabilities that seem magical when they are described, but represent technology at work to make our lives easier and better. Because consumers already understand the value of movies and are used to paying to watch them, video-on-demand will be an important application on the information highway. It won't be the first, however. We already know that PCs will be connected long before television sets and that the quality of movies shown on early systems will not be very high. The systems will be able to offer other applications such as games, electronic mail, and home banking. When high-quality video can be transmitted, there won't be any intermediary VCR; you'll simply request what you want from a long list of available programs.

Television shows will continue to be broadcast as they are today for synchronous 10 consumption—at the same time they are first broadcast. After they air, these shows—as well as thousands of movies and virtually all other kinds of video—will be available whenever you want to view them. You'll be able to watch the new episode of "Seinfeld" at 9:00 P.M. on Thursday night, or at 9:13 P.M., or at 9:45 P.M., or at 11:00 A.M. on Saturday. If you don't care for his brand of humor, there will be thousands of other choices. Even if a show is being broadcast live, you'll be able to use your infrared remote control to start, stop, or go to any previous part of the program, at any time. If someone comes to your door, you'll be able to pause the program for as long as you like. You'll be in absolute control.

Your television set will not look like a computer and won't have a keyboard, but additional electronics inside or attached will make it architecturally like a PC. Television sets will connect to the highway via a set-top box similar to ones supplied today by most cable TV companies.

A World of "E-Books"

On the information highway, rich electronic documents will be able to do things no piece of paper can. The highway's powerful database technology will allow them to be indexed and retrieved using interactive exploration. It will be extremely cheap and easy to distribute them. In short, these new digital documents will replace many printed paper ones because they will be able to help us in new ways.

Ultimately, incremental improvements in computer and screen technology will give us a lightweight, universal electronic book or "e-book," which will approximate today's paperback book. Inside a case roughly the same size and weight as today's hardcover or paperback book, you'll have a display that can show high-resolution text, pictures, and video. You'll be able to flip pages with your finger or use voice commands.

The real point of electronic documents is not simply that we will read them on hardware devices. Going from paper book to e-book is just the final stage of a process already well under way. The exciting aspect of digital documentation is the redefinition of the document itself.

By the end of the decade a significant percentage of documents, even in offices, 15 won't even be fully printable on paper. They will be like a movie or a song is today. You will still be able to print a two-dimensional view of its content, but it will be like reading a musical score instead of experiencing an audio recording.

Electronic documents will be interactive. Request a kind of information, and the document responds. Indicate that you've changed your mind, and the document responds again. Once you get used to this sort of system, you find that being able to look at information in different ways makes that information more valuable. The flexibility invites exploration, and the exploration is rewarded with discovery.

You'll be able to get your daily news in a similar way. You'll be able to specify how long you want your newscast to last because you'll be able to have each of the news stories selected individually. The newscast assembled for and delivered only to you might include world news from NBC, the BBC, CNN, or the *Los Angeles Times*, with a weather report from a favorite local TV meteorologist—or from any private meteorologist who wanted to offer his or her own service. You will be able to request longer stories on the subjects that particularly interest you and just highlights on others. If, while you are watching the newscast, you want more than has been put together, you will easily be able to request more background or detail, either from another news broadcast or from file information.

Among all the types of paper documents, narrative fiction is one of the few that will not benefit from electronic organization. Almost every reference book has an index, but novels don't because there is no need to be able to look something up in a novel. Novels are linear. Likewise, we'll continue to watch most movies from start to finish. This isn't a technological judgment—it is an artistic one: Their linearity is intrinsic to the storytelling process.

The success of CD-ROM games has encouraged authors to begin to create interactive novels and movies in which they introduce the characters and the general outline of the plot, then the reader/player makes decisions that change the outcome of the story. No one suggests that every book or movie should allow the reader or viewer to influence its outcome. A good story that makes you just want to sit there for a few hours and enjoy it is wonderful entertainment. I don't want to choose an ending for "The Great Gatsby"[1] or "La Dolce Vita."[2] F. Scott Fitzgerald and Federico Fellini[3] have done that for me.

Significant investments will be required to develop great on-line content that will   20
delight and excite PC users and raise the number on-line from 10 percent up to 50 percent, or even the 90 percent I believe it will become. Part of the reason this sort of investment isn't happening today is that simple mechanisms for authors and publishers to charge their users or to be paid by advertisers are just being developed.

As the fidelity of visual and audio elements improves, reality in all its aspects will be more closely simulated. This "virtual reality," or VR, will allow us to "go" places and "do" things we never would be able to otherwise.

In order to work, VR needs two different sets of technology: software that creates the scene and makes it respond to new information, and devices that allow the computer to transmit the information to our senses. The software will have to figure out how to describe the look, sound, and feel of the artificial world down to the smallest detail. That might sound overwhelmingly difficult but actually it's the easy part. We could write the software for VR today, but we need far more computer power to make it truly believable. At the pace technology is moving, though, that power will be available soon.

---

[1]*The Great Gatsby:* 1925 novel acclaimed as a classic depiction of the Roaring Twenties, by American writer F. Scott Fitzgerald (1896–1940).   [2]*La Dolce Vita (1960):* celebrated Fellini film.   [3]*Frederico Fellini (1920–1993):* Italian film director whose works are known for their extravagant visual fantasy.

Inevitably, there has been more speculation (and wishful thinking) about virtual sex than about any other use for VR. Sexually explicit content is as old as information itself. If historical patterns are a guide, a big early market for advanced virtual-reality documents will be virtual sex. But again, historically, as each of these markets grew, explicit material became a smaller and smaller factor.

The Importance of Education

More than ever, an education that emphasizes general problem-solving skills will be important. In a changing world, education is the best preparation for being able to adapt. As the economy shifts, people and societies who are appropriately educated will tend to do best. The premium that society pays for skills is going to climb, so my advice is to get a good formal education and then keep on learning. Acquire new interests and skills throughout your life.

Some fear that technology will dehumanize formal education. But anyone who has seen kids working together around a computer, the way my friends and I first did in 1968, or watched exchanges between students in classrooms separated by oceans, knows that technology can humanize the educational environment. The same technological forces that will make learning so necessary will also make it practical and enjoyable. Just as information technology now allows Levi Strauss & Co. to offer jeans that are both mass-produced and custom fitted, information technology will bring mass customization to learning. Multimedia documents and easy-to-use authoring tools will enable teachers to "mass-customize" a curriculum for each student: computers will fine-tune the product—educational material, in this case—to allow students to follow somewhat divergent paths and learn at their own rates.

There is an often-expressed fear that technology will replace teachers. I can say emphatically and unequivocally, IT WON'T. The information highway won't replace or devalue any of the human educational talent needed for the challenges ahead: committed teachers, creative administrators, involved parents, and, of course, diligent students. However, technology will be pivotal in the future role of teachers.

Before the benefits of these advances can be realized, though, the way computers in the classroom are thought about will have to change. A lot of people are cynical about educational technology because it has been overhyped and has failed to deliver on its promises. Many of the PCs in schools today are not powerful enough to be easy to use, and they don't have the storage capacity or network connections to permit them to respond to a child's curiosity with much information.

When teachers do excellent work and prepare wonderful materials now, only their few dozen students benefit each year. The network will enable teachers to share lessons and materials, so that the best educational practices can spread. The interactive network also will allow students to quiz themselves any time, in a risk-free environment. A self-administered quiz is a form of self-exploration. Testing will become a positive part of the learning process. A mistake won't call forth a reprimand; it will trigger the system to help the student overcome his misunderstanding. The highway will also make home schooling easier. It will allow parents to select some classes from a range of quality possibilities and still maintain control over content.

The Impact on Society

Just because I'm optimistic doesn't mean I don't have concerns about what is going to happen to all of us. The broad benefits of advancing productivity are no solace for someone whose job is on the line. When a person has been trained for a job that is no longer needed, you can't just suggest he go out and learn something else. Adjustments aren't that simple or fast, but ultimately they are necessary

The fully developed information highway will be affordable—almost by defini- 30 tion. An expensive system that connected a few big corporations and wealthy people simply would not be the information highway—it would be the information private road. The network will not attract enough great content to thrive if only the most affluent 10 percent of society choose to avail themselves of it. There are fixed costs to authoring material; so to make them affordable, a large audience is required. Advertising revenue won't support the highway if a majority of eligible people don't embrace it. If that is the case, the price for connecting will have to be cut or deployment delayed while the system is redesigned to be more attractive. The information highway is a mass phenomenon, or it is nothing.

The net effect will be a wealthier world, which should be stabilizing. Developed nations, and workers in those nations, are likely to maintain a sizable economic lead. However, the gap between the have and have-not nations will diminish. Starting out behind is sometimes an advantage. Those who adopt late skip steps, and avoid the mistakes of the trailblazers. Some countries will never have industrialization but will move directly into the Information Age.

The information highway is going to break down boundaries and may promote a world culture, or at least a sharing of cultural activities and values. The highway will also make it easy for patriots, even expatriates, deeply involved in their own ethnic communities to reach out to others with similar interests no matter where they may be located. This may strengthen cultural diversity and counter the tendency toward a single world culture.

A complete failure of the information highway is worth worrying about. Because the system will be thoroughly decentralized, any single outage is unlikely to have a widespread effect. If an individual server falls, it will be replaced and its data restored. But the system could be susceptible to assault. As the system becomes more important, we will have to design in more redundancy. One area of vulnerability is the system's reliance on cryptography—the mathematical locks that keep information safe. None of the protection systems that exist today, whether steering-wheel locks or steel vaults, are completely fail-safe. The best we can do is make it as difficult as possible for somebody to break in. Still, popular opinions to the contrary, computer security has a very good record.

Loss of privacy is another major concern about the highway. A great deal of information is already being gathered about each of us, by private companies as well as by government agencies, and we often have no idea how it is used or whether it is accurate. As more business is transacted using the highway and the amount of information stored there accrues, governments will consciously set policies regarding privacy and access to information. The potential problem is abuse, not the mere existence of information.

These privacy fears revolve around the possibility that someone else is keeping 35 track of information about you. But the highway will also make it possible for an individual to keep track of his or her own whereabouts—to lead what we might call "a documented life." Your wallet PC will be able to keep audio, time, location, and eventually even video records of everything that happens to you. It will be able to record every word you say and every word said to you, as well as body temperature, blood pressure, barometric pressure, and a variety of other data about you and your surroundings. It will be able to track your interactions with the highway—all of the commands you issue, the messages you send, and the people you call or who call you. The resulting record will be the ultimate diary and autobiography, if you want one.

I find the prospect of documented lives a little chilling, but some people will warm to the idea. One reason for documenting a life will be defensive. If someone ever accused you of something, you could retort: "Hey, buddy, I have a documented life. These bits are stored away. I can play back anything I've ever said. So don't play games with me." Medical malpractice insurance might be cheaper, or only available, for doctors who record surgical procedures or even office visits. I can imagine proposals that every automobile, including yours and mine, be outfitted not only with a recorder but also with a transmitter that identifies the car and its location. If a car was reported stolen, its location would be known immediately. After a hit-and-run accident or a drive-by shooting, a judge could authorize a query: "What vehicles were in the following two-block area during this thirty-minute period?" The black box could record your speed and location, which would allow for the perfect enforcement of speeding laws. I would vote against that.

Even if the model of political decision making does not change explicitly, the highway will bestow power on groups who want to organize to promote causes or candidates. This could lead to an increased number of special-interest groups and political parties. Someone will doubtless propose total "direct democracy," having all issues put to a vote. Personally, I don't think direct voting would be a good way to run a government. There is a place in governance for representatives—middlemen—to add value. They are the ones who understand all the nuances of complicated issues. Politics involves compromise, which is nearly impossible without a relatively small number of representatives making decisions on behalf of the people who elected them.

We are watching something historic happen, and it will affect the world seismically, the same way the scientific method, the invention of printing, and the arrival of the Industrial Age did. Big changes used to take generations or centuries. This one won't happen overnight, but it will move much faster. The first manifestations of the information highway will be apparent in the United States by the millennium. Within a decade there will be widespread effects. If I had to guess which applications of the network will be embraced quickly and which will take a long time, I'd certainly get some wrong. Within twenty years virtually everything I've talked about will be broadly available in developed countries and in businesses and schools in developing countries.

Questions for Discussion and Writing

1. Considering Gates's role as visionary for the software industry, take a close look at his predictions about the transforming effects of the Internet. Which of these predictions have materialized and which have not since he wrote this piece in 1995?

2. What aspects of Gates's analysis might be intended to reply to fears about the downside of the electronic revolution?

3. What changes have you observed that Gates does not mention? What do you think "the next technological revolution" will be, and how will it affect our society?

4. Design a business card for yourself, an organization, a club, or a team that provides information with distinctive typeface and graphic elements. Also, make up a bumper sticker that expresses a message that includes words and images that work together to get your message across.

Henry Petroski

• •

Henry Petroski (b. 1942) is a professor of civil and environmental engineering at Duke University. His works explore engineering achievements from bridges to pencils in Engineers of Dreams: Great Bridge Builders and the Spanning of America *(1995),* Remaking the World: Adventures in Engineering (1997), Paper Boy: Confessions of a Future Engineer *(2002), and* The Pencil: A History of Design and Circumstance *(1990), in which the following selection first appeared.*

THE PENCIL

Henry David Thoreau seemed to think of everything when he made a list of essential supplies for a twelve-day excursion into the Maine woods. He included pins, needles, and thread among the items to be carried in an India-rubber knapsack, and he even gave the dimensions of an ample tent: "six by seven feet, and four feet high in the middle, will do." He wanted to be doubly sure to be able to start a fire and to wash up, and so he listed: "matches (some also in a small vial in the waist-coat pocket); soap, two pieces." He specified the number of old newspapers (three or four, presumably to be used for cleaning chores), the length of strong cord (twenty feet), the size of his blanket (seven feet long), and the amount of "soft hardbread" (twenty-eight pounds!). He even noted something to leave behind: "A gun is not worth the carriage, unless you go as a huntsman."

Thoreau actually was a huntsman of sorts, but the insects and botanical specimens that he hunted could be taken without a gun and could be brought back in the knapsack. Thoreau also went into the woods as an observer. He observed the big and the little, and he advised like-minded observers to carry a small spyglass for birds and a pocket microscope for smaller objects. And to capture the true dimensions of those objects that might be too big to be brought back, Thoreau advised carrying a tape measure. The inveterate measurer, note taker, and list maker also reminded other travelers to take paper and stamps, to mail letters back to civilization.

But there is one object that Thoreau neglected to mention, one that he most certainly carried himself. For without this object Thoreau could not have sketched either the fleeting fauna he would not shoot or the larger flora he could not uproot. Without it he could not label his blotting paper pressing leaves or his insect boxes holding beetles; without it he could not record the measurements he made; without it he could not write home on the paper he brought; without it he could not make his list. Without a pencil Thoreau would have been lost in the Maine woods.

According to his friend Ralph Waldo Emerson, Thoreau seems always to have carried, "in his pocket, his diary and pencil." So why did Thoreau—who had worked with his father to produce the very best lead pencils manufactured in America in the 1840s—neglect to list even one among the essential things to take on an excursion? Perhaps the very object with which he may have been drafting his list was too close to him, too familiar a part of his own everyday outfit, too integral a part of his livelihood, too common a thing for him to think to mention.

Henry Thoreau seems not to be alone in forgetting about the pencil. A shop in   5
London specializes in old carpenter's tools. There are tools everywhere, from floor to ceiling and spilling out of baskets on the sidewalk outside. The shop seems to have an example of every kind of saw used in recent centuries; there are shelves of braces and bins of chisels and piles of levels and rows of planes—everything for the carpenter, or so it seems. What the shop does not have, however, are old carpenter's pencils, items that once got equal billing in Thoreau & Company advertisements with drawing pencils for artists and engineers. The implement that was necessary to draw sketches of the carpentry job, to figure the quantities of materials needed, to mark the length of wood to be cut, to indicate the locations of holes to be drilled, to highlight the edges of wood to be planed, is nowhere to be seen. When asked where he keeps the pencils, the shopkeeper replies that he does not think there are any about. Pencils, he admits, are often found in the toolboxes acquired by the shop, but they are thrown out with the sawdust.

In an American antique shop that deals in, among other things, old scientific and engineering instruments, there is a grand display of polished brass microscopes, telescopes, levels, balances, and scales; there are the precision instruments of physicians, navigators, surveyors, draftsmen, and engineers. The shop also has a collection of old jewelry and silverware and, behind the saltcellars, some old mechanical pencils, which appear to be there for their metal and mystery and not their utility. There are a clever Victorian combination pen and pencil in a single slender, if ornate, gold case; an unassuming little tube of brass less than two inches long that telescopes out to become a mechanical pencil of twice that length; a compact silver pencil case containing points in three colors—black, red, and blue—that can be slid into writing position; and a heavy silver pencil case that hides the half-inch stub of a still-sharpened yellow pencil of high quality. The shopkeeper will proudly show how all these work, but when asked if she has any plain wood-cased drawing pencils that the original owners of the drafting instruments must certainly have used, she will confess that she would not even know what distinguished a nineteenth-century pencil from any other kind.

Not only shops that purport to trade in the past but also museums that ostensibly preserve and display the past can seem to forget or merely ignore the indispensable role of simple objects like the pencil. Recently the Smithsonian Institution's National Museum of American History produced "After the Revolution: Everyday Life in America, 1780–1800," and one group of exhibits in the show consisted of separate worktables on which were displayed the tools of many crafts of the period: cabinet-maker and chairmaker, carpenter and joiner, shipwright, cooper, wheelwright, and others. Besides tools, many of the displays included pieces of work in progress, and a few even had wood shavings scattered about the work space, to add a sense of authenticity. Yet there was not a pencil to be seen.

While many early American craftsmen would have used sharp-pointed metal scribers to mark their work, pencils would also certainly have been used when they were available. And although there was no domestic pencil industry in America in the years immediately following the Revolution, that is not to say that pencils could not be gotten. A father, writing in 1774 from England to his daughter in what were still the colonies, sent her "one dozen Middleton's best Pencils," and in the last part of the century, even after the Revolution, English pencils like Middleton's were regularly advertised for sale in the larger cities. Imported pencils or homemade pencils fashioned from reclaimed pieces of broken lead would have been the proud possessions of wood-workers especially, for carpenters, cabinetmakers, and joiners possessed the craft skill to work wood into a form that could hold pieces of graphite in a comfortable and useful way. Not only would early American woodworkers have known about, admired, wanted to possess, and tried to imitate European pencils, but also they would have prized and cared for them as they prized and cared for the kinds of tools displayed two centuries later in the Smithsonian.

These stories of absence are interesting not so much because of what they say about the lowly status of the wood-cased pencil as an artifact as because of what they say about our awareness of and our attitudes toward common things, processes, events, or even ideas that appear to have little intrinsic, permanent, or special value. An object like the pencil is generally considered unremarkable, and it is taken for granted. It is taken for granted because it is abundant, inexpensive, and as familiar as speech.

Yet the pencil need be no cliché. It can be as powerful a metaphor as the pen, as 10 rich a symbol as the flag. Artists have long counted the pencil among the tools of their trade, and have even identified with the drawing medium. Andrew Wyeth described his pencil as a fencer's foil; Toulouse-Lautrec said of himself, "I am a pencil"; and the Moscow-born Paris illustrator and caricaturist Emmanuel Poiré took his pseudonym from the Russian word for pencil, *karandash*. In turn, the Swiss pencil-making firm of Caran d'Ache was named after this artist, and a stylized version of his signature is now used as a company logo.

The pencil, the tool of doodlers, stands for thinking and creativity, but at the same time, as the toy of children, it symbolizes spontaneity and immaturity. Yet the pencil's graphite is also the ephemeral medium of thinkers, planners, drafters, architects, and engineers, the medium to be erased, revised, smudged, obliterated, lost—or inked over. Ink, on the other hand, whether in a book or on plans or on a contract, signifies finality and supersedes the pencil drafts and sketches. If early pencilings interest collectors, it is often because of their association with the permanent success written or drawn in ink. Unlike graphite, to which paper is like sandpaper, ink flows smoothly and fills in the nooks and crannies of creation. Ink is the cosmetic that ideas will wear when they go out in public. Graphite is their dirty truth.

A glance at the index to any book of familiar quotations will corroborate the fact that there are scores of quotations extolling the pen for every one, if that, mentioning the pencil. Yet, while the conventional wisdom may be that the pen is mightier than the sword, the pencil has come to be the weapon of choice of those wishing to make better pens as well as better swords. It is often said that "everything begins with a pencil," and indeed it is the preferred medium of designers. In one recent study of the nature of the design process, engineers balked when they were asked to record their thought processes with a pen. While the directors of the study did not want the subjects to be able to erase their false starts or alter their records of creativity, the engineers did not feel comfortable or natural without a pencil in their hands when asked to comment on designing a new bridge or a better mousetrap.

Leonardo da Vinci seems to have wished to make a better everything, as his notebooks demonstrate. And when he wanted to set down his ideas for some new device, or when he merely wanted to record the state of the art of Renaissance engineering, he employed a drawing. Leonardo also used drawings to preserve his observations of natural facts, artifacts, and assorted phenomena, and he even sketched his own hand sketching. This sketch is usually identified as Leonardo's left hand, consistent with the widely held belief that the genius was left-handed. This trait in turn has been given as a reason for his mirror writing. However, it has also been convincingly argued that Leonardo was basically right-handed and was forced to use his left hand because his right was crippled in an accident. Thus Leonardo's sketch may really be of his maimed right hand as seen in a mirror by the artist drawing with his fully functioning left hand. The shortened and twisted middle finger in the sketch supports this view.

The precise nature of the drawing instrument in Leonardo's hand may also be open to some interpretation, but it appears most likely to be a small brush known from Roman times as a pencil. The lead pencil as we know it today does not seem to have existed in Leonardo's lifetime (1452–1519). Some of his sketches were done in metal point, but drawing with a pointed rod of silver or some alloy usually had to done on specially coated paper so that an otherwise faint mark would be enhanced. Some drawings were first outlined in metalpoint and then more or less traced over with a pen or a fine-pointed brush dipped in ink. This was the only kind of pencil Leonardo knew.

Questions for Discussion and Writing

1. Why is it significant that Henry David Thoreau, of all people, should have neglected to mention the pencil when he was listing items needed for a twelve-day camping trip?

2. How do Petroski's anecdotes illustrate the fact that the pencil is so common that it has become all but invisible and a special effort is needed to discover how truly indispensable it has always been?

3. Discuss the distinction Petroski makes between what we write using a pencil and using a pen. What other items that are overlooked and taken for granted are really quite successful engineering achievements (for example, zippers, safety pins,

paper clips, sticky notes, and pop-top aluminum cans)? Research the history of any of these and write up your findings.

4. Is there a product or invention that you wish existed? Describe it, and create an advertising campaign that extolls its virtues.

FICTION

Chet Williamson

Chet Williamson was born in 1948 in Lancaster, Pennsylvania, and received a B.S. degree in 1970 from Indiana University (in Pennsylvania). After teaching public school in Cleveland and working as a professional actor, he became a freelance writer in 1986. Since then he has published nearly twenty books in the fields of science fiction and fantasy. Nearly a hundred of his short stories have appeared in magazines such as the New Yorker, Esquire, *and* Playboy, *where this story was first published in 1983. His novels include* Hell: A Cyberpunk Thriller *(1995),* Clash by Night *(1998), and* Pennsylvania Dutch Night Before Christmas *(2002). If you have ever wished you could delete your name from computerized mailing lists and spam e-mail, this amusing story will confirm your worst fears.*

THE PERSONAL TOUCH

Seed catalog—toss; Acme flier—keep for Mary; *Sports Illustrated*—keep; phone bill, electric bill, gas bill—keep, keep, keep. Damn it. Subscription-renewal notice to *Snoop*—toss. . . .

Joe Priddy tossed, but the envelope landed face up, balanced on the edge of the wastebasket. He was about to tip it in when he noticed the words PERSONAL MESSAGE INSIDE on the lower-left front.

Personal, my ass, he thought, but he picked it up and read it.

Dear **Mr. Pridy,**

We have not yet received your subscription renewal to SNOOP, the Magazine of Electronic and Personal Surveillance. We trust that, after having been a loyal subscriber for 9 months, you will renew your subscription so that we may continue to send SNOOP to you at **19 Merrydale Drive.**

We do not have to remind you, **Mr. Pridy,** of the constant changes in surveillance technology and techniques. We are sure that in your own town of **Sidewheel, NY,** you have seen the consequences for yourself. So keep up to date on the latest in surveillance, **Mr. Pridy,** by sending **$11.95** in the enclosed prepaid envelope today. As one involved and/or interested in the field of law enforcement, you cannot afford to be without SNOOP, **Mr. Pridy.**

Best Regards,

David Michaelson
Subscription Director

P.S.: If you choose not to resubscribe, **Mr. Pridy,** would you please take a moment and tell us why, using the enclosed post-paid envelope? Thank you, **Mr. Pridy.**

Joe shook his head. Who did they think they were fooling? "Pridy," said Joe to himself. "Jesus."

Mary's brother Hank had given Joe the subscription to *Snoop* for his birthday.   5
"As a joke," he'd said, winking at Joe lasciviously, a reference to the evening he and Hank had watched the Quincy girl undress in the apartment across the courtyard with the aid of Joe's binoculars. It had taken some imagination to satisfy Mary's curiosity about Hank's joke, and Joe still felt uncomfortable each time *Snoop* hit his mailbox. And now they wanted him to resubscribe?

He was about to toss the letter again when he thought about the P.S. "Tell us why." Maybe he'd do just that. It would get all his feelings about *Snoop* out of his system to let them know just how he felt about their "personal message."

Dear MR. MICHELSON,

I have chosen not to resubscribe to SNOOP after having received it for 9 MONTHS because I am sick and tired of computer-typed messages that try to appear personal. I would much rather receive an honest request to "Dear Subscriber" than the phony garbage that keeps turning up in my mailbox. So do us both a favor and don't send any more subscription renewal notices to me at 19 MERRYDALE DRIVE in my lovely town of SIDEWHEEL, NY. OK?

Worst regards,

Joseph H. Priddy

P.S.: And it's Priddy, not Pridy. Teach your word processor to spell.

Joe pulled the page out of the typewriter and stuffed it into the postpaid envelope.

Two weeks later, he received another subscription-renewal notice. As before, PERSONAL MESSAGE INSIDE was printed on the envelope. He was about to throw it away without opening it when he noticed his name was spelled correctly. "Small favors," he muttered, sitting on the couch with Mary and tearing the envelope open. Could they, he wondered, be responding to his letter?

Dear **Mr. Priddy,**

Christ, another word-processor job. . . . At least they got the name right. . . .

We received your recent letter and are sorry that you have chosen not to resubscribe to SNOOP, the Magazine of Electronic and Personal Surveillance. We hope, however, that you will reconsider, for if you resubscribe now at the low price of **$427.85** for the next nine issues

$427.85? What the hell? What happened to $11.95?   10

we will be able to continue your subscription uninterrupted, bringing you all the latest news and updates on surveillance technology and techniques. And in today's world, ***Mr. Priddy,*** such knowledge should not be taken lightly. You'll learn techniques similar to those that led New York City law-enforcement officials to the biggest heroin bust in history, that told members of the FBI of a plan to overthrow the state government of Montana by force, that alerted us to your own four-month affair with **Rayette Squires.**

Wha—Joe could feel the blood leave his face.

You'll get tips on photographic surveillance, as well, and learn techniques that will let your own efforts equal that of the enclosed 2 by 2 showing you and **Miss Squires at The Sidewheel Motel** in the lovely town of **Sidewheel, NY.**

Joe dove for the envelope, which was lying dangerously close to Mary's *McCall's*. He peeked as surreptitiously as possible into the envelope and found, between the slick paper flier and the return envelope, a well-lit color photo of him and Rayette in a compromising and fatiguing position. His wife looked up in response to his high-pitched whine, and he smacked the envelope shut, giggled weakly, and finished the letter.

We sincerely hope, **Mr. Priddy,** that you'll rejoin our family of informed subscribers by mailing your check for **$427.85** very soon. Shall we say within 10 days?

Regards,

David Michaelson
Subscription Director

Joe got up, envelope and letter in hand, and went to the bedroom to get out the shoe box he'd hidden—the one with the money he'd been squirreling away for an outboard motor, the money even Mary didn't know about.

When he counted it, it totaled $428.05. Which made sense. This time, the return envelope wasn't prepaid.

Questions for Discussion and Writing

1. How would you characterize the narrator? How is the story shaped as a confrontation between the narrator and the mail-order company?
2. How does Williamson structure his story so that the stakes escalate for Joe Priddy, the narrator? Why is the amount of $427.85 significant? What exactly is being satirized—computerized mass mailings, the narrator's naïveté, or something else?
3. Describe your own experiences with mass marketing by phone, fax, letter, or spam e-mail. For example, have you ever responded to a notification that you have won a prize or a vacation? What happened?

POETRY

Walt Whitman

* *

Walt Whitman (1819–1892) was born in then-rural Huntington, Long Island, into a family of Quakers. The family later moved to Brooklyn, then a city of fewer than 10,000, where he worked as a carpenter. He attended school briefly and in 1830 went to work as an office boy but soon turned to printing and journalism. Until the 1850s he worked as a newspaperman. He was the editor of the Brooklyn Eagle *from 1846 to 1848. In 1855, Whitman published the first of many editions of* Leaves of Grass, *a work that was to prove to be of unparalleled influence in establishing him as one of the most innovative figures of nineteenth-century poetry. In subsequent editions, he showed himself capable of writing long, intricately orchestrated poems that embrace the ideals of working-class democracy expressed in experimental free-verse rhythms and realistic imagery. When the Civil War broke out, Whitman was too old to enlist but went to the front in 1862 to be with his brother George, who had been reported wounded. During the remainder of the war, Whitman served as a nurse tending wounded soldiers, Union and Confederate alike. In "When I Heard the Learn'd Astronomer" (1865), Whitman contrasts the poet's disenchantment with the impersonal coldness of rational science with a mystical appreciation of nature.*

WHEN I HEARD THE LEARN'D ASTRONOMER

When I heard the learn'd astronomer,
When the proofs, the figures, were ranged in columns before me,
When I was shown the charts and diagrams, to add, divide, and measure them,
When I sitting heard the astronomer where he lectured with much applause in
   the lecture-room,
How soon unaccountable I became tired and sick,   5
Till rising and gliding out I wander'd off by myself,
In the mystical moist night-air, and from time to time,
Look'd up in perfect silence at the stars.

Questions for Discussion and Writing

1. How is Whitman's description of what the astronomer is trying to do critical of the scientist's approach? How does he feel listening to the astronomer's lecture?
2. What feelings does the speaker get from looking at the stars? What words best reflect this mood?
3. In a short essay, discuss Whitman's attitudes toward science and nature as expressed in this poem.

Peggy Seeger

* * * * * * * * * * * * * * * * * * *

Peggy Seeger was born in New York in 1935. She received training in both folk and classical music as a child and studied music at Radcliffe College, where she began performing folk songs publicly. After graduation, she traveled throughout Europe and China from 1955 to 1956, moved to Britain in 1956, and became a British subject in 1959. As a solo performer and with her husband, James Henry Miller, she played an important role in leading a British folk music revival. They have written music for radio, films, and television; made many records; and compiled scholarly anthologies of folk songs. "I'm Gonna Be an Engineer" (1970) brings together her many roles as folksinger, song collector, and songwriter as she adapts a traditional style of folk song to modern themes. A recent work is The Peggy Seeger Songbook: Warts and All: Forty Years of Songmaking *(1998).*

I'M GONNA BE AN ENGINEER

When I was a little girl, I wished I was a boy,
I tagged along behind the gang and wore my corduroys,
Everybody said I only did it to annoy
But I was gonna be an engineer.

Mamma told me, "Can't you be a lady?   5
Your duty is to make me the mother of a pearl.
Wait until you're older, dear, and maybe
You'll be glad that you're a girl."

    DAINTY AS A DRESDEN STATUE.
    GENTLE AS A JERSEY COW.   10
    SMOOTH AS SILK, GIVES CREAMY MILK
    LEARN TO COO, LEARN TO MOO,
    THAT'S WHAT YOU DO TO BE A LADY NOW—

When I went to school I learned to write and how to read,
Some history, geography, and home economy.   15
And typing is a skill that every girl is sure to need,
To while away the extra time until the time to breed,
And then they had the nerve to say, "What would you like to be?"
I says, "I'm gonna be an engineer!"
    No, you only need to learn to be a lady,   20
    The duty isn't yours for to try and run the world,
    An engineer could never have a baby!
    Remember, dear, that you're a girl.

    SHE'S SMART (FOR A WOMAN).
    I WONDER HOW SHE GOT THAT WAY?   25
    YOU GET NO CHOICE, YOU GET NO VOICE

JUST STAY MUM, PRETEND YOU'RE DUMB
AND THAT'S HOW YOU COME TO BE A LADY TODAY—

Then Jimmy come along and we set up a conjugation,
We were busy every night with loving recreation.   30
I spent my day at work so HE could get his education,
Well, now he's an engineer.
   He says, "I know you'll always be a lady,
   It's the duty of my darling to love me all her life,
   Could an *engineer* look after or obey me?   35
   Remember, dear, that you're my wife."

Well, as soon as Jimmy got a job, I began again,
Then, happy at my turret-lathe a year or so, and then:
The morning that the twins were born, Jimmy says to them,
"Kids, your mother *was* an engineer."   40
   You owe it to the kids to be a lady,
   Dainty as a dishrag, faithful as a chow,
   Stay at home, you got to mind the baby,
   Remember you're a mother now.

Well, every time I turn around it's something else to do,   45
It's cook a meal, mend a sock, sweep a floor or two,
I listen in to Jimmy Young, it makes me want to spew,
I WAS GONNA BE AN ENGINEER!
   Don't I really wish that I could be a lady?
   I could do the lovely things that a lady's 'sposed to do,   50
   I wouldn't even mind, if only they would pay me,
   And I could be a person too.

WHAT PRICE—FOR A WOMAN?
YOU CAN BUY HER FOR A RING OF GOLD.
TO LOVE AND OBEY (WITHOUT ANY PAY)   55
YOU GET A COOK AND A NURSE (FOR BETTER OR WORSE)
YOU DON'T NEED A PURSE WHEN THE LADY IS SOLD.

Ah, but now that times are harder and my Jimmy's got the sack,
I went down to Vicker's, they were glad to have me back,
But I'm a third-class citizen, my wages tell me that,   60
And I'm a first-class engineer.
   The boss he says, "We pay you as a lady,
   You only got the job 'cause I can't afford a man,
   With you I keep the profits high as may be,
   You're just a cheaper pair of hands."   65

YOU GOT ONE FAULT—YOU'RE A WOMAN.
YOU'RE NOT WORTH THE EQUAL PAY.
A BITCH OR A TART, YOU'RE NOTHING BUT HEART,

SHALLOW AND VAIN, YOU GOT NO BRAIN,
YOU EVEN GO DOWN THE DRAIN LIKE A LADY TODAY—   70

Well, I listened to my mother and I joined a typing-pool,
I listened to my lover and I put him through his school,
But if I listen to the boss, I'm just a bloody fool
And an underpaid engineer!
    I been a sucker ever since I was a baby,   75
    As a daughter, as a wife, as a mother and a "dear"—
    But I'll fight them as a woman, not a lady,
    Fight them as an engineer!

Questions for Discussion and Writing

1. What images challenge assumptions that women are intrinsically less capable of becoming engineers than are men?
2. How do images of the speaker performing different socially expected roles contrast with those of her taking on roles traditionally associated with men?
3. What function do the refrains play as an expression of society's expectations? How do these contrast with the speaker's own personal story and the decision she reaches?
4. How does this photo of an engineer at work update Seeger's poem?

Thinking Critically About the Image

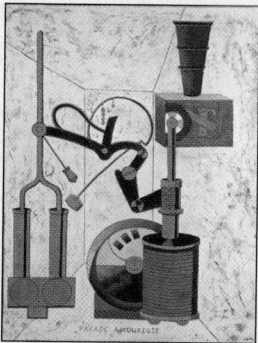

Francis Picabia (1878–1953), French painter, poet, and pamphleteer, was associated with Impressionism, Cubism, and Surrealism and was one of the first European exponents of Dada, an international movement among artists and writers that stresses absurdity and the unpredictable in artistic creation. In *Parade Amoureuse* (*Amorous Parade*, 1917, oil on board), Picabia inaugurates a style that blends a machinist aesthetic with representations of humans in a witty visual metaphor. The painting prefigures current technology questions and takes us to the edge of cybernetic eroticism (do we love our machines, do they love us, do they love each other)?

1. How does the very dry, "laid back" minimalist style of Picabia create a story of eroticism that breaks down the barriers between fantasy and reality?
2. How does the cryptic imagery in this painting suggest that we, in modern culture, are now part of a technological dream in which machines have displaced the romantic and idealized view of humans?
3. When you consider the technological appurtenances (Palm Pilots, laptop computers, cell phones) with which the average person is encumbered, how prescient do you find Picabia's vision of the electronically aided person?

Connections

Chapter 9: The Impact of Technology

David Ewing Duncan, *DNA as Destiny*
Compare the social implications of the discoveries at the frontiers of genetic research as discussed by Duncan and Lawrence Osborne.

LynNell Hancock, *The Haves and the Have-Nots*
Compare Bill Gates's optimism that technology will close the gap between the haves and the have-nots with Hancock's assessment.

Constance Holden, *Identical Twins Reared Apart*
How does the research Holden reports strengthen the "biology is destiny" theme of David Ewing Duncan's article?

Lawrence Osborne, *Got Silk*
How has hybridizing become a dominant idea in scientific developments as depicted by Osborne and Bill McKibben in "It's Easy Being Green"?

Umberto Eco, *How Not to Use the Fax Machine and the Cellular Phone*
Compare Eco's characterization of modern gadgets that symbolize success in a consumer culture with George Carlin's characterization of the "stuff" we think we need in "A Place for Your Stuff" (Ch. 2).

Bill McKibben, *It's Easy Being Green*
If adopted, would McKibben's suggestions mean the end of the "culture of consumerism" described by Juliet B. Schor (Ch. 5)? Why or why not?

Bill Gates, From *The Road Ahead*
To what extent has Gates's prediction of an overdocumented life become the basis of Chet Williamson's story "The Personal Touch"?

Henry Petroski, *The Pencil*
How is the lowly, taken-for-granted pencil as important as the computers described by Bill Gates?

Chet Williamson, *The Personal Touch*
How are both this story and Aldous Huxley's essay "Propaganda Under a Dictatorship" (Ch. 4) based on the concept of a "Big Brother" type of intrusiveness into the private life of the average citizen?

Walt Whitman, *When I Heard the Learn'd Astronomer*
Compare the ways Whitman and William Zinsser in "Niagara Falls" (Ch. 2) recover a sense of awe for nature that has been diminished by civilization.

Peggy Seeger, *I'm Gonna Be an Engineer*
How is the theme of empowerment developed in the poems by Seeger and Francis E. W. Harper in "Learning to Read" (Ch. 3)?

Gustav Klimt, **The Kiss,** *1907-1908.*
Oil on canvas. 180 × 180 cm. Erich Lessing/Art Resource, NY. Oesterreichische Galerie, Vienna, Austria.

The Artistic Impulse

One's destination is never a place, but rather a new way of looking at things.
—HENRY MILLER, "THE ORANGES OF THE MILLENNIUM"

ALTHOUGH THE CRITERIA FOR WHAT CONSTITUTES ART change from age to age and culture to culture, artists deepen, enrich, and extend our knowledge of human nature and experience. The pleasures we derive from listening to music, reading, looking at paintings, and engaging in other creative endeavors add immeasurably to our appreciation of life. Essays by Kurt Vonnegut, Jr., Fran Lebowitz, and Stephen King bring different perspectives to the question of what constitutes good writing, whether writing is an inborn talent, and how to learn from the works of great writers of the past.

Roger Ebert, a film critic, argues for watching older, and foreign films as well as current favorites. Agnes De Mille describes the influence of the Russian ballerina Anna Pavlova on her life and art. The American composer Aaron Copland takes us behind the scenes in a recording studio to reveal techniques used in scoring music for films. Lance Morrow examines the role photography has played in shaping our perception of key moments in history. David Brooks speculates why The Sims, a virtual reality game, provides an outlet for creativity for millions of players.

Carson McCullers tells the whimsical story of a music teacher whose lively imagination transforms her world and touches the lives of all who know her.

Poems by Anne Bradstreet and Emily Dickinson suggest that artists are never satisfied with their creations and that poetry creates its effects through indirect means. Paul Simon and Art Garfunkel in their song lyrics "The Sound of Silence" create an anthem for songwriters everywhere who want to make a difference.

NONFICTION

Kurt Vonnegut, Jr.

Kurt Vonnegut, Jr. (b. 1922) is the author of such iconoclastic masterpieces as Cat's Cradle *(1963),* Slaughterhouse Five *(1969),* Sirens of Titan *(1971),* Breakfast of Champions *(1973), and* Timequake *(1993) as well as innumerable short stories written for magazines. He is well qualified to offer practical advice on writing with style, as the unique voice Vonnegut creates in his fiction makes his work a joy to read. In 1999 he wrote a book with Lee Stringer about writing,* Like Shaking Hands with God: A Conversation About Writing. God Bless You, Dr. Kevorkian *(2000) is an ironic allusion to his 1965 novel* God Bless You, Mr. Rosewater.

As you read Vonnegut's essay, consider whether you would visualize the author in the same way as the caricaturist does.

HOW TO WRITE WITH STYLE

Newspaper reporters and technical writers are trained to reveal almost nothing about themselves in their writings. This makes them freaks in the world of writers, since almost all of the other ink-stained wretches in that world reveal a lot about themselves to readers. We call these revelations, accidental and intentional, elements of style.

These revelations tell us as readers what sort of person it is with whom we are spending time. Does the writer sound ignorant or informed, stupid or bright, crooked or honest, humorless or playful—? And on and on.

Why should you examine your writing style with the idea of improving it? Do so as a mark of respect for your readers, whatever you're writing. If you scribble your thoughts any which way, your readers will surely feel that you care nothing about them. They will mark you down as an egomaniac or a chowder head—or worse, they will stop reading you.

The most damning revelation you can make about yourself is that you do not know what is interesting and what is not. Don't you yourself like or dislike writers mainly for what they choose to show you or make you think about? Did you ever admire an empty-headed writer for his or her mastery of the language? No.

So your own winning style must begin with ideas in your head.   5

1. Find a Subject You Care About

Find a subject you care about and which you in your heart feel others should care about. It is this genuine caring, and not your games with language, which will be the most compelling and seductive element in your style.

I am not urging you to write a novel, by the way—although I would not be sorry if you wrote one, provided you genuinely cared about something. A petition to the mayor about a pothole in front of your house or a love letter to the girl next door will do.

2. Do Not Ramble, Though

I won't ramble on about that.

3. Keep It Simple

As for your use of language: Remember that two great masters of language, William Shakespeare and James Joyce, wrote sentences which were almost childlike when their subjects were most profound. "To be or not to be?" asks Shakespeare's Hamlet. The longest word is three letters long. Joyce, when he was frisky, could put together a sentence as intricate and as glittering as a necklace for Cleopatra, but my favorite sentence in his short story "Eveline" is this one: "She was tired." At that point in the story, no other words could break the heart of a reader as those three words do.

Simplicity of language is not only reputable, but perhaps even sacred. The *Bible*   10 opens with a sentence well within the writing skills of a lively fourteen-year-old: "In the beginning God created the heaven and the earth."

4. Have the Guts to Cut

It may be that you, too, are capable of making necklaces for Cleopatra, so to speak. But your eloquence should be the servant of the ideas in your head. Your rule might be this: If a sentence, no matter how excellent, does not illuminate your subject in some new and useful way, scratch it out.

5. Sound Like Yourself

The writing style which is most natural for you is bound to echo the speech you heard when a child. English was the novelist Joseph Conrad's third language, and much that seems piquant in his use of English was no doubt colored by his first language, which was Polish. And lucky indeed is the writer who has grown up in Ireland, for the English spoken there is so amusing and musical. I myself grew up in Indianapolis, where common speech sounds like a band saw cutting galvanized tin, and employs a vocabulary as unornamental as a monkey wrench.

In some of the more remote hollows of Appalachia, children still grow up hearing songs and locutions of Elizabethan times. Yes, and many Americans grow up hearing a language other than English, or an English dialect a majority of Americans cannot understand.

All these varieties of speech are beautiful, just as the varieties of butterflies are beautiful. No matter what your first language, you should treasure it all your life. If it happens not to be standard English, and if it shows itself when you write standard English, the result is usually delightful, like a very pretty girl with one eye that is green and one that is blue.

I myself find that I trust my own writing most, and others seem to trust it most, too, when I sound most like a person from Indianapolis, which is what I am. What alternatives do I have? The one most vehemently recommended by teachers has no doubt been pressed on you, as well: to write like cultivated Englishmen of a century or more ago.   15

6. Say What You Mean to Say

I used to be exasperated by such teachers, but am no more. I understand now that all those antique essays and stories with which I was to compare my own work were not magnificent for their datedness or foreignness, but for saying precisely what their authors meant them to say. My teachers wished me to write accurately, always selecting the most effective words, and relating the words to one another unambiguously, rigidly, like parts of a machine. The teachers did not want to turn me into an Englishman after all. They hoped that I would become understandable—and therefore understood. And there went my dream of doing with words what Pablo Picasso did with paint or what any number of jazz idols did with music. If I broke all the rules of punctuation, had words mean whatever I wanted them to mean, and strung them together higgledy-piggledy, I would simply not be understood. So you, too, had better avoid Picasso-style or jazz-style-writing, if you have something worth saying and wish to be understood.

Readers want our pages to look very much like pages they have seen before. Why? This is because they themselves have a tough job to do, and they need all the help they can get from us.

7. Pity the Readers

They have to identify thousands of little marks on paper, and make sense of them immediately. They have to *read,* an art so difficult that most people don't really master it even after having studied it all through grade school and high school—twelve long years.

So this discussion must finally acknowledge that our stylistic options as writers are neither numerous nor glamorous, since our readers are bound to be such imperfect artists. Our audience requires us to be sympathetic and patient teachers, even willing to simplify and clarify—whereas we would rather soar high above the crowd, singing like nightingales.

That is the bad news. The good news is that we Americans are governed under a 20 unique Constitution, which allows us to write whatever we please without fear of punishment. So the most meaningful aspect of our styles, which is what we choose to write about, is utterly unlimited.

8. For Really Detailed Advice

For a discussion of literary style in a narrower sense, in a more technical sense, I commend to your attention *The Elements of Style,* by William Strunk, Jr., and E. B. White (Macmillan, 1979). E. B. White is, of course, one of the most admirable literary stylists this country has so far produced.

You should realize, too, that no one would care how well or badly Mr. White expressed himself, if he did not have perfectly enchanting things to say.

Questions for Discussion and Writing

1. To what extent has Vonnegut followed his own advice? How would you characterize the voice he creates in this essay?
2. Why does Vonnegut use Shakespeare and Joyce as examples to illustrate the value of simplicity in language? Did you find the similes and metaphors Vonnegut uses to be particularly effective in getting his ideas across?
3. Rewrite a paragraph or two from a recent essay of yours following Vonnegut's seven suggestions. Which version did you prefer and why? You might wish to read any of Vonnegut's novels to see whether he follows his own advice.

Fran Lebowitz

Fran Lebowitz (b. 1951) is an acerbic humorist who has written on cultural manners and mores in Metropolitan Life *(1978),* Social Studies *(1981),* Mr. Chas and Lisa Sue Meet the Pandas *(1994), and* The Fran Lebowitz Reader *(1994), from which the following selection is reprinted. If you have ever wondered if writers were born or made, Lebowitz amusingly resolves the issue once and for all.*

HOW TO TELL IF YOUR CHILD IS A WRITER

Your child is a writer if one or more of the following statements are applicable. Truthfulness is advised—no amount of fudging will alter the grim reality.

1. Prenatal
   A. You have morning sickness at night because the fetus finds it too distracting to work during the day.
   B. You develop a craving for answering services and typists.
   C. When your obstetrician applies his stethoscope to your abdomen he hears excuses.

2. Birth
   A. The baby is at least three weeks late because he had a lot of trouble with the ending.
   B. You are in labor for twenty-seven hours because the baby left everything until the last minute and spent an inordinate amount of time trying to grow his toes in a more interesting order.
   C. When the doctor spanks the baby the baby is not at all surprised.
   D. It is definitely a single birth because the baby has dismissed being twins as too obvious.

3. Infancy
   A. The baby refuses both breast and bottle, preferring instead Perrier with a twist in preparation for giving up drinking.
   B. The baby sleeps through the night almost immediately. Also through the day.
   C. The baby's first words, uttered at the age of four days, are "Next week."
   D. The baby uses teething as an excuse not to learn to gurgle.
   E. The baby sucks his forefinger out of a firm conviction that the thumb's been done to death.

4. Toddlerhood
   A. He rejects teddy bears as derivative.
   B. He arranges his alphabet blocks so as to spell out derisive puns on the names of others.
   C. When he is lonely he does not ask his mother for a baby brother or sister but rather for a protégé.
   D. When he reaches the age of three he considers himself a trilogy.
   E. His mother is afraid to remove his crayoned handiwork from the living room walls lest she be accused of excessive editing.

F. When he is read his bedtime story he makes sarcastic remarks about style.
5. Childhood
A. At age seven he begins to think about changing his name. Also his sex.
B. He balks at going to summer camp because he is aware that there may be children there who have never heard of him.
C. He tells his teachers that he didn't do his homework because he was blocked.
D. He refuses to learn how to write a Friendly Letter because he knows he never will.
E. With an eye to a possible movie deal, he insists upon changing the title of his composition "What I Did on My Summer Vacation" to the far snappier "Vacation."
F. He is thoroughly hypochondriac and is convinced that his chicken pox is really leprosy.
G. On Halloween he goes out trick-or-treating dressed as Harold Acton.[1]

By the time this unfortunate child has reached puberty there is no longer any hope that he will outgrow being a writer and become something more appealing—like a kidnap victim.

Questions for Discussion and Writing

1. In what ways are the tendency to procrastinate and a desire for originality dominant themes in Lebowitz's analysis?
2. How is the use of lists intended to parody conventional baby books?
3. Lebowitz appears to view the innate predisposition to become a writer as something not to be desired. Have your own experiences in writing supported her assessment? Did you discover in yourself any of the same traits she identifies? Explain your answer.

Stephen King

* *

Stephen King (b. 1947) is a successful author of innumerable works in the fantasy, supernatural, and horror genres. Most of his books have been made into popular movies. A few of these works have attained the status of classics, including Carrie *(1974),* The Shining *(1977),* Misery *(1987), and* Cujo *(1991). He has also written dramatic novellas such as* Rita Hayworth and the Shawshank Redemption *(1982) and* Stand By Me *(1982), both of which became films. In June 1999, King was gravely injured by a van that sideswiped him as he walked down a country road in Maine where he lives. After intensive therapy he has almost completely recovered. He described his experiences in* On Writing *(2000), from which the following selection (a compendium of useful advice to would-be*

[1]*Harold Acton:* Sir Harold Acton (1904–1994) was a notable figure at Oxford University in the 1920s; he taught at the National University in Peking, and after World War II, his family home, La Pietra, in Florence, Italy, became a center for artists and literati.

writers) is drawn. His latest works include The Gunslinger *(2003),* Wolves of the Calla *(2003), and* the Dark Tower *(2004).*

ON WRITING

If you want to be a writer, you must do two things above all others: read a lot and write a lot. There's no way around these two things that I'm aware of, no shortcut.

I'm a slow reader, but I usually get through seventy or eighty books a year, mostly fiction. I don't read in order to study the craft; I read because I like to read. It's what I do at night, kicked back in my blue chair. Similarly, I don't read fiction to study the art of fiction, but simply because I like stories. Yet there is a learning process going on. Every book you pick up has its own lesson or lessons, and quite often the bad books have more to teach than the good ones.

When I was in the eighth grade, I happened upon a paperback novel by Murray Leinster, a science fiction pulp writer who did most of his work during the forties and fifties, when magazines like *Amazing Stories* paid a penny a word. I had read other books by Mr. Leinster, enough to know that the quality of his writing was uneven. This particular tale, which was about mining in the asteroid belt, was one of his less successful efforts. Only that's too kind. It was terrible, actually, a story populated by paper-thin characters and driven by outlandish plot developments. Worst of all (or so it seemed to me at the time), Leinster had fallen in love with the word *zestful*.

Characters watched the approach of ore-bearing asteroids with *zestful smiles*. Characters sat down to supper aboard their mining ship with *zestful anticipation*. Near the end of the book, the hero swept the large-breasted, blonde heroine into a *zestful embrace*. For me, it was the literary equivalent of a smallpox vaccination: I have never, so far as I know, used the word *zestful* in a novel or a story. God willing, I never will.

Asteroid Miners (which wasn't the title, but that's close enough) was an important book in my life as a reader. Almost everyone can remember losing his or her virginity, and most writers can remember the first book he/she put down thinking: *I can do better than this. Hell, I am doing better than this!* What could be more encouraging to the struggling writer than to realize his/her work is unquestionably better than that of someone who actually got paid for his/her stuff?

One learns most clearly what not to do by reading bad prose—one novel like *Asteroid Miners* (or *Valley of the Dolls, Flowers in the Attic,* and *The Bridges of Madison County,* to name just a few) is worth a semester at a good writing school, even with the superstar guest lecturers thrown in.

Good writing, on the other hand, teaches the learning writer about style, graceful narration, plot development, the creation of believable characters, and truth-telling. A novel like *The Grapes of Wrath* may fill a new writer with feelings of despair and good old-fashioned jealousy—"I'll never be able to write anything that good, not if I live to be a thousand"—but such feelings can also serve as a spur, goading the writer to work harder and aim higher. Being swept away by a combination of great story and great writing—of being flattened, in fact—is part of every writer's necessary formation. You cannot hope to sweep someone else away by the force of your writing until it has been done to you.

5

So we read to experience the mediocre and the outright rotten; such experience helps us to recognize those things when they begin to creep into our own work, and to steer clear of them. We also read in order to measure ourselves against the good and the great, to get a sense of all that can be done. And we read in order to experience different styles.

You may find yourself adopting a style you find particularly exciting, and there's nothing wrong with that. When I read Ray Bradbury as a kid, I wrote like Ray Bradbury—everything green and wondrous and seen through a lens smeared with the grease of nostalgia. When I read James M. Cain, everything I wrote came out clipped and stripped and hard-boiled. When I read Lovecraft, my prose became luxurious and Byzantine. I wrote stories in my teenage years where all these styles merged, creating a kind of hilarious stew. This sort of stylistic blending is a necessary part of developing one's own style, but it doesn't occur in a vacuum. You have to read widely, constantly refining (and redefining) your own work as you do so. It's hard for me to believe that people who read very little (or not at all in some cases) should presume to write and expect people to like what they have written, but I know it's true. If I had a nickel for every person who ever told me he/she wanted to become a writer but "didn't have time to read," I could buy myself a pretty good steak dinner. Can I be blunt on this subject? If you don't have time to read, you don't have the time (or the tools) to write. Simple as that.

Reading is the creative center of a writer's life. I take a book with me everywhere   10
I go, and find there are all sorts of opportunities to dip in. The trick is to teach yourself to read in small sips as well as in long swallows. Waiting rooms were made for books—of course! But so are theater lobbies before the show, long and boring checkout lines, and everyone's favorite, the john. You can even read while you're driving, thanks to the audiobook revolution. Of the books I read each year, anywhere from six to a dozen are on tape. As for all the wonderful radio you will be missing, come on— how many times can you listen to Deep Purple sing "Highway Star"?

Reading at meals is considered rude in polite society, but if you expect to succeed as a writer, rudeness should be the second-to-least of your concerns. The least of all should be polite society and what it expects. If you intend to write as truthfully as you can, your days as a member of polite society are numbered, anyway.

Where else can you read? There's always the treadmill, or whatever you use down at the local health club to get aerobic. I try to spend an hour doing that every day, and I think I'd go mad without a good novel to keep me company. Most exercise facilities (at home as well as outside it) are now equipped with TVs, but TV—while working out or anywhere else—really is about the last thing an aspiring writer needs. If you feel you must have the news analyst blowhards on CNN while you exercise, or the stock market blowhards on MSNBC, or the sports blowhards on ESPN, it's time for you to question how serious you really are about becoming a writer. You must be prepared to do some serious turning inward toward the life of the imagination, and that means, I'm afraid, that Geraldo, Keith Obermann, and Jay Leno must go. Reading takes time, and the glass teat takes too much of it.

Once weaned from the ephemeral craving for TV, most people will find they enjoy the time they spend reading. I'd like to suggest that turning off that endlessly quacking box is apt to improve the quality of your life as well as the quality of your writing. And how much of a sacrifice are we talking about here? How many *Frasier* and *ER* reruns does it take to make one American life complete? How many Richard Simmons infomercials? How many whiteboy/fatboy Beltway insiders on CNN? Oh man, don't get me started. Jerry-Springer-Dr.-Dre-Judge-Judy-Jerry-Falwell-Donny-and-Marie, I rest my case.

When my son Owen was seven or so, he fell in love with Bruce Springsteen's E Street Band, particularly with Clarence Clemons, the band's burly sax player. Owen decided he wanted to learn to play like Clarence. My wife and I were amused and delighted by this ambition. We were also hopeful, as any parent would be, that our kid would turn out to be talented, perhaps even some sort of prodigy. We got Owen a tenor saxophone for Christmas and lessons with Gordon Bowie, one of the local music men. Then we crossed our fingers and hoped for the best.

Seven months later I suggested to my wife that it was time to discontinue the sax   15 lessons, if Owen concurred. Owen did, and with palpable relief—he hadn't wanted to say it himself, especially not after asking for the sax in the first place, but seven months had been long enough for him to realize that, while he might love Clarence Clemons's big sound, the saxophone was simply not for him—God had not given him that particular talent.

I knew, not because Owen stopped practicing, but because he was practicing only during the periods Mr. Bowie had set for him: half an hour after school four days a week, plus an hour on the weekends. Owen mastered the scales and the notes—nothing wrong with his memory, his lungs, or his eye-hand coordination—but we never heard him taking off, surprising himself with something new, blissing himself out. And as soon as his practice time was over, it was back into the case with the horn, and there it stayed until the next lesson or practice-time. What this suggested to me was that when it came to the sax and my son, there was never going to be any real play-time; it was all going to be rehearsal. That's no good. If there's no joy in it, it's just no good. It's best to go on to some other area, where the deposits of talent may be richer and the fun quotient higher.

Talent renders the whole idea of rehearsal meaningless; when you find something at which you are talented, you do it (whatever *it* is) until your fingers bleed or your eyes are ready to fall out of your head. Even when no one is listening (or reading, or watching), every outing is a bravura performance, because you as the creator are happy. Perhaps even ecstatic. That goes for reading and writing as well as for playing a musical instrument, hitting a baseball, or running the four-forty. The sort of strenuous reading and writing program I advocate—four to six hours a day, every day—will not seem strenuous if you really enjoy doing these things and have an aptitude for them; in fact, you may be following such a program already. If you feel you need permission to do all the reading and writing your little heart desires, however, consider it hereby granted by yours truly.

The real importance of reading is that it creates an ease and intimacy with the process of writing; one comes to the country of the writer with one's papers and identification pretty much in order. Constant reading will pull you into a place (a mind-set, if you like the phrase) where you can write eagerly and without self-consciousness. It also offers you a constantly growing knowledge of what has been done and what hasn't, what is trite and what is fresh, what works and what just lies there dying (or dead) on the page. The more you read, the less apt you are to make a fool of yourself with your pen or word processor.

Questions for Discussion and Writing

1. According to King, why must apprentice writers read everything they can? What can they learn even from reading bad writing?
2. How does the example of his son Owen taking up the saxophone illustrate King's belief that writing should be a consuming passion?
3. Would you consider making any of the trade-offs that King describes (for example, less television watching for more reading time) to become a better writer? Why or why not?
4. How does this film still of Jack Nicholson as the crazed writer in *The Shining* suggest the unwholesome transformation of the main character when he appears through a door he has shattered and says, "Here's Johnny"?

Roger Ebert

Roger Ebert (b. 1942) is widely known for his television program Ebert and Roeper *and for his columns on film for the* Chicago Sun-Times, *where he has been on the staff since 1967. He won a Pulitizer Prize in 1975 for film criticism and has written, among other books,* A Kiss Is Still a Kiss *(1985),* Behind the Phantom's Mask *(1993), and* The Great Movies *(2002), from which the following selection is reprinted.*

GREAT MOVIES

Every other week I visit a film classic from the past and write about it. My "Great Movies" series began in the autumn of 1996 and now reaches a landmark of 100 titles with today's review of Federico Fellini's "8 1/2," which is, appropriately, a film about a film director. I love my job, and this is the part I love the most.

We have completed the first century of film. Too many moviegoers are stuck in the present and recent past. When people tell me that "Ferris Bueller's Day Off" or "Total Recall" are their favorite films, I wonder: Have they tasted the joys of Welles, Bunuel, Ford, Murnau, Keaton, Hitchcock, Wilder or Kurosawa? If they like Ferris Bueller, what would they think of Jacques Tati's "Mr. Hulot's Holiday," also about a strange day of misadventures? If they like "Total Recall," have they seen Fritz Lang's "Metropolis," also about an artificial city ruled by fear?

I ask not because I am a film snob. I like to sit in the dark and enjoy movies. I think of old films as a resource of treasures. Movies have been made for 100 years, in color and black and white, in sound and silence, in wide-screen and the classic frame, in English and every other language. To limit yourself to popular hits and recent years is like being Ferris Bueller but staying home all day.

I believe we are born with our minds open to wonderful experiences, and only slowly learn to limit ourselves to narrow tastes. We are taught to lose our curiosity by the bludgeon-blows of mass marketing, which brainwash us to see "hits," and discourage exploration.

I know that many people dislike subtitled films, and that few people reading this   5
article will have ever seen a film from Iran, for example. And yet a few weeks ago at my Overlooked Film Festival at the University of Illinois, the free kiddie matinee was "Children of Heaven," from Iran. It was a story about a boy who loses his sister's sneakers through no fault of his own, and is afraid to tell his parents. So he and his sister secretly share the same pair of shoes. Then he learns of a footrace where third prize is . . . a pair of sneakers.

"Anyone who can read at the third-grade level can read these subtitles," I told the audience of 1,000 kids and some parents. "If you can't, it's OK for your parents or older kids to read them aloud—just not too loudly."

The lights went down and the movie began. I expected a lot of reading aloud. There was none. Not all of the kids were old enough to read, but apparently they were picking up the story just by watching and using their intelligence. The audience was spellbound. No noise, restlessness, punching, kicking, running down the aisles. Just eyes lifted up to a fascinating story. Afterward, we asked kids up on the stage to ask questions or talk about the film. What they said indicated how involved they had become.

Kids. And yet most adults will not go to a movie from Iran, Japan, France or Brazil. They will, however, go to any movie that has been plugged with a $30 million ad campaign and sanctified as a "box-office winner." Yes, some of these big hits are good, and a few of them are great. But what happens between the time we are 8 and the time we are 20 that robs us of our curiosity? What turns movie lovers into consumers? What does it say about you if you only want to see what everybody else is seeing?

I don't know. What I do know is that if you love horror movies, your life as a film-goer is not complete until you see "Nosferatu." I know that once you see Orson Welles appear in the doorway in "The Third Man," you will never forget his curious little smile. And that the life and death of the old man in "Ikiru" will be an inspiration every time you remember it.

I have not written any of the 100 Great Movies reviews from memory. Every film has   10
been seen fresh, right before writing. When I'm at home, I often watch them on Sunday mornings. It's a form of prayer: The greatest films are meditations on why we are here. When I'm on the road, there's no telling where I'll see them. I saw "Written on the Wind" on a cold January night at the Everyman Cinema in Hampstead, north of London. I saw "Last Year at Marienbad" on a DVD on my PowerBook while at the Cannes Film Festival. I saw "2001: A Space Odyssey" in 70mm at Cyberfest, the celebration of HAL 9000's birthday, at the University of Illinois. I saw "Battleship Potemkin" projected on a sheet on the outside wall of the Vickers Theater in Three Oaks, Mich., while three young musicians played the score they had written for it. And Ozu's "Floating Weeds" at the Hawaii Film Festival, as part of a shot-by-shot seminar that took four days.

When people asked me where they should begin in looking at classic films, I never knew what to say. Now I can say, "Plunge into these Great Movies, and go where they lead you."

There's a next step. If you're really serious about the movies, get together with two or three friends who care as much as you do. Watch the film all the way through on video. Then start again at the top. Whenever anyone sees anything they want to comment on, freeze the frame. Talk about what you're looking at. The story, the performances, the sets, the locations. The camera movement, the lighting, the composition, the special effects. The color, the shadows, the sound, the music. The themes, the tone, the mood, the style.

There are no right answers. The questions are the point. They make you an active movie watcher, not a passive one. You should not be a witness at a movie, but a collaborator. Directors cannot make the film without you. Together, you can accomplish amazing things. The more you learn, the quicker you'll know when the director is not doing his share of the job. That's the whole key to being a great moviegoer. There's nothing else to it.

Questions for Discussion and Writing

1. How has Ebert's lifelong obsession with movies taught him to value out-of-the-way foreign films and underappreciated classics?
2. How does Ebert's example about free kiddie matinee films illustrate his thesis that great films stand on their own and audiences do not need to limit themselves to preapproved "hits"?
3. What factors have made audiences into consumers rather than movie lovers? Have you ever sought out unfamiliar foreign or older films instead of the "hyped" film of the moment? Describe your experiences.
4. Draw on the discussion in "Reading and Analyzing Visual Texts" (pages 23–27 in the Introduction) and study any of the following posters and movie stills

1922

1956

1968

1925

1997

that Ebert mentions as examples of "great movies." Analyze how the basic principles of design operate to create effective images (the last is from *Children of Heaven*).

Agnes De Mille

Agnes De Mille (1908–1993), a principal figure in American dance, was born in New York City. She created distinctive American ballets such as Rodeo *(1942) and* Tally-Ho *(1944) and brought her talents as an innovative choreographer to* Oklahoma! *(1943 and 1980),* Carousel *(1945),* Brigadoon *(1947),* Paint Your Wagon *(1951),* Gentlemen Prefer Blondes *(1949), and other musicals. De Mille's entertaining autobiographies,* Dance to the Piper *(1952) and* Reprieve: A Memoir *(1981), describe many exciting moments in her life. "Pavlova," from* Dance to the Piper, *contains De Mille's recollection of what she felt when she saw Anna Pavlova, the famed Russian ballerina, for the first time.*

PAVLOVA

Anna Pavlova! My life stops as I write that name. Across the daily preoccupation of lessons, lunch boxes, tooth brushings and quarrelings with Margaret flashed this bright, unworldly experience and burned in a single afternoon a path over which I could never retrace my steps. I had witnessed the power of beauty, and in some chamber of my heart I lost forever my irresponsibility. I was as clearly marked as though she had looked me in the face and called my name. For generations my father's family had loved and served the theater. All my life I had seen actors and actresses and had heard theater jargon at the dinner table and business talk of box-office grosses. I had thrilled at Father's projects and watched fascinated his picturesque occupations. I took a proprietary pride in the profitable and hasty growth of "The Industry." But nothing in his world or my uncle's prepared me for theater as I saw it that Saturday afternoon.

Since that day I have gained some knowledge in my trade and I recognize that her technique was limited; that her arabesques were not as pure or classically correct as Markova's, that her jumps and batterie were paltry, her turns not to be compared in strength and number with the strenuous durability of Baronova or Toumanova. I know that her scenery was designed by second-rate artists, her music was on a level with restaurant orchestrations, her company definitely inferior to all the standards we insist on today, and her choreography mostly hack. And yet I say that she was in her person the quintessence of theatrical excitement.

As her little bird body revealed itself on the scene, either immobile in trembling mystery or tense in the incredible arc which was her lift, her instep stretched ahead in an arch never before seen, the tiny bones of her hands in ceaseless vibration, her face radiant, diamonds glittering under her dark hair, her little waist encased in silk, the great tutu balancing, quickening and flashing over her beating, flashing, quivering legs, every man and woman sat forward, every pulse quickened. She never appeared to rest static, some part of her trembled, vibrated, beat like a heart. Before our dazzled eyes, she flashed with the sudden sweetness of a hummingbird in action too quick for understanding by our gross utilitarian standards, in action sensed rather than seen. The movie cameras of her day could not record her allegro. Her feet and hands photographed as a blur.

Bright little bird bones, delicate bird sinews! She was all fire and steel wire. There was not an ounce of spare flesh on her skeleton, and the life force used and used her body until she died of the fever of moving, gasping for breath, much too young.

She was small, about five feet. She wore a size one and a half slipper, but her feet 5 and hands were large in proportion to her height. Her hand could cover her whole face. Her trunk was small and stripped of all anatomy but the ciphers of adolescence, her arms and legs relatively long, the neck extraordinarily long and mobile. All her gestures were liquid and possessed of an inner rhythm that flowed to inevitable completion with the finality of architecture or music. Her arms seemed to lift not from the elbow or the arm socket, but from the base of the spine. Her legs seemed to function from the waist. When she bent her head her whole spine moved and the motion was completed the length of the arm through the elongation of her slender hand and the quivering reaching fingers. I believe there has never been a foot like hers, slender, delicate and of such an astonishing aggressiveness when arched as to suggest the ultimate in human vitality. Without in any way being sensual, being, in fact, almost sexless, she suggested all exhilaration, gaiety and delight. She jumped, and we broke bonds with reality. We flew. We hung over the earth, spread in the air as we do in dreams, our hands turning in the air as in water—the strong forthright taut plunging leg balanced on the poised arc of the foot, the other leg stretched to the horizon like the wing of a bird. We lay balancing, quivering, turning, and all things were possible, even to us, the ordinary people.

I have seen two dancers as great or greater since, Alicia Markova and Margot Fonteyn, and many other women who have kicked higher, balanced longer or turned faster. These are poor substitutes for passion. In spite of her flimsy dances, the bald and blatant virtuosity, there was an intoxicated rapture, a focus of energy, Dionysian in its physical intensity, that I have never seen equaled by a performer in any theater of the world. Also she was the *first* of the truly great in our experience.

I sat with the blood beating in my throat. As I walked into the bright glare of the afternoon, my head ached and I could scarcely swallow. I didn't wish to cry. I certainly couldn't speak. I sat in a daze in the car oblivious to the grownups' ceaseless prattle. At home I climbed the stairs slowly to my bedroom and, shutting myself in, placed both hands on the brass rail at the foot of my bed, then rising laboriously to the tips of my white buttoned shoes I stumped the width of the bed and back again. My toes throbbed with pain, my knees shook, my legs quivered with weakness. I repeated the exercise. The blessed, relieving tears stuck at last on my lashes. Only by hurting my feet could I ease the pain in my throat.

Standing on Ninth Avenue under the El, I saw the headlines on the front page of the *New York Times*. It did not seem possible. She was in essence the denial of death. My own life was rooted to her in a deep spiritual sense and had been during the whole of my growing up. It mattered not that I had only spoken to her once and that my work lay in a different direction. She was the vision and the impulse and the goal.

Questions for Discussion and Writing

1. What features of Pavlova's appearance and dance does De Mille find so enthralling? How did seeing Pavlova's performance change De Mille's life?

2. What details does De Mille include to focus the reader's attention on Pavlova's diminuative size and her ability to express emotion through gesture?

3. Describe a performance you have seen that you would call inspiring. What made it so? Organize your description and main impression by using specific details that will allow your readers to share your experience.

4. If you could appear on the cover of any magazine for an achievement for which you are celebrated, what would it be—*Sports Illustrated, Time, Rolling Stone, Business Week, Gourmet?*

5. How does this image of Pavlova illustrate how she was publicized?

Aaron Copland

* *

Aaron Copland (1900–1990), one of the most influential American composers of the twentieth century, was born in Brooklyn, New York. He studied with Nadia Boulanger in Paris (1921–1924) and taught at the New School for Social Research (1927–1937). He developed a distinctly American sound and style, incorporating not only Stravinsky's influence but jazz, folk songs, cowboy tunes, and Shaker hymns in works such as Billy the Kid *(1940),* Rodeo *(1942),* Fanfare for the Common Man *(1943), and the Pulitzer Prize–winning ballet* Appalachian Spring *(1944). He continued to compose music for orchestra, ballet, stage, films, chamber groups, and voice and to conduct, lecture, and write books, including* Music and Imagination *(1952). He won an Academy Award in 1950 for the musical score he wrote for the film* The Heiress. *In the following selection (from* What to Listen for in Music, *1957) we can appreciate Copland's engaging explanation of the qualities of effective music scored for films.*

FILM MUSIC

Film music constitutes a new musical medium that exerts a fascination of its own. Actually, it is a new form of dramatic music—related to opera, ballet, incidental theater music—in contradistinction to concert music of the symphonic or chamber-music kind. As a new form it opens up unexplored possibilities for composers and poses some interesting questions for the musical film patron.

Millions of movie-goers take the musical accompaniment to a dramatic film entirely too much for granted. Five minutes after the termination of a picture they couldn't tell you whether they had heard music or not. To ask whether they thought the score exciting or merely adequate or downright awful would be to give them a musical inferiority complex. But, on second thought, and possibly in self-protection, comes the query: "Isn't it true that one isn't supposed to be listening to the music? Isn't it supposed to work on you unconsciously without being listened to directly as you would listen at a concert?"

No discussion of movie music ever gets very far without having to face this problem: Should one hear a movie score? If you are a musician there is no problem because the chances are you can't help but listen. More than once a good picture has been ruined for me by an inferior score. Have you had the same experience? Yes? Then you may congratulate yourself: you are definitely musical.

But it's the average spectator, so absorbed in the dramatic action that he fails to take in the background music, who wants to know whether he is missing anything. The answer is bound up with the degree of your general musical perception. It is the degree to which you are aurally minded that will determine how much pleasure you may derive by absorbing the background musical accompaniment as an integral part of the combined impression made by the film.

Knowing more of what goes into the scoring of a picture may help the movie listener to get more out of it. Fortunately, the process is not so complex that it cannot be briefly outlined. 5

In preparation for composing the music, the first thing the composer must do, of course, is to see the picture. Almost all musical scores are written *after* the film itself is completed. The only exception to this is when the script calls for realistic music—that is, music which is visually sung or played or danced to on the screen. In that case the music must be composed before the scene is photographed. It will then be recorded and the scene in question shot to a playback of the recording. Thus, when you see an actor singing or playing or dancing, he is only making believe as far as the sound goes, for the music had previously been put down in recorded form.

The first run-through of the film for the composer is usually a solemn moment. After all, he must live with it for several weeks. The solemnity of the occasion is emphasized by the exclusive audience that views it with him: the producer, the director, the music head of the studio, the picture editor, the music cutter, the conductor, the orchestrater—in fact, anyone involved with the scoring of the picture.

The purpose of the run-through is to decide how much music is needed and where it should be. (In technical jargon this is called "to spot" the picture.) Since no background score is continuous throughout the full length of a film (that would constitute a motion-picture opera, an almost unexploited cinema form), the score will normally consist of separate sequences, each lasting from a few seconds to several minutes in duration. A sequence as long as seven minutes would be exceptional. The entire score, made up of perhaps thirty or more such sequences, may add up to from forty to ninety minutes of music.

Much discussion, much give-and-take may be necessary before final decisions are reached regarding the "spotting" of the picture. It is wise to make use of music's power sparingly, saving it for absolutely essential points. A composer knows how to play with silences—knows that to take music out can at times be more effective than any use of it on the sound track might be.

The producer-director, on the other hand, is more prone to think of music in terms of its immediate functional usage. Sometimes he has ulterior motives: anything wrong with a scene—a poor bit of acting, a badly read line, an embarrassing pause—he secretly hopes will be covered up by a clever composer. Producers have been known to hope that an entire picture would be saved by a good score. But the composer is not a 10 magician; he can hardly be expected to do more than to make potent through music the film's dramatic and emotional values.

When well-contrived, there is no question but that a musical score can be of enormous help to a picture. One can prove that point, laboratory-fashion, by showing an audience a climactic scene with the sound turned off and then once again with the sound track turned on. Here briefly are listed a number of ways in which music serves the screen:

Creating a more convincing atmosphere of time and place. Not all Hollywood composers bother about this nicety. Too often, their scores are interchangeable: a thirteenth-century Gothic drama and a hardboiled modern battle of the sexes get similar treatment. The lush symphonic texture of late nineteenth-century music remains the dominating influence. But there are exceptions. Recently, the higher-grade horse opera has begun to have its own musical flavor, mostly a folksong derivative.

Underlining psychological refinements—the unspoken thoughts of a character or the unseen implications of a situation. Music can play upon the emotions of the spectator, sometimes counterpointing the thing seen with an aural image that implies the contrary of the thing seen. This is not as subtle as it sounds. A well-placed dissonant chord can stop an audience cold in the middle of a sentimental scene, or a calculated woodwind passage can turn what appears to be a solemn moment into a belly laugh.

Serving as a kind of neutral background filler. This is really the music one isn't supposed to hear, the sort that helps to fill the empty spots, such as pauses in a conversation. It's the movie composer's most ungrateful task. But at times, though no one else may notice, he will get private satisfaction from the thought that music of little intrinsic value, through professional manipulation, has enlivened and made more human the deathly pallor of a screen shadow. This is hardest to do, as any film composer will attest, when the neutral filler type of music must weave its way underneath dialogue.

Building a sense of continuity. The picture editor knows better than anyone how [15] serviceable music can be in tying together a visual medium which is, by its very nature, continually in danger of falling apart. One sees this most obviously in montage scenes where the use of a unifying musical idea may save the quick flashes of disconnected scenes from seeming merely chaotic.

Underpinning the theatrical build-up of a scene, and rounding it off with a sense of finality. The first instance that comes to mind is the music that blares out at the end of a film. Certain producers have boasted their picture's lack of a musical score, but I never saw or heard of a picture that ended in silence.

We have merely skimmed the surface, without mentioning the innumerable examples of utilitarian music—offstage street bands, the barn dance, merry-go-rounds, circus music, café music, the neighbor's girl practicing her piano, and the like. All these, and many others, introduced with apparent naturalistic intent, serve to vary subtly the aural interest of the sound track.

But now let us return to our hypothetical composer. Having determined where the separate musical sequences will begin and end, he turns the film over to the music cutter, who prepares a so-called cue sheet. The cue sheet provides the composer with a detailed description of the physical action in each sequence, plus the exact timings in thirds of seconds of that action, thereby making it possible for a practiced composer to write an entire score without ever again referring to the picture.

The layman usually imagines that the most difficult part of the job in composing for the films has to do with the precise "fitting" of the music to the action. Doesn't that kind of timing strait-jacket the composer? The answer is no, for two reasons: First, having to compose music to accompany specific action is a help rather than a hindrance, since the action itself induces music in a composer of theatrical imagination, whereas he has no such visual stimulus in writing absolute music. Secondly, the timing is mostly a matter of minor adjustments, since the over-all musical fabric will have already been determined.

For the composer of concert music, changing to the medium of celluloid does bring 20 certain special pitfalls. For example, melodic invention, highly prized in the concert hall, may at times be distracting in certain film situations. Even phrasing in the concert manner, which would normally emphasize the independence of separate contrapuntal lines, may be distracting when applied to screen accompaniments. In orchestration there are many subtleties of timbre—distinctions meant to be listened to for their own expressive quality in an auditorium—which are completely wasted on sound track.

As compensation for these losses, the composer has other possibilities, some of them tricks, which are unobtainable in Carnegie Hall. In scoring one section of *The Heiress,* for example, I was able to superimpose two orchestras, one upon another. Both recorded the same music at different times, one orchestra consisting of strings alone, the other constituted normally. Later these were combined by simultaneously rerecording the original tracks, thereby producing a highly expressive orchestral texture. Bernard Herrmann,[1] one of the most ingenious of screen composers, called for (and got) eight celestas—an unheard-of combination on 57th Street—to suggest a winter's sleigh ride. Miklos Rozsa's[2] use of the "echo chamber"—a device to give normal tone a ghostlike aura—was widely remarked, and subsequently done to death.

Unusual effects are obtainable through overlapping incoming and outgoing music tracks. Like two trains passing one another, it is possible to bring in and take out at the same time two different musics. *The Red Pony*[3] gave me an opportunity to use this cinema specialty. When the daydreaming imagination of a little boy turns white chickens into white circus horses the visual image is mirrored in an aural image by having the chicken music transform itself into circus music, a device only obtainable by means of the overlap.

Let us now assume that the musical score has been completed and is ready for recording. The scoring stage is a happy-making place for the composer. Hollywood has gathered to itself some of America's finest performers; the music will be

---

[1]*Bernard Herrmann (1911–1975):* composed the music for *Citizen Kane* (1941) and many Alfred Hitchcock films, including *Psycho* (1960).   [2]*Miklos Rozsa (1907–1995):* Hungarian composer who wrote the film score for *Ben Hur* (1959).   [3]*The Red Pony:* 1948 film for which Copland wrote the music.

beautifully played and recorded with a technical perfection not to be matched anywhere else.

Most composers like to invite their friends to be present at the recording session of important sequences. The reason is that neither the composer nor his friends are ever again likely to hear the music sound out in concert style. For when it is combined with the picture most of the dynamic levels will be changed. Otherwise the finished product might sound like a concert with pictures. In lowering dynamic levels niceties of shading, some inner voices and bass parts may be lost. Erich Korngold[4] put it well when he said: "A movie composer's immortality lasts from the recording stage to the dubbing room."

The dubbing room is where all the tracks involving sound of any kind, including   25
dialogue, are put through the machines to obtain one master sound track. This is a delicate process as far as the music is concerned, for it is only a hairbreadth that separates the "too loud" from the "too soft." Sound engineers, working the dials that control volume, are not always as musically sensitive as composers would like them to be. What is called for is a new species, a sound mixer who is half musician and half engineer; and even then, the mixing of dialogue, music, and realistic sounds of all kinds must always remain problematical.

In view of these drawbacks to the full sounding out of his music, it is only natural that the composer often hopes to be able to extract a viable concert suite from his film score. There is a current tendency to believe that movie scores are not proper material for concert music. The argument is that, separated from its visual justification, the music falls flat.

Personally, I doubt very much that any hard and fast rule can be made that will cover all cases. Each score will have to be judged on its merits, and, no doubt, stories that require a more continuous type of musical development in a unified atmosphere will lend themselves better than others to reworking for concert purposes. Rarely is it conceivable that the music of a film might be extracted without much reworking. But I fail to see why, if successful suites like Grieg's[5] *Peer Gynt*[6] can be made from nineteenth-century incidental stage music, a twentieth-century composer can't be expected to do as well with a film score.

As for the picture score, it is only in the motion-picture theater that the composer for the first time gets the full impact of what he has accomplished, tests the dramatic punch of his favorite spot, appreciates the curious importance and unimportance of detail, wishes that he had done certain things differently, and is surprised that others came off better than he had hoped. For when all is said and done, the art of combining moving pictures with musical tones is still a mysterious art. Not the least mysterious element is the theatergoers' reaction: Millions will be listening but one never knows how many will be really hearing. The next time you go to the movies, remember to be on the composer's side.

---

[4]*Erich Korngold (1897–1957):* Austrian composer who wrote the film score for *The Adventures of Robin Hood* (1938).   [5]*Edvard Grieg (1843–1907):* Norway's greatest composer.   [6]*Peer Gynt:* incidental music composed by Grieg for Henrik Ibsen's 1875 play.

How does this album cover suggest that recordings of film scores were starting to achieve recognition in their own right? Does the image imply that Copland's film score for Something Wild *(1961) was as important as the movie itself?*

Questions for Discussion and Writing

1. In what ways can a musical score enhance a film? What qualities in film music that would be applauded in a concert would prove distracting for a movie audience?
2. What examples best illustrate that the role of film music must be subordinated to the images on the screen? How does Copland's personal experience enhance the credibility of his analysis?
3. Analyze one of your favorite films by paying particular attention to the ways in which music achieves some of the objectives Copland describes. Is there any movie score that you would consider owning for its intrinsic musical value? Explain why you like it.

Lance Morrow

• • • • • • • • • • • • • • • • • • •

Lance Morrow was born in Philadelphia in 1939, received his B.A. from Harvard in 1963, and joined the staff of Time *magazine shortly after graduation. As one of the magazine's regular contributors, he has written articles on a broad range of topics. Among his published works are* The Chief: A Memoir of Fathers and Sons *(1985),* America: A Rediscovery *(1987),* Fishing in the Tiber *(1989),* Safari: Experiencing the Wild *(with Neil Leifer, 1992),* Heart: A Memoir *(1995), and* Evil: An Investigation *(2003). "Imprisoning Time in a Rectangle" first appeared in a special issue of* Time *(Fall 1989) devoted to photojournalism.*

IMPRISONING TIME IN A RECTANGLE

Balzac[1] had a "vague dread" of being photographed. Like some primitive peoples, he thought the camera steals something of the soul—that, as he told a friend "every body in its natural state is made up of a series of ghostly images superimposed in layers to infinity, wrapped in infinitesimal films." Each time a photograph was made, he believed, another thin layer of the subject's being would be stripped off to become not life as before but a membrane of memory in a sort of translucent antiworld.

If that is what photography is up to, then the onion of the world is being peeled away, layer by layer—lenses like black holes gobbling up life's emanations. Mere images proliferate, while history pares down to a phosphorescence of itself.

The idea catches something of the superstition (sometimes justified, if you think about it) and the spooky metaphysics that go ghosting around photography. Taking pictures is a transaction that snatches instants away from time and imprisons them in rectangles. These rectangles become a collective public memory and an image-world that is located usually on the verge of tears, often on the edge of a moral mess.

It is possible to be entranced by photography and at the same time disquieted by its powerful capacity to bypass thought. Photography, as the critic Susan Sontag has pointed out, is an elegiac, nostalgic phenomenon. No one photographs the future. The instants that the photographer freezes are ever the past, ever receding. They have about them the brilliance or instancy of their moment but also the cello sound of loss that life makes when going irrecoverably away and lodging at last in the dreamworks.

The pictures made by photojournalists have the legitimacy of being news, fresh   5
information. They slice along the hard edge of the present. Photojournalism is not self-conscious, since it first enters the room (the brain) as a battle report from the far-flung Now. It is only later that the artifacts of photojournalism sink into the textures of the civilization and tincture its memory: Jack Ruby shooting Lee Harvey Oswald,[2] an image so raw and shocking, subsides at last into the ecology of memory where we also

---

[1] *Honoré de Balzac (born Honoré Balssa, 1799–1850):* French writer, best known for the novels and short stories of *La Comédie Humaine (The Human Comedy).*   [2] *Jack L. Ruby (1911–1967):* shot and killed Lee Harvey Oswald (1939–1963), the accused assassin of President John F. Kennedy, on November 24, 1963, two days after Kennedy was shot, in the Dallas County Jail, where Oswald was being held under arrest. A national television audience witnessed the event.

find thousands of other oddments from the time—John John saluting at the funeral, Jack and Jackie on Cape Cod, who knows?—bright shards that stimulate old feelings (ghost pangs, ghost tendernesses, wistfulness) but not thought really. The shocks turn into dreams. The memory of such pictures, flipped through like a disordered Rolodex, makes at last a cultural tapestry, an inventory of the kind that brothers and sisters and distant cousins may rummage through at family reunions, except that the greatest photojournalism has given certain memories the emotional prestige of icons.

If journalism—the kind done with words—is the first draft of history, what is photojournalism? Is it the first impression of history, the first graphic flash? Yes, but it is also (and this is the disturbing thing) history's lasting visual impression. The service that the pictures perform is splendid, and so powerful as to seem preternatural. But sometimes the power they possess is more than they deserve.

Call up Eddie Adams's 1968 photo of General Nguyen Ngoc Loan, the police chief of Saigon, firing his snub-nosed revolver into the temple of a Viet Cong officer. Bright sunlight, Saigon: the scrawny police chief's arm, outstretched, goes by extension through the trigger finger into the V.C.'s brain. That photograph, and another in 1972 showing a naked young Vietnamese girl running in armsoutstretched terror up a road away from American napalm, outmanned the force of three U.S. Presidents and the most powerful Army in the world. The photographs were considered, quite ridiculously, to be a portrait of America's moral disgrace. Freudians spend years trying to call up the primal image-memories, turned to trauma, that distort a neurotic patient's psyche. Photographs sometimes have a way of installing the image and legitimizing the trauma: the very vividness of the image, the greatness of the photograph as journalism or even as art, forestalls examination.

Adams has always felt uncomfortable about his picture of Loan executing the Viet Cong officer. What the picture does not show is that a few moments earlier the Viet Cong had slaughtered the family of Loan's best friend in a house just up the road. All this occurred during the Tet offensive, a state of general mayhem all over South Vietnam. The Communists in similar circumstances would not have had qualms about summary execution.

But Loan shot the man; Adams took the picture. The image went firing around the world and lodged in the conscience. Photography is the very dream of the Heisenberg[3] uncertainty principle, which holds that the act of observing a physical event inevitably changes it. War is merciless, bloody, and by definition it occurs outside the orbit of due process. Loan's Viet Cong did not have a trial. He did have a photographer. The photographer's picture took on a life of its own and changed history.

All great photographs have lives of their own, but they can be as false as dreams. 10 Somehow the mind knows that and sorts out the matter, and permits itself to enjoy the pictures without getting sunk in the really mysterious business that they involve.

Still, a puritan conscience recoils a little from the sheer power of photographs. They have lingering about them the ghost of the golden calf—the bright object too much admired, without God's abstract difficulties. Great photographs bring the mind

[3] *Werner Heisenberg (1901–1976):* German physicist famous for formulating the quantum theory, which converted the laws of physics into statements about relative, instead of absolute, certainties. He received the 1932 Nobel Prize in physics.

alive. Photographs are magic things that traffic in mystery. They float on the surface, and they have a strange life in the depths of the mind. They bear watching.

Questions for Discussion and Writing

1. How, in Morrow's view, does photojournalism go beyond merely recording events in history to help create history itself?
2. How does Morrow use photos of Jack Ruby shooting Lee Harvey Oswald and a police chief in Saigon shooting a Viet Cong prisoner to illustrate the power of photojournalism to affect history?
3. In your opinion, will this image of an Iraqi prisoner at Abu Ghraib prison, come to represent the war in Iraq as the photo by Eddie Adams did for the war in Vietnam? Why or why not?

David Brooks

· ·

David Brooks (b. 1961) is a graduate of the University of Chicago and is a senior editor of The Weekly Standard *and a twice-weekly columnist for the* New York Times. *He serves as a commentator on National Public Radio and CNN. His witty dissections of the American lifestyle include* Bobos in Paradise: The New Upper Class and How They Got There *(2000) and, most recently,* On Paradise Drive *(2004). In "Oversimulated Suburbia," which first appeared in the* New York Times Magazine *(November 2000), Brooks explores the cultural implications of* The Sims *and other virtual reality video games that invite players to release their suppressed artistic impulses. In cybersociety, players can design completely customized environments, take glamorous vacations, mix and mingle with other players, and produce outcomes unavailable in real life.*

OVERSIMULATED SUBURBIA

I don't know if it strikes you as odd that of all the arenas of human endeavor, the one that has produced the best-selling computer game of all time *is* the American suburb. There are other games about intergalactic warfare, supersonic-jet dogfights, and inner-city car theft, but none of them attract the same fanatical following—and no game attracts any sort of following among women—as *The Sims*.

You install *The Sims* on your computer and you begin the game, and what do you see? A subdivision. There's a little ranch home over there, a colonial over there, a larger McMansion up the hill. And the object of the game? Suburban conquest in its rawest form. You've got to get the kids scrubbed and fed by the time the school bus comes around in the morning. You have to select the right coffee table to go with your love seat. You have to remember to turn off the TV if you want to take a nap, because the noise will keep you up. There's no winning and losing in *The Sims*. No points, no end. In the game, as in life, you just keep doing the dishes until you die.

It's all about time management. You want to throw a dinner party for your friends, and you'd also like to do some gardening, but you've got to take out the garbage and pick up the paper from the front yard, and you notice your bladder is alarmingly full and you won't be at your best unless you head to the bathroom to relieve yourself. This is the epic heroism of everyday life! The most mundane tasks—the ones that actually bore the hell out of you in reality—come at you in the computer game with relentless insistence, and if you are going to be a happy Sim, master of your tract home, lord of your lawn, sultan of your suburb, you have to get organized. You have to impose order on chaos. You have to stay cool and go with the flow. In this way you can achieve split-level greatness.

The Sims is the brainchild of Will Wright. In the early 1980s, Wright was a programmer for a company that made conventional bullets-and-bombs PC games. For one game, Wright was told to design some enemy islands for warplanes to destroy. He discovered he was more interested in the islands—with refineries, buildings and streets—than the bombers, so he developed a computer game, *Sim City,* that lets players build their own cities. His employer, Broderbund, resisted the idea, so he went off to help found a company and in 1989 introduced the fantastically successful *SimCity* line of games.

Wright went on to design *SimEarth, SimHealth,* and *SimTower,* and, influenced by the work of the architectural theorist Christopher Alexander (the author of *A Pattern Language: Towns, Buildings, Construction*), he decided to build a game in which players would try to design the perfect home. He created abstract characters to live in the homes, but he quickly discovered that the characters were more fun than the residences. *The Sims* was released in February 2000; soon thereafter it was followed by expansion packs that allow you to take your characters, or Sims, out on dates, to resort hotels or nightclubs. Last year, Sims-related games occupied 5 of the top 10 spots on the computer-game best-seller chart. (Keep in mind, when weighing the social importance of these things, that in the United States, computer- and video-game revenues are greater than movie box-office receipts. Almost 20 million copies of *The Sims* and its add-ons have been sold.)

And next month, an online version of *The Sims* goes on sale ($50 for the game; $10 per month in subscription fees). In other words, in addition to the regular suburbia all around us, there will be a massive new cybersociety, filled with little computer-generated people with a passion for Barcaloungers.

· · ·

The Sims allows you to create your own characters, and the first thing many players do is base characters on themselves and their families. You can choose personality traits, skin shades, and wardrobes—all to reincarnate you and your loved ones on-screen. Then you have to buy things for them. As with any good bourgeois society, Sims society is built around interior decorating. You have to furnish your home, and the game itself offers a dazzling array of dining-room-table sets, recliners for every price point, party balloons, and sconces.

But, of course, as in American life generally, a mind-numbing array of choices is never enough. On the Internet are hundreds, if not thousands, of sites put up by free-lancers who have designed clothing, furnishings, and fashion accessories that you can download and import into your Sims game. There is Mall of the Sims, with more than 50 stores, where you can browse for paintings for your Sims walls and swimwear for your Sims selves. There is a Sims Thrift Mart, Yuppie Sims, and Historic Sims Houses, for those tired of the game's mostly contemporary architecture options. The designers sometimes charge a fee for their products; others, like philanthropic Ralph Laurens, make free Sims necklaces, Sims reading lamps, Sims tattoos, lingerie, and carpets just for the joy of creating new fashions.

And see how the public bubbles with enthusiasm! In Sims sites devoted to fashion discussions, you find yourself among people in a shopping frenzy. Authentic Victorian wallpaper is now available! Here's a new site with pet gyms for your little Sims gerbils to run around in! "Oh! And something very very very very very very special!" one Sims nut enthuses on <partysims.com>. "A brand-new portable-TV collection! . . . The base was made from a person named 'm.' . . . Big thanks and praise to you!"

You give a bunch of mostly young and, more often than not, female Sims players the chance through a make-believe computer world to do anything they want, to ex-plore any reality or set of interactions, and what do they do first? They consume! They nest and decorate! It's not exactly a materialistic fever they're stoking, because none of the Sims stuff is actually material. Instead it's a virtual hedonism that consumes them, a delicious set of pleasures and sensations that apparently come from imagining what floorings would go with what wall surfaces, from selecting blouses and boleros, from mixing and matching and combining. Human beings, at least in our culture, truly are consuming creatures.

But they are also social creatures. On the official Sims site, thousands of Sims lovers have posted Sims novellas—a sort of folk literature that future historians, zeitgeist hunters, and museum curators are going to go for in a big way. These novellas look like storyboards, with pictures of Sims interiors and characters, above written stories and dialogue. A typical novella may stretch for 64 to 200 pictures and thousands of words. Some of them are just *Architectural Digest* in digital form, involving dinner parties and room-by-room house tours. But most of the novellas are more substantial, and after you've read through a hundred or so of these things, they all blend into one vast modern cultural landscape in which *Oprah* meets *Friends*, *Terms of Endearment* and MTV's *Real World*.

Here's a bit from a story about a teenage single mom who lives with her alcoholic father, Shane, who beats her child, May:

> "Who the hell do you think you are!!!!" I yelled at Shane after telling May to go in the bed-room. "What the hell are you talking about?!" Shane yelled. "I saw you hit May you bas-tard!" . . . Shane just glared at me.

At the end of the story the single mom meets a hunky boyfriend who beats up the dad near the backyard swing set.

Some of the stories end badly. It occurs to some players that they don't have to play by the rules of normal society, so they start killing people. They invite neighbors over to their backyard pools and then pull up the exit ladders and watch them drown. Or they kill off husbands. But the striking thing about these stories is that most of them do end happily, the abusive relationships, dysfunctional families, drug and alcohol addictions are overcome and careers are put on track, just like at the ending of all those *Behind the Music* rockumentaries. Interestingly, the stories generally don't seem to regard marriage as the happily-ever-after ideal. Instead, cliques are the key to paradise. In story after story, the happy denouement comes when the main character settles into her new home, furnishes it to her taste and then invites 5 to 10 people over, and they surround her with companionship and celebrate her triumphs.

In this way, too, the Sims world reflects, anticipates and parodies the real world.   15 Specifically, it reflects the social inversion that has taken place over the past decade. If you came of age before, say, 1985, then your social life probably followed the 1950s pattern: you had a group of friends and also a relationship with your special boyfriend or girlfriend that was understood to be higher and more intense than that with the rest of the gang. There was a distinct line between "going out" and not "going out."

But for many American young people, the friendship relationship is more important than the sexual relationship. That's the model you see in the Sims world and the Sims literature. People go out in groups, rather than on one-on-one dates. In the new pattern, no one sits around by the phone waiting for the boy to ask the girl out, which is nice, but on the other hand, every serious or possibly serious relationship is plagued by ambiguity. There's a pervasive level of sexual tension, but also a new sort of anxiety, because without the formal dating rituals, it's hard to know where anyone stands.

Will Wright says that one of the things that has amazed him most about the online Sims—more than 35,000 people have been testing the system before its official launch—is the passionate energy people put into acquiring and cultivating roommates. People set up a home and then invite groups of people to come live and share resources with them. These social pods are like yuppie kibbutzim in which every woman is Jennifer Aniston and every guy is Matthew Perry, and so each anomic individual is surrounded in all directions by a supportive clique of happy singles for flirting and reinforcement. If you grew up in the bowling-alone world, maybe this is your idea of heaven.

So far, there are two basic types of players. First, there are the highly driven players obsessed with making Sims money and becoming masters of the Sims universe. (Already one player has become the Donald Trump of the online Sims world, acquiring enough money and property to open a string of coffee shops, stores and clubs.) Then there is another set of players who are mostly interested in building intimacies and relationships. (Draw your own sexist conclusions about which sort of person creates which type of Sim.) These people are interested in creating bonds, giving hugs, and building a clique. In the Sims world, of course, you can be as obnoxious as you want to be, with no real cost, but Wright says he's been impressed by the spirit of attentive camaraderie that so far prevails. "People are polite and social with each other," he says. (While there are many fantastic monsters and other bizarre personas available to them, most players are content to create normal, humanlike Sims beings.) There is no government yet in the online *Sims* game. It's a Hobbesian state of nature. And yet most people are cooperative and friendly—perhaps slightly more flamboyant than the average person you see in the Safeway, but not much.

The relationship players tend to create what Wright calls a mythos. They start with names like Backseat Betty, Tokyo Rose, the Lady of Prose, and Dean Martinez Bravo and create a back story to explain their characters. They want their Sims lives to be legible to the characters around them, so the other characters know how to approach and relate to them. The Sims players who thrive, according to Wright, are the ones who can build the abstract computer characters into distinct personalities. They can project a clear persona while also reading the moods of the other Sims.

The online world, which can accommodate a million players, is a vast society with   20 Internet cafes, investment banks, B & B's, parties, pizzerias, and homes, apartments, and condos. Aside from making money, the main activity is schmoozing. One player complained recently that he created a beauty pageant but that a character named Cheerleader Sue came in dressed as a hillbilly and ruined the talent competition with a flatulent version of "Camptown Races"; he had to block Cheerleader Sue from his environment. The online game allows you to register your displeasure with others by putting them in wrestling holds or by stomping on them. (This is only symbolic and doesn't kill them.) You can also die by your own hand—by starving or drowning yourself, at which point you wander around as a ghost until another player agrees to resurrect you.

But dealing grief is relatively rare. Many people compete to make the Top 100 Most Liked list. That means trying to invite hundreds of players over to your house to make friends, sometimes by having parties, quiz-show games, or offering bribes. (Every 24 hours, the game dispenses money to players depending on how many people have visited their homes.) If you walk into, say, somebody's backyard barbecue, you'll find a dozen Sims hanging out in the Jacuzzi or dancing by the stereo. The male characters are all ripped, and the female characters have bikini-perfect bodies, inevitably with humongous breasts. Mostly they're exchanging banal pleasantries. "This barbecue is such a good way to start the season!" enthuses one young woman in a short skirt with breasts that would have her tipping over if she existed in real life. "Burgers and hot dogs, grilled how you like 'em!" announces the host at the grill. "Sounds mouth-watering, but I know they'll just go straight to my thighs," says an African American Sim.

This isn't exactly Dostoyevsky material, so you head over to a futuristic nightclub with another clique of beautiful people, steel floors and weird twenty-third-century molded furniture that looks like Frank Gehry crossed with the design sensibility of Woody Allen's *Sleeper*. But again you detect a gap between the amazing visual sophistication of the place and the barely literate conversation. One beautiful guy is standing in the middle of the room saying, "Boy, these long silences are almost unbearable." So you move on to find a woman, again in a bikini, saying, "I need something to lift me up," and a *Saturday Night Fever* disco man with his shirt open to his navel responds, "I think I can provide that lift, young lady."

Another devastating come-on line.

I confess I sometimes don't know whether to be happy or depressed when I dip into Sims world. Sometimes you get the sense that these Sims fanatics are compensating online for the needs that aren't met in their real lives. If you read through the Sims discussion rooms, you find a lot of people who seem to spend a lot of time alone in their rooms thinking, often not terribly positively, about their own lives. "My family has been having a lot of problems lately," one teenager writes. "My sisters . . . have been fighting nonstop, which puts my mother in a bad mood, so she nags everyone, which puts me in a bad mood, and then my dad comes home drunk every night, which puts everyone in a worse mood. . . . I'll do anything to get away from home."

Others use it as the one place they can be in charge. "Hi, I'm a mom of four very 25 busy boys, 16, 13, 11, and 4. I'm always on the run with basketball. The Sims keep me sane, and they are my downtime."

But the other and more positive sensation you get in Sims world is that some mass creative process is going on, like the writing of a joint novel with millions of collaborative and competitive authors. We generally don't think that John Updike or Saul Bellow or Cynthia Ozick are pathetic because they escape from reality into richly populated fantasy worlds. We regard that process of creativity as something that enriches a life and yields deeper understandings about the real world. And the Sims players are doing something like that at their keyboards. The game is a superstructure for fantasy. The players become emotionally involved with their characters, celebrating their friendships and mourning them when they die. They engage in long debates about the virtual morality of Sims world and Sims fate. When Will Wright introduced a plague into the game, characters who bought a guinea pig but who didn't clean its cage got sick and sometimes died. The Sims fanatics had to figure out how to deal with this "reality."

Their fantasy, when you step back and look at it, is a remarkably realistic fantasy. The Sims is the most realistic computer game by far, but it is also more realistic than most contemporary novels that get produced by writing workshops. Unlike the fictional worlds that flow from the precious prose academies, the Sims world has the feel of real suburban life. It has the same emphasis on money making, shopping, coupling, and party throwing. The *Sims* characters have real-estate fantasies, just as real people do. They have consumer longings. And most of all, they have this desperate need to carve out a place for themselves amid the sprawl.

Unlike people, say, in a traditional Italian village, Sims characters have weak bonds—if any—to extended family or past generations, and they feel this intense need to tie themselves to others, to create some local community in which they can be happy. And all the shopping and decorating and party giving and bonding is part of that quest—the need to create your own roots in a mobile and individualistic world. That doesn't sound so strange for anybody living in modern America. Indeed, it's kind of inspiring. The creative process isn't just for art students and design professionals. It's alive out there amid the subdivisions.

Questions for Discussion and Writing

1. What distinction does Brooks draw between the two basic types of Sims players? What is the intrinsic appeal of this game? How does it permit its players to exercise latent abilities for design in homes and fashion, to be creative in projecting characters into intriguing situations, and to control the outcome?

2. How do the examples that Brooks uses illustrate that the world of The Sims offers a strangely compelling creative outlet that differs qualitatively from other forms of artistic expressions such as painting, writing, and participating in theater groups?

3. In your opinion, what therapeutic values does this game possess for its players? Have you ever played any of the Sims games, and if so, how did the game tap into your artistic impulses? How do other video games compare with The Sims?

4. What does this image of a virtual reality arcade in Tokyo say about how games will be played in the future?

FICTION

Carson McCullers

Carson McCullers (1917–1967) was born in Columbus, Georgia, as Lula Carson Smith. Although she moved from the South in 1934 (with intentions of studying music at Julliard), her writing is deeply embedded in the southern literary tradition and emphasizes loneliness and desire. This blend of the real and dramatic with the poetic and symbolic can be seen in her novels The Heart Is a Lonely Hunter *(1940), a touching portrait of an adolescent girl, and* The Member of the Wedding *(1946), in which the twelve-year-old main character's wishes to become part of the social community are rejected. This novel was adapted for the stage in 1950 and became a successful Broadway play as well as a motion picture in 1952.* The Ballad of the Sad Café *was published as a novella in 1951 and was adapted by Edward Albee for the stage in 1963. In addition to her five novels and two plays, she also wrote essays, poetry, and numerous short stories, including "Madame Zilensky and the King of Finland" with its uncharacteristically whimsical ending. The main character imbues everyday reality with fantasy and fable conveyed through McCullers's cool and engaging prose.*

MADAME ZILENSKY AND THE KING OF FINLAND

To Mr. Brook, the head of the music department at Ryder College, was due all the credit for getting Madame Zilensky on the faculty. The college considered itself fortunate; her reputation was impressive, both as a composer and as a pedagogue. Mr. Brook took on himself the responsibility of finding a house for Madame Zilensky, a comfortable place with a garden, which was convenient to the college and next to the apartment house where he himself lived.

No one in Westbridge had known Madame Zilensky before she came. Mr. Brook had seen her pictures in musical journals, and once he had written to her about the authenticity of a certain Buxtehude manuscript. Also, when it was being settled that she was to join the faculty, they had exchanged a few cables and letters on practical affairs. She wrote in a clear, square hand, and the only thing out of the ordinary in these letters was the fact that they contained an occasional reference to objects and persons altogether unknown to Mr. Brook, such as "the yellow cat in Lisbon" or "poor Heinrich." These lapses Mr. Brook put down to the confusion of getting herself and her family out of Europe.

Mr. Brook was a somewhat pastel person; years of Mozart minuets, of explanations about diminished sevenths and minor triads, had given him a watchful vocational patience. For the most part, he kept to himself. He loathed academic fiddle-faddle and committees. Years before, when the music department had decided to gang together and spend the summer in Salzburg, Mr. Brook sneaked out of the arrangement at the last moment and took a solitary trip to Peru. He had a few eccentricities himself and was tolerant of the peculiarities of others; indeed, he rather relished the ridiculous. Often, when confronted with some grave and incongruous situation, he would feel a little inside tickle, which stiffened his long, mild face and sharpened the light in his gray eyes.

Mr. Brook met Madame Zilensky at the Westbridge station a week before the beginning of the fall semester. He recognized her instantly. She was a tall, straight woman with a pale and haggard face. Her eyes were deeply shadowed and she wore her dark, ragged hair pushed back from her forehead. She had large, delicate hands, which were very grubby. About her person as a whole there was something noble and abstract that made Mr. Brook draw back for a moment and stand nervously undoing his cuff links. In spite of her clothes—a long, black skirt and a broken-down old leather jacket—she made an impression of vague elegance. With Madame Zilensky were three children, boys between the ages of ten and six, all blond, blank-eyed, and beautiful. There was one other person, an old woman who turned out later to be the Finnish servant.

This was the group he found at the station. The only luggage they had with them 5
was two immense boxes of manuscripts, the rest of their paraphernalia having been forgotten in the station at Springfield when they changed trains. That is the sort of thing that can happen to anyone. When Mr. Brook got them all into a taxi, he thought the worst difficulties were over, but Madame Zilensky suddenly tried to scramble over his knees and get out of the door.

"My God!" she said. "I left my—how do you say?—my tick-tick-tick—"

"Your watch?" asked Mr. Brook.

"Oh no!" she said vehemently. "You know, my tick-tick-tick," and she waved her forefinger from side to side, pendulum fashion.

"Tick-tick," said Mr. Brook, putting his hands to his forehead and closing his eyes. "Could you possibly mean a metronome?"

"Yes! Yes! I think I must have lost it there where we changed trains." 10

Mr. Brook managed to quiet her. He even said, with a kind of dazed gallantry, that he would get her another one the next day. But at the time he was bound to admit to himself that there was something curious about this panic over a metronome when there was all the rest of the lost luggage to consider.

The Zilensky ménage moved into the house next door, and on the surface everything was all right. The boys were quiet children. Their names were Sigmund, Boris, and Sammy. They were always together and they followed each other around Indian file, Sigmund usually the first. Among themselves they spoke a desperate-sounding family Esperanto made up of Russian, French, Finnish, German, and English; when other people were around, they were strangely silent. It was not any one thing that the Zilenskys did or said that made Mr. Brook uneasy. There were just little incidents. For example, something about the Zilensky children subconsciously bothered him when they were in a house, and finally he realized that what troubled him was the fact that the Zilensky boys never walked on a rug; they skirted it single file on the bare floor, and if a room was carpeted, they stood in the doorway and did not go inside. Another thing was this: Weeks passed and Madame Zilensky seemed to make no effort to get settled or to furnish the house with anything more than a table and some beds. The front door was left open day and night, and soon the house began to take on a queer, bleak look like that of a place abandoned for years.

The college had every reason to be satisfied with Madame Zilensky. She taught with a fierce insistence. She could become deeply indignant if some Mary Owens or Bernadine Smith would not clean up her Scarlatti trills. She got hold of four pianos for her college studio and set four dazed students to playing Bach fugues together. The racket that came from her end of the department was extraordinary, but Madame Zilensky did not seem to have a nerve in her, and if pure will and effort can get over a musical idea, then Ryder College could not have done better. At night Madame Zilensky worked on her twelfth symphony. She seemed never to sleep; no matter what time of night Mr. Brook happened to look out of his sitting-room window, the light in her studio was always on. No, it was not because of any professional consideration that Mr. Brook became so dubious.

It was in late October when he felt for the first time that something was unmistakably wrong. He had lunched with Madame Zilensky and had enjoyed himself, as she had given him a very detailed account of an African safari she had made in 1928. Later in the afternoon she stopped in at his office and stood rather abstractly in the doorway.

Mr. Brook looked up from his desk and asked, "Is there anything you want?"   15

"No, thank you," said Madame Zilensky. She had a low, beautiful, sombre voice. "I was only just wondering. You recall the metronome. Do you think perhaps that I might have left it with that French?"

"Who?" asked Mr. Brook.

"Why, that French I was married to," she answered.

"Frenchman," Mr. Brook said mildly. He tried to imagine the husband of Madame Zilensky, but his mind refused. He muttered half to himself, "The father of the children."

"But no," said Madame Zilensky with decision. "The father of Sammy."   20

Mr. Brook had a swift prescience. His deepest instincts warned him to say nothing further. Still, his respect for order, his conscience, demanded that he ask, "And the father of the other two?"

Madame Zilensky put her hand to the back of her head and ruffled up her short, cropped hair. Her face was dreamy, and for several moments she did not answer. Then she said gently, "Boris is of a Pole who played the piccolo."

"And Sigmund?" he asked. Mr. Brook looked over his orderly desk, with the stack of corrected papers, the three sharpened pencils, the ivory-elephant paperweight. When he glanced up at Madame Zilensky, she was obviously thinking hard. She gazed around at the corners of the room, her brows lowered and her jaw moving from side to side. At last she said, "We were discussing the father of Sigmund?"

"Why, no," said Mr. Brook. "There is no need to do that."

Madame Zilensky answered in a voice both dignified and final. "He was a fellow-   25
countryman."

Mr. Brook really did not care one way or the other. He had no prejudices; people could marry seventeen times and have Chinese children so far as he was concerned. But there was something about this conversation with Madame Zilensky that bothered him. Suddenly he understood. The children didn't look at all like Madame Zilensky, but they looked exactly like each other, and as they all had different fathers, Mr. Brook thought the resemblance astonishing.

But Madame Zilensky had finished with the subject. She zipped up her leather jacket and turned away.

"That is exactly where I left it," she said, with a quick nod. "*Chez* that French."

Affairs in the music department were running smoothly. Mr. Brook did not have any serious embarrassments to deal with, such as the harp teacher last year who had finally eloped with a garage mechanic. There was only this nagging apprehension about Madame Zilensky. He could not make out what was wrong in his relations with her or why his feelings were so mixed. To begin with, she was a great globe-trotter, and her conversations were incongruously seasoned with references to far-fetched places. She would go along for days without opening her mouth, prowling through the corridor with her hands in the pockets of her jacket and her face locked in meditation. Then suddenly she would buttonhole Mr. Brook and launch out on a long, volatile monologue, her eyes reckless and bright and her voice warm with eagerness. She would talk about anything or nothing at all. Yet, without exception, there was something queer, in a slanted sort of way, about every episode she ever mentioned. If she spoke of taking Sammy to the barbershop, the impression she created was just as foreign as if she were telling of an afternoon in Bagdad. Mr. Brook could not make it out.

The truth came to him very suddenly, and the truth made everything perfectly clear,   30
or at least clarified the situation. Mr. Brook had come home early and lighted a fire in the little grate in his sitting room. He felt comfortable and at peace that evening. He sat before the fire in his stocking feet, with a volume of William Blake on the table by his side, and he had poured himself a half-glass of apricot brandy. At ten o'clock he was drowsing cozily before the fire, his mind full of cloudy phrases of Mahler[1] and floating half-thoughts. Then all at once, out of this delicate stupor, four words came to his mind: "The King of Finland." The words seemed familiar, but for the first moment he could not place them. Then all at once he tracked them down. He had been walking across the campus that afternoon when Madame Zilensky stopped him and began some preposterous rigmarole, to which he had only half listened; he was thinking about

---

[1]*Mahler:* Gustav Mahler (1860–1911), renowned Austrian composer.

the stack of canons turned in by his counterpoint class. Now the words, the inflections of her voice, came back to him with insidious exactitude. Madame Zilensky had started off with the following remark: "One day, when I was standing in front of a *pâtisserie*, the King of Finland came by in a sled."

Mr. Brook jerked himself up straight in his chair and put down his glass of brandy. The woman was a pathological liar. Almost every word she uttered outside of class was an untruth. If she worked all night, she would go out of her way to tell you she spent the evening at the cinema. If she ate lunch at the Old Tavern, she would be sure to mention that she had lunched with her children at home. The woman was simply a pathological liar, and that accounted for everything.

Mr. Brook cracked his knuckles and got up from his chair. His first reaction was one of exasperation. That day after day Madame Zilensky would have the gall to sit there in his office and deluge him with her outrageous falsehoods! Mr. Brook was intensely provoked. He walked up and down the room, then he went into his kitchenette and made himself a sardine sandwich.

An hour later, as he sat before the fire, his irritation had changed to a scholarly and thoughtful wonder. What he must do, he told himself, was to regard the whole situation impersonally and look on Madame Zilensky as a doctor looks on a sick patient. Her lies were of the guileless sort. She did not dissimulate with any intention to deceive, and the untruths she told were never used to any possible advantage. That was the maddening thing; there was simply no motive behind it all.

Mr. Brook finished off the rest of the brandy. And slowly, when it was almost midnight, a further understanding came to him. The reason for the lies of Madame Zilensky was painful and plain. All her life long Madame Zilensky had worked—at the piano, teaching, and writing those beautiful and immense twelve symphonies. Day and night she had drudged and struggled and thrown her soul into her work, and there was not much of her left over for anything else. Being human, she suffered from this lack and did what she could to make up for it. If she passed the evening bent over a table in the library and later declared that she had spent that time playing cards, it was as though she had managed to do both those things. Through the lies, she lived vicariously. The lie doubled the little of her existence that was left over from work and augmented the little rag end of her personal life.

Mr. Brook looked into the fire, and the face of Madame Zilensky was in his mind— 35 a severe face, with dark, weary eyes and delicately disciplined mouth. He was conscious of a warmth in his chest, and a feeling of pity, protectiveness, and dreadful understanding. For a while he was in a state of lovely confusion.

Later on he brushed his teeth and got into his pajamas. He must be practical. What did this clear up? That French, the Pole with the piccolo, Bagdad? And the children, Sigmund, Boris, and Sammy—who were they? Were they really her children after all, or had she simply rounded them up from somewhere? Mr. Brook polished his spectacles and put them on the table by his bed. He must come to an immediate understanding with her. Otherwise, there would exist in the department a situation which could become most problematical. It was two o'clock. He glanced out of his window and saw that the light in Madame Zilensky's workroom was still on. Mr. Brook got into bed, made terrible faces in the dark, and tried to plan what he would say next day.

Mr. Brook was in his office by eight o'clock. He sat hunched up behind his desk, ready to trap Madame Zilensky as she passed down the corridor. He did not have to wait long, and as soon as he heard her footsteps he called out her name.

Madame Zilensky stood in the doorway. She looked vague and jaded. "How are you? I had such a fine night's rest," she said.

"Pray be seated, if you please," said Mr. Brook. "I would like a word with you."

Madame Zilensky put aside her portfolio and leaned back wearily in the armchair 40
across from him. "Yes?" she asked.

"Yesterday you spoke to me as I was walking across the campus," he said slowly. "And if I am not mistaken, I believe you said something about a pastry shop and the King of Finland. Is that correct?"

Madame Zilensky turned her head to one side and stared retrospectively at a corner of the window sill.

"Something about a pastry shop," he repeated.

Her tired face brightened. "But of course," she said eagerly. "I told you about the time I was standing in front of this shop and the King of Finland—"

"Madame Zilensky!" Mr. Brook cried. "There *is* no King of Finland." 45

Madame Zilensky looked absolutely blank. Then, after an instant, she started off again. "I was standing in front of Bjarne's *pâtisserie* when I turned away from the cakes and suddenly saw the King of Finland—"

"Madame Zilensky, I just told you that there is no King of Finland."

"In Helsingfors," she started off again desperately, and again he let her get as far as the King, and then no further.

"Finland is a democracy," he said. "You could not possibly have seen the King of Finland. Therefore, what you have just said is an untruth. A pure untruth."

Never afterward could Mr. Brook forget the face of Madame Zilensky at that mo- 50
ment. In her eyes there was astonishment, dismay, and a sort of cornered horror. She had the look of one who watches his whole interior world split open and disintegrate.

"It is a pity," said Mr. Brook with real sympathy.

But Madame Zilensky pulled herself together. She raised her chin and said coldly, "I am a Finn."

"That I do not question," answered Mr. Brook. On second thought, he did question it a little.

"I was born in Finland and I am a Finnish citizen."

"That may very well be," said Mr. Brook in a rising voice. 55

"In the war," she continued passionately, "I rode a motorcycle and was a messenger."

"Your patriotism does not enter into it."

"Just because I am getting out the first papers—"

"Madame Zilensky!" said Mr. Brook. His hands grasped the edge of the desk. "That is only an irrelevant issue. The point is that you maintained and testified that you saw—that you saw—" But he could not finish. Her face stopped him. She was deadly pale and there were shadows around her mouth. Her eyes were wide open, doomed, and proud. And Mr. Brook felt suddenly like a murderer. A great commotion of feelings—understanding, remorse, and unreasonable love—made him cover his face with his hands. He could not speak until this agitation in his insides quieted down, and then he said very faintly, "Yes. Of course. The King of Finland. And was he nice?"

An hour later, Mr. Brook sat looking out of the window of his office. The trees   60
along the quiet Westbridge street were almost bare, and the gray buildings of the college had a calm, sad look. As he idly took in the familiar scene, he noticed the Drakes' old Airedale waddling along down the street. It was a thing he had watched a hundred times before, so what was it that struck him as strange? Then he realized with a kind of cold surprise that the old dog was running along backward. Mr. Brook watched the Airedale until he was out of sight, then resumed his work on the canons which had been turned in by the class in counterpoint.

Questions for Discussion and Writing

1. What clues make Mr. Brook suspect that Madame Zilensky has fabricated a good deal of her past experiences? Why does he back down when he finally confronts her, and with what effect?
2. How does McCullers emphasize the uniqueness of Madame Zilensky and the positive effect she has on Mr. Brook and her students?
3. What is the point of the ending of the story, and how is it connected to the events that precede it? Did you find Madame Zilensky an appealing character or merely a somewhat sad lunatic?

POETRY

Anne Bradstreet

· ·

Anne Bradstreet (1612–1672) was born in England and came to the American colonies when she was eighteen. She had eight children and wrote poems for herself that her brother-in-law published in London, without her knowledge, in 1650. This volume, The Tenth Muse, *was the first book of poetry published in England by anyone living in colonial America. The following poem was composed in anticipation of a second edition of this volume (which appeared six years after her death).*

THE AUTHOR TO HER BOOK

Thou ill-formed offspring of my feeble brain,
Who after birth did'st by my side remain,
Till snatched from thence by friends, less wise than true,
Who thee abroad exposed to public view;
Made thee in rags, halting, to the press to trudge,   5
Where errors were not lessened, all my judge.

At thy return my blushing was not small,
My rambling brat[1] (in print) should mother call;
I cast thee by as one unfit for light,
Thy visage was so irksome in my sight;   10
Yet being mine own, at length affection would
Thy blemishes amend, if so I could:
I washed thy face, but more defects I saw,
And rubbing off a spot, still made a flaw.
I stretched thy joints to make thee even feet,[2]   15
Yet still thou run'st more hobbling than is meet;
In better dress to trim thee was my mind,
But nought save homespun cloth, in the house I find.
In this array, 'mongst vulgars may'st thou roam;
In the critics' hands beware thou dost not come;   20
And take thy way where yet thou art not known.
If for thy Father asked, say thou had'st none;
And for thy Mother, she alas is poor,
Which caused her thus to send thee out of door.

Questions for Discussion and Writing

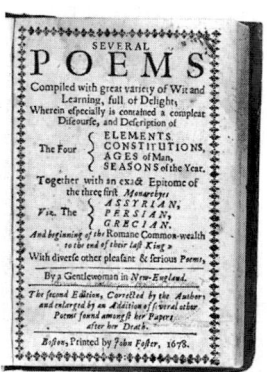

1. What is Bradstreet's attitude toward her "child," that is, her book of poetry, and to its initial publication without her consent?
2. What inferences can you draw about her everyday life from the homespun metaphors she applies to her writing?
3. Bradstreet refers to her work as if it were a child. In what sense do writers often think of their work as a kind of creation?
4. Why is it significant that the book cover for Anne Bradstreet's poems did not mention her name and simply referred to her as a "Gentlewoman in New-England"?

Emily Dickinson

* *

Emily Dickinson (1830–1886) was born in Amherst, Massachusetts, and spent her entire life there. She attended Mount Holyoke Female Seminary, where she quarreled frequently with the school's headmistress, who wanted her to accept Calvinist views. Dickinson became more reclusive in her mid-twenties, retired to the seclusion of her family, and in 1861 began writing poetry that was strongly influenced by the ideas of Ralph Waldo Emerson. She maintained a correspondence with Thomas Wentworth Higginson, an

---

[1]*brat:* the word here emphasizes the insignificance rather than the unpleasant aspects of a child. [2]*even feet:* Bradstreet is referring to her revision of the original poem to make the number of feet in each line match.

abolitionist editor who encouraged her to write poetry. During her life, she published only seven of the nearly eighteen hundred poems that she wrote. After her death, a selection of her work aroused public interest, and her stature as one of the great American poets is now unquestioned. "Tell All the Truth but Tell It Slant" expresses her artistic credo.

TELL ALL THE TRUTH BUT TELL IT SLANT

Tell all the Truth but tell it slant—
Success in Circuit lies
Too bright for our infirm Delight
The Truth's superb surprise
As Lightning to the Children eased   5
With explanation kind
The Truth must dazzle gradually
Or every man be blind—

Questions for Discussion and Writing

1. How might the quality of Dickinson's personal reticence lead some readers to perceive her poetry as obscure?
2. How does the metaphor that Dickinson uses to explain her reasons for telling the truth indirectly illuminate her choice?
3. In your experiences, have there been circumstances in which the truth was too strong and could be approached only indirectly? Describe these circumstances.

Paul Simon and Art Garfunkel

Paul Simon (b. 1941) has remained an innovative and popular musician since he achieved success as half of the Simon and Garfunkel team in the 1960s. The duo received Grammy Awards for the soundtrack recording for the film The Graduate *(1968) and for the record album* Bridge Over Troubled Water. *As a solo performer Simon received Grammy awards for the record albums* Still Crazy After All These Years *(1975) and* Graceland *(1987). Simon was inducted along with Art Garfunkel into the Rock and Roll Hall of Fame in 1990.*

Art Garfunkel (b. 1941) has an instantly recognizable tenor voice that has been heard since he began performing with Paul Simon during the folk music renaissance in the 1960s. He has also appeared as an actor in the films Catch 22 *(1969) and* Carnal Knowledge *(1971). Over half a million fans crowded Central Park in 1981 for an open-air concert when he reunited with Simon. The resulting record,* Simon and Garfunkel, the Concert in Central Park, *became an immediate hit. He recently cowrote (with Maia Sharp and Buddy Mondlock) six of the songs for the CD* Everything Waits To Be Noticed *(2002).*

The following song lyrics are accompanied by music featuring an overdubbed electric guitar, bass, and drums which were added to an earlier recording that had only vocals and an acoustic guitar. These lyrics, from The Sound of Silence *(1966), blend seamlessly with the music to create a timeless mood for generations of listeners.*

THE SOUND OF SILENCE

Hello darkness, my old friend. I've come to talk with you again.
Because a vision softly creeping left its seeds while I was sleeping
and the vision that was planted in my brain still remains within the sound of silence.

In restless dreams I walked alone, narrow streets of cobblestone
'neath the halo of a street lamp, I turned my collar to the cold and damp   5
when my eyes were stabbed by the flash of a neon light
that split the night and touched the sound of silence.

And in the naked light I saw ten thousand people, maybe more.
People talking without speaking, people hearing without listening.
People writing songs that voices never shared, no one dared disturb the sound of silence.   10

"Fools," said I, "you do not know, Silence like a cancer grows.
Hear my words that I might teach you, take my arms that I might reach you."
But my words like silent raindrops fell and echoed in the wells of silence.

And the people bowed and prayed to the neon god they made
and the sign flashed out its warning in the words that it was forming.   15
And the sign said "The words of the prophets are written on the subway walls
and tenement halls and whispered in the sound of silence."

Questions for Discussion and Writing

1. How do these song lyrics address the issue of the void at the center of communication? What change and impact does the singer wish to make through his **lyrics?**
2. What role does the "neon god" and its proclamation play in the drama the song describes? Why is it significant that it is the people themselves who have created this neon god?
3. To what extent does the song suggest that the real messages, the ones that are unheard, are silenced because they would prove disconcerting? In what ways could silence be like a growing cancer that destroys even as it conceals?

Thinking Critically About the Image

Gustav Klimt (1862–1918), Austrian painter, was the foremost exponent of Art Noveau (a decorative art movement that lasted from the 1880s to World War I, characterized by a richly ornamental asymmetrical style in furniture, jewelry, and book design and illustration). His greatest works are portraits and landscapes of erotic and exotic sensibilities with symbolic themes. In *The Kiss* (1908, oil on canvas) we see the brilliant colors and eerie dream-like state characteristic of the Symbolists. Symbolism was a movement in art and literature that sought to convey impressions by suggestion rather than by direct statement. The figures are depicted realistically in a highly stylized jewel-like surface that reflects the Byzantine mosaics Klimt had seen in Ravenna, Italy. This is one of the world's most reproduced images and communicates, as few paintings can, a feeling of rapture.

1. How does the setting suggest a timeless story whose mythic quality is enhanced by the garlands both the man and woman wear and by the flowery green platform that could be a magical carpet?
2. How does Klimt use whirls and spirals in the woman's robe to contrast with the upright black rectangles with which the man is emblazoned to underscore the archetypal nature of their story?
3. What other features of this work give it a timeless quality, as if it has come to us from far away and long ago?

Connections

Chapter 10: The Artistic Impulse

Kurt Vonnegut, Jr., *How to Write with Style*
Compare the different emphases of Vonnegut and Stephen King in their advice to would-be writers.

Fran Lebowitz, *How to Tell if Your Child Is a Writer*
Discuss the unexpected similarities between Lebowitz and Marcel Proust in "The Bodily Memory" (Ch. 1) in terms of the personality of the writer.

Stephen King,   *On Writing*
To what extent is King's approach to writing the same as Roger Ebert's approach to developing critical skills in appreciating films?

Roger Ebert,   *Great Movies*
Which of the films Ebert mentions are enhanced through their musical scores for the reasons discussed by Aaron Copland?

Agnes De Mille,   *Pavlova*
Is seeing the performance of a great dancer as inspirational in another dancer's career (as described by De Mille) as reading a great book for an aspiring writer is according to Kurt Vonnegut, Jr.?

Aaron Copland,   *Film Music*
Does film music enhance a film in the same way that music enhances the lyrics of a song such as "The Sound of Silence"? Why or why not?

Lance Morrow,   *Imprisoning Time in a Rectangle*
Discuss how the Vietnam era photographs described by Morrow place violent events in perspective just as Steven E. Barkan and Lynne L. Snowden achieve this goal in "Defining and Countering Terrorism" (Ch. 8).

David Brooks,   *Oversimulated Suburbia*
In what way is the impulse behind The Sims similar to that of the characters in Raymond Carver's story "Neighbors" (Ch. 2)?

Carson McCullers,   *Madame Zilensky and the King of Finland*
How does the ending of McCullers's story illustrate "The Road Not Taken" (Ch. 11) as Robert Frost uses the phrase?

Anne Bradstreet,   *The Author to Her Book*
What insights do Bradstreet and Charlotte Perkins Gilman in "The Yellow Wallpaper" (Ch. 1) offer into the social pressures on women who wish to write?

Emily Dickinson,   *Tell All the Truth but Tell It Slant*
In what sense do Dickinson and Carson McCullers in her story express views on how to reach audiences through less than obvious methods?

Paul Simon and Art Garfunkel,   *The Sound of Silence*
In what respects does Simon and Garfunkel's song attempt to awaken us in the same way that Plato intends to do in "The Allegory of the Cave" (Ch. 11)?

Edvard Munch, **The Scream,** *1893.*
Oil on canvas. © ARS, NY. Erich Lessing/Art Resource, NY. National Gallery, Oslo, Norway.

Matters of Ethics, Philosophy, and Religion

Is there any thing beyond?—Who knows?

—LORD BYRON, *LETTERS AND JOURNALS*

Essays in this chapter offer a vivid and extensive range of responses to universal questions of good and evil and life and death. Philip Wheelwright recommends a systematic approach to the ethical problems of everyday life. The Dalai Lama suggests developing tolerance toward the teachings of other religious faiths. Garrett Hardin investigates the ethical criteria by which actions are judged to be right or wrong and the trade-offs that must be accepted in some situations.

Paired selections by Marya Mannes and Richard Selzer illustrate very different reactions to abortion. Stanley Milgram, in his classic experiment, investigates why moral constraints fail to operate in the presence of authority figures. Tim O'Brien confronts the dilemma of whether or not to serve in the United States Army during the Vietnam War, and Langston Hughes amusingly addresses the issue of hypocrisy and religious faith.

Plato's "Allegory of the Cave" and parables drawn from the New Testament and from Buddhist and Islamic traditions use analogies and innovative storytelling techniques to transform philosophical issues into accessible and relevant anecdotes.

In her story Joyce Carol Oates creates a moral dilemma that requires the main character to make a life-or-death decision.

The poets in this chapter—Robert Frost, Linda Pastan, and Lisel Mueller—struggle with life choices that we all confront and remind us not to lose sight of important values.

NONFICTION

Philip Wheelwright

Philip Wheelwright (1901–1970) was born in Elizabeth, New Jersey, and earned a Ph.D. from Princeton University in 1924. He was professor of philosophy at Princeton, Dartmouth, and the University of California at Riverside. His many influential studies of philosophy and ethics include A Critical Introduction to Ethics *(1959);* The Burning Fountain: A Study in the Language of Symbolism *(1954);* Philosophy as the Art of Living *(1956), which was first given as the Tully Cleon Knoles lectures;* Heraclitus *(1959); and* Valid Thinking *(1962). In "The Meaning of Ethics," from* A Critical Introduction to Ethics, *Wheelwright discusses the essential elements involved in solving ethical problems.*

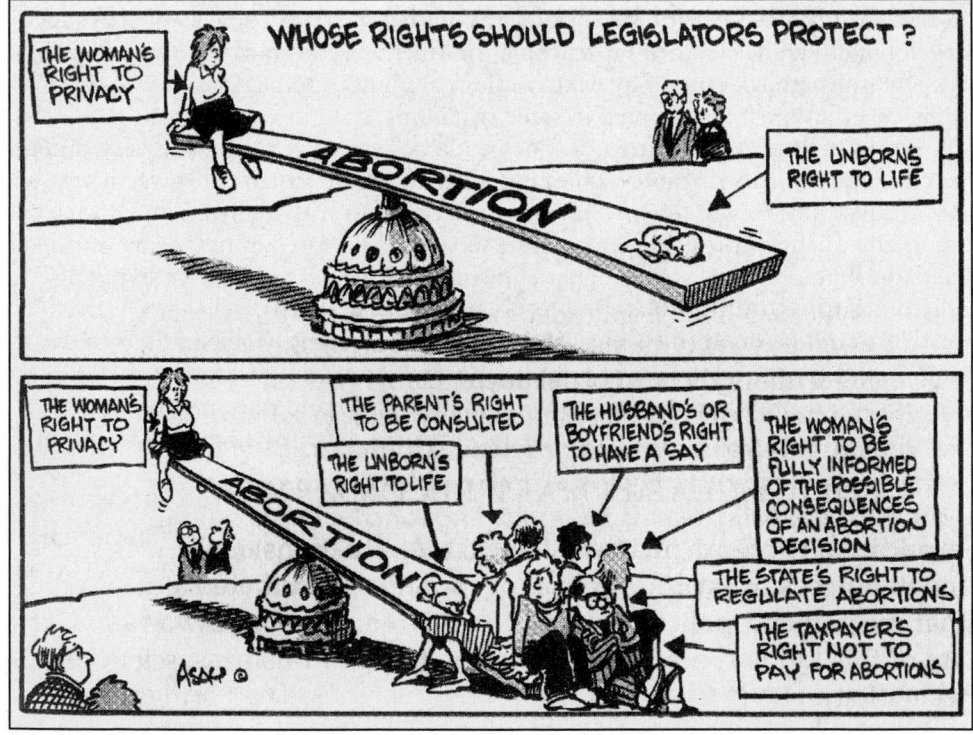

How does this cartoon by Chuck Asay reflect the ethical and legal dilemmas connected with abortion? How could Wheelwright's analysis of ethical inquiry be applied to this controversial issue?

THE MEANING OF ETHICS

For you see, Callicles, our discussion is concerned with a matter in which even a man of slight intelligence must take the profoundest interest—namely, what course of life is best.
                                                                —SOCRATES, *in Plato's* Gorgias

Man is the animal who can reflect. Like other animals, no doubt, he spends much of his time in merely reacting to the pressures and urgencies of his environment. But being a man he has moments also of conscious stock-taking, when he becomes aware not only of his world but of himself confronting his world, evaluating it, and making choices with regard to it. It is this ability to know himself and on the basis of self-knowledge to make evaluations and reflective choices that differentiates man from his subhuman cousins.

There are, as Aristotle has pointed out, two main ways in which man's power of reflection becomes active. They are called, in Aristotle's language, *theoretikos* and *praktikos* respectively; which is to say, thinking about what is actually the case and thinking about what had better be done. In English translation the words *contemplative* and *operative* probably come closest to Aristotle's intent. To think contemplatively is to ask oneself what *is;* to think operatively is to ask oneself what to *do.* These are the two modes of serious, one might even say of genuine thought—as distinguished from daydreams, emotional vaporizings, laryngeal chatter, and the repetition of clichés. To think seriously is to think either for the sake of knowing things as they are or for the sake of acting upon, and producing or helping to produce, things as they might be.

Although in practice the two types of thinking are much interrelated, it is operative thinking with which our present study is primarily concerned. Ethics, although it must be guided, limited, and qualified constantly by considerations of what is actually the case, is focused upon questions of what should be done. The converse, however, does not follow. Not all questions about what should be done are ethical questions. Much of our operative thinking is given to more immediate needs—to means whereby some given end can be achieved. A person who deliberates as to the most effective way of making money, or of passing a course, or of winning a battle, or of achieving popularity, is thinking operatively, but if that is as far as his planning goes it cannot be called ethical. Such deliberations about adapting means to an end would acquire an ethical character only if some thought were given to the nature and value of the end itself. Ethics cannot dispense with questions of means, but neither can it stop there.

Accordingly, ethics may be defined as that branch of philosophy which is the systematic study of reflective choice, of the standards of right and wrong by which it is to be guided, and of the goods toward which it may ultimately be directed. The relation between the parts of this definition, particularly between standards of right and wrong on the one hand and ultimately desirable goods on the other, will be an important part of the forthcoming study.

The Nature of Moral Deliberation

The soundest approach to ethical method is through reflection on our experience of   5
moral situations which from time to time we have had occasion to face, or through an
imagined confrontation of situations which others have faced and which we can thus
make sympathetically real to ourselves. For instance:

> Arthur Ames is a rising young district attorney engaged on his most important case. A
> prominent political boss has been murdered. Suspicion points at a certain ex-convict, known
> to have borne the politician a grudge. Aided by the newspapers, which have reported the
> murder in such a way as to persuade the public of the suspect's guilt, Ames feels certain
> that he can secure a conviction on the circumstantial evidence in his possession. If he suc-
> ceeds in sending the man to the chair he will become a strong candidate for governor at the
> next election.
>
> During the course of the trial, however, he accidentally stumbles on some fresh evidence,
> known only to himself and capable of being destroyed if he chooses, which appears to es-
> tablish the ex-convict's innocence. If this new evidence were to be introduced at the trial an
> acquittal would be practically certain. What ought the District Attorney to do? Surrender
> the evidence to the defence, in order that, as a matter of fair play, the accused might be
> given every legitimate chance of establishing his innocence? But to do that will mean the loss
> of a case that has received enormous publicity; the District Attorney will lose the backing
> of the press; he will appear to have failed, and his political career may be blocked. In that
> event not only will he himself suffer disappointment, but his ample plans for bestowing
> comforts on his family and for giving his children the benefits of a superior education may
> have to be curtailed. On the other hand, ought he to be instrumental in sending a man to
> the chair for a crime that in all probability he did not commit? And yet the ex-convict is a
> bad lot; even if innocent in the present case he has doubtless committed many other crimes
> in which he has escaped detection. Is a fellow like that worth the sacrifice of one's career?
> Still, there is no proof that he has ever committed a crime punishable by death. Until a man
> had been proved guilty he must be regarded, by a sound principle of American legal the-
> ory, as innocent. To conceal and destroy the new evidence, then, is not that tantamount to
> railroading an innocent man to the chair?
>
> So District Attorney Ames reasons back and forth. He knows that it is a widespread cus-
> tom for a district attorney to conceal evidence prejudicial to his side of a case. But is the cus-
> tom, particularly when a human life is at stake, morally right? A district attorney is an agent
> of the government, and his chief aim in that capacity should be to present his accusations
> in such a way as to ensure for the accused not condemnation but justice. The question,
> then, cannot be answered by appealing simply to law or to legal practice. It is a moral one:
> *What is Arthur Ames' duty? What ought he to do?*
>
> Benjamin Bates has a friend who lies in a hospital, slowly dying of a painful and incurable
> disease. Although there is no hope of recovery, the disease sometimes permits its victim to
> linger on for many months, in ever greater torment and with threatened loss of sanity. The
> dying man, apprised of the outcome and knowing that the hospital expenses are a severe
> drain on his family's limited financial resources, decides that death had better come at once.
> His physician, he knows, will not run the risk of providing him with the necessary drug.
> There is only his friend Bates to appeal to.
>
> How shall Bates decide? Dare he be instrumental in hastening another's death? Has he a
> moral right to be an accessory to the taking of a human life? Besides, suspicion would point
> his way, and his honorable motives would not avert a charge of murder. On the other hand,

can he morally refuse to alleviate a friend's suffering and the financial distress of a family when the means of doing so are in his hands? And has he not an obligation to respect a friend's declared will in the matter? To acquiesce and to refuse seem both somehow in different ways wrong, yet one course or the other must be chosen. *What ought Bates to do? Which way does his duty lie?*

In the city occupied by Crampton College a strike is declared by the employees of all the public-transit lines. Their wages have not been increased to meet the rising cost of living, and the justice of their grievance is rather widely admitted by neutral observers. The strike ties up business and causes much general inconvenience; except for the people who have cars of their own or can afford taxi fare, there is no way of getting from one part of the city to another. Labor being at this period scarce, an appeal is made by the mayor to college students to serve the community by acting in their spare time as motormen and drivers. The appeal is backed by a promise of lucrative wages and by the college administration's agreement to cooperate by permitting necessary absences from classes.

What ought the students of Crampton College to do? If they act as strikebreakers, they aid in forcing the employees back to work on the corporation's own terms. Have they any right to interfere so drastically and one-sidedly in the lives and happiness of others? On the other hand, if they turn down the mayor's request the community will continue to suffer grave inconveniences until the fight is somehow settled. *What is the students' duty in the matter? What is the right course for them to follow?*

These three situations, although perhaps unusual in the severity of their challenge, offer examples of problems distinctively moral. When the act of moral deliberation implicit in each of them is fully carried out, certain characteristic phases can be discerned.

(i) Examination and clarification of the alternatives. What are the relevant possibilities of action in the situation confronting me? Am I clear about the nature of each? Have I clearly distinguished them from one another? And are they mutually exhaustive, or would a more attentive search reveal others? In the case of District Attorney Ames, for example, a third alternative might have been to make a private deal with the ex-convict by which, in exchange for his acquittal, the District Attorney would receive the profits from some lucrative racket of which the ex-convict had control. No doubt to a reputable public servant this line of conduct would be too repugnant for consideration; it exemplifies, nevertheless, the ever-present logical possibility of going "between the horns"[1] of the original dilemma.

(ii) Rational elaboration of consequences. The next step is to think out the probable consequences of each of the alternatives in question. As this step involves predictions about a hypothetical future, the conclusions can have, at most, a high degree of probability, never certainty. The degree of probability is heightened accordingly as there is found some precedent in past experience for each of the proposed choices. Even if the present situation seems wholly new, analysis will always reveal *some* particulars for which analogies in past experience can be found or to which known laws of causal sequence are applicable. Such particulars will be dealt with partly by analogy (an act similar to the one now being deliberated about had on a previous occasion

---

[1] *"between the horns"*: In essence, finding a viable third alternative.

such and such consequences) and partly by the inductive-deductive method: appealing to general laws (deduction) which in turn have been built up as generalizations from observed particulars (induction). Mr. Ames, we may suppose, found the materials for this step in his professional knowledge of law and legal precedent, as well as in his more general knowledge of the policies of the press, the gullibility of its readers, and the high cost of domestic luxuries.

(iii) Imaginative projection of the self into the predicted situation.   It is not enough to reason out the probable consequences of a choice. In a moral deliberation the chief interests involved are not scientific but human and practical. The only way to judge the comparative desirability of two possible futures is to live through them both in imagination. The third step, then, is to project oneself imaginatively into the future; i.e. establish a dramatic identification of the present self with that future self to which the now merely imagined experiences may become real. Few persons, unfortunately, are capable of an imaginative identification forceful enough to give the claims of the future self an even break. Present goods loom larger than future goods, and goods in the immediate future than goods that are remote. The trained ethical thinker must have a sound *temporal perspective,* the acquisition of which is to be sought by a frequent, orderly, and detailed exercise of the imagination with respect to not yet actual situations.

(iv) Imaginative identification of the self with the points of view of those persons whom the proposed act will most seriously affect.   What decision I make here and now, if of any importance, is likely to have consequences, in varying degrees, for persons other than myself. An important part of a moral inquiry is to envisage the results of a proposed act as they will appear to those other persons affected by them. I must undertake, then, a dramatic identification of my own self with the selves of other persons. The possibility of doing this is evident from a consideration of how anyone's dramatic imagination works in the reading of a novel or the witnessing of a play. If the persons in the novel or play are dramatically convincing it is not because their characters and actions have been established by logical proof, but because they are presented so as to provoke in the reader an impulse to project himself into the world of the novel or play, to identify himself with this and that character in it, to share their feelings and moods, to get their slant on things.

In most persons, even very benevolent ones, the social consciousness works by fits   10 and starts. To examine fairly the needs and claims of other selves is no less hard and is often harder than to perform a similar task with regard to one's future self. Accordingly the ethical thinker must develop *social perspective*—that balanced appreciation of others' needs and claims which is the basis of justice.

In this fourth, as in the third step, the imaginative projection is to be carried out for each of the alternatives, according as their consequences shall have been predicted by Step ii.

(v) Estimation and comparison of the values involved.   Implicit in the third and fourth steps is a recognition that certain values both positive and negative are latent in each of the hypothetical situations to which moral choice may lead. The values must be made explicit in order that they may be justly compared, for it is as a result of their comparison that a choice is to be made. To make values explicit is to give them a relatively abstract formulation; they still, however, derive concrete significance from their imagined exemplifications. District Attorney Ames, for example, might have envisaged his dilemma as a choice between family happiness and worldly success on the one hand as against professional honor on the other. Each of these is undoubtedly good, that is to say a value, but the values cannot be reduced to a common denominator. Family happiness enters as a factor into Benjamin Bates's dilemma no less than into that of Arthur Ames, but it stands to be affected in a different way and therefore, in spite of the identical words by which our linguistic poverty forces us to describe it, it does not mean the same thing. Family happiness may mean any number of things; so may success, and honor—although these different meanings have, of course, an intelligible bond of unity. Arthur Ames's task is to compare not just any family happiness with any professional honor but the particular exemplifications of each that enter into his problem. The comparison is not a simple calculation but an imaginative deliberation, in which the abstract values that serve as the logical ground of the comparison are continuous with, and interactive with, the concrete particulars that serve as its starting-point.

(vi) Decision. Comparison of the alternative future situations and the values embodied in each must terminate in a decision. Which of the possible situations do I deem it better to bring into existence? There are no rules for the making of this decision. I must simply decide as wisely and as fairly and as relevantly to the total comparison as I can. Every moral decision is a risk, for the way in which a person decides is a factor in determining the kind of self he is going to become.

(vii) Action. The probable means of carrying out the decision have been established by Step ii. The wished-for object or situation is an end, certain specific means toward the fulfillment of which lie here and now within my power. These conditions supply the premises for an ethical syllogism. When a certain end, *x*, is recognized as the best of the available alternatives, and when the achievement of it is seen to be possible through a set of means *a, b, c* . . . which lie within my power, then whichever of the means *a, b, c* . . . is an action that can here and now be performed becomes at just this point my duty. If the deliberative process has been carried out forcefully and wisely it will have supplied a categorical answer to the question, What ought I to do?—even though the answer in some cases may be, Do nothing.

Naturally, not all experiences of moral deliberation and choice reveal these seven 15 phases in a distinct, clear-cut way. Nor is the order here given always the actual order. Sometimes we may begin by deliberating about the relative merits of two ends, seeking the means simultaneously with this abstract inquiry, or after its completion. The foregoing analysis does, however, throw some light on the nature of a moral problem, and may be tested by applying it to the three cases described at the beginning of the chapter.

Questions for Discussion and Writing

1. Why does solving an ethical problem always involve an examination of alternatives and a consideration of consequences? How is Wheelwright's emphasis on fair consideration of the effect of proposed actions on others an essential component of ethical inquiry?

2. What kinds of ethical dilemmas do Wheelwright's three hypothetical situations illustrate? Why is the ability to create hypothetical situations so important in the process of ethical inquiry?
3. Choose one of Wheelwright's three hypothetical cases and, using his outline of stages in the process of ethical inquiry, describe what you would do in each situation and why.

Marya Mannes

. . . .

Marya Mannes (1904–1990) was born in New York City to David Mannes and Clara Damrosch, the founders of the Mannes College of Music. Her major works of fiction and nonfiction include Message from a Stranger *(1948);* More in Anger *(1958);* The New York I Know *(1961);* Out of My Time *(1971), her autobiography;* Uncoupling: The Art of Coming Apart *(1972), a guide to divorce; and* Last Rights *(1974), a powerful and explicit plea for laws to ensure death with dignity. In the following excerpt from* Last Rights, *"The Unwilled," Mannes argues that a quality-of-life standard (rather than sanctity-of-life criteria) should be applied in those situations where an abortion is being considered.*

THE UNWILLED

Those who so passionately uphold the "sanctity of life" do not ask "what life?" nor see themselves as retarded and crippled in an institution for the rest of that life. Nor do they choose to see, to think of, the tens of thousands of lives born crippled and retarded, who, without will or choice, were allowed to be born as, presumably, the "right" of the damaged fetus *to* life.

Rather than seeing the many tangible horrors of that life, the sanctity people choose to emphasize the maternal love and care transcending the agony of a malformed or mindless presence, day after day and year after year. Or they point to those few institutions where a dedicated staff and the latest therapies bring these children or adults to a minimal level of competence: dressing themselves, cleaning themselves, learning small tasks. Since these "inmates" sometimes play and sometimes smile, they are, of course, "happy." They know no other existence, they act on reflexes, not will.

Certainly, love is the prime need of these incomplete beings, whether born that way or the victims of violent and crippling accident. Two middle-aged couples I know who cannot give such grown sons or daughters the special help they need, visit them where they live every week, stay with them for hours. "Ben is such a beautiful young man," said one father. "It's still hard to believe that his fine face and body can exist without thought processes or directions. The circuits in his brain just don't connect."

Certainly, there are parents who love their mongoloid and retarded children, accept them with their siblings as part of the family. But the "sanctity of life" people forget what an enormous toll it takes of the mother especially, who bore this child before the relatively new science of fetology could have given her the alternative choice: not to bear a permanently deformed or retarded being. For it has now become possible, with extremely delicate instruments and techniques, to establish deformation and brain damage, among other serious handicaps, in the unborn fetus when suspicions of malfunctioning exist.

Yet to the antiabortionists, any birth is presumably better than no birth. They seem   5
to forget that millions of unwanted children all over this world are not only destined for an uncherished and mean existence, but swell a population already threatening the resources of this planet, let alone its bare amenities.

They also choose to ignore the kind of "homes" in every large community where the pitiful accidents of biology sit half-naked on floors strewn with feces, autistic and motionless, or banging their swollen heads against peeling walls.

If the concept of "sanctity" does not include "quality," then the word has no meaning and less humanity. The rights of birth and death, of life itself, require both.

Above all, how can the sanctity-of-life argument prevail in a society that condones death in war of young men who want to live, but will not permit the old and hopelessly ill, craving release, to die?

Questions for Discussion and Writing

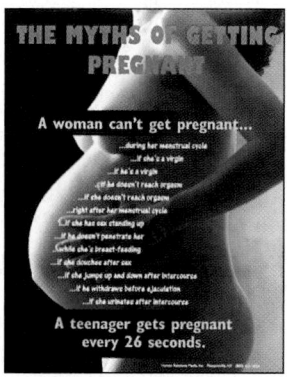

1. Why in Mannes's view should quality-of-life considerations overrule sanctity-of-life criteria with respect to those who would be born crippled or retarded and spend their lives in substandard institutions?
2. To what extent do Mannes's hypothetical examples support her assertion better than less extreme illustrations would have?
3. Does severe impairment necessarily exclude the capacity to love or to be loved? Who should have an absolute right to decide whether an abortion should be performed—the doctor, the mother, a hospital ethics committee, or some other agency? In a page or two, explain your answer.
4. How does the very public nature of this poster and its message suggest that pregnancy is now a social concern rather than simply a private matter?

Richard Selzer

• •

Richard Selzer was born in 1928 in Troy, New York. After receiving his M.D. from Albany Medical College in 1953, Selzer completed postdoctoral study at Yale (1957–1960) and is now a professor of surgery at the Yale University School of Medicine. Selzer's skill as a surgeon is matched by his skill as a writer; in 1975 he received the National Magazine Award from Columbia's School of Journalism for essays published in Esquire. *In his many books, including* Mortal Lessons *(1977),* Confessions of a Knife *(1979),* Letters to a Young Doctor *(1982),* Raising the Dead *(1993), and* The Exact Location of the Soul *(2001), Selzer draws on his experiences as a surgeon to take a hard look at the realities of illness, death, and disease that doctors must confront daily. "What I Saw at the Abortion," from* Mortal Lessons, *is characteristic of the way Selzer grapples with the actual conditions surgeons encounter; here, he describes the unexpected result and emotional impact of witnessing an abortion.*

WHAT I SAW AT THE ABORTION

I am a surgeon. Particularities of sick flesh is everyday news. Escaping blood, all the outpourings of disease—phlegm, pus, vomitus, even those occult meaty tumors that terrify—I see as blood, disease, phlegm, and so on. I touch them to destroy them. But I do not make symbols of them.

What I am saying is that I have seen and I am used to seeing. We are talking about a man who has a trade, who has practiced it long enough to see no news in any of it. Picture this man, then. A professional. In his forties. Three children. Lives in a university town—so, necessarily, well—enlightened? Enough, anyhow. Successful in his work, yes. No overriding religious posture. Nothing special, then, your routine fellow, trying to do his work and doing it well enough. Picture him, this professional, a sort of scientist, if you please, in possession of the standard admirable opinions, positions, convictions, and so on—on this and that matter—on *abortion,* for example.

All right.
Now listen.

It is the western wing of the fourth floor of a great university hospital. I am pres-   5
ent because I asked to be present. I wanted to see what I had never seen. An abortion.

The patient is Jamaican. She lies on the table in that state of notable submissiveness I have always seen in patients. Now and then she smiles at one of the nurses as though acknowledging a secret.

A nurse draws down the sheet, lays bare the abdomen. The belly mounds gently in the twenty-fourth week of pregnancy. The chief surgeon paints it with a sponge soaked in red antiseptic. He does this three times, each time a fresh sponge. He covers the area with a sterile sheet, an aperture in its center. He is a kindly man who teaches as he works, who pauses to reassure the woman.

He begins.

A little pinprick, he says to the woman.

He inserts the point of a tiny needle at the midline of the lower portion of her ab-   10
domen, on the downslope. He infiltrates local anesthetic into the skin, where it forms a small white bubble.

The woman grimaces.

That is all you will feel the doctor says. Except for a little pressure. But no more pain.

She smiles again. She seems to relax. She settles comfortably on the table. The worst is over.

The doctor selects a three-and-one-half-inch needle bearing a central stylet. He places the point at the site of the previous injection. He aims it straight up and down, perpendicular. Next he takes hold of her abdomen with his left hand, palming the womb, steadying it. He thrusts with his right hand. The needle sinks into the abdominal wall.

Oh, says the woman quietly. 15

But I guess it is not pain that she feels. It is more a recognition that the deed is being done.

Another thrust and he has spread the uterus.

We are in, he says.

He has felt the muscular wall of the organ gripping the shaft of his needle. A further slight pressure on the needle advances it a bit more. He takes his left hand from the woman's abdomen. He retracts the filament of the stylet from the barrel of the needle. A small geyser of pale yellow fluid erupts.

We are in the right place, says the doctor. Are you feeling any pain? he says. 20

She smiles, shakes her head. She gazes at the ceiling.

In the room we are six: two physicians, two nurses, the patient, and me.

The participants are busy, very attentive. I am not at all busy—but I am no less attentive. I want to see.

I see something!

It is unexpected, utterly unexpected, like a disturbance in the earth, a tumultuous 25 jarring. I see something other than what I expected here. I see a movement—a small one. But I have seen it.

And then I see it again. And now I see that it is the hub of the needle in the woman's belly that has jerked. First to one side. Then to the other side. Once more it wobbles, is *tugged,* like a fishing line nibbled by a sunfish.

Again! And I *know!*

It is the *fetus* that worries thus. It is the fetus struggling against the needle. Struggling? How can that be? I think: *that cannot be.* I think: the fetus feels no pain, cannot feel fear, has no *motivation.* It is merely reflex.

I point to the needle.

It is a reflex, says the doctor. 30

By the end of the fifth month, the fetus weighs about one pound, is about twelve inches long. Hair is on the head. There are eyebrows, eyelashes. Pale pink nipples show on the chest. Nails are present, at the fingertips, at the toes.

At the beginning of the sixth month, the fetus can cry, can suck, can make a fist. He kicks, he punches. The mother can feel this, can *see* this. His eyelids, until now closed, can open. He may look up, down, sideways. His grip is very strong. He could support his weight by holding with one hand.

A reflex, the doctor says.

I hear him. But I saw something. I saw *something* in that mass of cells *understand* that it must bob and butt. And I see it again! I have an impulse to shove to the table— it is just a step—seize that needle, pull it out.

We are not six, I think. I think we are *seven.* 35

Something strangles *there.* An effort, its effort, binds me to it.

I do not shove to the table. I take no little step. It would be . . . well, madness. Everyone here wants the needle where it is. Six do. No, *five* do.

I close my eyes. I see the inside of the uterus. It is bathed in ruby gloom. I see the creature curled upon itself. Its knees are flexed. Its head is bent upon its chest. It is in fluid and gently rocks to the rhythm of the distant heartbeat.

It resembles . . . a sleeping infant.

Its place is entered by something. It is sudden. A point coming. A needle!   40

A spike of *daylight* pierces the chamber. Now the light is extinguished. The needle comes closer in the pool. The point grazes the thigh, and I, stir. Perhaps I wake from dozing. The light is there again. I twist and straighten. My arms and legs *push*. My hand finds the shaft—grabs! I *grab*. I bend the needle this way and that. The point probes, touches on my belly. My mouth opens. Could I cry out? All is a commotion and a churning. There is a presence in the pool. An activity! The pool colors, reddens, darkens.

I open my eyes to see the doctor feeding a small plastic tube through the barrel of the needle into the uterus. Drops of pink fluid overrun the rim and spill onto the sheet. He withdraws the needle from around the plastic tubing. Now only the little tube protrudes from the woman's body. A nurse hands the physician a syringe loaded with a colorless liquid. He attaches it to the end of the tubing and injects it.

Prostaglandin, he says.

Ah, well, prostaglandin—a substance found normally in the body. When given in concentrated dosage, it throws the uterus into vigorous contraction. In eight to twelve hours, the woman will expel the fetus.

The doctor detaches the syringe but does not remove the tubing.   45

In case we must do it over, he says.

He takes away the sheet. He places gauze pads over the tubing. Over all this he applies adhesive tape.

I know. We cannot feed the great numbers. There is no more room. I know, I know. It is woman's right to refuse the risk, to decline the pain of childbirth. And an unwanted child is a very great burden. An unwanted child is a burden to himself. I know.

And yet . . . there is the flick of that needle. I *saw* it. I saw . . . I *felt*—in that room, a pace away, life prodded, life fending off, I saw life avulsed—swept by flood, blackening—then *out*.

There says the doctor, It's all over. It wasn't too bad, was it? he says to the woman.   50
She smiles. It is all over. Oh, yes.

And who would care to imagine that from a moist and dark commencement six months before there would ripen the cluster and globule, the sprout and pouch of man?

And who would care to imagine that trapped within the laked pearl and a dowry of yolk would lie the earliest stuff of dream and memory?

It is a persona carried here as well as person, I think. I think it is a signed piece, engraved with a hieroglyph of human genes.

I did not think this until I saw. The flick. The fending off.   55

We leave the room, the three of us, the doctors.

"Routine procedure," the chief surgeon says.

"All right," I say.

"Scrub nurse says first time you've seen one, Dick. First look at a purge," the surgeon says.

"That's right," I say. "First look."   60

"Oh, well," he says, "I guess you've seen everything else."

"Pretty much," I say.

"I'm not prying, Doctor," he says, "but was there something on your mind? I'd be delighted to field any questions . . ."

"No," I say. "No, thanks. Just simple curiosity."

"Okay," he says, and we all shake hands, scrub, change, and go to our calls.   65

I know, I know. The thing is normally done at sixteen weeks. Well, I've seen it performed at that stage, too. And seen . . . the flick. But I also know that in the sovereign state of my residence it is hospital policy to warrant the procedure at twenty-four weeks. And that in the great state that is adjacent, policy is enlarged to twenty-eight weeks.

Does this sound like argument? I hope not. I am not trying to argue. I am only saying I've *seen*. The flick. Whatever else may be said in abortion's defense, the vision of that other defense will not vanish from my eyes.

What I saw I saw as that: a *defense,* a motion *from,* an effort *away.* And it has happened that you cannot reason with me now. For what can language do against the truth of what I saw?

Questions for Discussion and Writing

1. How does Selzer's experience penetrate the usual objective stance he claims to maintain as a surgeon observing in the operating room? How do his reactions contrast with those of the doctor who actually performs the operation?
2. In what way are the details in this account structured to emphasize Selzer's unwilling recognition of what he is seeing? Why is it significant that medical terminology traditionally equates an abortion with the removal of a diseased part of the body?
3. Does Selzer's shift from an objective to a subjective viewpoint of the operation as experienced by the fetus detract from his account? Why or why not?

Garrett Hardin

•   •

Garrett Hardin was born in 1915 in Dallas, Texas. He graduated from the University of Chicago in 1936 and received a Ph.D. from Stanford University in 1941. A biologist, he was a professor of human ecology at the University of California at Santa Barbara until 1978. He is the author of many books and over two hundred articles, including Nature and Man's Fate *(1959), "The Tragedy of the Commons" in* Science *(December 1968), and* Exploring New Ethics for Survival *(1972). His latest works are* Stalking the Wild Taboo *(1996) and* The Ostrich Factor: Our Population Myopia *(1998). "Lifeboat Ethics: The Case against Helping the Poor" first appeared in the September 1974 issue of* Psychology Today. *In this article, Hardin compares a country that is well off to a lifeboat that is already almost full of people. Outside the lifeboat are the poor and needy, who*

How does this photo of a lifeboat holding Haitian refugees provide a concrete image that balances Garrett Hardin's abstract argument?

desperately wish to get in. Hardin claims that an ill-considered ethic of sharing will lead to the swamping of the lifeboat unless its occupants maintain a margin of safety by keeping people out.

LIFEBOAT ETHICS: THE CASE AGAINST HELPING THE POOR

Environmentalists use the metaphor of the earth as a "spaceship" in trying to persuade countries, industries and people to stop wasting and polluting our natural resources. Since we all share life on this planet, they argue, no single person or institution has the right to destroy, waste or use more than a fair share of its resources.

But does everyone on earth have an equal right to an equal share of its resources? The spaceship metaphor can be dangerous when used by misguided idealists to justify suicidal policies for sharing our resources through uncontrolled immigration and foreign aid. In their enthusiastic but unrealistic generosity, they confuse the ethics of a spaceship with those of a lifeboat.

A true spaceship would have to be under the control of a captain, since no ship could possibly survive if its course were determined by committee. Spaceship Earth certainly has no captain; the United Nations is merely a toothless tiger, with little power to enforce any policy upon its bickering members.

If we divide the world crudely into rich nations and poor nations, two thirds of them are desperately poor, and only one third comparatively rich, with the United

States the wealthiest of all. Metaphorically each nation can be seen as a lifeboat full of comparatively rich people. In the ocean outside each lifeboat swim the poor of the world, who would like to get in, or at least to share some of the wealth. What should the lifeboat passengers do?

First, we must recognize the limited capacity of any lifeboat. For example, a nation's   5 land has a limited capacity to support a population and as the current energy crisis has shown us, in some ways we have already exceeded the carrying capacity of our land.

Adrift in a Moral Sea

So here we sit, say fifty people in our lifeboat. To be generous, let us assume it has room for ten more, making a total capacity of sixty. Suppose the fifty of us in the lifeboat see 100 others swimming in the water outside, begging for admission to our boat or for handouts. We have several options: We may be tempted to try to live by the Christian ideal of being "our brother's keeper," or by the Marxist ideal of "to each according to his needs." Since the needs of all in the water are the same, and since they can all be seen as "our brothers," we could take them all into our boat, making a total of 150 in a boat designed for sixty. The boat swamps, everyone drowns. Complete justice, complete catastrophe.

Since the boat has an unused excess capacity of ten more passengers, we could admit just ten more to it. But which ten do we let in? How do we choose? Do we pick the best ten, the neediest ten, "first come, first served"? And what do we say to the ninety we exclude? If we do let an extra ten into our lifeboat, we will have lost our "safety factor," an engineering principle of critical importance. For example, if we don't leave room for excess capacity as a safety factor in our country's agriculture, a new plant disease or a bad change in the weather could have disastrous consequences.

Suppose we decide to preserve our small safety factor and admit no more to the lifeboat. Our survival is then possible, although we shall have to be constantly on guard against boarding parties.

While this last solution clearly offers the only means of our survival, it is morally abhorrent to many people. Some say they feel guilty about their good luck. My reply is simple: "Get out and yield your place to others." This may solve the problem of the guilt-ridden person's conscience, but it does not change the ethics of the lifeboat. The needy person to whom the guilt-ridden person yields his place will not himself feel guilty about his good luck. If he did, he would not climb aboard. The net result of conscience-stricken people giving up their unjustly held seats is the elimination of that sort of conscience from the lifeboat.

This is the basic metaphor within which we must work out our solutions. Let us   10 now enrich the image, step by step, with substantive additions from the real world, a world that must solve real and pressing problems of overpopulation and hunger.

The harsh ethics of the lifeboat become even harsher when we consider the reproductive differences between the rich nations and the poor nations. The people inside the lifeboats are doubling in numbers every eighty-seven years; those swimming around outside are doubling, on the average, every thirty-five years, more than twice as fast as the rich. And since the world's resources are dwindling, the difference in prosperity between the rich and the poor can only increase.

As of 1973, the U.S had a population of 210 million people, who were increasing by 0.8 percent per year. Outside our lifeboat, let us imagine another 210 million people (say the combined populations of Colombia, Ecuador, Venezuela, Morocco, Pakistan, Thailand and the Philippines), who are increasing at a rate of 3.3 percent per year. Put differently, the doubling time for this aggregate population is twenty-one years, compared to eighty-seven years for the U.S.

Multiplying the Rich and the Poor

Now suppose the U.S. agreed to pool its resources with those seven countries, with everyone receiving an equal share. Initially the ratio of Americans to non-Americans in this model would be one-to-one. But consider what the ratio would be after eighty-seven years, by which time the Americans would have doubled to a population of 420 million. By then, doubling every twenty-one years, the other group would have swollen to 354 billion. Each American would have to share the available resources with more than eight people.

But, one could argue, this discussion assumes that current population trends will continue, and they may not. Quite so. Most likely the rate of population increase will decline much faster in the U.S. than it will in the other countries, and there does not seem to be much we can do about it. In sharing with "each according to his needs," we must recognize that needs are determined by population size, which is determined by the rate of reproduction, which at present is regarded as a sovereign right of every nation, poor or not. This being so, the philanthropic load created by the sharing ethic of the spaceship can only increase.

The Tragedy of the Commons

The fundamental error of spaceship ethics, and the sharing it requires, is that it leads   15
to what I call "the tragedy of the commons." Under a system of private property, the men who own property recognize their responsibility to care for it, for if they don't they will eventually suffer. A farmer, for instance, will allow no more cattle in a pasture than its carrying capacity justifies. If he overloads it, erosion sets in, weeds take over, and he loses the use of the pasture.

If a pasture becomes a commons open to all, the right of each to use it may not be matched by a corresponding responsibility to protect it. Asking everyone to use it with discretion will hardly do, for the considerate herdsman who refrains from overloading the commons suffers more than a selfish one who says his needs are greater. If everyone would restrain himself, all would be well; but it takes only one less than everyone to ruin a system of voluntary restraint. In a crowded world of less than perfect human beings, mutual ruin is inevitable if there are no controls. This is the tragedy of the commons.

One of the major tasks of education today should be the creation of such an acute awareness of the dangers of the commons that people will recognize its many varieties. For example, the air and water have become polluted because they are treated as commons. Further growth in the population or per-capita conversion of natural resources into pollutants will only make the problem worse. The same holds true for the fish of the oceans. Fishing fleets have nearly disappeared in many parts of the world, technological improvements in the art of fishing are hastening the day of complete ruin. Only the replacement of the system of the commons with a responsible system of control will save the land, air, water and oceanic fisheries.

The World Food Bank

In recent years there has been a push to create a new commons called a World Food Bank, an international depository of food reserves to which nations would contribute according to their abilities and from which they would draw according to their needs. This humanitarian proposal has received support from many liberal international groups, and from such prominent citizens as Margaret Mead, U.N. Secretary General Kurt Waldheim, and Senators Edward Kennedy and George McGovern.

A world food bank appeals powerfully to our humanitarian impulses. But before we rush ahead with such a plan, let us recognize where the greatest political push comes from, lest we be disillusioned later. Our experience with the "Food for Peace program," or Public Law 480, gives us the answer. This program moved billions of dollars' worth of U.S. surplus grain to food-short, population-long countries during the past two decades. But when P.L. 480 first became law, a headline in the business magazine *Forbes* revealed the real power behind it: "Feeding the World's Hungry Millions: How It Will Mean Billions for U.S. Business."

And indeed it did. In the years 1960 to 1970, U.S. taxpayers spent a total of $7.9   20 billion on the Food for Peace program. Between 1948 and 1970, they also paid an additional $50 billion for other economic-aid programs, some of which went for food and food-producing machinery and technology. Though all U.S. taxpayers were forced to contribute to the cost of P.L. 480, certain special interest groups gained handsomely under the program. Farmers did not have to contribute the grain; the Government, or rather the taxpayers, bought it from them at full market prices. The increased demand raised prices of farm products generally. The manufacturers of farm machinery, fertilizers and pesticides benefited by the farmers' extra efforts to grow more food. Grain elevators profited from storing the surplus until it could be shipped. Railroads made money hauling it to ports, and shipping lines profited from carrying it overseas. The implementation of P.L. 480 required the creation of a vast Government bureaucracy, which then acquired its own vested interest in continuing the program regardless of its merits.

Extracting Dollars

Those who proposed and defended the Food for Peace program in public rarely mentioned its importance to any of these special interests. The public emphasis was always on its humanitarian effects. The combination of silent selfish interests and highly vocal humanitarian apologists made a powerful and successful lobby for extracting money from taxpayers. We can expect the same lobby to push now for the creation of a World Food Bank.

However great the potential benefit to selfish interests, it should not be a decisive argument against a truly humanitarian program. We must ask if such a program would actually do more good than harm, not only momentarily but also in the long run. Those who propose the food bank usually refer to a current "emergency" or "crisis" in terms of world food supply. But what is an emergency? Although they may be infrequent and sudden, everyone knows that emergencies will occur from time to time. A well-run family, company, organization or country prepares for the likelihood of accidents and emergencies. It expects them, it budgets for them, it saves for them.

Learning the Hard Way

What happens if some organizations or countries budget for accidents and others do not? If each country is solely responsible for its own well-being, poorly managed ones will suffer. But they can learn from experience. They may mend their ways, and learn to budget for infrequent but certain emergencies. For example, the weather varies from year to year, and periodic crop failures are certain. A wise and competent government saves out of the production of the good years in anticipation of bad years to come. Joseph taught this policy to Pharaoh in Egypt more than 2,000 years ago. Yet the great majority of the governments in the world today do not follow such a policy. They lack either the wisdom or the competence, or both. Should those nations that do manage to put something aside be forced to come to the rescue each time an emergency occurs among the poor nations?

"But it isn't their fault!" some kindhearted liberals argue. "How can we blame the poor people who are caught in an emergency? Why must they suffer for the sins of their governments?" The concept of blame is simply not relevant here. The real question is, what are the operational consequences of establishing a world food bank? If it is open to every country every time a need develops, slovenly rulers will not be motivated to take Joseph's advice. Someone will always come to their aid. Some countries will deposit food in the world food bank, and others will withdraw it. There will be almost no overlap. As a result of such solutions to food shortage emergencies, the poor countries will not learn to mend their ways, and will suffer progressively greater emergencies as their populations grow.

Population Control the Crude Way

On the average, poor countries undergo a 2.5 percent increase in population each year; 25 rich countries, about 0.8 percent. Only rich countries have anything in the way of food reserves set aside, and even they do not have as much as they should. Poor countries have none. If poor countries received no food from the outside, the rate of their population growth would be periodically checked by crop failures and famines. But if they can always draw on a world food bank in time of need, their populations can grow unchecked, and so will the "need" for aid. In the short run, a world food bank may diminish that need, but in the long run it actually increases the need without limit.

Without some system of worldwide food sharing, the proportion of people in the rich and poor nations might eventually stabilize. The overpopulated poor countries would decrease in numbers, while the rich countries that had room for more people would increase. But with a well-meaning system of sharing, such as a world food bank, the growth differential between the rich and the poor countries will not only persist, it will increase. Because of the higher rate of population growth in the poor countries of the world, 88 percent of today's children are born poor, and only 12 percent rich. Year by year the ratio becomes worse, as the fast-reproducing poor outnumber the slow-reproducing rich.

A world food bank is thus a commons in disguise. People will have more motivation to draw from it than to add to any common store. The less provident and less able will multiply at the expense of the abler and more provident, bringing eventual ruin upon all who share in the commons. Besides, any system of "sharing" that amounts to foreign aid from the rich nations to the poor nations will carry the taint of charity, which will contribute little to the world peace so devoutly desired by those who support the idea of a world food bank.

As past U.S. foreign-aid programs have amply and depressingly demonstrated, international charity frequently inspires mistrust and antagonism rather than gratitude on the part of the recipient nation.

Chinese Fish and Miracle Rice

The modern approach to foreign aid stresses the export of technology and advice, rather than money and food. As an ancient Chinese proverb goes: "Give a man a fish and he will eat for a day; teach him how to fish and he will eat for the rest of his days." Acting on this advice, the Rockefeller and Ford Foundations have financed a number of programs for improving agriculture in the hungry nations. Known as the "Green Revolution," these programs have led to the development of "miracle rice" and "miracle wheat," new strains that offer bigger harvests and greater resistance to crop damage. Norman Borlaug, the Nobel Prize–winning agronomist who, supported by the Rockefeller Foundation, developed "miracle wheat," is one of the most prominent advocates of a world food bank.

Whether or not the Green Revolution can increase food production as much as its   30 champions claim is a debatable but possibly irrelevant point. Those who support this well-intended humanitarian effort should first consider some of the fundamentals of human ecology. Ironically, one man who did was the late Alan Gregg, a vice president of the Rockefeller Foundation. Two decades ago he expressed strong doubts about the wisdom of such attempts to increase food production. He likened the growth and spread of humanity over the surface of the earth to the spread of cancer in the human body, remarking that "cancerous growths demand food; but, as far as I know, they have never been cured by getting it."

Overloading the Environment

Every human born constitutes a draft on all aspects of the environment: food, air, water, forests, beaches, wildlife, scenery and solitude. Food can, perhaps, be significantly increased to meet a growing demand. But what about clean beaches, unspoiled forests and solitude? If we satisfy a growing population's need for food, we necessarily decrease its per-capita supply of the other resources needed by men.

India, for example, now has a population of 600 million, which increases by 15 million each year. This population already puts a huge load on a relatively impoverished environment. The country's forests are now only a small fraction of what they were three centuries ago, and floods and erosion continually destroy the insufficient farmland that remains. Every one of the 15 million new lives added to India's population puts an additional burden on the environment, and increases the economic and social costs of crowding. However humanitarian our intent, every Indian life saved through medical or nutritional assistance from abroad diminishes the quality of life for those who remain, and for subsequent generations. If rich countries make it possible, through foreign aid, for 600 million Indians to swell to 1.2 billion in a mere twenty-eight years, as their current growth rate threatens, will future generations of Indians thank us for hastening the destruction of their environment? Will our good intentions be sufficient excuse for the consequences of our actions?

My final example of a commons in action is one for which the public has the least desire for rational discussion—immigration. Anyone who publicly questions the wisdom of current U.S. immigration policy is promptly charged with bigotry, prejudice, ethnocentrism, chauvinism, isolationism or selfishness. Rather than encounter such accusations, one would rather talk about other matters, leaving immigration policy to wallow in the crosscurrents of special interests that take no account of the good of the whole, or the interest of posterity.

Perhaps we still feel guilty about things we said in the past. Two generations ago the popular press frequently referred to Dagos, Wops, Polacks, Chinks and Krauts, in articles about how America was being "overrun" by foreigners of supposedly inferior genetic stock. But because the implied inferiority of foreigners was used then as justification for keeping them out, people now assume that restrictive policies could only be based on such misguided notions. There are no other grounds.

A Nation of Immigrants

Just consider the numbers involved. Our Government acknowledges a net inflow of 400,000 immigrants a year. While we have no hard data on the extent of illegal entries, educated guesses put the figure at about 600,000 a year. Since the natural increase (excess of births over deaths) of the resident population now runs about 1.7 million per year, the yearly gain from immigration amounts to at least 19 percent of the total annual increase, and may be as much as 37 percent if we include the estimate for illegal immigrants. Considering the growing use of birth-control devices, the potential effect of educational campaigns by such organizations as Planned Parenthood Federation of America and Zero Population Growth, and the influence of inflation and the housing shortage, the fertility rate of American women may decline so much that immigration could account for all the yearly increase in population. Should we not at least ask if that is what we want?

For the sake of those who worry about whether the "quality" of the average immigrant compares favorably with the quality of the average resident, let us assume that immigrants and native born citizens are of exactly equal quality, however one defines that term. We will focus here only on quantity; and since our conclusions will depend on nothing else, all charges of bigotry and chauvinism become irrelevant.

Immigration vs. Food Supply

World food banks *move food to the people,* hastening the exhaustion of the environment of the poor countries. Unrestricted immigration, on the other hand, *moves people to the food,* thus speeding up the destruction of the environment of the rich countries. We can easily understand why poor people should want to make this latter transfer, but why should rich hosts encourage it?

As in the case of foreign-aid programs, immigration receives support from selfish interests and humanitarian impulses. The primary selfish interest in unimpeded immigration is the desire of employers for cheap labor, particularly in industries and trades that offer degrading work. In the past, one wave of foreigners after another was brought into the U.S. to work at wretched jobs for wretched wages. In recent years, the Cubans, Puerto Ricans and Mexicans have had this dubious honor. The interests of the employers of cheap labor mesh well with the guilty silence of the country's liberal intelligentsia. White Anglo-Saxon Protestants are particularly reluctant to call for a closing of the doors to immigration for fear of being called bigots.

But not all countries have such reluctant leadership. Most educated Hawaiians, for example, are keenly aware of the limits of their environment, particularly in terms of population growth. There is only so much room on the islands, and the islanders know it. To Hawaiians, immigrants from the other forty-nine states present as great a threat as those from other nations. At a recent meeting of Hawaiian government officials in Honolulu, I had the ironic delight of hearing a speaker, who like most of his audience was of Japanese ancestry, ask how the country might practically and constitutionally close its doors to further immigration. One member of the audience countered: "How can we shut the doors now? We have many friends and relatives in Japan that we'd like to bring here some day so that they can enjoy Hawaii too." The Japanese-American speaker smiled sympathetically and answered: "Yes, but we have children now, and someday we'll have grandchildren too. We can bring more people here from Japan only by giving away some of the land that we hope to pass on to our grandchildren some day. What right do we have to do that?"

At this point, I can hear U.S. liberals asking: "How can you justify slamming   40
the door once you're inside? You say that immigrants should be kept out. But aren't we all immigrants, or the descendants of immigrants? If we insist on staying, must we not admit all others?" Our craving for intellectual order leads us to seek and prefer symmetrical rules and morals: a single rule for me and everybody else; the same rule yesterday, today, and tomorrow. Justice, we feel, should not change with time and place.

We Americans of non-Indian ancestry can look upon ourselves as the descendants of thieves who are guilty morally, if not legally, of stealing this land from its Indian owners. Should we then give back the land to the now living American descendants of those Indians? However morally or logically sound this proposal may be, I, for one, am unwilling to live by it and I know no one else who is. Besides, the logical consequence would be absurd. Suppose that, intoxicated with a sense of pure justice, we should decide to turn our land over to the Indians. Since all our wealth has also been derived from the land, wouldn't we be morally obliged to give that back to the Indians too?

Pure Justice vs. Reality

Clearly, the concept of pure justice produces an infinite regression to absurdity. Centuries ago, wise men invented statutes of limitations to justify the rejection of such pure justice, in the interest of preventing continual disorder. The law zealously defends property rights, but only relatively recent property rights. Drawing a line after an arbitrary time has elapsed may be unjust, but the alternatives are worse.

We are all descendants of thieves, and the world's resources are inequitably distributed. But we must begin the journey to tomorrow from the point where we are today. We cannot remake the past. We cannot safely divide the wealth equitably among all peoples so long as people reproduce at different rates. To do so would guarantee that our grandchildren, and everyone else's grandchildren, would have only a ruined world to inhabit.

To be generous with one's own possessions is quite different from being generous with those of posterity. We should call this point to the attention of those who, from a commendable love of justice and equality, would institute a system of the commons, either in the form of a world food bank, or of unrestricted immigration. We must convince them if we wish to save at least some parts of the world from environmental ruin.

Without a true world government to control reproduction and the use of available resources, the sharing ethic of the spaceship is impossible. For the foreseeable future, our survival demands that we govern our actions by the ethics of a lifeboat, harsh though they may be. Posterity will be satisfied with nothing less.   45

Questions for Discussion and Writing

1. What does Hardin mean by the expression "the tragedy of the commons"? How does the idea underlying this phrase rest on the assumption that human beings are not capable of responsible, voluntary restraint in using resources?

2. How does the analogy of the lifeboat support Hardin's contention that affluent nations have no obligation to share their food and resources with the world's starving masses? Evaluate Hardin's argument that our obligation to future generations should override our desire to help starving masses in the present.

3. To put Hardin's scenario in terms of personal moral choice, consider the following dilemmas and write a short essay on either (a) or (b) or both, and discuss the reasons for your answer(s):

   a. Would you be willing to add five years to your life even though it would mean taking five years away from the life of someone else you do not know? Would your decision be changed if you knew who the person was?

   b. If you had a child who was dying and the only thing that could save him or her was the bone marrow of a sibling, would you consider having another baby in order to facilitate what was almost sure to be a positive bone marrow transplant?

Tim O'Brien

Tim O'Brien was born in 1946 in Austin, Minnesota, and was educated at Macalester College and Harvard University. Drafted into the army during the Vietnam War, he attained the rank of sergeant and received the Purple Heart. His first published work, If I Die in a Combat Zone, Box Me Up and Ship Me Home *(1973), relates his experiences in Vietnam. This book is an innovative mixture of alternating chapters of fiction and autobiography in which the following nonfiction account first appeared.*

O'Brien's novel Northern Lights *(1974) was followed by the acclaimed work* Going After Cacciato *(1978), which won the National Book Award. Other works include* The Nuclear Age *(1985), a collection of stories titled* The Things They Carried *(1990),* Tomcat in Love *(1998), and most recently* July, July *(2002).*

IF I DIE IN A COMBAT ZONE

The summer of 1968, the summer I turned into a soldier, was a good time for talking about war and peace. Eugene McCarthy was bringing quiet thought to the subject. He was winning votes in the primaries. College students were listening to him, and some of us tried to help out. Lyndon Johnson was almost forgotten, no longer forbidding or feared; Robert Kennedy was dead but not quite forgotten; Richard Nixon looked like a loser. With all the tragedy and change that summer, it was fine weather for discussion.

And, with all of this, there was an induction notice tucked into a corner of my billfold.

So with friends and acquaintances and townspeople, I spent the summer in Fred's antiseptic cafe, drinking coffee and mapping out arguments on Fred's napkins. Or I sat in Chic's tavern, drinking beer with kids from the farms. I played some golf and tore up the pool table down at the bowling alley, keeping an eye open for likely-looking high school girls.

Late at night, the town deserted, two or three of us would drive a car around and around the town's lake, talking about the war, very seriously, moving with care from one argument to the next, trying to make it a dialogue and not a debate. We covered all the big questions: justice, tyranny, self-determination, conscience and the state, God and war and love.

College friends came to visit: "Too bad, I hear you're drafted. What will you do?" 5

I said I didn't know, that I'd let time decide. Maybe something would change, maybe the war would end. Then we'd turn to discuss the matter, talking long, trying out the questions, sleeping late in the mornings.

The summer conversations, spiked with plenty of references to the philosophers and academicians of war, were thoughtful and long and complex and careful. But, in the end, careful and precise argumentation hurt me. It was painful to tread deliberately over all the axioms and assumptions and corollaries when the people on the town's draft board were calling me to duty, smiling so nicely.

"It won't be bad at all," they said. "Stop in and see us when it's over."

So to bring the conversations to a focus and also to try out in real words my secret fears, I argued for running away.

I was persuaded then, and I remain persuaded now, that the war was wrong. And   10
since it was wrong and since people were dying as a result of it, it was evil. Doubts, of
course, hedged all this: I had neither the expertise nor the wisdom to synthesize answers;
most of the facts were clouded, and there was no certainty as to the kind of government that would follow a North Vietnamese victory or, for that matter, an American
victory, and the specifics of the conflict were hidden away—partly in men's minds,
partly in the archives of government, and partly in buried, irretrievable history. The war,
I thought, was wrongly conceived and poorly justified. But perhaps I was mistaken, and
who really knew, anyway?

Piled on top of this was the town, my family, my teachers, a whole history of the
prairie. Like magnets, these things pulled in one direction or the other, almost physical forces weighting the problem, so that, in the end, it was less reason and more gravity that was the final influence.

My family was careful that summer. The decision was mine and it was not talked
about. The town lay there, spread out in the corn and watching me, the mouths of old
women and Country Club men poised in a kind of eternal readiness to find fault. It was
not a town, not a Minneapolis or New York, where the son of a father can sometimes
escape scrutiny. More, I owed the prairie something. For twenty-one years I'd lived
under its laws, accepted its education, eaten its food, wasted and guzzled its water,
slept well at night, driven across its highways, dirtied and breathed its air, wallowed
in its luxuries. I'd played on its Little League teams. I remembered Plato's *Crito*, when
Socrates, facing certain death—execution, not war—had the chance to escape. But he
reminded himself that he had seventy years in which he could have left the country, if
he were not satisfied or felt the agreements he'd made with it were unfair. He had not
chosen Sparta or Crete. And, I reminded myself, I hadn't thought much about Canada
until that summer.

The summer passed this way. Gold afternoons on the golf course, a comforting
feeling that the matter of war would never touch me, nights in the pool hall or drug store,
talking with townsfolk, turning the questions over and over, being a philosopher.

Near the end of that summer the time came to go to the war. The family indulged
in a cautious sort of Last Supper together, and afterward my father, who is brave, said
it was time to report at the bus depot. I moped down to my bedroom and looked the
place over, feeling quite stupid, thinking that my mother would come in there in a day
or two and probably cry a little. I trudged back up to the kitchen and put my satchel
down. Everyone gathered around, saying so long and good health and write and let us
know if you want anything. My father took up the induction papers, checking on times
and dates and all the last-minute things, and when I pecked my mother's face and
grabbed the satchel for comfort, he told me to put it down, that I wasn't supposed to
report until tomorrow.

After laughing about the mistake, after a flush of red color and a flood of ribbing   15
and a wave of relief had come and gone, I took a long drive around the lake, looking
again at the place. Sunset Park, with its picnic table and little beach and a brown wood
shelter and some families swimming. The Crippled Children's School. Slater Park, more
kids. A long string of split level houses, painted every color.

The war and my person seemed like twins as I went around the town's lake. Twins
grafted together and forever together, as if a separation would kill them both.

The thought made me angry.

In the basement of my house I found some scraps of cardboard and paper. With devilish flair, I printed obscene words on them, declaring my intention to have no part of Vietnam. With delightful viciousness, a secret will, I declared the war evil, the draft board evil, the town evil in its lethargic acceptance of it all. For many minutes, making up the signs, making up my mind, I was outside the town. I was outside the law, all my old ties to my loves and family broken by the old crayon in my hand. I imagined strutting up and down the sidewalks outside the depot, the bus waiting and the driver blaring his horn, the *Daily Globe* photographer trying to push me into line with the other draftees, the frantic telephone calls, my head buzzing at the deed.

On the cardboard, my strokes of bright red were big and ferocious looking. The language was clear and certain and burned with a hard, defiant, criminal, blasphemous sound. I tried reading it aloud.

Later in the evening I tore the signs into pieces and put the shreds in the garbage   20
can outside, clanging the gray cover down and trapping the messages inside. I went back into the basement. I slipped the crayons into their box, the same stubs of color I'd used a long time before to chalk in reds and greens on Roy Rogers' cowboy boots.

I'd never been a demonstrator, except in the loose sense. True, I'd taken a stand in the school newspaper on the war, trying to show why it seemed wrong. But, mostly, I'd just listened.

"No war is worth losing your life for," a college acquaintance used to argue. "The issue isn't a moral one. It's a matter of efficiency: what's the most efficient way to stay alive when your nation is at war? That's the issue."

But others argued that no war is worth losing your country for, and when asked about the case when a country fights a wrong war, those people just shrugged.

Most of my college friends found easy paths away from the problem, all to their credit. Deferments for this and that. Letters from doctors or chaplains. It was hard to find people who had to think much about the problem. Counsel came from two main quarters, pacifists and veterans of foreign wars.

But neither camp had much to offer. It wasn't a matter of peace, as the pacifists argued, but rather a matter of when and when not to join others in making war. And it wasn't a matter of listening to an ex-lieutenant colonel talk about serving in a right war, when the question was whether to serve in what seemed a wrong one.

On August 13, I went to the bus depot. A Worthington *Daily Globe* photographer took my picture standing by a rail fence with four other draftees.

Then the bus took us through corn fields, to little towns along the way—Lismore and Rushmore and Adrian—where other recruits came aboard. With some of the tough guys drinking beer and howling in the back seats, brandishing their empty cans and calling one another "scum" and "trainee" and "GI Joe," with all this noise and hearty farewelling, we went to Sioux Falls. We spent the night in a YMCA. I went out alone for a beer, drank it in a corner booth, then I bought a book and read it in my room.

By noon the next day our hands were in the air, even the tough guys. We recited the proper words, some of us loudly and daringly and others in bewilderment. It was a brightly lighted room, wood paneled. A flag gave the place the right colors, there was some smoke in the air. We said the words, and we were soldiers.

I'd never been much of a fighter. I was afraid of bullies. Their ripe muscles made me angry: a frustrated anger. Still, I deferred to no one. Positively lorded myself over inferiors. And on top of that was the matter of conscience and conviction, uncertain and surface-deep but pure nonetheless: I was a confirmed liberal, not a pacifist; but I would have cast my ballot to end the Vietnam war immediately, I would have voted for Eugene McCarthy, hoping he would make peace. I was not soldier material, that was certain.

But I submitted. All the personal history, all the midnight conversations and books   30
and beliefs and learning, were crumpled by abstention, extinguished by forfeiture, for lack of oxygen, by a sort of sleepwalking default. It was no decision, no chain of ideas or reasons, that steered me into the war.

It was an intellectual and physical stand-off, and I did not have the energy to see it to an end. I did not want to be a soldier, not even an observer to war. But neither did I want to upset a peculiar balance between the order I knew, the people I knew, and my own private world. It was not that I valued that order. But I feared its opposite, in- evitable chaos, censure, embarrassment, the end of everything that had happened in my life, the end of it all.

And the stand-off is still there. I would wish this book could take the form of a plea for everlasting peace, a plea from one who knows, from one who's been there and come back, an old soldier looking back at a dying war.

That would be good. It would be fine to integrate it all to persuade my younger brother and perhaps some others to say no to wars and other battles.

Or it would be fine to confirm the odd beliefs about war: it's horrible, but it's a cru- cible of men and events and, in the end, it makes more of a man out of you.

But, still, none of these notions seems right. Men are killed, dead human beings are   35
heavy and awkward to carry, things smell different in Vietnam, soldiers are afraid and often brave, drill sergeants are boors, some men think the war is proper and just and others don't and most don't care. Is that the stuff for a morality lesson, even for a theme?

Do dreams offer lessons? Do nightmares have themes, do we awaken and analyze them and live our lives and advise others as a result? Can the foot soldier teach any- thing important about war, merely for having been there? I think not. He can tell war stories.

Questions for Discussion and Writing

1. What conflicting sets of values weighed on O'Brien when he learned he was drafted? Of these, which was the most significant in determining his ultimate decision?
2. Which features of this account provide insight into a Tim O'Brien who was very different from the one townspeople knew?
3. What do you think you would have done if you were in the same situation as O'Brien?

Stanley Milgram

· ·

Stanley Milgram (1933–1984) was born in New York, received his Ph.D. from Harvard in 1960, and taught at Yale, Harvard, and the City University of New York. His research into human conformity and aggression, the results of which were published in 1974 as Obedience to Authority, *began a national debate. Milgram's thesis cast new light on the Holocaust, the 1972 My Lai massacres in Vietnam, and the Watergate incident. Milgram also wrote* Psychology in Today's World *(1975) and* The Individual in a Social World: Essays and Experiments *(1977).*

THE PERILS OF OBEDIENCE

Obedience is as basic an element in the structure of social life as one can point to. Some system of authority is a requirement of all communal living, and it is only the person dwelling in isolation who is not forced to respond, with defiance or submission, to the commands of others. For many people, obedience is a deeply ingrained behavior tendency, indeed a potent impulse overriding training in ethics, sympathy, and moral conduct.

The dilemma inherent in submission to authority is ancient, as old as the story of Abraham, and the question of whether one should obey when commands conflict with conscience has been argued by Plato, dramatized in *Antigone*,[1] and treated to philosophic analysis in almost every historical epoch. Conservative philosophers argue that the very fabric of society is threatened by disobedience, while humanists stress the primacy of the individual conscience.

The legal and philosophic aspects of obedience are of enormous import, but they say very little about how most people behave in concrete situations. I set up a simple experiment at Yale University to test how much pain an ordinary citizen would inflict on another person simply because he was ordered to by an experimental scientist. Stark authority was pitted against the subjects' strongest moral imperatives against hurting others, and, with the subjects' ears ringing with the screams of the victims, authority won more often than not. The extreme willingness of adults to go to almost any lengths on the command of an authority constitutes the chief finding of the study and the fact most urgently demanding explanation.

In the basic experimental design, two people come to a psychology laboratory to take part in a study of memory and learning. One of them is designated as a "teacher" and the other a "learner." The experimenter explains that the study is concerned with the effects of punishment on learning. The learner is conducted into a room, seated in a kind of miniature electric chair; his arms are strapped to prevent excessive movement, and an electrode is attached to his wrist. He is told that he will be read lists of simple word pairs, and that he will then be tested on his ability to remember the second word of a pair when he hears the first one again. Whenever he makes an error, he will receive electric shocks of increasing intensity.

---

[1]*Antigone:* a play by Sophocles that depicts the confrontation between an individual and the state (in the person of Creon).

The real focus of the experiment is the teacher. After watching the learner being   5
strapped into place, he is seated before an impressive shock generator. The instrument
panel consists of thirty lever switches set in a horizontal line. Each switch is clearly labeled with a voltage designation ranging from 15 to 450 volts. The following desig-
nations are clearly indicated for groups of four switches, going from left to right: Slight
Shock, Moderate Shock, Strong Shock, Very Strong Shock, Intense Shock, Extreme Intensity Shock, Danger: Severe Shock. (Two switches after this last designation are simply marked XXX.)

When a switch is depressed, a pilot light corresponding to each switch is illumi-
nated in bright red; an electric buzzing is heard; a blue light, labeled "voltage ener-
gizer," flashes; the dial on the voltage meter swings to the right; and various relay clicks
sound off.

The upper left-hand corner of the generator is labeled SHOCK GENERATOR, TYPE ZLB,
DYSON INSTRUMENT COMPANY, WALTHAM, MASS. OUTPUT 15 VOLTS–450 VOLTS.

Each subject is given a sample 45-volt shock from the generator before his run as
teacher, and the jolt strengthens his belief in the authenticity of the machine.

The teacher is a genuinely naïve subject who has come to the laboratory for the experiment. The learner, or victim, is actually an actor who receives no shock at all. The
point of the experiment is to see how far a person will proceed in a concrete and measurable situation in which he is ordered to inflict increasing pain on a protesting victim.

Conflict arises when the man receiving the shock begins to show that he is expe-   10
riencing discomfort. At 75 volts, he grunts; at 120 volts, he complains loudly; at 150,
he demands to be released from the experiment. As the voltage increases, his protests
become more vehement and emotional. At 285 volts, his response can be described
only as an agonized scream. Soon thereafter, he makes no sound at all.

For the teacher, the situation quickly becomes one of gripping tension. It is not a
game for him; conflict is intense and obvious. The manifest suffering of the learner
presses him to quit; but each time he hesitates to administer a shock, the experimenter
orders him to continue. To extricate himself from this plight, the subject must make a
clear break with authority.

The subject, Gretchen Brandt,[2] is an attractive thirty-one-year-old medical technician who works at the Yale Medical School. She had emigrated from Germany five
years before.

On several occasions when the learner complains, she [Gretchen] turns to the experimenter coolly and inquires, "Shall I continue?" She promptly returns to her task
when the experimenter asks her to do so. At the administration of 210 volts, she turns
to the experimenter, remarking firmly, "Well, I'm sorry, I don't think we should
continue."

EXPERIMENTER: The experiment requires that you go on until he has learned all the
    word pairs correctly.
BRANDT: He has a heart condition, I'm sorry. He told you that before.   15
EXPERIMENTER: The shocks may be painful but they are not dangerous.

---

[2]*Gretchen Brandt:* Names of subjects described in this piece have been changed.

BRANDT: Well, I'm sorry, I think when shocks continue like this, they *are* danger-
ous. You ask him if he wants to get out. It's his free will.
EXPERIMENTER: It is absolutely essential that we continue. . . .
BRANDT: I'd like you to ask him. We came here of our free will. If he wants to continue I'll go ahead. He told you he had a heart condition. I'm sorry. I don't want
to be responsible for anything happening to him. I wouldn't like it for me either.
EXPERIMENTER: You have no other choice.   20
BRANDT: I think we are here on our own free will. I don't want to be responsible if
anything happens to him. Please understand that.

She refuses to go further and the experiment is terminated.

The woman is firm and resolute throughout. She indicates in the interview that
she was in no way tense or nervous, and this corresponds to her controlled appearance during the experiment. She feels that the last shock she administered to the learner
was extremely painful and reiterates that she "did not want to be responsible for any
harm to him."

The woman's straightforward, courteous behavior in the experiment, lack of tension, and total control of her own action seem to make disobedience a simple and rational deed. Her behavior is the very embodiment of what I envisioned would be true
for almost all subjects.

An Unexpected Outcome

Before the experiments, I sought predictions about the outcome from various kinds of   25
people—psychiatrists, college sophomores, middle-class adults, graduate students and
faculty in the behavioral sciences. With remarkable similarity, they predicted that virtually all subjects would refuse to obey the experimenter. The psychiatrists, specifically, predicted that most subjects would not go beyond 150 volts, when the victim
makes his first explicit demand to be freed. They expected that only 4 percent would
reach 300 volts, and that only a pathological fringe of about one in a thousand would
administer the highest shock on the board.

These predictions were unequivocally wrong. Of the forty subjects in the first experiment, twenty-five obeyed the orders of the experimenter to the end, punishing the
victim until they reached the most potent shock available on the generator. After 450
volts were administered three times, the experimenter called a halt to the session. Many
obedient subjects then heaved sighs of relief, mopped their brows, rubbed their fingers
over their eyes, or nervously fumbled cigarettes. Others displayed only minimal signs
of tension from beginning to end.

When the very first experiments were carried out, Yale undergraduates were used
as subjects, and about 60 percent of them were fully obedient. A colleague of mine immediately dismissed these findings as having no relevance to "ordinary" people, asserting that Yale undergraduates are a highly aggressive, competitive bunch who step
on each other's necks on the slightest provocation. He assured me that when "ordinary" people were tested, the results would be quite different. As we moved from the
pilot studies to the regular experimental series, people drawn from every stratum of New
Haven life came to be employed in the experiment: professionals, white-collar workers,

unemployed persons, and industrial workers. *The experiment's total outcome was the same as we had observed among the students.*

Moreover, when the experiments were repeated in Princeton, Munich, Rome, South Africa, and Australia, the level of obedience was invariably somewhat *higher* than found in the investigation reported in this article. Thus one scientist in Munich found 85 percent of his subjects obedient.

Fred Prozi's reactions, if more dramatic than most, illuminate the conflicts experienced by others in less visible form. About fifty years old and unemployed at the time of the experiment, he has a good-natured, if slightly dissolute, appearance, and he strikes people as a rather ordinary fellow. He begins the session calmly but becomes tense as it proceeds. After delivering the 180-volt shock, he pivots around in his chair and, shaking his head, addresses the experimenter in agitated tones:

PROZI: I can't stand it. I'm not going to kill that man in there. You hear him hollering?   30
EXPERIMENTER: As I told you before, the shocks may be painful, but. . . .
PROZI: But he's hollering. He can't stand it. What's going to happen to him?
EXPERIMENTER (his voice is patient, matter-of-fact):   The experiment requires that you continue, Teacher.
PROZI: Aaah, but, unh, I'm not going to get that man sick in there—know what I mean?
EXPERIMENTER: Whether the learner likes it or not, we must go on, through all the   35
    word pairs.
PROZI: I refuse to take the responsibility. He's in there hollering!
EXPERIMENTER: It's absolutely essential that you continue, Prozi.
PROZI: (indicating the unused questions): There's too many left here, I mean, Jeez, if he gets them wrong, there's too many of them left. I mean, who's going to take the responsibility if anything happens to that gentleman?
EXPERIMENTER: I'm responsible for anything that happens to him. Continue, please.
PROZI: All right. (Consults list of words.) The next one's "Slow—walk, truck,   40
    dance, music." Answer, please. (A buzzing sound indicates the learner has signaled his answer.) Wrong. A hundred and ninety-five volts. "Dance." (Zzumph!)
LEARNER (yelling):   Let me out of here! My heart's bothering me! (Teacher looks at experimenter.)
EXPERIMENTER: Continue, please.
LEARNER (screaming):   Let me out of here! You have no right to keep me here! Let me out of here, my heart's bothering me, let me out!
PROZI (shakes head, pats the table nervously):   You see, he's hollering. Hear that? Gee, I don't know.
EXPERIMENTER: The experiment requires . . .   45
PROZI (interrupting):   I know it does, sir, but I mean—hunh! He don't know what he's getting in for. He's up to 195 volts! (Experiment continues, through 210 volts, 225 volts, 240 volts, 255 volts, 270 volts, at which point Prozi, with evident relief, runs out of word-pair questions.)
EXPERIMENTER: You'll have to go back to the beginning of that page and go through them again until he's learned them all correctly.

PROZI: Aw, no. I'm not going to kill that man. You mean I've got to keep going up with the scale? No sir. He's hollering in there. I'm not going to give him 450 volts.

EXPERIMENTER: The experiment requires that you go on.

LEARNER: Ohhh. I absolutely refuse to answer anymore. (Shouting urgently now.)   50 Let me out of here! You can't hold me here! Get me out. Get-me-out-of-here!

EXPERIMENTER: Continue. The next word is "Green," please.

PROZI: "Green—grass, hat, ink, apple." (Nothing happens. No answering buzz. Just gloomy silence.)

PROZI: I don't think he is going to answer.

EXPERIMENTER: If the learner doesn't answer in a reasonable time, about four or five seconds, consider the answer wrong. And follow the same procedures you have been doing for wrong answers. Say, "Wrong," tell him the number of volts, give him the punishment, read him the correct answer. Continue, please.

PROZI: "Green—grass, hat, ink, apple." Answer, please. (More silence. Subject just   55 sits there.)

EXPERIMENTER: Go on with the procedure, please.

PROZI: Three hundred and fifteen volts. The answer is "ink." (Zzumph!)

LEARNER: Ohh. Ooohh.

PROZI (relieved to hear response):   Next one . . .

LEARNER: I absolutely refuse to answer.   60

PROZI: You got to. You get a shock if you don't answer. (Experiment continues with learner refusing to answer, and, finally, failing even to grunt or groan. At 375 volts, the subject stands up.)

PROZI: I think something's happened to that fellow in there. I don't get no answer. He was hollering at less voltage. Can't you check in and see if he's all right, please?

EXPERIMENTER (with same detached calm):   Not once we've started. Please continue, Teacher.

PROZI (sits down, sighs deeply):   "Cool—day, shade, water, paint." Answer, please. Are you all right in there? Are you all right?

EXPERIMENTER: Please continue, Teacher. Continue, please. (Subject pushes   65 lever. Zzumph!)

PROZI (swiveling around in his chair):   Something's happened to that man in there. (Swiveling back.) Next one. "Low—dollar, necklace, moon, paint." (Turning around again.) Something's happened to that man in there. You better check in on him, sir. He won't answer or nothing.

EXPERIMENTER: Continue. Go on, please.

PROZI: You accept all responsibility?

EXPERIMENTER: The responsibility is mine. Correct. Please go on. (Subject returns to his list, starts running through words as rapidly as he can read them, works through to 450 volts.)

PROZI: That's that.   70

EXPERIMENTER: Continue using the 450 switch for each wrong answer. Continue, please.

PROZI: But I don't get anything!

EXPERIMENTER: Please continue. The next word is "white."

PROZI: Don't you think you should look in on him, please?

EXPERIMENTER: Not once we've started the experiment.   75

PROZI: What if he's dead in there? (Gestures toward the room with the electric chair.) I mean, he told me he can't stand the shock, sir. I don't mean to be rude, but I think you should look in on him. All you have to do is look in on him. All you have to do is look in the door. I don't get no answer, no noise. Something might have happened to the gentleman in there, sir.

EXPERIMENTER: We must continue. Go on, please.

PROZI: You mean keep giving him what? Four-hundred-fifty volts, what he's got now?

EXPERIMENTER: That's correct. Continue. The next word is "white."

PROZI (now at a furious pace):   "White—cloud, horse, rock, house." Answer,   80 please. The answer is "horse." Four hundred and fifty volts. (Zzumph!) Next word, "Bag—paint, music, clown, girl." The answer is "paint." Four hundred and fifty volts. (Zzumph!) Next word is "Short—sentence, movie . . ."

EXPERIMENTER: Excuse me, Teacher. We'll have to discontinue the experiment.

Peculiar Reactions

Morris Braverman, another subject, is a thirty-nine-year-old social worker. He looks older than his years because of his bald head and serious demeanor. His brow is furrowed, as if all the world's burdens were carried on his face. He appears intelligent and concerned.

When the learner refuses to answer and the experimenter instructs Braverman to treat the absence of an answer as equivalent to a wrong answer, he takes his instruction to heart. Before administering 300 volts he asserts officiously to the victim, "Mr. Wallace, your silence has to be considered as a wrong answer." Then he administers the shock. He offers halfheartedly to change places with the learner, then asks the experimenter, "Do I have to follow these instructions literally?" He is satisfied with the experimenter's answer that he does. His very refined and authoritative manner of speaking is increasingly broken up by wheezing laughter.

The experimenter's notes on Mr. Braverman at the last few shocks are:

- Almost breaking up now each time gives shock. Rubbing face to hide laughter.
- Squinting, trying to hide face with hand, still laughing.
- Cannot control his laughter at this point no matter what he does.
- Clenching fist, pushing it onto table.

In an interview after the session, Mr. Braverman summarizes the experiment with   85 impressive fluency and intelligence. He feels the experiment may have been designed also to "test the effects on the teacher of being in an essentially sadistic role, as well as the reactions of a student to a learning situation that was authoritative and punitive." When asked how painful the last few shocks administered to the learner were, he indicates that the most extreme category on the scale is not adequate (it read EXTREMELY PAINFUL) and places his mark at the edge of the scale with an arrow carrying it beyond the scale.

It is almost impossible to convey the greatly relaxed, sedate quality of his conversation in the interview. In the most relaxed terms, he speaks about his severe inner tension.

EXPERIMENTER: At what point were you most tense or nervous?

MR. BRAVERMAN: Well, when he first began to cry out in pain, and I realized this
   was hurting him. This got worse when he just blocked and refused to answer.
   There was I. I'm a nice person, I think, hurting somebody, and caught up in
   what seemed a mad situation . . . and in the interest of science, one goes
   through with it.

When the interviewer pursues the general question of tension, Mr. Braverman spontaneously mentions his laughter.

"My reactions were awfully peculiar. I don't know if you were watching me, but   90
my reactions were giggly, and trying to stifle laughter. This isn't the way I usually am.
This was a sheer reaction to a totally impossible situation. And my reaction was to the
situation of having to hurt somebody. And being totally helpless and caught up in a
set of circumstances where I just couldn't deviate and I couldn't try to help. This is
what got me."

Mr. Braverman, like all subjects, was told the actual nature and purpose of the experiment, and a year later he affirmed in a questionnaire that he had learned something of personal importance: "What appalled me was that I could possess this capacity
for obedience and compliance to a central idea, i.e., the value of a memory experiment,
even after it became clear that continued adherence to this value was at the expense of
violation of another value, i.e., don't hurt someone who is helpless and not hurting
you. As my wife said, 'You can call yourself Eichmann.' I hope I deal more effectively
with any future conflicts of values I encounter."

The Etiquette of Submission

One theoretical interpretation of this behavior holds that all people harbor deeply aggressive instincts continually pressing for expression, and that the experiment provides
institutional justification for the release of these impulses. According to this view, if a
person is placed in a situation in which he has complete power over another individual, whom he may punish as much as he likes, all that is sadistic and bestial in man
comes to the fore. The impulse to shock the victim is seen to flow from the potent aggressive tendencies, which are part of the motivational life of the individual, and the experiment, because it provides social legitimacy, simply opens the door to their expression.

It becomes vital, therefore, to compare the subject's performance when he is under
orders and when he is allowed to choose the shock level.

The procedure was identical to our standard experiment, except that the teacher
was told that he was free to select any shock level on any of the trials. (The experimenter
took pains to point out that the teacher could use the highest levels on the generator,
the lowest, any in between, or any combination of levels.) Each subject proceeded for
thirty critical trials. The learner's protests were coordinated to standard shock levels,
his first grunt coming at 75 volts, his first vehement protest at 150 volts.

The average shock used during the thirty critical trials was less than 60 volts—   95
lower than the point at which the victim showed the first signs of discomfort. Three
of the forty subjects did not go beyond the very lowest level on the board, twenty-eight
went no higher than 75 volts, and thirty-eight did not go beyond the first loud protest

at 150 volts. Two subjects provided the exception, administering up to 325 and 450 volts, but the overall result was that the great majority of people delivered very low, usually painless, shocks when the choice was explicitly up to them.

This condition of the experiment undermines another commonly offered explanation of the subjects' behavior—that those who shocked the victim at the most severe levels came only from the sadistic fringe of society. If one considers that almost two-thirds of the participants fall into the category of "obedient" subjects, and that they represented ordinary people drawn from working, managerial, and professional classes, the argument becomes very shaky. Indeed, it is highly reminiscent of the issue that arose in connection with Hannah Arendt's 1963 book, *Eichmann in Jerusalem*. Arendt contended that the prosecution's effort to depict Eichmann as a sadistic monster was fundamentally wrong, that he came closer to being an uninspired bureaucrat who simply sat at his desk and did his job. For asserting her views, Arendt became the object of considerable scorn, even calumny. Somehow, it was felt that the monstrous deeds carried out by Eichmann required a brutal, twisted personality, evil incarnate. After witnessing hundreds of ordinary persons submit to the authority in our own experiments, I must conclude that Arendt's conception of the banality of evil comes closer to the truth than one might dare imagine. The ordinary person who shocked the victim did so out of a sense of obligation—an impression of his duties as a subject—and not from any peculiarly aggressive tendencies.

This is, perhaps, the most fundamental lesson of our study: ordinary people, simply doing their jobs, and without any particular hostility on their part, can become agents in a terrible destructive process. Moreover, even when the destructive effects of their work become patently clear, and they are asked to carry out actions incompatible with fundamental standards of morality, relatively few people have the resources needed to resist authority.

Many of the people were in some sense against what they did to the learner, and many protested even while they obeyed. Some were totally convinced of the wrongness of their actions but could not bring themselves to make an open break with authority. They often derived satisfaction from their thoughts and felt that—within themselves, at least—they had been on the side of the angels. They tried to reduce strain by obeying the experimenter but "only slightly," encouraging the learner, touching the generator switches gingerly. When interviewed, such a subject would stress that he had "asserted my humanity" by administering the briefest shock possible. Handling the conflict in this manner was easier than defiance.

The situation is constructed so that there is no way the subject can stop shocking the learner without violating the experimenter's definitions of his own competence. The subject fears that he will appear arrogant, untoward, and rude if he breaks off. Although these inhibiting emotions appear small in scope alongside the violence being done to the learner, they suffuse the mind and feelings of the subject, who is miserable at the prospect of having to repudiate the authority to his face. (When the experiment was altered so that the experimenter gave his instructions by telephone instead of in person, only a third as many people were fully obedient through 450 volts.) It is a curious thing that a measure of compassion on the part of the subject—an unwillingness to "hurt" the experimenter's feelings—is part of those binding forces inhibiting his disobedience. The withdrawal of such deference may be as painful to the subject as to the authority he defies.

Duty Without Conflict

The subjects do not derive satisfaction from inflicting pain, but they often like the feel- 100
ing they get from pleasing the experimenter. They are proud of doing a good job, obeying the experimenter under difficult circumstances. While the subjects administered only mild shocks on their own initiative, one experimental variation showed that, under orders, 30 percent of them were willing to deliver 450 volts even when they had to forcibly push the learner's hand down on the electrode.

Bruno Batta is a thirty-seven-year-old welder who took part in the variation requiring the use of force. He was born in New Haven, his parents in Italy. He has a rough-hewn face that conveys a conspicuous lack of alertness. He has some difficulty in mastering the experimental procedure and needs to be corrected by the experimenter several times. He shows appreciation for the help and willingness to do what is required. After the 150-volt level, Batta has to force the learner's hand down on the shock plate, since the learner himself refuses to touch it.

When the learner first complains, Mr. Batta pays no attention to him. His face remains impassive, as if to dissociate himself from the learner's disruptive behavior. When the experimenter instructs him to force the learner's hand down, he adopts a rigid, mechanical procedure. He tests the generator switch. When it fails to function, he immediately forces the learner's hand onto the shock plate. All the while he maintains the same rigid mask. The learner, seated alongside him, begs him to stop, but with robotic impassivity he continues the procedure.

What is extraordinary is his apparent total indifference to the learner; he hardly takes cognizance of him as a human being. Meanwhile, he relates to the experimenter in a submissive and courteous fashion.

At the 330-volt level, the learner refuses not only to touch the shock plate but also to provide any answers. Annoyed, Batta turns to him, and chastises him: "You better answer and get it over with. We can't stay here all night." These are the only words he directs to the learner in the course of an hour. Never again does he speak to him. The scene is brutal and depressing, his hard, impassive face showing total indifference as he subdues the screaming learner and gives him shocks. He seems to derive no pleasure from the act itself, only quiet satisfaction at doing his job properly.

When he administers 450 volts, he turns to the experimenter and asks, "Where 105
do we go from here, Professor?" His tone is deferential and expresses his willingness to be a cooperative subject, in contrast to the learner's obstinacy.

At the end of the session he tells the experimenter how honored he has been to help him, and in a moment of contrition, remarks, "Sir, sorry it couldn't have been a full experiment."

He has done his honest best. It is only the deficient behavior of the learner that has denied the experimenter full satisfaction.

The essence of obedience is that a person comes to view himself as the instrument for carrying out another person's wishes, and he therefore no longer regards himself as responsible for his actions. Once this critical shift of viewpoint has occurred, all of the essential features of obedience follow. The most far-reaching consequence is that the person feels responsible *to* the authority directing him but feels no responsibility *for* the content of the actions that the authority prescribes. Morality does not disappear—it acquires a radically different focus: the subordinate person feels shame or pride depending on how adequately he has performed the actions called for by authority.

Language provides numerous terms to pinpoint this type of morality: *loyalty, duty, discipline* all are terms heavily saturated with moral meaning and refer to the degree to which a person fulfills his obligations to authority. They refer not to the "goodness" of the person per se but to the adequacy with which a subordinate fulfills his socially defined role. The most frequent defense of the individual who has performed a heinous act under command of authority is that he has simply done his duty. In asserting this defense, the individual is not introducing an alibi concocted for the moment but is reporting honestly on the psychological attitude induced by submission to authority.

For a person to feel responsible for his actions, he must sense that the behavior   110 has flowed from "the self." In the situation we have studied, subjects have precisely the opposite view of their actions—namely, they see them as originating in the motives of some other person. Subjects in the experiment frequently said, "If it were up to me, I would not have administered shocks to the learner."

Once authority has been isolated as the cause of the subject's behavior, it is legitimate to inquire into the necessary elements of authority and how it must be perceived in order to gain his compliance. We conducted some investigations into the kinds of changes that would cause the experimenter to lose his power and to be disobeyed by the subject. Some of the variations revealed that:

- *The experimenter's physical presence has a marked impact on his authority.* As cited earlier, obedience dropped off sharply when orders were given by telephone. The experimenter could often induce a disobedient subject to go on by returning to the laboratory.
- *Conflicting authority severely paralyzes action.* When two experimenters of equal status, both seated at the command desk, gave incompatible orders, no shocks were delivered past the point of their disagreement.
- *The rebellious action of others severely undermines authority.* In one variation, three teachers (two actors and a real subject) administered a test and shocks. When the two actors disobeyed the experimenter and refused to go beyond a certain shock level, thirty-six of forty subjects joined their disobedient peers and refused as well.

Although the experimenter's authority was fragile in some respects, it is also true that he had almost none of the tools used in ordinary command structures. For example, the experimenter did not threaten the subjects with punishment—such as loss of income, community ostracism, or jail—for failure to obey. Neither could he offer incentives. Indeed, we should expect the experimenter's authority to be much less than that of someone like a general, since the experimenter has no power to enforce his imperatives, and since participation in a psychological experiment scarcely evokes the sense of urgency and dedication found in warfare. Despite these limitations, he still managed to command a dismaying degree of obedience.

I will cite one final variation of the experiment that depicts a dilemma that is more common in everyday life. The subject was not ordered to pull the lever that shocked the victim, but merely to perform a subsidiary task (administering the word-pair test) while another person administered the shock. In this situation, thirty-seven of forty adults continued to the highest level on the shock generator. Predictably, they excused their behavior by saying that the responsibility belonged to the man who actually pulled the switch. This may illustrate a dangerously typical arrangement in a complex society: it is easy to ignore responsibility when one is only an intermediate link in a chain of action.

The problem of obedience is not wholly psychological. The form and shape of society and the way it is developing have much to do with it. There was a time, perhaps, when people were able to give a fully human response to any situation because they were fully absorbed in it as human beings. But as soon as there was a division of labor things changed. Beyond a certain point, the breaking up of society into people carrying out narrow and very special jobs takes away from the human quality of work and life. A person does not get to see the whole situation but only a small part of it, and is thus unable to act without some kind of overall direction. He yields to authority but in doing so is alienated from his own actions.

Even Eichmann was sickened when he toured the concentration camps, but he   115 had only to sit at a desk and shuffle papers. At the same time the man in the camp who actually dropped Cyclon-b into the gas chambers was able to justify *his* behavior on the ground that he was only following orders from above. Thus there is a fragmentation of the total human act; no one is confronted with the consequences of his decision to carry out the evil act. The person who assumes responsibility has evaporated. Perhaps this is the most common characteristic of socially organized evil in modern society.

Questions for Discussion and Writing

1. How is Milgram's experiment designed to test how far people will go in obeying orders from authority figures? Why are terms such as *loyalty, duty, discipline,* and *obligation* important in Milgram's studies?
2. How does Milgram's inclusion of the actual transcript of Mr. Prozi's experience (instead of a summary) enable you to identify with the subject and therefore better understand the entire experiment?
3. Have you ever found yourself in a situation in which you were ordered by an authority figure to do something you thought might be wrong? How did you react? Describe your experience. Did your experience give you insight into Milgram's research?

Dalai Lama

. . . .

Lhamo Dhondup was born in 1935 to a poor farming family in northeastern Tibet. At the age of two, he was renamed Tenzin Gyatso (which means "ocean of wisdom") when he was recognized as the incarnation of the thirteenth Dalai Lama. He underwent eighteen years of religious and philosophical studies leading to the Tibetan equivalent of a Ph.D. in Buddhist studies. In 1950, when he was sixteen, the Chinese army invaded Tibet, and he assumed full political powers and attempted to negotiate with Mao Zedong. He escaped into exile in 1959, along with eighty thousand Tibetans, to Dharamasala in northern India, where he still resides. From there, he has waged a nonviolent campaign to free Tibet from the Chinese; he received the Nobel Peace Prize in 1989. His published works include Freedom in Exile: The Autobiography of the Dalai Lama *(1990) and the best-selling* Ethics for a New Millennium *(1999), in which the following essay first appeared.*

THE ROLE OF RELIGION IN MODERN SOCIETY

It is a sad fact of human history that religion has been a major source of conflict. Even today, individuals are killed, communities destroyed, and societies destabilized as a result of religious bigotry and hatred. It is no wonder that many question the place of religion in human society. Yet when we think carefully, we find that conflict in the name of religion arises from two principal sources. There is that which arises simply as a result of religious diversity—the doctrinal, cultural, and practical differences between one religion and another. Then there is the conflict that arises in the context of political, economic, and other factors, mainly at the institutional level. Interreligious harmony is the key to overcoming conflict of the first sort. In the case of the second, some other solution must be found. Secularization and in particular the separation of the religious hierarchy from the institutions of the state may go some way to reducing such institutional problems. Our concern in this chapter is with interreligious harmony, however.

This is an important aspect of what I have called universal responsibility. But before examining the matter in detail, it is perhaps worth considering the question of whether religion is really relevant in the modern world. Many people argue that it is not. Now I have observed that religious belief is not a precondition either of ethical conduct or of happiness itself. I have also suggested that whether a person practices religion or not, the spiritual qualities of love and compassion, patience, tolerance, forgiveness, humility, and so on are indispensable. At the same time, I should make it clear that I believe that these are most easily and effectively developed within the context of religious practice. I also believe that when an individual sincerely practices religion, that individual will benefit enormously. People who have developed a firm faith, grounded in understanding and rooted in daily practice, are in general much better at coping with adversity than those who have not. I am convinced, therefore, that religion has enormous potential to benefit humanity. Properly employed, it is an extremely effective instrument for establishing human happiness. In particular, it can play a leading role in encouraging people to develop a sense of responsibility toward others and of the need to be ethically disciplined.

On these grounds, therefore, I believe that religion is still relevant today. But consider this too: some years ago, the body of a Stone Age man was recovered from the ice of the European Alps. Despite being more than five thousand years old, it was perfectly preserved. Even its clothes were largely intact. I remember thinking at the time that were it possible to bring this individual back to life for a day, we would find that we have much in common with him. No doubt we would find that he too was concerned for his family and loved ones, for his health and so on. Differences of culture and expression notwithstanding, we would still be able to identify with one another on the level of feeling. And there could be no reason to suppose any less concern with finding happiness and avoiding suffering on his part than on ours. If religion, with its emphasis on overcoming suffering through the practice of ethical discipline and cultivation of love and compassion, can be conceived of as relevant in the past, it is hard to see why it should not be equally so today. Granted that in the past the value of religion may have been more obvious, in that human suffering was more explicit due to the lack of modern facilities. But because we humans still suffer, albeit today this is experienced more internally as mental and emotional affliction, and because religion in addition to its salvific truth claims is concerned to help us overcome suffering, surely it must still be relevant.

How then might we bring about the harmony that is necessary to overcome interreligious conflict? As in the case of individuals engaged in the discipline of restraining their response to negative thoughts and emotions and cultivating spiritual qualities, the key lies in developing understanding. We must first identify the factors that obstruct it. Then we must find ways to overcome them.

Perhaps the most significant obstruction to interreligious harmony is lack of appreciation of the value of others' faith traditions. Until comparatively recently, communication between different cultures, even different communities, was slow or nonexistent. For this reason, sympathy for other faith traditions was not necessarily very important—except of course where members of different religions lived side by side. But this attitude is no longer viable. In today's increasingly complex and interdependent world, we are compelled to acknowledge the existence of other cultures, different ethnic groups, and, of course, other religious faiths. Whether we like it or not, most of us now experience this diversity on a daily basis. 5

I believe that the best way to overcome ignorance and bring about understanding is through dialogue with members of other faith traditions. This I see occurring in a number of different ways. Discussions among scholars in which the convergence and perhaps more importantly the divergence between different faith traditions are explored and appreciated are very valuable. On another level, it is helpful when there are encounters between ordinary but practicing followers of different religions in which each shares their experiences. This is perhaps the most effective way of appreciating others' teachings. In my own case, for example, my meetings with the late Thomas Merton, a Catholic monk of the Cistercian order, were deeply inspiring. They helped me develop a profound admiration for the teachings of Christianity. I also feel that occasional meetings between religious leaders joining together to pray for a common cause are extremely useful. The gathering at Assisi in Italy in 1986, when representatives of the world's major religions gathered to pray for peace, was, I believe, tremendously beneficial to many religious believers insofar as it symbolized the solidarity and a commitment to peace of all those taking part.

Finally, I feel that the practice of members of different faith traditions going on joint pilgrimages together can be very helpful. It was in this spirit that in 1993 I went to Lourdes, and then to Jerusalem, a site holy to three of the world's great religions. I have also paid visits to various Hindu, Islamic, Jain, and Sikh shrines both in India and abroad. More recently, following a seminar devoted to discussing and practicing meditation in the Christian and Buddhist traditions, I joined an historic pilgrimage of practitioners of both traditions in a program of prayers, meditation, and dialogue under the Bodhi tree at Bodh Gaya in India. This is one of Buddhism's most important shrines.

When exchanges like these occur, followers of one tradition will find that, just as in the case of their own, the teachings of others' faiths are a source both of spiritual inspiration and of ethical guidance to their followers. It will also become clear that irrespective of doctrinal and other differences, all the major world religions are concerned with helping individuals to become good human beings. All emphasize love and compassion, patience, tolerance, forgiveness, humility, and so on, and all are capable of helping individuals to develop these. Moreover, the example given by the founders of each major religion clearly demonstrates a concern for helping others find happiness through developing these qualities. So far as their own lives were concerned, each conducted themselves with great simplicity. Ethical discipline and love for all others was the hallmark of their lives. They did not live luxuriously like emperors and kings. Instead, they voluntarily accepted suffering—without consideration of the hardships involved—in order to benefit humanity as a whole. In their teachings, all placed special emphasis on developing love and compassion and renouncing selfish desires. And each of them called on us to transform our hearts and minds. Indeed, whether we have faith or not, all are worthy of our profound admiration.

At the same time as engaging in dialogue with followers of other religions, we must, of course, implement in our daily life the teachings of our own religion. Once we have experienced the benefit of love and compassion, and of ethical discipline, we will easily recognize the value of other's teachings. But for this, it is essential to realize that religious practice entails a lot more than merely saying, "I believe" or, as in Buddhism, "I take refuge." There is also more to it than just visiting temples, or shrines, or churches. And taking religious teachings is of little benefit if they do not enter the heart but remain at the level of intellect alone. Simply relying on faith without understanding and without implementation is of limited value. I often tell Tibetans that carrying a *mala* (something like a rosary) does not make a person a genuine religious practitioner. The efforts we make sincerely to transform ourselves spiritually are what make us genuine religious practitioners.

We come to see the overriding importance of genuine practice when we recognize   10
that, along with ignorance, individuals' unhealthy relationships with their beliefs is the other major factor in religious disharmony. Far from applying the teachings of their religion in our personal lives, we have a tendency to use them to reinforce our self-centered attitudes. We relate to our religion as something we own or as a label that separates us from others. Surely this is misguided? Instead of using the nectar of religion to purify the poisonous elements of our hearts and minds, there is a danger when we think like this of using these negative elements to poison the nectar of religion.

Yet we must acknowledge that this reflects another problem, one which is implicit in all religions. I refer to the claims each has of being the one "true" religion. How are we to resolve this difficulty? It is true that from the point of view of the individual practitioner, it is essential to have a single-pointed commitment to one's own faith. It is also true that this depends on the deep conviction that one's own path is the sole mediator of truth. But at the same time, we have to find some means of reconciling this belief with the reality of a multiplicity of similar claims. In practical terms, this involves individual practitioners finding a way at least to accept the validity of the teachings of other religions while maintaining a wholehearted commitment to their own. As far as the validity of the metaphysical truth claims of a given religion is concerned, that is of course the internal business of that particular tradition.

In my own case, I am convinced that Buddhism provides me with the most effective framework within which to situate my efforts to develop spiritually through cultivating love and compassion. At the same time, I must acknowledge that while Buddhism represents the best path for me—that is, it suits my character, my temperament, my inclinations, and my cultural background—the same will be true of Christianity for Christians. For them, Christianity is the best way. On the basis of my conviction, I cannot, therefore, say that Buddhism is best for everyone.

I sometimes think of religion in terms of medicine for the human spirit. Independent of its usage and suitability to a particular individual in a particular condition, we really cannot judge a medicine's efficacy. We are not justified in saying this medicine is very good because of such and such ingredients. If you take the patient and the medicine's effect on that person out of the equation, it hardly makes sense. What is relevant is to say that in the case of this particular patient with its particular illness, this medicine is the most effective. Similarly with different religious traditions, we can say that this one is most effective for this particular individual. But it is unhelpful to try to argue on the basis of philosophy or metaphysics that one religion is better than another. The important thing is surely its effectiveness in individual cases.

My way to resolve the seeming contradiction between each religion's claim to "one truth and one religion" and the reality of the multiplicity of faiths is thus to understand that in the case of a single individual, there can indeed be only one truth, one religion. However, from the perspective of human society at large, we must accept the concept of "many truths, many religions." To continue with our medical analogy, in the case of one particular patient, the suitable medicine is in fact the one medicine. But clearly that does not mean that there may not be other medicines suitable to other patients.

To my way of thinking, the diversity that exists among the various religious traditions is enormously enriching. There is thus no need to try to find ways of saying that ultimately all religions are the same. They are similar in that they all emphasize the indispensability of love and compassion in the context of ethical discipline. But to say this is not to say that they are all essentially one. The contradictory understanding of creation and beginninglessness articulated by Buddhism, Christianity, and Hinduism, for example, means that in the end we have to part company when it comes to metaphysical claims, in spite of the many practical similarities that undoubtedly exist. These contradictions may not be very important in the beginning stages of religious practice. But as we advance along the path of one tradition or another, we are compelled at some point to acknowledge fundamental differences. For example, the concept of rebirth in Buddhism and various other ancient Indian traditions may turn out to be incompatible with the Christian idea of salvation. This need not be a cause for dismay, however. Even within Buddhism itself, in the realm of metaphysics there are diametrically opposing views. At the very least, such diversity means that we have different frameworks within which to locate ethical discipline and the development of spiritual values. That is why I do not advocate a super or a new world religion. It would mean that we would lose the unique characteristics of the different faith traditions.

Some people, it is true, hold that the Buddhist concept of *shunyata*, or emptiness, is ultimately the same as certain approaches to understanding the concept of God. Nevertheless, there remain difficulties with this. The first is that while of course we can interpret these concepts, to what extent can we be faithful to the original teachings if we do so? There are compelling similarities between the Mahayana Buddhist concept of *Dharmakaya, Sambogakaya,* and *Nirmanakaya* and the Christian trinity of God as Father, Son, and Holy Spirit. But to say, on the basis of this, that Buddhism and Christianity are ultimately the same is to go a bit far, I think! As an old Tibetan saying goes, we must beware of trying to put a yak's head on a sheep's body—or vice versa.

What is required instead is that we develop a genuine sense of religious pluralism in spite of the different claims of different faith traditions. This is especially true if we are serious in our respect for human rights as a universal principle. In this regard, I find the concept of a world parliament of religions very appealing. To begin with, the word "parliament" conveys a sense of democracy, while the plural "religions" underlines the importance of the principle of a multiplicity of faith traditions. The truly pluralist perspective on religion which the idea of such a parliament suggests could, I believe be, of great help. It would avoid the extremes of religious bigotry on the one hand, and the urge toward unnecessary syncretism on the other.

Connected with this issue of interreligious harmony, I should perhaps say something about religious conversion. This is a question which must be taken extremely seriously. It is essential to realize that the mere fact of conversion alone will not make an individual a better person, that is to say, a more disciplined, a more compassionate, and a warm-hearted person. Much more helpful, therefore, is for the individual to concentrate on transforming themselves spiritually through the practice of restraint, virtue, and compassion. To the extent that the insights or practices of other religions are useful or relevant to our own faith, it is valuable to learn from others. In some cases, it may even be helpful to adopt certain of them. Yet when this is done wisely, we can remain firmly committed to our own faith. This way is best because it carries with it no danger of confusion, especially with respect to the different ways of life that tend to go with different faith traditions.

Given the diversity to be found among individual human beings, it is of course bound to be the case that out of many millions of practitioners of a particular religion, a handful will find that another religion's approach to ethics and spiritual development is more satisfactory. For some, the concept of rebirth and karma will seem highly effective in inspiring the aspiration to develop love and compassion within the context of responsibility. For others, the concept of a transcendent, loving creator will come to seem more so. In such circumstances, it is crucial for those individuals to question themselves again and again. They must ask, "Am I attracted to this other religion for the right reasons? Is it merely the cultural and ritual aspects that are appealing? Or is it the essential teachings? Do I suppose that if I convert to this new religion it will be less demanding than my present one?" I say this because it has often struck me that when people do convert to a religion outside their own heritage, quite often they adopt certain superficial aspects of the culture to which their new faith belongs. But their practice may not go very much deeper than that.

In the case of a person who decides after a process of long and mature reflection   20
to adopt a different religion, it is very important that they remember the positive contribution to humanity of each religious tradition. The danger is that the individual may, in seeking to justify their decision to others, criticize their previous faith. It is essential to avoid this. Just because that tradition is no longer effective in the case of one individual does not mean it is no longer of benefit to humanity. On the contrary, we can be certain that it has been an inspiration to millions of people in the past, that it inspires millions today, and that it will inspire millions in the path of love and compassion in the future.

The important point to keep in mind is that ultimately the whole purpose of religion is to facilitate love and compassion, patience, tolerance, humility, forgiveness, and so on. If we neglect these, changing our religion will be of no help. In the same way, even if we are fervent believers in our own faith, it will avail us nothing if we neglect to implement these qualities in our daily lives. Such a believer is no better off than a patient with some fatal illness who merely reads a medical treatise but fails to undertake the treatment prescribed.

Moreover, if we who are practitioners of religion are not compassionate and disciplined, how can we expect it of others? If we can establish genuine harmony derived from mutual respect and understanding, religion has enormous potential to speak with authority on such vital moral questions as peace and disarmament, social and political justice, the natural environment, and many other matters affecting all humanity. But until we put our own spiritual teachings into practice, we will never be taken seriously. And this means, among other things, setting a good example through developing good relations with other faith traditions.

Questions for Discussion and Writing

1. How does the Dalai Lama suggest that we overcome one of the main obstructions to religious harmony—that is, the claim of each religion of being the one "true" religion? Why is compassion the essential quality in developing interreligious harmony?

2. How does the Dalai Lama use an analogy drawn from medicine to promote tolerance toward the teachings and practices of others' faiths?

3. The Dalai Lama believes that spiritual qualities are "most easily and effectively developed within the context of religious practice"; would it be possible to develop these qualities in a secular context? Would this essay have been as effective if you did not know that the author is a great religious leader? Explain your answers.

Langston Hughes

Langston Hughes (1902–1967) was born in Joplin, Missouri, and started writing poetry as a student in Central High School in Cleveland. After graduation he worked his way through Africa and Europe on cargo ships. In 1925, while he was working as a busboy in Washington, D.C., he encountered the poet Vachel Lindsay, who after reading Hughes's poems helped him publish his works. After the publication of his first book, The Weary Blues *(1926), Hughes toured the country giving poetry readings and became a leading figure in the Harlem Renaissance. He graduated from Lincoln University in Pennsylvania in 1929, returned to Harlem, and provided invaluable guidance to young writers. In "Salvation," which first appeared in his autobiography,* The Big Sea *(1940), Hughes reveals his uncanny gift for dialogue and irony, as he re-creates a revival meeting that played a crucial role in his life.*

SALVATION

I was saved from sin when I was going on thirteen. But not really saved. It happened like this. There was a big revival at my Auntie Reed's church. Every night for weeks there had been much preaching, singing, praying, and shouting, and some very hardened sinners had been brought to Christ, and the membership of the church had grown by leaps and bounds. Then just before the revival ended, they held a special meeting for children, "to bring the young lambs to the fold." My aunt spoke of it for days ahead. That night I was escorted to the front row and placed on the mourners' bench with all the other young sinners, who had not yet been brought to Jesus.

My aunt told me that when you were saved you saw a light, and something happened to you inside! And Jesus came into your life! And God was with you from then on! She said you could see and hear and feel Jesus in your soul. I believed her. I had heard a great many old people say that same thing and it seemed to me they ought to know. So I sat there calmly in the hot, crowded church, waiting for Jesus to come to me.

The preacher preached a wonderful rhythmical sermon, all moans and shouts and lonely cries and dire pictures of hell, and then he sang a song about the ninety and nine safe in the fold, but one little lamb was left out in the cold. Then he said: "Won't you come? Won't you come to Jesus? Young lambs, won't you come?" And he held out his arms to all us young sinners there on the mourners' bench. And the little girls cried. And some of them jumped up and went to Jesus right away. But most of us just sat there.

A great many old people came and knelt around us and prayed, old women with jet-black faces and braided hair, old men with work-gnarled hands. And the church sang a song about the lower lights are burning, some poor sinners to be saved. And the whole building rocked with prayer and song.

Still I kept waiting to *see* Jesus.   5

Finally all the young people had gone to the altar and were saved, but one boy and me. He was a rounder's son named Westley. Westley and I were surrounded by sisters and deacons praying. It was very hot in the church, and getting late now. Finally Westley said to me in a whisper: "God damn! I'm tired o' sitting here. Let's get up and be saved." So he got up and was saved.

Then I was left all alone on the mourners' bench. My aunt came and knelt at my knees and cried, while prayers and song swirled all around me in the little church. The whole congregation prayed for me alone in a mighty wail of moans and voices. And I kept waiting serenely for Jesus, waiting, waiting—but he didn't come. I wanted to see him, but nothing happened to me. Nothing! I wanted something to happen to me, but nothing happened.

I heard the songs and the minister saying: "Why don't you come? My dear child, why don't you come to Jesus? Jesus is waiting for you. He wants you. Why don't you come? Sister Reed, what is this child's name?"

"Langston," my aunt sobbed.

"Langston, why don't you come? Why don't you come and be saved? Oh, Lamb 10 of God! Why don't you come?"

Now it was really getting late. I began to be ashamed of myself, holding everything up so long. I began to wonder what God thought about Westley, who certainly hadn't seen Jesus either, but who was now sitting proudly on the platform, swinging his knickerbockered legs and grinning down at me, surrounded by deacons and old women on their knees praying. God had not struck Westley dead for taking his name in vain or for lying in the temple. So I decided that maybe to save further trouble, I'd better lie, too, and say that Jesus had come, and get up and be saved.

So I got up.

Suddenly the whole room broke into a sea of shouting, as they saw me rise. Waves of rejoicing swept the place. Women leaped in the air. My aunt threw her arms around me. The minister took me by the hand and led me to the platform.

When things quieted down, in a hushed silence, punctuated by a few ecstatic "Amens," all the new young lambs were blessed in the name of God. Then joyous singing filled the room.

That night, for the last time in my life but one—for I was a big boy twelve years 15 old—I cried. I cried, in bed alone, and couldn't stop. I buried my head under the quilts, but my aunt heard me. She woke up and told my uncle I was crying because the Holy Ghost had come into my life, and because I had seen Jesus. But I was really crying because I couldn't bear to tell her that I had lied, that I had deceived everybody in the church, that I hadn't seen Jesus, and that now I didn't believe there was a Jesus any more, since he didn't come to help me.

Questions for Discussion and Writing

1. Who are some of the people who have an interest in "saving" the young Langston Hughes? In each case, how would his salvation serve their interests?

2. What ultimately tips the balance and impels Hughes to declare himself saved? How does he use imagery and figurative language to intensify a sense of drama?

3. Have you ever been in a situation in which others tried to manipulate you into doing or saying something you would not have done otherwise? Describe the circumstances and what was at stake. How do you now feel in retrospect about that experience?

FICTION

Joyce Carol Oates

• •

Joyce Carol Oates was born in Lockport, New York, in 1938 and was raised on her grandparents' farm in Erie County, New York. She graduated from Syracuse University in 1960 and earned an M.A. at the University of Wisconsin. She has taught writing and literature at Princeton University since 1978. Oates received the O. Henry Special Award for Continuing Achievement and the National Book Award in 1970 for her novel them. *Oates is a prolific author who has published (on average) two books a year and has written countless essays and reviews. Her work covers the spectrum from novels and short fiction, poetry, plays, and criticism to nonfiction works on topics ranging from the poetry of D. H. Lawrence to boxing. "Where Are You Going, Where Have You Been?" first appeared in* The Wheel of Love *(1965). This story was inspired by an article in* Life *magazine titled "The Pied Piper of Tucson," about a twenty-three-year-old man who frequented teenage hangouts, picked up girls, took them for rides in his gold convertible, and ultimately was convicted for murdering three of them. Her recent works include* Faithless: Tales of Transgression *(2001);* The Tattooed Girl *(2003);* I Am No One You Know: Stories *(2004); and* Sexy *(2005).*

WHERE ARE YOU GOING, WHERE HAVE YOU BEEN?

For Bob Dylan[1]

Her name was Connie. She was fifteen and she had a quick nervous giggling habit of craning her neck to glance into mirrors, or checking other people's faces to make sure her own was all right. Her mother, who noticed everything and knew everything and who hadn't much reason any longer to look at her own face, always scolded Connie about it. "Stop gawking at yourself, who are you? You think you're so pretty?" she would say. Connie would raise her eyebrows at these familiar complaints and look right through her mother, into a shadowy vision of herself as she was right at that moment: she knew she was pretty and that was everything. Her mother had been pretty once too, if you could believe those old snapshots in the album, but now her looks were gone and that was why she was always after Connie.

"Why don't you keep your room clean like your sister? How've you got your hair fixed—what the hell stinks? Hair spray? You don't see your sister using that junk."

Her sister June was twenty-four and still lived at home. She was a secretary in the high school Connie attended, and if that wasn't bad enough—with her in the same building—she was so plain and chunky and steady that Connie had to hear her praised all the time by her mother and her mother's sisters. June did this, June did that, she saved money and helped clean the house and cooked and Connie couldn't do a thing, her

---

[1]*Bob Dylan (b. 1941):* a composer, author, and singer who created and popularized folk rock during the 1960s.

mind was all filled with trashy daydreams. Their father was away at work most of the time and when he came home he wanted supper and he read the newspaper at supper and after supper he went to bed. He didn't bother talking much to them, but around his bent head Connie's mother kept picking at her until Connie wished her mother was dead and she herself was dead and it was all over. "She makes me want to throw up sometimes," she complained to her friends. She had a high, breathless, amused voice which made everything she said a little forced, whether it was sincere or not.

There was one good thing: June went places with girl friends of hers, girls who were just as plain and steady as she, and so when Connie wanted to do that her mother had no objections. The father of Connie's best girl friend drove the girls the three miles to town and left them off at a shopping plaza, so that they could walk through the stores or go to a movie, and when he came to pick them up again at eleven he never bothered to ask what they had done.

They must have been familiar sights, walking around that shopping plaza in their   5
shorts and flat ballerina slippers that always scuffed the sidewalk, with charm bracelets jingling on their thin wrists; they would lean together to whisper and laugh secretly if someone passed by who amused or interested them. Connie had long dark blond hair that drew anyone's eye to it, and she wore part of it pulled up on her head and puffed out and the rest of it she let fall down her back. She wore a pullover jersey blouse that looked one way when she was at home and another way when she was away from home. Everything about her had two sides to it, one for home and one for anywhere that was not home: her walk that could be childlike and bobbing, or languid enough to make anyone think she was hearing music in her head, her mouth which was pale and smirking most of the time, but bright and pink on these evenings out, her laugh which was cynical and drawling at home—"Ha, ha, very funny"—but high-pitched and nervous anywhere else, like the jingling of the charms on her bracelet.

Sometimes they did go shopping or to a movie, but sometimes they went across the highway, ducking fast across the busy road, to a drive-in restaurant where older kids hung out. The restaurant was shaped like a big bottle, though squatter than a real bottle, and on its cap was a revolving figure of a grinning boy who held a hamburger aloft. One night in midsummer they ran across, breathless with daring, and right away someone leaned out a car window and invited them over, but it was just a boy from high school they didn't like. It made them feel good to be able to ignore him. They went up through the maze of parked and cruising cars to the bright-lit, fly-infested restaurant, their faces pleased and expectant as if they were entering a sacred building that loomed out of the night to give them what haven and what blessing they yearned for. They sat at the counter and crossed their legs at the ankles, their thin shoulders rigid with excitement and listened to the music that made everything so good: the music was always in the background like music at a church service, it was something to depend upon.

A boy named Eddie came in to talk with them. He sat backwards on his stool, turning himself jerkily around in semi-circles and then stopping and turning again, and after a while he asked Connie if she would like something to eat. She said she did and so she tapped her friend's arm on her way out—her friend pulled her face up into a brave droll look—and Connie said she would meet her at eleven, across the way. "I just hate to leave her like that," Connie said earnestly, but the boy said that she wouldn't be alone for long. So they went out to his car and on the way Connie couldn't help but let her eyes wander over the windshields and faces all around her, her face gleaming with the joy that had nothing to do with Eddie or even this place; it might have been the music. She drew her shoulders up and sucked in her breath with the pure pleasure of being alive, and just at that moment she happened to glance at a face just a few feet from hers. It was a boy with shaggy black hair, in a convertible jalopy painted gold. He stared at her and then his lips widened into a grin. Connie slit her eyes at him and turned away, but she couldn't help glancing back and there he was still watching her. He wagged a finger and laughed and said, "Gonna get you, baby," and Connie turned away again without Eddie noticing anything.

She spent three hours with him, at the restaurant where they ate hamburgers and drank Cokes in wax cups that were always sweating, and then down an alley a mile or so away, and when he left her off at five to eleven only the movie house was still open at the plaza. Her girl friend was there, talking with a boy. When Connie came up the two girls smiled at each other and Connie said, "How was the movie?" and the girl said, "*You* should know." They rode off with the girl's father, sleepy and pleased, and Connie couldn't help but look at the darkened shopping plaza with its big empty parking lot and its signs that were faded and ghostly now, and over at the drive-in restaurant where cars were still circling tirelessly. She couldn't hear the music at this distance.

Next morning June asked her how the movie was and Connie said, "So-so."

She and that girl and occasionally another girl went out several times a week that   10
way, and the rest of the time Connie spent around the house—it was summer vacation—getting in her mother's way and thinking, dreaming, about the boys she met. But all the boys fell back and dissolved into a single face that was not even a face, but an idea, a feeling, mixed up with the urgent insistent pounding of the music and the humid night air of July. Connie's mother kept dragging her back to the daylight by finding things for her to do or saying suddenly, "What's this about the Pettinger girl?"

And Connie would say nervously, "Oh, her. That dope." She always drew thick clear lines between herself and such girls, and her mother was simple and kindly enough to believe her. Her mother was so simple, Connie thought, that it was maybe cruel to fool her so much. Her mother went scuffling around the house in old bedroom slippers and complained over the telephone to one sister about the other, then the other called up and the two of them complained about the third one. If June's name was mentioned her mother's tone was approving, and if Connie's name was mentioned it was disapproving. This did not really mean she disliked Connie and actually Connie thought that her mother preferred her to June because she was prettier, but the two of them kept up a pretense of exasperation, a sense that they were tugging and struggling over something of little value to either of them. Sometimes, over coffee, they were almost friends, but something would come up—some vexation that was like a fly buzzing suddenly around their heads—and their faces went hard with contempt.

One Sunday Connie got up at eleven—none of them bothered with church—and washed her hair so that it could dry all day long, in the sun. Her parents and sister were going to a barbecue at an aunt's house and Connie said no, she wasn't interested, rolling her eyes, to let mother know just what she thought of it. "Stay home alone then," her mother said sharply. Connie sat out back in a lawn chair and watched them drive away, her father quiet and bald, hunched around so that he could back the car out, her mother with a look that was still angry and not at all softened through the windshield, and in the back seat poor old June all dressed up as if she didn't know what a barbecue was, with all the running yelling kids and the flies. Connie sat with her eyes closed in the sun, dreaming and dazed with the warmth about her as if this were a kind of love, the caresses of love, and her mind slipped over onto thoughts of the boy she had been with the night before and how nice he had been, how sweet it always was, not the way someone like June would suppose but sweet, gentle, the way it was in movies and promised in songs; and when she opened her eyes she hardly knew where she was, the back yard ran off into weeds and a fenceline of trees and behind it the sky was perfectly blue and still. The asbestos "ranch house" that was now three years old startled her—it looked small. She shook her head as if to get awake.

It was too hot. She went inside the house and turned on the radio to drown out the quiet. She sat on the edge of her bed, barefoot, and listened for an hour and a half to a program called XYZ Sunday Jamboree, record after record of hard, fast, shrieking songs she sang along with, interspersed by exclamations from "Bobby King": "An' look here you girls at Napoleon's—Son and Charley want you to pay real close attention to this song coming up!"

And Connie paid close attention herself, bathed in a glow of slow-pulsed joy that seemed to rise mysteriously out of the music itself and lay languidly about the airless little room, breathed in and breathed out with each gentle rise and fall of her chest.

After a while she heard a car coming up the drive. She sat up at once, startled, because it couldn't be her father so soon. The gravel kept crunching all the way in from the road—the driveway was long—and Connie ran to the window. It was a car she didn't know. It was an open jalopy, painted a bright gold that caught the sun opaquely. Her heart began to pound and her fingers snatched at her hair, checking it, and she whispered "Christ. Christ," wondering how bad she looked. The car came to a stop at the side door and the horn sounded four short taps as if this were a signal Connie knew.   15

She went into the kitchen and approaching the door slowly, then hung out the screen door, her bare toes curling down off the step. There were two boys in the car and now she recognized the driver: he had shaggy, shabby black hair that looked crazy as a wig and he was grinning at her.

"I ain't late, am I?" he said.

"Who the hell do you think you are?" Connie said.

"Toldja I'd be out, didn't I?"

"I don't even know who you are."   20

She spoke sullenly, careful to show no interest or pleasure, and he spoke in a fast bright monotone. Connie looked past him to the other boy, taking her time. He had fair brown hair, with a lock that fell onto his forehead. His sideburns gave him a fierce, embarrassed look, but so far he hadn't even bothered to glance at her. Both boys wore sunglasses. The driver's glasses were metallic and mirrored everything in miniature.

"You wanta come for a ride?" he said.

Connie smirked and let her hair fall loose over one shoulder.

"Don'tcha like my car? New paint job," he said. "Hey."

"What?"   25

"You're cute."

She pretended to fidget, chasing flies away from the door.

"Don'tcha believe me, or what?" he said.

"Look, I don't even know who you are," Connie said in disgust.

"Hey, Ellie's got a radio, see. Mine's broke down." He lifted his friend's arm and   30
showed her the little transistor the boy was holding, and now Connie began to hear
the music. It was the same program that was playing inside the house.

"Bobby King?" she said.

"I listen to him all the time. I think he's great."

"He's kind of great," Connie said reluctantly.

"Listen, that guy's *great*. He knows where the action is."

Connie blushed a little, because the glasses made it impossible for her to see just   35
what this boy was looking at. She couldn't decide if she liked him or if he was just a
jerk, and so she dawdled in the doorway and wouldn't come down or go back inside.
She said, "What's all that stuff painted on your car?"

"Can'tcha read it?" He opened the door very carefully, as if he was afraid it might
fall off. He slid out just as carefully, planting his feet firmly on the ground, the tiny
metallic world in his glasses slowing down like gelatine hardening and in the midst of
it Connie's bright green blouse. "This here is my name, to begin with," he said.
ARNOLD FRIEND was written in tar-like black letters on the side, with a drawing of
a round grinning face that reminded Connie of a pumpkin, except it wore sunglasses.
"I wanta introduce myself, I'm Arnold Friend and that's my real name and I'm gonna
be your friend, honey, and inside the car's Ellie Oscar, he's kinda shy." Ellie brought
his transistor up to his shoulder and balanced it there. "Now these numbers are a secret code, honey," Arnold Friend explained. He read off the numbers 33, 19, 17 and
raised his eyebrows at her to see what she thought of that, but she didn't think much
of it. The left rear fender had been smashed and around it was written, on the gleaming gold background: DONE BY CRAZY WOMAN DRIVER. Connie had to laugh
at that. Arnold Friend was pleased at her laughter and looked up at her. "Around the
other side's a lot more—you wanta come and see them?"

"No."

"Why not?"

"Why should I?"

"Don'tcha wanta see what's on the car? Don'tcha wanta go for a ride?"   40

"I don't know."

"Why not?"

"I got things to do."

"Like what?"

"Things."   45

He laughed as if she had said something funny. He slapped his thighs. He was
standing in a strange way, leaning back against the car as if he were balancing himself.
He wasn't tall, only an inch or so taller than she would be if she came down to him.
Connie liked the way he was dressed, which was the way all of them dressed: tight
faded jeans stuffed into black, scuffed boots, a belt that pulled his waist in and showed
how lean he was, and a white pull-over shirt that was a little soiled and showed the
hard small muscles of his arms and shoulders. He looked as if he probably did hard
work, lifting and carrying things. Even his neck looked muscular. And his face was a
familiar face, somehow: the jaw and chin and cheeks slightly darkened, because he

hadn't shaved for a day or two, and the nose long and hawklike, sniffing as if she were a treat he was going to gobble up and it was all a joke.

"Connie, you ain't telling the truth. This is your day set aside for a ride with me and you know it," he said, still laughing. The way he straightened and recovered from his fit of laughing showed that it had been all fake.

"How do you know what my name is?" she said suspiciously.

"It's Connie."

"Maybe and maybe not."   50

"I know my Connie," he said, wagging his finger. Now she remembered him even better, back at the restaurant, and her cheeks warmed at the thought of how she sucked in her breath just at the moment she passed him—how she must have looked to him. And he had remembered her. "Ellie and I come out here especially for you," he said. "Ellie can sit in back. How about it?"

"Where?"

"Where what?"

"Where're we going?"

He looked at her. He took off the sunglasses and she saw how pale the skin around   55
his eyes was, like holes that were not in shadow but instead in light. His eyes were like chips of broken glass that catch the light in an amiable way. He smiled. It was as if the idea of going for a ride somewhere, to some place, was a new idea to him.

"Just for a ride, Connie sweetheart."

"I never said my name was Connie," she said.

"But I know what it is. I know your name and all about you, lots of things," Arnold Friend said. He had not moved yet but stood still leaning back against the side of his jalopy. "I took a special interest in you, such a pretty girl, and found out all about you like I know your parents and sister are gone somewheres and I know where and how long they're going to be gone, and I know who you were with last night, and your best friend's name is Betty. Right?"

He spoke in a simple lilting voice, exactly as if he were reciting the words to a song. His smile assured her that everything was fine. In the car Ellie turned up the volume on his radio and did not bother to look around at them.

"Ellie can sit in the back seat," Arnold Friend said. He indicated his friend with a   60
casual jerk of his chin, as if Ellie did not count and she could not bother with him.

"How'd you find out all that stuff?" Connie said.

"Listen? Betty Schultz and Tony Fitch and Jimmy Pettinger and Nancy Pettinger," he said, in a chant. "Raymond Stanley and Bob Hutter—"

"Do you know all those kids?"

"I know everybody."

"Look, you're kidding. You're not from around here."   65

"Sure."

"But—how come we never saw you before?"

"Sure you saw me before," he said. He looked down at his boots, as if he were a little offended. "You just don't remember."

"I guess I'd remember you," Connie said.

"Yeah?" He looked up at this, beaming. He was pleased. He began to mark time   70
with the music from Ellie's radio, tapping his fists lightly together. Connie looked away

from his smile to the car, which was painted so bright it almost hurt her eyes to look at it. She looked at that name, ARNOLD FRIEND. And up at the front fender was an expression that was familiar—MAN THE FLYING SAUCERS. It was an expression kids had used the year before, but didn't use this year. She looked at it for a while as if the words meant something to her that she did not yet know.

"What're you thinking about? Huh?" Arnold Friend demanded. "Not worried about your hair blowing around in the car, are you?"

"No."

"Think I maybe can't drive good?"

"How do I know?"

"You're a hard girl to handle. How come?" he said. "Don't you know I'm your   75 friend? Didn't you see me put my sign in the air when you walked by?"

"What sign?"

"My sign." And he drew an X in the air, leaning out toward her. They were maybe ten feet apart. After his hand fell back to his side the X was still in the air, almost visible. Connie let the screen door close and stood perfectly still inside it, listening to the music from her radio and the boy's blend together. She stared at Arnold Friend. He stood there so stiffly relaxed, pretending to be relaxed, with one hand idly on the door handle as if he were keeping himself up that way and had no intention of ever moving again. She recognized most things about him, the tight jeans that showed his thighs and buttocks and the greasy leather boots and the tight shirt, and even that slippery friendly smile of his, that sleepy dreamy smile that all the boys used to get across ideas they didn't want to put into words. She recognized all this and also the singsong way he talked, slightly mocking, kidding, but serious and a little melancholy, and she recognized the way he tapped one fist against the other in homage to the perpetual music behind him. But all these things did not come together.

She said suddenly, "Hey, how old are you?"

His smile faded. She could see then that he wasn't a kid, he was much older—thirty, maybe more. At this knowledge her heart began to pound faster.

"That's a crazy thing to ask. Can'tcha see I'm your own age?"   80

"Like hell you are."

"Or maybe a coupla years older, I'm eighteen."

"Eighteen?" she said doubtfully.

He grinned to reassure her and lines appeared at the corners of his mouth. His teeth were big and white. He grinned so broadly his eyes became slits and she saw how thick the lashes were, thick and black as if painted with a black tar-like material. Then he seemed to become embarrassed, abruptly, and looked over his shoulder at Ellie. "*Him,* he's crazy," he said. "Ain't he a riot, he's a nut, a real character." Ellie was still listening to the music. His sunglasses told nothing about what he was thinking. He wore a bright orange shirt unbuttoned halfway to show his chest, which was a pale, bluish chest and not muscular like Arnold Friend's. His shirt collar was turned up all around and the very tips of the collar pointed out past his chin as if they were protecting him. He was pressing the transistor radio up against his ear and sat there in a kind of daze, right in the sun.

"He's kinda strange," Connie said.   85

"Hey, she says you're kinda strange! Kinda strange!" Arnold Friend cried. He pounded on the car to get Ellie's attention. Ellie turned for the first time and Connie saw with shock that he wasn't a kid either—he had a fair, hairless face, cheeks reddened slightly as if the veins grew too close to the surface of his skin, the face of a forty-year-old baby. Connie felt a wave of dizziness rise in her at this sight and she stared at him as if waiting for something to change the shock of the moment, make it all right again. Ellie's lips kept shaping words, mumbling along with the words blasting his ear.

"Maybe you two better go away," Connie said faintly.

"What? How come?" Arnold Friend cried. "We come out here to take you for a ride. It's Sunday." He had the voice of the man on the radio now. It was the same voice, Connie thought. "Don'tcha know it's Sunday all day and honey, no matter who you were with last night today you're with Arnold Friend and don't you forget it!—Maybe you better step out here," he said, and this last was in a different voice. It was a little flatter, as if the heat was finally getting to him.

"No. I got things to do."

"Hey."   90

"You two better leave."

"We ain't leaving until you come with us."

"Like hell I am—"

"Connie, don't fool around with me. I mean, I mean, don't fool *around,*" he said, shaking his head. He laughed incredulously. He placed his sunglasses on top of his head, carefully, as if he were indeed wearing a wig, and brought the stems down behind his ears. Connie stared at him, another wave of dizziness and fear rising in her so that for a moment he wasn't even in focus but was just a blur, standing there against his gold car, and she had the idea that he had driven up the driveway all right but had come from nowhere before that and belonged nowhere and that everything about him and even the music that was so familiar to her was only half real.

"If my father comes and sees you—"   95

"He ain't coming. He's at a barbecue."

"How do you know that?"

"Aunt Tillie's. Right now they're—uh—they're drinking. Sitting around," he said vaguely, squinting as if he were staring all the way to town and over to Aunt Tillie's back yard. Then the vision seemed to clear and he nodded energetically. "Yeah. Sitting around. There's your sister in a blue dress, huh? And high heels, the poor sad bitch—nothing like you, sweetheart! And your mother's helping some fat woman with the corn, they're cleaning the corn—husking the corn—"

"What fat woman?" Connie cried.

"How do I know what fat woman. I don't know every goddamn fat woman in the   100
world!" Arnold Friend laughed.

"Oh, that's Mrs. Hornby. . . . Who invited her?" Connie said. She felt a little light-headed. Her breath was coming quickly.

"She's too fat. I don't like them fat. I like them the way you are, honey," he said, smiling sleepily at her. They stared at each other for a while, through the screen door. He said softly, "Now what you're going to do is this: you're going to come out that door. You're going to sit up front with me and Ellie's going to sit in the back, the hell with Ellie, right? This isn't Ellie's date. You're my date. I'm your lover, honey."

"What? You're crazy—"

"Yes, I'm your lover. You don't know what that is but you will," he said. "I know that too. I know all about you. But look: it's real nice and you couldn't ask for nobody better than me, or more polite. I always keep my word. I'll tell you how it is, I'm always nice at first, the first time. I'll hold you so tight you won't think you have to try to get away or pretend anything because you'll know you can't. And I'll come inside you where it's all secret and you'll give in to me and you'll love me—"

"Shut up! You're crazy!" Connie said. She backed away from the door. She put her   105 hands against her ears as if she'd heard something terrible, something not meant for her. "People don't talk like that, you're crazy," she muttered. Her heart was almost too big now for her chest and its pumping made sweat break out all over her. She looked out to see Arnold Friend pause and then take a step toward the porch lurching. He almost fell. But, like a clever drunken man, he managed to catch his balance. He wobbled in his high boots and grabbed hold of one of the porch posts.

"Honey?" he said. "You still listening?"

"Get the hell out of here!"

"Be nice, honey. Listen."

"I'm going to call the police—"

He wobbled again and out of the side of his mouth came a fast spat curse, an aside   110 not meant for her to hear. But even this "Christ!" sounded forced. Then he began to smile again. She watched this smile come, awkward as if he were smiling from inside a mask. His whole face was a mask, she thought wildly, tanned down onto his throat but then running out as if he had plastered make-up on his face but had forgotten about his throat.

"Honey—? Listen, here's how it is. I always tell the truth and I promise you this: I ain't coming in that house after you."

"You better not! I'm going to call the police if you—if you don't—"

"Honey," he said, talking right through her voice, "honey, I'm not coming in there but you are coming out here. You know why?"

She was panting. The kitchen looked like a place she had never seen before, some room she had run inside but which wasn't good enough, wasn't going to help her. The kitchen window had never had a curtain, after three years, and there were dishes in the sink for her to do—probably—and if you ran your hand across the table you'd probably feel something sticky there.

"You listening, honey? Hey?"   115

"—going to call the police—"

"Soon as you touch the phone I don't need to keep my promise and can come inside. You won't want that."

She rushed forward and tried to lock the door. Her fingers were shaking. "But why lock it," Arnold Friend said gently, talking right into her face. "It's just a screen door. It's just nothing." One of his boots was at a strange angle, as if his foot wasn't in it. It pointed out to the left, bent at the ankle. "I mean, anybody can break through a screen door and glass and wood and iron or anything else if he needs to, anybody at all and specially Arnold Friend. If the place got lit up with a fire, honey, you'd come running out into my arms, right into my arms and safe at home—like you knew I was your lover and'd stopped fooling around, I don't mind a nice shy girl but I don't like no fooling around." Part of those words were spoken with a slightly rhythmic lilt, and

Connie somehow recognized them—the echo of a song from last year, about a girl rushing into her boy friend's arms and coming home again—

Connie stood barefoot on the linoleum floor, staring at him. "What do you want?" she whispered.

"I want you," he said.   120

"What?"

"Seen you that night and thought, that's the one, yes sir. I never needed to look any more."

"But my father's coming back. He's coming to get me. I had to wash my hair first—" She spoke in a dry, rapid voice, hardly raising it for him to hear.

"No, your daddy is not coming and yes, you had to wash your hair and you washed it for me. It's nice and shining and all for me, I thank you, sweetheart," he said, with a mock bow, but again he almost lost his balance. He had to bend and adjust his boots. Evidently his feet did not go all the way down; the boots must have been stuffed with something so that he would seem taller. Connie stared out at him and behind him Ellie in the car, who seemed to be looking off toward Connie's right, into nothing. This Ellie said, pulling the words out of the air one after another as if he were just discovering them, "You want me to pull out the phone?"

"Shut your mouth and keep it shut," Arnold Friend said, his face red from bend-   125
ing over or maybe from embarrassment because Connie had seen his boots. "This ain't none of your business."

"What—what are you doing? What do you want?" Connie said. "If I call the police they'll get you, they'll arrest you—"

"Promise was not to come in unless you touch that phone, and I'll keep that promise," he said. He resumed his erect position and tried to force his shoulders back. He sounded like a hero in a movie, declaring something important. He spoke too loudly and it was as if he were speaking to someone behind Connie. "I ain't made plans for coming in that house where I don't belong but just for you to come out to me, the way you should. Don't you know who I am?"

"You're crazy," she whispered. She backed away from the door but did not want to go into another part of the house, as if this would give him permission to come through the door. "What do you. . . . You're crazy, you. . . ."

"Huh? What're you saying, honey?"

Her eyes darted everywhere in the kitchen. She could not remember what it   130
was, this room.

"This is how it is, honey: you come out and we'll drive away, have a nice ride. But if you don't come out we're gonna wait till your people come home and then they're all going to get it."

"You want that telephone pulled out?" Ellie said. He held the radio away from his ear and grimaced, as if without the radio the air was too much for him.

"I toldja shut up, Ellie." Arnold Friend said, "You're deaf, get a hearing aid, right? Fix yourself up. This little girl's no trouble and's gonna be nice to me, so Ellie keep to yourself, this ain't your date—right? Don't hem in on me. Don't hog. Don't crush. Don't bird dog. Don't trail me," he said in a rapid meaningless voice, as if he were running through all the expressions he'd learned but was no longer sure which one of them was in style, then rushing on to new ones, making them up with his eyes closed,

"Don't crawl under my fence, don't squeeze in my chipmunk hole, don't sniff my glue, suck my popsicle, keep your own greasy fingers on yourself!" He shaded his eyes and peered in at Connie, who was backed against the kitchen table. "Don't mind him, honey, he's just a creep. He's a dope. Right? I'm the boy for you and like I said you come out here nice like a lady and give me your hand, and nobody else gets hurt, I mean, your nice old bald-headed daddy and your mummy and your sister in her high heels. Because listen: why bring them in this?"

"Leave me alone," Connie whispered.

"Hey, you know that old woman down the road, the one with the chickens and   135
stuff—you know her?"

"She's dead!"

"Dead? What? You know her?" Arnold Friend said.

"She's dead—"

"Don't you like her?"

"She's dead—she's—she isn't here any more—"   140

"But don't you like her, I mean, you got something against her? Some grudge or something?" Then his voice dipped as if he were conscious of rudeness. He touched the sunglasses on top of his head as if to make sure they were still there. "Now you be a good girl."

"What are you going to do?"

"Just two things, or maybe three," Arnold Friend said. "But I promise it won't last long and you'll like me that way you get to like people you're close to. You will. It's all over for you here, so come on out. You don't want your people in any trouble, do you?"

She turned and bumped against a chair or something, hurting her leg, but she ran into the back room and picked up the telephone. Something roared in her ear, a tiny roaring, and she was so sick with fear that she could do nothing but listen to it—the telephone was clammy and very heavy and her fingers groped down to the dial but were too weak to touch it. She began to scream into the phone, into the roaring. She cried out, she cried for her mother, she felt her breath start jerking back and forth in her lungs as if it were something Arnold Friend were stabbing her with again and again with no tenderness. A noisy sorrowful wailing rose all about her and she was locked inside it the way she was locked inside this house.

After a while she could hear again. She was sitting on the floor, with her wet back   145
against the wall.

Arnold Friend was saying from the door, "That's a good girl. Put the phone back."

She kicked the phone away from her.

"No, honey. Pick it up. Put it back right."

She picked it up and put it back. The dial tone stopped.

"That's a good girl. Now you come outside."   150

She was hollow with what had been fear, but what was now just an emptiness. All that screaming had blasted it out of her. She sat, one leg cramped under her, and deep inside her brain was something like a pinpoint of light that kept going and would not let her relax. She thought, I'm not going to see my mother again. She thought, I'm not going to sleep in my bed again. Her bright green blouse was all wet.

Arnold Friend said, in a gentle-loud voice that was like a stage voice. "The place where you came from ain't there any more, and where you had in mind to go is cancelled out. This place you are now—inside your daddy's house—is nothing but a cardboard box I can knock down any time. You know that and always did know it. You hear me?"

She thought, I have got to think. I have to know what to do.

"We'll go out to a nice field, out in the country here where it smells so nice and it's sunny," Arnold Friend said. "I'll have my arms tight around you so you won't need to try to get away and I'll show you what love is like, what it does. The hell with this house! It looks solid all right," he said. He ran a fingernail down the screen and the noise did not make Connie shiver, as it would have the day before. "Now put your hand on your heart, honey. Feel that? That feels solid too but we know better, be nice to me, be sweet like you can because what else is there for a girl like you but to be sweet and pretty and give in?—and get away before her people come back?"

She felt her pounding heart. Her hands seemed to enclose it. She thought for the 155 first time in her life that it was nothing that was hers, that belonged to her, but just a pounding, living thing inside this body that wasn't hers either.

"You don't want them to get hurt," Arnold Friend went on. "Now get up, honey. Get up all by yourself."

She stood.

"Now turn this way. That's right. Come over to me—Ellie, put that away, didn't I tell you? You dope. You miserable creep dope," Arnold Friend said. His words were not angry but only part of an incantation. The incantation was kindly. "Now come out through the kitchen to me honey and let's see a smile, try it, you're a brave sweet little girl and now they're eating corn and hotdogs cooked to bursting over an outdoor fire, and they don't know one thing about you and never did and honey you're better than them because not one of them would have done this for you."

Connie felt the linoleum under her feet; it was cool. She brushed her hair back out of her eyes. Arnold Friend let go of the post tentatively and opened his arms for her, his elbows pointing up toward each other and his wrist limp, to show that this was an embarrassed embrace and a little mocking, he didn't want to make her self-conscious.

She put out her hand against the screen. She watched herself push the door slowly 160 open as if she were safe back somewhere in the other doorway, watching this body and this head of long hair moving out into the sunlight where Arnold Friend waited.

"My sweet little blue-eyed girl," he said, in a half-sung sigh that had nothing to do with her brown eyes but was taken up just the same by the vast sunlit reaches of the land behind him and on all sides of him, so much land that Connie had ever seen before and did not recognize except to know that she was going to it.

Questions for Discussion and Writing

1. Why is it significant that everything about Connie "had two sides to it"? How does Connie see herself as being different from both her mother and her sister?
2. How does the description of Arnold Friend—his unusual hair, pale skin, awkward way of walking in his boots, out-of-date expressions, and car—suggest he is not what he appears to be? Who do you think he really is, or what do you think he represents?

3. What do you think Friend means when he says at the end, "Not a one of them would have done this for you"? In your opinion, does Connie really have a choice, and if so, what is it?

PARABLES

Plato

• •

Plato (428–347 B.C.), the philosopher who was a pupil of Socrates and the teacher of Aristotle, went into exile after the death of Socrates in 399 B.C. Plato returned to Athens in 380 B.C. to establish his school, known as the Academy, where he taught for the next forty years. Most of Plato's works are cast in the form of dialogues between Socrates and his students. The earliest of these, the Ion, Euthyphro, Protagoras, *and* Gorgias, *illustrate the so-called Socratic method, in which questions are asked until contradictions in the answers disclose the truth. Later in his life, Plato also wrote* Crito, Apology, Phaedo, Symposium, *and* Timaeus, *among other dialogues, as well as his influential treatises* The Republic *and* The Laws. *Plato's formative influence on Western thought can be traced to his belief that the soul and body have distinct and separate existences and that beyond the world of the senses exists an eternal order of ideal Forms.*

In "The Allegory of the Cave," from The Republic, *Plato creates an extended analogy to dramatize the importance of recognizing that the "unreal" world of the senses and physical phenomena are merely shadows cast by the immortal life of the "real" world of ideal Forms.*

THE ALLEGORY OF THE CAVE

Socrates: And now, I said, let me show in a figure[1] how far our nature is enlightened or unenlightened:—Behold! human beings living in an underground den, which has a mouth open towards the light and reaching all along the den: here they have been from their childhood, and have their legs and necks chained so that they cannot move, and can only see before them, being prevented by the chains from turning round their heads. Above and behind them a fire is blazing at a distance, and between the fire and the prisoners there is a raised way; and you will see, if you look, a low wall built along the way, like the screen which marionette players have in front of them, over which they show the puppets.

The den, the prisoners: the light at a distance;

Glaucon: I see.

And do you see, I said, men passing along the wall carrying all sorts of vessels, and statues and figures of animals made

---

[1]*figure:* a picture or image.

of wood and stone and various materials, which appear over the wall? Some of them are talking, others silent.

You have shown me a strange image, and they are strange prisoners.

Like ourselves, I replied; and they see only their own shadows, or the shadows of one another, which the fire throws on the opposite wall of cave?

The low wall, and the 5 moving figures of which the shadows are seen on the opposite wall of the den.

True, he said; how could they see anything but the shadows if they were never allowed to move their heads?

And of the objects which are being carried in like manner they would only see the shadows?

Yes, he said.

And if they were able to converse with one another, would they not suppose that they were naming what was actually before them?

Very true.

The prisoners would mistake the shadows for realities.

And suppose further that the prison had an echo which came from the other side, would they not be sure to fancy when one of the passers-by spoke that the voice which they heard came from the passing shadow?

No question, he replied.

To them, I said, the truth would be literally nothing but the shadows of the images.

That is certain.

And now look again, and see what will naturally follow if the prisoners are released and disabused of their error. At first, when any of them is liberated and compelled suddenly to stand up and turn his neck round and walk and look towards the light, he will suffer sharp pains; the glare will distress him, and he will be unable to see the realities of which in his former state he had seen the shadows; and then conceive some one saying to him, that what he saw before was an illusion, but that now, when he is approaching nearer to being and his eye is turned towards more real existence, he has a clearer vision,— what will be his reply? And you may further imagine that his instructor is pointing to the objects as they pass and requiring him to name them,—will he not be perplexed? Will he not fancy that the shadows which he formerly saw are truer than the objects which are now shown to him?

And when released, they 15 would still persist in maintaining the superior truth of the shadows.

Far truer.

And if he is compelled to look straight at the light, will he not have a pain in his eyes which will make him turn away to take refuge in the objects of vision which he can see, and which he will conceive to be in reality clearer than the things which are now being shown to him?

True, he said.

And suppose once more, that he is reluctantly dragged up a steep and rugged ascent, and held fast until he is forced into the presence of the sun himself, is he not likely to be pained and irritated. When he approaches the light his eyes will be dazzled, and he will not be able to see anything at all of what are now called realities.

When dragged upwards, they would be dazzled by excess of light.

Not all in a moment, he said.

20

He will require to grow accustomed to the sight of the upper world. And first he will see the shadows best, next the reflections of men and other objects in the water, and then the objects themselves; then he will gaze upon the light of the moon and the stars and the spangled heaven; and he will see the sky and the stars by night better than the sun or the light of the sun by day?

Certainly.

Last of all he will be able to see the sun, and not mere reflections of him in the water, but he will see him in his own proper place, and not in another; and he will contemplate him as he is.

At length they will see the sun and understand his nature.

Certainly.

He will then proceed to argue that this is he who gives the season and the years, and is the guardian of all that is in the visible world, and in a certain way the cause of all things which he and his fellows have been accustomed to behold?

25

Clearly, he said, he would first see the sun and then reason about him.

And when he remembered his old habitation, and the wisdom of the den and his fellow-prisoners, do you not suppose that he would felicitate himself on the change, and pity them?

They would then pity their old companions of the den.

Certainly, he would.

And if they were in the habit of conferring honours among themselves on those who were quickest to observe the passing shadows and to remark which of them went before, and which followed after, and which were together; and who were therefore best able to draw conclusions as to the future, do you think that he would care for such honours and glories, or envy the possessors of them? Would he not say with Homer, "Better to be the poor servant of a poor master," and to endure anything, rather than think as they do and live after their manner?

Yes, he said, I think that he would rather suffer anything than entertain those false notions and live in this miserable manner.

30

Imagine once more, I said, such an one coming suddenly out of the sun to be replaced in his old situation; would he not be certain to have his eyes full of darkness?

To be sure, he said.

And if there were a contest, and he had to compete in measuring the shadows with the prisoners who had never

But when they returned to the den they would see much worse than those who had never left it.

moved out of the den, while his sight was still weak, and before his eyes had become steady (and the time which would
be needed to acquire this new habit of sight might be very
considerable), would he not be ridiculous? Men would say
of him that up he went and down he came without his eyes;
and that it was better not even to think of ascending; and if
any one tried to loose another and lead him up to the light,
let them only catch the offender, and they would put him to
death.

No question, he said.

This entire allegory, I said, you may not append, dear
Glaucon, to the previous argument; the prison-house is the
world of sight, the light of the fire is the sun, and you will not
misapprehend me if you interpret the journey upwards to be
the ascent of the soul into the intellectual world according to
my poor belief, which, at your desire, I have expressed—
whether rightly or wrongly God knows. But, whether true or
false, my opinion is that in the world of knowledge the idea of
good appears last of all, and is seen only with an effort; and
when seen, is also inferred to be the universal author of all
things beautiful and right, parent of light and of the lord of
light in this visible world, and the immediate source of reason
and truth in the intellectual; and that this is the power upon
which he who would act rationally either in public or private
life must have his eye fixed.

*The prison is the world of   35
sight, the light of the fire is
the sun.*

I agree, he said, as far as I am able to understand you.

Questions for Discussion and Writing

1. Why do the prisoners in the cave believe the shadows on the wall are real? Why
   would a prisoner who was released and allowed to leave the cave be unwilling to
   believe that what he is seeing is real? After his eyes adjust to the light, what will
   he think about his former life inside the cave?
2. If the prisoner returns to the cave and is unable to see in the dark as well as the
   others, how would they respond to his report of a greater light outside? Why
   would they be unwilling to allow other prisoners to follow him outside?
3. Plato used this **allegory** as a teaching tool. If you were one of his philosophy students, what would the allegorical equivalence or meaning of the cave, the prisoners, the fire, the shadow, and the sun make you realize about the human
   condition? What do you think Plato means when he says that the sun is like the
   "idea of good" that "appears last of all, and is seen only with an effort"?
4. Plato's allegory is particularly well suited to describe "deprogramming" experiences, whether in a state or a cult. Apply his method to any form of propaganda
   or advertising in which one must sift through lies, deceptions, and misrepresen-
   tations in order to discover the truth (as in *the Matrix* movie trilogy).

Matthew

In the Gospels—that is, in the four biographies of Jesus in the New Testament that are at-tributed to Matthew, Mark, Luke, and John—parables are short illustrative narratives and figurative statements. The teaching that Christ gives in the New Testament takes different forms. The form in which the language of parables is cast is designed to create a bridge be-tween the part of the mind that responds to the literal and the normally undeveloped capaci-ties for spiritual reflection. The fact that the language in parables can be taken in two ways is meant to stimulate an awareness of this higher dimension. In the thirteenth chapter of Matthew,[1] Christ begins to speak in parables to the multitude. His disciples ask why he sud-denly has begun to use parables, and he responds that it is because he is speaking about the kingdom of heaven—that is, about a spiritual reality that would be impossible to grasp oth-erwise. The Parable of the Sower and the Seed is the starting point of Christ's teaching about the kingdom of heaven. Not surprisingly, this master parable is about the way people differ in their capacity to understand this teaching. Differences in receptivity are presented in the parable by analogy as differences in the kinds of ground or earth into which the seed is sown: the wayside, stony places, ground where the seed does not take root, seed planted among thorns, and varying quantities of harvest grown from the seed. From this analysis of capacity for receiving the teachings, there follow parables about the Grain of Mustard Seed, the Woman and the Leaven, the Wheat and the Tares, the Net, the Pearl of Great Price, and the Net Cast into the Sea. Each in its own way deals with the kingdom of heaven and the teaching concerning it. The twentieth chapter of Matthew, in the Parable of the Laborers in the Vineyard, presents a seemingly paradoxical idea that challenges conventional concepts of what is just and what is unjust. Laborers who have spent a whole day in the scorching heat of the fields are aghast that those who have simply labored one hour are paid the same. The parable teaches that the kingdom of heaven cannot be thought of in terms of conventional rewards. The seeming injustice of the parable—that those who work longer do not gain a greater reward—hints that the kingdom of heaven has to do with eternity. The context in which the parable is given suggests that it is meant as an answer to the disciples who have abandoned all they had to follow Jesus and now want a reward in the conventional sense.

PARABLES IN THE NEW TESTAMENT

Chapter 13

The same day went Jesus out of the house, and sat by the sea side.

2 And great multitudes were gathered together unto him, so that he went into a ship, and sat; and the whole multitude stood on the shore.

3 And he spake many things unto them in parables, saying, Behold, a sower went forth to sow:

---

[1]The Gospel According to St. Matthew is one of the first four books of the New Testament, a collection of documents from the early Christian community written in the first two centuries after Jesus. The Gospel of St. Matthew, believed to have been written between A.D. 80 and 95, stresses the ways in which Jesus fulfills the prophecies of the Old Testament. This Gospel also contains the Sermon on the Mount.

4 And when he sowed, some seeds fell by the way side, and the fowls came and devoured them up.

5 Some fell upon stony places, where they had not much earth: and forthwith they sprung up, because they had no deepness of earth.

6 And when the sun was up, they were scorched; and because they had no root, they withered away.

7 And some fell among thorns; and the thorns sprung up, and choked them;

8 But other fell into good ground, and brought forth fruit, some an hundredfold, some sixtyfold, some thirtyfold.

9 Who hath ears to hear, let him hear.

10 And the disciples came, and said unto him, Why speakest thou unto them in parables?

11 He answered and said unto them: Because it is given unto you to know the mysteries of the kingdom of heaven, but to them it is not given.

12 For whosoever hath, to him shall be given, and he shall have more abundance, but whosoever hath not, from him shall be taken away even that he hath.

13 Therefore speak I to them in parables: because they seeing see not; and hearing they hear not, neither do they understand.

14 And in them is fulfilled the prophecy of Esaias[2] which saith: By hearing ye shall hear, and shall not understand; and seeing ye shall see, and shall not perceive.

15 For this people's heart is waxed gross, and their ears are dull of hearing, and their eyes they have closed; lest at any time they should see with their eyes, and hear with their ears, and should understand with their heart, and should be converted, and I should heal them.

16 But blessed are your eyes, for they see; and your ears, for they hear.

17 For verily I say unto you, That many prophets and righteous men have desired to see those things which ye see, and have not seen them; and to hear those things which ye hear, and have not heard them.

18 Hear ye therefore the parable of the sower.

19 When any one heareth the word of the kingdom, and understandeth it not, then cometh the wicked one, and catcheth away that which was sown in his heart. This is he which received seed by the way side.

20 But he that received the seed into stony places, the same is he that heareth the word, and anon with joy receiveth it;

21 Yet hath he not root in himself, but dureth for a while: for when tribulation or persecution ariseth because of the word, by and by he is offended.[3]

22 He also that received seed among the thorns is he that heareth the word; and the care of this world, and the deceitfulness of riches, choke the word, and he becometh unfruitful.

23 But he that received seed into the good ground is he that heareth the word, and understandeth it; which also beareth fruit, and bringeth forth, some an hundredfold, some sixty, some thirty.

---

[2]*Esaias:* Isaiah 5:9–10.   [3]*offended:* falls away.

24 Another parable put he forth unto them, saying, The kingdom of heaven is likened unto a man which sowed good seed in his field.

25 But while men slept, his enemy came and sowed tares[4] among the wheat, and went his way.

26 But when the blade was sprung up, and brought forth fruit, then appeared the tares also.

27 So the servants of the householder came and said unto him, Sir, didst not thou sow good seed in thy field? from whence then hath it tares?

28 He said unto them, An enemy hath done this. The servants said unto him, Wilt thou then that we go and gather them up?

29 But he said, Nay; lest while ye gather up the tares, ye root up also the wheat with them.

30 Let both grow together until the harvest; and in the time of harvest I will say to the reapers, Gather ye together first the tares, and bind them in bundles to burn them: but gather the wheat into my barn.

31 Another parable put he forth unto them, saying, The kingdom of heaven is like to a grain of mustard seed, which a man took, and sowed in his field:

32 Which indeed is the least of all seeds: but when it is grown, it is the greatest among herbs, and becometh a tree, so that the birds of the air come and lodge in the branches thereof.

33 Another parable spake he unto them: The kingdom of heaven is like unto leaven, which a woman took, and hid in three measures of meal, till the whole was leavened.

34 All these things spake Jesus unto the multitude in parables; and without a parable spake he not unto them,

35 That it might be fulfilled which was spoken by the prophet, saying, I will open my mouth in parables; I will utter things which have been kept secret from the foundation of the world.

36 Then Jesus sent the multitude away, and went into the house: and his disciples came unto him, saying, Declare unto us the parable of the tares of the field.

37 He answered and said unto them; He that soweth the good seed is the Son of man;

38 The field is the world; the good seed are the children of the kingdom; but the tares are the children of the wicked one.

39 The enemy that sowed them is the devil; the harvest is the end of the world; and the reapers are the angels.

40 As therefore the tares are gathered and burned in the fire; so shall it be in the end of this world.

41 The Son of man shall send forth his angels, and they shall gather out of his kingdom all things that offend, and them which do iniquity;

42 And shall cast them into a furnace of fire: there shall be wailing and gnashing of teeth.

43 Then shall the righteous shine forth as the sun in the kingdom of their Father. Who hath ears to hear, let him hear.

---

[4]*tares:* a noxious weed, probably the darnel.

44 Again, the kingdom of heaven is like unto treasure hid in a field; the which when a man hath found, he hideth, and for joy thereof goeth and selleth all that he hath, and buyeth that field.

45 Again, the kingdom of heaven is like unto a merchant man, seeking goodly pearls:

46 Who, when he had found one pearl of great price, went and sold all that he had, and bought it.

47 Again, the kingdom of heaven is like unto a net, that was cast into the sea, and gathered of every kind:

48 Which, when it was full, they drew to shore, and sat down, and gathered the good into vessels, but cast the bad away.

49 So shall it be at the end of the world: the angels shall come forth, and sever the wicked from among the just,

50 And shall cast them into the furnace of fire: there shall be wailing and gnashing of teeth.

51 Jesus saith unto them, Have ye understood all these things? They say unto him, Yea, Lord.

52 Then said he unto them, Therefore every scribe which is instructed unto the kingdom of heaven is like unto a man that is an householder, which bringeth forth out of his treasure things new and old.

53 And it came to pass, that when Jesus had finished these parables, he departed thence.

54 And when he was come into his own country, he taught them in their synagogue, insomuch that they were astonished, and said, Whence hath this man this wisdom, and these mighty works?

55 Is not this the carpenter's son? is not his mother called Mary? and his brethren, James, and Joses, and Simon, and Judas?

56 And his sisters, are they not all with us? Whence then hath this man all these things?

57 And they were offended in him. But Jesus said unto them, A prophet is not without honour, save in his own country, and in his own house.

58 And he did not many mighty works there because of their unbelief.

Chapter 20

For the kingdom of heaven is like unto a man that is an householder, which went out early in the morning to hire labourers into his vineyard.

2 And when he had agreed with the labourers for a penny a day, he sent them into his vineyard.

3 And he went out about the third hour, and saw others standing idle in the marketplace,

4 And said unto them; Go ye also into the vineyard, and whatsoever is right I will give you. And they went their way.

5 Again he went out about the sixth and ninth hour, and did likewise.

6 And about the eleventh hour he went out, and found others standing idle, and saith unto them, Why stand ye here all the day idle?

7 They say unto him, Because no man hath hired us. He saith unto them, Go ye also into the vineyard; and whatsoever is right, that shall ye receive.

8 So when even was come, the lord of the vineyard saith unto his steward, Call the labourers, and give them their hire, beginning from the last unto the first.

9 And when they came that were hired about the eleventh hour, they received every man a penny.

10 But when the first came, they supposed that they should have received more; and they likewise received every man a penny.

11 And when they had received it, they murmured against the goodman of the house,

12 Saying, These last have wrought but one hour, and thou hast made them equal unto us, which have borne the burden and heat of the day.

13 But he answered one of them, and said, Friend, I do thee no wrong: didst not thou agree with me for a penny?

14 Take that thine is, and go thy way: I will give unto this last, even as unto thee.

15 Is it not lawful for me to do what I will with mine own? Is thine eye evil, because I am good?

16 So the last shall be first, and the first last: for many be called, but few chosen.

Questions for Discussion and Writing

1. What differences can you discover between the four kinds of ground described in the Parable of the Sower and the Seed and the response to Christ's teaching that is implied by each of these categories? Why would this master parable be an important starting point for an attempt to understand the other parables?
2. How does the Parable of the Laborers in the Vineyard contradict conventional ideas about justice and injustice?
3. Pick any of the parables in the preceding selection or any other in the New Testament, and write an essay exploring how the language of the parable functions as a bridge between literal and spiritual meanings.
4. Create your own parable to express your understanding of what the kingdom of heaven means and how it might be obtained.

The Buddha

The Buddha is the title given to the founder of Buddhism, Siddhartha Gautama (563–483 B.C.), who was born into a family of great wealth and power in southern Nepal. Although reared in luxury, Siddhartha renounced this life of privilege at the age of twenty-nine to become a wandering ascetic and to seek an answer to the problems of death and human suffering. After six years of intense spiritual discipline, he achieved enlightenment while meditating under a pipal tree at Bodh Gaya. He spent the remainder of his life teaching, and he established a community of monks to carry on his work. In the Buddha's view, bondage to the repeating cycles of birth and death and the consequent suffering are caused by desire. The method of breaking this cycle is the eightfold noble path that encompasses right views, right resolve, right speech, right action, right livelihood, right effort, right mindfulness, and right concentration. Buddhist parables are well suited to communicate important lessons or moral truths.

PARABLES OF BUDDHA

Buddha-Nature

Once upon a time a king gathered some blind men about an elephant and asked them to tell him what an elephant was like. The first man felt a tusk and said an elephant was like a giant carrot; another happened to touch an ear and said it was like a big fan; another touched its trunk and said it was like a pestle; still another, who happened to feel its leg, said it was like a mortar; and another, who grasped its tail, said it was like a rope. Not one of them was able to tell the king the elephant's real form.

In like manner, one might partially describe the nature of man but would not be able to describe the true nature of a human being, the Buddha-nature.

There is only one possible way by which the everlasting nature of man, his Buddha-nature, that can not be disturbed by worldly desires or destroyed by death, can be realized, and that is by the Buddha and the Buddha's noble teaching.

The Way of Purification

At one time there lived in the Himalayas a bird with one body and two heads. Once one of the heads noticed the other head eating some sweet fruit and felt jealous and said to itself: "I will then eat poison fruit." So it ate poison and the whole bird died.

Questions for Discussion and Writing

1. How do the many different conclusions the blind men reach about the nature of the elephant reveal the partial, limited, and contradictory perceptions that are the result of their being unable to see the whole elephant? In this case, what might being blind mean in relation to the Buddha-nature of humans?
2. What aspect of human nature is illustrated in the story of the bird with one body and two heads?
3. Have you ever had an experience whose meaning could be understood more clearly in light of either of these parables? Describe this experience and what you learned about yourself from it.
4. To gain more insight into Buddha's first parable find an interesting photo and crop it (electronically using an image editor, or by cutting and pasting) to select at least three different elements as focal points. Describe how the meaning changes according to the way the photo is cropped.

Nasreddin Hodja

Nasreddin Hodja was born in Sivrihisar, Turkey, in the early thirteenth century and died in 1284 near present-day Kenya. His father was the religious leader, the imam, of his village, and Hodja, too, served as imam. Later he traveled to Aksehir, where he became a dervish and was associated with a famous Islamic mystical sect. He also served as a judge and university professor. The stories that have made Hodja immortal blend wit, common sense, ingenuousness, and ridicule to reveal certain aspects of human psychology. Today, Hodja's stories are widely known throughout Turkey, Hungary, Siberia, North Africa, and the Middle East. They are told in teahouses, schools, and caravansaries and are even broadcast on the radio. Each tale is a certain kind of joke, a joke with a moral that has long been associated with the Sufi tradition of Islamic teaching. Unlike the philosophical allegories of Plato or the spiritual parables recorded in the New Testament, Hodja's stories use humor to surreptitiously bypass habitual patterns of thought in order to reveal a central truth about the human condition. Hodja very frequently uses the dervish technique of playing the fool. At other times, he is the embodiment of wisdom. All his stories are designed to sharpen our perceptions.

ISLAMIC FOLK STORIES

We Are Even

One day, Hodja went to a Turkish bath but nobody paid him much attention. They gave him an old bath robe and a towel. Hodja said nothing and on his way out he left a big tip. A week later, when he went back to the same bath, he was very well received. Everybody tried to help him and offered him extra services. On his way out, he left a very small tip.

"But, Hodja," they said, "Is it fair to leave such a small tip for all the attention and extra services you received?"

What impression do you get of Hodja's unique perspective from this statue?

Hodja answered,
"Today's tip is for last week's services and last week's tip was for today's services. Now we are even."

Do As You Please

Hodja and his son were going to another village. His son was riding the donkey and Hodja was walking along. A few people were coming down the road. They stopped and pointing at his son they muttered, "Look at that! The poor old man is walking and the young boy is riding the donkey. The youth of today has no consideration!" Hodja was irritated. He told his son to come down, and he began to ride the donkey himself. Then, they saw another group of people, who remarked, "Look at that man! On a hot day like this, he is riding the donkey and the poor boy is walking." 5

So, Hodja pulled his son on the donkey, too. After awhile, they saw a few more people coming down the road.

"Poor animal! Both of them are riding on it and it is about to pass out."

Hodja was fed up. He and his son got down and started walking behind the donkey. Soon, they heard a few people say,

"Look at those stupid people. They have a donkey but won't ride it."

Finally, Hodja lost his patience. He turned to his son and said, "You see, you can never please people and everybody says something behind your back. So, always do as you please." 10

You Believed That It Gave Birth

Hodja had borrowed his neighbour's cauldron. A few days later, he put a bowl in it and returned it. When his neighbour saw the bowl, he asked,

"What is this?"

Hodja answered,

"Your cauldron gave birth!"

His neighbour was very happy. He thanked Hodja and took the cauldron and the bowl. 15

A few weeks later, Hodja borrowed the cauldron again but this time he didn't return it. When his neighbour came to ask for it, Hodja said,

"Your cauldron died. I am sorry."

The man was surprised.

"Oh, come on!" he said, "Cauldrons don't die."

Hodja snapped back, "Well, you believed that it gave birth, then why don't you believe that it died?" 20

Questions for Discussion and Writing

1. How does the story "We Are Even" suggest that we should not be concerned about how others view our actions so long as we are aware of what we are doing and why we are doing it?

2. What do the experiences of Hodja and his son in "Do As You Please" tell us about human nature? Have you ever had a similar experience that led you to the same conclusion? Describe the circumstances.

3. In your view, what is the point of "You Believed That It Gave Birth"? Discuss your interpretation in a short essay. How is this or any of Hodja's stories designed to awaken people from the bonds of conditioning?

POETRY

Linda Pastan

Linda Pastan was born in 1932 in New York and was educated at Radcliffe (B.A., 1954), Simmons College (M.L.S., 1955), and Brandeis University (M.A., 1957). Her poetry explores the metaphysical implications of ordinary life and the mystery of what we take for granted. Her collected poems include Carnival Evening: New and Selected Poems—1968–1998 (1998) *and* PM/AM: New and Selected Poems (1981), *in which "Ethics" first appeared. A recent collection is* The Last Uncle: Poems (2002).

ETHICS

In ethics class so many years ago
our teacher asked this question every fall:
if there were a fire in a museum
which would you save, a Rembrandt painting
or an old woman who hadn't many   5
years left anyhow? Restless on hard chairs
caring little for pictures or old age
we'd opt one year for life, the next for art
and always half-heartedly. Sometimes
the woman borrowed my grandmother's face   10
leaving her usual kitchen to wander
some drafty, half-imagined museum.
One year, feeling clever, I replied
why not let the woman decide herself?
Linda, the teacher would report, eschews   15
the burdens of responsibility.
This fall in a real museum I stand
before a real Rembrandt, old woman,
or nearly so, myself. The colors
within this frame are darker than autumn,   20
darker even than winter—the browns of earth,
though earth's most radiant elements burn

through the canvas. I know now that woman
and painting and season are almost one
and all beyond saving by children.

25

Questions for Discussion and Writing

1. How has the speaker's understanding of the hypothetical dilemma proposed to her by her teacher altered with the passage of time?
2. How does Pastan make the theme of the poem more apparent through contrasting situations and time periods? How is the impact of the poem strengthened by the associations of fall and winter?
3. In your opinion, is the speaker's problem a failure to take responsibility when she was young and even now that she is an "old woman"? Why or why not?

Robert Frost

Robert Frost (1874–1963) was born in San Francisco and lived there until the age of eleven, although most people think of him as having grown up in New England. He spent his high school years in a Massachusetts mill town and studied at Harvard for two years. He worked a farm in New Hampshire that he had acquired in 1900, took a teaching job at the Pinkerton Academy, and wrote poetry that he had no luck in getting published. In 1912 he moved with his wife and five children to England, rented a farm, and met with success in publishing A Boy's Will *(1913) and* North of Boston *(1914). After the outbreak of World War I, he returned to the United States, where he was increasingly accorded recognition. He taught at Amherst College sporadically for many years. Frost won the Pulitzer Prize for poetry four times. He was a friend of John F. Kennedy, who invited him to read a poem at the presidential inauguration in 1961. Many of the qualities that made Frost's poetry so popular can be seen in "The Road Not Taken" (1916).*

THE ROAD NOT TAKEN

Two roads diverged in a yellow wood,
And sorry I could not travel both
And be one traveler, long I stood
And looked down one as far as I could
To where it bent in the undergrowth;

5

Then took the other, as just as fair,
And having perhaps the better claim,
Because it was grassy and wanted wear;
Though as for that the passing there
Had worn them really about the same,

10

And both that morning equally lay
In leaves no step had trodden black.

Oh, I kept the first for another day!
Yet knowing how way leads on to way,
I doubted if I should ever come back.   15

I shall be telling this with a sigh
Somewhere ages and ages hence:
Two roads diverged in a wood, and I—
I took the one less traveled by,
And that has made all the difference.   20

Questions for Discussion and Writing

1. How does Frost use a simple subject as a springboard to express a profound insight?
2. What prevents the speaker from berating himself for not having chosen a different, possibly easier, road?
3. In what way is it implied that the psychological sensibility of the speaker is more sophisticated than the anecdotal manner in which the poem is written?

Lisel Mueller

* *

Lisel Mueller (b. 1924) came to the United States from Germany in 1939. She studied at the University of Indiana and has taught at Goddard College in Vermont. Volumes of her poems include Dependencies *(1965; reissued 1998) and* Alive Together: New and Selected Poems *(1996), which won the Pulitzer Prize and in which "Hope" first appeared. Her honors include the Carl Sandburg Award and a National Endowment for the Arts fellowship.*

HOPE

It hovers in dark corners
before the lights are turned on,
    it shakes sleep from its eyes
    and drops from mushroom gills,
        it explodes in the starry heads   5
        of dandelions turned sages,
            it sticks to the wings of green angels
            that sail from the tops of maples.

It sprouts in each occluded eye
of the many-eyed potato,   10
    it lives in each earthworm segment
    surviving cruelty,

        it is the motion that runs
        from the eyes to the tail of a dog,
            it is the mouth that inflates the lungs   15
            of the child that has just been born.

It is the singular gift
We cannot destroy in ourselves,
The argument that refutes death,
The genius that invents the future,
All we know of God.

20

It is the serum which makes us swear
Not to betray one another;
It is in this poem, trying to speak.

Questions for Discussion and Writing

1. Hope is usually thought of in the abstract, but Mueller reveals its presence in a multitude of ordinary circumstances. What are some of these? Do you find her choices compelling? Why or why not?
2. Mueller makes a number of statements that would seem to require further exploration. Select one of these (for example, hope is a "serum which makes us swear / Not to betray one another"), and elaborate on her idea.
3. Discuss a few additional locations where "hope" may be found.

Thinking Critically About the Image

Edvard Munch (1863–1944) was a Norwegian painter and graphic artist whose violent, exciting, and emotionally charged style expressed his sense of isolation. In *The Scream* (1893, tempera and pastels on cardboard), Munch communicates the fear and existential anguish of the human condition. The absence of a specific cause and the undulating lines that transmit the echo of the scream into every part of the picture enhance the shocking effect. In 2003, astronomers established that the blood-red sky (which Munch described as a "great unending scream piercing through nature") depicted in the painting was the vivid sunset caused by debris from the great volcanic eruption in the island of Krakatoa in Indonesia in 1883, as Munch remembered it ten years later. Another version of this painting (valued at $70 million) was stolen in August 2004 from Oslo's Munch Museum.

1. How does the central distorted figure in the work, clutching his skull-like head between his hands as he mouths a scream that you can almost hear, communicate existential angst?
2. Munch aimed for an art that would transmit the innermost emotions of experience—love, death, anxiety—through a distinctly private symbolism stemming

from his own traumatic experiences. Why is the seemingly unfinished nature of the painting more effective in communicating an impossible feeling than a more polished presentation would have been?

3. How do the Halloween masks in the film *Scream* (and its sequel) tap into Munch's archetype and evoke a similar reaction?

Connections

Chapter 11: Matters of Ethics, Philosophy, and Religion

Philip Wheelwright,   *The Meaning of Ethics*
Does Linda Pastan's poem point out the limits of the kind of ethical analysis described by Wheelwright? Why or why not?

Marya Mannes,   *The Unwilled*
How might Mannes meet objections to her argument posed by such noteworthy exceptions as Helen Keller in "The Day Language Came into My Life" (Ch. 4)?

Richard Selzer,   *What I Saw at the Abortion*
Discuss Selzer's observations in light of Marya Mannes's argument.

Garrett Hardin,   *Lifeboat Ethics: The Case Against Helping the Poor*
To what extent does the conflict between self-preservation and consideration of others that Hardin sees as the crux of the lifeboat dilemma enter into "Report from Ground Zero" by Dennis Smith (Ch. 7), and with what surprising outcome?

Tim O'Brien,   *If I Die in a Combat Zone*
In what respects do O'Brien and the narrator in Panos Ioannides's story "Gregory" (Ch. 8) confront similar choices as to the extent of the allegiance that they owe the state?

Stanley Milgram,   *The Perils of Obedience*
How do Milgram's subjects react in similar ways to the narrator in Langston Hughes's essay to social pressure?

Dalai Lama,   *The Role of Religion in Modern Society*
Discuss how the Dalai Lama and Steven E. Barkan and Lynne L. Snowden adopt surprisingly similar methods for gaining objectivity on highly emotional issues—religion and terrorism (see "Defining and Countering Terrorism," Ch. 8).

Langston Hughes,   *Salvation*
Gayle Pemberton's grandmother, described in "Antidisestablishmentarianism" (Ch. 2), and Hughes's aunt greatly influenced their young relatives. Compare the lessons the authors learned from these adults.

Joyce Carol Oates,   *Where Are You Going, Where Have You Been?*
In what sense has Connie evoked her own version of the "rough beast" portrayed by W. B. Yeats in "The Second Coming" (Ch. 7)? What role does religious symbolism play in both works?

Plato,   *The Allegory of the Cave*
Compare Plato's allegory (as a method for teaching about the nature of absolute good) with the parables in the New Testament as to the nature of the kingdom of heaven. How do both works convey subtle concepts that are hard to grasp?

Matthew,   *Parables in the New Testament*
What similarities can you discover between any of the parables and Anna Kamieńska's depiction of the human condition in her poem "Funny" (Ch. 1)?

The Buddha,   *Parables of Buddha*
How do the Buddha's parables illuminate the experiences of Bill and Arlene in Raymond Carver's story "Neighbors" (Ch. 2)?

Nasreddin Hodja,   *Islamic Folk Stories*
What similarities can you discover between Hodja's teaching methods and those of George Gurdjieff as described by Fritz Peters in "Boyhood with Gurdjieff" (Ch. 1)?

Linda Pastan,   *Ethics*
Compare the real moral dilemma of Sabine Reichel in "Learning What Was Never Taught" (Ch. 3) with the choice that confronts the speaker in Pastan's poem.

Robert Frost,   *The Road Not Taken*
Could Linda Pastan's poem be considered a rebuttal to Frost's poem? Why or why not?

Lisel Mueller,   *Hope*
How is Joyce Carol Oates's story about hope in the sense that Mueller means it in her poem?

GLOSSARY

Advertisement   A public announcement of a product, service, or event, designed to promote awareness and sales.   26

Allegory   A type of narrative in which characters, events, and even the setting represent particular qualities, ideas, or concepts. See *fable, parable,* and *symbol.*   687

Alliteration   The repetition of similar or identical sounds at the beginning of words or in accented syllables. Alliteration is used to underscore similarities and contrasts (e.g., "from stem to stern").   20

Allusion   A brief reference in a literary work to a real or fictional person, place, thing, or event that the reader might be expected to recognize. For example, Edgar Allan Poe's story alludes to Shakespeare's play *The Tempest.* See *context.*   23

Ambiguity   A phrase, statement, or situation that may be understood in two or more ways. The title of Liliana Heker's story "The Stolen Party" has several meanings, for example.   6

Analogy   A comparison drawn between two basically different things that have some points in common; often used to explain a more complex idea in terms of a simpler and more familiar one. Barbara Kingsolver draws an analogy between the speaker's self and a dwelling in "This House I Cannot Leave." See *metaphor* and *symbol.*   9

Antagonist   A character who opposes the protagonist's completion of his or her goal. In Joyce Carol Oates's "Where Are You Going, Where Have You Been?" Arnold Friend is the antagonist to Connie.   21

Argument   A process of reasoning and putting forth evidence to support an interpretation, as in William A. Henry III's essay "In Defense of Elitism."   12

Assonance   The repetition of vowel sounds in a line, stanza, or sentence.   20

Assumptions   The knowledge, values, and beliefs a reader brings to a text.   14

Audience   The group of spectators, listeners, viewers, or readers that a performance or written work reaches.   2

Autobiography   An author's own life history or memoir. For example, Maya Angelou's "Liked for Myself" is drawn from her memoir *I Know Why the Caged Bird Sings* (1970).   5

Biographical context   The facts and circumstances of the author's life that are relevant to the work.   22

Case history   An in-depth account of the experience of one person that typifies the experience of many people in the same situation; used to substantiate a claim.   6

Causal analysis   A method of analysis that seeks to discover why something happened or will happen.   10

Character(s)   Fictional personalities created by the writer.   18

Claim   The assertion or interpretation the writer puts forward and supports with evidence and reasons. See *thesis.*   12

Classification and division   A method of sorting, grouping, collecting, and analyzing things by categories based on features shared by all members of a class or group. Division is a method of breaking down an entire whole into separate parts, or sorting a group of items into nonoverlapping categories; arguments can use classification as part of the writer's analysis in making a case.   7

Climax   The decisive or turning point of emotional intensity in a work of literature. For example, the climax in Carson McCuller's "Madame Zilensky and the King of Finland" occurs when Mr. Brook confronts Madame Zilensky.   21

Comparison and contrast   Rhetorical technique for pointing out similarities or differences; writers may use a point-by-point or subject-by-subject approach.   7

Conclusion   The end or closing; the last main division of a discourse, usually containing summation and a statement of opinion or decisions reached.   3

Conflict   The opposition between a character or narrator and an obstacle (another character, society, or fate) or within this person's mind.   21

Connotation   The emotional implications a word may suggest, as opposed to its literal meaning. The word *fireplace,* for example, might *connote* feelings of warmth, hospitality, and comfort, whereas it *denotes* the portion of a chimney in which fuel is burned. See *denotation.*   6

Consonance   Repetition of the final consonant sounds and stressed syllables that are preceded by a different vowel sound, as in "pain of a thorn."   20

Context   The surrounding situation that affects a literary work, including the writer's life and the political, historical, and social environment. See *biographical context, historical context,* and *social context.*   22

Controlling image   A dominant image or metaphor that determines the theme or organization of an entire poem. For example, Marge Piercy's poem "Barbie Doll" uses this figure as a controlling image. See *figurative language* and *metaphor*.   307

Crisis   The point of highest tension in a work that precipitates an irrevocable outcome; often the result of a choice made by the protagonist. For example, in Panos Ioannides's story "Gregory" the narrator chooses to follow orders to shoot his prisoner. See *climax*.   21

Culture   The totality of practices and institutions and the entire way of life of the people who produce them. In a narrow sense, specific aesthetic productions of literature, art, and music.   24

Deductive reasoning   A form of argument that applies a set of principles to specific cases and draws logical conclusions. For example, John Milton's argument in "Areopagitica" is based on deductive reasoning.   2

Definition   A method for specifying the basic nature of any phenomenon, idea, or thing. Dictionaries place the subject to be defined in the context of the general class to which it belongs and give distinguishing features that differentiate it from other things in its class.   6

Denotation   The explicit, primary, or literal meaning of a word as found in the dictionary, as distinct from its associative meanings. See *connotation*.   6

Description   Writing that reports how a person, place, or thing is perceived by the senses. *Objective* description recreates the appearance of objects, events, scenes, or people. *Subjective* description emphasizes the writer's feelings and reactions to a subject.   4

Dialogue   A conversation between characters. Dialogue can serve to characterize the speakers, create a mood or atmosphere, advance the plot, or develop the theme or main idea of the work. See *monologue*.   20

Division   See *classification and division*.   7

Drama   A literary work written to be acted on a stage.   20

Essay   A relatively brief prose discussion on a particular theme or subject.   1

Evidence   All material, including testimony of experts, statistics, cases (whether real, hypothetical, or analogical), and reasons brought forward to support a claim.   2

Examples   Specific incidents that clarify, illustrate, or support a writer's thesis or claim.   6

Exposition   The presentation of background material about the characters or the situation in a story, play, or poem, which supplies information necessary to understand events that follow; may appear either at the beginning or progressively throughout the work.   21

Fable   A short tale that illustrates a moral; the characters are frequently animals who speak and act like human beings.   18

Fairy tale   A story, frequently from the oral tradition, that involves the help or hindrance of magical persons such as fairies, goblins, trolls, and witches.   18

Farce   A type of comedy, usually satiric, that relies on exaggerated character types, slapstick, and other types of ridiculous behavior and situations resulting from a contrived plot that makes use of surprises and coincidences, as in David Ives's play *Sure Thing*.   311

Fiction   A mode of writing that constructs models of reality in the form of imaginative experiences that are not literally true in the sense that they did not actually occur in the "real" world.   19

Figurative language   The use of words outside their literal or usual meanings in order to add freshness and suggest associations and comparisons that create effective images; includes figures of speech such as metaphor, personification, and simile.   8

First-person narrator   A narrator who is part of the story and refers to himself or herself as "I."   5

Flashback   An interruption in the major action of a story, play, or essay to show an episode that happened at an earlier time; used to shed light on characters and events in the present by providing background information. Ambrose Bierce uses a flashback in "An Occurrence at Owl Creek Bridge."   441

Folktale   A traditional story about common people from a culture's oral tradition.   18

Foreshadowing   The technique of giving the reader, listener, or viewer of a story or play a hint or clue about what is to come next.   303

Free verse   Poetry that follows no set patterns of rhyme, meter, or line length but uses rhythm and other poetic devices, as in Linda Pastan's "Ethics."   19

Genre   A type of literary work defined by particular characteristics of form or technique—for example, the short story, novel, screenplay, poem, play, or essay.   1

Historical context   Applies to when the work was written and the time period in which the work is set in terms of economic, social, political, and cultural values.   22

Humor   Writing that expresses the faculty of perceiving or appreciating what is amusing or comical, often consisting of the recognition and expression of incongruities in a situation or character.   694

Hypothesis   (plural is *hypotheses*) The reader's provisional conjecture or anticipation of what will happen next; an essential element in the reader's interaction with the text.   19

Imagery   The use of language to convey sensory experience in order to arouse emotions or feelings that abstract language cannot accomplish; most often refers to a creation of pictoral images through figurative language. See *figurative language*.   9

Inductive reasoning   A form of argument that draws inferences from particular cases to support a generalization. Jonathan Kozol in "The Human Cost of an Illiterate Society" uses inductive reasoning.   2

Introduction   A preliminary part (as of a book) leading to the main part. The function of the introduction is to engage the reader in the central issue and present the thesis regarding the question at hand.   3

Irony, ironic   (from the Greek *eiron,* a stock comic character who misled his listeners). A contrast between appearance and reality, what is and what ought to be. *Dramatic irony* occurs when the reader or viewer can derive meaning from a character's words or actions that are unintended by the character, as in Raymond Carver's "Neighbors." *Verbal irony* is the contrast between what is said and what is actually meant; frequently used as a device in satire, as in Jonathan Swift's "A Modest Proposal."   14

Literature   A term that has come to stand for imaginative writing of high quality, although it should be recognized that "literature" is an evaluative designation, not an absolute category.   22

Lyric   A short poem or song expressing an intense, basic personal emotion, such as grief, happiness, or love. See Paul Simon and Art Garfunkel's "The Sound of Silence."   623

Metaphor   A figure of speech that implies comparison between two fundamentally different things without the use of *like* or *as*. It works by ascribing the qualities of one to the other, linking different meanings together, such as abstract and concrete, and literal and figurative. Anne Bradstreet in "The Author to Her Book" compares her book to a child. See *figurative language*.   8

Meter   Recurrent patterns of accented and unaccented or stressed and unstressed syllables that create patterns of rhythm and emphasis. Meter is measured in units called feet of which the most typical type in English is *iambic* (in which an accented or stressed syllable is preceded by an unaccented or unstressed syllable). Poetry without a recognizable metrical pattern is called *free verse*.   20

Monologue   A long speech by one character in a literary work.   20

Myth   Ancient stories that set out a society's religious or social beliefs, which often embody and express a culture's assumptions and values through characters and images that are universal symbols.   18

Narration   A true or made-up story that relates events and/or experiences in either poetry or prose. Narrations tell what happened, when it happened, and to whom; relate events from a consistent point of view; organize a story with a clear beginning, middle, and end; and use events and incidents to dramatize important moments in the action. See *plot*.   5

Narrator   The ostensible teller of a story, who may be a character in the story (as Macedo is in "A Canary's Ideas") or an anonymous voice outside the story (as in Kate Chopin's "Désirée's Baby"). The narrator's attitude toward the events gives rise to the work's *tone*. See *persona* and *point of view*.   5

Organization   The order of presentation that best fulfills the writer's purpose; may be chronological, least familiar to most familiar, simple to complex, or arranged according to some other rhetorical principle (such as comparison/contrast, classification, definition, cause and effect, process analysis, or problem and solution).   1

Parable   A short, simple story that is designed to teach a lesson, truth, or moral; unlike a fable, in which the characters are animals, or an allegory, where the characters represent abstract qualities. St. Matthew's Parables of "The Sower and the Seed" and "The Laborers in the Vineyard" from the New Testament are renowned examples.   18

Paradox   A seemingly self-contradictory statement that may nevertheless be true.   3

Parody   A composition that imitates the defining features of a serious piece of writing for comic or satiric effect. W. H. Auden's poem "The Unknown Citizen" parodies bureaucratic memorials.   8

Persona   (literally, "actor's mask") Refers to the voice and implied personality the author chooses to adopt in order to tell the story in poetry or fiction. The persona may serve as a projection of views quite different from the author's. Jonathan Swift uses this technique in "A Modest Proposal"; Bruce Springsteen adopts a persona in "Streets of Philadelphia." See *speaker* and *voice*.   14

Personification   A figure of speech that endows abstractions, ideas, animals, or inanimate objects with human characteristics, as in Lisel Mueller's poem "Hope."   20

Persuasion   The winning of the acceptance of a claim achieved through the combined effects of the audience's confidence in the speaker's character, appeals to reason, and the audience's emotional needs and values.   12

Plot   A series of related events organized around a conflict that builds to a climax followed by a resolution. Conflicts may be between two or more characters (as between Louise and Richard in Andre

Debus's story "The Fat Girl"); between a character and society (Alec in Anthony Burgess's "A Clock-work Orange") or the forces of nature (such as drought in Bessie Head's "Looking for a Rain God"); or internal, between opposing emotions, such as duty and conscience (as in Panos Ioannides's story "Gregory"). See *conflict, crisis, exposition,* and *structure.* 17

Poem A literary form that emphasizes rhythm and figurative language. Often used to express emotions. See *lyric, meter,* and *rhyme.* 19

Point of view The perspective from which the events in a story are related. A story may be related in either the first person (*I*) or the third person (*he, she,* or *they*). A first-person *narrator* is a character who tells the story he or she participated in or directly observed, as in Irene Zabytko's "Home Soil." The observations and inferences of such a narrator may be reliable, as far as they go, or unreliable, as with the narrator in Charlotte Perkins Gilman's "The Yellow Wallpaper." A third-person *omniscient narrator* stands outside the events of the story but allows the reader unlimited access to the characters' thoughts and feelings and may comment on the story or characters, as in Kate Chopin's "Désirée's Baby." So too, the third-person *limited omniscient narrator* is not directly involved in the story but restricts the reader's access to the thoughts of one or two of the characters, as does the narrator in Liliana Heker's "The Stolen Party." 5

Popular culture Those aspects of a culture—chiefly, the artifacts and icons displayed in its forms of entertainment, consumer goods, and means of communication—that have mass appeal. 307

Postmodernist Refers to works that undercut or subvert traditional models of unity and coherence, employing irony and allusion to create a sense of discontinuity, as in Raymond Carver's "Neighbors." 19

Premise An assumption from which deductive reasoning proceeds in an argument. 15

Problem solving A process writers use to identify problems, search for solutions, and verify them; an indispensable part of all academic and professional research. An argument that proposes a solution will often incorporate problem solving. 11

Process analysis A method of clarifying the nature of something by explaining how it works in separate, easy-to-understand steps. 10

Propaganda Information or ideas methodically spread to promote or injure a cause, group, or nation. 11

Protagonist The main character in a short story, play, or novel, opposed by an adversary, or antagonist, who may be another character, the forces of fate, chance, nature, or any combination of these. See *antagonist.* 21

Pseudonym ("false name") An alias used by a writer who does not desire to use his or her real name. Sometimes called a nom de plume or pen name. 324

Purpose The writer's objective; also, the goals of the four types of prose writing: narration (to tell or relate), description (to represent or delineate), exposition (to explain or clarify), and argument (to persuade). 15

Read In the language of semiotics, to decipher the latent social meanings governing the way people dress, what they eat, how they socialize and speak, and other cultural phenomena. 24

Realism A nineteenth-century literary movement that aims to depict life as it is, without artificiality or exaggeration. It uses ordinary language and focuses on ordinary people, events, and settings, all of which are described in great detail, as in Kate Chopin's "Désirée's Baby." 18

Rhetoric, rhetorical modes In ancient Greece and Rome, rhetoric was the art of using language to influence or persuade others. Today, the term also refers to the specialized literary uses of language to express oneself effectively and the study of elements of visual persuasion. 4

Rhyme The exact repetition of similar or identical sounds to unify parts of a poem to emphasize important words or lines, such as "alone" and "stone" in Sara Teasdale's "The Solitary." 20

Rhythm The arrangement of stressed and unstressed sounds into patterns in speech and writing. Rhythm, or meter, may be regular, or it may vary within a line or work. See *meter.* 20

Satire A technique that ridicules both people and societal institutions, often in an effort to bring about social reform. Exaggeration, wit, and irony are frequent devices used by satirists. George Carlin in "A Place for Your Stuff," Mark Twain in "The Lowest Animal," and Jonathan Swift in "A Modest Proposal" employ satiric techniques. 14

Scene A division of an act in a play that may be long or short, serve as a transition, or even have an inner dramatic structure. 21

Science fiction Works of fiction usually set in the future or some remote region of the universe that use scientific discoveries or advanced technology, real or imaginary, in the plot, as, for example, Anthony Burgess in "A Clockwork Orange." 246

Script The printed text of a play, including dialogue and stage directions. 20

Semiotics The study of linguistic, cultural, and behavioral sign systems. 25

Setting The time period and location in which the action of a story or play takes place. It may serve simply as a background, or it may help create the atmosphere from which the story evolves and may even affect the plot's development. Setting plays a crucial role in Bessie Head's story "Looking for a Rain God." 18

Short story A short work of narrative prose fiction that generally involves a small number of characters in a limited number of settings. 18

Sign A word, object, image, form of behavior, or anything whose meaning is conditioned by and can be interpreted according to an underlying code. See *code*. 25

Simile A figure of speech involving a direct comparison between two unlike things and using the word *like* or *as* (e.g., "passengers crammed *like* sardines in a can".) See *metaphor*. 8

Social context The relevant social conditions and the effect of social forces as they influence the depiction of characters and classes of people in literary works; includes economic and political circumstances as well as the effects of culture, race, class, power, and gender. 22

Sonnet A lyric poem of fourteen lines written in iambic pentameter. The English sonnet develops an idea in three stages and brings it to a conclusion in a couplet, as does Shakespeare in Sonnet 30, "When to the Sessions of Sweet Silent Thought." 87

Speaker The narrator of a poem; often a separate character created for the purpose of relating the events in a poem from a consistent point of view. See *persona*. 20

Stanza The grouping of a fixed number of verse lines in a recurring metrical and rhyme pattern. 19

Stereotype A conventional character who is defined in terms of one oversimplified, often exaggerated, personality trait. 35

Structure The fundamental organization or framework of a piece of writing, including both the principles underlying the form and the form itself. For example, in stories, the plot is the structural element; in plays, the divisions into acts and scenes express the inner dramatic structure; and in poetry, the formal arrangement into stanzas that develop a specific sequence of images and ideas forms the structure. 21

Style The author's characteristic manner of expression. Style includes the types of words used, their placement, and the distinctive features of tone, imagery, figurative language, sound, and rhythm. 20

Support In argument, all the evidence the writer brings forward to enhance the probability of a claim being accepted; can include evidence in the form of summary, paraphrases, quotations drawn from the text, examples from personal experience, hypothetical cases, the testimony of experts, appeals to the audience's emotions and values, and the writer's own character or personality. 3

Surrealism A movement in modern literature and art that emphasizes the expression of the imagination as manifested in dreams; stresses the subconscious, often through the unexpected juxtaposition of symbolic objects in mundane settings. 92

Suspense The feeling of psychological tension experienced by the reader or spectator in anticipation of learning the outcome of a developing sequence of events. 4

Symbol Something concrete, such as an object, person, place, or event, that stands for or represents something abstract, such as an idea, quality, concept, or condition. In Barbara Kingsolver's poem "This House I Cannot Leave" the house symbolizes the speaker's self. 90

Theme An underlying important idea, either stated or implied, in a nonfiction or literary work that may be mythical, moral, or psychological. Literary works commonly have more than one theme. The reader's reactions determine in large part which themes are perceived as important. The loss of identity is an important theme in Bruce Springsteen's song lyrics. 310

Thesis The position taken by a writer, often expressed in a single sentence, that an essay develops or supports. See *claim*. 1

Tone The writer's attitude toward the subject, expressed in style and word choice; the voice the writer chooses to project—for example, serious, lighthearted, matter-of-fact—to relate to readers. 13

Topic The subject the writer addresses, as distinct from the writer's thesis (opinion) about the subject. In Kelly Cherry's poem "Alzheimer's," the topic or subject is Alzheimer's disease, whereas the thesis might be "Identity is equal to memory." 2

Transition A signal word or phrase that connects two sentences, paragraphs, or sections of an essay to produce coherence. Can include pronoun references, parallel clauses, conjunctions, restatements of key ideas, and terms such as *furthermore, moreover, by contrast, therefore, consequently, accordingly,* or *thus*. 2

Understatement A form of verbal irony, often used for humorous effect, in which an opinion is expressed less emphatically than it might be. See *irony*. 474

Values   Moral or ethical principles or beliefs that express standards or criteria for judging actions right or wrong, good or bad, acceptable or unacceptable, appropriate or unseemly; an indispensable component of value arguments.   14

Voice   An imagined projection of a speaker in a literary work (usually in a poem), sometimes identified with the author. See *persona, speaker,* and *tone.*   13

Wit   Purely intellectual manifestation of cleverness and quick thinking, chiefly in discovering analogies between things that are unlike each other and expressing them in brief sharp observations as does Humbert Wolfe in "The Gray Squirrel."   371

CREDITS

Text

Arthur Ashe, "The Burden of Race" from Arthur Ashe and Arnold Rampersad, *Days of Grace: A Memoir.* Copyright © 1993 by Jeanne Moutoussamy-Ashe and Arnold Rampersad. Reprinted with the permission of Alfred A. Knopf, a division of Random House, Inc.

Margaret Atwood, "Fiction: Happy Endings" from *Good Bones and Simple Murders.* Copyright © 1983 by O. W. Toad, Inc. Reprinted with the permission of Doubleday, a division of Random House, Inc. and McClelland & Stewart, Ltd., *The Canadian Publishers.*

W. H. Auden, "The Unknown Citizen" from *W. B. Auden: Collected Poems,* edited by Edward Mendelson. Copyright 1940 and renewed © 1968 by W. H. Auden. Reprinted with the permission of Random House, Inc.

Hanson W. Baldwin, "R.M.S. Titanic" from *Harper's Magazine* (January 1934). Copyright 1933 by Hanson W. Baldwin. Reprinted by permission of Curtis Brown, Ltd.

Steven E. Barkan and Lynne L. Snowden, "Defining and Countering Terrorism" from Chapter 5: "Terrorism" from *Collective Violence.* Copyright © 2001 by Pearson Education. Reprinted by permission of the publisher.

Donald Barthelme, "The School" from *Sixty Stories.* Originally published in *The New Yorker.* Copyright © 1982 by Donald Barthelme. Reprinted with the permission of The Wylie Agency, Inc.

Judy Blume, "Is Harry Potter Evil?" from *The New York Times* (October 22, 1999). Copyright © 1999 by Judy Blume. Reprinted with the permission of William Morris Agency, Inc. on behalf of the author.

Bertolt Brecht, "A Worker Reads History" from *Selected Poems,* translated by H. R. Hays. Copyright 1947 by Bertolt Brecht and H. R. Hays and renewed © 1975 by H. R. Hays and Stefan S. Brecht. Reprinted with the permission of Harcourt, Inc.

David Brooks, "Oversimulated Suburbia" from *The New York Times Magazine* (November 24, 2002). Copyright © 2002 by David Brooks. Reprinted with the permission of the author.

Jan Harold Brunvand, "The Boyfriend's Death" from *The Vanishing Hitchhiker.* Copyright © 1981 by Jan Harold Brunvand. Reprinted with the permission of W. W. Norton & Company, Inc.

Anthony Burgess, excerpt from *A Clockwork Orange.* Copyright © 1962, 1989 and renewed 1990 by Anthony Burgess. Reprinted with the permission of W. W. Norton & Company, Inc. and William Heinemann, Ltd.

George Carlin, "A Place for My Stuff" from *Braindroppings.* Copyright © 1997 by Comedy Concepts, Inc. Reprinted with the permission of Hyperion.

Raymond Carver, "Neighbors" from *Where I'm Calling From: New and Selected Stories.* Copyright © 1976 by Raymond Carver. Reprinted with the permission of Grove/Atlantic, Inc.

John Cheever, "Reunion" from *The Stories of John Cheever.* Copyright © 1978 by John Cheever. Reprinted with the permission of Alfred A. Knopf, a division of Random House, Inc.

Kim Chernin, "The Flesh and the Devil" from *The Obsession: Reflections on the Tyranny of Slenderness.* Copyright © 1981 by Kim Chernin. Reprinted with the permission of HarperCollins Publishers, Inc.

Kelly Cherry, "Alzheimer's" from *Death and Transfigurations.* Copyright © 1997 by Kelly Cherry. Reprinted with the permission of Louisiana State University Press.

Maurizio Chierici, "The Man from Hiroshima," translated by Wallis Wilde-Menozzi, from *Granta* 22 (Autumn 1987). Reprinted with the permission of the author and translator.

Judith Ortiz Cofer, "The Myth of the Latin Woman: I Just Met a Girl Named Maria" from *The Latin Deli: Prose & Poetry.* Copyright © 1993 by Judith Ortiz Cofer. Reprinted with the permission of The University of Georgia Press.

Aaron Copland, "Film Music" from *What to Listen for in Music* (New York: McGraw-Hill, 1957), pp. 252-263. Reprinted by permission of the Aaron Copland Fund for Music, Inc., copyright holder.

Rosalind Coward, "The Body Beautiful" from *Female Desires.* Copyright © 1985 by Roseline Coward. Reprinted with the permission of Grove/Atlantic, Inc. and HarperCollins Publishers, Ltd.

Luis Sepulveda, excerpt from *Full Circle: A South American Journey,* translated by Chris Andrews (Oakland: Lonely Planet Publications, 1996). Copyright © 1996. Reprinted with the permission of Ray-Gude Mertin.

Paul Simon, "Sounds of Silence." Copyright © 1968 by Paul Simon. Used by permission of the Publisher, Paul Simon Music.

Richard Keller Simon, "The Shopping Mall and the Formal Garden" from *Trash Culture: Popular Culture and the Great Tradition.* Copyright © 1999 by The Regents of the University of California. Reprinted with the permission of the University of California Press.

Gunjan Sinha, "You Dirty Vole" from *Popular Science* (2002). Copyright © 2002 by Time, Inc. Reprinted with permission.

David R. Slavitt, "Titanic" from *Big Nose.* Copyright © 1981 by David R. Slavitt. Reprinted with the permission of Louisiana State University Press.

Dennis Smith, "Chief Joe Pfeifer" from *Report from Ground Zero.* Copyright © 2002 by Dennis Smith. Reprinted with the permission of Viking Penguin, a division of Penguin Group (USA) Inc.

Cathy Song, "The Youngest Daughter" from *Picture Bride.* Copyright © 1983 by Cathy Song. Reprinted with the permission of Yale University Press.

Bruce Springsteen, "Streets of Philadelphia." Copyright © 1993 by Bruce Springsteen (ASCAP). Reprinted by permission.

Kenneth M. Stampp, "To Make Them Stand in Fear" from *The Peculiar Institution.* Copyright © 1956 by Kenneth M. Stampp. Reprinted with the permission of Alfred A. Knopf, a division of Random House, Inc.

Olaf Stapleton, "The Ultimate Cosmos and the Eternal Spirit" from *Star Maker.* Copyright 1937 by Olaf Stapleton. Reprinted with the permission of Methuen & Co./International Thomson Publishing Services, Ltd.

Lin Sutherland, "A River Ran Over Me" from *A Different Angle,* edited by Holly Morris. Copyright © 1995 by Lynn Sutherland. Reprinted with the permission of Seal Press.

Deborah Tannen, "Sex, Lies and Conversations" from *You Just Don't Understand.* Copyright © 1990 by Deborah Tannen. Reprinted with the permission of HarperCollins Publishers, Inc.

Dylan Thomas, "Do Not Go Gentle into That Good Night" from *The Poems of Dylan Thomas.* Copyright 1946 by New Directions Publishing Corporation. Copyright 1952 by Dylan Thomas. Reprinted with the permission of New Directions Publishing Corporation.

Anne Tyler, "Still Just Writing" from *The Writer on Her Work, Volume I,* edited by Janet Sternburg. Copyright © 1980 by Janet Sternburg. Reprinted with the permission of W. W. Norton & Company, Inc.

Luisa Valenzuela, "The Censors," translated by David Unger, from *Short Shorts* (Boston: David R. Godine, Publisher, 1982). Translation copyright © 1982 by David Unger. Reprinted with the permission of the translator.

Kurt Vonnegut, "How to Write with Style" from *Palm Sunday.* Copyright © 1981 by the Ramjac Corporation. Reprinted with the permission of Dell Publishing, a division of Random House, Inc.

Philip Wheelwright, "The Meaning of Ethics" from *A Critical Introduction to Ethics, Third Edition.* Copyright © 1959 by Philip Wheelwright. Reprinted with the permission of Pearson Education, Inc., Upper Saddle River, New Jersey.

Sheila Whiteley, "Mick Jagger, Sexuality, Style and Image" from *Sexing the Groove,* edited by Sheila Whiteley. Copyright © 1997. Reprinted with the permission of Routledge.

Chet Williamson, "Personal Touch" from *Playboy* (August 1983). Reprinted with the permission of the author.

Rae Yang, "At the Center of the Storm" from *Spider Eaters.* Copyright © 1997 by The Regents of the University of California. Reprinted with the permission of the University of California Press.

William Zinsser, "Niagara Falls" from *American Places* (New York: HarperCollins Publishers, 1992). Copyright © 1992 by William Zinsser. Reprinted with the permission of the author.

Photos

Introduction: Page 25, Columbia Tristar Motion Picture Group. **P. 26,** Chris Pizzello/AP Wide World Photos. **P. 27,** Reproduced with permission of Yahoo! Inc. © 2004 by Yahoo! Inc. All rights reserved. YAHOO! And the YAHOO! Logo are trademarks of YAHOO! Inc.

Chap. 1:   **Page 28,** Pablo Picasso, *The Dream (La Reve),* January 24, 1932. Oil on canvas, 130 X 97 cm. Private collection. Art Resource, NY. © ARS, NY. **P. 37,** The Granger Collection, New York. **P. 49,** Dean Conger/CORBIS-NY. **P. 55,** Paul Kaleja.

Chap. 2:   **Page 94,** Vincent van Gogh (1853–1890). *Café—Terrace at Night (Place du Forum in Arles),* 1988. Oil on canvas. Cat. 232. Erich Lessing/Art Resource, NY. Rijksmuseum Kroeller—Mueller, Otterio, The Netherlands. **P. 115,** Vanni/Art Resource, NY. **P. 124,** Nick Wheeler/CORBIS-NY. **P. 131,** Tom Nebbia/CORBIS-NY. **P. 132,** Bettman/CORBIS-NY. **P. 133,** John Britton, *The Ames Tribune*/APWide World Photos. **P. 136,** Peter Krogh. **P. 148,** Jeremy Horner/CORBIS-NY.

Chap. 3:   **Page 152,** Jean-Honore Fragonard (French, 1732–1806), *A Young Girl Reading,* c. 1776. Gift of Mrs. Mellon Bruce in memory of her father, Andrew W. Mellon. Photograph © 2004 Board ofTrustees, National Gallery of Art, Washington, DC. Oil on canvas, .811 X .648 in. (32 X 25 1/2 cm.); framed: 1.049 X 895 X .022 in. (41 5/16 X 35 1/4 X 7/8 cm). **P. 169,** The Cartoon Bank. **P. 193,** Chris Columbus/Photofest.

Chap. 4:   **Page 204,** Paul Gauguin (1848–1903), *Ta Matete.* Canvas. Erich Lessing/Art Resource, NY. Kunstmuseum, Basel, Switzerland. **P. 211,** Steve Liss/Getty Images, Inc. **P. 234,** Tim Olin/National Organization on Disability. **P. 243, top left,** Church & Dwight Co., Inc. All rights reserved. **P. 243, top right,** reprinted with the permission of Mammoth. **P. 243, bottom left,** featuring Kim Cattrall. © 2002 America's Dairy Farmers and Milk Processors; Lowe New York. **P. 243, bottom right,** Copyright 1943 Colgate-Palmolive Company. All rights reserved. **P. 251,** Picture Desk, Inc./Kobal Collection.

Chap. 5:   **Page 254,** Grace Hartigan (American, b. 1922), *Billboard,* 1957. Painting, oil on canvas. Abstraction. 78 1/2 X 87 in. (199.4 X 221.0 cm.) LR in black: [Hartigan '57]. The Minneapolis Institute of Arts, The Julia B. Bigelow Fund. **P. 268,** Vincent van Gogh, *Skull with Cigarette, Antwerp,* 1885. Oil on canvas. Van Gogh Museum, Amsterdam, The Netherlands. Art Resource, NY. **P. 276, top,** Mobilization Recording, Inc. **P. 276, bottom,** NON SEQUITAR © 1998 Wiley Miller. Dist. By UNIVERSAL PRESS SYNDICATE. Reprinted with permission. All rights reserved. **P. 285,** Damian Dovarganes/AP Wide World Photos. **P. 290,** Reuters/CORBIS-NY. **P. 291,** © Reprinted with special permission of King Syndicate Features. **P. 307,** CORBIS-NY. **P. 312,** Copyright © 2003 Eight Minute Date. Edmonton. Alberta, Canada. All rights reserved. Site design: LastWords Desktop Publishing.

Chap. 6:   **Page 322,** Claude Monet (1840–1926), *The Artist's Garden at Giverny,* 1902. Oil on canvas, 89.5 X 92.3 cm. Inv. 3889. Nimatallah/Art Resource, NY. Oesterreichische Galerie, Vienna, Austria. **P. 348,** Coastal California Commission. **P. 356,** Bruce Beehler/Photo Researchers, Inc. **P. 369,** Picture Desk, Inc./Kobal Collection. **P. 371,** Corbis/Bettman.

Chap. 7:   **Page 374,** Scala/Art Resource, NY. Museo del Prado, Madrid, Spain. **P. 376,** Erich Lessing/Art Resource, NY. Deir el-Medina, Tombs of the Nobles, Thebes, Egypt. **P. 385,** Terry Hirschberg. **P. 386,** *The Far Side* ® by Gary Larson. © 1984 Farworks, Inc. All Rights Reserved. Used with Permission. **P. 420,** Bettman/Corbis/Bettmann. **P. 434,** courtesy of Arab American Institute. **P. 450, left & right,** from *Last Dinner on the Titanic: Menus & Recipes from the Legendary Liner,* ed. Dana McCauley, Rick Archbold, & Walter Lord. © 1997 Hyperion/Disney Publishing.

Chap. 8:   **Page 454,** Ben Shahn, *Riot on Carol Street,* 1944. Tempera on board, 71 X 51 cm.; framed: 83 X 63 X 5 cm. Thyssen-Bornemisza Collections. **P. 474,** James Leynse/CORBIS-NY. **P. 497,** Sergio Perez/ReutersAmerica, Inc.

Chap. 9:   **Page 530,** Francis Picabia (1879–1953), *Parade Amoureuse,* 1917. © ARS, NY. Bridgenman-Giraudon/Art Resource, NY. Private Collection, Chicago, USA. **P. 549,** Lucy Nicholson/CORBIS-NY. **P. 550,** Sean O'Neill/Nexia Biotechnologies. **P. 564,** Reuters/CORBIS-NY. **P. 581,** Michael Newman/PhotoEdit.

Chap. 10:   **Page 584,** Gustav Klimt (1862–1918), *The Kiss,* 1907-1908. Oil on canvas, 180 X 180 cm. Erich Lessing/Art Resource, NY. Oesterreichische Galerie, Vienna, Austria. **P. 586,** Luke A. Meeken. **P. 595,** Picture Desk, Inc./Kobal Collection. **P. 597, top left,** Photofest. **P. 597, top center,** Picture Desk, Inc./Kobal Collection. **P. 597, top right,** Photofest. **P. 597, bottom left,** Picture Desk, Inc./Kobal Collection. **P. 597, bottom right,** Photofest. **P. 600,** Mary Evans Picture Library Ltd. **P. 605,** Photofest. **P. 608, right,** Eddie Adams/AP/Wide World Photos; **left,** Getty Images, Inc. **P. 614,** Bob Krist/CORBIS-NY. **P. 621,** Courtesy of the Library of Congress.

Chap. 11:   **Page 626,** Edvard Munch (1863–1944), *The Scream,* 1893. Oil on canvas. © ARS, NY. Erich Lessing/Art Resource, NY. National Gallery, Oslo, Norway. **P. 628,** *Colorado Springs Gazette Telegraph.* **P. 635,** Bill Aron/PhotoEdit. **P. 640,** Nathan Benn/CORBIS-NY. **P. 694,** Chris Hellier/CORBIS-NY.

INDEX OF FIRST LINES OF POEMS

INDEX OF AUTHORS AND TITLES